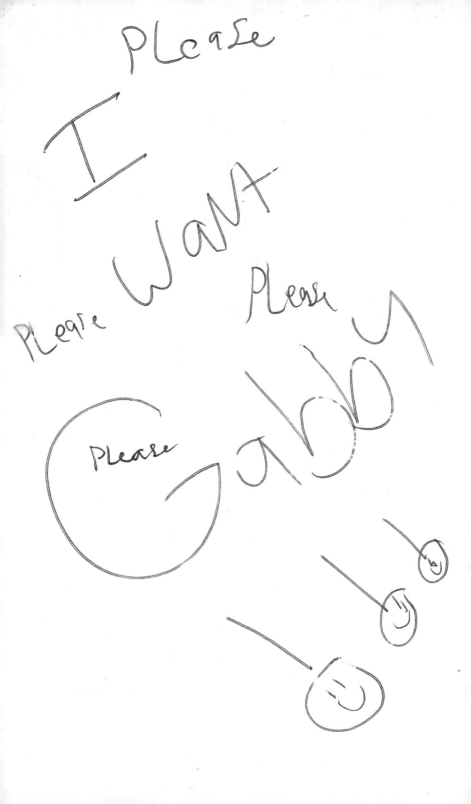

Presented to

Madison Begin

On

November 6, 2016

From

East Auburn Baptist Church

Welcome!

Welcome to a very special book—the Bible! Maybe you have read storybook Bibles before, but this might be your first "real" Bible. The Bible is made up of 66 books from Genesis to Revelation. Altogether these books are known as God's Word. Each book is broken into numbered chapters (just like many other books), and each chapter is made up of numbered verses.

Bible verses are located by book, chapter, and verse. They are written out like this: Genesis 3:2. That means you can find this verse in the book of Genesis, chapter 3, verse 2. Now try it on your own by searching for John 3:16. There is a table of contents in the front of your Bible, just a few pages after this page, to help you. (Hint: John is in the New Testament.)

We are excited for you to explore this Bible and discover just how much God loves you!

Creation

GENESIS 1:1–31

Noah's Ark

GENESIS 7:1–24

NEW INTERNATIONAL VERSION

HOLY BIBLE

ZONDERVAN®

Library of Congress Catalog Card Number 2010939325

Biblica provides God's Word to people through translation, publishing and Bible engagement in Africa, Asia Pacific, Europe, Latin America, Middle East, and North America. Through its worldwide reach, Biblica engages people with God's Word so that their lives are transformed through a relationship with Jesus Christ.

Table of Contents

Books of the Bible in Alphabetical Order iv
Preface v

The Old Testament

BOOK	ABBREVIATION	PAGE
Genesis	Ge	1
Exodus	Ex	86
Leviticus	Lev	153
Numbers	Nu.	202
Deuteronomy	Dt	272
Joshua	Jos.	330
Judges	Jdg	369
Ruth	Ru	408
1 Samuel	1Sa	415
2 Samuel	2Sa	467
1 Kings	1Ki	513
2 Kings	2Ki	565
1 Chronicles	1Ch	615
2 Chronicles	2Ch	670
Ezra	Ezr	728
Nehemiah	Ne	746
Esther	Est.	771
Job	Job	784
Psalms	Ps	840
Proverbs	Pr	984

BOOK	ABBREVIATION	PAGE
Ecclesiastes	Ecc	1035
Song of Songs	SS	1050
Isaiah	Isa	1060
Jeremiah	Jer	1170
Lamentations	La	1276
Ezekiel	Eze	1288
Daniel	Da	1374
Hosea	Hos	1400
Joel	Joel	1417
Amos	Am	1424
Obadiah	Ob	1438
Jonah	Jnh	1441
Micah	Mic	1445
Nahum	Na	1456
Habakkuk	Hab	1461
Zephaniah	Zep	1467
Haggai	Hag	1473
Zechariah	Zec	1476
Malachi	Mal	1491

The New Testament

BOOK	ABBREVIATION	PAGE
Matthew	Mt	1499
Mark	Mk	1555
Luke	Lk	1589
John	Jn	1646
Acts	Ac	1689
Romans	Ro	1744
1 Corinthians	1Co	1769
2 Corinthians	2Co	1792
Galatians	Gal	1806
Ephesians	Eph	1814
Philippians	Php	1822
Colossians	Col	1828
1 Thessalonians	1Th	1834
2 Thessalonians	2Th	1839

BOOK	ABBREVIATION	PAGE
1 Timothy	1Ti	1843
2 Timothy	2Ti	1850
Titus	Titus	1855
Philemon	Phm	1858
Hebrews	Heb	1860
James	Jas	1879
1 Peter	1Pe	1886
2 Peter	2Pe	1893
1 John	1Jn	1898
2 John	2Jn	1905
3 John	3Jn	1907
Jude	Jude	1909
Revelation	Rev	1912

Table of Weights and Measures.................... 1941

Alphabetical Order of the Books of the Bible

The books of the New Testament are indicated by *italics*.

Acts	1689	Judges	369
Amos	1424	1 Kings	513
1 Chronicles	615	2 Kings	565
2 Chronicles	670	Lamentations	1276
Colossians	1828	Leviticus	153
1 Corinthians	1769	*Luke*	1589
2 Corinthians	1792	Malachi	1491
Daniel	1374	*Mark*	1555
Deuteronomy	272	*Matthew*	1499
Ecclesiastes	1035	Micah	1445
Ephesians	1814	Nahum	1456
Esther	771	Nehemiah	746
Exodus	86	Numbers	202
Ezekiel	1288	Obadiah	1438
Ezra	728	*1 Peter*	1886
Galatians	1806	*2 Peter*	1893
Genesis	1	*Philemon*	1858
Habakkuk	1461	*Philippians*	1822
Haggai	1473	Proverbs	984
Hebrews	1860	Psalms	840
Hosea	1400	*Revelation*	1912
Isaiah	1060	*Romans*	1744
James	1879	Ruth	408
Jeremiah	1170	1 Samuel	415
Job	784	2 Samuel	467
Joel	1417	Song of Songs	1050
John	1646	*1 Thessalonians*	1834
1 John	1898	*2 Thessalonians*	1839
2 John	1905	*1 Timothy*	1843
3 John	1907	*2 Timothy*	1850
Jonah	1441	*Titus*	1855
Joshua	330	Zechariah	1476
Jude	1909	Zephaniah	1467

The goal of the New International Version (NIV) is to enable English-speaking people from around the world to read and hear God's eternal Word in their own language. Our work as translators is motivated by our conviction that the Bible is God's Word in written form. We believe that the Bible contains the divine answer to the deepest needs of humanity, sheds unique light on our path in a dark world and sets forth the way to our eternal well-being. Out of these deep convictions, we have sought to recreate as far as possible the experience of the original audience — blending transparency to the original text with accessibility for the millions of English speakers around the world. We have prioritized accuracy, clarity and literary quality with the goal of creating a translation suitable for public and private reading, evangelism, teaching, preaching, memorizing and liturgical use. We have also sought to preserve a measure of continuity with the long tradition of translating the Scriptures into English.

The complete NIV Bible was first published in 1978. It was a completely new translation made by over a hundred scholars working directly from the best available Hebrew, Aramaic and Greek texts. The translators came from the United States, Great Britain, Canada, Australia and New Zealand, giving the translation an international scope. They were from many denominations and churches — including Anglican, Assemblies of God, Baptist, Brethren, Christian Reformed, Church of Christ, Evangelical Covenant, Evangelical Free, Lutheran, Mennonite, Methodist, Nazarene, Presbyterian, Wesleyan and others. This breadth of denominational and theological perspective helped to safeguard the translation from sectarian bias. For these reasons, and by the grace of God, the NIV has gained a wide readership in all parts of the English-speaking world.

The work of translating the Bible is never finished. As good as they are, English translations must be regularly updated so that they will continue to communicate accurately the meaning of God's Word. Updates are needed in order to reflect the latest developments in our understanding of the biblical world and its languages and to keep pace with changes in English usage. Recognizing, then, that the NIV would retain its ability to communicate God's Word accurately only if it were regularly updated, the original translators established The Committee on Bible Translation (CBT). The committee is a self-perpetuating group of biblical scholars charged with keeping abreast of advances in biblical scholarship and changes in English and issuing periodic updates to the NIV. CBT is an independent, self-governing body and has sole responsibility for the NIV text. The committee mirrors the original group of translators in its diverse international and denominational makeup and in its unifying commitment to the Bible as God's inspired Word.

In obedience to its mandate, the committee has issued periodic updates to the NIV. An initial revision was released in 1984. A more thorough revision process was completed in 2005, resulting in the separately published Today's New International Version (TNIV). The updated NIV you now have in your hands builds on both the original NIV and the TNIV and represents the latest effort of the committee to articulate God's unchanging Word in the way the original authors might have said it had they been speaking in English to the global English-speaking audience today.

The first concern of the translators has continued to be the accuracy of the translation and its faithfulness to the intended meaning of the biblical writers. This has moved the translators to go beyond a formal word-for-word rendering of the original texts. Because thought patterns and syntax differ from language to language, accurate communication of the meaning of the biblical authors demands constant regard for varied contextual uses of words and idioms and for frequent modifications in sentence structures.

As an aid to the reader, sectional headings have been inserted. They are not to be regarded as part of the biblical text and are not intended for oral reading. It is the committee's hope that these headings may prove more helpful to the reader than the traditional chapter divisions, which were introduced long after the Bible was written.

For the Old Testament the standard Hebrew text, the Masoretic Text as published in the latest edition of *Biblia Hebraica,* has been used throughout. The Masoretic Text tradition contains marginal notations that offer variant readings. These have sometimes been followed instead of the text itself. Because such instances involve variants within the Masoretic tradition, they have not been indicated in the textual notes. In a few cases, words in the basic consonantal text have been divided differently than in the Masoretic Text. Such cases are usually indicated in the textual footnotes. The Dead Sea Scrolls contain biblical texts that represent an earlier stage of the transmission of the Hebrew text. They have been consulted, as have been the Samaritan Pentateuch and the ancient scribal traditions concerning deliberate textual changes. The translators also consulted the more important early versions — the Greek Septuagint, Aquila, Symmachus and Theodotion, the Latin Vulgate, the Syriac Peshitta, the Aramaic Targums and, for the Psalms, the *Juxta Hebraica* of Jerome. Readings from these versions, the Dead Sea Scrolls and the scribal traditions were occasionally followed where the Masoretic Text seemed doubtful and where accepted principles of textual criticism showed that one or more of these textual witnesses appeared to provide the correct reading. In rare cases, the committee has emended the Hebrew text where it appears to have become corrupted at an even earlier stage of its transmission. These departures from the Masoretic Text are also indicated in the textual footnotes. Sometimes the vowel indicators (which are later additions to the basic consonantal text) found in the Masoretic Text did not, in the judgment of the committee, represent the correct vowels for the original text. Accordingly, some words have been read with a different set of vowels. These instances are usually not indicated in the footnotes.

The Greek text used in translating the New Testament is an eclectic one, based on the latest editions of the Nestle-Aland/United Bible Societies' Greek New Testament. The committee has made its choices among the variant readings in accordance with widely accepted principles of New Testament textual criticism. Footnotes call attention to places where uncertainty remains.

The New Testament authors, writing in Greek, often quote the Old Testament from its ancient Greek version, the Septuagint. This is one reason why some of the Old Testament quotations in the NIV New Testament are not identical to the corresponding passages in the NIV Old Testament. Such quotations in the New Testament are indicated with the footnote "(see Septuagint)."

Other footnotes in this version are of several kinds, most of which need no explanation. Those giving alternative translations begin with "Or" and generally introduce the alternative with the last word preceding it in the text, except when it is a single-word alternative. When poetry is quoted in a footnote, a slash mark indicates a line division.

It should be noted that references to diseases, minerals, flora and fauna, architectural details, clothing, jewelry, musical instruments and other articles cannot always be identified with precision. Also, linear measurements and measures of capacity can only be approximated (see the Table of Weights and Measures). Although *Selah,* used mainly in the Psalms, is probably a musical term, its meaning is uncertain. Since it may interrupt reading and distract the reader, this word has not been kept in the English text, but every occurrence has been signaled by a footnote.

One of the main reasons the task of Bible translation is never finished is the change in our own language, English. Although a basic core of the language remains relatively stable, many diverse and complex linguistic factors continue to bring about subtle shifts in the meanings and/or connotations of even old, well-established words and phrases. One of the shifts that creates particular challenges to writers and translators alike is the manner in which gender is presented. The original NIV (1978) was published in a time when "a man" would naturally be understood, in many contexts, to be referring to a person, whether male or female. But most English speakers today tend to hear a distinctly male connotation in this word. In recognition of this change in English, this edition of the NIV, along with almost all other recent English translations, substitutes other expressions when the original text intends to refer generically to men and women equally. Thus, for instance, the NIV (1984) rendering of 1 Corinthians 8:3, "But the man who loves God is known by God" becomes in this edition "But whoever loves God is known by God." On the other hand, "man" and "mankind," as ways of denoting the human race, are still widely used. This edition of the NIV therefore continues to use these words, along with other expressions, in this way.

A related shift in English creates a greater challenge for modern translations: the move away from using the third-person masculine singular pronouns — "he/him/his" — to refer to men and women equally. This usage does persist at a low level in some forms of English, and this revision therefore occasionally uses these pronouns in a generic sense. But the tendency, recognized in day-to-day usage and confirmed by extensive research, is away from the generic use of "he," "him" and "his." In recognition of this shift in language and in an effort to translate into the "common"

English that people are actually using, this revision of the NIV generally uses other constructions when the biblical text is plainly addressed to men and women equally. The reader will frequently encounter a "they," "them" or "their" to express a generic singular idea. Thus, for instance, Mark 8:36 reads: "What good is it for someone to gain the whole world, yet forfeit their soul?" This generic use of the "indefinite" or "singular" "they/them/their" has a venerable place in English idiom and has quickly become established as standard English, spoken and written, all over the world. Where an individual emphasis is deemed to be present, "anyone" or "everyone" or some other equivalent is generally used as the antecedent of such pronouns.

Sometimes the chapter and/or verse numbering in English translations of the Old Testament differs from that found in published Hebrew texts. This is particularly the case in the Psalms, where the traditional titles are often included in the Hebrew verse numbering. Such differences are indicated in the footnotes at the bottom of the page. In the New Testament, verse numbers that marked off portions of the traditional English text not supported by the best Greek manuscripts now appear in brackets, with a footnote indicating the text that has been omitted (see, for example, Matthew 17:[21]).

Mark 16:9–20 and John 7:53–8:11, although long accorded virtually equal status with the rest of the Gospels in which they stand, have a very questionable — and confused — standing in the textual history of the New Testament, as noted in the bracketed annotations with which they are set off. A different typeface has been chosen for these passages to indicate even more clearly their uncertain status.

Basic formatting of the text, such as lining the poetry, paragraphing (both prose and poetry), setting up of (administrative-like) lists, indenting letters and lengthy prayers within narratives and the insertion of sectional headings, has been the work of the committee. However, the choice between single-column and double-column formats has been left to the publishers. Also the issuing of "red-letter" editions is a publisher's choice — one the committee does not endorse.

The committee has again been reminded that every human effort is flawed — including this revision of the NIV. We trust, however, that many will find in it an improved representation of the Word of God, through which they hear his call to faith in our Lord Jesus Christ and to service in his kingdom. We offer this version of the Bible to him in whose name and for whose glory it has been made.

The Committee on Bible Translation
September 2010

The Old Testament

Genesis

Introduction:

The word Genesis means "beginnings." The book of Genesis is about many beginnings — the beginning of the universe, the beginning of man and woman, the beginning of human sin, the beginning of God's promises and plans for salvation, and the beginning of a special relationship between Abraham and God. Genesis tells us about God's special people and his plan for their lives. Some of these people are: Adam and Eve, Noah, Abraham, Isaac, Jacob, and Joseph and his brothers.

Genesis is the first book in the Pentateuch — a word that means five books, and includes the first five books of the Bible. These books are also known as the books of the law because they contain God's instructions and laws for the people of Israel. Genesis is included because it tells the history of how Israel became God's special people. These five books were most likely written by Moses, except for the last chapter of Deuteronomy which tells about Moses' death.

Outline of contents:

The universe, the earth and human beings (1:1–2:25)
The Fall and the results of sin (3:1–5:32)
The story of Noah (6:1–9:29)
The scattering of the human race (10:1–11:32)
The life of Abraham (12:1–25:18)
Isaac and his family (25:19–26:35)
Jacob and his sons (27:1–37:1)
The life of Joseph (37:2–50:26)

The Beginning

1 In the beginning God created the heavens and the earth. ² Now the earth was formless and empty, darkness was over the surface of the deep, and the Spirit of God was hovering over the waters.

³ And God said, "Let there be light," and there was light. ⁴ God saw that the light was good, and he separated the light from the darkness. ⁵ God called the light "day," and the darkness he called "night." And there was evening, and

there was morning—the first day.

⁶And God said, "Let there be a vault between the waters to separate water from water." ⁷So God made the vault and separated the water under the vault from the water above it. And it was so. ⁸God called the vault "sky." And there was evening, and there was morning—the second day.

⁹And God said, "Let the water under the sky be gathered to one place, and let dry ground appear." And it was so. ¹⁰God called the dry ground "land," and the gathered waters he called "seas." And God saw that it was good.

¹¹Then God said, "Let the land produce vegetation: seed-bearing plants and trees on the land that bear fruit with seed in it, according to their various kinds." And it was so. ¹²The land produced vegetation: plants bearing seed according to their kinds and trees bearing fruit with seed in it according to their kinds. And God saw that it was good. ¹³And there was evening, and there was morning—the third day.

¹⁴And God said, "Let there be lights in the vault of the sky to separate the day from the night, and let them serve as signs to mark sacred times, and days and years, ¹⁵and let them be lights in the vault of the sky to give light on the earth." And it was so. ¹⁶God made two great lights—the greater light to govern the day and the lesser light to govern the night. He also made the stars. ¹⁷God set them in the vault of the sky to give light on the earth, ¹⁸to govern the day and the night, and to separate light from darkness. And God saw that it was good. ¹⁹And there was evening, and there was morning—the fourth day.

²⁰And God said, "Let the water teem with living creatures, and let birds fly above the earth across the vault of the sky." ²¹So God created the great creatures of the sea and every living thing with which the water teems and that moves about in it, according to their kinds, and every winged bird according to its kind. And God saw that it was good. ²²God blessed them and said, "Be fruitful and increase in number and fill the water in the seas, and let the birds increase on the earth." ²³And there was evening, and there was morning—the fifth day.

²⁴And God said, "Let the land produce living creatures according to their kinds: the livestock, the creatures that

move along the ground, and the wild animals, each according to its kind." And it was so. ²⁵God made the wild animals according to their kinds, the livestock according to their kinds, and all the creatures that move along the ground according to their kinds. And God saw that it was good.

²⁶Then God said, "Let us make mankind in our image, in our likeness, so that they may rule over the fish in the sea and the birds in the sky, over the livestock and all the wild animals,*a* and over all the creatures that move along the ground."

²⁷So God created mankind in
 his own image,
in the image of God he
 created them;
male and female he created
 them.

²⁸God blessed them and said to them, "Be fruitful and increase in number; fill the earth and subdue it. Rule over the fish in the sea and the birds in the sky and over every living creature that moves on the ground."

²⁹Then God said, "I give you every seed-bearing plant on the face of the whole earth and every tree that has fruit with seed in it. They will be yours for food. ³⁰And to all the beasts of the earth and all the birds in the sky and all the creatures that move along the ground—everything that has the breath of life in it—I give every green plant for food." And it was so.

³¹God saw all that he had made, and it was very good. And there was evening, and there was morning—the sixth day.

2 Thus the heavens and the earth were completed in all their vast array.

²By the seventh day God had finished the work he had been doing; so on the seventh day he rested from all his work. ³Then God blessed the seventh day and made it holy, because on it he rested from all the work of creating that he had done.

Adam and Eve

⁴This is the account of the heavens and the earth when they were created, when the LORD God made the earth and the heavens.

⁵Now no shrub had yet appeared on the earth*b* and no plant had yet sprung up, for the LORD God had not sent rain on the earth and there was no one to work the ground, ⁶but streams*c*

a 26 Probable reading of the original Hebrew text (see Syriac); Masoretic Text *the earth* *b 5* Or *land*; also in verse 6 *c 6* Or *mist* came up from the earth and watered the whole surface of the ground. **7** Then the LORD God formed a man*a* from the dust of the ground and breathed into his nostrils the breath of life, and the man became a living being.

8 Now the LORD God had planted a garden in the east, in Eden; and there he put the man he had formed. **9** The LORD God made all kinds of trees grow out of the ground — trees that were pleasing to the eye and good for food. In the middle of the garden were the tree of life and the tree of the knowledge of good and evil.

10 A river watering the garden flowed from Eden; from there it was separated into four headwaters. **11** The name of the first is the Pishon; it winds through the entire land of Havilah, where there is gold. **12** (The gold of that land is good; aromatic resin*b* and onyx are also there.) **13** The name of the second river is the Gihon; it winds through the entire land of Cush.*c* **14** The name of the third river is the Tigris; it runs along the east side of Ashur. And the fourth river is the Euphrates.

15 The LORD God took the man and put him in the Garden of Eden to work it and take care of it. **16** And the LORD God commanded the man, "You are free to eat from any tree in the garden; **17** but you must not eat from the tree of the knowledge of good and evil, for when you eat from it you will certainly die."

18 The LORD God said, "It is not good for the man to be alone. I will make a helper suitable for him."

19 Now the LORD God had formed out of the ground all the wild animals and all the birds in the sky. He brought them to the man to see what he would name them; and whatever the man called each living creature, that was its name. **20** So the man gave names to all the livestock, the birds in the sky and all the wild animals.

But for Adam*d* no suitable helper was found. **21** So the LORD God caused the man to fall into a deep sleep; and while he was sleeping, he took one of the man's ribs*e* and then closed up the place with flesh. **22** Then the LORD God made a woman from the rib*f* he had taken out of the man, and he brought her to the man.

23 The man said,

"This is now bone of my bones
  and flesh of my flesh;
she shall be called 'woman,'
  for she was taken out of
    man."

24 That is why a man leaves his father and mother and is united

---

a 7 The Hebrew for *man (adam)* sounds like and may be related to the Hebrew for *ground (adamah)*; it is also the name *Adam* (see verse 20).   *b 12* Or *good; pearls*
c 13 Possibly southeast Mesopotamia   *d 20* Or *the man*   *e 21* Or *took part of the man's side*   *f 22* Or *part*

to his wife, and they become one flesh. ²⁵Adam and his wife were both naked, and they felt no shame.

The Fall

3 Now the serpent was more crafty than any of the wild animals the LORD God had made. He said to the woman, "Did God really say, 'You must not eat from any tree in the garden'?"

²The woman said to the serpent, "We may eat fruit from the trees in the garden, ³but God did say, 'You must not eat fruit from the tree that is in the middle of the garden, and you must not touch it, or you will die.'"

⁴"You will not certainly die," the serpent said to the woman. ⁵"For God knows that when you eat from it your eyes will be opened, and you will be like God, knowing good and evil."

⁶When the woman saw that the fruit of the tree was good for food and pleasing to the eye, and also desirable for gaining wisdom, she took some and ate it. She also gave some to her husband, who was with her, and he ate it. ⁷Then the eyes of both of them were opened, and they realized they were naked; so they sewed fig leaves together and made coverings for themselves.

⁸Then the man and his wife heard the sound of the LORD God as he was walking in the garden in the cool of the day, and they hid from the LORD God among the trees of the garden. ⁹But the LORD God called to the man, "Where are you?"

¹⁰He answered, "I heard you in the garden, and I was afraid because I was naked; so I hid."

¹¹And he said, "Who told you that you were naked? Have you eaten from the tree that I commanded you not to eat from?"

¹²The man said, "The woman you put here with me — she gave me some fruit from the tree, and I ate it."

¹³Then the LORD God said to the woman, "What is this you have done?"

The woman said, "The serpent deceived me, and I ate."

¹⁴So the LORD God said to the serpent, "Because you have done this,

"Cursed are you above all
    livestock
    and all wild animals!
You will crawl on your
    belly
    and you will eat dust
    all the days of your life.
¹⁵And I will put enmity
    between you and the
        woman,
    and between your offspring*ᵃ*
        and hers;
he will crush*ᵇ* your head,
    and you will strike his
        heel."

ᵃ 15 Or *seed* *ᵇ* 15 Or *strike*

16 To the woman he said,

> "I will make your pains in
>   childbearing very severe;
>   with painful labor you will
>   give birth to children.
> Your desire will be for your
>   husband,
>   and he will rule over you."

17 To Adam he said, "Because you listened to your wife and ate fruit from the tree about which I commanded you, 'You must not eat from it,'

> "Cursed is the ground because
>   of you;
>   through painful toil you will
>   eat food from it
>   all the days of your life.
> **18** It will produce thorns and
>   thistles for you,
>   and you will eat the plants of
>   the field.
> **19** By the sweat of your brow
>   you will eat your food
> until you return to the ground,
>   since from it you were taken;
> for dust you are
>   and to dust you will return."

20 Adam[a] named his wife Eve,[b] because she would become the mother of all the living.

21 The LORD God made garments of skin for Adam and his wife and clothed them. **22** And the LORD God said, "The man has now become like one of us, knowing good and evil. He must not be allowed to reach out his hand and take also from the tree of life and eat, and live forever." **23** So the LORD God banished him from the Garden of Eden to work the ground from which he had been taken. **24** After he drove the man out, he placed on the east side[c] of the Garden of Eden cherubim and a flaming sword flashing back and forth to guard the way to the tree of life.

Cain and Abel

4 Adam[a] made love to his wife Eve, and she became pregnant and gave birth to Cain.[d] She said, "With the help of the LORD I have brought forth[e] a man." **2** Later she gave birth to his brother Abel.

Now Abel kept flocks, and Cain worked the soil. **3** In the course of time Cain brought some of the fruits of the soil as an offering to the LORD. **4** And Abel also brought an offering—fat portions from some of the firstborn of his flock. The LORD looked with favor on Abel and his offering, **5** but on Cain and his offering he did not look with favor. So Cain was very angry, and his face was downcast.

6 Then the LORD said to Cain, "Why are you angry? Why is your face downcast? **7** If you do what is

---

a 20,1 Or The man   *b 20 Eve probably means living.*   *c 24 Or placed in front*
d 1 Cain sounds like the Hebrew for brought forth or acquired.   *e 1 Or have acquired*

right, will you not be accepted? But if you do not do what is right, sin is crouching at your door; it desires to have you, but you must rule over it."

[8] Now Cain said to his brother Abel, "Let's go out to the field."[a] While they were in the field, Cain attacked his brother Abel and killed him.

[9] Then the LORD said to Cain, "Where is your brother Abel?"

"I don't know," he replied. "Am I my brother's keeper?"

[10] The LORD said, "What have you done? Listen! Your brother's blood cries out to me from the ground. [11] Now you are under a curse and driven from the ground, which opened its mouth to receive your brother's blood from your hand. [12] When you work the ground, it will no longer yield its crops for you. You will be a restless wanderer on the earth."

[13] Cain said to the LORD, "My punishment is more than I can bear. [14] Today you are driving me from the land, and I will be hidden from your presence; I will be a restless wanderer on the earth, and whoever finds me will kill me."

[15] But the LORD said to him, "Not so[b]; anyone who kills Cain will suffer vengeance seven times over." Then the LORD put a mark on Cain so that no one who found him would kill him. [16] So Cain went out from the LORD's presence and lived in the land of Nod,[c] east of Eden.

[17] Cain made love to his wife, and she became pregnant and gave birth to Enoch. Cain was then building a city, and he named it after his son Enoch. [18] To Enoch was born Irad, and Irad was the father of Mehujael, and Mehujael was the father of Methushael, and Methushael was the father of Lamech.

[19] Lamech married two women, one named Adah and the other Zillah. [20] Adah gave birth to Jabal; he was the father of those who live in tents and raise livestock. [21] His brother's name was Jubal; he was the father of all who play stringed instruments and pipes. [22] Zillah also had a son, Tubal-Cain, who forged all kinds of tools out of[d] bronze and iron. Tubal-Cain's sister was Naamah.

[23] Lamech said to his wives,

"Adah and Zillah, listen to me;
   wives of Lamech, hear my
      words.
I have killed a man for
      wounding me,
   a young man for injuring me.
[24] If Cain is avenged seven times,
   then Lamech seventy-seven
      times."

---

[a] 8 Samaritan Pentateuch, Septuagint, Vulgate and Syriac; Masoretic Text does not have *"Let's go out to the field."*   [b] 15 Septuagint, Vulgate and Syriac; Hebrew *Very well*   [c] 16 *Nod* means *wandering* (see verses 12 and 14).   [d] 22 Or *who instructed all who work in*

²⁵Adam made love to his wife again, and she gave birth to a son and named him Seth,ᵃ saying, "God has granted me another child in place of Abel, since Cain killed him." ²⁶Seth also had a son, and he named him Enosh.

At that time people began to call onᵇ the name of the LORD.

From Adam to Noah

5 This is the written account of Adam's family line.

When God created mankind, he made them in the likeness of God. ²He created them male and female and blessed them. And he named them "Mankind"ᶜ when they were created.

³When Adam had lived 130 years, he had a son in his own likeness, in his own image; and he named him Seth. ⁴After Seth was born, Adam lived 800 years and had other sons and daughters. ⁵Altogether, Adam lived a total of 930 years, and then he died.

⁶When Seth had lived 105 years, he became the fatherᵈ of Enosh. ⁷After he became the father of Enosh, Seth lived 807 years and had other sons and daughters. ⁸Altogether, Seth lived a total of 912 years, and then he died.

⁹When Enosh had lived 90 years, he became the father of Kenan. ¹⁰After he became the father of Kenan, Enosh lived 815 years and had other sons and daughters. ¹¹Altogether, Enosh lived a total of 905 years, and then he died.

¹²When Kenan had lived 70 years, he became the father of Mahalalel. ¹³After he became the father of Mahalalel, Kenan lived 840 years and had other sons and daughters. ¹⁴Altogether, Kenan lived a total of 910 years, and then he died.

¹⁵When Mahalalel had lived 65 years, he became the father of Jared. ¹⁶After he became the father of Jared, Mahalalel lived 830 years and had other sons and daughters. ¹⁷Altogether, Mahalalel lived a total of 895 years, and then he died.

¹⁸When Jared had lived 162 years, he became the father of Enoch. ¹⁹After he became the father of Enoch, Jared lived 800 years and had other sons and daughters. ²⁰Altogether, Jared lived a total of 962 years, and then he died.

²¹When Enoch had lived 65 years, he became the father of Methuselah. ²²After he became the father of Methuselah, Enoch walked faithfully with God 300 years and had other sons and daughters. ²³Altogether, Enoch lived a total of 365 years. ²⁴Enoch walked faithfully with God; then he was no more, because God took him away.

ᵃ 25 *Seth* probably means *granted*.   ᵇ 26 Or *to proclaim*   ᶜ 2 Hebrew *adam*
ᵈ 6 *Father* may mean *ancestor*; also in verses 7-26.

²⁵When Methuselah had lived 187 years, he became the father of Lamech. ²⁶After he became the father of Lamech, Methuselah lived 782 years and had other sons and daughters. ²⁷Altogether, Methuselah lived a total of 969 years, and then he died.

²⁸When Lamech had lived 182 years, he had a son. ²⁹He named him Noah[a] and said, "He will comfort us in the labor and painful toil of our hands caused by the ground the LORD has cursed." ³⁰After Noah was born, Lamech lived 595 years and had other sons and daughters. ³¹Altogether, Lamech lived a total of 777 years, and then he died.

³²After Noah was 500 years old, he became the father of Shem, Ham and Japheth.

Wickedness in the World

6 When human beings began to increase in number on the earth and daughters were born to them, ²the sons of God saw that the daughters of humans were beautiful, and they married any of them they chose. ³Then the LORD said, "My Spirit will not contend with[b] humans forever, for they are mortal[c]; their days will be a hundred and twenty years."

⁴The Nephilim were on the earth in those days—and also afterward—when the sons of God went to the daughters of humans and had children by them. They were the heroes of old, men of renown.

⁵The LORD saw how great the wickedness of the human race had become on the earth, and that every inclination of the thoughts of the human heart was only evil all the time. ⁶The LORD regretted that he had made human beings on the earth, and his heart was deeply troubled. ⁷So the LORD said, "I will wipe from the face of the earth the human race I have created—and with them the animals, the birds and the creatures that move along the ground—for I regret that I have made them." ⁸But Noah found favor in the eyes of the LORD.

Noah and the Flood

⁹This is the account of Noah and his family.

Noah was a righteous man, blameless among the people of his time, and he walked faithfully with God. ¹⁰Noah had three sons: Shem, Ham and Japheth.

¹¹Now the earth was corrupt in God's sight and was full of violence. ¹²God saw how corrupt the earth had become, for all the people on earth had corrupted their ways. ¹³So God said to Noah, "I am going to put an end to all people, for the earth is filled with violence because of them. I am surely

---

[a] 29 *Noah* sounds like the Hebrew for *comfort.*   [b] 3 Or *My spirit will not remain in*   [c] 3 Or *corrupt*

going to destroy both them and the earth. **14**So make yourself an ark of cypress*a* wood; make rooms in it and coat it with pitch inside and out. **15**This is how you are to build it: The ark is to be three hundred cubits long, fifty cubits wide and thirty cubits high.*b* **16**Make a roof for it, leaving below the roof an opening one cubit*c* high all around.*d* Put a door in the side of the ark and make lower, middle and upper decks. **17**I am going to bring floodwaters on the earth to destroy all life under the heavens, every creature that has the breath of life in it. Everything on earth will perish. **18**But I will establish my covenant with you, and you will enter the ark—you and your sons and your wife and your sons' wives with you. **19**You are to bring into the ark two of all living creatures, male and female, to keep them alive with you. **20**Two of every kind of bird, of every kind of animal and of every kind of creature that moves along the ground will come to you to be kept alive. **21**You are to take every kind of food that is to be eaten and store it away as food for you and for them."

22Noah did everything just as God commanded him.

7 The LORD then said to Noah, "Go into the ark, you and your whole family, because I have found you righteous in this generation. **2**Take with you seven pairs of every kind of clean animal, a male and its mate, and one pair of every kind of unclean animal, a male and its mate, **3**and also seven pairs of every kind of bird, male and female, to keep their various kinds alive throughout the earth. **4**Seven days from now I will send rain on the earth for forty days and forty nights, and I will wipe from the face of the earth every living creature I have made."

5And Noah did all that the LORD commanded him.

6Noah was six hundred years old when the floodwaters came on the earth. **7**And Noah and his sons and his wife and his sons' wives entered the ark to escape the waters of the flood. **8**Pairs of clean and unclean animals, of birds and of all creatures that move along the ground, **9**male and female, came to Noah and entered the ark, as God had commanded Noah. **10**And after the seven days the floodwaters came on the earth.

11In the six hundredth year of Noah's life, on the seventeenth day of the second month—on that day all the springs of the great deep burst forth, and the floodgates of the heavens were

---

a 14 The meaning of the Hebrew for this word is uncertain.   *b* 15 That is, about 450 feet long, 75 feet wide and 45 feet high or about 135 meters long, 23 meters wide and 14 meters high   *c* 16 That is, about 18 inches or about 45 centimeters   *d* 16 The meaning of the Hebrew for this clause is uncertain.

opened. [12]And rain fell on the earth forty days and forty nights.

[13]On that very day Noah and his sons, Shem, Ham and Japheth, together with his wife and the wives of his three sons, entered the ark. [14]They had with them every wild animal according to its kind, all livestock according to their kinds, every creature that moves along the ground according to its kind and every bird according to its kind, everything with wings. [15]Pairs of all creatures that have the breath of life in them came to Noah and entered the ark. [16]The animals going in were male and female of every living thing, as God had commanded Noah. Then the LORD shut him in.

[17]For forty days the flood kept coming on the earth, and as the waters increased they lifted the ark high above the earth. [18]The waters rose and increased greatly on the earth, and the ark floated on the surface of the water. [19]They rose greatly on the earth, and all the high mountains under the entire heavens were covered. [20]The waters rose and covered the mountains to a depth of more than fifteen cubits.[a,b] [21]Every living thing that moved on land perished—birds, livestock, wild animals, all the creatures that swarm over the earth, and all mankind. [22]Everything on dry land that had the breath of life in its nostrils died. [23]Every living thing on the face of the earth was wiped out; people and animals and the creatures that move along the ground and the birds were wiped from the earth. Only Noah was left, and those with him in the ark.

[24]The waters flooded the earth for a hundred and fifty days.

8 But God remembered Noah and all the wild animals and the livestock that were with him in the ark, and he sent a wind over the earth, and the waters receded. [2]Now the springs of the deep and the floodgates of the heavens had been closed, and the rain had stopped falling from the sky. [3]The water receded steadily from the earth. At the end of the hundred and fifty days the water had gone down, [4]and on the seventeenth day of the seventh month the ark came to rest on the mountains of Ararat. [5]The waters continued to recede until the tenth month, and on the first day of the tenth month the tops of the mountains became visible.

[6]After forty days Noah opened a window he had made in the ark [7]and sent out a raven, and it kept flying back and forth until the water had dried up from the earth. [8]Then he sent out a dove to see if the water had receded from the surface of the ground. [9]But the dove could find nowhere to

---

[a] 20 That is, about 23 feet or about 6.8 meters   [b] 20 Or *rose more than fifteen*
cubits, and the mountains were covered

perch because there was water over all the surface of the earth; so it returned to Noah in the ark. He reached out his hand and took the dove and brought it back to himself in the ark. ¹⁰He waited seven more days and again sent out the dove from the ark. ¹¹When the dove returned to him in the evening, there in its beak was a freshly plucked olive leaf! Then Noah knew that the water had receded from the earth. ¹²He waited seven more days and sent the dove out again, but this time it did not return to him.

¹³By the first day of the first month of Noah's six hundred and first year, the water had dried up from the earth. Noah then removed the covering from the ark and saw that the surface of the ground was dry. ¹⁴By the twenty-seventh day of the second month the earth was completely dry.

¹⁵Then God said to Noah, ¹⁶"Come out of the ark, you and your wife and your sons and their wives. ¹⁷Bring out every kind of living creature that is with you — the birds, the animals, and all the creatures that move along the ground — so they can multiply on the earth and be fruitful and increase in number on it."

¹⁸So Noah came out, together with his sons and his wife and his sons' wives. ¹⁹All the animals and all the creatures that move along the ground and all the birds — everything that moves on land — came out of the ark, one kind after another.

²⁰Then Noah built an altar to the LORD and, taking some of all the clean animals and clean birds, he sacrificed burnt offerings on it. ²¹The LORD smelled the pleasing aroma and said in his heart: "Never again will I curse the ground because of humans, even though[a] every inclination of the human heart is evil from childhood. And never again will I destroy all living creatures, as I have done.

²² "As long as the earth endures,
    seedtime and harvest,
    cold and heat,
    summer and winter,
    day and night
    will never cease."

God's Covenant With Noah

9 Then God blessed Noah and his sons, saying to them, "Be fruitful and increase in number and fill the earth. ²The fear and dread of you will fall on all the beasts of the earth, and on all the birds in the sky, on every creature that moves along the ground, and on all the fish in the sea; they are given into your hands. ³Everything that lives and moves about will be food for you. Just as I gave you the green plants, I now give you everything.

⁴"But you must not eat meat that has its lifeblood still in it.

---

[a] 21 Or humans, for

[5]And for your lifeblood I will surely demand an accounting. I will demand an accounting from every animal. And from each human being, too, I will demand an accounting for the life of another human being.

[6] "Whoever sheds human blood,
　by humans shall their blood
　　be shed;
　for in the image of God
　　has God made mankind.

[7]As for you, be fruitful and increase in number; multiply on the earth and increase upon it."

[8]Then God said to Noah and to his sons with him: [9]"I now establish my covenant with you and with your descendants after you [10]and with every living creature that was with you—the birds, the livestock and all the wild animals, all those that came out of the ark with you—every living creature on earth. [11]I establish my covenant with you: Never again will all life be destroyed by the waters of a flood; never again will there be a flood to destroy the earth."

[12]And God said, "This is the sign of the covenant I am making between me and you and every living creature with you, a covenant for all generations to come: [13]I have set my rainbow in the clouds, and it will be the sign of the covenant between me and the earth. [14]Whenever I bring clouds over the earth and the rainbow appears in the clouds, [15]I will remember my covenant between me and you and all living creatures of every kind. Never again will the waters become a flood to destroy all life. [16]Whenever the rainbow appears in the clouds, I will see it and remember the everlasting covenant between God and all living creatures of every kind on the earth."

[17]So God said to Noah, "This is the sign of the covenant I have established between me and all life on the earth."

The Sons of Noah

[18]The sons of Noah who came out of the ark were Shem, Ham and Japheth. (Ham was the father of Canaan.) [19]These were the three sons of Noah, and from them came the people who were scattered over the whole earth.

[20]Noah, a man of the soil, proceeded[a] to plant a vineyard. [21]When he drank some of its wine, he became drunk and lay uncovered inside his tent. [22]Ham, the father of Canaan, saw his father naked and told his two brothers outside. [23]But Shem and Japheth took a garment and laid it across their shoulders; then they walked in backward and covered their father's naked body. Their faces were turned the other way so that they would not see their father naked.

---

[a] 20 Or *soil, was the first*

²⁴When Noah awoke from his wine and found out what his youngest son had done to him, ²⁵he said,

"Cursed be Canaan!
    The lowest of slaves
    will he be to his brothers."

²⁶He also said,

"Praise be to the LORD, the
        God of Shem!
    May Canaan be the slave of
        Shem.
²⁷May God extend Japheth's*ᵃ*
        territory;
    may Japheth live in the tents
        of Shem,
    and may Canaan be the
        slave of Japheth."

²⁸After the flood Noah lived 350 years. ²⁹Noah lived a total of 950 years, and then he died.

The Table of Nations

10 This is the account of Shem, Ham and Japheth, Noah's sons, who themselves had sons after the flood.

The Japhethites

²The sonsᵇ of Japheth:
    Gomer, Magog, Madai, Javan, Tubal, Meshek and Tiras.

³The sons of Gomer:
    Ashkenaz, Riphath and Togarmah.
⁴The sons of Javan:
    Elishah, Tarshish, the Kittites and the Rodanites.ᶜ
⁵(From these the maritime peoples spread out into their territories by their clans within their nations, each with its own language.)

The Hamites

⁶The sons of Ham:
    Cush, Egypt, Put and Canaan.
⁷The sons of Cush:
    Seba, Havilah, Sabtah, Raamah and Sabteka.
The sons of Raamah:
    Sheba and Dedan.

⁸Cush was the fatherᵈ of Nimrod, who became a mighty warrior on the earth. ⁹He was a mighty hunter before the LORD; that is why it is said, "Like Nimrod, a mighty hunter before the LORD." ¹⁰The first centers of his kingdom were Babylon, Uruk, Akkad and Kalneh, inᵉ Shinar.ᶠ ¹¹From that land he went to Assyria, where he built Nineveh, Rehoboth Ir,ᵍ Calah ¹²and Resen, which is between Nineveh and Calah—which is the great city.

ᵃ 27 *Japheth* sounds like the Hebrew for *extend.*   ᵇ 2 *Sons* may mean *descendants* or *successors* or *nations*; also in verses 3, 4, 6, 7, 20-23, 29 and 31.
ᶜ 4 Some manuscripts of the Masoretic Text and Samaritan Pentateuch (see also Septuagint and 1 Chron. 1:7); most manuscripts of the Masoretic Text *Dodanites*
ᵈ 8 *Father* may mean *ancestor* or *predecessor* or *founder*; also in verses 13, 15, 24 and 26.   ᵉ 10 Or *Uruk and Akkad—all of them in*   ᶠ 10 That is, Babylonia
ᵍ 11 Or *Nineveh with its city squares*

¹³Egypt was the father of
the Ludites, Anamites,
Lehabites, Naphtuhites,
¹⁴Pathrusites, Kasluhites
(from whom the Philistines
came) and Caphtorites.

¹⁵Canaan was the father of
Sidon his firstborn,ᵃ and of
the Hittites, ¹⁶Jebusites, Am-
orites, Girgashites, ¹⁷Hivites,
Arkites, Sinites, ¹⁸Arvadites,
Zemarites and Hamathites.

Later the Canaanite clans scattered ¹⁹and the borders of Canaan reached from Sidon toward
Gerar as far as Gaza, and then toward Sodom, Gomorrah, Admah
and Zeboyim, as far as Lasha.

²⁰These are the sons of Ham
by their clans and languages, in
their territories and nations.

The Semites

²¹Sons were also born to Shem,
whose older brother wasᵇ Japheth; Shem was the ancestor of
all the sons of Eber.

²²The sons of Shem:
Elam, Ashur, Arphaxad,
Lud and Aram.

²³The sons of Aram:
Uz, Hul, Gether and Me-
shek.ᶜ

²⁴Arphaxad was the father ofᵈ
Shelah,
and Shelah the father of
Eber.

²⁵Two sons were born to Eber:
One was named Peleg,ᵉ be-
cause in his time the earth
was divided; his brother
was named Joktan.

²⁶Joktan was the father of
Almodad, Sheleph, Ha-
zarmaveth, Jerah, ²⁷Hado-
ram, Uzal, Diklah, ²⁸Obal,
Abimael, Sheba, ²⁹Ophir,
Havilah and Jobab. All
these were sons of Joktan.

³⁰The region where they lived
stretched from Mesha toward Se-
phar, in the eastern hill country.

³¹These are the sons of Shem
by their clans and languages, in
their territories and nations.

³²These are the clans of Noah's sons, according to their lines
of descent, within their nations.
From these the nations spread
out over the earth after the flood.

The Tower of Babel

11 Now the whole world had
one language and a com-
mon speech. ²As people moved
eastward,ᶠ they found a plain in
Shinarᵍ and settled there.

³They said to each other,
"Come, let's make bricks and
bake them thoroughly." They
used brick instead of stone, and
tar for mortar. ⁴Then they said,
"Come, let us build ourselves a
city, with a tower that reaches to

ᵃ 15 Or *of the Sidonians, the foremost*   ᵇ 21 Or *Shem, the older brother of*
ᶜ 23 See Septuagint and 1 Chron. 1:17; Hebrew *Mash.*   ᵈ 24 Hebrew; Septuagint
father of Cainan, and Cainan was the father of   ᵉ 25 *Peleg* means *division.*
ᶠ 2 Or *from the east;* or *in the east*   ᵍ 2 That is, Babylonia

the heavens, so that we may make a name for ourselves; otherwise we will be scattered over the face of the whole earth."

⁵But the LORD came down to see the city and the tower the people were building. ⁶The LORD said, "If as one people speaking the same language they have begun to do this, then nothing they plan to do will be impossible for them. ⁷Come, let us go down and confuse their language so they will not understand each other."

⁸So the LORD scattered them from there over all the earth, and they stopped building the city. ⁹That is why it was called Babel^a—because there the LORD confused the language of the whole world. From there the LORD scattered them over the face of the whole earth.

From Shem to Abram

¹⁰This is the account of Shem's family line.

Two years after the flood, when Shem was 100 years old, he became the father^b of Arphaxad. ¹¹And after he became the father of Arphaxad, Shem lived 500 years and had other sons and daughters.

¹²When Arphaxad had lived 35 years, he became the father of Shelah. ¹³And after he became the father of Shelah, Arphaxad lived 403 years and had other sons and daughters.^c

¹⁴When Shelah had lived 30 years, he became the father of Eber. ¹⁵And after he became the father of Eber, Shelah lived 403 years and had other sons and daughters.

¹⁶When Eber had lived 34 years, he became the father of Peleg. ¹⁷And after he became the father of Peleg, Eber lived 430 years and had other sons and daughters.

¹⁸When Peleg had lived 30 years, he became the father of Reu. ¹⁹And after he became the father of Reu, Peleg lived 209 years and had other sons and daughters.

²⁰When Reu had lived 32 years, he became the father of Serug. ²¹And after he became the father of Serug, Reu lived 207 years and had other sons and daughters.

²²When Serug had lived 30 years, he became the father of Nahor. ²³And after he became the father of Nahor, Serug lived 200 years and had other sons and daughters.

²⁴When Nahor had lived 29 years, he became the father of Terah. ²⁵And after he became

---

^a 9 That is, Babylon; *Babel* sounds like the Hebrew for *confused.* ^b 10 *Father* may mean *ancestor*; also in verses 11-25. ^c 12,13 Hebrew; Septuagint (see also Luke 3:35, 36 and note at Gen. 10:24) *35 years, he became the father of Cainan.* ¹³*And after he became the father of Cainan, Arphaxad lived 430 years and had other sons and daughters, and then he died. When Cainan had lived 130 years, he became the father of Shelah. And after he became the father of Shelah, Cainan lived 330 years and had other sons and daughters* the father of Terah, Nahor lived 119 years and had other sons and daughters.

²⁶ After Terah had lived 70 years, he became the father of Abram, Nahor and Haran.

Abram's Family

²⁷ This is the account of Terah's family line.

Terah became the father of Abram, Nahor and Haran. And Haran became the father of Lot. ²⁸ While his father Terah was still alive, Haran died in Ur of the Chaldeans, in the land of his birth. ²⁹ Abram and Nahor both married. The name of Abram's wife was Sarai, and the name of Nahor's wife was Milkah; she was the daughter of Haran, the father of both Milkah and Iskah. ³⁰ Now Sarai was childless because she was not able to conceive.

³¹ Terah took his son Abram, his grandson Lot son of Haran, and his daughter-in-law Sarai, the wife of his son Abram, and together they set out from Ur of the Chaldeans to go to Canaan. But when they came to Harran, they settled there.

³² Terah lived 205 years, and he died in Harran.

The Call of Abram

12 The LORD had said to Abram, "Go from your country, your people and your fa-ther's household to the land I will show you.

² "I will make you into a great nation,
    and I will bless you;
I will make your name great,
    and you will be a blessing.ᵃ
³ I will bless those who bless you,
    and whoever curses you I will curse;
and all peoples on earth
    will be blessed through you."ᵇ

⁴ So Abram went, as the LORD had told him; and Lot went with him. Abram was seventy-five years old when he set out from Harran. ⁵ He took his wife Sarai, his nephew Lot, all the possessions they had accumulated and the people they had acquired in Harran, and they set out for the land of Canaan, and they arrived there.

⁶ Abram traveled through the land as far as the site of the great tree of Moreh at Shechem. At that time the Canaanites were in the land. ⁷ The LORD appeared to Abram and said, "To your off-springᶜ I will give this land." So he built an altar there to the LORD, who had appeared to him.

⁸ From there he went on to-ward the hills east of Bethel and pitched his tent, with Bethel on the west and Ai on the east. Ther

---

ᵃ 2 Or *be seen as blessed*   ᵇ 3 Or *earth / will use your name in blessings* (see 48:20)   ᶜ 7 Or *seed* he built an altar to the Lord and called on the name of the Lord.

⁹Then Abram set out and continued toward the Negev.

Abram in Egypt

¹⁰Now there was a famine in the land, and Abram went down to Egypt to live there for a while because the famine was severe. ¹¹As he was about to enter Egypt, he said to his wife Sarai, "I know what a beautiful woman you are. ¹²When the Egyptians see you, they will say, 'This is his wife.' Then they will kill me but will let you live. ¹³Say you are my sister, so that I will be treated well for your sake and my life will be spared because of you."

¹⁴When Abram came to Egypt, the Egyptians saw that Sarai was a very beautiful woman. ¹⁵And when Pharaoh's officials saw her, they praised her to Pharaoh, and she was taken into his palace. ¹⁶He treated Abram well for her sake, and Abram acquired sheep and cattle, male and female donkeys, male and female servants, and camels.

¹⁷But the Lord inflicted serious diseases on Pharaoh and his household because of Abram's wife Sarai. ¹⁸So Pharaoh summoned Abram. "What have you done to me?" he said. "Why didn't you tell me she was your wife? ¹⁹Why did you say, 'She is my sister,' so that I took her to be my wife? Now then, here is your wife. Take her and go!" ²⁰Then Pharaoh gave orders about Abram to his men, and they sent him on his way, with his wife and everything he had.

Abram and Lot Separate

13 So Abram went up from Egypt to the Negev, with his wife and everything he had, and Lot went with him. ²Abram had become very wealthy in livestock and in silver and gold.

³From the Negev he went from place to place until he came to Bethel, to the place between Bethel and Ai where his tent had been earlier ⁴and where he had first built an altar. There Abram called on the name of the Lord.

⁵Now Lot, who was moving about with Abram, also had flocks and herds and tents. ⁶But the land could not support them while they stayed together, for their possessions were so great that they were not able to stay together. ⁷And quarreling arose between Abram's herders and Lot's. The Canaanites and Perizzites were also living in the land at that time.

⁸So Abram said to Lot, "Let's not have any quarreling between you and me, or between your herders and mine, for we are close relatives. ⁹Is not the whole land before you? Let's part company. If you go to the left, I'll go to the right; if you go to the right, I'll go to the left."

¹⁰Lot looked around and saw that the whole plain of the Jordan toward Zoar was well watered, like the garden of the LORD, like the land of Egypt. (This was before the LORD destroyed Sodom and Gomorrah.) ¹¹So Lot chose for himself the whole plain of the Jordan and set out toward the east. The two men parted company: ¹²Abram lived in the land of Canaan, while Lot lived among the cities of the plain and pitched his tents near Sodom. ¹³Now the people of Sodom were wicked and were sinning greatly against the LORD.

¹⁴The LORD said to Abram after Lot had parted from him, "Look around from where you are, to the north and south, to the east and west. ¹⁵All the land that you see I will give to you and your offspring[a] forever. ¹⁶I will make your offspring like the dust of the earth, so that if anyone could count the dust, then your offspring could be counted. ¹⁷Go, walk through the length and breadth of the land, for I am giving it to you."

¹⁸So Abram went to live near the great trees of Mamre at Hebron, where he pitched his tents. There he built an altar to the LORD.

Abram Rescues Lot

14 At the time when Amraphel was king of Shinar,[b] Arioch king of Ellasar, Kedorlao-mer king of Elam and Tidal king of Goyim, ²these kings went to war against Bera king of Sodom, Birsha king of Gomorrah, Shinab king of Admah, Shemeber king of Zeboyim, and the king of Bela (that is, Zoar). ³All these latter kings joined forces in the Valley of Siddim (that is, the Dead Sea Valley). ⁴For twelve years they had been subject to Kedorlaomer, but in the thirteenth year they rebelled.

⁵In the fourteenth year, Kedorlaomer and the kings allied with him went out and defeated the Rephaites in Ashteroth Karnaim, the Zuzites in Ham, the Emites in Shaveh Kiriathaim ⁶and the Horites in the hill country of Seir, as far as El Paran near the desert. ⁷Then they turned back and went to En Mishpat (that is, Kadesh), and they conquered the whole territory of the Amalekites, as well as the Amorites who were living in Hazezon Tamar.

⁸Then the king of Sodom, the king of Gomorrah, the king of Admah, the king of Zeboyim and the king of Bela (that is, Zoar) marched out and drew up their battle lines in the Valley of Siddim ⁹against Kedorlaomer king of Elam, Tidal king of Goyim, Amraphel king of Shinar and Arioch king of Ellasar—four kings against five. ¹⁰Now the Valley of Siddim was full of tar pits, and when the kings of Sodom

---

[a] 15 Or *seed*; also in verse 16   [b] 1 That is, Babylonia; also in verse 9

Gomorrah fled, some of the men fell into them and the rest fled to the hills. **11** The four kings seized all the goods of Sodom and Gomorrah and all their food; then they went away. **12** They also carried off Abram's nephew Lot and his possessions, since he was living in Sodom.

13 A man who had escaped came and reported this to Abram the Hebrew. Now Abram was living near the great trees of Mamre the Amorite, a brother*a* of Eshkol and Aner, all of whom were allied with Abram. **14** When Abram heard that his relative had been taken captive, he called out the 318 trained men born in his household and went in pursuit as far as Dan. **15** During the night Abram divided his men to attack them and he routed them, pursuing them as far as Hobah, north of Damascus. **16** He recovered all the goods and brought back his relative Lot and his possessions, together with the women and the other people.

17 After Abram returned from defeating Kedorlaomer and the kings allied with him, the king of Sodom came out to meet him in the Valley of Shaveh (that is, the King's Valley).

18 Then Melchizedek king of Salem brought out bread and wine. He was priest of God Most High, **19** and he blessed Abram, saying,

"Blessed be Abram by God
   Most High,
  Creator of heaven and earth.
20 And praise be to God Most
   High,
  who delivered your enemies
   into your hand."

Then Abram gave him a tenth of everything.

21 The king of Sodom said to Abram, "Give me the people and keep the goods for yourself."

22 But Abram said to the king of Sodom, "With raised hand I have sworn an oath to the LORD, God Most High, Creator of heaven and earth, **23** that I will accept nothing belonging to you, not even a thread or the strap of a sandal, so that you will never be able to say, 'I made Abram rich.' **24** I will accept nothing but what my men have eaten and the share that belongs to the men who went with me — to Aner, Eshkol and Mamre. Let them have their share."

The LORD's Covenant With Abram

15 After this, the word of the LORD came to Abram in a vision:

"Do not be afraid, Abram.
  I am your shield,*b*
  your very great reward.*c*"

2 But Abram said, "Sovereign LORD, what can you give me since

---

a 13 Or *a relative*; or *an ally*   *b* 1 Or *sovereign*   *c* 1 Or *shield; / your reward will be very great*

I remain childless and the one who will inherit[a] my estate is Eliezer of Damascus?" ³And Abram said, "You have given me no children; so a servant in my household will be my heir."

⁴Then the word of the LORD came to him: "This man will not be your heir, but a son who is your own flesh and blood will be your heir." ⁵He took him outside and said, "Look up at the sky and count the stars—if indeed you can count them." Then he said to him, "So shall your offspring[b] be."

⁶Abram believed the LORD, and he credited it to him as righteousness.

⁷He also said to him, "I am the LORD, who brought you out of Ur of the Chaldeans to give you this land to take possession of it."

⁸But Abram said, "Sovereign LORD, how can I know that I will gain possession of it?"

⁹So the LORD said to him, "Bring me a heifer, a goat and a ram, each three years old, along with a dove and a young pigeon." ¹⁰Abram brought all these to him, cut them in two and arranged the halves opposite each other; the birds, however, he did not cut in half. ¹¹Then birds of prey came down on the carcasses, but Abram drove them away.

¹²As the sun was setting, Abram fell into a deep sleep, and a thick and dreadful darkness came over him. ¹³Then the LORD said to him, "Know for certain that for four hundred years your descendants will be strangers in a country not their own and that they will be enslaved and mistreated there. ¹⁴But I will punish the nation they serve as slaves, and afterward they will come out with great possessions. ¹⁵You, however, will go to your ancestors in peace and be buried at a good old age. ¹⁶In the fourth generation your descendants will come back here, for the sin of the Amorites has not yet reached its full measure."

¹⁷When the sun had set and darkness had fallen, a smoking firepot with a blazing torch appeared and passed between the pieces. ¹⁸On that day the LORD made a covenant with Abram and said, "To your descendants I give this land, from the Wadi[c] of Egypt to the great river, the Euphrates— ¹⁹the land of the Kenites, Kenizzites, Kadmonites, ²⁰Hittites, Perizzites, Rephaites, ²¹Amorites, Canaanites, Girgashites and Jebusites."

Hagar and Ishmael

16 Now Sarai, Abram's wife, had borne him no children. But she had an Egyptian slave named Hagar; ²so she said to Abram, "The LORD has kept me

---

[a] 2 The meaning of the Hebrew for this phrase is uncertain.   [b] 5 Or *seed*
[c] 18 Or *river*

from having children. Go, sleep with my slave; perhaps I can build a family through her."

Abram agreed to what Sarai said. ³So after Abram had been living in Canaan ten years, Sarai his wife took her Egyptian slave Hagar and gave her to her husband to be his wife. ⁴He slept with Hagar, and she conceived.

When she knew she was pregnant, she began to despise her mistress. ⁵Then Sarai said to Abram, "You are responsible for the wrong I am suffering. I put my slave in your arms, and now that she knows she is pregnant, she despises me. May the LORD judge between you and me."

⁶"Your slave is in your hands," Abram said. "Do with her whatever you think best." Then Sarai mistreated Hagar; so she fled from her.

⁷The angel of the LORD found Hagar near a spring in the desert; it was the spring that is beside the road to Shur. ⁸And he said, "Hagar, slave of Sarai, where have you come from, and where are you going?"

"I'm running away from my mistress Sarai," she answered.

⁹Then the angel of the LORD told her, "Go back to your mistress and submit to her." ¹⁰The angel added, "I will increase your descendants so much that they will be too numerous to count."

¹¹The angel of the LORD also said to her:

"You are now pregnant
    and you will give birth to a
        son.
You shall name him Ishmael,ᵃ
    for the LORD has heard of
        your misery.
¹²He will be a wild donkey of a
        man;
    his hand will be against
        everyone
    and everyone's hand against
        him,
and he will live in hostility
    towardᵇ all his brothers."

¹³She gave this name to the LORD who spoke to her: "You are the God who sees me," for she said, "I have now seenᶜ the One who sees me." ¹⁴That is why the well was called Beer Lahai Roiᵈ; it is still there, between Kadesh and Bered.

¹⁵So Hagar bore Abram a son, and Abram gave the name Ishmael to the son she had borne. ¹⁶Abram was eighty-six years old when Hagar bore him Ishmael.

The Covenant of Circumcision

17 When Abram was ninety-nine years old, the LORD appeared to him and said, "I am God Almightyᵉ; walk before

---

ᵃ 11 Ishmael means God hears.   ᵇ 12 Or live to the east / of   ᶜ 13 Or seen the back of   ᵈ 14 Beer Lahai Roi means well of the Living One who sees me.
ᵉ 1 Hebrew El-Shaddai

me faithfully and be blameless. ²Then I will make my covenant between me and you and will greatly increase your numbers."

³Abram fell facedown, and God said to him, ⁴"As for me, this is my covenant with you: You will be the father of many nations. ⁵No longer will you be called Abram*a*; your name will be Abraham,*b* for I have made you a father of many nations. ⁶I will make you very fruitful; I will make nations of you, and kings will come from you. ⁷I will establish my covenant as an everlasting covenant between me and you and your descendants after you for the generations to come, to be your God and the God of your descendants after you. ⁸The whole land of Canaan, where you now reside as a foreigner, I will give as an everlasting possession to you and your descendants after you; and I will be their God."

⁹Then God said to Abraham, "As for you, you must keep my covenant, you and your descendants after you for the generations to come. ¹⁰This is my covenant with you and your descendants after you, the covenant you are to keep: Every male among you shall be circumcised. ¹¹You are to undergo circumcision, and it will be the sign of the covenant between me and you. ¹²For the generations to come every male among you who is eight days old must be circumcised, including those born in your household or bought with money from a foreigner — those who are not your offspring. ¹³Whether born in your household or bought with your money, they must be circumcised. My covenant in your flesh is to be an everlasting covenant. ¹⁴Any uncircumcised male, who has not been circumcised in the flesh, will be cut off from his people; he has broken my covenant."

¹⁵God also said to Abraham, "As for Sarai your wife, you are no longer to call her Sarai; her name will be Sarah. ¹⁶I will bless her and will surely give you a son by her. I will bless her so that she will be the mother of nations; kings of peoples will come from her."

¹⁷Abraham fell facedown; he laughed and said to himself, "Will a son be born to a man a hundred years old? Will Sarah bear a child at the age of ninety?" ¹⁸And Abraham said to God, "If only Ishmael might live under your blessing!"

¹⁹Then God said, "Yes, but your wife Sarah will bear you a son, and you will call him Isaac.*c* I will establish my covenant with him as an everlasting covenant for his descendants after him. ²⁰And as for Ishmael, I have heard you: I

---

a 5 *Abram* means *exalted father.*   *b* 5 *Abraham* probably means *father of many.*
c 19 *Isaac* means *he laughs.*

will surely bless him; I will make him fruitful and will greatly increase his numbers. He will be the father of twelve rulers, and I will make him into a great nation. ²¹ But my covenant I will establish with Isaac, whom Sarah will bear to you by this time next year." ²² When he had finished speaking with Abraham, God went up from him.

²³ On that very day Abraham took his son Ishmael and all those born in his household or bought with his money, every male in his household, and circumcised them, as God told him. ²⁴ Abraham was ninety-nine years old when he was circumcised, ²⁵ and his son Ishmael was thirteen; ²⁶ Abraham and his son Ishmael were both circumcised on that very day. ²⁷ And every male in Abraham's household, including those born in his household or bought from a foreigner, was circumcised with him.

The Three Visitors

18 The LORD appeared to Abraham near the great trees of Mamre while he was sitting at the entrance to his tent in the heat of the day. ² Abraham looked up and saw three men standing nearby. When he saw them, he hurried from the entrance of his tent to meet them and bowed low to the ground.

³ He said, "If I have found favor in your eyes, my lord,^a do not pass your servant by. ⁴ Let a little water be brought, and then you may all wash your feet and rest under this tree. ⁵ Let me get you something to eat, so you can be refreshed and then go on your way — now that you have come to your servant."

"Very well," they answered, "do as you say."

⁶ So Abraham hurried into the tent to Sarah. "Quick," he said, "get three seahs^b of the finest flour and knead it and bake some bread."

⁷ Then he ran to the herd and selected a choice, tender calf and gave it to a servant, who hurried to prepare it. ⁸ He then brought some curds and milk and the calf that had been prepared, and set these before them. While they ate, he stood near them under a tree.

⁹ "Where is your wife Sarah?" they asked him.

"There, in the tent," he said.

¹⁰ Then one of them said, "I will surely return to you about this time next year, and Sarah your wife will have a son."

Now Sarah was listening at the entrance to the tent, which was behind him. ¹¹ Abraham and Sarah were already very old, and Sarah was past the age of childbearing. ¹² So Sarah laughed to herself as she thought, "After I am worn out and my lord is old, will I now have this pleasure?"

---

^a 3 Or eyes, Lord   ^b 6 That is, probably about 36 pounds or about 16 kilograms

¹³Then the LORD said to Abraham, "Why did Sarah laugh and say, 'Will I really have a child, now that I am old?' ¹⁴Is anything too hard for the LORD? I will return to you at the appointed time next year, and Sarah will have a son."

¹⁵Sarah was afraid, so she lied and said, "I did not laugh."

But he said, "Yes, you did laugh."

Abraham Pleads for Sodom

¹⁶When the men got up to leave, they looked down toward Sodom, and Abraham walked along with them to see them on their way. ¹⁷Then the LORD said, "Shall I hide from Abraham what I am about to do? ¹⁸Abraham will surely become a great and powerful nation, and all nations on earth will be blessed through him.^a ¹⁹For I have chosen him, so that he will direct his children and his household after him to keep the way of the LORD by doing what is right and just, so that the LORD will bring about for Abraham what he has promised him."

²⁰Then the LORD said, "The outcry against Sodom and Gomorrah is so great and their sin so grievous ²¹that I will go down and see if what they have done is as bad as the outcry that has reached me. If not, I will know."

²²The men turned away and went toward Sodom, but Abraham remained standing before the LORD.^b ²³Then Abraham approached him and said: "Will you sweep away the righteous with the wicked? ²⁴What if there are fifty righteous people in the city? Will you really sweep it away and not spare^c the place for the sake of the fifty righteous people in it? ²⁵Far be it from you to do such a thing—to kill the righteous with the wicked, treating the righteous and the wicked alike. Far be it from you! Will not the Judge of all the earth do right?"

²⁶The LORD said, "If I find fifty righteous people in the city of Sodom, I will spare the whole place for their sake."

²⁷Then Abraham spoke up again: "Now that I have been so bold as to speak to the Lord, though I am nothing but dust and ashes, ²⁸what if the number of the righteous is five less than fifty? Will you destroy the whole city for lack of five people?"

"If I find forty-five there," he said, "I will not destroy it."

²⁹Once again he spoke to him, "What if only forty are found there?"

He said, "For the sake of forty, I will not do it."

³⁰Then he said, "May the Lord not be angry, but let me speak.

---

^a 18 Or *will use his name in blessings* (see 48:20) ^b 22 Masoretic Text; an ancient Hebrew scribal tradition *but the* LORD *remained standing before Abraham* ^c 24 Or *forgive*; also in verse 26

What if only thirty can be found there?"

He answered, "I will not do it if I find thirty there."

³¹ Abraham said, "Now that I have been so bold as to speak to the Lord, what if only twenty can be found there?"

He said, "For the sake of twenty, I will not destroy it."

³² Then he said, "May the Lord not be angry, but let me speak just once more. What if only ten can be found there?"

He answered, "For the sake of ten, I will not destroy it."

³³ When the LORD had finished speaking with Abraham, he left, and Abraham returned home.

Sodom and Gomorrah Destroyed

19 The two angels arrived at Sodom in the evening, and Lot was sitting in the gateway of the city. When he saw them, he got up to meet them and bowed down with his face to the ground. ² "My lords," he said, "please turn aside to your servant's house. You can wash your feet and spend the night and then go on your way early in the morning."

"No," they answered, "we will spend the night in the square."

³ But he insisted so strongly that they did go with him and entered his house. He prepared a meal for them, baking bread without yeast, and they ate. ⁴ Before they had gone to bed, all the men from every part of the city of Sodom — both young and old — surrounded the house. ⁵ They called to Lot, "Where are the men who came to you tonight? Bring them out to us so that we can have sex with them."

⁶ Lot went outside to meet them and shut the door behind him ⁷ and said, "No, my friends. Don't do this wicked thing. ⁸ Look, I have two daughters who have never slept with a man. Let me bring them out to you, and you can do what you like with them. But don't do anything to these men, for they have come under the protection of my roof."

⁹ "Get out of our way," they replied. "This fellow came here as a foreigner, and now he wants to play the judge! We'll treat you worse than them." They kept bringing pressure on Lot and moved forward to break down the door.

¹⁰ But the men inside reached out and pulled Lot back into the house and shut the door. ¹¹ Then they struck the men who were at the door of the house, young and old, with blindness so that they could not find the door.

¹² The two men said to Lot, "Do you have anyone else here — sons-in-law, sons or daughters, or anyone else in the city who belongs to you? Get them out of here, ¹³ because we are going to destroy this place. The outcry to the LORD against its people is so great that he has sent us to destroy it."

¹⁴So Lot went out and spoke to his sons-in-law, who were pledged to marry*ª* his daughters. He said, "Hurry and get out of this place, because the LORD is about to destroy the city!" But his sons-in-law thought he was joking.

¹⁵With the coming of dawn, the angels urged Lot, saying, "Hurry! Take your wife and your two daughters who are here, or you will be swept away when the city is punished."

¹⁶When he hesitated, the men grasped his hand and the hands of his wife and of his two daughters and led them safely out of the city, for the LORD was merciful to them. ¹⁷As soon as they had brought them out, one of them said, "Flee for your lives! Don't look back, and don't stop anywhere in the plain! Flee to the mountains or you will be swept away!"

¹⁸But Lot said to them, "No, my lords,*ᵇ* please! ¹⁹Your*ᶜ* servant has found favor in your*ᶜ* eyes, and you*ᶜ* have shown great kindness to me in sparing my life. But I can't flee to the mountains; this disaster will overtake me, and I'll die. ²⁰Look, here is a town near enough to run to, and it is small. Let me flee to it—it is very small, isn't it? Then my life will be spared."

²¹He said to him, "Very well, I will grant this request too; I will not overthrow the town you speak of. ²²But flee there quickly, because I cannot do anything until you reach it." (That is why the town was called Zoar.*ᵈ*)

²³By the time Lot reached Zoar, the sun had risen over the land. ²⁴Then the LORD rained down burning sulfur on Sodom and Gomorrah—from the LORD out of the heavens. ²⁵Thus he overthrew those cities and the entire plain, destroying all those living in the cities—and also the vegetation in the land. ²⁶But Lot's wife looked back, and she became a pillar of salt.

²⁷Early the next morning Abraham got up and returned to the place where he had stood before the LORD. ²⁸He looked down toward Sodom and Gomorrah, toward all the land of the plain, and he saw dense smoke rising from the land, like smoke from a furnace.

²⁹So when God destroyed the cities of the plain, he remembered Abraham, and he brought Lot out of the catastrophe that overthrew the cities where Lot had lived.

Lot and His Daughters

³⁰Lot and his two daughters left Zoar and settled in the mountains, for he was afraid to stay in Zoar. He and his two daughters lived in a cave. ³¹One day the older daughter said to the younger

---

ª 14 Or *were married to*   *ᵇ 18* Or *No, Lord*; or *No, my lord*   *ᶜ 19* The He*
singular.   *ᵈ 22* Zoar means *small.*

"Our father is old, and there is no man around here to give us children — as is the custom all over the earth. ³²Let's get our father to drink wine and then sleep with him and preserve our family line through our father."

³³That night they got their father to drink wine, and the older daughter went in and slept with him. He was not aware of it when she lay down or when she got up.

³⁴The next day the older daughter said to the younger, "Last night I slept with my father. Let's get him to drink wine again tonight, and you go in and sleep with him so we can preserve our family line through our father." ³⁵So they got their father to drink wine that night also, and the younger daughter went in and slept with him. Again he was not aware of it when she lay down or when she got up.

³⁶So both of Lot's daughters became pregnant by their father. ³⁷The older daughter had a son, and she named him Moab[a]; he is the father of the Moabites of today. ³⁸The younger daughter also had a son, and she named him Ben-Ammi[b]; he is the father of the Ammonites[c] of today.

Abraham and Abimelek

20 Now Abraham moved on from there into the region of the Negev and lived between Kadesh and Shur. For a while he stayed in Gerar, ²and there Abraham said of his wife Sarah, "She is my sister." Then Abimelek king of Gerar sent for Sarah and took her.

³But God came to Abimelek in a dream one night and said to him, "You are as good as dead because of the woman you have taken; she is a married woman."

⁴Now Abimelek had not gone near her, so he said, "Lord, will you destroy an innocent nation? ⁵Did he not say to me, 'She is my sister,' and didn't she also say, 'He is my brother'? I have done this with a clear conscience and clean hands."

⁶Then God said to him in the dream, "Yes, I know you did this with a clear conscience, and so I have kept you from sinning against me. That is why I did not let you touch her. ⁷Now return the man's wife, for he is a prophet, and he will pray for you and you will live. But if you do not return her, you may be sure that you and all who belong to you will die."

⁸Early the next morning Abimelek summoned all his officials, and when he told them all that had happened, they were very much afraid. ⁹Then Abimelek called Abraham in and said, "What have you done to us? How have I wronged you that you have

---

a 37 Moab sounds like the Hebrew for *from father.*   *b 38* Ben-Ammi means *son*
c my father's people.   *c 38* Hebrew Bene-Ammon

brought such great guilt upon me and my kingdom? You have done things to me that should never be done." ¹⁰And Abimelek asked Abraham, "What was your reason for doing this?"

¹¹Abraham replied, "I said to myself, 'There is surely no fear of God in this place, and they will kill me because of my wife.' ¹²Besides, she really is my sister, the daughter of my father though not of my mother; and she became my wife. ¹³And when God had me wander from my father's household, I said to her, 'This is how you can show your love to me: Everywhere we go, say of me, "He is my brother."'"

¹⁴Then Abimelek brought sheep and cattle and male and female slaves and gave them to Abraham, and he returned Sarah his wife to him. ¹⁵And Abimelek said, "My land is before you; live wherever you like."

¹⁶To Sarah he said, "I am giving your brother a thousand shekels[a] of silver. This is to cover the offense against you before all who are with you; you are completely vindicated."

¹⁷Then Abraham prayed to God, and God healed Abimelek, his wife and his female slaves so they could have children again, ¹⁸for the LORD had kept all the women in Abimelek's household from conceiving because of Abraham's wife Sarah.

The Birth of Isaac

21 Now the LORD was gracious to Sarah as he had said, and the LORD did for Sarah what he had promised. ²Sarah became pregnant and bore a son to Abraham in his old age, at the very time God had promised him. ³Abraham gave the name Isaac[b] to the son Sarah bore him. ⁴When his son Isaac was eight days old, Abraham circumcised him, as God commanded him. ⁵Abraham was a hundred years old when his son Isaac was born to him.

⁶Sarah said, "God has brought me laughter, and everyone who hears about this will laugh with me." ⁷And she added, "Who would have said to Abraham that Sarah would nurse children? Yet I have borne him a son in his old age."

Hagar and Ishmael Sent Away

⁸The child grew and was weaned, and on the day Isaac was weaned Abraham held a great feast. ⁹But Sarah saw that the son whom Hagar the Egyptian had borne to Abraham was mocking, ¹⁰and she said to Abraham, "Get rid of that slave woman and her son, for that woman's son will never share in the inheritance with my son Isaac."

¹¹The matter distressed Abraham greatly because it concerned his son. ¹²But God said to him, "Do not be so distressed about

---

^a 16 That is, about 25 pounds or about 12 kilograms   ^b 3 Isaac means he laughs.

the boy and your slave woman. Listen to whatever Sarah tells you, because it is through Isaac that your offspring*a* will be reckoned. ¹³I will make the son of the slave into a nation also, because he is your offspring."

¹⁴Early the next morning Abraham took some food and a skin of water and gave them to Hagar. He set them on her shoulders and then sent her off with the boy. She went on her way and wandered in the Desert of Beersheba.

¹⁵When the water in the skin was gone, she put the boy under one of the bushes. ¹⁶Then she went off and sat down about a bowshot away, for she thought, "I cannot watch the boy die." And as she sat there, she*b* began to sob.

¹⁷God heard the boy crying, and the angel of God called to Hagar from heaven and said to her, "What is the matter, Hagar? Do not be afraid; God has heard the boy crying as he lies there. ¹⁸Lift the boy up and take him by the hand, for I will make him into a great nation."

¹⁹Then God opened her eyes and she saw a well of water. So she went and filled the skin with water and gave the boy a drink. ²⁰God was with the boy as he grew up. He lived in the desert and became an archer. ²¹While he was living in the Desert of Paran, his mother got a wife for him from Egypt.

The Treaty at Beersheba

²²At that time Abimelek and Phicol the commander of his forces said to Abraham, "God is with you in everything you do. ²³Now swear to me here before God that you will not deal falsely with me or my children or my descendants. Show to me and the country where you now reside as a foreigner the same kindness I have shown to you."

²⁴Abraham said, "I swear it."

²⁵Then Abraham complained to Abimelek about a well of water that Abimelek's servants had seized. ²⁶But Abimelek said, "I don't know who has done this. You did not tell me, and I heard about it only today."

²⁷So Abraham brought sheep and cattle and gave them to Abimelek, and the two men made a treaty. ²⁸Abraham set apart seven ewe lambs from the flock, ²⁹and Abimelek asked Abraham, "What is the meaning of these seven ewe lambs you have set apart by themselves?"

³⁰He replied, "Accept these seven lambs from my hand as a witness that I dug this well."

³¹So that place was called Beersheba,*c* because the two men swore an oath there.

³²After the treaty had been

---

a 12 Or *seed*   *b* 16 Hebrew; Septuagint *the child*   *c* 31 *Beersheba* can mean *well of seven* and *well of the oath.*

made at Beersheba, Abimelek and Phicol the commander of his forces returned to the land of the Philistines. ³³ Abraham planted a tamarisk tree in Beersheba, and there he called on the name of the LORD, the Eternal God. ³⁴ And Abraham stayed in the land of the Philistines for a long time.

Abraham Tested

22 Some time later God tested Abraham. He said to him, "Abraham!"

"Here I am," he replied.

² Then God said, "Take your son, your only son, whom you love — Isaac — and go to the region of Moriah. Sacrifice him there as a burnt offering on a mountain I will show you."

³ Early the next morning Abraham got up and loaded his donkey. He took with him two of his servants and his son Isaac. When he had cut enough wood for the burnt offering, he set out for the place God had told him about. ⁴ On the third day Abraham looked up and saw the place in the distance. ⁵ He said to his servants, "Stay here with the donkey while I and the boy go over there. We will worship and then we will come back to you."

⁶ Abraham took the wood for the burnt offering and placed it on his son Isaac, and he himself carried the fire and the knife. As the two of them went on together, ⁷ Isaac spoke up and said to his father Abraham, "Father?"

"Yes, my son?" Abraham replied.

"The fire and wood are here," Isaac said, "but where is the lamb for the burnt offering?"

⁸ Abraham answered, "God himself will provide the lamb for the burnt offering, my son." And the two of them went on together.

⁹ When they reached the place God had told him about, Abraham built an altar there and arranged the wood on it. He bound his son Isaac and laid him on the altar, on top of the wood. ¹⁰ Then he reached out his hand and took the knife to slay his son. ¹¹ But the angel of the LORD called out to him from heaven, "Abraham! Abraham!"

"Here I am," he replied.

¹² "Do not lay a hand on the boy," he said. "Do not do anything to him. Now I know that you fear God, because you have not withheld from me your son, your only son."

¹³ Abraham looked up and there in a thicket he saw a ram*a* caught by its horns. He went over and took the ram and sacrificed it as a burnt offering instead of his son. ¹⁴ So Abraham called that place The LORD Will Provide. And to this day it is said, "On the mountain of the LORD it will be provided."

---

a 13 Many manuscripts of the Masoretic Text, Samaritan Pentateuch, Sept and Syriac; most manuscripts of the Masoretic Text *a ram behind him*

¹⁵The angel of the LORD called to Abraham from heaven a second time ¹⁶and said, "I swear by myself, declares the LORD, that because you have done this and have not withheld your son, your only son, ¹⁷I will surely bless you and make your descendants as numerous as the stars in the sky and as the sand on the seashore. Your descendants will take possession of the cities of their enemies, ¹⁸and through your offspring[a] all nations on earth will be blessed,[b] because you have obeyed me."

¹⁹Then Abraham returned to his servants, and they set off together for Beersheba. And Abraham stayed in Beersheba.

Nahor's Sons

²⁰Some time later Abraham was told, "Milkah is also a mother; she has borne sons to your brother Nahor: ²¹Uz the firstborn, Buz his brother, Kemuel (the father of Aram), ²²Kesed, Hazo, Pildash, Jidlaph and Bethuel." ²³Bethuel became the father of Rebekah. Milkah bore these eight sons to Abraham's brother Nahor. ²⁴His concubine, whose name was Reumah, also had sons: Tebah, Gaham, Tahash and Maakah.

The Death of Sarah

23 Sarah lived to be a hundred and twenty-seven years old. ²She died at Kiriath Arba (that is, Hebron) in the land of Canaan, and Abraham went to mourn for Sarah and to weep over her.

³Then Abraham rose from beside his dead wife and spoke to the Hittites.[c] He said, ⁴"I am a foreigner and stranger among you. Sell me some property for a burial site here so I can bury my dead."

⁵The Hittites replied to Abraham, ⁶"Sir, listen to us. You are a mighty prince among us. Bury your dead in the choicest of our tombs. None of us will refuse you his tomb for burying your dead."

⁷Then Abraham rose and bowed down before the people of the land, the Hittites. ⁸He said to them, "If you are willing to let me bury my dead, then listen to me and intercede with Ephron son of Zohar on my behalf ⁹so he will sell me the cave of Machpelah, which belongs to him and is at the end of his field. Ask him to sell it to me for the full price as a burial site among you."

¹⁰Ephron the Hittite was sitting among his people and he replied to Abraham in the hearing of all the Hittites who had come to the gate of his city. ¹¹"No, my lord," he said. "Listen to me; I give[d] you the field, and I give[d] you the cave that is in it. I give[d] it to you in the presence of my people. Bury your dead."

¹²Again Abraham bowed down

---

[a] 18 Or *seed*   [b] 18 Or *and all nations on earth will use the name of your offspring in blessings* (see 48:20)   [c] 3 Or *the descendants of Heth*; also in verses 5, 7, 10, 16, 8 and 20   [d] 11 Or *sell*

before the people of the land ¹³and he said to Ephron in their hearing, "Listen to me, if you will. I will pay the price of the field. Accept it from me so I can bury my dead there."

¹⁴Ephron answered Abraham, ¹⁵"Listen to me, my lord; the land is worth four hundred shekels*a* of silver, but what is that between you and me? Bury your dead."

¹⁶Abraham agreed to Ephron's terms and weighed out for him the price he had named in the hearing of the Hittites: four hundred shekels of silver, according to the weight current among the merchants.

¹⁷So Ephron's field in Machpelah near Mamre — both the field and the cave in it, and all the trees within the borders of the field — was deeded ¹⁸to Abraham as his property in the presence of all the Hittites who had come to the gate of the city. ¹⁹Afterward Abraham buried his wife Sarah in the cave in the field of Machpelah near Mamre (which is at Hebron) in the land of Canaan. ²⁰So the field and the cave in it were deeded to Abraham by the Hittites as a burial site.

Isaac and Rebekah

24 Abraham was now very old, and the LORD had blessed him in every way. ²He said to the senior servant in his household, the one in charge of all that he had, "Put your hand under my thigh. ³I want you to swear by the LORD, the God of heaven and the God of earth, that you will not get a wife for my son from the daughters of the Canaanites, among whom I am living, ⁴but will go to my country and my own relatives and get a wife for my son Isaac."

⁵The servant asked him, "What if the woman is unwilling to come back with me to this land? Shall I then take your son back to the country you came from?"

⁶"Make sure that you do not take my son back there," Abraham said. ⁷"The LORD, the God of heaven, who brought me out of my father's household and my native land and who spoke to me and promised me on oath, saying, 'To your offspring*b* I will give this land' — he will send his angel before you so that you can get a wife for my son from there. ⁸If the woman is unwilling to come back with you, then you will be released from this oath of mine. Only do not take my son back there." ⁹So the servant put his hand under the thigh of his master Abraham and swore an oath to him concerning this matter.

¹⁰Then the servant left, taking with him ten of his master's camels loaded with all kinds of good things from his master. He set out for Aram Naharaim*c* and mad

---

a 15 That is, about 10 pounds or about 4.6 kilograms   *b 7* Or *seed*   *c 10* is, Northwest Mesopotamia his way to the town of Nahor. [11] He had the camels kneel down near the well outside the town; it was toward evening, the time the women go out to draw water.

[12] Then he prayed, "LORD, God of my master Abraham, make me successful today, and show kindness to my master Abraham. [13] See, I am standing beside this spring, and the daughters of the townspeople are coming out to draw water. [14] May it be that when I say to a young woman, 'Please let down your jar that I may have a drink,' and she says, 'Drink, and I'll water your camels too'—let her be the one you have chosen for your servant Isaac. By this I will know that you have shown kindness to my master."

[15] Before he had finished praying, Rebekah came out with her jar on her shoulder. She was the daughter of Bethuel son of Milkah, who was the wife of Abraham's brother Nahor. [16] The woman was very beautiful, a virgin; no man had ever slept with her. She went down to the spring, filled her jar and came up again.

[17] The servant hurried to meet her and said, "Please give me a little water from your jar."

[18] "Drink, my lord," she said, and quickly lowered the jar to her hands and gave him a drink.

[19] After she had given him a drink, she said, "I'll draw water for your camels too, until they have had enough to drink." [20] So she quickly emptied her jar into the trough, ran back to the well to draw more water, and drew enough for all his camels. [21] Without saying a word, the man watched her closely to learn whether or not the LORD had made his journey successful.

[22] When the camels had finished drinking, the man took out a gold nose ring weighing a beka[a] and two gold bracelets weighing ten shekels.[b] [23] Then he asked, "Whose daughter are you? Please tell me, is there room in your father's house for us to spend the night?"

[24] She answered him, "I am the daughter of Bethuel, the son that Milkah bore to Nahor." [25] And she added, "We have plenty of straw and fodder, as well as room for you to spend the night."

[26] Then the man bowed down and worshiped the LORD, [27] saying, "Praise be to the LORD, the God of my master Abraham, who has not abandoned his kindness and faithfulness to my master. As for me, the LORD has led me on the journey to the house of my master's relatives."

[28] The young woman ran and told her mother's household about these things. [29] Now Rebekah had a brother named Laban, and he hurried out to the man at the

---

[a] 22 That is, about 1/5 ounce or about 5.7 grams   [b] 22 That is, about 4 ounces or bout 115 grams

spring. [30]As soon as he had seen the nose ring, and the bracelets on his sister's arms, and had heard Rebekah tell what the man said to her, he went out to the man and found him standing by the camels near the spring. [31]"Come, you who are blessed by the LORD," he said. "Why are you standing out here? I have prepared the house and a place for the camels."

[32]So the man went to the house, and the camels were unloaded. Straw and fodder were brought for the camels, and water for him and his men to wash their feet. [33]Then food was set before him, but he said, "I will not eat until I have told you what I have to say."

"Then tell us," Laban said.

[34]So he said, "I am Abraham's servant. [35]The LORD has blessed my master abundantly, and he has become wealthy. He has given him sheep and cattle, silver and gold, male and female servants, and camels and donkeys. [36]My master's wife Sarah has borne him a son in her old age, and he has given him everything he owns. [37]And my master made me swear an oath, and said, 'You must not get a wife for my son from the daughters of the Canaanites, in whose land I live, [38]but go to my father's family and to my own clan, and get a wife for my son.'

[39]"Then I asked my master, 'What if the woman will not come back with me?'

[40]"He replied, 'The LORD, before whom I have walked faithfully, will send his angel with you and make your journey a success, so that you can get a wife for my son from my own clan and from my father's family. [41]You will be released from my oath if, when you go to my clan, they refuse to give her to you — then you will be released from my oath.'

[42]"When I came to the spring today, I said, 'LORD, God of my master Abraham, if you will, please grant success to the journey on which I have come. [43]See, I am standing beside this spring. If a young woman comes out to draw water and I say to her, "Please let me drink a little water from your jar," [44]and if she says to me, "Drink, and I'll draw water for your camels too," let her be the one the LORD has chosen for my master's son.'

[45]"Before I finished praying in my heart, Rebekah came out, with her jar on her shoulder. She went down to the spring and drew water, and I said to her, 'Please give me a drink.'

[46]"She quickly lowered her jar from her shoulder and said, 'Drink, and I'll water your camels too.' So I drank, and she watered the camels also.

[47]"I asked her, 'Whose daughter are you?'

"She said, 'The daughter of Bethuel son of Nahor, whom Milkah bore to him.'

"Then I put the ring in her nose and the bracelets on her arms, [48] and I bowed down and worshiped the LORD. I praised the LORD, the God of my master Abraham, who had led me on the right road to get the granddaughter of my master's brother for his son. [49] Now if you will show kindness and faithfulness to my master, tell me; and if not, tell me, so I may know which way to turn."

[50] Laban and Bethuel answered, "This is from the LORD; we can say nothing to you one way or the other. [51] Here is Rebekah; take her and go, and let her become the wife of your master's son, as the LORD has directed."

[52] When Abraham's servant heard what they said, he bowed down to the ground before the LORD. [53] Then the servant brought out gold and silver jewelry and articles of clothing and gave them to Rebekah; he also gave costly gifts to her brother and to her mother. [54] Then he and the men who were with him ate and drank and spent the night there.

When they got up the next morning, he said, "Send me on my way to my master."

[55] But her brother and her mother replied, "Let the young woman remain with us ten days or so; then you[a] may go."

[56] But he said to them, "Do not detain me, now that the LORD has granted success to my journey. Send me on my way so I may go to my master."

[57] Then they said, "Let's call the young woman and ask her about it." [58] So they called Rebekah and asked her, "Will you go with this man?"

"I will go," she said.

[59] So they sent their sister Rebekah on her way, along with her nurse and Abraham's servant and his men. [60] And they blessed Rebekah and said to her,

"Our sister, may you increase
    to thousands upon
        thousands;
may your offspring possess
    the cities of their enemies."

[61] Then Rebekah and her attendants got ready and mounted the camels and went back with the man. So the servant took Rebekah and left.

[62] Now Isaac had come from Beer Lahai Roi, for he was living in the Negev. [63] He went out to the field one evening to meditate,[b] and as he looked up, he saw camels approaching. [64] Rebekah also looked up and saw Isaac. She got down from her camel [65] and asked the servant, "Who is that man in the field coming to meet us?"

"He is my master," the servant answered. So she took her veil and covered herself.

[66] Then the servant told Isaac all he had done. [67] Isaac brought her into the tent of his mother

---

[a] 55 Or she   [b] 63 The meaning of the Hebrew for this word is uncertain.

Sarah, and he married Rebekah. So she became his wife, and he loved her; and Isaac was comforted after his mother's death.

The Death of Abraham

25 Abraham had taken another wife, whose name was Keturah. ²She bore him Zimran, Jokshan, Medan, Midian, Ishbak and Shuah. ³Jokshan was the father of Sheba and Dedan; the descendants of Dedan were the Ashurites, the Letushites and the Leummites. ⁴The sons of Midian were Ephah, Epher, Hanok, Abida and Eldaah. All these were descendants of Keturah.

⁵Abraham left everything he owned to Isaac. ⁶But while he was still living, he gave gifts to the sons of his concubines and sent them away from his son Isaac to the land of the east.

⁷Abraham lived a hundred and seventy-five years. ⁸Then Abraham breathed his last and died at a good old age, an old man and full of years; and he was gathered to his people. ⁹His sons Isaac and Ishmael buried him in the cave of Machpelah near Mamre, in the field of Ephron son of Zohar the Hittite, ¹⁰the field Abraham had bought from the Hittites.ᵃ There Abraham was buried with his wife Sarah. ¹¹After Abraham's death, God blessed his son Isaac, who then lived near Beer Lahai Roi.

Ishmael's Sons

¹²This is the account of the family line of Abraham's son Ishmael, whom Sarah's slave, Hagar the Egyptian, bore to Abraham.

¹³These are the names of the sons of Ishmael, listed in the order of their birth: Nebaioth the firstborn of Ishmael, Kedar, Adbeel, Mibsam, ¹⁴Mishma, Dumah, Massa, ¹⁵Hadad, Tema, Jetur, Naphish and Kedemah. ¹⁶These were the sons of Ishmael, and these are the names of the twelve tribal rulers according to their settlements and camps. ¹⁷Ishmael lived a hundred and thirty-seven years. He breathed his last and died, and he was gathered to his people. ¹⁸His descendants settled in the area from Havilah to Shur, near the eastern border of Egypt, as you go toward Ashur. And they lived in hostility towardᵇ all the tribes related to them.

Jacob and Esau

¹⁹This is the account of the family line of Abraham's son Isaac.

Abraham became the father of Isaac, ²⁰and Isaac was forty years old when he married Rebekah daughter of Bethuel the Aramean from Paddan Aramᶜ and sister of Laban the Aramean.

²¹Isaac prayed to the LORD on behalf of his wife, because she

---

ᵃ 10 Or *the descendants of Heth*   ᵇ 18 Or *lived to the east of*   ᶜ 20 That is, Northwest Mesopotamia was childless. The LORD answered his prayer, and his wife Rebekah became pregnant. **22** The babies jostled each other within her, and she said, "Why is this happening to me?" So she went to inquire of the LORD.

23 The LORD said to her,

"Two nations are in your womb,
    and two peoples from within
        you will be separated;
one people will be stronger
        than the other,
    and the older will serve the
        younger."

24 When the time came for her to give birth, there were twin boys in her womb. **25** The first to come out was red, and his whole body was like a hairy garment; so they named him Esau.*a* **26** After this, his brother came out, with his hand grasping Esau's heel; so he was named Jacob.*b* Isaac was sixty years old when Rebekah gave birth to them.

27 The boys grew up, and Esau became a skillful hunter, a man of the open country, while Jacob was content to stay at home among the tents. **28** Isaac, who had a taste for wild game, loved Esau, but Rebekah loved Jacob.

29 Once when Jacob was cooking some stew, Esau came in from the open country, famished. **30** He said to Jacob, "Quick, let me have some of that red stew! I'm famished!" (That is why he was also called Edom.*c*)

31 Jacob replied, "First sell me your birthright."

32 "Look, I am about to die," Esau said. "What good is the birthright to me?"

33 But Jacob said, "Swear to me first." So he swore an oath to him, selling his birthright to Jacob.

34 Then Jacob gave Esau some bread and some lentil stew. He ate and drank, and then got up and left.

So Esau despised his birthright.

Isaac and Abimelek

26 Now there was a famine in the land — besides the previous famine in Abraham's time — and Isaac went to Abimelek king of the Philistines in Gerar. **2** The LORD appeared to Isaac and said, "Do not go down to Egypt; live in the land where I tell you to live. **3** Stay in this land for a while, and I will be with you and will bless you. For to you and your descendants I will give all these lands and will confirm the oath I swore to your father Abraham. **4** I will make your descendants as numerous as the stars in the sky and will give them all these lands, and through your offspring*d* all nations on earth will be blessed,*e* **5** because Abra-

---

a 25 Esau may mean *hairy.*   *b 26 Jacob* means *he grasps the heel,* a Hebrew idiom for *he deceives.*   *c 30 Edom* means *red.*   *d 4* Or *seed*   *e 4* Or *and all nations on earth will use the name of your offspring in blessings* (see 48:20) ham obeyed me and did everything I required of him, keeping my commands, my decrees and my instructions." **6**So Isaac stayed in Gerar.

7When the men of that place asked him about his wife, he said, "She is my sister," because he was afraid to say, "She is my wife." He thought, "The men of this place might kill me on account of Rebekah, because she is beautiful."

8When Isaac had been there a long time, Abimelek king of the Philistines looked down from a window and saw Isaac caressing his wife Rebekah. **9**So Abimelek summoned Isaac and said, "She is really your wife! Why did you say, 'She is my sister'?"

Isaac answered him, "Because I thought I might lose my life on account of her."

10Then Abimelek said, "What is this you have done to us? One of the men might well have slept with your wife, and you would have brought guilt upon us."

11So Abimelek gave orders to all the people: "Anyone who harms this man or his wife shall surely be put to death."

12Isaac planted crops in that land and the same year reaped a hundredfold, because the LORD blessed him. **13**The man became rich, and his wealth continued to grow until he became very wealthy. **14**He had so many flocks and herds and servants that the Philistines envied him. **15**So all the wells that his father's servants had dug in the time of his father Abraham, the Philistines stopped up, filling them with earth.

16Then Abimelek said to Isaac, "Move away from us; you have become too powerful for us."

17So Isaac moved away from there and encamped in the Valley of Gerar, where he settled. **18**Isaac reopened the wells that had been dug in the time of his father Abraham, which the Philistines had stopped up after Abraham died, and he gave them the same names his father had given them.

19Isaac's servants dug in the valley and discovered a well of fresh water there. **20**But the herders of Gerar quarreled with those of Isaac and said, "The water is ours!" So he named the well Esek,*a* because they disputed with him. **21**Then they dug another well, but they quarreled over that one also; so he named it Sitnah.*b* **22**He moved on from there and dug another well, and no one quarreled over it. He named it Rehoboth,*c* saying, "Now the LORD has given us room and we will flourish in the land."

23From there he went up to Beersheba. **24**That night the LORD appeared to him and said, "I am

---

a 20 Esek means *dispute.*   *b 21 Sitnah* means *opposition.*   *c 22 Rehoboth* means *room.*

the God of your father Abraham. Do not be afraid, for I am with you; I will bless you and will increase the number of your descendants for the sake of my servant Abraham."

²⁵ Isaac built an altar there and called on the name of the LORD. There he pitched his tent, and there his servants dug a well.

²⁶ Meanwhile, Abimelek had come to him from Gerar, with Ahuzzath his personal adviser and Phicol the commander of his forces. ²⁷ Isaac asked them, "Why have you come to me, since you were hostile to me and sent me away?"

²⁸ They answered, "We saw clearly that the LORD was with you; so we said, 'There ought to be a sworn agreement between us'—between us and you. Let us make a treaty with you ²⁹ that you will do us no harm, just as we did not harm you but always treated you well and sent you away peacefully. And now you are blessed by the LORD."

³⁰ Isaac then made a feast for them, and they ate and drank. ³¹ Early the next morning the men swore an oath to each other. Then Isaac sent them on their way, and they went away peacefully.

³² That day Isaac's servants came and told him about the well they had dug. They said, "We've found water!" ³³ He called it Shibah,ᵃ and to this day the name of the town has been Beersheba.ᵇ

Jacob Takes Esau's Blessing

³⁴ When Esau was forty years old, he married Judith daughter of Beeri the Hittite, and also Basemath daughter of Elon the Hittite. ³⁵ They were a source of grief to Isaac and Rebekah.

27 When Isaac was old and his eyes were so weak that he could no longer see, he called for Esau his older son and said to him, "My son."

"Here I am," he answered.

² Isaac said, "I am now an old man and don't know the day of my death. ³ Now then, get your equipment—your quiver and bow—and go out to the open country to hunt some wild game for me. ⁴ Prepare me the kind of tasty food I like and bring it to me to eat, so that I may give you my blessing before I die."

⁵ Now Rebekah was listening as Isaac spoke to his son Esau. When Esau left for the open country to hunt game and bring it back, ⁶ Rebekah said to her son Jacob, "Look, I overheard your father say to your brother Esau, ⁷ 'Bring me some game and prepare me some tasty food to eat, so that I may give you my blessing in the presence of the LORD before I die.' ⁸ Now, my son, listen carefully and do what I tell you:

ᵃ 33 Shibah can mean oath or seven.   ᵇ 33 Beersheba can mean well of the oath and well of seven.

⁹Go out to the flock and bring me two choice young goats, so I can prepare some tasty food for your father, just the way he likes it. ¹⁰Then take it to your father to eat, so that he may give you his blessing before he dies."

¹¹Jacob said to Rebekah his mother, "But my brother Esau is a hairy man while I have smooth skin. ¹²What if my father touches me? I would appear to be tricking him and would bring down a curse on myself rather than a blessing."

¹³His mother said to him, "My son, let the curse fall on me. Just do what I say; go and get them for me."

¹⁴So he went and got them and brought them to his mother, and she prepared some tasty food, just the way his father liked it. ¹⁵Then Rebekah took the best clothes of Esau her older son, which she had in the house, and put them on her younger son Jacob. ¹⁶She also covered his hands and the smooth part of his neck with the goatskins. ¹⁷Then she handed to her son Jacob the tasty food and the bread she had made.

¹⁸He went to his father and said, "My father."

"Yes, my son," he answered. "Who is it?"

¹⁹Jacob said to his father, "I am Esau your firstborn. I have done as you told me. Please sit up and eat some of my game, so that you may give me your blessing."

²⁰Isaac asked his son, "How did you find it so quickly, my son?"

"The Lord your God gave me success," he replied.

²¹Then Isaac said to Jacob, "Come near so I can touch you, my son, to know whether you really are my son Esau or not."

²²Jacob went close to his father Isaac, who touched him and said, "The voice is the voice of Jacob, but the hands are the hands of Esau." ²³He did not recognize him, for his hands were hairy like those of his brother Esau; so he proceeded to bless him. ²⁴"Are you really my son Esau?" he asked.

"I am," he replied.

²⁵Then he said, "My son, bring me some of your game to eat, so that I may give you my blessing."

Jacob brought it to him and he ate; and he brought some wine and he drank. ²⁶Then his father Isaac said to him, "Come here, my son, and kiss me."

²⁷So he went to him and kissed him. When Isaac caught the smell of his clothes, he blessed him and said,

"Ah, the smell of my son
    is like the smell of a field
    that the Lord has blessed.
²⁸May God give you heaven's
        dew
    and earth's richness —
    an abundance of grain and
        new wine.
²⁹May nations serve you
    and peoples bow down to
        you.

> Be lord over your brothers,
>> and may the sons of your
>> mother bow down to
>> you.
> May those who curse you be
>> cursed
>> and those who bless you be
>> blessed."

³⁰After Isaac finished blessing him, and Jacob had scarcely left his father's presence, his brother Esau came in from hunting. ³¹He too prepared some tasty food and brought it to his father. Then he said to him, "My father, please sit up and eat some of my game, so that you may give me your blessing."

³²His father Isaac asked him, "Who are you?"

"I am your son," he answered, "your firstborn, Esau."

³³Isaac trembled violently and said, "Who was it, then, that hunted game and brought it to me? I ate it just before you came and I blessed him—and indeed he will be blessed!"

³⁴When Esau heard his father's words, he burst out with a loud and bitter cry and said to his father, "Bless me—me too, my father!"

³⁵But he said, "Your brother came deceitfully and took your blessing."

³⁶Esau said, "Isn't he rightly named Jacob*ᵃ*? This is the second time he has taken advantage of me: He took my birthright, and now he's taken my blessing!" Then he asked, "Haven't you reserved any blessing for me?"

³⁷Isaac answered Esau, "I have made him lord over you and have made all his relatives his servants, and I have sustained him with grain and new wine. So what can I possibly do for you, my son?"

³⁸Esau said to his father, "Do you have only one blessing, my father? Bless me too, my father!" Then Esau wept aloud.

³⁹His father Isaac answered him,

> "Your dwelling will be
>> away from the earth's
>> richness,
>> away from the dew of heaven
>> above.
> ⁴⁰You will live by the sword
>> and you will serve your
>> brother.
> But when you grow restless,
>> you will throw his yoke
>> from off your neck."

⁴¹Esau held a grudge against Jacob because of the blessing his father had given him. He said to himself, "The days of mourning for my father are near; then I will kill my brother Jacob."

⁴²When Rebekah was told what her older son Esau had said, she sent for her younger son Jacob and said to him, "Your brother

---

ᵃ *36* *Jacob* means *he grasps the heel,* a Hebrew idiom for *he takes advantage of* or *he deceives.*

Esau is planning to avenge himself by killing you. **43**Now then, my son, do what I say: Flee at once to my brother Laban in Harran. **44**Stay with him for a while until your brother's fury subsides. **45**When your brother is no longer angry with you and forgets what you did to him, I'll send word for you to come back from there. Why should I lose both of you in one day?"

46Then Rebekah said to Isaac, "I'm disgusted with living because of these Hittite women. If Jacob takes a wife from among the women of this land, from Hittite women like these, my life will not be worth living."

28 So Isaac called for Jacob and blessed him. Then he commanded him: "Do not marry a Canaanite woman. **2**Go at once to Paddan Aram,*ᵃ* to the house of your mother's father Bethuel. Take a wife for yourself there, from among the daughters of Laban, your mother's brother. **3**May God Almighty*ᵇ* bless you and make you fruitful and increase your numbers until you become a community of peoples. **4**May he give you and your descendants the blessing given to Abraham, so that you may take possession of the land where you now reside as a foreigner, the land God gave to Abraham." **5**Then Isaac sent Jacob on his way, and he went to Paddan Aram, to Laban son of Bethuel the Aramean, the brother of Rebekah, who was the mother of Jacob and Esau.

6Now Esau learned that Isaac had blessed Jacob and had sent him to Paddan Aram to take a wife from there, and that when he blessed him he commanded him, "Do not marry a Canaanite woman," **7**and that Jacob had obeyed his father and mother and had gone to Paddan Aram. **8**Esau then realized how displeasing the Canaanite women were to his father Isaac; **9**so he went to Ishmael and married Mahalath, the sister of Nebaioth and daughter of Ishmael son of Abraham, in addition to the wives he already had.

Jacob's Dream at Bethel

10Jacob left Beersheba and set out for Harran. **11**When he reached a certain place, he stopped for the night because the sun had set. Taking one of the stones there, he put it under his head and lay down to sleep. **12**He had a dream in which he saw a stairway resting on the earth, with its top reaching to heaven, and the angels of God were ascending and descending on it. **13**There above it*ᶜ* stood the LORD, and he said: "I am the LORD, the God of your father Abraham and the God of Isaac. I will give you and your descendants the land

ᵃ 2 That is, Northwest Mesopotamia; also in verses 5, 6 and 7   *ᵇ 3* Hebrew *El Shaddai*   *ᶜ 13* Or *There beside him* on which you are lying. ¹⁴Your descendants will be like the dust of the earth, and you will spread out to the west and to the east, to the north and to the south. All peoples on earth will be blessed through you and your offspring.ᵃ ¹⁵I am with you and will watch over you wherever you go, and I will bring you back to this land. I will not leave you until I have done what I have promised you."

¹⁶When Jacob awoke from his sleep, he thought, "Surely the LORD is in this place, and I was not aware of it." ¹⁷He was afraid and said, "How awesome is this place! This is none other than the house of God; this is the gate of heaven."

¹⁸Early the next morning Jacob took the stone he had placed under his head and set it up as a pillar and poured oil on top of it. ¹⁹He called that place Bethel,ᵇ though the city used to be called Luz.

²⁰Then Jacob made a vow, saying, "If God will be with me and will watch over me on this journey I am taking and will give me food to eat and clothes to wear ²¹so that I return safely to my father's household, then the LORDᶜ will be my God ²²andᵈ this stone that I have set up as a pillar will be God's house, and of all that you give me I will give you a tenth."

Jacob Arrives in Paddan Aram

29 Then Jacob continued on his journey and came to the land of the eastern peoples. ²There he saw a well in the open country, with three flocks of sheep lying near it because the flocks were watered from that well. The stone over the mouth of the well was large. ³When all the flocks were gathered there, the shepherds would roll the stone away from the well's mouth and water the sheep. Then they would return the stone to its place over the mouth of the well.

⁴Jacob asked the shepherds, "My brothers, where are you from?"

"We're from Harran," they replied.

⁵He said to them, "Do you know Laban, Nahor's grandson?"

"Yes, we know him," they answered.

⁶Then Jacob asked them, "Is he well?"

"Yes, he is," they said, "and here comes his daughter Rachel with the sheep."

⁷"Look," he said, "the sun is still high; it is not time for the flocks to be gathered. Water the sheep and take them back to pasture."

⁸"We can't," they replied, "until all the flocks are gathered and the stone has been rolled away

---

ᵃ 14 Or *will use your name and the name of your offspring in blessings* (see 48:20)
ᵇ 19 *Bethel* means *house of God.* ᶜ 20,21 Or *Since God . . . father's household, the* LORD ᵈ 21,22 Or *household, and the* LORD *will be my God,* ²²*then*

from the mouth of the well. Then we will water the sheep."

⁹While he was still talking with them, Rachel came with her father's sheep, for she was a shepherd. ¹⁰When Jacob saw Rachel daughter of his uncle Laban, and Laban's sheep, he went over and rolled the stone away from the mouth of the well and watered his uncle's sheep. ¹¹Then Jacob kissed Rachel and began to weep aloud. ¹²He had told Rachel that he was a relative of her father and a son of Rebekah. So she ran and told her father.

¹³As soon as Laban heard the news about Jacob, his sister's son, he hurried to meet him. He embraced him and kissed him and brought him to his home, and there Jacob told him all these things. ¹⁴Then Laban said to him, "You are my own flesh and blood."

Jacob Marries Leah and Rachel

After Jacob had stayed with him for a whole month, ¹⁵Laban said to him, "Just because you are a relative of mine, should you work for me for nothing? Tell me what your wages should be."

¹⁶Now Laban had two daughters; the name of the older was Leah, and the name of the younger was Rachel. ¹⁷Leah had weak*a* eyes, but Rachel had a lovely figure and was beautiful. ¹⁸Jacob was in love with Rachel and said,

"I'll work for you seven years in return for your younger daughter Rachel."

¹⁹Laban said, "It's better that I give her to you than to some other man. Stay here with me." ²⁰So Jacob served seven years to get Rachel, but they seemed like only a few days to him because of his love for her.

²¹Then Jacob said to Laban, "Give me my wife. My time is completed, and I want to make love to her."

²²So Laban brought together all the people of the place and gave a feast. ²³But when evening came, he took his daughter Leah and brought her to Jacob, and Jacob made love to her. ²⁴And Laban gave his servant Zilpah to his daughter as her attendant.

²⁵When morning came, there was Leah! So Jacob said to Laban, "What is this you have done to me? I served you for Rachel, didn't I? Why have you deceived me?"

²⁶Laban replied, "It is not our custom here to give the younger daughter in marriage before the older one. ²⁷Finish this daughter's bridal week; then we will give you the younger one also, in return for another seven years of work."

²⁸And Jacob did so. He finished the week with Leah, and then Laban gave him his daughter Rachel to be his wife. ²⁹Laban gave his servant Bilhah to his daughter

a 17 Or *delicate*

Rachel as her attendant. ³⁰Jacob made love to Rachel also, and his love for Rachel was greater than his love for Leah. And he worked for Laban another seven years.

Jacob's Children

³¹When the LORD saw that Leah was not loved, he enabled her to conceive, but Rachel remained childless. ³²Leah became pregnant and gave birth to a son. She named him Reuben,ᵃ for she said, "It is because the LORD has seen my misery. Surely my husband will love me now."

³³She conceived again, and when she gave birth to a son she said, "Because the LORD heard that I am not loved, he gave me this one too." So she named him Simeon.ᵇ

³⁴Again she conceived, and when she gave birth to a son she said, "Now at last my husband will become attached to me, because I have borne him three sons." So he was named Levi.ᶜ

³⁵She conceived again, and when she gave birth to a son she said, "This time I will praise the LORD." So she named him Judah.ᵈ Then she stopped having children.

30 When Rachel saw that she was not bearing Jacob any children, she became jealous of her sister. So she said to Jacob, "Give me children, or I'll die!"

²Jacob became angry with her and said, "Am I in the place of God, who has kept you from having children?"

³Then she said, "Here is Bilhah, my servant. Sleep with her so that she can bear children for me and I too can build a family through her."

⁴So she gave him her servant Bilhah as a wife. Jacob slept with her, ⁵and she became pregnant and bore him a son. ⁶Then Rachel said, "God has vindicated me; he has listened to my plea and given me a son." Because of this she named him Dan.ᵉ

⁷Rachel's servant Bilhah conceived again and bore Jacob a second son. ⁸Then Rachel said, "I have had a great struggle with my sister, and I have won." So she named him Naphtali.ᶠ

⁹When Leah saw that she had stopped having children, she took her servant Zilpah and gave her to Jacob as a wife. ¹⁰Leah's servant Zilpah bore Jacob a son. ¹¹Then Leah said, "What good fortune!"ᵍ So she named him Gad.ʰ

¹²Leah's servant Zilpah bore Jacob a second son. ¹³Then Leah

ᵃ 32 *Reuben* sounds like the Hebrew for *he has seen my misery*; the name means *see, a son.*   ᵇ 33 *Simeon* probably means *one who hears.*   ᶜ 34 *Levi* sounds like and may be derived from the Hebrew for *attached.*   ᵈ 35 *Judah* sounds like and may be derived from the Hebrew for *praise.*   ᵉ 6 *Dan* here means *he has vindicated.*   ᶠ 8 *Naphtali* means *my struggle.*   ᵍ 11 Or *"A troop is coming!"*   ʰ 11 *Gad* can mean *good fortune* or *a troop.*

said, "How happy I am! The women will call me happy." So she named him Asher.[a]

[14] During wheat harvest, Reuben went out into the fields and found some mandrake plants, which he brought to his mother Leah. Rachel said to Leah, "Please give me some of your son's mandrakes."

[15] But she said to her, "Wasn't it enough that you took away my husband? Will you take my son's mandrakes too?"

"Very well," Rachel said, "he can sleep with you tonight in return for your son's mandrakes."

[16] So when Jacob came in from the fields that evening, Leah went out to meet him. "You must sleep with me," she said. "I have hired you with my son's mandrakes." So he slept with her that night.

[17] God listened to Leah, and she became pregnant and bore Jacob a fifth son. [18] Then Leah said, "God has rewarded me for giving my servant to my husband." So she named him Issachar.[b]

[19] Leah conceived again and bore Jacob a sixth son. [20] Then Leah said, "God has presented me with a precious gift. This time my husband will treat me with honor, because I have borne him six sons." So she named him Zebulun.[c]

[21] Some time later she gave birth to a daughter and named her Dinah.

[22] Then God remembered Rachel; he listened to her and enabled her to conceive. [23] She became pregnant and gave birth to a son and said, "God has taken away my disgrace." [24] She named him Joseph,[d] and said, "May the LORD add to me another son."

Jacob's Flocks Increase

[25] After Rachel gave birth to Joseph, Jacob said to Laban, "Send me on my way so I can go back to my own homeland. [26] Give me my wives and children, for whom I have served you, and I will be on my way. You know how much work I've done for you."

[27] But Laban said to him, "If I have found favor in your eyes, please stay. I have learned by divination that the LORD has blessed me because of you." [28] He added, "Name your wages, and I will pay them."

[29] Jacob said to him, "You know how I have worked for you and how your livestock has fared under my care. [30] The little you had before I came has increased greatly, and the LORD has blessed you wherever I have been. But now, when may I do something for my own household?"

[31] "What shall I give you?" he asked.

"Don't give me anything," Jacob replied. "But if you will do this one thing for me, I will go on tending your flocks and watching

---

[a] 13 *Asher* means *happy*. [b] 18 *Issachar* sounds like the Hebrew for *reward*.
[c] 20 *Zebulun* probably means *honor*. [d] 24 *Joseph* means *may he add*.

over them: **32**Let me go through all your flocks today and remove from them every speckled or spotted sheep, every dark-colored lamb and every spotted or speckled goat. They will be my wages. **33**And my honesty will testify for me in the future, whenever you check on the wages you have paid me. Any goat in my possession that is not speckled or spotted, or any lamb that is not dark-colored, will be considered stolen."

34"Agreed," said Laban. "Let it be as you have said." **35**That same day he removed all the male goats that were streaked or spotted, and all the speckled or spotted female goats (all that had white on them) and all the dark-colored lambs, and he placed them in the care of his sons. **36**Then he put a three-day journey between himself and Jacob, while Jacob continued to tend the rest of Laban's flocks.

37Jacob, however, took fresh-cut branches from poplar, almond and plane trees and made white stripes on them by peeling the bark and exposing the white inner wood of the branches. **38**Then he placed the peeled branches in all the watering troughs, so that they would be directly in front of the flocks when they came to drink. When the flocks were in heat and came to drink, **39**they mated in front of the branches. And they bore young that were streaked or speckled or spotted. **40**Jacob set apart the young of the flock by themselves, but made the rest face the streaked and dark-colored animals that belonged to Laban. Thus he made separate flocks for himself and did not put them with Laban's animals. **41**Whenever the stronger females were in heat, Jacob would place the branches in the troughs in front of the animals so they would mate near the branches, **42**but if the animals were weak, he would not place them there. So the weak animals went to Laban and the strong ones to Jacob. **43**In this way the man grew exceedingly prosperous and came to own large flocks, and female and male servants, and camels and donkeys.

Jacob Flees From Laban

31 Jacob heard that Laban's sons were saying, "Jacob has taken everything our father owned and has gained all this wealth from what belonged to our father." **2**And Jacob noticed that Laban's attitude toward him was not what it had been.

3Then the LORD said to Jacob, "Go back to the land of your fathers and to your relatives, and I will be with you."

4So Jacob sent word to Rachel and Leah to come out to the fields where his flocks were. **5**He said to them, "I see that your father's attitude toward me is not what it was before, but the God of my father has been with me. **6**You know that I've worked for your father with all my strength,

[7] yet your father has cheated me by changing my wages ten times. However, God has not allowed him to harm me. [8] If he said, 'The speckled ones will be your wages,' then all the flocks gave birth to speckled young; and if he said, 'The streaked ones will be your wages,' then all the flocks bore streaked young. [9] So God has taken away your father's livestock and has given them to me.

[10] "In breeding season I once had a dream in which I looked up and saw that the male goats mating with the flock were streaked, speckled or spotted. [11] The angel of God said to me in the dream, 'Jacob.' I answered, 'Here I am.' [12] And he said, 'Look up and see that all the male goats mating with the flock are streaked, speckled or spotted, for I have seen all that Laban has been doing to you. [13] I am the God of Bethel, where you anointed a pillar and where you made a vow to me. Now leave this land at once and go back to your native land.'"

[14] Then Rachel and Leah replied, "Do we still have any share in the inheritance of our father's estate? [15] Does he not regard us as foreigners? Not only has he sold us, but he has used up what was paid for us. [16] Surely all the wealth that God took away from our father belongs to us and our children. So do whatever God has told you."

[17] Then Jacob put his children and his wives on camels, [18] and he drove all his livestock ahead of him, along with all the goods he had accumulated in Paddan Aram,[a] to go to his father Isaac in the land of Canaan.

[19] When Laban had gone to shear his sheep, Rachel stole her father's household gods. [20] Moreover, Jacob deceived Laban the Aramean by not telling him he was running away. [21] So he fled with all he had, crossed the Euphrates River, and headed for the hill country of Gilead.

Laban Pursues Jacob

[22] On the third day Laban was told that Jacob had fled. [23] Taking his relatives with him, he pursued Jacob for seven days and caught up with him in the hill country of Gilead. [24] Then God came to Laban the Aramean in a dream at night and said to him, "Be careful not to say anything to Jacob, either good or bad."

[25] Jacob had pitched his tent in the hill country of Gilead when Laban overtook him, and Laban and his relatives camped there too. [26] Then Laban said to Jacob, "What have you done? You've deceived me, and you've carried off my daughters like captives in war. [27] Why did you run off secretly and deceive me? Why didn't you tell me, so I could send you away with joy and singing to

---

[a] 18 That is, Northwest Mesopotamia

the music of timbrels and harps? **28**You didn't even let me kiss my grandchildren and my daughters goodbye. You have done a foolish thing. **29**I have the power to harm you; but last night the God of your father said to me, 'Be careful not to say anything to Jacob, either good or bad.' **30**Now you have gone off because you longed to return to your father's household. But why did you steal my gods?"

31Jacob answered Laban, "I was afraid, because I thought you would take your daughters away from me by force. **32**But if you find anyone who has your gods, that person shall not live. In the presence of our relatives, see for yourself whether there is anything of yours here with me; and if so, take it." Now Jacob did not know that Rachel had stolen the gods.

33So Laban went into Jacob's tent and into Leah's tent and into the tent of the two female servants, but he found nothing. After he came out of Leah's tent, he entered Rachel's tent. **34**Now Rachel had taken the household gods and put them inside her camel's saddle and was sitting on them. Laban searched through everything in the tent but found nothing.

35Rachel said to her father, "Don't be angry, my lord, that I cannot stand up in your presence; I'm having my period." So he searched but could not find the household gods.

36Jacob was angry and took Laban to task. "What is my crime?" he asked Laban. "How have I wronged you that you hunt me down? **37**Now that you have searched through all my goods, what have you found that belongs to your household? Put it here in front of your relatives and mine, and let them judge between the two of us.

38"I have been with you for twenty years now. Your sheep and goats have not miscarried, nor have I eaten rams from your flocks. **39**I did not bring you animals torn by wild beasts; I bore the loss myself. And you demanded payment from me for whatever was stolen by day or night. **40**This was my situation: The heat consumed me in the daytime and the cold at night, and sleep fled from my eyes. **41**It was like this for the twenty years I was in your household. I worked for you fourteen years for your two daughters and six years for your flocks, and you changed my wages ten times. **42**If the God of my father, the God of Abraham and the Fear of Isaac, had not been with me, you would surely have sent me away empty-handed. But God has seen my hardship and the toil of my hands, and last night he rebuked you."

43Laban answered Jacob, "The women are my daughters, the children are my children, and the flocks are my flocks. All you see is mine. Yet what can I do today about these daughters of mine, or about the children they have borne? **44** Come now, let's make a covenant, you and I, and let it serve as a witness between us."

45 So Jacob took a stone and set it up as a pillar. **46** He said to his relatives, "Gather some stones." So they took stones and piled them in a heap, and they ate there by the heap. **47** Laban called it Jegar Sahadutha, and Jacob called it Galeed.*a*

48 Laban said, "This heap is a witness between you and me today." That is why it was called Galeed. **49** It was also called Mizpah,*b* because he said, "May the LORD keep watch between you and me when we are away from each other. **50** If you mistreat my daughters or if you take any wives besides my daughters, even though no one is with us, remember that God is a witness between you and me."

51 Laban also said to Jacob, "Here is this heap, and here is this pillar I have set up between you and me. **52** This heap is a witness, and this pillar is a witness, that I will not go past this heap to your side to harm you and that you will not go past this heap and pillar to my side to harm me. **53** May the God of Abraham and the God of Nahor, the God of their father, judge between us."

So Jacob took an oath in the name of the Fear of his father Isaac. **54** He offered a sacrifice there in the hill country and invited his relatives to a meal. After they had eaten, they spent the night there.

55 Early the next morning Laban kissed his grandchildren and his daughters and blessed them. Then he left and returned home.*c*

Jacob Prepares to Meet Esau

32*d* Jacob also went on his way, and the angels of God met him. **2** When Jacob saw them, he said, "This is the camp of God!" So he named that place Mahanaim.*e*

3 Jacob sent messengers ahead of him to his brother Esau in the land of Seir, the country of Edom. **4** He instructed them: "This is what you are to say to my lord Esau: 'Your servant Jacob says, I have been staying with Laban and have remained there till now. **5** I have cattle and donkeys, sheep and goats, male and female servants. Now I am sending this message to my lord, that I may find favor in your eyes.'"

6 When the messengers returned to Jacob, they said, "We went to your brother Esau, and now he is coming to meet you, and four hundred men are with him."

---

a 47 The Aramaic *Jegar Sahadutha* and the Hebrew *Galeed* both mean *witness heap.*   *b* 49 *Mizpah* means *watchtower.*   *c* 55 In Hebrew texts this verse (31:55) is numbered 32:1.   *d* In Hebrew texts 32:1-32 is numbered 32:2-33.
e 2 *Mahanaim* means *two camps.*

⁷In great fear and distress Jacob divided the people who were with him into two groups,ᵃ and the flocks and herds and camels as well. ⁸He thought, "If Esau comes and attacks one group,ᵇ the groupᵇ that is left may escape."

⁹Then Jacob prayed, "O God of my father Abraham, God of my father Isaac, LORD, you who said to me, 'Go back to your country and your relatives, and I will make you prosper,' ¹⁰I am unworthy of all the kindness and faithfulness you have shown your servant. I had only my staff when I crossed this Jordan, but now I have become two camps. ¹¹Save me, I pray, from the hand of my brother Esau, for I am afraid he will come and attack me, and also the mothers with their children. ¹²But you have said, 'I will surely make you prosper and will make your descendants like the sand of the sea, which cannot be counted.'"

¹³He spent the night there, and from what he had with him he selected a gift for his brother Esau: ¹⁴two hundred female goats and twenty male goats, two hundred ewes and twenty rams, ¹⁵thirty female camels with their young, forty cows and ten bulls, and twenty female donkeys and ten male donkeys. ¹⁶He put them in the care of his servants, each herd by itself, and said to his servants, "Go ahead of me, and keep some space between the herds."

¹⁷He instructed the one in the lead: "When my brother Esau meets you and asks, 'Who do you belong to, and where are you going, and who owns all these animals in front of you?' ¹⁸then you are to say, 'They belong to your servant Jacob. They are a gift sent to my lord Esau, and he is coming behind us.'"

¹⁹He also instructed the second, the third and all the others who followed the herds: "You are to say the same thing to Esau when you meet him. ²⁰And be sure to say, 'Your servant Jacob is coming behind us.'" For he thought, "I will pacify him with these gifts I am sending on ahead; later, when I see him, perhaps he will receive me." ²¹So Jacob's gifts went on ahead of him, but he himself spent the night in the camp.

Jacob Wrestles With God

²²That night Jacob got up and took his two wives, his two female servants and his eleven sons and crossed the ford of the Jabbok. ²³After he had sent them across the stream, he sent over all his possessions. ²⁴So Jacob was left alone, and a man wrestled with him till daybreak. ²⁵When the man saw that he could not overpower him, he touched the socket of Jacob's hip so that his hip was

---

ᵃ 7 Or *camps*   ᵇ 8 Or *camp*

wrenched as he wrestled with the man. **26** Then the man said, "Let me go, for it is daybreak."

But Jacob replied, "I will not let you go unless you bless me."

27 The man asked him, "What is your name?"

"Jacob," he answered.

28 Then the man said, "Your name will no longer be Jacob, but Israel,*a* because you have struggled with God and with humans and have overcome."

29 Jacob said, "Please tell me your name."

But he replied, "Why do you ask my name?" Then he blessed him there.

30 So Jacob called the place Peniel,*b* saying, "It is because I saw God face to face, and yet my life was spared."

31 The sun rose above him as he passed Peniel,*c* and he was limping because of his hip. **32** Therefore to this day the Israelites do not eat the tendon attached to the socket of the hip, because the socket of Jacob's hip was touched near the tendon.

Jacob Meets Esau

33 Jacob looked up and there was Esau, coming with his four hundred men; so he divided the children among Leah, Rachel and the two female servants. **2** He put the female servants and their children in front, Leah and her children next, and Rachel and Joseph in the rear. **3** He himself went on ahead and bowed down to the ground seven times as he approached his brother.

4 But Esau ran to meet Jacob and embraced him; he threw his arms around his neck and kissed him. And they wept. **5** Then Esau looked up and saw the women and children. "Who are these with you?" he asked.

Jacob answered, "They are the children God has graciously given your servant."

6 Then the female servants and their children approached and bowed down. **7** Next, Leah and her children came and bowed down. Last of all came Joseph and Rachel, and they too bowed down.

8 Esau asked, "What's the meaning of all these flocks and herds I met?"

"To find favor in your eyes, my lord," he said.

9 But Esau said, "I already have plenty, my brother. Keep what you have for yourself."

10 "No, please!" said Jacob. "If I have found favor in your eyes, accept this gift from me. For to see your face is like seeing the face of God, now that you have received me favorably. **11** Please accept the present that was brought to you, for God has been gracious

---

a 28 Israel probably means *he struggles with God.*   *b 30 Peniel* means *face of God.*   *c 31* Hebrew *Penuel,* a variant of *Peniel* to me and I have all I need." And because Jacob insisted, Esau accepted it.

¹²Then Esau said, "Let us be on our way; I'll accompany you."

¹³But Jacob said to him, "My lord knows that the children are tender and that I must care for the ewes and cows that are nursing their young. If they are driven hard just one day, all the animals will die. ¹⁴So let my lord go on ahead of his servant, while I move along slowly at the pace of the flocks and herds before me and the pace of the children, until I come to my lord in Seir."

¹⁵Esau said, "Then let me leave some of my men with you."

"But why do that?" Jacob asked. "Just let me find favor in the eyes of my lord."

¹⁶So that day Esau started on his way back to Seir. ¹⁷Jacob, however, went to Sukkoth, where he built a place for himself and made shelters for his livestock. That is why the place is called Sukkoth.ᵃ

¹⁸After Jacob came from Paddan Aram,ᵇ he arrived safely at the city of Shechem in Canaan and camped within sight of the city. ¹⁹For a hundred pieces of silver,ᶜ he bought from the sons of Hamor, the father of Shechem, the plot of ground where he pitched his tent. ²⁰There he set up an altar and called it El Elohe Israel.ᵈ

Dinah and the Shechemites

34 Now Dinah, the daughter Leah had borne to Jacob, went out to visit the women of the land. ²When Shechem son of Hamor the Hivite, the ruler of that area, saw her, he took her and raped her. ³His heart was drawn to Dinah daughter of Jacob; he loved the young woman and spoke tenderly to her. ⁴And Shechem said to his father Hamor, "Get me this girl as my wife."

⁵When Jacob heard that his daughter Dinah had been defiled, his sons were in the fields with his livestock; so he did nothing about it until they came home.

⁶Then Shechem's father Hamor went out to talk with Jacob. ⁷Meanwhile, Jacob's sons had come in from the fields as soon as they heard what had happened. They were shocked and furious, because Shechem had done an outrageous thing inᵉ Israel by sleeping with Jacob's daughter — a thing that should not be done.

⁸But Hamor said to them, "My son Shechem has his heart set on your daughter. Please give her to him as his wife. ⁹Intermarry with us; give us your daughters and take our daughters for your-

---

ᵃ 17 Sukkoth means shelters.   ᵇ 18 That is, Northwest Mesopotamia
ᶜ 19 Hebrew hundred kesitahs; a kesitah was a unit of money of unknown weight and value.   ᵈ 20 El Elohe Israel can mean El is the God of Israel or mighty is the God of Israel.   ᵉ 7 Or against

selves. [10] You can settle among us; the land is open to you. Live in it, trade[a] in it, and acquire property in it."

[11] Then Shechem said to Dinah's father and brothers, "Let me find favor in your eyes, and I will give you whatever you ask. [12] Make the price for the bride and the gift I am to bring as great as you like, and I'll pay whatever you ask me. Only give me the young woman as my wife."

[13] Because their sister Dinah had been defiled, Jacob's sons replied deceitfully as they spoke to Shechem and his father Hamor. [14] They said to them, "We can't do such a thing; we can't give our sister to a man who is not circumcised. That would be a disgrace to us. [15] We will enter into an agreement with you on one condition only: that you become like us by circumcising all your males. [16] Then we will give you our daughters and take your daughters for ourselves. We'll settle among you and become one people with you. [17] But if you will not agree to be circumcised, we'll take our sister and go."

[18] Their proposal seemed good to Hamor and his son Shechem. [19] The young man, who was the most honored of all his father's family, lost no time in doing what they said, because he was delighted with Jacob's daughter. [20] So Hamor and his son Shechem went to the gate of their city to speak to the men of their city. [21] "These men are friendly toward us," they said. "Let them live in our land and trade in it; the land has plenty of room for them. We can marry their daughters and they can marry ours. [22] But the men will agree to live with us as one people only on the condition that our males be circumcised, as they themselves are. [23] Won't their livestock, their property and all their other animals become ours? So let us agree to their terms, and they will settle among us."

[24] All the men who went out of the city gate agreed with Hamor and his son Shechem, and every male in the city was circumcised.

[25] Three days later, while all of them were still in pain, two of Jacob's sons, Simeon and Levi, Dinah's brothers, took their swords and attacked the unsuspecting city, killing every male. [26] They put Hamor and his son Shechem to the sword and took Dinah from Shechem's house and left. [27] The sons of Jacob came upon the dead bodies and looted the city where[b] their sister had been defiled. [28] They seized their flocks and herds and donkeys and everything else of theirs in the city and out in the fields. [29] They carried off all their wealth and all their women and children, taking as plunder everything in the houses.

[30] Then Jacob said to Simeon

---

[a] 10 Or *move about freely*; also in verse 21   [b] 27 Or *because*

and Levi, "You have brought trouble on me by making me obnoxious to the Canaanites and Perizzites, the people living in this land. We are few in number, and if they join forces against me and attack me, I and my household will be destroyed."

³¹But they replied, "Should he have treated our sister like a prostitute?"

Jacob Returns to Bethel

35 Then God said to Jacob, "Go up to Bethel and settle there, and build an altar there to God, who appeared to you when you were fleeing from your brother Esau."

²So Jacob said to his household and to all who were with him, "Get rid of the foreign gods you have with you, and purify yourselves and change your clothes. ³Then come, let us go up to Bethel, where I will build an altar to God, who answered me in the day of my distress and who has been with me wherever I have gone." ⁴So they gave Jacob all the foreign gods they had and the rings in their ears, and Jacob buried them under the oak at Shechem. ⁵Then they set out, and the terror of God fell on the towns all around them so that no one pursued them.

⁶Jacob and all the people with him came to Luz (that is, Bethel) in the land of Canaan. ⁷There he built an altar, and he called the place El Bethel,ᵃ because it was there that God revealed himself to him when he was fleeing from his brother.

⁸Now Deborah, Rebekah's nurse, died and was buried under the oak outside Bethel. So it was named Allon Bakuth.ᵇ

⁹After Jacob returned from Paddan Aram,ᶜ God appeared to him again and blessed him. ¹⁰God said to him, "Your name is Jacob,ᵈ but you will no longer be called Jacob; your name will be Israel.ᵉ" So he named him Israel.

¹¹And God said to him, "I am God Almighty ᶠ; be fruitful and increase in number. A nation and a community of nations will come from you, and kings will be among your descendants. ¹²The land I gave to Abraham and Isaac I also give to you, and I will give this land to your descendants after you." ¹³Then God went up from him at the place where he had talked with him.

¹⁴Jacob set up a stone pillar at the place where God had talked with him, and he poured out a drink offering on it; he also poured oil on it. ¹⁵Jacob called the place where God had talked with him Bethel.ᵍ

ᵃ 7 *El Bethel* means *God of Bethel*.   ᵇ 8 *Allon Bakuth* means *oak of weeping*.
ᶜ 9 That is, Northwest Mesopotamia; also in verse 26   ᵈ 10 *Jacob* means *he grasps the heel*, a Hebrew idiom for *he deceives*.   ᵉ 10 *Israel* probably means *he struggles with God*.   ᶠ 11 Hebrew *El-Shaddai*   ᵍ 15 *Bethel* means *house of God*.

The Deaths of Rachel and Isaac

[16]Then they moved on from Bethel. While they were still some distance from Ephrath, Rachel began to give birth and had great difficulty. [17]And as she was having great difficulty in childbirth, the midwife said to her, "Don't despair, for you have another son." [18]As she breathed her last—for she was dying—she named her son Ben-Oni.[a] But his father named him Benjamin.[b]

[19]So Rachel died and was buried on the way to Ephrath (that is, Bethlehem). [20]Over her tomb Jacob set up a pillar, and to this day that pillar marks Rachel's tomb.

[21]Israel moved on again and pitched his tent beyond Migdal Eder. [22]While Israel was living in that region, Reuben went in and slept with his father's concubine Bilhah, and Israel heard of it.

Jacob had twelve sons:
[23]The sons of Leah:
> Reuben the firstborn of Jacob,
> Simeon, Levi, Judah, Issachar and Zebulun.
[24]The sons of Rachel:
> Joseph and Benjamin.
[25]The sons of Rachel's servant Bilhah:
> Dan and Naphtali.
[26]The sons of Leah's servant Zilpah:
> Gad and Asher.

These were the sons of Jacob, who were born to him in Paddan Aram.

[27]Jacob came home to his father Isaac in Mamre, near Kiriath Arba (that is, Hebron), where Abraham and Isaac had stayed. [28]Isaac lived a hundred and eighty years. [29]Then he breathed his last and died and was gathered to his people, old and full of years. And his sons Esau and Jacob buried him.

Esau's Descendants

36
[1]This is the account of the family line of Esau (that is, Edom).

[2]Esau took his wives from the women of Canaan: Adah daughter of Elon the Hittite, and Oholibamah daughter of Anah and granddaughter of Zibeon the Hivite — [3]also Basemath daughter of Ishmael and sister of Nebaioth.

[4]Adah bore Eliphaz to Esau, Basemath bore Reuel, [5]and Oholibamah bore Jeush, Jalam and Korah. These were the sons of Esau, who were born to him in Canaan.

[6]Esau took his wives and sons and daughters and all the members of his household, as well as his livestock and all his other animals and all the goods he had acquired in Canaan, and moved to a

---

[a] 18 Ben-Oni means son of my trouble.   [b] 18 Benjamin means son of my right hand.

land some distance from his brother Jacob. **7** Their possessions were too great for them to remain together; the land where they were staying could not support them both because of their livestock. **8** So Esau (that is, Edom) settled in the hill country of Seir.

9 This is the account of the family line of Esau the father of the Edomites in the hill country of Seir.

10 These are the names of Esau's sons:

Eliphaz, the son of Esau's wife Adah, and Reuel, the son of Esau's wife Basemath.
11 The sons of Eliphaz:
Teman, Omar, Zepho, Gatam and Kenaz.
12 Esau's son Eliphaz also had a concubine named Timna, who bore him Amalek. These were grandsons of Esau's wife Adah.
13 The sons of Reuel:
Nahath, Zerah, Shammah and Mizzah. These were grandsons of Esau's wife Basemath.
14 The sons of Esau's wife Oholibamah daughter of Anah and granddaughter of Zibeon, whom she bore to Esau:
Jeush, Jalam and Korah.

15 These were the chiefs among Esau's descendants:

The sons of Eliphaz the firstborn of Esau:
Chiefs Teman, Omar, Zepho, Kenaz, **16** Korah,*a* Gatam and Amalek. These were the chiefs descended from Eliphaz in Edom; they were grandsons of Adah.
17 The sons of Esau's son Reuel:
Chiefs Nahath, Zerah, Shammah and Mizzah. These were the chiefs descended from Reuel in Edom; they were grandsons of Esau's wife Basemath.
18 The sons of Esau's wife Oholibamah:
Chiefs Jeush, Jalam and Korah. These were the chiefs descended from Esau's wife Oholibamah daughter of Anah.

19 These were the sons of Esau (that is, Edom), and these were their chiefs.

20 These were the sons of Seir the Horite, who were living in the region:

Lotan, Shobal, Zibeon, Anah, **21** Dishon, Ezer and Dishan. These sons of Seir in Edom were Horite chiefs.
22 The sons of Lotan:
Hori and Homam.*b* Timna was Lotan's sister.

---

a 16 Masoretic Text; Samaritan Pentateuch (also verse 11 and 1 Chron. 1:36) does not have *Korah*.   *b 22* Hebrew *Hemam,* a variant of *Homam* (see 1 Chron. 1:39)

²³The sons of Shobal:
Alvan, Manahath, Ebal, Shepho and Onam.

²⁴The sons of Zibeon:
Aiah and Anah. This is the Anah who discovered the hot springs^a in the desert while he was grazing the donkeys of his father Zibeon.

²⁵The children of Anah:
Dishon and Oholibamah daughter of Anah.

²⁶The sons of Dishon^b:
Hemdan, Eshban, Ithran and Keran.

²⁷The sons of Ezer:
Bilhan, Zaavan and Akan.

²⁸The sons of Dishan:
Uz and Aran.

²⁹These were the Horite chiefs:
Lotan, Shobal, Zibeon, Anah, ³⁰Dishon, Ezer and Dishan. These were the Horite chiefs, according to their divisions, in the land of Seir.

The Rulers of Edom

³¹These were the kings who reigned in Edom before any Israelite king reigned:

³²Bela son of Beor became king of Edom. His city was named Dinhabah.

³³When Bela died, Jobab son of Zerah from Bozrah succeeded him as king.

³⁴When Jobab died, Husham from the land of the Temanites succeeded him as king.

³⁵When Husham died, Hadad son of Bedad, who defeated Midian in the country of Moab, succeeded him as king. His city was named Avith.

³⁶When Hadad died, Samlah from Masrekah succeeded him as king.

³⁷When Samlah died, Shaul from Rehoboth on the river succeeded him as king.

³⁸When Shaul died, Baal-Hanan son of Akbor succeeded him as king.

³⁹When Baal-Hanan son of Akbor died, Hadad^c succeeded him as king. His city was named Pau, and his wife's name was Mehetabel daughter of Matred, the daughter of Me-Zahab.

⁴⁰These were the chiefs descended from Esau, by name, according to their clans and regions:

Timna, Alvah, Jetheth, ⁴¹Oholibamah, Elah, Pinon, ⁴²Kenaz, Teman, Mibzar, ⁴³Magdiel and Iram. These were the chiefs of Edom, according to their settlements in the land they occupied.

---

^a 24 Vulgate; Syriac *discovered water;* the meaning of the Hebrew for this word is uncertain.   ^b 26 Hebrew *Dishan,* a variant of *Dishon*   ^c 39 Many manuscripts of the Masoretic Text, Samaritan Pentateuch and Syriac (see also 1 Chron. 1:50); most manuscripts of the Masoretic Text *Hadar*

This is the family line of Esau, the father of the Edomites.

Joseph's Dreams

37 Jacob lived in the land where his father had stayed, the land of Canaan.

²This is the account of Jacob's family line.

Joseph, a young man of seventeen, was tending the flocks with his brothers, the sons of Bilhah and the sons of Zilpah, his father's wives, and he brought their father a bad report about them.

³Now Israel loved Joseph more than any of his other sons, because he had been born to him in his old age; and he made an ornate*ᵃ* robe for him. ⁴When his brothers saw that their father loved him more than any of them, they hated him and could not speak a kind word to him.

⁵Joseph had a dream, and when he told it to his brothers, they hated him all the more. ⁶He said to them, "Listen to this dream I had: ⁷We were binding sheaves of grain out in the field when suddenly my sheaf rose and stood upright, while your sheaves gathered around mine and bowed down to it."

⁸His brothers said to him, "Do you intend to reign over us? Will you actually rule us?" And they hated him all the more because of his dream and what he had said.

⁹Then he had another dream, and he told it to his brothers. "Listen," he said, "I had another dream, and this time the sun and moon and eleven stars were bowing down to me."

¹⁰When he told his father as well as his brothers, his father rebuked him and said, "What is this dream you had? Will your mother and I and your brothers actually come and bow down to the ground before you?" ¹¹His brothers were jealous of him, but his father kept the matter in mind.

Joseph Sold by His Brothers

¹²Now his brothers had gone to graze their father's flocks near Shechem, ¹³and Israel said to Joseph, "As you know, your brothers are grazing the flocks near Shechem. Come, I am going to send you to them."

"Very well," he replied.

¹⁴So he said to him, "Go and see if all is well with your brothers and with the flocks, and bring word back to me." Then he sent him off from the Valley of Hebron.

When Joseph arrived at Shechem, ¹⁵a man found him wandering around in the fields and asked him, "What are you looking for?"

ᵃ 3 The meaning of the Hebrew for this word is uncertain; also in verses 23 and 32.

16 He replied, "I'm looking for my brothers. Can you tell me where they are grazing their flocks?"

17 "They have moved on from here," the man answered. "I heard them say, 'Let's go to Dothan.'"

So Joseph went after his brothers and found them near Dothan. 18 But they saw him in the distance, and before he reached them, they plotted to kill him.

19 "Here comes that dreamer!" they said to each other. 20 "Come now, let's kill him and throw him into one of these cisterns and say that a ferocious animal devoured him. Then we'll see what comes of his dreams."

21 When Reuben heard this, he tried to rescue him from their hands. "Let's not take his life," he said. 22 "Don't shed any blood. Throw him into this cistern here in the wilderness, but don't lay a hand on him." Reuben said this to rescue him from them and take him back to his father.

23 So when Joseph came to his brothers, they stripped him of his robe—the ornate robe he was wearing— 24 and they took him and threw him into the cistern. The cistern was empty; there was no water in it.

25 As they sat down to eat their meal, they looked up and saw a caravan of Ishmaelites coming from Gilead. Their camels were loaded with spices, balm and myrrh, and they were on their way to take them down to Egypt.

26 Judah said to his brothers, "What will we gain if we kill our brother and cover up his blood? 27 Come, let's sell him to the Ishmaelites and not lay our hands on him; after all, he is our brother, our own flesh and blood." His brothers agreed.

28 So when the Midianite merchants came by, his brothers pulled Joseph up out of the cistern and sold him for twenty shekels[a] of silver to the Ishmaelites, who took him to Egypt.

29 When Reuben returned to the cistern and saw that Joseph was not there, he tore his clothes. 30 He went back to his brothers and said, "The boy isn't there! Where can I turn now?"

31 Then they got Joseph's robe, slaughtered a goat and dipped the robe in the blood. 32 They took the ornate robe back to their father and said, "We found this. Examine it to see whether it is your son's robe."

33 He recognized it and said, "It is my son's robe! Some ferocious animal has devoured him. Joseph has surely been torn to pieces."

34 Then Jacob tore his clothes, put on sackcloth and mourned for his son many days. 35 All his sons and daughters came to comfort him, but he refused to be

---

a 28 That is, about 8 ounces or about 230 grams

comforted. "No," he said, "I will continue to mourn until I join my son in the grave." So his father wept for him.

³⁶Meanwhile, the Midianites*ᵃ* sold Joseph in Egypt to Potiphar, one of Pharaoh's officials, the captain of the guard.

Judah and Tamar

38 At that time, Judah left his brothers and went down to stay with a man of Adullam named Hirah. ²There Judah met the daughter of a Canaanite man named Shua. He married her and made love to her; ³she became pregnant and gave birth to a son, who was named Er. ⁴She conceived again and gave birth to a son and named him Onan. ⁵She gave birth to still another son and named him Shelah. It was at Kezib that she gave birth to him.

⁶Judah got a wife for Er, his firstborn, and her name was Tamar. ⁷But Er, Judah's firstborn, was wicked in the LORD's sight; so the LORD put him to death.

⁸Then Judah said to Onan, "Sleep with your brother's wife and fulfill your duty to her as a brother-in-law to raise up offspring for your brother." ⁹But Onan knew that the child would not be his; so whenever he slept with his brother's wife, he spilled his semen on the ground to keep from providing offspring for his brother. ¹⁰What he did was wicked in the LORD's sight; so the LORD put him to death also.

¹¹Judah then said to his daughter-in-law Tamar, "Live as a widow in your father's household until my son Shelah grows up." For he thought, "He may die too, just like his brothers." So Tamar went to live in her father's household.

¹²After a long time Judah's wife, the daughter of Shua, died. When Judah had recovered from his grief, he went up to Timnah, to the men who were shearing his sheep, and his friend Hirah the Adullamite went with him.

¹³When Tamar was told, "Your father-in-law is on his way to Timnah to shear his sheep," ¹⁴she took off her widow's clothes, covered herself with a veil to disguise herself, and then sat down at the entrance to Enaim, which is on the road to Timnah. For she saw that, though Shelah had now grown up, she had not been given to him as his wife.

¹⁵When Judah saw her, he thought she was a prostitute, for she had covered her face. ¹⁶Not realizing that she was his daughter-in-law, he went over to her by the roadside and said, "Come now, let me sleep with you."

"And what will you give me to sleep with you?" she asked.

¹⁷"I'll send you a young goat from my flock," he said.

ᵃ 36 Samaritan Pentateuch, Septuagint, Vulgate and Syriac (see also verse 28); Masoretic Text *Medanites*

"Will you give me something as a pledge until you send it?" she asked.

¹⁸He said, "What pledge should I give you?"

"Your seal and its cord, and the staff in your hand," she answered. So he gave them to her and slept with her, and she became pregnant by him. ¹⁹After she left, she took off her veil and put on her widow's clothes again.

²⁰Meanwhile Judah sent the young goat by his friend the Adullamite in order to get his pledge back from the woman, but he did not find her. ²¹He asked the men who lived there, "Where is the shrine prostitute who was beside the road at Enaim?"

"There hasn't been any shrine prostitute here," they said.

²²So he went back to Judah and said, "I didn't find her. Besides, the men who lived there said, 'There hasn't been any shrine prostitute here.'"

²³Then Judah said, "Let her keep what she has, or we will become a laughingstock. After all, I did send her this young goat, but you didn't find her."

²⁴About three months later Judah was told, "Your daughter-in-law Tamar is guilty of prostitution, and as a result she is now pregnant."

Judah said, "Bring her out and have her burned to death!"

²⁵As she was being brought out, she sent a message to her father-in-law. "I am pregnant by the man who owns these," she said. And she added, "See if you recognize whose seal and cord and staff these are."

²⁶Judah recognized them and said, "She is more righteous than I, since I wouldn't give her to my son Shelah." And he did not sleep with her again.

²⁷When the time came for her to give birth, there were twin boys in her womb. ²⁸As she was giving birth, one of them put out his hand; so the midwife took a scarlet thread and tied it on his wrist and said, "This one came out first." ²⁹But when he drew back his hand, his brother came out, and she said, "So this is how you have broken out!" And he was named Perez.ᵃ ³⁰Then his brother, who had the scarlet thread on his wrist, came out. And he was named Zerah.ᵇ

Joseph and Potiphar's Wife

39
Now Joseph had been taken down to Egypt. Potiphar, an Egyptian who was one of Pharaoh's officials, the captain of the guard, bought him from the Ishmaelites who had taken him there.

²The LORD was with Joseph so that he prospered, and he lived in the house of his Egyptian master. ³When his master saw that the LORD was with him and that the

---

ᵃ 29 Perez means breaking out.   ᵇ 30 Zerah can mean scarlet or brightness.

LORD gave him success in everything he did, ⁴Joseph found favor in his eyes and became his attendant. Potiphar put him in charge of his household, and he entrusted to his care everything he owned. ⁵From the time he put him in charge of his household and of all that he owned, the LORD blessed the household of the Egyptian because of Joseph. The blessing of the LORD was on everything Potiphar had, both in the house and in the field. ⁶So Potiphar left everything he had in Joseph's care; with Joseph in charge, he did not concern himself with anything except the food he ate.

Now Joseph was well-built and handsome, ⁷and after a while his master's wife took notice of Joseph and said, "Come to bed with me!"

⁸But he refused. "With me in charge," he told her, "my master does not concern himself with anything in the house; everything he owns he has entrusted to my care. ⁹No one is greater in this house than I am. My master has withheld nothing from me except you, because you are his wife. How then could I do such a wicked thing and sin against God?" ¹⁰And though she spoke to Joseph day after day, he refused to go to bed with her or even be with her.

¹¹One day he went into the house to attend to his duties, and none of the household servants was inside. ¹²She caught him by his cloak and said, "Come to bed with me!" But he left his cloak in her hand and ran out of the house.

¹³When she saw that he had left his cloak in her hand and had run out of the house, ¹⁴she called her household servants. "Look," she said to them, "this Hebrew has been brought to us to make sport of us! He came in here to sleep with me, but I screamed. ¹⁵When he heard me scream for help, he left his cloak beside me and ran out of the house."

¹⁶She kept his cloak beside her until his master came home. ¹⁷Then she told him this story: "That Hebrew slave you brought us came to me to make sport of me. ¹⁸But as soon as I screamed for help, he left his cloak beside me and ran out of the house."

¹⁹When his master heard the story his wife told him, saying, "This is how your slave treated me," he burned with anger. ²⁰Joseph's master took him and put him in prison, the place where the king's prisoners were confined.

But while Joseph was there in the prison, ²¹the LORD was with him; he showed him kindness and granted him favor in the eyes of the prison warden. ²²So the warden put Joseph in charge of all those held in the prison, and he was made responsible for all that was done there. ²³The warden paid no attention to anything under Joseph's care, because the LORD was with Joseph and gave him success in whatever he did.

The Cupbearer and the Baker

40 Some time later, the cupbearer and the baker of the king of Egypt offended their master, the king of Egypt. ²Pharaoh was angry with his two officials, the chief cupbearer and the chief baker, ³and put them in custody in the house of the captain of the guard, in the same prison where Joseph was confined. ⁴The captain of the guard assigned them to Joseph, and he attended them.

After they had been in custody for some time, ⁵each of the two men—the cupbearer and the baker of the king of Egypt, who were being held in prison—had a dream the same night, and each dream had a meaning of its own.

⁶When Joseph came to them the next morning, he saw that they were dejected. ⁷So he asked Pharaoh's officials who were in custody with him in his master's house, "Why do you look so sad today?"

⁸"We both had dreams," they answered, "but there is no one to interpret them."

Then Joseph said to them, "Do not interpretations belong to God? Tell me your dreams."

⁹So the chief cupbearer told Joseph his dream. He said to him, "In my dream I saw a vine in front of me, ¹⁰and on the vine were three branches. As soon as it budded, it blossomed, and its clusters ripened into grapes. ¹¹Pharaoh's cup was in my hand, and I took the grapes, squeezed them into Pharaoh's cup and put the cup in his hand."

¹²"This is what it means," Joseph said to him. "The three branches are three days. ¹³Within three days Pharaoh will lift up your head and restore you to your position, and you will put Pharaoh's cup in his hand, just as you used to do when you were his cupbearer. ¹⁴But when all goes well with you, remember me and show me kindness; mention me to Pharaoh and get me out of this prison. ¹⁵I was forcibly carried off from the land of the Hebrews, and even here I have done nothing to deserve being put in a dungeon."

¹⁶When the chief baker saw that Joseph had given a favorable interpretation, he said to Joseph, "I too had a dream: On my head were three baskets of bread.^a ¹⁷In the top basket were all kinds of baked goods for Pharaoh, but the birds were eating them out of the basket on my head."

¹⁸"This is what it means," Joseph said. "The three baskets are three days. ¹⁹Within three days

^a 16 Or *three wicker baskets*

Pharaoh will lift off your head and impale your body on a pole. And the birds will eat away your flesh."

²⁰ Now the third day was Pharaoh's birthday, and he gave a feast for all his officials. He lifted up the heads of the chief cupbearer and the chief baker in the presence of his officials: ²¹ He restored the chief cupbearer to his position, so that he once again put the cup into Pharaoh's hand — ²² but he impaled the chief baker, just as Joseph had said to them in his interpretation.

²³ The chief cupbearer, however, did not remember Joseph; he forgot him.

Pharaoh's Dreams

41 When two full years had passed, Pharaoh had a dream: He was standing by the Nile, ² when out of the river there came up seven cows, sleek and fat, and they grazed among the reeds. ³ After them, seven other cows, ugly and gaunt, came up out of the Nile and stood beside those on the riverbank. ⁴ And the cows that were ugly and gaunt ate up the seven sleek, fat cows. Then Pharaoh woke up.

⁵ He fell asleep again and had a second dream: Seven heads of grain, healthy and good, were growing on a single stalk. ⁶ After them, seven other heads of grain sprouted — thin and scorched by the east wind. ⁷ The thin heads of grain swallowed up the seven healthy, full heads. Then Pharaoh woke up; it had been a dream.

⁸ In the morning his mind was troubled, so he sent for all the magicians and wise men of Egypt. Pharaoh told them his dreams, but no one could interpret them for him.

⁹ Then the chief cupbearer said to Pharaoh, "Today I am reminded of my shortcomings. ¹⁰ Pharaoh was once angry with his servants, and he imprisoned me and the chief baker in the house of the captain of the guard. ¹¹ Each of us had a dream the same night, and each dream had a meaning of its own. ¹² Now a young Hebrew was there with us, a servant of the captain of the guard. We told him our dreams, and he interpreted them for us, giving each man the interpretation of his dream. ¹³ And things turned out exactly as he interpreted them to us: I was restored to my position, and the other man was impaled."

¹⁴ So Pharaoh sent for Joseph, and he was quickly brought from the dungeon. When he had shaved and changed his clothes, he came before Pharaoh.

¹⁵ Pharaoh said to Joseph, "I had a dream, and no one can interpret it. But I have heard it said of you that when you hear a dream you can interpret it."

¹⁶ "I cannot do it," Joseph replied to Pharaoh, "but God will give Pharaoh the answer he desires."

opened all the storehouses and sold grain to the Egyptians, for the famine was severe throughout Egypt. ⁵⁷And all the world came to Egypt to buy grain from Joseph, because the famine was severe everywhere.

Joseph's Brothers Go to Egypt

42 When Jacob learned that there was grain in Egypt, he said to his sons, "Why do you just keep looking at each other?" ²He continued, "I have heard that there is grain in Egypt. Go down there and buy some for us, so that we may live and not die."

³Then ten of Joseph's brothers went down to buy grain from Egypt. ⁴But Jacob did not send Benjamin, Joseph's brother, with the others, because he was afraid that harm might come to him. ⁵So Israel's sons were among those who went to buy grain, for there was famine in the land of Canaan also.

⁶Now Joseph was the governor of the land, the person who sold grain to all its people. So when Joseph's brothers arrived, they bowed down to him with their faces to the ground. ⁷As soon as Joseph saw his brothers, he recognized them, but he pretended to be a stranger and spoke harshly to them. "Where do you come from?" he asked.

"From the land of Canaan," they replied, "to buy food."

⁸Although Joseph recognized his brothers, they did not recognize him. ⁹Then he remembered his dreams about them and said to them, "You are spies! You have come to see where our land is unprotected."

¹⁰"No, my lord," they answered. "Your servants have come to buy food. ¹¹We are all the sons of one man. Your servants are honest men, not spies."

¹²"No!" he said to them. "You have come to see where our land is unprotected."

¹³But they replied, "Your servants were twelve brothers, the sons of one man, who lives in the land of Canaan. The youngest is now with our father, and one is no more."

¹⁴Joseph said to them, "It is just as I told you: You are spies! ¹⁵And this is how you will be tested: As surely as Pharaoh lives, you will not leave this place unless your youngest brother comes here. ¹⁶Send one of your number to get your brother; the rest of you will be kept in prison, so that your words may be tested to see if you are telling the truth. If you are not, then as surely as Pharaoh lives, you are spies!" ¹⁷And he put them all in custody for three days.

¹⁸On the third day, Joseph said to them, "Do this and you will live, for I fear God: ¹⁹If you are honest men, let one of your brothers stay here in prison, while the rest of you go and take grain back

for your starving households. **20** But you must bring your youngest brother to me, so that your words may be verified and that you may not die." This they proceeded to do.

21 They said to one another, "Surely we are being punished because of our brother. We saw how distressed he was when he pleaded with us for his life, but we would not listen; that's why this distress has come on us."

22 Reuben replied, "Didn't I tell you not to sin against the boy? But you wouldn't listen! Now we must give an accounting for his blood." **23** They did not realize that Joseph could understand them, since he was using an interpreter.

24 He turned away from them and began to weep, but then came back and spoke to them again. He had Simeon taken from them and bound before their eyes.

25 Joseph gave orders to fill their bags with grain, to put each man's silver back in his sack, and to give them provisions for their journey. After this was done for them, **26** they loaded their grain on their donkeys and left.

27 At the place where they stopped for the night one of them opened his sack to get feed for his donkey, and he saw his silver in the mouth of his sack. **28** "My silver has been returned," he said to his brothers. "Here it is in my sack."

Their hearts sank and they turned to each other trembling and said, "What is this that God has done to us?"

29 When they came to their father Jacob in the land of Canaan, they told him all that had happened to them. They said, **30** "The man who is lord over the land spoke harshly to us and treated us as though we were spying on the land. **31** But we said to him, 'We are honest men; we are not spies. **32** We were twelve brothers, sons of one father. One is no more, and the youngest is now with our father in Canaan.'

33 "Then the man who is lord over the land said to us, 'This is how I will know whether you are honest men: Leave one of your brothers here with me, and take food for your starving households and go. **34** But bring your youngest brother to me so I will know that you are not spies but honest men. Then I will give your brother back to you, and you can trade*a* in the land.'"

35 As they were emptying their sacks, there in each man's sack was his pouch of silver! When they and their father saw the money pouches, they were frightened. **36** Their father Jacob said to them, "You have deprived me of my children. Joseph is no more and Simeon is no more, and now you want to take Benjamin. Everything is against me!"

---

a 34 Or *move about freely*

37 Then Reuben said to his father, "You may put both of my sons to death if I do not bring him back to you. Entrust him to my care, and I will bring him back."

38 But Jacob said, "My son will not go down there with you; his brother is dead and he is the only one left. If harm comes to him on the journey you are taking, you will bring my gray head down to the grave in sorrow."

The Second Journey to Egypt

43 Now the famine was still severe in the land. **2** So when they had eaten all the grain they had brought from Egypt, their father said to them, "Go back and buy us a little more food."

3 But Judah said to him, "The man warned us solemnly, 'You will not see my face again unless your brother is with you.' **4** If you will send our brother along with us, we will go down and buy food for you. **5** But if you will not send him, we will not go down, because the man said to us, 'You will not see my face again unless your brother is with you.'"

6 Israel asked, "Why did you bring this trouble on me by telling the man you had another brother?"

7 They replied, "The man questioned us closely about ourselves and our family. 'Is your father still living?' he asked us. 'Do you have another brother?' We simply answered his questions. How were we to know he would say, 'Bring your brother down here'?"

8 Then Judah said to Israel his father, "Send the boy along with me and we will go at once, so that we and you and our children may live and not die. **9** I myself will guarantee his safety; you can hold me personally responsible for him. If I do not bring him back to you and set him here before you, I will bear the blame before you all my life. **10** As it is, if we had not delayed, we could have gone and returned twice."

11 Then their father Israel said to them, "If it must be, then do this: Put some of the best products of the land in your bags and take them down to the man as a gift—a little balm and a little honey, some spices and myrrh, some pistachio nuts and almonds. **12** Take double the amount of silver with you, for you must return the silver that was put back into the mouths of your sacks. Perhaps it was a mistake. **13** Take your brother also and go back to the man at once. **14** And may God Almighty[a] grant you mercy before the man so that he will let your other brother and Benjamin come back with you. As for me, if I am bereaved, I am bereaved."

15 So the men took the gifts and double the amount of silver, and

---

a 14 Hebrew *El-Shaddai*

Benjamin also. They hurried down to Egypt and presented themselves to Joseph. ¹⁶When Joseph saw Benjamin with them, he said to the steward of his house, "Take these men to my house, slaughter an animal and prepare a meal; they are to eat with me at noon."

¹⁷The man did as Joseph told him and took the men to Joseph's house. ¹⁸Now the men were frightened when they were taken to his house. They thought, "We were brought here because of the silver that was put back into our sacks the first time. He wants to attack us and overpower us and seize us as slaves and take our donkeys."

¹⁹So they went up to Joseph's steward and spoke to him at the entrance to the house. ²⁰"We beg your pardon, our lord," they said, "we came down here the first time to buy food. ²¹But at the place where we stopped for the night we opened our sacks and each of us found his silver — the exact weight — in the mouth of his sack. So we have brought it back with us. ²²We have also brought additional silver with us to buy food. We don't know who put our silver in our sacks."

²³"It's all right," he said. "Don't be afraid. Your God, the God of your father, has given you treasure in your sacks; I received your silver." Then he brought Simeon out to them.

²⁴The steward took the men into Joseph's house, gave them water to wash their feet and provided fodder for their donkeys. ²⁵They prepared their gifts for Joseph's arrival at noon, because they had heard that they were to eat there.

²⁶When Joseph came home, they presented to him the gifts they had brought into the house, and they bowed down before him to the ground. ²⁷He asked them how they were, and then he said, "How is your aged father you told me about? Is he still living?"

²⁸They replied, "Your servant our father is still alive and well." And they bowed down, prostrating themselves before him.

²⁹As he looked about and saw his brother Benjamin, his own mother's son, he asked, "Is this your youngest brother, the one you told me about?" And he said, "God be gracious to you, my son." ³⁰Deeply moved at the sight of his brother, Joseph hurried out and looked for a place to weep. He went into his private room and wept there.

³¹After he had washed his face, he came out and, controlling himself, said, "Serve the food."

³²They served him by himself, the brothers by themselves, and the Egyptians who ate with him by themselves, because Egyptians could not eat with Hebrews, for that is detestable to Egyptians. ³³The men had been seated be-

fore him in the order of their ages, from the firstborn to the youngest; and they looked at each other in astonishment. ³⁴When portions were served to them from Joseph's table, Benjamin's portion was five times as much as anyone else's. So they feasted and drank freely with him.

A Silver Cup in a Sack

44 Now Joseph gave these instructions to the steward of his house: "Fill the men's sacks with as much food as they can carry, and put each man's silver in the mouth of his sack. ²Then put my cup, the silver one, in the mouth of the youngest one's sack, along with the silver for his grain." And he did as Joseph said.

³As morning dawned, the men were sent on their way with their donkeys. ⁴They had not gone far from the city when Joseph said to his steward, "Go after those men at once, and when you catch up with them, say to them, 'Why have you repaid good with evil? ⁵Isn't this the cup my master drinks from and also uses for divination? This is a wicked thing you have done.'"

⁶When he caught up with them, he repeated these words to them. ⁷But they said to him, "Why does my lord say such things? Far be it from your servants to do anything like that! ⁸We even brought back to you from the land of Ca-naan the silver we found inside the mouths of our sacks. So why would we steal silver or gold from your master's house? ⁹If any of your servants is found to have it, he will die; and the rest of us will become my lord's slaves."

¹⁰"Very well, then," he said, "let it be as you say. Whoever is found to have it will become my slave; the rest of you will be free from blame."

¹¹Each of them quickly lowered his sack to the ground and opened it. ¹²Then the steward proceeded to search, beginning with the oldest and ending with the youngest. And the cup was found in Benjamin's sack. ¹³At this, they tore their clothes. Then they all loaded their donkeys and returned to the city.

¹⁴Joseph was still in the house when Judah and his brothers came in, and they threw themselves to the ground before him. ¹⁵Joseph said to them, "What is this you have done? Don't you know that a man like me can find things out by divination?"

¹⁶"What can we say to my lord?" Judah replied. "What can we say? How can we prove our innocence? God has uncovered your servants' guilt. We are now my lord's slaves—we ourselves and the one who was found to have the cup."

¹⁷But Joseph said, "Far be it from me to do such a thing! Only the man who was found to have

the cup will become my slave. The rest of you, go back to your father in peace."

18 Then Judah went up to him and said: "Pardon your servant, my lord, let me speak a word to my lord. Do not be angry with your servant, though you are equal to Pharaoh himself. **19** My lord asked his servants, 'Do you have a father or a brother?' **20** And we answered, 'We have an aged father, and there is a young son born to him in his old age. His brother is dead, and he is the only one of his mother's sons left, and his father loves him.'

21 "Then you said to your servants, 'Bring him down to me so I can see him for myself.' **22** And we said to my lord, 'The boy cannot leave his father; if he leaves him, his father will die.' **23** But you told your servants, 'Unless your youngest brother comes down with you, you will not see my face again.' **24** When we went back to your servant my father, we told him what my lord had said.

25 "Then our father said, 'Go back and buy a little more food.' **26** But we said, 'We cannot go down. Only if our youngest brother is with us will we go. We cannot see the man's face unless our youngest brother is with us.'

27 "Your servant my father said to us, 'You know that my wife bore me two sons. **28** One of them went away from me, and I said, "He has surely been torn to pieces." And I have not seen him since. **29** If you take this one from me too and harm comes to him, you will bring my gray head down to the grave in misery.'

30 "So now, if the boy is not with us when I go back to your servant my father, and if my father, whose life is closely bound up with the boy's life, **31** sees that the boy isn't there, he will die. Your servants will bring the gray head of our father down to the grave in sorrow. **32** Your servant guaranteed the boy's safety to my father. I said, 'If I do not bring him back to you, I will bear the blame before you, my father, all my life!'

33 "Now then, please let your servant remain here as my lord's slave in place of the boy, and let the boy return with his brothers. **34** How can I go back to my father if the boy is not with me? No! Do not let me see the misery that would come on my father."

Joseph Makes Himself Known

45 Then Joseph could no longer control himself before all his attendants, and he cried out, "Have everyone leave my presence!" So there was no one with Joseph when he made himself known to his brothers. **2** And he wept so loudly that the Egyptians heard him, and Pharaoh's household heard about it.

3 Joseph said to his brothers, "I am Joseph! Is my father still living?" But his brothers were not able to answer him, because they were terrified at his presence.

4 Then Joseph said to his brothers, "Come close to me." When they had done so, he said, "I am your brother Joseph, the one you sold into Egypt! ⁵And now, do not be distressed and do not be angry with yourselves for selling me here, because it was to save lives that God sent me ahead of you. ⁶For two years now there has been famine in the land, and for the next five years there will be no plowing and reaping. ⁷But God sent me ahead of you to preserve for you a remnant on earth and to save your lives by a great deliverance.ᵃ

⁸"So then, it was not you who sent me here, but God. He made me father to Pharaoh, lord of his entire household and ruler of all Egypt. ⁹Now hurry back to my father and say to him, 'This is what your son Joseph says: God has made me lord of all Egypt. Come down to me; don't delay. ¹⁰You shall live in the region of Goshen and be near me—you, your children and grandchildren, your flocks and herds, and all you have. ¹¹I will provide for you there, because five years of famine are still to come. Otherwise you and your household and all who belong to you will become destitute.'

¹²"You can see for yourselves, and so can my brother Benjamin, that it is really I who am speaking to you. ¹³Tell my father about all the honor accorded me in Egypt and about everything you have seen. And bring my father down here quickly."

¹⁴Then he threw his arms around his brother Benjamin and wept, and Benjamin embraced him, weeping. ¹⁵And he kissed all his brothers and wept over them. Afterward his brothers talked with him.

¹⁶When the news reached Pharaoh's palace that Joseph's brothers had come, Pharaoh and all his officials were pleased. ¹⁷Pharaoh said to Joseph, "Tell your brothers, 'Do this: Load your animals and return to the land of Canaan, ¹⁸and bring your father and your families back to me. I will give you the best of the land of Egypt and you can enjoy the fat of the land.'

¹⁹"You are also directed to tell them, 'Do this: Take some carts from Egypt for your children and your wives, and get your father and come. ²⁰Never mind about your belongings, because the best of all Egypt will be yours.' "

²¹So the sons of Israel did this. Joseph gave them carts, as Pharaoh had commanded, and he also gave them provisions for their journey. ²²To each of them he gave new clothing, but to Benjamin he gave three hundred shekelsᵇ of silver and five sets of clothes. ²³And this is what he sent to his father: ten donkeys loaded with the best things of Egypt, and

---

ᵃ 7 Or *save you as a great band of survivors* about 3.5 kilograms

ᵇ 22 That is, about 7 1/2 pounds or

ten female donkeys loaded with grain and bread and other provisions for his journey. **24**Then he sent his brothers away, and as they were leaving he said to them, "Don't quarrel on the way!"

25So they went up out of Egypt and came to their father Jacob in the land of Canaan. **26**They told him, "Joseph is still alive! In fact, he is ruler of all Egypt." Jacob was stunned; he did not believe them. **27**But when they told him everything Joseph had said to them, and when he saw the carts Joseph had sent to carry him back, the spirit of their father Jacob revived. **28**And Israel said, "I'm convinced! My son Joseph is still alive. I will go and see him before I die."

Jacob Goes to Egypt

46 So Israel set out with all that was his, and when he reached Beersheba, he offered sacrifices to the God of his father Isaac.

2And God spoke to Israel in a vision at night and said, "Jacob! Jacob!"

"Here I am," he replied.

3"I am God, the God of your father," he said. "Do not be afraid to go down to Egypt, for I will make you into a great nation there. **4**I will go down to Egypt with you, and I will surely bring you back again. And Joseph's own hand will close your eyes."

5Then Jacob left Beersheba, and Israel's sons took their father Jacob and their children and their wives in the carts that Pharaoh had sent to transport him. **6**So Jacob and all his offspring went to Egypt, taking with them their livestock and the possessions they had acquired in Canaan. **7**Jacob brought with him to Egypt his sons and grandsons and his daughters and granddaughters — all his offspring.

8These are the names of the sons of Israel (Jacob and his descendants) who went to Egypt:

Reuben the firstborn of Jacob.

9The sons of Reuben:

Hanok, Pallu, Hezron and Karmi.

10The sons of Simeon:

Jemuel, Jamin, Ohad, Jakin, Zohar and Shaul the son of a Canaanite woman.

11The sons of Levi:

Gershon, Kohath and Merari.

12The sons of Judah:

Er, Onan, Shelah, Perez and Zerah (but Er and Onan had died in the land of Canaan).

The sons of Perez:

Hezron and Hamul.

13The sons of Issachar:

Tola, Puah,[a] Jashub[b] and Shimron.

---

[a] 13 Samaritan Pentateuch and Syriac (see also 1 Chron. 7:1); Masoretic Text *Puvah*   [b] 13 Samaritan Pentateuch and some Septuagint manuscripts (see also Num. 26:24 and 1 Chron. 7:1); Masoretic Text *Iob*

14The sons of Zebulun:

Sered, Elon and Jahleel.

15These were the sons Leah bore to Jacob in Paddan Aram,*a* besides his daughter Dinah. These sons and daughters of his were thirty-three in all.

16The sons of Gad:

Zephon,*b* Haggi, Shuni, Ezbon, Eri, Arodi and Areli.

17The sons of Asher:

Imnah, Ishvah, Ishvi and Beriah.

Their sister was Serah.

The sons of Beriah:

Heber and Malkiel.

18These were the children born to Jacob by Zilpah, whom Laban had given to his daughter Leah — sixteen in all.

19The sons of Jacob's wife Rachel:

Joseph and Benjamin.

20In Egypt, Manasseh and Ephraim were born to Joseph by Asenath daughter of Potiphera, priest of On.*c*

21The sons of Benjamin:

Bela, Beker, Ashbel, Gera, Naaman, Ehi, Rosh, Muppim, Huppim and Ard.

22These were the sons of Rachel who were born to Jacob — fourteen in all.

23The son of Dan:

Hushim.

24The sons of Naphtali:

Jahziel, Guni, Jezer and Shillem.

25These were the sons born to Jacob by Bilhah, whom Laban had given to his daughter Rachel — seven in all.

26All those who went to Egypt with Jacob — those who were his direct descendants, not counting his sons' wives — numbered sixty-six persons. **27**With the two sons*d* who had been born to Joseph in Egypt, the members of Jacob's family, which went to Egypt, were seventy*e* in all.

28Now Jacob sent Judah ahead of him to Joseph to get directions to Goshen. When they arrived in the region of Goshen, **29**Joseph had his chariot made ready and went to Goshen to meet his father Israel. As soon as Joseph appeared before him, he threw his arms around his father*f* and wept for a long time.

30Israel said to Joseph, "Now I am ready to die, since I have seen for myself that you are still alive."

31Then Joseph said to his brothers and to his father's household, "I will go up and speak to Pharaoh and will say to him, 'My brothers and my father's household, who were living in the land of Canaan, have come to me. **32**The men are

---

a 15 That is, Northwest Mesopotamia Septuagint (see also Num. 26:15); Masoretic Text *Ziphion*   *b 16* Samaritan Pentateuch and   *c 20* That is, Heliopolis   *d 27* Hebrew; Septuagint *the nine children* note); Septuagint (see also Acts 7:14) *seventy-five*   *e 27* Hebrew (see also Exodus 1:5 and   *f 29* Hebrew *around him* shepherds; they tend livestock, and they have brought along their flocks and herds and everything they own.' **33** When Pharaoh calls you in and asks, 'What is your occupation?' **34** you should answer, 'Your servants have tended livestock from our boyhood on, just as our fathers did.' Then you will be allowed to settle in the region of Goshen, for all shepherds are detestable to the Egyptians."

47 Joseph went and told Pharaoh, "My father and brothers, with their flocks and herds and everything they own, have come from the land of Canaan and are now in Goshen." **2** He chose five of his brothers and presented them before Pharaoh.

3 Pharaoh asked the brothers, "What is your occupation?"

"Your servants are shepherds," they replied to Pharaoh, "just as our fathers were." **4** They also said to him, "We have come to live here for a while, because the famine is severe in Canaan and your servants' flocks have no pasture. So now, please let your servants settle in Goshen."

5 Pharaoh said to Joseph, "Your father and your brothers have come to you, **6** and the land of Egypt is before you; settle your father and your brothers in the best part of the land. Let them live in Goshen. And if you know of any among them with special abili-

ty, put them in charge of my own livestock."

7 Then Joseph brought his father Jacob in and presented him before Pharaoh. After Jacob blessed[a] Pharaoh, **8** Pharaoh asked him, "How old are you?"

9 And Jacob said to Pharaoh, "The years of my pilgrimage are a hundred and thirty. My years have been few and difficult, and they do not equal the years of the pilgrimage of my fathers." **10** Then Jacob blessed[b] Pharaoh and went out from his presence.

11 So Joseph settled his father and his brothers in Egypt and gave them property in the best part of the land, the district of Rameses, as Pharaoh directed. **12** Joseph also provided his father and his brothers and all his father's household with food, according to the number of their children.

Joseph and the Famine

13 There was no food, however, in the whole region because the famine was severe; both Egypt and Canaan wasted away because of the famine. **14** Joseph collected all the money that was to be found in Egypt and Canaan in payment for the grain they were buying, and he brought it to Pharaoh's palace. **15** When the money of the people of Egypt and Canaan was gone, all Egypt came to Joseph and said, "Give us food.

---

a 7 Or *greeted*   *b* 10 Or *said farewell to*

Why should we die before your eyes? Our money is all gone."

16 "Then bring your livestock," said Joseph. "I will sell you food in exchange for your livestock, since your money is gone." 17 So they brought their livestock to Joseph, and he gave them food in exchange for their horses, their sheep and goats, their cattle and donkeys. And he brought them through that year with food in exchange for all their livestock.

18 When that year was over, they came to him the following year and said, "We cannot hide from our lord the fact that since our money is gone and our livestock belongs to you, there is nothing left for our lord except our bodies and our land. 19 Why should we perish before your eyes — we and our land as well? Buy us and our land in exchange for food, and we with our land will be in bondage to Pharaoh. Give us seed so that we may live and not die, and that the land may not become desolate."

20 So Joseph bought all the land in Egypt for Pharaoh. The Egyptians, one and all, sold their fields, because the famine was too severe for them. The land became Pharaoh's, 21 and Joseph reduced the people to servitude,*a* from one end of Egypt to the other. 22 However, he did not buy the land of the priests, because they received a regular allotment from Pharaoh and had food enough from the allotment Pharaoh gave them. That is why they did not sell their land.

23 Joseph said to the people, "Now that I have bought you and your land today for Pharaoh, here is seed for you so you can plant the ground. 24 But when the crop comes in, give a fifth of it to Pharaoh. The other four-fifths you may keep as seed for the fields and as food for yourselves and your households and your children."

25 "You have saved our lives," they said. "May we find favor in the eyes of our lord; we will be in bondage to Pharaoh."

26 So Joseph established it as a law concerning land in Egypt — still in force today — that a fifth of the produce belongs to Pharaoh. It was only the land of the priests that did not become Pharaoh's.

27 Now the Israelites settled in Egypt in the region of Goshen. They acquired property there and were fruitful and increased greatly in number.

28 Jacob lived in Egypt seventeen years, and the years of his life were a hundred and forty-seven. 29 When the time drew near for Israel to die, he called for his son Joseph and said to him, "If I have found favor in your eyes, put your hand under my thigh

---

a 21 Samaritan Pentateuch and Septuagint (see also Vulgate); Masoretic Text *and he moved the people into the cities* and promise that you will show me kindness and faithfulness. Do not bury me in Egypt, **30**but when I rest with my fathers, carry me out of Egypt and bury me where they are buried."

"I will do as you say," he said.

31"Swear to me," he said. Then Joseph swore to him, and Israel worshiped as he leaned on the top of his staff.*a*

Manasseh and Ephraim

48 Some time later Joseph was told, "Your father is ill." So he took his two sons Manasseh and Ephraim along with him. **2**When Jacob was told, "Your son Joseph has come to you," Israel rallied his strength and sat up on the bed.

3Jacob said to Joseph, "God Almighty*b* appeared to me at Luz in the land of Canaan, and there he blessed me **4**and said to me, 'I am going to make you fruitful and increase your numbers. I will make you a community of peoples, and I will give this land as an everlasting possession to your descendants after you.'

5"Now then, your two sons born to you in Egypt before I came to you here will be reckoned as mine; Ephraim and Manasseh will be mine, just as Reuben and Simeon are mine. **6**Any children born to you after them will be yours; in the territory they inherit they will be reckoned under the names of their brothers. **7**As I was returning from Paddan,*c* to my sorrow Rachel died in the land of Canaan while we were still on the way, a little distance from Ephrath. So I buried her there beside the road to Ephrath" (that is, Bethlehem).

8When Israel saw the sons of Joseph, he asked, "Who are these?"

9"They are the sons God has given me here," Joseph said to his father.

Then Israel said, "Bring them to me so I may bless them."

10Now Israel's eyes were failing because of old age, and he could hardly see. So Joseph brought his sons close to him, and his father kissed them and embraced them.

11Israel said to Joseph, "I never expected to see your face again, and now God has allowed me to see your children too."

12Then Joseph removed them from Israel's knees and bowed down with his face to the ground. **13**And Joseph took both of them, Ephraim on his right toward Israel's left hand and Manasseh on his left toward Israel's right hand, and brought them close to him. **14**But Israel reached out his right hand and put it on Ephraim's head, though he was the younger, and crossing his arms, he put his left hand on Manasseh's head,

---

a 31   Or *Israel bowed down at the head of his bed*   *b* 3   Hebrew *El-Shaddai*
c 7   That is, Northwest Mesopotamia

even though Manasseh was the firstborn.

¹⁵ Then he blessed Joseph and said,

"May the God before whom
    my fathers
  Abraham and Isaac walked
    faithfully,
the God who has been my
    shepherd
all my life to this day,
¹⁶ the Angel who has delivered
    me from all harm
  —may he bless these
    boys.
May they be called by my
    name
  and the names of my fathers
    Abraham and Isaac,
and may they increase
    greatly
  on the earth."

¹⁷ When Joseph saw his father placing his right hand on Ephraim's head he was displeased; so he took hold of his father's hand to move it from Ephraim's head to Manasseh's head. ¹⁸ Joseph said to him, "No, my father, this one is the firstborn; put your right hand on his head."

¹⁹ But his father refused and said, "I know, my son, I know. He too will become a people, and he too will become great. Nevertheless, his younger brother will be greater than he, and his descendants will become a group of na-tions." ²⁰ He blessed them that day and said,

"In your[a] name will Israel
    pronounce this blessing:
  'May God make you
    like Ephraim and
    Manasseh.'"

So he put Ephraim ahead of Ma-nasseh.

²¹ Then Israel said to Joseph, "I am about to die, but God will be with you[b] and take you[b] back to the land of your[b] fathers. ²² And to you I give one more ridge of land[c] than to your brothers, the ridge I took from the Amorites with my sword and my bow."

Jacob Blesses His Sons

49 Then Jacob called for his sons and said: "Gather around so I can tell you what will happen to you in days to come.

² "Assemble and listen, sons of
    Jacob;
  listen to your father Israel.

³ "Reuben, you are my firstborn,
  my might, the first sign of my
    strength,
  excelling in honor, excelling
    in power.
⁴ Turbulent as the waters, you
    will no longer excel,
  for you went up onto your
    father's bed,
  onto my couch and
    defiled it.

---

[a] 20 The Hebrew is singular.   [b] 21 The Hebrew is plural.   [c] 22 The Hebrew for *ridge of land* is identical with the place name Shechem.

5 "Simeon and Levi are
        brothers—
    their swords[a] are weapons of
        violence.
6 Let me not enter their council,
    let me not join their assembly,
  for they have killed men in
        their anger
    and hamstrung oxen as they
        pleased.
7 Cursed be their anger, so
        fierce,
    and their fury, so cruel!
  I will scatter them in Jacob
    and disperse them in Israel.

8 "Judah,[b] your brothers will
        praise you;
    your hand will be on the
        neck of your enemies;
    your father's sons will bow
        down to you.
9 You are a lion's cub, Judah;
    you return from the prey, my
        son.
  Like a lion he crouches and
        lies down,
    like a lioness—who dares to
        rouse him?
10 The scepter will not depart
        from Judah,
    nor the ruler's staff from
        between his feet,[c]
  until he to whom it belongs[d]
        shall come
    and the obedience of the
        nations shall be his.

11 He will tether his donkey to a
        vine,
    his colt to the choicest
        branch;
  he will wash his garments in
        wine,
    his robes in the blood of
        grapes.
12 His eyes will be darker than
        wine,
    his teeth whiter than
        milk.[e]

13 "Zebulun will live by the
        seashore
    and become a haven for
        ships;
    his border will extend
        toward Sidon.

14 "Issachar is a rawboned[f]
        donkey
    lying down among the sheep
        pens.[g]
15 When he sees how good is his
        resting place
    and how pleasant is his
        land,
  he will bend his shoulder to
        the burden
    and submit to forced labor.

16 "Dan[h] will provide justice for
        his people
    as one of the tribes of Israel.
17 Dan will be a snake by the
        roadside,
    a viper along the path,

---

a 5 The meaning of the Hebrew for this word is uncertain.   b 8 Judah
sounds like and may be derived from the Hebrew for praise.   c 10 Or from his
descendants   d 10 Or to whom tribute belongs; the meaning of the Hebrew for
this phrase is uncertain.   e 12 Or will be dull from wine, / his teeth white from
milk   f 14 Or strong   g 14 Or the campfires; or the saddlebags   h 16 Dan
here means he provides justice.

that bites the horse's heels
so that its rider tumbles
backward.

[18] "I look for your deliverance,
LORD.

[19] "Gad[a] will be attacked by a
band of raiders,
but he will attack them at
their heels.

[20] "Asher's food will be rich;
he will provide delicacies fit
for a king.

[21] "Naphtali is a doe set free
that bears beautiful fawns.[b]

[22] "Joseph is a fruitful vine,
a fruitful vine near a
spring,
whose branches climb over a
wall.[c]

[23] With bitterness archers
attacked him;
they shot at him with
hostility.

[24] But his bow remained
steady,
his strong arms stayed[d]
limber,
because of the hand of the
Mighty One of Jacob,
because of the Shepherd, the
Rock of Israel,

[25] because of your father's God,
who helps you,
because of the Almighty,[e]
who blesses you

with blessings of the skies
above,
blessings of the deep springs
below,
blessings of the breast and
womb.

[26] Your father's blessings are
greater
than the blessings of the
ancient mountains,
than[f] the bounty of the age-
old hills.
Let all these rest on the head of
Joseph,
on the brow of the prince
among[g] his brothers.

[27] "Benjamin is a ravenous wolf;
in the morning he devours
the prey,
in the evening he divides the
plunder."

[28] All these are the twelve tribes
of Israel, and this is what their father said to them when he blessed
them, giving each the blessing
appropriate to him.

The Death of Jacob

[29] Then he gave them these instructions: "I am about to be gathered to my people. Bury me with
my fathers in the cave in the field
of Ephron the Hittite, [30] the cave
in the field of Machpelah, near
Mamre in Canaan, which Abraham bought along with the field

---

[a] 19 Gad sounds like the Hebrew for attack and also for band of raiders.
[b] 21 Or free; / he utters beautiful words
wild colt near a spring, / a wild donkey on a terraced hill   [d] 23,24 Or archers
will attack . . . will shoot . . . will remain . . . will stay   [e] 25 Hebrew Shaddai
[f] 26 Or of my progenitors, / as great as   [g] 26 Or of the one separated from
[c] 22 Or Joseph is a wild colt, / a

as a burial place from Ephron the Hittite. [31] There Abraham and his wife Sarah were buried, there Isaac and his wife Rebekah were buried, and there I buried Leah. [32] The field and the cave in it were bought from the Hittites.[a]"

[33] When Jacob had finished giving instructions to his sons, he drew his feet up into the bed, breathed his last and was gathered to his people.

50 Joseph threw himself on his father and wept over him and kissed him. [2] Then Joseph directed the physicians in his service to embalm his father Israel. So the physicians embalmed him, [3] taking a full forty days, for that was the time required for embalming. And the Egyptians mourned for him seventy days.

[4] When the days of mourning had passed, Joseph said to Pharaoh's court, "If I have found favor in your eyes, speak to Pharaoh for me. Tell him, [5] 'My father made me swear an oath and said, "I am about to die; bury me in the tomb I dug for myself in the land of Canaan." Now let me go up and bury my father; then I will return.'"

[6] Pharaoh said, "Go up and bury your father, as he made you swear to do."

[7] So Joseph went up to bury his father. All Pharaoh's officials accompanied him — the dignitaries of his court and all the dignitaries of Egypt — [8] besides all the members of Joseph's household and his brothers and those belonging to his father's household. Only their children and their flocks and herds were left in Goshen. [9] Chariots and horsemen[b] also went up with him. It was a very large company.

[10] When they reached the threshing floor of Atad, near the Jordan, they lamented loudly and bitterly; and there Joseph observed a seven-day period of mourning for his father. [11] When the Canaanites who lived there saw the mourning at the threshing floor of Atad, they said, "The Egyptians are holding a solemn ceremony of mourning." That is why that place near the Jordan is called Abel Mizraim.[c]

[12] So Jacob's sons did as he had commanded them: [13] They carried him to the land of Canaan and buried him in the cave in the field of Machpelah, near Mamre, which Abraham had bought along with the field as a burial place from Ephron the Hittite. [14] After burying his father, Joseph returned to Egypt, together with his brothers and all the others who had gone with him to bury his father.

Joseph Reassures His Brothers

[15] When Joseph's brothers saw that their father was dead, they

---

[a] 32 Or *the descendants of Heth*   [b] 9 Or *charioteers*   [c] 11 *Abel Mizraim* means *mourning of the Egyptians.*

said, "What if Joseph holds a grudge against us and pays us back for all the wrongs we did to him?" 16So they sent word to Joseph, saying, "Your father left these instructions before he died: 17'This is what you are to say to Joseph: I ask you to forgive your brothers the sins and the wrongs they committed in treating you so badly.' Now please forgive the sins of the servants of the God of your father." When their message came to him, Joseph wept.

18His brothers then came and threw themselves down before him. "We are your slaves," they said.

19But Joseph said to them, "Don't be afraid. Am I in the place of God? 20You intended to harm me, but God intended it for good to accomplish what is now being done, the saving of many lives. 21So then, don't be afraid. I will provide for you and your children." And he reassured them and spoke kindly to them.

The Death of Joseph

22Joseph stayed in Egypt, along with all his father's family. He lived a hundred and ten years 23and saw the third generation of Ephraim's children. Also the children of Makir son of Manasseh were placed at birth on Joseph's knees.a

24Then Joseph said to his brothers, "I am about to die. But God will surely come to your aid and take you up out of this land to the land he promised on oath to Abraham, Isaac and Jacob." 25And Joseph made the Israelites swear an oath and said, "God will surely come to your aid, and then you must carry my bones up from this place."

26So Joseph died at the age of a hundred and ten. And after they embalmed him, he was placed in a coffin in Egypt.

a 23 That is, were counted as his

Exodus

Introduction:

The book of Exodus continues the story of God's people that began with Abraham in the book of Genesis. Exodus means "exit" or "departure." The title of this book comes from the story that demonstrates God's care for his chosen people in the Old Testament — the Israelites as they are freed from slavery and exit Egypt.

From Moses' birth, God chose him for a special task — to lead the Israelites out of Egypt and to the land God had promised them, Canaan. Moses is the main character and author of this book. Although he didn't think he was strong, God made him strong with his power and encouragement (7:6–11). God showed his power to the Israelites and the Egyptians in the ten plagues (7:14–11:10); the last plague made it possible for the Israelites to leave Egypt. Before leaving Egypt they celebrated the Passover (12:1–51).

The Israelites began their journey protected and guided by God in a pillar of cloud during the day and a pillar of fire at night. With Moses leading them they crossed the Red Sea (Sea of Reeds) and settled in the desert at the foot of Mount Sinai for about one year. In the desert of Sinai God set up his covenant with the Israelites by giving them laws to help them live and worship as his holy people.

The covenant between God and Israel began a relationship in which Israel was identified as God's holy nation. God gave his people the Ten Commandments, priests, and the tabernacle to help them live lives that showed they were truly God's people.

Outline of contents:

Moses, God's leader (1:1–4:31)
The contest with Pharaoh (5:1–13:19)
From Egypt to Mount Sinai (13:20–19:2)
God's covenant and laws (19:3–24:8)
The tabernacle for worship (24:9–40:38)

The Israelites Oppressed

1 These are the names of the sons of Israel who went to Egypt with Jacob, each with his family: **2**Reuben, Simeon, Levi and Judah; **3**Issachar, Zebulun and Benjamin; **4**Dan and Naphtali; Gad and Asher. **5**The descendants of Jacob numbered seventy[a] in all; Joseph was already in Egypt.

6Now Joseph and all his brothers and all that generation died, **7**but the Israelites were exceedingly fruitful; they multiplied greatly, increased in numbers and became so numerous that the land was filled with them.

8Then a new king, to whom Joseph meant nothing, came to power in Egypt. **9**"Look," he said to his people, "the Israelites have become far too numerous for us. **10**Come, we must deal shrewdly with them or they will become even more numerous and, if war breaks out, will join our enemies, fight against us and leave the country."

11So they put slave masters over them to oppress them with forced labor, and they built Pithom and Rameses as store cities for Pharaoh. **12**But the more they were oppressed, the more they multiplied and spread; so the Egyptians came to dread the Israelites **13**and worked them ruthlessly. **14**They made their lives bitter with harsh labor in brick and mortar and with all kinds of work in the fields; in all their harsh labor the Egyptians worked them ruthlessly.

15The king of Egypt said to the Hebrew midwives, whose names were Shiphrah and Puah, **16**"When you are helping the Hebrew women during childbirth on the delivery stool, if you see that the baby is a boy, kill him; but if it is a girl, let her live." **17**The midwives, however, feared God and did not do what the king of Egypt had told them to do; they let the boys live. **18**Then the king of Egypt summoned the midwives and asked them, "Why have you done this? Why have you let the boys live?"

19The midwives answered Pharaoh, "Hebrew women are not like Egyptian women; they are vigorous and give birth before the midwives arrive."

20So God was kind to the midwives and the people increased and became even more numerous. **21**And because the midwives feared God, he gave them families of their own.

22Then Pharaoh gave this order to all his people: "Every Hebrew boy that is born you must throw into the Nile, but let every girl live."

The Birth of Moses

2 Now a man of the tribe of Levi married a Levite woman, **2**and she became pregnant and gave birth to a son. When

---

a 5 Masoretic Text (see also Gen. 46:27); Dead Sea Scrolls and Septuagint (see also Acts 7:14 and note at Gen. 46:27) *seventy-five* she saw that he was a fine child, she hid him for three months. [3]But when she could hide him no longer, she got a papyrus basket[a] for him and coated it with tar and pitch. Then she placed the child in it and put it among the reeds along the bank of the Nile. [4]His sister stood at a distance to see what would happen to him.

[5]Then Pharaoh's daughter went down to the Nile to bathe, and her attendants were walking along the riverbank. She saw the basket among the reeds and sent her female slave to get it. [6]She opened it and saw the baby. He was crying, and she felt sorry for him. "This is one of the Hebrew babies," she said.

[7]Then his sister asked Pharaoh's daughter, "Shall I go and get one of the Hebrew women to nurse the baby for you?"

[8]"Yes, go," she answered. So the girl went and got the baby's mother. [9]Pharaoh's daughter said to her, "Take this baby and nurse him for me, and I will pay you." So the woman took the baby and nursed him. [10]When the child grew older, she took him to Pharaoh's daughter and he became her son. She named him Moses,[b] saying, "I drew him out of the water."

Moses Flees to Midian

[11]One day, after Moses had grown up, he went out to where his own people were and watched them at their hard labor. He saw an Egyptian beating a Hebrew, one of his own people. [12]Looking this way and that and seeing no one, he killed the Egyptian and hid him in the sand. [13]The next day he went out and saw two Hebrews fighting. He asked the one in the wrong, "Why are you hitting your fellow Hebrew?"

[14]The man said, "Who made you ruler and judge over us? Are you thinking of killing me as you killed the Egyptian?" Then Moses was afraid and thought, "What I did must have become known."

[15]When Pharaoh heard of this, he tried to kill Moses, but Moses fled from Pharaoh and went to live in Midian, where he sat down by a well. [16]Now a priest of Midian had seven daughters, and they came to draw water and fill the troughs to water their father's flock. [17]Some shepherds came along and drove them away, but Moses got up and came to their rescue and watered their flock.

[18]When the girls returned to Reuel their father, he asked them, "Why have you returned so early today?"

[19]They answered, "An Egyptian rescued us from the shepherds. He even drew water for us and watered the flock."

---

[a] 3 The Hebrew can also mean *ark*, as in Gen. 6:14.   [b] 10 *Moses* sounds like the Hebrew for *draw out*.

20 "And where is he?" Reuel asked his daughters. "Why did you leave him? Invite him to have something to eat."

21 Moses agreed to stay with the man, who gave his daughter Zipporah to Moses in marriage. 22 Zipporah gave birth to a son, and Moses named him Gershom,[a] saying, "I have become a foreigner in a foreign land."

23 During that long period, the king of Egypt died. The Israelites groaned in their slavery and cried out, and their cry for help because of their slavery went up to God. 24 God heard their groaning and he remembered his covenant with Abraham, with Isaac and with Jacob. 25 So God looked on the Israelites and was concerned about them.

Moses and the Burning Bush

3 Now Moses was tending the flock of Jethro his father-in-law, the priest of Midian, and he led the flock to the far side of the wilderness and came to Horeb, the mountain of God. 2 There the angel of the LORD appeared to him in flames of fire from within a bush. Moses saw that though the bush was on fire it did not burn up. 3 So Moses thought, "I will go over and see this strange sight — why the bush does not burn up."

4 When the LORD saw that he had gone over to look, God called to him from within the bush, "Moses! Moses!"

And Moses said, "Here I am."

5 "Do not come any closer," God said. "Take off your sandals, for the place where you are standing is holy ground." 6 Then he said, "I am the God of your father,[b] the God of Abraham, the God of Isaac and the God of Jacob." At this, Moses hid his face, because he was afraid to look at God.

7 The LORD said, "I have indeed seen the misery of my people in Egypt. I have heard them crying out because of their slave drivers, and I am concerned about their suffering. 8 So I have come down to rescue them from the hand of the Egyptians and to bring them up out of that land into a good and spacious land, a land flowing with milk and honey — the home of the Canaanites, Hittites, Amorites, Perizzites, Hivites and Jebusites. 9 And now the cry of the Israelites has reached me, and I have seen the way the Egyptians are oppressing them. 10 So now, go. I am sending you to Pharaoh to bring my people the Israelites out of Egypt."

11 But Moses said to God, "Who am I that I should go to Pharaoh and bring the Israelites out of Egypt?"

12 And God said, "I will be with you. And this will be the sign to you that it is I who have sent you:

a 22 Gershom sounds like the Hebrew for a foreigner there.   b 6 Masoretic Text; Samaritan Pentateuch (see Acts 7:32) fathers

When you have brought the people out of Egypt, you[a] will worship God on this mountain."

¹³Moses said to God, "Suppose I go to the Israelites and say to them, 'The God of your fathers has sent me to you,' and they ask me, 'What is his name?' Then what shall I tell them?"

¹⁴God said to Moses, "I AM WHO I AM.[b] This is what you are to say to the Israelites: 'I AM has sent me to you.'"

¹⁵God also said to Moses, "Say to the Israelites, 'The LORD,[c] the God of your fathers—the God of Abraham, the God of Isaac and the God of Jacob—has sent me to you.'

"This is my name forever,
    the name you shall call me
    from generation to
        generation.

¹⁶"Go, assemble the elders of Israel and say to them, 'The LORD, the God of your fathers—the God of Abraham, Isaac and Jacob—appeared to me and said: I have watched over you and have seen what has been done to you in Egypt. ¹⁷And I have promised to bring you up out of your misery in Egypt into the land of the Canaanites, Hittites, Amorites, Perizzites, Hivites and Jebusites—a land flowing with milk and honey.'

¹⁸"The elders of Israel will listen to you. Then you and the elders are to go to the king of Egypt and say to him, 'The LORD, the God of the Hebrews, has met with us. Let us take a three-day journey into the wilderness to offer sacrifices to the LORD our God.' ¹⁹But I know that the king of Egypt will not let you go unless a mighty hand compels him. ²⁰So I will stretch out my hand and strike the Egyptians with all the wonders that I will perform among them. After that, he will let you go.

²¹"And I will make the Egyptians favorably disposed toward this people, so that when you leave you will not go empty-handed. ²²Every woman is to ask her neighbor and any woman living in her house for articles of silver and gold and for clothing, which you will put on your sons and daughters. And so you will plunder the Egyptians."

Signs for Moses

4 Moses answered, "What if they do not believe me or listen to me and say, 'The LORD did not appear to you'?"

²Then the LORD said to him, "What is that in your hand?"

"A staff," he replied.

³The LORD said, "Throw it on the ground."

Moses threw it on the ground and it became a snake, and he ran from it. ⁴Then the LORD said

---

[a] 12 The Hebrew is plural.   [b] 14 Or I WILL BE WHAT I WILL BE   [c] 15 The Hebrew for LORD sounds like and may be related to the Hebrew for I AM in verse 14.

to him, "Reach out your hand and take it by the tail." So Moses reached out and took hold of the snake and it turned back into a staff in his hand. ⁵ "This," said the LORD, "is so that they may believe that the LORD, the God of their fathers — the God of Abraham, the God of Isaac and the God of Jacob — has appeared to you."

⁶ Then the LORD said, "Put your hand inside your cloak." So Moses put his hand into his cloak, and when he took it out, the skin was leprous*ᵃ* — it had become as white as snow.

⁷ "Now put it back into your cloak," he said. So Moses put his hand back into his cloak, and when he took it out, it was restored, like the rest of his flesh.

⁸ Then the LORD said, "If they do not believe you or pay attention to the first sign, they may believe the second. ⁹ But if they do not believe these two signs or listen to you, take some water from the Nile and pour it on the dry ground. The water you take from the river will become blood on the ground."

¹⁰ Moses said to the LORD, "Pardon your servant, Lord. I have never been eloquent, neither in the past nor since you have spoken to your servant. I am slow of speech and tongue."

¹¹ The LORD said to him, "Who gave human beings their mouths? Who makes them deaf or mute? Who gives them sight or makes them blind? Is it not I, the LORD? ¹² Now go; I will help you speak and will teach you what to say."

¹³ But Moses said, "Pardon your servant, Lord. Please send someone else."

¹⁴ Then the LORD's anger burned against Moses and he said, "What about your brother, Aaron the Levite? I know he can speak well. He is already on his way to meet you, and he will be glad to see you. ¹⁵ You shall speak to him and put words in his mouth; I will help both of you speak and will teach you what to do. ¹⁶ He will speak to the people for you, and it will be as if he were your mouth and as if you were God to him. ¹⁷ But take this staff in your hand so you can perform the signs with it."

Moses Returns to Egypt

¹⁸ Then Moses went back to Jethro his father-in-law and said to him, "Let me return to my own people in Egypt to see if any of them are still alive."

Jethro said, "Go, and I wish you well."

¹⁹ Now the LORD had said to Moses in Midian, "Go back to Egypt, for all those who wanted to kill you are dead." ²⁰ So Moses took his wife and sons, put them on a donkey and started back to Egypt. And he took the staff of God in his hand.

ᵃ 6 The Hebrew word for *leprous* was used for various diseases affecting the skin.

²¹The LORD said to Moses, "When you return to Egypt, see that you perform before Pharaoh all the wonders I have given you the power to do. But I will harden his heart so that he will not let the people go. ²²Then say to Pharaoh, 'This is what the LORD says: Israel is my firstborn son, ²³and I told you, "Let my son go, so he may worship me." But you refused to let him go; so I will kill your firstborn son.'"

²⁴At a lodging place on the way, the LORD met Moses[a] and was about to kill him. ²⁵But Zipporah took a flint knife, cut off her son's foreskin and touched Moses' feet with it.[b] "Surely you are a bridegroom of blood to me," she said. ²⁶So the LORD let him alone. (At that time she said "bridegroom of blood," referring to circumcision.)

²⁷The LORD said to Aaron, "Go into the wilderness to meet Moses." So he met Moses at the mountain of God and kissed him. ²⁸Then Moses told Aaron everything the LORD had sent him to say, and also about all the signs he had commanded him to perform.

²⁹Moses and Aaron brought together all the elders of the Israelites, ³⁰and Aaron told them everything the LORD had said to Moses. He also performed the signs before the people, ³¹and they believed. And when they heard that the LORD was concerned about them and had seen their misery, they bowed down and worshiped.

Bricks Without Straw

5 Afterward Moses and Aaron went to Pharaoh and said, "This is what the LORD, the God of Israel, says: 'Let my people go, so that they may hold a festival to me in the wilderness.'"

²Pharaoh said, "Who is the LORD, that I should obey him and let Israel go? I do not know the LORD and I will not let Israel go."

³Then they said, "The God of the Hebrews has met with us. Now let us take a three-day journey into the wilderness to offer sacrifices to the LORD our God, or he may strike us with plagues or with the sword."

⁴But the king of Egypt said, "Moses and Aaron, why are you taking the people away from their labor? Get back to your work!" ⁵Then Pharaoh said, "Look, the people of the land are now numerous, and you are stopping them from working."

⁶That same day Pharaoh gave this order to the slave drivers and overseers in charge of the people: ⁷"You are no longer to supply the people with straw for making bricks; let them go and gather their own straw. ⁸But require them to make the same number of bricks as before; don't reduce

---

[a] 24 Hebrew *him*   [b] 25 The meaning of the Hebrew for this clause is uncertain.

the quota. They are lazy; that is why they are crying out, 'Let us go and sacrifice to our God.' ⁹Make the work harder for the people so that they keep working and pay no attention to lies."

¹⁰Then the slave drivers and the overseers went out and said to the people, "This is what Pharaoh says: 'I will not give you any more straw. ¹¹Go and get your own straw wherever you can find it, but your work will not be reduced at all.'" ¹²So the people scattered all over Egypt to gather stubble to use for straw. ¹³The slave drivers kept pressing them, saying, "Complete the work required of you for each day, just as when you had straw." ¹⁴And Pharaoh's slave drivers beat the Israelite overseers they had appointed, demanding, "Why haven't you met your quota of bricks yesterday or today, as before?"

¹⁵Then the Israelite overseers went and appealed to Pharaoh: "Why have you treated your servants this way? ¹⁶Your servants are given no straw, yet we are told, 'Make bricks!' Your servants are being beaten, but the fault is with your own people."

¹⁷Pharaoh said, "Lazy, that's what you are — lazy! That is why you keep saying, 'Let us go and sacrifice to the LORD.' ¹⁸Now get to work. You will not be given any straw, yet must produce your full quota of bricks."

¹⁹The Israelite overseers realized they were in trouble when they were told, "You are not to reduce the number of bricks required of you for each day." ²⁰When they left Pharaoh, they found Moses and Aaron waiting to meet them, ²¹and they said, "May the LORD look on you and judge you! You have made us obnoxious to Pharaoh and his officials and have put a sword in their hand to kill us."

God Promises Deliverance

²²Moses returned to the LORD and said, "Why, Lord, why have you brought trouble on this people? Is this why you sent me? ²³Ever since I went to Pharaoh to speak in your name, he has brought trouble on this people, and you have not rescued your people at all."

6 Then the LORD said to Moses, "Now you will see what I will do to Pharaoh: Because of my mighty hand he will let them go; because of my mighty hand he will drive them out of his country."

²God also said to Moses, "I am the LORD. ³I appeared to Abraham, to Isaac and to Jacob as God Almighty,ᵃ but by my name the LORDᵇ I did not make myself fully known to them. ⁴I also established my covenant with them to give them the land of Canaan, where they resided as foreigners. ⁵Moreover, I have heard the

---

ᵃ 3 Hebrew *El-Shaddai*   ᵇ 3 See note at 3:15.

groaning of the Israelites, whom the Egyptians are enslaving, and I have remembered my covenant.

[6] "Therefore, say to the Israelites: 'I am the LORD, and I will bring you out from under the yoke of the Egyptians. I will free you from being slaves to them, and I will redeem you with an outstretched arm and with mighty acts of judgment. [7] I will take you as my own people, and I will be your God. Then you will know that I am the LORD your God, who brought you out from under the yoke of the Egyptians. [8] And I will bring you to the land I swore with uplifted hand to give to Abraham, to Isaac and to Jacob. I will give it to you as a possession. I am the LORD.'"

[9] Moses reported this to the Israelites, but they did not listen to him because of their discouragement and harsh labor.

[10] Then the LORD said to Moses, [11] "Go, tell Pharaoh king of Egypt to let the Israelites go out of his country."

[12] But Moses said to the LORD, "If the Israelites will not listen to me, why would Pharaoh listen to me, since I speak with faltering lips[a]?"

Family Record of Moses and Aaron

[13] Now the LORD spoke to Moses and Aaron about the Israelites and Pharaoh king of Egypt, and he commanded them to bring the Israelites out of Egypt.

[14] These were the heads of their families[b]:

The sons of Reuben the firstborn son of Israel were Hanok and Pallu, Hezron and Karmi. These were the clans of Reuben.

[15] The sons of Simeon were Jemuel, Jamin, Ohad, Jakin, Zohar and Shaul the son of a Canaanite woman. These were the clans of Simeon.

[16] These were the names of the sons of Levi according to their records: Gershon, Kohath and Merari. Levi lived 137 years.

[17] The sons of Gershon, by clans, were Libni and Shimei.

[18] The sons of Kohath were Amram, Izhar, Hebron and Uzziel. Kohath lived 133 years.

[19] The sons of Merari were Mahli and Mushi.

These were the clans of Levi according to their records.

[20] Amram married his father's sister Jochebed, who bore him Aaron and Moses. Amram lived 137 years.

[21] The sons of Izhar were Korah, Nepheg and Zikri.

[22] The sons of Uzziel were Mishael, Elzaphan and Sithri.

---

[a] 12 Hebrew *I am uncircumcised of lips*; also in verse 30   [b] 14 The Hebrew for *families* here and in verse 25 refers to units larger than clans.

²³Aaron married Elisheba, daughter of Amminadab and sister of Nahshon, and she bore him Nadab and Abihu, Eleazar and Ithamar.

²⁴The sons of Korah were Assir, Elkanah and Abiasaph. These were the Korahite clans.

²⁵Eleazar son of Aaron married one of the daughters of Putiel, and she bore him Phinehas.

These were the heads of the Levite families, clan by clan.

²⁶It was this Aaron and Moses to whom the LORD said, "Bring the Israelites out of Egypt by their divisions." ²⁷They were the ones who spoke to Pharaoh king of Egypt about bringing the Israelites out of Egypt — this same Moses and Aaron.

Aaron to Speak for Moses

²⁸Now when the LORD spoke to Moses in Egypt, ²⁹he said to him, "I am the LORD. Tell Pharaoh king of Egypt everything I tell you."

³⁰But Moses said to the LORD, "Since I speak with faltering lips, why would Pharaoh listen to me?"

7 Then the LORD said to Moses, "See, I have made you like God to Pharaoh, and your brother Aaron will be your prophet. ²You are to say everything I command you, and your brother Aaron is to tell Pharaoh to let the Israelites go out of his country. ³But I will harden Pharaoh's heart, and though I multiply my signs and wonders in Egypt, ⁴he will not listen to you. Then I will lay my hand on Egypt and with mighty acts of judgment I will bring out my divisions, my people the Israelites. ⁵And the Egyptians will know that I am the LORD when I stretch out my hand against Egypt and bring the Israelites out of it."

⁶Moses and Aaron did just as the LORD commanded them. ⁷Moses was eighty years old and Aaron eighty-three when they spoke to Pharaoh.

Aaron's Staff Becomes a Snake

⁸The LORD said to Moses and Aaron, ⁹"When Pharaoh says to you, 'Perform a miracle,' then say to Aaron, 'Take your staff and throw it down before Pharaoh,' and it will become a snake."

¹⁰So Moses and Aaron went to Pharaoh and did just as the LORD commanded. Aaron threw his staff down in front of Pharaoh and his officials, and it became a snake. ¹¹Pharaoh then summoned wise men and sorcerers, and the Egyptian magicians also did the same things by their secret arts: ¹²Each one threw down his staff and it became a snake. But Aaron's staff swallowed up their staffs. ¹³Yet Pharaoh's heart became hard and he would not listen to them, just as the LORD had said.

The Plague of Blood

14Then the LORD said to Moses, "Pharaoh's heart is unyielding; he refuses to let the people go. **15**Go to Pharaoh in the morning as he goes out to the river. Confront him on the bank of the Nile, and take in your hand the staff that was changed into a snake. **16**Then say to him, 'The LORD, the God of the Hebrews, has sent me to say to you: Let my people go, so that they may worship me in the wilderness. But until now you have not listened. **17**This is what the LORD says: By this you will know that I am the LORD: With the staff that is in my hand I will strike the water of the Nile, and it will be changed into blood. **18**The fish in the Nile will die, and the river will stink; the Egyptians will not be able to drink its water.'"

19The LORD said to Moses, "Tell Aaron, 'Take your staff and stretch out your hand over the waters of Egypt — over the streams and canals, over the ponds and all the reservoirs — and they will turn to blood.' Blood will be everywhere in Egypt, even in vessels*a* of wood and stone."

20Moses and Aaron did just as the LORD had commanded. He raised his staff in the presence of Pharaoh and his officials and struck the water of the Nile, and all the water was changed into blood. **21**The fish in the Nile died, and the river smelled so bad that the Egyptians could not drink its water. Blood was everywhere in Egypt.

22But the Egyptian magicians did the same things by their secret arts, and Pharaoh's heart became hard; he would not listen to Moses and Aaron, just as the LORD had said. **23**Instead, he turned and went into his palace, and did not take even this to heart. **24**And all the Egyptians dug along the Nile to get drinking water, because they could not drink the water of the river.

The Plague of Frogs

25Seven days passed after the LORD struck the Nile. **8** *b* **1**Then the LORD said to Moses, "Go to Pharaoh and say to him, 'This is what the LORD says: Let my people go, so that they may worship me. **2**If you refuse to let them go, I will send a plague of frogs on your whole country. **3**The Nile will teem with frogs. They will come up into your palace and your bedroom and onto your bed, into the houses of your officials and on your people, and into your ovens and kneading troughs. **4**The frogs will come up on you and your people and all your officials.'"

5Then the LORD said to Moses, "Tell Aaron, 'Stretch out your hand with your staff over the

---

a 19 Or *even on their idols*   *b* In Hebrew texts 8:1-4 is numbered 7:26-29, and 8:5-32 is numbered 8:1-28.

streams and canals and ponds, and make frogs come up on the land of Egypt.'"

[6] So Aaron stretched out his hand over the waters of Egypt, and the frogs came up and covered the land. [7] But the magicians did the same things by their secret arts; they also made frogs come up on the land of Egypt.

[8] Pharaoh summoned Moses and Aaron and said, "Pray to the LORD to take the frogs away from me and my people, and I will let your people go to offer sacrifices to the LORD."

[9] Moses said to Pharaoh, "I leave to you the honor of setting the time for me to pray for you and your officials and your people that you and your houses may be rid of the frogs, except for those that remain in the Nile."

[10] "Tomorrow," Pharaoh said.

Moses replied, "It will be as you say, so that you may know there is no one like the LORD our God. [11] The frogs will leave you and your houses, your officials and your people; they will remain only in the Nile."

[12] After Moses and Aaron left Pharaoh, Moses cried out to the LORD about the frogs he had brought on Pharaoh. [13] And the LORD did what Moses asked. The frogs died in the houses, in the courtyards and in the fields. [14] They were piled into heaps, and the land reeked of them. [15] But when Pharaoh saw that there was

relief, he hardened his heart and would not listen to Moses and Aaron, just as the LORD had said.

The Plague of Gnats

[16] Then the LORD said to Moses, "Tell Aaron, 'Stretch out your staff and strike the dust of the ground,' and throughout the land of Egypt the dust will become gnats." [17] They did this, and when Aaron stretched out his hand with the staff and struck the dust of the ground, gnats came on people and animals. All the dust throughout the land of Egypt became gnats. [18] But when the magicians tried to produce gnats by their secret arts, they could not.

Since the gnats were on people and animals everywhere, [19] the magicians said to Pharaoh, "This is the finger of God." But Pharaoh's heart was hard and he would not listen, just as the LORD had said.

The Plague of Flies

[20] Then the LORD said to Moses, "Get up early in the morning and confront Pharaoh as he goes to the river and say to him, 'This is what the LORD says: Let my people go, so that they may worship me. [21] If you do not let my people go, I will send swarms of flies on you and your officials, on your people and into your houses. The houses of the Egyptians will be full of flies; even the ground will be covered with them.

22 " 'But on that day I will deal differently with the land of Goshen, where my people live; no swarms of flies will be there, so that you will know that I, the LORD, am in this land. 23 I will make a distinction[a] between my people and your people. This sign will occur tomorrow.' "

24 And the LORD did this. Dense swarms of flies poured into Pharaoh's palace and into the houses of his officials; throughout Egypt the land was ruined by the flies.

25 Then Pharaoh summoned Moses and Aaron and said, "Go, sacrifice to your God here in the land."

26 But Moses said, "That would not be right. The sacrifices we offer the LORD our God would be detestable to the Egyptians. And if we offer sacrifices that are detestable in their eyes, will they not stone us? 27 We must take a three-day journey into the wilderness to offer sacrifices to the LORD our God, as he commands us."

28 Pharaoh said, "I will let you go to offer sacrifices to the LORD your God in the wilderness, but you must not go very far. Now pray for me."

29 Moses answered, "As soon as I leave you, I will pray to the LORD, and tomorrow the flies will leave Pharaoh and his officials and his people. Only let Pharaoh be sure that he does not act deceitfully again by not letting the people go to offer sacrifices to the LORD."

30 Then Moses left Pharaoh and prayed to the LORD, 31 and the LORD did what Moses asked. The flies left Pharaoh and his officials and his people; not a fly remained. 32 But this time also Pharaoh hardened his heart and would not let the people go.

The Plague on Livestock

9 Then the LORD said to Moses, "Go to Pharaoh and say to him, 'This is what the LORD, the God of the Hebrews, says: "Let my people go, so that they may worship me." 2 If you refuse to let them go and continue to hold them back, 3 the hand of the LORD will bring a terrible plague on your livestock in the field — on your horses, donkeys and camels and on your cattle, sheep and goats. 4 But the LORD will make a distinction between the livestock of Israel and that of Egypt, so that no animal belonging to the Israelites will die.' "

5 The LORD set a time and said, "Tomorrow the LORD will do this in the land." 6 And the next day the LORD did it: All the livestock of the Egyptians died, but not one animal belonging to the Israelites died. 7 Pharaoh investigated and found that not even one of the animals of the Israelites had died. Yet his heart was unyielding and he would not let the people go.

---

[a] 23 Septuagint and Vulgate; Hebrew *will put a deliverance*

The Plague of Boils

⁸Then the LORD said to Moses and Aaron, "Take handfuls of soot from a furnace and have Moses toss it into the air in the presence of Pharaoh. ⁹It will become fine dust over the whole land of Egypt, and festering boils will break out on people and animals throughout the land."

¹⁰So they took soot from a furnace and stood before Pharaoh. Moses tossed it into the air, and festering boils broke out on people and animals. ¹¹The magicians could not stand before Moses because of the boils that were on them and on all the Egyptians. ¹²But the LORD hardened Pharaoh's heart and he would not listen to Moses and Aaron, just as the LORD had said to Moses.

The Plague of Hail

¹³Then the LORD said to Moses, "Get up early in the morning, confront Pharaoh and say to him, 'This is what the LORD, the God of the Hebrews, says: Let my people go, so that they may worship me, ¹⁴or this time I will send the full force of my plagues against you and against your officials and your people, so you may know that there is no one like me in all the earth. ¹⁵For by now I could have stretched out my hand and struck you and your people with a plague that would have wiped you off the earth.

¹⁶But I have raised you up^a for this very purpose, that I might show you my power and that my name might be proclaimed in all the earth. ¹⁷You still set yourself against my people and will not let them go. ¹⁸Therefore, at this time tomorrow I will send the worst hailstorm that has ever fallen on Egypt, from the day it was founded till now. ¹⁹Give an order now to bring your livestock and everything you have in the field to a place of shelter, because the hail will fall on every person and animal that has not been brought in and is still out in the field, and they will die.'"

²⁰Those officials of Pharaoh who feared the word of the LORD hurried to bring their slaves and their livestock inside. ²¹But those who ignored the word of the LORD left their slaves and livestock in the field.

²²Then the LORD said to Moses, "Stretch out your hand toward the sky so that hail will fall all over Egypt—on people and animals and on everything growing in the fields of Egypt." ²³When Moses stretched out his staff toward the sky, the LORD sent thunder and hail, and lightning flashed down to the ground. So the LORD rained hail on the land of Egypt; ²⁴hail fell and lightning flashed back and forth. It was the worst storm in all the land of Egypt since it had become a

^{a} 16 Or have spared you

nation. ²⁵Throughout Egypt hail struck everything in the fields — both people and animals; it beat down everything growing in the fields and stripped every tree. ²⁶The only place it did not hail was the land of Goshen, where the Israelites were.

²⁷Then Pharaoh summoned Moses and Aaron. "This time I have sinned," he said to them. "The LORD is in the right, and I and my people are in the wrong. ²⁸Pray to the LORD, for we have had enough thunder and hail. I will let you go; you don't have to stay any longer."

²⁹Moses replied, "When I have gone out of the city, I will spread out my hands in prayer to the LORD. The thunder will stop and there will be no more hail, so you may know that the earth is the LORD's. ³⁰But I know that you and your officials still do not fear the LORD God."

³¹(The flax and barley were destroyed, since the barley had headed and the flax was in bloom. ³²The wheat and spelt, however, were not destroyed, because they ripen later.)

³³Then Moses left Pharaoh and went out of the city. He spread out his hands toward the LORD; the thunder and hail stopped, and the rain no longer poured down on the land. ³⁴When Pharaoh saw that the rain and hail and thunder had stopped, he sinned again: He and his officials hardened their hearts. ³⁵So Pharaoh's heart was hard and he would not let the Israelites go, just as the LORD had said through Moses.

The Plague of Locusts

10 Then the LORD said to Moses, "Go to Pharaoh, for I have hardened his heart and the hearts of his officials so that I may perform these signs of mine among them ²that you may tell your children and grandchildren how I dealt harshly with the Egyptians and how I performed my signs among them, and that you may know that I am the LORD."

³So Moses and Aaron went to Pharaoh and said to him, "This is what the LORD, the God of the Hebrews, says: 'How long will you refuse to humble yourself before me? Let my people go, so that they may worship me. ⁴If you refuse to let them go, I will bring locusts into your country tomorrow. ⁵They will cover the face of the ground so that it cannot be seen. They will devour what little you have left after the hail, including every tree that is growing in your fields. ⁶They will fill your houses and those of all your officials and all the Egyptians — something neither your parents nor your ancestors have ever seen from the day they settled in this land till now.'" Then Moses turned and left Pharaoh.

⁷Pharaoh's officials said to him, "How long will this man be a

snare to us? Let the people go, so that they may worship the LORD their God. Do you not yet realize that Egypt is ruined?"

8 Then Moses and Aaron were brought back to Pharaoh. "Go, worship the LORD your God," he said. "But tell me who will be going."

9 Moses answered, "We will go with our young and our old, with our sons and our daughters, and with our flocks and herds, because we are to celebrate a festival to the LORD."

10 Pharaoh said, "The LORD be with you — if I let you go, along with your women and children! Clearly you are bent on evil.*a* **11** No! Have only the men go and worship the LORD, since that's what you have been asking for." Then Moses and Aaron were driven out of Pharaoh's presence.

12 And the LORD said to Moses, "Stretch out your hand over Egypt so that locusts swarm over the land and devour everything growing in the fields, everything left by the hail."

13 So Moses stretched out his staff over Egypt, and the LORD made an east wind blow across the land all that day and all that night. By morning the wind had brought the locusts; **14** they invaded all Egypt and settled down in every area of the country in great numbers. Never before had there been such a plague of locusts, nor

will there ever be again. **15** They covered all the ground until it was black. They devoured all that was left after the hail — everything growing in the fields and the fruit on the trees. Nothing green remained on tree or plant in all the land of Egypt.

16 Pharaoh quickly summoned Moses and Aaron and said, "I have sinned against the LORD your God and against you. **17** Now forgive my sin once more and pray to the LORD your God to take this deadly plague away from me."

18 Moses then left Pharaoh and prayed to the LORD. **19** And the LORD changed the wind to a very strong west wind, which caught up the locusts and carried them into the Red Sea.*b* Not a locust was left anywhere in Egypt. **20** But the LORD hardened Pharaoh's heart, and he would not let the Israelites go.

The Plague of Darkness

21 Then the LORD said to Moses, "Stretch out your hand toward the sky so that darkness spreads over Egypt — darkness that can be felt." **22** So Moses stretched out his hand toward the sky, and total darkness covered all Egypt for three days. **23** No one could see anyone else or move about for three days. Yet all the Israelites had light in the places where they lived.

---

a 10 Or *Be careful, trouble is in store for you!*   *b* 19 Or *the Sea of Reeds*

²⁴Then Pharaoh summoned Moses and said, "Go, worship the LORD. Even your women and children may go with you; only leave your flocks and herds behind."

²⁵But Moses said, "You must allow us to have sacrifices and burnt offerings to present to the LORD our God. ²⁶Our livestock too must go with us; not a hoof is to be left behind. We have to use some of them in worshiping the LORD our God, and until we get there we will not know what we are to use to worship the LORD."

²⁷But the LORD hardened Pharaoh's heart, and he was not willing to let them go. ²⁸Pharaoh said to Moses, "Get out of my sight! Make sure you do not appear before me again! The day you see my face you will die."

²⁹"Just as you say," Moses replied. "I will never appear before you again."

The Plague on the Firstborn

11 Now the LORD had said to Moses, "I will bring one more plague on Pharaoh and on Egypt. After that, he will let you go from here, and when he does, he will drive you out completely. ²Tell the people that men and women alike are to ask their neighbors for articles of silver and gold." ³(The LORD made the Egyptians favorably disposed toward the people, and Moses himself was highly regarded in Egypt by Pharaoh's officials and by the people.)

⁴So Moses said, "This is what the LORD says: 'About midnight I will go throughout Egypt. ⁵Every firstborn son in Egypt will die, from the firstborn son of Pharaoh, who sits on the throne, to the firstborn son of the female slave, who is at her hand mill, and all the firstborn of the cattle as well. ⁶There will be loud wailing throughout Egypt—worse than there has ever been or ever will be again. ⁷But among the Israelites not a dog will bark at any person or animal.' Then you will know that the LORD makes a distinction between Egypt and Israel. ⁸All these officials of yours will come to me, bowing down before me and saying, 'Go, you and all the people who follow you!' After that I will leave." Then Moses, hot with anger, left Pharaoh.

⁹The LORD had said to Moses, "Pharaoh will refuse to listen to you—so that my wonders may be multiplied in Egypt." ¹⁰Moses and Aaron performed all these wonders before Pharaoh, but the LORD hardened Pharaoh's heart, and he would not let the Israelites go out of his country.

The Passover and the Festival of Unleavened Bread

12 The LORD said to Moses and Aaron in Egypt, ²"This month is to be for you the first month, the first month of your year. ³Tell the whole community of Israel that on the tenth day of this month each man is to take a lamb*a* for his family, one for each household. ⁴If any household is too small for a whole lamb, they must share one with their nearest neighbor, having taken into account the number of people there are. You are to determine the amount of lamb needed in accordance with what each person will eat. ⁵The animals you choose must be year-old males without defect, and you may take them from the sheep or the goats. ⁶Take care of them until the fourteenth day of the month, when all the members of the community of Israel must slaughter them at twilight. ⁷Then they are to take some of the blood and put it on the sides and tops of the doorframes of the houses where they eat the lambs. ⁸That same night they are to eat the meat roasted over the fire, along with bitter herbs, and bread made without yeast. ⁹Do not eat the meat raw or boiled in water, but roast it over a fire—with the head, legs and internal organs. ¹⁰Do not leave any of it till morning; if some is left till morning, you must burn it. ¹¹This is how you are to eat it: with your cloak tucked into your belt, your sandals on your feet and your staff in your hand. Eat it in haste; it is the LORD's Passover.

¹²"On that same night I will pass through Egypt and strike down every firstborn of both people and animals, and I will bring judgment on all the gods of Egypt. I am the LORD. ¹³The blood will be a sign for you on the houses where you are, and when I see the blood, I will pass over you. No destructive plague will touch you when I strike Egypt.

¹⁴"This is a day you are to commemorate; for the generations to come you shall celebrate it as a festival to the LORD—a lasting ordinance. ¹⁵For seven days you are to eat bread made without yeast. On the first day remove the yeast from your houses, for whoever eats anything with yeast in it from the first day through the seventh must be cut off from Israel. ¹⁶On the first day hold a sacred assembly, and another one on the seventh day. Do no work at all on these days, except to prepare food for everyone to eat; that is all you may do.

¹⁷"Celebrate the Festival of Unleavened Bread, because it was on this very day that I brought your divisions out of Egypt. Celebrate this day as a lasting ordinance for the generations to come. ¹⁸In the first month you are to eat bread made without yeast, from the evening of the fourteenth day until the evening of the twenty-first day. ¹⁹For seven days no yeast is to be found in your houses. And anyone, whether foreigner or native-born,

a 3 The Hebrew word can mean *lamb* or *kid*; also in verse 4.

who eats anything with yeast in it must be cut off from the community of Israel. ²⁰Eat nothing made with yeast. Wherever you live, you must eat unleavened bread."

²¹Then Moses summoned all the elders of Israel and said to them, "Go at once and select the animals for your families and slaughter the Passover lamb. ²²Take a bunch of hyssop, dip it into the blood in the basin and put some of the blood on the top and on both sides of the doorframe. None of you shall go out of the door of your house until morning. ²³When the LORD goes through the land to strike down the Egyptians, he will see the blood on the top and sides of the doorframe and will pass over that doorway, and he will not permit the destroyer to enter your houses and strike you down.

²⁴"Obey these instructions as a lasting ordinance for you and your descendants. ²⁵When you enter the land that the LORD will give you as he promised, observe this ceremony. ²⁶And when your children ask you, 'What does this ceremony mean to you?' ²⁷then tell them, 'It is the Passover sacrifice to the LORD, who passed over the houses of the Israelites in Egypt and spared our homes when he struck down the Egyptians.'" Then the people bowed down and worshiped. ²⁸The Israelites did just what the LORD commanded Moses and Aaron.

²⁹At midnight the LORD struck down all the firstborn in Egypt, from the firstborn of Pharaoh, who sat on the throne, to the firstborn of the prisoner, who was in the dungeon, and the firstborn of all the livestock as well. ³⁰Pharaoh and all his officials and all the Egyptians got up during the night, and there was loud wailing in Egypt, for there was not a house without someone dead.

The Exodus

³¹During the night Pharaoh summoned Moses and Aaron and said, "Up! Leave my people, you and the Israelites! Go, worship the LORD as you have requested. ³²Take your flocks and herds, as you have said, and go. And also bless me."

³³The Egyptians urged the people to hurry and leave the country. "For otherwise," they said, "we will all die!" ³⁴So the people took their dough before the yeast was added, and carried it on their shoulders in kneading troughs wrapped in clothing. ³⁵The Israelites did as Moses instructed and asked the Egyptians for articles of silver and gold and for clothing. ³⁶The LORD had made the Egyptians favorably disposed toward the people, and they gave them what they asked for; so they plundered the Egyptians.

³⁷The Israelites journeyed from Rameses to Sukkoth. There were about six hundred thousand men

on foot, besides women and children. **38** Many other people went up with them, and also large droves of livestock, both flocks and herds. **39** With the dough the Israelites had brought from Egypt, they baked loaves of unleavened bread. The dough was without yeast because they had been driven out of Egypt and did not have time to prepare food for themselves.

40 Now the length of time the Israelite people lived in Egypt*a* was 430 years. **41** At the end of the 430 years, to the very day, all the LORD's divisions left Egypt. **42** Because the LORD kept vigil that night to bring them out of Egypt, on this night all the Israelites are to keep vigil to honor the LORD for the generations to come.

Passover Restrictions

43 The LORD said to Moses and Aaron, "These are the regulations for the Passover meal:

"No foreigner may eat it. **44** Any slave you have bought may eat it after you have circumcised him, **45** but a temporary resident or a hired worker may not eat it.

46 "It must be eaten inside the house; take none of the meat outside the house. Do not break any of the bones. **47** The whole community of Israel must celebrate it.

48 "A foreigner residing among you who wants to celebrate the LORD's Passover must have all the males in his household circumcised; then he may take part like one born in the land. No uncircumcised male may eat it. **49** The same law applies both to the native-born and to the foreigner residing among you."

50 All the Israelites did just what the LORD had commanded Moses and Aaron. **51** And on that very day the LORD brought the Israelites out of Egypt by their divisions.

Consecration of the Firstborn

13 The LORD said to Moses, **2** "Consecrate to me every firstborn male. The first offspring of every womb among the Israelites belongs to me, whether human or animal."

3 Then Moses said to the people, "Commemorate this day, the day you came out of Egypt, out of the land of slavery, because the LORD brought you out of it with a mighty hand. Eat nothing containing yeast. **4** Today, in the month of Aviv, you are leaving. **5** When the LORD brings you into the land of the Canaanites, Hittites, Amorites, Hivites and Jebusites — the land he swore to your ancestors to give you, a land flowing with milk and honey — you are to observe this ceremony in this month: **6** For seven days eat bread made without yeast and on the seventh day hold a festival to

---

a 40 Masoretic Text; Samaritan Pentateuch and Septuagint *Egypt and Canaan* the LORD. ⁷Eat unleavened bread during those seven days; nothing with yeast in it is to be seen among you, nor shall any yeast be seen anywhere within your borders. ⁸On that day tell your son, 'I do this because of what the LORD did for me when I came out of Egypt.' ⁹This observance will be for you like a sign on your hand and a reminder on your forehead that this law of the LORD is to be on your lips. For the LORD brought you out of Egypt with his mighty hand. ¹⁰You must keep this ordinance at the appointed time year after year.

¹¹"After the LORD brings you into the land of the Canaanites and gives it to you, as he promised on oath to you and your ancestors, ¹²you are to give over to the LORD the first offspring of every womb. All the firstborn males of your livestock belong to the LORD. ¹³Redeem with a lamb every firstborn donkey, but if you do not redeem it, break its neck. Redeem every firstborn among your sons.

¹⁴"In days to come, when your son asks you, 'What does this mean?' say to him, 'With a mighty hand the LORD brought us out of Egypt, out of the land of slavery. ¹⁵When Pharaoh stubbornly refused to let us go, the LORD killed the firstborn of both people and animals in Egypt. This is why I sacrifice to the LORD the first male offspring of every womb

and redeem each of my firstborn sons.' ¹⁶And it will be like a sign on your hand and a symbol on your forehead that the LORD brought us out of Egypt with his mighty hand."

Crossing the Sea

¹⁷When Pharaoh let the people go, God did not lead them on the road through the Philistine country, though that was shorter. For God said, "If they face war, they might change their minds and return to Egypt." ¹⁸So God led the people around by the desert road toward the Red Sea.ᵃ The Israelites went up out of Egypt ready for battle.

¹⁹Moses took the bones of Joseph with him because Joseph had made the Israelites swear an oath. He had said, "God will surely come to your aid, and then you must carry my bones up with you from this place."ᵇ

²⁰After leaving Sukkoth they camped at Etham on the edge of the desert. ²¹By day the LORD went ahead of them in a pillar of cloud to guide them on their way and by night in a pillar of fire to give them light, so that they could travel by day or night. ²²Neither the pillar of cloud by day nor the pillar of fire by night left its place in front of the people.

14 Then the LORD said to Moses, ²"Tell the Israelites to turn back and encamp near Pi

---

ᵃ 18 Or *the Sea of Reeds*   ᵇ 19 See Gen. 50:25.

Hahiroth, between Migdol and the sea. They are to encamp by the sea, directly opposite Baal Zephon. ³Pharaoh will think, 'The Israelites are wandering around the land in confusion, hemmed in by the desert.' ⁴And I will harden Pharaoh's heart, and he will pursue them. But I will gain glory for myself through Pharaoh and all his army, and the Egyptians will know that I am the LORD." So the Israelites did this.

⁵When the king of Egypt was told that the people had fled, Pharaoh and his officials changed their minds about them and said, "What have we done? We have let the Israelites go and have lost their services!" ⁶So he had his chariot made ready and took his army with him. ⁷He took six hundred of the best chariots, along with all the other chariots of Egypt, with officers over all of them. ⁸The LORD hardened the heart of Pharaoh king of Egypt, so that he pursued the Israelites, who were marching out boldly. ⁹The Egyptians—all Pharaoh's horses and chariots, horsemen[a] and troops—pursued the Israelites and overtook them as they camped by the sea near Pi Hahiroth, opposite Baal Zephon.

¹⁰As Pharaoh approached, the Israelites looked up, and there were the Egyptians, marching after them. They were terrified and cried out to the LORD. ¹¹They said to Moses, "Was it because there were no graves in Egypt that you brought us to the desert to die? What have you done to us by bringing us out of Egypt? ¹²Didn't we say to you in Egypt, 'Leave us alone; let us serve the Egyptians'? It would have been better for us to serve the Egyptians than to die in the desert!"

¹³Moses answered the people, "Do not be afraid. Stand firm and you will see the deliverance the LORD will bring you today. The Egyptians you see today you will never see again. ¹⁴The LORD will fight for you; you need only to be still."

¹⁵Then the LORD said to Moses, "Why are you crying out to me? Tell the Israelites to move on. ¹⁶Raise your staff and stretch out your hand over the sea to divide the water so that the Israelites can go through the sea on dry ground. ¹⁷I will harden the hearts of the Egyptians so that they will go in after them. And I will gain glory through Pharaoh and all his army, through his chariots and his horsemen. ¹⁸The Egyptians will know that I am the LORD when I gain glory through Pharaoh, his chariots and his horsemen."

¹⁹Then the angel of God, who had been traveling in front of Israel's army, withdrew and went behind them. The pillar of cloud also moved from in front and

---

[a] 9 Or charioteers; also in verses 17, 18, 23, 26 and 28

stood behind them, ²⁰coming between the armies of Egypt and Israel. Throughout the night the cloud brought darkness to the one side and light to the other side; so neither went near the other all night long.

²¹Then Moses stretched out his hand over the sea, and all that night the LORD drove the sea back with a strong east wind and turned it into dry land. The waters were divided, ²²and the Israelites went through the sea on dry ground, with a wall of water on their right and on their left.

²³The Egyptians pursued them, and all Pharaoh's horses and chariots and horsemen followed them into the sea. ²⁴During the last watch of the night the LORD looked down from the pillar of fire and cloud at the Egyptian army and threw it into confusion. ²⁵He jammed[a] the wheels of their chariots so that they had difficulty driving. And the Egyptians said, "Let's get away from the Israelites! The LORD is fighting for them against Egypt."

²⁶Then the LORD said to Moses, "Stretch out your hand over the sea so that the waters may flow back over the Egyptians and their chariots and horsemen." ²⁷Moses stretched out his hand over the sea, and at daybreak the sea went back to its place. The Egyptians were fleeing toward[b]

it, and the LORD swept them into the sea. ²⁸The water flowed back and covered the chariots and horsemen—the entire army of Pharaoh that had followed the Israelites into the sea. Not one of them survived.

²⁹But the Israelites went through the sea on dry ground, with a wall of water on their right and on their left. ³⁰That day the LORD saved Israel from the hands of the Egyptians, and Israel saw the Egyptians lying dead on the shore. ³¹And when the Israelites saw the mighty hand of the LORD displayed against the Egyptians, the people feared the LORD and put their trust in him and in Moses his servant.

The Song of Moses and Miriam

15 Then Moses and the Israelites sang this song to the LORD:

"I will sing to the LORD,
    for he is highly exalted.
Both horse and driver
    he has hurled into the sea.

²"The LORD is my strength and
    my defense[c];
    he has become my salvation.
He is my God, and I will praise
    him,
    my father's God, and I will
    exalt him.
³The LORD is a warrior;
    the LORD is his name.

---

[a] 25 See Samaritan Pentateuch, Septuagint and Syriac; Masoretic Text *removed*
[b] 27 Or *from*   [c] 2 Or *song*

4 Pharaoh's chariots and his
    army
    he has hurled into the sea.
The best of Pharaoh's officers
    are drowned in the Red Sea.[a]
5 The deep waters have covered
    them;
    they sank to the depths like a
    stone.
6 Your right hand, LORD,
    was majestic in power.
Your right hand, LORD,
    shattered the enemy.

7 "In the greatness of your
    majesty
    you threw down those who
    opposed you.
You unleashed your burning
    anger;
    it consumed them like
    stubble.
8 By the blast of your nostrils
    the waters piled up.
The surging waters stood up
    like a wall;
    the deep waters congealed in
    the heart of the sea.
9 The enemy boasted,
    'I will pursue, I will overtake
    them.
I will divide the spoils;
    I will gorge myself on them.
I will draw my sword
    and my hand will destroy
    them.'
10 But you blew with your
    breath,
    and the sea covered them.
They sank like lead
    in the mighty waters.

11 Who among the gods
    is like you, LORD?
Who is like you—
    majestic in holiness,
awesome in glory,
    working wonders?

12 "You stretch out your right
    hand,
    and the earth swallows your
    enemies.
13 In your unfailing love you will
    lead
    the people you have
    redeemed.
In your strength you will guide
    them
    to your holy dwelling.
14 The nations will hear and
    tremble;
    anguish will grip the people
    of Philistia.
15 The chiefs of Edom will be
    terrified,
    the leaders of Moab will be
    seized with trembling,
    the people[b] of Canaan will
    melt away;
16   terror and dread will fall on
    them.
By the power of your arm
    they will be as still as a
    stone—
until your people pass by,
    LORD,
    until the people you bought[c]
    pass by.
17 You will bring them in and
    plant them
    on the mountain of your
    inheritance—

---

[a] 4 Or *the Sea of Reeds*; also in verse 22   [b] 15 Or *rulers*   [c] 16 Or *created*

the place, LORD, you made for
your dwelling,
the sanctuary, Lord, your
hands established.

18 "The LORD reigns
for ever and ever."

19 When Pharaoh's horses, chariots and horsemen[a] went into the sea, the LORD brought the waters of the sea back over them, but the Israelites walked through the sea on dry ground. 20 Then Miriam the prophet, Aaron's sister, took a timbrel in her hand, and all the women followed her, with timbrels and dancing. 21 Miriam sang to them:

"Sing to the LORD,
for he is highly exalted.
Both horse and driver
he has hurled into the sea."

The Waters of Marah and Elim

22 Then Moses led Israel from the Red Sea and they went into the Desert of Shur. For three days they traveled in the desert without finding water. 23 When they came to Marah, they could not drink its water because it was bitter. (That is why the place is called Marah.[b]) 24 So the people grumbled against Moses, saying, "What are we to drink?"

25 Then Moses cried out to the LORD, and the LORD showed him a piece of wood. He threw it into the water, and the water became fit to drink.

There the LORD issued a ruling and instruction for them and put them to the test. 26 He said, "If you listen carefully to the LORD your God and do what is right in his eyes, if you pay attention to his commands and keep all his decrees, I will not bring on you any of the diseases I brought on the Egyptians, for I am the LORD, who heals you."

27 Then they came to Elim, where there were twelve springs and seventy palm trees, and they camped there near the water.

Manna and Quail

16 The whole Israelite community set out from Elim and came to the Desert of Sin, which is between Elim and Sinai, on the fifteenth day of the second month after they had come out of Egypt. 2 In the desert the whole community grumbled against Moses and Aaron. 3 The Israelites said to them, "If only we had died by the LORD's hand in Egypt! There we sat around pots of meat and ate all the food we wanted, but you have brought us out into this desert to starve this entire assembly to death."

4 Then the LORD said to Moses, "I will rain down bread from heaven for you. The people are to go out each day and gather enough for that day. In this way I will test them and see whether they will follow my instructions.

---

[a] 19 Or charioteers   [b] 23 Marah means bitter.

⁵On the sixth day they are to prepare what they bring in, and that is to be twice as much as they gather on the other days."

⁶So Moses and Aaron said to all the Israelites, "In the evening you will know that it was the LORD who brought you out of Egypt, ⁷and in the morning you will see the glory of the LORD, because he has heard your grumbling against him. Who are we, that you should grumble against us?" ⁸Moses also said, "You will know that it was the LORD when he gives you meat to eat in the evening and all the bread you want in the morning, because he has heard your grumbling against him. Who are we? You are not grumbling against us, but against the LORD."

⁹Then Moses told Aaron, "Say to the entire Israelite community, 'Come before the LORD, for he has heard your grumbling.'"

¹⁰While Aaron was speaking to the whole Israelite community, they looked toward the desert, and there was the glory of the LORD appearing in the cloud.

¹¹The LORD said to Moses, ¹²"I have heard the grumbling of the Israelites. Tell them, 'At twilight you will eat meat, and in the morning you will be filled with bread. Then you will know that I am the LORD your God.'"

¹³That evening quail came and covered the camp, and in the morning there was a layer of dew around the camp. ¹⁴When the dew was gone, thin flakes like frost on the ground appeared on the desert floor. ¹⁵When the Israelites saw it, they said to each other, "What is it?" For they did not know what it was.

Moses said to them, "It is the bread the LORD has given you to eat. ¹⁶This is what the LORD has commanded: 'Everyone is to gather as much as they need. Take an omer[a] for each person you have in your tent.'"

¹⁷The Israelites did as they were told; some gathered much, some little. ¹⁸And when they measured it by the omer, the one who gathered much did not have too much, and the one who gathered little did not have too little. Everyone had gathered just as much as they needed.

¹⁹Then Moses said to them, "No one is to keep any of it until morning."

²⁰However, some of them paid no attention to Moses; they kept part of it until morning, but it was full of maggots and began to smell. So Moses was angry with them.

²¹Each morning everyone gathered as much as they needed, and when the sun grew hot, it melted away. ²²On the sixth day, they gathered twice as much—two omers[b] for each person—and

---

[a] 16 That is, possibly about 3 pounds or about 1.4 kilograms; also in verses 18, 32, 33 and 36   [b] 22 That is, possibly about 6 pounds or about 2.8 kilograms

the leaders of the community came and reported this to Moses. **23** He said to them, "This is what the Lord commanded: 'Tomorrow is to be a day of sabbath rest, a holy sabbath to the Lord. So bake what you want to bake and boil what you want to boil. Save whatever is left and keep it until morning.'"

24 So they saved it until morning, as Moses commanded, and it did not stink or get maggots in it. **25** "Eat it today," Moses said, "because today is a sabbath to the Lord. You will not find any of it on the ground today. **26** Six days you are to gather it, but on the seventh day, the Sabbath, there will not be any."

27 Nevertheless, some of the people went out on the seventh day to gather it, but they found none. **28** Then the Lord said to Moses, "How long will you*a* refuse to keep my commands and my instructions? **29** Bear in mind that the Lord has given you the Sabbath; that is why on the sixth day he gives you bread for two days. Everyone is to stay where they are on the seventh day; no one is to go out." **30** So the people rested on the seventh day.

31 The people of Israel called the bread manna.*b* It was white like coriander seed and tasted like wafers made with honey. **32** Moses said, "This is what the Lord has commanded: 'Take an omer of manna and keep it for the generations to come, so they can see the bread I gave you to eat in the wilderness when I brought you out of Egypt.'"

33 So Moses said to Aaron, "Take a jar and put an omer of manna in it. Then place it before the Lord to be kept for the generations to come."

34 As the Lord commanded Moses, Aaron put the manna with the tablets of the covenant law, so that it might be preserved. **35** The Israelites ate manna forty years, until they came to a land that was settled; they ate manna until they reached the border of Canaan.

36 (An omer is one-tenth of an ephah.)

Water From the Rock

17 The whole Israelite community set out from the Desert of Sin, traveling from place to place as the Lord commanded. They camped at Rephidim, but there was no water for the people to drink. **2** So they quarreled with Moses and said, "Give us water to drink."

Moses replied, "Why do you quarrel with me? Why do you put the Lord to the test?"

3 But the people were thirsty for water there, and they grumbled against Moses. They said, "Why

---

a 28 The Hebrew is plural.   *b 31 Manna* sounds like the Hebrew for *What is it?* (see verse 15).

did you bring us up out of Egypt to make us and our children and livestock die of thirst?"

⁴Then Moses cried out to the LORD, "What am I to do with these people? They are almost ready to stone me."

⁵The LORD answered Moses, "Go out in front of the people. Take with you some of the elders of Israel and take in your hand the staff with which you struck the Nile, and go. ⁶I will stand there before you by the rock at Horeb. Strike the rock, and water will come out of it for the people to drink." So Moses did this in the sight of the elders of Israel. ⁷And he called the place Massah*a* and Meribah*b* because the Israelites quarreled and because they tested the LORD saying, "Is the LORD among us or not?"

The Amalekites Defeated

⁸The Amalekites came and attacked the Israelites at Rephidim. ⁹Moses said to Joshua, "Choose some of our men and go out to fight the Amalekites. Tomorrow I will stand on top of the hill with the staff of God in my hands."

¹⁰So Joshua fought the Amalekites as Moses had ordered, and Moses, Aaron and Hur went to the top of the hill. ¹¹As long as Moses held up his hands, the Israelites were winning, but whenever he lowered his hands, the Amalekites were winning. ¹²When Moses' hands grew tired, they took a stone and put it under him and he sat on it. Aaron and Hur held his hands up — one on one side, one on the other — so that his hands remained steady till sunset. ¹³So Joshua overcame the Amalekite army with the sword.

¹⁴Then the LORD said to Moses, "Write this on a scroll as something to be remembered and make sure that Joshua hears it, because I will completely blot out the name of Amalek from under heaven."

¹⁵Moses built an altar and called it The LORD is my Banner. ¹⁶He said, "Because hands were lifted up against*c* the throne of the LORD,*d* the LORD will be at war against the Amalekites from generation to generation."

Jethro Visits Moses

18 Now Jethro, the priest of Midian and father-in-law of Moses, heard of everything God had done for Moses and for his people Israel, and how the LORD had brought Israel out of Egypt.

²After Moses had sent away his wife Zipporah, his father-in-law Jethro received her ³and her two sons. One son was named Gershom,*e* for Moses said, "I have

---

a 7 Massah means *testing.* *b 7* Meribah means *quarreling.* *c 16* Or *to*
d 16 The meaning of the Hebrew for this clause is uncertain. *e 3* Gershom
sounds like the Hebrew for *a foreigner there.*

become a foreigner in a foreign land"; [4] and the other was named Eliezer,[a] for he said, "My father's God was my helper; he saved me from the sword of Pharaoh."

[5] Jethro, Moses' father-in-law, together with Moses' sons and wife, came to him in the wilderness, where he was camped near the mountain of God. [6] Jethro had sent word to him, "I, your father-in-law Jethro, am coming to you with your wife and her two sons."

[7] So Moses went out to meet his father-in-law and bowed down and kissed him. They greeted each other and then went into the tent. [8] Moses told his father-in-law about everything the LORD had done to Pharaoh and the Egyptians for Israel's sake and about all the hardships they had met along the way and how the LORD had saved them.

[9] Jethro was delighted to hear about all the good things the LORD had done for Israel in rescuing them from the hand of the Egyptians. [10] He said, "Praise be to the LORD, who rescued you from the hand of the Egyptians and of Pharaoh, and who rescued the people from the hand of the Egyptians. [11] Now I know that the LORD is greater than all other gods, for he did this to those who had treated Israel arrogantly." [12] Then Jethro, Moses' father-in-law, brought a burnt offering and other sacrifices to God, and

Aaron came with all the elders of Israel to eat a meal with Moses' father-in-law in the presence of God.

[13] The next day Moses took his seat to serve as judge for the people, and they stood around him from morning till evening. [14] When his father-in-law saw all that Moses was doing for the people, he said, "What is this you are doing for the people? Why do you alone sit as judge, while all these people stand around you from morning till evening?"

[15] Moses answered him, "Because the people come to me to seek God's will. [16] Whenever they have a dispute, it is brought to me, and I decide between the parties and inform them of God's decrees and instructions."

[17] Moses' father-in-law replied, "What you are doing is not good. [18] You and these people who come to you will only wear yourselves out. The work is too heavy for you; you cannot handle it alone. [19] Listen now to me and I will give you some advice, and may God be with you. You must be the people's representative before God and bring their disputes to him. [20] Teach them his decrees and instructions, and show them the way they are to live and how they are to behave. [21] But select capable men from all the people—men who fear God, trustworthy men who hate dishonest gain—

---

[a] 4 *Eliezer* means *my God is helper.*

and appoint them as officials over thousands, hundreds, fifties and tens. ²²Have them serve as judges for the people at all times, but have them bring every difficult case to you; the simple cases they can decide themselves. That will make your load lighter, because they will share it with you. ²³If you do this and God so commands, you will be able to stand the strain, and all these people will go home satisfied."

²⁴Moses listened to his father-in-law and did everything he said. ²⁵He chose capable men from all Israel and made them leaders of the people, officials over thousands, hundreds, fifties and tens. ²⁶They served as judges for the people at all times. The difficult cases they brought to Moses, but the simple ones they decided themselves.

²⁷Then Moses sent his father-in-law on his way, and Jethro returned to his own country.

At Mount Sinai

19 On the first day of the third month after the Israelites left Egypt—on that very day—they came to the Desert of Sinai. ²After they set out from Rephidim, they entered the Desert of Sinai, and Israel camped there in the desert in front of the mountain.

³Then Moses went up to God, and the LORD called to him from the mountain and said, "This is what you are to say to the descendants of Jacob and what you are to tell the people of Israel: ⁴'You yourselves have seen what I did to Egypt, and how I carried you on eagles' wings and brought you to myself. ⁵Now if you obey me fully and keep my covenant, then out of all nations you will be my treasured possession. Although the whole earth is mine, ⁶you*a* will be for me a kingdom of priests and a holy nation.' These are the words you are to speak to the Israelites."

⁷So Moses went back and summoned the elders of the people and set before them all the words the LORD had commanded him to speak. ⁸The people all responded together, "We will do everything the LORD has said." So Moses brought their answer back to the LORD.

⁹The LORD said to Moses, "I am going to come to you in a dense cloud, so that the people will hear me speaking with you and will always put their trust in you." Then Moses told the LORD what the people had said.

¹⁰And the LORD said to Moses, "Go to the people and consecrate them today and tomorrow. Have them wash their clothes ¹¹and be ready by the third day, because on that day the LORD will come down on Mount Sinai in the sight of all the people. ¹²Put limits for

a 5,6 Or *possession, for the whole earth is mine.* ⁶*You* the people around the mountain and tell them, 'Be careful that you do not approach the mountain or touch the foot of it. Whoever touches the mountain is to be put to death. ¹³They are to be stoned or shot with arrows; not a hand is to be laid on them. No person or animal shall be permitted to live.' Only when the ram's horn sounds a long blast may they approach the mountain."

¹⁴After Moses had gone down the mountain to the people, he consecrated them, and they washed their clothes. ¹⁵Then he said to the people, "Prepare yourselves for the third day. Abstain from sexual relations."

¹⁶On the morning of the third day there was thunder and lightning, with a thick cloud over the mountain, and a very loud trumpet blast. Everyone in the camp trembled. ¹⁷Then Moses led the people out of the camp to meet with God, and they stood at the foot of the mountain. ¹⁸Mount Sinai was covered with smoke, because the LORD descended on it in fire. The smoke billowed up from it like smoke from a furnace, and the whole mountain*a* trembled violently. ¹⁹As the sound of the trumpet grew louder and louder, Moses spoke and the voice of God answered him.*b*

²⁰The LORD descended to the top of Mount Sinai and called Moses to the top of the mountain. So Moses went up ²¹and the LORD said to him, "Go down and warn the people so they do not force their way through to see the LORD and many of them perish. ²²Even the priests, who approach the LORD, must consecrate themselves, or the LORD will break out against them."

²³Moses said to the LORD, "The people cannot come up Mount Sinai, because you yourself warned us, 'Put limits around the mountain and set it apart as holy.' "

²⁴The LORD replied, "Go down and bring Aaron up with you. But the priests and the people must not force their way through to come up to the LORD, or he will break out against them."

²⁵So Moses went down to the people and told them.

The Ten Commandments

20 And God spoke all these words:

²"I am the LORD your God, who brought you out of Egypt, out of the land of slavery.

³"You shall have no other gods before*c* me.

⁴"You shall not make for yourself an image in the form of anything in heaven above or on the earth beneath or in the waters be-

---

a 18 Most Hebrew manuscripts; a few Hebrew manuscripts and Septuagint *and all the people*   *b 19* Or *and God answered him with thunder*   *c 3* Or *besides* low. ⁵You shall not bow down to them or worship them; for I, the LORD your God, am a jealous God, punishing the children for the sin of the parents to the third and fourth generation of those who hate me, ⁶but showing love to a thousand generations of those who love me and keep my commandments.

⁷"You shall not misuse the name of the LORD your God, for the LORD will not hold anyone guiltless who misuses his name.

⁸"Remember the Sabbath day by keeping it holy. ⁹Six days you shall labor and do all your work, ¹⁰but the seventh day is a sabbath to the LORD your God. On it you shall not do any work, neither you, nor your son or daughter, nor your male or female servant, nor your animals, nor any foreigner residing in your towns. ¹¹For in six days the LORD made the heavens and the earth, the sea, and all that is in them, but he rested on the seventh day. Therefore the LORD blessed the Sabbath day and made it holy.

¹²"Honor your father and your mother, so that you may live long in the land the LORD your God is giving you.

¹³"You shall not murder.

¹⁴"You shall not commit adultery.

¹⁵"You shall not steal.

¹⁶"You shall not give false testimony against your neighbor.

¹⁷"You shall not covet your neighbor's house. You shall not covet your neighbor's wife, or his male or female servant, his ox or donkey, or anything that belongs to your neighbor."

¹⁸When the people saw the thunder and lightning and heard the trumpet and saw the mountain in smoke, they trembled with fear. They stayed at a distance ¹⁹and said to Moses, "Speak to us yourself and we will listen. But do not have God speak to us or we will die."

²⁰Moses said to the people, "Do not be afraid. God has come to test you, so that the fear of God will be with you to keep you from sinning."

²¹The people remained at a distance, while Moses approached the thick darkness where God was.

Idols and Altars

²²Then the LORD said to Moses, "Tell the Israelites this: 'You have seen for yourselves that I

have spoken to you from heaven: **23** Do not make any gods to be alongside me; do not make for yourselves gods of silver or gods of gold.

24 " 'Make an altar of earth for me and sacrifice on it your burnt offerings and fellowship offerings, your sheep and goats and your cattle. Wherever I cause my name to be honored, I will come to you and bless you. **25** If you make an altar of stones for me, do not build it with dressed stones, for you will defile it if you use a tool on it. **26** And do not go up to my altar on steps, or your private parts may be exposed.'

21

"These are the laws you are to set before them:

Hebrew Servants

2 "If you buy a Hebrew servant, he is to serve you for six years. But in the seventh year, he shall go free, without paying anything. **3** If he comes alone, he is to go free alone; but if he has a wife when he comes, she is to go with him. **4** If his master gives him a wife and she bears him sons or daughters, the woman and her children shall belong to her master, and only the man shall go free.

5 "But if the servant declares, 'I love my master and my wife and children and do not want to go free,' **6** then his master must take him before the judges.[a] He shall take him to the door or the doorpost and pierce his ear with an awl. Then he will be his servant for life.

7 "If a man sells his daughter as a servant, she is not to go free as male servants do. **8** If she does not please the master who has selected her for himself,[b] he must let her be redeemed. He has no right to sell her to foreigners, because he has broken faith with her. **9** If he selects her for his son, he must grant her the rights of a daughter. **10** If he marries another woman, he must not deprive the first one of her food, clothing and marital rights. **11** If he does not provide her with these three things, she is to go free, without any payment of money.

Personal Injuries

12 "Anyone who strikes a person with a fatal blow is to be put to death. **13** However, if it is not done intentionally, but God lets it happen, they are to flee to a place I will designate. **14** But if anyone schemes and kills someone deliberately, that person is to be taken from my altar and put to death.

15 "Anyone who attacks[c] their father or mother is to be put to death.

16 "Anyone who kidnaps someone is to be put to death, whether the victim has been sold or is still in the kidnapper's possession.

---

[a] 6 Or *before God*   [b] 8 Or *master so that he does not choose her*   [c] 15 Or *kills*

¹⁷"Anyone who curses their father or mother is to be put to death.

¹⁸"If people quarrel and one person hits another with a stone or with their fist^a and the victim does not die but is confined to bed, ¹⁹the one who struck the blow will not be held liable if the other can get up and walk around outside with a staff; however, the guilty party must pay the injured person for any loss of time and see that the victim is completely healed.

²⁰"Anyone who beats their male or female slave with a rod must be punished if the slave dies as a direct result, ²¹but they are not to be punished if the slave recovers after a day or two, since the slave is their property.

²²"If people are fighting and hit a pregnant woman and she gives birth prematurely^b but there is no serious injury, the offender must be fined whatever the woman's husband demands and the court allows. ²³But if there is serious injury, you are to take life for life, ²⁴eye for eye, tooth for tooth, hand for hand, foot for foot, ²⁵burn for burn, wound for wound, bruise for bruise.

²⁶"An owner who hits a male or female slave in the eye and destroys it must let the slave go free to compensate for the eye. ²⁷And an owner who knocks out the tooth of a male or female slave must let the slave go free to compensate for the tooth.

²⁸"If a bull gores a man or woman to death, the bull is to be stoned to death, and its meat must not be eaten. But the owner of the bull will not be held responsible. ²⁹If, however, the bull has had the habit of goring and the owner has been warned but has not kept it penned up and it kills a man or woman, the bull is to be stoned and its owner also is to be put to death. ³⁰However, if payment is demanded, the owner may redeem his life by the payment of whatever is demanded. ³¹This law also applies if the bull gores a son or daughter. ³²If the bull gores a male or female slave, the owner must pay thirty shekels^c of silver to the master of the slave, and the bull is to be stoned to death.

³³"If anyone uncovers a pit or digs one and fails to cover it and an ox or a donkey falls into it, ³⁴the one who opened the pit must pay the owner for the loss and take the dead animal in exchange.

³⁵"If anyone's bull injures someone else's bull and it dies, the two parties are to sell the live one and divide both the money and the dead animal equally. ³⁶However, if it was known that the bull had the habit of goring,

---

^a 18 Or *with a tool*   ^b 22 Or *she has a miscarriage*   ^c 32 That is, about 12 ounces or about 345 grams

yet the owner did not keep it penned up, the owner must pay, animal for animal, and take the dead animal in exchange.

Protection of Property

22 [a] "Whoever steals an ox or a sheep and slaughters it or sells it must pay back five head of cattle for the ox and four sheep for the sheep.

2 "If a thief is caught breaking in at night and is struck a fatal blow, the defender is not guilty of bloodshed; 3 but if it happens after sunrise, the defender is guilty of bloodshed.

"Anyone who steals must certainly make restitution, but if they have nothing, they must be sold to pay for their theft. 4 If the stolen animal is found alive in their possession—whether ox or donkey or sheep—they must pay back double.

5 "If anyone grazes their livestock in a field or vineyard and lets them stray and they graze in someone else's field, the offender must make restitution from the best of their own field or vineyard.

6 "If a fire breaks out and spreads into thornbushes so that it burns shocks of grain or standing grain or the whole field, the one who started the fire must make restitution.

7 "If anyone gives a neighbor silver or goods for safekeeping and they are stolen from the neighbor's house, the thief, if caught, must pay back double. 8 But if the thief is not found, the owner of the house must appear before the judges, and they must [b] determine whether the owner of the house has laid hands on the other person's property. 9 In all cases of illegal possession of an ox, a donkey, a sheep, a garment, or any other lost property about which somebody says, 'This is mine,' both parties are to bring their cases before the judges. [c] The one whom the judges declare [d] guilty must pay back double to the other.

10 "If anyone gives a donkey, an ox, a sheep or any other animal to their neighbor for safekeeping and it dies or is injured or is taken away while no one is looking, 11 the issue between them will be settled by the taking of an oath before the Lord that the neighbor did not lay hands on the other person's property. The owner is to accept this, and no restitution is required. 12 But if the animal was stolen from the neighbor, restitution must be made to the owner. 13 If it was torn to pieces by a wild animal, the neighbor shall bring in the remains as evidence and shall not be required to pay for the torn animal.

14 "If anyone borrows an animal from their neighbor and it is injured or dies while the owner

[a] In Hebrew texts 22:1 is numbered 21:37, and 22:2-31 is numbered 22:1-30.
[b] 8 Or before God, and he will   [c] 9 Or before God   [d] 9 Or whom God declares

is not present, they must make restitution. **15**But if the owner is with the animal, the borrower will not have to pay. If the animal was hired, the money paid for the hire covers the loss.

Social Responsibility

16"If a man seduces a virgin who is not pledged to be married and sleeps with her, he must pay the bride-price, and she shall be his wife. **17**If her father absolutely refuses to give her to him, he must still pay the bride-price for virgins.

18"Do not allow a sorceress to live.

19"Anyone who has sexual relations with an animal is to be put to death.

20"Whoever sacrifices to any god other than the LORD must be destroyed.*a*

21"Do not mistreat or oppress a foreigner, for you were foreigners in Egypt.

22"Do not take advantage of the widow or the fatherless. **23**If you do and they cry out to me, I will certainly hear their cry. **24**My anger will be aroused, and I will kill you with the sword; your wives will become widows and your children fatherless.

25"If you lend money to one of my people among you who is needy, do not treat it like a business deal; charge no interest. **26**If

you take your neighbor's cloak as a pledge, return it by sunset, **27**because that cloak is the only covering your neighbor has. What else can they sleep in? When they cry out to me, I will hear, for I am compassionate.

28"Do not blaspheme God*b* or curse the ruler of your people.

29"Do not hold back offerings from your granaries or your vats.*c*

"You must give me the firstborn of your sons. **30**Do the same with your cattle and your sheep. Let them stay with their mothers for seven days, but give them to me on the eighth day.

31"You are to be my holy people. So do not eat the meat of an animal torn by wild beasts; throw it to the dogs.

Laws of Justice and Mercy

23 "Do not spread false reports. Do not help a guilty person by being a malicious witness.

2"Do not follow the crowd in doing wrong. When you give testimony in a lawsuit, do not pervert justice by siding with the crowd, **3**and do not show favoritism to a poor person in a lawsuit.

4"If you come across your enemy's ox or donkey wandering off, be sure to return it. **5**If you see the donkey of someone who hates you fallen down under its load,

---

a 20 The Hebrew term refers to the irrevocable giving over of things or persons to the LORD, often by totally destroying them.   *b 28* Or *Do not revile the judges*
c 29 The meaning of the Hebrew for this phrase is uncertain.

do not leave it there; be sure you help them with it.

⁶"Do not deny justice to your poor people in their lawsuits. ⁷Have nothing to do with a false charge and do not put an innocent or honest person to death, for I will not acquit the guilty.

⁸"Do not accept a bribe, for a bribe blinds those who see and twists the words of the innocent.

⁹"Do not oppress a foreigner; you yourselves know how it feels to be foreigners, because you were foreigners in Egypt.

Sabbath Laws

¹⁰"For six years you are to sow your fields and harvest the crops, ¹¹but during the seventh year let the land lie unplowed and unused. Then the poor among your people may get food from it, and the wild animals may eat what is left. Do the same with your vineyard and your olive grove.

¹²"Six days do your work, but on the seventh day do not work, so that your ox and your donkey may rest, and so that the slave born in your household and the foreigner living among you may be refreshed.

¹³"Be careful to do everything I have said to you. Do not invoke the names of other gods; do not let them be heard on your lips.

The Three Annual Festivals

¹⁴"Three times a year you are to celebrate a festival to me.

¹⁵"Celebrate the Festival of Unleavened Bread; for seven days eat bread made without yeast, as I commanded you. Do this at the appointed time in the month of Aviv, for in that month you came out of Egypt.

"No one is to appear before me empty-handed.

¹⁶"Celebrate the Festival of Harvest with the firstfruits of the crops you sow in your field.

"Celebrate the Festival of Ingathering at the end of the year, when you gather in your crops from the field.

¹⁷"Three times a year all the men are to appear before the Sovereign LORD.

¹⁸"Do not offer the blood of a sacrifice to me along with anything containing yeast.

"The fat of my festival offerings must not be kept until morning.

¹⁹"Bring the best of the firstfruits of your soil to the house of the LORD your God.

"Do not cook a young goat in its mother's milk.

God's Angel to Prepare the Way

²⁰"See, I am sending an angel ahead of you to guard you along the way and to bring you to the place I have prepared. ²¹Pay attention to him and listen to what he says. Do not rebel against him; he will not forgive your rebellion, since my Name is in him. ²²If you listen carefully to what he says and do all that I say, I will be an

enemy to your enemies and will oppose those who oppose you. 23 My angel will go ahead of you and bring you into the land of the Amorites, Hittites, Perizzites, Canaanites, Hivites and Jebusites, and I will wipe them out. 24 Do not bow down before their gods or worship them or follow their practices. You must demolish them and break their sacred stones to pieces. 25 Worship the LORD your God, and his blessing will be on your food and water. I will take away sickness from among you, 26 and none will miscarry or be barren in your land. I will give you a full life span.

27 "I will send my terror ahead of you and throw into confusion every nation you encounter. I will make all your enemies turn their backs and run. 28 I will send the hornet ahead of you to drive the Hivites, Canaanites and Hittites out of your way. 29 But I will not drive them out in a single year, because the land would become desolate and the wild animals too numerous for you. 30 Little by little I will drive them out before you, until you have increased enough to take possession of the land.

31 "I will establish your borders from the Red Sea*a* to the Mediterranean Sea,*b* and from the desert to the Euphrates River. I will give into your hands the people who live in the land, and you will drive them out before you. 32 Do not make a covenant with them or with their gods. 33 Do not let them live in your land or they will cause you to sin against me, because the worship of their gods will certainly be a snare to you."

The Covenant Confirmed

24 Then the LORD said to Moses, "Come up to the LORD, you and Aaron, Nadab and Abihu, and seventy of the elders of Israel. You are to worship at a distance, 2 but Moses alone is to approach the LORD; the others must not come near. And the people may not come up with him."

3 When Moses went and told the people all the LORD's words and laws, they responded with one voice, "Everything the LORD has said we will do." 4 Moses then wrote down everything the LORD had said.

He got up early the next morning and built an altar at the foot of the mountain and set up twelve stone pillars representing the twelve tribes of Israel. 5 Then he sent young Israelite men, and they offered burnt offerings and sacrificed young bulls as fellowship offerings to the LORD. 6 Moses took half of the blood and put it in bowls, and the other half he splashed against the altar. 7 Then he took the Book of the Covenant and read it to the people. They responded, "We will do

---

a 31 Or *the Sea of Reeds*   *b 31* Hebrew *to the Sea of the Philistines* everything the LORD has said; we will obey."

⁸Moses then took the blood, sprinkled it on the people and said, "This is the blood of the covenant that the LORD has made with you in accordance with all these words."

⁹Moses and Aaron, Nadab and Abihu, and the seventy elders of Israel went up ¹⁰and saw the God of Israel. Under his feet was something like a pavement made of lapis lazuli, as bright blue as the sky. ¹¹But God did not raise his hand against these leaders of the Israelites; they saw God, and they ate and drank.

¹²The LORD said to Moses, "Come up to me on the mountain and stay here, and I will give you the tablets of stone with the law and commandments I have written for their instruction."

¹³Then Moses set out with Joshua his aide, and Moses went up on the mountain of God. ¹⁴He said to the elders, "Wait here for us until we come back to you. Aaron and Hur are with you, and anyone involved in a dispute can go to them."

¹⁵When Moses went up on the mountain, the cloud covered it, ¹⁶and the glory of the LORD settled on Mount Sinai. For six days the cloud covered the mountain, and on the seventh day the LORD called to Moses from within the cloud. ¹⁷To the Israelites the glory of the LORD looked like a consuming fire on top of the mountain. ¹⁸Then Moses entered the cloud as he went on up the mountain. And he stayed on the mountain forty days and forty nights.

Offerings for the Tabernacle

25 The LORD said to Moses, ²"Tell the Israelites to bring me an offering. You are to receive the offering for me from everyone whose heart prompts them to give. ³These are the offerings you are to receive from them: gold, silver and bronze; ⁴blue, purple and scarlet yarn and fine linen; goat hair; ⁵ram skins dyed red and another type of durable leather*ᵃ*; acacia wood; ⁶olive oil for the light; spices for the anointing oil and for the fragrant incense; ⁷and onyx stones and other gems to be mounted on the ephod and breastpiece.

⁸"Then have them make a sanctuary for me, and I will dwell among them. ⁹Make this tabernacle and all its furnishings exactly like the pattern I will show you.

The Ark

¹⁰"Have them make an ark*ᵇ* of acacia wood — two and a half cubits long, a cubit and a half wide, and a cubit and a half high.*ᶜ*

ᵃ 5 Possibly the hides of large aquatic mammals   *ᵇ 10* That is, a chest
ᶜ 10 That is, about 3 3/4 feet long and 2 1/4 feet wide and high or about 1.1 meters long and 68 centimeters wide and high; similarly in verse 17

¹¹Overlay it with pure gold, both inside and out, and make a gold molding around it. ¹²Cast four gold rings for it and fasten them to its four feet, with two rings on one side and two rings on the other. ¹³Then make poles of acacia wood and overlay them with gold. ¹⁴Insert the poles into the rings on the sides of the ark to carry it. ¹⁵The poles are to remain in the rings of this ark; they are not to be removed. ¹⁶Then put in the ark the tablets of the covenant law, which I will give you.

¹⁷"Make an atonement cover of pure gold—two and a half cubits long and a cubit and a half wide. ¹⁸And make two cherubim out of hammered gold at the ends of the cover. ¹⁹Make one cherub on one end and the second cherub on the other; make the cherubim of one piece with the cover, at the two ends. ²⁰The cherubim are to have their wings spread upward, overshadowing the cover with them. The cherubim are to face each other, looking toward the cover. ²¹Place the cover on top of the ark and put in the ark the tablets of the covenant law that I will give you. ²²There, above the cover between the two cherubim that are over the ark of the covenant law, I will meet with you and give you all my commands for the Israelites.

The Table

²³"Make a table of acacia wood—two cubits long, a cubit wide and a cubit and a half high.^a ²⁴Overlay it with pure gold and make a gold molding around it. ²⁵Also make around it a rim a handbreadth^b wide and put a gold molding on the rim. ²⁶Make four gold rings for the table and fasten them to the four corners, where the four legs are. ²⁷The rings are to be close to the rim to hold the poles used in carrying the table. ²⁸Make the poles of acacia wood, overlay them with gold and carry the table with them. ²⁹And make its plates and dishes of pure gold, as well as its pitchers and bowls for the pouring out of offerings. ³⁰Put the bread of the Presence on this table to be before me at all times.

The Lampstand

³¹"Make a lampstand of pure gold. Hammer out its base and shaft, and make its flowerlike cups, buds and blossoms of one piece with them. ³²Six branches are to extend from the sides of the lampstand—three on one side and three on the other. ³³Three cups shaped like almond flowers with buds and blossoms are to be on one branch, three on the next branch, and the same for all six branches extending from

---

^a 23 That is, about 3 feet long, 1 1/2 feet wide and 2 1/4 feet high or about 90 centimeters long, 45 centimeters wide and 68 centimeters high   ^b 25 That is, about 3 inches or about 7.5 centimeters

the lampstand. ³⁴And on the lampstand there are to be four cups shaped like almond flowers with buds and blossoms. ³⁵One bud shall be under the first pair of branches extending from the lampstand, a second bud under the second pair, and a third bud under the third pair—six branches in all. ³⁶The buds and branches shall all be of one piece with the lampstand, hammered out of pure gold.

³⁷"Then make its seven lamps and set them up on it so that they light the space in front of it. ³⁸Its wick trimmers and trays are to be of pure gold. ³⁹A talent^a of pure gold is to be used for the lampstand and all these accessories. ⁴⁰See that you make them according to the pattern shown you on the mountain.

The Tabernacle

26 "Make the tabernacle with ten curtains of finely twisted linen and blue, purple and scarlet yarn, with cherubim woven into them by a skilled worker. ²All the curtains are to be the same size—twenty-eight cubits long and four cubits wide.^b ³Join five of the curtains together, and do the same with the other five. ⁴Make loops of blue material along the edge of the end curtain in one set, and do the same with the end curtain in the other set. ⁵Make fifty loops on one curtain and fifty loops on the end curtain of the other set, with the loops opposite each other. ⁶Then make fifty gold clasps and use them to fasten the curtains together so that the tabernacle is a unit.

⁷"Make curtains of goat hair for the tent over the tabernacle—eleven altogether. ⁸All eleven curtains are to be the same size—thirty cubits long and four cubits wide.^c ⁹Join five of the curtains together into one set and the other six into another set. Fold the sixth curtain double at the front of the tent. ¹⁰Make fifty loops along the edge of the end curtain in one set and also along the edge of the end curtain in the other set. ¹¹Then make fifty bronze clasps and put them in the loops to fasten the tent together as a unit. ¹²As for the additional length of the tent curtains, the half curtain that is left over is to hang down at the rear of the tabernacle. ¹³The tent curtains will be a cubit^d longer on both sides; what is left will hang over the sides of the tabernacle so as to cover it. ¹⁴Make for the tent a covering of ram skins dyed red, and over that a covering of the other durable leather.^e

---

^a 39 That is, about 75 pounds or about 34 kilograms   ^b 2 That is, about 42 feet long and 6 feet wide or about 13 meters long and 1.8 meters wide   ^c 8 That is, about 45 feet long and 6 feet wide or about 13.5 meters long and 1.8 meters wide   ^d 13 That is, about 18 inches or about 45 centimeters   ^e 14 Possibly the hides of large aquatic mammals (see 25:5)

¹⁵"Make upright frames of acacia wood for the tabernacle. ¹⁶Each frame is to be ten cubits long and a cubit and a half wide,ᵃ ¹⁷with two projections set parallel to each other. Make all the frames of the tabernacle in this way. ¹⁸Make twenty frames for the south side of the tabernacle ¹⁹and make forty silver bases to go under them—two bases for each frame, one under each projection. ²⁰For the other side, the north side of the tabernacle, make twenty frames ²¹and forty silver bases—two under each frame. ²²Make six frames for the far end, that is, the west end of the tabernacle, ²³and make two frames for the corners at the far end. ²⁴At these two corners they must be double from the bottom all the way to the top and fitted into a single ring; both shall be like that. ²⁵So there will be eight frames and sixteen silver bases—two under each frame.

²⁶"Also make crossbars of acacia wood: five for the frames on one side of the tabernacle, ²⁷five for those on the other side, and five for the frames on the west, at the far end of the tabernacle. ²⁸The center crossbar is to extend from end to end at the middle of the frames. ²⁹Overlay the frames with gold and make gold rings to hold the crossbars. Also overlay the crossbars with gold.

³⁰"Set up the tabernacle according to the plan shown you on the mountain.

³¹"Make a curtain of blue, purple and scarlet yarn and finely twisted linen, with cherubim woven into it by a skilled worker. ³²Hang it with gold hooks on four posts of acacia wood overlaid with gold and standing on four silver bases. ³³Hang the curtain from the clasps and place the ark of the covenant law behind the curtain. The curtain will separate the Holy Place from the Most Holy Place. ³⁴Put the atonement cover on the ark of the covenant law in the Most Holy Place. ³⁵Place the table outside the curtain on the north side of the tabernacle and put the lampstand opposite it on the south side.

³⁶"For the entrance to the tent make a curtain of blue, purple and scarlet yarn and finely twisted linen—the work of an embroiderer. ³⁷Make gold hooks for this curtain and five posts of acacia wood overlaid with gold. And cast five bronze bases for them.

The Altar of Burnt Offering

27 "Build an altar of acacia wood, three cubitsᵇ high; it is to be square, five cubits long and five cubits wide.ᶜ ²Make a horn at each of the four corners, so that the horns and the altar

---

ᵃ 16 That is, about 15 feet long and 2 1/4 feet wide or about 4.5 meters long and 68 centimeters wide   ᵇ 1 That is, about 4 1/2 feet or about 1.4 meters   ᶜ 1 That is, about 7 1/2 feet or about 2.3 meters long and wide are of one piece, and overlay the altar with bronze. ³Make all its utensils of bronze—its pots to remove the ashes, and its shovels, sprinkling bowls, meat forks and firepans. ⁴Make a grating for it, a bronze network, and make a bronze ring at each of the four corners of the network. ⁵Put it under the ledge of the altar so that it is halfway up the altar. ⁶Make poles of acacia wood for the altar and overlay them with bronze. ⁷The poles are to be inserted into the rings so they will be on two sides of the altar when it is carried. ⁸Make the altar hollow, out of boards. It is to be made just as you were shown on the mountain.

The Courtyard

⁹"Make a courtyard for the tabernacle. The south side shall be a hundred cubits*ᵃ* long and is to have curtains of finely twisted linen, ¹⁰with twenty posts and twenty bronze bases and with silver hooks and bands on the posts. ¹¹The north side shall also be a hundred cubits long and is to have curtains, with twenty posts and twenty bronze bases and with silver hooks and bands on the posts.

¹²"The west end of the courtyard shall be fifty cubits*ᵇ* wide and have curtains, with ten posts and ten bases. ¹³On the east end, toward the sunrise, the courtyard shall also be fifty cubits wide. ¹⁴Curtains fifteen cubits*ᶜ* long are to be on one side of the entrance, with three posts and three bases, ¹⁵and curtains fifteen cubits long are to be on the other side, with three posts and three bases.

¹⁶"For the entrance to the courtyard, provide a curtain twenty cubits*ᵈ* long, of blue, purple and scarlet yarn and finely twisted linen—the work of an embroiderer—with four posts and four bases. ¹⁷All the posts around the courtyard are to have silver bands and hooks, and bronze bases. ¹⁸The courtyard shall be a hundred cubits long and fifty cubits wide,*ᵉ* with curtains of finely twisted linen five cubits*ᶠ* high, and with bronze bases. ¹⁹All the other articles used in the service of the tabernacle, whatever their function, including all the tent pegs for it and those for the courtyard, are to be of bronze.

Oil for the Lampstand

²⁰"Command the Israelites to bring you clear oil of pressed olives for the light so that the lamps may be kept burning. ²¹In the

---

ᵃ 9 That is, about 150 feet or about 45 meters; also in verse 11   *ᵇ 12* That is, about 75 feet or about 23 meters; also in verse 13   *ᶜ 14* That is, about 23 feet or about 6.8 meters; also in verse 15   *ᵈ 16* That is, about 30 feet or about 9 meters   *ᵉ 18* That is, about 150 feet long and 75 feet wide or about 45 meters long and 23 meters wide   *ᶠ 18* That is, about 7 1/2 feet or about 2.3 meters tent of meeting, outside the curtain that shields the ark of the covenant law, Aaron and his sons are to keep the lamps burning before the LORD from evening till morning. This is to be a lasting ordinance among the Israelites for the generations to come.

The Priestly Garments

28 "Have Aaron your brother brought to you from among the Israelites, along with his sons Nadab and Abihu, Eleazar and Ithamar, so they may serve me as priests. ²Make sacred garments for your brother Aaron to give him dignity and honor. ³Tell all the skilled workers to whom I have given wisdom in such matters that they are to make garments for Aaron, for his consecration, so he may serve me as priest. ⁴These are the garments they are to make: a breastpiece, an ephod, a robe, a woven tunic, a turban and a sash. They are to make these sacred garments for your brother Aaron and his sons, so they may serve me as priests. ⁵Have them use gold, and blue, purple and scarlet yarn, and fine linen.

The Ephod

⁶"Make the ephod of gold, and of blue, purple and scarlet yarn, and of finely twisted linen—the work of skilled hands. ⁷It is to have two shoulder pieces attached to two of its corners, so it can be fastened. ⁸Its skillfully woven waistband is to be like it—of one piece with the ephod and made with gold, and with blue, purple and scarlet yarn, and with finely twisted linen.

⁹"Take two onyx stones and engrave on them the names of the sons of Israel ¹⁰in the order of their birth—six names on one stone and the remaining six on the other. ¹¹Engrave the names of the sons of Israel on the two stones the way a gem cutter engraves a seal. Then mount the stones in gold filigree settings ¹²and fasten them on the shoulder pieces of the ephod as memorial stones for the sons of Israel. Aaron is to bear the names on his shoulders as a memorial before the LORD. ¹³Make gold filigree settings ¹⁴and two braided chains of pure gold, like a rope, and attach the chains to the settings.

The Breastpiece

¹⁵"Fashion a breastpiece for making decisions—the work of skilled hands. Make it like the ephod: of gold, and of blue, purple and scarlet yarn, and of finely twisted linen. ¹⁶It is to be square—a span*a* long and a span wide—and folded double. ¹⁷Then mount four rows of precious stones on it. The first row shall be carnelian, chrysolite and

---

a 16 That is, about 9 inches or about 23 centimeters

beryl; [18] the second row shall be turquoise, lapis lazuli and emerald; [19] the third row shall be jacinth, agate and amethyst; [20] the fourth row shall be topaz, onyx and jasper.[a] Mount them in gold filigree settings. [21] There are to be twelve stones, one for each of the names of the sons of Israel, each engraved like a seal with the name of one of the twelve tribes.

[22] "For the breastpiece make braided chains of pure gold, like a rope. [23] Make two gold rings for it and fasten them to two corners of the breastpiece. [24] Fasten the two gold chains to the rings at the corners of the breastpiece, [25] and the other ends of the chains to the two settings, attaching them to the shoulder pieces of the ephod at the front. [26] Make two gold rings and attach them to the other two corners of the breastpiece on the inside edge next to the ephod. [27] Make two more gold rings and attach them to the bottom of the shoulder pieces on the front of the ephod, close to the seam just above the waistband of the ephod. [28] The rings of the breastpiece are to be tied to the rings of the ephod with blue cord, connecting it to the waistband, so that the breastpiece will not swing out from the ephod.

[29] "Whenever Aaron enters the Holy Place, he will bear the names of the sons of Israel over his heart on the breastpiece of decision as a continuing memorial before the LORD. [30] Also put the Urim and the Thummim in the breastpiece, so they may be over Aaron's heart whenever he enters the presence of the LORD. Thus Aaron will always bear the means of making decisions for the Israelites over his heart before the LORD.

Other Priestly Garments

[31] "Make the robe of the ephod entirely of blue cloth, [32] with an opening for the head in its center. There shall be a woven edge like a collar[b] around this opening, so that it will not tear. [33] Make pomegranates of blue, purple and scarlet yarn around the hem of the robe, with gold bells between them. [34] The gold bells and the pomegranates are to alternate around the hem of the robe. [35] Aaron must wear it when he ministers. The sound of the bells will be heard when he enters the Holy Place before the LORD and when he comes out, so that he will not die.

[36] "Make a plate of pure gold and engrave on it as on a seal: HOLY TO THE LORD. [37] Fasten a blue cord to it to attach it to the turban; it is to be on the front of the turban. [38] It will be on Aaron's forehead, and he will bear the guilt involved in the sacred gifts the Israelites con-

---

[a] 20 The precise identification of some of these precious stones is uncertain.
[b] 32 The meaning of the Hebrew for this word is uncertain.

secrate, whatever their gifts may be. It will be on Aaron's forehead continually so that they will be acceptable to the LORD.

³⁹ "Weave the tunic of fine linen and make the turban of fine linen. The sash is to be the work of an embroiderer. ⁴⁰ Make tunics, sashes and caps for Aaron's sons to give them dignity and honor. ⁴¹ After you put these clothes on your brother Aaron and his sons, anoint and ordain them. Consecrate them so they may serve me as priests.

⁴² "Make linen undergarments as a covering for the body, reaching from the waist to the thigh. ⁴³ Aaron and his sons must wear them whenever they enter the tent of meeting or approach the altar to minister in the Holy Place, so that they will not incur guilt and die.

"This is to be a lasting ordinance for Aaron and his descendants.

Consecration of the Priests

29 "This is what you are to do to consecrate them, so they may serve me as priests: Take a young bull and two rams without defect. ² And from the finest wheat flour make round loaves without yeast, thick loaves without yeast and with olive oil mixed in, and thin loaves without yeast and brushed with olive oil.

³ Put them in a basket and present them along with the bull and the two rams. ⁴ Then bring Aaron and his sons to the entrance to the tent of meeting and wash them with water. ⁵ Take the garments and dress Aaron with the tunic, the robe of the ephod, the ephod itself and the breastpiece. Fasten the ephod on him by its skillfully woven waistband. ⁶ Put the turban on his head and attach the sacred emblem to the turban. ⁷ Take the anointing oil and anoint him by pouring it on his head. ⁸ Bring his sons and dress them in tunics ⁹ and fasten caps on them. Then tie sashes on Aaron and his sons.ᵃ The priesthood is theirs by a lasting ordinance.

"Then you shall ordain Aaron and his sons.

¹⁰ "Bring the bull to the front of the tent of meeting, and Aaron and his sons shall lay their hands on its head. ¹¹ Slaughter it in the LORD's presence at the entrance to the tent of meeting. ¹² Take some of the bull's blood and put it on the horns of the altar with your finger, and pour out the rest of it at the base of the altar. ¹³ Then take all the fat on the internal organs, the long lobe of the liver, and both kidneys with the fat on them, and burn them on the altar. ¹⁴ But burn the bull's flesh and its hide and its intestines outside the camp. It is a sin offering.ᵇ

ᵃ 9 Hebrew; Septuagint *on them*   ᵇ 14 Or *purification offering*; also in verse 36

¹⁵"Take one of the rams, and Aaron and his sons shall lay their hands on its head. ¹⁶Slaughter it and take the blood and splash it against the sides of the altar. ¹⁷Cut the ram into pieces and wash the internal organs and the legs, putting them with the head and the other pieces. ¹⁸Then burn the entire ram on the altar. It is a burnt offering to the LORD, a pleasing aroma, a food offering presented to the LORD.

¹⁹"Take the other ram, and Aaron and his sons shall lay their hands on its head. ²⁰Slaughter it, take some of its blood and put it on the lobes of the right ears of Aaron and his sons, on the thumbs of their right hands, and on the big toes of their right feet. Then splash blood against the sides of the altar. ²¹And take some blood from the altar and some of the anointing oil and sprinkle it on Aaron and his garments and on his sons and their garments. Then he and his sons and their garments will be consecrated.

²²"Take from this ram the fat, the fat tail, the fat on the internal organs, the long lobe of the liver, both kidneys with the fat on them, and the right thigh. (This is the ram for the ordination.) ²³From the basket of bread made without yeast, which is before the LORD, take one round loaf, one thick loaf with olive oil mixed in, and one thin loaf. ²⁴Put all these in the hands of Aaron and his sons and have them wave them before the LORD as a wave offering. ²⁵Then take them from their hands and burn them on the altar along with the burnt offering for a pleasing aroma to the LORD, a food offering presented to the LORD. ²⁶After you take the breast of the ram for Aaron's ordination, wave it before the LORD as a wave offering, and it will be your share.

²⁷"Consecrate those parts of the ordination ram that belong to Aaron and his sons: the breast that was waved and the thigh that was presented. ²⁸This is always to be the perpetual share from the Israelites for Aaron and his sons. It is the contribution the Israelites are to make to the LORD from their fellowship offerings.

²⁹"Aaron's sacred garments will belong to his descendants so that they can be anointed and ordained in them. ³⁰The son who succeeds him as priest and comes to the tent of meeting to minister in the Holy Place is to wear them seven days.

³¹"Take the ram for the ordination and cook the meat in a sacred place. ³²At the entrance to the tent of meeting, Aaron and his sons are to eat the meat of the ram and the bread that is in the basket. ³³They are to eat these offerings by which atonement was made for their ordination and consecration. But no one else may eat them, because they are

sacred. [34] And if any of the meat of the ordination ram or any bread is left over till morning, burn it up. It must not be eaten, because it is sacred.

[35] "Do for Aaron and his sons everything I have commanded you, taking seven days to ordain them. [36] Sacrifice a bull each day as a sin offering to make atonement. Purify the altar by making atonement for it, and anoint it to consecrate it. [37] For seven days make atonement for the altar and consecrate it. Then the altar will be most holy, and whatever touches it will be holy.

[38] "This is what you are to offer on the altar regularly each day: two lambs a year old. [39] Offer one in the morning and the other at twilight. [40] With the first lamb offer a tenth of an ephah[a] of the finest flour mixed with a quarter of a hin[b] of oil from pressed olives, and a quarter of a hin of wine as a drink offering. [41] Sacrifice the other lamb at twilight with the same grain offering and its drink offering as in the morning—a pleasing aroma, a food offering presented to the LORD.

[42] "For the generations to come this burnt offering is to be made regularly at the entrance to the tent of meeting, before the LORD. There I will meet you and speak to you; [43] there also I will meet with the Israelites, and the place will be consecrated by my glory.

[44] "So I will consecrate the tent of meeting and the altar and will consecrate Aaron and his sons to serve me as priests. [45] Then I will dwell among the Israelites and be their God. [46] They will know that I am the LORD their God, who brought them out of Egypt so that I might dwell among them. I am the LORD their God.

The Altar of Incense

30 "Make an altar of acacia wood for burning incense. [2] It is to be square, a cubit long and a cubit wide, and two cubits high[c]—its horns of one piece with it. [3] Overlay the top and all the sides and the horns with pure gold, and make a gold molding around it. [4] Make two gold rings for the altar below the molding—two on each of the opposite sides—to hold the poles used to carry it. [5] Make the poles of acacia wood and overlay them with gold. [6] Put the altar in front of the curtain that shields the ark of the covenant law—before the atonement cover that is over the tablets of the covenant law—where I will meet with you.

[7] "Aaron must burn fragrant incense on the altar every morning when he tends the lamps. [8] He must burn incense again when

---

[a] 40 That is, probably about 3 1/2 pounds or about 1.6 kilograms   [b] 40 That is, probably about 1 quart or about 1 liter   [c] 2 That is, about 1 1/2 feet long and wide and 3 feet high or about 45 centimeters long and wide and 90 centimeters high

he lights the lamps at twilight so incense will burn regularly before the LORD for the generations to come. ⁹Do not offer on this altar any other incense or any burnt offering or grain offering, and do not pour a drink offering on it. ¹⁰Once a year Aaron shall make atonement on its horns. This annual atonement must be made with the blood of the atoning sin offering[a] for the generations to come. It is most holy to the LORD."

Atonement Money

¹¹Then the LORD said to Moses, ¹²"When you take a census of the Israelites to count them, each one must pay the LORD a ransom for his life at the time he is counted. Then no plague will come on them when you number them. ¹³Each one who crosses over to those already counted is to give a half shekel,[b] according to the sanctuary shekel, which weighs twenty gerahs. This half shekel is an offering to the LORD. ¹⁴All who cross over, those twenty years old or more, are to give an offering to the LORD. ¹⁵The rich are not to give more than a half shekel and the poor are not to give less when you make the offering to the LORD to atone for your lives. ¹⁶Receive the atonement money from the Israelites and use it for the service of the tent of meeting. It will be a memorial for the Israelites before the LORD, making atonement for your lives."

Basin for Washing

¹⁷Then the LORD said to Moses, ¹⁸"Make a bronze basin, with its bronze stand, for washing. Place it between the tent of meeting and the altar, and put water in it. ¹⁹Aaron and his sons are to wash their hands and feet with water from it. ²⁰Whenever they enter the tent of meeting, they shall wash with water so that they will not die. Also, when they approach the altar to minister by presenting a food offering to the LORD, ²¹they shall wash their hands and feet so that they will not die. This is to be a lasting ordinance for Aaron and his descendants for the generations to come."

Anointing Oil

²²Then the LORD said to Moses, ²³"Take the following fine spices: 500 shekels[c] of liquid myrrh, half as much (that is, 250 shekels) of fragrant cinnamon, 250 shekels[d] of fragrant calamus, ²⁴500 shekels of cassia—all according to the sanctuary shekel—and a hin[e] of olive oil. ²⁵Make these into a sacred anointing oil, a fragrant blend, the work of a perfumer. It

---

[a] 10 Or *purification offering*   [b] 13 That is, about 1/5 ounce or about 5.8 grams; also in verse 15   [c] 23 That is, about 12 1/2 pounds or about 5.8 kilograms; also in verse 24   [d] 23 That is, about 6 1/4 pounds or about 2.9 kilograms
[e] 24 That is, probably about 1 gallon or about 3.8 liters

will be the sacred anointing oil. ²⁶Then use it to anoint the tent of meeting, the ark of the covenant law, ²⁷the table and all its articles, the lampstand and its accessories, the altar of incense, ²⁸the altar of burnt offering and all its utensils, and the basin with its stand. ²⁹You shall consecrate them so they will be most holy, and whatever touches them will be holy.

³⁰"Anoint Aaron and his sons and consecrate them so they may serve me as priests. ³¹Say to the Israelites, 'This is to be my sacred anointing oil for the generations to come. ³²Do not pour it on anyone else's body and do not make any other oil using the same formula. It is sacred, and you are to consider it sacred. ³³Whoever makes perfume like it and puts it on anyone other than a priest must be cut off from their people.'"

Incense

³⁴Then the LORD said to Moses, "Take fragrant spices — gum resin, onycha and galbanum — and pure frankincense, all in equal amounts, ³⁵and make a fragrant blend of incense, the work of a perfumer. It is to be salted and pure and sacred. ³⁶Grind some of it to powder and place it in front of the ark of the covenant law in the tent of meeting, where I will meet with you. It shall be most holy to you. ³⁷Do not make any incense with this formula for yourselves; consider it holy to the LORD. ³⁸Whoever makes incense like it to enjoy its fragrance must be cut off from their people."

Bezalel and Oholiab

31 Then the LORD said to Moses, ²"See, I have chosen Bezalel son of Uri, the son of Hur, of the tribe of Judah, ³and I have filled him with the Spirit of God, with wisdom, with understanding, with knowledge and with all kinds of skills — ⁴to make artistic designs for work in gold, silver and bronze, ⁵to cut and set stones, to work in wood, and to engage in all kinds of crafts. ⁶Moreover, I have appointed Oholiab son of Ahisamak, of the tribe of Dan, to help him. Also I have given ability to all the skilled workers to make everything I have commanded you: ⁷the tent of meeting, the ark of the covenant law with the atonement cover on it, and all the other furnishings of the tent — ⁸the table and its articles, the pure gold lampstand and all its accessories, the altar of incense, ⁹the altar of burnt offering and all its utensils, the basin with its stand — ¹⁰and also the woven garments, both the sacred garments for Aaron the priest and the garments for his sons when they serve as priests, ¹¹and the anointing oil and fragrant incense for the Holy Place. They are to make them just as I commanded you."

The Sabbath

¹²Then the LORD said to Moses, ¹³"Say to the Israelites, 'You must observe my Sabbaths. This will be a sign between me and you for the generations to come, so you may know that I am the LORD, who makes you holy.

¹⁴"'Observe the Sabbath, because it is holy to you. Anyone who desecrates it is to be put to death; those who do any work on that day must be cut off from their people. ¹⁵For six days work is to be done, but the seventh day is a day of sabbath rest, holy to the LORD. Whoever does any work on the Sabbath day is to be put to death. ¹⁶The Israelites are to observe the Sabbath, celebrating it for the generations to come as a lasting covenant. ¹⁷It will be a sign between me and the Israelites forever, for in six days the LORD made the heavens and the earth, and on the seventh day he rested and was refreshed.'"

¹⁸When the LORD finished speaking to Moses on Mount Sinai, he gave him the two tablets of the covenant law, the tablets of stone inscribed by the finger of God.

The Golden Calf

32 When the people saw that Moses was so long in coming down from the mountain, they gathered around Aaron and said, "Come, make us gods[a] who will go before us. As for this fellow Moses who brought us up out of Egypt, we don't know what has happened to him."

²Aaron answered them, "Take off the gold earrings that your wives, your sons and your daughters are wearing, and bring them to me." ³So all the people took off their earrings and brought them to Aaron. ⁴He took what they handed him and made it into an idol cast in the shape of a calf, fashioning it with a tool. Then they said, "These are your gods,[b] Israel, who brought you up out of Egypt."

⁵When Aaron saw this, he built an altar in front of the calf and announced, "Tomorrow there will be a festival to the LORD." ⁶So the next day the people rose early and sacrificed burnt offerings and presented fellowship offerings. Afterward they sat down to eat and drink and got up to indulge in revelry.

⁷Then the LORD said to Moses, "Go down, because your people, whom you brought up out of Egypt, have become corrupt. ⁸They have been quick to turn away from what I commanded them and have made themselves an idol cast in the shape of a calf. They have bowed down to it and sacrificed to it and have said, 'These are your gods, Israel, who brought you up out of Egypt.'

⁹"I have seen these people," the LORD said to Moses, "and they

---

[a] 1 Or *a god*; also in verses 23 and 31   [b] 4 Or *This is your god*; also in verse 8

are a stiff-necked people. ¹⁰Now leave me alone so that my anger may burn against them and that I may destroy them. Then I will make you into a great nation."

¹¹But Moses sought the favor of the LORD his God. "LORD," he said, "why should your anger burn against your people, whom you brought out of Egypt with great power and a mighty hand? ¹²Why should the Egyptians say, 'It was with evil intent that he brought them out, to kill them in the mountains and to wipe them off the face of the earth'? Turn from your fierce anger; relent and do not bring disaster on your people. ¹³Remember your servants Abraham, Isaac and Israel, to whom you swore by your own self: 'I will make your descendants as numerous as the stars in the sky and I will give your descendants all this land I promised them, and it will be their inheritance forever.'" ¹⁴Then the LORD relented and did not bring on his people the disaster he had threatened.

¹⁵Moses turned and went down the mountain with the two tablets of the covenant law in his hands. They were inscribed on both sides, front and back. ¹⁶The tablets were the work of God; the writing was the writing of God, engraved on the tablets.

¹⁷When Joshua heard the noise of the people shouting, he said to Moses, "There is the sound of war in the camp."

¹⁸Moses replied:

"It is not the sound of
    victory,
  it is not the sound of
    defeat;
  it is the sound of singing that
    I hear."

¹⁹When Moses approached the camp and saw the calf and the dancing, his anger burned and he threw the tablets out of his hands, breaking them to pieces at the foot of the mountain. ²⁰And he took the calf the people had made and burned it in the fire; then he ground it to powder, scattered it on the water and made the Israelites drink it.

²¹He said to Aaron, "What did these people do to you, that you led them into such great sin?"

²²"Do not be angry, my lord," Aaron answered. "You know how prone these people are to evil. ²³They said to me, 'Make us gods who will go before us. As for this fellow Moses who brought us up out of Egypt, we don't know what has happened to him.' ²⁴So I told them, 'Whoever has any gold jewelry, take it off.' Then they gave me the gold, and I threw it into the fire, and out came this calf!"

²⁵Moses saw that the people were running wild and that Aaron had let them get out of control and so become a laughingstock to their enemies. ²⁶So he stood at the entrance to the camp and said, "Whoever is for the LORD,

come to me." And all the Levites rallied to him.

²⁷Then he said to them, "This is what the LORD, the God of Israel, says: 'Each man strap a sword to his side. Go back and forth through the camp from one end to the other, each killing his brother and friend and neighbor.'" ²⁸The Levites did as Moses commanded, and that day about three thousand of the people died. ²⁹Then Moses said, "You have been set apart to the LORD today, for you were against your own sons and brothers, and he has blessed you this day."

³⁰The next day Moses said to the people, "You have committed a great sin. But now I will go up to the LORD; perhaps I can make atonement for your sin."

³¹So Moses went back to the LORD and said, "Oh, what a great sin these people have committed! They have made themselves gods of gold. ³²But now, please forgive their sin—but if not, then blot me out of the book you have written."

³³The LORD replied to Moses, "Whoever has sinned against me I will blot out of my book. ³⁴Now go, lead the people to the place I spoke of, and my angel will go before you. However, when the time comes for me to punish, I will punish them for their sin."

³⁵And the LORD struck the people with a plague because of what they did with the calf Aaron had made.

33 Then the LORD said to Moses, "Leave this place, you and the people you brought up out of Egypt, and go up to the land I promised on oath to Abraham, Isaac and Jacob, saying, 'I will give it to your descendants.' ²I will send an angel before you and drive out the Canaanites, Amorites, Hittites, Perizzites, Hivites and Jebusites. ³Go up to the land flowing with milk and honey. But I will not go with you, because you are a stiff-necked people and I might destroy you on the way."

⁴When the people heard these distressing words, they began to mourn and no one put on any ornaments. ⁵For the LORD had said to Moses, "Tell the Israelites, 'You are a stiff-necked people. If I were to go with you even for a moment, I might destroy you. Now take off your ornaments and I will decide what to do with you.'" ⁶So the Israelites stripped off their ornaments at Mount Horeb.

The Tent of Meeting

⁷Now Moses used to take a tent and pitch it outside the camp some distance away, calling it the "tent of meeting." Anyone inquiring of the LORD would go to the tent of meeting outside the camp. ⁸And whenever Moses went out to the tent, all the people rose and stood at the entrances to their tents, watching Moses until he entered the tent. ⁹As Mo-

ses went into the tent, the pillar of cloud would come down and stay at the entrance, while the LORD spoke with Moses. **10**Whenever the people saw the pillar of cloud standing at the entrance to the tent, they all stood and worshiped, each at the entrance to their tent. **11**The LORD would speak to Moses face to face, as one speaks to a friend. Then Moses would return to the camp, but his young aide Joshua son of Nun did not leave the tent.

Moses and the Glory of the LORD

12Moses said to the LORD, "You have been telling me, 'Lead these people,' but you have not let me know whom you will send with me. You have said, 'I know you by name and you have found favor with me.' **13**If you are pleased with me, teach me your ways so I may know you and continue to find favor with you. Remember that this nation is your people."

14The LORD replied, "My Presence will go with you, and I will give you rest."

15Then Moses said to him, "If your Presence does not go with us, do not send us up from here. **16**How will anyone know that you are pleased with me and with your people unless you go with us? What else will distinguish me and your people from all the other people on the face of the earth?"

17And the LORD said to Moses, "I will do the very thing you have asked, because I am pleased with you and I know you by name."

18Then Moses said, "Now show me your glory."

19And the LORD said, "I will cause all my goodness to pass in front of you, and I will proclaim my name, the LORD, in your presence. I will have mercy on whom I will have mercy, and I will have compassion on whom I will have compassion. **20**But," he said, "you cannot see my face, for no one may see me and live."

21Then the LORD said, "There is a place near me where you may stand on a rock. **22**When my glory passes by, I will put you in a cleft in the rock and cover you with my hand until I have passed by. **23**Then I will remove my hand and you will see my back; but my face must not be seen."

The New Stone Tablets

34 The LORD said to Moses, "Chisel out two stone tablets like the first ones, and I will write on them the words that were on the first tablets, which you broke. **2**Be ready in the morning, and then come up on Mount Sinai. Present yourself to me there on top of the mountain. **3**No one is to come with you or be seen anywhere on the mountain; not even the flocks and herds may graze in front of the mountain."

⁴So Moses chiseled out two stone tablets like the first ones and went up Mount Sinai early in the morning, as the LORD had commanded him; and he carried the two stone tablets in his hands. ⁵Then the LORD came down in the cloud and stood there with him and proclaimed his name, the LORD. ⁶And he passed in front of Moses, proclaiming, "The LORD, the LORD, the compassionate and gracious God, slow to anger, abounding in love and faithfulness, ⁷maintaining love to thousands, and forgiving wickedness, rebellion and sin. Yet he does not leave the guilty unpunished; he punishes the children and their children for the sin of the parents to the third and fourth generation."

⁸Moses bowed to the ground at once and worshiped. ⁹"Lord," he said, "if I have found favor in your eyes, then let the Lord go with us. Although this is a stiff-necked people, forgive our wickedness and our sin, and take us as your inheritance."

¹⁰Then the LORD said: "I am making a covenant with you. Before all your people I will do wonders never before done in any nation in all the world. The people you live among will see how awesome is the work that I, the LORD, will do for you. ¹¹Obey what I command you today. I will drive out before you the Amorites, Canaanites, Hittites, Perizzites, Hivites and Jebusites. ¹²Be careful not to make a treaty with those who live in the land where you are going, or they will be a snare among you. ¹³Break down their altars, smash their sacred stones and cut down their Asherah poles.ᵃ ¹⁴Do not worship any other god, for the LORD, whose name is Jealous, is a jealous God.

¹⁵"Be careful not to make a treaty with those who live in the land; for when they prostitute themselves to their gods and sacrifice to them, they will invite you and you will eat their sacrifices. ¹⁶And when you choose some of their daughters as wives for your sons and those daughters prostitute themselves to their gods, they will lead your sons to do the same.

¹⁷"Do not make any idols.

¹⁸"Celebrate the Festival of Unleavened Bread. For seven days eat bread made without yeast, as I commanded you. Do this at the appointed time in the month of Aviv, for in that month you came out of Egypt.

¹⁹"The first offspring of every womb belongs to me, including all the firstborn males of your livestock, whether from herd or flock. ²⁰Redeem the firstborn donkey with a lamb, but if you do not redeem it, break its neck. Redeem all your firstborn sons.

"No one is to appear before me empty-handed.

²¹"Six days you shall labor, but

ᵃ 13 That is, wooden symbols of the goddess Asherah

on the seventh day you shall rest; even during the plowing season and harvest you must rest.

²²"Celebrate the Festival of Weeks with the firstfruits of the wheat harvest, and the Festival of Ingathering at the turn of the year.[a] ²³Three times a year all your men are to appear before the Sovereign Lord, the God of Israel. ²⁴I will drive out nations before you and enlarge your territory, and no one will covet your land when you go up three times each year to appear before the Lord your God.

²⁵"Do not offer the blood of a sacrifice to me along with anything containing yeast, and do not let any of the sacrifice from the Passover Festival remain until morning.

²⁶"Bring the best of the firstfruits of your soil to the house of the Lord your God.

"Do not cook a young goat in its mother's milk."

²⁷Then the Lord said to Moses, "Write down these words, for in accordance with these words I have made a covenant with you and with Israel." ²⁸Moses was there with the Lord forty days and forty nights without eating bread or drinking water. And he wrote on the tablets the words of the covenant—the Ten Commandments.

The Radiant Face of Moses

²⁹When Moses came down from Mount Sinai with the two tablets of the covenant law in his hands, he was not aware that his face was radiant because he had spoken with the Lord. ³⁰When Aaron and all the Israelites saw Moses, his face was radiant, and they were afraid to come near him. ³¹But Moses called to them; so Aaron and all the leaders of the community came back to him, and he spoke to them. ³²Afterward all the Israelites came near him, and he gave them all the commands the Lord had given him on Mount Sinai.

³³When Moses finished speaking to them, he put a veil over his face. ³⁴But whenever he entered the Lord's presence to speak with him, he removed the veil until he came out. And when he came out and told the Israelites what he had been commanded, ³⁵they saw that his face was radiant. Then Moses would put the veil back over his face until he went in to speak with the Lord.

Sabbath Regulations

35 Moses assembled the whole Israelite community and said to them, "These are the things the Lord has commanded you to do: ²For six days, work is to be done, but the seventh day shall be your holy day, a day of sabbath rest to the Lord. Whoever does any work on it is to be put to death. ³Do not light a fire in any of your dwellings on the Sabbath day."

---

[a] 22 That is, in the autumn

Materials for the Tabernacle

⁴Moses said to the whole Israelite community, "This is what the LORD has commanded: ⁵From what you have, take an offering for the LORD. Everyone who is willing is to bring to the LORD an offering of gold, silver and bronze; ⁶blue, purple and scarlet yarn and fine linen; goat hair; ⁷ram skins dyed red and another type of durable leatherᵃ; acacia wood; ⁸olive oil for the light; spices for the anointing oil and for the fragrant incense; ⁹and onyx stones and other gems to be mounted on the ephod and breastpiece.

¹⁰"All who are skilled among you are to come and make everything the LORD has commanded: ¹¹the tabernacle with its tent and its covering, clasps, frames, crossbars, posts and bases; ¹²the ark with its poles and the atonement cover and the curtain that shields it; ¹³the table with its poles and all its articles and the bread of the Presence; ¹⁴the lampstand that is for light with its accessories, lamps and oil for the light; ¹⁵the altar of incense with its poles, the anointing oil and the fragrant incense; the curtain for the doorway at the entrance to the tabernacle; ¹⁶the altar of burnt offering with its bronze grating, its poles and all its utensils; the bronze basin with its stand; ¹⁷the curtains of the courtyard with its posts and bases, and the curtain for the entrance to the courtyard; ¹⁸the tent pegs for the tabernacle and for the courtyard, and their ropes; ¹⁹the woven garments worn for ministering in the sanctuary—both the sacred garments for Aaron the priest and the garments for his sons when they serve as priests."

²⁰Then the whole Israelite community withdrew from Moses' presence, ²¹and everyone who was willing and whose heart moved them came and brought an offering to the LORD for the work on the tent of meeting, for all its service, and for the sacred garments. ²²All who were willing, men and women alike, came and brought gold jewelry of all kinds: brooches, earrings, rings and ornaments. They all presented their gold as a wave offering to the LORD. ²³Everyone who had blue, purple or scarlet yarn or fine linen, or goat hair, ram skins dyed red or the other durable leather brought them. ²⁴Those presenting an offering of silver or bronze brought it as an offering to the LORD, and everyone who had acacia wood for any part of the work brought it. ²⁵Every skilled woman spun with her hands and brought what she had spun—blue, purple or scarlet yarn or fine linen. ²⁶And all the women who were willing and had the skill spun the goat hair. ²⁷The leaders brought onyx stones and other gems to

---

ᵃ 7 Possibly the hides of large aquatic mammals; also in verse 23 be mounted on the ephod and breastpiece. ²⁸They also brought spices and olive oil for the light and for the anointing oil and for the fragrant incense. ²⁹All the Israelite men and women who were willing brought to the LORD freewill offerings for all the work the LORD through Moses had commanded them to do.

Bezalel and Oholiab

³⁰Then Moses said to the Israelites, "See, the LORD has chosen Bezalel son of Uri, the son of Hur, of the tribe of Judah, ³¹and he has filled him with the Spirit of God, with wisdom, with understanding, with knowledge and with all kinds of skills— ³²to make artistic designs for work in gold, silver and bronze, ³³to cut and set stones, to work in wood and to engage in all kinds of artistic crafts. ³⁴And he has given both him and Oholiab son of Ahisamak, of the tribe of Dan, the ability to teach others. ³⁵He has filled them with skill to do all kinds of work as engravers, designers, embroiderers in blue, purple and scarlet yarn and fine linen, and weavers—all of them

36 skilled workers and designers. ¹So Bezalel, Oholiab and every skilled person to whom the LORD has given skill and ability to know how to carry out all the work of constructing the sanctuary are to do the work just as the LORD has commanded."

²Then Moses summoned Bezalel and Oholiab and every skilled person to whom the LORD had given ability and who was willing to come and do the work. ³They received from Moses all the offerings the Israelites had brought to carry out the work of constructing the sanctuary. And the people continued to bring freewill offerings morning after morning. ⁴So all the skilled workers who were doing all the work on the sanctuary left what they were doing ⁵and said to Moses, "The people are bringing more than enough for doing the work the LORD commanded to be done."

⁶Then Moses gave an order and they sent this word throughout the camp: "No man or woman is to make anything else as an offering for the sanctuary." And so the people were restrained from bringing more, ⁷because what they already had was more than enough to do all the work.

The Tabernacle

⁸All those who were skilled among the workers made the tabernacle with ten curtains of finely twisted linen and blue, purple and scarlet yarn, with cherubim woven into them by expert hands. ⁹All the curtains were the same size—twenty-eight cubits long and four cubits wide.ᵃ ¹⁰They joined five of the curtains together and did the same with

---

ᵃ 9 That is, about 42 feet long and 6 feet wide or about 13 meters long and 1.8 meters wide the other five. **11** Then they made loops of blue material along the edge of the end curtain in one set, and the same was done with the end curtain in the other set. **12** They also made fifty loops on one curtain and fifty loops on the end curtain of the other set, with the loops opposite each other. **13** Then they made fifty gold clasps and used them to fasten the two sets of curtains together so that the tabernacle was a unit.

14 They made curtains of goat hair for the tent over the tabernacle — eleven altogether. **15** All eleven curtains were the same size — thirty cubits long and four cubits wide.*a* **16** They joined five of the curtains into one set and the other six into another set. **17** Then they made fifty loops along the edge of the end curtain in one set and also along the edge of the end curtain in the other set. **18** They made fifty bronze clasps to fasten the tent together as a unit. **19** Then they made for the tent a covering of ram skins dyed red, and over that a covering of the other durable leather.*b*

20 They made upright frames of acacia wood for the tabernacle. **21** Each frame was ten cubits long and a cubit and a half wide,*c* **22** with two projections set parallel to each other. They made all the frames of the tabernacle

in this way. **23** They made twenty frames for the south side of the tabernacle **24** and made forty silver bases to go under them — two bases for each frame, one under each projection. **25** For the other side, the north side of the tabernacle, they made twenty frames **26** and forty silver bases — two under each frame. **27** They made six frames for the far end, that is, the west end of the tabernacle, **28** and two frames were made for the corners of the tabernacle at the far end. **29** At these two corners the frames were double from the bottom all the way to the top and fitted into a single ring; both were made alike. **30** So there were eight frames and sixteen silver bases — two under each frame.

31 They also made crossbars of acacia wood: five for the frames on one side of the tabernacle, **32** five for those on the other side, and five for the frames on the west, at the far end of the tabernacle. **33** They made the center crossbar so that it extended from end to end at the middle of the frames. **34** They overlaid the frames with gold and made gold rings to hold the crossbars. They also overlaid the crossbars with gold.

35 They made the curtain of blue, purple and scarlet yarn and finely twisted linen, with cher-

---

a 15 That is, about 45 feet long and 6 feet wide or about 14 meters long and 1.8 meters wide   *b 19* Possibly the hides of large aquatic mammals (see 35:7)
c 21 That is, about 15 feet long and 2 1/4 feet wide or about 4.5 meters long and 68 centimeters wide

ubim woven into it by a skilled worker. ³⁶They made four posts of acacia wood for it and overlaid them with gold. They made gold hooks for them and cast their four silver bases. ³⁷For the entrance to the tent they made a curtain of blue, purple and scarlet yarn and finely twisted linen — the work of an embroiderer; ³⁸and they made five posts with hooks for them. They overlaid the tops of the posts and their bands with gold and made their five bases of bronze.

The Ark

37 Bezalel made the ark of acacia wood — two and a half cubits long, a cubit and a half wide, and a cubit and a half high.ᵃ ²He overlaid it with pure gold, both inside and out, and made a gold molding around it. ³He cast four gold rings for it and fastened them to its four feet, with two rings on one side and two rings on the other. ⁴Then he made poles of acacia wood and overlaid them with gold. ⁵And he inserted the poles into the rings on the sides of the ark to carry it.

⁶He made the atonement cover of pure gold — two and a half cubits long and a cubit and a half wide. ⁷Then he made two cherubim out of hammered gold at the ends of the cover. ⁸He made one cherub on one end and the second cherub on the other; at the two ends he made them of one piece with the cover. ⁹The cherubim had their wings spread upward, overshadowing the cover with them. The cherubim faced each other, looking toward the cover.

The Table

¹⁰Theyᵇ made the table of acacia wood — two cubits long, a cubit wide and a cubit and a half high.ᶜ ¹¹Then they overlaid it with pure gold and made a gold molding around it. ¹²They also made around it a rim a handbreadthᵈ wide and put a gold molding on the rim. ¹³They cast four gold rings for the table and fastened them to the four corners, where the four legs were. ¹⁴The rings were put close to the rim to hold the poles used in carrying the table. ¹⁵The poles for carrying the table were made of acacia wood and were overlaid with gold. ¹⁶And they made from pure gold the articles for the table — its plates and dishes and bowls and its pitchers for the pouring out of drink offerings.

The Lampstand

¹⁷They made the lampstand of pure gold. They hammered out its base and shaft, and

---

ᵃ *1* That is, about 3 3/4 feet long and 2 1/4 feet wide and high or about 1.1 meters long and 68 centimeters wide and high; similarly in verse 6   ᵇ *10* Or *He*; also in verses 11-29   ᶜ *10* That is, about 3 feet long, 1 1/2 feet wide and 2 1/4 feet high or about 90 centimeters long, 45 centimeters wide and 68 centimeters high   ᵈ *12* That is, about 3 inches or about 7.5 centimeters made its flowerlike cups, buds and blossoms of one piece with them. ¹⁸Six branches extended from the sides of the lampstand—three on one side and three on the other. ¹⁹Three cups shaped like almond flowers with buds and blossoms were on one branch, three on the next branch and the same for all six branches extending from the lampstand. ²⁰And on the lampstand were four cups shaped like almond flowers with buds and blossoms. ²¹One bud was under the first pair of branches extending from the lampstand, a second bud under the second pair, and a third bud under the third pair—six branches in all. ²²The buds and the branches were all of one piece with the lampstand, hammered out of pure gold.

²³They made its seven lamps, as well as its wick trimmers and trays, of pure gold. ²⁴They made the lampstand and all its accessories from one talent[a] of pure gold.

The Altar of Incense

²⁵They made the altar of incense out of acacia wood. It was square, a cubit long and a cubit wide and two cubits high[b]—its horns of one piece with it. ²⁶They overlaid the top and all the sides and the horns with pure gold,

and made a gold molding around it. ²⁷They made two gold rings below the molding—two on each of the opposite sides—to hold the poles used to carry it. ²⁸They made the poles of acacia wood and overlaid them with gold.

²⁹They also made the sacred anointing oil and the pure, fragrant incense—the work of a perfumer.

The Altar of Burnt Offering

38 They[c] built the altar of burnt offering of acacia wood, three cubits[d] high; it was square, five cubits long and five cubits wide.[e] ²They made a horn at each of the four corners, so that the horns and the altar were of one piece, and they overlaid the altar with bronze. ³They made all its utensils of bronze—its pots, shovels, sprinkling bowls, meat forks and firepans. ⁴They made a grating for the altar, a bronze network, to be under its ledge, halfway up the altar. ⁵They cast bronze rings to hold the poles for the four corners of the bronze grating. ⁶They made the poles of acacia wood and overlaid them with bronze. ⁷They inserted the poles into the rings so they would be on the sides of the altar for carrying it. They made it hollow, out of boards.

---

a 24 That is, about 75 pounds or about 34 kilograms   *b 25* That is, about 1 1/2 feet long and wide and 3 feet high or about 45 centimeters long and wide and 90 centimeters high   *c 1* Or *He*; also in verses 2-9   *d 1* That is, about 4 1/2 feet or about 1.4 meters   *e 1* That is, about 7 1/2 feet or about 2.3 meters long and wide

The Basin for Washing

8They made the bronze basin and its bronze stand from the mirrors of the women who served at the entrance to the tent of meeting.

The Courtyard

9Next they made the courtyard. The south side was a hundred cubits[a] long and had curtains of finely twisted linen, **10**with twenty posts and twenty bronze bases, and with silver hooks and bands on the posts. **11**The north side was also a hundred cubits long and had twenty posts and twenty bronze bases, with silver hooks and bands on the posts.

12The west end was fifty cubits[b] wide and had curtains, with ten posts and ten bases, with silver hooks and bands on the posts. **13**The east end, toward the sunrise, was also fifty cubits wide. **14**Curtains fifteen cubits[c] long were on one side of the entrance, with three posts and three bases, **15**and curtains fifteen cubits long were on the other side of the entrance to the courtyard, with three posts and three bases. **16**All the curtains around the courtyard were of finely twisted linen. **17**The bases for the posts were bronze. The hooks and bands on the posts were silver, and their tops were overlaid with silver; so all the posts of the courtyard had silver bands.

18The curtain for the entrance to the courtyard was made of blue, purple and scarlet yarn and finely twisted linen — the work of an embroiderer. It was twenty cubits[d] long and, like the curtains of the courtyard, five cubits[e] high, **19**with four posts and four bronze bases. Their hooks and bands were silver, and their tops were overlaid with silver. **20**All the tent pegs of the tabernacle and of the surrounding courtyard were bronze.

The Materials Used

21These are the amounts of the materials used for the tabernacle, the tabernacle of the covenant law, which were recorded at Moses' command by the Levites under the direction of Ithamar son of Aaron, the priest. **22**(Bezalel son of Uri, the son of Hur, of the tribe of Judah, made everything the LORD commanded Moses; **23**with him was Oholiab son of Ahisamak, of the tribe of Dan — an engraver and designer, and an embroiderer in blue, purple and scarlet yarn and fine linen.) **24**The total amount of the gold from the wave offering used for all the work on the sanctuary was 29 talents and 730 shekels,[f] according to the sanctuary shekel.

---

[a] 9 That is, about 150 feet or about 45 meters   [b] 12 That is, about 75 feet or about 23 meters   [c] 14 That is, about 22 feet or about 6.8 meters   [d] 18 That is, about 30 feet or about 9 meters   [e] 18 That is, about 7 1/2 feet or about 2.3 meters   [f] 24 The weight of the gold was a little over a ton or about 1 metric ton.

²⁵The silver obtained from those of the community who were counted in the census was 100 talents[a] and 1,775 shekels,[b] according to the sanctuary shekel — ²⁶one beka per person, that is, half a shekel,[c] according to the sanctuary shekel, from everyone who had crossed over to those counted, twenty years old or more, a total of 603,550 men. ²⁷The 100 talents of silver were used to cast the bases for the sanctuary and for the curtain — 100 bases from the 100 talents, one talent for each base. ²⁸They used the 1,775 shekels to make the hooks for the posts, to overlay the tops of the posts, and to make their bands.

²⁹The bronze from the wave offering was 70 talents and 2,400 shekels.[d] ³⁰They used it to make the bases for the entrance to the tent of meeting, the bronze altar with its bronze grating and all its utensils, ³¹the bases for the surrounding courtyard and those for its entrance and all the tent pegs for the tabernacle and those for the surrounding courtyard.

The Priestly Garments

39 From the blue, purple and scarlet yarn they made woven garments for ministering in the sanctuary. They also made sacred garments for Aaron, as the LORD commanded Moses.

The Ephod

²They[e] made the ephod of gold, and of blue, purple and scarlet yarn, and of finely twisted linen. ³They hammered out thin sheets of gold and cut strands to be worked into the blue, purple and scarlet yarn and fine linen — the work of skilled hands. ⁴They made shoulder pieces for the ephod, which were attached to two of its corners, so it could be fastened. ⁵Its skillfully woven waistband was like it — of one piece with the ephod and made with gold, and with blue, purple and scarlet yarn, and with finely twisted linen, as the LORD commanded Moses.

⁶They mounted the onyx stones in gold filigree settings and engraved them like a seal with the names of the sons of Israel. ⁷Then they fastened them on the shoulder pieces of the ephod as memorial stones for the sons of Israel, as the LORD commanded Moses.

The Breastpiece

⁸They fashioned the breastpiece — the work of a skilled craftsman. They made it like the ephod: of gold, and of blue, purple and scarlet yarn, and of finely

---

[a] 25 That is, about 3 3/4 tons or about 3.4 metric tons; also in verse 27   [b] 25 That is, about 44 pounds or about 20 kilograms; also in verse 28   [c] 26 That is, about 1/5 ounce or about 5.7 grams   [d] 29 The weight of the bronze was about 2 1/2 tons or about 2.4 metric tons.   [e] 2 Or He; also in verses 7, 8 and 22

twisted linen. ⁹It was square — a span*^a* long and a span wide — and folded double. ¹⁰Then they mounted four rows of precious stones on it. The first row was carnelian, chrysolite and beryl; ¹¹the second row was turquoise, lapis lazuli and emerald; ¹²the third row was jacinth, agate and amethyst; ¹³the fourth row was topaz, onyx and jasper.*^b* They were mounted in gold filigree settings. ¹⁴There were twelve stones, one for each of the names of the sons of Israel, each engraved like a seal with the name of one of the twelve tribes.

¹⁵For the breastpiece they made braided chains of pure gold, like a rope. ¹⁶They made two gold filigree settings and two gold rings, and fastened the rings to two of the corners of the breastpiece. ¹⁷They fastened the two gold chains to the rings at the corners of the breastpiece, ¹⁸and the other ends of the chains to the two settings, attaching them to the shoulder pieces of the ephod at the front. ¹⁹They made two gold rings and attached them to the other two corners of the breastpiece on the inside edge next to the ephod. ²⁰Then they made two more gold rings and attached them to the bottom of the shoulder pieces on the front of the ephod, close to the seam just above the waistband of the ephod. ²¹They tied the rings of the breastpiece to the rings of the ephod with blue cord, connecting it to the waistband so that the breastpiece would not swing out from the ephod — as the Lord commanded Moses.

Other Priestly Garments

²²They made the robe of the ephod entirely of blue cloth — the work of a weaver — ²³with an opening in the center of the robe like the opening of a collar,*^c* and a band around this opening, so that it would not tear. ²⁴They made pomegranates of blue, purple and scarlet yarn and finely twisted linen around the hem of the robe. ²⁵And they made bells of pure gold and attached them around the hem between the pomegranates. ²⁶The bells and pomegranates alternated around the hem of the robe to be worn for ministering, as the Lord commanded Moses.

²⁷For Aaron and his sons, they made tunics of fine linen — the work of a weaver — ²⁸and the turban of fine linen, the linen caps and the undergarments of finely twisted linen. ²⁹The sash was made of finely twisted linen and blue, purple and scarlet yarn — the work of an embroiderer — as the Lord commanded Moses.

---

^a 9 That is, about 9 inches or about 23 centimeters   *^b 13* The precise identification of some of these precious stones is uncertain.   *^c 23* The meaning of the Hebrew for this word is uncertain.

[30]They made the plate, the sacred emblem, out of pure gold and engraved on it, like an inscription on a seal: HOLY TO THE LORD. [31]Then they fastened a blue cord to it to attach it to the turban, as the LORD commanded Moses.

Moses Inspects the Tabernacle

[32]So all the work on the tabernacle, the tent of meeting, was completed. The Israelites did everything just as the LORD commanded Moses. [33]Then they brought the tabernacle to Moses: the tent and all its furnishings, its clasps, frames, crossbars, posts and bases; [34]the covering of ram skins dyed red and the covering of another durable leather[a] and the shielding curtain; [35]the ark of the covenant law with its poles and the atonement cover; [36]the table with all its articles and the bread of the Presence; [37]the pure gold lampstand with its row of lamps and all its accessories, and the olive oil for the light; [38]the gold altar, the anointing oil, the fragrant incense, and the curtain for the entrance to the tent; [39]the bronze altar with its bronze grating, its poles and all its utensils; the basin with its stand; [40]the curtains of the courtyard with its posts and bases, and the curtain for the entrance to the courtyard; the ropes and tent pegs for the courtyard; all the furnishings for the tabernacle, the tent of meeting; [41]and the woven garments worn for ministering in the sanctuary, both the sacred garments for Aaron the priest and the garments for his sons when serving as priests.

[42]The Israelites had done all the work just as the LORD had commanded Moses. [43]Moses inspected the work and saw that they had done it just as the LORD had commanded. So Moses blessed them.

Setting Up the Tabernacle

40 Then the LORD said to Moses: [2]"Set up the tabernacle, the tent of meeting, on the first day of the first month. [3]Place the ark of the covenant law in it and shield the ark with the curtain. [4]Bring in the table and set out what belongs on it. Then bring in the lampstand and set up its lamps. [5]Place the gold altar of incense in front of the ark of the covenant law and put the curtain at the entrance to the tabernacle.

[6]"Place the altar of burnt offering in front of the entrance to the tabernacle, the tent of meeting; [7]place the basin between the tent of meeting and the altar and put water in it. [8]Set up the courtyard around it and put the curtain at the entrance to the courtyard.

[9]"Take the anointing oil and anoint the tabernacle and ev-

---

[a] 34 Possibly the hides of large aquatic mammals

erything in it; consecrate it and all its furnishings, and it will be holy. ¹⁰Then anoint the altar of burnt offering and all its utensils; consecrate the altar, and it will be most holy. ¹¹Anoint the basin and its stand and consecrate them.

¹²"Bring Aaron and his sons to the entrance to the tent of meeting and wash them with water. ¹³Then dress Aaron in the sacred garments, anoint him and consecrate him so he may serve me as priest. ¹⁴Bring his sons and dress them in tunics. ¹⁵Anoint them just as you anointed their father, so they may serve me as priests. Their anointing will be to a priesthood that will continue throughout their generations." ¹⁶Moses did everything just as the LORD commanded him.

¹⁷So the tabernacle was set up on the first day of the first month in the second year. ¹⁸When Moses set up the tabernacle, he put the bases in place, erected the frames, inserted the crossbars and set up the posts. ¹⁹Then he spread the tent over the tabernacle and put the covering over the tent, as the LORD commanded him.

²⁰He took the tablets of the covenant law and placed them in the ark, attached the poles to the ark and put the atonement cover over it. ²¹Then he brought the ark into the tabernacle and hung the shielding curtain and shield-

ed the ark of the covenant law, as the LORD commanded him.

²²Moses placed the table in the tent of meeting on the north side of the tabernacle outside the curtain ²³and set out the bread on it before the LORD, as the LORD commanded him.

²⁴He placed the lampstand in the tent of meeting opposite the table on the south side of the tabernacle ²⁵and set up the lamps before the LORD, as the LORD commanded him.

²⁶Moses placed the gold altar in the tent of meeting in front of the curtain ²⁷and burned fragrant incense on it, as the LORD commanded him.

²⁸Then he put up the curtain at the entrance to the tabernacle. ²⁹He set the altar of burnt offering near the entrance to the tabernacle, the tent of meeting, and offered on it burnt offerings and grain offerings, as the LORD commanded him.

³⁰He placed the basin between the tent of meeting and the altar and put water in it for washing, ³¹and Moses and Aaron and his sons used it to wash their hands and feet. ³²They washed whenever they entered the tent of meeting or approached the altar, as the LORD commanded Moses.

³³Then Moses set up the courtyard around the tabernacle and altar and put up the curtain at the entrance to the courtyard. And so Moses finished the work.

The Glory of the LORD

34Then the cloud covered the tent of meeting, and the glory of the LORD filled the tabernacle. **35**Moses could not enter the tent of meeting because the cloud had settled on it, and the glory of the LORD filled the tabernacle.

36In all the travels of the Israelites, whenever the cloud lifted from above the tabernacle, they would set out; **37**but if the cloud did not lift, they did not set out—until the day it lifted. **38**So the cloud of the LORD was over the tabernacle by day, and fire was in the cloud by night, in the sight of all the Israelites during all their travels.

Leviticus

Introduction:

Leviticus means "about the Levites." The Levites were God's priests, and the book of Leviticus contains many of the rules they needed to do their work — rules for worshiping God, making sacrifices, and handling everyday problems concerning cleanliness. Although God gave many of the rules only to the Levites, his purpose for giving all the laws was to help the Israelites worship and live as his holy people. A key statement for the entire book is "Be holy, because I am holy" (11:44,45).

Outline of contents:

The laws and instructions for offerings (1:1–7:38)
The appointment of Aaron and his sons as God's
    priests (8:1–10:20)
Rules for holy living (11:1–15:33)
The Day of Atonement (16:1–34)
Practical holiness (17:1–22:33)
The Sabbath, festivals and seasons (23:1–25:55)
Conditions for God's blessings (26:1–27:34)

The Burnt Offering

1 The LORD called to Moses and spoke to him from the tent of meeting. He said, ² "Speak to the Israelites and say to them: 'When anyone among you brings an offering to the LORD, bring as your offering an animal from either the herd or the flock.

³ "'If the offering is a burnt offering from the herd, you are to offer a male without defect. You must present it at the entrance to the tent of meeting so that it will be acceptable to the LORD. ⁴ You are to lay your hand on the head of the burnt offering, and it will be accepted on your behalf to make atonement for you. ⁵ You are to slaughter the young bull before the LORD, and then Aaron's sons the priests shall bring the blood and splash it against the sides of the altar at the entrance to the tent of meeting. ⁶ You are to skin the burnt offering and cut it into pieces. ⁷ The sons of Aaron the priest are to put fire on the altar and arrange wood on the fire. ⁸ Then Aaron's sons the priests shall arrange the pieces, including the head and the fat, on the

wood that is burning on the altar. [9] You are to wash the internal organs and the legs with water, and the priest is to burn all of it on the altar. It is a burnt offering, a food offering, an aroma pleasing to the LORD.

[10] "'If the offering is a burnt offering from the flock, from either the sheep or the goats, you are to offer a male without defect. [11] You are to slaughter it at the north side of the altar before the LORD, and Aaron's sons the priests shall splash its blood against the sides of the altar. [12] You are to cut it into pieces, and the priest shall arrange them, including the head and the fat, on the wood that is burning on the altar. [13] You are to wash the internal organs and the legs with water, and the priest is to bring all of them and burn them on the altar. It is a burnt offering, a food offering, an aroma pleasing to the LORD.

[14] "'If the offering to the LORD is a burnt offering of birds, you are to offer a dove or a young pigeon. [15] The priest shall bring it to the altar, wring off the head and burn it on the altar; its blood shall be drained out on the side of the altar. [16] He is to remove the crop and the feathers[a] and throw them down east of the altar where the ashes are. [17] He shall tear it open by the wings, not dividing it completely, and then the priest shall burn it on the wood that is burning on the altar. It is a burnt offering, a food offering, an aroma pleasing to the LORD.

The Grain Offering

2 "'When anyone brings a grain offering to the LORD, their offering is to be of the finest flour. They are to pour olive oil on it, put incense on it [2] and take it to Aaron's sons the priests. The priest shall take a handful of the flour and oil, together with all the incense, and burn this as a memorial[b] portion on the altar, a food offering, an aroma pleasing to the LORD. [3] The rest of the grain offering belongs to Aaron and his sons; it is a most holy part of the food offerings presented to the LORD.

[4] "'If you bring a grain offering baked in an oven, it is to consist of the finest flour: either thick loaves made without yeast and with olive oil mixed in or thin loaves made without yeast and brushed with olive oil. [5] If your grain offering is prepared on a griddle, it is to be made of the finest flour mixed with oil, and without yeast. [6] Crumble it and pour oil on it; it is a grain offering. [7] If your grain offering is cooked in a pan, it is to be made of the finest flour and some olive oil. [8] Bring the grain offering made of these things to the LORD; present

---

[a] 16 Or *crop with its contents*; the meaning of the Hebrew for this word is uncertain.   [b] 2 Or *representative*; also in verses 9 and 16

it to the priest, who shall take it to the altar. **9**He shall take out the memorial portion from the grain offering and burn it on the altar as a food offering, an aroma pleasing to the LORD. **10**The rest of the grain offering belongs to Aaron and his sons; it is a most holy part of the food offerings presented to the LORD.

11 "'Every grain offering you bring to the LORD must be made without yeast, for you are not to burn any yeast or honey in a food offering presented to the LORD. **12**You may bring them to the LORD as an offering of the firstfruits, but they are not to be offered on the altar as a pleasing aroma. **13**Season all your grain offerings with salt. Do not leave the salt of the covenant of your God out of your grain offerings; add salt to all your offerings.

14 "'If you bring a grain offering of firstfruits to the LORD, offer crushed heads of new grain roasted in the fire. **15**Put oil and incense on it; it is a grain offering. **16**The priest shall burn the memorial portion of the crushed grain and the oil, together with all the incense, as a food offering presented to the LORD.

The Fellowship Offering

3 "'If your offering is a fellowship offering, and you offer an animal from the herd, whether male or female, you are to present before the LORD an animal with-

out defect. **2**You are to lay your hand on the head of your offering and slaughter it at the entrance to the tent of meeting. Then Aaron's sons the priests shall splash the blood against the sides of the altar. **3**From the fellowship offering you are to bring a food offering to the LORD: the internal organs and all the fat that is connected to them, **4**both kidneys with the fat on them near the loins, and the long lobe of the liver, which you will remove with the kidneys. **5**Then Aaron's sons are to burn it on the altar on top of the burnt offering that is lying on the burning wood; it is a food offering, an aroma pleasing to the LORD.

6 "'If you offer an animal from the flock as a fellowship offering to the LORD, you are to offer a male or female without defect. **7**If you offer a lamb, you are to present it before the LORD, **8**lay your hand on its head and slaughter it in front of the tent of meeting. Then Aaron's sons shall splash its blood against the sides of the altar. **9**From the fellowship offering you are to bring a food offering to the LORD: its fat, the entire fat tail cut off close to the backbone, the internal organs and all the fat that is connected to them, **10**both kidneys with the fat on them near the loins, and the long lobe of the liver, which you will remove with the kidneys. **11**The priest shall burn them on the altar as a food offering presented to the LORD.

¹² " 'If your offering is a goat, you are to present it before the Lord, ¹³ lay your hand on its head and slaughter it in front of the tent of meeting. Then Aaron's sons shall splash its blood against the sides of the altar. ¹⁴ From what you offer you are to present this food offering to the Lord: the internal organs and all the fat that is connected to them, ¹⁵ both kidneys with the fat on them near the loins, and the long lobe of the liver, which you will remove with the kidneys. ¹⁶ The priest shall burn them on the altar as a food offering, a pleasing aroma. All the fat is the Lord's.

¹⁷ " 'This is a lasting ordinance for the generations to come, wherever you live: You must not eat any fat or any blood.' "

The Sin Offering

4 The Lord said to Moses, ² "Say to the Israelites: 'When anyone sins unintentionally and does what is forbidden in any of the Lord's commands—

³ " 'If the anointed priest sins, bringing guilt on the people, he must bring to the Lord a young bull without defect as a sin offering*a* for the sin he has committed. ⁴ He is to present the bull at the entrance to the tent of meeting before the Lord. He is to lay his hand on its head and slaughter it there before the Lord. ⁵ Then the anointed priest shall take some of the bull's blood and carry it into the tent of meeting. ⁶ He is to dip his finger into the blood and sprinkle some of it seven times before the Lord, in front of the curtain of the sanctuary. ⁷ The priest shall then put some of the blood on the horns of the altar of fragrant incense that is before the Lord in the tent of meeting. The rest of the bull's blood he shall pour out at the base of the altar of burnt offering at the entrance to the tent of meeting. ⁸ He shall remove all the fat from the bull of the sin offering—all the fat that is connected to the internal organs, ⁹ both kidneys with the fat on them near the loins, and the long lobe of the liver, which he will remove with the kidneys— ¹⁰ just as the fat is removed from the ox*b* sacrificed as a fellowship offering. Then the priest shall burn them on the altar of burnt offering. ¹¹ But the hide of the bull and all its flesh, as well as the head and legs, the internal organs and the intestines— ¹² that is, all the rest of the bull—he must take outside the camp to a place ceremonially clean, where the ashes are thrown, and burn it there in a wood fire on the ash heap.

¹³ " 'If the whole Israelite community sins unintentionally and does what is forbidden in any of the Lord's commands, even

---

a 3 Or *purification offering*; here and throughout this chapter   *b 10* The Hebrew word can refer to either male or female.

though the community is unaware of the matter, when they realize their guilt [14] and the sin they committed becomes known, the assembly must bring a young bull as a sin offering and present it before the tent of meeting. [15] The elders of the community are to lay their hands on the bull's head before the LORD, and the bull shall be slaughtered before the LORD. [16] Then the anointed priest is to take some of the bull's blood into the tent of meeting. [17] He shall dip his finger into the blood and sprinkle it before the LORD seven times in front of the curtain. [18] He is to put some of the blood on the horns of the altar that is before the LORD in the tent of meeting. The rest of the blood he shall pour out at the base of the altar of burnt offering at the entrance to the tent of meeting. [19] He shall remove all the fat from it and burn it on the altar, [20] and do with this bull just as he did with the bull for the sin offering. In this way the priest will make atonement for the community, and they will be forgiven. [21] Then he shall take the bull outside the camp and burn it as he burned the first bull. This is the sin offering for the community.

[22] " 'When a leader sins unintentionally and does what is forbidden in any of the commands of the LORD his God, when he realizes his guilt [23] and the sin he has committed becomes known, he must bring as his offering a male goat without defect. [24] He is to lay his hand on the goat's head and slaughter it at the place where the burnt offering is slaughtered before the LORD. It is a sin offering. [25] Then the priest shall take some of the blood of the sin offering with his finger and put it on the horns of the altar of burnt offering and pour out the rest of the blood at the base of the altar. [26] He shall burn all the fat on the altar as he burned the fat of the fellowship offering. In this way the priest will make atonement for the leader's sin, and he will be forgiven.

[27] " 'If any member of the community sins unintentionally and does what is forbidden in any of the LORD's commands, when they realize their guilt [28] and the sin they have committed becomes known, they must bring as their offering for the sin they committed a female goat without defect. [29] They are to lay their hand on the head of the sin offering and slaughter it at the place of the burnt offering. [30] Then the priest is to take some of the blood with his finger and put it on the horns of the altar of burnt offering and pour out the rest of the blood at the base of the altar. [31] They shall remove all the fat, just as the fat is removed from the fellowship offering, and the priest shall burn it on the altar as an aroma pleasing to the LORD. In this way the priest will make atonement for them, and they will be forgiven.

³²"'If someone brings a lamb as their sin offering, they are to bring a female without defect. ³³They are to lay their hand on its head and slaughter it for a sin offering at the place where the burnt offering is slaughtered. ³⁴Then the priest shall take some of the blood of the sin offering with his finger and put it on the horns of the altar of burnt offering and pour out the rest of the blood at the base of the altar. ³⁵They shall remove all the fat, just as the fat is removed from the lamb of the fellowship offering, and the priest shall burn it on the altar on top of the food offerings presented to the LORD. In this way the priest will make atonement for them for the sin they have committed, and they will be forgiven.

5 "'If anyone sins because they do not speak up when they hear a public charge to testify regarding something they have seen or learned about, they will be held responsible.

²"'If anyone becomes aware that they are guilty—if they unwittingly touch anything ceremonially unclean (whether the carcass of an unclean animal, wild or domestic, or of any unclean creature that moves along the ground) and they are unaware that they have become unclean, but then they come to realize their guilt; ³or if they touch

human uncleanness (anything that would make them unclean) even though they are unaware of it, but then they learn of it and realize their guilt; ⁴or if anyone thoughtlessly takes an oath to do anything, whether good or evil (in any matter one might carelessly swear about) even though they are unaware of it, but then they learn of it and realize their guilt— ⁵when anyone becomes aware that they are guilty in any of these matters, they must confess in what way they have sinned. ⁶As a penalty for the sin they have committed, they must bring to the LORD a female lamb or goat from the flock as a sin offering[a]; and the priest shall make atonement for them for their sin.

⁷"'Anyone who cannot afford a lamb is to bring two doves or two young pigeons to the LORD as a penalty for their sin—one for a sin offering and the other for a burnt offering. ⁸They are to bring them to the priest, who shall first offer the one for the sin offering. He is to wring its head from its neck, not dividing it completely, ⁹and is to splash some of the blood of the sin offering against the side of the altar; the rest of the blood must be drained out at the base of the altar. It is a sin offering. ¹⁰The priest shall then offer the other as a burnt offering in the prescribed way and make atonement for them for the sin

---

ᵃ 6 Or *purification offering*; here and throughout this chapter they have committed, and they will be forgiven.

11 " 'If, however, they cannot afford two doves or two young pigeons, they are to bring as an offering for their sin a tenth of an ephah[a] of the finest flour for a sin offering. They must not put olive oil or incense on it, because it is a sin offering. **12** They are to bring it to the priest, who shall take a handful of it as a memorial[b] portion and burn it on the altar on top of the food offerings presented to the LORD. It is a sin offering. **13** In this way the priest will make atonement for them for any of these sins they have committed, and they will be forgiven. The rest of the offering will belong to the priest, as in the case of the grain offering.' "

The Guilt Offering

14 The LORD said to Moses: **15** "When anyone is unfaithful to the LORD by sinning unintentionally in regard to any of the LORD's holy things, they are to bring to the LORD as a penalty a ram from the flock, one without defect and of the proper value in silver, according to the sanctuary shekel.[c] It is a guilt offering. **16** They must make restitution for what they have failed to do in regard to the holy things, pay an additional penalty of a fifth of its value and give it all to the priest. The priest will make atonement for them with the ram as a guilt offering, and they will be forgiven.

17 "If anyone sins and does what is forbidden in any of the LORD's commands, even though they do not know it, they are guilty and will be held responsible. **18** They are to bring to the priest as a guilt offering a ram from the flock, one without defect and of the proper value. In this way the priest will make atonement for them for the wrong they have committed unintentionally, and they will be forgiven. **19** It is a guilt offering; they have been guilty of[d] wrongdoing against the LORD."

6 [e] The LORD said to Moses: **2** "If anyone sins and is unfaithful to the LORD by deceiving a neighbor about something entrusted to them or left in their care or about something stolen, or if they cheat their neighbor, **3** or if they find lost property and lie about it, or if they swear falsely about any such sin that people may commit— **4** when they sin in any of these ways and realize their guilt, they must return what they have stolen or taken by extortion, or what was entrusted to them, or the lost property they found, **5** or whatever it was they swore falsely about. They must make restitution in full, add a fifth of the value

---

[a] *11* That is, probably about 3 1/2 pounds or about 1.6 kilograms
[b] *12* Or *representative*   [c] *15* That is, about 2/5 ounce or about 12 grams
[d] *19* Or *offering; atonement has been made for their*   [e] In Hebrew texts 6:1-7 is numbered 5:20-26, and 6:8-30 is numbered 6:1-23.

to it and give it all to the owner on the day they present their guilt offering. ⁶And as a penalty they must bring to the priest, that is, to the LORD, their guilt offering, a ram from the flock, one without defect and of the proper value. ⁷In this way the priest will make atonement for them before the LORD, and they will be forgiven for any of the things they did that made them guilty.'"

The Burnt Offering

⁸The LORD said to Moses: ⁹"Give Aaron and his sons this command: 'These are the regulations for the burnt offering: The burnt offering is to remain on the altar hearth throughout the night, till morning, and the fire must be kept burning on the altar. ¹⁰The priest shall then put on his linen clothes, with linen undergarments next to his body, and shall remove the ashes of the burnt offering that the fire has consumed on the altar and place them beside the altar. ¹¹Then he is to take off these clothes and put on others, and carry the ashes outside the camp to a place that is ceremonially clean. ¹²The fire on the altar must be kept burning; it must not go out. Every morning the priest is to add firewood and arrange the burnt offering on the fire and burn the fat of the fel-

lowship offerings on it. ¹³The fire must be kept burning on the altar continuously; it must not go out.

The Grain Offering

¹⁴"'These are the regulations for the grain offering: Aaron's sons are to bring it before the LORD, in front of the altar. ¹⁵The priest is to take a handful of the finest flour and some olive oil, together with all the incense on the grain offering, and burn the memorial[a] portion on the altar as an aroma pleasing to the LORD. ¹⁶Aaron and his sons shall eat the rest of it, but it is to be eaten without yeast in the sanctuary area; they are to eat it in the courtyard of the tent of meeting. ¹⁷It must not be baked with yeast; I have given it as their share of the food offerings presented to me. Like the sin offering[b] and the guilt offering, it is most holy. ¹⁸Any male descendant of Aaron may eat it. For all generations to come it is his perpetual share of the food offerings presented to the LORD. Whatever touches them will become holy.[c]'"

¹⁹The LORD also said to Moses, ²⁰"This is the offering Aaron and his sons are to bring to the LORD on the day he[d] is anointed: a tenth of an ephah[e] of the finest flour as a regular grain offering, half of it in the morning and half in the evening. ²¹It must be pre-

---

[a] 15 Or *representative*   [b] 17 Or *purification offering*; also in verses 25 and 30   [c] 18 Or *Whoever touches them must be holy*; similarly in verse 27
[d] 20 Or *each*   [e] 20 That is, probably about 3 1/2 pounds or about 1.6 kilograms

pared with oil on a griddle; bring it well-mixed and present the grain offering broken[a] in pieces as an aroma pleasing to the LORD. [22] The son who is to succeed him as anointed priest shall prepare it. It is the LORD's perpetual share and is to be burned completely. [23] Every grain offering of a priest shall be burned completely; it must not be eaten."

The Sin Offering

[24] The LORD said to Moses, [25] "Say to Aaron and his sons: 'These are the regulations for the sin offering: The sin offering is to be slaughtered before the LORD in the place the burnt offering is slaughtered; it is most holy. [26] The priest who offers it shall eat it; it is to be eaten in the sanctuary area, in the courtyard of the tent of meeting. [27] Whatever touches any of the flesh will become holy, and if any of the blood is spattered on a garment, you must wash it in the sanctuary area. [28] The clay pot the meat is cooked in must be broken; but if it is cooked in a bronze pot, the pot is to be scoured and rinsed with water. [29] Any male in a priest's family may eat it; it is most holy. [30] But any sin offering whose blood is brought into the tent of meeting to make atonement in the Holy Place must not be eaten; it must be burned up.

The Guilt Offering

7 "'These are the regulations for the guilt offering, which is most holy: [2] The guilt offering is to be slaughtered in the place where the burnt offering is slaughtered, and its blood is to be splashed against the sides of the altar. [3] All its fat shall be offered: the fat tail and the fat that covers the internal organs, [4] both kidneys with the fat on them near the loins, and the long lobe of the liver, which is to be removed with the kidneys. [5] The priest shall burn them on the altar as a food offering presented to the LORD. It is a guilt offering. [6] Any male in a priest's family may eat it, but it must be eaten in the sanctuary area; it is most holy.

[7] "'The same law applies to both the sin offering[b] and the guilt offering: They belong to the priest who makes atonement with them. [8] The priest who offers a burnt offering for anyone may keep its hide for himself. [9] Every grain offering baked in an oven or cooked in a pan or on a griddle belongs to the priest who offers it, [10] and every grain offering, whether mixed with olive oil or dry, belongs equally to all the sons of Aaron.

The Fellowship Offering

[11] "'These are the regulations for the fellowship offering anyone may present to the LORD:

---

[a] 21 The meaning of the Hebrew for this word is uncertain.   [b] 7 Or *purification offering*; also in verse 37

12 " 'If they offer it as an expression of thankfulness, then along with this thank offering they are to offer thick loaves made without yeast and with olive oil mixed in, thin loaves made without yeast and brushed with oil, and thick loaves of the finest flour well-kneaded and with oil mixed in. 13 Along with their fellowship offering of thanksgiving they are to present an offering with thick loaves of bread made with yeast. 14 They are to bring one of each kind as an offering, a contribution to the LORD; it belongs to the priest who splashes the blood of the fellowship offering against the altar. 15 The meat of their fellowship offering of thanksgiving must be eaten on the day it is offered; they must leave none of it till morning.

16 " 'If, however, their offering is the result of a vow or is a freewill offering, the sacrifice shall be eaten on the day they offer it, but anything left over may be eaten on the next day. 17 Any meat of the sacrifice left over till the third day must be burned up. 18 If any meat of the fellowship offering is eaten on the third day, the one who offered it will not be accepted. It will not be reckoned to their credit, for it has become impure; the person who eats any of it will be held responsible.

19 " 'Meat that touches anything ceremonially unclean must not be eaten; it must be burned up. As for other meat, anyone ceremonially clean may eat it. 20 But if anyone who is unclean eats any meat of the fellowship offering belonging to the LORD, they must be cut off from their people. 21 Anyone who touches something unclean — whether human uncleanness or an unclean animal or any unclean creature that moves along the ground[a] — and then eats any of the meat of the fellowship offering belonging to the LORD must be cut off from their people.' "

Eating Fat and Blood Forbidden

22 The LORD said to Moses, 23 "Say to the Israelites: 'Do not eat any of the fat of cattle, sheep or goats. 24 The fat of an animal found dead or torn by wild animals may be used for any other purpose, but you must not eat it. 25 Anyone who eats the fat of an animal from which a food offering may be[b] presented to the LORD must be cut off from their people. 26 And wherever you live, you must not eat the blood of any bird or animal. 27 Anyone who eats blood must be cut off from their people.' "

The Priests' Share

28 The LORD said to Moses, 29 "Say to the Israelites: 'Anyone

a 21 A few Hebrew manuscripts, Samaritan Pentateuch, Syriac and Targum (see 5:2); most Hebrew manuscripts *any unclean, detestable thing*
b 25 Or *offering is*

who brings a fellowship offering to the LORD is to bring part of it as their sacrifice to the LORD. ³⁰With their own hands they are to present the food offering to the LORD; they are to bring the fat, together with the breast, and wave the breast before the LORD as a wave offering. ³¹The priest shall burn the fat on the altar, but the breast belongs to Aaron and his sons. ³²You are to give the right thigh of your fellowship offerings to the priest as a contribution. ³³The son of Aaron who offers the blood and the fat of the fellowship offering shall have the right thigh as his share. ³⁴From the fellowship offerings of the Israelites, I have taken the breast that is waved and the thigh that is presented and have given them to Aaron the priest and his sons as their perpetual share from the Israelites.' "

³⁵This is the portion of the food offerings presented to the LORD that were allotted to Aaron and his sons on the day they were presented to serve the LORD as priests. ³⁶On the day they were anointed, the LORD commanded that the Israelites give this to them as their perpetual share for the generations to come.

³⁷These, then, are the regulations for the burnt offering, the grain offering, the sin offering, the guilt offering, the ordination offering and the fellowship offering, ³⁸which the LORD gave Moses at Mount Sinai in the Desert of Sinai on the day he commanded the Israelites to bring their offerings to the LORD.

The Ordination of Aaron and His Sons

8 The LORD said to Moses, ²"Bring Aaron and his sons, their garments, the anointing oil, the bull for the sin offering,ᵃ the two rams and the basket containing bread made without yeast, ³and gather the entire assembly at the entrance to the tent of meeting." ⁴Moses did as the LORD commanded him, and the assembly gathered at the entrance to the tent of meeting.

⁵Moses said to the assembly, "This is what the LORD has commanded to be done." ⁶Then Moses brought Aaron and his sons forward and washed them with water. ⁷He put the tunic on Aaron, tied the sash around him, clothed him with the robe and put the ephod on him. He also fastened the ephod with a decorative waistband, which he tied around him. ⁸He placed the breastpiece on him and put the Urim and Thummim in the breastpiece. ⁹Then he placed the turban on Aaron's head and set the gold plate, the sacred emblem, on the front of it, as the LORD commanded Moses.

ᵃ 2 Or *purification offering*; also in verse 14

[10] Then Moses took the anointing oil and anointed the tabernacle and everything in it, and so consecrated them. [11] He sprinkled some of the oil on the altar seven times, anointing the altar and all its utensils and the basin with its stand, to consecrate them. [12] He poured some of the anointing oil on Aaron's head and anointed him to consecrate him. [13] Then he brought Aaron's sons forward, put tunics on them, tied sashes around them and fastened caps on them, as the LORD commanded Moses.

[14] He then presented the bull for the sin offering, and Aaron and his sons laid their hands on its head. [15] Moses slaughtered the bull and took some of the blood, and with his finger he put it on all the horns of the altar to purify the altar. He poured out the rest of the blood at the base of the altar. So he consecrated it to make atonement for it. [16] Moses also took all the fat around the internal organs, the long lobe of the liver, and both kidneys and their fat, and burned it on the altar. [17] But the bull with its hide and its flesh and its intestines he burned up outside the camp, as the LORD commanded Moses.

[18] He then presented the ram for the burnt offering, and Aaron and his sons laid their hands on its head. [19] Then Moses slaughtered the ram and splashed the blood against the sides of the al-

tar. [20] He cut the ram into pieces and burned the head, the pieces and the fat. [21] He washed the internal organs and the legs with water and burned the whole ram on the altar. It was a burnt offering, a pleasing aroma, a food offering presented to the LORD, as the LORD commanded Moses.

[22] He then presented the other ram, the ram for the ordination, and Aaron and his sons laid their hands on its head. [23] Moses slaughtered the ram and took some of its blood and put it on the lobe of Aaron's right ear, on the thumb of his right hand and on the big toe of his right foot. [24] Moses also brought Aaron's sons forward and put some of the blood on the lobes of their right ears, on the thumbs of their right hands and on the big toes of their right feet. Then he splashed blood against the sides of the altar. [25] After that, he took the fat, the fat tail, all the fat around the internal organs, the long lobe of the liver, both kidneys and their fat and the right thigh. [26] And from the basket of bread made without yeast, which was before the LORD, he took one thick loaf, one thick loaf with olive oil mixed in, and one thin loaf, and he put these on the fat portions and on the right thigh. [27] He put all these in the hands of Aaron and his sons, and they waved them before the LORD as a wave offering. [28] Then Moses took them from their hands and

burned them on the altar on top of the burnt offering as an ordination offering, a pleasing aroma, a food offering presented to the LORD. ²⁹Moses also took the breast, which was his share of the ordination ram, and waved it before the LORD as a wave offering, as the LORD commanded Moses.

³⁰Then Moses took some of the anointing oil and some of the blood from the altar and sprinkled them on Aaron and his garments and on his sons and their garments. So he consecrated Aaron and his garments and his sons and their garments.

³¹Moses then said to Aaron and his sons, "Cook the meat at the entrance to the tent of meeting and eat it there with the bread from the basket of ordination offerings, as I was commanded: 'Aaron and his sons are to eat it.' ³²Then burn up the rest of the meat and the bread. ³³Do not leave the entrance to the tent of meeting for seven days, until the days of your ordination are completed, for your ordination will last seven days. ³⁴What has been done today was commanded by the LORD to make atonement for you. ³⁵You must stay at the entrance to the tent of meeting day and night for seven days and do what the LORD requires, so you will not die; for that is what I have been commanded."

³⁶So Aaron and his sons did everything the LORD commanded through Moses.

The Priests Begin Their Ministry

9 On the eighth day Moses summoned Aaron and his sons and the elders of Israel. ²He said to Aaron, "Take a bull calf for your sin offering*a* and a ram for your burnt offering, both without defect, and present them before the LORD. ³Then say to the Israelites: 'Take a male goat for a sin offering, a calf and a lamb—both a year old and without defect—for a burnt offering, ⁴and an ox*b* and a ram for a fellowship offering to sacrifice before the LORD, together with a grain offering mixed with olive oil. For today the LORD will appear to you.'"

⁵They took the things Moses commanded to the front of the tent of meeting, and the entire assembly came near and stood before the LORD. ⁶Then Moses said, "This is what the LORD has commanded you to do, so that the glory of the LORD may appear to you."

⁷Moses said to Aaron, "Come to the altar and sacrifice your sin offering and your burnt offering and make atonement for yourself and the people; sacrifice the offering that is for the people and make atonement for them, as the LORD has commanded."

---

a 2 Or *purification offering*; here and throughout this chapter   *b* 4 The Hebrew word can refer to either male or female; also in verses 18 and 19.

[8] So Aaron came to the altar and slaughtered the calf as a sin offering for himself. [9] His sons brought the blood to him, and he dipped his finger into the blood and put it on the horns of the altar; the rest of the blood he poured out at the base of the altar. [10] On the altar he burned the fat, the kidneys and the long lobe of the liver from the sin offering, as the LORD commanded Moses; [11] the flesh and the hide he burned up outside the camp.

[12] Then he slaughtered the burnt offering. His sons handed him the blood, and he splashed it against the sides of the altar. [13] They handed him the burnt offering piece by piece, including the head, and he burned them on the altar. [14] He washed the internal organs and the legs and burned them on top of the burnt offering on the altar.

[15] Aaron then brought the offering that was for the people. He took the goat for the people's sin offering and slaughtered it and offered it for a sin offering as he did with the first one. [16] He brought the burnt offering and offered it in the prescribed way. [17] He also brought the grain offering, took a handful of it and burned it on the altar in addition to the morning's burnt offering.

[18] He slaughtered the ox and the ram as the fellowship offering for the people. His sons handed him the blood, and he splashed it against the sides of the altar. [19] But the fat portions of the ox and the ram — the fat tail, the layer of fat, the kidneys and the long lobe of the liver — [20] these they laid on the breasts, and then Aaron burned the fat on the altar. [21] Aaron waved the breasts and the right thigh before the LORD as a wave offering, as Moses commanded.

[22] Then Aaron lifted his hands toward the people and blessed them. And having sacrificed the sin offering, the burnt offering and the fellowship offering, he stepped down.

[23] Moses and Aaron then went into the tent of meeting. When they came out, they blessed the people; and the glory of the LORD appeared to all the people. [24] Fire came out from the presence of the LORD and consumed the burnt offering and the fat portions on the altar. And when all the people saw it, they shouted for joy and fell facedown.

The Death of Nadab and Abihu

10 Aaron's sons Nadab and Abihu took their censers, put fire in them and added incense; and they offered unauthorized fire before the LORD, contrary to his command. [2] So fire came out from the presence of the LORD and consumed them, and they died before the LORD. [3] Moses then said to Aaron, "This is what the LORD spoke of when he said:

" 'Among those who
approach me
I will be proved holy;
in the sight of all the people
I will be honored.' "

Aaron remained silent.

4 Moses summoned Mishael and Elzaphan, sons of Aaron's uncle Uzziel, and said to them, "Come here; carry your cousins outside the camp, away from the front of the sanctuary." **5** So they came and carried them, still in their tunics, outside the camp, as Moses ordered.

6 Then Moses said to Aaron and his sons Eleazar and Ithamar, "Do not let your hair become unkempt*a* and do not tear your clothes, or you will die and the LORD will be angry with the whole community. But your relatives, all the Israelites, may mourn for those the LORD has destroyed by fire. **7** Do not leave the entrance to the tent of meeting or you will die, because the LORD's anointing oil is on you." So they did as Moses said.

8 Then the LORD said to Aaron, **9** "You and your sons are not to drink wine or other fermented drink whenever you go into the tent of meeting, or you will die. This is a lasting ordinance for the generations to come, **10** so that you can distinguish between the holy and the common, between the unclean and the clean, **11** and

so you can teach the Israelites all the decrees the LORD has given them through Moses."

12 Moses said to Aaron and his remaining sons, Eleazar and Ithamar, "Take the grain offering left over from the food offerings prepared without yeast and presented to the LORD and eat it beside the altar, for it is most holy. **13** Eat it in the sanctuary area, because it is your share and your sons' share of the food offerings presented to the LORD; for so I have been commanded. **14** But you and your sons and your daughters may eat the breast that was waved and the thigh that was presented. Eat them in a ceremonially clean place; they have been given to you and your children as your share of the Israelites' fellowship offerings. **15** The thigh that was presented and the breast that was waved must be brought with the fat portions of the food offerings, to be waved before the LORD as a wave offering. This will be the perpetual share for you and your children, as the LORD has commanded."

16 When Moses inquired about the goat of the sin offering*b* and found that it had been burned up, he was angry with Eleazar and Ithamar, Aaron's remaining sons, and asked, **17** "Why didn't you eat the sin offering in the sanctuary area? It is most holy; it was given

---

a 6 Or *Do not uncover your heads*   *b* 16 Or *purification offering*; also in verses 17 and 19 to you to take away the guilt of the community by making atonement for them before the LORD. [18] Since its blood was not taken into the Holy Place, you should have eaten the goat in the sanctuary area, as I commanded."

[19] Aaron replied to Moses, "Today they sacrificed their sin offering and their burnt offering before the LORD, but such things as this have happened to me. Would the LORD have been pleased if I had eaten the sin offering today?" [20] When Moses heard this, he was satisfied.

Clean and Unclean Food

11 The LORD said to Moses and Aaron, [2] "Say to the Israelites: 'Of all the animals that live on land, these are the ones you may eat: [3] You may eat any animal that has a divided hoof and that chews the cud.

[4] "There are some that only chew the cud or only have a divided hoof, but you must not eat them. The camel, though it chews the cud, does not have a divided hoof; it is ceremonially unclean for you. [5] The hyrax, though it chews the cud, does not have a divided hoof; it is unclean for you. [6] The rabbit, though it chews the cud, does not have a divided hoof; it is unclean for you. [7] And the pig, though it has a divided hoof, does not chew the cud; it is

unclean for you. [8] You must not eat their meat or touch their carcasses; they are unclean for you.

[9] "'Of all the creatures living in the water of the seas and the streams you may eat any that have fins and scales. [10] But all creatures in the seas or streams that do not have fins and scales — whether among all the swarming things or among all the other living creatures in the water — you are to regard as unclean. [11] And since you are to regard them as unclean, you must not eat their meat; you must regard their carcasses as unclean. [12] Anything living in the water that does not have fins and scales is to be regarded as unclean by you.

[13] "'These are the birds you are to regard as unclean and not eat because they are unclean: the eagle,[a] the vulture, the black vulture, [14] the red kite, any kind of black kite, [15] any kind of raven, [16] the horned owl, the screech owl, the gull, any kind of hawk, [17] the little owl, the cormorant, the great owl, [18] the white owl, the desert owl, the osprey, [19] the stork, any kind of heron, the hoopoe and the bat.

[20] "'All flying insects that walk on all fours are to be regarded as unclean by you. [21] There are, however, some flying insects that walk on all fours that you may eat: those that have jointed legs

---

[a] 13 The precise identification of some of the birds, insects and animals in this chapter is uncertain.

for hopping on the ground. ²²Of these you may eat any kind of locust, katydid, cricket or grasshopper. ²³But all other flying insects that have four legs you are to regard as unclean.

²⁴"'You will make yourselves unclean by these; whoever touches their carcasses will be unclean till evening. ²⁵Whoever picks up one of their carcasses must wash their clothes, and they will be unclean till evening.

²⁶"'Every animal that does not have a divided hoof or that does not chew the cud is unclean for you; whoever touches the carcass of any of them will be unclean. ²⁷Of all the animals that walk on all fours, those that walk on their paws are unclean for you; whoever touches their carcasses will be unclean till evening. ²⁸Anyone who picks up their carcasses must wash their clothes, and they will be unclean till evening. These animals are unclean for you.

²⁹"'Of the animals that move along the ground, these are unclean for you: the weasel, the rat, any kind of great lizard, ³⁰the gecko, the monitor lizard, the wall lizard, the skink and the chameleon. ³¹Of all those that move along the ground, these are unclean for you. Whoever touches them when they are dead will be unclean till evening. ³²When one of them dies and falls on something, that article, whatever its use, will be unclean, whether it is made of wood, cloth, hide or sackcloth. Put it in water; it will be unclean till evening, and then it will be clean. ³³If one of them falls into a clay pot, everything in it will be unclean, and you must break the pot. ³⁴Any food you are allowed to eat that has come into contact with water from any such pot is unclean, and any liquid that is drunk from such a pot is unclean. ³⁵Anything that one of their carcasses falls on becomes unclean; an oven or cooking pot must be broken up. They are unclean, and you are to regard them as unclean. ³⁶A spring, however, or a cistern for collecting water remains clean, but anyone who touches one of these carcasses is unclean. ³⁷If a carcass falls on any seeds that are to be planted, they remain clean. ³⁸But if water has been put on the seed and a carcass falls on it, it is unclean for you.

³⁹"'If an animal that you are allowed to eat dies, anyone who touches its carcass will be unclean till evening. ⁴⁰Anyone who eats some of its carcass must wash their clothes, and they will be unclean till evening. Anyone who picks up the carcass must wash their clothes, and they will be unclean till evening.

⁴¹"'Every creature that moves along the ground is to be regarded as unclean; it is not to be eaten. ⁴²You are not to eat any creature

that moves along the ground, whether it moves on its belly or walks on all fours or on many feet; it is unclean. ⁴³ Do not defile yourselves by any of these creatures. Do not make yourselves unclean by means of them or be made unclean by them. ⁴⁴ I am the LORD your God; consecrate yourselves and be holy, because I am holy. Do not make yourselves unclean by any creature that moves along the ground. ⁴⁵ I am the LORD, who brought you up out of Egypt to be your God; therefore be holy, because I am holy.

⁴⁶ "'These are the regulations concerning animals, birds, every living thing that moves about in the water and every creature that moves along the ground. ⁴⁷ You must distinguish between the unclean and the clean, between living creatures that may be eaten and those that may not be eaten.'"

Purification After Childbirth

12 The LORD said to Moses, ² "Say to the Israelites: 'A woman who becomes pregnant and gives birth to a son will be ceremonially unclean for seven days, just as she is unclean during her monthly period. ³ On the eighth day the boy is to be circumcised. ⁴ Then the woman must wait thirty-three days to be purified from her bleeding. She must not touch anything sacred or go to the sanctuary until the days of her purification are over. ⁵ If she gives birth to a daughter, for two weeks the woman will be unclean, as during her period. Then she must wait sixty-six days to be purified from her bleeding.

⁶ "'When the days of her purification for a son or daughter are over, she is to bring to the priest at the entrance to the tent of meeting a year-old lamb for a burnt offering and a young pigeon or a dove for a sin offering.ᵃ ⁷ He shall offer them before the LORD to make atonement for her, and then she will be ceremonially clean from her flow of blood.

"'These are the regulations for the woman who gives birth to a boy or a girl. ⁸ But if she cannot afford a lamb, she is to bring two doves or two young pigeons, one for a burnt offering and the other for a sin offering. In this way the priest will make atonement for her, and she will be clean.'"

Regulations About Defiling Skin Diseases

13 The LORD said to Moses and Aaron, ² "When anyone has a swelling or a rash or a shiny spot on their skin that may be a defiling skin disease,ᵇ they must be brought to Aaron the priest or to one of his sonsᶜ who

---

ᵃ 6 Or *purification offering*; also in verse 8   ᵇ 2 The Hebrew word for *defiling skin disease*, traditionally translated "leprosy," was used for various diseases affecting the skin; here and throughout verses 3-46.   ᶜ 2 Or *descendants* is a priest. ³The priest is to examine the sore on the skin, and if the hair in the sore has turned white and the sore appears to be more than skin deep, it is a defiling skin disease. When the priest examines that person, he shall pronounce them ceremonially unclean. ⁴If the shiny spot on the skin is white but does not appear to be more than skin deep and the hair in it has not turned white, the priest is to isolate the affected person for seven days. ⁵On the seventh day the priest is to examine them, and if he sees that the sore is unchanged and has not spread in the skin, he is to isolate them for another seven days. ⁶On the seventh day the priest is to examine them again, and if the sore has faded and has not spread in the skin, the priest shall pronounce them clean; it is only a rash. They must wash their clothes, and they will be clean. ⁷But if the rash does spread in their skin after they have shown themselves to the priest to be pronounced clean, they must appear before the priest again. ⁸The priest is to examine that person, and if the rash has spread in the skin, he shall pronounce them unclean; it is a defiling skin disease.

⁹"When anyone has a defiling skin disease, they must be brought to the priest. ¹⁰The priest is to examine them, and if there is a white swelling in the skin that has turned the hair white and if there is raw flesh in the swelling, ¹¹it is a chronic skin disease and the priest shall pronounce them unclean. He is not to isolate them, because they are already unclean.

¹²"If the disease breaks out all over their skin and, so far as the priest can see, it covers all the skin of the affected person from head to foot, ¹³the priest is to examine them, and if the disease has covered their whole body, he shall pronounce them clean. Since it has all turned white, they are clean. ¹⁴But whenever raw flesh appears on them, they will be unclean. ¹⁵When the priest sees the raw flesh, he shall pronounce them unclean. The raw flesh is unclean; they have a defiling disease. ¹⁶If the raw flesh changes and turns white, they must go to the priest. ¹⁷The priest is to examine them, and if the sores have turned white, the priest shall pronounce the affected person clean; then they will be clean.

¹⁸"When someone has a boil on their skin and it heals, ¹⁹and in the place where the boil was, a white swelling or reddish-white spot appears, they must present themselves to the priest. ²⁰The priest is to examine it, and if it appears to be more than skin deep and the hair in it has turned white, the priest shall pronounce that person unclean. It is a defiling skin disease that has broken

out where the boil was. **21** But if, when the priest examines it, there is no white hair in it and it is not more than skin deep and has faded, then the priest is to isolate them for seven days. **22** If it is spreading in the skin, the priest shall pronounce them unclean; it is a defiling disease. **23** But if the spot is unchanged and has not spread, it is only a scar from the boil, and the priest shall pronounce them clean.

24 "When someone has a burn on their skin and a reddish-white or white spot appears in the raw flesh of the burn, **25** the priest is to examine the spot, and if the hair in it has turned white, and it appears to be more than skin deep, it is a defiling disease that has broken out in the burn. The priest shall pronounce them unclean; it is a defiling skin disease. **26** But if the priest examines it and there is no white hair in the spot and if it is not more than skin deep and has faded, then the priest is to isolate them for seven days. **27** On the seventh day the priest is to examine that person, and if it is spreading in the skin, the priest shall pronounce them unclean; it is a defiling skin disease. **28** If, however, the spot is unchanged and has not spread in the skin but has faded, it is a swelling from the burn, and the priest shall pronounce them clean; it is only a scar from the burn.

29 "If a man or woman has a sore on their head or chin, **30** the priest is to examine the sore, and if it appears to be more than skin deep and the hair in it is yellow and thin, the priest shall pronounce them unclean; it is a defiling skin disease on the head or chin. **31** But if, when the priest examines the sore, it does not seem to be more than skin deep and there is no black hair in it, then the priest is to isolate the affected person for seven days. **32** On the seventh day the priest is to examine the sore, and if it has not spread and there is no yellow hair in it and it does not appear to be more than skin deep, **33** then the man or woman must shave themselves, except for the affected area, and the priest is to keep them isolated another seven days. **34** On the seventh day the priest is to examine the sore, and if it has not spread in the skin and appears to be no more than skin deep, the priest shall pronounce them clean. They must wash their clothes, and they will be clean. **35** But if the sore does spread in the skin after they are pronounced clean, **36** the priest is to examine them, and if he finds that the sore has spread in the skin, he does not need to look for yellow hair; they are unclean. **37** If, however, the sore is unchanged so far as the priest can see, and if black hair has grown in it, the affected person is healed. They are clean, and the priest shall pronounce them clean.

38 "When a man or woman has white spots on the skin, 39 the priest is to examine them, and if the spots are dull white, it is a harmless rash that has broken out on the skin; they are clean.

40 "A man who has lost his hair and is bald is clean. 41 If he has lost his hair from the front of his scalp and has a bald forehead, he is clean. 42 But if he has a reddish-white sore on his bald head or forehead, it is a defiling disease breaking out on his head or forehead. 43 The priest is to examine him, and if the swollen sore on his head or forehead is reddish-white like a defiling skin disease, 44 the man is diseased and is unclean. The priest shall pronounce him unclean because of the sore on his head.

45 "Anyone with such a defiling disease must wear torn clothes, let their hair be unkempt,[a] cover the lower part of their face and cry out, 'Unclean! Unclean!' 46 As long as they have the disease they remain unclean. They must live alone; they must live outside the camp.

Regulations About Defiling Molds

47 "As for any fabric that is spoiled with a defiling mold—any woolen or linen clothing, 48 any woven or knitted material of linen or wool, any leather or anything made of leather— 49 if the affected area in the fabric, the leather, the woven or knitted material, or any leather article, is greenish or reddish, it is a defiling mold and must be shown to the priest. 50 The priest is to examine the affected area and isolate the article for seven days. 51 On the seventh day he is to examine it, and if the mold has spread in the fabric, the woven or knitted material, or the leather, whatever its use, it is a persistent defiling mold; the article is unclean. 52 He must burn the fabric, the woven or knitted material of wool or linen, or any leather article that has been spoiled; because the defiling mold is persistent, the article must be burned.

53 "But if, when the priest examines it, the mold has not spread in the fabric, the woven or knitted material, or the leather article, 54 he shall order that the spoiled article be washed. Then he is to isolate it for another seven days. 55 After the article has been washed, the priest is to examine it again, and if the mold has not changed its appearance, even though it has not spread, it is unclean. Burn it, no matter which side of the fabric has been spoiled. 56 If, when the priest examines it, the mold has faded after the article has been washed, he is to tear the spoiled part out of the fabric, the leather, or the woven or knitted material. 57 But

a 45 Or clothes, uncover their head

if it reappears in the fabric, in the woven or knitted material, or in the leather article, it is a spreading mold; whatever has the mold must be burned. ⁵⁸Any fabric, woven or knitted material, or any leather article that has been washed and is rid of the mold, must be washed again. Then it will be clean."

⁵⁹These are the regulations concerning defiling molds in woolen or linen clothing, woven or knitted material, or any leather article, for pronouncing them clean or unclean.

Cleansing From Defiling Skin Diseases

14 The LORD said to Moses, ²"These are the regulations for any diseased person at the time of their ceremonial cleansing, when they are brought to the priest: ³The priest is to go outside the camp and examine them. If they have been healed of their defiling skin disease,ᵃ ⁴the priest shall order that two live clean birds and some cedar wood, scarlet yarn and hyssop be brought for the person to be cleansed. ⁵Then the priest shall order that one of the birds be killed over fresh water in a clay pot. ⁶He is then to take the live bird and dip it, together with the cedar wood, the scarlet yarn

and the hyssop, into the blood of the bird that was killed over the fresh water. ⁷Seven times he shall sprinkle the one to be cleansed of the defiling disease, and then pronounce them clean. After that, he is to release the live bird in the open fields.

⁸"The person to be cleansed must wash their clothes, shave off all their hair and bathe with water; then they will be ceremonially clean. After this they may come into the camp, but they must stay outside their tent for seven days. ⁹On the seventh day they must shave off all their hair; they must shave their head, their beard, their eyebrows and the rest of their hair. They must wash their clothes and bathe themselves with water, and they will be clean.

¹⁰"On the eighth day they must bring two male lambs and one ewe lamb a year old, each without defect, along with three-tenths of an ephahᵇ of the finest flour mixed with olive oil for a grain offering, and one logᶜ of oil. ¹¹The priest who pronounces them clean shall present both the one to be cleansed and their offerings before the LORD at the entrance to the tent of meeting.

¹²"Then the priest is to take one of the male lambs and offer it as a guilt offering, along with the

---

ᵃ 3 The Hebrew word for *defiling skin disease*, traditionally translated "leprosy," was used for various diseases affecting the skin; also in verses 7, 32, 54 and 57. ᵇ 10 That is, probably about 11 pounds or about 5 kilograms ᶜ 10 That is, about 1/3 quart or about 0.3 liter; also in verses 12, 15, 21 and 24 log of oil; he shall wave them before the LORD as a wave offering. ¹³He is to slaughter the lamb in the sanctuary area where the sin offering*ᵃ* and the burnt offering are slaughtered. Like the sin offering, the guilt offering belongs to the priest; it is most holy. ¹⁴The priest is to take some of the blood of the guilt offering and put it on the lobe of the right ear of the one to be cleansed, on the thumb of their right hand and on the big toe of their right foot. ¹⁵The priest shall then take some of the log of oil, pour it in the palm of his own left hand, ¹⁶dip his right forefinger into the oil in his palm, and with his finger sprinkle some of it before the LORD seven times. ¹⁷The priest is to put some of the oil remaining in his palm on the lobe of the right ear of the one to be cleansed, on the thumb of their right hand and on the big toe of their right foot, on top of the blood of the guilt offering. ¹⁸The rest of the oil in his palm the priest shall put on the head of the one to be cleansed and make atonement for them before the LORD.

¹⁹ "Then the priest is to sacrifice the sin offering and make atonement for the one to be cleansed from their uncleanness. After that, the priest shall slaughter the burnt offering ²⁰and offer it on the altar, together with the grain offering, and make atonement for them, and they will be clean.

²¹ "If, however, they are poor and cannot afford these, they must take one male lamb as a guilt offering to be waved to make atonement for them, together with a tenth of an ephah*ᵇ* of the finest flour mixed with olive oil for a grain offering, a log of oil, ²²and two doves or two young pigeons, such as they can afford, one for a sin offering and the other for a burnt offering.

²³ "On the eighth day they must bring them for their cleansing to the priest at the entrance to the tent of meeting, before the LORD. ²⁴The priest is to take the lamb for the guilt offering, together with the log of oil, and wave them before the LORD as a wave offering. ²⁵He shall slaughter the lamb for the guilt offering and take some of its blood and put it on the lobe of the right ear of the one to be cleansed, on the thumb of their right hand and on the big toe of their right foot. ²⁶The priest is to pour some of the oil into the palm of his own left hand, ²⁷and with his right forefinger sprinkle some of the oil from his palm seven times before the LORD. ²⁸Some of the oil in his palm he is to put on the same places he put the blood of the guilt offering — on the lobe of the right ear of the one to be cleansed, on the thumb

---

ᵃ 13 Or *purification offering*; also in verses 19, 22 and 31   *ᵇ 21* That is, probably about 3 1/2 pounds or about 1.6 kilograms of their right hand and on the big toe of their right foot. ²⁹The rest of the oil in his palm the priest shall put on the head of the one to be cleansed, to make atonement for them before the LORD. ³⁰Then he shall sacrifice the doves or the young pigeons, such as the person can afford, ³¹one as a sin offering and the other as a burnt offering, together with the grain offering. In this way the priest will make atonement before the LORD on behalf of the one to be cleansed."

³²These are the regulations for anyone who has a defiling skin disease and who cannot afford the regular offerings for their cleansing.

Cleansing From Defiling Molds

³³The LORD said to Moses and Aaron, ³⁴"When you enter the land of Canaan, which I am giving you as your possession, and I put a spreading mold in a house in that land, ³⁵the owner of the house must go and tell the priest, 'I have seen something that looks like a defiling mold in my house.' ³⁶The priest is to order the house to be emptied before he goes in to examine the mold, so that nothing in the house will be pronounced unclean. After this the priest is to go in and inspect the house. ³⁷He is to examine the mold on the walls, and if it has greenish or reddish depressions that appear to be deeper than the surface of the wall, ³⁸the priest shall go out the doorway of the house and close it up for seven days. ³⁹On the seventh day the priest shall return to inspect the house. If the mold has spread on the walls, ⁴⁰he is to order that the contaminated stones be torn out and thrown into an unclean place outside the town. ⁴¹He must have all the inside walls of the house scraped and the material that is scraped off dumped into an unclean place outside the town. ⁴²Then they are to take other stones to replace these and take new clay and plaster the house.

⁴³"If the defiling mold reappears in the house after the stones have been torn out and the house scraped and plastered, ⁴⁴the priest is to go and examine it and, if the mold has spread in the house, it is a persistent defiling mold; the house is unclean. ⁴⁵It must be torn down—its stones, timbers and all the plaster—and taken out of the town to an unclean place.

⁴⁶"Anyone who goes into the house while it is closed up will be unclean till evening. ⁴⁷Anyone who sleeps or eats in the house must wash their clothes.

⁴⁸"But if the priest comes to examine it and the mold has not spread after the house has been plastered, he shall pronounce the house clean, because the defiling mold is gone. ⁴⁹To purify the

house he is to take two birds and some cedar wood, scarlet yarn and hyssop. ⁵⁰He shall kill one of the birds over fresh water in a clay pot. ⁵¹Then he is to take the cedar wood, the hyssop, the scarlet yarn and the live bird, dip them into the blood of the dead bird and the fresh water, and sprinkle the house seven times. ⁵²He shall purify the house with the bird's blood, the fresh water, the live bird, the cedar wood, the hyssop and the scarlet yarn. ⁵³Then he is to release the live bird in the open fields outside the town. In this way he will make atonement for the house, and it will be clean."

⁵⁴These are the regulations for any defiling skin disease, for a sore, ⁵⁵for defiling molds in fabric or in a house, ⁵⁶and for a swelling, a rash or a shiny spot, ⁵⁷to determine when something is clean or unclean.

These are the regulations for defiling skin diseases and defiling molds.

Discharges Causing Uncleanness

15 The Lord said to Moses and Aaron, ²"Speak to the Israelites and say to them: 'When any man has an unusual bodily discharge, such a discharge is unclean. ³Whether it continues flowing from his body or is blocked, it will make him unclean. This is how his discharge will bring about uncleanness:

⁴"'Any bed the man with a discharge lies on will be unclean, and anything he sits on will be unclean. ⁵Anyone who touches his bed must wash their clothes and bathe with water, and they will be unclean till evening. ⁶Whoever sits on anything that the man with a discharge sat on must wash their clothes and bathe with water, and they will be unclean till evening.

⁷"'Whoever touches the man who has a discharge must wash their clothes and bathe with water, and they will be unclean till evening.

⁸"'If the man with the discharge spits on anyone who is clean, they must wash their clothes and bathe with water, and they will be unclean till evening.

⁹"'Everything the man sits on when riding will be unclean, ¹⁰and whoever touches any of the things that were under him will be unclean till evening; whoever picks up those things must wash their clothes and bathe with water, and they will be unclean till evening.

¹¹"'Anyone the man with a discharge touches without rinsing his hands with water must wash their clothes and bathe with water, and they will be unclean till evening.

¹²"'A clay pot that the man touches must be broken, and any wooden article is to be rinsed with water.

¹³ "'When a man is cleansed from his discharge, he is to count off seven days for his ceremonial cleansing; he must wash his clothes and bathe himself with fresh water, and he will be clean. ¹⁴ On the eighth day he must take two doves or two young pigeons and come before the LORD to the entrance to the tent of meeting and give them to the priest. ¹⁵ The priest is to sacrifice them, the one for a sin offering^a and the other for a burnt offering. In this way he will make atonement before the LORD for the man because of his discharge.

¹⁶ "'When a man has an emission of semen, he must bathe his whole body with water, and he will be unclean till evening. ¹⁷ Any clothing or leather that has semen on it must be washed with water, and it will be unclean till evening. ¹⁸ When a man has sexual relations with a woman and there is an emission of semen, both of them must bathe with water, and they will be unclean till evening.

¹⁹ "'When a woman has her regular flow of blood, the impurity of her monthly period will last seven days, and anyone who touches her will be unclean till evening.

²⁰ "'Anything she lies on during her period will be unclean, and anything she sits on will be unclean. ²¹ Anyone who touches her bed will be unclean; they must wash their clothes and bathe with water, and they will be unclean till evening. ²² Anyone who touches anything she sits on will be unclean; they must wash their clothes and bathe with water, and they will be unclean till evening. ²³ Whether it is the bed or anything she was sitting on, when anyone touches it, they will be unclean till evening.

²⁴ "'If a man has sexual relations with her and her monthly flow touches him, he will be unclean for seven days; any bed he lies on will be unclean.

²⁵ "'When a woman has a discharge of blood for many days at a time other than her monthly period or has a discharge that continues beyond her period, she will be unclean as long as she has the discharge, just as in the days of her period. ²⁶ Any bed she lies on while her discharge continues will be unclean, as is her bed during her monthly period, and anything she sits on will be unclean, as during her period. ²⁷ Anyone who touches them will be unclean; they must wash their clothes and bathe with water, and they will be unclean till evening.

²⁸ "'When she is cleansed from her discharge, she must count off seven days, and after that she will be ceremonially clean. ²⁹ On the eighth day she must take two doves or two young pigeons and bring them to the priest at the

^a 15 Or *purification offering*; also in verse 30

entrance to the tent of meeting. [30] The priest is to sacrifice one for a sin offering and the other for a burnt offering. In this way he will make atonement for her before the Lord for the uncleanness of her discharge.

[31] "'You must keep the Israelites separate from things that make them unclean, so they will not die in their uncleanness for defiling my dwelling place,[a] which is among them.'"

[32] These are the regulations for a man with a discharge, for anyone made unclean by an emission of semen, [33] for a woman in her monthly period, for a man or a woman with a discharge, and for a man who has sexual relations with a woman who is ceremonially unclean.

The Day of Atonement

16 The Lord spoke to Moses after the death of the two sons of Aaron who died when they approached the Lord. [2] The Lord said to Moses: "Tell your brother Aaron that he is not to come whenever he chooses into the Most Holy Place behind the curtain in front of the atonement cover on the ark, or else he will die. For I will appear in the cloud over the atonement cover.

[3] "This is how Aaron is to enter the Most Holy Place: He must first bring a young bull for a sin offering[b] and a ram for a burnt offering. [4] He is to put on the sacred linen tunic, with linen undergarments next to his body; he is to tie the linen sash around him and put on the linen turban. These are sacred garments; so he must bathe himself with water before he puts them on. [5] From the Israelite community he is to take two male goats for a sin offering and a ram for a burnt offering.

[6] "Aaron is to offer the bull for his own sin offering to make atonement for himself and his household. [7] Then he is to take the two goats and present them before the Lord at the entrance to the tent of meeting. [8] He is to cast lots for the two goats — one lot for the Lord and the other for the scapegoat.[c] [9] Aaron shall bring the goat whose lot falls to the Lord and sacrifice it for a sin offering. [10] But the goat chosen by lot as the scapegoat shall be presented alive before the Lord to be used for making atonement by sending it into the wilderness as a scapegoat.

[11] "Aaron shall bring the bull for his own sin offering to make atonement for himself and his household, and he is to slaughter the bull for his own sin offering. [12] He is to take a censer full of burning coals from the altar

---

[a] 31 Or my tabernacle   [b] 3 Or purification offering; here and throughout this chapter   [c] 8 The meaning of the Hebrew for this word is uncertain; also in verses 10 and 26.

before the LORD and two handfuls of finely ground fragrant incense and take them behind the curtain. ¹³ He is to put the incense on the fire before the LORD, and the smoke of the incense will conceal the atonement cover above the tablets of the covenant law, so that he will not die. ¹⁴ He is to take some of the bull's blood and with his finger sprinkle it on the front of the atonement cover; then he shall sprinkle some of it with his finger seven times before the atonement cover.

¹⁵ "He shall then slaughter the goat for the sin offering for the people and take its blood behind the curtain and do with it as he did with the bull's blood: He shall sprinkle it on the atonement cover and in front of it. ¹⁶ In this way he will make atonement for the Most Holy Place because of the uncleanness and rebellion of the Israelites, whatever their sins have been. He is to do the same for the tent of meeting, which is among them in the midst of their uncleanness. ¹⁷ No one is to be in the tent of meeting from the time Aaron goes in to make atonement in the Most Holy Place until he comes out, having made atonement for himself, his household and the whole community of Israel.

¹⁸ "Then he shall come out to the altar that is before the LORD and make atonement for it. He shall take some of the bull's blood and some of the goat's blood and put it on all the horns of the altar. ¹⁹ He shall sprinkle some of the blood on it with his finger seven times to cleanse it and to consecrate it from the uncleanness of the Israelites.

²⁰ "When Aaron has finished making atonement for the Most Holy Place, the tent of meeting and the altar, he shall bring forward the live goat. ²¹ He is to lay both hands on the head of the live goat and confess over it all the wickedness and rebellion of the Israelites — all their sins — and put them on the goat's head. He shall send the goat away into the wilderness in the care of someone appointed for the task. ²² The goat will carry on itself all their sins to a remote place; and the man shall release it in the wilderness.

²³ "Then Aaron is to go into the tent of meeting and take off the linen garments he put on before he entered the Most Holy Place, and he is to leave them there. ²⁴ He shall bathe himself with water in the sanctuary area and put on his regular garments. Then he shall come out and sacrifice the burnt offering for himself and the burnt offering for the people, to make atonement for himself and for the people. ²⁵ He shall also burn the fat of the sin offering on the altar.

²⁶ "The man who releases the goat as a scapegoat must wash his

clothes and bathe himself with water; afterward he may come into the camp. **27** The bull and the goat for the sin offerings, whose blood was brought into the Most Holy Place to make atonement, must be taken outside the camp; their hides, flesh and intestines are to be burned up. **28** The man who burns them must wash his clothes and bathe himself with water; afterward he may come into the camp.

29 "This is to be a lasting ordinance for you: On the tenth day of the seventh month you must deny yourselves[a] and not do any work — whether native-born or a foreigner residing among you — **30** because on this day atonement will be made for you, to cleanse you. Then, before the Lord, you will be clean from all your sins. **31** It is a day of sabbath rest, and you must deny yourselves; it is a lasting ordinance. **32** The priest who is anointed and ordained to succeed his father as high priest is to make atonement. He is to put on the sacred linen garments **33** and make atonement for the Most Holy Place, for the tent of meeting and the altar, and for the priests and all the members of the community.

34 "This is to be a lasting ordinance for you: Atonement is to be made once a year for all the sins of the Israelites."

And it was done, as the Lord commanded Moses.

Eating Blood Forbidden

17 The Lord said to Moses, **2** "Speak to Aaron and his sons and to all the Israelites and say to them: 'This is what the Lord has commanded: **3** Any Israelite who sacrifices an ox,[b] a lamb or a goat in the camp or outside of it **4** instead of bringing it to the entrance to the tent of meeting to present it as an offering to the Lord in front of the tabernacle of the Lord — that person shall be considered guilty of bloodshed; they have shed blood and must be cut off from their people. **5** This is so the Israelites will bring to the Lord the sacrifices they are now making in the open fields. They must bring them to the priest, that is, to the Lord, at the entrance to the tent of meeting and sacrifice them as fellowship offerings. **6** The priest is to splash the blood against the altar of the Lord at the entrance to the tent of meeting and burn the fat as an aroma pleasing to the Lord. **7** They must no longer offer any of their sacrifices to the goat idols[c] to whom they prostitute themselves. This is to be a lasting ordinance for them and for the generations to come.'

8 "Say to them: 'Any Israelite or any foreigner residing among

---

[a] 29 Or *must fast*; also in verse 31   [b] 3 The Hebrew word can refer to either male or female.   [c] 7 Or *the demons*

them who offers a burnt offering or sacrifice ⁹and does not bring it to the entrance to the tent of meeting to sacrifice it to the LORD must be cut off from the people of Israel.

¹⁰ " 'I will set my face against any Israelite or any foreigner residing among them who eats blood, and I will cut them off from the people. ¹¹For the life of a creature is in the blood, and I have given it to you to make atonement for yourselves on the altar; it is the blood that makes atonement for one's life.ᵃ ¹²Therefore I say to the Israelites, "None of you may eat blood, nor may any foreigner residing among you eat blood."

¹³ " 'Any Israelite or any foreigner residing among you who hunts any animal or bird that may be eaten must drain out the blood and cover it with earth, ¹⁴because the life of every creature is its blood. That is why I have said to the Israelites, "You must not eat the blood of any creature, because the life of every creature is its blood; anyone who eats it must be cut off."

¹⁵ " 'Anyone, whether native-born or foreigner, who eats anything found dead or torn by wild animals must wash their clothes and bathe with water, and they will be ceremonially unclean till evening; then they will be clean. ¹⁶But if they do not wash their clothes and bathe themselves, they will be held responsible.' "

Unlawful Sexual Relations

18 The LORD said to Moses, ²"Speak to the Israelites and say to them: 'I am the LORD your God. ³You must not do as they do in Egypt, where you used to live, and you must not do as they do in the land of Canaan, where I am bringing you. Do not follow their practices. ⁴You must obey my laws and be careful to follow my decrees. I am the LORD your God. ⁵Keep my decrees and laws, for the person who obeys them will live by them. I am the LORD.

⁶ " 'No one is to approach any close relative to have sexual relations. I am the LORD.

⁷ " 'Do not dishonor your father by having sexual relations with your mother. She is your mother; do not have relations with her.

⁸ " 'Do not have sexual relations with your father's wife; that would dishonor your father.

⁹ " 'Do not have sexual relations with your sister, either your father's daughter or your mother's daughter, whether she was born in the same home or elsewhere.

¹⁰ " 'Do not have sexual relations with your son's daughter or your daughter's daughter; that would dishonor you.

¹¹ " 'Do not have sexual relations with the daughter of your father's wife, born to your father; she is your sister.

¹² " 'Do not have sexual rela-

ᵃ 11 Or *atonement by the life in the blood*

tions with your father's sister; she is your father's close relative.

13 " 'Do not have sexual relations with your mother's sister, because she is your mother's close relative.

14 " 'Do not dishonor your father's brother by approaching his wife to have sexual relations; she is your aunt.

15 " 'Do not have sexual relations with your daughter-in-law. She is your son's wife; do not have relations with her.

16 " 'Do not have sexual relations with your brother's wife; that would dishonor your brother.

17 " 'Do not have sexual relations with both a woman and her daughter. Do not have sexual relations with either her son's daughter or her daughter's daughter; they are her close relatives. That is wickedness.

18 " 'Do not take your wife's sister as a rival wife and have sexual relations with her while your wife is living.

19 " 'Do not approach a woman to have sexual relations during the uncleanness of her monthly period.

20 " 'Do not have sexual relations with your neighbor's wife and defile yourself with her.

21 " 'Do not give any of your children to be sacrificed to Molek, for you must not profane the name of your God. I am the LORD.

22 " 'Do not have sexual relations with a man as one does with a woman; that is detestable.

23 " 'Do not have sexual relations with an animal and defile yourself with it. A woman must not present herself to an animal to have sexual relations with it; that is a perversion.

24 " 'Do not defile yourselves in any of these ways, because this is how the nations that I am going to drive out before you became defiled. **25** Even the land was defiled; so I punished it for its sin, and the land vomited out its inhabitants. **26** But you must keep my decrees and my laws. The native-born and the foreigners residing among you must not do any of these detestable things, **27** for all these things were done by the people who lived in the land before you, and the land became defiled. **28** And if you defile the land, it will vomit you out as it vomited out the nations that were before you.

29 " 'Everyone who does any of these detestable things — such persons must be cut off from their people. **30** Keep my requirements and do not follow any of the detestable customs that were practiced before you came and do not defile yourselves with them. I am the LORD your God.' "

Various Laws

19 The LORD said to Moses, **2** "Speak to the entire assembly of Israel and say to them: 'Be holy because I, the LORD your God, am holy.

³ " 'Each of you must respect your mother and father, and you must observe my Sabbaths. I am the LORD your God.

⁴ " 'Do not turn to idols or make metal gods for yourselves. I am the LORD your God.

⁵ " 'When you sacrifice a fellowship offering to the LORD, sacrifice it in such a way that it will be accepted on your behalf. ⁶ It shall be eaten on the day you sacrifice it or on the next day; anything left over until the third day must be burned up. ⁷ If any of it is eaten on the third day, it is impure and will not be accepted. ⁸ Whoever eats it will be held responsible because they have desecrated what is holy to the LORD; they must be cut off from their people.

⁹ " 'When you reap the harvest of your land, do not reap to the very edges of your field or gather the gleanings of your harvest. ¹⁰ Do not go over your vineyard a second time or pick up the grapes that have fallen. Leave them for the poor and the foreigner. I am the LORD your God.

¹¹ " 'Do not steal.

" 'Do not lie.

" 'Do not deceive one another.

¹² " 'Do not swear falsely by my name and so profane the name of your God. I am the LORD.

¹³ " 'Do not defraud or rob your neighbor.

" 'Do not hold back the wages of a hired worker overnight.

¹⁴ " 'Do not curse the deaf or put a stumbling block in front of the blind, but fear your God. I am the LORD.

¹⁵ " 'Do not pervert justice; do not show partiality to the poor or favoritism to the great, but judge your neighbor fairly.

¹⁶ " 'Do not go about spreading slander among your people.

" 'Do not do anything that endangers your neighbor's life. I am the LORD.

¹⁷ " 'Do not hate a fellow Israelite in your heart. Rebuke your neighbor frankly so you will not share in their guilt.

¹⁸ " 'Do not seek revenge or bear a grudge against anyone among your people, but love your neighbor as yourself. I am the LORD.

¹⁹ " 'Keep my decrees.

" 'Do not mate different kinds of animals.

" 'Do not plant your field with two kinds of seed.

" 'Do not wear clothing woven of two kinds of material.

²⁰ " 'If a man sleeps with a female slave who is promised to another man but who has not been ransomed or given her freedom, there must be due punishment.[a] Yet they are not to be put to death, because she had not been freed. ²¹ The man, however, must bring a ram to the entrance to the tent of meeting for a guilt offering to the LORD. ²² With the ram of the guilt offering the

---

[a] 20 Or *be an inquiry*

priest is to make atonement for him before the LORD for the sin he has committed, and his sin will be forgiven.

23 " 'When you enter the land and plant any kind of fruit tree, regard its fruit as forbidden.ᵃ For three years you are to consider it forbiddenᵃ; it must not be eaten. 24 In the fourth year all its fruit will be holy, an offering of praise to the LORD. 25 But in the fifth year you may eat its fruit. In this way your harvest will be increased. I am the LORD your God.

26 " 'Do not eat any meat with the blood still in it.

" 'Do not practice divination or seek omens.

27 " 'Do not cut the hair at the sides of your head or clip off the edges of your beard.

28 " 'Do not cut your bodies for the dead or put tattoo marks on yourselves. I am the LORD.

29 " 'Do not degrade your daughter by making her a prostitute, or the land will turn to prostitution and be filled with wickedness.

30 " 'Observe my Sabbaths and have reverence for my sanctuary. I am the LORD.

31 " 'Do not turn to mediums or seek out spiritists, for you will be defiled by them. I am the LORD your God.

32 " 'Stand up in the presence of the aged, show respect for the el-

derly and revere your God. I am the LORD.

33 " 'When a foreigner resides among you in your land, do not mistreat them. 34 The foreigner residing among you must be treated as your native-born. Love them as yourself, for you were foreigners in Egypt. I am the LORD your God.

35 " 'Do not use dishonest standards when measuring length, weight or quantity. 36 Use honest scales and honest weights, an honest ephahᵇ and an honest hin.ᶜ I am the LORD your God, who brought you out of Egypt.

37 " 'Keep all my decrees and all my laws and follow them. I am the LORD.' "

Punishments for Sin

20 The LORD said to Moses, 2 "Say to the Israelites: 'Any Israelite or any foreigner residing in Israel who sacrifices any of his children to Molek is to be put to death. The members of the community are to stone him. 3 I myself will set my face against him and will cut him off from his people; for by sacrificing his children to Molek, he has defiled my sanctuary and profaned my holy name. 4 If the members of the community close their eyes when that man sacrifices one of his children to Molek and if they

---

ᵃ 23 Hebrew uncircumcised   ᵇ 36 An ephah was a dry measure having the capacity of about 3/5 of a bushel or about 22 liters.   ᶜ 36 A hin was a liquid measure having the capacity of about 1 gallon or about 3.8 liters.

fail to put him to death, ⁵I myself will set my face against him and his family and will cut them off from their people together with all who follow him in prostituting themselves to Molek.

⁶ " 'I will set my face against anyone who turns to mediums and spiritists to prostitute themselves by following them, and I will cut them off from their people.

⁷ " 'Consecrate yourselves and be holy, because I am the LORD your God. ⁸Keep my decrees and follow them. I am the LORD, who makes you holy.

⁹ " 'Anyone who curses their father or mother is to be put to death. Because they have cursed their father or mother, their blood will be on their own head.

¹⁰ " 'If a man commits adultery with another man's wife — with the wife of his neighbor — both the adulterer and the adulteress are to be put to death.

¹¹ " 'If a man has sexual relations with his father's wife, he has dishonored his father. Both the man and the woman are to be put to death; their blood will be on their own heads.

¹² " 'If a man has sexual relations with his daughter-in-law, both of them are to be put to death. What they have done is a perversion; their blood will be on their own heads.

¹³ " 'If a man has sexual relations with a man as one does with a woman, both of them have done what is detestable. They are to be put to death; their blood will be on their own heads.

¹⁴ " 'If a man marries both a woman and her mother, it is wicked. Both he and they must be burned in the fire, so that no wickedness will be among you.

¹⁵ " 'If a man has sexual relations with an animal, he is to be put to death, and you must kill the animal.

¹⁶ " 'If a woman approaches an animal to have sexual relations with it, kill both the woman and the animal. They are to be put to death; their blood will be on their own heads.

¹⁷ " 'If a man marries his sister, the daughter of either his father or his mother, and they have sexual relations, it is a disgrace. They are to be publicly removed from their people. He has dishonored his sister and will be held responsible.

¹⁸ " 'If a man has sexual relations with a woman during her monthly period, he has exposed the source of her flow, and she has also uncovered it. Both of them are to be cut off from their people.

¹⁹ " 'Do not have sexual relations with the sister of either your mother or your father, for that would dishonor a close relative; both of you would be held responsible.

²⁰ " 'If a man has sexual relations with his aunt, he has dishonored his uncle. They will be held responsible; they will die childless.

21 " 'If a man marries his brother's wife, it is an act of impurity; he has dishonored his brother. They will be childless.

22 " 'Keep all my decrees and laws and follow them, so that the land where I am bringing you to live may not vomit you out. 23 You must not live according to the customs of the nations I am going to drive out before you. Because they did all these things, I abhorred them. 24 But I said to you, "You will possess their land; I will give it to you as an inheritance, a land flowing with milk and honey." I am the LORD your God, who has set you apart from the nations.

25 " 'You must therefore make a distinction between clean and unclean animals and between unclean and clean birds. Do not defile yourselves by any animal or bird or anything that moves along the ground—those that I have set apart as unclean for you. 26 You are to be holy to me because I, the LORD, am holy, and I have set you apart from the nations to be my own.

27 " 'A man or woman who is a medium or spiritist among you must be put to death. You are to stone them; their blood will be on their own heads.' "

Rules for Priests

21 The LORD said to Moses, "Speak to the priests, the sons of Aaron, and say to them: 'A priest must not make himself ceremonially unclean for any of his people who die, 2 except for a close relative, such as his mother or father, his son or daughter, his brother, 3 or an unmarried sister who is dependent on him since she has no husband—for her he may make himself unclean. 4 He must not make himself unclean for people related to him by marriage,[a] and so defile himself.

5 " 'Priests must not shave their heads or shave off the edges of their beards or cut their bodies. 6 They must be holy to their God and must not profane the name of their God. Because they present the food offerings to the LORD, the food of their God, they are to be holy.

7 " 'They must not marry women defiled by prostitution or divorced from their husbands, because priests are holy to their God. 8 Regard them as holy, because they offer up the food of your God. Consider them holy, because I the LORD am holy—I who make you holy.

9 " 'If a priest's daughter defiles herself by becoming a prostitute, she disgraces her father; she must be burned in the fire.

10 " 'The high priest, the one among his brothers who has had the anointing oil poured on his head and who has been ordained to wear the priestly garments, must not let his hair become

---

a 4 Or unclean as a leader among his people

unkempt[a] or tear his clothes. [11]He must not enter a place where there is a dead body. He must not make himself unclean, even for his father or mother, [12]nor leave the sanctuary of his God or desecrate it, because he has been dedicated by the anointing oil of his God. I am the LORD.

[13]"'The woman he marries must be a virgin. [14]He must not marry a widow, a divorced woman, or a woman defiled by prostitution, but only a virgin from his own people, [15]so that he will not defile his offspring among his people. I am the LORD, who makes him holy.'"

[16]The LORD said to Moses, [17]"Say to Aaron: 'For the generations to come none of your descendants who has a defect may come near to offer the food of his God. [18]No man who has any defect may come near: no man who is blind or lame, disfigured or deformed; [19]no man with a crippled foot or hand, [20]or who is a hunchback or a dwarf, or who has any eye defect, or who has festering or running sores or damaged testicles. [21]No descendant of Aaron the priest who has any defect is to come near to present the food offerings to the LORD. He has a defect; he must not come near to offer the food of his God. [22]He may eat the most holy food of his God, as well as the holy food; [23]yet because of his defect, he must not go near the curtain or approach the altar, and so desecrate my sanctuary. I am the LORD, who makes them holy.'"

[24]So Moses told this to Aaron and his sons and to all the Israelites.

22

The LORD said to Moses, [2]"Tell Aaron and his sons to treat with respect the sacred offerings the Israelites consecrate to me, so they will not profane my holy name. I am the LORD.

[3]"Say to them: 'For the generations to come, if any of your descendants is ceremonially unclean and yet comes near the sacred offerings that the Israelites consecrate to the LORD, that person must be cut off from my presence. I am the LORD.

[4]"'If a descendant of Aaron has a defiling skin disease[b] or a bodily discharge, he may not eat the sacred offerings until he is cleansed. He will also be unclean if he touches something defiled by a corpse or by anyone who has an emission of semen, [5]or if he touches any crawling thing that makes him unclean, or any person who makes him unclean, whatever the uncleanness may be. [6]The one who touches any such thing will be unclean till evening. He must not eat any of the sacred offerings unless he has bathed himself with water.

---

[a] 10 Or not uncover his head   [b] 4 The Hebrew word for defiling skin disease, traditionally translated "leprosy," was used for various diseases affecting the skin.

7When the sun goes down, he will be clean, and after that he may eat the sacred offerings, for they are his food. 8He must not eat anything found dead or torn by wild animals, and so become unclean through it. I am the LORD.

9 " 'The priests are to perform my service in such a way that they do not become guilty and die for treating it with contempt. I am the LORD, who makes them holy.

10 " 'No one outside a priest's family may eat the sacred offering, nor may the guest of a priest or his hired worker eat it. 11But if a priest buys a slave with money, or if slaves are born in his household, they may eat his food. 12If a priest's daughter marries anyone other than a priest, she may not eat any of the sacred contributions. 13But if a priest's daughter becomes a widow or is divorced, yet has no children, and she returns to live in her father's household as in her youth, she may eat her father's food. No unauthorized person, however, may eat it.

14 " 'Anyone who eats a sacred offering by mistake must make restitution to the priest for the offering and add a fifth of the value to it. 15The priests must not desecrate the sacred offerings the Israelites present to the LORD 16by allowing them to eat the sacred offerings and so bring upon them guilt requiring payment. I am the LORD, who makes them holy.' "

Unacceptable Sacrifices

17The LORD said to Moses, 18"Speak to Aaron and his sons and to all the Israelites and say to them: 'If any of you — whether an Israelite or a foreigner residing in Israel — presents a gift for a burnt offering to the LORD, either to fulfill a vow or as a freewill offering, 19you must present a male without defect from the cattle, sheep or goats in order that it may be accepted on your behalf. 20Do not bring anything with a defect, because it will not be accepted on your behalf. 21When anyone brings from the herd or flock a fellowship offering to the LORD to fulfill a special vow or as a freewill offering, it must be without defect or blemish to be acceptable. 22Do not offer to the LORD the blind, the injured or the maimed, or anything with warts or festering or running sores. Do not place any of these on the altar as a food offering presented to the LORD. 23You may, however, present as a freewill offering an ox[a] or a sheep that is deformed or stunted, but it will not be accepted in fulfillment of a vow. 24You must not offer to the LORD an animal whose testicles are bruised, crushed, torn or cut. You must not do this in your own land, 25and you must not accept such animals

---

[a] 23 The Hebrew word can refer to either male or female.

from the hand of a foreigner and offer them as the food of your God. They will not be accepted on your behalf, because they are deformed and have defects.'"

²⁶The LORD said to Moses, ²⁷"When a calf, a lamb or a goat is born, it is to remain with its mother for seven days. From the eighth day on, it will be acceptable as a food offering presented to the LORD. ²⁸Do not slaughter a cow or a sheep and its young on the same day.

²⁹"When you sacrifice a thank offering to the LORD, sacrifice it in such a way that it will be accepted on your behalf. ³⁰It must be eaten that same day; leave none of it till morning. I am the LORD.

³¹"Keep my commands and follow them. I am the LORD. ³²Do not profane my holy name, for I must be acknowledged as holy by the Israelites. I am the LORD, who made you holy ³³and who brought you out of Egypt to be your God. I am the LORD."

The Appointed Festivals

23 The LORD said to Moses, ²"Speak to the Israelites and say to them: 'These are my appointed festivals, the appointed festivals of the LORD, which you are to proclaim as sacred assemblies.

The Sabbath

³"'There are six days when you may work, but the seventh day is a day of sabbath rest, a day of sacred assembly. You are not to do any work; wherever you live, it is a sabbath to the LORD.

The Passover and the Festival of Unleavened Bread

⁴"'These are the LORD's appointed festivals, the sacred assemblies you are to proclaim at their appointed times: ⁵The LORD's Passover begins at twilight on the fourteenth day of the first month. ⁶On the fifteenth day of that month the LORD's Festival of Unleavened Bread begins; for seven days you must eat bread made without yeast. ⁷On the first day hold a sacred assembly and do no regular work. ⁸For seven days present a food offering to the LORD. And on the seventh day hold a sacred assembly and do no regular work.'"

Offering the Firstfruits

⁹The LORD said to Moses, ¹⁰"Speak to the Israelites and say to them: 'When you enter the land I am going to give you and you reap its harvest, bring to the priest a sheaf of the first grain you harvest. ¹¹He is to wave the sheaf before the LORD so it will be accepted on your behalf; the priest is to wave it on the day after the Sabbath. ¹²On the day you wave the sheaf, you must sacrifice as a burnt offering to the LORD a lamb a year old without defect, ¹³together with its grain offering of two-tenths of an

ephah[a] of the finest flour mixed with olive oil—a food offering presented to the LORD, a pleasing aroma—and its drink offering of a quarter of a hin[b] of wine. [14]You must not eat any bread, or roasted or new grain, until the very day you bring this offering to your God. This is to be a lasting ordinance for the generations to come, wherever you live.

The Festival of Weeks

[15]"'From the day after the Sabbath, the day you brought the sheaf of the wave offering, count off seven full weeks. [16]Count off fifty days up to the day after the seventh Sabbath, and then present an offering of new grain to the LORD. [17]From wherever you live, bring two loaves made of two-tenths of an ephah of the finest flour, baked with yeast, as a wave offering of firstfruits to the LORD. [18]Present with this bread seven male lambs, each a year old and without defect, one young bull and two rams. They will be a burnt offering to the LORD, together with their grain offerings and drink offerings—a food offering, an aroma pleasing to the LORD. [19]Then sacrifice one male goat for a sin offering[c] and two lambs, each a year old, for a fellowship offering. [20]The priest is to wave the two lambs before the LORD as a wave offering, together with the bread of the firstfruits. They are a sacred offering to the LORD for the priest. [21]On that same day you are to proclaim a sacred assembly and do no regular work. This is to be a lasting ordinance for the generations to come, wherever you live.

[22]"'When you reap the harvest of your land, do not reap to the very edges of your field or gather the gleanings of your harvest. Leave them for the poor and for the foreigner residing among you. I am the LORD your God.'"

The Festival of Trumpets

[23]The LORD said to Moses, [24]"Say to the Israelites: 'On the first day of the seventh month you are to have a day of sabbath rest, a sacred assembly commemorated with trumpet blasts. [25]Do no regular work, but present a food offering to the LORD.'"

The Day of Atonement

[26]The LORD said to Moses, [27]"The tenth day of this seventh month is the Day of Atonement. Hold a sacred assembly and deny yourselves,[d] and present a food offering to the LORD. [28]Do not do any work on that day, because it is the Day of Atonement, when atonement is made for you before the LORD your God. [29]Those who do not deny themselves on that day must be cut off from

---

[a] 13 That is, probably about 7 pounds or about 3.2 kilograms; also in verse 17
[b] 13 That is, about 1 quart or about 1 liter   [c] 19 Or purification offering
[d] 27 Or and fast; similarly in verses 29 and 32

their people. **30** I will destroy from among their people anyone who does any work on that day. **31** You shall do no work at all. This is to be a lasting ordinance for the generations to come, wherever you live. **32** It is a day of sabbath rest for you, and you must deny yourselves. From the evening of the ninth day of the month until the following evening you are to observe your sabbath."

The Festival of Tabernacles

33 The LORD said to Moses, **34** "Say to the Israelites: 'On the fifteenth day of the seventh month the LORD's Festival of Tabernacles begins, and it lasts for seven days. **35** The first day is a sacred assembly; do no regular work. **36** For seven days present food offerings to the LORD, and on the eighth day hold a sacred assembly and present a food offering to the LORD. It is the closing special assembly; do no regular work.

37 ("'These are the LORD's appointed festivals, which you are to proclaim as sacred assemblies for bringing food offerings to the LORD — the burnt offerings and grain offerings, sacrifices and drink offerings required for each day. **38** These offerings are in addition to those for the LORD's Sabbaths and*a* in addition to your gifts and whatever you have vowed and all the freewill offerings you give to the LORD.)

39 "'So beginning with the fifteenth day of the seventh month, after you have gathered the crops of the land, celebrate the festival to the LORD for seven days; the first day is a day of sabbath rest, and the eighth day also is a day of sabbath rest. **40** On the first day you are to take branches from luxuriant trees — from palms, willows and other leafy trees — and rejoice before the LORD your God for seven days. **41** Celebrate this as a festival to the LORD for seven days each year. This is to be a lasting ordinance for the generations to come; celebrate it in the seventh month. **42** Live in temporary shelters for seven days: All native-born Israelites are to live in such shelters **43** so your descendants will know that I had the Israelites live in temporary shelters when I brought them out of Egypt. I am the LORD your God.'"

44 So Moses announced to the Israelites the appointed festivals of the LORD.

Olive Oil and Bread Set Before the LORD

24 The LORD said to Moses, **2** "Command the Israelites to bring you clear oil of pressed olives for the light so that the lamps may be kept burning continually. **3** Outside the curtain that shields the ark of the covenant law in the tent of meet-

---

a 38 Or *These festivals are in addition to the LORD's Sabbaths, and these offerings are* ing, Aaron is to tend the lamps before the LORD from evening till morning, continually. This is to be a lasting ordinance for the generations to come. [4] The lamps on the pure gold lampstand before the LORD must be tended continually.

[5] "Take the finest flour and bake twelve loaves of bread, using two-tenths of an ephah[a] for each loaf. [6] Arrange them in two stacks, six in each stack, on the table of pure gold before the LORD. [7] By each stack put some pure incense as a memorial[b] portion to represent the bread and to be a food offering presented to the LORD. [8] This bread is to be set out before the LORD regularly, Sabbath after Sabbath, on behalf of the Israelites, as a lasting covenant. [9] It belongs to Aaron and his sons, who are to eat it in the sanctuary area, because it is a most holy part of their perpetual share of the food offerings presented to the LORD."

A Blasphemer Put to Death

[10] Now the son of an Israelite mother and an Egyptian father went out among the Israelites, and a fight broke out in the camp between him and an Israelite. [11] The son of the Israelite woman blasphemed the Name with a curse; so they brought him to Moses. (His mother's name was Shelomith, the daughter of Dibri the Danite.) [12] They put him in custody until the will of the LORD should be made clear to them.

[13] Then the LORD said to Moses: [14] "Take the blasphemer outside the camp. All those who heard him are to lay their hands on his head, and the entire assembly is to stone him. [15] Say to the Israelites: 'Anyone who curses their God will be held responsible; [16] anyone who blasphemes the name of the LORD is to be put to death. The entire assembly must stone them. Whether foreigner or native-born, when they blaspheme the Name they are to be put to death.

[17] "'Anyone who takes the life of a human being is to be put to death. [18] Anyone who takes the life of someone's animal must make restitution—life for life. [19] Anyone who injures their neighbor is to be injured in the same manner: [20] fracture for fracture, eye for eye, tooth for tooth. The one who has inflicted the injury must suffer the same injury. [21] Whoever kills an animal must make restitution, but whoever kills a human being is to be put to death. [22] You are to have the same law for the foreigner and the native-born. I am the LORD your God.'"

[23] Then Moses spoke to the Israelites, and they took the blasphemer outside the camp and stoned him. The Israelites did as the LORD commanded Moses.

---

[a] 5 That is, probably about 7 pounds or about 3.2 kilograms   [b] 7 Or representative

The Sabbath Year

25 The LORD said to Moses at Mount Sinai, ²"Speak to the Israelites and say to them: 'When you enter the land I am going to give you, the land itself must observe a sabbath to the LORD. ³For six years sow your fields, and for six years prune your vineyards and gather their crops. ⁴But in the seventh year the land is to have a year of sabbath rest, a sabbath to the LORD. Do not sow your fields or prune your vineyards. ⁵Do not reap what grows of itself or harvest the grapes of your untended vines. The land is to have a year of rest. ⁶Whatever the land yields during the sabbath year will be food for you — for yourself, your male and female servants, and the hired worker and temporary resident who live among you, ⁷as well as for your livestock and the wild animals in your land. Whatever the land produces may be eaten.

The Year of Jubilee

⁸"'Count off seven sabbath years — seven times seven years — so that the seven sabbath years amount to a period of forty-nine years. ⁹Then have the trumpet sounded everywhere on the tenth day of the seventh month; on the Day of Atonement sound the trumpet throughout your land. ¹⁰Consecrate the fiftieth year and proclaim liberty throughout the land to all its inhabitants. It shall be a jubilee for you; each of you is to return to your family property and to your own clan. ¹¹The fiftieth year shall be a jubilee for you; do not sow and do not reap what grows of itself or harvest the untended vines. ¹²For it is a jubilee and is to be holy for you; eat only what is taken directly from the fields.

¹³"'In this Year of Jubilee everyone is to return to their own property.

¹⁴"'If you sell land to any of your own people or buy land from them, do not take advantage of each other. ¹⁵You are to buy from your own people on the basis of the number of years since the Jubilee. And they are to sell to you on the basis of the number of years left for harvesting crops. ¹⁶When the years are many, you are to increase the price, and when the years are few, you are to decrease the price, because what is really being sold to you is the number of crops. ¹⁷Do not take advantage of each other, but fear your God. I am the LORD your God.

¹⁸"'Follow my decrees and be careful to obey my laws, and you will live safely in the land. ¹⁹Then the land will yield its fruit, and you will eat your fill and live there in safety. ²⁰You may ask, "What will we eat in the seventh year if we do not plant or harvest our crops?" ²¹I will send you such a blessing in the sixth year that the

land will yield enough for three years. ²²While you plant during the eighth year, you will eat from the old crop and will continue to eat from it until the harvest of the ninth year comes in.

²³ " 'The land must not be sold permanently, because the land is mine and you reside in my land as foreigners and strangers. ²⁴Throughout the land that you hold as a possession, you must provide for the redemption of the land.

²⁵ " 'If one of your fellow Israelites becomes poor and sells some of their property, their nearest relative is to come and redeem what they have sold. ²⁶If, however, there is no one to redeem it for them but later on they prosper and acquire sufficient means to redeem it themselves, ²⁷they are to determine the value for the years since they sold it and refund the balance to the one to whom they sold it; they can then go back to their own property. ²⁸But if they do not acquire the means to repay, what was sold will remain in the possession of the buyer until the Year of Jubilee. It will be returned in the Jubilee, and they can then go back to their property.

²⁹ " 'Anyone who sells a house in a walled city retains the right of redemption a full year after its sale. During that time the seller may redeem it. ³⁰If it is not redeemed before a full year has passed, the house in the walled city shall belong permanently to the buyer and the buyer's descendants. It is not to be returned in the Jubilee. ³¹But houses in villages without walls around them are to be considered as belonging to the open country. They can be redeemed, and they are to be returned in the Jubilee.

³² " 'The Levites always have the right to redeem their houses in the Levitical towns, which they possess. ³³So the property of the Levites is redeemable — that is, a house sold in any town they hold — and is to be returned in the Jubilee, because the houses in the towns of the Levites are their property among the Israelites. ³⁴But the pastureland belonging to their towns must not be sold; it is their permanent possession.

³⁵ " 'If any of your fellow Israelites become poor and are unable to support themselves among you, help them as you would a foreigner and stranger, so they can continue to live among you. ³⁶Do not take interest or any profit from them, but fear your God, so that they may continue to live among you. ³⁷You must not lend them money at interest or sell them food at a profit. ³⁸I am the LORD your God, who brought you out of Egypt to give you the land of Canaan and to be your God.

³⁹ " 'If any of your fellow Israelites become poor and sell themselves to you, do not make them

work as slaves. **40**They are to be treated as hired workers or temporary residents among you; they are to work for you until the Year of Jubilee. **41**Then they and their children are to be released, and they will go back to their own clans and to the property of their ancestors. **42**Because the Israelites are my servants, whom I brought out of Egypt, they must not be sold as slaves. **43**Do not rule over them ruthlessly, but fear your God.

44"'Your male and female slaves are to come from the nations around you; from them you may buy slaves. **45**You may also buy some of the temporary residents living among you and members of their clans born in your country, and they will become your property. **46**You can bequeath them to your children as inherited property and can make them slaves for life, but you must not rule over your fellow Israelites ruthlessly.

47"'If a foreigner residing among you becomes rich and any of your fellow Israelites become poor and sell themselves to the foreigner or to a member of the foreigner's clan, **48**they retain the right of redemption after they have sold themselves. One of their relatives may redeem them: **49**An uncle or a cousin or any blood relative in their clan may redeem them. Or if they prosper, they may redeem themselves. **50**They and their buyer are to count the time from the year they sold themselves up to the Year of Jubilee. The price for their release is to be based on the rate paid to a hired worker for that number of years. **51**If many years remain, they must pay for their redemption a larger share of the price paid for them. **52**If only a few years remain until the Year of Jubilee, they are to compute that and pay for their redemption accordingly. **53**They are to be treated as workers hired from year to year; you must see to it that those to whom they owe service do not rule over them ruthlessly.

54"'Even if someone is not redeemed in any of these ways, they and their children are to be released in the Year of Jubilee, **55**for the Israelites belong to me as servants. They are my servants, whom I brought out of Egypt. I am the LORD your God.

Reward for Obedience

26 "'Do not make idols or set up an image or a sacred stone for yourselves, and do not place a carved stone in your land to bow down before it. I am the LORD your God.

2"'Observe my Sabbaths and have reverence for my sanctuary. I am the LORD.

3"'If you follow my decrees and are careful to obey my commands, **4**I will send you rain in its season, and the ground will yield its crops and the trees their fruit. **5**Your threshing will continue until grape harvest and the grape harvest will continue until planting, and you will eat all the food you want and live in safety in your land.

6"'I will grant peace in the land, and you will lie down and no one will make you afraid. I will remove wild beasts from the land, and the sword will not pass through your country. **7**You will pursue your enemies, and they will fall by the sword before you. **8**Five of you will chase a hundred, and a hundred of you will chase ten thousand, and your enemies will fall by the sword before you.

9"'I will look on you with favor and make you fruitful and increase your numbers, and I will keep my covenant with you. **10**You will still be eating last year's harvest when you will have to move it out to make room for the new. **11**I will put my dwelling place*a* among you, and I will not abhor you. **12**I will walk among you and be your God, and you will be my people. **13**I am the LORD your God, who brought you out of Egypt so that you would no longer be slaves to the Egyptians; I broke the bars of your yoke and enabled you to walk with heads held high.

Punishment for Disobedience

14"'But if you will not listen to me and carry out all these commands, **15**and if you reject my decrees and abhor my laws and fail to carry out all my commands and so violate my covenant, **16**then I will do this to you: I will bring on you sudden terror, wasting diseases and fever that will destroy your sight and sap your strength. You will plant seed in vain, because your enemies will eat it. **17**I will set my face against you so that you will be defeated by your enemies; those who hate you will rule over you, and you will flee even when no one is pursuing you.

18"'If after all this you will not listen to me, I will punish you for your sins seven times over. **19**I will break down your stubborn pride and make the sky above you like iron and the ground beneath you like bronze. **20**Your strength will be spent in vain, because your soil will not yield its crops, nor will the trees of your land yield their fruit.

21"'If you remain hostile toward me and refuse to listen to me, I will multiply your afflictions seven times over, as your sins deserve. **22**I will send wild animals against you, and they will rob you of your children, destroy your cattle and make you so few in number that your roads will be deserted.

23"'If in spite of these things you do not accept my correction but continue to be hostile toward me, **24**I myself will be hostile

a 11 Or *my tabernacle*

toward you and will afflict you for your sins seven times over. ²⁵ And I will bring the sword on you to avenge the breaking of the covenant. When you withdraw into your cities, I will send a plague among you, and you will be given into enemy hands. ²⁶ When I cut off your supply of bread, ten women will be able to bake your bread in one oven, and they will dole out the bread by weight. You will eat, but you will not be satisfied.

²⁷ "'If in spite of this you still do not listen to me but continue to be hostile toward me, ²⁸ then in my anger I will be hostile toward you, and I myself will punish you for your sins seven times over. ²⁹ You will eat the flesh of your sons and the flesh of your daughters. ³⁰ I will destroy your high places, cut down your incense altars and pile your dead bodies[a] on the lifeless forms of your idols, and I will abhor you. ³¹ I will turn your cities into ruins and lay waste your sanctuaries, and I will take no delight in the pleasing aroma of your offerings. ³² I myself will lay waste the land, so that your enemies who live there will be appalled. ³³ I will scatter you among the nations and will draw out my sword and pursue you. Your land will be laid waste, and your cities will lie in ruins. ³⁴ Then the land will enjoy its sabbath years all the time that it lies desolate and you are in the country of your enemies; then the land will rest and enjoy its sabbaths. ³⁵ All the time that it lies desolate, the land will have the rest it did not have during the sabbaths you lived in it.

³⁶ "'As for those of you who are left, I will make their hearts so fearful in the lands of their enemies that the sound of a wind-blown leaf will put them to flight. They will run as though fleeing from the sword, and they will fall, even though no one is pursuing them. ³⁷ They will stumble over one another as though fleeing from the sword, even though no one is pursuing them. So you will not be able to stand before your enemies. ³⁸ You will perish among the nations; the land of your enemies will devour you. ³⁹ Those of you who are left will waste away in the lands of their enemies because of their sins; also because of their ancestors' sins they will waste away.

⁴⁰ "'But if they will confess their sins and the sins of their ancestors—their unfaithfulness and their hostility toward me, ⁴¹ which made me hostile toward them so that I sent them into the land of their enemies—then when their uncircumcised hearts are humbled and they pay for their sin, ⁴² I will remember my covenant with Jacob and my covenant with Isaac and my covenant with Abraham, and I will remember

---

[a] 30 Or *your funeral offerings*

the land. **43**For the land will be deserted by them and will enjoy its sabbaths while it lies desolate without them. They will pay for their sins because they rejected my laws and abhorred my decrees. **44**Yet in spite of this, when they are in the land of their enemies, I will not reject them or abhor them so as to destroy them completely, breaking my covenant with them. I am the LORD their God. **45**But for their sake I will remember the covenant with their ancestors whom I brought out of Egypt in the sight of the nations to be their God. I am the LORD.'"

46These are the decrees, the laws and the regulations that the LORD established at Mount Sinai between himself and the Israelites through Moses.

Redeeming What Is the LORD's

27 The LORD said to Moses, **2**"Speak to the Israelites and say to them: 'If anyone makes a special vow to dedicate a person to the LORD by giving the equivalent value, **3**set the value of a male between the ages of twenty and sixty at fifty shekels*a* of silver, according to the sanctuary shekel*b*; **4**for a female, set her value at thirty shekels*c*; **5**for a person between the ages of five and twenty, set the value of a male at twenty shekels*d* and of a female at ten shekels*e*; **6**for a person between one month and five years, set the value of a male at five shekels*f* of silver and that of a female at three shekels*g* of silver; **7**for a person sixty years old or more, set the value of a male at fifteen shekels*h* and of a female at ten shekels. **8**If anyone making the vow is too poor to pay the specified amount, the person being dedicated is to be presented to the priest, who will set the value according to what the one making the vow can afford.

9"'If what they vowed is an animal that is acceptable as an offering to the LORD, such an animal given to the LORD becomes holy. **10**They must not exchange it or substitute a good one for a bad one, or a bad one for a good one; if they should substitute one animal for another, both it and the substitute become holy. **11**If what they vowed is a ceremonially unclean animal—one that is not acceptable as an offering to the LORD—the animal must be presented to the priest, **12**who will judge its quality as good or bad. Whatever value the priest then sets, that is what it will be.

---

a 3 That is, about 1 1/4 pounds or about 575 grams; also in verse 16   *b 3* That is, about 2/5 ounce or about 12 grams; also in verse 25   *c 4* That is, about 12 ounces or about 345 grams   *d 5* That is, about 8 ounces or about 230 grams   *e 5* That is, about 4 ounces or about 115 grams; also in verse 7   *f 6* That is, about 2 ounces or about 58 grams   *g 6* That is, about 1 1/4 ounces or about 35 grams   *h 7* That is, about 6 ounces or about 175 grams

¹³If the owner wishes to redeem the animal, a fifth must be added to its value.

¹⁴"'If anyone dedicates their house as something holy to the LORD, the priest will judge its quality as good or bad. Whatever value the priest then sets, so it will remain. ¹⁵If the one who dedicates their house wishes to redeem it, they must add a fifth to its value, and the house will again become theirs.

¹⁶"'If anyone dedicates to the LORD part of their family land, its value is to be set according to the amount of seed required for it—fifty shekels of silver to a homer^a of barley seed. ¹⁷If they dedicate a field during the Year of Jubilee, the value that has been set remains. ¹⁸But if they dedicate a field after the Jubilee, the priest will determine the value according to the number of years that remain until the next Year of Jubilee, and its set value will be reduced. ¹⁹If the one who dedicates the field wishes to redeem it, they must add a fifth to its value, and the field will again become theirs. ²⁰If, however, they do not redeem the field, or if they have sold it to someone else, it can never be redeemed. ²¹When the field is released in the Jubilee, it will become holy, like a field devoted to the LORD; it will become priestly property.

²²"'If anyone dedicates to the LORD a field they have bought, which is not part of their family land, ²³the priest will determine its value up to the Year of Jubilee, and the owner must pay its value on that day as something holy to the LORD. ²⁴In the Year of Jubilee the field will revert to the person from whom it was bought, the one whose land it was. ²⁵Every value is to be set according to the sanctuary shekel, twenty gerahs to the shekel.

²⁶"'No one, however, may dedicate the firstborn of an animal, since the firstborn already belongs to the LORD; whether an ox^b or a sheep, it is the LORD's. ²⁷If it is one of the unclean animals, it may be bought back at its set value, adding a fifth of the value to it. If it is not redeemed, it is to be sold at its set value.

²⁸"'But nothing that a person owns and devotes^c to the LORD—whether a human being or an animal or family land—may be sold or redeemed; everything so devoted is most holy to the LORD.

²⁹"'No person devoted to destruction^d may be ransomed; they are to be put to death.

³⁰"'A tithe of everything from the land, whether grain from the

---

^a 16 That is, probably about 300 pounds or about 135 kilograms
^b 26 The Hebrew word can refer to either male or female.   ^c 28 The Hebrew term refers to the irrevocable giving over of things or persons to the LORD.
^d 29 The Hebrew term refers to the irrevocable giving over of things or persons to the LORD, often by totally destroying them.

soil or fruit from the trees, belongs to the LORD; it is holy to the LORD. ³¹ Whoever would redeem any of their tithe must add a fifth of the value to it. ³² Every tithe of the herd and flock—every tenth animal that passes under the shepherd's rod—will be holy to the LORD. ³³ No one may pick out the good from the bad or make any substitution. If anyone does make a substitution, both the animal and its substitute become holy and cannot be redeemed.'"

³⁴ These are the commands the LORD gave Moses at Mount Sinai for the Israelites.

Numbers

Introduction:

Numbers gets its name from the two accounts in chapters 1 and 26 of the numberings or countings of the people of Israel. Moses is the author of this book as well as the leader of the Israelites.

The first part of the book tells about Israel's year while camped at the foot of Mount Sinai. The second part of the book tells of Israel's journey from Mount Sinai to the east side of the Dead Sea. The third part of the book tells of the preparations for entering and conquering the land of Canaan.

Throughout the years of wandering in the desert, the Israelites were constantly reminded of one thing — God's care for them. He miraculously supplied the Israelites with manna, water and quails for their forty years in the desert. God loved and forgave his people continually even though they rebelled against him and their leaders.

Outline of contents:

Instructions for camping and marching (1:1–10:10)
From Sinai to the plains of Moab (10:11–21:35)
Balaam, Balak and Israel (22:1–25:18)
Instructions for conquest and possession of the land
    of Canaan (26:1–36:13)

The Census

1 The LORD spoke to Moses in the tent of meeting in the Desert of Sinai on the first day of the second month of the second year after the Israelites came out of Egypt. He said: 2 "Take a census of the whole Israelite community by their clans and families, listing every man by name, one by one. 3 You and Aaron are to count according to their divisions all the men in Israel who are twenty years old or more and able to serve in the army. 4 One man from each tribe, each of them the head of his family, is to help you. 5 These are the names of the men who are to assist you:

from Reuben, Elizur son of
    Shedeur;
6 from Simeon, Shelumiel son
    of Zurishaddai;
7 from Judah, Nahshon son of
    Amminadab;
8 from Issachar, Nethanel son
    of Zuar;

⁹from Zebulun, Eliab son of Helon;

¹⁰from the sons of Joseph:
from Ephraim, Elishama son of Ammihud;
from Manasseh, Gamaliel son of Pedahzur;

¹¹from Benjamin, Abidan son of Gideoni;

¹²from Dan, Ahiezer son of Ammishaddai;

¹³from Asher, Pagiel son of Okran;

¹⁴from Gad, Eliasaph son of Deuel;

¹⁵from Naphtali, Ahira son of Enan."

¹⁶These were the men appointed from the community, the leaders of their ancestral tribes. They were the heads of the clans of Israel.

¹⁷Moses and Aaron took these men whose names had been specified, ¹⁸and they called the whole community together on the first day of the second month. The people registered their ancestry by their clans and families, and the men twenty years old or more were listed by name, one by one, ¹⁹as the LORD commanded Moses. And so he counted them in the Desert of Sinai:

²⁰From the descendants of Reuben the firstborn son of Israel:
All the men twenty years old or more who were able to serve in the army were listed by name, one by one, according to the records of their clans and families.
²¹The number from the tribe of Reuben was 46,500.

²²From the descendants of Simeon:
All the men twenty years old or more who were able to serve in the army were counted and listed by name, one by one, according to the records of their clans and families. ²³The number from the tribe of Simeon was 59,300.

²⁴From the descendants of Gad:
All the men twenty years old or more who were able to serve in the army were listed by name, according to the records of their clans and families. ²⁵The number from the tribe of Gad was 45,650.

²⁶From the descendants of Judah:
All the men twenty years old or more who were able to serve in the army were listed by name, according to the records of their clans and families. ²⁷The number from the tribe of Judah was 74,600.

²⁸From the descendants of Issachar:
All the men twenty years old or more who were able to serve in the army were listed by name, according

to the records of their clans and families. **29** The number from the tribe of Issachar was 54,400.

30 From the descendants of Zebulun:

All the men twenty years old or more who were able to serve in the army were listed by name, according to the records of their clans and families. **31** The number from the tribe of Zebulun was 57,400.

32 From the sons of Joseph:

From the descendants of Ephraim:

All the men twenty years old or more who were able to serve in the army were listed by name, according to the records of their clans and families. **33** The number from the tribe of Ephraim was 40,500.

34 From the descendants of Manasseh:

All the men twenty years old or more who were able to serve in the army were listed by name, according to the records of their clans and families. **35** The number from the tribe of Manasseh was 32,200.

36 From the descendants of Benjamin:

All the men twenty years old or more who were able to serve in the army were listed by name, according to the records of their clans and families. **37** The number from the tribe of Benjamin was 35,400.

38 From the descendants of Dan:

All the men twenty years old or more who were able to serve in the army were listed by name, according to the records of their clans and families. **39** The number from the tribe of Dan was 62,700.

40 From the descendants of Asher:

All the men twenty years old or more who were able to serve in the army were listed by name, according to the records of their clans and families. **41** The number from the tribe of Asher was 41,500.

42 From the descendants of Naphtali:

All the men twenty years old or more who were able to serve in the army were listed by name, according to the records of their clans and families. **43** The number from the tribe of Naphtali was 53,400.

44 These were the men counted by Moses and Aaron and the twelve leaders of Israel, each one representing his family. **45** All the Israelites twenty years old or more who were able to serve in Israel's army were counted according to their families. ⁴⁶The total number was 603,550.

⁴⁷The ancestral tribe of the Levites, however, was not counted along with the others. ⁴⁸The LORD had said to Moses: ⁴⁹"You must not count the tribe of Levi or include them in the census of the other Israelites. ⁵⁰Instead, appoint the Levites to be in charge of the tabernacle of the covenant law—over all its furnishings and everything belonging to it. They are to carry the tabernacle and all its furnishings; they are to take care of it and encamp around it. ⁵¹Whenever the tabernacle is to move, the Levites are to take it down, and whenever the tabernacle is to be set up, the Levites shall do it. Anyone else who approaches it is to be put to death. ⁵²The Israelites are to set up their tents by divisions, each of them in their own camp under their standard. ⁵³The Levites, however, are to set up their tents around the tabernacle of the covenant law so that my wrath will not fall on the Israelite community. The Levites are to be responsible for the care of the tabernacle of the covenant law."

⁵⁴The Israelites did all this just as the LORD commanded Moses.

The Arrangement of the Tribal Camps

2 The LORD said to Moses and Aaron: ²"The Israelites are to camp around the tent of meeting some distance from it, each of them under their standard and holding the banners of their family."

³On the east, toward the sunrise, the divisions of the camp of Judah are to encamp under their standard. The leader of the people of Judah is Nahshon son of Amminadab. ⁴His division numbers 74,600.

⁵The tribe of Issachar will camp next to them. The leader of the people of Issachar is Nethanel son of Zuar. ⁶His division numbers 54,400.

⁷The tribe of Zebulun will be next. The leader of the people of Zebulun is Eliab son of Helon. ⁸His division numbers 57,400.

⁹All the men assigned to the camp of Judah, according to their divisions, number 186,400. They will set out first.

¹⁰On the south will be the divisions of the camp of Reuben under their standard. The leader of the people of Reuben is Elizur son of Shedeur. ¹¹His division numbers 46,500.

¹²The tribe of Simeon will camp next to them. The leader of the people of Simeon is Shelumiel son of Zurishaddai. ¹³His division numbers 59,300.

¹⁴The tribe of Gad will be next. The leader of the people of Gad is Eliasaph son of Deuel.ᵃ ¹⁵His division numbers 45,650.

¹⁶All the men assigned to the camp of Reuben, according to their divisions, number 151,450. They will set out second.

¹⁷Then the tent of meeting and the camp of the Levites will set out in the middle of the camps. They will set out in the same order as they encamp, each in their own place under their standard.

¹⁸On the west will be the divisions of the camp of Ephraim under their standard. The leader of the people of Ephraim is Elishama son of Ammihud. ¹⁹His division numbers 40,500.

²⁰The tribe of Manasseh will be next to them. The leader of the people of Manasseh is Gamaliel son of Pedahzur. ²¹His division numbers 32,200.

²²The tribe of Benjamin will be next. The leader of the people of Benjamin is Abidan son of Gideoni. ²³His division numbers 35,400.

²⁴All the men assigned to the camp of Ephraim, according to their divisions, number 108,100. They will set out third.

²⁵On the north will be the divisions of the camp of Dan under their standard. The leader of the people of Dan is Ahiezer son of Ammishaddai. ²⁶His division numbers 62,700.

²⁷The tribe of Asher will camp next to them. The leader of the people of Asher is Pagiel son of Okran. ²⁸His division numbers 41,500.

²⁹The tribe of Naphtali will be next. The leader of the people of Naphtali is Ahira son of Enan. ³⁰His division numbers 53,400.

³¹All the men assigned to the camp of Dan number 157,600. They will set out last, under their standards.

³²These are the Israelites, counted according to their families. All the men in the camps, by their divisions, number 603,550. ³³The Levites, however, were not counted along with the other Israelites, as the LORD commanded Moses.

³⁴So the Israelites did everything the LORD commanded Moses; that is the way they encamped under their standards, and that is the way they set out, each of them with their clan and family.

ᵃ 14 Many manuscripts of the Masoretic Text, Samaritan Pentateuch and Vulgate (see also 1:14); most manuscripts of the Masoretic Text *Reuel*

The Levites

3 This is the account of the family of Aaron and Moses at the time the LORD spoke to Moses at Mount Sinai.

[2] The names of the sons of Aaron were Nadab the firstborn and Abihu, Eleazar and Ithamar. [3] Those were the names of Aaron's sons, the anointed priests, who were ordained to serve as priests. [4] Nadab and Abihu, however, died before the LORD when they made an offering with unauthorized fire before him in the Desert of Sinai. They had no sons, so Eleazar and Ithamar served as priests during the lifetime of their father Aaron.

[5] The LORD said to Moses, [6] "Bring the tribe of Levi and present them to Aaron the priest to assist him. [7] They are to perform duties for him and for the whole community at the tent of meeting by doing the work of the tabernacle. [8] They are to take care of all the furnishings of the tent of meeting, fulfilling the obligations of the Israelites by doing the work of the tabernacle. [9] Give the Levites to Aaron and his sons; they are the Israelites who are to be given wholly to him. [a] [10] Appoint Aaron and his sons to serve as priests; anyone else who approaches the sanctuary is to be put to death."

[11] The LORD also said to Moses, [12] "I have taken the Levites from among the Israelites in place of the first male offspring of every Israelite woman. The Levites are mine, [13] for all the firstborn are mine. When I struck down all the firstborn in Egypt, I set apart for myself every firstborn in Israel, whether human or animal. They are to be mine. I am the LORD."

[14] The LORD said to Moses in the Desert of Sinai, [15] "Count the Levites by their families and clans. Count every male a month old or more." [16] So Moses counted them, as he was commanded by the word of the LORD.

[17] These were the names of the sons of Levi:

Gershon, Kohath and Merari.

[18] These were the names of the Gershonite clans:

Libni and Shimei.

[19] The Kohathite clans:

Amram, Izhar, Hebron and Uzziel.

[20] The Merarite clans:

Mahli and Mushi.

These were the Levite clans, according to their families.

[21] To Gershon belonged the clans of the Libnites and Shimeites; these were the Gershonite clans. [22] The number of all the males a month old or more who were counted was 7,500. [23] The Gershonite clans were to camp on the west, behind the tabernacle. [24] The leader of the families of

a 9 Most manuscripts of the Masoretic Text; some manuscripts of the Masoretic Text, Samaritan Pentateuch and Septuagint (see also 8:16) *to me* the Gershonites was Eliasaph son of Lael. 25 At the tent of meeting the Gershonites were responsible for the care of the tabernacle and tent, its coverings, the curtain at the entrance to the tent of meeting, 26 the curtains of the courtyard, the curtain at the entrance to the courtyard surrounding the tabernacle and altar, and the ropes—and everything related to their use.

27 To Kohath belonged the clans of the Amramites, Izharites, Hebronites and Uzzielites; these were the Kohathite clans. 28 The number of all the males a month old or more was 8,600.ª The Kohathites were responsible for the care of the sanctuary. 29 The Kohathite clans were to camp on the south side of the tabernacle. 30 The leader of the families of the Kohathite clans was Elizaphan son of Uzziel. 31 They were responsible for the care of the ark, the table, the lampstand, the altars, the articles of the sanctuary used in ministering, the curtain, and everything related to their use. 32 The chief leader of the Levites was Eleazar son of Aaron, the priest. He was appointed over those who were responsible for the care of the sanctuary.

33 To Merari belonged the clans of the Mahlites and the Mushites; these were the Merarite clans.

34 The number of all the males a month old or more who were counted was 6,200. 35 The leader of the families of the Merarite clans was Zuriel son of Abihail; they were to camp on the north side of the tabernacle. 36 The Merarites were appointed to take care of the frames of the tabernacle, its crossbars, posts, bases, all its equipment, and everything related to their use, 37 as well as the posts of the surrounding courtyard with their bases, tent pegs and ropes.

38 Moses and Aaron and his sons were to camp to the east of the tabernacle, toward the sunrise, in front of the tent of meeting. They were responsible for the care of the sanctuary on behalf of the Israelites. Anyone else who approached the sanctuary was to be put to death.

39 The total number of Levites counted at the LORD's command by Moses and Aaron according to their clans, including every male a month old or more, was 22,000.

40 The LORD said to Moses, "Count all the firstborn Israelite males who are a month old or more and make a list of their names. 41 Take the Levites for me in place of all the firstborn of the Israelites, and the livestock of the Levites in place of all the first-

---

ª 28 Hebrew; some Septuagint manuscripts 8,300

born of the livestock of the Israelites. I am the LORD."

⁴²So Moses counted all the firstborn of the Israelites, as the LORD commanded him. ⁴³The total number of firstborn males a month old or more, listed by name, was 22,273.

⁴⁴The LORD also said to Moses, ⁴⁵"Take the Levites in place of all the firstborn of Israel, and the livestock of the Levites in place of their livestock. The Levites are to be mine. I am the LORD. ⁴⁶To redeem the 273 firstborn Israelites who exceed the number of the Levites, ⁴⁷collect five shekelsᵃ for each one, according to the sanctuary shekel, which weighs twenty gerahs. ⁴⁸Give the money for the redemption of the additional Israelites to Aaron and his sons."

⁴⁹So Moses collected the redemption money from those who exceeded the number redeemed by the Levites. ⁵⁰From the firstborn of the Israelites he collected silver weighing 1,365 shekels,ᵇ according to the sanctuary shekel. ⁵¹Moses gave the redemption money to Aaron and his sons, as he was commanded by the word of the LORD.

The Kohathites

4 The LORD said to Moses and Aaron: ²"Take a census of the Kohathite branch of the Levites by their clans and families. ³Count all the men from thirty to fifty years of age who come to serve in the work at the tent of meeting.

⁴"This is the work of the Kohathites at the tent of meeting: the care of the most holy things. ⁵When the camp is to move, Aaron and his sons are to go in and take down the shielding curtain and put it over the ark of the covenant law. ⁶Then they are to cover the curtain with a durable leather,ᶜ spread a cloth of solid blue over that and put the poles in place.

⁷"Over the table of the Presence they are to spread a blue cloth and put on it the plates, dishes and bowls, and the jars for drink offerings; the bread that is continually there is to remain on it. ⁸They are to spread a scarlet cloth over them, cover that with the durable leather and put the poles in place.

⁹"They are to take a blue cloth and cover the lampstand that is for light, together with its lamps, its wick trimmers and trays, and all its jars for the olive oil used to supply it. ¹⁰Then they are to wrap it and all its accessories in a covering of the durable leather and put it on a carrying frame.

¹¹"Over the gold altar they are to spread a blue cloth and cover

---

ᵃ 47 That is, about 2 ounces or about 58 grams   ᵇ 50 That is, about 35 pounds or about 16 kilograms   ᶜ 6 Possibly the hides of large aquatic mammals; also in verses 8, 10, 11, 12, 14 and 25 that with the durable leather and put the poles in place.

¹² "They are to take all the articles used for ministering in the sanctuary, wrap them in a blue cloth, cover that with the durable leather and put them on a carrying frame.

¹³ "They are to remove the ashes from the bronze altar and spread a purple cloth over it. ¹⁴ Then they are to place on it all the utensils used for ministering at the altar, including the firepans, meat forks, shovels and sprinkling bowls. Over it they are to spread a covering of the durable leather and put the poles in place.

¹⁵ "After Aaron and his sons have finished covering the holy furnishings and all the holy articles, and when the camp is ready to move, only then are the Kohathites to come and do the carrying. But they must not touch the holy things or they will die. The Kohathites are to carry those things that are in the tent of meeting.

¹⁶ "Eleazar son of Aaron, the priest, is to have charge of the oil for the light, the fragrant incense, the regular grain offering and the anointing oil. He is to be in charge of the entire tabernacle and everything in it, including its holy furnishings and articles."

¹⁷ The LORD said to Moses and Aaron, ¹⁸ "See that the Kohathite tribal clans are not destroyed from among the Levites. ¹⁹ So that they may live and not die when they come near the most holy things, do this for them: Aaron and his sons are to go into the sanctuary and assign to each man his work and what he is to carry. ²⁰ But the Kohathites must not go in to look at the holy things, even for a moment, or they will die."

The Gershonites

²¹ The LORD said to Moses, ²² "Take a census also of the Gershonites by their families and clans. ²³ Count all the men from thirty to fifty years of age who come to serve in the work at the tent of meeting.

²⁴ "This is the service of the Gershonite clans in their carrying and their other work: ²⁵ They are to carry the curtains of the tabernacle, that is, the tent of meeting, its covering and its outer covering of durable leather, the curtains for the entrance to the tent of meeting, ²⁶ the curtains of the courtyard surrounding the tabernacle and altar, the curtain for the entrance to the courtyard, the ropes and all the equipment used in the service of the tent. The Gershonites are to do all that needs to be done with these things. ²⁷ All their service, whether carrying or doing other work, is to be done under the direction of Aaron and his sons. You shall assign to them as their responsibility all they are to carry. ²⁸ This is the service of

the Gershonite clans at the tent of meeting. Their duties are to be under the direction of Ithamar son of Aaron, the priest.

The Merarites

29 "Count the Merarites by their clans and families. 30 Count all the men from thirty to fifty years of age who come to serve in the work at the tent of meeting. 31 As part of all their service at the tent, they are to carry the frames of the tabernacle, its crossbars, posts and bases, 32 as well as the posts of the surrounding courtyard with their bases, tent pegs, ropes, all their equipment and everything related to their use. Assign to each man the specific things he is to carry. 33 This is the service of the Merarite clans as they work at the tent of meeting under the direction of Ithamar son of Aaron, the priest."

The Numbering of the Levite Clans

34 Moses, Aaron and the leaders of the community counted the Kohathites by their clans and families. 35 All the men from thirty to fifty years of age who came to serve in the work at the tent of meeting, 36 counted by clans, were 2,750. 37 This was the total of all those in the Kohathite clans who served at the tent of meeting. Moses and Aaron counted them according to the LORD's command through Moses.

38 The Gershonites were counted by their clans and families. 39 All the men from thirty to fifty years of age who came to serve in the work at the tent of meeting, 40 counted by their clans and families, were 2,630. 41 This was the total of those in the Gershonite clans who served at the tent of meeting. Moses and Aaron counted them according to the LORD's command.

42 The Merarites were counted by their clans and families. 43 All the men from thirty to fifty years of age who came to serve in the work at the tent of meeting, 44 counted by their clans, were 3,200. 45 This was the total of those in the Merarite clans. Moses and Aaron counted them according to the LORD's command through Moses.

46 So Moses, Aaron and the leaders of Israel counted all the Levites by their clans and families. 47 All the men from thirty to fifty years of age who came to do the work of serving and carrying the tent of meeting 48 numbered 8,580. 49 At the LORD's command through Moses, each was assigned his work and told what to carry.

Thus they were counted, as the LORD commanded Moses.

The Purity of the Camp

5 The LORD said to Moses, 2 "Command the Israelites to send away from the camp anyone

who has a defiling skin disease[a] or a discharge of any kind, or who is ceremonially unclean because of a dead body. [3] Send away male and female alike; send them outside the camp so they will not defile their camp, where I dwell among them." [4] The Israelites did so; they sent them outside the camp. They did just as the LORD had instructed Moses.

Restitution for Wrongs

[5] The LORD said to Moses, [6] "Say to the Israelites: 'Any man or woman who wrongs another in any way[b] and so is unfaithful to the LORD is guilty [7] and must confess the sin they have committed. They must make full restitution for the wrong they have done, add a fifth of the value to it and give it all to the person they have wronged. [8] But if that person has no close relative to whom restitution can be made for the wrong, the restitution belongs to the LORD and must be given to the priest, along with the ram with which atonement is made for the wrongdoer. [9] All the sacred contributions the Israelites bring to a priest will belong to him. [10] Sacred things belong to their owners, but what they give to the priest will belong to the priest.'"

The Test for an Unfaithful Wife

[11] Then the LORD said to Moses, [12] "Speak to the Israelites and say to them: 'If a man's wife goes astray and is unfaithful to him [13] so that another man has sexual relations with her, and this is hidden from her husband and her impurity is undetected (since there is no witness against her and she has not been caught in the act), [14] and if feelings of jealousy come over her husband and he suspects his wife and she is impure — or if he is jealous and suspects her even though she is not impure — [15] then he is to take his wife to the priest. He must also take an offering of a tenth of an ephah[c] of barley flour on her behalf. He must not pour olive oil on it or put incense on it, because it is a grain offering for jealousy, a reminder-offering to draw attention to wrongdoing.

[16] "'The priest shall bring her and have her stand before the LORD. [17] Then he shall take some holy water in a clay jar and put some dust from the tabernacle floor into the water. [18] After the priest has had the woman stand before the LORD, he shall loosen her hair and place in her hands the reminder-offering, the grain offering for jealousy, while he himself holds the bitter water

---

[a] 2 The Hebrew word for *defiling skin disease*, traditionally translated "leprosy," was used for various diseases affecting the skin.   [b] 6 Or *woman who commits any wrong common to mankind*   [c] 15 That is, probably about 3 1/2 pounds or about 1.6 kilograms

that brings a curse. ¹⁹Then the priest shall put the woman under oath and say to her, "If no other man has had sexual relations with you and you have not gone astray and become impure while married to your husband, may this bitter water that brings a curse not harm you. ²⁰But if you have gone astray while married to your husband and you have made yourself impure by having sexual relations with a man other than your husband"— ²¹here the priest is to put the woman under this curse — "may the LORD cause you to become a curse[a] among your people when he makes your womb miscarry and your abdomen swell. ²²May this water that brings a curse enter your body so that your abdomen swells or your womb miscarries."

"'Then the woman is to say, "Amen. So be it."

²³"'The priest is to write these curses on a scroll and then wash them off into the bitter water. ²⁴He shall make the woman drink the bitter water that brings a curse, and this water that brings a curse and causes bitter suffering will enter her. ²⁵The priest is to take from her hands the grain offering for jealousy, wave it before the LORD and bring it to the altar. ²⁶The priest is then to take a handful of the grain offering as a memorial[b] offering and burn it on

the altar; after that, he is to have the woman drink the water. ²⁷If she has made herself impure and been unfaithful to her husband, this will be the result: When she is made to drink the water that brings a curse and causes bitter suffering, it will enter her, her abdomen will swell and her womb will miscarry, and she will become a curse. ²⁸If, however, the woman has not made herself impure, but is clean, she will be cleared of guilt and will be able to have children.

²⁹"'This, then, is the law of jealousy when a woman goes astray and makes herself impure while married to her husband, ³⁰or when feelings of jealousy come over a man because he suspects his wife. The priest is to have her stand before the LORD and is to apply this entire law to her. ³¹The husband will be innocent of any wrongdoing, but the woman will bear the consequences of her sin.'"

The Nazirite

6 The LORD said to Moses, ²"Speak to the Israelites and say to them: 'If a man or woman wants to make a special vow, a vow of dedication to the LORD as a Nazirite, ³they must abstain from wine and other fermented drink and must not drink vinegar made from wine or other

---

[a] 21 That is, may he cause your name to be used in cursing (see Jer. 29:22); or, may others see that you are cursed; similarly in verse 27.   [b] 26 Or representative

fermented drink. They must not drink grape juice or eat grapes or raisins. [4] As long as they remain under their Nazirite vow, they must not eat anything that comes from the grapevine, not even the seeds or skins.

[5] "'During the entire period of their Nazirite vow, no razor may be used on their head. They must be holy until the period of their dedication to the LORD is over; they must let their hair grow long.

[6] "'Throughout the period of their dedication to the LORD, the Nazirite must not go near a dead body. [7] Even if their own father or mother or brother or sister dies, they must not make themselves ceremonially unclean on account of them, because the symbol of their dedication to God is on their head. [8] Throughout the period of their dedication, they are consecrated to the LORD.

[9] "'If someone dies suddenly in the Nazirite's presence, thus defiling the hair that symbolizes their dedication, they must shave their head on the seventh day — the day of their cleansing. [10] Then on the eighth day they must bring two doves or two young pigeons to the priest at the entrance to the tent of meeting. [11] The priest is to offer one as a sin offering[a] and the other as a burnt offering to make atonement for the Nazirite because they sinned by being in the presence of the dead body. That same day they are to consecrate their head again. [12] They must rededicate themselves to the LORD for the same period of dedication and must bring a year-old male lamb as a guilt offering. The previous days do not count, because they became defiled during their period of dedication.

[13] "'Now this is the law of the Nazirite when the period of their dedication is over. They are to be brought to the entrance to the tent of meeting. [14] There they are to present their offerings to the LORD: a year-old male lamb without defect for a burnt offering, a year-old ewe lamb without defect for a sin offering, a ram without defect for a fellowship offering, [15] together with their grain offerings and drink offerings, and a basket of bread made with the finest flour and without yeast — thick loaves with olive oil mixed in, and thin loaves brushed with olive oil.

[16] "'The priest is to present all these before the LORD and make the sin offering and the burnt offering. [17] He is to present the basket of unleavened bread and is to sacrifice the ram as a fellowship offering to the LORD, together with its grain offering and drink offering.

[18] "'Then at the entrance to the tent of meeting, the Nazirite must shave off the hair that symbolizes their dedication. They are to take

---

[a] 11 Or *purification offering*; also in verses 14 and 16

the hair and put it in the fire that is under the sacrifice of the fellowship offering.

19 " 'After the Nazirite has shaved off the hair that symbolizes their dedication, the priest is to place in their hands a boiled shoulder of the ram, and one thick loaf and one thin loaf from the basket, both made without yeast. 20 The priest shall then wave these before the LORD as a wave offering; they are holy and belong to the priest, together with the breast that was waved and the thigh that was presented. After that, the Nazirite may drink wine.

21 " 'This is the law of the Nazirite who vows offerings to the LORD in accordance with their dedication, in addition to whatever else they can afford. They must fulfill the vows they have made, according to the law of the Nazirite.' "

The Priestly Blessing

22 The LORD said to Moses, 23 "Tell Aaron and his sons, 'This is how you are to bless the Israelites. Say to them:

24 " ' "The LORD bless you
    and keep you;
25 the LORD make his face shine
    on you
    and be gracious to you;
26 the LORD turn his face toward
    you
    and give you peace." '

27 "So they will put my name on the Israelites, and I will bless them."

Offerings at the Dedication of the Tabernacle

7 When Moses finished setting up the tabernacle, he anointed and consecrated it and all its furnishings. He also anointed and consecrated the altar and all its utensils. 2 Then the leaders of Israel, the heads of families who were the tribal leaders in charge of those who were counted, made offerings. 3 They brought as their gifts before the LORD six covered carts and twelve oxen — an ox from each leader and a cart from every two. These they presented before the tabernacle.

4 The LORD said to Moses, 5 "Accept these from them, that they may be used in the work at the tent of meeting. Give them to the Levites as each man's work requires."

6 So Moses took the carts and oxen and gave them to the Levites. 7 He gave two carts and four oxen to the Gershonites, as their work required, 8 and he gave four carts and eight oxen to the Merarites, as their work required. They were all under the direction of Ithamar son of Aaron, the priest. 9 But Moses did not give any to the Kohathites, because they were to carry on their shoulders the holy things, for which they were responsible.

10 When the altar was anointed, the leaders brought their offerings for its dedication and presented them before the altar.

¹¹ For the LORD had said to Moses, "Each day one leader is to bring his offering for the dedication of the altar."

¹² The one who brought his offering on the first day was Nahshon son of Amminadab of the tribe of Judah.

¹³ His offering was one silver plate weighing a hundred and thirty shekels[a] and one silver sprinkling bowl weighing seventy shekels,[b] both according to the sanctuary shekel, each filled with the finest flour mixed with olive oil as a grain offering; ¹⁴ one gold dish weighing ten shekels,[c] filled with incense; ¹⁵ one young bull, one ram and one male lamb a year old for a burnt offering; ¹⁶ one male goat for a sin offering[d]; ¹⁷ and two oxen, five rams, five male goats and five male lambs a year old to be sacrificed as a fellowship offering. This was the offering of Nahshon son of Amminadab.

¹⁸ On the second day Nethanel son of Zuar, the leader of Issachar, brought his offering.

¹⁹ The offering he brought was one silver plate weighing a hundred and thirty shekels and one silver sprinkling bowl weighing seventy shek-els, both according to the sanctuary shekel, each filled with the finest flour mixed with olive oil as a grain offering; ²⁰ one gold dish weighing ten shekels, filled with incense; ²¹ one young bull, one ram and one male lamb a year old for a burnt offering; ²² one male goat for a sin offering; ²³ and two oxen, five rams, five male goats and five male lambs a year old to be sacrificed as a fellowship offering. This was the offering of Nethanel son of Zuar.

²⁴ On the third day, Eliab son of Helon, the leader of the people of Zebulun, brought his offering.

²⁵ His offering was one silver plate weighing a hundred and thirty shekels and one silver sprinkling bowl weighing seventy shekels, both according to the sanctuary shekel, each filled with the finest flour mixed with olive oil as a grain offering; ²⁶ one gold dish weighing ten shekels, filled with incense; ²⁷ one young bull, one ram and one male lamb a year old for a burnt offering; ²⁸ one male goat for a sin offering; ²⁹ and two oxen, five rams, five male goats and five male lambs a year old to be sacrificed as a

---

[a] 13 That is, about 3 1/4 pounds or about 1.5 kilograms; also elsewhere in this chapter   [b] 13 That is, about 1 3/4 pounds or about 800 grams; also elsewhere in this chapter   [c] 14 That is, about 4 ounces or about 115 grams; also elsewhere in this chapter   [d] 16 Or *purification offering*; also elsewhere in this chapter

fellowship offering. This was the offering of Eliab son of Helon.

30 On the fourth day Elizur son of Shedeur, the leader of the people of Reuben, brought his offering. 31 His offering was one silver plate weighing a hundred and thirty shekels and one silver sprinkling bowl weighing seventy shekels, both according to the sanctuary shekel, each filled with the finest flour mixed with olive oil as a grain offering; 32 one gold dish weighing ten shekels, filled with incense; 33 one young bull, one ram and one male lamb a year old for a burnt offering; 34 one male goat for a sin offering; 35 and two oxen, five rams, five male goats and five male lambs a year old to be sacrificed as a fellowship offering. This was the offering of Elizur son of Shedeur.

36 On the fifth day Shelumiel son of Zurishaddai, the leader of the people of Simeon, brought his offering. 37 His offering was one silver plate weighing a hundred and thirty shekels and one silver sprinkling bowl weighing seventy shekels, both according to the sanctuary shekel, each filled with the finest flour mixed with olive oil as a grain offering; 38 one gold dish weighing ten shekels, filled with incense; 39 one young bull, one ram and one male lamb a year old for a burnt offering; 40 one male goat for a sin offering; 41 and two oxen, five rams, five male goats and five male lambs a year old to be sacrificed as a fellowship offering. This was the offering of Shelumiel son of Zurishaddai.

42 On the sixth day Eliasaph son of Deuel, the leader of the people of Gad, brought his offering. 43 His offering was one silver plate weighing a hundred and thirty shekels and one silver sprinkling bowl weighing seventy shekels, both according to the sanctuary shekel, each filled with the finest flour mixed with olive oil as a grain offering; 44 one gold dish weighing ten shekels, filled with incense; 45 one young bull, one ram and one male lamb a year old for a burnt offering; 46 one male goat for a sin offering; 47 and two oxen, five rams, five male goats and five male lambs a year old to be sacrificed as a fellowship offering. This was the offering of Eliasaph son of Deuel.

48 On the seventh day Elishama son of Ammihud, the leader of the people of Ephraim, brought his offering.

⁴⁹His offering was one silver plate weighing a hundred and thirty shekels and one silver sprinkling bowl weighing seventy shekels, both according to the sanctuary shekel, each filled with the finest flour mixed with olive oil as a grain offering; ⁵⁰one gold dish weighing ten shekels, filled with incense; ⁵¹one young bull, one ram and one male lamb a year old for a burnt offering; ⁵²one male goat for a sin offering; ⁵³and two oxen, five rams, five male goats and five male lambs a year old to be sacrificed as a fellowship offering. This was the offering of Elishama son of Ammihud.

⁵⁴On the eighth day Gamaliel son of Pedahzur, the leader of the people of Manasseh, brought his offering.

⁵⁵His offering was one silver plate weighing a hundred and thirty shekels and one silver sprinkling bowl weighing seventy shekels, both according to the sanctuary shekel, each filled with the finest flour mixed with olive oil as a grain offering; ⁵⁶one gold dish weighing ten shekels, filled with incense; ⁵⁷one young bull, one ram and one male lamb a year old for a burnt offering; ⁵⁸one male goat for a sin offering; ⁵⁹and two oxen, five rams, five male goats and five male lambs a year old to be sacrificed as a fellowship offering. This was the offering of Gamaliel son of Pedahzur.

⁶⁰On the ninth day Abidan son of Gideoni, the leader of the people of Benjamin, brought his offering.

⁶¹His offering was one silver plate weighing a hundred and thirty shekels and one silver sprinkling bowl weighing seventy shekels, both according to the sanctuary shekel, each filled with the finest flour mixed with olive oil as a grain offering; ⁶²one gold dish weighing ten shekels, filled with incense; ⁶³one young bull, one ram and one male lamb a year old for a burnt offering; ⁶⁴one male goat for a sin offering; ⁶⁵and two oxen, five rams, five male goats and five male lambs a year old to be sacrificed as a fellowship offering. This was the offering of Abidan son of Gideoni.

⁶⁶On the tenth day Ahiezer son of Ammishaddai, the leader of the people of Dan, brought his offering.

⁶⁷His offering was one silver plate weighing a hundred and thirty shekels and one silver sprinkling bowl weighing seventy shekels, both according to the sanctuary shekel, each filled with the finest flour mixed with olive oil as a grain offering; ⁶⁸one

gold dish weighing ten shekels, filled with incense; [69] one young bull, one ram and one male lamb a year old for a burnt offering; [70] one male goat for a sin offering; [71] and two oxen, five rams, five male goats and five male lambs a year old to be sacrificed as a fellowship offering. This was the offering of Ahiezer son of Ammishaddai.

[72] On the eleventh day Pagiel son of Okran, the leader of the people of Asher, brought his offering.

[73] His offering was one silver plate weighing a hundred and thirty shekels and one silver sprinkling bowl weighing seventy shekels, both according to the sanctuary shekel, each filled with the finest flour mixed with olive oil as a grain offering; [74] one gold dish weighing ten shekels, filled with incense; [75] one young bull, one ram and one male lamb a year old for a burnt offering; [76] one male goat for a sin offering; [77] and two oxen, five rams, five male goats and five male lambs a year old to be sacrificed as a fellowship offering. This was the offering of Pagiel son of Okran.

[78] On the twelfth day Ahira son of Enan, the leader of the people of Naphtali, brought his offering.

[79] His offering was one silver plate weighing a hundred and thirty shekels and one silver sprinkling bowl weighing seventy shekels, both according to the sanctuary shekel, each filled with the finest flour mixed with olive oil as a grain offering; [80] one gold dish weighing ten shekels, filled with incense; [81] one young bull, one ram and one male lamb a year old for a burnt offering; [82] one male goat for a sin offering; [83] and two oxen, five rams, five male goats and five male lambs a year old to be sacrificed as a fellowship offering. This was the offering of Ahira son of Enan.

[84] These were the offerings of the Israelite leaders for the dedication of the altar when it was anointed: twelve silver plates, twelve silver sprinkling bowls and twelve gold dishes. [85] Each silver plate weighed a hundred and thirty shekels, and each sprinkling bowl seventy shekels. Altogether, the silver dishes weighed two thousand four hundred shekels,[a] according to the sanctuary shekel. [86] The twelve gold dishes filled with incense weighed ten shekels each, according to the sanctuary shekel. Altogether, the gold dishes weighed a hundred and twenty shekels.[b] [87] The total number of animals for the burnt offering came to

---

[a] 85 That is, about 60 pounds or about 28 kilograms   [b] 86 That is, about 3 pounds or about 1.4 kilograms

twelve young bulls, twelve rams and twelve male lambs a year old, together with their grain offering. Twelve male goats were used for the sin offering. **88** The total number of animals for the sacrifice of the fellowship offering came to twenty-four oxen, sixty rams, sixty male goats and sixty male lambs a year old. These were the offerings for the dedication of the altar after it was anointed.

89 When Moses entered the tent of meeting to speak with the LORD, he heard the voice speaking to him from between the two cherubim above the atonement cover on the ark of the covenant law. In this way the LORD spoke to him.

Setting Up the Lamps

8 The LORD said to Moses, **2** "Speak to Aaron and say to him, 'When you set up the lamps, see that all seven light up the area in front of the lampstand.'"

3 Aaron did so; he set up the lamps so that they faced forward on the lampstand, just as the LORD commanded Moses. **4** This is how the lampstand was made: It was made of hammered gold— from its base to its blossoms. The lampstand was made exactly like the pattern the LORD had shown Moses.

The Setting Apart of the Levites

5 The LORD said to Moses: **6** "Take the Levites from among all the Is- raelites and make them ceremonially clean. **7** To purify them, do this: Sprinkle the water of cleansing on them; then have them shave their whole bodies and wash their clothes. And so they will purify themselves. **8** Have them take a young bull with its grain offering of the finest flour mixed with olive oil; then you are to take a second young bull for a sin offering.*a* **9** Bring the Levites to the front of the tent of meeting and assemble the whole Israelite community. **10** You are to bring the Levites before the LORD, and the Israelites are to lay their hands on them. **11** Aaron is to present the Levites before the LORD as a wave offering from the Israelites, so that they may be ready to do the work of the LORD.

12 "Then the Levites are to lay their hands on the heads of the bulls, using one for a sin offering to the LORD and the other for a burnt offering, to make atonement for the Levites. **13** Have the Levites stand in front of Aaron and his sons and then present them as a wave offering to the LORD. **14** In this way you are to set the Levites apart from the other Israelites, and the Levites will be mine.

15 "After you have purified the Levites and presented them as a wave offering, they are to come to do their work at the tent of meeting. **16** They are the Israel-

---

a 8 Or *purification offering*; also in verse 12

ites who are to be given wholly to me. I have taken them as my own in place of the firstborn, the first male offspring from every Israelite woman. [17]Every firstborn male in Israel, whether human or animal, is mine. When I struck down all the firstborn in Egypt, I set them apart for myself. [18]And I have taken the Levites in place of all the firstborn sons in Israel. [19]From among all the Israelites, I have given the Levites as gifts to Aaron and his sons to do the work at the tent of meeting on behalf of the Israelites and to make atonement for them so that no plague will strike the Israelites when they go near the sanctuary."

[20]Moses, Aaron and the whole Israelite community did with the Levites just as the LORD commanded Moses. [21]The Levites purified themselves and washed their clothes. Then Aaron presented them as a wave offering before the LORD and made atonement for them to purify them. [22]After that, the Levites came to do their work at the tent of meeting under the supervision of Aaron and his sons. They did with the Levites just as the LORD commanded Moses.

[23]The LORD said to Moses, [24]"This applies to the Levites: Men twenty-five years old or more shall come to take part in the work at the tent of meeting, [25]but at the age of fifty, they must retire from their regular service and work no longer. [26]They

may assist their brothers in performing their duties at the tent of meeting, but they themselves must not do the work. This, then, is how you are to assign the responsibilities of the Levites."

The Passover

9 The LORD spoke to Moses in the Desert of Sinai in the first month of the second year after they came out of Egypt. He said, [2]"Have the Israelites celebrate the Passover at the appointed time. [3]Celebrate it at the appointed time, at twilight on the fourteenth day of this month, in accordance with all its rules and regulations."

[4]So Moses told the Israelites to celebrate the Passover, [5]and they did so in the Desert of Sinai at twilight on the fourteenth day of the first month. The Israelites did everything just as the LORD commanded Moses.

[6]But some of them could not celebrate the Passover on that day because they were ceremonially unclean on account of a dead body. So they came to Moses and Aaron that same day [7]and said to Moses, "We have become unclean because of a dead body, but why should we be kept from presenting the LORD's offering with the other Israelites at the appointed time?"

[8]Moses answered them, "Wait until I find out what the LORD commands concerning you."

⁹Then the LORD said to Moses, ¹⁰"Tell the Israelites: 'When any of you or your descendants are unclean because of a dead body or are away on a journey, they are still to celebrate the LORD's Passover, ¹¹but they are to do it on the fourteenth day of the second month at twilight. They are to eat the lamb, together with unleavened bread and bitter herbs. ¹²They must not leave any of it till morning or break any of its bones. When they celebrate the Passover, they must follow all the regulations. ¹³But if anyone who is ceremonially clean and not on a journey fails to celebrate the Passover, they must be cut off from their people for not presenting the LORD's offering at the appointed time. They will bear the consequences of their sin.

¹⁴"'A foreigner residing among you is also to celebrate the LORD's Passover in accordance with its rules and regulations. You must have the same regulations for both the foreigner and the native-born.'"

The Cloud Above the Tabernacle

¹⁵On the day the tabernacle, the tent of the covenant law, was set up, the cloud covered it. From evening till morning the cloud above the tabernacle looked like fire. ¹⁶That is how it continued to be; the cloud covered it, and at night it looked like fire. ¹⁷Whenever the cloud lifted from above the tent, the Israelites set out; wherever the cloud settled, the Israelites encamped. ¹⁸At the LORD's command the Israelites set out, and at his command they encamped. As long as the cloud stayed over the tabernacle, they remained in camp. ¹⁹When the cloud remained over the tabernacle a long time, the Israelites obeyed the LORD's order and did not set out. ²⁰Sometimes the cloud was over the tabernacle only a few days; at the LORD's command they would encamp, and then at his command they would set out. ²¹Sometimes the cloud stayed only from evening till morning, and when it lifted in the morning, they set out. Whether by day or by night, whenever the cloud lifted, they set out. ²²Whether the cloud stayed over the tabernacle for two days or a month or a year, the Israelites would remain in camp and not set out; but when it lifted, they would set out. ²³At the LORD's command they encamped, and at the LORD's command they set out. They obeyed the LORD's order, in accordance with his command through Moses.

The Silver Trumpets

10 The LORD said to Moses: ²"Make two trumpets of hammered silver, and use them

for calling the community together and for having the camps set out. ³When both are sounded, the whole community is to assemble before you at the entrance to the tent of meeting. ⁴If only one is sounded, the leaders—the heads of the clans of Israel—are to assemble before you. ⁵When a trumpet blast is sounded, the tribes camping on the east are to set out. ⁶At the sounding of a second blast, the camps on the south are to set out. The blast will be the signal for setting out. ⁷To gather the assembly, blow the trumpets, but not with the signal for setting out.

⁸"The sons of Aaron, the priests, are to blow the trumpets. This is to be a lasting ordinance for you and the generations to come. ⁹When you go into battle in your own land against an enemy who is oppressing you, sound a blast on the trumpets. Then you will be remembered by the LORD your God and rescued from your enemies. ¹⁰Also at your times of rejoicing—your appointed festivals and New Moon feasts—you are to sound the trumpets over your burnt offerings and fellowship offerings, and they will be a memorial for you before your God. I am the LORD your God."

The Israelites Leave Sinai

¹¹On the twentieth day of the second month of the second year, the cloud lifted from above the tabernacle of the covenant law. ¹²Then the Israelites set out from the Desert of Sinai and traveled from place to place until the cloud came to rest in the Desert of Paran. ¹³They set out, this first time, at the LORD's command through Moses.

¹⁴The divisions of the camp of Judah went first, under their standard. Nahshon son of Amminadab was in command. ¹⁵Nethanel son of Zuar was over the division of the tribe of Issachar, ¹⁶and Eliab son of Helon was over the division of the tribe of Zebulun. ¹⁷Then the tabernacle was taken down, and the Gershonites and Merarites, who carried it, set out.

¹⁸The divisions of the camp of Reuben went next, under their standard. Elizur son of Shedeur was in command. ¹⁹Shelumiel son of Zurishaddai was over the division of the tribe of Simeon, ²⁰and Eliasaph son of Deuel was over the division of the tribe of Gad. ²¹Then the Kohathites set out, carrying the holy things. The tabernacle was to be set up before they arrived.

²²The divisions of the camp of Ephraim went next, under their standard. Elishama son of Ammihud was in command. ²³Gamaliel son of Pedahzur was over the division of the tribe of Manasseh, ²⁴and Abidan son of Gideoni was over the division of the tribe of Benjamin.

²⁵ Finally, as the rear guard for all the units, the divisions of the camp of Dan set out under their standard. Ahiezer son of Ammishaddai was in command. ²⁶ Pagiel son of Okran was over the division of the tribe of Asher, ²⁷ and Ahira son of Enan was over the division of the tribe of Naphtali. ²⁸ This was the order of march for the Israelite divisions as they set out.

²⁹ Now Moses said to Hobab son of Reuel the Midianite, Moses' father-in-law, "We are setting out for the place about which the LORD said, 'I will give it to you.' Come with us and we will treat you well, for the LORD has promised good things to Israel."

³⁰ He answered, "No, I will not go; I am going back to my own land and my own people."

³¹ But Moses said, "Please do not leave us. You know where we should camp in the wilderness, and you can be our eyes. ³² If you come with us, we will share with you whatever good things the LORD gives us."

³³ So they set out from the mountain of the LORD and traveled for three days. The ark of the covenant of the LORD went before them during those three days to find them a place to rest. ³⁴ The cloud of the LORD was over them by day when they set out from the camp.

³⁵ Whenever the ark set out, Moses said,

"Rise up, LORD!
May your enemies be
    scattered;
may your foes flee before
    you."

³⁶ Whenever it came to rest, he said,

"Return, LORD,
    to the countless thousands
    of Israel."

Fire From the LORD

11 Now the people complained about their hardships in the hearing of the LORD, and when he heard them his anger was aroused. Then fire from the LORD burned among them and consumed some of the outskirts of the camp. ² When the people cried out to Moses, he prayed to the LORD and the fire died down. ³ So that place was called Taberah,ᵃ because fire from the LORD had burned among them.

Quail From the LORD

⁴ The rabble with them began to crave other food, and again the Israelites started wailing and said, "If only we had meat to eat! ⁵ We remember the fish we ate in Egypt at no cost—also the cucumbers, melons, leeks, onions and garlic. ⁶ But now we have lost our appetite; we never see anything but this manna!"

ᵃ 3 *Taberah* means *burning.*

[7] The manna was like coriander seed and looked like resin. [8] The people went around gathering it, and then ground it in a hand mill or crushed it in a mortar. They cooked it in a pot or made it into loaves. And it tasted like something made with olive oil. [9] When the dew settled on the camp at night, the manna also came down.

[10] Moses heard the people of every family wailing at the entrance to their tents. The LORD became exceedingly angry, and Moses was troubled. [11] He asked the LORD, "Why have you brought this trouble on your servant? What have I done to displease you that you put the burden of all these people on me? [12] Did I conceive all these people? Did I give them birth? Why do you tell me to carry them in my arms, as a nurse carries an infant, to the land you promised on oath to their ancestors? [13] Where can I get meat for all these people? They keep wailing to me, 'Give us meat to eat!' [14] I cannot carry all these people by myself; the burden is too heavy for me. [15] If this is how you are going to treat me, please go ahead and kill me — if I have found favor in your eyes — and do not let me face my own ruin."

[16] The LORD said to Moses: "Bring me seventy of Israel's elders who are known to you as leaders and officials among the people. Have them come to the tent of meeting, that they may stand there with you. [17] I will come down and speak with you there, and I will take some of the power of the Spirit that is on you and put it on them. They will share the burden of the people with you so that you will not have to carry it alone.

[18] "Tell the people: 'Consecrate yourselves in preparation for tomorrow, when you will eat meat. The LORD heard you when you wailed, "If only we had meat to eat! We were better off in Egypt!" Now the LORD will give you meat, and you will eat it. [19] You will not eat it for just one day, or two days, or five, ten or twenty days, [20] but for a whole month — until it comes out of your nostrils and you loathe it — because you have rejected the LORD, who is among you, and have wailed before him, saying, "Why did we ever leave Egypt?" ' "

[21] But Moses said, "Here I am among six hundred thousand men on foot, and you say, 'I will give them meat to eat for a whole month!' [22] Would they have enough if flocks and herds were slaughtered for them? Would they have enough if all the fish in the sea were caught for them?"

[23] The LORD answered Moses, "Is the LORD's arm too short? Now you will see whether or not what I say will come true for you."

[24] So Moses went out and told the people what the LORD had

said. He brought together seventy of their elders and had them stand around the tent. ²⁵Then the LORD came down in the cloud and spoke with him, and he took some of the power of the Spirit that was on him and put it on the seventy elders. When the Spirit rested on them, they prophesied — but did not do so again.

²⁶However, two men, whose names were Eldad and Medad, had remained in the camp. They were listed among the elders, but did not go out to the tent. Yet the Spirit also rested on them, and they prophesied in the camp. ²⁷A young man ran and told Moses, "Eldad and Medad are prophesying in the camp."

²⁸Joshua son of Nun, who had been Moses' aide since youth, spoke up and said, "Moses, my lord, stop them!"

²⁹But Moses replied, "Are you jealous for my sake? I wish that all the LORD's people were prophets and that the LORD would put his Spirit on them!" ³⁰Then Moses and the elders of Israel returned to the camp.

³¹Now a wind went out from the LORD and drove quail in from the sea. It scattered them up to two cubits^a deep all around the camp, as far as a day's walk in any direction. ³²All that day and night and all the next day the people went out and gathered quail. No one gathered less than ten homers.^b Then they spread them out all around the camp. ³³But while the meat was still between their teeth and before it could be consumed, the anger of the LORD burned against the people, and he struck them with a severe plague. ³⁴Therefore the place was named Kibroth Hattaavah,^c because there they buried the people who had craved other food.

³⁵From Kibroth Hattaavah the people traveled to Hazeroth and stayed there.

Miriam and Aaron Oppose Moses

12 Miriam and Aaron began to talk against Moses because of his Cushite wife, for he had married a Cushite. ²"Has the LORD spoken only through Moses?" they asked. "Hasn't he also spoken through us?" And the LORD heard this.

³(Now Moses was a very humble man, more humble than anyone else on the face of the earth.)

⁴At once the LORD said to Moses, Aaron and Miriam, "Come out to the tent of meeting, all three of you." So the three of them went out. ⁵Then the LORD came down in a pillar of cloud; he stood at the entrance to the

---

^a 31 That is, about 3 feet or about 90 centimeters   ^b 32 That is, possibly about 1 3/4 tons or about 1.6 metric tons   ^c 34 Kibroth Hattaavah means graves of craving.

tent and summoned Aaron and Miriam. When the two of them stepped forward, ⁶he said, "Listen to my words:

"When there is a prophet
  among you,
 I, the LORD, reveal myself to
  them in visions,
 I speak to them in dreams.
⁷But this is not true of my
  servant Moses;
 he is faithful in all my house.
⁸With him I speak face to face,
  clearly and not in riddles;
 he sees the form of the LORD.
 Why then were you not afraid
  to speak against my servant
  Moses?"

⁹The anger of the LORD burned against them, and he left them.

¹⁰When the cloud lifted from above the tent, Miriam's skin was leprous*ᵃ*—it became as white as snow. Aaron turned toward her and saw that she had a defiling skin disease, ¹¹and he said to Moses, "Please, my lord, I ask you not to hold against us the sin we have so foolishly committed. ¹²Do not let her be like a stillborn infant coming from its mother's womb with its flesh half eaten away."

¹³So Moses cried out to the LORD, "Please, God, heal her!"

¹⁴The LORD replied to Moses, "If her father had spit in her face, would she not have been in disgrace for seven days? Confine her outside the camp for seven days;

after that she can be brought back." ¹⁵So Miriam was confined outside the camp for seven days, and the people did not move on till she was brought back.

¹⁶After that, the people left Hazeroth and encamped in the Desert of Paran.

Exploring Canaan

13 The LORD said to Moses, ²"Send some men to explore the land of Canaan, which I am giving to the Israelites. From each ancestral tribe send one of its leaders."

³So at the LORD's command Moses sent them out from the Desert of Paran. All of them were leaders of the Israelites. ⁴These are their names:

from the tribe of Reuben,
  Shammua son of Zakkur;
⁵from the tribe of Simeon,
  Shaphat son of Hori;
⁶from the tribe of Judah, Caleb
  son of Jephunneh;
⁷from the tribe of Issachar,
  Igal son of Joseph;
⁸from the tribe of Ephraim,
  Hoshea son of Nun;
⁹from the tribe of Benjamin,
  Palti son of Raphu;
¹⁰from the tribe of Zebulun,
  Gaddiel son of Sodi;
¹¹from the tribe of Manasseh (a
  tribe of Joseph), Gaddi son
  of Susi;
¹²from the tribe of Dan, Ammiel son of Gemalli;

ᵃ 10 The Hebrew for *leprous* was used for various diseases affecting the skin.

13from the tribe of Asher, Sethur son of Michael;

14from the tribe of Naphtali, Nahbi son of Vophsi;

15from the tribe of Gad, Geuel son of Maki.

16These are the names of the men Moses sent to explore the land. (Moses gave Hoshea son of Nun the name Joshua.)

17When Moses sent them to explore Canaan, he said, "Go up through the Negev and on into the hill country. 18See what the land is like and whether the people who live there are strong or weak, few or many. 19What kind of land do they live in? Is it good or bad? What kind of towns do they live in? Are they unwalled or fortified? 20How is the soil? Is it fertile or poor? Are there trees in it or not? Do your best to bring back some of the fruit of the land." (It was the season for the first ripe grapes.)

21So they went up and explored the land from the Desert of Zin as far as Rehob, toward Lebo Hamath. 22They went up through the Negev and came to Hebron, where Ahiman, Sheshai and Talmai, the descendants of Anak, lived. (Hebron had been built seven years before Zoan in Egypt.) 23When they reached the Valley of Eshkol,ᵃ they cut off a branch bearing a single cluster of grapes. Two of them carried it on a pole between them, along with some pomegranates and figs. 24That place was called the Valley of Eshkol because of the cluster of grapes the Israelites cut off there. 25At the end of forty days they returned from exploring the land.

Report on the Exploration

26They came back to Moses and Aaron and the whole Israelite community at Kadesh in the Desert of Paran. There they reported to them and to the whole assembly and showed them the fruit of the land. 27They gave Moses this account: "We went into the land to which you sent us, and it does flow with milk and honey! Here is its fruit. 28But the people who live there are powerful, and the cities are fortified and very large. We even saw descendants of Anak there. 29The Amalekites live in the Negev; the Hittites, Jebusites and Amorites live in the hill country; and the Canaanites live near the sea and along the Jordan."

30Then Caleb silenced the people before Moses and said, "We should go up and take possession of the land, for we can certainly do it."

31But the men who had gone up with him said, "We can't attack those people; they are stronger than we are." 32And they spread among the Israelites a bad report about the land they had ex-

ᵃ 23 *Eshkol* means *cluster*; also in verse 24.

plored. They said, "The land we explored devours those living in it. All the people we saw there are of great size. ³³We saw the Nephilim there (the descendants of Anak come from the Nephilim). We seemed like grasshoppers in our own eyes, and we looked the same to them."

The People Rebel

14 That night all the members of the community raised their voices and wept aloud. ²All the Israelites grumbled against Moses and Aaron, and the whole assembly said to them, "If only we had died in Egypt! Or in this wilderness! ³Why is the LORD bringing us to this land only to let us fall by the sword? Our wives and children will be taken as plunder. Wouldn't it be better for us to go back to Egypt?" ⁴And they said to each other, "We should choose a leader and go back to Egypt."

⁵Then Moses and Aaron fell facedown in front of the whole Israelite assembly gathered there. ⁶Joshua son of Nun and Caleb son of Jephunneh, who were among those who had explored the land, tore their clothes ⁷and said to the entire Israelite assembly, "The land we passed through and explored is exceedingly good. ⁸If the LORD is pleased with us, he will lead us into that land, a land flowing with milk and honey, and will give it to us. ⁹Only do not rebel against the LORD. And do not be afraid of the people of the land, because we will devour them. Their protection is gone, but the LORD is with us. Do not be afraid of them."

¹⁰But the whole assembly talked about stoning them. Then the glory of the LORD appeared at the tent of meeting to all the Israelites. ¹¹The LORD said to Moses, "How long will these people treat me with contempt? How long will they refuse to believe in me, in spite of all the signs I have performed among them? ¹²I will strike them down with a plague and destroy them, but I will make you into a nation greater and stronger than they."

¹³Moses said to the LORD, "Then the Egyptians will hear about it! By your power you brought these people up from among them. ¹⁴And they will tell the inhabitants of this land about it. They have already heard that you, LORD, are with these people and that you, LORD, have been seen face to face, that your cloud stays over them, and that you go before them in a pillar of cloud by day and a pillar of fire by night. ¹⁵If you put all these people to death, leaving none alive, the nations who have heard this report about you will say, ¹⁶'The LORD was not able to bring these people into the land he promised them on oath, so he slaughtered them in the wilderness.'

¹⁷"Now may the Lord's strength be displayed, just as you have declared: ¹⁸'The LORD is slow to anger, abounding in love and forgiving sin and rebellion. Yet he does not leave the guilty unpunished; he punishes the children for the sin of the parents to the third and fourth generation.' ¹⁹In accordance with your great love, forgive the sin of these people, just as you have pardoned them from the time they left Egypt until now."

²⁰The LORD replied, "I have forgiven them, as you asked. ²¹Nevertheless, as surely as I live and as surely as the glory of the LORD fills the whole earth, ²²not one of those who saw my glory and the signs I performed in Egypt and in the wilderness but who disobeyed me and tested me ten times— ²³not one of them will ever see the land I promised on oath to their ancestors. No one who has treated me with contempt will ever see it. ²⁴But because my servant Caleb has a different spirit and follows me wholeheartedly, I will bring him into the land he went to, and his descendants will inherit it. ²⁵Since the Amalekites and the Canaanites are living in the valleys, turn back tomorrow and set out toward the desert along the route to the Red Sea.ᵃ"

²⁶The LORD said to Moses and Aaron: ²⁷"How long will this wicked community grumble against me? I have heard the complaints of these grumbling Israelites. ²⁸So tell them, 'As surely as I live, declares the LORD, I will do to you the very thing I heard you say: ²⁹In this wilderness your bodies will fall—every one of you twenty years old or more who was counted in the census and who has grumbled against me. ³⁰Not one of you will enter the land I swore with uplifted hand to make your home, except Caleb son of Jephunneh and Joshua son of Nun. ³¹As for your children that you said would be taken as plunder, I will bring them in to enjoy the land you have rejected. ³²But as for you, your bodies will fall in this wilderness. ³³Your children will be shepherds here for forty years, suffering for your unfaithfulness, until the last of your bodies lies in the wilderness. ³⁴For forty years—one year for each of the forty days you explored the land—you will suffer for your sins and know what it is like to have me against you.' ³⁵I, the LORD, have spoken, and I will surely do these things to this whole wicked community, which has banded together against me. They will meet their end in this wilderness; here they will die."

³⁶So the men Moses had sent to explore the land, who returned and made the whole community grumble against him by

ᵃ 25 Or *the Sea of Reeds*

spreading a bad report about it— ³⁷ these men who were responsible for spreading the bad report about the land were struck down and died of a plague before the LORD. ³⁸ Of the men who went to explore the land, only Joshua son of Nun and Caleb son of Jephunneh survived.

³⁹ When Moses reported this to all the Israelites, they mourned bitterly. ⁴⁰ Early the next morning they set out for the highest point in the hill country, saying, "Now we are ready to go up to the land the LORD promised. Surely we have sinned!"

⁴¹ But Moses said, "Why are you disobeying the LORD's command? This will not succeed! ⁴² Do not go up, because the LORD is not with you. You will be defeated by your enemies, ⁴³ for the Amalekites and the Canaanites will face you there. Because you have turned away from the LORD, he will not be with you and you will fall by the sword."

⁴⁴ Nevertheless, in their presumption they went up toward the highest point in the hill country, though neither Moses nor the ark of the LORD's covenant moved from the camp. ⁴⁵ Then the Amalekites and the Canaanites who lived in that hill country came down and attacked them and beat them down all the way to Hormah.

Supplementary Offerings

15 The LORD said to Moses, ² Speak to the Israelites and say to them: 'After you enter the land I am giving you as a home ³ and you present to the LORD food offerings from the herd or the flock, as an aroma pleasing to the LORD—whether burnt offerings or sacrifices, for special vows or freewill offerings or festival offerings— ⁴ then the person who brings an offering shall present to the LORD a grain offering of a tenth of an ephah*a* of the finest flour mixed with a quarter of a hin*b* of olive oil. ⁵ With each lamb for the burnt offering or the sacrifice, prepare a quarter of a hin of wine as a drink offering.

⁶ " 'With a ram prepare a grain offering of two-tenths of an ephah*c* of the finest flour mixed with a third of a hin*d* of olive oil, ⁷ and a third of a hin of wine as a drink offering. Offer it as an aroma pleasing to the LORD.

⁸ " 'When you prepare a young bull as a burnt offering or sacrifice, for a special vow or a fellowship offering to the LORD, ⁹ bring with the bull a grain offering of three-tenths of an ephah*e* of the

---

a 4 That is, probably about 3 1/2 pounds or about 1.6 kilograms   *b* 4 That is, about 1 quart or about 1 liter; also in verse 5   *c* 6 That is, probably about 7 pounds or about 3.2 kilograms   *d* 6 That is, about 1 1/3 quarts or about 1.3 liters; also in verse 7   *e* 9 That is, probably about 11 pounds or about 5 kilograms finest flour mixed with half a hin*ᵃ* of olive oil, ¹⁰and also bring half a hin of wine as a drink offering. This will be a food offering, an aroma pleasing to the LORD. ¹¹Each bull or ram, each lamb or young goat, is to be prepared in this manner. ¹²Do this for each one, for as many as you prepare.

¹³"'Everyone who is native-born must do these things in this way when they present a food offering as an aroma pleasing to the LORD. ¹⁴For the generations to come, whenever a foreigner or anyone else living among you presents a food offering as an aroma pleasing to the LORD, they must do exactly as you do. ¹⁵The community is to have the same rules for you and for the foreigner residing among you; this is a lasting ordinance for the generations to come. You and the foreigner shall be the same before the LORD: ¹⁶The same laws and regulations will apply both to you and to the foreigner residing among you.'"

¹⁷The LORD said to Moses, ¹⁸"Speak to the Israelites and say to them: 'When you enter the land to which I am taking you ¹⁹and you eat the food of the land, present a portion as an offering to the LORD. ²⁰Present a loaf from the first of your ground meal and present it as an offering from the threshing floor. ²¹Throughout the generations to come you are to give this offering to the LORD from the first of your ground meal.

Offerings for Unintentional Sins

²²"'Now if you as a community unintentionally fail to keep any of these commands the LORD gave Moses — ²³any of the LORD's commands to you through him, from the day the LORD gave them and continuing through the generations to come — ²⁴and if this is done unintentionally without the community being aware of it, then the whole community is to offer a young bull for a burnt offering as an aroma pleasing to the LORD, along with its prescribed grain offering and drink offering, and a male goat for a sin offering.*ᵇ* ²⁵The priest is to make atonement for the whole Israelite community, and they will be forgiven, for it was not intentional and they have presented to the LORD for their wrong a food offering and a sin offering. ²⁶The whole Israelite community and the foreigners residing among them will be forgiven, because all the people were involved in the unintentional wrong.

²⁷"'But if just one person sins unintentionally, that person must bring a year-old female goat for a sin offering. ²⁸The priest is to make atonement before the LORD for the one who erred by sinning

---

ᵃ 9 That is, about 2 quarts or about 1.9 liters; also in verse 10   *ᵇ 24* Or *purification offering*; also in verses 25 and 27 unintentionally, and when atonement has been made, that person will be forgiven. [29] One and the same law applies to everyone who sins unintentionally, whether a native-born Israelite or a foreigner residing among you.

[30] " 'But anyone who sins defiantly, whether native-born or foreigner, blasphemes the LORD and must be cut off from the people of Israel. [31] Because they have despised the LORD's word and broken his commands, they must surely be cut off; their guilt remains on them.' "

The Sabbath-Breaker Put to Death

[32] While the Israelites were in the wilderness, a man was found gathering wood on the Sabbath day. [33] Those who found him gathering wood brought him to Moses and Aaron and the whole assembly, [34] and they kept him in custody, because it was not clear what should be done to him. [35] Then the LORD said to Moses, "The man must die. The whole assembly must stone him outside the camp." [36] So the assembly took him outside the camp and stoned him to death, as the LORD commanded Moses.

Tassels on Garments

[37] The LORD said to Moses, [38] "Speak to the Israelites and say to them: 'Throughout the generations to come you are to make tassels on the corners of your garments, with a blue cord on each tassel. [39] You will have these tassels to look at and so you will remember all the commands of the LORD, that you may obey them and not prostitute yourselves by chasing after the lusts of your own hearts and eyes. [40] Then you will remember to obey all my commands and will be consecrated to your God. [41] I am the LORD your God, who brought you out of Egypt to be your God. I am the LORD your God.' "

Korah, Dathan and Abiram

16 Korah son of Izhar, the son of Kohath, the son of Levi, and certain Reubenites—Dathan and Abiram, sons of Eliab, and On son of Peleth— became insolent[a] [2] and rose up against Moses. With them were 250 Israelite men, well-known community leaders who had been appointed members of the council. [3] They came as a group to oppose Moses and Aaron and said to them, "You have gone too far! The whole community is holy, every one of them, and the LORD is with them. Why then do you set yourselves above the LORD's assembly?"

[4] When Moses heard this, he fell facedown. [5] Then he said to Korah and all his followers: "In the morning the LORD will show who

---

[a] 1 Or *Peleth* —*took men*

belongs to him and who is holy, and he will have that person come near him. The man he chooses he will cause to come near him. **6** You, Korah, and all your followers are to do this: Take censers **7** and tomorrow put burning coals and incense in them before the LORD. The man the LORD chooses will be the one who is holy. You Levites have gone too far!"

8 Moses also said to Korah, "Now listen, you Levites! **9** Isn't it enough for you that the God of Israel has separated you from the rest of the Israelite community and brought you near himself to do the work at the LORD's tabernacle and to stand before the community and minister to them? **10** He has brought you and all your fellow Levites near himself, but now you are trying to get the priesthood too. **11** It is against the LORD that you and all your followers have banded together. Who is Aaron that you should grumble against him?"

12 Then Moses summoned Dathan and Abiram, the sons of Eliab. But they said, "We will not come! **13** Isn't it enough that you have brought us up out of a land flowing with milk and honey to kill us in the wilderness? And now you also want to lord it over us! **14** Moreover, you haven't brought us into a land flowing with milk and honey or given us an inheritance of fields and vineyards. Do

you want to treat these men like slaves*a*? No, we will not come!"

15 Then Moses became very angry and said to the LORD, "Do not accept their offering. I have not taken so much as a donkey from them, nor have I wronged any of them."

16 Moses said to Korah, "You and all your followers are to appear before the LORD tomorrow—you and they and Aaron. **17** Each man is to take his censer and put incense in it—250 censers in all—and present it before the LORD. You and Aaron are to present your censers also." **18** So each of them took his censer, put burning coals and incense in it, and stood with Moses and Aaron at the entrance to the tent of meeting. **19** When Korah had gathered all his followers in opposition to them at the entrance to the tent of meeting, the glory of the LORD appeared to the entire assembly. **20** The LORD said to Moses and Aaron, **21** "Separate yourselves from this assembly so I can put an end to them at once."

22 But Moses and Aaron fell facedown and cried out, "O God, the God who gives breath to all living things, will you be angry with the entire assembly when only one man sins?"

23 Then the LORD said to Moses, **24** "Say to the assembly, 'Move away from the tents of Korah, Dathan and Abiram.'"

---

a 14 Or *to deceive these men*; Hebrew *Will you gouge out the eyes of these men*

25Moses got up and went to Dathan and Abiram, and the elders of Israel followed him. **26**He warned the assembly, "Move back from the tents of these wicked men! Do not touch anything belonging to them, or you will be swept away because of all their sins." **27**So they moved away from the tents of Korah, Dathan and Abiram. Dathan and Abiram had come out and were standing with their wives, children and little ones at the entrances to their tents.

28Then Moses said, "This is how you will know that the LORD has sent me to do all these things and that it was not my idea: **29**If these men die a natural death and suffer the fate of all mankind, then the LORD has not sent me. **30**But if the LORD brings about something totally new, and the earth opens its mouth and swallows them, with everything that belongs to them, and they go down alive into the realm of the dead, then you will know that these men have treated the LORD with contempt."

31As soon as he finished saying all this, the ground under them split apart **32**and the earth opened its mouth and swallowed them and their households, and all those associated with Korah, together with their possessions. **33**They went down alive into the realm of the dead, with everything they owned; the earth closed over them, and they perished and were gone from the community. **34**At their cries, all the Israelites around them fled, shouting, "The earth is going to swallow us too!"

35And fire came out from the LORD and consumed the 250 men who were offering the incense.

36The LORD said to Moses, **37**"Tell Eleazar son of Aaron, the priest, to remove the censers from the charred remains and scatter the coals some distance away, for the censers are holy— **38**the censers of the men who sinned at the cost of their lives. Hammer the censers into sheets to overlay the altar, for they were presented before the LORD and have become holy. Let them be a sign to the Israelites."

39So Eleazar the priest collected the bronze censers brought by those who had been burned to death, and he had them hammered out to overlay the altar, **40**as the LORD directed him through Moses. This was to remind the Israelites that no one except a descendant of Aaron should come to burn incense before the LORD, or he would become like Korah and his followers.

41The next day the whole Israelite community grumbled against Moses and Aaron. "You have killed the LORD's people," they said.

42But when the assembly gathered in opposition to Moses and

Aaron and turned toward the tent of meeting, suddenly the cloud covered it and the glory of the LORD appeared. ⁴³Then Moses and Aaron went to the front of the tent of meeting, ⁴⁴and the LORD said to Moses, ⁴⁵"Get away from this assembly so I can put an end to them at once." And they fell facedown.

⁴⁶Then Moses said to Aaron, "Take your censer and put incense in it, along with burning coals from the altar, and hurry to the assembly to make atonement for them. Wrath has come out from the LORD; the plague has started." ⁴⁷So Aaron did as Moses said, and ran into the midst of the assembly. The plague had already started among the people, but Aaron offered the incense and made atonement for them. ⁴⁸He stood between the living and the dead, and the plague stopped. ⁴⁹But 14,700 people died from the plague, in addition to those who had died because of Korah. ⁵⁰Then Aaron returned to Moses at the entrance to the tent of meeting, for the plague had stopped.[a]

The Budding of Aaron's Staff

17[b] The LORD said to Moses, ²"Speak to the Israelites and get twelve staffs from them, one from the leader of each of their ancestral tribes. Write the name of each man on his staff. ³On the staff of Levi write Aaron's name, for there must be one staff for the head of each ancestral tribe. ⁴Place them in the tent of meeting in front of the ark of the covenant law, where I meet with you. ⁵The staff belonging to the man I choose will sprout, and I will rid myself of this constant grumbling against you by the Israelites."

⁶So Moses spoke to the Israelites, and their leaders gave him twelve staffs, one for the leader of each of their ancestral tribes, and Aaron's staff was among them. ⁷Moses placed the staffs before the LORD in the tent of the covenant law.

⁸The next day Moses entered the tent and saw that Aaron's staff, which represented the tribe of Levi, had not only sprouted but had budded, blossomed and produced almonds. ⁹Then Moses brought out all the staffs from the LORD's presence to all the Israelites. They looked at them, and each of the leaders took his own staff. ¹⁰The LORD said to Moses, "Put back Aaron's staff in front of the ark of the covenant law, to be kept as a sign to the rebellious. This will put an end to their grumbling against me, so that they will not die." ¹¹Moses did just as the LORD commanded him.

---

[a] 50 In Hebrew texts 16:36-50 is numbered 17:1-15.   [b] In Hebrew texts 17:1-13 is numbered 17:16-28.

¹²The Israelites said to Moses, "We will die! We are lost, we are all lost! ¹³Anyone who even comes near the tabernacle of the LORD will die. Are we all going to die?"

Duties of Priests and Levites

18 The LORD said to Aaron, "You, your sons and your family are to bear the responsibility for offenses connected with the sanctuary, and you and your sons alone are to bear the responsibility for offenses connected with the priesthood. ²Bring your fellow Levites from your ancestral tribe to join you and assist you when you and your sons minister before the tent of the covenant law. ³They are to be responsible to you and are to perform all the duties of the tent, but they must not go near the furnishings of the sanctuary or the altar. Otherwise both they and you will die. ⁴They are to join you and be responsible for the care of the tent of meeting—all the work at the tent—and no one else may come near where you are.

⁵"You are to be responsible for the care of the sanctuary and the altar, so that my wrath will not fall on the Israelites again. ⁶I myself have selected your fellow Levites from among the Israelites as a gift to you, dedicated to the LORD to do the work at the tent of meeting. ⁷But only you and your sons may serve as priests in connection with everything at the altar and inside the curtain. I am giving you the service of the priesthood as a gift. Anyone else who comes near the sanctuary is to be put to death."

Offerings for Priests and Levites

⁸Then the LORD said to Aaron, "I myself have put you in charge of the offerings presented to me; all the holy offerings the Israelites give me I give to you and your sons as your portion, your perpetual share. ⁹You are to have the part of the most holy offerings that is kept from the fire. From all the gifts they bring me as most holy offerings, whether grain or sinᵃ or guilt offerings, that part belongs to you and your sons. ¹⁰Eat it as something most holy; every male shall eat it. You must regard it as holy.

¹¹"This also is yours: whatever is set aside from the gifts of all the wave offerings of the Israelites. I give this to you and your sons and daughters as your perpetual share. Everyone in your household who is ceremonially clean may eat it.

¹²"I give you all the finest olive oil and all the finest new wine and grain they give the LORD as the firstfruits of their harvest. ¹³All the land's firstfruits that they bring to the LORD will be yours. Everyone in your

ᵃ 9 Or *purification*

household who is ceremonially clean may eat it.

¹⁴"Everything in Israel that is devoted*ᵃ* to the LORD is yours. ¹⁵The first offspring of every womb, both human and animal, that is offered to the LORD is yours. But you must redeem every firstborn son and every firstborn male of unclean animals. ¹⁶When they are a month old, you must redeem them at the redemption price set at five shekels*ᵇ* of silver, according to the sanctuary shekel, which weighs twenty gerahs.

¹⁷"But you must not redeem the firstborn of a cow, a sheep or a goat; they are holy. Splash their blood against the altar and burn their fat as a food offering, an aroma pleasing to the LORD. ¹⁸Their meat is to be yours, just as the breast of the wave offering and the right thigh are yours. ¹⁹Whatever is set aside from the holy offerings the Israelites present to the LORD I give to you and your sons and daughters as your perpetual share. It is an everlasting covenant of salt before the LORD for both you and your offspring."

²⁰The LORD said to Aaron, "You will have no inheritance in their land, nor will you have any share among them; I am your share and your inheritance among the Israelites.

²¹"I give to the Levites all the tithes in Israel as their inheritance in return for the work they do while serving at the tent of meeting. ²²From now on the Israelites must not go near the tent of meeting, or they will bear the consequences of their sin and will die. ²³It is the Levites who are to do the work at the tent of meeting and bear the responsibility for any offenses they commit against it. This is a lasting ordinance for the generations to come. They will receive no inheritance among the Israelites. ²⁴Instead, I give to the Levites as their inheritance the tithes that the Israelites present as an offering to the LORD. That is why I said concerning them: 'They will have no inheritance among the Israelites.'"

²⁵The LORD said to Moses, ²⁶"Speak to the Levites and say to them: 'When you receive from the Israelites the tithe I give you as your inheritance, you must present a tenth of that tithe as the LORD's offering. ²⁷Your offering will be reckoned to you as grain from the threshing floor or juice from the winepress. ²⁸In this way you also will present an offering to the LORD from all the tithes you receive from the Israelites. From these tithes you must give the LORD's portion to Aaron the priest. ²⁹You must present as the LORD's portion the best and

---

ᵃ 14 The Hebrew term refers to the irrevocable giving over of things or persons to the LORD.   *ᵇ 16* That is, about 2 ounces or about 58 grams holiest part of everything given to you.'

³⁰ "Say to the Levites: 'When you present the best part, it will be reckoned to you as the product of the threshing floor or the winepress. ³¹ You and your households may eat the rest of it anywhere, for it is your wages for your work at the tent of meeting. ³² By presenting the best part of it you will not be guilty in this matter; then you will not defile the holy offerings of the Israelites, and you will not die.' "

The Water of Cleansing

19 The LORD said to Moses and Aaron: ² "This is a requirement of the law that the LORD has commanded: Tell the Israelites to bring you a red heifer without defect or blemish and that has never been under a yoke. ³ Give it to Eleazar the priest; it is to be taken outside the camp and slaughtered in his presence. ⁴ Then Eleazar the priest is to take some of its blood on his finger and sprinkle it seven times toward the front of the tent of meeting. ⁵ While he watches, the heifer is to be burned — its hide, flesh, blood and intestines. ⁶ The priest is to take some cedar wood, hyssop and scarlet wool and throw them onto the burning heifer. ⁷ After that, the priest must wash his clothes and bathe himself with water. He may then come into the camp, but he will be cer-

emonially unclean till evening. ⁸ The man who burns it must also wash his clothes and bathe with water, and he too will be unclean till evening.

⁹ "A man who is clean shall gather up the ashes of the heifer and put them in a ceremonially clean place outside the camp. They are to be kept by the Israelite community for use in the water of cleansing; it is for purification from sin. ¹⁰ The man who gathers up the ashes of the heifer must also wash his clothes, and he too will be unclean till evening. This will be a lasting ordinance both for the Israelites and for the foreigners residing among them.

¹¹ "Whoever touches a human corpse will be unclean for seven days. ¹² They must purify themselves with the water on the third day and on the seventh day; then they will be clean. But if they do not purify themselves on the third and seventh days, they will not be clean. ¹³ If they fail to purify themselves after touching a human corpse, they defile the LORD's tabernacle. They must be cut off from Israel. Because the water of cleansing has not been sprinkled on them, they are unclean; their uncleanness remains on them.

¹⁴ "This is the law that applies when a person dies in a tent: Anyone who enters the tent and anyone who is in it will be unclean

for seven days, ¹⁵ and every open container without a lid fastened on it will be unclean.

¹⁶ "Anyone out in the open who touches someone who has been killed with a sword or someone who has died a natural death, or anyone who touches a human bone or a grave, will be unclean for seven days.

¹⁷ "For the unclean person, put some ashes from the burned purification offering into a jar and pour fresh water over them. ¹⁸ Then a man who is ceremonially clean is to take some hyssop, dip it in the water and sprinkle the tent and all the furnishings and the people who were there. He must also sprinkle anyone who has touched a human bone or a grave or anyone who has been killed or anyone who has died a natural death. ¹⁹ The man who is clean is to sprinkle those who are unclean on the third and seventh days, and on the seventh day he is to purify them. Those who are being cleansed must wash their clothes and bathe with water, and that evening they will be clean. ²⁰ But if those who are unclean do not purify themselves, they must be cut off from the community, because they have defiled the sanctuary of the LORD. The water of cleansing has not been sprinkled on them, and they are unclean. ²¹ This is a lasting ordinance for them.

"The man who sprinkles the water of cleansing must also wash his clothes, and anyone who touches the water of cleansing will be unclean till evening. ²² Anything that an unclean person touches becomes unclean, and anyone who touches it becomes unclean till evening."

Water From the Rock

20 In the first month the whole Israelite community arrived at the Desert of Zin, and they stayed at Kadesh. There Miriam died and was buried.

² Now there was no water for the community, and the people gathered in opposition to Moses and Aaron. ³ They quarreled with Moses and said, "If only we had died when our brothers fell dead before the LORD! ⁴ Why did you bring the LORD's community into this wilderness, that we and our livestock should die here? ⁵ Why did you bring us up out of Egypt to this terrible place? It has no grain or figs, grapevines or pomegranates. And there is no water to drink!"

⁶ Moses and Aaron went from the assembly to the entrance to the tent of meeting and fell facedown, and the glory of the LORD appeared to them. ⁷ The LORD said to Moses, ⁸ "Take the staff, and you and your brother Aaron gather the assembly together. Speak to that rock before their eyes and it will pour out its water. You will bring water out of the rock for the community so they and their livestock can drink."

⁹So Moses took the staff from the LORD's presence, just as he commanded him. ¹⁰He and Aaron gathered the assembly together in front of the rock and Moses said to them, "Listen, you rebels, must we bring you water out of this rock?" ¹¹Then Moses raised his arm and struck the rock twice with his staff. Water gushed out, and the community and their livestock drank.

¹²But the LORD said to Moses and Aaron, "Because you did not trust in me enough to honor me as holy in the sight of the Israelites, you will not bring this community into the land I give them."

¹³These were the waters of Meribah,ᵃ where the Israelites quarreled with the LORD and where he was proved holy among them.

Edom Denies Israel Passage

¹⁴Moses sent messengers from Kadesh to the king of Edom, saying:

"This is what your brother Israel says: You know about all the hardships that have come on us. ¹⁵Our ancestors went down into Egypt, and we lived there many years. The Egyptians mistreated us and our ancestors, ¹⁶but when we cried out to the LORD, he heard our cry and sent an angel and brought us out of Egypt.

"Now we are here at Kadesh, a town on the edge of your territory. ¹⁷Please let us pass through your country. We will not go through any field or vineyard, or drink water from any well. We will travel along the King's Highway and not turn to the right or to the left until we have passed through your territory."

¹⁸But Edom answered:

"You may not pass through here; if you try, we will march out and attack you with the sword."

¹⁹The Israelites replied:

"We will go along the main road, and if we or our livestock drink any of your water, we will pay for it. We only want to pass through on foot — nothing else."

²⁰Again they answered:

"You may not pass through."

Then Edom came out against them with a large and powerful army. ²¹Since Edom refused to let them go through their territory, Israel turned away from them.

The Death of Aaron

²²The whole Israelite community set out from Kadesh and came to Mount Hor. ²³At Mount Hor, near the border of Edom, the LORD said to Moses and Aaron, ²⁴"Aaron will be gathered to his people. He will not enter the

ᵃ 13 *Meribah* means *quarreling*.

land I give the Israelites, because both of you rebelled against my command at the waters of Meribah. ²⁵Get Aaron and his son Eleazar and take them up Mount Hor. ²⁶Remove Aaron's garments and put them on his son Eleazar, for Aaron will be gathered to his people; he will die there."

²⁷Moses did as the LORD commanded: They went up Mount Hor in the sight of the whole community. ²⁸Moses removed Aaron's garments and put them on his son Eleazar. And Aaron died there on top of the mountain. Then Moses and Eleazar came down from the mountain, ²⁹and when the whole community learned that Aaron had died, all the Israelites mourned for him thirty days.

Arad Destroyed

21 When the Canaanite king of Arad, who lived in the Negev, heard that Israel was coming along the road to Atharim, he attacked the Israelites and captured some of them. ²Then Israel made this vow to the LORD: "If you will deliver these people into our hands, we will totally destroy[a] their cities." ³The LORD listened to Israel's plea and gave the Canaanites over to them. They completely destroyed them and their towns; so the place was named Hormah.[b]

The Bronze Snake

⁴They traveled from Mount Hor along the route to the Red Sea,[c] to go around Edom. But the people grew impatient on the way; ⁵they spoke against God and against Moses, and said, "Why have you brought us up out of Egypt to die in the wilderness? There is no bread! There is no water! And we detest this miserable food!"

⁶Then the LORD sent venomous snakes among them; they bit the people and many Israelites died. ⁷The people came to Moses and said, "We sinned when we spoke against the LORD and against you. Pray that the LORD will take the snakes away from us." So Moses prayed for the people.

⁸The LORD said to Moses, "Make a snake and put it up on a pole; anyone who is bitten can look at it and live." ⁹So Moses made a bronze snake and put it up on a pole. Then when anyone was bitten by a snake and looked at the bronze snake, they lived.

The Journey to Moab

¹⁰The Israelites moved on and camped at Oboth. ¹¹Then they set out from Oboth and camped in Iye Abarim, in the wilderness that faces Moab toward the sunrise. ¹²From there they moved on and camped in the Zered Valley. ¹³They set out from there and

---

^a 2 The Hebrew term refers to the irrevocable giving over of things or persons to the LORD, often by totally destroying them; also in verse 3.   ^b 3 *Hormah* means *destruction*.   ^c 4 Or *the Sea of Reeds*

camped alongside the Arnon, which is in the wilderness extending into Amorite territory. The Arnon is the border of Moab, between Moab and the Amorites. ¹⁴That is why the Book of the Wars of the LORD says:

> ". . . Zahab[a] in Suphah and the
>   ravines,
>   the Arnon ¹⁵and[b] the slopes
>   of the ravines
> that lead to the settlement
>   of Ar
>   and lie along the border of
>   Moab."

¹⁶From there they continued on to Beer, the well where the LORD said to Moses, "Gather the people together and I will give them water."

¹⁷Then Israel sang this song:

> "Spring up, O well!
>   Sing about it,
> ¹⁸about the well that the princes
>   dug,
>   that the nobles of the people
>   sank—
>   the nobles with scepters and
>   staffs."

Then they went from the wilderness to Mattanah, ¹⁹from Mattanah to Nahaliel, from Nahaliel to Bamoth, ²⁰and from Bamoth to the valley in Moab where the top of Pisgah overlooks the wasteland.

Defeat of Sihon and Og

²¹Israel sent messengers to say to Sihon king of the Amorites:

²²"Let us pass through your country. We will not turn aside into any field or vineyard, or drink water from any well. We will travel along the King's Highway until we have passed through your territory."

²³But Sihon would not let Israel pass through his territory. He mustered his entire army and marched out into the wilderness against Israel. When he reached Jahaz, he fought with Israel. ²⁴Israel, however, put him to the sword and took over his land from the Arnon to the Jabbok, but only as far as the Ammonites, because their border was fortified. ²⁵Israel captured all the cities of the Amorites and occupied them, including Heshbon and all its surrounding settlements. ²⁶Heshbon was the city of Sihon king of the Amorites, who had fought against the former king of Moab and had taken from him all his land as far as the Arnon.

²⁷That is why the poets say:

> "Come to Heshbon and let it be
>   rebuilt;
>   let Sihon's city be restored.

> ²⁸"Fire went out from
>   Heshbon,
>   a blaze from the city of
>   Sihon.
> It consumed Ar of Moab,
>   the citizens of Arnon's
>   heights.

---

[a] 14 Septuagint; Hebrew *Waheb*   [b] 14,15 Or *"I have been given from Suphah and the ravines / of the Arnon ¹⁵to*

²⁹Woe to you, Moab!
　　You are destroyed, people of
　　　Chemosh!
　　He has given up his sons as
　　　fugitives
　　and his daughters as
　　　captives
　　to Sihon king of the
　　　Amorites.
³⁰"But we have overthrown
　　them;
　　Heshbon's dominion has
　　　been destroyed all the
　　　way to Dibon.
　　We have demolished them as
　　　far as Nophah,
　　which extends to Medeba."

³¹So Israel settled in the land of the Amorites.

³²After Moses had sent spies to Jazer, the Israelites captured its surrounding settlements and drove out the Amorites who were there. ³³Then they turned and went up along the road toward Bashan, and Og king of Bashan and his whole army marched out to meet them in battle at Edrei.

³⁴The LORD said to Moses, "Do not be afraid of him, for I have delivered him into your hands, along with his whole army and his land. Do to him what you did to Sihon king of the Amorites, who reigned in Heshbon."

³⁵So they struck him down, together with his sons and his whole army, leaving them no survivors. And they took possession of his land.

Balak Summons Balaam

22 Then the Israelites traveled to the plains of Moab and camped along the Jordan across from Jericho.

²Now Balak son of Zippor saw all that Israel had done to the Amorites, ³and Moab was terrified because there were so many people. Indeed, Moab was filled with dread because of the Israelites.

⁴The Moabites said to the elders of Midian, "This horde is going to lick up everything around us, as an ox licks up the grass of the field."

So Balak son of Zippor, who was king of Moab at that time, ⁵sent messengers to summon Balaam son of Beor, who was at Pethor, near the Euphrates River, in his native land. Balak said:

　"A people has come out of Egypt; they cover the face of the land and have settled next to me. ⁶Now come and put a curse on these people, because they are too powerful for me. Perhaps then I will be able to defeat them and drive them out of the land. For I know that whoever you bless is blessed, and whoever you curse is cursed."

⁷The elders of Moab and Midian left, taking with them the fee for divination. When they came to Balaam, they told him what Balak had said.

8 "Spend the night here," Balaam said to them, "and I will report back to you with the answer the LORD gives me." So the Moabite officials stayed with him.

9 God came to Balaam and asked, "Who are these men with you?"

10 Balaam said to God, "Balak son of Zippor, king of Moab, sent me this message: 11 'A people that has come out of Egypt covers the face of the land. Now come and put a curse on them for me. Perhaps then I will be able to fight them and drive them away.' "

12 But God said to Balaam, "Do not go with them. You must not put a curse on those people, because they are blessed."

13 The next morning Balaam got up and said to Balak's officials, "Go back to your own country, for the LORD has refused to let me go with you."

14 So the Moabite officials returned to Balak and said, "Balaam refused to come with us."

15 Then Balak sent other officials, more numerous and more distinguished than the first. 16 They came to Balaam and said:

"This is what Balak son of Zippor says: Do not let anything keep you from coming to me, 17 because I will reward you handsomely and do whatever you say. Come and put a curse on these people for me."

18 But Balaam answered them, "Even if Balak gave me all the silver and gold in his palace, I could not do anything great or small to go beyond the command of the LORD my God. 19 Now spend the night here so that I can find out what else the LORD will tell me."

20 That night God came to Balaam and said, "Since these men have come to summon you, go with them, but do only what I tell you."

Balaam's Donkey

21 Balaam got up in the morning, saddled his donkey and went with the Moabite officials. 22 But God was very angry when he went, and the angel of the LORD stood in the road to oppose him. Balaam was riding on his donkey, and his two servants were with him. 23 When the donkey saw the angel of the LORD standing in the road with a drawn sword in his hand, it turned off the road into a field. Balaam beat it to get it back on the road.

24 Then the angel of the LORD stood in a narrow path through the vineyards, with walls on both sides. 25 When the donkey saw the angel of the LORD, it pressed close to the wall, crushing Balaam's foot against it. So he beat the donkey again.

26 Then the angel of the LORD moved on ahead and stood in a narrow place where there was no room to turn, either to the right or to the left. 27 When the donkey saw the angel of the LORD, it

lay down under Balaam, and he was angry and beat it with his staff. **28**Then the LORD opened the donkey's mouth, and it said to Balaam, "What have I done to you to make you beat me these three times?"

29Balaam answered the donkey, "You have made a fool of me! If only I had a sword in my hand, I would kill you right now."

30The donkey said to Balaam, "Am I not your own donkey, which you have always ridden, to this day? Have I been in the habit of doing this to you?"

"No," he said.

31Then the LORD opened Balaam's eyes, and he saw the angel of the LORD standing in the road with his sword drawn. So he bowed low and fell facedown.

32The angel of the LORD asked him, "Why have you beaten your donkey these three times? I have come here to oppose you because your path is a reckless one before me.*a* **33**The donkey saw me and turned away from me these three times. If it had not turned away, I would certainly have killed you by now, but I would have spared it."

34Balaam said to the angel of the LORD, "I have sinned. I did not realize you were standing in the road to oppose me. Now if you are displeased, I will go back."

35The angel of the LORD said to Balaam, "Go with the men, but speak only what I tell you." So Balaam went with Balak's officials.

36When Balak heard that Balaam was coming, he went out to meet him at the Moabite town on the Arnon border, at the edge of his territory. **37**Balak said to Balaam, "Did I not send you an urgent summons? Why didn't you come to me? Am I really not able to reward you?"

38"Well, I have come to you now," Balaam replied. "But I can't say whatever I please. I must speak only what God puts in my mouth."

39Then Balaam went with Balak to Kiriath Huzoth. **40**Balak sacrificed cattle and sheep, and gave some to Balaam and the officials who were with him. **41**The next morning Balak took Balaam up to Bamoth Baal, and from there he could see the outskirts of the Israelite camp.

Balaam's First Message

23 Balaam said, "Build me seven altars here, and prepare seven bulls and seven rams for me." **2**Balak did as Balaam said, and the two of them offered a bull and a ram on each altar.

3Then Balaam said to Balak, "Stay here beside your offering while I go aside. Perhaps the LORD will come to meet with me. Whatever he reveals to me I will tell you." Then he went off to a barren height.

---

a 32 The meaning of the Hebrew for this clause is uncertain.

Joseph and His Beautiful Robe

GENESIS 37:1–4

Baby Moses in a Basket

EXODUS 2:1–10

Ten Commandments
for Kids

1 You may not love anyone or anything more than you love God.

2 You may not worship or put more importance on any person or thing other than God. You must worship only the Lord, not a friend, not a movie star or sports hero, not a car or skateboard.

3 You may not swear. Use God's holy name in a loving way, never to express anger or frustration.

4 One day of your week should be set aside for resting and worshiping God.

5 Respect your parents. Love them, and the Lord will reward you in your life.

6 You may not hate other people; don't think of hurting someone else in any way.

7 Keep your thoughts and actions pure. Husbands and wives should share their special love only with each other.

8 Do not take anything that does not belong to you.

9 You may not tell lies, especially when that lie will hurt someone else.

10 Do not be jealous of what others have. You may not be jealous of your friend's new toy or clothes or the big house your neighbor lives in. Be satisfied with what you have.

BASED ON EXODUS 20:1–17 AND DEUTERONOMY 5:7–21

Moses Receives the Ten Commandments
EXODUS 24:12–18

⁴God met with him, and Balaam said, "I have prepared seven altars, and on each altar I have offered a bull and a ram."

⁵The LORD put a word in Balaam's mouth and said, "Go back to Balak and give him this word."

⁶So he went back to him and found him standing beside his offering, with all the Moabite officials. ⁷Then Balaam spoke his message:

"Balak brought me from Aram,
  the king of Moab from the
    eastern mountains.
'Come,' he said, 'curse Jacob
  for me;
  come, denounce Israel.'
⁸How can I curse
  those whom God has not
    cursed?
How can I denounce
  those whom the LORD has
    not denounced?
⁹From the rocky peaks I see
    them,
  from the heights I view
    them.
I see a people who live
    apart
  and do not consider
    themselves one of the
    nations.
¹⁰Who can count the dust of
    Jacob
  or number even a fourth of
    Israel?
Let me die the death of the
    righteous,
  and may my final end be like
    theirs!"

¹¹Balak said to Balaam, "What have you done to me? I brought you to curse my enemies, but you have done nothing but bless them!"

¹²He answered, "Must I not speak what the LORD puts in my mouth?"

Balaam's Second Message

¹³Then Balak said to him, "Come with me to another place where you can see them; you will not see them all but only the outskirts of their camp. And from there, curse them for me." ¹⁴So he took him to the field of Zophim on the top of Pisgah, and there he built seven altars and offered a bull and a ram on each altar.

¹⁵Balaam said to Balak, "Stay here beside your offering while I meet with him over there."

¹⁶The LORD met with Balaam and put a word in his mouth and said, "Go back to Balak and give him this word."

¹⁷So he went to him and found him standing beside his offering, with the Moabite officials. Balak asked him, "What did the LORD say?"

¹⁸Then he spoke his message:

"Arise, Balak, and listen;
  hear me, son of Zippor.
¹⁹God is not human, that he
    should lie,
  not a human being, that he
    should change his mind.

Does he speak and then not act?
Does he promise and not
fulfill?
²⁰I have received a command to
bless;
he has blessed, and I cannot
change it.

²¹"No misfortune is seen in Jacob,
no misery observed^a in
Israel.
The LORD their God is with
them;
the shout of the King is
among them.
²²God brought them out of
Egypt;
they have the strength of a
wild ox.
²³There is no divination against^b
Jacob,
no evil omens against^b
Israel.
It will now be said of Jacob
and of Israel, 'See what God
has done!'
²⁴The people rise like a lioness;
they rouse themselves like a
lion
that does not rest till it devours
its prey
and drinks the blood of its
victims."

²⁵Then Balak said to Balaam,
"Neither curse them at all nor
bless them at all!"
²⁶Balaam answered, "Did I not
tell you I must do whatever the
LORD says?"

Balaam's Third Message

²⁷Then Balak said to Balaam,
"Come, let me take you to another
place. Perhaps it will please God
to let you curse them for me from
there." ²⁸And Balak took Balaam
to the top of Peor, overlooking the
wasteland.

²⁹Balaam said, "Build me seven altars here, and prepare seven bulls and seven rams for me."
³⁰Balak did as Balaam had said,
and offered a bull and a ram on
each altar.

24 Now when Balaam saw
that it pleased the LORD
to bless Israel, he did not resort to
divination as at other times, but
turned his face toward the wilderness. ²When Balaam looked out
and saw Israel encamped tribe by
tribe, the Spirit of God came on
him ³and he spoke his message:

"The prophecy of Balaam son
of Beor,
the prophecy of one whose
eye sees clearly,
⁴the prophecy of one who hears
the words of God,
who sees a vision from the
Almighty,^c
who falls prostrate, and
whose eyes are opened:

⁵"How beautiful are your tents,
Jacob,
your dwelling places, Israel!

⁶"Like valleys they spread out,
like gardens beside a river,

---

^a 21 Or *He has not looked on Jacob's offenses / or on the wrongs found*   ^b 23 Or *in*
^c 4 Hebrew *Shaddai*; also in verse 16

like aloes planted by the LORD,
    like cedars beside the waters.
⁷Water will flow from their
    buckets;
  their seed will have
    abundant water.

"Their king will be greater
    than Agag;
  their kingdom will be
    exalted.

⁸"God brought them out of
    Egypt;
  they have the strength of a
    wild ox.
They devour hostile nations
  and break their bones in
    pieces;
  with their arrows they pierce
    them.
⁹Like a lion they crouch and lie
    down,
  like a lioness — who dares to
    rouse them?

"May those who bless you be
    blessed
  and those who curse you be
    cursed!"

¹⁰Then Balak's anger burned against Balaam. He struck his hands together and said to him, "I summoned you to curse my enemies, but you have blessed them these three times. ¹¹Now leave at once and go home! I said I would reward you handsomely, but the LORD has kept you from being rewarded."

¹²Balaam answered Balak, "Did I not tell the messengers you sent me, ¹³'Even if Balak gave me all the silver and gold in his palace, I could not do anything of my own accord, good or bad, to go beyond the command of the LORD — and I must say only what the LORD says'? ¹⁴Now I am going back to my people, but come, let me warn you of what this people will do to your people in days to come."

Balaam's Fourth Message

¹⁵Then he spoke his message:

"The prophecy of Balaam son
    of Beor,
  the prophecy of one whose
    eye sees clearly,
¹⁶the prophecy of one who hears
    the words of God,
  who has knowledge from the
    Most High,
who sees a vision from the
    Almighty,
  who falls prostrate, and
    whose eyes are opened:

¹⁷"I see him, but not now;
  I behold him, but not near.
A star will come out of Jacob;
  a scepter will rise out of
    Israel.
He will crush the foreheads of
    Moab,
  the skulls^a of^b all the people
    of Sheth.^c

---

^a 17 Samaritan Pentateuch (see also Jer. 48:45); the meaning of the word in the Masoretic Text is uncertain.   ^b 17 Or possibly *Moab, / batter*   ^c 17 Or *all the noisy boasters*

¹⁸Edom will be conquered;
　　Seir, his enemy, will be
　　　conquered,
　but Israel will grow strong.
¹⁹A ruler will come out of Jacob
　　and destroy the survivors of
　　　the city."

Balaam's Fifth Message

²⁰Then Balaam saw Amalek
and spoke his message:

"Amalek was first among the
　　nations,
　but their end will be utter
　　　destruction."

Balaam's Sixth Message

²¹Then he saw the Kenites and
spoke his message:

"Your dwelling place is secure,
　　your nest is set in a rock;
²²yet you Kenites will be
　　destroyed
　　when Ashur takes you
　　　captive."

Balaam's Seventh Message

²³Then he spoke his message:

"Alas! Who can live when God
　　does this?[a]
²⁴　Ships will come from the
　　　shores of Cyprus;
　they will subdue Ashur and
　　　Eber,
　　but they too will come to
　　　ruin."

²⁵Then Balaam got up and returned home, and Balak went his
own way.

Moab Seduces Israel

25 While Israel was stay-
ing in Shittim, the men
began to indulge in sexual immorality with Moabite women,
²who invited them to the sacrifices to their gods. The people ate
the sacrificial meal and bowed
down before these gods. ³So Israel yoked themselves to the Baal
of Peor. And the LORD's anger
burned against them.

⁴The LORD said to Moses, "Take
all the leaders of these people, kill
them and expose them in broad
daylight before the LORD, so that
the LORD's fierce anger may turn
away from Israel."

⁵So Moses said to Israel's judges, "Each of you must put to death
those of your people who have
yoked themselves to the Baal of
Peor."

⁶Then an Israelite man brought
into the camp a Midianite woman right before the eyes of Moses
and the whole assembly of Israel
while they were weeping at the
entrance to the tent of meeting.
⁷When Phinehas son of Eleazar,
the son of Aaron, the priest, saw
this, he left the assembly, took
a spear in his hand ⁸and followed the Israelite into the tent.
He drove the spear into both of
them, right through the Israelite

---

[a] 23 Masoretic Text; with a different word division of the Hebrew *The people from
the islands will gather from the north.*

man and into the woman's stomach. Then the plague against the Israelites was stopped; [9]but those who died in the plague numbered 24,000.

[10]The LORD said to Moses, [11]"Phinehas son of Eleazar, the son of Aaron, the priest, has turned my anger away from the Israelites. Since he was as zealous for my honor among them as I am, I did not put an end to them in my zeal. [12]Therefore tell him I am making my covenant of peace with him. [13]He and his descendants will have a covenant of a lasting priesthood, because he was zealous for the honor of his God and made atonement for the Israelites."

[14]The name of the Israelite who was killed with the Midianite woman was Zimri son of Salu, the leader of a Simeonite family. [15]And the name of the Midianite woman who was put to death was Kozbi daughter of Zur, a tribal chief of a Midianite family.

[16]The LORD said to Moses, [17]"Treat the Midianites as enemies and kill them. [18]They treated you as enemies when they deceived you in the Peor incident involving their sister Kozbi, the daughter of a Midianite leader, the woman who was killed when the plague came as a result of that incident."

The Second Census

26 After the plague the LORD said to Moses and Eleazar son of Aaron, the priest, [2]"Take a census of the whole Israelite community by families—all those twenty years old or more who are able to serve in the army of Israel." [3]So on the plains of Moab by the Jordan across from Jericho, Moses and Eleazar the priest spoke with them and said, [4]"Take a census of the men twenty years old or more, as the LORD commanded Moses."

These were the Israelites who came out of Egypt:

[5]The descendants of Reuben, the firstborn son of Israel, were:

through Hanok, the Hanokite clan;

through Pallu, the Palluite clan;

[6]through Hezron, the Hezronite clan;

through Karmi, the Karmite clan.

[7]These were the clans of Reuben; those numbered were 43,730.

[8]The son of Pallu was Eliab, [9]and the sons of Eliab were Nemuel, Dathan and Abiram. The same Dathan and Abiram were the community officials who rebelled against Moses and Aaron and were among Korah's followers when they rebelled against the LORD. [10]The earth opened its mouth and swallowed them along with Korah, whose followers died when the fire devoured the 250 men. And they served as a warning sign. [11]The line of Korah, however, did not die out.

[12]The descendants of Simeon by their clans were:

through Nemuel, the Nemuelite clan;

through Jamin, the Jaminite clan;

through Jakin, the Jakinite clan;

13 through Zerah, the Zerahite clan;

through Shaul, the Shaulite clan.

14 These were the clans of Simeon; those numbered were 22,200.

15 The descendants of Gad by their clans were:

through Zephon, the Zephonite clan;

through Haggi, the Haggite clan;

through Shuni, the Shunite clan;

16 through Ozni, the Oznite clan;

through Eri, the Erite clan;

17 through Arodi,^a the Arodite clan;

through Areli, the Arelite clan.

18 These were the clans of Gad; those numbered were 40,500.

19 Er and Onan were sons of Judah, but they died in Canaan.

20 The descendants of Judah by their clans were:

through Shelah, the Shelanite clan;

through Perez, the Perezite clan;

through Zerah, the Zerahite clan.

21 The descendants of Perez were:

through Hezron, the Hezronite clan;

through Hamul, the Hamulite clan.

22 These were the clans of Judah; those numbered were 76,500.

23 The descendants of Issachar by their clans were:

through Tola, the Tolaite clan;

through Puah, the Puite^b clan;

24 through Jashub, the Jashubite clan;

through Shimron, the Shimronite clan.

25 These were the clans of Issachar; those numbered were 64,300.

26 The descendants of Zebulun by their clans were:

through Sered, the Seredite clan;

through Elon, the Elonite clan;

through Jahleel, the Jahleelite clan.

27 These were the clans of Zebulun; those numbered were 60,500.

28 The descendants of Joseph by their clans through Manasseh and Ephraim were:

---

^a 17 Samaritan Pentateuch and Syriac (see also Gen. 46:16); Masoretic Text *Arod*
^b 23 Samaritan Pentateuch, Septuagint, Vulgate and Syriac (see also 1 Chron. 7:1); Masoretic Text *through Puvah, the Punite*

²⁹The descendants of Manasseh:

through Makir, the Makirite clan (Makir was the father of Gilead);

through Gilead, the Gileadite clan.

³⁰These were the descendants of Gilead:

through Iezer, the Iezerite clan;

through Helek, the Helekite clan;

³¹through Asriel, the Asrielite clan;

through Shechem, the Shechemite clan;

³²through Shemida, the Shemidaite clan;

through Hepher, the Hepherite clan.

³³(Zelophehad son of Hepher had no sons; he had only daughters, whose names were Mahlah, Noah, Hoglah, Milkah and Tirzah.)

³⁴These were the clans of Manasseh; those numbered were 52,700.

³⁵These were the descendants of Ephraim by their clans:

through Shuthelah, the Shuthelahite clan;

through Beker, the Bekerite clan;

through Tahan, the Tahanite clan.

³⁶These were the descendants of Shuthelah:

through Eran, the Eranite clan.

³⁷These were the clans of Ephraim; those numbered were 32,500.

These were the descendants of Joseph by their clans.

³⁸The descendants of Benjamin by their clans were:

through Bela, the Belaite clan;

through Ashbel, the Ashbelite clan;

through Ahiram, the Ahiramite clan;

³⁹through Shupham,^{*a*} the Shuphamite clan;

through Hupham, the Huphamite clan.

⁴⁰The descendants of Bela through Ard and Naaman were:

through Ard,^{*b*} the Ardite clan;

through Naaman, the Naamite clan.

⁴¹These were the clans of Benjamin; those numbered were 45,600.

⁴²These were the descendants of Dan by their clans:

through Shuham, the Shuhamite clan.

These were the clans of Dan:
⁴³All of them were Shuhamite clans; and those numbered were 64,400.

---

a 39 A few manuscripts of the Masoretic Text, Samaritan Pentateuch, Vulgate and Syriac (see also Septuagint); most manuscripts of the Masoretic Text *Shephupham*
b 40 Samaritan Pentateuch and Vulgate (see also Septuagint); Masoretic Text does not have *through Ard*.

44 The descendants of Asher by their clans were:

through Imnah, the Imnite clan;

through Ishvi, the Ishvite clan;

through Beriah, the Beriite clan;

45 and through the descendants of Beriah:

through Heber, the Heberite clan;

through Malkiel, the Malkielite clan.

46 (Asher had a daughter named Serah.)

47 These were the clans of Asher; those numbered were 53,400.

48 The descendants of Naphtali by their clans were:

through Jahzeel, the Jahzeelite clan;

through Guni, the Gunite clan;

49 through Jezer, the Jezerite clan;

through Shillem, the Shillemite clan.

50 These were the clans of Naphtali; those numbered were 45,400.

51 The total number of the men of Israel was 601,730.

52 The LORD said to Moses, **53** "The land is to be allotted to them as an inheritance based on the number of names. **54** To a larger group give a larger inheritance, and to a smaller group a smaller one; each is to receive its inheritance according to the number of those listed. **55** Be sure that the land is distributed by lot. What each group inherits will be according to the names for its ancestral tribe. **56** Each inheritance is to be distributed by lot among the larger and smaller groups."

57 These were the Levites who were counted by their clans:

through Gershon, the Gershonite clan;

through Kohath, the Kohathite clan;

through Merari, the Merarite clan.

58 These also were Levite clans:

the Libnite clan,

the Hebronite clan,

the Mahlite clan,

the Mushite clan,

the Korahite clan.

(Kohath was the forefather of Amram; **59** the name of Amram's wife was Jochebed, a descendant of Levi, who was born to the Levites[a] in Egypt. To Amram she bore Aaron, Moses and their sister Miriam. **60** Aaron was the father of Nadab and Abihu, Eleazar and Ithamar. **61** But Nadab and Abihu died when they made an offering before the LORD with unauthorized fire.)

62 All the male Levites a month old or more numbered 23,000. They were not counted along

---

a 59 Or *Jochebed, a daughter of Levi, who was born to Levi* with the other Israelites because they received no inheritance among them.

⁶³These are the ones counted by Moses and Eleazar the priest when they counted the Israelites on the plains of Moab by the Jordan across from Jericho. ⁶⁴Not one of them was among those counted by Moses and Aaron the priest when they counted the Israelites in the Desert of Sinai. ⁶⁵For the LORD had told those Israelites they would surely die in the wilderness, and not one of them was left except Caleb son of Jephunneh and Joshua son of Nun.

Zelophehad's Daughters

27 The daughters of Zelophehad son of Hepher, the son of Gilead, the son of Makir, the son of Manasseh, belonged to the clans of Manasseh son of Joseph. The names of the daughters were Mahlah, Noah, Hoglah, Milkah and Tirzah. They came forward ²and stood before Moses, Eleazar the priest, the leaders and the whole assembly at the entrance to the tent of meeting and said, ³"Our father died in the wilderness. He was not among Korah's followers, who banded together against the LORD, but he died for his own sin and left no sons. ⁴Why should our father's name disappear from his clan because he had no son? Give us property among our father's relatives."

⁵So Moses brought their case before the LORD, ⁶and the LORD said to him, ⁷"What Zelophehad's daughters are saying is right. You must certainly give them property as an inheritance among their father's relatives and give their father's inheritance to them.

⁸"Say to the Israelites, 'If a man dies and leaves no son, give his inheritance to his daughter. ⁹If he has no daughter, give his inheritance to his brothers. ¹⁰If he has no brothers, give his inheritance to his father's brothers. ¹¹If his father had no brothers, give his inheritance to the nearest relative in his clan, that he may possess it. This is to have the force of law for the Israelites, as the LORD commanded Moses.'"

Joshua to Succeed Moses

¹²Then the LORD said to Moses, "Go up this mountain in the Abarim Range and see the land I have given the Israelites. ¹³After you have seen it, you too will be gathered to your people, as your brother Aaron was, ¹⁴for when the community rebelled at the waters in the Desert of Zin, both of you disobeyed my command to honor me as holy before their eyes." (These were the waters of Meribah Kadesh, in the Desert of Zin.)

¹⁵Moses said to the LORD, ¹⁶"May the LORD, the God who gives breath to all living things, appoint someone over this community ¹⁷to go out and come in

before them, one who will lead them out and bring them in, so the LORD's people will not be like sheep without a shepherd."

18So the LORD said to Moses, "Take Joshua son of Nun, a man in whom is the spirit of leadership,^a and lay your hand on him. **19**Have him stand before Eleazar the priest and the entire assembly and commission him in their presence. **20**Give him some of your authority so the whole Israelite community will obey him. **21**He is to stand before Eleazar the priest, who will obtain decisions for him by inquiring of the Urim before the LORD. At his command he and the entire community of the Israelites will go out, and at his command they will come in."

22Moses did as the LORD commanded him. He took Joshua and had him stand before Eleazar the priest and the whole assembly. **23**Then he laid his hands on him and commissioned him, as the LORD instructed through Moses.

Daily Offerings

28 The LORD said to Moses, **2**"Give this command to the Israelites and say to them: 'Make sure that you present to me at the appointed time my food offerings, as an aroma pleasing to me.' **3**Say to them: 'This is the food offering you are to present to the LORD: two lambs a year old without defect, as a regular burnt offering each day. **4**Offer one lamb in the morning and the other at twilight, **5**together with a grain offering of a tenth of an ephah^b of the finest flour mixed with a quarter of a hin^c of oil from pressed olives. **6**This is the regular burnt offering instituted at Mount Sinai as a pleasing aroma, a food offering presented to the LORD. **7**The accompanying drink offering is to be a quarter of a hin of fermented drink with each lamb. Pour out the drink offering to the LORD at the sanctuary. **8**Offer the second lamb at twilight, along with the same kind of grain offering and drink offering that you offer in the morning. This is a food offering, an aroma pleasing to the LORD.

Sabbath Offerings

9"On the Sabbath day, make an offering of two lambs a year old without defect, together with its drink offering and a grain offering of two-tenths of an ephah^d of the finest flour mixed with olive oil. **10**This is the burnt offering for every Sabbath, in addition to the regular burnt offering and its drink offering.

---

^a *18* Or *the Spirit*   ^b *5* That is, probably about 3 1/2 pounds or about 1.6 kilograms; also in verses 13, 21 and 29   ^c *5* That is, about 1 quart or about 1 liter; also in verses 7 and 14   ^d *9* That is, probably about 7 pounds or about 3.2 kilograms; also in verses 12, 20 and 28

Monthly Offerings

11 "'On the first of every month, present to the LORD a burnt offering of two young bulls, one ram and seven male lambs a year old, all without defect. **12** With each bull there is to be a grain offering of three-tenths of an ephah[a] of the finest flour mixed with oil; with the ram, a grain offering of two-tenths of an ephah of the finest flour mixed with oil; **13** and with each lamb, a grain offering of a tenth of an ephah of the finest flour mixed with oil. This is for a burnt offering, a pleasing aroma, a food offering presented to the LORD. **14** With each bull there is to be a drink offering of half a hin[b] of wine; with the ram, a third of a hin[c]; and with each lamb, a quarter of a hin. This is the monthly burnt offering to be made at each new moon during the year. **15** Besides the regular burnt offering with its drink offering, one male goat is to be presented to the LORD as a sin offering.[d]

The Passover

16 "'On the fourteenth day of the first month the LORD's Passover is to be held. **17** On the fifteenth day of this month there is to be a festival; for seven days eat bread made without yeast. **18** On the first day hold a sacred assembly and do no regular work.

19 Present to the LORD a food offering consisting of a burnt offering of two young bulls, one ram and seven male lambs a year old, all without defect. **20** With each bull offer a grain offering of three-tenths of an ephah of the finest flour mixed with oil; with the ram, two-tenths; **21** and with each of the seven lambs, one-tenth. **22** Include one male goat as a sin offering to make atonement for you. **23** Offer these in addition to the regular morning burnt offering. **24** In this way present the food offering every day for seven days as an aroma pleasing to the LORD; it is to be offered in addition to the regular burnt offering and its drink offering. **25** On the seventh day hold a sacred assembly and do no regular work.

The Festival of Weeks

26 "'On the day of firstfruits, when you present to the LORD an offering of new grain during the Festival of Weeks, hold a sacred assembly and do no regular work. **27** Present a burnt offering of two young bulls, one ram and seven male lambs a year old as an aroma pleasing to the LORD. **28** With each bull there is to be a grain offering of three-tenths of an ephah of the finest flour mixed with oil; with the ram, two-tenths; **29** and with each of the seven lambs,

---

a 12 That is, probably about 11 pounds or about 5 kilograms; also in verses 20 and 28   *b 14* That is, about 2 quarts or about 1.9 liters   *c 14* That is, about 1 1/3 quarts or about 1.3 liters   *d 15* Or *purification offering*; also in verse 22 one-tenth. ³⁰Include one male goat to make atonement for you. ³¹Offer these together with their drink offerings, in addition to the regular burnt offering and its grain offering. Be sure the animals are without defect.

The Festival of Trumpets

29 "'On the first day of the seventh month hold a sacred assembly and do no regular work. It is a day for you to sound the trumpets. ²As an aroma pleasing to the LORD, offer a burnt offering of one young bull, one ram and seven male lambs a year old, all without defect. ³With the bull offer a grain offering of three-tenths of an ephah^a of the finest flour mixed with olive oil; with the ram, two-tenths^b; ⁴and with each of the seven lambs, one-tenth.^c ⁵Include one male goat as a sin offering^d to make atonement for you. ⁶These are in addition to the monthly and daily burnt offerings with their grain offerings and drink offerings as specified. They are food offerings presented to the LORD, a pleasing aroma.

The Day of Atonement

⁷"'On the tenth day of this seventh month hold a sacred assembly. You must deny yourselves^e and do no work. ⁸Present as an aroma pleasing to the LORD a burnt offering of one young bull, one ram and seven male lambs a year old, all without defect. ⁹With the bull offer a grain offering of three-tenths of an ephah of the finest flour mixed with oil; with the ram, two-tenths; ¹⁰and with each of the seven lambs, one-tenth. ¹¹Include one male goat as a sin offering, in addition to the sin offering for atonement and the regular burnt offering with its grain offering, and their drink offerings.

The Festival of Tabernacles

¹²"'On the fifteenth day of the seventh month, hold a sacred assembly and do no regular work. Celebrate a festival to the LORD for seven days. ¹³Present as an aroma pleasing to the LORD a food offering consisting of a burnt offering of thirteen young bulls, two rams and fourteen male lambs a year old, all without defect. ¹⁴With each of the thirteen bulls offer a grain offering of three-tenths of an ephah of the finest flour mixed with oil; with each of the two rams, two-tenths; ¹⁵and with each of the fourteen lambs, one-tenth. ¹⁶Include one male goat as a sin offering, in addition to the regular burnt offering with its grain offering and drink offering.

---

^a 3 That is, probably about 11 pounds or about 5 kilograms; also in verses 9 and 14   ^b 3 That is, probably about 7 pounds or about 3.2 kilograms; also in verses 9 and 14   ^c 4 That is, probably about 3 1/2 pounds or about 1.6 kilograms; also in verses 10 and 15   ^d 5 Or *purification offering*; also elsewhere in this chapter   ^e 7 Or *must fast*

¹⁷ " 'On the second day offer twelve young bulls, two rams and fourteen male lambs a year old, all without defect. ¹⁸With the bulls, rams and lambs, offer their grain offerings and drink offerings according to the number specified. ¹⁹Include one male goat as a sin offering, in addition to the regular burnt offering with its grain offering, and their drink offerings.

²⁰ " 'On the third day offer eleven bulls, two rams and fourteen male lambs a year old, all without defect. ²¹With the bulls, rams and lambs, offer their grain offerings and drink offerings according to the number specified. ²²Include one male goat as a sin offering, in addition to the regular burnt offering with its grain offering and drink offering.

²³ " 'On the fourth day offer ten bulls, two rams and fourteen male lambs a year old, all without defect. ²⁴With the bulls, rams and lambs, offer their grain offerings and drink offerings according to the number specified. ²⁵Include one male goat as a sin offering, in addition to the regular burnt offering with its grain offering and drink offering.

²⁶ " 'On the fifth day offer nine bulls, two rams and fourteen male lambs a year old, all without defect. ²⁷With the bulls, rams and lambs, offer their grain offerings and drink offerings according to the number specified.

²⁸Include one male goat as a sin offering, in addition to the regular burnt offering with its grain offering and drink offering.

²⁹ " 'On the sixth day offer eight bulls, two rams and fourteen male lambs a year old, all without defect. ³⁰With the bulls, rams and lambs, offer their grain offerings and drink offerings according to the number specified. ³¹Include one male goat as a sin offering, in addition to the regular burnt offering with its grain offering and drink offering.

³² " 'On the seventh day offer seven bulls, two rams and fourteen male lambs a year old, all without defect. ³³With the bulls, rams and lambs, offer their grain offerings and drink offerings according to the number specified. ³⁴Include one male goat as a sin offering, in addition to the regular burnt offering with its grain offering and drink offering.

³⁵ " 'On the eighth day hold a closing special assembly and do no regular work. ³⁶Present as an aroma pleasing to the LORD a food offering consisting of a burnt offering of one bull, one ram and seven male lambs a year old, all without defect. ³⁷With the bull, the ram and the lambs, offer their grain offerings and drink offerings according to the number specified. ³⁸Include one male goat as a sin offering, in addition to the regular burnt offering with its grain offering and drink offering.

³⁹ "'In addition to what you vow and your freewill offerings, offer these to the LORD at your appointed festivals: your burnt offerings, grain offerings, drink offerings and fellowship offerings.'"

⁴⁰ Moses told the Israelites all that the LORD commanded him.^a

Vows

30 ^b Moses said to the heads of the tribes of Israel: "This is what the LORD commands: ² When a man makes a vow to the LORD or takes an oath to obligate himself by a pledge, he must not break his word but must do everything he said.

³ "When a young woman still living in her father's household makes a vow to the LORD or obligates herself by a pledge ⁴ and her father hears about her vow or pledge but says nothing to her, then all her vows and every pledge by which she obligated herself will stand. ⁵ But if her father forbids her when he hears about it, none of her vows or the pledges by which she obligated herself will stand; the LORD will release her because her father has forbidden her.

⁶ "If she marries after she makes a vow or after her lips utter a rash promise by which she obligates herself ⁷ and her husband hears about it but says nothing to her, then her vows or the pledges by which she obligated herself will stand. ⁸ But if her husband forbids her when he hears about it, he nullifies the vow that obligates her or the rash promise by which she obligates herself, and the LORD will release her.

⁹ "Any vow or obligation taken by a widow or divorced woman will be binding on her.

¹⁰ "If a woman living with her husband makes a vow or obligates herself by a pledge under oath ¹¹ and her husband hears about it but says nothing to her and does not forbid her, then all her vows or the pledges by which she obligated herself will stand. ¹² But if her husband nullifies them when he hears about them, then none of the vows or pledges that came from her lips will stand. Her husband has nullified them, and the LORD will release her. ¹³ Her husband may confirm or nullify any vow she makes or any sworn pledge to deny herself.^c ¹⁴ But if her husband says nothing to her about it from day to day, then he confirms all her vows or the pledges binding on her. He confirms them by saying nothing to her when he hears about them. ¹⁵ If, however, he nullifies them some time after he hears about them, then he must bear the consequences of her wrongdoing."

---

^a 40 In Hebrew texts this verse (29:40) is numbered 30:1.   ^b In Hebrew texts 30:1-16 is numbered 30:2-17.   ^c 13 Or to fast

16 These are the regulations the LORD gave Moses concerning relationships between a man and his wife, and between a father and his young daughter still living at home.

Vengeance on the Midianites

31 The LORD said to Moses, 2 "Take vengeance on the Midianites for the Israelites. After that, you will be gathered to your people."

3 So Moses said to the people, "Arm some of your men to go to war against the Midianites so that they may carry out the LORD's vengeance on them. 4 Send into battle a thousand men from each of the tribes of Israel." 5 So twelve thousand men armed for battle, a thousand from each tribe, were supplied from the clans of Israel. 6 Moses sent them into battle, a thousand from each tribe, along with Phinehas son of Eleazar, the priest, who took with him articles from the sanctuary and the trumpets for signaling.

7 They fought against Midian, as the LORD commanded Moses, and killed every man. 8 Among their victims were Evi, Rekem, Zur, Hur and Reba — the five kings of Midian. They also killed Balaam son of Beor with the sword. 9 The Israelites captured the Midianite women and children and took all the Midianite herds, flocks and goods as plunder. 10 They burned all the towns where the Midianites had settled, as well as all their camps. 11 They took all the plunder and spoils, including the people and animals, 12 and brought the captives, spoils and plunder to Moses and Eleazar the priest and the Israelite assembly at their camp on the plains of Moab, by the Jordan across from Jericho.

13 Moses, Eleazar the priest and all the leaders of the community went to meet them outside the camp. 14 Moses was angry with the officers of the army — the commanders of thousands and commanders of hundreds — who returned from the battle.

15 "Have you allowed all the women to live?" he asked them. 16 "They were the ones who followed Balaam's advice and enticed the Israelites to be unfaithful to the LORD in the Peor incident, so that a plague struck the LORD's people. 17 Now kill all the boys. And kill every woman who has slept with a man, 18 but save for yourselves every girl who has never slept with a man.

19 "Anyone who has killed someone or touched someone who was killed must stay outside the camp seven days. On the third and seventh days you must purify yourselves and your captives. 20 Purify every garment as well as everything made of leather, goat hair or wood."

21 Then Eleazar the priest said to the soldiers who had gone into

battle, "This is what is required by the law that the LORD gave Moses: ²²Gold, silver, bronze, iron, tin, lead ²³and anything else that can withstand fire must be put through the fire, and then it will be clean. But it must also be purified with the water of cleansing. And whatever cannot withstand fire must be put through that water. ²⁴On the seventh day wash your clothes and you will be clean. Then you may come into the camp."

Dividing the Spoils

²⁵The LORD said to Moses, ²⁶"You and Eleazar the priest and the family heads of the community are to count all the people and animals that were captured. ²⁷Divide the spoils equally between the soldiers who took part in the battle and the rest of the community. ²⁸From the soldiers who fought in the battle, set apart as tribute for the LORD one out of every five hundred, whether people, cattle, donkeys or sheep. ²⁹Take this tribute from their half share and give it to Eleazar the priest as the LORD's part. ³⁰From the Israelites' half, select one out of every fifty, whether people, cattle, donkeys, sheep or other animals. Give them to the Levites, who are responsible for the care of the LORD's tabernacle." ³¹So Moses and Eleazar the priest did as the LORD commanded Moses.

³²The plunder remaining from the spoils that the soldiers took was 675,000 sheep, ³³72,000 cattle, ³⁴61,000 donkeys ³⁵and 32,000 women who had never slept with a man.

³⁶The half share of those who fought in the battle was:

337,500 sheep, ³⁷of which the tribute for the LORD was 675;

³⁸36,000 cattle, of which the tribute for the LORD was 72;

³⁹30,500 donkeys, of which the tribute for the LORD was 61;

⁴⁰16,000 people, of whom the tribute for the LORD was 32.

⁴¹Moses gave the tribute to Eleazar the priest as the LORD's part, as the LORD commanded Moses.

⁴²The half belonging to the Israelites, which Moses set apart from that of the fighting men — ⁴³the community's half — was 337,500 sheep, ⁴⁴36,000 cattle, ⁴⁵30,500 donkeys ⁴⁶and 16,000 people. ⁴⁷From the Israelites' half, Moses selected one out of every fifty people and animals, as the LORD commanded him, and gave them to the Levites, who were responsible for the care of the LORD's tabernacle.

⁴⁸Then the officers who were over the units of the army — the commanders of thousands and commanders of hundreds —

went to Moses [49] and said to him, "Your servants have counted the soldiers under our command, and not one is missing. [50] So we have brought as an offering to the LORD the gold articles each of us acquired — armlets, bracelets, signet rings, earrings and necklaces — to make atonement for ourselves before the LORD."

[51] Moses and Eleazar the priest accepted from them the gold — all the crafted articles. [52] All the gold from the commanders of thousands and commanders of hundreds that Moses and Eleazar presented as a gift to the LORD weighed 16,750 shekels.[a] [53] Each soldier had taken plunder for himself. [54] Moses and Eleazar the priest accepted the gold from the commanders of thousands and commanders of hundreds and brought it into the tent of meeting as a memorial for the Israelites before the LORD.

The Transjordan Tribes

32 The Reubenites and Gadites, who had very large herds and flocks, saw that the lands of Jazer and Gilead were suitable for livestock. [2] So they came to Moses and Eleazar the priest and to the leaders of the community, and said, [3] "Ataroth, Dibon, Jazer, Nimrah, Heshbon, Elealeh, Sebam, Nebo and Beon — [4] the land the LORD subdued before the people of Israel — are suitable for livestock, and your servants have livestock. [5] If we have found favor in your eyes," they said, "let this land be given to your servants as our possession. Do not make us cross the Jordan."

[6] Moses said to the Gadites and Reubenites, "Should your fellow Israelites go to war while you sit here? [7] Why do you discourage the Israelites from crossing over into the land the LORD has given them? [8] This is what your fathers did when I sent them from Kadesh Barnea to look over the land. [9] After they went up to the Valley of Eshkol and viewed the land, they discouraged the Israelites from entering the land the LORD had given them. [10] The LORD's anger was aroused that day and he swore this oath: [11] 'Because they have not followed me wholeheartedly, not one of those who were twenty years old or more when they came up out of Egypt will see the land I promised on oath to Abraham, Isaac and Jacob — [12] not one except Caleb son of Jephunneh the Kenizzite and Joshua son of Nun, for they followed the LORD wholeheartedly.' [13] The LORD's anger burned against Israel and he made them wander in the wilderness forty years, until the whole generation of those who had done evil in his sight was gone.

[14] "And here you are, a brood of sinners, standing in the place of

[a] 52 That is, about 420 pounds or about 190 kilograms

your fathers and making the LORD even more angry with Israel. ¹⁵If you turn away from following him, he will again leave all this people in the wilderness, and you will be the cause of their destruction."

¹⁶Then they came up to him and said, "We would like to build pens here for our livestock and cities for our women and children. ¹⁷But we will arm ourselves for battle*a* and go ahead of the Israelites until we have brought them to their place. Meanwhile our women and children will live in fortified cities, for protection from the inhabitants of the land. ¹⁸We will not return to our homes until each of the Israelites has received their inheritance. ¹⁹We will not receive any inheritance with them on the other side of the Jordan, because our inheritance has come to us on the east side of the Jordan."

²⁰Then Moses said to them, "If you will do this — if you will arm yourselves before the LORD for battle ²¹and if all of you who are armed cross over the Jordan before the LORD until he has driven his enemies out before him — ²²then when the land is subdued before the LORD, you may return and be free from your obligation to the LORD and to Israel. And this land will be your possession before the LORD.

²³"But if you fail to do this, you will be sinning against the LORD; and you may be sure that your sin will find you out. ²⁴Build cities for your women and children, and pens for your flocks, but do what you have promised."

²⁵The Gadites and Reubenites said to Moses, "We your servants will do as our lord commands. ²⁶Our children and wives, our flocks and herds will remain here in the cities of Gilead. ²⁷But your servants, every man who is armed for battle, will cross over to fight before the LORD, just as our lord says."

²⁸Then Moses gave orders about them to Eleazar the priest and Joshua son of Nun and to the family heads of the Israelite tribes. ²⁹He said to them, "If the Gadites and Reubenites, every man armed for battle, cross over the Jordan with you before the LORD, then when the land is subdued before you, you must give them the land of Gilead as their possession. ³⁰But if they do not cross over with you armed, they must accept their possession with you in Canaan."

³¹The Gadites and Reubenites answered, "Your servants will do what the LORD has said. ³²We will cross over before the LORD into Canaan armed, but the property we inherit will be on this side of the Jordan."

³³Then Moses gave to the Gadites, the Reubenites and the half-tribe of Manasseh son of Joseph the kingdom of Sihon king of the

a 17 Septuagint; Hebrew will be quick to arm ourselves

Amorites and the kingdom of Og king of Bashan — the whole land with its cities and the territory around them.

³⁴ The Gadites built up Dibon, Ataroth, Aroer, ³⁵ Atroth Shophan, Jazer, Jogbehah, ³⁶ Beth Nimrah and Beth Haran as fortified cities, and built pens for their flocks. ³⁷ And the Reubenites rebuilt Heshbon, Elealeh and Kiriathaim, ³⁸ as well as Nebo and Baal Meon (these names were changed) and Sibmah. They gave names to the cities they rebuilt.

³⁹ The descendants of Makir son of Manasseh went to Gilead, captured it and drove out the Amorites who were there. ⁴⁰ So Moses gave Gilead to the Makirites, the descendants of Manasseh, and they settled there. ⁴¹ Jair, a descendant of Manasseh, captured their settlements and called them Havvoth Jair.^a ⁴² And Nobah captured Kenath and its surrounding settlements and called it Nobah after himself.

Stages in Israel's Journey

33 Here are the stages in the journey of the Israelites when they came out of Egypt by divisions under the leadership of Moses and Aaron. ² At the LORD's command Moses recorded the stages in their journey. This is their journey by stages:

³ The Israelites set out from Rameses on the fifteenth day of the first month, the day after the Passover. They marched out defiantly in full view of all the Egyptians, ⁴ who were burying all their firstborn, whom the LORD had struck down among them; for the LORD had brought judgment on their gods.

⁵ The Israelites left Rameses and camped at Sukkoth.

⁶ They left Sukkoth and camped at Etham, on the edge of the desert.

⁷ They left Etham, turned back to Pi Hahiroth, to the east of Baal Zephon, and camped near Migdol.

⁸ They left Pi Hahiroth^b and passed through the sea into the desert, and when they had traveled for three days in the Desert of Etham, they camped at Marah.

⁹ They left Marah and went to Elim, where there were twelve springs and seventy palm trees, and they camped there.

¹⁰ They left Elim and camped by the Red Sea.^c

¹¹ They left the Red Sea and camped in the Desert of Sin.

¹² They left the Desert of Sin and camped at Dophkah.

---

^a 41 Or *them the settlements of Jair*   ^b 8 Many manuscripts of the Masoretic Text, Samaritan Pentateuch and Vulgate; most manuscripts of the Masoretic Text *left from before Hahiroth*   ^c 10 Or *the Sea of Reeds*; also in verse 11

¹³They left Dophkah and camped at Alush.

¹⁴They left Alush and camped at Rephidim, where there was no water for the people to drink.

¹⁵They left Rephidim and camped in the Desert of Sinai.

¹⁶They left the Desert of Sinai and camped at Kibroth Hattaavah.

¹⁷They left Kibroth Hattaavah and camped at Hazeroth.

¹⁸They left Hazeroth and camped at Rithmah.

¹⁹They left Rithmah and camped at Rimmon Perez.

²⁰They left Rimmon Perez and camped at Libnah.

²¹They left Libnah and camped at Rissah.

²²They left Rissah and camped at Kehelathah.

²³They left Kehelathah and camped at Mount Shepher.

²⁴They left Mount Shepher and camped at Haradah.

²⁵They left Haradah and camped at Makheloth.

²⁶They left Makheloth and camped at Tahath.

²⁷They left Tahath and camped at Terah.

²⁸They left Terah and camped at Mithkah.

²⁹They left Mithkah and camped at Hashmonah.

³⁰They left Hashmonah and camped at Moseroth.

³¹They left Moseroth and camped at Bene Jaakan.

³²They left Bene Jaakan and camped at Hor Haggidgad.

³³They left Hor Haggidgad and camped at Jotbathah.

³⁴They left Jotbathah and camped at Abronah.

³⁵They left Abronah and camped at Ezion Geber.

³⁶They left Ezion Geber and camped at Kadesh, in the Desert of Zin.

³⁷They left Kadesh and camped at Mount Hor, on the border of Edom. ³⁸At the LORD's command Aaron the priest went up Mount Hor, where he died on the first day of the fifth month of the fortieth year after the Israelites came out of Egypt. ³⁹Aaron was a hundred and twenty-three years old when he died on Mount Hor.

⁴⁰The Canaanite king of Arad, who lived in the Negev of Canaan, heard that the Israelites were coming.

⁴¹They left Mount Hor and camped at Zalmonah.

⁴²They left Zalmonah and camped at Punon.

⁴³They left Punon and camped at Oboth.

⁴⁴They left Oboth and camped at Iye Abarim, on the border of Moab.

⁴⁵They left Iye Abarim and camped at Dibon Gad.

⁴⁶They left Dibon Gad and camped at Almon Diblathaim.

⁴⁷They left Almon Diblathaim and camped in the mountains of Abarim, near Nebo.

⁴⁸They left the mountains of Abarim and camped on the plains of Moab by the Jordan across from Jericho. ⁴⁹There on the plains of Moab they camped along the Jordan from Beth Jeshimoth to Abel Shittim.

⁵⁰On the plains of Moab by the Jordan across from Jericho the LORD said to Moses, ⁵¹"Speak to the Israelites and say to them: 'When you cross the Jordan into Canaan, ⁵²drive out all the inhabitants of the land before you. Destroy all their carved images and their cast idols, and demolish all their high places. ⁵³Take possession of the land and settle in it, for I have given you the land to possess. ⁵⁴Distribute the land by lot, according to your clans. To a larger group give a larger inheritance, and to a smaller group a smaller one. Whatever falls to them by lot will be theirs. Distribute it according to your ancestral tribes.

⁵⁵"'But if you do not drive out the inhabitants of the land, those you allow to remain will become barbs in your eyes and thorns in your sides. They will give you trouble in the land where you will live. ⁵⁶And then I will do to you what I plan to do to them.'"

Boundaries of Canaan

34 The LORD said to Moses, ²"Command the Israelites and say to them: 'When you enter Canaan, the land that will be allotted to you as an inheritance is to have these boundaries:

³"'Your southern side will include some of the Desert of Zin along the border of Edom. Your southern boundary will start in the east from the southern end of the Dead Sea, ⁴cross south of Scorpion Pass, continue on to Zin and go south of Kadesh Barnea. Then it will go to Hazar Addar and over to Azmon, ⁵where it will turn, join the Wadi of Egypt and end at the Mediterranean Sea.

⁶"'Your western boundary will be the coast of the Mediterranean Sea. This will be your boundary on the west.

⁷"'For your northern boundary, run a line from the Mediterranean Sea to Mount Hor ⁸and from Mount Hor to Lebo Hamath. Then the boundary will go to Zedad, ⁹continue to Ziphron and end at Hazar Enan. This will be your boundary on the north.

¹⁰"'For your eastern boundary, run a line from Hazar Enan to Shepham. ¹¹The boundary will go down from Shepham to Riblah on the east side of Ain and continue along the slopes east of the Sea of Galilee.ᵃ ¹²Then the

ᵃ 11 Hebrew *Kinnereth*

boundary will go down along the Jordan and end at the Dead Sea.

"'This will be your land, with its boundaries on every side.'"

¹³Moses commanded the Israelites: "Assign this land by lot as an inheritance. The LORD has ordered that it be given to the nine and a half tribes, ¹⁴because the families of the tribe of Reuben, the tribe of Gad and the half-tribe of Manasseh have received their inheritance. ¹⁵These two and a half tribes have received their inheritance east of the Jordan across from Jericho, toward the sunrise."

¹⁶The LORD said to Moses, ¹⁷"These are the names of the men who are to assign the land for you as an inheritance: Eleazar the priest and Joshua son of Nun. ¹⁸And appoint one leader from each tribe to help assign the land. ¹⁹These are their names:

Caleb son of Jephunneh,
    from the tribe of Judah;
²⁰Shemuel son of Ammihud,
    from the tribe of Simeon;
²¹Elidad son of Kislon,
    from the tribe of Benjamin;
²²Bukki son of Jogli,
    the leader from the tribe of Dan;
²³Hanniel son of Ephod,
    the leader from the tribe of Manasseh son of Joseph;
²⁴Kemuel son of Shiphtan,
    the leader from the tribe of Ephraim son of Joseph;

²⁵Elizaphan son of Parnak,
    the leader from the tribe of Zebulun;
²⁶Paltiel son of Azzan,
    the leader from the tribe of Issachar;
²⁷Ahihud son of Shelomi,
    the leader from the tribe of Asher;
²⁸Pedahel son of Ammihud,
    the leader from the tribe of Naphtali."

²⁹These are the men the LORD commanded to assign the inheritance to the Israelites in the land of Canaan.

Towns for the Levites

35 On the plains of Moab by the Jordan across from Jericho, the LORD said to Moses, ²"Command the Israelites to give the Levites towns to live in from the inheritance the Israelites will possess. And give them pasturelands around the towns. ³Then they will have towns to live in and pasturelands for the cattle they own and all their other animals.

⁴"The pasturelands around the towns that you give the Levites will extend a thousand cubits[a] from the town wall. ⁵Outside the town, measure two thousand cubits[b] on the east side, two thousand on the south side, two thousand on the west and two thousand on the north, with

---

[a] 4 That is, about 1,500 feet or about 450 meters   [b] 5 That is, about 3,000 feet or about 900 meters

the town in the center. They will have this area as pastureland for the towns.

Cities of Refuge

6 "Six of the towns you give the Levites will be cities of refuge, to which a person who has killed someone may flee. In addition, give them forty-two other towns. 7 In all you must give the Levites forty-eight towns, together with their pasturelands. 8 The towns you give the Levites from the land the Israelites possess are to be given in proportion to the inheritance of each tribe: Take many towns from a tribe that has many, but few from one that has few."

9 Then the LORD said to Moses: 10 "Speak to the Israelites and say to them: 'When you cross the Jordan into Canaan, 11 select some towns to be your cities of refuge, to which a person who has killed someone accidentally may flee. 12 They will be places of refuge from the avenger, so that anyone accused of murder may not die before they stand trial before the assembly. 13 These six towns you give will be your cities of refuge. 14 Give three on this side of the Jordan and three in Canaan as cities of refuge. 15 These six towns will be a place of refuge for Israelites and for foreigners residing among them, so that anyone who has killed another accidentally can flee there.

16 "'If anyone strikes someone a fatal blow with an iron object, that person is a murderer; the murderer is to be put to death. 17 Or if anyone is holding a stone and strikes someone a fatal blow with it, that person is a murderer; the murderer is to be put to death. 18 Or if anyone is holding a wooden object and strikes someone a fatal blow with it, that person is a murderer; the murderer is to be put to death. 19 The avenger of blood shall put the murderer to death; when the avenger comes upon the murderer, the avenger shall put the murderer to death. 20 If anyone with malice aforethought shoves another or throws something at them intentionally so that they die 21 or if out of enmity one person hits another with their fist so that the other dies, that person is to be put to death; that person is a murderer. The avenger of blood shall put the murderer to death when they meet.

22 "'But if without enmity someone suddenly pushes another or throws something at them unintentionally 23 or, without seeing them, drops on them a stone heavy enough to kill them, and they die, then since that other person was not an enemy and no harm was intended, 24 the assembly must judge between the accused and the avenger of blood according to these regulations. 25 The assembly must protect the

one accused of murder from the avenger of blood and send the accused back to the city of refuge to which they fled. The accused must stay there until the death of the high priest, who was anointed with the holy oil.

26 " 'But if the accused ever goes outside the limits of the city of refuge to which they fled 27 and the avenger of blood finds them outside the city, the avenger of blood may kill the accused without being guilty of murder. 28 The accused must stay in the city of refuge until the death of the high priest; only after the death of the high priest may they return to their own property.

29 " 'This is to have the force of law for you throughout the generations to come, wherever you live.

30 " 'Anyone who kills a person is to be put to death as a murderer only on the testimony of witnesses. But no one is to be put to death on the testimony of only one witness.

31 " 'Do not accept a ransom for the life of a murderer, who deserves to die. They are to be put to death.

32 " 'Do not accept a ransom for anyone who has fled to a city of refuge and so allow them to go back and live on their own land before the death of the high priest.

33 " 'Do not pollute the land where you are. Bloodshed pollutes the land, and atonement cannot be made for the land on which blood has been shed, except by the blood of the one who shed it. 34 Do not defile the land where you live and where I dwell, for I, the LORD, dwell among the Israelites.' "

Inheritance of Zelophehad's Daughters

36 The family heads of the clan of Gilead son of Makir, the son of Manasseh, who were from the clans of the descendants of Joseph, came and spoke before Moses and the leaders, the heads of the Israelite families. 2 They said, "When the LORD commanded my lord to give the land as an inheritance to the Israelites by lot, he ordered you to give the inheritance of our brother Zelophehad to his daughters. 3 Now suppose they marry men from other Israelite tribes; then their inheritance will be taken from our ancestral inheritance and added to that of the tribe they marry into. And so part of the inheritance allotted to us will be taken away. 4 When the Year of Jubilee for the Israelites comes, their inheritance will be added to that of the tribe into which they marry, and their property will be taken from the tribal inheritance of our ancestors."

5 Then at the LORD's command Moses gave this order to the Israelites: "What the tribe of the

descendants of Joseph is saying is right. **6**This is what the LORD commands for Zelophehad's daughters: They may marry anyone they please as long as they marry within their father's tribal clan. **7**No inheritance in Israel is to pass from one tribe to another, for every Israelite shall keep the tribal inheritance of their ancestors. **8**Every daughter who inherits land in any Israelite tribe must marry someone in her father's tribal clan, so that every Israelite will possess the inheritance of their ancestors. **9**No inheritance may pass from one tribe to another, for each Is-

raelite tribe is to keep the land it inherits."

10So Zelophehad's daughters did as the LORD commanded Moses. **11**Zelophehad's daughters—Mahlah, Tirzah, Hoglah, Milkah and Noah—married their cousins on their father's side. **12**They married within the clans of the descendants of Manasseh son of Joseph, and their inheritance remained in their father's tribe and clan.

13These are the commands and regulations the LORD gave through Moses to the Israelites on the plains of Moab by the Jordan across from Jericho.

Deuteronomy

Introduction:

Deuteronomy means "second law." After forty years the Israelites were about to enter the Promised Land of Canaan. But before they did, Moses wanted to remind them of their history, all that God had done for them, and the laws they had to continue to obey as God's chosen people.

His first speech reminded the people of God's goodness to them through their journey and God's gift of the land of Canaan. Moses' second speech was a summary of God's laws including the Ten Commandments. Moses told the people to "love the LORD your God with all your heart and with all your soul and with all your strength" in order to continue to enjoy God's blessing. Moses also emphasized that the people had to teach their children to love the Lord and obey his commandments.

Deuteronomy ends with Moses' reminding the people of the covenant God had made with them (29:1–29), Joshua's appointment to be the new leader (31:1–8), and Moses' death (34:1–8). It is generally accepted that Moses wrote Deuteronomy except for the chapter about his death.

Outline of contents:

Moses' first speech: Israel's history (1:1–4:43)
Moses' second speech: review of the law (4:44–11:32)
Rules for daily living (12:1–26:19)
The results of obedience and disobedience (27:1–28:68)
The renewal of the covenant (29:1–30:20)
Moses' blessing on Israel and his death (31:1–34:12)

The Command to Leave Horeb

1 These are the words Moses spoke to all Israel in the wilderness east of the Jordan — that is, in the Arabah — opposite Suph, between Paran and Tophel, Laban, Hazeroth and Dizahab. ² (It takes eleven days to go from Horeb to Kadesh Barnea by the Mount Seir road.)

³ In the fortieth year, on the first day of the eleventh month, Moses proclaimed to the Israelites all that the LORD had commanded him concerning them. ⁴ This was after he had defeated Sihon king of the Amorites, who reigned in Heshbon, and at Edrei had defeated Og king of Bashan, who reigned in Ashtaroth.

[5] East of the Jordan in the territory of Moab, Moses began to expound this law, saying:

[6] The LORD our God said to us at Horeb, "You have stayed long enough at this mountain. [7] Break camp and advance into the hill country of the Amorites; go to all the neighboring peoples in the Arabah, in the mountains, in the western foothills, in the Negev and along the coast, to the land of the Canaanites and to Lebanon, as far as the great river, the Euphrates. [8] See, I have given you this land. Go in and take possession of the land the LORD swore he would give to your fathers — to Abraham, Isaac and Jacob — and to their descendants after them."

The Appointment of Leaders

[9] At that time I said to you, "You are too heavy a burden for me to carry alone. [10] The LORD your God has increased your numbers so that today you are as numerous as the stars in the sky. [11] May the LORD, the God of your ancestors, increase you a thousand times and bless you as he has promised! [12] But how can I bear your problems and your burdens and your disputes all by myself? [13] Choose some wise, understanding and respected men from each of your tribes, and I will set them over you."

[14] You answered me, "What you propose to do is good."

[15] So I took the leading men of your tribes, wise and respected men, and appointed them to have authority over you — as commanders of thousands, of hundreds, of fifties and of tens and as tribal officials. [16] And I charged your judges at that time, "Hear the disputes between your people and judge fairly, whether the case is between two Israelites or between an Israelite and a foreigner residing among you. [17] Do not show partiality in judging; hear both small and great alike. Do not be afraid of anyone, for judgment belongs to God. Bring me any case too hard for you, and I will hear it." [18] And at that time I told you everything you were to do.

Spies Sent Out

[19] Then, as the LORD our God commanded us, we set out from Horeb and went toward the hill country of the Amorites through all that vast and dreadful wilderness that you have seen, and so we reached Kadesh Barnea. [20] Then I said to you, "You have reached the hill country of the Amorites, which the LORD our God is giving us. [21] See, the LORD your God has given you the land. Go up and take possession of it as the LORD, the God of your ancestors, told you. Do not be afraid; do not be discouraged."

[22] Then all of you came to me and said, "Let us send men ahead to spy out the land for us

and bring back a report about the route we are to take and the towns we will come to."

²³ The idea seemed good to me; so I selected twelve of you, one man from each tribe. ²⁴ They left and went up into the hill country, and came to the Valley of Eshkol and explored it. ²⁵ Taking with them some of the fruit of the land, they brought it down to us and reported, "It is a good land that the LORD our God is giving us."

Rebellion Against the LORD

²⁶ But you were unwilling to go up; you rebelled against the command of the LORD your God. ²⁷ You grumbled in your tents and said, "The LORD hates us; so he brought us out of Egypt to deliver us into the hands of the Amorites to destroy us. ²⁸ Where can we go? Our brothers have made our hearts melt in fear. They say, 'The people are stronger and taller than we are; the cities are large, with walls up to the sky. We even saw the Anakites there.' "

²⁹ Then I said to you, "Do not be terrified; do not be afraid of them. ³⁰ The LORD your God, who is going before you, will fight for you, as he did for you in Egypt, before your very eyes, ³¹ and in the wilderness. There you saw how the LORD your God carried you, as a father carries his son, all the way you went until you reached this place."

³² In spite of this, you did not trust in the LORD your God, ³³ who went ahead of you on your journey, in fire by night and in a cloud by day, to search out places for you to camp and to show you the way you should go.

³⁴ When the LORD heard what you said, he was angry and solemnly swore: ³⁵ "No one from this evil generation shall see the good land I swore to give your ancestors, ³⁶ except Caleb son of Jephunneh. He will see it, and I will give him and his descendants the land he set his feet on, because he followed the LORD wholeheartedly."

³⁷ Because of you the LORD became angry with me also and said, "You shall not enter it, either. ³⁸ But your assistant, Joshua son of Nun, will enter it. Encourage him, because he will lead Israel to inherit it. ³⁹ And the little ones that you said would be taken captive, your children who do not yet know good from bad — they will enter the land. I will give it to them and they will take possession of it. ⁴⁰ But as for you, turn around and set out toward the desert along the route to the Red Sea.ᵃ"

⁴¹ Then you replied, "We have sinned against the LORD. We will go up and fight, as the LORD our God commanded us." So every one of you put on his weapons, thinking it easy to go up into the hill country.

ᵃ 40 Or *the Sea of Reeds*

42 But the LORD said to me, "Tell them, 'Do not go up and fight, because I will not be with you. You will be defeated by your enemies.'"

43 So I told you, but you would not listen. You rebelled against the LORD's command and in your arrogance you marched up into the hill country. 44 The Amorites who lived in those hills came out against you; they chased you like a swarm of bees and beat you down from Seir all the way to Hormah. 45 You came back and wept before the LORD, but he paid no attention to your weeping and turned a deaf ear to you. 46 And so you stayed in Kadesh many days — all the time you spent there.

Wanderings in the Wilderness

2 Then we turned back and set out toward the wilderness along the route to the Red Sea,[a] as the LORD had directed me. For a long time we made our way around the hill country of Seir.

2 Then the LORD said to me, 3 "You have made your way around this hill country long enough; now turn north. 4 Give the people these orders: 'You are about to pass through the territory of your relatives the descendants of Esau, who live in Seir. They will be afraid of you, but be very careful. 5 Do not provoke them to war, for I will not give you any of their land, not even enough to put your foot on. I have given Esau the hill country of Seir as his own. 6 You are to pay them in silver for the food you eat and the water you drink.'"

7 The LORD your God has blessed you in all the work of your hands. He has watched over your journey through this vast wilderness. These forty years the LORD your God has been with you, and you have not lacked anything.

8 So we went on past our relatives the descendants of Esau, who live in Seir. We turned from the Arabah road, which comes up from Elath and Ezion Geber, and traveled along the desert road of Moab.

9 Then the LORD said to me, "Do not harass the Moabites or provoke them to war, for I will not give you any part of their land. I have given Ar to the descendants of Lot as a possession."

10 (The Emites used to live there — a people strong and numerous, and as tall as the Anakites. 11 Like the Anakites, they too were considered Rephaites, but the Moabites called them Emites. 12 Horites used to live in Seir, but the descendants of Esau drove them out. They destroyed the Horites from before them and settled in their place, just as Israel did in the land the LORD gave them as their possession.)

13 And the LORD said, "Now get

a 1 Or the Sea of Reeds

up and cross the Zered Valley." So we crossed the valley.

¹⁴Thirty-eight years passed from the time we left Kadesh Barnea until we crossed the Zered Valley. By then, that entire generation of fighting men had perished from the camp, as the LORD had sworn to them. ¹⁵The LORD's hand was against them until he had completely eliminated them from the camp.

¹⁶Now when the last of these fighting men among the people had died, ¹⁷the LORD said to me, ¹⁸"Today you are to pass by the region of Moab at Ar. ¹⁹When you come to the Ammonites, do not harass them or provoke them to war, for I will not give you possession of any land belonging to the Ammonites. I have given it as a possession to the descendants of Lot."

²⁰(That too was considered a land of the Rephaites, who used to live there; but the Ammonites called them Zamzummites. ²¹They were a people strong and numerous, and as tall as the Anakites. The LORD destroyed them from before the Ammonites, who drove them out and settled in their place. ²²The LORD had done the same for the descendants of Esau, who lived in Seir, when he destroyed the Horites from before them. They drove them out and have lived in their place to this day. ²³And as for the Avvites who lived in villages as far as Gaza, the Caphtorites coming out from Caphtorᵃ destroyed them and settled in their place.)

Defeat of Sihon King of Heshbon

²⁴"Set out now and cross the Arnon Gorge. See, I have given into your hand Sihon the Amorite, king of Heshbon, and his country. Begin to take possession of it and engage him in battle. ²⁵This very day I will begin to put the terror and fear of you on all the nations under heaven. They will hear reports of you and will tremble and be in anguish because of you."

²⁶From the Desert of Kedemoth I sent messengers to Sihon king of Heshbon offering peace and saying, ²⁷"Let us pass through your country. We will stay on the main road; we will not turn aside to the right or to the left. ²⁸Sell us food to eat and water to drink for their price in silver. Only let us pass through on foot— ²⁹as the descendants of Esau, who live in Seir, and the Moabites, who live in Ar, did for us— until we cross the Jordan into the land the LORD our God is giving us." ³⁰But Sihon king of Heshbon refused to let us pass through. For the LORD your God had made his spirit stubborn and his heart obstinate in order to give him into your hands, as he has now done.

ᵃ 23 That is, Crete

³¹The LORD said to me, "See, I have begun to deliver Sihon and his country over to you. Now begin to conquer and possess his land."

³²When Sihon and all his army came out to meet us in battle at Jahaz, ³³the LORD our God delivered him over to us and we struck him down, together with his sons and his whole army. ³⁴At that time we took all his towns and completely destroyed*a* them — men, women and children. We left no survivors. ³⁵But the livestock and the plunder from the towns we had captured we carried off for ourselves. ³⁶From Aroer on the rim of the Arnon Gorge, and from the town in the gorge, even as far as Gilead, not one town was too strong for us. The LORD our God gave us all of them. ³⁷But in accordance with the command of the LORD our God, you did not encroach on any of the land of the Ammonites, neither the land along the course of the Jabbok nor that around the towns in the hills.

Defeat of Og King of Bashan

3 Next we turned and went up along the road toward Bashan, and Og king of Bashan with his whole army marched out to meet us in battle at Edrei. ²The LORD said to me, "Do not be afraid of him, for I have delivered him into your hands, along with his whole army and his land. Do to him what you did to Sihon king of the Amorites, who reigned in Heshbon."

³So the LORD our God also gave into our hands Og king of Bashan and all his army. We struck them down, leaving no survivors. ⁴At that time we took all his cities. There was not one of the sixty cities that we did not take from them — the whole region of Argob, Og's kingdom in Bashan. ⁵All these cities were fortified with high walls and with gates and bars, and there were also a great many unwalled villages. ⁶We completely destroyed*a* them, as we had done with Sihon king of Heshbon, destroying*a* every city — men, women and children. ⁷But all the livestock and the plunder from their cities we carried off for ourselves.

⁸So at that time we took from these two kings of the Amorites the territory east of the Jordan, from the Arnon Gorge as far as Mount Hermon. ⁹(Hermon is called Sirion by the Sidonians; the Amorites call it Senir.) ¹⁰We took all the towns on the plateau, and all Gilead, and all Bashan as far as Salekah and Edrei, towns of Og's kingdom in Bashan. ¹¹(Og king of Bashan was the last of the Rephaites. His bed was decorated with iron and was more than

---

a 34,6 The Hebrew term refers to the irrevocable giving over of things or persons to the LORD, often by totally destroying them.

nine cubits long and four cubits wide.[a] It is still in Rabbah of the Ammonites.)

Division of the Land

¹²Of the land that we took over at that time, I gave the Reubenites and the Gadites the territory north of Aroer by the Arnon Gorge, including half the hill country of Gilead, together with its towns. ¹³The rest of Gilead and also all of Bashan, the kingdom of Og, I gave to the half-tribe of Manasseh. (The whole region of Argob in Bashan used to be known as a land of the Rephaites. ¹⁴Jair, a descendant of Manasseh, took the whole region of Argob as far as the border of the Geshurites and the Maakathites; it was named after him, so that to this day Bashan is called Havvoth Jair.[b]) ¹⁵And I gave Gilead to Makir. ¹⁶But to the Reubenites and the Gadites I gave the territory extending from Gilead down to the Arnon Gorge (the middle of the gorge being the border) and out to the Jabbok River, which is the border of the Ammonites. ¹⁷Its western border was the Jordan in the Arabah, from Kinnereth to the Sea of the Arabah (that is, the Dead Sea), below the slopes of Pisgah.

¹⁸I commanded you at that time: "The LORD your God has given you this land to take possession of it. But all your able-bodied men, armed for battle, must cross over ahead of the other Israelites. ¹⁹However, your wives, your children and your livestock (I know you have much livestock) may stay in the towns I have given you, ²⁰until the LORD gives rest to your fellow Israelites as he has to you, and they too have taken over the land that the LORD your God is giving them across the Jordan. After that, each of you may go back to the possession I have given you."

Moses Forbidden to Cross the Jordan

²¹At that time I commanded Joshua: "You have seen with your own eyes all that the LORD your God has done to these two kings. The LORD will do the same to all the kingdoms over there where you are going. ²²Do not be afraid of them; the LORD your God himself will fight for you."

²³At that time I pleaded with the LORD: ²⁴"Sovereign LORD, you have begun to show to your servant your greatness and your strong hand. For what god is there in heaven or on earth who can do the deeds and mighty works you do? ²⁵Let me go over and see the good land beyond the Jordan—that fine hill country and Lebanon."

²⁶But because of you the LORD was angry with me and would not

---

[a] 11 That is, about 14 feet long and 6 feet wide or about 4 meters long and 1.8 meters wide   [b] 14 Or called the settlements of Jair

listen to me. "That is enough," the Lord said. "Do not speak to me anymore about this matter. ²⁷ Go up to the top of Pisgah and look west and north and south and east. Look at the land with your own eyes, since you are not going to cross this Jordan. ²⁸ But commission Joshua, and encourage and strengthen him, for he will lead this people across and will cause them to inherit the land that you will see." ²⁹ So we stayed in the valley near Beth Peor.

Obedience Commanded

4 Now, Israel, hear the decrees and laws I am about to teach you. Follow them so that you may live and may go in and take possession of the land the Lord, the God of your ancestors, is giving you. ² Do not add to what I command you and do not subtract from it, but keep the commands of the Lord your God that I give you.

³ You saw with your own eyes what the Lord did at Baal Peor. The Lord your God destroyed from among you everyone who followed the Baal of Peor, ⁴ but all of you who held fast to the Lord your God are still alive today.

⁵ See, I have taught you decrees and laws as the Lord my God commanded me, so that you may follow them in the land you are entering to take possession of it. ⁶ Observe them carefully, for this will show your wisdom and understanding to the nations, who will hear about all these decrees and say, "Surely this great nation is a wise and understanding people." ⁷ What other nation is so great as to have their gods near them the way the Lord our God is near us whenever we pray to him? ⁸ And what other nation is so great as to have such righteous decrees and laws as this body of laws I am setting before you today?

⁹ Only be careful, and watch yourselves closely so that you do not forget the things your eyes have seen or let them fade from your heart as long as you live. Teach them to your children and to their children after them. ¹⁰ Remember the day you stood before the Lord your God at Horeb, when he said to me, "Assemble the people before me to hear my words so that they may learn to revere me as long as they live in the land and may teach them to their children." ¹¹ You came near and stood at the foot of the mountain while it blazed with fire to the very heavens, with black clouds and deep darkness. ¹² Then the Lord spoke to you out of the fire. You heard the sound of words but saw no form; there was only a voice. ¹³ He declared to you his covenant, the Ten Commandments, which he commanded you to follow and then wrote them on two stone tablets. ¹⁴ And the Lord directed me at

that time to teach you the decrees and laws you are to follow in the land that you are crossing the Jordan to possess.

Idolatry Forbidden

¹⁵You saw no form of any kind the day the LORD spoke to you at Horeb out of the fire. Therefore watch yourselves very carefully, ¹⁶so that you do not become corrupt and make for yourselves an idol, an image of any shape, whether formed like a man or a woman, ¹⁷or like any animal on earth or any bird that flies in the air, ¹⁸or like any creature that moves along the ground or any fish in the waters below. ¹⁹And when you look up to the sky and see the sun, the moon and the stars — all the heavenly array — do not be enticed into bowing down to them and worshiping things the LORD your God has apportioned to all the nations under heaven. ²⁰But as for you, the LORD took you and brought you out of the iron-smelting furnace, out of Egypt, to be the people of his inheritance, as you now are.

²¹The LORD was angry with me because of you, and he solemnly swore that I would not cross the Jordan and enter the good land the LORD your God is giving you as your inheritance. ²²I will die in this land; I will not cross the Jordan; but you are about to cross over and take possession of that good land. ²³Be careful not to forget the covenant of the LORD your God that he made with you; do not make for yourselves an idol in the form of anything the LORD your God has forbidden. ²⁴For the LORD your God is a consuming fire, a jealous God.

²⁵After you have had children and grandchildren and have lived in the land a long time — if you then become corrupt and make any kind of idol, doing evil in the eyes of the LORD your God and arousing his anger, ²⁶I call the heavens and the earth as witnesses against you this day that you will quickly perish from the land that you are crossing the Jordan to possess. You will not live there long but will certainly be destroyed. ²⁷The LORD will scatter you among the peoples, and only a few of you will survive among the nations to which the LORD will drive you. ²⁸There you will worship man-made gods of wood and stone, which cannot see or hear or eat or smell. ²⁹But if from there you seek the LORD your God, you will find him if you seek him with all your heart and with all your soul. ³⁰When you are in distress and all these things have happened to you, then in later days you will return to the LORD your God and obey him. ³¹For the LORD your God is a merciful God; he will not abandon or destroy you or forget the covenant with your ancestors, which he confirmed to them by oath.

The LORD Is God

32 Ask now about the former days, long before your time, from the day God created human beings on the earth; ask from one end of the heavens to the other. Has anything so great as this ever happened, or has anything like it ever been heard of? **33** Has any other people heard the voice of God[a] speaking out of fire, as you have, and lived? **34** Has any god ever tried to take for himself one nation out of another nation, by testings, by signs and wonders, by war, by a mighty hand and an outstretched arm, or by great and awesome deeds, like all the things the LORD your God did for you in Egypt before your very eyes?

35 You were shown these things so that you might know that the LORD is God; besides him there is no other. **36** From heaven he made you hear his voice to discipline you. On earth he showed you his great fire, and you heard his words from out of the fire. **37** Because he loved your ancestors and chose their descendants after them, he brought you out of Egypt by his Presence and his great strength, **38** to drive out before you nations greater and stronger than you and to bring you into their land to give it to you for your inheritance, as it is today.

39 Acknowledge and take to heart this day that the LORD is God in heaven above and on the earth below. There is no other. **40** Keep his decrees and commands, which I am giving you today, so that it may go well with you and your children after you and that you may live long in the land the LORD your God gives you for all time.

Cities of Refuge

41 Then Moses set aside three cities east of the Jordan, **42** to which anyone who had killed a person could flee if they had unintentionally killed a neighbor without malice aforethought. They could flee into one of these cities and save their life. **43** The cities were these: Bezer in the wilderness plateau, for the Reubenites; Ramoth in Gilead, for the Gadites; and Golan in Bashan, for the Manassites.

Introduction to the Law

44 This is the law Moses set before the Israelites. **45** These are the stipulations, decrees and laws Moses gave them when they came out of Egypt **46** and were in the valley near Beth Peor east of the Jordan, in the land of Sihon king of the Amorites, who reigned in Heshbon and was defeated by Moses and the Israelites as they came out of Egypt. **47** They took possession of his land and the land of Og king of Bashan, the two Amorite kings east of the Jordan. **48** This land extended from Aroer on the rim of the Arnon Gorge to Mount Sirion[b] (that

---

[a] 33 Or *of a god*   [b] 48 Syriac (see also 3:9); Hebrew *Siyon*

is, Hermon), [49] and included all the Arabah east of the Jordan, as far as the Dead Sea,[a] below the slopes of Pisgah.

The Ten Commandments

5 Moses summoned all Israel and said:

Hear, Israel, the decrees and laws I declare in your hearing today. Learn them and be sure to follow them. [2] The LORD our God made a covenant with us at Horeb. [3] It was not with our ancestors[b] that the LORD made this covenant, but with us, with all of us who are alive here today. [4] The LORD spoke to you face to face out of the fire on the mountain. [5] (At that time I stood between the LORD and you to declare to you the word of the LORD, because you were afraid of the fire and did not go up the mountain.) And he said:

[6] "I am the LORD your God, who brought you out of Egypt, out of the land of slavery.

[7] "You shall have no other gods before[c] me.

[8] "You shall not make for yourself an image in the form of anything in heaven above or on the earth beneath or in the waters below. [9] You shall not bow down to them or worship them; for I, the LORD your God, am a jealous God, punishing the children for the sin of the parents to the third and fourth generation of those who hate me, [10] but showing love to a thousand generations of those who love me and keep my commandments.

[11] "You shall not misuse the name of the LORD your God, for the LORD will not hold anyone guiltless who misuses his name.

[12] "Observe the Sabbath day by keeping it holy, as the LORD your God has commanded you. [13] Six days you shall labor and do all your work, [14] but the seventh day is a sabbath to the LORD your God. On it you shall not do any work, neither you, nor your son or daughter, nor your male or female servant, nor your ox, your donkey or any of your animals, nor any foreigner residing in your towns, so that your male and female servants may rest, as you do. [15] Remember that you were slaves in Egypt and that the LORD your God brought you out of there with a mighty hand and an outstretched arm. Therefore the LORD

---

[a] 49 Hebrew *the Sea of the Arabah*   [b] 3 Or *not only with our parents*
[c] 7 Or *besides*

your God has commanded you to observe the Sabbath day.

16 "Honor your father and your mother, as the LORD your God has commanded you, so that you may live long and that it may go well with you in the land the LORD your God is giving you.

17 "You shall not murder.

18 "You shall not commit adultery.

19 "You shall not steal.

20 "You shall not give false testimony against your neighbor.

21 "You shall not covet your neighbor's wife. You shall not set your desire on your neighbor's house or land, his male or female servant, his ox or donkey, or anything that belongs to your neighbor."

22 These are the commandments the LORD proclaimed in a loud voice to your whole assembly there on the mountain from out of the fire, the cloud and the deep darkness; and he added nothing more. Then he wrote them on two stone tablets and gave them to me.

23 When you heard the voice out of the darkness, while the mountain was ablaze with fire, all the leaders of your tribes and your elders came to me. 24 And you said, "The LORD our God has shown us his glory and his majesty, and we have heard his voice from the fire. Today we have seen that a person can live even if God speaks with them. 25 But now, why should we die? This great fire will consume us, and we will die if we hear the voice of the LORD our God any longer. 26 For what mortal has ever heard the voice of the living God speaking out of fire, as we have, and survived? 27 Go near and listen to all that the LORD our God says. Then tell us whatever the LORD our God tells you. We will listen and obey."

28 The LORD heard you when you spoke to me, and the LORD said to me, "I have heard what this people said to you. Everything they said was good. 29 Oh, that their hearts would be inclined to fear me and keep all my commands always, so that it might go well with them and their children forever!

30 "Go, tell them to return to their tents. 31 But you stay here with me so that I may give you all the commands, decrees and laws you are to teach them to follow in the land I am giving them to possess."

32 So be careful to do what the LORD your God has commanded you; do not turn aside to the right or to the left. 33 Walk in obedience to all that the LORD your God has commanded you, so that you may live and prosper and prolong your days in the land that you will possess.

Love the LORD Your God

6 These are the commands, decrees and laws the LORD your God directed me to teach you to observe in the land that you are crossing the Jordan to possess, ²so that you, your children and their children after them may fear the LORD your God as long as you live by keeping all his decrees and commands that I give you, and so that you may enjoy long life. ³Hear, Israel, and be careful to obey so that it may go well with you and that you may increase greatly in a land flowing with milk and honey, just as the LORD, the God of your ancestors, promised you.

⁴Hear, O Israel: The LORD our God, the LORD is one.ᵃ ⁵Love the LORD your God with all your heart and with all your soul and with all your strength. ⁶These commandments that I give you today are to be on your hearts. ⁷Impress them on your children. Talk about them when you sit at home and when you walk along the road, when you lie down and when you get up. ⁸Tie them as symbols on your hands and bind them on your foreheads. ⁹Write them on the doorframes of your houses and on your gates.

¹⁰When the LORD your God brings you into the land he swore to your fathers, to Abraham, Isaac and Jacob, to give you—a land with large, flourishing cities you did not build, ¹¹houses filled with all kinds of good things you did not provide, wells you did not dig, and vineyards and olive groves you did not plant—then when you eat and are satisfied, ¹²be careful that you do not forget the LORD, who brought you out of Egypt, out of the land of slavery.

¹³Fear the LORD your God, serve him only and take your oaths in his name. ¹⁴Do not follow other gods, the gods of the peoples around you; ¹⁵for the LORD your God, who is among you, is a jealous God and his anger will burn against you, and he will destroy you from the face of the land. ¹⁶Do not put the LORD your God to the test as you did at Massah. ¹⁷Be sure to keep the commands of the LORD your God and the stipulations and decrees he has given you. ¹⁸Do what is right and good in the LORD's sight, so that it may go well with you and you may go in and take over the good land the LORD promised on oath to your ancestors, ¹⁹thrusting out all your enemies before you, as the LORD said.

²⁰In the future, when your son asks you, "What is the meaning of the stipulations, decrees and laws the LORD our God has commanded you?" ²¹tell him: "We were slaves of Pharaoh in Egypt, but the LORD brought us

---

ᵃ 4 Or The LORD our God is one LORD; or The LORD is our God, the LORD is one; or The LORD is our God, the LORD alone out of Egypt with a mighty hand. **22** Before our eyes the Lord sent signs and wonders — great and terrible — on Egypt and Pharaoh and his whole household. **23** But he brought us out from there to bring us in and give us the land he promised on oath to our ancestors. **24** The Lord commanded us to obey all these decrees and to fear the Lord our God, so that we might always prosper and be kept alive, as is the case today. **25** And if we are careful to obey all this law before the Lord our God, as he has commanded us, that will be our righteousness."

Driving Out the Nations

7 When the Lord your God brings you into the land you are entering to possess and drives out before you many nations — the Hittites, Girgashites, Amorites, Canaanites, Perizzites, Hivites and Jebusites, seven nations larger and stronger than you — **2** and when the Lord your God has delivered them over to you and you have defeated them, then you must destroy them totally.*a* Make no treaty with them, and show them no mercy. **3** Do not intermarry with them. Do not give your daughters to their sons or take their daughters for your sons, **4** for they will turn your chil-

dren away from following me to serve other gods, and the Lord's anger will burn against you and will quickly destroy you. **5** This is what you are to do to them: Break down their altars, smash their sacred stones, cut down their Asherah poles*b* and burn their idols in the fire. **6** For you are a people holy to the Lord your God. The Lord your God has chosen you out of all the peoples on the face of the earth to be his people, his treasured possession.

7 The Lord did not set his affection on you and choose you because you were more numerous than other peoples, for you were the fewest of all peoples. **8** But it was because the Lord loved you and kept the oath he swore to your ancestors that he brought you out with a mighty hand and redeemed you from the land of slavery, from the power of Pharaoh king of Egypt. **9** Know therefore that the Lord your God is God; he is the faithful God, keeping his covenant of love to a thousand generations of those who love him and keep his commandments. **10** But

those who hate him he will
    repay to their face by
    destruction;
he will not be slow to repay
    to their face those who
    hate him.

---

a 2 The Hebrew term refers to the irrevocable giving over of things or persons to the Lord, often by totally destroying them; also in verse 26.   *b 5* That is, wooden symbols of the goddess Asherah; here and elsewhere in Deuteronomy

[11] Therefore, take care to follow the commands, decrees and laws I give you today.

[12] If you pay attention to these laws and are careful to follow them, then the LORD your God will keep his covenant of love with you, as he swore to your ancestors. [13] He will love you and bless you and increase your numbers. He will bless the fruit of your womb, the crops of your land—your grain, new wine and olive oil—the calves of your herds and the lambs of your flocks in the land he swore to your ancestors to give you. [14] You will be blessed more than any other people; none of your men or women will be childless, nor will any of your livestock be without young. [15] The LORD will keep you free from every disease. He will not inflict on you the horrible diseases you knew in Egypt, but he will inflict them on all who hate you. [16] You must destroy all the peoples the LORD your God gives over to you. Do not look on them with pity and do not serve their gods, for that will be a snare to you.

[17] You may say to yourselves, "These nations are stronger than we are. How can we drive them out?" [18] But do not be afraid of them; remember well what the LORD your God did to Pharaoh and to all Egypt. [19] You saw with your own eyes the great trials, the signs and wonders, the mighty hand and outstretched arm, with which the LORD your God brought you out. The LORD your God will do the same to all the peoples you now fear. [20] Moreover, the LORD your God will send the hornet among them until even the survivors who hide from you have perished. [21] Do not be terrified by them, for the LORD your God, who is among you, is a great and awesome God. [22] The LORD your God will drive out those nations before you, little by little. You will not be allowed to eliminate them all at once, or the wild animals will multiply around you. [23] But the LORD your God will deliver them over to you, throwing them into great confusion until they are destroyed. [24] He will give their kings into your hand, and you will wipe out their names from under heaven. No one will be able to stand up against you; you will destroy them. [25] The images of their gods you are to burn in the fire. Do not covet the silver and gold on them, and do not take it for yourselves, or you will be ensnared by it, for it is detestable to the LORD your God. [26] Do not bring a detestable thing into your house or you, like it, will be set apart for destruction. Regard it as vile and utterly detest it, for it is set apart for destruction.

Do Not Forget the LORD

8 Be careful to follow every command I am giving you today, so that you may live and increase and may enter and possess the land the LORD promised on oath to your ancestors. ²Remember how the LORD your God led you all the way in the wilderness these forty years, to humble and test you in order to know what was in your heart, whether or not you would keep his commands. ³He humbled you, causing you to hunger and then feeding you with manna, which neither you nor your ancestors had known, to teach you that man does not live on bread alone but on every word that comes from the mouth of the LORD. ⁴Your clothes did not wear out and your feet did not swell during these forty years. ⁵Know then in your heart that as a man disciplines his son, so the LORD your God disciplines you.

⁶Observe the commands of the LORD your God, walking in obedience to him and revering him. ⁷For the LORD your God is bringing you into a good land—a land with brooks, streams, and deep springs gushing out into the valleys and hills; ⁸a land with wheat and barley, vines and fig trees, pomegranates, olive oil and honey; ⁹a land where bread will not be scarce and you will lack nothing; a land where the rocks are iron and you can dig copper out of the hills.

¹⁰When you have eaten and are satisfied, praise the LORD your God for the good land he has given you. ¹¹Be careful that you do not forget the LORD your God, failing to observe his commands, his laws and his decrees that I am giving you this day. ¹²Otherwise, when you eat and are satisfied, when you build fine houses and settle down, ¹³and when your herds and flocks grow large and your silver and gold increase and all you have is multiplied, ¹⁴then your heart will become proud and you will forget the LORD your God, who brought you out of Egypt, out of the land of slavery. ¹⁵He led you through the vast and dreadful wilderness, that thirsty and waterless land, with its venomous snakes and scorpions. He brought you water out of hard rock. ¹⁶He gave you manna to eat in the wilderness, something your ancestors had never known, to humble and test you so that in the end it might go well with you. ¹⁷You may say to yourself, "My power and the strength of my hands have produced this wealth for me." ¹⁸But remember the LORD your God, for it is he who gives you the ability to produce wealth, and so confirms his covenant, which he swore to your ancestors, as it is today.

¹⁹If you ever forget the LORD your God and follow other gods and worship and bow down to them, I testify against you today that you will surely be destroyed. ²⁰Like the nations the LORD destroyed before you, so you will be destroyed for not obeying the LORD your God.

Not Because of Israel's Righteousness

9 Hear, Israel: You are now about to cross the Jordan to go in and dispossess nations greater and stronger than you, with large cities that have walls up to the sky. **2** The people are strong and tall—Anakites! You know about them and have heard it said: "Who can stand up against the Anakites?" **3** But be assured today that the LORD your God is the one who goes across ahead of you like a devouring fire. He will destroy them; he will subdue them before you. And you will drive them out and annihilate them quickly, as the LORD has promised you.

4 After the LORD your God has driven them out before you, do not say to yourself, "The LORD has brought me here to take possession of this land because of my righteousness." No, it is on account of the wickedness of these nations that the LORD is going to drive them out before you. **5** It is not because of your righteousness or your integrity that you are going in to take possession of their land; but on account of the wickedness of these nations, the LORD your God will drive them out before you, to accomplish what he swore to your fathers, to Abraham, Isaac and Jacob. **6** Understand, then, that it is not because of your righteousness that the LORD your God is giving you this good land to possess, for you are a stiff-necked people.

The Golden Calf

7 Remember this and never forget how you aroused the anger of the LORD your God in the wilderness. From the day you left Egypt until you arrived here, you have been rebellious against the LORD. **8** At Horeb you aroused the LORD's wrath so that he was angry enough to destroy you. **9** When I went up on the mountain to receive the tablets of stone, the tablets of the covenant that the LORD had made with you, I stayed on the mountain forty days and forty nights; I ate no bread and drank no water. **10** The LORD gave me two stone tablets inscribed by the finger of God. On them were all the commandments the LORD proclaimed to you on the mountain out of the fire, on the day of the assembly.

11 At the end of the forty days and forty nights, the LORD gave me the two stone tablets, the tablets of the covenant. **12** Then the LORD told me, "Go down from here at once, because your people whom you brought out of Egypt have become corrupt. They have turned away quickly from what I commanded them and have made an idol for themselves."

13 And the LORD said to me, "I have seen this people, and they are a stiff-necked people indeed! **14** Let me alone, so that I may destroy them and blot out their name from under heaven. And I will make you into a nation stronger and more numerous than they."

¹⁵So I turned and went down from the mountain while it was ablaze with fire. And the two tablets of the covenant were in my hands. ¹⁶When I looked, I saw that you had sinned against the LORD your God; you had made for yourselves an idol cast in the shape of a calf. You had turned aside quickly from the way that the LORD had commanded you. ¹⁷So I took the two tablets and threw them out of my hands, breaking them to pieces before your eyes.

¹⁸Then once again I fell prostrate before the LORD for forty days and forty nights; I ate no bread and drank no water, because of all the sin you had committed, doing what was evil in the LORD's sight and so arousing his anger. ¹⁹I feared the anger and wrath of the LORD, for he was angry enough with you to destroy you. But again the LORD listened to me. ²⁰And the LORD was angry enough with Aaron to destroy him, but at that time I prayed for Aaron too. ²¹Also I took that sinful thing of yours, the calf you had made, and burned it in the fire. Then I crushed it and ground it to powder as fine as dust and threw the dust into a stream that flowed down the mountain.

²²You also made the LORD angry at Taberah, at Massah and at Kibroth Hattaavah.

²³And when the LORD sent you out from Kadesh Barnea, he said, "Go up and take possession of the land I have given you." But you rebelled against the command of the LORD your God. You did not trust him or obey him. ²⁴You have been rebellious against the LORD ever since I have known you.

²⁵I lay prostrate before the LORD those forty days and forty nights because the LORD had said he would destroy you. ²⁶I prayed to the LORD and said, "Sovereign LORD, do not destroy your people, your own inheritance that you redeemed by your great power and brought out of Egypt with a mighty hand. ²⁷Remember your servants Abraham, Isaac and Jacob. Overlook the stubbornness of this people, their wickedness and their sin. ²⁸Otherwise, the country from which you brought us will say, 'Because the LORD was not able to take them into the land he had promised them, and because he hated them, he brought them out to put them to death in the wilderness.' ²⁹But they are your people, your inheritance that you brought out by your great power and your outstretched arm."

Tablets Like the First Ones

10 At that time the LORD said to me, "Chisel out two stone tablets like the first ones and come up to me on the mountain. Also make a wooden ark.[a] [2]I will write on the tablets the words that were on the first tablets, which you broke. Then you are to put them in the ark."

[3]So I made the ark out of acacia wood and chiseled out two stone tablets like the first ones, and I went up on the mountain with the two tablets in my hands. [4]The LORD wrote on these tablets what he had written before, the Ten Commandments he had proclaimed to you on the mountain, out of the fire, on the day of the assembly. And the LORD gave them to me. [5]Then I came back down the mountain and put the tablets in the ark I had made, as the LORD commanded me, and they are there now.

[6](The Israelites traveled from the wells of Bene Jaakan to Moserah. There Aaron died and was buried, and Eleazar his son succeeded him as priest. [7]From there they traveled to Gudgodah and on to Jotbathah, a land with streams of water. [8]At that time the LORD set apart the tribe of Levi to carry the ark of the covenant of the LORD, to stand before the LORD to minister and to pronounce blessings in his name, as they still do today. [9]That is why the Levites have no share or inheritance among their fellow Israelites; the LORD is their inheritance, as the LORD your God told them.)

[10]Now I had stayed on the mountain forty days and forty nights, as I did the first time, and the LORD listened to me at this time also. It was not his will to destroy you. [11]"Go," the LORD said to me, "and lead the people on their way, so that they may enter and possess the land I swore to their ancestors to give them."

Fear the LORD

[12]And now, Israel, what does the LORD your God ask of you but to fear the LORD your God, to walk in obedience to him, to love him, to serve the LORD your God with all your heart and with all your soul, [13]and to observe the LORD's commands and decrees that I am giving you today for your own good?

[14]To the LORD your God belong the heavens, even the highest heavens, the earth and everything in it. [15]Yet the LORD set his affection on your ancestors and loved them, and he chose you, their descendants, above all the nations—as it is today. [16]Circumcise your hearts, therefore, and do not be stiff-necked any longer. [17]For the LORD your God is God of gods and Lord of lords, the great God, mighty and awesome, who shows no partiality and accepts no bribes. [18]He defends the cause of the fatherless and the widow, and loves the foreigner residing among you, giving them food

---

[a] 1 That is, a chest

and clothing. ¹⁹And you are to love those who are foreigners, for you yourselves were foreigners in Egypt. ²⁰Fear the LORD your God and serve him. Hold fast to him and take your oaths in his name. ²¹He is the one you praise; he is your God, who performed for you those great and awesome wonders you saw with your own eyes. ²²Your ancestors who went down into Egypt were seventy in all, and now the LORD your God has made you as numerous as the stars in the sky.

Love and Obey the LORD

11 Love the LORD your God and keep his requirements, his decrees, his laws and his commands always. ²Remember today that your children were not the ones who saw and experienced the discipline of the LORD your God: his majesty, his mighty hand, his outstretched arm; ³the signs he performed and the things he did in the heart of Egypt, both to Pharaoh king of Egypt and to his whole country; ⁴what he did to the Egyptian army, to its horses and chariots, how he overwhelmed them with the waters of the Red Sea*a* as they were pursuing you, and how the LORD brought lasting ruin on them. ⁵It was not your children who saw what he did for you in the wilderness until you arrived at this place, ⁶and what he did

to Dathan and Abiram, sons of Eliab the Reubenite, when the earth opened its mouth right in the middle of all Israel and swallowed them up with their households, their tents and every living thing that belonged to them. ⁷But it was your own eyes that saw all these great things the LORD has done.

⁸Observe therefore all the commands I am giving you today, so that you may have the strength to go in and take over the land that you are crossing the Jordan to possess, ⁹and so that you may live long in the land the LORD swore to your ancestors to give to them and their descendants, a land flowing with milk and honey. ¹⁰The land you are entering to take over is not like the land of Egypt, from which you have come, where you planted your seed and irrigated it by foot as in a vegetable garden. ¹¹But the land you are crossing the Jordan to take possession of is a land of mountains and valleys that drinks rain from heaven. ¹²It is a land the LORD your God cares for; the eyes of the LORD your God are continually on it from the beginning of the year to its end.

¹³So if you faithfully obey the commands I am giving you today — to love the LORD your God and to serve him with all your heart and with all your soul — ¹⁴then I will send rain on your

---

a 4 Or *the Sea of Reeds*

land in its season, both autumn and spring rains, so that you may gather in your grain, new wine and olive oil. **15** I will provide grass in the fields for your cattle, and you will eat and be satisfied.

16 Be careful, or you will be enticed to turn away and worship other gods and bow down to them. **17** Then the LORD's anger will burn against you, and he will shut up the heavens so that it will not rain and the ground will yield no produce, and you will soon perish from the good land the LORD is giving you. **18** Fix these words of mine in your hearts and minds; tie them as symbols on your hands and bind them on your foreheads. **19** Teach them to your children, talking about them when you sit at home and when you walk along the road, when you lie down and when you get up. **20** Write them on the doorframes of your houses and on your gates, **21** so that your days and the days of your children may be many in the land the LORD swore to give your ancestors, as many as the days that the heavens are above the earth.

22 If you carefully observe all these commands I am giving you to follow — to love the LORD your God, to walk in obedience to him and to hold fast to him — **23** then the LORD will drive out all these nations before you, and you will dispossess nations larger and

stronger than you. **24** Every place where you set your foot will be yours: Your territory will extend from the desert to Lebanon, and from the Euphrates River to the Mediterranean Sea. **25** No one will be able to stand against you. The LORD your God, as he promised you, will put the terror and fear of you on the whole land, wherever you go.

26 See, I am setting before you today a blessing and a curse — **27** the blessing if you obey the commands of the LORD your God that I am giving you today; **28** the curse if you disobey the commands of the LORD your God and turn from the way that I command you today by following other gods, which you have not known. **29** When the LORD your God has brought you into the land you are entering to possess, you are to proclaim on Mount Gerizim the blessings, and on Mount Ebal the curses. **30** As you know, these mountains are across the Jordan, westward, toward the setting sun, near the great trees of Moreh, in the territory of those Canaanites living in the Arabah in the vicinity of Gilgal. **31** You are about to cross the Jordan to enter and take possession of the land the LORD your God is giving you. When you have taken it over and are living there, **32** be sure that you obey all the decrees and laws I am setting before you today.

The One Place of Worship

12 These are the decrees and laws you must be careful to follow in the land that the LORD, the God of your ancestors, has given you to possess—as long as you live in the land. ²Destroy completely all the places on the high mountains, on the hills and under every spreading tree, where the nations you are dispossessing worship their gods. ³Break down their altars, smash their sacred stones and burn their Asherah poles in the fire; cut down the idols of their gods and wipe out their names from those places.

⁴You must not worship the LORD your God in their way. ⁵But you are to seek the place the LORD your God will choose from among all your tribes to put his Name there for his dwelling. To that place you must go; ⁶there bring your burnt offerings and sacrifices, your tithes and special gifts, what you have vowed to give and your freewill offerings, and the firstborn of your herds and flocks. ⁷There, in the presence of the LORD your God, you and your families shall eat and shall rejoice in everything you have put your hand to, because the LORD your God has blessed you.

⁸You are not to do as we do here today, everyone doing as they see fit, ⁹since you have not yet reached the resting place and the inheritance the LORD your God is giving you. ¹⁰But you will cross the Jordan and settle in the land the LORD your God is giving you as an inheritance, and he will give you rest from all your enemies around you so that you will live in safety. ¹¹Then to the place the LORD your God will choose as a dwelling for his Name—there you are to bring everything I command you: your burnt offerings and sacrifices, your tithes and special gifts, and all the choice possessions you have vowed to the LORD. ¹²And there rejoice before the LORD your God—you, your sons and daughters, your male and female servants, and the Levites from your towns who have no allotment or inheritance of their own. ¹³Be careful not to sacrifice your burnt offerings anywhere you please. ¹⁴Offer them only at the place the LORD will choose in one of your tribes, and there observe everything I command you.

¹⁵Nevertheless, you may slaughter your animals in any of your towns and eat as much of the meat as you want, as if it were gazelle or deer, according to the blessing the LORD your God gives you. Both the ceremonially unclean and the clean may eat it. ¹⁶But you must not eat the blood; pour it out on the ground like water. ¹⁷You must not eat in your own towns the tithe of your grain and new wine and olive oil, or the firstborn of your herds

and flocks, or whatever you have vowed to give, or your freewill offerings or special gifts. [18]Instead, you are to eat them in the presence of the LORD your God at the place the LORD your God will choose — you, your sons and daughters, your male and female servants, and the Levites from your towns — and you are to rejoice before the LORD your God in everything you put your hand to. [19]Be careful not to neglect the Levites as long as you live in your land.

[20]When the LORD your God has enlarged your territory as he promised you, and you crave meat and say, "I would like some meat," then you may eat as much of it as you want. [21]If the place where the LORD your God chooses to put his Name is too far away from you, you may slaughter animals from the herds and flocks the LORD has given you, as I have commanded you, and in your own towns you may eat as much of them as you want. [22]Eat them as you would gazelle or deer. Both the ceremonially unclean and the clean may eat. [23]But be sure you do not eat the blood, because the blood is the life, and you must not eat the life with the meat. [24]You must not eat the blood; pour it out on the ground like water. [25]Do not eat it, so that it may go well with you and your children after you, because you will be doing what is right in the eyes of the LORD.

[26]But take your consecrated things and whatever you have vowed to give, and go to the place the LORD will choose. [27]Present your burnt offerings on the altar of the LORD your God, both the meat and the blood. The blood of your sacrifices must be poured beside the altar of the LORD your God, but you may eat the meat. [28]Be careful to obey all these regulations I am giving you, so that it may always go well with you and your children after you, because you will be doing what is good and right in the eyes of the LORD your God.

[29]The LORD your God will cut off before you the nations you are about to invade and dispossess. But when you have driven them out and settled in their land, [30]and after they have been destroyed before you, be careful not to be ensnared by inquiring about their gods, saying, "How do these nations serve their gods? We will do the same." [31]You must not worship the LORD your God in their way, because in worshiping their gods, they do all kinds of detestable things the LORD hates. They even burn their sons and daughters in the fire as sacrifices to their gods.

[32]See that you do all I command you; do not add to it or take away from it.[a]

---

[a] 32 In Hebrew texts this verse (12:32) is numbered 13:1.

Worshiping Other Gods

13 [a] If a prophet, or one who foretells by dreams, appears among you and announces to you a sign or wonder, **2** and if the sign or wonder spoken of takes place, and the prophet says, "Let us follow other gods" (gods you have not known) "and let us worship them," **3** you must not listen to the words of that prophet or dreamer. The LORD your God is testing you to find out whether you love him with all your heart and with all your soul. **4** It is the LORD your God you must follow, and him you must revere. Keep his commands and obey him; serve him and hold fast to him. **5** That prophet or dreamer must be put to death for inciting rebellion against the LORD your God, who brought you out of Egypt and redeemed you from the land of slavery. That prophet or dreamer tried to turn you from the way the LORD your God commanded you to follow. You must purge the evil from among you.

6 If your very own brother, or your son or daughter, or the wife you love, or your closest friend secretly entices you, saying, "Let us go and worship other gods" (gods that neither you nor your ancestors have known, **7** gods of the peoples around you, whether near or far, from one end of the land to the other), **8** do not yield to them or listen to them. Show them no pity. Do not spare them or shield them. **9** You must certainly put them to death. Your hand must be the first in putting them to death, and then the hands of all the people. **10** Stone them to death, because they tried to turn you away from the LORD your God, who brought you out of Egypt, out of the land of slavery. **11** Then all Israel will hear and be afraid, and no one among you will do such an evil thing again.

12 If you hear it said about one of the towns the LORD your God is giving you to live in **13** that troublemakers have arisen among you and have led the people of their town astray, saying, "Let us go and worship other gods" (gods you have not known), **14** then you must inquire, probe and investigate it thoroughly. And if it is true and it has been proved that this detestable thing has been done among you, **15** you must certainly put to the sword all who live in that town. You must destroy it completely,[b] both its people and its livestock. **16** You are to gather all the plunder of the town into the middle of the public square and completely burn the town and all its plunder as a whole burnt offering to the LORD your God. That town is to remain a ruin forever, never to

---

[a] In Hebrew texts 13:1-18 is numbered 13:2-19.   [b] 15 The Hebrew term refers to the irrevocable giving over of things or persons to the LORD, often by totally destroying them.

be rebuilt, [17] and none of the condemned things[a] are to be found in your hands. Then the LORD will turn from his fierce anger, will show you mercy, and will have compassion on you. He will increase your numbers, as he promised on oath to your ancestors— [18] because you obey the LORD your God by keeping all his commands that I am giving you today and doing what is right in his eyes.

Clean and Unclean Food

14 You are the children of the LORD your God. Do not cut yourselves or shave the front of your heads for the dead, [2] for you are a people holy to the LORD your God. Out of all the peoples on the face of the earth, the LORD has chosen you to be his treasured possession.

[3] Do not eat any detestable thing. [4] These are the animals you may eat: the ox, the sheep, the goat, [5] the deer, the gazelle, the roe deer, the wild goat, the ibex, the antelope and the mountain sheep.[b] [6] You may eat any animal that has a divided hoof and that chews the cud. [7] However, of those that chew the cud or that have a divided hoof you may not eat the camel, the rabbit or the hyrax. Although they chew the cud, they do not have a divided hoof; they are ceremonially unclean for you. [8] The pig is also unclean; although it has a divided hoof, it does not chew the cud. You are not to eat their meat or touch their carcasses.

[9] Of all the creatures living in the water, you may eat any that has fins and scales. [10] But anything that does not have fins and scales you may not eat; for you it is unclean.

[11] You may eat any clean bird. [12] But these you may not eat: the eagle, the vulture, the black vulture, [13] the red kite, the black kite, any kind of falcon, [14] any kind of raven, [15] the horned owl, the screech owl, the gull, any kind of hawk, [16] the little owl, the great owl, the white owl, [17] the desert owl, the osprey, the cormorant, [18] the stork, any kind of heron, the hoopoe and the bat.

[19] All flying insects are unclean to you; do not eat them. [20] But any winged creature that is clean you may eat.

[21] Do not eat anything you find already dead. You may give it to the foreigner residing in any of your towns, and they may eat it, or you may sell it to any other foreigner. But you are a people holy to the LORD your God.

Do not cook a young goat in its mother's milk.

Tithes

[22] Be sure to set aside a tenth of all that your fields produce each

---

[a] 17 The Hebrew term refers to the irrevocable giving over of things or persons to the LORD, often by totally destroying them.   [b] 5 The precise identification of some of the birds and animals in this chapter is uncertain.

year. **²³**Eat the tithe of your grain, new wine and olive oil, and the firstborn of your herds and flocks in the presence of the LORD your God at the place he will choose as a dwelling for his Name, so that you may learn to revere the LORD your God always. **²⁴**But if that place is too distant and you have been blessed by the LORD your God and cannot carry your tithe (because the place where the LORD will choose to put his Name is so far away), **²⁵**then exchange your tithe for silver, and take the silver with you and go to the place the LORD your God will choose. **²⁶**Use the silver to buy whatever you like: cattle, sheep, wine or other fermented drink, or anything you wish. Then you and your household shall eat there in the presence of the LORD your God and rejoice. **²⁷**And do not neglect the Levites living in your towns, for they have no allotment or inheritance of their own.

²⁸At the end of every three years, bring all the tithes of that year's produce and store it in your towns, **²⁹**so that the Levites (who have no allotment or inheritance of their own) and the foreigners, the fatherless and the widows who live in your towns may come and eat and be satisfied, and so that the LORD your God may bless you in all the work of your hands.

The Year for Canceling Debts

15 At the end of every seven years you must cancel debts. **²**This is how it is to be done: Every creditor shall cancel any loan they have made to a fellow Israelite. They shall not require payment from anyone among their own people, because the LORD's time for canceling debts has been proclaimed. **³**You may require payment from a foreigner, but you must cancel any debt your fellow Israelite owes you. **⁴**However, there need be no poor people among you, for in the land the LORD your God is giving you to possess as your inheritance, he will richly bless you, **⁵**if only you fully obey the LORD your God and are careful to follow all these commands I am giving you today. **⁶**For the LORD your God will bless you as he has promised, and you will lend to many nations but will borrow from none. You will rule over many nations but none will rule over you.

⁷If anyone is poor among your fellow Israelites in any of the towns of the land the LORD your God is giving you, do not be hard-hearted or tightfisted toward them. **⁸**Rather, be openhanded and freely lend them whatever they need. **⁹**Be careful not to harbor this wicked thought: "The seventh year, the year for canceling debts, is near," so that you do not show ill will toward the needy among your fellow Israelites and give them nothing. They may then appeal to the LORD against you, and you will be found guilty of sin. **¹⁰**Give generously to them and do so without a grudging heart; then because of this the LORD your God will bless you in all your work and in everything you put your hand to. ¹¹ There will always be poor people in the land. Therefore I command you to be openhanded toward your fellow Israelites who are poor and needy in your land.

Freeing Servants

¹² If any of your people — Hebrew men or women — sell themselves to you and serve you six years, in the seventh year you must let them go free. ¹³ And when you release them, do not send them away empty-handed. ¹⁴ Supply them liberally from your flock, your threshing floor and your winepress. Give to them as the LORD your God has blessed you. ¹⁵ Remember that you were slaves in Egypt and the LORD your God redeemed you. That is why I give you this command today.

¹⁶ But if your servant says to you, "I do not want to leave you," because he loves you and your family and is well off with you, ¹⁷ then take an awl and push it through his earlobe into the door, and he will become your servant for life. Do the same for your female servant.

¹⁸ Do not consider it a hardship to set your servant free, because their service to you these six years has been worth twice as much as that of a hired hand. And the LORD your God will bless you in everything you do.

The Firstborn Animals

¹⁹ Set apart for the LORD your God every firstborn male of your herds and flocks. Do not put the firstborn of your cows to work, and do not shear the firstborn of your sheep. ²⁰ Each year you and your family are to eat them in the presence of the LORD your God at the place he will choose. ²¹ If an animal has a defect, is lame or blind, or has any serious flaw, you must not sacrifice it to the LORD your God. ²² You are to eat it in your own towns. Both the ceremonially unclean and the clean may eat it, as if it were gazelle or deer. ²³ But you must not eat the blood; pour it out on the ground like water.

The Passover

16 Observe the month of Aviv and celebrate the Passover of the LORD your God, because in the month of Aviv he brought you out of Egypt by night. ² Sacrifice as the Passover to the LORD your God an animal from your flock or herd at the place the LORD will choose as a dwelling for his Name. ³ Do not eat it with bread made with yeast, but for seven days eat unleavened bread, the bread of affliction, because you left Egypt in haste — so that all the days of your life you may remember the time of your

departure from Egypt. ⁴Let no yeast be found in your possession in all your land for seven days. Do not let any of the meat you sacrifice on the evening of the first day remain until morning.

⁵You must not sacrifice the Passover in any town the LORD your God gives you ⁶except in the place he will choose as a dwelling for his Name. There you must sacrifice the Passover in the evening, when the sun goes down, on the anniversary*ᵃ* of your departure from Egypt. ⁷Roast it and eat it at the place the LORD your God will choose. Then in the morning return to your tents. ⁸For six days eat unleavened bread and on the seventh day hold an assembly to the LORD your God and do no work.

The Festival of Weeks

⁹Count off seven weeks from the time you begin to put the sickle to the standing grain. ¹⁰Then celebrate the Festival of Weeks to the LORD your God by giving a freewill offering in proportion to the blessings the LORD your God has given you. ¹¹And rejoice before the LORD your God at the place he will choose as a dwelling for his Name — you, your sons and daughters, your male and female servants, the Levites in your towns, and the foreigners, the fatherless and the widows living among you. ¹²Remember that

you were slaves in Egypt, and follow carefully these decrees.

The Festival of Tabernacles

¹³Celebrate the Festival of Tabernacles for seven days after you have gathered the produce of your threshing floor and your winepress. ¹⁴Be joyful at your festival — you, your sons and daughters, your male and female servants, and the Levites, the foreigners, the fatherless and the widows who live in your towns. ¹⁵For seven days celebrate the festival to the LORD your God at the place the LORD will choose. For the LORD your God will bless you in all your harvest and in all the work of your hands, and your joy will be complete.

¹⁶Three times a year all your men must appear before the LORD your God at the place he will choose: at the Festival of Unleavened Bread, the Festival of Weeks and the Festival of Tabernacles. No one should appear before the LORD empty-handed: ¹⁷Each of you must bring a gift in proportion to the way the LORD your God has blessed you.

Judges

¹⁸Appoint judges and officials for each of your tribes in every town the LORD your God is giving you, and they shall judge the people fairly. ¹⁹Do not pervert justice or show partiality. Do not accept

---

ᵃ 6 Or *down, at the time of day*

a bribe, for a bribe blinds the eyes of the wise and twists the words of the innocent. ²⁰Follow justice and justice alone, so that you may live and possess the land the LORD your God is giving you.

Worshiping Other Gods

²¹Do not set up any wooden Asherah pole beside the altar you build to the LORD your God, ²²and do not erect a sacred stone, for these the LORD your God hates.

17 Do not sacrifice to the LORD your God an ox or a sheep that has any defect or flaw in it, for that would be detestable to him.

²If a man or woman living among you in one of the towns the LORD gives you is found doing evil in the eyes of the LORD your God in violation of his covenant, ³and contrary to my command has worshiped other gods, bowing down to them or to the sun or the moon or the stars in the sky, ⁴and this has been brought to your attention, then you must investigate it thoroughly. If it is true and it has been proved that this detestable thing has been done in Israel, ⁵take the man or woman who has done this evil deed to your city gate and stone that person to death. ⁶On the testimony of two or three witnesses a person is to be put to death, but no one is to be put to death on the testimony of only one witness.

⁷The hands of the witnesses must be the first in putting that person to death, and then the hands of all the people. You must purge the evil from among you.

Law Courts

⁸If cases come before your courts that are too difficult for you to judge—whether bloodshed, lawsuits or assaults—take them to the place the LORD your God will choose. ⁹Go to the Levitical priests and to the judge who is in office at that time. Inquire of them and they will give you the verdict. ¹⁰You must act according to the decisions they give you at the place the LORD will choose. Be careful to do everything they instruct you to do. ¹¹Act according to whatever they teach you and the decisions they give you. Do not turn aside from what they tell you, to the right or to the left. ¹²Anyone who shows contempt for the judge or for the priest who stands ministering there to the LORD your God is to be put to death. You must purge the evil from Israel. ¹³All the people will hear and be afraid, and will not be contemptuous again.

The King

¹⁴When you enter the land the LORD your God is giving you and have taken possession of it and settled in it, and you say, "Let us set a king over us like all the nations around us," ¹⁵be sure to ap-

point over you a king the LORD your God chooses. He must be from among your fellow Israelites. Do not place a foreigner over you, one who is not an Israelite. ¹⁶The king, moreover, must not acquire great numbers of horses for himself or make the people return to Egypt to get more of them, for the LORD has told you, "You are not to go back that way again." ¹⁷He must not take many wives, or his heart will be led astray. He must not accumulate large amounts of silver and gold.

¹⁸When he takes the throne of his kingdom, he is to write for himself on a scroll a copy of this law, taken from that of the Levitical priests. ¹⁹It is to be with him, and he is to read it all the days of his life so that he may learn to revere the LORD his God and follow carefully all the words of this law and these decrees ²⁰and not consider himself better than his fellow Israelites and turn from the law to the right or to the left. Then he and his descendants will reign a long time over his kingdom in Israel.

Offerings for Priests and Levites

18 The Levitical priests — indeed, the whole tribe of Levi — are to have no allotment or inheritance with Israel. They shall live on the food offerings presented to the LORD, for that is their inheritance. ²They shall have no inheritance among their fellow Israelites; the LORD is their inheritance, as he promised them.

³This is the share due the priests from the people who sacrifice a bull or a sheep: the shoulder, the internal organs and the meat from the head. ⁴You are to give them the firstfruits of your grain, new wine and olive oil, and the first wool from the shearing of your sheep, ⁵for the LORD your God has chosen them and their descendants out of all your tribes to stand and minister in the LORD's name always.

⁶If a Levite moves from one of your towns anywhere in Israel where he is living, and comes in all earnestness to the place the LORD will choose, ⁷he may minister in the name of the LORD his God like all his fellow Levites who serve there in the presence of the LORD. ⁸He is to share equally in their benefits, even though he has received money from the sale of family possessions.

Occult Practices

⁹When you enter the land the LORD your God is giving you, do not learn to imitate the detestable ways of the nations there. ¹⁰Let no one be found among you who sacrifices their son or daughter in the fire, who practices divination or sorcery, interprets omens, engages in witchcraft, ¹¹or casts spells, or who is a medium or spiritist or who consults the

dead. [12] Anyone who does these things is detestable to the LORD; because of these same detestable practices the LORD your God will drive out those nations before you. [13] You must be blameless before the LORD your God.

The Prophet

[14] The nations you will dispossess listen to those who practice sorcery or divination. But as for you, the LORD your God has not permitted you to do so. [15] The LORD your God will raise up for you a prophet like me from among you, from your fellow Israelites. You must listen to him. [16] For this is what you asked of the LORD your God at Horeb on the day of the assembly when you said, "Let us not hear the voice of the LORD our God nor see this great fire anymore, or we will die."

[17] The LORD said to me: "What they say is good. [18] I will raise up for them a prophet like you from among their fellow Israelites, and I will put my words in his mouth. He will tell them everything I command him. [19] I myself will call to account anyone who does not listen to my words that the prophet speaks in my name. [20] But a prophet who presumes to speak in my name anything I have not commanded, or a prophet who speaks in the name of other gods, is to be put to death."

[21] You may say to yourselves, "How can we know when a message has not been spoken by the LORD?" [22] If what a prophet proclaims in the name of the LORD does not take place or come true, that is a message the LORD has not spoken. That prophet has spoken presumptuously, so do not be alarmed.

Cities of Refuge

19 When the LORD your God has destroyed the nations whose land he is giving you, and when you have driven them out and settled in their towns and houses, [2] then set aside for yourselves three cities in the land the LORD your God is giving you to possess. [3] Determine the distances involved and divide into three parts the land the LORD your God is giving you as an inheritance, so that a person who kills someone may flee for refuge to one of these cities.

[4] This is the rule concerning anyone who kills a person and flees there for safety—anyone who kills a neighbor unintentionally, without malice aforethought. [5] For instance, a man may go into the forest with his neighbor to cut wood, and as he swings his ax to fell a tree, the head may fly off and hit his neighbor and kill him. That man may flee to one of these cities and save his life. [6] Otherwise, the avenger of blood might pursue him in a rage, overtake him if the distance is too great, and

kill him even though he is not deserving of death, since he did it to his neighbor without malice aforethought. ⁷This is why I command you to set aside for yourselves three cities.

⁸If the LORD your God enlarges your territory, as he promised on oath to your ancestors, and gives you the whole land he promised them, ⁹because you carefully follow all these laws I command you today—to love the LORD your God and to walk always in obedience to him—then you are to set aside three more cities. ¹⁰Do this so that innocent blood will not be shed in your land, which the LORD your God is giving you as your inheritance, and so that you will not be guilty of bloodshed.

¹¹But if out of hate someone lies in wait, assaults and kills a neighbor, and then flees to one of these cities, ¹²the killer shall be sent for by the town elders, be brought back from the city, and be handed over to the avenger of blood to die. ¹³Show no pity. You must purge from Israel the guilt of shedding innocent blood, so that it may go well with you.

¹⁴Do not move your neighbor's boundary stone set up by your predecessors in the inheritance you receive in the land the LORD your God is giving you to possess.

Witnesses

¹⁵One witness is not enough to convict anyone accused of any crime or offense they may have committed. A matter must be established by the testimony of two or three witnesses.

¹⁶If a malicious witness takes the stand to accuse someone of a crime, ¹⁷the two people involved in the dispute must stand in the presence of the LORD before the priests and the judges who are in office at the time. ¹⁸The judges must make a thorough investigation, and if the witness proves to be a liar, giving false testimony against a fellow Israelite, ¹⁹then do to the false witness as that witness intended to do to the other party. You must purge the evil from among you. ²⁰The rest of the people will hear of this and be afraid, and never again will such an evil thing be done among you. ²¹Show no pity: life for life, eye for eye, tooth for tooth, hand for hand, foot for foot.

Going to War

20 When you go to war against your enemies and see horses and chariots and an army greater than yours, do not be afraid of them, because the LORD your God, who brought you up out of Egypt, will be with you. ²When you are about to go into battle, the priest shall come forward and address the army. ³He shall say: "Hear, Israel: Today you are going into battle against your enemies. Do not be fainthearted or afraid; do not panic or be

terrified by them. **4**For the LORD your God is the one who goes with you to fight for you against your enemies to give you victory."

5The officers shall say to the army: "Has anyone built a new house and not yet begun to live in it? Let him go home, or he may die in battle and someone else may begin to live in it. **6**Has anyone planted a vineyard and not begun to enjoy it? Let him go home, or he may die in battle and someone else enjoy it. **7**Has anyone become pledged to a woman and not married her? Let him go home, or he may die in battle and someone else marry her." **8**Then the officers shall add, "Is anyone afraid or fainthearted? Let him go home so that his fellow soldiers will not become disheartened too." **9**When the officers have finished speaking to the army, they shall appoint commanders over it.

10When you march up to attack a city, make its people an offer of peace. **11**If they accept and open their gates, all the people in it shall be subject to forced labor and shall work for you. **12**If they refuse to make peace and they engage you in battle, lay siege to that city. **13**When the LORD your God delivers it into your hand, put to the sword all the men in it. **14**As for the women, the children, the livestock and everything else in the city, you may take these as plunder for yourselves. And you may use the plunder the LORD your God gives you from your enemies. **15**This is how you are to treat all the cities that are at a distance from you and do not belong to the nations nearby.

16However, in the cities of the nations the LORD your God is giving you as an inheritance, do not leave alive anything that breathes. **17**Completely destroy*a* them — the Hittites, Amorites, Canaanites, Perizzites, Hivites and Jebusites — as the LORD your God has commanded you. **18**Otherwise, they will teach you to follow all the detestable things they do in worshiping their gods, and you will sin against the LORD your God.

19When you lay siege to a city for a long time, fighting against it to capture it, do not destroy its trees by putting an ax to them, because you can eat their fruit. Do not cut them down. Are the trees people, that you should besiege them?*b* **20**However, you may cut down trees that you know are not fruit trees and use them to build siege works until the city at war with you falls.

Atonement for an Unsolved Murder

21 If someone is found slain, lying in a field in the land the LORD your God is giving you to possess, and it is not known

---

a 17 The Hebrew term refers to the irrevocable giving over of things or persons to the LORD, often by totally destroying them.   *b 19* Or *down to use in the siege, for the fruit trees are for the benefit of people.*

who the killer was, ²your elders and judges shall go out and measure the distance from the body to the neighboring towns. ³Then the elders of the town nearest the body shall take a heifer that has never been worked and has never worn a yoke ⁴and lead it down to a valley that has not been plowed or planted and where there is a flowing stream. There in the valley they are to break the heifer's neck. ⁵The Levitical priests shall step forward, for the LORD your God has chosen them to minister and to pronounce blessings in the name of the LORD and to decide all cases of dispute and assault. ⁶Then all the elders of the town nearest the body shall wash their hands over the heifer whose neck was broken in the valley, ⁷and they shall declare: "Our hands did not shed this blood, nor did our eyes see it done. ⁸Accept this atonement for your people Israel, whom you have redeemed, LORD, and do not hold your people guilty of the blood of an innocent person." Then the bloodshed will be atoned for, ⁹and you will have purged from yourselves the guilt of shedding innocent blood, since you have done what is right in the eyes of the LORD.

Marrying a Captive Woman

¹⁰When you go to war against your enemies and the LORD your God delivers them into your hands and you take captives, ¹¹if you notice among the captives a beautiful woman and are attracted to her, you may take her as your wife. ¹²Bring her into your home and have her shave her head, trim her nails ¹³and put aside the clothes she was wearing when captured. After she has lived in your house and mourned her father and mother for a full month, then you may go to her and be her husband and she shall be your wife. ¹⁴If you are not pleased with her, let her go wherever she wishes. You must not sell her or treat her as a slave, since you have dishonored her.

The Right of the Firstborn

¹⁵If a man has two wives, and he loves one but not the other, and both bear him sons but the firstborn is the son of the wife he does not love, ¹⁶when he wills his property to his sons, he must not give the rights of the firstborn to the son of the wife he loves in preference to his actual firstborn, the son of the wife he does not love. ¹⁷He must acknowledge the son of his unloved wife as the firstborn by giving him a double share of all he has. That son is the first sign of his father's strength. The right of the firstborn belongs to him.

A Rebellious Son

¹⁸If someone has a stubborn and rebellious son who does not obey his father and mother and will not listen to them when they

discipline him, [19]his father and mother shall take hold of him and bring him to the elders at the gate of his town. [20]They shall say to the elders, "This son of ours is stubborn and rebellious. He will not obey us. He is a glutton and a drunkard." [21]Then all the men of his town are to stone him to death. You must purge the evil from among you. All Israel will hear of it and be afraid.

Various Laws

[22]If someone guilty of a capital offense is put to death and their body is exposed on a pole, [23]you must not leave the body hanging on the pole overnight. Be sure to bury it that same day, because anyone who is hung on a pole is under God's curse. You must not desecrate the land the LORD your God is giving you as an inheritance.

22 If you see your fellow Israelite's ox or sheep straying, do not ignore it but be sure to take it back to its owner. [2]If they do not live near you or if you do not know who owns it, take it home with you and keep it until they come looking for it. Then give it back. [3]Do the same if you find their donkey or cloak or anything else they have lost. Do not ignore it.

[4]If you see your fellow Israelite's donkey or ox fallen on the road, do not ignore it. Help the owner get it to its feet.

[5]A woman must not wear men's clothing, nor a man wear women's clothing, for the LORD your God detests anyone who does this.

[6]If you come across a bird's nest beside the road, either in a tree or on the ground, and the mother is sitting on the young or on the eggs, do not take the mother with the young. [7]You may take the young, but be sure to let the mother go, so that it may go well with you and you may have a long life.

[8]When you build a new house, make a parapet around your roof so that you may not bring the guilt of bloodshed on your house if someone falls from the roof.

[9]Do not plant two kinds of seed in your vineyard; if you do, not only the crops you plant but also the fruit of the vineyard will be defiled.[a]

[10]Do not plow with an ox and a donkey yoked together.

[11]Do not wear clothes of wool and linen woven together.

[12]Make tassels on the four corners of the cloak you wear.

Marriage Violations

[13]If a man takes a wife and, after sleeping with her, dislikes her [14]and slanders her and gives her a bad name, saying, "I married this woman, but when I approached her, I did not find proof of her virginity," [15]then the young woman's father and mother shall

---

[a] 9 Or *be forfeited to the sanctuary*

bring to the town elders at the gate proof that she was a virgin. [16]Her father will say to the elders, "I gave my daughter in marriage to this man, but he dislikes her. [17]Now he has slandered her and said, 'I did not find your daughter to be a virgin.' But here is the proof of my daughter's virginity." Then her parents shall display the cloth before the elders of the town, [18]and the elders shall take the man and punish him. [19]They shall fine him a hundred shekels[a] of silver and give them to the young woman's father, because this man has given an Israelite virgin a bad name. She shall continue to be his wife; he must not divorce her as long as he lives.

[20]If, however, the charge is true and no proof of the young woman's virginity can be found, [21]she shall be brought to the door of her father's house and there the men of her town shall stone her to death. She has done an outrageous thing in Israel by being promiscuous while still in her father's house. You must purge the evil from among you.

[22]If a man is found sleeping with another man's wife, both the man who slept with her and the woman must die. You must purge the evil from Israel.

[23]If a man happens to meet in a town a virgin pledged to be married and he sleeps with her, [24]you shall take both of them to the gate of that town and stone them to death — the young woman because she was in a town and did not scream for help, and the man because he violated another man's wife. You must purge the evil from among you.

[25]But if out in the country a man happens to meet a young woman pledged to be married and rapes her, only the man who has done this shall die. [26]Do nothing to the woman; she has committed no sin deserving death. This case is like that of someone who attacks and murders a neighbor, [27]for the man found the young woman out in the country, and though the betrothed woman screamed, there was no one to rescue her.

[28]If a man happens to meet a virgin who is not pledged to be married and rapes her and they are discovered, [29]he shall pay her father fifty shekels[b] of silver. He must marry the young woman, for he has violated her. He can never divorce her as long as he lives.

[30]A man is not to marry his father's wife; he must not dishonor his father's bed.[c]

Exclusion From the Assembly

23[d] No one who has been emasculated by crushing or cutting may enter the assembly of the LORD.

---

[a] 19 That is, about 2 1/2 pounds or about 1.2 kilograms   [b] 29 That is, about 1 1/4 pounds or about 575 grams   [c] 30 In Hebrew texts this verse (22:30) is numbered 23:1.   [d] In Hebrew texts 23:1-25 is numbered 23:2-26.

²No one born of a forbidden marriage*a* nor any of their descendants may enter the assembly of the LORD, not even in the tenth generation.

³No Ammonite or Moabite or any of their descendants may enter the assembly of the LORD, not even in the tenth generation. ⁴For they did not come to meet you with bread and water on your way when you came out of Egypt, and they hired Balaam son of Beor from Pethor in Aram Naharaim*b* to pronounce a curse on you. ⁵However, the LORD your God would not listen to Balaam but turned the curse into a blessing for you, because the LORD your God loves you. ⁶Do not seek a treaty of friendship with them as long as you live.

⁷Do not despise an Edomite, for the Edomites are related to you. Do not despise an Egyptian, because you resided as foreigners in their country. ⁸The third generation of children born to them may enter the assembly of the LORD.

Uncleanness in the Camp

⁹When you are encamped against your enemies, keep away from everything impure. ¹⁰If one of your men is unclean because of a nocturnal emission, he is to go outside the camp and stay there. ¹¹But as evening approaches he is to wash himself, and at sunset he may return to the camp.

¹²Designate a place outside the camp where you can go to relieve yourself. ¹³As part of your equipment have something to dig with, and when you relieve yourself, dig a hole and cover up your excrement. ¹⁴For the LORD your God moves about in your camp to protect you and to deliver your enemies to you. Your camp must be holy, so that he will not see among you anything indecent and turn away from you.

Miscellaneous Laws

¹⁵If a slave has taken refuge with you, do not hand them over to their master. ¹⁶Let them live among you wherever they like and in whatever town they choose. Do not oppress them.

¹⁷No Israelite man or woman is to become a shrine prostitute. ¹⁸You must not bring the earnings of a female prostitute or of a male prostitute*c* into the house of the LORD your God to pay any vow, because the LORD your God detests them both.

¹⁹Do not charge a fellow Israelite interest, whether on money or food or anything else that may earn interest. ²⁰You may charge a foreigner interest, but not a fellow Israelite, so that the LORD your God may bless you in everything you put your hand to in the land you are entering to possess.

²¹If you make a vow to the LORD your God, do not be slow to

---

a 2 Or *one of illegitimate birth*   *b 4* That is, Northwest Mesopotamia
c 18 Hebrew *of a dog*

pay it, for the LORD your God will certainly demand it of you and you will be guilty of sin. ²²But if you refrain from making a vow, you will not be guilty. ²³Whatever your lips utter you must be sure to do, because you made your vow freely to the LORD your God with your own mouth.

²⁴If you enter your neighbor's vineyard, you may eat all the grapes you want, but do not put any in your basket. ²⁵If you enter your neighbor's grainfield, you may pick kernels with your hands, but you must not put a sickle to their standing grain.

24 If a man marries a woman who becomes displeasing to him because he finds something indecent about her, and he writes her a certificate of divorce, gives it to her and sends her from his house, ²and if after she leaves his house she becomes the wife of another man, ³and her second husband dislikes her and writes her a certificate of divorce, gives it to her and sends her from his house, or if he dies, ⁴then her first husband, who divorced her, is not allowed to marry her again after she has been defiled. That would be detestable in the eyes of the LORD. Do not bring sin upon the land the LORD your God is giving you as an inheritance.

⁵If a man has recently married, he must not be sent to war or have any other duty laid on him. For one year he is to be free to stay at home and bring happiness to the wife he has married.

⁶Do not take a pair of millstones — not even the upper one — as security for a debt, because that would be taking a person's livelihood as security.

⁷If someone is caught kidnapping a fellow Israelite and treating or selling them as a slave, the kidnapper must die. You must purge the evil from among you.

⁸In cases of defiling skin diseases,[a] be very careful to do exactly as the Levitical priests instruct you. You must follow carefully what I have commanded them. ⁹Remember what the LORD your God did to Miriam along the way after you came out of Egypt.

¹⁰When you make a loan of any kind to your neighbor, do not go into their house to get what is offered to you as a pledge. ¹¹Stay outside and let the neighbor to whom you are making the loan bring the pledge out to you. ¹²If the neighbor is poor, do not go to sleep with their pledge in your possession. ¹³Return their cloak by sunset so that your neighbor may sleep in it. Then they will thank you, and it will be regarded as a righteous act in the sight of the LORD your God.

¹⁴Do not take advantage of a hired worker who is poor and needy, whether that worker is a

---

[a] 8 The Hebrew word for *defiling skin diseases*, traditionally translated "leprosy," was used for various diseases affecting the skin.

fellow Israelite or a foreigner residing in one of your towns. ¹⁵ Pay them their wages each day before sunset, because they are poor and are counting on it. Otherwise they may cry to the LORD against you, and you will be guilty of sin.

¹⁶ Parents are not to be put to death for their children, nor children put to death for their parents; each will die for their own sin.

¹⁷ Do not deprive the foreigner or the fatherless of justice, or take the cloak of the widow as a pledge. ¹⁸ Remember that you were slaves in Egypt and the LORD your God redeemed you from there. That is why I command you to do this.

¹⁹ When you are harvesting in your field and you overlook a sheaf, do not go back to get it. Leave it for the foreigner, the fatherless and the widow, so that the LORD your God may bless you in all the work of your hands. ²⁰ When you beat the olives from your trees, do not go over the branches a second time. Leave what remains for the foreigner, the fatherless and the widow. ²¹ When you harvest the grapes in your vineyard, do not go over the vines again. Leave what remains for the foreigner, the fatherless and the widow. ²² Remember that you were slaves in Egypt. That is why I command you to do this.

25 When people have a dispute, they are to take it to court and the judges will decide the case, acquitting the innocent and condemning the guilty. ² If the guilty person deserves to be beaten, the judge shall make them lie down and have them flogged in his presence with the number of lashes the crime deserves, ³ but the judge must not impose more than forty lashes. If the guilty party is flogged more than that, your fellow Israelite will be degraded in your eyes.

⁴ Do not muzzle an ox while it is treading out the grain.

⁵ If brothers are living together and one of them dies without a son, his widow must not marry outside the family. Her husband's brother shall take her and marry her and fulfill the duty of a brother-in-law to her. ⁶ The first son she bears shall carry on the name of the dead brother so that his name will not be blotted out from Israel.

⁷ However, if a man does not want to marry his brother's wife, she shall go to the elders at the town gate and say, "My husband's brother refuses to carry on his brother's name in Israel. He will not fulfill the duty of a brother-in-law to me." ⁸ Then the elders of his town shall summon him and talk to him. If he persists in saying, "I do not want to marry her," ⁹ his brother's widow shall go up to him in the presence of the elders, take off one of his sandals, spit in his face and say, "This is what is done to the man who will not build up his brother's family

line." ¹⁰That man's line shall be known in Israel as The Family of the Unsandaled.

¹¹If two men are fighting and the wife of one of them comes to rescue her husband from his assailant, and she reaches out and seizes him by his private parts, ¹²you shall cut off her hand. Show her no pity.

¹³Do not have two differing weights in your bag — one heavy, one light. ¹⁴Do not have two differing measures in your house — one large, one small. ¹⁵You must have accurate and honest weights and measures, so that you may live long in the land the LORD your God is giving you. ¹⁶For the LORD your God detests anyone who does these things, anyone who deals dishonestly.

¹⁷Remember what the Amalekites did to you along the way when you came out of Egypt. ¹⁸When you were weary and worn out, they met you on your journey and attacked all who were lagging behind; they had no fear of God. ¹⁹When the LORD your God gives you rest from all the enemies around you in the land he is giving you to possess as an inheritance, you shall blot out the name of Amalek from under heaven. Do not forget!

Firstfruits and Tithes

26 When you have entered the land the LORD your God is giving you as an inheritance and have taken possession of it and settled in it, ²take some of the firstfruits of all that you produce from the soil of the land the LORD your God is giving you and put them in a basket. Then go to the place the LORD your God will choose as a dwelling for his Name ³and say to the priest in office at the time, "I declare today to the LORD your God that I have come to the land the LORD swore to our ancestors to give us." ⁴The priest shall take the basket from your hands and set it down in front of the altar of the LORD your God. ⁵Then you shall declare before the LORD your God: "My father was a wandering Aramean, and he went down into Egypt with a few people and lived there and became a great nation, powerful and numerous. ⁶But the Egyptians mistreated us and made us suffer, subjecting us to harsh labor. ⁷Then we cried out to the LORD, the God of our ancestors, and the LORD heard our voice and saw our misery, toil and oppression. ⁸So the LORD brought us out of Egypt with a mighty hand and an outstretched arm, with great terror and with signs and wonders. ⁹He brought us to this place and gave us this land, a land flowing with milk and honey; ¹⁰and now I bring the firstfruits of the soil that you, LORD, have given me." Place the basket before the LORD your God and bow down before him. ¹¹Then you and the Levites and the foreigners residing among you shall rejoice in all the good things the LORD your God has given to you and your household.

¹²When you have finished setting aside a tenth of all your produce in the third year, the year of the tithe, you shall give it to the Levite, the foreigner, the fatherless and the widow, so that they may eat in your towns and be satisfied. ¹³Then say to the LORD your God: "I have removed from my house the sacred portion and have given it to the Levite, the foreigner, the fatherless and the widow, according to all you commanded. I have not turned aside from your commands nor have I forgotten any of them. ¹⁴I have not eaten any of the sacred portion while I was in mourning, nor have I removed any of it while I was unclean, nor have I offered any of it to the dead. I have obeyed the LORD my God; I have done everything you commanded me. ¹⁵Look down from heaven, your holy dwelling place, and bless your people Israel and the land you have given us as you promised on oath to our ancestors, a land flowing with milk and honey."

Follow the LORD's Commands

¹⁶The LORD your God commands you this day to follow these decrees and laws; carefully observe them with all your heart and with all your soul. ¹⁷You have declared this day that the LORD is your God and that you will walk in obedience to him, that you will keep his decrees, commands and laws—that you will listen to him. ¹⁸And the LORD has declared this day that you are his people, his treasured possession as he promised, and that you are to keep all his commands. ¹⁹He has declared that he will set you in praise, fame and honor high above all the nations he has made and that you will be a people holy to the LORD your God, as he promised.

The Altar on Mount Ebal

27 Moses and the elders of Israel commanded the people: "Keep all these commands that I give you today. ²When you have crossed the Jordan into the land the LORD your God is giving you, set up some large stones and coat them with plaster. ³Write on them all the words of this law when you have crossed over to enter the land the LORD your God is giving you, a land flowing with milk and honey, just as the LORD, the God of your ancestors, promised you. ⁴And when you have crossed the Jordan, set up these stones on Mount Ebal, as I command you today, and coat them with plaster. ⁵Build there an altar to the LORD your God, an altar of stones. Do not use any iron tool

on them. ⁶Build the altar of the LORD your God with fieldstones and offer burnt offerings on it to the LORD your God. ⁷Sacrifice fellowship offerings there, eating them and rejoicing in the presence of the LORD your God. ⁸And you shall write very clearly all the words of this law on these stones you have set up."

Curses From Mount Ebal

⁹Then Moses and the Levitical priests said to all Israel, "Be silent, Israel, and listen! You have now become the people of the LORD your God. ¹⁰Obey the LORD your God and follow his commands and decrees that I give you today."

¹¹On the same day Moses commanded the people:

¹²When you have crossed the Jordan, these tribes shall stand on Mount Gerizim to bless the people: Simeon, Levi, Judah, Issachar, Joseph and Benjamin. ¹³And these tribes shall stand on Mount Ebal to pronounce curses: Reuben, Gad, Asher, Zebulun, Dan and Naphtali.

¹⁴The Levites shall recite to all the people of Israel in a loud voice:

¹⁵"Cursed is anyone who makes an idol—a thing detestable to the LORD, the work of skilled hands—and sets it up in secret."

Then all the people shall say, "Amen!"

¹⁶"Cursed is anyone who dishonors their father or mother."

Then all the people shall say, "Amen!"

¹⁷"Cursed is anyone who moves their neighbor's boundary stone."

Then all the people shall say, "Amen!"

¹⁸"Cursed is anyone who leads the blind astray on the road."

Then all the people shall say, "Amen!"

¹⁹"Cursed is anyone who withholds justice from the foreigner, the fatherless or the widow."

Then all the people shall say, "Amen!"

²⁰"Cursed is anyone who sleeps with his father's wife, for he dishonors his father's bed."

Then all the people shall say, "Amen!"

²¹"Cursed is anyone who has sexual relations with any animal."

Then all the people shall say, "Amen!"

²²"Cursed is anyone who sleeps with his sister, the daughter of his father or the daughter of his mother."

Then all the people shall say, "Amen!"

²³"Cursed is anyone who sleeps with his mother-in-law."

Then all the people shall say, "Amen!"

24 "Cursed is anyone who kills their neighbor secretly."

Then all the people shall say, "Amen!"

25 "Cursed is anyone who accepts a bribe to kill an innocent person."

Then all the people shall say, "Amen!"

26 "Cursed is anyone who does not uphold the words of this law by carrying them out."

Then all the people shall say, "Amen!"

Blessings for Obedience

28 If you fully obey the LORD your God and carefully follow all his commands I give you today, the LORD your God will set you high above all the nations on earth. **2** All these blessings will come on you and accompany you if you obey the LORD your God:

3 You will be blessed in the city and blessed in the country.

4 The fruit of your womb will be blessed, and the crops of your land and the young of your livestock — the calves of your herds and the lambs of your flocks.

5 Your basket and your kneading trough will be blessed.

6 You will be blessed when you come in and blessed when you go out.

7 The LORD will grant that the enemies who rise up against you will be defeated before you. They will come at you from one direction but flee from you in seven.

8 The LORD will send a blessing on your barns and on everything you put your hand to. The LORD your God will bless you in the land he is giving you.

9 The LORD will establish you as his holy people, as he promised you on oath, if you keep the commands of the LORD your God and walk in obedience to him. **10** Then all the peoples on earth will see that you are called by the name of the LORD, and they will fear you. **11** The LORD will grant you abundant prosperity — in the fruit of your womb, the young of your livestock and the crops of your ground — in the land he swore to your ancestors to give you.

12 The LORD will open the heavens, the storehouse of his bounty, to send rain on your land in season and to bless all the work of your hands. You will lend to many nations but will borrow from none. **13** The LORD will make you the head, not the tail. If you pay attention to the commands of the LORD your God that I give you this day and carefully follow them, you will always be at the top, never at the bottom. **14** Do not turn aside from any of the commands I give you today, to the right or to the left, following other gods and serving them.

Curses for Disobedience

15 However, if you do not obey the LORD your God and do not carefully follow all his commands and decrees I am giving you today, all these curses will come on you and overtake you:

16 You will be cursed in the city and cursed in the country.

17 Your basket and your kneading trough will be cursed.

18 The fruit of your womb will be cursed, and the crops of your land, and the calves of your herds and the lambs of your flocks.

19 You will be cursed when you come in and cursed when you go out.

20 The LORD will send on you curses, confusion and rebuke in everything you put your hand to, until you are destroyed and come to sudden ruin because of the evil you have done in forsaking him.*a* **21** The LORD will plague you with diseases until he has destroyed you from the land you are entering to possess. **22** The LORD will strike you with wasting disease, with fever and inflammation, with scorching heat and drought, with blight and mildew, which will plague you until you perish. **23** The sky over your head will be bronze, the ground beneath you iron. **24** The LORD will turn the rain of your country into dust and powder; it will come down from the skies until you are destroyed.

25 The LORD will cause you to be defeated before your enemies. You will come at them from one direction but flee from them in seven, and you will become a thing of horror to all the kingdoms on earth. **26** Your carcasses will be food for all the birds and the wild animals, and there will be no one to frighten them away. **27** The LORD will afflict you with the boils of Egypt and with tumors, festering sores and the itch, from which you cannot be cured. **28** The LORD will afflict you with madness, blindness and confusion of mind. **29** At midday you will grope about like a blind person in the dark. You will be unsuccessful in everything you do; day after day you will be oppressed and robbed, with no one to rescue you.

30 You will be pledged to be married to a woman, but another will take her and rape her. You will build a house, but you will not live in it. You will plant a vineyard, but you will not even begin to enjoy its fruit. **31** Your ox will be slaughtered before your eyes, but you will eat none of it. Your donkey will be forcibly taken from you and will not be returned. Your sheep will be given to your enemies, and no one will

a 20 Hebrew *me*

rescue them. ³²Your sons and daughters will be given to another nation, and you will wear out your eyes watching for them day after day, powerless to lift a hand. ³³A people that you do not know will eat what your land and labor produce, and you will have nothing but cruel oppression all your days. ³⁴The sights you see will drive you mad. ³⁵The LORD will afflict your knees and legs with painful boils that cannot be cured, spreading from the soles of your feet to the top of your head.

³⁶The LORD will drive you and the king you set over you to a nation unknown to you or your ancestors. There you will worship other gods, gods of wood and stone. ³⁷You will become a thing of horror, a byword and an object of ridicule among all the peoples where the LORD will drive you.

³⁸You will sow much seed in the field but you will harvest little, because locusts will devour it. ³⁹You will plant vineyards and cultivate them but you will not drink the wine or gather the grapes, because worms will eat them. ⁴⁰You will have olive trees throughout your country but you will not use the oil, because the olives will drop off. ⁴¹You will have sons and daughters but you will not keep them, because they will go into captivity. ⁴²Swarms of locusts will take over all your trees and the crops of your land.

⁴³The foreigners who reside among you will rise above you higher and higher, but you will sink lower and lower. ⁴⁴They will lend to you, but you will not lend to them. They will be the head, but you will be the tail.

⁴⁵All these curses will come on you. They will pursue you and overtake you until you are destroyed, because you did not obey the LORD your God and observe the commands and decrees he gave you. ⁴⁶They will be a sign and a wonder to you and your descendants forever. ⁴⁷Because you did not serve the LORD your God joyfully and gladly in the time of prosperity, ⁴⁸therefore in hunger and thirst, in nakedness and dire poverty, you will serve the enemies the LORD sends against you. He will put an iron yoke on your neck until he has destroyed you.

⁴⁹The LORD will bring a nation against you from far away, from the ends of the earth, like an eagle swooping down, a nation whose language you will not understand, ⁵⁰a fierce-looking nation without respect for the old or pity for the young. ⁵¹They will devour the young of your livestock and the crops of your land until you are destroyed. They will leave you no grain, new wine or olive oil, nor any calves of your herds or lambs of your flocks until you are ruined. ⁵²They will lay siege to all the cities throughout your land until the high forti-

fied walls in which you trust fall down. They will besiege all the cities throughout the land the LORD your God is giving you.

⁵³Because of the suffering your enemy will inflict on you during the siege, you will eat the fruit of the womb, the flesh of the sons and daughters the LORD your God has given you. ⁵⁴Even the most gentle and sensitive man among you will have no compassion on his own brother or the wife he loves or his surviving children, ⁵⁵and he will not give to one of them any of the flesh of his children that he is eating. It will be all he has left because of the suffering your enemy will inflict on you during the siege of all your cities. ⁵⁶The most gentle and sensitive woman among you—so sensitive and gentle that she would not venture to touch the ground with the sole of her foot—will begrudge the husband she loves and her own son or daughter ⁵⁷the afterbirth from her womb and the children she bears. For in her dire need she intends to eat them secretly because of the suffering your enemy will inflict on you during the siege of your cities.

⁵⁸If you do not carefully follow all the words of this law, which are written in this book, and do not revere this glorious and awesome name—the LORD your God—⁵⁹the LORD will send fearful plagues on you and your descendants, harsh and prolonged disasters, and severe and lingering illnesses. ⁶⁰He will bring on you all the diseases of Egypt that you dreaded, and they will cling to you. ⁶¹The LORD will also bring on you every kind of sickness and disaster not recorded in this Book of the Law, until you are destroyed. ⁶²You who were as numerous as the stars in the sky will be left but few in number, because you did not obey the LORD your God. ⁶³Just as it pleased the LORD to make you prosper and increase in number, so it will please him to ruin and destroy you. You will be uprooted from the land you are entering to possess.

⁶⁴Then the LORD will scatter you among all nations, from one end of the earth to the other. There you will worship other gods—gods of wood and stone, which neither you nor your ancestors have known. ⁶⁵Among those nations you will find no repose, no resting place for the sole of your foot. There the LORD will give you an anxious mind, eyes weary with longing, and a despairing heart. ⁶⁶You will live in constant suspense, filled with dread both night and day, never sure of your life. ⁶⁷In the morning you will say, "If only it were evening!" and in the evening, "If only it were morning!"—because of the terror that will fill your hearts and the sights that your eyes will see. ⁶⁸The LORD will send you

back in ships to Egypt on a journey I said you should never make again. There you will offer yourselves for sale to your enemies as male and female slaves, but no one will buy you.

Renewal of the Covenant

29 ^a These are the terms of the covenant the LORD commanded Moses to make with the Israelites in Moab, in addition to the covenant he had made with them at Horeb.

² Moses summoned all the Israelites and said to them:

Your eyes have seen all that the LORD did in Egypt to Pharaoh, to all his officials and to all his land. ³ With your own eyes you saw those great trials, those signs and great wonders. ⁴ But to this day the LORD has not given you a mind that understands or eyes that see or ears that hear. ⁵ Yet the LORD says, "During the forty years that I led you through the wilderness, your clothes did not wear out, nor did the sandals on your feet. ⁶ You ate no bread and drank no wine or other fermented drink. I did this so that you might know that I am the LORD your God."

⁷ When you reached this place, Sihon king of Heshbon and Og king of Bashan came out to fight against us, but we defeated them. ⁸ We took their land and gave it as an inheritance to the Reubenites, the Gadites and the half-tribe of Manasseh.

⁹ Carefully follow the terms of this covenant, so that you may prosper in everything you do. ¹⁰ All of you are standing today in the presence of the LORD your God—your leaders and chief men, your elders and officials, and all the other men of Israel, ¹¹ together with your children and your wives, and the foreigners living in your camps who chop your wood and carry your water. ¹² You are standing here in order to enter into a covenant with the LORD your God, a covenant the LORD is making with you this day and sealing with an oath, ¹³ to confirm you this day as his people, that he may be your God as he promised you and as he swore to your fathers, Abraham, Isaac and Jacob. ¹⁴ I am making this covenant, with its oath, not only with you ¹⁵ who are standing here with us today in the presence of the LORD our God but also with those who are not here today.

¹⁶ You yourselves know how we lived in Egypt and how we passed through the countries on the way here. ¹⁷ You saw among them their detestable images and idols of wood and stone, of silver and gold. ¹⁸ Make sure there is no man or woman, clan or tribe among you today whose heart turns away from the LORD our

---

^a In Hebrew texts 29:1 is numbered 28:69, and 29:2-29 is numbered 29:1-28.

God to go and worship the gods of those nations; make sure there is no root among you that produces such bitter poison.

¹⁹When such a person hears the words of this oath and they invoke a blessing on themselves, thinking, "I will be safe, even though I persist in going my own way," they will bring disaster on the watered land as well as the dry. ²⁰The LORD will never be willing to forgive them; his wrath and zeal will burn against them. All the curses written in this book will fall on them, and the LORD will blot out their names from under heaven. ²¹The LORD will single them out from all the tribes of Israel for disaster, according to all the curses of the covenant written in this Book of the Law.

²²Your children who follow you in later generations and foreigners who come from distant lands will see the calamities that have fallen on the land and the diseases with which the LORD has afflicted it. ²³The whole land will be a burning waste of salt and sulfur — nothing planted, nothing sprouting, no vegetation growing on it. It will be like the destruction of Sodom and Gomorrah, Admah and Zeboyim, which the LORD overthrew in fierce anger. ²⁴All the nations will ask: "Why has the LORD done this to this land? Why this fierce, burning anger?"

²⁵And the answer will be: "It is because this people abandoned the covenant of the LORD, the God of their ancestors, the covenant he made with them when he brought them out of Egypt. ²⁶They went off and worshiped other gods and bowed down to them, gods they did not know, gods he had not given them. ²⁷Therefore the LORD's anger burned against this land, so that he brought on it all the curses written in this book. ²⁸In furious anger and in great wrath the LORD uprooted them from their land and thrust them into another land, as it is now."

²⁹The secret things belong to the LORD our God, but the things revealed belong to us and to our children forever, that we may follow all the words of this law.

Prosperity After Turning to the LORD

30 When all these blessings and curses I have set before you come on you and you take them to heart wherever the LORD your God disperses you among the nations, ²and when you and your children return to the LORD your God and obey him with all your heart and with all your soul according to everything I command you today, ³then the LORD your God will restore your fortunes^a and have compassion on you and gather you again from all the nations

^a 3 Or *will bring you back from captivity*

where he scattered you. ⁴Even if you have been banished to the most distant land under the heavens, from there the LORD your God will gather you and bring you back. ⁵He will bring you to the land that belonged to your ancestors, and you will take possession of it. He will make you more prosperous and numerous than your ancestors. ⁶The LORD your God will circumcise your hearts and the hearts of your descendants, so that you may love him with all your heart and with all your soul, and live. ⁷The LORD your God will put all these curses on your enemies who hate and persecute you. ⁸You will again obey the LORD and follow all his commands I am giving you today. ⁹Then the LORD your God will make you most prosperous in all the work of your hands and in the fruit of your womb, the young of your livestock and the crops of your land. The LORD will again delight in you and make you prosperous, just as he delighted in your ancestors, ¹⁰if you obey the LORD your God and keep his commands and decrees that are written in this Book of the Law and turn to the LORD your God with all your heart and with all your soul.

The Offer of Life or Death

¹¹Now what I am commanding you today is not too difficult for you or beyond your reach. ¹²It is not up in heaven, so that you have to ask, "Who will ascend into heaven to get it and proclaim it to us so we may obey it?" ¹³Nor is it beyond the sea, so that you have to ask, "Who will cross the sea to get it and proclaim it to us so we may obey it?" ¹⁴No, the word is very near you; it is in your mouth and in your heart so you may obey it.

¹⁵See, I set before you today life and prosperity, death and destruction. ¹⁶For I command you today to love the LORD your God, to walk in obedience to him, and to keep his commands, decrees and laws; then you will live and increase, and the LORD your God will bless you in the land you are entering to possess.

¹⁷But if your heart turns away and you are not obedient, and if you are drawn away to bow down to other gods and worship them, ¹⁸I declare to you this day that you will certainly be destroyed. You will not live long in the land you are crossing the Jordan to enter and possess.

¹⁹This day I call the heavens and the earth as witnesses against you that I have set before you life and death, blessings and curses. Now choose life, so that you and your children may live ²⁰and that you may love the LORD your God, listen to his voice, and hold fast to him. For the LORD is your life, and he will give you many years in the land he swore

to give to your fathers, Abraham, Isaac and Jacob.

Joshua to Succeed Moses

31 Then Moses went out and spoke these words to all Israel: ² "I am now a hundred and twenty years old and I am no longer able to lead you. The LORD has said to me, 'You shall not cross the Jordan.' ³ The LORD your God himself will cross over ahead of you. He will destroy these nations before you, and you will take possession of their land. Joshua also will cross over ahead of you, as the LORD said. ⁴ And the LORD will do to them what he did to Sihon and Og, the kings of the Amorites, whom he destroyed along with their land. ⁵ The LORD will deliver them to you, and you must do to them all that I have commanded you. ⁶ Be strong and courageous. Do not be afraid or terrified because of them, for the LORD your God goes with you; he will never leave you nor forsake you."

⁷ Then Moses summoned Joshua and said to him in the presence of all Israel, "Be strong and courageous, for you must go with this people into the land that the LORD swore to their ancestors to give them, and you must divide it among them as their inheritance. ⁸ The LORD himself goes before you and will be with you; he will never leave you nor forsake you. Do not be afraid; do not be discouraged."

Public Reading of the Law

⁹ So Moses wrote down this law and gave it to the Levitical priests, who carried the ark of the covenant of the LORD, and to all the elders of Israel. ¹⁰ Then Moses commanded them: "At the end of every seven years, in the year for canceling debts, during the Festival of Tabernacles, ¹¹ when all Israel comes to appear before the LORD your God at the place he will choose, you shall read this law before them in their hearing. ¹² Assemble the people — men, women and children, and the foreigners residing in your towns — so they can listen and learn to fear the LORD your God and follow carefully all the words of this law. ¹³ Their children, who do not know this law, must hear it and learn to fear the LORD your God as long as you live in the land you are crossing the Jordan to possess."

Israel's Rebellion Predicted

¹⁴ The LORD said to Moses, "Now the day of your death is near. Call Joshua and present yourselves at the tent of meeting, where I will commission him." So Moses and Joshua came and presented themselves at the tent of meeting. ¹⁵ Then the LORD appeared at the tent in a pillar of cloud, and the cloud stood over the entrance to the tent. ¹⁶ And the LORD said to Moses: "You are going to rest with your ancestors, and these people will soon prostitute themselves to

the foreign gods of the land they are entering. They will forsake me and break the covenant I made with them. [17] And in that day I will become angry with them and forsake them; I will hide my face from them, and they will be destroyed. Many disasters and calamities will come on them, and in that day they will ask, 'Have not these disasters come on us because our God is not with us?' [18] And I will certainly hide my face in that day because of all their wickedness in turning to other gods.

[19] "Now write down this song and teach it to the Israelites and have them sing it, so that it may be a witness for me against them. [20] When I have brought them into the land flowing with milk and honey, the land I promised on oath to their ancestors, and when they eat their fill and thrive, they will turn to other gods and worship them, rejecting me and breaking my covenant. [21] And when many disasters and calamities come on them, this song will testify against them, because it will not be forgotten by their descendants. I know what they are disposed to do, even before I bring them into the land I promised them on oath." [22] So Moses wrote down this song that day and taught it to the Israelites.

[23] The LORD gave this command to Joshua son of Nun: "Be strong and courageous, for you will bring the Israelites into the land I promised them on oath, and I myself will be with you."

[24] After Moses finished writing in a book the words of this law from beginning to end, [25] he gave this command to the Levites who carried the ark of the covenant of the LORD: [26] "Take this Book of the Law and place it beside the ark of the covenant of the LORD your God. There it will remain as a witness against you. [27] For I know how rebellious and stiff-necked you are. If you have been rebellious against the LORD while I am still alive and with you, how much more will you rebel after I die! [28] Assemble before me all the elders of your tribes and all your officials, so that I can speak these words in their hearing and call the heavens and the earth to testify against them. [29] For I know that after my death you are sure to become utterly corrupt and to turn from the way I have commanded you. In days to come, disaster will fall on you because you will do evil in the sight of the LORD and arouse his anger by what your hands have made."

The Song of Moses

[30] And Moses recited the words of this song from beginning to end in the hearing of the whole assembly of Israel:

32 Listen, you heavens, and I will speak;
hear, you earth, the words of my mouth.

²Let my teaching fall like
    rain
  and my words descend like
    dew,
like showers on new
    grass,
  like abundant rain on tender
    plants.

³I will proclaim the name of the
    LORD.
  Oh, praise the greatness of
    our God!
⁴He is the Rock, his works are
    perfect,
  and all his ways are just.
A faithful God who does no
    wrong,
  upright and just is he.

⁵They are corrupt and not his
    children;
  to their shame they are a
    warped and crooked
    generation.
⁶Is this the way you repay the
    LORD,
  you foolish and unwise
    people?
Is he not your Father, your
    Creator,ᵃ
  who made you and formed
    you?

⁷Remember the days of old;
  consider the generations
    long past.
Ask your father and he will tell
    you,
  your elders, and they will
    explain to you.

⁸When the Most High gave the
    nations their inheritance,
  when he divided all
    mankind,
he set up boundaries for the
    peoples
  according to the number of
    the sons of Israel.ᵇ
⁹For the LORD's portion is his
    people,
  Jacob his allotted inheritance.

¹⁰In a desert land he found him,
  in a barren and howling
    waste.
He shielded him and cared for
    him;
  he guarded him as the apple
    of his eye,
¹¹like an eagle that stirs up its
    nest
  and hovers over its young,
that spreads its wings to catch
    them
  and carries them aloft.
¹²The LORD alone led him;
  no foreign god was with him.

¹³He made him ride on the
    heights of the land
  and fed him with the fruit of
    the fields.
He nourished him with honey
    from the rock,
  and with oil from the flinty
    crag,
¹⁴with curds and milk from herd
    and flock
  and with fattened lambs and
    goats,

ᵃ 6 Or *Father, who bought you*
Septuagint) *sons of God*

ᵇ 8 Masoretic Text; Dead Sea Scrolls (see also

with choice rams of Bashan
and the finest kernels of
wheat.
You drank the foaming blood
of the grape.

¹⁵ Jeshurun*ᵃ* grew fat and kicked;
filled with food, they
became heavy and
sleek.
They abandoned the God who
made them
and rejected the Rock their
Savior.
¹⁶ They made him jealous with
their foreign gods
and angered him with their
detestable idols.
¹⁷ They sacrificed to false gods,
which are not God —
gods they had not known,
gods that recently appeared,
gods your ancestors did not
fear.
¹⁸ You deserted the Rock, who
fathered you;
you forgot the God who gave
you birth.

¹⁹ The LORD saw this and
rejected them
because he was angered by
his sons and daughters.
²⁰ "I will hide my face from
them," he said,
"and see what their end
will be;
for they are a perverse
generation,
children who are
unfaithful.

²¹ They made me jealous by what
is no god
and angered me with their
worthless idols.
I will make them envious
by those who are not a
people;
I will make them angry by
a nation that has no
understanding.
²² For a fire will be kindled by my
wrath,
one that burns down to the
realm of the dead
below.
It will devour the earth and its
harvests
and set afire the foundations
of the mountains.

²³ "I will heap calamities on
them
and spend my arrows
against them.
²⁴ I will send wasting famine
against them,
consuming pestilence and
deadly plague;
I will send against them the
fangs of wild beasts,
the venom of vipers that
glide in the dust.
²⁵ In the street the sword will
make them childless;
in their homes terror will
reign.
The young men and young
women will perish,
the infants and those with
gray hair.

ᵃ 15 *Jeshurun* means *the upright one*, that is, Israel.

²⁶I said I would scatter them
and erase their name from
human memory,
²⁷but I dreaded the taunt of the
enemy,
lest the adversary
misunderstand
and say, 'Our hand has
triumphed;
the LORD has not done all
this.'"

²⁸They are a nation without
sense,
there is no discernment in
them.
²⁹If only they were wise and
would understand this
and discern what their end
will be!
³⁰How could one man chase a
thousand,
or two put ten thousand to
flight,
unless their Rock had sold
them,
unless the LORD had given
them up?
³¹For their rock is not like our
Rock,
as even our enemies
concede.
³²Their vine comes from the
vine of Sodom
and from the fields of
Gomorrah.
Their grapes are filled with
poison,
and their clusters with
bitterness.

³³Their wine is the venom of
serpents,
the deadly poison of cobras.

³⁴"Have I not kept this in
reserve
and sealed it in my vaults?
³⁵It is mine to avenge; I will
repay.
In due time their foot will
slip;
their day of disaster is near
and their doom rushes upon
them."

³⁶The LORD will vindicate his
people
and relent concerning his
servants
when he sees their strength is
gone
and no one is left, slave or
free.ᵃ
³⁷He will say: "Now where are
their gods,
the rock they took refuge in,
³⁸the gods who ate the fat of
their sacrifices
and drank the wine of their
drink offerings?
Let them rise up to help you!
Let them give you shelter!

³⁹"See now that I myself am he!
There is no god besides me.
I put to death and I bring to
life,
I have wounded and I will
heal,
and no one can deliver out of
my hand.

ᵃ 36 Or *and they are without a ruler or leader*

⁴⁰I lift my hand to heaven and
solemnly swear:
  As surely as I live forever,
⁴¹when I sharpen my flashing
sword
  and my hand grasps it in
judgment,
  I will take vengeance on my
adversaries
  and repay those who
hate me.
⁴²I will make my arrows drunk
with blood,
  while my sword devours
flesh:
  the blood of the slain and the
captives,
  the heads of the enemy
leaders."

⁴³Rejoice, you nations, with his
people,ᵃ,ᵇ
  for he will avenge the blood
of his servants;
  he will take vengeance on his
enemies
  and make atonement for his
land and people.

⁴⁴Moses came with Joshuaᶜ son
of Nun and spoke all the words of
this song in the hearing of the
people. ⁴⁵When Moses finished
reciting all these words to all Israel, ⁴⁶he said to them, "Take to
heart all the words I have solemnly declared to you this day,
so that you may command your
children to obey carefully all the
words of this law. ⁴⁷They are not
just idle words for you — they are
your life. By them you will live
long in the land you are crossing
the Jordan to possess."

Moses to Die on Mount Nebo

⁴⁸On that same day the LORD
told Moses, ⁴⁹"Go up into the Abarim Range to Mount Nebo in
Moab, across from Jericho, and
view Canaan, the land I am giving the Israelites as their own possession. ⁵⁰There on the mountain
that you have climbed you will die
and be gathered to your people,
just as your brother Aaron died on
Mount Hor and was gathered to
his people. ⁵¹This is because both
of you broke faith with me in the
presence of the Israelites at the
waters of Meribah Kadesh in the
Desert of Zin and because you did
not uphold my holiness among
the Israelites. ⁵²Therefore, you
will see the land only from a distance; you will not enter the land I
am giving to the people of Israel."

Moses Blesses the Tribes

33 This is the blessing that
Moses the man of God
pronounced on the Israelites before his death. ²He said:

"The LORD came from Sinai
  and dawned over them from
Seir;
  he shone forth from Mount
Paran.

ᵃ 43 Or *Make his people rejoice, you nations*   ᵇ 43 Masoretic Text; Dead
Sea Scrolls (see also Septuagint) *people, / and let all the angels worship him, /*
ᶜ 44 Hebrew *Hoshea,* a variant of *Joshua*

He came with[a] myriads of holy
   ones
  from the south, from his
   mountain slopes.[b]
3 Surely it is you who love the
  people;
  all the holy ones are in your
   hand.
At your feet they all bow
  down,
  and from you receive
   instruction,
4 the law that Moses gave us,
  the possession of the
   assembly of Jacob.
5 He was king over Jeshurun[c]
  when the leaders of the
   people assembled,
  along with the tribes of
   Israel.

6 "Let Reuben live and not die,
  nor[d] his people be few."

7 And this he said about Judah:

"Hear, LORD, the cry of
  Judah;
  bring him to his people.
With his own hands he
  defends his cause.
  Oh, be his help against his
   foes!"

8 About Levi he said:

"Your Thummim and Urim
  belong
  to your faithful servant.
You tested him at Massah;
  you contended with him at
   the waters of Meribah.

9 He said of his father and
  mother,
  'I have no regard for them.'
He did not recognize his
  brothers
  or acknowledge his own
   children,
but he watched over your
  word
  and guarded your covenant.
10 He teaches your precepts to
  Jacob
  and your law to Israel.
He offers incense before you
  and whole burnt offerings on
   your altar.
11 Bless all his skills, LORD,
  and be pleased with the
   work of his hands.
Strike down those who rise
  against him,
  his foes till they rise no
   more."

12 About Benjamin he said:

"Let the beloved of the LORD
  rest secure in him,
  for he shields him all day
   long,
  and the one the LORD
   loves rests between his
   shoulders."

13 About Joseph he said:

"May the LORD bless his land
  with the precious dew from
   heaven above
  and with the deep waters
   that lie below;

---

[a] 2 Or *from*   [b] 2 The meaning of the Hebrew for this phrase is uncertain.
[c] 5 *Jeshurun* means *the upright one,* that is, Israel; also in verse 26.   [d] 6 Or *but let*

¹⁴with the best the sun brings
forth
and the finest the moon can
yield;
¹⁵with the choicest gifts of the
ancient mountains
and the fruitfulness of the
everlasting hills;
¹⁶with the best gifts of the earth
and its fullness
and the favor of him who
dwelt in the burning
bush.
Let all these rest on the head of
Joseph,
on the brow of the prince
among^a his brothers.
¹⁷In majesty he is like a firstborn
bull;
his horns are the horns of a
wild ox.
With them he will gore the
nations,
even those at the ends of the
earth.
Such are the ten thousands of
Ephraim;
such are the thousands of
Manasseh."

¹⁸About Zebulun he said:

"Rejoice, Zebulun, in your
going out,
and you, Issachar, in your
tents.
¹⁹They will summon peoples to
the mountain
and there offer the sacrifices
of the righteous;
they will feast on the
abundance of the seas,

on the treasures hidden in
the sand."

²⁰About Gad he said:

"Blessed is he who enlarges
Gad's domain!
Gad lives there like a
lion,
tearing at arm or head.
²¹He chose the best land for
himself;
the leader's portion was kept
for him.
When the heads of the people
assembled,
he carried out the LORD's
righteous will,
and his judgments
concerning Israel."

²²About Dan he said:

"Dan is a lion's cub,
springing out of Bashan."

²³About Naphtali he said:

"Naphtali is abounding with
the favor of the LORD
and is full of his blessing;
he will inherit southward to
the lake."

²⁴About Asher he said:

"Most blessed of sons is Asher;
let him be favored by his
brothers,
and let him bathe his feet in
oil.
²⁵The bolts of your gates will be
iron and bronze,
and your strength will equal
your days.

^a 16 Or of the one separated from

²⁶ "There is no one like the God
of Jeshurun,
who rides across the heavens
to help you
and on the clouds in his
majesty.
²⁷ The eternal God is your refuge,
and underneath are the
everlasting arms.
He will drive out your enemies
before you,
saying, 'Destroy them!'
²⁸ So Israel will live in safety;
Jacob will dwell*a* secure
in a land of grain and new wine,
where the heavens drop dew.
²⁹ Blessed are you, Israel!
Who is like you,
a people saved by the LORD?
He is your shield and helper
and your glorious sword.
Your enemies will cower
before you,
and you will tread on their
heights."

The Death of Moses

34 Then Moses climbed
Mount Nebo from the
plains of Moab to the top of Pisgah, across from Jericho. There
the LORD showed him the whole
land — from Gilead to Dan, ²all of
Naphtali, the territory of Ephraim and Manasseh, all the land
of Judah as far as the Mediterranean Sea, ³the Negev and the
whole region from the Valley of
Jericho, the City of Palms, as far
as Zoar. ⁴Then the LORD said to
him, "This is the land I promised
on oath to Abraham, Isaac and
Jacob when I said, 'I will give it to
your descendants.' I have let you
see it with your eyes, but you will
not cross over into it."

⁵ And Moses the servant of the
LORD died there in Moab, as the
LORD had said. ⁶He buried him*b*
in Moab, in the valley opposite
Beth Peor, but to this day no one
knows where his grave is. ⁷Moses
was a hundred and twenty years
old when he died, yet his eyes
were not weak nor his strength
gone. ⁸The Israelites grieved for
Moses in the plains of Moab thirty days, until the time of weeping
and mourning was over.

⁹ Now Joshua son of Nun was
filled with the spirit*c* of wisdom because Moses had laid his
hands on him. So the Israelites
listened to him and did what the
LORD had commanded Moses.

¹⁰ Since then, no prophet has
risen in Israel like Moses, whom
the LORD knew face to face, ¹¹who
did all those signs and wonders the LORD sent him to do in
Egypt — to Pharaoh and to all his
officials and to his whole land.
¹² For no one has ever shown the
mighty power or performed the
awesome deeds that Moses did
in the sight of all Israel.

a 28 Septuagint; Hebrew *Jacob's spring is*   *b 6* Or *He was buried*   *c 9* Or *Spirit*

Joshua

Introduction:

Joshua had been chosen and appointed by God just before Moses' death to be Israel's leader. This book uses his name as its title because Joshua is the leading character.

The book of Joshua is the story of both Joshua and Israel as they, with God's help, conquered the Promised Land — Canaan. The people miraculously crossed the Jordan River and conquered the town of Jericho. Then, with God's help again, they quickly took possession of all the main areas of Canaan.

Before Joshua died, he reminded the people of God's covenant promises to them. He instructed the people to keep on loving and obeying God. Publicly, he spoke of his own willingness to serve God when he said, "Choose for yourselves this day whom you will serve, . . . but as for me and my household, we will serve the LORD" (24:15).

Outline of contents:

Preparation for possession of Canaan (1:1–5:15)
The conquest of Canaan (6:1–12:24)
The division of land by tribes (13:1–21:45)
Farewell and death of Joshua (22:1–24:33)

Joshua Installed as Leader

1 After the death of Moses the servant of the LORD, the LORD said to Joshua son of Nun, Moses' aide: ²"Moses my servant is dead. Now then, you and all these people, get ready to cross the Jordan River into the land I am about to give to them — to the Israelites. ³I will give you every place where you set your foot, as I promised Moses. ⁴Your territory will extend from the desert to Lebanon, and from the great river, the Euphrates — all the Hittite country — to the Mediterranean Sea in the west. ⁵No one will be able to stand against you all the days of your life. As I was with Moses, so I will be with you; I will never leave you nor forsake you. ⁶Be strong and courageous, because you will lead these people to inherit the land I swore to their ancestors to give them.

⁷"Be strong and very courageous. Be careful to obey all the law my servant Moses gave you;

do not turn from it to the right or to the left, that you may be successful wherever you go. **8** Keep this Book of the Law always on your lips; meditate on it day and night, so that you may be careful to do everything written in it. Then you will be prosperous and successful. **9** Have I not commanded you? Be strong and courageous. Do not be afraid; do not be discouraged, for the LORD your God will be with you wherever you go."

10 So Joshua ordered the officers of the people: **11** "Go through the camp and tell the people, 'Get your provisions ready. Three days from now you will cross the Jordan here to go in and take possession of the land the LORD your God is giving you for your own.'"

12 But to the Reubenites, the Gadites and the half-tribe of Manasseh, Joshua said, **13** "Remember the command that Moses the servant of the LORD gave you after he said, 'The LORD your God will give you rest by giving you this land.' **14** Your wives, your children and your livestock may stay in the land that Moses gave you east of the Jordan, but all your fighting men, ready for battle, must cross over ahead of your fellow Israelites. You are to help them **15** until the LORD gives them rest, as he has done for you, and until they too have taken possession of the land the LORD your God is giving them. After that,

you may go back and occupy your own land, which Moses the servant of the LORD gave you east of the Jordan toward the sunrise."

16 Then they answered Joshua, "Whatever you have commanded us we will do, and wherever you send us we will go. **17** Just as we fully obeyed Moses, so we will obey you. Only may the LORD your God be with you as he was with Moses. **18** Whoever rebels against your word and does not obey it, whatever you may command them, will be put to death. Only be strong and courageous!"

Rahab and the Spies

2 Then Joshua son of Nun secretly sent two spies from Shittim. "Go, look over the land," he said, "especially Jericho." So they went and entered the house of a prostitute named Rahab and stayed there.

2 The king of Jericho was told, "Look, some of the Israelites have come here tonight to spy out the land." **3** So the king of Jericho sent this message to Rahab: "Bring out the men who came to you and entered your house, because they have come to spy out the whole land."

4 But the woman had taken the two men and hidden them. She said, "Yes, the men came to me, but I did not know where they had come from. **5** At dusk, when it was time to close the city gate, they left. I don't know which way they went. Go after them quickly. You may catch up with them." ⁶(But she had taken them up to the roof and hidden them under the stalks of flax she had laid out on the roof.) ⁷So the men set out in pursuit of the spies on the road that leads to the fords of the Jordan, and as soon as the pursuers had gone out, the gate was shut.

⁸Before the spies lay down for the night, she went up on the roof ⁹and said to them, "I know that the LORD has given you this land and that a great fear of you has fallen on us, so that all who live in this country are melting in fear because of you. ¹⁰We have heard how the LORD dried up the water of the Red Sea^a for you when you came out of Egypt, and what you did to Sihon and Og, the two kings of the Amorites east of the Jordan, whom you completely destroyed.^b ¹¹When we heard of it, our hearts melted in fear and everyone's courage failed because of you, for the LORD your God is God in heaven above and on the earth below.

¹²"Now then, please swear to me by the LORD that you will show kindness to my family, because I have shown kindness to you. Give me a sure sign ¹³that you will spare the lives of my father and mother, my brothers and sisters, and all who belong to them — and that you will save us from death."

¹⁴"Our lives for your lives!" the men assured her. "If you don't tell what we are doing, we will treat you kindly and faithfully when the LORD gives us the land."

¹⁵So she let them down by a rope through the window, for the house she lived in was part of the city wall. ¹⁶She said to them, "Go to the hills so the pursuers will not find you. Hide yourselves there three days until they return, and then go on your way."

¹⁷Now the men had said to her, "This oath you made us swear will not be binding on us ¹⁸unless, when we enter the land, you have tied this scarlet cord in the window through which you let us down, and unless you have brought your father and mother, your brothers and all your family into your house. ¹⁹If any of them go outside your house into the street, their blood will be on their own heads; we will not be responsible. As for those who are in the house with you, their blood will be on our head if a hand is laid on them. ²⁰But if you tell what we are doing, we will be released from the oath you made us swear."

²¹"Agreed," she replied. "Let it be as you say."

So she sent them away, and they departed. And she tied the scarlet cord in the window.

²²When they left, they went into the hills and stayed there

---

^a 10 Or *the Sea of Reeds*   ^b 10 The Hebrew term refers to the irrevocable giving over of things or persons to the LORD, often by totally destroying them.

three days, until the pursuers had searched all along the road and returned without finding them. ²³ Then the two men started back. They went down out of the hills, forded the river and came to Joshua son of Nun and told him everything that had happened to them. ²⁴ They said to Joshua, "The LORD has surely given the whole land into our hands; all the people are melting in fear because of us."

Crossing the Jordan

3 Early in the morning Joshua and all the Israelites set out from Shittim and went to the Jordan, where they camped before crossing over. ² After three days the officers went throughout the camp, ³ giving orders to the people: "When you see the ark of the covenant of the LORD your God, and the Levitical priests carrying it, you are to move out from your positions and follow it. ⁴ Then you will know which way to go, since you have never been this way before. But keep a distance of about two thousand cubits*ᵃ* between you and the ark; do not go near it."

⁵ Joshua told the people, "Consecrate yourselves, for tomorrow the LORD will do amazing things among you."

⁶ Joshua said to the priests, "Take up the ark of the covenant and pass on ahead of the people."

So they took it up and went ahead of them.

⁷ And the LORD said to Joshua, "Today I will begin to exalt you in the eyes of all Israel, so they may know that I am with you as I was with Moses. ⁸ Tell the priests who carry the ark of the covenant: 'When you reach the edge of the Jordan's waters, go and stand in the river.'"

⁹ Joshua said to the Israelites, "Come here and listen to the words of the LORD your God. ¹⁰ This is how you will know that the living God is among you and that he will certainly drive out before you the Canaanites, Hittites, Hivites, Perizzites, Girgashites, Amorites and Jebusites. ¹¹ See, the ark of the covenant of the Lord of all the earth will go into the Jordan ahead of you. ¹² Now then, choose twelve men from the tribes of Israel, one from each tribe. ¹³ And as soon as the priests who carry the ark of the LORD — the Lord of all the earth — set foot in the Jordan, its waters flowing downstream will be cut off and stand up in a heap."

¹⁴ So when the people broke camp to cross the Jordan, the priests carrying the ark of the covenant went ahead of them. ¹⁵ Now the Jordan is at flood stage all during harvest. Yet as soon as the priests who carried the ark reached the Jordan and their feet touched the water's edge, ¹⁶ the

ᵃ 4 That is, about 3,000 feet or about 900 meters

water from upstream stopped flowing. It piled up in a heap a great distance away, at a town called Adam in the vicinity of Zarethan, while the water flowing down to the Sea of the Arabah (that is, the Dead Sea) was completely cut off. So the people crossed over opposite Jericho. ¹⁷The priests who carried the ark of the covenant of the LORD stopped in the middle of the Jordan and stood on dry ground, while all Israel passed by until the whole nation had completed the crossing on dry ground.

4 When the whole nation had finished crossing the Jordan, the LORD said to Joshua, ²"Choose twelve men from among the people, one from each tribe, ³and tell them to take up twelve stones from the middle of the Jordan, from right where the priests are standing, and carry them over with you and put them down at the place where you stay tonight."

⁴So Joshua called together the twelve men he had appointed from the Israelites, one from each tribe, ⁵and said to them, "Go over before the ark of the LORD your God into the middle of the Jordan. Each of you is to take up a stone on his shoulder, according to the number of the tribes of the Israelites, ⁶to serve as a sign among you. In the future, when your children ask you, 'What do these stones mean?' ⁷tell them that the flow of the Jordan was cut off before the ark of the covenant of the LORD. When it crossed the Jordan, the waters of the Jordan were cut off. These stones are to be a memorial to the people of Israel forever."

⁸So the Israelites did as Joshua commanded them. They took twelve stones from the middle of the Jordan, according to the number of the tribes of the Israelites, as the LORD had told Joshua; and they carried them over with them to their camp, where they put them down. ⁹Joshua set up the twelve stones that had been[a] in the middle of the Jordan at the spot where the priests who carried the ark of the covenant had stood. And they are there to this day.

¹⁰Now the priests who carried the ark remained standing in the middle of the Jordan until everything the LORD had commanded Joshua was done by the people, just as Moses had directed Joshua. The people hurried over, ¹¹and as soon as all of them had crossed, the ark of the LORD and the priests came to the other side while the people watched. ¹²The men of Reuben, Gad and the half-tribe of Manasseh crossed over, ready for battle, in front of the Israelites, as Moses had directed them. ¹³About forty thousand armed for battle crossed over before the LORD to the plains of Jericho for war.

---

[a] 9 Or Joshua also set up twelve stones

¹⁴That day the LORD exalted Joshua in the sight of all Israel; and they stood in awe of him all the days of his life, just as they had stood in awe of Moses.

¹⁵Then the LORD said to Joshua, ¹⁶"Command the priests carrying the ark of the covenant law to come up out of the Jordan."

¹⁷So Joshua commanded the priests, "Come up out of the Jordan."

¹⁸And the priests came up out of the river carrying the ark of the covenant of the LORD. No sooner had they set their feet on the dry ground than the waters of the Jordan returned to their place and ran at flood stage as before.

¹⁹On the tenth day of the first month the people went up from the Jordan and camped at Gilgal on the eastern border of Jericho. ²⁰And Joshua set up at Gilgal the twelve stones they had taken out of the Jordan. ²¹He said to the Israelites, "In the future when your descendants ask their parents, 'What do these stones mean?' ²²tell them, 'Israel crossed the Jordan on dry ground.' ²³For the LORD your God dried up the Jordan before you until you had crossed over. The LORD your God did to the Jordan what he had done to the Red Sea[a] when he dried it up before us until we had crossed over. ²⁴He did this so that all the peoples of the earth might know that the hand of the LORD is powerful and so that you might always fear the LORD your God."

5 Now when all the Amorite kings west of the Jordan and all the Canaanite kings along the coast heard how the LORD had dried up the Jordan before the Israelites until they[b] had crossed over, their hearts melted in fear and they no longer had the courage to face the Israelites.

Circumcision and Passover at Gilgal

²At that time the LORD said to Joshua, "Make flint knives and circumcise the Israelites again." ³So Joshua made flint knives and circumcised the Israelites at Gibeath Haaraloth.[c]

⁴Now this is why he did so: All those who came out of Egypt—all the men of military age—died in the wilderness on the way after leaving Egypt. ⁵All the people that came out had been circumcised, but all the people born in the wilderness during the journey from Egypt had not. ⁶The Israelites had moved about in the wilderness forty years until all the men who were of military age when they left Egypt had died, since they had not obeyed the LORD. For the LORD had sworn to them that they would not see the land he had solemnly promised their ancestors to give us, a land

ᵃ 23 Or *the Sea of Reeds*   ᵇ 1 Another textual tradition *we*   ᶜ 3 *Gibeath Haaraloth* means *the hill of foreskins*.

flowing with milk and honey. **7**So he raised up their sons in their place, and these were the ones Joshua circumcised. They were still uncircumcised because they had not been circumcised on the way. **8**And after the whole nation had been circumcised, they remained where they were in camp until they were healed.

9Then the LORD said to Joshua, "Today I have rolled away the reproach of Egypt from you." So the place has been called Gilgal*a* to this day.

10On the evening of the fourteenth day of the month, while camped at Gilgal on the plains of Jericho, the Israelites celebrated the Passover. **11**The day after the Passover, that very day, they ate some of the produce of the land: unleavened bread and roasted grain. **12**The manna stopped the day after*b* they ate this food from the land; there was no longer any manna for the Israelites, but that year they ate the produce of Canaan.

The Fall of Jericho

13Now when Joshua was near Jericho, he looked up and saw a man standing in front of him with a drawn sword in his hand. Joshua went up to him and asked, "Are you for us or for our enemies?"

14"Neither," he replied, "but as commander of the army of the LORD I have now come." Then Joshua fell facedown to the ground in reverence, and asked him, "What message does my Lord*c* have for his servant?"

15The commander of the LORD's army replied, "Take off your sandals, for the place where you are standing is holy." And Joshua did so.

6 Now the gates of Jericho were securely barred because of the Israelites. No one went out and no one came in.

2Then the LORD said to Joshua, "See, I have delivered Jericho into your hands, along with its king and its fighting men. **3**March around the city once with all the armed men. Do this for six days. **4**Have seven priests carry trumpets of rams' horns in front of the ark. On the seventh day, march around the city seven times, with the priests blowing the trumpets. **5**When you hear them sound a long blast on the trumpets, have the whole army give a loud shout; then the wall of the city will collapse and the army will go up, everyone straight in."

6So Joshua son of Nun called the priests and said to them, "Take up the ark of the covenant of the LORD and have seven priests carry trumpets in front of it." **7**And he ordered the army, "Advance! March around the city, with an armed guard going ahead of the ark of the LORD."

---

a 9 *Gilgal* sounds like the Hebrew for *roll*.   *b* 12 Or *the day*   *c* 14 Or *lord*

⁸When Joshua had spoken to the people, the seven priests carrying the seven trumpets before the LORD went forward, blowing their trumpets, and the ark of the LORD's covenant followed them. ⁹The armed guard marched ahead of the priests who blew the trumpets, and the rear guard followed the ark. All this time the trumpets were sounding. ¹⁰But Joshua had commanded the army, "Do not give a war cry, do not raise your voices, do not say a word until the day I tell you to shout. Then shout!" ¹¹So he had the ark of the LORD carried around the city, circling it once. Then the army returned to camp and spent the night there.

¹²Joshua got up early the next morning and the priests took up the ark of the LORD. ¹³The seven priests carrying the seven trumpets went forward, marching before the ark of the LORD and blowing the trumpets. The armed men went ahead of them and the rear guard followed the ark of the LORD, while the trumpets kept sounding. ¹⁴So on the second day they marched around the city once and returned to the camp. They did this for six days.

¹⁵On the seventh day, they got up at daybreak and marched around the city seven times in the same manner, except that on that day they circled the city seven times. ¹⁶The seventh time around, when the priests sounded the trumpet blast, Joshua commanded the army, "Shout! For the LORD has given you the city! ¹⁷The city and all that is in it are to be devoted*ᵃ* to the LORD. Only Rahab the prostitute and all who are with her in her house shall be spared, because she hid the spies we sent. ¹⁸But keep away from the devoted things, so that you will not bring about your own destruction by taking any of them. Otherwise you will make the camp of Israel liable to destruction and bring trouble on it. ¹⁹All the silver and gold and the articles of bronze and iron are sacred to the LORD and must go into his treasury."

²⁰When the trumpets sounded, the army shouted, and at the sound of the trumpet, when the men gave a loud shout, the wall collapsed; so everyone charged straight in, and they took the city. ²¹They devoted the city to the LORD and destroyed with the sword every living thing in it — men and women, young and old, cattle, sheep and donkeys.

²²Joshua said to the two men who had spied out the land, "Go into the prostitute's house and bring her out and all who belong to her, in accordance with your oath to her." ²³So the young men who had done the spying went

---

ᵃ 17 The Hebrew term refers to the irrevocable giving over of things or persons to the LORD, often by totally destroying them; also in verses 18 and 21.

in and brought out Rahab, her father and mother, her brothers and sisters and all who belonged to her. They brought out her entire family and put them in a place outside the camp of Israel.

²⁴Then they burned the whole city and everything in it, but they put the silver and gold and the articles of bronze and iron into the treasury of the LORD's house. ²⁵But Joshua spared Rahab the prostitute, with her family and all who belonged to her, because she hid the men Joshua had sent as spies to Jericho — and she lives among the Israelites to this day.

²⁶At that time Joshua pronounced this solemn oath: "Cursed before the LORD is the one who undertakes to rebuild this city, Jericho:

"At the cost of his firstborn
 son
  he will lay its foundations;
at the cost of his youngest
  he will set up its gates."

²⁷So the LORD was with Joshua, and his fame spread throughout the land.

Achan's Sin

7 But the Israelites were unfaithful in regard to the devoted things^a; Achan son of Karmi, the son of Zimri,^b the son of Zerah, of the tribe of Judah, took some of them. So the LORD's anger burned against Israel.

²Now Joshua sent men from Jericho to Ai, which is near Beth Aven to the east of Bethel, and told them, "Go up and spy out the region." So the men went up and spied out Ai.

³When they returned to Joshua, they said, "Not all the army will have to go up against Ai. Send two or three thousand men to take it and do not weary the whole army, for only a few people live there." ⁴So about three thousand went up; but they were routed by the men of Ai, ⁵who killed about thirty-six of them. They chased the Israelites from the city gate as far as the stone quarries and struck them down on the slopes. At this the hearts of the people melted in fear and became like water.

⁶Then Joshua tore his clothes and fell facedown to the ground before the ark of the LORD, remaining there till evening. The elders of Israel did the same, and sprinkled dust on their heads. ⁷And Joshua said, "Alas, Sovereign LORD, why did you ever bring this people across the Jordan to deliver us into the hands of the Amorites to destroy us? If only we had been content to stay on the other side of the Jordan! ⁸Pardon your servant, Lord.

---

^a 1 The Hebrew term refers to the irrevocable giving over of things or persons to the LORD, often by totally destroying them; also in verses 11, 12, 13 and 15.
^b 1 See Septuagint and 1 Chron. 2:6; Hebrew *Zabdi*; also in verses 17 and 18.

What can I say, now that Israel has been routed by its enemies? ⁹The Canaanites and the other people of the country will hear about this and they will surround us and wipe out our name from the earth. What then will you do for your own great name?"

¹⁰The LORD said to Joshua, "Stand up! What are you doing down on your face? ¹¹Israel has sinned; they have violated my covenant, which I commanded them to keep. They have taken some of the devoted things; they have stolen, they have lied, they have put them with their own possessions. ¹²That is why the Israelites cannot stand against their enemies; they turn their backs and run because they have been made liable to destruction. I will not be with you anymore unless you destroy whatever among you is devoted to destruction.

¹³"Go, consecrate the people. Tell them, 'Consecrate yourselves in preparation for tomorrow; for this is what the LORD, the God of Israel, says: There are devoted things among you, Israel. You cannot stand against your enemies until you remove them.

¹⁴"'In the morning, present yourselves tribe by tribe. The tribe the LORD chooses shall come forward clan by clan; the clan the LORD chooses shall come forward family by family; and the family the LORD chooses shall come forward man by man. ¹⁵Whoever is caught with the devoted things shall be destroyed by fire, along with all that belongs to him. He has violated the covenant of the LORD and has done an outrageous thing in Israel!'"

¹⁶Early the next morning Joshua had Israel come forward by tribes, and Judah was chosen. ¹⁷The clans of Judah came forward, and the Zerahites were chosen. He had the clan of the Zerahites come forward by families, and Zimri was chosen. ¹⁸Joshua had his family come forward man by man, and Achan son of Karmi, the son of Zimri, the son of Zerah, of the tribe of Judah, was chosen.

¹⁹Then Joshua said to Achan, "My son, give glory to the LORD, the God of Israel, and honor him. Tell me what you have done; do not hide it from me."

²⁰Achan replied, "It is true! I have sinned against the LORD, the God of Israel. This is what I have done: ²¹When I saw in the plunder a beautiful robe from Babylonia,ᵃ two hundred shekelsᵇ of silver and a bar of gold weighing fifty shekels,ᶜ I coveted them and took them. They are hidden in the ground inside my tent, with the silver underneath."

²²So Joshua sent messengers, and they ran to the tent, and there

---

ᵃ 21 Hebrew *Shinar*   ᵇ 21 That is, about 5 pounds or about 2.3 kilograms
ᶜ 21 That is, about 1 1/4 pounds or about 575 grams

it was, hidden in his tent, with the silver underneath. ²³They took the things from the tent, brought them to Joshua and all the Israelites and spread them out before the LORD.

²⁴Then Joshua, together with all Israel, took Achan son of Zerah, the silver, the robe, the gold bar, his sons and daughters, his cattle, donkeys and sheep, his tent and all that he had, to the Valley of Achor. ²⁵Joshua said, "Why have you brought this trouble on us? The LORD will bring trouble on you today."

Then all Israel stoned him, and after they had stoned the rest, they burned them. ²⁶Over Achan they heaped up a large pile of rocks, which remains to this day. Then the LORD turned from his fierce anger. Therefore that place has been called the Valley of Achor[a] ever since.

Ai Destroyed

8 Then the LORD said to Joshua, "Do not be afraid; do not be discouraged. Take the whole army with you, and go up and attack Ai. For I have delivered into your hands the king of Ai, his people, his city and his land. ²You shall do to Ai and its king as you did to Jericho and its king, except that you may carry off their plunder and livestock for yourselves. Set an ambush behind the city."

³So Joshua and the whole army moved out to attack Ai. He chose thirty thousand of his best fighting men and sent them out at night ⁴with these orders: "Listen carefully. You are to set an ambush behind the city. Don't go very far from it. All of you be on the alert. ⁵I and all those with me will advance on the city, and when the men come out against us, as they did before, we will flee from them. ⁶They will pursue us until we have lured them away from the city, for they will say, 'They are running away from us as they did before.' So when we flee from them, ⁷you are to rise up from ambush and take the city. The LORD your God will give it into your hand. ⁸When you have taken the city, set it on fire. Do what the LORD has commanded. See to it; you have my orders."

⁹Then Joshua sent them off, and they went to the place of ambush and lay in wait between Bethel and Ai, to the west of Ai — but Joshua spent that night with the people.

¹⁰Early the next morning Joshua mustered his army, and he and the leaders of Israel marched before them to Ai. ¹¹The entire force that was with him marched up and approached the city and arrived in front of it. They set up camp north of Ai, with the valley between them and the city. ¹²Joshua had taken about five thousand men and set them in

---

[a] 26 Achor means trouble.

ambush between Bethel and Ai, to the west of the city. ¹³So the soldiers took up their positions — with the main camp to the north of the city and the ambush to the west of it. That night Joshua went into the valley.

¹⁴When the king of Ai saw this, he and all the men of the city hurried out early in the morning to meet Israel in battle at a certain place overlooking the Arabah. But he did not know that an ambush had been set against him behind the city. ¹⁵Joshua and all Israel let themselves be driven back before them, and they fled toward the wilderness. ¹⁶All the men of Ai were called to pursue them, and they pursued Joshua and were lured away from the city. ¹⁷Not a man remained in Ai or Bethel who did not go after Israel. They left the city open and went in pursuit of Israel.

¹⁸Then the LORD said to Joshua, "Hold out toward Ai the javelin that is in your hand, for into your hand I will deliver the city." So Joshua held out toward the city the javelin that was in his hand. ¹⁹As soon as he did this, the men in the ambush rose quickly from their position and rushed forward. They entered the city and captured it and quickly set it on fire.

²⁰The men of Ai looked back and saw the smoke of the city rising up into the sky, but they had no chance to escape in any direction; the Israelites who had been fleeing toward the wilderness had turned back against their pursuers. ²¹For when Joshua and all Israel saw that the ambush had taken the city and that smoke was going up from it, they turned around and attacked the men of Ai. ²²Those in the ambush also came out of the city against them, so that they were caught in the middle, with Israelites on both sides. Israel cut them down, leaving them neither survivors nor fugitives. ²³But they took the king of Ai alive and brought him to Joshua.

²⁴When Israel had finished killing all the men of Ai in the fields and in the wilderness where they had chased them, and when every one of them had been put to the sword, all the Israelites returned to Ai and killed those who were in it. ²⁵Twelve thousand men and women fell that day — all the people of Ai. ²⁶For Joshua did not draw back the hand that held out his javelin until he had destroyed[a] all who lived in Ai. ²⁷But Israel did carry off for themselves the livestock and plunder of this city, as the LORD had instructed Joshua.

²⁸So Joshua burned Ai[b] and made it a permanent heap of ruins, a desolate place to this day. ²⁹He impaled the body of the

---

[a] 26 The Hebrew term refers to the irrevocable giving over of things or persons to the LORD, often by totally destroying them.   [b] 28 Ai means the ruin.

king of Ai on a pole and left it there until evening. At sunset, Joshua ordered them to take the body from the pole and throw it down at the entrance of the city gate. And they raised a large pile of rocks over it, which remains to this day.

The Covenant Renewed at Mount Ebal

³⁰ Then Joshua built on Mount Ebal an altar to the LORD, the God of Israel, ³¹ as Moses the servant of the LORD had commanded the Israelites. He built it according to what is written in the Book of the Law of Moses — an altar of uncut stones, on which no iron tool had been used. On it they offered to the LORD burnt offerings and sacrificed fellowship offerings. ³² There, in the presence of the Israelites, Joshua wrote on stones a copy of the law of Moses. ³³ All the Israelites, with their elders, officials and judges, were standing on both sides of the ark of the covenant of the LORD, facing the Levitical priests who carried it. Both the foreigners living among them and the native-born were there. Half of the people stood in front of Mount Gerizim and half of them in front of Mount Ebal, as Moses the servant of the LORD had formerly commanded when he gave instructions to bless the people of Israel.

³⁴ Afterward, Joshua read all the words of the law — the blessings and the curses — just as it is written in the Book of the Law. ³⁵ There was not a word of all that Moses had commanded that Joshua did not read to the whole assembly of Israel, including the women and children, and the foreigners who lived among them.

The Gibeonite Deception

9 Now when all the kings west of the Jordan heard about these things — the kings in the hill country, in the western foothills, and along the entire coast of the Mediterranean Sea as far as Lebanon (the kings of the Hittites, Amorites, Canaanites, Perizzites, Hivites and Jebusites) — ² they came together to wage war against Joshua and Israel.

³ However, when the people of Gibeon heard what Joshua had done to Jericho and Ai, ⁴ they resorted to a ruse: They went as a delegation whose donkeys were loaded*a* with worn-out sacks and old wineskins, cracked and mended. ⁵ They put worn and patched sandals on their feet and wore old clothes. All the bread of their food supply was dry and moldy. ⁶ Then they went to Joshua in the camp at Gilgal and said to him and the Israelites, "We have come from a distant country; make a treaty with us."

a 4 Most Hebrew manuscripts; some Hebrew manuscripts, Vulgate and Syriac (see also Septuagint) *They prepared provisions and loaded their donkeys*

⁷The Israelites said to the Hivites, "But perhaps you live near us, so how can we make a treaty with you?"

⁸"We are your servants," they said to Joshua.

But Joshua asked, "Who are you and where do you come from?"

⁹They answered: "Your servants have come from a very distant country because of the fame of the LORD your God. For we have heard reports of him: all that he did in Egypt, ¹⁰and all that he did to the two kings of the Amorites east of the Jordan — Sihon king of Heshbon, and Og king of Bashan, who reigned in Ashtaroth. ¹¹And our elders and all those living in our country said to us, 'Take provisions for your journey; go and meet them and say to them, "We are your servants; make a treaty with us."' ¹²This bread of ours was warm when we packed it at home on the day we left to come to you. But now see how dry and moldy it is. ¹³And these wineskins that we filled were new, but see how cracked they are. And our clothes and sandals are worn out by the very long journey."

¹⁴The Israelites sampled their provisions but did not inquire of the LORD. ¹⁵Then Joshua made a treaty of peace with them to let them live, and the leaders of the assembly ratified it by oath.

¹⁶Three days after they made the treaty with the Gibeonites, the Israelites heard that they were neighbors, living near them. ¹⁷So the Israelites set out and on the third day came to their cities: Gibeon, Kephirah, Beeroth and Kiriath Jearim. ¹⁸But the Israelites did not attack them, because the leaders of the assembly had sworn an oath to them by the LORD, the God of Israel.

The whole assembly grumbled against the leaders, ¹⁹but all the leaders answered, "We have given them our oath by the LORD, the God of Israel, and we cannot touch them now. ²⁰This is what we will do to them: We will let them live, so that God's wrath will not fall on us for breaking the oath we swore to them." ²¹They continued, "Let them live, but let them be woodcutters and water carriers in the service of the whole assembly." So the leaders' promise to them was kept.

²²Then Joshua summoned the Gibeonites and said, "Why did you deceive us by saying, 'We live a long way from you,' while actually you live near us? ²³You are now under a curse: You will never be released from service as woodcutters and water carriers for the house of my God."

²⁴They answered Joshua, "Your servants were clearly told how the LORD your God had commanded his servant Moses to give you the whole land and to wipe out all its inhabitants from before you. So we feared for our lives because of you, and that is why we did this.

²⁵We are now in your hands. Do to us whatever seems good and right to you."

²⁶So Joshua saved them from the Israelites, and they did not kill them. ²⁷That day he made the Gibeonites woodcutters and water carriers for the assembly, to provide for the needs of the altar of the LORD at the place the LORD would choose. And that is what they are to this day.

The Sun Stands Still

10 Now Adoni-Zedek king of Jerusalem heard that Joshua had taken Ai and totally destroyed[a] it, doing to Ai and its king as he had done to Jericho and its king, and that the people of Gibeon had made a treaty of peace with Israel and had become their allies. ²He and his people were very much alarmed at this, because Gibeon was an important city, like one of the royal cities; it was larger than Ai, and all its men were good fighters. ³So Adoni-Zedek king of Jerusalem appealed to Hoham king of Hebron, Piram king of Jarmuth, Japhia king of Lachish and Debir king of Eglon. ⁴"Come up and help me attack Gibeon," he said, "because it has made peace with Joshua and the Israelites."

⁵Then the five kings of the Amorites — the kings of Jerusalem, Hebron, Jarmuth, Lachish and Eglon — joined forces. They moved up with all their troops and took up positions against Gibeon and attacked it.

⁶The Gibeonites then sent word to Joshua in the camp at Gilgal: "Do not abandon your servants. Come up to us quickly and save us! Help us, because all the Amorite kings from the hill country have joined forces against us."

⁷So Joshua marched up from Gilgal with his entire army, including all the best fighting men. ⁸The LORD said to Joshua, "Do not be afraid of them; I have given them into your hand. Not one of them will be able to withstand you."

⁹After an all-night march from Gilgal, Joshua took them by surprise. ¹⁰The LORD threw them into confusion before Israel, so Joshua and the Israelites defeated them completely at Gibeon. Israel pursued them along the road going up to Beth Horon and cut them down all the way to Azekah and Makkedah. ¹¹As they fled before Israel on the road down from Beth Horon to Azekah, the LORD hurled large hailstones down on them, and more of them died from the hail than were killed by the swords of the Israelites.

¹²On the day the LORD gave the Amorites over to Israel, Joshua said to the LORD in the presence of Israel:

---

[a] 1 The Hebrew term refers to the irrevocable giving over of things or persons to the LORD, often by totally destroying them; also in verses 28, 35, 37, 39 and 40.

"Sun, stand still over
 Gibeon,
 and you, moon, over the
 Valley of Aijalon."
¹³ So the sun stood still,
 and the moon stopped,
 till the nation avenged itself
 on^a its enemies,

as it is written in the Book of Jashar.

The sun stopped in the middle of the sky and delayed going down about a full day. ¹⁴ There has never been a day like it before or since, a day when the LORD listened to a human being. Surely the LORD was fighting for Israel!

¹⁵ Then Joshua returned with all Israel to the camp at Gilgal.

Five Amorite Kings Killed

¹⁶ Now the five kings had fled and hidden in the cave at Makkedah. ¹⁷ When Joshua was told that the five kings had been found hiding in the cave at Makkedah, ¹⁸ he said, "Roll large rocks up to the mouth of the cave, and post some men there to guard it. ¹⁹ But don't stop; pursue your enemies! Attack them from the rear and don't let them reach their cities, for the LORD your God has given them into your hand."

²⁰ So Joshua and the Israelites defeated them completely, but a few survivors managed to reach their fortified cities. ²¹ The whole army then returned safely to Joshua in the camp at Makkedah, and no one uttered a word against the Israelites.

²² Joshua said, "Open the mouth of the cave and bring those five kings out to me." ²³ So they brought the five kings out of the cave — the kings of Jerusalem, Hebron, Jarmuth, Lachish and Eglon. ²⁴ When they had brought these kings to Joshua, he summoned all the men of Israel and said to the army commanders who had come with him, "Come here and put your feet on the necks of these kings." So they came forward and placed their feet on their necks.

²⁵ Joshua said to them, "Do not be afraid; do not be discouraged. Be strong and courageous. This is what the LORD will do to all the enemies you are going to fight." ²⁶ Then Joshua put the kings to death and exposed their bodies on five poles, and they were left hanging on the poles until evening.

²⁷ At sunset Joshua gave the order and they took them down from the poles and threw them into the cave where they had been hiding. At the mouth of the cave they placed large rocks, which are there to this day.

Southern Cities Conquered

²⁸ That day Joshua took Makkedah. He put the city and its king to the sword and totally destroyed everyone in it. He left no

^a 13 Or *nation triumphed over*

survivors. And he did to the king of Makkedah as he had done to the king of Jericho.

²⁹Then Joshua and all Israel with him moved on from Makkedah to Libnah and attacked it. ³⁰The LORD also gave that city and its king into Israel's hand. The city and everyone in it Joshua put to the sword. He left no survivors there. And he did to its king as he had done to the king of Jericho.

³¹Then Joshua and all Israel with him moved on from Libnah to Lachish; he took up positions against it and attacked it. ³²The LORD gave Lachish into Israel's hands, and Joshua took it on the second day. The city and everyone in it he put to the sword, just as he had done to Libnah. ³³Meanwhile, Horam king of Gezer had come up to help Lachish, but Joshua defeated him and his army—until no survivors were left.

³⁴Then Joshua and all Israel with him moved on from Lachish to Eglon; they took up positions against it and attacked it. ³⁵They captured it that same day and put it to the sword and totally destroyed everyone in it, just as they had done to Lachish.

³⁶Then Joshua and all Israel with him went up from Eglon to Hebron and attacked it. ³⁷They took the city and put it to the sword, together with its king, its villages and everyone in it. They left no survivors. Just as at Eglon, they totally destroyed it and everyone in it.

³⁸Then Joshua and all Israel with him turned around and attacked Debir. ³⁹They took the city, its king and its villages, and put them to the sword. Everyone in it they totally destroyed. They left no survivors. They did to Debir and its king as they had done to Libnah and its king and to Hebron.

⁴⁰So Joshua subdued the whole region, including the hill country, the Negev, the western foothills and the mountain slopes, together with all their kings. He left no survivors. He totally destroyed all who breathed, just as the LORD, the God of Israel, had commanded. ⁴¹Joshua subdued them from Kadesh Barnea to Gaza and from the whole region of Goshen to Gibeon. ⁴²All these kings and their lands Joshua conquered in one campaign, because the LORD, the God of Israel, fought for Israel.

⁴³Then Joshua returned with all Israel to the camp at Gilgal.

Northern Kings Defeated

11 When Jabin king of Hazor heard of this, he sent word to Jobab king of Madon, to the kings of Shimron and Akshaph, ²and to the northern kings who were in the mountains, in the Arabah south of Kinnereth, in the western foothills and in Naphoth Dor on the west; ³to the Canaanites in the east and west; to the Amorites, Hittites, Perizzites and

Jebusites in the hill country; and to the Hivites below Hermon in the region of Mizpah. ⁴They came out with all their troops and a large number of horses and chariots—a huge army, as numerous as the sand on the seashore. ⁵All these kings joined forces and made camp together at the Waters of Merom to fight against Israel.

⁶The LORD said to Joshua, "Do not be afraid of them, because by this time tomorrow I will hand all of them, slain, over to Israel. You are to hamstring their horses and burn their chariots."

⁷So Joshua and his whole army came against them suddenly at the Waters of Merom and attacked them, ⁸and the LORD gave them into the hand of Israel. They defeated them and pursued them all the way to Greater Sidon, to Misrephoth Maim, and to the Valley of Mizpah on the east, until no survivors were left. ⁹Joshua did to them as the LORD had directed: He hamstrung their horses and burned their chariots.

¹⁰At that time Joshua turned back and captured Hazor and put its king to the sword. (Hazor had been the head of all these kingdoms.) ¹¹Everyone in it they put to the sword. They totally destroyed*ᵃ* them, not sparing anyone that breathed, and he burned Hazor itself.

¹²Joshua took all these royal cities and their kings and put them to the sword. He totally destroyed them, as Moses the servant of the LORD had commanded. ¹³Yet Israel did not burn any of the cities built on their mounds—except Hazor, which Joshua burned. ¹⁴The Israelites carried off for themselves all the plunder and livestock of these cities, but all the people they put to the sword until they completely destroyed them, not sparing anyone that breathed. ¹⁵As the LORD commanded his servant Moses, so Moses commanded Joshua, and Joshua did it; he left nothing undone of all that the LORD commanded Moses.

¹⁶So Joshua took this entire land: the hill country, all the Negev, the whole region of Goshen, the western foothills, the Arabah and the mountains of Israel with their foothills, ¹⁷from Mount Halak, which rises toward Seir, to Baal Gad in the Valley of Lebanon below Mount Hermon. He captured all their kings and put them to death. ¹⁸Joshua waged war against all these kings for a long time. ¹⁹Except for the Hivites living in Gibeon, not one city made a treaty of peace with the Israelites, who took them all in battle. ²⁰For it was the LORD himself who hardened their hearts to wage war against Israel, so that he might destroy them totally, exterminating them without mercy, as the LORD had commanded Moses.

²¹At that time Joshua went and

ᵃ 11 The Hebrew term refers to the irrevocable giving over of things or persons to the LORD, often by totally destroying them; also in verses 12, 20 and 21.

destroyed the Anakites from the hill country: from Hebron, Debir and Anab, from all the hill country of Judah, and from all the hill country of Israel. Joshua totally destroyed them and their towns. ²²No Anakites were left in Israelite territory; only in Gaza, Gath and Ashdod did any survive.

²³So Joshua took the entire land, just as the LORD had directed Moses, and he gave it as an inheritance to Israel according to their tribal divisions. Then the land had rest from war.

List of Defeated Kings

12 These are the kings of the land whom the Israelites had defeated and whose territory they took over east of the Jordan, from the Arnon Gorge to Mount Hermon, including all the eastern side of the Arabah:

²Sihon king of the Amorites, who reigned in Heshbon.

He ruled from Aroer on the rim of the Arnon Gorge—from the middle of the gorge—to the Jabbok River, which is the border of the Ammonites. This included half of Gilead. ³He also ruled over the eastern Arabah from the Sea of Galilee[a] to the Sea of the Arabah (that is, the Dead Sea), to Beth Jeshimoth, and then southward below the slopes of Pisgah.

⁴And the territory of Og king of Bashan, one of the last of the Rephaites, who reigned in Ashtaroth and Edrei. ⁵He ruled over Mount Hermon, Salekah, all of Bashan to the border of the people of Geshur and Maakah, and half of Gilead to the border of Sihon king of Heshbon.

⁶Moses, the servant of the LORD, and the Israelites conquered them. And Moses the servant of the LORD gave their land to the Reubenites, the Gadites and the half-tribe of Manasseh to be their possession.

⁷Here is a list of the kings of the land that Joshua and the Israelites conquered on the west side of the Jordan, from Baal Gad in the Valley of Lebanon to Mount Halak, which rises toward Seir. Joshua gave their lands as an inheritance to the tribes of Israel according to their tribal divisions. ⁸The lands included the hill country, the western foothills, the Arabah, the mountain slopes, the wilderness and the Negev. These were the lands of the Hittites, Amorites, Canaanites, Perizzites, Hivites and Jebusites. These were the kings:

⁹the king of Jericho   one
the king of Ai
  (near Bethel)   one
¹⁰the king of Jerusalem   one
the king of Hebron   one

^a 3 Hebrew *Kinnereth*

¹¹the king of Jarmuth   one
the king of Lachish   one
¹²the king of Eglon   one
the king of Gezer   one
¹³the king of Debir   one
the king of Geder   one
¹⁴the king of Hormah   one
the king of Arad   one
¹⁵the king of Libnah   one
the king of Adullam   one
¹⁶the king of
Makkedah   one
the king of Bethel   one
¹⁷the king of Tappuah   one
the king of Hepher   one
¹⁸the king of Aphek   one
the king of Lasharon   one
¹⁹the king of Madon   one
the king of Hazor   one
²⁰the king of Shimron
Meron   one
the king of Akshaph   one
²¹the king of Taanach   one
the king of Megiddo   one
²²the king of Kedesh   one
the king of Jokneam
in Carmel   one
²³the king of Dor (in
Naphoth Dor)   one
the king of Goyim in
Gilgal   one
²⁴the king of Tirzah   one
thirty-one kings in all.

Land Still to Be Taken

13 When Joshua had grown old, the LORD said to him, "You are now very old, and there are still very large areas of land to be taken over.

²"This is the land that remains: all the regions of the Philistines and Geshurites, ³from the Shihor River on the east of Egypt to the territory of Ekron on the north, all of it counted as Canaanite though held by the five Philistine rulers in Gaza, Ashdod, Ashkelon, Gath and Ekron; the territory of the Avvites ⁴on the south; all the land of the Canaanites, from Arah of the Sidonians as far as Aphek and the border of the Amorites; ⁵the area of Byblos; and all Lebanon to the east, from Baal Gad below Mount Hermon to Lebo Hamath.

⁶"As for all the inhabitants of the mountain regions from Lebanon to Misrephoth Maim, that is, all the Sidonians, I myself will drive them out before the Israelites. Be sure to allocate this land to Israel for an inheritance, as I have instructed you, ⁷and divide it as an inheritance among the nine tribes and half of the tribe of Manasseh."

Division of the Land East of the Jordan

⁸The other half of Manasseh,ᵃ the Reubenites and the Gadites had received the inheritance that Moses had given them east of the Jordan, as he, the servant of the LORD, had assigned it to them.

⁹It extended from Aroer on the rim of the Arnon Gorge,

ᵃ 8 Hebrew *With it* (that is, with the other half of Manasseh) and from the town in the middle of the gorge, and included the whole plateau of Medeba as far as Dibon, [10] and all the towns of Sihon king of the Amorites, who ruled in Heshbon, out to the border of the Ammonites. [11] It also included Gilead, the territory of the people of Geshur and Maakah, all of Mount Hermon and all Bashan as far as Salekah — [12] that is, the whole kingdom of Og in Bashan, who had reigned in Ashtaroth and Edrei. (He was the last of the Rephaites.) Moses had defeated them and taken over their land. [13] But the Israelites did not drive out the people of Geshur and Maakah, so they continue to live among the Israelites to this day.

[14] But to the tribe of Levi he gave no inheritance, since the food offerings presented to the LORD, the God of Israel, are their inheritance, as he promised them.

[15] This is what Moses had given to the tribe of Reuben, according to its clans:

[16] The territory from Aroer on the rim of the Arnon Gorge, and from the town in the middle of the gorge, and the whole plateau past Medeba [17] to Heshbon and all its towns on the plateau, including Dibon, Bamoth Baal, Beth Baal Meon, [18] Jahaz, Kedemoth, Mephaath, [19] Kiriathaim, Sibmah, Zereth Shahar on the hill in the valley, [20] Beth Peor, the slopes of Pisgah, and Beth Jeshimoth — [21] all the towns on the plateau and the entire realm of Sihon king of the Amorites, who ruled at Heshbon. Moses had defeated him and the Midianite chiefs, Evi, Rekem, Zur, Hur and Reba — princes allied with Sihon — who lived in that country. [22] In addition to those slain in battle, the Israelites had put to the sword Balaam son of Beor, who practiced divination. [23] The boundary of the Reubenites was the bank of the Jordan. These towns and their villages were the inheritance of the Reubenites, according to their clans.

[24] This is what Moses had given to the tribe of Gad, according to its clans:

[25] The territory of Jazer, all the towns of Gilead and half the Ammonite country as far as Aroer, near Rabbah; [26] and from Heshbon to Ramath Mizpah and Betonim, and from Mahanaim to the territory of Debir; [27] and in the valley, Beth Haram, Beth Nimrah, Sukkoth and Zaphon with the rest of the realm of Sihon king of Heshbon (the east side of the Jor-

dan, the territory up to the end of the Sea of Galilee[a]). [28] These towns and their villages were the inheritance of the Gadites, according to their clans.

[29] This is what Moses had given to the half-tribe of Manasseh, that is, to half the family of the descendants of Manasseh, according to its clans:

[30] The territory extending from Mahanaim and including all of Bashan, the entire realm of Og king of Bashan — all the settlements of Jair in Bashan, sixty towns, [31] half of Gilead, and Ashtaroth and Edrei (the royal cities of Og in Bashan). This was for the descendants of Makir son of Manasseh — for half of the sons of Makir, according to their clans.

[32] This is the inheritance Moses had given when he was in the plains of Moab across the Jordan east of Jericho. [33] But to the tribe of Levi, Moses had given no inheritance; the LORD, the God of Israel, is their inheritance, as he promised them.

Division of the Land West of the Jordan

14 Now these are the areas the Israelites received as an inheritance in the land of Canaan, which Eleazar the priest, Joshua son of Nun and the heads of the tribal clans of Israel allotted to them. [2] Their inheritances were assigned by lot to the nine and a half tribes, as the LORD had commanded through Moses. [3] Moses had granted the two and a half tribes their inheritance east of the Jordan but had not granted the Levites an inheritance among the rest, [4] for Joseph's descendants had become two tribes — Manasseh and Ephraim. The Levites received no share of the land but only towns to live in, with pasturelands for their flocks and herds. [5] So the Israelites divided the land, just as the LORD had commanded Moses.

Allotment for Caleb

[6] Now the people of Judah approached Joshua at Gilgal, and Caleb son of Jephunneh the Kenizzite said to him, "You know what the LORD said to Moses the man of God at Kadesh Barnea about you and me. [7] I was forty years old when Moses the servant of the LORD sent me from Kadesh Barnea to explore the land. And I brought him back a report according to my convictions, [8] but my fellow Israelites who went up with me made the hearts of the people melt in fear. I, however, followed the LORD my God wholeheartedly. [9] So on that day Moses swore to me, 'The land

on which your feet have walked will be your inheritance and that of your children forever, because you have followed the LORD my God wholeheartedly.'[a]

¹⁰ "Now then, just as the LORD promised, he has kept me alive for forty-five years since the time he said this to Moses, while Israel moved about in the wilderness. So here I am today, eighty-five years old! ¹¹ I am still as strong today as the day Moses sent me out; I'm just as vigorous to go out to battle now as I was then. ¹² Now give me this hill country that the LORD promised me that day. You yourself heard then that the Anakites were there and their cities were large and fortified, but, the LORD helping me, I will drive them out just as he said."

¹³ Then Joshua blessed Caleb son of Jephunneh and gave him Hebron as his inheritance. ¹⁴ So Hebron has belonged to Caleb son of Jephunneh the Kenizzite ever since, because he followed the LORD, the God of Israel, wholeheartedly. ¹⁵ (Hebron used to be called Kiriath Arba after Arba, who was the greatest man among the Anakites.)

Then the land had rest from war.

Allotment for Judah

15 The allotment for the tribe of Judah, according to its clans, extended down to the territory of Edom, to the Desert of Zin in the extreme south.

² Their southern boundary started from the bay at the southern end of the Dead Sea, ³ crossed south of Scorpion Pass, continued on to Zin and went over to the south of Kadesh Barnea. Then it ran past Hezron up to Addar and curved around to Karka. ⁴ It then passed along to Azmon and joined the Wadi of Egypt, ending at the Mediterranean Sea. This is their[b] southern boundary.

⁵ The eastern boundary is the Dead Sea as far as the mouth of the Jordan.

The northern boundary started from the bay of the sea at the mouth of the Jordan, ⁶ went up to Beth Hoglah and continued north of Beth Arabah to the Stone of Bohan son of Reuben. ⁷ The boundary then went up to Debir from the Valley of Achor and turned north to Gilgal, which faces the Pass of Adummim south of the gorge. It continued along to the waters of En Shemesh and came out at En Rogel. ⁸ Then it ran up the Valley of Ben Hinnom along the southern slope of the Jebusite city (that is, Jerusalem). From there it climbed to the top of the hill west of the Hinnom Valley at the north-

---

[a] 9 Deut. 1:36   [b] 4 Septuagint; Hebrew *your*

ern end of the Valley of Reph-aim. **9**From the hilltop the boundary headed toward the spring of the waters of Neph-toah, came out at the towns of Mount Ephron and went down toward Baalah (that is, Kiriath Jearim). **10**Then it curved westward from Baal-ah to Mount Seir, ran along the northern slope of Mount Jearim (that is, Kesalon), continued down to Beth She-mesh and crossed to Tim-nah. **11**It went to the north-ern slope of Ekron, turned toward Shikkeron, passed along to Mount Baalah and reached Jabneel. The bound-ary ended at the sea.

12The western boundary is the coastline of the Mediter-ranean Sea.

These are the boundaries around the people of Judah by their clans.

13In accordance with the LORD's command to him, Joshua gave to Caleb son of Jephunneh a portion in Judah — Kiriath Arba, that is, Hebron. (Arba was the forefather of Anak.) **14**From He-bron Caleb drove out the three Anakites — Sheshai, Ahiman and Talmai, the sons of Anak. **15**From there he marched against the people living in Debir (formerly called Kiriath Sepher). **16**And Ca-leb said, "I will give my daughter Aksah in marriage to the man who attacks and captures Kiriath Sepher." **17**Othniel son of Kenaz, Caleb's brother, took it; so Caleb gave his daughter Aksah to him in marriage.

18One day when she came to Othniel, she urged him*a* to ask her father for a field. When she got off her donkey, Caleb asked her, "What can I do for you?"

19She replied, "Do me a special favor. Since you have given me land in the Negev, give me also springs of water." So Caleb gave her the upper and lower springs.

20This is the inheritance of the tribe of Judah, according to its clans:

21The southernmost towns of the tribe of Judah in the Negev toward the boundary of Edom were:

Kabzeel, Eder, Jagur, **22**Ki-nah, Dimonah, Adadah, **23**Kedesh, Hazor, Ithnan, **24**Ziph, Telem, Bealoth, **25**Ha-zor Hadattah, Kerioth Hez-ron (that is, Hazor), **26**Amam, Shema, Moladah, **27**Hazar Gaddah, Heshmon, Beth Pelet, **28**Hazar Shual, Beer-sheba, Biziothiah, **29**Baalah, Iyim, Ezem, **30**Eltolad, Kesil, Hormah, **31**Ziklag, Madman-nah, Sansannah, **32**Lebaoth, Shilhim, Ain and Rimmon —

---

a 18 Hebrew and some Septuagint manuscripts; other Septuagint manuscripts (see also note at Judges 1:14) *Othniel, he urged her* a total of twenty-nine towns and their villages.

³³ In the western foothills:

Eshtaol, Zorah, Ashnah, ³⁴ Zanoah, En Gannim, Tappuah, Enam, ³⁵ Jarmuth, Adullam, Sokoh, Azekah, ³⁶ Shaaraim, Adithaim and Gederah (or Gederothaim)^a — fourteen towns and their villages.

³⁷ Zenan, Hadashah, Migdal Gad, ³⁸ Dilean, Mizpah, Joktheel, ³⁹ Lachish, Bozkath, Eglon, ⁴⁰ Kabbon, Lahmas, Kitlish, ⁴¹ Gederoth, Beth Dagon, Naamah and Makkedah — sixteen towns and their villages.

⁴² Libnah, Ether, Ashan, ⁴³ Iphtah, Ashnah, Nezib, ⁴⁴ Keilah, Akzib and Mareshah — nine towns and their villages.

⁴⁵ Ekron, with its surrounding settlements and villages; ⁴⁶ west of Ekron, all that were in the vicinity of Ashdod, together with their villages; ⁴⁷ Ashdod, its surrounding settlements and villages; and Gaza, its settlements and villages, as far as the Wadi of Egypt and the coastline of the Mediterranean Sea.

⁴⁸ In the hill country:

Shamir, Jattir, Sokoh, ⁴⁹ Dannah, Kiriath Sannah (that is, Debir), ⁵⁰ Anab, Eshtemoh, Anim, ⁵¹ Goshen, Holon and Giloh — eleven towns and their villages.

⁵² Arab, Dumah, Eshan, ⁵³ Janim, Beth Tappuah, Aphekah, ⁵⁴ Humtah, Kiriath Arba (that is, Hebron) and Zior — nine towns and their villages.

⁵⁵ Maon, Carmel, Ziph, Juttah, ⁵⁶ Jezreel, Jokdeam, Zanoah, ⁵⁷ Kain, Gibeah and Timnah — ten towns and their villages.

⁵⁸ Halhul, Beth Zur, Gedor, ⁵⁹ Maarath, Beth Anoth and Eltekon — six towns and their villages.^b

⁶⁰ Kiriath Baal (that is, Kiriath Jearim) and Rabbah — two towns and their villages.

⁶¹ In the wilderness:

Beth Arabah, Middin, Sekakah, ⁶² Nibshan, the City of Salt and En Gedi — six towns and their villages.

⁶³ Judah could not dislodge the Jebusites, who were living in Jerusalem; to this day the Jebusites live there with the people of Judah.

Allotment for Ephraim and Manasseh

16 The allotment for Joseph began at the Jordan, east of the springs of Jericho, and went up from there through the desert into the hill country of Bethel. ² It

---

^a 36 Or *Gederah and Gederothaim*   ^b 59 The Septuagint adds another district of eleven towns, including Tekoa and Ephrathah (Bethlehem).

went on from Bethel (that is, Luz),[a] crossed over to the territory of the Arkites in Ataroth, ³descended westward to the territory of the Japhletites as far as the region of Lower Beth Horon and on to Gezer, ending at the Mediterranean Sea.

⁴So Manasseh and Ephraim, the descendants of Joseph, received their inheritance.

⁵This was the territory of Ephraim, according to its clans:

The boundary of their inheritance went from Ataroth Addar in the east to Upper Beth Horon ⁶and continued to the Mediterranean Sea. From Mikmethath on the north it curved eastward to Taanath Shiloh, passing by it to Janoah on the east. ⁷Then it went down from Janoah to Ataroth and Naarah, touched Jericho and came out at the Jordan. ⁸From Tappuah the border went west to the Kanah Ravine and ended at the Mediterranean Sea. This was the inheritance of the tribe of the Ephraimites, according to its clans. ⁹It also included all the towns and their villages that were set aside for the Ephraimites within the inheritance of the Manassites.

¹⁰They did not dislodge the Canaanites living in Gezer; to this day the Canaanites live among the people of Ephraim but are required to do forced labor.

17 This was the allotment for the tribe of Manasseh as Joseph's firstborn, that is, for Makir, Manasseh's firstborn. Makir was the ancestor of the Gileadites, who had received Gilead and Bashan because the Makirites were great soldiers. ²So this allotment was for the rest of the people of Manasseh — the clans of Abiezer, Helek, Asriel, Shechem, Hepher and Shemida. These are the other male descendants of Manasseh son of Joseph by their clans.

³Now Zelophehad son of Hepher, the son of Gilead, the son of Makir, the son of Manasseh, had no sons but only daughters, whose names were Mahlah, Noah, Hoglah, Milkah and Tirzah. ⁴They went to Eleazar the priest, Joshua son of Nun, and the leaders and said, "The LORD commanded Moses to give us an inheritance among our relatives." So Joshua gave them an inheritance along with the brothers of their father, according to the LORD's command. ⁵Manasseh's share consisted of ten tracts of land besides Gilead and Bashan east of the Jordan, ⁶because the daughters of the tribe of Manasseh received an inheritance among the sons. The land of Gilead belonged to the rest of the descendants of Manasseh.

---

[a] 2 Septuagint; Hebrew *Bethel to Luz*

[7]The territory of Manasseh extended from Asher to Mikmethath east of Shechem. The boundary ran southward from there to include the people living at En Tappuah. [8](Manasseh had the land of Tappuah, but Tappuah itself, on the boundary of Manasseh, belonged to the Ephraimites.) [9]Then the boundary continued south to the Kanah Ravine. There were towns belonging to Ephraim lying among the towns of Manasseh, but the boundary of Manasseh was the northern side of the ravine and ended at the Mediterranean Sea. [10]On the south the land belonged to Ephraim, on the north to Manasseh. The territory of Manasseh reached the Mediterranean Sea and bordered Asher on the north and Issachar on the east.

[11]Within Issachar and Asher, Manasseh also had Beth Shan, Ibleam and the people of Dor, Endor, Taanach and Megiddo, together with their surrounding settlements (the third in the list is Naphoth[a]). [12]Yet the Manassites were not able to occupy these towns, for the Canaanites were determined to live in that region. [13]However, when the Israelites grew stronger, they subjected the Canaanites to forced labor but did not drive them out completely.

[14]The people of Joseph said to Joshua, "Why have you given us only one allotment and one portion for an inheritance? We are a numerous people, and the Lord has blessed us abundantly."

[15]"If you are so numerous," Joshua answered, "and if the hill country of Ephraim is too small for you, go up into the forest and clear land for yourselves there in the land of the Perizzites and Rephaites."

[16]The people of Joseph replied, "The hill country is not enough for us, and all the Canaanites who live in the plain have chariots fitted with iron, both those in Beth Shan and its settlements and those in the Valley of Jezreel."

[17]But Joshua said to the tribes of Joseph — to Ephraim and Manasseh — "You are numerous and very powerful. You will have not only one allotment [18]but the forested hill country as well. Clear it, and its farthest limits will be yours; though the Canaanites have chariots fitted with iron and though they are strong, you can drive them out."

Division of the Rest of the Land

18 The whole assembly of the Israelites gathered at Shiloh and set up the tent of meeting there. The country was brought under their control, [2]but

---

[a] 11 That is, Naphoth Dor

there were still seven Israelite tribes who had not yet received their inheritance.

³So Joshua said to the Israelites: "How long will you wait before you begin to take possession of the land that the LORD, the God of your ancestors, has given you? ⁴Appoint three men from each tribe. I will send them out to make a survey of the land and to write a description of it, according to the inheritance of each. Then they will return to me. ⁵You are to divide the land into seven parts. Judah is to remain in its territory on the south and the tribes of Joseph in their territory on the north. ⁶After you have written descriptions of the seven parts of the land, bring them here to me and I will cast lots for you in the presence of the LORD our God. ⁷The Levites, however, do not get a portion among you, because the priestly service of the LORD is their inheritance. And Gad, Reuben and the half-tribe of Manasseh have already received their inheritance on the east side of the Jordan. Moses the servant of the LORD gave it to them."

⁸As the men started on their way to map out the land, Joshua instructed them, "Go and make a survey of the land and write a description of it. Then return to me, and I will cast lots for you here at Shiloh in the presence of the LORD." ⁹So the men left and went through the land. They wrote its description on a scroll, town by town, in seven parts, and returned to Joshua in the camp at Shiloh. ¹⁰Joshua then cast lots for them in Shiloh in the presence of the LORD, and there he distributed the land to the Israelites according to their tribal divisions.

Allotment for Benjamin

¹¹The first lot came up for the tribe of Benjamin according to its clans. Their allotted territory lay between the tribes of Judah and Joseph:

¹²On the north side their boundary began at the Jordan, passed the northern slope of Jericho and headed west into the hill country, coming out at the wilderness of Beth Aven. ¹³From there it crossed to the south slope of Luz (that is, Bethel) and went down to Ataroth Addar on the hill south of Lower Beth Horon.

¹⁴From the hill facing Beth Horon on the south the boundary turned south along the western side and came out at Kiriath Baal (that is, Kiriath Jearim), a town of the people of Judah. This was the western side.

¹⁵The southern side began at the outskirts of Kiriath Jearim on the west, and the boundary came out at the spring of the waters of Nephtoah. ¹⁶The boundary went

down to the foot of the hill facing the Valley of Ben Hinnom, north of the Valley of Rephaim. It continued down the Hinnom Valley along the southern slope of the Jebusite city and so to En Rogel. [17] It then curved north, went to En Shemesh, continued to Geliloth, which faces the Pass of Adummim, and ran down to the Stone of Bohan son of Reuben. [18] It continued to the northern slope of Beth Arabah[a] and on down into the Arabah. [19] It then went to the northern slope of Beth Hoglah and came out at the northern bay of the Dead Sea, at the mouth of the Jordan in the south. This was the southern boundary.

[20] The Jordan formed the boundary on the eastern side.

These were the boundaries that marked out the inheritance of the clans of Benjamin on all sides.

[21] The tribe of Benjamin, according to its clans, had the following towns:

Jericho, Beth Hoglah, Emek Keziz, [22] Beth Arabah, Zemaraim, Bethel, [23] Avvim, Parah, Ophrah, [24] Kephar Ammoni, Ophni and Geba — twelve towns and their villages.

[25] Gibeon, Ramah, Beeroth, [26] Mizpah, Kephirah, Mozah, [27] Rekem, Irpeel, Taralah, [28] Zelah, Haeleph, the Jebusite city (that is, Jerusalem), Gibeah and Kiriath — fourteen towns and their villages.

This was the inheritance of Benjamin for its clans.

Allotment for Simeon

19 The second lot came out for the tribe of Simeon according to its clans. Their inheritance lay within the territory of Judah. [2] It included:

Beersheba (or Sheba),[b] Moladah, [3] Hazar Shual, Balah, Ezem, [4] Eltolad, Bethul, Hormah, [5] Ziklag, Beth Markaboth, Hazar Susah, [6] Beth Lebaoth and Sharuhen — thirteen towns and their villages;

[7] Ain, Rimmon, Ether and Ashan — four towns and their villages — [8] and all the villages around these towns as far as Baalath Beer (Ramah in the Negev).

This was the inheritance of the tribe of the Simeonites, according to its clans. [9] The inheritance of the Simeonites was taken from the share of Judah, because Judah's portion was more than they needed. So the Simeonites received their inheritance within the territory of Judah.

Allotment for Zebulun

[10] The third lot came up for Zebulun according to its clans:

---

[a] 18 Septuagint; Hebrew *slope facing the Arabah*   [b] 2 Or *Beersheba, Sheba*;
1 Chron. 4:28 does not have *Sheba*.

The boundary of their inheritance went as far as Sarid. **11** Going west it ran to Maralah, touched Dabbesheth, and extended to the ravine near Jokneam. **12** It turned east from Sarid toward the sunrise to the territory of Kisloth Tabor and went on to Daberath and up to Japhia. **13** Then it continued eastward to Gath Hepher and Eth Kazin; it came out at Rimmon and turned toward Neah. **14** There the boundary went around on the north to Hannathon and ended at the Valley of Iphtah El. **15** Included were Kattath, Nahalal, Shimron, Idalah and Bethlehem. There were twelve towns and their villages.

16 These towns and their villages were the inheritance of Zebulun, according to its clans.

Allotment for Issachar

17 The fourth lot came out for Issachar according to its clans. **18** Their territory included:

Jezreel, Kesulloth, Shunem, **19** Hapharaim, Shion, Anaharath, **20** Rabbith, Kishion, Ebez, **21** Remeth, En Gannim, En Haddah and Beth Pazzez. **22** The boundary touched Tabor, Shahazumah and Beth Shemesh, and ended at the Jordan. There were sixteen towns and their villages.

23 These towns and their villages were the inheritance of the tribe of Issachar, according to its clans.

Allotment for Asher

24 The fifth lot came out for the tribe of Asher according to its clans. **25** Their territory included:

Helkath, Hali, Beten, Akshaph, **26** Allammelek, Amad and Mishal. On the west the boundary touched Carmel and Shihor Libnath. **27** It then turned east toward Beth Dagon, touched Zebulun and the Valley of Iphtah El, and went north to Beth Emek and Neiel, passing Kabul on the left. **28** It went to Abdon,*a* Rehob, Hammon and Kanah, as far as Greater Sidon. **29** The boundary then turned back toward Ramah and went to the fortified city of Tyre, turned toward Hosah and came out at the Mediterranean Sea in the region of Akzib, **30** Ummah, Aphek and Rehob. There were twenty-two towns and their villages.

31 These towns and their villages were the inheritance of the tribe of Asher, according to its clans.

Allotment for Naphtali

32 The sixth lot came out for Naphtali according to its clans:

33 Their boundary went from Heleph and the large tree in Zaanannim, passing

a 28 Some Hebrew manuscripts (see also 21:30); most Hebrew manuscripts *Ebron*

Adami Nekeb and Jabneel to Lakkum and ending at the Jordan. ³⁴The boundary ran west through Aznoth Tabor and came out at Hukkok. It touched Zebulun on the south, Asher on the west and the Jordan^a on the east. ³⁵The fortified towns were Ziddim, Zer, Hammath, Rakkath, Kinnereth, ³⁶Adamah, Ramah, Hazor, ³⁷Kedesh, Edrei, En Hazor, ³⁸Iron, Migdal El, Horem, Beth Anath and Beth Shemesh. There were nineteen towns and their villages.

³⁹These towns and their villages were the inheritance of the tribe of Naphtali, according to its clans.

Allotment for Dan

⁴⁰The seventh lot came out for the tribe of Dan according to its clans. ⁴¹The territory of their inheritance included:

Zorah, Eshtaol, Ir Shemesh, ⁴²Shaalabbin, Aijalon, Ithlah, ⁴³Elon, Timnah, Ekron, ⁴⁴Eltekeh, Gibbethon, Baalath, ⁴⁵Jehud, Bene Berak, Gath Rimmon, ⁴⁶Me Jarkon and Rakkon, with the area facing Joppa.

⁴⁷(When the territory of the Danites was lost to them, they went up and attacked Leshem, took it, put it to the sword and occupied it. They settled in Leshem and named it Dan after their ancestor.)

⁴⁸These towns and their villages were the inheritance of the tribe of Dan, according to its clans.

Allotment for Joshua

⁴⁹When they had finished dividing the land into its allotted portions, the Israelites gave Joshua son of Nun an inheritance among them, ⁵⁰as the LORD had commanded. They gave him the town he asked for — Timnath Serah^b in the hill country of Ephraim. And he built up the town and settled there.

⁵¹These are the territories that Eleazar the priest, Joshua son of Nun and the heads of the tribal clans of Israel assigned by lot at Shiloh in the presence of the LORD at the entrance to the tent of meeting. And so they finished dividing the land.

Cities of Refuge

20 Then the LORD said to Joshua: ²"Tell the Israelites to designate the cities of refuge, as I instructed you through Moses, ³so that anyone who kills a person accidentally and unintentionally may flee there and find protection from the avenger of blood. ⁴When they flee to one of these cities, they are to stand in the entrance of the city gate and state their case before the el-

---

^a 34 Septuagint; Hebrew *west, and Judah, the Jordan,*   ^b 50 Also known as *Timnath Heres* (see Judges 2:9)

ders of that city. Then the elders are to admit the fugitive into their city and provide a place to live among them. ⁵ If the avenger of blood comes in pursuit, the elders must not surrender the fugitive, because the fugitive killed their neighbor unintentionally and without malice aforethought. ⁶ They are to stay in that city until they have stood trial before the assembly and until the death of the high priest who is serving at that time. Then they may go back to their own home in the town from which they fled."

⁷ So they set apart Kedesh in Galilee in the hill country of Naphtali, Shechem in the hill country of Ephraim, and Kiriath Arba (that is, Hebron) in the hill country of Judah. ⁸ East of the Jordan (on the other side from Jericho) they designated Bezer in the wilderness on the plateau in the tribe of Reuben, Ramoth in Gilead in the tribe of Gad, and Golan in Bashan in the tribe of Manasseh. ⁹ Any of the Israelites or any foreigner residing among them who killed someone accidentally could flee to these designated cities and not be killed by the avenger of blood prior to standing trial before the assembly.

Towns for the Levites

21 Now the family heads of the Levites approached Eleazar the priest, Joshua son of Nun, and the heads of the other tribal families of Israel ² at Shiloh in Canaan and said to them, "The LORD commanded through Moses that you give us towns to live in, with pasturelands for our livestock." ³ So, as the LORD had commanded, the Israelites gave the Levites the following towns and pasturelands out of their own inheritance:

⁴ The first lot came out for the Kohathites, according to their clans. The Levites who were descendants of Aaron the priest were allotted thirteen towns from the tribes of Judah, Simeon and Benjamin. ⁵ The rest of Kohath's descendants were allotted ten towns from the clans of the tribes of Ephraim, Dan and half of Manasseh.

⁶ The descendants of Gershon were allotted thirteen towns from the clans of the tribes of Issachar, Asher, Naphtali and the half-tribe of Manasseh in Bashan.

⁷ The descendants of Merari, according to their clans, received twelve towns from the tribes of Reuben, Gad and Zebulun.

⁸ So the Israelites allotted to the Levites these towns and their pasturelands, as the LORD had commanded through Moses.

⁹ From the tribes of Judah and Simeon they allotted the following towns by name ¹⁰ (these towns were assigned to the descendants of Aaron who were

from the Kohathite clans of the Levites, because the first lot fell to them):

¹¹They gave them Kiriath Arba (that is, Hebron), with its surrounding pastureland, in the hill country of Judah. (Arba was the forefather of Anak.) ¹²But the fields and villages around the city they had given to Caleb son of Jephunneh as his possession.

¹³So to the descendants of Aaron the priest they gave Hebron (a city of refuge for one accused of murder), Libnah, ¹⁴Jattir, Eshtemoa, ¹⁵Holon, Debir, ¹⁶Ain, Juttah and Beth Shemesh, together with their pasturelands — nine towns from these two tribes.

¹⁷And from the tribe of Benjamin they gave them Gibeon, Geba, ¹⁸Anathoth and Almon, together with their pasturelands — four towns.

¹⁹The total number of towns for the priests, the descendants of Aaron, came to thirteen, together with their pasturelands.

²⁰The rest of the Kohathite clans of the Levites were allotted towns from the tribe of Ephraim:

²¹In the hill country of Ephraim they were given Shechem (a city of refuge for one accused of murder) and Gezer, ²²Kibzaim and Beth Horon, together with their pasturelands — four towns.

²³Also from the tribe of Dan they received Eltekeh, Gibbethon, ²⁴Aijalon and Gath Rimmon, together with their pasturelands — four towns.

²⁵From half the tribe of Manasseh they received Taanach and Gath Rimmon, together with their pasturelands — two towns.

²⁶All these ten towns and their pasturelands were given to the rest of the Kohathite clans.

²⁷The Levite clans of the Gershonites were given:

from the half-tribe of Manasseh,

Golan in Bashan (a city of refuge for one accused of murder) and Be Eshterah, together with their pasturelands — two towns;

²⁸from the tribe of Issachar, Kishion, Daberath, ²⁹Jarmuth and En Gannim, together with their pasturelands — four towns;

³⁰from the tribe of Asher, Mishal, Abdon, ³¹Helkath and Rehob, together with their pasturelands — four towns;

³²from the tribe of Naphtali, Kedesh in Galilee (a city of refuge for one accused of murder), Hammoth Dor and Kartan, together with their pasturelands — three towns.

³³The total number of towns of the Gershonite clans came to thirteen, together with their pasturelands.

³⁴The Merarite clans (the rest of the Levites) were given:

from the tribe of Zebulun, Jokneam, Kartah, ³⁵Dimnah and Nahalal, together with their pasturelands—four towns;

³⁶from the tribe of Reuben, Bezer, Jahaz, ³⁷Kedemoth and Mephaath, together with their pasturelands—four towns;

³⁸from the tribe of Gad, Ramoth in Gilead (a city of refuge for one accused of murder), Mahanaim, ³⁹Heshbon and Jazer, together with their pasturelands—four towns in all.

⁴⁰The total number of towns allotted to the Merarite clans, who were the rest of the Levites, came to twelve.

⁴¹The towns of the Levites in the territory held by the Israelites were forty-eight in all, together with their pasturelands. ⁴²Each of these towns had pasturelands surrounding it; this was true for all these towns.

⁴³So the LORD gave Israel all the land he had sworn to give their ancestors, and they took possession of it and settled there. ⁴⁴The LORD gave them rest on every side, just as he had sworn to their ancestors. Not one of their enemies withstood them; the LORD gave all their enemies into their hands. ⁴⁵Not one of all the LORD's good promises to Israel failed; every one was fulfilled.

Eastern Tribes Return Home

22 Then Joshua summoned the Reubenites, the Gadites and the half-tribe of Manasseh ²and said to them, "You have done all that Moses the servant of the LORD commanded, and you have obeyed me in everything I commanded. ³For a long time now—to this very day—you have not deserted your fellow Israelites but have carried out the mission the LORD your God gave you. ⁴Now that the LORD your God has given them rest as he promised, return to your homes in the land that Moses the servant of the LORD gave you on the other side of the Jordan. ⁵But be very careful to keep the commandment and the law that Moses the servant of the LORD gave you: to love the LORD your God, to walk in obedience to him, to keep his commands, to hold fast to him and to serve him with all your heart and with all your soul."

⁶Then Joshua blessed them and sent them away, and they went to their homes. ⁷(To the half-tribe of Manasseh Moses had given land in Bashan, and to the other half of the tribe Joshua gave land on the west side of the Jordan along with their fellow Israelites.) When Joshua sent them home, he blessed them, ⁸saying, "Return to your homes with your great wealth—with large herds of livestock, with silver, gold, bronze

and iron, and a great quantity of clothing—and divide the plunder from your enemies with your fellow Israelites."

⁹So the Reubenites, the Gadites and the half-tribe of Manasseh left the Israelites at Shiloh in Canaan to return to Gilead, their own land, which they had acquired in accordance with the command of the LORD through Moses.

¹⁰When they came to Geliloth near the Jordan in the land of Canaan, the Reubenites, the Gadites and the half-tribe of Manasseh built an imposing altar there by the Jordan. ¹¹And when the Israelites heard that they had built the altar on the border of Canaan at Geliloth near the Jordan on the Israelite side, ¹²the whole assembly of Israel gathered at Shiloh to go to war against them.

¹³So the Israelites sent Phinehas son of Eleazar, the priest, to the land of Gilead—to Reuben, Gad and the half-tribe of Manasseh. ¹⁴With him they sent ten of the chief men, one from each of the tribes of Israel, each the head of a family division among the Israelite clans.

¹⁵When they went to Gilead—to Reuben, Gad and the half-tribe of Manasseh—they said to them: ¹⁶"The whole assembly of the LORD says: 'How could you break faith with the God of Israel like this? How could you turn away from the LORD and build yourselves an altar in rebellion against him now? ¹⁷Was not the sin of Peor enough for us? Up to this very day we have not cleansed ourselves from that sin, even though a plague fell on the community of the LORD! ¹⁸And are you now turning away from the LORD?

"'If you rebel against the LORD today, tomorrow he will be angry with the whole community of Israel. ¹⁹If the land you possess is defiled, come over to the LORD's land, where the LORD's tabernacle stands, and share the land with us. But do not rebel against the LORD or against us by building an altar for yourselves, other than the altar of the LORD our God. ²⁰When Achan son of Zerah was unfaithful in regard to the devoted things,ᵃ did not wrath come on the whole community of Israel? He was not the only one who died for his sin.'"

²¹Then Reuben, Gad and the half-tribe of Manasseh replied to the heads of the clans of Israel: ²²"The Mighty One, God, the LORD! The Mighty One, God, the LORD! He knows! And let Israel know! If this has been in rebellion or disobedience to the LORD, do not spare us this day. ²³If we have built our own altar to turn away from the LORD and to offer burnt offerings and grain offerings, or to sacrifice fellowship of-

ᵃ 20 The Hebrew term refers to the irrevocable giving over of things or persons to the LORD, often by totally destroying them.

ferings on it, may the LORD himself call us to account.

24 "No! We did it for fear that some day your descendants might say to ours, 'What do you have to do with the LORD, the God of Israel? 25 The LORD has made the Jordan a boundary between us and you—you Reubenites and Gadites! You have no share in the LORD.' So your descendants might cause ours to stop fearing the LORD.

26 "That is why we said, 'Let us get ready and build an altar—but not for burnt offerings or sacrifices.' 27 On the contrary, it is to be a witness between us and you and the generations that follow, that we will worship the LORD at his sanctuary with our burnt offerings, sacrifices and fellowship offerings. Then in the future your descendants will not be able to say to ours, 'You have no share in the LORD.'

28 "And we said, 'If they ever say this to us, or to our descendants, we will answer: Look at the replica of the LORD's altar, which our ancestors built, not for burnt offerings and sacrifices, but as a witness between us and you.'

29 "Far be it from us to rebel against the LORD and turn away from him today by building an altar for burnt offerings, grain offerings and sacrifices, other than the altar of the LORD our God that stands before his tabernacle."

30 When Phinehas the priest and the leaders of the community—the heads of the clans of the Israelites—heard what Reuben, Gad and Manasseh had to say, they were pleased. 31 And Phinehas son of Eleazar, the priest, said to Reuben, Gad and Manasseh, "Today we know that the LORD is with us, because you have not been unfaithful to the LORD in this matter. Now you have rescued the Israelites from the LORD's hand."

32 Then Phinehas son of Eleazar, the priest, and the leaders returned to Canaan from their meeting with the Reubenites and Gadites in Gilead and reported to the Israelites. 33 They were glad to hear the report and praised God. And they talked no more about going to war against them to devastate the country where the Reubenites and the Gadites lived.

34 And the Reubenites and the Gadites gave the altar this name: A Witness Between Us—that the LORD is God.

Joshua's Farewell to the Leaders

23 After a long time had passed and the LORD had given Israel rest from all their enemies around them, Joshua, by then a very old man, 2 summoned all Israel—their elders, leaders, judges and officials—and said to them: "I am very old. 3 You yourselves have seen everything the LORD your God has done to all these nations for your sake; it was the LORD your God who fought

for you. ⁴Remember how I have allotted as an inheritance for your tribes all the land of the nations that remain — the nations I conquered — between the Jordan and the Mediterranean Sea in the west. ⁵The LORD your God himself will push them out for your sake. He will drive them out before you, and you will take possession of their land, as the LORD your God promised you.

⁶"Be very strong; be careful to obey all that is written in the Book of the Law of Moses, without turning aside to the right or to the left. ⁷Do not associate with these nations that remain among you; do not invoke the names of their gods or swear by them. You must not serve them or bow down to them. ⁸But you are to hold fast to the LORD your God, as you have until now.

⁹"The LORD has driven out before you great and powerful nations; to this day no one has been able to withstand you. ¹⁰One of you routs a thousand, because the LORD your God fights for you, just as he promised. ¹¹So be very careful to love the LORD your God.

¹²"But if you turn away and ally yourselves with the survivors of these nations that remain among you and if you intermarry with them and associate with them, ¹³then you may be sure that the LORD your God will no longer drive out these nations before you. Instead, they will become snares and traps for you, whips on your backs and thorns in your eyes, until you perish from this good land, which the LORD your God has given you.

¹⁴"Now I am about to go the way of all the earth. You know with all your heart and soul that not one of all the good promises the LORD your God gave you has failed. Every promise has been fulfilled; not one has failed. ¹⁵But just as all the good things the LORD your God has promised you have come to you, so he will bring on you all the evil things he has threatened, until the LORD your God has destroyed you from this good land he has given you. ¹⁶If you violate the covenant of the LORD your God, which he commanded you, and go and serve other gods and bow down to them, the LORD's anger will burn against you, and you will quickly perish from the good land he has given you."

The Covenant Renewed at Shechem

24 Then Joshua assembled all the tribes of Israel at Shechem. He summoned the elders, leaders, judges and officials of Israel, and they presented themselves before God.

²Joshua said to all the people, "This is what the LORD, the God of Israel, says: 'Long ago your ancestors, including Terah the father of Abraham and Nahor, lived beyond the Euphrates River and wor-

shiped other gods. ³But I took your father Abraham from the land beyond the Euphrates and led him throughout Canaan and gave him many descendants. I gave him Isaac, ⁴and to Isaac I gave Jacob and Esau. I assigned the hill country of Seir to Esau, but Jacob and his family went down to Egypt.

⁵"'Then I sent Moses and Aaron, and I afflicted the Egyptians by what I did there, and I brought you out. ⁶When I brought your people out of Egypt, you came to the sea, and the Egyptians pursued them with chariots and horsemen*a* as far as the Red Sea.*b* ⁷But they cried to the LORD for help, and he put darkness between you and the Egyptians; he brought the sea over them and covered them. You saw with your own eyes what I did to the Egyptians. Then you lived in the wilderness for a long time.

⁸"'I brought you to the land of the Amorites who lived east of the Jordan. They fought against you, but I gave them into your hands. I destroyed them from before you, and you took possession of their land. ⁹When Balak son of Zippor, the king of Moab, prepared to fight against Israel, he sent for Balaam son of Beor to put a curse on you. ¹⁰But I would not listen to Balaam, so he blessed you again and again, and I delivered you out of his hand.

¹¹"'Then you crossed the Jordan and came to Jericho. The citizens of Jericho fought against you, as did also the Amorites, Perizzites, Canaanites, Hittites, Girgashites, Hivites and Jebusites, but I gave them into your hands. ¹²I sent the hornet ahead of you, which drove them out before you—also the two Amorite kings. You did not do it with your own sword and bow. ¹³So I gave you a land on which you did not toil and cities you did not build; and you live in them and eat from vineyards and olive groves that you did not plant.'

¹⁴"Now fear the LORD and serve him with all faithfulness. Throw away the gods your ancestors worshiped beyond the Euphrates River and in Egypt, and serve the LORD. ¹⁵But if serving the LORD seems undesirable to you, then choose for yourselves this day whom you will serve, whether the gods your ancestors served beyond the Euphrates, or the gods of the Amorites, in whose land you are living. But as for me and my household, we will serve the LORD."

¹⁶Then the people answered, "Far be it from us to forsake the LORD to serve other gods! ¹⁷It was the LORD our God himself who brought us and our parents up out of Egypt, from that land of slavery, and performed those great signs before our eyes. He protected us on our entire journey and among all the nations through which we traveled.

a 6 Or *charioteers*   *b* 6 Or *the Sea of Reeds*

¹⁸And the LORD drove out before us all the nations, including the Amorites, who lived in the land. We too will serve the LORD, because he is our God."

¹⁹Joshua said to the people, "You are not able to serve the LORD. He is a holy God; he is a jealous God. He will not forgive your rebellion and your sins. ²⁰If you forsake the LORD and serve foreign gods, he will turn and bring disaster on you and make an end of you, after he has been good to you."

²¹But the people said to Joshua, "No! We will serve the LORD."

²²Then Joshua said, "You are witnesses against yourselves that you have chosen to serve the LORD."

"Yes, we are witnesses," they replied.

²³"Now then," said Joshua, "throw away the foreign gods that are among you and yield your hearts to the LORD, the God of Israel."

²⁴And the people said to Joshua, "We will serve the LORD our God and obey him."

²⁵On that day Joshua made a covenant for the people, and there at Shechem he reaffirmed for them decrees and laws. ²⁶And Joshua recorded these things in the Book of the Law of God. Then he took a large stone and set it up there under the oak near the holy place of the LORD.

²⁷"See!" he said to all the people. "This stone will be a witness against us. It has heard all the words the LORD has said to us. It will be a witness against you if you are untrue to your God."

²⁸Then Joshua dismissed the people, each to their own inheritance.

Buried in the Promised Land

²⁹After these things, Joshua son of Nun, the servant of the LORD, died at the age of a hundred and ten. ³⁰And they buried him in the land of his inheritance, at Timnath Serah^a in the hill country of Ephraim, north of Mount Gaash.

³¹Israel served the LORD throughout the lifetime of Joshua and of the elders who outlived him and who had experienced everything the LORD had done for Israel.

³²And Joseph's bones, which the Israelites had brought up from Egypt, were buried at Shechem in the tract of land that Jacob bought for a hundred pieces of silver^b from the sons of Hamor, the father of Shechem. This became the inheritance of Joseph's descendants.

³³And Eleazar son of Aaron died and was buried at Gibeah, which had been allotted to his son Phinehas in the hill country of Ephraim.

---

^a 30 Also known as *Timnath Heres* (see Judges 2:9)   ^b 32 Hebrew *hundred kesitahs*; a kesitah was a unit of money of unknown weight and value.

Judges

Introduction:

The book of Judges tells the stories of Israel's history for the years between the death of Joshua and the ministry of Samuel. This time period was known for its heroes — called judges — who ruled the tribes of Israel. A total of fifteen judges are listed for their leadership. The best-known judges are Deborah, Gideon and Samson.

The events in Judges followed a certain pattern:

1. The Israelites lived in peace while serving and loving God.
2. The Israelites forgot God and worshiped idols.
3. God punished his people by sending a neighboring nation to fight and rule over them.
4. The Israelites turned to God and asked for forgiveness.
5. God forgave his people and saved them by sending a judge to help conquer their enemy.

This pattern of events repeated itself over and over during this time in Israel's history.

Outline of contents:

Conditions during the time of the judges (1:1–3:6)
Conquering nations and ruling judges (3:7–16:31)
Idolatry and civil war (17:1–21:35)

Israel Fights the Remaining Canaanites

1 After the death of Joshua, the Israelites asked the LORD, "Who of us is to go up first to fight against the Canaanites?"

²The LORD answered, "Judah shall go up; I have given the land into their hands."

³The men of Judah then said to the Simeonites their fellow Israelites, "Come up with us into the territory allotted to us, to fight against the Canaanites. We in turn will go with you into yours." So the Simeonites went with them.

⁴When Judah attacked, the LORD gave the Canaanites and Perizzites into their hands, and they struck down ten thousand men at Bezek. ⁵It was there that they found Adoni-Bezek and fought against him, putting to rout the Canaanites and Perizzites. ⁶Adoni-Bezek fled, but they chased him and caught him, and cut off his thumbs and big toes.

⁷Then Adoni-Bezek said, "Seventy kings with their thumbs and big toes cut off have picked up scraps under my table. Now God has paid me back for what I did to them." They brought him to Jerusalem, and he died there.

⁸The men of Judah attacked Jerusalem also and took it. They put the city to the sword and set it on fire.

⁹After that, Judah went down to fight against the Canaanites living in the hill country, the Negev and the western foothills. ¹⁰They advanced against the Canaanites living in Hebron (formerly called Kiriath Arba) and defeated Sheshai, Ahiman and Talmai. ¹¹From there they advanced against the people living in Debir (formerly called Kiriath Sepher).

¹²And Caleb said, "I will give my daughter Aksah in marriage to the man who attacks and captures Kiriath Sepher." ¹³Othniel son of Kenaz, Caleb's younger brother, took it; so Caleb gave his daughter Aksah to him in marriage.

¹⁴One day when she came to Othniel, she urged him[a] to ask her father for a field. When she got off her donkey, Caleb asked her, "What can I do for you?"

¹⁵She replied, "Do me a special favor. Since you have given me land in the Negev, give me also springs of water." So Caleb gave her the upper and lower springs.

¹⁶The descendants of Moses' father-in-law, the Kenite, went up from the City of Palms[b] with the people of Judah to live among the inhabitants of the Desert of Judah in the Negev near Arad.

¹⁷Then the men of Judah went with the Simeonites their fellow Israelites and attacked the Canaanites living in Zephath, and they totally destroyed[c] the city. Therefore it was called Hormah.[d] ¹⁸Judah also took[e] Gaza, Ashkelon and Ekron—each city with its territory.

¹⁹The Lord was with the men of Judah. They took possession of the hill country, but they were unable to drive the people from the plains, because they had chariots fitted with iron. ²⁰As Moses had promised, Hebron was given to Caleb, who drove from it the three sons of Anak. ²¹The Benjamites, however, did not drive out the Jebusites, who were living in Jerusalem; to this day the Jebusites live there with the Benjamites.

²²Now the tribes of Joseph attacked Bethel, and the Lord was with them. ²³When they sent men to spy out Bethel (formerly called Luz), ²⁴the spies saw a man coming out of the city and they said to him, "Show us how to get into

---

[a] 14 Hebrew; Septuagint and Vulgate *Othniel, he urged her*   [b] 16 That is, Jericho
[c] 17 The Hebrew term refers to the irrevocable giving over of things or persons to the Lord, often by totally destroying them.   [d] 17 *Hormah* means *destruction*.
[e] 18 Hebrew; Septuagint *Judah did not take*

the city and we will see that you are treated well." ²⁵So he showed them, and they put the city to the sword but spared the man and his whole family. ²⁶He then went to the land of the Hittites, where he built a city and called it Luz, which is its name to this day.

²⁷But Manasseh did not drive out the people of Beth Shan or Taanach or Dor or Ibleam or Megiddo and their surrounding settlements, for the Canaanites were determined to live in that land. ²⁸When Israel became strong, they pressed the Canaanites into forced labor but never drove them out completely. ²⁹Nor did Ephraim drive out the Canaanites living in Gezer, but the Canaanites continued to live there among them. ³⁰Neither did Zebulun drive out the Canaanites living in Kitron or Nahalol, so these Canaanites lived among them, but Zebulun did subject them to forced labor. ³¹Nor did Asher drive out those living in Akko or Sidon or Ahlab or Akzib or Helbah or Aphek or Rehob. ³²The Asherites lived among the Canaanite inhabitants of the land because they did not drive them out. ³³Neither did Naphtali drive out those living in Beth Shemesh or Beth Anath; but the Naphtalites too lived among the Canaanite inhabitants of the land, and those living in Beth Shemesh and Beth Anath became forced

laborers for them. ³⁴The Amorites confined the Danites to the hill country, not allowing them to come down into the plain. ³⁵And the Amorites were determined also to hold out in Mount Heres, Aijalon and Shaalbim, but when the power of the tribes of Joseph increased, they too were pressed into forced labor. ³⁶The boundary of the Amorites was from Scorpion Pass to Sela and beyond.

The Angel of the LORD at Bokim

2 The angel of the LORD went up from Gilgal to Bokim and said, "I brought you up out of Egypt and led you into the land I swore to give to your ancestors. I said, 'I will never break my covenant with you, ²and you shall not make a covenant with the people of this land, but you shall break down their altars.' Yet you have disobeyed me. Why have you done this? ³And I have also said, 'I will not drive them out before you; they will become traps for you, and their gods will become snares to you.'"

⁴When the angel of the LORD had spoken these things to all the Israelites, the people wept aloud, ⁵and they called that place Bokim.ᵃ There they offered sacrifices to the LORD.

Disobedience and Defeat

⁶After Joshua had dismissed the Israelites, they went to take

---

ᵃ 5 *Bokim* means *weepers*.

possession of the land, each to their own inheritance. ⁷The people served the LORD throughout the lifetime of Joshua and of the elders who outlived him and who had seen all the great things the LORD had done for Israel.

⁸Joshua son of Nun, the servant of the LORD, died at the age of a hundred and ten. ⁹And they buried him in the land of his inheritance, at Timnath Heres*a* in the hill country of Ephraim, north of Mount Gaash.

¹⁰After that whole generation had been gathered to their ancestors, another generation grew up who knew neither the LORD nor what he had done for Israel. ¹¹Then the Israelites did evil in the eyes of the LORD and served the Baals. ¹²They forsook the LORD, the God of their ancestors, who had brought them out of Egypt. They followed and worshiped various gods of the peoples around them. They aroused the LORD's anger ¹³because they forsook him and served Baal and the Ashtoreths. ¹⁴In his anger against Israel the LORD gave them into the hands of raiders who plundered them. He sold them into the hands of their enemies all around, whom they were no longer able to resist. ¹⁵Whenever Israel went out to fight, the hand of the LORD was against them to defeat them, just as he had sworn to them. They were in great distress.

¹⁶Then the LORD raised up judges,*b* who saved them out of the hands of these raiders. ¹⁷Yet they would not listen to their judges but prostituted themselves to other gods and worshiped them. They quickly turned from the ways of their ancestors, who had been obedient to the LORD's commands. ¹⁸Whenever the LORD raised up a judge for them, he was with the judge and saved them out of the hands of their enemies as long as the judge lived; for the LORD relented because of their groaning under those who oppressed and afflicted them. ¹⁹But when the judge died, the people returned to ways even more corrupt than those of their ancestors, following other gods and serving and worshiping them. They refused to give up their evil practices and stubborn ways.

²⁰Therefore the LORD was very angry with Israel and said, "Because this nation has violated the covenant I ordained for their ancestors and has not listened to me, ²¹I will no longer drive out before them any of the nations Joshua left when he died. ²²I will use them to test Israel and see whether they will keep the way of the LORD and walk in it as their ancestors did." ²³The LORD had

---

a 9 Also known as *Timnath Serah* (see Joshua 19:50 and 24:30)   *b* 16 Or *leaders*; similarly in verses 17-19 allowed those nations to remain; he did not drive them out at once by giving them into the hands of Joshua.

3 These are the nations the LORD left to test all those Israelites who had not experienced any of the wars in Canaan ²(he did this only to teach warfare to the descendants of the Israelites who had not had previous battle experience): ³the five rulers of the Philistines, all the Canaanites, the Sidonians, and the Hivites living in the Lebanon mountains from Mount Baal Hermon to Lebo Hamath. ⁴They were left to test the Israelites to see whether they would obey the LORD's commands, which he had given their ancestors through Moses.

⁵The Israelites lived among the Canaanites, Hittites, Amorites, Perizzites, Hivites and Jebusites. ⁶They took their daughters in marriage and gave their own daughters to their sons, and served their gods.

Othniel

⁷The Israelites did evil in the eyes of the LORD; they forgot the LORD their God and served the Baals and the Asherahs. ⁸The anger of the LORD burned against Israel so that he sold them into the hands of Cushan-Rishathaim king of Aram Naharaim,[a] to whom the Israelites were subject for eight years. ⁹But when they cried out to the LORD, he raised up for them a deliverer, Othniel son of Kenaz, Caleb's younger brother, who saved them. ¹⁰The Spirit of the LORD came on him, so that he became Israel's judge[b] and went to war. The LORD gave Cushan-Rishathaim king of Aram into the hands of Othniel, who overpowered him. ¹¹So the land had peace for forty years, until Othniel son of Kenaz died.

Ehud

¹²Again the Israelites did evil in the eyes of the LORD, and because they did this evil the LORD gave Eglon king of Moab power over Israel. ¹³Getting the Ammonites and Amalekites to join him, Eglon came and attacked Israel, and they took possession of the City of Palms.[c] ¹⁴The Israelites were subject to Eglon king of Moab for eighteen years.

¹⁵Again the Israelites cried out to the LORD, and he gave them a deliverer—Ehud, a left-handed man, the son of Gera the Benjamite. The Israelites sent him with tribute to Eglon king of Moab. ¹⁶Now Ehud had made a double-edged sword about a cubit[d] long, which he strapped to his right thigh under his clothing. ¹⁷He presented the tribute to Eglon king of Moab, who was a very fat man. ¹⁸After Ehud had presented

---

[a] 8 That is, Northwest Mesopotamia   [b] 10 Or leader   [c] 13 That is, Jericho
[d] 16 That is, about 18 inches or about 45 centimeters

the tribute, he sent on their way those who had carried it. ¹⁹But on reaching the stone images near Gilgal he himself went back to Eglon and said, "Your Majesty, I have a secret message for you."

The king said to his attendants, "Leave us!" And they all left.

²⁰Ehud then approached him while he was sitting alone in the upper room of his palace^a and said, "I have a message from God for you." As the king rose from his seat, ²¹Ehud reached with his left hand, drew the sword from his right thigh and plunged it into the king's belly. ²²Even the handle sank in after the blade, and his bowels discharged. Ehud did not pull the sword out, and the fat closed in over it. ²³Then Ehud went out to the porch^b; he shut the doors of the upper room behind him and locked them.

²⁴After he had gone, the servants came and found the doors of the upper room locked. They said, "He must be relieving himself in the inner room of the palace." ²⁵They waited to the point of embarrassment, but when he did not open the doors of the room, they took a key and unlocked them. There they saw their lord fallen to the floor, dead.

²⁶While they waited, Ehud got away. He passed by the stone images and escaped to Seirah. ²⁷When he arrived there, he blew a trumpet in the hill country of Ephraim, and the Israelites went down with him from the hills, with him leading them.

²⁸"Follow me," he ordered, "for the LORD has given Moab, your enemy, into your hands." So they followed him down and took possession of the fords of the Jordan that led to Moab; they allowed no one to cross over. ²⁹At that time they struck down about ten thousand Moabites, all vigorous and strong; not one escaped. ³⁰That day Moab was made subject to Israel, and the land had peace for eighty years.

Shamgar

³¹After Ehud came Shamgar son of Anath, who struck down six hundred Philistines with an oxgoad. He too saved Israel.

Deborah

4 Again the Israelites did evil in the eyes of the LORD, now that Ehud was dead. ²So the LORD sold them into the hands of Jabin king of Canaan, who reigned in Hazor. Sisera, the commander of his army, was based in Harosheth Haggoyim. ³Because he had nine hundred chariots fitted with iron and had cruelly oppressed the Israelites for twenty years, they cried to the LORD for help.

⁴Now Deborah, a prophet, the wife of Lappidoth, was leading^c

---

^a 20 The meaning of the Hebrew for this word is uncertain; also in verse 24.   ^b 23 The meaning of the Hebrew for this word is uncertain.   ^c 4 Traditionally judging

Israel at that time. ⁵She held court under the Palm of Deborah between Ramah and Bethel in the hill country of Ephraim, and the Israelites went up to her to have their disputes decided. ⁶She sent for Barak son of Abinoam from Kedesh in Naphtali and said to him, "The LORD, the God of Israel, commands you: 'Go, take with you ten thousand men of Naphtali and Zebulun and lead them up to Mount Tabor. ⁷I will lead Sisera, the commander of Jabin's army, with his chariots and his troops to the Kishon River and give him into your hands.'"

⁸Barak said to her, "If you go with me, I will go; but if you don't go with me, I won't go."

⁹"Certainly I will go with you," said Deborah. "But because of the course you are taking, the honor will not be yours, for the LORD will deliver Sisera into the hands of a woman." So Deborah went with Barak to Kedesh. ¹⁰There Barak summoned Zebulun and Naphtali, and ten thousand men went up under his command. Deborah also went up with him.

¹¹Now Heber the Kenite had left the other Kenites, the descendants of Hobab, Moses' brother-in-law,ᵃ and pitched his tent by the great tree in Zaanannim near Kedesh.

¹²When they told Sisera that Barak son of Abinoam had gone up to Mount Tabor, ¹³Sisera summoned from Harosheth Haggoyim to the Kishon River all his men and his nine hundred chariots fitted with iron.

¹⁴Then Deborah said to Barak, "Go! This is the day the LORD has given Sisera into your hands. Has not the LORD gone ahead of you?" So Barak went down Mount Tabor, with ten thousand men following him. ¹⁵At Barak's advance, the LORD routed Sisera and all his chariots and army by the sword, and Sisera got down from his chariot and fled on foot.

¹⁶Barak pursued the chariots and army as far as Harosheth Haggoyim, and all Sisera's troops fell by the sword; not a man was left. ¹⁷Sisera, meanwhile, fled on foot to the tent of Jael, the wife of Heber the Kenite, because there was an alliance between Jabin king of Hazor and the family of Heber the Kenite.

¹⁸Jael went out to meet Sisera and said to him, "Come, my lord, come right in. Don't be afraid." So he entered her tent, and she covered him with a blanket.

¹⁹"I'm thirsty," he said. "Please give me some water." She opened a skin of milk, gave him a drink, and covered him up.

²⁰"Stand in the doorway of the tent," he told her. "If someone comes by and asks you, 'Is anyone in there?' say 'No.'"

²¹But Jael, Heber's wife, picked up a tent peg and a hammer and

ᵃ 11 Or *father-in-law*

went quietly to him while he lay fast asleep, exhausted. She drove the peg through his temple into the ground, and he died.

²²Just then Barak came by in pursuit of Sisera, and Jael went out to meet him. "Come," she said, "I will show you the man you're looking for." So he went in with her, and there lay Sisera with the tent peg through his temple — dead.

²³On that day God subdued Jabin king of Canaan before the Israelites. ²⁴And the hand of the Israelites pressed harder and harder against Jabin king of Canaan until they destroyed him.

The Song of Deborah

5 On that day Deborah and Barak son of Abinoam sang this song:

²"When the princes in Israel
  take the lead,
when the people willingly
    offer themselves —
praise the LORD!

³"Hear this, you kings! Listen,
  you rulers!
I, even I, will sing to^a the
    LORD;
I will praise the LORD, the
    God of Israel, in song.

⁴"When you, LORD, went out
  from Seir,
when you marched from the
    land of Edom,

the earth shook, the heavens
  poured,
the clouds poured down
    water.
⁵The mountains quaked before
  the LORD, the One of
    Sinai,
before the LORD, the God of
    Israel.

⁶"In the days of Shamgar son of
  Anath,
in the days of Jael, the
    highways were
    abandoned;
travelers took to winding
    paths.
⁷Villagers in Israel would not
  fight;
they held back until I,
    Deborah, arose,
until I arose, a mother in
    Israel.
⁸God chose new leaders
when war came to the city
    gates,
but not a shield or spear was
    seen
among forty thousand in
    Israel.
⁹My heart is with Israel's princes,
with the willing volunteers
    among the people.
Praise the LORD!

¹⁰"You who ride on white
  donkeys,
sitting on your saddle
    blankets,
and you who walk along the
    road,

^a 3 Or of

consider ¹¹the voice of the
singers^a at the watering
places.
They recite the victories of
the LORD,
the victories of his villagers
in Israel.

"Then the people of the LORD
went down to the city gates.
¹²'Wake up, wake up, Deborah!
Wake up, wake up, break out
in song!
Arise, Barak!
Take captive your captives,
son of Abinoam.'

¹³"The remnant of the nobles
came down;
the people of the LORD came
down to me against the
mighty.
¹⁴Some came from Ephraim,
whose roots were in
Amalek;
Benjamin was with the
people who followed
you.
From Makir captains came
down,
from Zebulun those who
bear a commander's^a
staff.
¹⁵The princes of Issachar were
with Deborah;
yes, Issachar was with Barak,
sent under his command
into the valley.
In the districts of Reuben
there was much searching of
heart.

¹⁶Why did you stay among the
sheep pens^b
to hear the whistling for the
flocks?
In the districts of Reuben
there was much searching of
heart.
¹⁷Gilead stayed beyond the
Jordan.
And Dan, why did he linger
by the ships?
Asher remained on the coast
and stayed in his coves.
¹⁸The people of Zebulun risked
their very lives;
so did Naphtali on the
terraced fields.

¹⁹"Kings came, they fought,
the kings of Canaan fought.
At Taanach, by the waters of
Megiddo,
they took no plunder of
silver.
²⁰From the heavens the stars
fought,
from their courses they
fought against Sisera.
²¹The river Kishon swept them
away,
the age-old river, the river
Kishon.
March on, my soul; be strong!
²²Then thundered the horses'
hooves —
galloping, galloping go his
mighty steeds.
²³'Curse Meroz,' said the angel
of the LORD.
'Curse its people bitterly,

---

^a 11,14 The meaning of the Hebrew for this word is uncertain.   ^b 16 Or the
campfires; or the saddlebags

because they did not come to
help the LORD,
to help the LORD against the
mighty.'

²⁴ "Most blessed of women be
Jael,
the wife of Heber the
Kenite,
most blessed of tent-
dwelling women.
²⁵ He asked for water, and she
gave him milk;
in a bowl fit for nobles she
brought him curdled
milk.
²⁶ Her hand reached for the tent
peg,
her right hand for the
workman's hammer.
She struck Sisera, she crushed
his head,
she shattered and pierced
his temple.
²⁷ At her feet he sank,
he fell; there he lay.
At her feet he sank, he fell;
where he sank, there he
fell — dead.

²⁸ "Through the window peered
Sisera's mother;
behind the lattice she cried
out,
'Why is his chariot so long in
coming?
Why is the clatter of his
chariots delayed?'
²⁹ The wisest of her ladies answer
her;
indeed, she keeps saying to
herself,

³⁰ 'Are they not finding and
dividing the spoils:
a woman or two for each
man,
colorful garments as plunder
for Sisera,
colorful garments
embroidered,
highly embroidered garments
for my neck —
all this as plunder?'

³¹ "So may all your enemies
perish, LORD!
But may all who love you be
like the sun
when it rises in its strength."

Then the land had peace forty
years.

Gideon

6 The Israelites did evil in the
eyes of the LORD, and for
seven years he gave them into
the hands of the Midianites. ² Because the power of Midian was
so oppressive, the Israelites prepared shelters for themselves
in mountain clefts, caves and
strongholds. ³ Whenever the Israelites planted their crops, the
Midianites, Amalekites and other eastern peoples invaded the
country. ⁴ They camped on the
land and ruined the crops all the
way to Gaza and did not spare
a living thing for Israel, neither
sheep nor cattle nor donkeys.
⁵ They came up with their livestock and their tents like swarms
of locusts. It was impossible to

count them or their camels; they invaded the land to ravage it. [6]Midian so impoverished the Israelites that they cried out to the LORD for help.

[7]When the Israelites cried out to the LORD because of Midian, [8]he sent them a prophet, who said, "This is what the LORD, the God of Israel, says: I brought you up out of Egypt, out of the land of slavery. [9]I rescued you from the hand of the Egyptians. And I delivered you from the hand of all your oppressors; I drove them out before you and gave you their land. [10]I said to you, 'I am the LORD your God; do not worship the gods of the Amorites, in whose land you live.' But you have not listened to me."

[11]The angel of the LORD came and sat down under the oak in Ophrah that belonged to Joash the Abiezrite, where his son Gideon was threshing wheat in a winepress to keep it from the Midianites. [12]When the angel of the LORD appeared to Gideon, he said, "The LORD is with you, mighty warrior."

[13]"Pardon me, my lord," Gideon replied, "but if the LORD is with us, why has all this happened to us? Where are all his wonders that our ancestors told us about when they said, 'Did not the LORD bring us up out of Egypt?' But now the LORD has abandoned us and given us into the hand of Midian."

[14]The LORD turned to him and said, "Go in the strength you have and save Israel out of Midian's hand. Am I not sending you?"

[15]"Pardon me, my lord," Gideon replied, "but how can I save Israel? My clan is the weakest in Manasseh, and I am the least in my family."

[16]The LORD answered, "I will be with you, and you will strike down all the Midianites, leaving none alive."

[17]Gideon replied, "If now I have found favor in your eyes, give me a sign that it is really you talking to me. [18]Please do not go away until I come back and bring my offering and set it before you."

And the LORD said, "I will wait until you return."

[19]Gideon went inside, prepared a young goat, and from an ephah[a] of flour he made bread without yeast. Putting the meat in a basket and its broth in a pot, he brought them out and offered them to him under the oak.

[20]The angel of God said to him, "Take the meat and the unleavened bread, place them on this rock, and pour out the broth." And Gideon did so. [21]Then the angel of the LORD touched the meat and the unleavened bread with the tip of the staff that was in his hand. Fire flared from the rock, consuming the meat and the bread. And the angel of the LORD disappeared. [22]When Gideon realized

---

[a] 19 That is, probably about 36 pounds or about 16 kilograms

that it was the angel of the LORD, he exclaimed, "Alas, Sovereign LORD! I have seen the angel of the LORD face to face!"

²³ But the LORD said to him, "Peace! Do not be afraid. You are not going to die."

²⁴ So Gideon built an altar to the LORD there and called it The LORD Is Peace. To this day it stands in Ophrah of the Abiezrites.

²⁵ That same night the LORD said to him, "Take the second bull from your father's herd, the one seven years old.ᵃ Tear down your father's altar to Baal and cut down the Asherah poleᵇ beside it. ²⁶ Then build a proper kind ofᶜ altar to the LORD your God on the top of this height. Using the wood of the Asherah pole that you cut down, offer the secondᵈ bull as a burnt offering."

²⁷ So Gideon took ten of his servants and did as the LORD told him. But because he was afraid of his family and the townspeople, he did it at night rather than in the daytime.

²⁸ In the morning when the people of the town got up, there was Baal's altar, demolished, with the Asherah pole beside it cut down and the second bull sacrificed on the newly built altar!

²⁹ They asked each other, "Who did this?"

When they carefully investigated, they were told, "Gideon son of Joash did it."

³⁰ The people of the town demanded of Joash, "Bring out your son. He must die, because he has broken down Baal's altar and cut down the Asherah pole beside it."

³¹ But Joash replied to the hostile crowd around him, "Are you going to plead Baal's cause? Are you trying to save him? Whoever fights for him shall be put to death by morning! If Baal really is a god, he can defend himself when someone breaks down his altar." ³² So because Gideon broke down Baal's altar, they gave him the name Jerub-Baalᵉ that day, saying, "Let Baal contend with him."

³³ Now all the Midianites, Amalekites and other eastern peoples joined forces and crossed over the Jordan and camped in the Valley of Jezreel. ³⁴ Then the Spirit of the LORD came on Gideon, and he blew a trumpet, summoning the Abiezrites to follow him. ³⁵ He sent messengers throughout Manasseh, calling them to arms, and also into Asher, Zebulun and Naphtali, so that they too went up to meet them.

³⁶ Gideon said to God, "If you will save Israel by my hand as you have promised— ³⁷ look, I will place a wool fleece on the thresh-

---

ᵃ 25 Or *Take a full-grown, mature bull from your father's herd*   ᵇ 25 That is, a wooden symbol of the goddess Asherah; also in verses 26, 28 and 30
ᶜ 26 Or *build with layers of stone an*   ᵈ 26 Or *full-grown*; also in verse 28
ᵉ 32 *Jerub-Baal* probably means *let Baal contend*.

ing floor. If there is dew only on the fleece and all the ground is dry, then I will know that you will save Israel by my hand, as you said." ³⁸ And that is what happened. Gideon rose early the next day; he squeezed the fleece and wrung out the dew — a bowlful of water.

³⁹ Then Gideon said to God, "Do not be angry with me. Let me make just one more request. Allow me one more test with the fleece, but this time make the fleece dry and let the ground be covered with dew." ⁴⁰ That night God did so. Only the fleece was dry; all the ground was covered with dew.

Gideon Defeats the Midianites

7 Early in the morning, Jerub-Baal (that is, Gideon) and all his men camped at the spring of Harod. The camp of Midian was north of them in the valley near the hill of Moreh. ² The LORD said to Gideon, "You have too many men. I cannot deliver Midian into their hands, or Israel would boast against me, 'My own strength has saved me.' ³ Now announce to the army, 'Anyone who trembles with fear may turn back and leave Mount Gilead.'" So twenty-two thousand men left, while ten thousand remained.

⁴ But the LORD said to Gideon, "There are still too many men. Take them down to the water, and I will thin them out for you there. If I say, 'This one shall go

with you,' he shall go; but if I say, 'This one shall not go with you,' he shall not go."

⁵ So Gideon took the men down to the water. There the LORD told him, "Separate those who lap the water with their tongues as a dog laps from those who kneel down to drink." ⁶ Three hundred of them drank from cupped hands, lapping like dogs. All the rest got down on their knees to drink.

⁷ The LORD said to Gideon, "With the three hundred men that lapped I will save you and give the Midianites into your hands. Let all the others go home." ⁸ So Gideon sent the rest of the Israelites home but kept the three hundred, who took over the provisions and trumpets of the others.

Now the camp of Midian lay below him in the valley. ⁹ During that night the LORD said to Gideon, "Get up, go down against the camp, because I am going to give it into your hands. ¹⁰ If you are afraid to attack, go down to the camp with your servant Purah ¹¹ and listen to what they are saying. Afterward, you will be encouraged to attack the camp." So he and Purah his servant went down to the outposts of the camp. ¹² The Midianites, the Amalekites and all the other eastern peoples had settled in the valley, thick as locusts. Their camels could no more be counted than the sand on the seashore.

¹³Gideon arrived just as a man was telling a friend his dream. "I had a dream," he was saying. "A round loaf of barley bread came tumbling into the Midianite camp. It struck the tent with such force that the tent overturned and collapsed."

¹⁴His friend responded, "This can be nothing other than the sword of Gideon son of Joash, the Israelite. God has given the Midianites and the whole camp into his hands."

¹⁵When Gideon heard the dream and its interpretation, he bowed down and worshiped. He returned to the camp of Israel and called out, "Get up! The LORD has given the Midianite camp into your hands." ¹⁶Dividing the three hundred men into three companies, he placed trumpets and empty jars in the hands of all of them, with torches inside.

¹⁷"Watch me," he told them. "Follow my lead. When I get to the edge of the camp, do exactly as I do. ¹⁸When I and all who are with me blow our trumpets, then from all around the camp blow yours and shout, 'For the LORD and for Gideon.'"

¹⁹Gideon and the hundred men with him reached the edge of the camp at the beginning of the middle watch, just after they had changed the guard. They blew their trumpets and broke the jars that were in their hands. ²⁰The three companies blew the trumpets and smashed the jars. Grasping the torches in their left hands and holding in their right hands the trumpets they were to blow, they shouted, "A sword for the LORD and for Gideon!" ²¹While each man held his position around the camp, all the Midianites ran, crying out as they fled.

²²When the three hundred trumpets sounded, the LORD caused the men throughout the camp to turn on each other with their swords. The army fled to Beth Shittah toward Zererah as far as the border of Abel Meholah near Tabbath. ²³Israelites from Naphtali, Asher and all Manasseh were called out, and they pursued the Midianites. ²⁴Gideon sent messengers throughout the hill country of Ephraim, saying, "Come down against the Midianites and seize the waters of the Jordan ahead of them as far as Beth Barah."

So all the men of Ephraim were called out and they seized the waters of the Jordan as far as Beth Barah. ²⁵They also captured two of the Midianite leaders, Oreb and Zeeb. They killed Oreb at the rock of Oreb, and Zeeb at the winepress of Zeeb. They pursued the Midianites and brought the heads of Oreb and Zeeb to Gideon, who was by the Jordan.

Zebah and Zalmunna

8 Now the Ephraimites asked Gideon, "Why have you treated us like this? Why didn't you call us when you went to fight

Midian?" And they challenged him vigorously.

²But he answered them, "What have I accomplished compared to you? Aren't the gleanings of Ephraim's grapes better than the full grape harvest of Abiezer? ³God gave Oreb and Zeeb, the Midianite leaders, into your hands. What was I able to do compared to you?" At this, their resentment against him subsided.

⁴Gideon and his three hundred men, exhausted yet keeping up the pursuit, came to the Jordan and crossed it. ⁵He said to the men of Sukkoth, "Give my troops some bread; they are worn out, and I am still pursuing Zebah and Zalmunna, the kings of Midian."

⁶But the officials of Sukkoth said, "Do you already have the hands of Zebah and Zalmunna in your possession? Why should we give bread to your troops?"

⁷Then Gideon replied, "Just for that, when the LORD has given Zebah and Zalmunna into my hand, I will tear your flesh with desert thorns and briers."

⁸From there he went up to Peniel[a] and made the same request of them, but they answered as the men of Sukkoth had. ⁹So he said to the men of Peniel, "When I return in triumph, I will tear down this tower."

¹⁰Now Zebah and Zalmunna were in Karkor with a force of about fifteen thousand men, all that were left of the armies of the eastern peoples; a hundred and twenty thousand swordsmen had fallen. ¹¹Gideon went up by the route of the nomads east of Nobah and Jogbehah and attacked the unsuspecting army. ¹²Zebah and Zalmunna, the two kings of Midian, fled, but he pursued them and captured them, routing their entire army.

¹³Gideon son of Joash then returned from the battle by the Pass of Heres. ¹⁴He caught a young man of Sukkoth and questioned him, and the young man wrote down for him the names of the seventy-seven officials of Sukkoth, the elders of the town. ¹⁵Then Gideon came and said to the men of Sukkoth, "Here are Zebah and Zalmunna, about whom you taunted me by saying, 'Do you already have the hands of Zebah and Zalmunna in your possession? Why should we give bread to your exhausted men?'" ¹⁶He took the elders of the town and taught the men of Sukkoth a lesson by punishing them with desert thorns and briers. ¹⁷He also pulled down the tower of Peniel and killed the men of the town.

¹⁸Then he asked Zebah and Zalmunna, "What kind of men did you kill at Tabor?"

"Men like you," they answered, "each one with the bearing of a prince."

¹⁹Gideon replied, "Those were

ᵃ 8 Hebrew *Penuel,* a variant of *Peniel;* also in verses 9 and 17 my brothers, the sons of my own mother. As surely as the LORD lives, if you had spared their lives, I would not kill you." [20]Turning to Jether, his oldest son, he said, "Kill them!" But Jether did not draw his sword, because he was only a boy and was afraid.

[21]Zebah and Zalmunna said, "Come, do it yourself. 'As is the man, so is his strength.' " So Gideon stepped forward and killed them, and took the ornaments off their camels' necks.

Gideon's Ephod

[22]The Israelites said to Gideon, "Rule over us — you, your son and your grandson — because you have saved us from the hand of Midian."

[23]But Gideon told them, "I will not rule over you, nor will my son rule over you. The LORD will rule over you." [24]And he said, "I do have one request, that each of you give me an earring from your share of the plunder." (It was the custom of the Ishmaelites to wear gold earrings.)

[25]They answered, "We'll be glad to give them." So they spread out a garment, and each of them threw a ring from his plunder onto it. [26]The weight of the gold rings he asked for came to seventeen hundred shekels,[a] not counting the ornaments, the pendants and the purple garments worn by the kings of Midian or the chains that were on their camels' necks. [27]Gideon made the gold into an ephod, which he placed in Ophrah, his town. All Israel prostituted themselves by worshiping it there, and it became a snare to Gideon and his family.

Gideon's Death

[28]Thus Midian was subdued before the Israelites and did not raise its head again. During Gideon's lifetime, the land had peace forty years.

[29]Jerub-Baal son of Joash went back home to live. [30]He had seventy sons of his own, for he had many wives. [31]His concubine, who lived in Shechem, also bore him a son, whom he named Abimelek. [32]Gideon son of Joash died at a good old age and was buried in the tomb of his father Joash in Ophrah of the Abiezrites.

[33]No sooner had Gideon died than the Israelites again prostituted themselves to the Baals. They set up Baal-Berith as their god [34]and did not remember the LORD their God, who had rescued them from the hands of all their enemies on every side. [35]They also failed to show any loyalty to the family of Jerub-Baal (that is, Gideon) in spite of all the good things he had done for them.

Abimelek

9 Abimelek son of Jerub-Baal went to his mother's broth-

---

[a] 26 That is, about 43 pounds or about 20 kilograms

ers in Shechem and said to them and to all his mother's clan, ² "Ask all the citizens of Shechem, 'Which is better for you: to have all seventy of Jerub-Baal's sons rule over you, or just one man?' Remember, I am your flesh and blood."

³ When the brothers repeated all this to the citizens of Shechem, they were inclined to follow Abimelek, for they said, "He is related to us." ⁴ They gave him seventy shekels*a* of silver from the temple of Baal-Berith, and Abimelek used it to hire reckless scoundrels, who became his followers. ⁵ He went to his father's home in Ophrah and on one stone murdered his seventy brothers, the sons of Jerub-Baal. But Jotham, the youngest son of Jerub-Baal, escaped by hiding. ⁶ Then all the citizens of Shechem and Beth Millo gathered beside the great tree at the pillar in Shechem to crown Abimelek king.

⁷ When Jotham was told about this, he climbed up on the top of Mount Gerizim and shouted to them, "Listen to me, citizens of Shechem, so that God may listen to you. ⁸ One day the trees went out to anoint a king for themselves. They said to the olive tree, 'Be our king.'

⁹ "But the olive tree answered, 'Should I give up my oil, by which both gods and humans are honored, to hold sway over the trees?'

¹⁰ "Next, the trees said to the fig tree, 'Come and be our king.'

¹¹ "But the fig tree replied, 'Should I give up my fruit, so good and sweet, to hold sway over the trees?'

¹² "Then the trees said to the vine, 'Come and be our king.'

¹³ "But the vine answered, 'Should I give up my wine, which cheers both gods and humans, to hold sway over the trees?'

¹⁴ "Finally all the trees said to the thornbush, 'Come and be our king.'

¹⁵ "The thornbush said to the trees, 'If you really want to anoint me king over you, come and take refuge in my shade; but if not, then let fire come out of the thornbush and consume the cedars of Lebanon!'

¹⁶ "Have you acted honorably and in good faith by making Abimelek king? Have you been fair to Jerub-Baal and his family? Have you treated him as he deserves? ¹⁷ Remember that my father fought for you and risked his life to rescue you from the hand of Midian. ¹⁸ But today you have revolted against my father's family. You have murdered his seventy sons on a single stone and have made Abimelek, the son of his female slave, king over the citizens of Shechem because he is related to you. ¹⁹ So have you acted honorably and in good faith toward Jerub-Baal and his family

---

a 4 That is, about 1 3/4 pounds or about 800 grams

today? If you have, may Abimelek be your joy, and may you be his, too! **20** But if you have not, let fire come out from Abimelek and consume you, the citizens of Shechem and Beth Millo, and let fire come out from you, the citizens of Shechem and Beth Millo, and consume Abimelek!"

21 Then Jotham fled, escaping to Beer, and he lived there because he was afraid of his brother Abimelek.

22 After Abimelek had governed Israel three years, **23** God stirred up animosity between Abimelek and the citizens of Shechem so that they acted treacherously against Abimelek. **24** God did this in order that the crime against Jerub-Baal's seventy sons, the shedding of their blood, might be avenged on their brother Abimelek and on the citizens of Shechem, who had helped him murder his brothers. **25** In opposition to him these citizens of Shechem set men on the hilltops to ambush and rob everyone who passed by, and this was reported to Abimelek.

26 Now Gaal son of Ebed moved with his clan into Shechem, and its citizens put their confidence in him. **27** After they had gone out into the fields and gathered the grapes and trodden them, they held a festival in the temple of their god. While they were eating and drinking, they cursed Abimelek. **28** Then Gaal son of Ebed said, "Who is Abimelek, and why should we Shechemites be subject to him? Isn't he Jerub-Baal's son, and isn't Zebul his deputy? Serve the family of Hamor, Shechem's father! Why should we serve Abimelek? **29** If only this people were under my command! Then I would get rid of him. I would say to Abimelek, 'Call out your whole army!'" *a*

30 When Zebul the governor of the city heard what Gaal son of Ebed said, he was very angry. **31** Under cover he sent messengers to Abimelek, saying, "Gaal son of Ebed and his clan have come to Shechem and are stirring up the city against you. **32** Now then, during the night you and your men should come and lie in wait in the fields. **33** In the morning at sunrise, advance against the city. When Gaal and his men come out against you, seize the opportunity to attack them."

34 So Abimelek and all his troops set out by night and took up concealed positions near Shechem in four companies. **35** Now Gaal son of Ebed had gone out and was standing at the entrance of the city gate just as Abimelek and his troops came out from their hiding place.

36 When Gaal saw them, he said to Zebul, "Look, people are com-

---

a **29** Septuagint; Hebrew *him." Then he said to Abimelek, "Call out your whole army!"*

ing down from the tops of the mountains!"

Zebul replied, "You mistake the shadows of the mountains for men."

³⁷ But Gaal spoke up again: "Look, people are coming down from the central hill,^a and a company is coming from the direction of the diviners' tree."

³⁸ Then Zebul said to him, "Where is your big talk now, you who said, 'Who is Abimelek that we should be subject to him?' Aren't these the men you ridiculed? Go out and fight them!"

³⁹ So Gaal led out^b the citizens of Shechem and fought Abimelek. ⁴⁰ Abimelek chased him all the way to the entrance of the gate, and many were killed as they fled. ⁴¹ Then Abimelek stayed in Arumah, and Zebul drove Gaal and his clan out of Shechem.

⁴² The next day the people of Shechem went out to the fields, and this was reported to Abimelek. ⁴³ So he took his men, divided them into three companies and set an ambush in the fields. When he saw the people coming out of the city, he rose to attack them. ⁴⁴ Abimelek and the companies with him rushed forward to a position at the entrance of the city gate. Then two companies attacked those in the fields and struck them down. ⁴⁵ All that day Abimelek pressed his attack against the city until he had captured it and killed its people. Then he destroyed the city and scattered salt over it.

⁴⁶ On hearing this, the citizens in the tower of Shechem went into the stronghold of the temple of El-Berith. ⁴⁷ When Abimelek heard that they had assembled there, ⁴⁸ he and all his men went up Mount Zalmon. He took an ax and cut off some branches, which he lifted to his shoulders. He ordered the men with him, "Quick! Do what you have seen me do!" ⁴⁹ So all the men cut branches and followed Abimelek. They piled them against the stronghold and set it on fire with the people still inside. So all the people in the tower of Shechem, about a thousand men and women, also died.

⁵⁰ Next Abimelek went to Thebez and besieged it and captured it. ⁵¹ Inside the city, however, was a strong tower, to which all the men and women — all the people of the city — had fled. They had locked themselves in and climbed up on the tower roof. ⁵² Abimelek went to the tower and attacked it. But as he approached the entrance to the tower to set it on fire, ⁵³ a woman dropped an upper millstone on his head and cracked his skull.

⁵⁴ Hurriedly he called to his armor-bearer, "Draw your sword

---

^a 37 The Hebrew for this phrase means *the navel of the earth.*   ^b 39 Or *Gaal went out in the sight of*

and kill me, so that they can't say, 'A woman killed him.'" So his servant ran him through, and he died. [55]When the Israelites saw that Abimelek was dead, they went home.

[56]Thus God repaid the wickedness that Abimelek had done to his father by murdering his seventy brothers. [57]God also made the people of Shechem pay for all their wickedness. The curse of Jotham son of Jerub-Baal came on them.

Tola

10 After the time of Abimelek, a man of Issachar named Tola son of Puah, the son of Dodo, rose to save Israel. He lived in Shamir, in the hill country of Ephraim. [2]He led[a] Israel twenty-three years; then he died, and was buried in Shamir.

Jair

[3]He was followed by Jair of Gilead, who led Israel twenty-two years. [4]He had thirty sons, who rode thirty donkeys. They controlled thirty towns in Gilead, which to this day are called Havvoth Jair.[b] [5]When Jair died, he was buried in Kamon.

Jephthah

[6]Again the Israelites did evil in the eyes of the LORD. They served the Baals and the Ashtoreths, and the gods of Aram, the gods of Sidon, the gods of Moab, the gods of the Ammonites and the gods of the Philistines. And because the Israelites forsook the LORD and no longer served him, [7]he became angry with them. He sold them into the hands of the Philistines and the Ammonites, [8]who that year shattered and crushed them. For eighteen years they oppressed all the Israelites on the east side of the Jordan in Gilead, the land of the Amorites. [9]The Ammonites also crossed the Jordan to fight against Judah, Benjamin and Ephraim; Israel was in great distress. [10]Then the Israelites cried out to the LORD, "We have sinned against you, forsaking our God and serving the Baals."

[11]The LORD replied, "When the Egyptians, the Amorites, the Ammonites, the Philistines, [12]the Sidonians, the Amalekites and the Maonites[c] oppressed you and you cried to me for help, did I not save you from their hands? [13]But you have forsaken me and served other gods, so I will no longer save you. [14]Go and cry out to the gods you have chosen. Let them save you when you are in trouble!"

[15]But the Israelites said to the LORD, "We have sinned. Do with us whatever you think best, but please rescue us now." [16]Then they got rid of the foreign gods among them and served the

---

[a] 2 Traditionally *judged*; also in verse 3   [b] 4 Or *called the settlements of Jair*
[c] 12 Hebrew; some Septuagint manuscripts *Midianites*

LORD. And he could bear Israel's misery no longer.

¹⁷When the Ammonites were called to arms and camped in Gilead, the Israelites assembled and camped at Mizpah. ¹⁸The leaders of the people of Gilead said to each other, "Whoever will take the lead in attacking the Ammonites will be head over all who live in Gilead."

11 Jephthah the Gileadite was a mighty warrior. His father was Gilead; his mother was a prostitute. ²Gilead's wife also bore him sons, and when they were grown up, they drove Jephthah away. "You are not going to get any inheritance in our family," they said, "because you are the son of another woman." ³So Jephthah fled from his brothers and settled in the land of Tob, where a gang of scoundrels gathered around him and followed him.

⁴Some time later, when the Ammonites were fighting against Israel, ⁵the elders of Gilead went to get Jephthah from the land of Tob. ⁶"Come," they said, "be our commander, so we can fight the Ammonites."

⁷Jephthah said to them, "Didn't you hate me and drive me from my father's house? Why do you come to me now, when you're in trouble?"

⁸The elders of Gilead said to him, "Nevertheless, we are turning to you now; come with us to fight the Ammonites, and you will be head over all of us who live in Gilead."

⁹Jephthah answered, "Suppose you take me back to fight the Ammonites and the LORD gives them to me — will I really be your head?"

¹⁰The elders of Gilead replied, "The LORD is our witness; we will certainly do as you say." ¹¹So Jephthah went with the elders of Gilead, and the people made him head and commander over them. And he repeated all his words before the LORD in Mizpah.

¹²Then Jephthah sent messengers to the Ammonite king with the question: "What do you have against me that you have attacked my country?"

¹³The king of the Ammonites answered Jephthah's messengers, "When Israel came up out of Egypt, they took away my land from the Arnon to the Jabbok, all the way to the Jordan. Now give it back peaceably."

¹⁴Jephthah sent back messengers to the Ammonite king, ¹⁵saying:

"This is what Jephthah says: Israel did not take the land of Moab or the land of the Ammonites. ¹⁶But when they came up out of Egypt, Israel went through the wilderness to the Red Sea[a] and on to Kadesh. ¹⁷Then Israel sent

---

a 16 Or *the Sea of Reeds*

messengers to the king of Edom, saying, 'Give us permission to go through your country,' but the king of Edom would not listen. They sent also to the king of Moab, and he refused. So Israel stayed at Kadesh.

¹⁸ "Next they traveled through the wilderness, skirted the lands of Edom and Moab, passed along the eastern side of the country of Moab, and camped on the other side of the Arnon. They did not enter the territory of Moab, for the Arnon was its border.

¹⁹ "Then Israel sent messengers to Sihon king of the Amorites, who ruled in Heshbon, and said to him, 'Let us pass through your country to our own place.' ²⁰ Sihon, however, did not trust Israel*a* to pass through his territory. He mustered all his troops and encamped at Jahaz and fought with Israel.

²¹ "Then the LORD, the God of Israel, gave Sihon and his whole army into Israel's hands, and they defeated them. Israel took over all the land of the Amorites who lived in that country, ²² capturing all of it from the Arnon to the Jabbok and from the desert to the Jordan.

²³ "Now since the LORD, the God of Israel, has driven the Amorites out before his people Israel, what right have you to take it over? ²⁴ Will you not take what your god Chemosh gives you? Likewise, whatever the LORD our God has given us, we will possess. ²⁵ Are you any better than Balak son of Zippor, king of Moab? Did he ever quarrel with Israel or fight with them? ²⁶ For three hundred years Israel occupied Heshbon, Aroer, the surrounding settlements and all the towns along the Arnon. Why didn't you retake them during that time? ²⁷ I have not wronged you, but you are doing me wrong by waging war against me. Let the LORD, the Judge, decide the dispute this day between the Israelites and the Ammonites.' "

²⁸ The king of Ammon, however, paid no attention to the message Jephthah sent him.

²⁹ Then the Spirit of the LORD came on Jephthah. He crossed Gilead and Manasseh, passed through Mizpah of Gilead, and from there he advanced against the Ammonites. ³⁰ And Jephthah made a vow to the LORD: "If you give the Ammonites into my hands, ³¹ whatever comes out of the door of my house to meet me when I return in triumph from the Ammonites will be the

---

a 20 Or however, would not make an agreement for Israel

LORD's, and I will sacrifice it as a burnt offering."

³²Then Jephthah went over to fight the Ammonites, and the LORD gave them into his hands. ³³He devastated twenty towns from Aroer to the vicinity of Minnith, as far as Abel Keramim. Thus Israel subdued Ammon.

³⁴When Jephthah returned to his home in Mizpah, who should come out to meet him but his daughter, dancing to the sound of timbrels! She was an only child. Except for her he had neither son nor daughter. ³⁵When he saw her, he tore his clothes and cried, "Oh no, my daughter! You have brought me down and I am devastated. I have made a vow to the LORD that I cannot break."

³⁶"My father," she replied, "you have given your word to the LORD. Do to me just as you promised, now that the LORD has avenged you of your enemies, the Ammonites. ³⁷But grant me this one request," she said. "Give me two months to roam the hills and weep with my friends, because I will never marry."

³⁸"You may go," he said. And he let her go for two months. She and her friends went into the hills and wept because she would never marry. ³⁹After the two months, she returned to her father, and he did to her as he had vowed. And she was a virgin.

From this comes the Israelite tradition ⁴⁰that each year the young women of Israel go out for four days to commemorate the daughter of Jephthah the Gileadite.

Jephthah and Ephraim

12 The Ephraimite forces were called out, and they crossed over to Zaphon. They said to Jephthah, "Why did you go to fight the Ammonites without calling us to go with you? We're going to burn down your house over your head."

²Jephthah answered, "I and my people were engaged in a great struggle with the Ammonites, and although I called, you didn't save me out of their hands. ³When I saw that you wouldn't help, I took my life in my hands and crossed over to fight the Ammonites, and the LORD gave me the victory over them. Now why have you come up today to fight me?"

⁴Jephthah then called together the men of Gilead and fought against Ephraim. The Gileadites struck them down because the Ephraimites had said, "You Gileadites are renegades from Ephraim and Manasseh." ⁵The Gileadites captured the fords of the Jordan leading to Ephraim, and whenever a survivor of Ephraim said, "Let me cross over," the men of Gilead asked him, "Are you an Ephraimite?" If he replied, "No," ⁶they said, "All right, say 'Shibboleth.'" If he said, "Sibboleth,"

because he could not pronounce the word correctly, they seized him and killed him at the fords of the Jordan. Forty-two thousand Ephraimites were killed at that time.

⁷Jephthah led*a* Israel six years. Then Jephthah the Gileadite died and was buried in a town in Gilead.

Ibzan, Elon and Abdon

⁸After him, Ibzan of Bethlehem led Israel. ⁹He had thirty sons and thirty daughters. He gave his daughters away in marriage to those outside his clan, and for his sons he brought in thirty young women as wives from outside his clan. Ibzan led Israel seven years. ¹⁰Then Ibzan died and was buried in Bethlehem.

¹¹After him, Elon the Zebulunite led Israel ten years. ¹²Then Elon died and was buried in Aijalon in the land of Zebulun.

¹³After him, Abdon son of Hillel, from Pirathon, led Israel. ¹⁴He had forty sons and thirty grandsons, who rode on seventy donkeys. He led Israel eight years. ¹⁵Then Abdon son of Hillel died and was buried at Pirathon in Ephraim, in the hill country of the Amalekites.

The Birth of Samson

13 Again the Israelites did evil in the eyes of the LORD, so the LORD delivered them into the hands of the Philistines for forty years.

²A certain man of Zorah, named Manoah, from the clan of the Danites, had a wife who was childless, unable to give birth. ³The angel of the LORD appeared to her and said, "You are barren and childless, but you are going to become pregnant and give birth to a son. ⁴Now see to it that you drink no wine or other fermented drink and that you do not eat anything unclean. ⁵You will become pregnant and have a son whose head is never to be touched by a razor because the boy is to be a Nazirite, dedicated to God from the womb. He will take the lead in delivering Israel from the hands of the Philistines."

⁶Then the woman went to her husband and told him, "A man of God came to me. He looked like an angel of God, very awesome. I didn't ask him where he came from, and he didn't tell me his name. ⁷But he said to me, 'You will become pregnant and have a son. Now then, drink no wine or other fermented drink and do not eat anything unclean, because the boy will be a Nazirite of God from the womb until the day of his death.'"

⁸Then Manoah prayed to the LORD: "Pardon your servant, Lord. I beg you to let the man of God you sent to us come again to

---

a 7 Traditionally *judged*; also in verses 8-14

teach us how to bring up the boy who is to be born."

⁹God heard Manoah, and the angel of God came again to the woman while she was out in the field; but her husband Manoah was not with her. ¹⁰The woman hurried to tell her husband, "He's here! The man who appeared to me the other day!"

¹¹Manoah got up and followed his wife. When he came to the man, he said, "Are you the man who talked to my wife?"

"I am," he said.

¹²So Manoah asked him, "When your words are fulfilled, what is to be the rule that governs the boy's life and work?"

¹³The angel of the LORD answered, "Your wife must do all that I have told her. ¹⁴She must not eat anything that comes from the grapevine, nor drink any wine or other fermented drink nor eat anything unclean. She must do everything I have commanded her."

¹⁵Manoah said to the angel of the LORD, "We would like you to stay until we prepare a young goat for you."

¹⁶The angel of the LORD replied, "Even though you detain me, I will not eat any of your food. But if you prepare a burnt offering, offer it to the LORD." (Manoah did not realize that it was the angel of the LORD.)

¹⁷Then Manoah inquired of the angel of the LORD, "What is your name, so that we may honor you when your word comes true?"

¹⁸He replied, "Why do you ask my name? It is beyond understanding.ᵃ" ¹⁹Then Manoah took a young goat, together with the grain offering, and sacrificed it on a rock to the LORD. And the LORD did an amazing thing while Manoah and his wife watched: ²⁰As the flame blazed up from the altar toward heaven, the angel of the LORD ascended in the flame. Seeing this, Manoah and his wife fell with their faces to the ground. ²¹When the angel of the LORD did not show himself again to Manoah and his wife, Manoah realized that it was the angel of the LORD.

²²"We are doomed to die!" he said to his wife. "We have seen God!"

²³But his wife answered, "If the LORD had meant to kill us, he would not have accepted a burnt offering and grain offering from our hands, nor shown us all these things or now told us this."

²⁴The woman gave birth to a boy and named him Samson. He grew and the LORD blessed him, ²⁵and the Spirit of the LORD began to stir him while he was in Mahaneh Dan, between Zorah and Eshtaol.

Samson's Marriage

14 Samson went down to Timnah and saw there a young Philistine woman. ²When

---

ᵃ 18 Or *is wonderful*

he returned, he said to his father and mother, "I have seen a Philistine woman in Timnah; now get her for me as my wife."

³His father and mother replied, "Isn't there an acceptable woman among your relatives or among all our people? Must you go to the uncircumcised Philistines to get a wife?"

But Samson said to his father, "Get her for me. She's the right one for me." ⁴(His parents did not know that this was from the LORD, who was seeking an occasion to confront the Philistines; for at that time they were ruling over Israel.)

⁵Samson went down to Timnah together with his father and mother. As they approached the vineyards of Timnah, suddenly a young lion came roaring toward him. ⁶The Spirit of the LORD came powerfully upon him so that he tore the lion apart with his bare hands as he might have torn a young goat. But he told neither his father nor his mother what he had done. ⁷Then he went down and talked with the woman, and he liked her.

⁸Some time later, when he went back to marry her, he turned aside to look at the lion's carcass, and in it he saw a swarm of bees and some honey. ⁹He scooped out the honey with his hands and ate as he went along. When he rejoined his parents, he gave them some, and they too ate it. But he did not tell them that he had taken the honey from the lion's carcass.

¹⁰Now his father went down to see the woman. And there Samson held a feast, as was customary for young men. ¹¹When the people saw him, they chose thirty men to be his companions.

¹²"Let me tell you a riddle," Samson said to them. "If you can give me the answer within the seven days of the feast, I will give you thirty linen garments and thirty sets of clothes. ¹³If you can't tell me the answer, you must give me thirty linen garments and thirty sets of clothes."

"Tell us your riddle," they said. "Let's hear it."

¹⁴He replied,

"Out of the eater, something to eat;
    out of the strong, something sweet."

For three days they could not give the answer.

¹⁵On the fourth*a* day, they said to Samson's wife, "Coax your husband into explaining the riddle for us, or we will burn you and your father's household to death. Did you invite us here to steal our property?"

¹⁶Then Samson's wife threw herself on him, sobbing, "You hate me! You don't really love me. You've given my people a riddle, but you haven't told me the answer."

---

a 15 Some Septuagint manuscripts and Syriac; Hebrew *seventh*

"I haven't even explained it to my father or mother," he replied, "so why should I explain it to you?" **17**She cried the whole seven days of the feast. So on the seventh day he finally told her, because she continued to press him. She in turn explained the riddle to her people.

18Before sunset on the seventh day the men of the town said to him,

"What is sweeter than honey?
  What is stronger than a lion?"

Samson said to them,

"If you had not plowed with
    my heifer,
  you would not have solved
    my riddle."

19Then the Spirit of the LORD came powerfully upon him. He went down to Ashkelon, struck down thirty of their men, stripped them of everything and gave their clothes to those who had explained the riddle. Burning with anger, he returned to his father's home. **20**And Samson's wife was given to one of his companions who had attended him at the feast.

Samson's Vengeance on the Philistines

15 Later on, at the time of wheat harvest, Samson took a young goat and went to visit his wife. He said, "I'm going to my wife's room." But her father would not let him go in.

2"I was so sure you hated her," he said, "that I gave her to your companion. Isn't her younger sister more attractive? Take her instead."

3Samson said to them, "This time I have a right to get even with the Philistines; I will really harm them." **4**So he went out and caught three hundred foxes and tied them tail to tail in pairs. He then fastened a torch to every pair of tails, **5**lit the torches and let the foxes loose in the standing grain of the Philistines. He burned up the shocks and standing grain, together with the vineyards and olive groves.

6When the Philistines asked, "Who did this?" they were told, "Samson, the Timnite's son-in-law, because his wife was given to his companion."

So the Philistines went up and burned her and her father to death. **7**Samson said to them, "Since you've acted like this, I swear that I won't stop until I get my revenge on you." **8**He attacked them viciously and slaughtered many of them. Then he went down and stayed in a cave in the rock of Etam.

9The Philistines went up and camped in Judah, spreading out near Lehi. **10**The people of Judah asked, "Why have you come to fight us?"

"We have come to take Samson prisoner," they answered, "to do to him as he did to us."

¹¹Then three thousand men from Judah went down to the cave in the rock of Etam and said to Samson, "Don't you realize that the Philistines are rulers over us? What have you done to us?"

He answered, "I merely did to them what they did to me."

¹²They said to him, "We've come to tie you up and hand you over to the Philistines."

Samson said, "Swear to me that you won't kill me yourselves."

¹³"Agreed," they answered. "We will only tie you up and hand you over to them. We will not kill you." So they bound him with two new ropes and led him up from the rock. ¹⁴As he approached Lehi, the Philistines came toward him shouting. The Spirit of the LORD came powerfully upon him. The ropes on his arms became like charred flax, and the bindings dropped from his hands. ¹⁵Finding a fresh jawbone of a donkey, he grabbed it and struck down a thousand men.

¹⁶Then Samson said,

"With a donkey's jawbone
    I have made donkeys of
        them.ᵃ
With a donkey's jawbone
    I have killed a thousand
        men."

¹⁷When he finished speaking, he threw away the jawbone; and the place was called Ramath Lehi.ᵇ

¹⁸Because he was very thirsty, he cried out to the LORD, "You have given your servant this great victory. Must I now die of thirst and fall into the hands of the uncircumcised?" ¹⁹Then God opened up the hollow place in Lehi, and water came out of it. When Samson drank, his strength returned and he revived. So the spring was called En Hakkore,ᶜ and it is still there in Lehi.

²⁰Samson ledᵈ Israel for twenty years in the days of the Philistines.

Samson and Delilah

16 One day Samson went to Gaza, where he saw a prostitute. He went in to spend the night with her. ²The people of Gaza were told, "Samson is here!" So they surrounded the place and lay in wait for him all night at the city gate. They made no move during the night, saying, "At dawn we'll kill him."

³But Samson lay there only until the middle of the night. Then he got up and took hold of the doors of the city gate, together with the two posts, and tore them loose, bar and all. He lifted them to his shoulders and carried them to the top of the hill that faces Hebron.

⁴Some time later, he fell in love with a woman in the Valley of Sorek whose name was Delilah.

ᵃ 16 Or *made a heap or two*; the Hebrew for *donkey* sounds like the Hebrew for *heap*.   ᵇ 17 *Ramath Lehi* means *jawbone hill*.   ᶜ 19 *En Hakkore* means *caller's spring*.   ᵈ 20 Traditionally *judged*

⁵The rulers of the Philistines went to her and said, "See if you can lure him into showing you the secret of his great strength and how we can overpower him so we may tie him up and subdue him. Each one of us will give you eleven hundred shekels*ᵃ* of silver."

⁶So Delilah said to Samson, "Tell me the secret of your great strength and how you can be tied up and subdued."

⁷Samson answered her, "If anyone ties me with seven fresh bowstrings that have not been dried, I'll become as weak as any other man."

⁸Then the rulers of the Philistines brought her seven fresh bowstrings that had not been dried, and she tied him with them. ⁹With men hidden in the room, she called to him, "Samson, the Philistines are upon you!" But he snapped the bowstrings as easily as a piece of string snaps when it comes close to a flame. So the secret of his strength was not discovered.

¹⁰Then Delilah said to Samson, "You have made a fool of me; you lied to me. Come now, tell me how you can be tied."

¹¹He said, "If anyone ties me securely with new ropes that have never been used, I'll become as weak as any other man."

¹²So Delilah took new ropes and tied him with them. Then, with men hidden in the room, she called to him, "Samson, the Philistines are upon you!" But he snapped the ropes off his arms as if they were threads.

¹³Delilah then said to Samson, "All this time you have been making a fool of me and lying to me. Tell me how you can be tied."

He replied, "If you weave the seven braids of my head into the fabric on the loom and tighten it with the pin, I'll become as weak as any other man." So while he was sleeping, Delilah took the seven braids of his head, wove them into the fabric ¹⁴and*ᵇ* tightened it with the pin.

Again she called to him, "Samson, the Philistines are upon you!" He awoke from his sleep and pulled up the pin and the loom, with the fabric.

¹⁵Then she said to him, "How can you say, 'I love you,' when you won't confide in me? This is the third time you have made a fool of me and haven't told me the secret of your great strength." ¹⁶With such nagging she prodded him day after day until he was sick to death of it.

¹⁷So he told her everything. "No razor has ever been used on my head," he said, "because I have been a Nazirite dedicated to God from my mother's

---

ᵃ 5 That is, about 28 pounds or about 13 kilograms   *ᵇ* 13,14 Some Septuagint manuscripts; Hebrew *replied, "I can if you weave the seven braids of my head into the fabric on the loom." ¹⁴So she* womb. If my head were shaved, my strength would leave me, and I would become as weak as any other man."

¹⁸When Delilah saw that he had told her everything, she sent word to the rulers of the Philistines, "Come back once more; he has told me everything." So the rulers of the Philistines returned with the silver in their hands. ¹⁹After putting him to sleep on her lap, she called for someone to shave off the seven braids of his hair, and so began to subdue him.ᵃ And his strength left him.

²⁰Then she called, "Samson, the Philistines are upon you!"

He awoke from his sleep and thought, "I'll go out as before and shake myself free." But he did not know that the LORD had left him.

²¹Then the Philistines seized him, gouged out his eyes and took him down to Gaza. Binding him with bronze shackles, they set him to grinding grain in the prison. ²²But the hair on his head began to grow again after it had been shaved.

The Death of Samson

²³Now the rulers of the Philistines assembled to offer a great sacrifice to Dagon their god and to celebrate, saying, "Our god has delivered Samson, our enemy, into our hands."

²⁴When the people saw him, they praised their god, saying,

"Our god has delivered our enemy
    into our hands,
the one who laid waste our land
    and multiplied our slain."

²⁵While they were in high spirits, they shouted, "Bring out Samson to entertain us." So they called Samson out of the prison, and he performed for them.

When they stood him among the pillars, ²⁶Samson said to the servant who held his hand, "Put me where I can feel the pillars that support the temple, so that I may lean against them." ²⁷Now the temple was crowded with men and women; all the rulers of the Philistines were there, and on the roof were about three thousand men and women watching Samson perform. ²⁸Then Samson prayed to the LORD, "Sovereign LORD, remember me. Please, God, strengthen me just once more, and let me with one blow get revenge on the Philistines for my two eyes." ²⁹Then Samson reached toward the two central pillars on which the temple stood. Bracing himself against them, his right hand on the one and his left hand on the other, ³⁰Samson said, "Let me die with the Philistines!" Then he pushed with all his might, and down came the temple on the rulers and all the people in it. Thus he killed many more when he died than while he lived.

ᵃ 19 Hebrew; some Septuagint manuscripts *and he began to weaken*

31 Then his brothers and his father's whole family went down to get him. They brought him back and buried him between Zorah and Eshtaol in the tomb of Manoah his father. He had led[a] Israel twenty years.

Micah's Idols

17 Now a man named Micah from the hill country of Ephraim **2** said to his mother, "The eleven hundred shekels[b] of silver that were taken from you and about which I heard you utter a curse—I have that silver with me; I took it."

Then his mother said, "The LORD bless you, my son!"

3 When he returned the eleven hundred shekels of silver to his mother, she said, "I solemnly consecrate my silver to the LORD for my son to make an image overlaid with silver. I will give it back to you."

4 So after he returned the silver to his mother, she took two hundred shekels[c] of silver and gave them to a silversmith, who used them to make the idol. And it was put in Micah's house.

5 Now this man Micah had a shrine, and he made an ephod and some household gods and installed one of his sons as his priest. **6** In those days Israel had no king; everyone did as they saw fit.

7 A young Levite from Bethlehem in Judah, who had been living within the clan of Judah, **8** left that town in search of some other place to stay. On his way[d] he came to Micah's house in the hill country of Ephraim.

9 Micah asked him, "Where are you from?"

"I'm a Levite from Bethlehem in Judah," he said, "and I'm looking for a place to stay."

10 Then Micah said to him, "Live with me and be my father and priest, and I'll give you ten shekels[e] of silver a year, your clothes and your food." **11** So the Levite agreed to live with him, and the young man became like one of his sons to him. **12** Then Micah installed the Levite, and the young man became his priest and lived in his house. **13** And Micah said, "Now I know that the LORD will be good to me, since this Levite has become my priest."

The Danites Settle in Laish

18 In those days Israel had no king.

And in those days the tribe of the Danites was seeking a place of their own where they might settle, because they had not yet come into an inheritance among the tribes of Israel. **2** So the Danites sent five of their leading men from Zorah and Eshtaol to spy

---

[a] 31 Traditionally *judged*   [b] 2 That is, about 28 pounds or about 13 kilograms
[c] 4 That is, about 5 pounds or about 2.3 kilograms   [d] 8 Or *To carry on his profession*   [e] 10 That is, about 4 ounces or about 115 grams

out the land and explore it. These men represented all the Danites. They told them, "Go, explore the land."

So they entered the hill country of Ephraim and came to the house of Micah, where they spent the night. ³When they were near Micah's house, they recognized the voice of the young Levite; so they turned in there and asked him, "Who brought you here? What are you doing in this place? Why are you here?"

⁴He told them what Micah had done for him, and said, "He has hired me and I am his priest."

⁵Then they said to him, "Please inquire of God to learn whether our journey will be successful."

⁶The priest answered them, "Go in peace. Your journey has the LORD's approval."

⁷So the five men left and came to Laish, where they saw that the people were living in safety, like the Sidonians, at peace and secure. And since their land lacked nothing, they were prosperous.ᵃ Also, they lived a long way from the Sidonians and had no relationship with anyone else.ᵇ

⁸When they returned to Zorah and Eshtaol, their fellow Danites asked them, "How did you find things?"

⁹They answered, "Come on, let's attack them! We have seen the land, and it is very good. Aren't you going to do something? Don't hesitate to go there and take it over. ¹⁰When you get there, you will find an unsuspecting people and a spacious land that God has put into your hands, a land that lacks nothing whatever."

¹¹Then six hundred men of the Danites, armed for battle, set out from Zorah and Eshtaol. ¹²On their way they set up camp near Kiriath Jearim in Judah. This is why the place west of Kiriath Jearim is called Mahaneh Danᶜ to this day. ¹³From there they went on to the hill country of Ephraim and came to Micah's house.

¹⁴Then the five men who had spied out the land of Laish said to their fellow Danites, "Do you know that one of these houses has an ephod, some household gods and an image overlaid with silver? Now you know what to do." ¹⁵So they turned in there and went to the house of the young Levite at Micah's place and greeted him. ¹⁶The six hundred Danites, armed for battle, stood at the entrance of the gate. ¹⁷The five men who had spied out the land went inside and took the idol, the ephod and the household gods while the priest and the six hundred armed men stood at the entrance of the gate.

ᵃ 7 The meaning of the Hebrew for this clause is uncertain.   ᵇ 7 Hebrew; some Septuagint manuscripts *with the Arameans*   ᶜ 12 *Mahaneh Dan* means *Dan's camp.*

[18] When the five men went into Micah's house and took the idol, the ephod and the household gods, the priest said to them, "What are you doing?"

[19] They answered him, "Be quiet! Don't say a word. Come with us, and be our father and priest. Isn't it better that you serve a tribe and clan in Israel as priest rather than just one man's household?" [20] The priest was very pleased. He took the ephod, the household gods and the idol and went along with the people. [21] Putting their little children, their livestock and their possessions in front of them, they turned away and left.

[22] When they had gone some distance from Micah's house, the men who lived near Micah were called together and overtook the Danites. [23] As they shouted after them, the Danites turned and said to Micah, "What's the matter with you that you called out your men to fight?"

[24] He replied, "You took the gods I made, and my priest, and went away. What else do I have? How can you ask, 'What's the matter with you?'"

[25] The Danites answered, "Don't argue with us, or some of the men may get angry and attack you, and you and your family will lose your lives." [26] So the Danites went their way, and Micah, seeing that they were too strong for him, turned around and went back home.

[27] Then they took what Micah had made, and his priest, and went on to Laish, against a people at peace and secure. They attacked them with the sword and burned down their city. [28] There was no one to rescue them because they lived a long way from Sidon and had no relationship with anyone else. The city was in a valley near Beth Rehob.

The Danites rebuilt the city and settled there. [29] They named it Dan after their ancestor Dan, who was born to Israel—though the city used to be called Laish. [30] There the Danites set up for themselves the idol, and Jonathan son of Gershom, the son of Moses,[a] and his sons were priests for the tribe of Dan until the time of the captivity of the land. [31] They continued to use the idol Micah had made, all the time the house of God was in Shiloh.

A Levite and His Concubine

19

In those days Israel had no king.

Now a Levite who lived in a remote area in the hill country of Ephraim took a concubine from Bethlehem in Judah. [2] But she was unfaithful to him. She left him and went back to her

---

[a] 30 Many Hebrew manuscripts, some Septuagint manuscripts and Vulgate; many other Hebrew manuscripts and some other Septuagint manuscripts *Manasseh*

parents' home in Bethlehem, Judah. After she had been there four months, **3**her husband went to her to persuade her to return. He had with him his servant and two donkeys. She took him into her parents' home, and when her father saw him, he gladly welcomed him. **4**His father-in-law, the woman's father, prevailed on him to stay; so he remained with him three days, eating and drinking, and sleeping there.

5On the fourth day they got up early and he prepared to leave, but the woman's father said to his son-in-law, "Refresh yourself with something to eat; then you can go." **6**So the two of them sat down to eat and drink together. Afterward the woman's father said, "Please stay tonight and enjoy yourself." **7**And when the man got up to go, his father-in-law persuaded him, so he stayed there that night. **8**On the morning of the fifth day, when he rose to go, the woman's father said, "Refresh yourself. Wait till afternoon!" So the two of them ate together.

9Then when the man, with his concubine and his servant, got up to leave, his father-in-law, the woman's father, said, "Now look, it's almost evening. Spend the night here; the day is nearly over. Stay and enjoy yourself. Early tomorrow morning you can get up and be on your way home." **10**But,

unwilling to stay another night, the man left and went toward Jebus (that is, Jerusalem), with his two saddled donkeys and his concubine.

11When they were near Jebus and the day was almost gone, the servant said to his master, "Come, let's stop at this city of the Jebusites and spend the night."

12His master replied, "No. We won't go into any city whose people are not Israelites. We will go on to Gibeah." **13**He added, "Come, let's try to reach Gibeah or Ramah and spend the night in one of those places." **14**So they went on, and the sun set as they neared Gibeah in Benjamin. **15**There they stopped to spend the night. They went and sat in the city square, but no one took them in for the night.

16That evening an old man from the hill country of Ephraim, who was living in Gibeah (the inhabitants of the place were Benjamites), came in from his work in the fields. **17**When he looked and saw the traveler in the city square, the old man asked, "Where are you going? Where did you come from?"

18He answered, "We are on our way from Bethlehem in Judah to a remote area in the hill country of Ephraim where I live. I have been to Bethlehem in Judah and now I am going to the house of the LORD.*ᵃ* No one has taken me

---

ᵃ 18 Hebrew, Vulgate, Syriac and Targum; Septuagint *going home* in for the night. **¹⁹**We have both straw and fodder for our donkeys and bread and wine for ourselves your servants—me, the woman and the young man with us. We don't need anything."

²⁰"You are welcome at my house," the old man said. "Let me supply whatever you need. Only don't spend the night in the square." **²¹**So he took him into his house and fed his donkeys. After they had washed their feet, they had something to eat and drink.

²²While they were enjoying themselves, some of the wicked men of the city surrounded the house. Pounding on the door, they shouted to the old man who owned the house, "Bring out the man who came to your house so we can have sex with him."

²³The owner of the house went outside and said to them, "No, my friends, don't be so vile. Since this man is my guest, don't do this outrageous thing. **²⁴**Look, here is my virgin daughter, and his concubine. I will bring them out to you now, and you can use them and do to them whatever you wish. But as for this man, don't do such an outrageous thing."

²⁵But the men would not listen to him. So the man took his concubine and sent her outside to them, and they raped her and abused her throughout the night, and at dawn they let her go. **²⁶**At daybreak the woman went back to the house where her master was staying, fell down at the door and lay there until daylight.

²⁷When her master got up in the morning and opened the door of the house and stepped out to continue on his way, there lay his concubine, fallen in the doorway of the house, with her hands on the threshold. **²⁸**He said to her, "Get up; let's go." But there was no answer. Then the man put her on his donkey and set out for home.

²⁹When he reached home, he took a knife and cut up his concubine, limb by limb, into twelve parts and sent them into all the areas of Israel. **³⁰**Everyone who saw it was saying to one another, "Such a thing has never been seen or done, not since the day the Israelites came up out of Egypt. Just imagine! We must do something! So speak up!"

The Israelites Punish the Benjamites

20 Then all Israel from Dan to Beersheba and from the land of Gilead came together as one and assembled before the LORD in Mizpah. **²**The leaders of all the people of the tribes of Israel took their places in the assembly of God's people, four hundred thousand men armed with swords. **³**(The Benjamites heard that the Israelites had gone up to Mizpah.) Then the Israelites said, "Tell us how this awful thing happened."

[4]So the Levite, the husband of the murdered woman, said, "I and my concubine came to Gibeah in Benjamin to spend the night. [5]During the night the men of Gibeah came after me and surrounded the house, intending to kill me. They raped my concubine, and she died. [6]I took my concubine, cut her into pieces and sent one piece to each region of Israel's inheritance, because they committed this lewd and outrageous act in Israel. [7]Now, all you Israelites, speak up and tell me what you have decided to do."

[8]All the men rose up together as one, saying, "None of us will go home. No, not one of us will return to his house. [9]But now this is what we'll do to Gibeah: We'll go up against it in the order decided by casting lots. [10]We'll take ten men out of every hundred from all the tribes of Israel, and a hundred from a thousand, and a thousand from ten thousand, to get provisions for the army. Then, when the army arrives at Gibeah[a] in Benjamin, it can give them what they deserve for this outrageous act done in Israel." [11]So all the Israelites got together and united as one against the city.

[12]The tribes of Israel sent messengers throughout the tribe of Benjamin, saying, "What about this awful crime that was committed among you? [13]Now turn those wicked men of Gibeah over to us so that we may put them to death and purge the evil from Israel."

But the Benjamites would not listen to their fellow Israelites. [14]From their towns they came together at Gibeah to fight against the Israelites. [15]At once the Benjamites mobilized twenty-six thousand swordsmen from their towns, in addition to seven hundred able young men from those living in Gibeah. [16]Among all these soldiers there were seven hundred select troops who were left-handed, each of whom could sling a stone at a hair and not miss.

[17]Israel, apart from Benjamin, mustered four hundred thousand swordsmen, all of them fit for battle.

[18]The Israelites went up to Bethel[b] and inquired of God. They said, "Who of us is to go up first to fight against the Benjamites?"

The LORD replied, "Judah shall go first."

[19]The next morning the Israelites got up and pitched camp near Gibeah. [20]The Israelites went out to fight the Benjamites and took up battle positions against them at Gibeah. [21]The Benjamites came out of Gibeah and cut down twenty-two thousand Israelites on the battlefield that day. [22]But

---

[a] 10 One Hebrew manuscript; most Hebrew manuscripts *Geba*, a variant of *Gibeah*   [b] 18 Or *to the house of God*; also in verse 26

the Israelites encouraged one another and again took up their positions where they had stationed themselves the first day. ²³ The Israelites went up and wept before the LORD until evening, and they inquired of the LORD. They said, "Shall we go up again to fight against the Benjamites, our fellow Israelites?"

The LORD answered, "Go up against them."

²⁴ Then the Israelites drew near to Benjamin the second day. ²⁵ This time, when the Benjamites came out from Gibeah to oppose them, they cut down another eighteen thousand Israelites, all of them armed with swords.

²⁶ Then all the Israelites, the whole army, went up to Bethel, and there they sat weeping before the LORD. They fasted that day until evening and presented burnt offerings and fellowship offerings to the LORD. ²⁷ And the Israelites inquired of the LORD. (In those days the ark of the covenant of God was there, ²⁸ with Phinehas son of Eleazar, the son of Aaron, ministering before it.) They asked, "Shall we go up again to fight against the Benjamites, our fellow Israelites, or not?"

The LORD responded, "Go, for tomorrow I will give them into your hands."

²⁹ Then Israel set an ambush around Gibeah. ³⁰ They went up against the Benjamites on the third day and took up positions against Gibeah as they had done before. ³¹ The Benjamites came out to meet them and were drawn away from the city. They began to inflict casualties on the Israelites as before, so that about thirty men fell in the open field and on the roads — the one leading to Bethel and the other to Gibeah. ³² While the Benjamites were saying, "We are defeating them as before," the Israelites were saying, "Let's retreat and draw them away from the city to the roads."

³³ All the men of Israel moved from their places and took up positions at Baal Tamar, and the Israelite ambush charged out of its place on the west[a] of Gibeah.[b] ³⁴ Then ten thousand of Israel's able young men made a frontal attack on Gibeah. The fighting was so heavy that the Benjamites did not realize how near disaster was. ³⁵ The LORD defeated Benjamin before Israel, and on that day the Israelites struck down 25,100 Benjamites, all armed with swords. ³⁶ Then the Benjamites saw that they were beaten.

Now the men of Israel had given way before Benjamin, because they relied on the ambush they had set near Gibeah. ³⁷ Those who had been in ambush made a sudden dash into Gibeah, spread out and put the whole city to the

---

[a] 33 Some Septuagint manuscripts and Vulgate; the meaning of the Hebrew for this word is uncertain.   [b] 33 Hebrew Geba, a variant of Gibeah

sword. **38**The Israelites had arranged with the ambush that they should send up a great cloud of smoke from the city, **39**and then the Israelites would counterattack.

The Benjamites had begun to inflict casualties on the Israelites (about thirty), and they said, "We are defeating them as in the first battle." **40**But when the column of smoke began to rise from the city, the Benjamites turned and saw the whole city going up in smoke. **41**Then the Israelites counterattacked, and the Benjamites were terrified, because they realized that disaster had come on them. **42**So they fled before the Israelites in the direction of the wilderness, but they could not escape the battle. And the Israelites who came out of the towns cut them down there. **43**They surrounded the Benjamites, chased them and easily*a* overran them in the vicinity of Gibeah on the east. **44**Eighteen thousand Benjamites fell, all of them valiant fighters. **45**As they turned and fled toward the wilderness to the rock of Rimmon, the Israelites cut down five thousand men along the roads. They kept pressing after the Benjamites as far as Gidom and struck down two thousand more.

46On that day twenty-five thousand Benjamite swordsmen fell, all of them valiant fighters. **47**But six hundred of them turned and fled into the wilderness to the rock of Rimmon, where they stayed four months. **48**The men of Israel went back to Benjamin and put all the towns to the sword, including the animals and everything else they found. All the towns they came across they set on fire.

Wives for the Benjamites

21 The men of Israel had taken an oath at Mizpah: "Not one of us will give his daughter in marriage to a Benjamite."

2The people went to Bethel,*b* where they sat before God until evening, raising their voices and weeping bitterly. **3**"Lord, God of Israel," they cried, "why has this happened to Israel? Why should one tribe be missing from Israel today?"

4Early the next day the people built an altar and presented burnt offerings and fellowship offerings.

5Then the Israelites asked, "Who from all the tribes of Israel has failed to assemble before the Lord?" For they had taken a solemn oath that anyone who failed to assemble before the Lord at Mizpah was to be put to death.

6Now the Israelites grieved for the tribe of Benjamin, their fellow Israelites. "Today one tribe is cut off from Israel," they said. **7**"How can we provide wives for those who are left, since we have taken

---

a 43 The meaning of the Hebrew for this word is uncertain.   *b* 2 Or *to the house of God* an oath by the LORD not to give them any of our daughters in marriage?" **8**Then they asked, "Which one of the tribes of Israel failed to assemble before the LORD at Mizpah?" They discovered that no one from Jabesh Gilead had come to the camp for the assembly. **9**For when they counted the people, they found that none of the people of Jabesh Gilead were there.

10So the assembly sent twelve thousand fighting men with instructions to go to Jabesh Gilead and put to the sword those living there, including the women and children. **11**"This is what you are to do," they said. "Kill every male and every woman who is not a virgin." **12**They found among the people living in Jabesh Gilead four hundred young women who had never slept with a man, and they took them to the camp at Shiloh in Canaan.

13Then the whole assembly sent an offer of peace to the Benjamites at the rock of Rimmon. **14**So the Benjamites returned at that time and were given the women of Jabesh Gilead who had been spared. But there were not enough for all of them.

15The people grieved for Benjamin, because the LORD had made a gap in the tribes of Israel. **16**And the elders of the assembly said, "With the women of Benjamin destroyed, how shall we provide wives for the men who are left? **17**The Benjamite survivors must have heirs," they said, "so that a tribe of Israel will not be wiped out. **18**We can't give them our daughters as wives, since we Israelites have taken this oath: 'Cursed be anyone who gives a wife to a Benjamite.' **19**But look, there is the annual festival of the LORD in Shiloh, which lies north of Bethel, east of the road that goes from Bethel to Shechem, and south of Lebonah."

20So they instructed the Benjamites, saying, "Go and hide in the vineyards **21**and watch. When the young women of Shiloh come out to join in the dancing, rush from the vineyards and each of you seize one of them to be your wife. Then return to the land of Benjamin. **22**When their fathers or brothers complain to us, we will say to them, 'Do us the favor of helping them, because we did not get wives for them during the war. You will not be guilty of breaking your oath because you did not give your daughters to them.'"

23So that is what the Benjamites did. While the young women were dancing, each man caught one and carried her off to be his wife. Then they returned to their inheritance and rebuilt the towns and settled in them.

24At that time the Israelites left that place and went home to their tribes and clans, each to his own inheritance.

25In those days Israel had no king; everyone did as they saw fit.

Ruth

Introduction:

The book of Ruth is named after the leading character whose story is told here. It may have been written during the reign of David, whose ancestry is traced in the final verses to his great-grandfather Boaz, whose wife was Ruth.

The story begins with an Israelite couple who moved to Moab during a famine in Canaan. The husband and his two sons died, leaving the mother (Naomi) alone with her two daughters-in-law (Orpah and Ruth). Naomi decided to move back to Israel and Ruth insisted on going back with her. Back in Israel, they looked to their relative Boaz for help and Ruth finally married Boaz. The royal family of King David and the Messiah, Jesus Christ, came from their family.

This book teaches us about love and devotion. It also teaches us of God's concern for our everyday needs and that he is working out his plan for salvation.

Outline of contents:

Naomi's departure from Israel and her return (1:1–22)
Ruth's welcome (2:1–3:18)
Boaz and Ruth (4:1–22)

Naomi Loses Her Husband and Sons

1 In the days when the judges ruled,[a] there was a famine in the land. So a man from Bethlehem in Judah, together with his wife and two sons, went to live for a while in the country of Moab. ²The man's name was Elimelek, his wife's name was Naomi, and the names of his two sons were Mahlon and Kilion. They were Ephrathites from Bethlehem, Judah. And they went to Moab and lived there.

³Now Elimelek, Naomi's husband, died, and she was left with her two sons. ⁴They married Moabite women, one named Orpah and the other Ruth. After they had lived there about ten years, ⁵both Mahlon and Kilion also died, and Naomi was left without her two sons and her husband.

Naomi and Ruth Return to Bethlehem

⁶When Naomi heard in Moab that the LORD had come to the aid of his people by providing food for them, she and her daughters-in-law prepared to return home from there. ⁷With her two daughters-in-law she left the place where she had been living and set out on the road that would take them back to the land of Judah.

⁸Then Naomi said to her two daughters-in-law, "Go back, each of you, to your mother's home. May the LORD show you kindness, as you have shown kindness to your dead husbands and to me. ⁹May the LORD grant that each of you will find rest in the home of another husband."

Then she kissed them goodbye and they wept aloud ¹⁰and said to her, "We will go back with you to your people."

¹¹But Naomi said, "Return home, my daughters. Why would you come with me? Am I going to have any more sons, who could become your husbands? ¹²Return home, my daughters; I am too old to have another husband. Even if I thought there was still hope for me — even if I had a husband tonight and then gave birth to sons — ¹³would you wait until they grew up? Would you remain unmarried for them? No, my daughters. It is more bitter for me than for you, because the LORD's hand has turned against me!"

¹⁴At this they wept aloud again. Then Orpah kissed her mother-in-law goodbye, but Ruth clung to her.

¹⁵"Look," said Naomi, "your sister-in-law is going back to her people and her gods. Go back with her."

¹⁶But Ruth replied, "Don't urge me to leave you or to turn back from you. Where you go I will go, and where you stay I will stay. Your people will be my people and your God my God. ¹⁷Where you die I will die, and there I will be buried. May the LORD deal with me, be it ever so severely, if even death separates you and me." ¹⁸When Naomi realized that Ruth was determined to go with her, she stopped urging her.

¹⁹So the two women went on until they came to Bethlehem. When they arrived in Bethlehem, the whole town was stirred because of them, and the women exclaimed, "Can this be Naomi?"

²⁰"Don't call me Naomi,ᵃ" she told them. "Call me Mara,ᵇ because the Almightyᶜ has made my life very bitter. ²¹I went away full, but the LORD has brought me back empty. Why call me Naomi? The LORD has afflictedᵈ me; the Almighty has brought misfortune upon me."

ᵃ 20 Naomi means pleasant.   ᵇ 20 Mara means bitter.   ᶜ 20 Hebrew Shaddai; also in verse 21   ᵈ 21 Or has testified against

²²So Naomi returned from Moab accompanied by Ruth the Moabite, her daughter-in-law, arriving in Bethlehem as the barley harvest was beginning.

Ruth Meets Boaz in the Grain Field

2 Now Naomi had a relative on her husband's side, a man of standing from the clan of Elimelek, whose name was Boaz.

²And Ruth the Moabite said to Naomi, "Let me go to the fields and pick up the leftover grain behind anyone in whose eyes I find favor."

Naomi said to her, "Go ahead, my daughter." ³So she went out, entered a field and began to glean behind the harvesters. As it turned out, she was working in a field belonging to Boaz, who was from the clan of Elimelek.

⁴Just then Boaz arrived from Bethlehem and greeted the harvesters, "The LORD be with you!"

"The LORD bless you!" they answered.

⁵Boaz asked the overseer of his harvesters, "Who does that young woman belong to?"

⁶The overseer replied, "She is the Moabite who came back from Moab with Naomi. ⁷She said, 'Please let me glean and gather among the sheaves behind the harvesters.' She came into the field and has remained here from morning till now, except for a short rest in the shelter."

⁸So Boaz said to Ruth, "My daughter, listen to me. Don't go and glean in another field and don't go away from here. Stay here with the women who work for me. ⁹Watch the field where the men are harvesting, and follow along after the women. I have told the men not to lay a hand on you. And whenever you are thirsty, go and get a drink from the water jars the men have filled."

¹⁰At this, she bowed down with her face to the ground. She asked him, "Why have I found such favor in your eyes that you notice me — a foreigner?"

¹¹Boaz replied, "I've been told all about what you have done for your mother-in-law since the death of your husband — how you left your father and mother and your homeland and came to live with a people you did not know before. ¹²May the LORD repay you for what you have done. May you be richly rewarded by the LORD, the God of Israel, under whose wings you have come to take refuge."

¹³"May I continue to find favor in your eyes, my lord," she said. "You have put me at ease by speaking kindly to your servant — though I do not have the standing of one of your servants."

¹⁴At mealtime Boaz said to her, "Come over here. Have some bread and dip it in the wine vinegar."

When she sat down with the harvesters, he offered her some roasted grain. She ate all she wanted and had some left over. [15] As she got up to glean, Boaz gave orders to his men, "Let her gather among the sheaves and don't reprimand her. [16] Even pull out some stalks for her from the bundles and leave them for her to pick up, and don't rebuke her."

[17] So Ruth gleaned in the field until evening. Then she threshed the barley she had gathered, and it amounted to about an ephah.[a] [18] She carried it back to town, and her mother-in-law saw how much she had gathered. Ruth also brought out and gave her what she had left over after she had eaten enough.

[19] Her mother-in-law asked her, "Where did you glean today? Where did you work? Blessed be the man who took notice of you!"

Then Ruth told her mother-in-law about the one at whose place she had been working. "The name of the man I worked with today is Boaz," she said.

[20] "The LORD bless him!" Naomi said to her daughter-in-law. "He has not stopped showing his kindness to the living and the dead." She added, "That man is our close relative; he is one of our guardian-redeemers.[b]"

[21] Then Ruth the Moabite said, "He even said to me, 'Stay with my workers until they finish harvesting all my grain.'"

[22] Naomi said to Ruth her daughter-in-law, "It will be good for you, my daughter, to go with the women who work for him, because in someone else's field you might be harmed."

[23] So Ruth stayed close to the women of Boaz to glean until the barley and wheat harvests were finished. And she lived with her mother-in-law.

Ruth and Boaz at the Threshing Floor

3 One day Ruth's mother-in-law Naomi said to her, "My daughter, I must find a home[c] for you, where you will be well provided for. [2] Now Boaz, with whose women you have worked, is a relative of ours. Tonight he will be winnowing barley on the threshing floor. [3] Wash, put on perfume, and get dressed in your best clothes. Then go down to the threshing floor, but don't let him know you are there until he has finished eating and drinking. [4] When he lies down, note the place where he is lying. Then go and uncover his feet and lie down. He will tell you what to do."

[5] "I will do whatever you say," Ruth answered. [6] So she went down to the threshing floor and

---

[a] 17 That is, probably about 30 pounds or about 13 kilograms   [b] 20 The Hebrew word for *guardian-redeemer* is a legal term for one who has the obligation to redeem a relative in serious difficulty (see Lev. 25:25-55).   [c] 1 Hebrew *find rest* (see 1:9)

did everything her mother-in-law told her to do.

⁷When Boaz had finished eating and drinking and was in good spirits, he went over to lie down at the far end of the grain pile. Ruth approached quietly, uncovered his feet and lay down. ⁸In the middle of the night something startled the man; he turned — and there was a woman lying at his feet!

⁹"Who are you?" he asked.

"I am your servant Ruth," she said. "Spread the corner of your garment over me, since you are a guardian-redeemer*a* of our family."

¹⁰"The LORD bless you, my daughter," he replied. "This kindness is greater than that which you showed earlier: You have not run after the younger men, whether rich or poor. ¹¹And now, my daughter, don't be afraid. I will do for you all you ask. All the people of my town know that you are a woman of noble character. ¹²Although it is true that I am a guardian-redeemer of our family, there is another who is more closely related than I. ¹³Stay here for the night, and in the morning if he wants to do his duty as your guardian-redeemer, good; let him redeem you. But if he is not willing, as surely as the LORD lives I will do it. Lie here until morning."

¹⁴So she lay at his feet until morning, but got up before anyone could be recognized; and he said, "No one must know that a woman came to the threshing floor."

¹⁵He also said, "Bring me the shawl you are wearing and hold it out." When she did so, he poured into it six measures of barley and placed the bundle on her. Then he*b* went back to town.

¹⁶When Ruth came to her mother-in-law, Naomi asked, "How did it go, my daughter?"

Then she told her everything Boaz had done for her ¹⁷and added, "He gave me these six measures of barley, saying, 'Don't go back to your mother-in-law empty-handed.'"

¹⁸Then Naomi said, "Wait, my daughter, until you find out what happens. For the man will not rest until the matter is settled today."

Boaz Marries Ruth

4 Meanwhile Boaz went up to the town gate and sat down there just as the guardian-redeemer*c* he had mentioned came along. Boaz said, "Come over

---

a 9 The Hebrew word for *guardian-redeemer* is a legal term for one who has the obligation to redeem a relative in serious difficulty (see Lev. 25:25-55); also in verses 12 and 13.   *b* 15 Most Hebrew manuscripts; many Hebrew manuscripts, Vulgate and Syriac *she*   *c* 1 The Hebrew word for *guardian-redeemer* is a legal term for one who has the obligation to redeem a relative in serious difficulty (see Lev. 25:25-55); also in verses 3, 6, 8 and 14.

here, my friend, and sit down." So he went over and sat down.

²Boaz took ten of the elders of the town and said, "Sit here," and they did so. ³Then he said to the guardian-redeemer, "Naomi, who has come back from Moab, is selling the piece of land that belonged to our relative Elimelek. ⁴I thought I should bring the matter to your attention and suggest that you buy it in the presence of these seated here and in the presence of the elders of my people. If you will redeem it, do so. But if you*ᵃ* will not, tell me, so I will know. For no one has the right to do it except you, and I am next in line."

"I will redeem it," he said.

⁵Then Boaz said, "On the day you buy the land from Naomi, you also acquire Ruth the Moabite, theᵇ dead man's widow, in order to maintain the name of the dead with his property."

⁶At this, the guardian-redeemer said, "Then I cannot redeem it because I might endanger my own estate. You redeem it yourself. I cannot do it."

⁷(Now in earlier times in Israel, for the redemption and transfer of property to become final, one party took off his sandal and gave it to the other. This was the method of legalizing transactions in Israel.)

⁸So the guardian-redeemer said to Boaz, "Buy it yourself." And he removed his sandal.

⁹Then Boaz announced to the elders and all the people, "Today you are witnesses that I have bought from Naomi all the property of Elimelek, Kilion and Mahlon. ¹⁰I have also acquired Ruth the Moabite, Mahlon's widow, as my wife, in order to maintain the name of the dead with his property, so that his name will not disappear from among his family or from his hometown. Today you are witnesses!"

¹¹Then the elders and all the people at the gate said, "We are witnesses. May the Lᴏʀᴅ make the woman who is coming into your home like Rachel and Leah, who together built up the family of Israel. May you have standing in Ephrathah and be famous in Bethlehem. ¹²Through the offspring the Lᴏʀᴅ gives you by this young woman, may your family be like that of Perez, whom Tamar bore to Judah."

Naomi Gains a Son

¹³So Boaz took Ruth and she became his wife. When he made love to her, the Lᴏʀᴅ enabled her to conceive, and she gave birth to a son. ¹⁴The women said to Naomi: "Praise be to the Lᴏʀᴅ, who this day has not left you without a guardian-redeemer. May he become famous throughout Israel! ¹⁵He will renew your life and sustain you in your old age. For

---

ᵃ 4 Many Hebrew manuscripts, Septuagint, Vulgate and Syriac; most Hebrew manuscripts *he*   ᵇ 5 Vulgate and Syriac; Hebrew (see also Septuagint) *Naomi and from Ruth the Moabite, you acquire the* your daughter-in-law, who loves you and who is better to you than seven sons, has given him birth."

[16]Then Naomi took the child in her arms and cared for him. [17]The women living there said, "Naomi has a son!" And they named him Obed. He was the father of Jesse, the father of David.

The Genealogy of David

[18]This, then, is the family line of Perez:

Perez was the father of Hezron,
[19]Hezron the father of Ram,
Ram the father of Amminadab,
[20]Amminadab the father of Nahshon,
Nahshon the father of Salmon,[a]
[21]Salmon the father of Boaz,
Boaz the father of Obed,
[22]Obed the father of Jesse,
and Jesse the father of David.

---

[a] 20 A few Hebrew manuscripts, some Septuagint manuscripts and Vulgate (see also verse 21 and Septuagint of 1 Chron. 2:11); most Hebrew manuscripts Salma

1 Samuel

Introduction:

The book of 1 Samuel records the lives of Samuel and Saul, and much of the life of David. First Samuel begins with the birth of Samuel and his training in the house of the LORD. It describes how he led Israel as prophet, priest and judge.

When the people of Israel demanded a king, Samuel, by God's leading, anointed Saul to be the first king of Israel. But Saul was disobedient to God and God rejected him as king. Then Samuel secretly anointed David to take Saul's place. The struggles between Saul and David make up the rest of this book. Although the stories of these people's disobedience are included, there is a stronger emphasis on their goodness and obedience to God.

Samuel, as prophet, priest and judge, had a great deal of influence throughout this time period. During this part of Israel's history the nation changed from the leadership of judges to the leadership of a king, which is what the people wanted. The Israelites were now ruled like their neighboring nations.

Outline of contents:

Eli as priest and judge (1:1–4:22)
Samuel as leader of Israel (5:1–8:22)
Saul the first king of Israel (9:1–15:35)
David and Saul (16:1–30:31)
Death of Saul (31:1–13)

The Birth of Samuel

1 There was a certain man from Ramathaim, a Zuphite[a] from the hill country of Ephraim, whose name was Elkanah son of Jeroham, the son of Elihu, the son of Tohu, the son of Zuph, an Ephraimite. ²He had two wives; one was called Hannah and the other Peninnah. Peninnah had children, but Hannah had none.

³Year after year this man went up from his town to worship and sacrifice to the LORD Almighty at Shiloh, where Hophni and Phinehas, the two sons of Eli, were priests of the LORD. ⁴Whenever the day came for Elkanah to sacrifice, he would give portions of

---

a 1 See Septuagint and 1 Chron. 6:26-27,33-35; or *from Ramathaim Zuphim.*

the meat to his wife Peninnah and to all her sons and daughters. ⁵But to Hannah he gave a double portion because he loved her, and the LORD had closed her womb. ⁶Because the LORD had closed Hannah's womb, her rival kept provoking her in order to irritate her. ⁷This went on year after year. Whenever Hannah went up to the house of the LORD, her rival provoked her till she wept and would not eat. ⁸Her husband Elkanah would say to her, "Hannah, why are you weeping? Why don't you eat? Why are you downhearted? Don't I mean more to you than ten sons?"

⁹Once when they had finished eating and drinking in Shiloh, Hannah stood up. Now Eli the priest was sitting on his chair by the doorpost of the LORD's house. ¹⁰In her deep anguish Hannah prayed to the LORD, weeping bitterly. ¹¹And she made a vow, saying, "LORD Almighty, if you will only look on your servant's misery and remember me, and not forget your servant but give her a son, then I will give him to the LORD for all the days of his life, and no razor will ever be used on his head."

¹²As she kept on praying to the LORD, Eli observed her mouth. ¹³Hannah was praying in her heart, and her lips were moving but her voice was not heard. Eli thought she was drunk ¹⁴and said to her, "How long are you going to stay drunk? Put away your wine."

¹⁵"Not so, my lord," Hannah replied, "I am a woman who is deeply troubled. I have not been drinking wine or beer; I was pouring out my soul to the LORD. ¹⁶Do not take your servant for a wicked woman; I have been praying here out of my great anguish and grief."

¹⁷Eli answered, "Go in peace, and may the God of Israel grant you what you have asked of him."

¹⁸She said, "May your servant find favor in your eyes." Then she went her way and ate something, and her face was no longer downcast.

¹⁹Early the next morning they arose and worshiped before the LORD and then went back to their home at Ramah. Elkanah made love to his wife Hannah, and the LORD remembered her. ²⁰So in the course of time Hannah became pregnant and gave birth to a son. She named him Samuel,ᵃ saying, "Because I asked the LORD for him."

Hannah Dedicates Samuel

²¹When her husband Elkanah went up with all his family to offer the annual sacrifice to the LORD and to fulfill his vow, ²²Hannah did not go. She said to her husband, "After the boy is weaned, I will take him and pre-

---

ᵃ 20 Samuel sounds like the Hebrew for heard by God.

sent him before the LORD, and he will live there always."[a]

23 "Do what seems best to you," her husband Elkanah told her. "Stay here until you have weaned him; only may the LORD make good his[b] word." So the woman stayed at home and nursed her son until she had weaned him.

24 After he was weaned, she took the boy with her, young as he was, along with a three-year-old bull,[c] an ephah[d] of flour and a skin of wine, and brought him to the house of the LORD at Shiloh. 25 When the bull had been sacrificed, they brought the boy to Eli, 26 and she said to him, "Pardon me, my lord. As surely as you live, I am the woman who stood here beside you praying to the LORD. 27 I prayed for this child, and the LORD has granted me what I asked of him. 28 So now I give him to the LORD. For his whole life he will be given over to the LORD." And he worshiped the LORD there.

Hannah's Prayer

2 Then Hannah prayed and said:

"My heart rejoices in the
LORD;
in the LORD my horn[e] is
lifted high.

My mouth boasts over my
enemies,
for I delight in your
deliverance.

2 "There is no one holy like the
LORD;
there is no one besides you;
there is no Rock like our God.

3 "Do not keep talking so
proudly
or let your mouth speak such
arrogance,
for the LORD is a God who
knows,
and by him deeds are
weighed.

4 "The bows of the warriors are
broken,
but those who stumbled are
armed with strength.
5 Those who were full hire
themselves out for food,
but those who were hungry
are hungry no more.
She who was barren has borne
seven children,
but she who has had many
sons pines away.

6 "The LORD brings death and
makes alive;
he brings down to the grave
and raises up.
7 The LORD sends poverty and
wealth;
he humbles and he exalts.

---

[a] 22 Masoretic Text; Dead Sea Scrolls *always. I have dedicated him as a Nazirite — all the days of his life."* [b] 23 Masoretic Text; Dead Sea Scrolls, Septuagint and Syriac *your* [c] 24 Dead Sea Scrolls, Septuagint and Syriac; Masoretic Text *with three bulls* [d] 24 That is, probably about 36 pounds or about 16 kilograms [e] 1 *Horn* here symbolizes strength; also in verse 10.

⁸He raises the poor from the
　　dust
　　and lifts the needy from the
　　　ash heap;
he seats them with princes
　　and has them inherit a
　　　throne of honor.

"For the foundations of the
　　earth are the LORD's;
　on them he has set the
　　　world.
⁹He will guard the feet of his
　　faithful servants,
　but the wicked will be
　　silenced in the place
　　　of darkness.

"It is not by strength that one
　　prevails;
¹⁰ 　those who oppose the LORD
　　　will be broken.
The Most High will thunder
　　from heaven;
　the LORD will judge the ends
　　　of the earth.

"He will give strength to his
　　king
　and exalt the horn of his
　　anointed."

¹¹Then Elkanah went home to
Ramah, but the boy ministered
before the LORD under Eli the
priest.

Eli's Wicked Sons

¹²Eli's sons were scoundrels;
they had no regard for the LORD.
¹³Now it was the practice of the
priests that, whenever any of the
people offered a sacrifice, the
priest's servant would come with
a three-pronged fork in his hand
while the meat was being boiled
¹⁴and would plunge the fork into
the pan or kettle or caldron or pot.
Whatever the fork brought up the
priest would take for himself. This
is how they treated all the Israelites who came to Shiloh. ¹⁵But
even before the fat was burned, the
priest's servant would come and
say to the person who was sacrificing, "Give the priest some meat to
roast; he won't accept boiled meat
from you, but only raw."

¹⁶If the person said to him, "Let
the fat be burned first, and then
take whatever you want," the servant would answer, "No, hand it
over now; if you don't, I'll take it
by force."

¹⁷This sin of the young men was
very great in the LORD's sight, for
theyᵃ were treating the LORD's offering with contempt.

¹⁸But Samuel was ministering
before the LORD—a boy wearing a linen ephod. ¹⁹Each year
his mother made him a little
robe and took it to him when she
went up with her husband to offer
the annual sacrifice. ²⁰Eli would
bless Elkanah and his wife, saying, "May the LORD give you children by this woman to take the
place of the one she prayed for
and gave toᵇ the LORD." Then

ᵃ 17 Dead Sea Scrolls and Septuagint; Masoretic Text *people*　　ᵇ 20 Dead Sea
Scrolls; Masoretic Text *and asked from*

they would go home. ²¹And the LORD was gracious to Hannah; she gave birth to three sons and two daughters. Meanwhile, the boy Samuel grew up in the presence of the LORD.

²²Now Eli, who was very old, heard about everything his sons were doing to all Israel and how they slept with the women who served at the entrance to the tent of meeting. ²³So he said to them, "Why do you do such things? I hear from all the people about these wicked deeds of yours. ²⁴No, my sons; the report I hear spreading among the LORD's people is not good. ²⁵If one person sins against another, God*ᵃ* may mediate for the offender; but if anyone sins against the LORD, who will intercede for them?" His sons, however, did not listen to their father's rebuke, for it was the LORD's will to put them to death.

²⁶And the boy Samuel continued to grow in stature and in favor with the LORD and with people.

Prophecy Against the House of Eli

²⁷Now a man of God came to Eli and said to him, "This is what the LORD says: 'Did I not clearly reveal myself to your ancestor's family when they were in Egypt under Pharaoh? ²⁸I chose your ancestor out of all the tribes of Israel to be my priest, to go up to my altar, to burn incense, and to wear an ephod in my presence. I also gave your ancestor's family all the food offerings presented by the Israelites. ²⁹Why do you*ᵇ* scorn my sacrifice and offering that I prescribed for my dwelling? Why do you honor your sons more than me by fattening yourselves on the choice parts of every offering made by my people Israel?'

³⁰"Therefore the LORD, the God of Israel, declares: 'I promised that members of your family would minister before me forever.' But now the LORD declares: 'Far be it from me! Those who honor me I will honor, but those who despise me will be disdained. ³¹The time is coming when I will cut short your strength and the strength of your priestly house, so that no one in it will reach old age, ³²and you will see distress in my dwelling. Although good will be done to Israel, no one in your family line will ever reach old age. ³³Every one of you that I do not cut off from serving at my altar I will spare only to destroy your sight and sap your strength, and all your descendants will die in the prime of life.

³⁴"'And what happens to your two sons, Hophni and Phinehas, will be a sign to you — they will both die on the same day. ³⁵I will raise up for myself a faithful priest, who will do according to what is in my heart and mind. I

ᵃ 25 Or *the judges*   *ᵇ* 29 The Hebrew is plural.

will firmly establish his priestly house, and they will minister before my anointed one always. ³⁶Then everyone left in your family line will come and bow down before him for a piece of silver and a loaf of bread and plead, "Appoint me to some priestly office so I can have food to eat." ' "

The LORD Calls Samuel

3 The boy Samuel ministered before the LORD under Eli. In those days the word of the LORD was rare; there were not many visions.

²One night Eli, whose eyes were becoming so weak that he could barely see, was lying down in his usual place. ³The lamp of God had not yet gone out, and Samuel was lying down in the house of the LORD, where the ark of God was. ⁴Then the LORD called Samuel.

Samuel answered, "Here I am." ⁵And he ran to Eli and said, "Here I am; you called me."

But Eli said, "I did not call; go back and lie down." So he went and lay down.

⁶Again the LORD called, "Samuel!" And Samuel got up and went to Eli and said, "Here I am; you called me."

"My son," Eli said, "I did not call; go back and lie down."

⁷Now Samuel did not yet know the LORD: The word of the LORD had not yet been revealed to him.

⁸A third time the LORD called, "Samuel!" And Samuel got up and went to Eli and said, "Here I am; you called me."

Then Eli realized that the LORD was calling the boy. ⁹So Eli told Samuel, "Go and lie down, and if he calls you, say, 'Speak, LORD, for your servant is listening.' " So Samuel went and lay down in his place.

¹⁰The LORD came and stood there, calling as at the other times, "Samuel! Samuel!"

Then Samuel said, "Speak, for your servant is listening."

¹¹And the LORD said to Samuel: "See, I am about to do something in Israel that will make the ears of everyone who hears about it tingle. ¹²At that time I will carry out against Eli everything I spoke against his family — from beginning to end. ¹³For I told him that I would judge his family forever because of the sin he knew about; his sons blasphemed God,^a and he failed to restrain them. ¹⁴Therefore I swore to the house of Eli, 'The guilt of Eli's house will never be atoned for by sacrifice or offering.' "

¹⁵Samuel lay down until morning and then opened the doors of the house of the LORD. He was afraid to tell Eli the vision, ¹⁶but Eli called him and said, "Samuel, my son."

Samuel answered, "Here I am."

¹⁷"What was it he said to you?"

---

^a 13 An ancient Hebrew scribal tradition (see also Septuagint); Masoretic Text *sons made themselves contemptible*

Eli asked. "Do not hide it from me. May God deal with you, be it ever so severely, if you hide from me anything he told you." ¹⁸So Samuel told him everything, hiding nothing from him. Then Eli said, "He is the LORD; let him do what is good in his eyes."

¹⁹The LORD was with Samuel as he grew up, and he let none of Samuel's words fall to the ground. ²⁰And all Israel from Dan to Beersheba recognized that Samuel was attested as a prophet of the LORD. ²¹The LORD continued to appear at Shiloh, and there he revealed himself to Samuel through his word.

4 And Samuel's word came to all Israel.

The Philistines Capture the Ark

Now the Israelites went out to fight against the Philistines. The Israelites camped at Ebenezer, and the Philistines at Aphek. ²The Philistines deployed their forces to meet Israel, and as the battle spread, Israel was defeated by the Philistines, who killed about four thousand of them on the battlefield. ³When the soldiers returned to camp, the elders of Israel asked, "Why did the LORD bring defeat on us today before the Philistines? Let us bring the ark of the LORD's covenant from Shiloh, so that he may go with us and save us from the hand of our enemies."

⁴So the people sent men to Shiloh, and they brought back the ark of the covenant of the LORD Almighty, who is enthroned between the cherubim. And Eli's two sons, Hophni and Phinehas, were there with the ark of the covenant of God.

⁵When the ark of the LORD's covenant came into the camp, all Israel raised such a great shout that the ground shook. ⁶Hearing the uproar, the Philistines asked, "What's all this shouting in the Hebrew camp?"

When they learned that the ark of the LORD had come into the camp, ⁷the Philistines were afraid. "A god has^a come into the camp," they said. "Oh no! Nothing like this has happened before. ⁸We're doomed! Who will deliver us from the hand of these mighty gods? They are the gods who struck the Egyptians with all kinds of plagues in the wilderness. ⁹Be strong, Philistines! Be men, or you will be subject to the Hebrews, as they have been to you. Be men, and fight!"

¹⁰So the Philistines fought, and the Israelites were defeated and every man fled to his tent. The slaughter was very great; Israel lost thirty thousand foot soldiers. ¹¹The ark of God was captured, and Eli's two sons, Hophni and Phinehas, died.

Death of Eli

¹²That same day a Benjamite ran from the battle line and went

---

^a 7 Or "Gods have (see Septuagint)

to Shiloh with his clothes torn and dust on his head. ¹³When he arrived, there was Eli sitting on his chair by the side of the road, watching, because his heart feared for the ark of God. When the man entered the town and told what had happened, the whole town sent up a cry.

¹⁴Eli heard the outcry and asked, "What is the meaning of this uproar?"

The man hurried over to Eli, ¹⁵who was ninety-eight years old and whose eyes had failed so that he could not see. ¹⁶He told Eli, "I have just come from the battle line; I fled from it this very day."

Eli asked, "What happened, my son?"

¹⁷The man who brought the news replied, "Israel fled before the Philistines, and the army has suffered heavy losses. Also your two sons, Hophni and Phinehas, are dead, and the ark of God has been captured."

¹⁸When he mentioned the ark of God, Eli fell backward off his chair by the side of the gate. His neck was broken and he died, for he was an old man, and he was heavy. He had led*ᵃ* Israel forty years.

¹⁹His daughter-in-law, the wife of Phinehas, was pregnant and near the time of delivery. When she heard the news that the ark of God had been captured and that her father-in-law and her husband were dead, she went into labor and gave birth, but was overcome by her labor pains. ²⁰As she was dying, the women attending her said, "Don't despair; you have given birth to a son." But she did not respond or pay any attention.

²¹She named the boy Ichabod,*ᵇ* saying, "The Glory has departed from Israel" — because of the capture of the ark of God and the deaths of her father-in-law and her husband. ²²She said, "The Glory has departed from Israel, for the ark of God has been captured."

The Ark in Ashdod and Ekron

5 After the Philistines had captured the ark of God, they took it from Ebenezer to Ashdod. ²Then they carried the ark into Dagon's temple and set it beside Dagon. ³When the people of Ashdod rose early the next day, there was Dagon, fallen on his face on the ground before the ark of the LORD! They took Dagon and put him back in his place. ⁴But the following morning when they rose, there was Dagon, fallen on his face on the ground before the ark of the LORD! His head and hands had been broken off and were lying on the threshold; only his body remained. ⁵That is why to this day neither the priests of Dagon nor any others who enter Dagon's temple at Ashdod step on the threshold.

ᵃ 18 Traditionally *judged*   ᵇ 21 *Ichabod* means *no glory*.

[6] The Lord's hand was heavy on the people of Ashdod and its vicinity; he brought devastation on them and afflicted them with tumors.[a] [7] When the people of Ashdod saw what was happening, they said, "The ark of the god of Israel must not stay here with us, because his hand is heavy on us and on Dagon our god." [8] So they called together all the rulers of the Philistines and asked them, "What shall we do with the ark of the god of Israel?"

They answered, "Have the ark of the god of Israel moved to Gath." So they moved the ark of the God of Israel.

[9] But after they had moved it, the Lord's hand was against that city, throwing it into a great panic. He afflicted the people of the city, both young and old, with an outbreak of tumors.[b] [10] So they sent the ark of God to Ekron.

As the ark of God was entering Ekron, the people of Ekron cried out, "They have brought the ark of the god of Israel around to us to kill us and our people." [11] So they called together all the rulers of the Philistines and said, "Send the ark of the god of Israel away; let it go back to its own place, or it[c] will kill us and our people." For death had filled the city with panic; God's hand was very heavy on it. [12] Those who did not die were afflicted with tumors, and the outcry of the city went up to heaven.

The Ark Returned to Israel

6 When the ark of the Lord had been in Philistine territory seven months, [2] the Philistines called for the priests and the diviners and said, "What shall we do with the ark of the Lord? Tell us how we should send it back to its place."

[3] They answered, "If you return the ark of the god of Israel, do not send it back to him without a gift; by all means send a guilt offering to him. Then you will be healed, and you will know why his hand has not been lifted from you."

[4] The Philistines asked, "What guilt offering should we send to him?"

They replied, "Five gold tumors and five gold rats, according to the number of the Philistine rulers, because the same plague has struck both you and your rulers. [5] Make models of the tumors and of the rats that are destroying the country, and give glory to Israel's god. Perhaps he will lift his hand from you and your gods and your land. [6] Why do you harden your hearts as the Egyptians and Pharaoh did? When Israel's god dealt harshly with them, did they not send the Israelites out so they could go on their way?

---

[a] 6 Hebrew; Septuagint and Vulgate *tumors. And rats appeared in their land, and there was death and destruction throughout the city* [b] 9 Or *with tumors in the groin* (see Septuagint) [c] 11 Or *he*

[7] "Now then, get a new cart ready, with two cows that have calved and have never been yoked. Hitch the cows to the cart, but take their calves away and pen them up. [8] Take the ark of the LORD and put it on the cart, and in a chest beside it put the gold objects you are sending back to him as a guilt offering. Send it on its way, [9] but keep watching it. If it goes up to its own territory, toward Beth Shemesh, then the LORD has brought this great disaster on us. But if it does not, then we will know that it was not his hand that struck us but that it happened to us by chance."

[10] So they did this. They took two such cows and hitched them to the cart and penned up their calves. [11] They placed the ark of the LORD on the cart and along with it the chest containing the gold rats and the models of the tumors. [12] Then the cows went straight up toward Beth Shemesh, keeping on the road and lowing all the way; they did not turn to the right or to the left. The rulers of the Philistines followed them as far as the border of Beth Shemesh.

[13] Now the people of Beth Shemesh were harvesting their wheat in the valley, and when they looked up and saw the ark, they rejoiced at the sight. [14] The cart came to the field of Joshua of Beth Shemesh, and there it stopped beside a large rock. The people chopped up the wood of the cart and sacrificed the cows as a burnt offering to the LORD. [15] The Levites took down the ark of the LORD, together with the chest containing the gold objects, and placed them on the large rock. On that day the people of Beth Shemesh offered burnt offerings and made sacrifices to the LORD. [16] The five rulers of the Philistines saw all this and then returned that same day to Ekron.

[17] These are the gold tumors the Philistines sent as a guilt offering to the LORD — one each for Ashdod, Gaza, Ashkelon, Gath and Ekron. [18] And the number of the gold rats was according to the number of Philistine towns belonging to the five rulers — the fortified towns with their country villages. The large rock on which the Levites set the ark of the LORD is a witness to this day in the field of Joshua of Beth Shemesh.

[19] But God struck down some of the inhabitants of Beth Shemesh, putting seventy[a] of them to death because they looked into the ark of the LORD. The people mourned because of the heavy blow the LORD had dealt them. [20] And the people of Beth Shemesh asked, "Who can stand in the presence of the LORD, this holy God? To whom will the ark go up from here?"

[21] Then they sent messengers to the people of Kiriath Jearim,

---

[a] 19 A few Hebrew manuscripts; most Hebrew manuscripts and Septuagint 50,070

saying, "The Philistines have returned the ark of the LORD. Come down and take it up to your town." **1** So the men of Kiriath Jearim came and took up the ark of the LORD. They brought it to Abinadab's house on the hill and consecrated Eleazar his son to guard the ark of the LORD. **2** The ark remained at Kiriath Jearim a long time — twenty years in all.

Samuel Subdues the Philistines at Mizpah

Then all the people of Israel turned back to the LORD. **3** So Samuel said to all the Israelites, "If you are returning to the LORD with all your hearts, then rid yourselves of the foreign gods and the Ashtoreths and commit yourselves to the LORD and serve him only, and he will deliver you out of the hand of the Philistines." **4** So the Israelites put away their Baals and Ashtoreths, and served the LORD only.

5 Then Samuel said, "Assemble all Israel at Mizpah, and I will intercede with the LORD for you." **6** When they had assembled at Mizpah, they drew water and poured it out before the LORD. On that day they fasted and there they confessed, "We have sinned against the LORD." Now Samuel was serving as leader*a* of Israel at Mizpah.

7 When the Philistines heard that Israel had assembled at Miz-

pah, the rulers of the Philistines came up to attack them. When the Israelites heard of it, they were afraid because of the Philistines. **8** They said to Samuel, "Do not stop crying out to the LORD our God for us, that he may rescue us from the hand of the Philistines." **9** Then Samuel took a suckling lamb and sacrificed it as a whole burnt offering to the LORD. He cried out to the LORD on Israel's behalf, and the LORD answered him.

10 While Samuel was sacrificing the burnt offering, the Philistines drew near to engage Israel in battle. But that day the LORD thundered with loud thunder against the Philistines and threw them into such a panic that they were routed before the Israelites. **11** The men of Israel rushed out of Mizpah and pursued the Philistines, slaughtering them along the way to a point below Beth Kar.

12 Then Samuel took a stone and set it up between Mizpah and Shen. He named it Ebenezer,*b* saying, "Thus far the LORD has helped us."

13 So the Philistines were subdued and they stopped invading Israel's territory. Throughout Samuel's lifetime, the hand of the LORD was against the Philistines. **14** The towns from Ekron to Gath that the Philistines had captured from Israel were restored to Israel, and Israel delivered the neighboring territory from the hands

---

a 6 Traditionally *judge*; also in verse 15

b 12 *Ebenezer* means *stone of help.*

of the Philistines. And there was peace between Israel and the Amorites.

¹⁵Samuel continued as Israel's leader all the days of his life. ¹⁶From year to year he went on a circuit from Bethel to Gilgal to Mizpah, judging Israel in all those places. ¹⁷But he always went back to Ramah, where his home was, and there he also held court for Israel. And he built an altar there to the LORD.

Israel Asks for a King

8 When Samuel grew old, he appointed his sons as Israel's leaders.ᵃ ²The name of his firstborn was Joel and the name of his second was Abijah, and they served at Beersheba. ³But his sons did not follow his ways. They turned aside after dishonest gain and accepted bribes and perverted justice.

⁴So all the elders of Israel gathered together and came to Samuel at Ramah. ⁵They said to him, "You are old, and your sons do not follow your ways; now appoint a king to leadᵇ us, such as all the other nations have."

⁶But when they said, "Give us a king to lead us," this displeased Samuel; so he prayed to the LORD. ⁷And the LORD told him: "Listen to all that the people are saying to you; it is not you they have rejected, but they have rejected me

as their king. ⁸As they have done from the day I brought them up out of Egypt until this day, forsaking me and serving other gods, so they are doing to you. ⁹Now listen to them; but warn them solemnly and let them know what the king who will reign over them will claim as his rights."

¹⁰Samuel told all the words of the LORD to the people who were asking him for a king. ¹¹He said, "This is what the king who will reign over you will claim as his rights: He will take your sons and make them serve with his chariots and horses, and they will run in front of his chariots. ¹²Some he will assign to be commanders of thousands and commanders of fifties, and others to plow his ground and reap his harvest, and still others to make weapons of war and equipment for his chariots. ¹³He will take your daughters to be perfumers and cooks and bakers. ¹⁴He will take the best of your fields and vineyards and olive groves and give them to his attendants. ¹⁵He will take a tenth of your grain and of your vintage and give it to his officials and attendants. ¹⁶Your male and female servants and the best of your cattleᶜ and donkeys he will take for his own use. ¹⁷He will take a tenth of your flocks, and you yourselves will become his slaves. ¹⁸When that day comes,

---

ᵃ 1 Traditionally *judges*   ᵇ 5 Traditionally *judge*; also in verses 6 and 20
ᶜ 16 Septuagint; Hebrew *young men*

you will cry out for relief from the king you have chosen, but the LORD will not answer you in that day."

¹⁹ But the people refused to listen to Samuel. "No!" they said. "We want a king over us. ²⁰ Then we will be like all the other nations, with a king to lead us and to go out before us and fight our battles."

²¹ When Samuel heard all that the people said, he repeated it before the LORD. ²² The LORD answered, "Listen to them and give them a king."

Then Samuel said to the Israelites, "Everyone go back to your own town."

Samuel Anoints Saul

9 There was a Benjamite, a man of standing, whose name was Kish son of Abiel, the son of Zeror, the son of Bekorath, the son of Aphiah of Benjamin. ² Kish had a son named Saul, as handsome a young man as could be found anywhere in Israel, and he was a head taller than anyone else.

³ Now the donkeys belonging to Saul's father Kish were lost, and Kish said to his son Saul, "Take one of the servants with you and go and look for the donkeys." ⁴ So he passed through the hill country of Ephraim and through the area around Shalisha, but they did not find them. They went on into the district of Shaalim, but

the donkeys were not there. Then he passed through the territory of Benjamin, but they did not find them.

⁵ When they reached the district of Zuph, Saul said to the servant who was with him, "Come, let's go back, or my father will stop thinking about the donkeys and start worrying about us."

⁶ But the servant replied, "Look, in this town there is a man of God; he is highly respected, and everything he says comes true. Let's go there now. Perhaps he will tell us what way to take."

⁷ Saul said to his servant, "If we go, what can we give the man? The food in our sacks is gone. We have no gift to take to the man of God. What do we have?"

⁸ The servant answered him again. "Look," he said, "I have a quarter of a shekel[a] of silver. I will give it to the man of God so that he will tell us what way to take." ⁹ (Formerly in Israel, if someone went to inquire of God, they would say, "Come, let us go to the seer," because the prophet of today used to be called a seer.)

¹⁰ "Good," Saul said to his servant. "Come, let's go." So they set out for the town where the man of God was.

¹¹ As they were going up the hill to the town, they met some young women coming out to draw water, and they asked them, "Is the seer here?"

---

[a] 8 That is, about 1/10 ounce or about 3 grams

¹²"He is," they answered. "He's ahead of you. Hurry now; he has just come to our town today, for the people have a sacrifice at the high place. ¹³As soon as you enter the town, you will find him before he goes up to the high place to eat. The people will not begin eating until he comes, because he must bless the sacrifice; afterward, those who are invited will eat. Go up now; you should find him about this time."

¹⁴They went up to the town, and as they were entering it, there was Samuel, coming toward them on his way up to the high place.

¹⁵Now the day before Saul came, the LORD had revealed this to Samuel: ¹⁶"About this time tomorrow I will send you a man from the land of Benjamin. Anoint him ruler over my people Israel; he will deliver them from the hand of the Philistines. I have looked on my people, for their cry has reached me."

¹⁷When Samuel caught sight of Saul, the LORD said to him, "This is the man I spoke to you about; he will govern my people."

¹⁸Saul approached Samuel in the gateway and asked, "Would you please tell me where the seer's house is?"

¹⁹"I am the seer," Samuel replied. "Go up ahead of me to the high place, for today you are to eat with me, and in the morning I will send you on your way

and will tell you all that is in your heart. ²⁰As for the donkeys you lost three days ago, do not worry about them; they have been found. And to whom is all the desire of Israel turned, if not to you and your whole family line?"

²¹Saul answered, "But am I not a Benjamite, from the smallest tribe of Israel, and is not my clan the least of all the clans of the tribe of Benjamin? Why do you say such a thing to me?"

²²Then Samuel brought Saul and his servant into the hall and seated them at the head of those who were invited — about thirty in number. ²³Samuel said to the cook, "Bring the piece of meat I gave you, the one I told you to lay aside."

²⁴So the cook took up the thigh with what was on it and set it in front of Saul. Samuel said, "Here is what has been kept for you. Eat, because it was set aside for you for this occasion from the time I said, 'I have invited guests.'" And Saul dined with Samuel that day.

²⁵After they came down from the high place to the town, Samuel talked with Saul on the roof of his house. ²⁶They rose about daybreak, and Samuel called to Saul on the roof, "Get ready, and I will send you on your way." When Saul got ready, he and Samuel went outside together. ²⁷As they were going down to the edge of the town, Samuel said to Saul, "Tell the servant to go on ahead

of us" — and the servant did so — "but you stay here for a while, so that I may give you a message from God."

10 Then Samuel took a flask of olive oil and poured it on Saul's head and kissed him, saying, "Has not the LORD anointed you ruler over his inheritance?[a] ²When you leave me today, you will meet two men near Rachel's tomb, at Zelzah on the border of Benjamin. They will say to you, 'The donkeys you set out to look for have been found. And now your father has stopped thinking about them and is worried about you. He is asking, "What shall I do about my son?"'

³"Then you will go on from there until you reach the great tree of Tabor. Three men going up to worship God at Bethel will meet you there. One will be carrying three young goats, another three loaves of bread, and another a skin of wine. ⁴They will greet you and offer you two loaves of bread, which you will accept from them.

⁵"After that you will go to Gibeah of God, where there is a Philistine outpost. As you approach the town, you will meet a procession of prophets coming down from the high place with lyres, timbrels, pipes and harps being played before them, and they will be prophesying. ⁶The Spirit of the LORD will come powerfully upon you, and you will prophesy with them; and you will be changed into a different person. ⁷Once these signs are fulfilled, do whatever your hand finds to do, for God is with you.

⁸"Go down ahead of me to Gilgal. I will surely come down to you to sacrifice burnt offerings and fellowship offerings, but you must wait seven days until I come to you and tell you what you are to do."

Saul Made King

⁹As Saul turned to leave Samuel, God changed Saul's heart, and all these signs were fulfilled that day. ¹⁰When he and his servant arrived at Gibeah, a procession of prophets met him; the Spirit of God came powerfully upon him, and he joined in their prophesying. ¹¹When all those who had formerly known him saw him prophesying with the prophets, they asked each other, "What is this that has happened to the son of Kish? Is Saul also among the prophets?"

¹²A man who lived there answered, "And who is their father?" So it became a saying: "Is Saul also among the prophets?" ¹³After Saul stopped prophesying, he went to the high place.

---

[a] 1 Hebrew; Septuagint and Vulgate *over his people Israel? You will reign over the LORD's people and save them from the power of their enemies round about. And this will be a sign to you that the LORD has anointed you ruler over his inheritance:*

14 Now Saul's uncle asked him and his servant, "Where have you been?"

"Looking for the donkeys," he said. "But when we saw they were not to be found, we went to Samuel."

15 Saul's uncle said, "Tell me what Samuel said to you."

16 Saul replied, "He assured us that the donkeys had been found." But he did not tell his uncle what Samuel had said about the kingship.

17 Samuel summoned the people of Israel to the LORD at Mizpah 18 and said to them, "This is what the LORD, the God of Israel, says: 'I brought Israel up out of Egypt, and I delivered you from the power of Egypt and all the kingdoms that oppressed you.' 19 But you have now rejected your God, who saves you out of all your disasters and calamities. And you have said, 'No, appoint a king over us.' So now present yourselves before the LORD by your tribes and clans."

20 When Samuel had all Israel come forward by tribes, the tribe of Benjamin was taken by lot. 21 Then he brought forward the tribe of Benjamin, clan by clan, and Matri's clan was taken. Finally Saul son of Kish was taken. But when they looked for him, he was not to be found. 22 So they inquired further of the LORD, "Has the man come here yet?"

And the LORD said, "Yes, he has hidden himself among the supplies."

23 They ran and brought him out, and as he stood among the people he was a head taller than any of the others. 24 Samuel said to all the people, "Do you see the man the LORD has chosen? There is no one like him among all the people."

Then the people shouted, "Long live the king!"

25 Samuel explained to the people the rights and duties of kingship. He wrote them down on a scroll and deposited it before the LORD. Then Samuel dismissed the people to go to their own homes.

26 Saul also went to his home in Gibeah, accompanied by valiant men whose hearts God had touched. 27 But some scoundrels said, "How can this fellow save us?" They despised him and brought him no gifts. But Saul kept silent.

Saul Rescues the City of Jabesh

11 Nahash[a] the Ammonite went up and besieged Jabesh Gilead. And all the men of

---

[a] 1 Masoretic Text; Dead Sea Scrolls *gifts. Now Nahash king of the Ammonites oppressed the Gadites and Reubenites severely. He gouged out all their right eyes and struck terror and dread in Israel. Not a man remained among the Israelites beyond the Jordan whose right eye was not gouged out by Nahash king of the Ammonites, except that seven thousand men fled from the Ammonites and entered Jabesh Gilead. About a month later,* ¹Nahash

Jabesh said to him, "Make a treaty with us, and we will be subject to you."

² But Nahash the Ammonite replied, "I will make a treaty with you only on the condition that I gouge out the right eye of every one of you and so bring disgrace on all Israel."

³ The elders of Jabesh said to him, "Give us seven days so we can send messengers throughout Israel; if no one comes to rescue us, we will surrender to you."

⁴ When the messengers came to Gibeah of Saul and reported these terms to the people, they all wept aloud. ⁵ Just then Saul was returning from the fields, behind his oxen, and he asked, "What is wrong with everyone? Why are they weeping?" Then they repeated to him what the men of Jabesh had said.

⁶ When Saul heard their words, the Spirit of God came powerfully upon him, and he burned with anger. ⁷ He took a pair of oxen, cut them into pieces, and sent the pieces by messengers throughout Israel, proclaiming, "This is what will be done to the oxen of anyone who does not follow Saul and Samuel." Then the terror of the LORD fell on the people, and they came out together as one. ⁸ When Saul mustered them at Bezek, the men of Israel numbered three hundred thousand and those of Judah thirty thousand.

⁹ They told the messengers who had come, "Say to the men of Ja-besh Gilead, 'By the time the sun is hot tomorrow, you will be rescued.'" When the messengers went and reported this to the men of Jabesh, they were elated. ¹⁰ They said to the Ammonites, "Tomorrow we will surrender to you, and you can do to us whatever you like."

¹¹ The next day Saul separated his men into three divisions; during the last watch of the night they broke into the camp of the Ammonites and slaughtered them until the heat of the day. Those who survived were scattered, so that no two of them were left together.

Saul Confirmed as King

¹² The people then said to Samuel, "Who was it that asked, 'Shall Saul reign over us?' Turn these men over to us so that we may put them to death."

¹³ But Saul said, "No one will be put to death today, for this day the LORD has rescued Israel."

¹⁴ Then Samuel said to the people, "Come, let us go to Gilgal and there renew the kingship." ¹⁵ So all the people went to Gilgal and made Saul king in the presence of the LORD. There they sacrificed fellowship offerings before the LORD, and Saul and all the Israelites held a great celebration.

Samuel's Farewell Speech

12 Samuel said to all Israel, "I have listened to everything you said to me and have set

a king over you. ²Now you have a king as your leader. As for me, I am old and gray, and my sons are here with you. I have been your leader from my youth until this day. ³Here I stand. Testify against me in the presence of the LORD and his anointed. Whose ox have I taken? Whose donkey have I taken? Whom have I cheated? Whom have I oppressed? From whose hand have I accepted a bribe to make me shut my eyes? If I have done any of these things, I will make it right."

⁴"You have not cheated or oppressed us," they replied. "You have not taken anything from anyone's hand."

⁵Samuel said to them, "The LORD is witness against you, and also his anointed is witness this day, that you have not found anything in my hand."

"He is witness," they said.

⁶Then Samuel said to the people, "It is the LORD who appointed Moses and Aaron and brought your ancestors up out of Egypt. ⁷Now then, stand here, because I am going to confront you with evidence before the LORD as to all the righteous acts performed by the LORD for you and your ancestors.

⁸"After Jacob entered Egypt, they cried to the LORD for help, and the LORD sent Moses and Aaron, who brought your ancestors out of Egypt and settled them in this place.

⁹"But they forgot the LORD their God; so he sold them into the hand of Sisera, the commander of the army of Hazor, and into the hands of the Philistines and the king of Moab, who fought against them. ¹⁰They cried out to the LORD and said, 'We have sinned; we have forsaken the LORD and served the Baals and the Ashtoreths. But now deliver us from the hands of our enemies, and we will serve you.' ¹¹Then the LORD sent Jerub-Baal,ᵃ Barak,ᵇ Jephthah and Samuel,ᶜ and he delivered you from the hands of your enemies all around you, so that you lived in safety.

¹²"But when you saw that Nahash king of the Ammonites was moving against you, you said to me, 'No, we want a king to rule over us'—even though the LORD your God was your king. ¹³Now here is the king you have chosen, the one you asked for; see, the LORD has set a king over you. ¹⁴If you fear the LORD and serve and obey him and do not rebel against his commands, and if both you and the king who reigns over you follow the LORD your God—good! ¹⁵But if you do not obey the LORD, and if you rebel against his commands, his hand will be against you, as it was against your ancestors.

ᵃ 11 Also called *Gideon*   ᵇ 11 Some Septuagint manuscripts and Syriac; Hebrew *Bedan*   ᶜ 11 Hebrew; some Septuagint manuscripts and Syriac *Samson*

[16] "Now then, stand still and see this great thing the LORD is about to do before your eyes! [17] Is it not wheat harvest now? I will call on the LORD to send thunder and rain. And you will realize what an evil thing you did in the eyes of the LORD when you asked for a king."

[18] Then Samuel called on the LORD, and that same day the LORD sent thunder and rain. So all the people stood in awe of the LORD and of Samuel.

[19] The people all said to Samuel, "Pray to the LORD your God for your servants so that we will not die, for we have added to all our other sins the evil of asking for a king."

[20] "Do not be afraid," Samuel replied. "You have done all this evil; yet do not turn away from the LORD, but serve the LORD with all your heart. [21] Do not turn away after useless idols. They can do you no good, nor can they rescue you, because they are useless. [22] For the sake of his great name the LORD will not reject his people, because the LORD was pleased to make you his own. [23] As for me, far be it from me that I should sin against the LORD by failing to pray for you. And I will teach you the way that is good and right. [24] But be sure to fear the LORD and serve him faithfully with all your heart; consider what great things he has done for you. [25] Yet if you persist in doing evil, both you and your king will perish."

Samuel Rebukes Saul

13 Saul was thirty[a] years old when he became king, and he reigned over Israel forty-[b] two years.

[2] Saul chose three thousand men from Israel; two thousand were with him at Mikmash and in the hill country of Bethel, and a thousand were with Jonathan at Gibeah in Benjamin. The rest of the men he sent back to their homes.

[3] Jonathan attacked the Philistine outpost at Geba, and the Philistines heard about it. Then Saul had the trumpet blown throughout the land and said, "Let the Hebrews hear!" [4] So all Israel heard the news: "Saul has attacked the Philistine outpost, and now Israel has become obnoxious to the Philistines." And the people were summoned to join Saul at Gilgal.

[5] The Philistines assembled to fight Israel, with three thousand[c] chariots, six thousand charioteers, and soldiers as numerous as the sand on the seashore. They went up and camped at Mikmash, east of Beth Aven. [6] When

---

[a] 1 A few late manuscripts of the Septuagint; Hebrew does not have *thirty*.
[b] 1 Probable reading of the original Hebrew text (see Acts 13:21); Masoretic Text does not have *forty-*. [c] 5 Some Septuagint manuscripts and Syriac; Hebrew *thirty thousand*

the Israelites saw that their situation was critical and that their army was hard pressed, they hid in caves and thickets, among the rocks, and in pits and cisterns. [7] Some Hebrews even crossed the Jordan to the land of Gad and Gilead.

Saul remained at Gilgal, and all the troops with him were quaking with fear. [8] He waited seven days, the time set by Samuel; but Samuel did not come to Gilgal, and Saul's men began to scatter. [9] So he said, "Bring me the burnt offering and the fellowship offerings." And Saul offered up the burnt offering. [10] Just as he finished making the offering, Samuel arrived, and Saul went out to greet him.

[11] "What have you done?" asked Samuel.

Saul replied, "When I saw that the men were scattering, and that you did not come at the set time, and that the Philistines were assembling at Mikmash, [12] I thought, 'Now the Philistines will come down against me at Gilgal, and I have not sought the LORD's favor.' So I felt compelled to offer the burnt offering."

[13] "You have done a foolish thing," Samuel said. "You have not kept the command the LORD your God gave you; if you had, he would have established your kingdom over Israel for all time. [14] But now your kingdom will not endure; the LORD has sought out a man after his own heart and appointed him ruler of his people, because you have not kept the LORD's command."

[15] Then Samuel left Gilgal[a] and went up to Gibeah in Benjamin, and Saul counted the men who were with him. They numbered about six hundred.

Israel Without Weapons

[16] Saul and his son Jonathan and the men with them were staying in Gibeah[b] in Benjamin, while the Philistines camped at Mikmash. [17] Raiding parties went out from the Philistine camp in three detachments. One turned toward Ophrah in the vicinity of Shual, [18] another toward Beth Horon, and the third toward the borderland overlooking the Valley of Zeboyim facing the wilderness.

[19] Not a blacksmith could be found in the whole land of Israel, because the Philistines had said, "Otherwise the Hebrews will make swords or spears!" [20] So all Israel went down to the Philistines to have their plow points, mattocks, axes and sickles[c] sharpened. [21] The price was two-thirds of a shekel[d] for sharpening plow points and mattocks, and a

---

[a] 15 Hebrew; Septuagint *Gilgal and went his way; the rest of the people went after Saul to meet the army, and they went out of Gilgal*   [b] 16 Two Hebrew manuscripts; most Hebrew manuscripts *Geba,* a variant of *Gibeah*   [c] 20 Septuagint; Hebrew *plow points*   [d] 21 That is, about 1/4 ounce or about 8 grams

third of a shekel[a] for sharpening forks and axes and for repointing goads.

²² So on the day of the battle not a soldier with Saul and Jonathan had a sword or spear in his hand; only Saul and his son Jonathan had them.

Jonathan Attacks the Philistines

²³ Now a detachment of Philistines had gone out to the pass at

14 Mikmash. ¹ One day Jonathan son of Saul said to his young armor-bearer, "Come, let's go over to the Philistine outpost on the other side." But he did not tell his father.

² Saul was staying on the outskirts of Gibeah under a pomegranate tree in Migron. With him were about six hundred men, ³ among whom was Ahijah, who was wearing an ephod. He was a son of Ichabod's brother Ahitub son of Phinehas, the son of Eli, the LORD's priest in Shiloh. No one was aware that Jonathan had left.

⁴ On each side of the pass that Jonathan intended to cross to reach the Philistine outpost was a cliff; one was called Bozez and the other Seneh. ⁵ One cliff stood to the north toward Mikmash, the other to the south toward Geba.

⁶ Jonathan said to his young armor-bearer, "Come, let's go over to the outpost of those uncircumcised men. Perhaps the LORD will

act in our behalf. Nothing can hinder the LORD from saving, whether by many or by few."

⁷ "Do all that you have in mind," his armor-bearer said. "Go ahead; I am with you heart and soul."

⁸ Jonathan said, "Come on, then; we will cross over toward them and let them see us. ⁹ If they say to us, 'Wait there until we come to you,' we will stay where we are and not go up to them. ¹⁰ But if they say, 'Come up to us,' we will climb up, because that will be our sign that the LORD has given them into our hands."

¹¹ So both of them showed themselves to the Philistine outpost. "Look!" said the Philistines. "The Hebrews are crawling out of the holes they were hiding in." ¹² The men of the outpost shouted to Jonathan and his armor-bearer, "Come up to us and we'll teach you a lesson."

So Jonathan said to his armor-bearer, "Climb up after me; the LORD has given them into the hand of Israel."

¹³ Jonathan climbed up, using his hands and feet, with his armor-bearer right behind him. The Philistines fell before Jonathan, and his armor-bearer followed and killed behind him. ¹⁴ In that first attack Jonathan and his armor-bearer killed some twenty men in an area of about half an acre.

---

[a] 21 That is, about 1/8 ounce or about 4 grams

Israel Routs the Philistines

15 Then panic struck the whole army — those in the camp and field, and those in the outposts and raiding parties — and the ground shook. It was a panic sent by God.*a*

16 Saul's lookouts at Gibeah in Benjamin saw the army melting away in all directions. **17** Then Saul said to the men who were with him, "Muster the forces and see who has left us." When they did, it was Jonathan and his armor-bearer who were not there.

18 Saul said to Ahijah, "Bring the ark of God." (At that time it was with the Israelites.)*b* **19** While Saul was talking to the priest, the tumult in the Philistine camp increased more and more. So Saul said to the priest, "Withdraw your hand."

20 Then Saul and all his men assembled and went to the battle. They found the Philistines in total confusion, striking each other with their swords. **21** Those Hebrews who had previously been with the Philistines and had gone up with them to their camp went over to the Israelites who were with Saul and Jonathan. **22** When all the Israelites who had hidden in the hill country of Ephraim heard that the Philistines were on the run, they joined the battle in hot pursuit. **23** So on that day the LORD saved Israel, and the battle moved on beyond Beth Aven.

Jonathan Eats Honey

24 Now the Israelites were in distress that day, because Saul had bound the people under an oath, saying, "Cursed be anyone who eats food before evening comes, before I have avenged myself on my enemies!" So none of the troops tasted food.

25 The entire army entered the woods, and there was honey on the ground. **26** When they went into the woods, they saw the honey oozing out; yet no one put his hand to his mouth, because they feared the oath. **27** But Jonathan had not heard that his father had bound the people with the oath, so he reached out the end of the staff that was in his hand and dipped it into the honeycomb. He raised his hand to his mouth, and his eyes brightened.*c* **28** Then one of the soldiers told him, "Your father bound the army under a strict oath, saying, 'Cursed be anyone who eats food today!' That is why the men are faint."

29 Jonathan said, "My father has made trouble for the country. See how my eyes brightened when I tasted a little of this honey. **30** How much better it would have been if the men had eaten today some of the plunder they took from their

---

a 15 Or *a terrible panic*   *b* 18 Hebrew; Septuagint *"Bring the ephod." (At that time he wore the ephod before the Israelites.)*   *c* 27 Or *his strength was renewed*; similarly in verse 29 enemies. Would not the slaughter of the Philistines have been even greater?"

³¹ That day, after the Israelites had struck down the Philistines from Mikmash to Aijalon, they were exhausted. ³² They pounced on the plunder and, taking sheep, cattle and calves, they butchered them on the ground and ate them, together with the blood. ³³ Then someone said to Saul, "Look, the men are sinning against the LORD by eating meat that has blood in it."

"You have broken faith," he said. "Roll a large stone over here at once." ³⁴ Then he said, "Go out among the men and tell them, 'Each of you bring me your cattle and sheep, and slaughter them here and eat them. Do not sin against the LORD by eating meat with blood still in it.'"

So everyone brought his ox that night and slaughtered it there. ³⁵ Then Saul built an altar to the LORD; it was the first time he had done this.

³⁶ Saul said, "Let us go down and pursue the Philistines by night and plunder them till dawn, and let us not leave one of them alive."

"Do whatever seems best to you," they replied.

But the priest said, "Let us inquire of God here."

³⁷ So Saul asked God, "Shall I go down and pursue the Philistines? Will you give them into Israel's hand?" But God did not answer him that day.

³⁸ Saul therefore said, "Come here, all you who are leaders of the army, and let us find out what sin has been committed today. ³⁹ As surely as the LORD who rescues Israel lives, even if the guilt lies with my son Jonathan, he must die." But not one of them said a word.

⁴⁰ Saul then said to all the Israelites, "You stand over there; I and Jonathan my son will stand over here."

"Do what seems best to you," they replied.

⁴¹ Then Saul prayed to the LORD, the God of Israel, "Why have you not answered your servant today? If the fault is in me or my son Jonathan, respond with Urim, but if the men of Israel are at fault,^a respond with Thummim." Jonathan and Saul were taken by lot, and the men were cleared. ⁴² Saul said, "Cast the lot between me and Jonathan my son." And Jonathan was taken.

⁴³ Then Saul said to Jonathan, "Tell me what you have done."

So Jonathan told him, "I tasted a little honey with the end of my staff. And now I must die!"

⁴⁴ Saul said, "May God deal with me, be it ever so severely, if you do not die, Jonathan."

⁴⁵ But the men said to Saul, "Should Jonathan die — he who

---

^a 41 Septuagint; Hebrew does not have "Why . . . at fault."

has brought about this great deliverance in Israel? Never! As surely as the LORD lives, not a hair of his head will fall to the ground, for he did this today with God's help." So the men rescued Jonathan, and he was not put to death.

⁴⁶ Then Saul stopped pursuing the Philistines, and they withdrew to their own land.

⁴⁷ After Saul had assumed rule over Israel, he fought against their enemies on every side: Moab, the Ammonites, Edom, the kings*a* of Zobah, and the Philistines. Wherever he turned, he inflicted punishment on them.*b* ⁴⁸ He fought valiantly and defeated the Amalekites, delivering Israel from the hands of those who had plundered them.

Saul's Family

⁴⁹ Saul's sons were Jonathan, Ishvi and Malki-Shua. The name of his older daughter was Merab, and that of the younger was Michal. ⁵⁰ His wife's name was Ahinoam daughter of Ahimaaz. The name of the commander of Saul's army was Abner son of Ner, and Ner was Saul's uncle. ⁵¹ Saul's father Kish and Abner's father Ner were sons of Abiel.

⁵² All the days of Saul there was bitter war with the Philistines, and whenever Saul saw a mighty or brave man, he took him into his service.

The LORD Rejects Saul as King

15 Samuel said to Saul, "I am the one the LORD sent to anoint you king over his people Israel; so listen now to the message from the LORD. ²This is what the LORD Almighty says: 'I will punish the Amalekites for what they did to Israel when they waylaid them as they came up from Egypt. ³Now go, attack the Amalekites and totally destroy*c* all that belongs to them. Do not spare them; put to death men and women, children and infants, cattle and sheep, camels and donkeys.'"

⁴ So Saul summoned the men and mustered them at Telaim — two hundred thousand foot soldiers and ten thousand from Judah. ⁵ Saul went to the city of Amalek and set an ambush in the ravine. ⁶ Then he said to the Kenites, "Go away, leave the Amalekites so that I do not destroy you along with them; for you showed kindness to all the Israelites when they came up out of Egypt." So the Kenites moved away from the Amalekites.

⁷ Then Saul attacked the Amalekites all the way from Havilah to Shur, near the eastern border

---

a 47 Masoretic Text; Dead Sea Scrolls and Septuagint *king*   *b 47* Hebrew; Septuagint *he was victorious*   *c 3* The Hebrew term refers to the irrevocable giving over of things or persons to the LORD, often by totally destroying them; also in verses 8, 9, 15, 18, 20 and 21.

of Egypt. **8**He took Agag king of the Amalekites alive, and all his people he totally destroyed with the sword. **9**But Saul and the army spared Agag and the best of the sheep and cattle, the fat calves*a* and lambs — everything that was good. These they were unwilling to destroy completely, but everything that was despised and weak they totally destroyed.

10Then the word of the LORD came to Samuel: **11**"I regret that I have made Saul king, because he has turned away from me and has not carried out my instructions." Samuel was angry, and he cried out to the LORD all that night.

12Early in the morning Samuel got up and went to meet Saul, but he was told, "Saul has gone to Carmel. There he has set up a monument in his own honor and has turned and gone on down to Gilgal."

13When Samuel reached him, Saul said, "The LORD bless you! I have carried out the LORD's instructions."

14But Samuel said, "What then is this bleating of sheep in my ears? What is this lowing of cattle that I hear?"

15Saul answered, "The soldiers brought them from the Amalekites; they spared the best of the sheep and cattle to sacrifice to the LORD your God, but we totally destroyed the rest."

16"Enough!" Samuel said to Saul. "Let me tell you what the LORD said to me last night."

"Tell me," Saul replied.

17Samuel said, "Although you were once small in your own eyes, did you not become the head of the tribes of Israel? The LORD anointed you king over Israel. **18**And he sent you on a mission, saying, 'Go and completely destroy those wicked people, the Amalekites; wage war against them until you have wiped them out.' **19**Why did you not obey the LORD? Why did you pounce on the plunder and do evil in the eyes of the LORD?"

20"But I did obey the LORD," Saul said. "I went on the mission the LORD assigned me. I completely destroyed the Amalekites and brought back Agag their king. **21**The soldiers took sheep and cattle from the plunder, the best of what was devoted to God, in order to sacrifice them to the LORD your God at Gilgal."

22But Samuel replied:

"Does the LORD delight in
      burnt offerings and
      sacrifices
   as much as in obeying the
      LORD?
To obey is better than
      sacrifice,
   and to heed is better than
      the fat of rams.
23For rebellion is like the sin of
      divination,
   and arrogance like the evil
      of idolatry.

a 9 Or *the grown bulls*; the meaning of the Hebrew for this phrase is uncertain.

Because you have rejected the
word of the LORD,
he has rejected you as king."

²⁴ Then Saul said to Samuel, "I have sinned. I violated the LORD's command and your instructions. I was afraid of the men and so I gave in to them. ²⁵ Now I beg you, forgive my sin and come back with me, so that I may worship the LORD."

²⁶ But Samuel said to him, "I will not go back with you. You have rejected the word of the LORD, and the LORD has rejected you as king over Israel!"

²⁷ As Samuel turned to leave, Saul caught hold of the hem of his robe, and it tore. ²⁸ Samuel said to him, "The LORD has torn the kingdom of Israel from you today and has given it to one of your neighbors—to one better than you. ²⁹ He who is the Glory of Israel does not lie or change his mind; for he is not a human being, that he should change his mind."

³⁰ Saul replied, "I have sinned. But please honor me before the elders of my people and before Israel; come back with me, so that I may worship the LORD your God." ³¹ So Samuel went back with Saul, and Saul worshiped the LORD.

³² Then Samuel said, "Bring me Agag king of the Amalekites."

Agag came to him in chains.ᵃ

And he thought, "Surely the bitterness of death is past."

³³ But Samuel said,

"As your sword has made
women childless,
so will your mother be
childless among
women."

And Samuel put Agag to death before the LORD at Gilgal.

³⁴ Then Samuel left for Ramah, but Saul went up to his home in Gibeah of Saul. ³⁵ Until the day Samuel died, he did not go to see Saul again, though Samuel mourned for him. And the LORD regretted that he had made Saul king over Israel.

Samuel Anoints David

16 The LORD said to Samuel, "How long will you mourn for Saul, since I have rejected him as king over Israel? Fill your horn with oil and be on your way; I am sending you to Jesse of Bethlehem. I have chosen one of his sons to be king."

² But Samuel said, "How can I go? If Saul hears about it, he will kill me."

The LORD said, "Take a heifer with you and say, 'I have come to sacrifice to the LORD.' ³ Invite Jesse to the sacrifice, and I will show you what to do. You are to anoint for me the one I indicate."

⁴ Samuel did what the LORD said. When he arrived at Bethle-

ᵃ 32 The meaning of the Hebrew for this phrase is uncertain.

hem, the elders of the town trembled when they met him. They asked, "Do you come in peace?"

⁵Samuel replied, "Yes, in peace; I have come to sacrifice to the LORD. Consecrate yourselves and come to the sacrifice with me." Then he consecrated Jesse and his sons and invited them to the sacrifice.

⁶When they arrived, Samuel saw Eliab and thought, "Surely the LORD's anointed stands here before the LORD."

⁷But the LORD said to Samuel, "Do not consider his appearance or his height, for I have rejected him. The LORD does not look at the things people look at. People look at the outward appearance, but the LORD looks at the heart."

⁸Then Jesse called Abinadab and had him pass in front of Samuel. But Samuel said, "The LORD has not chosen this one either." ⁹Jesse then had Shammah pass by, but Samuel said, "Nor has the LORD chosen this one." ¹⁰Jesse had seven of his sons pass before Samuel, but Samuel said to him, "The LORD has not chosen these." ¹¹So he asked Jesse, "Are these all the sons you have?"

"There is still the youngest," Jesse answered. "He is tending the sheep."

Samuel said, "Send for him; we will not sit down until he arrives."

¹²So he sent for him and had him brought in. He was glowing with health and had a fine appearance and handsome features.

Then the LORD said, "Rise and anoint him; this is the one."

¹³So Samuel took the horn of oil and anointed him in the presence of his brothers, and from that day on the Spirit of the LORD came powerfully upon David. Samuel then went to Ramah.

David in Saul's Service

¹⁴Now the Spirit of the LORD had departed from Saul, and an evil*ᵃ* spirit from the LORD tormented him.

¹⁵Saul's attendants said to him, "See, an evil spirit from God is tormenting you. ¹⁶Let our lord command his servants here to search for someone who can play the lyre. He will play when the evil spirit from God comes on you, and you will feel better."

¹⁷So Saul said to his attendants, "Find someone who plays well and bring him to me."

¹⁸One of the servants answered, "I have seen a son of Jesse of Bethlehem who knows how to play the lyre. He is a brave man and a warrior. He speaks well and is a fine-looking man. And the LORD is with him."

¹⁹Then Saul sent messengers to Jesse and said, "Send me your son David, who is with the sheep." ²⁰So Jesse took a donkey loaded with bread, a skin of wine

---

ᵃ 14 Or *and a harmful*; similarly in verses 15, 16 and 23 and a young goat and sent them with his son David to Saul.

²¹ David came to Saul and entered his service. Saul liked him very much, and David became one of his armor-bearers. ²² Then Saul sent word to Jesse, saying, "Allow David to remain in my service, for I am pleased with him."

²³ Whenever the spirit from God came on Saul, David would take up his lyre and play. Then relief would come to Saul; he would feel better, and the evil spirit would leave him.

David and Goliath

17 Now the Philistines gathered their forces for war and assembled at Sokoh in Judah. They pitched camp at Ephes Dammim, between Sokoh and Azekah. ² Saul and the Israelites assembled and camped in the Valley of Elah and drew up their battle line to meet the Philistines. ³ The Philistines occupied one hill and the Israelites another, with the valley between them.

⁴ A champion named Goliath, who was from Gath, came out of the Philistine camp. His height was six cubits and a span.ᵃ ⁵ He had a bronze helmet on his head and wore a coat of scale armor of bronze weighing five thousand shekelsᵇ; ⁶ on his legs he wore bronze greaves, and a bronze javelin was slung on his back. ⁷ His spear shaft was like a weaver's rod, and its iron point weighed six hundred shekels.ᶜ His shield bearer went ahead of him.

⁸ Goliath stood and shouted to the ranks of Israel, "Why do you come out and line up for battle? Am I not a Philistine, and are you not the servants of Saul? Choose a man and have him come down to me. ⁹ If he is able to fight and kill me, we will become your subjects; but if I overcome him and kill him, you will become our subjects and serve us." ¹⁰ Then the Philistine said, "This day I defy the armies of Israel! Give me a man and let us fight each other." ¹¹ On hearing the Philistine's words, Saul and all the Israelites were dismayed and terrified.

¹² Now David was the son of an Ephrathite named Jesse, who was from Bethlehem in Judah. Jesse had eight sons, and in Saul's time he was very old. ¹³ Jesse's three oldest sons had followed Saul to the war: The firstborn was Eliab; the second, Abinadab; and the third, Shammah. ¹⁴ David was the youngest. The three oldest followed Saul, ¹⁵ but David went back and forth from Saul to tend his father's sheep at Bethlehem.

¹⁶ For forty days the Philistine came forward every morning and evening and took his stand.

ᵃ 4 That is, about 9 feet 9 inches or about 3 meters   ᵇ 5 That is, about 125 pounds or about 58 kilograms   ᶜ 7 That is, about 15 pounds or about 6.9 kilograms

¹⁷Now Jesse said to his son David, "Take this ephah^d of roasted grain and these ten loaves of bread for your brothers and hurry to their camp. ¹⁸Take along these ten cheeses to the commander of their unit. See how your brothers are and bring back some assurance^e from them. ¹⁹They are with Saul and all the men of Israel in the Valley of Elah, fighting against the Philistines."

²⁰Early in the morning David left the flock in the care of a shepherd, loaded up and set out, as Jesse had directed. He reached the camp as the army was going out to its battle positions, shouting the war cry. ²¹Israel and the Philistines were drawing up their lines facing each other. ²²David left his things with the keeper of supplies, ran to the battle lines and asked his brothers how they were. ²³As he was talking with them, Goliath, the Philistine champion from Gath, stepped out from his lines and shouted his usual defiance, and David heard it. ²⁴Whenever the Israelites saw the man, they all fled from him in great fear.

²⁵Now the Israelites had been saying, "Do you see how this man keeps coming out? He comes out to defy Israel. The king will give great wealth to the man who kills him. He will also give him his daughter in marriage and will exempt his family from taxes in Israel."

²⁶David asked the men standing near him, "What will be done for the man who kills this Philistine and removes this disgrace from Israel? Who is this uncircumcised Philistine that he should defy the armies of the living God?"

²⁷They repeated to him what they had been saying and told him, "This is what will be done for the man who kills him."

²⁸When Eliab, David's oldest brother, heard him speaking with the men, he burned with anger at him and asked, "Why have you come down here? And with whom did you leave those few sheep in the wilderness? I know how conceited you are and how wicked your heart is; you came down only to watch the battle."

²⁹"Now what have I done?" said David. "Can't I even speak?" ³⁰He then turned away to someone else and brought up the same matter, and the men answered him as before. ³¹What David said was overheard and reported to Saul, and Saul sent for him.

³²David said to Saul, "Let no one lose heart on account of this Philistine; your servant will go and fight him."

³³Saul replied, "You are not able to go out against this Philistine and fight him; you are only

---

^a 17 That is, probably about 36 pounds or about 16 kilograms   ^b 18 Or some token; or some pledge of spoils a young man, and he has been a warrior from his youth."

³⁴But David said to Saul, "Your servant has been keeping his father's sheep. When a lion or a bear came and carried off a sheep from the flock, ³⁵I went after it, struck it and rescued the sheep from its mouth. When it turned on me, I seized it by its hair, struck it and killed it. ³⁶Your servant has killed both the lion and the bear; this uncircumcised Philistine will be like one of them, because he has defied the armies of the living God. ³⁷The LORD who rescued me from the paw of the lion and the paw of the bear will rescue me from the hand of this Philistine."

Saul said to David, "Go, and the LORD be with you."

³⁸Then Saul dressed David in his own tunic. He put a coat of armor on him and a bronze helmet on his head. ³⁹David fastened on his sword over the tunic and tried walking around, because he was not used to them.

"I cannot go in these," he said to Saul, "because I am not used to them." So he took them off. ⁴⁰Then he took his staff in his hand, chose five smooth stones from the stream, put them in the pouch of his shepherd's bag and, with his sling in his hand, approached the Philistine.

⁴¹Meanwhile, the Philistine, with his shield bearer in front of him, kept coming closer to David. ⁴²He looked David over and saw that he was little more than a boy, glowing with health and handsome, and he despised him. ⁴³He said to David, "Am I a dog, that you come at me with sticks?" And the Philistine cursed David by his gods. ⁴⁴"Come here," he said, "and I'll give your flesh to the birds and the wild animals!"

⁴⁵David said to the Philistine, "You come against me with sword and spear and javelin, but I come against you in the name of the LORD Almighty, the God of the armies of Israel, whom you have defied. ⁴⁶This day the LORD will deliver you into my hands, and I'll strike you down and cut off your head. This very day I will give the carcasses of the Philistine army to the birds and the wild animals, and the whole world will know that there is a God in Israel. ⁴⁷All those gathered here will know that it is not by sword or spear that the LORD saves; for the battle is the LORD's, and he will give all of you into our hands."

⁴⁸As the Philistine moved closer to attack him, David ran quickly toward the battle line to meet him. ⁴⁹Reaching into his bag and taking out a stone, he slung it and struck the Philistine on the forehead. The stone sank into his forehead, and he fell facedown on the ground.

⁵⁰So David triumphed over the Philistine with a sling and

a stone; without a sword in his hand he struck down the Philistine and killed him.

⁵¹David ran and stood over him. He took hold of the Philistine's sword and drew it from the sheath. After he killed him, he cut off his head with the sword.

When the Philistines saw that their hero was dead, they turned and ran. ⁵²Then the men of Israel and Judah surged forward with a shout and pursued the Philistines to the entrance of Gath*a* and to the gates of Ekron. Their dead were strewn along the Shaaraim road to Gath and Ekron. ⁵³When the Israelites returned from chasing the Philistines, they plundered their camp.

⁵⁴David took the Philistine's head and brought it to Jerusalem; he put the Philistine's weapons in his own tent.

⁵⁵As Saul watched David going out to meet the Philistine, he said to Abner, commander of the army, "Abner, whose son is that young man?"

Abner replied, "As surely as you live, Your Majesty, I don't know."

⁵⁶The king said, "Find out whose son this young man is."

⁵⁷As soon as David returned from killing the Philistine, Abner took him and brought him before Saul, with David still holding the Philistine's head.

⁵⁸"Whose son are you, young man?" Saul asked him.

David said, "I am the son of your servant Jesse of Bethlehem."

Saul's Growing Fear of David

18 After David had finished talking with Saul, Jonathan became one in spirit with David, and he loved him as himself. ²From that day Saul kept David with him and did not let him return home to his family. ³And Jonathan made a covenant with David because he loved him as himself. ⁴Jonathan took off the robe he was wearing and gave it to David, along with his tunic, and even his sword, his bow and his belt.

⁵Whatever mission Saul sent him on, David was so successful that Saul gave him a high rank in the army. This pleased all the troops, and Saul's officers as well.

⁶When the men were returning home after David had killed the Philistine, the women came out from all the towns of Israel to meet King Saul with singing and dancing, with joyful songs and with timbrels and lyres. ⁷As they danced, they sang:

"Saul has slain his thousands,
    and David his tens of
        thousands."

⁸Saul was very angry; this refrain displeased him greatly. "They have credited David with tens of thousands," he thought, "but me with only thousands.

---

a 52 Some Septuagint manuscripts; Hebrew *of a valley*

What more can he get but the kingdom?" ⁹And from that time on Saul kept a close eye on David.

¹⁰The next day an evil^a spirit from God came forcefully on Saul. He was prophesying in his house, while David was playing the lyre, as he usually did. Saul had a spear in his hand ¹¹and he hurled it, saying to himself, "I'll pin David to the wall." But David eluded him twice.

¹²Saul was afraid of David, because the LORD was with David but had departed from Saul. ¹³So he sent David away from him and gave him command over a thousand men, and David led the troops in their campaigns. ¹⁴In everything he did he had great success, because the LORD was with him. ¹⁵When Saul saw how successful he was, he was afraid of him. ¹⁶But all Israel and Judah loved David, because he led them in their campaigns.

¹⁷Saul said to David, "Here is my older daughter Merab. I will give her to you in marriage; only serve me bravely and fight the battles of the LORD." For Saul said to himself, "I will not raise a hand against him. Let the Philistines do that!"

¹⁸But David said to Saul, "Who am I, and what is my family or my clan in Israel, that I should become the king's son-in-law?" ¹⁹So^b when the time came for Merab, Saul's daughter, to be given to David, she was given in marriage to Adriel of Meholah.

²⁰Now Saul's daughter Michal was in love with David, and when they told Saul about it, he was pleased. ²¹"I will give her to him," he thought, "so that she may be a snare to him and so that the hand of the Philistines may be against him." So Saul said to David, "Now you have a second opportunity to become my son-in-law."

²²Then Saul ordered his attendants: "Speak to David privately and say, 'Look, the king likes you, and his attendants all love you; now become his son-in-law.'"

²³They repeated these words to David. But David said, "Do you think it is a small matter to become the king's son-in-law? I'm only a poor man and little known."

²⁴When Saul's servants told him what David had said, ²⁵Saul replied, "Say to David, 'The king wants no other price for the bride than a hundred Philistine foreskins, to take revenge on his enemies.'" Saul's plan was to have David fall by the hands of the Philistines.

²⁶When the attendants told David these things, he was pleased to become the king's son-in-law. So before the allotted time elapsed, ²⁷David took his men with him and went out and killed two hundred Philistines and brought back their

^a 10 Or *a harmful*   ^b 19 Or *However,*

foreskins. They counted out the full number to the king so that David might become the king's son-in-law. Then Saul gave him his daughter Michal in marriage.

28 When Saul realized that the LORD was with David and that his daughter Michal loved David, **29** Saul became still more afraid of him, and he remained his enemy the rest of his days.

30 The Philistine commanders continued to go out to battle, and as often as they did, David met with more success than the rest of Saul's officers, and his name became well known.

Saul Tries to Kill David

19 Saul told his son Jonathan and all the attendants to kill David. But Jonathan had taken a great liking to David **2** and warned him, "My father Saul is looking for a chance to kill you. Be on your guard tomorrow morning; go into hiding and stay there. **3** I will go out and stand with my father in the field where you are. I'll speak to him about you and will tell you what I find out."

4 Jonathan spoke well of David to Saul his father and said to him, "Let not the king do wrong to his servant David; he has not wronged you, and what he has done has benefited you greatly. **5** He took his life in his hands when he killed the Philistine. The LORD won a great victory for all Israel, and you saw it and were glad. Why then would you do wrong to an innocent man like David by killing him for no reason?"

6 Saul listened to Jonathan and took this oath: "As surely as the LORD lives, David will not be put to death."

7 So Jonathan called David and told him the whole conversation. He brought him to Saul, and David was with Saul as before.

8 Once more war broke out, and David went out and fought the Philistines. He struck them with such force that they fled before him.

9 But an evil[a] spirit from the LORD came on Saul as he was sitting in his house with his spear in his hand. While David was playing the lyre, **10** Saul tried to pin him to the wall with his spear, but David eluded him as Saul drove the spear into the wall. That night David made good his escape.

11 Saul sent men to David's house to watch it and to kill him in the morning. But Michal, David's wife, warned him, "If you don't run for your life tonight, tomorrow you'll be killed." **12** So Michal let David down through a window, and he fled and escaped. **13** Then Michal took an idol and laid it on the bed, covering it with a garment and putting some goats' hair at the head.

---

[a] 9 Or *But a harmful*

¹⁴When Saul sent the men to capture David, Michal said, "He is ill."

¹⁵Then Saul sent the men back to see David and told them, "Bring him up to me in his bed so that I may kill him." ¹⁶But when the men entered, there was the idol in the bed, and at the head was some goats' hair.

¹⁷Saul said to Michal, "Why did you deceive me like this and send my enemy away so that he escaped?"

Michal told him, "He said to me, 'Let me get away. Why should I kill you?'"

¹⁸When David had fled and made his escape, he went to Samuel at Ramah and told him all that Saul had done to him. Then he and Samuel went to Naioth and stayed there. ¹⁹Word came to Saul: "David is in Naioth at Ramah"; ²⁰so he sent men to capture him. But when they saw a group of prophets prophesying, with Samuel standing there as their leader, the Spirit of God came on Saul's men, and they also prophesied. ²¹Saul was told about it, and he sent more men, and they prophesied too. Saul sent men a third time, and they also prophesied. ²²Finally, he himself left for Ramah and went to the great cistern at Seku. And he asked, "Where are Samuel and David?"

"Over in Naioth at Ramah," they said.

²³So Saul went to Naioth at Ramah. But the Spirit of God came even on him, and he walked along prophesying until he came to Naioth. ²⁴He stripped off his garments, and he too prophesied in Samuel's presence. He lay naked all that day and all that night. This is why people say, "Is Saul also among the prophets?"

David and Jonathan

20 Then David fled from Naioth at Ramah and went to Jonathan and asked, "What have I done? What is my crime? How have I wronged your father, that he is trying to kill me?"

²"Never!" Jonathan replied. "You are not going to die! Look, my father doesn't do anything, great or small, without letting me know. Why would he hide this from me? It isn't so!"

³But David took an oath and said, "Your father knows very well that I have found favor in your eyes, and he has said to himself, 'Jonathan must not know this or he will be grieved.' Yet as surely as the LORD lives and as you live, there is only a step between me and death."

⁴Jonathan said to David, "Whatever you want me to do, I'll do for you."

⁵So David said, "Look, tomorrow is the New Moon feast, and I am supposed to dine with the king; but let me go and hide in the

field until the evening of the day after tomorrow. ⁶If your father misses me at all, tell him, 'David earnestly asked my permission to hurry to Bethlehem, his hometown, because an annual sacrifice is being made there for his whole clan.' ⁷If he says, 'Very well,' then your servant is safe. But if he loses his temper, you can be sure that he is determined to harm me. ⁸As for you, show kindness to your servant, for you have brought him into a covenant with you before the LORD. If I am guilty, then kill me yourself! Why hand me over to your father?"

⁹"Never!" Jonathan said. "If I had the least inkling that my father was determined to harm you, wouldn't I tell you?"

¹⁰David asked, "Who will tell me if your father answers you harshly?"

¹¹"Come," Jonathan said, "let's go out into the field." So they went there together.

¹²Then Jonathan said to David, "I swear by the LORD, the God of Israel, that I will surely sound out my father by this time the day after tomorrow! If he is favorably disposed toward you, will I not send you word and let you know? ¹³But if my father intends to harm you, may the LORD deal with Jonathan, be it ever so severely, if I do not let you know and send you away in peace. May the LORD be with you as he has been with my father. ¹⁴But show me unfailing kindness like the LORD's kindness as long as I live, so that I may not be killed, ¹⁵and do not ever cut off your kindness from my family—not even when the LORD has cut off every one of David's enemies from the face of the earth."

¹⁶So Jonathan made a covenant with the house of David, saying, "May the LORD call David's enemies to account." ¹⁷And Jonathan had David reaffirm his oath out of love for him, because he loved him as he loved himself.

¹⁸Then Jonathan said to David, "Tomorrow is the New Moon feast. You will be missed, because your seat will be empty. ¹⁹The day after tomorrow, toward evening, go to the place where you hid when this trouble began, and wait by the stone Ezel. ²⁰I will shoot three arrows to the side of it, as though I were shooting at a target. ²¹Then I will send a boy and say, 'Go, find the arrows.' If I say to him, 'Look, the arrows are on this side of you; bring them here,' then come, because, as surely as the LORD lives, you are safe; there is no danger. ²²But if I say to the boy, 'Look, the arrows are beyond you,' then you must go, because the LORD has sent you away. ²³And about the matter you and I discussed—remember, the LORD is witness between you and me forever."

²⁴So David hid in the field, and when the New Moon feast

came, the king sat down to eat. ²⁵He sat in his customary place by the wall, opposite Jonathan,ᵃ and Abner sat next to Saul, but David's place was empty. ²⁶Saul said nothing that day, for he thought, "Something must have happened to David to make him ceremonially unclean—surely he is unclean." ²⁷But the next day, the second day of the month, David's place was empty again. Then Saul said to his son Jonathan, "Why hasn't the son of Jesse come to the meal, either yesterday or today?"

²⁸Jonathan answered, "David earnestly asked me for permission to go to Bethlehem. ²⁹He said, 'Let me go, because our family is observing a sacrifice in the town and my brother has ordered me to be there. If I have found favor in your eyes, let me get away to see my brothers.' That is why he has not come to the king's table."

³⁰Saul's anger flared up at Jonathan and he said to him, "You son of a perverse and rebellious woman! Don't I know that you have sided with the son of Jesse to your own shame and to the shame of the mother who bore you? ³¹As long as the son of Jesse lives on this earth, neither you nor your kingdom will be established. Now send someone to bring him to me, for he must die!"

³²"Why should he be put to death? What has he done?" Jonathan asked his father. ³³But Saul hurled his spear at him to kill him. Then Jonathan knew that his father intended to kill David.

³⁴Jonathan got up from the table in fierce anger; on that second day of the feast he did not eat, because he was grieved at his father's shameful treatment of David.

³⁵In the morning Jonathan went out to the field for his meeting with David. He had a small boy with him, ³⁶and he said to the boy, "Run and find the arrows I shoot." As the boy ran, he shot an arrow beyond him. ³⁷When the boy came to the place where Jonathan's arrow had fallen, Jonathan called out after him, "Isn't the arrow beyond you?" ³⁸Then he shouted, "Hurry! Go quickly! Don't stop!" The boy picked up the arrow and returned to his master. ³⁹(The boy knew nothing about all this; only Jonathan and David knew.) ⁴⁰Then Jonathan gave his weapons to the boy and said, "Go, carry them back to town."

⁴¹After the boy had gone, David got up from the south side of the stone and bowed down before Jonathan three times, with his face to the ground. Then they kissed each other and wept together—but David wept the most.

⁴²Jonathan said to David, "Go in peace, for we have sworn

ᵃ 25 Septuagint; Hebrew *wall. Jonathan arose*

friendship with each other in the name of the LORD, saying, 'The LORD is witness between you and me, and between your descendants and my descendants forever.'" Then David left, and Jonathan went back to the town.[a]

David at Nob

21 [b] David went to Nob, to Ahimelek the priest. Ahimelek trembled when he met him, and asked, "Why are you alone? Why is no one with you?"

[2] David answered Ahimelek the priest, "The king sent me on a mission and said to me, 'No one is to know anything about the mission I am sending you on.' As for my men, I have told them to meet me at a certain place. [3] Now then, what do you have on hand? Give me five loaves of bread, or whatever you can find."

[4] But the priest answered David, "I don't have any ordinary bread on hand; however, there is some consecrated bread here — provided the men have kept themselves from women."

[5] David replied, "Indeed women have been kept from us, as usual whenever[c] I set out. The men's bodies are holy even on missions that are not holy. How much more so today!" [6] So the priest gave him the consecrated bread, since there was no bread there except the bread of the Presence that had been removed from before the LORD and replaced by hot bread on the day it was taken away.

[7] Now one of Saul's servants was there that day, detained before the LORD; he was Doeg the Edomite, Saul's chief shepherd.

[8] David asked Ahimelek, "Don't you have a spear or a sword here? I haven't brought my sword or any other weapon, because the king's mission was urgent."

[9] The priest replied, "The sword of Goliath the Philistine, whom you killed in the Valley of Elah, is here; it is wrapped in a cloth behind the ephod. If you want it, take it; there is no sword here but that one."

David said, "There is none like it; give it to me."

David at Gath

[10] That day David fled from Saul and went to Achish king of Gath. [11] But the servants of Achish said to him, "Isn't this David, the king of the land? Isn't he the one they sing about in their dances:

> "'Saul has slain his thousands,
>   and David his tens of
>   thousands'?"

[12] David took these words to heart and was very much afraid of Achish king of Gath. [13] So he pretended to be insane in their presence; and while he was in

---

[a] 42 In Hebrew texts this sentence (20:42b) is numbered 21:1.   [b] In Hebrew texts 21:1-15 is numbered 21:2-16.   [c] 5 Or *from us in the past few days since*

their hands he acted like a mad-man, making marks on the doors of the gate and letting saliva run down his beard.

[14] Achish said to his servants, "Look at the man! He is insane! Why bring him to me? [15] Am I so short of madmen that you have to bring this fellow here to carry on like this in front of me? Must this man come into my house?"

David at Adullam and Mizpah

22 David left Gath and escaped to the cave of Adullam. When his brothers and his father's household heard about it, they went down to him there. [2] All those who were in distress or in debt or discontented gathered around him, and he became their commander. About four hundred men were with him.

[3] From there David went to Mizpah in Moab and said to the king of Moab, "Would you let my father and mother come and stay with you until I learn what God will do for me?" [4] So he left them with the king of Moab, and they stayed with him as long as David was in the stronghold.

[5] But the prophet Gad said to David, "Do not stay in the stronghold. Go into the land of Judah." So David left and went to the forest of Hereth.

Saul Kills the Priests of Nob

[6] Now Saul heard that David and his men had been discov-ered. And Saul was seated, spear in hand, under the tamarisk tree on the hill at Gibeah, with all his officials standing at his side. [7] He said to them, "Listen, men of Benjamin! Will the son of Jes-se give all of you fields and vine-yards? Will he make all of you commanders of thousands and commanders of hundreds? [8] Is that why you have all conspired against me? No one tells me when my son makes a covenant with the son of Jesse. None of you is concerned about me or tells me that my son has incited my servant to lie in wait for me, as he does today."

[9] But Doeg the Edomite, who was standing with Saul's offi-cials, said, "I saw the son of Jesse come to Ahimelek son of Ahitub at Nob. [10] Ahimelek inquired of the LORD for him; he also gave him provisions and the sword of Goliath the Philistine."

[11] Then the king sent for the priest Ahimelek son of Ahitub and all the men of his family, who were the priests at Nob, and they all came to the king. [12] Saul said, "Listen now, son of Ahitub."

"Yes, my lord," he answered.

[13] Saul said to him, "Why have you conspired against me, you and the son of Jesse, giving him bread and a sword and inquiring of God for him, so that he has re-belled against me and lies in wait for me, as he does today?"

[14] Ahimelek answered the king,

"Who of all your servants is as loyal as David, the king's son-in-law, captain of your bodyguard and highly respected in your household? ¹⁵Was that day the first time I inquired of God for him? Of course not! Let not the king accuse your servant or any of his father's family, for your servant knows nothing at all about this whole affair."

¹⁶But the king said, "You will surely die, Ahimelek, you and your whole family."

¹⁷Then the king ordered the guards at his side: "Turn and kill the priests of the LORD, because they too have sided with David. They knew he was fleeing, yet they did not tell me."

But the king's officials were unwilling to raise a hand to strike the priests of the LORD.

¹⁸The king then ordered Doeg, "You turn and strike down the priests." So Doeg the Edomite turned and struck them down. That day he killed eighty-five men who wore the linen ephod. ¹⁹He also put to the sword Nob, the town of the priests, with its men and women, its children and infants, and its cattle, donkeys and sheep.

²⁰But one son of Ahimelek son of Ahitub, named Abiathar, escaped and fled to join David. ²¹He told David that Saul had killed the priests of the LORD. ²²Then David said to Abiathar, "That day, when Doeg the Edom-ite was there, I knew he would be sure to tell Saul. I am responsible for the death of your whole family. ²³Stay with me; don't be afraid. The man who wants to kill you is trying to kill me too. You will be safe with me."

David Saves Keilah

23 When David was told, "Look, the Philistines are fighting against Keilah and are looting the threshing floors," ²he inquired of the LORD, saying, "Shall I go and attack these Philistines?"

The LORD answered him, "Go, attack the Philistines and save Keilah."

³But David's men said to him, "Here in Judah we are afraid. How much more, then, if we go to Keilah against the Philistine forces!"

⁴Once again David inquired of the LORD, and the LORD answered him, "Go down to Keilah, for I am going to give the Philistines into your hand." ⁵So David and his men went to Keilah, fought the Philistines and carried off their livestock. He inflicted heavy losses on the Philistines and saved the people of Keilah. ⁶(Now Abiathar son of Ahimelek had brought the ephod down with him when he fled to David at Keilah.)

Saul Pursues David

⁷Saul was told that David had gone to Keilah, and he said, "God

has delivered him into my hands, for David has imprisoned himself by entering a town with gates and bars." ⁸And Saul called up all his forces for battle, to go down to Keilah to besiege David and his men.

⁹When David learned that Saul was plotting against him, he said to Abiathar the priest, "Bring the ephod." ¹⁰David said, "LORD, God of Israel, your servant has heard definitely that Saul plans to come to Keilah and destroy the town on account of me. ¹¹Will the citizens of Keilah surrender me to him? Will Saul come down, as your servant has heard? LORD, God of Israel, tell your servant."

And the LORD said, "He will."

¹²Again David asked, "Will the citizens of Keilah surrender me and my men to Saul?"

And the LORD said, "They will."

¹³So David and his men, about six hundred in number, left Keilah and kept moving from place to place. When Saul was told that David had escaped from Keilah, he did not go there.

¹⁴David stayed in the wilderness strongholds and in the hills of the Desert of Ziph. Day after day Saul searched for him, but God did not give David into his hands.

¹⁵While David was at Horesh in the Desert of Ziph, he learned that[a] Saul had come out to take his life. ¹⁶And Saul's son Jona-

than went to David at Horesh and helped him find strength in God. ¹⁷"Don't be afraid," he said. "My father Saul will not lay a hand on you. You will be king over Israel, and I will be second to you. Even my father Saul knows this." ¹⁸The two of them made a covenant before the LORD. Then Jonathan went home, but David remained at Horesh.

¹⁹The Ziphites went up to Saul at Gibeah and said, "Is not David hiding among us in the strongholds at Horesh, on the hill of Hakilah, south of Jeshimon? ²⁰Now, Your Majesty, come down whenever it pleases you to do so, and we will be responsible for giving him into your hands."

²¹Saul replied, "The LORD bless you for your concern for me. ²²Go and get more information. Find out where David usually goes and who has seen him there. They tell me he is very crafty. ²³Find out about all the hiding places he uses and come back to me with definite information. Then I will go with you; if he is in the area, I will track him down among all the clans of Judah."

²⁴So they set out and went to Ziph ahead of Saul. Now David and his men were in the Desert of Maon, in the Arabah south of Jeshimon. ²⁵Saul and his men began the search, and when David was told about it, he went down to the rock and stayed in the Des-

---

a 15 Or *he was afraid because*

ert of Maon. When Saul heard this, he went into the Desert of Maon in pursuit of David.

²⁶Saul was going along one side of the mountain, and David and his men were on the other side, hurrying to get away from Saul. As Saul and his forces were closing in on David and his men to capture them, ²⁷a messenger came to Saul, saying, "Come quickly! The Philistines are raiding the land." ²⁸Then Saul broke off his pursuit of David and went to meet the Philistines. That is why they call this place Sela Hammahlekoth.ᵃ ²⁹And David went up from there and lived in the strongholds of En Gedi.ᵇ

David Spares Saul's Life

24 ᶜ After Saul returned from pursuing the Philistines, he was told, "David is in the Desert of En Gedi." ²So Saul took three thousand able young men from all Israel and set out to look for David and his men near the Crags of the Wild Goats.

³He came to the sheep pens along the way; a cave was there, and Saul went in to relieve himself. David and his men were far back in the cave. ⁴The men said, "This is the day the LORD spoke of when he saidᵈ to you, 'I will give your enemy into your hands for you to deal with as you wish.'"

Then David crept up unnoticed and cut off a corner of Saul's robe.

⁵Afterward, David was conscience-stricken for having cut off a corner of his robe. ⁶He said to his men, "The LORD forbid that I should do such a thing to my master, the LORD's anointed, or lay my hand on him; for he is the anointed of the LORD." ⁷With these words David sharply rebuked his men and did not allow them to attack Saul. And Saul left the cave and went his way.

⁸Then David went out of the cave and called out to Saul, "My lord the king!" When Saul looked behind him, David bowed down and prostrated himself with his face to the ground. ⁹He said to Saul, "Why do you listen when men say, 'David is bent on harming you'? ¹⁰This day you have seen with your own eyes how the LORD delivered you into my hands in the cave. Some urged me to kill you, but I spared you; I said, 'I will not lay my hand on my lord, because he is the LORD's anointed.' ¹¹See, my father, look at this piece of your robe in my hand! I cut off the corner of your robe but did not kill you. See that there is nothing in my hand to indicate that I am guilty of wrongdoing or rebellion. I have not wronged you, but you are hunting me down to take my life. ¹²May

---

ᵃ 28 *Sela Hammahlekoth* means *rock of parting.*   ᵇ 29 In Hebrew texts this verse (23:29) is numbered 24:1.   ᶜ In Hebrew texts 24:1-22 is numbered 24:2-23.
ᵈ 4 Or *"Today the LORD is saying*

the LORD judge between you and me. And may the LORD avenge the wrongs you have done to me, but my hand will not touch you. ¹³As the old saying goes, 'From evildoers come evil deeds,' so my hand will not touch you.

¹⁴"Against whom has the king of Israel come out? Who are you pursuing? A dead dog? A flea? ¹⁵May the LORD be our judge and decide between us. May he consider my cause and uphold it; may he vindicate me by delivering me from your hand."

¹⁶When David finished saying this, Saul asked, "Is that your voice, David my son?" And he wept aloud. ¹⁷"You are more righteous than I," he said. "You have treated me well, but I have treated you badly. ¹⁸You have just now told me about the good you did to me; the LORD delivered me into your hands, but you did not kill me. ¹⁹When a man finds his enemy, does he let him get away unharmed? May the LORD reward you well for the way you treated me today. ²⁰I know that you will surely be king and that the kingdom of Israel will be established in your hands. ²¹Now swear to me by the LORD that you will not kill off my descendants or wipe out my name from my father's family."

²²So David gave his oath to Saul. Then Saul returned home, but David and his men went up to the stronghold.

David, Nabal and Abigail

25 Now Samuel died, and all Israel assembled and mourned for him; and they buried him at his home in Ramah. Then David moved down into the Desert of Paran.ᵃ

²A certain man in Maon, who had property there at Carmel, was very wealthy. He had a thousand goats and three thousand sheep, which he was shearing in Carmel. ³His name was Nabal and his wife's name was Abigail. She was an intelligent and beautiful woman, but her husband was surly and mean in his dealings — he was a Calebite.

⁴While David was in the wilderness, he heard that Nabal was shearing sheep. ⁵So he sent ten young men and said to them, "Go up to Nabal at Carmel and greet him in my name. ⁶Say to him: 'Long life to you! Good health to you and your household! And good health to all that is yours!

⁷"'Now I hear that it is sheep-shearing time. When your shepherds were with us, we did not mistreat them, and the whole time they were at Carmel nothing of theirs was missing. ⁸Ask your own servants and they will tell you. Therefore be favorable toward my men, since we come at a

---

ᵃ 1 Hebrew and some Septuagint manuscripts; other Septuagint manuscripts *Maon* festive time. Please give your servants and your son David whatever you can find for them.' "

⁹When David's men arrived, they gave Nabal this message in David's name. Then they waited.

¹⁰Nabal answered David's servants, "Who is this David? Who is this son of Jesse? Many servants are breaking away from their masters these days. ¹¹Why should I take my bread and water, and the meat I have slaughtered for my shearers, and give it to men coming from who knows where?"

¹²David's men turned around and went back. When they arrived, they reported every word. ¹³David said to his men, "Each of you strap on your sword!" So they did, and David strapped his on as well. About four hundred men went up with David, while two hundred stayed with the supplies.

¹⁴One of the servants told Abigail, Nabal's wife, "David sent messengers from the wilderness to give our master his greetings, but he hurled insults at them. ¹⁵Yet these men were very good to us. They did not mistreat us, and the whole time we were out in the fields near them nothing was missing. ¹⁶Night and day they were a wall around us the whole time we were herding our sheep near them. ¹⁷Now think it over and see what you can do, because disaster is hanging over our master and his whole household. He is such a wicked man that no one can talk to him."

¹⁸Abigail acted quickly. She took two hundred loaves of bread, two skins of wine, five dressed sheep, five seahs*ᵃ* of roasted grain, a hundred cakes of raisins and two hundred cakes of pressed figs, and loaded them on donkeys. ¹⁹Then she told her servants, "Go on ahead; I'll follow you." But she did not tell her husband Nabal.

²⁰As she came riding her donkey into a mountain ravine, there were David and his men descending toward her, and she met them. ²¹David had just said, "It's been useless — all my watching over this fellow's property in the wilderness so that nothing of his was missing. He has paid me back evil for good. ²²May God deal with David,*ᵇ* be it ever so severely, if by morning I leave alive one male of all who belong to him!"

²³When Abigail saw David, she quickly got off her donkey and bowed down before David with her face to the ground. ²⁴She fell at his feet and said: "Pardon your servant, my lord, and let me speak to you; hear what your servant has to say. ²⁵Please pay no attention, my lord, to that wicked

---

ᵃ 18 That is, probably about 60 pounds or about 27 kilograms   *ᵇ 22* Some Septuagint manuscripts; Hebrew *with David's enemies* man Nabal. He is just like his name — his name means Fool, and folly goes with him. And as for me, your servant, I did not see the men my lord sent. ²⁶ And now, my lord, as surely as the LORD your God lives and as you live, since the LORD has kept you from bloodshed and from avenging yourself with your own hands, may your enemies and all who are intent on harming my lord be like Nabal. ²⁷ And let this gift, which your servant has brought to my lord, be given to the men who follow you.

²⁸ "Please forgive your servant's presumption. The LORD your God will certainly make a lasting dynasty for my lord, because you fight the LORD's battles, and no wrongdoing will be found in you as long as you live. ²⁹ Even though someone is pursuing you to take your life, the life of my lord will be bound securely in the bundle of the living by the LORD your God, but the lives of your enemies he will hurl away as from the pocket of a sling. ³⁰ When the LORD has fulfilled for my lord every good thing he promised concerning him and has appointed him ruler over Israel, ³¹ my lord will not have on his conscience the staggering burden of needless bloodshed or of having avenged himself. And when the LORD your God has brought my lord success, remember your servant."

³² David said to Abigail, "Praise be to the LORD, the God of Israel, who has sent you today to meet me. ³³ May you be blessed for your good judgment and for keeping me from bloodshed this day and from avenging myself with my own hands. ³⁴ Otherwise, as surely as the LORD, the God of Israel, lives, who has kept me from harming you, if you had not come quickly to meet me, not one male belonging to Nabal would have been left alive by daybreak."

³⁵ Then David accepted from her hand what she had brought him and said, "Go home in peace. I have heard your words and granted your request."

³⁶ When Abigail went to Nabal, he was in the house holding a banquet like that of a king. He was in high spirits and very drunk. So she told him nothing at all until daybreak. ³⁷ Then in the morning, when Nabal was sober, his wife told him all these things, and his heart failed him and he became like a stone. ³⁸ About ten days later, the LORD struck Nabal and he died.

³⁹ When David heard that Nabal was dead, he said, "Praise be to the LORD, who has upheld my cause against Nabal for treating me with contempt. He has kept his servant from doing wrong and has brought Nabal's wrongdoing down on his own head."

Then David sent word to Abigail, asking her to become his wife. ⁴⁰ His servants went to Carmel and said to Abigail, "David has sent us to you to take you to become his wife."

⁴¹She bowed down with her face to the ground and said, "I am your servant and am ready to serve you and wash the feet of my lord's servants." ⁴²Abigail quickly got on a donkey and, attended by her five female servants, went with David's messengers and became his wife. ⁴³David had also married Ahinoam of Jezreel, and they both were his wives. ⁴⁴But Saul had given his daughter Michal, David's wife, to Paltiel*a* son of Laish, who was from Gallim.

David Again Spares Saul's Life

26 The Ziphites went to Saul at Gibeah and said, "Is not David hiding on the hill of Hakilah, which faces Jeshimon?" ²So Saul went down to the Desert of Ziph, with his three thousand select Israelite troops, to search there for David. ³Saul made his camp beside the road on the hill of Hakilah facing Jeshimon, but David stayed in the wilderness. When he saw that Saul had followed him there, ⁴he sent out scouts and learned that Saul had definitely arrived.

⁵Then David set out and went to the place where Saul had camped. He saw where Saul and Abner son of Ner, the commander of the army, had lain down. Saul was lying inside the camp, with the army encamped around him.

⁶David then asked Ahimelek the Hittite and Abishai son of Zeruiah, Joab's brother, "Who will go down into the camp with me to Saul?"

"I'll go with you," said Abishai.

⁷So David and Abishai went to the army by night, and there was Saul, lying asleep inside the camp with his spear stuck in the ground near his head. Abner and the soldiers were lying around him.

⁸Abishai said to David, "Today God has delivered your enemy into your hands. Now let me pin him to the ground with one thrust of the spear; I won't strike him twice."

⁹But David said to Abishai, "Don't destroy him! Who can lay a hand on the LORD's anointed and be guiltless? ¹⁰As surely as the LORD lives," he said, "the LORD himself will strike him, or his time will come and he will die, or he will go into battle and perish. ¹¹But the LORD forbid that I should lay a hand on the LORD's anointed. Now get the spear and water jug that are near his head, and let's go."

¹²So David took the spear and water jug near Saul's head, and they left. No one saw or knew about it, nor did anyone wake up. They were all sleeping, because the LORD had put them into a deep sleep.

---

a 44 Hebrew *Palti*, a variant of *Paltiel*

¹³Then David crossed over to the other side and stood on top of the hill some distance away; there was a wide space between them. ¹⁴He called out to the army and to Abner son of Ner, "Aren't you going to answer me, Abner?"

Abner replied, "Who are you who calls to the king?"

¹⁵David said, "You're a man, aren't you? And who is like you in Israel? Why didn't you guard your lord the king? Someone came to destroy your lord the king. ¹⁶What you have done is not good. As surely as the LORD lives, you and your men must die, because you did not guard your master, the LORD's anointed. Look around you. Where are the king's spear and water jug that were near his head?"

¹⁷Saul recognized David's voice and said, "Is that your voice, David my son?"

David replied, "Yes it is, my lord the king." ¹⁸And he added, "Why is my lord pursuing his servant? What have I done, and what wrong am I guilty of? ¹⁹Now let my lord the king listen to his servant's words. If the LORD has incited you against me, then may he accept an offering. If, however, people have done it, may they be cursed before the LORD! They have driven me today from my share in the LORD's inheritance and have said, 'Go, serve other gods.' ²⁰Now do not let my blood fall to the ground far from the presence of the LORD. The king of Israel has come out to look for a flea—as one hunts a partridge in the mountains."

²¹Then Saul said, "I have sinned. Come back, David my son. Because you considered my life precious today, I will not try to harm you again. Surely I have acted like a fool and have been terribly wrong."

²²"Here is the king's spear," David answered. "Let one of your young men come over and get it. ²³The LORD rewards everyone for their righteousness and faithfulness. The LORD delivered you into my hands today, but I would not lay a hand on the LORD's anointed. ²⁴As surely as I valued your life today, so may the LORD value my life and deliver me from all trouble."

²⁵Then Saul said to David, "May you be blessed, David my son; you will do great things and surely triumph."

So David went on his way, and Saul returned home.

David Among the Philistines

27 But David thought to himself, "One of these days I will be destroyed by the hand of Saul. The best thing I can do is to escape to the land of the Philistines. Then Saul will give up searching for me anywhere in Israel, and I will slip out of his hand."

²So David and the six hundred men with him left and went over

to Achish son of Maok king of Gath. ³David and his men settled in Gath with Achish. Each man had his family with him, and David had his two wives: Ahinoam of Jezreel and Abigail of Carmel, the widow of Nabal. ⁴When Saul was told that David had fled to Gath, he no longer searched for him.

⁵Then David said to Achish, "If I have found favor in your eyes, let a place be assigned to me in one of the country towns, that I may live there. Why should your servant live in the royal city with you?"

⁶So on that day Achish gave him Ziklag, and it has belonged to the kings of Judah ever since. ⁷David lived in Philistine territory a year and four months.

⁸Now David and his men went up and raided the Geshurites, the Girzites and the Amalekites. (From ancient times these peoples had lived in the land extending to Shur and Egypt.) ⁹Whenever David attacked an area, he did not leave a man or woman alive, but took sheep and cattle, donkeys and camels, and clothes. Then he returned to Achish.

¹⁰When Achish asked, "Where did you go raiding today?" David would say, "Against the Negev of Judah" or "Against the Negev of Jerahmeel" or "Against the Negev of the Kenites." ¹¹He did not leave a man or woman alive to be brought to Gath, for he thought, "They might inform on us and say, 'This is what David did.'" And such was his practice as long as he lived in Philistine territory. ¹²Achish trusted David and said to himself, "He has become so obnoxious to his people, the Israelites, that he will be my servant for life."

28

In those days the Philistines gathered their forces to fight against Israel. Achish said to David, "You must understand that you and your men will accompany me in the army."

²David said, "Then you will see for yourself what your servant can do."

Achish replied, "Very well, I will make you my bodyguard for life."

Saul and the Medium at Endor

³Now Samuel was dead, and all Israel had mourned for him and buried him in his own town of Ramah. Saul had expelled the mediums and spiritists from the land.

⁴The Philistines assembled and came and set up camp at Shunem, while Saul gathered all Israel and set up camp at Gilboa. ⁵When Saul saw the Philistine army, he was afraid; terror filled his heart. ⁶He inquired of the LORD, but the LORD did not answer him by dreams or Urim or prophets. ⁷Saul then said to his attendants, "Find me a woman who is a medium, so I may go and inquire of her."

"There is one in Endor," they said.

8 So Saul disguised himself, putting on other clothes, and at night he and two men went to the woman. "Consult a spirit for me," he said, "and bring up for me the one I name."

9 But the woman said to him, "Surely you know what Saul has done. He has cut off the mediums and spiritists from the land. Why have you set a trap for my life to bring about my death?"

10 Saul swore to her by the LORD, "As surely as the LORD lives, you will not be punished for this."

11 Then the woman asked, "Whom shall I bring up for you?"

"Bring up Samuel," he said.

12 When the woman saw Samuel, she cried out at the top of her voice and said to Saul, "Why have you deceived me? You are Saul!"

13 The king said to her, "Don't be afraid. What do you see?"

The woman said, "I see a ghostly figure*a* coming up out of the earth."

14 "What does he look like?" he asked.

"An old man wearing a robe is coming up," she said.

Then Saul knew it was Samuel, and he bowed down and prostrated himself with his face to the ground.

15 Samuel said to Saul, "Why have you disturbed me by bringing me up?"

"I am in great distress," Saul said. "The Philistines are fighting against me, and God has departed from me. He no longer answers me, either by prophets or by dreams. So I have called on you to tell me what to do."

16 Samuel said, "Why do you consult me, now that the LORD has departed from you and become your enemy? **17** The LORD has done what he predicted through me. The LORD has torn the kingdom out of your hands and given it to one of your neighbors — to David. **18** Because you did not obey the LORD or carry out his fierce wrath against the Amalekites, the LORD has done this to you today. **19** The LORD will deliver both Israel and you into the hands of the Philistines, and tomorrow you and your sons will be with me. The LORD will also give the army of Israel into the hands of the Philistines."

20 Immediately Saul fell full length on the ground, filled with fear because of Samuel's words. His strength was gone, for he had eaten nothing all that day and all that night.

21 When the woman came to Saul and saw that he was greatly shaken, she said, "Look, your servant has obeyed you. I took my life in my hands and did what you told me to do. **22** Now please listen to your servant and let me give you some food so you may

a 13 Or *see spirits;* or *see gods*

eat and have the strength to go on your way."

²³He refused and said, "I will not eat."

But his men joined the woman in urging him, and he listened to them. He got up from the ground and sat on the couch.

²⁴The woman had a fattened calf at the house, which she butchered at once. She took some flour, kneaded it and baked bread without yeast. ²⁵Then she set it before Saul and his men, and they ate. That same night they got up and left.

Achish Sends David Back to Ziklag

29 The Philistines gathered all their forces at Aphek, and Israel camped by the spring in Jezreel. ²As the Philistine rulers marched with their units of hundreds and thousands, David and his men were marching at the rear with Achish. ³The commanders of the Philistines asked, "What about these Hebrews?"

Achish replied, "Is this not David, who was an officer of Saul king of Israel? He has already been with me for over a year, and from the day he left Saul until now, I have found no fault in him."

⁴But the Philistine commanders were angry with Achish and said, "Send the man back, that he may return to the place you assigned him. He must not go with us into battle, or he will turn against us during the fighting. How better could he regain his master's favor than by taking the heads of our own men? ⁵Isn't this the David they sang about in their dances:

"'Saul has slain his thousands,
and David his tens of
thousands'?"

⁶So Achish called David and said to him, "As surely as the LORD lives, you have been reliable, and I would be pleased to have you serve with me in the army. From the day you came to me until today, I have found no fault in you, but the rulers don't approve of you. ⁷Now turn back and go in peace; do nothing to displease the Philistine rulers."

⁸"But what have I done?" asked David. "What have you found against your servant from the day I came to you until now? Why can't I go and fight against the enemies of my lord the king?"

⁹Achish answered, "I know that you have been as pleasing in my eyes as an angel of God; nevertheless, the Philistine commanders have said, 'He must not go up with us into battle.' ¹⁰Now get up early, along with your master's servants who have come with you, and leave in the morning as soon as it is light."

¹¹So David and his men got up early in the morning to go back to the land of the Philistines, and the Philistines went up to Jezreel.

David Destroys the Amalekites

30 David and his men reached Ziklag on the third day. Now the Amalekites had raided the Negev and Ziklag. They had attacked Ziklag and burned it, ²and had taken captive the women and everyone else in it, both young and old. They killed none of them, but carried them off as they went on their way.

³When David and his men reached Ziklag, they found it destroyed by fire and their wives and sons and daughters taken captive. ⁴So David and his men wept aloud until they had no strength left to weep. ⁵David's two wives had been captured — Ahinoam of Jezreel and Abigail, the widow of Nabal of Carmel. ⁶David was greatly distressed because the men were talking of stoning him; each one was bitter in spirit because of his sons and daughters. But David found strength in the LORD his God.

⁷Then David said to Abiathar the priest, the son of Ahimelek, "Bring me the ephod." Abiathar brought it to him, ⁸and David inquired of the LORD, "Shall I pursue this raiding party? Will I overtake them?"

"Pursue them," he answered. "You will certainly overtake them and succeed in the rescue."

⁹David and the six hundred men with him came to the Besor Valley, where some stayed behind. ¹⁰Two hundred of them were too exhausted to cross the valley, but David and the other four hundred continued the pursuit.

¹¹They found an Egyptian in a field and brought him to David. They gave him water to drink and food to eat — ¹²part of a cake of pressed figs and two cakes of raisins. He ate and was revived, for he had not eaten any food or drunk any water for three days and three nights.

¹³David asked him, "Who do you belong to? Where do you come from?"

He said, "I am an Egyptian, the slave of an Amalekite. My master abandoned me when I became ill three days ago. ¹⁴We raided the Negev of the Kerethites, some territory belonging to Judah and the Negev of Caleb. And we burned Ziklag."

¹⁵David asked him, "Can you lead me down to this raiding party?"

He answered, "Swear to me before God that you will not kill me or hand me over to my master, and I will take you down to them."

¹⁶He led David down, and there they were, scattered over the countryside, eating, drinking and reveling because of the great amount of plunder they had taken from the land of the Philistines and from Judah. ¹⁷David fought them from dusk until the evening

of the next day, and none of them got away, except four hundred young men who rode off on camels and fled. ¹⁸David recovered everything the Amalekites had taken, including his two wives. ¹⁹Nothing was missing: young or old, boy or girl, plunder or anything else they had taken. David brought everything back. ²⁰He took all the flocks and herds, and his men drove them ahead of the other livestock, saying, "This is David's plunder."

²¹Then David came to the two hundred men who had been too exhausted to follow him and who were left behind at the Besor Valley. They came out to meet David and the men with him. As David and his men approached, he asked them how they were. ²²But all the evil men and troublemakers among David's followers said, "Because they did not go out with us, we will not share with them the plunder we recovered. However, each man may take his wife and children and go."

²³David replied, "No, my brothers, you must not do that with what the LORD has given us. He has protected us and delivered into our hands the raiding party that came against us. ²⁴Who will listen to what you say? The share of the man who stayed with the supplies is to be the same as that of him who went down to the battle. All will share alike." ²⁵David made this a statute and ordi-nance for Israel from that day to this.

²⁶When David reached Ziklag, he sent some of the plunder to the elders of Judah, who were his friends, saying, "Here is a gift for you from the plunder of the LORD's enemies."

²⁷David sent it to those who were in Bethel, Ramoth Negev and Jattir; ²⁸to those in Aroer, Siphmoth, Eshtemoa ²⁹and Rakal; to those in the towns of the Jerahmeelites and the Kenites; ³⁰to those in Hormah, Bor Ashan, Athak ³¹and Hebron; and to those in all the other places where he and his men had roamed.

Saul Takes His Life

31 Now the Philistines fought against Israel; the Israelites fled before them, and many fell dead on Mount Gilboa. ²The Philistines were in hot pursuit of Saul and his sons, and they killed his sons Jonathan, Abinadab and Malki-Shua. ³The fighting grew fierce around Saul, and when the archers overtook him, they wounded him critically.

⁴Saul said to his armor-bearer, "Draw your sword and run me through, or these uncircumcised fellows will come and run me through and abuse me."

But his armor-bearer was terrified and would not do it; so Saul took his own sword and fell on it. ⁵When the armor-bearer saw that Saul was dead, he too fell on his sword and died with him. [6]So Saul and his three sons and his armor-bearer and all his men died together that same day.

[7]When the Israelites along the valley and those across the Jordan saw that the Israelite army had fled and that Saul and his sons had died, they abandoned their towns and fled. And the Philistines came and occupied them.

[8]The next day, when the Philistines came to strip the dead, they found Saul and his three sons fallen on Mount Gilboa. [9]They cut off his head and stripped off his armor, and they sent messengers throughout the land of the Philistines to proclaim the news in the temple of their idols and among their people. [10]They put his armor in the temple of the Ashtoreths and fastened his body to the wall of Beth Shan.

[11]When the people of Jabesh Gilead heard what the Philistines had done to Saul, [12]all their valiant men marched through the night to Beth Shan. They took down the bodies of Saul and his sons from the wall of Beth Shan and went to Jabesh, where they burned them. [13]Then they took their bones and buried them under a tamarisk tree at Jabesh, and they fasted seven days.

2 Samuel

Introduction:

Second Samuel continues the story of the kingdom of Israel. It begins with the death of the very first king, King Saul. Then it describes David's forty-year reign. Some of the best-known stories are the capture of Jerusalem, David's sin with Bathsheba, and Absalom's rebellion.

Outline of contents:

David as king of Judah (1:1–4:12)
David unites Israel (5:1–24:25)

David Hears of Saul's Death

1 After the death of Saul, David returned from striking down the Amalekites and stayed in Ziklag two days. **2** On the third day a man arrived from Saul's camp with his clothes torn and dust on his head. When he came to David, he fell to the ground to pay him honor.

3 "Where have you come from?" David asked him.

He answered, "I have escaped from the Israelite camp."

4 "What happened?" David asked. "Tell me."

"The men fled from the battle," he replied. "Many of them fell and died. And Saul and his son Jonathan are dead."

5 Then David said to the young man who brought him the report, "How do you know that Saul and his son Jonathan are dead?"

6 "I happened to be on Mount Gilboa," the young man said, "and there was Saul, leaning on his spear, with the chariots and their drivers in hot pursuit. **7** When he turned around and saw me, he called out to me, and I said, 'What can I do?'

8 "He asked me, 'Who are you?'

" 'An Amalekite,' I answered.

9 "Then he said to me, 'Stand here by me and kill me! I'm in the throes of death, but I'm still alive.'

10 "So I stood beside him and killed him, because I knew that after he had fallen he could not survive. And I took the crown that was on his head and the band on his arm and have brought them here to my lord."

11 Then David and all the men with him took hold of their clothes and tore them. **12** They mourned and wept and fasted till evening for Saul and his son Jonathan, and for the army of the LORD and for the nation of Israel, because they had fallen by the sword.

¹³ David said to the young man who brought him the report, "Where are you from?"

"I am the son of a foreigner, an Amalekite," he answered.

¹⁴ David asked him, "Why weren't you afraid to lift your hand to destroy the LORD's anointed?"

¹⁵ Then David called one of his men and said, "Go, strike him down!" So he struck him down, and he died. ¹⁶ For David had said to him, "Your blood be on your own head. Your own mouth testified against you when you said, 'I killed the LORD's anointed.'"

David's Lament for Saul and Jonathan

¹⁷ David took up this lament concerning Saul and his son Jonathan, ¹⁸ and he ordered that the people of Judah be taught this lament of the bow (it is written in the Book of Jashar):

¹⁹ "A gazelle*ᵃ* lies slain on your heights, Israel.
   How the mighty have fallen!

²⁰ "Tell it not in Gath,
   proclaim it not in the streets of Ashkelon,
lest the daughters of the Philistines be glad,
   lest the daughters of the uncircumcised rejoice.

²¹ "Mountains of Gilboa,
   may you have neither dew nor rain,
   may no showers fall on your terraced fields.*ᵇ*
For there the shield of the mighty was despised,
   the shield of Saul—no longer rubbed with oil.

²² "From the blood of the slain,
   from the flesh of the mighty,
the bow of Jonathan did not turn back,
   the sword of Saul did not return unsatisfied.
²³ Saul and Jonathan—
   in life they were loved and admired,
   and in death they were not parted.
They were swifter than eagles,
   they were stronger than lions.

²⁴ "Daughters of Israel,
   weep for Saul,
who clothed you in scarlet and finery,
   who adorned your garments with ornaments of gold.

²⁵ "How the mighty have fallen in battle!
   Jonathan lies slain on your heights.

ᵃ 19 Gazelle here symbolizes a human dignitary.   *ᵇ 21* Or / nor fields that yield grain for offerings

26 I grieve for you, Jonathan my
    brother;
  you were very dear to me.
  Your love for me was
    wonderful,
    more wonderful than that of
    women.

27 "How the mighty have fallen!
  The weapons of war have
    perished!"

David Anointed King Over Judah

2 In the course of time, David
inquired of the LORD. "Shall
I go up to one of the towns of Judah?" he asked.

The LORD said, "Go up."

David asked, "Where shall
I go?"

"To Hebron," the LORD an-
swered.

2 So David went up there with
his two wives, Ahinoam of Jezreel
and Abigail, the widow of Nabal of
Carmel. 3 David also took the men
who were with him, each with his
family, and they settled in Hebron
and its towns. 4 Then the men of
Judah came to Hebron, and there
they anointed David king over the
tribe of Judah.

When David was told that it was
the men from Jabesh Gilead who
had buried Saul, 5 he sent messengers to them to say to them, "The
LORD bless you for showing this
kindness to Saul your master by
burying him. 6 May the LORD now
show you kindness and faithfulness, and I too will show you the
same favor because you have done
this. 7 Now then, be strong and
brave, for Saul your master is dead,
and the people of Judah have
anointed me king over them."

War Between the Houses of David and Saul

8 Meanwhile, Abner son of Ner,
the commander of Saul's army,
had taken Ish-Bosheth son of
Saul and brought him over to
Mahanaim. 9 He made him king
over Gilead, Ashuri and Jezreel,
and also over Ephraim, Benjamin and all Israel.

10 Ish-Bosheth son of Saul was
forty years old when he became
king over Israel, and he reigned
two years. The tribe of Judah,
however, remained loyal to David. 11 The length of time David
was king in Hebron over Judah
was seven years and six months.

12 Abner son of Ner, together
with the men of Ish-Bosheth son
of Saul, left Mahanaim and went
to Gibeon. 13 Joab son of Zeruiah
and David's men went out and
met them at the pool of Gibeon.
One group sat down on one side
of the pool and one group on the
other side.

14 Then Abner said to Joab,
"Let's have some of the young
men get up and fight hand to
hand in front of us."

"All right, let them do it," Joab
said.

15 So they stood up and were
counted off—twelve men for

Benjamin and Ish-Bosheth son of Saul, and twelve for David. [16]Then each man grabbed his opponent by the head and thrust his dagger into his opponent's side, and they fell down together. So that place in Gibeon was called Helkath Hazzurim.[a]

[17]The battle that day was very fierce, and Abner and the Israelites were defeated by David's men.

[18]The three sons of Zeruiah were there: Joab, Abishai and Asahel. Now Asahel was as fleet-footed as a wild gazelle. [19]He chased Abner, turning neither to the right nor to the left as he pursued him. [20]Abner looked behind him and asked, "Is that you, Asahel?"

"It is," he answered.

[21]Then Abner said to him, "Turn aside to the right or to the left; take on one of the young men and strip him of his weapons." But Asahel would not stop chasing him.

[22]Again Abner warned Asahel, "Stop chasing me! Why should I strike you down? How could I look your brother Joab in the face?"

[23]But Asahel refused to give up the pursuit; so Abner thrust the butt of his spear into Asahel's stomach, and the spear came out through his back. He fell there and died on the spot. And every man stopped when he came to the place where Asahel had fallen and died.

[24]But Joab and Abishai pursued Abner, and as the sun was setting, they came to the hill of Ammah, near Giah on the way to the wasteland of Gibeon. [25]Then the men of Benjamin rallied behind Abner. They formed themselves into a group and took their stand on top of a hill.

[26]Abner called out to Joab, "Must the sword devour forever? Don't you realize that this will end in bitterness? How long before you order your men to stop pursuing their fellow Israelites?"

[27]Joab answered, "As surely as God lives, if you had not spoken, the men would have continued pursuing them until morning."

[28]So Joab blew the trumpet, and all the troops came to a halt; they no longer pursued Israel, nor did they fight anymore.

[29]All that night Abner and his men marched through the Arabah. They crossed the Jordan, continued through the morning hours[b] and came to Mahanaim.

[30]Then Joab stopped pursuing Abner and assembled the whole army. Besides Asahel, nineteen of David's men were found missing. [31]But David's men had killed three hundred and sixty Benjamites who were with Abner. [32]They took Asahel and buried

---

[a] 16 *Helkath Hazzurim* means *field of daggers* or *field of hostilities.*   [b] 29 See Septuagint; the meaning of the Hebrew for this phrase is uncertain.

him in his father's tomb at Bethlehem. Then Joab and his men marched all night and arrived at Hebron by daybreak.

3 The war between the house of Saul and the house of David lasted a long time. David grew stronger and stronger, while the house of Saul grew weaker and weaker.

2 Sons were born to David in Hebron:

His firstborn was Amnon the son of Ahinoam of Jezreel;

3 his second, Kileab the son of Abigail the widow of Nabal of Carmel;

the third, Absalom the son of Maakah daughter of Talmai king of Geshur;

4 the fourth, Adonijah the son of Haggith;

the fifth, Shephatiah the son of Abital;

5 and the sixth, Ithream the son of David's wife Eglah.

These were born to David in Hebron.

Abner Goes Over to David

6 During the war between the house of Saul and the house of David, Abner had been strengthening his own position in the house of Saul. 7 Now Saul had had a concubine named Rizpah daughter of Aiah. And Ish-Bosheth said to Abner, "Why did you sleep with my father's concubine?"

8 Abner was very angry because of what Ish-Bosheth said. So he answered, "Am I a dog's head — on Judah's side? This very day I am loyal to the house of your father Saul and to his family and friends. I haven't handed you over to David. Yet now you accuse me of an offense involving this woman! 9 May God deal with Abner, be it ever so severely, if I do not do for David what the LORD promised him on oath 10 and transfer the kingdom from the house of Saul and establish David's throne over Israel and Judah from Dan to Beersheba." 11 Ish-Bosheth did not dare to say another word to Abner, because he was afraid of him.

12 Then Abner sent messengers on his behalf to say to David, "Whose land is it? Make an agreement with me, and I will help you bring all Israel over to you."

13 "Good," said David. "I will make an agreement with you. But I demand one thing of you: Do not come into my presence unless you bring Michal daughter of Saul when you come to see me." 14 Then David sent messengers to Ish-Bosheth son of Saul, demanding, "Give me my wife Michal, whom I betrothed to myself for the price of a hundred Philistine foreskins."

15 So Ish-Bosheth gave orders and had her taken away from her husband Paltiel son of Laish. 16 Her husband, however, went

with her, weeping behind her all the way to Bahurim. Then Abner said to him, "Go back home!" So he went back.

¹⁷ Abner conferred with the elders of Israel and said, "For some time you have wanted to make David your king. ¹⁸ Now do it! For the LORD promised David, 'By my servant David I will rescue my people Israel from the hand of the Philistines and from the hand of all their enemies.'"

¹⁹ Abner also spoke to the Benjamites in person. Then he went to Hebron to tell David everything that Israel and the whole tribe of Benjamin wanted to do. ²⁰ When Abner, who had twenty men with him, came to David at Hebron, David prepared a feast for him and his men. ²¹ Then Abner said to David, "Let me go at once and assemble all Israel for my lord the king, so that they may make a covenant with you, and that you may rule over all that your heart desires." So David sent Abner away, and he went in peace.

Joab Murders Abner

²² Just then David's men and Joab returned from a raid and brought with them a great deal of plunder. But Abner was no longer with David in Hebron, because David had sent him away, and he had gone in peace. ²³ When Joab and all the soldiers with him arrived, he was told that Abner son of Ner had come to the king and that the king had sent him away and that he had gone in peace.

²⁴ So Joab went to the king and said, "What have you done? Look, Abner came to you. Why did you let him go? Now he is gone! ²⁵ You know Abner son of Ner; he came to deceive you and observe your movements and find out everything you are doing."

²⁶ Joab then left David and sent messengers after Abner, and they brought him back from the cistern at Sirah. But David did not know it. ²⁷ Now when Abner returned to Hebron, Joab took him aside into an inner chamber, as if to speak with him privately. And there, to avenge the blood of his brother Asahel, Joab stabbed him in the stomach, and he died.

²⁸ Later, when David heard about this, he said, "I and my kingdom are forever innocent before the LORD concerning the blood of Abner son of Ner. ²⁹ May his blood fall on the head of Joab and on his whole family! May Joab's family never be without someone who has a running sore or leprosy*a* or who leans on a crutch or who falls by the sword or who lacks food."

³⁰ (Joab and his brother Abishai murdered Abner because he had killed their brother Asahel in the battle at Gibeon.)

³¹ Then David said to Joab and all the people with him, "Tear

---

a 29 The Hebrew for *leprosy* was used for various diseases affecting the skin.

your clothes and put on sackcloth and walk in mourning in front of Abner." King David himself walked behind the bier. ³²They buried Abner in Hebron, and the king wept aloud at Abner's tomb. All the people wept also.

³³The king sang this lament for Abner:

"Should Abner have died as
  the lawless die?
³⁴ Your hands were not bound,
  your feet were not fettered.
You fell as one falls before the
  wicked."

And all the people wept over him again.

³⁵Then they all came and urged David to eat something while it was still day; but David took an oath, saying, "May God deal with me, be it ever so severely, if I taste bread or anything else before the sun sets!"

³⁶All the people took note and were pleased; indeed, everything the king did pleased them. ³⁷So on that day all the people there and all Israel knew that the king had no part in the murder of Abner son of Ner.

³⁸Then the king said to his men, "Do you not realize that a commander and a great man has fallen in Israel this day? ³⁹And today, though I am the anointed king, I am weak, and these sons of Zeruiah are too strong for me. May the LORD repay the evildoer according to his evil deeds!"

Ish-Bosheth Murdered

4 When Ish-Bosheth son of Saul heard that Abner had died in Hebron, he lost courage, and all Israel became alarmed. ²Now Saul's son had two men who were leaders of raiding bands. One was named Baanah and the other Rekab; they were sons of Rimmon the Beerothite from the tribe of Benjamin — Beeroth is considered part of Benjamin, ³because the people of Beeroth fled to Gittaim and have resided there as foreigners to this day.

⁴(Jonathan son of Saul had a son who was lame in both feet. He was five years old when the news about Saul and Jonathan came from Jezreel. His nurse picked him up and fled, but as she hurried to leave, he fell and became disabled. His name was Mephibosheth.)

⁵Now Rekab and Baanah, the sons of Rimmon the Beerothite, set out for the house of Ish-Bosheth, and they arrived there in the heat of the day while he was taking his noonday rest. ⁶They went into the inner part of the house as if to get some wheat, and they stabbed him in the stomach. Then Rekab and his brother Baanah slipped away.

⁷They had gone into the house while he was lying on the bed in his bedroom. After they stabbed and killed him, they cut off his head. Taking it with them, they

traveled all night by way of the Arabah. **8**They brought the head of Ish-Bosheth to David at Hebron and said to the king, "Here is the head of Ish-Bosheth son of Saul, your enemy, who tried to kill you. This day the LORD has avenged my lord the king against Saul and his offspring."

9David answered Rekab and his brother Baanah, the sons of Rimmon the Beerothite, "As surely as the LORD lives, who has delivered me out of every trouble, **10**when someone told me, 'Saul is dead,' and thought he was bringing good news, I seized him and put him to death in Ziklag. That was the reward I gave him for his news! **11**How much more — when wicked men have killed an innocent man in his own house and on his own bed — should I not now demand his blood from your hand and rid the earth of you!"

12So David gave an order to his men, and they killed them. They cut off their hands and feet and hung the bodies by the pool in Hebron. But they took the head of Ish-Bosheth and buried it in Abner's tomb at Hebron.

David Becomes King Over Israel

5 All the tribes of Israel came to David at Hebron and said, "We are your own flesh and blood. **2**In the past, while Saul was king over us, you were the one who led Israel on their military campaigns. And the LORD said to you, 'You will shepherd my people Israel, and you will become their ruler.'"

3When all the elders of Israel had come to King David at Hebron, the king made a covenant with them at Hebron before the LORD, and they anointed David king over Israel.

4David was thirty years old when he became king, and he reigned forty years. **5**In Hebron he reigned over Judah seven years and six months, and in Jerusalem he reigned over all Israel and Judah thirty-three years.

David Conquers Jerusalem

6The king and his men marched to Jerusalem to attack the Jebusites, who lived there. The Jebusites said to David, "You will not get in here; even the blind and the lame can ward you off." They thought, "David cannot get in here." **7**Nevertheless, David captured the fortress of Zion — which is the City of David.

8On that day David had said, "Anyone who conquers the Jebusites will have to use the water shaft to reach those 'lame and blind' who are David's enemies.[a]" That is why they say, "The 'blind and lame' will not enter the palace."

9David then took up residence in the fortress and called it the City of David. He built up the area

---

[a] 8 Or *are hated by David*

around it, from the terraces[a] inward. [10]And he became more and more powerful, because the LORD God Almighty was with him.

[11]Now Hiram king of Tyre sent envoys to David, along with cedar logs and carpenters and stonemasons, and they built a palace for David. [12]Then David knew that the LORD had established him as king over Israel and had exalted his kingdom for the sake of his people Israel.

[13]After he left Hebron, David took more concubines and wives in Jerusalem, and more sons and daughters were born to him. [14]These are the names of the children born to him there: Shammua, Shobab, Nathan, Solomon, [15]Ibhar, Elishua, Nepheg, Japhia, [16]Elishama, Eliada and Eliphelet.

David Defeats the Philistines

[17]When the Philistines heard that David had been anointed king over Israel, they went up in full force to search for him, but David heard about it and went down to the stronghold. [18]Now the Philistines had come and spread out in the Valley of Rephaim; [19]so David inquired of the LORD, "Shall I go and attack the Philistines? Will you deliver them into my hands?"

The LORD answered him, "Go,

for I will surely deliver the Philistines into your hands."

[20]So David went to Baal Perazim, and there he defeated them. He said, "As waters break out, the LORD has broken out against my enemies before me." So that place was called Baal Perazim.[b] [21]The Philistines abandoned their idols there, and David and his men carried them off.

[22]Once more the Philistines came up and spread out in the Valley of Rephaim; [23]so David inquired of the LORD, and he answered, "Do not go straight up, but circle around behind them and attack them in front of the poplar trees. [24]As soon as you hear the sound of marching in the tops of the poplar trees, move quickly, because that will mean the LORD has gone out in front of you to strike the Philistine army." [25]So David did as the LORD commanded him, and he struck down the Philistines all the way from Gibeon[c] to Gezer.

The Ark Brought to Jerusalem

6 David again brought together all the able young men of Israel — thirty thousand. [2]He and all his men went to Baalah[d] in Judah to bring up from there the ark of God, which is called by the Name,[e] the name of the LORD Almighty, who is enthroned between the

---

[a] 9 Or *the Millo*   [b] 20 *Baal Perazim* means *the lord who breaks out.*
[c] 25 Septuagint (see also 1 Chron. 14:16); Hebrew *Geba*   [d] 2 That is, Kiriath Jearim (see 1 Chron. 13:6)   [e] 2 Hebrew; Septuagint and Vulgate do not have *the Name.*

cherubim on the ark. ³They set the ark of God on a new cart and brought it from the house of Abinadab, which was on the hill. Uzzah and Ahio, sons of Abinadab, were guiding the new cart ⁴with the ark of God on it,ᵃ and Ahio was walking in front of it. ⁵David and all Israel were celebrating with all their might before the Lord, with castanets,ᵇ harps, lyres, timbrels, sistrums and cymbals.

⁶When they came to the threshing floor of Nakon, Uzzah reached out and took hold of the ark of God, because the oxen stumbled. ⁷The Lord's anger burned against Uzzah because of his irreverent act; therefore God struck him down, and he died there beside the ark of God.

⁸Then David was angry because the Lord's wrath had broken out against Uzzah, and to this day that place is called Perez Uzzah.ᶜ

⁹David was afraid of the Lord that day and said, "How can the ark of the Lord ever come to me?" ¹⁰He was not willing to take the ark of the Lord to be with him in the City of David. Instead, he took it to the house of Obed-Edom the Gittite. ¹¹The ark of the Lord remained in the house of Obed-Edom the Gittite for three months, and the Lord blessed him and his entire household.

¹²Now King David was told, "The Lord has blessed the household of Obed-Edom and everything he has, because of the ark of God." So David went to bring up the ark of God from the house of Obed-Edom to the City of David with rejoicing. ¹³When those who were carrying the ark of the Lord had taken six steps, he sacrificed a bull and a fattened calf. ¹⁴Wearing a linen ephod, David was dancing before the Lord with all his might, ¹⁵while he and all Israel were bringing up the ark of the Lord with shouts and the sound of trumpets.

¹⁶As the ark of the Lord was entering the City of David, Michal daughter of Saul watched from a window. And when she saw King David leaping and dancing before the Lord, she despised him in her heart.

¹⁷They brought the ark of the Lord and set it in its place inside the tent that David had pitched for it, and David sacrificed burnt offerings and fellowship offerings before the Lord. ¹⁸After he had finished sacrificing the burnt offerings and fellowship offerings, he blessed the people in the name of the Lord Almighty. ¹⁹Then he gave a loaf of bread, a cake of dates and a cake of raisins to each person in the whole crowd of Israelites, both men and

---

ᵃ 3,4 Dead Sea Scrolls and some Septuagint manuscripts; Masoretic Text *cart* ⁴*and they brought it with the ark of God from the house of Abinadab, which was on the hill* ᵇ 5 Masoretic Text; Dead Sea Scrolls and Septuagint (see also 1 Chron. 13:8) *songs* ᶜ 8 *Perez Uzzah* means *outbreak against Uzzah.*

women. And all the people went to their homes.

²⁰When David returned home to bless his household, Michal daughter of Saul came out to meet him and said, "How the king of Israel has distinguished himself today, going around half-naked in full view of the slave girls of his servants as any vulgar fellow would!"

²¹David said to Michal, "It was before the LORD, who chose me rather than your father or anyone from his house when he appointed me ruler over the LORD's people Israel — I will celebrate before the LORD. ²²I will become even more undignified than this, and I will be humiliated in my own eyes. But by these slave girls you spoke of, I will be held in honor."

²³And Michal daughter of Saul had no children to the day of her death.

God's Promise to David

7 After the king was settled in his palace and the LORD had given him rest from all his enemies around him, ²he said to Nathan the prophet, "Here I am, living in a house of cedar, while the ark of God remains in a tent."

³Nathan replied to the king, "Whatever you have in mind, go ahead and do it, for the LORD is with you."

⁴But that night the word of the LORD came to Nathan, saying:

⁵"Go and tell my servant David, 'This is what the LORD says: Are you the one to build me a house to dwell in? ⁶I have not dwelt in a house from the day I brought the Israelites up out of Egypt to this day. I have been moving from place to place with a tent as my dwelling. ⁷Wherever I have moved with all the Israelites, did I ever say to any of their rulers whom I commanded to shepherd my people Israel, "Why have you not built me a house of cedar?"'

⁸"Now then, tell my servant David, 'This is what the LORD Almighty says: I took you from the pasture, from tending the flock, and appointed you ruler over my people Israel. ⁹I have been with you wherever you have gone, and I have cut off all your enemies from before you. Now I will make your name great, like the names of the greatest men on earth. ¹⁰And I will provide a place for my people Israel and will plant them so that they can have a home of their own and no longer be disturbed. Wicked people will not oppress them anymore, as they did at the beginning ¹¹and have done ever since the time I appointed leaders*a* over my people Israel. I will also give you rest from all your enemies.

a 11 Traditionally judges

" 'The LORD declares to you that the LORD himself will establish a house for you: ¹²When your days are over and you rest with your ancestors, I will raise up your offspring to succeed you, your own flesh and blood, and I will establish his kingdom. ¹³He is the one who will build a house for my Name, and I will establish the throne of his kingdom forever. ¹⁴I will be his father, and he will be my son. When he does wrong, I will punish him with a rod wielded by men, with floggings inflicted by human hands. ¹⁵But my love will never be taken away from him, as I took it away from Saul, whom I removed from before you. ¹⁶Your house and your kingdom will endure forever before me[a]; your throne will be established forever.' "

¹⁷Nathan reported to David all the words of this entire revelation.

David's Prayer

¹⁸Then King David went in and sat before the LORD, and he said:

"Who am I, Sovereign LORD, and what is my family, that you have brought me this far? ¹⁹And as if this were not enough in your sight, Sovereign LORD, you have also spoken about the future of the house of your servant—and this decree, Sovereign LORD, is for a mere human![b]

²⁰"What more can David say to you? For you know your servant, Sovereign LORD. ²¹For the sake of your word and according to your will, you have done this great thing and made it known to your servant.

²²"How great you are, Sovereign LORD! There is no one like you, and there is no God but you, as we have heard with our own ears. ²³And who is like your people Israel—the one nation on earth that God went out to redeem as a people for himself, and to make a name for himself, and to perform great and awesome wonders by driving out nations and their gods from before your people, whom you redeemed from Egypt?[c] ²⁴You have established your people Israel as your very own forever, and you, LORD, have become their God.

²⁵"And now, LORD God, keep forever the promise you have made concerning your servant and his house. Do as

---

[a] 16 Some Hebrew manuscripts and Septuagint; most Hebrew manuscripts *you*   [b] 19 Or *for the human race*   [c] 23 See Septuagint and 1 Chron. 17:21; Hebrew *wonders for your land and before your people, whom you redeemed from Egypt, from the nations and their gods.*

you promised, **26**so that your name will be great forever. Then people will say, 'The LORD Almighty is God over Israel!' And the house of your servant David will be established in your sight.

27"LORD Almighty, God of Israel, you have revealed this to your servant, saying, 'I will build a house for you.' So your servant has found courage to pray this prayer to you. **28**Sovereign LORD, you are God! Your covenant is trustworthy, and you have promised these good things to your servant. **29**Now be pleased to bless the house of your servant, that it may continue forever in your sight; for you, Sovereign LORD, have spoken, and with your blessing the house of your servant will be blessed forever."

David's Victories

8 In the course of time, David defeated the Philistines and subdued them, and he took Metheg Ammah from the control of the Philistines.

2David also defeated the Moabites. He made them lie down on the ground and measured them off with a length of cord. Every two lengths of them were put to death, and the third length was allowed to live. So the Moabites became subject to David and brought him tribute.

3Moreover, David defeated Hadadezer son of Rehob, king of Zobah, when he went to restore his monument at*ᵃ* the Euphrates River. **4**David captured a thousand of his chariots, seven thousand charioteers*ᵇ* and twenty thousand foot soldiers. He hamstrung all but a hundred of the chariot horses.

5When the Arameans of Damascus came to help Hadadezer king of Zobah, David struck down twenty-two thousand of them. **6**He put garrisons in the Aramean kingdom of Damascus, and the Arameans became subject to him and brought tribute. The LORD gave David victory wherever he went.

7David took the gold shields that belonged to the officers of Hadadezer and brought them to Jerusalem. **8**From Tebah*ᶜ* and Berothai, towns that belonged to Hadadezer, King David took a great quantity of bronze.

9When Tou*ᵈ* king of Hamath heard that David had defeated the entire army of Hadadezer, **10**he sent his son Joram*ᵉ* to King David to greet him and congratulate him on his victory in battle over Hadadezer, who had been at war with Tou. Joram brought

---

ᵃ 3 Or *his control along*   *ᵇ 4* Septuagint (see also Dead Sea Scrolls and 1 Chron. 18:4); Masoretic Text *captured seventeen hundred of his charioteers*
ᶜ 8 See some Septuagint manuscripts (see also 1 Chron. 18:8); Hebrew *Betah*.
ᵈ 9 Hebrew *Toi*, a variant of *Tou*; also in verse 10   *ᵉ 10* A variant of *Hadoram*

with him articles of silver, of gold and of bronze.

¹¹ King David dedicated these articles to the LORD, as he had done with the silver and gold from all the nations he had subdued: ¹²Edom*a* and Moab, the Ammonites and the Philistines, and Amalek. He also dedicated the plunder taken from Hadadezer son of Rehob, king of Zobah.

¹³ And David became famous after he returned from striking down eighteen thousand Edomites*b* in the Valley of Salt.

¹⁴ He put garrisons throughout Edom, and all the Edomites became subject to David. The LORD gave David victory wherever he went.

David's Officials

¹⁵ David reigned over all Israel, doing what was just and right for all his people. ¹⁶ Joab son of Zeruiah was over the army; Jehoshaphat son of Ahilud was recorder; ¹⁷ Zadok son of Ahitub and Ahimelek son of Abiathar were priests; Seraiah was secretary; ¹⁸ Benaiah son of Jehoiada was over the Kerethites and Pelethites; and David's sons were priests.*c*

David and Mephibosheth

9 David asked, "Is there anyone still left of the house of Saul to whom I can show kindness for Jonathan's sake?"

²Now there was a servant of Saul's household named Ziba. They summoned him to appear before David, and the king said to him, "Are you Ziba?"

"At your service," he replied.

³The king asked, "Is there no one still alive from the house of Saul to whom I can show God's kindness?"

Ziba answered the king, "There is still a son of Jonathan; he is lame in both feet."

⁴"Where is he?" the king asked.

Ziba answered, "He is at the house of Makir son of Ammiel in Lo Debar."

⁵So King David had him brought from Lo Debar, from the house of Makir son of Ammiel.

⁶When Mephibosheth son of Jonathan, the son of Saul, came to David, he bowed down to pay him honor.

David said, "Mephibosheth!"

"At your service," he replied.

⁷"Don't be afraid," David said to him, "for I will surely show you kindness for the sake of your father Jonathan. I will restore to you all the land that belonged to your grandfather Saul, and you will always eat at my table."

⁸Mephibosheth bowed down and said, "What is your servant,

---

a 12 Some Hebrew manuscripts, Septuagint and Syriac (see also 1 Chron. 18:11); most Hebrew manuscripts *Aram*   *b 13* A few Hebrew manuscripts, Septuagint and Syriac (see also 1 Chron. 18:12); most Hebrew manuscripts *Aram* (that is, Arameans)   *c 18* Or *were chief officials* (see Septuagint and Targum; see also 1 Chron. 18:17) that you should notice a dead dog like me?"

⁹Then the king summoned Ziba, Saul's steward, and said to him, "I have given your master's grandson everything that belonged to Saul and his family. ¹⁰You and your sons and your servants are to farm the land for him and bring in the crops, so that your master's grandson may be provided for. And Mephibosheth, grandson of your master, will always eat at my table." (Now Ziba had fifteen sons and twenty servants.)

¹¹Then Ziba said to the king, "Your servant will do whatever my lord the king commands his servant to do." So Mephibosheth ate at David's[a] table like one of the king's sons.

¹²Mephibosheth had a young son named Mika, and all the members of Ziba's household were servants of Mephibosheth. ¹³And Mephibosheth lived in Jerusalem, because he always ate at the king's table; he was lame in both feet.

David Defeats the Ammonites

10 In the course of time, the king of the Ammonites died, and his son Hanun succeeded him as king. ²David thought, "I will show kindness to Hanun son of Nahash, just as his father showed kindness to me." So David sent a delegation to express his sympathy to Hanun concerning his father.

When David's men came to the land of the Ammonites, ³the Ammonite commanders said to Hanun their lord, "Do you think David is honoring your father by sending envoys to you to express sympathy? Hasn't David sent them to you only to explore the city and spy it out and overthrow it?" ⁴So Hanun seized David's envoys, shaved off half of each man's beard, cut off their garments at the buttocks, and sent them away.

⁵When David was told about this, he sent messengers to meet the men, for they were greatly humiliated. The king said, "Stay at Jericho till your beards have grown, and then come back."

⁶When the Ammonites realized that they had become obnoxious to David, they hired twenty thousand Aramean foot soldiers from Beth Rehob and Zobah, as well as the king of Maakah with a thousand men, and also twelve thousand men from Tob.

⁷On hearing this, David sent Joab out with the entire army of fighting men. ⁸The Ammonites came out and drew up in battle formation at the entrance of their city gate, while the Arameans of Zobah and Rehob and the men of Tob and Maakah were by themselves in the open country.

⁹Joab saw that there were battle lines in front of him and behind

---

[a] 11 Septuagint; Hebrew *my*

him; so he selected some of the best troops in Israel and deployed them against the Arameans. ¹⁰He put the rest of the men under the command of Abishai his brother and deployed them against the Ammonites. ¹¹Joab said, "If the Arameans are too strong for me, then you are to come to my rescue; but if the Ammonites are too strong for you, then I will come to rescue you. ¹²Be strong, and let us fight bravely for our people and the cities of our God. The LORD will do what is good in his sight."

¹³Then Joab and the troops with him advanced to fight the Arameans, and they fled before him. ¹⁴When the Ammonites realized that the Arameans were fleeing, they fled before Abishai and went inside the city. So Joab returned from fighting the Ammonites and came to Jerusalem.

¹⁵After the Arameans saw that they had been routed by Israel, they regrouped. ¹⁶Hadadezer had Arameans brought from beyond the Euphrates River; they went to Helam, with Shobak the commander of Hadadezer's army leading them.

¹⁷When David was told of this, he gathered all Israel, crossed the Jordan and went to Helam. The Arameans formed their battle lines to meet David and fought against him. ¹⁸But they fled before Israel, and David killed seven hundred of their charioteers and forty thousand of their foot soldiers.[a] He also struck down Shobak the commander of their army, and he died there. ¹⁹When all the kings who were vassals of Hadadezer saw that they had been routed by Israel, they made peace with the Israelites and became subject to them.

So the Arameans were afraid to help the Ammonites anymore.

David and Bathsheba

11 In the spring, at the time when kings go off to war, David sent Joab out with the king's men and the whole Israelite army. They destroyed the Ammonites and besieged Rabbah. But David remained in Jerusalem.

²One evening David got up from his bed and walked around on the roof of the palace. From the roof he saw a woman bathing. The woman was very beautiful, ³and David sent someone to find out about her. The man said, "She is Bathsheba, the daughter of Eliam and the wife of Uriah the Hittite." ⁴Then David sent messengers to get her. She came to him, and he slept with her. (Now she was purifying herself from her monthly uncleanness.) Then she went back home. ⁵The woman conceived and sent word to David, saying, "I am pregnant."

⁶So David sent this word to

ᵃ 18 Some Septuagint manuscripts (see also 1 Chron. 19:18); Hebrew *horsemen*

Joab: "Send me Uriah the Hittite." And Joab sent him to David. ⁷When Uriah came to him, David asked him how Joab was, how the soldiers were and how the war was going. ⁸Then David said to Uriah, "Go down to your house and wash your feet." So Uriah left the palace, and a gift from the king was sent after him. ⁹But Uriah slept at the entrance to the palace with all his master's servants and did not go down to his house.

¹⁰David was told, "Uriah did not go home." So he asked Uriah, "Haven't you just come from a military campaign? Why didn't you go home?"

¹¹Uriah said to David, "The ark and Israel and Judah are staying in tents,ᵃ and my commander Joab and my lord's men are camped in the open country. How could I go to my house to eat and drink and make love to my wife? As surely as you live, I will not do such a thing!"

¹²Then David said to him, "Stay here one more day, and tomorrow I will send you back." So Uriah remained in Jerusalem that day and the next. ¹³At David's invitation, he ate and drank with him, and David made him drunk. But in the evening Uriah went out to sleep on his mat among his master's servants; he did not go home.

¹⁴In the morning David wrote a letter to Joab and sent it with Uriah. ¹⁵In it he wrote, "Put Uriah out in front where the fighting is fiercest. Then withdraw from him so he will be struck down and die."

¹⁶So while Joab had the city under siege, he put Uriah at a place where he knew the strongest defenders were. ¹⁷When the men of the city came out and fought against Joab, some of the men in David's army fell; moreover, Uriah the Hittite died.

¹⁸Joab sent David a full account of the battle. ¹⁹He instructed the messenger: "When you have finished giving the king this account of the battle, ²⁰the king's anger may flare up, and he may ask you, 'Why did you get so close to the city to fight? Didn't you know they would shoot arrows from the wall? ²¹Who killed Abimelek son of Jerub-Beshethᵇ? Didn't a woman drop an upper millstone on him from the wall, so that he died in Thebez? Why did you get so close to the wall?' If he asks you this, then say to him, 'Moreover, your servant Uriah the Hittite is dead.'"

²²The messenger set out, and when he arrived he told David everything Joab had sent him to say. ²³The messenger said to David, "The men overpowered us and came out against us in the open, but we drove them back to the entrance of the city gate. ²⁴Then the archers shot arrows

---

ᵃ 11 Or *staying at Sukkoth*   ᵇ 21 Also known as *Jerub-Baal* (that is, Gideon) at your servants from the wall, and some of the king's men died. Moreover, your servant Uriah the Hittite is dead."

25 David told the messenger, "Say this to Joab: 'Don't let this upset you; the sword devours one as well as another. Press the attack against the city and destroy it.' Say this to encourage Joab."

26 When Uriah's wife heard that her husband was dead, she mourned for him. 27 After the time of mourning was over, David had her brought to his house, and she became his wife and bore him a son. But the thing David had done displeased the LORD.

Nathan Rebukes David

12 The LORD sent Nathan to David. When he came to him, he said, "There were two men in a certain town, one rich and the other poor. 2 The rich man had a very large number of sheep and cattle, 3 but the poor man had nothing except one little ewe lamb he had bought. He raised it, and it grew up with him and his children. It shared his food, drank from his cup and even slept in his arms. It was like a daughter to him.

4 "Now a traveler came to the rich man, but the rich man refrained from taking one of his own sheep or cattle to prepare a meal for the traveler who had come to him. Instead, he took the ewe lamb that belonged to the poor man and prepared it for the one who had come to him."

5 David burned with anger against the man and said to Nathan, "As surely as the LORD lives, the man who did this must die! 6 He must pay for that lamb four times over, because he did such a thing and had no pity."

7 Then Nathan said to David, "You are the man! This is what the LORD, the God of Israel, says: 'I anointed you king over Israel, and I delivered you from the hand of Saul. 8 I gave your master's house to you, and your master's wives into your arms. I gave you all Israel and Judah. And if all this had been too little, I would have given you even more. 9 Why did you despise the word of the LORD by doing what is evil in his eyes? You struck down Uriah the Hittite with the sword and took his wife to be your own. You killed him with the sword of the Ammonites. 10 Now, therefore, the sword will never depart from your house, because you despised me and took the wife of Uriah the Hittite to be your own.'

11 "This is what the LORD says: 'Out of your own household I am going to bring calamity on you. Before your very eyes I will take your wives and give them to one who is close to you, and he will sleep with your wives in broad daylight. 12 You did it in secret, but I will do this thing in broad daylight before all Israel.'"

¹³Then David said to Nathan, "I have sinned against the LORD."

Nathan replied, "The LORD has taken away your sin. You are not going to die. ¹⁴But because by doing this you have shown utter contempt for*ᵃ* the LORD, the son born to you will die."

¹⁵After Nathan had gone home, the LORD struck the child that Uriah's wife had borne to David, and he became ill. ¹⁶David pleaded with God for the child. He fasted and spent the nights lying in sackcloth*ᵇ* on the ground. ¹⁷The elders of his household stood beside him to get him up from the ground, but he refused, and he would not eat any food with them.

¹⁸On the seventh day the child died. David's attendants were afraid to tell him that the child was dead, for they thought, "While the child was still living, he wouldn't listen to us when we spoke to him. How can we now tell him the child is dead? He may do something desperate."

¹⁹David noticed that his attendants were whispering among themselves, and he realized the child was dead. "Is the child dead?" he asked.

"Yes," they replied, "he is dead."

²⁰Then David got up from the ground. After he had washed, put on lotions and changed his clothes, he went into the house of the LORD and worshiped. Then he went to his own house, and at his request they served him food, and he ate.

²¹His attendants asked him, "Why are you acting this way? While the child was alive, you fasted and wept, but now that the child is dead, you get up and eat!"

²²He answered, "While the child was still alive, I fasted and wept. I thought, 'Who knows? The LORD may be gracious to me and let the child live.' ²³But now that he is dead, why should I go on fasting? Can I bring him back again? I will go to him, but he will not return to me."

²⁴Then David comforted his wife Bathsheba, and he went to her and made love to her. She gave birth to a son, and they named him Solomon. The LORD loved him; ²⁵and because the LORD loved him, he sent word through Nathan the prophet to name him Jedidiah.*ᶜ*

²⁶Meanwhile Joab fought against Rabbah of the Ammonites and captured the royal citadel. ²⁷Joab then sent messengers to David, saying, "I have fought against Rabbah and taken its water supply. ²⁸Now muster the rest of the troops and besiege the city and capture it. Otherwise I will take the city, and it will be named after me."

ᵃ 14 An ancient Hebrew scribal tradition; Masoretic Text *for the enemies of*
ᵇ 16 Dead Sea Scrolls and Septuagint; Masoretic Text does not have *in sackcloth.*
ᶜ 25 *Jedidiah* means *loved by the LORD.*

²⁹ So David mustered the entire army and went to Rabbah, and attacked and captured it. ³⁰ David took the crown from their king's*a* head, and it was placed on his own head. It weighed a talent*b* of gold, and it was set with precious stones. David took a great quantity of plunder from the city ³¹ and brought out the people who were there, consigning them to labor with saws and with iron picks and axes, and he made them work at brickmaking.*c* David did this to all the Ammonite towns. Then he and his entire army returned to Jerusalem.

Amnon and Tamar

13 In the course of time, Amnon son of David fell in love with Tamar, the beautiful sister of Absalom son of David.

² Amnon became so obsessed with his sister Tamar that he made himself ill. She was a virgin, and it seemed impossible for him to do anything to her.

³ Now Amnon had an adviser named Jonadab son of Shimeah, David's brother. Jonadab was a very shrewd man. ⁴ He asked Amnon, "Why do you, the king's son, look so haggard morning after morning? Won't you tell me?"

Amnon said to him, "I'm in love with Tamar, my brother Absalom's sister."

⁵ "Go to bed and pretend to be ill," Jonadab said. "When your father comes to see you, say to him, 'I would like my sister Tamar to come and give me something to eat. Let her prepare the food in my sight so I may watch her and then eat it from her hand.'"

⁶ So Amnon lay down and pretended to be ill. When the king came to see him, Amnon said to him, "I would like my sister Tamar to come and make some special bread in my sight, so I may eat from her hand."

⁷ David sent word to Tamar at the palace: "Go to the house of your brother Amnon and prepare some food for him." ⁸ So Tamar went to the house of her brother Amnon, who was lying down. She took some dough, kneaded it, made the bread in his sight and baked it. ⁹ Then she took the pan and served him the bread, but he refused to eat.

"Send everyone out of here," Amnon said. So everyone left him. ¹⁰ Then Amnon said to Tamar, "Bring the food here into my bedroom so I may eat from your hand." And Tamar took the bread she had prepared and brought it to her brother Amnon in his bedroom. ¹¹ But when she took it to him to eat, he grabbed her and said, "Come to bed with me, my sister."

¹² "No, my brother!" she said to him. "Don't force me! Such a

---

a 30 Or *from Milkom's* (that is, Molek's)   *b 30* That is, about 75 pounds or about 34 kilograms   *c 31* The meaning of the Hebrew for this clause is uncertain.

thing should not be done in Israel! Don't do this wicked thing. [13]What about me? Where could I get rid of my disgrace? And what about you? You would be like one of the wicked fools in Israel. Please speak to the king; he will not keep me from being married to you." [14]But he refused to listen to her, and since he was stronger than she, he raped her.

[15]Then Amnon hated her with intense hatred. In fact, he hated her more than he had loved her. Amnon said to her, "Get up and get out!"

[16]"No!" she said to him. "Sending me away would be a greater wrong than what you have already done to me."

But he refused to listen to her. [17]He called his personal servant and said, "Get this woman out of my sight and bolt the door after her." [18]So his servant put her out and bolted the door after her. She was wearing an ornate[a] robe, for this was the kind of garment the virgin daughters of the king wore. [19]Tamar put ashes on her head and tore the ornate robe she was wearing. She put her hands on her head and went away, weeping aloud as she went.

[20]Her brother Absalom said to her, "Has that Amnon, your brother, been with you? Be quiet for now, my sister; he is your brother. Don't take this thing to heart." And Tamar lived in her brother Absalom's house, a desolate woman.

[21]When King David heard all this, he was furious. [22]And Absalom never said a word to Amnon, either good or bad; he hated Amnon because he had disgraced his sister Tamar.

Absalom Kills Amnon

[23]Two years later, when Absalom's sheepshearers were at Baal Hazor near the border of Ephraim, he invited all the king's sons to come there. [24]Absalom went to the king and said, "Your servant has had shearers come. Will the king and his attendants please join me?"

[25]"No, my son," the king replied. "All of us should not go; we would only be a burden to you." Although Absalom urged him, he still refused to go but gave him his blessing.

[26]Then Absalom said, "If not, please let my brother Amnon come with us."

The king asked him, "Why should he go with you?" [27]But Absalom urged him, so he sent with him Amnon and the rest of the king's sons.

[28]Absalom ordered his men, "Listen! When Amnon is in high spirits from drinking wine and I say to you, 'Strike Amnon down,' then kill him. Don't be afraid. Haven't I given you this order? Be strong and brave." [29]So Absalom's

---

[a] 18 The meaning of the Hebrew for this word is uncertain; also in verse 19.

men did to Amnon what Absalom had ordered. Then all the king's sons got up, mounted their mules and fled.

30 While they were on their way, the report came to David: "Absalom has struck down all the king's sons; not one of them is left." **31** The king stood up, tore his clothes and lay down on the ground; and all his attendants stood by with their clothes torn.

32 But Jonadab son of Shimeah, David's brother, said, "My lord should not think that they killed all the princes; only Amnon is dead. This has been Absalom's express intention ever since the day Amnon raped his sister Tamar. **33** My lord the king should not be concerned about the report that all the king's sons are dead. Only Amnon is dead."

34 Meanwhile, Absalom had fled.

Now the man standing watch looked up and saw many people on the road west of him, coming down the side of the hill. The watchman went and told the king, "I see men in the direction of Horonaim, on the side of the hill."*a*

35 Jonadab said to the king, "See, the king's sons have come; it has happened just as your servant said."

36 As he finished speaking, the king's sons came in, wailing loudly. The king, too, and all his attendants wept very bitterly.

37 Absalom fled and went to Talmai son of Ammihud, the king of Geshur. But King David mourned many days for his son.

38 After Absalom fled and went to Geshur, he stayed there three years. **39** And King David longed to go to Absalom, for he was consoled concerning Amnon's death.

Absalom Returns to Jerusalem

14 Joab son of Zeruiah knew that the king's heart longed for Absalom. **2** So Joab sent someone to Tekoa and had a wise woman brought from there. He said to her, "Pretend you are in mourning. Dress in mourning clothes, and don't use any cosmetic lotions. Act like a woman who has spent many days grieving for the dead. **3** Then go to the king and speak these words to him." And Joab put the words in her mouth.

4 When the woman from Tekoa went*b* to the king, she fell with her face to the ground to pay him honor, and she said, "Help me, Your Majesty!"

5 The king asked her, "What is troubling you?"

She said, "I am a widow; my husband is dead. **6** I your servant had two sons. They got into a fight with each other in the field, and no one was there to separate

---

a 34 Septuagint; Hebrew does not have this sentence.   *b 4* Many Hebrew manuscripts, Septuagint, Vulgate and Syriac; most Hebrew manuscripts *spoke* them. One struck the other and killed him. ⁷Now the whole clan has risen up against your servant; they say, 'Hand over the one who struck his brother down, so that we may put him to death for the life of his brother whom he killed; then we will get rid of the heir as well.' They would put out the only burning coal I have left, leaving my husband neither name nor descendant on the face of the earth."

⁸The king said to the woman, "Go home, and I will issue an order in your behalf."

⁹But the woman from Tekoa said to him, "Let my lord the king pardon me and my family, and let the king and his throne be without guilt."

¹⁰The king replied, "If anyone says anything to you, bring them to me, and they will not bother you again."

¹¹She said, "Then let the king invoke the Lord his God to prevent the avenger of blood from adding to the destruction, so that my son will not be destroyed."

"As surely as the Lord lives," he said, "not one hair of your son's head will fall to the ground."

¹²Then the woman said, "Let your servant speak a word to my lord the king."

"Speak," he replied.

¹³The woman said, "Why then have you devised a thing like this against the people of God? When the king says this, does he not convict himself, for the king has not brought back his banished son? ¹⁴Like water spilled on the ground, which cannot be recovered, so we must die. But that is not what God desires; rather, he devises ways so that a banished person does not remain banished from him.

¹⁵"And now I have come to say this to my lord the king because the people have made me afraid. Your servant thought, 'I will speak to the king; perhaps he will grant his servant's request. ¹⁶Perhaps the king will agree to deliver his servant from the hand of the man who is trying to cut off both me and my son from God's inheritance.'

¹⁷"And now your servant says, 'May the word of my lord the king secure my inheritance, for my lord the king is like an angel of God in discerning good and evil. May the Lord your God be with you.'"

¹⁸Then the king said to the woman, "Don't keep from me the answer to what I am going to ask you."

"Let my lord the king speak," the woman said.

¹⁹The king asked, "Isn't the hand of Joab with you in all this?"

The woman answered, "As surely as you live, my lord the king, no one can turn to the right or to the left from anything my lord the king says. Yes, it was your servant Joab who instructed me to do this and who put all these words into the mouth of your servant. **20**Your servant Joab did this to change the present situation. My lord has wisdom like that of an angel of God — he knows everything that happens in the land."

21The king said to Joab, "Very well, I will do it. Go, bring back the young man Absalom."

22Joab fell with his face to the ground to pay him honor, and he blessed the king. Joab said, "Today your servant knows that he has found favor in your eyes, my lord the king, because the king has granted his servant's request."

23Then Joab went to Geshur and brought Absalom back to Jerusalem. **24**But the king said, "He must go to his own house; he must not see my face." So Absalom went to his own house and did not see the face of the king.

25In all Israel there was not a man so highly praised for his handsome appearance as Absalom. From the top of his head to the sole of his foot there was no blemish in him. **26**Whenever he cut the hair of his head — he used to cut his hair once a year because it became too heavy for him — he would weigh it, and its weight was two hundred shekels*a* by the royal standard.

27Three sons and a daughter were born to Absalom. His daughter's name was Tamar, and she became a beautiful woman.

28Absalom lived two years in Jerusalem without seeing the king's face. **29**Then Absalom sent for Joab in order to send him to the king, but Joab refused to come to him. So he sent a second time, but he refused to come. **30**Then he said to his servants, "Look, Joab's field is next to mine, and he has barley there. Go and set it on fire." So Absalom's servants set the field on fire.

31Then Joab did go to Absalom's house, and he said to him, "Why have your servants set my field on fire?"

32Absalom said to Joab, "Look, I sent word to you and said, 'Come here so I can send you to the king to ask, "Why have I come from Geshur? It would be better for me if I were still there!"' Now then, I want to see the king's face, and if I am guilty of anything, let him put me to death."

33So Joab went to the king and told him this. Then the king summoned Absalom, and he came in and bowed down with his face to the ground before the king. And the king kissed Absalom.

Absalom's Conspiracy

15 In the course of time, Absalom provided himself with a chariot and horses and with fifty men to run ahead of him. **2**He would get up early and stand by

---

a 26 That is, about 5 pounds or about 2.3 kilograms

the side of the road leading to the city gate. Whenever anyone came with a complaint to be placed before the king for a decision, Absalom would call out to him, "What town are you from?" He would answer, "Your servant is from one of the tribes of Israel." ³Then Absalom would say to him, "Look, your claims are valid and proper, but there is no representative of the king to hear you." ⁴And Absalom would add, "If only I were appointed judge in the land! Then everyone who has a complaint or case could come to me and I would see that they receive justice."

⁵Also, whenever anyone approached him to bow down before him, Absalom would reach out his hand, take hold of him and kiss him. ⁶Absalom behaved in this way toward all the Israelites who came to the king asking for justice, and so he stole the hearts of the people of Israel.

⁷At the end of four*a* years, Absalom said to the king, "Let me go to Hebron and fulfill a vow I made to the Lord. ⁸While your servant was living at Geshur in Aram, I made this vow: 'If the Lord takes me back to Jerusalem, I will worship the Lord in Hebron.*b*'"

⁹The king said to him, "Go in peace." So he went to Hebron.

¹⁰Then Absalom sent secret messengers throughout the tribes of Israel to say, "As soon as you hear the sound of the trumpets, then say, 'Absalom is king in Hebron.'" ¹¹Two hundred men from Jerusalem had accompanied Absalom. They had been invited as guests and went quite innocently, knowing nothing about the matter. ¹²While Absalom was offering sacrifices, he also sent for Ahithophel the Gilonite, David's counselor, to come from Giloh, his hometown. And so the conspiracy gained strength, and Absalom's following kept on increasing.

David Flees

¹³A messenger came and told David, "The hearts of the people of Israel are with Absalom."

¹⁴Then David said to all his officials who were with him in Jerusalem, "Come! We must flee, or none of us will escape from Absalom. We must leave immediately, or he will move quickly to overtake us and bring ruin on us and put the city to the sword."

¹⁵The king's officials answered him, "Your servants are ready to do whatever our lord the king chooses."

¹⁶The king set out, with his entire household following him; but he left ten concubines to take care of the palace. ¹⁷So the king set out, with all the people following him, and they halted at the edge of the city. ¹⁸All his men

a 7 Some Septuagint manuscripts, Syriac and Josephus; Hebrew *forty*
b 8 Some Septuagint manuscripts; Hebrew does not have *in Hebron*.

marched past him, along with all the Kerethites and Pelethites; and all the six hundred Gittites who had accompanied him from Gath marched before the king.

¹⁹The king said to Ittai the Gittite, "Why should you come along with us? Go back and stay with King Absalom. You are a foreigner, an exile from your homeland. ²⁰You came only yesterday. And today shall I make you wander about with us, when I do not know where I am going? Go back, and take your people with you. May the LORD show you kindness and faithfulness."^a

²¹But Ittai replied to the king, "As surely as the LORD lives, and as my lord the king lives, wherever my lord the king may be, whether it means life or death, there will your servant be."

²²David said to Ittai, "Go ahead, march on." So Ittai the Gittite marched on with all his men and the families that were with him.

²³The whole countryside wept aloud as all the people passed by. The king also crossed the Kidron Valley, and all the people moved on toward the wilderness.

²⁴Zadok was there, too, and all the Levites who were with him were carrying the ark of the covenant of God. They set down the ark of God, and Abiathar offered sacrifices until all the people had finished leaving the city.

²⁵Then the king said to Zadok, "Take the ark of God back into the city. If I find favor in the LORD's eyes, he will bring me back and let me see it and his dwelling place again. ²⁶But if he says, 'I am not pleased with you,' then I am ready; let him do to me whatever seems good to him."

²⁷The king also said to Zadok the priest, "Do you understand? Go back to the city with my blessing. Take your son Ahimaaz with you, and also Abiathar's son Jonathan. You and Abiathar return with your two sons. ²⁸I will wait at the fords in the wilderness until word comes from you to inform me." ²⁹So Zadok and Abiathar took the ark of God back to Jerusalem and stayed there.

³⁰But David continued up the Mount of Olives, weeping as he went; his head was covered and he was barefoot. All the people with him covered their heads too and were weeping as they went up. ³¹Now David had been told, "Ahithophel is among the conspirators with Absalom." So David prayed, "LORD, turn Ahithophel's counsel into foolishness."

³²When David arrived at the summit, where people used to worship God, Hushai the Arkite was there to meet him, his robe torn and dust on his head. ³³David said to him, "If you go with me, you will be a burden to me. ³⁴But if you return to the city and say to Absalom, 'Your Majesty, I

^a 20 Septuagint; Hebrew *May kindness and faithfulness be with you*

will be your servant; I was your father's servant in the past, but now I will be your servant,' then you can help me by frustrating Ahithophel's advice. ³⁵Won't the priests Zadok and Abiathar be there with you? Tell them anything you hear in the king's palace. ³⁶Their two sons, Ahimaaz son of Zadok and Jonathan son of Abiathar, are there with them. Send them to me with anything you hear."

³⁷So Hushai, David's confidant, arrived at Jerusalem as Absalom was entering the city.

David and Ziba

16 When David had gone a short distance beyond the summit, there was Ziba, the steward of Mephibosheth, waiting to meet him. He had a string of donkeys saddled and loaded with two hundred loaves of bread, a hundred cakes of raisins, a hundred cakes of figs and a skin of wine.

²The king asked Ziba, "Why have you brought these?"

Ziba answered, "The donkeys are for the king's household to ride on, the bread and fruit are for the men to eat, and the wine is to refresh those who become exhausted in the wilderness."

³The king then asked, "Where is your master's grandson?"

Ziba said to him, "He is staying in Jerusalem, because he thinks, 'Today the Israelites will restore to me my grandfather's kingdom.'"

⁴Then the king said to Ziba, "All that belonged to Mephibosheth is now yours."

"I humbly bow," Ziba said. "May I find favor in your eyes, my lord the king."

Shimei Curses David

⁵As King David approached Bahurim, a man from the same clan as Saul's family came out from there. His name was Shimei son of Gera, and he cursed as he came out. ⁶He pelted David and all the king's officials with stones, though all the troops and the special guard were on David's right and left. ⁷As he cursed, Shimei said, "Get out, get out, you murderer, you scoundrel! ⁸The LORD has repaid you for all the blood you shed in the household of Saul, in whose place you have reigned. The LORD has given the kingdom into the hands of your son Absalom. You have come to ruin because you are a murderer!"

⁹Then Abishai son of Zeruiah said to the king, "Why should this dead dog curse my lord the king? Let me go over and cut off his head."

¹⁰But the king said, "What does this have to do with you, you sons of Zeruiah? If he is cursing because the LORD said to him, 'Curse David,' who can ask, 'Why do you do this?'"

¹¹David then said to Abishai

and all his officials, "My son, my own flesh and blood, is trying to kill me. How much more, then, this Benjamite! Leave him alone; let him curse, for the LORD has told him to. [12]It may be that the LORD will look upon my misery and restore to me his covenant blessing instead of his curse today."

[13]So David and his men continued along the road while Shimei was going along the hillside opposite him, cursing as he went and throwing stones at him and showering him with dirt. [14]The king and all the people with him arrived at their destination exhausted. And there he refreshed himself.

The Advice of Ahithophel and Hushai

[15]Meanwhile, Absalom and all the men of Israel came to Jerusalem, and Ahithophel was with him. [16]Then Hushai the Arkite, David's confidant, went to Absalom and said to him, "Long live the king! Long live the king!"

[17]Absalom said to Hushai, "So this is the love you show your friend? If he's your friend, why didn't you go with him?"

[18]Hushai said to Absalom, "No, the one chosen by the LORD, by these people, and by all the men of Israel — his I will be, and I will remain with him. [19]Furthermore, whom should I serve? Should I

not serve the son? Just as I served your father, so I will serve you."

[20]Absalom said to Ahithophel, "Give us your advice. What should we do?"

[21]Ahithophel answered, "Sleep with your father's concubines whom he left to take care of the palace. Then all Israel will hear that you have made yourself obnoxious to your father, and the hands of everyone with you will be more resolute." [22]So they pitched a tent for Absalom on the roof, and he slept with his father's concubines in the sight of all Israel.

[23]Now in those days the advice Ahithophel gave was like that of one who inquires of God. That was how both David and Absalom regarded all of Ahithophel's advice.

17 Ahithophel said to Absalom, "I would[a] choose twelve thousand men and set out tonight in pursuit of David. [2]I would attack him while he is weary and weak. I would strike him with terror, and then all the people with him will flee. I would strike down only the king [3]and bring all the people back to you. The death of the man you seek will mean the return of all; all the people will be unharmed." [4]This plan seemed good to Absalom and to all the elders of Israel.

[5]But Absalom said, "Summon also Hushai the Arkite, so we can

[a] 1 Or Let me

hear what he has to say as well." ⁶When Hushai came to him, Absalom said, "Ahithophel has given this advice. Should we do what he says? If not, give us your opinion."

⁷Hushai replied to Absalom, "The advice Ahithophel has given is not good this time. ⁸You know your father and his men; they are fighters, and as fierce as a wild bear robbed of her cubs. Besides, your father is an experienced fighter; he will not spend the night with the troops. ⁹Even now, he is hidden in a cave or some other place. If he should attack your troops first,ᵃ whoever hears about it will say, 'There has been a slaughter among the troops who follow Absalom.' ¹⁰Then even the bravest soldier, whose heart is like the heart of a lion, will melt with fear, for all Israel knows that your father is a fighter and that those with him are brave.

¹¹"So I advise you: Let all Israel, from Dan to Beersheba — as numerous as the sand on the seashore — be gathered to you, with you yourself leading them into battle. ¹²Then we will attack him wherever he may be found, and we will fall on him as dew settles on the ground. Neither he nor any of his men will be left alive. ¹³If he withdraws into a city, then all Israel will bring ropes to that city, and we will drag it down to the valley until not so much as a pebble is left."

¹⁴Absalom and all the men of Israel said, "The advice of Hushai the Arkite is better than that of Ahithophel." For the Lord had determined to frustrate the good advice of Ahithophel in order to bring disaster on Absalom.

¹⁵Hushai told Zadok and Abiathar, the priests, "Ahithophel has advised Absalom and the elders of Israel to do such and such, but I have advised them to do so and so. ¹⁶Now send a message at once and tell David, 'Do not spend the night at the fords in the wilderness; cross over without fail, or the king and all the people with him will be swallowed up.'"

¹⁷Jonathan and Ahimaaz were staying at En Rogel. A female servant was to go and inform them, and they were to go and tell King David, for they could not risk being seen entering the city. ¹⁸But a young man saw them and told Absalom. So the two of them left at once and went to the house of a man in Bahurim. He had a well in his courtyard, and they climbed down into it. ¹⁹His wife took a covering and spread it out over the opening of the well and scattered grain over it. No one knew anything about it.

²⁰When Absalom's men came to the woman at the house, they asked, "Where are Ahimaaz and Jonathan?"

ᵃ 9 Or *When some of the men fall at the first attack*

The woman answered them, "They crossed over the brook."[a] The men searched but found no one, so they returned to Jerusalem.

[21] After they had gone, the two climbed out of the well and went to inform King David. They said to him, "Set out and cross the river at once; Ahithophel has advised such and such against you." [22] So David and all the people with him set out and crossed the Jordan. By daybreak, no one was left who had not crossed the Jordan.

[23] When Ahithophel saw that his advice had not been followed, he saddled his donkey and set out for his house in his hometown. He put his house in order and then hanged himself. So he died and was buried in his father's tomb.

Absalom's Death

[24] David went to Mahanaim, and Absalom crossed the Jordan with all the men of Israel. [25] Absalom had appointed Amasa over the army in place of Joab. Amasa was the son of Jether,[b] an Ishmaelite[c] who had married Abigail,[d] the daughter of Nahash and sister of Zeruiah the mother of Joab. [26] The Israelites and Absalom camped in the land of Gilead.

[27] When David came to Mahanaim, Shobi son of Nahash from Rabbah of the Ammonites, and Makir son of Ammiel from Lo Debar, and Barzillai the Gileadite from Rogelim [28] brought bedding and bowls and articles of pottery. They also brought wheat and barley, flour and roasted grain, beans and lentils,[e] [29] honey and curds, sheep, and cheese from cows' milk for David and his people to eat. For they said, "The people have become exhausted and hungry and thirsty in the wilderness."

18 David mustered the men who were with him and appointed over them commanders of thousands and commanders of hundreds. [2] David sent out his troops, a third under the command of Joab, a third under Joab's brother Abishai son of Zeruiah, and a third under Ittai the Gittite. The king told the troops, "I myself will surely march out with you."

[3] But the men said, "You must not go out; if we are forced to flee, they won't care about us. Even if half of us die, they won't care; but you are worth ten thousand of us.[f] It would be better now for you to give us support from the city."

---

[a] 20 Or *"They passed by the sheep pen toward the water."*   [b] 25 Hebrew *Ithra*, a variant of *Jether*   [c] 25 Some Septuagint manuscripts (see also 1 Chron. 2:17); Hebrew and other Septuagint manuscripts *Israelite*   [d] 25 Hebrew *Abigal*, a variant of *Abigail*   [e] 28 Most Septuagint manuscripts and Syriac; Hebrew *lentils, and roasted grain*   [f] 3 Two Hebrew manuscripts, some Septuagint manuscripts and Vulgate; most Hebrew manuscripts *care; for now there are ten thousand like us*

⁴The king answered, "I will do whatever seems best to you."

So the king stood beside the gate while all his men marched out in units of hundreds and of thousands. ⁵The king commanded Joab, Abishai and Ittai, "Be gentle with the young man Absalom for my sake." And all the troops heard the king giving orders concerning Absalom to each of the commanders.

⁶David's army marched out of the city to fight Israel, and the battle took place in the forest of Ephraim. ⁷There Israel's troops were routed by David's men, and the casualties that day were great—twenty thousand men. ⁸The battle spread out over the whole countryside, and the forest swallowed up more men that day than the sword.

⁹Now Absalom happened to meet David's men. He was riding his mule, and as the mule went under the thick branches of a large oak, Absalom's hair got caught in the tree. He was left hanging in midair, while the mule he was riding kept on going.

¹⁰When one of the men saw what had happened, he told Joab, "I just saw Absalom hanging in an oak tree."

¹¹Joab said to the man who had told him this, "What! You saw him? Why didn't you strike him

to the ground right there? Then I would have had to give you ten shekelsᵃ of silver and a warrior's belt."

¹²But the man replied, "Even if a thousand shekelsᵇ were weighed out into my hands, I would not lay a hand on the king's son. In our hearing the king commanded you and Abishai and Ittai, 'Protect the young man Absalom for my sake.ᶜ' ¹³And if I had put my life in jeopardyᵈ—and nothing is hidden from the king—you would have kept your distance from me."

¹⁴Joab said, "I'm not going to wait like this for you." So he took three javelins in his hand and plunged them into Absalom's heart while Absalom was still alive in the oak tree. ¹⁵And ten of Joab's armor-bearers surrounded Absalom, struck him and killed him.

¹⁶Then Joab sounded the trumpet, and the troops stopped pursuing Israel, for Joab halted them. ¹⁷They took Absalom, threw him into a big pit in the forest and piled up a large heap of rocks over him. Meanwhile, all the Israelites fled to their homes.

¹⁸During his lifetime Absalom had taken a pillar and erected it in the King's Valley as a monument to himself, for he thought, "I have no son to carry on the

---

ᵃ 11 That is, about 4 ounces or about 115 grams   ᵇ 12 That is, about 25 pounds or about 12 kilograms   ᶜ 12 A few Hebrew manuscripts, Septuagint, Vulgate and Syriac; most Hebrew manuscripts may be translated *Absalom, whoever you may be.*   ᵈ 13 Or *Otherwise, if I had acted treacherously toward him* memory of my name." He named the pillar after himself, and it is called Absalom's Monument to this day.

David Mourns

19 Now Ahimaaz son of Zadok said, "Let me run and take the news to the king that the LORD has vindicated him by delivering him from the hand of his enemies."

20 "You are not the one to take the news today," Joab told him. "You may take the news another time, but you must not do so today, because the king's son is dead."

21 Then Joab said to a Cushite, "Go, tell the king what you have seen." The Cushite bowed down before Joab and ran off.

22 Ahimaaz son of Zadok again said to Joab, "Come what may, please let me run behind the Cushite."

But Joab replied, "My son, why do you want to go? You don't have any news that will bring you a reward."

23 He said, "Come what may, I want to run."

So Joab said, "Run!" Then Ahimaaz ran by way of the plain[a] and outran the Cushite.

24 While David was sitting between the inner and outer gates, the watchman went up to the roof of the gateway by the wall. As he looked out, he saw a man running alone. 25 The watchman called out to the king and reported it.

The king said, "If he is alone, he must have good news." And the runner came closer and closer.

26 Then the watchman saw another runner, and he called down to the gatekeeper, "Look, another man running alone!"

The king said, "He must be bringing good news, too."

27 The watchman said, "It seems to me that the first one runs like Ahimaaz son of Zadok."

"He's a good man," the king said. "He comes with good news."

28 Then Ahimaaz called out to the king, "All is well!" He bowed down before the king with his face to the ground and said, "Praise be to the LORD your God! He has delivered up those who lifted their hands against my lord the king."

29 The king asked, "Is the young man Absalom safe?"

Ahimaaz answered, "I saw great confusion just as Joab was about to send the king's servant and me, your servant, but I don't know what it was."

30 The king said, "Stand aside and wait here." So he stepped aside and stood there.

31 Then the Cushite arrived and said, "My lord the king, hear the good news! The LORD has vindicated you today by delivering you from the hand of all who rose up against you."

a 23 That is, the plain of the Jordan

[32]The king asked the Cushite, "Is the young man Absalom safe?"

The Cushite replied, "May the enemies of my lord the king and all who rise up to harm you be like that young man."

[33]The king was shaken. He went up to the room over the gateway and wept. As he went, he said: "O my son Absalom! My son, my son Absalom! If only I had died instead of you—O Absalom, my son, my son!"[a]

19 [b]Joab was told, "The king is weeping and mourning for Absalom." [2]And for the whole army the victory that day was turned into mourning, because on that day the troops heard it said, "The king is grieving for his son." [3]The men stole into the city that day as men steal in who are ashamed when they flee from battle. [4]The king covered his face and cried aloud, "O my son Absalom! O Absalom, my son, my son!"

[5]Then Joab went into the house to the king and said, "Today you have humiliated all your men, who have just saved your life and the lives of your sons and daughters and the lives of your wives and concubines. [6]You love those who hate you and hate those who love you. You have made it clear today that the commanders and their men mean nothing to you. I see that you would be pleased if Absalom were alive today and all of us were dead. [7]Now go out and encourage your men. I swear by the LORD that if you don't go out, not a man will be left with you by nightfall. This will be worse for you than all the calamities that have come on you from your youth till now."

[8]So the king got up and took his seat in the gateway. When the men were told, "The king is sitting in the gateway," they all came before him.

Meanwhile, the Israelites had fled to their homes.

David Returns to Jerusalem

[9]Throughout the tribes of Israel, all the people were arguing among themselves, saying, "The king delivered us from the hand of our enemies; he is the one who rescued us from the hand of the Philistines. But now he has fled the country to escape from Absalom; [10]and Absalom, whom we anointed to rule over us, has died in battle. So why do you say nothing about bringing the king back?"

[11]King David sent this message to Zadok and Abiathar, the priests: "Ask the elders of Judah, 'Why should you be the last to bring the king back to his palace, since what is being said throughout Israel has reached the king at his quarters? [12]You are my relatives, my own flesh and blood. So why should you be

a 33 In Hebrew texts this verse (18:33) is numbered 19:1.   b In Hebrew texts 19:1-43 is numbered 19:2-44.

the last to bring back the king?' ¹³And say to Amasa, 'Are you not my own flesh and blood? May God deal with me, be it ever so severely, if you are not the commander of my army for life in place of Joab.'"

¹⁴He won over the hearts of the men of Judah so that they were all of one mind. They sent word to the king, "Return, you and all your men." ¹⁵Then the king returned and went as far as the Jordan.

Now the men of Judah had come to Gilgal to go out and meet the king and bring him across the Jordan. ¹⁶Shimei son of Gera, the Benjamite from Bahurim, hurried down with the men of Judah to meet King David. ¹⁷With him were a thousand Benjamites, along with Ziba, the steward of Saul's household, and his fifteen sons and twenty servants. They rushed to the Jordan, where the king was. ¹⁸They crossed at the ford to take the king's household over and to do whatever he wished.

When Shimei son of Gera crossed the Jordan, he fell prostrate before the king ¹⁹and said to him, "May my lord not hold me guilty. Do not remember how your servant did wrong on the day my lord the king left Jerusalem. May the king put it out of his mind. ²⁰For I your servant know that I have sinned, but today I have come here as the first from the tribes of Joseph to come down and meet my lord the king."

²¹Then Abishai son of Zeruiah said, "Shouldn't Shimei be put to death for this? He cursed the LORD's anointed."

²²David replied, "What does this have to do with you, you sons of Zeruiah? What right do you have to interfere? Should anyone be put to death in Israel today? Don't I know that today I am king over Israel?" ²³So the king said to Shimei, "You shall not die." And the king promised him on oath.

²⁴Mephibosheth, Saul's grandson, also went down to meet the king. He had not taken care of his feet or trimmed his mustache or washed his clothes from the day the king left until the day he returned safely. ²⁵When he came from Jerusalem to meet the king, the king asked him, "Why didn't you go with me, Mephibosheth?"

²⁶He said, "My lord the king, since I your servant am lame, I said, 'I will have my donkey saddled and will ride on it, so I can go with the king.' But Ziba my servant betrayed me. ²⁷And he has slandered your servant to my lord the king. My lord the king is like an angel of God; so do whatever you wish. ²⁸All my grandfather's descendants deserved nothing but death from my lord the king, but you gave your servant a place among those who eat at your table. So what right do I

have to make any more appeals to the king?"

29 The king said to him, "Why say more? I order you and Ziba to divide the land."

30 Mephibosheth said to the king, "Let him take everything, now that my lord the king has returned home safely."

31 Barzillai the Gileadite also came down from Rogelim to cross the Jordan with the king and to send him on his way from there. **32** Now Barzillai was very old, eighty years of age. He had provided for the king during his stay in Mahanaim, for he was a very wealthy man. **33** The king said to Barzillai, "Cross over with me and stay with me in Jerusalem, and I will provide for you."

34 But Barzillai answered the king, "How many more years will I live, that I should go up to Jerusalem with the king? **35** I am now eighty years old. Can I tell the difference between what is enjoyable and what is not? Can your servant taste what he eats and drinks? Can I still hear the voices of male and female singers? Why should your servant be an added burden to my lord the king? **36** Your servant will cross over the Jordan with the king for a short distance, but why should the king reward me in this way? **37** Let your servant return, that I may die in my own town near the tomb of my father and mother. But here is your servant Kim-ham. Let him cross over with my lord the king. Do for him whatever you wish."

38 The king said, "Kimham shall cross over with me, and I will do for him whatever you wish. And anything you desire from me I will do for you."

39 So all the people crossed the Jordan, and then the king crossed over. The king kissed Barzillai and bid him farewell, and Barzillai returned to his home.

40 When the king crossed over to Gilgal, Kimham crossed with him. All the troops of Judah and half the troops of Israel had taken the king over.

41 Soon all the men of Israel were coming to the king and saying to him, "Why did our brothers, the men of Judah, steal the king away and bring him and his household across the Jordan, together with all his men?"

42 All the men of Judah answered the men of Israel, "We did this because the king is closely related to us. Why are you angry about it? Have we eaten any of the king's provisions? Have we taken anything for ourselves?"

43 Then the men of Israel answered the men of Judah, "We have ten shares in the king; so we have a greater claim on David than you have. Why then do you treat us with contempt? Weren't we the first to speak of bringing back our king?"

But the men of Judah pre

their claims even more forcefully than the men of Israel.

Sheba Rebels Against David

20 Now a troublemaker named Sheba son of Bikri, a Benjamite, happened to be there. He sounded the trumpet and shouted,

> "We have no share in David,
>   no part in Jesse's son!
> Every man to his tent, Israel!"

²So all the men of Israel deserted David to follow Sheba son of Bikri. But the men of Judah stayed by their king all the way from the Jordan to Jerusalem.

³When David returned to his palace in Jerusalem, he took the ten concubines he had left to take care of the palace and put them in a house under guard. He provided for them but had no sexual relations with them. They were kept in confinement till the day of their death, living as widows.

⁴Then the king said to Amasa, "Summon the men of Judah to come to me within three days, and be here yourself." ⁵But when Amasa went to summon Judah, he took longer than the time the king had set for him.

⁶David said to Abishai, "Now Sheba son of Bikri will do us more harm than Absalom did. Take your master's men and pursue him, or he will find fortified cities and escape from us."*ᵃ* ⁷So Joab's men and the Kerethites and Pelethites and all the mighty warriors went out under the command of Abishai. They marched out from Jerusalem to pursue Sheba son of Bikri.

⁸While they were at the great rock in Gibeon, Amasa came to meet them. Joab was wearing his military tunic, and strapped over it at his waist was a belt with a dagger in its sheath. As he stepped forward, it dropped out of its sheath.

⁹Joab said to Amasa, "How are you, my brother?" Then Joab took Amasa by the beard with his right hand to kiss him. ¹⁰Amasa was not on his guard against the dagger in Joab's hand, and Joab plunged it into his belly, and his intestines spilled out on the ground. Without being stabbed again, Amasa died. Then Joab and his brother Abishai pursued Sheba son of Bikri.

¹¹One of Joab's men stood beside Amasa and said, "Whoever favors Joab, and whoever is for David, let him follow Joab!" ¹²Amasa lay wallowing in his blood in the middle of the road, and the man saw that all the troops came to a halt there. When he realized that everyone who came up to Amasa stopped, he dragged him from the road into a field and threw a garment over him. ¹³After Amasa had been removed from the road, everyone

---

ᵃ Or *and do us serious injury*

Balaam's Talking Donkey
NUMBERS 22:21–41

The Walls of Jericho Fall Down

JOSHUA 6:1–21

Famous People of the Bible

Abraham	Genesis 12:1—25:10
Adam and Eve	Genesis 2:21—3:19
David	1 Samuel 16–17; 2 Samuel 1–6; 11–12
Deborah	Judges 4–5
Esau	Genesis 25:29–34; 27; Malachi 1:2–3
Esther	Esther 3–8
Gideon	Judges 6–7
Hannah	1 Samuel 1:1—2:21
Isaac	Genesis 24–27
Jacob	Genesis 27–33
Job	Job 1:1—2:13; 42:7–17
John	John 19:26–27; Acts 4:1–31
John the Baptist	Matthew 3; 14:1–12
Joseph	Genesis 37; 39–50
Joshua	Numbers 13:1—14:38; Joshua 1–6
Lazarus	John 11:1–44
Mary the mother of Jesus	Luke 1:26—2:52
Mary and Martha	Luke 10:38–42; John 11:1–5, 19–33
Mary Magdalene	John 20:1–18
Matthew	Mark 2:13–14
Miriam	Exodus 2:1–10; Numbers 12:1–15
Moses	Exodus 2–4; 14–15
Naomi	Ruth 1–4
Noah	Genesis 6:9—9:17
Paul (Saul)	Acts 9:1–19; 21–28
Peter	Matthew 14:22–33; Acts 3:1–10
Philip	Acts 8:4–7, 26–40
Ruth	Ruth 1–4
Samson	Judges 13–16
Samuel	1 Samuel 1–3; 8; 16
Sarah	Genesis 11:29—23:20
Solomon	1 Kings 2:1—3:28; 4:20–34; 10
Timothy	Acts 16:1; 17:14–15; 1 Timothy 1:1–2

David and Goliath
1 SAMUEL 17

went on with Joab to pursue Sheba son of Bikri.

[14] Sheba passed through all the tribes of Israel to Abel Beth Maakah and through the entire region of the Bikrites,[a] who gathered together and followed him. [15] All the troops with Joab came and besieged Sheba in Abel Beth Maakah. They built a siege ramp up to the city, and it stood against the outer fortifications. While they were battering the wall to bring it down, [16] a wise woman called from the city, "Listen! Listen! Tell Joab to come here so I can speak to him." [17] He went toward her, and she asked, "Are you Joab?"

"I am," he answered.

She said, "Listen to what your servant has to say."

"I'm listening," he said.

[18] She continued, "Long ago they used to say, 'Get your answer at Abel,' and that settled it. [19] We are the peaceful and faithful in Israel. You are trying to destroy a city that is a mother in Israel. Why do you want to swallow up the LORD's inheritance?"

[20] "Far be it from me!" Joab replied, "Far be it from me to swallow up or destroy! [21] That is not the case. A man named Sheba son of Bikri, from the hill country of Ephraim, has lifted up his hand against the king, against David. Hand over this one man, and I'll withdraw from the city."

The woman said to Joab, "His head will be thrown to you from the wall."

[22] Then the woman went to all the people with her wise advice, and they cut off the head of Sheba son of Bikri and threw it to Joab. So he sounded the trumpet, and his men dispersed from the city, each returning to his home. And Joab went back to the king in Jerusalem.

David's Officials

[23] Joab was over Israel's entire army; Benaiah son of Jehoiada was over the Kerethites and Pelethites; [24] Adoniram[b] was in charge of forced labor; Jehoshaphat son of Ahilud was recorder; [25] Sheva was secretary; Zadok and Abiathar were priests; [26] and Ira the Jairite[c] was David's priest.

The Gibeonites Avenged

21 During the reign of David, there was a famine for three successive years; so David sought the face of the LORD. The LORD said, "It is on account of Saul and his blood-stained house; it is because he put the Gibeonites to death."

[2] The king summoned the Gibeonites and spoke to them. (Now the Gibeonites were not a part

---

[a] 14 See Septuagint and Vulgate; Hebrew *Berites*. [b] 24 Some Septuagint manuscripts (see also 1 Kings 4:6 and 5:14); Hebrew *Adoram* [c] 26 Hebrew; some Septuagint manuscripts and Syriac (see also 23:38) *Ithrite*

of Israel but were survivors of the Amorites; the Israelites had sworn to spare them, but Saul in his zeal for Israel and Judah had tried to annihilate them.) ³David asked the Gibeonites, "What shall I do for you? How shall I make atonement so that you will bless the Lord's inheritance?"

⁴The Gibeonites answered him, "We have no right to demand silver or gold from Saul or his family, nor do we have the right to put anyone in Israel to death."

"What do you want me to do for you?" David asked.

⁵They answered the king, "As for the man who destroyed us and plotted against us so that we have been decimated and have no place anywhere in Israel, ⁶let seven of his male descendants be given to us to be killed and their bodies exposed before the Lord at Gibeah of Saul—the Lord's chosen one."

So the king said, "I will give them to you."

⁷The king spared Mephibosheth son of Jonathan, the son of Saul, because of the oath before the Lord between David and Jonathan son of Saul. ⁸But the king took Armoni and Mephibosheth, the two sons of Aiah's daughter Rizpah, whom she had borne to Saul, together with the five sons of Saul's daughter Merab,ᵃ whom she had borne to

Adriel son of Barzillai the Meholathite. ⁹He handed them over to the Gibeonites, who killed them and exposed their bodies on a hill before the Lord. All seven of them fell together; they were put to death during the first days of the harvest, just as the barley harvest was beginning.

¹⁰Rizpah daughter of Aiah took sackcloth and spread it out for herself on a rock. From the beginning of the harvest till the rain poured down from the heavens on the bodies, she did not let the birds touch them by day or the wild animals by night. ¹¹When David was told what Aiah's daughter Rizpah, Saul's concubine, had done, ¹²he went and took the bones of Saul and his son Jonathan from the citizens of Jabesh Gilead. (They had stolen their bodies from the public square at Beth Shan, where the Philistines had hung them after they struck Saul down on Gilboa.) ¹³David brought the bones of Saul and his son Jonathan from there, and the bones of those who had been killed and exposed were gathered up.

¹⁴They buried the bones of Saul and his son Jonathan in the tomb of Saul's father Kish, at Zela in Benjamin, and did everything the king commanded. After that, God answered prayer in behalf of the land.

ᵃ 8 Two Hebrew manuscripts, some Septuagint manuscripts and Syriac (see also 1 Samuel 18:19); most Hebrew and Septuagint manuscripts *Michal*

Wars Against the Philistines

15 Once again there was a battle between the Philistines and Israel. David went down with his men to fight against the Philistines, and he became exhausted. **16** And Ishbi-Benob, one of the descendants of Rapha, whose bronze spearhead weighed three hundred shekels[a] and who was armed with a new sword, said he would kill David. **17** But Abishai son of Zeruiah came to David's rescue; he struck the Philistine down and killed him. Then David's men swore to him, saying, "Never again will you go out with us to battle, so that the lamp of Israel will not be extinguished."

18 In the course of time, there was another battle with the Philistines, at Gob. At that time Sibbekai the Hushathite killed Saph, one of the descendants of Rapha.

19 In another battle with the Philistines at Gob, Elhanan son of Jair[b] the Bethlehemite killed the brother of[c] Goliath the Gittite, who had a spear with a shaft like a weaver's rod.

20 In still another battle, which took place at Gath, there was a huge man with six fingers on each hand and six toes on each foot — twenty-four in all. He also was descended from Rapha. **21** When he taunted Israel, Jonathan son of Shimeah, David's brother, killed him.

22 These four were descendants of Rapha in Gath, and they fell at the hands of David and his men.

David's Song of Praise

22 David sang to the LORD the words of this song when the LORD delivered him from the hand of all his enemies and from the hand of Saul. **2** He said:

"The LORD is my rock,
   my fortress and my
   deliverer;
3 my God is my rock, in whom
   I take refuge,
my shield[d] and the horn[e] of
   my salvation.
He is my stronghold, my refuge
   and my savior —
from violent people you
   save me.

4 "I called to the LORD, who is
   worthy of praise,
and have been saved from
   my enemies.
5 The waves of death swirled
   about me;
the torrents of destruction
   overwhelmed me.
6 The cords of the grave coiled
   around me;
the snares of death
   confronted me.

7 "In my distress I called to the
   LORD;
I called out to my God.

---

[a] *16* That is, about 7 1/2 pounds or about 3.5 kilograms   [b] *19* See 1 Chron. 20:5; Hebrew *Jaare-Oregim*.   [c] *19* See 1 Chron. 20:5; Hebrew does not have *the brother of*.   [d] *3* Or *sovereign*   [e] *3* *Horn* here symbolizes strength.

From his temple he heard my
     voice;
  my cry came to his ears.
⁸The earth trembled and
     quaked,
  the foundations of the
     heavens*a* shook;
  they trembled because he
     was angry.
⁹Smoke rose from his nostrils;
  consuming fire came from
     his mouth,
  burning coals blazed out
     of it.
¹⁰He parted the heavens and
     came down;
  dark clouds were under his
     feet.
¹¹He mounted the cherubim and
     flew;
  he soared*b* on the wings of
     the wind.
¹²He made darkness his canopy
     around him —
  the dark*c* rain clouds of the
     sky.
¹³Out of the brightness of his
     presence
  bolts of lightning blazed
     forth.
¹⁴The LORD thundered from
     heaven;
  the voice of the Most High
     resounded.
¹⁵He shot his arrows and
     scattered the enemy,
  with great bolts of lightning
     he routed them.

¹⁶The valleys of the sea were
     exposed
  and the foundations of the
     earth laid bare
at the rebuke of the LORD,
  at the blast of breath from
     his nostrils.

¹⁷"He reached down from on
     high and took hold
     of me;
  he drew me out of deep
     waters.
¹⁸He rescued me from my
     powerful enemy,
  from my foes, who were too
     strong for me.
¹⁹They confronted me in the day
     of my disaster,
  but the LORD was my
     support.
²⁰He brought me out into a
     spacious place;
  he rescued me because he
     delighted in me.

²¹"The LORD has dealt with
     me according to my
     righteousness;
  according to the cleanness
     of my hands he has
     rewarded me.
²²For I have kept the ways of the
     LORD;
  I am not guilty of turning
     from my God.
²³All his laws are before me;
  I have not turned away from
     his decrees.

---

a 8 Hebrew; Vulgate and Syriac (see also Psalm 18:7) *mountains* *b* 11 Many
Hebrew manuscripts (see also Psalm 18:10); most Hebrew manuscripts *appeared*
c 12 Septuagint (see also Psalm 18:11); Hebrew *massed*

²⁴I have been blameless before
  him
  and have kept myself from
  sin.
²⁵The Lord has rewarded
  me according to my
  righteousness,
  according to my cleanness*a*
  in his sight.

²⁶"To the faithful you show
  yourself faithful,
  to the blameless you show
  yourself blameless,
²⁷to the pure you show yourself
  pure,
  but to the devious you show
  yourself shrewd.
²⁸You save the humble,
  but your eyes are on the
  haughty to bring them
  low.
²⁹You, Lord, are my lamp;
  the Lord turns my darkness
  into light.
³⁰With your help I can advance
  against a troop*b*;
  with my God I can scale a
  wall.

³¹"As for God, his way is perfect:
  The Lord's word is flawless;
  he shields all who take
  refuge in him.
³²For who is God besides the
  Lord?
  And who is the Rock except
  our God?

³³It is God who arms me with
  strength*c*
  and keeps my way secure.
³⁴He makes my feet like the feet
  of a deer;
  he causes me to stand on the
  heights.
³⁵He trains my hands for battle;
  my arms can bend a bow of
  bronze.
³⁶You make your saving help my
  shield;
  your help has made*d* me
  great.
³⁷You provide a broad path for
  my feet,
  so that my ankles do not give
  way.

³⁸"I pursued my enemies and
  crushed them;
  I did not turn back till they
  were destroyed.
³⁹I crushed them completely,
  and they could not rise;
  they fell beneath my feet.
⁴⁰You armed me with strength
  for battle;
  you humbled my adversaries
  before me.
⁴¹You made my enemies turn
  their backs in flight,
  and I destroyed my foes.
⁴²They cried for help, but there
  was no one to save
  them—
  to the Lord, but he did not
  answer.

---

a 25 Hebrew; Septuagint and Vulgate (see also Psalm 18:24) *to the cleanness of my hands*   *b* 30 Or *can run through a barricade*   *c* 33 Dead Sea Scrolls, some Septuagint manuscripts, Vulgate and Syriac (see also Psalm 18:32); Masoretic Text *who is my strong refuge*   *d* 36 Dead Sea Scrolls; Masoretic Text *shield; / you stoop down to make*

⁴³I beat them as fine as the dust
    of the earth;
  I pounded and trampled
    them like mud in the
    streets.

⁴⁴"You have delivered me
    from the attacks of the
    peoples;
  you have preserved me as
    the head of nations.
People I did not know now
    serve me,
⁴⁵ foreigners cower before me;
  as soon as they hear of me,
    they obey me.
⁴⁶They all lose heart;
  they come trembling*ᵃ* from
    their strongholds.

⁴⁷"The Lᴏʀᴅ lives! Praise be to
    my Rock!
  Exalted be my God, the
    Rock, my Savior!
⁴⁸He is the God who avenges me,
  who puts the nations
    under me,
⁴⁹ who sets me free from my
    enemies.
You exalted me above my
    foes;
  from a violent man you
    rescued me.
⁵⁰Therefore I will praise you,
  Lᴏʀᴅ, among the
    nations;
  I will sing the praises of your
    name.

⁵¹"He gives his king great
    victories;

he shows unfailing kindness
    to his anointed,
  to David and his
    descendants forever."

David's Last Words

23 These are the last words
of David:

"The inspired utterance of
    David son of Jesse,
  the utterance of the man
    exalted by the Most
    High,
the man anointed by the God
    of Jacob,
  the hero of Israel's songs:

²"The Spirit of the Lᴏʀᴅ spoke
    through me;
  his word was on my tongue.
³The God of Israel spoke,
  the Rock of Israel said to me:
'When one rules over people
    in righteousness,
  when he rules in the fear of
    God,
⁴he is like the light of morning
    at sunrise
  on a cloudless morning,
like the brightness after rain
    that brings grass from the
    earth.'

⁵"If my house were not right
    with God,
  surely he would not have
    made with me an
    everlasting covenant,
arranged and secured in
    every part;

ᵃ 46 Some Septuagint manuscripts and Vulgate (see also Psalm 18:45); Masoretic
Text *they arm themselves*

surely he would not bring to
    fruition my salvation
  and grant me my every
    desire.
6 But evil men are all to be cast
    aside like thorns,
  which are not gathered with
    the hand.
7 Whoever touches thorns
  uses a tool of iron or the
    shaft of a spear;
  they are burned up where
    they lie."

David's Mighty Warriors

8 These are the names of David's mighty warriors:

Josheb-Basshebeth,[a] a Tahkemonite,[b] was chief of the Three; he raised his spear against eight hundred men, whom he killed[c] in one encounter.

9 Next to him was Eleazar son of Dodai the Ahohite. As one of the three mighty warriors, he was with David when they taunted the Philistines gathered at Pas Dammim[d] for battle. Then the Israelites retreated, 10 but Eleazar stood his ground and struck down the Philistines till his hand grew tired and froze to the sword. The LORD brought about a great victory that day. The troops returned to Eleazar, but only to strip the dead.

11 Next to him was Shammah son of Agee the Hararite. When the Philistines banded together at a place where there was a field full of lentils, Israel's troops fled from them. 12 But Shammah took his stand in the middle of the field. He defended it and struck the Philistines down, and the LORD brought about a great victory.

13 During harvest time, three of the thirty chief warriors came down to David at the cave of Adullam, while a band of Philistines was encamped in the Valley of Rephaim. 14 At that time David was in the stronghold, and the Philistine garrison was at Bethlehem. 15 David longed for water and said, "Oh, that someone would get me a drink of water from the well near the gate of Bethlehem!" 16 So the three mighty warriors broke through the Philistine lines, drew water from the well near the gate of Bethlehem and carried it back to David. But he refused to drink it; instead, he poured it out before the LORD. 17 "Far be it from me, LORD, to do this!" he said. "Is it not the blood of men who went at the risk of their lives?" And David would not drink it.

Such were the exploits of the three mighty warriors.

18 Abishai the brother of Joab son of Zeruiah was chief of the

---

[a] 8 Hebrew; some Septuagint manuscripts suggest *Ish-Bosheth,* that is, *Esh-Baal* (see also 1 Chron. 11:11 *Jashobeam*).   [b] 8 Probably a variant of *Hakmonite* (see 1 Chron. 11:11)   [c] 8 Some Septuagint manuscripts (see also 1 Chron. 11:11); Hebrew and other Septuagint manuscripts *Three; it was Adino the Eznite who killed eight hundred men*   [d] 9 See 1 Chron. 11:13; Hebrew *gathered there.*

Three.[a] He raised his spear against three hundred men, whom he killed, and so he became as famous as the Three. [19]Was he not held in greater honor than the Three? He became their commander, even though he was not included among them.

[20]Benaiah son of Jehoiada, a valiant fighter from Kabzeel, performed great exploits. He struck down Moab's two mightiest warriors. He also went down into a pit on a snowy day and killed a lion. [21]And he struck down a huge Egyptian. Although the Egyptian had a spear in his hand, Benaiah went against him with a club. He snatched the spear from the Egyptian's hand and killed him with his own spear. [22]Such were the exploits of Benaiah son of Jehoiada; he too was as famous as the three mighty warriors. [23]He was held in greater honor than any of the Thirty, but he was not included among the Three. And David put him in charge of his bodyguard.

[24]Among the Thirty were:
Asahel the brother of Joab,
Elhanan son of Dodo from Bethlehem,
[25]Shammah the Harodite,
Elika the Harodite,
[26]Helez the Paltite,
Ira son of Ikkesh from Tekoa,
[27]Abiezer from Anathoth,
Sibbekai[b] the Hushathite,
[28]Zalmon the Ahohite,
Maharai the Netophathite,
[29]Heled[c] son of Baanah the Netophathite,
Ithai son of Ribai from Gibeah in Benjamin,
[30]Benaiah the Pirathonite,
Hiddai[d] from the ravines of Gaash,
[31]Abi-Albon the Arbathite,
Azmaveth the Barhumite,
[32]Eliahba the Shaalbonite,
the sons of Jashen,
Jonathan [33]son of[e] Shammah the Hararite,
Ahiam son of Sharar[f] the Hararite,
[34]Eliphelet son of Ahasbai the Maakathite,
Eliam son of Ahithophel the Gilonite,
[35]Hezro the Carmelite,
Paarai the Arbite,
[36]Igal son of Nathan from Zobah,
the son of Hagri,[g]
[37]Zelek the Ammonite,
Naharai the Beerothite, the armor-bearer of Joab son of Zeruiah,

---

[a] 18 Most Hebrew manuscripts (see also 1 Chron. 11:20); two Hebrew manuscripts and Syriac *Thirty*   [b] 27 Some Septuagint manuscripts (see also 21:18; 1 Chron. 11:29); Hebrew *Mebunnai*   [c] 29 Some Hebrew manuscripts and Vulgate (see also 1 Chron. 11:30); most Hebrew manuscripts *Heleb*   [d] 30 Hebrew; some Septuagint manuscripts (see also 1 Chron. 11:32) *Hurai*   [e] 33 Some Septuagint manuscripts (see also 1 Chron. 11:34); Hebrew does not have *son of*.   [f] 33 Hebrew; some Septuagint manuscripts (see also 1 Chron. 11:35) *Sakar*   [g] 36 Some Septuagint manuscripts (see also 1 Chron. 11:38); Hebrew *Haggadi*

³⁸Ira the Ithrite,
Gareb the Ithrite
³⁹and Uriah the Hittite.
There were thirty-seven in all.

David Enrolls the Fighting Men

24 Again the anger of the LORD burned against Israel, and he incited David against them, saying, "Go and take a census of Israel and Judah."

²So the king said to Joab and the army commanders^a with him, "Go throughout the tribes of Israel from Dan to Beersheba and enroll the fighting men, so that I may know how many there are."

³But Joab replied to the king, "May the LORD your God multiply the troops a hundred times over, and may the eyes of my lord the king see it. But why does my lord the king want to do such a thing?"

⁴The king's word, however, overruled Joab and the army commanders; so they left the presence of the king to enroll the fighting men of Israel.

⁵After crossing the Jordan, they camped near Aroer, south of the town in the gorge, and then went through Gad and on to Jazer. ⁶They went to Gilead and the region of Tahtim Hodshi, and on to Dan Jaan and around toward Sidon. ⁷Then they went toward the fortress of Tyre and all the towns of the Hivites and Canaanites. Finally, they went on to Beersheba in the Negev of Judah.

⁸After they had gone through the entire land, they came back to Jerusalem at the end of nine months and twenty days.

⁹Joab reported the number of the fighting men to the king: In Israel there were eight hundred thousand able-bodied men who could handle a sword, and in Judah five hundred thousand.

¹⁰David was conscience-stricken after he had counted the fighting men, and he said to the LORD, "I have sinned greatly in what I have done. Now, LORD, I beg you, take away the guilt of your servant. I have done a very foolish thing."

¹¹Before David got up the next morning, the word of the LORD had come to Gad the prophet, David's seer: ¹²"Go and tell David, 'This is what the LORD says: I am giving you three options. Choose one of them for me to carry out against you.'"

¹³So Gad went to David and said to him, "Shall there come on you three^b years of famine in your land? Or three months of fleeing from your enemies while they pursue you? Or three days of plague in your land? Now then, think it over and decide how I should answer the one who sent me."

---

^a 2 Septuagint (see also verse 4 and 1 Chron. 21:2); Hebrew *Joab the army commander*   ^b 13 Septuagint (see also 1 Chron. 21:12); Hebrew *seven*

[14]David said to Gad, "I am in deep distress. Let us fall into the hands of the LORD, for his mercy is great; but do not let me fall into human hands."

[15]So the LORD sent a plague on Israel from that morning until the end of the time designated, and seventy thousand of the people from Dan to Beersheba died. [16]When the angel stretched out his hand to destroy Jerusalem, the LORD relented concerning the disaster and said to the angel who was afflicting the people, "Enough! Withdraw your hand." The angel of the LORD was then at the threshing floor of Araunah the Jebusite.

[17]When David saw the angel who was striking down the people, he said to the LORD, "I have sinned; I, the shepherd,[a] have done wrong. These are but sheep. What have they done? Let your hand fall on me and my family."

David Builds an Altar

[18]On that day Gad went to David and said to him, "Go up and build an altar to the LORD on the threshing floor of Araunah the Jebusite." [19]So David went up, as the LORD had commanded through Gad. [20]When Araunah looked and saw the king and his officials coming toward him, he went out and bowed down before the king with his face to the ground.

[21]Araunah said, "Why has my lord the king come to his servant?"

"To buy your threshing floor," David answered, "so I can build an altar to the LORD, that the plague on the people may be stopped."

[22]Araunah said to David, "Let my lord the king take whatever he wishes and offer it up. Here are oxen for the burnt offering, and here are threshing sledges and ox yokes for the wood. [23]Your Majesty, Araunah[b] gives all this to the king." Araunah also said to him, "May the LORD your God accept you."

[24]But the king replied to Araunah, "No, I insist on paying you for it. I will not sacrifice to the LORD my God burnt offerings that cost me nothing."

So David bought the threshing floor and the oxen and paid fifty shekels[c] of silver for them. [25]David built an altar to the LORD there and sacrificed burnt offerings and fellowship offerings. Then the LORD answered his prayer in behalf of the land, and the plague on Israel was stopped.

---

[a] 17 Dead Sea Scrolls and Septuagint; Masoretic Text does not have *the shepherd*.
[b] 23 Some Hebrew manuscripts and Septuagint; most Hebrew manuscripts *King Araunah*   [c] 24 That is, about 1 1/4 pounds or about 575 grams

1 Kings

Introduction:

Beginning with Solomon's reign (about 971 BC) 1 Kings records the history of Israel through the divided kingdom to the death of Ahaziah, the son of Ahab. Chapters 3 through 11 describe Solomon's reign, including the building of the temple and the palace in Jerusalem.

Rehoboam, Solomon's son, took the throne after Solomon's death but lost the northern part of the kingdom to Jeroboam. After this the northern kingdom was known as Israel, and the southern kingdom was called Judah. The last chapters of 1 Kings tell about the evil King Ahab and God's prophet Elijah, who condemned Ahab's wickedness and Israel's disobedience.

Because the author of 1 and 2 Kings was interested in Israel's faithfulness to God and his covenant he recorded how each king was faithful or unfaithful to God. The author often used the phrase, "did what was right in the eyes of the LORD," or "did evil in the eyes of the LORD," to describe the goodness or wickedness of the king.

The same pattern as in the time of the judges repeats itself during the time of the kings: God brought peace to the land when Israel was obedient, but Israel suffered wars and other disasters when the people were disobedient and worshiped idols.

Outline of contents:

The reign of Solomon (1:1–11:43)
Rehoboam and Jeroboam (12:1–14:31)
Kings of Israel and Judah (15:1–16:34)
Elijah and Ahab (17:1–19:21)
The reign of Ahab and Jezebel (20:1–22:53)

Adonijah Sets Himself Up as King

1 When King David was very old, he could not keep warm even when they put covers over him. ²So his attendants said to him, "Let us look for a young virgin to serve the king and take care of him. She can lie beside him so that our lord the king may keep warm."

³Then they searched throughout Israel for a beautiful young woman and found Abishag, a Shunammite, and brought her to the king. ⁴The woman was very

beautiful; she took care of the king and waited on him, but the king had no sexual relations with her.

⁵Now Adonijah, whose mother was Haggith, put himself forward and said, "I will be king." So he got chariots and horses*a* ready, with fifty men to run ahead of him. ⁶(His father had never rebuked him by asking, "Why do you behave as you do?" He was also very handsome and was born next after Absalom.)

⁷Adonijah conferred with Joab son of Zeruiah and with Abiathar the priest, and they gave him their support. ⁸But Zadok the priest, Benaiah son of Jehoiada, Nathan the prophet, Shimei and Rei and David's special guard did not join Adonijah.

⁹Adonijah then sacrificed sheep, cattle and fattened calves at the Stone of Zoheleth near En Rogel. He invited all his brothers, the king's sons, and all the royal officials of Judah, ¹⁰but he did not invite Nathan the prophet or Benaiah or the special guard or his brother Solomon.

¹¹Then Nathan asked Bathsheba, Solomon's mother, "Have you not heard that Adonijah, the son of Haggith, has become king, and our lord David knows nothing about it? ¹²Now then, let me advise you how you can save your own life and the life of your son Solomon. ¹³Go in to King David and say to him, 'My lord the king, did you not swear to me your servant: "Surely Solomon your son shall be king after me, and he will sit on my throne"? Why then has Adonijah become king?' ¹⁴While you are still there talking to the king, I will come in and add my word to what you have said."

¹⁵So Bathsheba went to see the aged king in his room, where Abishag the Shunammite was attending him. ¹⁶Bathsheba bowed down, prostrating herself before the king.

"What is it you want?" the king asked.

¹⁷She said to him, "My lord, you yourself swore to me your servant by the LORD your God: 'Solomon your son shall be king after me, and he will sit on my throne.' ¹⁸But now Adonijah has become king, and you, my lord the king, do not know about it. ¹⁹He has sacrificed great numbers of cattle, fattened calves, and sheep, and has invited all the king's sons, Abiathar the priest and Joab the commander of the army, but he has not invited Solomon your servant. ²⁰My lord the king, the eyes of all Israel are on you, to learn from you who will sit on the throne of my lord the king after him. ²¹Otherwise, as soon as my lord the king is laid to rest with his ancestors, I and my son Solomon will be treated as criminals."

---

a 5 Or charioteers

²²While she was still speaking with the king, Nathan the prophet arrived. ²³And the king was told, "Nathan the prophet is here." So he went before the king and bowed with his face to the ground.

²⁴Nathan said, "Have you, my lord the king, declared that Adonijah shall be king after you, and that he will sit on your throne? ²⁵Today he has gone down and sacrificed great numbers of cattle, fattened calves, and sheep. He has invited all the king's sons, the commanders of the army and Abiathar the priest. Right now they are eating and drinking with him and saying, 'Long live King Adonijah!' ²⁶But me your servant, and Zadok the priest, and Benaiah son of Jehoiada, and your servant Solomon he did not invite. ²⁷Is this something my lord the king has done without letting his servants know who should sit on the throne of my lord the king after him?"

David Makes Solomon King

²⁸Then King David said, "Call in Bathsheba." So she came into the king's presence and stood before him. ²⁹The king then took an oath: "As surely as the Lord lives, who has delivered me out of every trouble, ³⁰I will surely carry out this very day what I swore to you by the Lord, the God of Israel: Solomon your son shall be king after me, and he will sit on my throne in my place."

³¹Then Bathsheba bowed down with her face to the ground, prostrating herself before the king, and said, "May my lord King David live forever!"

³²King David said, "Call in Zadok the priest, Nathan the prophet and Benaiah son of Jehoiada." When they came before the king, ³³he said to them: "Take your lord's servants with you and have Solomon my son mount my own mule and take him down to Gihon. ³⁴There have Zadok the priest and Nathan the prophet anoint him king over Israel. Blow the trumpet and shout, 'Long live King Solomon!' ³⁵Then you are to go up with him, and he is to come and sit on my throne and reign in my place. I have appointed him ruler over Israel and Judah."

³⁶Benaiah son of Jehoiada answered the king, "Amen! May the Lord, the God of my lord the king, so declare it. ³⁷As the Lord was with my lord the king, so may he be with Solomon to make his throne even greater than the throne of my lord King David!"

³⁸So Zadok the priest, Nathan the prophet, Benaiah son of Jehoiada, the Kerethites and the Pelethites went down and had Solomon mount King David's mule, and they escorted him to Gihon. ³⁹Zadok the priest took the horn of oil from the sacred tent and anointed Solomon.

Then they sounded the trumpet and all the people shouted, "Long live King Solomon!" [40] And all the people went up after him, playing pipes and rejoicing greatly, so that the ground shook with the sound.

[41] Adonijah and all the guests who were with him heard it as they were finishing their feast. On hearing the sound of the trumpet, Joab asked, "What's the meaning of all the noise in the city?"

[42] Even as he was speaking, Jonathan son of Abiathar the priest arrived. Adonijah said, "Come in. A worthy man like you must be bringing good news."

[43] "Not at all!" Jonathan answered. "Our lord King David has made Solomon king. [44] The king has sent with him Zadok the priest, Nathan the prophet, Benaiah son of Jehoiada, the Kerethites and the Pelethites, and they have put him on the king's mule, [45] and Zadok the priest and Nathan the prophet have anointed him king at Gihon. From there they have gone up cheering, and the city resounds with it. That's the noise you hear. [46] Moreover, Solomon has taken his seat on the royal throne. [47] Also, the royal officials have come to congratulate our lord King David, saying, 'May your God make Solomon's name more famous than yours and his throne greater than yours!' And the king bowed in worship on his bed [48] and said, 'Praise be to the LORD, the God of Israel, who has allowed my eyes to see a successor on my throne today.'"

[49] At this, all Adonijah's guests rose in alarm and dispersed. [50] But Adonijah, in fear of Solomon, went and took hold of the horns of the altar. [51] Then Solomon was told, "Adonijah is afraid of King Solomon and is clinging to the horns of the altar. He says, 'Let King Solomon swear to me today that he will not put his servant to death with the sword.'"

[52] Solomon replied, "If he shows himself to be worthy, not a hair of his head will fall to the ground; but if evil is found in him, he will die." [53] Then King Solomon sent men, and they brought him down from the altar. And Adonijah came and bowed down to King Solomon, and Solomon said, "Go to your home."

David's Charge to Solomon

2 When the time drew near for David to die, he gave a charge to Solomon his son.

[2] "I am about to go the way of all the earth," he said. "So be strong, act like a man, [3] and observe what the LORD your God requires: Walk in obedience to him, and keep his decrees and commands, his laws and regulations, as written in the Law of Moses. Do this so that you may prosper in all you do and wherever you go [4] and that the LORD may keep his promise

to me: 'If your descendants watch how they live, and if they walk faithfully before me with all their heart and soul, you will never fail to have a successor on the throne of Israel.'

⁵"Now you yourself know what Joab son of Zeruiah did to me — what he did to the two commanders of Israel's armies, Abner son of Ner and Amasa son of Jether. He killed them, shedding their blood in peacetime as if in battle, and with that blood he stained the belt around his waist and the sandals on his feet. ⁶Deal with him according to your wisdom, but do not let his gray head go down to the grave in peace.

⁷"But show kindness to the sons of Barzillai of Gilead and let them be among those who eat at your table. They stood by me when I fled from your brother Absalom.

⁸"And remember, you have with you Shimei son of Gera, the Benjamite from Bahurim, who called down bitter curses on me the day I went to Mahanaim. When he came down to meet me at the Jordan, I swore to him by the LORD: 'I will not put you to death by the sword.' ⁹But now, do not consider him innocent. You are a man of wisdom; you will know what to do to him. Bring his gray head down to the grave in blood."

¹⁰Then David rested with his ancestors and was buried in the City of David. ¹¹He had reigned forty years over Israel — seven years in Hebron and thirty-three in Jerusalem. ¹²So Solomon sat on the throne of his father David, and his rule was firmly established.

Solomon's Throne Established

¹³Now Adonijah, the son of Haggith, went to Bathsheba, Solomon's mother. Bathsheba asked him, "Do you come peacefully?"

He answered, "Yes, peacefully." ¹⁴Then he added, "I have something to say to you."

"You may say it," she replied.

¹⁵"As you know," he said, "the kingdom was mine. All Israel looked to me as their king. But things changed, and the kingdom has gone to my brother; for it has come to him from the LORD. ¹⁶Now I have one request to make of you. Do not refuse me."

"You may make it," she said.

¹⁷So he continued, "Please ask King Solomon — he will not refuse you — to give me Abishag the Shunammite as my wife."

¹⁸"Very well," Bathsheba replied, "I will speak to the king for you."

¹⁹When Bathsheba went to King Solomon to speak to him for Adonijah, the king stood up to meet her, bowed down to her and sat down on his throne. He had a throne brought for the king's mother, and she sat down at his right hand.

²⁰"I have one small request to

make of you," she said. "Do not refuse me."

The king replied, "Make it, my mother; I will not refuse you."

²¹ So she said, "Let Abishag the Shunammite be given in marriage to your brother Adonijah."

²² King Solomon answered his mother, "Why do you request Abishag the Shunammite for Adonijah? You might as well request the kingdom for him — after all, he is my older brother — yes, for him and for Abiathar the priest and Joab son of Zeruiah!"

²³ Then King Solomon swore by the LORD: "May God deal with me, be it ever so severely, if Adonijah does not pay with his life for this request! ²⁴ And now, as surely as the LORD lives — he who has established me securely on the throne of my father David and has founded a dynasty for me as he promised — Adonijah shall be put to death today!" ²⁵ So King Solomon gave orders to Benaiah son of Jehoiada, and he struck down Adonijah and he died.

²⁶ To Abiathar the priest the king said, "Go back to your fields in Anathoth. You deserve to die, but I will not put you to death now, because you carried the ark of the Sovereign LORD before my father David and shared all my father's hardships." ²⁷ So Solomon removed Abiathar from the priesthood of the LORD, fulfilling the word the LORD had spoken at Shiloh about the house of Eli.

²⁸ When the news reached Joab, who had conspired with Adonijah though not with Absalom, he fled to the tent of the LORD and took hold of the horns of the altar. ²⁹ King Solomon was told that Joab had fled to the tent of the LORD and was beside the altar. Then Solomon ordered Benaiah son of Jehoiada, "Go, strike him down!"

³⁰ So Benaiah entered the tent of the LORD and said to Joab, "The king says, 'Come out!'"

But he answered, "No, I will die here."

Benaiah reported to the king, "This is how Joab answered me."

³¹ Then the king commanded Benaiah, "Do as he says. Strike him down and bury him, and so clear me and my whole family of the guilt of the innocent blood that Joab shed. ³² The LORD will repay him for the blood he shed, because without my father David knowing it he attacked two men and killed them with the sword. Both of them — Abner son of Ner, commander of Israel's army, and Amasa son of Jether, commander of Judah's army — were better men and more upright than he. ³³ May the guilt of their blood rest on the head of Joab and his descendants forever. But on David and his descendants, his house and his throne, may there be the LORD's peace forever."

³⁴ So Benaiah son of Jehoiada went up and struck down Joab

and killed him, and he was buried at his home out in the country. **35** The king put Benaiah son of Jehoiada over the army in Joab's position and replaced Abiathar with Zadok the priest.

36 Then the king sent for Shimei and said to him, "Build yourself a house in Jerusalem and live there, but do not go anywhere else. **37** The day you leave and cross the Kidron Valley, you can be sure you will die; your blood will be on your own head."

38 Shimei answered the king, "What you say is good. Your servant will do as my lord the king has said." And Shimei stayed in Jerusalem for a long time.

39 But three years later, two of Shimei's slaves ran off to Achish son of Maakah, king of Gath, and Shimei was told, "Your slaves are in Gath." **40** At this, he saddled his donkey and went to Achish at Gath in search of his slaves. So Shimei went away and brought the slaves back from Gath.

41 When Solomon was told that Shimei had gone from Jerusalem to Gath and had returned, **42** the king summoned Shimei and said to him, "Did I not make you swear by the LORD and warn you, 'On the day you leave to go anywhere else, you can be sure you will die'? At that time you said to me, 'What you say is good. I will obey.' **43** Why then did you not keep your oath to the LORD and obey the command I gave you?"

44 The king also said to Shimei, "You know in your heart all the wrong you did to my father David. Now the LORD will repay you for your wrongdoing. **45** But King Solomon will be blessed, and David's throne will remain secure before the LORD forever."

46 Then the king gave the order to Benaiah son of Jehoiada, and he went out and struck Shimei down and he died.

The kingdom was now established in Solomon's hands.

Solomon Asks for Wisdom

3 Solomon made an alliance with Pharaoh king of Egypt and married his daughter. He brought her to the City of David until he finished building his palace and the temple of the LORD, and the wall around Jerusalem. **2** The people, however, were still sacrificing at the high places, because a temple had not yet been built for the Name of the LORD. **3** Solomon showed his love for the LORD by walking according to the instructions given him by his father David, except that he offered sacrifices and burned incense on the high places.

4 The king went to Gibeon to offer sacrifices, for that was the most important high place, and Solomon offered a thousand burnt offerings on that altar. **5** At Gibeon the LORD appeared to Solomon during the night in a dream, and God said, "Ask for whatever you want me to give you."

⁶ Solomon answered, "You have shown great kindness to your servant, my father David, because he was faithful to you and righteous and upright in heart. You have continued this great kindness to him and have given him a son to sit on his throne this very day.

⁷ "Now, LORD my God, you have made your servant king in place of my father David. But I am only a little child and do not know how to carry out my duties. ⁸ Your servant is here among the people you have chosen, a great people, too numerous to count or number. ⁹ So give your servant a discerning heart to govern your people and to distinguish between right and wrong. For who is able to govern this great people of yours?"

¹⁰ The Lord was pleased that Solomon had asked for this. ¹¹ So God said to him, "Since you have asked for this and not for long life or wealth for yourself, nor have asked for the death of your enemies but for discernment in administering justice, ¹² I will do what you have asked. I will give you a wise and discerning heart, so that there will never have been anyone like you, nor will there ever be. ¹³ Moreover, I will give you what you have not asked for — both wealth and honor — so that in your lifetime you will have

no equal among kings. ¹⁴ And if you walk in obedience to me and keep my decrees and commands as David your father did, I will give you a long life." ¹⁵ Then Solomon awoke — and he realized it had been a dream.

He returned to Jerusalem, stood before the ark of the Lord's covenant and sacrificed burnt offerings and fellowship offerings. Then he gave a feast for all his court.

A Wise Ruling

¹⁶ Now two prostitutes came to the king and stood before him. ¹⁷ One of them said, "Pardon me, my lord. This woman and I live in the same house, and I had a baby while she was there with me. ¹⁸ The third day after my child was born, this woman also had a baby. We were alone; there was no one in the house but the two of us.

¹⁹ "During the night this woman's son died because she lay on him. ²⁰ So she got up in the middle of the night and took my son from my side while I your servant was asleep. She put him by her breast and put her dead son by my breast. ²¹ The next morning, I got up to nurse my son — and he was dead! But when I looked at him closely in the morning light, I saw that it wasn't the son I had borne."

²² The other woman said, "No! The living one is my son; the dead one is yours."

But the first one insisted, "No!

The dead one is yours; the living one is mine." And so they argued before the king.

²³ The king said, "This one says, 'My son is alive and your son is dead,' while that one says, 'No! Your son is dead and mine is alive.'"

²⁴ Then the king said, "Bring me a sword." So they brought a sword for the king. ²⁵ He then gave an order: "Cut the living child in two and give half to one and half to the other."

²⁶ The woman whose son was alive was deeply moved out of love for her son and said to the king, "Please, my lord, give her the living baby! Don't kill him!"

But the other said, "Neither I nor you shall have him. Cut him in two!"

²⁷ Then the king gave his ruling: "Give the living baby to the first woman. Do not kill him; she is his mother."

²⁸ When all Israel heard the verdict the king had given, they held the king in awe, because they saw that he had wisdom from God to administer justice.

Solomon's Officials and Governors

4 So King Solomon ruled over all Israel. ² And these were his chief officials:

Azariah son of Zadok — the priest;

³ Elihoreph and Ahijah, sons of Shisha — secretaries;

Jehoshaphat son of Ahilud — recorder;

⁴ Benaiah son of Jehoiada — commander in chief;

Zadok and Abiathar — priests;

⁵ Azariah son of Nathan — in charge of the district governors;

Zabud son of Nathan — a priest and adviser to the king;

⁶ Ahishar — palace administrator;

Adoniram son of Abda — in charge of forced labor.

⁷ Solomon had twelve district governors over all Israel, who supplied provisions for the king and the royal household. Each one had to provide supplies for one month in the year. ⁸ These are their names:

Ben-Hur — in the hill country of Ephraim;

⁹ Ben-Deker — in Makaz, Shaalbim, Beth Shemesh and Elon Bethhanan;

¹⁰ Ben-Hesed — in Arubboth (Sokoh and all the land of Hepher were his);

¹¹ Ben-Abinadab — in Naphoth Dor (he was married to Taphath daughter of Solomon);

¹² Baana son of Ahilud — in Taanach and Megiddo, and in all of Beth Shan next to Zarethan below Jezreel, from Beth Shan to Abel Meholah across to Jokmeam;

¹³Ben-Geber—in Ramoth Gilead (the settlements of Jair son of Manasseh in Gilead were his, as well as the region of Argob in Bashan and its sixty large walled cities with bronze gate bars);

¹⁴Ahinadab son of Iddo—in Mahanaim;

¹⁵Ahimaaz—in Naphtali (he had married Basemath daughter of Solomon);

¹⁶Baana son of Hushai—in Asher and in Aloth;

¹⁷Jehoshaphat son of Paruah—in Issachar;

¹⁸Shimei son of Ela—in Benjamin;

¹⁹Geber son of Uri—in Gilead (the country of Sihon king of the Amorites and the country of Og king of Bashan). He was the only governor over the district.

Solomon's Daily Provisions

²⁰The people of Judah and Israel were as numerous as the sand on the seashore; they ate, they drank and they were happy. ²¹And Solomon ruled over all the kingdoms from the Euphrates River to the land of the Philistines, as far as the border of Egypt. These countries brought tribute and were Solomon's subjects all his life.

²²Solomon's daily provisions were thirty cors[a] of the finest flour and sixty cors[b] of meal, ²³ten head of stall-fed cattle, twenty of pasture-fed cattle and a hundred sheep and goats, as well as deer, gazelles, roebucks and choice fowl. ²⁴For he ruled over all the kingdoms west of the Euphrates River, from Tiphsah to Gaza, and had peace on all sides. ²⁵During Solomon's lifetime Judah and Israel, from Dan to Beersheba, lived in safety, everyone under their own vine and under their own fig tree.

²⁶Solomon had four[c] thousand stalls for chariot horses, and twelve thousand horses.[d]

²⁷The district governors, each in his month, supplied provisions for King Solomon and all who came to the king's table. They saw to it that nothing was lacking. ²⁸They also brought to the proper place their quotas of barley and straw for the chariot horses and the other horses.

Solomon's Wisdom

²⁹God gave Solomon wisdom and very great insight, and a breadth of understanding as measureless as the sand on the seashore. ³⁰Solomon's wisdom was greater than the wisdom of all the people of the East, and greater than all the wisdom of

---

[a] 22 That is, probably about 5 1/2 tons or about 5 metric tons   [b] 22 That is, probably about 11 tons or about 10 metric tons   [c] 26 Some Septuagint manuscripts (see also 2 Chron. 9:25); Hebrew *forty*   [d] 26 Or *charioteers*

Egypt. [31] He was wiser than anyone else, including Ethan the Ezrahite — wiser than Heman, Kalkol and Darda, the sons of Mahol. And his fame spread to all the surrounding nations. [32] He spoke three thousand proverbs and his songs numbered a thousand and five. [33] He spoke about plant life, from the cedar of Lebanon to the hyssop that grows out of walls. He also spoke about animals and birds, reptiles and fish. [34] From all nations people came to listen to Solomon's wisdom, sent by all the kings of the world, who had heard of his wisdom.[a]

Preparations for Building the Temple

5[b] When Hiram king of Tyre heard that Solomon had been anointed king to succeed his father David, he sent his envoys to Solomon, because he had always been on friendly terms with David. [2] Solomon sent back this message to Hiram:

[3] "You know that because of the wars waged against my father David from all sides, he could not build a temple for the Name of the LORD his God until the LORD put his enemies under his feet. [4] But now the LORD my God has given me rest on every side, and there is no adversary or disaster. [5] I intend, therefore, to build a temple for the Name of the LORD my God, as the LORD told my father David, when he said, 'Your son whom I will put on the throne in your place will build the temple for my Name.'

[6] "So give orders that cedars of Lebanon be cut for me. My men will work with yours, and I will pay you for your men whatever wages you set. You know that we have no one so skilled in felling timber as the Sidonians."

[7] When Hiram heard Solomon's message, he was greatly pleased and said, "Praise be to the LORD today, for he has given David a wise son to rule over this great nation."

[8] So Hiram sent word to Solomon:

"I have received the message you sent me and will do all you want in providing the cedar and juniper logs. [9] My men will haul them down from Lebanon to the Mediterranean Sea, and I will float them as rafts by sea to the place you specify. There I will separate them and you can take them away. And you are to grant my wish by providing food for my royal household."

[10] In this way Hiram kept Solomon supplied with all the cedar

---

[a] 34 In Hebrew texts 4:21-34 is numbered 5:1-14.   [b] In Hebrew texts 5:1-18 is numbered 5:15-32.

and juniper logs he wanted, **11** and Solomon gave Hiram twenty thousand cors*a* of wheat as food for his household, in addition to twenty thousand baths*b,c* of pressed olive oil. Solomon continued to do this for Hiram year after year. **12** The LORD gave Solomon wisdom, just as he had promised him. There were peaceful relations between Hiram and Solomon, and the two of them made a treaty.

13 King Solomon conscripted laborers from all Israel — thirty thousand men. **14** He sent them off to Lebanon in shifts of ten thousand a month, so that they spent one month in Lebanon and two months at home. Adoniram was in charge of the forced labor. **15** Solomon had seventy thousand carriers and eighty thousand stonecutters in the hills, **16** as well as thirty-three hundred*d* foremen who supervised the project and directed the workers. **17** At the king's command they removed from the quarry large blocks of high-grade stone to provide a foundation of dressed stone for the temple. **18** The craftsmen of Solomon and Hiram and workers from Byblos cut and prepared the timber and stone for the building of the temple.

Solomon Builds the Temple

6 In the four hundred and eightieth*e* year after the Israelites came out of Egypt, in the fourth year of Solomon's reign over Israel, in the month of Ziv, the second month, he began to build the temple of the LORD.

2 The temple that King Solomon built for the LORD was sixty cubits long, twenty wide and thirty high.*f* **3** The portico at the front of the main hall of the temple extended the width of the temple, that is twenty cubits,*g* and projected ten cubits*h* from the front of the temple. **4** He made narrow windows high up in the temple walls. **5** Against the walls of the main hall and inner sanctuary he built a structure around the building, in which there were side rooms. **6** The lowest floor was five cubits*i* wide, the middle floor six cubits*j* and the third floor seven.*k* He made offset ledges around the outside of the temple so that nothing would be inserted into the temple walls.

7 In building the temple, only

---

a 11 That is, probably about 3,600 tons or about 3,250 metric tons
b 11 Septuagint (see also 2 Chron. 2:10); Hebrew *twenty cors*   *c 11* That is, about 120,000 gallons or about 440,000 liters   *d 16* Hebrew; some Septuagint manuscripts (see also 2 Chron. 2:2,18) *thirty-six hundred*   *e 1* Hebrew; Septuagint *four hundred and fortieth*   *f 2* That is, about 90 feet long, 30 feet wide and 45 feet high or about 27 meters long, 9 meters wide and 14 meters high
g 3 That is, about 30 feet or about 9 meters; also in verses 16 and 20   *h 3* That is, about 15 feet or about 4.5 meters; also in verses 23-26   *i 6* That is, about 7 1/2 feet or about 2.3 meters; also in verses 10 and 24   *j 6* That is, about 9 feet or about 2.7 meters   *k 6* That is, about 11 feet or about 3.2 meters

blocks dressed at the quarry were used, and no hammer, chisel or any other iron tool was heard at the temple site while it was being built.

8 The entrance to the lowest[a] floor was on the south side of the temple; a stairway led up to the middle level and from there to the third. **9** So he built the temple and completed it, roofing it with beams and cedar planks. **10** And he built the side rooms all along the temple. The height of each was five cubits, and they were attached to the temple by beams of cedar.

11 The word of the LORD came to Solomon: **12** "As for this temple you are building, if you follow my decrees, observe my laws and keep all my commands and obey them, I will fulfill through you the promise I gave to David your father. **13** And I will live among the Israelites and will not abandon my people Israel."

14 So Solomon built the temple and completed it. **15** He lined its interior walls with cedar boards, paneling them from the floor of the temple to the ceiling, and covered the floor of the temple with planks of juniper. **16** He partitioned off twenty cubits at the rear of the temple with cedar boards from floor to ceiling to form within the temple an inner sanctuary, the Most Holy Place. **17** The main hall in front of this room was forty cubits[b] long.

18 The inside of the temple was cedar, carved with gourds and open flowers. Everything was cedar; no stone was to be seen.

19 He prepared the inner sanctuary within the temple to set the ark of the covenant of the LORD there. **20** The inner sanctuary was twenty cubits long, twenty wide and twenty high. He overlaid the inside with pure gold, and he also overlaid the altar of cedar. **21** Solomon covered the inside of the temple with pure gold, and he extended gold chains across the front of the inner sanctuary, which was overlaid with gold. **22** So he overlaid the whole interior with gold. He also overlaid with gold the altar that belonged to the inner sanctuary.

23 For the inner sanctuary he made a pair of cherubim out of olive wood, each ten cubits high. **24** One wing of the first cherub was five cubits long, and the other wing five cubits—ten cubits from wing tip to wing tip. **25** The second cherub also measured ten cubits, for the two cherubim were identical in size and shape. **26** The height of each cherub was ten cubits. **27** He placed the cherubim inside the innermost room of the temple, with their wings spread out. The wing of one cherub touched one wall, while the wing of the other touched the other wall, and their wings touched each other in the middle

---

[a] *8* Septuagint; Hebrew *middle*   [b] *17* That is, about 60 feet or about 18 meters

of the room. ²⁸He overlaid the cherubim with gold.

²⁹On the walls all around the temple, in both the inner and outer rooms, he carved cherubim, palm trees and open flowers. ³⁰He also covered the floors of both the inner and outer rooms of the temple with gold.

³¹For the entrance to the inner sanctuary he made doors out of olive wood that were one fifth of the width of the sanctuary. ³²And on the two olive-wood doors he carved cherubim, palm trees and open flowers, and overlaid the cherubim and palm trees with hammered gold. ³³In the same way, for the entrance to the main hall he made doorframes out of olive wood that were one fourth of the width of the hall. ³⁴He also made two doors out of juniper wood, each having two leaves that turned in sockets. ³⁵He carved cherubim, palm trees and open flowers on them and overlaid them with gold hammered evenly over the carvings.

³⁶And he built the inner courtyard of three courses of dressed stone and one course of trimmed cedar beams.

³⁷The foundation of the temple of the LORD was laid in the fourth year, in the month of Ziv. ³⁸In the eleventh year in the month of Bul, the eighth month, the temple was finished in all its details according to its specifications. He had spent seven years building it.

Solomon Builds His Palace

7 It took Solomon thirteen years, however, to complete the construction of his palace. ²He built the Palace of the Forest of Lebanon a hundred cubits long, fifty wide and thirty high,^a with four rows of cedar columns supporting trimmed cedar beams. ³It was roofed with cedar above the beams that rested on the columns — forty-five beams, fifteen to a row. ⁴Its windows were placed high in sets of three, facing each other. ⁵All the doorways had rectangular frames; they were in the front part in sets of three, facing each other.^b

⁶He made a colonnade fifty cubits long and thirty wide.^c In front of it was a portico, and in front of that were pillars and an overhanging roof.

⁷He built the throne hall, the Hall of Justice, where he was to judge, and he covered it with cedar from floor to ceiling.^d ⁸And the palace in which he was to live, set farther back, was similar in design. Solomon also made a palace like this hall for Pharaoh's daughter, whom he had married.

⁹All these structures, from the outside to the great court-

---

^a 2 That is, about 150 feet long, 75 feet wide and 45 feet high or about 45 meters long, 23 meters wide and 14 meters high   ^b 5 The meaning of the Hebrew for this verse is uncertain.   ^c 6 That is, about 75 feet long and 45 feet wide or about 23 meters long and 14 meters wide   ^d 7 Vulgate and Syriac; Hebrew *floor*

yard and from foundation to eaves, were made of blocks of high-grade stone cut to size and smoothed on their inner and outer faces. [10]The foundations were laid with large stones of good quality, some measuring ten cubits[a] and some eight.[b] [11]Above were high-grade stones, cut to size, and cedar beams. [12]The great courtyard was surrounded by a wall of three courses of dressed stone and one course of trimmed cedar beams, as was the inner courtyard of the temple of the LORD with its portico.

The Temple's Furnishings

[13]King Solomon sent to Tyre and brought Huram,[c] [14]whose mother was a widow from the tribe of Naphtali and whose father was from Tyre and a skilled craftsman in bronze. Huram was filled with wisdom, with understanding and with knowledge to do all kinds of bronze work. He came to King Solomon and did all the work assigned to him.

[15]He cast two bronze pillars, each eighteen cubits high and twelve cubits in circumference.[d] [16]He also made two capitals of cast bronze to set on the tops of the pillars; each capital was five cubits[e] high. [17]A network of interwoven chains adorned the capitals on top of the pillars, seven for each capital. [18]He made pomegranates in two rows[f] encircling each network to decorate the capitals on top of the pillars.[g] He did the same for each capital. [19]The capitals on top of the pillars in the portico were in the shape of lilies, four cubits[h] high. [20]On the capitals of both pillars, above the bowl-shaped part next to the network, were the two hundred pomegranates in rows all around. [21]He erected the pillars at the portico of the temple. The pillar to the south he named Jakin[i] and the one to the north Boaz.[j] [22]The capitals on top were in the shape of lilies. And so the work on the pillars was completed.

[23]He made the Sea of cast metal, circular in shape, measuring ten cubits from rim to rim and five cubits high. It took a line of thirty cubits[k] to measure around it. [24]Below the rim, gourds encircled it — ten to a cubit. The gourds were cast in two rows in one piece with the Sea.

---

[a] 10 That is, about 15 feet or about 4.5 meters; also in verse 23   [b] 10 That is, about 12 feet or about 3.6 meters   [c] 13 Hebrew *Hiram*, a variant of *Huram*; also in verses 40 and 45   [d] 15 That is, about 27 feet high and 18 feet in circumference or about 8.1 meters high and 5.4 meters in circumference   [e] 16 That is, about 7 1/2 feet or about 2.3 meters; also in verse 23   [f] 18 Two Hebrew manuscripts and Septuagint; most Hebrew manuscripts *made the pillars, and there were two rows*   [g] 18 Many Hebrew manuscripts and Syriac; most Hebrew manuscripts *pomegranates*   [h] 19 That is, about 6 feet or about 1.8 meters; also in verse 38   [i] 21 *Jakin* probably means *he establishes*.   [j] 21 *Boaz* probably means *in him is strength*.   [k] 23 That is, about 45 feet or about 14 meters

²⁵The Sea stood on twelve bulls, three facing north, three facing west, three facing south and three facing east. The Sea rested on top of them, and their hindquarters were toward the center. ²⁶It was a handbreadth^a in thickness, and its rim was like the rim of a cup, like a lily blossom. It held two thousand baths.^b

²⁷He also made ten movable stands of bronze; each was four cubits long, four wide and three high.^c ²⁸This is how the stands were made: They had side panels attached to uprights. ²⁹On the panels between the uprights were lions, bulls and cherubim — and on the uprights as well. Above and below the lions and bulls were wreaths of hammered work. ³⁰Each stand had four bronze wheels with bronze axles, and each had a basin resting on four supports, cast with wreaths on each side. ³¹On the inside of the stand there was an opening that had a circular frame one cubit^d deep. This opening was round, and with its basework it measured a cubit and a half.^e Around its opening there was engraving. The panels of the stands were square, not round. ³²The four wheels were under the panels, and the axles of the wheels were attached to the stand. The diameter of each wheel was a cubit and a half. ³³The wheels were made like chariot wheels; the axles, rims, spokes and hubs were all of cast metal.

³⁴Each stand had four handles, one on each corner, projecting from the stand. ³⁵At the top of the stand there was a circular band half a cubit^f deep. The supports and panels were attached to the top of the stand. ³⁶He engraved cherubim, lions and palm trees on the surfaces of the supports and on the panels, in every available space, with wreaths all around. ³⁷This is the way he made the ten stands. They were all cast in the same molds and were identical in size and shape.

³⁸He then made ten bronze basins, each holding forty baths^g and measuring four cubits across, one basin to go on each of the ten stands. ³⁹He placed five of the stands on the south side of the temple and five on the north. He placed the Sea on the south side, at the southeast corner of the temple. ⁴⁰He also made the pots^h and shovels and sprinkling bowls.

---

^a 26 That is, about 3 inches or about 7.5 centimeters   ^b 26 That is, about 12,000 gallons or about 44,000 liters; the Septuagint does not have this sentence.   ^c 27 That is, about 6 feet long and wide and about 4 1/2 feet high or about 1.8 meters long and wide and 1.4 meters high   ^d 31 That is, about 18 inches or about 45 centimeters   ^e 31 That is, about 2 1/4 feet or about 68 centimeters; also in verse 32   ^f 35 That is, about 9 inches or about 23 centimeters   ^g 38 That is, about 240 gallons or about 880 liters   ^h 40 Many Hebrew manuscripts, Septuagint, Syriac and Vulgate (see also verse 45 and 2 Chron. 4:11); many other Hebrew manuscripts basins

So Huram finished all the work he had undertaken for King Solomon in the temple of the LORD:

⁴¹the two pillars;

the two bowl-shaped capitals on top of the pillars;

the two sets of network decorating the two bowl-shaped capitals on top of the pillars;

⁴²the four hundred pomegranates for the two sets of network (two rows of pomegranates for each network decorating the bowl-shaped capitals on top of the pillars);

⁴³the ten stands with their ten basins;

⁴⁴the Sea and the twelve bulls under it;

⁴⁵the pots, shovels and sprinkling bowls.

All these objects that Huram made for King Solomon for the temple of the LORD were of burnished bronze. ⁴⁶The king had them cast in clay molds in the plain of the Jordan between Sukkoth and Zarethan. ⁴⁷Solomon left all these things unweighed, because there were so many; the weight of the bronze was not determined.

⁴⁸Solomon also made all the furnishings that were in the LORD's temple:

the golden altar;

the golden table on which was the bread of the Presence;

⁴⁹the lampstands of pure gold (five on the right and five on the left, in front of the inner sanctuary);

the gold floral work and lamps and tongs;

⁵⁰the pure gold basins, wick trimmers, sprinkling bowls, dishes and censers;

and the gold sockets for the doors of the innermost room, the Most Holy Place, and also for the doors of the main hall of the temple.

⁵¹When all the work King Solomon had done for the temple of the LORD was finished, he brought in the things his father David had dedicated—the silver and gold and the furnishings—and he placed them in the treasuries of the LORD's temple.

The Ark Brought to the Temple

8 Then King Solomon summoned into his presence at Jerusalem the elders of Israel, all the heads of the tribes and the chiefs of the Israelite families, to bring up the ark of the LORD's covenant from Zion, the City of David. ²All the Israelites came together to King Solomon at the time of the festival in the month of Ethanim, the seventh month.

³When all the elders of Israel had arrived, the priests took up the ark, ⁴and they brought up the ark of the LORD and the tent of meeting and all the sacred furnishings in it. The priests and

Levites carried them up, ⁵and King Solomon and the entire assembly of Israel that had gathered about him were before the ark, sacrificing so many sheep and cattle that they could not be recorded or counted.

⁶The priests then brought the ark of the Lord's covenant to its place in the inner sanctuary of the temple, the Most Holy Place, and put it beneath the wings of the cherubim. ⁷The cherubim spread their wings over the place of the ark and overshadowed the ark and its carrying poles. ⁸These poles were so long that their ends could be seen from the Holy Place in front of the inner sanctuary, but not from outside the Holy Place; and they are still there today. ⁹There was nothing in the ark except the two stone tablets that Moses had placed in it at Horeb, where the Lord made a covenant with the Israelites after they came out of Egypt.

¹⁰When the priests withdrew from the Holy Place, the cloud filled the temple of the Lord. ¹¹And the priests could not perform their service because of the cloud, for the glory of the Lord filled his temple.

¹²Then Solomon said, "The Lord has said that he would dwell in a dark cloud; ¹³I have indeed built a magnificent temple for you, a place for you to dwell forever."

¹⁴While the whole assembly of Israel was standing there, the king turned around and blessed them. ¹⁵Then he said:

"Praise be to the Lord, the God of Israel, who with his own hand has fulfilled what he promised with his own mouth to my father David. For he said, ¹⁶'Since the day I brought my people Israel out of Egypt, I have not chosen a city in any tribe of Israel to have a temple built so that my Name might be there, but I have chosen David to rule my people Israel.'

¹⁷"My father David had it in his heart to build a temple for the Name of the Lord, the God of Israel. ¹⁸But the Lord said to my father David, 'You did well to have it in your heart to build a temple for my Name. ¹⁹Nevertheless, you are not the one to build the temple, but your son, your own flesh and blood—he is the one who will build the temple for my Name.'

²⁰"The Lord has kept the promise he made: I have succeeded David my father and now I sit on the throne of Israel, just as the Lord promised, and I have built the temple for the Name of the Lord, the God of Israel. ²¹I have provided a place there for the ark, in which is the covenant of the Lord that he made with our ancestors when he brought them out of Egypt."

Solomon's Prayer of Dedication

²²Then Solomon stood before the altar of the LORD in front of the whole assembly of Israel, spread out his hands toward heaven ²³and said:

"LORD, the God of Israel, there is no God like you in heaven above or on earth below—you who keep your covenant of love with your servants who continue wholeheartedly in your way. ²⁴You have kept your promise to your servant David my father; with your mouth you have promised and with your hand you have fulfilled it—as it is today.

²⁵"Now LORD, the God of Israel, keep for your servant David my father the promises you made to him when you said, 'You shall never fail to have a successor to sit before me on the throne of Israel, if only your descendants are careful in all they do to walk before me faithfully as you have done.' ²⁶And now, God of Israel, let your word that you promised your servant David my father come true.

²⁷"But will God really dwell on earth? The heavens, even the highest heaven, cannot contain you. How much less this temple I have built! ²⁸Yet give attention to your servant's prayer and his plea for mercy, LORD my God. Hear the cry and the prayer that your servant is praying in your presence this day. ²⁹May your eyes be open toward this temple night and day, this place of which you said, 'My Name shall be there,' so that you will hear the prayer your servant prays toward this place. ³⁰Hear the supplication of your servant and of your people Israel when they pray toward this place. Hear from heaven, your dwelling place, and when you hear, forgive.

³¹"When anyone wrongs their neighbor and is required to take an oath and they come and swear the oath before your altar in this temple, ³²then hear from heaven and act. Judge between your servants, condemning the guilty by bringing down on their heads what they have done, and vindicating the innocent by treating them in accordance with their innocence.

³³"When your people Israel have been defeated by an enemy because they have sinned against you, and when they turn back to you and give praise to your name, praying and making supplication to you in this temple, ³⁴then hear from heaven and forgive the sin of your people

Israel and bring them back to the land you gave to their ancestors.

³⁵"When the heavens are shut up and there is no rain because your people have sinned against you, and when they pray toward this place and give praise to your name and turn from their sin because you have afflicted them, ³⁶then hear from heaven and forgive the sin of your servants, your people Israel. Teach them the right way to live, and send rain on the land you gave your people for an inheritance.

³⁷"When famine or plague comes to the land, or blight or mildew, locusts or grasshoppers, or when an enemy besieges them in any of their cities, whatever disaster or disease may come, ³⁸and when a prayer or plea is made by anyone among your people Israel—being aware of the afflictions of their own hearts, and spreading out their hands toward this temple— ³⁹then hear from heaven, your dwelling place. Forgive and act; deal with everyone according to all they do, since you know their hearts (for you alone know every human heart), ⁴⁰so that they will fear you all the time they live in the land you gave our ancestors.

⁴¹"As for the foreigner who does not belong to your people Israel but has come from a distant land because of your name— ⁴²for they will hear of your great name and your mighty hand and your outstretched arm—when they come and pray toward this temple, ⁴³then hear from heaven, your dwelling place. Do whatever the foreigner asks of you, so that all the peoples of the earth may know your name and fear you, as do your own people Israel, and may know that this house I have built bears your Name.

⁴⁴"When your people go to war against their enemies, wherever you send them, and when they pray to the LORD toward the city you have chosen and the temple I have built for your Name, ⁴⁵then hear from heaven their prayer and their plea, and uphold their cause.

⁴⁶"When they sin against you—for there is no one who does not sin—and you become angry with them and give them over to their enemies, who take them captive to their own lands, far away or near; ⁴⁷and if they have a change of heart in the land where they are held captive, and repent and plead with you in the land of their cap-

tors and say, 'We have sinned, we have done wrong, we have acted wickedly'; **48** and if they turn back to you with all their heart and soul in the land of their enemies who took them captive, and pray to you toward the land you gave their ancestors, toward the city you have chosen and the temple I have built for your Name; **49** then from heaven, your dwelling place, hear their prayer and their plea, and uphold their cause. **50** And forgive your people, who have sinned against you; forgive all the offenses they have committed against you, and cause their captors to show them mercy; **51** for they are your people and your inheritance, whom you brought out of Egypt, out of that iron-smelting furnace.

52 "May your eyes be open to your servant's plea and to the plea of your people Israel, and may you listen to them whenever they cry out to you. **53** For you singled them out from all the nations of the world to be your own inheritance, just as you declared through your servant Moses when you, Sovereign LORD, brought our ancestors out of Egypt."

54 When Solomon had finished all these prayers and supplications to the LORD, he rose from before the altar of the LORD, where he had been kneeling with his hands spread out toward heaven. **55** He stood and blessed the whole assembly of Israel in a loud voice, saying:

56 "Praise be to the LORD, who has given rest to his people Israel just as he promised. Not one word has failed of all the good promises he gave through his servant Moses. **57** May the LORD our God be with us as he was with our ancestors; may he never leave us nor forsake us. **58** May he turn our hearts to him, to walk in obedience to him and keep the commands, decrees and laws he gave our ancestors. **59** And may these words of mine, which I have prayed before the LORD, be near to the LORD our God day and night, that he may uphold the cause of his servant and the cause of his people Israel according to each day's need, **60** so that all the peoples of the earth may know that the LORD is God and that there is no other. **61** And may your hearts be fully committed to the LORD our God, to live by his decrees and obey his commands, as at this time."

The Dedication of the Temple

62 Then the king and all Israel with him offered sacrifices before the LORD. **63** Solomon offered a sacrifice of fellowship offerings to the LORD: twenty-two thousand cattle and a hundred and twenty thousand sheep and goats. So the king and all the Israelites dedicated the temple of the LORD.

⁶⁴On that same day the king consecrated the middle part of the courtyard in front of the temple of the LORD, and there he offered burnt offerings, grain offerings and the fat of the fellowship offerings, because the bronze altar that stood before the LORD was too small to hold the burnt offerings, the grain offerings and the fat of the fellowship offerings.

⁶⁵So Solomon observed the festival at that time, and all Israel with him — a vast assembly, people from Lebo Hamath to the Wadi of Egypt. They celebrated it before the LORD our God for seven days and seven days more, fourteen days in all. ⁶⁶On the following day he sent the people away. They blessed the king and then went home, joyful and glad in heart for all the good things the LORD had done for his servant David and his people Israel.

The LORD Appears to Solomon

9 When Solomon had finished building the temple of the LORD and the royal palace, and had achieved all he had desired to do, ²the LORD appeared to him a second time, as he had appeared to him at Gibeon. ³The LORD said to him:

"I have heard the prayer and plea you have made before me; I have consecrated this temple, which you have built, by putting my Name there forever. My eyes and my heart will always be there.

⁴"As for you, if you walk before me faithfully with integrity of heart and uprightness, as David your father did, and do all I command and observe my decrees and laws, ⁵I will establish your royal throne over Israel forever, as I promised David your father when I said, 'You shall never fail to have a successor on the throne of Israel.'

⁶"But if you*ᵃ* or your descendants turn away from me and do not observe the commands and decrees I have given you*ᵃ* and go off to serve other gods and worship them, ⁷then I will cut off Israel from the land I have given them and will reject this temple I have consecrated for my Name. Israel will then become a byword and an object of ridicule among all peoples. ⁸This temple will become a heap of rubble. All*ᵇ* who pass by will be appalled and will scoff and say, 'Why has the LORD done such a

---

ᵃ 6 The Hebrew is plural.　　*ᵇ 8* See some Septuagint manuscripts, Old Latin, Syriac, Arabic and Targum; Hebrew *And though this temple is now imposing, all* thing to this land and to this temple?' ⁹People will answer, 'Because they have forsaken the LORD their God, who brought their ancestors out of Egypt, and have embraced other gods, worshiping and serving them—that is why the LORD brought all this disaster on them.' "

Solomon's Other Activities

¹⁰At the end of twenty years, during which Solomon built these two buildings—the temple of the LORD and the royal palace— ¹¹King Solomon gave twenty towns in Galilee to Hiram king of Tyre, because Hiram had supplied him with all the cedar and juniper and gold he wanted. ¹²But when Hiram went from Tyre to see the towns that Solomon had given him, he was not pleased with them. ¹³"What kind of towns are these you have given me, my brother?" he asked. And he called them the Land of Kabul,ᵃ a name they have to this day. ¹⁴Now Hiram had sent to the king 120 talentsᵇ of gold.

¹⁵Here is the account of the forced labor King Solomon conscripted to build the LORD's temple, his own palace, the terraces,ᶜ the wall of Jerusalem, and Hazor, Megiddo and Gezer. ¹⁶(Phar-aoh king of Egypt had attacked and captured Gezer. He had set it on fire. He killed its Canaanite inhabitants and then gave it as a wedding gift to his daughter, Solomon's wife. ¹⁷And Solomon rebuilt Gezer.) He built up Lower Beth Horon, ¹⁸Baalath, and Tadmorᵈ in the desert, within his land, ¹⁹as well as all his store cities and the towns for his chariots and for his horsesᵉ—whatever he desired to build in Jerusalem, in Lebanon and throughout all the territory he ruled.

²⁰There were still people left from the Amorites, Hittites, Perizzites, Hivites and Jebusites (these peoples were not Israelites). ²¹Solomon conscripted the descendants of all these peoples remaining in the land—whom the Israelites could not exterminateᶠ—to serve as slave labor, as it is to this day. ²²But Solomon did not make slaves of any of the Israelites; they were his fighting men, his government officials, his officers, his captains, and the commanders of his chariots and charioteers. ²³They were also the chief officials in charge of Solomon's projects—550 officials supervising those who did the work.

²⁴After Pharaoh's daughter had come up from the City of David to

---

ᵃ 13 *Kabul* sounds like the Hebrew for *good-for-nothing.*   ᵇ 14 That is, about 4 1/2 tons or about 4 metric tons   ᶜ 15 Or *the Millo*; also in verse 24   ᵈ 18 The Hebrew may also be read *Tamar.*   ᵉ 19 Or *charioteers*
ᶠ 21 The Hebrew term refers to the irrevocable giving over of things or persons to the LORD, often by totally destroying them.

the palace Solomon had built for her, he constructed the terraces.

²⁵Three times a year Solomon sacrificed burnt offerings and fellowship offerings on the altar he had built for the LORD, burning incense before the LORD along with them, and so fulfilled the temple obligations.

²⁶King Solomon also built ships at Ezion Geber, which is near Elath in Edom, on the shore of the Red Sea.ᵃ ²⁷And Hiram sent his men—sailors who knew the sea—to serve in the fleet with Solomon's men. ²⁸They sailed to Ophir and brought back 420 talentsᵇ of gold, which they delivered to King Solomon.

The Queen of Sheba Visits Solomon

10 When the queen of Sheba heard about the fame of Solomon and his relationship to the LORD, she came to test Solomon with hard questions. ²Arriving at Jerusalem with a very great caravan—with camels carrying spices, large quantities of gold, and precious stones—she came to Solomon and talked with him about all that she had on her mind. ³Solomon answered all her questions; nothing was too hard for the king to explain to her. ⁴When the queen of Sheba saw all the wisdom of Solomon and the palace he had built, ⁵the food on his table, the seating of his officials, the attending servants in their robes, his cupbearers, and the burnt offerings he made atᶜ the temple of the LORD, she was overwhelmed.

⁶She said to the king, "The report I heard in my own country about your achievements and your wisdom is true. ⁷But I did not believe these things until I came and saw with my own eyes. Indeed, not even half was told me; in wisdom and wealth you have far exceeded the report I heard. ⁸How happy your people must be! How happy your officials, who continually stand before you and hear your wisdom! ⁹Praise be to the LORD your God, who has delighted in you and placed you on the throne of Israel. Because of the LORD's eternal love for Israel, he has made you king to maintain justice and righteousness."

¹⁰And she gave the king 120 talentsᵈ of gold, large quantities of spices, and precious stones. Never again were so many spices brought in as those the queen of Sheba gave to King Solomon.

¹¹(Hiram's ships brought gold from Ophir; and from there they brought great cargoes of almugwoodᵉ and precious stones. ¹²The king used the almugwood

---

ᵃ 26 Or *the Sea of Reeds*   ᵇ 28 That is, about 16 tons or about 14 metric tons
ᶜ 5 Or *the ascent by which he went up to*   ᵈ 10 That is, about 4 1/2 tons or
about 4 metric tons   ᵉ 11 Probably a variant of *algumwood*; also in verse 12

to make supports[a] for the temple of the LORD and for the royal palace, and to make harps and lyres for the musicians. So much almugwood has never been imported or seen since that day.)

¹³King Solomon gave the queen of Sheba all she desired and asked for, besides what he had given her out of his royal bounty. Then she left and returned with her retinue to her own country.

Solomon's Splendor

¹⁴The weight of the gold that Solomon received yearly was 666 talents,[b] ¹⁵not including the revenues from merchants and traders and from all the Arabian kings and the governors of the territories.

¹⁶King Solomon made two hundred large shields of hammered gold; six hundred shekels[c] of gold went into each shield. ¹⁷He also made three hundred small shields of hammered gold, with three minas[d] of gold in each shield. The king put them in the Palace of the Forest of Lebanon.

¹⁸Then the king made a great throne covered with ivory and overlaid with fine gold. ¹⁹The throne had six steps, and its back had a rounded top. On both sides of the seat were armrests, with a lion standing beside each of them. ²⁰Twelve lions stood on the six steps, one at either end of each step. Nothing like it had ever been made for any other kingdom. ²¹All King Solomon's goblets were gold, and all the household articles in the Palace of the Forest of Lebanon were pure gold. Nothing was made of silver, because silver was considered of little value in Solomon's days. ²²The king had a fleet of trading ships[e] at sea along with the ships of Hiram. Once every three years it returned, carrying gold, silver and ivory, and apes and baboons.

²³King Solomon was greater in riches and wisdom than all the other kings of the earth. ²⁴The whole world sought audience with Solomon to hear the wisdom God had put in his heart. ²⁵Year after year, everyone who came brought a gift — articles of silver and gold, robes, weapons and spices, and horses and mules.

²⁶Solomon accumulated chariots and horses; he had fourteen hundred chariots and twelve thousand horses,[f] which he kept in the chariot cities and also with him in Jerusalem. ²⁷The king made silver as common in Jerusalem as stones, and cedar as plentiful as sycamore-fig trees in the foothills. ²⁸Solomon's horses were imported from Egypt and

---

[a] 12 The meaning of the Hebrew for this word is uncertain.   [b] 14 That is, about 25 tons or about 23 metric tons   [c] 16 That is, about 15 pounds or about 6.9 kilograms; also in verse 29   [d] 17 That is, about 3 3/4 pounds or about 1.7 kilograms; or perhaps reference is to double minas, that is, about 7 1/2 pounds or about 3.5 kilograms.   [e] 22 Hebrew of ships of Tarshish   [f] 26 Or charioteers

from Kue[a] — the royal merchants purchased them from Kue at the current price. ²⁹They imported a chariot from Egypt for six hundred shekels of silver, and a horse for a hundred and fifty.[b] They also exported them to all the kings of the Hittites and of the Arameans.

Solomon's Wives

11 King Solomon, however, loved many foreign women besides Pharaoh's daughter — Moabites, Ammonites, Edomites, Sidonians and Hittites. ²They were from nations about which the LORD had told the Israelites, "You must not intermarry with them, because they will surely turn your hearts after their gods." Nevertheless, Solomon held fast to them in love. ³He had seven hundred wives of royal birth and three hundred concubines, and his wives led him astray. ⁴As Solomon grew old, his wives turned his heart after other gods, and his heart was not fully devoted to the LORD his God, as the heart of David his father had been. ⁵He followed Ashtoreth the goddess of the Sidonians, and Molek the detestable god of the Ammonites. ⁶So Solomon did evil in the eyes of the LORD; he did not follow the LORD completely, as David his father had done.

⁷On a hill east of Jerusalem, Solomon built a high place for Chemosh the detestable god of Moab, and for Molek the detestable god of the Ammonites. ⁸He did the same for all his foreign wives, who burned incense and offered sacrifices to their gods.

⁹The LORD became angry with Solomon because his heart had turned away from the LORD, the God of Israel, who had appeared to him twice. ¹⁰Although he had forbidden Solomon to follow other gods, Solomon did not keep the LORD's command. ¹¹So the LORD said to Solomon, "Since this is your attitude and you have not kept my covenant and my decrees, which I commanded you, I will most certainly tear the kingdom away from you and give it to one of your subordinates. ¹²Nevertheless, for the sake of David your father, I will not do it during your lifetime. I will tear it out of the hand of your son. ¹³Yet I will not tear the whole kingdom from him, but will give him one tribe for the sake of David my servant and for the sake of Jerusalem, which I have chosen."

Solomon's Adversaries

¹⁴Then the LORD raised up against Solomon an adversary, Hadad the Edomite, from the royal line of Edom. ¹⁵Earlier when David was fighting with Edom, Joab the commander of the army, who had gone up to bury the dead, had struck down

---

^a 28 Probably *Cilicia*   ^b 29 That is, about 3 3/4 pounds or about 1.7 kilograms

all the men in Edom. ¹⁶Joab and all the Israelites stayed there for six months, until they had destroyed all the men in Edom. ¹⁷But Hadad, still only a boy, fled to Egypt with some Edomite officials who had served his father. ¹⁸They set out from Midian and went to Paran. Then taking people from Paran with them, they went to Egypt, to Pharaoh king of Egypt, who gave Hadad a house and land and provided him with food.

¹⁹Pharaoh was so pleased with Hadad that he gave him a sister of his own wife, Queen Tahpenes, in marriage. ²⁰The sister of Tahpenes bore him a son named Genubath, whom Tahpenes brought up in the royal palace. There Genubath lived with Pharaoh's own children.

²¹While he was in Egypt, Hadad heard that David rested with his ancestors and that Joab the commander of the army was also dead. Then Hadad said to Pharaoh, "Let me go, that I may return to my own country."

²²"What have you lacked here that you want to go back to your own country?" Pharaoh asked.

"Nothing," Hadad replied, "but do let me go!"

²³And God raised up against Solomon another adversary, Rezon son of Eliada, who had fled from his master, Hadadezer king of Zobah. ²⁴When David destroyed Zobah's army, Rezon gathered a band of men around him and became their leader; they went to Damascus, where they settled and took control. ²⁵Rezon was Israel's adversary as long as Solomon lived, adding to the trouble caused by Hadad. So Rezon ruled in Aram and was hostile toward Israel.

Jeroboam Rebels Against Solomon

²⁶Also, Jeroboam son of Nebat rebelled against the king. He was one of Solomon's officials, an Ephraimite from Zeredah, and his mother was a widow named Zeruah.

²⁷Here is the account of how he rebelled against the king: Solomon had built the terraces^a and had filled in the gap in the wall of the city of David his father. ²⁸Now Jeroboam was a man of standing, and when Solomon saw how well the young man did his work, he put him in charge of the whole labor force of the tribes of Joseph.

²⁹About that time Jeroboam was going out of Jerusalem, and Ahijah the prophet of Shiloh met him on the way, wearing a new cloak. The two of them were alone out in the country, ³⁰and Ahijah took hold of the new cloak he was wearing and tore it into twelve pieces. ³¹Then he said to Jeroboam, "Take ten pieces for yourself, for this is what the

^a 27 Or *the Millo*

LORD, the God of Israel, says: 'See, I am going to tear the kingdom out of Solomon's hand and give you ten tribes. ³²But for the sake of my servant David and the city of Jerusalem, which I have chosen out of all the tribes of Israel, he will have one tribe. ³³I will do this because they have*ᵃ* forsaken me and worshiped Ashtoreth the goddess of the Sidonians, Chemosh the god of the Moabites, and Molek the god of the Ammonites, and have not walked in obedience to me, nor done what is right in my eyes, nor kept my decrees and laws as David, Solomon's father, did.

³⁴ " 'But I will not take the whole kingdom out of Solomon's hand; I have made him ruler all the days of his life for the sake of David my servant, whom I chose and who obeyed my commands and decrees. ³⁵I will take the kingdom from his son's hands and give you ten tribes. ³⁶I will give one tribe to his son so that David my servant may always have a lamp before me in Jerusalem, the city where I chose to put my Name. ³⁷However, as for you, I will take you, and you will rule over all that your heart desires; you will be king over Israel. ³⁸If you do whatever I command you and walk in obedience to me and do what is right in my eyes by obeying my decrees and commands, as Da-

vid my servant did, I will be with you. I will build you a dynasty as enduring as the one I built for David and will give Israel to you. ³⁹I will humble David's descendants because of this, but not forever.' "

⁴⁰Solomon tried to kill Jeroboam, but Jeroboam fled to Egypt, to Shishak the king, and stayed there until Solomon's death.

Solomon's Death

⁴¹As for the other events of Solomon's reign — all he did and the wisdom he displayed — are they not written in the book of the annals of Solomon? ⁴²Solomon reigned in Jerusalem over all Israel forty years. ⁴³Then he rested with his ancestors and was buried in the city of David his father. And Rehoboam his son succeeded him as king.

Israel Rebels Against Rehoboam

12 Rehoboam went to Shechem, for all Israel had gone there to make him king. ²When Jeroboam son of Nebat heard this (he was still in Egypt, where he had fled from King Solomon), he returned from*ᵇ* Egypt. ³So they sent for Jeroboam, and he and the whole assembly of Israel went to Rehoboam and said to him: ⁴"Your father put a heavy yoke on us, but now lighten the harsh labor and the heavy yoke he put on us, and we will serve you."

ᵃ 33 Hebrew; Septuagint, Vulgate and Syriac *because he has remained in*   ᵇ 2 Or *he*

⁵Rehoboam answered, "Go away for three days and then come back to me." So the people went away.

⁶Then King Rehoboam consulted the elders who had served his father Solomon during his lifetime. "How would you advise me to answer these people?" he asked.

⁷They replied, "If today you will be a servant to these people and serve them and give them a favorable answer, they will always be your servants."

⁸But Rehoboam rejected the advice the elders gave him and consulted the young men who had grown up with him and were serving him. ⁹He asked them, "What is your advice? How should we answer these people who say to me, 'Lighten the yoke your father put on us'?"

¹⁰The young men who had grown up with him replied, "These people have said to you, 'Your father put a heavy yoke on us, but make our yoke lighter.' Now tell them, 'My little finger is thicker than my father's waist. ¹¹My father laid on you a heavy yoke; I will make it even heavier. My father scourged you with whips; I will scourge you with scorpions.'"

¹²Three days later Jeroboam and all the people returned to Rehoboam, as the king had said, "Come back to me in three days."

¹³The king answered the people harshly. Rejecting the advice given him by the elders, ¹⁴he followed the advice of the young men and said, "My father made your yoke heavy; I will make it even heavier. My father scourged you with whips; I will scourge you with scorpions." ¹⁵So the king did not listen to the people, for this turn of events was from the LORD, to fulfill the word the LORD had spoken to Jeroboam son of Nebat through Ahijah the Shilonite.

¹⁶When all Israel saw that the king refused to listen to them, they answered the king:

"What share do we have in
    David,
  what part in Jesse's son?
To your tents, Israel!
  Look after your own house,
    David!"

So the Israelites went home. ¹⁷But as for the Israelites who were living in the towns of Judah, Rehoboam still ruled over them.

¹⁸King Rehoboam sent out Adoniram,ᵃ who was in charge of forced labor, but all Israel stoned him to death. King Rehoboam, however, managed to get into his chariot and escape to Jerusalem. ¹⁹So Israel has been in rebellion against the house of David to this day.

²⁰When all the Israelites heard that Jeroboam had returned, they

---

ᵃ 18 Some Septuagint manuscripts and Syriac (see also 4:6 and 5:14); Hebrew *Adoram* sent and called him to the assembly and made him king over all Israel. Only the tribe of Judah remained loyal to the house of David.

²¹ When Rehoboam arrived in Jerusalem, he mustered all Judah and the tribe of Benjamin — a hundred and eighty thousand able young men — to go to war against Israel and to regain the kingdom for Rehoboam son of Solomon.

²² But this word of God came to Shemaiah the man of God: ²³ "Say to Rehoboam son of Solomon king of Judah, to all Judah and Benjamin, and to the rest of the people, ²⁴ 'This is what the LORD says: Do not go up to fight against your brothers, the Israelites. Go home, every one of you, for this is my doing.'" So they obeyed the word of the LORD and went home again, as the LORD had ordered.

Golden Calves at Bethel and Dan

²⁵ Then Jeroboam fortified Shechem in the hill country of Ephraim and lived there. From there he went out and built up Peniel.ᵃ

²⁶ Jeroboam thought to himself, "The kingdom will now likely revert to the house of David. ²⁷ If these people go up to offer sacrifices at the temple of the LORD in Jerusalem, they will again give their allegiance to their lord, Re-

hoboam king of Judah. They will kill me and return to King Rehoboam."

²⁸ After seeking advice, the king made two golden calves. He said to the people, "It is too much for you to go up to Jerusalem. Here are your gods, Israel, who brought you up out of Egypt." ²⁹ One he set up in Bethel, and the other in Dan. ³⁰ And this thing became a sin; the people came to worship the one at Bethel and went as far as Dan to worship the other.ᵇ

³¹ Jeroboam built shrines on high places and appointed priests from all sorts of people, even though they were not Levites. ³² He instituted a festival on the fifteenth day of the eighth month, like the festival held in Judah, and offered sacrifices on the altar. This he did in Bethel, sacrificing to the calves he had made. And at Bethel he also installed priests at the high places he had made. ³³ On the fifteenth day of the eighth month, a month of his own choosing, he offered sacrifices on the altar he had built at Bethel. So he instituted the festival for the Israelites and went up to the altar to make offerings.

The Man of God From Judah

13 By the word of the LORD a man of God came from Judah to Bethel, as Jeroboam was

---

ᵃ 25 Hebrew *Penuel*, a variant of *Peniel*   ᵇ 30 Probable reading of the original Hebrew text; Masoretic Text *people went to the one as far as Dan* standing by the altar to make an offering. **2** By the word of the LORD he cried out against the altar: "Altar, altar! This is what the LORD says: 'A son named Josiah will be born to the house of David. On you he will sacrifice the priests of the high places who make offerings here, and human bones will be burned on you.'" **3** That same day the man of God gave a sign: "This is the sign the LORD has declared: The altar will be split apart and the ashes on it will be poured out."

4 When King Jeroboam heard what the man of God cried out against the altar at Bethel, he stretched out his hand from the altar and said, "Seize him!" But the hand he stretched out toward the man shriveled up, so that he could not pull it back. **5** Also, the altar was split apart and its ashes poured out according to the sign given by the man of God by the word of the LORD.

6 Then the king said to the man of God, "Intercede with the LORD your God and pray for me that my hand may be restored." So the man of God interceded with the LORD, and the king's hand was restored and became as it was before.

7 The king said to the man of God, "Come home with me for a meal, and I will give you a gift."

8 But the man of God answered the king, "Even if you were to give me half your possessions, I would not go with you, nor would I eat bread or drink water here. **9** For I was commanded by the word of the LORD: 'You must not eat bread or drink water or return by the way you came.'" **10** So he took another road and did not return by the way he had come to Bethel.

11 Now there was a certain old prophet living in Bethel, whose sons came and told him all that the man of God had done there that day. They also told their father what he had said to the king. **12** Their father asked them, "Which way did he go?" And his sons showed him which road the man of God from Judah had taken. **13** So he said to his sons, "Saddle the donkey for me." And when they had saddled the donkey for him, he mounted it **14** and rode after the man of God. He found him sitting under an oak tree and asked, "Are you the man of God who came from Judah?"

"I am," he replied.

15 So the prophet said to him, "Come home with me and eat."

16 The man of God said, "I cannot turn back and go with you, nor can I eat bread or drink water with you in this place. **17** I have been told by the word of the LORD: 'You must not eat bread or drink water there or return by the way you came.'"

18 The old prophet answered, "I too am a prophet, as you are. And an angel said to me by the word of the LORD: 'Bring him back with you to your house so that he may eat bread and drink water.' " (But he was lying to him.) **19** So the man of God returned with him and ate and drank in his house.

20 While they were sitting at the table, the word of the LORD came to the old prophet who had brought him back. **21** He cried out to the man of God who had come from Judah, "This is what the LORD says: 'You have defied the word of the LORD and have not kept the command the LORD your God gave you. **22** You came back and ate bread and drank water in the place where he told you not to eat or drink. Therefore your body will not be buried in the tomb of your ancestors.' "

23 When the man of God had finished eating and drinking, the prophet who had brought him back saddled his donkey for him. **24** As he went on his way, a lion met him on the road and killed him, and his body was left lying on the road, with both the donkey and the lion standing beside it. **25** Some people who passed by saw the body lying there, with the lion standing beside the body, and they went and reported it in the city where the old prophet lived.

26 When the prophet who had brought him back from his journey heard of it, he said, "It is the man of God who defied the word of the LORD. The LORD has given him over to the lion, which has mauled him and killed him, as the word of the LORD had warned him."

27 The prophet said to his sons, "Saddle the donkey for me," and they did so. **28** Then he went out and found the body lying on the road, with the donkey and the lion standing beside it. The lion had neither eaten the body nor mauled the donkey. **29** So the prophet picked up the body of the man of God, laid it on the donkey, and brought it back to his own city to mourn for him and bury him. **30** Then he laid the body in his own tomb, and they mourned over him and said, "Alas, my brother!"

31 After burying him, he said to his sons, "When I die, bury me in the grave where the man of God is buried; lay my bones beside his bones. **32** For the message he declared by the word of the LORD against the altar in Bethel and against all the shrines on the high places in the towns of Samaria will certainly come true."

33 Even after this, Jeroboam did not change his evil ways, but once more appointed priests for the high places from all sorts of people. Anyone who wanted to become a priest he consecrated for the high places. **34** This was the sin of the house of Jeroboam that led to its downfall and to its destruction from the face of the earth.

Ahijah's Prophecy Against Jeroboam

14 At that time Abijah son of Jeroboam became ill, ² and Jeroboam said to his wife, "Go, disguise yourself, so you won't be recognized as the wife of Jeroboam. Then go to Shiloh. Ahijah the prophet is there — the one who told me I would be king over this people. ³ Take ten loaves of bread with you, some cakes and a jar of honey, and go to him. He will tell you what will happen to the boy." ⁴ So Jeroboam's wife did what he said and went to Ahijah's house in Shiloh.

Now Ahijah could not see; his sight was gone because of his age. ⁵ But the LORD had told Ahijah, "Jeroboam's wife is coming to ask you about her son, for he is ill, and you are to give her such and such an answer. When she arrives, she will pretend to be someone else."

⁶ So when Ahijah heard the sound of her footsteps at the door, he said, "Come in, wife of Jeroboam. Why this pretense? I have been sent to you with bad news. ⁷ Go, tell Jeroboam that this is what the LORD, the God of Israel, says: 'I raised you up from among the people and appointed you ruler over my people Israel. ⁸ I tore the kingdom away from the house of David and gave it to you, but you have not been like my servant David, who kept my commands and followed me with all his heart, doing only what was right in my eyes. ⁹ You have done more evil than all who lived before you. You have made for yourself other gods, idols made of metal; you have aroused my anger and turned your back on me.

¹⁰ "'Because of this, I am going to bring disaster on the house of Jeroboam. I will cut off from Jeroboam every last male in Israel — slave or free.ᵃ I will burn up the house of Jeroboam as one burns dung, until it is all gone. ¹¹ Dogs will eat those belonging to Jeroboam who die in the city, and the birds will feed on those who die in the country. The LORD has spoken!'

¹² "As for you, go back home. When you set foot in your city, the boy will die. ¹³ All Israel will mourn for him and bury him. He is the only one belonging to Jeroboam who will be buried, because he is the only one in the house of Jeroboam in whom the LORD, the God of Israel, has found anything good.

¹⁴ "The LORD will raise up for himself a king over Israel who will cut off the family of Jeroboam. Even now this is beginning to happen.ᵇ ¹⁵ And the LORD will strike Israel, so that it will be like a reed swaying in the water. He will uproot Israel from this good

---

ᵃ 10 Or Israel — every ruler or leader   ᵇ 14 The meaning of the Hebrew for this sentence is uncertain.

land that he gave to their ancestors and scatter them beyond the Euphrates River, because they aroused the LORD's anger by making Asherah poles.[a] ¹⁶And he will give Israel up because of the sins Jeroboam has committed and has caused Israel to commit."

¹⁷Then Jeroboam's wife got up and left and went to Tirzah. As soon as she stepped over the threshold of the house, the boy died. ¹⁸They buried him, and all Israel mourned for him, as the LORD had said through his servant the prophet Ahijah.

¹⁹The other events of Jeroboam's reign, his wars and how he ruled, are written in the book of the annals of the kings of Israel. ²⁰He reigned for twenty-two years and then rested with his ancestors. And Nadab his son succeeded him as king.

Rehoboam King of Judah

²¹Rehoboam son of Solomon was king in Judah. He was forty-one years old when he became king, and he reigned seventeen years in Jerusalem, the city the LORD had chosen out of all the tribes of Israel in which to put his Name. His mother's name was Naamah; she was an Ammonite.

²²Judah did evil in the eyes of the LORD. By the sins they committed they stirred up his jealous anger more than those who were before them had done. ²³They also set up for themselves high places, sacred stones and Asherah poles on every high hill and under every spreading tree. ²⁴There were even male shrine prostitutes in the land; the people engaged in all the detestable practices of the nations the LORD had driven out before the Israelites.

²⁵In the fifth year of King Rehoboam, Shishak king of Egypt attacked Jerusalem. ²⁶He carried off the treasures of the temple of the LORD and the treasures of the royal palace. He took everything, including all the gold shields Solomon had made. ²⁷So King Rehoboam made bronze shields to replace them and assigned these to the commanders of the guard on duty at the entrance to the royal palace. ²⁸Whenever the king went to the LORD's temple, the guards bore the shields, and afterward they returned them to the guardroom.

²⁹As for the other events of Rehoboam's reign, and all he did, are they not written in the book of the annals of the kings of Judah? ³⁰There was continual warfare between Rehoboam and Jeroboam. ³¹And Rehoboam rested with his ancestors and was buried with them in the City of David. His mother's name was Naamah; she was an Ammonite. And

---

[a] 15 That is, wooden symbols of the goddess Asherah; here and elsewhere in 1 Kings

Abijah[a] his son succeeded him as king.

Abijah King of Judah

15 In the eighteenth year of the reign of Jeroboam son of Nebat, Abijah[b] became king of Judah, **2** and he reigned in Jerusalem three years. His mother's name was Maakah daughter of Abishalom.[c]

3 He committed all the sins his father had done before him; his heart was not fully devoted to the LORD his God, as the heart of David his forefather had been. **4** Nevertheless, for David's sake the LORD his God gave him a lamp in Jerusalem by raising up a son to succeed him and by making Jerusalem strong. **5** For David had done what was right in the eyes of the LORD and had not failed to keep any of the LORD's commands all the days of his life — except in the case of Uriah the Hittite.

6 There was war between Abijah[d] and Jeroboam throughout Abijah's lifetime. **7** As for the other events of Abijah's reign, and all he did, are they not written in the book of the annals of the kings of Judah? There was war between Abijah and Jeroboam. **8** And Abijah rested with his ancestors and was buried in the City of David. And Asa his son succeeded him as king.

Asa King of Judah

9 In the twentieth year of Jeroboam king of Israel, Asa became king of Judah, **10** and he reigned in Jerusalem forty-one years. His grandmother's name was Maakah daughter of Abishalom.

11 Asa did what was right in the eyes of the LORD, as his father David had done. **12** He expelled the male shrine prostitutes from the land and got rid of all the idols his ancestors had made. **13** He even deposed his grandmother Maakah from her position as queen mother, because she had made a repulsive image for the worship of Asherah. Asa cut it down and burned it in the Kidron Valley. **14** Although he did not remove the high places, Asa's heart was fully committed to the LORD all his life. **15** He brought into the temple of the LORD the silver and gold and the articles that he and his father had dedicated.

16 There was war between Asa and Baasha king of Israel throughout their reigns. **17** Baasha king of Israel went up against Judah and fortified Ramah to prevent anyone from leaving or entering the territory of Asa king of Judah.

---

[a] 31 Some Hebrew manuscripts and Septuagint (see also 2 Chron. 12:16); most Hebrew manuscripts *Abijam*   [b] 1 Some Hebrew manuscripts and Septuagint (see also 2 Chron. 12:16); most Hebrew manuscripts *Abijam*; also in verses 7 and 8   [c] 2 A variant of *Absalom*; also in verse 10   [d] 6 Some Hebrew manuscripts and Syriac *Abijam* (that is, Abijah); most Hebrew manuscripts *Rehoboam*

¹⁸Asa then took all the silver and gold that was left in the treasuries of the LORD's temple and of his own palace. He entrusted it to his officials and sent them to Ben-Hadad son of Tabrimmon, the son of Hezion, the king of Aram, who was ruling in Damascus. ¹⁹"Let there be a treaty between me and you," he said, "as there was between my father and your father. See, I am sending you a gift of silver and gold. Now break your treaty with Baasha king of Israel so he will withdraw from me."

²⁰Ben-Hadad agreed with King Asa and sent the commanders of his forces against the towns of Israel. He conquered Ijon, Dan, Abel Beth Maakah and all Kinnereth in addition to Naphtali. ²¹When Baasha heard this, he stopped building Ramah and withdrew to Tirzah. ²²Then King Asa issued an order to all Judah — no one was exempt — and they carried away from Ramah the stones and timber Baasha had been using there. With them King Asa built up Geba in Benjamin, and also Mizpah.

²³As for all the other events of Asa's reign, all his achievements, all he did and the cities he built, are they not written in the book of the annals of the kings of Judah? In his old age, however, his feet became diseased. ²⁴Then Asa rested with his ancestors and was buried with them in the city of his father David. And Jehoshaphat his son succeeded him as king.

Nadab King of Israel

²⁵Nadab son of Jeroboam became king of Israel in the second year of Asa king of Judah, and he reigned over Israel two years. ²⁶He did evil in the eyes of the LORD, following the ways of his father and committing the same sin his father had caused Israel to commit.

²⁷Baasha son of Ahijah from the tribe of Issachar plotted against him, and he struck him down at Gibbethon, a Philistine town, while Nadab and all Israel were besieging it. ²⁸Baasha killed Nadab in the third year of Asa king of Judah and succeeded him as king.

²⁹As soon as he began to reign, he killed Jeroboam's whole family. He did not leave Jeroboam anyone that breathed, but destroyed them all, according to the word of the LORD given through his servant Ahijah the Shilonite. ³⁰This happened because of the sins Jeroboam had committed and had caused Israel to commit, and because he aroused the anger of the LORD, the God of Israel.

³¹As for the other events of Nadab's reign, and all he did, are they not written in the book of the annals of the kings of Israel? ³²There was war between Asa and Baasha king of Israel throughout their reigns.

Baasha King of Israel

33In the third year of Asa king of Judah, Baasha son of Ahijah became king of all Israel in Tirzah, and he reigned twenty-four years. **34**He did evil in the eyes of the LORD, following the ways of Jeroboam and committing the same sin Jeroboam had caused Israel to commit.

16
Then the word of the LORD came to Jehu son of Hanani concerning Baasha: **2**"I lifted you up from the dust and appointed you ruler over my people Israel, but you followed the ways of Jeroboam and caused my people Israel to sin and to arouse my anger by their sins. **3**So I am about to wipe out Baasha and his house, and I will make your house like that of Jeroboam son of Nebat. **4**Dogs will eat those belonging to Baasha who die in the city, and birds will feed on those who die in the country."

5As for the other events of Baasha's reign, what he did and his achievements, are they not written in the book of the annals of the kings of Israel? **6**Baasha rested with his ancestors and was buried in Tirzah. And Elah his son succeeded him as king.

7Moreover, the word of the LORD came through the prophet Jehu son of Hanani to Baasha and his house, because of all the evil he had done in the eyes of the LORD, arousing his anger by the things he did, becoming like the house of Jeroboam—and also because he destroyed it.

Elah King of Israel

8In the twenty-sixth year of Asa king of Judah, Elah son of Baasha became king of Israel, and he reigned in Tirzah two years.

9Zimri, one of his officials, who had command of half his chariots, plotted against him. Elah was in Tirzah at the time, getting drunk in the home of Arza, the palace administrator at Tirzah. **10**Zimri came in, struck him down and killed him in the twenty-seventh year of Asa king of Judah. Then he succeeded him as king.

11As soon as he began to reign and was seated on the throne, he killed off Baasha's whole family. He did not spare a single male, whether relative or friend. **12**So Zimri destroyed the whole family of Baasha, in accordance with the word of the LORD spoken against Baasha through the prophet Jehu— **13**because of all the sins Baasha and his son Elah had committed and had caused Israel to commit, so that they aroused the anger of the LORD, the God of Israel, by their worthless idols.

14As for the other events of Elah's reign, and all he did, are they not written in the book of the annals of the kings of Israel?

Zimri King of Israel

15In the twenty-seventh year of Asa king of Judah, Zimri reigned in Tirzah seven days. The army was encamped near Gibbethon, a Philistine town. [16]When the Israelites in the camp heard that Zimri had plotted against the king and murdered him, they proclaimed Omri, the commander of the army, king over Israel that very day there in the camp. [17]Then Omri and all the Israelites with him withdrew from Gibbethon and laid siege to Tirzah. [18]When Zimri saw that the city was taken, he went into the citadel of the royal palace and set the palace on fire around him. So he died, [19]because of the sins he had committed, doing evil in the eyes of the LORD and following the ways of Jeroboam and committing the same sin Jeroboam had caused Israel to commit.

[20]As for the other events of Zimri's reign, and the rebellion he carried out, are they not written in the book of the annals of the kings of Israel?

Omri King of Israel

[21]Then the people of Israel were split into two factions; half supported Tibni son of Ginath for king, and the other half supported Omri. [22]But Omri's followers proved stronger than those of Tibni son of Ginath. So Tibni died and Omri became king.

[23]In the thirty-first year of Asa king of Judah, Omri became king of Israel, and he reigned twelve years, six of them in Tirzah. [24]He bought the hill of Samaria from Shemer for two talents[a] of silver and built a city on the hill, calling it Samaria, after Shemer, the name of the former owner of the hill.

[25]But Omri did evil in the eyes of the LORD and sinned more than all those before him. [26]He followed completely the ways of Jeroboam son of Nebat, committing the same sin Jeroboam had caused Israel to commit, so that they aroused the anger of the LORD, the God of Israel, by their worthless idols.

[27]As for the other events of Omri's reign, what he did and the things he achieved, are they not written in the book of the annals of the kings of Israel? [28]Omri rested with his ancestors and was buried in Samaria. And Ahab his son succeeded him as king.

Ahab Becomes King of Israel

[29]In the thirty-eighth year of Asa king of Judah, Ahab son of Omri became king of Israel, and he reigned in Samaria over Israel twenty-two years. [30]Ahab son of Omri did more evil in the eyes of the LORD than any of those before him. [31]He not only considered it trivial to commit the sins of Jeroboam son of Nebat, but he also married Jezebel daughter of Ethbaal king of the Sidonians, and began to serve Baal and wor-

---

[a] 24 That is, about 150 pounds or about 68 kilograms

ship him. ³²He set up an altar for Baal in the temple of Baal that he built in Samaria. ³³Ahab also made an Asherah pole and did more to arouse the anger of the LORD, the God of Israel, than did all the kings of Israel before him.

³⁴In Ahab's time, Hiel of Bethel rebuilt Jericho. He laid its foundations at the cost of his firstborn son Abiram, and he set up its gates at the cost of his youngest son Segub, in accordance with the word of the LORD spoken by Joshua son of Nun.

Elijah Announces a Great Drought

17 Now Elijah the Tishbite, from Tishbe*ᵃ* in Gilead, said to Ahab, "As the LORD, the God of Israel, lives, whom I serve, there will be neither dew nor rain in the next few years except at my word."

Elijah Fed by Ravens

²Then the word of the LORD came to Elijah: ³"Leave here, turn eastward and hide in the Kerith Ravine, east of the Jordan. ⁴You will drink from the brook, and I have directed the ravens to supply you with food there."

⁵So he did what the LORD had told him. He went to the Kerith Ravine, east of the Jordan, and stayed there. ⁶The ravens brought him bread and meat in the morning and bread and meat

in the evening, and he drank from the brook.

Elijah and the Widow at Zarephath

⁷Some time later the brook dried up because there had been no rain in the land. ⁸Then the word of the LORD came to him: ⁹"Go at once to Zarephath in the region of Sidon and stay there. I have directed a widow there to supply you with food." ¹⁰So he went to Zarephath. When he came to the town gate, a widow was there gathering sticks. He called to her and asked, "Would you bring me a little water in a jar so I may have a drink?" ¹¹As she was going to get it, he called, "And bring me, please, a piece of bread."

¹²"As surely as the LORD your God lives," she replied, "I don't have any bread — only a handful of flour in a jar and a little olive oil in a jug. I am gathering a few sticks to take home and make a meal for myself and my son, that we may eat it — and die."

¹³Elijah said to her, "Don't be afraid. Go home and do as you have said. But first make a small loaf of bread for me from what you have and bring it to me, and then make something for yourself and your son. ¹⁴For this is what the LORD, the God of Israel, says: 'The jar of flour will not be used up and the jug of oil will not

run dry until the day the LORD sends rain on the land.'"

¹⁵She went away and did as Elijah had told her. So there was food every day for Elijah and for the woman and her family. ¹⁶For the jar of flour was not used up and the jug of oil did not run dry, in keeping with the word of the LORD spoken by Elijah.

¹⁷Some time later the son of the woman who owned the house became ill. He grew worse and worse, and finally stopped breathing. ¹⁸She said to Elijah, "What do you have against me, man of God? Did you come to remind me of my sin and kill my son?"

¹⁹"Give me your son," Elijah replied. He took him from her arms, carried him to the upper room where he was staying, and laid him on his bed. ²⁰Then he cried out to the LORD, "LORD my God, have you brought tragedy even on this widow I am staying with, by causing her son to die?" ²¹Then he stretched himself out on the boy three times and cried out to the LORD, "LORD my God, let this boy's life return to him!"

²²The LORD heard Elijah's cry, and the boy's life returned to him, and he lived. ²³Elijah picked up the child and carried him down from the room into the house. He gave him to his mother and said, "Look, your son is alive!"

²⁴Then the woman said to Elijah, "Now I know that you are a man of God and that the word of the LORD from your mouth is the truth."

Elijah and Obadiah

18 After a long time, in the third year, the word of the LORD came to Elijah: "Go and present yourself to Ahab, and I will send rain on the land." ²So Elijah went to present himself to Ahab.

Now the famine was severe in Samaria, ³and Ahab had summoned Obadiah, his palace administrator. (Obadiah was a devout believer in the LORD. ⁴While Jezebel was killing off the LORD's prophets, Obadiah had taken a hundred prophets and hidden them in two caves, fifty in each, and had supplied them with food and water.) ⁵Ahab had said to Obadiah, "Go through the land to all the springs and valleys. Maybe we can find some grass to keep the horses and mules alive so we will not have to kill any of our animals." ⁶So they divided the land they were to cover, Ahab going in one direction and Obadiah in another.

⁷As Obadiah was walking along, Elijah met him. Obadiah recognized him, bowed down to the ground, and said, "Is it really you, my lord Elijah?"

⁸"Yes," he replied. "Go tell your master, 'Elijah is here.'"

⁹"What have I done wrong," asked Obadiah, "that you are

handing your servant over to Ahab to be put to death? ¹⁰As surely as the LORD your God lives, there is not a nation or kingdom where my master has not sent someone to look for you. And whenever a nation or kingdom claimed you were not there, he made them swear they could not find you. ¹¹But now you tell me to go to my master and say, 'Elijah is here.' ¹²I don't know where the Spirit of the LORD may carry you when I leave you. If I go and tell Ahab and he doesn't find you, he will kill me. Yet I your servant have worshiped the LORD since my youth. ¹³Haven't you heard, my lord, what I did while Jezebel was killing the prophets of the LORD? I hid a hundred of the LORD's prophets in two caves, fifty in each, and supplied them with food and water. ¹⁴And now you tell me to go to my master and say, 'Elijah is here.' He will kill me!"

¹⁵Elijah said, "As the LORD Almighty lives, whom I serve, I will surely present myself to Ahab today."

Elijah on Mount Carmel

¹⁶So Obadiah went to meet Ahab and told him, and Ahab went to meet Elijah. ¹⁷When he saw Elijah, he said to him, "Is that you, you troubler of Israel?"

¹⁸"I have not made trouble for Israel," Elijah replied. "But you and your father's family have. You have abandoned the LORD's commands and have followed the Baals. ¹⁹Now summon the people from all over Israel to meet me on Mount Carmel. And bring the four hundred and fifty prophets of Baal and the four hundred prophets of Asherah, who eat at Jezebel's table."

²⁰So Ahab sent word throughout all Israel and assembled the prophets on Mount Carmel. ²¹Elijah went before the people and said, "How long will you waver between two opinions? If the LORD is God, follow him; but if Baal is God, follow him."

But the people said nothing.

²²Then Elijah said to them, "I am the only one of the LORD's prophets left, but Baal has four hundred and fifty prophets. ²³Get two bulls for us. Let Baal's prophets choose one for themselves, and let them cut it into pieces and put it on the wood but not set fire to it. I will prepare the other bull and put it on the wood but not set fire to it. ²⁴Then you call on the name of your god, and I will call on the name of the LORD. The god who answers by fire—he is God."

Then all the people said, "What you say is good."

²⁵Elijah said to the prophets of Baal, "Choose one of the bulls and prepare it first, since there are so many of you. Call on the name of your god, but do not light the fire." ²⁶So they took the bull given them and prepared it.

Then they called on the name of Baal from morning till noon. "Baal, answer us!" they shouted. But there was no response; no one answered. And they danced around the altar they had made.

²⁷At noon Elijah began to taunt them. "Shout louder!" he said. "Surely he is a god! Perhaps he is deep in thought, or busy, or traveling. Maybe he is sleeping and must be awakened." ²⁸So they shouted louder and slashed themselves with swords and spears, as was their custom, until their blood flowed. ²⁹Midday passed, and they continued their frantic prophesying until the time for the evening sacrifice. But there was no response, no one answered, no one paid attention.

³⁰Then Elijah said to all the people, "Come here to me." They came to him, and he repaired the altar of the LORD, which had been torn down. ³¹Elijah took twelve stones, one for each of the tribes descended from Jacob, to whom the word of the LORD had come, saying, "Your name shall be Israel." ³²With the stones he built an altar in the name of the LORD, and he dug a trench around it large enough to hold two seahs*a* of seed. ³³He arranged the wood, cut the bull into pieces and laid it on the wood. Then he said to them, "Fill four large jars with water and pour it on the offering and on the wood."

³⁴"Do it again," he said, and they did it again.

"Do it a third time," he ordered, and they did it the third time. ³⁵The water ran down around the altar and even filled the trench.

³⁶At the time of sacrifice, the prophet Elijah stepped forward and prayed: "LORD, the God of Abraham, Isaac and Israel, let it be known today that you are God in Israel and that I am your servant and have done all these things at your command. ³⁷Answer me, LORD, answer me, so these people will know that you, LORD, are God, and that you are turning their hearts back again."

³⁸Then the fire of the LORD fell and burned up the sacrifice, the wood, the stones and the soil, and also licked up the water in the trench.

³⁹When all the people saw this, they fell prostrate and cried, "The LORD—he is God! The LORD—he is God!"

⁴⁰Then Elijah commanded them, "Seize the prophets of Baal. Don't let anyone get away!" They seized them, and Elijah had them brought down to the Kishon Valley and slaughtered there.

⁴¹And Elijah said to Ahab, "Go, eat and drink, for there is the sound of a heavy rain." ⁴²So Ahab went off to eat and drink, but Elijah climbed to the top of Carmel, bent down to the ground and put his face between his knees.

---

a 32 That is, probably about 24 pounds or about 11 kilograms

⁴³"Go and look toward the sea," he told his servant. And he went up and looked.

"There is nothing there," he said.

Seven times Elijah said, "Go back."

⁴⁴The seventh time the servant reported, "A cloud as small as a man's hand is rising from the sea."

So Elijah said, "Go and tell Ahab, 'Hitch up your chariot and go down before the rain stops you.'"

⁴⁵Meanwhile, the sky grew black with clouds, the wind rose, a heavy rain started falling and Ahab rode off to Jezreel. ⁴⁶The power of the LORD came on Elijah and, tucking his cloak into his belt, he ran ahead of Ahab all the way to Jezreel.

Elijah Flees to Horeb

19 Now Ahab told Jezebel everything Elijah had done and how he had killed all the prophets with the sword. ²So Jezebel sent a messenger to Elijah to say, "May the gods deal with me, be it ever so severely, if by this time tomorrow I do not make your life like that of one of them."

³Elijah was afraid[a] and ran for his life. When he came to Beersheba in Judah, he left his servant there, ⁴while he himself went a day's journey into the wilderness. He came to a broom bush, sat down under it and prayed that he might die. "I have had enough, LORD," he said. "Take my life; I am no better than my ancestors." ⁵Then he lay down under the bush and fell asleep.

All at once an angel touched him and said, "Get up and eat." ⁶He looked around, and there by his head was some bread baked over hot coals, and a jar of water. He ate and drank and then lay down again.

⁷The angel of the LORD came back a second time and touched him and said, "Get up and eat, for the journey is too much for you." ⁸So he got up and ate and drank. Strengthened by that food, he traveled forty days and forty nights until he reached Horeb, the mountain of God. ⁹There he went into a cave and spent the night.

The LORD Appears to Elijah

And the word of the LORD came to him: "What are you doing here, Elijah?"

¹⁰He replied, "I have been very zealous for the LORD God Almighty. The Israelites have rejected your covenant, torn down your altars, and put your prophets to death with the sword. I am the only one left, and now they are trying to kill me too."

¹¹The LORD said, "Go out and stand on the mountain in the presence of the LORD, for the LORD is about to pass by."

---

[a] 3 Or Elijah saw

Then a great and powerful wind tore the mountains apart and shattered the rocks before the LORD, but the LORD was not in the wind. After the wind there was an earthquake, but the LORD was not in the earthquake. ¹²After the earthquake came a fire, but the LORD was not in the fire. And after the fire came a gentle whisper. ¹³When Elijah heard it, he pulled his cloak over his face and went out and stood at the mouth of the cave.

Then a voice said to him, "What are you doing here, Elijah?"

¹⁴He replied, "I have been very zealous for the LORD God Almighty. The Israelites have rejected your covenant, torn down your altars, and put your prophets to death with the sword. I am the only one left, and now they are trying to kill me too."

¹⁵The LORD said to him, "Go back the way you came, and go to the Desert of Damascus. When you get there, anoint Hazael king over Aram. ¹⁶Also, anoint Jehu son of Nimshi king over Israel, and anoint Elisha son of Shaphat from Abel Meholah to succeed you as prophet. ¹⁷Jehu will put to death any who escape the sword of Hazael, and Elisha will put to death any who escape the sword of Jehu. ¹⁸Yet I reserve seven thousand in Israel — all whose knees have not bowed down to Baal and whose mouths have not kissed him."

The Call of Elisha

¹⁹So Elijah went from there and found Elisha son of Shaphat. He was plowing with twelve yoke of oxen, and he himself was driving the twelfth pair. Elijah went up to him and threw his cloak around him. ²⁰Elisha then left his oxen and ran after Elijah. "Let me kiss my father and mother goodbye," he said, "and then I will come with you."

"Go back," Elijah replied. "What have I done to you?"

²¹So Elisha left him and went back. He took his yoke of oxen and slaughtered them. He burned the plowing equipment to cook the meat and gave it to the people, and they ate. Then he set out to follow Elijah and became his servant.

Ben-Hadad Attacks Samaria

20 Now Ben-Hadad king of Aram mustered his entire army. Accompanied by thirty-two kings with their horses and chariots, he went up and besieged Samaria and attacked it. ²He sent messengers into the city to Ahab king of Israel, saying, "This is what Ben-Hadad says: ³'Your silver and gold are mine, and the best of your wives and children are mine.'"

⁴The king of Israel answered, "Just as you say, my lord the king. I and all I have are yours."

⁵The messengers came again and said, "This is what Ben-Hadad says: 'I sent to demand your silver

and gold, your wives and your children. **6**But about this time tomorrow I am going to send my officials to search your palace and the houses of your officials. They will seize everything you value and carry it away.' "

7The king of Israel summoned all the elders of the land and said to them, "See how this man is looking for trouble! When he sent for my wives and my children, my silver and my gold, I did not refuse him."

8The elders and the people all answered, "Don't listen to him or agree to his demands."

9So he replied to Ben-Hadad's messengers, "Tell my lord the king, 'Your servant will do all you demanded the first time, but this demand I cannot meet.' " They left and took the answer back to Ben-Hadad.

10Then Ben-Hadad sent another message to Ahab: "May the gods deal with me, be it ever so severely, if enough dust remains in Samaria to give each of my men a handful."

11The king of Israel answered, "Tell him: 'One who puts on his armor should not boast like one who takes it off.' "

12Ben-Hadad heard this message while he and the kings were drinking in their tents,*a* and he ordered his men: "Prepare to attack." So they prepared to attack the city.

Ahab Defeats Ben-Hadad

13Meanwhile a prophet came to Ahab king of Israel and announced, "This is what the LORD says: 'Do you see this vast army? I will give it into your hand today, and then you will know that I am the LORD.' "

14"But who will do this?" asked Ahab.

The prophet replied, "This is what the LORD says: 'The junior officers under the provincial commanders will do it.' "

"And who will start the battle?" he asked.

The prophet answered, "You will."

15So Ahab summoned the 232 junior officers under the provincial commanders. Then he assembled the rest of the Israelites, 7,000 in all. **16**They set out at noon while Ben-Hadad and the 32 kings allied with him were in their tents getting drunk. **17**The junior officers under the provincial commanders went out first.

Now Ben-Hadad had dispatched scouts, who reported, "Men are advancing from Samaria."

18He said, "If they have come out for peace, take them alive; if they have come out for war, take them alive."

19The junior officers under the provincial commanders marched out of the city with the army behind them **20**and each one struck

---

a 12 Or *in Sukkoth*; also in verse 16

down his opponent. At that, the Arameans fled, with the Israelites in pursuit. But Ben-Hadad king of Aram escaped on horseback with some of his horsemen. ²¹ The king of Israel advanced and overpowered the horses and chariots and inflicted heavy losses on the Arameans.

²² Afterward, the prophet came to the king of Israel and said, "Strengthen your position and see what must be done, because next spring the king of Aram will attack you again."

²³ Meanwhile, the officials of the king of Aram advised him, "Their gods are gods of the hills. That is why they were too strong for us. But if we fight them on the plains, surely we will be stronger than they. ²⁴ Do this: Remove all the kings from their commands and replace them with other officers. ²⁵ You must also raise an army like the one you lost—horse for horse and chariot for chariot—so we can fight Israel on the plains. Then surely we will be stronger than they." He agreed with them and acted accordingly.

²⁶ The next spring Ben-Hadad mustered the Arameans and went up to Aphek to fight against Israel. ²⁷ When the Israelites were also mustered and given provisions, they marched out to meet them. The Israelites camped opposite them like two small flocks of goats, while the Arameans covered the countryside.

²⁸ The man of God came up and told the king of Israel, "This is what the LORD says: 'Because the Arameans think the LORD is a god of the hills and not a god of the valleys, I will deliver this vast army into your hands, and you will know that I am the LORD.'"

²⁹ For seven days they camped opposite each other, and on the seventh day the battle was joined. The Israelites inflicted a hundred thousand casualties on the Aramean foot soldiers in one day. ³⁰ The rest of them escaped to the city of Aphek, where the wall collapsed on twenty-seven thousand of them. And Ben-Hadad fled to the city and hid in an inner room.

³¹ His officials said to him, "Look, we have heard that the kings of Israel are merciful. Let us go to the king of Israel with sackcloth around our waists and ropes around our heads. Perhaps he will spare your life."

³² Wearing sackcloth around their waists and ropes around their heads, they went to the king of Israel and said, "Your servant Ben-Hadad says: 'Please let me live.'"

The king answered, "Is he still alive? He is my brother."

³³ The men took this as a good sign and were quick to pick up his word. "Yes, your brother Ben-Hadad!" they said.

"Go and get him," the king said. When Ben-Hadad came out,

Ahab had him come up into his chariot.

³⁴"I will return the cities my father took from your father," Ben-Hadad offered. "You may set up your own market areas in Damascus, as my father did in Samaria."

Ahab said, "On the basis of a treaty I will set you free." So he made a treaty with him, and let him go.

A Prophet Condemns Ahab

³⁵By the word of the LORD one of the company of the prophets said to his companion, "Strike me with your weapon," but he refused.

³⁶So the prophet said, "Because you have not obeyed the LORD, as soon as you leave me a lion will kill you." And after the man went away, a lion found him and killed him.

³⁷The prophet found another man and said, "Strike me, please." So the man struck him and wounded him. ³⁸Then the prophet went and stood by the road waiting for the king. He disguised himself with his headband down over his eyes. ³⁹As the king passed by, the prophet called out to him, "Your servant went into the thick of the battle, and someone came to me with a captive and said, 'Guard this

man. If he is missing, it will be your life for his life, or you must pay a talent^a of silver.' ⁴⁰While your servant was busy here and there, the man disappeared."

"That is your sentence," the king of Israel said. "You have pronounced it yourself."

⁴¹Then the prophet quickly removed the headband from his eyes, and the king of Israel recognized him as one of the prophets. ⁴²He said to the king, "This is what the LORD says: 'You have set free a man I had determined should die.^b Therefore it is your life for his life, your people for his people.'" ⁴³Sullen and angry, the king of Israel went to his palace in Samaria.

Naboth's Vineyard

21 Some time later there was an incident involving a vineyard belonging to Naboth the Jezreelite. The vineyard was in Jezreel, close to the palace of Ahab king of Samaria. ²Ahab said to Naboth, "Let me have your vineyard to use for a vegetable garden, since it is close to my palace. In exchange I will give you a better vineyard or, if you prefer, I will pay you whatever it is worth."

³But Naboth replied, "The LORD forbid that I should give you the inheritance of my ancestors."

---

^a 39 That is, about 75 pounds or about 34 kilograms   ^b 42 The Hebrew term refers to the irrevocable giving over of things or persons to the LORD, often by totally destroying them.

⁴So Ahab went home, sullen and angry because Naboth the Jezreelite had said, "I will not give you the inheritance of my ancestors." He lay on his bed sulking and refused to eat.

⁵His wife Jezebel came in and asked him, "Why are you so sullen? Why won't you eat?"

⁶He answered her, "Because I said to Naboth the Jezreelite, 'Sell me your vineyard; or if you prefer, I will give you another vineyard in its place.' But he said, 'I will not give you my vineyard.'"

⁷Jezebel his wife said, "Is this how you act as king over Israel? Get up and eat! Cheer up. I'll get you the vineyard of Naboth the Jezreelite."

⁸So she wrote letters in Ahab's name, placed his seal on them, and sent them to the elders and nobles who lived in Naboth's city with him. ⁹In those letters she wrote:

"Proclaim a day of fasting and seat Naboth in a prominent place among the people. ¹⁰But seat two scoundrels opposite him and have them bring charges that he has cursed both God and the king. Then take him out and stone him to death."

¹¹So the elders and nobles who lived in Naboth's city did as Jezebel directed in the letters she had written to them. ¹²They proclaimed a fast and seated Naboth in a prominent place among the people. ¹³Then two scoundrels came and sat opposite him and brought charges against Naboth before the people, saying, "Naboth has cursed both God and the king." So they took him outside the city and stoned him to death. ¹⁴Then they sent word to Jezebel: "Naboth has been stoned to death."

¹⁵As soon as Jezebel heard that Naboth had been stoned to death, she said to Ahab, "Get up and take possession of the vineyard of Naboth the Jezreelite that he refused to sell you. He is no longer alive, but dead." ¹⁶When Ahab heard that Naboth was dead, he got up and went down to take possession of Naboth's vineyard.

¹⁷Then the word of the LORD came to Elijah the Tishbite: ¹⁸"Go down to meet Ahab king of Israel, who rules in Samaria. He is now in Naboth's vineyard, where he has gone to take possession of it. ¹⁹Say to him, 'This is what the LORD says: Have you not murdered a man and seized his property?' Then say to him, 'This is what the LORD says: In the place where dogs licked up Naboth's blood, dogs will lick up your blood — yes, yours!'"

²⁰Ahab said to Elijah, "So you have found me, my enemy!"

"I have found you," he answered, "because you have sold yourself to do evil in the eyes of the LORD. ²¹He says, 'I am going to bring disaster on you. I will wipe out your descendants and cut off from Ahab every last male in Israel — slave or free.*[a] 22 I will make your house like that of Jeroboam son of Nebat and that of Baasha son of Ahijah, because you have aroused my anger and have caused Israel to sin.'

23 "And also concerning Jezebel the LORD says: 'Dogs will devour Jezebel by the wall of[b] Jezreel.'

24 "Dogs will eat those belonging to Ahab who die in the city, and the birds will feed on those who die in the country."

25 (There was never anyone like Ahab, who sold himself to do evil in the eyes of the LORD, urged on by Jezebel his wife. 26 He behaved in the vilest manner by going after idols, like the Amorites the LORD drove out before Israel.)

27 When Ahab heard these words, he tore his clothes, put on sackcloth and fasted. He lay in sackcloth and went around meekly.

28 Then the word of the LORD came to Elijah the Tishbite: 29 "Have you noticed how Ahab has humbled himself before me? Because he has humbled himself, I will not bring this disaster in his day, but I will bring it on his house in the days of his son."

Micaiah Prophesies Against Ahab

22 For three years there was no war between Aram and Israel. 2 But in the third year Jehoshaphat king of Judah went down to see the king of Israel. 3 The king of Israel had said to his officials, "Don't you know that Ramoth Gilead belongs to us and yet we are doing nothing to retake it from the king of Aram?"

4 So he asked Jehoshaphat, "Will you go with me to fight against Ramoth Gilead?"

Jehoshaphat replied to the king of Israel, "I am as you are, my people as your people, my horses as your horses." 5 But Jehoshaphat also said to the king of Israel, "First seek the counsel of the LORD."

6 So the king of Israel brought together the prophets — about four hundred men — and asked them, "Shall I go to war against Ramoth Gilead, or shall I refrain?"

"Go," they answered, "for the Lord will give it into the king's hand."

7 But Jehoshaphat asked, "Is there no longer a prophet of the LORD here whom we can inquire of?"

8 The king of Israel answered Jehoshaphat, "There is still one prophet through whom we can inquire of the LORD, but I hate him because he never prophesies anything good about me, but always bad. He is Micaiah son of Imlah."

"The king should not say such a thing," Jehoshaphat replied.

a 21 Or Israel — every ruler or leader   *b 23 Most Hebrew manuscripts; a few Hebrew manuscripts, Vulgate and Syriac (see also 2 Kings 9:26) the plot of ground at*

⁹ So the king of Israel called one of his officials and said, "Bring Micaiah son of Imlah at once."

¹⁰ Dressed in their royal robes, the king of Israel and Jehoshaphat king of Judah were sitting on their thrones at the threshing floor by the entrance of the gate of Samaria, with all the prophets prophesying before them. ¹¹ Now Zedekiah son of Kenaanah had made iron horns and he declared, "This is what the LORD says: 'With these you will gore the Arameans until they are destroyed.'"

¹² All the other prophets were prophesying the same thing. "Attack Ramoth Gilead and be victorious," they said, "for the LORD will give it into the king's hand."

¹³ The messenger who had gone to summon Micaiah said to him, "Look, the other prophets without exception are predicting success for the king. Let your word agree with theirs, and speak favorably."

¹⁴ But Micaiah said, "As surely as the LORD lives, I can tell him only what the LORD tells me."

¹⁵ When he arrived, the king asked him, "Micaiah, shall we go to war against Ramoth Gilead, or not?"

"Attack and be victorious," he answered, "for the LORD will give it into the king's hand."

¹⁶ The king said to him, "How many times must I make you swear to tell me nothing but the truth in the name of the LORD?"

¹⁷ Then Micaiah answered, "I saw all Israel scattered on the hills like sheep without a shepherd, and the LORD said, 'These people have no master. Let each one go home in peace.'"

¹⁸ The king of Israel said to Jehoshaphat, "Didn't I tell you that he never prophesies anything good about me, but only bad?"

¹⁹ Micaiah continued, "Therefore hear the word of the LORD: I saw the LORD sitting on his throne with all the multitudes of heaven standing around him on his right and on his left. ²⁰ And the LORD said, 'Who will entice Ahab into attacking Ramoth Gilead and going to his death there?'

"One suggested this, and another that. ²¹ Finally, a spirit came forward, stood before the LORD and said, 'I will entice him.'

²² "'By what means?' the LORD asked.

"'I will go out and be a deceiving spirit in the mouths of all his prophets,' he said.

"'You will succeed in enticing him,' said the LORD. 'Go and do it.'

²³ "So now the LORD has put a deceiving spirit in the mouths of all these prophets of yours. The LORD has decreed disaster for you."

²⁴ Then Zedekiah son of Kenaanah went up and slapped Micaiah in the face. "Which way did the spirit from*a* the LORD go

a 24 Or *Spirit of*

when he went from me to speak to you?" he asked.

²⁵Micaiah replied, "You will find out on the day you go to hide in an inner room."

²⁶The king of Israel then ordered, "Take Micaiah and send him back to Amon the ruler of the city and to Joash the king's son ²⁷and say, 'This is what the king says: Put this fellow in prison and give him nothing but bread and water until I return safely.'"

²⁸Micaiah declared, "If you ever return safely, the LORD has not spoken through me." Then he added, "Mark my words, all you people!"

Ahab Killed at Ramoth Gilead

²⁹So the king of Israel and Jehoshaphat king of Judah went up to Ramoth Gilead. ³⁰The king of Israel said to Jehoshaphat, "I will enter the battle in disguise, but you wear your royal robes." So the king of Israel disguised himself and went into battle.

³¹Now the king of Aram had ordered his thirty-two chariot commanders, "Do not fight with anyone, small or great, except the king of Israel." ³²When the chariot commanders saw Jehoshaphat, they thought, "Surely this is the king of Israel." So they turned to attack him, but when Jehoshaphat cried out, ³³the chariot commanders saw that he was not the king of Israel and stopped pursuing him.

³⁴But someone drew his bow at random and hit the king of Israel between the sections of his armor. The king told his chariot driver, "Wheel around and get me out of the fighting. I've been wounded." ³⁵All day long the battle raged, and the king was propped up in his chariot facing the Arameans. The blood from his wound ran onto the floor of the chariot, and that evening he died. ³⁶As the sun was setting, a cry spread through the army: "Every man to his town. Every man to his land!"

³⁷So the king died and was brought to Samaria, and they buried him there. ³⁸They washed the chariot at a pool in Samaria (where the prostitutes bathed),ᵃ and the dogs licked up his blood, as the word of the LORD had declared.

³⁹As for the other events of Ahab's reign, including all he did, the palace he built and adorned with ivory, and the cities he fortified, are they not written in the book of the annals of the kings of Israel? ⁴⁰Ahab rested with his ancestors. And Ahaziah his son succeeded him as king.

Jehoshaphat King of Judah

⁴¹Jehoshaphat son of Asa became king of Judah in the fourth year of Ahab king of Israel. ⁴²Jehoshaphat was thirty-five years old when he became king, and

---

ᵃ 38 Or *Samaria and cleaned the weapons*

he reigned in Jerusalem twenty-five years. His mother's name was Azubah daughter of Shilhi. [43] In everything he followed the ways of his father Asa and did not stray from them; he did what was right in the eyes of the LORD. The high places, however, were not removed, and the people continued to offer sacrifices and burn incense there.[a] [44] Jehoshaphat was also at peace with the king of Israel.

[45] As for the other events of Jehoshaphat's reign, the things he achieved and his military exploits, are they not written in the book of the annals of the kings of Judah? [46] He rid the land of the rest of the male shrine prostitutes who remained there even after the reign of his father Asa. [47] There was then no king in Edom; a provincial governor ruled.

[48] Now Jehoshaphat built a fleet of trading ships[b] to go to Ophir for gold, but they never set sail— they were wrecked at Ezion Geber. [49] At that time Ahaziah son of Ahab said to Jehoshaphat, "Let my men sail with yours," but Jehoshaphat refused.

[50] Then Jehoshaphat rested with his ancestors and was buried with them in the city of David his father. And Jehoram his son succeeded him as king.

Ahaziah King of Israel

[51] Ahaziah son of Ahab became king of Israel in Samaria in the seventeenth year of Jehoshaphat king of Judah, and he reigned over Israel two years. [52] He did evil in the eyes of the LORD, because he followed the ways of his father and mother and of Jeroboam son of Nebat, who caused Israel to sin. [53] He served and worshiped Baal and aroused the anger of the LORD, the God of Israel, just as his father had done.

---

[a] 43 In Hebrew texts this sentence (22:43b) is numbered 22:44, and 22:44-53 is numbered 22:45-54.   [b] 48 Hebrew *of ships of Tarshish*

2 Kings

Introduction:

Second Kings continues the stories of the great prophets Elijah and Elisha. It records the history of the northern kingdom of Israel and the southern kingdom of Judah until they were both finally conquered. Israel was conquered by Assyria in 722 BC and Judah was conquered by the Babylonians in 586 BC. In both kingdoms God's prophets continually warned the people that God would punish them if they did not repent from their sins.

Outline of contents:

Elijah and Elisha (1:1–8:15)
Kings of Israel and Judah (8:16–17:6)
Israel taken captive to Assyria (17:7–41)
Judah survives Assyrian rule (18:1–23:37)
Judah taken captive to Babylonia (24:1–25:30)

The LORD's Judgment on Ahaziah

1 After Ahab's death, Moab rebelled against Israel. ²Now Ahaziah had fallen through the lattice of his upper room in Samaria and injured himself. So he sent messengers, saying to them, "Go and consult Baal-Zebub, the god of Ekron, to see if I will recover from this injury."

³But the angel of the LORD said to Elijah the Tishbite, "Go up and meet the messengers of the king of Samaria and ask them, 'Is it because there is no God in Israel that you are going off to consult Baal-Zebub, the god of Ekron?' ⁴Therefore this is what the LORD says: 'You will not leave the bed you are lying on. You will certainly die!' " So Elijah went.

⁵When the messengers returned to the king, he asked them, "Why have you come back?"

⁶"A man came to meet us," they replied. "And he said to us, 'Go back to the king who sent you and tell him, "This is what the LORD says: Is it because there is no God in Israel that you are sending messengers to consult Baal-Zebub, the god of Ekron? Therefore you will not leave the bed you are lying on. You will certainly die!" ' "

⁷The king asked them, "What kind of man was it who came to meet you and told you this?"

⁸They replied, "He had a garment of hair[a] and had a leather belt around his waist."

The king said, "That was Elijah the Tishbite."

⁹Then he sent to Elijah a captain with his company of fifty men. The captain went up to Elijah, who was sitting on the top of a hill, and said to him, "Man of God, the king says, 'Come down!'"

¹⁰Elijah answered the captain, "If I am a man of God, may fire come down from heaven and consume you and your fifty men!" Then fire fell from heaven and consumed the captain and his men.

¹¹At this the king sent to Elijah another captain with his fifty men. The captain said to him, "Man of God, this is what the king says, 'Come down at once!'"

¹²"If I am a man of God," Elijah replied, "may fire come down from heaven and consume you and your fifty men!" Then the fire of God fell from heaven and consumed him and his fifty men.

¹³So the king sent a third captain with his fifty men. This third captain went up and fell on his knees before Elijah. "Man of God," he begged, "please have respect for my life and the lives of these fifty men, your servants! ¹⁴See, fire has fallen from heaven and consumed the first two captains and all their men. But now have respect for my life!"

¹⁵The angel of the LORD said to Elijah, "Go down with him; do not be afraid of him." So Elijah got up and went down with him to the king.

¹⁶He told the king, "This is what the LORD says: Is it because there is no God in Israel for you to consult that you have sent messengers to consult Baal-Zebub, the god of Ekron? Because you have done this, you will never leave the bed you are lying on. You will certainly die!" ¹⁷So he died, according to the word of the LORD that Elijah had spoken.

Because Ahaziah had no son, Joram[b] succeeded him as king in the second year of Jehoram son of Jehoshaphat king of Judah. ¹⁸As for all the other events of Ahaziah's reign, and what he did, are they not written in the book of the annals of the kings of Israel?

Elijah Taken Up to Heaven

2 When the LORD was about to take Elijah up to heaven in a whirlwind, Elijah and Elisha were on their way from Gilgal. ²Elijah said to Elisha, "Stay here; the LORD has sent me to Bethel."

But Elisha said, "As surely as the LORD lives and as you live, I will not leave you." So they went down to Bethel.

³The company of the prophets at Bethel came out to Elisha and asked, "Do you know that the

---

[a] 8 Or *He was a hairy man*   [b] 17 Hebrew *Jehoram,* a variant of *Joram*

LORD is going to take your master from you today?"

"Yes, I know," Elisha replied, "so be quiet."

⁴Then Elijah said to him, "Stay here, Elisha; the LORD has sent me to Jericho."

And he replied, "As surely as the LORD lives and as you live, I will not leave you." So they went to Jericho.

⁵The company of the prophets at Jericho went up to Elisha and asked him, "Do you know that the LORD is going to take your master from you today?"

"Yes, I know," he replied, "so be quiet."

⁶Then Elijah said to him, "Stay here; the LORD has sent me to the Jordan."

And he replied, "As surely as the LORD lives and as you live, I will not leave you." So the two of them walked on.

⁷Fifty men from the company of the prophets went and stood at a distance, facing the place where Elijah and Elisha had stopped at the Jordan. ⁸Elijah took his cloak, rolled it up and struck the water with it. The water divided to the right and to the left, and the two of them crossed over on dry ground.

⁹When they had crossed, Elijah said to Elisha, "Tell me, what can I do for you before I am taken from you?"

"Let me inherit a double portion of your spirit," Elisha replied.

¹⁰"You have asked a difficult thing," Elijah said, "yet if you see me when I am taken from you, it will be yours—otherwise, it will not."

¹¹As they were walking along and talking together, suddenly a chariot of fire and horses of fire appeared and separated the two of them, and Elijah went up to heaven in a whirlwind. ¹²Elisha saw this and cried out, "My father! My father! The chariots and horsemen of Israel!" And Elisha saw him no more. Then he took hold of his garment and tore it in two.

¹³Elisha then picked up Elijah's cloak that had fallen from him and went back and stood on the bank of the Jordan. ¹⁴He took the cloak that had fallen from Elijah and struck the water with it. "Where now is the LORD, the God of Elijah?" he asked. When he struck the water, it divided to the right and to the left, and he crossed over.

¹⁵The company of the prophets from Jericho, who were watching, said, "The spirit of Elijah is resting on Elisha." And they went to meet him and bowed to the ground before him. ¹⁶"Look," they said, "we your servants have fifty able men. Let them go and look for your master. Perhaps the Spirit of the LORD has picked him up and set him down on some mountain or in some valley."

"No," Elisha replied, "do not send them."

[17] But they persisted until he was too embarrassed to refuse. So he said, "Send them." And they sent fifty men, who searched for three days but did not find him. [18] When they returned to Elisha, who was staying in Jericho, he said to them, "Didn't I tell you not to go?"

Healing of the Water

[19] The people of the city said to Elisha, "Look, our lord, this town is well situated, as you can see, but the water is bad and the land is unproductive."

[20] "Bring me a new bowl," he said, "and put salt in it." So they brought it to him.

[21] Then he went out to the spring and threw the salt into it, saying, "This is what the LORD says: 'I have healed this water. Never again will it cause death or make the land unproductive.'" [22] And the water has remained pure to this day, according to the word Elisha had spoken.

Elisha Is Jeered

[23] From there Elisha went up to Bethel. As he was walking along the road, some boys came out of the town and jeered at him. "Get out of here, baldy!" they said. "Get out of here, baldy!" [24] He turned around, looked at them and called down a curse on them in the name of the LORD. Then two bears came out of the woods and mauled forty-two of the boys. [25] And he went on to Mount Carmel and from there returned to Samaria.

Moab Revolts

3 Joram[a] son of Ahab became king of Israel in Samaria in the eighteenth year of Jehoshaphat king of Judah, and he reigned twelve years. [2] He did evil in the eyes of the LORD, but not as his father and mother had done. He got rid of the sacred stone of Baal that his father had made. [3] Nevertheless he clung to the sins of Jeroboam son of Nebat, which he had caused Israel to commit; he did not turn away from them.

[4] Now Mesha king of Moab raised sheep, and he had to pay the king of Israel a tribute of a hundred thousand lambs and the wool of a hundred thousand rams. [5] But after Ahab died, the king of Moab rebelled against the king of Israel. [6] So at that time King Joram set out from Samaria and mobilized all Israel. [7] He also sent this message to Jehoshaphat king of Judah: "The king of Moab has rebelled against me. Will you go with me to fight against Moab?"

"I will go with you," he replied. "I am as you are, my people as your people, my horses as your horses."

[a] 1 Hebrew *Jehoram*, a variant of *Joram*; also in verse 6

⁸"By what route shall we attack?" he asked.

"Through the Desert of Edom," he answered.

⁹So the king of Israel set out with the king of Judah and the king of Edom. After a roundabout march of seven days, the army had no more water for themselves or for the animals with them.

¹⁰"What!" exclaimed the king of Israel. "Has the Lord called us three kings together only to deliver us into the hands of Moab?"

¹¹But Jehoshaphat asked, "Is there no prophet of the Lord here, through whom we may inquire of the Lord?"

An officer of the king of Israel answered, "Elisha son of Shaphat is here. He used to pour water on the hands of Elijah.ᵃ"

¹²Jehoshaphat said, "The word of the Lord is with him." So the king of Israel and Jehoshaphat and the king of Edom went down to him.

¹³Elisha said to the king of Israel, "Why do you want to involve me? Go to the prophets of your father and the prophets of your mother."

"No," the king of Israel answered, "because it was the Lord who called us three kings together to deliver us into the hands of Moab."

¹⁴Elisha said, "As surely as the Lord Almighty lives, whom I serve, if I did not have respect for the presence of Jehoshaphat king of Judah, I would not pay any attention to you. ¹⁵But now bring me a harpist."

While the harpist was playing, the hand of the Lord came on Elisha ¹⁶and he said, "This is what the Lord says: I will fill this valley with pools of water. ¹⁷For this is what the Lord says: You will see neither wind nor rain, yet this valley will be filled with water, and you, your cattle and your other animals will drink. ¹⁸This is an easy thing in the eyes of the Lord; he will also deliver Moab into your hands. ¹⁹You will overthrow every fortified city and every major town. You will cut down every good tree, stop up all the springs, and ruin every good field with stones."

²⁰The next morning, about the time for offering the sacrifice, there it was—water flowing from the direction of Edom! And the land was filled with water.

²¹Now all the Moabites had heard that the kings had come to fight against them; so every man, young and old, who could bear arms was called up and stationed on the border. ²²When they got up early in the morning, the sun was shining on the water. To the Moabites across the way, the water looked red—like blood. ²³"That's blood!" they said. "Those kings must have fought and slaughtered each other. Now to the plunder, Moab!"

ᵃ 11 That is, he was Elijah's personal servant.

²⁴But when the Moabites came to the camp of Israel, the Israelites rose up and fought them until they fled. And the Israelites invaded the land and slaughtered the Moabites. ²⁵They destroyed the towns, and each man threw a stone on every good field until it was covered. They stopped up all the springs and cut down every good tree. Only Kir Hareseth was left with its stones in place, but men armed with slings surrounded it and attacked it.

²⁶When the king of Moab saw that the battle had gone against him, he took with him seven hundred swordsmen to break through to the king of Edom, but they failed. ²⁷Then he took his firstborn son, who was to succeed him as king, and offered him as a sacrifice on the city wall. The fury against Israel was great; they withdrew and returned to their own land.

The Widow's Olive Oil

4 The wife of a man from the company of the prophets cried out to Elisha, "Your servant my husband is dead, and you know that he revered the LORD. But now his creditor is coming to take my two boys as his slaves."

²Elisha replied to her, "How can I help you? Tell me, what do you have in your house?"

"Your servant has nothing there at all," she said, "except a small jar of olive oil."

³Elisha said, "Go around and ask all your neighbors for empty jars. Don't ask for just a few. ⁴Then go inside and shut the door behind you and your sons. Pour oil into all the jars, and as each is filled, put it to one side."

⁵She left him and shut the door behind her and her sons. They brought the jars to her and she kept pouring. ⁶When all the jars were full, she said to her son, "Bring me another one."

But he replied, "There is not a jar left." Then the oil stopped flowing.

⁷She went and told the man of God, and he said, "Go, sell the oil and pay your debts. You and your sons can live on what is left."

The Shunammite's Son Restored to Life

⁸One day Elisha went to Shunem. And a well-to-do woman was there, who urged him to stay for a meal. So whenever he came by, he stopped there to eat. ⁹She said to her husband, "I know that this man who often comes our way is a holy man of God. ¹⁰Let's make a small room on the roof and put in it a bed and a table, a chair and a lamp for him. Then he can stay there whenever he comes to us."

¹¹One day when Elisha came, he went up to his room and lay down there. ¹²He said to his servant Gehazi, "Call the Shunammite." So he called her, and she

stood before him. **13**Elisha said to him, "Tell her, 'You have gone to all this trouble for us. Now what can be done for you? Can we speak on your behalf to the king or the commander of the army?'"

She replied, "I have a home among my own people."

14"What can be done for her?" Elisha asked.

Gehazi said, "She has no son, and her husband is old."

15Then Elisha said, "Call her." So he called her, and she stood in the doorway. **16**"About this time next year," Elisha said, "you will hold a son in your arms."

"No, my lord!" she objected. "Please, man of God, don't mislead your servant!"

17But the woman became pregnant, and the next year about that same time she gave birth to a son, just as Elisha had told her.

18The child grew, and one day he went out to his father, who was with the reapers. **19**He said to his father, "My head! My head!"

His father told a servant, "Carry him to his mother." **20**After the servant had lifted him up and carried him to his mother, the boy sat on her lap until noon, and then he died. **21**She went up and laid him on the bed of the man of God, then shut the door and went out.

22She called her husband and said, "Please send me one of the servants and a donkey so I can go to the man of God quickly and return."

23"Why go to him today?" he asked. "It's not the New Moon or the Sabbath."

"That's all right," she said.

24She saddled the donkey and said to her servant, "Lead on; don't slow down for me unless I tell you." **25**So she set out and came to the man of God at Mount Carmel.

When he saw her in the distance, the man of God said to his servant Gehazi, "Look! There's the Shunammite! **26**Run to meet her and ask her, 'Are you all right? Is your husband all right? Is your child all right?'"

"Everything is all right," she said.

27When she reached the man of God at the mountain, she took hold of his feet. Gehazi came over to push her away, but the man of God said, "Leave her alone! She is in bitter distress, but the LORD has hidden it from me and has not told me why."

28"Did I ask you for a son, my lord?" she said. "Didn't I tell you, 'Don't raise my hopes'?"

29Elisha said to Gehazi, "Tuck your cloak into your belt, take my staff in your hand and run. Don't greet anyone you meet, and if anyone greets you, do not answer. Lay my staff on the boy's face."

30But the child's mother said, "As surely as the LORD lives and as you live, I will not leave you." So he got up and followed her.

³¹Gehazi went on ahead and laid the staff on the boy's face, but there was no sound or response. So Gehazi went back to meet Elisha and told him, "The boy has not awakened."

³²When Elisha reached the house, there was the boy lying dead on his couch. ³³He went in, shut the door on the two of them and prayed to the LORD. ³⁴Then he got on the bed and lay on the boy, mouth to mouth, eyes to eyes, hands to hands. As he stretched himself out on him, the boy's body grew warm. ³⁵Elisha turned away and walked back and forth in the room and then got on the bed and stretched out on him once more. The boy sneezed seven times and opened his eyes.

³⁶Elisha summoned Gehazi and said, "Call the Shunammite." And he did. When she came, he said, "Take your son." ³⁷She came in, fell at his feet and bowed to the ground. Then she took her son and went out.

Death in the Pot

³⁸Elisha returned to Gilgal and there was a famine in that region. While the company of the prophets was meeting with him, he said to his servant, "Put on the large pot and cook some stew for these prophets."

³⁹One of them went out into the fields to gather herbs and found a wild vine and picked as many of its gourds as his garment could hold. When he returned, he cut them up into the pot of stew, though no one knew what they were. ⁴⁰The stew was poured out for the men, but as they began to eat it, they cried out, "Man of God, there is death in the pot!" And they could not eat it.

⁴¹Elisha said, "Get some flour." He put it into the pot and said, "Serve it to the people to eat." And there was nothing harmful in the pot.

Feeding of a Hundred

⁴²A man came from Baal Shalishah, bringing the man of God twenty loaves of barley bread baked from the first ripe grain, along with some heads of new grain. "Give it to the people to eat," Elisha said.

⁴³"How can I set this before a hundred men?" his servant asked.

But Elisha answered, "Give it to the people to eat. For this is what the LORD says: 'They will eat and have some left over.'" ⁴⁴Then he set it before them, and they ate and had some left over, according to the word of the LORD.

Naaman Healed of Leprosy

5 Now Naaman was commander of the army of the king of Aram. He was a great man in the sight of his master and highly regarded, because through him the LORD had given

victory to Aram. He was a valiant soldier, but he had leprosy.*

2 Now bands of raiders from Aram had gone out and had taken captive a young girl from Israel, and she served Naaman's wife. **3** She said to her mistress, "If only my master would see the prophet who is in Samaria! He would cure him of his leprosy."

4 Naaman went to his master and told him what the girl from Israel had said. **5** "By all means, go," the king of Aram replied. "I will send a letter to the king of Israel." So Naaman left, taking with him ten talents[b] of silver, six thousand shekels[c] of gold and ten sets of clothing. **6** The letter that he took to the king of Israel read: "With this letter I am sending my servant Naaman to you so that you may cure him of his leprosy."

7 As soon as the king of Israel read the letter, he tore his robes and said, "Am I God? Can I kill and bring back to life? Why does this fellow send someone to me to be cured of his leprosy? See how he is trying to pick a quarrel with me!"

8 When Elisha the man of God heard that the king of Israel had torn his robes, he sent him this message: "Why have you torn your robes? Have the man come to me and he will know that there is a prophet in Israel." **9** So Naaman went with his horses and chariots and stopped at the door of Elisha's house. **10** Elisha sent a messenger to say to him, "Go, wash yourself seven times in the Jordan, and your flesh will be restored and you will be cleansed."

11 But Naaman went away angry and said, "I thought that he would surely come out to me and stand and call on the name of the LORD his God, wave his hand over the spot and cure me of my leprosy. **12** Are not Abana and Pharpar, the rivers of Damascus, better than all the waters of Israel? Couldn't I wash in them and be cleansed?" So he turned and went off in a rage.

13 Naaman's servants went to him and said, "My father, if the prophet had told you to do some great thing, would you not have done it? How much more, then, when he tells you, 'Wash and be cleansed'!" **14** So he went down and dipped himself in the Jordan seven times, as the man of God had told him, and his flesh was restored and became clean like that of a young boy.

15 Then Naaman and all his attendants went back to the man of God. He stood before him and said, "Now I know that there is no God in all the world except in Israel. So please accept a gift from your servant."

---

a 1 The Hebrew for *leprosy* was used for various diseases affecting the skin; also in verses 3, 6, 7, 11 and 27.   *b* 5 That is, about 750 pounds or about 340 kilograms
c 5 That is, about 150 pounds or about 69 kilograms

¹⁶The prophet answered, "As surely as the LORD lives, whom I serve, I will not accept a thing." And even though Naaman urged him, he refused.

¹⁷"If you will not," said Naaman, "please let me, your servant, be given as much earth as a pair of mules can carry, for your servant will never again make burnt offerings and sacrifices to any other god but the LORD. ¹⁸But may the LORD forgive your servant for this one thing: When my master enters the temple of Rimmon to bow down and he is leaning on my arm and I have to bow there also—when I bow down in the temple of Rimmon, may the LORD forgive your servant for this."

¹⁹"Go in peace," Elisha said.

After Naaman had traveled some distance, ²⁰Gehazi, the servant of Elisha the man of God, said to himself, "My master was too easy on Naaman, this Aramean, by not accepting from him what he brought. As surely as the LORD lives, I will run after him and get something from him."

²¹So Gehazi hurried after Naaman. When Naaman saw him running toward him, he got down from the chariot to meet him. "Is everything all right?" he asked.

²²"Everything is all right," Gehazi answered. "My master sent me to say, 'Two young men from the company of the prophets have just come to me from the hill country of Ephraim. Please give them a talent^a of silver and two sets of clothing.'"

²³"By all means, take two talents," said Naaman. He urged Gehazi to accept them, and then tied up the two talents of silver in two bags, with two sets of clothing. He gave them to two of his servants, and they carried them ahead of Gehazi. ²⁴When Gehazi came to the hill, he took the things from the servants and put them away in the house. He sent the men away and they left.

²⁵When he went in and stood before his master, Elisha asked him, "Where have you been, Gehazi?"

"Your servant didn't go anywhere," Gehazi answered.

²⁶But Elisha said to him, "Was not my spirit with you when the man got down from his chariot to meet you? Is this the time to take money or to accept clothes—or olive groves and vineyards, or flocks and herds, or male and female slaves? ²⁷Naaman's leprosy will cling to you and to your descendants forever." Then Gehazi went from Elisha's presence and his skin was leprous—it had become as white as snow.

An Axhead Floats

6 The company of the prophets said to Elisha, "Look, the place where we meet with you is too small for us. ²Let us go to the

---

^{a} 22 That is, about 75 pounds or about 34 kilograms

Jordan, where each of us can get a pole; and let us build a place there for us to meet."

And he said, "Go."

³Then one of them said, "Won't you please come with your servants?"

"I will," Elisha replied. ⁴And he went with them.

They went to the Jordan and began to cut down trees. ⁵As one of them was cutting down a tree, the iron axhead fell into the water. "Oh no, my lord!" he cried out. "It was borrowed!"

⁶The man of God asked, "Where did it fall?" When he showed him the place, Elisha cut a stick and threw it there, and made the iron float. ⁷"Lift it out," he said. Then the man reached out his hand and took it.

Elisha Traps Blinded Arameans

⁸Now the king of Aram was at war with Israel. After conferring with his officers, he said, "I will set up my camp in such and such a place."

⁹The man of God sent word to the king of Israel: "Beware of passing that place, because the Arameans are going down there." ¹⁰So the king of Israel checked on the place indicated by the man of God. Time and again Elisha warned the king, so that he was on his guard in such places.

¹¹This enraged the king of Aram. He summoned his officers and demanded of them, "Tell me! Which of us is on the side of the king of Israel?"

¹²"None of us, my lord the king," said one of his officers, "but Elisha, the prophet who is in Israel, tells the king of Israel the very words you speak in your bedroom."

¹³"Go, find out where he is," the king ordered, "so I can send men and capture him." The report came back: "He is in Dothan." ¹⁴Then he sent horses and chariots and a strong force there. They went by night and surrounded the city.

¹⁵When the servant of the man of God got up and went out early the next morning, an army with horses and chariots had surrounded the city. "Oh no, my lord! What shall we do?" the servant asked.

¹⁶"Don't be afraid," the prophet answered. "Those who are with us are more than those who are with them."

¹⁷And Elisha prayed, "Open his eyes, LORD, so that he may see." Then the LORD opened the servant's eyes, and he looked and saw the hills full of horses and chariots of fire all around Elisha.

¹⁸As the enemy came down toward him, Elisha prayed to the LORD, "Strike this army with blindness." So he struck them with blindness, as Elisha had asked.

¹⁹Elisha told them, "This is not the road and this is not the city.

Follow me, and I will lead you to the man you are looking for." And he led them to Samaria.

²⁰After they entered the city, Elisha said, "Lord, open the eyes of these men so they can see." Then the Lord opened their eyes and they looked, and there they were, inside Samaria.

²¹When the king of Israel saw them, he asked Elisha, "Shall I kill them, my father? Shall I kill them?"

²²"Do not kill them," he answered. "Would you kill those you have captured with your own sword or bow? Set food and water before them so that they may eat and drink and then go back to their master." ²³So he prepared a great feast for them, and after they had finished eating and drinking, he sent them away, and they returned to their master. So the bands from Aram stopped raiding Israel's territory.

Famine in Besieged Samaria

²⁴Some time later, Ben-Hadad king of Aram mobilized his entire army and marched up and laid siege to Samaria. ²⁵There was a great famine in the city; the siege lasted so long that a donkey's head sold for eighty shekels*a* of silver, and a quarter of a cab*b* of seed pods*c* for five shekels.*d*

²⁶As the king of Israel was passing by on the wall, a woman cried to him, "Help me, my lord the king!"

²⁷The king replied, "If the Lord does not help you, where can I get help for you? From the threshing floor? From the winepress?" ²⁸Then he asked her, "What's the matter?"

She answered, "This woman said to me, 'Give up your son so we may eat him today, and tomorrow we'll eat my son.' ²⁹So we cooked my son and ate him. The next day I said to her, 'Give up your son so we may eat him,' but she had hidden him."

³⁰When the king heard the woman's words, he tore his robes. As he went along the wall, the people looked, and they saw that, under his robes, he had sackcloth on his body. ³¹He said, "May God deal with me, be it ever so severely, if the head of Elisha son of Shaphat remains on his shoulders today!"

³²Now Elisha was sitting in his house, and the elders were sitting with him. The king sent a messenger ahead, but before he arrived, Elisha said to the elders, "Don't you see how this murderer is sending someone to cut off my head? Look, when the messenger comes, shut the door and hold it shut against him. Is not the sound of his master's footsteps behind

---

a 25 That is, about 2 pounds or about 920 grams   *b 25* That is, probably about 1/4 pound or about 100 grams   *c 25* Or *of doves' dung*   *d 25* That is, about 2 ounces or about 58 grams him?" ³³While he was still talking to them, the messenger came down to him.

The king said, "This disaster is from the LORD. Why should I wait for the LORD any longer?"

7 Elisha replied, "Hear the word of the LORD. This is what the LORD says: About this time tomorrow, a seah^a of the finest flour will sell for a shekel^b and two seahs^c of barley for a shekel at the gate of Samaria."

²The officer on whose arm the king was leaning said to the man of God, "Look, even if the LORD should open the floodgates of the heavens, could this happen?"

"You will see it with your own eyes," answered Elisha, "but you will not eat any of it!"

The Siege Lifted

³Now there were four men with leprosy^d at the entrance of the city gate. They said to each other, "Why stay here until we die? ⁴If we say, 'We'll go into the city' — the famine is there, and we will die. And if we stay here, we will die. So let's go over to the camp of the Arameans and surrender. If they spare us, we live; if they kill us, then we die."

⁵At dusk they got up and went to the camp of the Arameans. When they reached the edge of the camp, no one was there, ⁶for the Lord had caused the Arameans to hear the sound of chariots and horses and a great army, so that they said to one another, "Look, the king of Israel has hired the Hittite and Egyptian kings to attack us!" ⁷So they got up and fled in the dusk and abandoned their tents and their horses and donkeys. They left the camp as it was and ran for their lives.

⁸The men who had leprosy reached the edge of the camp, entered one of the tents and ate and drank. Then they took silver, gold and clothes, and went off and hid them. They returned and entered another tent and took some things from it and hid them also.

⁹Then they said to each other, "What we're doing is not right. This is a day of good news and we are keeping it to ourselves. If we wait until daylight, punishment will overtake us. Let's go at once and report this to the royal palace."

¹⁰So they went and called out to the city gatekeepers and told them, "We went into the Aramean camp and no one was there — not a sound of anyone — only tethered horses and donkeys, and the tents left just as they were." ¹¹The gatekeepers shout-

---

^a 1 That is, probably about 12 pounds or about 5.5 kilograms of flour; also in verses 16 and 18   ^b 1 That is, about 2/5 ounce or about 12 grams; also in verses 16 and 18   ^c 1 That is, probably about 20 pounds or about 9 kilograms of barley; also in verses 16 and 18   ^d 3 The Hebrew for leprosy was used for various diseases affecting the skin; also in verse 8.

ed the news, and it was reported within the palace.

¹²The king got up in the night and said to his officers, "I will tell you what the Arameans have done to us. They know we are starving; so they have left the camp to hide in the countryside, thinking, 'They will surely come out, and then we will take them alive and get into the city.' "

¹³One of his officers answered, "Have some men take five of the horses that are left in the city. Their plight will be like that of all the Israelites left here — yes, they will only be like all these Israelites who are doomed. So let us send them to find out what happened."

¹⁴So they selected two chariots with their horses, and the king sent them after the Aramean army. He commanded the drivers, "Go and find out what has happened." ¹⁵They followed them as far as the Jordan, and they found the whole road strewn with the clothing and equipment the Arameans had thrown away in their headlong flight. So the messengers returned and reported to the king. ¹⁶Then the people went out and plundered the camp of the Arameans. So a seah of the finest flour sold for a shekel, and two seahs of barley sold for a shekel, as the LORD had said.

¹⁷Now the king had put the officer on whose arm he leaned in charge of the gate, and the people trampled him in the gateway, and he died, just as the man of God had foretold when the king came down to his house. ¹⁸It happened as the man of God had said to the king: "About this time tomorrow, a seah of the finest flour will sell for a shekel and two seahs of barley for a shekel at the gate of Samaria."

¹⁹The officer had said to the man of God, "Look, even if the LORD should open the floodgates of the heavens, could this happen?" The man of God had replied, "You will see it with your own eyes, but you will not eat any of it!" ²⁰And that is exactly what happened to him, for the people trampled him in the gateway, and he died.

The Shunammite's Land Restored

8 Now Elisha had said to the woman whose son he had restored to life, "Go away with your family and stay for a while wherever you can, because the LORD has decreed a famine in the land that will last seven years." ²The woman proceeded to do as the man of God said. She and her family went away and stayed in the land of the Philistines seven years.

³At the end of the seven years she came back from the land of the Philistines and went to appeal to the king for her house and land. ⁴The king was talk-

ing to Gehazi, the servant of the man of God, and had said, "Tell me about all the great things Elisha has done." ⁵Just as Gehazi was telling the king how Elisha had restored the dead to life, the woman whose son Elisha had brought back to life came to appeal to the king for her house and land.

Gehazi said, "This is the woman, my lord the king, and this is her son whom Elisha restored to life." ⁶The king asked the woman about it, and she told him.

Then he assigned an official to her case and said to him, "Give back everything that belonged to her, including all the income from her land from the day she left the country until now."

Hazael Murders Ben-Hadad

⁷Elisha went to Damascus, and Ben-Hadad king of Aram was ill. When the king was told, "The man of God has come all the way up here," ⁸he said to Hazael, "Take a gift with you and go to meet the man of God. Consult the LORD through him; ask him, 'Will I recover from this illness?'"

⁹Hazael went to meet Elisha, taking with him as a gift forty camel-loads of all the finest wares of Damascus. He went in and stood before him, and said, "Your son Ben-Hadad king of Aram has sent me to ask, 'Will I recover from this illness?'"

¹⁰Elisha answered, "Go and say to him, 'You will certainly recover.' Nevertheless,ᵃ the LORD has revealed to me that he will in fact die." ¹¹He stared at him with a fixed gaze until Hazael was embarrassed. Then the man of God began to weep.

¹²"Why is my lord weeping?" asked Hazael.

"Because I know the harm you will do to the Israelites," he answered. "You will set fire to their fortified places, kill their young men with the sword, dash their little children to the ground, and rip open their pregnant women."

¹³Hazael said, "How could your servant, a mere dog, accomplish such a feat?"

"The LORD has shown me that you will become king of Aram," answered Elisha.

¹⁴Then Hazael left Elisha and returned to his master. When Ben-Hadad asked, "What did Elisha say to you?" Hazael replied, "He told me that you would certainly recover." ¹⁵But the next day he took a thick cloth, soaked it in water and spread it over the king's face, so that he died. Then Hazael succeeded him as king.

Jehoram King of Judah

¹⁶In the fifth year of Joram son of Ahab king of Israel, when Jehoshaphat was king of Judah, Jehoram son of Jehoshaphat began his reign as king of Judah. ¹⁷He

---

ᵃ 10 The Hebrew may also be read *Go and say, 'You will certainly not recover,'* for.

was thirty-two years old when he became king, and he reigned in Jerusalem eight years. ¹⁸He followed the ways of the kings of Israel, as the house of Ahab had done, for he married a daughter of Ahab. He did evil in the eyes of the LORD. ¹⁹Nevertheless, for the sake of his servant David, the LORD was not willing to destroy Judah. He had promised to maintain a lamp for David and his descendants forever.

²⁰In the time of Jehoram, Edom rebelled against Judah and set up its own king. ²¹So Jehoram*ᵃ* went to Zair with all his chariots. The Edomites surrounded him and his chariot commanders, but he rose up and broke through by night; his army, however, fled back home. ²²To this day Edom has been in rebellion against Judah. Libnah revolted at the same time.

²³As for the other events of Jehoram's reign, and all he did, are they not written in the book of the annals of the kings of Judah? ²⁴Jehoram rested with his ancestors and was buried with them in the City of David. And Ahaziah his son succeeded him as king.

Ahaziah King of Judah

²⁵In the twelfth year of Joram son of Ahab king of Israel, Ahaziah son of Jehoram king of Judah began to reign. ²⁶Ahaziah was twenty-two years old when he became king, and he reigned in Jerusalem one year. His mother's name was Athaliah, a granddaughter of Omri king of Israel. ²⁷He followed the ways of the house of Ahab and did evil in the eyes of the LORD, as the house of Ahab had done, for he was related by marriage to Ahab's family.

²⁸Ahaziah went with Joram son of Ahab to war against Hazael king of Aram at Ramoth Gilead. The Arameans wounded Joram; ²⁹so King Joram returned to Jezreel to recover from the wounds the Arameans had inflicted on him at Ramoth*ᵇ* in his battle with Hazael king of Aram.

Then Ahaziah son of Jehoram king of Judah went down to Jezreel to see Joram son of Ahab, because he had been wounded.

Jehu Anointed King of Israel

9 The prophet Elisha summoned a man from the company of the prophets and said to him, "Tuck your cloak into your belt, take this flask of olive oil with you and go to Ramoth Gilead. ²When you get there, look for Jehu son of Jehoshaphat, the son of Nimshi. Go to him, get him away from his companions and take him into an inner room. ³Then take the flask and pour the oil on his head and declare, 'This is what the LORD says: I anoint

ᵃ 21 Hebrew *Joram,* a variant of *Jehoram*; also in verses 23 and 24   *ᵇ 29* Hebrew *Ramah,* a variant of *Ramoth* you king over Israel.' Then open the door and run; don't delay!"

⁴So the young prophet went to Ramoth Gilead. ⁵When he arrived, he found the army officers sitting together. "I have a message for you, commander," he said.

"For which of us?" asked Jehu.

"For you, commander," he replied.

⁶Jehu got up and went into the house. Then the prophet poured the oil on Jehu's head and declared, "This is what the LORD, the God of Israel, says: 'I anoint you king over the LORD's people Israel. ⁷You are to destroy the house of Ahab your master, and I will avenge the blood of my servants the prophets and the blood of all the LORD's servants shed by Jezebel. ⁸The whole house of Ahab will perish. I will cut off from Ahab every last male in Israel—slave or free.ᵃ ⁹I will make the house of Ahab like the house of Jeroboam son of Nebat and like the house of Baasha son of Ahijah. ¹⁰As for Jezebel, dogs will devour her on the plot of ground at Jezreel, and no one will bury her.'" Then he opened the door and ran.

¹¹When Jehu went out to his fellow officers, one of them asked him, "Is everything all right? Why did this maniac come to you?"

"You know the man and the sort of things he says," Jehu replied.

¹²"That's not true!" they said. "Tell us."

Jehu said, "Here is what he told me: 'This is what the LORD says: I anoint you king over Israel.'"

¹³They quickly took their cloaks and spread them under him on the bare steps. Then they blew the trumpet and shouted, "Jehu is king!"

Jehu Kills Joram and Ahaziah

¹⁴So Jehu son of Jehoshaphat, the son of Nimshi, conspired against Joram. (Now Joram and all Israel had been defending Ramoth Gilead against Hazael king of Aram, ¹⁵but King Joramᵇ had returned to Jezreel to recover from the wounds the Arameans had inflicted on him in the battle with Hazael king of Aram.) Jehu said, "If you desire to make me king, don't let anyone slip out of the city to go and tell the news in Jezreel." ¹⁶Then he got into his chariot and rode to Jezreel, because Joram was resting there and Ahaziah king of Judah had gone down to see him.

¹⁷When the lookout standing on the tower in Jezreel saw Jehu's troops approaching, he called out, "I see some troops coming."

"Get a horseman," Joram ordered. "Send him to meet them and ask, 'Do you come in peace?'"

¹⁸The horseman rode off to meet Jehu and said, "This is what

ᵃ 8 Or Israel—every ruler or leader; also in verses 17 and 21-24   ᵇ 15 Hebrew Jehoram, a variant of Joram;

the king says: 'Do you come in peace?'"

"What do you have to do with peace?" Jehu replied. "Fall in behind me."

The lookout reported, "The messenger has reached them, but he isn't coming back."

¹⁹So the king sent out a second horseman. When he came to them he said, "This is what the king says: 'Do you come in peace?'"

Jehu replied, "What do you have to do with peace? Fall in behind me."

²⁰The lookout reported, "He has reached them, but he isn't coming back either. The driving is like that of Jehu son of Nimshi—he drives like a maniac."

²¹"Hitch up my chariot," Joram ordered. And when it was hitched up, Joram king of Israel and Ahaziah king of Judah rode out, each in his own chariot, to meet Jehu. They met him at the plot of ground that had belonged to Naboth the Jezreelite. ²²When Joram saw Jehu he asked, "Have you come in peace, Jehu?"

"How can there be peace," Jehu replied, "as long as all the idolatry and witchcraft of your mother Jezebel abound?"

²³Joram turned about and fled, calling out to Ahaziah, "Treachery, Ahaziah!"

²⁴Then Jehu drew his bow and shot Joram between the shoulders. The arrow pierced his heart and he slumped down in his chariot. ²⁵Jehu said to Bidkar, his chariot officer, "Pick him up and throw him on the field that belonged to Naboth the Jezreelite. Remember how you and I were riding together in chariots behind Ahab his father when the LORD spoke this prophecy against him: ²⁶'Yesterday I saw the blood of Naboth and the blood of his sons, declares the LORD, and I will surely make you pay for it on this plot of ground, declares the LORD.'ᵃ Now then, pick him up and throw him on that plot, in accordance with the word of the LORD."

²⁷When Ahaziah king of Judah saw what had happened, he fled up the road to Beth Haggan.ᵇ Jehu chased him, shouting, "Kill him too!" They wounded him in his chariot on the way up to Gur near Ibleam, but he escaped to Megiddo and died there. ²⁸His servants took him by chariot to Jerusalem and buried him with his ancestors in his tomb in the City of David. ²⁹(In the eleventh year of Joram son of Ahab, Ahaziah had become king of Judah.)

Jezebel Killed

³⁰Then Jehu went to Jezreel. When Jezebel heard about it, she put on eye makeup, arranged her hair and looked out of a window. ³¹As Jehu entered the gate, she

---

ᵃ 26 See 1 Kings 21:19.　ᵇ 27 Or *fled by way of the garden house* asked, "Have you come in peace, you Zimri, you murderer of your master?"*a*

32 He looked up at the window and called out, "Who is on my side? Who?" Two or three eunuchs looked down at him. **33** "Throw her down!" Jehu said. So they threw her down, and some of her blood spattered the wall and the horses as they trampled her underfoot.

34 Jehu went in and ate and drank. "Take care of that cursed woman," he said, "and bury her, for she was a king's daughter." **35** But when they went out to bury her, they found nothing except her skull, her feet and her hands. **36** They went back and told Jehu, who said, "This is the word of the LORD that he spoke through his servant Elijah the Tishbite: On the plot of ground at Jezreel dogs will devour Jezebel's flesh.*b* **37** Jezebel's body will be like dung on the ground in the plot at Jezreel, so that no one will be able to say, 'This is Jezebel.'"

Ahab's Family Killed

10 Now there were in Samaria seventy sons of the house of Ahab. So Jehu wrote letters and sent them to Samaria: to the officials of Jezreel,*c* to the elders and to the guardians of Ahab's children. He said, **2** "You have your master's sons with you and you have chariots and horses, a fortified city and weapons. Now as soon as this letter reaches you, **3** choose the best and most worthy of your master's sons and set him on his father's throne. Then fight for your master's house."

4 But they were terrified and said, "If two kings could not resist him, how can we?"

5 So the palace administrator, the city governor, the elders and the guardians sent this message to Jehu: "We are your servants and we will do anything you say. We will not appoint anyone as king; you do whatever you think best."

6 Then Jehu wrote them a second letter, saying, "If you are on my side and will obey me, take the heads of your master's sons and come to me in Jezreel by this time tomorrow."

Now the royal princes, seventy of them, were with the leading men of the city, who were rearing them. **7** When the letter arrived, these men took the princes and slaughtered all seventy of them. They put their heads in baskets and sent them to Jehu in Jezreel. **8** When the messenger arrived, he told Jehu, "They have brought the heads of the princes."

Then Jehu ordered, "Put them in two piles at the entrance of the city gate until morning."

9 The next morning Jehu went

---

a 31 Or *"Was there peace for Zimri, who murdered his master?"*   *b 36* See 1 Kings 21:23.   *c 1* Hebrew; some Septuagint manuscripts and Vulgate *of the city* out. He stood before all the people and said, "You are innocent. It was I who conspired against my master and killed him, but who killed all these? ¹⁰Know, then, that not a word the LORD has spoken against the house of Ahab will fail. The LORD has done what he announced through his servant Elijah." ¹¹So Jehu killed everyone in Jezreel who remained of the house of Ahab, as well as all his chief men, his close friends and his priests, leaving him no survivor.

¹²Jehu then set out and went toward Samaria. At Beth Eked of the Shepherds, ¹³he met some relatives of Ahaziah king of Judah and asked, "Who are you?"

They said, "We are relatives of Ahaziah, and we have come down to greet the families of the king and of the queen mother."

¹⁴"Take them alive!" he ordered. So they took them alive and slaughtered them by the well of Beth Eked — forty-two of them. He left no survivor.

¹⁵After he left there, he came upon Jehonadab son of Rekab, who was on his way to meet him. Jehu greeted him and said, "Are you in accord with me, as I am with you?"

"I am," Jehonadab answered.

"If so," said Jehu, "give me your hand." So he did, and Jehu helped him up into the chariot. ¹⁶Jehu said, "Come with me and see my zeal for the LORD." Then he had him ride along in his chariot.

¹⁷When Jehu came to Samaria, he killed all who were left there of Ahab's family; he destroyed them, according to the word of the LORD spoken to Elijah.

Servants of Baal Killed

¹⁸Then Jehu brought all the people together and said to them, "Ahab served Baal a little; Jehu will serve him much. ¹⁹Now summon all the prophets of Baal, all his servants and all his priests. See that no one is missing, because I am going to hold a great sacrifice for Baal. Anyone who fails to come will no longer live." But Jehu was acting deceptively in order to destroy the servants of Baal.

²⁰Jehu said, "Call an assembly in honor of Baal." So they proclaimed it. ²¹Then he sent word throughout Israel, and all the servants of Baal came; not one stayed away. They crowded into the temple of Baal until it was full from one end to the other. ²²And Jehu said to the keeper of the wardrobe, "Bring robes for all the servants of Baal." So he brought out robes for them.

²³Then Jehu and Jehonadab son of Rekab went into the temple of Baal. Jehu said to the servants of Baal, "Look around and see that no one who serves the LORD is here with you — only servants of Baal." ²⁴So they went in to make sacrifices and burnt offerings. Now Jehu had posted eighty

men outside with this warning: "If one of you lets any of the men I am placing in your hands escape, it will be your life for his life."

²⁵As soon as Jehu had finished making the burnt offering, he ordered the guards and officers: "Go in and kill them; let no one escape." So they cut them down with the sword. The guards and officers threw the bodies out and then entered the inner shrine of the temple of Baal. ²⁶They brought the sacred stone out of the temple of Baal and burned it. ²⁷They demolished the sacred stone of Baal and tore down the temple of Baal, and people have used it for a latrine to this day.

²⁸So Jehu destroyed Baal worship in Israel. ²⁹However, he did not turn away from the sins of Jeroboam son of Nebat, which he had caused Israel to commit — the worship of the golden calves at Bethel and Dan.

³⁰The LORD said to Jehu, "Because you have done well in accomplishing what is right in my eyes and have done to the house of Ahab all I had in mind to do, your descendants will sit on the throne of Israel to the fourth generation." ³¹Yet Jehu was not careful to keep the law of the LORD, the God of Israel, with all his heart. He did not turn away from the sins of Jeroboam, which he had caused Israel to commit.

³²In those days the LORD began to reduce the size of Israel. Hazael overpowered the Israelites throughout their territory ³³east of the Jordan in all the land of Gilead (the region of Gad, Reuben and Manasseh), from Aroer by the Arnon Gorge through Gilead to Bashan.

³⁴As for the other events of Jehu's reign, all he did, and all his achievements, are they not written in the book of the annals of the kings of Israel?

³⁵Jehu rested with his ancestors and was buried in Samaria. And Jehoahaz his son succeeded him as king. ³⁶The time that Jehu reigned over Israel in Samaria was twenty-eight years.

Athaliah and Joash

11 When Athaliah the mother of Ahaziah saw that her son was dead, she proceeded to destroy the whole royal family. ²But Jehosheba, the daughter of King Jehoram*ᵃ* and sister of Ahaziah, took Joash son of Ahaziah and stole him away from among the royal princes, who were about to be murdered. She put him and his nurse in a bedroom to hide him from Athaliah; so he was not killed. ³He remained hidden with his nurse at the temple of the LORD for six years while Athaliah ruled the land.

⁴In the seventh year Jehoiada sent for the commanders of units of a hundred, the Carites and the

---

ᵃ 2 Hebrew *Joram,* a variant of *Jehoram*

guards and had them brought to him at the temple of the LORD. He made a covenant with them and put them under oath at the temple of the LORD. Then he showed them the king's son. ⁵He commanded them, saying, "This is what you are to do: You who are in the three companies that are going on duty on the Sabbath — a third of you guarding the royal palace, ⁶a third at the Sur Gate, and a third at the gate behind the guard, who take turns guarding the temple — ⁷and you who are in the other two companies that normally go off Sabbath duty are all to guard the temple for the king. ⁸Station yourselves around the king, each of you with weapon in hand. Anyone who approaches your ranks*a* is to be put to death. Stay close to the king wherever he goes."

⁹The commanders of units of a hundred did just as Jehoiada the priest ordered. Each one took his men — those who were going on duty on the Sabbath and those who were going off duty — and came to Jehoiada the priest. ¹⁰Then he gave the commanders the spears and shields that had belonged to King David and that were in the temple of the LORD. ¹¹The guards, each with weapon in hand, stationed themselves around the king — near the altar and the temple, from the south side to the north side of the temple.

¹²Jehoiada brought out the king's son and put the crown on him; he presented him with a copy of the covenant and proclaimed him king. They anointed him, and the people clapped their hands and shouted, "Long live the king!"

¹³When Athaliah heard the noise made by the guards and the people, she went to the people at the temple of the LORD. ¹⁴She looked and there was the king, standing by the pillar, as the custom was. The officers and the trumpeters were beside the king, and all the people of the land were rejoicing and blowing trumpets. Then Athaliah tore her robes and called out, "Treason! Treason!"

¹⁵Jehoiada the priest ordered the commanders of units of a hundred, who were in charge of the troops: "Bring her out between the ranks*b* and put to the sword anyone who follows her." For the priest had said, "She must not be put to death in the temple of the LORD." ¹⁶So they seized her as she reached the place where the horses enter the palace grounds, and there she was put to death.

¹⁷Jehoiada then made a covenant between the LORD and the king and people that they would be the LORD's people. He also made a covenant between the king and the people. ¹⁸All

---

a 8 Or *approaches the precincts*   *b* 15 Or *out from the precincts* the people of the land went to the temple of Baal and tore it down. They smashed the altars and idols to pieces and killed Mattan the priest of Baal in front of the altars.

Then Jehoiada the priest posted guards at the temple of the LORD. ¹⁹He took with him the commanders of hundreds, the Carites, the guards and all the people of the land, and together they brought the king down from the temple of the LORD and went into the palace, entering by way of the gate of the guards. The king then took his place on the royal throne. ²⁰All the people of the land rejoiced, and the city was calm, because Athaliah had been slain with the sword at the palace.

²¹Joash*ᵃ* was seven years old when he began to reign.*ᵇ*

Joash Repairs the Temple

12ᶜ In the seventh year of Jehu, Joash*ᵈ* became king, and he reigned in Jerusalem forty years. His mother's name was Zibiah; she was from Beersheba. ²Joash did what was right in the eyes of the LORD all the years Jehoiada the priest instructed him. ³The high places, however, were not removed; the people continued to offer sacrifices and burn incense there.

⁴Joash said to the priests, "Collect all the money that is brought as sacred offerings to the temple of the LORD — the money collected in the census, the money received from personal vows and the money brought voluntarily to the temple. ⁵Let every priest receive the money from one of the treasurers, then use it to repair whatever damage is found in the temple."

⁶But by the twenty-third year of King Joash the priests still had not repaired the temple. ⁷Therefore King Joash summoned Jehoiada the priest and the other priests and asked them, "Why aren't you repairing the damage done to the temple? Take no more money from your treasurers, but hand it over for repairing the temple." ⁸The priests agreed that they would not collect any more money from the people and that they would not repair the temple themselves.

⁹Jehoiada the priest took a chest and bored a hole in its lid. He placed it beside the altar, on the right side as one enters the temple of the LORD. The priests who guarded the entrance put into the chest all the money that was brought to the temple of the LORD. ¹⁰Whenever they saw that there was a large amount of money in the chest, the royal

---

ᵃ 21 Hebrew *Jehoash,* a variant of *Joash* (11:21) is numbered 12:1.   ᶜ In Hebrew texts 12:1-21 is numbered 12:2-22.
ᵇ 21 In Hebrew texts this verse
ᵈ 1 Hebrew *Jehoash,* a variant of *Joash*; also in verses 2, 4, 6, 7 and 18

secretary and the high priest came, counted the money that had been brought into the temple of the LORD and put it into bags. [11]When the amount had been determined, they gave the money to the men appointed to supervise the work on the temple. With it they paid those who worked on the temple of the LORD — the carpenters and builders, [12]the masons and stonecutters. They purchased timber and blocks of dressed stone for the repair of the temple of the LORD, and met all the other expenses of restoring the temple.

[13]The money brought into the temple was not spent for making silver basins, wick trimmers, sprinkling bowls, trumpets or any other articles of gold or silver for the temple of the LORD; [14]it was paid to the workers, who used it to repair the temple. [15]They did not require an accounting from those to whom they gave the money to pay the workers, because they acted with complete honesty. [16]The money from the guilt offerings and sin offerings[a] was not brought into the temple of the LORD; it belonged to the priests.

[17]About this time Hazael king of Aram went up and attacked Gath and captured it. Then he turned to attack Jerusalem. [18]But Joash king of Judah took all the sacred objects dedicated by his predecessors — Jehoshaphat, Jehoram and Ahaziah, the kings of Judah — and the gifts he himself had dedicated and all the gold found in the treasuries of the temple of the LORD and of the royal palace, and he sent them to Hazael king of Aram, who then withdrew from Jerusalem.

[19]As for the other events of the reign of Joash, and all he did, are they not written in the book of the annals of the kings of Judah? [20]His officials conspired against him and assassinated him at Beth Millo, on the road down to Silla. [21]The officials who murdered him were Jozabad son of Shimeath and Jehozabad son of Shomer. He died and was buried with his ancestors in the City of David. And Amaziah his son succeeded him as king.

Jehoahaz King of Israel

13 In the twenty-third year of Joash son of Ahaziah king of Judah, Jehoahaz son of Jehu became king of Israel in Samaria, and he reigned seventeen years. [2]He did evil in the eyes of the LORD by following the sins of Jeroboam son of Nebat, which he had caused Israel to commit, and he did not turn away from them. [3]So the LORD's anger burned against Israel, and for a long time he kept them under the power of Hazael king of Aram and Ben-Hadad his son.

---

[a] 16 Or *purification offerings*

⁴Then Jehoahaz sought the LORD's favor, and the LORD listened to him, for he saw how severely the king of Aram was oppressing Israel. ⁵The LORD provided a deliverer for Israel, and they escaped from the power of Aram. So the Israelites lived in their own homes as they had before. ⁶But they did not turn away from the sins of the house of Jeroboam, which he had caused Israel to commit; they continued in them. Also, the Asherah pole*ᵃ* remained standing in Samaria.

⁷Nothing had been left of the army of Jehoahaz except fifty horsemen, ten chariots and ten thousand foot soldiers, for the king of Aram had destroyed the rest and made them like the dust at threshing time.

⁸As for the other events of the reign of Jehoahaz, all he did and his achievements, are they not written in the book of the annals of the kings of Israel? ⁹Jehoahaz rested with his ancestors and was buried in Samaria. And Jehoash*ᵇ* his son succeeded him as king.

Jehoash King of Israel

¹⁰In the thirty-seventh year of Joash king of Judah, Jehoash son of Jehoahaz became king of Israel in Samaria, and he reigned sixteen years. ¹¹He did evil in the eyes of the LORD and did not turn away from any of the sins of Jeroboam son of Nebat, which he had caused Israel to commit; he continued in them.

¹²As for the other events of the reign of Jehoash, all he did and his achievements, including his war against Amaziah king of Judah, are they not written in the book of the annals of the kings of Israel? ¹³Jehoash rested with his ancestors, and Jeroboam succeeded him on the throne. Jehoash was buried in Samaria with the kings of Israel.

¹⁴Now Elisha had been suffering from the illness from which he died. Jehoash king of Israel went down to see him and wept over him. "My father! My father!" he cried. "The chariots and horsemen of Israel!"

¹⁵Elisha said, "Get a bow and some arrows," and he did so. ¹⁶"Take the bow in your hands," he said to the king of Israel. When he had taken it, Elisha put his hands on the king's hands.

¹⁷"Open the east window," he said, and he opened it. "Shoot!" Elisha said, and he shot. "The LORD's arrow of victory, the arrow of victory over Aram!" Elisha declared. "You will completely destroy the Arameans at Aphek." ¹⁸Then he said, "Take the arrows," and the king took them. Elisha told him, "Strike the ground." He struck it three times and stopped. ¹⁹The man of God was

---

ᵃ 6 That is, a wooden symbol of the goddess Asherah; here and elsewhere in 2 Kings   *ᵇ 9* Hebrew *Joash,* a variant of *Jehoash;* also in verses 12-14 and 25 angry with him and said, "You should have struck the ground five or six times; then you would have defeated Aram and completely destroyed it. But now you will defeat it only three times."

²⁰ Elisha died and was buried.

Now Moabite raiders used to enter the country every spring. ²¹ Once while some Israelites were burying a man, suddenly they saw a band of raiders; so they threw the man's body into Elisha's tomb. When the body touched Elisha's bones, the man came to life and stood up on his feet.

²² Hazael king of Aram oppressed Israel throughout the reign of Jehoahaz. ²³ But the LORD was gracious to them and had compassion and showed concern for them because of his covenant with Abraham, Isaac and Jacob. To this day he has been unwilling to destroy them or banish them from his presence.

²⁴ Hazael king of Aram died, and Ben-Hadad his son succeeded him as king. ²⁵ Then Jehoash son of Jehoahaz recaptured from Ben-Hadad son of Hazael the towns he had taken in battle from his father Jehoahaz. Three times Jehoash defeated him, and so he recovered the Israelite towns.

Amaziah King of Judah

14 In the second year of Jehoash[a] son of Jehoahaz king of Israel, Amaziah son of Joash king of Judah began to reign. ² He was twenty-five years old when he became king, and he reigned in Jerusalem twenty-nine years. His mother's name was Jehoaddan; she was from Jerusalem. ³ He did what was right in the eyes of the LORD, but not as his father David had done. In everything he followed the example of his father Joash. ⁴ The high places, however, were not removed; the people continued to offer sacrifices and burn incense there.

⁵ After the kingdom was firmly in his grasp, he executed the officials who had murdered his father the king. ⁶ Yet he did not put the children of the assassins to death, in accordance with what is written in the Book of the Law of Moses where the LORD commanded: "Parents are not to be put to death for their children, nor children put to death for their parents; each will die for their own sin."[b]

⁷ He was the one who defeated ten thousand Edomites in the Valley of Salt and captured Sela in battle, calling it Joktheel, the name it has to this day.

⁸ Then Amaziah sent messengers to Jehoash son of Jehoahaz, the son of Jehu, king of Israel, with the challenge: "Come, let us face each other in battle."

⁹ But Jehoash king of Israel replied to Amaziah king of Judah:

---

[a] 1 Hebrew *Joash*, a variant of *Jehoash*; also in verses 13, 23 and 27   [b] 6 Deut. 24:16

"A thistle in Lebanon sent a message to a cedar in Lebanon, 'Give your daughter to my son in marriage.' Then a wild beast in Lebanon came along and trampled the thistle underfoot. [10] You have indeed defeated Edom and now you are arrogant. Glory in your victory, but stay at home! Why ask for trouble and cause your own downfall and that of Judah also?"

[11] Amaziah, however, would not listen, so Jehoash king of Israel attacked. He and Amaziah king of Judah faced each other at Beth Shemesh in Judah. [12] Judah was routed by Israel, and every man fled to his home. [13] Jehoash king of Israel captured Amaziah king of Judah, the son of Joash, the son of Ahaziah, at Beth Shemesh. Then Jehoash went to Jerusalem and broke down the wall of Jerusalem from the Ephraim Gate to the Corner Gate—a section about four hundred cubits long.[a] [14] He took all the gold and silver and all the articles found in the temple of the LORD and in the treasuries of the royal palace. He also took hostages and returned to Samaria.

[15] As for the other events of the reign of Jehoash, what he did and his achievements, including his war against Amaziah king of Judah, are they not written in the book of the annals of the kings of Israel? [16] Jehoash rested with his ancestors and was buried in Samaria with the kings of Israel. And Jeroboam his son succeeded him as king.

[17] Amaziah son of Joash king of Judah lived for fifteen years after the death of Jehoash son of Jehoahaz king of Israel. [18] As for the other events of Amaziah's reign, are they not written in the book of the annals of the kings of Judah?

[19] They conspired against him in Jerusalem, and he fled to Lachish, but they sent men after him to Lachish and killed him there. [20] He was brought back by horse and was buried in Jerusalem with his ancestors, in the City of David.

[21] Then all the people of Judah took Azariah,[b] who was sixteen years old, and made him king in place of his father Amaziah. [22] He was the one who rebuilt Elath and restored it to Judah after Amaziah rested with his ancestors.

Jeroboam II King of Israel

[23] In the fifteenth year of Amaziah son of Joash king of Judah, Jeroboam son of Jehoash king of Israel became king in Samaria, and he reigned forty-one years. [24] He did evil in the eyes of the LORD and did not turn away from any of the sins of Jeroboam son of Nebat, which he had caused Israel to commit. [25] He was the one who restored the boundaries

[a] 13 That is, about 600 feet or about 180 meters   [b] 21 Also called Uzziah

of Israel from Lebo Hamath to the Dead Sea,[a] in accordance with the word of the LORD, the God of Israel, spoken through his servant Jonah son of Amittai, the prophet from Gath Hepher.

[26] The LORD had seen how bitterly everyone in Israel, whether slave or free, was suffering;[b] there was no one to help them. [27] And since the LORD had not said he would blot out the name of Israel from under heaven, he saved them by the hand of Jeroboam son of Jehoash.

[28] As for the other events of Jeroboam's reign, all he did, and his military achievements, including how he recovered for Israel both Damascus and Hamath, which had belonged to Judah, are they not written in the book of the annals of the kings of Israel? [29] Jeroboam rested with his ancestors, the kings of Israel. And Zechariah his son succeeded him as king.

Azariah King of Judah

15 In the twenty-seventh year of Jeroboam king of Israel, Azariah[c] son of Amaziah king of Judah began to reign. [2] He was sixteen years old when he became king, and he reigned in Jerusalem fifty-two years. His mother's name was Jekoliah; she was from Jerusalem. [3] He did what was right in the eyes of the LORD, just as his father Amaziah had done. [4] The high places, however, were not removed; the people continued to offer sacrifices and burn incense there.

[5] The LORD afflicted the king with leprosy[d] until the day he died, and he lived in a separate house.[e] Jotham the king's son had charge of the palace and governed the people of the land.

[6] As for the other events of Azariah's reign, and all he did, are they not written in the book of the annals of the kings of Judah? [7] Azariah rested with his ancestors and was buried near them in the City of David. And Jotham his son succeeded him as king.

Zechariah King of Israel

[8] In the thirty-eighth year of Azariah king of Judah, Zechariah son of Jeroboam became king of Israel in Samaria, and he reigned six months. [9] He did evil in the eyes of the LORD, as his predecessors had done. He did not turn away from the sins of Jeroboam son of Nebat, which he had caused Israel to commit.

[10] Shallum son of Jabesh conspired against Zechariah. He attacked him in front of the people,[f] assassinated him and succeeded

---

[a] 25 Hebrew *the Sea of the Arabah*   [b] 26 Or *Israel was suffering. They were without a ruler or leader, and*   [c] 1 Also called *Uzziah*; also in verses 6, 7, 8, 17, 23 and 27   [d] 5 The Hebrew for *leprosy* was used for various diseases affecting the skin.   [e] 5 Or *in a house where he was relieved of responsibilities*   [f] 10 Hebrew; some Septuagint manuscripts *in Ibleam*

him as king. [11] The other events of Zechariah's reign are written in the book of the annals of the kings of Israel. [12] So the word of the LORD spoken to Jehu was fulfilled: "Your descendants will sit on the throne of Israel to the fourth generation."[a]

Shallum King of Israel

[13] Shallum son of Jabesh became king in the thirty-ninth year of Uzziah king of Judah, and he reigned in Samaria one month. [14] Then Menahem son of Gadi went from Tirzah up to Samaria. He attacked Shallum son of Jabesh in Samaria, assassinated him and succeeded him as king.

[15] The other events of Shallum's reign, and the conspiracy he led, are written in the book of the annals of the kings of Israel.

[16] At that time Menahem, starting out from Tirzah, attacked Tiphsah and everyone in the city and its vicinity, because they refused to open their gates. He sacked Tiphsah and ripped open all the pregnant women.

Menahem King of Israel

[17] In the thirty-ninth year of Azariah king of Judah, Menahem son of Gadi became king of Israel, and he reigned in Samaria ten years. [18] He did evil in the eyes of the LORD. During his entire reign he did not turn away from the sins of Jeroboam son of Nebat, which he had caused Israel to commit.

[19] Then Pul[b] king of Assyria invaded the land, and Menahem gave him a thousand talents[c] of silver to gain his support and strengthen his own hold on the kingdom. [20] Menahem exacted this money from Israel. Every wealthy person had to contribute fifty shekels[d] of silver to be given to the king of Assyria. So the king of Assyria withdrew and stayed in the land no longer.

[21] As for the other events of Menahem's reign, and all he did, are they not written in the book of the annals of the kings of Israel? [22] Menahem rested with his ancestors. And Pekahiah his son succeeded him as king.

Pekahiah King of Israel

[23] In the fiftieth year of Azariah king of Judah, Pekahiah son of Menahem became king of Israel in Samaria, and he reigned two years. [24] Pekahiah did evil in the eyes of the LORD. He did not turn away from the sins of Jeroboam son of Nebat, which he had caused Israel to commit. [25] One of his chief officers, Pekah son of Remaliah, conspired against him. Taking fifty men of Gilead with him, he assassinated Pekahiah, along with Argob and

---

[a] 12 2 Kings 10:30   [b] 19 Also called *Tiglath-Pileser*   [c] 19 That is, about 38 tons or about 34 metric tons   [d] 20 That is, about 1 1/4 pounds or about 575 grams

Arieh, in the citadel of the royal palace at Samaria. So Pekah killed Pekahiah and succeeded him as king.

²⁶The other events of Pekahiah's reign, and all he did, are written in the book of the annals of the kings of Israel.

Pekah King of Israel

²⁷In the fifty-second year of Azariah king of Judah, Pekah son of Remaliah became king of Israel in Samaria, and he reigned twenty years. ²⁸He did evil in the eyes of the LORD. He did not turn away from the sins of Jeroboam son of Nebat, which he had caused Israel to commit.

²⁹In the time of Pekah king of Israel, Tiglath-Pileser king of Assyria came and took Ijon, Abel Beth Maakah, Janoah, Kedesh and Hazor. He took Gilead and Galilee, including all the land of Naphtali, and deported the people to Assyria. ³⁰Then Hoshea son of Elah conspired against Pekah son of Remaliah. He attacked and assassinated him, and then succeeded him as king in the twentieth year of Jotham son of Uzziah.

³¹As for the other events of Pekah's reign, and all he did, are they not written in the book of the annals of the kings of Israel?

Jotham King of Judah

³²In the second year of Pekah son of Remaliah king of Israel, Jotham son of Uzziah king of Judah began to reign. ³³He was twenty-five years old when he became king, and he reigned in Jerusalem sixteen years. His mother's name was Jerusha daughter of Zadok. ³⁴He did what was right in the eyes of the LORD, just as his father Uzziah had done. ³⁵The high places, however, were not removed; the people continued to offer sacrifices and burn incense there. Jotham rebuilt the Upper Gate of the temple of the LORD.

³⁶As for the other events of Jotham's reign, and what he did, are they not written in the book of the annals of the kings of Judah? ³⁷(In those days the LORD began to send Rezin king of Aram and Pekah son of Remaliah against Judah.) ³⁸Jotham rested with his ancestors and was buried with them in the City of David, the city of his father. And Ahaz his son succeeded him as king.

Ahaz King of Judah

16 In the seventeenth year of Pekah son of Remaliah, Ahaz son of Jotham king of Judah began to reign. ²Ahaz was twenty years old when he became king, and he reigned in Jerusalem sixteen years. Unlike David his father, he did not do what was right in the eyes of the LORD his God. ³He followed the ways of the kings of Israel and even sacrificed his son in the fire, engaging in the detestable practices of the

nations the LORD had driven out before the Israelites. [4]He offered sacrifices and burned incense at the high places, on the hilltops and under every spreading tree.

[5]Then Rezin king of Aram and Pekah son of Remaliah king of Israel marched up to fight against Jerusalem and besieged Ahaz, but they could not overpower him. [6]At that time, Rezin king of Aram recovered Elath for Aram by driving out the people of Judah. Edomites then moved into Elath and have lived there to this day.

[7]Ahaz sent messengers to say to Tiglath-Pileser king of Assyria, "I am your servant and vassal. Come up and save me out of the hand of the king of Aram and of the king of Israel, who are attacking me." [8]And Ahaz took the silver and gold found in the temple of the LORD and in the treasuries of the royal palace and sent it as a gift to the king of Assyria. [9]The king of Assyria complied by attacking Damascus and capturing it. He deported its inhabitants to Kir and put Rezin to death.

[10]Then King Ahaz went to Damascus to meet Tiglath-Pileser king of Assyria. He saw an altar in Damascus and sent to Uriah the priest a sketch of the altar, with detailed plans for its construction. [11]So Uriah the priest built an altar in accordance with all the plans that King Ahaz had sent from Damascus and fin-ished it before King Ahaz re-turned. [12]When the king came back from Damascus and saw the altar, he approached it and presented offerings[a] on it. [13]He offered up his burnt offering and grain offering, poured out his drink offering, and splashed the blood of his fellowship offer-ings against the altar. [14]As for the bronze altar that stood before the LORD, he brought it from the front of the temple — from between the new altar and the temple of the LORD — and put it on the north side of the new altar.

[15]King Ahaz then gave these or-ders to Uriah the priest: "On the large new altar, offer the morning burnt offering and the evening grain offering, the king's burnt offering and his grain offering, and the burnt offering of all the people of the land, and their grain offering and their drink of-fering. Splash against this altar the blood of all the burnt offer-ings and sacrifices. But I will use the bronze altar for seeking guid-ance." [16]And Uriah the priest did just as King Ahaz had ordered.

[17]King Ahaz cut off the side panels and removed the basins from the movable stands. He re-moved the Sea from the bronze bulls that supported it and set it on a stone base. [18]He took away the Sabbath canopy[b] that had been built at the temple and removed the royal entryway

[a] 12 Or *and went up*   [b] 18 Or *the dais of his throne* (see Septuagint)

outside the temple of the LORD, in deference to the king of Assyria.

¹⁹As for the other events of the reign of Ahaz, and what he did, are they not written in the book of the annals of the kings of Judah? ²⁰Ahaz rested with his ancestors and was buried with them in the City of David. And Hezekiah his son succeeded him as king.

Hoshea Last King of Israel

17 In the twelfth year of Ahaz king of Judah, Hoshea son of Elah became king of Israel in Samaria, and he reigned nine years. ²He did evil in the eyes of the LORD, but not like the kings of Israel who preceded him.

³Shalmaneser king of Assyria came up to attack Hoshea, who had been Shalmaneser's vassal and had paid him tribute. ⁴But the king of Assyria discovered that Hoshea was a traitor, for he had sent envoys to So^a king of Egypt, and he no longer paid tribute to the king of Assyria, as he had done year by year. Therefore Shalmaneser seized him and put him in prison. ⁵The king of Assyria invaded the entire land, marched against Samaria and laid siege to it for three years. ⁶In the ninth year of Hoshea, the king of Assyria captured Samaria and deported the Israelites to Assyria. He settled them in Halah, in Gozan on the Habor River and in the towns of the Medes.

Israel Exiled Because of Sin

⁷All this took place because the Israelites had sinned against the LORD their God, who had brought them up out of Egypt from under the power of Pharaoh king of Egypt. They worshiped other gods ⁸and followed the practices of the nations the LORD had driven out before them, as well as the practices that the kings of Israel had introduced. ⁹The Israelites secretly did things against the LORD their God that were not right. From watchtower to fortified city they built themselves high places in all their towns. ¹⁰They set up sacred stones and Asherah poles on every high hill and under every spreading tree. ¹¹At every high place they burned incense, as the nations whom the LORD had driven out before them had done. They did wicked things that aroused the LORD's anger. ¹²They worshiped idols, though the LORD had said, "You shall not do this."^b ¹³The LORD warned Israel and Judah through all his prophets and seers: "Turn from your evil ways. Observe my commands and decrees, in accordance with the entire Law that I commanded your ancestors to obey and that I delivered to you through my servants the prophets."

¹⁴But they would not listen and were as stiff-necked as their ancestors, who did not trust in the

---

^a 4 *So* is probably an abbreviation for *Osorkon.*   ^b 12 Exodus 20:4,5

LORD their God. ¹⁵They rejected his decrees and the covenant he had made with their ancestors and the statutes he had warned them to keep. They followed worthless idols and themselves became worthless. They imitated the nations around them although the LORD had ordered them, "Do not do as they do."

¹⁶They forsook all the commands of the LORD their God and made for themselves two idols cast in the shape of calves, and an Asherah pole. They bowed down to all the starry hosts, and they worshiped Baal. ¹⁷They sacrificed their sons and daughters in the fire. They practiced divination and sought omens and sold themselves to do evil in the eyes of the LORD, arousing his anger.

¹⁸So the LORD was very angry with Israel and removed them from his presence. Only the tribe of Judah was left, ¹⁹and even Judah did not keep the commands of the LORD their God. They followed the practices Israel had introduced. ²⁰Therefore the LORD rejected all the people of Israel; he afflicted them and gave them into the hands of plunderers, until he thrust them from his presence.

²¹When he tore Israel away from the house of David, they made Jeroboam son of Nebat their king. Jeroboam enticed Israel away from following the LORD and caused them to commit a great sin. ²²The Israelites persisted in all the sins of Jeroboam and did not turn away from them ²³until the LORD removed them from his presence, as he had warned through all his servants the prophets. So the people of Israel were taken from their homeland into exile in Assyria, and they are still there.

Samaria Resettled

²⁴The king of Assyria brought people from Babylon, Kuthah, Avva, Hamath and Sepharvaim and settled them in the towns of Samaria to replace the Israelites. They took over Samaria and lived in its towns. ²⁵When they first lived there, they did not worship the LORD; so he sent lions among them and they killed some of the people. ²⁶It was reported to the king of Assyria: "The people you deported and resettled in the towns of Samaria do not know what the god of that country requires. He has sent lions among them, which are killing them off, because the people do not know what he requires."

²⁷Then the king of Assyria gave this order: "Have one of the priests you took captive from Samaria go back to live there and teach the people what the god of the land requires." ²⁸So one of the priests who had been exiled from Samaria came to live in Bethel and taught them how to worship the LORD.

²⁹Nevertheless, each national group made its own gods in the

several towns where they settled, and set them up in the shrines the people of Samaria had made at the high places. **30** The people from Babylon made Sukkoth Benoth, those from Kuthah made Nergal, and those from Hamath made Ashima; **31** the Avvites made Nibhaz and Tartak, and the Sepharvites burned their children in the fire as sacrifices to Adrammelek and Anammelek, the gods of Sepharvaim. **32** They worshiped the LORD, but they also appointed all sorts of their own people to officiate for them as priests in the shrines at the high places. **33** They worshiped the LORD, but they also served their own gods in accordance with the customs of the nations from which they had been brought.

34 To this day they persist in their former practices. They neither worship the LORD nor adhere to the decrees and regulations, the laws and commands that the LORD gave the descendants of Jacob, whom he named Israel. **35** When the LORD made a covenant with the Israelites, he commanded them: "Do not worship any other gods or bow down to them, serve them or sacrifice to them. **36** But the LORD, who brought you up out of Egypt with mighty power and outstretched arm, is the one you must worship. To him you shall bow down and to him offer sacrifices. **37** You must always be careful to keep the decrees and regulations, the laws and commands he wrote for you. Do not worship other gods. **38** Do not forget the covenant I have made with you, and do not worship other gods. **39** Rather, worship the LORD your God; it is he who will deliver you from the hand of all your enemies."

40 They would not listen, however, but persisted in their former practices. **41** Even while these people were worshiping the LORD, they were serving their idols. To this day their children and grandchildren continue to do as their ancestors did.

Hezekiah King of Judah

18 In the third year of Hoshea son of Elah king of Israel, Hezekiah son of Ahaz king of Judah began to reign. **2** He was twenty-five years old when he became king, and he reigned in Jerusalem twenty-nine years. His mother's name was Abijah[a] daughter of Zechariah. **3** He did what was right in the eyes of the LORD, just as his father David had done. **4** He removed the high places, smashed the sacred stones and cut down the Asherah poles. He broke into pieces the bronze snake Moses had made, for up to that time the Israelites had been burning incense to it. (It was called Nehushtan.[b])

[a] 2 Hebrew *Abi*, a variant of *Abijah* [b] 4 *Nehushtan* sounds like the Hebrew for both *bronze* and *snake*.

⁵Hezekiah trusted in the LORD, the God of Israel. There was no one like him among all the kings of Judah, either before him or after him. ⁶He held fast to the LORD and did not stop following him; he kept the commands the LORD had given Moses. ⁷And the LORD was with him; he was successful in whatever he undertook. He rebelled against the king of Assyria and did not serve him. ⁸From watchtower to fortified city, he defeated the Philistines, as far as Gaza and its territory.

⁹In King Hezekiah's fourth year, which was the seventh year of Hoshea son of Elah king of Israel, Shalmaneser king of Assyria marched against Samaria and laid siege to it. ¹⁰At the end of three years the Assyrians took it. So Samaria was captured in Hezekiah's sixth year, which was the ninth year of Hoshea king of Israel. ¹¹The king of Assyria deported Israel to Assyria and settled them in Halah, in Gozan on the Habor River and in towns of the Medes. ¹²This happened because they had not obeyed the LORD their God, but had violated his covenant — all that Moses the servant of the LORD commanded. They neither listened to the commands nor carried them out.

¹³In the fourteenth year of King Hezekiah's reign, Sennacherib king of Assyria attacked all the fortified cities of Judah and captured them. ¹⁴So Hezekiah king of Judah sent this message to the king of Assyria at Lachish: "I have done wrong. Withdraw from me, and I will pay whatever you demand of me." The king of Assyria exacted from Hezekiah king of Judah three hundred talents*a* of silver and thirty talents*b* of gold. ¹⁵So Hezekiah gave him all the silver that was found in the temple of the LORD and in the treasuries of the royal palace.

¹⁶At this time Hezekiah king of Judah stripped off the gold with which he had covered the doors and doorposts of the temple of the LORD, and gave it to the king of Assyria.

Sennacherib Threatens Jerusalem

¹⁷The king of Assyria sent his supreme commander, his chief officer and his field commander with a large army, from Lachish to King Hezekiah at Jerusalem. They came up to Jerusalem and stopped at the aqueduct of the Upper Pool, on the road to the Washerman's Field. ¹⁸They called for the king; and Eliakim son of Hilkiah the palace administrator, Shebna the secretary, and Joah son of Asaph the recorder went out to them.

¹⁹The field commander said to them, "Tell Hezekiah:

---

a 14 That is, about 11 tons or about 10 metric tons or about 1 metric ton

b 14 That is, about 1 ton or

"'This is what the great king, the king of Assyria, says: On what are you basing this confidence of yours? ²⁰You say you have the counsel and the might for war—but you speak only empty words. On whom are you depending, that you rebel against me? ²¹Look, I know you are depending on Egypt, that splintered reed of a staff, which pierces the hand of anyone who leans on it! Such is Pharaoh king of Egypt to all who depend on him. ²²But if you say to me, "We are depending on the LORD our God"—isn't he the one whose high places and altars Hezekiah removed, saying to Judah and Jerusalem, "You must worship before this altar in Jerusalem"?

²³"'Come now, make a bargain with my master, the king of Assyria: I will give you two thousand horses—if you can put riders on them! ²⁴How can you repulse one officer of the least of my master's officials, even though you are depending on Egypt for chariots and horsemen*a*? ²⁵Furthermore, have I come to attack and destroy this place without word from the LORD? The LORD himself told me to march against this country and destroy it.'"

²⁶Then Eliakim son of Hilkiah, and Shebna and Joah said to the field commander, "Please speak to your servants in Aramaic, since we understand it. Don't speak to us in Hebrew in the hearing of the people on the wall."

²⁷But the commander replied, "Was it only to your master and you that my master sent me to say these things, and not to the people sitting on the wall—who, like you, will have to eat their own excrement and drink their own urine?"

²⁸Then the commander stood and called out in Hebrew, "Hear the word of the great king, the king of Assyria! ²⁹This is what the king says: Do not let Hezekiah deceive you. He cannot deliver you from my hand. ³⁰Do not let Hezekiah persuade you to trust in the LORD when he says, 'The LORD will surely deliver us; this city will not be given into the hand of the king of Assyria.'

³¹"Do not listen to Hezekiah. This is what the king of Assyria says: Make peace with me and come out to me. Then each of you will eat fruit from your own vine and fig tree and drink water from your own cistern, ³²until I come and take you to a land like your own—a land of grain and new wine, a land of bread and vineyards, a land of olive trees and honey. Choose life and not death!

a 24 Or *charioteers*

"Do not listen to Hezekiah, for he is misleading you when he says, 'The LORD will deliver us.' ³³Has the god of any nation ever delivered his land from the hand of the king of Assyria? ³⁴Where are the gods of Hamath and Arpad? Where are the gods of Sepharvaim, Hena and Ivvah? Have they rescued Samaria from my hand? ³⁵Who of all the gods of these countries has been able to save his land from me? How then can the LORD deliver Jerusalem from my hand?"

³⁶But the people remained silent and said nothing in reply, because the king had commanded, "Do not answer him."

³⁷Then Eliakim son of Hilkiah the palace administrator, Shebna the secretary, and Joah son of Asaph the recorder went to Hezekiah, with their clothes torn, and told him what the field commander had said.

Jerusalem's Deliverance Foretold

19 When King Hezekiah heard this, he tore his clothes and put on sackcloth and went into the temple of the LORD. ²He sent Eliakim the palace administrator, Shebna the secretary and the leading priests, all wearing sackcloth, to the prophet Isaiah son of Amoz. ³They told him, "This is what Hezekiah says: This day is a day of distress and rebuke and disgrace, as when children come to the moment of birth and there is no strength to deliver them. ⁴It may be that the LORD your God will hear all the words of the field commander, whom his master, the king of Assyria, has sent to ridicule the living God, and that he will rebuke him for the words the LORD your God has heard. Therefore pray for the remnant that still survives."

⁵When King Hezekiah's officials came to Isaiah, ⁶Isaiah said to them, "Tell your master, 'This is what the LORD says: Do not be afraid of what you have heard— those words with which the underlings of the king of Assyria have blasphemed me. ⁷Listen! When he hears a certain report, I will make him want to return to his own country, and there I will have him cut down with the sword.' "

⁸When the field commander heard that the king of Assyria had left Lachish, he withdrew and found the king fighting against Libnah.

⁹Now Sennacherib received a report that Tirhakah, the king of Cush,ᵃ was marching out to fight against him. So he again sent messengers to Hezekiah with this word: ¹⁰"Say to Hezekiah king of Judah: Do not let the god you depend on deceive you when he says, 'Jerusalem will not be given into the hands of the king

ᵃ 9 That is, the upper Nile region

of Assyria.' ¹¹Surely you have heard what the kings of Assyria have done to all the countries, destroying them completely. And will you be delivered? ¹²Did the gods of the nations that were destroyed by my predecessors deliver them — the gods of Gozan, Harran, Rezeph and the people of Eden who were in Tel Assar? ¹³Where is the king of Hamath or the king of Arpad? Where are the kings of Lair, Sepharvaim, Hena and Ivvah?"

Hezekiah's Prayer

¹⁴Hezekiah received the letter from the messengers and read it. Then he went up to the temple of the LORD and spread it out before the LORD. ¹⁵And Hezekiah prayed to the LORD: "LORD, the God of Israel, enthroned between the cherubim, you alone are God over all the kingdoms of the earth. You have made heaven and earth. ¹⁶Give ear, LORD, and hear; open your eyes, LORD, and see; listen to the words Sennacherib has sent to ridicule the living God.

¹⁷"It is true, LORD, that the Assyrian kings have laid waste these nations and their lands. ¹⁸They have thrown their gods into the fire and destroyed them, for they were not gods but only wood and stone, fashioned by human hands. ¹⁹Now, LORD our God, deliver us from his hand, so that all the kingdoms of the earth may know that you alone, LORD, are God."

Isaiah Prophesies Sennacherib's Fall

²⁰Then Isaiah son of Amoz sent a message to Hezekiah: "This is what the LORD, the God of Israel, says: I have heard your prayer concerning Sennacherib king of Assyria. ²¹This is the word that the LORD has spoken against him:

" 'Virgin Daughter Zion
    despises you and mocks you.
Daughter Jerusalem
    tosses her head as you flee.
²²Who is it you have ridiculed
        and blasphemed?
    Against whom have you
        raised your voice
and lifted your eyes in pride?
    Against the Holy One of
        Israel!
²³By your messengers
    you have ridiculed the Lord.
And you have said,
    "With my many chariots
I have ascended the heights of
        the mountains,
    the utmost heights of
        Lebanon.
I have cut down its tallest
        cedars,
    the choicest of its junipers.
I have reached its remotest
        parts,
    the finest of its forests.
²⁴I have dug wells in foreign
        lands
    and drunk the water there.

With the soles of my feet
I have dried up all the
streams of Egypt."

25 " 'Have you not heard?
Long ago I ordained it.
In days of old I planned it;
now I have brought it to pass,
that you have turned fortified
cities
into piles of stone.
26 Their people, drained of
power,
are dismayed and put to
shame.
They are like plants in the
field,
like tender green shoots,
like grass sprouting on the
roof,
scorched before it grows up.

27 " 'But I know where you are
and when you come and go
and how you rage against me.
28 Because you rage against me
and because your insolence
has reached my ears,
I will put my hook in your nose
and my bit in your mouth,
and I will make you return
by the way you came.'

29 "This will be the sign for you,
Hezekiah:

"This year you will eat what
grows by itself,
and the second year what
springs from that.
But in the third year sow and
reap,
plant vineyards and eat their
fruit.

30 Once more a remnant of the
kingdom of Judah
will take root below and bear
fruit above.
31 For out of Jerusalem will come
a remnant,
and out of Mount Zion a
band of survivors.

"The zeal of the LORD Almighty
will accomplish this.

32 "Therefore this is what the
LORD says concerning the king of
Assyria:

" 'He will not enter this city
or shoot an arrow here.
He will not come before it with
shield
or build a siege ramp
against it.
33 By the way that he came he
will return;
he will not enter this city,
declares the LORD.
34 I will defend this city and
save it,
for my sake and for the sake
of David my servant.' "

35 That night the angel of the
LORD went out and put to death
a hundred and eighty-five thousand in the Assyrian camp.
When the people got up the next
morning—there were all the
dead bodies! 36 So Sennacherib
king of Assyria broke camp and
withdrew. He returned to Nineveh and stayed there.

37 One day, while he was worshiping in the temple of his god

Nisrok, his sons Adrammelek and Sharezer killed him with the sword, and they escaped to the land of Ararat. And Esarhaddon his son succeeded him as king.

Hezekiah's Illness

20 In those days Hezekiah became ill and was at the point of death. The prophet Isaiah son of Amoz went to him and said, "This is what the LORD says: Put your house in order, because you are going to die; you will not recover."

2 Hezekiah turned his face to the wall and prayed to the LORD, 3 "Remember, LORD, how I have walked before you faithfully and with wholehearted devotion and have done what is good in your eyes." And Hezekiah wept bitterly.

4 Before Isaiah had left the middle court, the word of the LORD came to him: 5 "Go back and tell Hezekiah, the ruler of my people, 'This is what the LORD, the God of your father David, says: I have heard your prayer and seen your tears; I will heal you. On the third day from now you will go up to the temple of the LORD. 6 I will add fifteen years to your life. And I will deliver you and this city from the hand of the king of Assyria. I will defend this city for my sake and for the sake of my servant David.'"

7 Then Isaiah said, "Prepare a poultice of figs." They did so and applied it to the boil, and he recovered.

8 Hezekiah had asked Isaiah, "What will be the sign that the LORD will heal me and that I will go up to the temple of the LORD on the third day from now?"

9 Isaiah answered, "This is the LORD's sign to you that the LORD will do what he has promised: Shall the shadow go forward ten steps, or shall it go back ten steps?"

10 "It is a simple matter for the shadow to go forward ten steps," said Hezekiah. "Rather, have it go back ten steps."

11 Then the prophet Isaiah called on the LORD, and the LORD made the shadow go back the ten steps it had gone down on the stairway of Ahaz.

Envoys From Babylon

12 At that time Marduk-Baladan son of Baladan king of Babylon sent Hezekiah letters and a gift, because he had heard of Hezekiah's illness. 13 Hezekiah received the envoys and showed them all that was in his storehouses — the silver, the gold, the spices and the fine olive oil — his armory and everything found among his treasures. There was nothing in his palace or in all his kingdom that Hezekiah did not show them.

14 Then Isaiah the prophet went to King Hezekiah and asked, "What did those men say, and where did they come from?"

"From a distant land," Hezekiah replied. "They came from Babylon."

¹⁵The prophet asked, "What did they see in your palace?"

"They saw everything in my palace," Hezekiah said. "There is nothing among my treasures that I did not show them."

¹⁶Then Isaiah said to Hezekiah, "Hear the word of the LORD: ¹⁷The time will surely come when everything in your palace, and all that your predecessors have stored up until this day, will be carried off to Babylon. Nothing will be left, says the LORD. ¹⁸And some of your descendants, your own flesh and blood who will be born to you, will be taken away, and they will become eunuchs in the palace of the king of Babylon."

¹⁹"The word of the LORD you have spoken is good," Hezekiah replied. For he thought, "Will there not be peace and security in my lifetime?"

²⁰As for the other events of Hezekiah's reign, all his achievements and how he made the pool and the tunnel by which he brought water into the city, are they not written in the book of the annals of the kings of Judah? ²¹Hezekiah rested with his ancestors. And Manasseh his son succeeded him as king.

Manasseh King of Judah

21 Manasseh was twelve years old when he became king, and he reigned in Jerusalem fifty-five years. His mother's name was Hephzibah. ²He did evil in the eyes of the LORD, following the detestable practices of the nations the LORD had driven out before the Israelites. ³He rebuilt the high places his father Hezekiah had destroyed; he also erected altars to Baal and made an Asherah pole, as Ahab king of Israel had done. He bowed down to all the starry hosts and worshiped them. ⁴He built altars in the temple of the LORD, of which the LORD had said, "In Jerusalem I will put my Name." ⁵In the two courts of the temple of the LORD, he built altars to all the starry hosts. ⁶He sacrificed his own son in the fire, practiced divination, sought omens, and consulted mediums and spiritists. He did much evil in the eyes of the LORD, arousing his anger.

⁷He took the carved Asherah pole he had made and put it in the temple, of which the LORD had said to David and to his son Solomon, "In this temple and in Jerusalem, which I have chosen out of all the tribes of Israel, I will put my Name forever. ⁸I will not again make the feet of the Israelites wander from the land I gave their ancestors, if only they will be careful to do everything I commanded them and will keep the whole Law that my servant Moses gave them." ⁹But the people did not listen. Manasseh led them astray, so that they did more evil than the nations the

LORD had destroyed before the Israelites.

¹⁰The LORD said through his servants the prophets: ¹¹"Manasseh king of Judah has committed these detestable sins. He has done more evil than the Amorites who preceded him and has led Judah into sin with his idols. ¹²Therefore this is what the LORD, the God of Israel, says: I am going to bring such disaster on Jerusalem and Judah that the ears of everyone who hears of it will tingle. ¹³I will stretch out over Jerusalem the measuring line used against Samaria and the plumb line used against the house of Ahab. I will wipe out Jerusalem as one wipes a dish, wiping it and turning it upside down. ¹⁴I will forsake the remnant of my inheritance and give them into the hands of enemies. They will be looted and plundered by all their enemies; ¹⁵they have done evil in my eyes and have aroused my anger from the day their ancestors came out of Egypt until this day."

¹⁶Moreover, Manasseh also shed so much innocent blood that he filled Jerusalem from end to end — besides the sin that he had caused Judah to commit, so that they did evil in the eyes of the LORD.

¹⁷As for the other events of Manasseh's reign, and all he did, including the sin he committed, are they not written in the book of the annals of the kings of Judah? ¹⁸Manasseh rested with his ancestors and was buried in his palace garden, the garden of Uzza. And Amon his son succeeded him as king.

Amon King of Judah

¹⁹Amon was twenty-two years old when he became king, and he reigned in Jerusalem two years. His mother's name was Meshullemeth daughter of Haruz; she was from Jotbah. ²⁰He did evil in the eyes of the LORD, as his father Manasseh had done. ²¹He followed completely the ways of his father, worshiping the idols his father had worshiped, and bowing down to them. ²²He forsook the LORD, the God of his ancestors, and did not walk in obedience to him.

²³Amon's officials conspired against him and assassinated the king in his palace. ²⁴Then the people of the land killed all who had plotted against King Amon, and they made Josiah his son king in his place.

²⁵As for the other events of Amon's reign, and what he did, are they not written in the book of the annals of the kings of Judah? ²⁶He was buried in his tomb in the garden of Uzza. And Josiah his son succeeded him as king.

The Book of the Law Found

22 Josiah was eight years old when he became king, and he reigned in Jerusalem thir-

ty-one years. His mother's name was Jedidah daughter of Adaiah; she was from Bozkath. ²He did what was right in the eyes of the LORD and followed completely the ways of his father David, not turning aside to the right or to the left.

³In the eighteenth year of his reign, King Josiah sent the secretary, Shaphan son of Azaliah, the son of Meshullam, to the temple of the LORD. He said: ⁴"Go up to Hilkiah the high priest and have him get ready the money that has been brought into the temple of the LORD, which the doorkeepers have collected from the people. ⁵Have them entrust it to the men appointed to supervise the work on the temple. And have these men pay the workers who repair the temple of the LORD — ⁶the carpenters, the builders and the masons. Also have them purchase timber and dressed stone to repair the temple. ⁷But they need not account for the money entrusted to them, because they are honest in their dealings."

⁸Hilkiah the high priest said to Shaphan the secretary, "I have found the Book of the Law in the temple of the LORD." He gave it to Shaphan, who read it. ⁹Then Shaphan the secretary went to the king and reported to him: "Your officials have paid out the money that was in the temple of the LORD and have entrusted it to the workers and supervisors at the temple." ¹⁰Then Shaphan the secretary informed the king, "Hilkiah the priest has given me a book." And Shaphan read from it in the presence of the king.

¹¹When the king heard the words of the Book of the Law, he tore his robes. ¹²He gave these orders to Hilkiah the priest, Ahikam son of Shaphan, Akbor son of Micaiah, Shaphan the secretary and Asaiah the king's attendant: ¹³"Go and inquire of the LORD for me and for the people and for all Judah about what is written in this book that has been found. Great is the LORD's anger that burns against us because those who have gone before us have not obeyed the words of this book; they have not acted in accordance with all that is written there concerning us."

¹⁴Hilkiah the priest, Ahikam, Akbor, Shaphan and Asaiah went to speak to the prophet Huldah, who was the wife of Shallum son of Tikvah, the son of Harhas, keeper of the wardrobe. She lived in Jerusalem, in the New Quarter.

¹⁵She said to them, "This is what the LORD, the God of Israel, says: Tell the man who sent you to me, ¹⁶'This is what the LORD says: I am going to bring disaster on this place and its people, according to everything written in the book the king of Judah has read. ¹⁷Because they have forsaken me and burned incense to other gods and aroused my anger by all the

idols their hands have made,ᵃ my anger will burn against this place and will not be quenched.' **¹⁸**Tell the king of Judah, who sent you to inquire of the LORD, 'This is what the LORD, the God of Israel, says concerning the words you heard: **¹⁹**Because your heart was responsive and you humbled yourself before the LORD when you heard what I have spoken against this place and its people — that they would become a curseᵇ and be laid waste — and because you tore your robes and wept in my presence, I also have heard you, declares the LORD. **²⁰**Therefore I will gather you to your ancestors, and you will be buried in peace. Your eyes will not see all the disaster I am going to bring on this place.' "

So they took her answer back to the king.

Josiah Renews the Covenant

23 Then the king called together all the elders of Judah and Jerusalem. **²**He went up to the temple of the LORD with the people of Judah, the inhabitants of Jerusalem, the priests and the prophets — all the people from the least to the greatest. He read in their hearing all the words of the Book of the Covenant, which had been found in the temple of the LORD. **³**The king stood by the pillar and renewed the covenant in the presence of the LORD — to follow the LORD and keep his commands, statutes and decrees with all his heart and all his soul, thus confirming the words of the covenant written in this book. Then all the people pledged themselves to the covenant.

⁴The king ordered Hilkiah the high priest, the priests next in rank and the doorkeepers to remove from the temple of the LORD all the articles made for Baal and Asherah and all the starry hosts. He burned them outside Jerusalem in the fields of the Kidron Valley and took the ashes to Bethel. **⁵**He did away with the idolatrous priests appointed by the kings of Judah to burn incense on the high places of the towns of Judah and on those around Jerusalem — those who burned incense to Baal, to the sun and moon, to the constellations and to all the starry hosts. **⁶**He took the Asherah pole from the temple of the LORD to the Kidron Valley outside Jerusalem and burned it there. He ground it to powder and scattered the dust over the graves of the common people. **⁷**He also tore down the quarters of the male shrine prostitutes that were in the temple of the LORD, the quarters where women did weaving for Asherah.

⁸Josiah brought all the priests from the towns of Judah and des-

---

ᵃ **17** Or *by everything they have done*   ᵇ **19** That is, their names would be used in cursing (see Jer. 29:22); or, others would see that they are cursed.

ecrated the high places, from Geba to Beersheba, where the priests had burned incense. He broke down the gateway at the entrance of the Gate of Joshua, the city governor, which was on the left of the city gate. ⁹ Although the priests of the high places did not serve at the altar of the LORD in Jerusalem, they ate unleavened bread with their fellow priests.

¹⁰ He desecrated Topheth, which was in the Valley of Ben Hinnom, so no one could use it to sacrifice their son or daughter in the fire to Molek. ¹¹ He removed from the entrance to the temple of the LORD the horses that the kings of Judah had dedicated to the sun. They were in the court*a* near the room of an official named Nathan-Melek. Josiah then burned the chariots dedicated to the sun.

¹² He pulled down the altars the kings of Judah had erected on the roof near the upper room of Ahaz, and the altars Manasseh had built in the two courts of the temple of the LORD. He removed them from there, smashed them to pieces and threw the rubble into the Kidron Valley. ¹³ The king also desecrated the high places that were east of Jerusalem on the south of the Hill of Corruption — the ones Solomon king of Israel had built for Ashtoreth the

vile goddess of the Sidonians, for Chemosh the vile god of Moab, and for Molek the detestable god of the people of Ammon. ¹⁴ Josiah smashed the sacred stones and cut down the Asherah poles and covered the sites with human bones.

¹⁵ Even the altar at Bethel, the high place made by Jeroboam son of Nebat, who had caused Israel to sin — even that altar and high place he demolished. He burned the high place and ground it to powder, and burned the Asherah pole also. ¹⁶ Then Josiah looked around, and when he saw the tombs that were there on the hillside, he had the bones removed from them and burned on the altar to defile it, in accordance with the word of the LORD proclaimed by the man of God who foretold these things.

¹⁷ The king asked, "What is that tombstone I see?"

The people of the city said, "It marks the tomb of the man of God who came from Judah and pronounced against the altar of Bethel the very things you have done to it."

¹⁸ "Leave it alone," he said. "Don't let anyone disturb his bones." So they spared his bones and those of the prophet who had come from Samaria.

¹⁹ Just as he had done at Bethel, Josiah removed all the shrines

---

a 11 The meaning of the Hebrew for this word is uncertain.

at the high places that the kings of Israel had built in the towns of Samaria and that had aroused the LORD's anger. ²⁰ Josiah slaughtered all the priests of those high places on the altars and burned human bones on them. Then he went back to Jerusalem.

²¹ The king gave this order to all the people: "Celebrate the Passover to the LORD your God, as it is written in this Book of the Covenant." ²² Neither in the days of the judges who led Israel nor in the days of the kings of Israel and the kings of Judah had any such Passover been observed. ²³ But in the eighteenth year of King Josiah, this Passover was celebrated to the LORD in Jerusalem.

²⁴ Furthermore, Josiah got rid of the mediums and spiritists, the household gods, the idols and all the other detestable things seen in Judah and Jerusalem. This he did to fulfill the requirements of the law written in the book that Hilkiah the priest had discovered in the temple of the LORD. ²⁵ Neither before nor after Josiah was there a king like him who turned to the LORD as he did—with all his heart and with all his soul and with all his strength, in accordance with all the Law of Moses.

²⁶ Nevertheless, the LORD did not turn away from the heat of his fierce anger, which burned against Judah because of all that Manasseh had done to arouse his anger. ²⁷ So the LORD said, "I will remove Judah also from my presence as I removed Israel, and I will reject Jerusalem, the city I chose, and this temple, about which I said, 'My Name shall be there.'ᵃ"

²⁸ As for the other events of Josiah's reign, and all he did, are they not written in the book of the annals of the kings of Judah?

²⁹ While Josiah was king, Pharaoh Necho king of Egypt went up to the Euphrates River to help the king of Assyria. King Josiah marched out to meet him in battle, but Necho faced him and killed him at Megiddo. ³⁰ Josiah's servants brought his body in a chariot from Megiddo to Jerusalem and buried him in his own tomb. And the people of the land took Jehoahaz son of Josiah and anointed him and made him king in place of his father.

Jehoahaz King of Judah

³¹ Jehoahaz was twenty-three years old when he became king, and he reigned in Jerusalem three months. His mother's name was Hamutal daughter of Jeremiah; she was from Libnah. ³² He did evil in the eyes of the LORD, just as his predecessors had done. ³³ Pharaoh Necho put him in chains at Riblah in the land of Hamath so that he might not reign in Jerusalem, and he imposed on Judah a levy of a

ᵃ 27 1 Kings 8:29

hundred talents[a] of silver and a talent[b] of gold. ³⁴Pharaoh Necho made Eliakim son of Josiah king in place of his father Josiah and changed Eliakim's name to Jehoiakim. But he took Jehoahaz and carried him off to Egypt, and there he died. ³⁵Jehoiakim paid Pharaoh Necho the silver and gold he demanded. In order to do so, he taxed the land and exacted the silver and gold from the people of the land according to their assessments.

Jehoiakim King of Judah

³⁶Jehoiakim was twenty-five years old when he became king, and he reigned in Jerusalem eleven years. His mother's name was Zebidah daughter of Pedaiah; she was from Rumah. ³⁷And he did evil in the eyes of the LORD, just as his predecessors had done.

24 During Jehoiakim's reign, Nebuchadnezzar king of Babylon invaded the land, and Jehoiakim became his vassal for three years. But then he turned against Nebuchadnezzar and rebelled. ²The LORD sent Babylonian,[c] Aramean, Moabite and Ammonite raiders against him to destroy Judah, in accordance with the word of the LORD proclaimed by his servants the prophets. ³Surely these things happened to Judah according to

the LORD's command, in order to remove them from his presence because of the sins of Manasseh and all he had done, ⁴including the shedding of innocent blood. For he had filled Jerusalem with innocent blood, and the LORD was not willing to forgive.

⁵As for the other events of Jehoiakim's reign, and all he did, are they not written in the book of the annals of the kings of Judah? ⁶Jehoiakim rested with his ancestors. And Jehoiachin his son succeeded him as king.

⁷The king of Egypt did not march out from his own country again, because the king of Babylon had taken all his territory, from the Wadi of Egypt to the Euphrates River.

Jehoiachin King of Judah

⁸Jehoiachin was eighteen years old when he became king, and he reigned in Jerusalem three months. His mother's name was Nehushta daughter of Elnathan; she was from Jerusalem. ⁹He did evil in the eyes of the LORD, just as his father had done.

¹⁰At that time the officers of Nebuchadnezzar king of Babylon advanced on Jerusalem and laid siege to it, ¹¹and Nebuchadnezzar himself came up to the city while his officers were besieging it. ¹²Jehoiachin king of Judah, his mother, his attendants, his

---

[a] 33 That is, about 3 3/4 tons or about 3.4 metric tons   [b] 33 That is, about 75 pounds or about 34 kilograms   [c] 2 Or *Chaldean*

nobles and his officials all surrendered to him.

In the eighth year of the reign
of the king of Babylon, he took Jehoiachin prisoner. [13] As the LORD
had declared, Nebuchadnezzar
removed the treasures from the
temple of the LORD and from the
royal palace, and cut up the gold
articles that Solomon king of Israel had made for the temple of
the LORD. [14] He carried all Jerusalem into exile: all the officers and
fighting men, and all the skilled
workers and artisans — a total of
ten thousand. Only the poorest
people of the land were left.

[15] Nebuchadnezzar took Jehoiachin captive to Babylon. He also
took from Jerusalem to Babylon
the king's mother, his wives, his
officials and the prominent people of the land. [16] The king of Babylon also deported to Babylon
the entire force of seven thousand fighting men, strong and fit
for war, and a thousand skilled
workers and artisans. [17] He made
Mattaniah, Jehoiachin's uncle,
king in his place and changed his
name to Zedekiah.

Zedekiah King of Judah

[18] Zedekiah was twenty-one
years old when he became king,
and he reigned in Jerusalem elev-
en years. His mother's name was
Hamutal daughter of Jeremiah;
she was from Libnah. [19] He did
evil in the eyes of the LORD, just
as Jehoiakim had done. [20] It was
because of the LORD's anger that
all this happened to Jerusalem
and Judah, and in the end he
thrust them from his presence.

The Fall of Jerusalem

Now Zedekiah rebelled against
the king of Babylon.

25 So in the ninth year of
Zedekiah's reign, on the
tenth day of the tenth month,
Nebuchadnezzar king of Babylon
marched against Jerusalem with
his whole army. He encamped
outside the city and built siege
works all around it. [2] The city was
kept under siege until the eleventh year of King Zedekiah.

[3] By the ninth day of the fourth[a]
month the famine in the city had
become so severe that there was
no food for the people to eat.
[4] Then the city wall was broken
through, and the whole army
fled at night through the gate
between the two walls near the
king's garden, though the Babylonians[b] were surrounding the
city. They fled toward the Arabah,[c] [5] but the Babylonian[d] army
pursued the king and overtook
him in the plains of Jericho. All
his soldiers were separated from
him and scattered, [6] and he was
captured.

---

[a] 3 Probable reading of the original Hebrew text (see Jer. 52:6); Masoretic
Text does not have *fourth*.   [b] 4 Or *Chaldeans*; also in verses 13, 25 and 26
[c] 4 Or *the Jordan Valley*   [d] 5 Or *Chaldean*; also in verses 10 and 24

He was taken to the king of Babylon at Riblah, where sentence was pronounced on him. [7]They killed the sons of Zedekiah before his eyes. Then they put out his eyes, bound him with bronze shackles and took him to Babylon.

[8]On the seventh day of the fifth month, in the nineteenth year of Nebuchadnezzar king of Babylon, Nebuzaradan commander of the imperial guard, an official of the king of Babylon, came to Jerusalem. [9]He set fire to the temple of the LORD, the royal palace and all the houses of Jerusalem. Every important building he burned down. [10]The whole Babylonian army under the commander of the imperial guard broke down the walls around Jerusalem. [11]Nebuzaradan the commander of the guard carried into exile the people who remained in the city, along with the rest of the populace and those who had deserted to the king of Babylon. [12]But the commander left behind some of the poorest people of the land to work the vineyards and fields.

[13]The Babylonians broke up the bronze pillars, the movable stands and the bronze Sea that were at the temple of the LORD and they carried the bronze to Babylon. [14]They also took away the pots, shovels, wick trimmers, dishes and all the bronze arti-cles used in the temple service. [15]The commander of the imperial guard took away the censers and sprinkling bowls — all that were made of pure gold or silver.

[16]The bronze from the two pillars, the Sea and the movable stands, which Solomon had made for the temple of the LORD, was more than could be weighed. [17]Each pillar was eighteen cubits[a] high. The bronze capital on top of one pillar was three cubits[b] high and was decorated with a network and pomegranates of bronze all around. The other pillar, with its network, was similar.

[18]The commander of the guard took as prisoners Seraiah the chief priest, Zephaniah the priest next in rank and the three doorkeepers. [19]Of those still in the city, he took the officer in charge of the fighting men, and five royal advisers. He also took the secretary who was chief officer in charge of conscripting the people of the land and sixty of the conscripts who were found in the city. [20]Nebuzaradan the commander took them all and brought them to the king of Babylon at Riblah. [21]There at Riblah, in the land of Hamath, the king had them executed.

So Judah went into captivity, away from her land.

[22]Nebuchadnezzar king of Babylon appointed Gedaliah son

_____

[a] 17 That is, about 27 feet or about 8.1 meters [b] 17 That is, about 4 1/2 feet or about 1.4 meters

of Ahikam, the son of Shaphan, to be over the people he had left behind in Judah. **23** When all the army officers and their men heard that the king of Babylon had appointed Gedaliah as governor, they came to Gedaliah at Mizpah—Ishmael son of Nethaniah, Johanan son of Kareah, Seraiah son of Tanhumeth the Netophathite, Jaazaniah the son of the Maakathite, and their men. **24** Gedaliah took an oath to reassure them and their men. "Do not be afraid of the Babylonian officials," he said. "Settle down in the land and serve the king of Babylon, and it will go well with you."

25 In the seventh month, however, Ishmael son of Nethaniah, the son of Elishama, who was of royal blood, came with ten men and assassinated Gedaliah and also the men of Judah and the Babylonians who were with him at Mizpah. **26** At this, all the people from the least to the greatest, together with the army officers, fled to Egypt for fear of the Babylonians.

Jehoiachin Released

27 In the thirty-seventh year of the exile of Jehoiachin king of Judah, in the year Awel-Marduk became king of Babylon, he released Jehoiachin king of Judah from prison. He did this on the twenty-seventh day of the twelfth month. **28** He spoke kindly to him and gave him a seat of honor higher than those of the other kings who were with him in Babylon. **29** So Jehoiachin put aside his prison clothes and for the rest of his life ate regularly at the king's table. **30** Day by day the king gave Jehoiachin a regular allowance as long as he lived.

1 Chronicles

Introduction:

Although the books of Chronicles seem like a repeat of Samuel and Kings, they aren't. The Chronicles were written for the exiles who had returned to Israel after the Babylonian captivity to remind them they were from the royal line of David and were God's chosen people. The main theme is that God is always faithful to his covenant.

For these reasons 1 Chronicles begins with an outline of history from Adam through the death of King Saul. The rest of the book is about the reign of King David. These books serve as both a warning and encouragement to the Jews to be faithful to the covenant.

Outline of contents:

List of generations (1:1 – 9:44)
The reign of David (10:1 – 29:30)

Historical Records From Adam to Abraham

To Noah's Sons

1 Adam, Seth, Enosh, **2**Kenan, Mahalalel, Jared, **3**Enoch, Methuselah, Lamech, Noah.

4The sons of Noah:*a*
Shem, Ham and Japheth.

The Japhethites

5The sons*b* of Japheth:
Gomer, Magog, Madai, Javan, Tubal, Meshek and Tiras.
6The sons of Gomer:
Ashkenaz, Riphath*c* and Togarmah.

7The sons of Javan:
Elishah, Tarshish, the Kittites and the Rodanites.

The Hamites

8The sons of Ham:
Cush, Egypt, Put and Canaan.
9The sons of Cush:
Seba, Havilah, Sabta, Raamah and Sabteka.
The sons of Raamah:
Sheba and Dedan.
10Cush was the father*d* of Nimrod, who became a mighty warrior on earth.
11Egypt was the father of the Ludites, Anamites,

---

a 4 Septuagint; Hebrew does not have this line.   *b 5 Sons* may mean *descendants* or *successors* or *nations*; also in verses 6-9, 17 and 23.   *c 6* Many Hebrew manuscripts and Vulgate (see also Septuagint and Gen. 10:3); most Hebrew manuscripts *Diphath*   *d 10 Father* may mean *ancestor* or *predecessor* or *founder*; also in verses 11, 13, 18 and 20.

Lehabites, Naphtuhites, [12]Pathrusites, Kasluhites (from whom the Philistines came) and Caphtorites.

[13]Canaan was the father of Sidon his firstborn,[a] and of the Hittites, [14]Jebusites, Amorites, Girgashites, [15]Hivites, Arkites, Sinites, [16]Arvadites, Zemarites and Hamathites.

The Semites

[17]The sons of Shem:

Elam, Ashur, Arphaxad, Lud and Aram.

The sons of Aram:[b]

Uz, Hul, Gether and Meshek.

[18]Arphaxad was the father of Shelah,

and Shelah the father of Eber.

[19]Two sons were born to Eber:

One was named Peleg,[c] because in his time the earth was divided; his brother was named Joktan.

[20]Joktan was the father of Almodad, Sheleph, Hazarmaveth, Jerah, [21]Hadoram, Uzal, Diklah, [22]Obal,[d] Abimael, Sheba, [23]Ophir, Havilah and Jobab. All these were sons of Joktan.

[24]Shem, Arphaxad,[e] Shelah,

[25]Eber, Peleg, Reu,

[26]Serug, Nahor, Terah

[27]and Abram (that is, Abraham).

The Family of Abraham

[28]The sons of Abraham:

Isaac and Ishmael.

Descendants of Hagar

[29]These were their descendants:

Nebaioth the firstborn of Ishmael, Kedar, Adbeel, Mibsam, [30]Mishma, Dumah, Massa, Hadad, Tema, [31]Jetur, Naphish and Kedemah. These were the sons of Ishmael.

Descendants of Keturah

[32]The sons born to Keturah, Abraham's concubine:

Zimran, Jokshan, Medan, Midian, Ishbak and Shuah.

The sons of Jokshan:

Sheba and Dedan.

[33]The sons of Midian:

Ephah, Epher, Hanok, Abida and Eldaah.

All these were descendants of Keturah.

Descendants of Sarah

[34]Abraham was the father of Isaac.

The sons of Isaac:

Esau and Israel.

---

[a] 13 Or of the Sidonians, the foremost   [b] 17 One Hebrew manuscript and some Septuagint manuscripts (see also Gen. 10:23); most Hebrew manuscripts do not have this line.   [c] 19 Peleg means division.   [d] 22 Some Hebrew manuscripts and Syriac (see also Gen. 10:28); most Hebrew manuscripts Ebal   [e] 24 Hebrew; some Septuagint manuscripts Arphaxad, Cainan (see also note at Gen. 11:10)

Esau's Sons

35 The sons of Esau:

Eliphaz, Reuel, Jeush, Jalam and Korah.

36 The sons of Eliphaz:

Teman, Omar, Zepho,[a] Gatam and Kenaz;

by Timna: Amalek.[b]

37 The sons of Reuel:

Nahath, Zerah, Shammah and Mizzah.

The People of Seir in Edom

38 The sons of Seir:

Lotan, Shobal, Zibeon, Anah, Dishon, Ezer and Dishan.

39 The sons of Lotan:

Hori and Homam. Timna was Lotan's sister.

40 The sons of Shobal:

Alvan,[c] Manahath, Ebal, Shepho and Onam.

The sons of Zibeon:

Aiah and Anah.

41 The son of Anah:

Dishon.

The sons of Dishon:

Hemdan,[d] Eshban, Ithran and Keran.

42 The sons of Ezer:

Bilhan, Zaavan and Akan.[e]

The sons of Dishan[f]:

Uz and Aran.

The Rulers of Edom

43 These were the kings who reigned in Edom before any Israelite king reigned:

Bela son of Beor, whose city was named Dinhabah.

44 When Bela died, Jobab son of Zerah from Bozrah succeeded him as king.

45 When Jobab died, Husham from the land of the Temanites succeeded him as king.

46 When Husham died, Hadad son of Bedad, who defeated Midian in the country of Moab, succeeded him as king. His city was named Avith.

47 When Hadad died, Samlah from Masrekah succeeded him as king.

48 When Samlah died, Shaul from Rehoboth on the river[g] succeeded him as king.

49 When Shaul died, Baal-Hanan son of Akbor succeeded him as king.

50 When Baal-Hanan died, Hadad succeeded him as king. His city was named Pau,[h]

---

a 36 Many Hebrew manuscripts, some Septuagint manuscripts and Syriac (see also Gen. 36:11); most Hebrew manuscripts *Zephi*   *b 36* Some Septuagint manuscripts (see also Gen. 36:12); Hebrew *Gatam, Kenaz, Timna and Amalek*   *c 40* Many Hebrew manuscripts and some Septuagint manuscripts (see also Gen. 36:23); most Hebrew manuscripts *Alian*   *d 41* Many Hebrew manuscripts and some Septuagint manuscripts (see also Gen. 36:26); most Hebrew manuscripts *Hamran*   *e 42* Many Hebrew and Septuagint manuscripts (see also Gen. 36:27); most Hebrew manuscripts *Zaavan, Jaakan*   *f 42* See Gen. 36:28; Hebrew *Dishon*, a variant of *Dishan*   *g 48* Possibly the Euphrates   *h 50* Many Hebrew manuscripts, some Septuagint manuscripts, Vulgate and Syriac (see also Gen. 36:39); most Hebrew manuscripts *Pai* and his wife's name was Mehetabel daughter of Matred, the daughter of Me-Zahab. **51** Hadad also died.

The chiefs of Edom were:
Timna, Alvah, Jetheth, **52** Oholibamah, Elah, Pinon, **53** Kenaz, Teman, Mibzar, **54** Magdiel and Iram. These were the chiefs of Edom.

Israel's Sons

2 These were the sons of Israel: Reuben, Simeon, Levi, Judah, Issachar, Zebulun, **2** Dan, Joseph, Benjamin, Naphtali, Gad and Asher.

Judah

To Hezron's Sons

3 The sons of Judah:
Er, Onan and Shelah. These three were born to him by a Canaanite woman, the daughter of Shua. Er, Judah's firstborn, was wicked in the LORD's sight; so the LORD put him to death. **4** Judah's daughter-in-law Tamar bore Perez and Zerah to Judah. He had five sons in all.

5 The sons of Perez:
Hezron and Hamul.

6 The sons of Zerah:
Zimri, Ethan, Heman, Kalkol and Darda[a] — five in all.

7 The son of Karmi:
Achar,[b] who brought trouble on Israel by violating the ban on taking devoted things.[c]

8 The son of Ethan:
Azariah.

9 The sons born to Hezron were:
Jerahmeel, Ram and Caleb.[d]

From Ram Son of Hezron

10 Ram was the father of Amminadab, and Amminadab the father of Nahshon, the leader of the people of Judah. **11** Nahshon was the father of Salmon,[e] Salmon the father of Boaz, **12** Boaz the father of Obed and Obed the father of Jesse.

13 Jesse was the father of Eliab his firstborn; the second son was Abinadab, the third Shimea, **14** the fourth Nethanel, the fifth Raddai, **15** the sixth Ozem and the seventh David. **16** Their sisters were Zeruiah and Abigail. Zeruiah's three sons were Abishai, Joab and Asahel. **17** Abigail was the mother of Amasa, whose father was Jether the Ishmaelite.

---

[a] 6 Many Hebrew manuscripts, some Septuagint manuscripts and Syriac (see also 1 Kings 4:31); most Hebrew manuscripts *Dara*   [b] 7 *Achar* means *trouble*; *Achar* is called *Achan* in Joshua.   [c] 7 The Hebrew term refers to the irrevocable giving over of things or persons to the LORD, often by totally destroying them.   [d] 9 Hebrew *Kelubai*, a variant of *Caleb*   [e] 11 Septuagint (see also Ruth 4:21); Hebrew *Salma*

Caleb Son of Hezron

¹⁸ Caleb son of Hezron had children by his wife Azubah (and by Jerioth). These were her sons: Jesher, Shobab and Ardon. ¹⁹ When Azubah died, Caleb married Ephrath, who bore him Hur. ²⁰ Hur was the father of Uri, and Uri the father of Bezalel.

²¹ Later, Hezron, when he was sixty years old, married the daughter of Makir the father of Gilead. He made love to her, and she bore him Segub. ²² Segub was the father of Jair, who controlled twenty-three towns in Gilead. ²³ (But Geshur and Aram captured Havvoth Jair,ᵃ as well as Kenath with its surrounding settlements — sixty towns.) All these were descendants of Makir the father of Gilead.

²⁴ After Hezron died in Caleb Ephrathah, Abijah the wife of Hezron bore him Ashhur the fatherᵇ of Tekoa.

Jerahmeel Son of Hezron

²⁵ The sons of Jerahmeel the firstborn of Hezron:
Ram his firstborn, Bunah, Oren, Ozem andᶜ Ahijah. ²⁶ Jerahmeel had another wife, whose name was Atarah; she was the mother of Onam.

²⁷ The sons of Ram the firstborn of Jerahmeel:
Maaz, Jamin and Eker.
²⁸ The sons of Onam:
Shammai and Jada.
The sons of Shammai:
Nadab and Abishur.
²⁹ Abishur's wife was named Abihail, who bore him Ahban and Molid.
³⁰ The sons of Nadab:
Seled and Appaim. Seled died without children.
³¹ The son of Appaim:
Ishi, who was the father of Sheshan.
Sheshan was the father of Ahlai.
³² The sons of Jada, Shammai's brother:
Jether and Jonathan. Jether died without children.
³³ The sons of Jonathan:
Peleth and Zaza.
These were the descendants of Jerahmeel.
³⁴ Sheshan had no sons — only daughters.
He had an Egyptian servant named Jarha. ³⁵ Sheshan gave his daughter in marriage to his servant Jarha, and she bore him Attai.
³⁶ Attai was the father of Nathan,
Nathan the father of Zabad,
³⁷ Zabad the father of Ephlal,
Ephlal the father of Obed,

ᵃ 23 Or *captured the settlements of Jair*
leader or *military leader*; also in verses 42, 45, 49-52 and possibly elsewhere.
ᶜ 25 Or *Oren and Ozem, by*
ᵇ 24 *Father* may mean *civic*

³⁸Obed the father of Jehu,
Jehu the father of Azariah,
³⁹Azariah the father of Helez,
Helez the father of Eleasah,
⁴⁰Eleasah the father of Sismai,
Sismai the father of Shallum,
⁴¹Shallum the father of Jekamiah,
and Jekamiah the father of
Elishama.

The Clans of Caleb

⁴²The sons of Caleb the brother of Jerahmeel:
Mesha his firstborn, who was the father of Ziph, and his son Mareshah,ᵃ who was the father of Hebron.
⁴³The sons of Hebron:
Korah, Tappuah, Rekem and Shema. ⁴⁴Shema was the father of Raham, and Raham the father of Jorkeam. Rekem was the father of Shammai. ⁴⁵The son of Shammai was Maon, and Maon was the father of Beth Zur.
⁴⁶Caleb's concubine Ephah was the mother of Haran, Moza and Gazez. Haran was the father of Gazez.
⁴⁷The sons of Jahdai:
Regem, Jotham, Geshan, Pelet, Ephah and Shaaph.
⁴⁸Caleb's concubine Maakah was the mother of Sheber and Tirhanah. ⁴⁹She also gave birth to Shaaph the father of Madmannah and to Sheva the father of Makbenah and Gibea. Caleb's daughter was Aksah. ⁵⁰These were the descendants of Caleb.

The sons of Hur the firstborn of Ephrathah:
Shobal the father of Kiriath Jearim, ⁵¹Salma the father of Bethlehem, and Hareph the father of Beth Gader.
⁵²The descendants of Shobal the father of Kiriath Jearim were:
Haroeh, half the Manahathites, ⁵³and the clans of Kiriath Jearim: the Ithrites, Puthites, Shumathites and Mishraites. From these descended the Zorathites and Eshtaolites.
⁵⁴The descendants of Salma:
Bethlehem, the Netophathites, Atroth Beth Joab, half the Manahathites, the Zorites, ⁵⁵and the clans of scribesᵇ who lived at Jabez: the Tirathites, Shimeathites and Sucathites. These are the Kenites who came from Hammath, the father of the Rekabites.ᶜ

The Sons of David

3 These were the sons of David born to him in Hebron:

ᵃ 42 The meaning of the Hebrew for this phrase is uncertain.   ᵇ 55 Or *of the Sopherites*   ᶜ 55 Or *father of Beth Rekab*

The firstborn was Amnon the son of Ahinoam of Jezreel;

the second, Daniel the son of Abigail of Carmel;

²the third, Absalom the son of Maakah daughter of Talmai king of Geshur;

the fourth, Adonijah the son of Haggith;

³the fifth, Shephatiah the son of Abital;

and the sixth, Ithream, by his wife Eglah.

⁴These six were born to David in Hebron, where he reigned seven years and six months.

David reigned in Jerusalem thirty-three years, ⁵and these were the children born to him there:

Shammua,ᵃ Shobab, Nathan and Solomon. These four were by Bathshebaᵇ daughter of Ammiel.

⁶There were also Ibhar, Elishua,ᶜ Eliphelet, ⁷Nogah, Nepheg, Japhia, ⁸Elishama, Eliada and Eliphelet — nine in all. ⁹All these were the sons of David, besides his sons by his concubines. And Tamar was their sister.

The Kings of Judah

¹⁰Solomon's son was Rehoboam,
Abijah his son,
Asa his son,
Jehoshaphat his son,
¹¹Jehoramᵈ his son,
Ahaziah his son,
Joash his son,
¹²Amaziah his son,
Azariah his son,
Jotham his son,
¹³Ahaz his son,
Hezekiah his son,
Manasseh his son,
¹⁴Amon his son,
Josiah his son.
¹⁵The sons of Josiah:
Johanan the firstborn,
Jehoiakim the second son,
Zedekiah the third,
Shallum the fourth.
¹⁶The successors of Jehoiakim:
Jehoiachinᵉ his son,
and Zedekiah.

The Royal Line After the Exile

¹⁷The descendants of Jehoiachin the captive:
Shealtiel his son, ¹⁸Malkiram, Pedaiah, Shenazzar, Jekamiah, Hoshama and Nedabiah.
¹⁹The sons of Pedaiah:
Zerubbabel and Shimei.
The sons of Zerubbabel:
Meshullam and Hananiah. Shelomith was their sister.
²⁰There were also five others:
Hashubah, Ohel, Berekiah, Hasadiah and Jushab-Hesed.

ᵃ 5 Hebrew *Shimea,* a variant of *Shammua* (see also Septuagint and 2 Samuel 11:3); most Hebrew manuscripts *Bathshua* ᵇ 5 One Hebrew manuscript and Vulgate (see also Septuagint and 2 Samuel 11:3); most Hebrew manuscripts ᶜ 6 Two Hebrew manuscripts (see also 2 Samuel 5:15 and 1 Chron. 14:5); most Hebrew manuscripts *Elishama* ᵈ 11 Hebrew *Joram,* a variant of *Jehoram* ᵉ 16 Hebrew *Jeconiah,* a variant of *Jehoiachin*; also in verse 17

21 The descendants of Hananiah:

Pelatiah and Jeshaiah, and the sons of Rephaiah, of Arnan, of Obadiah and of Shekaniah.

22 The descendants of Shekaniah:

Shemaiah and his sons:

Hattush, Igal, Bariah, Neariah and Shaphat — six in all.

23 The sons of Neariah:

Elioenai, Hizkiah and Azrikam — three in all.

24 The sons of Elioenai:

Hodaviah, Eliashib, Pelaiah, Akkub, Johanan, Delaiah and Anani — seven in all.

Other Clans of Judah

4 The descendants of Judah:

Perez, Hezron, Karmi, Hur and Shobal.

2 Reaiah son of Shobal was the father of Jahath, and Jahath the father of Ahumai and Lahad. These were the clans of the Zorathites.

3 These were the sons*a* of Etam:

Jezreel, Ishma and Idbash. Their sister was named Hazzelelponi. 4 Penuel was the father of Gedor, and Ezer the father of Hushah.

These were the descendants of Hur, the firstborn of Ephrathah and father*b* of Bethlehem.

5 Ashhur the father of Tekoa had two wives, Helah and Naarah.

6 Naarah bore him Ahuzzam, Hepher, Temeni and Haahashtari. These were the descendants of Naarah.

7 The sons of Helah:

Zereth, Zohar, Ethnan, 8 and Koz, who was the father of Anub and Hazzobebah and of the clans of Aharhel son of Harum.

9 Jabez was more honorable than his brothers. His mother had named him Jabez,*c* saying, "I gave birth to him in pain." 10 Jabez cried out to the God of Israel, "Oh, that you would bless me and enlarge my territory! Let your hand be with me, and keep me from harm so that I will be free from pain." And God granted his request.

11 Kelub, Shuhah's brother, was the father of Mehir, who was the father of Eshton. 12 Eshton was the father of Beth Rapha, Paseah and Tehinnah the father of Ir Nahash.*d* These were the men of Rekah.

13 The sons of Kenaz:

Othniel and Seraiah.

---

a 3 Some Septuagint manuscripts (see also Vulgate); Hebrew *father*   *b 4* *Father* may mean *civic leader* or *military leader*; also in verses 12, 14, 17, 18 and possibly elsewhere.   *c 9* *Jabez* sounds like the Hebrew for *pain*.   *d 12* Or *of the city of Nahash*

The sons of Othniel:
Hathath and Meonothai.[a]
[14] Meonothai was the father of Ophrah.

Seraiah was the father of Joab, the father of Ge Harashim.[b] It was called this because its people were skilled workers.

[15] The sons of Caleb son of Jephunneh:
Iru, Elah and Naam.

The son of Elah:
Kenaz.

[16] The sons of Jehallelel:
Ziph, Ziphah, Tiria and Asarel.

[17] The sons of Ezrah:
Jether, Mered, Epher and Jalon. One of Mered's wives gave birth to Miriam, Shammai and Ishbah the father of Eshtemoa. [18] (His wife from the tribe of Judah gave birth to Jered the father of Gedor, Heber the father of Soko, and Jekuthiel the father of Zanoah.) These were the children of Pharaoh's daughter Bithiah, whom Mered had married.

[19] The sons of Hodiah's wife, the sister of Naham:
the father of Keilah the Garmite, and Eshtemoa the Maakathite.

[20] The sons of Shimon:
Amnon, Rinnah, Ben-Hanan and Tilon.

The descendants of Ishi:
Zoheth and Ben-Zoheth.

[21] The sons of Shelah son of Judah:
Er the father of Lekah, Laadah the father of Mareshah and the clans of the linen workers at Beth Ashbea, [22] Jokim, the men of Kozeba, and Joash and Saraph, who ruled in Moab and Jashubi Lehem. (These records are from ancient times.) [23] They were the potters who lived at Netaim and Gederah; they stayed there and worked for the king.

Simeon

[24] The descendants of Simeon:
Nemuel, Jamin, Jarib, Zerah and Shaul;
[25] Shallum was Shaul's son, Mibsam his son and Mishma his son.

[26] The descendants of Mishma:
Hammuel his son, Zakkur his son and Shimei his son.

[27] Shimei had sixteen sons and six daughters, but his brothers did not have many children; so their entire clan did not become as numerous as the people of Judah. [28] They lived in Beersheba, Moladah, Hazar Shual, [29] Bilhah, Ezem, Tolad, [30] Bethuel, Hormah, Ziklag, [31] Beth Markaboth, Hazar Susim, Beth Biri and Shaaraim. These

---

[a] 13 Some Septuagint manuscripts and Vulgate; Hebrew does not have *and Meonothai.* [b] 14 *Ge Harashim* means *valley of skilled workers.*

were their towns until the reign of David. [32] Their surrounding villages were Etam, Ain, Rimmon, Token and Ashan—five towns— [33] and all the villages around these towns as far as Baalath.[a] These were their settlements. And they kept a genealogical record.

[34] Meshobab, Jamlech, Joshah son of Amaziah, [35] Joel, Jehu son of Joshibiah, the son of Seraiah, the son of Asiel, [36] also Elioenai, Jaakobah, Jeshohaiah, Asaiah, Adiel, Jesimiel, Benaiah, [37] and Ziza son of Shiphi, the son of Allon, the son of Jedaiah, the son of Shimri, the son of Shemaiah.

[38] The men listed above by name were leaders of their clans. Their families increased greatly, [39] and they went to the outskirts of Gedor to the east of the valley in search of pasture for their flocks. [40] They found rich, good pasture, and the land was spacious, peaceful and quiet. Some Hamites had lived there formerly.

[41] The men whose names were listed came in the days of Hezekiah king of Judah. They attacked the Hamites in their dwellings and also the Meunites who were there and completely destroyed[b] them, as is evident to this day. Then they settled in their place, because there was pasture for their flocks. [42] And five hundred of these Simeonites, led by Pelatiah, Neariah, Rephaiah and Uzziel, the sons of Ishi, invaded the hill country of Seir. [43] They killed the remaining Amalekites who had escaped, and they have lived there to this day.

Reuben

5 The sons of Reuben the firstborn of Israel (he was the firstborn, but when he defiled his father's marriage bed, his rights as firstborn were given to the sons of Joseph son of Israel; so he could not be listed in the genealogical record in accordance with his birthright, [2] and though Judah was the strongest of his brothers and a ruler came from him, the rights of the firstborn belonged to Joseph)— [3] the sons of Reuben the firstborn of Israel:

Hanok, Pallu, Hezron and Karmi.

[4] The descendants of Joel:

Shemaiah his son, Gog his son,

Shimei his son, [5] Micah his son,

Reaiah his son, Baal his son,

[6] and Beerah his son, whom Tiglath-Pileser[c] king of Assyria took into exile. Beerah was a leader of the Reubenites.

---

[a] 33 Some Septuagint manuscripts (see also Joshua 19:8); Hebrew *Baal*
[b] 41 The Hebrew term refers to the irrevocable giving over of things or persons to the LORD, often by totally destroying them.   [c] 6 Hebrew *Tilgath-Pilneser*, a variant of *Tiglath-Pileser*; also in verse 26

[7] Their relatives by clans, listed according to their genealogical records:

Jeiel the chief, Zechariah, [8] and Bela son of Azaz, the son of Shema, the son of Joel. They settled in the area from Aroer to Nebo and Baal Meon. [9] To the east they occupied the land up to the edge of the desert that extends to the Euphrates River, because their livestock had increased in Gilead.

[10] During Saul's reign they waged war against the Hagrites, who were defeated at their hands; they occupied the dwellings of the Hagrites throughout the entire region east of Gilead.

Gad

[11] The Gadites lived next to them in Bashan, as far as Salekah:

[12] Joel was the chief, Shapham the second, then Janai and Shaphat, in Bashan.

[13] Their relatives, by families, were:

Michael, Meshullam, Sheba, Jorai, Jakan, Zia and Eber — seven in all.

[14] These were the sons of Abihail son of Huri, the son of Jaroah, the son of Gilead, the son of Michael, the son of Jeshishai, the son of Jahdo, the son of Buz.

[15] Ahi son of Abdiel, the son of Guni, was head of their family.

[16] The Gadites lived in Gilead, in Bashan and its outlying villages, and on all the pasturelands of Sharon as far as they extended.

[17] All these were entered in the genealogical records during the reigns of Jotham king of Judah and Jeroboam king of Israel.

[18] The Reubenites, the Gadites and the half-tribe of Manasseh had 44,760 men ready for military service — able-bodied men who could handle shield and sword, who could use a bow, and who were trained for battle. [19] They waged war against the Hagrites, Jetur, Naphish and Nodab. [20] They were helped in fighting them, and God delivered the Hagrites and all their allies into their hands, because they cried out to him during the battle. He answered their prayers, because they trusted in him. [21] They seized the livestock of the Hagrites — fifty thousand camels, two hundred fifty thousand sheep and two thousand donkeys. They also took one hundred thousand people captive, [22] and many others fell slain, because the battle was God's. And they occupied the land until the exile.

The Half-Tribe of Manasseh

[23] The people of the half-tribe of Manasseh were numerous; they

settled in the land from Bashan to Baal Hermon, that is, to Senir (Mount Hermon).

24 These were the heads of their families: Epher, Ishi, Eliel, Azriel, Jeremiah, Hodaviah and Jahdiel. They were brave warriors, famous men, and heads of their families. 25 But they were unfaithful to the God of their ancestors and prostituted themselves to the gods of the peoples of the land, whom God had destroyed before them. 26 So the God of Israel stirred up the spirit of Pul king of Assyria (that is, Tiglath-Pileser king of Assyria), who took the Reubenites, the Gadites and the half-tribe of Manasseh into exile. He took them to Halah, Habor, Hara and the river of Gozan, where they are to this day.

Levi

6 *a* The sons of Levi:
  Gershon, Kohath and Merari.
2 The sons of Kohath:
  Amram, Izhar, Hebron and Uzziel.
3 The children of Amram:
  Aaron, Moses and Miriam.
  The sons of Aaron:
  Nadab, Abihu, Eleazar and Ithamar.
4 Eleazar was the father of Phinehas,
  Phinehas the father of Abishua,

5 Abishua the father of Bukki,
  Bukki the father of Uzzi,
6 Uzzi the father of Zerahiah,
  Zerahiah the father of Meraioth,
7 Meraioth the father of Amariah,
  Amariah the father of Ahitub,
8 Ahitub the father of Zadok,
  Zadok the father of Ahimaaz,
9 Ahimaaz the father of Azariah,
  Azariah the father of Johanan,
10 Johanan the father of Azariah (it was he who served as priest in the temple Solomon built in Jerusalem),
11 Azariah the father of Amariah,
  Amariah the father of Ahitub,
12 Ahitub the father of Zadok,
  Zadok the father of Shallum,
13 Shallum the father of Hilkiah,
  Hilkiah the father of Azariah,
14 Azariah the father of Seraiah,
  and Seraiah the father of Jozadak. *b*
15 Jozadak was deported when the Lord sent Judah and Jerusalem into exile by the hand of Nebuchadnezzar.

---

a In Hebrew texts 6:1-15 is numbered 5:27-41, and 6:16-81 is numbered 6:1-66.
b 14 Hebrew *Jehozadak*, a variant of *Jozadak*; also in verse 15

¹⁶The sons of Levi:

Gershon,^{*a*} Kohath and Merari.

¹⁷These are the names of the sons of Gershon:

Libni and Shimei.

¹⁸The sons of Kohath:

Amram, Izhar, Hebron and Uzziel.

¹⁹The sons of Merari:

Mahli and Mushi.

These are the clans of the Levites listed according to their fathers:

²⁰Of Gershon:

Libni his son, Jahath his son,

Zimmah his son, ²¹Joah his son,

Iddo his son, Zerah his son and Jeatherai his son.

²²The descendants of Kohath:

Amminadab his son, Korah his son,

Assir his son, ²³Elkanah his son,

Ebiasaph his son, Assir his son,

²⁴Tahath his son, Uriel his son,

Uzziah his son and Shaul his son.

²⁵The descendants of Elkanah:

Amasai, Ahimoth,

²⁶Elkanah his son,^{*b*} Zophai his son,

Nahath his son, ²⁷Eliab his son,

Jeroham his son, Elkanah his son

and Samuel his son.^{*c*}

²⁸The sons of Samuel:

Joel^{*d*} the firstborn

and Abijah the second son.

²⁹The descendants of Merari:

Mahli, Libni his son,

Shimei his son, Uzzah his son,

³⁰Shimea his son, Haggiah his son

and Asaiah his son.

The Temple Musicians

³¹These are the men David put in charge of the music in the house of the LORD after the ark came to rest there. ³²They ministered with music before the tabernacle, the tent of meeting, until Solomon built the temple of the LORD in Jerusalem. They performed their duties according to the regulations laid down for them.

³³Here are the men who served, together with their sons:

From the Kohathites:

Heman, the musician,

the son of Joel, the son of Samuel,

³⁴the son of Elkanah, the son of Jeroham,

---

^{*a*} 16 Hebrew *Gershom,* a variant of *Gershon;* also in verses 17, 20, 43, 62 and 71
^{*b*} 26 Some Hebrew manuscripts, Septuagint and Syriac; most Hebrew manuscripts *Ahimoth* ²⁶*and Elkanah. The sons of Elkanah:* ^{*c*} 27 Some Septuagint manuscripts (see also 1 Samuel 1:19,20 and 1 Chron. 6:33,34); Hebrew does not have *and Samuel his son.* ^{*d*} 28 Some Septuagint manuscripts and Syriac (see also 1 Samuel 8:2 and 1 Chron. 6:33); Hebrew does not have *Joel.*

the son of Eliel, the son of
Toah,
³⁵ the son of Zuph, the son of
Elkanah,
the son of Mahath, the son
of Amasai,
³⁶ the son of Elkanah, the son
of Joel,
the son of Azariah, the son
of Zephaniah,
³⁷ the son of Tahath, the son
of Assir,
the son of Ebiasaph, the son
of Korah,
³⁸ the son of Izhar, the son of
Kohath,
the son of Levi, the son of
Israel;
³⁹ and Heman's associate
Asaph, who served at his
right hand:
Asaph son of Berekiah, the
son of Shimea,
⁴⁰ the son of Michael, the son
of Baaseiah,^a
the son of Malkijah, ⁴¹ the
son of Ethni,
the son of Zerah, the son of
Adaiah,
⁴² the son of Ethan, the son of
Zimmah,
the son of Shimei, ⁴³ the son
of Jahath,
the son of Gershon, the son
of Levi;
⁴⁴ and from their associates, the
Merarites, at his left hand:
Ethan son of Kishi, the son
of Abdi,

the son of Malluk, ⁴⁵ the son
of Hashabiah,
the son of Amaziah, the son
of Hilkiah,
⁴⁶ the son of Amzi, the son of
Bani,
the son of Shemer, ⁴⁷ the
son of Mahli,
the son of Mushi, the son of
Merari,
the son of Levi.

⁴⁸ Their fellow Levites were assigned to all the other duties of the tabernacle, the house of God. ⁴⁹ But Aaron and his descendants were the ones who presented offerings on the altar of burnt offering and on the altar of incense in connection with all that was done in the Most Holy Place, making atonement for Israel, in accordance with all that Moses the servant of God had commanded.

⁵⁰ These were the descendants
of Aaron:
Eleazar his son, Phinehas
his son,
Abishua his son, ⁵¹ Bukki
his son,
Uzzi his son, Zerahiah his
son,
⁵² Meraioth his son, Amariah
his son,
Ahitub his son, ⁵³ Zadok his
son
and Ahimaaz his son.

⁵⁴ These were the locations of
their settlements allotted as their

^a 40 Most Hebrew manuscripts; some Hebrew manuscripts, one Septuagint manuscript and Syriac *Maaseiah*

territory (they were assigned to the descendants of Aaron who were from the Kohathite clan, because the first lot was for them):

55 They were given Hebron in Judah with its surrounding pasturelands. **56** But the fields and villages around the city were given to Caleb son of Jephunneh.

57 So the descendants of Aaron were given Hebron (a city of refuge), and Libnah,[a] Jattir, Eshtemoa, **58** Hilen, Debir, **59** Ashan, Juttah[b] and Beth Shemesh, together with their pasturelands. **60** And from the tribe of Benjamin they were given Gibeon,[c] Geba, Alemeth and Anathoth, together with their pasturelands.

The total number of towns distributed among the Kohathite clans came to thirteen.

61 The rest of Kohath's descendants were allotted ten towns from the clans of half the tribe of Manasseh.

62 The descendants of Gershon, clan by clan, were allotted thirteen towns from the tribes of Issachar, Asher and Naphtali, and from the part of the tribe of Manasseh that is in Bashan.

63 The descendants of Merari, clan by clan, were allotted twelve towns from the tribes of Reuben, Gad and Zebulun.

64 So the Israelites gave the Levites these towns and their pasturelands. **65** From the tribes of Judah, Simeon and Benjamin they allotted the previously named towns.

66 Some of the Kohathite clans were given as their territory towns from the tribe of Ephraim.

67 In the hill country of Ephraim they were given Shechem (a city of refuge), and Gezer,[d] **68** Jokmeam, Beth Horon, **69** Aijalon and Gath Rimmon, together with their pasturelands.

70 And from half the tribe of Manasseh the Israelites gave Aner and Bileam, together with their pasturelands, to the rest of the Kohathite clans.

71 The Gershonites received the following:

From the clan of the half-tribe of Manasseh
they received Golan in Bashan and also Ashtaroth, together with their pasturelands;
72 from the tribe of Issachar
they received Kedesh, Daberath, **73** Ramoth and Anem, together with their pasturelands;
74 from the tribe of Asher
they received Mashal,

---

[a] 57 See Joshua 21:13; Hebrew *given the cities of refuge: Hebron, Libnah.*
[b] 59 Syriac (see also Septuagint and Joshua 21:16); Hebrew does not have *Juttah*.
[c] 60 See Joshua 21:17; Hebrew does not have *Gibeon*. [d] 67 See Joshua 21:21; Hebrew *given the cities of refuge: Shechem, Gezer.*

Abdon, [75]Hukok and Rehob, together with their pasturelands;

[76]and from the tribe of Naphtali they received Kedesh in Galilee, Hammon and Kiriathaim, together with their pasturelands.

[77]The Merarites (the rest of the Levites) received the following:

From the tribe of Zebulun they received Jokneam, Kartah,[a] Rimmono and Tabor, together with their pasturelands;

[78]from the tribe of Reuben across the Jordan east of Jericho

they received Bezer in the wilderness, Jahzah, [79]Kedemoth and Mephaath, together with their pasturelands;

[80]and from the tribe of Gad they received Ramoth in Gilead, Mahanaim, [81]Heshbon and Jazer, together with their pasturelands.

Issachar

7 The sons of Issachar:
Tola, Puah, Jashub and Shimron — four in all.
[2]The sons of Tola:
Uzzi, Rephaiah, Jeriel, Jahmai, Ibsam and Samuel — heads of their families. During the reign of David, the descendants of Tola listed as fighting men in their genealogy numbered 22,600.

[3]The son of Uzzi:
Izrahiah.
The sons of Izrahiah:
Michael, Obadiah, Joel and Ishiah. All five of them were chiefs. [4]According to their family genealogy, they had 36,000 men ready for battle, for they had many wives and children.

[5]The relatives who were fighting men belonging to all the clans of Issachar, as listed in their genealogy, were 87,000 in all.

Benjamin

[6]Three sons of Benjamin:
Bela, Beker and Jediael.
[7]The sons of Bela:
Ezbon, Uzzi, Uzziel, Jerimoth and Iri, heads of families — five in all. Their genealogical record listed 22,034 fighting men.

[8]The sons of Beker:
Zemirah, Joash, Eliezer, Elioenai, Omri, Jeremoth, Abijah, Anathoth and Alemeth. All these were the sons of Beker. [9]Their genealogical record listed the heads of families and 20,200 fighting men.

[10]The son of Jediael:
Bilhan.

---

[a] 77 See Septuagint and Joshua 21:34; Hebrew does not have *Jokneam, Kartah*.

The sons of Bilhan:

Jeush, Benjamin, Ehud, Kenaanah, Zethan, Tarshish and Ahishahar. [11]All these sons of Jediael were heads of families. There were 17,200 fighting men ready to go out to war. [12]The Shuppites and Huppites were the descendants of Ir, and the Hushites[a] the descendants of Aher.

Naphtali

[13]The sons of Naphtali:

Jahziel, Guni, Jezer and Shillem[b] — the descendants of Bilhah.

Manasseh

[14]The descendants of Manasseh:

Asriel was his descendant through his Aramean concubine. She gave birth to Makir the father of Gilead. [15]Makir took a wife from among the Huppites and Shuppites. His sister's name was Maakah.

Another descendant was named Zelophehad, who had only daughters.

[16]Makir's wife Maakah gave birth to a son and named him Peresh. His brother was named Sheresh, and his sons were Ulam and Rakem.

[17]The son of Ulam:

Bedan.

These were the sons of Gilead son of Makir, the son of Manasseh. [18]His sister Hammoleketh gave birth to Ishhod, Abiezer and Mahlah.

[19]The sons of Shemida were:

Ahian, Shechem, Likhi and Aniam.

Ephraim

[20]The descendants of Ephraim:

Shuthelah, Bered his son,
Tahath his son, Eleadah his son,
Tahath his son, [21]Zabad his son
and Shuthelah his son.

Ezer and Elead were killed by the native-born men of Gath, when they went down to seize their livestock. [22]Their father Ephraim mourned for them many days, and his relatives came to comfort him. [23]Then he made love to his wife again, and she became pregnant and gave birth to a son. He named him Beriah,[c] because there had been misfortune in his family. [24]His daughter was Sheerah, who built Lower and Upper Beth Horon as well as Uzzen Sheerah.

---

[a] 12 Or *Ir. The sons of Dan: Hushim,* (see Gen. 46:23); Hebrew does not have *The sons of Dan.*   [b] 13 Some Hebrew and Septuagint manuscripts (see also Gen. 46:24 and Num. 26:49); most Hebrew manuscripts *Shallum*   [c] 23 *Beriah* sounds like the Hebrew for *misfortune.*

²⁵Rephah was his son, Resheph his son,[a]
Telah his son, Tahan his son,
²⁶Ladan his son, Ammihud his son,
Elishama his son, ²⁷Nun his son
and Joshua his son.

²⁸Their lands and settlements included Bethel and its surrounding villages, Naaran to the east, Gezer and its villages to the west, and Shechem and its villages all the way to Ayyah and its villages. ²⁹Along the borders of Manasseh were Beth Shan, Taanach, Megiddo and Dor, together with their villages. The descendants of Joseph son of Israel lived in these towns.

Asher

³⁰The sons of Asher:
Imnah, Ishvah, Ishvi and Beriah. Their sister was Serah.
³¹The sons of Beriah:
Heber and Malkiel, who was the father of Birzaith.
³²Heber was the father of Japhlet, Shomer and Hotham and of their sister Shua.
³³The sons of Japhlet:
Pasak, Bimhal and Ashvath.
These were Japhlet's sons.
³⁴The sons of Shomer:
Ahi, Rohgah,[b] Hubbah and Aram.

³⁵The sons of his brother Helem:
Zophah, Imna, Shelesh and Amal.
³⁶The sons of Zophah:
Suah, Harnepher, Shual, Beri, Imrah, ³⁷Bezer, Hod, Shamma, Shilshah, Ithran[c] and Beera.
³⁸The sons of Jether:
Jephunneh, Pispah and Ara.
³⁹The sons of Ulla:
Arah, Hanniel and Rizia.

⁴⁰All these were descendants of Asher—heads of families, choice men, brave warriors and outstanding leaders. The number of men ready for battle, as listed in their genealogy, was 26,000.

The Genealogy of Saul the Benjamite

8 Benjamin was the father of Bela his firstborn,
Ashbel the second son, Aharah the third,
²Nohah the fourth and Rapha the fifth.
³The sons of Bela were:
Addar, Gera, Abihud,[d]
⁴Abishua, Naaman, Ahoah,
⁵Gera, Shephuphan and Huram.
⁶These were the descendants of Ehud, who were heads of families of those living in Geba and were deported to Manahath:

---

[a] 25 Some Septuagint manuscripts; Hebrew does not have *his son.*   [b] 34 Or *of his brother Shomer: Rohgah*   [c] 37 Possibly a variant of *Jether*   [d] 3 Or *Gera the father of Ehud*

[7]Naaman, Ahijah, and Gera, who deported them and who was the father of Uzza and Ahihud.

[8]Sons were born to Shaharaim in Moab after he had divorced his wives Hushim and Baara. [9]By his wife Hodesh he had Jobab, Zibia, Mesha, Malkam, [10]Jeuz, Sakia and Mirmah. These were his sons, heads of families. [11]By Hushim he had Abitub and Elpaal.

[12]The sons of Elpaal:

Eber, Misham, Shemed (who built Ono and Lod with its surrounding villages), [13]and Beriah and Shema, who were heads of families of those living in Aijalon and who drove out the inhabitants of Gath.

[14]Ahio, Shashak, Jeremoth, [15]Zebadiah, Arad, Eder, [16]Michael, Ishpah and Joha were the sons of Beriah.

[17]Zebadiah, Meshullam, Hizki, Heber, [18]Ishmerai, Izliah and Jobab were the sons of Elpaal.

[19]Jakim, Zikri, Zabdi, [20]Elienai, Zillethai, Eliel, [21]Adaiah, Beraiah and Shimrath were the sons of Shimei.

[22]Ishpan, Eber, Eliel, [23]Abdon, Zikri, Hanan, [24]Hananiah, Elam, Anthothijah, [25]Iphdeiah and Penuel were the sons of Shashak.

[26]Shamsherai, Shehariah, Athaliah, [27]Jaareshiah, Elijah and Zikri were the sons of Jeroham.

[28]All these were heads of families, chiefs as listed in their genealogy, and they lived in Jerusalem.

[29]Jeiel[a] the father[b] of Gibeon lived in Gibeon.

His wife's name was Maakah, [30]and his firstborn son was Abdon, followed by Zur, Kish, Baal, Ner,[c] Nadab, [31]Gedor, Ahio, Zeker [32]and Mikloth, who was the father of Shimeah. They too lived near their relatives in Jerusalem.

[33]Ner was the father of Kish, Kish the father of Saul, and Saul the father of Jonathan, Malki-Shua, Abinadab and Esh-Baal.[d]

[34]The son of Jonathan:

Merib-Baal,[e] who was the father of Micah.

[35]The sons of Micah:

Pithon, Melek, Tarea and Ahaz.

[36]Ahaz was the father of Jehoaddah, Jehoaddah was the father of Alemeth, Azmaveth and Zimri, and Zimri was the father of Moza.

---

[a] 29 Some Septuagint manuscripts (see also 9:35); Hebrew does not have *Jeiel*.
[b] 29 *Father* may mean *civic leader* or *military leader*.   [c] 30 Some Septuagint manuscripts (see also 9:36); Hebrew does not have *Ner*.   [d] 33 Also known as *Ish-Bosheth*   [e] 34 Also known as *Mephibosheth*

37 Moza was the father of Binea; Raphah was his son, Eleasah his son and Azel his son.

38 Azel had six sons, and these were their names:

Azrikam, Bokeru, Ishmael, Sheariah, Obadiah and Hanan. All these were the sons of Azel.

39 The sons of his brother Eshek:

Ulam his firstborn, Jeush the second son and Eliphelet the third. **40** The sons of Ulam were brave warriors who could handle the bow. They had many sons and grandsons — 150 in all.

All these were the descendants of Benjamin.

9 All Israel was listed in the genealogies recorded in the book of the kings of Israel and Judah. They were taken captive to Babylon because of their unfaithfulness.

The People in Jerusalem

2 Now the first to resettle on their own property in their own towns were some Israelites, priests, Levites and temple servants.

3 Those from Judah, from Benjamin, and from Ephraim and Manasseh who lived in Jerusalem were:

4 Uthai son of Ammihud, the son of Omri, the son of Imri, the son of Bani, a descendant of Perez son of Judah.

5 Of the Shelanites[a]:

Asaiah the firstborn and his sons.

6 Of the Zerahites:

Jeuel.

The people from Judah numbered 690.

7 Of the Benjamites:

Sallu son of Meshullam, the son of Hodaviah, the son of Hassenuah;

8 Ibneiah son of Jeroham; Elah son of Uzzi, the son of Mikri; and Meshullam son of Shephatiah, the son of Reuel, the son of Ibnijah.

9 The people from Benjamin, as listed in their genealogy, numbered 956. All these men were heads of their families.

10 Of the priests:

Jedaiah; Jehoiarib; Jakin;

11 Azariah son of Hilkiah, the son of Meshullam, the son of Zadok, the son of Meraioth, the son of Ahitub, the official in charge of the house of God;

12 Adaiah son of Jeroham, the son of Pashhur, the son of Malkijah; and Maasai son of Adiel, the son of Jahzerah, the son of Meshullam, the son of Meshillemith, the son of Immer.

13 The priests, who were heads of families, num-

---

a 5 See Num. 26:20; Hebrew *Shilonites*.

bered 1,760. They were able men, responsible for ministering in the house of God.

¹⁴Of the Levites:

Shemaiah son of Hasshub, the son of Azrikam, the son of Hashabiah, a Merarite; ¹⁵Bakbakkar, Heresh, Galal and Mattaniah son of Mika, the son of Zikri, the son of Asaph; ¹⁶Obadiah son of Shemaiah, the son of Galal, the son of Jeduthun; and Berekiah son of Asa, the son of Elkanah, who lived in the villages of the Netophathites.

¹⁷The gatekeepers:

Shallum, Akkub, Talmon, Ahiman and their fellow Levites, Shallum their chief ¹⁸being stationed at the King's Gate on the east, up to the present time. These were the gatekeepers belonging to the camp of the Levites. ¹⁹Shallum son of Kore, the son of Ebiasaph, the son of Korah, and his fellow gatekeepers from his family (the Korahites) were responsible for guarding the thresholds of the tent just as their ancestors had been responsible for guarding the entrance to the dwelling of the LORD. ²⁰In earlier times Phinehas son of Eleazar was the official in charge of the gatekeepers, and the LORD was

with him. ²¹Zechariah son of Meshelemiah was the gatekeeper at the entrance to the tent of meeting.

²²Altogether, those chosen to be gatekeepers at the thresholds numbered 212. They were registered by genealogy in their villages. The gatekeepers had been assigned to their positions of trust by David and Samuel the seer. ²³They and their descendants were in charge of guarding the gates of the house of the LORD — the house called the tent of meeting. ²⁴The gatekeepers were on the four sides: east, west, north and south. ²⁵Their fellow Levites in their villages had to come from time to time and share their duties for seven-day periods. ²⁶But the four principal gatekeepers, who were Levites, were entrusted with the responsibility for the rooms and treasuries in the house of God. ²⁷They would spend the night stationed around the house of God, because they had to guard it; and they had charge of the key for opening it each morning.

²⁸Some of them were in charge of the articles used in the temple service; they counted them when they were brought in and when they were taken out. ²⁹Others were assigned to take care of the furnishings and all the other articles of the sanctuary, as well as the special flour and wine, and the olive oil, incense and

spices. ³⁰But some of the priests took care of mixing the spices. ³¹A Levite named Mattithiah, the firstborn son of Shallum the Korahite, was entrusted with the responsibility for baking the offering bread. ³²Some of the Kohathites, their fellow Levites, were in charge of preparing for every Sabbath the bread set out on the table.

³³Those who were musicians, heads of Levite families, stayed in the rooms of the temple and were exempt from other duties because they were responsible for the work day and night.

³⁴All these were heads of Levite families, chiefs as listed in their genealogy, and they lived in Jerusalem.

The Genealogy of Saul

³⁵Jeiel the father*a* of Gibeon lived in Gibeon.

His wife's name was Maakah, ³⁶and his firstborn son was Abdon, followed by Zur, Kish, Baal, Ner, Nadab, ³⁷Gedor, Ahio, Zechariah and Mikloth. ³⁸Mikloth was the father of Shimeam. They too lived near their relatives in Jerusalem.

³⁹Ner was the father of Kish, Kish the father of Saul, and Saul the father of Jonathan, Malki-Shua, Abinadab and Esh-Baal.*b*

⁴⁰The son of Jonathan:
Merib-Baal,*c* who was the father of Micah.

⁴¹The sons of Micah:
Pithon, Melek, Tahrea and Ahaz.*d*

⁴²Ahaz was the father of Jadah, Jadah*e* was the father of Alemeth, Azmaveth and Zimri, and Zimri was the father of Moza. ⁴³Moza was the father of Binea; Rephaiah was his son, Eleasah his son and Azel his son.

⁴⁴Azel had six sons, and these were their names:
Azrikam, Bokeru, Ishmael, Sheariah, Obadiah and Hanan. These were the sons of Azel.

Saul Takes His Life

10 Now the Philistines fought against Israel; the Israelites fled before them, and many fell dead on Mount Gilboa. ²The Philistines were in hot pursuit of Saul and his sons, and they killed his sons Jonathan, Abinadab and Malki-Shua. ³The fighting grew fierce around Saul, and when the archers overtook him, they wounded him.

⁴Saul said to his armor-bearer, "Draw your sword and run me

---

a 35 *Father* may mean *civic leader* or *military leader.*   *b* 39 Also known as *Ish-Bosheth*   *c* 40 Also known as *Mephibosheth*   *d* 41 Vulgate and Syriac (see also Septuagint and 8:35); Hebrew does not have *and Ahaz.*   *e* 42 Some Hebrew manuscripts and Septuagint (see also 8:36); most Hebrew manuscripts *Jarah, Jarah* through, or these uncircumcised fellows will come and abuse me."

But his armor-bearer was terrified and would not do it; so Saul took his own sword and fell on it. ⁵When the armor-bearer saw that Saul was dead, he too fell on his sword and died. ⁶So Saul and his three sons died, and all his house died together.

⁷When all the Israelites in the valley saw that the army had fled and that Saul and his sons had died, they abandoned their towns and fled. And the Philistines came and occupied them.

⁸The next day, when the Philistines came to strip the dead, they found Saul and his sons fallen on Mount Gilboa. ⁹They stripped him and took his head and his armor, and sent messengers throughout the land of the Philistines to proclaim the news among their idols and their people. ¹⁰They put his armor in the temple of their gods and hung up his head in the temple of Dagon.

¹¹When all the inhabitants of Jabesh Gilead heard what the Philistines had done to Saul, ¹²all their valiant men went and took the bodies of Saul and his sons and brought them to Jabesh. Then they buried their bones under the great tree in Jabesh, and they fasted seven days.

¹³Saul died because he was unfaithful to the LORD; he did not keep the word of the LORD and even consulted a medium for guidance, ¹⁴and did not inquire of the LORD. So the LORD put him to death and turned the kingdom over to David son of Jesse.

David Becomes King Over Israel

11 All Israel came together to David at Hebron and said, "We are your own flesh and blood. ²In the past, even while Saul was king, you were the one who led Israel on their military campaigns. And the LORD your God said to you, 'You will shepherd my people Israel, and you will become their ruler.'"

³When all the elders of Israel had come to King David at Hebron, he made a covenant with them at Hebron before the LORD, and they anointed David king over Israel, as the LORD had promised through Samuel.

David Conquers Jerusalem

⁴David and all the Israelites marched to Jerusalem (that is, Jebus). The Jebusites who lived there ⁵said to David, "You will not get in here." Nevertheless, David captured the fortress of Zion—which is the City of David.

⁶David had said, "Whoever leads the attack on the Jebusites will become commander-in-chief." Joab son of Zeruiah went up first, and so he received the command.

⁷David then took up residence in the fortress, and so it was called the City of David. ⁸He

built up the city around it, from the terraces*a* to the surrounding wall, while Joab restored the rest of the city. **9** And David became more and more powerful, because the LORD Almighty was with him.

David's Mighty Warriors

10 These were the chiefs of David's mighty warriors — they, together with all Israel, gave his kingship strong support to extend it over the whole land, as the LORD had promised — **11** this is the list of David's mighty warriors:

Jashobeam,*b* a Hakmonite, was chief of the officers*c*; he raised his spear against three hundred men, whom he killed in one encounter.

12 Next to him was Eleazar son of Dodai the Ahohite, one of the three mighty warriors. **13** He was with David at Pas Dammim when the Philistines gathered there for battle. At a place where there was a field full of barley, the troops fled from the Philistines. **14** But they took their stand in the middle of the field. They defended it and struck the Philistines down, and the LORD brought about a great victory.

15 Three of the thirty chiefs came down to David to the rock at the cave of Adullam, while a band of Philistines was encamped in the Valley of Rephaim. **16** At that time David was in the stronghold, and the Philistine garrison was at Bethlehem. **17** David longed for water and said, "Oh, that someone would get me a drink of water from the well near the gate of Bethlehem!" **18** So the Three broke through the Philistine lines, drew water from the well near the gate of Bethlehem and carried it back to David. But he refused to drink it; instead, he poured it out to the LORD. **19** "God forbid that I should do this!" he said. "Should I drink the blood of these men who went at the risk of their lives?" Because they risked their lives to bring it back, David would not drink it.

Such were the exploits of the three mighty warriors.

20 Abishai the brother of Joab was chief of the Three. He raised his spear against three hundred men, whom he killed, and so he became as famous as the Three. **21** He was doubly honored above the Three and became their commander, even though he was not included among them.

22 Benaiah son of Jehoiada, a valiant fighter from Kabzeel, performed great exploits. He struck down Moab's two mightiest warriors. He also went down into a pit on a snowy day and killed a lion. **23** And he struck down an Egyptian who was five cubits*d* tall. Although

---

a 8 Or *the Millo*   *b 11* Possibly a variant of *Jashob-Baal*   *c 11* Or *Thirty*; some Septuagint manuscripts *Three* (see also 2 Samuel 23:8)   *d 23* That is, about 7 feet 6 inches or about 2.3 meters the Egyptian had a spear like a weaver's rod in his hand, Benaiah went against him with a club. He snatched the spear from the Egyptian's hand and killed him with his own spear. ²⁴Such were the exploits of Benaiah son of Jehoiada; he too was as famous as the three mighty warriors. ²⁵He was held in greater honor than any of the Thirty, but he was not included among the Three. And David put him in charge of his bodyguard.

²⁶The mighty warriors were:
 Asahel the brother of Joab,
 Elhanan son of Dodo from Bethlehem,
²⁷Shammoth the Harorite,
 Helez the Pelonite,
²⁸Ira son of Ikkesh from Tekoa,
 Abiezer from Anathoth,
²⁹Sibbekai the Hushathite,
 Ilai the Ahohite,
³⁰Maharai the Netophathite,
 Heled son of Baanah the Netophathite,
³¹Ithai son of Ribai from Gibeah in Benjamin,
 Benaiah the Pirathonite,
³²Hurai from the ravines of Gaash,
 Abiel the Arbathite,
³³Azmaveth the Baharumite,
 Eliahba the Shaalbonite,
³⁴the sons of Hashem the Gizonite,
 Jonathan son of Shagee the Hararite,
³⁵Ahiam son of Sakar the Hararite,

Eliphal son of Ur,
³⁶Hepher the Mekerathite,
 Ahijah the Pelonite,
³⁷Hezro the Carmelite,
 Naarai son of Ezbai,
³⁸Joel the brother of Nathan,
 Mibhar son of Hagri,
³⁹Zelek the Ammonite,
 Naharai the Berothite, the armor-bearer of Joab son of Zeruiah,
⁴⁰Ira the Ithrite,
 Gareb the Ithrite,
⁴¹Uriah the Hittite,
 Zabad son of Ahlai,
⁴²Adina son of Shiza the Reubenite, who was chief of the Reubenites, and the thirty with him,
⁴³Hanan son of Maakah,
 Joshaphat the Mithnite,
⁴⁴Uzzia the Ashterathite,
 Shama and Jeiel the sons of Hotham the Aroerite,
⁴⁵Jediael son of Shimri,
 his brother Joha the Tizite,
⁴⁶Eliel the Mahavite,
 Jeribai and Joshaviah the sons of Elnaam,
 Ithmah the Moabite,
⁴⁷Eliel, Obed and Jaasiel the Mezobaite.

Warriors Join David

12 These were the men who came to David at Ziklag, while he was banished from the presence of Saul son of Kish (they were among the warriors who helped him in battle; ²they were armed with bows and were able to shoot arrows or to sling stones right-handed or left-handed; they were relatives of Saul from the tribe of Benjamin):

³Ahiezer their chief and Joash the sons of Shemaah the Gibeathite; Jeziel and Pelet the sons of Azmaveth; Berakah, Jehu the Anathothite, ⁴and Ishmaiah the Gibeonite, a mighty warrior among the Thirty, who was a leader of the Thirty; Jeremiah, Jahaziel, Johanan, Jozabad the Gederathite,ᵃ ⁵Eluzai, Jerimoth, Bealiah, Shemariah and Shephatiah the Haruphite; ⁶Elkanah, Ishiah, Azarel, Joezer and Jashobeam the Korahites; ⁷and Joelah and Zebadiah the sons of Jeroham from Gedor.

⁸Some Gadites defected to David at his stronghold in the wilderness. They were brave warriors, ready for battle and able to handle the shield and spear. Their faces were the faces of lions, and they were as swift as gazelles in the mountains.

⁹Ezer was the chief,
Obadiah the second in command, Eliab the third,
¹⁰Mishmannah the fourth, Jeremiah the fifth,
¹¹Attai the sixth, Eliel the seventh,
¹²Johanan the eighth, Elzabad the ninth,
¹³Jeremiah the tenth and Makbannai the eleventh.

¹⁴These Gadites were army commanders; the least was a match for a hundred, and the greatest for a thousand. ¹⁵It was they who crossed the Jordan in the first month when it was overflowing all its banks, and they put to flight everyone living in the valleys, to the east and to the west.

¹⁶Other Benjamites and some men from Judah also came to David in his stronghold. ¹⁷David went out to meet them and said to them, "If you have come to me in peace to help me, I am ready for you to join me. But if you have come to betray me to my enemies when my hands are free from violence, may the God of our ancestors see it and judge you."

¹⁸Then the Spirit came on Amasai, chief of the Thirty, and he said:

"We are yours, David!
  We are with you, son of Jesse!
Success, success to you,
  and success to those who
    help you,
    for your God will help
      you."

So David received them and made them leaders of his raiding bands.

¹⁹Some of the tribe of Manasseh defected to David when he

ᵃ 4 In Hebrew texts the second half of this verse (*Jeremiah . . . Gederathite*) is numbered 12:5, and 12:5-40 is numbered 12:6-41.

went with the Philistines to fight against Saul. (He and his men did not help the Philistines because, after consultation, their rulers sent him away. They said, "It will cost us our heads if he deserts to his master Saul.") **20**When David went to Ziklag, these were the men of Manasseh who defected to him: Adnah, Jozabad, Jediael, Michael, Jozabad, Elihu and Zillethai, leaders of units of a thousand in Manasseh. **21**They helped David against raiding bands, for all of them were brave warriors, and they were commanders in his army. **22**Day after day men came to help David, until he had a great army, like the army of God.[a]

Others Join David at Hebron

23These are the numbers of the men armed for battle who came to David at Hebron to turn Saul's kingdom over to him, as the Lord had said:

24from Judah, carrying shield and spear — 6,800 armed for battle;

25from Simeon, warriors ready for battle — 7,100;

26from Levi — 4,600, **27**including Jehoiada, leader of the family of Aaron, with 3,700 men, **28**and Zadok, a brave young warrior, with 22 officers from his family;

29from Benjamin, Saul's tribe — 3,000, most of whom had

remained loyal to Saul's house until then;

30from Ephraim, brave warriors, famous in their own clans — 20,800;

31from half the tribe of Manasseh, designated by name to come and make David king — 18,000;

32from Issachar, men who understood the times and knew what Israel should do — 200 chiefs, with all their relatives under their command;

33from Zebulun, experienced soldiers prepared for battle with every type of weapon, to help David with undivided loyalty — 50,000;

34from Naphtali — 1,000 officers, together with 37,000 men carrying shields and spears;

35from Dan, ready for battle — 28,600;

36from Asher, experienced soldiers prepared for battle — 40,000;

37and from east of the Jordan, from Reuben, Gad and the half-tribe of Manasseh, armed with every type of weapon — 120,000.

38All these were fighting men who volunteered to serve in the ranks. They came to Hebron fully determined to make David king over all Israel. All the rest of the Israelites were also of one

[a] 22 Or *a great and mighty army*

mind to make David king. ³⁹ The men spent three days there with David, eating and drinking, for their families had supplied provisions for them. ⁴⁰ Also, their neighbors from as far away as Issachar, Zebulun and Naphtali came bringing food on donkeys, camels, mules and oxen. There were plentiful supplies of flour, fig cakes, raisin cakes, wine, olive oil, cattle and sheep, for there was joy in Israel.

Bringing Back the Ark

13 David conferred with each of his officers, the commanders of thousands and commanders of hundreds. ² He then said to the whole assembly of Israel, "If it seems good to you and if it is the will of the LORD our God, let us send word far and wide to the rest of our people throughout the territories of Israel, and also to the priests and Levites who are with them in their towns and pasturelands, to come and join us. ³ Let us bring the ark of our God back to us, for we did not inquire of ᵃ it ᵇ during the reign of Saul." ⁴ The whole assembly agreed to do this, because it seemed right to all the people.

⁵ So David assembled all Israel, from the Shihor River in Egypt to Lebo Hamath, to bring the ark of God from Kiriath Jearim. ⁶ David and all Israel went to Baalah of Judah (Kiriath Jearim) to bring up from there the ark of God the LORD, who is enthroned between the cherubim—the ark that is called by the Name.

⁷ They moved the ark of God from Abinadab's house on a new cart, with Uzzah and Ahio guiding it. ⁸ David and all the Israelites were celebrating with all their might before God, with songs and with harps, lyres, timbrels, cymbals and trumpets.

⁹ When they came to the threshing floor of Kidon, Uzzah reached out his hand to steady the ark, because the oxen stumbled. ¹⁰ The LORD's anger burned against Uzzah, and he struck him down because he had put his hand on the ark. So he died there before God.

¹¹ Then David was angry because the LORD's wrath had broken out against Uzzah, and to this day that place is called Perez Uzzah.ᶜ

¹² David was afraid of God that day and asked, "How can I ever bring the ark of God to me?" ¹³ He did not take the ark to be with him in the City of David. Instead, he took it to the house of Obed-Edom the Gittite. ¹⁴ The ark of God remained with the family of Obed-Edom in his house for three months, and the LORD blessed his household and everything he had.

ᵃ 3 Or *we neglected*   ᵇ 3 Or *him*   ᶜ 11 *Perez Uzzah* means *outbreak against Uzzah.*

David's House and Family

14 Now Hiram king of Tyre sent messengers to David, along with cedar logs, stonemasons and carpenters to build a palace for him. ²And David knew that the LORD had established him as king over Israel and that his kingdom had been highly exalted for the sake of his people Israel.

³In Jerusalem David took more wives and became the father of more sons and daughters. ⁴These are the names of the children born to him there: Shammua, Shobab, Nathan, Solomon, ⁵Ibhar, Elishua, Elpelet, ⁶Nogah, Nepheg, Japhia, ⁷Elishama, Beeliada*a* and Eliphelet.

David Defeats the Philistines

⁸When the Philistines heard that David had been anointed king over all Israel, they went up in full force to search for him, but David heard about it and went out to meet them. ⁹Now the Philistines had come and raided the Valley of Rephaim; ¹⁰so David inquired of God: "Shall I go and attack the Philistines? Will you deliver them into my hands?"

The LORD answered him, "Go, I will deliver them into your hands."

¹¹So David and his men went up to Baal Perazim, and there he defeated them. He said, "As waters break out, God has broken out against my enemies by my hand." So that place was called Baal Perazim.*b* ¹²The Philistines had abandoned their gods there, and David gave orders to burn them in the fire.

¹³Once more the Philistines raided the valley; ¹⁴so David inquired of God again, and God answered him, "Do not go directly after them, but circle around them and attack them in front of the poplar trees. ¹⁵As soon as you hear the sound of marching in the tops of the poplar trees, move out to battle, because that will mean God has gone out in front of you to strike the Philistine army." ¹⁶So David did as God commanded him, and they struck down the Philistine army, all the way from Gibeon to Gezer.

¹⁷So David's fame spread throughout every land, and the LORD made all the nations fear him.

The Ark Brought to Jerusalem

15 After David had constructed buildings for himself in the City of David, he prepared a place for the ark of God and pitched a tent for it. ²Then David said, "No one but the Levites may carry the ark of God, because the LORD chose them to carry the ark of the LORD and to minister before him forever."

---

a 7 A variant of *Eliada*   *b 11* *Baal Perazim* means *the lord who breaks out.*

³David assembled all Israel in Jerusalem to bring up the ark of the LORD to the place he had prepared for it. ⁴He called together the descendants of Aaron and the Levites:

⁵From the descendants of Kohath,
Uriel the leader and 120 relatives;
⁶from the descendants of Merari,
Asaiah the leader and 220 relatives;
⁷from the descendants of Gershon,ᵃ
Joel the leader and 130 relatives;
⁸from the descendants of Elizaphan,
Shemaiah the leader and 200 relatives;
⁹from the descendants of Hebron,
Eliel the leader and 80 relatives;
¹⁰from the descendants of Uzziel,
Amminadab the leader and 112 relatives.

¹¹Then David summoned Zadok and Abiathar the priests, and Uriel, Asaiah, Joel, Shemaiah, Eliel and Amminadab the Levites. ¹²He said to them, "You are the heads of the Levitical families; you and your fellow Levites are to consecrate yourselves and bring up the ark of the LORD, the God of Israel, to the place I have prepared for it. ¹³It was because you, the Levites, did not bring it up the first time that the LORD our God broke out in anger against us. We did not inquire of him about how to do it in the prescribed way." ¹⁴So the priests and Levites consecrated themselves in order to bring up the ark of the LORD, the God of Israel. ¹⁵And the Levites carried the ark of God with the poles on their shoulders, as Moses had commanded in accordance with the word of the LORD.

¹⁶David told the leaders of the Levites to appoint their fellow Levites as musicians to make a joyful sound with musical instruments: lyres, harps and cymbals.

¹⁷So the Levites appointed Heman son of Joel; from his relatives, Asaph son of Berekiah; and from their relatives the Merarites, Ethan son of Kushaiah; ¹⁸and with them their relatives next in rank: Zechariah,ᵇ Jaaziel, Shemiramoth, Jehiel, Unni, Eliab, Benaiah, Maaseiah, Mattithiah, Eliphelehu, Mikneiah, Obed-Edom and Jeiel,ᶜ the gatekeepers. ¹⁹The musicians Heman, Asaph and Ethan were to sound the bronze cymbals; ²⁰Zechariah, Jaaziel,ᵈ Shemiramoth, Jehiel, Unni,

---

ᵃ 7 Hebrew *Gershom*, a variant of *Gershon*   ᵇ 18 Three Hebrew manuscripts and most Septuagint manuscripts (see also verse 20 and 16:5); most Hebrew manuscripts *Zechariah son and* or *Zechariah, Ben and*   ᶜ 18 Hebrew; Septuagint (see also verse 21) *Jeiel and Azaziah*   ᵈ 20 See verse 18; Hebrew *Aziel*, a variant of *Jaaziel*.

Eliab, Maaseiah and Benaiah were to play the lyres according to *alamoth*,[a] 21 and Mattithiah, Eliphelehu, Mikneiah, Obed-Edom, Jeiel and Azaziah were to play the harps, directing according to *sheminith*.[a] 22 Kenaniah the head Levite was in charge of the singing; that was his responsibility because he was skillful at it.

23 Berekiah and Elkanah were to be doorkeepers for the ark. 24 Shebaniah, Joshaphat, Nethanel, Amasai, Zechariah, Benaiah and Eliezer the priests were to blow trumpets before the ark of God. Obed-Edom and Jehiah were also to be doorkeepers for the ark.

25 So David and the elders of Israel and the commanders of units of a thousand went to bring up the ark of the covenant of the LORD from the house of Obed-Edom, with rejoicing. 26 Because God had helped the Levites who were carrying the ark of the covenant of the LORD, seven bulls and seven rams were sacrificed. 27 Now David was clothed in a robe of fine linen, as were all the Levites who were carrying the ark, and as were the musicians, and Kenaniah, who was in charge of the singing of the choirs. David also wore a linen ephod. 28 So all Israel brought up the ark of the covenant of the LORD with shouts, with the sounding of rams' horns and trumpets, and of cymbals, and the playing of lyres and harps.

29 As the ark of the covenant of the LORD was entering the City of David, Michal daughter of Saul watched from a window. And when she saw King David dancing and celebrating, she despised him in her heart.

Ministering Before the Ark

16 They brought the ark of God and set it inside the tent that David had pitched for it, and they presented burnt offerings and fellowship offerings before God. 2 After David had finished sacrificing the burnt offerings and fellowship offerings, he blessed the people in the name of the LORD. 3 Then he gave a loaf of bread, a cake of dates and a cake of raisins to each Israelite man and woman.

4 He appointed some of the Levites to minister before the ark of the LORD, to extol,[b] thank, and praise the LORD, the God of Israel: 5 Asaph was the chief, and next to him in rank were Zechariah, then Jaaziel,[c] Shemiramoth, Jehiel, Mattithiah, Eliab, Benaiah, Obed-Edom and Jeiel. They were to play the lyres and harps, Asaph was to sound the cymbals, 6 and Benaiah and Jahaziel the priests were to blow the trumpets

---

[a] 20,21 Probably a musical term   [b] 4 Or *petition*; or *invoke*   [c] 5 See 15:18,20; Hebrew *Jeiel*, possibly another name for *Jaaziel*.

regularly before the ark of the covenant of God.

7 That day David first appointed Asaph and his associates to give praise to the LORD in this manner:

8 Give praise to the LORD,
    proclaim his name;
make known among the
    nations what he has done.
9 Sing to him, sing praise to him;
    tell of all his wonderful acts.
10 Glory in his holy name;
    let the hearts of those who
        seek the LORD rejoice.
11 Look to the LORD and his
        strength;
    seek his face always.

12 Remember the wonders he has
        done,
    his miracles, and the
        judgments he
        pronounced,
13 you his servants, the
        descendants of Israel,
    his chosen ones, the
        children of Jacob.
14 He is the LORD our God;
    his judgments are in all the
        earth.
15 He remembers[a] his covenant
        forever,
    the promise he made, for a
        thousand generations,
16 the covenant he made with
        Abraham,
    the oath he swore to Isaac.

17 He confirmed it to Jacob as a
        decree,
    to Israel as an everlasting
        covenant:
18 "To you I will give the land of
        Canaan
    as the portion you will
        inherit."

19 When they were but few in
        number,
    few indeed, and strangers in
        it,
20 they[b] wandered from nation to
        nation,
    from one kingdom to
        another.
21 He allowed no one to oppress
        them;
    for their sake he rebuked
        kings:
22 "Do not touch my anointed
        ones;
    do my prophets no harm."

23 Sing to the LORD, all the earth;
    proclaim his salvation day
        after day.
24 Declare his glory among the
        nations,
    his marvelous deeds among
        all peoples.

25 For great is the LORD and most
        worthy of praise;
    he is to be feared above all
        gods.
26 For all the gods of the nations
        are idols,

a 15 Some Septuagint manuscripts (see also Psalm 105:8); Hebrew Remember
b 18-20 One Hebrew manuscript, Septuagint and Vulgate (see also Psalm 105:12); most Hebrew manuscripts inherit, / 19though you are but few in number, / few indeed, and strangers in it." / 20They

but the Lord made the
heavens.
²⁷Splendor and majesty are
before him;
strength and joy are in his
dwelling place.

²⁸Ascribe to the Lord, all you
families of nations,
ascribe to the Lord glory
and strength.
²⁹Ascribe to the Lord the glory
due his name;
bring an offering and come
before him.
Worship the Lord in the
splendor of his*ᵃ holiness.
³⁰ Tremble before him, all the
earth!
The world is firmly
established; it cannot be
moved.

³¹Let the heavens rejoice, let the
earth be glad;
let them say among the
nations, "The Lord
reigns!"
³²Let the sea resound, and all
that is in it;
let the fields be jubilant, and
everything in them!
³³Let the trees of the forest sing,
let them sing for joy before
the Lord,
for he comes to judge the
earth.
³⁴Give thanks to the Lord, for he
is good;
his love endures forever.

³⁵Cry out, "Save us, God our
Savior;
gather us and deliver us from
the nations,
that we may give thanks to
your holy name,
and glory in your praise."
³⁶Praise be to the Lord, the God
of Israel,
from everlasting to
everlasting.

Then all the people said "Amen"
and "Praise the Lord."

³⁷David left Asaph and his associates before the ark of the covenant of the Lord to minister
there regularly, according to each
day's requirements. ³⁸He also left
Obed-Edom and his sixty-eight
associates to minister with them.
Obed-Edom son of Jeduthun, and
also Hosah, were gatekeepers.

³⁹David left Zadok the priest
and his fellow priests before the
tabernacle of the Lord at the
high place in Gibeon ⁴⁰to present burnt offerings to the Lord
on the altar of burnt offering regularly, morning and evening, in
accordance with everything written in the Law of the Lord, which
he had given Israel. ⁴¹With them
were Heman and Jeduthun and
the rest of those chosen and designated by name to give thanks
to the Lord, "for his love endures
forever." ⁴²Heman and Jeduthun
were responsible for the sounding of the trumpets and cymbals

ᵃ 29 Or Lord with the splendor of

and for the playing of the other instruments for sacred song. The sons of Jeduthun were stationed at the gate.

⁴³ Then all the people left, each for their own home, and David returned home to bless his family.

God's Promise to David

17 After David was settled in his palace, he said to Nathan the prophet, "Here I am, living in a house of cedar, while the ark of the covenant of the LORD is under a tent."

² Nathan replied to David, "Whatever you have in mind, do it, for God is with you."

³ But that night the word of God came to Nathan, saying:

⁴ "Go and tell my servant David, 'This is what the LORD says: You are not the one to build me a house to dwell in. ⁵ I have not dwelt in a house from the day I brought Israel up out of Egypt to this day. I have moved from one tent site to another, from one dwelling place to another. ⁶ Wherever I have moved with all the Israelites, did I ever say to any of their leaders*a* whom I commanded to shepherd my people, "Why have you not built me a house of cedar?"'

⁷ "Now then, tell my servant David, 'This is what the LORD Almighty says: I took you

from the pasture, from tending the flock, and appointed you ruler over my people Israel. ⁸ I have been with you wherever you have gone, and I have cut off all your enemies from before you. Now I will make your name like the names of the greatest men on earth. ⁹ And I will provide a place for my people Israel and will plant them so that they can have a home of their own and no longer be disturbed. Wicked people will not oppress them anymore, as they did at the beginning ¹⁰ and have done ever since the time I appointed leaders over my people Israel. I will also subdue all your enemies.

" 'I declare to you that the LORD will build a house for you: ¹¹ When your days are over and you go to be with your ancestors, I will raise up your offspring to succeed you, one of your own sons, and I will establish his kingdom. ¹² He is the one who will build a house for me, and I will establish his throne forever. ¹³ I will be his father, and he will be my son. I will never take my love away from him, as I took it away from your predecessor. ¹⁴ I will set him over my house and my kingdom forever; his throne will be established forever.' "

a 6 Traditionally *judges*; also in verse 10

[15] Nathan reported to David all the words of this entire revelation.

David's Prayer

[16] Then King David went in and sat before the LORD, and he said:

"Who am I, LORD God, and what is my family, that you have brought me this far? [17] And as if this were not enough in your sight, my God, you have spoken about the future of the house of your servant. You, LORD God, have looked on me as though I were the most exalted of men.

[18] "What more can David say to you for honoring your servant? For you know your servant, [19] LORD. For the sake of your servant and according to your will, you have done this great thing and made known all these great promises.

[20] "There is no one like you, LORD, and there is no God but you, as we have heard with our own ears. [21] And who is like your people Israel — the one nation on earth whose God went out to redeem a people for himself, and to make a name for yourself, and to perform great and awesome wonders by driving out nations from before your people, whom you redeemed from Egypt? [22] You made your people Israel your very own forever, and you, LORD, have become their God.

[23] "And now, LORD, let the promise you have made concerning your servant and his house be established forever. Do as you promised, [24] so that it will be established and that your name will be great forever. Then people will say, 'The LORD Almighty, the God over Israel, is Israel's God!' And the house of your servant David will be established before you.

[25] "You, my God, have revealed to your servant that you will build a house for him. So your servant has found courage to pray to you. [26] You, LORD, are God! You have promised these good things to your servant. [27] Now you have been pleased to bless the house of your servant, that it may continue forever in your sight; for you, LORD, have blessed it, and it will be blessed forever."

David's Victories

18 In the course of time, David defeated the Philistines and subdued them, and he took Gath and its surrounding villages from the control of the Philistines.

[2] David also defeated the Moabites, and they became subject to him and brought him tribute.

³Moreover, David defeated Hadadezer king of Zobah, in the vicinity of Hamath, when he went to set up his monument at[a] the Euphrates River. ⁴David captured a thousand of his chariots, seven thousand charioteers and twenty thousand foot soldiers. He hamstrung all but a hundred of the chariot horses.

⁵When the Arameans of Damascus came to help Hadadezer king of Zobah, David struck down twenty-two thousand of them. ⁶He put garrisons in the Aramean kingdom of Damascus, and the Arameans became subject to him and brought him tribute. The Lᴏʀᴅ gave David victory wherever he went.

⁷David took the gold shields carried by the officers of Hadadezer and brought them to Jerusalem. ⁸From Tebah[b] and Kun, towns that belonged to Hadadezer, David took a great quantity of bronze, which Solomon used to make the bronze Sea, the pillars and various bronze articles.

⁹When Tou king of Hamath heard that David had defeated the entire army of Hadadezer king of Zobah, ¹⁰he sent his son Hadoram to King David to greet him and congratulate him on his victory in battle over Hadadezer, who had been at war with Tou. Hadoram brought all kinds of articles of gold, of silver and of bronze.

¹¹King David dedicated these articles to the Lᴏʀᴅ, as he had done with the silver and gold he had taken from all these nations: Edom and Moab, the Ammonites and the Philistines, and Amalek.

¹²Abishai son of Zeruiah struck down eighteen thousand Edomites in the Valley of Salt. ¹³He put garrisons in Edom, and all the Edomites became subject to David. The Lᴏʀᴅ gave David victory wherever he went.

David's Officials

¹⁴David reigned over all Israel, doing what was just and right for all his people. ¹⁵Joab son of Zeruiah was over the army; Jehoshaphat son of Ahilud was recorder; ¹⁶Zadok son of Ahitub and Ahimelek[c] son of Abiathar were priests; Shavsha was secretary; ¹⁷Benaiah son of Jehoiada was over the Kerethites and Pelethites; and David's sons were chief officials at the king's side.

David Defeats the Ammonites

19 In the course of time, Nahash king of the Ammonites died, and his son succeeded him as king. ²David thought, "I will show kindness to Hanun son of Nahash, because his father showed kindness to me." So Da-

---

[a] 3 Or *to restore his control over*   [b] 8 Hebrew *Tibhath,* a variant of *Tebah*
[c] 16 Some Hebrew manuscripts, Vulgate and Syriac (see also 2 Samuel 8:17); most Hebrew manuscripts *Abimelek*

vid sent a delegation to express his sympathy to Hanun concerning his father.

When David's envoys came to Hanun in the land of the Ammonites to express sympathy to him, ³the Ammonite commanders said to Hanun, "Do you think David is honoring your father by sending envoys to you to express sympathy? Haven't his envoys come to you only to explore and spy out the country and overthrow it?" ⁴So Hanun seized David's envoys, shaved them, cut off their garments at the buttocks, and sent them away.

⁵When someone came and told David about the men, he sent messengers to meet them, for they were greatly humiliated. The king said, "Stay at Jericho till your beards have grown, and then come back."

⁶When the Ammonites realized that they had become obnoxious to David, Hanun and the Ammonites sent a thousand talents[a] of silver to hire chariots and charioteers from Aram Naharaim,[b] Aram Maakah and Zobah. ⁷They hired thirty-two thousand chariots and charioteers, as well as the king of Maakah with his troops, who came and camped near Medeba, while the Ammonites were mustered from their towns and moved out for battle.

⁸On hearing this, David sent Joab out with the entire army of fighting men. ⁹The Ammonites came out and drew up in battle formation at the entrance to their city, while the kings who had come were by themselves in the open country.

¹⁰Joab saw that there were battle lines in front of him and behind him; so he selected some of the best troops in Israel and deployed them against the Arameans. ¹¹He put the rest of the men under the command of Abishai his brother, and they were deployed against the Ammonites. ¹²Joab said, "If the Arameans are too strong for me, then you are to rescue me; but if the Ammonites are too strong for you, then I will rescue you. ¹³Be strong, and let us fight bravely for our people and the cities of our God. The LORD will do what is good in his sight."

¹⁴Then Joab and the troops with him advanced to fight the Arameans, and they fled before him. ¹⁵When the Ammonites realized that the Arameans were fleeing, they too fled before his brother Abishai and went inside the city. So Joab went back to Jerusalem.

¹⁶After the Arameans saw that they had been routed by Israel, they sent messengers and had Arameans brought from beyond the Euphrates River, with Shophak

---

[a] 6 That is, about 38 tons or about 34 metric tons   [b] 6 That is, Northwest Mesopotamia

the commander of Hadadezer's army leading them.

[17] When David was told of this, he gathered all Israel and crossed the Jordan; he advanced against them and formed his battle lines opposite them. David formed his lines to meet the Arameans in battle, and they fought against him. [18] But they fled before Israel, and David killed seven thousand of their charioteers and forty thousand of their foot soldiers. He also killed Shophak the commander of their army.

[19] When the vassals of Hadadezer saw that they had been routed by Israel, they made peace with David and became subject to him.

So the Arameans were not willing to help the Ammonites anymore.

The Capture of Rabbah

20 In the spring, at the time when kings go off to war, Joab led out the armed forces. He laid waste the land of the Ammonites and went to Rabbah and besieged it, but David remained in Jerusalem. Joab attacked Rabbah and left it in ruins. [2] David took the crown from the head of their king[a] — its weight was found to be a talent[b] of gold, and it was set with precious stones — and it was placed on David's head. He took a great quantity of plunder from the city [3] and brought out the people who were there, consigning them to labor with saws and with iron picks and axes. David did this to all the Ammonite towns. Then David and his entire army returned to Jerusalem.

War With the Philistines

[4] In the course of time, war broke out with the Philistines, at Gezer. At that time Sibbekai the Hushathite killed Sippai, one of the descendants of the Rephaites, and the Philistines were subjugated.

[5] In another battle with the Philistines, Elhanan son of Jair killed Lahmi the brother of Goliath the Gittite, who had a spear with a shaft like a weaver's rod.

[6] In still another battle, which took place at Gath, there was a huge man with six fingers on each hand and six toes on each foot — twenty-four in all. He also was descended from Rapha. [7] When he taunted Israel, Jonathan son of Shimea, David's brother, killed him.

[8] These were descendants of Rapha in Gath, and they fell at the hands of David and his men.

David Counts the Fighting Men

21 Satan rose up against Israel and incited David to take a census of Israel. [2] So David said to Joab and the commanders

---

[a] 2 Or *of Milkom,* that is, Molek   [b] 2 That is, about 75 pounds or about 34 kilograms

of the troops, "Go and count the Israelites from Beersheba to Dan. Then report back to me so that I may know how many there are."

³But Joab replied, "May the LORD multiply his troops a hundred times over. My lord the king, are they not all my lord's subjects? Why does my lord want to do this? Why should he bring guilt on Israel?"

⁴The king's word, however, overruled Joab; so Joab left and went throughout Israel and then came back to Jerusalem. ⁵Joab reported the number of the fighting men to David: In all Israel there were one million one hundred thousand men who could handle a sword, including four hundred and seventy thousand in Judah.

⁶But Joab did not include Levi and Benjamin in the numbering, because the king's command was repulsive to him. ⁷This command was also evil in the sight of God; so he punished Israel.

⁸Then David said to God, "I have sinned greatly by doing this. Now, I beg you, take away the guilt of your servant. I have done a very foolish thing."

⁹The LORD said to Gad, David's seer, ¹⁰"Go and tell David, 'This is what the LORD says: I am giving you three options. Choose one of them for me to carry out against you.'"

¹¹So Gad went to David and said to him, "This is what the LORD says: 'Take your choice: ¹²three years of famine, three months of being swept away*a* before your enemies, with their swords overtaking you, or three days of the sword of the LORD — days of plague in the land, with the angel of the LORD ravaging every part of Israel.' Now then, decide how I should answer the one who sent me."

¹³David said to Gad, "I am in deep distress. Let me fall into the hands of the LORD, for his mercy is very great; but do not let me fall into human hands."

¹⁴So the LORD sent a plague on Israel, and seventy thousand men of Israel fell dead. ¹⁵And God sent an angel to destroy Jerusalem. But as the angel was doing so, the LORD saw it and relented concerning the disaster and said to the angel who was destroying the people, "Enough! Withdraw your hand." The angel of the LORD was then standing at the threshing floor of Araunah*b* the Jebusite.

¹⁶David looked up and saw the angel of the LORD standing between heaven and earth, with a drawn sword in his hand extended over Jerusalem. Then David and the elders, clothed in sackcloth, fell facedown.

¹⁷David said to God, "Was it not I who ordered the fighting men

a 12 Hebrew; Septuagint and Vulgate (see also 2 Samuel 24:13) *of fleeing*
b 15 Hebrew *Ornan,* a variant of *Araunah;* also in verses 18-28

to be counted? I, the shepherd,[a] have sinned and done wrong. These are but sheep. What have they done? LORD my God, let your hand fall on me and my family, but do not let this plague remain on your people."

David Builds an Altar

[18] Then the angel of the LORD ordered Gad to tell David to go up and build an altar to the LORD on the threshing floor of Araunah the Jebusite. [19] So David went up in obedience to the word that Gad had spoken in the name of the LORD.

[20] While Araunah was threshing wheat, he turned and saw the angel; his four sons who were with him hid themselves. [21] Then David approached, and when Araunah looked and saw him, he left the threshing floor and bowed down before David with his face to the ground.

[22] David said to him, "Let me have the site of your threshing floor so I can build an altar to the LORD, that the plague on the people may be stopped. Sell it to me at the full price."

[23] Araunah said to David, "Take it! Let my lord the king do whatever pleases him. Look, I will give the oxen for the burnt offerings, the threshing sledges for the wood, and the wheat for the grain offering. I will give all this."

[24] But King David replied to Araunah, "No, I insist on paying the full price. I will not take for the LORD what is yours, or sacrifice a burnt offering that costs me nothing."

[25] So David paid Araunah six hundred shekels[b] of gold for the site. [26] David built an altar to the LORD there and sacrificed burnt offerings and fellowship offerings. He called on the LORD, and the LORD answered him with fire from heaven on the altar of burnt offering.

[27] Then the LORD spoke to the angel, and he put his sword back into its sheath. [28] At that time, when David saw that the LORD had answered him on the threshing floor of Araunah the Jebusite, he offered sacrifices there. [29] The tabernacle of the LORD, which Moses had made in the wilderness, and the altar of burnt offering were at that time on the high place at Gibeon. [30] But David could not go before it to inquire of God, because he was afraid of the sword of the angel of the LORD.

22 Then David said, "The house of the LORD God is to be here, and also the altar of burnt offering for Israel."

Preparations for the Temple

[2] So David gave orders to assemble the foreigners residing

---

[a] 17 Probable reading of the original Hebrew text (see 2 Samuel 24:17 and note); Masoretic Text does not have *the shepherd*.   [b] 25 That is, about 15 pounds or about 6.9 kilograms

in Israel, and from among them he appointed stonecutters to prepare dressed stone for building the house of God. ³He provided a large amount of iron to make nails for the doors of the gateways and for the fittings, and more bronze than could be weighed. ⁴He also provided more cedar logs than could be counted, for the Sidonians and Tyrians had brought large numbers of them to David.

⁵David said, "My son Solomon is young and inexperienced, and the house to be built for the LORD should be of great magnificence and fame and splendor in the sight of all the nations. Therefore I will make preparations for it." So David made extensive preparations before his death.

⁶Then he called for his son Solomon and charged him to build a house for the LORD, the God of Israel. ⁷David said to Solomon: "My son, I had it in my heart to build a house for the Name of the LORD my God. ⁸But this word of the LORD came to me: 'You have shed much blood and have fought many wars. You are not to build a house for my Name, because you have shed much blood on the earth in my sight. ⁹But you will have a son who will be a man of peace and rest, and I will give him rest from all his enemies on every side. His name will be Solomon,ᵃ and I will grant Israel peace and quiet during his reign. ¹⁰He is the one who will build a house for my Name. He will be my son, and I will be his father. And I will establish the throne of his kingdom over Israel forever.'

¹¹"Now, my son, the LORD be with you, and may you have success and build the house of the LORD your God, as he said you would. ¹²May the LORD give you discretion and understanding when he puts you in command over Israel, so that you may keep the law of the LORD your God. ¹³Then you will have success if you are careful to observe the decrees and laws that the LORD gave Moses for Israel. Be strong and courageous. Do not be afraid or discouraged.

¹⁴"I have taken great pains to provide for the temple of the LORD a hundred thousand talentsᵇ of gold, a million talentsᶜ of silver, quantities of bronze and iron too great to be weighed, and wood and stone. And you may add to them. ¹⁵You have many workers: stonecutters, masons and carpenters, as well as those skilled in every kind of work ¹⁶in gold and silver, bronze and iron—craftsmen beyond number. Now begin the work, and the LORD be with you."

ᵃ 9 *Solomon* sounds like and may be derived from the Hebrew for *peace*.
ᵇ 14 That is, about 3,750 tons or about 3,400 metric tons   ᶜ 14 That is, about 37,500 tons or about 34,000 metric tons

[17]Then David ordered all the leaders of Israel to help his son Solomon. [18]He said to them, "Is not the LORD your God with you? And has he not granted you rest on every side? For he has given the inhabitants of the land into my hands, and the land is subject to the LORD and to his people. [19]Now devote your heart and soul to seeking the LORD your God. Begin to build the sanctuary of the LORD God, so that you may bring the ark of the covenant of the LORD and the sacred articles belonging to God into the temple that will be built for the Name of the LORD."

The Levites

23 When David was old and full of years, he made his son Solomon king over Israel.

[2]He also gathered together all the leaders of Israel, as well as the priests and Levites. [3]The Levites thirty years old or more were counted, and the total number of men was thirty-eight thousand. [4]David said, "Of these, twenty-four thousand are to be in charge of the work of the temple of the LORD and six thousand are to be officials and judges. [5]Four thousand are to be gatekeepers and four thousand are to praise the LORD with the musical instruments I have provided for that purpose."

[6]David separated the Levites into divisions corresponding to the sons of Levi: Gershon, Kohath and Merari.

Gershonites

[7]Belonging to the Gershonites:
  Ladan and Shimei.
[8]The sons of Ladan:
  Jehiel the first, Zetham and Joel—three in all.
[9]The sons of Shimei:
  Shelomoth, Haziel and Haran—three in all.
  These were the heads of the families of Ladan.
[10]And the sons of Shimei:
  Jahath, Ziza,[a] Jeush and Beriah.
  These were the sons of Shimei—four in all.
[11]Jahath was the first and Ziza the second, but Jeush and Beriah did not have many sons; so they were counted as one family with one assignment.

Kohathites

[12]The sons of Kohath:
  Amram, Izhar, Hebron and Uzziel—four in all.
[13]The sons of Amram:
  Aaron and Moses.
  Aaron was set apart, he and his descendants forever, to consecrate the most holy things, to offer sacrifices before the LORD, to minis-

---

[a] 10 One Hebrew manuscript, Septuagint and Vulgate (see also verse 11); most Hebrew manuscripts *Zina*

ter before him and to pronounce blessings in his
name forever. ¹⁴The sons of
Moses the man of God were
counted as part of the tribe
of Levi.

¹⁵The sons of Moses:
Gershom and Eliezer.

¹⁶The descendants of Gershom:
Shubael was the first.

¹⁷The descendants of Eliezer:
Rehabiah was the first.
Eliezer had no other sons,
but the sons of Rehabiah
were very numerous.

¹⁸The sons of Izhar:
Shelomith was the first.

¹⁹The sons of Hebron:
Jeriah the first, Amariah
the second, Jahaziel the
third and Jekameam the
fourth.

²⁰The sons of Uzziel:
Micah the first and Ishiah
the second.

Merarites

²¹The sons of Merari:
Mahli and Mushi.
The sons of Mahli:
Eleazar and Kish.

²²Eleazar died without having sons: he had only
daughters. Their cousins,
the sons of Kish, married
them.

²³The sons of Mushi:
Mahli, Eder and Jerimoth —
three in all.

²⁴These were the descendants
of Levi by their families — the
heads of families as they were
registered under their names
and counted individually, that is,
the workers twenty years old or
more who served in the temple of
the LORD. ²⁵For David had said,
"Since the LORD, the God of Israel, has granted rest to his people
and has come to dwell in Jerusalem forever, ²⁶the Levites no longer need to carry the tabernacle
or any of the articles used in its
service." ²⁷According to the last
instructions of David, the Levites
were counted from those twenty
years old or more.

²⁸The duty of the Levites was to
help Aaron's descendants in the
service of the temple of the LORD:
to be in charge of the courtyards,
the side rooms, the purification
of all sacred things and the per-
formance of other duties at the
house of God. ²⁹They were in
charge of the bread set out on
the table, the special flour for the
grain offerings, the thin loaves
made without yeast, the baking
and the mixing, and all measurements of quantity and size.
³⁰They were also to stand every
morning to thank and praise the
LORD. They were to do the same
in the evening ³¹and whenever
burnt offerings were presented
to the LORD on the Sabbaths, at
the New Moon feasts and at the
appointed festivals. They were to
serve before the LORD regularly
in the proper number and in the
way prescribed for them.

³²And so the Levites carried out their responsibilities for the tent of meeting, for the Holy Place and, under their relatives the descendants of Aaron, for the service of the temple of the LORD.

The Divisions of Priests

24 These were the divisions of the descendants of Aaron:

The sons of Aaron were Nadab, Abihu, Eleazar and Ithamar. ²But Nadab and Abihu died before their father did, and they had no sons; so Eleazar and Ithamar served as the priests. ³With the help of Zadok a descendant of Eleazar and Ahimelek a descendant of Ithamar, David separated them into divisions for their appointed order of ministering. ⁴A larger number of leaders were found among Eleazar's descendants than among Ithamar's, and they were divided accordingly: sixteen heads of families from Eleazar's descendants and eight heads of families from Ithamar's descendants. ⁵They divided them impartially by casting lots, for there were officials of the sanctuary and officials of God among the descendants of both Eleazar and Ithamar.

⁶The scribe Shemaiah son of Nethanel, a Levite, recorded their names in the presence of the king and of the officials: Zadok the priest, Ahimelek son of Abiathar and the heads of families of the priests and of the Levites—one family being taken from Eleazar and then one from Ithamar.

⁷The first lot fell to Jehoiarib,
  the second to Jedaiah,
⁸the third to Harim,
  the fourth to Seorim,
⁹the fifth to Malkijah,
  the sixth to Mijamin,
¹⁰the seventh to Hakkoz,
  the eighth to Abijah,
¹¹the ninth to Jeshua,
  the tenth to Shekaniah,
¹²the eleventh to Eliashib,
  the twelfth to Jakim,
¹³the thirteenth to Huppah,
  the fourteenth to Jeshebeab,
¹⁴the fifteenth to Bilgah,
  the sixteenth to Immer,
¹⁵the seventeenth to Hezir,
  the eighteenth to Happizzez,
¹⁶the nineteenth to Pethahiah,
  the twentieth to Jehezkel,
¹⁷the twenty-first to Jakin,
  the twenty-second to Gamul,
¹⁸the twenty-third to Delaiah
  and the twenty-fourth to Maaziah.

¹⁹This was their appointed order of ministering when they entered the temple of the LORD, according to the regulations prescribed for them by their ancestor Aaron, as the LORD, the God of Israel, had commanded him.

The Rest of the Levites

²⁰As for the rest of the descendants of Levi:

from the sons of Amram: Shubael;

from the sons of Shubael: Jehdeiah.

²¹ As for Rehabiah, from his sons:

Ishiah was the first.

²² From the Izharites: Shelomoth;

from the sons of Shelomoth: Jahath.

²³ The sons of Hebron: Jeriah the first,ᵃ Amariah the second, Jahaziel the third and Jekameam the fourth.

²⁴ The son of Uzziel: Micah;

from the sons of Micah: Shamir.

²⁵ The brother of Micah: Ishiah;

from the sons of Ishiah: Zechariah.

²⁶ The sons of Merari: Mahli and Mushi.

The son of Jaaziah: Beno.

²⁷ The sons of Merari:

from Jaaziah: Beno, Shoham, Zakkur and Ibri.

²⁸ From Mahli: Eleazar, who had no sons.

²⁹ From Kish: the son of Kish: Jerahmeel.

³⁰ And the sons of Mushi: Mahli, Eder and Jerimoth.

These were the Levites, according to their families. ³¹ They also cast lots, just as their relatives the descendants of Aaron did, in the presence of King David and of Zadok, Ahimelek, and the heads of families of the priests and of the Levites. The families of the oldest brother were treated the same as those of the youngest.

The Musicians

25 David, together with the commanders of the army, set apart some of the sons of Asaph, Heman and Jeduthun for the ministry of prophesying, accompanied by harps, lyres and cymbals. Here is the list of the men who performed this service:

² From the sons of Asaph:

Zakkur, Joseph, Nethaniah and Asarelah. The sons of Asaph were under the supervision of Asaph, who prophesied under the king's supervision.

³ As for Jeduthun, from his sons:

Gedaliah, Zeri, Jeshaiah, Shimei,ᵇ Hashabiah and Mattithiah, six in all, under the supervision of their father Jeduthun, who prophesied, using the harp in thanking and praising the LORD.

⁴ As for Heman, from his sons:

Bukkiah, Mattaniah, Uzziel, Shubael and Jerimoth; Hananiah, Hanani, Eliathah, Giddalti and Romamti-Ezer; Joshbekashah, Mallothi, Hothir and Mahazioth. ⁵ (All

---

ᵃ 23 Two Hebrew manuscripts and some Septuagint manuscripts (see also 23:19); most Hebrew manuscripts *The sons of Jeriah:*   ᵇ 3 One Hebrew manuscript and some Septuagint manuscripts (see also verse 17); most Hebrew manuscripts do not have *Shimei.*

these were sons of Heman the king's seer. They were given him through the promises of God to exalt him. God gave Heman fourteen sons and three daughters.)

⁶All these men were under the supervision of their father for the music of the temple of the LORD, with cymbals, lyres and harps, for the ministry at the house of God.

Asaph, Jeduthun and Heman were under the supervision of the king. ⁷Along with their relatives — all of them trained and skilled in music for the LORD — they numbered 288. ⁸Young and old alike, teacher as well as student, cast lots for their duties.

⁹The first lot, which was for
    Asaph, fell to Joseph,
    his sons and relatives^a 12^b
  the second to Gedaliah,
    him and his relatives
    and sons 12
¹⁰the third to Zakkur,
    his sons and relatives 12
¹¹the fourth to Izri,^c
    his sons and relatives 12
¹²the fifth to Nethaniah,
    his sons and relatives 12
¹³the sixth to Bukkiah,
    his sons and relatives 12
¹⁴the seventh to
    Jesarelah,^d
    his sons and relatives 12

¹⁵the eighth to Jeshaiah,
    his sons and relatives 12
¹⁶the ninth to Mattaniah,
    his sons and relatives 12
¹⁷the tenth to Shimei,
    his sons and relatives 12
¹⁸the eleventh to Azarel,^e
    his sons and relatives 12
¹⁹the twelfth to
    Hashabiah,
    his sons and relatives 12
²⁰the thirteenth to
    Shubael,
    his sons and relatives 12
²¹the fourteenth to
    Mattithiah,
    his sons and relatives 12
²²the fifteenth to
    Jerimoth,
    his sons and relatives 12
²³the sixteenth to
    Hananiah,
    his sons and relatives 12
²⁴the seventeenth to
    Joshbekashah,
    his sons and relatives 12
²⁵the eighteenth to
    Hanani,
    his sons and relatives 12
²⁶the nineteenth to
    Mallothi,
    his sons and relatives 12
²⁷the twentieth to
    Eliathah,
    his sons and relatives 12
²⁸the twenty-first to
    Hothir,
    his sons and relatives 12

---

^a 9 See Septuagint; Hebrew does not have *his sons and relatives.*   ^b 9 See the total in verse 7; Hebrew does not have *twelve.*   ^c 11 A variant of *Zeri*
^d 14 A variant of *Asarelah*   ^e 18 A variant of *Uzziel*

29 the twenty-second to
Giddalti,
his sons and relatives 12
30 the twenty-third to
Mahazioth,
his sons and relatives 12
31 the twenty-fourth to
Romamti-Ezer,
his sons and relatives 12.

The Gatekeepers

26 The divisions of the gatekeepers:

From the Korahites: Meshele-
miah son of Kore, one of the
sons of Asaph.
2 Meshelemiah had sons:
Zechariah the firstborn,
Jediael the second,
Zebadiah the third,
Jathniel the fourth,
3 Elam the fifth,
Jehohanan the sixth
and Eliehoenai the sev-
enth.
4 Obed-Edom also had sons:
Shemaiah the firstborn,
Jehozabad the second,
Joah the third,
Sakar the fourth,
Nethanel the fifth,
5 Ammiel the sixth,
Issachar the seventh
and Peullethai the eighth.
(For God had blessed Obed-
Edom.)
6 Obed-Edom's son Shemaiah
also had sons, who were
leaders in their father's

family because they were
very capable men. **7** The
sons of Shemaiah: Othni,
Rephael, Obed and Elza-
bad; his relatives Elihu and
Semakiah were also able
men. **8** All these were descendants of Obed-Edom;
they and their sons and
their relatives were capable
men with the strength to do
the work — descendants of
Obed-Edom, 62 in all.
9 Meshelemiah had sons and
relatives, who were able
men — 18 in all.

10 Hosah the Merarite had sons:
Shimri the first (although
he was not the firstborn,
his father had appointed
him the first), **11** Hilkiah the
second, Tabaliah the third
and Zechariah the fourth.
The sons and relatives of
Hosah were 13 in all.

12 These divisions of the gatekeepers, through their leaders,
had duties for ministering in the
temple of the LORD, just as their
relatives had. **13** Lots were cast for
each gate, according to their families, young and old alike.
14 The lot for the East Gate fell
to Shelemiah.[a] Then lots were
cast for his son Zechariah, a wise
counselor, and the lot for the
North Gate fell to him. **15** The lot
for the South Gate fell to Obed-
Edom, and the lot for the storehouse fell to his sons. **16** The lots

---

a 14 A variant of *Meshelemiah*

for the West Gate and the Shalleketh Gate on the upper road fell to Shuppim and Hosah.

Guard was alongside of guard: ¹⁷There were six Levites a day on the east, four a day on the north, four a day on the south and two at a time at the storehouse. ¹⁸As for the court*ᵃ* to the west, there were four at the road and two at the court*ᵃ* itself.

¹⁹These were the divisions of the gatekeepers who were descendants of Korah and Merari.

The Treasurers and Other Officials

²⁰Their fellow Levites were*ᵇ* in charge of the treasuries of the house of God and the treasuries for the dedicated things.

²¹The descendants of Ladan, who were Gershonites through Ladan and who were heads of families belonging to Ladan the Gershonite, were Jehieli, ²²the sons of Jehieli, Zetham and his brother Joel. They were in charge of the treasuries of the temple of the LORD.

²³From the Amramites, the Izharites, the Hebronites and the Uzzielites:

²⁴Shubael, a descendant of Gershom son of Moses, was the official in charge of the treasuries. ²⁵His relatives through Eliezer: Rehabiah his son, Jeshaiah his son, Joram his son, Zikri his son and Shelomith his son. ²⁶Shelomith and his relatives were in charge of all the treasuries for the things dedicated by King David, by the heads of families who were the commanders of thousands and commanders of hundreds, and by the other army commanders. ²⁷Some of the plunder taken in battle they dedicated for the repair of the temple of the LORD. ²⁸And everything dedicated by Samuel the seer and by Saul son of Kish, Abner son of Ner and Joab son of Zeruiah, and all the other dedicated things were in the care of Shelomith and his relatives.

²⁹From the Izharites: Kenaniah and his sons were assigned duties away from the temple, as officials and judges over Israel.

³⁰From the Hebronites: Hashabiah and his relatives — seventeen hundred able men — were responsible in Israel west of the Jordan for all the work of the LORD and for the king's service. ³¹As for the Hebronites, Jeriah was their chief according to the genealogical records of their families. In the fortieth year of David's

ᵃ 18 The meaning of the Hebrew for this word is uncertain.   *ᵇ 20* Septuagint;
Hebrew *As for the Levites, Ahijah was*

reign a search was made in the records, and capable men among the Hebronites were found at Jazer in Gilead. ³²Jeriah had twenty-seven hundred relatives, who were able men and heads of families, and King David put them in charge of the Reubenites, the Gadites and the half-tribe of Manasseh for every matter pertaining to God and for the affairs of the king.

Army Divisions

27 This is the list of the Israelites — heads of families, commanders of thousands and commanders of hundreds, and their officers, who served the king in all that concerned the army divisions that were on duty month by month throughout the year. Each division consisted of 24,000 men.

²In charge of the first division, for the first month, was Jashobeam son of Zabdiel. There were 24,000 men in his division. ³He was a descendant of Perez and chief of all the army officers for the first month.

⁴In charge of the division for the second month was Dodai the Ahohite; Mikloth was the leader of his division. There were 24,000 men in his division.

⁵The third army commander, for the third month, was Benaiah son of Jehoiada the priest. He was chief and there were 24,000 men in his division. ⁶This was the Benaiah who was a mighty warrior among the Thirty and was over the Thirty. His son Ammizabad was in charge of his division.

⁷The fourth, for the fourth month, was Asahel the brother of Joab; his son Zebadiah was his successor. There were 24,000 men in his division.

⁸The fifth, for the fifth month, was the commander Shamhuth the Izrahite. There were 24,000 men in his division.

⁹The sixth, for the sixth month, was Ira the son of Ikkesh the Tekoite. There were 24,000 men in his division.

¹⁰The seventh, for the seventh month, was Helez the Pelonite, an Ephraimite. There were 24,000 men in his division.

¹¹The eighth, for the eighth month, was Sibbekai the Hushathite, a Zerahite. There were 24,000 men in his division.

¹²The ninth, for the ninth month, was Abiezer the Anathothite, a Benjamite. There were 24,000 men in his division.

¹³The tenth, for the tenth month, was Maharai the Netophathite, a Zerahite. There were 24,000 men in his division.

¹⁴The eleventh, for the eleventh month, was Benaiah the Pirathonite, an Ephraimite. There were 24,000 men in his division.

¹⁵The twelfth, for the twelfth month, was Heldai the Netophathite, from the family of Othniel. There were 24,000 men in his division.

Leaders of the Tribes

¹⁶The leaders of the tribes of Israel:

over the Reubenites: Eliezer son of Zikri;

over the Simeonites: Shephatiah son of Maakah;

¹⁷over Levi: Hashabiah son of Kemuel;

over Aaron: Zadok;

¹⁸over Judah: Elihu, a brother of David;

over Issachar: Omri son of Michael;

¹⁹over Zebulun: Ishmaiah son of Obadiah;

over Naphtali: Jerimoth son of Azriel;

²⁰over the Ephraimites: Hoshea son of Azaziah;

over half the tribe of Manasseh: Joel son of Pedaiah;

²¹over the half-tribe of Manasseh in Gilead: Iddo son of Zechariah;

over Benjamin: Jaasiel son of Abner;

²²over Dan: Azarel son of Jeroham.

These were the leaders of the tribes of Israel.

²³David did not take the number of the men twenty years old or less, because the LORD had promised to make Israel as numerous as the stars in the sky. ²⁴Joab son of Zeruiah began to count the men but did not finish. God's wrath came on Israel on account of this numbering, and the number was not entered in the book[a] of the annals of King David.

The King's Overseers

²⁵Azmaveth son of Adiel was in charge of the royal storehouses.

Jonathan son of Uzziah was in charge of the storehouses in the outlying districts, in the towns, the villages and the watchtowers.

²⁶Ezri son of Kelub was in charge of the workers who farmed the land.

²⁷Shimei the Ramathite was in charge of the vineyards.

Zabdi the Shiphmite was in charge of the produce of the vineyards for the wine vats.

²⁸Baal-Hanan the Gederite was in charge of the olive and sycamore-fig trees in the western foothills.

Joash was in charge of the supplies of olive oil.

²⁹Shitrai the Sharonite was in charge of the herds grazing in Sharon.

_____
[a] 24 Septuagint; Hebrew *number*

Shaphat son of Adlai was in charge of the herds in the valleys. [30]Obil the Ishmaelite was in charge of the camels.

Jehdeiah the Meronothite was in charge of the donkeys. [31]Jaziz the Hagrite was in charge of the flocks.

All these were the officials in charge of King David's property.

[32]Jonathan, David's uncle, was a counselor, a man of insight and a scribe. Jehiel son of Hakmoni took care of the king's sons. [33]Ahithophel was the king's counselor.

Hushai the Arkite was the king's confidant. [34]Ahithophel was succeeded by Jehoiada son of Benaiah and by Abiathar.

Joab was the commander of the royal army.

David's Plans for the Temple

28 David summoned all the officials of Israel to assemble at Jerusalem: the officers over the tribes, the commanders of the divisions in the service of the king, the commanders of thousands and commanders of hundreds, and the officials in charge of all the property and livestock belonging to the king and his sons, together with the palace officials, the warriors and all the brave fighting men.

[2]King David rose to his feet and said: "Listen to me, my fellow Israelites, my people. I had it in my heart to build a house as a place of rest for the ark of the covenant of the LORD, for the footstool of our God, and I made plans to build it. [3]But God said to me, 'You are not to build a house for my Name, because you are a warrior and have shed blood.'

[4]"Yet the LORD, the God of Israel, chose me from my whole family to be king over Israel forever. He chose Judah as leader, and from the tribe of Judah he chose my family, and from my father's sons he was pleased to make me king over all Israel. [5]Of all my sons — and the LORD has given me many — he has chosen my son Solomon to sit on the throne of the kingdom of the LORD over Israel. [6]He said to me: 'Solomon your son is the one who will build my house and my courts, for I have chosen him to be my son, and I will be his father. [7]I will establish his kingdom forever if he is unswerving in carrying out my commands and laws, as is being done at this time.'

[8]"So now I charge you in the sight of all Israel and of the assembly of the LORD, and in the hearing of our God: Be careful to follow all the commands of the LORD your God, that you may possess this good land and pass it on as an inheritance to your descendants forever.

[9]"And you, my son Solomon, acknowledge the God of your father, and serve him with wholehearted devotion and with a willing

mind, for the LORD searches every heart and understands every desire and every thought. If you seek him, he will be found by you; but if you forsake him, he will reject you forever. ¹⁰Consider now, for the LORD has chosen you to build a house as the sanctuary. Be strong and do the work."

¹¹Then David gave his son Solomon the plans for the portico of the temple, its buildings, its storerooms, its upper parts, its inner rooms and the place of atonement. ¹²He gave him the plans of all that the Spirit had put in his mind for the courts of the temple of the LORD and all the surrounding rooms, for the treasuries of the temple of God and for the treasuries for the dedicated things. ¹³He gave him instructions for the divisions of the priests and Levites, and for all the work of serving in the temple of the LORD, as well as for all the articles to be used in its service. ¹⁴He designated the weight of gold for all the gold articles to be used in various kinds of service, and the weight of silver for all the silver articles to be used in various kinds of service: ¹⁵the weight of gold for the gold lampstands and their lamps, with the weight for each lampstand and its lamps; and the weight of silver for each silver lampstand and its lamps, according to the use of each lampstand; ¹⁶the weight of gold for each table for conse-

crated bread; the weight of silver for the silver tables; ¹⁷the weight of pure gold for the forks, sprinkling bowls and pitchers; the weight of gold for each gold dish; the weight of silver for each silver dish; ¹⁸and the weight of the refined gold for the altar of incense. He also gave him the plan for the chariot, that is, the cherubim of gold that spread their wings and overshadow the ark of the covenant of the LORD.

¹⁹"All this," David said, "I have in writing as a result of the LORD's hand on me, and he enabled me to understand all the details of the plan."

²⁰David also said to Solomon his son, "Be strong and courageous, and do the work. Do not be afraid or discouraged, for the LORD God, my God, is with you. He will not fail you or forsake you until all the work for the service of the temple of the LORD is finished. ²¹The divisions of the priests and Levites are ready for all the work on the temple of God, and every willing person skilled in any craft will help you in all the work. The officials and all the people will obey your every command."

Gifts for Building the Temple

29 Then King David said to the whole assembly: "My son Solomon, the one whom God has chosen, is young and inexperienced. The task is great, because this palatial structure is not for man but for the LORD God. ²With all my resources I have provided for the temple of my God — gold for the gold work, silver for the silver, bronze for the bronze, iron for the iron and wood for the wood, as well as onyx for the settings, turquoise,ᵃ stones of various colors, and all kinds of fine stone and marble — all of these in large quantities. ³Besides, in my devotion to the temple of my God I now give my personal treasures of gold and silver for the temple of my God, over and above everything I have provided for this holy temple: ⁴three thousand talentsᵇ of gold (gold of Ophir) and seven thousand talentsᶜ of refined silver, for the overlaying of the walls of the buildings, ⁵for the gold work and the silver work, and for all the work to be done by the craftsmen. Now, who is willing to consecrate themselves to the LORD today?"

⁶Then the leaders of families, the officers of the tribes of Israel, the commanders of thousands and commanders of hundreds, and the officials in charge of the king's work gave willingly. ⁷They gave toward the work on the temple of God five thousand talentsᵈ and ten thousand daricsᵉ of gold, ten thousand talentsᶠ of silver, eighteen thousand talentsᵍ of bronze and a hundred thousand talentsʰ of iron. ⁸Anyone who had precious stones gave them to the treasury of the temple of the LORD in the custody of Jehiel the Gershonite. ⁹The people rejoiced at the willing response of their leaders, for they had given freely and wholeheartedly to the LORD. David the king also rejoiced greatly.

David's Prayer

¹⁰David praised the LORD in the presence of the whole assembly, saying,

"Praise be to you, LORD,
  the God of our father Israel,
  from everlasting to
  everlasting.
¹¹Yours, LORD, is the greatness
  and the power
  and the glory and the
  majesty and the
  splendor,
  for everything in heaven and
  earth is yours.
Yours, LORD, is the kingdom;
  you are exalted as head over
  all.
¹²Wealth and honor come from
  you;
  you are the ruler of all
  things.

ᵃ 2 The meaning of the Hebrew for this word is uncertain.   ᵇ 4 That is, about 110 tons or about 100 metric tons   ᶜ 4 That is, about 260 tons or about 235 metric tons   ᵈ 7 That is, about 190 tons or about 170 metric tons   ᵉ 7 That is, about 185 pounds or about 84 kilograms   ᶠ 7 That is, about 380 tons or about 340 metric tons   ᵍ 7 That is, about 675 tons or about 610 metric tons   ʰ 7 That is, about 3,800 tons or about 3,400 metric tons

In your hands are strength and
power
to exalt and give strength to
all.
¹³Now, our God, we give you
thanks,
and praise your glorious
name.

¹⁴"But who am I, and who are
my people, that we should be
able to give as generously as this?
Everything comes from you, and
we have given you only what
comes from your hand. ¹⁵We
are foreigners and strangers in
your sight, as were all our ancestors. Our days on earth are like
a shadow, without hope. ¹⁶LORD
our God, all this abundance that
we have provided for building
you a temple for your Holy Name
comes from your hand, and all
of it belongs to you. ¹⁷I know, my
God, that you test the heart and
are pleased with integrity. All
these things I have given willingly and with honest intent. And
now I have seen with joy how
willingly your people who are
here have given to you. ¹⁸LORD,
the God of our fathers Abraham,
Isaac and Israel, keep these desires and thoughts in the hearts
of your people forever, and keep
their hearts loyal to you. ¹⁹And
give my son Solomon the wholehearted devotion to keep your
commands, statutes and decrees
and to do everything to build
the palatial structure for which I
have provided."

²⁰Then David said to the whole
assembly, "Praise the LORD your
God." So they all praised the
LORD, the God of their fathers;
they bowed down, prostrating
themselves before the LORD and
the king.

Solomon Acknowledged as King

²¹The next day they made sacrifices to the LORD and presented
burnt offerings to him: a thousand bulls, a thousand rams and
a thousand male lambs, together
with their drink offerings, and
other sacrifices in abundance for
all Israel. ²²They ate and drank
with great joy in the presence of
the LORD that day.

Then they acknowledged Solomon son of David as king a second time, anointing him before
the LORD to be ruler and Zadok
to be priest. ²³So Solomon sat on
the throne of the LORD as king
in place of his father David. He
prospered and all Israel obeyed
him. ²⁴All the officers and warriors, as well as all of King David's
sons, pledged their submission to
King Solomon.

²⁵The LORD highly exalted Solomon in the sight of all Israel and
bestowed on him royal splendor
such as no king over Israel ever
had before.

The Death of David

²⁶David son of Jesse was king
over all Israel. ²⁷He ruled over
Israel forty years—seven in He-

bron and thirty-three in Jerusalem. [28] He died at a good old age, having enjoyed long life, wealth and honor. His son Solomon succeeded him as king.

[29] As for the events of King David's reign, from beginning to end, they are written in the records of Samuel the seer, the records of Nathan the prophet and the records of Gad the seer, [30] together with the details of his reign and power, and the circumstances that surrounded him and Israel and the kingdoms of all the other lands.

2 Chronicles

Introduction:

Second Chronicles continues the history of David's royal line. Chapters 1–9 describe the building of the temple during Solomon's reign. Chapters 10–36 follow the history of the southern kingdom of Judah to the final destruction of Jerusalem and the people being captured and taken to Babylon.

This book, like 1 Chronicles, shows that the people's relationship to God was most important. When the author wrote about the kings he measured them on the basis of their faithfulness to God. The reigns of evil kings are reported by the author quickly, while the reigns of good kings are described in more detail.

Outline of contents:

The reign of Solomon (1:1–9:31)
The kings of Judah (10:1–36:14)
The destruction of Jerusalem (36:15–23)

Solomon Asks for Wisdom

1 Solomon son of David established himself firmly over his kingdom, for the LORD his God was with him and made him exceedingly great.

² Then Solomon spoke to all Israel — to the commanders of thousands and commanders of hundreds, to the judges and to all the leaders in Israel, the heads of families — ³ and Solomon and the whole assembly went to the high place at Gibeon, for God's tent of meeting was there, which Moses the LORD's servant had made in the wilderness. ⁴ Now David had brought up the ark of God from Kiriath Jearim to the place he had prepared for it, because he had pitched a tent for it in Jerusalem. ⁵ But the bronze altar that Bezalel son of Uri, the son of Hur, had made was in Gibeon in front of the tabernacle of the LORD; so Solomon and the assembly inquired of him there. ⁶ Solomon went up to the bronze altar before the LORD in the tent of meeting and offered a thousand burnt offerings on it.

⁷ That night God appeared to Solomon and said to him, "Ask for whatever you want me to give you."

⁸ Solomon answered God, "You have shown great kindness to David my father and have made

me king in his place. ⁹Now, LORD God, let your promise to my father David be confirmed, for you have made me king over a people who are as numerous as the dust of the earth. ¹⁰Give me wisdom and knowledge, that I may lead this people, for who is able to govern this great people of yours?"

¹¹God said to Solomon, "Since this is your heart's desire and you have not asked for wealth, possessions or honor, nor for the death of your enemies, and since you have not asked for a long life but for wisdom and knowledge to govern my people over whom I have made you king, ¹²therefore wisdom and knowledge will be given you. And I will also give you wealth, possessions and honor, such as no king who was before you ever had and none after you will have."

¹³Then Solomon went to Jerusalem from the high place at Gibeon, from before the tent of meeting. And he reigned over Israel.

¹⁴Solomon accumulated chariots and horses; he had fourteen hundred chariots and twelve thousand horses,ᵃ which he kept in the chariot cities and also with him in Jerusalem. ¹⁵The king made silver and gold as common in Jerusalem as stones, and cedar as plentiful as sycamore-fig trees in the foothills. ¹⁶Solomon's hors-

es were imported from Egypt and from Kueᵇ — the royal merchants purchased them from Kue at the current price. ¹⁷They imported a chariot from Egypt for six hundred shekelsᶜ of silver, and a horse for a hundred and fifty.ᵈ They also exported them to all the kings of the Hittites and of the Arameans.

Preparations for Building the Temple

2ᵉ Solomon gave orders to build a temple for the Name of the LORD and a royal palace for himself. ²He conscripted 70,000 men as carriers and 80,000 as stonecutters in the hills and 3,600 as foremen over them.

³Solomon sent this message to Hiramᶠ king of Tyre:

"Send me cedar logs as you did for my father David when you sent him cedar to build a palace to live in. ⁴Now I am about to build a temple for the Name of the LORD my God and to dedicate it to him for burning fragrant incense before him, for setting out the consecrated bread regularly, and for making burnt offerings every morning and evening and on the Sabbaths, at the New Moons and at the appointed festivals of the

---

ᵃ 14 Or charioteers   ᵇ 16 Probably Cilicia   ᶜ 17 That is, about 15 pounds or about 6.9 kilograms   ᵈ 17 That is, about 3 3/4 pounds or about 1.7 kilograms   ᵉ In Hebrew texts 2:1 is numbered 1:18, and 2:2-18 is numbered 2:1-17.   ᶠ 3 Hebrew Huram, a variant of Hiram; also in verses 11 and 12

Lord our God. This is a lasting ordinance for Israel.

⁵ "The temple I am going to build will be great, because our God is greater than all other gods. ⁶ But who is able to build a temple for him, since the heavens, even the highest heavens, cannot contain him? Who then am I to build a temple for him, except as a place to burn sacrifices before him?

⁷ "Send me, therefore, a man skilled to work in gold and silver, bronze and iron, and in purple, crimson and blue yarn, and experienced in the art of engraving, to work in Judah and Jerusalem with my skilled workers, whom my father David provided.

⁸ "Send me also cedar, juniper and algum*ᵃ* logs from Lebanon, for I know that your servants are skilled in cutting timber there. My servants will work with yours ⁹ to provide me with plenty of lumber, because the temple I build must be large and magnificent. ¹⁰ I will give your servants, the woodsmen who cut the timber, twenty thousand cors*ᵇ* of ground wheat, twenty thousand cors*ᶜ* of barley, twenty thousand baths*ᵈ*

of wine and twenty thousand baths of olive oil."

¹¹ Hiram king of Tyre replied by letter to Solomon:

"Because the Lord loves his people, he has made you their king."

¹² And Hiram added:

"Praise be to the Lord, the God of Israel, who made heaven and earth! He has given King David a wise son, endowed with intelligence and discernment, who will build a temple for the Lord and a palace for himself.

¹³ "I am sending you Huram-Abi, a man of great skill, ¹⁴ whose mother was from Dan and whose father was from Tyre. He is trained to work in gold and silver, bronze and iron, stone and wood, and with purple and blue and crimson yarn and fine linen. He is experienced in all kinds of engraving and can execute any design given to him. He will work with your skilled workers and with those of my lord, David your father.

¹⁵ "Now let my lord send his servants the wheat and barley and the olive oil and wine

---

ᵃ 8 Probably a variant of *almug*   *ᵇ 10* That is, probably about 3,600 tons or about 3,200 metric tons of wheat   *ᶜ 10* That is, probably about 3,000 tons or about 2,700 metric tons of barley   *ᵈ 10* That is, about 120,000 gallons or about 440,000 liters he promised, ¹⁶and we will cut all the logs from Lebanon that you need and will float them as rafts by sea down to Joppa. You can then take them up to Jerusalem."

¹⁷Solomon took a census of all the foreigners residing in Israel, after the census his father David had taken; and they were found to be 153,600. ¹⁸He assigned 70,000 of them to be carriers and 80,000 to be stonecutters in the hills, with 3,600 foremen over them to keep the people working.

Solomon Builds the Temple

3 Then Solomon began to build the temple of the LORD in Jerusalem on Mount Moriah, where the LORD had appeared to his father David. It was on the threshing floor of Araunah^a the Jebusite, the place provided by David. ²He began building on the second day of the second month in the fourth year of his reign.

³The foundation Solomon laid for building the temple of God was sixty cubits long and twenty cubits wide^b (using the cubit of the old standard). ⁴The portico at the front of the temple was twenty cubits^c long across the width of the building and twenty^d cubits high.

He overlaid the inside with pure gold. ⁵He paneled the main hall with juniper and covered it with fine gold and decorated it with palm tree and chain designs. ⁶He adorned the temple with precious stones. And the gold he used was gold of Parvaim. ⁷He overlaid the ceiling beams, doorframes, walls and doors of the temple with gold, and he carved cherubim on the walls.

⁸He built the Most Holy Place, its length corresponding to the width of the temple — twenty cubits long and twenty cubits wide. He overlaid the inside with six hundred talents^e of fine gold. ⁹The gold nails weighed fifty shekels.^f He also overlaid the upper parts with gold.

¹⁰For the Most Holy Place he made a pair of sculptured cherubim and overlaid them with gold. ¹¹The total wingspan of the cherubim was twenty cubits. One wing of the first cherub was five cubits^g long and touched the temple wall, while its other wing, also five cubits long, touched the wing of the other cherub. ¹²Similarly one wing of the second cherub was five cubits long and touched the other temple wall, and its other wing, also five

^a 1 Hebrew Ornan, a variant of Araunah ^b 3 That is, about 90 feet long and 30 feet wide or about 27 meters long and 9 meters wide ^c 4 That is, about 30 feet or about 9 meters; also in verses 8, 11 and 13 ^d 4 Some Septuagint and Syriac manuscripts; Hebrew and a hundred and twenty ^e 8 That is, about 23 tons or about 21 metric tons ^f 9 That is, about 1 1/4 pounds or about 575 grams ^g 11 That is, about 7 1/2 feet or about 2.3 meters; also in verse 15

cubits long, touched the wing of the first cherub. ¹³The wings of these cherubim extended twenty cubits. They stood on their feet, facing the main hall.ᵃ

¹⁴He made the curtain of blue, purple and crimson yarn and fine linen, with cherubim worked into it.

¹⁵For the front of the temple he made two pillars, which together were thirty-five cubitsᵇ long, each with a capital five cubits high. ¹⁶He made interwoven chainsᶜ and put them on top of the pillars. He also made a hundred pomegranates and attached them to the chains. ¹⁷He erected the pillars in the front of the temple, one to the south and one to the north. The one to the south he named Jakinᵈ and the one to the north Boaz.ᵉ

The Temple's Furnishings

4 He made a bronze altar twenty cubits long, twenty cubits wide and ten cubits high.ᶠ ²He made the Sea of cast metal, circular in shape, measuring ten cubits from rim to rim and five cubitsᵍ high. It took a line of thirty cubitsʰ to measure around it. ³Below the rim, figures of bulls encircled it—ten to a cubit.ⁱ The bulls were cast in two rows in one piece with the Sea.

⁴The Sea stood on twelve bulls, three facing north, three facing west, three facing south and three facing east. The Sea rested on top of them, and their hindquarters were toward the center. ⁵It was a handbreadthʲ in thickness, and its rim was like the rim of a cup, like a lily blossom. It held three thousand baths.ᵏ

⁶He then made ten basins for washing and placed five on the south side and five on the north. In them the things to be used for the burnt offerings were rinsed, but the Sea was to be used by the priests for washing.

⁷He made ten gold lampstands according to the specifications for them and placed them in the temple, five on the south side and five on the north.

⁸He made ten tables and placed them in the temple, five on the south side and five on the north. He also made a hundred gold sprinkling bowls.

⁹He made the courtyard of the priests, and the large court and the doors for the court, and overlaid the doors with bronze. ¹⁰He

---

placed the Sea on the south side, at the southeast corner.

¹¹ And Huram also made the pots and shovels and sprinkling bowls.

So Huram finished the work he had undertaken for King Solomon in the temple of God:

¹² the two pillars;

the two bowl-shaped capitals on top of the pillars;

the two sets of network decorating the two bowl-shaped capitals on top of the pillars;

¹³ the four hundred pomegranates for the two sets of network (two rows of pomegranates for each network, decorating the bowl-shaped capitals on top of the pillars);

¹⁴ the stands with their basins;

¹⁵ the Sea and the twelve bulls under it;

¹⁶ the pots, shovels, meat forks and all related articles.

All the objects that Huram-Abi made for King Solomon for the temple of the LORD were of polished bronze. ¹⁷ The king had them cast in clay molds in the plain of the Jordan between Sukkoth and Zarethan.ᵃ ¹⁸ All these things that Solomon made amounted to so much that the weight of the bronze could not be calculated.

¹⁹ Solomon also made all the furnishings that were in God's temple:

the golden altar;

the tables on which was the bread of the Presence;

²⁰ the lampstands of pure gold with their lamps, to burn in front of the inner sanctuary as prescribed;

²¹ the gold floral work and lamps and tongs (they were solid gold);

²² the pure gold wick trimmers, sprinkling bowls, dishes and censers; and the gold doors of the temple: the inner doors to the Most Holy Place and the doors of the main hall.

5 When all the work Solomon had done for the temple of the LORD was finished, he brought in the things his father David had dedicated—the silver and gold and all the furnishings—and he placed them in the treasuries of God's temple.

The Ark Brought to the Temple

² Then Solomon summoned to Jerusalem the elders of Israel, all the heads of the tribes and the chiefs of the Israelite families, to bring up the ark of the LORD's covenant from Zion, the City of David. ³ And all the Israelites came together to the king at the time of the festival in the seventh month.

⁴ When all the elders of Israel had arrived, the Levites took up

ᵃ 17 Hebrew *Zeredatha*, a variant of *Zarethan*

the ark, [5]and they brought up the ark and the tent of meeting and all the sacred furnishings in it. The Levitical priests carried them up; [6]and King Solomon and the entire assembly of Israel that had gathered about him were before the ark, sacrificing so many sheep and cattle that they could not be recorded or counted.

[7]The priests then brought the ark of the LORD's covenant to its place in the inner sanctuary of the temple, the Most Holy Place, and put it beneath the wings of the cherubim. [8]The cherubim spread their wings over the place of the ark and covered the ark and its carrying poles. [9]These poles were so long that their ends, extending from the ark, could be seen from in front of the inner sanctuary, but not from outside the Holy Place; and they are still there today. [10]There was nothing in the ark except the two tablets that Moses had placed in it at Horeb, where the LORD made a covenant with the Israelites after they came out of Egypt.

[11]The priests then withdrew from the Holy Place. All the priests who were there had consecrated themselves, regardless of their divisions. [12]All the Levites who were musicians—Asaph, Heman, Jeduthun and their sons and relatives—stood on the east side of the altar, dressed in fine linen and playing cymbals, harps and lyres. They were accompanied by 120 priests sounding trumpets. [13]The trumpeters and musicians joined in unison to give praise and thanks to the LORD. Accompanied by trumpets, cymbals and other instruments, the singers raised their voices in praise to the LORD and sang:

"He is good;
his love endures forever."

Then the temple of the LORD was filled with the cloud, [14]and the priests could not perform their service because of the cloud, for the glory of the LORD filled the temple of God.

6 Then Solomon said, "The LORD has said that he would dwell in a dark cloud; [2]I have built a magnificent temple for you, a place for you to dwell forever."

[3]While the whole assembly of Israel was standing there, the king turned around and blessed them. [4]Then he said:

"Praise be to the LORD, the God of Israel, who with his hands has fulfilled what he promised with his mouth to my father David. For he said, [5]'Since the day I brought my people out of Egypt, I have not chosen a city in any tribe of Israel to have a temple built so that my Name might be there, nor have I chosen anyone to be ruler over my people Israel. [6]But now I have chosen Jerusalem for my Name to be there, and I have chosen David to rule my people Israel.'

⁷ "My father David had it in his heart to build a temple for the Name of the LORD, the God of Israel. ⁸ But the LORD said to my father David, 'You did well to have it in your heart to build a temple for my Name. ⁹ Nevertheless, you are not the one to build the temple, but your son, your own flesh and blood—he is the one who will build the temple for my Name.'

¹⁰ "The LORD has kept the promise he made. I have succeeded David my father and now I sit on the throne of Israel, just as the LORD promised, and I have built the temple for the Name of the LORD, the God of Israel. ¹¹ There I have placed the ark, in which is the covenant of the LORD that he made with the people of Israel."

Solomon's Prayer of Dedication

¹² Then Solomon stood before the altar of the LORD in front of the whole assembly of Israel and spread out his hands. ¹³ Now he had made a bronze platform, five cubits long, five cubits wide and three cubits high,ᵃ and had placed it in the center of the out-er court. He stood on the platform and then knelt down before the whole assembly of Israel and spread out his hands toward heaven. ¹⁴ He said:

"LORD, the God of Israel, there is no God like you in heaven or on earth—you who keep your covenant of love with your servants who continue wholeheartedly in your way. ¹⁵ You have kept your promise to your servant David my father; with your mouth you have promised and with your hand you have fulfilled it—as it is today.

¹⁶ "Now, LORD, the God of Israel, keep for your servant David my father the promises you made to him when you said, 'You shall never fail to have a successor to sit before me on the throne of Israel, if only your descendants are careful in all they do to walk before me according to my law, as you have done.' ¹⁷ And now, LORD, the God of Israel, let your word that you promised your servant David come true.

¹⁸ "But will God really dwell on earth with humans? The heavens, even the highest heavens, cannot contain you. How much less this temple I have built! ¹⁹ Yet, LORD my God, give attention to your

---

ᵃ 13 That is, about 7 1/2 feet long and wide and 4 1/2 feet high or about 2.3 meters long and wide and 1.4 meters high servant's prayer and his plea for mercy. Hear the cry and the prayer that your servant is praying in your presence. [20]May your eyes be open toward this temple day and night, this place of which you said you would put your Name there. May you hear the prayer your servant prays toward this place. [21]Hear the supplications of your servant and of your people Israel when they pray toward this place. Hear from heaven, your dwelling place; and when you hear, forgive.

[22]"When anyone wrongs their neighbor and is required to take an oath and they come and swear the oath before your altar in this temple, [23]then hear from heaven and act. Judge between your servants, condemning the guilty and bringing down on their heads what they have done, and vindicating the innocent by treating them in accordance with their innocence.

[24]"When your people Israel have been defeated by an enemy because they have sinned against you and when they turn back and give praise to your name, praying and making supplication before you in this temple, [25]then hear from heaven and forgive the sin of your people Israel and bring them back to the land you gave to them and their ancestors.

[26]"When the heavens are shut up and there is no rain because your people have sinned against you, and when they pray toward this place and give praise to your name and turn from their sin because you have afflicted them, [27]then hear from heaven and forgive the sin of your servants, your people Israel. Teach them the right way to live, and send rain on the land you gave your people for an inheritance.

[28]"When famine or plague comes to the land, or blight or mildew, locusts or grasshoppers, or when enemies besiege them in any of their cities, whatever disaster or disease may come, [29]and when a prayer or plea is made by anyone among your people Israel—being aware of their afflictions and pains, and spreading out their hands toward this temple— [30]then hear from heaven, your dwelling place. Forgive, and deal with everyone according to all they do, since you know their hearts (for you alone know the human heart), [31]so that they will fear you and walk in obedience to you all the time they live in the land you gave our ancestors.

[32] "As for the foreigner who does not belong to your people Israel but has come from a distant land because of your great name and your mighty hand and your outstretched arm — when they come and pray toward this temple, [33] then hear from heaven, your dwelling place. Do whatever the foreigner asks of you, so that all the peoples of the earth may know your name and fear you, as do your own people Israel, and may know that this house I have built bears your Name.

[34] "When your people go to war against their enemies, wherever you send them, and when they pray to you toward this city you have chosen and the temple I have built for your Name, [35] then hear from heaven their prayer and their plea, and uphold their cause.

[36] "When they sin against you — for there is no one who does not sin — and you become angry with them and give them over to the enemy, who takes them captive to a land far away or near; [37] and if they have a change of heart in the land where they are held captive, and repent and plead with you in the land of their captivity and say, 'We have sinned, we have done wrong and acted wickedly'; [38] and if they turn back to you with all their heart and soul in the land of their captivity where they were taken, and pray toward the land you gave their ancestors, toward the city you have chosen and toward the temple I have built for your Name; [39] then from heaven, your dwelling place, hear their prayer and their pleas, and uphold their cause. And forgive your people, who have sinned against you.

[40] "Now, my God, may your eyes be open and your ears attentive to the prayers offered in this place.

[41] "Now arise, LORD God, and come to your resting place,
you and the ark of your might.
May your priests, LORD God, be clothed with salvation,
may your faithful people rejoice in your goodness.
[42] LORD God, do not reject your anointed one.
Remember the great love promised to David your servant."

The Dedication of the Temple

7 When Solomon finished praying, fire came down from heaven and consumed the burnt offering and the sacrifices, and the glory of the LORD filled the temple. [2] The priests could

not enter the temple of the LORD because the glory of the LORD filled it. ³When all the Israelites saw the fire coming down and the glory of the LORD above the temple, they knelt on the pavement with their faces to the ground, and they worshiped and gave thanks to the LORD, saying,

"He is good;
his love endures forever."

⁴Then the king and all the people offered sacrifices before the LORD. ⁵And King Solomon offered a sacrifice of twenty-two thousand head of cattle and a hundred and twenty thousand sheep and goats. So the king and all the people dedicated the temple of God. ⁶The priests took their positions, as did the Levites with the LORD's musical instruments, which King David had made for praising the LORD and which were used when he gave thanks, saying, "His love endures forever." Opposite the Levites, the priests blew their trumpets, and all the Israelites were standing.

⁷Solomon consecrated the middle part of the courtyard in front of the temple of the LORD, and there he offered burnt offerings and the fat of the fellowship offerings, because the bronze altar he had made could not hold the burnt offerings, the grain offerings and the fat portions.

⁸So Solomon observed the festival at that time for seven days, and all Israel with him — a vast assembly, people from Lebo Hamath to the Wadi of Egypt. ⁹On the eighth day they held an assembly, for they had celebrated the dedication of the altar for seven days and the festival for seven days more. ¹⁰On the twenty-third day of the seventh month he sent the people to their homes, joyful and glad in heart for the good things the LORD had done for David and Solomon and for his people Israel.

The LORD Appears to Solomon

¹¹When Solomon had finished the temple of the LORD and the royal palace, and had succeeded in carrying out all he had in mind to do in the temple of the LORD and in his own palace, ¹²the LORD appeared to him at night and said:

"I have heard your prayer and have chosen this place for myself as a temple for sacrifices.

¹³"When I shut up the heavens so that there is no rain, or command locusts to devour the land or send a plague among my people, ¹⁴if my people, who are called by my name, will humble themselves and pray and seek my face and turn from their wicked ways, then I will hear from heaven, and I will forgive their sin and will heal their land. ¹⁵Now my eyes will be open and my ears at-

tentive to the prayers offered in this place. **16**I have chosen and consecrated this temple so that my Name may be there forever. My eyes and my heart will always be there.

17"As for you, if you walk before me faithfully as David your father did, and do all I command, and observe my decrees and laws, **18**I will establish your royal throne, as I covenanted with David your father when I said, 'You shall never fail to have a successor to rule over Israel.'

19"But if you*a* turn away and forsake the decrees and commands I have given you*a* and go off to serve other gods and worship them, **20**then I will uproot Israel from my land, which I have given them, and will reject this temple I have consecrated for my Name. I will make it a byword and an object of ridicule among all peoples. **21**This temple will become a heap of rubble. All*b* who pass by will be appalled and say, 'Why has the LORD done such a thing to this land and to this temple?' **22**People will answer, 'Because they have forsaken the LORD, the God of their ancestors, who brought them out of Egypt, and have

embraced other gods, worshiping and serving them — that is why he brought all this disaster on them.' "

Solomon's Other Activities

8 At the end of twenty years, during which Solomon built the temple of the LORD and his own palace, **2**Solomon rebuilt the villages that Hiram*c* had given him, and settled Israelites in them. **3**Solomon then went to Hamath Zobah and captured it. **4**He also built up Tadmor in the desert and all the store cities he had built in Hamath. **5**He rebuilt Upper Beth Horon and Lower Beth Horon as fortified cities, with walls and with gates and bars, **6**as well as Baalath and all his store cities, and all the cities for his chariots and for his horses*d* — whatever he desired to build in Jerusalem, in Lebanon and throughout all the territory he ruled.

7There were still people left from the Hittites, Amorites, Perizzites, Hivites and Jebusites (these people were not Israelites). **8**Solomon conscripted the descendants of all these people remaining in the land — whom the Israelites had not destroyed — to serve as slave labor, as it is to this day. **9**But Solomon did not make slaves of the Israelites for his

---

a 19 The Hebrew is plural. *b 21* See some Septuagint manuscripts, Old Latin, Syriac, Arabic and Targum; Hebrew *And though this temple is now so imposing, all*
c 2 Hebrew *Huram,* a variant of *Hiram*; also in verse 18 *d 6* Or *charioteers*

work; they were his fighting men, commanders of his captains, and commanders of his chariots and charioteers. [10]They were also King Solomon's chief officials — two hundred and fifty officials supervising the men.

[11]Solomon brought Pharaoh's daughter up from the City of David to the palace he had built for her, for he said, "My wife must not live in the palace of David king of Israel, because the places the ark of the LORD has entered are holy."

[12]On the altar of the LORD that he had built in front of the portico, Solomon sacrificed burnt offerings to the LORD, [13]according to the daily requirement for offerings commanded by Moses for the Sabbaths, the New Moons and the three annual festivals — the Festival of Unleavened Bread, the Festival of Weeks and the Festival of Tabernacles. [14]In keeping with the ordinance of his father David, he appointed the divisions of the priests for their duties, and the Levites to lead the praise and to assist the priests according to each day's requirement. He also appointed the gatekeepers by divisions for the various gates, because this was what David the man of God had ordered. [15]They did not deviate from the king's commands to the priests or to the Levites in any matter, including that of the treasuries.

[16]All Solomon's work was carried out, from the day the foundation of the temple of the LORD was laid until its completion. So the temple of the LORD was finished.

[17]Then Solomon went to Ezion Geber and Elath on the coast of Edom. [18]And Hiram sent him ships commanded by his own men, sailors who knew the sea. These, with Solomon's men, sailed to Ophir and brought back four hundred and fifty talents[a] of gold, which they delivered to King Solomon.

The Queen of Sheba Visits Solomon

9 When the queen of Sheba heard of Solomon's fame, she came to Jerusalem to test him with hard questions. Arriving with a very great caravan — with camels carrying spices, large quantities of gold, and precious stones — she came to Solomon and talked with him about all she had on her mind. [2]Solomon answered all her questions; nothing was too hard for him to explain to her. [3]When the queen of Sheba saw the wisdom of Solomon, as well as the palace he had built, [4]the food on his table, the seating of his officials, the attending servants in their robes, the cupbearers in their robes and the burnt offerings he made at[b] the temple of the LORD, she was overwhelmed.

---

[a] 18 That is, about 17 tons or about 15 metric tons   [b] 4 Or *and the ascent by which he went up to*

⁵She said to the king, "The report I heard in my own country about your achievements and your wisdom is true. ⁶But I did not believe what they said until I came and saw with my own eyes. Indeed, not even half the greatness of your wisdom was told me; you have far exceeded the report I heard. ⁷How happy your people must be! How happy your officials, who continually stand before you and hear your wisdom! ⁸Praise be to the LORD your God, who has delighted in you and placed you on his throne as king to rule for the LORD your God. Because of the love of your God for Israel and his desire to uphold them forever, he has made you king over them, to maintain justice and righteousness."

⁹Then she gave the king 120 talents[a] of gold, large quantities of spices, and precious stones. There had never been such spices as those the queen of Sheba gave to King Solomon.

¹⁰(The servants of Hiram and the servants of Solomon brought gold from Ophir; they also brought algumwood[b] and precious stones. ¹¹The king used the algumwood to make steps for the temple of the LORD and for the royal palace, and to make harps and lyres for the musicians. Nothing like them had ever been seen in Judah.)

¹²King Solomon gave the queen of Sheba all she desired and asked for; he gave her more than she had brought to him. Then she left and returned with her retinue to her own country.

Solomon's Splendor

¹³The weight of the gold that Solomon received yearly was 666 talents,[c] ¹⁴not including the revenues brought in by merchants and traders. Also all the kings of Arabia and the governors of the territories brought gold and silver to Solomon.

¹⁵King Solomon made two hundred large shields of hammered gold; six hundred shekels[d] of hammered gold went into each shield. ¹⁶He also made three hundred small shields of hammered gold, with three hundred shekels[e] of gold in each shield. The king put them in the Palace of the Forest of Lebanon.

¹⁷Then the king made a great throne covered with ivory and overlaid with pure gold. ¹⁸The throne had six steps, and a footstool of gold was attached to it. On both sides of the seat were armrests, with a lion standing beside each of them. ¹⁹Twelve lions stood on the six steps, one at either end of each step. Nothing like it had ever been made for any other kingdom. ²⁰All King Solomon's goblets were

---

[a] 9 That is, about 4 1/2 tons or about 4 metric tons   [b] 10 Probably a variant of *almugwood*   [c] 13 That is, about 25 tons or about 23 metric tons   [d] 15 That is, about 15 pounds or about 6.9 kilograms   [e] 16 That is, about 7 1/2 pounds or about 3.5 kilograms

gold, and all the household articles in the Palace of the Forest of Lebanon were pure gold. Nothing was made of silver, because silver was considered of little value in Solomon's day. ²¹The king had a fleet of trading ships*ᵃ* manned by Hiram's*ᵇ* servants. Once every three years it returned, carrying gold, silver and ivory, and apes and baboons.

²²King Solomon was greater in riches and wisdom than all the other kings of the earth. ²³All the kings of the earth sought audience with Solomon to hear the wisdom God had put in his heart. ²⁴Year after year, everyone who came brought a gift—articles of silver and gold, and robes, weapons and spices, and horses and mules.

²⁵Solomon had four thousand stalls for horses and chariots, and twelve thousand horses,*ᶜ* which he kept in the chariot cities and also with him in Jerusalem. ²⁶He ruled over all the kings from the Euphrates River to the land of the Philistines, as far as the border of Egypt. ²⁷The king made silver as common in Jerusalem as stones, and cedar as plentiful as sycamore-fig trees in the foothills. ²⁸Solomon's horses were imported from Egypt and from all other countries.

Solomon's Death

²⁹As for the other events of Solomon's reign, from beginning to end, are they not written in the records of Nathan the prophet, in the prophecy of Ahijah the Shilonite and in the visions of Iddo the seer concerning Jeroboam son of Nebat? ³⁰Solomon reigned in Jerusalem over all Israel forty years. ³¹Then he rested with his ancestors and was buried in the city of David his father. And Rehoboam his son succeeded him as king.

Israel Rebels Against Rehoboam

10 Rehoboam went to Shechem, for all Israel had gone there to make him king. ²When Jeroboam son of Nebat heard this (he was in Egypt, where he had fled from King Solomon), he returned from Egypt. ³So they sent for Jeroboam, and he and all Israel went to Rehoboam and said to him: ⁴"Your father put a heavy yoke on us, but now lighten the harsh labor and the heavy yoke he put on us, and we will serve you."

⁵Rehoboam answered, "Come back to me in three days." So the people went away.

⁶Then King Rehoboam consulted the elders who had served his father Solomon during his lifetime. "How would you advise me to answer these people?" he asked.

⁷They replied, "If you will be kind to these people and please

---

ᵃ 21 Hebrew *of ships that could go to Tarshish*   *ᵇ 21* Hebrew *Huram,* a variant of *Hiram*   *ᶜ 25* Or *charioteers* them and give them a favorable answer, they will always be your servants."

8 But Rehoboam rejected the advice the elders gave him and consulted the young men who had grown up with him and were serving him. 9 He asked them, "What is your advice? How should we answer these people who say to me, 'Lighten the yoke your father put on us'?"

10 The young men who had grown up with him replied, "The people have said to you, 'Your father put a heavy yoke on us, but make our yoke lighter.' Now tell them, 'My little finger is thicker than my father's waist. 11 My father laid on you a heavy yoke; I will make it even heavier. My father scourged you with whips; I will scourge you with scorpions.'"

12 Three days later Jeroboam and all the people returned to Rehoboam, as the king had said, "Come back to me in three days." 13 The king answered them harshly. Rejecting the advice of the elders, 14 he followed the advice of the young men and said, "My father made your yoke heavy; I will make it even heavier. My father scourged you with whips; I will scourge you with scorpions." 15 So the king did not listen to the people, for this turn of events was from God, to fulfill the word the LORD had spoken to Jeroboam son of Nebat through Ahijah the Shilonite.

16 When all Israel saw that the king refused to listen to them, they answered the king:

"What share do we have in
    David,
    what part in Jesse's son?
To your tents, Israel!
    Look after your own house,
    David!"

So all the Israelites went home. 17 But as for the Israelites who were living in the towns of Judah, Rehoboam still ruled over them.

18 King Rehoboam sent out Adoniram,[a] who was in charge of forced labor, but the Israelites stoned him to death. King Rehoboam, however, managed to get into his chariot and escape to Jerusalem. 19 So Israel has been in rebellion against the house of David to this day.

11 When Rehoboam arrived in Jerusalem, he mustered Judah and Benjamin—a hundred and eighty thousand able young men—to go to war against Israel and to regain the kingdom for Rehoboam.

2 But this word of the LORD came to Shemaiah the man of God: 3 "Say to Rehoboam son of Solomon king of Judah and to all Israel in Judah and Benjamin, 4 'This is what the LORD says: Do not go up to fight against your fellow Israelites. Go home, every

---

a 18 Hebrew *Hadoram*, a variant of *Adoniram*

one of you, for this is my doing.'" So they obeyed the words of the LORD and turned back from marching against Jeroboam.

Rehoboam Fortifies Judah

⁵Rehoboam lived in Jerusalem and built up towns for defense in Judah: ⁶Bethlehem, Etam, Tekoa, ⁷Beth Zur, Soko, Adullam, ⁸Gath, Mareshah, Ziph, ⁹Adoraim, Lachish, Azekah, ¹⁰Zorah, Aijalon and Hebron. These were fortified cities in Judah and Benjamin. ¹¹He strengthened their defenses and put commanders in them, with supplies of food, olive oil and wine. ¹²He put shields and spears in all the cities, and made them very strong. So Judah and Benjamin were his.

¹³The priests and Levites from all their districts throughout Israel sided with him. ¹⁴The Levites even abandoned their pasturelands and property and came to Judah and Jerusalem, because Jeroboam and his sons had rejected them as priests of the LORD ¹⁵when he appointed his own priests for the high places and for the goat and calf idols he had made. ¹⁶Those from every tribe of Israel who set their hearts on seeking the LORD, the God of Israel, followed the Levites to Jerusalem to offer sacrifices to the LORD, the God of their ancestors. ¹⁷They strengthened the kingdom of Judah and supported Rehoboam son of Solomon three years, following the ways of David and Solomon during this time.

Rehoboam's Family

¹⁸Rehoboam married Mahalath, who was the daughter of David's son Jerimoth and of Abihail, the daughter of Jesse's son Eliab. ¹⁹She bore him sons: Jeush, Shemariah and Zaham. ²⁰Then he married Maakah daughter of Absalom, who bore him Abijah, Attai, Ziza and Shelomith. ²¹Rehoboam loved Maakah daughter of Absalom more than any of his other wives and concubines. In all, he had eighteen wives and sixty concubines, twenty-eight sons and sixty daughters.

²²Rehoboam appointed Abijah son of Maakah as crown prince among his brothers, in order to make him king. ²³He acted wisely, dispersing some of his sons throughout the districts of Judah and Benjamin, and to all the fortified cities. He gave them abundant provisions and took many wives for them.

Shishak Attacks Jerusalem

12 After Rehoboam's position as king was established and he had become strong, he and all Israel[a] with him abandoned the law of the LORD. ²Because they had been unfaithful to the LORD, Shishak

---

[a] 1 That is, Judah, as frequently in 2 Chronicles

king of Egypt attacked Jerusalem in the fifth year of King Rehoboam. ³With twelve hundred chariots and sixty thousand horsemen and the innumerable troops of Libyans, Sukkites and Cushites*a* that came with him from Egypt, ⁴he captured the fortified cities of Judah and came as far as Jerusalem.

⁵Then the prophet Shemaiah came to Rehoboam and to the leaders of Judah who had assembled in Jerusalem for fear of Shishak, and he said to them, "This is what the Lord says, 'You have abandoned me; therefore, I now abandon you to Shishak.'"

⁶The leaders of Israel and the king humbled themselves and said, "The Lord is just."

⁷When the Lord saw that they humbled themselves, this word of the Lord came to Shemaiah: "Since they have humbled themselves, I will not destroy them but will soon give them deliverance. My wrath will not be poured out on Jerusalem through Shishak. ⁸They will, however, become subject to him, so that they may learn the difference between serving me and serving the kings of other lands."

⁹When Shishak king of Egypt attacked Jerusalem, he carried off the treasures of the temple of the Lord and the treasures of the royal palace. He took everything, including the gold shields Solomon had made. ¹⁰So King Rehoboam made bronze shields to replace them and assigned these to the commanders of the guard on duty at the entrance to the royal palace. ¹¹Whenever the king went to the Lord's temple, the guards went with him, bearing the shields, and afterward they returned them to the guardroom.

¹²Because Rehoboam humbled himself, the Lord's anger turned from him, and he was not totally destroyed. Indeed, there was some good in Judah.

¹³King Rehoboam established himself firmly in Jerusalem and continued as king. He was forty-one years old when he became king, and he reigned seventeen years in Jerusalem, the city the Lord had chosen out of all the tribes of Israel in which to put his Name. His mother's name was Naamah; she was an Ammonite. ¹⁴He did evil because he had not set his heart on seeking the Lord.

¹⁵As for the events of Rehoboam's reign, from beginning to end, are they not written in the records of Shemaiah the prophet and of Iddo the seer that deal with genealogies? There was continual warfare between Rehoboam and Jeroboam. ¹⁶Rehoboam rested with his ancestors and was buried in the City of David. And Abijah his son succeeded him as king.

---

a 3 That is, people from the upper Nile region

Abijah King of Judah

13 In the eighteenth year of the reign of Jeroboam, Abijah became king of Judah, ²and he reigned in Jerusalem three years. His mother's name was Maakah,ᵃ a daughterᵇ of Uriel of Gibeah.

There was war between Abijah and Jeroboam. ³Abijah went into battle with an army of four hundred thousand able fighting men, and Jeroboam drew up a battle line against him with eight hundred thousand able troops.

⁴Abijah stood on Mount Zemaraim, in the hill country of Ephraim, and said, "Jeroboam and all Israel, listen to me! ⁵Don't you know that the LORD, the God of Israel, has given the kingship of Israel to David and his descendants forever by a covenant of salt? ⁶Yet Jeroboam son of Nebat, an official of Solomon son of David, rebelled against his master. ⁷Some worthless scoundrels gathered around him and opposed Rehoboam son of Solomon when he was young and indecisive and not strong enough to resist them.

⁸"And now you plan to resist the kingdom of the LORD, which is in the hands of David's descendants. You are indeed a vast army and have with you the golden calves that Jeroboam made to be your gods. ⁹But didn't you drive out the priests of the LORD, the sons of Aaron, and the Levites, and make priests of your own as the peoples of other lands do? Whoever comes to consecrate himself with a young bull and seven rams may become a priest of what are not gods.

¹⁰"As for us, the LORD is our God, and we have not forsaken him. The priests who serve the LORD are sons of Aaron, and the Levites assist them. ¹¹Every morning and evening they present burnt offerings and fragrant incense to the LORD. They set out the bread on the ceremonially clean table and light the lamps on the gold lampstand every evening. We are observing the requirements of the LORD our God. But you have forsaken him. ¹²God is with us; he is our leader. His priests with their trumpets will sound the battle cry against you. People of Israel, do not fight against the LORD, the God of your ancestors, for you will not succeed."

¹³Now Jeroboam had sent troops around to the rear, so that while he was in front of Judah the ambush was behind them. ¹⁴Judah turned and saw that they were being attacked at both front and rear. Then they cried out to the LORD. The priests blew their trumpets ¹⁵and the men of Judah raised the battle cry. At the sound of their battle cry, God routed Jeroboam and all Israel before

---

ᵃ 2 Most Septuagint manuscripts and Syriac (see also 11:20 and 1 Kings 15:2); Hebrew *Micaiah*   ᵇ 2 Or *granddaughter*

Abijah and Judah. ¹⁶The Israelites fled before Judah, and God delivered them into their hands. ¹⁷Abijah and his troops inflicted heavy losses on them, so that there were five hundred thousand casualties among Israel's able men. ¹⁸The Israelites were subdued on that occasion, and the people of Judah were victorious because they relied on the LORD, the God of their ancestors.

¹⁹Abijah pursued Jeroboam and took from him the towns of Bethel, Jeshanah and Ephron, with their surrounding villages. ²⁰Jeroboam did not regain power during the time of Abijah. And the LORD struck him down and he died.

²¹But Abijah grew in strength. He married fourteen wives and had twenty-two sons and sixteen daughters.

²²The other events of Abijah's reign, what he did and what he said, are written in the annotations of the prophet Iddo.

14 ᵃ And Abijah rested with his ancestors and was buried in the City of David. Asa his son succeeded him as king, and in his days the country was at peace for ten years.

Asa King of Judah

²Asa did what was good and right in the eyes of the LORD his God. ³He removed the foreign altars and the high places, smashed the sacred stones and cut down the Asherah poles.ᵇ ⁴He commanded Judah to seek the LORD, the God of their ancestors, and to obey his laws and commands. ⁵He removed the high places and incense altars in every town in Judah, and the kingdom was at peace under him. ⁶He built up the fortified cities of Judah, since the land was at peace. No one was at war with him during those years, for the LORD gave him rest.

⁷"Let us build up these towns," he said to Judah, "and put walls around them, with towers, gates and bars. The land is still ours, because we have sought the LORD our God; we sought him and he has given us rest on every side." So they built and prospered.

⁸Asa had an army of three hundred thousand men from Judah, equipped with large shields and with spears, and two hundred and eighty thousand from Benjamin, armed with small shields and with bows. All these were brave fighting men.

⁹Zerah the Cushite marched out against them with an army of thousands upon thousands and three hundred chariots, and came as far as Mareshah. ¹⁰Asa went out to meet him, and they took up battle positions in the Valley of Zephathah near Mareshah.

ᵃ In Hebrew texts 14:1 is numbered 13:23, and 14:2-15 is numbered 14:1-14.
ᵇ 3 That is, wooden symbols of the goddess Asherah; here and elsewhere in 2 Chronicles

[11]Then Asa called to the LORD his God and said, "LORD, there is no one like you to help the powerless against the mighty. Help us, LORD our God, for we rely on you, and in your name we have come against this vast army. LORD, you are our God; do not let mere mortals prevail against you."

[12]The LORD struck down the Cushites before Asa and Judah. The Cushites fled, [13]and Asa and his army pursued them as far as Gerar. Such a great number of Cushites fell that they could not recover; they were crushed before the LORD and his forces. The men of Judah carried off a large amount of plunder. [14]They destroyed all the villages around Gerar, for the terror of the LORD had fallen on them. They looted all these villages, since there was much plunder there. [15]They also attacked the camps of the herders and carried off droves of sheep and goats and camels. Then they returned to Jerusalem.

Asa's Reform

15 The Spirit of God came on Azariah son of Oded. [2]He went out to meet Asa and said to him, "Listen to me, Asa and all Judah and Benjamin. The LORD is with you when you are with him. If you seek him, he will be found by you, but if you forsake him, he will forsake you. [3]For a long time Israel was without the true God, without a priest to teach and without the law. [4]But in their distress they turned to the LORD, the God of Israel, and sought him, and he was found by them. [5]In those days it was not safe to travel about, for all the inhabitants of the lands were in great turmoil. [6]One nation was being crushed by another and one city by another, because God was troubling them with every kind of distress. [7]But as for you, be strong and do not give up, for your work will be rewarded."

[8]When Asa heard these words and the prophecy of Azariah son of[a] Oded the prophet, he took courage. He removed the detestable idols from the whole land of Judah and Benjamin and from the towns he had captured in the hills of Ephraim. He repaired the altar of the LORD that was in front of the portico of the LORD's temple.

[9]Then he assembled all Judah and Benjamin and the people from Ephraim, Manasseh and Simeon who had settled among them, for large numbers had come over to him from Israel when they saw that the LORD his God was with him.

[10]They assembled at Jerusalem in the third month of the fifteenth year of Asa's reign. [11]At that time they sacrificed to the LORD seven

---

[a] 8 Vulgate and Syriac (see also Septuagint and verse 1); Hebrew does not have *Azariah son of.*

hundred head of cattle and seven thousand sheep and goats from the plunder they had brought back. [12]They entered into a covenant to seek the LORD, the God of their ancestors, with all their heart and soul. [13]All who would not seek the LORD, the God of Israel, were to be put to death, whether small or great, man or woman. [14]They took an oath to the LORD with loud acclamation, with shouting and with trumpets and horns. [15]All Judah rejoiced about the oath because they had sworn it wholeheartedly. They sought God eagerly, and he was found by them. So the LORD gave them rest on every side.

[16]King Asa also deposed his grandmother Maakah from her position as queen mother, because she had made a repulsive image for the worship of Asherah. Asa cut it down, broke it up and burned it in the Kidron Valley. [17]Although he did not remove the high places from Israel, Asa's heart was fully committed to the LORD all his life. [18]He brought into the temple of God the silver and gold and the articles that he and his father had dedicated.

[19]There was no more war until the thirty-fifth year of Asa's reign.

Asa's Last Years

16 In the thirty-sixth year of Asa's reign Baasha king of Israel went up against Judah and fortified Ramah to prevent anyone from leaving or entering the territory of Asa king of Judah.

[2]Asa then took the silver and gold out of the treasuries of the LORD's temple and of his own palace and sent it to Ben-Hadad king of Aram, who was ruling in Damascus. [3]"Let there be a treaty between me and you," he said, "as there was between my father and your father. See, I am sending you silver and gold. Now break your treaty with Baasha king of Israel so he will withdraw from me."

[4]Ben-Hadad agreed with King Asa and sent the commanders of his forces against the towns of Israel. They conquered Ijon, Dan, Abel Maim[a] and all the store cities of Naphtali. [5]When Baasha heard this, he stopped building Ramah and abandoned his work. [6]Then King Asa brought all the men of Judah, and they carried away from Ramah the stones and timber Baasha had been using. With them he built up Geba and Mizpah.

[7]At that time Hanani the seer came to Asa king of Judah and said to him: "Because you relied on the king of Aram and not on the LORD your God, the army of the king of Aram has escaped from your hand. [8]Were not the Cushites[b] and Libyans a mighty

---

[a] 4 Also known as *Abel Beth Maakah* region   [b] 8 That is, people from the upper Nile

army with great numbers of chariots and horsemen[a]? Yet when you relied on the LORD, he delivered them into your hand. [9]For the eyes of the LORD range throughout the earth to strengthen those whose hearts are fully committed to him. You have done a foolish thing, and from now on you will be at war."

[10]Asa was angry with the seer because of this; he was so enraged that he put him in prison. At the same time Asa brutally oppressed some of the people.

[11]The events of Asa's reign, from beginning to end, are written in the book of the kings of Judah and Israel. [12]In the thirty-ninth year of his reign Asa was afflicted with a disease in his feet. Though his disease was severe, even in his illness he did not seek help from the LORD, but only from the physicians. [13]Then in the forty-first year of his reign Asa died and rested with his ancestors. [14]They buried him in the tomb that he had cut out for himself in the City of David. They laid him on a bier covered with spices and various blended perfumes, and they made a huge fire in his honor.

Jehoshaphat King of Judah

17 Jehoshaphat his son succeeded him as king and strengthened himself against Israel. [2]He stationed troops in all the fortified cities of Judah and put garrisons in Judah and in the towns of Ephraim that his father Asa had captured.

[3]The LORD was with Jehoshaphat because he followed the ways of his father David before him. He did not consult the Baals [4]but sought the God of his father and followed his commands rather than the practices of Israel. [5]The LORD established the kingdom under his control; and all Judah brought gifts to Jehoshaphat, so that he had great wealth and honor. [6]His heart was devoted to the ways of the LORD; furthermore, he removed the high places and the Asherah poles from Judah.

[7]In the third year of his reign he sent his officials Ben-Hail, Obadiah, Zechariah, Nethanel and Micaiah to teach in the towns of Judah. [8]With them were certain Levites — Shemaiah, Nethaniah, Zebadiah, Asahel, Shemiramoth, Jehonathan, Adonijah, Tobijah and Tob-Adonijah — and the priests Elishama and Jehoram. [9]They taught throughout Judah, taking with them the Book of the Law of the LORD; they went around to all the towns of Judah and taught the people.

[10]The fear of the LORD fell on all the kingdoms of the lands surrounding Judah, so that they did not go to war against Jehoshaphat. [11]Some Philistines brought Jehoshaphat gifts and silver as tribute, and the Arabs brought

---

[a] 8 Or *charioteers*

him flocks: seven thousand seven hundred rams and seven thousand seven hundred goats.

¹²Jehoshaphat became more and more powerful; he built forts and store cities in Judah ¹³and had large supplies in the towns of Judah. He also kept experienced fighting men in Jerusalem. ¹⁴Their enrollment by families was as follows:

From Judah, commanders of units of 1,000:

Adnah the commander, with 300,000 fighting men;

¹⁵next, Jehohanan the commander, with 280,000;

¹⁶next, Amasiah son of Zikri, who volunteered himself for the service of the Lord, with 200,000.

¹⁷From Benjamin:

Eliada, a valiant soldier, with 200,000 men armed with bows and shields;

¹⁸next, Jehozabad, with 180,000 men armed for battle.

¹⁹These were the men who served the king, besides those he stationed in the fortified cities throughout Judah.

Micaiah Prophesies Against Ahab

18 Now Jehoshaphat had great wealth and honor, and he allied himself with Ahab by marriage. ²Some years later he went down to see Ahab in Samaria. Ahab slaughtered many sheep and cattle for him and the people with him and urged him to attack Ramoth Gilead. ³Ahab king of Israel asked Jehoshaphat king of Judah, "Will you go with me against Ramoth Gilead?"

Jehoshaphat replied, "I am as you are, and my people as your people; we will join you in the war." ⁴But Jehoshaphat also said to the king of Israel, "First seek the counsel of the Lord."

⁵So the king of Israel brought together the prophets — four hundred men — and asked them, "Shall we go to war against Ramoth Gilead, or shall I not?"

"Go," they answered, "for God will give it into the king's hand."

⁶But Jehoshaphat asked, "Is there no longer a prophet of the Lord here whom we can inquire of?"

⁷The king of Israel answered Jehoshaphat, "There is still one prophet through whom we can inquire of the Lord, but I hate him because he never prophesies anything good about me, but always bad. He is Micaiah son of Imlah."

"The king should not say such a thing," Jehoshaphat replied.

⁸So the king of Israel called one of his officials and said, "Bring Micaiah son of Imlah at once."

⁹Dressed in their royal robes, the king of Israel and Jehoshaphat king of Judah were sitting

on their thrones at the threshing floor by the entrance of the gate of Samaria, with all the prophets prophesying before them. [10] Now Zedekiah son of Kenaanah had made iron horns, and he declared, "This is what the LORD says: 'With these you will gore the Arameans until they are destroyed.'"

[11] All the other prophets were prophesying the same thing. "Attack Ramoth Gilead and be victorious," they said, "for the LORD will give it into the king's hand."

[12] The messenger who had gone to summon Micaiah said to him, "Look, the other prophets without exception are predicting success for the king. Let your word agree with theirs, and speak favorably."

[13] But Micaiah said, "As surely as the LORD lives, I can tell him only what my God says."

[14] When he arrived, the king asked him, "Micaiah, shall we go to war against Ramoth Gilead, or shall I not?"

"Attack and be victorious," he answered, "for they will be given into your hand."

[15] The king said to him, "How many times must I make you swear to tell me nothing but the truth in the name of the LORD?"

[16] Then Micaiah answered, "I saw all Israel scattered on the hills like sheep without a shepherd, and the LORD said, 'These people have no master. Let each one go home in peace.'"

[17] The king of Israel said to Jehoshaphat, "Didn't I tell you that he never prophesies anything good about me, but only bad?"

[18] Micaiah continued, "Therefore hear the word of the LORD: I saw the LORD sitting on his throne with all the multitudes of heaven standing on his right and on his left. [19] And the LORD said, 'Who will entice Ahab king of Israel into attacking Ramoth Gilead and going to his death there?'

"One suggested this, and another that. [20] Finally, a spirit came forward, stood before the LORD and said, 'I will entice him.'

"'By what means?' the LORD asked.

[21] "'I will go and be a deceiving spirit in the mouths of all his prophets,' he said.

"'You will succeed in enticing him,' said the LORD. 'Go and do it.'

[22] "So now the LORD has put a deceiving spirit in the mouths of these prophets of yours. The LORD has decreed disaster for you."

[23] Then Zedekiah son of Kenaanah went up and slapped Micaiah in the face. "Which way did the spirit from[a] the LORD go when he went from me to speak to you?" he asked.

[24] Micaiah replied, "You will find out on the day you go to hide in an inner room."

---

[a] 23 Or Spirit of

²⁵The king of Israel then ordered, "Take Micaiah and send him back to Amon the ruler of the city and to Joash the king's son, ²⁶and say, 'This is what the king says: Put this fellow in prison and give him nothing but bread and water until I return safely.'"

²⁷Micaiah declared, "If you ever return safely, the LORD has not spoken through me." Then he added, "Mark my words, all you people!"

Ahab Killed at Ramoth Gilead

²⁸So the king of Israel and Jehoshaphat king of Judah went up to Ramoth Gilead. ²⁹The king of Israel said to Jehoshaphat, "I will enter the battle in disguise, but you wear your royal robes." So the king of Israel disguised himself and went into battle.

³⁰Now the king of Aram had ordered his chariot commanders, "Do not fight with anyone, small or great, except the king of Israel." ³¹When the chariot commanders saw Jehoshaphat, they thought, "This is the king of Israel." So they turned to attack him, but Jehoshaphat cried out, and the LORD helped him. God drew them away from him, ³²for when the chariot commanders saw that he was not the king of Israel, they stopped pursuing him.

³³But someone drew his bow at random and hit the king of Israel between the breastplate and the scale armor. The king told the chariot driver, "Wheel around and get me out of the fighting. I've been wounded." ³⁴All day long the battle raged, and the king of Israel propped himself up in his chariot facing the Arameans until evening. Then at sunset he died.

19 When Jehoshaphat king of Judah returned safely to his palace in Jerusalem, ²Jehu the seer, the son of Hanani, went out to meet him and said to the king, "Should you help the wicked and love*ᵃ* those who hate the LORD? Because of this, the wrath of the LORD is on you. ³There is, however, some good in you, for you have rid the land of the Asherah poles and have set your heart on seeking God."

Jehoshaphat Appoints Judges

⁴Jehoshaphat lived in Jerusalem, and he went out again among the people from Beersheba to the hill country of Ephraim and turned them back to the LORD, the God of their ancestors. ⁵He appointed judges in the land, in each of the fortified cities of Judah. ⁶He told them, "Consider carefully what you do, because you are not judging for mere mortals but for the LORD, who is with you whenever you give a verdict. ⁷Now let the fear of the LORD be on you. Judge carefully, for with the LORD our God there is no injustice or partiality or bribery."

ᵃ 2 Or *and make alliances with*

⁸In Jerusalem also, Jehoshaphat appointed some of the Levites, priests and heads of Israelite families to administer the law of the LORD and to settle disputes. And they lived in Jerusalem. ⁹He gave them these orders: "You must serve faithfully and wholeheartedly in the fear of the LORD. ¹⁰In every case that comes before you from your people who live in the cities—whether bloodshed or other concerns of the law, commands, decrees or regulations—you are to warn them not to sin against the LORD; otherwise his wrath will come on you and your people. Do this, and you will not sin.

¹¹ "Amariah the chief priest will be over you in any matter concerning the LORD, and Zebadiah son of Ishmael, the leader of the tribe of Judah, will be over you in any matter concerning the king, and the Levites will serve as officials before you. Act with courage, and may the LORD be with those who do well."

Jehoshaphat Defeats Moab and Ammon

20 After this, the Moabites and Ammonites with some of the Meunites*ᵃ* came to wage war against Jehoshaphat.

²Some people came and told Jehoshaphat, "A vast army is coming against you from Edom,*ᵇ* from the other side of the Dead Sea. It is already in Hazezon Tamar" (that is, En Gedi). ³Alarmed, Jehoshaphat resolved to inquire of the LORD, and he proclaimed a fast for all Judah. ⁴The people of Judah came together to seek help from the LORD; indeed, they came from every town in Judah to seek him.

⁵Then Jehoshaphat stood up in the assembly of Judah and Jerusalem at the temple of the LORD in the front of the new courtyard ⁶and said:

"LORD, the God of our ancestors, are you not the God who is in heaven? You rule over all the kingdoms of the nations. Power and might are in your hand, and no one can withstand you. ⁷Our God, did you not drive out the inhabitants of this land before your people Israel and give it forever to the descendants of Abraham your friend? ⁸They have lived in it and have built in it a sanctuary for your Name, saying, ⁹'If calamity comes upon us, whether the sword of judgment, or plague or famine, we will stand in your presence before this temple that bears your Name and will cry out to you in our distress, and you will hear us and save us.'

¹⁰"But now here are men from Ammon, Moab and

ᵃ 1 Some Septuagint manuscripts; Hebrew *Ammonites*   *ᵇ 2* One Hebrew manuscript; most Hebrew manuscripts, Septuagint and Vulgate *Aram*

Mount Seir, whose territory you would not allow Israel to invade when they came from Egypt; so they turned away from them and did not destroy them. ¹¹See how they are repaying us by coming to drive us out of the possession you gave us as an inheritance. ¹²Our God, will you not judge them? For we have no power to face this vast army that is attacking us. We do not know what to do, but our eyes are on you."

¹³All the men of Judah, with their wives and children and little ones, stood there before the LORD.

¹⁴Then the Spirit of the LORD came on Jahaziel son of Zechariah, the son of Benaiah, the son of Jeiel, the son of Mattaniah, a Levite and descendant of Asaph, as he stood in the assembly.

¹⁵He said: "Listen, King Jehoshaphat and all who live in Judah and Jerusalem! This is what the LORD says to you: 'Do not be afraid or discouraged because of this vast army. For the battle is not yours, but God's. ¹⁶Tomorrow march down against them. They will be climbing up by the Pass of Ziz, and you will find them at the end of the gorge in the Desert of Jeruel. ¹⁷You will not have to fight this battle. Take up your positions; stand firm and see the deliverance the LORD will give you, Judah and Jerusalem. Do not be afraid; do not be discouraged. Go out to face them tomorrow, and the LORD will be with you.'"

¹⁸Jehoshaphat bowed down with his face to the ground, and all the people of Judah and Jerusalem fell down in worship before the LORD. ¹⁹Then some Levites from the Kohathites and Korahites stood up and praised the LORD, the God of Israel, with a very loud voice.

²⁰Early in the morning they left for the Desert of Tekoa. As they set out, Jehoshaphat stood and said, "Listen to me, Judah and people of Jerusalem! Have faith in the LORD your God and you will be upheld; have faith in his prophets and you will be successful." ²¹After consulting the people, Jehoshaphat appointed men to sing to the LORD and to praise him for the splendor of his*a* holiness as they went out at the head of the army, saying:

"Give thanks to the LORD,
    for his love endures forever."

²²As they began to sing and praise, the LORD set ambushes against the men of Ammon and Moab and Mount Seir who were invading Judah, and they were defeated. ²³The Ammonites and Moabites rose up against the men from Mount Seir to destroy and annihilate them. After they finished slaughtering the men from

---

a 21 Or *him with the splendor of*

Seir, they helped to destroy one another.

²⁴When the men of Judah came to the place that overlooks the desert and looked toward the vast army, they saw only dead bodies lying on the ground; no one had escaped. ²⁵So Jehoshaphat and his men went to carry off their plunder, and they found among them a great amount of equipment and clothing*a* and also articles of value — more than they could take away. There was so much plunder that it took three days to collect it. ²⁶On the fourth day they assembled in the Valley of Berakah, where they praised the LORD. This is why it is called the Valley of Berakah*b* to this day.

²⁷Then, led by Jehoshaphat, all the men of Judah and Jerusalem returned joyfully to Jerusalem, for the LORD had given them cause to rejoice over their enemies. ²⁸They entered Jerusalem and went to the temple of the LORD with harps and lyres and trumpets.

²⁹The fear of God came on all the surrounding kingdoms when they heard how the LORD had fought against the enemies of Israel. ³⁰And the kingdom of Jehoshaphat was at peace, for his God had given him rest on every side.

The End of Jehoshaphat's Reign

³¹So Jehoshaphat reigned over Judah. He was thirty-five years old when he became king of Judah, and he reigned in Jerusalem twenty-five years. His mother's name was Azubah daughter of Shilhi. ³²He followed the ways of his father Asa and did not stray from them; he did what was right in the eyes of the LORD. ³³The high places, however, were not removed, and the people still had not set their hearts on the God of their ancestors.

³⁴The other events of Jehoshaphat's reign, from beginning to end, are written in the annals of Jehu son of Hanani, which are recorded in the book of the kings of Israel.

³⁵Later, Jehoshaphat king of Judah made an alliance with Ahaziah king of Israel, whose ways were wicked. ³⁶He agreed with him to construct a fleet of trading ships.*c* After these were built at Ezion Geber, ³⁷Eliezer son of Dodavahu of Mareshah prophesied against Jehoshaphat, saying, "Because you have made an alliance with Ahaziah, the LORD will destroy what you have made." The ships were wrecked and were not able to set sail to trade.*d*

21 Then Jehoshaphat rested with his ancestors and was buried with them in the

---

a 25 Some Hebrew manuscripts and Vulgate; most Hebrew manuscripts *corpses*
b 26 *Berakah* means *praise.* *c 36* Hebrew *of ships that could go to Tarshish*
d 37 Hebrew *sail for Tarshish*

City of David. And Jehoram his son succeeded him as king. ²Jehoram's brothers, the sons of Jehoshaphat, were Azariah, Jehiel, Zechariah, Azariahu, Michael and Shephatiah. All these were sons of Jehoshaphat king of Israel.*ª* ³Their father had given them many gifts of silver and gold and articles of value, as well as fortified cities in Judah, but he had given the kingdom to Jehoram because he was his firstborn son.

Jehoram King of Judah

⁴When Jehoram established himself firmly over his father's kingdom, he put all his brothers to the sword along with some of the officials of Israel. ⁵Jehoram was thirty-two years old when he became king, and he reigned in Jerusalem eight years. ⁶He followed the ways of the kings of Israel, as the house of Ahab had done, for he married a daughter of Ahab. He did evil in the eyes of the LORD. ⁷Nevertheless, because of the covenant the LORD had made with David, the LORD was not willing to destroy the house of David. He had promised to maintain a lamp for him and his descendants forever.

⁸In the time of Jehoram, Edom rebelled against Judah and set up its own king. ⁹So Jehoram went there with his officers and all his chariots. The Edomites surrounded him and his chariot commanders, but he rose up and broke through by night. ¹⁰To this day Edom has been in rebellion against Judah.

Libnah revolted at the same time, because Jehoram had forsaken the LORD, the God of his ancestors. ¹¹He had also built high places on the hills of Judah and had caused the people of Jerusalem to prostitute themselves and had led Judah astray.

¹²Jehoram received a letter from Elijah the prophet, which said:

"This is what the LORD, the God of your father David, says: 'You have not followed the ways of your father Jehoshaphat or of Asa king of Judah. ¹³But you have followed the ways of the kings of Israel, and you have led Judah and the people of Jerusalem to prostitute themselves, just as the house of Ahab did. You have also murdered your own brothers, members of your own family, men who were better than you. ¹⁴So now the LORD is about to strike your people, your sons, your wives and everything that is yours, with a heavy blow. ¹⁵You yourself will be very ill with a lingering disease of the bowels, until the disease causes your bowels to come out.'"

¹⁶The LORD aroused against Jehoram the hostility of the

ª 2 That is, Judah, as frequently in 2 Chronicles

Philistines and of the Arabs who lived near the Cushites. ¹⁷They attacked Judah, invaded it and carried off all the goods found in the king's palace, together with his sons and wives. Not a son was left to him except Ahaziah,ᵃ the youngest.

¹⁸After all this, the LORD afflicted Jehoram with an incurable disease of the bowels. ¹⁹In the course of time, at the end of the second year, his bowels came out because of the disease, and he died in great pain. His people made no funeral fire in his honor, as they had for his predecessors.

²⁰Jehoram was thirty-two years old when he became king, and he reigned in Jerusalem eight years. He passed away, to no one's regret, and was buried in the City of David, but not in the tombs of the kings.

Ahaziah King of Judah

22 The people of Jerusalem made Ahaziah, Jehoram's youngest son, king in his place, since the raiders, who came with the Arabs into the camp, had killed all the older sons. So Ahaziah son of Jehoram king of Judah began to reign.

²Ahaziah was twenty-twoᵇ years old when he became king,

and he reigned in Jerusalem one year. His mother's name was Athaliah, a granddaughter of Omri.

³He too followed the ways of the house of Ahab, for his mother encouraged him to act wickedly. ⁴He did evil in the eyes of the LORD, as the house of Ahab had done, for after his father's death they became his advisers, to his undoing. ⁵He also followed their counsel when he went with Joramᶜ son of Ahab king of Israel to wage war against Hazael king of Aram at Ramoth Gilead. The Arameans wounded Joram; ⁶so he returned to Jezreel to recover from the wounds they had inflicted on him at Ramothᵈ in his battle with Hazael king of Aram.

Then Ahaziahᵉ son of Jehoram king of Judah went down to Jezreel to see Joram son of Ahab because he had been wounded.

⁷Through Ahaziah's visit to Joram, God brought about Ahaziah's downfall. When Ahaziah arrived, he went out with Joram to meet Jehu son of Nimshi, whom the LORD had anointed to destroy the house of Ahab. ⁸While Jehu was executing judgment on the house of Ahab, he found the officials of Judah and the sons of Ahaziah's relatives, who had been attending Ahaziah, and he killed them. ⁹He then went in

---

ᵃ 17 Hebrew *Jehoahaz*, a variant of *Ahaziah*   ᵇ 2 Some Septuagint manuscripts and Syriac (see also 2 Kings 8:26); Hebrew *forty-two*   ᶜ 5 Hebrew *Jehoram*, a variant of *Joram*; also in verses 6 and 7   ᵈ 6 Hebrew *Ramah*, a variant of *Ramoth*   ᵉ 6 Some Hebrew manuscripts, Septuagint, Vulgate and Syriac (see also 2 Kings 8:29); most Hebrew manuscripts *Azariah* search of Ahaziah, and his men captured him while he was hiding in Samaria. He was brought to Jehu and put to death. They buried him, for they said, "He was a son of Jehoshaphat, who sought the LORD with all his heart." So there was no one in the house of Ahaziah powerful enough to retain the kingdom.

Athaliah and Joash

¹⁰When Athaliah the mother of Ahaziah saw that her son was dead, she proceeded to destroy the whole royal family of the house of Judah. ¹¹But Jehosheba,ᵃ the daughter of King Jehoram, took Joash son of Ahaziah and stole him away from among the royal princes who were about to be murdered and put him and his nurse in a bedroom. Because Jehosheba,ᵃ the daughter of King Jehoram and wife of the priest Jehoiada, was Ahaziah's sister, she hid the child from Athaliah so she could not kill him. ¹²He remained hidden with them at the temple of God for six years while Athaliah ruled the land.

23 In the seventh year Jehoiada showed his strength. He made a covenant with the commanders of units of a hundred: Azariah son of Jeroham, Ishmael son of Jehohanan, Azariah son of Obed, Maaseiah son of Adaiah, and Elishaphat son

of Zikri. ²They went throughout Judah and gathered the Levites and the heads of Israelite families from all the towns. When they came to Jerusalem, ³the whole assembly made a covenant with the king at the temple of God.

Jehoiada said to them, "The king's son shall reign, as the LORD promised concerning the descendants of David. ⁴Now this is what you are to do: A third of you priests and Levites who are going on duty on the Sabbath are to keep watch at the doors, ⁵a third of you at the royal palace and a third at the Foundation Gate, and all the others are to be in the courtyards of the temple of the LORD. ⁶No one is to enter the temple of the LORD except the priests and Levites on duty; they may enter because they are consecrated, but all the others are to observe the LORD's command not to enter.ᵇ ⁷The Levites are to station themselves around the king, each with weapon in hand. Anyone who enters the temple is to be put to death. Stay close to the king wherever he goes."

⁸The Levites and all the men of Judah did just as Jehoiada the priest ordered. Each one took his men—those who were going on duty on the Sabbath and those who were going off duty—for Jehoiada the priest had not released any of the divisions. ⁹Then

---

ᵃ 11 Hebrew *Jehoshabeath*, a variant of *Jehosheba*   ᵇ 6 Or *are to stand guard*
where the LORD has assigned them

he gave the commanders of units of a hundred the spears and the large and small shields that had belonged to King David and that were in the temple of God. ¹⁰He stationed all the men, each with his weapon in his hand, around the king—near the altar and the temple, from the south side to the north side of the temple.

¹¹Jehoiada and his sons brought out the king's son and put the crown on him; they presented him with a copy of the covenant and proclaimed him king. They anointed him and shouted, "Long live the king!"

¹²When Athaliah heard the noise of the people running and cheering the king, she went to them at the temple of the LORD. ¹³She looked, and there was the king, standing by his pillar at the entrance. The officers and the trumpeters were beside the king, and all the people of the land were rejoicing and blowing trumpets, and musicians with their instruments were leading the praises. Then Athaliah tore her robes and shouted, "Treason! Treason!"

¹⁴Jehoiada the priest sent out the commanders of units of a hundred, who were in charge of the troops, and said to them: "Bring her out between the ranks*ᵃ* and put to the sword anyone who follows her." For the priest had said, "Do not put her to death at the temple of the LORD." ¹⁵So they seized her as she reached the entrance of the Horse Gate on the palace grounds, and there they put her to death.

¹⁶Jehoiada then made a covenant that he, the people and the king*ᵇ* would be the LORD's people. ¹⁷All the people went to the temple of Baal and tore it down. They smashed the altars and idols and killed Mattan the priest of Baal in front of the altars.

¹⁸Then Jehoiada placed the oversight of the temple of the LORD in the hands of the Levitical priests, to whom David had made assignments in the temple, to present the burnt offerings of the LORD as written in the Law of Moses, with rejoicing and singing, as David had ordered. ¹⁹He also stationed gatekeepers at the gates of the LORD's temple so that no one who was in any way unclean might enter.

²⁰He took with him the commanders of hundreds, the nobles, the rulers of the people and all the people of the land and brought the king down from the temple of the LORD. They went into the palace through the Upper Gate and seated the king on the royal throne. ²¹All the people of the land rejoiced, and the city was calm, because Athaliah had been slain with the sword.

ᵃ 14 Or *out from the precincts*   *ᵇ 16* Or *covenant between the LORD and the people and the king that they* (see 2 Kings 11:17)

Joash Repairs the Temple

24 Joash was seven years old when he became king, and he reigned in Jerusalem forty years. His mother's name was Zibiah; she was from Beersheba. ²Joash did what was right in the eyes of the LORD all the years of Jehoiada the priest. ³Jehoiada chose two wives for him, and he had sons and daughters.

⁴Some time later Joash decided to restore the temple of the LORD. ⁵He called together the priests and Levites and said to them, "Go to the towns of Judah and collect the money due annually from all Israel, to repair the temple of your God. Do it now." But the Levites did not act at once.

⁶Therefore the king summoned Jehoiada the chief priest and said to him, "Why haven't you required the Levites to bring in from Judah and Jerusalem the tax imposed by Moses the servant of the LORD and by the assembly of Israel for the tent of the covenant law?"

⁷Now the sons of that wicked woman Athaliah had broken into the temple of God and had used even its sacred objects for the Baals.

⁸At the king's command, a chest was made and placed outside, at the gate of the temple of the LORD. ⁹A proclamation was then issued in Judah and Jerusalem that they should bring to the LORD the tax that Moses the servant of God had required of Israel in the wilderness. ¹⁰All the officials and all the people brought their contributions gladly, dropping them into the chest until it was full. ¹¹Whenever the chest was brought in by the Levites to the king's officials and they saw that there was a large amount of money, the royal secretary and the officer of the chief priest would come and empty the chest and carry it back to its place. They did this regularly and collected a great amount of money. ¹²The king and Jehoiada gave it to those who carried out the work required for the temple of the LORD. They hired masons and carpenters to restore the LORD's temple, and also workers in iron and bronze to repair the temple.

¹³The men in charge of the work were diligent, and the repairs progressed under them. They rebuilt the temple of God according to its original design and reinforced it. ¹⁴When they had finished, they brought the rest of the money to the king and Jehoiada, and with it were made articles for the LORD's temple: articles for the service and for the burnt offerings, and also dishes and other objects of gold and silver. As long as Jehoiada lived, burnt offerings were presented continually in the temple of the LORD.

¹⁵Now Jehoiada was old and full of years, and he died at the

age of a hundred and thirty. [16]He
was buried with the kings in the
City of David, because of the good
he had done in Israel for God and
his temple.

The Wickedness of Joash

[17]After the death of Jehoiada,
the officials of Judah came and
paid homage to the king, and he
listened to them. [18]They abandoned the temple of the LORD,
the God of their ancestors, and
worshiped Asherah poles and
idols. Because of their guilt, God's
anger came on Judah and Jerusalem. [19]Although the LORD sent
prophets to the people to bring
them back to him, and though
they testified against them, they
would not listen.

[20]Then the Spirit of God came
on Zechariah son of Jehoiada the
priest. He stood before the people
and said, "This is what God says:
'Why do you disobey the LORD's
commands? You will not prosper. Because you have forsaken
the LORD, he has forsaken you.'"

[21]But they plotted against him,
and by order of the king they
stoned him to death in the courtyard of the LORD's temple. [22]King
Joash did not remember the
kindness Zechariah's father Jehoiada had shown him but killed
his son, who said as he lay dying,
"May the LORD see this and call
you to account."

[23]At the turn of the year,[a] the
army of Aram marched against
Joash; it invaded Judah and Jerusalem and killed all the leaders
of the people. They sent all the
plunder to their king in Damascus. [24]Although the Aramean
army had come with only a few
men, the LORD delivered into
their hands a much larger army.
Because Judah had forsaken the
LORD, the God of their ancestors,
judgment was executed on Joash.
[25]When the Arameans withdrew,
they left Joash severely wounded.
His officials conspired against
him for murdering the son of Jehoiada the priest, and they killed
him in his bed. So he died and
was buried in the City of David,
but not in the tombs of the kings.

[26]Those who conspired against
him were Zabad,[b] son of Shimeath an Ammonite woman, and
Jehozabad, son of Shimrith[c] a
Moabite woman. [27]The account
of his sons, the many prophecies
about him, and the record of the
restoration of the temple of God
are written in the annotations on
the book of the kings. And Amaziah his son succeeded him as
king.

Amaziah King of Judah

25 Amaziah was twenty-
five years old when he
became king, and he reigned in
Jerusalem twenty-nine years. His

[a] 23 Probably in the spring   [b] 26 A variant of *Jozabad*   [c] 26 A variant of
Shomer

mother's name was Jehoaddan; she was from Jerusalem. ²He did what was right in the eyes of the LORD, but not wholeheartedly. ³After the kingdom was firmly in his control, he executed the officials who had murdered his father the king. ⁴Yet he did not put their children to death, but acted in accordance with what is written in the Law, in the Book of Moses, where the LORD commanded: "Parents shall not be put to death for their children, nor children be put to death for their parents; each will die for their own sin."ᵃ

⁵Amaziah called the people of Judah together and assigned them according to their families to commanders of thousands and commanders of hundreds for all Judah and Benjamin. He then mustered those twenty years old or more and found that there were three hundred thousand men fit for military service, able to handle the spear and shield. ⁶He also hired a hundred thousand fighting men from Israel for a hundred talentsᵇ of silver.

⁷But a man of God came to him and said, "Your Majesty, these troops from Israel must not march with you, for the LORD is not with Israel—not with any of the people of Ephraim. ⁸Even if you go and fight courageously in battle, God will overthrow you before the enemy, for God has the power to help or to overthrow."

⁹Amaziah asked the man of God, "But what about the hundred talents I paid for these Israelite troops?"

The man of God replied, "The LORD can give you much more than that."

¹⁰So Amaziah dismissed the troops who had come to him from Ephraim and sent them home. They were furious with Judah and left for home in a great rage.

¹¹Amaziah then marshaled his strength and led his army to the Valley of Salt, where he killed ten thousand men of Seir. ¹²The army of Judah also captured ten thousand men alive, took them to the top of a cliff and threw them down so that all were dashed to pieces.

¹³Meanwhile the troops that Amaziah had sent back and had not allowed to take part in the war raided towns belonging to Judah from Samaria to Beth Horon. They killed three thousand people and carried off great quantities of plunder.

¹⁴When Amaziah returned from slaughtering the Edomites, he brought back the gods of the people of Seir. He set them up as his own gods, bowed down to them and burned sacrifices to them. ¹⁵The anger of the LORD

ᵃ 4 Deut. 24:16   ᵇ 6 That is, about 3 3/4 tons or about 3.4 metric tons; also in verse 9 burned against Amaziah, and he sent a prophet to him, who said, "Why do you consult this people's gods, which could not save their own people from your hand?"

16While he was still speaking, the king said to him, "Have we appointed you an adviser to the king? Stop! Why be struck down?"

So the prophet stopped but said, "I know that God has determined to destroy you, because you have done this and have not listened to my counsel."

17After Amaziah king of Judah consulted his advisers, he sent this challenge to Jehoash*a* son of Jehoahaz, the son of Jehu, king of Israel: "Come, let us face each other in battle."

18But Jehoash king of Israel replied to Amaziah king of Judah: "A thistle in Lebanon sent a message to a cedar in Lebanon, 'Give your daughter to my son in marriage.' Then a wild beast in Lebanon came along and trampled the thistle underfoot. **19**You say to yourself that you have defeated Edom, and now you are arrogant and proud. But stay at home! Why ask for trouble and cause your own downfall and that of Judah also?"

20Amaziah, however, would not listen, for God so worked that he might deliver them into the hands of Jehoash, because they sought the gods of Edom. **21**So Jehoash king of Israel attacked. He and Amaziah king of Judah faced each other at Beth Shemesh in Judah. **22**Judah was routed by Israel, and every man fled to his home. **23**Jehoash king of Israel captured Amaziah king of Judah, the son of Joash, the son of Ahaziah,*b* at Beth Shemesh. Then Jehoash brought him to Jerusalem and broke down the wall of Jerusalem from the Ephraim Gate to the Corner Gate—a section about four hundred cubits*c* long. **24**He took all the gold and silver and all the articles found in the temple of God that had been in the care of Obed-Edom, together with the palace treasures and the hostages, and returned to Samaria.

25Amaziah son of Joash king of Judah lived for fifteen years after the death of Jehoash son of Jehoahaz king of Israel. **26**As for the other events of Amaziah's reign, from beginning to end, are they not written in the book of the kings of Judah and Israel? **27**From the time that Amaziah turned away from following the LORD, they conspired against him in Jerusalem and he fled to Lachish, but they sent men after him to Lachish and killed him there.

---

a 17 Hebrew *Joash,* a variant of *Jehoash;* also in verses 18, 21, 23 and 25
b 23 Hebrew *Jehoahaz,* a variant of *Ahaziah*   *c 23* That is, about 600 feet or about 180 meters

²⁸He was brought back by horse and was buried with his ancestors in the City of Judah.[a]

Uzziah King of Judah

26 Then all the people of Judah took Uzziah,[b] who was sixteen years old, and made him king in place of his father Amaziah. ²He was the one who rebuilt Elath and restored it to Judah after Amaziah rested with his ancestors.

³Uzziah was sixteen years old when he became king, and he reigned in Jerusalem fifty-two years. His mother's name was Jekoliah; she was from Jerusalem. ⁴He did what was right in the eyes of the LORD, just as his father Amaziah had done. ⁵He sought God during the days of Zechariah, who instructed him in the fear[c] of God. As long as he sought the LORD, God gave him success.

⁶He went to war against the Philistines and broke down the walls of Gath, Jabneh and Ashdod. He then rebuilt towns near Ashdod and elsewhere among the Philistines. ⁷God helped him against the Philistines and against the Arabs who lived in Gur Baal and against the Meunites. ⁸The Ammonites brought tribute to Uzziah, and his fame spread as far as the border of Egypt, because he had become very powerful.

⁹Uzziah built towers in Jerusalem at the Corner Gate, at the Valley Gate and at the angle of the wall, and he fortified them. ¹⁰He also built towers in the wilderness and dug many cisterns, because he had much livestock in the foothills and in the plain. He had people working his fields and vineyards in the hills and in the fertile lands, for he loved the soil.

¹¹Uzziah had a well-trained army, ready to go out by divisions according to their numbers as mustered by Jeiel the secretary and Maaseiah the officer under the direction of Hananiah, one of the royal officials. ¹²The total number of family leaders over the fighting men was 2,600. ¹³Under their command was an army of 307,500 men trained for war, a powerful force to support the king against his enemies. ¹⁴Uzziah provided shields, spears, helmets, coats of armor, bows and slingstones for the entire army. ¹⁵In Jerusalem he made devices invented for use on the towers and on the corner defenses so that soldiers could shoot arrows and hurl large stones from the walls. His fame spread far and wide, for he was greatly helped until he became powerful.

¹⁶But after Uzziah became powerful, his pride led to his

---

[a] 28 Most Hebrew manuscripts; some Hebrew manuscripts, Septuagint, Vulgate and Syriac (see also 2 Kings 14:20) *David*   [b] 1 Also called *Azariah*   [c] 5 Many Hebrew manuscripts, Septuagint and Syriac; other Hebrew manuscripts *vision*

downfall. He was unfaithful to the LORD his God, and entered the temple of the LORD to burn incense on the altar of incense. [17]Azariah the priest with eighty other courageous priests of the LORD followed him in. [18]They confronted King Uzziah and said, "It is not right for you, Uzziah, to burn incense to the LORD. That is for the priests, the descendants of Aaron, who have been consecrated to burn incense. Leave the sanctuary, for you have been unfaithful; and you will not be honored by the LORD God."

[19]Uzziah, who had a censer in his hand ready to burn incense, became angry. While he was raging at the priests in their presence before the incense altar in the LORD's temple, leprosy[a] broke out on his forehead. [20]When Azariah the chief priest and all the other priests looked at him, they saw that he had leprosy on his forehead, so they hurried him out. Indeed, he himself was eager to leave, because the LORD had afflicted him.

[21]King Uzziah had leprosy until the day he died. He lived in a separate house[b] — leprous, and banned from the temple of the LORD. Jotham his son had charge of the palace and governed the people of the land.

[22]The other events of Uzziah's reign, from beginning to end, are recorded by the prophet Isaiah son of Amoz. [23]Uzziah rested with his ancestors and was buried near them in a cemetery that belonged to the kings, for people said, "He had leprosy." And Jotham his son succeeded him as king.

Jotham King of Judah

27 Jotham was twenty-five years old when he became king, and he reigned in Jerusalem sixteen years. His mother's name was Jerusha daughter of Zadok. [2]He did what was right in the eyes of the LORD, just as his father Uzziah had done, but unlike him he did not enter the temple of the LORD. The people, however, continued their corrupt practices. [3]Jotham rebuilt the Upper Gate of the temple of the LORD and did extensive work on the wall at the hill of Ophel. [4]He built towns in the hill country of Judah and forts and towers in the wooded areas.

[5]Jotham waged war against the king of the Ammonites and conquered them. That year the Ammonites paid him a hundred talents[c] of silver, ten thousand cors[d] of wheat and ten thousand cors[e] of barley. The Ammonites

---

[a] 19 The Hebrew for leprosy was used for various diseases affecting the skin; also in verses 20, 21 and 23.   [b] 21 Or in a house where he was relieved of responsibilities   [c] 5 That is, about 3 3/4 tons or about 3.4 metric tons   [d] 5 That is, probably about 1,800 tons or about 1,600 metric tons of wheat   [e] 5 That is, probably about 1,500 tons or about 1,350 metric tons of barley

brought him the same amount also in the second and third years.

⁶Jotham grew powerful because he walked steadfastly before the LORD his God.

⁷The other events in Jotham's reign, including all his wars and the other things he did, are written in the book of the kings of Israel and Judah. ⁸He was twenty-five years old when he became king, and he reigned in Jerusalem sixteen years. ⁹Jotham rested with his ancestors and was buried in the City of David. And Ahaz his son succeeded him as king.

Ahaz King of Judah

28 Ahaz was twenty years old when he became king, and he reigned in Jerusalem sixteen years. Unlike David his father, he did not do what was right in the eyes of the LORD. ²He followed the ways of the kings of Israel and also made idols for worshiping the Baals. ³He burned sacrifices in the Valley of Ben Hinnom and sacrificed his children in the fire, engaging in the detestable practices of the nations the LORD had driven out before the Israelites. ⁴He offered sacrifices and burned incense at the high places, on the hilltops and under every spreading tree.

⁵Therefore the LORD his God delivered him into the hands of the king of Aram. The Arameans defeated him and took many of his people as prisoners and brought them to Damascus.

He was also given into the hands of the king of Israel, who inflicted heavy casualties on him. ⁶In one day Pekah son of Remaliah killed a hundred and twenty thousand soldiers in Judah—because Judah had forsaken the LORD, the God of their ancestors. ⁷Zikri, an Ephraimite warrior, killed Maaseiah the king's son, Azrikam the officer in charge of the palace, and Elkanah, second to the king. ⁸The men of Israel took captive from their fellow Israelites who were from Judah two hundred thousand wives, sons and daughters. They also took a great deal of plunder, which they carried back to Samaria.

⁹But a prophet of the LORD named Oded was there, and he went out to meet the army when it returned to Samaria. He said to them, "Because the LORD, the God of your ancestors, was angry with Judah, he gave them into your hand. But you have slaughtered them in a rage that reaches to heaven. ¹⁰And now you intend to make the men and women of Judah and Jerusalem your slaves. But aren't you also guilty of sins against the LORD your God? ¹¹Now listen to me! Send back your fellow Israelites you have taken as prisoners, for the LORD's fierce anger rests on you."

¹²Then some of the leaders in Ephraim—Azariah son of Jehohanan, Berekiah son of Meshillemoth, Jehizkiah son of Shallum, and Amasa son of Hadlai—confronted those who were arriving from the war. ¹³"You must not bring those prisoners here," they said, "or we will be guilty before the LORD. Do you intend to add to our sin and guilt? For our guilt is already great, and his fierce anger rests on Israel."

¹⁴So the soldiers gave up the prisoners and plunder in the presence of the officials and all the assembly. ¹⁵The men designated by name took the prisoners, and from the plunder they clothed all who were naked. They provided them with clothes and sandals, food and drink, and healing balm. All those who were weak they put on donkeys. So they took them back to their fellow Israelites at Jericho, the City of Palms, and returned to Samaria.

¹⁶At that time King Ahaz sent to the kings*a* of Assyria for help. ¹⁷The Edomites had again come and attacked Judah and carried away prisoners, ¹⁸while the Philistines had raided towns in the foothills and in the Negev of Judah. They captured and occupied Beth Shemesh, Aijalon and Gederoth, as well as Soko, Timnah and Gimzo, with their sur-rounding villages. ¹⁹The LORD had humbled Judah because of Ahaz king of Israel,*b* for he had promoted wickedness in Judah and had been most unfaithful to the LORD. ²⁰Tiglath-Pileser*c* king of Assyria came to him, but he gave him trouble instead of help. ²¹Ahaz took some of the things from the temple of the LORD and from the royal palace and from the officials and presented them to the king of Assyria, but that did not help him.

²²In his time of trouble King Ahaz became even more un-faithful to the LORD. ²³He offered sacrifices to the gods of Damascus, who had defeated him; for he thought, "Since the gods of the kings of Aram have helped them, I will sacrifice to them so they will help me." But they were his downfall and the downfall of all Israel.

²⁴Ahaz gathered together the furnishings from the temple of God and cut them in pieces. He shut the doors of the LORD's temple and set up altars at every street corner in Jerusalem. ²⁵In every town in Judah he built high places to burn sacrifices to other gods and aroused the anger of the LORD, the God of his ancestors.

²⁶The other events of his reign and all his ways, from beginning

---

a 16 Most Hebrew manuscripts; one Hebrew manuscript, Septuagint and Vulgate (see also 2 Kings 16:7) *king*   *b 19* That is, Judah, as frequently in 2 Chronicles
c 20 Hebrew *Tilgath-Pilneser*, a variant of *Tiglath-Pileser*

to end, are written in the book of the kings of Judah and Israel. ²⁷Ahaz rested with his ancestors and was buried in the city of Jerusalem, but he was not placed in the tombs of the kings of Israel. And Hezekiah his son succeeded him as king.

Hezekiah Purifies the Temple

29 Hezekiah was twenty-five years old when he became king, and he reigned in Jerusalem twenty-nine years. His mother's name was Abijah daughter of Zechariah. ²He did what was right in the eyes of the LORD, just as his father David had done.

³In the first month of the first year of his reign, he opened the doors of the temple of the LORD and repaired them. ⁴He brought in the priests and the Levites, assembled them in the square on the east side ⁵and said: "Listen to me, Levites! Consecrate yourselves now and consecrate the temple of the LORD, the God of your ancestors. Remove all defilement from the sanctuary. ⁶Our parents were unfaithful; they did evil in the eyes of the LORD our God and forsook him. They turned their faces away from the LORD's dwelling place and turned their backs on him. ⁷They also shut the doors of the portico and put out the lamps. They did not burn incense or present any burnt offerings at the sanctuary to the God of Israel. ⁸Therefore, the anger of the LORD has fallen on Judah and Jerusalem; he has made them an object of dread and horror and scorn, as you can see with your own eyes. ⁹This is why our fathers have fallen by the sword and why our sons and daughters and our wives are in captivity. ¹⁰Now I intend to make a covenant with the LORD, the God of Israel, so that his fierce anger will turn away from us. ¹¹My sons, do not be negligent now, for the LORD has chosen you to stand before him and serve him, to minister before him and to burn incense."

¹²Then these Levites set to work:

from the Kohathites,
Mahath son of Amasai and Joel son of Azariah;
from the Merarites,
Kish son of Abdi and Azariah son of Jehallelel;
from the Gershonites,
Joah son of Zimmah and Eden son of Joah;
¹³from the descendants of Elizaphan,
Shimri and Jeiel;
from the descendants of Asaph,
Zechariah and Mattaniah;
¹⁴from the descendants of Heman,
Jehiel and Shimei;
from the descendants of Jeduthun,
Shemaiah and Uzziel.

¹⁵When they had assembled their fellow Levites and consecrated themselves, they went in to purify the temple of the LORD, as the king had ordered, following the word of the LORD. ¹⁶The priests went into the sanctuary of the LORD to purify it. They brought out to the courtyard of the LORD's temple everything unclean that they found in the temple of the LORD. The Levites took it and carried it out to the Kidron Valley. ¹⁷They began the consecration on the first day of the first month, and by the eighth day of the month they reached the portico of the LORD. For eight more days they consecrated the temple of the LORD itself, finishing on the sixteenth day of the first month.

¹⁸Then they went in to King Hezekiah and reported: "We have purified the entire temple of the LORD, the altar of burnt offering with all its utensils, and the table for setting out the consecrated bread, with all its articles. ¹⁹We have prepared and consecrated all the articles that King Ahaz removed in his unfaithfulness while he was king. They are now in front of the LORD's altar."

²⁰Early the next morning King Hezekiah gathered the city officials together and went up to the temple of the LORD. ²¹They brought seven bulls, seven rams, seven male lambs and seven male goats as a sin offering*a* for the kingdom, for the sanctuary and for Judah. The king commanded the priests, the descendants of Aaron, to offer these on the altar of the LORD. ²²So they slaughtered the bulls, and the priests took the blood and splashed it against the altar; next they slaughtered the rams and splashed their blood against the altar; then they slaughtered the lambs and splashed their blood against the altar. ²³The goats for the sin offering were brought before the king and the assembly, and they laid their hands on them. ²⁴The priests then slaughtered the goats and presented their blood on the altar for a sin offering to atone for all Israel, because the king had ordered the burnt offering and the sin offering for all Israel.

²⁵He stationed the Levites in the temple of the LORD with cymbals, harps and lyres in the way prescribed by David and Gad the king's seer and Nathan the prophet; this was commanded by the LORD through his prophets. ²⁶So the Levites stood ready with David's instruments, and the priests with their trumpets.

²⁷Hezekiah gave the order to sacrifice the burnt offering on the altar. As the offering began, singing to the LORD began also, accompanied by trumpets and the instruments of David king of Israel. ²⁸The whole assembly

---

a 21 Or *purification offering*; also in verses 23 and 24

bowed in worship, while the musicians played and the trumpets sounded. All this continued until the sacrifice of the burnt offering was completed.

²⁹When the offerings were finished, the king and everyone present with him knelt down and worshiped. ³⁰King Hezekiah and his officials ordered the Levites to praise the LORD with the words of David and of Asaph the seer. So they sang praises with gladness and bowed down and worshiped.

³¹Then Hezekiah said, "You have now dedicated yourselves to the LORD. Come and bring sacrifices and thank offerings to the temple of the LORD." So the assembly brought sacrifices and thank offerings, and all whose hearts were willing brought burnt offerings.

³²The number of burnt offerings the assembly brought was seventy bulls, a hundred rams and two hundred male lambs—all of them for burnt offerings to the LORD. ³³The animals consecrated as sacrifices amounted to six hundred bulls and three thousand sheep and goats. ³⁴The priests, however, were too few to skin all the burnt offerings; so their relatives the Levites helped them until the task was finished and until other priests had been consecrated, for the Levites had been more conscientious in consecrating themselves than the priests had been. ³⁵There were

burnt offerings in abundance, together with the fat of the fellowship offerings and the drink offerings that accompanied the burnt offerings.

So the service of the temple of the LORD was reestablished. ³⁶Hezekiah and all the people rejoiced at what God had brought about for his people, because it was done so quickly.

Hezekiah Celebrates the Passover

30 Hezekiah sent word to all Israel and Judah and also wrote letters to Ephraim and Manasseh, inviting them to come to the temple of the LORD in Jerusalem and celebrate the Passover to the LORD, the God of Israel. ²The king and his officials and the whole assembly in Jerusalem decided to celebrate the Passover in the second month. ³They had not been able to celebrate it at the regular time because not enough priests had consecrated themselves and the people had not assembled in Jerusalem. ⁴The plan seemed right both to the king and to the whole assembly. ⁵They decided to send a proclamation throughout Israel, from Beersheba to Dan, calling the people to come to Jerusalem and celebrate the Passover to the LORD, the God of Israel. It had not been celebrated in large numbers according to what was written.

⁶At the king's command, couriers went throughout Israel and Judah with letters from the king and from his officials, which read:

"People of Israel, return to the LORD, the God of Abraham, Isaac and Israel, that he may return to you who are left, who have escaped from the hand of the kings of Assyria. ⁷Do not be like your parents and your fellow Israelites, who were unfaithful to the LORD, the God of their ancestors, so that he made them an object of horror, as you see. ⁸Do not be stiff-necked, as your ancestors were; submit to the LORD. Come to his sanctuary, which he has consecrated forever. Serve the LORD your God, so that his fierce anger will turn away from you. ⁹If you return to the LORD, then your fellow Israelites and your children will be shown compassion by their captors and will return to this land, for the LORD your God is gracious and compassionate. He will not turn his face from you if you return to him."

¹⁰The couriers went from town to town in Ephraim and Manasseh, as far as Zebulun, but people scorned and ridiculed them. ¹¹Nevertheless, some from Asher, Manasseh and Zebulun humbled themselves and went to Jerusalem. ¹²Also in Judah the hand of God was on the people to give them unity of mind to carry out what the king and his officials had ordered, following the word of the LORD.

¹³A very large crowd of people assembled in Jerusalem to celebrate the Festival of Unleavened Bread in the second month. ¹⁴They removed the altars in Jerusalem and cleared away the incense altars and threw them into the Kidron Valley.

¹⁵They slaughtered the Passover lamb on the fourteenth day of the second month. The priests and the Levites were ashamed and consecrated themselves and brought burnt offerings to the temple of the LORD. ¹⁶Then they took up their regular positions as prescribed in the Law of Moses the man of God. The priests splashed against the altar the blood handed to them by the Levites. ¹⁷Since many in the crowd had not consecrated themselves, the Levites had to kill the Passover lambs for all those who were not ceremonially clean and could not consecrate their lambs[a] to the LORD. ¹⁸Although most of the many people who came from Ephraim, Manasseh, Issachar and Zebulun had not purified themselves, yet they ate the Passover, contrary to what was

---

[a] 17 Or *consecrate themselves*

written. But Hezekiah prayed for them, saying, "May the LORD, who is good, pardon everyone [19] who sets their heart on seeking God — the LORD, the God of their ancestors — even if they are not clean according to the rules of the sanctuary." [20] And the LORD heard Hezekiah and healed the people.

[21] The Israelites who were present in Jerusalem celebrated the Festival of Unleavened Bread for seven days with great rejoicing, while the Levites and priests praised the LORD every day with resounding instruments dedicated to the LORD.[a]

[22] Hezekiah spoke encouragingly to all the Levites, who showed good understanding of the service of the LORD. For the seven days they ate their assigned portion and offered fellowship offerings and praised[b] the LORD, the God of their ancestors.

[23] The whole assembly then agreed to celebrate the festival seven more days; so for another seven days they celebrated joyfully. [24] Hezekiah king of Judah provided a thousand bulls and seven thousand sheep and goats for the assembly, and the officials provided them with a thousand bulls and ten thousand sheep and goats. A great number of priests consecrated themselves. [25] The entire assembly of Judah rejoiced, along with the priests and Levites and all who had assembled from Israel, including the foreigners who had come from Israel and also those who resided in Judah. [26] There was great joy in Jerusalem, for since the days of Solomon son of David king of Israel there had been nothing like this in Jerusalem. [27] The priests and the Levites stood to bless the people, and God heard them, for their prayer reached heaven, his holy dwelling place.

31 When all this had ended, the Israelites who were there went out to the towns of Judah, smashed the sacred stones and cut down the Asherah poles. They destroyed the high places and the altars throughout Judah and Benjamin and in Ephraim and Manasseh. After they had destroyed all of them, the Israelites returned to their own towns and to their own property.

Contributions for Worship

[2] Hezekiah assigned the priests and Levites to divisions — each of them according to their duties as priests or Levites — to offer burnt offerings and fellowship offerings, to minister, to give thanks and to sing praises at the gates of the LORD's dwelling. [3] The king contributed from his own possessions for the morning and evening burnt offerings and for

---

[a] 21 Or *priests sang to the LORD every day, accompanied by the LORD's instruments of praise*   [b] 22 Or *and confessed their sins to*

the burnt offerings on the Sabbaths, at the New Moons and at the appointed festivals as written in the Law of the LORD. ⁴He ordered the people living in Jerusalem to give the portion due the priests and Levites so they could devote themselves to the Law of the LORD. ⁵As soon as the order went out, the Israelites generously gave the firstfruits of their grain, new wine, olive oil and honey and all that the fields produced. They brought a great amount, a tithe of everything. ⁶The people of Israel and Judah who lived in the towns of Judah also brought a tithe of their herds and flocks and a tithe of the holy things dedicated to the LORD their God, and they piled them in heaps. ⁷They began doing this in the third month and finished in the seventh month. ⁸When Hezekiah and his officials came and saw the heaps, they praised the LORD and blessed his people Israel.

⁹Hezekiah asked the priests and Levites about the heaps; ¹⁰and Azariah the chief priest, from the family of Zadok, answered, "Since the people began to bring their contributions to the temple of the LORD, we have had enough to eat and plenty to spare, because the LORD has blessed his people, and this great amount is left over."

¹¹Hezekiah gave orders to prepare storerooms in the temple of the LORD, and this was done. ¹²Then they faithfully brought in the contributions, tithes and dedicated gifts. Konaniah, a Levite, was the overseer in charge of these things, and his brother Shimei was next in rank. ¹³Jehiel, Azaziah, Nahath, Asahel, Jerimoth, Jozabad, Eliel, Ismakiah, Mahath and Benaiah were assistants of Konaniah and Shimei his brother. All these served by appointment of King Hezekiah and Azariah the official in charge of the temple of God.

¹⁴Kore son of Imnah the Levite, keeper of the East Gate, was in charge of the freewill offerings given to God, distributing the contributions made to the LORD and also the consecrated gifts. ¹⁵Eden, Miniamin, Jeshua, Shemaiah, Amariah and Shekaniah assisted him faithfully in the towns of the priests, distributing to their fellow priests according to their divisions, old and young alike.

¹⁶In addition, they distributed to the males three years old or more whose names were in the genealogical records—all who would enter the temple of the LORD to perform the daily duties of their various tasks, according to their responsibilities and their divisions. ¹⁷And they distributed to the priests enrolled by their families in the genealogical records and likewise to the Levites twenty years old or more, accord-

ing to their responsibilities and their divisions. **18** They included all the little ones, the wives, and the sons and daughters of the whole community listed in these genealogical records. For they were faithful in consecrating themselves.

19 As for the priests, the descendants of Aaron, who lived on the farmlands around their towns or in any other towns, men were designated by name to distribute portions to every male among them and to all who were recorded in the genealogies of the Levites.

20 This is what Hezekiah did throughout Judah, doing what was good and right and faithful before the LORD his God. **21** In everything that he undertook in the service of God's temple and in obedience to the law and the commands, he sought his God and worked wholeheartedly. And so he prospered.

Sennacherib Threatens Jerusalem

32 After all that Hezekiah had so faithfully done, Sennacherib king of Assyria came and invaded Judah. He laid siege to the fortified cities, thinking to conquer them for himself. **2** When Hezekiah saw that Sennacherib had come and that he intended to wage war against Jerusalem, **3** he consult-

ed with his officials and military staff about blocking off the water from the springs outside the city, and they helped him. **4** They gathered a large group of people who blocked all the springs and the stream that flowed through the land. "Why should the kings*a* of Assyria come and find plenty of water?" they said. **5** Then he worked hard repairing all the broken sections of the wall and building towers on it. He built another wall outside that one and reinforced the terraces*b* of the City of David. He also made large numbers of weapons and shields.

6 He appointed military officers over the people and assembled them before him in the square at the city gate and encouraged them with these words: **7** "Be strong and courageous. Do not be afraid or discouraged because of the king of Assyria and the vast army with him, for there is a greater power with us than with him. **8** With him is only the arm of flesh, but with us is the LORD our God to help us and to fight our battles." And the people gained confidence from what Hezekiah the king of Judah said.

9 Later, when Sennacherib king of Assyria and all his forces were laying siege to Lachish, he sent his officers to Jerusalem with this message for Hezekiah king of Judah and for all the people of Judah who were there:

---

a 4 Hebrew; Septuagint and Syriac *king*   *b* 5 Or *the Millo*

¹⁰"This is what Sennacherib king of Assyria says: On what are you basing your confidence, that you remain in Jerusalem under siege? ¹¹When Hezekiah says, 'The LORD our God will save us from the hand of the king of Assyria,' he is misleading you, to let you die of hunger and thirst. ¹²Did not Hezekiah himself remove this god's high places and altars, saying to Judah and Jerusalem, 'You must worship before one altar and burn sacrifices on it'?

¹³"Do you not know what I and my predecessors have done to all the peoples of the other lands? Were the gods of those nations ever able to deliver their land from my hand? ¹⁴Who of all the gods of these nations that my predecessors destroyed has been able to save his people from me? How then can your god deliver you from my hand? ¹⁵Now do not let Hezekiah deceive you and mislead you like this. Do not believe him, for no god of any nation or kingdom has been able to deliver his people from my hand or the hand of my predecessors. How much less will your god deliver you from my hand!"

¹⁶Sennacherib's officers spoke further against the LORD God and against his servant Hezekiah. ¹⁷The king also wrote letters ridiculing the LORD, the God of Israel, and saying this against him: "Just as the gods of the peoples of the other lands did not rescue their people from my hand, so the god of Hezekiah will not rescue his people from my hand." ¹⁸Then they called out in Hebrew to the people of Jerusalem who were on the wall, to terrify them and make them afraid in order to capture the city. ¹⁹They spoke about the God of Jerusalem as they did about the gods of the other peoples of the world — the work of human hands.

²⁰King Hezekiah and the prophet Isaiah son of Amoz cried out in prayer to heaven about this. ²¹And the LORD sent an angel, who annihilated all the fighting men and the commanders and officers in the camp of the Assyrian king. So he withdrew to his own land in disgrace. And when he went into the temple of his god, some of his sons, his own flesh and blood, cut him down with the sword.

²²So the LORD saved Hezekiah and the people of Jerusalem from the hand of Sennacherib king of Assyria and from the hand of all others. He took care of them[a] on every side. ²³Many brought offerings to Jerusalem for the LORD and valuable gifts for Hezekiah king of Judah. From then on he was highly regarded by all the nations.

---

[a] 22 Hebrew; Septuagint and Vulgate *He gave them rest*

Hezekiah's Pride, Success and Death

24 In those days Hezekiah became ill and was at the point of death. He prayed to the LORD, who answered him and gave him a miraculous sign. **25** But Hezekiah's heart was proud and he did not respond to the kindness shown him; therefore the LORD's wrath was on him and on Judah and Jerusalem. **26** Then Hezekiah repented of the pride of his heart, as did the people of Jerusalem; therefore the LORD's wrath did not come on them during the days of Hezekiah. **27** Hezekiah had very great wealth and honor, and he made treasuries for his silver and gold and for his precious stones, spices, shields and all kinds of valuables. **28** He also made buildings to store the harvest of grain, new wine and olive oil; and he made stalls for various kinds of cattle, and pens for the flocks. **29** He built villages and acquired great numbers of flocks and herds, for God had given him very great riches.

30 It was Hezekiah who blocked the upper outlet of the Gihon spring and channeled the water down to the west side of the City of David. He succeeded in everything he undertook. **31** But when envoys were sent by the rulers of Babylon to ask him about the miraculous sign that had occurred in the land, God left him to test him and to know everything that was in his heart.

32 The other events of Hezekiah's reign and his acts of devotion are written in the vision of the prophet Isaiah son of Amoz in the book of the kings of Judah and Israel. **33** Hezekiah rested with his ancestors and was buried on the hill where the tombs of David's descendants are. All Judah and the people of Jerusalem honored him when he died. And Manasseh his son succeeded him as king.

Manasseh King of Judah

33 Manasseh was twelve years old when he became king, and he reigned in Jerusalem fifty-five years. **2** He did evil in the eyes of the LORD, following the detestable practices of the nations the LORD had driven out before the Israelites. **3** He rebuilt the high places his father Hezekiah had demolished; he also erected altars to the Baals and made Asherah poles. He bowed down to all the starry hosts and worshiped them. **4** He built altars in the temple of the LORD, of which the LORD had said, "My Name will remain in Jerusalem forever." **5** In both courts of the temple of the LORD, he built altars to all the starry hosts. **6** He sacrificed his children in the fire in the Valley of Ben Hinnom, practiced divination and witchcraft, sought omens, and consulted mediums and spiritists. He did much evil in the eyes of the LORD, arousing his anger.

⁷He took the image he had made and put it in God's temple, of which God had said to David and to his son Solomon, "In this temple and in Jerusalem, which I have chosen out of all the tribes of Israel, I will put my Name forever. ⁸I will not again make the feet of the Israelites leave the land I assigned to your ancestors, if only they will be careful to do everything I commanded them concerning all the laws, decrees and regulations given through Moses." ⁹But Manasseh led Judah and the people of Jerusalem astray, so that they did more evil than the nations the LORD had destroyed before the Israelites.

¹⁰The LORD spoke to Manasseh and his people, but they paid no attention. ¹¹So the LORD brought against them the army commanders of the king of Assyria, who took Manasseh prisoner, put a hook in his nose, bound him with bronze shackles and took him to Babylon. ¹²In his distress he sought the favor of the LORD his God and humbled himself greatly before the God of his ancestors. ¹³And when he prayed to him, the LORD was moved by his entreaty and listened to his plea; so he brought him back to Jerusalem and to his kingdom. Then Manasseh knew that the LORD is God.

¹⁴Afterward he rebuilt the outer wall of the City of David, west of the Gihon spring in the valley, as far as the entrance of the Fish Gate and encircling the hill of Ophel; he also made it much higher. He stationed military commanders in all the fortified cities in Judah.

¹⁵He got rid of the foreign gods and removed the image from the temple of the LORD, as well as all the altars he had built on the temple hill and in Jerusalem; and he threw them out of the city. ¹⁶Then he restored the altar of the LORD and sacrificed fellowship offerings and thank offerings on it, and told Judah to serve the LORD, the God of Israel. ¹⁷The people, however, continued to sacrifice at the high places, but only to the LORD their God.

¹⁸The other events of Manasseh's reign, including his prayer to his God and the words the seers spoke to him in the name of the LORD, the God of Israel, are written in the annals of the kings of Israel.ᵃ ¹⁹His prayer and how God was moved by his entreaty, as well as all his sins and unfaithfulness, and the sites where he built high places and set up Asherah poles and idols before he humbled himself—all these are written in the records of the seers.ᵇ ²⁰Manasseh rested with his ancestors and was buried in his palace. And Amon his son succeeded him as king.

ᵃ 18 That is, Judah, as frequently in 2 Chronicles   ᵇ 19 One Hebrew manuscript and Septuagint; most Hebrew manuscripts *of Hozai*

Amon King of Judah

²¹ Amon was twenty-two years old when he became king, and he reigned in Jerusalem two years. ²² He did evil in the eyes of the LORD, as his father Manasseh had done. Amon worshiped and offered sacrifices to all the idols Manasseh had made. ²³ But unlike his father Manasseh, he did not humble himself before the LORD; Amon increased his guilt.

²⁴ Amon's officials conspired against him and assassinated him in his palace. ²⁵ Then the people of the land killed all who had plotted against King Amon, and they made Josiah his son king in his place.

Josiah's Reforms

34 Josiah was eight years old when he became king, and he reigned in Jerusalem thirty-one years. ² He did what was right in the eyes of the LORD and followed the ways of his father David, not turning aside to the right or to the left.

³ In the eighth year of his reign, while he was still young, he began to seek the God of his father David. In his twelfth year he began to purge Judah and Jerusalem of high places, Asherah poles and idols. ⁴ Under his direction the altars of the Baals were torn down; he cut to pieces the incense altars that were above them, and smashed the Asherah poles and the idols. These he broke to piec-

es and scattered over the graves of those who had sacrificed to them. ⁵ He burned the bones of the priests on their altars, and so he purged Judah and Jerusalem. ⁶ In the towns of Manasseh, Ephraim and Simeon, as far as Naphtali, and in the ruins around them, ⁷ he tore down the altars and the Asherah poles and crushed the idols to powder and cut to pieces all the incense altars throughout Israel. Then he went back to Jerusalem.

⁸ In the eighteenth year of Josiah's reign, to purify the land and the temple, he sent Shaphan son of Azaliah and Maaseiah the ruler of the city, with Joah son of Joahaz, the recorder, to repair the temple of the LORD his God.

⁹ They went to Hilkiah the high priest and gave him the money that had been brought into the temple of God, which the Levites who were the gatekeepers had collected from the people of Manasseh, Ephraim and the entire remnant of Israel and from all the people of Judah and Benjamin and the inhabitants of Jerusalem. ¹⁰ Then they entrusted it to the men appointed to supervise the work on the LORD's temple. These men paid the workers who repaired and restored the temple. ¹¹ They also gave money to the carpenters and builders to purchase dressed stone, and timber for joists and beams for the buildings that the kings of Judah had allowed to fall into ruin.

12 The workers labored faithfully. Over them to direct them were Jahath and Obadiah, Levites descended from Merari, and Zechariah and Meshullam, descended from Kohath. The Levites — all who were skilled in playing musical instruments — 13 had charge of the laborers and supervised all the workers from job to job. Some of the Levites were secretaries, scribes and gatekeepers.

The Book of the Law Found

14 While they were bringing out the money that had been taken into the temple of the LORD, Hilkiah the priest found the Book of the Law of the LORD that had been given through Moses. 15 Hilkiah said to Shaphan the secretary, "I have found the Book of the Law in the temple of the LORD." He gave it to Shaphan.

16 Then Shaphan took the book to the king and reported to him: "Your officials are doing everything that has been committed to them. 17 They have paid out the money that was in the temple of the LORD and have entrusted it to the supervisors and workers." 18 Then Shaphan the secretary informed the king, "Hilkiah the priest has given me a book." And Shaphan read from it in the presence of the king.

19 When the king heard the words of the Law, he tore his robes. 20 He gave these orders to Hilkiah, Ahikam son of Shaphan, Abdon son of Micah,[a] Shaphan the secretary and Asaiah the king's attendant: 21 "Go and inquire of the LORD for me and for the remnant in Israel and Judah about what is written in this book that has been found. Great is the LORD's anger that is poured out on us because those who have gone before us have not kept the word of the LORD; they have not acted in accordance with all that is written in this book."

22 Hilkiah and those the king had sent with him[b] went to speak to the prophet Huldah, who was the wife of Shallum son of Tokhath,[c] the son of Hasrah,[d] keeper of the wardrobe. She lived in Jerusalem, in the New Quarter.

23 She said to them, "This is what the LORD, the God of Israel, says: Tell the man who sent you to me, 24 'This is what the LORD says: I am going to bring disaster on this place and its people — all the curses written in the book that has been read in the presence of the king of Judah. 25 Because they have forsaken me and burned incense to other gods and aroused my anger by all that their hands have made,[e] my anger will be poured out on this place and will not be quenched.'

---

[26] Tell the king of Judah, who sent you to inquire of the LORD, 'This is what the LORD, the God of Israel, says concerning the words you heard: [27] Because your heart was responsive and you humbled yourself before God when you heard what he spoke against this place and its people, and because you humbled yourself before me and tore your robes and wept in my presence, I have heard you, declares the LORD. [28] Now I will gather you to your ancestors, and you will be buried in peace. Your eyes will not see all the disaster I am going to bring on this place and on those who live here.' "

So they took her answer back to the king.

[29] Then the king called together all the elders of Judah and Jerusalem. [30] He went up to the temple of the LORD with the people of Judah, the inhabitants of Jerusalem, the priests and the Levites — all the people from the least to the greatest. He read in their hearing all the words of the Book of the Covenant, which had been found in the temple of the LORD. [31] The king stood by his pillar and renewed the covenant in the presence of the LORD — to follow the LORD and keep his commands, statutes and decrees with all his heart and all his soul, and to obey the words of the covenant written in this book.

[32] Then he had everyone in Jerusalem and Benjamin pledge themselves to it; the people of Jerusalem did this in accordance with the covenant of God, the God of their ancestors.

[33] Josiah removed all the detestable idols from all the territory belonging to the Israelites, and he had all who were present in Israel serve the LORD their God. As long as he lived, they did not fail to follow the LORD, the God of their ancestors.

Josiah Celebrates the Passover

35 Josiah celebrated the Passover to the LORD in Jerusalem, and the Passover lamb was slaughtered on the fourteenth day of the first month. [2] He appointed the priests to their duties and encouraged them in the service of the LORD's temple. [3] He said to the Levites, who instructed all Israel and who had been consecrated to the LORD: "Put the sacred ark in the temple that Solomon son of David king of Israel built. It is not to be carried about on your shoulders. Now serve the LORD your God and his people Israel. [4] Prepare yourselves by families in your divisions, according to the instructions written by David king of Israel and by his son Solomon.

[5] "Stand in the holy place with a group of Levites for each subdivision of the families of your fellow Israelites, the lay people. [6] Slaughter the Passover lambs, consecrate yourselves and prepare the

lambs for your fellow Israelites, doing what the LORD commanded through Moses."

⁷Josiah provided for all the lay people who were there a total of thirty thousand lambs and goats for the Passover offerings, and also three thousand cattle—all from the king's own possessions.

⁸His officials also contributed voluntarily to the people and the priests and Levites. Hilkiah, Zechariah and Jehiel, the officials in charge of God's temple, gave the priests twenty-six hundred Passover offerings and three hundred cattle. ⁹Also Konaniah along with Shemaiah and Nethanel, his brothers, and Hashabiah, Jeiel and Jozabad, the leaders of the Levites, provided five thousand Passover offerings and five hundred head of cattle for the Levites.

¹⁰The service was arranged and the priests stood in their places with the Levites in their divisions as the king had ordered. ¹¹The Passover lambs were slaughtered, and the priests splashed against the altar the blood handed to them, while the Levites skinned the animals. ¹²They set aside the burnt offerings to give them to the subdivisions of the families of the people to offer to the LORD, as it is written in the Book of Moses. They did the same with the cattle. ¹³They roasted the Passover animals over the fire as prescribed, and boiled the holy offerings in pots, caldrons and pans and served them quickly to all the people. ¹⁴After this, they made preparations for themselves and for the priests, because the priests, the descendants of Aaron, were sacrificing the burnt offerings and the fat portions until nightfall. So the Levites made preparations for themselves and for the Aaronic priests.

¹⁵The musicians, the descendants of Asaph, were in the places prescribed by David, Asaph, Heman and Jeduthun the king's seer. The gatekeepers at each gate did not need to leave their posts, because their fellow Levites made the preparations for them.

¹⁶So at that time the entire service of the LORD was carried out for the celebration of the Passover and the offering of burnt offerings on the altar of the LORD, as King Josiah had ordered. ¹⁷The Israelites who were present celebrated the Passover at that time and observed the Festival of Unleavened Bread for seven days. ¹⁸The Passover had not been observed like this in Israel since the days of the prophet Samuel; and none of the kings of Israel had ever celebrated such a Passover as did Josiah, with the priests, the Levites and all Judah and Israel who were there with the people of Jerusalem. ¹⁹This Passover was celebrated in the eighteenth year of Josiah's reign.

The Death of Josiah

20 After all this, when Josiah had set the temple in order, Necho king of Egypt went up to fight at Carchemish on the Euphrates, and Josiah marched out to meet him in battle. 21 But Necho sent messengers to him, saying, "What quarrel is there, king of Judah, between you and me? It is not you I am attacking at this time, but the house with which I am at war. God has told me to hurry; so stop opposing God, who is with me, or he will destroy you."

22 Josiah, however, would not turn away from him, but disguised himself to engage him in battle. He would not listen to what Necho had said at God's command but went to fight him on the plain of Megiddo.

23 Archers shot King Josiah, and he told his officers, "Take me away; I am badly wounded." 24 So they took him out of his chariot, put him in his other chariot and brought him to Jerusalem, where he died. He was buried in the tombs of his ancestors, and all Judah and Jerusalem mourned for him.

25 Jeremiah composed laments for Josiah, and to this day all the male and female singers commemorate Josiah in the laments. These became a tradition in Israel and are written in the Laments.

26 The other events of Josiah's reign and his acts of devotion in accordance with what is written in the Law of the LORD— 27 all the events, from beginning to end, are written in the book of

36 the kings of Israel and Judah. 1 And the people of the land took Jehoahaz son of Josiah and made him king in Jerusalem in place of his father.

Jehoahaz King of Judah

2 Jehoahaz[a] was twenty-three years old when he became king, and he reigned in Jerusalem three months. 3 The king of Egypt dethroned him in Jerusalem and imposed on Judah a levy of a hundred talents[b] of silver and a talent[c] of gold. 4 The king of Egypt made Eliakim, a brother of Jehoahaz, king over Judah and Jerusalem and changed Eliakim's name to Jehoiakim. But Necho took Eliakim's brother Jehoahaz and carried him off to Egypt.

Jehoiakim King of Judah

5 Jehoiakim was twenty-five years old when he became king, and he reigned in Jerusalem eleven years. He did evil in the eyes of the LORD his God. 6 Nebuchadnezzar king of Babylon attacked him and bound him with bronze shackles to take him to Babylon. 7 Nebuchadnezzar also took to

---

a 2 Hebrew *Joahaz*, a variant of *Jehoahaz*; also in verse 4   *b* 3 That is, about 3 3/4 tons or about 3.4 metric tons   *c* 3 That is, about 75 pounds or about 34 kilograms

Babylon articles from the temple of the LORD and put them in his temple[a] there.

8 The other events of Jehoiakim's reign, the detestable things he did and all that was found against him, are written in the book of the kings of Israel and Judah. And Jehoiachin his son succeeded him as king.

Jehoiachin King of Judah

9 Jehoiachin was eighteen[b] years old when he became king, and he reigned in Jerusalem three months and ten days. He did evil in the eyes of the LORD. 10 In the spring, King Nebuchadnezzar sent for him and brought him to Babylon, together with articles of value from the temple of the LORD, and he made Jehoiachin's uncle,[c] Zedekiah, king over Judah and Jerusalem.

Zedekiah King of Judah

11 Zedekiah was twenty-one years old when he became king, and he reigned in Jerusalem eleven years. 12 He did evil in the eyes of the LORD his God and did not humble himself before Jeremiah the prophet, who spoke the word of the LORD. 13 He also rebelled against King Nebuchadnezzar, who had made him take an oath in God's name. He became stiff-necked and hardened his heart and would not turn to the LORD, the God of Israel. 14 Furthermore, all the leaders of the priests and the people became more and more unfaithful, following all the detestable practices of the nations and defiling the temple of the LORD, which he had consecrated in Jerusalem.

The Fall of Jerusalem

15 The LORD, the God of their ancestors, sent word to them through his messengers again and again, because he had pity on his people and on his dwelling place. 16 But they mocked God's messengers, despised his words and scoffed at his prophets until the wrath of the LORD was aroused against his people and there was no remedy. 17 He brought up against them the king of the Babylonians,[d] who killed their young men with the sword in the sanctuary, and did not spare young men or young women, the elderly or the infirm. God gave them all into the hands of Nebuchadnezzar. 18 He carried to Babylon all the articles from the temple of God, both large and small, and the treasures of the LORD's temple and the treasures of the king and his officials. 19 They set fire to God's temple and broke down the wall of Jerusalem; they burned all the palac-

---

a 7 Or *palace*   *b* 9 One Hebrew manuscript, some Septuagint manuscripts and Syriac (see also 2 Kings 24:8); most Hebrew manuscripts *eight*   *c* 10 Hebrew *brother*, that is, relative (see 2 Kings 24:17)   *d* 17 Or *Chaldeans* es and destroyed everything of value there.

20 He carried into exile to Babylon the remnant, who escaped from the sword, and they became servants to him and his successors until the kingdom of Persia came to power. **21** The land enjoyed its sabbath rests; all the time of its desolation it rested, until the seventy years were completed in fulfillment of the word of the LORD spoken by Jeremiah.

22 In the first year of Cyrus king of Persia, in order to fulfill the word of the LORD spoken by Jeremiah, the LORD moved the heart of Cyrus king of Persia to make a proclamation throughout his realm and also to put it in writing:

23 "This is what Cyrus king of Persia says:

"'The LORD, the God of heaven, has given me all the kingdoms of the earth and he has appointed me to build a temple for him at Jerusalem in Judah. Any of his people among you may go up, and may the LORD their God be with them.'"

Ezra

Introduction:

The book of Ezra tells about the return of the Jews from exile in Babylon. It begins in 539 BC with the decree of Cyrus, king of Persia, which allowed the people to go back to Jerusalem under the leadership of Zerubbabel. The people enthusiastically began rebuilding the temple and resumed making sacrifices. But for eighteen years they were delayed by their enemies from the north. Finally, in 521 BC a decree from Darius, king of Persia, let them continue the building project. The people completed and dedicated the temple in 515 BC.

In 458 BC, Ezra, the priest, returned to Jerusalem with another group of Babylonian exiles. He taught the people the law and reformed their religious life so the other nations around them could see they were God's chosen nation.

Ezra is the author of the books of Ezra and Nehemiah.

Outline of contents:

The first exiles return to the land of Judah (1:1–2:70)
The temple is rebuilt (3:1–6:22)
Ezra's return and ministry (7:1–10:44)

Cyrus Helps the Exiles to Return

1 In the first year of Cyrus king of Persia, in order to fulfill the word of the LORD spoken by Jeremiah, the LORD moved the heart of Cyrus king of Persia to make a proclamation throughout his realm and also to put it in writing:

² "This is what Cyrus king of Persia says:

"'The LORD, the God of heaven, has given me all the kingdoms of the earth and he has appointed me to build a temple for him at Jerusalem in Judah. ³ Any of his people among you may go up to Jerusalem in Judah and build the temple of the LORD, the God of Israel, the God who is in Jerusalem, and may their God be with them. ⁴ And in any locality where survivors may now be living, the people are to provide them with silver and gold, with goods and livestock, and with freewill offerings for the temple of God in Jerusalem.'"

⁵ Then the family heads of Judah and Benjamin, and the

priests and Levites—everyone whose heart God had moved—prepared to go up and build the house of the LORD in Jerusalem. ⁶All their neighbors assisted them with articles of silver and gold, with goods and livestock, and with valuable gifts, in addition to all the freewill offerings.

⁷Moreover, King Cyrus brought out the articles belonging to the temple of the LORD, which Nebuchadnezzar had carried away from Jerusalem and had placed in the temple of his god.*a* ⁸Cyrus king of Persia had them brought by Mithredath the treasurer, who counted them out to Sheshbazzar the prince of Judah.

⁹This was the inventory:

gold dishes	30
silver dishes	1,000
silver pans*b*	29
¹⁰gold bowls	30
matching silver bowls	410
other articles	1,000

¹¹In all, there were 5,400 articles of gold and of silver. Sheshbazzar brought all these along with the exiles when they came up from Babylon to Jerusalem.

The List of the Exiles Who Returned

2 Now these are the people of the province who came up from the captivity of the exiles, whom Nebuchadnezzar king

of Babylon had taken captive to Babylon (they returned to Jerusalem and Judah, each to their own town, ²in company with Zerubbabel, Joshua, Nehemiah, Seraiah, Reelaiah, Mordecai, Bilshan, Mispar, Bigvai, Rehum and Baanah):

The list of the men of the people of Israel:

³the descendants of Parosh	2,172
⁴of Shephatiah	372
⁵of Arah	775
⁶of Pahath-Moab (through the line of Jeshua and Joab)	2,812
⁷of Elam	1,254
⁸of Zattu	945
⁹of Zakkai	760
¹⁰of Bani	642
¹¹of Bebai	623
¹²of Azgad	1,222
¹³of Adonikam	666
¹⁴of Bigvai	2,056
¹⁵of Adin	454
¹⁶of Ater (through Hezekiah)	98
¹⁷of Bezai	323
¹⁸of Jorah	112
¹⁹of Hashum	223
²⁰of Gibbar	95
²¹the men of Bethlehem	123
²²of Netophah	56
²³of Anathoth	128
²⁴of Azmaveth	42

a 7 Or *gods*   *b 9* The meaning of the Hebrew for this word is uncertain.

25 of Kiriath Jearim,[a] Kephirah and Beeroth   743

26 of Ramah and Geba   621

27 of Mikmash   122

28 of Bethel and Ai   223

29 of Nebo   52

30 of Magbish   156

31 of the other Elam   1,254

32 of Harim   320

33 of Lod, Hadid and Ono   725

34 of Jericho   345

35 of Senaah   3,630

36 The priests:

the descendants of Jedaiah (through the family of Jeshua)   973

37 of Immer   1,052

38 of Pashhur   1,247

39 of Harim   1,017

40 The Levites:

the descendants of Jeshua and Kadmiel (of the line of Hodaviah)   74

41 The musicians:

the descendants of Asaph   128

42 The gatekeepers of the temple:

the descendants of Shallum, Ater, Talmon, Akkub, Hatita and Shobai   139

43 The temple servants:

the descendants of Ziha, Hasupha, Tabbaoth,

44 Keros, Siaha, Padon,

45 Lebanah, Hagabah, Akkub,

46 Hagab, Shalmai, Hanan,

47 Giddel, Gahar, Reaiah,

48 Rezin, Nekoda, Gazzam,

49 Uzza, Paseah, Besai,

50 Asnah, Meunim, Nephusim,

51 Bakbuk, Hakupha, Harhur,

52 Bazluth, Mehida, Harsha,

53 Barkos, Sisera, Temah,

54 Neziah and Hatipha

55 The descendants of the servants of Solomon:

the descendants of Sotai, Hassophereth, Peruda,

56 Jaala, Darkon, Giddel,

57 Shephatiah, Hattil, Pokereth-Hazzebaim and Ami

58 The temple servants and the descendants of the servants of Solomon   392

59 The following came up from the towns of Tel Melah, Tel Harsha, Kerub, Addon and Immer, but they could not show that their families were descended from Israel:

---

[a] 25 See Septuagint (see also Neh. 7:29); Hebrew *Kiriath Arim*.

60 The descendants of
     Delaiah, Tobiah
     and Nekoda   652

61 And from among the
priests:

The descendants of
     Hobaiah, Hakkoz and
     Barzillai (a man who had
     married a daughter of
     Barzillai the Gileadite
     and was called by that
     name).
62 These searched for their
family records, but they
could not find them and
so were excluded from the
priesthood as unclean. 63 The
governor ordered them not
to eat any of the most sacred
food until there was a priest
ministering with the Urim
and Thummim.

64 The whole company
numbered 42,360, 65 besides
their 7,337 male and female
slaves; and they also had
200 male and female sing-
ers. 66 They had 736 horses,
245 mules, 67 435 camels and
6,720 donkeys.

68 When they arrived at the
house of the LORD in Jerusalem,
some of the heads of the families
gave freewill offerings toward the
rebuilding of the house of God on
its site. 69 According to their ability they gave to the treasury for
this work 61,000 darics[a] of gold,
5,000 minas[b] of silver and 100
priestly garments.

70 The priests, the Levites, the
musicians, the gatekeepers and
the temple servants settled in
their own towns, along with
some of the other people, and
the rest of the Israelites settled in
their towns.

Rebuilding the Altar

3 When the seventh month
came and the Israelites had
settled in their towns, the people assembled together as one
in Jerusalem. 2 Then Joshua son
of Jozadak and his fellow priests
and Zerubbabel son of Shealtiel
and his associates began to build
the altar of the God of Israel to
sacrifice burnt offerings on it, in
accordance with what is written
in the Law of Moses the man of
God. 3 Despite their fear of the
peoples around them, they built
the altar on its foundation and
sacrificed burnt offerings on it
to the LORD, both the morning
and evening sacrifices. 4 Then in
accordance with what is written, they celebrated the Festival
of Tabernacles with the required
number of burnt offerings prescribed for each day. 5 After that,
they presented the regular burnt
offerings, the New Moon sacrifices and the sacrifices for all the
appointed sacred festivals of the

a 69 That is, about 1,100 pounds or about 500 kilograms   b 69 That is, about
3 tons or about 2.8 metric tons

LORD, as well as those brought as freewill offerings to the LORD. [6]On the first day of the seventh month they began to offer burnt offerings to the LORD, though the foundation of the LORD's temple had not yet been laid.

Rebuilding the Temple

[7]Then they gave money to the masons and carpenters, and gave food and drink and olive oil to the people of Sidon and Tyre, so that they would bring cedar logs by sea from Lebanon to Joppa, as authorized by Cyrus king of Persia.

[8]In the second month of the second year after their arrival at the house of God in Jerusalem, Zerubbabel son of Shealtiel, Joshua son of Jozadak and the rest of the people (the priests and the Levites and all who had returned from the captivity to Jerusalem) began the work. They appointed Levites twenty years old and older to supervise the building of the house of the LORD. [9]Joshua and his sons and brothers and Kadmiel and his sons (descendants of Hodaviah[a]) and the sons of Henadad and their sons and brothers — all Levites — joined together in supervising those working on the house of God.

[10]When the builders laid the foundation of the temple of the LORD, the priests in their vestments and with trumpets, and the Levites (the sons of Asaph) with cymbals, took their places to praise the LORD, as prescribed by David king of Israel. [11]With praise and thanksgiving they sang to the LORD:

> "He is good;
>   his love toward Israel
>   endures forever."

And all the people gave a great shout of praise to the LORD, because the foundation of the house of the LORD was laid. [12]But many of the older priests and Levites and family heads, who had seen the former temple, wept aloud when they saw the foundation of this temple being laid, while many others shouted for joy. [13]No one could distinguish the sound of the shouts of joy from the sound of weeping, because the people made so much noise. And the sound was heard far away.

Opposition to the Rebuilding

4 When the enemies of Judah and Benjamin heard that the exiles were building a temple for the LORD, the God of Israel, [2]they came to Zerubbabel and to the heads of the families and said, "Let us help you build because, like you, we seek your God and have been sacrificing to him since the time of Esarhaddon king of Assyria, who brought us here."

[3]But Zerubbabel, Joshua and the rest of the heads of the fami-

---

[a] 9 Hebrew *Yehudah*, a variant of *Hodaviah*

lies of Israel answered, "You have no part with us in building a temple to our God. We alone will build it for the LORD, the God of Israel, as King Cyrus, the king of Persia, commanded us."

⁴Then the peoples around them set out to discourage the people of Judah and make them afraid to go on building.ᵃ ⁵They bribed officials to work against them and frustrate their plans during the entire reign of Cyrus king of Persia and down to the reign of Darius king of Persia.

Later Opposition Under Xerxes and Artaxerxes

⁶At the beginning of the reign of Xerxes,ᵇ they lodged an accusation against the people of Judah and Jerusalem.

⁷And in the days of Artaxerxes king of Persia, Bishlam, Mithredath, Tabeel and the rest of his associates wrote a letter to Artaxerxes. The letter was written in Aramaic script and in the Aramaic language.ᶜ,ᵈ

⁸Rehum the commanding officer and Shimshai the secretary wrote a letter against Jerusalem to Artaxerxes the king as follows:

⁹Rehum the commanding officer and Shimshai the secretary, together with the rest of their associates — the judges, officials and administrators over the people from Persia, Uruk and Babylon, the Elamites of Susa, ¹⁰and the other people whom the great and honorable Ashurbanipal deported and settled in the city of Samaria and elsewhere in Trans-Euphrates.

¹¹(This is a copy of the letter they sent him.)

To King Artaxerxes,

From your servants in Trans-Euphrates:

¹²The king should know that the people who came up to us from you have gone to Jerusalem and are rebuilding that rebellious and wicked city. They are restoring the walls and repairing the foundations.

¹³Furthermore, the king should know that if this city is built and its walls are restored, no more taxes, tribute or duty will be paid, and eventually the royal revenues will suffer.ᵉ ¹⁴Now since we are under obligation to the palace and it is not proper for us to see the king dishonored, we are sending this message to inform the king, ¹⁵so that a search may be made in the archives of your predecessors. In these records you will find that this

---

ᵃ 4 Or *and troubled them as they built in Aramaic and translated*   ᵇ 6 Hebrew *Ahasuerus*   ᶜ 7 Or *written*   ᵈ 7 The text of 4:8–6:18 is in Aramaic.   ᵉ 13 The meaning of the Aramaic for this clause is uncertain.

city is a rebellious city, troublesome to kings and provinces, a place with a long history of sedition. That is why this city was destroyed. [16] We inform the king that if this city is built and its walls are restored, you will be left with nothing in Trans-Euphrates.

[17] The king sent this reply:

To Rehum the commanding officer, Shimshai the secretary and the rest of their associates living in Samaria and elsewhere in Trans-Euphrates:

Greetings.

[18] The letter you sent us has been read and translated in my presence. [19] I issued an order and a search was made, and it was found that this city has a long history of revolt against kings and has been a place of rebellion and sedition. [20] Jerusalem has had powerful kings ruling over the whole of Trans-Euphrates, and taxes, tribute and duty were paid to them. [21] Now issue an order to these men to stop work, so that this city will not be rebuilt until I so order. [22] Be careful not to neglect this matter. Why let this threat grow, to the detriment of the royal interests?

[23] As soon as the copy of the letter of King Artaxerxes was read to Rehum and Shimshai the secretary and their associates, they went immediately to the Jews in Jerusalem and compelled them by force to stop.

[24] Thus the work on the house of God in Jerusalem came to a standstill until the second year of the reign of Darius king of Persia.

Tattenai's Letter to Darius

5 Now Haggai the prophet and Zechariah the prophet, a descendant of Iddo, prophesied to the Jews in Judah and Jerusalem in the name of the God of Israel, who was over them. [2] Then Zerubbabel son of Shealtiel and Joshua son of Jozadak set to work to rebuild the house of God in Jerusalem. And the prophets of God were with them, supporting them.

[3] At that time Tattenai, governor of Trans-Euphrates, and Shethar-Bozenai and their associates went to them and asked, "Who authorized you to rebuild this temple and to finish it?" [4] They[a] also asked, "What are the names of those who are constructing this building?" [5] But the eye of their God was watching over the elders of the Jews, and they were not stopped until a report could go to Darius and his written reply be received.

<hr>

a 4 See Septuagint; Aramaic *We.*

⁶This is a copy of the letter that Tattenai, governor of Trans-Euphrates, and Shethar-Bozenai and their associates, the officials of Trans-Euphrates, sent to King Darius. ⁷The report they sent him read as follows:

To King Darius:

Cordial greetings.

⁸The king should know that we went to the district of Judah, to the temple of the great God. The people are building it with large stones and placing the timbers in the walls. The work is being carried on with diligence and is making rapid progress under their direction.

⁹We questioned the elders and asked them, "Who authorized you to rebuild this temple and to finish it?" ¹⁰We also asked them their names, so that we could write down the names of their leaders for your information.

¹¹This is the answer they gave us:

"We are the servants of the God of heaven and earth, and we are rebuilding the temple that was built many years ago, one that a great king of Israel built and finished. ¹²But because our ancestors angered the God of heaven, he gave them into the hands of Nebuchadnezzar the Chaldean, king of Babylon, who destroyed this temple and deported the people to Babylon.

¹³"However, in the first year of Cyrus king of Babylon, King Cyrus issued a decree to rebuild this house of God. ¹⁴He even removed from the temple^a of Babylon the gold and silver articles of the house of God, which Nebuchadnezzar had taken from the temple in Jerusalem and brought to the temple^a in Babylon. Then King Cyrus gave them to a man named Sheshbazzar, whom he had appointed governor, ¹⁵and he told him, 'Take these articles and go and deposit them in the temple in Jerusalem. And rebuild the house of God on its site.'

¹⁶"So this Sheshbazzar came and laid the foundations of the house of God in Jerusalem. From that day to the present it has been under construction but is not yet finished."

¹⁷Now if it pleases the king, let a search be made in the royal archives of Babylon to see if King Cyrus did in fact issue a decree to rebuild this house of God in Jerusalem. Then let the king send us his decision in this matter.

---

^a 14 Or *palace*

The Decree of Darius

6 King Darius then issued an order, and they searched in the archives stored in the treasury at Babylon. ²A scroll was found in the citadel of Ecbatana in the province of Media, and this was written on it:

Memorandum:

³In the first year of King Cyrus, the king issued a decree concerning the temple of God in Jerusalem:

Let the temple be rebuilt as a place to present sacrifices, and let its foundations be laid. It is to be sixty cubits*a* high and sixty cubits wide, ⁴with three courses of large stones and one of timbers. The costs are to be paid by the royal treasury. ⁵Also, the gold and silver articles of the house of God, which Nebuchadnezzar took from the temple in Jerusalem and brought to Babylon, are to be returned to their places in the temple in Jerusalem; they are to be deposited in the house of God.

⁶Now then, Tattenai, governor of Trans-Euphrates, and Shethar-Bozenai and you other officials of that province, stay away from there. ⁷Do not interfere with the work on this temple of God. Let the governor of the Jews and the Jewish elders rebuild this house of God on its site.

⁸Moreover, I hereby decree what you are to do for these elders of the Jews in the construction of this house of God:

Their expenses are to be fully paid out of the royal treasury, from the revenues of Trans-Euphrates, so that the work will not stop. ⁹Whatever is needed — young bulls, rams, male lambs for burnt offerings to the God of heaven, and wheat, salt, wine and olive oil, as requested by the priests in Jerusalem — must be given them daily without fail, ¹⁰so that they may offer sacrifices pleasing to the God of heaven and pray for the well-being of the king and his sons.

¹¹Furthermore, I decree that if anyone defies this edict, a beam is to be pulled from their house and they are to be impaled on it. And for this crime their house is to be made a pile of rubble. ¹²May God, who has caused his Name to dwell there, overthrow any king or people who lifts a hand to change this decree or to destroy this temple in Jerusalem.

I Darius have decreed it. Let it be carried out with diligence.

a 3 That is, about 90 feet or about 27 meters

Completion and Dedication of the Temple

¹³Then, because of the decree King Darius had sent, Tattenai, governor of Trans-Euphrates, and Shethar-Bozenai and their associates carried it out with diligence. ¹⁴So the elders of the Jews continued to build and prosper under the preaching of Haggai the prophet and Zechariah, a descendant of Iddo. They finished building the temple according to the command of the God of Israel and the decrees of Cyrus, Darius and Artaxerxes, kings of Persia. ¹⁵The temple was completed on the third day of the month Adar, in the sixth year of the reign of King Darius.

¹⁶Then the people of Israel— the priests, the Levites and the rest of the exiles—celebrated the dedication of the house of God with joy. ¹⁷For the dedication of this house of God they offered a hundred bulls, two hundred rams, four hundred male lambs and, as a sin offering[a] for all Israel, twelve male goats, one for each of the tribes of Israel. ¹⁸And they installed the priests in their divisions and the Levites in their groups for the service of God at Jerusalem, according to what is written in the Book of Moses.

The Passover

¹⁹On the fourteenth day of the first month, the exiles celebrated the Passover. ²⁰The priests and Levites had purified themselves and were all ceremonially clean. The Levites slaughtered the Passover lamb for all the exiles, for their relatives the priests and for themselves. ²¹So the Israelites who had returned from the exile ate it, together with all who had separated themselves from the unclean practices of their Gentile neighbors in order to seek the Lord, the God of Israel. ²²For seven days they celebrated with joy the Festival of Unleavened Bread, because the Lord had filled them with joy by changing the attitude of the king of Assyria so that he assisted them in the work on the house of God, the God of Israel.

Ezra Comes to Jerusalem

7 After these things, during the reign of Artaxerxes king of Persia, Ezra son of Seraiah, the son of Azariah, the son of Hilkiah, ²the son of Shallum, the son of Zadok, the son of Ahitub, ³the son of Amariah, the son of Azariah, the son of Meraioth, ⁴the son of Zerahiah, the son of Uzzi, the son of Bukki, ⁵the son of Abishua, the son of Phinehas, the son of Eleazar, the son of Aaron the chief priest— ⁶this Ezra came up from Babylon. He was a teacher well versed in the Law of Moses, which the Lord, the God of Israel, had given. The king had granted him everything he asked, for

---

a 17 Or *purification offering*

the hand of the LORD his God was on him. [7] Some of the Israelites, including priests, Levites, musicians, gatekeepers and temple servants, also came up to Jerusalem in the seventh year of King Artaxerxes.

[8] Ezra arrived in Jerusalem in the fifth month of the seventh year of the king. [9] He had begun his journey from Babylon on the first day of the first month, and he arrived in Jerusalem on the first day of the fifth month, for the gracious hand of his God was on him. [10] For Ezra had devoted himself to the study and observance of the Law of the LORD, and to teaching its decrees and laws in Israel.

King Artaxerxes' Letter to Ezra

[11] This is a copy of the letter King Artaxerxes had given to Ezra the priest, a teacher of the Law, a man learned in matters concerning the commands and decrees of the LORD for Israel:

[12] Artaxerxes, king of kings,

To Ezra the priest, teacher of the Law of the God of heaven:

Greetings.

[13] Now I decree that any of the Israelites in my kingdom, including priests and Levites, who volunteer to go to Jerusalem with you, may go. [14] You are sent by the king and his seven advisers to inquire about Judah and Jerusalem with regard to the Law of your God, which is in your hand. [15] Moreover, you are to take with you the silver and gold that the king and his advisers have freely given to the God of Israel, whose dwelling is in Jerusalem, [16] together with all the silver and gold you may obtain from the province of Babylon, as well as the freewill offerings of the people and priests for the temple of their God in Jerusalem. [17] With this money be sure to buy bulls, rams and male lambs, together with their grain offerings and drink offerings, and sacrifice them on the altar of the temple of your God in Jerusalem.

[18] You and your fellow Israelites may then do whatever seems best with the rest of the silver and gold, in accordance with the will of your God. [19] Deliver to the God of Jerusalem all the articles entrusted to you for worship in the temple of your God. [20] And anything else needed for the temple of your God that you are responsible to supply, you may provide from the royal treasury.

[21] Now I, King Artaxerxes, decree that all the treasurers of Trans-Euphrates are to provide with diligence whatever Ezra the priest, the teacher of the Law of the God of heaven, may ask of you—

²²up to a hundred talents*ᵃ* of silver, a hundred cors*ᵇ* of wheat, a hundred baths*ᶜ* of wine, a hundred baths*ᶜ* of olive oil, and salt without limit. ²³Whatever the God of heaven has prescribed, let it be done with diligence for the temple of the God of heaven. Why should his wrath fall on the realm of the king and of his sons? ²⁴You are also to know that you have no authority to impose taxes, tribute or duty on any of the priests, Levites, musicians, gatekeepers, temple servants or other workers at this house of God.

²⁵And you, Ezra, in accordance with the wisdom of your God, which you possess, appoint magistrates and judges to administer justice to all the people of Trans-Euphrates — all who know the laws of your God. And you are to teach any who do not know them. ²⁶Whoever does not obey the law of your God and the law of the king must surely be punished by death, banishment, confiscation of property, or imprisonment.*ᵈ*

²⁷Praise be to the LORD, the God of our ancestors, who has put it into the king's heart to bring honor to the house of the LORD in Jerusalem in this way ²⁸and who has extended his good favor to me before the king and his advisers and all the king's powerful officials. Because the hand of the LORD my God was on me, I took courage and gathered leaders from Israel to go up with me.

List of the Family Heads Returning With Ezra

8 These are the family heads and those registered with them who came up with me from Babylon during the reign of King Artaxerxes:

²of the descendants of Phinehas, Gershom;
  of the descendants of Ithamar, Daniel;
  of the descendants of David, Hattush ³of the descendants of Shekaniah;

  of the descendants of Parosh, Zechariah, and with him were registered 150 men;
⁴of the descendants of Pahath-Moab, Eliehoenai son of Zerahiah, and with him 200 men;
⁵of the descendants of Zattu,*ᵉ* Shekaniah son of Jahaziel, and with him 300 men;
⁶of the descendants of Adin, Ebed son of Jonathan, and with him 50 men;

ᵃ 22 That is, about 3 3/4 tons or about 3.4 metric tons   *ᵇ* 22 That is, probably about 18 tons or about 16 metric tons   *ᶜ* 22 That is, about 600 gallons or about 2,200 liters   *ᵈ* 26 The text of 7:12-26 is in Aramaic.   *ᵉ* 5 Some Septuagint manuscripts (also 1 Esdras 8:32); Hebrew does not have *Zattu*.

[7] of the descendants of Elam, Jeshaiah son of Athaliah, and with him 70 men;

[8] of the descendants of Shephatiah, Zebadiah son of Michael, and with him 80 men;

[9] of the descendants of Joab, Obadiah son of Jehiel, and with him 218 men;

[10] of the descendants of Bani,[a] Shelomith son of Josiphiah, and with him 160 men;

[11] of the descendants of Bebai, Zechariah son of Bebai, and with him 28 men;

[12] of the descendants of Azgad, Johanan son of Hakkatan, and with him 110 men;

[13] of the descendants of Adonikam, the last ones, whose names were Eliphelet, Jeuel and Shemaiah, and with them 60 men;

[14] of the descendants of Bigvai, Uthai and Zakkur, and with them 70 men.

The Return to Jerusalem

[15] I assembled them at the canal that flows toward Ahava, and we camped there three days. When I checked among the people and the priests, I found no Levites there. [16] So I summoned Eliezer, Ariel, Shemaiah, Elnathan, Jarib, Elnathan, Nathan, Zechariah and Meshullam, who were leaders, and Joiarib and Elnathan, who were men of learning, [17] and I ordered them to go to Iddo, the leader in Kasiphia. I told them what to say to Iddo and his fellow Levites, the temple servants in Kasiphia, so that they might bring attendants to us for the house of our God. [18] Because the gracious hand of our God was on us, they brought us Sherebiah, a capable man, from the descendants of Mahli son of Levi, the son of Israel, and Sherebiah's sons and brothers, 18 in all; [19] and Hashabiah, together with Jeshaiah from the descendants of Merari, and his brothers and nephews, 20 in all. [20] They also brought 220 of the temple servants—a body that David and the officials had established to assist the Levites. All were registered by name.

[21] There, by the Ahava Canal, I proclaimed a fast, so that we might humble ourselves before our God and ask him for a safe journey for us and our children, with all our possessions. [22] I was ashamed to ask the king for soldiers and horsemen to protect us from enemies on the road, because we had told the king, "The gracious hand of our God is on everyone who looks to him, but his great anger is against all who forsake him." [23] So we fasted and petitioned our God about this, and he answered our prayer.

---

[a] 10 Some Septuagint manuscripts (also 1 Esdras 8:36); Hebrew does not have Bani.

²⁴Then I set apart twelve of the leading priests, namely, Sherebiah, Hashabiah and ten of their brothers, ²⁵and I weighed out to them the offering of silver and gold and the articles that the king, his advisers, his officials and all Israel present there had donated for the house of our God. ²⁶I weighed out to them 650 talents[a] of silver, silver articles weighing 100 talents,[b] 100 talents[b] of gold, ²⁷20 bowls of gold valued at 1,000 darics,[c] and two fine articles of polished bronze, as precious as gold.

²⁸I said to them, "You as well as these articles are consecrated to the LORD. The silver and gold are a freewill offering to the LORD, the God of your ancestors. ²⁹Guard them carefully until you weigh them out in the chambers of the house of the LORD in Jerusalem before the leading priests and the Levites and the family heads of Israel." ³⁰Then the priests and Levites received the silver and gold and sacred articles that had been weighed out to be taken to the house of our God in Jerusalem.

³¹On the twelfth day of the first month we set out from the Ahava Canal to go to Jerusalem. The hand of our God was on us, and he protected us from enemies and bandits along the way. ³²So we arrived in Jerusalem, where we rested three days.

³³On the fourth day, in the house of our God, we weighed out the silver and gold and the sacred articles into the hands of Meremoth son of Uriah, the priest. Eleazar son of Phinehas was with him, and so were the Levites Jozabad son of Jeshua and Noadiah son of Binnui. ³⁴Everything was accounted for by number and weight, and the entire weight was recorded at that time.

³⁵Then the exiles who had returned from captivity sacrificed burnt offerings to the God of Israel: twelve bulls for all Israel, ninety-six rams, seventy-seven male lambs and, as a sin offering,[d] twelve male goats. All this was a burnt offering to the LORD. ³⁶They also delivered the king's orders to the royal satraps and to the governors of Trans-Euphrates, who then gave assistance to the people and to the house of God.

Ezra's Prayer About Intermarriage

9 After these things had been done, the leaders came to me and said, "The people of Israel, including the priests and the Levites, have not kept themselves separate from the neighboring peoples with their detestable

---

[a] 26 That is, about 24 tons or about 22 metric tons   [b] 26 That is, about 3 3/4 tons or about 3.4 metric tons   [c] 27 That is, about 19 pounds or about 8.4 kilograms   [d] 35 Or purification offering

practices, like those of the Canaanites, Hittites, Perizzites, Jebusites, Ammonites, Moabites, Egyptians and Amorites. ²They have taken some of their daughters as wives for themselves and their sons, and have mingled the holy race with the peoples around them. And the leaders and officials have led the way in this unfaithfulness."

³When I heard this, I tore my tunic and cloak, pulled hair from my head and beard and sat down appalled. ⁴Then everyone who trembled at the words of the God of Israel gathered around me because of this unfaithfulness of the exiles. And I sat there appalled until the evening sacrifice.

⁵Then, at the evening sacrifice, I rose from my self-abasement, with my tunic and cloak torn, and fell on my knees with my hands spread out to the LORD my God ⁶and prayed:

"I am too ashamed and disgraced, my God, to lift up my face to you, because our sins are higher than our heads and our guilt has reached to the heavens. ⁷From the days of our ancestors until now, our guilt has been great. Because of our sins, we and our kings and our priests have been subjected to the sword and captivity, to pillage and humiliation at the hand of foreign kings, as it is today.

⁸"But now, for a brief moment, the LORD our God has been gracious in leaving us a remnant and giving us a firm place*ᵃ* in his sanctuary, and so our God gives light to our eyes and a little relief in our bondage. ⁹Though we are slaves, our God has not forsaken us in our bondage. He has shown us kindness in the sight of the kings of Persia: He has granted us new life to rebuild the house of our God and repair its ruins, and he has given us a wall of protection in Judah and Jerusalem.

¹⁰"But now, our God, what can we say after this? For we have forsaken the commands ¹¹you gave through your servants the prophets when you said: 'The land you are entering to possess is a land polluted by the corruption of its peoples. By their detestable practices they have filled it with their impurity from one end to the other. ¹²Therefore, do not give your daughters in marriage to their sons or take their daughters for your sons. Do not seek a treaty of friendship with them at any time, that you may be strong and eat the good things of the land and leave it to your children as an everlasting inheritance.'

¹³"What has happened to us is a result of our evil deeds

ᵃ 8 Or *a foothold*

and our great guilt, and yet, our God, you have punished us less than our sins deserved and have given us a remnant like this. ¹⁴Shall we then break your commands again and intermarry with the peoples who commit such detestable practices? Would you not be angry enough with us to destroy us, leaving us no remnant or survivor? ¹⁵LORD, the God of Israel, you are righteous! We are left this day as a remnant. Here we are before you in our guilt, though because of it not one of us can stand in your presence."

The People's Confession of Sin

10 While Ezra was praying and confessing, weeping and throwing himself down before the house of God, a large crowd of Israelites — men, women and children — gathered around him. They too wept bitterly. ²Then Shekaniah son of Jehiel, one of the descendants of Elam, said to Ezra, "We have been unfaithful to our God by marrying foreign women from the peoples around us. But in spite of this, there is still hope for Israel. ³Now let us make a covenant before our God to send away all these women and their children, in accordance with the counsel of my lord and of those who fear the commands of our God. Let it be done according to the Law. ⁴Rise up; this matter is in your hands. We will support you, so take courage and do it."

⁵So Ezra rose up and put the leading priests and Levites and all Israel under oath to do what had been suggested. And they took the oath. ⁶Then Ezra withdrew from before the house of God and went to the room of Jehohanan son of Eliashib. While he was there, he ate no food and drank no water, because he continued to mourn over the unfaithfulness of the exiles.

⁷A proclamation was then issued throughout Judah and Jerusalem for all the exiles to assemble in Jerusalem. ⁸Anyone who failed to appear within three days would forfeit all his property, in accordance with the decision of the officials and elders, and would himself be expelled from the assembly of the exiles.

⁹Within the three days, all the men of Judah and Benjamin had gathered in Jerusalem. And on the twentieth day of the ninth month, all the people were sitting in the square before the house of God, greatly distressed by the occasion and because of the rain. ¹⁰Then Ezra the priest stood up and said to them, "You have been unfaithful; you have married foreign women, adding to Israel's guilt. ¹¹Now honor[a] the LORD,

---

[a] 11 Or *Now make confession to*

the God of your ancestors, and do his will. Separate yourselves from the peoples around you and from your foreign wives."

¹²The whole assembly responded with a loud voice: "You are right! We must do as you say. ¹³But there are many people here and it is the rainy season; so we cannot stand outside. Besides, this matter cannot be taken care of in a day or two, because we have sinned greatly in this thing. ¹⁴Let our officials act for the whole assembly. Then let everyone in our towns who has married a foreign woman come at a set time, along with the elders and judges of each town, until the fierce anger of our God in this matter is turned away from us." ¹⁵Only Jonathan son of Asahel and Jahzeiah son of Tikvah, supported by Meshullam and Shabbethai the Levite, opposed this.

¹⁶So the exiles did as was proposed. Ezra the priest selected men who were family heads, one from each family division, and all of them designated by name. On the first day of the tenth month they sat down to investigate the cases, ¹⁷and by the first day of the first month they finished dealing with all the men who had married foreign women.

Those Guilty of Intermarriage

¹⁸Among the descendants of the priests, the following had married foreign women:

From the descendants of Joshua son of Jozadak, and his brothers: Maaseiah, Eliezer, Jarib and Gedaliah. ¹⁹(They all gave their hands in pledge to put away their wives, and for their guilt they each presented a ram from the flock as a guilt offering.)

²⁰From the descendants of Immer:
Hanani and Zebadiah.
²¹From the descendants of Harim:
Maaseiah, Elijah, Shemaiah, Jehiel and Uzziah.
²²From the descendants of Pashhur:
Elioenai, Maaseiah, Ishmael, Nethanel, Jozabad and Elasah.

²³Among the Levites:

Jozabad, Shimei, Kelaiah (that is, Kelita), Pethahiah, Judah and Eliezer.
²⁴From the musicians:
Eliashib.
From the gatekeepers:
Shallum, Telem and Uri.

²⁵And among the other Israelites:

From the descendants of Parosh:
Ramiah, Izziah, Malkijah, Mijamin, Eleazar, Malkijah and Benaiah.
²⁶From the descendants of Elam:

Mattaniah, Zechariah, Jehiel, Abdi, Jeremoth and Elijah.

²⁷ From the descendants of Zattu:

Elioenai, Eliashib, Mattaniah, Jeremoth, Zabad and Aziza.

²⁸ From the descendants of Bebai:

Jehohanan, Hananiah, Zabbai and Athlai.

²⁹ From the descendants of Bani:

Meshullam, Malluk, Adaiah, Jashub, Sheal and Jeremoth.

³⁰ From the descendants of Pahath-Moab:

Adna, Kelal, Benaiah, Maaseiah, Mattaniah, Bezalel, Binnui and Manasseh.

³¹ From the descendants of Harim:

Eliezer, Ishijah, Malkijah, Shemaiah, Shimeon, ³² Benjamin, Malluk and Shemariah.

³³ From the descendants of Hashum:

Mattenai, Mattattah, Zabad, Eliphelet, Jeremai, Manasseh and Shimei.

³⁴ From the descendants of Bani:

Maadai, Amram, Uel, ³⁵ Benaiah, Bedeiah, Keluhi, ³⁶ Vaniah, Meremoth, Eliashib, ³⁷ Mattaniah, Mattenai and Jaasu.

³⁸ From the descendants of Binnui:ᵃ

Shimei, ³⁹ Shelemiah, Nathan, Adaiah, ⁴⁰ Maknadebai, Shashai, Sharai, ⁴¹ Azarel, Shelemiah, Shemariah, ⁴² Shallum, Amariah and Joseph.

⁴³ From the descendants of Nebo:

Jeiel, Mattithiah, Zabad, Zebina, Jaddai, Joel and Benaiah.

⁴⁴ All these had married foreign women, and some of them had children by these wives.ᵇ

ᵃ 37,38 See Septuagint (also 1 Esdras 9:34); Hebrew *Jaasu* ³⁸ *and Bani and Binnui,*
ᵇ 44 Or *and they sent them away with their children*

Nehemiah

Introduction:

The book of Nehemiah continues the history of the Jews who returned from exile in Babylon. Nehemiah gave up his job as cupbearer to Artaxerxes, the Persian king, to become governor of Jerusalem. Nehemiah went to Jerusalem in 444 BC, almost 100 years after the return of the first exiles. Nehemiah led the people in repairing the walls of Jerusalem and with Ezra provided leadership for the people. An important part of this book is the description of the importance of prayer to Nehemiah.

Outline of contents:

Nehemiah rebuilds the walls (1:1–7:3)
Change under Ezra (7:4–10:39)
Nehemiah's plans (11:1–13:31)

Nehemiah's Prayer

1 The words of Nehemiah son of Hakaliah:

In the month of Kislev in the twentieth year, while I was in the citadel of Susa, ²Hanani, one of my brothers, came from Judah with some other men, and I questioned them about the Jewish remnant that had survived the exile, and also about Jerusalem.

³They said to me, "Those who survived the exile and are back in the province are in great trouble and disgrace. The wall of Jerusalem is broken down, and its gates have been burned with fire."

⁴When I heard these things, I sat down and wept. For some days I mourned and fasted and prayed before the God of heaven. ⁵Then I said:

"LORD, the God of heaven, the great and awesome God, who keeps his covenant of love with those who love him and keep his commandments, ⁶let your ear be attentive and your eyes open to hear the prayer your servant is praying before you day and night for your servants, the people of Israel. I confess the sins we Israelites, including myself and my father's family, have committed against you. ⁷We have acted very wickedly toward you. We have not obeyed the commands, decrees and laws you gave your servant Moses.

⁸"Remember the instruction you gave your servant Moses, saying, 'If you are unfaithful, I will scatter you among the nations, ⁹but if you return to me and obey my commands, then even if your exiled people are at the farthest horizon, I will gather them from there and bring them to the place I have chosen as a dwelling for my Name.'

¹⁰"They are your servants and your people, whom you redeemed by your great strength and your mighty hand. ¹¹Lord, let your ear be attentive to the prayer of this your servant and to the prayer of your servants who delight in revering your name. Give your servant success today by granting him favor in the presence of this man."

I was cupbearer to the king.

Artaxerxes Sends Nehemiah to Jerusalem

2 In the month of Nisan in the twentieth year of King Artaxerxes, when wine was brought for him, I took the wine and gave it to the king. I had not been sad in his presence before, ²so the king asked me, "Why does your face look so sad when you are not ill? This can be nothing but sadness of heart."

I was very much afraid, ³but I said to the king, "May the king live forever! Why should my face not look sad when the city where my ancestors are buried lies in ruins, and its gates have been destroyed by fire?"

⁴The king said to me, "What is it you want?"

Then I prayed to the God of heaven, ⁵and I answered the king, "If it pleases the king and if your servant has found favor in his sight, let him send me to the city in Judah where my ancestors are buried so that I can rebuild it."

⁶Then the king, with the queen sitting beside him, asked me, "How long will your journey take, and when will you get back?" It pleased the king to send me; so I set a time.

⁷I also said to him, "If it pleases the king, may I have letters to the governors of Trans-Euphrates, so that they will provide me safe-conduct until I arrive in Judah? ⁸And may I have a letter to Asaph, keeper of the royal park, so he will give me timber to make beams for the gates of the citadel by the temple and for the city wall and for the residence I will occupy?" And because the gracious hand of my God was on me, the king granted my requests. ⁹So I went to the governors of Trans-Euphrates and gave them the king's letters. The king had also sent army officers and cavalry with me.

¹⁰When Sanballat the Horonite and Tobiah the Ammonite

official heard about this, they were very much disturbed that someone had come to promote the welfare of the Israelites.

Nehemiah Inspects Jerusalem's Walls

¹¹I went to Jerusalem, and after staying there three days ¹²I set out during the night with a few others. I had not told anyone what my God had put in my heart to do for Jerusalem. There were no mounts with me except the one I was riding on. ¹³By night I went out through the Valley Gate toward the Jackal[a] Well and the Dung Gate, examining the walls of Jerusalem, which had been broken down, and its gates, which had been destroyed by fire. ¹⁴Then I moved on toward the Fountain Gate and the King's Pool, but there was not enough room for my mount to get through; ¹⁵so I went up the valley by night, examining the wall. Finally, I turned back and reentered through the Valley Gate. ¹⁶The officials did not know where I had gone or what I was doing, because as yet I had said nothing to the Jews or the priests or nobles or officials or any others who would be doing the work. ¹⁷Then I said to them, "You see the trouble we are in: Jerusalem lies in ruins, and its gates have been burned with fire. Come, let us rebuild the wall of Jerusalem, and we will no longer be in disgrace." ¹⁸I also told them about the gracious hand of my God on me and what the king had said to me.

They replied, "Let us start rebuilding." So they began this good work.

¹⁹But when Sanballat the Horonite, Tobiah the Ammonite official and Geshem the Arab heard about it, they mocked and ridiculed us. "What is this you are doing?" they asked. "Are you rebelling against the king?"

²⁰I answered them by saying, "The God of heaven will give us success. We his servants will start rebuilding, but as for you, you have no share in Jerusalem or any claim or historic right to it."

Builders of the Wall

3 Eliashib the high priest and his fellow priests went to work and rebuilt the Sheep Gate. They dedicated it and set its doors in place, building as far as the Tower of the Hundred, which they dedicated, and as far as the Tower of Hananel. ²The men of Jericho built the adjoining section, and Zakkur son of Imri built next to them.

³The Fish Gate was rebuilt by the sons of Hassenaah. They laid its beams and put its doors and bolts and bars in place. ⁴Meremoth son of Uriah, the son of Hakkoz, repaired the next sec-

---

[a] 13 Or *Serpent* or *Fig*

tion. Next to him Meshullam son of Berekiah, the son of Meshezabel, made repairs, and next to him Zadok son of Baana also made repairs. **5** The next section was repaired by the men of Tekoa, but their nobles would not put their shoulders to the work under their supervisors.*a*

6 The Jeshanah*b* Gate was repaired by Joiada son of Paseah and Meshullam son of Besodeiah. They laid its beams and put its doors with their bolts and bars in place. **7** Next to them, repairs were made by men from Gibeon and Mizpah—Melatiah of Gibeon and Jadon of Meronoth—places under the authority of the governor of Trans-Euphrates. **8** Uzziel son of Harhaiah, one of the goldsmiths, repaired the next section; and Hananiah, one of the perfume-makers, made repairs next to that. They restored Jerusalem as far as the Broad Wall. **9** Rephaiah son of Hur, ruler of a half-district of Jerusalem, repaired the next section. **10** Adjoining this, Jedaiah son of Harumaph made repairs opposite his house, and Hattush son of Hashabneiah made repairs next to him. **11** Malkijah son of Harim and Hasshub son of Pahath-Moab repaired another section and the Tower of the Ovens. **12** Shallum son of Hallohesh, rul-

er of a half-district of Jerusalem, repaired the next section with the help of his daughters.

13 The Valley Gate was repaired by Hanun and the residents of Zanoah. They rebuilt it and put its doors with their bolts and bars in place. They also repaired a thousand cubits*c* of the wall as far as the Dung Gate.

14 The Dung Gate was repaired by Malkijah son of Rekab, ruler of the district of Beth Hakkerem. He rebuilt it and put its doors with their bolts and bars in place.

15 The Fountain Gate was repaired by Shallun son of Kol-Hozeh, ruler of the district of Mizpah. He rebuilt it, roofing it over and putting its doors and bolts and bars in place. He also repaired the wall of the Pool of Siloam,*d* by the King's Garden, as far as the steps going down from the City of David. **16** Beyond him, Nehemiah son of Azbuk, ruler of a half-district of Beth Zur, made repairs up to a point opposite the tombs*e* of David, as far as the artificial pool and the House of the Heroes.

17 Next to him, the repairs were made by the Levites under Rehum son of Bani. Beside him, Hashabiah, ruler of half the district of Keilah, carried out repairs for his district. **18** Next to him, the

a 5 Or *their Lord* or *the governor*   *b 6* Or *Old*   *c 13* That is, about 1,500 feet or about 450 meters   *d 15* Hebrew *Shelah,* a variant of *Shiloah,* that is, Siloam   *e 16* Hebrew; Septuagint, some Vulgate manuscripts and Syriac *tomb* repairs were made by their fellow Levites under Binnui[a] son of Henadad, ruler of the other half-district of Keilah. **19**Next to him, Ezer son of Jeshua, ruler of Mizpah, repaired another section, from a point facing the ascent to the armory as far as the angle of the wall. **20**Next to him, Baruch son of Zabbai zealously repaired another section, from the angle to the entrance of the house of Eliashib the high priest. **21**Next to him, Meremoth son of Uriah, the son of Hakkoz, repaired another section, from the entrance of Eliashib's house to the end of it.

22The repairs next to him were made by the priests from the surrounding region. **23**Beyond them, Benjamin and Hasshub made repairs in front of their house; and next to them, Azariah son of Maaseiah, the son of Ananiah, made repairs beside his house. **24**Next to him, Binnui son of Henadad repaired another section, from Azariah's house to the angle and the corner, **25**and Palal son of Uzai worked opposite the angle and the tower projecting from the upper palace near the court of the guard. Next to him, Pedaiah son of Parosh **26**and the temple servants living on the hill of Ophel made repairs up to a point opposite the Water Gate toward the east and the projecting tower. **27**Next to them, the men of Tekoa repaired another section, from the great projecting tower to the wall of Ophel.

28Above the Horse Gate, the priests made repairs, each in front of his own house. **29**Next to them, Zadok son of Immer made repairs opposite his house. Next to him, Shemaiah son of Shekaniah, the guard at the East Gate, made repairs. **30**Next to him, Hananiah son of Shelemiah, and Hanun, the sixth son of Zalaph, repaired another section. Next to them, Meshullam son of Berekiah made repairs opposite his living quarters. **31**Next to him, Malkijah, one of the goldsmiths, made repairs as far as the house of the temple servants and the merchants, opposite the Inspection Gate, and as far as the room above the corner; **32**and between the room above the corner and the Sheep Gate the goldsmiths and merchants made repairs.

Opposition to the Rebuilding

4[b] When Sanballat heard that we were rebuilding the wall, he became angry and was greatly incensed. He ridiculed the Jews, **2**and in the presence of his associates and the army of Samaria, he said, "What are those feeble Jews doing? Will they restore their wall? Will they offer sacrifices? Will they finish in a day?

---

[a] 18 Two Hebrew manuscripts and Syriac (see also Septuagint and verse 24); most Hebrew manuscripts *Bavvai*   [b] In Hebrew texts 4:1-6 is numbered 3:33-38, and 4:7-23 is numbered 4:1-17.

Can they bring the stones back to life from those heaps of rubble — burned as they are?"

³Tobiah the Ammonite, who was at his side, said, "What they are building — even a fox climbing up on it would break down their wall of stones!"

⁴Hear us, our God, for we are despised. Turn their insults back on their own heads. Give them over as plunder in a land of captivity. ⁵Do not cover up their guilt or blot out their sins from your sight, for they have thrown insults in the face of[a] the builders.

⁶So we rebuilt the wall till all of it reached half its height, for the people worked with all their heart.

⁷But when Sanballat, Tobiah, the Arabs, the Ammonites and the people of Ashdod heard that the repairs to Jerusalem's walls had gone ahead and that the gaps were being closed, they were very angry. ⁸They all plotted together to come and fight against Jerusalem and stir up trouble against it. ⁹But we prayed to our God and posted a guard day and night to meet this threat.

¹⁰Meanwhile, the people in Judah said, "The strength of the laborers is giving out, and there is so much rubble that we cannot rebuild the wall."

¹¹Also our enemies said, "Before they know it or see us, we will be right there among them and will kill them and put an end to the work."

¹²Then the Jews who lived near them came and told us ten times over, "Wherever you turn, they will attack us."

¹³Therefore I stationed some of the people behind the lowest points of the wall at the exposed places, posting them by families, with their swords, spears and bows. ¹⁴After I looked things over, I stood up and said to the nobles, the officials and the rest of the people, "Don't be afraid of them. Remember the Lord, who is great and awesome, and fight for your families, your sons and your daughters, your wives and your homes."

¹⁵When our enemies heard that we were aware of their plot and that God had frustrated it, we all returned to the wall, each to our own work.

¹⁶From that day on, half of my men did the work, while the other half were equipped with spears, shields, bows and armor. The officers posted themselves behind all the people of Judah ¹⁷who were building the wall. Those who carried materials did their work with one hand and held a weapon in the other, ¹⁸and each of the builders wore his sword at his side as he worked. But the man who sounded the trumpet stayed with me.

---

[a] 5 Or *have aroused your anger before*

¹⁹Then I said to the nobles, the officials and the rest of the people, "The work is extensive and spread out, and we are widely separated from each other along the wall. ²⁰Wherever you hear the sound of the trumpet, join us there. Our God will fight for us!"

²¹So we continued the work with half the men holding spears, from the first light of dawn till the stars came out. ²²At that time I also said to the people, "Have every man and his helper stay inside Jerusalem at night, so they can serve us as guards by night and as workers by day." ²³Neither I nor my brothers nor my men nor the guards with me took off our clothes; each had his weapon, even when he went for water.ᵃ

Nehemiah Helps the Poor

5 Now the men and their wives raised a great outcry against their fellow Jews. ²Some were saying, "We and our sons and daughters are numerous; in order for us to eat and stay alive, we must get grain."

³Others were saying, "We are mortgaging our fields, our vineyards and our homes to get grain during the famine."

⁴Still others were saying, "We have had to borrow money to pay the king's tax on our fields and vineyards. ⁵Although we are of the same flesh and blood as our fellow Jews and though our chil-

dren are as good as theirs, yet we have to subject our sons and daughters to slavery. Some of our daughters have already been enslaved, but we are powerless, because our fields and our vineyards belong to others."

⁶When I heard their outcry and these charges, I was very angry. ⁷I pondered them in my mind and then accused the nobles and officials. I told them, "You are charging your own people interest!" So I called together a large meeting to deal with them ⁸and said: "As far as possible, we have bought back our fellow Jews who were sold to the Gentiles. Now you are selling your own people, only for them to be sold back to us!" They kept quiet, because they could find nothing to say.

⁹So I continued, "What you are doing is not right. Shouldn't you walk in the fear of our God to avoid the reproach of our Gentile enemies? ¹⁰I and my brothers and my men are also lending the people money and grain. But let us stop charging interest! ¹¹Give back to them immediately their fields, vineyards, olive groves and houses, and also the interest you are charging them — one percent of the money, grain, new wine and olive oil."

¹²"We will give it back," they said. "And we will not demand anything more from them. We will do as you say."

ᵃ 23 The meaning of the Hebrew for this clause is uncertain.

Then I summoned the priests and made the nobles and officials take an oath to do what they had promised. [13]I also shook out the folds of my robe and said, "In this way may God shake out of their house and possessions anyone who does not keep this promise. So may such a person be shaken out and emptied!"

At this the whole assembly said, "Amen," and praised the LORD. And the people did as they had promised.

[14]Moreover, from the twentieth year of King Artaxerxes, when I was appointed to be their governor in the land of Judah, until his thirty-second year—twelve years—neither I nor my brothers ate the food allotted to the governor. [15]But the earlier governors—those preceding me—placed a heavy burden on the people and took forty shekels[a] of silver from them in addition to food and wine. Their assistants also lorded it over the people. But out of reverence for God I did not act like that. [16]Instead, I devoted myself to the work on this wall. All my men were assembled there for the work; we[b] did not acquire any land.

[17]Furthermore, a hundred and fifty Jews and officials ate at my table, as well as those who came to us from the surrounding nations. [18]Each day one ox, six choice sheep and some poultry were prepared for me, and every ten days an abundant supply of wine of all kinds. In spite of all this, I never demanded the food allotted to the governor, because the demands were heavy on these people.

[19]Remember me with favor, my God, for all I have done for these people.

Further Opposition to the Rebuilding

6 When word came to Sanballat, Tobiah, Geshem the Arab and the rest of our enemies that I had rebuilt the wall and not a gap was left in it—though up to that time I had not set the doors in the gates— [2]Sanballat and Geshem sent me this message: "Come, let us meet together in one of the villages[c] on the plain of Ono."

But they were scheming to harm me; [3]so I sent messengers to them with this reply: "I am carrying on a great project and cannot go down. Why should the work stop while I leave it and go down to you?" [4]Four times they sent me the same message, and each time I gave them the same answer.

[5]Then, the fifth time, Sanballat sent his aide to me with the same message, and in his hand was an

---

[a] 15 That is, about 1 pound or about 460 grams   [b] 16 Most Hebrew manuscripts; some Hebrew manuscripts, Septuagint, Vulgate and Syriac *I*
[c] 2 Or *in Kephirim*

unsealed letter [6]in which was written:

"It is reported among the nations—and Geshem[a] says it is true—that you and the Jews are plotting to revolt, and therefore you are building the wall. Moreover, according to these reports you are about to become their king [7]and have even appointed prophets to make this proclamation about you in Jerusalem: 'There is a king in Judah!' Now this report will get back to the king; so come, let us meet together."

[8]I sent him this reply: "Nothing like what you are saying is happening; you are just making it up out of your head."

[9]They were all trying to frighten us, thinking, "Their hands will get too weak for the work, and it will not be completed."

But I prayed, "Now strengthen my hands."

[10]One day I went to the house of Shemaiah son of Delaiah, the son of Mehetabel, who was shut in at his home. He said, "Let us meet in the house of God, inside the temple, and let us close the temple doors, because men are coming to kill you—by night they are coming to kill you."

[11]But I said, "Should a man like me run away? Or should someone like me go into the temple to save his life? I will not go!" [12]I realized that God had not sent him, but that he had prophesied against me because Tobiah and Sanballat had hired him. [13]He had been hired to intimidate me so that I would commit a sin by doing this, and then they would give me a bad name to discredit me.

[14]Remember Tobiah and Sanballat, my God, because of what they have done; remember also the prophet Noadiah and how she and the rest of the prophets have been trying to intimidate me. [15]So the wall was completed on the twenty-fifth of Elul, in fifty-two days.

Opposition to the Completed Wall

[16]When all our enemies heard about this, all the surrounding nations were afraid and lost their self-confidence, because they realized that this work had been done with the help of our God.

[17]Also, in those days the nobles of Judah were sending many letters to Tobiah, and replies from Tobiah kept coming to them. [18]For many in Judah were under oath to him, since he was son-in-law to Shekaniah son of Arah, and his son Jehohanan had married the daughter of Meshullam son of Berekiah. [19]Moreover, they kept reporting to me his good deeds and then telling him what

I said. And Tobiah sent letters to intimidate me.

7 After the wall had been rebuilt and I had set the doors in place, the gatekeepers, the musicians and the Levites were appointed. ²I put in charge of Jerusalem my brother Hanani, along with Hananiah the commander of the citadel, because he was a man of integrity and feared God more than most people do. ³I said to them, "The gates of Jerusalem are not to be opened until the sun is hot. While the gatekeepers are still on duty, have them shut the doors and bar them. Also appoint residents of Jerusalem as guards, some at their posts and some near their own houses."

The List of the Exiles Who Returned

⁴Now the city was large and spacious, but there were few people in it, and the houses had not yet been rebuilt. ⁵So my God put it into my heart to assemble the nobles, the officials and the common people for registration by families. I found the genealogical record of those who had been the first to return. This is what I found written there:

⁶These are the people of the province who came up from the captivity of the exiles whom Nebuchadnezzar king of Babylon had taken captive (they returned to Jerusalem and Judah, each to his own town, ⁷in company with Zerubbabel, Joshua, Nehemiah, Azariah, Raamiah, Nahamani, Mordecai, Bilshan, Mispereth, Bigvai, Nehum and Baanah):

The list of the men of Israel:

⁸the descendants of Parosh	2,172
⁹of Shephatiah	372
¹⁰of Arah	652
¹¹of Pahath-Moab (through the line of Jeshua and Joab)	2,818
¹²of Elam	1,254
¹³of Zattu	845
¹⁴of Zakkai	760
¹⁵of Binnui	648
¹⁶of Bebai	628
¹⁷of Azgad	2,322
¹⁸of Adonikam	667
¹⁹of Bigvai	2,067
²⁰of Adin	655
²¹of Ater (through Hezekiah)	98
²²of Hashum	328
²³of Bezai	324
²⁴of Hariph	112
²⁵of Gibeon	95
²⁶the men of Bethlehem and Netophah	188
²⁷of Anathoth	128
²⁸of Beth Azmaveth	42
²⁹of Kiriath Jearim, Kephirah and Beeroth	743
³⁰of Ramah and Geba	621
³¹of Mikmash	122
³²of Bethel and Ai	123
³³of the other Nebo	52

³⁴ of the other
  Elam   1,254
³⁵ of Harim   320
³⁶ of Jericho   345
³⁷ of Lod, Hadid
  and Ono   721
³⁸ of Senaah   3,930

³⁹ The priests:

the descendants of
  Jedaiah (through
  the family of Jeshua)   973
⁴⁰ of Immer   1,052
⁴¹ of Pashhur   1,247
⁴² of Harim   1,017

⁴³ The Levites:

the descendants of
  Jeshua (through
  Kadmiel through
  the line of Hodaviah)   74

⁴⁴ The musicians:

the descendants
  of Asaph   148

⁴⁵ The gatekeepers:

the descendants of
  Shallum, Ater,
  Talmon, Akkub,
  Hatita and Shobai   138

⁴⁶ The temple servants:

the descendants of
  Ziha, Hasupha,
  Tabbaoth,
⁴⁷ Keros, Sia, Padon,
⁴⁸ Lebana, Hagaba,
  Shalmai,
⁴⁹ Hanan, Giddel, Gahar,
⁵⁰ Reaiah, Rezin, Nekoda,
⁵¹ Gazzam, Uzza, Paseah,
⁵² Besai, Meunim,
  Nephusim,
⁵³ Bakbuk, Hakupha,
  Harhur,
⁵⁴ Bazluth, Mehida, Harsha,
⁵⁵ Barkos, Sisera, Temah,
⁵⁶ Neziah and Hatipha

⁵⁷ The descendants of the servants of Solomon:

the descendants of
  Sotai, Sophereth, Perida,
⁵⁸ Jaala, Darkon, Giddel,
⁵⁹ Shephatiah, Hattil,
  Pokereth-Hazzebaim
  and Amon

⁶⁰ The temple servants and
  the descendants of the
  servants of Solomon   392

⁶¹ The following came up from the towns of Tel Melah, Tel Harsha, Kerub, Addon and Immer, but they could not show that their families were descended from Israel:

⁶² the descendants of
  Delaiah, Tobiah and
  Nekoda   642
⁶³ And from among the priests:

the descendants of
  Hobaiah, Hakkoz and
  Barzillai (a man who had
  married a daughter of
  Barzillai the Gileadite
  and was called by that
  name).
⁶⁴ These searched for their family records, but they could

not find them and so were excluded from the priesthood as unclean. ⁶⁵The governor, therefore, ordered them not to eat any of the most sacred food until there should be a priest ministering with the Urim and Thummim.

⁶⁶The whole company numbered 42,360, ⁶⁷besides their 7,337 male and female slaves; and they also had 245 male and female singers. ⁶⁸There were 736 horses, 245 mules,^a ⁶⁹435 camels and 6,720 donkeys.

⁷⁰Some of the heads of the families contributed to the work. The governor gave to the treasury 1,000 darics^b of gold, 50 bowls and 530 garments for priests. ⁷¹Some of the heads of the families gave to the treasury for the work 20,000 darics^c of gold and 2,200 minas^d of silver. ⁷²The total given by the rest of the people was 20,000 darics of gold, 2,000 minas^e of silver and 67 garments for priests.

⁷³The priests, the Levites, the gatekeepers, the musicians and the temple servants, along with certain of the people and the rest of the Israelites, settled in their own towns.

Ezra Reads the Law

When the seventh month came and the Israelites had settled in 8 their towns, ¹all the people came together as one in the square before the Water Gate. They told Ezra the teacher of the Law to bring out the Book of the Law of Moses, which the LORD had commanded for Israel.

²So on the first day of the seventh month Ezra the priest brought the Law before the assembly, which was made up of men and women and all who were able to understand. ³He read it aloud from daybreak till noon as he faced the square before the Water Gate in the presence of the men, women and others who could understand. And all the people listened attentively to the Book of the Law.

⁴Ezra the teacher of the Law stood on a high wooden platform built for the occasion. Beside him on his right stood Mattithiah, Shema, Anaiah, Uriah, Hilkiah and Maaseiah; and on his left were Pedaiah, Mishael, Malkijah, Hashum, Hashbaddanah, Zechariah and Meshullam.

⁵Ezra opened the book. All the people could see him because he

---

^a 68 Some Hebrew manuscripts (see also Ezra 2:66); most Hebrew manuscripts do not have this verse.   ^b 70 That is, about 19 pounds or about 8.4 kilograms
^c 71 That is, about 375 pounds or about 170 kilograms; also in verse 72
^d 71 That is, about 1 1/3 tons or about 1.2 metric tons   ^e 72 That is, about 1 1/4 tons or about 1.1 metric tons

was standing above them; and as he opened it, the people all stood up. **6**Ezra praised the LORD, the great God; and all the people lifted their hands and responded, "Amen! Amen!" Then they bowed down and worshiped the LORD with their faces to the ground.

7The Levites—Jeshua, Bani, Sherebiah, Jamin, Akkub, Shabbethai, Hodiah, Maaseiah, Kelita, Azariah, Jozabad, Hanan and Pelaiah—instructed the people in the Law while the people were standing there. **8**They read from the Book of the Law of God, making it clear*a* and giving the meaning so that the people understood what was being read.

9Then Nehemiah the governor, Ezra the priest and teacher of the Law, and the Levites who were instructing the people said to them all, "This day is holy to the LORD your God. Do not mourn or weep." For all the people had been weeping as they listened to the words of the Law.

10Nehemiah said, "Go and enjoy choice food and sweet drinks, and send some to those who have nothing prepared. This day is holy to our Lord. Do not grieve, for the joy of the LORD is your strength."

11The Levites calmed all the people, saying, "Be still, for this is a holy day. Do not grieve."

12Then all the people went away to eat and drink, to send portions of food and to celebrate with great joy, because they now understood the words that had been made known to them.

13On the second day of the month, the heads of all the families, along with the priests and the Levites, gathered around Ezra the teacher to give attention to the words of the Law. **14**They found written in the Law, which the LORD had commanded through Moses, that the Israelites were to live in temporary shelters during the festival of the seventh month **15**and that they should proclaim this word and spread it throughout their towns and in Jerusalem: "Go out into the hill country and bring back branches from olive and wild olive trees, and from myrtles, palms and shade trees, to make temporary shelters"—as it is written.*b*

16So the people went out and brought back branches and built themselves temporary shelters on their own roofs, in their courtyards, in the courts of the house of God and in the square by the Water Gate and the one by the Gate of Ephraim. **17**The whole company that had returned from exile built temporary shelters and lived in them. From the days of Joshua son of Nun until that day, the Israelites had not celebrated it like this. And their joy was very great.

18Day after day, from the first

---

a 8 Or *God, translating it*   *b 15* See Lev. 23:37-40.

Elijah Is Taken Up to Heaven

2 KINGS 2:1–14

Daniel in the Lions' Den

DANIEL 6

Jonah and the Big Fish
JONAH 1:1-17

Reading the Bible

People read the Bible in different ways. Some people like to read it like any other book, from the beginning to the end. Other people like to read one book at a time, like the Gospel of Mark. Still others choose to read about a special theme in the Bible, like Jesus' life. Here's an example you might want to try:

The Life and Teachings of Jesus

❏ Luke 1: Preparing for Jesus' arrival

❏ Luke 2: The story of Jesus' birth

❏ Mark 1: The beginning of Jesus' ministry

❏ Mark 9: A day in the life of Jesus

❏ Matthew 5: The Sermon on the Mount

❏ Matthew 6: The Sermon on the Mount (continued)

❏ Luke 15: Parables of Jesus

❏ John 3: A conversation with Jesus

❏ John 14: Jesus' final instructions

❏ John 17: Jesus' prayer for his disciples

❏ Matthew 26: Jesus' betrayal and arrest

❏ Matthew 27: Jesus dies on a cross

❏ John 20: Jesus' resurrection

❏ Luke 24: Jesus appears after his resurrection

day to the last, Ezra read from the Book of the Law of God. They celebrated the festival for seven days, and on the eighth day, in accordance with the regulation, there was an assembly.

The Israelites Confess Their Sins

9 On the twenty-fourth day of the same month, the Israelites gathered together, fasting and wearing sackcloth and putting dust on their heads. ²Those of Israelite descent had separated themselves from all foreigners. They stood in their places and confessed their sins and the sins of their ancestors. ³They stood where they were and read from the Book of the Law of the LORD their God for a quarter of the day, and spent another quarter in confession and in worshiping the LORD their God. ⁴Standing on the stairs of the Levites were Jeshua, Bani, Kadmiel, Shebaniah, Bunni, Sherebiah, Bani and Kenani. They cried out with loud voices to the LORD their God. ⁵And the Levites—Jeshua, Kadmiel, Bani, Hashabneiah, Sherebiah, Hodiah, Shebaniah and Pethahiah—said: "Stand up and praise the LORD your God, who is from everlasting to everlasting.ᵃ"

"Blessed be your glorious name, and may it be exalted above all blessing and praise. ⁶You alone are the LORD. You made the heavens, even the highest heavens, and all their starry host, the earth and all that is on it, the seas and all that is in them. You give life to everything, and the multitudes of heaven worship you.

⁷"You are the LORD God, who chose Abram and brought him out of Ur of the Chaldeans and named him Abraham. ⁸You found his heart faithful to you, and you made a covenant with him to give to his descendants the land of the Canaanites, Hittites, Amorites, Perizzites, Jebusites and Girgashites. You have kept your promise because you are righteous.

⁹"You saw the suffering of our ancestors in Egypt; you heard their cry at the Red Sea.ᵇ ¹⁰You sent signs and wonders against Pharaoh, against all his officials and all the people of his land, for you knew how arrogantly the Egyptians treated them. You made a name for yourself, which remains to this day. ¹¹You divided the sea before them, so that they passed through it on dry ground, but you hurled their pursuers into the depths, like a stone into mighty waters. ¹²By day you led them with a pillar of cloud, and by night with a pillar of fire to give them light on the way they were to take.

ᵃ 5 Or *God for ever and ever*   ᵇ 9 Or *the Sea of Reeds*

13 "You came down on Mount Sinai; you spoke to them from heaven. You gave them regulations and laws that are just and right, and decrees and commands that are good. 14 You made known to them your holy Sabbath and gave them commands, decrees and laws through your servant Moses. 15 In their hunger you gave them bread from heaven and in their thirst you brought them water from the rock; you told them to go in and take possession of the land you had sworn with uplifted hand to give them.

16 "But they, our ancestors, became arrogant and stiff-necked, and they did not obey your commands. 17 They refused to listen and failed to remember the miracles you performed among them. They became stiff-necked and in their rebellion appointed a leader in order to return to their slavery. But you are a forgiving God, gracious and compassionate, slow to anger and abounding in love. Therefore you did not desert them, 18 even when they cast for themselves an image of a calf and said, 'This is your god, who brought you up out of Egypt,' or when they committed awful blasphemies.

19 "Because of your great compassion you did not abandon them in the wilderness. By day the pillar of cloud did not fail to guide them on their path, nor the pillar of fire by night to shine on the way they were to take. 20 You gave your good Spirit to instruct them. You did not withhold your manna from their mouths, and you gave them water for their thirst. 21 For forty years you sustained them in the wilderness; they lacked nothing, their clothes did not wear out nor did their feet become swollen.

22 "You gave them kingdoms and nations, allotting to them even the remotest frontiers. They took over the country of Sihon[a] king of Heshbon and the country of Og king of Bashan. 23 You made their children as numerous as the stars in the sky, and you brought them into the land that you told their parents to enter and possess. 24 Their children went in and took possession of the land. You subdued before them the Canaanites, who lived in the land; you gave the Canaanites into their hands, along

---

[a] 22 One Hebrew manuscript and Septuagint; most Hebrew manuscripts *Sihon, that is, the country of the*

with their kings and the peoples of the land, to deal with them as they pleased. ²⁵ They captured fortified cities and fertile land; they took possession of houses filled with all kinds of good things, wells already dug, vineyards, olive groves and fruit trees in abundance. They ate to the full and were well-nourished; they reveled in your great goodness.

²⁶ "But they were disobedient and rebelled against you; they turned their backs on your law. They killed your prophets, who had warned them in order to turn them back to you; they committed awful blasphemies. ²⁷ So you delivered them into the hands of their enemies, who oppressed them. But when they were oppressed they cried out to you. From heaven you heard them, and in your great compassion you gave them deliverers, who rescued them from the hand of their enemies.

²⁸ "But as soon as they were at rest, they again did what was evil in your sight. Then you abandoned them to the hand of their enemies so that they ruled over them. And when they cried out to you again, you heard from heaven, and in your compassion you delivered them time after time.

²⁹ "You warned them in order to turn them back to your law, but they became arrogant and disobeyed your commands. They sinned against your ordinances, of which you said, 'The person who obeys them will live by them.' Stubbornly they turned their backs on you, became stiff-necked and refused to listen. ³⁰ For many years you were patient with them. By your Spirit you warned them through your prophets. Yet they paid no attention, so you gave them into the hands of the neighboring peoples. ³¹ But in your great mercy you did not put an end to them or abandon them, for you are a gracious and merciful God.

³² "Now therefore, our God, the great God, mighty and awesome, who keeps his covenant of love, do not let all this hardship seem trifling in your eyes — the hardship that has come on us, on our kings and leaders, on our priests and prophets, on our ancestors and all your people, from the days of the kings of Assyria until today. ³³ In all that has happened to us, you have remained righteous; you have acted faithfully, while we acted wickedly. ³⁴ Our kings, our leaders, our priests and our ancestors did not follow your

law; they did not pay attention to your commands or the statutes you warned them to keep. **35** Even while they were in their kingdom, enjoying your great goodness to them in the spacious and fertile land you gave them, they did not serve you or turn from their evil ways.

36 "But see, we are slaves today, slaves in the land you gave our ancestors so they could eat its fruit and the other good things it produces. **37** Because of our sins, its abundant harvest goes to the kings you have placed over us. They rule over our bodies and our cattle as they please. We are in great distress.

The Agreement of the People

38 "In view of all this, we are making a binding agreement, putting it in writing, and our leaders, our Levites and our priests are affixing their seals to it." [a]

10 [b] Those who sealed it were:

Nehemiah the governor, the son of Hakaliah.

Zedekiah, **2** Seraiah, Azariah, Jeremiah,
3 Pashhur, Amariah, Malkijah,
4 Hattush, Shebaniah, Malluk,
5 Harim, Meremoth, Obadiah,
6 Daniel, Ginnethon, Baruch,
7 Meshullam, Abijah, Mijamin,
8 Maaziah, Bilgai and Shemaiah.

These were the priests.

9 The Levites:

Jeshua son of Azaniah, Binnui of the sons of Henadad, Kadmiel,
10 and their associates: Shebaniah,

Hodiah, Kelita, Pelaiah, Hanan,
11 Mika, Rehob, Hashabiah,
12 Zakkur, Sherebiah, Shebaniah,
13 Hodiah, Bani and Beninu.

14 The leaders of the people:

Parosh, Pahath-Moab, Elam, Zattu, Bani,
15 Bunni, Azgad, Bebai,
16 Adonijah, Bigvai, Adin,
17 Ater, Hezekiah, Azzur,
18 Hodiah, Hashum, Bezai,
19 Hariph, Anathoth, Nebai,
20 Magpiash, Meshullam, Hezir,
21 Meshezabel, Zadok, Jaddua,
22 Pelatiah, Hanan, Anaiah,
23 Hoshea, Hananiah, Hasshub,
24 Hallohesh, Pilha, Shobek,
25 Rehum, Hashabnah, Maaseiah,
26 Ahiah, Hanan, Anan,
27 Malluk, Harim and Baanah.

28 "The rest of the people — priests, Levites, gatekeepers, musicians, temple servants

---

[a] **38** In Hebrew texts this verse (9:38) is numbered 10:1.   [b] In Hebrew texts 10:1-39 is numbered 10:2-40.

and all who separated themselves from the neighboring peoples for the sake of the Law of God, together with their wives and all their sons and daughters who are able to understand— ²⁹ all these now join their fellow Israelites the nobles, and bind themselves with a curse and an oath to follow the Law of God given through Moses the servant of God and to obey carefully all the commands, regulations and decrees of the LORD our Lord.

³⁰ "We promise not to give our daughters in marriage to the peoples around us or take their daughters for our sons.

³¹ "When the neighboring peoples bring merchandise or grain to sell on the Sabbath, we will not buy from them on the Sabbath or on any holy day. Every seventh year we will forgo working the land and will cancel all debts.

³² "We assume the responsibility for carrying out the commands to give a third of a shekel*ᵃ* each year for the service of the house of our God: ³³ for the bread set out on the table; for the regular grain offerings and burnt offerings; for the offerings on the Sabbaths, at the New Moon feasts and at the appointed festivals; for the holy offerings; for sin offerings*ᵇ* to make atonement for Israel; and for all the duties of the house of our God.

³⁴ "We — the priests, the Levites and the people — have cast lots to determine when each of our families is to bring to the house of our God at set times each year a contribution of wood to burn on the altar of the LORD our God, as it is written in the Law.

³⁵ "We also assume responsibility for bringing to the house of the LORD each year the firstfruits of our crops and of every fruit tree.

³⁶ "As it is also written in the Law, we will bring the firstborn of our sons and of our cattle, of our herds and of our flocks to the house of our God, to the priests ministering there.

³⁷ "Moreover, we will bring to the storerooms of the house of our God, to the priests, the first of our ground meal, of our grain offerings, of the fruit of all our trees and of our new wine and olive oil. And we will bring a tithe of our crops to the Levites, for it is the Levites who collect the tithes in all the towns where we work. ³⁸ A priest descended from Aaron is to accompany the Levites when they receive the

---

ᵃ 32 That is, about 1/8 ounce or about 4 grams *ᵇ* 33 Or *purification offerings* tithes, and the Levites are to bring a tenth of the tithes up to the house of our God, to the storerooms of the treasury. **39** The people of Israel, including the Levites, are to bring their contributions of grain, new wine and olive oil to the storerooms, where the articles for the sanctuary and for the ministering priests, the gatekeepers and the musicians are also kept.

"We will not neglect the house of our God."

The New Residents of Jerusalem

11 Now the leaders of the people settled in Jerusalem. The rest of the people cast lots to bring one out of every ten of them to live in Jerusalem, the holy city, while the remaining nine were to stay in their own towns. **2** The people commended all who volunteered to live in Jerusalem.

3 These are the provincial leaders who settled in Jerusalem (now some Israelites, priests, Levites, temple servants and descendants of Solomon's servants lived in the towns of Judah, each on their own property in the various towns, **4** while other people from both Judah and Benjamin lived in Jerusalem):

From the descendants of Judah:

Athaiah son of Uzziah, the son of Zechariah, the son of Amariah, the son of Shephatiah, the son of Mahalalel, a descendant of Perez; **5** and Maaseiah son of Baruch, the son of Kol-Hozeh, the son of Hazaiah, the son of Adaiah, the son of Joiarib, the son of Zechariah, a descendant of Shelah. **6** The descendants of Perez who lived in Jerusalem totaled 468 men of standing.

7 From the descendants of Benjamin:

Sallu son of Meshullam, the son of Joed, the son of Pedaiah, the son of Kolaiah, the son of Maaseiah, the son of Ithiel, the son of Jeshaiah, **8** and his followers, Gabbai and Sallai — 928 men. **9** Joel son of Zikri was their chief officer, and Judah son of Hassenuah was over the New Quarter of the city.

10 From the priests:

Jedaiah; the son of Joiarib; Jakin; **11** Seraiah son of Hilkiah, the son of Meshullam, the son of Zadok, the son of Meraioth, the son of Ahitub, the official in charge of the house of God, **12** and their associates, who carried on work for the temple — 822 men; Adaiah son of Jeroham, the son of Pelaliah, the son of Amzi, the son of Zechariah, the son of Pashhur, the son of Malkijah, **13** and his associates, who were heads of families — 242 men; Amashsai son of Azarel, the son of Ahzai, the son of Meshillemoth, the son of Immer, [14]and his[a] associates, who were men of standing — 128. Their chief officer was Zabdiel son of Haggedolim.

[15]From the Levites:

Shemaiah son of Hasshub, the son of Azrikam, the son of Hashabiah, the son of Bunni; [16]Shabbethai and Jozabad, two of the heads of the Levites, who had charge of the outside work of the house of God; [17]Mattaniah son of Mika, the son of Zabdi, the son of Asaph, the director who led in thanksgiving and prayer; Bakbukiah, second among his associates; and Abda son of Shammua, the son of Galal, the son of Jeduthun. [18]The Levites in the holy city totaled 284.

[19]The gatekeepers:

Akkub, Talmon and their associates, who kept watch at the gates — 172 men.

[20]The rest of the Israelites, with the priests and Levites, were in all the towns of Judah, each on their ancestral property. [21]The temple servants lived on the hill of Ophel, and Ziha and Gishpa were in charge of them.

[22]The chief officer of the Levites in Jerusalem was Uzzi son of Bani, the son of Hashabiah, the son of Mattaniah, the son of Mika. Uzzi was one of Asaph's descendants, who were the musicians responsible for the service of the house of God. [23]The musicians were under the king's orders, which regulated their daily activity.

[24]Pethahiah son of Meshezabel, one of the descendants of Zerah son of Judah, was the king's agent in all affairs relating to the people.

[25]As for the villages with their fields, some of the people of Judah lived in Kiriath Arba and its surrounding settlements, in Dibon and its settlements, in Jekabzeel and its villages, [26]in Jeshua, in Moladah, in Beth Pelet, [27]in Hazar Shual, in Beersheba and its settlements, [28]in Ziklag, in Mekonah and its settlements, [29]in En Rimmon, in Zorah, in Jarmuth, [30]Zanoah, Adullam and their villages, in Lachish and its fields, and in Azekah and its settlements. So they were living all the way from Beersheba to the Valley of Hinnom.

[31]The descendants of the Benjamites from Geba lived in Mikmash, Aija, Bethel and its settlements, [32]in Anathoth, Nob and Ananiah, [33]in Hazor, Ramah and Gittaim, [34]in Hadid, Zeboim and Neballat, [35]in Lod and Ono, and in Ge Harashim.

---

[a] 14 Most Septuagint manuscripts; Hebrew *their*

³⁶Some of the divisions of the Levites of Judah settled in Benjamin.

Priests and Levites

12 These were the priests and Levites who returned with Zerubbabel son of Shealtiel and with Joshua:

Seraiah, Jeremiah, Ezra, ²Amariah, Malluk, Hattush, ³Shekaniah, Rehum, Meremoth, ⁴Iddo, Ginnethon,ᵃ Abijah, ⁵Mijamin,ᵇ Moadiah, Bilgah, ⁶Shemaiah, Joiarib, Jedaiah, ⁷Sallu, Amok, Hilkiah and Jedaiah.

These were the leaders of the priests and their associates in the days of Joshua.

⁸The Levites were Jeshua, Binnui, Kadmiel, Sherebiah, Judah, and also Mattaniah, who, together with his associates, was in charge of the songs of thanksgiving. ⁹Bakbukiah and Unni, their associates, stood opposite them in the services.

¹⁰Joshua was the father of Joiakim, Joiakim the father of Eliashib, Eliashib the father of Joiada, ¹¹Joiada the father of Jonathan, and Jonathan the father of Jaddua.

¹²In the days of Joiakim, these were the heads of the priestly families:

of Seraiah's family, Meraiah;
of Jeremiah's, Hananiah;
¹³of Ezra's, Meshullam;
of Amariah's, Jehohanan;
¹⁴of Malluk's, Jonathan;
of Shekaniah's,ᶜ Joseph;
¹⁵of Harim's, Adna;
of Meremoth's,ᵈ Helkai;
¹⁶of Iddo's, Zechariah;
of Ginnethon's, Meshullam;
¹⁷of Abijah's, Zikri;
of Miniamin's and of Moadiah's, Piltai;
¹⁸of Bilgah's, Shammua;
of Shemaiah's, Jehonathan;
¹⁹of Joiarib's, Mattenai;
of Jedaiah's, Uzzi;
²⁰of Sallu's, Kallai;
of Amok's, Eber;
²¹of Hilkiah's, Hashabiah;
of Jedaiah's, Nethanel.

²²The family heads of the Levites in the days of Eliashib, Joiada, Johanan and Jaddua, as well as those of the priests, were recorded in the reign of Darius the Persian. ²³The family heads among the descendants of Levi up to the time of Johanan son of Eliashib were recorded in the book of the annals. ²⁴And the leaders of the Levites were Hashabiah, Sherebiah, Jeshua son of Kadmiel, and their associates, who stood opposite them to give praise and thanksgiving, one section responding to the other,

---

ᵃ 4 Many Hebrew manuscripts and Vulgate (see also verse 16); most Hebrew manuscripts *Ginnethoi*   ᵇ 5 A variant of *Miniamin*   ᶜ 14 Very many Hebrew manuscripts, some Septuagint manuscripts and Syriac (see also verse 3); most Hebrew manuscripts *Shebaniah's*   ᵈ 15 Some Septuagint manuscripts (see also verse 3); Hebrew *Meraioth's* as prescribed by David the man of God.

[25] Mattaniah, Bakbukiah, Obadiah, Meshullam, Talmon and Akkub were gatekeepers who guarded the storerooms at the gates. [26] They served in the days of Joiakim son of Joshua, the son of Jozadak, and in the days of Nehemiah the governor and of Ezra the priest, the teacher of the Law.

Dedication of the Wall of Jerusalem

[27] At the dedication of the wall of Jerusalem, the Levites were sought out from where they lived and were brought to Jerusalem to celebrate joyfully the dedication with songs of thanksgiving and with the music of cymbals, harps and lyres. [28] The musicians also were brought together from the region around Jerusalem—from the villages of the Netophathites, [29] from Beth Gilgal, and from the area of Geba and Azmaveth, for the musicians had built villages for themselves around Jerusalem. [30] When the priests and Levites had purified themselves ceremonially, they purified the people, the gates and the wall.

[31] I had the leaders of Judah go up on top of[a] the wall. I also assigned two large choirs to give thanks. One was to proceed on top of[b] the wall to the right, toward the Dung Gate. [32] Hoshaiah and half the leaders of Judah followed them, [33] along with Azariah, Ezra, Meshullam, [34] Judah, Benjamin, Shemaiah, Jeremiah, [35] as well as some priests with trumpets, and also Zechariah son of Jonathan, the son of Shemaiah, the son of Mattaniah, the son of Micaiah, the son of Zakkur, the son of Asaph, [36] and his associates—Shemaiah, Azarel, Milalai, Gilalai, Maai, Nethanel, Judah and Hanani—with musical instruments prescribed by David the man of God. Ezra the teacher of the Law led the procession. [37] At the Fountain Gate they continued directly up the steps of the City of David on the ascent to the wall and passed above the site of David's palace to the Water Gate on the east.

[38] The second choir proceeded in the opposite direction. I followed them on top of[c] the wall, together with half the people—past the Tower of the Ovens to the Broad Wall, [39] over the Gate of Ephraim, the Jeshanah[d] Gate, the Fish Gate, the Tower of Hananel and the Tower of the Hundred, as far as the Sheep Gate. At the Gate of the Guard they stopped.

[40] The two choirs that gave thanks then took their places in the house of God; so did I, together with half the officials, [41] as well as the priests—Eliakim, Maaseiah, Miniamin, Micaiah,

---

[a] 31 Or go alongside   [b] 31 Or proceed alongside   [c] 38 Or them alongside
[d] 39 Or Old

Elioenai, Zechariah and Hananiah with their trumpets— ⁴²and also Maaseiah, Shemaiah, Eleazar, Uzzi, Jehohanan, Malkijah, Elam and Ezer. The choirs sang under the direction of Jezrahiah. ⁴³And on that day they offered great sacrifices, rejoicing because God had given them great joy. The women and children also rejoiced. The sound of rejoicing in Jerusalem could be heard far away.

⁴⁴At that time men were appointed to be in charge of the storerooms for the contributions, firstfruits and tithes. From the fields around the towns they were to bring into the storerooms the portions required by the Law for the priests and the Levites, for Judah was pleased with the ministering priests and Levites. ⁴⁵They performed the service of their God and the service of purification, as did also the musicians and gatekeepers, according to the commands of David and his son Solomon. ⁴⁶For long ago, in the days of David and Asaph, there had been directors for the musicians and for the songs of praise and thanksgiving to God. ⁴⁷So in the days of Zerubbabel and of Nehemiah, all Israel contributed the daily portions for the musicians and the gatekeepers. They also set aside the portion for the other Levites, and the Levites set aside the portion for the descendants of Aaron.

Nehemiah's Final Reforms

13 On that day the Book of Moses was read aloud in the hearing of the people and there it was found written that no Ammonite or Moabite should ever be admitted into the assembly of God, ²because they had not met the Israelites with food and water but had hired Balaam to call a curse down on them. (Our God, however, turned the curse into a blessing.) ³When the people heard this law, they excluded from Israel all who were of foreign descent.

⁴Before this, Eliashib the priest had been put in charge of the storerooms of the house of our God. He was closely associated with Tobiah, ⁵and he had provided him with a large room formerly used to store the grain offerings and incense and temple articles, and also the tithes of grain, new wine and olive oil prescribed for the Levites, musicians and gatekeepers, as well as the contributions for the priests.

⁶But while all this was going on, I was not in Jerusalem, for in the thirty-second year of Artaxerxes king of Babylon I had returned to the king. Some time later I asked his permission ⁷and came back to Jerusalem. Here I learned about the evil thing Eliashib had done in providing Tobiah a room in the courts of the house of God. ⁸I was greatly displeased and threw all Tobiah's household goods out of

the room. ⁹I gave orders to purify the rooms, and then I put back into them the equipment of the house of God, with the grain offerings and the incense.

¹⁰I also learned that the portions assigned to the Levites had not been given to them, and that all the Levites and musicians responsible for the service had gone back to their own fields. ¹¹So I rebuked the officials and asked them, "Why is the house of God neglected?" Then I called them together and stationed them at their posts.

¹²All Judah brought the tithes of grain, new wine and olive oil into the storerooms. ¹³I put Shelemiah the priest, Zadok the scribe, and a Levite named Pedaiah in charge of the storerooms and made Hanan son of Zakkur, the son of Mattaniah, their assistant, because they were considered trustworthy. They were made responsible for distributing the supplies to their fellow Levites.

¹⁴Remember me for this, my God, and do not blot out what I have so faithfully done for the house of my God and its services.

¹⁵In those days I saw people in Judah treading winepresses on the Sabbath and bringing in grain and loading it on donkeys, together with wine, grapes, figs and all other kinds of loads. And they were bringing all this into Jerusalem on the Sabbath. Therefore I warned them against selling food on that day. ¹⁶People from Tyre who lived in Jerusalem were bringing in fish and all kinds of merchandise and selling them in Jerusalem on the Sabbath to the people of Judah. ¹⁷I rebuked the nobles of Judah and said to them, "What is this wicked thing you are doing—desecrating the Sabbath day? ¹⁸Didn't your ancestors do the same things, so that our God brought all this calamity on us and on this city? Now you are stirring up more wrath against Israel by desecrating the Sabbath."

¹⁹When evening shadows fell on the gates of Jerusalem before the Sabbath, I ordered the doors to be shut and not opened until the Sabbath was over. I stationed some of my own men at the gates so that no load could be brought in on the Sabbath day. ²⁰Once or twice the merchants and sellers of all kinds of goods spent the night outside Jerusalem. ²¹But I warned them and said, "Why do you spend the night by the wall? If you do this again, I will arrest you." From that time on they no longer came on the Sabbath. ²²Then I commanded the Levites to purify themselves and go and guard the gates in order to keep the Sabbath day holy.

Remember me for this also, my God, and show mercy to me according to your great love.

²³Moreover, in those days I saw men of Judah who had married women from Ashdod, Ammon and Moab. ²⁴Half of their children spoke the language of Ashdod or the language of one of the other peoples, and did not know how to speak the language of Judah. ²⁵I rebuked them and called curses down on them. I beat some of the men and pulled out their hair. I made them take an oath in God's name and said: "You are not to give your daughters in marriage to their sons, nor are you to take their daughters in marriage for your sons or for yourselves. ²⁶Was it not because of marriages like these that Solomon king of Israel sinned? Among the many nations there was no king like him. He was loved by his God, and God made him king over all Israel, but even he was led into sin by foreign women. ²⁷Must we hear now that you too are doing all this terrible wickedness and are being unfaithful to our God by marrying foreign women?"

²⁸One of the sons of Joiada son of Eliashib the high priest was son-in-law to Sanballat the Horonite. And I drove him away from me.

²⁹Remember them, my God, because they defiled the priestly office and the covenant of the priesthood and of the Levites.

³⁰So I purified the priests and the Levites of everything foreign, and assigned them duties, each to his own task. ³¹I also made provision for contributions of wood at designated times, and for the firstfruits.

Remember me with favor, my God.

Esther

Introduction:

The setting for the book of Esther is Susa, the capital city of Persia. It takes place during the time of King Xerxes, who ruled Persia from 486 to 465 BC. The book tells the story of a beautiful Jewish girl whom King Xerxes chose to be his queen. When Haman plotted to murder all the Jews, Queen Esther's cousin Mordecai persuaded Esther to try to save her people. Risking her own life, she appealed to the king and rescued the Jews.

Although the name of God does not appear in this book, his care for his chosen people is clearly shown. The annual days of Purim celebrate this exciting story of the rescue of the Jews. During the days of celebration the Jews read the book of Esther out loud.

Outline of contents:

Esther made queen (1:1–2:23)
Haman's plot to destroy the Jews (3:1–5:14)
The Jews win (6:1–10:3)

Queen Vashti Deposed

1 This is what happened during the time of Xerxes,*a* the Xerxes who ruled over 127 provinces stretching from India to Cush*b*: ² At that time King Xerxes reigned from his royal throne in the citadel of Susa, ³ and in the third year of his reign he gave a banquet for all his nobles and officials. The military leaders of Persia and Media, the princes, and the nobles of the provinces were present.

⁴ For a full 180 days he displayed the vast wealth of his kingdom and the splendor and glory of his majesty. ⁵ When these days were over, the king gave a banquet, lasting seven days, in the enclosed garden of the king's palace, for all the people from the least to the greatest who were in the citadel of Susa. ⁶ The garden had hangings of white and blue linen, fastened with cords of white linen and purple material to silver rings on marble pillars. There were couches of gold and silver on a mosaic pavement of porphyry, marble, mother-of-pearl and other costly stones.

a 1 Hebrew *Ahasuerus*; here and throughout Esther   *b 1* That is, the upper Nile region

⁷Wine was served in goblets of gold, each one different from the other, and the royal wine was abundant, in keeping with the king's liberality. ⁸By the king's command each guest was allowed to drink with no restrictions, for the king instructed all the wine stewards to serve each man what he wished.

⁹Queen Vashti also gave a banquet for the women in the royal palace of King Xerxes.

¹⁰On the seventh day, when King Xerxes was in high spirits from wine, he commanded the seven eunuchs who served him—Mehuman, Biztha, Harbona, Bigtha, Abagtha, Zethar and Karkas— ¹¹to bring before him Queen Vashti, wearing her royal crown, in order to display her beauty to the people and nobles, for she was lovely to look at. ¹²But when the attendants delivered the king's command, Queen Vashti refused to come. Then the king became furious and burned with anger.

¹³Since it was customary for the king to consult experts in matters of law and justice, he spoke with the wise men who understood the times ¹⁴and were closest to the king—Karshena, Shethar, Admatha, Tarshish, Meres, Marsena and Memukan, the seven nobles of Persia and Media who had special access to the king and were highest in the kingdom. ¹⁵"According to law, what must be done to Queen Vashti?" he asked. "She has not obeyed the command of King Xerxes that the eunuchs have taken to her."

¹⁶Then Memukan replied in the presence of the king and the nobles, "Queen Vashti has done wrong, not only against the king but also against all the nobles and the peoples of all the provinces of King Xerxes. ¹⁷For the queen's conduct will become known to all the women, and so they will despise their husbands and say, 'King Xerxes commanded Queen Vashti to be brought before him, but she would not come.' ¹⁸This very day the Persian and Median women of the nobility who have heard about the queen's conduct will respond to all the king's nobles in the same way. There will be no end of disrespect and discord.

¹⁹"Therefore, if it pleases the king, let him issue a royal decree and let it be written in the laws of Persia and Media, which cannot be repealed, that Vashti is never again to enter the presence of King Xerxes. Also let the king give her royal position to someone else who is better than she. ²⁰Then when the king's edict is proclaimed throughout all his vast realm, all the women will respect their husbands, from the least to the greatest."

²¹The king and his nobles were pleased with this advice, so the king did as Memukan proposed. ²²He sent dispatches to all parts

of the kingdom, to each province in its own script and to each people in their own language, proclaiming that every man should be ruler over his own household, using his native tongue.

Esther Made Queen

2 Later when King Xerxes' fury had subsided, he remembered Vashti and what she had done and what he had decreed about her. ²Then the king's personal attendants proposed, "Let a search be made for beautiful young virgins for the king. ³Let the king appoint commissioners in every province of his realm to bring all these beautiful young women into the harem at the citadel of Susa. Let them be placed under the care of Hegai, the king's eunuch, who is in charge of the women; and let beauty treatments be given to them. ⁴Then let the young woman who pleases the king be queen instead of Vashti." This advice appealed to the king, and he followed it.

⁵Now there was in the citadel of Susa a Jew of the tribe of Benjamin, named Mordecai son of Jair, the son of Shimei, the son of Kish, ⁶who had been carried into exile from Jerusalem by Nebuchadnezzar king of Babylon, among those taken captive with Jehoiachin*a* king of Judah. ⁷Mordecai had a cousin named Hadassah, whom he had brought up be-

cause she had neither father nor mother. This young woman, who was also known as Esther, had a lovely figure and was beautiful. Mordecai had taken her as his own daughter when her father and mother died.

⁸When the king's order and edict had been proclaimed, many young women were brought to the citadel of Susa and put under the care of Hegai. Esther also was taken to the king's palace and entrusted to Hegai, who had charge of the harem. ⁹She pleased him and won his favor. Immediately he provided her with her beauty treatments and special food. He assigned to her seven female attendants selected from the king's palace and moved her and her attendants into the best place in the harem.

¹⁰Esther had not revealed her nationality and family background, because Mordecai had forbidden her to do so. ¹¹Every day he walked back and forth near the courtyard of the harem to find out how Esther was and what was happening to her.

¹²Before a young woman's turn came to go in to King Xerxes, she had to complete twelve months of beauty treatments prescribed for the women, six months with oil of myrrh and six with perfumes and cosmetics. ¹³And this is how she would go to the king: Anything she wanted was given

---

a 6 Hebrew *Jeconiah*, a variant of *Jehoiachin*

her to take with her from the harem to the king's palace. ¹⁴ In the evening she would go there and in the morning return to another part of the harem to the care of Shaashgaz, the king's eunuch who was in charge of the concubines. She would not return to the king unless he was pleased with her and summoned her by name.

¹⁵ When the turn came for Esther (the young woman Mordecai had adopted, the daughter of his uncle Abihail) to go to the king, she asked for nothing other than what Hegai, the king's eunuch who was in charge of the harem, suggested. And Esther won the favor of everyone who saw her. ¹⁶ She was taken to King Xerxes in the royal residence in the tenth month, the month of Tebeth, in the seventh year of his reign.

¹⁷ Now the king was attracted to Esther more than to any of the other women, and she won his favor and approval more than any of the other virgins. So he set a royal crown on her head and made her queen instead of Vashti. ¹⁸ And the king gave a great banquet, Esther's banquet, for all his nobles and officials. He proclaimed a holiday throughout the provinces and distributed gifts with royal liberality.

Mordecai Uncovers a Conspiracy

¹⁹ When the virgins were assembled a second time, Mordecai was sitting at the king's gate. ²⁰ But Esther had kept secret her family background and nationality just as Mordecai had told her to do, for she continued to follow Mordecai's instructions as she had done when he was bringing her up.

²¹ During the time Mordecai was sitting at the king's gate, Bigthana[a] and Teresh, two of the king's officers who guarded the doorway, became angry and conspired to assassinate King Xerxes. ²² But Mordecai found out about the plot and told Queen Esther, who in turn reported it to the king, giving credit to Mordecai. ²³ And when the report was investigated and found to be true, the two officials were impaled on poles. All this was recorded in the book of the annals in the presence of the king.

Haman's Plot to Destroy the Jews

3 After these events, King Xerxes honored Haman son of Hammedatha, the Agagite, elevating him and giving him a seat of honor higher than that of all the other nobles. ² All the royal officials at the king's gate knelt down and paid honor to Haman, for the king had commanded this concerning him. But Mordecai would not kneel down or pay him honor. ³ Then the royal officials at the king's gate asked Mordecai, "Why do you disobey the king's

---

command?" ⁴Day after day they spoke to him but he refused to comply. Therefore they told Haman about it to see whether Mordecai's behavior would be tolerated, for he had told them he was a Jew.

⁵When Haman saw that Mordecai would not kneel down or pay him honor, he was enraged. ⁶Yet having learned who Mordecai's people were, he scorned the idea of killing only Mordecai. Instead Haman looked for a way to destroy all Mordecai's people, the Jews, throughout the whole kingdom of Xerxes.

⁷In the twelfth year of King Xerxes, in the first month, the month of Nisan, the *pur* (that is, the lot) was cast in the presence of Haman to select a day and month. And the lot fell on*ᵃ* the twelfth month, the month of Adar.

⁸Then Haman said to King Xerxes, "There is a certain people dispersed among the peoples in all the provinces of your kingdom who keep themselves separate. Their customs are different from those of all other people, and they do not obey the king's laws; it is not in the king's best interest to tolerate them. ⁹If it pleases the king, let a decree be issued to destroy them, and I will give ten thousand talents*ᵇ* of silver to the king's administrators for the royal treasury."

¹⁰So the king took his signet ring from his finger and gave it to Haman son of Hammedatha, the Agagite, the enemy of the Jews. ¹¹"Keep the money," the king said to Haman, "and do with the people as you please."

¹²Then on the thirteenth day of the first month the royal secretaries were summoned. They wrote out in the script of each province and in the language of each people all Haman's orders to the king's satraps, the governors of the various provinces and the nobles of the various peoples. These were written in the name of King Xerxes himself and sealed with his own ring. ¹³Dispatches were sent by couriers to all the king's provinces with the order to destroy, kill and annihilate all the Jews — young and old, women and children — on a single day, the thirteenth day of the twelfth month, the month of Adar, and to plunder their goods. ¹⁴A copy of the text of the edict was to be issued as law in every province and made known to the people of every nationality so they would be ready for that day.

¹⁵The couriers went out, spurred on by the king's command, and the edict was issued in the citadel of Susa. The king and Haman sat down to drink, but the city of Susa was bewildered.

ᵃ 7 Septuagint; Hebrew does not have *And the lot fell on.*   *ᵇ* 9 That is, about 375 tons or about 340 metric tons

Mordecai Persuades Esther to Help

4 When Mordecai learned of all that had been done, he tore his clothes, put on sackcloth and ashes, and went out into the city, wailing loudly and bitterly. ²But he went only as far as the king's gate, because no one clothed in sackcloth was allowed to enter it. ³In every province to which the edict and order of the king came, there was great mourning among the Jews, with fasting, weeping and wailing. Many lay in sackcloth and ashes.

⁴When Esther's eunuchs and female attendants came and told her about Mordecai, she was in great distress. She sent clothes for him to put on instead of his sackcloth, but he would not accept them. ⁵Then Esther summoned Hathak, one of the king's eunuchs assigned to attend her, and ordered him to find out what was troubling Mordecai and why.

⁶So Hathak went out to Mordecai in the open square of the city in front of the king's gate. ⁷Mordecai told him everything that had happened to him, including the exact amount of money Haman had promised to pay into the royal treasury for the destruction of the Jews. ⁸He also gave him a copy of the text of the edict for their annihilation, which had been published in Susa, to show to Esther and explain it to her, and he told him to instruct her to go into the king's presence to beg for mercy and plead with him for her people.

⁹Hathak went back and reported to Esther what Mordecai had said. ¹⁰Then she instructed him to say to Mordecai, ¹¹"All the king's officials and the people of the royal provinces know that for any man or woman who approaches the king in the inner court without being summoned the king has but one law: that they be put to death unless the king extends the gold scepter to them and spares their lives. But thirty days have passed since I was called to go to the king."

¹²When Esther's words were reported to Mordecai, ¹³he sent back this answer: "Do not think that because you are in the king's house you alone of all the Jews will escape. ¹⁴For if you remain silent at this time, relief and deliverance for the Jews will arise from another place, but you and your father's family will perish. And who knows but that you have come to your royal position for such a time as this?"

¹⁵Then Esther sent this reply to Mordecai: ¹⁶"Go, gather together all the Jews who are in Susa, and fast for me. Do not eat or drink for three days, night or day. I and my attendants will fast as you do. When this is done, I will go to the king, even though it is against the law. And if I perish, I perish."

¹⁷So Mordecai went away and

carried out all of Esther's instructions.

Esther's Request to the King

5 On the third day Esther put on her royal robes and stood in the inner court of the palace, in front of the king's hall. The king was sitting on his royal throne in the hall, facing the entrance. [2]When he saw Queen Esther standing in the court, he was pleased with her and held out to her the gold scepter that was in his hand. So Esther approached and touched the tip of the scepter.

[3]Then the king asked, "What is it, Queen Esther? What is your request? Even up to half the kingdom, it will be given you."

[4]"If it pleases the king," replied Esther, "let the king, together with Haman, come today to a banquet I have prepared for him."

[5]"Bring Haman at once," the king said, "so that we may do what Esther asks."

So the king and Haman went to the banquet Esther had prepared. [6]As they were drinking wine, the king again asked Esther, "Now what is your petition? It will be given you. And what is your request? Even up to half the kingdom, it will be granted."

[7]Esther replied, "My petition and my request is this: [8]If the king regards me with favor and if it pleases the king to grant my petition and fulfill my request, let the king and Haman come tomorrow to the banquet I will prepare for them. Then I will answer the king's question."

Haman's Rage Against Mordecai

[9]Haman went out that day happy and in high spirits. But when he saw Mordecai at the king's gate and observed that he neither rose nor showed fear in his presence, he was filled with rage against Mordecai. [10]Nevertheless, Haman restrained himself and went home.

Calling together his friends and Zeresh, his wife, [11]Haman boasted to them about his vast wealth, his many sons, and all the ways the king had honored him and how he had elevated him above the other nobles and officials. [12]"And that's not all," Haman added. "I'm the only person Queen Esther invited to accompany the king to the banquet she gave. And she has invited me along with the king tomorrow. [13]But all this gives me no satisfaction as long as I see that Jew Mordecai sitting at the king's gate."

[14]His wife Zeresh and all his friends said to him, "Have a pole set up, reaching to a height of fifty cubits,[a] and ask the king in the morning to have Mordecai impaled on it. Then go with the king to the banquet and enjoy

---

[a] 14 That is, about 75 feet or about 23 meters

yourself." This suggestion delighted Haman, and he had the pole set up.

Mordecai Honored

6 That night the king could not sleep; so he ordered the book of the chronicles, the record of his reign, to be brought in and read to him. [2]It was found recorded there that Mordecai had exposed Bigthana and Teresh, two of the king's officers who guarded the doorway, who had conspired to assassinate King Xerxes.

[3]"What honor and recognition has Mordecai received for this?" the king asked.

"Nothing has been done for him," his attendants answered.

[4]The king said, "Who is in the court?" Now Haman had just entered the outer court of the palace to speak to the king about impaling Mordecai on the pole he had set up for him.

[5]His attendants answered, "Haman is standing in the court."

"Bring him in," the king ordered.

[6]When Haman entered, the king asked him, "What should be done for the man the king delights to honor?"

Now Haman thought to himself, "Who is there that the king would rather honor than me?" [7]So he answered the king, "For the man the king delights to honor, [8]have them bring a royal robe the king has worn and a horse the king has ridden, one with a royal crest placed on its head. [9]Then let the robe and horse be entrusted to one of the king's most noble princes. Let them robe the man the king delights to honor, and lead him on the horse through the city streets, proclaiming before him, 'This is what is done for the man the king delights to honor!'"

[10]"Go at once," the king commanded Haman. "Get the robe and the horse and do just as you have suggested for Mordecai the Jew, who sits at the king's gate. Do not neglect anything you have recommended."

[11]So Haman got the robe and the horse. He robed Mordecai, and led him on horseback through the city streets, proclaiming before him, "This is what is done for the man the king delights to honor!"

[12]Afterward Mordecai returned to the king's gate. But Haman rushed home, with his head covered in grief, [13]and told Zeresh his wife and all his friends everything that had happened to him.

His advisers and his wife Zeresh said to him, "Since Mordecai, before whom your downfall has started, is of Jewish origin, you cannot stand against him—you will surely come to ruin!" [14]While they were still talking with him, the king's eunuchs arrived and hurried Haman away to the banquet Esther had prepared.

Haman Impaled

7 So the king and Haman went to Queen Esther's banquet, **2** and as they were drinking wine on the second day, the king again asked, "Queen Esther, what is your petition? It will be given you. What is your request? Even up to half the kingdom, it will be granted."

3 Then Queen Esther answered, "If I have found favor with you, Your Majesty, and if it pleases you, grant me my life — this is my petition. And spare my people — this is my request. **4** For I and my people have been sold to be destroyed, killed and annihilated. If we had merely been sold as male and female slaves, I would have kept quiet, because no such distress would justify disturbing the king.*a*"

5 King Xerxes asked Queen Esther, "Who is he? Where is he — the man who has dared to do such a thing?"

6 Esther said, "An adversary and enemy! This vile Haman!"

Then Haman was terrified before the king and queen. **7** The king got up in a rage, left his wine and went out into the palace garden. But Haman, realizing that the king had already decided his fate, stayed behind to beg Queen Esther for his life.

8 Just as the king returned from the palace garden to the banquet hall, Haman was falling on the couch where Esther was reclining.

The king exclaimed, "Will he even molest the queen while she is with me in the house?"

As soon as the word left the king's mouth, they covered Haman's face. **9** Then Harbona, one of the eunuchs attending the king, said, "A pole reaching to a height of fifty cubits*b* stands by Haman's house. He had it set up for Mordecai, who spoke up to help the king."

The king said, "Impale him on it!" **10** So they impaled Haman on the pole he had set up for Mordecai. Then the king's fury subsided.

The King's Edict in Behalf of the Jews

8 That same day King Xerxes gave Queen Esther the estate of Haman, the enemy of the Jews. And Mordecai came into the presence of the king, for Esther had told how he was related to her. **2** The king took off his signet ring, which he had reclaimed from Haman, and presented it to Mordecai. And Esther appointed him over Haman's estate.

3 Esther again pleaded with the king, falling at his feet and weeping. She begged him to put an end to the evil plan of Haman the Agagite, which he had devised

---

a 4 Or *quiet, but the compensation our adversary offers cannot be compared with the loss the king would suffer*   *b* 9 That is, about 75 feet or about 23 meters against the Jews. **4** Then the king extended the gold scepter to Esther and she arose and stood before him.

5 "If it pleases the king," she said, "and if he regards me with favor and thinks it the right thing to do, and if he is pleased with me, let an order be written overruling the dispatches that Haman son of Hammedatha, the Agagite, devised and wrote to destroy the Jews in all the king's provinces. **6** For how can I bear to see disaster fall on my people? How can I bear to see the destruction of my family?"

7 King Xerxes replied to Queen Esther and to Mordecai the Jew, "Because Haman attacked the Jews, I have given his estate to Esther, and they have impaled him on the pole he set up. **8** Now write another decree in the king's name in behalf of the Jews as seems best to you, and seal it with the king's signet ring— for no document written in the king's name and sealed with his ring can be revoked."

9 At once the royal secretaries were summoned—on the twenty-third day of the third month, the month of Sivan. They wrote out all Mordecai's orders to the Jews, and to the satraps, governors and nobles of the 127 provinces stretching from India to Cush.*a* These orders were written in the script of each province and the language of each people and also to the Jews in their own script and language. **10** Mordecai wrote in the name of King Xerxes, sealed the dispatches with the king's signet ring, and sent them by mounted couriers, who rode fast horses especially bred for the king.

11 The king's edict granted the Jews in every city the right to assemble and protect themselves; to destroy, kill and annihilate the armed men of any nationality or province who might attack them and their women and children,*b* and to plunder the property of their enemies. **12** The day appointed for the Jews to do this in all the provinces of King Xerxes was the thirteenth day of the twelfth month, the month of Adar. **13** A copy of the text of the edict was to be issued as law in every province and made known to the people of every nationality so that the Jews would be ready on that day to avenge themselves on their enemies.

14 The couriers, riding the royal horses, went out, spurred on by the king's command, and the edict was issued in the citadel of Susa.

The Triumph of the Jews

15 When Mordecai left the king's presence, he was wearing roy-

---

a 9 That is, the upper Nile region   *b* 11 Or *province, together with their women and children, who might attack them;*

al garments of blue and white, a large crown of gold and a purple robe of fine linen. And the city of Susa held a joyous celebration. ¹⁶For the Jews it was a time of happiness and joy, gladness and honor. ¹⁷In every province and in every city to which the edict of the king came, there was joy and gladness among the Jews, with feasting and celebrating. And many people of other nationalities became Jews because fear of the Jews had seized them.

9 On the thirteenth day of the twelfth month, the month of Adar, the edict commanded by the king was to be carried out. On this day the enemies of the Jews had hoped to overpower them, but now the tables were turned and the Jews got the upper hand over those who hated them. ²The Jews assembled in their cities in all the provinces of King Xerxes to attack those determined to destroy them. No one could stand against them, because the people of all the other nationalities were afraid of them. ³And all the nobles of the provinces, the satraps, the governors and the king's administrators helped the Jews, because fear of Mordecai had seized them. ⁴Mordecai was prominent in the palace; his reputation spread throughout the provinces, and he became more and more powerful.

⁵The Jews struck down all their enemies with the sword, killing and destroying them, and they did what they pleased to those who hated them. ⁶In the citadel of Susa, the Jews killed and destroyed five hundred men. ⁷They also killed Parshandatha, Dalphon, Aspatha, ⁸Poratha, Adalia, Aridatha, ⁹Parmashta, Arisai, Aridai and Vaizatha, ¹⁰the ten sons of Haman son of Hammedatha, the enemy of the Jews. But they did not lay their hands on the plunder.

¹¹The number of those killed in the citadel of Susa was reported to the king that same day. ¹²The king said to Queen Esther, "The Jews have killed and destroyed five hundred men and the ten sons of Haman in the citadel of Susa. What have they done in the rest of the king's provinces? Now what is your petition? It will be given you. What is your request? It will also be granted."

¹³"If it pleases the king," Esther answered, "give the Jews in Susa permission to carry out this day's edict tomorrow also, and let Haman's ten sons be impaled on poles."

¹⁴So the king commanded that this be done. An edict was issued in Susa, and they impaled the ten sons of Haman. ¹⁵The Jews in Susa came together on the fourteenth day of the month of Adar, and they put to death in Susa three hundred men, but they did not lay their hands on the plunder.

¹⁶Meanwhile, the remainder of the Jews who were in the king's

provinces also assembled to protect themselves and get relief from their enemies. They killed seventy-five thousand of them but did not lay their hands on the plunder. ¹⁷This happened on the thirteenth day of the month of Adar, and on the fourteenth they rested and made it a day of feasting and joy.

¹⁸The Jews in Susa, however, had assembled on the thirteenth and fourteenth, and then on the fifteenth they rested and made it a day of feasting and joy.

¹⁹That is why rural Jews—those living in villages—observe the fourteenth of the month of Adar as a day of joy and feasting, a day for giving presents to each other.

Purim Established

²⁰Mordecai recorded these events, and he sent letters to all the Jews throughout the provinces of King Xerxes, near and far, ²¹to have them celebrate annually the fourteenth and fifteenth days of the month of Adar ²²as the time when the Jews got relief from their enemies, and as the month when their sorrow was turned into joy and their mourning into a day of celebration. He wrote them to observe the days as days of feasting and joy and giving presents of food to one another and gifts to the poor.

²³So the Jews agreed to continue the celebration they had begun, doing what Mordecai had written to them. ²⁴For Haman son of Hammedatha, the Agagite, the enemy of all the Jews, had plotted against the Jews to destroy them and had cast the *pur* (that is, the lot) for their ruin and destruction. ²⁵But when the plot came to the king's attention,ᵃ he issued written orders that the evil scheme Haman had devised against the Jews should come back onto his own head, and that he and his sons should be impaled on poles. ²⁶(Therefore these days were called Purim, from the word *pur*.) Because of everything written in this letter and because of what they had seen and what had happened to them, ²⁷the Jews took it on themselves to establish the custom that they and their descendants and all who join them should without fail observe these two days every year, in the way prescribed and at the time appointed. ²⁸These days should be remembered and observed in every generation by every family, and in every province and in every city. And these days of Purim should never fail to be celebrated by the Jews—nor should the memory of these days die out among their descendants.

²⁹So Queen Esther, daughter of Abihail, along with Mordecai the Jew, wrote with full author-

ᵃ 25 Or *when Esther came before the king*

ity to confirm this second letter concerning Purim. **30**And Mordecai sent letters to all the Jews in the 127 provinces of Xerxes' kingdom — words of goodwill and assurance — **31**to establish these days of Purim at their designated times, as Mordecai the Jew and Queen Esther had decreed for them, and as they had established for themselves and their descendants in regard to their times of fasting and lamentation. **32**Esther's decree confirmed these regulations about Purim, and it was written down in the records.

The Greatness of Mordecai

10 King Xerxes imposed tribute throughout the empire, to its distant shores. **2**And all his acts of power and might, together with a full account of the greatness of Mordecai, whom the king had promoted, are they not written in the book of the annals of the kings of Media and Persia? **3**Mordecai the Jew was second in rank to King Xerxes, preeminent among the Jews, and held in high esteem by his many fellow Jews, because he worked for the good of his people and spoke up for the welfare of all the Jews.

Job

Introduction:

The book of Job is named for its main character, a righteous man who was very rich. Even after losing everything he owned and suffering from a terrible sickness, Job still confessed his love for God.

The book questions the reasons for suffering, especially why good people or those who love God suffer. Job's friends insist he was suffering as punishment for his sin. Job defends himself by insisting that he has done nothing seriously wrong and then expresses his trust in God.

Finally God speaks and shows his mighty power. Job then admits that God is too great and wonderful for us to understand. Because Job remains faithful to God through his ordeal, God blesses him and rebuilds his family and restores his wealth.

Outline of contents:

Setting and background (1:1–3:26)
Job's discussions with his three friends (4:1–31:40)
  How is God related to Job's suffering? (4:1–14:22)
  Do wicked people always suffer? (15:1–21:34)
  Is Job guilty of secret sins? (22:1–31:40)
Elihu's speech (32:1–37:24)
God speaks (38:1–41:34)
Ending (42:1–17)

Prologue

1 In the land of Uz there lived a man whose name was Job. This man was blameless and upright; he feared God and shunned evil. ²He had seven sons and three daughters, ³and he owned seven thousand sheep, three thousand camels, five hundred yoke of oxen and five hundred donkeys, and had a large number of servants. He was the greatest man among all the people of the East.

⁴His sons used to hold feasts in their homes on their birthdays, and they would invite their three sisters to eat and drink with them. ⁵When a period of feasting had run its course, Job would make arrangements for them to be purified. Early in the morning he would sacrifice a burnt offering for each of them, thinking, "Per-

haps my children have sinned and cursed God in their hearts." This was Job's regular custom.

⁶One day the angels*ᵃ* came to present themselves before the Lord, and Satan*ᵇ* also came with them. ⁷The Lord said to Satan, "Where have you come from?"

Satan answered the Lord, "From roaming throughout the earth, going back and forth on it."

⁸Then the Lord said to Satan, "Have you considered my servant Job? There is no one on earth like him; he is blameless and upright, a man who fears God and shuns evil."

⁹"Does Job fear God for nothing?" Satan replied. ¹⁰"Have you not put a hedge around him and his household and everything he has? You have blessed the work of his hands, so that his flocks and herds are spread throughout the land. ¹¹But now stretch out your hand and strike everything he has, and he will surely curse you to your face."

¹²The Lord said to Satan, "Very well, then, everything he has is in your power, but on the man himself do not lay a finger."

Then Satan went out from the presence of the Lord.

¹³One day when Job's sons and daughters were feasting and drinking wine at the oldest brother's house, ¹⁴a messenger came to Job and said, "The oxen were plowing and the donkeys were grazing nearby, ¹⁵and the Sabeans attacked and made off with them. They put the servants to the sword, and I am the only one who has escaped to tell you!"

¹⁶While he was still speaking, another messenger came and said, "The fire of God fell from the heavens and burned up the sheep and the servants, and I am the only one who has escaped to tell you!"

¹⁷While he was still speaking, another messenger came and said, "The Chaldeans formed three raiding parties and swept down on your camels and made off with them. They put the servants to the sword, and I am the only one who has escaped to tell you!"

¹⁸While he was still speaking, yet another messenger came and said, "Your sons and daughters were feasting and drinking wine at the oldest brother's house, ¹⁹when suddenly a mighty wind swept in from the desert and struck the four corners of the house. It collapsed on them and they are dead, and I am the only one who has escaped to tell you!"

²⁰At this, Job got up and tore his robe and shaved his head. Then he fell to the ground in worship ²¹and said:

"Naked I came from my
    mother's womb,
    and naked I will depart.*ᶜ*

ᵃ 6 Hebrew *the sons of God*   *ᵇ* 6 Hebrew *satan* means *adversary*.   *ᶜ* 21 Or *will return there*

The LORD gave and the LORD
has taken away;
may the name of the LORD
be praised."

²²In all this, Job did not sin by charging God with wrongdoing.

2 On another day the angels[a] came to present themselves before the LORD, and Satan also came with them to present himself before him. ²And the LORD said to Satan, "Where have you come from?"

Satan answered the LORD, "From roaming throughout the earth, going back and forth on it."

³Then the LORD said to Satan, "Have you considered my servant Job? There is no one on earth like him; he is blameless and upright, a man who fears God and shuns evil. And he still maintains his integrity, though you incited me against him to ruin him without any reason."

⁴"Skin for skin!" Satan replied. "A man will give all he has for his own life. ⁵But now stretch out your hand and strike his flesh and bones, and he will surely curse you to your face."

⁶The LORD said to Satan, "Very well, then, he is in your hands; but you must spare his life."

⁷So Satan went out from the presence of the LORD and afflicted Job with painful sores from the soles of his feet to the crown of his head. ⁸Then Job took a piece of broken pottery and scraped himself with it as he sat among the ashes.

⁹His wife said to him, "Are you still maintaining your integrity? Curse God and die!"

¹⁰He replied, "You are talking like a foolish[b] woman. Shall we accept good from God, and not trouble?"

In all this, Job did not sin in what he said.

¹¹When Job's three friends, Eliphaz the Temanite, Bildad the Shuhite and Zophar the Naamathite, heard about all the troubles that had come upon him, they set out from their homes and met together by agreement to go and sympathize with him and comfort him. ¹²When they saw him from a distance, they could hardly recognize him; they began to weep aloud, and they tore their robes and sprinkled dust on their heads. ¹³Then they sat on the ground with him for seven days and seven nights. No one said a word to him, because they saw how great his suffering was.

Job Speaks

3 After this, Job opened his mouth and cursed the day of his birth. ²He said:

³"May the day of my birth
perish,
and the night that said, 'A
boy is conceived!'

---

[a] 1 Hebrew *the sons of God*   [b] 10 The Hebrew word rendered *foolish* denotes moral deficiency.

⁴That day — may it turn to
darkness;
may God above not care
about it;
may no light shine on it.
⁵May gloom and utter darkness
claim it once more;
may a cloud settle over it;
may blackness overwhelm it.
⁶That night — may thick
darkness seize it;
may it not be included
among the days of the
year
nor be entered in any of the
months.
⁷May that night be barren;
may no shout of joy be heard
in it.
⁸May those who curse days*a*
curse that day,
those who are ready to rouse
Leviathan.
⁹May its morning stars become
dark;
may it wait for daylight in
vain
and not see the first rays of
dawn,
¹⁰for it did not shut the doors of
the womb on me
to hide trouble from my eyes.

¹¹"Why did I not perish at
birth,
and die as I came from the
womb?
¹²Why were there knees to
receive me
and breasts that I might be
nursed?

¹³For now I would be lying down
in peace;
I would be asleep and at rest
¹⁴with kings and rulers of the
earth,
who built for themselves
places now lying in
ruins,
¹⁵with princes who had gold,
who filled their houses with
silver.
¹⁶Or why was I not hidden away
in the ground like a
stillborn child,
like an infant who never saw
the light of day?
¹⁷There the wicked cease from
turmoil,
and there the weary are at
rest.
¹⁸Captives also enjoy their ease;
they no longer hear the slave
driver's shout.
¹⁹The small and the great are
there,
and the slaves are freed from
their owners.

²⁰"Why is light given to those in
misery,
and life to the bitter of soul,
²¹to those who long for death
that does not come,
who search for it more than
for hidden treasure,
²²who are filled with gladness
and rejoice when they reach
the grave?
²³Why is life given to a man
whose way is hidden,
whom God has hedged in?

---

a 8 Or *curse the sea*

²⁴For sighing has become my
daily food;
my groans pour out like
water.
²⁵What I feared has come
upon me;
what I dreaded has
happened to me.
²⁶I have no peace, no
quietness;
I have no rest, but only
turmoil."

Eliphaz

4 Then Eliphaz the Temanite
replied:

² "If someone ventures a word
with you, will you be
impatient?
But who can keep from
speaking?
³Think how you have
instructed many,
how you have strengthened
feeble hands.
⁴Your words have supported
those who stumbled;
you have strengthened
faltering knees.
⁵But now trouble comes to you,
and you are discouraged;
it strikes you, and you are
dismayed.
⁶Should not your piety be your
confidence
and your blameless ways
your hope?

⁷ "Consider now: Who, being
innocent, has ever
perished?

Where were the upright ever
destroyed?
⁸As I have observed, those who
plow evil
and those who sow trouble
reap it.
⁹At the breath of God they
perish;
at the blast of his anger they
are no more.
¹⁰The lions may roar and growl,
yet the teeth of the great
lions are broken.
¹¹The lion perishes for lack of
prey,
and the cubs of the lioness
are scattered.

¹² "A word was secretly brought
to me,
my ears caught a whisper
of it.
¹³Amid disquieting dreams in
the night,
when deep sleep falls on
people,
¹⁴fear and trembling seized me
and made all my bones
shake.
¹⁵A spirit glided past my face,
and the hair on my body
stood on end.
¹⁶It stopped,
but I could not tell what it
was.
A form stood before my eyes,
and I heard a hushed voice:
¹⁷'Can a mortal be more
righteous than God?
Can even a strong man be
more pure than his
Maker?

¹⁸ If God places no trust in his
servants,
if he charges his angels with
error,
¹⁹ how much more those who
live in houses of clay,
whose foundations are in the
dust,
who are crushed more
readily than a moth!
²⁰ Between dawn and dusk they
are broken to pieces;
unnoticed, they perish
forever.
²¹ Are not the cords of their tent
pulled up,
so that they die without
wisdom?'

5 "Call if you will, but who
will answer you?
To which of the holy ones
will you turn?
² Resentment kills a fool,
and envy slays the
simple.
³ I myself have seen a fool
taking root,
but suddenly his house was
cursed.
⁴ His children are far from
safety,
crushed in court without a
defender.
⁵ The hungry consume his
harvest,
taking it even from among
thorns,
and the thirsty pant after his
wealth.
⁶ For hardship does not spring
from the soil,

nor does trouble sprout from
the ground.
⁷ Yet man is born to trouble
as surely as sparks fly
upward.

⁸ "But if I were you, I would
appeal to God;
I would lay my cause before
him.
⁹ He performs wonders that
cannot be fathomed,
miracles that cannot be
counted.
¹⁰ He provides rain for the
earth;
he sends water on the
countryside.
¹¹ The lowly he sets on high,
and those who mourn are
lifted to safety.
¹² He thwarts the plans of the
crafty,
so that their hands achieve
no success.
¹³ He catches the wise in their
craftiness,
and the schemes of the wily
are swept away.
¹⁴ Darkness comes upon them in
the daytime;
at noon they grope as in the
night.
¹⁵ He saves the needy from
the sword in their
mouth;
he saves them from the
clutches of the
powerful.
¹⁶ So the poor have hope,
and injustice shuts its
mouth.

17 "Blessed is the one whom God
        corrects;
    so do not despise the
        discipline of the
        Almighty.*a*

18 For he wounds, but he also
        binds up;
    he injures, but his hands
        also heal.

19 From six calamities he will
        rescue you;
    in seven no harm will touch
        you.

20 In famine he will deliver you
        from death,
    and in battle from the stroke
        of the sword.

21 You will be protected from the
        lash of the tongue,
    and need not fear when
        destruction comes.

22 You will laugh at destruction
        and famine,
    and need not fear the wild
        animals.

23 For you will have a covenant
        with the stones of the
        field,
    and the wild animals will be
        at peace with you.

24 You will know that your tent is
        secure;
    you will take stock of your
        property and find
        nothing missing.

25 You will know that your
        children will be many,
    and your descendants like
        the grass of the earth.

26 You will come to the grave in
        full vigor,
    like sheaves gathered in
        season.

27 "We have examined this, and
        it is true.
    So hear it and apply it to
        yourself."

Job

6 Then Job replied:

2 "If only my anguish could be
        weighed
    and all my misery be placed
        on the scales!

3 It would surely outweigh the
        sand of the seas —
    no wonder my words have
        been impetuous.

4 The arrows of the Almighty
        are in me,
    my spirit drinks in their
        poison;
    God's terrors are marshaled
        against me.

5 Does a wild donkey bray when
        it has grass,
    or an ox bellow when it has
        fodder?

6 Is tasteless food eaten without
        salt,
    or is there flavor in the sap of
        the mallow*b*?

7 I refuse to touch it;
    such food makes me ill.

8 "Oh, that I might have my
        request,

a 17 Hebrew *Shaddai*; here and throughout Job   *b 6* The meaning of the
Hebrew for this phrase is uncertain.

that God would grant what I
hope for,
⁹that God would be willing to
crush me,
to let loose his hand and cut
off my life!
¹⁰Then I would still have this
consolation —
my joy in unrelenting
pain —
that I had not denied the
words of the Holy One.

¹¹"What strength do I have, that
I should still hope?
What prospects, that I
should be patient?
¹²Do I have the strength of
stone?
Is my flesh bronze?
¹³Do I have any power to help
myself,
now that success has been
driven from me?

¹⁴"Anyone who withholds
kindness from a friend
forsakes the fear of the
Almighty.
¹⁵But my brothers are as
undependable as
intermittent streams,
as the streams that overflow
¹⁶when darkened by thawing
ice
and swollen with melting
snow,
¹⁷but that stop flowing in the dry
season,
and in the heat vanish from
their channels.
¹⁸Caravans turn aside from their
routes;

they go off into the
wasteland and perish.
¹⁹The caravans of Tema look for
water,
the traveling merchants of
Sheba look in hope.
²⁰They are distressed, because
they had been confident;
they arrive there, only to be
disappointed.
²¹Now you too have proved to be
of no help;
you see something dreadful
and are afraid.
²²Have I ever said, 'Give
something on my behalf,
pay a ransom for me from
your wealth,
²³deliver me from the hand of
the enemy,
rescue me from the clutches
of the ruthless'?

²⁴"Teach me, and I will be
quiet;
show me where I have been
wrong.
²⁵How painful are honest words!
But what do your arguments
prove?
²⁶Do you mean to correct what I
say,
and treat my desperate
words as wind?
²⁷You would even cast lots for
the fatherless
and barter away your
friend.

²⁸"But now be so kind as to look
at me.
Would I lie to your face?

²⁹Relent, do not be unjust;
  reconsider, for my integrity
    is at stake.^a
³⁰Is there any wickedness on my
    lips?
  Can my mouth not discern
    malice?

7 "Do not mortals have hard
    service on earth?
  Are not their days like those
    of hired laborers?
²Like a slave longing for the
    evening shadows,
  or a hired laborer waiting to
    be paid,
³so I have been allotted months
    of futility,
  and nights of misery have
    been assigned to me.
⁴When I lie down I think, 'How
    long before I get up?'
  The night drags on, and I
    toss and turn until dawn.
⁵My body is clothed with
    worms and scabs,
  my skin is broken and
    festering.

⁶"My days are swifter than a
    weaver's shuttle,
  and they come to an end
    without hope.
⁷Remember, O God, that my life
    is but a breath;
  my eyes will never see
    happiness again.
⁸The eye that now sees me will
    see me no longer;
  you will look for me, but I
    will be no more.

⁹As a cloud vanishes and is gone,
  so one who goes down to the
    grave does not return.
¹⁰He will never come to his
    house again;
  his place will know him no
    more.

¹¹"Therefore I will not keep
    silent;
  I will speak out in the
    anguish of my spirit,
  I will complain in the
    bitterness of my soul.
¹²Am I the sea, or the monster of
    the deep,
  that you put me under guard?
¹³When I think my bed will
    comfort me
  and my couch will ease my
    complaint,
¹⁴even then you frighten me
    with dreams
  and terrify me with visions,
¹⁵so that I prefer strangling and
    death,
  rather than this body of
    mine.
¹⁶I despise my life; I would not
    live forever.
  Let me alone; my days have
    no meaning.

¹⁷"What is mankind that you
    make so much of them,
  that you give them so much
    attention,
¹⁸that you examine them every
    morning
  and test them every
    moment?

---

^a 29 Or *my righteousness still stands*

¹⁹Will you never look away
from me,
or let me alone even for an
instant?
²⁰If I have sinned, what have I
done to you,
you who see everything
we do?
Why have you made me your
target?
Have I become a burden to
you?^a
²¹Why do you not pardon my
offenses
and forgive my sins?
For I will soon lie down in the
dust;
you will search for me, but I
will be no more."

Bildad

8 Then Bildad the Shuhite replied:

²"How long will you say such
things?
Your words are a blustering
wind.
³Does God pervert justice?
Does the Almighty pervert
what is right?
⁴When your children sinned
against him,
he gave them over to the
penalty of their sin.
⁵But if you will seek God
earnestly
and plead with the Almighty,

⁶if you are pure and upright,
even now he will rouse
himself on your
behalf
and restore you to your
prosperous state.
⁷Your beginnings will seem
humble,
so prosperous will your
future be.

⁸"Ask the former generation
and find out what their
ancestors learned,
⁹for we were born only
yesterday and know
nothing,
and our days on earth are
but a shadow.
¹⁰Will they not instruct you and
tell you?
Will they not bring forth
words from their
understanding?
¹¹Can papyrus grow tall where
there is no marsh?
Can reeds thrive without
water?
¹²While still growing and
uncut,
they wither more quickly
than grass.
¹³Such is the destiny of all who
forget God;
so perishes the hope of the
godless.
¹⁴What they trust in is fragile^b;
what they rely on is a spider's
web.

---

^a 20 A few manuscripts of the Masoretic Text, an ancient Hebrew scribal tradition
and Septuagint; most manuscripts of the Masoretic Text *I have become a burden to
myself.* ^b 14 The meaning of the Hebrew for this word is uncertain.

¹⁵They lean on the web, but it
     gives way;
  they cling to it, but it does
     not hold.
¹⁶They are like a well-watered
     plant in the sunshine,
  spreading its shoots over the
     garden;
¹⁷it entwines its roots around a
     pile of rocks
  and looks for a place among
     the stones.
¹⁸But when it is torn from its
     spot,
  that place disowns it and
     says, 'I never saw you.'
¹⁹Surely its life withers away,
  and^a from the soil other
     plants grow.
²⁰"Surely God does not reject
     one who is blameless
  or strengthen the hands of
     evildoers.
²¹He will yet fill your mouth
     with laughter
  and your lips with shouts of
     joy.
²²Your enemies will be clothed
     in shame,
  and the tents of the wicked
     will be no more."

Job

9 Then Job replied:

²"Indeed, I know that this is
     true.
  But how can mere mortals
     prove their innocence
     before God?

³Though they wished to dispute
     with him,
  they could not answer
     him one time out of a
     thousand.
⁴His wisdom is profound, his
     power is vast.
  Who has resisted him and
     come out unscathed?
⁵He moves mountains without
     their knowing it
  and overturns them in his
     anger.
⁶He shakes the earth from its
     place
  and makes its pillars
     tremble.
⁷He speaks to the sun and it
     does not shine;
  he seals off the light of the
     stars.
⁸He alone stretches out the
     heavens
  and treads on the waves of
     the sea.
⁹He is the Maker of the Bear^b
     and Orion,
  the Pleiades and the
     constellations of the
     south.
¹⁰He performs wonders that
     cannot be fathomed,
  miracles that cannot be
     counted.
¹¹When he passes me, I cannot
     see him;
  when he goes by, I cannot
     perceive him.
¹²If he snatches away, who can
     stop him?

---

^a 19 Or *Surely all the joy it has / is that*   ^b 9 Or *of Leo*

Who can say to him, 'What
are you doing?'
[13] God does not restrain his
anger;
even the cohorts of Rahab
cowered at his feet.

[14] "How then can I dispute with
him?
How can I find words to
argue with him?
[15] Though I were innocent, I
could not answer him;
I could only plead with my
Judge for mercy.
[16] Even if I summoned him and
he responded,
I do not believe he would
give me a hearing.
[17] He would crush me with a
storm
and multiply my wounds for
no reason.
[18] He would not let me catch my
breath
but would overwhelm me
with misery.
[19] If it is a matter of strength, he
is mighty!
And if it is a matter of justice,
who can challenge
him[a]?
[20] Even if I were innocent,
my mouth would
condemn me;
if I were blameless, it would
pronounce me guilty.

[21] "Although I am blameless,
I have no concern for myself;
I despise my own life.

[22] It is all the same; that is why I
say,
'He destroys both the
blameless and the
wicked.'
[23] When a scourge brings sudden
death,
he mocks the despair of the
innocent.
[24] When a land falls into the
hands of the wicked,
he blindfolds its judges.
If it is not he, then who is it?

[25] "My days are swifter than a
runner;
they fly away without a
glimpse of joy.
[26] They skim past like boats of
papyrus,
like eagles swooping down
on their prey.
[27] If I say, 'I will forget my
complaint,
I will change my expression,
and smile,'
[28] I still dread all my sufferings,
for I know you will not hold
me innocent.
[29] Since I am already found
guilty,
why should I struggle in
vain?
[30] Even if I washed myself with
soap
and my hands with
cleansing powder,
[31] you would plunge me into a
slime pit
so that even my clothes
would detest me.

[a] 19 See Septuagint; Hebrew *me*.

³²"He is not a mere mortal like
    me that I might answer
    him,
    that we might confront each
      other in court.
³³If only there were someone to
    mediate between us,
    someone to bring us
      together,
³⁴someone to remove God's rod
    from me,
    so that his terror would
      frighten me no more.
³⁵Then I would speak up without
    fear of him,
    but as it now stands with me,
      I cannot.

10

"I loathe my very life;
therefore I will give free
rein to my complaint
and speak out in the
    bitterness of my soul.
²I say to God: Do not declare
    me guilty,
    but tell me what charges you
      have against me.
³Does it please you to
    oppress me,
    to spurn the work of your
      hands,
    while you smile on the plans
      of the wicked?
⁴Do you have eyes of flesh?
    Do you see as a mortal
      sees?
⁵Are your days like those of a
    mortal
    or your years like those of a
      strong man,

⁶that you must search out my
    faults
    and probe after my sin —
⁷though you know that I am not
    guilty
    and that no one can rescue
      me from your hand?

⁸"Your hands shaped me and
    made me.
    Will you now turn and
      destroy me?
⁹Remember that you molded
    me like clay.
    Will you now turn me to dust
      again?
¹⁰Did you not pour me out like
    milk
    and curdle me like cheese,
¹¹clothe me with skin and flesh
    and knit me together with
      bones and sinews?
¹²You gave me life and showed
    me kindness,
    and in your providence
      watched over my spirit.

¹³"But this is what you
    concealed in your heart,
    and I know that this was in
      your mind:
¹⁴If I sinned, you would be
    watching me
    and would not let my offense
      go unpunished.
¹⁵If I am guilty — woe to me!
    Even if I am innocent, I
      cannot lift my head,
    for I am full of shame
    and drowned in^a my
      affliction.

^a 15 Or *and aware of*

¹⁶ If I hold my head high, you
    stalk me like a lion
  and again display your
    awesome power
    against me.
¹⁷ You bring new witnesses
    against me
  and increase your anger
    toward me;
  your forces come against me
    wave upon wave.

¹⁸ "Why then did you bring me
    out of the womb?
  I wish I had died before any
    eye saw me.
¹⁹ If only I had never come into
    being,
  or had been carried straight
    from the womb to the
    grave!
²⁰ Are not my few days almost
    over?
  Turn away from me so I can
    have a moment's joy
²¹ before I go to the place of no
    return,
  to the land of gloom and
    utter darkness,
²² to the land of deepest night,
  of utter darkness and
    disorder,
  where even the light is like
    darkness."

Zophar

11 Then Zophar the Naamathite replied:

² "Are all these words to go
    unanswered?
  Is this talker to be vindicated?

³ Will your idle talk reduce
    others to silence?
  Will no one rebuke you when
    you mock?
⁴ You say to God, 'My beliefs are
    flawless
  and I am pure in your
    sight.'
⁵ Oh, how I wish that God would
    speak,
  that he would open his lips
    against you
⁶ and disclose to you the secrets
    of wisdom,
  for true wisdom has two
    sides.
  Know this: God has even
    forgotten some of your
    sin.

⁷ "Can you fathom the mysteries
    of God?
  Can you probe the limits of
    the Almighty?
⁸ They are higher than the
    heavens above — what
    can you do?
  They are deeper than the
    depths below — what can
    you know?
⁹ Their measure is longer than
    the earth
  and wider than the sea.

¹⁰ "If he comes along and
    confines you in prison
  and convenes a court, who
    can oppose him?
¹¹ Surely he recognizes
    deceivers;
  and when he sees evil, does
    he not take note?

¹²But the witless can no more
become wise
than a wild donkey's colt can
be born human.ᵃ

¹³"Yet if you devote your heart to
him
and stretch out your hands
to him,
¹⁴if you put away the sin that is
in your hand
and allow no evil to dwell in
your tent,
¹⁵then, free of fault, you will lift
up your face;
you will stand firm and
without fear.
¹⁶You will surely forget your
trouble,
recalling it only as waters
gone by.
¹⁷Life will be brighter than
noonday,
and darkness will become
like morning.
¹⁸You will be secure, because
there is hope;
you will look about you
and take your rest in
safety.
¹⁹You will lie down, with no one
to make you afraid,
and many will court your
favor.
²⁰But the eyes of the wicked will
fail,
and escape will elude
them;
their hope will become a
dying gasp."

Job

12
Then Job replied:

²"Doubtless you are the only
people who matter,
and wisdom will die with
you!
³But I have a mind as well as
you;
I am not inferior to you.
Who does not know all these
things?

⁴"I have become a
laughingstock to my
friends,
though I called on God and
he answered—
a mere laughingstock,
though righteous and
blameless!
⁵Those who are at ease have
contempt for misfortune
as the fate of those whose
feet are slipping.
⁶The tents of marauders are
undisturbed,
and those who provoke God
are secure—
those God has in his
hand.ᵇ

⁷"But ask the animals, and they
will teach you,
or the birds in the sky, and
they will tell you;
⁸or speak to the earth, and it
will teach you,
or let the fish in the sea
inform you.

ᵃ 12 Or *wild donkey can be born tame
hand*

ᵇ 6 Or *those whose god is in their own*
hand

⁹Which of all these does not
    know
    that the hand of the LORD
        has done this?
¹⁰In his hand is the life of every
    creature
    and the breath of all
        mankind.
¹¹Does not the ear test words
    as the tongue tastes food?
¹²Is not wisdom found among
    the aged?
    Does not long life bring
        understanding?

¹³"To God belong wisdom and
    power;
    counsel and understanding
        are his.
¹⁴What he tears down cannot be
    rebuilt;
    those he imprisons cannot
        be released.
¹⁵If he holds back the waters,
    there is drought;
    if he lets them loose, they
        devastate the land.
¹⁶To him belong strength and
    insight;
    both deceived and deceiver
        are his.
¹⁷He leads rulers away stripped
    and makes fools of judges.
¹⁸He takes off the shackles put
    on by kings
    and ties a loincloth[a] around
        their waist.
¹⁹He leads priests away stripped
    and overthrows officials long
        established.

²⁰He silences the lips of trusted
    advisers
    and takes away the
        discernment of elders.
²¹He pours contempt on nobles
    and disarms the mighty.
²²He reveals the deep things of
    darkness
    and brings utter darkness
        into the light.
²³He makes nations great, and
    destroys them;
    he enlarges nations, and
        disperses them.
²⁴He deprives the leaders of the
    earth of their reason;
    he makes them wander in a
        trackless waste.
²⁵They grope in darkness with
    no light;
    he makes them stagger like
        drunkards.

13 "My eyes have seen all
    this,
    my ears have heard and
        understood it.
²What you know, I also know;
    I am not inferior to you.
³But I desire to speak to the
    Almighty
    and to argue my case with
        God.
⁴You, however, smear me with
    lies;
    you are worthless
        physicians, all of you!
⁵If only you would be altogether
    silent!
    For you, that would be
        wisdom.

---

a 18 Or *shackles of kings / and ties a belt*

⁶Hear now my argument;
 listen to the pleas of my lips.
⁷Will you speak wickedly on
  God's behalf?
 Will you speak deceitfully for
  him?
⁸Will you show him partiality?
 Will you argue the case for
  God?
⁹Would it turn out well if he
  examined you?
 Could you deceive him as
  you might deceive a
  mortal?
¹⁰He would surely call you to
  account
 if you secretly showed
  partiality.
¹¹Would not his splendor terrify
  you?
 Would not the dread of him
  fall on you?
¹²Your maxims are proverbs of
  ashes;
 your defenses are defenses of
  clay.
¹³"Keep silent and let me speak;
 then let come to me what
  may.
¹⁴Why do I put myself in
  jeopardy
 and take my life in my
  hands?
¹⁵Though he slay me, yet will I
  hope in him;
 I will surely*ᵃ* defend my ways
  to his face.
¹⁶Indeed, this will turn out for
  my deliverance,

for no godless person would
  dare come before him!
¹⁷Listen carefully to what I say;
 let my words ring in your
  ears.
¹⁸Now that I have prepared my
  case,
 I know I will be vindicated.
¹⁹Can anyone bring charges
  against me?
 If so, I will be silent and die.

²⁰"Only grant me these two
  things, God,
 and then I will not hide from
  you:
²¹Withdraw your hand far
  from me,
 and stop frightening me with
  your terrors.
²²Then summon me and I will
  answer,
 or let me speak, and you
  reply to me.
²³How many wrongs and sins
  have I committed?
 Show me my offense and my
  sin.
²⁴Why do you hide your
  face
 and consider me your
  enemy?
²⁵Will you torment a windblown
  leaf?
 Will you chase after dry
  chaff?
²⁶For you write down bitter
  things against me
 and make me reap the sins
  of my youth.

ᵃ 15 Or *He will surely slay me; I have no hope — / yet I will*

²⁷You fasten my feet in shackles;
    you keep close watch on all
      my paths
    by putting marks on the
      soles of my feet.

²⁸"So man wastes away like
      something rotten,
    like a garment eaten by
      moths.

14 "Mortals, born of
      woman,
    are of few days and full of
      trouble.
²They spring up like flowers
      and wither away;
    like fleeting shadows, they
      do not endure.
³Do you fix your eye on them?
    Will you bring them*ᵃ* before
      you for judgment?
⁴Who can bring what is pure
      from the impure?
    No one!
⁵A person's days are
      determined;
    you have decreed the
      number of his months
    and have set limits he
      cannot exceed.
⁶So look away from him and let
      him alone,
    till he has put in his time like
      a hired laborer.

⁷"At least there is hope for a
      tree:
    If it is cut down, it will sprout
      again,
    and its new shoots will not
      fail.

⁸Its roots may grow old in the
      ground
    and its stump die in the soil,
⁹yet at the scent of water it will
      bud
    and put forth shoots like a
      plant.
¹⁰But a man dies and is laid low;
    he breathes his last and is no
      more.
¹¹As the water of a lake dries up
    or a riverbed becomes
      parched and dry,
¹²so he lies down and does not
      rise;
    till the heavens are no more,
      people will not awake
    or be roused from their
      sleep.

¹³"If only you would hide me in
      the grave
    and conceal me till your
      anger has passed!
    If only you would set me a
      time
    and then remember me!
¹⁴If someone dies, will they live
      again?
    All the days of my hard
      service
    I will wait for my renewalᵇ to
      come.
¹⁵You will call and I will answer
      you;
    you will long for the creature
      your hands have made.
¹⁶Surely then you will count my
      steps
    but not keep track of my sin.

ᵃ 3 Septuagint, Vulgate and Syriac; Hebrew *me*   *ᵇ 14* Or *release*

¹⁷My offenses will be sealed up
in a bag;
you will cover over my sin.

¹⁸"But as a mountain erodes and
crumbles
and as a rock is moved from
its place,
¹⁹as water wears away stones
and torrents wash away the
soil,
so you destroy a person's
hope.
²⁰You overpower them once for
all, and they are gone;
you change their
countenance and send
them away.
²¹If their children are honored,
they do not know it;
if their offspring are brought
low, they do not see it.
²²They feel but the pain of their
own bodies
and mourn only for
themselves."

Eliphaz

15 Then Eliphaz the Temanite replied:

²"Would a wise person answer
with empty notions
or fill their belly with the hot
east wind?
³Would they argue with useless
words,
with speeches that have no
value?
⁴But you even undermine piety
and hinder devotion
to God.

⁵Your sin prompts your mouth;
you adopt the tongue of the
crafty.
⁶Your own mouth condemns
you, not mine;
your own lips testify against
you.

⁷"Are you the first man ever
born?
Were you brought forth
before the hills?
⁸Do you listen in on God's
council?
Do you have a monopoly on
wisdom?
⁹What do you know that we do
not know?
What insights do you have
that we do not have?
¹⁰The gray-haired and the aged
are on our side,
men even older than your
father.
¹¹Are God's consolations not
enough for you,
words spoken gently to you?
¹²Why has your heart carried
you away,
and why do your eyes flash,
¹³so that you vent your rage
against God
and pour out such words
from your mouth?

¹⁴"What are mortals, that they
could be pure,
or those born of woman, that
they could be righteous?
¹⁵If God places no trust in his
holy ones,
if even the heavens are not
pure in his eyes,

¹⁶how much less mortals, who
are vile and corrupt,
who drink up evil like water!

¹⁷"Listen to me and I will
explain to you;
let me tell you what I have
seen,
¹⁸what the wise have declared,
hiding nothing received
from their ancestors
¹⁹(to whom alone the land was
given
when no foreigners moved
among them):
²⁰All his days the wicked man
suffers torment,
the ruthless man through all
the years stored up for
him.
²¹Terrifying sounds fill his ears;
when all seems well,
marauders attack him.
²²He despairs of escaping the
realm of darkness;
he is marked for the sword.
²³He wanders about for food like
a vulture;
he knows the day of
darkness is at hand.
²⁴Distress and anguish fill him
with terror;
troubles overwhelm him,
like a king poised to
attack,
²⁵because he shakes his fist at
God
and vaunts himself against
the Almighty,
²⁶defiantly charging against him
with a thick, strong
shield.

²⁷"Though his face is covered
with fat
and his waist bulges with
flesh,
²⁸he will inhabit ruined towns
and houses where no one
lives,
houses crumbling to
rubble.
²⁹He will no longer be rich
and his wealth will not
endure,
nor will his possessions
spread over the land.
³⁰He will not escape the
darkness;
a flame will wither his
shoots,
and the breath of God's
mouth will carry him
away.
³¹Let him not deceive himself
by trusting what is
worthless,
for he will get nothing in
return.
³²Before his time he will wither,
and his branches will not
flourish.
³³He will be like a vine stripped
of its unripe grapes,
like an olive tree shedding
its blossoms.
³⁴For the company of the godless
will be barren,
and fire will consume the
tents of those who love
bribes.
³⁵They conceive trouble and
give birth to evil;
their womb fashions deceit."

Job

16

Then Job replied:

2 "I have heard many things like these;
    you are miserable
        comforters, all of you!
3 Will your long-winded
        speeches never end?
    What ails you that you keep
        on arguing?
4 I also could speak like you,
    if you were in my place;
    I could make fine speeches
        against you
    and shake my head at you.
5 But my mouth would
        encourage you;
    comfort from my lips would
        bring you relief.

6 "Yet if I speak, my pain is not
        relieved;
    and if I refrain, it does not go
        away.
7 Surely, God, you have worn me
        out;
    you have devastated my
        entire household.
8 You have shriveled me up —
    and it has become a
        witness;
    my gauntness rises up and
        testifies against me.
9 God assails me and tears me
        in his anger
    and gnashes his teeth at me;
    my opponent fastens on me
        his piercing eyes.
10 People open their mouths to
        jeer at me;
    they strike my cheek in
        scorn
    and unite together
        against me.
11 God has turned me over to the
        ungodly
    and thrown me into the
        clutches of the wicked.
12 All was well with me, but he
        shattered me;
    he seized me by the neck
        and crushed me.
    He has made me his target;
13   his archers surround me.
    Without pity, he pierces my
        kidneys
    and spills my gall on the
        ground.
14 Again and again he bursts
        upon me;
    he rushes at me like a
        warrior.

15 "I have sewed sackcloth over
        my skin
    and buried my brow in the
        dust.
16 My face is red with weeping,
    dark shadows ring my eyes;
17 yet my hands have been free of
        violence
    and my prayer is pure.

18 "Earth, do not cover my blood;
    may my cry never be laid to
        rest!
19 Even now my witness is in
        heaven;
    my advocate is on high.
20 My intercessor is my friend[a]
    as my eyes pour out tears to
        God;

---

[a] 20 Or *My friends treat me with scorn*

²¹ on behalf of a man he pleads
with God
as one pleads for a friend.

²² "Only a few years will pass
before I take the path of no
return.

17 ¹ My spirit is broken,
my days are cut short,
the grave awaits me.
² Surely mockers surround me;
my eyes must dwell on their
hostility.

³ "Give me, O God, the pledge
you demand.
Who else will put up security
for me?
⁴ You have closed their minds to
understanding;
therefore you will not let
them triumph.
⁵ If anyone denounces their
friends for reward,
the eyes of their children
will fail.

⁶ "God has made me a byword
to everyone,
a man in whose face people
spit.
⁷ My eyes have grown dim with
grief;
my whole frame is but a
shadow.
⁸ The upright are appalled at
this;
the innocent are aroused
against the ungodly.
⁹ Nevertheless, the righteous
will hold to their ways,
and those with clean hands
will grow stronger.

¹⁰ "But come on, all of you, try
again!
I will not find a wise man
among you.
¹¹ My days have passed, my
plans are shattered.
Yet the desires of my heart
¹² turn night into day;
in the face of the darkness
light is near.
¹³ If the only home I hope for is
the grave,
if I spread out my bed in the
realm of darkness,
¹⁴ if I say to corruption, 'You are
my father,'
and to the worm, 'My
mother' or 'My sister,'
¹⁵ where then is my hope —
who can see any hope for me?
¹⁶ Will it go down to the gates of
death?
Will we descend together
into the dust?"

Bildad

18 Then Bildad the Shuhite
replied:

² "When will you end these
speeches?
Be sensible, and then we can
talk.
³ Why are we regarded as cattle
and considered stupid in
your sight?
⁴ You who tear yourself to pieces
in your anger,
is the earth to be abandoned
for your sake?
Or must the rocks be moved
from their place?

5 "The lamp of a wicked man is
    snuffed out;
  the flame of his fire stops
    burning.
6 The light in his tent becomes
    dark;
  the lamp beside him goes out.
7 The vigor of his step is
    weakened;
  his own schemes throw him
    down.
8 His feet thrust him into a net;
  he wanders into its mesh.
9 A trap seizes him by the heel;
  a snare holds him fast.
10 A noose is hidden for him on
    the ground;
  a trap lies in his path.
11 Terrors startle him on every
    side
  and dog his every step.
12 Calamity is hungry for him;
  disaster is ready for him
    when he falls.
13 It eats away parts of his skin;
  death's firstborn devours his
    limbs.
14 He is torn from the security of
    his tent
  and marched off to the king
    of terrors.
15 Fire resides*a* in his tent;
  burning sulfur is scattered
    over his dwelling.
16 His roots dry up below
  and his branches wither
    above.
17 The memory of him perishes
    from the earth;
  he has no name in the land.

18 He is driven from light into the
    realm of darkness
  and is banished from the
    world.
19 He has no offspring or
    descendants among his
    people,
  no survivor where once he
    lived.
20 People of the west are appalled
    at his fate;
  those of the east are seized
    with horror.
21 Surely such is the dwelling of
    an evil man;
  such is the place of one who
    does not know God."

Job

19

Then Job replied:

2 "How long will you torment
    me
  and crush me with
    words?
3 Ten times now you have
    reproached me;
  shamelessly you attack me.
4 If it is true that I have gone
    astray,
  my error remains my
    concern alone.
5 If indeed you would exalt
    yourselves above me
  and use my humiliation
    against me,
6 then know that God has
    wronged me
  and drawn his net
    around me.

---

a 15 Or *Nothing he had remains*

7 "Though I cry, 'Violence!' I get
no response;
though I call for help, there
is no justice.
8 He has blocked my way so I
cannot pass;
he has shrouded my paths in
darkness.
9 He has stripped me of my
honor
and removed the crown
from my head.
10 He tears me down on every
side till I am gone;
he uproots my hope like a
tree.
11 His anger burns against me;
he counts me among his
enemies.
12 His troops advance in
force;
they build a siege ramp
against me
and encamp around
my tent.

13 "He has alienated my family
from me;
my acquaintances are
completely estranged
from me.
14 My relatives have gone
away;
my closest friends have
forgotten me.
15 My guests and my female
servants count me a
foreigner;
they look on me as on a
stranger.

16 I summon my servant, but he
does not answer,
though I beg him with my
own mouth.
17 My breath is offensive to my
wife;
I am loathsome to my own
family.
18 Even the little boys scorn me;
when I appear, they
ridicule me.
19 All my intimate friends
detest me;
those I love have turned
against me.
20 I am nothing but skin and
bones;
I have escaped only by the
skin of my teeth.ᵃ

21 "Have pity on me, my friends,
have pity,
for the hand of God has
struck me.
22 Why do you pursue me as God
does?
Will you never get enough of
my flesh?

23 "Oh, that my words were
recorded,
that they were written on a
scroll,
24 that they were inscribed with
an iron tool onᵇ lead,
or engraved in rock forever!
25 I know that my redeemerᶜ
lives,
and that in the end he will
stand on the earth.ᵈ

ᵃ 20 Or only by my gums   ᵇ 24 Or and   ᶜ 25 Or vindicator   ᵈ 25 Or on my
grave

²⁶And after my skin has been
destroyed,
    yet*a* in*b* my flesh I will see
    God;
²⁷I myself will see him
    with my own eyes — I, and
    not another.
    How my heart yearns within
    me!

²⁸"If you say, 'How we will
    hound him,
    since the root of the trouble
    lies in him,'*c'*
²⁹you should fear the sword
    yourselves;
    for wrath will bring
    punishment by the
    sword,
    and then you will know that
    there is judgment.*d*"

Zophar

20 Then Zophar the Naama-
thite replied:

²"My troubled thoughts prompt
    me to answer
    because I am greatly
    disturbed.
³I hear a rebuke that
    dishonors me,
    and my understanding
    inspires me to reply.

⁴"Surely you know how it has
    been from of old,
    ever since mankind*e* was
    placed on the earth,

⁵that the mirth of the wicked is
    brief,
    the joy of the godless lasts
    but a moment.
⁶Though the pride of the
    godless person reaches
    to the heavens
    and his head touches the
    clouds,
⁷he will perish forever, like his
    own dung;
    those who have seen him
    will say, 'Where is he?'
⁸Like a dream he flies away, no
    more to be found,
    banished like a vision of the
    night.
⁹The eye that saw him will not
    see him again;
    his place will look on him no
    more.
¹⁰His children must make
    amends to the poor;
    his own hands must give
    back his wealth.
¹¹The youthful vigor that fills his
    bones
    will lie with him in the
    dust.

¹²"Though evil is sweet in his
    mouth
    and he hides it under his
    tongue,
¹³though he cannot bear to let it
    go
    and lets it linger in his
    mouth,

---

a 26 Or *And after I awake, / though this body has been destroyed, / then*
b 26 Or *destroyed, / apart from*   *c* 28 Many Hebrew manuscripts, Septuagint
and Vulgate; most Hebrew manuscripts *me*   *d* 29 Or *sword, / that you may come
to know the Almighty*   *e* 4 Or *Adam*

¹⁴yet his food will turn sour in
  his stomach;
    it will become the venom of
    serpents within him.
¹⁵He will spit out the riches he
  swallowed;
    God will make his stomach
    vomit them up.
¹⁶He will suck the poison of
  serpents;
    the fangs of an adder will kill
    him.
¹⁷He will not enjoy the streams,
  the rivers flowing with
  honey and cream.
¹⁸What he toiled for he must give
  back uneaten;
    he will not enjoy the profit
    from his trading.
¹⁹For he has oppressed the poor
  and left them destitute;
    he has seized houses he did
    not build.
²⁰"Surely he will have no respite
  from his craving;
    he cannot save himself by
    his treasure.
²¹Nothing is left for him to
  devour;
    his prosperity will not endure.
²²In the midst of his plenty,
  distress will overtake
  him;
    the full force of misery will
    come upon him.
²³When he has filled his belly,
  God will vent his burning
  anger against him
    and rain down his blows on
    him.

²⁴Though he flees from an iron
  weapon,
    a bronze-tipped arrow
    pierces him.
²⁵He pulls it out of his back,
  the gleaming point out of his
  liver.
  Terrors will come over him;
²⁶ total darkness lies in wait for
    his treasures.
  A fire unfanned will consume
  him
    and devour what is left in his
    tent.
²⁷The heavens will expose his
  guilt;
    the earth will rise up against
    him.
²⁸A flood will carry off his house,
  rushing waters*ᵃ* on the day
  of God's wrath.
²⁹Such is the fate God allots the
  wicked,
    the heritage appointed for
    them by God."

Job

21

Then Job replied:

²"Listen carefully to my words;
  let this be the consolation
  you give me.
³Bear with me while I speak,
  and after I have spoken,
  mock on.
⁴"Is my complaint directed to a
  human being?
    Why should I not be
    impatient?

ᵃ 28 Or *The possessions in his house will be carried off, / washed away*

⁵Look at me and be appalled;
   clap your hand over your
      mouth.
⁶When I think about this, I am
      terrified;
   trembling seizes my body.
⁷Why do the wicked live on,
   growing old and increasing
      in power?
⁸They see their children
      established around
      them,
   their offspring before their
      eyes.
⁹Their homes are safe and free
      from fear;
   the rod of God is not on
      them.
¹⁰Their bulls never fail to breed;
   their cows calve and do not
      miscarry.
¹¹They send forth their children
      as a flock;
   their little ones dance about.
¹²They sing to the music of
      timbrel and lyre;
   they make merry to the
      sound of the pipe.
¹³They spend their years in
      prosperity
   and go down to the grave in
      peace.ᵃ
¹⁴Yet they say to God, 'Leave us
      alone!
   We have no desire to know
      your ways.
¹⁵Who is the Almighty, that we
      should serve him?
   What would we gain by
      praying to him?'

¹⁶But their prosperity is not in
      their own hands,
   so I stand aloof from the
      plans of the wicked.

¹⁷"Yet how often is the lamp of
      the wicked snuffed out?
   How often does calamity
      come upon them,
   the fate God allots in his
      anger?
¹⁸How often are they like straw
      before the wind,
   like chaff swept away by a
      gale?
¹⁹It is said, 'God stores up
      the punishment of
      the wicked for their
      children.'
   Let him repay the wicked, so
      that they themselves will
      experience it!
²⁰Let their own eyes see their
      destruction;
   let them drink the cup of the
      wrath of the Almighty.
²¹For what do they care about
      the families they leave
      behind
   when their allotted months
      come to an end?

²²"Can anyone teach knowledge
      to God,
   since he judges even the
      highest?
²³One person dies in full vigor,
   completely secure and at
      ease,
²⁴well nourished in body,ᵇ
   bones rich with marrow.

ᵃ 13 Or in an instant   ᵇ 24 The meaning of the Hebrew for this word is uncertain.

25 Another dies in bitterness of
soul,
    never having enjoyed
    anything good.
26 Side by side they lie in the
dust,
    and worms cover them both.

27 "I know full well what you are
thinking,
    the schemes by which you
    would wrong me.
28 You say, 'Where now is the
house of the great,
    the tents where the wicked
    lived?'
29 Have you never questioned
those who travel?
    Have you paid no regard to
    their accounts —
30 that the wicked are spared
from the day of calamity,
    that they are delivered from*a*
    the day of wrath?
31 Who denounces their conduct
to their face?
    Who repays them for what
    they have done?
32 They are carried to the grave,
    and watch is kept over their
    tombs.
33 The soil in the valley is sweet
to them;
    everyone follows after them,
    and a countless throng goes*b*
    before them.

34 "So how can you console me
with your nonsense?
    Nothing is left of your
    answers but falsehood!"

Eliphaz

22 Then Eliphaz the Temanite replied:

2 "Can a man be of benefit to
God?
    Can even a wise person
    benefit him?
3 What pleasure would it give
the Almighty if you were
righteous?
    What would he gain if your
    ways were blameless?

4 "Is it for your piety that he
rebukes you
    and brings charges against
    you?
5 Is not your wickedness great?
    Are not your sins endless?
6 You demanded security from
your relatives for no
reason;
    you stripped people of their
    clothing, leaving them
    naked.
7 You gave no water to the weary
    and you withheld food from
    the hungry,
8 though you were a powerful
man, owning land —
    an honored man, living on it.
9 And you sent widows away
empty-handed
    and broke the strength of the
    fatherless.
10 That is why snares are all
around you,
    why sudden peril terrifies
    you,

---

a 30 Or *wicked are reserved for the day of calamity, / that they are brought forth to*
b 33 Or *them, / as a countless throng went*

¹¹ why it is so dark you cannot
see,
and why a flood of water
covers you.

¹² "Is not God in the heights of
heaven?
And see how lofty are the
highest stars!
¹³ Yet you say, 'What does God
know?
Does he judge through such
darkness?
¹⁴ Thick clouds veil him, so he
does not see us
as he goes about in the
vaulted heavens.'
¹⁵ Will you keep to the old
path
that the wicked have
trod?
¹⁶ They were carried off before
their time,
their foundations washed
away by a flood.
¹⁷ They said to God, 'Leave us
alone!
What can the Almighty do to
us?'
¹⁸ Yet it was he who filled their
houses with good
things,
so I stand aloof from the
plans of the wicked.
¹⁹ The righteous see their ruin
and rejoice;
the innocent mock them,
saying,
²⁰ 'Surely our foes are
destroyed,
and fire devours their
wealth.'

²¹ "Submit to God and be at
peace with him;
in this way prosperity will
come to you.
²² Accept instruction from his
mouth
and lay up his words in your
heart.
²³ If you return to the Almighty,
you will be restored:
If you remove wickedness far
from your tent
²⁴ and assign your nuggets to the
dust,
your gold of Ophir to the
rocks in the ravines,
²⁵ then the Almighty will be your
gold,
the choicest silver for you.
²⁶ Surely then you will find
delight in the Almighty
and will lift up your face to
God.
²⁷ You will pray to him, and he
will hear you,
and you will fulfill your
vows.
²⁸ What you decide on will be
done,
and light will shine on your
ways.
²⁹ When people are brought
low and you say, 'Lift
them up!'
then he will save the
downcast.
³⁰ He will deliver even one who is
not innocent,
who will be delivered
through the cleanness of
your hands."

Job

23

Then Job replied:

² "Even today my complaint is
bitter;
his hand*a* is heavy in spite
of*b* my groaning.
³ If only I knew where to find
him;
if only I could go to his
dwelling!
⁴ I would state my case before
him
and fill my mouth with
arguments.
⁵ I would find out what he would
answer me,
and consider what he would
say to me.
⁶ Would he vigorously
oppose me?
No, he would not press
charges against me.
⁷ There the upright can
establish their innocence
before him,
and there I would be
delivered forever from
my judge.

⁸ "But if I go to the east, he is not
there;
if I go to the west, I do not
find him.
⁹ When he is at work in the
north, I do not see him;
when he turns to the south, I
catch no glimpse of him.
¹⁰ But he knows the way that I
take;

when he has tested me, I will
come forth as gold.
¹¹ My feet have closely followed
his steps;
I have kept to his way
without turning aside.
¹² I have not departed from the
commands of his lips;
I have treasured the words of
his mouth more than my
daily bread.

¹³ "But he stands alone, and who
can oppose him?
He does whatever he pleases.
¹⁴ He carries out his decree
against me,
and many such plans he still
has in store.
¹⁵ That is why I am terrified
before him;
when I think of all this, I fear
him.
¹⁶ God has made my heart faint;
the Almighty has
terrified me.
¹⁷ Yet I am not silenced by the
darkness,
by the thick darkness that
covers my face.

24

"Why does the Almighty
not set times for
judgment?
Why must those who know
him look in vain for such
days?
² There are those who move
boundary stones;
they pasture flocks they
have stolen.

---

a 2 Septuagint and Syriac; Hebrew / *the hand on me*   *b* 2 Or *heavy on me in*

³ They drive away the orphan's
    donkey
  and take the widow's ox in
    pledge.
⁴ They thrust the needy from
    the path
  and force all the poor of the
    land into hiding.
⁵ Like wild donkeys in the desert,
  the poor go about their labor
    of foraging food;
  the wasteland provides food
    for their children.
⁶ They gather fodder in the
    fields
  and glean in the vineyards of
    the wicked.
⁷ Lacking clothes, they spend
    the night naked;
  they have nothing to cover
    themselves in the cold.
⁸ They are drenched by
    mountain rains
  and hug the rocks for lack of
    shelter.
⁹ The fatherless child is
    snatched from the
    breast;
  the infant of the poor is
    seized for a debt.
¹⁰ Lacking clothes, they go about
    naked;
  they carry the sheaves, but
    still go hungry.
¹¹ They crush olives among the
    terraces*a*;
  they tread the winepresses,
    yet suffer thirst.
¹² The groans of the dying rise
    from the city,

and the souls of the
    wounded cry out for
    help.
  But God charges no one with
    wrongdoing.

¹³ "There are those who rebel
    against the light,
  who do not know its ways
  or stay in its paths.
¹⁴ When daylight is gone, the
    murderer rises up,
  kills the poor and needy,
  and in the night steals forth
    like a thief.
¹⁵ The eye of the adulterer
    watches for dusk;
  he thinks, 'No eye will
    see me,'
  and he keeps his face
    concealed.
¹⁶ In the dark, thieves break into
    houses,
  but by day they shut
    themselves in;
  they want nothing to do with
    the light.
¹⁷ For all of them, midnight is
    their morning;
  they make friends with the
    terrors of darkness.

¹⁸ "Yet they are foam on the
    surface of the water;
  their portion of the land is
    cursed,
  so that no one goes to the
    vineyards.
¹⁹ As heat and drought snatch
    away the melted snow,
  so the grave snatches away
    those who have sinned.

a 11 The meaning of the Hebrew for this word is uncertain.

20 The womb forgets them,
  the worm feasts on them;
the wicked are no longer
    remembered
  but are broken like a tree.
21 They prey on the barren and
    childless woman,
  and to the widow they show
    no kindness.
22 But God drags away the
    mighty by his power;
  though they become
    established, they have no
    assurance of life.
23 He may let them rest in a
    feeling of security,
  but his eyes are on their
    ways.
24 For a little while they are
    exalted, and then they
    are gone;
  they are brought low and
    gathered up like all
    others;
  they are cut off like heads of
    grain.

25 "If this is not so, who can prove
    me false
  and reduce my words to
    nothing?"

Bildad

25 Then Bildad the Shuhite
    replied:

2 "Dominion and awe belong to
    God;
  he establishes order in the
    heights of heaven.

3 Can his forces be numbered?
  On whom does his light not
    rise?
4 How then can a mortal be
    righteous before God?
  How can one born of woman
    be pure?
5 If even the moon is not
    bright
  and the stars are not pure in
    his eyes,
6 how much less a mortal, who
    is but a maggot—
  a human being, who is only
    a worm!"

Job

26 Then Job replied:

2 "How you have helped the
    powerless!
  How you have saved the arm
    that is feeble!
3 What advice you have offered
    to one without wisdom!
  And what great insight you
    have displayed!
4 Who has helped you utter
    these words?
  And whose spirit spoke from
    your mouth?

5 "The dead are in deep
    anguish,
  those beneath the waters
    and all that live in
    them.
6 The realm of the dead is naked
    before God;
  Destruction[a] lies uncovered.

a 6 Hebrew *Abaddon*

⁷ He spreads out the northern
  skies over empty space;
he suspends the earth over
  nothing.
⁸ He wraps up the waters in his
  clouds,
yet the clouds do not burst
  under their weight.
⁹ He covers the face of the full
  moon,
spreading his clouds over it.
¹⁰ He marks out the horizon on
  the face of the waters
for a boundary between light
  and darkness.
¹¹ The pillars of the heavens
  quake,
aghast at his rebuke.
¹² By his power he churned up
  the sea;
by his wisdom he cut Rahab
  to pieces.
¹³ By his breath the skies became
  fair;
his hand pierced the gliding
  serpent.
¹⁴ And these are but the outer
  fringe of his works;
how faint the whisper we
  hear of him!
Who then can understand
  the thunder of his
  power?"

Job's Final Word to His Friends

27 And Job continued his
discourse:

² "As surely as God lives, who
  has denied me justice,
the Almighty, who has made
  my life bitter,

³ as long as I have life
  within me,
the breath of God in my
  nostrils,
⁴ my lips will not say anything
  wicked,
and my tongue will not utter
  lies.
⁵ I will never admit you are in
  the right;
till I die, I will not deny my
  integrity.
⁶ I will maintain my innocence
  and never let go of it;
my conscience will not
  reproach me as long as I
  live.

⁷ "May my enemy be like the
  wicked,
my adversary like the unjust!
⁸ For what hope have the
  godless when they are
  cut off,
when God takes away their
  life?
⁹ Does God listen to their cry
  when distress comes upon
  them?
¹⁰ Will they find delight in the
  Almighty?
Will they call on God at all
  times?

¹¹ "I will teach you about the
  power of God;
the ways of the Almighty I
  will not conceal.
¹² You have all seen this
  yourselves.
Why then this meaningless
  talk?

13 "Here is the fate God allots to
the wicked,
the heritage a ruthless
man receives from the
Almighty:
14 However many his children,
their fate is the sword;
his offspring will never have
enough to eat.
15 The plague will bury those
who survive him,
and their widows will not
weep for them.
16 Though he heaps up silver like
dust
and clothes like piles of
clay,
17 what he lays up the righteous
will wear,
and the innocent will divide
his silver.
18 The house he builds is like a
moth's cocoon,
like a hut made by a
watchman.
19 He lies down wealthy, but will
do so no more;
when he opens his eyes, all is
gone.
20 Terrors overtake him like a
flood;
a tempest snatches him
away in the night.
21 The east wind carries him off,
and he is gone;
it sweeps him out of his
place.
22 It hurls itself against him
without mercy
as he flees headlong from its
power.

23 It claps its hands in derision
and hisses him out of his
place."

Interlude: Where Wisdom Is Found

28 There is a mine for silver
and a place where gold is
refined.
2 Iron is taken from the earth,
and copper is smelted from
ore.
3 Mortals put an end to the
darkness;
they search out the farthest
recesses
for ore in the blackest
darkness.
4 Far from human dwellings
they cut a shaft,
in places untouched by
human feet;
far from other people they
dangle and sway.
5 The earth, from which food
comes,
is transformed below as by
fire;
6 lapis lazuli comes from its
rocks,
and its dust contains nuggets
of gold.
7 No bird of prey knows that
hidden path,
no falcon's eye has seen it.
8 Proud beasts do not set foot
on it,
and no lion prowls there.
9 People assault the flinty rock
with their hands
and lay bare the roots of the
mountains.

¹⁰They tunnel through the rock;
      their eyes see all its
         treasures.
¹¹They search*a* the sources of
         the rivers
      and bring hidden things to
         light.

¹²But where can wisdom be
         found?
      Where does understanding
         dwell?
¹³No mortal comprehends its
         worth;
      it cannot be found in the
         land of the living.
¹⁴The deep says, "It is not
         in me";
      the sea says, "It is not
         with me."
¹⁵It cannot be bought with the
         finest gold,
      nor can its price be weighed
         out in silver.
¹⁶It cannot be bought with the
         gold of Ophir,
      with precious onyx or lapis
         lazuli.
¹⁷Neither gold nor crystal can
         compare with it,
      nor can it be had for jewels of
         gold.
¹⁸Coral and jasper are not
         worthy of mention;
      the price of wisdom is
         beyond rubies.
¹⁹The topaz of Cush cannot
         compare with it;
      it cannot be bought with
         pure gold.

²⁰Where then does wisdom
         come from?
      Where does understanding
         dwell?
²¹It is hidden from the eyes of
         every living thing,
      concealed even from the
         birds in the sky.
²²Destruction*b* and Death say,
      "Only a rumor of it has
         reached our ears."
²³God understands the way to it
      and he alone knows where it
         dwells,
²⁴for he views the ends of the
         earth
      and sees everything under
         the heavens.
²⁵When he established the force
         of the wind
      and measured out the
         waters,
²⁶when he made a decree for the
         rain
      and a path for the
         thunderstorm,
²⁷then he looked at wisdom and
         appraised it;
      he confirmed it and tested it.
²⁸And he said to the human
         race,
      "The fear of the Lord — that
         is wisdom,
      and to shun evil is
         understanding."

Job's Final Defense

29 Job continued his dis-
         course:

---

a 11 Septuagint, Aquila and Vulgate; Hebrew *They dam up*   *b 22* Hebrew
Abaddon

2 "How I long for the months
    gone by,
  for the days when God
    watched over me,
3 when his lamp shone on my
    head
  and by his light I walked
    through darkness!
4 Oh, for the days when I was in
    my prime,
  when God's intimate
    friendship blessed my
    house,
5 when the Almighty was still
    with me
  and my children were
    around me,
6 when my path was drenched
    with cream
  and the rock poured out for
    me streams of olive oil.

7 "When I went to the gate of the
    city
  and took my seat in the
    public square,
8 the young men saw me and
    stepped aside
  and the old men rose to their
    feet;
9 the chief men refrained from
    speaking
  and covered their mouths
    with their hands;
10 the voices of the nobles were
    hushed,
  and their tongues stuck to
    the roof of their mouths.
11 Whoever heard me spoke well
    of me,
  and those who saw me
    commended me,

12 because I rescued the poor
    who cried for help,
  and the fatherless who had
    none to assist them.
13 The one who was dying
    blessed me;
  I made the widow's heart
    sing.
14 I put on righteousness as my
    clothing;
  justice was my robe and my
    turban.
15 I was eyes to the blind
  and feet to the lame.
16 I was a father to the needy;
  I took up the case of the
    stranger.
17 I broke the fangs of the
    wicked
  and snatched the victims
    from their teeth.

18 "I thought, 'I will die in my
    own house,
  my days as numerous as the
    grains of sand.
19 My roots will reach to the
    water,
  and the dew will lie all night
    on my branches.
20 My glory will not fade;
  the bow will be ever new in
    my hand.'

21 "People listened to me
    expectantly,
  waiting in silence for my
    counsel.
22 After I had spoken, they spoke
    no more;
  my words fell gently on their
    ears.

²³They waited for me as for
    showers
and drank in my words as
    the spring rain.
²⁴When I smiled at them, they
    scarcely believed it;
the light of my face was
    precious to them.ᵃ
²⁵I chose the way for them and
    sat as their chief;
I dwelt as a king among his
    troops;
I was like one who comforts
    mourners.

30 "But now they mock me,
    men younger than I,
whose fathers I would have
    disdained
to put with my sheep dogs.
²Of what use was the strength
    of their hands to me,
since their vigor had gone
    from them?
³Haggard from want and
    hunger,
they roamedᵇ the parched
    land
in desolate wastelands at
    night.
⁴In the brush they gathered salt
    herbs,
and their foodᶜ was the root
    of the broom bush.
⁵They were banished from
    human society,
shouted at as if they were
    thieves.
⁶They were forced to live in the
    dry stream beds,

among the rocks and in
    holes in the ground.
⁷They brayed among the
    bushes
and huddled in the
    undergrowth.
⁸A base and nameless brood,
    they were driven out of the
    land.

⁹"And now those young men
    mock me in song;
I have become a byword
    among them.
¹⁰They detest me and keep their
    distance;
they do not hesitate to spit in
    my face.
¹¹Now that God has unstrung
    my bow and afflicted me,
they throw off restraint in
    my presence.
¹²On my right the tribeᵈ attacks;
    they lay snares for my feet,
they build their siege ramps
    against me.
¹³They break up my road;
    they succeed in
    destroying me.
'No one can help him,' they
    say.
¹⁴They advance as through a
    gaping breach;
amid the ruins they come
    rolling in.
¹⁵Terrors overwhelm me;
    my dignity is driven away as
    by the wind,
my safety vanishes like a
    cloud.

ᵃ 24 The meaning of the Hebrew for this clause is uncertain.   ᵇ 3 Or gnawed
ᶜ 4 Or fuel   ᵈ 12 The meaning of the Hebrew for this word is uncertain.

16 "And now my life ebbs away;
    days of suffering grip me.
17 Night pierces my bones;
    my gnawing pains never
        rest.
18 In his great power God
        becomes like clothing
        to me*a*;
    he binds me like the neck of
        my garment.
19 He throws me into the mud,
    and I am reduced to dust
        and ashes.

20 "I cry out to you, God, but you
        do not answer;
    I stand up, but you merely
        look at me.
21 You turn on me ruthlessly;
    with the might of your hand
        you attack me.
22 You snatch me up and drive
        me before the wind;
    you toss me about in the
        storm.
23 I know you will bring me down
        to death,
    to the place appointed for all
        the living.

24 "Surely no one lays a hand on
        a broken man
    when he cries for help in his
        distress.
25 Have I not wept for those in
        trouble?
    Has not my soul grieved for
        the poor?
26 Yet when I hoped for good, evil
        came;
    when I looked for light, then
        came darkness.

27 The churning inside me never
        stops;
    days of suffering
        confront me.
28 I go about blackened, but not
        by the sun;
    I stand up in the assembly
        and cry for help.
29 I have become a brother of
        jackals,
    a companion of owls.
30 My skin grows black and
        peels;
    my body burns with
        fever.
31 My lyre is tuned to mourning,
    and my pipe to the sound of
        wailing.

31 "I made a covenant with
    my eyes
    not to look lustfully at a
        young woman.
2 For what is our lot from God
        above,
    our heritage from the
        Almighty on high?
3 Is it not ruin for the wicked,
    disaster for those who do
        wrong?
4 Does he not see my ways
    and count my every step?

5 "If I have walked with
        falsehood
    or my foot has hurried after
        deceit —
6 let God weigh me in honest
        scales
    and he will know that I am
        blameless —

a 18 Hebrew; Septuagint *power he grasps my clothing*

⁷if my steps have turned from
the path,
if my heart has been led by
my eyes,
or if my hands have been
defiled,
⁸then may others eat what I
have sown,
and may my crops be
uprooted.

⁹"If my heart has been enticed
by a woman,
or if I have lurked at my
neighbor's door,
¹⁰then may my wife grind
another man's grain,
and may other men sleep
with her.
¹¹For that would have been
wicked,
a sin to be judged.
¹²It is a fire that burns to
Destruction*ᵃ*;
it would have uprooted my
harvest.

¹³"If I have denied justice to any
of my servants,
whether male or female,
when they had a grievance
against me,
¹⁴what will I do when God
confronts me?
What will I answer when
called to account?
¹⁵Did not he who made me in
the womb make them?
Did not the same one form
us both within our
mothers?

¹⁶"If I have denied the desires of
the poor
or let the eyes of the widow
grow weary,
¹⁷if I have kept my bread to
myself,
not sharing it with the
fatherless—
¹⁸but from my youth I reared
them as a father would,
and from my birth I guided
the widow—
¹⁹if I have seen anyone perishing
for lack of clothing,
or the needy without
garments,
²⁰and their hearts did not
bless me
for warming them with the
fleece from my sheep,
²¹if I have raised my hand
against the fatherless,
knowing that I had influence
in court,
²²then let my arm fall from the
shoulder,
let it be broken off at the
joint.
²³For I dreaded destruction from
God,
and for fear of his splendor I
could not do such things.

²⁴"If I have put my trust in gold
or said to pure gold, 'You are
my security,'
²⁵if I have rejoiced over my great
wealth,
the fortune my hands had
gained,

ᵃ 12 Hebrew *Abaddon*

²⁶if I have regarded the sun in its
radiance
or the moon moving in
splendor,
²⁷so that my heart was secretly
enticed
and my hand offered them a
kiss of homage,
²⁸then these also would be sins
to be judged,
for I would have been
unfaithful to God on
high.

²⁹"If I have rejoiced at my
enemy's misfortune
or gloated over the trouble
that came to him —
³⁰I have not allowed my mouth
to sin
by invoking a curse against
their life —
³¹if those of my household have
never said,
'Who has not been filled
with Job's meat?' —
³²but no stranger had to spend
the night in the street,
for my door was always open
to the traveler —
³³if I have concealed my sin as
people do,ᵃ
by hiding my guilt in my
heart
³⁴because I so feared the
crowd
and so dreaded the
contempt of the clans
that I kept silent and would
not go outside —

³⁵("Oh, that I had someone to
hear me!
I sign now my defense — let
the Almighty answer me;
let my accuser put his
indictment in writing.
³⁶Surely I would wear it on my
shoulder,
I would put it on like a
crown.
³⁷I would give him an account of
my every step;
I would present it to him as
to a ruler.) —

³⁸"if my land cries out against me
and all its furrows are wet
with tears,
³⁹if I have devoured its yield
without payment
or broken the spirit of its
tenants,
⁴⁰then let briers come up instead
of wheat
and stinkweed instead of
barley."
The words of Job are ended.

Elihu

32 So these three men
stopped answering Job,
because he was righteous in his
own eyes. ²But Elihu son of Barakel the Buzite, of the family of
Ram, became very angry with
Job for justifying himself rather than God. ³He was also angry
with the three friends, because
they had found no way to refute
Job, and yet had condemned

ᵃ 33 Or *as Adam did*

him.[a] [4] Now Elihu had waited before speaking to Job because they were older than he. [5] But when he saw that the three men had nothing more to say, his anger was aroused.

[6] So Elihu son of Barakel the Buzite said:

"I am young in years,
    and you are old;
that is why I was fearful,
    not daring to tell you what I
        know.
[7] I thought, 'Age should speak;
    advanced years should teach
        wisdom.'
[8] But it is the spirit[b] in a person,
    the breath of the Almighty,
        that gives them
            understanding.
[9] It is not only the old[c] who are
        wise,
    not only the aged who
        understand what is right.

[10] "Therefore I say: Listen to me;
    I too will tell you what I
        know.
[11] I waited while you spoke,
    I listened to your reasoning;
    while you were searching for
        words,
[12] I gave you my full attention.
    But not one of you has proved
        Job wrong;
    none of you has answered
        his arguments.
[13] Do not say, 'We have found
        wisdom;

let God, not a man, refute
        him.'
[14] But Job has not marshaled his
        words against me,
    and I will not answer him
        with your arguments.

[15] "They are dismayed and have
        no more to say;
    words have failed them.
[16] Must I wait, now that they are
        silent,
    now that they stand there
        with no reply?
[17] I too will have my say;
    I too will tell what I know.
[18] For I am full of words,
    and the spirit within me
        compels me;
[19] inside I am like bottled-up
        wine,
    like new wineskins ready to
        burst.
[20] I must speak and find relief;
    I must open my lips and
        reply.
[21] I will show no partiality,
    nor will I flatter anyone;
[22] for if I were skilled in
        flattery,
    my Maker would soon take
        me away.

33 "But now, Job, listen to
    my words;
    pay attention to everything I
        say.
[2] I am about to open my mouth;
    my words are on the tip of
        my tongue.

---

[a] 3 Masoretic Text; an ancient Hebrew scribal tradition *Job, and so had condemned God*   [b] 8 Or *Spirit*; also in verse 18   [c] 9 Or *many*; or *great*

³My words come from an
  upright heart;
    my lips sincerely speak what
      I know.
⁴The Spirit of God has
  made me;
    the breath of the Almighty
      gives me life.
⁵Answer me then, if you can;
  stand up and argue your
    case before me.
⁶I am the same as you in God's
  sight;
    I too am a piece of clay.
⁷No fear of me should alarm
  you,
    nor should my hand be
      heavy on you.

⁸"But you have said in my
  hearing —
    I heard the very words —
⁹'I am pure, I have done no
  wrong;
    I am clean and free from
      sin.
¹⁰Yet God has found fault
  with me;
    he considers me his enemy.
¹¹He fastens my feet in shackles;
  he keeps close watch on all
    my paths.'

¹²"But I tell you, in this you are
  not right,
    for God is greater than any
      mortal.
¹³Why do you complain to him
  that he responds to no one's
    words*a*?

¹⁴For God does speak — now one
  way, now another —
    though no one perceives it.
¹⁵In a dream, in a vision of the
  night,
    when deep sleep falls on
      people
        as they slumber in their
          beds,
¹⁶he may speak in their ears
  and terrify them with
    warnings,
¹⁷to turn them from wrongdoing
  and keep them from pride,
¹⁸to preserve them from the pit,
  their lives from perishing by
    the sword.*b*

¹⁹"Or someone may be
  chastened on a bed of
    pain
      with constant distress in
        their bones,
²⁰so that their body finds food
  repulsive
    and their soul loathes the
      choicest meal.
²¹Their flesh wastes away to
  nothing,
    and their bones, once
      hidden, now stick out.
²²They draw near to the pit,
  and their life to the
    messengers of death.*c*
²³Yet if there is an angel at their
  side,
    a messenger, one out of a
      thousand,
        sent to tell them how to be
          upright,

---

a 13 Or *that he does not answer for any of his actions*   *b* 18 Or *from crossing the river*   *c* 22 Or *to the place of the dead*

24and he is gracious to that
    person and says to God,
  'Spare them from going
    down to the pit;
  I have found a ransom for
    them —
25let their flesh be renewed like
    a child's;
  let them be restored as in the
    days of their youth' —
26then that person can pray to
    God and find favor with
    him,
  they will see God's face and
    shout for joy;
  he will restore them to full
    well-being.
27And they will go to others and
    say,
  'I have sinned, I have
    perverted what is right,
  but I did not get what I
    deserved.
28God has delivered me from
    going down to the pit,
  and I shall live to enjoy the
    light of life.'

29"God does all these things to a
    person —
  twice, even three times —
30to turn them back from the pit,
  that the light of life may
    shine on them.

31"Pay attention, Job, and listen
    to me;
  be silent, and I will speak.
32If you have anything to say,
    answer me;
  speak up, for I want to
    vindicate you.

33But if not, then listen to me;
  be silent, and I will teach you
    wisdom."

34 Then Elihu said:

2"Hear my words, you wise
    men;
  listen to me, you men of
    learning.
3For the ear tests words
  as the tongue tastes food.
4Let us discern for ourselves
    what is right;
  let us learn together what is
    good.

5"Job says, 'I am innocent,
  but God denies me justice.
6Although I am right,
  I am considered a liar;
  although I am guiltless,
    his arrow inflicts an
    incurable wound.'
7Is there anyone like Job,
  who drinks scorn like water?
8He keeps company with
    evildoers;
  he associates with the
    wicked.
9For he says, 'There is no profit
  in trying to please God.'

10"So listen to me, you men of
    understanding.
  Far be it from God to do evil,
  from the Almighty to do
    wrong.
11He repays everyone for what
    they have done;
  he brings on them what their
    conduct deserves.

¹²It is unthinkable that God
would do wrong,
that the Almighty would
pervert justice.
¹³Who appointed him over the
earth?
Who put him in charge of
the whole world?
¹⁴If it were his intention
and he withdrew his spirit*a*
and breath,
¹⁵all humanity would perish
together
and mankind would return
to the dust.

¹⁶"If you have understanding,
hear this;
listen to what I say.
¹⁷Can someone who hates
justice govern?
Will you condemn the just
and mighty One?
¹⁸Is he not the One who says
to kings, 'You are
worthless,'
and to nobles, 'You are
wicked,'
¹⁹who shows no partiality to
princes
and does not favor the rich
over the poor,
for they are all the work of
his hands?
²⁰They die in an instant, in the
middle of the night;
the people are shaken and
they pass away;
the mighty are removed
without human hand.

²¹"His eyes are on the ways of
mortals;
he sees their every step.
²²There is no deep shadow, no
utter darkness,
where evildoers can hide.
²³God has no need to examine
people further,
that they should come before
him for judgment.
²⁴Without inquiry he shatters
the mighty
and sets up others in their
place.
²⁵Because he takes note of their
deeds,
he overthrows them in
the night and they are
crushed.
²⁶He punishes them for their
wickedness
where everyone can see them,
²⁷because they turned from
following him
and had no regard for any of
his ways.
²⁸They caused the cry of the
poor to come before him,
so that he heard the cry of
the needy.
²⁹But if he remains silent, who
can condemn him?
If he hides his face, who can
see him?
Yet he is over individual and
nation alike,
³⁰   to keep the godless from
ruling,
from laying snares for the
people.

a 14 Or *Spirit*

³¹ "Suppose someone says to God,
    'I am guilty but will offend
        no more.
³² Teach me what I cannot see;
    if I have done wrong, I will
        not do so again.'
³³ Should God then reward you
        on your terms,
    when you refuse to repent?
    You must decide, not I;
        so tell me what you know.

³⁴ "Men of understanding
        declare,
    wise men who hear me say
        to me,
³⁵ 'Job speaks without
        knowledge;
    his words lack insight.'
³⁶ Oh, that Job might be tested to
        the utmost
    for answering like a wicked
        man!
³⁷ To his sin he adds rebellion;
    scornfully he claps his hands
        among us
    and multiplies his words
        against God."

35

Then Elihu said:

² "Do you think this is just?
    You say, 'I am in the right,
        not God.'
³ Yet you ask him, 'What profit is
        it to me,ᵃ
    and what do I gain by not
        sinning?'

⁴ "I would like to reply to you
    and to your friends with you.

⁵ Look up at the heavens and
        see;
    gaze at the clouds so high
        above you.
⁶ If you sin, how does that affect
        him?
    If your sins are many, what
        does that do to him?
⁷ If you are righteous, what do
        you give to him,
    or what does he receive from
        your hand?
⁸ Your wickedness only affects
        humans like yourself,
    and your righteousness only
        other people.

⁹ "People cry out under a load of
        oppression;
    they plead for relief from the
        arm of the powerful.
¹⁰ But no one says, 'Where is God
        my Maker,
    who gives songs in the night,
¹¹ who teaches us more than he
        teachesᵇ the beasts of the
            earth
    and makes us wiser thanᶜ
        the birds in the sky?'
¹² He does not answer when
        people cry out
    because of the arrogance of
        the wicked.
¹³ Indeed, God does not listen to
        their empty plea;
    the Almighty pays no
        attention to it.
¹⁴ How much less, then, will he
        listen
    when you say that you do not
        see him,

that your case is before him
and you must wait for him,
¹⁵ and further, that his anger
never punishes
and he does not take
the least notice of
wickedness.ᵃ
¹⁶ So Job opens his mouth with
empty talk;
without knowledge he
multiplies words."

36 Elihu continued:
² "Bear with me a little longer
and I will show you
that there is more to be said
in God's behalf.
³ I get my knowledge from
afar;
I will ascribe justice to my
Maker.
⁴ Be assured that my words are
not false;
one who has perfect
knowledge is with you.

⁵ "God is mighty, but despises
no one;
he is mighty, and firm in his
purpose.
⁶ He does not keep the wicked
alive
but gives the afflicted their
rights.
⁷ He does not take his eyes off
the righteous;
he enthrones them with
kings
and exalts them forever.

⁸ But if people are bound in
chains,
held fast by cords of
affliction,
⁹ he tells them what they have
done —
that they have sinned
arrogantly.
¹⁰ He makes them listen to
correction
and commands them to
repent of their evil.
¹¹ If they obey and serve him,
they will spend the rest of
their days in prosperity
and their years in
contentment.
¹² But if they do not listen,
they will perish by the swordᵇ
and die without knowledge.

¹³ "The godless in heart harbor
resentment;
even when he fetters them,
they do not cry for help.
¹⁴ They die in their youth,
among male prostitutes of
the shrines.
¹⁵ But those who suffer he
delivers in their
suffering;
he speaks to them in their
affliction.

¹⁶ "He is wooing you from the
jaws of distress
to a spacious place free from
restriction,
to the comfort of your table
laden with choice food.

ᵃ 15 Symmachus, Theodotion and Vulgate; the meaning of the Hebrew for this word is uncertain.   ᵇ 12 Or *will cross the river*

¹⁷But now you are laden with
the judgment due the
wicked;
judgment and justice have
taken hold of you.
¹⁸Be careful that no one entices
you by riches;
do not let a large bribe turn
you aside.
¹⁹Would your wealth or even all
your mighty efforts
sustain you so you would not
be in distress?
²⁰Do not long for the night,
to drag people away from
their homes.^a
²¹Beware of turning to evil,
which you seem to prefer to
affliction.

²² "God is exalted in his power.
Who is a teacher like him?
²³Who has prescribed his ways
for him,
or said to him, 'You have
done wrong'?
²⁴Remember to extol his work,
which people have praised
in song.
²⁵All humanity has seen it;
mortals gaze on it from afar.
²⁶How great is God — beyond
our understanding!
The number of his years is
past finding out.

²⁷ "He draws up the drops of
water,
which distill as rain to the
streams^b;

²⁸the clouds pour down their
moisture
and abundant showers fall
on mankind.
²⁹Who can understand how he
spreads out the clouds,
how he thunders from his
pavilion?
³⁰See how he scatters his
lightning about him,
bathing the depths of the
sea.
³¹This is the way he governs^c the
nations
and provides food in
abundance.
³²He fills his hands with lightning
and commands it to strike its
mark.
³³His thunder announces the
coming storm;
even the cattle make known
its approach.^d

37

"At this my heart pounds
and leaps from its place.
²Listen! Listen to the roar of his
voice,
to the rumbling that comes
from his mouth.
³He unleashes his lightning
beneath the whole
heaven
and sends it to the ends of
the earth.
⁴After that comes the sound of
his roar;
he thunders with his
majestic voice.

---

^a 20 The meaning of the Hebrew for verses 18-20 is uncertain.   ^b 27 Or distill
from the mist as rain   ^c 31 Or nourishes   ^d 33 Or announces his coming — /
the One zealous against evil

When his voice resounds,
  he holds nothing back.
⁵God's voice thunders in
    marvelous ways;
  he does great things beyond
    our understanding.
⁶He says to the snow, 'Fall on
    the earth,'
  and to the rain shower, 'Be a
    mighty downpour.'
⁷So that everyone he has made
    may know his work,
  he stops all people from their
    labor.ᵃ
⁸The animals take cover;
  they remain in their dens.
⁹The tempest comes out from
    its chamber,
  the cold from the driving
    winds.
¹⁰The breath of God produces ice,
  and the broad waters
    become frozen.
¹¹He loads the clouds with
    moisture;
  he scatters his lightning
    through them.
¹²At his direction they swirl
    around
  over the face of the whole
    earth
  to do whatever he
    commands them.
¹³He brings the clouds to punish
    people,
  or to water his earth and
    show his love.

¹⁴"Listen to this, Job;
  stop and consider God's
    wonders.
¹⁵Do you know how God
    controls the clouds
  and makes his lightning
    flash?
¹⁶Do you know how the clouds
    hang poised,
  those wonders of him who
    has perfect knowledge?
¹⁷You who swelter in your
    clothes
  when the land lies hushed
    under the south wind,
¹⁸can you join him in spreading
    out the skies,
  hard as a mirror of cast
    bronze?

¹⁹"Tell us what we should say to
    him;
  we cannot draw up our case
    because of our darkness.
²⁰Should he be told that I want
    to speak?
  Would anyone ask to be
    swallowed up?
²¹Now no one can look at the
    sun,
  bright as it is in the skies
  after the wind has swept
    them clean.
²²Out of the north he comes in
    golden splendor;
  God comes in awesome
    majesty.
²³The Almighty is beyond our
    reach and exalted in
    power;
  in his justice and great
    righteousness, he does
    not oppress.

ᵃ 7 Or *work, / he fills all people with fear by his power*

²⁴Therefore, people revere him,
  for does he not have regard
    for all the wise in
    heart?ᵃ"

The LORD Speaks

38 Then the LORD spoke to
Job out of the storm. He
said:

²"Who is this that obscures my
    plans
  with words without
    knowledge?
³Brace yourself like a man;
  I will question you,
  and you shall answer me.

⁴"Where were you when I laid
    the earth's foundation?
  Tell me, if you understand.
⁵Who marked off its
    dimensions? Surely you
    know!
  Who stretched a measuring
    line across it?
⁶On what were its footings set,
  or who laid its cornerstone —
⁷while the morning stars sang
    together
  and all the angelsᵇ shouted
    for joy?

⁸"Who shut up the sea behind
    doors
  when it burst forth from the
    womb,
⁹when I made the clouds its
    garment
  and wrapped it in thick
    darkness,

¹⁰when I fixed limits for it
  and set its doors and bars in
    place,
¹¹when I said, 'This far you may
    come and no farther;
  here is where your proud
    waves halt'?

¹²"Have you ever given orders to
    the morning,
  or shown the dawn its place,
¹³that it might take the earth by
    the edges
  and shake the wicked out
    of it?
¹⁴The earth takes shape like clay
    under a seal;
  its features stand out like
    those of a garment.
¹⁵The wicked are denied their
    light,
  and their upraised arm is
    broken.

¹⁶"Have you journeyed to the
    springs of the sea
  or walked in the recesses of
    the deep?
¹⁷Have the gates of death been
    shown to you?
  Have you seen the gates of
    the deepest darkness?
¹⁸Have you comprehended the
    vast expanses of the
    earth?
  Tell me, if you know all this.

¹⁹"What is the way to the abode
    of light?
  And where does darkness
    reside?

ᵃ 24 Or *for he does not have regard for any who think they are wise.*   ᵇ 7 Hebrew
the sons of God

²⁰Can you take them to their
places?
Do you know the paths to
their dwellings?
²¹Surely you know, for you were
already born!
You have lived so many years!

²²"Have you entered the
storehouses of the snow
or seen the storehouses of
the hail,
²³which I reserve for times of
trouble,
for days of war and battle?
²⁴What is the way to the place
where the lightning is
dispersed,
or the place where the east
winds are scattered over
the earth?
²⁵Who cuts a channel for the
torrents of rain,
and a path for the
thunderstorm,
²⁶to water a land where no one
lives,
an uninhabited desert,
²⁷to satisfy a desolate wasteland
and make it sprout with
grass?
²⁸Does the rain have a father?
Who fathers the drops of
dew?
²⁹From whose womb comes the
ice?
Who gives birth to the frost
from the heavens

³⁰when the waters become hard
as stone,
when the surface of the deep
is frozen?
³¹"Can you bind the chains[a] of
the Pleiades?
Can you loosen Orion's
belt?
³²Can you bring forth the
constellations in their
seasons[b]
or lead out the Bear[c] with its
cubs?
³³Do you know the laws of the
heavens?
Can you set up God's[d]
dominion over the
earth?
³⁴"Can you raise your voice to
the clouds
and cover yourself with a
flood of water?
³⁵Do you send the lightning
bolts on their way?
Do they report to you, 'Here
we are'?
³⁶Who gives the ibis wisdom[e]
or gives the rooster
understanding?[f]
³⁷Who has the wisdom to count
the clouds?
Who can tip over the water
jars of the heavens
³⁸when the dust becomes
hard
and the clods of earth stick
together?

---

[a] 31 Septuagint; Hebrew *beauty*   [b] 32 Or *the morning star in its season*
[c] 32 Or *out Leo*   [d] 33 Or *their*   [e] 36 That is, wisdom about the flooding of the
Nile   [f] 36 That is, understanding of when to crow; the meaning of the Hebrew
for this verse is uncertain.

³⁹"Do you hunt the prey for the
   lioness
   and satisfy the hunger of the
      lions
⁴⁰when they crouch in their dens
   or lie in wait in a thicket?
⁴¹Who provides food for the
   raven
   when its young cry out to
      God
   and wander about for lack of
      food?

39

"Do you know when the
mountain goats give
birth?
   Do you watch when the doe
      bears her fawn?
²Do you count the months till
   they bear?
   Do you know the time they
      give birth?
³They crouch down and bring
   forth their young;
   their labor pains are ended.
⁴Their young thrive and grow
   strong in the wilds;
   they leave and do not return.

⁵"Who let the wild donkey go
   free?
   Who untied its ropes?
⁶I gave it the wasteland as its
   home,
   the salt flats as its habitat.
⁷It laughs at the commotion in
   the town;
   it does not hear a driver's
      shout.
⁸It ranges the hills for its
   pasture
   and searches for any green
      thing.

⁹"Will the wild ox consent to
   serve you?
   Will it stay by your manger at
      night?
¹⁰Can you hold it to the furrow
   with a harness?
   Will it till the valleys behind
      you?
¹¹Will you rely on it for its great
   strength?
   Will you leave your heavy
      work to it?
¹²Can you trust it to haul in your
   grain
   and bring it to your
      threshing floor?

¹³"The wings of the ostrich flap
   joyfully,
   though they cannot compare
   with the wings and feathers
      of the stork.
¹⁴She lays her eggs on the
   ground
   and lets them warm in the
      sand,
¹⁵unmindful that a foot may
   crush them,
   that some wild animal may
      trample them.
¹⁶She treats her young harshly,
   as if they were not hers;
   she cares not that her labor
      was in vain,
¹⁷for God did not endow her
   with wisdom
   or give her a share of good
      sense.
¹⁸Yet when she spreads her
   feathers to run,
   she laughs at horse and
      rider.

19 "Do you give the horse its
strength
    or clothe its neck with a
    flowing mane?
20 Do you make it leap like a
locust,
    striking terror with its proud
    snorting?
21 It paws fiercely, rejoicing in its
strength,
    and charges into the fray.
22 It laughs at fear, afraid of
nothing;
    it does not shy away from the
    sword.
23 The quiver rattles against its
side,
    along with the flashing spear
    and lance.
24 In frenzied excitement it eats
up the ground;
    it cannot stand still when the
    trumpet sounds.
25 At the blast of the trumpet it
snorts, 'Aha!'
    It catches the scent of battle
    from afar,
    the shout of commanders
    and the battle cry.

26 "Does the hawk take flight by
your wisdom
    and spread its wings toward
    the south?
27 Does the eagle soar at your
command
    and build its nest on high?
28 It dwells on a cliff and stays
there at night;
    a rocky crag is its stronghold.
29 From there it looks for food;
    its eyes detect it from afar.

30 Its young ones feast on blood,
    and where the slain are,
    there it is."

40

The LORD said to Job:

2 "Will the one who contends
    with the Almighty
    correct him?
    Let him who accuses God
    answer him!"

3 Then Job answered the LORD:

4 "I am unworthy — how can I
reply to you?
    I put my hand over my
    mouth.
5 I spoke once, but I have no
answer —
    twice, but I will say no
    more."

6 Then the LORD spoke to Job
out of the storm:

7 "Brace yourself like a man;
    I will question you,
    and you shall answer me.

8 "Would you discredit my
justice?
    Would you condemn me to
    justify yourself?
9 Do you have an arm like God's,
    and can your voice thunder
    like his?
10 Then adorn yourself with glory
and splendor,
    and clothe yourself in honor
    and majesty.
11 Unleash the fury of your
wrath,
    look at all who are proud and
    bring them low,

¹²look at all who are proud and
    humble them,
  crush the wicked where they
    stand.
¹³Bury them all in the dust
    together;
  shroud their faces in the
    grave.
¹⁴Then I myself will admit to you
  that your own right hand
    can save you.

¹⁵"Look at Behemoth,
  which I made along with you
  and which feeds on grass
    like an ox.
¹⁶What strength it has in its
    loins,
  what power in the muscles of
    its belly!
¹⁷Its tail sways like a cedar;
  the sinews of its thighs are
    close-knit.
¹⁸Its bones are tubes of bronze,
  its limbs like rods of iron.
¹⁹It ranks first among the works
    of God,
  yet its Maker can approach it
    with his sword.
²⁰The hills bring it their
    produce,
  and all the wild animals play
    nearby.
²¹Under the lotus plants it lies,
  hidden among the reeds in
    the marsh.
²²The lotuses conceal it in their
    shadow;
  the poplars by the stream
    surround it.

²³A raging river does not
    alarm it;
  it is secure, though the
    Jordan should surge
    against its mouth.
²⁴Can anyone capture it by the
    eyes,
  or trap it and pierce its nose?

41 ᵃ "Can you pull in
      Leviathan with a
      fishhook
  or tie down its tongue with a
    rope?
²Can you put a cord through its
    nose
  or pierce its jaw with a hook?
³Will it keep begging you for
    mercy?
  Will it speak to you with
    gentle words?
⁴Will it make an agreement
    with you
  for you to take it as your
    slave for life?
⁵Can you make a pet of it like a
    bird
  or put it on a leash for the
    young women in your
    house?
⁶Will traders barter for it?
  Will they divide it up among
    the merchants?
⁷Can you fill its hide with
    harpoons
  or its head with fishing
    spears?
⁸If you lay a hand on it,
  you will remember the
    struggle and never do it
    again!

ᵃ In Hebrew texts 41:1-8 is numbered 40:25-32, and 41:9-34 is numbered 41:1-26.

⁹Any hope of subduing it is
    false;
  the mere sight of it is
    overpowering.
¹⁰No one is fierce enough to
    rouse it.
  Who then is able to stand
    against me?
¹¹Who has a claim against me
    that I must pay?
  Everything under heaven
    belongs to me.

¹²"I will not fail to speak of
    Leviathan's limbs,
  its strength and its graceful
    form.
¹³Who can strip off its outer
    coat?
  Who can penetrate its
    double coat of armor*?
¹⁴Who dares open the doors of
    its mouth,
  ringed about with fearsome
    teeth?
¹⁵Its back has* rows of shields
    tightly sealed together;
¹⁶each is so close to the next
    that no air can pass
      between.
¹⁷They are joined fast to one
    another;
  they cling together and
    cannot be parted.
¹⁸Its snorting throws out flashes
    of light;
  its eyes are like the rays of
    dawn.
¹⁹Flames stream from its mouth;
  sparks of fire shoot out.

²⁰Smoke pours from its nostrils
  as from a boiling pot over
    burning reeds.
²¹Its breath sets coals ablaze,
  and flames dart from its
    mouth.
²²Strength resides in its neck;
  dismay goes before it.
²³The folds of its flesh are tightly
    joined;
  they are firm and
    immovable.
²⁴Its chest is hard as rock,
  hard as a lower millstone.
²⁵When it rises up, the mighty
    are terrified;
  they retreat before its
    thrashing.
²⁶The sword that reaches it has
    no effect,
  nor does the spear or the
    dart or the javelin.
²⁷Iron it treats like straw
  and bronze like rotten
    wood.
²⁸Arrows do not make it flee;
  slingstones are like chaff
    to it.
²⁹A club seems to it but a piece
    of straw;
  it laughs at the rattling of the
    lance.
³⁰Its undersides are jagged
    potsherds,
  leaving a trail in the mud
    like a threshing sledge.
³¹It makes the depths churn like
    a boiling caldron
  and stirs up the sea like a pot
    of ointment.

---

a 13 Septuagint; Hebrew *double bridle*   *b* 15 Or *Its pride is its*

³² It leaves a glistening wake
   behind it;
   one would think the deep
   had white hair.
³³ Nothing on earth is its equal —
   a creature without fear.
³⁴ It looks down on all that are
   haughty;
   it is king over all that are
   proud."

Job

42 Then Job replied to the
   LORD:

² "I know that you can do all
   things;
   no purpose of yours can be
   thwarted.
³ You asked, 'Who is this that
   obscures my plans
   without knowledge?'
   Surely I spoke of things I did
   not understand,
   things too wonderful for me
   to know.

⁴ "You said, 'Listen now, and I
   will speak;
   I will question you,
   and you shall answer me.'
⁵ My ears had heard of you
   but now my eyes have seen
   you.
⁶ Therefore I despise myself
   and repent in dust and ashes."

Epilogue

⁷ After the LORD had said these
things to Job, he said to Eliphaz
the Temanite, "I am angry with
you and your two friends, because you have not spoken the
truth about me, as my servant
Job has. ⁸ So now take seven bulls
and seven rams and go to my servant Job and sacrifice a burnt offering for yourselves. My servant
Job will pray for you, and I will
accept his prayer and not deal
with you according to your folly. You have not spoken the truth
about me, as my servant Job has."
⁹ So Eliphaz the Temanite, Bildad
the Shuhite and Zophar the Naamathite did what the LORD told
them; and the LORD accepted
Job's prayer.

¹⁰ After Job had prayed for his
friends, the LORD restored his
fortunes and gave him twice as
much as he had before. ¹¹ All his
brothers and sisters and everyone who had known him before
came and ate with him in his
house. They comforted and consoled him over all the trouble the
LORD had brought on him, and
each one gave him a piece of sil-
verᵃ and a gold ring.

¹² The LORD blessed the latter
part of Job's life more than the
former part. He had fourteen
thousand sheep, six thousand
camels, a thousand yoke of oxen
and a thousand donkeys. ¹³ And
he also had seven sons and three
daughters. ¹⁴ The first daughter
he named Jemimah, the second

ᵃ 11 Hebrew *him a kesitah*; a kesitah was a unit of money of unknown weight and
value.

Keziah and the third Keren-Happuch. ¹⁵Nowhere in all the land were there found women as beautiful as Job's daughters, and their father granted them an inheritance along with their brothers.

¹⁶After this, Job lived a hundred and forty years; he saw his children and their children to the fourth generation. ¹⁷And so Job died, an old man and full of years.

Psalms

Introduction:

The Psalms are poems or songs of praise, worship, thankfulness and repentance. They show a variety of emotions, attitudes and interests, and vary in length from a few verses (Psalm 117) to many parts with 176 verses (Psalm 119). Hebrew poetry often uses pairs of lines. The second line either repeats the thought of the first or gives an opposite. Look for these pairs of lines as you read the Psalms.

Of the 150 Psalms, one hundred of them are thought to be written by the following authors: David — 73; Asaph — 12; Sons of Korah — 10; Moses — 1; Heman the Ezrahite — 1; Ethan the Ezrahite — 1; and one or two by Solomon. The rest of the Psalms have no recorded author.

These poems have a world-wide appeal and are familiar and loved by many people because they were written by many authors, from different time periods, and show a variety of emotions.

Outline of contents:

Book I: Psalms 1–41
Book II: Psalms 42–72
Book III: Psalms 73–89
Book IV: Psalms 90–106
Book V: Psalms 107–150

BOOK I

Psalms 1–41

Psalm 1

¹ Blessed is the one
     who does not walk in step
          with the wicked
     or stand in the way that
          sinners take
     or sit in the company of
          mockers,
² but whose delight is in the law
          of the LORD,
     and who meditates on his
          law day and night.
³ That person is like a tree
          planted by streams of
               water,
     which yields its fruit in
          season
     and whose leaf does not
          wither —
     whatever they do
          prospers.

4 Not so the wicked!
  They are like chaff
    that the wind blows away.
5 Therefore the wicked will not
    stand in the judgment,
  nor sinners in the assembly
    of the righteous.

6 For the LORD watches over the
    way of the righteous,
  but the way of the wicked
    leads to destruction.

Psalm 2

1 Why do the nations conspire[a]
  and the peoples plot in vain?
2 The kings of the earth rise up
  and the rulers band together
    against the LORD and
    against his anointed,
    saying,
3 "Let us break their chains
  and throw off their shackles."

4 The One enthroned in heaven
    laughs;
  the Lord scoffs at them.
5 He rebukes them in his anger
  and terrifies them in his
    wrath, saying,
6 "I have installed my king
  on Zion, my holy mountain."

7 I will proclaim the LORD's decree:

He said to me, "You are my son;
  today I have become your
    father.

8 Ask me,
  and I will make the nations
    your inheritance,
  the ends of the earth your
    possession.
9 You will break them with a rod
    of iron[b];
  you will dash them to pieces
    like pottery."

10 Therefore, you kings, be wise;
  be warned, you rulers of the
    earth.
11 Serve the LORD with fear
  and celebrate his rule with
    trembling.
12 Kiss his son, or he will be
    angry
  and your way will lead to
    your destruction,
  for his wrath can flare up in a
    moment.
  Blessed are all who take
    refuge in him.

Psalm 3[c]

*A psalm of David. When he fled
  from his son Absalom.*

1 LORD, how many are my foes!
  How many rise up against me!
2 Many are saying of me,
  "God will not deliver him."[d]

3 But you, LORD, are a shield
    around me,
  my glory, the One who lifts
    my head high.

---

[a] 1 Hebrew; Septuagint *rage*   [b] 9 Or *will rule them with an iron scepter* (see
Septuagint and Syriac)   [c] In Hebrew texts 3:1-8 is numbered 3:2-9.   [d] 2 The
Hebrew has *Selah* (a word of uncertain meaning) here and at the end of verses 4
and 8.

⁴I call out to the LORD,
  and he answers me from his
    holy mountain.

⁵I lie down and sleep;
  I wake again, because the
    LORD sustains me.
⁶I will not fear though tens of
    thousands
  assail me on every side.

⁷Arise, LORD!
  Deliver me, my God!
Strike all my enemies on the
    jaw;
  break the teeth of the wicked.

⁸From the LORD comes
    deliverance.
  May your blessing be on
    your people.

Psalm 4[a]

For the director of music.
With stringed instruments.
A psalm of David.

¹Answer me when I call to you,
  my righteous God.
Give me relief from my distress;
  have mercy on me and hear
    my prayer.

²How long will you people turn
    my glory into shame?
How long will you love
    delusions and seek false
    gods[b]?[c]
³Know that the LORD has set
    apart his faithful servant
    for himself;

the LORD hears when I call
  to him.

⁴Tremble and[d] do not sin;
  when you are on your
    beds,
  search your hearts and be
    silent.
⁵Offer the sacrifices of the
    righteous
  and trust in the LORD.

⁶Many, LORD, are asking, "Who
    will bring us prosperity?"
  Let the light of your face
    shine on us.
⁷Fill my heart with joy
  when their grain and new
    wine abound.

⁸In peace I will lie down and
    sleep,
  for you alone, LORD,
  make me dwell in safety.

Psalm 5[e]

For the director of music.
For pipes. A psalm of David.

¹Listen to my words, LORD,
  consider my lament.
²Hear my cry for help,
  my King and my God,
  for to you I pray.

³In the morning, LORD, you
    hear my voice;
  in the morning I lay my
    requests before you
  and wait expectantly.

---

[a] In Hebrew texts 4:1-8 is numbered 4:2-9.   [b] 2 Or *seek lies*   [c] 2 The Hebrew has *Selah* (a word of uncertain meaning) here and at the end of verse 4.   [d] 4 Or *In your anger* (see Septuagint)   [e] In Hebrew texts 5:1-12 is numbered 5:2-13.

⁴For you are not a God
who is pleased with
wickedness;
with you, evil people are not
welcome.
⁵The arrogant cannot stand
in your presence.
You hate all who do wrong;
⁶ you destroy those who tell
lies.
The bloodthirsty and
deceitful
you, LORD, detest.
⁷But I, by your great love,
can come into your house;
in reverence I bow down
toward your holy temple.

⁸Lead me, LORD, in your
righteousness
because of my enemies —
make your way straight
before me.
⁹Not a word from their mouth
can be trusted;
their heart is filled with
malice.
Their throat is an open grave;
with their tongues they tell
lies.
¹⁰Declare them guilty, O God!
Let their intrigues be their
downfall.
Banish them for their many
sins,
for they have rebelled
against you.
¹¹But let all who take refuge in
you be glad;
let them ever sing for joy.

Spread your protection over
them,
that those who love your
name may rejoice in you.

¹²Surely, LORD, you bless the
righteous;
you surround them with your
favor as with a shield.

Psalm 6^a

For the director of music.
With stringed instruments.
According to sheminith.^b
A psalm of David.

¹LORD, do not rebuke me in
your anger
or discipline me in your
wrath.
²Have mercy on me, LORD, for I
am faint;
heal me, LORD, for my bones
are in agony.
³My soul is in deep anguish.
How long, LORD, how long?

⁴Turn, LORD, and deliver me;
save me because of your
unfailing love.
⁵Among the dead no one
proclaims your name.
Who praises you from the
grave?

⁶I am worn out from my
groaning.

All night long I flood my bed
with weeping
and drench my couch with
tears.

^a In Hebrew texts 6:1-10 is numbered 6:2-11.   ^b Title: Probably a musical term

⁷My eyes grow weak with
    sorrow;
  they fail because of all my
    foes.

⁸Away from me, all you who do
    evil,
  for the LORD has heard my
    weeping.
⁹The LORD has heard my cry for
    mercy;
  the LORD accepts my prayer.
¹⁰All my enemies will be
    overwhelmed with
    shame and anguish;
  they will turn back and
    suddenly be put to
    shame.

Psalm 7ᵃ

*A shiggaionᵇ of David, which he
sang to the LORD concerning
Cush, a Benjamite.*

¹LORD my God, I take refuge in
    you;
  save and deliver me from all
    who pursue me,
²or they will tear me apart like a
    lion
  and rip me to pieces with no
    one to rescue me.

³LORD my God, if I have done
    this
  and there is guilt on my
    hands —
⁴if I have repaid my ally with
    evil

or without cause have
    robbed my foe —
⁵then let my enemy pursue and
    overtake me;
  let him trample my life to the
    ground
  and make me sleep in the
    dust.ᶜ

⁶Arise, LORD, in your anger;
  rise up against the rage of
    my enemies.
  Awake, my God; decree
    justice.
⁷Let the assembled peoples
    gather around you,
  while you sit enthroned over
    them on high.
⁸ Let the LORD judge the
    peoples.
Vindicate me, LORD,
    according to my
    righteousness,
  according to my integrity,
    O Most High.
⁹Bring to an end the violence of
    the wicked
  and make the righteous
    secure —
you, the righteous God
  who probes minds and
    hearts.

¹⁰My shieldᵈ is God Most High,
  who saves the upright in
    heart.
¹¹God is a righteous judge,
  a God who displays his
    wrath every day.

ᵃ In Hebrew texts 7:1-17 is numbered 7:2-18.   ᵇ Title: Probably a literary or
musical term   ᶜ 5 The Hebrew has *Selah* (a word of uncertain meaning) here.
ᵈ 10 Or *sovereign*

¹²If he does not relent,
he^a will sharpen his sword;
he will bend and string his
bow.
¹³He has prepared his deadly
weapons;
he makes ready his flaming
arrows.

¹⁴Whoever is pregnant with
evil
conceives trouble and
gives birth to
disillusionment.
¹⁵Whoever digs a hole and
scoops it out
falls into the pit they have
made.
¹⁶The trouble they cause recoils
on them;
their violence comes down
on their own heads.

¹⁷I will give thanks to the
LORD because of his
righteousness;
I will sing the praises of the
name of the LORD Most
High.

Psalm 8^b

*For the director of music.
According to* gittith.^c
A psalm of David.

¹LORD, our Lord,
how majestic is your name in
all the earth!

You have set your glory
in the heavens.
²Through the praise of children
and infants
you have established a
stronghold against your
enemies,
to silence the foe and the
avenger.
³When I consider your
heavens,
the work of your fingers,
the moon and the stars,
which you have set in
place,
⁴what is mankind that you are
mindful of them,
human beings that you care
for them?^d

⁵You have made them^e a little
lower than the angels^f
and crowned them^e with
glory and honor.
⁶You made them rulers over the
works of your hands;
you put everything under
their^g feet:
⁷all flocks and herds,
and the animals of the
wild,
⁸the birds in the sky,
and the fish in the sea,
all that swim the paths of the
seas.

⁹LORD, our Lord,
how majestic is your name in
all the earth!

---

^a 12 Or *If anyone does not repent, / God*
8:2-10.   ^c Title: Probably a musical term
that you are mindful of him, / a son of man that you care for him?   ^b In Hebrew texts 8:1-9 is numbered
^d 4 Or *what is a human being*
^e 5 Or *him*
^f 5 Or *than God*   ^g 6 Or *made him ruler . . . ; / . . . his*

Psalm 9[a,b]

For the director of music. To the tune of "The Death of the Son." A psalm of David.

[1] I will give thanks to you, LORD,
    with all my heart;
  I will tell of all your
    wonderful deeds.
[2] I will be glad and rejoice in you;
  I will sing the praises of your
    name, O Most High.

[3] My enemies turn back;
  they stumble and perish
    before you.
[4] For you have upheld my right
    and my cause,
  sitting enthroned as the
    righteous judge.
[5] You have rebuked the nations
    and destroyed the
    wicked;
  you have blotted out their
    name for ever and ever.
[6] Endless ruin has overtaken my
    enemies,
  you have uprooted their cities;
  even the memory of them
    has perished.

[7] The LORD reigns forever;
  he has established his
    throne for judgment.
[8] He rules the world in
    righteousness
  and judges the peoples with
    equity.

[9] The LORD is a refuge for the
    oppressed,
  a stronghold in times of
    trouble.
[10] Those who know your name
    trust in you,
  for you, LORD, have never
    forsaken those who seek
    you.

[11] Sing the praises of the LORD,
    enthroned in Zion;
  proclaim among the nations
    what he has done.
[12] For he who avenges blood
    remembers;
  he does not ignore the cries
    of the afflicted.

[13] LORD, see how my enemies
    persecute me!
  Have mercy and lift me up
    from the gates of death,
[14] that I may declare your
    praises
  in the gates of Daughter
    Zion,
  and there rejoice in your
    salvation.

[15] The nations have fallen into
    the pit they have dug;
  their feet are caught in the
    net they have hidden.
[16] The LORD is known by his acts
    of justice;
  the wicked are ensnared by
    the work of their hands.[c]

[a] Psalms 9 and 10 may originally have been a single acrostic poem in which alternating lines began with the successive letters of the Hebrew alphabet. In the Septuagint they constitute one psalm.   [b] In Hebrew texts 9:1-20 is numbered 9:2-21.   [c] 16 The Hebrew has *Higgaion* and *Selah* (words of uncertain meaning) here; *Selah* occurs also at the end of verse 20.

¹⁷The wicked go down to the
realm of the dead,
all the nations that forget
God.
¹⁸But God will never forget the
needy;
the hope of the afflicted will
never perish.

¹⁹Arise, LORD, do not let mortals
triumph;
let the nations be judged in
your presence.
²⁰Strike them with terror, LORD;
let the nations know they are
only mortal.

Psalm 10^a

¹Why, LORD, do you stand far
off?
Why do you hide yourself in
times of trouble?

²In his arrogance the wicked
man hunts down the
weak,
who are caught in the
schemes he devises.
³He boasts about the cravings
of his heart;
he blesses the greedy and
reviles the LORD.
⁴In his pride the wicked man
does not seek him;
in all his thoughts there is no
room for God.
⁵His ways are always
prosperous;

your laws are rejected by^b
him;
he sneers at all his
enemies.
⁶He says to himself, "Nothing
will ever shake me."
He swears, "No one will ever
do me harm."

⁷His mouth is full of lies and
threats;
trouble and evil are under
his tongue.
⁸He lies in wait near the
villages;
from ambush he murders
the innocent.
His eyes watch in secret for his
victims;
⁹   like a lion in cover he lies in
wait.
He lies in wait to catch the
helpless;
he catches the helpless and
drags them off in his
net.
¹⁰His victims are crushed, they
collapse;
they fall under his
strength.
¹¹He says to himself, "God will
never notice;
he covers his face and never
sees."

¹²Arise, LORD! Lift up your hand,
O God.
Do not forget the helpless.

---

^a Psalms 9 and 10 may originally have been a single acrostic poem in which
alternating lines began with the successive letters of the Hebrew alphabet. In the
Septuagint they constitute one psalm.   ^b 5 See Septuagint; Hebrew / *they are
haughty, and your laws are far from*

¹³Why does the wicked man
    revile God?
  Why does he say to himself,
  "He won't call me to
    account"?
¹⁴But you, God, see the trouble
    of the afflicted;
  you consider their grief and
    take it in hand.
  The victims commit
    themselves to you;
  you are the helper of the
    fatherless.
¹⁵Break the arm of the wicked
    man;
  call the evildoer to account
    for his wickedness
  that would not otherwise be
    found out.

¹⁶The LORD is King for ever and
    ever;
  the nations will perish from
    his land.
¹⁷You, LORD, hear the desire of
    the afflicted;
  you encourage them, and
    you listen to their cry,
¹⁸defending the fatherless and
    the oppressed,
  so that mere earthly mortals
  will never again strike
    terror.

Psalm 11

For the director of music.
Of David.

¹In the LORD I take refuge.
  How then can you say to me:

"Flee like a bird to your
    mountain.
²For look, the wicked bend their
    bows;
  they set their arrows against
    the strings
  to shoot from the shadows
    at the upright in heart.
³When the foundations are
    being destroyed,
  what can the righteous do?"

⁴The LORD is in his holy
    temple;
  the LORD is on his heavenly
    throne.
  He observes everyone on
    earth;
  his eyes examine them.
⁵The LORD examines the
    righteous,
  but the wicked, those who
    love violence,
  he hates with a passion.
⁶On the wicked he will rain
    fiery coals and burning
    sulfur;
  a scorching wind will be
    their lot.

⁷For the LORD is righteous,
  he loves justice;
  the upright will see his face.

Psalm 12ᵃ

For the director of music.
According to sheminith.ᵇ
A psalm of David.

¹Help, LORD, for no one is
  faithful anymore;

ᵃ In Hebrew texts 12:1-8 is numbered 12:2-9.   ᵇ Title: Probably a musical term

those who are loyal have
   vanished from the
   human race.
[2] Everyone lies to their
   neighbor;
they flatter with their lips
   but harbor deception in their
   hearts.

[3] May the LORD silence all
   flattering lips
   and every boastful tongue —
[4] those who say,
   "By our tongues we will
   prevail;
   our own lips will defend
   us — who is lord over
   us?"

[5] "Because the poor are
   plundered and the needy
   groan,
   I will now arise," says the
   LORD.
   "I will protect them from
   those who malign them."
[6] And the words of the LORD are
   flawless,
   like silver purified in a
   crucible,
   like gold[a] refined seven
   times.

[7] You, LORD, will keep the needy
   safe
   and will protect us forever
   from the wicked,
[8] who freely strut about
   when what is vile is honored
   by the human race.

Psalm 13[b]

*For the director of music.
A psalm of David.*

[1] How long, LORD? Will you
   forget me forever?
How long will you hide your
   face from me?
[2] How long must I wrestle with
   my thoughts
   and day after day have
   sorrow in my heart?
How long will my enemy
   triumph over me?

[3] Look on me and answer, LORD
   my God.
Give light to my eyes, or I
   will sleep in death,
[4] and my enemy will say, "I have
   overcome him,"
   and my foes will rejoice
   when I fall.

[5] But I trust in your unfailing
   love;
   my heart rejoices in your
   salvation.
[6] I will sing the LORD's
   praise,
   for he has been good
   to me.

Psalm 14

*For the director of music.
Of David.*

[1] The fool[c] says in his heart,
   "There is no God."

---

[a] 6 Probable reading of the original Hebrew text; Masoretic Text *earth*   [b] In
Hebrew texts 13:1-6 is numbered 13:2-6.   [c] 1 The Hebrew words rendered *fool*
in Psalms denote one who is morally deficient.

They are corrupt, their deeds
are vile;
there is no one who does
good.

²The Lord looks down from
heaven
on all mankind
to see if there are any who
understand,
any who seek God.
³All have turned away, all have
become corrupt;
there is no one who does
good,
not even one.

⁴Do all these evildoers know
nothing?

They devour my people as
though eating bread;
they never call on the
Lord.
⁵But there they are,
overwhelmed with
dread,
for God is present in
the company of the
righteous.
⁶You evildoers frustrate the
plans of the poor,
but the Lord is their
refuge.

⁷Oh, that salvation for Israel
would come out of
Zion!
When the Lord restores his
people,
let Jacob rejoice and Israel be
glad!

ª Title: Probably a literary or musical term

Psalm 15

A psalm of David.

¹Lord, who may dwell in your
sacred tent?
Who may live on your holy
mountain?

²The one whose walk is
blameless,
who does what is righteous,
who speaks the truth from
their heart;
³whose tongue utters no slander,
who does no wrong to a
neighbor,
and casts no slur on others;
⁴who despises a vile person
but honors those who fear
the Lord;
who keeps an oath even when
it hurts,
and does not change their
mind;
⁵who lends money to the poor
without interest;
who does not accept a bribe
against the innocent.

Whoever does these things
will never be shaken.

Psalm 16

A miktam[a] of David.

¹Keep me safe, my God,
for in you I take refuge.

²I say to the Lord, "You are my
Lord;
apart from you I have no
good thing."

³I say of the holy people who
are in the land,
"They are the noble ones in
whom is all my delight."
⁴Those who run after other
gods will suffer more
and more.
I will not pour out libations
of blood to such gods
or take up their names on
my lips.

⁵Lord, you alone are my
portion and my cup;
you make my lot secure.
⁶The boundary lines have fallen
for me in pleasant places;
surely I have a delightful
inheritance.
⁷I will praise the Lord, who
counsels me;
even at night my heart
instructs me.
⁸I keep my eyes always on the
Lord.
With him at my right hand, I
will not be shaken.

⁹Therefore my heart is glad and
my tongue rejoices;
my body also will rest secure,
¹⁰because you will not abandon
me to the realm of the
dead,
nor will you let your faithful[a]
one see decay.
¹¹You make known to me the
path of life;
you will fill me with joy in
your presence,
with eternal pleasures at
your right hand.

[a] 10 Or *holy*

Psalm 17

A prayer of David.

¹Hear me, Lord, my plea is just;
listen to my cry.
Hear my prayer—
it does not rise from
deceitful lips.
²Let my vindication come from
you;
may your eyes see what is
right.

³Though you probe my
heart,
though you examine me at
night and test me,
you will find that I have
planned no evil;
my mouth has not
transgressed.
⁴Though people tried to
bribe me,
I have kept myself from the
ways of the violent
through what your lips have
commanded.
⁵My steps have held to your
paths;
my feet have not stumbled.

⁶I call on you, my God, for you
will answer me;
turn your ear to me and hear
my prayer.
⁷Show me the wonders of your
great love,
you who save by your right
hand
those who take refuge in you
from their foes.

8 Keep me as the apple of your
  eye;
    hide me in the shadow of
    your wings
9 from the wicked who are out to
  destroy me,
    from my mortal enemies
    who surround me.

10 They close up their callous
  hearts,
    and their mouths speak with
    arrogance.
11 They have tracked me down,
  they now surround me,
    with eyes alert, to throw me
    to the ground.
12 They are like a lion hungry for
  prey,
    like a fierce lion crouching in
    cover.

13 Rise up, LORD, confront them,
  bring them down;
    with your sword rescue me
    from the wicked.
14 By your hand save me from
  such people, LORD,
    from those of this world
    whose reward is in this
    life.
  May what you have stored up
    for the wicked fill their
    bellies;
    may their children gorge
    themselves on it,
    and may there be leftovers
    for their little ones.

15 As for me, I will be vindicated
  and will see your face;

when I awake, I will be
  satisfied with seeing
  your likeness.

Psalm 18[a]

For the director of music.
Of David the servant of the LORD.
He sang to the LORD the words
  of this song when the LORD
  delivered him from the hand
  of all his enemies and from
  the hand of Saul. He said:

1 I love you, LORD, my
  strength.

2 The LORD is my rock, my
  fortress and my
  deliverer;
    my God is my rock, in whom
    I take refuge,
    my shield[b] and the horn[c]
    of my salvation, my
    stronghold.

3 I called to the LORD, who is
  worthy of praise,
    and I have been saved from
    my enemies.
4 The cords of death
  entangled me;
    the torrents of destruction
    overwhelmed me.
5 The cords of the grave coiled
  around me;
    the snares of death
    confronted me.
6 In my distress I called to the
  LORD;
    I cried to my God for help.

---

a In Hebrew texts 18:1-50 is numbered 18:2-51.   *b* 2 Or *sovereign*   *c* 2 *Horn*
here symbolizes strength.

From his temple he heard my
voice;
my cry came before him,
into his ears.
⁷The earth trembled and
quaked,
and the foundations of the
mountains shook;
they trembled because he
was angry.
⁸Smoke rose from his nostrils;
consuming fire came from
his mouth,
burning coals blazed out
of it.
⁹He parted the heavens and
came down;
dark clouds were under his
feet.
¹⁰He mounted the cherubim and
flew;
he soared on the wings of
the wind.
¹¹He made darkness his
covering, his canopy
around him —
the dark rain clouds of the
sky.
¹²Out of the brightness of
his presence clouds
advanced,
with hailstones and bolts of
lightning.
¹³The Lord thundered from
heaven;
the voice of the Most High
resounded.ᵃ
¹⁴He shot his arrows and
scattered the enemy,

with great bolts of lightning
he routed them.
¹⁵The valleys of the sea were
exposed
and the foundations of the
earth laid bare
at your rebuke, Lord,
at the blast of breath from
your nostrils.

¹⁶He reached down from on high
and took hold of me;
he drew me out of deep
waters.
¹⁷He rescued me from my
powerful enemy,
from my foes, who were too
strong for me.
¹⁸They confronted me in the day
of my disaster,
but the Lord was my
support.
¹⁹He brought me out into a
spacious place;
he rescued me because he
delighted in me.
²⁰The Lord has dealt with
me according to my
righteousness;
according to the cleanness
of my hands he has
rewarded me.
²¹For I have kept the ways of the
Lord;
I am not guilty of turning
from my God.
²²All his laws are before me;
I have not turned away from
his decrees.

ᵃ 13 Some Hebrew manuscripts and Septuagint (see also 2 Samuel 22:14); most
Hebrew manuscripts *resounded, / amid hailstones and bolts of lightning*

²³I have been blameless before
    him
    and have kept myself from
        sin.
²⁴The LORD has rewarded
    me according to my
    righteousness,
    according to the cleanness of
    my hands in his sight.

²⁵To the faithful you show
    yourself faithful,
    to the blameless you show
    yourself blameless,
²⁶to the pure you show yourself
        pure,
    but to the devious you show
    yourself shrewd.
²⁷You save the humble
    but bring low those whose
    eyes are haughty.
²⁸You, LORD, keep my lamp
        burning;
    my God turns my darkness
    into light.
²⁹With your help I can advance
    against a troop*ᵃ*;
    with my God I can scale a
        wall.

³⁰As for God, his way is perfect:
    The LORD's word is flawless;
    he shields all who take
    refuge in him.
³¹For who is God besides the
        LORD?
    And who is the Rock except
    our God?
³²It is God who arms me with
        strength
    and keeps my way secure.

ᵃ 29 Or *can run through a barricade*

³³He makes my feet like the feet
    of a deer;
    he causes me to stand on the
        heights.
³⁴He trains my hands for
        battle;
    my arms can bend a bow of
    bronze.
³⁵You make your saving help my
        shield,
    and your right hand
    sustains me;
    your help has made me
        great.
³⁶You provide a broad path for
    my feet,
    so that my ankles do not give
        way.

³⁷I pursued my enemies and
    overtook them;
    I did not turn back till they
    were destroyed.
³⁸I crushed them so that they
    could not rise;
    they fell beneath my
        feet.
³⁹You armed me with strength
    for battle;
    you humbled my adversaries
    before me.
⁴⁰You made my enemies turn
    their backs in flight,
    and I destroyed my
        foes.
⁴¹They cried for help, but there
    was no one to save
    them —
    to the LORD, but he did not
    answer.

⁴²I beat them as fine as
 windblown dust;
 I trampled them*a* like mud
 in the streets.
⁴³You have delivered me from
 the attacks of the people;
 you have made me the head
 of nations.
 People I did not know now
 serve me,
⁴⁴ foreigners cower before me;
 as soon as they hear of me,
 they obey me.
⁴⁵They all lose heart;
 they come trembling from
 their strongholds.

⁴⁶The LORD lives! Praise be to
 my Rock!
 Exalted be God my Savior!
⁴⁷He is the God who avenges me,
 who subdues nations
 under me,
⁴⁸ who saves me from my
 enemies.
 You exalted me above my foes;
 from a violent man you
 rescued me.
⁴⁹Therefore I will praise you,
 LORD, among the nations;
 I will sing the praises of your
 name.

⁵⁰He gives his king great
 victories;
 he shows unfailing love to
 his anointed,
 to David and to his
 descendants forever.

Psalm 19*b*

*For the director of music.
A psalm of David.*

¹The heavens declare the glory
 of God;
 the skies proclaim the work
 of his hands.
²Day after day they pour forth
 speech;
 night after night they reveal
 knowledge.
³They have no speech, they use
 no words;
 no sound is heard from them.
⁴Yet their voice*c* goes out into
 all the earth,
 their words to the ends of the
 world.
 In the heavens God has
 pitched a tent for the
 sun.
⁵ It is like a bridegroom
 coming out of his
 chamber,
 like a champion rejoicing to
 run his course.
⁶It rises at one end of the heavens
 and makes its circuit to the
 other;
 nothing is deprived of its
 warmth.

⁷The law of the LORD is perfect,
 refreshing the soul.
 The statutes of the LORD are
 trustworthy,
 making wise the simple.

---

a 42 Many Hebrew manuscripts, Septuagint, Syriac and Targum (see also
2 Samuel 22:43); Masoretic Text *I poured them out*   *b* In Hebrew texts 19:1-14 is
numbered 19:2-15.   *c 4* Septuagint, Jerome and Syriac; Hebrew *measuring line*

⁸The precepts of the LORD are
right,
  giving joy to the heart.
The commands of the LORD
  are radiant,
  giving light to the eyes.
⁹The fear of the LORD is pure,
  enduring forever.
The decrees of the LORD are
  firm,
  and all of them are
  righteous.

¹⁰They are more precious than
  gold,
  than much pure gold;
they are sweeter than
  honey,
  than honey from the
  honeycomb.
¹¹By them your servant is
  warned;
  in keeping them there is
  great reward.
¹²But who can discern their own
  errors?
  Forgive my hidden faults.
¹³Keep your servant also from
  willful sins;
  may they not rule over me.
Then I will be blameless,
  innocent of great
  transgression.

¹⁴May these words of my mouth
  and this meditation of
  my heart
  be pleasing in your sight,
LORD, my Rock and my
  Redeemer.

Psalm 20ᵃ

*For the director of music.
A psalm of David.*

¹May the LORD answer you
  when you are in
  distress;
  may the name of the God of
  Jacob protect you.
²May he send you help from the
  sanctuary
  and grant you support from
  Zion.
³May he remember all your
  sacrifices
  and accept your burnt
  offerings.ᵇ
⁴May he give you the desire of
  your heart
  and make all your plans
  succeed.
⁵May we shout for joy over your
  victory
  and lift up our banners in
  the name of our God.

May the LORD grant all your
  requests.

⁶Now this I know:
  The LORD gives victory to his
  anointed.
He answers him from his
  heavenly sanctuary
  with the victorious power of
  his right hand.
⁷Some trust in chariots and
  some in horses,
  but we trust in the name of
  the LORD our God.

ᵃ In Hebrew texts 20:1-9 is numbered 20:2-10.   ᵇ 3 The Hebrew has *Selah*
(a word of uncertain meaning) here.

⁸They are brought to their
    knees and fall,
but we rise up and stand
    firm.
⁹LORD, give victory to the king!
    Answer us when we call!

Psalm 21ᵃ

*For the director of music.
A psalm of David.*

¹The king rejoices in your
    strength, LORD.
How great is his joy in the
    victories you give!

²You have granted him his
    heart's desire
and have not withheld the
    request of his lips.ᵇ
³You came to greet him with
    rich blessings
and placed a crown of pure
    gold on his head.
⁴He asked you for life, and you
    gave it to him —
length of days, for ever and
    ever.
⁵Through the victories you
    gave, his glory is great;
you have bestowed on him
    splendor and majesty.
⁶Surely you have granted him
    unending blessings
and made him glad with the
    joy of your presence.
⁷For the king trusts in the LORD;
    through the unfailing love of
    the Most High
he will not be shaken.

⁸Your hand will lay hold on all
    your enemies;
your right hand will seize
    your foes.
⁹When you appear for battle,
    you will burn them up as in
    a blazing furnace.
The LORD will swallow them
    up in his wrath,
and his fire will consume
    them.
¹⁰You will destroy their
    descendants from the
    earth,
their posterity from mankind.
¹¹Though they plot evil against
    you
and devise wicked schemes,
    they cannot succeed.
¹²You will make them turn their
    backs
when you aim at them with
    drawn bow.
¹³Be exalted in your strength,
    LORD;
we will sing and praise your
    might.

Psalm 22ᶜ

*For the director of music.
To the tune of "The Doe of the
Morning." A psalm of David.*

¹My God, my God, why have
    you forsaken me?
Why are you so far from
    saving me,
so far from my cries of
    anguish?

ᵃ In Hebrew texts 21:1-13 is numbered 21:2-14.   ᵇ 2 The Hebrew has *Selah* (a word
of uncertain meaning) here.   ᶜ In Hebrew texts 22:1-31 is numbered 22:2-32.

[2] My God, I cry out by day, but
   you do not answer,
   by night, but I find no rest.[a]

[3] Yet you are enthroned as the
   Holy One;
   you are the one Israel
   praises.[b]
[4] In you our ancestors put their
   trust;
   they trusted and you
   delivered them.
[5] To you they cried out and were
   saved;
   in you they trusted and were
   not put to shame.

[6] But I am a worm and not a
   man,
   scorned by everyone,
   despised by the
   people.
[7] All who see me mock me;
   they hurl insults, shaking
   their heads.
[8] "He trusts in the Lord," they
   say,
   "let the Lord rescue him.
   Let him deliver him,
   since he delights in him."

[9] Yet you brought me out of the
   womb;
   you made me trust in you,
   even at my mother's
   breast.
[10] From birth I was cast on you;
   from my mother's womb you
   have been my God.

[11] Do not be far from me,
   for trouble is near
   and there is no one to help.

[12] Many bulls surround me;
   strong bulls of Bashan
   encircle me.
[13] Roaring lions that tear their
   prey
   open their mouths wide
   against me.
[14] I am poured out like water,
   and all my bones are out of
   joint.
   My heart has turned to wax;
   it has melted within me.
[15] My mouth[c] is dried up like a
   potsherd,
   and my tongue sticks to the
   roof of my mouth;
   you lay me in the dust of
   death.

[16] Dogs surround me,
   a pack of villains
   encircles me;
   they pierce[d] my hands and
   my feet.
[17] All my bones are on display;
   people stare and gloat
   over me.
[18] They divide my clothes among
   them
   and cast lots for my garment.

[19] But you, Lord, do not be far
   from me.
   You are my strength; come
   quickly to help me.

---

[a] 2 Or *night, and am not silent*   [b] 3 Or *Yet you are holy, / enthroned on the praises
of Israel*   [c] 15 Probable reading of the original Hebrew text; Masoretic Text
strength   [d] 16 Dead Sea Scrolls and some manuscripts of the Masoretic Text,
Septuagint and Syriac; most manuscripts of the Masoretic Text *me, / like a lion*

20 Deliver me from the sword,
my precious life from the
power of the dogs.
21 Rescue me from the mouth of
the lions;
save me from the horns of
the wild oxen.

22 I will declare your name to my
people;
in the assembly I will praise
you.
23 You who fear the LORD, praise
him!
All you descendants of Jacob,
honor him!
Revere him, all you
descendants of Israel!
24 For he has not despised or
scorned
the suffering of the afflicted
one;
he has not hidden his face
from him
but has listened to his cry for
help.

25 From you comes the theme of
my praise in the great
assembly;
before those who fear you[a] I
will fulfill my vows.
26 The poor will eat and be
satisfied;
those who seek the LORD
will praise him —
may your hearts live
forever!

27 All the ends of the earth
will remember and turn to
the LORD,

and all the families of the
nations
will bow down before him,
28 for dominion belongs to the
LORD
and he rules over the
nations.

29 All the rich of the earth will
feast and worship;
all who go down to the dust
will kneel before him —
those who cannot keep
themselves alive.
30 Posterity will serve him;
future generations will be
told about the Lord.
31 They will proclaim his
righteousness,
declaring to a people yet
unborn:
He has done it!

Psalm 23

A psalm of David.

1 The LORD is my shepherd, I
lack nothing.
2 He makes me lie down in
green pastures,
he leads me beside quiet
waters,
3 he refreshes my soul.
He guides me along the right
paths
for his name's sake.
4 Even though I walk
through the darkest valley,[b]
I will fear no evil,
for you are with me;

---

a 25 Hebrew *him*   *b 4* Or *the valley of the shadow of death*

your rod and your staff,
  they comfort me.
⁵ You prepare a table before me
    in the presence of my
    enemies.
You anoint my head with oil;
  my cup overflows.
⁶ Surely your goodness and love
    will follow me
all the days of my life,
and I will dwell in the house of
    the LORD
  forever.

Psalm 24

Of David. A psalm.

¹ The earth is the LORD's, and
    everything in it,
  the world, and all who live
    in it;
² for he founded it on the seas
  and established it on the
    waters.

³ Who may ascend the
    mountain of the LORD?
  Who may stand in his holy
    place?
⁴ The one who has clean hands
    and a pure heart,
  who does not trust in an idol
  or swear by a false god.ᵃ

⁵ They will receive blessing from
    the LORD
  and vindication from God
    their Savior.

⁶ Such is the generation of those
    who seek him,
  who seek your face, God of
    Jacob.ᵇ,ᶜ

⁷ Lift up your heads, you
    gates;
  be lifted up, you ancient
    doors,
  that the King of glory may
    come in.
⁸ Who is this King of glory?
  The LORD strong and
    mighty,
  the LORD mighty in battle.
⁹ Lift up your heads, you
    gates;
  lift them up, you ancient
    doors,
  that the King of glory may
    come in.
¹⁰ Who is he, this King of glory?
  The LORD Almighty—
  he is the King of glory.

Psalm 25ᵈ

Of David.

¹ In you, LORD my God,
  I put my trust.

² I trust in you;
  do not let me be put to
    shame,
  nor let my enemies triumph
    over me.
³ No one who hopes in you
  will ever be put to shame,

ᵃ 4 Or *swear falsely*   ᵇ 6 Two Hebrew manuscripts and Syriac (see also
Septuagint); most Hebrew manuscripts *face, Jacob*   ᶜ 6 The Hebrew has *Selah* (a
word of uncertain meaning) here and at the end of verse 10.   ᵈ This psalm is an
acrostic poem, the verses of which begin with the successive letters of the Hebrew
alphabet.

but shame will come on those
who are treacherous without
cause.

⁴Show me your ways, LORD,
teach me your paths.
⁵Guide me in your truth and
teach me,
for you are God my Savior,
and my hope is in you all day
long.
⁶Remember, LORD, your great
mercy and love,
for they are from of old.
⁷Do not remember the sins of
my youth
and my rebellious ways;
according to your love
remember me,
for you, LORD, are good.

⁸Good and upright is the LORD;
therefore he instructs
sinners in his ways.
⁹He guides the humble in what
is right
and teaches them his way.
¹⁰All the ways of the LORD are
loving and faithful
toward those who keep
the demands of his
covenant.
¹¹For the sake of your name,
LORD,
forgive my iniquity, though it
is great.
¹²Who, then, are those who fear
the LORD?
He will instruct them in
the ways they should
choose.ᵃ

¹³They will spend their days in
prosperity,
and their descendants will
inherit the land.
¹⁴The LORD confides in those
who fear him;
he makes his covenant
known to them.
¹⁵My eyes are ever on the
LORD,
for only he will release my
feet from the snare.

¹⁶Turn to me and be gracious
to me,
for I am lonely and
afflicted.
¹⁷Relieve the troubles of my
heart
and free me from my
anguish.
¹⁸Look on my affliction and my
distress
and take away all my
sins.
¹⁹See how numerous are my
enemies
and how fiercely they
hate me!
²⁰Guard my life and
rescue me;
do not let me be put to
shame,
for I take refuge in you.
²¹May integrity and uprightness
protect me,
because my hope, LORD,ᵇ is
in you.

²²Deliver Israel, O God,
from all their troubles!

ᵃ 12 Or *ways he chooses*   ᵇ 21 Septuagint; Hebrew does not have LORD.

Psalm 26

Of David.

¹ Vindicate me, LORD,
for I have led a blameless
life;
I have trusted in the LORD
and have not faltered.
² Test me, LORD, and try me,
examine my heart and my
mind;
³ for I have always been mindful
of your unfailing love
and have lived in reliance on
your faithfulness.

⁴ I do not sit with the deceitful,
nor do I associate with
hypocrites.
⁵ I abhor the assembly of
evildoers
and refuse to sit with the
wicked.
⁶ I wash my hands in innocence,
and go about your altar, LORD,
⁷ proclaiming aloud your praise
and telling of all your
wonderful deeds.

⁸ LORD, I love the house where
you live,
the place where your glory
dwells.
⁹ Do not take away my soul
along with sinners,
my life with those who are
bloodthirsty,
¹⁰ in whose hands are wicked
schemes,
whose right hands are full of
bribes.

¹¹ I lead a blameless life;
deliver me and be merciful
to me.
¹² My feet stand on level ground;
in the great congregation I
will praise the LORD.

Psalm 27

Of David.

¹ The LORD is my light and my
salvation —
whom shall I fear?
The LORD is the stronghold of
my life —
of whom shall I be afraid?

² When the wicked advance
against me
to devour[a] me,
it is my enemies and my foes
who will stumble and fall.
³ Though an army besiege me,
my heart will not fear;
though war break out
against me,
even then I will be confident.

⁴ One thing I ask from the LORD,
this only do I seek:
that I may dwell in the house
of the LORD
all the days of my life,
to gaze on the beauty of the
LORD
and to seek him in his
temple.
⁵ For in the day of trouble
he will keep me safe in his
dwelling;

---

a 2 Or *slander*

he will hide me in the shelter
of his sacred tent
and set me high upon a rock.

6 Then my head will be exalted
above the enemies who
surround me;
at his sacred tent I will
sacrifice with shouts of
joy;
I will sing and make music
to the LORD.

7 Hear my voice when I call,
LORD;
be merciful to me and
answer me.
8 My heart says of you, "Seek his
face!"
Your face, LORD, I will seek.
9 Do not hide your face from me,
do not turn your servant
away in anger;
you have been my helper.
Do not reject me or forsake me,
God my Savior.
10 Though my father and mother
forsake me,
the LORD will receive me.
11 Teach me your way, LORD;
lead me in a straight path
because of my oppressors.
12 Do not turn me over to the
desire of my foes,
for false witnesses rise up
against me,
spouting malicious
accusations.

13 I remain confident of this:
I will see the goodness of the
LORD
in the land of the living.

14 Wait for the LORD;
be strong and take heart
and wait for the LORD.

Psalm 28

Of David.

1 To you, LORD, I call;
you are my Rock,
do not turn a deaf ear to me.
For if you remain silent,
I will be like those who go
down to the pit.
2 Hear my cry for mercy
as I call to you for help,
as I lift up my hands
toward your Most Holy Place.

3 Do not drag me away with the
wicked,
with those who do evil,
who speak cordially with their
neighbors
but harbor malice in their
hearts.
4 Repay them for their deeds
and for their evil work;
repay them for what their
hands have done
and bring back on them
what they deserve.

5 Because they have no regard
for the deeds of the LORD
and what his hands have
done,
he will tear them down
and never build them up
again.

6 Praise be to the LORD,
for he has heard my cry for
mercy.

7 The LORD is my strength and
 my shield;
 my heart trusts in him, and
 he helps me.
My heart leaps for joy,
 and with my song I praise
 him.

8 The LORD is the strength of his
 people,
 a fortress of salvation for his
 anointed one.
9 Save your people and bless
 your inheritance;
 be their shepherd and carry
 them forever.

Psalm 29

A psalm of David.

1 Ascribe to the LORD, you
 heavenly beings,
 ascribe to the LORD glory
 and strength.
2 Ascribe to the LORD the glory
 due his name;
 worship the LORD in the
 splendor of his*a* holiness.

3 The voice of the LORD is over
 the waters;
 the God of glory thunders,
 the LORD thunders over the
 mighty waters.
4 The voice of the LORD is
 powerful;
 the voice of the LORD is
 majestic.
5 The voice of the LORD breaks
 the cedars;

the LORD breaks in pieces
 the cedars of Lebanon.
6 He makes Lebanon leap like a
 calf,
 Sirion*b* like a young wild ox.
7 The voice of the LORD strikes
 with flashes of lightning.
8 The voice of the LORD shakes
 the desert;
 the LORD shakes the Desert
 of Kadesh.
9 The voice of the LORD twists
 the oaks*c*
 and strips the forests bare.
And in his temple all cry,
 "Glory!"

10 The LORD sits enthroned over
 the flood;
 the LORD is enthroned as
 King forever.
11 The LORD gives strength to his
 people;
 the LORD blesses his people
 with peace.

Psalm 30*d*

*A psalm. A song. For the
dedication of the temple.*e
Of David.

1 I will exalt you, LORD,
 for you lifted me out of the
 depths
 and did not let my enemies
 gloat over me.
2 LORD my God, I called to you
 for help,
 and you healed me.

---

a 2 Or LORD *with the splendor of*   *b* 6 That is, Mount Hermon   *c* 9 Or LORD
makes the deer give birth   *d* In Hebrew texts 30:1-12 is numbered 30:2-13.
e Title: Or *palace*

³You, Lord, brought me up
from the realm of the
dead;
you spared me from going
down to the pit.

⁴Sing the praises of the Lord,
you his faithful people;
praise his holy name.
⁵For his anger lasts only a
moment,
but his favor lasts a lifetime;
weeping may stay for the
night,
but rejoicing comes in the
morning.

⁶When I felt secure, I said,
"I will never be shaken."
⁷Lord, when you favored me,
you made my royal
mountainᵃ stand firm;
but when you hid your face,
I was dismayed.

⁸To you, Lord, I called;
to the Lord I cried for
mercy:
⁹"What is gained if I am
silenced,
if I go down to the pit?
Will the dust praise you?
Will it proclaim your
faithfulness?
¹⁰Hear, Lord, and be merciful
to me;
Lord, be my help."

¹¹You turned my wailing into
dancing;
you removed my sackcloth
and clothed me with joy,

¹²that my heart may sing your
praises and not be silent.
Lord my God, I will praise
you forever.

Psalm 31ᵇ

*For the director of music.
A psalm of David.*

¹In you, Lord, I have taken
refuge;
let me never be put to
shame;
deliver me in your
righteousness.
²Turn your ear to me,
come quickly to my rescue;
be my rock of refuge,
a strong fortress to save me.
³Since you are my rock and my
fortress,
for the sake of your name
lead and guide me.
⁴Keep me free from the trap
that is set for me,
for you are my refuge.
⁵Into your hands I commit my
spirit;
deliver me, Lord, my
faithful God.

⁶I hate those who cling to
worthless idols;
as for me, I trust in the
Lord.
⁷I will be glad and rejoice in
your love,
for you saw my affliction
and knew the anguish of my
soul.

ᵃ 7 That is, Mount Zion   ᵇ In Hebrew texts 31:1-24 is numbered 31:2-25.

⁸You have not given me into the
hands of the enemy
  but have set my feet in a
    spacious place.

⁹Be merciful to me, LORD, for I
am in distress;
  my eyes grow weak with
    sorrow,
  my soul and body with
    grief.
¹⁰My life is consumed by
anguish
  and my years by groaning;
  my strength fails because of
    my affliction,ᵃ
  and my bones grow weak.
¹¹Because of all my enemies,
I am the utter contempt of
    my neighbors
  and an object of dread to my
    closest friends —
  those who see me on the
    street flee from me.
¹²I am forgotten as though I
were dead;
  I have become like broken
    pottery.
¹³For I hear many whispering,
  "Terror on every side!"
  They conspire against me
  and plot to take my life.

¹⁴But I trust in you, LORD;
  I say, "You are my God."
¹⁵My times are in your hands;
  deliver me from the hands of
    my enemies,
  from those who pursue me.
¹⁶Let your face shine on your
servant;

save me in your unfailing
love.
¹⁷Let me not be put to shame,
LORD,
  for I have cried out to you;
  but let the wicked be put to
    shame
  and be silent in the realm of
    the dead.
¹⁸Let their lying lips be silenced,
  for with pride and contempt
  they speak arrogantly
    against the righteous.

¹⁹How abundant are the good
things
  that you have stored up for
    those who fear you,
  that you bestow in the sight of
    all,
  on those who take refuge in
    you.
²⁰In the shelter of your presence
you hide them
  from all human intrigues;
  you keep them safe in your
    dwelling
  from accusing tongues.

²¹Praise be to the LORD,
  for he showed me the
    wonders of his love
  when I was in a city under
    siege.
²²In my alarm I said,
  "I am cut off from your sight!"
  Yet you heard my cry for mercy
  when I called to you for help.

²³Love the LORD, all his faithful
people!

ᵃ 10 Or guilt

The LORD preserves those
who are true to him,
but the proud he pays back
in full.
²⁴Be strong and take heart,
all you who hope in the
LORD.

Psalm 32

Of David. A maskil.ᵃ

¹Blessed is the one
whose transgressions are
forgiven,
whose sins are covered.
²Blessed is the one
whose sin the LORD does not
count against them
and in whose spirit is no
deceit.

³When I kept silent,
my bones wasted away
through my groaning all day
long.
⁴For day and night
your hand was heavy
on me;
my strength was sapped
as in the heat of summer.ᵇ

⁵Then I acknowledged my sin
to you
and did not cover up my
iniquity.
I said, "I will confess
my transgressions to the
LORD."
And you forgave
the guilt of my sin.

⁶Therefore let all the faithful
pray to you
while you may be found;
surely the rising of the mighty
waters
will not reach them.
⁷You are my hiding place;
you will protect me from
trouble
and surround me with songs
of deliverance.

⁸I will instruct you and teach
you in the way you
should go;
I will counsel you with my
loving eye on you.
⁹Do not be like the horse or the
mule,
which have no understanding
but must be controlled by bit
and bridle
or they will not come to you.
¹⁰Many are the woes of the
wicked,
but the LORD's unfailing love
surrounds the one who
trusts in him.

¹¹Rejoice in the LORD and be
glad, you righteous;
sing, all you who are upright
in heart!

Psalm 33

¹Sing joyfully to the LORD, you
righteous;
it is fitting for the upright to
praise him.

ᵃ Title: Probably a literary or musical term
uncertain meaning) here and at the end of verses 5 and 7.   ᵇ 4 The Hebrew has *Selah* (a word of

²Praise the LORD with the harp;
 make music to him on the
  ten-stringed lyre.
³Sing to him a new song;
 play skillfully, and shout for
  joy.

⁴For the word of the LORD is
  right and true;
 he is faithful in all he does.
⁵The LORD loves
  righteousness and
  justice;
 the earth is full of his
  unfailing love.

⁶By the word of the LORD the
  heavens were made,
 their starry host by the
  breath of his mouth.
⁷He gathers the waters of the
  sea into jars*a*;
 he puts the deep into
  storehouses.
⁸Let all the earth fear the
  LORD;
 let all the people of the world
  revere him.
⁹For he spoke, and it came
  to be;
 he commanded, and it stood
  firm.

¹⁰The LORD foils the plans of the
  nations;
 he thwarts the purposes of
  the peoples.
¹¹But the plans of the LORD
  stand firm forever,
 the purposes of his heart
  through all generations.

¹²Blessed is the nation whose
  God is the LORD,
 the people he chose for his
  inheritance.
¹³From heaven the LORD looks
  down
 and sees all mankind;
¹⁴from his dwelling place he
  watches
 all who live on earth—
¹⁵he who forms the hearts
  of all,
 who considers everything
  they do.

¹⁶No king is saved by the size of
  his army;
 no warrior escapes by his
  great strength.
¹⁷A horse is a vain hope for
  deliverance;
 despite all its great strength
  it cannot save.
¹⁸But the eyes of the LORD are on
  those who fear him,
 on those whose hope is in
  his unfailing love,
¹⁹to deliver them from death
 and keep them alive in
  famine.

²⁰We wait in hope for the LORD;
 he is our help and our
  shield.
²¹In him our hearts rejoice,
 for we trust in his holy
  name.
²²May your unfailing love be
  with us, LORD,
 even as we put our hope in
  you.

a 7 Or sea as into a heap

Psalm 34 [a,b]

Of David. When he pretended to be insane before Abimelek, who drove him away, and he left.

¹ I will extol the LORD at all
    times;
  his praise will always be on
    my lips.
² I will glory in the LORD;
  let the afflicted hear and
    rejoice.
³ Glorify the LORD with me;
  let us exalt his name
    together.

⁴ I sought the LORD, and he
    answered me;
  he delivered me from all my
    fears.
⁵ Those who look to him are
    radiant;
  their faces are never covered
    with shame.
⁶ This poor man called, and the
    LORD heard him;
  he saved him out of all his
    troubles.
⁷ The angel of the LORD
    encamps around those
    who fear him,
  and he delivers them.

⁸ Taste and see that the LORD is
    good;
  blessed is the one who takes
    refuge in him.
⁹ Fear the LORD, you his holy
    people,
  for those who fear him lack
    nothing.

¹⁰ The lions may grow weak and
    hungry,
  but those who seek the LORD
    lack no good thing.
¹¹ Come, my children, listen
    to me;
  I will teach you the fear of
    the LORD.
¹² Whoever of you loves life
  and desires to see many
    good days,
¹³ keep your tongue from evil
  and your lips from telling
    lies.
¹⁴ Turn from evil and do
    good;
  seek peace and pursue it.

¹⁵ The eyes of the LORD are on
    the righteous,
  and his ears are attentive to
    their cry;
¹⁶ but the face of the LORD is
    against those who do
    evil,
  to blot out their name from
    the earth.

¹⁷ The righteous cry out, and the
    LORD hears them;
  he delivers them from all
    their troubles.
¹⁸ The LORD is close to the
    brokenhearted
  and saves those who are
    crushed in spirit.

¹⁹ The righteous person may
    have many troubles,
  but the LORD delivers him
    from them all;

---

[a] This psalm is an acrostic poem, the verses of which begin with the successive letters of the Hebrew alphabet.   [b] In Hebrew texts 34:1-22 is numbered 34:2-23.

²⁰ he protects all his bones,
    not one of them will be
    broken.

²¹ Evil will slay the wicked;
    the foes of the righteous will
    be condemned.
²² The LORD will rescue his
    servants;
    no one who takes refuge in
    him will be condemned.

Psalm 35

Of David.

¹ Contend, LORD, with those
    who contend with me;
    fight against those who fight
    against me.
² Take up shield and armor;
    arise and come to my aid.
³ Brandish spear and javelin*ᵃ*
    against those who
    pursue me.
    Say to me,
    "I am your salvation."

⁴ May those who seek my life
    be disgraced and put to
    shame;
    may those who plot my ruin
    be turned back in dismay.
⁵ May they be like chaff before
    the wind,
    with the angel of the LORD
    driving them away;
⁶ may their path be dark and
    slippery,
    with the angel of the LORD
    pursuing them.

⁷ Since they hid their net for me
    without cause
    and without cause dug a pit
    for me,
⁸ may ruin overtake them by
    surprise —
    may the net they hid
    entangle them,
    may they fall into the pit, to
    their ruin.
⁹ Then my soul will rejoice in
    the LORD
    and delight in his salvation.
¹⁰ My whole being will exclaim,
    "Who is like you, LORD?
    You rescue the poor from
    those too strong for
    them,
    the poor and needy from
    those who rob them."

¹¹ Ruthless witnesses come
    forward;
    they question me on things I
    know nothing about.
¹² They repay me evil for good
    and leave me like one
    bereaved.
¹³ Yet when they were ill, I put on
    sackcloth
    and humbled myself with
    fasting.
    When my prayers returned to
    me unanswered,
¹⁴   I went about mourning
    as though for my friend or
    brother.
    I bowed my head in grief
    as though weeping for my
    mother.

ᵃ 3 Or *and block the way*

15 But when I stumbled, they
gathered in glee;
assailants gathered
against me without my
knowledge.
They slandered me without
ceasing.
16 Like the ungodly they
maliciously mocked;^a
they gnashed their teeth
at me.

17 How long, Lord, will you
look on?
Rescue me from their
ravages,
my precious life from these
lions.
18 I will give you thanks in the
great assembly;
among the throngs I will
praise you.
19 Do not let those gloat over me
who are my enemies without
cause;
do not let those who hate me
without reason
maliciously wink the eye.
20 They do not speak peaceably,
but devise false accusations
against those who live
quietly in the land.
21 They sneer at me and say,
"Aha! Aha!
With our own eyes we have
seen it."

22 LORD, you have seen this; do
not be silent.
Do not be far from me, Lord.

23 Awake, and rise to my defense!
Contend for me, my God and
Lord.
24 Vindicate me in your
righteousness, LORD my
God;
do not let them gloat
over me.
25 Do not let them think, "Aha,
just what we wanted!"
or say, "We have swallowed
him up."

26 May all who gloat over my
distress
be put to shame and
confusion;
may all who exalt themselves
over me
be clothed with shame and
disgrace.
27 May those who delight in my
vindication
shout for joy and gladness;
may they always say, "The
LORD be exalted,
who delights in the well-
being of his servant."

28 My tongue will proclaim your
righteousness,
your praises all day long.

Psalm 36^b

*For the director of music.
Of David the servant
of the LORD.*

1 I have a message from God in
my heart

---

^a *16* Septuagint; Hebrew may mean *Like an ungodly circle of mockers,*   ^b In Hebrew texts 36:1-12 is numbered 36:2-13.

concerning the sinfulness of
the wicked:[a]
There is no fear of God
before their eyes.

2 In their own eyes they flatter
themselves
too much to detect or hate
their sin.
3 The words of their mouths are
wicked and deceitful;
they fail to act wisely or do
good.
4 Even on their beds they plot
evil;
they commit themselves to a
sinful course
and do not reject what is
wrong.

5 Your love, LORD, reaches to the
heavens,
your faithfulness to the skies.
6 Your righteousness is like the
highest mountains,
your justice like the great
deep.
You, LORD, preserve both
people and animals.
7 How priceless is your unfailing
love, O God!
People take refuge in the
shadow of your wings.
8 They feast on the abundance
of your house;
you give them drink from
your river of delights.
9 For with you is the fountain of
life;
in your light we see light.

10 Continue your love to those
who know you,
your righteousness to the
upright in heart.
11 May the foot of the proud not
come against me,
nor the hand of the wicked
drive me away.
12 See how the evildoers lie
fallen —
thrown down, not able to
rise!

Psalm 37[b]

Of David.

1 Do not fret because of those
who are evil
or be envious of those who
do wrong;
2 for like the grass they will soon
wither,
like green plants they will
soon die away.

3 Trust in the LORD and do good;
dwell in the land and enjoy
safe pasture.
4 Take delight in the LORD,
and he will give you the
desires of your heart.

5 Commit your way to the LORD;
trust in him and he will do
this:
6 He will make your righteous
reward shine like the
dawn,
your vindication like the
noonday sun.

---

[a] 1 Or *A message from God: The transgression of the wicked / resides in their hearts.*
[b] This psalm is an acrostic poem, the stanzas of which begin with the successive letters of the Hebrew alphabet.

7 Be still before the LORD
and wait patiently for
him;
do not fret when people
succeed in their
ways,
when they carry out their
wicked schemes.

8 Refrain from anger and turn
from wrath;
do not fret — it leads only to
evil.
9 For those who are evil will be
destroyed,
but those who hope in the
LORD will inherit the
land.

10 A little while, and the wicked
will be no more;
though you look for them,
they will not be found.
11 But the meek will inherit the
land
and enjoy peace and
prosperity.

12 The wicked plot against the
righteous
and gnash their teeth at
them;
13 but the Lord laughs at the
wicked,
for he knows their day is
coming.

14 The wicked draw the sword
and bend the bow
to bring down the poor and
needy,
to slay those whose ways are
upright.

15 But their swords will pierce
their own hearts,
and their bows will be
broken.

16 Better the little that the
righteous have
than the wealth of many
wicked;
17 for the power of the wicked
will be broken,
but the LORD upholds the
righteous.

18 The blameless spend their
days under the LORD's
care,
and their inheritance will
endure forever.
19 In times of disaster they will
not wither;
in days of famine they will
enjoy plenty.

20 But the wicked will perish:
Though the LORD's enemies
are like the flowers of the
field,
they will be consumed, they
will go up in smoke.

21 The wicked borrow and do not
repay,
but the righteous give
generously;
22 those the LORD blesses will
inherit the land,
but those he curses will be
destroyed.

23 The LORD makes firm the
steps
of the one who delights in
him;

²⁴though he may stumble, he
    will not fall,
  for the LORD upholds him
    with his hand.

²⁵I was young and now I am
    old,
  yet I have never seen the
    righteous forsaken
  or their children begging
    bread.
²⁶They are always generous and
    lend freely;
  their children will be a
    blessing.ᵃ

²⁷Turn from evil and do
    good;
  then you will dwell in the
    land forever.
²⁸For the LORD loves the just
  and will not forsake his
    faithful ones.

  Wrongdoers will be completely
    destroyedᵇ;
  the offspring of the wicked
    will perish.
²⁹The righteous will inherit the
    land
  and dwell in it forever.

³⁰The mouths of the righteous
    utter wisdom,
  and their tongues speak
    what is just.
³¹The law of their God is in their
    hearts;
  their feet do not slip.

³²The wicked lie in wait for the
    righteous,
  intent on putting them to
    death;
³³but the LORD will not leave
    them in the power of the
    wicked
  or let them be condemned
    when brought to trial.

³⁴Hope in the LORD
  and keep his way.
  He will exalt you to inherit the
    land;
  when the wicked are
    destroyed, you will see it.

³⁵I have seen a wicked and
    ruthless man
  flourishing like a luxuriant
    native tree,
³⁶but he soon passed away and
    was no more;
  though I looked for him, he
    could not be found.

³⁷Consider the blameless,
    observe the upright;
  a future awaits those who
    seek peace.ᶜ
³⁸But all sinners will be
    destroyed;
  there will be no futureᵈ for
    the wicked.

³⁹The salvation of the righteous
    comes from the LORD;
  he is their stronghold in time
    of trouble.

ᵃ 26 Or *freely; / the names of their children will be used in blessings* (see Gen. 48:20); or *freely; / others will see that their children are blessed*   ᵇ 28 See Septuagint; Hebrew *They will be protected forever*   ᶜ 37 Or *upright; / those who seek peace will have posterity*   ᵈ 38 Or *posterity*

⁴⁰The LORD helps them and
delivers them;
he delivers them from the
wicked and saves them,
because they take refuge in
him.

Psalm 38*a*

A psalm of David. A petition.

¹LORD, do not rebuke me in
your anger
or discipline me in your
wrath.
²Your arrows have pierced me,
and your hand has come
down on me.
³Because of your wrath there is
no health in my body;
there is no soundness in my
bones because of my
sin.
⁴My guilt has overwhelmed me
like a burden too heavy to
bear.

⁵My wounds fester and are
loathsome
because of my sinful folly.
⁶I am bowed down and brought
very low;
all day long I go about
mourning.
⁷My back is filled with searing
pain;
there is no health in my
body.
⁸I am feeble and utterly
crushed;
I groan in anguish of heart.

⁹All my longings lie open before
you, Lord;
my sighing is not hidden
from you.
¹⁰My heart pounds, my strength
fails me;
even the light has gone from
my eyes.
¹¹My friends and companions
avoid me because of my
wounds;
my neighbors stay far
away.
¹²Those who want to kill me set
their traps,
those who would harm me
talk of my ruin;
all day long they scheme and
lie.

¹³I am like the deaf, who cannot
hear,
like the mute, who cannot
speak;
¹⁴I have become like one who
does not hear,
whose mouth can offer no
reply.
¹⁵LORD, I wait for you;
you will answer, Lord my
God.
¹⁶For I said, "Do not let them
gloat
or exalt themselves over me
when my feet slip."

¹⁷For I am about to fall,
and my pain is ever
with me.
¹⁸I confess my iniquity;
I am troubled by my sin.

a In Hebrew texts 38:1-22 is numbered 38:2-23.

[19] Many have become my
   enemies without cause[a];
those who hate me without
   reason are numerous.
[20] Those who repay my good
   with evil
lodge accusations against me,
   though I seek only to do
   what is good.

[21] LORD, do not forsake me;
   do not be far from me, my
   God.
[22] Come quickly to help me,
   my Lord and my Savior.

Psalm 39[b]

*For the director of music. For
Jeduthun. A psalm of David.*

[1] I said, "I will watch my ways
   and keep my tongue from sin;
I will put a muzzle on my
   mouth
   while in the presence of the
   wicked."
[2] So I remained utterly silent,
   not even saying anything
   good.
But my anguish increased;
[3]   my heart grew hot within me.
While I meditated, the fire
   burned;
   then I spoke with my tongue:

[4] "Show me, LORD, my life's end
   and the number of my days;
   let me know how fleeting my
   life is.

[5] You have made my days a
   mere handbreadth;
   the span of my years is as
   nothing before you.
Everyone is but a breath,
   even those who seem
   secure.[c]

[6] "Surely everyone goes around
   like a mere phantom;
in vain they rush about,
   heaping up wealth
   without knowing whose it
   will finally be.

[7] "But now, Lord, what do I look
   for?
   My hope is in you.
[8] Save me from all my
   transgressions;
   do not make me the scorn of
   fools.
[9] I was silent; I would not open
   my mouth,
   for you are the one who has
   done this.
[10] Remove your scourge from me;
   I am overcome by the blow
   of your hand.
[11] When you rebuke and
   discipline anyone for
   their sin,
you consume their wealth
   like a moth —
   surely everyone is but a
   breath.

[12] "Hear my prayer, LORD,
   listen to my cry for help;
   do not be deaf to my
   weeping.

---

[a] 19 One Dead Sea Scrolls manuscript; Masoretic Text *my vigorous enemies*   [b] In Hebrew texts 39:1-13 is numbered 39:2-14.   [c] 5 The Hebrew has *Selah* (a word of uncertain meaning) here and at the end of verse 11.

I dwell with you as a foreigner,
   a stranger, as all my
      ancestors were.
¹³ Look away from me, that I may
   enjoy life again
      before I depart and am no
         more."

Psalm 40ᵃ

For the director of music.
Of David. A psalm.

¹ I waited patiently for the LORD;
   he turned to me and heard
      my cry.
² He lifted me out of the slimy
   pit,
      out of the mud and mire;
   he set my feet on a rock
      and gave me a firm place to
         stand.
³ He put a new song in my
   mouth,
      a hymn of praise to our God.
   Many will see and fear the
      LORD
      and put their trust in him.

⁴ Blessed is the one
   who trusts in the LORD,
   who does not look to the
      proud,
      to those who turn aside to
         false gods.ᵇ
⁵ Many, LORD my God,
   are the wonders you have
      done,
      the things you planned
         for us.

None can compare with you;
   were I to speak and tell of
      your deeds,
      they would be too many to
         declare.

⁶ Sacrifice and offering you did
   not desire —
      but my ears you have
         openedᶜ —
   burnt offerings and sin
      offeringsᵈ you did not
         require.
⁷ Then I said, "Here I am, I have
   come —
      it is written about me in the
         scroll.ᵉ
⁸ I desire to do your will, my
   God;
      your law is within my
         heart."

⁹ I proclaim your saving acts in
   the great assembly;
   I do not seal my lips, LORD,
      as you know.
¹⁰ I do not hide your
      righteousness in my
         heart;
   I speak of your faithfulness
      and your saving help.
   I do not conceal your love and
      your faithfulness
      from the great assembly.

¹¹ Do not withhold your mercy
   from me, LORD;
   may your love and
      faithfulness always
         protect me.

ᵃ In Hebrew texts 40:1-17 is numbered 40:2-18.   ᵇ 4 Or *to lies*   ᶜ 6 Hebrew;
some Septuagint manuscripts *but a body you have prepared for me*
ᵈ 6 Or *purification offerings*   ᵉ 7 Or *come / with the scroll written for me*

¹²For troubles without number
surround me;
my sins have overtaken me,
and I cannot see.
They are more than the hairs
of my head,
and my heart fails within me.
¹³Be pleased to save me, LORD;
come quickly, LORD, to
help me.

¹⁴May all who want to take my
life
be put to shame and
confusion;
may all who desire my ruin
be turned back in disgrace.
¹⁵May those who say to me,
"Aha! Aha!"
be appalled at their own
shame.
¹⁶But may all who seek you
rejoice and be glad in you;
may those who long for your
saving help always say,
"The LORD is great!"

¹⁷But as for me, I am poor and
needy;
may the Lord think of me.
You are my help and my
deliverer;
you are my God, do not
delay.

Psalm 41 ᵃ

*For the director of music.
A psalm of David.*

¹Blessed are those who have
regard for the weak;

the LORD delivers them in
times of trouble.
²The LORD protects and
preserves them—
they are counted among the
blessed in the land—
he does not give them over to
the desire of their foes.
³The LORD sustains them on
their sickbed
and restores them from their
bed of illness.

⁴I said, "Have mercy on me,
LORD;
heal me, for I have sinned
against you."
⁵My enemies say of me in
malice,
"When will he die and his
name perish?"
⁶When one of them comes to
see me,
he speaks falsely, while his
heart gathers slander;
then he goes out and spreads
it around.

⁷All my enemies whisper
together against me;
they imagine the worst for
me, saying,
⁸"A vile disease has afflicted
him;
he will never get up from the
place where he lies."
⁹Even my close friend,
someone I trusted,
one who shared my
bread,
has turned ᵇ against me.

ᵃ In Hebrew texts 41:1-13 is numbered 41:2-14.   ᵇ 9 Hebrew *has lifted up his heel*

10 But may you have mercy on
       me, LORD;
    raise me up, that I may repay
       them.
11 I know that you are pleased
       with me,
    for my enemy does not
       triumph over me.
12 Because of my integrity you
       uphold me
    and set me in your presence
       forever.

13 Praise be to the LORD, the God
       of Israel,
    from everlasting to
       everlasting.
              Amen and Amen.

BOOK II

Psalms 42–72

Psalm 42[a,b]

*For the director of music.
A maskil[c] of the Sons of Korah.*

1 As the deer pants for streams
       of water,
    so my soul pants for you, my
       God.
2 My soul thirsts for God, for the
       living God.
    When can I go and meet
       with God?
3 My tears have been my food
       day and night,

while people say to me all day
       long,
    "Where is your God?"
4 These things I remember
    as I pour out my soul:
how I used to go to the house
       of God
under the protection of the
       Mighty One[d]
with shouts of joy and praise
    among the festive throng.

5 Why, my soul, are you
       downcast?
    Why so disturbed within me?
Put your hope in God,
    for I will yet praise him,
    my Savior and my God.

6 My soul is downcast within me;
    therefore I will remember
       you
from the land of the Jordan,
    the heights of Hermon —
       from Mount Mizar.
7 Deep calls to deep
    in the roar of your
       waterfalls;
all your waves and breakers
    have swept over me.

8 By day the LORD directs his
       love,
    at night his song is with
       me —
    a prayer to the God of my
       life.

9 I say to God my Rock,
    "Why have you forgotten me?

---

[a] In many Hebrew manuscripts Psalms 42 and 43 constitute one psalm.   [b] In Hebrew texts 42:1-11 is numbered 42:2-12.   [c] Title: Probably a literary or musical term   [d] 4 See Septuagint and Syriac; the meaning of the Hebrew for this line is uncertain.

Why must I go about
mourning,
oppressed by the enemy?"
¹⁰ My bones suffer mortal agony
as my foes taunt me,
saying to me all day long,
"Where is your God?"

¹¹ Why, my soul, are you
downcast?
Why so disturbed within
me?
Put your hope in God,
for I will yet praise him,
my Savior and my God.

Psalm 43[a]

¹ Vindicate me, my God,
and plead my cause
against an unfaithful nation.
Rescue me from those who are
deceitful and wicked.
² You are God my stronghold.
Why have you rejected me?
Why must I go about
mourning,
oppressed by the enemy?
³ Send me your light and your
faithful care,
let them lead me;
let them bring me to your holy
mountain,
to the place where you dwell.
⁴ Then I will go to the altar of
God,
to God, my joy and my
delight.

I will praise you with the lyre,
O God, my God.
⁵ Why, my soul, are you
downcast?
Why so disturbed
within me?
Put your hope in God,
for I will yet praise him,
my Savior and my God.

Psalm 44[b]

*For the director of music. Of the
Sons of Korah. A maskil.[c]*

¹ We have heard it with our ears,
O God;
our ancestors have told us
what you did in their days,
in days long ago.
² With your hand you drove out
the nations
and planted our ancestors;
you crushed the peoples
and made our ancestors
flourish.
³ It was not by their sword that
they won the land,
nor did their arm bring them
victory;
it was your right hand, your
arm,
and the light of your face, for
you loved them.
⁴ You are my King and my God,
who decrees[d] victories for
Jacob.

---

[a] In many Hebrew manuscripts Psalms 42 and 43 constitute one psalm.   [b] In
Hebrew texts 44:1-26 is numbered 44:2-27.   [c] Title: Probably a literary or
musical term   [d] 4 Septuagint, Aquila and Syriac; Hebrew *King, O God; /
command*

⁵Through you we push back our
enemies;
through your name we
trample our foes.
⁶I put no trust in my bow,
my sword does not bring me
victory;
⁷but you give us victory over
our enemies,
you put our adversaries to
shame.
⁸In God we make our boast all
day long,
and we will praise your
name forever.ᵃ

⁹But now you have rejected and
humbled us;
you no longer go out with
our armies.
¹⁰You made us retreat before the
enemy,
and our adversaries have
plundered us.
¹¹You gave us up to be devoured
like sheep
and have scattered us among
the nations.
¹²You sold your people for a
pittance,
gaining nothing from their
sale.
¹³You have made us a reproach
to our neighbors,
the scorn and derision of
those around us.
¹⁴You have made us a byword
among the nations;
the peoples shake their
heads at us.

¹⁵I live in disgrace all day long,
and my face is covered with
shame
¹⁶at the taunts of those who
reproach and revile me,
because of the enemy, who is
bent on revenge.

¹⁷All this came upon us,
though we had not forgotten
you;
we had not been false to your
covenant.
¹⁸Our hearts had not turned
back;
our feet had not strayed from
your path.
¹⁹But you crushed us and made
us a haunt for jackals;
you covered us over with
deep darkness.

²⁰If we had forgotten the name
of our God
or spread out our hands to a
foreign god,
²¹would not God have
discovered it,
since he knows the secrets of
the heart?
²²Yet for your sake we face death
all day long;
we are considered as sheep
to be slaughtered.

²³Awake, Lord! Why do you
sleep?
Rouse yourself! Do not reject
us forever.
²⁴Why do you hide your face
and forget our misery and
oppression?

ᵃ 8 The Hebrew has *Selah* (a word of uncertain meaning) here.

25We are brought down to the
    dust;
  our bodies cling to the
    ground.
26Rise up and help us;
  rescue us because of your
    unfailing love.

Psalm 45[a]

*For the director of music. To the
tune of "Lilies." Of the Sons of
Korah. A maskil.[b] A wedding song.*

1My heart is stirred by a noble
    theme
  as I recite my verses for the
    king;
  my tongue is the pen of a
    skillful writer.

2You are the most excellent of
    men
  and your lips have been
    anointed with grace,
  since God has blessed you
    forever.

3Gird your sword on your side,
    you mighty one;
  clothe yourself with splendor
    and majesty.
4In your majesty ride forth
    victoriously
  in the cause of truth,
    humility and justice;
  let your right hand achieve
    awesome deeds.
5Let your sharp arrows pierce
    the hearts of the king's
    enemies;

let the nations fall beneath
    your feet.
6Your throne, O God,[c] will last
    for ever and ever;
  a scepter of justice will
    be the scepter of your
    kingdom.
7You love righteousness and
    hate wickedness;
  therefore God, your God,
    has set you above your
    companions
  by anointing you with the oil
    of joy.
8All your robes are fragrant
    with myrrh and aloes
    and cassia;
  from palaces adorned with
    ivory
  the music of the strings
    makes you glad.
9Daughters of kings are among
    your honored women;
  at your right hand is the
    royal bride in gold of
    Ophir.
10Listen, daughter, and pay
    careful attention:
  Forget your people and your
    father's house.
11Let the king be enthralled by
    your beauty;
  honor him, for he is your
    lord.
12The city of Tyre will come with
    a gift,[d]
  people of wealth will seek
    your favor.

[a] In Hebrew texts 45:1-17 is numbered 45:2-18.   [b] Title: Probably a literary
or musical term   [c] 6 Here the king is addressed as God's representative.
[d] 12 Or *A Tyrian robe is among the gifts*

[13] All glorious is the princess
within her chamber;
her gown is interwoven with
gold.
[14] In embroidered garments she
is led to the king;
her virgin companions
follow her —
those brought to be with
her.
[15] Led in with joy and gladness,
they enter the palace of the
king.
[16] Your sons will take the place of
your fathers;
you will make them princes
throughout the land.
[17] I will perpetuate your memory
through all generations;
therefore the nations will
praise you for ever and
ever.

Psalm 46[a]

*For the director of music. Of the
Sons of Korah. According
to alamoth.[b] A song.*

[1] God is our refuge and
strength,
an ever-present help in
trouble.
[2] Therefore we will not fear,
though the earth give
way
and the mountains fall into
the heart of the sea,

[3] though its waters roar and
foam
and the mountains quake
with their surging.[c]

[4] There is a river whose streams
make glad the city of
God,
the holy place where the
Most High dwells.
[5] God is within her, she will not
fall;
God will help her at break of
day.
[6] Nations are in uproar,
kingdoms fall;
he lifts his voice, the earth
melts.

[7] The LORD Almighty is
with us;
the God of Jacob is our
fortress.

[8] Come and see what the LORD
has done,
the desolations he has
brought on the earth.
[9] He makes wars cease
to the ends of the earth.
He breaks the bow and
shatters the spear;
he burns the shields[d] with
fire.
[10] He says, "Be still, and know
that I am God;
I will be exalted among the
nations,
I will be exalted in the
earth."

---

[a] In Hebrew texts 46:1-11 is numbered 46:2-12.   [b] Title: Probably a musical term
[c] 3 The Hebrew has *Selah* (a word of uncertain meaning) here and at the end of
verses 7 and 11.   [d] 9 Or *chariots*

11 The LORD Almighty is with us;
　　the God of Jacob is our
　　　fortress.

Psalm 47[a]

*For the director of music. Of the
Sons of Korah. A psalm.*

1 Clap your hands, all you
　　nations;
　　shout to God with cries of
　　　joy.

2 For the LORD Most High is
　　awesome,
　　the great King over all the
　　　earth.
3 He subdued nations under us,
　　peoples under our feet.
4 He chose our inheritance for us,
　　the pride of Jacob, whom he
　　　loved.[b]

5 God has ascended amid
　　shouts of joy,
　　the LORD amid the sounding
　　　of trumpets.
6 Sing praises to God, sing
　　praises;
　　sing praises to our King, sing
　　　praises.
7 For God is the King of all the
　　earth;
　　sing to him a psalm of
　　　praise.
8 God reigns over the nations;
　　God is seated on his holy
　　　throne.

9 The nobles of the nations
　　assemble
　　as the people of the God of
　　　Abraham,
　　for the kings[c] of the earth
　　　belong to God;
　　he is greatly exalted.

Psalm 48[d]

*A song. A psalm of the
Sons of Korah.*

1 Great is the LORD, and most
　　worthy of praise,
　　in the city of our God, his
　　　holy mountain.

2 Beautiful in its loftiness,
　　the joy of the whole earth,
　　like the heights of Zaphon[e] is
　　　Mount Zion,
　　the city of the Great King.
3 God is in her citadels;
　　he has shown himself to be
　　　her fortress.

4 When the kings joined forces,
　　when they advanced
　　　together,
5 they saw her and were
　　astounded;
　　they fled in terror.
6 Trembling seized them there,
　　pain like that of a woman in
　　　labor.
7 You destroyed them like ships
　　of Tarshish
　　shattered by an east wind.

---

a In Hebrew texts 47:1-9 is numbered 47:2-10.　b 4 The Hebrew has *Selah* (a word
of uncertain meaning) here.　c 9 Or *shields*　d In Hebrew texts 48:1-14 is
numbered 48:2-15.　e 2 *Zaphon* was the most sacred mountain of the Canaanites.

8 As we have heard,
    so we have seen
in the city of the LORD
        Almighty,
    in the city of our God:
God makes her secure
        forever.[a]

9 Within your temple, O God,
    we meditate on your
        unfailing love.
10 Like your name, O God,
    your praise reaches to the
        ends of the earth;
    your right hand is filled with
        righteousness.
11 Mount Zion rejoices,
    the villages of Judah are glad
    because of your judgments.

12 Walk about Zion, go around
        her,
    count her towers,
13 consider well her ramparts,
    view her citadels,
    that you may tell of them
    to the next generation.

14 For this God is our God for
        ever and ever;
    he will be our guide even to
        the end.

Psalm 49[b]

*For the director of music. Of the
Sons of Korah. A psalm.*

1 Hear this, all you peoples;
    listen, all who live in this
        world,

2 both low and high,
    rich and poor alike:
3 My mouth will speak words of
        wisdom;
    the meditation of my
        heart will give you
        understanding.
4 I will turn my ear to a
        proverb;
    with the harp I will expound
        my riddle:

5 Why should I fear when evil
        days come,
    when wicked deceivers
        surround me —
6 those who trust in their wealth
    and boast of their great
        riches?
7 No one can redeem the life of
        another
    or give to God a ransom for
        them —
8 the ransom for a life is costly,
    no payment is ever
        enough —
9 so that they should live on
        forever
    and not see decay.
10 For all can see that the wise
        die,
    that the foolish and the
        senseless also perish,
    leaving their wealth to
        others.
11 Their tombs will remain their
        houses[c] forever,
    their dwellings for endless
        generations,

---

[a] 8 The Hebrew has *Selah* (a word of uncertain meaning) here.   [b] In Hebrew
texts 49:1-20 is numbered 49:2-21.   [c] 11 Septuagint and Syriac; Hebrew *In their
thoughts their houses will remain*

though they had[a] named
lands after themselves.

12 People, despite their wealth,
do not endure;
they are like the beasts that
perish.

13 This is the fate of those who
trust in themselves,
and of their followers, who
approve their sayings.[b]

14 They are like sheep and are
destined to die;
death will be their shepherd
(but the upright will prevail
over them in the
morning).
Their forms will decay in the
grave,
far from their princely
mansions.

15 But God will redeem me from
the realm of the dead;
he will surely take me to
himself.

16 Do not be overawed when
others grow rich,
when the splendor of their
houses increases;

17 for they will take nothing with
them when they die,
their splendor will not
descend with them.

18 Though while they live they
count themselves
blessed —
and people praise you when
you prosper —

19 they will join those who have
gone before them,
who will never again see the
light of life.

20 People who have wealth but
lack understanding
are like the beasts that
perish.

Psalm 50

A psalm of Asaph.

1 The Mighty One, God, the
Lord,
speaks and summons the
earth
from the rising of the sun to
where it sets.

2 From Zion, perfect in beauty,
God shines forth.

3 Our God comes
and will not be silent;
a fire devours before him,
and around him a tempest
rages.

4 He summons the heavens
above,
and the earth, that he may
judge his people:

5 "Gather to me this consecrated
people,
who made a covenant with
me by sacrifice."

6 And the heavens proclaim his
righteousness,
for he is a God of justice.[c,d]

---

[a] 11 Or *generations, / for they have*   [b] 13 The Hebrew has *Selah* (a word of
uncertain meaning) here and at the end of verse 15.   [c] 6 With a different word
division of the Hebrew; Masoretic Text *for God himself is judge*   [d] 6 The Hebrew
has *Selah* (a word of uncertain meaning) here.

7 "Listen, my people, and I will
    speak;
  I will testify against you,
    Israel:
  I am God, your God.
8 I bring no charges against
    you concerning your
    sacrifices
  or concerning your burnt
    offerings, which are ever
    before me.
9 I have no need of a bull from
    your stall
  or of goats from your
    pens,
10 for every animal of the forest is
    mine,
  and the cattle on a thousand
    hills.
11 I know every bird in the
    mountains,
  and the insects in the fields
    are mine.
12 If I were hungry I would not
    tell you,
  for the world is mine, and all
    that is in it.
13 Do I eat the flesh of
    bulls
  or drink the blood of
    goats?

14 "Sacrifice thank offerings to
    God,
  fulfill your vows to the Most
    High,
15 and call on me in the day of
    trouble;
  I will deliver you, and you
    will honor me."

16 But to the wicked person, God
    says:

  "What right have you to recite
    my laws
  or take my covenant on your
    lips?
17 You hate my instruction
  and cast my words behind
    you.
18 When you see a thief, you join
    with him;
  you throw in your lot with
    adulterers.
19 You use your mouth for
    evil
  and harness your tongue to
    deceit.
20 You sit and testify against your
    brother
  and slander your own
    mother's son.
21 When you did these things
    and I kept silent,
  you thought I was exactly[a]
    like you.
  But I now arraign you
  and set my accusations
    before you.

22 "Consider this, you who forget
    God,
  or I will tear you to pieces,
    with no one to rescue
    you:
23 Those who sacrifice thank
    offerings honor me,
  and to the blameless[b] I
    will show my
    salvation."

[a] 21 Or thought the 'I AM' was   [b] 23 Probable reading of the original Hebrew
text; the meaning of the Masoretic Text for this phrase is uncertain.

Psalm 51 [a]

For the director of music.
A psalm of David. When the
prophet Nathan came to him
after David had committed
adultery with Bathsheba.

¹ Have mercy on me, O God,
according to your unfailing
love;
according to your great
compassion
blot out my transgressions.
² Wash away all my iniquity
and cleanse me from my sin.

³ For I know my transgressions,
and my sin is always
before me.
⁴ Against you, you only, have I
sinned
and done what is evil in your
sight;
so you are right in your verdict
and justified when you
judge.
⁵ Surely I was sinful at birth,
sinful from the time my
mother conceived me.
⁶ Yet you desired faithfulness
even in the womb;
you taught me wisdom in
that secret place.

⁷ Cleanse me with hyssop, and I
will be clean;
wash me, and I will be
whiter than snow.
⁸ Let me hear joy and gladness;
let the bones you have
crushed rejoice.

⁹ Hide your face from my sins
and blot out all my iniquity.

¹⁰ Create in me a pure heart,
O God,
and renew a steadfast spirit
within me.
¹¹ Do not cast me from your
presence
or take your Holy Spirit
from me.
¹² Restore to me the joy of your
salvation
and grant me a willing spirit,
to sustain me.

¹³ Then I will teach transgressors
your ways,
so that sinners will turn back
to you.
¹⁴ Deliver me from the guilt of
bloodshed, O God,
you who are God my
Savior,
and my tongue will sing of
your righteousness.
¹⁵ Open my lips, Lord,
and my mouth will declare
your praise.
¹⁶ You do not delight in sacrifice,
or I would bring it;
you do not take pleasure in
burnt offerings.
¹⁷ My sacrifice, O God, is [b] a
broken spirit;
a broken and contrite heart
you, God, will not despise.

¹⁸ May it please you to prosper
Zion,
to build up the walls of
Jerusalem.

---

[a] In Hebrew texts 51:1-19 is numbered 51:3-21.   [b] 17 Or *The sacrifices of God are*

¹⁹Then you will delight in
the sacrifices of the
righteous,
in burnt offerings offered
whole;
then bulls will be offered on
your altar.

Psalm 52^a

*For the director of music.
A maskil^b of David. When
Doeg the Edomite had gone
to Saul and told him: "David
has gone to the house
of Ahimelek."*

¹Why do you boast of evil, you
mighty hero?
Why do you boast all day
long,
you who are a disgrace in the
eyes of God?
²You who practice deceit,
your tongue plots
destruction;
it is like a sharpened razor.
³You love evil rather than good,
falsehood rather than
speaking the truth.^c
⁴You love every harmful word,
you deceitful tongue!

⁵Surely God will bring you
down to everlasting ruin:
He will snatch you up and
pluck you from your tent;
he will uproot you from the
land of the living.

⁶The righteous will see and
fear;
they will laugh at you, saying,
⁷"Here now is the man
who did not make God his
stronghold
but trusted in his great wealth
and grew strong by
destroying others!"

⁸But I am like an olive tree
flourishing in the house of
God;
I trust in God's unfailing love
for ever and ever.
⁹For what you have done I will
always praise you
in the presence of your
faithful people.
And I will hope in your name,
for your name is good.

Psalm 53^d

*For the director of music.
According to* mahalath.^e
A maskil^b of David.

¹The fool says in his heart,
"There is no God."
They are corrupt, and their
ways are vile;
there is no one who does
good.

²God looks down from heaven
on all mankind
to see if there are any who
understand,
any who seek God.

---

^a In Hebrew texts 52:1-9 is numbered 52:3-11.   ^b Title: Probably a literary
or musical term   ^c 3 The Hebrew has *Selah* (a word of uncertain meaning)
here and at the end of verse 5.   ^d In Hebrew texts 53:1-6 is numbered 53:2-7.
^e Title: Probably a musical term

³Everyone has turned away, all
    have become corrupt;
there is no one who does
    good,
    not even one.

⁴Do all these evildoers know
    nothing?

They devour my people as
    though eating bread;
they never call on God.
⁵But there they are,
    overwhelmed with
    dread,
where there was nothing to
    dread.
God scattered the bones of
    those who attacked you;
you put them to shame, for
    God despised them.

⁶Oh, that salvation for Israel
    would come out of Zion!
When God restores his
    people,
    let Jacob rejoice and Israel be
    glad!

Psalm 54[a]

*For the director of music. With
stringed instruments. A maskil[b]
of David. When the Ziphites
had gone to Saul and said, "Is
not David hiding among us?"*

¹Save me, O God, by your
    name;
    vindicate me by your
    might.

²Hear my prayer, O God;
    listen to the words of my
    mouth.

³Arrogant foes are attacking me;
    ruthless people are trying to
    kill me —
    people without regard for
    God.[c]

⁴Surely God is my help;
    the Lord is the one who
    sustains me.

⁵Let evil recoil on those who
    slander me;
    in your faithfulness destroy
    them.

⁶I will sacrifice a freewill
    offering to you;
I will praise your name,
    Lᴏʀᴅ, for it is good.
⁷You have delivered me from all
    my troubles,
and my eyes have looked in
    triumph on my foes.

Psalm 55[d]

*For the director of music.
With stringed instruments.
A maskil[b] of David.*

¹Listen to my prayer, O God,
    do not ignore my plea;
²   hear me and answer me.
My thoughts trouble me and I
    am distraught
³   because of what my enemy is
    saying,

---

[a] In Hebrew texts 54:1-7 is numbered 54:3-9.   [b] Title: Probably a literary or
musical term   [c] 3 The Hebrew has *Selah* (a word of uncertain meaning) here.
[d] In Hebrew texts 55:1-23 is numbered 55:2-24.

because of the threats of the
  wicked;
for they bring down suffering
  on me
  and assail me in their anger.

⁴My heart is in anguish
  within me;
  the terrors of death have
  fallen on me.
⁵Fear and trembling have
  beset me;
  horror has overwhelmed me.
⁶I said, "Oh, that I had the
  wings of a dove!
  I would fly away and be at
  rest.
⁷I would flee far away
  and stay in the desert;ᵃ
⁸I would hurry to my place of
  shelter,
  far from the tempest and
  storm."

⁹Lord, confuse the wicked,
  confound their words,
  for I see violence and strife
  in the city.
¹⁰Day and night they prowl
  about on its walls;
  malice and abuse are
  within it.
¹¹Destructive forces are at work
  in the city;
  threats and lies never leave
  its streets.

¹²If an enemy were insulting me,
  I could endure it;
  if a foe were rising against me,
  I could hide.

¹³But it is you, a man like
  myself,
  my companion, my close
  friend,
¹⁴with whom I once enjoyed
  sweet fellowship
  at the house of God,
  as we walked about
  among the worshipers.

¹⁵Let death take my enemies by
  surprise;
  let them go down alive to the
  realm of the dead,
  for evil finds lodging among
  them.

¹⁶As for me, I call to God,
  and the LORD saves me.
¹⁷Evening, morning and noon
  I cry out in distress,
  and he hears my voice.
¹⁸He rescues me unharmed
  from the battle waged
  against me,
  even though many
  oppose me.
¹⁹God, who is enthroned from of
  old,
  who does not change—
  he will hear them and humble
  them,
  because they have no fear of
  God.

²⁰My companion attacks his
  friends;
  he violates his covenant.
²¹His talk is smooth as
  butter,
  yet war is in his heart;

ᵃ 7 The Hebrew has *Selah* (a word of uncertain meaning) here and in the middle
of verse 19.

his words are more soothing
than oil,
    yet they are drawn swords.

²² Cast your cares on the LORD
    and he will sustain you;
he will never let
    the righteous be shaken.
²³ But you, God, will bring down
    the wicked
into the pit of decay;
    the bloodthirsty and
        deceitful
    will not live out half their
        days.

But as for me, I trust in you.

Psalm 56[a]

*For the director of music. To
the tune of "A Dove on
Distant Oaks." Of David.
A miktam.[b] When the
Philistines had seized
him in Gath.*

¹ Be merciful to me, my God,
    for my enemies are in hot
        pursuit;
all day long they press their
    attack.
² My adversaries pursue me all
    day long;
in their pride many are
    attacking me.
³ When I am afraid, I put my
    trust in you.
⁴   In God, whose word I
        praise —

in God I trust and am not
    afraid.
    What can mere mortals do
        to me?

⁵ All day long they twist my
    words;
    all their schemes are for my
        ruin.
⁶ They conspire, they lurk,
    they watch my steps,
    hoping to take my life.
⁷ Because of their wickedness
        do not[c] let them escape;
    in your anger, God, bring the
        nations down.

⁸ Record my misery;
    list my tears on your
        scroll[d] —
    are they not in your record?
⁹ Then my enemies will turn
        back
    when I call for help.
    By this I will know that God
        is for me.

¹⁰ In God, whose word I praise,
    in the LORD, whose word I
        praise —
¹¹ in God I trust and am not
    afraid.
    What can man do to me?

¹² I am under vows to you, my
        God;
    I will present my thank
        offerings to you.
¹³ For you have delivered me
        from death
    and my feet from stumbling,

---

[a] In Hebrew texts 56:1-13 is numbered 56:2-14.   [b] Title: Probably a literary or
musical term   [c] 7 Probable reading of the original Hebrew text; Masoretic Text
does not have *do not*.   [d] 8 Or *misery; / put my tears in your wineskin*

that I may walk before God
in the light of life.

Psalm 57[a]

*For the director of music. To
the tune of "Do Not Destroy."
Of David. A miktam.[b] When
he had fled from Saul
into the cave.*

[1] Have mercy on me, my God,
have mercy on me,
for in you I take refuge.
I will take refuge in the
shadow of your
wings
until the disaster has
passed.

[2] I cry out to God Most High,
to God, who vindicates me.
[3] He sends from heaven and
saves me,
rebuking those who hotly
pursue me — [c]
God sends forth his love and
his faithfulness.

[4] I am in the midst of lions;
I am forced to dwell among
ravenous beasts —
men whose teeth are spears
and arrows,
whose tongues are sharp
swords.
[5] Be exalted, O God, above the
heavens;
let your glory be over all the
earth.

[6] They spread a net for my
feet —
I was bowed down in
distress.
They dug a pit in my path —
but they have fallen into it
themselves.

[7] My heart, O God, is steadfast,
my heart is steadfast;
I will sing and make music.
[8] Awake, my soul!
Awake, harp and lyre!
I will awaken the dawn.

[9] I will praise you, Lord, among
the nations;
I will sing of you among the
peoples.
[10] For great is your love, reaching
to the heavens;
your faithfulness reaches to
the skies.

[11] Be exalted, O God, above the
heavens;
let your glory be over all the
earth.

Psalm 58[d]

*For the director of music. To
the tune of "Do Not Destroy."
Of David. A miktam.[b]*

[1] Do you rulers indeed speak
justly?
Do you judge people with
equity?
[2] No, in your heart you devise
injustice,

---

[a] In Hebrew texts 57:1-11 is numbered 57:2-12.   [b] Title: Probably a literary or
musical term   [c] 3 The Hebrew has *Selah* (a word of uncertain meaning) here
and at the end of verse 6.   [d] In Hebrew texts 58:1-11 is numbered 58:2-12.

and your hands mete out
violence on the earth.

³ Even from birth the wicked go
astray;
from the womb they are
wayward, spreading lies.
⁴ Their venom is like the venom
of a snake,
like that of a cobra that has
stopped its ears,
⁵ that will not heed the tune of
the charmer,
however skillful the
enchanter may be.

⁶ Break the teeth in their
mouths, O God;
LORD, tear out the fangs of
those lions!
⁷ Let them vanish like water that
flows away;
when they draw the bow, let
their arrows fall short.
⁸ May they be like a slug that
melts away as it moves
along,
like a stillborn child that
never sees the sun.

⁹ Before your pots can feel the
heat of the thorns —
whether they be green or
dry — the wicked will be
swept away.ᵃ
¹⁰ The righteous will be glad
when they are avenged,
when they dip their feet in
the blood of the wicked.

¹¹ Then people will say,
"Surely the righteous still are
rewarded;
surely there is a God who
judges the earth."

Psalm 59ᵇ

*For the director of music. To
the tune of "Do Not Destroy."
Of David. A miktam.ᶜ When
Saul had sent men to watch
David's house in order
to kill him.*

¹ Deliver me from my enemies,
O God;
be my fortress against those
who are attacking me.
² Deliver me from evildoers
and save me from those who
are after my blood.

³ See how they lie in wait for me!
Fierce men conspire
against me
for no offense or sin of mine,
LORD.
⁴ I have done no wrong, yet they
are ready to attack me.
Arise to help me; look on my
plight!
⁵ You, LORD God Almighty,
you who are the God of
Israel,
rouse yourself to punish all the
nations;
show no mercy to wicked
traitors.ᵈ

ᵃ 9 The meaning of the Hebrew for this verse is uncertain.   ᵇ In Hebrew
texts 59:1-17 is numbered 59:2-18.   ᶜ Title: Probably a literary or musical term
ᵈ 5 The Hebrew has *Selah* (a word of uncertain meaning) here and at the end of
verse 13.

⁶They return at evening,
  snarling like dogs,
  and prowl about the city.
⁷See what they spew from their
    mouths —
  the words from their lips are
    sharp as swords,
  and they think, "Who can
    hear us?"
⁸But you laugh at them, LORD;
  you scoff at all those
    nations.

⁹You are my strength, I watch
    for you;
  you, God, are my fortress,
10 my God on whom I can
    rely.

God will go before me
  and will let me gloat over
    those who slander me.
¹¹But do not kill them, Lord our
    shield,ᵃ
  or my people will forget.
In your might uproot them
  and bring them down.
¹²For the sins of their mouths,
  for the words of their lips,
  let them be caught in their
    pride.
For the curses and lies they
    utter,
13 consume them in your
    wrath,
  consume them till they are
    no more.
Then it will be known to the
    ends of the earth
  that God rules over Jacob.

¹⁴They return at evening,
  snarling like dogs,
  and prowl about the city.
¹⁵They wander about for food
  and howl if not satisfied.
¹⁶But I will sing of your strength,
  in the morning I will sing of
    your love;
for you are my fortress,
  my refuge in times of trouble.

¹⁷You are my strength, I sing
    praise to you;
  you, God, are my fortress,
  my God on whom I can rely.

Psalm 60ᵇ

*For the director of music. To
the tune of "The Lily of the
Covenant." A miktamᶜ of David.
For teaching. When he fought
Aram Naharaimᵈ and Aram
Zobah,ᵉ and when Joab
returned and struck down
twelve thousand Edomites
in the Valley of Salt.*

¹You have rejected us, God, and
    burst upon us;
  you have been angry — now
    restore us!
²You have shaken the land and
    torn it open;
  mend its fractures, for it is
    quaking.
³You have shown your people
    desperate times;
  you have given us wine that
    makes us stagger.

ᵃ 11 Or *sovereign*   ᵇ In Hebrew texts 60:1-12 is numbered 60:3-14.   ᶜ Title: Probably a literary or musical term   ᵈ Title: That is, Arameans of Northwest Mesopotamia   ᵉ Title: That is, Arameans of central Syria

⁴ But for those who fear you, you
    have raised a banner
  to be unfurled against the
    bow.ᵃ

⁵ Save us and help us with your
    right hand,
  that those you love may be
    delivered.
⁶ God has spoken from his
    sanctuary:
  "In triumph I will parcel out
    Shechem
  and measure off the Valley of
    Sukkoth.
⁷ Gilead is mine, and Manasseh
    is mine;
  Ephraim is my helmet,
  Judah is my scepter.
⁸ Moab is my washbasin,
  on Edom I toss my
    sandal;
  over Philistia I shout in
    triumph."

⁹ Who will bring me to the
    fortified city?
  Who will lead me to Edom?
¹⁰ Is it not you, God, you who
    have now rejected us
  and no longer go out with
    our armies?
¹¹ Give us aid against the enemy,
  for human help is
    worthless.
¹² With God we will gain the
    victory,
  and he will trample down
    our enemies.

Psalm 61ᵇ

For the director of music.
With stringed instruments.
Of David.

¹ Hear my cry, O God;
  listen to my prayer.

² From the ends of the earth I
    call to you,
  I call as my heart grows
    faint;
  lead me to the rock that is
    higher than I.
³ For you have been my refuge,
  a strong tower against the foe.

⁴ I long to dwell in your tent
    forever
  and take refuge in the shelter
    of your wings.ᶜ
⁵ For you, God, have heard my
    vows;
  you have given me the
    heritage of those who
    fear your name.

⁶ Increase the days of the king's
    life,
  his years for many
    generations.
⁷ May he be enthroned in God's
    presence forever;
  appoint your love and
    faithfulness to protect
    him.

⁸ Then I will ever sing in praise
    of your name
  and fulfill my vows day after
    day.

ᵃ 4 The Hebrew has *Selah* (a word of uncertain meaning) here.   ᵇ In Hebrew texts 61:1-8 is numbered 61:2-9.   ᶜ 4 The Hebrew has *Selah* (a word of uncertain meaning) here.

Psalm 62[a]

For the director of music. For Jeduthun. A psalm of David.

[1] Truly my soul finds rest in
     God;
  my salvation comes from
     him.
[2] Truly he is my rock and my
     salvation;
  he is my fortress, I will never
     be shaken.

[3] How long will you assault me?
  Would all of you throw me
     down —
  this leaning wall, this
     tottering fence?
[4] Surely they intend to
     topple me
  from my lofty place;
  they take delight in lies.
  With their mouths they bless,
  but in their hearts they
     curse.[b]

[5] Yes, my soul, find rest in God;
  my hope comes from him.
[6] Truly he is my rock and my
     salvation;
  he is my fortress, I will not be
     shaken.
[7] My salvation and my honor
     depend on God[c];
  he is my mighty rock, my
     refuge.
[8] Trust in him at all times, you
     people;
  pour out your hearts to him,
  for God is our refuge.

[9] Surely the lowborn are but a
     breath,
  the highborn are but a lie.
  If weighed on a balance, they
     are nothing;
  together they are only a
     breath.
[10] Do not trust in extortion
  or put vain hope in stolen
     goods;
  though your riches increase,
  do not set your heart on
     them.

[11] One thing God has spoken,
  two things I have heard:
  "Power belongs to you, God,
[12]   and with you, Lord, is
     unfailing love";
  and, "You reward everyone
     according to what they have
     done."

Psalm 63[d]

*A psalm of David. When he was
in the Desert of Judah.*

[1] You, God, are my God,
  earnestly I seek you;
  I thirst for you,
  my whole being longs for
     you,
  in a dry and parched land
  where there is no water.

[2] I have seen you in the
     sanctuary
  and beheld your power and
     your glory.

---

[a] In Hebrew texts 62:1-12 is numbered 62:2-13.   [b] 4 The Hebrew has *Selah* (a word
of uncertain meaning) here and at the end of verse 8.   [c] 7 Or / *God Most High is
my salvation and my honor*   [d] In Hebrew texts 63:1-11 is numbered 63:2-12.

3 Because your love is better
    than life,
  my lips will glorify you.
4 I will praise you as long as I
    live,
  and in your name I will lift
    up my hands.
5 I will be fully satisfied as with
    the richest of foods;
  with singing lips my mouth
    will praise you.

6 On my bed I remember you;
  I think of you through the
    watches of the night.
7 Because you are my help,
  I sing in the shadow of your
    wings.
8 I cling to you;
  your right hand upholds me.

9 Those who want to kill me will
    be destroyed;
  they will go down to the
    depths of the earth.
10 They will be given over to the
    sword
  and become food for jackals.

11 But the king will rejoice in God;
  all who swear by God will
    glory in him,
  while the mouths of liars will
    be silenced.

Psalm 64[a]

For the director of music.
A psalm of David.

1 Hear me, my God, as I voice
    my complaint;

protect my life from the
    threat of the enemy.
2 Hide me from the conspiracy
    of the wicked,
  from the plots of
    evildoers.
3 They sharpen their tongues
    like swords
  and aim cruel words like
    deadly arrows.
4 They shoot from ambush at
    the innocent;
  they shoot suddenly, without
    fear.

5 They encourage each other in
    evil plans,
  they talk about hiding their
    snares;
  they say, "Who will see it[b]?"
6 They plot injustice and say,
  "We have devised a perfect
    plan!"
  Surely the human mind and
    heart are cunning.

7 But God will shoot them with
    his arrows;
  they will suddenly be struck
    down.
8 He will turn their own tongues
    against them
  and bring them to ruin;
  all who see them will shake
    their heads in scorn.
9 All people will fear;
  they will proclaim the works
    of God
  and ponder what he has
    done.

---

a In Hebrew texts 64:1-10 is numbered 64:2-11.   b 5 Or *us*

[10] The righteous will rejoice in
the LORD
and take refuge in him;
all the upright in heart will
glory in him!

Psalm 65[a]

For the director of music.
A psalm of David. A song.

[1] Praise awaits[b] you, our God, in
Zion;
to you our vows will be
fulfilled.
[2] You who answer prayer,
to you all people will come.
[3] When we were overwhelmed
by sins,
you forgave[c] our
transgressions.
[4] Blessed are those you
choose
and bring near to live in your
courts!
We are filled with the good
things of your house,
of your holy temple.

[5] You answer us with awesome
and righteous deeds,
God our Savior,
the hope of all the ends of the
earth
and of the farthest seas,
[6] who formed the mountains by
your power,
having armed yourself with
strength,

[7] who stilled the roaring of the
seas,
the roaring of their
waves,
and the turmoil of the
nations.
[8] The whole earth is filled with
awe at your wonders;
where morning dawns,
where evening fades,
you call forth songs
of joy.

[9] You care for the land and
water it;
you enrich it abundantly.
The streams of God are filled
with water
to provide the people with
grain,
for so you have ordained it.[d]
[10] You drench its furrows and
level its ridges;
you soften it with showers
and bless its crops.
[11] You crown the year with your
bounty,
and your carts overflow with
abundance.
[12] The grasslands of the
wilderness overflow;
the hills are clothed with
gladness.
[13] The meadows are covered
with flocks
and the valleys are mantled
with grain;
they shout for joy and
sing.

[a] In Hebrew texts 65:1-13 is numbered 65:2-14.   [b] 1 Or *befits*; the meaning of
the Hebrew for this word is uncertain.   [c] 3 Or *made atonement for*   [d] 9 Or *for
that is how you prepare the land*

Psalm 66

For the director of music.
A song. A psalm.

¹ Shout for joy to God, all the
earth!
² Sing the glory of his name;
make his praise glorious.
³ Say to God, "How awesome are
your deeds!
So great is your power
that your enemies cringe
before you.
⁴ All the earth bows down to
you;
they sing praise to you,
they sing the praises of your
name."ᵃ

⁵ Come and see what God has
done,
his awesome deeds for
mankind!
⁶ He turned the sea into dry
land,
they passed through the
waters on foot —
come, let us rejoice in him.
⁷ He rules forever by his
power,
his eyes watch the nations —
let not the rebellious rise up
against him.

⁸ Praise our God, all peoples,
let the sound of his praise be
heard;
⁹ he has preserved our lives
and kept our feet from
slipping.

¹⁰ For you, God, tested us;
you refined us like silver.
¹¹ You brought us into prison
and laid burdens on our
backs.
¹² You let people ride over our
heads;
we went through fire and
water,
but you brought us to a place
of abundance.

¹³ I will come to your temple with
burnt offerings
and fulfill my vows to
you —
¹⁴ vows my lips promised and my
mouth spoke
when I was in trouble.
¹⁵ I will sacrifice fat animals to
you
and an offering of rams;
I will offer bulls and
goats.

¹⁶ Come and hear, all you who
fear God;
let me tell you what he has
done for me.
¹⁷ I cried out to him with my
mouth;
his praise was on my
tongue.
¹⁸ If I had cherished sin in my
heart,
the Lord would not have
listened;
¹⁹ but God has surely listened
and has heard my prayer.

ᵃ 4 The Hebrew has *Selah* (a word of uncertain meaning) here and at the end of
verses 7 and 15.

²⁰Praise be to God,
  who has not rejected my
    prayer
  or withheld his love from
    me!

Psalm 67^a

For the director of music.
With stringed instruments.
A psalm. A song.

¹May God be gracious to us and
    bless us
  and make his face shine on
    us— ^b
²so that your ways may be
    known on earth,
  your salvation among all
    nations.

³May the peoples praise you,
    God;
  may all the peoples praise
    you.
⁴May the nations be glad and
    sing for joy,
  for you rule the peoples with
    equity
  and guide the nations of the
    earth.
⁵May the peoples praise you,
    God;
  may all the peoples praise
    you.

⁶The land yields its harvest;
  God, our God, blesses us.
⁷May God bless us still,

so that all the ends of the
    earth will fear him.

Psalm 68^c

For the director of music.
Of David. A psalm. A song.

¹May God arise, may his
    enemies be scattered;
  may his foes flee before him.
²May you blow them away like
    smoke—
  as wax melts before the fire,
  may the wicked perish
    before God.
³But may the righteous be glad
  and rejoice before God;
  may they be happy and
    joyful.

⁴Sing to God, sing in praise of
    his name,
  extol him who rides on the
    clouds^d;
  rejoice before him— his
    name is the LORD.
⁵A father to the fatherless, a
    defender of widows,
  is God in his holy dwelling.
⁶God sets the lonely in
    families,^e
  he leads out the prisoners
    with singing;
  but the rebellious live in a
    sun-scorched land.

⁷When you, God, went out
  before your people,

---

^a In Hebrew texts 67:1-7 is numbered 67:2-8.   ^b 1 The Hebrew has *Selah* (a word of uncertain meaning) here and at the end of verse 4.   ^c In Hebrew texts 68:1-35 is numbered 68:2-36.   ^d 4 Or *name, / prepare the way for him who rides through the deserts*   ^e 6 Or *the desolate in a homeland*

when you marched through
  the wilderness,*a*
⁸the earth shook, the heavens
  poured down rain,
  before God, the One of Sinai,
  before God, the God of
    Israel.
⁹You gave abundant showers,
    O God;
  you refreshed your weary
    inheritance.
¹⁰Your people settled in it,
  and from your bounty, God,
    you provided for the
    poor.

¹¹The Lord announces the word,
  and the women who
    proclaim it are a mighty
    throng:
¹²"Kings and armies flee in haste;
  the women at home divide
    the plunder.
¹³Even while you sleep among
    the sheep pens,*b*
  the wings of my dove are
    sheathed with silver,
  its feathers with shining
    gold."
¹⁴When the Almighty*c* scattered
    the kings in the land,
  it was like snow fallen on
    Mount Zalmon.

¹⁵Mount Bashan, majestic
    mountain,
  Mount Bashan, rugged
    mountain,
¹⁶why gaze in envy, you rugged
    mountain,
  at the mountain where God
    chooses to reign,
  where the LORD himself will
    dwell forever?
¹⁷The chariots of God are tens of
    thousands
  and thousands of thousands;
  the Lord has come from
    Sinai into his sanctuary.*d*
¹⁸When you ascended on high,
  you took many captives;
  you received gifts from
    people,
  even from*e* the rebellious—
  that you,*f* LORD God, might
    dwell there.

¹⁹Praise be to the Lord, to God
    our Savior,
  who daily bears our burdens.
²⁰Our God is a God who saves;
  from the Sovereign LORD
    comes escape from
    death.
²¹Surely God will crush the
    heads of his enemies,
  the hairy crowns of those
    who go on in their sins.
²²The Lord says, "I will bring
    them from Bashan;
  I will bring them from the
    depths of the sea,
²³that your feet may wade in the
    blood of your foes,
  while the tongues of your
    dogs have their share."

---

a 7 The Hebrew has *Selah* (a word of uncertain meaning) here and at the end
of verses 19 and 32.   *b* 13 Or *the campfires;* or *the saddlebags*   *c* 14 Hebrew
Shaddai   *d* 17 Probable reading of the original Hebrew text; Masoretic
Text *Lord is among them at Sinai in holiness*   *e* 18 Or *gifts for people, / even*
f 18 Or *they*

²⁴Your procession, God, has
come into view,
the procession of my God
and King into the
sanctuary.
²⁵In front are the singers, after
them the musicians;
with them are the young
women playing the
timbrels.
²⁶Praise God in the great
congregation;
praise the LORD in the
assembly of Israel.
²⁷There is the little tribe of
Benjamin, leading them,
there the great throng of
Judah's princes,
and there the princes of
Zebulun and of Naphtali.

²⁸Summon your power, God[a];
show us your strength, our
God, as you have done
before.
²⁹Because of your temple at
Jerusalem
kings will bring you gifts.
³⁰Rebuke the beast among the
reeds,
the herd of bulls among the
calves of the nations.
Humbled, may the beast bring
bars of silver.
Scatter the nations who
delight in war.
³¹Envoys will come from Egypt;
Cush[b] will submit herself to
God.

³²Sing to God, you kingdoms of
the earth,
sing praise to the Lord,
³³to him who rides across the
highest heavens, the
ancient heavens,
who thunders with mighty
voice.
³⁴Proclaim the power of God,
whose majesty is over
Israel,
whose power is in the
heavens.
³⁵You, God, are awesome in your
sanctuary;
the God of Israel gives power
and strength to his
people.

Praise be to God!

Psalm 69[c]

*For the director of music. To the
tune of "Lilies." Of David.*

¹Save me, O God,
for the waters have come up
to my neck.
²I sink in the miry depths,
where there is no foothold.
I have come into the deep
waters;
the floods engulf me.
³I am worn out calling for
help;
my throat is parched.
My eyes fail,
looking for my God.

---

[a] 28 Many Hebrew manuscripts, Septuagint and Syriac; most Hebrew
manuscripts *Your God has summoned power for you*   [b] 31 That is, the upper
Nile region   [c] In Hebrew texts 69:1-36 is numbered 69:2-37.

⁴Those who hate me without
    reason
    outnumber the hairs of my
        head;
many are my enemies without
    cause,
    those who seek to
        destroy me.
I am forced to restore
    what I did not steal.

⁵You, God, know my folly;
    my guilt is not hidden from
        you.

⁶Lord, the LORD Almighty,
    may those who hope in you
    not be disgraced because
        of me;
God of Israel,
    may those who seek you
    not be put to shame because
        of me.
⁷For I endure scorn for your
        sake,
    and shame covers my face.
⁸I am a foreigner to my own
        family,
    a stranger to my own
        mother's children;
⁹for zeal for your house
        consumes me,
    and the insults of those who
        insult you fall on me.
¹⁰When I weep and fast,
    I must endure scorn;
¹¹when I put on sackcloth,
    people make sport of me.
¹²Those who sit at the gate
        mock me,
    and I am the song of the
        drunkards.

¹³But I pray to you, LORD,
    in the time of your favor;
in your great love, O God,
    answer me with your sure
        salvation.
¹⁴Rescue me from the mire,
    do not let me sink;
deliver me from those who
        hate me,
    from the deep waters.
¹⁵Do not let the floodwaters
        engulf me
    or the depths swallow me up
    or the pit close its mouth
        over me.
¹⁶Answer me, LORD, out of the
        goodness of your love;
    in your great mercy turn
        to me.
¹⁷Do not hide your face from
        your servant;
    answer me quickly, for I am
        in trouble.
¹⁸Come near and rescue me;
    deliver me because of my
        foes.
¹⁹You know how I am scorned,
        disgraced and shamed;
    all my enemies are before
        you.
²⁰Scorn has broken my
        heart
    and has left me helpless;
I looked for sympathy, but
        there was none,
    for comforters, but I found
        none.
²¹They put gall in my food
    and gave me vinegar for my
        thirst.

²²May the table set before them
become a snare;
    may it become retribution
    and*ᵃ* a trap.
²³May their eyes be darkened so
they cannot see,
    and their backs be bent
    forever.
²⁴Pour out your wrath on them;
    let your fierce anger overtake
    them.
²⁵May their place be deserted;
    let there be no one to dwell
    in their tents.
²⁶For they persecute those you
wound
    and talk about the pain of
    those you hurt.
²⁷Charge them with crime upon
crime;
    do not let them share in your
    salvation.
²⁸May they be blotted out of the
book of life
    and not be listed with the
    righteous.

²⁹But as for me, afflicted and in
pain —
    may your salvation, God,
    protect me.

³⁰I will praise God's name in
song
    and glorify him with
    thanksgiving.
³¹This will please the LORD more
than an ox,
    more than a bull with its
    horns and hooves.

³²The poor will see and be
glad —
    you who seek God, may your
    hearts live!
³³The LORD hears the needy
    and does not despise his
    captive people.

³⁴Let heaven and earth praise
him,
    the seas and all that move in
    them,
³⁵for God will save Zion
    and rebuild the cities of
    Judah.
Then people will settle there
and possess it;
³⁶   the children of his servants
    will inherit it,
    and those who love his name
    will dwell there.

Psalm 70*ᵇ*

For the director of music.
Of David. A petition.

¹Hasten, O God, to save me;
    come quickly, LORD, to
    help me.

²May those who want to take
my life
    be put to shame and
    confusion;
may all who desire my ruin
    be turned back in disgrace.
³May those who say to me,
    "Aha! Aha!"
    turn back because of their
    shame.

ᵃ 22 Or *snare / and their fellowship become*
numbered 70:2-6.

ᵇ In Hebrew texts 70:1-5 is

⁴But may all who seek you
    rejoice and be glad in you;
may those who long for your
    saving help always say,
    "The Lord is great!"

⁵But as for me, I am poor and
    needy;
    come quickly to me, O God.
You are my help and my
    deliverer;
    Lord, do not delay.

Psalm 71

¹In you, Lord, I have taken
    refuge;
    let me never be put to
    shame.
²In your righteousness, rescue
    me and deliver me;
    turn your ear to me and
    save me.
³Be my rock of refuge,
    to which I can always go;
give the command to save me,
    for you are my rock and my
    fortress.
⁴Deliver me, my God, from the
    hand of the wicked,
    from the grasp of those who
    are evil and cruel.

⁵For you have been my hope,
    Sovereign Lord,
    my confidence since my
    youth.
⁶From birth I have relied on
    you;
    you brought me forth from
    my mother's womb.
I will ever praise you.

⁷I have become a sign to many;
    you are my strong refuge.
⁸My mouth is filled with your
    praise,
    declaring your splendor all
    day long.

⁹Do not cast me away when I
    am old;
    do not forsake me when my
    strength is gone.
¹⁰For my enemies speak
    against me;
    those who wait to kill me
    conspire together.
¹¹They say, "God has forsaken
    him;
    pursue him and seize
    him,
    for no one will rescue
    him."
¹²Do not be far from me, my
    God;
    come quickly, God, to
    help me.
¹³May my accusers perish in
    shame;
    may those who want to
    harm me
    be covered with scorn and
    disgrace.

¹⁴As for me, I will always have
    hope;
    I will praise you more and
    more.
¹⁵My mouth will tell of your
    righteous deeds,
    of your saving acts all day
    long—
    though I know not how to
    relate them all.

¹⁶ I will come and proclaim your
    mighty acts, Sovereign
    LORD;
  I will proclaim your
    righteous deeds, yours
    alone.
¹⁷ Since my youth, God, you have
    taught me,
  and to this day I declare your
    marvelous deeds.
¹⁸ Even when I am old and gray,
    do not forsake me, my God,
  till I declare your power to the
    next generation,
  your mighty acts to all who
    are to come.

¹⁹ Your righteousness, God,
    reaches to the heavens,
  you who have done great
    things.
  Who is like you, God?
²⁰ Though you have made me see
    troubles,
    many and bitter,
  you will restore my life
    again;
  from the depths of the earth
    you will again bring me up.
²¹ You will increase my honor
    and comfort me once more.

²² I will praise you with the harp
    for your faithfulness, my
    God;
  I will sing praise to you with
    the lyre,
  Holy One of Israel.
²³ My lips will shout for joy
    when I sing praise to you —
  I whom you have delivered.

²⁴ My tongue will tell of your
    righteous acts
  all day long,
  for those who wanted to
    harm me
  have been put to shame and
    confusion.

Psalm 72

Of Solomon.

¹ Endow the king with your
    justice, O God,
  the royal son with your
    righteousness.
² May he judge your people in
    righteousness,
  your afflicted ones with
    justice.
³ May the mountains bring
    prosperity to the people,
  the hills the fruit of
    righteousness.
⁴ May he defend the afflicted
    among the people
  and save the children of the
    needy;
  may he crush the oppressor.
⁵ May he endure*ᵃ* as long as the
    sun,
  as long as the moon, through
    all generations.
⁶ May he be like rain falling on a
    mown field,
  like showers watering the
    earth.
⁷ In his days may the righteous
    flourish
  and prosperity abound till
    the moon is no more.

ᵃ 5 Septuagint; Hebrew *You will be feared*

⁸May he rule from sea to sea
    and from the River*ᵃ* to the
        ends of the earth.
⁹May the desert tribes bow
        before him
    and his enemies lick the
        dust.
¹⁰May the kings of Tarshish and
        of distant shores
    bring tribute to him.
May the kings of Sheba and
        Seba
    present him gifts.
¹¹May all kings bow down to
        him
    and all nations serve him.

¹²For he will deliver the needy
        who cry out,
    the afflicted who have no
        one to help.
¹³He will take pity on the weak
        and the needy
    and save the needy from
        death.
¹⁴He will rescue them from
        oppression and violence,
    for precious is their blood in
        his sight.

¹⁵Long may he live!
    May gold from Sheba be
        given him.
May people ever pray for him
    and bless him all day long.
¹⁶May grain abound throughout
        the land;
    on the tops of the hills may it
        sway.

May the crops flourish like
        Lebanon
    and thrive*ᵇ* like the grass of
        the field.
¹⁷May his name endure
        forever;
    may it continue as long as
        the sun.

Then all nations will be
    blessed through him,*ᶜ*
and they will call him
    blessed.

¹⁸Praise be to the LORD God, the
        God of Israel,
    who alone does marvelous
        deeds.
¹⁹Praise be to his glorious name
        forever;
    may the whole earth be
        filled with his glory.
        Amen and Amen.

²⁰This concludes the prayers
        of David son of Jesse.

BOOK III

Psalms 73–89

Psalm 73

A psalm of Asaph.

¹Surely God is good to Israel,
    to those who are pure in
        heart.

ᵃ 8 That is, the Euphrates   *ᵇ 16* Probable reading of the original Hebrew text;
Masoretic Text *Lebanon, / from the city*   *ᶜ 17* Or *will use his name in blessings*
(see Gen. 48:20)

²But as for me, my feet had
  almost slipped;
  I had nearly lost my
    foothold.
³For I envied the arrogant
  when I saw the prosperity of
    the wicked.

⁴They have no struggles;
  their bodies are healthy and
    strong.^a
⁵They are free from common
    human burdens;
  they are not plagued by
    human ills.
⁶Therefore pride is their
    necklace;
  they clothe themselves with
    violence.
⁷From their callous hearts
    comes iniquity^b;
  their evil imaginations have
    no limits.
⁸They scoff, and speak with
    malice;
  with arrogance they
    threaten oppression.
⁹Their mouths lay claim to
    heaven,
  and their tongues take
    possession of the earth.
¹⁰Therefore their people turn to
    them
  and drink up waters in
    abundance.^c
¹¹They say, "How would God
    know?
  Does the Most High know
    anything?"

¹²This is what the wicked are
    like —
  always free of care, they go
    on amassing wealth.

¹³Surely in vain I have kept my
    heart pure
  and have washed my hands
    in innocence.
¹⁴All day long I have been
    afflicted,
  and every morning brings
    new punishments.

¹⁵If I had spoken out like that,
  I would have betrayed your
    children.
¹⁶When I tried to understand all
    this,
  it troubled me deeply
¹⁷till I entered the sanctuary of
    God;
  then I understood their final
    destiny.

¹⁸Surely you place them on
    slippery ground;
  you cast them down to ruin.
¹⁹How suddenly are they
    destroyed,
  completely swept away by
    terrors!
²⁰They are like a dream when
    one awakes;
  when you arise, Lord,
  you will despise them as
    fantasies.

²¹When my heart was grieved
  and my spirit embittered,

---

^a 4 With a different word division of the Hebrew; Masoretic Text *struggles at their death; / their bodies are healthy*   ^b 7 Syriac (see also Septuagint); Hebrew *Their eyes bulge with fat*   ^c 10 The meaning of the Hebrew for this verse is uncertain.

²²I was senseless and ignorant;
  I was a brute beast before
    you.

²³Yet I am always with you;
  you hold me by my right
    hand.
²⁴You guide me with your
    counsel,
  and afterward you will take
    me into glory.
²⁵Whom have I in heaven but
    you?
  And earth has nothing I
    desire besides you.
²⁶My flesh and my heart may
    fail,
  but God is the strength of my
    heart
  and my portion forever.

²⁷Those who are far from you
    will perish;
  you destroy all who are
    unfaithful to you.
²⁸But as for me, it is good to be
    near God.
  I have made the Sovereign
    LORD my refuge;
  I will tell of all your deeds.

Psalm 74

A maskil^a of Asaph.

¹O God, why have you rejected
    us forever?
  Why does your anger
    smolder against the
    sheep of your pasture?
²Remember the nation you
    purchased long ago,

the people of your
    inheritance, whom you
    redeemed —
  Mount Zion, where you
    dwelt.
³Turn your steps toward these
    everlasting ruins,
  all this destruction the
    enemy has brought on
    the sanctuary.

⁴Your foes roared in the place
    where you met with us;
  they set up their standards
    as signs.
⁵They behaved like men
    wielding axes
  to cut through a thicket of
    trees.
⁶They smashed all the carved
    paneling
  with their axes and hatchets.
⁷They burned your sanctuary
    to the ground;
  they defiled the dwelling
    place of your Name.
⁸They said in their hearts,
    "We will crush them
    completely!"
  They burned every place
    where God was
    worshiped in the land.

⁹We are given no signs from
    God;
  no prophets are left,
  and none of us knows how
    long this will be.
¹⁰How long will the enemy mock
    you, God?
  Will the foe revile your name
    forever?

^a Title: Probably a literary or musical term

¹¹ Why do you hold back your
    hand, your right hand?
Take it from the folds of your
    garment and destroy
    them!

¹² But God is my King from long
    ago;
he brings salvation on the
    earth.

¹³ It was you who split open the
    sea by your power;
you broke the heads of the
    monster in the waters.

¹⁴ It was you who crushed the
    heads of Leviathan
and gave it as food to the
    creatures of the desert.

¹⁵ It was you who opened up
    springs and streams;
you dried up the ever-
    flowing rivers.

¹⁶ The day is yours, and yours
    also the night;
you established the sun and
    moon.

¹⁷ It was you who set all the
    boundaries of the earth;
you made both summer and
    winter.

¹⁸ Remember how the enemy has
    mocked you, LORD,
how foolish people have
    reviled your name.

¹⁹ Do not hand over the life of
    your dove to wild beasts;
do not forget the lives of your
    afflicted people forever.

²⁰ Have regard for your covenant,
    because haunts of violence
    fill the dark places of the
    land.

²¹ Do not let the oppressed
    retreat in disgrace;
may the poor and needy
    praise your name.

²² Rise up, O God, and defend
    your cause;
remember how fools mock
    you all day long.

²³ Do not ignore the clamor of
    your adversaries,
the uproar of your enemies,
    which rises continually.

Psalm 75ᵃ

*For the director of music. To the
tune of "Do Not Destroy."
A psalm of Asaph. A song.*

¹ We praise you, God,
    we praise you, for your Name
    is near;
people tell of your wonderful
    deeds.

² You say, "I choose the
    appointed time;
it is I who judge with equity.

³ When the earth and all its
    people quake,
it is I who hold its pillars
    firm.ᵇ

⁴ To the arrogant I say, 'Boast no
    more,'
and to the wicked, 'Do not
    lift up your horns.ᶜ

ᵃ In Hebrew texts 75:1-10 is numbered 75:2-11.   ᵇ 3 The Hebrew has *Selah* (a
word of uncertain meaning) here.   ᶜ 4 *Horns* here symbolize strength; also in
verses 5 and 10.

⁵ Do not lift your horns against
heaven;
do not speak so defiantly.' "

⁶ No one from the east or the
west
or from the desert can exalt
themselves.
⁷ It is God who judges:
He brings one down, he
exalts another.
⁸ In the hand of the LORD is a
cup
full of foaming wine mixed
with spices;
he pours it out, and all the
wicked of the earth
drink it down to its very
dregs.

⁹ As for me, I will declare this
forever;
I will sing praise to the God
of Jacob,
¹⁰ who says, "I will cut off the
horns of all the wicked,
but the horns of the righteous
will be lifted up."

Psalm 76ᵃ

For the director of music.
With stringed instruments.
A psalm of Asaph. A song.

¹ God is renowned in Judah;
in Israel his name is great.
² His tent is in Salem,
his dwelling place in Zion.

³ There he broke the flashing
arrows,
the shields and the swords,
the weapons of war.ᵇ

⁴ You are radiant with light,
more majestic than
mountains rich with
game.
⁵ The valiant lie plundered,
they sleep their last sleep;
not one of the warriors
can lift his hands.
⁶ At your rebuke, God of Jacob,
both horse and chariot lie
still.

⁷ It is you alone who are to be
feared.
Who can stand before you
when you are angry?
⁸ From heaven you pronounced
judgment,
and the land feared and was
quiet—
⁹ when you, God, rose up to
judge,
to save all the afflicted of the
land.
¹⁰ Surely your wrath against
mankind brings you
praise,
and the survivors of your
wrath are restrained.ᶜ

¹¹ Make vows to the LORD your
God and fulfill them;
let all the neighboring lands
bring gifts to the One to be
feared.

ᵃ In Hebrew texts 76:1-12 is numbered 76:2-13.   ᵇ 3 The Hebrew has *Selah* (a
word of uncertain meaning) here and at the end of verse 9.   ᶜ 10 Or *Surely the
wrath of mankind brings you praise, / and with the remainder of wrath you arm
yourself*

¹²He breaks the spirit of rulers;
he is feared by the kings of
the earth.

Psalm 77ᵃ

*For the director of music. For
Jeduthun. Of Asaph. A psalm.*

¹I cried out to God for help;
I cried out to God to hear me.
²When I was in distress, I
sought the Lord;
at night I stretched out
untiring hands,
and I would not be
comforted.

³I remembered you, God, and I
groaned;
I meditated, and my spirit
grew faint.ᵇ
⁴You kept my eyes from
closing;
I was too troubled to
speak.
⁵I thought about the former
days,
the years of long ago;
⁶I remembered my songs in the
night.
My heart meditated and my
spirit asked:

⁷"Will the Lord reject forever?
Will he never show his favor
again?
⁸Has his unfailing love
vanished forever?
Has his promise failed for all
time?

⁹Has God forgotten to be
merciful?
Has he in anger withheld his
compassion?"

¹⁰Then I thought, "To this I will
appeal:
the years when the Most
High stretched out his
right hand.
¹¹I will remember the deeds of
the LORD;
yes, I will remember your
miracles of long ago.
¹²I will consider all your works
and meditate on all your
mighty deeds."

¹³Your ways, God, are holy.
What god is as great as our
God?
¹⁴You are the God who performs
miracles;
you display your power
among the peoples.
¹⁵With your mighty arm you
redeemed your people,
the descendants of Jacob
and Joseph.

¹⁶The waters saw you, God,
the waters saw you and
writhed;
the very depths were
convulsed.
¹⁷The clouds poured down
water,
the heavens resounded with
thunder;
your arrows flashed back
and forth.

ᵃ In Hebrew texts 77:1-20 is numbered 77:2-21.   ᵇ 3 The Hebrew has *Selah* (a
word of uncertain meaning) here and at the end of verses 9 and 15.

18 Your thunder was heard in the
  whirlwind,
    your lightning lit up the
      world;
    the earth trembled and
      quaked.
19 Your path led through the sea,
    your way through the mighty
      waters,
    though your footprints were
      not seen.

20 You led your people like a flock
    by the hand of Moses and
      Aaron.

Psalm 78

A maskil[a] *of Asaph.*

1 My people, hear my teaching;
    listen to the words of my
      mouth.
2 I will open my mouth with a
    parable;
    I will utter hidden things,
      things from of old —
3 things we have heard and
    known,
    things our ancestors have
      told us.
4 We will not hide them from
    their descendants;
    we will tell the next
      generation
  the praiseworthy deeds of the
    LORD,
    his power, and the wonders
      he has done.
5 He decreed statutes for Jacob
    and established the law in
      Israel,

which he commanded our
    ancestors
    to teach their children,
6 so the next generation would
    know them,
    even the children yet to be
      born,
    and they in turn would tell
      their children.
7 Then they would put their
    trust in God
  and would not forget his
    deeds
  but would keep his
    commands.
8 They would not be like their
    ancestors —
    a stubborn and rebellious
      generation,
  whose hearts were not loyal to
    God,
    whose spirits were not
      faithful to him.

9 The men of Ephraim, though
    armed with bows,
    turned back on the day of
      battle;
10 they did not keep God's
    covenant
    and refused to live by his
      law.
11 They forgot what he had
    done,
    the wonders he had shown
      them.
12 He did miracles in the sight of
    their ancestors
    in the land of Egypt, in the
      region of Zoan.

---

a Title: Probably a literary or musical term

¹³He divided the sea and led
    them through;
  he made the water stand up
    like a wall.
¹⁴He guided them with the cloud
    by day
  and with light from the fire
    all night.
¹⁵He split the rocks in the
    wilderness
  and gave them water as
    abundant as the seas;
¹⁶he brought streams out of a
    rocky crag
  and made water flow down
    like rivers.

¹⁷But they continued to sin
    against him,
  rebelling in the wilderness
    against the Most High.
¹⁸They willfully put God to the
    test
  by demanding the food they
    craved.
¹⁹They spoke against God;
  they said, "Can God really
    spread a table in the
    wilderness?
²⁰True, he struck the rock,
  and water gushed out,
  streams flowed abundantly,
  but can he also give us
    bread?
  Can he supply meat for his
    people?"
²¹When the LORD heard them,
    he was furious;
  his fire broke out against
    Jacob,
  and his wrath rose against
    Israel,

²²for they did not believe in God
  or trust in his deliverance.
²³Yet he gave a command to the
    skies above
  and opened the doors of the
    heavens;
²⁴he rained down manna for the
    people to eat,
  he gave them the grain of
    heaven.
²⁵Human beings ate the bread of
    angels;
  he sent them all the food
    they could eat.
²⁶He let loose the east wind from
    the heavens
  and by his power made the
    south wind blow.
²⁷He rained meat down on them
    like dust,
  birds like sand on the
    seashore.
²⁸He made them come down
    inside their camp,
  all around their tents.
²⁹They ate till they were gorged —
  he had given them what they
    craved.
³⁰But before they turned from
    what they craved,
  even while the food was still
    in their mouths,
³¹God's anger rose against them;
  he put to death the sturdiest
    among them,
  cutting down the young men
    of Israel.

³²In spite of all this, they kept on
    sinning;
  in spite of his wonders, they
    did not believe.

³³So he ended their days in
        futility
    and their years in terror.
³⁴Whenever God slew them,
        they would seek him;
    they eagerly turned to him
        again.
³⁵They remembered that God
        was their Rock,
    that God Most High was
        their Redeemer.
³⁶But then they would flatter
        him with their mouths,
    lying to him with their
        tongues;
³⁷their hearts were not loyal to
        him,
    they were not faithful to his
        covenant.
³⁸Yet he was merciful;
    he forgave their iniquities
    and did not destroy them.
    Time after time he restrained
        his anger
    and did not stir up his full
        wrath.
³⁹He remembered that they were
        but flesh,
    a passing breeze that does
        not return.

⁴⁰How often they rebelled
        against him in the
        wilderness
    and grieved him in the
        wasteland!
⁴¹Again and again they put God
        to the test;
    they vexed the Holy One of
        Israel.
⁴²They did not remember his
        power —

the day he redeemed them
        from the oppressor,
⁴³the day he displayed his signs
        in Egypt,
    his wonders in the region of
        Zoan.
⁴⁴He turned their river into
        blood;
    they could not drink from
        their streams.
⁴⁵He sent swarms of flies that
        devoured them,
    and frogs that devastated
        them.
⁴⁶He gave their crops to the
        grasshopper,
    their produce to the locust.
⁴⁷He destroyed their vines with
        hail
    and their sycamore-figs with
        sleet.
⁴⁸He gave over their cattle to the
        hail,
    their livestock to bolts of
        lightning.
⁴⁹He unleashed against them his
        hot anger,
    his wrath, indignation and
        hostility —
    a band of destroying
        angels.
⁵⁰He prepared a path for his
        anger;
    he did not spare them from
        death
    but gave them over to the
        plague.
⁵¹He struck down all the
        firstborn of Egypt,
    the firstfruits of manhood in
        the tents of Ham.

52 But he brought his people out
like a flock;
he led them like sheep
through the wilderness.
53 He guided them safely, so they
were unafraid;
but the sea engulfed their
enemies.
54 And so he brought them to the
border of his holy land,
to the hill country his right
hand had taken.
55 He drove out nations before
them
and allotted their lands to
them as an inheritance;
he settled the tribes of Israel
in their homes.
56 But they put God to the test
and rebelled against the
Most High;
they did not keep his
statutes.
57 Like their ancestors they were
disloyal and faithless,
as unreliable as a faulty bow.
58 They angered him with their
high places;
they aroused his jealousy
with their idols.
59 When God heard them, he was
furious;
he rejected Israel completely.
60 He abandoned the tabernacle
of Shiloh,
the tent he had set up among
humans.
61 He sent the ark of his might
into captivity,
his splendor into the hands
of the enemy.

62 He gave his people over to the
sword;
he was furious with his
inheritance.
63 Fire consumed their young
men,
and their young women had
no wedding songs;
64 their priests were put to the
sword,
and their widows could not
weep.

65 Then the Lord awoke as from
sleep,
as a warrior wakes from the
stupor of wine.
66 He beat back his enemies;
he put them to everlasting
shame.
67 Then he rejected the tents of
Joseph,
he did not choose the tribe of
Ephraim;
68 but he chose the tribe of Judah,
Mount Zion, which he loved.
69 He built his sanctuary like the
heights,
like the earth that he
established forever.
70 He chose David his servant
and took him from the sheep
pens;
71 from tending the sheep he
brought him
to be the shepherd of his
people Jacob,
of Israel his inheritance.
72 And David shepherded them
with integrity of heart;
with skillful hands he led
them.

Psalm 79

A psalm of Asaph.

¹O God, the nations have
    invaded your inheritance;
  they have defiled your holy
    temple,
  they have reduced Jerusalem
    to rubble.
²They have left the dead bodies
    of your servants
  as food for the birds of the
    sky,
  the flesh of your own people
    for the animals of the
    wild.
³They have poured out blood
    like water
  all around Jerusalem,
  and there is no one to bury
    the dead.
⁴We are objects of contempt to
    our neighbors,
  of scorn and derision to
    those around us.

⁵How long, LORD? Will you be
    angry forever?
  How long will your jealousy
    burn like fire?
⁶Pour out your wrath on the
    nations
  that do not acknowledge
    you,
 on the kingdoms
  that do not call on your
    name;
⁷for they have devoured Jacob
  and devastated his
    homeland.

⁸Do not hold against us the sins
    of past generations;
  may your mercy come
    quickly to meet us,
  for we are in desperate need.
⁹Help us, God our Savior,
  for the glory of your name;
 deliver us and forgive our sins
  for your name's sake.
¹⁰Why should the nations say,
  "Where is their God?"

Before our eyes, make known
    among the nations
  that you avenge the
    outpoured blood of your
    servants.
¹¹May the groans of the prisoners
    come before you;
  with your strong arm
    preserve those
    condemned to die.
¹²Pay back into the laps of our
    neighbors seven times
  the contempt they have
    hurled at you, Lord.
¹³Then we your people, the
    sheep of your pasture,
  will praise you forever;
 from generation to generation
  we will proclaim your praise.

Psalm 80[a]

For the director of music.
To the tune of "The Lilies of the
Covenant." Of Asaph. A psalm.

¹Hear us, Shepherd of Israel,
  you who lead Joseph like a
    flock.

---

[a] In Hebrew texts 80:1-19 is numbered 80:2-20.

You who sit enthroned
  between the cherubim,
shine forth ²before
  Ephraim, Benjamin and
  Manasseh.
Awaken your might;
  come and save us.

³Restore us, O God;
  make your face shine on us,
  that we may be saved.

⁴How long, LORD God
  Almighty,
  will your anger smolder
  against the prayers of your
  people?
⁵You have fed them with the
  bread of tears;
  you have made them drink
  tears by the bowlful.
⁶You have made us an object
  of derision*a* to our
  neighbors,
  and our enemies mock us.

⁷Restore us, God Almighty;
  make your face shine on us,
  that we may be saved.

⁸You transplanted a vine from
  Egypt;
  you drove out the nations
  and planted it.
⁹You cleared the ground
  for it,
  and it took root and filled the
  land.
¹⁰The mountains were covered
  with its shade,
the mighty cedars with its
  branches.
¹¹Its branches reached as far as
  the Sea,*b*
  its shoots as far as the
  River.*c*

¹²Why have you broken down its
  walls
  so that all who pass by pick
  its grapes?
¹³Boars from the forest ravage it,
  and insects from the fields
  feed on it.
¹⁴Return to us, God Almighty!
  Look down from heaven and
  see!
  Watch over this vine,
¹⁵ the root your right hand has
  planted,
  the son*d* you have raised up
  for yourself.

¹⁶Your vine is cut down, it is
  burned with fire;
  at your rebuke your people
  perish.
¹⁷Let your hand rest on the man
  at your right hand,
  the son of man you have
  raised up for yourself.
¹⁸Then we will not turn away
  from you;
  revive us, and we will call on
  your name.

¹⁹Restore us, LORD God
  Almighty;
  make your face shine on us,
  that we may be saved.

a 6 Probable reading of the original Hebrew text; Masoretic Text *contention*
b 11 Probably the Mediterranean   *c* 11 That is, the Euphrates
d 15 Or *branch*

Psalm 81[a]

For the director of music.
According to gittith.[b]
Of Asaph.

[1] Sing for joy to God our strength;
　　shout aloud to the God of
　　　　Jacob!
[2] Begin the music, strike the
　　　　timbrel,
　　play the melodious harp and
　　　　lyre.

[3] Sound the ram's horn at the
　　　　New Moon,
　　and when the moon is full,
　　　　on the day of our festival;
[4] this is a decree for Israel,
　　an ordinance of the God of
　　　　Jacob.
[5] When God went out against
　　　　Egypt,
　　he established it as a statute
　　　　for Joseph.

I heard an unknown voice say:

[6] "I removed the burden from
　　　　their shoulders;
　　their hands were set free
　　　　from the basket.
[7] In your distress you called and
　　　　I rescued you,
　　I answered you out of a
　　　　thundercloud;
　　I tested you at the waters of
　　　　Meribah.[c]
[8] Hear me, my people, and I will
　　　　warn you —
　　if you would only listen to
　　　　me, Israel!

[9] You shall have no foreign god
　　　　among you;
　　you shall not worship any
　　　　god other than me.
[10] I am the LORD your God,
　　who brought you up out of
　　　　Egypt.
　　Open wide your mouth and I
　　　　will fill it.
[11] "But my people would not
　　　　listen to me;
　　Israel would not submit to me.
[12] So I gave them over to their
　　　　stubborn hearts
　　to follow their own devices.

[13] "If my people would only listen
　　　　to me,
　　if Israel would only follow
　　　　my ways,
[14] how quickly I would subdue
　　　　their enemies
　　and turn my hand against
　　　　their foes!
[15] Those who hate the LORD
　　　　would cringe before him,
　　and their punishment would
　　　　last forever.
[16] But you would be fed with the
　　　　finest of wheat;
　　with honey from the rock I
　　　　would satisfy you."

Psalm 82

A psalm of Asaph.

[1] God presides in the great
　　　　assembly;
　　he renders judgment among
　　　　the "gods":

---

[a] In Hebrew texts 81:1-16 is numbered 81:2-17.　　[b] Title: Probably a musical term
[c] 7 The Hebrew has *Selah* (a word of uncertain meaning) here.

[2] "How long will you[a] defend the unjust
and show partiality to the wicked?[b]
[3] Defend the weak and the fatherless;
uphold the cause of the poor and the oppressed.
[4] Rescue the weak and the needy;
deliver them from the hand of the wicked.

[5] "The 'gods' know nothing, they understand nothing.
They walk about in darkness;
all the foundations of the earth are shaken.

[6] "I said, 'You are "gods"; you are all sons of the Most High.'
[7] But you will die like mere mortals;
you will fall like every other ruler."

[8] Rise up, O God, judge the earth,
for all the nations are your inheritance.

Psalm 83[c]

A song. A psalm of Asaph.

[1] O God, do not remain silent;
do not turn a deaf ear,
do not stand aloof, O God.

[2] See how your enemies growl,
how your foes rear their heads.
[3] With cunning they conspire against your people;
they plot against those you cherish.
[4] "Come," they say, "let us destroy them as a nation,
so that Israel's name is remembered no more."

[5] With one mind they plot together;
they form an alliance against you—
[6] the tents of Edom and the Ishmaelites,
of Moab and the Hagrites,
[7] Byblos, Ammon and Amalek,
Philistia, with the people of Tyre.
[8] Even Assyria has joined them to reinforce Lot's descendants.[b]

[9] Do to them as you did to Midian,
as you did to Sisera and Jabin at the river Kishon,
[10] who perished at Endor and became like dung on the ground.
[11] Make their nobles like Oreb and Zeeb,
all their princes like Zebah and Zalmunna,
[12] who said, "Let us take possession
of the pasturelands of God."

---

[a] 2 The Hebrew is plural.   [b] 2,8 The Hebrew has *Selah* (a word of uncertain meaning) here.   [c] In Hebrew texts 83:1-18 is numbered 83:2-19.

13 Make them like tumbleweed,
    my God,
  like chaff before the wind.
14 As fire consumes the forest
    or a flame sets the
      mountains ablaze,
15 so pursue them with your
      tempest
    and terrify them with your
      storm.
16 Cover their faces with shame,
    LORD,
  so that they will seek your
      name.

17 May they ever be ashamed and
      dismayed;
  may they perish in disgrace.
18 Let them know that you, whose
      name is the LORD —
  that you alone are the Most
      High over all the earth.

Psalm 84 [a]

*For the director of music.
According to* gittith.[b] *Of the
Sons of Korah. A psalm.*

1 How lovely is your dwelling
      place,
  LORD Almighty!
2 My soul yearns, even faints,
    for the courts of the LORD;
  my heart and my flesh cry out
    for the living God.
3 Even the sparrow has found a
      home,
  and the swallow a nest for
      herself,

where she may have her
      young —
  a place near your altar,
    LORD Almighty, my King and
      my God.
4 Blessed are those who dwell in
      your house;
  they are ever praising you.[c]

5 Blessed are those whose
      strength is in you,
  whose hearts are set on
      pilgrimage.
6 As they pass through the
      Valley of Baka,
  they make it a place of
      springs;
  the autumn rains also cover
    it with pools.[d]
7 They go from strength to
      strength,
  till each appears before God
    in Zion.

8 Hear my prayer, LORD God
      Almighty;
  listen to me, God of Jacob.
9 Look on our shield,[e] O God;
  look with favor on your
      anointed one.

10 Better is one day in your courts
    than a thousand elsewhere;
  I would rather be a doorkeeper
    in the house of my God
  than dwell in the tents of the
      wicked.
11 For the LORD God is a sun and
      shield;
  the LORD bestows favor and
      honor;

---

[a] In Hebrew texts 84:1-12 is numbered 84:2-13.   [b] Title: Probably a musical term
[c] 4 The Hebrew has *Selah* (a word of uncertain meaning) here and at the end of
verse 8.   [d] 6 Or *blessings*   [e] 9 Or *sovereign*

no good thing does he
withhold
from those whose walk is
blameless.

¹² Lord Almighty,
blessed is the one who trusts
in you.

Psalm 85[a]

*For the director of music. Of
the Sons of Korah. A psalm.*

¹ You, Lord, showed favor to
your land;
you restored the fortunes of
Jacob.
² You forgave the iniquity of
your people
and covered all their
sins.[b]
³ You set aside all your wrath
and turned from your fierce
anger.

⁴ Restore us again, God our
Savior,
and put away your
displeasure toward us.
⁵ Will you be angry with us
forever?
Will you prolong your anger
through all generations?
⁶ Will you not revive us again,
that your people may rejoice
in you?
⁷ Show us your unfailing love,
Lord,
and grant us your
salvation.

⁸ I will listen to what God the
Lord says;
he promises peace to his
people, his faithful
servants —
but let them not turn to folly.
⁹ Surely his salvation is near
those who fear him,
that his glory may dwell in
our land.

¹⁰ Love and faithfulness meet
together;
righteousness and peace kiss
each other.
¹¹ Faithfulness springs forth
from the earth,
and righteousness looks
down from heaven.
¹² The Lord will indeed give
what is good,
and our land will yield its
harvest.
¹³ Righteousness goes before him
and prepares the way for his
steps.

Psalm 86

A prayer of David.

¹ Hear me, Lord, and answer me,
for I am poor and needy.
² Guard my life, for I am faithful
to you;
save your servant who trusts
in you.
You are my God; ³ have mercy
on me, Lord,
for I call to you all day long.

---

a In Hebrew texts 85:1-13 is numbered 85:2-14.   *b* 2 The Hebrew has *Selah* (a
word of uncertain meaning) here.

⁴Bring joy to your servant,
  Lord,
    for I put my trust in you.

⁵You, Lord, are forgiving and
  good,
    abounding in love to all who
    call to you.
⁶Hear my prayer, LORD;
    listen to my cry for mercy.
⁷When I am in distress, I call to
  you,
    because you answer me.

⁸Among the gods there is none
  like you, Lord;
    no deeds can compare with
    yours.
⁹All the nations you have made
  will come and worship
    before you, Lord;
    they will bring glory to your
    name.
¹⁰For you are great and do
  marvelous deeds;
    you alone are God.

¹¹Teach me your way, LORD,
  that I may rely on your
  faithfulness;
    give me an undivided heart,
    that I may fear your name.
¹²I will praise you, Lord my God,
  with all my heart;
    I will glorify your name
    forever.
¹³For great is your love
  toward me;
    you have delivered me from
    the depths,
    from the realm of the dead.

¹⁴Arrogant foes are attacking
  me, O God;
    ruthless people are trying to
    kill me —
    they have no regard for you.
¹⁵But you, Lord, are a
  compassionate and
    gracious God,
    slow to anger, abounding in
    love and faithfulness.
¹⁶Turn to me and have mercy
  on me;
    show your strength in behalf
    of your servant;
  save me, because I serve you
    just as my mother did.
¹⁷Give me a sign of your
  goodness,
    that my enemies may see it
    and be put to shame,
    for you, LORD, have helped
    me and comforted me.

Psalm 87

*Of the Sons of Korah.
A psalm. A song.*

¹He has founded his city on the
  holy mountain.
²The LORD loves the gates of
  Zion
    more than all the other
    dwellings of Jacob.

³Glorious things are said of you,
  city of God:ᵃ
⁴"I will record Rahabᵇ and
  Babylon
    among those who
    acknowledge me —

ᵃ 3 The Hebrew has *Selah* (a word of uncertain meaning) here and at the end of
verse 6.   ᵇ 4 A poetic name for Egypt

Philistia too, and Tyre, along
with Cush[a] —
and will say, 'This one was
born in Zion.'"[b]
[5] Indeed, of Zion it will be said,
"This one and that one were
born in her,
and the Most High himself
will establish her."
[6] The LORD will write in the
register of the peoples:
"This one was born in Zion."

[7] As they make music they will
sing,
"All my fountains are in
you."

Psalm 88[c]

*A song. A psalm of the Sons
of Korah. For the director of
music. According to* mahalath
leannoth.[d] *A* maskil[e] *of
Heman the Ezrahite.*

[1] LORD, you are the God who
saves me;
day and night I cry out to
you.
[2] May my prayer come before
you;
turn your ear to my cry.

[3] I am overwhelmed with
troubles
and my life draws near to
death.

[4] I am counted among those
who go down to the pit;
I am like one without
strength.
[5] I am set apart with the dead,
like the slain who lie in the
grave,
whom you remember no
more,
who are cut off from your
care.

[6] You have put me in the lowest
pit,
in the darkest depths.
[7] Your wrath lies heavily on me;
you have overwhelmed me
with all your waves.[f]
[8] You have taken from me my
closest friends
and have made me repulsive
to them.
I am confined and cannot
escape;
[9] my eyes are dim with grief.

I call to you, LORD, every day;
I spread out my hands to
you.
[10] Do you show your wonders to
the dead?
Do their spirits rise up and
praise you?
[11] Is your love declared in the
grave,
your faithfulness in
Destruction[g]?

---

[a] 4 That is, the upper Nile region   [b] 4 Or *"I will record concerning those who
acknowledge me: / 'This one was born in Zion.' / Hear this, Rahab and Babylon, /
and you too, Philistia, Tyre and Cush."*   [c] In Hebrew texts 88:1-18 is numbered
88:2-19.   [d] Title: Possibly a tune, "The Suffering of Affliction"   [e] Title:
Probably a literary or musical term   [f] 7 The Hebrew has *Selah* (a word of
uncertain meaning) here and at the end of verse 10.   [g] 11 Hebrew *Abaddon*

¹² Are your wonders known in
the place of darkness,
or your righteous deeds in
the land of oblivion?

¹³ But I cry to you for help, LORD;
in the morning my prayer
comes before you.
¹⁴ Why, LORD, do you reject me
and hide your face from me?

¹⁵ From my youth I have suffered
and been close to death;
I have borne your terrors and
am in despair.
¹⁶ Your wrath has swept over me;
your terrors have
destroyed me.
¹⁷ All day long they surround me
like a flood;
they have completely
engulfed me.
¹⁸ You have taken from me friend
and neighbor —
darkness is my closest
friend.

Psalm 89^a

A maskil^b of Ethan the Ezrahite.

¹ I will sing of the LORD's great
love forever;
with my mouth I will make
your faithfulness known
through all generations.
² I will declare that your love
stands firm forever,
that you have established
your faithfulness in
heaven itself.

³ You said, "I have made a
covenant with my
chosen one,
I have sworn to David my
servant,
⁴ 'I will establish your line
forever
and make your throne
firm through all
generations.' "^c

⁵ The heavens praise your
wonders, LORD,
your faithfulness too, in the
assembly of the holy ones.
⁶ For who in the skies above can
compare with the LORD?
Who is like the LORD among
the heavenly beings?
⁷ In the council of the holy ones
God is greatly feared;
he is more awesome than all
who surround him.
⁸ Who is like you, LORD God
Almighty?
You, LORD, are mighty,
and your faithfulness
surrounds you.

⁹ You rule over the surging sea;
when its waves mount up,
you still them.
¹⁰ You crushed Rahab like one of
the slain;
with your strong arm you
scattered your enemies.
¹¹ The heavens are yours, and
yours also the earth;
you founded the world and
all that is in it.

^a In Hebrew texts 89:1-52 is numbered 89:2-53.   ^b Title: Probably a literary or
musical term   ^c 4 The Hebrew has *Selah* (a word of uncertain meaning) here
and at the end of verses 37, 45 and 48.

¹²You created the north and the
south;
Tabor and Hermon sing for
joy at your name.
¹³Your arm is endowed with
power;
your hand is strong, your
right hand exalted.

¹⁴Righteousness and justice are
the foundation of your
throne;
love and faithfulness go
before you.
¹⁵Blessed are those who have
learned to acclaim
you,
who walk in the light of your
presence, LORD.
¹⁶They rejoice in your name all
day long;
they celebrate your
righteousness.
¹⁷For you are their glory and
strength,
and by your favor you exalt
our horn.ᵃ
¹⁸Indeed, our shieldᵇ belongs to
the LORD,
our king to the Holy One of
Israel.

¹⁹Once you spoke in a vision,
to your faithful people you
said:
"I have bestowed strength on a
warrior;
I have raised up a young
man from among the
people.

²⁰I have found David my
servant;
with my sacred oil I have
anointed him.
²¹My hand will sustain him;
surely my arm will
strengthen him.
²²The enemy will not get the
better of him;
the wicked will not oppress
him.
²³I will crush his foes before
him
and strike down his
adversaries.
²⁴My faithful love will be with
him,
and through my name his
hornᶜ will be exalted.
²⁵I will set his hand over the sea,
his right hand over the
rivers.
²⁶He will call out to me, 'You are
my Father,
my God, the Rock my Savior.'
²⁷And I will appoint him to be
my firstborn,
the most exalted of the kings
of the earth.
²⁸I will maintain my love to him
forever,
and my covenant with him
will never fail.
²⁹I will establish his line forever,
his throne as long as the
heavens endure.

³⁰"If his sons forsake my law
and do not follow my
statutes,

ᵃ 17 *Horn* here symbolizes strong one.
symbolizes strength.   ᵇ 18 Or *sovereign*   ᶜ 24 *Horn* here

31 if they violate my decrees
    and fail to keep my
        commands,
32 I will punish their sin with the
        rod,
    their iniquity with flogging;
33 but I will not take my love from
        him,
    nor will I ever betray my
        faithfulness.
34 I will not violate my covenant
    or alter what my lips have
        uttered.
35 Once for all, I have sworn by
        my holiness—
    and I will not lie to David—
36 that his line will continue
        forever
    and his throne endure
        before me like the sun;
37 it will be established forever
        like the moon,
    the faithful witness in the
        sky."

38 But you have rejected, you
        have spurned,
    you have been very angry
        with your anointed one.
39 You have renounced the
        covenant with your
        servant
    and have defiled his crown
        in the dust.
40 You have broken through all
        his walls
    and reduced his strongholds
        to ruins.
41 All who pass by have
        plundered him;

he has become the scorn of
    his neighbors.
42 You have exalted the right
        hand of his foes;
    you have made all his
        enemies rejoice.
43 Indeed, you have turned back
        the edge of his sword
    and have not supported him
        in battle.
44 You have put an end to his
        splendor
    and cast his throne to the
        ground.
45 You have cut short the days of
        his youth;
    you have covered him with a
        mantle of shame.

46 How long, LORD? Will you hide
        yourself forever?
    How long will your wrath
        burn like fire?
47 Remember how fleeting is my
        life.
    For what futility you have
        created all humanity!
48 Who can live and not see
        death,
    or who can escape the power
        of the grave?
49 Lord, where is your former
        great love,
    which in your faithfulness
        you swore to David?
50 Remember, Lord, how your
        servant has[a] been
        mocked,
    how I bear in my heart the
        taunts of all the nations,

a 50 Or your servants have

51 the taunts with which your
    enemies, LORD, have
    mocked,
with which they have
    mocked every step of
    your anointed one.

52 Praise be to the LORD forever!
    Amen and Amen.

BOOK IV

Psalms 90–106

Psalm 90

*A prayer of Moses the
man of God.*

1 Lord, you have been our
    dwelling place
throughout all generations.
2 Before the mountains were
    born
or you brought forth the
    whole world,
from everlasting to
    everlasting you are
    God.

3 You turn people back to dust,
    saying, "Return to dust, you
    mortals."
4 A thousand years in your
    sight
are like a day that has just
    gone by,
or like a watch in the night.
5 Yet you sweep people away in
    the sleep of death —
they are like the new grass of
    the morning:

6 In the morning it springs up
    new,
but by evening it is dry and
    withered.
7 We are consumed by your
    anger
and terrified by your
    indignation.
8 You have set our iniquities
    before you,
our secret sins in the light of
    your presence.
9 All our days pass away under
    your wrath;
we finish our years with a
    moan.
10 Our days may come to seventy
    years,
or eighty, if our strength
    endures;
yet the best of them are but
    trouble and sorrow,
for they quickly pass, and we
    fly away.
11 If only we knew the power of
    your anger!
Your wrath is as great as the
    fear that is your due.
12 Teach us to number our
    days,
that we may gain a heart of
    wisdom.
13 Relent, LORD! How long will it
    be?
Have compassion on your
    servants.
14 Satisfy us in the morning with
    your unfailing love,
that we may sing for joy and
    be glad all our days.

¹⁵ Make us glad for as many days
as you have afflicted us,
for as many years as we have
seen trouble.
¹⁶ May your deeds be shown to
your servants,
your splendor to their
children.
¹⁷ May the favor^a of the Lord our
God rest on us;
establish the work of our
hands for us —
yes, establish the work of our
hands.

Psalm 91

¹ Whoever dwells in the shelter
of the Most High
will rest in the shadow of the
Almighty.^b
² I will say of the LORD, "He
is my refuge and my
fortress,
my God, in whom I trust."

³ Surely he will save you
from the fowler's snare
and from the deadly
pestilence.
⁴ He will cover you with his
feathers,
and under his wings you will
find refuge;
his faithfulness will be your
shield and rampart.
⁵ You will not fear the terror of
night,
nor the arrow that flies by
day,

⁶ nor the pestilence that stalks
in the darkness,
nor the plague that destroys
at midday.
⁷ A thousand may fall at your
side,
ten thousand at your right
hand,
but it will not come near you.
⁸ You will only observe with
your eyes
and see the punishment of
the wicked.

⁹ If you say, "The LORD is my
refuge,"
and you make the Most High
your dwelling,
¹⁰ no harm will overtake you,
no disaster will come near
your tent.
¹¹ For he will command his
angels concerning
you
to guard you in all your
ways;
¹² they will lift you up in their
hands,
so that you will not strike
your foot against a
stone.
¹³ You will tread on the lion and
the cobra;
you will trample the great
lion and the serpent.

¹⁴ "Because he^c loves me," says
the LORD, "I will rescue
him;
I will protect him, for he
acknowledges my name.

---

^a 17 Or beauty   ^b 1 Hebrew Shaddai   ^c 14 That is, probably the king

¹⁵He will call on me, and I will
    answer him;
  I will be with him in trouble,
  I will deliver him and honor
    him.
¹⁶With long life I will satisfy him
  and show him my salvation."

Psalm 92^a

*A psalm. A song. For
the Sabbath day.*

¹It is good to praise the LORD
  and make music to your
    name, O Most High,
²proclaiming your love in the
    morning
  and your faithfulness at
    night,
³to the music of the ten-
    stringed lyre
  and the melody of the harp.

⁴For you make me glad by your
    deeds, LORD;
  I sing for joy at what your
    hands have done.
⁵How great are your works,
    LORD,
  how profound your thoughts!
⁶Senseless people do not know,
  fools do not understand,
⁷that though the wicked spring
    up like grass
  and all evildoers flourish,
  they will be destroyed
    forever.

⁸But you, LORD, are forever
  exalted.

⁹For surely your enemies, LORD,
  surely your enemies will
    perish;
  all evildoers will be scattered.
¹⁰You have exalted my horn^b like
    that of a wild ox;
  fine oils have been poured
    on me.
¹¹My eyes have seen the defeat
    of my adversaries;
  my ears have heard the rout
    of my wicked foes.

¹²The righteous will flourish like
    a palm tree,
  they will grow like a cedar of
    Lebanon;
¹³planted in the house of the
    LORD,
  they will flourish in the
    courts of our God.
¹⁴They will still bear fruit in old
    age,
  they will stay fresh and
    green,
¹⁵proclaiming, "The LORD is
    upright;
  he is my Rock, and there is
    no wickedness in him."

Psalm 93

¹The LORD reigns, he is robed
    in majesty;
  the LORD is robed in
    majesty and armed with
    strength;
  indeed, the world is
    established, firm and
    secure.

---

^a In Hebrew texts 92:1-15 is numbered 92:2-16.
strength.   ^b 10 *Horn* here symbolizes

2 Your throne was established
long ago;
you are from all eternity.

3 The seas have lifted up, LORD,
the seas have lifted up their
voice;
the seas have lifted up their
pounding waves.
4 Mightier than the thunder of
the great waters,
mightier than the breakers
of the sea —
the LORD on high is mighty.

5 Your statutes, LORD, stand
firm;
holiness adorns your house
for endless days.

Psalm 94

1 The LORD is a God who
avenges.
O God who avenges, shine
forth.
2 Rise up, Judge of the earth;
pay back to the proud what
they deserve.
3 How long, LORD, will the
wicked,
how long will the wicked be
jubilant?

4 They pour out arrogant words;
all the evildoers are full of
boasting.
5 They crush your people, LORD;
they oppress your
inheritance.
6 They slay the widow and the
foreigner;
they murder the fatherless.

7 They say, "The LORD does not
see;
the God of Jacob takes no
notice."

8 Take notice, you senseless
ones among the people;
you fools, when will you
become wise?
9 Does he who fashioned the ear
not hear?
Does he who formed the eye
not see?
10 Does he who disciplines
nations not punish?
Does he who teaches
mankind lack
knowledge?
11 The LORD knows all human
plans;
he knows that they are futile.

12 Blessed is the one you
discipline, LORD,
the one you teach from your
law;
13 you grant them relief from
days of trouble,
till a pit is dug for the wicked.
14 For the LORD will not reject his
people;
he will never forsake his
inheritance.
15 Judgment will again
be founded on
righteousness,
and all the upright in heart
will follow it.

16 Who will rise up for me
against the wicked?
Who will take a stand for me
against evildoers?

¹⁷Unless the LORD had given me
help,
    I would soon have dwelt in
    the silence of death.
¹⁸When I said, "My foot is
slipping,"
    your unfailing love, LORD,
    supported me.
¹⁹When anxiety was great
within me,
    your consolation brought me
    joy.

²⁰Can a corrupt throne be allied
with you —
    a throne that brings on
    misery by its decrees?
²¹The wicked band together
against the righteous
    and condemn the innocent
    to death.
²²But the LORD has become my
fortress,
    and my God the rock in
    whom I take refuge.
²³He will repay them for their sins
    and destroy them for their
    wickedness;
    the LORD our God will
    destroy them.

Psalm 95

¹Come, let us sing for joy to the
LORD;
    let us shout aloud to the
    Rock of our salvation.
²Let us come before him with
thanksgiving
    and extol him with music
    and song.

³For the LORD is the great God,
    the great King above all
    gods.
⁴In his hand are the depths of
the earth,
    and the mountain peaks
    belong to him.
⁵The sea is his, for he made it,
    and his hands formed the
    dry land.

⁶Come, let us bow down in
worship,
    let us kneel before the LORD
    our Maker;
⁷for he is our God
    and we are the people of his
    pasture,
    the flock under his care.

Today, if only you would hear
his voice,
⁸"Do not harden your hearts as
you did at Meribah,^a
    as you did that day at
    Massah^b in the
    wilderness,
⁹where your ancestors
tested me;
    they tried me, though they
    had seen what I did.
¹⁰For forty years I was angry
with that generation;
    I said, 'They are a people
    whose hearts go astray,
    and they have not known my
    ways.'
¹¹So I declared on oath in my
anger,
    'They shall never enter my
    rest.'"

---

^a 8 *Meribah* means *quarreling.*   ^b 8 *Massah* means *testing.*

Psalm 96

1 Sing to the LORD a new song;
   sing to the LORD, all the
      earth.
2 Sing to the LORD, praise his
      name;
   proclaim his salvation day
      after day.
3 Declare his glory among the
      nations,
   his marvelous deeds among
      all peoples.

4 For great is the LORD and most
      worthy of praise;
   he is to be feared above all
      gods.
5 For all the gods of the nations
      are idols,
   but the LORD made the
      heavens.
6 Splendor and majesty are
      before him;
   strength and glory are in his
      sanctuary.

7 Ascribe to the LORD, all you
      families of nations,
   ascribe to the LORD glory
      and strength.
8 Ascribe to the LORD the glory
      due his name;
   bring an offering and come
      into his courts.
9 Worship the LORD in the
      splendor of his[a] holiness;
   tremble before him, all the
      earth.
10 Say among the nations, "The
      LORD reigns."

The world is firmly
      established, it cannot be
      moved;
   he will judge the peoples
      with equity.

11 Let the heavens rejoice, let the
      earth be glad;
   let the sea resound, and all
      that is in it.
12 Let the fields be jubilant, and
      everything in them;
   let all the trees of the forest
      sing for joy.
13 Let all creation rejoice before
      the LORD, for he
      comes,
   he comes to judge the
      earth.
He will judge the world in
      righteousness
   and the peoples in his
      faithfulness.

Psalm 97

1 The LORD reigns, let the earth
      be glad;
   let the distant shores
      rejoice.
2 Clouds and thick darkness
      surround him;
   righteousness and justice
      are the foundation of his
      throne.
3 Fire goes before him
   and consumes his foes on
      every side.
4 His lightning lights up the
      world;
   the earth sees and trembles.

a 9 Or LORD with the splendor of

⁵The mountains melt like wax
  before the Lord,
 before the Lord of all the
  earth.
⁶The heavens proclaim his
  righteousness,
 and all peoples see his glory.

⁷All who worship images are
  put to shame,
 those who boast in idols —
 worship him, all you gods!

⁸Zion hears and rejoices
 and the villages of Judah are
  glad
 because of your judgments,
  Lord.
⁹For you, Lord, are the Most
  High over all the earth;
 you are exalted far above all
  gods.
¹⁰Let those who love the Lord
  hate evil,
 for he guards the lives of his
  faithful ones
 and delivers them from the
  hand of the wicked.
¹¹Light shines*a* on the righteous
 and joy on the upright in
  heart.
¹²Rejoice in the Lord, you who
  are righteous,
 and praise his holy name.

Psalm 98

A psalm.

¹Sing to the Lord a new song,
 for he has done marvelous
  things;

his right hand and his holy
  arm
 have worked salvation for
  him.
²The Lord has made his
  salvation known
 and revealed his
  righteousness to the
  nations.
³He has remembered his love
 and his faithfulness to Israel;
 all the ends of the earth have
  seen
 the salvation of our God.

⁴Shout for joy to the Lord, all
  the earth,
 burst into jubilant song with
  music;
⁵make music to the Lord with
  the harp,
 with the harp and the sound
  of singing,
⁶with trumpets and the blast of
  the ram's horn —
 shout for joy before the
  Lord, the King.

⁷Let the sea resound, and
  everything in it,
 the world, and all who live
  in it.
⁸Let the rivers clap their hands,
 let the mountains sing
  together for joy;
⁹let them sing before the Lord,
 for he comes to judge the
  earth.
He will judge the world in
  righteousness
 and the peoples with equity.

---

a 11 One Hebrew manuscript and ancient versions (see also 112:4); most Hebrew
manuscripts *Light is sown*

Psalm 99

[1] The Lord reigns,
   let the nations tremble;
he sits enthroned between the
      cherubim,
   let the earth shake.
[2] Great is the Lord in Zion;
   he is exalted over all the
      nations.
[3] Let them praise your great and
      awesome name —
   he is holy.

[4] The King is mighty, he loves
      justice —
   you have established equity;
in Jacob you have done
   what is just and right.
[5] Exalt the Lord our God
   and worship at his footstool;
   he is holy.

[6] Moses and Aaron were among
      his priests,
   Samuel was among those
      who called on his name;
they called on the Lord
   and he answered them.
[7] He spoke to them from the
      pillar of cloud;
   they kept his statutes and
      the decrees he gave
      them.

[8] Lord our God,
   you answered them;
you were to Israel a forgiving
      God,
   though you punished their
      misdeeds.[a]
[9] Exalt the Lord our God

and worship at his holy
      mountain,
   for the Lord our God is holy.

Psalm 100

*A psalm. For giving grateful
praise.*

[1] Shout for joy to the Lord, all
      the earth.
[2]   Worship the Lord with
         gladness;
   come before him with joyful
      songs.
[3] Know that the Lord is God.
   It is he who made us, and we
      are his[b];
   we are his people, the sheep
      of his pasture.

[4] Enter his gates with
      thanksgiving
   and his courts with praise;
   give thanks to him and
      praise his name.
[5] For the Lord is good and his
      love endures forever;
   his faithfulness continues
      through all generations.

Psalm 101

Of David. A psalm.

[1] I will sing of your love and
      justice;
   to you, Lord, I will sing
      praise.
[2] I will be careful to lead a
      blameless life —
   when will you come to me?

---

[a] 8 Or *God, / an avenger of the wrongs done to them*   [b] 3 Or *and not we ourselves*

I will conduct the affairs of my
   house
   with a blameless heart.
³ I will not look with approval
   on anything that is vile.

I hate what faithless
   people do;
   I will have no part in it.
⁴ The perverse of heart shall be
   far from me;
   I will have nothing to do
   with what is evil.

⁵ Whoever slanders their
   neighbor in secret,
   I will put to silence;
whoever has haughty eyes and
   a proud heart,
   I will not tolerate.

⁶ My eyes will be on the faithful
   in the land,
   that they may dwell
   with me;
the one whose walk is
   blameless
   will minister to me.

⁷ No one who practices deceit
   will dwell in my
   house;
no one who speaks falsely
   will stand in my
   presence.

⁸ Every morning I will put to
   silence
   all the wicked in the
   land;
I will cut off every evildoer
   from the city of the LORD.

Psalm 102 ᵃ

*A prayer of an afflicted person
who has grown weak and pours
out a lament before the LORD.*

¹ Hear my prayer, LORD;
   let my cry for help come to
   you.
² Do not hide your face from me
   when I am in distress.
Turn your ear to me;
   when I call, answer me
   quickly.

³ For my days vanish like smoke;
   my bones burn like glowing
   embers.
⁴ My heart is blighted and
   withered like grass;
   I forget to eat my food.
⁵ In my distress I groan aloud
   and am reduced to skin and
   bones.
⁶ I am like a desert owl,
   like an owl among the ruins.
⁷ I lie awake; I have become
   like a bird alone on a roof.
⁸ All day long my enemies
   taunt me;
   those who rail against me
   use my name as a curse.
⁹ For I eat ashes as my food
   and mingle my drink with
   tears
¹⁰ because of your great wrath,
   for you have taken me up
   and thrown me aside.
¹¹ My days are like the evening
   shadow;
   I wither away like grass.

ᵃ In Hebrew texts 102:1-28 is numbered 102:2-29.

¹²But you, LORD, sit enthroned
    forever;
  your renown endures
    through all generations.
¹³You will arise and have
    compassion on Zion,
  for it is time to show favor to
    her;
  the appointed time has
    come.
¹⁴For her stones are dear to your
    servants;
  her very dust moves them to
    pity.
¹⁵The nations will fear the name
    of the LORD,
  all the kings of the earth will
    revere your glory.
¹⁶For the LORD will rebuild
    Zion
  and appear in his glory.
¹⁷He will respond to the prayer
    of the destitute;
  he will not despise their plea.

¹⁸Let this be written for a future
    generation,
  that a people not yet created
    may praise the LORD:
¹⁹"The LORD looked down from
    his sanctuary on high,
  from heaven he viewed the
    earth,
²⁰to hear the groans of the
    prisoners
  and release those
    condemned to death."
²¹So the name of the LORD will
    be declared in Zion
  and his praise in
    Jerusalem

²²when the peoples and the
    kingdoms
  assemble to worship the
    LORD.

²³In the course of my life[b] he
    broke my strength;
  he cut short my days.
²⁴So I said:
  "Do not take me away, my
    God, in the midst of my
    days;
  your years go on through all
    generations.
²⁵In the beginning you laid the
    foundations of the earth,
  and the heavens are the
    work of your hands.
²⁶They will perish, but you
    remain;
  they will all wear out like a
    garment.
  Like clothing you will change
    them
  and they will be discarded.
²⁷But you remain the same,
  and your years will never
    end.
²⁸The children of your servants
    will live in your
    presence;
  their descendants will be
    established before you."

Psalm 103

Of David.

¹Praise the LORD, my soul;
  all my inmost being, praise
    his holy name.

ᵇ 23 Or *By his power*

² Praise the LORD, my soul,
  and forget not all his
    benefits —
³ who forgives all your sins
  and heals all your
    diseases,
⁴ who redeems your life from
    the pit
  and crowns you with love
    and compassion,
⁵ who satisfies your desires with
    good things
  so that your youth is
    renewed like the eagle's.

⁶ The LORD works righteousness
  and justice for all the
    oppressed.

⁷ He made known his ways to
    Moses,
  his deeds to the people of
    Israel:
⁸ The LORD is compassionate
    and gracious,
  slow to anger, abounding in
    love.
⁹ He will not always accuse,
  nor will he harbor his anger
    forever;
¹⁰ he does not treat us as our sins
    deserve
  or repay us according to our
    iniquities.
¹¹ For as high as the heavens are
    above the earth,
  so great is his love for those
    who fear him;
¹² as far as the east is from the
    west,
  so far has he removed our
    transgressions from us.

¹³ As a father has compassion on
    his children,
  so the LORD has compassion
    on those who fear him;
¹⁴ for he knows how we are
    formed,
  he remembers that we are
    dust.
¹⁵ The life of mortals is like
    grass,
  they flourish like a flower of
    the field;
¹⁶ the wind blows over it and it is
    gone,
  and its place remembers it
    no more.
¹⁷ But from everlasting to
    everlasting
  the LORD's love is with those
    who fear him,
  and his righteousness
    with their children's
    children —
¹⁸ with those who keep his
    covenant
  and remember to obey his
    precepts.

¹⁹ The LORD has established his
    throne in heaven,
  and his kingdom rules over
    all.

²⁰ Praise the LORD, you his
    angels,
  you mighty ones who do his
    bidding,
  who obey his word.
²¹ Praise the LORD, all his
    heavenly hosts,
  you his servants who do his
    will.

²²Praise the LORD, all his
works
everywhere in his dominion.

Praise the LORD, my soul.

Psalm 104

¹Praise the LORD, my soul.

LORD my God, you are very
great;
you are clothed with
splendor and majesty.

²The LORD wraps himself in
light as with a garment;
he stretches out the heavens
like a tent
³ and lays the beams of his
upper chambers on their
waters.
He makes the clouds his
chariot
and rides on the wings of the
wind.
⁴He makes winds his
messengers,ᵃ
flames of fire his servants.

⁵He set the earth on its
foundations;
it can never be moved.
⁶You covered it with the
watery depths as with a
garment;
the waters stood above the
mountains.
⁷But at your rebuke the waters
fled,
at the sound of your thunder
they took to flight;

⁸they flowed over the
mountains,
they went down into the
valleys,
to the place you assigned for
them.
⁹You set a boundary they
cannot cross;
never again will they cover
the earth.

¹⁰He makes springs pour water
into the ravines;
it flows between the
mountains.
¹¹They give water to all the
beasts of the field;
the wild donkeys quench
their thirst.
¹²The birds of the sky nest by the
waters;
they sing among the
branches.
¹³He waters the mountains from
his upper chambers;
the land is satisfied by the
fruit of his work.
¹⁴He makes grass grow for the
cattle,
and plants for people to
cultivate —
bringing forth food from the
earth:
¹⁵wine that gladdens human
hearts,
oil to make their faces
shine,
and bread that sustains their
hearts.
¹⁶The trees of the LORD are well
watered,

ᵃ 4 Or *angels*

the cedars of Lebanon that
    he planted.
¹⁷There the birds make their
    nests;
  the stork has its home in the
    junipers.
¹⁸The high mountains belong to
    the wild goats;
  the crags are a refuge for the
    hyrax.

¹⁹He made the moon to mark
    the seasons,
  and the sun knows when to
    go down.
²⁰You bring darkness, it
    becomes night,
  and all the beasts of the
    forest prowl.
²¹The lions roar for their
    prey
  and seek their food from
    God.
²²The sun rises, and they steal
    away;
  they return and lie down in
    their dens.
²³Then people go out to their
    work,
  to their labor until
    evening.

²⁴How many are your works,
    Lord!
  In wisdom you made them
    all;
  the earth is full of your
    creatures.
²⁵There is the sea, vast and
    spacious,
  teeming with creatures
    beyond number —

living things both large and
    small.
²⁶There the ships go to and
    fro,
  and Leviathan, which you
    formed to frolic there.

²⁷All creatures look to you
  to give them their food at the
    proper time.
²⁸When you give it to them,
  they gather it up;
  when you open your hand,
  they are satisfied with good
    things.
²⁹When you hide your face,
  they are terrified;
  when you take away their
    breath,
  they die and return to the
    dust.
³⁰When you send your
    Spirit,
  they are created,
  and you renew the face of
    the ground.

³¹May the glory of the Lord
    endure forever;
  may the Lord rejoice in his
    works —
³²he who looks at the earth, and
    it trembles,
  who touches the mountains,
    and they smoke.

³³I will sing to the Lord all my
    life;
  I will sing praise to my God
    as long as I live.
³⁴May my meditation be
    pleasing to him,
  as I rejoice in the Lord.

35 But may sinners vanish from
    the earth
    and the wicked be no more.

Praise the LORD, my soul.

Praise the LORD.[a]

Psalm 105

1 Give praise to the LORD,
    proclaim his name;
    make known among the
    nations what he has
    done.
2 Sing to him, sing praise to him;
    tell of all his wonderful acts.
3 Glory in his holy name;
    let the hearts of those who
    seek the LORD rejoice.
4 Look to the LORD and his
    strength;
    seek his face always.

5 Remember the wonders he has
    done,
    his miracles, and the
    judgments he
    pronounced,
6 you his servants, the
    descendants of
    Abraham,
    his chosen ones, the
    children of Jacob.
7 He is the LORD our God;
    his judgments are in all the
    earth.
8 He remembers his covenant
    forever,
    the promise he made, for a
    thousand generations,

9 the covenant he made with
    Abraham,
    the oath he swore to
    Isaac.
10 He confirmed it to Jacob as a
    decree,
    to Israel as an everlasting
    covenant:
11 "To you I will give the land of
    Canaan
    as the portion you will
    inherit."

12 When they were but few in
    number,
    few indeed, and strangers
    in it,
13 they wandered from nation to
    nation,
    from one kingdom to
    another.
14 He allowed no one to oppress
    them;
    for their sake he rebuked
    kings:
15 "Do not touch my anointed
    ones;
    do my prophets no
    harm."

16 He called down famine on the
    land
    and destroyed all their
    supplies of food;
17 and he sent a man before
    them —
    Joseph, sold as a slave.
18 They bruised his feet with
    shackles,
    his neck was put in irons,

---

a 35 Hebrew *Hallelu Yah*; in the Septuagint this line stands at the beginning of
Psalm 105.

¹⁹till what he foretold came to
pass,
till the word of the LORD
proved him true.
²⁰The king sent and released
him,
the ruler of peoples set him
free.
²¹He made him master of his
household,
ruler over all he possessed,
²²to instruct his princes as he
pleased
and teach his elders wisdom.

²³Then Israel entered Egypt;
Jacob resided as a foreigner
in the land of Ham.
²⁴The LORD made his people
very fruitful;
he made them too numerous
for their foes,
²⁵whose hearts he turned to hate
his people,
to conspire against his
servants.
²⁶He sent Moses his servant,
and Aaron, whom he had
chosen.
²⁷They performed his signs
among them,
his wonders in the land of
Ham.
²⁸He sent darkness and made
the land dark —
for had they not rebelled
against his words?
²⁹He turned their waters into
blood,
causing their fish to die.
³⁰Their land teemed with
frogs,

which went up into the
bedrooms of their
rulers.
³¹He spoke, and there came
swarms of flies,
and gnats throughout their
country.
³²He turned their rain into hail,
with lightning throughout
their land;
³³he struck down their vines and
fig trees
and shattered the trees of
their country.
³⁴He spoke, and the locusts
came,
grasshoppers without
number;
³⁵they ate up every green thing
in their land,
ate up the produce of their
soil.
³⁶Then he struck down all the
firstborn in their land,
the firstfruits of all their
manhood.
³⁷He brought out Israel, laden
with silver and gold,
and from among their tribes
no one faltered.
³⁸Egypt was glad when they left,
because dread of Israel had
fallen on them.

³⁹He spread out a cloud as a
covering,
and a fire to give light at
night.
⁴⁰They asked, and he brought
them quail;
he fed them well with the
bread of heaven.

41 He opened the rock, and water
gushed out;
  it flowed like a river in the
    desert.
42 For he remembered his holy
promise
  given to his servant
    Abraham.
43 He brought out his people with
rejoicing,
  his chosen ones with shouts
    of joy;
44 he gave them the lands of the
nations,
  and they fell heir to what
    others had toiled for —
45 that they might keep his
precepts
  and observe his laws.

  Praise the LORD.[a]

Psalm 106

1 Praise the LORD.[b]

  Give thanks to the LORD, for he
    is good;
  his love endures forever.
2 Who can proclaim the mighty
acts of the LORD
  or fully declare his praise?
3 Blessed are those who act
justly,
  who always do what is right.
4 Remember me, LORD, when
  you show favor to your
    people,
  come to my aid when you
    save them,

5 that I may enjoy the prosperity
of your chosen ones,
  that I may share in the joy of
    your nation
  and join your inheritance in
    giving praise.

6 We have sinned, even as our
ancestors did;
  we have done wrong and
    acted wickedly.
7 When our ancestors were in
Egypt,
  they gave no thought to your
    miracles;
  they did not remember your
    many kindnesses,
  and they rebelled by the sea,
    the Red Sea.[c]
8 Yet he saved them for his
name's sake,
  to make his mighty power
    known.
9 He rebuked the Red Sea, and it
dried up;
  he led them through the
    depths as through a
    desert.
10 He saved them from the hand
of the foe;
  from the hand of the
    enemy he redeemed
    them.
11 The waters covered their
adversaries;
  not one of them
    survived.
12 Then they believed his
promises
  and sang his praise.

---

[a] 45 Hebrew *Hallelu Yah*   [b] 1 Hebrew *Hallelu Yah*; also in verse 48   [c] 7 Or *the Sea of Reeds*; also in verses 9 and 22

¹³ But they soon forgot what he
    had done
  and did not wait for his plan
    to unfold.
¹⁴ In the desert they gave in to
    their craving;
  in the wilderness they put
    God to the test.
¹⁵ So he gave them what they
    asked for,
  but sent a wasting disease
    among them.

¹⁶ In the camp they grew envious
    of Moses
  and of Aaron, who was
    consecrated to the
    LORD.
¹⁷ The earth opened up and
    swallowed Dathan;
  it buried the company of
    Abiram.
¹⁸ Fire blazed among their
    followers;
  a flame consumed the
    wicked.
¹⁹ At Horeb they made a calf
  and worshiped an idol cast
    from metal.
²⁰ They exchanged their glorious
    God
  for an image of a bull, which
    eats grass.
²¹ They forgot the God who saved
    them,
  who had done great things in
    Egypt,
²² miracles in the land of Ham
  and awesome deeds by the
    Red Sea.
²³ So he said he would destroy
    them —

had not Moses, his chosen
    one,
  stood in the breach before
    him
  to keep his wrath from
    destroying them.

²⁴ Then they despised the
    pleasant land;
  they did not believe his
    promise.
²⁵ They grumbled in their tents
  and did not obey the LORD.
²⁶ So he swore to them with
    uplifted hand
  that he would make them
    fall in the wilderness,
²⁷ make their descendants fall
    among the nations
  and scatter them throughout
    the lands.

²⁸ They yoked themselves to the
    Baal of Peor
  and ate sacrifices offered to
    lifeless gods;
²⁹ they aroused the LORD's anger
    by their wicked deeds,
  and a plague broke out
    among them.
³⁰ But Phinehas stood up and
    intervened,
  and the plague was
    checked.
³¹ This was credited to him as
    righteousness
  for endless generations to
    come.
³² By the waters of Meribah they
    angered the LORD,
  and trouble came to Moses
    because of them;

³³for they rebelled against the
  Spirit of God,
 and rash words came from
  Moses' lips.ᵃ

³⁴They did not destroy the
  peoples
 as the LORD had
  commanded them,
³⁵but they mingled with the
  nations
 and adopted their customs.
³⁶They worshiped their idols,
 which became a snare to
  them.
³⁷They sacrificed their sons
 and their daughters to false
  gods.
³⁸They shed innocent blood,
 the blood of their sons and
  daughters,
 whom they sacrificed to the
  idols of Canaan,
 and the land was desecrated
  by their blood.
³⁹They defiled themselves by
  what they did;
 by their deeds they
  prostituted themselves.

⁴⁰Therefore the LORD was angry
  with his people
 and abhorred his
  inheritance.
⁴¹He gave them into the hands
  of the nations,
 and their foes ruled over
  them.
⁴²Their enemies oppressed them
 and subjected them to their
  power.

⁴³Many times he delivered them,
 but they were bent on
  rebellion
 and they wasted away in
  their sin.
⁴⁴Yet he took note of their
  distress
 when he heard their cry;
⁴⁵for their sake he remembered
  his covenant
 and out of his great love he
  relented.
⁴⁶He caused all who held them
  captive
 to show them mercy.

⁴⁷Save us, LORD our God,
 and gather us from the
  nations,
 that we may give thanks to
  your holy name
 and glory in your praise.

⁴⁸Praise be to the LORD, the God
  of Israel,
 from everlasting to
  everlasting.

Let all the people say, "Amen!"

Praise the LORD.

BOOK V

Psalms 107–150

Psalm 107

¹Give thanks to the LORD, for he
  is good;
 his love endures forever.

ᵃ 33 Or *against his spirit, / and rash words came from his lips*

2 Let the redeemed of the LORD
tell their story —
those he redeemed from the
hand of the foe,
3 those he gathered from the
lands,
from east and west, from
north and south.ᵃ

4 Some wandered in desert
wastelands,
finding no way to a city
where they could settle.
5 They were hungry and thirsty,
and their lives ebbed away.
6 Then they cried out to the
LORD in their trouble,
and he delivered them from
their distress.
7 He led them by a straight way
to a city where they could
settle.
8 Let them give thanks to the
LORD for his unfailing
love
and his wonderful deeds for
mankind,
9 for he satisfies the thirsty
and fills the hungry with
good things.

10 Some sat in darkness, in utter
darkness,
prisoners suffering in iron
chains,
11 because they rebelled against
God's commands
and despised the plans of the
Most High.
12 So he subjected them to bitter
labor;

they stumbled, and there
was no one to help.
13 Then they cried to the LORD in
their trouble,
and he saved them from
their distress.
14 He brought them out of
darkness, the utter
darkness,
and broke away their chains.
15 Let them give thanks to the
LORD for his unfailing
love
and his wonderful deeds for
mankind,
16 for he breaks down gates of
bronze
and cuts through bars of
iron.

17 Some became fools through
their rebellious ways
and suffered affliction
because of their
iniquities.
18 They loathed all food
and drew near the gates of
death.
19 Then they cried to the LORD in
their trouble,
and he saved them from
their distress.
20 He sent out his word and
healed them;
he rescued them from the
grave.
21 Let them give thanks to the
LORD for his unfailing
love
and his wonderful deeds for
mankind.

ᵃ 3 Hebrew *north and the sea*

²²Let them sacrifice thank
offerings
and tell of his works with
songs of joy.

²³Some went out on the sea in
ships;
they were merchants on the
mighty waters.
²⁴They saw the works of the
LORD,
his wonderful deeds in the
deep.
²⁵For he spoke and stirred up a
tempest
that lifted high the waves.
²⁶They mounted up to the
heavens and went down
to the depths;
in their peril their courage
melted away.
²⁷They reeled and staggered like
drunkards;
they were at their wits' end.
²⁸Then they cried out to the
LORD in their trouble,
and he brought them out of
their distress.
²⁹He stilled the storm to a
whisper;
the waves of the sea^a were
hushed.
³⁰They were glad when it grew
calm,
and he guided them to their
desired haven.
³¹Let them give thanks to the
LORD for his unfailing
love
and his wonderful deeds for
mankind.

³²Let them exalt him in the
assembly of the people
and praise him in the
council of the elders.

³³He turned rivers into a
desert,
flowing springs into thirsty
ground,
³⁴and fruitful land into a salt
waste,
because of the wickedness of
those who lived there.
³⁵He turned the desert into
pools of water
and the parched ground into
flowing springs;
³⁶there he brought the hungry to
live,
and they founded a city
where they could
settle.
³⁷They sowed fields and planted
vineyards
that yielded a fruitful
harvest;
³⁸he blessed them, and their
numbers greatly
increased,
and he did not let their herds
diminish.

³⁹Then their numbers
decreased, and they
were humbled
by oppression, calamity and
sorrow;
⁴⁰he who pours contempt on
nobles
made them wander in a
trackless waste.

^a 29 Dead Sea Scrolls; Masoretic Text / *their waves*

41 But he lifted the needy out of
  their affliction
    and increased their families
    like flocks.
42 The upright see and rejoice,
    but all the wicked shut their
    mouths.

43 Let the one who is wise heed
  these things
    and ponder the loving deeds
    of the LORD.

Psalm 108[a]

A song. A psalm of David.

1 My heart, O God, is steadfast;
    I will sing and make music
    with all my soul.
2 Awake, harp and lyre!
    I will awaken the dawn.
3 I will praise you, LORD, among
  the nations;
    I will sing of you among the
    peoples.
4 For great is your love, higher
  than the heavens;
    your faithfulness reaches to
    the skies.
5 Be exalted, O God, above the
  heavens;
    let your glory be over all the
    earth.

6 Save us and help us with your
  right hand,
    that those you love may be
    delivered.
7 God has spoken from his
  sanctuary:

"In triumph I will parcel out
  Shechem
    and measure off the Valley of
    Sukkoth.
8 Gilead is mine, Manasseh is
  mine;
    Ephraim is my helmet,
    Judah is my scepter.
9 Moab is my washbasin,
    on Edom I toss my sandal;
    over Philistia I shout in
    triumph."

10 Who will bring me to the
  fortified city?
    Who will lead me to Edom?
11 Is it not you, God, you who
  have rejected us
    and no longer go out with
    our armies?
12 Give us aid against the
  enemy,
    for human help is worthless.
13 With God we will gain the
  victory,
    and he will trample down
    our enemies.

Psalm 109

*For the director of music.
Of David. A psalm.*

1 My God, whom I praise,
    do not remain silent,
2 for people who are wicked and
  deceitful
    have opened their mouths
    against me;
    they have spoken against me
    with lying tongues.

---

a In Hebrew texts 108:1-13 is numbered 108:2-14.

³With words of hatred they
surround me;
they attack me without
cause.
⁴In return for my friendship
they accuse me,
but I am a man of prayer.
⁵They repay me evil for good,
and hatred for my
friendship.

⁶Appoint someone evil to
oppose my enemy;
let an accuser stand at his
right hand.
⁷When he is tried, let him be
found guilty,
and may his prayers
condemn him.
⁸May his days be few;
may another take his place
of leadership.
⁹May his children be
fatherless
and his wife a widow.
¹⁰May his children be
wandering beggars;
may they be driven[a] from
their ruined homes.
¹¹May a creditor seize all he has;
may strangers plunder the
fruits of his labor.
¹²May no one extend kindness to
him
or take pity on his fatherless
children.
¹³May his descendants be cut
off,
their names blotted out from
the next generation.

¹⁴May the iniquity of his fathers
be remembered before
the LORD;
may the sin of his mother
never be blotted out.
¹⁵May their sins always remain
before the LORD,
that he may blot out their
name from the earth.

¹⁶For he never thought of doing
a kindness,
but hounded to death the
poor
and the needy and the
brokenhearted.
¹⁷He loved to pronounce a
curse—
may it come back on him.
He found no pleasure in
blessing—
may it be far from him.
¹⁸He wore cursing as his
garment;
it entered into his body like
water,
into his bones like oil.
¹⁹May it be like a cloak wrapped
about him,
like a belt tied forever
around him.
²⁰May this be the LORD's
payment to my accusers,
to those who speak evil
of me.

²¹But you, Sovereign LORD,
help me for your name's
sake;
out of the goodness of your
love, deliver me.

---

a 10 Septuagint; Hebrew *sought*

²²For I am poor and needy,
and my heart is wounded
within me.
²³I fade away like an evening
shadow;
I am shaken off like a locust.
²⁴My knees give way from
fasting;
my body is thin and gaunt.
²⁵I am an object of scorn to my
accusers;
when they see me, they
shake their heads.

²⁶Help me, Lord my God;
save me according to your
unfailing love.
²⁷Let them know that it is your
hand,
that you, Lord, have done it.
²⁸While they curse, may you
bless;
may those who attack me be
put to shame,
but may your servant rejoice.
²⁹May my accusers be clothed
with disgrace
and wrapped in shame as in
a cloak.

³⁰With my mouth I will greatly
extol the Lord;
in the great throng of
worshipers I will praise
him.
³¹For he stands at the right hand
of the needy,
to save their lives from those
who would condemn
them.

Psalm 110

Of David. A psalm.

¹The Lord says to my lord:[a]

"Sit at my right hand
until I make your enemies
a footstool for your feet."

²The Lord will extend your
mighty scepter from
Zion, saying,
"Rule in the midst of your
enemies!"
³Your troops will be willing
on your day of battle.
Arrayed in holy splendor,
your young men will come to
you
like dew from the morning's
womb.[b]

⁴The Lord has sworn
and will not change his
mind:
"You are a priest forever,
in the order of Melchizedek."

⁵The Lord is at your right
hand[c];
he will crush kings on the
day of his wrath.
⁶He will judge the nations,
heaping up the dead
and crushing the rulers of
the whole earth.
⁷He will drink from a brook
along the way,[d]
and so he will lift his head
high.

---

[a] 1 Or *Lord*   [b] 3 The meaning of the Hebrew for this sentence is uncertain.
[c] 5 Or *My lord is at your right hand*, Lord   [d] 7 The meaning of the Hebrew for
this clause is uncertain.

Psalm 111[a]

1 Praise the LORD.[b]

I will extol the LORD with all
my heart
in the council of the upright
and in the assembly.

2 Great are the works of the LORD;
they are pondered by all who
delight in them.

3 Glorious and majestic are his
deeds,
and his righteousness
endures forever.

4 He has caused his wonders to
be remembered;
the LORD is gracious and
compassionate.

5 He provides food for those
who fear him;
he remembers his covenant
forever.

6 He has shown his people the
power of his works,
giving them the lands of
other nations.

7 The works of his hands are
faithful and just;
all his precepts are
trustworthy.

8 They are established for ever
and ever,
enacted in faithfulness and
uprightness.

9 He provided redemption for
his people;
he ordained his covenant
forever —

holy and awesome is his
name.

10 The fear of the LORD is the
beginning of wisdom;
all who follow his
precepts have good
understanding.
To him belongs eternal
praise.

Psalm 112[a]

1 Praise the LORD.[b]

Blessed are those who fear the
LORD,
who find great delight in his
commands.

2 Their children will be mighty
in the land;
the generation of the upright
will be blessed.

3 Wealth and riches are in their
houses,
and their righteousness
endures forever.

4 Even in darkness light dawns
for the upright,
for those who are gracious
and compassionate and
righteous.

5 Good will come to those who
are generous and lend
freely,
who conduct their affairs
with justice.

6 Surely the righteous will never
be shaken;

---

[a] This psalm is an acrostic poem, the lines of which begin with the successive
letters of the Hebrew alphabet.   [b] 1 Hebrew *Hallelu Yah*

they will be remembered
forever.
⁷They will have no fear of bad
news;
their hearts are steadfast,
trusting in the LORD.
⁸Their hearts are secure, they
will have no fear;
in the end they will look in
triumph on their foes.
⁹They have freely scattered
their gifts to the poor,
their righteousness endures
forever;
their horn*a* will be lifted high
in honor.

¹⁰The wicked will see and be
vexed,
they will gnash their teeth
and waste away;
the longings of the wicked
will come to nothing.

Psalm 113

¹Praise the LORD.*b*

Praise the LORD, you his
servants;
praise the name of the LORD.
²Let the name of the LORD be
praised,
both now and forevermore.
³From the rising of the sun to
the place where it sets,
the name of the LORD is to be
praised.

⁴The LORD is exalted over all
the nations,
his glory above the heavens.

⁵Who is like the LORD our God,
the One who sits enthroned
on high,
⁶who stoops down to look
on the heavens and the
earth?

⁷He raises the poor from the
dust
and lifts the needy from the
ash heap;
⁸he seats them with princes,
with the princes of his
people.
⁹He settles the childless woman
in her home
as a happy mother of
children.

Praise the LORD.

Psalm 114

¹When Israel came out of Egypt,
Jacob from a people of
foreign tongue,
²Judah became God's
sanctuary,
Israel his dominion.

³The sea looked and fled,
the Jordan turned back;
⁴the mountains leaped like
rams,
the hills like lambs.

⁵Why was it, sea, that you fled?
Why, Jordan, did you turn
back?
⁶Why, mountains, did you leap
like rams,
you hills, like lambs?

---

a 9 *Horn* here symbolizes dignity.   *b* 1 Hebrew *Hallelu Yah*; also in verse 9

7Tremble, earth, at the presence
of the Lord,
at the presence of the God of
Jacob,
8who turned the rock into a
pool,
the hard rock into springs of
water.

Psalm 115

1Not to us, LORD, not to us
but to your name be the
glory,
because of your love and
faithfulness.

2Why do the nations say,
"Where is their God?"
3Our God is in heaven;
he does whatever pleases
him.
4But their idols are silver and
gold,
made by human hands.
5They have mouths, but cannot
speak,
eyes, but cannot see.
6They have ears, but cannot
hear,
noses, but cannot smell.
7They have hands, but cannot
feel,
feet, but cannot walk,
nor can they utter a sound
with their throats.
8Those who make them will be
like them,
and so will all who trust in
them.

9All you Israelites, trust in the
LORD—
he is their help and shield.
10House of Aaron, trust in the
LORD—
he is their help and shield.
11You who fear him, trust in the
LORD—
he is their help and shield.

12The LORD remembers us and
will bless us:
He will bless his people
Israel,
he will bless the house of
Aaron,
13he will bless those who fear
the LORD—
small and great alike.

14May the LORD cause you to
flourish,
both you and your
children.
15May you be blessed by the
LORD,
the Maker of heaven and
earth.

16The highest heavens belong to
the LORD,
but the earth he has given to
mankind.
17It is not the dead who praise
the LORD,
those who go down to the
place of silence;
18it is we who extol the
LORD,
both now and forevermore.

Praise the LORD.[a]

---

[a] 18 Hebrew *Hallelu Yah*

Psalm 116

¹ I love the LORD, for he heard
my voice;
he heard my cry for mercy.
² Because he turned his ear
to me,
I will call on him as long as I
live.

³ The cords of death entangled
me,
the anguish of the grave
came over me;
I was overcome by distress
and sorrow.
⁴ Then I called on the name of
the LORD:
"LORD, save me!"

⁵ The LORD is gracious and
righteous;
our God is full of
compassion.
⁶ The LORD protects the unwary;
when I was brought low, he
saved me.

⁷ Return to your rest, my soul,
for the LORD has been good
to you.

⁸ For you, LORD, have delivered
me from death,
my eyes from tears,
my feet from stumbling,
⁹ that I may walk before the
LORD
in the land of the living.

¹⁰ I trusted in the LORD when I
said,
"I am greatly afflicted";
¹¹ in my alarm I said,
"Everyone is a liar."

¹² What shall I return to the LORD
for all his goodness to me?

¹³ I will lift up the cup of salvation
and call on the name of the
LORD.
¹⁴ I will fulfill my vows to the
LORD
in the presence of all his
people.

¹⁵ Precious in the sight of the
LORD
is the death of his faithful
servants.
¹⁶ Truly I am your servant, LORD;
I serve you just as my mother
did;
you have freed me from my
chains.

¹⁷ I will sacrifice a thank offering
to you
and call on the name of the
LORD.
¹⁸ I will fulfill my vows to the
LORD
in the presence of all his
people,
¹⁹ in the courts of the house of
the LORD —
in your midst, Jerusalem.

Praise the LORD.^a

Psalm 117

¹ Praise the LORD, all you
nations;
extol him, all you peoples.

^a 19 Hebrew *Hallelu Yah*

² For great is his love toward us,
  and the faithfulness of the
    LORD endures forever.

Praise the LORD.ᵃ

Psalm 118

¹ Give thanks to the LORD, for he
    is good;
  his love endures forever.

² Let Israel say:
  "His love endures forever."
³ Let the house of Aaron say:
  "His love endures forever."
⁴ Let those who fear the LORD
    say:
  "His love endures forever."

⁵ When hard pressed, I cried to
    the LORD;
  he brought me into a
    spacious place.
⁶ The LORD is with me; I will not
    be afraid.
  What can mere mortals do
    to me?
⁷ The LORD is with me; he is my
    helper.
  I look in triumph on my
    enemies.

⁸ It is better to take refuge in the
    LORD
  than to trust in humans.
⁹ It is better to take refuge in the
    LORD
  than to trust in princes.
¹⁰ All the nations surrounded me,
  but in the name of the LORD
    I cut them down.

¹¹ They surrounded me on every
    side,
  but in the name of the LORD
    I cut them down.
¹² They swarmed around me like
    bees,
  but they were consumed
    as quickly as burning
    thorns;
  in the name of the LORD I cut
    them down.
¹³ I was pushed back and about
    to fall,
  but the LORD helped me.
¹⁴ The LORD is my strength and
    my defenseᵇ;
  he has become my salvation.

¹⁵ Shouts of joy and victory
  resound in the tents of the
    righteous:
  "The LORD's right hand has
    done mighty things!
¹⁶   The LORD's right hand is
    lifted high;
  the LORD's right hand has
    done mighty things!"
¹⁷ I will not die but live,
  and will proclaim what the
    LORD has done.
¹⁸ The LORD has chastened me
    severely,
  but he has not given me over
    to death.
¹⁹ Open for me the gates of the
    righteous;
  I will enter and give thanks
    to the LORD.
²⁰ This is the gate of the LORD
  through which the righteous
    may enter.

ᵃ 2 Hebrew *Hallelu Yah*   ᵇ 14 Or *song*

²¹ I will give you thanks, for you
　　answered me;
　you have become my
　　salvation.

²² The stone the builders
　　rejected
　has become the
　　cornerstone;
²³ the LORD has done this,
　and it is marvelous in our
　　eyes.
²⁴ The LORD has done it this very
　　day;
　let us rejoice today and be
　　glad.

²⁵ LORD, save us!
　LORD, grant us success!

²⁶ Blessed is he who comes in the
　　name of the LORD.
　From the house of the LORD
　　we bless you.ᵃ
²⁷ The LORD is God,
　and he has made his light
　　shine on us.
　With boughs in hand, join in
　　the festal procession
　upᵇ to the horns of the
　　altar.

²⁸ You are my God, and I will
　　praise you;
　you are my God, and I will
　　exalt you.

²⁹ Give thanks to the LORD, for he
　　is good;
　his love endures forever.

Psalm 119ᶜ

א Aleph

¹ Blessed are those whose ways
　　are blameless,
　who walk according to the
　　law of the LORD.
² Blessed are those who keep his
　　statutes
　and seek him with all their
　　heart —
³ they do no wrong
　but follow his ways.
⁴ You have laid down precepts
　that are to be fully obeyed.
⁵ Oh, that my ways were
　　steadfast
　in obeying your decrees!
⁶ Then I would not be put to
　　shame
　when I consider all your
　　commands.
⁷ I will praise you with an
　　upright heart
　as I learn your righteous
　　laws.
⁸ I will obey your decrees;
　do not utterly forsake me.

ב Beth

⁹ How can a young person stay
　　on the path of purity?
　By living according to your
　　word.
¹⁰ I seek you with all my heart;
　do not let me stray from your
　　commands.

ᵃ 26 The Hebrew is plural.　　ᵇ 27 Or *Bind the festal sacrifice with ropes / and take it*　　ᶜ This psalm is an acrostic poem, the stanzas of which begin with successive letters of the Hebrew alphabet; moreover, the verses of each stanza begin with the same letter of the Hebrew alphabet.

¹¹ I have hidden your word in my
heart
   that I might not sin against
   you.
¹² Praise be to you, LORD;
   teach me your decrees.
¹³ With my lips I recount
   all the laws that come from
   your mouth.
¹⁴ I rejoice in following your
statutes
   as one rejoices in great riches.
¹⁵ I meditate on your precepts
   and consider your ways.
¹⁶ I delight in your decrees;
   I will not neglect your word.

ג Gimel

¹⁷ Be good to your servant while I
live,
   that I may obey your word.
¹⁸ Open my eyes that I may see
   wonderful things in your law.
¹⁹ I am a stranger on earth;
   do not hide your commands
   from me.
²⁰ My soul is consumed with
longing
   for your laws at all times.
²¹ You rebuke the arrogant, who
are accursed,
   those who stray from your
   commands.
²² Remove from me their scorn
and contempt,
   for I keep your statutes.
²³ Though rulers sit together and
slander me,
   your servant will meditate
   on your decrees.

²⁴ Your statutes are my delight;
   they are my counselors.

ד Daleth

²⁵ I am laid low in the dust;
   preserve my life according to
   your word.
²⁶ I gave an account of my ways
   and you answered me;
   teach me your decrees.
²⁷ Cause me to understand the
   way of your precepts,
   that I may meditate on your
   wonderful deeds.
²⁸ My soul is weary with sorrow;
   strengthen me according to
   your word.
²⁹ Keep me from deceitful ways;
   be gracious to me and teach
   me your law.
³⁰ I have chosen the way of
faithfulness;
   I have set my heart on your
   laws.
³¹ I hold fast to your statutes,
LORD;
   do not let me be put to shame.
³² I run in the path of your
commands,
   for you have broadened my
   understanding.

ה He

³³ Teach me, LORD, the way of
   your decrees,
   that I may follow it to the
   end.ᵃ
³⁴ Give me understanding, so
   that I may keep your law
   and obey it with all my heart.

ᵃ 33 Or *follow it for its reward*

³⁵Direct me in the path of your
commands,
for there I find delight.
³⁶Turn my heart toward your
statutes
and not toward selfish gain.
³⁷Turn my eyes away from
worthless things;
preserve my life according to
your word.^a
³⁸Fulfill your promise to your
servant,
so that you may be feared.
³⁹Take away the disgrace I
dread,
for your laws are good.
⁴⁰How I long for your precepts!
In your righteousness
preserve my life.

ו Waw

⁴¹May your unfailing love come
to me, LORD,
your salvation, according to
your promise;
⁴²then I can answer anyone who
taunts me,
for I trust in your word.
⁴³Never take your word of truth
from my mouth,
for I have put my hope in
your laws.
⁴⁴I will always obey your law,
for ever and ever.
⁴⁵I will walk about in freedom,
for I have sought out your
precepts.
⁴⁶I will speak of your statutes
before kings

and will not be put to shame,
⁴⁷for I delight in your commands
because I love them.
⁴⁸I reach out for your
commands, which I love,
that I may meditate on your
decrees.

ז Zayin

⁴⁹Remember your word to your
servant,
for you have given me hope.
⁵⁰My comfort in my suffering is
this:
Your promise preserves my
life.
⁵¹The arrogant mock me
unmercifully,
but I do not turn from your
law.
⁵²I remember, LORD, your
ancient laws,
and I find comfort in them.
⁵³Indignation grips me because
of the wicked,
who have forsaken your law.
⁵⁴Your decrees are the theme of
my song
wherever I lodge.
⁵⁵In the night, LORD, I remember
your name,
that I may keep your law.
⁵⁶This has been my practice:
I obey your precepts.

ח Heth

⁵⁷You are my portion, LORD;
I have promised to obey your
words.

^a 37 Two manuscripts of the Masoretic Text and Dead Sea Scrolls; most
manuscripts of the Masoretic Text *life in your way*

58 I have sought your face with all
   my heart;
   be gracious to me according
   to your promise.
59 I have considered my ways
   and have turned my steps to
   your statutes.
60 I will hasten and not delay
   to obey your commands.
61 Though the wicked bind me
   with ropes,
   I will not forget your law.
62 At midnight I rise to give you
   thanks
   for your righteous laws.
63 I am a friend to all who fear
   you,
   to all who follow your
   precepts.
64 The earth is filled with your
   love, LORD;
   teach me your decrees.

ט Teth

65 Do good to your servant
   according to your word,
   LORD.
66 Teach me knowledge and good
   judgment,
   for I trust your commands.
67 Before I was afflicted I went
   astray,
   but now I obey your word.
68 You are good, and what you do
   is good;
   teach me your decrees.
69 Though the arrogant have
   smeared me with
   lies,
   I keep your precepts with all
   my heart.

70 Their hearts are callous and
   unfeeling,
   but I delight in your law.
71 It was good for me to be
   afflicted
   so that I might learn your
   decrees.
72 The law from your mouth is
   more precious to me
   than thousands of pieces of
   silver and gold.

י Yodh

73 Your hands made me and
   formed me;
   give me understanding to
   learn your commands.
74 May those who fear you rejoice
   when they see me,
   for I have put my hope in
   your word.
75 I know, LORD, that your laws
   are righteous,
   and that in faithfulness you
   have afflicted me.
76 May your unfailing love be my
   comfort,
   according to your promise to
   your servant.
77 Let your compassion come to
   me that I may live,
   for your law is my delight.
78 May the arrogant be put to
   shame for wronging me
   without cause;
   but I will meditate on your
   precepts.
79 May those who fear you turn
   to me,
   those who understand your
   statutes.

⁸⁰May I wholeheartedly follow
your decrees,
that I may not be put to
shame.

כ Kaph

⁸¹My soul faints with longing for
your salvation,
but I have put my hope in
your word.
⁸²My eyes fail, looking for your
promise;
I say, "When will you
comfort me?"
⁸³Though I am like a wineskin in
the smoke,
I do not forget your decrees.
⁸⁴How long must your servant
wait?
When will you punish my
persecutors?
⁸⁵The arrogant dig pits to
trap me,
contrary to your law.
⁸⁶All your commands are
trustworthy;
help me, for I am being
persecuted without
cause.
⁸⁷They almost wiped me from
the earth,
but I have not forsaken your
precepts.
⁸⁸In your unfailing love preserve
my life,
that I may obey the statutes
of your mouth.

ל Lamedh

⁸⁹Your word, LORD, is eternal;
it stands firm in the heavens.

⁹⁰Your faithfulness continues
through all generations;
you established the earth,
and it endures.
⁹¹Your laws endure to this day,
for all things serve you.
⁹²If your law had not been my
delight,
I would have perished in my
affliction.
⁹³I will never forget your
precepts,
for by them you have
preserved my life.
⁹⁴Save me, for I am yours;
I have sought out your
precepts.
⁹⁵The wicked are waiting to
destroy me,
but I will ponder your
statutes.
⁹⁶To all perfection I see a limit,
but your commands are
boundless.

מ Mem

⁹⁷Oh, how I love your law!
I meditate on it all day long.
⁹⁸Your commands are always
with me
and make me wiser than my
enemies.
⁹⁹I have more insight than all
my teachers,
for I meditate on your
statutes.
¹⁰⁰I have more understanding
than the elders,
for I obey your precepts.
¹⁰¹I have kept my feet from every
evil path

so that I might obey your
word.
¹⁰² I have not departed from your
laws,
for you yourself have
taught me.
¹⁰³ How sweet are your words to
my taste,
sweeter than honey to my
mouth!
¹⁰⁴ I gain understanding from
your precepts;
therefore I hate every wrong
path.

ב Nun

¹⁰⁵ Your word is a lamp for my
feet,
a light on my path.
¹⁰⁶ I have taken an oath and
confirmed it,
that I will follow your
righteous laws.
¹⁰⁷ I have suffered much;
preserve my life, LORD,
according to your
word.
¹⁰⁸ Accept, LORD, the willing
praise of my mouth,
and teach me your laws.
¹⁰⁹ Though I constantly take my
life in my hands,
I will not forget your law.
¹¹⁰ The wicked have set a snare
for me,
but I have not strayed from
your precepts.
¹¹¹ Your statutes are my heritage
forever;
they are the joy of my heart.

¹¹² My heart is set on keeping
your decrees
to the very end.^a

ס Samekh

¹¹³ I hate double-minded
people,
but I love your law.
¹¹⁴ You are my refuge and my
shield;
I have put my hope in your
word.
¹¹⁵ Away from me, you evildoers,
that I may keep the
commands of my God!
¹¹⁶ Sustain me, my God,
according to your
promise, and I will live;
do not let my hopes be
dashed.
¹¹⁷ Uphold me, and I will be
delivered;
I will always have regard for
your decrees.
¹¹⁸ You reject all who stray from
your decrees,
for their delusions come to
nothing.
¹¹⁹ All the wicked of the earth
you discard like dross;
therefore I love your statutes.
¹²⁰ My flesh trembles in fear of
you;
I stand in awe of your laws.

ע Ayin

¹²¹ I have done what is righteous
and just;
do not leave me to my
oppressors.

---

^a 112 Or decrees / for their enduring reward

¹²²Ensure your servant's well-
being;
do not let the arrogant
oppress me.
¹²³My eyes fail, looking for your
salvation,
looking for your righteous
promise.
¹²⁴Deal with your servant
according to your love
and teach me your decrees.
¹²⁵I am your servant; give me
discernment
that I may understand your
statutes.
¹²⁶It is time for you to act, LORD;
your law is being broken.
¹²⁷Because I love your
commands
more than gold, more than
pure gold,
¹²⁸and because I consider all
your precepts right,
I hate every wrong path.

פ Pe

¹²⁹Your statutes are wonderful;
therefore I obey them.
¹³⁰The unfolding of your words
gives light;
it gives understanding to the
simple.
¹³¹I open my mouth and pant,
longing for your commands.
¹³²Turn to me and have mercy
on me,
as you always do to those
who love your name.
¹³³Direct my footsteps according
to your word;
let no sin rule over me.

¹³⁴Redeem me from human
oppression,
that I may obey your
precepts.
¹³⁵Make your face shine on your
servant
and teach me your decrees.
¹³⁶Streams of tears flow from my
eyes,
for your law is not obeyed.

צ Tsadhe

¹³⁷You are righteous, LORD,
and your laws are right.
¹³⁸The statutes you have laid
down are righteous;
they are fully trustworthy.
¹³⁹My zeal wears me out,
for my enemies ignore your
words.
¹⁴⁰Your promises have been
thoroughly tested,
and your servant loves them.
¹⁴¹Though I am lowly and
despised,
I do not forget your precepts.
¹⁴²Your righteousness is
everlasting
and your law is true.
¹⁴³Trouble and distress have
come upon me,
but your commands give me
delight.
¹⁴⁴Your statutes are always
righteous;
give me understanding that I
may live.

ק Qoph

¹⁴⁵I call with all my heart;
answer me, LORD,
and I will obey your decrees.

¹⁴⁶ I call out to you; save me
and I will keep your statutes.
¹⁴⁷ I rise before dawn and cry for
help;
I have put my hope in your
word.
¹⁴⁸ My eyes stay open through
the watches of the night,
that I may meditate on your
promises.
¹⁴⁹ Hear my voice in accordance
with your love;
preserve my life, Lord,
according to your laws.
¹⁵⁰ Those who devise wicked
schemes are near,
but they are far from your
law.
¹⁵¹ Yet you are near, Lord,
and all your commands are
true.
¹⁵² Long ago I learned from your
statutes
that you established them to
last forever.

ר Resh

¹⁵³ Look on my suffering and
deliver me,
for I have not forgotten your
law.
¹⁵⁴ Defend my cause and
redeem me;
preserve my life according to
your promise.
¹⁵⁵ Salvation is far from the
wicked,
for they do not seek out your
decrees.
¹⁵⁶ Your compassion, Lord, is
great;

preserve my life according to
your laws.
¹⁵⁷ Many are the foes who
persecute me,
but I have not turned from
your statutes.
¹⁵⁸ I look on the faithless with
loathing,
for they do not obey your
word.
¹⁵⁹ See how I love your
precepts;
preserve my life, Lord, in
accordance with your
love.
¹⁶⁰ All your words are true;
all your righteous laws are
eternal.

ש Sin and Shin

¹⁶¹ Rulers persecute me without
cause,
but my heart trembles at
your word.
¹⁶² I rejoice in your promise
like one who finds great
spoil.
¹⁶³ I hate and detest falsehood
but I love your law.
¹⁶⁴ Seven times a day I praise
you
for your righteous
laws.
¹⁶⁵ Great peace have those who
love your law,
and nothing can make them
stumble.
¹⁶⁶ I wait for your salvation,
Lord,
and I follow your
commands.

167 I obey your statutes,
   for I love them greatly.
168 I obey your precepts and your
     statutes,
   for all my ways are known to
     you.

ת Taw

169 May my cry come before you,
   LORD;
   give me understanding
     according to your word.
170 May my supplication come
     before you;
   deliver me according to your
     promise.
171 May my lips overflow with
     praise,
   for you teach me your
     decrees.
172 May my tongue sing of your
     word,
   for all your commands are
     righteous.
173 May your hand be ready to
     help me,
   for I have chosen your
     precepts.
174 I long for your salvation,
   LORD,
   and your law gives me
     delight.
175 Let me live that I may praise
     you,
   and may your laws
     sustain me.
176 I have strayed like a lost
     sheep.
   Seek your servant,
   for I have not forgotten your
     commands.

Psalm 120

A song of ascents.

1 I call on the LORD in my
   distress,
   and he answers me.
2 Save me, LORD,
   from lying lips
   and from deceitful tongues.

3 What will he do to you,
   and what more besides,
   you deceitful tongue?
4 He will punish you with a
     warrior's sharp arrows,
   with burning coals of the
     broom bush.

5 Woe to me that I dwell in
     Meshek,
   that I live among the tents of
     Kedar!
6 Too long have I lived
   among those who hate
     peace.
7 I am for peace;
   but when I speak, they are
     for war.

Psalm 121

A song of ascents.

1 I lift up my eyes to the
     mountains —
   where does my help come
     from?
2 My help comes from the LORD,
   the Maker of heaven and
     earth.

3 He will not let your foot slip —
   he who watches over you
     will not slumber;

⁴indeed, he who watches over
Israel
will neither slumber nor
sleep.

⁵The Lord watches over you —
the Lord is your shade at
your right hand;
⁶the sun will not harm you by
day,
nor the moon by night.

⁷The Lord will keep you from
all harm —
he will watch over your life;
⁸the Lord will watch over your
coming and going
both now and forevermore.

Psalm 122

A song of ascents. Of David.

¹I rejoiced with those who said
to me,
"Let us go to the house of the
Lord."
²Our feet are standing
in your gates, Jerusalem.

³Jerusalem is built like a city
that is closely compacted
together.
⁴That is where the tribes
go up —
the tribes of the Lord —
to praise the name of the Lord
according to the statute
given to Israel.
⁵There stand the thrones for
judgment,
the thrones of the house
of David.

⁶Pray for the peace of
Jerusalem:
"May those who love you be
secure.
⁷May there be peace within
your walls
and security within your
citadels."
⁸For the sake of my family and
friends,
I will say, "Peace be within
you."
⁹For the sake of the house of the
Lord our God,
I will seek your prosperity.

Psalm 123

A song of ascents.

¹I lift up my eyes to you,
to you who sit enthroned in
heaven.
²As the eyes of slaves look to
the hand of their
master,
as the eyes of a female slave
look to the hand of her
mistress,
so our eyes look to the Lord
our God,
till he shows us his mercy.

³Have mercy on us, Lord, have
mercy on us,
for we have endured no end
of contempt.
⁴We have endured no end
of ridicule from the
arrogant,
of contempt from the
proud.

Psalm 124

A song of ascents. Of David.

¹ If the LORD had not been on
  our side —
  let Israel say —
² if the LORD had not been on
  our side
  when people attacked us,
³ they would have swallowed us
  alive
  when their anger flared
  against us;
⁴ the flood would have engulfed
  us,
  the torrent would have swept
  over us,
⁵ the raging waters
  would have swept us
  away.

⁶ Praise be to the LORD,
  who has not let us be torn by
  their teeth.
⁷ We have escaped like a bird
  from the fowler's snare;
  the snare has been broken,
  and we have escaped.
⁸ Our help is in the name of the
  LORD,
  the Maker of heaven and
  earth.

Psalm 125

A song of ascents.

¹ Those who trust in the LORD
  are like Mount Zion,
  which cannot be shaken but
  endures forever.

² As the mountains surround
  Jerusalem,
  so the LORD surrounds his
  people
  both now and
  forevermore.

³ The scepter of the wicked will
  not remain
  over the land allotted to the
  righteous,
  for then the righteous might
  use
  their hands to do evil.

⁴ LORD, do good to those who
  are good,
  to those who are upright in
  heart.
⁵ But those who turn to crooked
  ways
  the LORD will banish with
  the evildoers.

Peace be on Israel.

Psalm 126

A song of ascents.

¹ When the LORD restored the
  fortunes of*ᵃ* Zion,
  we were like those who
  dreamed.*ᵇ*
² Our mouths were filled with
  laughter,
  our tongues with songs of
  joy.
  Then it was said among the
  nations,
  "The LORD has done great
  things for them."

ᵃ 1 Or LORD *brought back the captives to*   ᵇ 1 Or *those restored to health*

3 The LORD has done great
     things for us,
   and we are filled with joy.

4 Restore our fortunes,*a* LORD,
   like streams in the Negev.
5 Those who sow with tears
   will reap with songs of joy.
6 Those who go out weeping,
   carrying seed to sow,
   will return with songs of joy,
     carrying sheaves with them.

Psalm 127

A song of ascents. Of Solomon.

1 Unless the LORD builds the
     house,
   the builders labor in vain.
   Unless the LORD watches over
     the city,
   the guards stand watch in
     vain.
2 In vain you rise early
   and stay up late,
   toiling for food to eat —
     for he grants sleep to*b* those
     he loves.

3 Children are a heritage from
     the LORD,
   offspring a reward from him.
4 Like arrows in the hands of a
     warrior
   are children born in one's
     youth.
5 Blessed is the man
   whose quiver is full of them.
   They will not be put to shame
   when they contend with
     their opponents in court.

Psalm 128

A song of ascents.

1 Blessed are all who fear the
     LORD,
   who walk in obedience to
     him.
2 You will eat the fruit of your
     labor;
   blessings and prosperity will
     be yours.
3 Your wife will be like a fruitful
     vine
   within your house;
   your children will be like olive
     shoots
     around your table.
4 Yes, this will be the blessing
   for the man who fears the
     LORD.

5 May the LORD bless you from
     Zion;
   may you see the prosperity
     of Jerusalem
   all the days of your life.
6 May you live to see your
     children's children —
   peace be on Israel.

Psalm 129

A song of ascents.

1 "They have greatly oppressed
     me from my youth,"
   let Israel say;
2 "they have greatly oppressed
     me from my youth,
   but they have not gained the
     victory over me.

a 4 Or *Bring back our captives*   *b* 2 Or *eat — / for while they sleep he **provides** for*

³ Plowmen have plowed my
　　back
　　and made their furrows
　　　long.
⁴ But the LORD is righteous;
　　he has cut me free from the
　　　cords of the wicked."

⁵ May all who hate Zion
　　be turned back in
　　　shame.
⁶ May they be like grass on the
　　roof,
　　which withers before it can
　　　grow;
⁷ a reaper cannot fill his hands
　　with it,
　　nor one who gathers fill his
　　　arms.
⁸ May those who pass by not say
　　to them,
　　"The blessing of the LORD be
　　　on you;
　　we bless you in the name of
　　　the LORD."

Psalm 130

A song of ascents.

¹ Out of the depths I cry to you,
　　LORD;
²　　Lord, hear my voice.
　Let your ears be attentive
　　to my cry for mercy.

³ If you, LORD, kept a record of
　　sins,
　　Lord, who could stand?
⁴ But with you there is
　　forgiveness,
　　so that we can, with
　　　reverence, serve you.

⁵ I wait for the LORD, my whole
　　being waits,
　　and in his word I put my
　　　hope.
⁶ I wait for the Lord
　　more than watchmen wait
　　　for the morning,
　　more than watchmen wait
　　　for the morning.

⁷ Israel, put your hope in the
　　LORD,
　　for with the LORD is
　　　unfailing love
　　and with him is full
　　　redemption.
⁸ He himself will redeem
　　Israel
　　from all their sins.

Psalm 131

A song of ascents. Of David.

¹ My heart is not proud,
　　LORD,
　　my eyes are not
　　　haughty;
　I do not concern myself with
　　great matters
　　or things too wonderful
　　　for me.
² But I have calmed and quieted
　　myself,
　　I am like a weaned child
　　　with its mother;
　　like a weaned child I am
　　　content.

³ Israel, put your hope in the
　　LORD
　　both now and forevermore.

Psalm 132

A song of ascents.

¹ LORD, remember David
and all his self-denial.

² He swore an oath to the
LORD,
he made a vow to the Mighty
One of Jacob:
³ "I will not enter my house
or go to my bed,
⁴ I will allow no sleep to my
eyes
or slumber to my eyelids,
⁵ till I find a place for the
LORD,
a dwelling for the Mighty
One of Jacob."

⁶ We heard it in Ephrathah,
we came upon it in the fields
of Jaar:ᵃ
⁷ "Let us go to his dwelling
place,
let us worship at his
footstool, saying,
⁸ 'Arise, LORD, and come to your
resting place,
you and the ark of your
might.
⁹ May your priests be clothed
with your righteousness;
may your faithful people
sing for joy.'"

¹⁰ For the sake of your servant
David,
do not reject your anointed
one.

¹¹ The LORD swore an oath to
David,
a sure oath he will not
revoke:
"One of your own descendants
I will place on your throne.
¹² If your sons keep my
covenant
and the statutes I teach
them,
then their sons will sit
on your throne for ever and
ever."

¹³ For the LORD has chosen
Zion,
he has desired it for his
dwelling, saying,
¹⁴ "This is my resting place for
ever and ever;
here I will sit enthroned, for I
have desired it.
¹⁵ I will bless her with abundant
provisions;
her poor I will satisfy with
food.
¹⁶ I will clothe her priests with
salvation,
and her faithful people will
ever sing for joy.

¹⁷ "Here I will make a hornᵇ grow
for David
and set up a lamp for my
anointed one.
¹⁸ I will clothe his enemies with
shame,
but his head will be adorned
with a radiant crown."

ᵃ 6 Or *heard of it in Ephrathah, / we found it in the fields of Jearim.* (See 1 Chron. 13:5,6) (And no quotation marks around verses 7-9)   ᵇ 17 *Horn* here symbolizes strong one, that is, king.

Psalm 133

A song of ascents. Of David.

[1] How good and pleasant it is
when God's people live
together in unity!

[2] It is like precious oil poured on
the head,
running down on the beard,
running down on Aaron's
beard,
down on the collar of his robe.
[3] It is as if the dew of Hermon
were falling on Mount Zion.
For there the LORD bestows his
blessing,
even life forevermore.

Psalm 134

A song of ascents.

[1] Praise the LORD, all you
servants of the LORD
who minister by night in the
house of the LORD.
[2] Lift up your hands in the
sanctuary
and praise the LORD.

[3] May the LORD bless you from
Zion,
he who is the Maker of
heaven and earth.

Psalm 135

[1] Praise the LORD.[a]

Praise the name of the LORD;
praise him, you servants of
the LORD,
[2] you who minister in the house
of the LORD,
in the courts of the house of
our God.

[3] Praise the LORD, for the LORD
is good;
sing praise to his name, for
that is pleasant.
[4] For the LORD has chosen Jacob
to be his own,
Israel to be his treasured
possession.

[5] I know that the LORD is great,
that our Lord is greater than
all gods.
[6] The LORD does whatever
pleases him,
in the heavens and on the
earth,
in the seas and all their
depths.
[7] He makes clouds rise from the
ends of the earth;
he sends lightning with the
rain
and brings out the wind
from his storehouses.

[8] He struck down the firstborn
of Egypt,
the firstborn of people and
animals.
[9] He sent his signs and wonders
into your midst, Egypt,
against Pharaoh and all his
servants.
[10] He struck down many nations
and killed mighty kings—
[11] Sihon king of the Amorites,
Og king of Bashan,

---

[a] 1 Hebrew *Hallelu Yah*; also in verses 3 and 21

and all the kings of Canaan—
¹² and he gave their land as an inheritance,
an inheritance to his people Israel.

¹³ Your name, LORD, endures forever,
your renown, LORD, through all generations.
¹⁴ For the LORD will vindicate his people
and have compassion on his servants.

¹⁵ The idols of the nations are silver and gold,
made by human hands.
¹⁶ They have mouths, but cannot speak,
eyes, but cannot see.
¹⁷ They have ears, but cannot hear,
nor is there breath in their mouths.
¹⁸ Those who make them will be like them,
and so will all who trust in them.

¹⁹ All you Israelites, praise the LORD;
house of Aaron, praise the LORD;
²⁰ house of Levi, praise the LORD;
you who fear him, praise the LORD.
²¹ Praise be to the LORD from Zion,
to him who dwells in Jerusalem.

Praise the LORD.

Psalm 136

¹ Give thanks to the LORD, for he is good.
His love endures forever.
² Give thanks to the God of gods.
His love endures forever.
³ Give thanks to the Lord of lords:
His love endures forever.

⁴ to him who alone does great wonders,
His love endures forever.
⁵ who by his understanding made the heavens,
His love endures forever.
⁶ who spread out the earth upon the waters,
His love endures forever.
⁷ who made the great lights—
His love endures forever.
⁸ the sun to govern the day,
His love endures forever.
⁹ the moon and stars to govern the night;
His love endures forever.

¹⁰ to him who struck down the firstborn of Egypt
His love endures forever.
¹¹ and brought Israel out from among them
His love endures forever.
¹² with a mighty hand and outstretched arm;
His love endures forever.
¹³ to him who divided the Red Sea[a] asunder
His love endures forever.

---

^a 13 Or *the Sea of Reeds*; also in verse 15

[14] and brought Israel through the
midst of it,
His love endures forever.
[15] but swept Pharaoh and his
army into the Red Sea;
His love endures forever.
[16] to him who led his people
through the wilderness;
His love endures forever.
[17] to him who struck down great
kings,
His love endures forever.
[18] and killed mighty kings —
His love endures forever.
[19] Sihon king of the Amorites
His love endures forever.
[20] and Og king of Bashan —
His love endures forever.
[21] and gave their land as an
inheritance,
His love endures forever.
[22] an inheritance to his servant
Israel.
His love endures forever.
[23] He remembered us in our low
estate
His love endures forever.
[24] and freed us from our enemies.
His love endures forever.
[25] He gives food to every
creature.
His love endures forever.
[26] Give thanks to the God of
heaven.
His love endures forever.

Psalm 137

[1] By the rivers of Babylon we sat
and wept
when we remembered Zion.

[2] There on the poplars
we hung our harps,
[3] for there our captors asked us
for songs,
our tormentors demanded
songs of joy;
they said, "Sing us one of the
songs of Zion!"
[4] How can we sing the songs of
the LORD
while in a foreign land?
[5] If I forget you, Jerusalem,
may my right hand forget its
skill.
[6] May my tongue cling to the
roof of my mouth
if I do not remember you,
if I do not consider Jerusalem
my highest joy.
[7] Remember, LORD, what the
Edomites did
on the day Jerusalem fell.
"Tear it down," they cried,
"tear it down to its
foundations!"
[8] Daughter Babylon, doomed to
destruction,
happy is the one who repays
you
according to what you have
done to us.
[9] Happy is the one who seizes
your infants
and dashes them against the
rocks.

Psalm 138

Of David.

[1] I will praise you, LORD, with all
my heart;

before the "gods" I will sing
  your praise.
²I will bow down toward your
  holy temple
  and will praise your name
  for your unfailing love and
    your faithfulness,
  for you have so exalted your
    solemn decree
  that it surpasses your
    fame.
³When I called, you
    answered me;
  you greatly emboldened me.

⁴May all the kings of the earth
    praise you, Lord,
  when they hear what you
    have decreed.
⁵May they sing of the ways of
    the Lord,
  for the glory of the Lord is
    great.
⁶Though the Lord is exalted,
    he looks kindly on the
    lowly;
  though lofty, he sees them
    from afar.
⁷Though I walk in the midst of
    trouble,
  you preserve my life.
  You stretch out your hand
    against the anger of my
    foes;
  with your right hand you
    save me.
⁸The Lord will vindicate me;
  your love, Lord, endures
    forever —
  do not abandon the works of
    your hands.

Psalm 139

For the director of music.
Of David. A psalm.

¹You have searched me, Lord,
  and you know me.
²You know when I sit and when
    I rise;
  you perceive my thoughts
    from afar.
³You discern my going out and
    my lying down;
  you are familiar with all my
    ways.
⁴Before a word is on my
    tongue
  you, Lord, know it
    completely.
⁵You hem me in behind and
    before,
  and you lay your hand
    upon me.
⁶Such knowledge is too
    wonderful for me,
  too lofty for me to attain.

⁷Where can I go from your
    Spirit?
  Where can I flee from your
    presence?
⁸If I go up to the heavens, you
    are there;
  if I make my bed in the
    depths, you are there.
⁹If I rise on the wings of the
    dawn,
  if I settle on the far side of
    the sea,
¹⁰even there your hand will
    guide me,
  your right hand will hold me
    fast.

¹¹ If I say, "Surely the darkness
will hide me
and the light become night
around me,"
¹² even the darkness will not be
dark to you;
the night will shine like the
day,
for darkness is as light to you.

¹³ For you created my inmost
being;
you knit me together in my
mother's womb.
¹⁴ I praise you because I
am fearfully and
wonderfully made;
your works are wonderful,
I know that full well.
¹⁵ My frame was not hidden from
you
when I was made in the
secret place,
when I was woven together
in the depths of the
earth.
¹⁶ Your eyes saw my unformed
body;
all the days ordained for
me were written in your
book
before one of them came
to be.
¹⁷ How precious to me are your
thoughts,ᵃ God!
How vast is the sum of them!
¹⁸ Were I to count them,
they would outnumber the
grains of sand —

when I awake, I am still with
you.
¹⁹ If only you, God, would slay
the wicked!
Away from me, you who are
bloodthirsty!
²⁰ They speak of you with evil
intent;
your adversaries misuse
your name.
²¹ Do I not hate those who hate
you, LORD,
and abhor those who are in
rebellion against you?
²² I have nothing but hatred for
them;
I count them my enemies.
²³ Search me, God, and know my
heart;
test me and know my
anxious thoughts.
²⁴ See if there is any offensive
way in me,
and lead me in the way
everlasting.

Psalm 140ᵇ

*For the director of music.
A psalm of David.*

¹ Rescue me, LORD, from
evildoers;
protect me from the violent,
² who devise evil plans in their
hearts
and stir up war every day.
³ They make their tongues as
sharp as a serpent's;

ᵃ 17 Or *How amazing are your thoughts concerning me*   ᵇ In Hebrew texts 140:1-13 is numbered 140:2-14.

the poison of vipers is on
their lips.*a*

⁴Keep me safe, LORD, from the
hands of the wicked;
protect me from the violent,
who devise ways to trip my
feet.
⁵The arrogant have hidden a
snare for me;
they have spread out the
cords of their net
and have set traps for me
along my path.

⁶I say to the LORD, "You are my
God."
Hear, LORD, my cry for mercy.
⁷Sovereign LORD, my strong
deliverer,
you shield my head in the
day of battle.
⁸Do not grant the wicked their
desires, LORD;
do not let their plans succeed.

⁹Those who surround me
proudly rear their heads;
may the mischief of their lips
engulf them.
¹⁰May burning coals fall on
them;
may they be thrown into the
fire,
into miry pits, never to rise.
¹¹May slanderers not be
established in the land;
may disaster hunt down the
violent.

¹²I know that the LORD secures
justice for the poor

and upholds the cause of the
needy.
¹³Surely the righteous will
praise your name,
and the upright will live in
your presence.

Psalm 141

A psalm of David.

¹I call to you, LORD, come
quickly to me;
hear me when I call to you.
²May my prayer be set before
you like incense;
may the lifting up of my
hands be like the
evening sacrifice.

³Set a guard over my mouth,
LORD;
keep watch over the door of
my lips.
⁴Do not let my heart be drawn
to what is evil
so that I take part in wicked
deeds
along with those who are
evildoers;
do not let me eat their
delicacies.

⁵Let a righteous man strike
me — that is a kindness;
let him rebuke me — that is
oil on my head.
My head will not refuse it,
for my prayer will still be
against the deeds of
evildoers.

---

a 3 The Hebrew has *Selah* (a word of uncertain meaning) here and at the end of
verses 5 and 8.

⁶Their rulers will be thrown
     down from the cliffs,
  and the wicked will learn
     that my words were well
     spoken.
⁷They will say, "As one plows
     and breaks up the earth,
  so our bones have been
     scattered at the mouth of
     the grave."

⁸But my eyes are fixed on you,
     Sovereign LORD;
  in you I take refuge — do not
     give me over to death.
⁹Keep me safe from the traps
     set by evildoers,
  from the snares they have
     laid for me.
¹⁰Let the wicked fall into their
     own nets,
  while I pass by in safety.

Psalm 142ᵃ

*A maskilᵇ of David. When he
was in the cave. A prayer.*

¹I cry aloud to the LORD;
  I lift up my voice to the LORD
     for mercy.
²I pour out before him my
     complaint;
  before him I tell my trouble.

³When my spirit grows faint
     within me,
  it is you who watch over my
     way.
 In the path where I walk
  people have hidden a snare
     for me.

⁴Look and see, there is no one
     at my right hand;
  no one is concerned for me.
 I have no refuge;
  no one cares for my life.

⁵I cry to you, LORD;
  I say, "You are my refuge,
     my portion in the land of the
     living."

⁶Listen to my cry,
  for I am in desperate need;
 rescue me from those who
     pursue me,
  for they are too strong for me.
⁷Set me free from my prison,
  that I may praise your name.
 Then the righteous will gather
     about me
  because of your goodness
     to me.

Psalm 143

A psalm of David.

¹LORD, hear my prayer,
  listen to my cry for mercy;
 in your faithfulness and
     righteousness
  come to my relief.
²Do not bring your servant into
     judgment,
  for no one living is righteous
     before you.
³The enemy pursues me,
  he crushes me to the ground;
 he makes me dwell in the
     darkness
  like those long dead.

ᵃ In Hebrew texts 142:1-7 is numbered 142:2-8.   ᵇ Title: Probably a literary or
musical term

⁴ So my spirit grows faint
    within me;
  my heart within me is
    dismayed.
⁵ I remember the days of long
    ago;
  I meditate on all your works
  and consider what your
    hands have done.
⁶ I spread out my hands to you;
  I thirst for you like a parched
    land.ᵃ

⁷ Answer me quickly, Lord;
  my spirit fails.
  Do not hide your face from me
    or I will be like those who go
    down to the pit.
⁸ Let the morning bring me
    word of your unfailing
    love,
  for I have put my trust in you.
  Show me the way I should go,
    for to you I entrust my life.
⁹ Rescue me from my enemies,
    Lord,
  for I hide myself in you.
¹⁰ Teach me to do your will,
    for you are my God;
  may your good Spirit
    lead me on level ground.

¹¹ For your name's sake, Lord,
    preserve my life;
  in your righteousness, bring
    me out of trouble.
¹² In your unfailing love, silence
    my enemies;
  destroy all my foes,
    for I am your servant.

Psalm 144

Of David.

¹ Praise be to the Lord my Rock,
  who trains my hands for war,
    my fingers for battle.
² He is my loving God and my
    fortress,
  my stronghold and my
    deliverer,
  my shield, in whom I take
    refuge,
  who subdues peoplesᵇ
    under me.

³ Lord, what are human beings
    that you care for them,
  mere mortals that you think
    of them?
⁴ They are like a breath;
  their days are like a fleeting
    shadow.

⁵ Part your heavens, Lord, and
    come down;
  touch the mountains, so that
    they smoke.
⁶ Send forth lightning and
    scatter the enemy;
  shoot your arrows and rout
    them.
⁷ Reach down your hand from
    on high;
  deliver me and rescue me
  from the mighty waters,
  from the hands of
    foreigners
⁸ whose mouths are full of lies,
  whose right hands are
    deceitful.

ᵃ 6 The Hebrew has *Selah* (a word of uncertain meaning) here. ᵇ 2 Many manuscripts of the Masoretic Text, Dead Sea Scrolls, Aquila, Jerome and Syriac; most manuscripts of the Masoretic Text *subdues my people*

⁹I will sing a new song to you,
my God;
on the ten-stringed lyre I will
make music to you,
¹⁰to the One who gives victory to
kings,
who delivers his servant
David.

From the deadly sword
¹¹deliver me;
rescue me from the hands of
foreigners
whose mouths are full of lies,
whose right hands are
deceitful.

¹²Then our sons in their youth
will be like well-nurtured
plants,
and our daughters will be like
pillars
carved to adorn a palace.
¹³Our barns will be filled
with every kind of provision.
Our sheep will increase by
thousands,
by tens of thousands in our
fields;
¹⁴ our oxen will draw heavy
loads.ᵃ
There will be no breaching of
walls,
no going into captivity,
no cry of distress in our
streets.
¹⁵Blessed is the people of whom
this is true;

blessed is the people whose
God is the LORD.

Psalm 145ᵇ

A psalm of praise. Of David.

¹I will exalt you, my God the
King;
I will praise your name for
ever and ever.
²Every day I will praise you
and extol your name for ever
and ever.

³Great is the LORD and most
worthy of praise;
his greatness no one can
fathom.
⁴One generation commends
your works to another;
they tell of your mighty acts.
⁵They speak of the glorious
splendor of your
majesty—
and I will meditate on your
wonderful works.ᶜ
⁶They tell of the power of your
awesome works—
and I will proclaim your
great deeds.
⁷They celebrate your abundant
goodness
and joyfully sing of your
righteousness.
⁸The LORD is gracious and
compassionate,

ᵃ 14 Or *our chieftains will be firmly established*   ᵇ This psalm is an acrostic
poem, the verses of which (including verse 13b) begin with the successive letters
of the Hebrew alphabet.   ᶜ 5 Dead Sea Scrolls and Syriac (see also Septuagint);
Masoretic Text *On the glorious splendor of your majesty / and on your wonderful
works I will meditate*

slow to anger and rich in
love.

⁹ The LORD is good to all;
  he has compassion on all he
  has made.
¹⁰ All your works praise you,
  LORD;
  your faithful people extol
  you.
¹¹ They tell of the glory of your
  kingdom
  and speak of your might,
¹² so that all people may know of
  your mighty acts
  and the glorious splendor of
  your kingdom.
¹³ Your kingdom is an everlasting
  kingdom,
  and your dominion endures
  through all generations.

The LORD is trustworthy in all
  he promises
  and faithful in all he does.ᵃ
¹⁴ The LORD upholds all who fall
  and lifts up all who are
  bowed down.
¹⁵ The eyes of all look to you,
  and you give them their food
  at the proper time.
¹⁶ You open your hand
  and satisfy the desires of
  every living thing.

¹⁷ The LORD is righteous in all
  his ways
  and faithful in all he does.
¹⁸ The LORD is near to all who
  call on him,
  to all who call on him in
  truth.
¹⁹ He fulfills the desires of those
  who fear him;
  he hears their cry and saves
  them.
²⁰ The LORD watches over all
  who love him,
  but all the wicked he will
  destroy.

²¹ My mouth will speak in praise
  of the LORD.
  Let every creature praise his
  holy name
  for ever and ever.

Psalm 146

¹ Praise the LORD.ᵇ

Praise the LORD, my soul.

² I will praise the LORD all my
  life;
  I will sing praise to my God
  as long as I live.
³ Do not put your trust in princes,
  in human beings, who
  cannot save.
⁴ When their spirit departs, they
  return to the ground;
  on that very day their plans
  come to nothing.
⁵ Blessed are those whose help
  is the God of Jacob,
  whose hope is in the LORD
  their God.
⁶ He is the Maker of heaven and
  earth,

ᵃ 13 One manuscript of the Masoretic Text, Dead Sea Scrolls and Syriac (see also
Septuagint); most manuscripts of the Masoretic Text do not have the last two lines
of verse 13.   ᵇ 1 Hebrew *Hallelu Yah*; also in verse 10

the sea, and everything in
them —
he remains faithful forever.
⁷He upholds the cause of the
oppressed
and gives food to the hungry.
The LORD sets prisoners free,
⁸ the LORD gives sight to the
blind,
the LORD lifts up those who
are bowed down,
the LORD loves the righteous.
⁹The LORD watches over the
foreigner
and sustains the fatherless
and the widow,
but he frustrates the ways of
the wicked.
¹⁰The LORD reigns forever,
your God, O Zion, for all
generations.

Praise the LORD.

Psalm 147

¹Praise the LORD.ᵃ

How good it is to sing praises
to our God,
how pleasant and fitting to
praise him!
²The LORD builds up Jerusalem;
he gathers the exiles of
Israel.
³He heals the brokenhearted
and binds up their wounds.
⁴He determines the number of
the stars
and calls them each by
name.

⁵Great is our Lord and mighty
in power;
his understanding has no
limit.
⁶The LORD sustains the
humble
but casts the wicked to the
ground.

⁷Sing to the LORD with grateful
praise;
make music to our God on
the harp.

⁸He covers the sky with clouds;
he supplies the earth with
rain
and makes grass grow on the
hills.
⁹He provides food for the cattle
and for the young ravens
when they call.

¹⁰His pleasure is not in the
strength of the horse,
nor his delight in the legs of
the warrior;
¹¹the LORD delights in those who
fear him,
who put their hope in his
unfailing love.

¹²Extol the LORD, Jerusalem;
praise your God, Zion.

¹³He strengthens the bars of
your gates
and blesses your people
within you.
¹⁴He grants peace to your
borders
and satisfies you with the
finest of wheat.

ᵃ 1 Hebrew *Hallelu Yah*; also in verse 20

15 He sends his command to the
　　earth;
　　his word runs swiftly.
16 He spreads the snow like
　　wool
　　and scatters the frost like
　　ashes.
17 He hurls down his hail like
　　pebbles.
　　Who can withstand his icy
　　blast?
18 He sends his word and melts
　　them;
　　he stirs up his breezes, and
　　the waters flow.

19 He has revealed his word to
　　Jacob,
　　his laws and decrees to
　　Israel.
20 He has done this for no other
　　nation;
　　they do not know his
　　laws.*a*

Praise the LORD.

Psalm 148

1 Praise the LORD.*b*

Praise the LORD from the
　　heavens;
　　praise him in the heights
　　above.
2 Praise him, all his angels;
　　praise him, all his heavenly
　　hosts.
3 Praise him, sun and moon;
　　praise him, all you shining
　　stars.

4 Praise him, you highest
　　heavens
　　and you waters above the
　　skies.

5 Let them praise the name of
　　the LORD,
　　for at his command they
　　were created,
6 and he established them for
　　ever and ever—
　　he issued a decree that will
　　never pass away.

7 Praise the LORD from the
　　earth,
　　you great sea creatures and
　　all ocean depths,
8 lightning and hail, snow and
　　clouds,
　　stormy winds that do his
　　bidding,
9 you mountains and all hills,
　　fruit trees and all cedars,
10 wild animals and all cattle,
　　small creatures and flying
　　birds,
11 kings of the earth and all
　　nations,
　　you princes and all rulers
　　on earth,
12 young men and women,
　　old men and children.

13 Let them praise the name of
　　the LORD,
　　for his name alone is
　　exalted;
　　his splendor is above the
　　earth and the heavens.

---

a 20 Masoretic Text; Dead Sea Scrolls and Septuagint *nation; / he has not made his laws known to them* 　　*b 1* Hebrew *Hallelu Yah;* also in verse 14

[14] And he has raised up for his
people a horn,[a]
the praise of all his faithful
servants,
of Israel, the people close to
his heart.

Praise the LORD.

Psalm 149

[1] Praise the LORD.[b]

Sing to the LORD a new song,
his praise in the assembly of
his faithful people.

[2] Let Israel rejoice in their
Maker;
let the people of Zion be glad
in their King.

[3] Let them praise his name with
dancing
and make music to him with
timbrel and harp.

[4] For the LORD takes delight in
his people;
he crowns the humble with
victory.

[5] Let his faithful people rejoice
in this honor
and sing for joy on their
beds.

[6] May the praise of God be in
their mouths
and a double-edged sword in
their hands,

[7] to inflict vengeance on the
nations

and punishment on the
peoples,

[8] to bind their kings with fetters,
their nobles with shackles of
iron,

[9] to carry out the sentence
written against them —
this is the glory of all his
faithful people.

Praise the LORD.

Psalm 150

[1] Praise the LORD.[c]

Praise God in his sanctuary;
praise him in his mighty
heavens.

[2] Praise him for his acts of
power;
praise him for his surpassing
greatness.

[3] Praise him with the sounding
of the trumpet,
praise him with the harp
and lyre,

[4] praise him with timbrel and
dancing,
praise him with the strings
and pipe,

[5] praise him with the clash of
cymbals,
praise him with resounding
cymbals.

[6] Let everything that has breath
praise the LORD.

Praise the LORD.

---

[a] 14 *Horn* here symbolizes strength.   [b] 1 Hebrew *Hallelu Yah*; also in verse 9
[c] 1 Hebrew *Hallelu Yah*; also in verse 6

Proverbs

Introduction:

Proverbs is a collection of wise sayings and good advice for daily living. The author begins by reminding us that "The fear of the LORD is the beginning of knowledge" (1:7). The first four chapters discuss the importance of wisdom.

The author also includes a collection of short and powerful two-line sayings that cover many different subjects including marriage, social behavior, friendship, justice, folly, poverty, wealth, family, love, laziness, and warnings against drinking and adultery.

Many of these proverbs were written by King Solomon. Others were copied by the men of Hezekiah. Agur and Lemuel wrote the last two chapters.

Outline of contents:

Instructions on wisdom and foolishness (1:1–9:18)
The proverbs of Solomon (10:1–22:16)
Sayings of the wise (22:17–24:34)
More proverbs of Solomon (25:1–29:27)
Sayings of Agur and Lemuel (30:1–31:31)

Purpose and Theme

1 The proverbs of Solomon son of David, king of Israel:

² for gaining wisdom and instruction;
    for understanding words of insight;
³ for receiving instruction in prudent behavior,
    doing what is right and just and fair;

⁴ for giving prudence to those who are simple,ᵃ
    knowledge and discretion to the young—
⁵ let the wise listen and add to their learning,
    and let the discerning get guidance—
⁶ for understanding proverbs and parables,
    the sayings and riddles of the wise.ᵇ

ᵃ 4 The Hebrew word rendered *simple* in Proverbs denotes a person who is gullible, without moral direction and inclined to evil.   ᵇ 6 Or *understanding a proverb, namely, a parable, / and the sayings of the wise, their riddles*

7 The fear of the LORD is the
    beginning of knowledge,
  but fools[a] despise wisdom
    and instruction.

Prologue: Exhortations to Embrace Wisdom

Warning Against the Invitation of Sinful Men

8 Listen, my son, to your father's
    instruction
  and do not forsake your
    mother's teaching.
9 They are a garland to grace
    your head
  and a chain to adorn your
    neck.

10 My son, if sinful men entice
    you,
  do not give in to them.
11 If they say, "Come along
    with us;
  let's lie in wait for innocent
    blood,
  let's ambush some harmless
    soul;
12 let's swallow them alive, like
    the grave,
  and whole, like those who go
    down to the pit;
13 we will get all sorts of valuable
    things
  and fill our houses with
    plunder;
14 cast lots with us;
  we will all share the
    loot"—

15 my son, do not go along with
    them,
  do not set foot on their
    paths;
16 for their feet rush into evil,
  they are swift to shed
    blood.
17 How useless to spread a net
  where every bird can see it!
18 These men lie in wait for their
    own blood;
  they ambush only
    themselves!
19 Such are the paths of all who
    go after ill-gotten gain;
  it takes away the life of those
    who get it.

Wisdom's Rebuke

20 Out in the open wisdom calls
    aloud,
  she raises her voice in the
    public square;
21 on top of the wall[b] she cries
    out,
  at the city gate she makes
    her speech:

22 "How long will you who are
    simple love your simple
    ways?
  How long will mockers
    delight in mockery
  and fools hate knowledge?
23 Repent at my rebuke!
  Then I will pour out my
    thoughts to you,
  I will make known to you my
    teachings.

---

a 7 The Hebrew words rendered *fool* in Proverbs, and often elsewhere in the Old
Testament, denote a person who is morally deficient.   b 21 Septuagint; Hebrew
/ at noisy street corners

24 But since you refuse to listen
        when I call
    and no one pays attention
        when I stretch out my
        hand,
25 since you disregard all my
        advice
    and do not accept my
        rebuke,
26 I in turn will laugh when
        disaster strikes you;
    I will mock when calamity
        overtakes you—
27 when calamity overtakes you
        like a storm,
    when disaster sweeps over
        you like a whirlwind,
    when distress and trouble
        overwhelm you.

28 "Then they will call to me but I
        will not answer;
    they will look for me but will
        not find me,
29 since they hated knowledge
    and did not choose to fear
        the LORD.
30 Since they would not accept
        my advice
    and spurned my rebuke,
31 they will eat the fruit of their
        ways
    and be filled with the fruit of
        their schemes.
32 For the waywardness of the
        simple will kill them,
    and the complacency of fools
        will destroy them;
33 but whoever listens to me will
        live in safety
    and be at ease, without fear
        of harm."

Moral Benefits of Wisdom

2 My son, if you accept my
        words
    and store up my commands
        within you,
2 turning your ear to wisdom
    and applying your heart to
        understanding—
3 indeed, if you call out for
        insight
    and cry aloud for
        understanding,
4 and if you look for it as for
        silver
    and search for it as for
        hidden treasure,
5 then you will understand the
        fear of the LORD
    and find the knowledge of
        God.
6 For the LORD gives wisdom;
    from his mouth come
        knowledge and
        understanding.
7 He holds success in store for
        the upright,
    he is a shield to those whose
        walk is blameless,
8 for he guards the course of the
        just
    and protects the way of his
        faithful ones.

9 Then you will understand
        what is right and just
    and fair—every good
        path.
10 For wisdom will enter your
        heart,
    and knowledge will be
        pleasant to your soul.

¹¹ Discretion will protect you,
and understanding will
guard you.

¹² Wisdom will save you from the
ways of wicked men,
from men whose words are
perverse,
¹³ who have left the straight
paths
to walk in dark ways,
¹⁴ who delight in doing wrong
and rejoice in the
perverseness of evil,
¹⁵ whose paths are crooked
and who are devious in their
ways.

¹⁶ Wisdom will save you also
from the adulterous
woman,
from the wayward woman
with her seductive
words,
¹⁷ who has left the partner of her
youth
and ignored the covenant
she made before
God.ᵃ
¹⁸ Surely her house leads down to
death
and her paths to the spirits of
the dead.
¹⁹ None who go to her return
or attain the paths of life.

²⁰ Thus you will walk in the ways
of the good
and keep to the paths of the
righteous.
²¹ For the upright will live in the
land,

and the blameless will
remain in it;
²² but the wicked will be cut off
from the land,
and the unfaithful will be
torn from it.

Wisdom Bestows Well-Being

3 My son, do not forget my
teaching,
but keep my commands in
your heart,
² for they will prolong your life
many years
and bring you peace and
prosperity.

³ Let love and faithfulness never
leave you;
bind them around your
neck,
write them on the tablet of
your heart.
⁴ Then you will win favor and a
good name
in the sight of God and man.

⁵ Trust in the LORD with all your
heart
and lean not on your own
understanding;
⁶ in all your ways submit to him,
and he will make your paths
straight.ᵇ

⁷ Do not be wise in your own
eyes;
fear the LORD and shun evil.
⁸ This will bring health to your
body
and nourishment to your
bones.

ᵃ 17 Or *covenant of her God*   ᵇ 6 Or *will direct your paths*

⁹ Honor the LORD with your
wealth,
    with the firstfruits of all your
    crops;
¹⁰ then your barns will be filled
to overflowing,
    and your vats will brim over
    with new wine.

¹¹ My son, do not despise the
LORD's discipline,
    and do not resent his rebuke,
¹² because the LORD disciplines
those he loves,
    as a father the son he
    delights in.ᵃ

¹³ Blessed are those who find
wisdom,
    those who gain
    understanding,
¹⁴ for she is more profitable than
silver
    and yields better returns
    than gold.
¹⁵ She is more precious than
rubies;
    nothing you desire can
    compare with her.
¹⁶ Long life is in her right hand;
    in her left hand are riches
    and honor.
¹⁷ Her ways are pleasant ways,
    and all her paths are peace.
¹⁸ She is a tree of life to those
who take hold of her;
    those who hold her fast will
    be blessed.

¹⁹ By wisdom the LORD laid the
earth's foundations,

by understanding he set the
    heavens in place;
²⁰ by his knowledge the watery
depths were divided,
    and the clouds let drop the
    dew.

²¹ My son, do not let wisdom and
understanding out of
your sight,
    preserve sound judgment
    and discretion;
²² they will be life for you,
    an ornament to grace your
    neck.
²³ Then you will go on your way
in safety,
    and your foot will not
    stumble.
²⁴ When you lie down, you will
not be afraid;
    when you lie down, your
    sleep will be sweet.
²⁵ Have no fear of sudden
disaster
    or of the ruin that overtakes
    the wicked,
²⁶ for the LORD will be at your
side
    and will keep your foot from
    being snared.

²⁷ Do not withhold good from
those to whom it is due,
    when it is in your power to
    act.
²⁸ Do not say to your neighbor,
    "Come back tomorrow and
    I'll give it to you" —
when you already have it
    with you.

ᵃ 12 Hebrew; Septuagint *loves, / and he chastens everyone he accepts as his child*

²⁹ Do not plot harm against your
neighbor,
who lives trustfully near
you.
³⁰ Do not accuse anyone for no
reason —
when they have done you no
harm.
³¹ Do not envy the violent
or choose any of their
ways.
³² For the LORD detests the
perverse
but takes the upright into his
confidence.
³³ The LORD's curse is on the
house of the wicked,
but he blesses the home of
the righteous.
³⁴ He mocks proud mockers
but shows favor to the
humble and oppressed.
³⁵ The wise inherit honor,
but fools get only shame.

Get Wisdom at Any Cost

4 Listen, my sons, to a father's
instruction;
pay attention and gain
understanding.
² I give you sound learning,
so do not forsake my
teaching.
³ For I too was a son to my
father,
still tender, and cherished by
my mother.
⁴ Then he taught me, and he
said to me,

"Take hold of my words with
all your heart;
keep my commands, and
you will live.
⁵ Get wisdom, get
understanding;
do not forget my words or
turn away from them.
⁶ Do not forsake wisdom, and
she will protect you;
love her, and she will watch
over you.
⁷ The beginning of wisdom is
this: Get^a wisdom.
Though it cost all you have,^{b}
get understanding.
⁸ Cherish her, and she will exalt
you;
embrace her, and she will
honor you.
⁹ She will give you a garland to
grace your head
and present you with a
glorious crown."
¹⁰ Listen, my son, accept what I
say,
and the years of your life will
be many.
¹¹ I instruct you in the way of
wisdom
and lead you along straight
paths.
¹² When you walk, your steps
will not be hampered;
when you run, you will not
stumble.
¹³ Hold on to instruction, do not
let it go;
guard it well, for it is your
life.

---

^{a} 7 Or *Wisdom is supreme; therefore get* ^{b} 7 Or *wisdom. / Whatever else you get*

¹⁴ Do not set foot on the path of
the wicked
or walk in the way of
evildoers.
¹⁵ Avoid it, do not travel on it;
turn from it and go on your
way.
¹⁶ For they cannot rest until they
do evil;
they are robbed of sleep
till they make someone
stumble.
¹⁷ They eat the bread of
wickedness
and drink the wine of
violence.
¹⁸ The path of the righteous is
like the morning sun,
shining ever brighter till the
full light of day.
¹⁹ But the way of the wicked is
like deep darkness;
they do not know what
makes them stumble.
²⁰ My son, pay attention to what I
say;
turn your ear to my words.
²¹ Do not let them out of your
sight,
keep them within your
heart;
²² for they are life to those who
find them
and health to one's whole
body.
²³ Above all else, guard your
heart,
for everything you do flows
from it.

²⁴ Keep your mouth free of
perversity;
keep corrupt talk far from
your lips.
²⁵ Let your eyes look straight
ahead;
fix your gaze directly before
you.
²⁶ Give careful thought to the*ᵃ*
paths for your feet
and be steadfast in all your
ways.
²⁷ Do not turn to the right or the
left;
keep your foot from evil.

Warning Against Adultery

5 My son, pay attention to my
wisdom,
turn your ear to my words of
insight,
² that you may maintain
discretion
and your lips may preserve
knowledge.
³ For the lips of the adulterous
woman drip honey,
and her speech is smoother
than oil;
⁴ but in the end she is bitter as
gall,
sharp as a double-edged
sword.
⁵ Her feet go down to death;
her steps lead straight to the
grave.
⁶ She gives no thought to the
way of life;
her paths wander aimlessly,
but she does not know it.

ᵃ 26 Or Make level

⁷Now then, my sons, listen
to me;
do not turn aside from what I
say.
⁸Keep to a path far from her,
do not go near the door of
her house,
⁹lest you lose your honor to
others
and your dignity*a* to one who
is cruel,
¹⁰lest strangers feast on your
wealth
and your toil enrich the
house of another.
¹¹At the end of your life you will
groan,
when your flesh and body
are spent.
¹²You will say, "How I hated
discipline!
How my heart spurned
correction!
¹³I would not obey my
teachers
or turn my ear to my
instructors.
¹⁴And I was soon in serious
trouble
in the assembly of God's
people."

¹⁵Drink water from your own
cistern,
running water from your
own well.
¹⁶Should your springs overflow
in the streets,
your streams of water in the
public squares?

¹⁷Let them be yours alone,
never to be shared with
strangers.
¹⁸May your fountain be blessed,
and may you rejoice in the
wife of your youth.
¹⁹A loving doe, a graceful
deer —
may her breasts satisfy you
always,
may you ever be intoxicated
with her love.
²⁰Why, my son, be intoxicated
with another man's wife?
Why embrace the bosom of a
wayward woman?
²¹For your ways are in full view
of the Lᴏʀᴅ,
and he examines all your
paths.
²²The evil deeds of the wicked
ensnare them;
the cords of their sins hold
them fast.
²³For lack of discipline they will
die,
led astray by their own great
folly.

Warnings Against Folly

6 My son, if you have put
up security for your
neighbor,
if you have shaken hands in
pledge for a stranger,
²you have been trapped by
what you said,
ensnared by the words of
your mouth.

---

a 9 Or *years*

³ So do this, my son, to free
yourself,
since you have fallen into
your neighbor's hands:
Go — to the point of
exhaustion — ^a
and give your neighbor no
rest!
⁴ Allow no sleep to your eyes,
no slumber to your eyelids.
⁵ Free yourself, like a gazelle
from the hand of the
hunter,
like a bird from the snare of
the fowler.

⁶ Go to the ant, you sluggard;
consider its ways and be
wise!
⁷ It has no commander,
no overseer or ruler,
⁸ yet it stores its provisions in
summer
and gathers its food at
harvest.

⁹ How long will you lie there,
you sluggard?
When will you get up from
your sleep?
¹⁰ A little sleep, a little slumber,
a little folding of the hands
to rest —
¹¹ and poverty will come on you
like a thief
and scarcity like an armed
man.

¹² A troublemaker and a villain,
who goes about with a
corrupt mouth,

¹³ who winks maliciously with
his eye,
signals with his feet
and motions with his fingers,
¹⁴ who plots evil with deceit in
his heart —
he always stirs up conflict.
¹⁵ Therefore disaster will
overtake him in an
instant;
he will suddenly be
destroyed — without
remedy.

¹⁶ There are six things the LORD
hates,
seven that are detestable to
him:
¹⁷ haughty eyes,
a lying tongue,
hands that shed innocent
blood,
¹⁸ a heart that devises wicked
schemes,
feet that are quick to rush
into evil,
¹⁹ a false witness who pours
out lies
and a person who stirs
up conflict in the
community.

Warning Against Adultery

²⁰ My son, keep your father's
command
and do not forsake your
mother's teaching.
²¹ Bind them always on your
heart;
fasten them around your
neck.

---

^a 3 Or *Go and humble yourself,*

²²When you walk, they will
    guide you;
  when you sleep, they will
    watch over you;
  when you awake, they will
    speak to you.
²³For this command is a
    lamp,
  this teaching is a light,
 and correction and
    instruction
  are the way to life,
²⁴keeping you from your
    neighbor's wife,
  from the smooth talk of a
    wayward woman.

²⁵Do not lust in your heart after
    her beauty
  or let her captivate you with
    her eyes.

²⁶For a prostitute can be had for
    a loaf of bread,
  but another man's wife preys
    on your very life.
²⁷Can a man scoop fire into his
    lap
  without his clothes being
    burned?
²⁸Can a man walk on hot
    coals
  without his feet being
    scorched?
²⁹So is he who sleeps with
    another man's wife;
  no one who touches her will
    go unpunished.

³⁰People do not despise a thief if
    he steals
  to satisfy his hunger when he
    is starving.

³¹Yet if he is caught, he must pay
    sevenfold,
  though it costs him all the
    wealth of his house.
³²But a man who commits
    adultery has no sense;
  whoever does so destroys
    himself.
³³Blows and disgrace are his lot,
  and his shame will never be
    wiped away.

³⁴For jealousy arouses a
    husband's fury,
  and he will show no mercy
    when he takes revenge.
³⁵He will not accept any
    compensation;
  he will refuse a bribe,
    however great it is.

Warning Against the Adulterous Woman

7 My son, keep my words
  and store up my commands
    within you.
²Keep my commands and you
    will live;
  guard my teachings as the
    apple of your eye.
³Bind them on your fingers;
  write them on the tablet of
    your heart.
⁴Say to wisdom, "You are my
    sister,"
  and to insight, "You are my
    relative."
⁵They will keep you from the
    adulterous woman,
  from the wayward woman
    with her seductive
    words.

⁶At the window of my house
  I looked down through the
    lattice.
⁷I saw among the simple,
  I noticed among the young
    men,
  a youth who had no sense.
⁸He was going down the street
    near her corner,
  walking along in the
    direction of her house
⁹at twilight, as the day was
    fading,
  as the dark of night set in.

¹⁰Then out came a woman to
    meet him,
  dressed like a prostitute and
    with crafty intent.
¹¹(She is unruly and defiant,
  her feet never stay at
    home;
¹²now in the street, now in the
    squares,
  at every corner she lurks.)
¹³She took hold of him and
    kissed him
  and with a brazen face she
    said:

¹⁴"Today I fulfilled my vows,
  and I have food from my
    fellowship offering at
    home.
¹⁵So I came out to meet you;
  I looked for you and have
    found you!
¹⁶I have covered my bed
  with colored linens from
    Egypt.

¹⁷I have perfumed my bed
  with myrrh, aloes and
    cinnamon.
¹⁸Come, let's drink deeply of
    love till morning;
  let's enjoy ourselves with
    love!
¹⁹My husband is not at home;
  he has gone on a long
    journey.
²⁰He took his purse filled with
    money
  and will not be home till full
    moon."

²¹With persuasive words she led
    him astray;
  she seduced him with her
    smooth talk.
²²All at once he followed her
  like an ox going to the
    slaughter,
  like a deer*ᵃ* stepping into a
    noose*ᵇ*
²³ till an arrow pierces his liver,
  like a bird darting into a
    snare,
  little knowing it will cost
    him his life.

²⁴Now then, my sons, listen to
    me;
  pay attention to what I say.
²⁵Do not let your heart turn to
    her ways
  or stray into her paths.
²⁶Many are the victims she has
    brought down;
  her slain are a mighty
    throng.

ᵃ 22 Syriac (see also Septuagint); Hebrew *fool*
for this line is uncertain.   *ᵇ 22* The meaning of the Hebrew

²⁷Her house is a highway to the
grave,
leading down to the
chambers of death.

Wisdom's Call

8 Does not wisdom call out?
Does not understanding
raise her voice?
²At the highest point along the
way,
where the paths meet, she
takes her stand;
³beside the gate leading into
the city,
at the entrance, she cries
aloud:
⁴"To you, O people, I call out;
I raise my voice to all
mankind.
⁵You who are simple, gain
prudence;
you who are foolish, set your
hearts on it.ᵃ
⁶Listen, for I have trustworthy
things to say;
I open my lips to speak what
is right.
⁷My mouth speaks what is true,
for my lips detest
wickedness.
⁸All the words of my mouth are
just;
none of them is crooked or
perverse.
⁹To the discerning all of them
are right;
they are upright to those
who have found
knowledge.

¹⁰Choose my instruction instead
of silver,
knowledge rather than
choice gold,
¹¹for wisdom is more precious
than rubies,
and nothing you desire can
compare with her.

¹²"I, wisdom, dwell together
with prudence;
I possess knowledge and
discretion.
¹³To fear the LORD is to hate evil;
I hate pride and arrogance,
evil behavior and perverse
speech.
¹⁴Counsel and sound judgment
are mine;
I have insight, I have power.
¹⁵By me kings reign
and rulers issue decrees that
are just;
¹⁶by me princes govern,
and nobles — all who rule on
earth.ᵇ
¹⁷I love those who love me,
and those who seek me
find me.
¹⁸With me are riches and
honor,
enduring wealth and
prosperity.
¹⁹My fruit is better than fine
gold;
what I yield surpasses choice
silver.
²⁰I walk in the way of
righteousness,
along the paths of justice,

ᵃ 5 Septuagint; Hebrew *foolish, instruct your minds*   ᵇ 16 Some Hebrew
manuscripts and Septuagint; other Hebrew manuscripts *all righteous rulers*

²¹ bestowing a rich inheritance
    on those who love me
  and making their treasuries
    full.

²² "The LORD brought me forth as
    the first of his works,*ᵃ,ᵇ*
  before his deeds of old;
²³ I was formed long ages ago,
    at the very beginning, when
    the world came to be.
²⁴ When there were no watery
    depths, I was given birth,
  when there were no springs
    overflowing with water;
²⁵ before the mountains were
    settled in place,
  before the hills, I was given
    birth,
²⁶ before he made the world or its
    fields
  or any of the dust of the
    earth.
²⁷ I was there when he set the
    heavens in place,
  when he marked out the
    horizon on the face of
    the deep,
²⁸ when he established the
    clouds above
  and fixed securely the
    fountains of the deep,
²⁹ when he gave the sea its
    boundary
  so the waters would not
    overstep his command,
  and when he marked out the
    foundations of the earth.

³⁰ Then I was constantlyᶜ at his
    side.
  I was filled with delight day
    after day,
  rejoicing always in his
    presence,
³¹ rejoicing in his whole world
  and delighting in mankind.

³² "Now then, my children, listen
    to me;
  blessed are those who keep
    my ways.
³³ Listen to my instruction and
    be wise;
  do not disregard it.
³⁴ Blessed are those who listen
    to me,
  watching daily at my doors,
  waiting at my doorway.
³⁵ For those who find me find life
  and receive favor from the
    LORD.
³⁶ But those who fail to find me
    harm themselves;
  all who hate me love death."

Invitations of Wisdom and Folly

9 Wisdom has built her house;
    she has set upᵈ its seven
    pillars.
² She has prepared her meat and
    mixed her wine;
  she has also set her table.
³ She has sent out her servants,
    and she calls
  from the highest point of the
    city,

ᵃ 22 Or *way*; or *dominion*   ᵇ 22 Or *The LORD possessed me at the beginning of his
work*; or *The LORD brought me forth at the beginning of his work*   ᶜ 30 Or *was the
artisan*; or *was a little child*   ᵈ 1 Septuagint, Syriac and Targum; Hebrew *has
hewn out*

4 "Let all who are simple come
  to my house!"
To those who have no sense
  she says,
5 "Come, eat my food
  and drink the wine I have
  mixed.
6 Leave your simple ways and
  you will live;
  walk in the way of insight."

7 Whoever corrects a mocker
  invites insults;
  whoever rebukes the wicked
  incurs abuse.
8 Do not rebuke mockers or they
  will hate you;
  rebuke the wise and they
  will love you.
9 Instruct the wise and they will
  be wiser still;
  teach the righteous and
  they will add to their
  learning.

10 The fear of the LORD is the
  beginning of wisdom,
  and knowledge of the Holy
  One is understanding.
11 For through wisdom[a] your
  days will be many,
  and years will be added to
  your life.
12 If you are wise, your wisdom
  will reward you;
  if you are a mocker, you
  alone will suffer.

13 Folly is an unruly woman;
  she is simple and knows
  nothing.

14 She sits at the door of her
  house,
  on a seat at the highest point
  of the city,
15 calling out to those who
  pass by,
  who go straight on their
  way,
16 "Let all who are simple come
  to my house!"
To those who have no sense
  she says,
17 "Stolen water is sweet;
  food eaten in secret is
  delicious!"
18 But little do they know that the
  dead are there,
  that her guests are deep in
  the realm of the dead.

Proverbs of Solomon

10

The proverbs of Solomon:

A wise son brings joy to his
  father,
  but a foolish son brings grief
  to his mother.

2 Ill-gotten treasures have no
  lasting value,
  but righteousness delivers
  from death.

3 The LORD does not let the
  righteous go hungry,
  but he thwarts the craving of
  the wicked.

4 Lazy hands make for poverty,
  but diligent hands bring
  wealth.

a 11 Septuagint, Syriac and Targum; Hebrew me

⁵He who gathers crops in
    summer is a prudent
    son,
but he who sleeps during
    harvest is a disgraceful
    son.

⁶Blessings crown the head of
    the righteous,
but violence overwhelms the
    mouth of the wicked.ᵃ

⁷The name of the righteous is
    used in blessings,ᵇ
but the name of the wicked
    will rot.

⁸The wise in heart accept
    commands,
but a chattering fool comes
    to ruin.

⁹Whoever walks in integrity
    walks securely,
but whoever takes crooked
    paths will be found out.

¹⁰Whoever winks maliciously
    causes grief,
and a chattering fool comes
    to ruin.

¹¹The mouth of the righteous is a
    fountain of life,
but the mouth of the wicked
    conceals violence.

¹²Hatred stirs up conflict,
but love covers over all
    wrongs.

¹³Wisdom is found on the lips of
    the discerning,

but a rod is for the back of
    one who has no sense.

¹⁴The wise store up knowledge,
but the mouth of a fool
    invites ruin.

¹⁵The wealth of the rich is their
    fortified city,
but poverty is the ruin of the
    poor.

¹⁶The wages of the righteous is
    life,
but the earnings of the
    wicked are sin and
    death.

¹⁷Whoever heeds discipline
    shows the way to life,
but whoever ignores
    correction leads others
    astray.

¹⁸Whoever conceals hatred with
    lying lips
and spreads slander is a
    fool.

¹⁹Sin is not ended by multiplying
    words,
but the prudent hold their
    tongues.

²⁰The tongue of the righteous is
    choice silver,
but the heart of the wicked is
    of little value.

²¹The lips of the righteous
    nourish many,
but fools die for lack of
    sense.

ᵃ 6 Or *righteous, / but the mouth of the wicked conceals violence*   ᵇ 7 See
Gen. 48:20.

²²The blessing of the LORD
    brings wealth,
    without painful toil for it.

²³A fool finds pleasure in wicked
    schemes,
    but a person of understanding
    delights in wisdom.

²⁴What the wicked dread will
    overtake them;
    what the righteous desire
    will be granted.

²⁵When the storm has swept by,
    the wicked are gone,
    but the righteous stand firm
    forever.

²⁶As vinegar to the teeth and
    smoke to the eyes,
    so are sluggards to those
    who send them.

²⁷The fear of the LORD adds
    length to life,
    but the years of the wicked
    are cut short.

²⁸The prospect of the righteous
    is joy,
    but the hopes of the wicked
    come to nothing.

²⁹The way of the LORD is a refuge
    for the blameless,
    but it is the ruin of those who
    do evil.

³⁰The righteous will never be
    uprooted,
    but the wicked will not
    remain in the land.

³¹From the mouth of the
    righteous comes the fruit
    of wisdom,

but a perverse tongue will be
    silenced.

³²The lips of the righteous know
    what finds favor,
    but the mouth of the wicked
    only what is perverse.

11 The LORD detests
    dishonest scales,
    but accurate weights find
    favor with him.

²When pride comes, then
    comes disgrace,
    but with humility comes
    wisdom.

³The integrity of the upright
    guides them,
    but the unfaithful are
    destroyed by their
    duplicity.

⁴Wealth is worthless in the day
    of wrath,
    but righteousness delivers
    from death.

⁵The righteousness of the
    blameless makes their
    paths straight,
    but the wicked are brought
    down by their own
    wickedness.

⁶The righteousness of the
    upright delivers
    them,
    but the unfaithful are
    trapped by evil
    desires.

⁷Hopes placed in mortals die
    with them;

all the promise of[a] their
   power comes to nothing.

8 The righteous person is
   rescued from trouble,
and it falls on the wicked
   instead.

9 With their mouths the godless
   destroy their neighbors,
but through knowledge the
   righteous escape.

10 When the righteous prosper,
   the city rejoices;
when the wicked perish,
   there are shouts of joy.

11 Through the blessing of the
   upright a city is exalted,
but by the mouth of the
   wicked it is destroyed.

12 Whoever derides their
   neighbor has no sense,
but the one who has
   understanding holds
   their tongue.

13 A gossip betrays a confidence,
but a trustworthy person
   keeps a secret.

14 For lack of guidance a nation
   falls,
but victory is won through
   many advisers.

15 Whoever puts up security for
   a stranger will surely
   suffer,
but whoever refuses to shake
   hands in pledge is safe.

16 A kindhearted woman gains
   honor,
but ruthless men gain only
   wealth.

17 Those who are kind benefit
   themselves,
but the cruel bring ruin on
   themselves.

18 A wicked person earns
   deceptive wages,
but the one who sows
   righteousness reaps a
   sure reward.

19 Truly the righteous attain life,
but whoever pursues evil
   finds death.

20 The LORD detests those whose
   hearts are perverse,
but he delights in those
   whose ways are
   blameless.

21 Be sure of this: The wicked will
   not go unpunished,
but those who are righteous
   will go free.

22 Like a gold ring in a pig's snout
   is a beautiful woman who
   shows no discretion.

23 The desire of the righteous
   ends only in good,
but the hope of the wicked
   only in wrath.

24 One person gives freely, yet
   gains even more;
another withholds unduly,
   but comes to poverty.

---

[a] 7 Two Hebrew manuscripts; most Hebrew manuscripts, Vulgate, Syriac and Targum *When the wicked die, their hope perishes; / all they expected from*

²⁵ A generous person will
    prosper;
  whoever refreshes others
    will be refreshed.

²⁶ People curse the one who
    hoards grain,
  but they pray God's blessing
    on the one who is willing
    to sell.

²⁷ Whoever seeks good finds
    favor,
  but evil comes to one who
    searches for it.

²⁸ Those who trust in their riches
    will fall,
  but the righteous will thrive
    like a green leaf.

²⁹ Whoever brings ruin on their
    family will inherit only
    wind,
  and the fool will be servant
    to the wise.

³⁰ The fruit of the righteous is a
    tree of life,
  and the one who is wise
    saves lives.

³¹ If the righteous receive their
    due on earth,
  how much more the ungodly
    and the sinner!

12 Whoever loves discipline
  loves knowledge,
  but whoever hates correction
    is stupid.

² Good people obtain favor from
    the LORD,
  but he condemns those who
    devise wicked schemes.

³ No one can be established
    through wickedness,
  but the righteous cannot be
    uprooted.

⁴ A wife of noble character is her
    husband's crown,
  but a disgraceful wife is like
    decay in his bones.

⁵ The plans of the righteous are
    just,
  but the advice of the wicked
    is deceitful.

⁶ The words of the wicked lie in
    wait for blood,
  but the speech of the upright
    rescues them.

⁷ The wicked are overthrown
    and are no more,
  but the house of the
    righteous stands firm.

⁸ A person is praised according
    to their prudence,
  and one with a warped mind
    is despised.

⁹ Better to be a nobody and yet
    have a servant
  than pretend to be
    somebody and have no
    food.

¹⁰ The righteous care for the
    needs of their animals,
  but the kindest acts of the
    wicked are cruel.

¹¹ Those who work their land will
    have abundant food,
  but those who chase
    fantasies have no sense.

¹²The wicked desire the
  stronghold of evildoers,
 but the root of the righteous
  endures.

¹³Evildoers are trapped by their
  sinful talk,
 and so the innocent escape
  trouble.

¹⁴From the fruit of their lips
  people are filled with
  good things,
 and the work of their hands
  brings them reward.

¹⁵The way of fools seems right to
  them,
 but the wise listen to advice.

¹⁶Fools show their annoyance at
  once,
 but the prudent overlook an
  insult.

¹⁷An honest witness tells the
  truth,
 but a false witness tells lies.

¹⁸The words of the reckless
  pierce like swords,
 but the tongue of the wise
  brings healing.

¹⁹Truthful lips endure forever,
 but a lying tongue lasts only
  a moment.

²⁰Deceit is in the hearts of those
  who plot evil,
 but those who promote
  peace have joy.

²¹No harm overtakes the
  righteous,

 but the wicked have their fill
  of trouble.

²²The LORD detests lying lips,
 but he delights in people
  who are trustworthy.

²³The prudent keep their
  knowledge to
  themselves,
 but a fool's heart blurts out
  folly.

²⁴Diligent hands will rule,
 but laziness ends in forced
  labor.

²⁵Anxiety weighs down the heart,
 but a kind word cheers it up.

²⁶The righteous choose their
  friends carefully,
 but the way of the wicked
  leads them astray.

²⁷The lazy do not roast*a* any
  game,
 but the diligent feed on the
  riches of the hunt.

²⁸In the way of righteousness
  there is life;
 along that path is
  immortality.

13 A wise son heeds his
  father's instruction,
 but a mocker does not
  respond to rebukes.

²From the fruit of their lips
  people enjoy good
  things,
 but the unfaithful have an
  appetite for violence.

---

a 27 The meaning of the Hebrew for this word is uncertain.

³Those who guard their lips
preserve their lives,
but those who speak rashly
will come to ruin.

⁴A sluggard's appetite is never
filled,
but the desires of the diligent
are fully satisfied.

⁵The righteous hate what is
false,
but the wicked make
themselves a stench
and bring shame on
themselves.

⁶Righteousness guards the
person of integrity,
but wickedness overthrows
the sinner.

⁷One person pretends to be
rich, yet has nothing;
another pretends to be poor,
yet has great wealth.

⁸A person's riches may ransom
their life,
but the poor cannot respond
to threatening rebukes.

⁹The light of the righteous
shines brightly,
but the lamp of the wicked is
snuffed out.

¹⁰Where there is strife, there is
pride,
but wisdom is found in those
who take advice.

¹¹Dishonest money dwindles
away,
but whoever gathers money
little by little makes it
grow.

¹²Hope deferred makes the heart
sick,
but a longing fulfilled is a
tree of life.

¹³Whoever scorns instruction
will pay for it,
but whoever respects a
command is rewarded.

¹⁴The teaching of the wise is a
fountain of life,
turning a person from the
snares of death.

¹⁵Good judgment wins favor,
but the way of the
unfaithful leads to their
destruction.ᵃ

¹⁶All who are prudent act withᵇ
knowledge,
but fools expose their folly.

¹⁷A wicked messenger falls into
trouble,
but a trustworthy envoy
brings healing.

¹⁸Whoever disregards discipline
comes to poverty and
shame,
but whoever heeds
correction is honored.

¹⁹A longing fulfilled is sweet to
the soul,
but fools detest turning from
evil.

ᵃ 15 Septuagint and Syriac; the meaning of the Hebrew for this phrase is
uncertain.   ᵇ 16 Or prudent protect themselves through

²⁰Walk with the wise and
　　become wise,
　for a companion of fools
　　suffers harm.
²¹Trouble pursues the sinner,
　but the righteous are
　　rewarded with good
　　things.
²²A good person leaves an
　　inheritance for their
　　children's children,
　but a sinner's wealth is stored
　　up for the righteous.

²³An unplowed field produces
　　food for the poor,
　but injustice sweeps it away.
²⁴Whoever spares the rod hates
　　their children,
　but the one who loves their
　　children is careful to
　　discipline them.
²⁵The righteous eat to their
　　hearts' content,
　but the stomach of the
　　wicked goes hungry.

14 The wise woman builds
　　her house,
　but with her own hands the
　　foolish one tears hers
　　down.

²Whoever fears the LORD walks
　　uprightly,
　but those who despise him
　　are devious in their ways.

³A fool's mouth lashes out with
　　pride,
　but the lips of the wise
　　protect them.

⁴Where there are no oxen, the
　　manger is empty,
　but from the strength of
　　an ox come abundant
　　harvests.
⁵An honest witness does not
　　deceive,
　but a false witness pours out
　　lies.

⁶The mocker seeks wisdom and
　　finds none,
　but knowledge comes easily
　　to the discerning.
⁷Stay away from a fool,
　for you will not find
　　knowledge on their lips.
⁸The wisdom of the prudent is
　　to give thought to their
　　ways,
　but the folly of fools is
　　deception.

⁹Fools mock at making amends
　　for sin,
　but goodwill is found among
　　the upright.
¹⁰Each heart knows its own
　　bitterness,
　and no one else can share its
　　joy.
¹¹The house of the wicked will
　　be destroyed,
　but the tent of the upright
　　will flourish.
¹²There is a way that appears to
　　be right,
　but in the end it leads to
　　death.

¹³ Even in laughter the heart may
ache,
and rejoicing may end in
grief.

¹⁴ The faithless will be fully
repaid for their ways,
and the good rewarded for
theirs.

¹⁵ The simple believe anything,
but the prudent give thought
to their steps.

¹⁶ The wise fear the LORD and
shun evil,
but a fool is hotheaded and
yet feels secure.

¹⁷ A quick-tempered person does
foolish things,
and the one who devises evil
schemes is hated.

¹⁸ The simple inherit folly,
but the prudent are crowned
with knowledge.

¹⁹ Evildoers will bow down in the
presence of the good,
and the wicked at the gates
of the righteous.

²⁰ The poor are shunned even by
their neighbors,
but the rich have many
friends.

²¹ It is a sin to despise one's
neighbor,
but blessed is the one who is
kind to the needy.

²² Do not those who plot evil go
astray?

But those who plan what
is good find^a love and
faithfulness.

²³ All hard work brings a profit,
but mere talk leads only to
poverty.

²⁴ The wealth of the wise is their
crown,
but the folly of fools yields
folly.

²⁵ A truthful witness saves lives,
but a false witness is
deceitful.

²⁶ Whoever fears the LORD has a
secure fortress,
and for their children it will
be a refuge.

²⁷ The fear of the LORD is a
fountain of life,
turning a person from the
snares of death.

²⁸ A large population is a king's
glory,
but without subjects a prince
is ruined.

²⁹ Whoever is patient has great
understanding,
but one who is quick-
tempered displays folly.

³⁰ A heart at peace gives life to
the body,
but envy rots the bones.

³¹ Whoever oppresses the poor
shows contempt for their
Maker,
but whoever is kind to the
needy honors God.

^a 22 Or *show*

32When calamity comes, the
    wicked are brought
    down,
  but even in death the
    righteous seek refuge in
    God.

33Wisdom reposes in the heart
    of the discerning
  and even among fools she
    lets herself be known.*a*

34Righteousness exalts a nation,
  but sin condemns any
    people.

35A king delights in a wise
    servant,
  but a shameful servant
    arouses his fury.

15 A gentle answer turns
    away wrath,
  but a harsh word stirs up
    anger.

2The tongue of the wise adorns
    knowledge,
  but the mouth of the fool
    gushes folly.

3The eyes of the LORD are
    everywhere,
  keeping watch on the wicked
    and the good.

4The soothing tongue is a tree
    of life,
  but a perverse tongue
    crushes the spirit.

5A fool spurns a parent's
    discipline,

  but whoever heeds
    correction shows
    prudence.

6The house of the righteous
    contains great treasure,
  but the income of the wicked
    brings ruin.

7The lips of the wise spread
    knowledge,
  but the hearts of fools are not
    upright.

8The LORD detests the sacrifice
    of the wicked,
  but the prayer of the upright
    pleases him.

9The LORD detests the way of
    the wicked,
  but he loves those who
    pursue righteousness.

10Stern discipline awaits anyone
    who leaves the path;
  the one who hates correction
    will die.

11Death and Destruction*b* lie
    open before the LORD —
  how much more do human
    hearts!

12Mockers resent correction,
  so they avoid the wise.

13A happy heart makes the face
    cheerful,
  but heartache crushes the
    spirit.

14The discerning heart seeks
    knowledge,

---

a 33 Hebrew; Septuagint and Syriac *discerning / but in the heart of fools she is not known*   *b 11* Hebrew *Abaddon*

but the mouth of a fool feeds
on folly.

¹⁵All the days of the oppressed
are wretched,
but the cheerful heart has a
continual feast.

¹⁶Better a little with the fear of
the LORD
than great wealth with
turmoil.

¹⁷Better a small serving of
vegetables with love
than a fattened calf with
hatred.

¹⁸A hot-tempered person stirs up
conflict,
but the one who is patient
calms a quarrel.

¹⁹The way of the sluggard is
blocked with thorns,
but the path of the upright is
a highway.

²⁰A wise son brings joy to his
father,
but a foolish man despises
his mother.

²¹Folly brings joy to one who has
no sense,
but whoever has
understanding keeps a
straight course.

²²Plans fail for lack of counsel,
but with many advisers they
succeed.

²³A person finds joy in giving an
apt reply —
and how good is a timely
word!

²⁴The path of life leads upward
for the prudent
to keep them from going
down to the realm of the
dead.

²⁵The LORD tears down the
house of the proud,
but he sets the widow's
boundary stones in
place.

²⁶The LORD detests the thoughts
of the wicked,
but gracious words are pure
in his sight.

²⁷The greedy bring ruin to their
households,
but the one who hates bribes
will live.

²⁸The heart of the righteous
weighs its answers,
but the mouth of the wicked
gushes evil.

²⁹The LORD is far from the
wicked,
but he hears the prayer of the
righteous.

³⁰Light in a messenger's eyes
brings joy to the heart,
and good news gives health
to the bones.

³¹Whoever heeds life-giving
correction
will be at home among the
wise.

³²Those who disregard
discipline despise
themselves,

but the one who heeds
   correction gains
   understanding.
³³Wisdom's instruction is to fear
   the LORD,
   and humility comes before
   honor.

16

To humans belong the
   plans of the heart,
but from the LORD comes
   the proper answer of the
   tongue.

²All a person's ways seem pure
   to them,
   but motives are weighed by
   the LORD.

³Commit to the LORD whatever
   you do,
   and he will establish your
   plans.

⁴The LORD works out
   everything to its proper
   end—
   even the wicked for a day of
   disaster.

⁵The LORD detests all the proud
   of heart.
   Be sure of this: They will not
   go unpunished.

⁶Through love and faithfulness
   sin is atoned for;
   through the fear of the LORD
   evil is avoided.

⁷When the LORD takes pleasure
   in anyone's way,
   he causes their enemies to
   make peace with them.

⁸Better a little with
   righteousness
   than much gain with
   injustice.

⁹In their hearts humans plan
   their course,
   but the LORD establishes
   their steps.

¹⁰The lips of a king speak as an
   oracle,
   and his mouth does not
   betray justice.

¹¹Honest scales and balances
   belong to the LORD;
   all the weights in the bag are
   of his making.

¹²Kings detest wrongdoing,
   for a throne is established
   through righteousness.

¹³Kings take pleasure in honest
   lips;
   they value the one who
   speaks what is right.

¹⁴A king's wrath is a messenger
   of death,
   but the wise will appease it.

¹⁵When a king's face brightens,
   it means life;
   his favor is like a rain cloud
   in spring.

¹⁶How much better to get
   wisdom than gold,
   to get insight rather than
   silver!

¹⁷The highway of the upright
   avoids evil;
   those who guard their ways
   preserve their lives.

18 Pride goes before destruction,
  a haughty spirit before a fall.

19 Better to be lowly in spirit
    along with the oppressed
  than to share plunder with
    the proud.

20 Whoever gives heed to
    instruction prospers,*a*
  and blessed is the one who
    trusts in the LORD.

21 The wise in heart are called
    discerning,
  and gracious words promote
    instruction.*b*

22 Prudence is a fountain of life
    to the prudent,
  but folly brings punishment
    to fools.

23 The hearts of the wise make
    their mouths prudent,
  and their lips promote
    instruction.*c*

24 Gracious words are a
    honeycomb,
  sweet to the soul and healing
    to the bones.

25 There is a way that appears to
    be right,
  but in the end it leads to
    death.

26 The appetite of laborers works
    for them;
  their hunger drives them on.

27 A scoundrel plots evil,
  and on their lips it is like a
    scorching fire.

28 A perverse person stirs up
    conflict,
  and a gossip separates close
    friends.

29 A violent person entices their
    neighbor
  and leads them down a path
    that is not good.

30 Whoever winks with their eye
    is plotting perversity;
  whoever purses their lips is
    bent on evil.

31 Gray hair is a crown of
    splendor;
  it is attained in the way of
    righteousness.

32 Better a patient person than a
    warrior,
  one with self-control than
    one who takes a city.

33 The lot is cast into the lap,
  but its every decision is from
    the LORD.

17 Better a dry crust with
  peace and quiet
than a house full of feasting,
  with strife.

2 A prudent servant will rule
    over a disgraceful son
and will share the
    inheritance as one of the
    family.

3 The crucible for silver and the
    furnace for gold,
  but the LORD tests the heart.

---

a 20 Or *whoever speaks prudently finds what is good*   *b* 21 Or *words make a person persuasive*   *c* 23 Or *prudent / and make their lips persuasive*

⁴A wicked person listens to
    deceitful lips;
a liar pays attention to a
    destructive tongue.

⁵Whoever mocks the poor
    shows contempt for their
    Maker;
whoever gloats over disaster
    will not go unpunished.

⁶Children's children are a
    crown to the aged,
and parents are the pride of
    their children.

⁷Eloquent lips are unsuited to a
    godless fool —
how much worse lying lips to
    a ruler!

⁸A bribe is seen as a charm by
    the one who gives it;
they think success will come
    at every turn.

⁹Whoever would foster love
    covers over an offense,
but whoever repeats the
    matter separates close
    friends.

¹⁰A rebuke impresses a
    discerning person
more than a hundred lashes
    a fool.

¹¹Evildoers foster rebellion
    against God;
the messenger of death will
    be sent against them.

¹²Better to meet a bear robbed of
    her cubs
than a fool bent on folly.

¹³Evil will never leave the house
    of one who pays back evil for
    good.

¹⁴Starting a quarrel is like
    breaching a dam;
so drop the matter before a
    dispute breaks out.

¹⁵Acquitting the guilty and
    condemning the
    innocent —
the LORD detests them both.

¹⁶Why should fools have money
    in hand to buy wisdom,
when they are not able to
    understand it?

¹⁷A friend loves at all times,
and a brother is born for a
    time of adversity.

¹⁸One who has no sense shakes
    hands in pledge
and puts up security for a
    neighbor.

¹⁹Whoever loves a quarrel loves
    sin;
whoever builds a high gate
    invites destruction.

²⁰One whose heart is corrupt
    does not prosper;
one whose tongue is
    perverse falls into
    trouble.

²¹To have a fool for a child brings
    grief;
there is no joy for the parent
    of a godless fool.

²²A cheerful heart is good
    medicine,

but a crushed spirit dries up
the bones.

23 The wicked accept bribes in
secret
to pervert the course of
justice.

24 A discerning person keeps
wisdom in view,
but a fool's eyes wander to
the ends of the earth.

25 A foolish son brings grief to his
father
and bitterness to the mother
who bore him.

26 If imposing a fine on the
innocent is not good,
surely to flog honest officials
is not right.

27 The one who has knowledge
uses words with
restraint,
and whoever has
understanding is even-
tempered.

28 Even fools are thought wise if
they keep silent,
and discerning if they hold
their tongues.

18 An unfriendly person
pursues selfish ends
and against all sound
judgment starts
quarrels.

2 Fools find no pleasure in
understanding
but delight in airing their
own opinions.

3 When wickedness comes, so
does contempt,
and with shame comes
reproach.

4 The words of the mouth are
deep waters,
but the fountain of wisdom
is a rushing stream.

5 It is not good to be partial to
the wicked
and so deprive the innocent
of justice.

6 The lips of fools bring them
strife,
and their mouths invite a
beating.

7 The mouths of fools are their
undoing,
and their lips are a snare to
their very lives.

8 The words of a gossip are like
choice morsels;
they go down to the inmost
parts.

9 One who is slack in his work
is brother to one who
destroys.

10 The name of the LORD is a
fortified tower;
the righteous run to it and
are safe.

11 The wealth of the rich is their
fortified city;
they imagine it a wall too
high to scale.

12 Before a downfall the heart is
haughty,

but humility comes before
honor.

¹³ To answer before listening —
that is folly and shame.

¹⁴ The human spirit can endure
in sickness,
but a crushed spirit who can
bear?

¹⁵ The heart of the discerning
acquires knowledge,
for the ears of the wise seek
it out.

¹⁶ A gift opens the way
and ushers the giver into the
presence of the great.

¹⁷ In a lawsuit the first to speak
seems right,
until someone comes
forward and cross-
examines.

¹⁸ Casting the lot settles disputes
and keeps strong opponents
apart.

¹⁹ A brother wronged is more
unyielding than a
fortified city;
disputes are like the barred
gates of a citadel.

²⁰ From the fruit of their mouth
a person's stomach is
filled;
with the harvest of their lips
they are satisfied.

²¹ The tongue has the power of
life and death,
and those who love it will eat
its fruit.

²² He who finds a wife finds what
is good
and receives favor from the
LORD.

²³ The poor plead for mercy,
but the rich answer
harshly.

²⁴ One who has unreliable
friends soon comes to
ruin,
but there is a friend who
sticks closer than a
brother.

19 Better the poor whose
walk is blameless
than a fool whose lips are
perverse.

² Desire without knowledge is
not good —
how much more will hasty
feet miss the way!

³ A person's own folly leads to
their ruin,
yet their heart rages against
the LORD.

⁴ Wealth attracts many
friends,
but even the closest friend of
the poor person deserts
them.

⁵ A false witness will not go
unpunished,
and whoever pours out lies
will not go free.

⁶ Many curry favor with a ruler,
and everyone is the friend of
one who gives gifts.

⁷The poor are shunned by all
    their relatives—
how much more do their
    friends avoid them!
Though the poor pursue them
    with pleading,
they are nowhere to be
    found.ᵃ

⁸The one who gets wisdom
    loves life;
the one who cherishes
    understanding will soon
    prosper.

⁹A false witness will not go
    unpunished,
and whoever pours out lies
    will perish.

¹⁰It is not fitting for a fool to live
    in luxury—
how much worse for a slave
    to rule over princes!

¹¹A person's wisdom yields
    patience;
it is to one's glory to overlook
    an offense.

¹²A king's rage is like the roar of
    a lion,
but his favor is like dew on
    the grass.

¹³A foolish child is a father's ruin,
and a quarrelsome wife is like
    the constant dripping of a
    leaky roof.

¹⁴Houses and wealth are
    inherited from parents,
but a prudent wife is from
    the LORD.

¹⁵Laziness brings on deep sleep,
and the shiftless go hungry.

¹⁶Whoever keeps
        commandments keeps
        their life,
but whoever shows
        contempt for their ways
        will die.

¹⁷Whoever is kind to the poor
        lends to the LORD,
and he will reward them for
        what they have done.

¹⁸Discipline your children, for in
        that there is hope;
do not be a willing party to
        their death.

¹⁹A hot-tempered person must
        pay the penalty;
rescue them, and you will
        have to do it again.

²⁰Listen to advice and accept
        discipline,
and at the end you will be
        counted among the wise.

²¹Many are the plans in a
        person's heart,
but it is the LORD's purpose
        that prevails.

²²What a person desires is
        unfailing loveᵇ;
better to be poor than a liar.

²³The fear of the LORD leads to
        life;
then one rests content,
        untouched by trouble.

ᵃ 7 The meaning of the Hebrew for this sentence is uncertain.   ᵇ 22 Or *Greed is a person's shame*

²⁴A sluggard buries his hand in
the dish;
he will not even bring it back
to his mouth!

²⁵Flog a mocker, and the simple
will learn prudence;
rebuke the discerning,
and they will gain
knowledge.

²⁶Whoever robs their father
and drives out their
mother
is a child who brings shame
and disgrace.

²⁷Stop listening to instruction,
my son,
and you will stray from the
words of knowledge.

²⁸A corrupt witness mocks at
justice,
and the mouth of the wicked
gulps down evil.

²⁹Penalties are prepared for
mockers,
and beatings for the backs of
fools.

20 Wine is a mocker and
beer a brawler;
whoever is led astray by
them is not wise.

²A king's wrath strikes terror
like the roar of a lion;
those who anger him forfeit
their lives.

³It is to one's honor to avoid
strife,
but every fool is quick to
quarrel.

⁴Sluggards do not plow in
season;
so at harvest time they look
but find nothing.

⁵The purposes of a person's
heart are deep waters,
but one who has insight
draws them out.

⁶Many claim to have unfailing
love,
but a faithful person who
can find?

⁷The righteous lead blameless
lives;
blessed are their children
after them.

⁸When a king sits on his throne
to judge,
he winnows out all evil with
his eyes.

⁹Who can say, "I have kept my
heart pure;
I am clean and without sin"?

¹⁰Differing weights and differing
measures—
the LORD detests them both.

¹¹Even small children are
known by their actions,
so is their conduct really
pure and upright?

¹²Ears that hear and eyes that
see—
the LORD has made them
both.

¹³Do not love sleep or you will
grow poor;
stay awake and you will have
food to spare.

The Birth of Jesus
LUKE 2:1–20

Jesus Walks on the Water
MATTHEW 14:22–23

The Lord's Prayer

Our Father which art in heaven,
Hallowed be thy name.

Thy kingdom come,
Thy will be done
On earth, as it is in heaven.

Give us this day our daily bread.
And forgive us our debts
As we forgive our debtors.

And lead us not into temptation,
But deliver us from evil.

For thine is the kingdom,
And the power,
And the glory, forever.

Amen.

*These words of the Lord's Prayer are found in Matthew 6:9–13 in the King James Version. Different Bible translations use different words, but this is the most commonly memorized version of this prayer.

Love Passage for Kids
Based on 1 Corinthians 13

If I can speak beautifully and sing like an angel but don't love others, I sound like a child banging on a piano or a screeching radio. If I'm very smart—almost a genius—but don't love others, I am nothing.

Love will stand in line and wait its turn.

Love looks for the good in others.

Love doesn't always want what others have, and it doesn't brag about what it does have.

Love is polite, even when the other person is rude.

Love doesn't have to be first.

Love doesn't get angry over small things, and it doesn't remember one reason after another to be hurt.

Love isn't happy when someone else fails but is happy with the truth.

Love will always protect others, especially those who are often picked on or teased.

Love always believes the best about others and is steady and true.

Love never gives up.

The three most important things to have
are faith, hope, and love.
But the greatest of these is love.

¹⁴ "It's no good, it's no good!"
  says the buyer —
  then goes off and boasts
  about the purchase.

¹⁵ Gold there is, and rubies in
  abundance,
  but lips that speak
  knowledge are a rare
  jewel.

¹⁶ Take the garment of one who
  puts up security for a
  stranger;
  hold it in pledge if it is done
  for an outsider.

¹⁷ Food gained by fraud tastes
  sweet,
  but one ends up with a
  mouth full of gravel.

¹⁸ Plans are established by
  seeking advice;
  so if you wage war, obtain
  guidance.

¹⁹ A gossip betrays a confidence;
  so avoid anyone who talks
  too much.

²⁰ If someone curses their father
  or mother,
  their lamp will be snuffed
  out in pitch darkness.

²¹ An inheritance claimed too
  soon
  will not be blessed at the
  end.

²² Do not say, "I'll pay you back
  for this wrong!"
  Wait for the LORD, and he
  will avenge you.

²³ The LORD detests differing
  weights,
  and dishonest scales do not
  please him.

²⁴ A person's steps are directed
  by the LORD.
  How then can anyone
  understand their own
  way?

²⁵ It is a trap to dedicate
  something rashly
  and only later to consider
  one's vows.

²⁶ A wise king winnows out the
  wicked;
  he drives the threshing
  wheel over them.

²⁷ The human spirit is[a] the lamp
  of the LORD
  that sheds light on one's
  inmost being.

²⁸ Love and faithfulness keep a
  king safe;
  through love his throne is
  made secure.

²⁹ The glory of young men is their
  strength,
  gray hair the splendor of the
  old.

³⁰ Blows and wounds scrub away
  evil,
  and beatings purge the
  inmost being.

21

In the LORD's hand the
  king's heart is a stream
  of water

---

[a] 27 Or *A person's words are*

that he channels toward all
who please him.

² A person may think their own
ways are right,
but the LORD weighs the
heart.

³ To do what is right and just
is more acceptable to the
LORD than sacrifice.

⁴ Haughty eyes and a proud
heart—
the unplowed field of the
wicked—produce sin.

⁵ The plans of the diligent lead
to profit
as surely as haste leads to
poverty.

⁶ A fortune made by a lying
tongue
is a fleeting vapor and a
deadly snare.ᵃ

⁷ The violence of the wicked will
drag them away,
for they refuse to do what is
right.

⁸ The way of the guilty is
devious,
but the conduct of the
innocent is upright.

⁹ Better to live on a corner of the
roof
than share a house with a
quarrelsome wife.

¹⁰ The wicked crave evil;
their neighbors get no mercy
from them.

¹¹ When a mocker is punished,
the simple gain wisdom;
by paying attention to the
wise they get knowledge.

¹² The Righteous Oneᵇ takes
note of the house of the
wicked
and brings the wicked to
ruin.

¹³ Whoever shuts their ears to
the cry of the poor
will also cry out and not be
answered.

¹⁴ A gift given in secret soothes
anger,
and a bribe concealed in
the cloak pacifies great
wrath.

¹⁵ When justice is done, it brings
joy to the righteous
but terror to evildoers.

¹⁶ Whoever strays from the path
of prudence
comes to rest in the
company of the dead.

¹⁷ Whoever loves pleasure will
become poor;
whoever loves wine and olive
oil will never be rich.

¹⁸ The wicked become a ransom
for the righteous,
and the unfaithful for the
upright.

¹⁹ Better to live in a desert
than with a quarrelsome and
nagging wife.

ᵃ 6 Some Hebrew manuscripts, Septuagint and Vulgate; most Hebrew
manuscripts *vapor for those who seek death*   ᵇ 12 Or *The righteous person*

²⁰The wise store up choice food
and olive oil,
but fools gulp theirs down.

²¹Whoever pursues
righteousness and love
finds life, prosperity*^a* and
honor.

²²One who is wise can go up
against the city of the
mighty
and pull down the
stronghold in which they
trust.

²³Those who guard their mouths
and their tongues
keep themselves from
calamity.

²⁴The proud and arrogant
person — "Mocker" is his
name —
behaves with insolent
fury.

²⁵The craving of a sluggard will
be the death of him,
because his hands refuse to
work.
²⁶All day long he craves for
more,
but the righteous give
without sparing.

²⁷The sacrifice of the wicked is
detestable —
how much more so when
brought with evil intent!

²⁸A false witness will perish,
but a careful listener will
testify successfully.

²⁹The wicked put up a bold
front,
but the upright give thought
to their ways.

³⁰There is no wisdom, no
insight, no plan
that can succeed against the
LORD.

³¹The horse is made ready for
the day of battle,
but victory rests with the
LORD.

22 A good name is more
desirable than great
riches;
to be esteemed is better than
silver or gold.

²Rich and poor have this in
common:
The LORD is the Maker of
them all.

³The prudent see danger and
take refuge,
but the simple keep going
and pay the penalty.

⁴Humility is the fear of the
LORD;
its wages are riches and
honor and life.

⁵In the paths of the wicked are
snares and pitfalls,
but those who would
preserve their life stay
far from them.

⁶Start children off on the way
they should go,

^a 21 Or *righteousness*

and even when they are old
    they will not turn from it.

7 The rich rule over the poor,
    and the borrower is slave to
    the lender.

8 Whoever sows injustice reaps
    calamity,
    and the rod they wield in
    fury will be broken.

9 The generous will themselves
    be blessed,
    for they share their food with
    the poor.

10 Drive out the mocker, and out
    goes strife;
    quarrels and insults are
    ended.

11 One who loves a pure heart
    and who speaks with
    grace
    will have the king for a
    friend.

12 The eyes of the LORD keep
    watch over knowledge,
    but he frustrates the words
    of the unfaithful.

13 The sluggard says, "There's a
    lion outside!
    I'll be killed in the public
    square!"

14 The mouth of an adulterous
    woman is a deep pit;
    a man who is under the
    LORD's wrath falls into it.

15 Folly is bound up in the heart
    of a child,
    but the rod of discipline will
    drive it far away.

16 One who oppresses the poor to
    increase his wealth
    and one who gives gifts to
    the rich — both come to
    poverty.

Thirty Sayings of the Wise

Saying 1

17 Pay attention and turn your
    ear to the sayings of the
    wise;
    apply your heart to what I
    teach,

18 for it is pleasing when you keep
    them in your heart
    and have all of them ready
    on your lips.

19 So that your trust may be in
    the LORD,
    I teach you today, even
    you.

20 Have I not written thirty
    sayings for you,
    sayings of counsel and
    knowledge,

21 teaching you to be honest and
    to speak the truth,
    so that you bring back
    truthful reports
    to those you serve?

Saying 2

22 Do not exploit the poor
    because they are
    poor
    and do not crush the needy
    in court,

23 for the LORD will take up their
    case
    and will exact life for
    life.

Saying 3

²⁴Do not make friends with a
hot-tempered person,
do not associate with one
easily angered,
²⁵or you may learn their ways
and get yourself ensnared.

Saying 4

²⁶Do not be one who shakes
hands in pledge
or puts up security for
debts;
²⁷if you lack the means to pay,
your very bed will be
snatched from under
you.

Saying 5

²⁸Do not move an ancient
boundary stone
set up by your ancestors.

Saying 6

²⁹Do you see someone skilled in
their work?
They will serve before
kings;
they will not serve before
officials of low rank.

Saying 7

23 When you sit to dine
with a ruler,
note well what[a] is before
you,
²and put a knife to your throat
if you are given to gluttony.
³Do not crave his delicacies,
for that food is deceptive.

Saying 8

⁴Do not wear yourself out to get
rich;
do not trust your own
cleverness.
⁵Cast but a glance at riches, and
they are gone,
for they will surely sprout
wings
and fly off to the sky like an
eagle.

Saying 9

⁶Do not eat the food of a
begrudging host,
do not crave his delicacies;
⁷for he is the kind of person
who is always thinking
about the cost.[b]
"Eat and drink," he says to
you,
but his heart is not with you.
⁸You will vomit up the little you
have eaten
and will have wasted your
compliments.

Saying 10

⁹Do not speak to fools,
for they will scorn your
prudent words.

Saying 11

¹⁰Do not move an ancient
boundary stone
or encroach on the fields of
the fatherless,
¹¹for their Defender is strong;
he will take up their case
against you.

---

^a 1 Or *who*   ^b 7 Or *for as he thinks within himself, / so he is*; or *for as he puts on a feast, / so he is*

Saying 12

¹²Apply your heart to instruction
and your ears to words of
knowledge.

Saying 13

¹³Do not withhold discipline
from a child;
if you punish them with the
rod, they will not die.
¹⁴Punish them with the rod
and save them from death.

Saying 14

¹⁵My son, if your heart is wise,
then my heart will be glad
indeed;
¹⁶my inmost being will rejoice
when your lips speak what is
right.

Saying 15

¹⁷Do not let your heart envy
sinners,
but always be zealous for the
fear of the Lord.
¹⁸There is surely a future hope
for you,
and your hope will not be cut
off.

Saying 16

¹⁹Listen, my son, and be wise,
and set your heart on the
right path:
²⁰Do not join those who drink
too much wine
or gorge themselves on meat,
²¹for drunkards and gluttons
become poor,
and drowsiness clothes them
in rags.

Saying 17

²²Listen to your father, who gave
you life,
and do not despise your
mother when she is
old.
²³Buy the truth and do not
sell it —
wisdom, instruction and
insight as well.
²⁴The father of a righteous child
has great joy;
a man who fathers a wise
son rejoices in him.
²⁵May your father and mother
rejoice;
may she who gave you birth
be joyful!

Saying 18

²⁶My son, give me your heart
and let your eyes delight in
my ways,
²⁷for an adulterous woman is a
deep pit,
and a wayward wife is a
narrow well.
²⁸Like a bandit she lies in wait
and multiplies the unfaithful
among men.

Saying 19

²⁹Who has woe? Who has
sorrow?
Who has strife? Who has
complaints?
Who has needless bruises?
Who has bloodshot
eyes?
³⁰Those who linger over wine,
who go to sample bowls of
mixed wine.

³¹ Do not gaze at wine when it is
  red,
    when it sparkles in the cup,
    when it goes down smoothly!
³² In the end it bites like a snake
    and poisons like a viper.
³³ Your eyes will see strange
    sights,
    and your mind will imagine
    confusing things.
³⁴ You will be like one sleeping
    on the high seas,
    lying on top of the rigging.
³⁵ "They hit me," you will say,
    "but I'm not hurt!
    They beat me, but I don't
    feel it!
  When will I wake up
    so I can find another drink?"

Saying 20

24 Do not envy the wicked,
    do not desire their
    company;
² for their hearts plot violence,
    and their lips talk about
    making trouble.

Saying 21

³ By wisdom a house is built,
    and through understanding
    it is established;
⁴ through knowledge its rooms
    are filled
    with rare and beautiful
    treasures.

Saying 22

⁵ The wise prevail through great
    power,
    and those who have
    knowledge muster their
    strength.

⁶ Surely you need guidance to
    wage war,
    and victory is won through
    many advisers.

Saying 23

⁷ Wisdom is too high for fools;
    in the assembly at the gate
    they must not open their
    mouths.

Saying 24

⁸ Whoever plots evil
    will be known as a schemer.
⁹ The schemes of folly are sin,
    and people detest a mocker.

Saying 25

¹⁰ If you falter in a time of
    trouble,
    how small is your strength!
¹¹ Rescue those being led away to
    death;
    hold back those staggering
    toward slaughter.
¹² If you say, "But we knew
    nothing about this,"
    does not he who weighs the
    heart perceive it?
  Does not he who guards your
    life know it?
    Will he not repay everyone
    according to what they
    have done?

Saying 26

¹³ Eat honey, my son, for it is
    good;
    honey from the comb is
    sweet to your taste.
¹⁴ Know also that wisdom is like
    honey for you:

If you find it, there is a future
hope for you,
and your hope will not be cut
off.

Saying 27

15 Do not lurk like a thief near the
house of the righteous,
do not plunder their
dwelling place;
16 for though the righteous fall
seven times, they rise
again,
but the wicked stumble
when calamity strikes.

Saying 28

17 Do not gloat when your enemy
falls;
when they stumble, do not
let your heart rejoice,
18 or the LORD will see and
disapprove
and turn his wrath away
from them.

Saying 29

19 Do not fret because of
evildoers
or be envious of the wicked,
20 for the evildoer has no future
hope,
and the lamp of the wicked
will be snuffed out.

Saying 30

21 Fear the LORD and the king,
my son,
and do not join with
rebellious officials,
22 for those two will send sudden
destruction on them,

and who knows what
calamities they can
bring?

Further Sayings of the Wise

23 These also are sayings of the
wise:

To show partiality in judging is
not good:
24 Whoever says to the guilty,
"You are innocent,"
will be cursed by peoples
and denounced by
nations.
25 But it will go well with those
who convict the guilty,
and rich blessing will come
on them.

26 An honest answer
is like a kiss on the lips.

27 Put your outdoor work in order
and get your fields ready;
after that, build your house.

28 Do not testify against your
neighbor without
cause —
would you use your lips to
mislead?
29 Do not say, "I'll do to them as
they have done to me;
I'll pay them back for what
they did."

30 I went past the field of a
sluggard,
past the vineyard of
someone who has no
sense;
31 thorns had come up
everywhere,

the ground was covered with weeds,
and the stone wall was in ruins.
32 I applied my heart to what I observed
and learned a lesson from what I saw:
33 A little sleep, a little slumber,
a little folding of the hands to rest —
34 and poverty will come on you like a thief
and scarcity like an armed man.

More Proverbs of Solomon

25 These are more proverbs of Solomon, compiled by the men of Hezekiah king of Judah:

2 It is the glory of God to conceal a matter;
to search out a matter is the glory of kings.
3 As the heavens are high and the earth is deep,
so the hearts of kings are unsearchable.

4 Remove the dross from the silver,
and a silversmith can produce a vessel;
5 remove wicked officials from the king's presence,
and his throne will be established through righteousness.

6 Do not exalt yourself in the king's presence,
and do not claim a place among his great men;
7 it is better for him to say to you, "Come up here,"
than for him to humiliate you before his nobles.

What you have seen with your eyes
8   do not bring[a] hastily to court,
for what will you do in the end if your neighbor puts you to shame?

9 If you take your neighbor to court,
do not betray another's confidence,
10 or the one who hears it may shame you
and the charge against you will stand.

11 Like apples[b] of gold in settings of silver
is a ruling rightly given.
12 Like an earring of gold or an ornament of fine gold
is the rebuke of a wise judge to a listening ear.

13 Like a snow-cooled drink at harvest time
is a trustworthy messenger to the one who sends him;
he refreshes the spirit of his master.

---

[a] 7,8 Or nobles / on whom you had set your eyes. / [8]Do not go   [b] 11 Or possibly apricots

¹⁴Like clouds and wind without
     rain
  is one who boasts of gifts
     never given.

¹⁵Through patience a ruler can
     be persuaded,
  and a gentle tongue can
     break a bone.

¹⁶If you find honey, eat just
     enough —
  too much of it, and you will
     vomit.

¹⁷Seldom set foot in your
     neighbor's house —
  too much of you, and they
     will hate you.

¹⁸Like a club or a sword or a
     sharp arrow
  is one who gives false
     testimony against a
     neighbor.

¹⁹Like a broken tooth or a lame
     foot
  is reliance on the unfaithful
     in a time of trouble.

²⁰Like one who takes away a
     garment on a cold day,
  or like vinegar poured on a
     wound,
  is one who sings songs to a
     heavy heart.

²¹If your enemy is hungry, give
     him food to eat;
  if he is thirsty, give him
     water to drink.

²²In doing this, you will heap
     burning coals on his
     head,
  and the Lord will reward
     you.

²³Like a north wind that brings
     unexpected rain
  is a sly tongue — which
     provokes a horrified
     look.

²⁴Better to live on a corner of the
     roof
  than share a house with a
     quarrelsome wife.

²⁵Like cold water to a weary soul
  is good news from a distant
     land.

²⁶Like a muddied spring or a
     polluted well
  are the righteous who give
     way to the wicked.

²⁷It is not good to eat too much
     honey,
  nor is it honorable to search
     out matters that are too
     deep.

²⁸Like a city whose walls are
     broken through
  is a person who lacks self-
     control.

26

  Like snow in summer or
     rain in harvest,
  honor is not fitting for a fool.
²Like a fluttering sparrow or a
     darting swallow,
  an undeserved curse does
     not come to rest.
³A whip for the horse, a bridle
     for the donkey,
  and a rod for the backs of
     fools!
⁴Do not answer a fool according
     to his folly,
  or you yourself will be just
     like him.

⁵Answer a fool according to his
     folly,
 or he will be wise in his own
     eyes.
⁶Sending a message by the
     hands of a fool
 is like cutting off one's feet or
     drinking poison.
⁷Like the useless legs of one
     who is lame
 is a proverb in the mouth of a
     fool.
⁸Like tying a stone in a sling
 is the giving of honor to a
     fool.
⁹Like a thornbush in a
     drunkard's hand
 is a proverb in the mouth of a
     fool.
¹⁰Like an archer who wounds at
     random
 is one who hires a fool or any
     passer-by.
¹¹As a dog returns to its vomit,
 so fools repeat their folly.
¹²Do you see a person wise in
     their own eyes?
 There is more hope for a fool
     than for them.
¹³A sluggard says, "There's a lion
     in the road,
 a fierce lion roaming the
     streets!"
¹⁴As a door turns on its hinges,
 so a sluggard turns on his
     bed.
¹⁵A sluggard buries his hand in
     the dish;
 he is too lazy to bring it back
     to his mouth.

¹⁶A sluggard is wiser in his own
     eyes
 than seven people who
     answer discreetly.

¹⁷Like one who grabs a stray dog
     by the ears
 is someone who rushes into
     a quarrel not their own.

¹⁸Like a maniac shooting
 flaming arrows of death
¹⁹is one who deceives their
     neighbor
 and says, "I was only
     joking!"

²⁰Without wood a fire goes out;
 without a gossip a quarrel
     dies down.
²¹As charcoal to embers and as
     wood to fire,
 so is a quarrelsome person
     for kindling strife.
²²The words of a gossip are like
     choice morsels;
 they go down to the inmost
     parts.

²³Like a coating of silver dross
     on earthenware
 are fervent*a* lips with an evil
     heart.
²⁴Enemies disguise themselves
     with their lips,
 but in their hearts they
     harbor deceit.
²⁵Though their speech is
     charming, do not believe
     them,
 for seven abominations fill
     their hearts.

a 23 Hebrew; Septuagint *smooth*

²⁶Their malice may be
    concealed by deception,
    but their wickedness will be
    exposed in the assembly.
²⁷Whoever digs a pit will fall
    into it;
    if someone rolls a stone, it
    will roll back on them.
²⁸A lying tongue hates those it
    hurts,
    and a flattering mouth works
    ruin.

27 Do not boast about
    tomorrow,
    for you do not know what a
    day may bring.

²Let someone else praise
    you, and not your own
    mouth;
    an outsider, and not your
    own lips.

³Stone is heavy and sand a
    burden,
    but a fool's provocation is
    heavier than both.

⁴Anger is cruel and fury
    overwhelming,
    but who can stand before
    jealousy?

⁵Better is open rebuke
    than hidden love.

⁶Wounds from a friend can be
    trusted,
    but an enemy multiplies
    kisses.

⁷One who is full loathes honey
    from the comb,
    but to the hungry even what
    is bitter tastes sweet.

⁸Like a bird that flees its nest
    is anyone who flees from
    home.

⁹Perfume and incense bring joy
    to the heart,
    and the pleasantness of a
    friend
    springs from their heartfelt
    advice.

¹⁰Do not forsake your friend or a
    friend of your family,
    and do not go to your
    relative's house when
    disaster strikes you —
    better a neighbor nearby
    than a relative far away.

¹¹Be wise, my son, and bring joy
    to my heart;
    then I can answer anyone
    who treats me with
    contempt.

¹²The prudent see danger and
    take refuge,
    but the simple keep going
    and pay the penalty.

¹³Take the garment of one who
    puts up security for a
    stranger;
    hold it in pledge if it is done
    for an outsider.

¹⁴If anyone loudly blesses their
    neighbor early in the
    morning,
    it will be taken as a curse.

¹⁵A quarrelsome wife is like the
    dripping
    of a leaky roof in a
    rainstorm;

16 restraining her is like
    restraining the wind
or grasping oil with the
    hand.

17 As iron sharpens iron,
so one person sharpens
    another.

18 The one who guards a fig tree
    will eat its fruit,
and whoever protects their
    master will be honored.

19 As water reflects the face,
so one's life reflects the
    heart.*a*

20 Death and Destruction*b* are
    never satisfied,
and neither are human
    eyes.

21 The crucible for silver and the
    furnace for gold,
but people are tested by their
    praise.

22 Though you grind a fool in a
    mortar,
grinding them like grain
    with a pestle,
you will not remove their
    folly from them.

23 Be sure you know the
    condition of your flocks,
give careful attention to your
    herds;
24 for riches do not endure
    forever,
and a crown is not secure for
    all generations.

25 When the hay is removed and
    new growth appears
and the grass from the hills
    is gathered in,
26 the lambs will provide you
    with clothing,
and the goats with the price
    of a field.
27 You will have plenty of goats'
    milk to feed your family
and to nourish your female
    servants.

28 The wicked flee though
    no one pursues,
but the righteous are as bold
    as a lion.

2 When a country is rebellious,
    it has many rulers,
but a ruler with discernment
    and knowledge
    maintains order.

3 A ruler*c* who oppresses the
    poor
is like a driving rain that
    leaves no crops.

4 Those who forsake instruction
    praise the wicked,
but those who heed it resist
    them.

5 Evildoers do not understand
    what is right,
but those who seek the LORD
    understand it fully.

6 Better the poor whose walk is
    blameless
than the rich whose ways are
    perverse.

---

a 19 Or *so others reflect your heart back to you*   *b 20* Hebrew *Abaddon*
c 3 Or *A poor person*

⁷A discerning son heeds
　　instruction,
　　but a companion of gluttons
　　　disgraces his father.

⁸Whoever increases wealth by
　　taking interest or profit
　　from the poor
　　amasses it for another, who
　　　will be kind to the poor.

⁹If anyone turns a deaf ear to
　　my instruction,
　　even their prayers are
　　　detestable.

¹⁰Whoever leads the upright
　　along an evil path
　　will fall into their own trap,
　　but the blameless will
　　　receive a good
　　　inheritance.

¹¹The rich are wise in their own
　　eyes;
　　one who is poor and
　　　discerning sees how
　　　deluded they are.

¹²When the righteous triumph,
　　there is great elation;
　　but when the wicked rise to
　　　power, people go into
　　　hiding.

¹³Whoever conceals their sins
　　does not prosper,
　　but the one who confesses
　　　and renounces them
　　　finds mercy.

¹⁴Blessed is the one who always
　　trembles before God,
　　but whoever hardens their
　　　heart falls into trouble.

¹⁵Like a roaring lion or a
　　charging bear
　　is a wicked ruler over a
　　　helpless people.

¹⁶A tyrannical ruler practices
　　extortion,
　　but one who hates ill-gotten
　　　gain will enjoy a long
　　　reign.

¹⁷Anyone tormented by the guilt
　　of murder
　　will seek refuge in the grave;
　　let no one hold them back.

¹⁸The one whose walk is
　　blameless is kept safe,
　　but the one whose ways are
　　　perverse will fall into the
　　　pit.ᵃ

¹⁹Those who work their land will
　　have abundant food,
　　but those who chase
　　　fantasies will have their
　　　fill of poverty.

²⁰A faithful person will be richly
　　blessed,
　　but one eager to get rich will
　　　not go unpunished.

²¹To show partiality is not
　　good—
　　yet a person will do wrong
　　　for a piece of bread.

²²The stingy are eager to get rich
　　and are unaware that
　　　poverty awaits them.

²³Whoever rebukes a person will
　　in the end gain favor

ᵃ 18 Syriac (see Septuagint); Hebrew *into one*

rather than one who has a
flattering tongue.

²⁴Whoever robs their father or
mother
and says, "It's not wrong,"
is partner to one who
destroys.

²⁵The greedy stir up conflict,
but those who trust in the
LORD will prosper.

²⁶Those who trust in themselves
are fools,
but those who walk in
wisdom are kept safe.

²⁷Those who give to the poor
will lack nothing,
but those who close their
eyes to them receive
many curses.

²⁸When the wicked rise to
power, people go into
hiding;
but when the wicked perish,
the righteous thrive.

29 Whoever remains stiff-
necked after many
rebukes
will suddenly be
destroyed — without
remedy.

²When the righteous thrive, the
people rejoice;
when the wicked rule, the
people groan.

³A man who loves wisdom
brings joy to his father,
but a companion of
prostitutes squanders his
wealth.

⁴By justice a king gives a
country stability,
but those who are greedy
for ᵃ bribes tear it down.

⁵Those who flatter their
neighbors
are spreading nets for their
feet.

⁶Evildoers are snared by their
own sin,
but the righteous shout for
joy and are glad.

⁷The righteous care about
justice for the poor,
but the wicked have no such
concern.

⁸Mockers stir up a city,
but the wise turn away
anger.

⁹If a wise person goes to court
with a fool,
the fool rages and scoffs, and
there is no peace.

¹⁰The bloodthirsty hate a person
of integrity
and seek to kill the upright.

¹¹Fools give full vent to their
rage,
but the wise bring calm in
the end.

¹²If a ruler listens to lies,
all his officials become
wicked.

13 The poor and the oppressor
    have this in common:
  The LORD gives sight to the
    eyes of both.

14 If a king judges the poor with
    fairness,
  his throne will be
    established forever.

15 A rod and a reprimand impart
    wisdom,
  but a child left undisciplined
    disgraces its mother.

16 When the wicked thrive, so
    does sin,
  but the righteous will see
    their downfall.

17 Discipline your children, and
    they will give you peace;
  they will bring you the
    delights you desire.

18 Where there is no revelation,
    people cast off restraint;
  but blessed is the one
    who heeds wisdom's
    instruction.

19 Servants cannot be corrected
    by mere words;
  though they understand,
    they will not respond.

20 Do you see someone who
    speaks in haste?
  There is more hope for a fool
    than for them.

21 A servant pampered from
    youth
  will turn out to be insolent.

22 An angry person stirs up
    conflict,
  and a hot-tempered person
    commits many sins.

23 Pride brings a person low,
  but the lowly in spirit gain
    honor.

24 The accomplices of thieves are
    their own enemies;
  they are put under oath and
    dare not testify.

25 Fear of man will prove to be a
    snare,
  but whoever trusts in the
    LORD is kept safe.

26 Many seek an audience with a
    ruler,
  but it is from the LORD that
    one gets justice.

27 The righteous detest the
    dishonest;
  the wicked detest the
    upright.

Sayings of Agur

30 The sayings of Agur son
    of Jakeh—an inspired
utterance.

  This man's utterance to
    Ithiel:

"I am weary, God,
  but I can prevail.*a*
2 Surely I am only a brute, not a
    man;
  I do not have human
    understanding.

---

a 1 With a different word division of the Hebrew; Masoretic Text *utterance to
Ithiel, / to Ithiel and Ukal:*

³I have not learned wisdom,
    nor have I attained to the
        knowledge of the Holy
        One.
⁴Who has gone up to heaven
        and come down?
    Whose hands have gathered
        up the wind?
Who has wrapped up the
        waters in a cloak?
    Who has established all the
        ends of the earth?
What is his name, and what is
        the name of his son?
    Surely you know!

⁵ "Every word of God is flawless;
    he is a shield to those who
        take refuge in him.
⁶Do not add to his words,
    or he will rebuke you and
        prove you a liar.

⁷ "Two things I ask of you, LORD;
    do not refuse me before I die:
⁸Keep falsehood and lies far
        from me;
    give me neither poverty nor
        riches,
    but give me only my daily
        bread.
⁹Otherwise, I may have too
        much and disown you
    and say, 'Who is the LORD?'
Or I may become poor and
        steal,
    and so dishonor the name of
        my God.

¹⁰ "Do not slander a servant to
        their master,
    or they will curse you, and
        you will pay for it.

¹¹ "There are those who curse
        their fathers
    and do not bless their
        mothers;
¹²those who are pure in their
        own eyes
    and yet are not cleansed of
        their filth;
¹³those whose eyes are ever so
        haughty,
    whose glances are so
        disdainful;
¹⁴those whose teeth are swords
    and whose jaws are set with
        knives
to devour the poor from the
        earth
    and the needy from among
        mankind.

¹⁵ "The leech has two daughters.
    'Give! Give!' they cry.

"There are three things that
        are never satisfied,
    four that never say,
        'Enough!':
¹⁶the grave, the barren womb,
    land, which is never satisfied
        with water,
    and fire, which never says,
        'Enough!'

¹⁷ "The eye that mocks a father,
    that scorns an aged mother,
will be pecked out by the
        ravens of the valley,
    will be eaten by the vultures.

¹⁸ "There are three things that
        are too amazing for me,
    four that I do not
        understand:

19 the way of an eagle in the sky,
   the way of a snake on a rock,
the way of a ship on the high
      seas,
   and the way of a man with a
      young woman.

20 "This is the way of an
      adulterous woman:
   She eats and wipes her
      mouth
   and says, 'I've done nothing
      wrong.'

21 "Under three things the earth
      trembles,
   under four it cannot bear up:
22 a servant who becomes king,
   a godless fool who gets
      plenty to eat,
23 a contemptible woman who
      gets married,
   and a servant who displaces
      her mistress.

24 "Four things on earth are
      small,
   yet they are extremely wise:
25 Ants are creatures of little
      strength,
   yet they store up their food
      in the summer;
26 hyraxes are creatures of little
      power,
   yet they make their home in
      the crags;
27 locusts have no king,
   yet they advance together in
      ranks;
28 a lizard can be caught with the
      hand,

   yet it is found in kings'
      palaces.

29 "There are three things that
      are stately in their stride,
   four that move with stately
      bearing:
30 a lion, mighty among beasts,
   who retreats before nothing;
31 a strutting rooster, a he-goat,
   and a king secure against
      revolt.ᵃ

32 "If you play the fool and exalt
      yourself,
   or if you plan evil,
   clap your hand over your
      mouth!
33 For as churning cream
      produces butter,
   and as twisting the nose
      produces blood,
   so stirring up anger
      produces strife."

Sayings of King Lemuel

31 The sayings of King Lemuel—an inspired utter-
ance his mother taught him.

2 Listen, my son! Listen, son of
      my womb!
   Listen, my son, the answer to
      my prayers!
3 Do not spend your strengthᵇ
      on women,
   your vigor on those who ruin
      kings.

4 It is not for kings, Lemuel—
   it is not for kings to drink
      wine,
   not for rulers to crave beer,

ᵃ 31 The meaning of the Hebrew for this phrase is uncertain.   ᵇ 3 Or *wealth*

⁵lest they drink and forget what
has been decreed,
and deprive all the
oppressed of their rights.
⁶Let beer be for those who are
perishing,
wine for those who are in
anguish!
⁷Let them drink and forget their
poverty
and remember their misery
no more.

⁸Speak up for those who cannot
speak for themselves,
for the rights of all who are
destitute.
⁹Speak up and judge fairly;
defend the rights of the poor
and needy.

Epilogue: The Wife of Noble Character

¹⁰[a]A wife of noble character who
can find?
She is worth far more than
rubies.
¹¹Her husband has full
confidence in her
and lacks nothing of value.
¹²She brings him good, not
harm,
all the days of her life.
¹³She selects wool and flax
and works with eager
hands.
¹⁴She is like the merchant
ships,
bringing her food from
afar.

¹⁵She gets up while it is still
night;
she provides food for her
family
and portions for her female
servants.
¹⁶She considers a field and
buys it;
out of her earnings she
plants a vineyard.
¹⁷She sets about her work
vigorously;
her arms are strong for her
tasks.
¹⁸She sees that her trading is
profitable,
and her lamp does not go out
at night.
¹⁹In her hand she holds the
distaff
and grasps the spindle with
her fingers.
²⁰She opens her arms to the
poor
and extends her hands to the
needy.
²¹When it snows, she has no fear
for her household;
for all of them are clothed in
scarlet.
²²She makes coverings for her
bed;
she is clothed in fine linen
and purple.
²³Her husband is respected at
the city gate,
where he takes his seat
among the elders of the
land.

---

[a] 10 Verses 10-31 are an acrostic poem, the verses of which begin with the
successive letters of the Hebrew alphabet.

24 She makes linen garments and
sells them,
and supplies the merchants
with sashes.
25 She is clothed with strength
and dignity;
she can laugh at the days to
come.
26 She speaks with wisdom,
and faithful instruction is on
her tongue.
27 She watches over the affairs of
her household
and does not eat the bread of
idleness.

28 Her children arise and call her
blessed;
her husband also, and he
praises her:
29 "Many women do noble
things,
but you surpass them all."
30 Charm is deceptive, and
beauty is fleeting;
but a woman who fears the
LORD is to be praised.
31 Honor her for all that her
hands have done,
and let her works bring her
praise at the city gate.

Ecclesiastes

Introduction:

Ecclesiastes studies the meaning of life. The Teacher looks at wisdom, pleasure, work, power, riches, religion and other things. All of these have some value and are useful in the proper time and place, but they have lasting value only if God is at the center of a person's life. Reverence and respect for God and a real devotion in serving God are the most important to make life meaningful. Without God, the Teacher says, "Everything is meaningless" (1:2).

Outline of contents:

Life is without meaning (1:1–11)
The limits of wisdom (1:12–2:26)
A time for everything (3:1–22)
Disappointments and contentment (4:1–5:20)
Satisfaction in this life is limited (6:1–8:17)
Life balanced with wisdom (9:1–10:20)
True wisdom — fear of God (11:1–12:14)

Everything Is Meaningless

1 The words of the Teacher,[a] son of David, king in Jerusalem:

² "Meaningless! Meaningless!"
    says the Teacher.
"Utterly meaningless!
    Everything is meaningless."

³ What do people gain from all
        their labors
    at which they toil under the
        sun?
⁴ Generations come and
        generations go,
    but the earth remains
        forever.

⁵ The sun rises and the sun sets,
    and hurries back to where it
        rises.
⁶ The wind blows to the south
    and turns to the north;
round and round it goes,
    ever returning on its course.
⁷ All streams flow into the sea,
    yet the sea is never full.
To the place the streams come
        from,
    there they return again.
⁸ All things are wearisome,
    more than one can say.
The eye never has enough of
        seeing,
    nor the ear its fill of hearing.

---

[a] 1 Or *the leader of the assembly*; also in verses 2 and 12

⁹What has been will be again,
  what has been done will be
    done again;
  there is nothing new under
    the sun.
¹⁰Is there anything of which one
    can say,
  "Look! This is something
    new"?
  It was here already, long ago;
    it was here before our time.
¹¹No one remembers the former
    generations,
  and even those yet to come
  will not be remembered
    by those who follow them.

Wisdom Is Meaningless

¹²I, the Teacher, was king over Israel in Jerusalem. ¹³I applied my mind to study and to explore by wisdom all that is done under the heavens. What a heavy burden God has laid on mankind! ¹⁴I have seen all the things that are done under the sun; all of them are meaningless, a chasing after the wind.

¹⁵What is crooked cannot be
    straightened;
  what is lacking cannot be
    counted.

¹⁶I said to myself, "Look, I have increased in wisdom more than anyone who has ruled over Jerusalem before me; I have experienced much of wisdom and knowledge." ¹⁷Then I applied myself to the understanding of wisdom, and also of madness and folly, but I learned that this, too, is a chasing after the wind.

¹⁸For with much wisdom comes
    much sorrow;
  the more knowledge, the
    more grief.

Pleasures Are Meaningless

2 I said to myself, "Come now, I will test you with pleasure to find out what is good." But that also proved to be meaningless. ²"Laughter," I said, "is madness. And what does pleasure accomplish?" ³I tried cheering myself with wine, and embracing folly— my mind still guiding me with wisdom. I wanted to see what was good for people to do under the heavens during the few days of their lives.

⁴I undertook great projects: I built houses for myself and planted vineyards. ⁵I made gardens and parks and planted all kinds of fruit trees in them. ⁶I made reservoirs to water groves of flourishing trees. ⁷I bought male and female slaves and had other slaves who were born in my house. I also owned more herds and flocks than anyone in Jerusalem before me. ⁸I amassed silver and gold for myself, and the treasure of kings and provinces. I acquired male and female singers, and a harem[a] as well—the delights of a man's heart. ⁹I became

---

[a] 8 The meaning of the Hebrew for this phrase is uncertain.

greater by far than anyone in Jerusalem before me. In all this my wisdom stayed with me.

¹⁰ I denied myself nothing my
    eyes desired;
  I refused my heart no
    pleasure.
  My heart took delight in all my
    labor,
    and this was the reward for
      all my toil.
¹¹ Yet when I surveyed all that
    my hands had done
    and what I had toiled to
      achieve,
  everything was meaningless, a
    chasing after the wind;
    nothing was gained under
      the sun.

Wisdom and Folly Are Meaningless

¹² Then I turned my thoughts to
    consider wisdom,
    and also madness and
      folly.
  What more can the king's
    successor do
    than what has already been
      done?
¹³ I saw that wisdom is better
    than folly,
    just as light is better than
      darkness.
¹⁴ The wise have eyes in their
    heads,
    while the fool walks in the
      darkness;
  but I came to realize
    that the same fate overtakes
      them both.

¹⁵ Then I said to myself,

  "The fate of the fool will
    overtake me also.
  What then do I gain by being
    wise?"
  I said to myself,
    "This too is meaningless."
¹⁶ For the wise, like the fool, will
    not be long remembered;
    the days have already come
      when both have been
      forgotten.
  Like the fool, the wise too must
    die!

Toil Is Meaningless

¹⁷ So I hated life, because the work that is done under the sun was grievous to me. All of it is meaningless, a chasing after the wind. ¹⁸ I hated all the things I had toiled for under the sun, because I must leave them to the one who comes after me. ¹⁹ And who knows whether that person will be wise or foolish? Yet they will have control over all the fruit of my toil into which I have poured my effort and skill under the sun. This too is meaningless. ²⁰ So my heart began to despair over all my toilsome labor under the sun. ²¹ For a person may labor with wisdom, knowledge and skill, and then they must leave all they own to another who has not toiled for it. This too is meaningless and a great misfortune. ²² What do people get for all the toil and anxious striving with which they labor under the

sun? **23** All their days their work is grief and pain; even at night their minds do not rest. This too is meaningless.

24 A person can do nothing better than to eat and drink and find satisfaction in their own toil. This too, I see, is from the hand of God, **25** for without him, who can eat or find enjoyment? **26** To the person who pleases him, God gives wisdom, knowledge and happiness, but to the sinner he gives the task of gathering and storing up wealth to hand it over to the one who pleases God. This too is meaningless, a chasing after the wind.

A Time for Everything

3 There is a time for everything,
and a season for every activity under the heavens:

2 a time to be born and a time to die,
a time to plant and a time to uproot,
3 a time to kill and a time to heal,
a time to tear down and a time to build,
4 a time to weep and a time to laugh,
a time to mourn and a time to dance,
5 a time to scatter stones and a time to gather them,
a time to embrace and a time to refrain from embracing,
6 a time to search and a time to give up,
a time to keep and a time to throw away,
7 a time to tear and a time to mend,
a time to be silent and a time to speak,
8 a time to love and a time to hate,
a time for war and a time for peace.

9 What do workers gain from their toil? **10** I have seen the burden God has laid on the human race. **11** He has made everything beautiful in its time. He has also set eternity in the human heart; yet[a] no one can fathom what God has done from beginning to end. **12** I know that there is nothing better for people than to be happy and to do good while they live. **13** That each of them may eat and drink, and find satisfaction in all their toil—this is the gift of God. **14** I know that everything God does will endure forever; nothing can be added to it and nothing taken from it. God does it so that people will fear him.

15 Whatever is has already been,
and what will be has been before;
and God will call the past to account.[b]

---

a 11 Or *also placed ignorance in the human heart, so that*   *b 15* Or *God calls back the past*

¹⁶And I saw something else under the sun:

In the place of judgment—
    wickedness was there,
in the place of justice—
    wickedness was there.

¹⁷I said to myself,

"God will bring into judgment
    both the righteous and the
        wicked,
for there will be a time for
        every activity,
    a time to judge every deed."

¹⁸I also said to myself, "As for humans, God tests them so that they may see that they are like the animals. ¹⁹Surely the fate of human beings is like that of the animals; the same fate awaits them both: As one dies, so dies the other. All have the same breath^a; humans have no advantage over animals. Everything is meaningless. ²⁰All go to the same place; all come from dust, and to dust all return. ²¹Who knows if the human spirit rises upward and if the spirit of the animal goes down into the earth?"

²²So I saw that there is nothing better for a person than to enjoy their work, because that is their lot. For who can bring them to see what will happen after them?

Oppression, Toil, Friendlessness

4 Again I looked and saw all the oppression that was taking place under the sun:

I saw the tears of the
        oppressed—
and they have no comforter;
power was on the side of their
        oppressors—
and they have no comforter.
²And I declared that the dead,
    who had already died,
are happier than the living,
    who are still alive.
³But better than both
    is the one who has never
        been born,
who has not seen the evil
    that is done under the sun.

⁴And I saw that all toil and all achievement spring from one person's envy of another. This too is meaningless, a chasing after the wind.

⁵Fools fold their hands
    and ruin themselves.
⁶Better one handful with
        tranquillity
    than two handfuls with toil
    and chasing after the wind.

⁷Again I saw something meaningless under the sun:

⁸There was a man all alone;
    he had neither son nor
        brother.
There was no end to his toil,
    yet his eyes were not content
        with his wealth.
"For whom am I toiling," he
        asked,
    "and why am I depriving
        myself of enjoyment?"

^a 19 Or *spirit*

This too is meaningless —
a miserable business!

⁹Two are better than one,
because they have a good
return for their labor:
¹⁰If either of them falls down,
one can help the other up.
But pity anyone who falls
and has no one to help
them up.
¹¹Also, if two lie down together,
they will keep warm.
But how can one keep warm
alone?
¹²Though one may be
overpowered,
two can defend themselves.
A cord of three strands is not
quickly broken.

Advancement Is Meaningless

¹³Better a poor but wise youth than an old but foolish king who no longer knows how to heed a warning. ¹⁴The youth may have come from prison to the kingship, or he may have been born in poverty within his kingdom. ¹⁵I saw that all who lived and walked under the sun followed the youth, the king's successor. ¹⁶There was no end to all the people who were before them. But those who came later were not pleased with the successor. This too is meaningless, a chasing after the wind.

Fulfill Your Vow to God

5 ᵃ Guard your steps when you go to the house of God. Go near to listen rather than to offer the sacrifice of fools, who do not know that they do wrong.

²Do not be quick with your
mouth,
do not be hasty in your
heart
to utter anything before
God.
God is in heaven
and you are on earth,
so let your words be few.
³A dream comes when there are
many cares,
and many words mark the
speech of a fool.

⁴When you make a vow to God, do not delay to fulfill it. He has no pleasure in fools; fulfill your vow. ⁵It is better not to make a vow than to make one and not fulfill it. ⁶Do not let your mouth lead you into sin. And do not protest to the temple messenger, "My vow was a mistake." Why should God be angry at what you say and destroy the work of your hands? ⁷Much dreaming and many words are meaningless. Therefore fear God.

Riches Are Meaningless

⁸If you see the poor oppressed in a district, and justice and rights denied, do not be surprised at such things; for one official is eyed by a higher one, and over them both are others higher still. ⁹The increase from the land

is taken by all; the king himself profits from the fields.

[10] Whoever loves money never
    has enough;
  whoever loves wealth is
    never satisfied with their
    income.
  This too is meaningless.

[11] As goods increase,
  so do those who consume
    them.
  And what benefit are they to
    the owners
  except to feast their eyes on
    them?

[12] The sleep of a laborer is
    sweet,
  whether they eat little or
    much,
  but as for the rich, their
    abundance
  permits them no sleep.

[13] I have seen a grievous evil
under the sun:

  wealth hoarded to the harm of
    its owners,
[14] or wealth lost through some
    misfortune,
  so that when they have
    children
  there is nothing left for them
    to inherit.
[15] Everyone comes naked from
    their mother's womb,
  and as everyone comes, so
    they depart.
  They take nothing from their
    toil
  that they can carry in their
    hands.

[16] This too is a grievous evil:

  As everyone comes, so they
    depart,
  and what do they gain,
  since they toil for the wind?
[17] All their days they eat in
    darkness,
  with great frustration,
    affliction and anger.

[18] This is what I have observed to be good: that it is appropriate for a person to eat, to drink and to find satisfaction in their toilsome labor under the sun during the few days of life God has given them—for this is their lot. [19] Moreover, when God gives someone wealth and possessions, and the ability to enjoy them, to accept their lot and be happy in their toil—this is a gift of God. [20] They seldom reflect on the days of their life, because God keeps them occupied with gladness of heart.

6 I have seen another evil under the sun, and it weighs heavily on mankind: [2] God gives some people wealth, possessions and honor, so that they lack nothing their hearts desire, but God does not grant them the ability to enjoy them, and strangers enjoy them instead. This is meaningless, a grievous evil.

[3] A man may have a hundred children and live many years; yet no matter how long he lives, if he cannot enjoy his prosperity and does not receive proper burial, I

say that a stillborn child is better off than he. ⁴It comes without meaning, it departs in darkness, and in darkness its name is shrouded. ⁵Though it never saw the sun or knew anything, it has more rest than does that man—⁶even if he lives a thousand years twice over but fails to enjoy his prosperity. Do not all go to the same place?

⁷Everyone's toil is for their
      mouth,
   yet their appetite is never
      satisfied.
⁸What advantage have the wise
      over fools?
   What do the poor gain
      by knowing how to conduct
      themselves before
      others?
⁹Better what the eye sees
      than the roving of the
      appetite.
   This too is meaningless,
      a chasing after the wind.

¹⁰Whatever exists has already
      been named,
   and what humanity is has
      been known;
   no one can contend
      with someone who is
      stronger.
¹¹The more the words,
      the less the meaning,
   and how does that profit
      anyone?

¹²For who knows what is good for a person in life, during the few and meaningless days they pass

through like a shadow? Who can tell them what will happen under the sun after they are gone?

Wisdom

7 A good name is better than
      fine perfume,
   and the day of death better
      than the day of birth.
²It is better to go to a house of
      mourning
   than to go to a house of
      feasting,
   for death is the destiny of
      everyone;
   the living should take this to
      heart.
³Frustration is better than
      laughter,
   because a sad face is good
      for the heart.
⁴The heart of the wise is in the
      house of mourning,
   but the heart of fools is in the
      house of pleasure.
⁵It is better to heed the rebuke
      of a wise person
   than to listen to the song of
      fools.
⁶Like the crackling of thorns
      under the pot,
   so is the laughter of fools.
   This too is meaningless.

⁷Extortion turns a wise person
      into a fool,
   and a bribe corrupts the
      heart.
⁸The end of a matter is better
      than its beginning,
   and patience is better than
      pride.

⁹Do not be quickly provoked in
    your spirit,
      for anger resides in the lap of
        fools.

¹⁰Do not say, "Why were the old
    days better than these?"
    For it is not wise to ask such
      questions.

¹¹Wisdom, like an inheritance,
    is a good thing
  and benefits those who see
    the sun.
¹²Wisdom is a shelter
  as money is a shelter,
but the advantage of
    knowledge is this:
  Wisdom preserves those
    who have it.

¹³Consider what God has done:

Who can straighten
  what he has made crooked?
¹⁴When times are good, be
    happy;
  but when times are bad,
    consider this:
God has made the one
  as well as the other.
Therefore, no one can discover
  anything about their future.

¹⁵In this meaningless life of
mine I have seen both of these:

  the righteous perishing in
    their righteousness,
  and the wicked living long in
    their wickedness.
¹⁶Do not be overrighteous,
  neither be overwise —

why destroy yourself?
¹⁷Do not be overwicked,
  and do not be a fool —
  why die before your time?
¹⁸It is good to grasp the one
  and not let go of the other.
  Whoever fears God will
    avoid all extremes.ᵃ

¹⁹Wisdom makes one wise
    person more powerful
  than ten rulers in a city.

²⁰Indeed, there is no one on
    earth who is righteous,
  no one who does what is
    right and never sins.

²¹Do not pay attention to every
    word people say,
  or you may hear your servant
    cursing you —
²²for you know in your heart
  that many times you yourself
    have cursed others.

²³All this I tested by wisdom
and I said,

"I am determined to be
    wise" —
but this was beyond me.
²⁴Whatever exists is far off and
    most profound —
  who can discover it?
²⁵So I turned my mind to
    understand,
  to investigate and to search
    out wisdom and the
    scheme of things
and to understand the
    stupidity of wickedness
    and the madness of folly.

ᵃ 18 Or *will follow them both*

²⁶I find more bitter than death
the woman who is a snare,
whose heart is a trap
and whose hands are chains.
The man who pleases God will
escape her,
but the sinner she will
ensnare.

²⁷"Look," says the Teacher,[a]
"this is what I have discovered:

"Adding one thing to another
to discover the scheme of
things—
²⁸ while I was still searching
but not finding—
I found one upright man
among a thousand,
but not one upright woman
among them all.
²⁹This only have I found:
God created mankind
upright,
but they have gone in search
of many schemes."

8 Who is like the wise?
Who knows the explanation
of things?
A person's wisdom brightens
their face
and changes its hard
appearance.

Obey the King

²Obey the king's command, I
say, because you took an oath before God. ³Do not be in a hurry
to leave the king's presence. Do
not stand up for a bad cause, for
he will do whatever he pleases.
⁴Since a king's word is supreme,
who can say to him, "What are
you doing?"

⁵Whoever obeys his command
will come to no harm,
and the wise heart will know
the proper time and
procedure.
⁶For there is a proper time and
procedure for every
matter,
though a person may be
weighed down by
misery.

⁷Since no one knows the
future,
who can tell someone else
what is to come?
⁸As no one has power over the
wind to contain it,
so[b] no one has power over
the time of their death.
As no one is discharged in
time of war,
so wickedness will not
release those who
practice it.

⁹All this I saw, as I applied my
mind to everything done under
the sun. There is a time when a
man lords it over others to his
own[c] hurt. ¹⁰Then too, I saw the
wicked buried—those who used
to come and go from the holy
place and receive praise[d] in the

---

[a] 27 Or *the leader of the assembly*   [b] 8 Or *over the human spirit to retain it, / and
so*   [c] 9 Or *to their*   [d] 10 Some Hebrew manuscripts and Septuagint (Aquila);
most Hebrew manuscripts *and are forgotten*

city where they did this. This too is meaningless.

¹¹When the sentence for a crime is not quickly carried out, people's hearts are filled with schemes to do wrong. ¹²Although a wicked person who commits a hundred crimes may live a long time, I know that it will go better with those who fear God, who are reverent before him. ¹³Yet because the wicked do not fear God, it will not go well with them, and their days will not lengthen like a shadow.

¹⁴There is something else meaningless that occurs on earth: the righteous who get what the wicked deserve, and the wicked who get what the righteous deserve. This too, I say, is meaningless. ¹⁵So I commend the enjoyment of life, because there is nothing better for a person under the sun than to eat and drink and be glad. Then joy will accompany them in their toil all the days of the life God has given them under the sun.

¹⁶When I applied my mind to know wisdom and to observe the labor that is done on earth — people getting no sleep day or night — ¹⁷then I saw all that God has done. No one can comprehend what goes on under the sun. Despite all their efforts to search it out, no one can discover its meaning. Even if the wise claim they know, they cannot really comprehend it.

A Common Destiny for All

9 So I reflected on all this and concluded that the righteous and the wise and what they do are in God's hands, but no one knows whether love or hate awaits them. ²All share a common destiny — the righteous and the wicked, the good and the bad,ᵃ the clean and the unclean, those who offer sacrifices and those who do not.

> As it is with the good,
>   so with the sinful;
> as it is with those who take
>   oaths,
>   so with those who are afraid
>   to take them.

³This is the evil in everything that happens under the sun: The same destiny overtakes all. The hearts of people, moreover, are full of evil and there is madness in their hearts while they live, and afterward they join the dead. ⁴Anyone who is among the living has hopeᵇ — even a live dog is better off than a dead lion!

> ⁵For the living know that they
>   will die,
>   but the dead know nothing;
> they have no further
>   reward,
>   and even their name is
>   forgotten.

ᵃ 2 Septuagint (Aquila), Vulgate and Syriac; Hebrew does not have *and the bad*.
ᵇ 4 Or *What then is to be chosen? With all who live, there is hope*

[6]Their love, their hate
and their jealousy have long
since vanished;
never again will they have a
part
in anything that happens
under the sun.

[7]Go, eat your food with gladness, and drink your wine with a joyful heart, for God has already approved what you do. [8]Always be clothed in white, and always anoint your head with oil. [9]Enjoy life with your wife, whom you love, all the days of this meaningless life that God has given you under the sun—all your meaningless days. For this is your lot in life and in your toilsome labor under the sun. [10]Whatever your hand finds to do, do it with all your might, for in the realm of the dead, where you are going, there is neither working nor planning nor knowledge nor wisdom.

[11]I have seen something else under the sun:

The race is not to the swift
or the battle to the strong,
nor does food come to the wise
or wealth to the brilliant
or favor to the learned;
but time and chance happen
to them all.

[12]Moreover, no one knows when their hour will come:

As fish are caught in a cruel
net,
or birds are taken in a snare,
so people are trapped by evil
times
that fall unexpectedly upon
them.

Wisdom Better Than Folly

[13]I also saw under the sun this example of wisdom that greatly impressed me: [14]There was once a small city with only a few people in it. And a powerful king came against it, surrounded it and built huge siege works against it. [15]Now there lived in that city a man poor but wise, and he saved the city by his wisdom. But nobody remembered that poor man. [16]So I said, "Wisdom is better than strength." But the poor man's wisdom is despised, and his words are no longer heeded.

[17]The quiet words of the wise are
more to be heeded
than the shouts of a ruler of
fools.
[18]Wisdom is better than
weapons of war,
but one sinner destroys
much good.

10 As dead flies give
perfume a bad smell,
so a little folly outweighs
wisdom and honor.
[2]The heart of the wise inclines
to the right,
but the heart of the fool to
the left.
[3]Even as fools walk along the
road,
they lack sense

and show everyone how
 stupid they are.
⁴If a ruler's anger rises against
 you,
 do not leave your post;
 calmness can lay great
  offenses to rest.

⁵There is an evil I have seen
 under the sun,
 the sort of error that arises
  from a ruler:
⁶Fools are put in many high
 positions,
 while the rich occupy the
  low ones.
⁷I have seen slaves on
 horseback,
 while princes go on foot like
  slaves.

⁸Whoever digs a pit may fall
 into it;
 whoever breaks through a
  wall may be bitten by a
  snake.
⁹Whoever quarries stones may
 be injured by them;
 whoever splits logs may be
  endangered by them.

¹⁰If the ax is dull
 and its edge unsharpened,
 more strength is needed,
 but skill will bring success.

¹¹If a snake bites before it is
 charmed,
 the charmer receives no fee.

¹²Words from the mouth of the
 wise are gracious,

but fools are consumed by
 their own lips.
¹³At the beginning their words
 are folly;
 at the end they are wicked
  madness—
¹⁴ and fools multiply words.

No one knows what is
 coming—
 who can tell someone else
  what will happen after
  them?

¹⁵The toil of fools wearies them;
 they do not know the way to
  town.

¹⁶Woe to the land whose king
 was a servant*ᵃ*
 and whose princes feast in
  the morning.
¹⁷Blessed is the land whose king
 is of noble birth
 and whose princes eat at a
  proper time—
 for strength and not for
  drunkenness.

¹⁸Through laziness, the rafters
 sag;
 because of idle hands, the
  house leaks.

¹⁹A feast is made for laughter,
 wine makes life merry,
 and money is the answer for
  everything.

²⁰Do not revile the king even in
 your thoughts,
 or curse the rich in your
  bedroom,

ᵃ 16 Or *king is a child*

because a bird in the sky may
    carry your words,
    and a bird on the wing may
    report what you say.

Invest in Many Ventures

11 Ship your grain across
    the sea;
    after many days you may
    receive a return.
[2] Invest in seven ventures, yes,
    in eight;
    you do not know what
    disaster may come upon
    the land.

[3] If clouds are full of water,
    they pour rain on the earth.
    Whether a tree falls to the
    south or to the north,
    in the place where it falls,
    there it will lie.
[4] Whoever watches the wind
    will not plant;
    whoever looks at the clouds
    will not reap.

[5] As you do not know the path of
    the wind,
    or how the body is formed[a]
    in a mother's womb,
    so you cannot understand the
    work of God,
    the Maker of all things.

[6] Sow your seed in the morning,
    and at evening let your
    hands not be idle,
    for you do not know which will
    succeed,
    whether this or that,

or whether both will do
    equally well.

Remember Your Creator While Young

[7] Light is sweet,
    and it pleases the eyes to see
    the sun.
[8] However many years anyone
    may live,
    let them enjoy them all.
    But let them remember the
    days of darkness,
    for there will be many.
    Everything to come is
    meaningless.

[9] You who are young, be happy
    while you are young,
    and let your heart give you
    joy in the days of your
    youth.
    Follow the ways of your heart
    and whatever your eyes see,
    but know that for all these
    things
    God will bring you into
    judgment.
[10] So then, banish anxiety from
    your heart
    and cast off the troubles of
    your body,
    for youth and vigor are
    meaningless.

12 Remember your Creator
    in the days of your youth,
    before the days of trouble
    come
    and the years approach
    when you will say,

---

[a] 5 Or *know how life* (or *the spirit*) / *enters the body being formed*

"I find no pleasure in
them" —
² before the sun and the light
and the moon and the stars
grow dark,
and the clouds return after
the rain;
³ when the keepers of the house
tremble,
and the strong men stoop,
when the grinders cease
because they are few,
and those looking through
the windows grow dim;
⁴ when the doors to the street
are closed
and the sound of grinding
fades;
when people rise up at the
sound of birds,
but all their songs grow faint;
⁵ when people are afraid of
heights
and of dangers in the streets;
when the almond tree blossoms
and the grasshopper drags
itself along
and desire no longer is stirred.
Then people go to their eternal
home
and mourners go about the
streets.

⁶ Remember him — before the
silver cord is severed,
and the golden bowl is
broken;
before the pitcher is shattered
at the spring,
and the wheel broken at the
well,

⁷ and the dust returns to the
ground it came from,
and the spirit returns to God
who gave it.

⁸ "Meaningless! Meaningless!"
says the Teacher.ᵃ
"Everything is meaningless!"

The Conclusion of the Matter

⁹ Not only was the Teacher wise,
but he also imparted knowledge
to the people. He pondered and
searched out and set in order
many proverbs. ¹⁰ The Teacher searched to find just the right
words, and what he wrote was
upright and true.

¹¹ The words of the wise are like
goads, their collected sayings like
firmly embedded nails — given
by one shepherd.ᵇ ¹² Be warned,
my son, of anything in addition
to them.

Of making many books there is
no end, and much study wearies
the body.

¹³ Now all has been heard;
here is the conclusion of the
matter:
Fear God and keep his
commandments,
for this is the duty of all
mankind.
¹⁴ For God will bring every deed
into judgment,
including every hidden
thing,
whether it is good or
evil.

ᵃ 8 Or *the leader of the assembly*; also in verses 9 and 10   ᵇ 11 Or *Shepherd*

Song of Songs

Introduction:

Although some scholars view Song of Songs as being a picture of Christ's love for his people, the more accepted view of Song of Songs is that it is a collection of love poems between a man and a woman. It is a beautiful picture of ideal human love and marriage.

Outline of contents:

The bride and the bridegroom (1:1–2:7)
The praise of her beloved (2:8–3:5)
In praise of the bride (3:6–5:1)
A troubled love (5:2–7:9)
The unbroken communion (7:10–8:14)

1

Solomon's Song of Songs.

She[a]

² Let him kiss me with the kisses
 of his mouth —
 for your love is more
 delightful than
 wine.
³ Pleasing is the fragrance of
 your perfumes;
 your name is like perfume
 poured out.
 No wonder the young
 women love you!
⁴ Take me away with you — let
 us hurry!
 Let the king bring me into
 his chambers.

Friends

We rejoice and delight in
 you[b];
 we will praise your love
 more than wine.

She

How right they are to adore
 you!

⁵ Dark am I, yet lovely,
 daughters of Jerusalem,
 dark like the tents of Kedar,
 like the tent curtains of
 Solomon.[c]
⁶ Do not stare at me because I
 am dark,
 because I am darkened by
 the sun.

---

[a] The main male and female speakers (identified primarily on the basis of the gender of the relevant Hebrew forms) are indicated by the captions *He* and *She* respectively. The words of others are marked *Friends*. In some instances the divisions and their captions are debatable.   [b] 4 The Hebrew is masculine singular.   [c] 5 Or *Salma*

My mother's sons were angry
with me
and made me take care of
the vineyards;
my own vineyard I had to
neglect.
⁷Tell me, you whom I love,
where you graze your flock
and where you rest your
sheep at midday.
Why should I be like a veiled
woman
beside the flocks of your
friends?

Friends

⁸If you do not know, most
beautiful of women,
follow the tracks of the sheep
and graze your young goats
by the tents of the
shepherds.

He

⁹I liken you, my darling, to a
mare
among Pharaoh's chariot
horses.
¹⁰Your cheeks are beautiful with
earrings,
your neck with strings of
jewels.
¹¹We will make you earrings of
gold,
studded with silver.

She

¹²While the king was at his table,
my perfume spread its
fragrance.

¹³My beloved is to me a sachet of
myrrh
resting between my
breasts.
¹⁴My beloved is to me a cluster
of henna blossoms
from the vineyards of En
Gedi.

He

¹⁵How beautiful you are, my
darling!
Oh, how beautiful!
Your eyes are doves.

She

¹⁶How handsome you are, my
beloved!
Oh, how charming!
And our bed is verdant.

He

¹⁷The beams of our house are
cedars;
our rafters are firs.

*She*ᵃ

2 I am a roseᵇ of Sharon,
a lily of the valleys.

He

²Like a lily among thorns
is my darling among the
young women.

She

³Like an appleᶜ tree among the
trees of the forest
is my beloved among the
young men.

ᵃ Or *He*   ᵇ *1* Probably a member of the crocus family   ᶜ *3* Or possibly *apricot*;
here and elsewhere in Song of Songs

I delight to sit in his shade,
and his fruit is sweet to my
taste.
⁴Let him lead me to the
banquet hall,
and let his banner over me
be love.
⁵Strengthen me with raisins,
refresh me with apples,
for I am faint with love.
⁶His left arm is under my
head,
and his right arm
embraces me.
⁷Daughters of Jerusalem, I
charge you
by the gazelles and by the
does of the field:
Do not arouse or awaken love
until it so desires.

⁸Listen! My beloved!
Look! Here he comes,
leaping across the mountains,
bounding over the hills.
⁹My beloved is like a gazelle or
a young stag.
Look! There he stands
behind our wall,
gazing through the windows,
peering through the lattice.
¹⁰My beloved spoke and said
to me,
"Arise, my darling,
my beautiful one, come
with me.
¹¹See! The winter is past;
the rains are over and gone.
¹²Flowers appear on the earth;
the season of singing has
come,

the cooing of doves
is heard in our land.
¹³The fig tree forms its early
fruit;
the blossoming vines spread
their fragrance.
Arise, come, my darling;
my beautiful one, come
with me."

He
¹⁴My dove in the clefts of the
rock,
in the hiding places on the
mountainside,
show me your face,
let me hear your voice;
for your voice is sweet,
and your face is lovely.
¹⁵Catch for us the foxes,
the little foxes
that ruin the vineyards,
our vineyards that are in
bloom.

She
¹⁶My beloved is mine and I am
his;
he browses among the lilies.
¹⁷Until the day breaks
and the shadows flee,
turn, my beloved,
and be like a gazelle
or like a young stag
on the rugged hills.*ᵃ*

3 All night long on my bed
I looked for the one my
heart loves;
I looked for him but did not
find him.

ᵃ 17 Or the hills of Bether

² I will get up now and go about
the city,
through its streets and
squares;
I will search for the one my
heart loves.
So I looked for him but did
not find him.
³ The watchmen found me
as they made their rounds in
the city.
"Have you seen the one my
heart loves?"
⁴ Scarcely had I passed them
when I found the one my
heart loves.
I held him and would not let
him go
till I had brought him to my
mother's house,
to the room of the one who
conceived me.
⁵ Daughters of Jerusalem, I
charge you
by the gazelles and by the
does of the field:
Do not arouse or awaken
love
until it so desires.

⁶ Who is this coming up from
the wilderness
like a column of smoke,
perfumed with myrrh and
incense
made from all the spices of
the merchant?
⁷ Look! It is Solomon's carriage,
escorted by sixty warriors,
the noblest of Israel,

⁸ all of them wearing the sword,
all experienced in battle,
each with his sword at his side,
prepared for the terrors of
the night.
⁹ King Solomon made for
himself the carriage;
he made it of wood from
Lebanon.
¹⁰ Its posts he made of silver,
its base of gold.
Its seat was upholstered with
purple,
its interior inlaid with love.
Daughters of Jerusalem,
¹¹ come out,
and look, you daughters of
Zion.
Look*a* on King Solomon
wearing a crown,
the crown with which his
mother crowned him
on the day of his wedding,
the day his heart rejoiced.

He

4 How beautiful you are, my
darling!
Oh, how beautiful!
Your eyes behind your veil
are doves.
Your hair is like a flock of goats
descending from the hills of
Gilead.
² Your teeth are like a flock of
sheep just shorn,
coming up from the
washing.
Each has its twin;
not one of them is alone.

---

a 10,11 Or *interior lovingly inlaid / by the daughters of Jerusalem. / ¹¹Come out, you
daughters of Zion, / and look*

³Your lips are like a scarlet
    ribbon;
  your mouth is lovely.
Your temples behind your veil
    are like the halves of a
      pomegranate.
⁴Your neck is like the tower of
    David,
  built with courses of stone^a;
on it hang a thousand
    shields,
  all of them shields of
    warriors.
⁵Your breasts are like two
    fawns,
  like twin fawns of a gazelle
  that browse among the lilies.
⁶Until the day breaks
  and the shadows flee,
I will go to the mountain of
    myrrh
  and to the hill of incense.
⁷You are altogether beautiful,
    my darling;
  there is no flaw in you.

⁸Come with me from Lebanon,
    my bride,
  come with me from
    Lebanon.
Descend from the crest of
    Amana,
  from the top of Senir, the
    summit of Hermon,
from the lions' dens
  and the mountain haunts of
    leopards.
⁹You have stolen my heart, my
    sister, my bride;
  you have stolen my heart

with one glance of your eyes,
  with one jewel of your
    necklace.
¹⁰How delightful is your love, my
    sister, my bride!
  How much more pleasing is
    your love than
    wine,
and the fragrance of your
    perfume
  more than any spice!
¹¹Your lips drop sweetness as
    the honeycomb, my
    bride;
  milk and honey are under
    your tongue.
The fragrance of your
    garments
  is like the fragrance of
    Lebanon.
¹²You are a garden locked up, my
    sister, my bride;
  you are a spring enclosed, a
    sealed fountain.
¹³Your plants are an orchard of
    pomegranates
  with choice fruits,
  with henna and nard,
¹⁴ nard and saffron,
  calamus and cinnamon,
  with every kind of incense
    tree,
  with myrrh and aloes
  and all the finest
    spices.
¹⁵You are^b a garden fountain,
  a well of flowing water
  streaming down from
    Lebanon.

She

16 Awake, north wind,
  and come, south wind!
Blow on my garden,
  that its fragrance may spread
    everywhere.
Let my beloved come into his
    garden
  and taste its choice fruits.

He

5 I have come into my garden,
  my sister, my bride;
I have gathered my myrrh
  with my spice.
I have eaten my honeycomb
  and my honey;
I have drunk my wine and
  my milk.

Friends

Eat, friends, and drink;
  drink your fill of love.

She

2 I slept but my heart was
    awake.
  Listen! My beloved is
    knocking:
"Open to me, my sister, my
    darling,
  my dove, my flawless one.
My head is drenched with
    dew,
  my hair with the dampness
    of the night."
3 I have taken off my robe —
  must I put it on again?
I have washed my feet —
  must I soil them again?

4 My beloved thrust his hand
    through the latch-
    opening;
  my heart began to pound for
    him.
5 I arose to open for my beloved,
  and my hands dripped with
    myrrh,
my fingers with flowing
    myrrh,
  on the handles of the bolt.
6 I opened for my beloved,
  but my beloved had left; he
    was gone.
  My heart sank at his
    departure.*a*
I looked for him but did not
    find him.
  I called him but he did not
    answer.
7 The watchmen found me
  as they made their rounds in
    the city.
  They beat me, they
    bruised me;
  they took away my cloak,
    those watchmen of the walls!
8 Daughters of Jerusalem, I
    charge you —
  if you find my beloved,
what will you tell him?
  Tell him I am faint with love.

Friends

9 How is your beloved better
    than others,
  most beautiful of women?
How is your beloved better
    than others,
  that you so charge us?

a 6 Or *heart had gone out to him when he spoke*

She

10 My beloved is radiant and
        ruddy,
    outstanding among ten
        thousand.
11 His head is purest gold;
    his hair is wavy
        and black as a raven.
12 His eyes are like doves
        by the water streams,
    washed in milk,
        mounted like jewels.
13 His cheeks are like beds of
        spice
    yielding perfume.
    His lips are like lilies
        dripping with myrrh.
14 His arms are rods of gold
        set with topaz.
    His body is like polished
        ivory
        decorated with lapis lazuli.
15 His legs are pillars of marble
        set on bases of pure gold.
    His appearance is like
        Lebanon,
        choice as its cedars.
16 His mouth is sweetness itself;
    he is altogether lovely.
    This is my beloved, this is my
        friend,
    daughters of Jerusalem.

Friends

6 Where has your beloved
        gone,
    most beautiful of women?
    Which way did your beloved
        turn,
    that we may look for him
        with you?

She

2 My beloved has gone down to
        his garden,
    to the beds of spices,
    to browse in the gardens
        and to gather lilies.
3 I am my beloved's and my
        beloved is mine;
    he browses among the lilies.

He

4 You are as beautiful as Tirzah,
        my darling,
    as lovely as Jerusalem,
        as majestic as troops with
        banners.
5 Turn your eyes from me;
    they overwhelm me.
    Your hair is like a flock of goats
        descending from Gilead.
6 Your teeth are like a flock of
        sheep
    coming up from the
        washing.
    Each has its twin,
        not one of them is missing.
7 Your temples behind your veil
    are like the halves of a
        pomegranate.
8 Sixty queens there may be,
    and eighty concubines,
    and virgins beyond number;
9 but my dove, my perfect one, is
        unique,
    the only daughter of her
        mother,
    the favorite of the one who
        bore her.
    The young women saw her and
        called her blessed;
    the queens and concubines
        praised her.

Friends

¹⁰Who is this that appears like
   the dawn,
      fair as the moon, bright as
         the sun,
      majestic as the stars in
         procession?

He

¹¹I went down to the grove of nut
   trees
      to look at the new growth in
         the valley,
   to see if the vines had budded
      or the pomegranates were in
         bloom.
¹²Before I realized it,
      my desire set me among
         the royal chariots of my
            people.ᵃ

Friends

¹³Come back, come back,
   O Shulammite;
      come back, come back, that
         we may gaze on you!

He

   Why would you gaze on the
      Shulammite
   as on the dance of
      Mahanaim?ᵇ

7ᶜ How beautiful your
      sandaled feet,
   O prince's daughter!
   Your graceful legs are like
      jewels,
      the work of an artist's hands.

²Your navel is a rounded goblet
   that never lacks blended
      wine.
   Your waist is a mound of wheat
      encircled by lilies.
³Your breasts are like two
      fawns,
      like twin fawns of a gazelle.
⁴Your neck is like an ivory
      tower.
   Your eyes are the pools of
      Heshbon
      by the gate of Bath Rabbim.
   Your nose is like the tower of
      Lebanon
      looking toward Damascus.
⁵Your head crowns you like
      Mount Carmel.
   Your hair is like royal
      tapestry;
      the king is held captive by its
         tresses.
⁶How beautiful you are and
      how pleasing,
      my love, with your delights!
⁷Your stature is like that of the
      palm,
      and your breasts like clusters
         of fruit.
⁸I said, "I will climb the palm
      tree;
      I will take hold of its fruit."
   May your breasts be like
      clusters of grapes on the
         vine,
      the fragrance of your breath
         like apples,
⁹ and your mouth like the best
      wine.

ᵃ 12 Or *among the chariots of Amminadab*; or *among the chariots of the people
of the prince*   ᵇ 13 In Hebrew texts this verse (6:13) is numbered 7:1.   ᶜ In
Hebrew texts 7:1-13 is numbered 7:2-14.

She

May the wine go straight to my
   beloved,
      flowing gently over lips and
      teeth.[a]
¹⁰ I belong to my beloved,
   and his desire is for me.
¹¹ Come, my beloved, let us go to
   the countryside,
      let us spend the night in the
      villages.[b]
¹² Let us go early to the vineyards
   to see if the vines have
   budded,
      if their blossoms have opened,
      and if the pomegranates are
      in bloom —
   there I will give you my
   love.
¹³ The mandrakes send out their
   fragrance,
      and at our door is every
      delicacy,
   both new and old,
      that I have stored up for you,
      my beloved.

8 If only you were to me like a
   brother,
      who was nursed at my
      mother's breasts!
   Then, if I found you outside,
      I would kiss you,
      and no one would
      despise me.
² I would lead you
      and bring you to my
      mother's house —
      she who has taught me.
I would give you spiced wine
   to drink,
      the nectar of my
      pomegranates.
³ His left arm is under my head
   and his right arm
      embraces me.
⁴ Daughters of Jerusalem, I
   charge you:
   Do not arouse or awaken love
   until it so desires.

Friends

⁵ Who is this coming up from
   the wilderness
      leaning on her beloved?

She

Under the apple tree I roused
   you;
      there your mother conceived
      you,
      there she who was in labor
      gave you birth.
⁶ Place me like a seal over your
   heart,
      like a seal on your arm;
   for love is as strong as death,
      its jealousy[c] unyielding as
      the grave.
   It burns like blazing fire,
      like a mighty flame.[d]
⁷ Many waters cannot quench
   love;
      rivers cannot sweep it away.
   If one were to give
      all the wealth of one's house
      for love,
      it[e] would be utterly scorned.

---

[a] 9 Septuagint, Aquila, Vulgate and Syriac; Hebrew *lips of sleepers*   [b] 11 Or *the henna bushes*   [c] 6 Or *ardor*   [d] 6 Or *fire, / like the very flame of the* Lord   [e] 7 Or *he*

Friends

⁸We have a little sister,
  and her breasts are not yet
    grown.
  What shall we do for our sister
    on the day she is spoken for?
⁹If she is a wall,
  we will build towers of silver
    on her.
  If she is a door,
  we will enclose her with
    panels of cedar.

She

¹⁰I am a wall,
  and my breasts are like
    towers.
  Thus I have become in his eyes
    like one bringing
      contentment.
¹¹Solomon had a vineyard in
    Baal Hamon;
  he let out his vineyard to
    tenants.
  Each was to bring for its fruit
    a thousand shekels*ᵃ* of silver.
¹²But my own vineyard is mine
    to give;
  the thousand shekels are for
    you, Solomon,
  and two hundred*ᵇ* are for
    those who tend its fruit.

He

¹³You who dwell in the gardens
  with friends in attendance,
  let me hear your voice!

She

¹⁴Come away, my beloved,
  and be like a gazelle
  or like a young stag
    on the spice-laden
      mountains.

ᵃ 11 That is, about 25 pounds or about 12 kilograms; also in verse 12   *ᵇ 12* That
is, about 5 pounds or about 2.3 kilograms

Isaiah

Introduction:

Isaiah prophesied in Judah during the reigns of Kings Uzziah, Jotham, Ahaz and Hezekiah. According to tradition Isaiah was martyred under Manasseh, the wicked son of Hezekiah, about 680 BC.

Isaiah repeatedly warned the people that Jerusalem and Judah would be judged because of their wickedness. In chapter 39 he predicted the Babylonian exile. But he also held to the hope that the kingdom would be restored again.

Beginning in chapter 40 Isaiah offered comfort with these promises from God: (1) Babylonian exiles would be allowed to return to Jerusalem; (2) a righteous, suffering servant would bring salvation; (3) God would set up a new, righteous kingdom.

Outline of contents:

Judgment and hope of restoration (1:1–6:13)
Hope in Assyria or hope in God (7:1–12:6)
Prophecies about nations (13:1–23:18)
Israel's judgment and deliverance (24:1–27:13)
Warnings and Zion restored (28:1–35:10)
King Hezekiah withstands Assyria (36:1–39:8)
Promises of divine deliverance (40:1–56:8)
The final kingdom established (56:9–66:24)

1 The vision concerning Judah and Jerusalem that Isaiah son of Amoz saw during the reigns of Uzziah, Jotham, Ahaz and Hezekiah, kings of Judah.

A Rebellious Nation

² Hear me, you heavens! Listen, earth!
  For the LORD has spoken:
"I reared children and brought them up,
  but they have rebelled against me.
³ The ox knows its master,
  the donkey its owner's manger,
but Israel does not know,
  my people do not understand."

⁴ Woe to the sinful nation,

a people whose guilt is great,
a brood of evildoers,
children given to corruption!
They have forsaken the LORD;
they have spurned the Holy
One of Israel
and turned their backs on
him.

⁵Why should you be beaten
anymore?
Why do you persist in
rebellion?
Your whole head is injured,
your whole heart afflicted.
⁶From the sole of your foot to
the top of your head
there is no soundness—
only wounds and welts
and open sores,
not cleansed or bandaged
or soothed with olive oil.

⁷Your country is desolate,
your cities burned with fire;
your fields are being stripped
by foreigners
right before you,
laid waste as when
overthrown by strangers.
⁸Daughter Zion is left
like a shelter in a vineyard,
like a hut in a cucumber field,
like a city under siege.
⁹Unless the LORD Almighty
had left us some survivors,
we would have become like
Sodom,
we would have been like
Gomorrah.

¹⁰Hear the word of the LORD,
you rulers of Sodom;

listen to the instruction of our
God,
you people of Gomorrah!
¹¹"The multitude of your
sacrifices—
what are they to me?" says
the LORD.
"I have more than enough of
burnt offerings,
of rams and the fat of
fattened animals;
I have no pleasure
in the blood of bulls and
lambs and goats.
¹²When you come to appear
before me,
who has asked this of you,
this trampling of my
courts?
¹³Stop bringing meaningless
offerings!
Your incense is detestable
to me.
New Moons, Sabbaths and
convocations—
I cannot bear your worthless
assemblies.
¹⁴Your New Moon feasts and
your appointed
festivals
I hate with all my being.
They have become a burden
to me;
I am weary of bearing them.
¹⁵When you spread out your
hands in prayer,
I hide my eyes from you;
even when you offer many
prayers,
I am not listening.

Your hands are full of blood!

¹⁶Wash and make yourselves
    clean.
  Take your evil deeds out of
    my sight;
  stop doing wrong.
¹⁷Learn to do right; seek
    justice.
  Defend the oppressed.ᵃ
  Take up the cause of the
    fatherless;
  plead the case of the widow.

¹⁸"Come now, let us settle the
    matter,"
  says the LORD.
  "Though your sins are like
    scarlet,
    they shall be as white as
      snow;
  though they are red as
    crimson,
    they shall be like wool.
¹⁹If you are willing and
    obedient,
  you will eat the good things
    of the land;
²⁰but if you resist and rebel,
  you will be devoured by the
    sword."
      For the mouth of the
        LORD has spoken.

²¹See how the faithful city
  has become a prostitute!
  She once was full of justice;
  righteousness used to dwell
    in her —
  but now murderers!
²²Your silver has become dross,
  your choice wine is diluted
    with water.

²³Your rulers are rebels,
  partners with thieves;
  they all love bribes
  and chase after gifts.
  They do not defend the cause
    of the fatherless;
  the widow's case does
    not come before
    them.
²⁴Therefore the Lord, the LORD
    Almighty,
  the Mighty One of Israel,
    declares:
  "Ah! I will vent my wrath on
    my foes
  and avenge myself on my
    enemies.
²⁵I will turn my hand against
    you;ᵇ
  I will thoroughly purge away
    your dross
  and remove all your
    impurities.
²⁶I will restore your leaders as in
    days of old,
  your rulers as at the
    beginning.
  Afterward you will be
    called
  the City of Righteousness,
  the Faithful City."

²⁷Zion will be delivered with
    justice,
  her penitent ones with
    righteousness.
²⁸But rebels and sinners will
    both be broken,
  and those who forsake the
    LORD will perish.

ᵃ 17 Or justice. / Correct the oppressor   ᵇ 25 That is, against Jerusalem

²⁹ "You will be ashamed because
of the sacred oaks
in which you have delighted;
you will be disgraced because
of the gardens
that you have chosen.
³⁰ You will be like an oak with
fading leaves,
like a garden without water.
³¹ The mighty man will become
tinder
and his work a spark;
both will burn together,
with no one to quench the
fire."

The Mountain of the LORD

2 This is what Isaiah son of
Amoz saw concerning Judah
and Jerusalem:

²In the last days

the mountain of the
LORD's temple will be
established
as the highest of the
mountains;
it will be exalted above the
hills,
and all nations will stream
to it.

³Many peoples will come and
say,

"Come, let us go up to the
mountain of the LORD,
to the temple of the God of
Jacob.
He will teach us his ways,
so that we may walk in his
paths."

The law will go out from Zion,
the word of the LORD from
Jerusalem.
⁴He will judge between the
nations
and will settle disputes for
many peoples.
They will beat their swords
into plowshares
and their spears into
pruning hooks.
Nation will not take up sword
against nation,
nor will they train for war
anymore.

⁵Come, descendants of Jacob,
let us walk in the light of the
LORD.

The Day of the LORD

⁶You, LORD, have abandoned
your people,
the descendants of Jacob.
They are full of superstitions
from the East;
they practice divination like
the Philistines
and embrace pagan
customs.
⁷Their land is full of silver and
gold;
there is no end to their
treasures.
Their land is full of horses;
there is no end to their
chariots.
⁸Their land is full of idols;
they bow down to the work
of their hands,
to what their fingers have
made.

⁹So people will be brought low
and everyone humbled —
do not forgive them.ᵃ

¹⁰Go into the rocks, hide in the
ground
from the fearful presence of
the Lord
and the splendor of his
majesty!
¹¹The eyes of the arrogant will
be humbled
and human pride brought
low;
the Lord alone will be exalted
in that day.

¹²The Lord Almighty has a day
in store
for all the proud and lofty,
for all that is exalted
(and they will be humbled),
¹³for all the cedars of Lebanon,
tall and lofty,
and all the oaks of Bashan,
¹⁴for all the towering mountains
and all the high hills,
¹⁵for every lofty tower
and every fortified wall,
¹⁶for every trading shipᵇ
and every stately vessel.
¹⁷The arrogance of man will be
brought low
and human pride humbled;
the Lord alone will be exalted
in that day,
¹⁸ and the idols will totally
disappear.

¹⁹People will flee to caves in the
rocks
and to holes in the ground

from the fearful presence of
the Lord
and the splendor of his
majesty,
when he rises to shake the
earth.
²⁰In that day people will throw
away
to the moles and bats
their idols of silver and idols of
gold,
which they made to
worship.
²¹They will flee to caverns in the
rocks
and to the overhanging
crags
from the fearful presence of
the Lord
and the splendor of his
majesty,
when he rises to shake the
earth.
²²Stop trusting in mere humans,
who have but a breath in
their nostrils.
Why hold them in esteem?

Judgment on Jerusalem and Judah

3 See now, the Lord,
the Lord Almighty,
is about to take from Jerusalem
and Judah
both supply and support:
all supplies of food and all
supplies of water,
² the hero and the warrior,
the judge and the prophet,
the diviner and the elder,

ᵃ 9 Or *not raise them up*   ᵇ 16 Hebrew *every ship of Tarshish*

³the captain of fifty and the
    man of rank,
  the counselor, skilled
    craftsman and clever
    enchanter.

⁴"I will make mere youths their
    officials;
  children will rule over
    them."

⁵People will oppress each
    other—
  man against man, neighbor
    against neighbor.
  The young will rise up against
    the old,
    the nobody against the
    honored.

⁶A man will seize one of his
    brothers
  in his father's house, and
    say,
  "You have a cloak, you be our
    leader;
  take charge of this heap of
    ruins!"

⁷But in that day he will cry
    out,
  "I have no remedy.
  I have no food or clothing in
    my house;
  do not make me the leader of
    the people."

⁸Jerusalem staggers,
    Judah is falling;
  their words and deeds are
    against the LORD,
  defying his glorious
    presence.

⁹The look on their faces testifies
    against them;

they parade their sin like
    Sodom;
  they do not hide it.
Woe to them!
  They have brought disaster
    upon themselves.

¹⁰Tell the righteous it will be
    well with them,
  for they will enjoy the fruit of
    their deeds.

¹¹Woe to the wicked!
  Disaster is upon them!
  They will be paid back
  for what their hands have
    done.

¹²Youths oppress my people,
  women rule over them.
  My people, your guides lead
    you astray;
  they turn you from the path.

¹³The LORD takes his place in
    court;
  he rises to judge the people.

¹⁴The LORD enters into
    judgment
  against the elders and
    leaders of his people:
  "It is you who have ruined my
    vineyard;
  the plunder from the poor is
    in your houses.

¹⁵What do you mean by
    crushing my people
  and grinding the faces of the
    poor?"

            declares the Lord,
            the LORD Almighty.

¹⁶The LORD says,
  "The women of Zion are
    haughty,

walking along with
　　outstretched necks,
　　flirting with their eyes,
strutting along with swaying
　　hips,
　　with ornaments jingling on
　　their ankles.
17 Therefore the Lord will bring
　　sores on the heads of the
　　women of Zion;
　　the LORD will make their
　　scalps bald."

18 In that day the Lord will snatch away their finery: the bangles and headbands and crescent necklaces, 19 the earrings and bracelets and veils, 20 the headdresses and anklets and sashes, the perfume bottles and charms, 21 the signet rings and nose rings, 22 the fine robes and the capes and cloaks, the purses 23 and mirrors, and the linen garments and tiaras and shawls.

24 Instead of fragrance there will
　　be a stench;
　　instead of a sash, a rope;
　instead of well-dressed hair,
　　baldness;
　　instead of fine clothing,
　　sackcloth;
　　instead of beauty, branding.
25 Your men will fall by the
　　sword,
　　your warriors in battle.
26 The gates of Zion will lament
　　and mourn;
　　destitute, she will sit on the
　　ground.

4 ¹ In that day seven women
will take hold of one man
and say, "We will eat our own
　　food
　　and provide our own
　　clothes;
only let us be called by your
　　name.
Take away our disgrace!"

The Branch of the LORD

² In that day the Branch of the LORD will be beautiful and glorious, and the fruit of the land will be the pride and glory of the survivors in Israel. ³ Those who are left in Zion, who remain in Jerusalem, will be called holy, all who are recorded among the living in Jerusalem. ⁴ The Lord will wash away the filth of the women of Zion; he will cleanse the bloodstains from Jerusalem by a spirit[a] of judgment and a spirit[a] of fire. ⁵ Then the LORD will create over all of Mount Zion and over those who assemble there a cloud of smoke by day and a glow of flaming fire by night; over everything the glory[b] will be a canopy. ⁶ It will be a shelter and shade from the heat of the day, and a refuge and hiding place from the storm and rain.

The Song of the Vineyard

5 I will sing for the one I love
a song about his vineyard:
My loved one had a vineyard
on a fertile hillside.

---

[a] 4 Or the Spirit   [b] 5 Or over all the glory there

2 He dug it up and cleared it of
   stones
   and planted it with the
   choicest vines.
He built a watchtower in it
   and cut out a winepress as
   well.
Then he looked for a crop of
   good grapes,
   but it yielded only bad fruit.

3 "Now you dwellers in
   Jerusalem and people of
   Judah,
   judge between me and my
   vineyard.
4 What more could have been
   done for my vineyard
   than I have done for it?
When I looked for good grapes,
   why did it yield only bad?
5 Now I will tell you
   what I am going to do to my
   vineyard:
I will take away its hedge,
   and it will be destroyed;
I will break down its wall,
   and it will be trampled.
6 I will make it a wasteland,
   neither pruned nor
   cultivated,
   and briers and thorns will
   grow there.
I will command the clouds
   not to rain on it."

7 The vineyard of the LORD
   Almighty
   is the nation of Israel,
and the people of Judah
   are the vines he delighted in.
And he looked for justice, but
   saw bloodshed;
   for righteousness, but heard
   cries of distress.

Woes and Judgments

8 Woe to you who add house to
   house
   and join field to field
till no space is left
   and you live alone in the
   land.

9 The LORD Almighty has declared in my hearing:

"Surely the great houses will
   become desolate,
   the fine mansions left
   without occupants.
10 A ten-acre vineyard will
   produce only a bath[a] of
   wine;
   a homer[b] of seed will yield
   only an ephah[c] of grain."

11 Woe to those who rise early in
   the morning
   to run after their drinks,
who stay up late at night
   till they are inflamed with
   wine.
12 They have harps and lyres at
   their banquets,
   pipes and timbrels and wine,
but they have no regard for the
   deeds of the LORD,
   no respect for the work of his
   hands.

---

[a] 10 That is, about 6 gallons or about 22 liters [b] 10 That is, probably about
360 pounds or about 160 kilograms [c] 10 That is, probably about 36 pounds or
about 16 kilograms

¹³Therefore my people will go
     into exile
   for lack of understanding;
   those of high rank will die of
     hunger
     and the common people will
       be parched with thirst.
¹⁴Therefore Death expands its
     jaws,
     opening wide its mouth;
   into it will descend their
     nobles and masses
     with all their brawlers and
       revelers.
¹⁵So people will be brought
     low
     and everyone humbled,
   the eyes of the arrogant
     humbled.
¹⁶But the LORD Almighty will be
     exalted by his justice,
   and the holy God will be
     proved holy by his
     righteous acts.
¹⁷Then sheep will graze as in
     their own pasture;
   lambs will feed[a] among the
     ruins of the rich.

¹⁸Woe to those who draw sin
     along with cords of
     deceit,
   and wickedness as with cart
     ropes,
¹⁹to those who say, "Let God
     hurry;
   let him hasten his work
     so we may see it.
   The plan of the Holy One of
     Israel —

let it approach, let it come
     into view,
   so we may know it."

²⁰Woe to those who call evil
     good
     and good evil,
   who put darkness for light
     and light for darkness,
   who put bitter for sweet
     and sweet for bitter.

²¹Woe to those who are wise in
     their own eyes
     and clever in their own sight.

²²Woe to those who are heroes at
     drinking wine
     and champions at mixing
       drinks,
²³who acquit the guilty for a
     bribe,
   but deny justice to the
     innocent.
²⁴Therefore, as tongues of fire
     lick up straw
   and as dry grass sinks down
     in the flames,
   so their roots will decay
     and their flowers blow away
       like dust;
   for they have rejected the law
     of the LORD Almighty
   and spurned the word of the
     Holy One of Israel.
²⁵Therefore the LORD's anger
     burns against his people;
   his hand is raised and he
     strikes them down.
   The mountains shake,
     and the dead bodies are like
       refuse in the streets.

---

a 17 Septuagint; Hebrew / *strangers will eat*

Yet for all this, his anger is not
 turned away,
 his hand is still upraised.

²⁶He lifts up a banner for the
 distant nations,
 he whistles for those at the
 ends of the earth.
 Here they come,
 swiftly and speedily!
²⁷Not one of them grows tired or
 stumbles,
 not one slumbers or sleeps;
 not a belt is loosened at the
 waist,
 not a sandal strap is broken.
²⁸Their arrows are sharp,
 all their bows are strung;
 their horses' hooves seem like
 flint,
 their chariot wheels like a
 whirlwind.
²⁹Their roar is like that of the
 lion,
 they roar like young lions;
 they growl as they seize their
 prey
 and carry it off with no one
 to rescue.
³⁰In that day they will roar
 over it
 like the roaring of the sea.
 And if one looks at the land,
 there is only darkness and
 distress;
 even the sun will be
 darkened by clouds.

Isaiah's Commission

6 In the year that King Uzziah died, I saw the Lord, high
and exalted, seated on a throne;
and the train of his robe filled the
temple. ²Above him were seraphim, each with six wings: With
two wings they covered their faces, with two they covered their
feet, and with two they were flying. ³And they were calling to
one another:

 "Holy, holy, holy is the LORD
 Almighty;
 the whole earth is full of his
 glory."

⁴At the sound of their voices the
doorposts and thresholds shook
and the temple was filled with
smoke.

⁵"Woe to me!" I cried. "I am ruined! For I am a man of unclean
lips, and I live among a people of unclean lips, and my eyes
have seen the King, the LORD Almighty."

⁶Then one of the seraphim
flew to me with a live coal in his
hand, which he had taken with
tongs from the altar. ⁷With it he
touched my mouth and said,
"See, this has touched your lips;
your guilt is taken away and your
sin atoned for."

⁸Then I heard the voice of the
Lord saying, "Whom shall I send?
And who will go for us?"

And I said, "Here am I. Send
me!"

⁹He said, "Go and tell this people:

 " 'Be ever hearing, but never
 understanding;
 be ever seeing, but never
 perceiving.'

¹⁰Make the heart of this people
  calloused;
  make their ears dull
  and close their eyes.ᵃ
Otherwise they might see with
    their eyes,
  hear with their ears,
  understand with their
    hearts,
and turn and be healed."

¹¹Then I said, "For how long,
Lord?"
And he answered:

"Until the cities lie ruined
  and without inhabitant,
until the houses are left
    deserted
  and the fields ruined and
    ravaged,
¹²until the LORD has sent
    everyone far away
  and the land is utterly
    forsaken.
¹³And though a tenth remains in
    the land,
  it will again be laid waste.
But as the terebinth and oak
  leave stumps when they are
    cut down,
  so the holy seed will be the
    stump in the land."

The Sign of Immanuel

7 When Ahaz son of Jotham,
the son of Uzziah, was king
of Judah, King Rezin of Aram and
Pekah son of Remaliah king of Israel marched up to fight against
Jerusalem, but they could not
overpower it.

²Now the house of David was
told, "Aram has allied itself withᵇ
Ephraim"; so the hearts of Ahaz
and his people were shaken, as
the trees of the forest are shaken
by the wind.

³Then the LORD said to Isaiah, "Go out, you and your son
Shear-Jashub,ᶜ to meet Ahaz at
the end of the aqueduct of the
Upper Pool, on the road to the
Launderer's Field. ⁴Say to him,
'Be careful, keep calm and don't
be afraid. Do not lose heart because of these two smoldering
stubs of firewood—because of
the fierce anger of Rezin and
Aram and of the son of Remaliah.
⁵Aram, Ephraim and Remaliah's
son have plotted your ruin, saying, ⁶"Let us invade Judah; let us
tear it apart and divide it among
ourselves, and make the son of
Tabeel king over it." ⁷Yet this is
what the Sovereign LORD says:

" 'It will not take place,
  it will not happen,
⁸for the head of Aram is
    Damascus,
  and the head of Damascus is
    only Rezin.
Within sixty-five years
  Ephraim will be too
    shattered to be a people.

ᵃ 9,10 Hebrew; Septuagint 'You will be ever hearing, but never understanding; /
you will be ever seeing, but never perceiving.' / ¹⁰This people's heart has become
calloused; / they hardly hear with their ears, / and they have closed their eyes
ᵇ 2 Or has set up camp in   ᶜ 3 Shear-Jashub means a remnant will return.

⁹The head of Ephraim is
  Samaria,
and the head of Samaria is
  only Remaliah's son.
If you do not stand firm in
  your faith,
you will not stand at all.' "

¹⁰Again the LORD spoke to Ahaz, ¹¹"Ask the LORD your God for a sign, whether in the deepest depths or in the highest heights."

¹²But Ahaz said, "I will not ask; I will not put the LORD to the test."

¹³Then Isaiah said, "Hear now, you house of David! Is it not enough to try the patience of humans? Will you try the patience of my God also? ¹⁴Therefore the Lord himself will give you[a] a sign: The virgin[b] will conceive and give birth to a son, and[c] will call him Immanuel.[d] ¹⁵He will be eating curds and honey when he knows enough to reject the wrong and choose the right, ¹⁶for before the boy knows enough to reject the wrong and choose the right, the land of the two kings you dread will be laid waste. ¹⁷The LORD will bring on you and on your people and on the house of your father a time unlike any since Ephraim broke away from Judah—he will bring the king of Assyria."

Assyria, the LORD's Instrument

¹⁸In that day the LORD will whistle for flies from the Nile delta in Egypt and for bees from the land of Assyria. ¹⁹They will all come and settle in the steep ravines and in the crevices in the rocks, on all the thornbushes and at all the water holes. ²⁰In that day the Lord will use a razor hired from beyond the Euphrates River—the king of Assyria—to shave your head and private parts, and to cut off your beard also. ²¹In that day, a person will keep alive a young cow and two goats. ²²And because of the abundance of the milk they give, there will be curds to eat. All who remain in the land will eat curds and honey. ²³In that day, in every place where there were a thousand vines worth a thousand silver shekels,[e] there will be only briers and thorns. ²⁴Hunters will go there with bow and arrow, for the land will be covered with briers and thorns. ²⁵As for all the hills once cultivated by the hoe, you will no longer go there for fear of the briers and thorns; they will become places where cattle are turned loose and where sheep run.

Isaiah and His Children as Signs

8 The LORD said to me, "Take a large scroll and write on it with an ordinary pen: Maher-Shalal-Hash-Baz."[f] ²So I called in Uriah the priest and Zechariah

---

[a] 14 The Hebrew is plural.   [b] 14 Or *young woman*   [c] 14 Masoretic Text; Dead Sea Scrolls *son, and he* or *son, and they*   [d] 14 *Immanuel* means *God with us.*
[e] 23 That is, about 25 pounds or about 12 kilograms   [f] 1 *Maher-Shalal-Hash-Baz* means *quick to the plunder, swift to the spoil*; also in verse 3.

son of Jeberekiah as reliable witnesses for me. **3**Then I made love to the prophetess, and she conceived and gave birth to a son. And the LORD said to me, "Name him Maher-Shalal-Hash-Baz. **4**For before the boy knows how to say 'My father' or 'My mother,' the wealth of Damascus and the plunder of Samaria will be carried off by the king of Assyria."

5The LORD spoke to me again:

6 "Because this people has
 rejected
  the gently flowing waters of
   Shiloah
 and rejoices over Rezin
  and the son of Remaliah,
7therefore the Lord is about to
  bring against them
 the mighty floodwaters of
  the Euphrates —
 the king of Assyria with all
  his pomp.
It will overflow all its
  channels,
 run over all its banks
8and sweep on into Judah,
  swirling over it,
 passing through it and
  reaching up to the neck.
Its outspread wings will cover
  the breadth of your land,
  Immanuel*a*!"

9Raise the war cry,*b* you
  nations, and be
  shattered!
Listen, all you distant lands.
Prepare for battle, and be
  shattered!
Prepare for battle, and be
  shattered!
10Devise your strategy, but it will
  be thwarted;
 propose your plan, but it will
  not stand,
 for God is with us.*c*

11This is what the LORD says to me with his strong hand upon me, warning me not to follow the way of this people:

12"Do not call conspiracy
 everything this people calls
  a conspiracy;
do not fear what they fear,
 and do not dread it.
13The LORD Almighty is the one
  you are to regard as holy,
 he is the one you are to fear,
 he is the one you are to
  dread.
14He will be a holy place;
 for both Israel and Judah he
  will be
a stone that causes people to
  stumble
 and a rock that makes them
  fall.
And for the people of
  Jerusalem he will be
a trap and a snare.
15Many of them will stumble;
 they will fall and be
  broken,
 they will be snared and
  captured."

---

a 8 Immanuel means *God with us.* *b 9* Or *Do your worst* *c 10* Hebrew *Immanuel*

¹⁶ Bind up this testimony of
warning
and seal up God's
instruction among my
disciples.
¹⁷ I will wait for the LORD,
who is hiding his face from
the descendants of Jacob.
I will put my trust in him.

¹⁸ Here am I, and the children
the LORD has given me. We are
signs and symbols in Israel from
the LORD Almighty, who dwells
on Mount Zion.

The Darkness Turns to Light

¹⁹ When someone tells you to
consult mediums and spiritists,
who whisper and mutter, should
not a people inquire of their God?
Why consult the dead on behalf
of the living? ²⁰ Consult God's
instruction and the testimony
of warning. If anyone does not
speak according to this word,
they have no light of dawn. ²¹ Distressed and hungry, they will
roam through the land; when
they are famished, they will become enraged and, looking upward, will curse their king and
their God. ²² Then they will look
toward the earth and see only
distress and darkness and fearful gloom, and they will be thrust
into utter darkness.

9ᵃ Nevertheless, there will be
no more gloom for those
who were in distress. In the past

he humbled the land of Zebulun
and the land of Naphtali, but in
the future he will honor Galilee
of the nations, by the Way of the
Sea, beyond the Jordan —

² The people walking in
darkness
have seen a great light;
on those living in the land of
deep darkness
a light has dawned.
³ You have enlarged the nation
and increased their joy;
they rejoice before you
as people rejoice at the
harvest,
as warriors rejoice
when dividing the plunder.
⁴ For as in the day of Midian's
defeat,
you have shattered
the yoke that burdens them,
the bar across their
shoulders,
the rod of their oppressor.
⁵ Every warrior's boot used in
battle
and every garment rolled in
blood
will be destined for burning,
will be fuel for the fire.
⁶ For to us a child is born,
to us a son is given,
and the government will be
on his shoulders.
And he will be called
Wonderful Counselor,
Mighty God,
Everlasting Father, Prince of
Peace.

ᵃ In Hebrew texts 9:1 is numbered 8:23, and 9:2-21 is numbered 9:1-20.

⁷Of the greatness of his
        government and peace
    there will be no end.
    He will reign on David's throne
        and over his kingdom,
    establishing and upholding it
        with justice and
        righteousness
    from that time on and
        forever.
    The zeal of the LORD Almighty
        will accomplish this.

The LORD's Anger Against Israel

⁸The Lord has sent a message
        against Jacob;
    it will fall on Israel.
⁹All the people will know it—
    Ephraim and the inhabitants
        of Samaria—
    who say with pride
    and arrogance of heart,
¹⁰"The bricks have fallen down,
    but we will rebuild with
        dressed stone;
    the fig trees have been felled,
    but we will replace them
        with cedars."
¹¹But the LORD has strengthened
    Rezin's foes against
        them
    and has spurred their
        enemies on.
¹²Arameans from the east and
    Philistines from the
        west
    have devoured Israel with
        open mouth.

    Yet for all this, his anger is not
        turned away,
    his hand is still upraised.

¹³But the people have not
        returned to him who
        struck them,
    nor have they sought the
        LORD Almighty.
¹⁴So the LORD will cut off from
        Israel both head and
        tail,
    both palm branch and reed
        in a single day;
¹⁵the elders and dignitaries are
        the head,
    the prophets who teach lies
        are the tail.
¹⁶Those who guide this people
        mislead them,
    and those who are guided
        are led astray.
¹⁷Therefore the Lord will take
        no pleasure in the young
        men,
    nor will he pity the fatherless
        and widows,
    for everyone is ungodly and
        wicked,
    every mouth speaks folly.

    Yet for all this, his anger is not
        turned away,
    his hand is still upraised.

¹⁸Surely wickedness burns like a
        fire;
    it consumes briers and
        thorns,
    it sets the forest thickets
        ablaze,
    so that it rolls upward in a
        column of smoke.
¹⁹By the wrath of the LORD
        Almighty
    the land will be scorched

and the people will be fuel for
the fire;
they will not spare one
another.
²⁰ On the right they will devour,
but still be hungry;
on the left they will eat,
but not be satisfied.
Each will feed on the flesh of
their own offspring*:
²¹ Manasseh will feed on
Ephraim, and Ephraim
on Manasseh;
together they will turn
against Judah.

Yet for all this, his anger is not
turned away,
his hand is still upraised.

10 Woe to those who make
unjust laws,
to those who issue
oppressive decrees,
² to deprive the poor of their
rights
and withhold justice from
the oppressed of my
people,
making widows their
prey
and robbing the
fatherless.
³ What will you do on the day of
reckoning,
when disaster comes from
afar?
To whom will you run for
help?
Where will you leave your
riches?

⁴ Nothing will remain but
to cringe among the
captives
or fall among the slain.

Yet for all this, his anger is not
turned away,
his hand is still upraised.

God's Judgment on Assyria

⁵ "Woe to the Assyrian, the rod
of my anger,
in whose hand is the club of
my wrath!
⁶ I send him against a godless
nation,
I dispatch him against a
people who anger me,
to seize loot and snatch
plunder,
and to trample them down
like mud in the streets.
⁷ But this is not what he intends,
this is not what he has in
mind;
his purpose is to destroy,
to put an end to many
nations.
⁸ 'Are not my commanders all
kings?' he says.
⁹ 'Has not Kalno fared like
Carchemish?
Is not Hamath like Arpad,
and Samaria like Damascus?
¹⁰ As my hand seized the
kingdoms of the idols,
kingdoms whose images
excelled those of
Jerusalem and
Samaria —

ª 20 Or *arm*

¹¹ shall I not deal with Jerusalem
and her images
as I dealt with Samaria and
her idols?' "

¹² When the Lord has finished
all his work against Mount Zion
and Jerusalem, he will say, "I will
punish the king of Assyria for the
willful pride of his heart and the
haughty look in his eyes. ¹³ For he
says:

" 'By the strength of my hand I
have done this,
and by my wisdom, because
I have understanding.
I removed the boundaries of
nations,
I plundered their treasures;
like a mighty one I subdued*a*
their kings.
¹⁴ As one reaches into a nest,
so my hand reached for the
wealth of the nations;
as people gather abandoned
eggs,
so I gathered all the
countries;
not one flapped a wing,
or opened its mouth to
chirp.' "

¹⁵ Does the ax raise itself above
the person who swings it,
or the saw boast against the
one who uses it?
As if a rod were to wield the
person who lifts it up,
or a club brandish the one
who is not wood!

¹⁶ Therefore, the Lord, the LORD
Almighty,
will send a wasting disease
upon his sturdy warriors;
under his pomp a fire will be
kindled
like a blazing flame.
¹⁷ The Light of Israel will become
a fire,
their Holy One a flame;
in a single day it will burn and
consume
his thorns and his briers.
¹⁸ The splendor of his forests and
fertile fields
it will completely destroy,
as when a sick person wastes
away.
¹⁹ And the remaining trees of his
forests will be so few
that a child could write them
down.

The Remnant of Israel

²⁰ In that day the remnant of
Israel,
the survivors of Jacob,
will no longer rely on him
who struck them down
but will truly rely on the LORD,
the Holy One of Israel.
²¹ A remnant will return,*b* a
remnant of Jacob
will return to the Mighty
God.
²² Though your people be like
the sand by the sea,
Israel,
only a remnant will return.

---

a 13 Or *treasures; / I subdued the mighty,*
and note); also in verse 22

b 21 Hebrew *shear-jashub* (see 7:3)

Destruction has been decreed,
  overwhelming and
  righteous.
²³The Lord, the LORD Almighty,
  will carry out
  the destruction decreed
  upon the whole land.

²⁴Therefore this is what the
Lord, the LORD Almighty, says:

"My people who live in Zion,
  do not be afraid of the
  Assyrians,
who beat you with a rod
  and lift up a club against
  you, as Egypt did.
²⁵Very soon my anger against
  you will end
  and my wrath will be
  directed to their
  destruction."

²⁶The LORD Almighty will lash
  them with a whip,
  as when he struck down
  Midian at the rock of
  Oreb;
and he will raise his staff over
  the waters,
  as he did in Egypt.
²⁷In that day their burden will
  be lifted from your
  shoulders,
  their yoke from your neck;
the yoke will be broken
  because you have grown so
  fat.ᵃ

²⁸They enter Aiath;
  they pass through Migron;
  they store supplies at
  Mikmash.

²⁹They go over the pass, and say,
  "We will camp overnight at
  Geba."
Ramah trembles;
  Gibeah of Saul flees.
³⁰Cry out, Daughter Gallim!
  Listen, Laishah!
  Poor Anathoth!
³¹Madmenah is in flight;
  the people of Gebim take
  cover.
³²This day they will halt at Nob;
  they will shake their fist
at the mount of Daughter Zion,
  at the hill of Jerusalem.

³³See, the Lord, the LORD
  Almighty,
  will lop off the boughs with
  great power.
The lofty trees will be felled,
  the tall ones will be brought
  low.
³⁴He will cut down the forest
  thickets with an ax;
  Lebanon will fall before the
  Mighty One.

The Branch From Jesse

11 A shoot will come up
   from the stump of Jesse;
from his roots a Branch will
  bear fruit.
²The Spirit of the LORD will rest
  on him —
the Spirit of wisdom and of
  understanding,
the Spirit of counsel and of
  might,
the Spirit of the knowledge
  and fear of the LORD —

ᵃ 27 Hebrew; Septuagint *broken / from your shoulders*

³and he will delight in the fear
of the Lord.

He will not judge by what he
sees with his eyes,
or decide by what he hears
with his ears;
⁴but with righteousness he will
judge the needy,
with justice he will give
decisions for the poor of
the earth.
He will strike the earth with
the rod of his mouth;
with the breath of his lips he
will slay the wicked.
⁵Righteousness will be his
belt
and faithfulness the sash
around his waist.

⁶The wolf will live with the
lamb,
the leopard will lie down
with the goat,
the calf and the lion and the
yearling*a* together;
and a little child will lead
them.
⁷The cow will feed with the
bear,
their young will lie down
together,
and the lion will eat straw
like the ox.
⁸The infant will play near the
cobra's den,
and the young child will put
its hand into the viper's
nest.

⁹They will neither harm nor
destroy
on all my holy mountain,
for the earth will be filled with
the knowledge of the
Lord
as the waters cover the sea.

¹⁰In that day the Root of Jesse
will stand as a banner for the peoples; the nations will rally to him,
and his resting place will be glorious. ¹¹In that day the Lord will
reach out his hand a second time
to reclaim the surviving remnant
of his people from Assyria, from
Lower Egypt, from Upper Egypt,
from Cush,*b* from Elam, from Babylonia,*c* from Hamath and from
the islands of the Mediterranean.

¹²He will raise a banner for the
nations
and gather the exiles of
Israel;
he will assemble the scattered
people of Judah
from the four quarters of the
earth.
¹³Ephraim's jealousy will vanish,
and Judah's enemies*d* will be
destroyed;
Ephraim will not be jealous of
Judah,
nor Judah hostile toward
Ephraim.
¹⁴They will swoop down on the
slopes of Philistia to the
west;
together they will plunder
the people to the east.

a 6 Hebrew; Septuagint *lion will feed*   *b 11* That is, the upper Nile region
c 11 Hebrew *Shinar*   *d 13* Or *hostility*

They will subdue Edom and
    Moab,
    and the Ammonites will be
        subject to them.
¹⁵The Lord will dry up
    the gulf of the Egyptian
        sea;
with a scorching wind he will
    sweep his hand
    over the Euphrates River.
He will break it up into seven
    streams
    so that anyone can cross
        over in sandals.
¹⁶There will be a highway for the
    remnant of his people
    that is left from Assyria,
as there was for Israel
    when they came up from
        Egypt.

Songs of Praise

12 In that day you will say:

"I will praise you, Lord.
    Although you were angry
        with me,
your anger has turned away
    and you have comforted me.
²Surely God is my salvation;
    I will trust and not be
        afraid.
The Lord, the Lord himself,
    is my strength and my
        defense^a;
    he has become my
        salvation."
³With joy you will draw
    water
    from the wells of salvation.

⁴In that day you will say:

"Give praise to the Lord,
    proclaim his name;
make known among the
    nations what he has
        done,
    and proclaim that his name
        is exalted.
⁵Sing to the Lord, for he has
    done glorious things;
    let this be known to all the
        world.
⁶Shout aloud and sing for joy,
    people of Zion,
    for great is the Holy One of
        Israel among you."

A Prophecy Against Babylon

13 A prophecy against Bab-
    ylon that Isaiah son of
Amoz saw:

²Raise a banner on a bare
    hilltop,
    shout to them;
beckon to them
    to enter the gates of the
        nobles.
³I have commanded those I
    prepared for battle;
    I have summoned my
        warriors to carry out my
        wrath —
    those who rejoice in my
        triumph.

⁴Listen, a noise on the
    mountains,
    like that of a great
        multitude!

---

^a 2 Or *song*

Listen, an uproar among the
kingdoms,
like nations massing
together!
The LORD Almighty is
mustering
an army for war.
⁵ They come from faraway lands,
from the ends of the
heavens —
the LORD and the weapons of
his wrath —
to destroy the whole country.

⁶ Wail, for the day of the LORD is
near;
it will come like destruction
from the Almighty.ᵃ
⁷ Because of this, all hands will
go limp,
every heart will melt with
fear.
⁸ Terror will seize them,
pain and anguish will grip
them;
they will writhe like a
woman in labor.
They will look aghast at each
other,
their faces aflame.

⁹ See, the day of the LORD is
coming
— a cruel day, with wrath
and fierce anger —
to make the land desolate
and destroy the sinners
within it.
¹⁰ The stars of heaven and their
constellations
will not show their light.

The rising sun will be
darkened
and the moon will not give
its light.
¹¹ I will punish the world for its
evil,
the wicked for their sins.
I will put an end to the
arrogance of the
haughty
and will humble the pride of
the ruthless.
¹² I will make people scarcer
than pure gold,
more rare than the gold of
Ophir.
¹³ Therefore I will make the
heavens tremble;
and the earth will shake
from its place
at the wrath of the LORD
Almighty,
in the day of his burning
anger.

¹⁴ Like a hunted gazelle,
like sheep without a
shepherd,
they will all return to their
own people,
they will flee to their native
land.
¹⁵ Whoever is captured will be
thrust through;
all who are caught will fall
by the sword.
¹⁶ Their infants will be dashed to
pieces before their eyes;
their houses will be looted
and their wives violated.

ᵃ 6 Hebrew *Shaddai*

¹⁷ See, I will stir up against them
    the Medes,
  who do not care for silver
  and have no delight in gold.
¹⁸ Their bows will strike down
    the young men;
  they will have no mercy on
    infants,
  nor will they look with
    compassion on children.
¹⁹ Babylon, the jewel of kingdoms,
  the pride and glory of the
    Babylonians,ᵃ
  will be overthrown by God
  like Sodom and Gomorrah.
²⁰ She will never be inhabited
  or lived in through all
    generations;
  there no nomads will pitch
    their tents,
  there no shepherds will rest
    their flocks.
²¹ But desert creatures will lie
    there,
  jackals will fill her houses;
  there the owls will dwell,
  and there the wild goats will
    leap about.
²² Hyenas will inhabit her
    strongholds,
  jackals her luxurious palaces.
  Her time is at hand,
  and her days will not be
    prolonged.

14 The LORD will have
    compassion on Jacob;
  once again he will choose
    Israel

and will settle them in their
    own land.
  Foreigners will join them
  and unite with the
    descendants of Jacob.
² Nations will take them
  and bring them to their own
    place.
  And Israel will take possession
    of the nations
  and make them male and
    female servants in the
    LORD's land.
  They will make captives of
    their captors
  and rule over their
    oppressors.

³ On the day the LORD gives you
relief from your suffering and
turmoil and from the harsh labor forced on you, ⁴ you will take
up this taunt against the king of
Babylon:

How the oppressor has come
    to an end!
  How his furyᵇ has ended!
⁵ The LORD has broken the rod
    of the wicked,
  the scepter of the rulers,
⁶ which in anger struck down
    peoples
  with unceasing blows,
  and in fury subdued
    nations
  with relentless aggression.
⁷ All the lands are at rest and at
    peace;
  they break into singing.

ᵃ 19 Or *Chaldeans*   ᵇ 4 Dead Sea Scrolls, Septuagint and Syriac; the meaning of
the word in the Masoretic Text is uncertain.

⁸Even the junipers and the
     cedars of Lebanon
  gloat over you and say,
  "Now that you have been laid
     low,
  no one comes to cut us
     down."

⁹The realm of the dead below is
     all astir
  to meet you at your coming;
  it rouses the spirits of the
     departed to greet you —
  all those who were leaders in
     the world;
  it makes them rise from their
     thrones —
  all those who were kings
     over the nations.
¹⁰They will all respond,
  they will say to you,
  "You also have become weak,
     as we are;
  you have become like us."
¹¹All your pomp has been
     brought down to the
     grave,
  along with the noise of your
     harps;
  maggots are spread out
     beneath you
  and worms cover you.

¹²How you have fallen from
     heaven,
  morning star, son of the
     dawn!
  You have been cast down to
     the earth,
  you who once laid low the
     nations!

¹³You said in your heart,
  "I will ascend to the
     heavens;
  I will raise my throne
     above the stars of God;
  I will sit enthroned on the
     mount of assembly,
  on the utmost heights of
     Mount Zaphon.ᵃ
¹⁴I will ascend above the tops of
     the clouds;
  I will make myself like the
     Most High."
¹⁵But you are brought down to
     the realm of the dead,
  to the depths of the pit.

¹⁶Those who see you stare at
     you,
  they ponder your fate:
  "Is this the man who shook the
     earth
  and made kingdoms
     tremble,
¹⁷the man who made the world a
     wilderness,
  who overthrew its cities
  and would not let his
     captives go home?"

¹⁸All the kings of the nations lie
     in state,
  each in his own tomb.
¹⁹But you are cast out of your
     tomb
  like a rejected branch;
  you are covered with the slain,
  with those pierced by the
     sword,
  those who descend to the
     stones of the pit.

ᵃ 13 Or *of the north*; Zaphon was the most sacred mountain of the Canaanites.

Like a corpse trampled
underfoot,
20 you will not join them in
burial,
for you have destroyed your
land
and killed your people.

Let the offspring of the wicked
never be mentioned again.
21 Prepare a place to slaughter
his children
for the sins of their
ancestors;
they are not to rise to inherit
the land
and cover the earth with
their cities.

22 "I will rise up against them,"
declares the LORD Almighty.
"I will wipe out Babylon's
name and survivors,
her offspring and
descendants,"
declares the LORD.
23 "I will turn her into a place for
owls
and into swampland;
I will sweep her with the
broom of destruction,"
declares the LORD Almighty.

24 The LORD Almighty has
sworn,

"Surely, as I have planned, so it
will be,
and as I have purposed, so it
will happen.
25 I will crush the Assyrian in my
land;
on my mountains I will
trample him down.

His yoke will be taken from my
people,
and his burden removed
from their shoulders."

26 This is the plan determined for
the whole world;
this is the hand stretched out
over all nations.
27 For the LORD Almighty has
purposed, and who can
thwart him?
His hand is stretched out,
and who can turn it
back?

A Prophecy Against the Philistines

28 This prophecy came in the
year King Ahaz died:

29 Do not rejoice, all you
Philistines,
that the rod that struck you
is broken;
from the root of that snake will
spring up a viper,
its fruit will be a darting,
venomous serpent.
30 The poorest of the poor will
find pasture,
and the needy will lie down
in safety.
But your root I will destroy by
famine;
it will slay your survivors.

31 Wail, you gate! Howl, you city!
Melt away, all you
Philistines!
A cloud of smoke comes from
the north,
and there is not a straggler in
its ranks.

32 What answer shall be given
    to the envoys of that nation?
"The LORD has established
    Zion,
  and in her his afflicted
    people will find refuge."

A Prophecy Against Moab

15 A prophecy against Moab:

Ar in Moab is ruined,
  destroyed in a night!
Kir in Moab is ruined,
  destroyed in a night!
2 Dibon goes up to its temple,
  to its high places to weep;
Moab wails over Nebo and
    Medeba.
Every head is shaved
  and every beard cut off.
3 In the streets they wear
    sackcloth;
  on the roofs and in the
    public squares
they all wail,
  prostrate with weeping.
4 Heshbon and Elealeh cry out,
  their voices are heard all the
    way to Jahaz.
Therefore the armed men of
    Moab cry out,
  and their hearts are faint.

5 My heart cries out over Moab;
  her fugitives flee as far as
    Zoar,
  as far as Eglath Shelishiyah.
They go up the hill to Luhith,
  weeping as they go;
on the road to Horonaim

they lament their
    destruction.
6 The waters of Nimrim are
    dried up
  and the grass is withered;
the vegetation is gone
  and nothing green is left.
7 So the wealth they have
    acquired and stored up
  they carry away over the
    Ravine of the Poplars.
8 Their outcry echoes along the
    border of Moab;
  their wailing reaches as far
    as Eglaim,
  their lamentation as far as
    Beer Elim.
9 The waters of Dimon[a] are full
    of blood,
  but I will bring still more
    upon Dimon[a] —
a lion upon the fugitives of
    Moab
  and upon those who remain
    in the land.

16 Send lambs as tribute
  to the ruler of the land,
from Sela, across the
    desert,
  to the mount of Daughter
    Zion.
2 Like fluttering birds
  pushed from the nest,
so are the women of Moab
  at the fords of the Arnon.

3 "Make up your mind," Moab
    says.
  "Render a decision.

---

[a] 9 *Dimon*, a wordplay on *Dibon* (see verse 2), sounds like the Hebrew for *blood*.

Make your shadow like
      night —
   at high noon.
Hide the fugitives,
   do not betray the refugees.
⁴Let the Moabite fugitives stay
      with you;
   be their shelter from the
      destroyer."

The oppressor will come to an
      end,
   and destruction will cease;
   the aggressor will vanish
      from the land.
⁵In love a throne will be
      established;
   in faithfulness a man will sit
      on it —
   one from the house*a* of
      David —
   one who in judging seeks
      justice
   and speeds the cause of
      righteousness.

⁶We have heard of Moab's
      pride —
   how great is her
      arrogance! —
   of her conceit, her pride and
      her insolence;
   but her boasts are empty.
⁷Therefore the Moabites wail,
      they wail together for
      Moab.
Lament and grieve
   for the raisin cakes of Kir
      Hareseth.
⁸The fields of Heshbon wither,
   the vines of Sibmah also.

The rulers of the nations
   have trampled down the
      choicest vines,
which once reached Jazer
   and spread toward the
      desert.
Their shoots spread out
   and went as far as the sea.*b*
⁹So I weep, as Jazer weeps,
   for the vines of Sibmah.
Heshbon and Elealeh,
   I drench you with tears!
The shouts of joy over your
      ripened fruit
   and over your harvests have
      been stilled.
¹⁰Joy and gladness are taken
      away from the orchards;
   no one sings or shouts in the
      vineyards;
no one treads out wine at the
      presses,
   for I have put an end to the
      shouting.
¹¹My heart laments for Moab
      like a harp,
   my inmost being for Kir
      Hareseth.
¹²When Moab appears at her
      high place,
   she only wears herself
      out;
when she goes to her shrine to
      pray,
   it is to no avail.

¹³This is the word the Lord
has already spoken concerning
Moab. ¹⁴But now the Lord says:
"Within three years, as a servant
bound by contract would count

---

a 5 Hebrew *tent*   *b 8* Probably the Dead Sea

them, Moab's splendor and all her many people will be despised, and her survivors will be very few and feeble."

A Prophecy Against Damascus

17 A prophecy against Damascus:

"See, Damascus will no longer
    be a city
  but will become a heap of
    ruins.
² The cities of Aroer will be
    deserted
  and left to flocks, which will
    lie down,
  with no one to make them
    afraid.
³ The fortified city will
    disappear from Ephraim,
  and royal power from
    Damascus;
  the remnant of Aram will be
    like the glory of the
    Israelites,"
            declares the LORD
            Almighty.

⁴ "In that day the glory of Jacob
    will fade;
  the fat of his body will waste
    away.
⁵ It will be as when reapers
    harvest the standing
    grain,
  gathering the grain in their
    arms —
  as when someone gleans
    heads of grain
  in the Valley of Rephaim.

⁶ Yet some gleanings will
    remain,
  as when an olive tree is
    beaten,
leaving two or three olives on
    the topmost branches,
  four or five on the fruitful
    boughs,"
            declares the LORD,
            the God of Israel.

⁷ In that day people will look to
    their Maker
  and turn their eyes to the
    Holy One of Israel.
⁸ They will not look to the altars,
    the work of their hands,
  and they will have no regard
    for the Asherah poles*ᵃ*
  and the incense altars their
    fingers have made.

⁹ In that day their strong cities, which they left because of the Israelites, will be like places abandoned to thickets and undergrowth. And all will be desolation.

¹⁰ You have forgotten God your
    Savior;
  you have not remembered
    the Rock, your fortress.
Therefore, though you set out
    the finest plants
  and plant imported vines,
¹¹ though on the day you set
    them out, you make
    them grow,
  and on the morning when
    you plant them, you
    bring them to bud,

ᵃ 8 That is, wooden symbols of the goddess Asherah

yet the harvest will be as
  nothing
  in the day of disease and
  incurable pain.

12 Woe to the many nations that
  rage —
  they rage like the raging sea!
Woe to the peoples who roar —
  they roar like the roaring of
  great waters!
13 Although the peoples roar
  like the roar of surging
  waters,
  when he rebukes them they
  flee far away,
driven before the wind like
  chaff on the hills,
  like tumbleweed before a
  gale.
14 In the evening, sudden terror!
  Before the morning, they are
  gone!
This is the portion of those
  who loot us,
  the lot of those who plunder
  us.

A Prophecy Against Cush

18 Woe to the land of
  whirring wings[a]
  along the rivers of Cush,[b]
2 which sends envoys by sea
  in papyrus boats over the
  water.

Go, swift messengers,
to a people tall and smooth-
  skinned,
  to a people feared far and
  wide,

an aggressive nation of strange
  speech,
  whose land is divided by
  rivers.

3 All you people of the world,
  you who live on the earth,
when a banner is raised on the
  mountains,
  you will see it,
and when a trumpet sounds,
  you will hear it.
4 This is what the LORD says
  to me:
  "I will remain quiet and
  will look on from my
  dwelling place,
like shimmering heat in the
  sunshine,
  like a cloud of dew in the
  heat of harvest."
5 For, before the harvest, when
  the blossom is gone
  and the flower becomes a
  ripening grape,
he will cut off the shoots with
  pruning knives,
  and cut down and take away
  the spreading branches.
6 They will all be left to the
  mountain birds of prey
  and to the wild animals;
the birds will feed on them all
  summer,
  the wild animals all winter.

7 At that time gifts will be
brought to the LORD Almighty

from a people tall and smooth-
  skinned,

---

^a 1 Or *of locusts*   ^b 1 That is, the upper Nile region

from a people feared far and
wide,
an aggressive nation of strange
speech,
whose land is divided by
rivers —
the gifts will be brought to Mount
Zion, the place of the Name of the
LORD Almighty.

A Prophecy Against Egypt

19 A prophecy against Egypt:

See, the LORD rides on a swift
cloud
and is coming to Egypt.
The idols of Egypt tremble
before him,
and the hearts of the
Egyptians melt with fear.

² "I will stir up Egyptian against
Egyptian —
brother will fight against
brother,
neighbor against neighbor,
city against city,
kingdom against kingdom.
³ The Egyptians will lose heart,
and I will bring their plans to
nothing;
they will consult the idols and
the spirits of the dead,
the mediums and the
spiritists.
⁴ I will hand the Egyptians over
to the power of a cruel
master,
and a fierce king will rule over
them,"
declares the Lord, the LORD
Almighty.

⁵ The waters of the river will
dry up,
and the riverbed will be
parched and dry.
⁶ The canals will stink;
the streams of Egypt will
dwindle and dry up.
The reeds and rushes will
wither,
⁷ also the plants along the
Nile,
at the mouth of the river.
Every sown field along the
Nile
will become parched, will
blow away and be no
more.
⁸ The fishermen will groan and
lament,
all who cast hooks into the
Nile;
those who throw nets on the
water
will pine away.
⁹ Those who work with combed
flax will despair,
the weavers of fine linen will
lose hope.
¹⁰ The workers in cloth will be
dejected,
and all the wage earners will
be sick at heart.

¹¹ The officials of Zoan are
nothing but fools;
the wise counselors of
Pharaoh give senseless
advice.
How can you say to Pharaoh,
"I am one of the wise men,
a disciple of the ancient
kings"?

¹²Where are your wise men
now?
Let them show you and
make known
what the Lord Almighty
has planned against Egypt.
¹³The officials of Zoan have
become fools,
the leaders of Memphis are
deceived;
the cornerstones of her
peoples
have led Egypt astray.
¹⁴The Lord has poured into
them
a spirit of dizziness;
they make Egypt stagger in all
that she does,
as a drunkard staggers
around in his vomit.
¹⁵There is nothing Egypt can
do —
head or tail, palm branch or
reed.

¹⁶In that day the Egyptians will become weaklings. They will shudder with fear at the uplifted hand that the Lord Almighty raises against them. ¹⁷And the land of Judah will bring terror to the Egyptians; everyone to whom Judah is mentioned will be terrified, because of what the Lord Almighty is planning against them.

¹⁸In that day five cities in Egypt will speak the language of Canaan and swear allegiance to the Lord Almighty. One of them will be called the City of the Sun.ᵃ

¹⁹In that day there will be an altar to the Lord in the heart of Egypt, and a monument to the Lord at its border. ²⁰It will be a sign and witness to the Lord Almighty in the land of Egypt. When they cry out to the Lord because of their oppressors, he will send them a savior and defender, and he will rescue them. ²¹So the Lord will make himself known to the Egyptians, and in that day they will acknowledge the Lord. They will worship with sacrifices and grain offerings; they will make vows to the Lord and keep them. ²²The Lord will strike Egypt with a plague; he will strike them and heal them. They will turn to the Lord, and he will respond to their pleas and heal them.

²³In that day there will be a highway from Egypt to Assyria. The Assyrians will go to Egypt and the Egyptians to Assyria. The Egyptians and Assyrians will worship together. ²⁴In that day Israel will be the third, along with Egypt and Assyria, a blessingᵇ on the earth. ²⁵The Lord Almighty will bless them, saying, "Blessed be Egypt my people, Assyria my handiwork, and Israel my inheritance."

ᵃ 18 Some manuscripts of the Masoretic Text, Dead Sea Scrolls, Symmachus and Vulgate; most manuscripts of the Masoretic Text *City of Destruction*
ᵇ 24 Or *Assyria, whose names will be used in blessings* (see Gen. 48:20); or *Assyria, who will be seen by others as blessed*

A Prophecy Against Egypt and Cush

20 In the year that the supreme commander, sent by Sargon king of Assyria, came to Ashdod and attacked and captured it — **2** at that time the LORD spoke through Isaiah son of Amoz. He said to him, "Take off the sackcloth from your body and the sandals from your feet." And he did so, going around stripped and barefoot.

3 Then the LORD said, "Just as my servant Isaiah has gone stripped and barefoot for three years, as a sign and portent against Egypt and Cush,*a* **4** so the king of Assyria will lead away stripped and barefoot the Egyptian captives and Cushite exiles, young and old, with buttocks bared — to Egypt's shame. **5** Those who trusted in Cush and boasted in Egypt will be dismayed and put to shame. **6** In that day the people who live on this coast will say, 'See what has happened to those we relied on, those we fled to for help and deliverance from the king of Assyria! How then can we escape?' "

A Prophecy Against Babylon

21 A prophecy against the Desert by the Sea:

Like whirlwinds sweeping
        through the southland,
an invader comes from the
        desert,
    from a land of terror.

2 A dire vision has been shown
        to me:
    The traitor betrays, the
        looter takes loot.
Elam, attack! Media, lay
        siege!
    I will bring to an end all the
        groaning she caused.

3 At this my body is racked with
        pain,
    pangs seize me, like those of
        a woman in labor;
I am staggered by what I
        hear,
    I am bewildered by what I
        see.
4 My heart falters,
    fear makes me tremble;
the twilight I longed for
    has become a horror
        to me.

5 They set the tables,
    they spread the rugs,
    they eat, they drink!
Get up, you officers,
    oil the shields!

6 This is what the Lord says
to me:

"Go, post a lookout
    and have him report what he
        sees.
7 When he sees chariots
    with teams of horses,
riders on donkeys
    or riders on camels,
let him be alert,
    fully alert."

---

a 3 That is, the upper Nile region; also in verse 5

[8]And the lookout[a] shouted,

"Day after day, my lord, I stand
  on the watchtower;
every night I stay at my post.
[9]Look, here comes a man in a
  chariot
with a team of horses.
And he gives back the answer:
  'Babylon has fallen, has
  fallen!
All the images of its gods
  lie shattered on the
  ground!' "

[10]My people who are crushed on
  the threshing floor,
I tell you what I have heard
from the LORD Almighty,
  from the God of Israel.

A Prophecy Against Edom

[11]A prophecy against Dumah[b]:

Someone calls to me from Seir,
  "Watchman, what is left of
  the night?
Watchman, what is left of the
  night?"
[12]The watchman replies,
  "Morning is coming, but also
  the night.
If you would ask, then ask;
  and come back yet again."

A Prophecy Against Arabia

[13]A prophecy against Arabia:

You caravans of Dedanites,
  who camp in the thickets of
  Arabia,
[14] bring water for the thirsty;

you who live in Tema,
  bring food for the fugitives.
[15]They flee from the sword,
  from the drawn sword,
from the bent bow
  and from the heat of battle.

[16]This is what the Lord says to
me: "Within one year, as a servant bound by contract would
count it, all the splendor of Kedar
will come to an end. [17]The survivors of the archers, the warriors
of Kedar, will be few." The LORD,
the God of Israel, has spoken.

A Prophecy About Jerusalem

22 A prophecy against the
Valley of Vision:

What troubles you now,
  that you have all gone up on
  the roofs,
[2]you town so full of commotion,
  you city of tumult and
  revelry?
Your slain were not killed by
  the sword,
  nor did they die in battle.
[3]All your leaders have fled
  together;
they have been captured
  without using the bow.
All you who were caught were
  taken prisoner together,
having fled while the enemy
  was still far away.
[4]Therefore I said, "Turn away
  from me;
  let me weep bitterly.

---

[a] 8 Dead Sea Scrolls and Syriac; Masoretic Text *A lion*   [b] 11 *Dumah*, a wordplay
on *Edom*, means *silence* or *stillness*.

Do not try to console me
over the destruction of my
people."

⁵The Lord, the LORD Almighty,
has a day
of tumult and trampling and
terror
˙in the Valley of Vision,
a day of battering down walls
and of crying out to the
mountains.
⁶Elam takes up the quiver,
with her charioteers and
horses;
Kir uncovers the shield.
⁷Your choicest valleys are full of
chariots,
and horsemen are posted at
the city gates.

⁸The Lord stripped away the
defenses of Judah,
and you looked in that day
to the weapons in the Palace
of the Forest.
⁹You saw that the walls of the
City of David
were broken through in
many places;
you stored up water
in the Lower Pool.
¹⁰You counted the buildings in
Jerusalem
and tore down houses to
strengthen the wall.
¹¹You built a reservoir between
the two walls
for the water of the Old Pool,
but you did not look to the One
who made it,
or have regard for the One
who planned it long ago.

¹²The Lord, the LORD
Almighty,
called you on that day
to weep and to wail,
to tear out your hair and put
on sackcloth.
¹³But see, there is joy and
revelry,
slaughtering of cattle and
killing of sheep,
eating of meat and drinking
of wine!
"Let us eat and drink," you
say,
"for tomorrow we die!"

¹⁴The LORD Almighty has revealed this in my hearing: "Till
your dying day this sin will not
be atoned for," says the Lord, the
LORD Almighty.

¹⁵This is what the Lord, the
LORD Almighty, says:

"Go, say to this steward,
to Shebna the palace
administrator:
¹⁶What are you doing here and
who gave you permission
to cut out a grave for yourself
here,
hewing your grave on the
height
and chiseling your resting
place in the rock?

¹⁷"Beware, the LORD is about to
take firm hold of you
and hurl you away, you
mighty man.
¹⁸He will roll you up tightly like
a ball

and throw you into a large
country.
There you will die
and there the chariots you
were so proud of
will become a disgrace to
your master's house.
19 I will depose you from your
office,
and you will be ousted from
your position.

20 "In that day I will summon
my servant, Eliakim son of Hilkiah. **21** I will clothe him with
your robe and fasten your sash
around him and hand your authority over to him. He will be a
father to those who live in Jerusalem and to the people of Judah.
22 I will place on his shoulder the
key to the house of David; what
he opens no one can shut, and
what he shuts no one can open.
23 I will drive him like a peg into
a firm place; he will become a
seat[a] of honor for the house of
his father. **24** All the glory of his
family will hang on him: its offspring and offshoots — all its
lesser vessels, from the bowls to
all the jars.

25 "In that day," declares the
Lord Almighty, "the peg driven
into the firm place will give way;
it will be sheared off and will fall,
and the load hanging on it will be
cut down." The Lord has spoken.

A Prophecy Against Tyre

23 A prophecy against Tyre:

Wail, you ships of Tarshish!
For Tyre is destroyed
and left without house or
harbor.
From the land of Cyprus
word has come to them.

2 Be silent, you people of the
island
and you merchants of Sidon,
whom the seafarers have
enriched.
3 On the great waters
came the grain of the Shihor;
the harvest of the Nile[b] was
the revenue of Tyre,
and she became the
marketplace of the
nations.

4 Be ashamed, Sidon, and you
fortress of the sea,
for the sea has spoken:
"I have neither been in labor
nor given birth;
I have neither reared
sons nor brought up
daughters."
5 When word comes to Egypt,
they will be in anguish at the
report from Tyre.

6 Cross over to Tarshish;
wail, you people of the
island.
7 Is this your city of revelry,
the old, old city,

---

[a] 23 Or *throne*   [b] 2,3 Masoretic Text; Dead Sea Scrolls *Sidon, / who cross over
the sea; / your envoys* [3]*are on the great waters. / The grain of the Shihor, / the
harvest of the Nile,*

whose feet have taken her
to settle in far-off lands?
⁸Who planned this against
Tyre,
the bestower of crowns,
whose merchants are princes,
whose traders are renowned
in the earth?
⁹The Lord Almighty planned it,
to bring down her pride in
all her splendor
and to humble all who are
renowned on the earth.

¹⁰Till*a* your land as they do
along the Nile,
Daughter Tarshish,
for you no longer have a
harbor.
¹¹The Lord has stretched out his
hand over the sea
and made its kingdoms
tremble.
He has given an order
concerning Phoenicia
that her fortresses be
destroyed.
¹²He said, "No more of your
reveling,
Virgin Daughter Sidon, now
crushed!

"Up, cross over to Cyprus;
even there you will find no
rest."
¹³Look at the land of the
Babylonians,*b*
this people that is now of no
account!
The Assyrians have made it
a place for desert creatures;
they raised up their siege
towers,
they stripped its fortresses
bare
and turned it into a ruin.

¹⁴Wail, you ships of Tarshish;
your fortress is destroyed!

¹⁵At that time Tyre will be forgotten for seventy years, the span of a king's life. But at the end of these seventy years, it will happen to Tyre as in the song of the prostitute:

¹⁶"Take up a harp, walk through
the city,
you forgotten prostitute;
play the harp well, sing many a
song,
so that you will be
remembered."

¹⁷At the end of seventy years, the Lord will deal with Tyre. She will return to her lucrative prostitution and will ply her trade with all the kingdoms on the face of the earth. ¹⁸Yet her profit and her earnings will be set apart for the Lord; they will not be stored up or hoarded. Her profits will go to those who live before the Lord, for abundant food and fine clothes.

The Lord's Devastation of the Earth

24 See, the Lord is going to
lay waste the earth
and devastate it;

---

a 10 Dead Sea Scrolls and some Septuagint manuscripts; Masoretic Text *Go through*   *b 13* Or *Chaldeans*

he will ruin its face
and scatter its inhabitants —
² it will be the same
for priest as for people,
for the master as for his
servant,
for the mistress as for her
servant,
for seller as for buyer,
for borrower as for lender,
for debtor as for creditor.
³ The earth will be completely
laid waste
and totally plundered.
The LORD has spoken
this word.

⁴ The earth dries up and withers,
the world languishes and
withers,
the heavens languish with
the earth.
⁵ The earth is defiled by its
people;
they have disobeyed the laws,
violated the statutes
and broken the everlasting
covenant.
⁶ Therefore a curse consumes
the earth;
its people must bear their
guilt.
Therefore earth's inhabitants
are burned up,
and very few are left.
⁷ The new wine dries up and the
vine withers;
all the merrymakers groan.
⁸ The joyful timbrels are stilled,
the noise of the revelers has
stopped,
the joyful harp is silent.

⁹ No longer do they drink wine
with a song;
the beer is bitter to its
drinkers.
¹⁰ The ruined city lies desolate;
the entrance to every house
is barred.
¹¹ In the streets they cry out for
wine;
all joy turns to gloom,
all joyful sounds are
banished from the earth.
¹² The city is left in ruins,
its gate is battered to pieces.
¹³ So will it be on the earth
and among the nations,
as when an olive tree is beaten,
or as when gleanings are left
after the grape harvest.

¹⁴ They raise their voices, they
shout for joy;
from the west they acclaim
the LORD's majesty.
¹⁵ Therefore in the east give glory
to the LORD;
exalt the name of the LORD,
the God of Israel,
in the islands of the sea.
¹⁶ From the ends of the earth we
hear singing:
"Glory to the Righteous One."

But I said, "I waste away, I
waste away!
Woe to me!
The treacherous betray!
With treachery the
treacherous betray!"
¹⁷ Terror and pit and snare await
you,
people of the earth.

18 Whoever flees at the sound of
terror
will fall into a pit;
whoever climbs out of the pit
will be caught in a snare.

The floodgates of the heavens
are opened,
the foundations of the earth
shake.
19 The earth is broken up,
the earth is split asunder,
the earth is violently shaken.
20 The earth reels like a
drunkard,
it sways like a hut in the
wind;
so heavy upon it is the guilt of
its rebellion
that it falls — never to rise
again.

21 In that day the LORD will
punish
the powers in the heavens
above
and the kings on the earth
below.
22 They will be herded together
like prisoners bound in a
dungeon;
they will be shut up in prison
and be punished[a] after
many days.
23 The moon will be dismayed,
the sun ashamed;
for the LORD Almighty will
reign
on Mount Zion and in
Jerusalem,
and before its elders — with
great glory.

---

a 22 Or *released*

Praise to the LORD

25 LORD, you are my God;
I will exalt you and
praise your name,
for in perfect faithfulness
you have done wonderful
things,
things planned long ago.
2 You have made the city a heap
of rubble,
the fortified town a ruin,
the foreigners' stronghold a
city no more;
it will never be rebuilt.
3 Therefore strong peoples will
honor you;
cities of ruthless nations will
revere you.
4 You have been a refuge for the
poor,
a refuge for the needy in
their distress,
a shelter from the storm
and a shade from the heat.
For the breath of the ruthless
is like a storm driving
against a wall
5 and like the heat of the
desert.
You silence the uproar of
foreigners;
as heat is reduced by the
shadow of a cloud,
so the song of the ruthless is
stilled.

6 On this mountain the LORD
Almighty will prepare
a feast of rich food for all
peoples,

a banquet of aged wine —
the best of meats and the
finest of wines.
⁷On this mountain he will
destroy
the shroud that enfolds all
peoples,
the sheet that covers all nations;
⁸   he will swallow up death
forever.
The Sovereign Lord will wipe
away the tears
from all faces;
he will remove his people's
disgrace
from all the earth.
The Lord has spoken.

⁹In that day they will say,

"Surely this is our God;
we trusted in him, and he
saved us.
This is the Lord, we trusted in
him;
let us rejoice and be glad in
his salvation."

¹⁰The hand of the Lord will rest
on this mountain;
but Moab will be trampled
in their land
as straw is trampled down in
the manure.
¹¹They will stretch out their
hands in it,
as swimmers stretch out
their hands to swim.
God will bring down their
pride
despite the cleverness[a] of
their hands.

¹²He will bring down your high
fortified walls
and lay them low;
he will bring them down to the
ground,
to the very dust.

A Song of Praise

26 In that day this song will
be sung in the land of Judah:

We have a strong city;
God makes salvation
its walls and ramparts.
²Open the gates
that the righteous nation
may enter,
the nation that keeps faith.
³You will keep in perfect peace
those whose minds are
steadfast,
because they trust in you.
⁴Trust in the Lord forever,
for the Lord, the Lord
himself, is the Rock
eternal.
⁵He humbles those who dwell
on high,
he lays the lofty city low;
he levels it to the ground
and casts it down to the dust.
⁶Feet trample it down —
the feet of the oppressed,
the footsteps of the poor.

⁷The path of the righteous is
level;
you, the Upright One, make
the way of the righteous
smooth.

ᵃ 11 The meaning of the Hebrew for this word is uncertain.

8 Yes, LORD, walking in the way
of your laws,*a*
we wait for you;
your name and renown
are the desire of our
hearts.
9 My soul yearns for you in the
night;
in the morning my spirit
longs for you.
When your judgments come
upon the earth,
the people of the world learn
righteousness.
10 But when grace is shown to the
wicked,
they do not learn
righteousness;
even in a land of uprightness
they go on doing evil
and do not regard the
majesty of the LORD.
11 LORD, your hand is lifted
high,
but they do not see it.
Let them see your zeal for your
people and be put to
shame;
let the fire reserved for your
enemies consume them.
12 LORD, you establish peace
for us;
all that we have
accomplished you have
done for us.
13 LORD our God, other lords
besides you have ruled
over us,
but your name alone do we
honor.

14 They are now dead, they live
no more;
their spirits do not rise.
You punished them and
brought them to ruin;
you wiped out all memory of
them.
15 You have enlarged the nation,
LORD;
you have enlarged the
nation.
You have gained glory for
yourself;
you have extended all the
borders of the land.

16 LORD, they came to you in
their distress;
when you disciplined
them,
they could barely whisper a
prayer.*b*
17 As a pregnant woman about to
give birth
writhes and cries out in her
pain,
so were we in your presence,
LORD.
18 We were with child, we
writhed in labor,
but we gave birth to wind.
We have not brought salvation
to the earth,
and the people of the world
have not come to life.
19 But your dead will live, LORD;
their bodies will rise —
let those who dwell in the
dust
wake up and shout for joy —

---

a 8 Or *judgments*   *b 16* The meaning of the Hebrew for this clause is uncertain.

your dew is like the dew of the
    morning;
    the earth will give birth to
      her dead.

20 Go, my people, enter your
    rooms
    and shut the doors behind
      you;
hide yourselves for a little
    while
    until his wrath has passed by.
21 See, the LORD is coming out of
    his dwelling
    to punish the people of the
      earth for their sins.
The earth will disclose the
    blood shed on it;
    the earth will conceal its
      slain no longer.

Deliverance of Israel

27 In that day,

the LORD will punish with his
    sword —
    his fierce, great and
      powerful sword —
Leviathan the gliding serpent,
    Leviathan the coiling
      serpent;
he will slay the monster of the
    sea.

2 In that day —

"Sing about a fruitful vineyard:
3   I, the LORD, watch over it;
    I water it continually.
I guard it day and night
    so that no one may harm it.

4   I am not angry.
If only there were briers and
    thorns confronting me!
I would march against them
    in battle;
    I would set them all on fire.
5 Or else let them come to me for
    refuge;
    let them make peace with me,
yes, let them make peace
    with me."

6 In days to come Jacob will take
    root,
    Israel will bud and blossom
and fill all the world with
    fruit.

7 Has the LORD struck her
    as he struck down those who
      struck her?
Has she been killed
    as those were killed who
      killed her?
8 By warfare[a] and exile you
    contend with her —
with his fierce blast he drives
    her out,
    as on a day the east wind
      blows.
9 By this, then, will Jacob's guilt
    be atoned for,
and this will be the full fruit
    of the removal of his sin:
When he makes all the altar
    stones
    to be like limestone crushed
      to pieces,
no Asherah poles[b] or incense
    altars
    will be left standing.

---

[a] 8 See Septuagint; the meaning of the Hebrew for this word is uncertain.
[b] 9 That is, wooden symbols of the goddess Asherah

¹⁰The fortified city stands
    desolate,
    an abandoned settlement,
    forsaken like the
    wilderness;
there the calves graze,
    there they lie down;
    they strip its branches bare.
¹¹When its twigs are dry, they
    are broken off
    and women come and make
    fires with them.
For this is a people without
    understanding;
    so their Maker has no
    compassion on them,
    and their Creator shows
    them no favor.

¹²In that day the LORD will
thresh from the flowing Euphrates to the Wadi of Egypt, and you,
Israel, will be gathered up one
by one. ¹³And in that day a great
trumpet will sound. Those who
were perishing in Assyria and
those who were exiled in Egypt
will come and worship the LORD
on the holy mountain in Jerusalem.

Woe to the Leaders of Ephraim and Judah

28 Woe to that wreath,
    the pride of Ephraim's
    drunkards,
    to the fading flower, his
    glorious beauty,
set on the head of a fertile
    valley—
    to that city, the pride of those
    laid low by wine!

²See, the Lord has one who is
    powerful and strong.
Like a hailstorm and a
    destructive wind,
    like a driving rain and a
    flooding downpour,
he will throw it forcefully to
    the ground.
³That wreath, the pride of
    Ephraim's drunkards,
    will be trampled underfoot.
⁴That fading flower, his glorious
    beauty,
    set on the head of a fertile
    valley,
will be like figs ripe before
    harvest—
    as soon as people see them
    and take them in hand,
    they swallow them.

⁵In that day the LORD
    Almighty
    will be a glorious crown,
    a beautiful wreath
    for the remnant of his
    people.
⁶He will be a spirit of justice
    to the one who sits in
    judgment,
    a source of strength
    to those who turn back the
    battle at the gate.

⁷And these also stagger from
    wine
    and reel from beer:
Priests and prophets stagger
    from beer
    and are befuddled with
    wine;
    they reel from beer,

they stagger when seeing
visions,
they stumble when
rendering decisions.
⁸All the tables are covered with
vomit
and there is not a spot
without filth.

⁹"Who is it he is trying to teach?
To whom is he explaining his
message?
To children weaned from their
milk,
to those just taken from the
breast?
¹⁰For it is:
Do this, do that,
a rule for this, a rule for that*a*;
a little here, a little there."

¹¹Very well then, with foreign
lips and strange tongues
God will speak to this
people,
¹²to whom he said,
"This is the resting place, let
the weary rest";
and, "This is the place of
repose" —
but they would not listen.
¹³So then, the word of the Lord
to them will become:
Do this, do that,
a rule for this, a rule for that;
a little here, a little there —
so that as they go they will fall
backward;
they will be injured and
snared and captured.

¹⁴Therefore hear the word of the
Lord, you scoffers
who rule this people in
Jerusalem.
¹⁵You boast, "We have entered
into a covenant with
death,
with the realm of the dead
we have made an
agreement.
When an overwhelming
scourge sweeps by,
it cannot touch us,
for we have made a lie our
refuge
and falsehood*b* our hiding
place."

¹⁶So this is what the Sovereign
Lord says:

"See, I lay a stone in Zion, a
tested stone,
a precious cornerstone for a
sure foundation;
the one who relies on it
will never be stricken with
panic.
¹⁷I will make justice the
measuring line
and righteousness the
plumb line;
hail will sweep away your
refuge, the lie,
and water will overflow your
hiding place.
¹⁸Your covenant with death will
be annulled;
your agreement with the
realm of the dead will
not stand.

a 10 Hebrew / *sav lasav sav lasav* / *kav lakav kav lakav* (probably meaningless
sounds mimicking the prophet's words); also in verse 13   *b* 15 Or *false gods*

When the overwhelming
    scourge sweeps by,
  you will be beaten down
    by it.
19 As often as it comes it will
    carry you away;
  morning after morning, by
    day and by night,
  it will sweep through."

The understanding of this
    message
  will bring sheer terror.
20 The bed is too short to stretch
    out on,
  the blanket too narrow to
    wrap around you.
21 The LORD will rise up as he did
    at Mount Perazim,
  he will rouse himself as in
    the Valley of Gibeon —
  to do his work, his strange
    work,
  and perform his task, his
    alien task.
22 Now stop your mocking,
  or your chains will become
    heavier;
  the Lord, the LORD Almighty,
    has told me
  of the destruction decreed
    against the whole land.

23 Listen and hear my voice;
  pay attention and hear what
    I say.
24 When a farmer plows for
    planting, does he plow
    continually?
  Does he keep on breaking up
    and working the soil?
25 When he has leveled the
    surface,
  does he not sow caraway and
    scatter cumin?
Does he not plant wheat in its
    place,[a]
  barley in its plot,[a]
  and spelt in its field?
26 His God instructs him
  and teaches him the right
    way.

27 Caraway is not threshed with a
    sledge,
  nor is the wheel of a cart
    rolled over cumin;
  caraway is beaten out with a
    rod,
  and cumin with a stick.
28 Grain must be ground to make
    bread;
  so one does not go on
    threshing it forever.
The wheels of a threshing cart
    may be rolled over it,
  but one does not use horses
    to grind grain.
29 All this also comes from the
    LORD Almighty,
  whose plan is wonderful,
  whose wisdom is
    magnificent.

Woe to David's City

29 Woe to you, Ariel, Ariel,
    the city where David
    settled!
Add year to year
  and let your cycle of festivals
    go on.

---

[a] 25 The meaning of the Hebrew for this word is uncertain.

2 Yet I will besiege Ariel;
she will mourn and lament,
she will be to me like an
altar hearth.[a]
3 I will encamp against you on
all sides;
I will encircle you with
towers
and set up my siege works
against you.
4 Brought low, you will speak
from the ground;
your speech will mumble out
of the dust.
Your voice will come ghostlike
from the earth;
out of the dust your speech
will whisper.

5 But your many enemies will
become like fine dust,
the ruthless hordes like
blown chaff.
Suddenly, in an instant,
6   the LORD Almighty will
come
with thunder and earthquake
and great noise,
with windstorm and
tempest and flames of a
devouring fire.
7 Then the hordes of all the
nations that fight against
Ariel,
that attack her and her
fortress and besiege her,
will be as it is with a dream,
with a vision in the night —
8 as when a hungry person
dreams of eating,
but awakens hungry still;

as when a thirsty person
dreams of drinking,
but awakens faint and
thirsty still.
So will it be with the hordes of
all the nations
that fight against Mount
Zion.

9 Be stunned and amazed,
blind yourselves and be
sightless;
be drunk, but not from
wine,
stagger, but not from
beer.
10 The LORD has brought over
you a deep sleep:
He has sealed your eyes (the
prophets);
he has covered your heads
(the seers).

11 For you this whole vision is
nothing but words sealed in a
scroll. And if you give the scroll
to someone who can read, and
say, "Read this, please," they will
answer, "I can't; it is sealed." **12** Or
if you give the scroll to someone
who cannot read, and say, "Read
this, please," they will answer, "I
don't know how to read."

13 The Lord says:

"These people come near to
me with their mouth
and honor me with their
lips,
but their hearts are far
from me.

---

[a] 2 The Hebrew for *altar hearth* sounds like the Hebrew for *Ariel*.

Their worship of me
　is based on merely human
　　rules they have been
　　taught.[a]
14 Therefore once more I will
　　astound these people
　with wonder upon wonder;
the wisdom of the wise will
　　perish,
　the intelligence of the
　　intelligent will vanish."
15 Woe to those who go to great
　　depths
　to hide their plans from the
　　LORD,
　who do their work in darkness
　　and think,
　　"Who sees us? Who will
　　know?"
16 You turn things upside down,
　　as if the potter were thought
　　to be like the clay!
　Shall what is formed say to the
　　one who formed it,
　　"You did not make me"?
　Can the pot say to the potter,
　　"You know nothing"?

17 In a very short time, will not
　　Lebanon be turned into
　　a fertile field
　and the fertile field seem like
　　a forest?
18 In that day the deaf will hear
　　the words of the scroll,
　and out of gloom and
　　darkness
　the eyes of the blind will see.
19 Once more the humble will
　　rejoice in the LORD;

the needy will rejoice in the
　　Holy One of Israel.
20 The ruthless will vanish,
　the mockers will disappear,
　and all who have an eye for
　　evil will be cut down—
21 those who with a word make
　　someone out to be guilty,
　who ensnare the defender in
　　court
　and with false testimony
　　deprive the innocent of
　　justice.

22 Therefore this is what the
LORD, who redeemed Abraham,
says to the descendants of Jacob:

"No longer will Jacob be
　　ashamed;
　no longer will their faces
　　grow pale.
23 When they see among them
　　their children,
　the work of my hands,
　they will keep my name holy;
　they will acknowledge the
　　holiness of the Holy One
　　of Jacob,
　and will stand in awe of the
　　God of Israel.
24 Those who are wayward
　　in spirit will gain
　　understanding;
　those who complain will
　　accept instruction."

Woe to the Obstinate Nation

30 "Woe to the obstinate
　　children,"
　declares the LORD,

---

[a] 13 Hebrew; Septuagint *They worship me in vain; / their teachings are merely human rules*

"to those who carry out plans
  that are not mine,
  forming an alliance, but not
    by my Spirit,
  heaping sin upon sin;
[2] who go down to Egypt
  without consulting me;
who look for help to Pharaoh's
    protection,
  to Egypt's shade for
    refuge.
[3] But Pharaoh's protection will
    be to your shame,
  Egypt's shade will bring you
    disgrace.
[4] Though they have officials in
    Zoan
  and their envoys have
    arrived in Hanes,
[5] everyone will be put to
    shame
  because of a people useless
    to them,
who bring neither help nor
    advantage,
  but only shame and
    disgrace."

[6] A prophecy concerning the
animals of the Negev:

Through a land of hardship
    and distress,
  of lions and lionesses,
  of adders and darting
    snakes,
the envoys carry their riches
    on donkeys' backs,
  their treasures on the humps
    of camels,
to that unprofitable nation,
[7]   to Egypt, whose help is
    utterly useless.

Therefore I call her
  Rahab the Do-Nothing.

[8] Go now, write it on a tablet for
    them,
  inscribe it on a scroll,
that for the days to come
  it may be an everlasting
    witness.
[9] For these are rebellious
    people, deceitful
    children,
  children unwilling to listen
    to the LORD's instruction.
[10] They say to the seers,
  "See no more visions!"
and to the prophets,
  "Give us no more visions of
    what is right!
Tell us pleasant things,
  prophesy illusions.
[11] Leave this way,
  get off this path,
and stop confronting us
  with the Holy One of
    Israel!"

[12] Therefore this is what the
Holy One of Israel says:

"Because you have rejected
    this message,
  relied on oppression
  and depended on deceit,
[13] this sin will become for
    you
  like a high wall, cracked and
    bulging,
  that collapses suddenly, in
    an instant.
[14] It will break in pieces like
    pottery,
  shattered so mercilessly

that among its pieces not a
    fragment will be found
  for taking coals from a
    hearth
  or scooping water out of a
    cistern."

15 This is what the Sovereign
Lord, the Holy One of Israel, says:

"In repentance and rest is your
    salvation,
  in quietness and trust is your
    strength,
  but you would have none of it.
16 You said, 'No, we will flee on
    horses.'
  Therefore you will flee!
You said, 'We will ride off on
    swift horses.'
  Therefore your pursuers will
    be swift!
17 A thousand will flee
    at the threat of one;
  at the threat of five
    you will all flee away,
  till you are left
    like a flagstaff on a
      mountaintop,
    like a banner on a hill."

18 Yet the Lord longs to be
    gracious to you;
  therefore he will rise up to
    show you compassion.
For the Lord is a God of
    justice.
  Blessed are all who wait for
    him!

19 People of Zion, who live in Jerusalem, you will weep no more. How gracious he will be when you cry for help! As soon as he hears, he will answer you. **20** Although the Lord gives you the bread of adversity and the water of affliction, your teachers will be hidden no more; with your own eyes you will see them. **21** Whether you turn to the right or to the left, your ears will hear a voice behind you, saying, "This is the way; walk in it." **22** Then you will desecrate your idols overlaid with silver and your images covered with gold; you will throw them away like a menstrual cloth and say to them, "Away with you!"

23 He will also send you rain for the seed you sow in the ground, and the food that comes from the land will be rich and plentiful. In that day your cattle will graze in broad meadows. **24** The oxen and donkeys that work the soil will eat fodder and mash, spread out with fork and shovel. **25** In the day of great slaughter, when the towers fall, streams of water will flow on every high mountain and every lofty hill. **26** The moon will shine like the sun, and the sunlight will be seven times brighter, like the light of seven full days, when the Lord binds up the bruises of his people and heals the wounds he inflicted.

27 See, the Name of the Lord
    comes from afar,
  with burning anger and
    dense clouds of smoke;
his lips are full of wrath,
  and his tongue is a
    consuming fire.

28 His breath is like a rushing
   torrent,
  rising up to the neck.
He shakes the nations in the
   sieve of destruction;
  he places in the jaws of the
   peoples
  a bit that leads them
   astray.
29 And you will sing
  as on the night you celebrate
   a holy festival;
your hearts will rejoice
  as when people playing
   pipes go up
to the mountain of the LORD,
  to the Rock of Israel.
30 The LORD will cause people to
   hear his majestic voice
  and will make them see his
   arm coming down
with raging anger and
   consuming fire,
  with cloudburst,
   thunderstorm and hail.
31 The voice of the LORD will
   shatter Assyria;
  with his rod he will strike
   them down.
32 Every stroke the LORD lays on
   them
  with his punishing club
will be to the music of timbrels
   and harps,
  as he fights them in battle
   with the blows of his
   arm.
33 Topheth has long been
   prepared;
  it has been made ready for
   the king.

Its fire pit has been made deep
   and wide,
  with an abundance of fire
   and wood;
the breath of the LORD,
  like a stream of burning
   sulfur,
  sets it ablaze.

Woe to Those Who Rely on Egypt

31 Woe to those who go
   down to Egypt for help,
who rely on horses,
who trust in the multitude of
   their chariots
  and in the great strength of
   their horsemen,
but do not look to the Holy One
   of Israel,
  or seek help from the
   LORD.
2 Yet he too is wise and can
   bring disaster;
  he does not take back his
   words.
He will rise up against that
   wicked nation,
  against those who help
   evildoers.
3 But the Egyptians are mere
   mortals and not God;
  their horses are flesh and not
   spirit.
When the LORD stretches out
   his hand,
  those who help will
   stumble,
  those who are helped will
   fall;
  all will perish together.

⁴This is what the LORD says to me:

"As a lion growls,
a great lion over its prey —
and though a whole band of
shepherds
is called together against it,
it is not frightened by their
shouts
or disturbed by their
clamor —
so the LORD Almighty will
come down
to do battle on Mount Zion
and on its heights.
⁵Like birds hovering overhead,
the LORD Almighty will
shield Jerusalem;
he will shield it and deliver it,
he will 'pass over' it and will
rescue it."

⁶Return, you Israelites, to the One you have so greatly revolted against. ⁷For in that day every one of you will reject the idols of silver and gold your sinful hands have made.

⁸"Assyria will fall by no human
sword;
a sword, not of mortals, will
devour them.
They will flee before the
sword
and their young men will be
put to forced labor.
⁹Their stronghold will fall
because of terror;
at the sight of the battle
standard their
commanders will panic,"

declares the LORD,
whose fire is in Zion,
whose furnace is in
Jerusalem.

The Kingdom of Righteousness

32 See, a king will reign in
righteousness
and rulers will rule with
justice.
²Each one will be like a shelter
from the wind
and a refuge from the storm,
like streams of water in the
desert
and the shadow of a great
rock in a thirsty land.

³Then the eyes of those who see
will no longer be closed,
and the ears of those who
hear will listen.
⁴The fearful heart will know
and understand,
and the stammering tongue
will be fluent and clear.
⁵No longer will the fool be
called noble
nor the scoundrel be highly
respected.
⁶For fools speak folly,
their hearts are bent on
evil:
They practice ungodliness
and spread error concerning
the LORD;
the hungry they leave empty
and from the thirsty they
withhold water.
⁷Scoundrels use wicked
methods,
they make up evil schemes

to destroy the poor with lies,
even when the plea of the
needy is just.
⁸ But the noble make noble
plans,
and by noble deeds they
stand.

The Women of Jerusalem

⁹ You women who are so
complacent,
rise up and listen to me;
you daughters who feel secure,
hear what I have to say!
¹⁰ In little more than a year
you who feel secure will
tremble;
the grape harvest will fail,
and the harvest of fruit will
not come.
¹¹ Tremble, you complacent
women;
shudder, you daughters who
feel secure!
Strip off your fine clothes
and wrap yourselves in rags.
¹² Beat your breasts for the
pleasant fields,
for the fruitful vines
¹³ and for the land of my people,
a land overgrown with
thorns and briers —
yes, mourn for all houses of
merriment
and for this city of revelry.
¹⁴ The fortress will be
abandoned,
the noisy city deserted;
citadel and watchtower will
become a wasteland
forever,

the delight of donkeys, a
pasture for flocks,
¹⁵ till the Spirit is poured on us
from on high,
and the desert becomes a
fertile field,
and the fertile field seems
like a forest.
¹⁶ The LORD's justice will dwell
in the desert,
his righteousness live in the
fertile field.
¹⁷ The fruit of that righteousness
will be peace;
its effect will be quietness
and confidence forever.
¹⁸ My people will live in peaceful
dwelling places,
in secure homes,
in undisturbed places of
rest.
¹⁹ Though hail flattens the forest
and the city is leveled
completely,
²⁰ how blessed you will be,
sowing your seed by every
stream,
and letting your cattle and
donkeys range free.

Distress and Help

33 Woe to you, destroyer,
you who have not been
destroyed!
Woe to you, betrayer,
you who have not been
betrayed!
When you stop destroying,
you will be destroyed;
when you stop betraying,
you will be betrayed.

²LORD, be gracious to us;
  we long for you.
 Be our strength every
    morning,
   our salvation in time of
    distress.
³At the uproar of your army, the
    peoples flee;
  when you rise up, the
    nations scatter.
⁴Your plunder, O nations, is
    harvested as by young
    locusts;
  like a swarm of locusts
    people pounce on it.

⁵The LORD is exalted, for he
    dwells on high;
  he will fill Zion with
    his justice and
    righteousness.
⁶He will be the sure foundation
    for your times,
  a rich store of salvation and
    wisdom and knowledge;
  the fear of the LORD is the
    key to this treasure.ᵃ

⁷Look, their brave men cry
    aloud in the streets;
  the envoys of peace weep
    bitterly.
⁸The highways are deserted,
  no travelers are on the roads.
  The treaty is broken,
   its witnessesᵇ are despised,
   no one is respected.
⁹The land dries up and wastes
    away,
  Lebanon is ashamed and
    withers;

Sharon is like the Arabah,
  and Bashan and Carmel
    drop their leaves.

¹⁰"Now will I arise," says the
    LORD.
 "Now will I be exalted;
   now will I be lifted up.
¹¹You conceive chaff,
  you give birth to straw;
  your breath is a fire that
    consumes you.
¹²The peoples will be burned to
    ashes;
  like cut thornbushes they
    will be set ablaze."

¹³You who are far away, hear
    what I have done;
  you who are near,
    acknowledge my power!
¹⁴The sinners in Zion are
    terrified;
  trembling grips the godless:
 "Who of us can dwell with the
    consuming fire?
  Who of us can dwell with
    everlasting burning?"
¹⁵Those who walk righteously
    and speak what is right,
  who reject gain from extortion
  and keep their hands from
    accepting bribes,
  who stop their ears against
    plots of murder
  and shut their eyes against
    contemplating evil—
¹⁶they are the ones who will
    dwell on the heights,
  whose refuge will be the
    mountain fortress.

ᵃ 6 Or *is a treasure from him*   ᵇ 8 Dead Sea Scrolls; Masoretic Text / *the cities*

Their bread will be supplied,
  and water will not fail them.

¹⁷Your eyes will see the king in
    his beauty
  and view a land that
    stretches afar.
¹⁸In your thoughts you will
    ponder the former terror:
  "Where is that chief officer?
  Where is the one who took the
    revenue?
  Where is the officer in
    charge of the towers?"
¹⁹You will see those arrogant
    people no more,
  people whose speech is
    obscure,
  whose language is strange
    and incomprehensible.

²⁰Look on Zion, the city of our
    festivals;
  your eyes will see Jerusalem,
  a peaceful abode, a tent that
    will not be moved;
  its stakes will never be
    pulled up,
  nor any of its ropes broken.
²¹There the LORD will be our
    Mighty One.
  It will be like a place of broad
    rivers and streams.
  No galley with oars will ride
    them,
  no mighty ship will sail
    them.
²²For the LORD is our judge,
  the LORD is our lawgiver,
  the LORD is our king;
  it is he who will save us.

²³Your rigging hangs loose:
  The mast is not held secure,
  the sail is not spread.
  Then an abundance of spoils
    will be divided
  and even the lame will carry
    off plunder.
²⁴No one living in Zion will say,
    "I am ill";
  and the sins of those who
    dwell there will be
    forgiven.

Judgment Against the Nations

34 Come near, you nations,
    and listen;
  pay attention, you peoples!
  Let the earth hear, and all that
    is in it,
  the world, and all that comes
    out of it!
²The LORD is angry with all
    nations;
  his wrath is on all their
    armies.
  He will totally destroy^a them,
  he will give them over to
    slaughter.
³Their slain will be thrown
    out,
  their dead bodies will
    stink;
  the mountains will be
    soaked with their blood.
⁴All the stars in the sky will be
    dissolved
  and the heavens rolled up
    like a scroll;
  all the starry host will fall

---

^a 2 The Hebrew term refers to the irrevocable giving over of things or persons to
the LORD, often by totally destroying them; also in verse 5.

like withered leaves from the
vine,
like shriveled figs from the
fig tree.

⁵My sword has drunk its fill in
the heavens;
see, it descends in judgment
on Edom,
the people I have totally
destroyed.

⁶The sword of the Lᴏʀᴅ is
bathed in blood,
it is covered with fat —
the blood of lambs and goats,
fat from the kidneys of rams.
For the Lᴏʀᴅ has a sacrifice in
Bozrah
and a great slaughter in the
land of Edom.

⁷And the wild oxen will fall
with them,
the bull calves and the great
bulls.
Their land will be drenched
with blood,
and the dust will be soaked
with fat.

⁸For the Lᴏʀᴅ has a day of
vengeance,
a year of retribution, to
uphold Zion's cause.

⁹Edom's streams will be turned
into pitch,
her dust into burning sulfur;
her land will become blazing
pitch!

¹⁰It will not be quenched night
or day;
its smoke will rise forever.

From generation to generation
it will lie desolate;
no one will ever pass
through it again.

¹¹The desert owl[a] and screech
owl[a] will possess it;
the great owl[a] and the raven
will nest there.
God will stretch out over
Edom
the measuring line of
chaos
and the plumb line of
desolation.

¹²Her nobles will have nothing
there to be called a
kingdom,
all her princes will vanish
away.

¹³Thorns will overrun her
citadels,
nettles and brambles her
strongholds.
She will become a haunt for
jackals,
a home for owls.

¹⁴Desert creatures will meet
with hyenas,
and wild goats will bleat to
each other;
there the night creatures will
also lie down
and find for themselves
places of rest.

¹⁵The owl will nest there and lay
eggs,
she will hatch them, and
care for her young
under the shadow of her
wings;

---

[a] 11 The precise identification of these birds is uncertain.

there also the falcons will
gather,
each with its mate.

[16] Look in the scroll of the LORD
and read:

None of these will be missing,
not one will lack her mate.
For it is his mouth that has
given the order,
and his Spirit will gather
them together.
[17] He allots their portions;
his hand distributes them by
measure.
They will possess it forever
and dwell there from
generation to generation.

Joy of the Redeemed

35 The desert and the
parched land will be
glad;
the wilderness will rejoice
and blossom.
Like the crocus, [2] it will burst
into bloom;
it will rejoice greatly and
shout for joy.
The glory of Lebanon will be
given to it,
the splendor of Carmel and
Sharon;
they will see the glory of the
LORD,
the splendor of our God.

[3] Strengthen the feeble hands,
steady the knees that give
way;
[4] say to those with fearful
hearts,
"Be strong, do not fear;

your God will come,
he will come with
vengeance;
with divine retribution
he will come to save you."

[5] Then will the eyes of the blind
be opened
and the ears of the deaf
unstopped.
[6] Then will the lame leap like a
deer,
and the mute tongue shout
for joy.
Water will gush forth in the
wilderness
and streams in the desert.
[7] The burning sand will become
a pool,
the thirsty ground bubbling
springs.
In the haunts where jackals
once lay,
grass and reeds and papyrus
will grow.

[8] And a highway will be there;
it will be called the Way of
Holiness;
it will be for those who walk
on that Way.
The unclean will not journey
on it;
wicked fools will not go
about on it.
[9] No lion will be there,
nor any ravenous beast;
they will not be found there.
But only the redeemed will
walk there,
[10] and those the LORD has
rescued will return.

They will enter Zion with
   singing;
  everlasting joy will crown
   their heads.
Gladness and joy will overtake
   them,
  and sorrow and sighing will
   flee away.

Sennacherib Threatens Jerusalem

36 In the fourteenth year of King Hezekiah's reign, Sennacherib king of Assyria attacked all the fortified cities of Judah and captured them. ²Then the king of Assyria sent his field commander with a large army from Lachish to King Hezekiah at Jerusalem. When the commander stopped at the aqueduct of the Upper Pool, on the road to the Launderer's Field, ³Eliakim son of Hilkiah the palace administrator, Shebna the secretary, and Joah son of Asaph the recorder went out to him.

⁴The field commander said to them, "Tell Hezekiah:

"'This is what the great king, the king of Assyria, says: On what are you basing this confidence of yours? ⁵You say you have counsel and might for war—but you speak only empty words. On whom are you depending, that you rebel against me? ⁶Look, I know you are depending on Egypt, that splintered reed of a staff, which pierces the hand of anyone who leans on it! Such is Pharaoh king of Egypt to all who depend on him. ⁷But if you say to me, "We are depending on the Lord our God"—isn't he the one whose high places and altars Hezekiah removed, saying to Judah and Jerusalem, "You must worship before this altar"?

⁸"'Come now, make a bargain with my master, the king of Assyria: I will give you two thousand horses—if you can put riders on them! ⁹How then can you repulse one officer of the least of my master's officials, even though you are depending on Egypt for chariots and horsemen*a*? ¹⁰Furthermore, have I come to attack and destroy this land without the Lord? The Lord himself told me to march against this country and destroy it.'"

¹¹Then Eliakim, Shebna and Joah said to the field commander, "Please speak to your servants in Aramaic, since we understand it. Don't speak to us in Hebrew in the hearing of the people on the wall."

¹²But the commander replied, "Was it only to your master and you that my master sent me to say these things, and not to the people sitting on the wall—who, like you, will have to eat their own

---

a 9 Or *charioteers*

excrement and drink their own urine?"

¹³Then the commander stood and called out in Hebrew, "Hear the words of the great king, the king of Assyria! ¹⁴This is what the king says: Do not let Hezekiah deceive you. He cannot deliver you! ¹⁵Do not let Hezekiah persuade you to trust in the Lord when he says, 'The Lord will surely deliver us; this city will not be given into the hand of the king of Assyria.'

¹⁶"Do not listen to Hezekiah. This is what the king of Assyria says: Make peace with me and come out to me. Then each of you will eat fruit from your own vine and fig tree and drink water from your own cistern, ¹⁷until I come and take you to a land like your own—a land of grain and new wine, a land of bread and vineyards.

¹⁸"Do not let Hezekiah mislead you when he says, 'The Lord will deliver us.' Have the gods of any nations ever delivered their lands from the hand of the king of Assyria? ¹⁹Where are the gods of Hamath and Arpad? Where are the gods of Sepharvaim? Have they rescued Samaria from my hand? ²⁰Who of all the gods of these countries have been able to save their lands from me? How then can the Lord deliver Jerusalem from my hand?"

²¹But the people remained silent and said nothing in reply, because the king had commanded, "Do not answer him."

²²Then Eliakim son of Hilkiah the palace administrator, Shebna the secretary and Joah son of Asaph the recorder went to Hezekiah, with their clothes torn, and told him what the field commander had said.

Jerusalem's Deliverance Foretold

37 When King Hezekiah heard this, he tore his clothes and put on sackcloth and went into the temple of the Lord. ²He sent Eliakim the palace administrator, Shebna the secretary, and the leading priests, all wearing sackcloth, to the prophet Isaiah son of Amoz. ³They told him, "This is what Hezekiah says: This day is a day of distress and rebuke and disgrace, as when children come to the moment of birth and there is no strength to deliver them. ⁴It may be that the Lord your God will hear the words of the field commander, whom his master, the king of Assyria, has sent to ridicule the living God, and that he will rebuke him for the words the Lord your God has heard. Therefore pray for the remnant that still survives."

⁵When King Hezekiah's officials came to Isaiah, ⁶Isaiah said to them, "Tell your master, 'This is what the Lord says: Do not be afraid of what you have heard—

those words with which the underlings of the king of Assyria have blasphemed me. [7] Listen! When he hears a certain report, I will make him want to return to his own country, and there I will have him cut down with the sword.'"

[8] When the field commander heard that the king of Assyria had left Lachish, he withdrew and found the king fighting against Libnah.

[9] Now Sennacherib received a report that Tirhakah, the king of Cush,[a] was marching out to fight against him. When he heard it, he sent messengers to Hezekiah with this word: [10] "Say to Hezekiah king of Judah: Do not let the god you depend on deceive you when he says, 'Jerusalem will not be given into the hands of the king of Assyria.' [11] Surely you have heard what the kings of Assyria have done to all the countries, destroying them completely. And will you be delivered? [12] Did the gods of the nations that were destroyed by my predecessors deliver them—the gods of Gozan, Harran, Rezeph and the people of Eden who were in Tel Assar? [13] Where is the king of Hamath or the king of Arpad? Where are the kings of Lair, Sepharvaim, Hena and Ivvah?"

Hezekiah's Prayer

[14] Hezekiah received the letter from the messengers and read it. Then he went up to the temple of the LORD and spread it out before the LORD. [15] And Hezekiah prayed to the LORD: [16] "LORD Almighty, the God of Israel, enthroned between the cherubim, you alone are God over all the kingdoms of the earth. You have made heaven and earth. [17] Give ear, LORD, and hear; open your eyes, LORD, and see; listen to all the words Sennacherib has sent to ridicule the living God.

[18] "It is true, LORD, that the Assyrian kings have laid waste all these peoples and their lands. [19] They have thrown their gods into the fire and destroyed them, for they were not gods but only wood and stone, fashioned by human hands. [20] Now, LORD our God, deliver us from his hand, so that all the kingdoms of the earth may know that you, LORD, are the only God.[b] —

Sennacherib's Fall

[21] Then Isaiah son of Amoz sent a message to Hezekiah: "This is what the LORD, the God of Israel, says: Because you have prayed to me concerning Sennacherib king of Assyria, [22] this is the word the LORD has spoken against him:

"Virgin Daughter Zion
    despises and mocks you.
Daughter Jerusalem
    tosses her head as you
        flee.

---

[a] 9 That is, the upper Nile region   [b] 20 Dead Sea Scrolls (see also 2 Kings 19:19); Masoretic Text *you alone are the LORD*

²³Who is it you have ridiculed
  and blasphemed?
  Against whom have you
    raised your voice
and lifted your eyes in pride?
  Against the Holy One of
    Israel!
²⁴By your messengers
  you have ridiculed the Lord.
And you have said,
  'With my many chariots
I have ascended the heights of
    the mountains,
  the utmost heights of
    Lebanon.
I have cut down its tallest
    cedars,
  the choicest of its junipers.
I have reached its remotest
    heights,
  the finest of its forests.
²⁵I have dug wells in foreign
    lands^a
  and drunk the water there.
With the soles of my feet
  I have dried up all the
    streams of Egypt.'

²⁶"Have you not heard?
  Long ago I ordained it.
In days of old I planned it;
  now I have brought it to pass,
that you have turned fortified
    cities
  into piles of stone.
²⁷Their people, drained of
    power,
  are dismayed and put to
    shame.

They are like plants in the
    field,
  like tender green shoots,
like grass sprouting on the
    roof,
  scorched^b before it grows up.
²⁸"But I know where you are
  and when you come and go
  and how you rage against
    me.
²⁹Because you rage against me
  and because your insolence
    has reached my ears,
I will put my hook in your nose
  and my bit in your mouth,
and I will make you return
  by the way you came.

³⁰"This will be the sign for you,
Hezekiah:

"This year you will eat what
    grows by itself,
  and the second year what
    springs from that.
But in the third year sow and
    reap,
  plant vineyards and eat their
    fruit.
³¹Once more a remnant of the
    kingdom of Judah
  will take root below and bear
    fruit above.
³²For out of Jerusalem will come
    a remnant,
  and out of Mount Zion a
    band of survivors.
The zeal of the LORD Almighty
  will accomplish this.

^a 25 Dead Sea Scrolls (see also 2 Kings 19:24); Masoretic Text does not have *in
foreign lands*.   ^b 27 Some manuscripts of the Masoretic Text, Dead Sea Scrolls
and some Septuagint manuscripts (see also 2 Kings 19:26); most manuscripts of
the Masoretic Text *roof / and terraced fields*

³³"Therefore this is what the LORD says concerning the king of Assyria:

"He will not enter this city
  or shoot an arrow here.
He will not come before it with shield
  or build a siege ramp
    against it.
³⁴By the way that he came he
    will return;
  he will not enter this city,"
            declares the LORD.
³⁵"I will defend this city and
    save it,
  for my sake and for the sake
    of David my servant!"

³⁶Then the angel of the LORD went out and put to death a hundred and eighty-five thousand in the Assyrian camp. When the people got up the next morning—there were all the dead bodies! ³⁷So Sennacherib king of Assyria broke camp and withdrew. He returned to Nineveh and stayed there.

³⁸One day, while he was worshiping in the temple of his god Nisrok, his sons Adrammelek and Sharezer killed him with the sword, and they escaped to the land of Ararat. And Esarhaddon his son succeeded him as king.

Hezekiah's Illness

38 In those days Hezekiah became ill and was at the point of death. The prophet Isaiah son of Amoz went to him and said, "This is what the LORD says: Put your house in order, because you are going to die; you will not recover."

²Hezekiah turned his face to the wall and prayed to the LORD, ³"Remember, LORD, how I have walked before you faithfully and with wholehearted devotion and have done what is good in your eyes." And Hezekiah wept bitterly.

⁴Then the word of the LORD came to Isaiah: ⁵"Go and tell Hezekiah, 'This is what the LORD, the God of your father David, says: I have heard your prayer and seen your tears; I will add fifteen years to your life. ⁶And I will deliver you and this city from the hand of the king of Assyria. I will defend this city.

⁷"'This is the LORD's sign to you that the LORD will do what he has promised: ⁸I will make the shadow cast by the sun go back the ten steps it has gone down on the stairway of Ahaz.'" So the sunlight went back the ten steps it had gone down.

⁹A writing of Hezekiah king of Judah after his illness and recovery:

¹⁰I said, "In the prime of my life
    must I go through the gates
      of death
  and be robbed of the rest of
      my years?"
¹¹I said, "I will not again see the
      LORD himself
  in the land of the living;

no longer will I look on my
    fellow man,
  or be with those who now
    dwell in this world.
¹²Like a shepherd's tent my
    house
  has been pulled down and
    taken from me.
Like a weaver I have rolled up
    my life,
  and he has cut me off from
    the loom;
  day and night you made an
    end of me.
¹³I waited patiently till dawn,
  but like a lion he broke all
    my bones;
  day and night you made an
    end of me.
¹⁴I cried like a swift or thrush,
  I moaned like a mourning
    dove.
My eyes grew weak as I looked
    to the heavens.
  I am being threatened; Lord,
    come to my aid!"

¹⁵But what can I say?
  He has spoken to me, and he
    himself has done this.
I will walk humbly all my
    years
  because of this anguish of
    my soul.
¹⁶Lord, by such things people
    live;
  and my spirit finds life in
    them too.
You restored me to health
  and let me live.
¹⁷Surely it was for my benefit
  that I suffered such anguish.

In your love you kept me
  from the pit of destruction;
you have put all my sins
  behind your back.
¹⁸For the grave cannot praise
    you,
  death cannot sing your
    praise;
those who go down to the pit
  cannot hope for your
    faithfulness.
¹⁹The living, the living — they
    praise you,
  as I am doing today;
parents tell their children
  about your faithfulness.

²⁰The LORD will save me,
  and we will sing with
    stringed instruments
all the days of our lives
  in the temple of the LORD.

²¹Isaiah had said, "Prepare a poultice of figs and apply it to the boil, and he will recover."

²²Hezekiah had asked, "What will be the sign that I will go up to the temple of the LORD?"

Envoys From Babylon

39 At that time Marduk-Baladan son of Baladan king of Babylon sent Hezekiah letters and a gift, because he had heard of his illness and recovery. ²Hezekiah received the envoys gladly and showed them what was in his storehouses — the silver, the gold, the spices, the fine olive oil — his entire armory and everything found among his treasures. There was nothing in his palace or in all his kingdom that Hezekiah did not show them.

³ Then Isaiah the prophet went to King Hezekiah and asked, "What did those men say, and where did they come from?"

"From a distant land," Hezekiah replied. "They came to me from Babylon."

⁴ The prophet asked, "What did they see in your palace?"

"They saw everything in my palace," Hezekiah said. "There is nothing among my treasures that I did not show them."

⁵ Then Isaiah said to Hezekiah, "Hear the word of the LORD Almighty: ⁶ The time will surely come when everything in your palace, and all that your predecessors have stored up until this day, will be carried off to Babylon. Nothing will be left, says the LORD. ⁷ And some of your descendants, your own flesh and blood who will be born to you, will be taken away, and they will become eunuchs in the palace of the king of Babylon."

⁸ "The word of the LORD you have spoken is good," Hezekiah replied. For he thought, "There will be peace and security in my lifetime."

Comfort for God's People

40 Comfort, comfort my people,
   says your God.
² Speak tenderly to Jerusalem,
   and proclaim to her
that her hard service has been
   completed,
   that her sin has been paid
   for,
that she has received from the
   LORD's hand
   double for all her sins.

³ A voice of one calling:
"In the wilderness prepare
   the way for the LORDᵃ;
make straight in the desert
   a highway for our God.ᵇ
⁴ Every valley shall be raised up,
   every mountain and hill
   made low;
the rough ground shall
   become level,
   the rugged places a plain.
⁵ And the glory of the LORD will
   be revealed,
   and all people will see it
   together.
   For the mouth of the LORD
   has spoken."

⁶ A voice says, "Cry out."
   And I said, "What shall I
   cry?"

"All people are like grass,
   and all their faithfulness is
   like the flowers of the
   field.
⁷ The grass withers and the
   flowers fall,
   because the breath of the
   LORD blows on them.
   Surely the people are grass.

ᵃ 3 Or A voice of one calling in the wilderness: / "Prepare the way for the LORD
ᵇ 3 Hebrew; Septuagint make straight the paths of our God

⁸The grass withers and the
flowers fall,
but the word of our God
endures forever."

⁹You who bring good news to
Zion,
go up on a high mountain.
You who bring good news to
Jerusalem,*ᵃ*
lift up your voice with a
shout,
lift it up, do not be afraid;
say to the towns of Judah,
"Here is your God!"
¹⁰See, the Sovereign LORD
comes with power,
and he rules with a mighty
arm.
See, his reward is with him,
and his recompense
accompanies him.
¹¹He tends his flock like a
shepherd:
He gathers the lambs in his
arms
and carries them close to his
heart;
he gently leads those that
have young.
¹²Who has measured the waters
in the hollow of his hand,
or with the breadth of his
hand marked off the
heavens?
Who has held the dust of the
earth in a basket,
or weighed the mountains
on the scales
and the hills in a balance?

¹³Who can fathom the Spirit*ᵇ* of
the LORD,
or instruct the LORD as his
counselor?
¹⁴Whom did the LORD consult to
enlighten him,
and who taught him the
right way?
Who was it that taught him
knowledge,
or showed him the path of
understanding?
¹⁵Surely the nations are like a
drop in a bucket;
they are regarded as dust on
the scales;
he weighs the islands as
though they were fine
dust.
¹⁶Lebanon is not sufficient for
altar fires,
nor its animals enough for
burnt offerings.
¹⁷Before him all the nations are
as nothing;
they are regarded by him as
worthless
and less than nothing.
¹⁸With whom, then, will you
compare God?
To what image will you liken
him?
¹⁹As for an idol, a metalworker
casts it,
and a goldsmith overlays it
with gold
and fashions silver chains
for it.

ᵃ 9 Or *Zion, bringer of good news, / go up on a high mountain. / Jerusalem, bringer
of good news* *ᵇ 13* Or *mind*

20 A person too poor to present
       such an offering
    selects wood that will not
       rot;
    they look for a skilled worker
       to set up an idol that will not
       topple.

21 Do you not know?
    Have you not heard?
    Has it not been told you from
       the beginning?
    Have you not understood
       since the earth was
       founded?
22 He sits enthroned above the
       circle of the earth,
    and its people are like
       grasshoppers.
    He stretches out the heavens
       like a canopy,
    and spreads them out like a
       tent to live in.
23 He brings princes to naught
    and reduces the rulers of this
       world to nothing.
24 No sooner are they planted,
    no sooner are they sown,
    no sooner do they take root
       in the ground,
    than he blows on them and
       they wither,
    and a whirlwind sweeps
       them away like chaff.

25 "To whom will you
       compare me?
    Or who is my equal?" says
       the Holy One.
26 Lift up your eyes and look to
       the heavens:
    Who created all these?

He who brings out the starry
    host one by one
    and calls forth each of them
       by name.
Because of his great power and
    mighty strength,
    not one of them is missing.

27 Why do you complain,
       Jacob?
    Why do you say, Israel,
    "My way is hidden from the
       Lord;
    my cause is disregarded by
       my God"?
28 Do you not know?
    Have you not heard?
    The Lord is the everlasting
       God,
    the Creator of the ends of the
       earth.
    He will not grow tired or
       weary,
    and his understanding no
       one can fathom.
29 He gives strength to the
       weary
    and increases the power of
       the weak.
30 Even youths grow tired and
       weary,
    and young men stumble and
       fall;
31 but those who hope in the
       Lord
    will renew their strength.
    They will soar on wings like
       eagles;
    they will run and not grow
       weary,
    they will walk and not be
       faint.

The Helper of Israel

41 "Be silent before me, you
islands!
Let the nations renew their
strength!
Let them come forward and
speak;
let us meet together at the
place of judgment.

2 "Who has stirred up one from
the east,
calling him in righteousness
to his service*a*?
He hands nations over to him
and subdues kings before
him.
He turns them to dust with his
sword,
to windblown chaff with his
bow.
3 He pursues them and moves
on unscathed,
by a path his feet have not
traveled before.
4 Who has done this and carried
it through,
calling forth the generations
from the beginning?
I, the LORD — with the first of
them
and with the last — I am he."

5 The islands have seen it and
fear;
the ends of the earth tremble.
They approach and come
forward;
6 they help each other
and say to their companions,
"Be strong!"

7 The metalworker encourages
the goldsmith,
and the one who smooths
with the hammer
spurs on the one who strikes
the anvil.
One says of the welding, "It is
good."
The other nails down the
idol so it will not topple.

8 "But you, Israel, my servant,
Jacob, whom I have
chosen,
you descendants of Abraham
my friend,
9 I took you from the ends of the
earth,
from its farthest corners I
called you.
I said, 'You are my servant';
I have chosen you and have
not rejected you.
10 So do not fear, for I am with
you;
do not be dismayed, for I am
your God.
I will strengthen you and help
you;
I will uphold you with my
righteous right hand.

11 "All who rage against you
will surely be ashamed and
disgraced;
those who oppose you
will be as nothing and
perish.
12 Though you search for your
enemies,
you will not find them.

a 2 Or *east, / whom victory meets at every step*

Those who wage war against
you
will be as nothing at all.
¹³ For I am the LORD your God
who takes hold of your right
hand
and says to you, Do not
fear;
I will help you.
¹⁴ Do not be afraid, you worm
Jacob,
little Israel, do not fear,
for I myself will help you,"
declares the LORD,
your Redeemer, the Holy
One of Israel.
¹⁵ "See, I will make you into a
threshing sledge,
new and sharp, with many
teeth.
You will thresh the mountains
and crush them,
and reduce the hills to
chaff.
¹⁶ You will winnow them, the
wind will pick them up,
and a gale will blow them
away.
But you will rejoice in the
LORD
and glory in the Holy One of
Israel.

¹⁷ "The poor and needy search
for water,
but there is none;
their tongues are parched
with thirst.
But I the LORD will answer
them;
I, the God of Israel, will not
forsake them.

¹⁸ I will make rivers flow on
barren heights,
and springs within the
valleys.
I will turn the desert into pools
of water,
and the parched ground into
springs.
¹⁹ I will put in the desert
the cedar and the acacia, the
myrtle and the olive.
I will set junipers in the
wasteland,
the fir and the cypress
together,
²⁰ so that people may see and
know,
may consider and
understand,
that the hand of the LORD has
done this,
that the Holy One of Israel
has created it.

²¹ "Present your case," says the
LORD.
"Set forth your arguments,"
says Jacob's King.
²² "Tell us, you idols,
what is going to happen.
Tell us what the former things
were,
so that we may consider
them
and know their final
outcome.
Or declare to us the things to
come,
²³ tell us what the future
holds,
so we may know that you are
gods.

Do something, whether good
or bad,
so that we will be dismayed
and filled with fear.
²⁴But you are less than nothing
and your works are utterly
worthless;
whoever chooses you is
detestable.

²⁵"I have stirred up one from the
north, and he comes—
one from the rising sun who
calls on my name.
He treads on rulers as if they
were mortar,
as if he were a potter
treading the clay.
²⁶Who told of this from the
beginning, so we could
know,
or beforehand, so we could
say, 'He was right'?
No one told of this,
no one foretold it,
no one heard any words
from you.
²⁷I was the first to tell Zion,
'Look, here they are!'
I gave to Jerusalem a
messenger of good
news.
²⁸I look but there is no one—
no one among the gods to
give counsel,
no one to give answer when I
ask them.
²⁹See, they are all false!
Their deeds amount to
nothing;
their images are but wind
and confusion.

The Servant of the LORD

42 "Here is my servant,
whom I uphold,
my chosen one in whom I
delight;
I will put my Spirit on him,
and he will bring justice to
the nations.
²He will not shout or cry out,
or raise his voice in the
streets.
³A bruised reed he will not
break,
and a smoldering wick he
will not snuff out.
In faithfulness he will bring
forth justice;
⁴ he will not falter or be
discouraged
till he establishes justice on
earth.
In his teaching the islands
will put their hope."

⁵This is what God the LORD
says—
the Creator of the heavens,
who stretches them
out,
who spreads out the earth
with all that springs
from it,
who gives breath to its
people,
and life to those who walk
on it:
⁶"I, the LORD, have called you
in righteousness;
I will take hold of your
hand.
I will keep you and will make
you

to be a covenant for the
people
and a light for the Gentiles,
⁷to open eyes that are blind,
to free captives from prison
and to release from the
dungeon those who sit in
darkness.

⁸"I am the LORD; that is my
name!
I will not yield my glory to
another
or my praise to idols.
⁹See, the former things have
taken place,
and new things I declare;
before they spring into
being
I announce them to you."

Song of Praise to the LORD

¹⁰Sing to the LORD a new song,
his praise from the ends of
the earth,
you who go down to the sea,
and all that is in it,
you islands, and all who live
in them.
¹¹Let the wilderness and its
towns raise their
voices;
let the settlements where
Kedar lives rejoice.
Let the people of Sela sing for
joy;
let them shout from the
mountaintops.
¹²Let them give glory to the
LORD
and proclaim his praise in
the islands.

¹³The LORD will march out like a
champion,
like a warrior he will stir up
his zeal;
with a shout he will raise the
battle cry
and will triumph over his
enemies.

¹⁴"For a long time I have kept
silent,
I have been quiet and held
myself back.
But now, like a woman in
childbirth,
I cry out, I gasp and pant.
¹⁵I will lay waste the mountains
and hills
and dry up all their
vegetation;
I will turn rivers into islands
and dry up the pools.
¹⁶I will lead the blind by ways
they have not known,
along unfamiliar paths I will
guide them;
I will turn the darkness into
light before them
and make the rough places
smooth.
These are the things I
will do;
I will not forsake them.
¹⁷But those who trust in idols,
who say to images, 'You are
our gods,'
will be turned back in utter
shame.

Israel Blind and Deaf

¹⁸"Hear, you deaf;
look, you blind, and see!

¹⁹Who is blind but my servant,
and deaf like the messenger
I send?
Who is blind like the one in
covenant with me,
blind like the servant of the
Lord?
²⁰You have seen many things,
but you pay no attention;
your ears are open, but you
do not listen."
²¹It pleased the Lord
for the sake of his
righteousness
to make his law great and
glorious.
²²But this is a people plundered
and looted,
all of them trapped in pits
or hidden away in prisons.
They have become plunder,
with no one to rescue them;
they have been made loot,
with no one to say, "Send
them back."

²³Which of you will listen to this
or pay close attention in time
to come?
²⁴Who handed Jacob over to
become loot,
and Israel to the plunderers?
Was it not the Lord,
against whom we have
sinned?
For they would not follow his
ways;
they did not obey his law.
²⁵So he poured out on them his
burning anger,
the violence of war.

It enveloped them in flames,
yet they did not
understand;
it consumed them, but they
did not take it to heart.

Israel's Only Savior

43 But now, this is what the
Lord says —
he who created you, Jacob,
he who formed you, Israel:
"Do not fear, for I have
redeemed you;
I have summoned you by
name; you are mine.
²When you pass through the
waters,
I will be with you;
and when you pass through
the rivers,
they will not sweep over
you.
When you walk through the
fire,
you will not be burned;
the flames will not set you
ablaze.
³For I am the Lord your God,
the Holy One of Israel, your
Savior;
I give Egypt for your ransom,
Cush^a and Seba in your
stead.
⁴Since you are precious and
honored in my sight,
and because I love you,
I will give people in exchange
for you,
nations in exchange for your
life.

^a 3 That is, the upper Nile region

⁵Do not be afraid, for I am with
      you;
   I will bring your children
      from the east
   and gather you from the
      west.
⁶I will say to the north, 'Give
      them up!'
   and to the south, 'Do not
      hold them back.'
Bring my sons from afar
   and my daughters from the
      ends of the earth —
⁷everyone who is called by my
      name,
   whom I created for my glory,
   whom I formed and made."

⁸Lead out those who have eyes
      but are blind,
   who have ears but are deaf.
⁹All the nations gather
      together
   and the peoples assemble.
Which of their gods foretold
      this
   and proclaimed to us the
      former things?
Let them bring in their
      witnesses to prove they
      were right,
   so that others may hear and
      say, "It is true."
¹⁰"You are my witnesses,"
      declares the LORD,
   "and my servant whom I
      have chosen,
   so that you may know and
      believe me
   and understand that I am he.

Before me no god was formed,
   nor will there be one after me.
¹¹I, even I, am the LORD,
   and apart from me there is
      no savior.
¹²I have revealed and saved and
      proclaimed —
   I, and not some foreign god
      among you.
You are my witnesses,"
   declares the LORD, "that
      I am God.
¹³   Yes, and from ancient days I
      am he.
No one can deliver out of my
      hand.
   When I act, who can
      reverse it?"

God's Mercy and Israel's Unfaithfulness

¹⁴This is what the LORD says —
   your Redeemer, the Holy
      One of Israel:
"For your sake I will send to
      Babylon
   and bring down as fugitives
      all the Babylonians,ᵃ
   in the ships in which they
      took pride.
¹⁵I am the LORD, your Holy
      One,
   Israel's Creator, your King."

¹⁶This is what the LORD says —
   he who made a way through
      the sea,
   a path through the mighty
      waters,
¹⁷who drew out the chariots and
      horses,

ᵃ 14 Or Chaldeans

the army and reinforcements
together,
and they lay there, never to
rise again,
extinguished, snuffed out
like a wick:
¹⁸ "Forget the former things;
do not dwell on the past.
¹⁹ See, I am doing a new thing!
Now it springs up; do you not
perceive it?
I am making a way in the
wilderness
and streams in the
wasteland.
²⁰ The wild animals honor me,
the jackals and the owls,
because I provide water in the
wilderness
and streams in the
wasteland,
to give drink to my people, my
chosen,
²¹   the people I formed for
myself
that they may proclaim my
praise.

²² "Yet you have not called on
me, Jacob,
you have not wearied
yourselves for^a me,
Israel.
²³ You have not brought me
sheep for burnt offerings,
nor honored me with your
sacrifices.
I have not burdened you with
grain offerings

nor wearied you with
demands for incense.
²⁴ You have not bought any
fragrant calamus for me,
or lavished on me the fat of
your sacrifices.
But you have burdened me
with your sins
and wearied me with your
offenses.

²⁵ "I, even I, am he who blots
out
your transgressions, for my
own sake,
and remembers your sins no
more.
²⁶ Review the past for me,
let us argue the matter
together;
state the case for your
innocence.
²⁷ Your first father sinned;
those I sent to teach you
rebelled against me.
²⁸ So I disgraced the dignitaries
of your temple;
I consigned Jacob to
destruction^b
and Israel to scorn.

Israel the Chosen

44 "But now listen, Jacob,
my servant,
Israel, whom I have chosen.
² This is what the LORD says —
he who made you, who
formed you in the womb,
and who will help you:

---

^a 22 Or *Jacob; / surely you have grown weary of*   ^b 28 The Hebrew term refers
to the irrevocable giving over of things or persons to the LORD, often by totally
destroying them.

Do not be afraid, Jacob, my
  servant,
  Jeshurun,[a] whom I have
  chosen.
³For I will pour water on the
  thirsty land,
  and streams on the dry
  ground;
I will pour out my Spirit on
  your offspring,
  and my blessing on your
  descendants.
⁴They will spring up like grass
  in a meadow,
  like poplar trees by flowing
  streams.
⁵Some will say, 'I belong to the
  LORD';
  others will call themselves
  by the name of Jacob;
still others will write on their
  hand, 'The LORD's,'
  and will take the name
  Israel.

The LORD, Not Idols

⁶"This is what the LORD says —
  Israel's King and Redeemer,
  the LORD Almighty:
I am the first and I am the last;
  apart from me there is no
  God.
⁷Who then is like me? Let him
  proclaim it.
  Let him declare and lay out
  before me
what has happened since I
  established my ancient
  people,
  and what is yet to come —

yes, let them foretell what
  will come.
⁸Do not tremble, do not be
  afraid.
Did I not proclaim this and
  foretell it long ago?
You are my witnesses. Is there
  any God besides me?
  No, there is no other Rock; I
  know not one."

⁹All who make idols are
  nothing,
  and the things they treasure
  are worthless.
Those who would speak up for
  them are blind;
  they are ignorant, to their
  own shame.
¹⁰Who shapes a god and casts an
  idol,
  which can profit nothing?
¹¹People who do that will be put
  to shame;
  such craftsmen are only
  human beings.
Let them all come together
  and take their stand;
  they will be brought down to
  terror and shame.

¹²The blacksmith takes a
  tool
  and works with it in the
  coals;
he shapes an idol with
  hammers,
  he forges it with the might of
  his arm.
He gets hungry and loses his
  strength;

---

[a] 2 *Jeshurun* means *the upright one*, that is, Israel.

he drinks no water and
grows faint.
13 The carpenter measures with
a line
and makes an outline with a
marker;
he roughs it out with chisels
and marks it with
compasses.
He shapes it in human form,
human form in all its glory,
that it may dwell in a shrine.
14 He cut down cedars,
or perhaps took a cypress or
oak.
He let it grow among the trees
of the forest,
or planted a pine, and the
rain made it grow.
15 It is used as fuel for burning;
some of it he takes and
warms himself,
he kindles a fire and bakes
bread.
But he also fashions a god and
worships it;
he makes an idol and bows
down to it.
16 Half of the wood he burns in
the fire;
over it he prepares his meal,
he roasts his meat and eats
his fill.
He also warms himself and
says,
"Ah! I am warm; I see the
fire."
17 From the rest he makes a god,
his idol;
he bows down to it and
worships.

He prays to it and says,
"Save me! You are my god!"
18 They know nothing, they
understand nothing;
their eyes are plastered over
so they cannot see,
and their minds closed so
they cannot understand.
19 No one stops to think,
no one has the knowledge or
understanding to say,
"Half of it I used for fuel;
I even baked bread over its
coals,
I roasted meat and I ate.
Shall I make a detestable thing
from what is left?
Shall I bow down to a block
of wood?"
20 Such a person feeds on ashes;
a deluded heart misleads
him;
he cannot save himself, or
say,
"Is not this thing in my right
hand a lie?"
21 "Remember these things, Jacob,
for you, Israel, are my
servant.
I have made you, you are my
servant;
Israel, I will not forget you.
22 I have swept away your
offenses like a cloud,
your sins like the morning
mist.
Return to me,
for I have redeemed you."
23 Sing for joy, you heavens, for
the LORD has done this;

shout aloud, you earth
beneath.
Burst into song, you
mountains,
you forests and all your
trees,
for the LORD has redeemed
Jacob,
he displays his glory in
Israel.

Jerusalem to Be Inhabited

24 "This is what the LORD says —
your Redeemer, who formed
you in the womb:

I am the LORD,
the Maker of all things,
who stretches out the
heavens,
who spreads out the earth by
myself,
25 who foils the signs of false
prophets
and makes fools of diviners,
who overthrows the learning
of the wise
and turns it into nonsense,
26 who carries out the words of
his servants
and fulfills the predictions of
his messengers,

who says of Jerusalem, 'It shall
be inhabited,'
of the towns of Judah, 'They
shall be rebuilt,'
and of their ruins, 'I will
restore them,'
27 who says to the watery deep,
'Be dry,

and I will dry up your
streams,'
28 who says of Cyrus, 'He is my
shepherd
and will accomplish all that I
please;
he will say of Jerusalem, "Let it
be rebuilt,"
and of the temple, "Let its
foundations be laid." '

45 "This is what the LORD
says to his anointed,
to Cyrus, whose right hand I
take hold of
to subdue nations before him
and to strip kings of their
armor,
to open doors before him
so that gates will not be
shut:
2 I will go before you
and will level the
mountains^a;
I will break down gates of
bronze
and cut through bars of
iron.
3 I will give you hidden
treasures,
riches stored in secret
places,
so that you may know that I
am the LORD,
the God of Israel, who
summons you by name.
4 For the sake of Jacob my
servant,
of Israel my chosen,

---

^a 2 Dead Sea Scrolls and Septuagint; the meaning of the word in the Masoretic
Text is uncertain.

I summon you by name
and bestow on you a title of
honor,
though you do not
acknowledge me.
⁵ I am the LORD, and there is no
other;
apart from me there is no
God.
I will strengthen you,
though you have not
acknowledged me,
⁶ so that from the rising of the
sun
to the place of its setting
people may know there is none
besides me.
I am the LORD, and there is
no other.
⁷ I form the light and create
darkness,
I bring prosperity and create
disaster;
I, the LORD, do all these
things.

⁸ "You heavens above, rain
down my righteousness;
let the clouds shower it
down.
Let the earth open wide,
let salvation spring up,
let righteousness flourish
with it;
I, the LORD, have created it.

⁹ "Woe to those who quarrel
with their Maker,
those who are nothing but
potsherds
among the potsherds on the
ground.

Does the clay say to the potter,
'What are you making?'
Does your work say,
'The potter has no hands'?
¹⁰ Woe to the one who says to a
father,
'What have you begotten?'
or to a mother,
'What have you brought to
birth?'

¹¹ "This is what the LORD says —
the Holy One of Israel, and
its Maker:
Concerning things to come,
do you question me about
my children,
or give me orders about the
work of my hands?
¹² It is I who made the earth
and created mankind on it.
My own hands stretched out
the heavens;
I marshaled their starry
hosts.
¹³ I will raise up Cyrusᵃ in my
righteousness:
I will make all his ways
straight.
He will rebuild my city
and set my exiles free,
but not for a price or reward,
says the LORD Almighty."

¹⁴ This is what the LORD says:

"The products of Egypt and
the merchandise of
Cush,ᵇ
and those tall Sabeans —
they will come over to you
and will be yours;

ᵃ 13 Hebrew *him*   ᵇ 14 That is, the upper Nile region

they will trudge behind you,
  coming over to you in
    chains.
They will bow down before
  you
  and plead with you, saying,
'Surely God is with you, and
    there is no other;
  there is no other god.'"

15 Truly you are a God who has
    been hiding himself,
  the God and Savior of Israel.
16 All the makers of idols will
    be put to shame and
      disgraced;
  they will go off into disgrace
    together.
17 But Israel will be saved by the
    LORD
  with an everlasting
    salvation;
  you will never be put to shame
    or disgraced,
  to ages everlasting.

18 For this is what the LORD
    says —
  he who created the heavens,
    he is God;
  he who fashioned and made
    the earth,
    he founded it;
  he did not create it to be
    empty,
    but formed it to be
      inhabited —
  he says:
  "I am the LORD,
    and there is no other.
19 I have not spoken in secret,
  from somewhere in a land of
    darkness;

I have not said to Jacob's
    descendants,
  'Seek me in vain.'
I, the LORD, speak the truth;
  I declare what is right.

20 "Gather together and come;
  assemble, you fugitives from
    the nations.
Ignorant are those who carry
    about idols of wood,
  who pray to gods that cannot
    save.
21 Declare what is to be, present
    it —
  let them take counsel
    together.
Who foretold this long ago,
  who declared it from the
    distant past?
Was it not I, the LORD?
  And there is no God apart
    from me,
a righteous God and a Savior;
  there is none but me.

22 "Turn to me and be saved,
  all you ends of the earth;
  for I am God, and there is no
    other.
23 By myself I have sworn,
  my mouth has uttered in all
    integrity
  a word that will not be
    revoked:
Before me every knee will
    bow;
  by me every tongue will
    swear.
24 They will say of me, 'In the
    LORD alone
  are deliverance and
    strength.'"

All who have raged against
    him
    will come to him and be put
      to shame.
25 But all the descendants of
    Israel
    will find deliverance in the
      LORD
    and will make their boast in
      him.

Gods of Babylon

46   Bel bows down, Nebo
    stoops low;
    their idols are borne by
      beasts of burden.*a*
The images that are carried
    about are burdensome,
    a burden for the weary.
2 They stoop and bow down
    together;
    unable to rescue the burden,
    they themselves go off into
      captivity.

3 "Listen to me, you descendants
    of Jacob,
    all the remnant of the people
      of Israel,
you whom I have upheld since
    your birth,
    and have carried since you
      were born.
4 Even to your old age and gray
    hairs
    I am he, I am he who will
      sustain you.
I have made you and I will
    carry you;
    I will sustain you and I will
      rescue you.

5 "With whom will you compare
    me or count me equal?
    To whom will you liken
      me that we may be
      compared?
6 Some pour out gold from their
    bags
    and weigh out silver on the
      scales;
they hire a goldsmith to make
    it into a god,
    and they bow down and
      worship it.
7 They lift it to their shoulders
    and carry it;
    they set it up in its place, and
      there it stands.
From that spot it cannot
    move.
Even though someone cries
    out to it, it cannot
      answer;
    it cannot save them from
      their troubles.

8 "Remember this, keep it in
    mind,
    take it to heart, you rebels.
9 Remember the former things,
    those of long ago;
    I am God, and there is no
      other;
    I am God, and there is none
      like me.
10 I make known the end from
    the beginning,
    from ancient times, what is
      still to come.
I say, 'My purpose will stand,
    and I will do all that I
      please.'

a 1 Or *are but beasts and cattle*

¹¹From the east I summon a bird
    of prey;
    from a far-off land, a man to
    fulfill my purpose.
What I have said, that I will
    bring about;
    what I have planned, that I
    will do.
¹²Listen to me, you stubborn-
    hearted,
    you who are now far from my
    righteousness.
¹³I am bringing my
    righteousness near,
    it is not far away;
    and my salvation will not be
    delayed.
I will grant salvation to
    Zion,
    my splendor to Israel.

The Fall of Babylon

47 "Go down, sit in the dust,
    Virgin Daughter Babylon;
sit on the ground without a
    throne,
    queen city of the
    Babylonians.^a
No more will you be called
    tender or delicate.
²Take millstones and grind
    flour;
    take off your veil.
Lift up your skirts, bare your
    legs,
    and wade through the
    streams.
³Your nakedness will be
    exposed
    and your shame uncovered.

I will take vengeance;
    I will spare no one."

⁴Our Redeemer — the LORD
    Almighty is his name —
    is the Holy One of Israel.

⁵"Sit in silence, go into
    darkness,
    queen city of the
    Babylonians;
no more will you be called
    queen of kingdoms.
⁶I was angry with my people
    and desecrated my
    inheritance;
I gave them into your hand,
    and you showed them no
    mercy.
Even on the aged
    you laid a very heavy yoke.
⁷You said, 'I am forever —
    the eternal queen!'
But you did not consider these
    things
    or reflect on what might
    happen.

⁸"Now then, listen, you lover of
    pleasure,
    lounging in your security
and saying to yourself,
    'I am, and there is none
    besides me.
I will never be a widow
    or suffer the loss of children.'
⁹Both of these will overtake
    you
    in a moment, on a single
    day:
    loss of children and
    widowhood.

---

^a 1 Or *Chaldeans*; also in verse 5

They will come upon you in
full measure,
in spite of your many
sorceries
and all your potent spells.
¹⁰You have trusted in your
wickedness
and have said, 'No one
sees me.'
Your wisdom and knowledge
mislead you
when you say to yourself,
'I am, and there is none
besides me.'
¹¹Disaster will come upon you,
and you will not know how
to conjure it away.
A calamity will fall upon you
that you cannot ward off
with a ransom;
a catastrophe you cannot
foresee
will suddenly come upon
you.

¹²"Keep on, then, with your
magic spells
and with your many
sorceries,
which you have labored at
since childhood.
Perhaps you will succeed,
perhaps you will cause
terror.
¹³All the counsel you have
received has only worn
you out!
Let your astrologers come
forward,
those stargazers who make
predictions month by
month,

let them save you from what
is coming upon you.
¹⁴Surely they are like stubble;
the fire will burn them up.
They cannot even save
themselves
from the power of the
flame.
These are not coals for
warmth;
this is not a fire to sit by.
¹⁵That is all they are to you —
these you have dealt with
and labored with since
childhood.
All of them go on in their
error;
there is not one that can save
you.

Stubborn Israel

48 "Listen to this, you
descendants of Jacob,
you who are called by the
name of Israel
and come from the line of
Judah,
you who take oaths in the
name of the LORD
and invoke the God of
Israel —
but not in truth or
righteousness —
²you who call yourselves
citizens of the holy city
and claim to rely on the God
of Israel —
the LORD Almighty is his
name:
³I foretold the former things
long ago,

my mouth announced them
and I made them known;
then suddenly I acted, and
they came to pass.
4 For I knew how stubborn you
were;
your neck muscles were
iron,
your forehead was bronze.
5 Therefore I told you these
things long ago;
before they happened I
announced them to you
so that you could not say,
'My images brought them
about;
my wooden image and metal
god ordained them.'
6 You have heard these things;
look at them all.
Will you not admit them?

"From now on I will tell you of
new things,
of hidden things unknown
to you.
7 They are created now, and not
long ago;
you have not heard of them
before today.
So you cannot say,
'Yes, I knew of them.'
8 You have neither heard nor
understood;
from of old your ears have
not been open.
Well do I know how
treacherous you are;
you were called a rebel from
birth.

9 For my own name's sake I
delay my wrath;
for the sake of my praise I
hold it back from you,
so as not to destroy you
completely.
10 See, I have refined you, though
not as silver;
I have tested you in the
furnace of affliction.
11 For my own sake, for my own
sake, I do this.
How can I let myself be
defamed?
I will not yield my glory to
another.

Israel Freed

12 "Listen to me, Jacob,
Israel, whom I have called:
I am he;
I am the first and I am the
last.
13 My own hand laid the
foundations of the earth,
and my right hand spread
out the heavens;
when I summon them,
they all stand up together.

14 "Come together, all of you, and
listen:
Which of the idols has
foretold these things?
The Lord's chosen ally
will carry out his purpose
against Babylon;
his arm will be against the
Babylonians.ᵃ
15 I, even I, have spoken;
yes, I have called him.

ᵃ 14 Or Chaldeans; also in verse 20

I will bring him,
and he will succeed in his
mission.

16 "Come near me and listen to
this:

"From the first announcement
I have not spoken in
secret;
at the time it happens, I am
there."

And now the Sovereign LORD
has sent me,
endowed with his Spirit.

17 This is what the LORD says —
your Redeemer, the Holy
One of Israel:
"I am the LORD your God,
who teaches you what is best
for you,
who directs you in the way
you should go.
18 If only you had paid attention
to my commands,
your peace would have been
like a river,
your well-being like the
waves of the sea.
19 Your descendants would have
been like the sand,
your children like its
numberless grains;
their name would never be
blotted out
nor destroyed from
before me."

20 Leave Babylon,
flee from the Babylonians!
Announce this with shouts of
joy
and proclaim it.

Send it out to the ends of the
earth;
say, "The LORD has
redeemed his servant
Jacob."
21 They did not thirst when he
led them through the
deserts;
he made water flow for them
from the rock;
he split the rock
and water gushed out.

22 "There is no peace," says the
LORD, "for the wicked."

The Servant of the LORD

49 Listen to me, you
islands;
hear this, you distant
nations:
Before I was born the LORD
called me;
from my mother's womb
he has spoken my
name.
2 He made my mouth like a
sharpened sword,
in the shadow of his hand he
hid me;
he made me into a polished
arrow
and concealed me in his
quiver.
3 He said to me, "You are my
servant,
Israel, in whom I will display
my splendor."
4 But I said, "I have labored in
vain;
I have spent my strength for
nothing at all.

Yet what is due me is in the
LORD's hand,
and my reward is with my
God."

⁵And now the LORD says —
he who formed me in the
womb to be his servant
to bring Jacob back to him
and gather Israel to
himself,
for I am*a* honored in the eyes
of the LORD
and my God has been my
strength —
⁶he says:
"It is too small a thing for you
to be my servant
to restore the tribes of Jacob
and bring back those of
Israel I have kept.
I will also make you a light for
the Gentiles,
that my salvation may reach
to the ends of the earth."

⁷This is what the LORD says —
the Redeemer and Holy One
of Israel —
to him who was despised and
abhorred by the nation,
to the servant of rulers:
"Kings will see you and
stand up,
princes will see and bow
down,
because of the LORD, who is
faithful,
the Holy One of Israel, who
has chosen you."

Restoration of Israel

⁸This is what the LORD says:

"In the time of my favor I will
answer you,
and in the day of salvation I
will help you;
I will keep you and will make
you
to be a covenant for the
people,
to restore the land
and to reassign its desolate
inheritances,
⁹to say to the captives, 'Come
out,'
and to those in darkness, 'Be
free!'

"They will feed beside the
roads
and find pasture on every
barren hill.
¹⁰They will neither hunger nor
thirst,
nor will the desert heat or the
sun beat down on them.
He who has compassion on
them will guide them
and lead them beside
springs of water.
¹¹I will turn all my mountains
into roads,
and my highways will be
raised up.
¹²See, they will come from afar —
some from the north, some
from the west,
some from the region of
Aswan.*b*"

---

a 5 Or *him, / but Israel would not be gathered; / yet I will be*   *b* 12 Dead Sea
Scrolls; Masoretic Text *Sinim*

¹³Shout for joy, you heavens;
rejoice, you earth;
burst into song, you
mountains!
For the LORD comforts his
people
and will have compassion on
his afflicted ones.

¹⁴But Zion said, "The LORD has
forsaken me,
the Lord has forgotten me."

¹⁵"Can a mother forget the baby
at her breast
and have no compassion on
the child she has borne?
Though she may forget,
I will not forget you!
¹⁶See, I have engraved you on
the palms of my hands;
your walls are ever
before me.
¹⁷Your children hasten back,
and those who laid you
waste depart from you.
¹⁸Lift up your eyes and look
around;
all your children gather and
come to you.
As surely as I live," declares
the LORD,
"you will wear them all as
ornaments;
you will put them on, like a
bride.

¹⁹"Though you were ruined and
made desolate
and your land laid waste,
now you will be too small for
your people,
and those who devoured you
will be far away.
²⁰The children born during your
bereavement
will yet say in your hearing,
'This place is too small
for us;
give us more space to
live in.'
²¹Then you will say in your
heart,
'Who bore me these?
I was bereaved and barren;
I was exiled and rejected.
Who brought these up?
I was left all alone,
but these — where have they
come from?'"

²²This is what the Sovereign
LORD says:

"See, I will beckon to the
nations,
I will lift up my banner to the
peoples;
they will bring your sons in
their arms
and carry your daughters on
their hips.
²³Kings will be your foster
fathers,
and their queens your
nursing mothers.
They will bow down before
you with their faces to
the ground;
they will lick the dust at your
feet.
Then you will know that I am
the LORD;
those who hope in me will
not be disappointed."

²⁴Can plunder be taken from
warriors,
or captives be rescued from
the fierce*ᵃ*?

²⁵But this is what the LORD
says:

"Yes, captives will be taken
from warriors,
and plunder retrieved from
the fierce;
I will contend with those who
contend with you,
and your children I will save.
²⁶I will make your oppressors
eat their own flesh;
they will be drunk on their
own blood, as with wine.
Then all mankind will know
that I, the LORD, am your
Savior,
your Redeemer, the Mighty
One of Jacob."

Israel's Sin and the Servant's Obedience

50 This is what the LORD
says:

"Where is your mother's
certificate of divorce
with which I sent her
away?
Or to which of my creditors
did I sell you?
Because of your sins you were
sold;
because of your
transgressions your
mother was sent away.

²When I came, why was there
no one?
When I called, why was
there no one to answer?
Was my arm too short to
deliver you?
Do I lack the strength to
rescue you?
By a mere rebuke I dry up the
sea,
I turn rivers into a desert;
their fish rot for lack of water
and die of thirst.
³I clothe the heavens with
darkness
and make sackcloth its
covering."

⁴The Sovereign LORD has given
me a well-instructed
tongue,
to know the word that
sustains the weary.
He wakens me morning by
morning,
wakens my ear to listen like
one being instructed.
⁵The Sovereign LORD has
opened my ears;
I have not been rebellious,
I have not turned away.
⁶I offered my back to those who
beat me,
my cheeks to those who
pulled out my beard;
I did not hide my face
from mocking and spitting.
⁷Because the Sovereign LORD
helps me,
I will not be disgraced.

ᵃ 24 Dead Sea Scrolls, Vulgate and Syriac (see also Septuagint and verse 25);
Masoretic Text *righteous*

Therefore have I set my face
like flint,
and I know I will not be put
to shame.
[8] He who vindicates me is near.
Who then will bring charges
against me?
Let us face each other!
Who is my accuser?
Let him confront me!
[9] It is the Sovereign LORD who
helps me.
Who will condemn me?
They will all wear out like a
garment;
the moths will eat them up.

[10] Who among you fears the
LORD
and obeys the word of his
servant?
Let the one who walks in the
dark,
who has no light,
trust in the name of the LORD
and rely on their God.
[11] But now, all you who light
fires
and provide yourselves with
flaming torches,
go, walk in the light of your
fires
and of the torches you have
set ablaze.
This is what you shall receive
from my hand:
You will lie down in torment.

Everlasting Salvation for Zion

51 "Listen to me, you who
pursue righteousness
and who seek the LORD:

Look to the rock from which
you were cut
and to the quarry from
which you were hewn;
[2] look to Abraham, your father,
and to Sarah, who gave you
birth.
When I called him he was only
one man,
and I blessed him and made
him many.
[3] The LORD will surely comfort
Zion
and will look with
compassion on all her
ruins;
he will make her deserts like
Eden,
her wastelands like the
garden of the LORD.
Joy and gladness will be found
in her,
thanksgiving and the sound
of singing.

[4] "Listen to me, my people;
hear me, my nation:
Instruction will go out
from me;
my justice will become a
light to the nations.
[5] My righteousness draws near
speedily,
my salvation is on the way,
and my arm will bring
justice to the nations.
The islands will look to me
and wait in hope for my
arm.
[6] Lift up your eyes to the
heavens,
look at the earth beneath;

the heavens will vanish like
smoke,
the earth will wear out like a
garment
and its inhabitants die like
flies.
But my salvation will last
forever,
my righteousness will never
fail.

7 "Hear me, you who know what
is right,
you people who have taken
my instruction to heart:
Do not fear the reproach of
mere mortals
or be terrified by their
insults.
8 For the moth will eat them up
like a garment;
the worm will devour them
like wool.
But my righteousness will last
forever,
my salvation through all
generations."

9 Awake, awake, arm of the
Lord,
clothe yourself with
strength!
Awake, as in days gone by,
as in generations of old.
Was it not you who cut Rahab
to pieces,
who pierced that monster
through?
10 Was it not you who dried up
the sea,
the waters of the great deep,
who made a road in the depths
of the sea

so that the redeemed might
cross over?
11 Those the Lord has rescued
will return.
They will enter Zion with
singing;
everlasting joy will crown
their heads.
Gladness and joy will overtake
them,
and sorrow and sighing will
flee away.

12 "I, even I, am he who comforts
you.
Who are you that you fear
mere mortals,
human beings who are but
grass,
13 that you forget the Lord your
Maker,
who stretches out the
heavens
and who lays the
foundations of the earth,
that you live in constant terror
every day
because of the wrath of the
oppressor,
who is bent on destruction?
For where is the wrath of the
oppressor?
14 The cowering prisoners will
soon be set free;
they will not die in their
dungeon,
nor will they lack bread.
15 For I am the Lord your God,
who stirs up the sea so that
its waves roar —
the Lord Almighty is his
name.

¹⁶ I have put my words in your
mouth
and covered you with the
shadow of my hand —
I who set the heavens in place,
who laid the foundations of
the earth,
and who say to Zion, 'You are
my people.'"

The Cup of the LORD's Wrath

¹⁷ Awake, awake!
Rise up, Jerusalem,
you who have drunk from the
hand of the LORD
the cup of his wrath,
you who have drained to its
dregs
the goblet that makes people
stagger.
¹⁸ Among all the children she
bore
there was none to guide her;
among all the children she
reared
there was none to take her by
the hand.
¹⁹ These double calamities have
come upon you —
who can comfort you? —
ruin and destruction, famine
and sword —
who can^a console you?
²⁰ Your children have fainted;
they lie at every street
corner,
like antelope caught in a net.
They are filled with the wrath
of the LORD,
with the rebuke of your God.

²¹ Therefore hear this, you
afflicted one,
made drunk, but not with
wine.
²² This is what your Sovereign
LORD says,
your God, who defends his
people:
"See, I have taken out of your
hand
the cup that made you
stagger;
from that cup, the goblet of my
wrath,
you will never drink again.
²³ I will put it into the hands of
your tormentors,
who said to you,
'Fall prostrate that we may
walk on you.'
And you made your back like
the ground,
like a street to be walked on."

52

Awake, awake, Zion,
clothe yourself with
strength!
Put on your garments of
splendor,
Jerusalem, the holy city.
The uncircumcised and
defiled
will not enter you again.
² Shake off your dust;
rise up, sit enthroned,
Jerusalem.
Free yourself from the chains
on your neck,
Daughter Zion, now a
captive.

---

^a 19 Dead Sea Scrolls, Septuagint, Vulgate and Syriac; Masoretic Text / how can I

³ For this is what the Lord says:

"You were sold for nothing,
  and without money you will
    be redeemed."

⁴ For this is what the Sovereign
Lord says:

"At first my people went down
    to Egypt to live;
  lately, Assyria has oppressed
    them.

⁵ "And now what do I have here?"
declares the Lord.

"For my people have been
    taken away for
    nothing,
  and those who rule them
    mock,ᵃ"
        declares the Lord.
"And all day long
  my name is constantly
    blasphemed.
⁶ Therefore my people will know
    my name;
  therefore in that day they
    will know
  that it is I who foretold it.
    Yes, it is I."

⁷ How beautiful on the
    mountains
  are the feet of those who
    bring good news,
who proclaim peace,
  who bring good tidings,
  who proclaim salvation,
who say to Zion,
  "Your God reigns!"

⁸ Listen! Your watchmen lift up
    their voices;
  together they shout for joy.
When the Lord returns to
    Zion,
  they will see it with their
    own eyes.
⁹ Burst into songs of joy
    together,
  you ruins of Jerusalem,
for the Lord has comforted his
    people,
  he has redeemed Jerusalem.
¹⁰ The Lord will lay bare his holy
    arm
  in the sight of all the nations,
and all the ends of the earth
    will see
  the salvation of our God.

¹¹ Depart, depart, go out from
    there!
  Touch no unclean thing!
Come out from it and be
    pure,
  you who carry the articles of
    the Lord's house.
¹² But you will not leave in haste
    or go in flight;
for the Lord will go before
    you,
  the God of Israel will be your
    rear guard.

The Suffering and Glory of the Servant

¹³ See, my servant will act
    wisely ᵇ;
  he will be raised and lifted
    up and highly exalted.

ᵃ 5 Dead Sea Scrolls and Vulgate; Masoretic Text *wail*   ᵇ 13 Or *will prosper*

¹⁴Just as there were many who
were appalled at him^a —
his appearance was so
disfigured beyond that of
any human being
and his form marred beyond
human likeness —
¹⁵so he will sprinkle many
nations,^b
and kings will shut their
mouths because of him.
For what they were not told,
they will see,
and what they have not
heard, they will
understand.

53

Who has believed our
message
and to whom has the arm of
the LORD been revealed?
²He grew up before him like a
tender shoot,
and like a root out of dry
ground.
He had no beauty or majesty to
attract us to him,
nothing in his appearance
that we should desire
him.
³He was despised and rejected
by mankind,
a man of suffering, and
familiar with pain.
Like one from whom people
hide their faces
he was despised, and we
held him in low esteem.

⁴Surely he took up our pain
and bore our suffering,
yet we considered him
punished by God,
stricken by him, and
afflicted.
⁵But he was pierced for our
transgressions,
he was crushed for our
iniquities;
the punishment that brought
us peace was on him,
and by his wounds we are
healed.
⁶We all, like sheep, have gone
astray,
each of us has turned to our
own way;
and the LORD has laid on him
the iniquity of us all.

⁷He was oppressed and
afflicted,
yet he did not open his mouth;
he was led like a lamb to the
slaughter,
and as a sheep before its
shearers is silent,
so he did not open his mouth.
⁸By oppression^c and judgment
he was taken away.
Yet who of his generation
protested?
For he was cut off from the
land of the living;
for the transgression of
my people he was
punished.^d

---

^a 14 Hebrew *you*   ^b 15 Or *so will many nations be amazed at him* (see also
Septuagint)   ^c 8 Or *From arrest*   ^d 8 Or *generation considered / that he was
cut off from the land of the living, / that he was punished for the transgression of my
people?*

⁹He was assigned a grave with
the wicked,
    and with the rich in his
    death,
though he had done no
    violence,
    nor was any deceit in his
    mouth.
¹⁰Yet it was the LORD's will to
    crush him and cause
    him to suffer,
    and though the LORD
    makes*a* his life an
    offering for sin,
he will see his offspring and
    prolong his days,
    and the will of the LORD will
    prosper in his hand.
¹¹After he has suffered,
    he will see the light of life*b*
    and be satisfied*c*;
by his knowledge*d* my
    righteous servant will
    justify many,
    and he will bear their
    iniquities.
¹²Therefore I will give him
    a portion among the
    great,*e*
and he will divide the spoils
    with the strong,*f*
because he poured out his life
    unto death,
    and was numbered with the
    transgressors.
For he bore the sin of many,
    and made intercession for
    the transgressors.

The Future Glory of Zion

54 "Sing, barren woman,
    you who never bore a
    child;
burst into song, shout for joy,
    you who were never in
    labor;
because more are the children
    of the desolate woman
    than of her who has a
    husband,"
        says the LORD.
²"Enlarge the place of your tent,
    stretch your tent curtains
    wide,
    do not hold back;
lengthen your cords,
    strengthen your stakes.
³For you will spread out to the
    right and to the left;
    your descendants will
    dispossess nations
    and settle in their desolate
    cities.

⁴"Do not be afraid; you will not
    be put to shame.
Do not fear disgrace; you
    will not be humiliated.
You will forget the shame of
    your youth
    and remember no more
    the reproach of your
    widowhood.
⁵For your Maker is your
    husband —
    the LORD Almighty is his
    name —

---

a 10 Hebrew *though you make*   *b 11* Dead Sea Scrolls (see also Septuagint);
Masoretic Text does not have *the light of life.*   *c 11* Or (with Masoretic Text) *¹¹He
will see the fruit of his suffering / and will be satisfied*   *d 11* Or *by knowledge of
him*   *e 12* Or *many*   *f 12* Or *numerous*

the Holy One of Israel is your
  Redeemer;
he is called the God of all the
  earth.
⁶The LORD will call you back
  as if you were a wife deserted
    and distressed in
    spirit —
a wife who married young,
  only to be rejected," says
    your God.
⁷"For a brief moment I
    abandoned you,
  but with deep compassion I
    will bring you back.
⁸In a surge of anger
I hid my face from you for a
  moment,
  but with everlasting kindness
  I will have compassion on
    you,"
  says the LORD your
    Redeemer.
⁹"To me this is like the days of
  Noah,
  when I swore that the waters
    of Noah would never
    again cover the earth.
So now I have sworn not to be
  angry with you,
  never to rebuke you again.
¹⁰Though the mountains be
  shaken
  and the hills be removed,
yet my unfailing love for you
  will not be shaken
  nor my covenant of peace be
    removed,"
  says the LORD, who has
    compassion on you.

¹¹"Afflicted city, lashed
  by storms and not
    comforted,
  I will rebuild you with stones
    of turquoise,ᵃ
  your foundations with lapis
    lazuli.
¹²I will make your battlements
    of rubies,
  your gates of sparkling
    jewels,
  and all your walls of
    precious stones.
¹³All your children will be
    taught by the LORD,
  and great will be their
    peace.
¹⁴In righteousness you will be
    established:
Tyranny will be far from you;
  you will have nothing to fear.
Terror will be far removed;
  it will not come near you.
¹⁵If anyone does attack you, it
    will not be my doing;
  whoever attacks you will
    surrender to you.

¹⁶"See, it is I who created the
    blacksmith
  who fans the coals into
    flame
  and forges a weapon fit for its
    work.
And it is I who have created
    the destroyer to wreak
    havoc;
¹⁷ no weapon forged against
    you will prevail,
  and you will refute every
    tongue that accuses you.

ᵃ 11 The meaning of the Hebrew for this word is uncertain.

This is the heritage of the
　　servants of the LORD,
　　and this is their vindication
　　　from me,"
　　　　　　declares the LORD.

Invitation to the Thirsty

55 "Come, all you who are
　　thirsty,
　　come to the waters;
　and you who have no money,
　　come, buy and eat!
　Come, buy wine and milk
　　without money and without
　　　cost.
2 Why spend money on what is
　　not bread,
　　and your labor on what does
　　　not satisfy?
　Listen, listen to me, and eat
　　what is good,
　　and you will delight in the
　　　richest of fare.
3 Give ear and come to me;
　　listen, that you may live.
　I will make an everlasting
　　covenant with you,
　　my faithful love promised to
　　　David.
4 See, I have made him a witness
　　to the peoples,
　　a ruler and commander of
　　　the peoples.
5 Surely you will summon
　　nations you know not,
　　and nations you do not know
　　　will come running to
　　　you,
　because of the LORD your God,
　　the Holy One of Israel,
　　for he has endowed you with
　　　splendor."

6 Seek the LORD while he may
　　be found;
　　call on him while he is
　　　near.
7 Let the wicked forsake their
　　ways
　　and the unrighteous their
　　　thoughts.
　Let them turn to the LORD, and
　　he will have mercy on
　　them,
　　and to our God, for he will
　　　freely pardon.

8 "For my thoughts are not your
　　thoughts,
　　neither are your ways my
　　　ways,"
　　　　　　declares the LORD.
9 "As the heavens are higher
　　than the earth,
　　so are my ways higher than
　　　your ways
　　and my thoughts than your
　　　thoughts.
10 As the rain and the snow
　　come down from heaven,
　and do not return to it
　　without watering the earth
　and making it bud and
　　　flourish,
　　so that it yields seed for the
　　　sower and bread for the
　　　eater,
11 so is my word that goes out
　　from my mouth:
　It will not return to me
　　empty,
　but will accomplish what I
　　desire
　　and achieve the purpose for
　　　which I sent it.

¹²You will go out in joy
and be led forth in peace;
the mountains and hills
will burst into song before
you,
and all the trees of the field
will clap their hands.
¹³Instead of the thornbush will
grow the juniper,
and instead of briers the
myrtle will grow.
This will be for the LORD's
renown,
for an everlasting sign,
that will endure forever."

Salvation for Others

56 This is what the LORD
says:

"Maintain justice
and do what is right,
for my salvation is close at
hand
and my righteousness will
soon be revealed.
²Blessed is the one who does
this—
the person who holds it
fast,
who keeps the Sabbath
without desecrating it,
and keeps their hands from
doing any evil."

³Let no foreigner who is bound
to the LORD say,
"The LORD will surely
exclude me from his
people."
And let no eunuch complain,
"I am only a dry tree."

⁴For this is what the LORD says:

"To the eunuchs who keep my
Sabbaths,
who choose what pleases me
and hold fast to my
covenant—
⁵to them I will give within my
temple and its walls
a memorial and a name
better than sons and
daughters;
I will give them an everlasting
name
that will endure forever.
⁶And foreigners who bind
themselves to the LORD
to minister to him,
to love the name of the LORD,
and to be his servants,
all who keep the Sabbath
without desecrating it
and who hold fast to my
covenant—
⁷these I will bring to my holy
mountain
and give them joy in my
house of prayer.
Their burnt offerings and
sacrifices
will be accepted on my altar;
for my house will be called
a house of prayer for all
nations."
⁸The Sovereign LORD
declares—
he who gathers the exiles of
Israel:
"I will gather still others to
them
besides those already
gathered."

God's Accusation Against the Wicked

⁹Come, all you beasts of the
field,
come and devour, all you
beasts of the forest!
¹⁰Israel's watchmen are blind,
they all lack knowledge;
they are all mute dogs,
they cannot bark;
they lie around and dream,
they love to sleep.
¹¹They are dogs with mighty
appetites;
they never have enough.
They are shepherds who lack
understanding;
they all turn to their own
way,
they seek their own gain.
¹²"Come," each one cries, "let
me get wine!
Let us drink our fill of beer!
And tomorrow will be like
today,
or even far better."

57 The righteous perish,
and no one takes it to
heart;
the devout are taken away,
and no one understands
that the righteous are taken
away
to be spared from evil.
²Those who walk uprightly
enter into peace;
they find rest as they lie in
death.

³"But you — come here, you
children of a sorceress,

you offspring of adulterers
and prostitutes!
⁴Who are you mocking?
At whom do you sneer
and stick out your tongue?
Are you not a brood of
rebels,
the offspring of liars?
⁵You burn with lust among the
oaks
and under every spreading
tree;
you sacrifice your children in
the ravines
and under the overhanging
crags.
⁶The idols among the smooth
stones of the ravines are
your portion;
indeed, they are your lot.
Yes, to them you have poured
out drink offerings
and offered grain offerings.
In view of all this, should I
relent?
⁷You have made your bed on a
high and lofty hill;
there you went up to offer
your sacrifices.
⁸Behind your doors and your
doorposts
you have put your pagan
symbols.
Forsaking me, you uncovered
your bed,
you climbed into it and
opened it wide;
you made a pact with those
whose beds you love,
and you looked with lust on
their naked bodies.

⁹You went to Molek[a] with olive
    oil
  and increased your
    perfumes.
You sent your ambassadors[b]
    far away;
  you descended to the very
    realm of the dead!
¹⁰You wearied yourself by such
    going about,
  but you would not say, 'It is
    hopeless.'
You found renewal of your
    strength,
  and so you did not faint.

¹¹ "Whom have you so dreaded
    and feared
  that you have not been true
    to me,
  and have neither
    remembered me
    nor taken this to heart?
Is it not because I have long
    been silent
  that you do not fear me?
¹²I will expose your
    righteousness and your
    works,
  and they will not benefit you.
¹³When you cry out for help,
  let your collection of idols
    save you!
The wind will carry all of them
    off,
  a mere breath will blow
    them away.
But whoever takes refuge
    in me
  will inherit the land

and possess my holy
    mountain."

Comfort for the Contrite

¹⁴And it will be said:

"Build up, build up, prepare
    the road!
  Remove the obstacles out of
    the way of my people."
¹⁵For this is what the high and
    exalted One says —
  he who lives forever, whose
    name is holy:
"I live in a high and holy
    place,
  but also with the one who
    is contrite and lowly in
    spirit,
to revive the spirit of the lowly
  and to revive the heart of the
    contrite.
¹⁶I will not accuse them
    forever,
  nor will I always be angry,
for then they would faint away
    because of me —
  the very people I have
    created.
¹⁷I was enraged by their sinful
    greed;
  I punished them, and hid my
    face in anger,
  yet they kept on in their
    willful ways.
¹⁸I have seen their ways, but I
    will heal them;
  I will guide them and restore
    comfort to Israel's
    mourners,
¹⁹ creating praise on their lips.

---

[a] 9 Or *to the king*   [b] 9 Or *idols*

Peace, peace, to those far and
      near,"
  says the LORD. "And I will
      heal them."
20 But the wicked are like the
      tossing sea,
  which cannot rest,
  whose waves cast up mire
      and mud.
21 "There is no peace," says my
      God, "for the wicked."

True Fasting

58 "Shout it aloud, do not
  hold back.
  Raise your voice like a
      trumpet.
  Declare to my people their
      rebellion
  and to the descendants of
      Jacob their sins.
2 For day after day they seek me
      out;
  they seem eager to know my
      ways,
  as if they were a nation that
      does what is right
  and has not forsaken the
      commands of its God.
  They ask me for just decisions
  and seem eager for God to
      come near them.
3 'Why have we fasted,' they
      say,
  'and you have not seen it?
  Why have we humbled
      ourselves,
  and you have not noticed?'

  "Yet on the day of your fasting,
      you do as you please
  and exploit all your workers.

4 Your fasting ends in quarreling
      and strife,
  and in striking each other
      with wicked fists.
  You cannot fast as you do
      today
  and expect your voice to be
      heard on high.
5 Is this the kind of fast I have
      chosen,
  only a day for people to
      humble themselves?
  Is it only for bowing one's head
      like a reed
  and for lying in sackcloth
      and ashes?
  Is that what you call a
      fast,
  a day acceptable to the
      LORD?

6 "Is not this the kind of fasting I
      have chosen:
  to loose the chains of
      injustice
  and untie the cords of the
      yoke,
  to set the oppressed free
  and break every yoke?
7 Is it not to share your food with
      the hungry
  and to provide the poor
      wanderer with shelter —
  when you see the naked, to
      clothe them,
  and not to turn away from
      your own flesh and
      blood?
8 Then your light will break
      forth like the dawn,
  and your healing will
      quickly appear;

then your righteousness[a] will
go before you,
and the glory of the LORD
will be your rear
guard.
⁹Then you will call, and the
LORD will answer;
you will cry for help, and he
will say: Here am I.

"If you do away with the yoke
of oppression,
with the pointing finger and
malicious talk,
¹⁰and if you spend yourselves in
behalf of the hungry
and satisfy the needs of the
oppressed,
then your light will rise in the
darkness,
and your night will become
like the noonday.
¹¹The LORD will guide you
always;
he will satisfy your needs in
a sun-scorched land
and will strengthen your
frame.
You will be like a well-watered
garden,
like a spring whose waters
never fail.
¹²Your people will rebuild the
ancient ruins
and will raise up the age-old
foundations;
you will be called Repairer of
Broken Walls,
Restorer of Streets with
Dwellings.

¹³"If you keep your feet from
breaking the Sabbath
and from doing as you please
on my holy day,
if you call the Sabbath a
delight
and the LORD's holy day
honorable,
and if you honor it by not going
your own way
and not doing as you please
or speaking idle words,
¹⁴then you will find your joy in
the LORD,
and I will cause you to
ride in triumph on the
heights of the land
and to feast on the
inheritance of your
father Jacob."
For the mouth of the
LORD has spoken.

Sin, Confession and Redemption

59 Surely the arm of the
LORD is not too short to
save,
nor his ear too dull to hear.
²But your iniquities have
separated
you from your God;
your sins have hidden his face
from you,
so that he will not hear.
³For your hands are stained
with blood,
your fingers with guilt.
Your lips have spoken falsely,
and your tongue mutters
wicked things.

⁴No one calls for justice;
 no one pleads a case with
  integrity.
They rely on empty
  arguments, they utter
   lies;
 they conceive trouble and
  give birth to evil.
⁵They hatch the eggs of vipers
 and spin a spider's web.
Whoever eats their eggs will
  die,
 and when one is broken, an
  adder is hatched.
⁶Their cobwebs are useless for
  clothing;
 they cannot cover
  themselves with what
   they make.
Their deeds are evil deeds,
 and acts of violence are in
  their hands.
⁷Their feet rush into sin;
 they are swift to shed
  innocent blood.
They pursue evil schemes;
 acts of violence mark their
  ways.
⁸The way of peace they do not
  know;
 there is no justice in their
  paths.
They have turned them into
  crooked roads;
 no one who walks along
  them will know peace.

⁹So justice is far from us,
 and righteousness does not
  reach us.
We look for light, but all is
  darkness;

for brightness, but we walk
 in deep shadows.
¹⁰Like the blind we grope along
  the wall,
 feeling our way like people
  without eyes.
At midday we stumble as if it
  were twilight;
 among the strong, we are
  like the dead.
¹¹We all growl like bears;
 we moan mournfully like
  doves.
We look for justice, but find
  none;
 for deliverance, but it is far
  away.
¹²For our offenses are many in
  your sight,
 and our sins testify
  against us.
Our offenses are ever with us,
 and we acknowledge our
  iniquities:
¹³rebellion and treachery
  against the Lord,
 turning our backs on our
   God,
 inciting revolt and
   oppression,
 uttering lies our hearts have
   conceived.
¹⁴So justice is driven back,
 and righteousness stands at
  a distance;
 truth has stumbled in the
  streets,
 honesty cannot enter.
¹⁵Truth is nowhere to be found,
 and whoever shuns evil
  becomes a prey.

The LORD looked and was
displeased
that there was no justice.
¹⁶ He saw that there was no one,
he was appalled that there
was no one to intervene;
so his own arm achieved
salvation for him,
and his own righteousness
sustained him.
¹⁷ He put on righteousness as his
breastplate,
and the helmet of salvation
on his head;
he put on the garments of
vengeance
and wrapped himself in zeal
as in a cloak.
¹⁸ According to what they have
done,
so will he repay
wrath to his enemies
and retribution to his foes;
he will repay the islands
their due.
¹⁹ From the west, people will fear
the name of the LORD,
and from the rising of the
sun, they will revere his
glory.
For he will come like a pent-up
flood
that the breath of the LORD
drives along.ᵃ

²⁰ "The Redeemer will come to
Zion,
to those in Jacob who repent
of their sins,"
declares the LORD.

²¹ "As for me, this is my covenant
with them," says the LORD. "My
Spirit, who is on you, will not depart from you, and my words that I
have put in your mouth will always
be on your lips, on the lips of your
children and on the lips of their
descendants—from this time on
and forever," says the LORD.

The Glory of Zion

60 "Arise, shine, for your
light has come,
and the glory of the LORD
rises upon you.
² See, darkness covers the earth
and thick darkness is over
the peoples,
but the LORD rises upon you
and his glory appears over
you.
³ Nations will come to your light,
and kings to the brightness
of your dawn.
⁴ "Lift up your eyes and look
about you:
All assemble and come to
you;
your sons come from afar,
and your daughters are
carried on the hip.
⁵ Then you will look and be
radiant,
your heart will throb and
swell with joy;
the wealth on the seas will be
brought to you,
to you the riches of the
nations will come.

ᵃ 19 Or *When enemies come in like a flood, / the Spirit of the LORD will put them to
flight*

⁶Herds of camels will cover
  your land,
    young camels of Midian and
      Ephah.
  And all from Sheba will
    come,
    bearing gold and incense
    and proclaiming the praise
      of the LORD.
⁷All Kedar's flocks will be
    gathered to you,
    the rams of Nebaioth will
      serve you;
  they will be accepted as
    offerings on my altar,
    and I will adorn my glorious
      temple.

⁸"Who are these that fly along
    like clouds,
    like doves to their nests?
⁹Surely the islands look to me;
  in the lead are the ships of
    Tarshish,ᵃ
  bringing your children from
    afar,
    with their silver and gold,
  to the honor of the LORD your
    God,
    the Holy One of Israel,
    for he has endowed you with
      splendor.

¹⁰"Foreigners will rebuild your
    walls,
    and their kings will serve
      you.
  Though in anger I struck you,
    in favor I will show you
      compassion.

¹¹Your gates will always stand
    open,
  they will never be shut, day
    or night,
  so that people may bring
    you the wealth of the
      nations —
  their kings led in triumphal
    procession.
¹²For the nation or kingdom that
    will not serve you will
      perish;
  it will be utterly ruined.

¹³"The glory of Lebanon will
    come to you,
    the juniper, the fir and the
      cypress together,
  to adorn my sanctuary;
    and I will glorify the place
    for my feet.
¹⁴The children of your
    oppressors will come
      bowing before you;
  all who despise you will bow
    down at your feet
  and will call you the City of the
    LORD,
    Zion of the Holy One of
      Israel.

¹⁵"Although you have been
    forsaken and hated,
    with no one traveling
      through,
  I will make you the everlasting
    pride
  and the joy of all
    generations.
¹⁶You will drink the milk of
    nations

ᵃ 9 Or *the trading ships*

and be nursed at royal
   breasts.
Then you will know that I, the
   LORD, am your Savior,
   your Redeemer, the Mighty
   One of Jacob.
¹⁷ Instead of bronze I will bring
   you gold,
   and silver in place of iron.
Instead of wood I will bring
   you bronze,
   and iron in place of stones.
I will make peace your
   governor
   and well-being your ruler.
¹⁸ No longer will violence be
   heard in your land,
   nor ruin or destruction
   within your borders,
but you will call your walls
   Salvation
   and your gates Praise.
¹⁹ The sun will no more be your
   light by day,
   nor will the brightness of the
   moon shine on you,
for the LORD will be your
   everlasting light,
   and your God will be your
   glory.
²⁰ Your sun will never set
   again,
   and your moon will wane no
   more;
the LORD will be your
   everlasting light,
   and your days of sorrow will
   end.
²¹ Then all your people will be
   righteous

and they will possess the
   land forever.
They are the shoot I have
   planted,
   the work of my hands,
   for the display of my
   splendor.
²² The least of you will become a
   thousand,
   the smallest a mighty nation.
I am the LORD;
   in its time I will do this
   swiftly."

The Year of the LORD's Favor

61 The Spirit of the
   Sovereign LORD is
   on me,
because the LORD has
   anointed me
to proclaim good news to the
   poor.
He has sent me to bind up the
   brokenhearted,
   to proclaim freedom for the
   captives
   and release from darkness
   for the prisoners,ᵃ
² to proclaim the year of the
   LORD's favor
   and the day of vengeance of
   our God,
to comfort all who mourn,
³   and provide for those who
   grieve in Zion —
to bestow on them a crown of
   beauty
   instead of ashes,
the oil of joy
   instead of mourning,

ᵃ 1 Hebrew; Septuagint the blind

and a garment of praise
   instead of a spirit of despair.
They will be called oaks of
   righteousness,
   a planting of the LORD
   for the display of his
   splendor.

⁴They will rebuild the ancient
   ruins
   and restore the places long
   devastated;
they will renew the ruined
   cities
   that have been devastated
   for generations.
⁵Strangers will shepherd your
   flocks;
   foreigners will work your
   fields and vineyards.
⁶And you will be called priests
   of the LORD,
   you will be named ministers
   of our God.
You will feed on the wealth of
   nations,
   and in their riches you will
   boast.

⁷Instead of your shame
   you will receive a double
   portion,
   and instead of disgrace
   you will rejoice in your
   inheritance.
And so you will inherit a
   double portion in your
   land,
   and everlasting joy will be
   yours.

⁸"For I, the LORD, love justice;
   I hate robbery and
   wrongdoing.

In my faithfulness I will
   reward my people
   and make an everlasting
   covenant with them.
⁹Their descendants will be
   known among the
   nations
   and their offspring among
   the peoples.
All who see them will
   acknowledge
   that they are a people the
   LORD has blessed."

¹⁰I delight greatly in the LORD;
   my soul rejoices in my God.
For he has clothed me with
   garments of salvation
   and arrayed me in a robe of
   his righteousness,
as a bridegroom adorns his
   head like a priest,
   and as a bride adorns herself
   with her jewels.
¹¹For as the soil makes the
   sprout come up
   and a garden causes seeds to
   grow,
so the Sovereign LORD will
   make righteousness
   and praise spring up before
   all nations.

Zion's New Name

62 For Zion's sake I will not
   keep silent,
   for Jerusalem's sake I will not
   remain quiet,
till her vindication shines out
   like the dawn,
   her salvation like a blazing
   torch.

2 The nations will see your
   vindication,
  and all kings your glory;
 you will be called by a new
   name
    that the mouth of the LORD
    will bestow.
3 You will be a crown of
   splendor in the LORD's
   hand,
  a royal diadem in the hand
   of your God.
4 No longer will they call you
   Deserted,
  or name your land Desolate.
 But you will be called
   Hephzibah,*a*
  and your land Beulah*b*;
 for the LORD will take delight
   in you,
  and your land will be
   married.
5 As a young man marries a
   young woman,
  so will your Builder marry
   you;
 as a bridegroom rejoices over
   his bride,
  so will your God rejoice over
   you.

6 I have posted watchmen on
   your walls, Jerusalem;
  they will never be silent day
   or night.
 You who call on the LORD,
  give yourselves no rest,
7 and give him no rest till he
   establishes Jerusalem
  and makes her the praise of
   the earth.

8 The LORD has sworn by his
   right hand
  and by his mighty arm:
 "Never again will I give your
   grain
  as food for your enemies,
 and never again will foreigners
   drink the new wine
  for which you have toiled;
9 but those who harvest it will
   eat it
  and praise the LORD,
 and those who gather the
   grapes will drink it
  in the courts of my
   sanctuary."

10 Pass through, pass through
    the gates!
  Prepare the way for the
   people.
 Build up, build up the
   highway!
  Remove the stones.
 Raise a banner for the
   nations.

11 The LORD has made
    proclamation
  to the ends of the earth:
 "Say to Daughter Zion,
  'See, your Savior comes!
 See, his reward is with him,
  and his recompense
   accompanies him.' "
12 They will be called the Holy
    People,
  the Redeemed of the LORD;
 and you will be called Sought
   After,
  the City No Longer Deserted.

---

a 4 *Hephzibah* means *my delight is in her.*   *b* 4 *Beulah* means *married.*

God's Day of Vengeance and Redemption

63 Who is this coming from
Edom,
from Bozrah, with his
garments stained
crimson?
Who is this, robed in splendor,
striding forward in the
greatness of his
strength?

"It is I, proclaiming victory,
mighty to save."

2 Why are your garments red,
like those of one treading the
winepress?

3 "I have trodden the winepress
alone;
from the nations no one was
with me.
I trampled them in my anger
and trod them down in my
wrath;
their blood spattered my
garments,
and I stained all my clothing.
4 It was for me the day of
vengeance;
the year for me to redeem
had come.
5 I looked, but there was no one
to help,
I was appalled that no one
gave support;
so my own arm achieved
salvation for me,
and my own wrath
sustained me.

6 I trampled the nations in my
anger;
in my wrath I made them
drunk
and poured their blood on
the ground."

Praise and Prayer

7 I will tell of the kindnesses of
the LORD,
the deeds for which he is to
be praised,
according to all the LORD
has done for us —
yes, the many good things
he has done for Israel,
according to his compassion
and many kindnesses.
8 He said, "Surely they are my
people,
children who will be true to
me";
and so he became their
Savior.
9 In all their distress he too was
distressed,
and the angel of his presence
saved them.[a]
In his love and mercy he
redeemed them;
he lifted them up and
carried them
all the days of old.
10 Yet they rebelled
and grieved his Holy Spirit.
So he turned and became their
enemy
and he himself fought
against them.

[a] 9 Or *Savior* 9 *in their distress. / It was no envoy or angel / but his own presence that saved them*

[11] Then his people recalled[a] the
days of old,
the days of Moses and his
people —
where is he who brought them
through the sea,
with the shepherd of his
flock?
Where is he who set
his Holy Spirit among them,
[12] who sent his glorious arm of
power
to be at Moses' right hand,
who divided the waters before
them,
to gain for himself
everlasting renown,
[13] who led them through the
depths?
Like a horse in open country,
they did not stumble;
[14] like cattle that go down to the
plain,
they were given rest by the
Spirit of the LORD.
This is how you guided your
people
to make for yourself a
glorious name.

[15] Look down from heaven and
see,
from your lofty throne, holy
and glorious.
Where are your zeal and your
might?
Your tenderness and
compassion are withheld
from us.

[16] But you are our Father,
though Abraham does not
know us
or Israel acknowledge us;
you, LORD, are our Father,
our Redeemer from of old is
your name.
[17] Why, LORD, do you make us
wander from your ways
and harden our hearts so we
do not revere you?
Return for the sake of your
servants,
the tribes that are your
inheritance.
[18] For a little while your people
possessed your holy
place,
but now our enemies have
trampled down your
sanctuary.
[19] We are yours from of old;
but you have not ruled over
them,
they have not been called[b]
by your name.

64 [c] Oh, that you would rend
the heavens and come
down,
that the mountains would
tremble before you!
[2] As when fire sets twigs ablaze
and causes water to boil,
come down to make your
name known to your
enemies
and cause the nations to
quake before you!

---

[a] 11 Or *But may he recall*   [b] 19 Or *We are like those you have never ruled, / like those never called*   [c] In Hebrew texts 64:1 is numbered 63:19b, and 64:2-12 is numbered 64:1-11.

³ For when you did awesome
      things that we did not
      expect,
   you came down, and the
      mountains trembled
      before you.
⁴ Since ancient times no one has
      heard,
   no ear has perceived,
 no eye has seen any God
      besides you,
   who acts on behalf of those
      who wait for him.
⁵ You come to the help of those
      who gladly do right,
   who remember your ways.
   But when we continued to sin
      against them,
      you were angry.
   How then can we be
      saved?
⁶ All of us have become like one
      who is unclean,
   and all our righteous acts are
      like filthy rags;
   we all shrivel up like a leaf,
      and like the wind our sins
      sweep us away.
⁷ No one calls on your name
   or strives to lay hold of
      you;
   for you have hidden your face
      from us
   and have given us over to*ᵃ*
      our sins.

⁸ Yet you, Lᴏʀᴅ, are our Father.
   We are the clay, you are the
      potter;
   we are all the work of your
      hand.

⁹ Do not be angry beyond
      measure, Lᴏʀᴅ;
   do not remember our sins
      forever.
   Oh, look on us, we pray,
   for we are all your people.
¹⁰ Your sacred cities have
      become a wasteland;
   even Zion is a wasteland,
      Jerusalem a desolation.
¹¹ Our holy and glorious temple,
      where our ancestors
      praised you,
   has been burned with fire,
   and all that we treasured lies
      in ruins.
¹² After all this, Lᴏʀᴅ, will you
      hold yourself back?
   Will you keep silent and
      punish us beyond
      measure?

Judgment and Salvation

65 "I revealed myself to
      those who did not ask
      for me;
   I was found by those who did
      not seek me.
   To a nation that did not call on
      my name,
   I said, 'Here am I, here am I.'
² All day long I have held out my
      hands
   to an obstinate people,
   who walk in ways not good,
      pursuing their own
      imaginations—
³ a people who continually
      provoke me
   to my very face,

ᵃ 7 Septuagint, Syriac and Targum; Hebrew *have made us melt because of*

offering sacrifices in gardens
and burning incense on
altars of brick;
[4] who sit among the graves
and spend their nights
keeping secret vigil;
who eat the flesh of pigs,
and whose pots hold broth of
impure meat;
[5] who say, 'Keep away; don't
come near me,
for I am too sacred for you!'
Such people are smoke in my
nostrils,
a fire that keeps burning all
day.

[6] "See, it stands written
before me:
I will not keep silent but will
pay back in full;
I will pay it back into their
laps —
[7] both your sins and the sins of
your ancestors,"
says the LORD.
"Because they burned
sacrifices on the
mountains
and defied me on the hills,
I will measure into their laps
the full payment for their
former deeds."

[8] This is what the LORD says:

"As when juice is still found in
a cluster of grapes
and people say, 'Don't
destroy it,
there is still a blessing in it,'
so will I do in behalf of my
servants;
I will not destroy them all.

[9] I will bring forth descendants
from Jacob,
and from Judah those
who will possess my
mountains;
my chosen people will inherit
them,
and there will my servants
live.
[10] Sharon will become a pasture
for flocks,
and the Valley of Achor a
resting place for herds,
for my people who seek me.

[11] "But as for you who forsake the
LORD
and forget my holy
mountain,
who spread a table for Fortune
and fill bowls of mixed wine
for Destiny,
[12] I will destine you for the
sword,
and all of you will fall in the
slaughter;
for I called but you did not
answer,
I spoke but you did not
listen.
You did evil in my sight
and chose what
displeases me."

[13] Therefore this is what the
Sovereign LORD says:

"My servants will eat,
but you will go hungry;
my servants will drink,
but you will go thirsty;
my servants will rejoice,
but you will be put to shame.

¹⁴My servants will sing
  out of the joy of their hearts,
but you will cry out
  from anguish of heart
  and wail in brokenness of
    spirit.
¹⁵You will leave your name
  for my chosen ones to use in
    their curses;
the Sovereign LORD will put
  you to death,
  but to his servants he will
    give another name.
¹⁶Whoever invokes a blessing in
    the land
  will do so by the one true
    God;
whoever takes an oath in the
    land
  will swear by the one true
    God.
For the past troubles will be
    forgotten
  and hidden from my eyes.

New Heavens and a New Earth

¹⁷"See, I will create
  new heavens and a new
    earth.
The former things will not be
    remembered,
  nor will they come to mind.
¹⁸But be glad and rejoice forever
  in what I will create,
for I will create Jerusalem to be
    a delight
  and its people a joy.
¹⁹I will rejoice over Jerusalem
  and take delight in my
    people;

the sound of weeping and of
    crying
  will be heard in it no more.

²⁰"Never again will there be in it
  an infant who lives but a few
    days,
  or an old man who does not
    live out his years;
the one who dies at a hundred
  will be thought a mere child;
the one who fails to reach*ᵃ* a
    hundred
  will be considered accursed.
²¹They will build houses and
    dwell in them;
  they will plant vineyards
    and eat their fruit.
²²No longer will they build
    houses and others live in
      them,
  or plant and others eat.
For as the days of a tree,
  so will be the days of my
    people;
my chosen ones will long enjoy
  the work of their hands.
²³They will not labor in vain,
  nor will they bear children
    doomed to misfortune;
for they will be a people
  blessed by the LORD,
  they and their descendants
    with them.
²⁴Before they call I will answer;
  while they are still speaking
    I will hear.
²⁵The wolf and the lamb will
    feed together,
  and the lion will eat straw
    like the ox,

ᵃ 20 Or the sinner who reaches

and dust will be the
    serpent's food.
They will neither harm nor
    destroy
on all my holy mountain,"
            says the LORD.

Judgment and Hope

66 This is what the LORD
    says:

"Heaven is my throne,
    and the earth is my footstool.
Where is the house you will
    build for me?
Where will my resting
    place be?
² Has not my hand made all
    these things,
and so they came into
    being?"
            declares the LORD.

"These are the ones I look on
    with favor:
    those who are humble and
        contrite in spirit,
    and who tremble at my
        word.
³ But whoever sacrifices a bull
    is like one who kills a person,
and whoever offers a lamb
    is like one who breaks a
        dog's neck;
whoever makes a grain
    offering
    is like one who presents pig's
        blood,
and whoever burns memorial
    incense
    is like one who worships an
        idol.

They have chosen their own
    ways,
    and they delight in their
        abominations;
⁴ so I also will choose harsh
    treatment for them
    and will bring on them what
        they dread.
For when I called, no one
    answered,
    when I spoke, no one
        listened.
They did evil in my sight
    and chose what
        displeases me."

⁵ Hear the word of the LORD,
    you who tremble at his word:
"Your own people who hate
    you,
    and exclude you because of
        my name, have said,
'Let the LORD be glorified,
    that we may see your joy!'
Yet they will be put to
    shame.
⁶ Hear that uproar from the city,
    hear that noise from the
        temple!
It is the sound of the LORD
    repaying his enemies all
        they deserve.

⁷ "Before she goes into labor,
    she gives birth;
before the pains come upon
    her,
    she delivers a son.
⁸ Who has ever heard of such
    things?
    Who has ever seen things
        like this?

Can a country be born in a day
   or a nation be brought forth
     in a moment?
Yet no sooner is Zion in labor
   than she gives birth to her
     children.
⁹ Do I bring to the moment of
     birth
   and not give delivery?" says
     the Lord.
"Do I close up the womb
   when I bring to delivery?"
   says your God.
¹⁰ "Rejoice with Jerusalem and
     be glad for her,
   all you who love her;
rejoice greatly with her,
   all you who mourn over
     her.
¹¹ For you will nurse and be
     satisfied
   at her comforting breasts;
you will drink deeply
   and delight in her
     overflowing abundance."

¹² For this is what the Lord
says:

"I will extend peace to her like
     a river,
   and the wealth of nations
     like a flooding stream;
you will nurse and be carried
     on her arm
   and dandled on her knees.
¹³ As a mother comforts her
     child,
   so will I comfort you;
   and you will be comforted
     over Jerusalem."

¹⁴ When you see this, your heart
     will rejoice
   and you will flourish like
     grass;
the hand of the Lord will
     be made known to his
     servants,
   but his fury will be shown to
     his foes.
¹⁵ See, the Lord is coming with
     fire,
   and his chariots are like a
     whirlwind;
he will bring down his anger
     with fury,
   and his rebuke with flames
     of fire.
¹⁶ For with fire and with his
     sword
   the Lord will execute
     judgment on all people,
   and many will be those slain
     by the Lord.

¹⁷ "Those who consecrate and purify themselves to go into the gardens, following one who is among those who eat the flesh of pigs, rats and other unclean things — they will meet their end together with the one they follow," declares the Lord.

¹⁸ "And I, because of what they have planned and done, am about to come*ᵃ* and gather the people of all nations and languages, and they will come and see my glory.

¹⁹ "I will set a sign among them, and I will send some of those who survive to the nations — to Tar-

---

ᵃ 18 The meaning of the Hebrew for this clause is uncertain.

shish, to the Libyans[a] and Lydians (famous as archers), to Tubal and Greece, and to the distant islands that have not heard of my fame or seen my glory. They will proclaim my glory among the nations. **20** And they will bring all your people, from all the nations, to my holy mountain in Jerusalem as an offering to the LORD — on horses, in chariots and wagons, and on mules and camels," says the LORD. "They will bring them, as the Israelites bring their grain offerings, to the temple of the LORD in ceremonially clean vessels. **21** And I will select some of them also to be priests and Levites," says the LORD.

22 "As the new heavens and the new earth that I make will endure before me," declares the LORD, "so will your name and descendants endure. **23** From one New Moon to another and from one Sabbath to another, all mankind will come and bow down before me," says the LORD. **24** "And they will go out and look on the dead bodies of those who rebelled against me; the worms that eat them will not die, the fire that burns them will not be quenched, and they will be loathsome to all mankind."

---

[a] *19* Some Septuagint manuscripts *Put* (Libyans); Hebrew *Pul*

Jeremiah

Introduction:

Jeremiah, like Isaiah, was a young man called by God to warn Judah about its wickedness. He spent the first twenty years of his ministry under Josiah, a good king who tried to bring the people of Judah back to God. Jeremiah was often in danger from political and religious leaders who were angry because of his messages. Through this entire ordeal God protected Jeremiah so he could continue to warn the wicked and comfort those who trusted in God.

After Jerusalem was destroyed in 586 BC., Jeremiah chose to remain with the people, and eventually went with them to Egypt.

Since the messages of Jeremiah are not arranged in chronological order, it is helpful to read the history of Judah as found in Kings and Chronicles to better understand Jeremiah's messages.

Outline of contents:

The call of Jeremiah (1:1–19)
The sinful condition of Judah (2:1–6:30)
The temple, the law and the covenant (7:1–12:17)
The certainty of captivity (13:1–18:23)
Jeremiah confronts the leaders (19:1–29:32)
The promise of restoration (30:1–33:26)
The kingdom falls apart (34:1–39:18)
The trip to Egypt (40:1–45:5)
Messages concerning foreign nations (46:1–51:64)
The fall of Jerusalem (52:1–34)

1 The words of Jeremiah son of Hilkiah, one of the priests at Anathoth in the territory of Benjamin. ²The word of the LORD came to him in the thirteenth year of the reign of Josiah son of Amon king of Judah, ³and through the reign of Jehoiakim son of Josiah king of Judah, down to the fifth month of the eleventh year of Zedekiah son of Josiah king of Judah, when the people of Jerusalem went into exile.

The Call of Jeremiah

⁴The word of the LORD came to me, saying,

⁵ "Before I formed you in the
    womb I knew*a* you,

a 5 Or *chose*

before you were born I set
    you apart;
I appointed you as a prophet
    to the nations."

⁶ "Alas, Sovereign LORD," I said, "I do not know how to speak; I am too young."

⁷ But the LORD said to me, "Do not say, 'I am too young.' You must go to everyone I send you to and say whatever I command you. ⁸ Do not be afraid of them, for I am with you and will rescue you," declares the LORD.

⁹ Then the LORD reached out his hand and touched my mouth and said to me, "I have put my words in your mouth. ¹⁰ See, today I appoint you over nations and kingdoms to uproot and tear down, to destroy and overthrow, to build and to plant."

¹¹ The word of the LORD came to me: "What do you see, Jeremiah?"

"I see the branch of an almond tree," I replied.

¹² The LORD said to me, "You have seen correctly, for I am watching[a] to see that my word is fulfilled."

¹³ The word of the LORD came to me again: "What do you see?"

"I see a pot that is boiling," I answered. "It is tilting toward us from the north."

¹⁴ The LORD said to me, "From the north disaster will be poured out on all who live in the land. ¹⁵ I am about to summon all the peo-

ples of the northern kingdoms," declares the LORD.

"Their kings will come and set
    up their thrones
  in the entrance of the gates
    of Jerusalem;
they will come against all her
    surrounding walls
  and against all the towns of
    Judah.
¹⁶ I will pronounce my
    judgments on my
    people
  because of their wickedness
    in forsaking me,
in burning incense to other
    gods
  and in worshiping what their
    hands have made.

¹⁷ "Get yourself ready! Stand up and say to them whatever I command you. Do not be terrified by them, or I will terrify you before them. ¹⁸ Today I have made you a fortified city, an iron pillar and a bronze wall to stand against the whole land — against the kings of Judah, its officials, its priests and the people of the land. ¹⁹ They will fight against you but will not overcome you, for I am with you and will rescue you," declares the LORD.

Israel Forsakes God

2 The word of the LORD came to me: ² "Go and proclaim in the hearing of Jerusalem:

---

[a] 12 The Hebrew for *watching* sounds like the Hebrew for *almond tree*.

"This is what the LORD says:

"'I remember the devotion of
    your youth,
    how as a bride you loved me
and followed me through the
    wilderness,
    through a land not sown.
³Israel was holy to the LORD,
    the firstfruits of his harvest;
all who devoured her were
    held guilty,
    and disaster overtook
        them,'"
                    declares the LORD.

⁴Hear the word of the LORD,
    you descendants of
        Jacob,
    all you clans of Israel.

⁵This is what the LORD says:

"What fault did your ancestors
    find in me,
    that they strayed so far from
        me?
They followed worthless idols
    and became worthless
        themselves.
⁶They did not ask, 'Where is the
    LORD,
    who brought us up out of
        Egypt
and led us through the barren
    wilderness,
    through a land of deserts
        and ravines,
a land of drought and utter
    darkness,
    a land where no one travels
        and no one lives?'

⁷I brought you into a fertile
    land
    to eat its fruit and rich
        produce.
But you came and defiled my
    land
    and made my inheritance
        detestable.
⁸The priests did not ask,
    'Where is the LORD?'
Those who deal with the law
    did not know me;
    the leaders rebelled against
        me.
The prophets prophesied by
    Baal,
    following worthless idols.

⁹"Therefore I bring charges
    against you again,"
                    declares the LORD.
"And I will bring charges
    against your children's
        children.
¹⁰Cross over to the coasts of
    Cyprus and look,
    send to Kedarᵃ and observe
        closely;
    see if there has ever been
        anything like this:
¹¹Has a nation ever changed its
    gods?
    (Yet they are not gods at all.)
But my people have exchanged
    their glorious God
    for worthless idols.
¹²Be appalled at this, you
    heavens,
    and shudder with great
        horror,"
                    declares the LORD.

ᵃ 10 In the Syro-Arabian desert

¹³"My people have committed
two sins:
They have forsaken me,
the spring of living water,
and have dug their own
cisterns,
broken cisterns that cannot
hold water.
¹⁴Is Israel a servant, a slave by
birth?
Why then has he become
plunder?
¹⁵Lions have roared;
they have growled at him.
They have laid waste his
land;
his towns are burned and
deserted.
¹⁶Also, the men of Memphis and
Tahpanhes
have cracked your skull.
¹⁷Have you not brought this on
yourselves
by forsaking the LORD your
God
when he led you in the
way?
¹⁸Now why go to Egypt
to drink water from the
Nile^a?
And why go to Assyria
to drink water from the
Euphrates?
¹⁹Your wickedness will punish
you;
your backsliding will rebuke
you.
Consider then and realize
how evil and bitter it is for
you

when you forsake the LORD
your God
and have no awe of me,"
declares the Lord,
the LORD Almighty.

²⁰"Long ago you broke off your
yoke
and tore off your bonds;
you said, 'I will not serve you!'
Indeed, on every high hill
and under every spreading
tree
you lay down as a prostitute.
²¹I had planted you like a choice
vine
of sound and reliable stock.
How then did you turn
against me
into a corrupt, wild vine?
²²Although you wash yourself
with soap
and use an abundance of
cleansing powder,
the stain of your guilt is still
before me,"
declares the Sovereign
LORD.
²³"How can you say, 'I am not
defiled;
I have not run after the
Baals'?
See how you behaved in the
valley;
consider what you have
done.
You are a swift she-camel
running here and there,
²⁴a wild donkey accustomed to
the desert,

^a 18 Hebrew *Shihor*; that is, a branch of the Nile

sniffing the wind in her
    craving —
in her heat who can restrain
    her?
Any males that pursue her
    need not tire
    themselves;
at mating time they will find
    her.
²⁵Do not run until your feet are
    bare
and your throat is dry.
But you said, 'It's no use!
I love foreign gods,
and I must go after them.'

²⁶"As a thief is disgraced when
    he is caught,
so the people of Israel are
    disgraced —
they, their kings and their
    officials,
their priests and their
    prophets.
²⁷They say to wood, 'You are my
    father,'
and to stone, 'You gave me
    birth.'
They have turned their backs
    to me
and not their faces;
yet when they are in trouble,
    they say,
'Come and save us!'
²⁸Where then are the gods you
    made for yourselves?
Let them come if they can
    save you
when you are in trouble!
For you, Judah, have as many
    gods
as you have towns.

²⁹"Why do you bring charges
    against me?
You have all rebelled
    against me,"
            declares the LORD.
³⁰"In vain I punished your
    people;
they did not respond to
    correction.
Your sword has devoured your
    prophets
like a ravenous lion.

³¹"You of this generation, consider the word of the LORD:

"Have I been a desert to Israel
or a land of great darkness?
Why do my people say, 'We are
    free to roam;
we will come to you no
    more'?
³²Does a young woman forget
    her jewelry,
a bride her wedding
    ornaments?
Yet my people have
    forgotten me,
days without number.
³³How skilled you are at
    pursuing love!
Even the worst of women
    can learn from your
    ways.
³⁴On your clothes is found
    the lifeblood of the innocent
    poor,
though you did not catch
    them breaking in.
Yet in spite of all this
³⁵   you say, 'I am innocent;
    he is not angry with me.'

But I will pass judgment on
you
because you say, 'I have not
sinned.'
³⁶Why do you go about so much,
changing your ways?
You will be disappointed by
Egypt
as you were by Assyria.
³⁷You will also leave that place
with your hands on your
head,
for the LORD has rejected those
you trust;
you will not be helped by
them.

3 "If a man divorces his wife
and she leaves him and
marries another man,
should he return to her
again?
Would not the land be
completely defiled?
But you have lived as a
prostitute with many
lovers —
would you now return
to me?"
declares the LORD.
²"Look up to the barren heights
and see.
Is there any place where you
have not been ravished?
By the roadside you sat waiting
for lovers,
sat like a nomad in the
desert.
You have defiled the land
with your prostitution and
wickedness.

³Therefore the showers have
been withheld,
and no spring rains have
fallen.
Yet you have the brazen look of
a prostitute;
you refuse to blush with
shame.
⁴Have you not just called to me:
'My Father, my friend from
my youth,
⁵will you always be angry?
Will your wrath continue
forever?'
This is how you talk,
but you do all the evil you
can."

Unfaithful Israel

⁶During the reign of King Josiah, the LORD said to me, "Have you seen what faithless Israel has done? She has gone up on every high hill and under every spreading tree and has committed adultery there. ⁷I thought that after she had done all this she would return to me but she did not, and her unfaithful sister Judah saw it. ⁸I gave faithless Israel her certificate of divorce and sent her away because of all her adulteries. Yet I saw that her unfaithful sister Judah had no fear; she also went out and committed adultery. ⁹Because Israel's immorality mattered so little to her, she defiled the land and committed adultery with stone and wood. ¹⁰In spite of all this, her unfaithful sister Judah did not return to

me with all her heart, but only in pretense," declares the LORD.

¹¹The LORD said to me, "Faithless Israel is more righteous than unfaithful Judah. ¹²Go, proclaim this message toward the north:

"'Return, faithless Israel,'
 declares the LORD,
'I will frown on you no
 longer,
for I am faithful,' declares the
 LORD,
'I will not be angry forever.
¹³Only acknowledge your
 guilt—
you have rebelled against
 the LORD your God,
you have scattered your favors
 to foreign gods
under every spreading tree,
and have not obeyed me,' "
 declares the LORD.

¹⁴"Return, faithless people," declares the LORD, "for I am your husband. I will choose you— one from a town and two from a clan—and bring you to Zion. ¹⁵Then I will give you shepherds after my own heart, who will lead you with knowledge and understanding. ¹⁶In those days, when your numbers have increased greatly in the land," declares the LORD, "people will no longer say, 'The ark of the covenant of the LORD.' It will never enter their minds or be remembered; it will not be missed, nor will another one be made. ¹⁷At that time they will call Jerusalem The Throne of the LORD, and all nations will gather in Jerusalem to honor the name of the LORD. No longer will they follow the stubbornness of their evil hearts. ¹⁸In those days the people of Judah will join the people of Israel, and together they will come from a northern land to the land I gave your ancestors as an inheritance.

¹⁹"I myself said,

"'How gladly would I treat you
 like my children
and give you a pleasant
 land,
the most beautiful
 inheritance of any
 nation.'
I thought you would call me
 'Father'
and not turn away from
 following me.
²⁰But like a woman unfaithful to
 her husband,
so you, Israel, have been
 unfaithful to me,"
 declares the LORD.

²¹A cry is heard on the barren
 heights,
the weeping and pleading of
 the people of Israel,
because they have perverted
 their ways
and have forgotten the LORD
 their God.

²²"Return, faithless people;
 I will cure you of
 backsliding."

"Yes, we will come to you,
 for you are the LORD our
 God.

²³Surely the idolatrous
      commotion on the hills
  and mountains is a
      deception;
surely in the LORD our God
  is the salvation of Israel.
²⁴From our youth shameful gods
      have consumed
  the fruits of our ancestors'
      labor —
their flocks and herds,
  their sons and daughters.
²⁵Let us lie down in our shame,
  and let our disgrace cover us.
We have sinned against the
      LORD our God,
  both we and our ancestors;
from our youth till this day
  we have not obeyed the
      LORD our God."

4   "If you, Israel, will return,
    then return to me,"
           declares the LORD.
"If you put your detestable
      idols out of my sight
and no longer go astray,
²and if in a truthful, just and
      righteous way
you swear, 'As surely as the
      LORD lives,'
then the nations will invoke
      blessings by him
  and in him they will boast."

³This is what the LORD says to
the people of Judah and to Jerusalem:

"Break up your unplowed
      ground
  and do not sow among
      thorns.
⁴Circumcise yourselves to the
      LORD,
  circumcise your hearts,
  you people of Judah and
      inhabitants of Jerusalem,
or my wrath will flare up and
      burn like fire
because of the evil you have
      done —
  burn with no one to
      quench it.

Disaster From the North

⁵"Announce in Judah and
      proclaim in Jerusalem
  and say:
  'Sound the trumpet
      throughout the land!'
Cry aloud and say:
  'Gather together!
  Let us flee to the fortified
      cities!'
⁶Raise the signal to go to
      Zion!
  Flee for safety without
      delay!
For I am bringing disaster
      from the north,
  even terrible destruction."

⁷A lion has come out of his
      lair;
  a destroyer of nations has set
      out.
He has left his place
  to lay waste your land.
Your towns will lie in ruins
  without inhabitant.
⁸So put on sackcloth,
  lament and wail,
for the fierce anger of the LORD
  has not turned away from us.

⁹ "In that day," declares the
LORD,
  "the king and the officials
    will lose heart,
the priests will be horrified,
  and the prophets will be
    appalled."

¹⁰ Then I said, "Alas, Sovereign
LORD! How completely you have
deceived this people and Jerusalem by saying, 'You will have
peace,' when the sword is at our
throats!"

¹¹ At that time this people and
Jerusalem will be told, "A scorching wind from the barren heights
in the desert blows toward my
people, but not to winnow or
cleanse; ¹² a wind too strong for
that comes from me. Now I pronounce my judgments against
them."

¹³ Look! He advances like the
    clouds,
  his chariots come like a
    whirlwind,
  his horses are swifter than
    eagles.
  Woe to us! We are ruined!
¹⁴ Jerusalem, wash the evil from
    your heart and be saved.
  How long will you harbor
    wicked thoughts?
¹⁵ A voice is announcing from
    Dan,
  proclaiming disaster from
    the hills of Ephraim.
¹⁶ "Tell this to the nations,
  proclaim concerning
    Jerusalem:

'A besieging army is coming
    from a distant land,
  raising a war cry against the
    cities of Judah.
¹⁷ They surround her like men
    guarding a field,
  because she has rebelled
    against me,' "
        declares the LORD.
¹⁸ "Your own conduct and
    actions
  have brought this on you.
  This is your punishment.
  How bitter it is!
  How it pierces to the
    heart!"

¹⁹ Oh, my anguish, my anguish!
  I writhe in pain.
  Oh, the agony of my heart!
  My heart pounds within me,
  I cannot keep silent.
  For I have heard the sound of
    the trumpet;
  I have heard the battle cry.
²⁰ Disaster follows disaster;
  the whole land lies in ruins.
  In an instant my tents are
    destroyed,
  my shelter in a moment.
²¹ How long must I see the battle
    standard
  and hear the sound of the
    trumpet?

²² "My people are fools;
  they do not know me.
  They are senseless children;
  they have no understanding.
  They are skilled in doing evil;
  they know not how to do
    good."

²³I looked at the earth,
    and it was formless and
        empty;
    and at the heavens,
        and their light was gone.
²⁴I looked at the mountains,
    and they were quaking;
    all the hills were swaying.
²⁵I looked, and there were no
        people;
    every bird in the sky had
        flown away.
²⁶I looked, and the fruitful land
        was a desert;
    all its towns lay in ruins
    before the LORD, before his
        fierce anger.

²⁷This is what the LORD says:

"The whole land will be
        ruined,
    though I will not destroy it
        completely.
²⁸Therefore the earth will
        mourn
    and the heavens above grow
        dark,
    because I have spoken and
        will not relent,
    I have decided and will not
        turn back."

²⁹At the sound of horsemen and
        archers
    every town takes to
        flight.
    Some go into the thickets;
        some climb up among the
        rocks.
    All the towns are deserted;
        no one lives in them.

³⁰What are you doing, you
        devastated one?
    Why dress yourself in scarlet
        and put on jewels of gold?
    Why highlight your eyes with
        makeup?
    You adorn yourself in vain.
    Your lovers despise you;
        they want to kill you.

³¹I hear a cry as of a woman in
        labor,
    a groan as of one bearing her
        first child—
    the cry of Daughter Zion
        gasping for breath,
    stretching out her hands and
        saying,
"Alas! I am fainting;
    my life is given over to
        murderers."

Not One Is Upright

5 "Go up and down the streets
        of Jerusalem,
    look around and consider,
        search through her squares.
If you can find but one person
    who deals honestly and
        seeks the truth,
    I will forgive this city.
²Although they say, 'As surely
        as the LORD lives,'
    still they are swearing
        falsely."

³LORD, do not your eyes look for
        truth?
    You struck them, but they
        felt no pain;
    you crushed them, but they
        refused correction.

They made their faces harder
than stone
and refused to repent.
⁴I thought, "These are only the
poor;
they are foolish,
for they do not know the way
of the LORD,
the requirements of their
God.
⁵So I will go to the leaders
and speak to them;
surely they know the way of
the LORD,
the requirements of their
God."
But with one accord they too
had broken off the
yoke
and torn off the bonds.
⁶Therefore a lion from the forest
will attack them,
a wolf from the desert will
ravage them,
a leopard will lie in wait near
their towns
to tear to pieces any who
venture out,
for their rebellion is great
and their backslidings
many.

⁷"Why should I forgive you?
Your children have
forsaken me
and sworn by gods that are
not gods.
I supplied all their needs,
yet they committed
adultery
and thronged to the houses
of prostitutes.

⁸They are well-fed, lusty
stallions,
each neighing for another
man's wife.
⁹Should I not punish them for
this?"
declares the LORD.
"Should I not avenge myself
on such a nation as this?

¹⁰"Go through her vineyards
and ravage them,
but do not destroy them
completely.
Strip off her branches,
for these people do not
belong to the LORD.
¹¹The people of Israel and the
people of Judah
have been utterly unfaithful
to me,"
declares the LORD.

¹²They have lied about the LORD;
they said, "He will do
nothing!
No harm will come to us;
we will never see sword or
famine.
¹³The prophets are but wind
and the word is not in
them;
so let what they say be done
to them."

¹⁴Therefore this is what the
LORD God Almighty says:

"Because the people have
spoken these words,
I will make my words in your
mouth a fire
and these people the wood it
consumes.

¹⁵ People of Israel," declares the
LORD,
"I am bringing a distant
nation against you —
an ancient and enduring
nation,
a people whose language
you do not know,
whose speech you do not
understand.
¹⁶ Their quivers are like an open
grave;
all of them are mighty
warriors.
¹⁷ They will devour your harvests
and food,
devour your sons and
daughters;
they will devour your flocks
and herds,
devour your vines and fig
trees.
With the sword they will
destroy
the fortified cities in which
you trust.

¹⁸ "Yet even in those days," declares the LORD, "I will not destroy you completely. ¹⁹ And when the people ask, 'Why has the LORD our God done all this to us?' you will tell them, 'As you have forsaken me and served foreign gods in your own land, so now you will serve foreigners in a land not your own.'

²⁰ "Announce this to the
descendants of Jacob
and proclaim it in Judah:
²¹ Hear this, you foolish and
senseless people,
who have eyes but do not
see,
who have ears but do not
hear:
²² Should you not fear me?"
declares the LORD.
"Should you not tremble in
my presence?
I made the sand a boundary
for the sea,
an everlasting barrier it
cannot cross.
The waves may roll, but they
cannot prevail;
they may roar, but they
cannot cross it.
²³ But these people have
stubborn and rebellious
hearts;
they have turned aside and
gone away.
²⁴ They do not say to themselves,
'Let us fear the LORD our
God,
who gives autumn and spring
rains in season,
who assures us of the regular
weeks of harvest.'
²⁵ Your wrongdoings have kept
these away;
your sins have deprived you
of good.

²⁶ "Among my people are the
wicked
who lie in wait like men who
snare birds
and like those who set traps
to catch people.
²⁷ Like cages full of birds,
their houses are full of
deceit;

they have become rich and
powerful
28 and have grown fat and
sleek.
Their evil deeds have no
limit;
they do not seek justice.
They do not promote the case
of the fatherless;
they do not defend the just
cause of the poor.
29 Should I not punish them for
this?"
declares the LORD.
"Should I not avenge myself
on such a nation as this?

30 "A horrible and shocking
thing
has happened in the land:
31 The prophets prophesy lies,
the priests rule by their own
authority,
and my people love it this
way.
But what will you do in the
end?

Jerusalem Under Siege

6 "Flee for safety, people of
Benjamin!
Flee from Jerusalem!
Sound the trumpet in Tekoa!
Raise the signal over Beth
Hakkerem!
For disaster looms out of the
north,
even terrible destruction.
2 I will destroy Daughter Zion,
so beautiful and delicate.
3 Shepherds with their flocks
will come against her;

they will pitch their tents
around her,
each tending his own
portion."

4 "Prepare for battle against
her!
Arise, let us attack at noon!
But, alas, the daylight is
fading,
and the shadows of evening
grow long.
5 So arise, let us attack at night
and destroy her fortresses!"

6 This is what the LORD Almighty says:

"Cut down the trees
and build siege ramps
against Jerusalem.
This city must be punished;
it is filled with oppression.
7 As a well pours out its water,
so she pours out her
wickedness.
Violence and destruction
resound in her;
her sickness and wounds are
ever before me.
8 Take warning, Jerusalem,
or I will turn away from you
and make your land desolate
so no one can live in it."

9 This is what the LORD Almighty says:

"Let them glean the remnant
of Israel
as thoroughly as a vine;
pass your hand over the
branches again,
like one gathering grapes."

¹⁰To whom can I speak and give
warning?
Who will listen to me?
Their ears are closed*ᵃ*
so they cannot hear.
The word of the Lᴏʀᴅ is
offensive to them;
they find no pleasure in it.
¹¹But I am full of the wrath of
the Lᴏʀᴅ,
and I cannot hold it in.

"Pour it out on the children in
the street
and on the young men
gathered together;
both husband and wife will be
caught in it,
and the old, those weighed
down with years.
¹²Their houses will be turned
over to others,
together with their fields and
their wives,
when I stretch out my hand
against those who live in the
land,"
declares the Lᴏʀᴅ.
¹³"From the least to the greatest,
all are greedy for gain;
prophets and priests alike,
all practice deceit.
¹⁴They dress the wound of my
people
as though it were not
serious.
'Peace, peace,' they say,
when there is no peace.
¹⁵Are they ashamed of their
detestable conduct?

No, they have no shame at all;
they do not even know how
to blush.
So they will fall among the
fallen;
they will be brought down
when I punish them,"
says the Lᴏʀᴅ.

¹⁶This is what the Lᴏʀᴅ says:

"Stand at the crossroads and
look;
ask for the ancient paths,
ask where the good way is, and
walk in it,
and you will find rest for
your souls.
But you said, 'We will not
walk in it.'
¹⁷I appointed watchmen over
you and said,
'Listen to the sound of the
trumpet!'
But you said, 'We will not
listen.'
¹⁸Therefore hear, you nations;
you who are witnesses,
observe what will happen to
them.
¹⁹Hear, you earth:
I am bringing disaster on
this people,
the fruit of their schemes,
because they have not listened
to my words
and have rejected my law.
²⁰What do I care about incense
from Sheba
or sweet calamus from a
distant land?

ᵃ 10 Hebrew *uncircumcised*

Your burnt offerings are not
    acceptable;
  your sacrifices do not
    please me."

21 Therefore this is what the
LORD says:

"I will put obstacles before this
    people.
  Parents and children alike
    will stumble over them;
  neighbors and friends will
    perish."

22 This is what the LORD says:

"Look, an army is coming
  from the land of the north;
a great nation is being
    stirred up
  from the ends of the earth.
23 They are armed with bow and
    spear;
  they are cruel and show no
    mercy.
They sound like the roaring
    sea
  as they ride on their horses;
they come like men in battle
    formation
  to attack you, Daughter
    Zion."

24 We have heard reports about
    them,
  and our hands hang limp.
Anguish has gripped us,
  pain like that of a woman in
    labor.
25 Do not go out to the fields
  or walk on the roads,
for the enemy has a sword,
  and there is terror on every
    side.

26 Put on sackcloth, my people,
  and roll in ashes;
mourn with bitter wailing
  as for an only son,
for suddenly the destroyer
  will come upon us.

27 "I have made you a tester of
    metals
  and my people the ore,
that you may observe
  and test their ways.
28 They are all hardened rebels,
  going about to slander.
They are bronze and iron;
  they all act corruptly.
29 The bellows blow fiercely
  to burn away the lead with
    fire,
but the refining goes on in
    vain;
  the wicked are not purged
    out.
30 They are called rejected silver,
  because the LORD has
    rejected them."

False Religion Worthless

7 This is the word that came
to Jeremiah from the LORD:
2 "Stand at the gate of the LORD's
house and there proclaim this
message:

"'Hear the word of the LORD,
all you people of Judah who come
through these gates to worship
the LORD. **3** This is what the LORD
Almighty, the God of Israel, says:
Reform your ways and your actions, and I will let you live in this
place. **4** Do not trust in deceptive
words and say, "This is the tem-

ple of the LORD, the temple of the LORD, the temple of the LORD!" ⁵If you really change your ways and your actions and deal with each other justly, ⁶if you do not oppress the foreigner, the fatherless or the widow and do not shed innocent blood in this place, and if you do not follow other gods to your own harm, ⁷then I will let you live in this place, in the land I gave your ancestors for ever and ever. ⁸But look, you are trusting in deceptive words that are worthless.

⁹" 'Will you steal and murder, commit adultery and perjury,ᵃ burn incense to Baal and follow other gods you have not known, ¹⁰and then come and stand before me in this house, which bears my Name, and say, "We are safe" — safe to do all these detestable things? ¹¹Has this house, which bears my Name, become a den of robbers to you? But I have been watching! declares the LORD.

¹²" 'Go now to the place in Shiloh where I first made a dwelling for my Name, and see what I did to it because of the wickedness of my people Israel. ¹³While you were doing all these things, declares the LORD, I spoke to you again and again, but you did not listen; I called you, but you did not answer. ¹⁴Therefore, what I did to Shiloh I will now do to the house that bears my Name, the temple you trust in, the place I gave to you and your ancestors. ¹⁵I will thrust you from my presence, just as I did all your fellow Israelites, the people of Ephraim.'

¹⁶"So do not pray for this people nor offer any plea or petition for them; do not plead with me, for I will not listen to you. ¹⁷Do you not see what they are doing in the towns of Judah and in the streets of Jerusalem? ¹⁸The children gather wood, the fathers light the fire, and the women knead the dough and make cakes to offer to the Queen of Heaven. They pour out drink offerings to other gods to arouse my anger. ¹⁹But am I the one they are provoking? declares the LORD. Are they not rather harming themselves, to their own shame?

²⁰" 'Therefore this is what the Sovereign LORD says: My anger and my wrath will be poured out on this place — on man and beast, on the trees of the field and on the crops of your land — and it will burn and not be quenched.

²¹" 'This is what the LORD Almighty, the God of Israel, says: Go ahead, add your burnt offerings to your other sacrifices and eat the meat yourselves! ²²For when I brought your ancestors out of Egypt and spoke to them, I did not just give them commands about burnt offerings and sacrifices, ²³but I gave them this command: Obey me, and I will

ᵃ 9 Or *and swear by false gods*

be your God and you will be my people. Walk in obedience to all I command you, that it may go well with you. **24**But they did not listen or pay attention; instead, they followed the stubborn inclinations of their evil hearts. They went backward and not forward. **25**From the time your ancestors left Egypt until now, day after day, again and again I sent you my servants the prophets. **26**But they did not listen to me or pay attention. They were stiff-necked and did more evil than their ancestors.'

27"When you tell them all this, they will not listen to you; when you call to them, they will not answer. **28**Therefore say to them, 'This is the nation that has not obeyed the LORD its God or responded to correction. Truth has perished; it has vanished from their lips.

29" 'Cut off your hair and throw it away; take up a lament on the barren heights, for the LORD has rejected and abandoned this generation that is under his wrath.

The Valley of Slaughter

30" 'The people of Judah have done evil in my eyes, declares the LORD. They have set up their detestable idols in the house that bears my Name and have defiled it. **31**They have built the high places of Topheth in the Valley of Ben Hinnom to burn their sons and daughters in the fire—something I did not command, nor did

it enter my mind. **32**So beware, the days are coming, declares the LORD, when people will no longer call it Topheth or the Valley of Ben Hinnom, but the Valley of Slaughter, for they will bury the dead in Topheth until there is no more room. **33**Then the carcasses of this people will become food for the birds and the wild animals, and there will be no one to frighten them away. **34**I will bring an end to the sounds of joy and gladness and to the voices of bride and bridegroom in the towns of Judah and the streets of Jerusalem, for the land will become desolate.

8 " 'At that time, declares the LORD, the bones of the kings and officials of Judah, the bones of the priests and prophets, and the bones of the people of Jerusalem will be removed from their graves. **2**They will be exposed to the sun and the moon and all the stars of the heavens, which they have loved and served and which they have followed and consulted and worshiped. They will not be gathered up or buried, but will be like dung lying on the ground. **3**Wherever I banish them, all the survivors of this evil nation will prefer death to life, declares the LORD Almighty.'

Sin and Punishment

4"Say to them, 'This is what the LORD says:

" 'When people fall down, do they not get up?

When someone turns away,
do they not return?
⁵Why then have these people
turned away?
Why does Jerusalem always
turn away?
They cling to deceit;
they refuse to return.
⁶I have listened attentively,
but they do not say what is
right.
None of them repent of their
wickedness,
saying, "What have I done?"
Each pursues their own course
like a horse charging into
battle.
⁷Even the stork in the sky
knows her appointed
seasons,
and the dove, the swift and the
thrush
observe the time of their
migration.
But my people do not know
the requirements of the
LORD.

⁸ " 'How can you say, "We are
wise,
for we have the law of the
LORD,"
when actually the lying pen of
the scribes
has handled it falsely?
⁹The wise will be put to shame;
they will be dismayed and
trapped.
Since they have rejected the
word of the LORD,

what kind of wisdom do they
have?
¹⁰Therefore I will give their
wives to other men
and their fields to new
owners.
From the least to the greatest,
all are greedy for gain;
prophets and priests alike,
all practice deceit.
¹¹They dress the wound of my
people
as though it were not
serious.
"Peace, peace," they say,
when there is no peace.
¹²Are they ashamed of their
detestable conduct?
No, they have no shame at
all;
they do not even know how
to blush.
So they will fall among the
fallen;
they will be brought down
when they are punished,
says the LORD.

¹³ " 'I will take away their
harvest,
declares the LORD.
There will be no grapes on
the vine.
There will be no figs on the
tree,
and their leaves will wither.
What I have given them
will be taken from them.ᵃ' "

¹⁴Why are we sitting here?
Gather together!

ᵃ 13 The meaning of the Hebrew for this sentence is uncertain.

Let us flee to the fortified
        cities
    and perish there!
For the LORD our God has
        doomed us to perish
    and given us poisoned water
        to drink,
    because we have sinned
        against him.
15 We hoped for peace
    but no good has come,
for a time of healing
    but there is only terror.
16 The snorting of the enemy's
        horses
    is heard from Dan;
at the neighing of their
        stallions
    the whole land trembles.
They have come to devour
    the land and everything
        in it,
    the city and all who live
        there.
17 "See, I will send venomous
        snakes among you,
    vipers that cannot be
        charmed,
    and they will bite you,"
            declares the LORD.
18 You who are my Comforter[a] in
        sorrow,
    my heart is faint within me.
19 Listen to the cry of my people
    from a land far away:
"Is the LORD not in Zion?
    Is her King no longer there?"

"Why have they aroused my
        anger with their images,
    with their worthless foreign
        idols?"

20 "The harvest is past,
    the summer has ended,
    and we are not saved."

21 Since my people are crushed, I
        am crushed;
    I mourn, and horror
        grips me.
22 Is there no balm in Gilead?
    Is there no physician there?
Why then is there no healing
    for the wound of my people?

9[b] 1 Oh, that my head were a
        spring of water
    and my eyes a fountain of
        tears!
I would weep day and night
    for the slain of my people.
2 Oh, that I had in the desert
    a lodging place for travelers,
so that I might leave my people
    and go away from them;
for they are all adulterers,
    a crowd of unfaithful people.

3 "They make ready their
        tongue
    like a bow, to shoot lies;
it is not by truth
    that they triumph[c] in the
        land.
They go from one sin to
        another;
    they do not acknowledge me,"
            declares the LORD.

---

[a] 18 The meaning of the Hebrew for this word is uncertain.   [b] In Hebrew texts
9:1 is numbered 8:23, and 9:2-26 is numbered 9:1-25.   [c] 3 Or lies; / they are not
valiant for truth

4 "Beware of your friends;
do not trust anyone in your
clan.
For every one of them is a
deceiver,*a*
and every friend a slanderer.
5 Friend deceives friend,
and no one speaks the truth.
They have taught their tongues
to lie;
they weary themselves with
sinning.
6 You*b* live in the midst of
deception;
in their deceit they refuse to
acknowledge me,"
declares the LORD.

7 Therefore this is what the
LORD Almighty says:

"See, I will refine and test
them,
for what else can I do
because of the sin of my
people?
8 Their tongue is a deadly arrow;
it speaks deceitfully.
With their mouths they all
speak cordially to their
neighbors,
but in their hearts they set
traps for them.
9 Should I not punish them for
this?"
declares the LORD.
"Should I not avenge myself
on such a nation as this?"

10 I will weep and wail for the
mountains
and take up a lament
concerning the
wilderness grasslands.
They are desolate and
untraveled,
and the lowing of cattle is
not heard.
The birds have all fled
and the animals are gone.

11 "I will make Jerusalem a heap
of ruins,
a haunt of jackals;
and I will lay waste the towns
of Judah
so no one can live there."

12 Who is wise enough to understand this? Who has been instructed by the LORD and can explain it? Why has the land been ruined and laid waste like a desert that no one can cross?

13 The LORD said, "It is because they have forsaken my law, which I set before them; they have not obeyed me or followed my law. **14** Instead, they have followed the stubbornness of their hearts; they have followed the Baals, as their ancestors taught them." **15** Therefore this is what the LORD Almighty, the God of Israel, says: "See, I will make this people eat bitter food and drink poisoned water. **16** I will scatter them among nations that neither they nor their ancestors have known, and I will pursue them with the sword until I have made an end of them."

a 4 Or *a deceiving Jacob*   *b 6* That is, Jeremiah (the Hebrew is singular)

¹⁷This is what the LORD Almighty says:

"Consider now! Call for the
wailing women to come;
send for the most skillful of
them.
¹⁸Let them come quickly
and wail over us
till our eyes overflow with
tears
and water streams from our
eyelids.
¹⁹The sound of wailing is heard
from Zion:
'How ruined we are!
How great is our shame!
We must leave our land
because our houses are in
ruins.'"

²⁰Now, you women, hear the
word of the LORD;
open your ears to the words
of his mouth.
Teach your daughters how to
wail;
teach one another a lament.
²¹Death has climbed in through
our windows
and has entered our
fortresses;
it has removed the children
from the streets
and the young men from the
public squares.

²²Say, "This is what the LORD
declares:

"'Dead bodies will lie
like dung on the open field,
like cut grain behind the
reaper,
with no one to gather them.'"

²³This is what the LORD says:

"Let not the wise boast of their
wisdom
or the strong boast of their
strength
or the rich boast of their
riches,
²⁴but let the one who boasts
boast about this:
that they have the
understanding to
know me,
that I am the LORD, who
exercises kindness,
justice and righteousness on
earth,
for in these I delight,"
declares the LORD.

²⁵"The days are coming," declares the LORD, "when I will punish all who are circumcised only in the flesh — ²⁶Egypt, Judah, Edom, Ammon, Moab and all who live in the wilderness in distant places.^a For all these nations are really uncircumcised, and even the whole house of Israel is uncircumcised in heart."

God and Idols

10
Hear what the LORD says
to you, people of Israel.
²This is what the LORD says:

"Do not learn the ways of the
nations

^a 26 Or *wilderness and who clip the hair by their foreheads*

or be terrified by signs in the
heavens,
though the nations are
terrified by them.
³For the practices of the peoples
are worthless;
they cut a tree out of the
forest,
and a craftsman shapes it
with his chisel.
⁴They adorn it with silver and
gold;
they fasten it with hammer
and nails
so it will not totter.
⁵Like a scarecrow in a
cucumber field,
their idols cannot speak;
they must be carried
because they cannot
walk.
Do not fear them;
they can do no harm
nor can they do any good."

⁶No one is like you, LORD;
you are great,
and your name is mighty in
power.
⁷Who should not fear you,
King of the nations?
This is your due.
Among all the wise leaders of
the nations
and in all their kingdoms,
there is no one like you.

⁸They are all senseless and
foolish;
they are taught by worthless
wooden idols.

⁹Hammered silver is brought
from Tarshish
and gold from Uphaz.
What the craftsman and
goldsmith have made
is then dressed in blue and
purple —
all made by skilled workers.
¹⁰But the LORD is the true God;
he is the living God, the
eternal King.
When he is angry, the earth
trembles;
the nations cannot endure
his wrath.

¹¹ "Tell them this: 'These gods, who did not make the heavens and the earth, will perish from the earth and from under the heavens.' "ᵃ

¹²But God made the earth by his
power;
he founded the world by his
wisdom
and stretched out the
heavens by his
understanding.
¹³When he thunders, the waters
in the heavens roar;
he makes clouds rise from
the ends of the earth.
He sends lightning with the
rain
and brings out the wind
from his storehouses.

¹⁴Everyone is senseless and
without knowledge;
every goldsmith is shamed
by his idols.

ᵃ 11 The text of this verse is in Aramaic.

The images he makes are a
fraud;
they have no breath in them.
¹⁵ They are worthless, the objects
of mockery;
when their judgment comes,
they will perish.
¹⁶ He who is the Portion of Jacob
is not like these,
for he is the Maker of all
things,
including Israel, the people of
his inheritance —
the LORD Almighty is his
name.

Coming Destruction

¹⁷ Gather up your belongings to
leave the land,
you who live under siege.
¹⁸ For this is what the LORD
says:
"At this time I will hurl out
those who live in this
land;
I will bring distress on them
so that they may be
captured."
¹⁹ Woe to me because of my
injury!
My wound is incurable!
Yet I said to myself,
"This is my sickness, and I
must endure it."
²⁰ My tent is destroyed;
all its ropes are snapped.
My children are gone from me
and are no more;
no one is left now to pitch my
tent
or to set up my shelter.

²¹ The shepherds are senseless
and do not inquire of the
LORD;
so they do not prosper
and all their flock is
scattered.
²² Listen! The report is coming —
a great commotion from the
land of the north!
It will make the towns of Judah
desolate,
a haunt of jackals.

Jeremiah's Prayer

²³ LORD, I know that people's
lives are not their own;
it is not for them to direct
their steps.
²⁴ Discipline me, LORD, but only
in due measure —
not in your anger,
or you will reduce me to
nothing.
²⁵ Pour out your wrath on the
nations
that do not acknowledge
you,
on the peoples who do not
call on your name.
For they have devoured Jacob;
they have devoured him
completely
and destroyed his homeland.

The Covenant Is Broken

11 This is the word that
came to Jeremiah from
the LORD: ² "Listen to the terms
of this covenant and tell them to
the people of Judah and to those
who live in Jerusalem. ³ Tell them

that this is what the LORD, the God of Israel, says: 'Cursed is the one who does not obey the terms of this covenant— ⁴the terms I commanded your ancestors when I brought them out of Egypt, out of the iron-smelting furnace.' I said, 'Obey me and do everything I command you, and you will be my people, and I will be your God. ⁵Then I will fulfill the oath I swore to your ancestors, to give them a land flowing with milk and honey'—the land you possess today."

I answered, "Amen, LORD."

⁶The LORD said to me, "Proclaim all these words in the towns of Judah and in the streets of Jerusalem: 'Listen to the terms of this covenant and follow them. ⁷From the time I brought your ancestors up from Egypt until today, I warned them again and again, saying, "Obey me." ⁸But they did not listen or pay attention; instead, they followed the stubbornness of their evil hearts. So I brought on them all the curses of the covenant I had commanded them to follow but that they did not keep.'"

⁹Then the LORD said to me, "There is a conspiracy among the people of Judah and those who live in Jerusalem. ¹⁰They have returned to the sins of their ancestors, who refused to listen to my words. They have followed other gods to serve them. Both Israel and Judah have broken the covenant I made with their ancestors. ¹¹Therefore this is what the LORD says: 'I will bring on them a disaster they cannot escape. Although they cry out to me, I will not listen to them. ¹²The towns of Judah and the people of Jerusalem will go and cry out to the gods to whom they burn incense, but they will not help them at all when disaster strikes. ¹³You, Judah, have as many gods as you have towns; and the altars you have set up to burn incense to that shameful god Baal are as many as the streets of Jerusalem.'

¹⁴"Do not pray for this people or offer any plea or petition for them, because I will not listen when they call to me in the time of their distress.

¹⁵"What is my beloved doing in
        my temple
    as she, with many others,
        works out her evil
        schemes?
    Can consecrated meat avert
        your punishment?
When you engage in your
        wickedness,
    then you rejoice.ᵃ"

¹⁶The LORD called you a thriving
        olive tree
    with fruit beautiful in form.
But with the roar of a mighty
        storm
    he will set it on fire,
    and its branches will be
        broken.

ᵃ 15 Or *Could consecrated meat avert your punishment? / Then you would rejoice*

17 The LORD Almighty, who planted you, has decreed disaster for you, because the people of both Israel and Judah have done evil and aroused my anger by burning incense to Baal.

Plot Against Jeremiah

18 Because the LORD revealed their plot to me, I knew it, for at that time he showed me what they were doing. **19** I had been like a gentle lamb led to the slaughter; I did not realize that they had plotted against me, saying,

"Let us destroy the tree and its
    fruit;
  let us cut him off from the
      land of the living,
  that his name be
      remembered no more."
20 But you, LORD Almighty, who
      judge righteously
  and test the heart and mind,
  let me see your vengeance on
      them,
  for to you I have committed
      my cause.

21 Therefore this is what the LORD says about the people of Anathoth who are threatening to kill you, saying, "Do not prophesy in the name of the LORD or you will die by our hands" — **22** therefore this is what the LORD Almighty says: "I will punish them. Their young men will die by the sword, their sons and daughters by famine. **23** Not even a remnant will be left to them, because I will bring disaster on the people of Anathoth in the year of their punishment."

Jeremiah's Complaint

12 You are always righteous,
      LORD,
  when I bring a case before
      you.
  Yet I would speak with you
      about your justice:
  Why does the way of the
      wicked prosper?
  Why do all the faithless live
      at ease?
2 You have planted them, and
      they have taken root;
  they grow and bear
      fruit.
  You are always on their
      lips
  but far from their
      hearts.
3 Yet you know me, LORD;
  you see me and test my
      thoughts about you.
  Drag them off like sheep to be
      butchered!
  Set them apart for the day of
      slaughter!
4 How long will the land lie
      parched
  and the grass in every field
      be withered?
  Because those who live in it
      are wicked,
  the animals and birds have
      perished.
  Moreover, the people are
      saying,
  "He will not see what
      happens to us."

God's Answer

5 "If you have raced with men
      on foot
   and they have worn you out,
   how can you compete with
      horses?
   If you stumble*a* in safe
      country,
   how will you manage in the
      thickets by*b* the Jordan?
6 Your relatives, members of
      your own family—
   even they have betrayed you;
   they have raised a loud cry
      against you.
   Do not trust them,
      though they speak well of
      you.

7 "I will forsake my house,
   abandon my inheritance;
   I will give the one I love
   into the hands of her
      enemies.
8 My inheritance has become
      to me
   like a lion in the forest.
   She roars at me;
      therefore I hate her.
9 Has not my inheritance
      become to me
   like a speckled bird of prey
   that other birds of prey
      surround and attack?
   Go and gather all the wild
      beasts;
   bring them to devour.
10 Many shepherds will ruin my
      vineyard
   and trample down my field;

they will turn my pleasant
      field
   into a desolate wasteland.
11 It will be made a wasteland,
   parched and desolate
      before me;
   the whole land will be laid
      waste
   because there is no one who
      cares.
12 Over all the barren heights in
      the desert
   destroyers will swarm,
   for the sword of the LORD will
      devour
   from one end of the land to
      the other;
   no one will be safe.
13 They will sow wheat but reap
      thorns;
   they will wear themselves
      out but gain nothing.
   They will bear the shame of
      their harvest
   because of the LORD's fierce
      anger."

14 This is what the LORD says:
"As for all my wicked neighbors
who seize the inheritance I gave
my people Israel, I will uproot
them from their lands and I will
uproot the people of Judah from
among them. 15 But after I uproot
them, I will again have compassion and will bring each of them
back to their own inheritance
and their own country. 16 And if
they learn well the ways of my
people and swear by my name,
saying, 'As surely as the LORD

---

a 5 Or *you feel secure only*   *b 5* Or *the flooding of* lives' — even as they once taught my people to swear by Baal — then they will be established among my people. [17]But if any nation does not listen, I will completely uproot and destroy it," declares the LORD.

A Linen Belt

13 This is what the LORD said to me: "Go and buy a linen belt and put it around your waist, but do not let it touch water." [2]So I bought a belt, as the LORD directed, and put it around my waist.

[3]Then the word of the LORD came to me a second time: [4]"Take the belt you bought and are wearing around your waist, and go now to Perath[a] and hide it there in a crevice in the rocks." [5]So I went and hid it at Perath, as the LORD told me.

[6]Many days later the LORD said to me, "Go now to Perath and get the belt I told you to hide there." [7]So I went to Perath and dug up the belt and took it from the place where I had hidden it, but now it was ruined and completely useless.

[8]Then the word of the LORD came to me: [9]"This is what the LORD says: 'In the same way I will ruin the pride of Judah and the great pride of Jerusalem. [10]These wicked people, who refuse to listen to my words, who follow the stubbornness of their hearts and go after other gods to serve and worship them, will be like this belt — completely useless! [11]For as a belt is bound around the waist, so I bound all the people of Israel and all the people of Judah to me,' declares the LORD, 'to be my people for my renown and praise and honor. But they have not listened.'

Wineskins

[12]"Say to them: 'This is what the LORD, the God of Israel, says: Every wineskin should be filled with wine.' And if they say to you, 'Don't we know that every wineskin should be filled with wine?' [13]then tell them, 'This is what the LORD says: I am going to fill with drunkenness all who live in this land, including the kings who sit on David's throne, the priests, the prophets and all those living in Jerusalem. [14]I will smash them one against the other, parents and children alike, declares the LORD. I will allow no pity or mercy or compassion to keep me from destroying them.'"

Threat of Captivity

[15]Hear and pay attention,
do not be arrogant,
for the LORD has spoken.
[16]Give glory to the LORD your
God
before he brings the
darkness,
before your feet stumble
on the darkening hills.

---

[a] 4 Or possibly *to the Euphrates*; similarly in verses 5-7

You hope for light,
  but he will turn it to utter
    darkness
  and change it to deep
    gloom.
¹⁷If you do not listen,
  I will weep in secret
  because of your pride;
my eyes will weep bitterly,
  overflowing with tears,
  because the LORD's flock will
    be taken captive.

¹⁸Say to the king and to the
    queen mother,
  "Come down from your
    thrones,
for your glorious crowns
  will fall from your heads."
¹⁹The cities in the Negev will be
    shut up,
  and there will be no one to
    open them.
All Judah will be carried into
    exile,
  carried completely away.

²⁰Look up and see
  those who are coming from
    the north.
Where is the flock that was
  entrusted to you,
  the sheep of which you
    boasted?
²¹What will you say when the
  LORD sets over you
  those you cultivated as your
    special allies?
Will not pain grip you
  like that of a woman in
    labor?

²²And if you ask yourself,
  "Why has this happened to
    me?" —
it is because of your many sins
  that your skirts have been
    torn off
  and your body mistreated.
²³Can an Ethiopian^a change his
    skin
  or a leopard its spots?
Neither can you do good
  who are accustomed to
    doing evil.

²⁴"I will scatter you like chaff
  driven by the desert wind.
²⁵This is your lot,
  the portion I have decreed
    for you,"
            declares the LORD,
  "because you have
    forgotten me
  and trusted in false gods.
²⁶I will pull up your skirts over
    your face
  that your shame may be
    seen —
²⁷your adulteries and lustful
    neighings,
  your shameless prostitution!
I have seen your detestable
    acts
  on the hills and in the fields.
Woe to you, Jerusalem!
  How long will you be
    unclean?"

Drought, Famine, Sword

14 This is the word of the
    LORD that came to Jere-
miah concerning the drought:

---

^a 23 Hebrew *Cushite* (probably a person from the upper Nile region)

2 "Judah mourns,
  her cities languish;
they wail for the land,
  and a cry goes up from
    Jerusalem.
3 The nobles send their servants
    for water;
  they go to the cisterns
    but find no water.
They return with their jars
    unfilled;
  dismayed and despairing,
    they cover their heads.
4 The ground is cracked
  because there is no rain in
    the land;
  the farmers are dismayed
    and cover their heads.
5 Even the doe in the field
  deserts her newborn fawn
    because there is no grass.
6 Wild donkeys stand on the
    barren heights
  and pant like jackals;
their eyes fail
  for lack of food."

7 Although our sins testify
    against us,
  do something, Lord, for the
    sake of your name.
For we have often rebelled;
  we have sinned against
    you.
8 You who are the hope of Israel,
  its Savior in times of
    distress,
why are you like a stranger in
    the land,
  like a traveler who stays only
    a night?

9 Why are you like a man taken
    by surprise,
  like a warrior powerless to
    save?
You are among us, Lord,
  and we bear your name;
  do not forsake us!

10 This is what the Lord says
about this people:

"They greatly love to wander;
  they do not restrain their
    feet.
So the Lord does not accept
    them;
  he will now remember their
    wickedness
  and punish them for their
    sins."

11 Then the Lord said to me, "Do
not pray for the well-being of this
people. 12 Although they fast, I will
not listen to their cry; though they
offer burnt offerings and grain offerings, I will not accept them. Instead, I will destroy them with the
sword, famine and plague."

13 But I said, "Alas, Sovereign
Lord! The prophets keep telling them, 'You will not see the
sword or suffer famine. Indeed, I
will give you lasting peace in this
place.'"

14 Then the Lord said to me,
"The prophets are prophesying
lies in my name. I have not sent
them or appointed them or spoken to them. They are prophesying to you false visions, divinations, idolatries*a* and the delusions

a 14 Or *visions, worthless divinations*

of their own minds. **15**Therefore this is what the LORD says about the prophets who are prophesying in my name: I did not send them, yet they are saying, 'No sword or famine will touch this land.' Those same prophets will perish by sword and famine. **16**And the people they are prophesying to will be thrown out into the streets of Jerusalem because of the famine and sword. There will be no one to bury them, their wives, their sons and their daughters. I will pour out on them the calamity they deserve.

17"Speak this word to them:

" 'Let my eyes overflow with
    tears
  night and day without
    ceasing;
for the Virgin Daughter, my
    people,
  has suffered a grievous
    wound,
  a crushing blow.
18If I go into the country,
  I see those slain by the sword;
if I go into the city,
  I see the ravages of famine.
Both prophet and priest
  have gone to a land they
    know not.' "

19Have you rejected Judah
    completely?
  Do you despise Zion?
Why have you afflicted us
  so that we cannot be healed?
We hoped for peace
  but no good has come,

for a time of healing
  but there is only terror.
20We acknowledge our
    wickedness, LORD,
  and the guilt of our
    ancestors;
we have indeed sinned
    against you.
21For the sake of your name do
    not despise us;
  do not dishonor your
    glorious throne.
Remember your covenant
    with us
  and do not break it.
22Do any of the worthless idols
    of the nations bring rain?
Do the skies themselves
    send down showers?
No, it is you, LORD our God.
  Therefore our hope is in you,
  for you are the one who does
    all this.

15 Then the LORD said to me: "Even if Moses and Samuel were to stand before me, my heart would not go out to this people. Send them away from my presence! Let them go! **2**And if they ask you, 'Where shall we go?' tell them, 'This is what the LORD says:

" 'Those destined for death, to
    death;
those for the sword, to the
    sword;
those for starvation, to
    starvation;
those for captivity, to
    captivity.'

³ "I will send four kinds of destroyers against them," declares the Lord, "the sword to kill and the dogs to drag away and the birds and the wild animals to devour and destroy. ⁴ I will make them abhorrent to all the kingdoms of the earth because of what Manasseh son of Hezekiah king of Judah did in Jerusalem.

⁵ "Who will have pity on you,
    Jerusalem?
Who will mourn for you?
Who will stop to ask how you
    are?
⁶ You have rejected me,"
    declares the Lord.
"You keep on backsliding.
So I will reach out and destroy
    you;
    I am tired of holding back.
⁷ I will winnow them with a
    winnowing fork
    at the city gates of the land.
I will bring bereavement
    and destruction on my
    people,
    for they have not changed
    their ways.
⁸ I will make their widows more
    numerous
    than the sand of the sea.
At midday I will bring a
    destroyer
    against the mothers of their
    young men;
suddenly I will bring down on
    them
    anguish and terror.

⁹ The mother of seven will grow
    faint
    and breathe her last.
Her sun will set while it is still
    day;
    she will be disgraced and
    humiliated.
I will put the survivors to the
    sword
    before their enemies,"
        declares the Lord.

¹⁰ Alas, my mother, that you gave
    me birth,
    a man with whom the
    whole land strives and
    contends!
I have neither lent nor
    borrowed,
    yet everyone curses me.

¹¹ The Lord said,

"Surely I will deliver you for a
    good purpose;
    surely I will make your
    enemies plead with you
in times of disaster and
    times of distress.

¹² "Can a man break iron —
    iron from the north — or
    bronze?

¹³ "Your wealth and your
    treasures
I will give as plunder,
    without charge,
because of all your sins
    throughout your country.
¹⁴ I will enslave you to your
    enemies
    in ᵃ a land you do not know,

ᵃ 14 Some Hebrew manuscripts, Septuagint and Syriac (see also 17:4); most Hebrew manuscripts *I will cause your enemies to bring you / into*

for my anger will kindle a
    fire
  that will burn against you."

[15] LORD, you understand;
  remember me and care
    for me.
Avenge me on my
    persecutors.
You are long-suffering — do
    not take me away;
  think of how I suffer
    reproach for your sake.
[16] When your words came, I ate
    them;
  they were my joy and my
    heart's delight,
for I bear your name,
  LORD God Almighty.
[17] I never sat in the company of
    revelers,
  never made merry with
    them;
I sat alone because your hand
    was on me
  and you had filled me with
    indignation.
[18] Why is my pain unending
  and my wound grievous and
    incurable?
You are to me like a deceptive
    brook,
  like a spring that fails.

[19] Therefore this is what the
LORD says:

  "If you repent, I will restore
    you
    that you may serve me;
if you utter worthy, not
    worthless, words,
  you will be my spokesman.

Let this people turn to you,
  but you must not turn to
    them.
[20] I will make you a wall to this
    people,
  a fortified wall of bronze;
they will fight against you
  but will not overcome you,
for I am with you
  to rescue and save you,"
      declares the LORD.
[21] "I will save you from the hands
    of the wicked
  and deliver you from the
    grasp of the cruel."

Day of Disaster

16 Then the word of the LORD came to me: [2] "You must not marry and have sons or daughters in this place." [3] For this is what the LORD says about the sons and daughters born in this land and about the women who are their mothers and the men who are their fathers: [4] "They will die of deadly diseases. They will not be mourned or buried but will be like dung lying on the ground. They will perish by sword and famine, and their dead bodies will become food for the birds and the wild animals."

[5] For this is what the LORD says: "Do not enter a house where there is a funeral meal; do not go to mourn or show sympathy, because I have withdrawn my blessing, my love and my pity from this people," declares the LORD. [6] "Both high and low will

die in this land. They will not be buried or mourned, and no one will cut themselves or shave their head for the dead. **7** No one will offer food to comfort those who mourn for the dead — not even for a father or a mother — nor will anyone give them a drink to console them.

8 "And do not enter a house where there is feasting and sit down to eat and drink. **9** For this is what the LORD Almighty, the God of Israel, says: Before your eyes and in your days I will bring an end to the sounds of joy and gladness and to the voices of bride and bridegroom in this place.

10 "When you tell these people all this and they ask you, 'Why has the LORD decreed such a great disaster against us? What wrong have we done? What sin have we committed against the LORD our God?' **11** then say to them, 'It is because your ancestors forsook me,' declares the LORD, 'and followed other gods and served and worshiped them. They forsook me and did not keep my law. **12** But you have behaved more wickedly than your ancestors. See how all of you are following the stubbornness of your evil hearts instead of obeying me. **13** So I will throw you out of this land into a land neither you nor your ancestors have known, and there you will serve other gods day and night, for I will show you no favor.'

14 "However, the days are coming," declares the LORD, "when it will no longer be said, 'As surely as the LORD lives, who brought the Israelites up out of Egypt,' **15** but it will be said, 'As surely as the LORD lives, who brought the Israelites up out of the land of the north and out of all the countries where he had banished them.' For I will restore them to the land I gave their ancestors.

16 "But now I will send for many fishermen," declares the LORD, "and they will catch them. After that I will send for many hunters, and they will hunt them down on every mountain and hill and from the crevices of the rocks. **17** My eyes are on all their ways; they are not hidden from me, nor is their sin concealed from my eyes. **18** I will repay them double for their wickedness and their sin, because they have defiled my land with the lifeless forms of their vile images and have filled my inheritance with their detestable idols."

19 LORD, my strength and my
> fortress,
>> my refuge in time of distress,
> to you the nations will come
>> from the ends of the earth
>> and say,
> "Our ancestors possessed
>> nothing but false gods,
>> worthless idols that did them
>> no good.
20 Do people make their own
>> gods?
>> Yes, but they are not gods!"

21 "Therefore I will teach them —
    this time I will teach them
    my power and might.
  Then they will know
    that my name is the LORD.

17 "Judah's sin is engraved
      with an iron tool,
    inscribed with a flint point,
  on the tablets of their hearts
    and on the horns of their
      altars.
2 Even their children remember
    their altars and Asherah
      poles[a]
  beside the spreading trees
    and on the high hills.
3 My mountain in the land
    and your[b] wealth and all
      your treasures
  I will give away as plunder,
    together with your high
      places,
  because of sin throughout
    your country.
4 Through your own fault you
      will lose
    the inheritance I gave you.
  I will enslave you to your
      enemies
    in a land you do not know,
  for you have kindled my
      anger,
    and it will burn forever."

5 This is what the LORD says:

"Cursed is the one who trusts
      in man,
    who draws strength from
      mere flesh

and whose heart turns away
    from the LORD.
6 That person will be like a bush
    in the wastelands;
  they will not see prosperity
    when it comes.
  They will dwell in the parched
    places of the desert,
  in a salt land where no one
    lives.

7 "But blessed is the one who
    trusts in the LORD,
  whose confidence is in him.
8 They will be like a tree planted
    by the water
  that sends out its roots by the
    stream.
  It does not fear when heat
    comes;
    its leaves are always green.
  It has no worries in a year of
    drought
    and never fails to bear fruit."

9 The heart is deceitful above all
    things
  and beyond cure.
    Who can understand it?

10 "I the LORD search the heart
    and examine the mind,
  to reward each person
      according to their
      conduct,
    according to what their
      deeds deserve."

11 Like a partridge that hatches
    eggs it did not lay
  are those who gain riches by
    unjust means.

---

a 2 That is, wooden symbols of the goddess Asherah   b 2,3 Or hills / 3 and the
mountains of the land. / Your

When their lives are half gone,
   their riches will desert
   them,
and in the end they will
   prove to be fools.

¹²A glorious throne, exalted
   from the beginning,
is the place of our sanctuary.
¹³LORD, you are the hope of
   Israel;
all who forsake you will be
   put to shame.
Those who turn away from
   you will be written in the
   dust
because they have forsaken
   the LORD,
the spring of living water.

¹⁴Heal me, LORD, and I will be
   healed;
save me and I will be
   saved,
for you are the one I praise.
¹⁵They keep saying to me,
   "Where is the word of the
   LORD?
Let it now be fulfilled!"
¹⁶I have not run away from
   being your shepherd;
you know I have not desired
   the day of despair.
What passes my lips is open
   before you.
¹⁷Do not be a terror to me;
   you are my refuge in the day
   of disaster.
¹⁸Let my persecutors be put to
   shame,
but keep me from shame;

let them be terrified,
   but keep me from terror.
Bring on them the day of
   disaster;
destroy them with double
   destruction.

Keeping the Sabbath Day Holy

¹⁹This is what the LORD said to me: "Go and stand at the Gate of the People,[a] through which the kings of Judah go in and out; stand also at all the other gates of Jerusalem. ²⁰Say to them, 'Hear the word of the LORD, you kings of Judah and all people of Judah and everyone living in Jerusalem who come through these gates. ²¹This is what the LORD says: Be careful not to carry a load on the Sabbath day or bring it through the gates of Jerusalem. ²²Do not bring a load out of your houses or do any work on the Sabbath, but keep the Sabbath day holy, as I commanded your ancestors. ²³Yet they did not listen or pay attention; they were stiff-necked and would not listen or respond to discipline. ²⁴But if you are careful to obey me, declares the LORD, and bring no load through the gates of this city on the Sabbath, but keep the Sabbath day holy by not doing any work on it, ²⁵then kings who sit on David's throne will come through the gates of this city with their officials. They and their officials will come riding in chariots and on horses, accompanied

by the men of Judah and those living in Jerusalem, and this city will be inhabited forever. ²⁶People will come from the towns of Judah and the villages around Jerusalem, from the territory of Benjamin and the western foothills, from the hill country and the Negev, bringing burnt offerings and sacrifices, grain offerings and incense, and bringing thank offerings to the house of the LORD. ²⁷But if you do not obey me to keep the Sabbath day holy by not carrying any load as you come through the gates of Jerusalem on the Sabbath day, then I will kindle an unquenchable fire in the gates of Jerusalem that will consume her fortresses.' "

At the Potter's House

18 This is the word that came to Jeremiah from the LORD: ²"Go down to the potter's house, and there I will give you my message." ³So I went down to the potter's house, and I saw him working at the wheel. ⁴But the pot he was shaping from the clay was marred in his hands; so the potter formed it into another pot, shaping it as seemed best to him.

⁵Then the word of the LORD came to me. ⁶He said, "Can I not do with you, Israel, as this potter does?" declares the LORD. "Like clay in the hand of the potter, so are you in my hand, Israel. ⁷If at any time I announce that a na-

tion or kingdom is to be uprooted, torn down and destroyed, ⁸and if that nation I warned repents of its evil, then I will relent and not inflict on it the disaster I had planned. ⁹And if at another time I announce that a nation or kingdom is to be built up and planted, ¹⁰and if it does evil in my sight and does not obey me, then I will reconsider the good I had intended to do for it.

¹¹"Now therefore say to the people of Judah and those living in Jerusalem, 'This is what the LORD says: Look! I am preparing a disaster for you and devising a plan against you. So turn from your evil ways, each one of you, and reform your ways and your actions.' ¹²But they will reply, 'It's no use. We will continue with our own plans; we will all follow the stubbornness of our evil hearts.' "

¹³Therefore this is what the LORD says:

"Inquire among the nations:
  Who has ever heard
    anything like this?
A most horrible thing has been done
  by Virgin Israel.
¹⁴Does the snow of Lebanon
  ever vanish from its rocky slopes?
Do its cool waters from distant sources
  ever stop flowing?ᵃ

ᵃ 14 The meaning of the Hebrew for this sentence is uncertain.

¹⁵Yet my people have
　　forgotten me;
　　they burn incense to
　　　worthless idols,
　which made them stumble in
　　their ways,
　　in the ancient paths.
　They made them walk in
　　byways,
　　on roads not built up.
¹⁶Their land will be an object of
　　horror
　　and of lasting scorn;
　all who pass by will be
　　appalled
　　and will shake their heads.
¹⁷Like a wind from the east,
　　I will scatter them before
　　　their enemies;
　I will show them my back and
　　not my face
　　in the day of their disaster."

¹⁸They said, "Come, let's make plans against Jeremiah; for the teaching of the law by the priest will not cease, nor will counsel from the wise, nor the word from the prophets. So come, let's attack him with our tongues and pay no attention to anything he says."

¹⁹Listen to me, LORD;
　　hear what my accusers are
　　　saying!
²⁰Should good be repaid with
　　evil?
　　Yet they have dug a pit for me.
　Remember that I stood before
　　you
　　and spoke in their behalf
　　to turn your wrath away
　　　from them.

²¹So give their children over to
　　famine;
　hand them over to the power
　　of the sword.
　Let their wives be made
　　childless and widows;
　　let their men be put to death,
　their young men slain by the
　　sword in battle.
²²Let a cry be heard from their
　　houses
　when you suddenly bring
　　invaders against them,
　for they have dug a pit to
　　capture me
　　and have hidden snares for
　　　my feet.
²³But you, LORD, know
　　all their plots to kill me.
　Do not forgive their crimes
　　or blot out their sins from
　　　your sight.
　Let them be overthrown
　　before you;
　　deal with them in the time of
　　　your anger.

19 This is what the LORD says: "Go and buy a clay jar from a potter. Take along some of the elders of the people and of the priests ²and go out to the Valley of Ben Hinnom, near the entrance of the Potsherd Gate. There proclaim the words I tell you, ³and say, 'Hear the word of the LORD, you kings of Judah and people of Jerusalem. This is what the LORD Almighty, the God of Israel, says: Listen! I am going to bring a disaster on this

place that will make the ears of everyone who hears of it tingle. ⁴For they have forsaken me and made this a place of foreign gods; they have burned incense in it to gods that neither they nor their ancestors nor the kings of Judah ever knew, and they have filled this place with the blood of the innocent. ⁵They have built the high places of Baal to burn their children in the fire as offerings to Baal — something I did not command or mention, nor did it enter my mind. ⁶So beware, the days are coming, declares the LORD, when people will no longer call this place Topheth or the Valley of Ben Hinnom, but the Valley of Slaughter.

⁷ " 'In this place I will ruin*a* the plans of Judah and Jerusalem. I will make them fall by the sword before their enemies, at the hands of those who want to kill them, and I will give their carcasses as food to the birds and the wild animals. ⁸I will devastate this city and make it an object of horror and scorn; all who pass by will be appalled and will scoff because of all its wounds. ⁹I will make them eat the flesh of their sons and daughters, and they will eat one another's flesh because their enemies will press the siege so hard against them to destroy them.'

¹⁰ "Then break the jar while those who go with you are watching, ¹¹and say to them, 'This is what the LORD Almighty says: I will smash this nation and this city just as this potter's jar is smashed and cannot be repaired. They will bury the dead in Topheth until there is no more room. ¹²This is what I will do to this place and to those who live here, declares the LORD. I will make this city like Topheth. ¹³The houses in Jerusalem and those of the kings of Judah will be defiled like this place, Topheth — all the houses where they burned incense on the roofs to all the starry hosts and poured out drink offerings to other gods.' "

¹⁴Jeremiah then returned from Topheth, where the LORD had sent him to prophesy, and stood in the court of the LORD's temple and said to all the people, ¹⁵"This is what the LORD Almighty, the God of Israel, says: 'Listen! I am going to bring on this city and all the villages around it every disaster I pronounced against them, because they were stiff-necked and would not listen to my words.' "

Jeremiah and Pashhur

20 When the priest Pashhur son of Immer, the official in charge of the temple of the LORD, heard Jeremiah prophesying these things, ²he had Jeremiah the prophet beaten and put in the stocks at the Upper Gate of

a 7 The Hebrew for *ruin* sounds like the Hebrew for *jar* (see verses 1 and 10).

Benjamin at the LORD's temple. ³The next day, when Pashhur released him from the stocks, Jeremiah said to him, "The LORD's name for you is not Pashhur, but Terror on Every Side. ⁴For this is what the LORD says: 'I will make you a terror to yourself and to all your friends; with your own eyes you will see them fall by the sword of their enemies. I will give all Judah into the hands of the king of Babylon, who will carry them away to Babylon or put them to the sword. ⁵I will deliver all the wealth of this city into the hands of their enemies — all its products, all its valuables and all the treasures of the kings of Judah. They will take it away as plunder and carry it off to Babylon. ⁶And you, Pashhur, and all who live in your house will go into exile to Babylon. There you will die and be buried, you and all your friends to whom you have prophesied lies.'"

Jeremiah's Complaint

⁷You deceived*a* me, LORD, and I
    was deceived*a*;
  you overpowered me and
    prevailed.
  I am ridiculed all day long;
    everyone mocks me.
⁸Whenever I speak, I cry out
    proclaiming violence and
    destruction.
  So the word of the LORD has
    brought me

insult and reproach all day
    long.
⁹But if I say, "I will not mention
    his word
  or speak anymore in his
    name,"
  his word is in my heart like a
    fire,
  a fire shut up in my bones.
  I am weary of holding it in;
    indeed, I cannot.
¹⁰I hear many whispering,
  "Terror on every side!
    Denounce him! Let's
    denounce him!"
  All my friends
    are waiting for me to slip,
    saying,
  "Perhaps he will be deceived;
    then we will prevail over
    him
  and take our revenge on
    him."
¹¹But the LORD is with me like a
    mighty warrior;
  so my persecutors will
    stumble and not prevail.
  They will fail and be
    thoroughly disgraced;
  their dishonor will never be
    forgotten.
¹²LORD Almighty, you who
    examine the righteous
  and probe the heart and
    mind,
  let me see your vengeance on
    them,
  for to you I have committed
    my cause.

---

a 7 Or *persuaded*

¹³Sing to the LORD!
  Give praise to the LORD!
  He rescues the life of the needy
    from the hands of the
      wicked.

¹⁴Cursed be the day I was born!
  May the day my mother bore
    me not be blessed!
¹⁵Cursed be the man who
    brought my father the
      news,
  who made him very glad,
    saying,
  "A child is born to you — a
    son!"
¹⁶May that man be like the
    towns
  the LORD overthrew without
    pity.
  May he hear wailing in the
    morning,
  a battle cry at noon.
¹⁷For he did not kill me in the
    womb,
  with my mother as my grave,
  her womb enlarged forever.
¹⁸Why did I ever come out of the
    womb
  to see trouble and sorrow
  and to end my days in
    shame?

God Rejects Zedekiah's Request

21 The word came to Jeremiah from the LORD when King Zedekiah sent to him Pashhur son of Malkijah and the priest Zephaniah son of Maaseiah. They said: ²"Inquire now of the LORD for us because Nebuchadnezzar[a] king of Babylon is attacking us. Perhaps the LORD will perform wonders for us as in times past so that he will withdraw from us."

³But Jeremiah answered them, "Tell Zedekiah, ⁴'This is what the LORD, the God of Israel, says: I am about to turn against you the weapons of war that are in your hands, which you are using to fight the king of Babylon and the Babylonians[b] who are outside the wall besieging you. And I will gather them inside this city. ⁵I myself will fight against you with an outstretched hand and a mighty arm in furious anger and in great wrath. ⁶I will strike down those who live in this city — both man and beast — and they will die of a terrible plague. ⁷After that, declares the LORD, I will give Zedekiah king of Judah, his officials and the people in this city who survive the plague, sword and famine, into the hands of Nebuchadnezzar king of Babylon and to their enemies who want to kill them. He will put them to the sword; he will show them no mercy or pity or compassion.'

⁸"Furthermore, tell the people, 'This is what the LORD says: See, I am setting before you the way of life and the way of death. ⁹Whoever stays in this city will die by the sword, famine or plague. But

---

[a] 2 Hebrew *Nebuchadrezzar*, of which *Nebuchadnezzar* is a variant; here and often in Jeremiah and Ezekiel   [b] 4 Or *Chaldeans*; also in verse 9

whoever goes out and surrenders to the Babylonians who are besieging you will live; they will escape with their lives. ¹⁰I have determined to do this city harm and not good, declares the LORD. It will be given into the hands of the king of Babylon, and he will destroy it with fire.'

¹¹ "Moreover, say to the royal house of Judah, 'Hear the word of the LORD. ¹²This is what the LORD says to you, house of David:

> " 'Administer justice every
>   morning;
>   rescue from the hand of the
>   oppressor
>   the one who has been
>   robbed,
> or my wrath will break out and
>   burn like fire
>   because of the evil you have
>   done —
>   burn with no one to
>   quench it.
> ¹³I am against you, Jerusalem,
>   you who live above this
>   valley
>   on the rocky plateau,
>   declares the LORD —
> you who say, "Who can come
>   against us?
>   Who can enter our refuge?"
> ¹⁴I will punish you as your deeds
>   deserve,
>   declares the LORD.
>   I will kindle a fire in your
>   forests
>   that will consume
>   everything around
>   you.' "

Judgment Against Wicked Kings

22 This is what the LORD says: "Go down to the palace of the king of Judah and proclaim this message there: ² 'Hear the word of the LORD to you, king of Judah, you who sit on David's throne — you, your officials and your people who come through these gates. ³This is what the LORD says: Do what is just and right. Rescue from the hand of the oppressor the one who has been robbed. Do no wrong or violence to the foreigner, the fatherless or the widow, and do not shed innocent blood in this place. ⁴For if you are careful to carry out these commands, then kings who sit on David's throne will come through the gates of this palace, riding in chariots and on horses, accompanied by their officials and their people. ⁵But if you do not obey these commands, declares the LORD, I swear by myself that this palace will become a ruin.' "

⁶For this is what the LORD says about the palace of the king of Judah:

> "Though you are like Gilead
>   to me,
>   like the summit of Lebanon,
> I will surely make you like a
>   wasteland,
>   like towns not inhabited.
> ⁷I will send destroyers against
>   you,
>   each man with his weapons,

and they will cut up your fine
   cedar beams
   and throw them into the fire.

8 "People from many nations
will pass by this city and will ask
one another, 'Why has the Lord
done such a thing to this great
city?' 9 And the answer will be:
'Because they have forsaken the
covenant of the Lord their God
and have worshiped and served
other gods.' "

10 Do not weep for the dead king
   or mourn his loss;
   rather, weep bitterly for him
   who is exiled,
   because he will never return
   nor see his native land
   again.

11 For this is what the Lord says
about Shallum[a] son of Josiah,
who succeeded his father as king
of Judah but has gone from this
place: "He will never return. 12 He
will die in the place where they
have led him captive; he will not
see this land again."

13 "Woe to him who builds
   his palace by
   unrighteousness,
   his upper rooms by injustice,
   making his own people work
   for nothing,
   not paying them for their
   labor.
14 He says, 'I will build myself a
   great palace
   with spacious upper rooms.'

So he makes large windows
   in it,
   panels it with cedar
   and decorates it in red.

15 "Does it make you a king
   to have more and more
   cedar?
   Did not your father have food
   and drink?
   He did what was right and
   just,
   so all went well with him.
16 He defended the cause of the
   poor and needy,
   and so all went well.
   Is that not what it means to
   know me?"
   declares the Lord.
17 "But your eyes and your
   heart
   are set only on dishonest
   gain,
   on shedding innocent blood
   and on oppression and
   extortion."

18 Therefore this is what the Lord
says about Jehoiakim son of Josiah king of Judah:

"They will not mourn for him:
   'Alas, my brother! Alas, my
   sister!'
They will not mourn for him:
   'Alas, my master! Alas, his
   splendor!'
19 He will have the burial of a
   donkey—
   dragged away and thrown
   outside the gates of
   Jerusalem."

---

a 11 Also called *Jehoahaz*

20 "Go up to Lebanon and cry
        out,
    let your voice be heard in
        Bashan,
  cry out from Abarim,
    for all your allies are
        crushed.
21 I warned you when you felt
        secure,
    but you said, 'I will not
        listen!'
  This has been your way from
        your youth;
    you have not obeyed me.
22 The wind will drive all your
        shepherds away,
    and your allies will go into
        exile.
  Then you will be ashamed and
        disgraced
    because of all your
        wickedness.
23 You who live in 'Lebanon,'*a*
    who are nestled in cedar
        buildings,
  how you will groan when
        pangs come upon you,
    pain like that of a woman in
        labor!

24 "As surely as I live," declares
the LORD, "even if you, Jehoiachin*b* son of Jehoiakim king
of Judah, were a signet ring on
my right hand, I would still pull
you off. 25 I will deliver you into
the hands of those who want to
kill you, those you fear — Nebuchadnezzar king of Babylon and
the Babylonians.*c* 26 I will hurl

you and the mother who gave
you birth into another country,
where neither of you was born,
and there you both will die. 27 You
will never come back to the land
you long to return to."

28 Is this man Jehoiachin a
        despised, broken pot,
    an object no one wants?
  Why will he and his children
        be hurled out,
    cast into a land they do not
        know?
29 O land, land, land,
    hear the word of the
        LORD!
30 This is what the LORD says:
  "Record this man as if
        childless,
    a man who will not prosper
        in his lifetime,
  for none of his offspring will
        prosper,
    none will sit on the throne of
        David
    or rule anymore in Judah."

The Righteous Branch

23 "Woe to the shepherds
who are destroying and
scattering the sheep of my pasture!" declares the LORD. 2 Therefore this is what the LORD, the
God of Israel, says to the shepherds who tend my people: "Because you have scattered my
flock and driven them away and
have not bestowed care on them,
I will bestow punishment on you

---

a 23 That is, the palace in Jerusalem (see 1 Kings 7:2)   *b 24* Hebrew *Koniah,* a
variant of *Jehoiachin*; also in verse 28   *c 25* Or *Chaldeans*

for the evil you have done," declares the LORD. ³"I myself will gather the remnant of my flock out of all the countries where I have driven them and will bring them back to their pasture, where they will be fruitful and increase in number. ⁴I will place shepherds over them who will tend them, and they will no longer be afraid or terrified, nor will any be missing," declares the LORD.

⁵ "The days are coming,"
      declares the LORD,
   "when I will raise up for
      David*ᵃ* a righteous
      Branch,
   a King who will reign wisely
      and do what is just and right
      in the land.
⁶In his days Judah will be
      saved
   and Israel will live in safety.
   This is the name by which he
      will be called:
   The LORD Our Righteous
      Savior.

⁷ "So then, the days are coming," declares the LORD, "when people will no longer say, 'As surely as the LORD lives, who brought the Israelites up out of Egypt,' ⁸but they will say, 'As surely as the LORD lives, who brought the descendants of Israel up out of the land of the north and out of all the countries where he had banished them.' Then they will live in their own land."

Lying Prophets

⁹Concerning the prophets:

My heart is broken within me;
   all my bones tremble.
I am like a drunken man,
   like a strong man overcome
      by wine,
because of the LORD
   and his holy words.
¹⁰The land is full of adulterers;
   because of the curse*ᵇ* the
      land lies parched
   and the pastures in the
      wilderness are withered.
The prophets follow an evil
      course
   and use their power
      unjustly.

¹¹ "Both prophet and priest are
      godless;
   even in my temple I find
      their wickedness,"
            declares the LORD.
¹² "Therefore their path will
      become slippery;
   they will be banished to
      darkness
   and there they will fall.
I will bring disaster on them
   in the year they are
      punished,"
            declares the LORD.

¹³ "Among the prophets of
      Samaria
   I saw this repulsive thing:
They prophesied by Baal
   and led my people Israel
      astray.

ᵃ 5 Or *up from David's line*   *ᵇ 10* Or *because of these things*

¹⁴And among the prophets of
  Jerusalem
    I have seen something
      horrible:
    They commit adultery and
      live a lie.
    They strengthen the hands of
      evildoers,
      so that not one of them turns
        from their wickedness.
    They are all like Sodom to me;
      the people of Jerusalem are
        like Gomorrah."

¹⁵Therefore this is what the
LORD Almighty says concerning
the prophets:

"I will make them eat bitter
  food
  and drink poisoned water,
because from the prophets of
  Jerusalem
  ungodliness has spread
    throughout the land."

¹⁶This is what the LORD Almighty says:

"Do not listen to what
  the prophets are
    prophesying to you;
  they fill you with false hopes.
They speak visions from their
  own minds,
  not from the mouth of the
    LORD.
¹⁷They keep saying to those who
  despise me,
  'The LORD says: You will
    have peace.'
And to all who follow the
  stubbornness of their
    hearts

they say, 'No harm will come
  to you.'
¹⁸But which of them has stood in
  the council of the LORD
  to see or to hear his word?
  Who has listened and heard
    his word?
¹⁹See, the storm of the LORD
  will burst out in wrath,
  a whirlwind swirling down
    on the heads of the wicked.
²⁰The anger of the LORD will not
  turn back
  until he fully accomplishes
    the purposes of his heart.
In days to come
  you will understand it
    clearly.
²¹I did not send these
  prophets,
  yet they have run with their
    message;
I did not speak to them,
  yet they have prophesied.
²²But if they had stood in my
  council,
  they would have proclaimed
    my words to my people
and would have turned them
  from their evil ways
  and from their evil deeds.

²³"Am I only a God nearby,"
  declares the LORD,
  "and not a God far away?
²⁴Who can hide in secret
  places
  so that I cannot see them?"
  declares the LORD.
  "Do not I fill heaven and
    earth?"
  declares the LORD.

25 "I have heard what the prophets say who prophesy lies in my name. They say, 'I had a dream! I had a dream!' **26** How long will this continue in the hearts of these lying prophets, who prophesy the delusions of their own minds? **27** They think the dreams they tell one another will make my people forget my name, just as their ancestors forgot my name through Baal worship. **28** Let the prophet who has a dream recount the dream, but let the one who has my word speak it faithfully. For what has straw to do with grain?" declares the Lord. **29** "Is not my word like fire," declares the Lord, "and like a hammer that breaks a rock in pieces?

30 "Therefore," declares the Lord, "I am against the prophets who steal from one another words supposedly from me. **31** Yes," declares the Lord, "I am against the prophets who wag their own tongues and yet declare, 'The Lord declares.' **32** Indeed, I am against those who prophesy false dreams," declares the Lord. "They tell them and lead my people astray with their reckless lies, yet I did not send or appoint them. They do not benefit these people in the least," declares the Lord.

False Prophecy

33 "When these people, or a prophet or a priest, ask you, 'What is the message from the Lord?' say to them, 'What message? I will forsake you, declares the Lord.' **34** If a prophet or a priest or anyone else claims, 'This is a message from the Lord,' I will punish them and their household. **35** This is what each of you keeps saying to your friends and other Israelites: 'What is the Lord's answer?' or 'What has the Lord spoken?' **36** But you must not mention 'a message from the Lord' again, because each one's word becomes their own message. So you distort the words of the living God, the Lord Almighty, our God. **37** This is what you keep saying to a prophet: 'What is the Lord's answer to you?' or 'What has the Lord spoken?' **38** Although you claim, 'This is a message from the Lord,' this is what the Lord says: You used the words, 'This is a message from the Lord,' even though I told you that you must not claim, 'This is a message from the Lord.' **39** Therefore, I will surely forget you and cast you out of my presence along with the city I gave to you and your ancestors. **40** I will bring on you everlasting disgrace — everlasting shame that will not be forgotten."

Two Baskets of Figs

24 After Jehoiachin[a] son of Jehoiakim king of Judah and the officials, the skilled

---

[a] 1 Hebrew *Jeconiah*, a variant of *Jehoiachin*

workers and the artisans of Judah were carried into exile from Jerusalem to Babylon by Nebuchadnezzar king of Babylon, the LORD showed me two baskets of figs placed in front of the temple of the LORD. [2]One basket had very good figs, like those that ripen early; the other basket had very bad figs, so bad they could not be eaten.

[3]Then the LORD asked me, "What do you see, Jeremiah?"

"Figs," I answered. "The good ones are very good, but the bad ones are so bad they cannot be eaten."

[4]Then the word of the LORD came to me: [5]"This is what the LORD, the God of Israel, says: 'Like these good figs, I regard as good the exiles from Judah, whom I sent away from this place to the land of the Babylonians.[a] [6]My eyes will watch over them for their good, and I will bring them back to this land. I will build them up and not tear them down; I will plant them and not uproot them. [7]I will give them a heart to know me, that I am the LORD. They will be my people, and I will be their God, for they will return to me with all their heart.

[8]" 'But like the bad figs, which are so bad they cannot be eaten,' says the LORD, 'so will I deal with Zedekiah king of Judah, his officials and the survivors from Jerusalem, whether they remain in this land or live in Egypt. [9]I will make them abhorrent and an offense to all the kingdoms of the earth, a reproach and a byword, a curse[b] and an object of ridicule, wherever I banish them. [10]I will send the sword, famine and plague against them until they are destroyed from the land I gave to them and their ancestors.' "

Seventy Years of Captivity

25 The word came to Jeremiah concerning all the people of Judah in the fourth year of Jehoiakim son of Josiah king of Judah, which was the first year of Nebuchadnezzar king of Babylon. [2]So Jeremiah the prophet said to all the people of Judah and to all those living in Jerusalem: [3]For twenty-three years—from the thirteenth year of Josiah son of Amon king of Judah until this very day—the word of the LORD has come to me and I have spoken to you again and again, but you have not listened.

[4]And though the LORD has sent all his servants the prophets to you again and again, you have not listened or paid any attention. [5]They said, "Turn now, each of you, from your evil ways and your evil practices, and you can stay in the land the LORD gave to

---

[a] 5 Or *Chaldeans*   [b] 9 That is, their names will be used in cursing (see 29:22); or, others will see that they are cursed.

you and your ancestors for ever and ever. ⁶Do not follow other gods to serve and worship them; do not arouse my anger with what your hands have made. Then I will not harm you."

⁷"But you did not listen to me," declares the LORD, "and you have aroused my anger with what your hands have made, and you have brought harm to yourselves."

⁸Therefore the LORD Almighty says this: "Because you have not listened to my words, ⁹I will summon all the peoples of the north and my servant Nebuchadnezzar king of Babylon," declares the LORD, "and I will bring them against this land and its inhabitants and against all the surrounding nations. I will completely destroy*ᵃ* them and make them an object of horror and scorn, and an everlasting ruin. ¹⁰I will banish from them the sounds of joy and gladness, the voices of bride and bridegroom, the sound of millstones and the light of the lamp. ¹¹This whole country will become a desolate wasteland, and these nations will serve the king of Babylon seventy years.

¹²"But when the seventy years are fulfilled, I will punish the king of Babylon and his nation, the land of the Babylonians,*ᵇ* for their guilt," declares the LORD,

"and will make it desolate forever. ¹³I will bring on that land all the things I have spoken against it, all that are written in this book and prophesied by Jeremiah against all the nations. ¹⁴They themselves will be enslaved by many nations and great kings; I will repay them according to their deeds and the work of their hands."

The Cup of God's Wrath

¹⁵This is what the LORD, the God of Israel, said to me: "Take from my hand this cup filled with the wine of my wrath and make all the nations to whom I send you drink it. ¹⁶When they drink it, they will stagger and go mad because of the sword I will send among them."

¹⁷So I took the cup from the LORD's hand and made all the nations to whom he sent me drink it: ¹⁸Jerusalem and the towns of Judah, its kings and officials, to make them a ruin and an object of horror and scorn, a curse*ᶜ*—as they are today; ¹⁹Pharaoh king of Egypt, his attendants, his officials and all his people, ²⁰and all the foreign people there; all the kings of Uz; all the kings of the Philistines (those of Ashkelon, Gaza, Ekron, and the people left at Ashdod); ²¹Edom, Moab and Ammon; ²²all the kings of

---

ᵃ 9 The Hebrew term refers to the irrevocable giving over of things or persons to the LORD, often by totally destroying them.   *ᵇ 12* Or *Chaldeans*   *ᶜ 18* That is, their names to be used in cursing (see 29:22); or, to be seen by others as cursed

Tyre and Sidon; the kings of the coastlands across the sea; [23] Dedan, Tema, Buz and all who are in distant places[a]; [24] all the kings of Arabia and all the kings of the foreign people who live in the wilderness; [25] all the kings of Zimri, Elam and Media; [26] and all the kings of the north, near and far, one after the other — all the kingdoms on the face of the earth. And after all of them, the king of Sheshak[b] will drink it too.

[27] "Then tell them, 'This is what the LORD Almighty, the God of Israel, says: Drink, get drunk and vomit, and fall to rise no more because of the sword I will send among you.' [28] But if they refuse to take the cup from your hand and drink, tell them, 'This is what the LORD Almighty says: You must drink it! [29] See, I am beginning to bring disaster on the city that bears my Name, and will you indeed go unpunished? You will not go unpunished, for I am calling down a sword on all who live on the earth, declares the LORD Almighty.'

[30] "Now prophesy all these words against them and say to them:

" 'The LORD will roar from on high;
    he will thunder from his holy dwelling
    and roar mightily against his land.

He will shout like those who tread the grapes,
    shout against all who live on the earth.
[31] The tumult will resound to the ends of the earth,
    for the LORD will bring charges against the nations;
he will bring judgment on all mankind
    and put the wicked to the sword,' "
        declares the LORD.

[32] This is what the LORD Almighty says:

"Look! Disaster is spreading
    from nation to nation;
a mighty storm is rising
    from the ends of the earth."

[33] At that time those slain by the LORD will be everywhere — from one end of the earth to the other. They will not be mourned or gathered up or buried, but will be like dung lying on the ground.

[34] Weep and wail, you shepherds;
    roll in the dust, you leaders of the flock.
For your time to be slaughtered has come;
    you will fall like the best of the rams.[c]
[35] The shepherds will have nowhere to flee,
    the leaders of the flock no place to escape.

---

[a] 23 Or *who clip the hair by their foreheads*   [b] 26 *Sheshak* is a cryptogram for Babylon.   [c] 34 Septuagint; Hebrew *fall and be shattered like fine pottery*

³⁶ Hear the cry of the shepherds,
    the wailing of the leaders of
        the flock,
    for the LORD is destroying
        their pasture.
³⁷ The peaceful meadows will be
    laid waste
    because of the fierce anger of
        the LORD.
³⁸ Like a lion he will leave his lair,
    and their land will become
        desolate
    because of the sword*a* of the
        oppressor
    and because of the LORD's
        fierce anger.

Jeremiah Threatened With Death

26 Early in the reign of Jehoiakim son of Josiah king of
Judah, this word came from the
LORD: ² "This is what the LORD
says: Stand in the courtyard of
the LORD's house and speak to
all the people of the towns of Judah who come to worship in the
house of the LORD. Tell them everything I command you; do not
omit a word. ³ Perhaps they will
listen and each will turn from
their evil ways. Then I will relent and not inflict on them the
disaster I was planning because
of the evil they have done. ⁴ Say
to them, 'This is what the LORD
says: If you do not listen to me
and follow my law, which I have

set before you, ⁵ and if you do not
listen to the words of my servants
the prophets, whom I have sent to
you again and again (though you
have not listened), ⁶ then I will
make this house like Shiloh and
this city a curse*b* among all the
nations of the earth.'"

⁷ The priests, the prophets and
all the people heard Jeremiah
speak these words in the house of
the LORD. ⁸ But as soon as Jeremiah finished telling all the people
everything the LORD had commanded him to say, the priests,
the prophets and all the people
seized him and said, "You must
die! ⁹ Why do you prophesy in the
LORD's name that this house will
be like Shiloh and this city will be
desolate and deserted?" And all
the people crowded around Jeremiah in the house of the LORD.

¹⁰ When the officials of Judah
heard about these things, they
went up from the royal palace to
the house of the LORD and took
their places at the entrance of the
New Gate of the LORD's house.
¹¹ Then the priests and the prophets said to the officials and all the
people, "This man should be sentenced to death because he has
prophesied against this city. You
have heard it with your own ears!"

¹² Then Jeremiah said to all the
officials and all the people: "The
LORD sent me to prophesy against

---

a 38 Some Hebrew manuscripts and Septuagint (see also 46:16 and 50:16); most
Hebrew manuscripts *anger*   *b 6* That is, its name will be used in cursing (see
29:22); or, others will see that it is cursed.

this house and this city all the things you have heard. [13] Now reform your ways and your actions and obey the LORD your God. Then the LORD will relent and not bring the disaster he has pronounced against you. [14] As for me, I am in your hands; do with me whatever you think is good and right. [15] Be assured, however, that if you put me to death, you will bring the guilt of innocent blood on yourselves and on this city and on those who live in it, for in truth the LORD has sent me to you to speak all these words in your hearing."

[16] Then the officials and all the people said to the priests and the prophets, "This man should not be sentenced to death! He has spoken to us in the name of the LORD our God."

[17] Some of the elders of the land stepped forward and said to the entire assembly of people, [18] "Micah of Moresheth prophesied in the days of Hezekiah king of Judah. He told all the people of Judah, 'This is what the LORD Almighty says:

"'Zion will be plowed like a
    field,
Jerusalem will become a
    heap of rubble,
the temple hill a mound
    overgrown with
    thickets.'[a]

[19] "Did Hezekiah king of Judah or anyone else in Judah put him to death? Did not Hezekiah fear the LORD and seek his favor? And did not the LORD relent, so that he did not bring the disaster he pronounced against them? We are about to bring a terrible disaster on ourselves!"

[20] (Now Uriah son of Shemaiah from Kiriath Jearim was another man who prophesied in the name of the LORD; he prophesied the same things against this city and this land as Jeremiah did. [21] When King Jehoiakim and all his officers and officials heard his words, the king was determined to put him to death. But Uriah heard of it and fled in fear to Egypt. [22] King Jehoiakim, however, sent Elnathan son of Akbor to Egypt, along with some other men. [23] They brought Uriah out of Egypt and took him to King Jehoiakim, who had him struck down with a sword and his body thrown into the burial place of the common people.)

[24] Furthermore, Ahikam son of Shaphan supported Jeremiah, and so he was not handed over to the people to be put to death.

Judah to Serve Nebuchadnezzar

27 Early in the reign of Zedekiah[b] son of Josiah king of Judah, this word came to Jer-

---

[a] 18 Micah 3:12   [b] 1 A few Hebrew manuscripts and Syriac (see also 27:3,12 and 28:1); most Hebrew manuscripts Jehoiakim (Most Septuagint manuscripts do not have this verse.)

emiah from the LORD: ²This is what the LORD said to me: "Make a yoke out of straps and crossbars and put it on your neck. ³Then send word to the kings of Edom, Moab, Ammon, Tyre and Sidon through the envoys who have come to Jerusalem to Zedekiah king of Judah. ⁴Give them a message for their masters and say, 'This is what the LORD Almighty, the God of Israel, says: "Tell this to your masters: ⁵With my great power and outstretched arm I made the earth and its people and the animals that are on it, and I give it to anyone I please. ⁶Now I will give all your countries into the hands of my servant Nebuchadnezzar king of Babylon; I will make even the wild animals subject to him. ⁷All nations will serve him and his son and his grandson until the time for his land comes; then many nations and great kings will subjugate him.

⁸" ' "If, however, any nation or kingdom will not serve Nebuchadnezzar king of Babylon or bow its neck under his yoke, I will punish that nation with the sword, famine and plague, declares the LORD, until I destroy it by his hand. ⁹So do not listen to your prophets, your diviners, your interpreters of dreams, your mediums or your sorcerers who tell you, 'You will not serve the king of Babylon.' ¹⁰They prophesy lies to you that will only serve to remove you far from your lands; I will banish you and you will perish. ¹¹But if any nation will bow its neck under the yoke of the king of Babylon and serve him, I will let that nation remain in its own land to till it and to live there, declares the LORD." ' "

¹²I gave the same message to Zedekiah king of Judah. I said, "Bow your neck under the yoke of the king of Babylon; serve him and his people, and you will live. ¹³Why will you and your people die by the sword, famine and plague with which the LORD has threatened any nation that will not serve the king of Babylon? ¹⁴Do not listen to the words of the prophets who say to you, 'You will not serve the king of Babylon,' for they are prophesying lies to you. ¹⁵'I have not sent them,' declares the LORD. 'They are prophesying lies in my name. Therefore, I will banish you and you will perish, both you and the prophets who prophesy to you.' "

¹⁶Then I said to the priests and all these people, "This is what the LORD says: Do not listen to the prophets who say, 'Very soon now the articles from the LORD's house will be brought back from Babylon.' They are prophesying lies to you. ¹⁷Do not listen to them. Serve the king of Babylon, and you will live. Why should this city become a ruin? ¹⁸If they are prophets and have the word of the LORD, let them plead with

the LORD Almighty that the articles remaining in the house of the LORD and in the palace of the king of Judah and in Jerusalem not be taken to Babylon. **19**For this is what the LORD Almighty says about the pillars, the bronze Sea, the movable stands and the other articles that are left in this city, **20**which Nebuchadnezzar king of Babylon did not take away when he carried Jehoiachin[a] son of Jehoiakim king of Judah into exile from Jerusalem to Babylon, along with all the nobles of Judah and Jerusalem — **21**yes, this is what the LORD Almighty, the God of Israel, says about the things that are left in the house of the LORD and in the palace of the king of Judah and in Jerusalem: **22**'They will be taken to Babylon and there they will remain until the day I come for them,' declares the LORD. 'Then I will bring them back and restore them to this place.' "

The False Prophet Hananiah

28 In the fifth month of that same year, the fourth year, early in the reign of Zedekiah king of Judah, the prophet Hananiah son of Azzur, who was from Gibeon, said to me in the house of the LORD in the presence of the priests and all the people: **2**"This is what the LORD Almighty, the God of Israel, says: 'I will break the yoke of the king of Babylon. **3**Within two years I will bring back to this place all the articles of the LORD's house that Nebuchadnezzar king of Babylon removed from here and took to Babylon. **4**I will also bring back to this place Jehoiachin[a] son of Jehoiakim king of Judah and all the other exiles from Judah who went to Babylon,' declares the LORD, 'for I will break the yoke of the king of Babylon.' "

5Then the prophet Jeremiah replied to the prophet Hananiah before the priests and all the people who were standing in the house of the LORD. **6**He said, "Amen! May the LORD do so! May the LORD fulfill the words you have prophesied by bringing the articles of the LORD's house and all the exiles back to this place from Babylon. **7**Nevertheless, listen to what I have to say in your hearing and in the hearing of all the people: **8**From early times the prophets who preceded you and me have prophesied war, disaster and plague against many countries and great kingdoms. **9**But the prophet who prophesies peace will be recognized as one truly sent by the LORD only if his prediction comes true."

10Then the prophet Hananiah took the yoke off the neck of the prophet Jeremiah and broke it, **11**and he said before all the people, "This is what the LORD says: 'In the same way I will break the

---

a 20,4 Hebrew *Jeconiah,* a variant of *Jehoiachin*

yoke of Nebuchadnezzar king of Babylon off the neck of all the nations within two years.'" At this, the prophet Jeremiah went on his way.

¹²After the prophet Hananiah had broken the yoke off the neck of the prophet Jeremiah, the word of the LORD came to Jeremiah: ¹³"Go and tell Hananiah, 'This is what the LORD says: You have broken a wooden yoke, but in its place you will get a yoke of iron. ¹⁴This is what the LORD Almighty, the God of Israel, says: I will put an iron yoke on the necks of all these nations to make them serve Nebuchadnezzar king of Babylon, and they will serve him. I will even give him control over the wild animals.'"

¹⁵Then the prophet Jeremiah said to Hananiah the prophet, "Listen, Hananiah! The LORD has not sent you, yet you have persuaded this nation to trust in lies. ¹⁶Therefore this is what the LORD says: 'I am about to remove you from the face of the earth. This very year you are going to die, because you have preached rebellion against the LORD.'"

¹⁷In the seventh month of that same year, Hananiah the prophet died.

A Letter to the Exiles

29 This is the text of the letter that the prophet Jeremiah sent from Jerusalem to the surviving elders among the exiles and to the priests, the prophets and all the other people Nebuchadnezzar had carried into exile from Jerusalem to Babylon. ²(This was after King Jehoiachin[a] and the queen mother, the court officials and the leaders of Judah and Jerusalem, the skilled workers and the artisans had gone into exile from Jerusalem.) ³He entrusted the letter to Elasah son of Shaphan and to Gemariah son of Hilkiah, whom Zedekiah king of Judah sent to King Nebuchadnezzar in Babylon. It said:

⁴This is what the LORD Almighty, the God of Israel, says to all those I carried into exile from Jerusalem to Babylon: ⁵"Build houses and settle down; plant gardens and eat what they produce. ⁶Marry and have sons and daughters; find wives for your sons and give your daughters in marriage, so that they too may have sons and daughters. Increase in number there; do not decrease. ⁷Also, seek the peace and prosperity of the city to which I have carried you into exile. Pray to the LORD for it, because if it prospers, you too will prosper." ⁸Yes, this is what the LORD Almighty, the God of Israel, says: "Do not let the prophets and diviners among you deceive you. Do not listen to the

---

[a] 2 Hebrew *Jeconiah*, a variant of *Jehoiachin*

dreams you encourage them to have. **9** They are prophesying lies to you in my name. I have not sent them," declares the LORD.

10 This is what the LORD says: "When seventy years are completed for Babylon, I will come to you and fulfill my good promise to bring you back to this place. **11** For I know the plans I have for you," declares the LORD, "plans to prosper you and not to harm you, plans to give you hope and a future. **12** Then you will call on me and come and pray to me, and I will listen to you. **13** You will seek me and find me when you seek me with all your heart. **14** I will be found by you," declares the LORD, "and will bring you back from captivity.*a* I will gather you from all the nations and places where I have banished you," declares the LORD, "and will bring you back to the place from which I carried you into exile."

15 You may say, "The LORD has raised up prophets for us in Babylon," **16** but this is what the LORD says about the king who sits on David's throne and all the people who remain in this city, your fellow citizens who did not go with you into exile— **17** yes, this is what the LORD Almighty says: "I will send the sword, famine and plague against them and I will make them like figs that are so bad they cannot be eaten. **18** I will pursue them with the sword, famine and plague and will make them abhorrent to all the kingdoms of the earth, a curse*b* and an object of horror, of scorn and reproach, among all the nations where I drive them. **19** For they have not listened to my words," declares the LORD, "words that I sent to them again and again by my servants the prophets. And you exiles have not listened either," declares the LORD.

20 Therefore, hear the word of the LORD, all you exiles whom I have sent away from Jerusalem to Babylon. **21** This is what the LORD Almighty, the God of Israel, says about Ahab son of Kolaiah and Zedekiah son of Maaseiah, who are prophesying lies to you in my name: "I will deliver them into the hands of Nebuchadnezzar king of Babylon, and he will put them to death before your very eyes. **22** Because of them, all the exiles from Judah who are in Babylon will use this curse: 'May the LORD treat you like Zedekiah and Ahab, whom the

---

a 14 Or *will restore your fortunes*   *b 18* That is, their names will be used in cursing (see verse 22); or, others will see that they are cursed.

king of Babylon burned in the fire.' ²³ For they have done outrageous things in Israel; they have committed adultery with their neighbors' wives, and in my name they have uttered lies—which I did not authorize. I know it and am a witness to it," declares the LORD.

Message to Shemaiah

²⁴ Tell Shemaiah the Nehelamite, ²⁵ "This is what the LORD Almighty, the God of Israel, says: You sent letters in your own name to all the people in Jerusalem, to the priest Zephaniah son of Maaseiah, and to all the other priests. You said to Zephaniah, ²⁶ 'The LORD has appointed you priest in place of Jehoiada to be in charge of the house of the LORD; you should put any maniac who acts like a prophet into the stocks and neck-irons. ²⁷ So why have you not reprimanded Jeremiah from Anathoth, who poses as a prophet among you? ²⁸ He has sent this message to us in Babylon: It will be a long time. Therefore build houses and settle down; plant gardens and eat what they produce.' "

²⁹ Zephaniah the priest, however, read the letter to Jeremiah the prophet. ³⁰ Then the word of the LORD came to Jeremiah: ³¹ "Send this message to all the exiles: 'This is what the LORD says about Shemaiah the Nehelamite: Because Shemaiah has prophesied to you, even though I did not send him, and has persuaded you to trust in lies, ³² this is what the LORD says: I will surely punish Shemaiah the Nehelamite and his descendants. He will have no one left among this people, nor will he see the good things I will do for my people, declares the LORD, because he has preached rebellion against me.' "

Restoration of Israel

30 This is the word that came to Jeremiah from the LORD: ² "This is what the LORD, the God of Israel, says: 'Write in a book all the words I have spoken to you. ³ The days are coming,' declares the LORD, 'when I will bring my people Israel and Judah back from captivity*a* and restore them to the land I gave their ancestors to possess,' says the LORD."

⁴ These are the words the LORD spoke concerning Israel and Judah: ⁵ "This is what the LORD says:

" 'Cries of fear are heard—
  terror, not peace.
⁶ Ask and see:
  Can a man bear children?
Then why do I see every strong man
  with his hands on his
    stomach like a woman in
    labor,

^a 3 Or *will restore the fortunes of my people Israel and Judah*

every face turned deathly
pale?
⁷ How awful that day will be!
No other will be like it.
It will be a time of trouble for
Jacob,
but he will be saved out
of it.

⁸ " 'In that day,' declares the
LORD Almighty,
'I will break the yoke off their
necks
and will tear off their bonds;
no longer will foreigners
enslave them.
⁹ Instead, they will serve the
LORD their God
and David their king,
whom I will raise up for
them.

¹⁰ " 'So do not be afraid, Jacob my
servant;
do not be dismayed, Israel,'
declares the LORD.
'I will surely save you out of a
distant place,
your descendants from the
land of their exile.
Jacob will again have peace
and security,
and no one will make him
afraid.
¹¹ I am with you and will save
you,'
declares the LORD.
'Though I completely destroy
all the nations
among which I scatter you,
I will not completely destroy
you.

I will discipline you but only in
due measure;
I will not let you go entirely
unpunished.'

¹² "This is what the LORD says:

" 'Your wound is incurable,
your injury beyond
healing.
¹³ There is no one to plead your
cause,
no remedy for your sore,
no healing for you.
¹⁴ All your allies have forgotten
you;
they care nothing for you.
I have struck you as an enemy
would
and punished you as would
the cruel,
because your guilt is so great
and your sins so many.
¹⁵ Why do you cry out over your
wound,
your pain that has no cure?
Because of your great guilt and
many sins
I have done these things to
you.

¹⁶ " 'But all who devour you will
be devoured;
all your enemies will go into
exile.
Those who plunder you will be
plundered;
all who make spoil of you I
will despoil.
¹⁷ But I will restore you to
health
and heal your wounds,'
declares the LORD,

'because you are called an
outcast,
Zion for whom no one cares.'

¹⁸"This is what the LORD says:

" 'I will restore the fortunes of
Jacob's tents
and have compassion on his
dwellings;
the city will be rebuilt on her
ruins,
and the palace will stand in
its proper place.
¹⁹From them will come songs of
thanksgiving
and the sound of rejoicing.
I will add to their numbers,
and they will not be
decreased;
I will bring them honor,
and they will not be
disdained.
²⁰Their children will be as in
days of old,
and their community will be
established before me;
I will punish all who oppress
them.
²¹Their leader will be one of
their own;
their ruler will arise from
among them.
I will bring him near and he
will come close to me —
for who is he who will devote
himself
to be close to me?'
declares the LORD.
²²" 'So you will be my people,
and I will be your God.' "

²³See, the storm of the LORD
will burst out in wrath,
a driving wind swirling down
on the heads of the wicked.
²⁴The fierce anger of the LORD
will not turn back
until he fully accomplishes
the purposes of his heart.
In days to come
you will understand this.

31

"At that time," declares
the LORD, "I will be the
God of all the families of Israel,
and they will be my people."
²This is what the LORD says:

"The people who survive the
sword
will find favor in the
wilderness;
I will come to give rest to
Israel."

³The LORD appeared to us in
the past,^a saying:

"I have loved you with an
everlasting love;
I have drawn you with
unfailing kindness.
⁴I will build you up again,
and you, Virgin Israel, will
be rebuilt.
Again you will take up your
timbrels
and go out to dance with the
joyful.
⁵Again you will plant vineyards
on the hills of Samaria;
the farmers will plant them
and enjoy their fruit.

---

^a 3 Or LORD *has appeared to us from afar*

⁶There will be a day when
    watchmen cry out
    on the hills of Ephraim,
'Come, let us go up to Zion,
    to the Lord our God.'"

⁷This is what the Lord says:

"Sing with joy for Jacob;
    shout for the foremost of the
    nations.
Make your praises heard, and
    say,
    'Lord, save your people,
    the remnant of Israel.'
⁸See, I will bring them from the
    land of the north
    and gather them from the
    ends of the earth.
Among them will be the blind
    and the lame,
    expectant mothers and
    women in labor;
    a great throng will return.
⁹They will come with weeping;
    they will pray as I bring
    them back.
I will lead them beside streams
    of water
    on a level path where they
    will not stumble,
because I am Israel's father,
    and Ephraim is my firstborn
    son.

¹⁰"Hear the word of the Lord,
    you nations;
    proclaim it in distant
    coastlands:
'He who scattered Israel will
    gather them
    and will watch over his flock
    like a shepherd.'

¹¹For the Lord will deliver
    Jacob
    and redeem them from the
    hand of those stronger
    than they.
¹²They will come and shout for
    joy on the heights of
    Zion;
    they will rejoice in the
    bounty of the Lord —
    the grain, the new wine and
    the olive oil,
    the young of the flocks and
    herds.
They will be like a well-
    watered garden,
    and they will sorrow no
    more.
¹³Then young women will dance
    and be glad,
    young men and old as
    well.
I will turn their mourning into
    gladness;
    I will give them comfort and
    joy instead of sorrow.
¹⁴I will satisfy the priests with
    abundance,
    and my people will be filled
    with my bounty,"
        declares the Lord.

¹⁵This is what the Lord says:

"A voice is heard in Ramah,
    mourning and great
    weeping,
Rachel weeping for her
    children
    and refusing to be
    comforted,
    because they are no more."

¹⁶This is what the LORD says:

"Restrain your voice from
        weeping
    and your eyes from tears,
for your work will be
        rewarded,"
            declares the LORD.
    "They will return from the
        land of the enemy.
¹⁷So there is hope for your
        descendants,"
            declares the LORD.
    "Your children will return to
        their own land.

¹⁸"I have surely heard Ephraim's
        moaning:
    'You disciplined me like an
        unruly calf,
    and I have been disciplined.
Restore me, and I will return,
    because you are the LORD
        my God.
¹⁹After I strayed,
    I repented;
after I came to understand,
    I beat my breast.
I was ashamed and humiliated
    because I bore the disgrace
        of my youth.'
²⁰Is not Ephraim my dear son,
    the child in whom I delight?
Though I often speak against
        him,
    I still remember him.
Therefore my heart yearns for
        him;
    I have great compassion for
        him,"
            declares the LORD.

²¹"Set up road signs;
    put up guideposts.
Take note of the highway,
    the road that you take.
Return, Virgin Israel,
    return to your towns.
²²How long will you wander,
    unfaithful Daughter Israel?
The LORD will create a new
        thing on earth —
    the woman will return to^a
        the man."

²³This is what the LORD Almighty, the God of Israel, says: "When I bring them back from captivity,^b the people in the land of Judah and in its towns will once again use these words: 'The LORD bless you, you prosperous city, you sacred mountain.' ²⁴People will live together in Judah and all its towns — farmers and those who move about with their flocks. ²⁵I will refresh the weary and satisfy the faint."

²⁶At this I awoke and looked around. My sleep had been pleasant to me.

²⁷"The days are coming," declares the LORD, "when I will plant the kingdoms of Israel and Judah with the offspring of people and of animals. ²⁸Just as I watched over them to uproot and tear down, and to overthrow, destroy and bring disaster, so I will watch over them to build and to plant," declares the LORD. ²⁹"In those days people will no longer say,

^a 22 Or *will protect*   ^b 23 Or *I restore their fortunes*

'The parents have eaten sour
  grapes,
  and the children's teeth are
  set on edge.'

³⁰ Instead, everyone will die for
their own sin; whoever eats sour
grapes — their own teeth will be
set on edge.

³¹ "The days are coming,"
  declares the LORD,
  "when I will make a new
  covenant
  with the people of Israel
  and with the people of
  Judah.
³² It will not be like the covenant
  I made with their ancestors
  when I took them by the hand
  to lead them out of Egypt,
  because they broke my
  covenant,
  though I was a husband to*ᵃ*
  them,*ᵇ*"
          declares the LORD.
³³ "This is the covenant I will
  make with the people of
  Israel
  after that time," declares the
  LORD.
  "I will put my law in their
  minds
  and write it on their hearts.
  I will be their God,
  and they will be my people.
³⁴ No longer will they teach their
  neighbor,
  or say to one another, 'Know
  the LORD,'

because they will all know me,
  from the least of them to the
  greatest,"
          declares the LORD.
"For I will forgive their
  wickedness
  and will remember their sins
  no more."

³⁵ This is what the LORD says,

he who appoints the sun
  to shine by day,
who decrees the moon and
  stars
  to shine by night,
who stirs up the sea
  so that its waves roar —
  the LORD Almighty is his
  name:
³⁶ "Only if these decrees vanish
  from my sight,"
  declares the LORD,
  "will Israel ever cease
  being a nation before me."

³⁷ This is what the LORD says:

"Only if the heavens above can
  be measured
  and the foundations of the
  earth below be searched
  out
will I reject all the descendants
  of Israel
  because of all they have
  done,"
          declares the LORD.

³⁸ "The days are coming," declares the LORD, "when this city
will be rebuilt for me from the

ᵃ 32 Hebrew; Septuagint and Syriac / *and I turned away from*   *ᵇ* 32 Or *was their master*

Tower of Hananel to the Corner Gate. ³⁹The measuring line will stretch from there straight to the hill of Gareb and then turn to Goah. ⁴⁰The whole valley where dead bodies and ashes are thrown, and all the terraces out to the Kidron Valley on the east as far as the corner of the Horse Gate, will be holy to the LORD. The city will never again be uprooted or demolished."

Jeremiah Buys a Field

32 This is the word that came to Jeremiah from the LORD in the tenth year of Zedekiah king of Judah, which was the eighteenth year of Nebuchadnezzar. ²The army of the king of Babylon was then besieging Jerusalem, and Jeremiah the prophet was confined in the courtyard of the guard in the royal palace of Judah.

³Now Zedekiah king of Judah had imprisoned him there, saying, "Why do you prophesy as you do? You say, 'This is what the LORD says: I am about to give this city into the hands of the king of Babylon, and he will capture it. ⁴Zedekiah king of Judah will not escape the Babylonians*ᵃ* but will certainly be given into the hands of the king of Babylon, and will speak with him face to face and see him with his own eyes. ⁵He will take Zedekiah to Babylon, where he will remain until I deal with him, declares the LORD. If you fight against the Babylonians, you will not succeed.'"

⁶Jeremiah said, "The word of the LORD came to me: ⁷Hanamel son of Shallum your uncle is going to come to you and say, 'Buy my field at Anathoth, because as nearest relative it is your right and duty to buy it.'

⁸"Then, just as the LORD had said, my cousin Hanamel came to me in the courtyard of the guard and said, 'Buy my field at Anathoth in the territory of Benjamin. Since it is your right to redeem it and possess it, buy it for yourself.'

"I knew that this was the word of the LORD; ⁹so I bought the field at Anathoth from my cousin Hanamel and weighed out for him seventeen shekels*ᵇ* of silver. ¹⁰I signed and sealed the deed, had it witnessed, and weighed out the silver on the scales. ¹¹I took the deed of purchase—the sealed copy containing the terms and conditions, as well as the unsealed copy— ¹²and I gave this deed to Baruch son of Neriah, the son of Mahseiah, in the presence of my cousin Hanamel and of the witnesses who had signed the deed and of all the Jews sitting in the courtyard of the guard.

¹³"In their presence I gave Baruch these instructions: ¹⁴'This is

---

ᵃ 4 Or *Chaldeans*; also in verses 5, 24, 25, 28, 29 and 43   *ᵇ 9* That is, about 7 ounces or about 200 grams what the Lord Almighty, the God of Israel, says: Take these documents, both the sealed and unsealed copies of the deed of purchase, and put them in a clay jar so they will last a long time. [15] For this is what the Lord Almighty, the God of Israel, says: Houses, fields and vineyards will again be bought in this land.'

[16] "After I had given the deed of purchase to Baruch son of Neriah, I prayed to the Lord:

[17] "Ah, Sovereign Lord, you have made the heavens and the earth by your great power and outstretched arm. Nothing is too hard for you. [18] You show love to thousands but bring the punishment for the parents' sins into the laps of their children after them. Great and mighty God, whose name is the Lord Almighty, [19] great are your purposes and mighty are your deeds. Your eyes are open to the ways of all mankind; you reward each person according to their conduct and as their deeds deserve. [20] You performed signs and wonders in Egypt and have continued them to this day, in Israel and among all mankind, and have gained the renown that is still yours. [21] You brought your people Israel out of Egypt with signs and wonders, by a mighty hand and an outstretched arm and with great terror.

[22] You gave them this land you had sworn to give their ancestors, a land flowing with milk and honey. [23] They came in and took possession of it, but they did not obey you or follow your law; they did not do what you commanded them to do. So you brought all this disaster on them.

[24] "See how the siege ramps are built up to take the city. Because of the sword, famine and plague, the city will be given into the hands of the Babylonians who are attacking it. What you said has happened, as you now see. [25] And though the city will be given into the hands of the Babylonians, you, Sovereign Lord, say to me, 'Buy the field with silver and have the transaction witnessed.'"

[26] Then the word of the Lord came to Jeremiah: [27] "I am the Lord, the God of all mankind. Is anything too hard for me? [28] Therefore this is what the Lord says: I am about to give this city into the hands of the Babylonians and to Nebuchadnezzar king of Babylon, who will capture it. [29] The Babylonians who are attacking this city will come in and set it on fire; they will burn it down, along with the houses where the people aroused my anger by burning incense on the roofs to Baal and by pouring out drink offerings to other gods.

30 "The people of Israel and Judah have done nothing but evil in my sight from their youth; indeed, the people of Israel have done nothing but arouse my anger with what their hands have made, declares the LORD. **31** From the day it was built until now, this city has so aroused my anger and wrath that I must remove it from my sight. **32** The people of Israel and Judah have provoked me by all the evil they have done — they, their kings and officials, their priests and prophets, the people of Judah and those living in Jerusalem. **33** They turned their backs to me and not their faces; though I taught them again and again, they would not listen or respond to discipline. **34** They set up their vile images in the house that bears my Name and defiled it. **35** They built high places for Baal in the Valley of Ben Hinnom to sacrifice their sons and daughters to Molek, though I never commanded — nor did it enter my mind — that they should do such a detestable thing and so make Judah sin.

36 "You are saying about this city, 'By the sword, famine and plague it will be given into the hands of the king of Babylon'; but this is what the LORD, the God of Israel, says: **37** I will surely gather them from all the lands where I banish them in my furious anger and great wrath; I will bring them back to this place and let them live in safety. **38** They will be my people, and I will be their God. **39** I will give them singleness of heart and action, so that they will always fear me and that all will then go well for them and for their children after them. **40** I will make an everlasting covenant with them: I will never stop doing good to them, and I will inspire them to fear me, so that they will never turn away from me. **41** I will rejoice in doing them good and will assuredly plant them in this land with all my heart and soul.

42 "This is what the LORD says: As I have brought all this great calamity on this people, so I will give them all the prosperity I have promised them. **43** Once more fields will be bought in this land of which you say, 'It is a desolate waste, without people or animals, for it has been given into the hands of the Babylonians.' **44** Fields will be bought for silver, and deeds will be signed, sealed and witnessed in the territory of Benjamin, in the villages around Jerusalem, in the towns of Judah and in the towns of the hill country, of the western foothills and of the Negev, because I will restore their fortunes,[a] declares the LORD."

Promise of Restoration

33 While Jeremiah was still confined in the courtyard of the guard, the word of the

---

[a] 44 Or *will bring them back from captivity*

LORD came to him a second time: ² "This is what the LORD says, he who made the earth, the LORD who formed it and established it — the LORD is his name: ³ 'Call to me and I will answer you and tell you great and unsearchable things you do not know.' ⁴ For this is what the LORD, the God of Israel, says about the houses in this city and the royal palaces of Judah that have been torn down to be used against the siege ramps and the sword ⁵ in the fight with the Babylonians[a]: 'They will be filled with the dead bodies of the people I will slay in my anger and wrath. I will hide my face from this city because of all its wickedness.

⁶ " 'Nevertheless, I will bring health and healing to it; I will heal my people and will let them enjoy abundant peace and security. ⁷ I will bring Judah and Israel back from captivity[b] and will rebuild them as they were before. ⁸ I will cleanse them from all the sin they have committed against me and will forgive all their sins of rebellion against me. ⁹ Then this city will bring me renown, joy, praise and honor before all nations on earth that hear of all the good things I do for it; and they will be in awe and will tremble at the abundant prosperity and peace I provide for it.'

¹⁰ "This is what the LORD says: 'You say about this place, "It is a desolate waste, without people or animals." Yet in the towns of Judah and the streets of Jerusalem that are deserted, inhabited by neither people nor animals, there will be heard once more ¹¹ the sounds of joy and gladness, the voices of bride and bridegroom, and the voices of those who bring thank offerings to the house of the LORD, saying,

"Give thanks to the LORD
    Almighty,
  for the LORD is good;
  his love endures forever."

For I will restore the fortunes of the land as they were before,' says the LORD.

¹² "This is what the LORD Almighty says: 'In this place, desolate and without people or animals — in all its towns there will again be pastures for shepherds to rest their flocks. ¹³ In the towns of the hill country, of the western foothills and of the Negev, in the territory of Benjamin, in the villages around Jerusalem and in the towns of Judah, flocks will again pass under the hand of the one who counts them,' says the LORD.

¹⁴ " 'The days are coming,' declares the LORD, 'when I will fulfill the good promise I made to the people of Israel and Judah.

¹⁵ " 'In those days and at that
      time
  I will make a righteous
      Branch sprout from
      David's line;

---

he will do what is just and
right in the land.
¹⁶ In those days Judah will be
saved
and Jerusalem will live in
safety.
This is the name by which it*
will be called:
The LORD Our Righteous
Savior.'

¹⁷ For this is what the LORD says: 'David will never fail to have a man to sit on the throne of Israel, ¹⁸ nor will the Levitical priests ever fail to have a man to stand before me continually to offer burnt offerings, to burn grain offerings and to present sacrifices.' "

¹⁹ The word of the LORD came to Jeremiah: ²⁰ "This is what the LORD says: 'If you can break my covenant with the day and my covenant with the night, so that day and night no longer come at their appointed time, ²¹ then my covenant with David my servant—and my covenant with the Levites who are priests ministering before me—can be broken and David will no longer have a descendant to reign on his throne. ²² I will make the descendants of David my servant and the Levites who minister before me as countless as the stars in the sky and as measureless as the sand on the seashore.' "

²³ The word of the LORD came to Jeremiah: ²⁴ "Have you not noticed that these people are saying, 'The LORD has rejected the two kingdoms* he chose'? So they despise my people and no longer regard them as a nation. ²⁵ This is what the LORD says: 'If I have not made my covenant with day and night and established the laws of heaven and earth, ²⁶ then I will reject the descendants of Jacob and David my servant and will not choose one of his sons to rule over the descendants of Abraham, Isaac and Jacob. For I will restore their fortunes* and have compassion on them.' "

Warning to Zedekiah

34 While Nebuchadnezzar king of Babylon and all his army and all the kingdoms and peoples in the empire he ruled were fighting against Jerusalem and all its surrounding towns, this word came to Jeremiah from the LORD: ² "This is what the LORD, the God of Israel, says: Go to Zedekiah king of Judah and tell him, 'This is what the LORD says: I am about to give this city into the hands of the king of Babylon, and he will burn it down. ³ You will not escape from his grasp but will surely be captured and given into his hands. You will see the king of Babylon with your own eyes, and he will speak with you face to face. And you will go to Babylon.

⁴ " 'Yet hear the LORD's promise to you, Zedekiah king of Judah.

---

a 16 Or *he*   *b 24* Or *families*   *c 26* Or *will bring them back from captivity*

This is what the LORD says concerning you: You will not die by the sword; [5] you will die peacefully. As people made a funeral fire in honor of your predecessors, the kings who ruled before you, so they will make a fire in your honor and lament, "Alas, master!" I myself make this promise, declares the LORD.'"

[6] Then Jeremiah the prophet told all this to Zedekiah king of Judah, in Jerusalem, [7] while the army of the king of Babylon was fighting against Jerusalem and the other cities of Judah that were still holding out—Lachish and Azekah. These were the only fortified cities left in Judah.

Freedom for Slaves

[8] The word came to Jeremiah from the LORD after King Zedekiah had made a covenant with all the people in Jerusalem to proclaim freedom for the slaves. [9] Everyone was to free their Hebrew slaves, both male and female; no one was to hold a fellow Hebrew in bondage. [10] So all the officials and people who entered into this covenant agreed that they would free their male and female slaves and no longer hold them in bondage. They agreed, and set them free. [11] But afterward they changed their minds and took back the slaves they had freed and enslaved them again.

[12] Then the word of the LORD came to Jeremiah: [13] "This is what the LORD, the God of Israel, says: I made a covenant with your ancestors when I brought them out of Egypt, out of the land of slavery. I said, [14] 'Every seventh year each of you must free any fellow Hebrews who have sold themselves to you. After they have served you six years, you must let them go free.'[a] Your ancestors, however, did not listen to me or pay attention to me. [15] Recently you repented and did what is right in my sight: Each of you proclaimed freedom to your own people. You even made a covenant before me in the house that bears my Name. [16] But now you have turned around and profaned my name; each of you has taken back the male and female slaves you had set free to go where they wished. You have forced them to become your slaves again.

[17] "Therefore this is what the LORD says: You have not obeyed me; you have not proclaimed freedom to your own people. So I now proclaim 'freedom' for you, declares the LORD—'freedom' to fall by the sword, plague and famine. I will make you abhorrent to all the kingdoms of the earth. [18] Those who have violated my covenant and have not fulfilled the terms of the covenant they made before me, I will treat like the calf they cut in two and then walked between its pieces.

[a] 14 Deut. 15:12

¹⁹The leaders of Judah and Jerusalem, the court officials, the priests and all the people of the land who walked between the pieces of the calf, ²⁰I will deliver into the hands of their enemies who want to kill them. Their dead bodies will become food for the birds and the wild animals.

²¹ "I will deliver Zedekiah king of Judah and his officials into the hands of their enemies who want to kill them, to the army of the king of Babylon, which has withdrawn from you. ²²I am going to give the order, declares the LORD, and I will bring them back to this city. They will fight against it, take it and burn it down. And I will lay waste the towns of Judah so no one can live there."

The Rekabites

35 This is the word that came to Jeremiah from the LORD during the reign of Jehoiakim son of Josiah king of Judah: ²"Go to the Rekabite family and invite them to come to one of the side rooms of the house of the LORD and give them wine to drink."

³So I went to get Jaazaniah son of Jeremiah, the son of Habazziniah, and his brothers and all his sons—the whole family of the Rekabites. ⁴I brought them into the house of the LORD, into the room of the sons of Hanan son of Igdaliah the man of God. It was next to the room of the officials, which was over that of Maaseiah son of Shallum the doorkeeper. ⁵Then I set bowls full of wine and some cups before the Rekabites and said to them, "Drink some wine."

⁶But they replied, "We do not drink wine, because our forefather Jehonadab[a] son of Rekab gave us this command: 'Neither you nor your descendants must ever drink wine. ⁷Also you must never build houses, sow seed or plant vineyards; you must never have any of these things, but must always live in tents. Then you will live a long time in the land where you are nomads.' ⁸We have obeyed everything our forefather Jehonadab son of Rekab commanded us. Neither we nor our wives nor our sons and daughters have ever drunk wine ⁹or built houses to live in or had vineyards, fields or crops. ¹⁰We have lived in tents and have fully obeyed everything our forefather Jehonadab commanded us. ¹¹But when Nebuchadnezzar king of Babylon invaded this land, we said, 'Come, we must go to Jerusalem to escape the Babylonian[b] and Aramean armies.' So we have remained in Jerusalem."

¹²Then the word of the LORD came to Jeremiah, saying: ¹³"This is what the LORD Almighty, the

---

a 6 Hebrew *Jonadab*, a variant of *Jehonadab*; here and often in this chapter
b 11 Or *Chaldean*

God of Israel, says: Go and tell the people of Judah and those living in Jerusalem, 'Will you not learn a lesson and obey my words?' declares the LORD. ¹⁴'Jehonadab son of Rekab ordered his descendants not to drink wine and this command has been kept. To this day they do not drink wine, because they obey their forefather's command. But I have spoken to you again and again, yet you have not obeyed me. ¹⁵Again and again I sent all my servants the prophets to you. They said, "Each of you must turn from your wicked ways and reform your actions; do not follow other gods to serve them. Then you will live in the land I have given to you and your ancestors." But you have not paid attention or listened to me. ¹⁶The descendants of Jehonadab son of Rekab have carried out the command their forefather gave them, but these people have not obeyed me.'

¹⁷"Therefore this is what the LORD God Almighty, the God of Israel, says: 'Listen! I am going to bring on Judah and on everyone living in Jerusalem every disaster I pronounced against them. I spoke to them, but they did not listen; I called to them, but they did not answer.'"

¹⁸Then Jeremiah said to the family of the Rekabites, "This is what the LORD Almighty, the God of Israel, says: 'You have obeyed the command of your forefather Jehonadab and have followed all his instructions and have done everything he ordered.' ¹⁹Therefore this is what the LORD Almighty, the God of Israel, says: 'Jehonadab son of Rekab will never fail to have a descendant to serve me.'"

Jehoiakim Burns Jeremiah's Scroll

36 In the fourth year of Jehoiakim son of Josiah king of Judah, this word came to Jeremiah from the LORD: ²"Take a scroll and write on it all the words I have spoken to you concerning Israel, Judah and all the other nations from the time I began speaking to you in the reign of Josiah till now. ³Perhaps when the people of Judah hear about every disaster I plan to inflict on them, they will each turn from their wicked ways; then I will forgive their wickedness and their sin."

⁴So Jeremiah called Baruch son of Neriah, and while Jeremiah dictated all the words the LORD had spoken to him, Baruch wrote them on the scroll. ⁵Then Jeremiah told Baruch, "I am restricted; I am not allowed to go to the LORD's temple. ⁶So you go to the house of the LORD on a day of fasting and read to the people from the scroll the words of the LORD that you wrote as I dictated. Read them to all the people of Judah who come in from their

towns. **7**Perhaps they will bring their petition before the Lord and will each turn from their wicked ways, for the anger and wrath pronounced against this people by the Lord are great."

8Baruch son of Neriah did everything Jeremiah the prophet told him to do; at the Lord's temple he read the words of the Lord from the scroll. **9**In the ninth month of the fifth year of Jehoiakim son of Josiah king of Judah, a time of fasting before the Lord was proclaimed for all the people in Jerusalem and those who had come from the towns of Judah. **10**From the room of Gemariah son of Shaphan the secretary, which was in the upper courtyard at the entrance of the New Gate of the temple, Baruch read to all the people at the Lord's temple the words of Jeremiah from the scroll.

11When Micaiah son of Gemariah, the son of Shaphan, heard all the words of the Lord from the scroll, **12**he went down to the secretary's room in the royal palace, where all the officials were sitting: Elishama the secretary, Delaiah son of Shemaiah, Elnathan son of Akbor, Gemariah son of Shaphan, Zedekiah son of Hananiah, and all the other officials. **13**After Micaiah told them everything he had heard Baruch read to the people from the scroll, **14**all the officials sent Jehudi son of Nethaniah, the son of Shelemiah, the son of Cushi, to say to Baruch, "Bring the scroll from which you have read to the people and come." So Baruch son of Neriah went to them with the scroll in his hand. **15**They said to him, "Sit down, please, and read it to us."

So Baruch read it to them. **16**When they heard all these words, they looked at each other in fear and said to Baruch, "We must report all these words to the king." **17**Then they asked Baruch, "Tell us, how did you come to write all this? Did Jeremiah dictate it?"

18"Yes," Baruch replied, "he dictated all these words to me, and I wrote them in ink on the scroll."

19Then the officials said to Baruch, "You and Jeremiah, go and hide. Don't let anyone know where you are."

20After they put the scroll in the room of Elishama the secretary, they went to the king in the courtyard and reported everything to him. **21**The king sent Jehudi to get the scroll, and Jehudi brought it from the room of Elishama the secretary and read it to the king and all the officials standing beside him. **22**It was the ninth month and the king was sitting in the winter apartment, with a fire burning in the firepot in front of him. **23**Whenever Jehudi had read three or four columns of the scroll, the king cut them off with a scribe's knife and threw them into the firepot, until the entire scroll was burned in the fire. ²⁴The king and all his attendants who heard all these words showed no fear, nor did they tear their clothes. ²⁵Even though Elnathan, Delaiah and Gemariah urged the king not to burn the scroll, he would not listen to them. ²⁶Instead, the king commanded Jerahmeel, a son of the king, Seraiah son of Azriel and Shelemiah son of Abdeel to arrest Baruch the scribe and Jeremiah the prophet. But the LORD had hidden them.

²⁷After the king burned the scroll containing the words that Baruch had written at Jeremiah's dictation, the word of the LORD came to Jeremiah: ²⁸"Take another scroll and write on it all the words that were on the first scroll, which Jehoiakim king of Judah burned up. ²⁹Also tell Jehoiakim king of Judah, 'This is what the LORD says: You burned that scroll and said, "Why did you write on it that the king of Babylon would certainly come and destroy this land and wipe from it both man and beast?" ³⁰Therefore this is what the LORD says about Jehoiakim king of Judah: He will have no one to sit on the throne of David; his body will be thrown out and exposed to the heat by day and the frost by night. ³¹I will punish him and his children and his attendants for their wickedness; I will bring on them and those living in Jerusalem and the people of Judah every disaster I pronounced against them, because they have not listened.'"

³²So Jeremiah took another scroll and gave it to the scribe Baruch son of Neriah, and as Jeremiah dictated, Baruch wrote on it all the words of the scroll that Jehoiakim king of Judah had burned in the fire. And many similar words were added to them.

Jeremiah in Prison

37 Zedekiah son of Josiah was made king of Judah by Nebuchadnezzar king of Babylon; he reigned in place of Jehoiachin[a] son of Jehoiakim. ²Neither he nor his attendants nor the people of the land paid any attention to the words the LORD had spoken through Jeremiah the prophet.

³King Zedekiah, however, sent Jehukal son of Shelemiah with the priest Zephaniah son of Maaseiah to Jeremiah the prophet with this message: "Please pray to the LORD our God for us."

⁴Now Jeremiah was free to come and go among the people, for he had not yet been put in prison. ⁵Pharaoh's army had marched out of Egypt, and when

---

ᵃ 1 Hebrew *Koniah*, a variant of *Jehoiachin*

the Babylonians[a] who were besieging Jerusalem heard the report about them, they withdrew from Jerusalem.

[6] Then the word of the LORD came to Jeremiah the prophet: [7] "This is what the LORD, the God of Israel, says: Tell the king of Judah, who sent you to inquire of me, 'Pharaoh's army, which has marched out to support you, will go back to its own land, to Egypt. [8] Then the Babylonians will return and attack this city; they will capture it and burn it down.'

[9] "This is what the LORD says: Do not deceive yourselves, thinking, 'The Babylonians will surely leave us.' They will not! [10] Even if you were to defeat the entire Babylonian[b] army that is attacking you and only wounded men were left in their tents, they would come out and burn this city down."

[11] After the Babylonian army had withdrawn from Jerusalem because of Pharaoh's army, [12] Jeremiah started to leave the city to go to the territory of Benjamin to get his share of the property among the people there. [13] But when he reached the Benjamin Gate, the captain of the guard, whose name was Irijah son of Shelemiah, the son of Hananiah, arrested him and said, "You are deserting to the Babylonians!"

[14] "That's not true!" Jeremiah said. "I am not deserting to the Babylonians." But Irijah would not listen to him; instead, he arrested Jeremiah and brought him to the officials. [15] They were angry with Jeremiah and had him beaten and imprisoned in the house of Jonathan the secretary, which they had made into a prison.

[16] Jeremiah was put into a vaulted cell in a dungeon, where he remained a long time. [17] Then King Zedekiah sent for him and had him brought to the palace, where he asked him privately, "Is there any word from the LORD?"

"Yes," Jeremiah replied, "you will be delivered into the hands of the king of Babylon."

[18] Then Jeremiah said to King Zedekiah, "What crime have I committed against you or your attendants or this people, that you have put me in prison? [19] Where are your prophets who prophesied to you, 'The king of Babylon will not attack you or this land'? [20] But now, my lord the king, please listen. Let me bring my petition before you: Do not send me back to the house of Jonathan the secretary, or I will die there."

[21] King Zedekiah then gave orders for Jeremiah to be placed in the courtyard of the guard and given a loaf of bread from the street of the bakers each day until all the bread in the city was gone. So Jeremiah remained in the courtyard of the guard.

---

[a] 5 Or *Chaldeans*; also in verses 8, 9, 13 and 14   [b] 10 Or *Chaldean*; also in verse 11

Jeremiah Thrown Into a Cistern

38 Shephatiah son of Mattan, Gedaliah son of Pashhur, Jehukal[a] son of Shelemiah, and Pashhur son of Malkijah heard what Jeremiah was telling all the people when he said, [2] "This is what the LORD says: 'Whoever stays in this city will die by the sword, famine or plague, but whoever goes over to the Babylonians[b] will live. They will escape with their lives; they will live.' [3] And this is what the LORD says: 'This city will certainly be given into the hands of the army of the king of Babylon, who will capture it.'"

[4] Then the officials said to the king, "This man should be put to death. He is discouraging the soldiers who are left in this city, as well as all the people, by the things he is saying to them. This man is not seeking the good of these people but their ruin."

[5] "He is in your hands," King Zedekiah answered. "The king can do nothing to oppose you."

[6] So they took Jeremiah and put him into the cistern of Malkijah, the king's son, which was in the courtyard of the guard. They lowered Jeremiah by ropes into the cistern; it had no water in it, only mud, and Jeremiah sank down into the mud.

[7] But Ebed-Melek, a Cushite,[c] an official[d] in the royal palace, heard that they had put Jeremiah into the cistern. While the king was sitting in the Benjamin Gate, [8] Ebed-Melek went out of the palace and said to him, [9] "My lord the king, these men have acted wickedly in all they have done to Jeremiah the prophet. They have thrown him into a cistern, where he will starve to death when there is no longer any bread in the city."

[10] Then the king commanded Ebed-Melek the Cushite, "Take thirty men from here with you and lift Jeremiah the prophet out of the cistern before he dies."

[11] So Ebed-Melek took the men with him and went to a room under the treasury in the palace. He took some old rags and worn-out clothes from there and let them down with ropes to Jeremiah in the cistern. [12] Ebed-Melek the Cushite said to Jeremiah, "Put these old rags and worn-out clothes under your arms to pad the ropes." Jeremiah did so, [13] and they pulled him up with the ropes and lifted him out of the cistern. And Jeremiah remained in the courtyard of the guard.

Zedekiah Questions Jeremiah Again

[14] Then King Zedekiah sent for Jeremiah the prophet and had him brought to the third entrance to the temple of the LORD.

---

[a] 1 Hebrew *Jukal,* a variant of *Jehukal* and 23   [c] 7 Probably from the upper Nile region   [b] 2 Or *Chaldeans*; also in verses 18, 19   [d] 7 Or *a eunuch*

"I am going to ask you something," the king said to Jeremiah. "Do not hide anything from me."

¹⁵Jeremiah said to Zedekiah, "If I give you an answer, will you not kill me? Even if I did give you counsel, you would not listen to me."

¹⁶But King Zedekiah swore this oath secretly to Jeremiah: "As surely as the LORD lives, who has given us breath, I will neither kill you nor hand you over to those who want to kill you."

¹⁷Then Jeremiah said to Zedekiah, "This is what the LORD God Almighty, the God of Israel, says: 'If you surrender to the officers of the king of Babylon, your life will be spared and this city will not be burned down; you and your family will live. ¹⁸But if you will not surrender to the officers of the king of Babylon, this city will be given into the hands of the Babylonians and they will burn it down; you yourself will not escape from them.'"

¹⁹King Zedekiah said to Jeremiah, "I am afraid of the Jews who have gone over to the Babylonians, for the Babylonians may hand me over to them and they will mistreat me."

²⁰"They will not hand you over," Jeremiah replied. "Obey the LORD by doing what I tell you. Then it will go well with you, and your life will be spared. ²¹But if you refuse to surrender, this is what the LORD has revealed to me: ²²All the women left in the palace of the king of Judah will be brought out to the officials of the king of Babylon. Those women will say to you:

"'They misled you and
    overcame you —
  those trusted friends of
    yours.
Your feet are sunk in the mud;
  your friends have deserted
  you.'

²³"All your wives and children will be brought out to the Babylonians. You yourself will not escape from their hands but will be captured by the king of Babylon; and this city will*a* be burned down."

²⁴Then Zedekiah said to Jeremiah, "Do not let anyone know about this conversation, or you may die. ²⁵If the officials hear that I talked with you, and they come to you and say, 'Tell us what you said to the king and what the king said to you; do not hide it from us or we will kill you,' ²⁶then tell them, 'I was pleading with the king not to send me back to Jonathan's house to die there.'"

²⁷All the officials did come to Jeremiah and question him, and he told them everything the king had ordered him to say. So they said no more to him, for no one had heard his conversation with the king.

---

a 23 Or *and you will cause this city to*

²⁸And Jeremiah remained in the courtyard of the guard until the day Jerusalem was captured.

The Fall of Jerusalem

This is how Jerusalem was taken:

39 ¹In the ninth year of Zedekiah king of Judah, in the tenth month, Nebuchadnezzar king of Babylon marched against Jerusalem with his whole army and laid siege to it. ²And on the ninth day of the fourth month of Zedekiah's eleventh year, the city wall was broken through. ³Then all the officials of the king of Babylon came and took seats in the Middle Gate: Nergal-Sharezer of Samgar, Nebo-Sarsekim a chief officer, Nergal-Sharezer a high official and all the other officials of the king of Babylon. ⁴When Zedekiah king of Judah and all the soldiers saw them, they fled; they left the city at night by way of the king's garden, through the gate between the two walls, and headed toward the Arabah.ᵃ

⁵But the Babylonianᵇ army pursued them and overtook Zedekiah in the plains of Jericho. They captured him and took him to Nebuchadnezzar king of Babylon at Riblah in the land of Hamath, where he pronounced sentence on him. ⁶There at Riblah the king of Babylon slaughtered the sons of Zedekiah before his eyes and also killed all the nobles of Judah. ⁷Then he put out Zedekiah's eyes and bound him with bronze shackles to take him to Babylon.

⁸The Babyloniansᶜ set fire to the royal palace and the houses of the people and broke down the walls of Jerusalem. ⁹Nebuzaradan commander of the imperial guard carried into exile to Babylon the people who remained in the city, along with those who had gone over to him, and the rest of the people. ¹⁰But Nebuzaradan the commander of the guard left behind in the land of Judah some of the poor people, who owned nothing; and at that time he gave them vineyards and fields.

¹¹Now Nebuchadnezzar king of Babylon had given these orders about Jeremiah through Nebuzaradan commander of the imperial guard: ¹²"Take him and look after him; don't harm him but do for him whatever he asks." ¹³So Nebuzaradan the commander of the guard, Nebushazban a chief officer, Nergal-Sharezer a high official and all the other officers of the king of Babylon ¹⁴sent and had Jeremiah taken out of the courtyard of the guard. They turned him over to Gedaliah son of Ahikam, the son of Shaphan, to take him back to his home. So he remained among his own people.

¹⁵While Jeremiah had been confined in the courtyard of the guard, the word of the LORD came to him: ¹⁶"Go and tell Ebed-

---

ᵃ 4 Or *the Jordan Valley*   ᵇ 5 Or *Chaldean*   ᶜ 8 Or *Chaldeans*

Melek the Cushite, 'This is what the LORD Almighty, the God of Israel, says: I am about to fulfill my words against this city—words concerning disaster, not prosperity. At that time they will be fulfilled before your eyes. **17**But I will rescue you on that day, declares the LORD; you will not be given into the hands of those you fear. **18**I will save you; you will not fall by the sword but will escape with your life, because you trust in me, declares the LORD.'"

Jeremiah Freed

40 The word came to Jeremiah from the LORD after Nebuzaradan commander of the imperial guard had released him at Ramah. He had found Jeremiah bound in chains among all the captives from Jerusalem and Judah who were being carried into exile to Babylon. **2**When the commander of the guard found Jeremiah, he said to him, "The LORD your God decreed this disaster for this place. **3**And now the LORD has brought it about; he has done just as he said he would. All this happened because you people sinned against the LORD and did not obey him. **4**But today I am freeing you from the chains on your wrists. Come with me to Babylon, if you like, and I will look after you; but if you do not want to, then don't come. Look, the whole country lies before you;

go wherever you please." **5**However, before Jeremiah turned to go,[a] Nebuzaradan added, "Go back to Gedaliah son of Ahikam, the son of Shaphan, whom the king of Babylon has appointed over the towns of Judah, and live with him among the people, or go anywhere else you please."

Then the commander gave him provisions and a present and let him go. **6**So Jeremiah went to Gedaliah son of Ahikam at Mizpah and stayed with him among the people who were left behind in the land.

Gedaliah Assassinated

7When all the army officers and their men who were still in the open country heard that the king of Babylon had appointed Gedaliah son of Ahikam as governor over the land and had put him in charge of the men, women and children who were the poorest in the land and who had not been carried into exile to Babylon, **8**they came to Gedaliah at Mizpah—Ishmael son of Nethaniah, Johanan and Jonathan the sons of Kareah, Seraiah son of Tanhumeth, the sons of Ephai the Netophathite, and Jaazaniah[b] the son of the Maakathite, and their men. **9**Gedaliah son of Ahikam, the son of Shaphan, took an oath to reassure them and their men. "Do not be afraid to serve the Babylonians,[a]" he said. "Settle down in the land and serve the king of Babylon, and it will go well with you. **10**I myself will stay at Mizpah to represent you before the Babylonians who come to us, but you are to harvest the wine, summer fruit and olive oil, and put them in your storage jars, and live in the towns you have taken over."

11When all the Jews in Moab, Ammon, Edom and all the other countries heard that the king of Babylon had left a remnant in Judah and had appointed Gedaliah son of Ahikam, the son of Shaphan, as governor over them, **12**they all came back to the land of Judah, to Gedaliah at Mizpah, from all the countries where they had been scattered. And they harvested an abundance of wine and summer fruit.

13Johanan son of Kareah and all the army officers still in the open country came to Gedaliah at Mizpah **14**and said to him, "Don't you know that Baalis king of the Ammonites has sent Ishmael son of Nethaniah to take your life?" But Gedaliah son of Ahikam did not believe them.

15Then Johanan son of Kareah said privately to Gedaliah in Mizpah, "Let me go and kill Ishmael son of Nethaniah, and no one will know it. Why should he take your life and cause all the Jews who are gathered around you to be scattered and the remnant of Judah to perish?"

16But Gedaliah son of Ahikam said to Johanan son of Kareah, "Don't do such a thing! What you are saying about Ishmael is not true."

41 In the seventh month Ishmael son of Nethaniah, the son of Elishama, who was of royal blood and had been one of the king's officers, came with ten men to Gedaliah son of Ahikam at Mizpah. While they were eating together there, **2**Ishmael son of Nethaniah and the ten men who were with him got up and struck down Gedaliah son of Ahikam, the son of Shaphan, with the sword, killing the one whom the king of Babylon had appointed as governor over the land. **3**Ishmael also killed all the men of Judah who were with Gedaliah at Mizpah, as well as the Babylonian*b* soldiers who were there.

4The day after Gedaliah's assassination, before anyone knew about it, **5**eighty men who had shaved off their beards, torn their clothes and cut themselves came from Shechem, Shiloh and Samaria, bringing grain offerings and incense with them to the house of the LORD. **6**Ishmael son of Nethaniah went out from Mizpah to meet them, weeping as he went. When he met them, he said, "Come to Gedaliah son of

---

a 9 Or *Chaldeans*; also in verse 10   *b* 3 Or *Chaldean*

Ahikam." **7**When they went into the city, Ishmael son of Nethaniah and the men who were with him slaughtered them and threw them into a cistern. **8**But ten of them said to Ishmael, "Don't kill us! We have wheat and barley, olive oil and honey, hidden in a field." So he let them alone and did not kill them with the others. **9**Now the cistern where he threw all the bodies of the men he had killed along with Gedaliah was the one King Asa had made as part of his defense against Baasha king of Israel. Ishmael son of Nethaniah filled it with the dead.

10Ishmael made captives of all the rest of the people who were in Mizpah—the king's daughters along with all the others who were left there, over whom Nebuzaradan commander of the imperial guard had appointed Gedaliah son of Ahikam. Ishmael son of Nethaniah took them captive and set out to cross over to the Ammonites.

11When Johanan son of Kareah and all the army officers who were with him heard about all the crimes Ishmael son of Nethaniah had committed, **12**they took all their men and went to fight Ishmael son of Nethaniah. They caught up with him near the great pool in Gibeon. **13**When all the people Ishmael had with him saw Johanan son of Kareah and the army officers who were

with him, they were glad. **14**All the people Ishmael had taken captive at Mizpah turned and went over to Johanan son of Kareah. **15**But Ishmael son of Nethaniah and eight of his men escaped from Johanan and fled to the Ammonites.

Flight to Egypt

16Then Johanan son of Kareah and all the army officers who were with him led away all the people of Mizpah who had survived, whom Johanan had recovered from Ishmael son of Nethaniah after Ishmael had assassinated Gedaliah son of Ahikam—the soldiers, women, children and court officials he had recovered from Gibeon. **17**And they went on, stopping at Geruth Kimham near Bethlehem on their way to Egypt **18**to escape the Babylonians.*a* They were afraid of them because Ishmael son of Nethaniah had killed Gedaliah son of Ahikam, whom the king of Babylon had appointed as governor over the land.

42 Then all the army officers, including Johanan son of Kareah and Jezaniah*b* son of Hoshaiah, and all the people from the least to the greatest approached **2**Jeremiah the prophet and said to him, "Please hear our petition and pray to the Lord your God for this entire remnant. For as you now see, though we

---

a 18 Or *Chaldeans*   *b 1* Hebrew; Septuagint (see also 43:2) *Azariah* were once many, now only a few are left. ³Pray that the LORD your God will tell us where we should go and what we should do."

⁴"I have heard you," replied Jeremiah the prophet. "I will certainly pray to the LORD your God as you have requested; I will tell you everything the LORD says and will keep nothing back from you."

⁵Then they said to Jeremiah, "May the LORD be a true and faithful witness against us if we do not act in accordance with everything the LORD your God sends you to tell us. ⁶Whether it is favorable or unfavorable, we will obey the LORD our God, to whom we are sending you, so that it will go well with us, for we will obey the LORD our God."

⁷Ten days later the word of the LORD came to Jeremiah. ⁸So he called together Johanan son of Kareah and all the army officers who were with him and all the people from the least to the greatest. ⁹He said to them, "This is what the LORD, the God of Israel, to whom you sent me to present your petition, says: ¹⁰'If you stay in this land, I will build you up and not tear you down; I will plant you and not uproot you, for I have relented concerning the disaster I have inflicted on you. ¹¹Do not be afraid of the king of Babylon, whom you now fear. Do not be afraid of him, declares the LORD, for I am with you and will save you and deliver you from his hands. ¹²I will show you compassion so that he will have compassion on you and restore you to your land.'

¹³"However, if you say, 'We will not stay in this land,' and so disobey the LORD your God, ¹⁴and if you say, 'No, we will go and live in Egypt, where we will not see war or hear the trumpet or be hungry for bread,' ¹⁵then hear the word of the LORD, you remnant of Judah. This is what the LORD Almighty, the God of Israel, says: 'If you are determined to go to Egypt and you do go to settle there, ¹⁶then the sword you fear will overtake you there, and the famine you dread will follow you into Egypt, and there you will die. ¹⁷Indeed, all who are determined to go to Egypt to settle there will die by the sword, famine and plague; not one of them will survive or escape the disaster I will bring on them.' ¹⁸This is what the LORD Almighty, the God of Israel, says: 'As my anger and wrath have been poured out on those who lived in Jerusalem, so will my wrath be poured out on you when you go to Egypt. You will be a curse*ᵃ* and an object of horror, a curse*ᵃ* and an object of reproach; you will never see this place again.'

ᵃ 18 That is, your name will be used in cursing (see 29:22); or, others will see that you are cursed.

[19] "Remnant of Judah, the LORD has told you, 'Do not go to Egypt.' Be sure of this: I warn you today [20] that you made a fatal mistake when you sent me to the LORD your God and said, 'Pray to the LORD our God for us; tell us everything he says and we will do it.' [21] I have told you today, but you still have not obeyed the LORD your God in all he sent me to tell you. [22] So now, be sure of this: You will die by the sword, famine and plague in the place where you want to go to settle."

43 When Jeremiah had finished telling the people all the words of the LORD their God — everything the LORD had sent him to tell them — [2] Azariah son of Hoshaiah and Johanan son of Kareah and all the arrogant men said to Jeremiah, "You are lying! The LORD our God has not sent you to say, 'You must not go to Egypt to settle there.' [3] But Baruch son of Neriah is inciting you against us to hand us over to the Babylonians,[a] so they may kill us or carry us into exile to Babylon."

[4] So Johanan son of Kareah and all the army officers and all the people disobeyed the LORD's command to stay in the land of Judah. [5] Instead, Johanan son of Kareah and all the army officers led away all the remnant of Judah who had come back to live in the land of Judah from all the nations where they had been scattered. [6] They also led away all those whom Nebuzaradan commander of the imperial guard had left with Gedaliah son of Ahikam, the son of Shaphan — the men, the women, the children and the king's daughters. And they took Jeremiah the prophet and Baruch son of Neriah along with them. [7] So they entered Egypt in disobedience to the LORD and went as far as Tahpanhes.

[8] In Tahpanhes the word of the LORD came to Jeremiah: [9] "While the Jews are watching, take some large stones with you and bury them in clay in the brick pavement at the entrance to Pharaoh's palace in Tahpanhes. [10] Then say to them, 'This is what the LORD Almighty, the God of Israel, says: I will send for my servant Nebuchadnezzar king of Babylon, and I will set his throne over these stones I have buried here; he will spread his royal canopy above them. [11] He will come and attack Egypt, bringing death to those destined for death, captivity to those destined for captivity, and the sword to those destined for the sword. [12] He will set fire to the temples of the gods of Egypt; he will burn their temples and take their gods captive. As a shepherd picks his garment clean of lice, so he will pick Egypt clean and depart. [13] There in the temple of the sun[b] in Egypt he will demolish the sacred pillars and will burn

---

[a] 3 Or *Chaldeans*   [b] 13 Or *in Heliopolis*

down the temples of the gods of Egypt.' "

Disaster Because of Idolatry

44 This word came to Jeremiah concerning all the Jews living in Lower Egypt — in Migdol, Tahpanhes and Memphis — and in Upper Egypt: ² "This is what the LORD Almighty, the God of Israel, says: You saw the great disaster I brought on Jerusalem and on all the towns of Judah. Today they lie deserted and in ruins ³ because of the evil they have done. They aroused my anger by burning incense to and worshiping other gods that neither they nor you nor your ancestors ever knew. ⁴ Again and again I sent my servants the prophets, who said, 'Do not do this detestable thing that I hate!' ⁵ But they did not listen or pay attention; they did not turn from their wickedness or stop burning incense to other gods. ⁶ Therefore, my fierce anger was poured out; it raged against the towns of Judah and the streets of Jerusalem and made them the desolate ruins they are today.

⁷ "Now this is what the LORD God Almighty, the God of Israel, says: Why bring such great disaster on yourselves by cutting off from Judah the men and women, the children and infants, and so leave yourselves without a rem-

nant? ⁸ Why arouse my anger with what your hands have made, burning incense to other gods in Egypt, where you have come to live? You will destroy yourselves and make yourselves a curse*a* and an object of reproach among all the nations on earth. ⁹ Have you forgotten the wickedness committed by your ancestors and by the kings and queens of Judah and the wickedness committed by you and your wives in the land of Judah and the streets of Jerusalem? ¹⁰ To this day they have not humbled themselves or shown reverence, nor have they followed my law and the decrees I set before you and your ancestors.

¹¹ "Therefore this is what the LORD Almighty, the God of Israel, says: I am determined to bring disaster on you and to destroy all Judah. ¹² I will take away the remnant of Judah who were determined to go to Egypt to settle there. They will all perish in Egypt; they will fall by the sword or die from famine. From the least to the greatest, they will die by sword or famine. They will become a curse and an object of horror, a curse and an object of reproach. ¹³ I will punish those who live in Egypt with the sword, famine and plague, as I punished Jerusalem. ¹⁴ None of the remnant of Judah who have gone to

---

a 8 That is, your name will be used in cursing (see 29:22); or, others will see that you are cursed; also in verse 12; similarly in verse 22.

live in Egypt will escape or survive to return to the land of Judah, to which they long to return and live; none will return except a few fugitives."

¹⁵Then all the men who knew that their wives were burning incense to other gods, along with all the women who were present — a large assembly — and all the people living in Lower and Upper Egypt, said to Jeremiah, ¹⁶"We will not listen to the message you have spoken to us in the name of the LORD! ¹⁷We will certainly do everything we said we would: We will burn incense to the Queen of Heaven and will pour out drink offerings to her just as we and our ancestors, our kings and our officials did in the towns of Judah and in the streets of Jerusalem. At that time we had plenty of food and were well off and suffered no harm. ¹⁸But ever since we stopped burning incense to the Queen of Heaven and pouring out drink offerings to her, we have had nothing and have been perishing by sword and famine."

¹⁹The women added, "When we burned incense to the Queen of Heaven and poured out drink offerings to her, did not our husbands know that we were making cakes impressed with her image and pouring out drink offerings to her?"

²⁰Then Jeremiah said to all the people, both men and women, who were answering him, ²¹"Did not the LORD remember and call to mind the incense burned in the towns of Judah and the streets of Jerusalem by you and your ancestors, your kings and your officials and the people of the land? ²²When the LORD could no longer endure your wicked actions and the detestable things you did, your land became a curse and a desolate waste without inhabitants, as it is today. ²³Because you have burned incense and have sinned against the LORD and have not obeyed him or followed his law or his decrees or his stipulations, this disaster has come upon you, as you now see."

²⁴Then Jeremiah said to all the people, including the women, "Hear the word of the LORD, all you people of Judah in Egypt. ²⁵This is what the LORD Almighty, the God of Israel, says: You and your wives have done what you said you would do when you promised, 'We will certainly carry out the vows we made to burn incense and pour out drink offerings to the Queen of Heaven.'

"Go ahead then, do what you promised! Keep your vows! ²⁶But hear the word of the LORD, all you Jews living in Egypt: 'I swear by my great name,' says the LORD, 'that no one from Judah living anywhere in Egypt will ever again invoke my name or swear, "As surely as the Sovereign LORD lives." ²⁷For I am watching over them for harm, not for good; the Jews in Egypt will perish by sword and famine until they are all destroyed. **28** Those who escape the sword and return to the land of Judah from Egypt will be very few. Then the whole remnant of Judah who came to live in Egypt will know whose word will stand — mine or theirs.

29 "'This will be the sign to you that I will punish you in this place,' declares the LORD, 'so that you will know that my threats of harm against you will surely stand.' **30** This is what the LORD says: 'I am going to deliver Pharaoh Hophra king of Egypt into the hands of his enemies who want to kill him, just as I gave Zedekiah king of Judah into the hands of Nebuchadnezzar king of Babylon, the enemy who wanted to kill him.'"

A Message to Baruch

45 When Baruch son of Neriah wrote on a scroll the words Jeremiah the prophet dictated in the fourth year of Jehoiakim son of Josiah king of Judah, Jeremiah said this to Baruch: **2** "This is what the LORD, the God of Israel, says to you, Baruch: **3** You said, 'Woe to me! The LORD has added sorrow to my pain; I am worn out with groaning and find no rest.' **4** But the LORD has told me to say to you, 'This is what the LORD says: I will overthrow what I have built and uproot what I have planted, throughout the earth. **5** Should you then seek great things for yourself? Do not seek them. For I will bring disaster on all people, declares the LORD, but wherever you go I will let you escape with your life.'"

A Message About Egypt

46 This is the word of the LORD that came to Jeremiah the prophet concerning the nations:

2 Concerning Egypt:

This is the message against the army of Pharaoh Necho king of Egypt, which was defeated at Carchemish on the Euphrates River by Nebuchadnezzar king of Babylon in the fourth year of Jehoiakim son of Josiah king of Judah:

3 "Prepare your shields, both
　　large and small,
　　and march out for battle!
4 Harness the horses,
　　mount the steeds!
Take your positions
　　with helmets on!
Polish your spears,
　　put on your armor!
5 What do I see?
　　They are terrified,
　　they are retreating,
　　their warriors are defeated.
They flee in haste
　　without looking back,
　　and there is terror on every
　　side,"
　　　　declares the LORD.

⁶ "The swift cannot flee
   nor the strong escape.
In the north by the River
      Euphrates
   they stumble and fall.

⁷ "Who is this that rises like the
      Nile,
   like rivers of surging
      waters?
⁸ Egypt rises like the Nile,
   like rivers of surging
      waters.
She says, 'I will rise and cover
      the earth;
   I will destroy cities and their
      people.'
⁹ Charge, you horses!
   Drive furiously, you
      charioteers!
March on, you warriors — men
      of Cush[a] and Put who
      carry shields,
   men of Lydia who draw the
      bow.
¹⁰ But that day belongs to
      the Lord, the LORD
      Almighty —
   a day of vengeance, for
      vengeance on his
      foes.
The sword will devour till it is
      satisfied,
   till it has quenched its thirst
      with blood.
For the Lord, the LORD
      Almighty, will offer
      sacrifice
   in the land of the north by
      the River Euphrates.

¹¹ "Go up to Gilead and get
      balm,
   Virgin Daughter Egypt.
But you try many medicines in
      vain;
   there is no healing for you.
¹² The nations will hear of your
      shame;
   your cries will fill the earth.
One warrior will stumble over
      another;
   both will fall down together."

¹³ This is the message the LORD
spoke to Jeremiah the prophet
about the coming of Nebuchadnezzar king of Babylon to attack
Egypt:

¹⁴ "Announce this in Egypt, and
      proclaim it in Migdol;
   proclaim it also in Memphis
      and Tahpanhes:
'Take your positions and get
      ready,
   for the sword devours those
      around you.'
¹⁵ Why will your warriors be laid
      low?
   They cannot stand, for the
      LORD will push them
      down.
¹⁶ They will stumble repeatedly;
   they will fall over each
      other.
They will say, 'Get up, let us go
      back
   to our own people and our
      native lands,
   away from the sword of the
      oppressor.'

---

a 9 That is, the upper Nile region

¹⁷ There they will exclaim,
'Pharaoh king of Egypt is
only a loud noise;
he has missed his
opportunity.'

¹⁸ "As surely as I live," declares
the King,
whose name is the LORD
Almighty,
"one will come who is like
Tabor among the
mountains,
like Carmel by the sea.
¹⁹ Pack your belongings for
exile,
you who live in Egypt,
for Memphis will be laid
waste
and lie in ruins without
inhabitant.

²⁰ "Egypt is a beautiful heifer,
but a gadfly is coming
against her from the north.
²¹ The mercenaries in her ranks
are like fattened calves.
They too will turn and flee
together,
they will not stand their
ground,
for the day of disaster is
coming upon them,
the time for them to be
punished.
²² Egypt will hiss like a fleeing
serpent
as the enemy advances in
force;
they will come against her
with axes,
like men who cut down
trees.

²³ They will chop down her
forest,"
declares the LORD,
"dense though it be.
They are more numerous than
locusts,
they cannot be counted.
²⁴ Daughter Egypt will be put to
shame,
given into the hands of the
people of the north."

²⁵ The LORD Almighty, the God of Israel, says: "I am about to bring punishment on Amon god of Thebes, on Pharaoh, on Egypt and her gods and her kings, and on those who rely on Pharaoh. ²⁶ I will give them into the hands of those who want to kill them — Nebuchadnezzar king of Babylon and his officers. Later, however, Egypt will be inhabited as in times past," declares the LORD.

²⁷ "Do not be afraid, Jacob my
servant;
do not be dismayed,
Israel.
I will surely save you out of a
distant place,
your descendants from the
land of their exile.
Jacob will again have peace
and security,
and no one will make him
afraid.
²⁸ Do not be afraid, Jacob my
servant,
for I am with you," declares
the LORD.

"Though I completely destroy
all the nations
among which I scatter you,
I will not completely destroy
you.
I will discipline you but only in
due measure;
I will not let you go entirely
unpunished."

A Message About the Philistines

47 This is the word of the
LORD that came to Jere-
miah the prophet concerning the
Philistines before Pharaoh attacked Gaza:

²This is what the LORD says:

"See how the waters are rising
in the north;
they will become an
overflowing torrent.
They will overflow the land
and everything in it,
the towns and those who live
in them.
The people will cry out;
all who dwell in the land will
wail
³at the sound of the hooves of
galloping steeds,
at the noise of enemy
chariots
and the rumble of their
wheels.
Parents will not turn to help
their children;
their hands will hang limp.
⁴For the day has come
to destroy all the Philistines

and to remove all survivors
who could help Tyre and
Sidon.
The LORD is about to destroy
the Philistines,
the remnant from the coasts
of Caphtor.*a*
⁵Gaza will shave her head in
mourning;
Ashkelon will be silenced.
You remnant on the plain,
how long will you cut
yourselves?

⁶" 'Alas, sword of the LORD,
how long till you rest?
Return to your sheath;
cease and be still.'
⁷But how can it rest
when the LORD has
commanded it,
when he has ordered it
to attack Ashkelon and the
coast?"

A Message About Moab

48 Concerning Moab:

This is what the LORD Al-
mighty, the God of Israel, says:

"Woe to Nebo, for it will be
ruined.
Kiriathaim will be disgraced
and captured;
the stronghold*b* will be
disgraced and shattered.
²Moab will be praised no more;
in Heshbon*c* people will plot
her downfall:

---

a 4 That is, Crete   *b* 1 Or *captured; / Misgab*   *c* 2 The Hebrew for *Heshbon*
sounds like the Hebrew for *plot*.

'Come, let us put an end to
that nation.'
You, the people of Madmen,*a*
will also be silenced;
the sword will pursue you.
³Cries of anguish arise from
Horonaim,
cries of great havoc and
destruction.
⁴Moab will be broken;
her little ones will cry out.*b*
⁵They go up the hill to Luhith,
weeping bitterly as they go;
on the road down to Horonaim
anguished cries over the
destruction are heard.
⁶Flee! Run for your lives;
become like a bush*c* in the
desert.
⁷Since you trust in your deeds
and riches,
you too will be taken captive,
and Chemosh will go into
exile,
together with his priests and
officials.
⁸The destroyer will come
against every town,
and not a town will escape.
The valley will be ruined
and the plateau destroyed,
because the LORD has
spoken.
⁹Put salt on Moab,
for she will be laid waste*d*;
her towns will become
desolate,
with no one to live in them.

¹⁰"A curse on anyone who is lax
in doing the LORD's work!
A curse on anyone who
keeps their sword from
bloodshed!

¹¹"Moab has been at rest from
youth,
like wine left on its dregs,
not poured from one jar to
another—
she has not gone into exile.
So she tastes as she did,
and her aroma is unchanged.
¹²But days are coming,"
declares the LORD,
"when I will send men who
pour from pitchers,
and they will pour her out;
they will empty her pitchers
and smash her jars.
¹³Then Moab will be ashamed of
Chemosh,
as Israel was ashamed
when they trusted in Bethel.

¹⁴"How can you say, 'We are
warriors,
men valiant in battle'?
¹⁵Moab will be destroyed and
her towns invaded;
her finest young men will go
down in the slaughter,"
declares the King, whose
name is the LORD
Almighty.
¹⁶"The fall of Moab is at hand;
her calamity will come
quickly.

---

a 2 The name of the Moabite town Madmen sounds like the Hebrew for *be silenced.*   *b* 4 Hebrew; Septuagint / *proclaim it to Zoar*   *c* 6 Or *like Aroer*
d 9 Or *Give wings to Moab, / for she will fly away*

17 Mourn for her, all who live
    around her,
  all who know her fame;
  say, 'How broken is the mighty
    scepter,
  how broken the glorious
    staff!'

18 "Come down from your glory
  and sit on the parched
    ground,
  you inhabitants of Daughter
    Dibon,
  for the one who destroys
    Moab
  will come up against you
  and ruin your fortified
    cities.

19 Stand by the road and
    watch,
  you who live in Aroer.
  Ask the man fleeing and the
    woman escaping,
  ask them, 'What has
    happened?'

20 Moab is disgraced, for she is
    shattered.
  Wail and cry out!
  Announce by the Arnon
  that Moab is destroyed.

21 Judgment has come to the
    plateau —
  to Holon, Jahzah and
    Mephaath,

22   to Dibon, Nebo and Beth
    Diblathaim,

23   to Kiriathaim, Beth Gamul
    and Beth Meon,

24   to Kerioth and Bozrah —
  to all the towns of Moab, far
    and near.

25 Moab's horn[a] is cut off;
  her arm is broken,"
    declares the LORD.

26 "Make her drunk,
  for she has defied the LORD.
  Let Moab wallow in her
    vomit;
  let her be an object of
    ridicule.

27 Was not Israel the object of
    your ridicule?
  Was she caught among
    thieves,
  that you shake your head in
    scorn
  whenever you speak of her?

28 Abandon your towns and
    dwell among the rocks,
  you who live in Moab.
  Be like a dove that makes its
    nest
  at the mouth of a cave.

29 "We have heard of Moab's
    pride —
  how great is her
    arrogance! —
  of her insolence, her pride, her
    conceit
  and the haughtiness of her
    heart.

30 I know her insolence but it is
    futile,"
    declares the LORD,
  "and her boasts accomplish
    nothing.

31 Therefore I wail over Moab,
  for all Moab I cry out,
  I moan for the people of Kir
    Hareseth.

a 25 *Horn* here symbolizes strength.

³²I weep for you, as Jazer weeps,
  you vines of Sibmah.
Your branches spread as far as
    the sea*a*;
  they reached as far as*b*
    Jazer.
The destroyer has fallen
  on your ripened fruit and
    grapes.
³³Joy and gladness are gone
  from the orchards and fields
    of Moab.
I have stopped the flow of wine
  from the presses;
  no one treads them with
    shouts of joy.
Although there are shouts,
  they are not shouts of joy.

³⁴"The sound of their cry rises
  from Heshbon to Elealeh
    and Jahaz,
  from Zoar as far as Horonaim
    and Eglath Shelishiyah,
  for even the waters of
    Nimrim are dried up.
³⁵In Moab I will put an end
  to those who make offerings
    on the high places
  and burn incense to their
    gods,"
          declares the LORD.
³⁶"So my heart laments for Moab
  like the music of a pipe;
  it laments like a pipe for the
    people of Kir Hareseth.
The wealth they acquired is
    gone.
³⁷Every head is shaved
  and every beard cut off;

every hand is slashed
  and every waist is covered
    with sackcloth.
³⁸On all the roofs in Moab
  and in the public squares
there is nothing but
    mourning,
  for I have broken Moab
  like a jar that no one wants,"
          declares the LORD.
³⁹"How shattered she is! How
    they wail!
  How Moab turns her back in
    shame!
Moab has become an object of
    ridicule,
  an object of horror to all
    those around her."

⁴⁰This is what the LORD says:

"Look! An eagle is swooping
    down,
  spreading its wings over
    Moab.
⁴¹Kerioth*c* will be captured
  and the strongholds taken.
In that day the hearts of
    Moab's warriors
  will be like the heart of a
    woman in labor.
⁴²Moab will be destroyed as a
    nation
  because she defied the LORD.
⁴³Terror and pit and snare await
    you,
  you people of Moab,"
          declares the LORD.
⁴⁴"Whoever flees from the terror
  will fall into a pit,

a 32 Probably the Dead Sea   *b* 32 Two Hebrew manuscripts and Septuagint;
most Hebrew manuscripts *as far as the Sea of*   *c* 41 Or *The cities*

whoever climbs out of the pit
will be caught in a snare;
for I will bring on Moab
the year of her punishment,"
declares the LORD.

⁴⁵ "In the shadow of Heshbon
the fugitives stand helpless,
for a fire has gone out from
Heshbon,
a blaze from the midst of
Sihon;
it burns the foreheads of Moab,
the skulls of the noisy
boasters.
⁴⁶ Woe to you, Moab!
The people of Chemosh are
destroyed;
your sons are taken into exile
and your daughters into
captivity.

⁴⁷ "Yet I will restore the fortunes
of Moab
in days to come,"
declares the LORD.

Here ends the judgment on
Moab.

A Message About Ammon

49 Concerning the Ammon-
ites:

This is what the LORD says:

"Has Israel no sons?
Has Israel no heir?
Why then has Molek[a] taken
possession of Gad?
Why do his people live in its
towns?

² But the days are coming,"
declares the LORD,
"when I will sound the battle
cry
against Rabbah of the
Ammonites;
it will become a mound of
ruins,
and its surrounding villages
will be set on fire.
Then Israel will drive out
those who drove her out,"
says the LORD.
³ "Wail, Heshbon, for Ai is
destroyed!
Cry out, you inhabitants of
Rabbah!
Put on sackcloth and mourn;
rush here and there inside
the walls,
for Molek will go into exile,
together with his priests and
officials.
⁴ Why do you boast of your
valleys,
boast of your valleys so
fruitful?
Unfaithful Daughter
Ammon,
you trust in your riches and
say,
'Who will attack me?'
⁵ I will bring terror on you
from all those around you,"
declares the Lord,
the LORD Almighty.
"Every one of you will be
driven away,
and no one will gather the
fugitives.

---

a 1 Or *their king*; also in verse 3

6 "Yet afterward, I will restore
the fortunes of the
Ammonites,"
declares the LORD.

A Message About Edom

7 Concerning Edom:

This is what the LORD Almighty
says:

"Is there no longer wisdom in
Teman?
Has counsel perished from
the prudent?
Has their wisdom decayed?
8 Turn and flee, hide in deep
caves,
you who live in Dedan,
for I will bring disaster on
Esau
at the time when I punish
him.
9 If grape pickers came to you,
would they not leave a few
grapes?
If thieves came during the
night,
would they not steal only as
much as they wanted?
10 But I will strip Esau bare;
I will uncover his hiding
places,
so that he cannot conceal
himself.
His armed men are
destroyed,
also his allies and
neighbors,
so there is no one to say,

11 'Leave your fatherless
children; I will keep
them alive.
Your widows too can depend
on me.' "

12 This is what the LORD says:
"If those who do not deserve to
drink the cup must drink it, why
should you go unpunished? You
will not go unpunished, but must
drink it. 13 I swear by myself," declares the LORD, "that Bozrah
will become a ruin and a curse,*a*
an object of horror and reproach;
and all its towns will be in ruins
forever."

14 I have heard a message from
the LORD;
an envoy was sent to the
nations to say,
"Assemble yourselves to
attack it!
Rise up for battle!"

15 "Now I will make you small
among the nations,
despised by mankind.
16 The terror you inspire
and the pride of your heart
have deceived you,
you who live in the clefts of the
rocks,
who occupy the heights of
the hill.
Though you build your nest as
high as the eagle's,
from there I will bring you
down,"
declares the LORD.

---

a 13 That is, its name will be used in cursing (see 29:22); or, others will see that it
is cursed.

17 "Edom will become an object
of horror;
all who pass by will be
appalled and will
scoff
because of all its wounds.
18 As Sodom and Gomorrah were
overthrown,
along with their neighboring
towns,"
says the LORD,
"so no one will live there;
no people will dwell in it.

19 "Like a lion coming up from
Jordan's thickets
to a rich pastureland,
I will chase Edom from its land
in an instant.
Who is the chosen one I will
appoint for this?
Who is like me and who can
challenge me?
And what shepherd can
stand against me?"

20 Therefore, hear what the LORD
has planned against
Edom,
what he has purposed
against those who live in
Teman:
The young of the flock will be
dragged away;
their pasture will be
appalled at their
fate.
21 At the sound of their fall the
earth will tremble;
their cry will resound to the
Red Sea.[a]

22 Look! An eagle will soar and
swoop down,
spreading its wings over
Bozrah.
In that day the hearts of
Edom's warriors
will be like the heart of a
woman in labor.

A Message About Damascus

23 Concerning Damascus:

"Hamath and Arpad are
dismayed,
for they have heard bad
news.
They are disheartened,
troubled like[b] the restless
sea.
24 Damascus has become
feeble,
she has turned to flee
and panic has gripped her;
anguish and pain have seized
her,
pain like that of a woman in
labor.
25 Why has the city of renown not
been abandoned,
the town in which I delight?
26 Surely, her young men will fall
in the streets;
all her soldiers will be
silenced in that day,"
declares the LORD
Almighty.
27 "I will set fire to the walls of
Damascus;
it will consume the
fortresses of Ben-
Hadad."

[a] 21 Or *the Sea of Reeds*   [b] 23 Hebrew *on* or *by*

A Message About Kedar and Hazor

28Concerning Kedar and the kingdoms of Hazor, which Nebuchadnezzar king of Babylon attacked:

This is what the Lord says:

"Arise, and attack Kedar
    and destroy the people of the
        East.
29Their tents and their flocks
        will be taken;
    their shelters will be carried
        off
    with all their goods and
        camels.
People will shout to them,
    'Terror on every side!'

30"Flee quickly away!
    Stay in deep caves, you who
        live in Hazor,"
            declares the Lord.
"Nebuchadnezzar king of
        Babylon has plotted
        against you;
    he has devised a plan
        against you.

31"Arise and attack a nation at
        ease,
    which lives in confidence,"
            declares the Lord,
"a nation that has neither gates
        nor bars;
    its people live far from danger.
32Their camels will become
        plunder,
    and their large herds will be
        spoils of war.

I will scatter to the winds
    those who are in distant
        places[a]
and will bring disaster on
    them from every side,"
            declares the Lord.
33"Hazor will become a haunt of
        jackals,
    a desolate place forever.
No one will live there;
    no people will dwell in it."

A Message About Elam

34This is the word of the Lord that came to Jeremiah the prophet concerning Elam, early in the reign of Zedekiah king of Judah:

35This is what the Lord Almighty says:

"See, I will break the bow of
        Elam,
    the mainstay of their might.
36I will bring against Elam the
        four winds
    from the four quarters of
        heaven;
I will scatter them to the four
        winds,
    and there will not be a
        nation
    where Elam's exiles do
        not go.
37I will shatter Elam before their
        foes,
    before those who want to kill
        them;
I will bring disaster on them,
    even my fierce anger,"
            declares the Lord.

---

[a] 32 Or *who clip the hair by their foreheads*

"I will pursue them with the
sword
until I have made an end of
them.
38 I will set my throne in Elam
and destroy her king and
officials,"
declares the LORD.

39 "Yet I will restore the fortunes
of Elam
in days to come,"
declares the LORD.

A Message About Babylon

50 This is the word the LORD
spoke through Jeremiah
the prophet concerning Babylon
and the land of the Babylonians[a]:

2 "Announce and proclaim
among the nations,
lift up a banner and
proclaim it;
keep nothing back, but
say,
'Babylon will be captured;
Bel will be put to shame,
Marduk filled with terror.
Her images will be put to
shame
and her idols filled with
terror.'
3 A nation from the north will
attack her
and lay waste her land.
No one will live in it;
both people and animals
will flee away.

4 "In those days, at that time,"
declares the LORD,

"the people of Israel and the
people of Judah together
will go in tears to seek the
LORD their God.
5 They will ask the way to Zion
and turn their faces toward it.
They will come and bind
themselves to the LORD
in an everlasting covenant
that will not be forgotten.

6 "My people have been lost
sheep;
their shepherds have led
them astray
and caused them to roam on
the mountains.
They wandered over mountain
and hill
and forgot their own resting
place.
7 Whoever found them
devoured them;
their enemies said, 'We are
not guilty,
for they sinned against the
LORD, their verdant
pasture,
the LORD, the hope of their
ancestors.'

8 "Flee out of Babylon;
leave the land of the
Babylonians,
and be like the goats that
lead the flock.
9 For I will stir up and bring
against Babylon
an alliance of great nations
from the land of the
north.

---

a 1 Or Chaldeans; also in verses 8, 25, 35 and 45

They will take up their
      positions against her,
   and from the north she will
      be captured.
Their arrows will be like
      skilled warriors
   who do not return empty-
      handed.
¹⁰ So Babylonia*ᵃ* will be
      plundered;
   all who plunder her will have
      their fill,"
            declares the LORD.

¹¹ "Because you rejoice and are
      glad,
   you who pillage my
      inheritance,
   because you frolic like a heifer
      threshing grain
   and neigh like stallions,
¹² your mother will be greatly
      ashamed;
   she who gave you birth will
      be disgraced.
She will be the least of the
      nations—
   a wilderness, a dry land, a
      desert.
¹³ Because of the LORD's anger
      she will not be inhabited
   but will be completely
      desolate.
All who pass Babylon will be
      appalled;
   they will scoff because of all
      her wounds.
¹⁴ "Take up your positions
      around Babylon,
   all you who draw the bow.

Shoot at her! Spare no arrows,
   for she has sinned against
      the LORD.
¹⁵ Shout against her on every
      side!
   She surrenders, her towers
      fall,
   her walls are torn down.
Since this is the vengeance of
      the LORD,
   take vengeance on her;
   do to her as she has done to
      others.
¹⁶ Cut off from Babylon the
      sower,
   and the reaper with his
      sickle at harvest.
Because of the sword of the
      oppressor
   let everyone return to their
      own people,
   let everyone flee to their own
      land.

¹⁷ "Israel is a scattered flock
   that lions have chased
      away.
The first to devour them
   was the king of Assyria;
   the last to crush their bones
      was Nebuchadnezzar king of
      Babylon."

¹⁸ Therefore this is what the
LORD Almighty, the God of Israel, says:

"I will punish the king of
      Babylon and his land
   as I punished the king of
      Assyria.

ᵃ 10 Or *Chaldea*

¹⁹But I will bring Israel back to
　　their own pasture,
　and they will graze on
　　Carmel and Bashan;
　their appetite will be satisfied
　　on the hills of Ephraim and
　　Gilead.
²⁰In those days, at that time,"
　declares the LORD,
　"search will be made for
　　Israel's guilt,
　but there will be none,
　and for the sins of Judah,
　but none will be found,
　for I will forgive the remnant
　　I spare.

²¹ "Attack the land of Merathaim
　and those who live in
　　Pekod.
　Pursue, kill and completely
　　destroy*ᵃ* them,"
　　　　　declares the LORD.
　"Do everything I have
　　commanded you.
²²The noise of battle is in the
　　land,
　the noise of great
　　destruction!
²³How broken and shattered
　　is the hammer of the whole
　　earth!
　How desolate is Babylon
　　among the nations!
²⁴I set a trap for you, Babylon,
　and you were caught before
　　you knew it;
　you were found and captured
　　because you opposed the
　　LORD.

²⁵The LORD has opened his
　　arsenal
　and brought out the
　　weapons of his wrath,
　for the Sovereign LORD
　　Almighty has work
　　to do
　in the land of the
　　Babylonians.
²⁶Come against her from afar.
　Break open her granaries;
　pile her up like heaps of
　　grain.
　Completely destroy her
　and leave her no remnant.
²⁷Kill all her young bulls;
　let them go down to the
　　slaughter!
　Woe to them! For their day has
　　come,
　the time for them to be
　　punished.
²⁸Listen to the fugitives and
　　refugees from Babylon
　declaring in Zion
　how the LORD our God has
　　taken vengeance,
　vengeance for his temple.

²⁹ "Summon archers against
　　Babylon,
　all those who draw the
　　bow.
　Encamp all around her;
　let no one escape.
　Repay her for her deeds;
　do to her as she has done.
　For she has defied the
　　LORD,
　the Holy One of Israel.

ᵃ *21* The Hebrew term refers to the irrevocable giving over of things or persons to
the LORD, often by totally destroying them; also in verse 26.

³⁰Therefore, her young men will
fall in the streets;
all her soldiers will be
silenced in that day,"
declares the Lord.
³¹ "See, I am against you, you
arrogant one,"
declares the Lord, the Lord
Almighty,
"for your day has come,
the time for you to be
punished.
³²The arrogant one will stumble
and fall
and no one will help her up;
I will kindle a fire in her towns
that will consume all who
are around her."

³³This is what the Lord Almighty says:

"The people of Israel are
oppressed,
and the people of Judah as
well.
All their captors hold them
fast,
refusing to let them go.
³⁴Yet their Redeemer is strong;
the Lord Almighty is his
name.
He will vigorously defend their
cause
so that he may bring rest to
their land,
but unrest to those who live
in Babylon.

³⁵ "A sword against the
Babylonians!"
declares the Lord —

"against those who live in
Babylon
and against her officials and
wise men!
³⁶A sword against her false
prophets!
They will become fools.
A sword against her warriors!
They will be filled with
terror.
³⁷A sword against her horses
and chariots
and all the foreigners in her
ranks!
They will become
weaklings.
A sword against her
treasures!
They will be plundered.
³⁸A drought on* her waters!
They will dry up.
For it is a land of idols,
idols that will go mad with
terror.

³⁹ "So desert creatures and
hyenas will live there,
and there the owl will
dwell.
It will never again be
inhabited
or lived in from generation
to generation.
⁴⁰As I overthrew Sodom and
Gomorrah
along with their neighboring
towns,"
declares the Lord,
"so no one will live there;
no people will dwell in it.

---

a 38 Or *A sword against*

41 "Look! An army is coming
        from the north;
    a great nation and many
        kings
    are being stirred up from the
        ends of the earth.
42 They are armed with bows and
        spears;
    they are cruel and without
        mercy.
    They sound like the roaring
        sea
    as they ride on their
        horses;
    they come like men in battle
        formation
    to attack you, Daughter
        Babylon.
43 The king of Babylon has heard
        reports about them,
    and his hands hang limp.
    Anguish has gripped him,
        pain like that of a woman in
        labor.
44 Like a lion coming up from
        Jordan's thickets
    to a rich pastureland,
    I will chase Babylon from its
        land in an instant.
    Who is the chosen one I will
        appoint for this?
    Who is like me and who can
        challenge me?
    And what shepherd can
        stand against me?"

45 Therefore, hear what the LORD
        has planned against
        Babylon,
what he has purposed
        against the land of the
        Babylonians:
    The young of the flock will be
        dragged away;
    their pasture will be
        appalled at their fate.
46 At the sound of Babylon's
        capture the earth will
        tremble;
    its cry will resound among
        the nations.

51 This is what the LORD
    says:

"See, I will stir up the spirit of
        a destroyer
    against Babylon and the
        people of Leb Kamai.[a]
2 I will send foreigners to
        Babylon
    to winnow her and to
        devastate her land;
    they will oppose her on every
        side
    in the day of her disaster.
3 Let not the archer string his
        bow,
    nor let him put on his
        armor.
    Do not spare her young
        men;
    completely destroy[b] her
        army.
4 They will fall down slain in
        Babylon,[c]
    fatally wounded in her
        streets.

---

[a] 1 *Leb Kamai* is a cryptogram for Chaldea, that is, Babylonia.   [b] 3 The Hebrew term refers to the irrevocable giving over of things or persons to the LORD, often by totally destroying them.   [c] 4 Or *Chaldea*

⁵For Israel and Judah have not
    been forsaken
  by their God, the Lord
    Almighty,
  though their land*a* is full of
    guilt
  before the Holy One of
    Israel.

⁶"Flee from Babylon!
  Run for your lives!
  Do not be destroyed because
    of her sins.
It is time for the Lord's
    vengeance;
  he will repay her what she
    deserves.
⁷Babylon was a gold cup in the
    Lord's hand;
  she made the whole earth
    drunk.
  The nations drank her
    wine;
  therefore they have now
    gone mad.
⁸Babylon will suddenly fall and
    be broken.
  Wail over her!
Get balm for her pain;
  perhaps she can be
    healed.

⁹" 'We would have healed
    Babylon,
  but she cannot be healed;
let us leave her and each go to
    our own land,
  for her judgment reaches to
    the skies,
  it rises as high as the
    heavens.'

¹⁰" 'The Lord has vindicated us;
  come, let us tell in Zion
  what the Lord our God has
    done.'

¹¹"Sharpen the arrows,
  take up the shields!
The Lord has stirred up the
    kings of the Medes,
  because his purpose is to
    destroy Babylon.
The Lord will take
    vengeance,
  vengeance for his temple.
¹²Lift up a banner against the
    walls of Babylon!
  Reinforce the guard,
station the watchmen,
  prepare an ambush!
The Lord will carry out his
    purpose,
  his decree against the people
    of Babylon.
¹³You who live by many
    waters
  and are rich in treasures,
your end has come,
  the time for you to be
    destroyed.
¹⁴The Lord Almighty has sworn
    by himself:
  I will surely fill you with
    troops, as with a swarm
    of locusts,
  and they will shout in
    triumph over you.

¹⁵"He made the earth by his
    power;
  he founded the world by his
    wisdom

a 5 Or Almighty, / and the land of the Babylonians

and stretched out the
heavens by his
understanding.
¹⁶When he thunders, the waters
in the heavens roar;
he makes clouds rise from
the ends of the earth.
He sends lightning with the
rain
and brings out the wind
from his storehouses.

¹⁷"Everyone is senseless and
without knowledge;
every goldsmith is shamed
by his idols.
The images he makes are a
fraud;
they have no breath in
them.
¹⁸They are worthless, the objects
of mockery;
when their judgment comes,
they will perish.
¹⁹He who is the Portion of Jacob
is not like these,
for he is the Maker of all
things,
including the people of his
inheritance —
the LORD Almighty is his
name.
²⁰"You are my war club,
my weapon for battle —
with you I shatter nations,
with you I destroy kingdoms,
²¹with you I shatter horse and
rider,
with you I shatter chariot
and driver,

²²with you I shatter man and
woman,
with you I shatter old man
and youth,
with you I shatter young
man and young
woman,
²³with you I shatter shepherd
and flock,
with you I shatter farmer and
oxen,
with you I shatter governors
and officials.

²⁴"Before your eyes I will repay Babylon and all who live in
Babylonia*ᵃ* for all the wrong they
have done in Zion," declares the
LORD.

²⁵"I am against you, you
destroying mountain,
you who destroy the whole
earth,"
declares the LORD.
"I will stretch out my hand
against you,
roll you off the cliffs,
and make you a burned-out
mountain.
²⁶No rock will be taken from you
for a cornerstone,
nor any stone for a
foundation,
for you will be desolate
forever,"
declares the LORD.

²⁷"Lift up a banner in the
land!
Blow the trumpet among the
nations!

ᵃ 24 Or *Chaldea*; also in verse 35

Prepare the nations for battle
against her;
summon against her these
kingdoms:
Ararat, Minni and Ashkenaz.
Appoint a commander against
her;
send up horses like a swarm
of locusts.
²⁸ Prepare the nations for battle
against her —
the kings of the Medes,
their governors and all their
officials,
and all the countries they
rule.
²⁹ The land trembles and
writhes,
for the Lord's purposes
against Babylon stand —
to lay waste the land of
Babylon
so that no one will live there.
³⁰ Babylon's warriors have
stopped fighting;
they remain in their
strongholds.
Their strength is exhausted;
they have become
weaklings.
Her dwellings are set on fire;
the bars of her gates are
broken.
³¹ One courier follows another
and messenger follows
messenger
to announce to the king of
Babylon
that his entire city is
captured,
³² the river crossings seized,
the marshes set on fire,
and the soldiers terrified."

³³ This is what the Lord Almighty, the God of Israel, says:

"Daughter Babylon is like a
threshing floor
at the time it is trampled;
the time to harvest her will
soon come."

³⁴ "Nebuchadnezzar king of
Babylon has devoured
us,
he has thrown us into
confusion,
he has made us an empty jar.
Like a serpent he has
swallowed us
and filled his stomach with
our delicacies,
and then has spewed us out.
³⁵ May the violence done to our
flesh^a be on Babylon,"
say the inhabitants of Zion.
"May our blood be on those
who live in Babylonia,"
says Jerusalem.

³⁶ Therefore this is what the
Lord says:

"See, I will defend your cause
and avenge you;
I will dry up her sea
and make her springs dry.
³⁷ Babylon will be a heap of
ruins,
a haunt of jackals,
an object of horror and scorn,
a place where no one lives.

^a 35 Or *done to us and to our children*

Parable of the Lost Sheep
LUKE 15:1–7

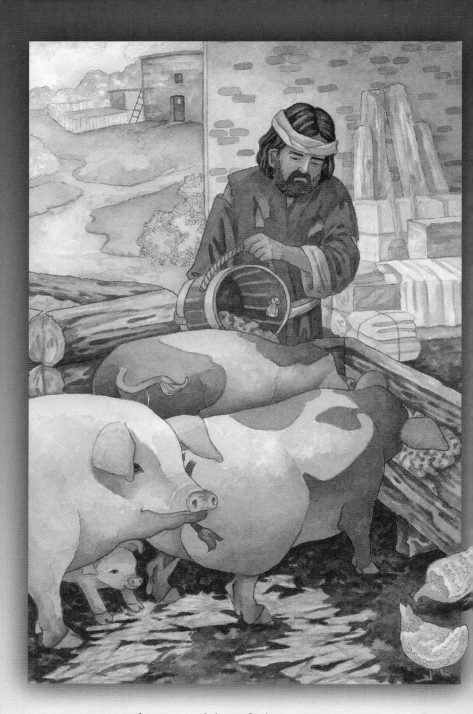

The Parable of the Lost Son
LUKE 15:11–32

Fruit of the Spirit

Galatians 5:22–23 tells us how God wants us to live. These are the things that God wants us to produce so that everyone around us can see the good fruit that he grows in us!

Love Joy

Peace

Patience
(Forbearance, Longsuffering)

Kindness

good-ness

FAITHFULNESS

Gentleness

Self-control
(Temperance)

The Little Children and Jesus
MARK 10:13–16

³⁸Her people all roar like young
lions,
they growl like lion cubs.
³⁹But while they are aroused,
I will set out a feast for them
and make them drunk,
so that they shout with
laughter —
then sleep forever and not
awake,"
declares the LORD.
⁴⁰"I will bring them down
like lambs to the slaughter,
like rams and goats.

⁴¹"How Sheshak^a will be
captured,
the boast of the whole earth
seized!
How desolate Babylon will be
among the nations!
⁴²The sea will rise over Babylon;
its roaring waves will cover
her.
⁴³Her towns will be desolate,
a dry and desert land,
a land where no one lives,
through which no one
travels.
⁴⁴I will punish Bel in Babylon
and make him spew out
what he has swallowed.
The nations will no longer
stream to him.
And the wall of Babylon will
fall.

⁴⁵"Come out of her, my people!
Run for your lives!
Run from the fierce anger of
the LORD.

⁴⁶Do not lose heart or be
afraid
when rumors are heard in
the land;
one rumor comes this year,
another the next,
rumors of violence in the
land
and of ruler against ruler.
⁴⁷For the time will surely come
when I will punish the idols
of Babylon;
her whole land will be
disgraced
and her slain will all lie
fallen within her.
⁴⁸Then heaven and earth and all
that is in them
will shout for joy over
Babylon,
for out of the north
destroyers will attack her,"
declares the LORD.

⁴⁹"Babylon must fall because of
Israel's slain,
just as the slain in all the
earth
have fallen because of
Babylon.
⁵⁰You who have escaped the
sword,
leave and do not linger!
Remember the LORD in a
distant land,
and call to mind Jerusalem."

⁵¹"We are disgraced,
for we have been insulted
and shame covers our
faces,

^a 41 *Sheshak* is a cryptogram for Babylon.

because foreigners have
entered
    the holy places of the LORD's
    house."

⁵²"But days are coming,"
    declares the LORD,
    "when I will punish her
    idols,
and throughout her land
    the wounded will groan.
⁵³Even if Babylon ascends to the
    heavens
    and fortifies her lofty
    stronghold,
    I will send destroyers against
    her,"
                declares the LORD.

⁵⁴"The sound of a cry comes
    from Babylon,
    the sound of great
    destruction
    from the land of the
    Babylonians.ᵃ
⁵⁵The LORD will destroy
    Babylon;
    he will silence her noisy din.
Waves of enemies will rage like
    great waters;
    the roar of their voices will
    resound.
⁵⁶A destroyer will come against
    Babylon;
    her warriors will be
    captured,
    and their bows will be
    broken.
For the LORD is a God of
    retribution;
    he will repay in full.

⁵⁷I will make her officials and
    wise men drunk,
    her governors, officers and
    warriors as well;
they will sleep forever and not
    awake,"
    declares the King, whose
    name is the LORD
    Almighty.

⁵⁸This is what the LORD Almighty says:

"Babylon's thick wall will be
    leveled
    and her high gates set on
    fire;
the peoples exhaust
    themselves for nothing,
    the nations' labor is only fuel
    for the flames."

⁵⁹This is the message Jeremiah the prophet gave to the staff officer Seraiah son of Neriah, the son of Mahseiah, when he went to Babylon with Zedekiah king of Judah in the fourth year of his reign. ⁶⁰Jeremiah had written on a scroll about all the disasters that would come upon Babylon—all that had been recorded concerning Babylon. ⁶¹He said to Seraiah, "When you get to Babylon, see that you read all these words aloud. ⁶²Then say, 'LORD, you have said you will destroy this place, so that neither people nor animals will live in it; it will be desolate forever.' ⁶³When you finish reading this scroll, tie a stone to it and throw it into the

ᵃ 54 Or Chaldeans

Euphrates. **64**Then say, 'So will Babylon sink to rise no more because of the disaster I will bring on her. And her people will fall.'"

The words of Jeremiah end here.

The Fall of Jerusalem

52 Zedekiah was twenty-one years old when he became king, and he reigned in Jerusalem eleven years. His mother's name was Hamutal daughter of Jeremiah; she was from Libnah. **2**He did evil in the eyes of the LORD, just as Jehoiakim had done. **3**It was because of the LORD's anger that all this happened to Jerusalem and Judah, and in the end he thrust them from his presence.

Now Zedekiah rebelled against the king of Babylon.

4So in the ninth year of Zedekiah's reign, on the tenth day of the tenth month, Nebuchadnezzar king of Babylon marched against Jerusalem with his whole army. They encamped outside the city and built siege works all around it. **5**The city was kept under siege until the eleventh year of King Zedekiah.

6By the ninth day of the fourth month the famine in the city had become so severe that there was no food for the people to eat. **7**Then the city wall was broken through, and the whole army fled.

They left the city at night through the gate between the two walls near the king's garden, though the Babylonians*a* were surrounding the city. They fled toward the Arabah,*b* **8**but the Babylonian*c* army pursued King Zedekiah and overtook him in the plains of Jericho. All his soldiers were separated from him and scattered, **9**and he was captured.

He was taken to the king of Babylon at Riblah in the land of Hamath, where he pronounced sentence on him. **10**There at Riblah the king of Babylon killed the sons of Zedekiah before his eyes; he also killed all the officials of Judah. **11**Then he put out Zedekiah's eyes, bound him with bronze shackles and took him to Babylon, where he put him in prison till the day of his death.

12On the tenth day of the fifth month, in the nineteenth year of Nebuchadnezzar king of Babylon, Nebuzaradan commander of the imperial guard, who served the king of Babylon, came to Jerusalem. **13**He set fire to the temple of the LORD, the royal palace and all the houses of Jerusalem. Every important building he burned down. **14**The whole Babylonian army, under the commander of the imperial guard, broke down all the walls around Jerusalem. **15**Nebuzaradan the commander of the guard carried into exile

---

a 7 Or *Chaldeans*; also in verse 17   *b* 7 Or *the Jordan Valley*   *c* 8 Or *Chaldean*; also in verse 14 some of the poorest people and those who remained in the city, along with the rest of the craftsmen[a] and those who had deserted to the king of Babylon. [16]But Nebuzaradan left behind the rest of the poorest people of the land to work the vineyards and fields.

[17]The Babylonians broke up the bronze pillars, the movable stands and the bronze Sea that were at the temple of the LORD and they carried all the bronze to Babylon. [18]They also took away the pots, shovels, wick trimmers, sprinkling bowls, dishes and all the bronze articles used in the temple service. [19]The commander of the imperial guard took away the basins, censers, sprinkling bowls, pots, lampstands, dishes and bowls used for drink offerings—all that were made of pure gold or silver.

[20]The bronze from the two pillars, the Sea and the twelve bronze bulls under it, and the movable stands, which King Solomon had made for the temple of the LORD, was more than could be weighed. [21]Each pillar was eighteen cubits high and twelve cubits in circumference[b]; each was four fingers thick, and hollow. [22]The bronze capital on top of one pillar was five cubits[c] high and was decorated with a network and pomegranates of bronze all around. The other pillar, with its pomegranates, was similar. [23]There were ninety-six pomegranates on the sides; the total number of pomegranates above the surrounding network was a hundred.

[24]The commander of the guard took as prisoners Seraiah the chief priest, Zephaniah the priest next in rank and the three doorkeepers. [25]Of those still in the city, he took the officer in charge of the fighting men, and seven royal advisers. He also took the secretary who was chief officer in charge of conscripting the people of the land, sixty of whom were found in the city. [26]Nebuzaradan the commander took them all and brought them to the king of Babylon at Riblah. [27]There at Riblah, in the land of Hamath, the king had them executed.

So Judah went into captivity, away from her land. [28]This is the number of the people Nebuchadnezzar carried into exile:

in the seventh year, 3,023 Jews;
[29]in Nebuchadnezzar's eighteenth year,
832 people from Jerusalem;
[30]in his twenty-third year,
745 Jews taken into exile by Nebuzaradan the commander of the imperial guard.
There were 4,600 people in all.

[a] 15 Or the populace   [b] 21 That is, about 27 feet high and 18 feet in circumference or about 8.1 meters high and 5.4 meters in circumference
[c] 22 That is, about 7 1/2 feet or about 2.3 meters

Jehoiachin Released

³¹ In the thirty-seventh year of the exile of Jehoiachin king of Judah, in the year Awel-Marduk became king of Babylon, on the twenty-fifth day of the twelfth month, he released Jehoiachin king of Judah and freed him from prison. ³² He spoke kindly to him and gave him a seat of honor higher than those of the other kings who were with him in Babylon. ³³ So Jehoiachin put aside his prison clothes and for the rest of his life ate regularly at the king's table. ³⁴ Day by day the king of Babylon gave Jehoiachin a regular allowance as long as he lived, till the day of his death.

Lamentations

Introduction:

The title of this book means "funeral songs." The author was probably Jeremiah, who was grieving about the destruction of Jerusalem.

In the original language, Hebrew, the twenty-two verses in each of chapters 1, 2, and 4 use the twenty-two letters of the Hebrew alphabet to start the verse. The third chapter has sixty-six verses and every third verse starts a new letter of the Hebrew alphabet. This is called an acrostic.

In this book Jeremiah reflects on the destruction of Jerusalem and the temple. But he recognizes that this disaster is the judgment of a righteous God. Knowing that God is merciful he appeals for mercy in prayer to God.

Outline of contents:

Jerusalem's total destruction (1:1–22)
God's anger — search for comfort (2:1–22)
Thoughts on suffering — hope in God (3:1–66)
The old glory of Jerusalem — present misery (4:1–22)
A prayer for God's mercy (5:1–22)

1 ^{a} How deserted lies the
city,
    once so full of people!
How like a widow is she,
    who once was great among
    the nations!
She who was queen among the
provinces
    has now become a slave.

2 Bitterly she weeps at night,
    tears are on her cheeks.
Among all her lovers
    there is no one to comfort
    her.
All her friends have betrayed
her;
    they have become her
    enemies.

3 After affliction and harsh
labor,
    Judah has gone into exile.
She dwells among the
nations;
    she finds no resting place.
All who pursue her have
overtaken her
    in the midst of her
    distress.

^{a} This chapter is an acrostic poem, the verses of which begin with the successive letters of the Hebrew alphabet.

⁴The roads to Zion mourn,
  for no one comes to her
    appointed festivals.
All her gateways are desolate,
  her priests groan,
her young women grieve,
  and she is in bitter anguish.

⁵Her foes have become her
    masters;
  her enemies are at ease.
The Lord has brought her
    grief
  because of her many sins.
Her children have gone into
    exile,
  captive before the foe.

⁶All the splendor has departed
    from Daughter Zion.
Her princes are like deer
  that find no pasture;
in weakness they have fled
  before the pursuer.

⁷In the days of her affliction
    and wandering
  Jerusalem remembers all the
    treasures
  that were hers in days of old.
When her people fell into
    enemy hands,
  there was no one to help
    her.
Her enemies looked at her
  and laughed at her
    destruction.

⁸Jerusalem has sinned greatly
  and so has become unclean.
All who honored her despise
    her,
  for they have all seen her
    naked;

she herself groans
  and turns away.

⁹Her filthiness clung to her
    skirts;
  she did not consider her
    future.
Her fall was astounding;
  there was none to comfort
    her.
"Look, Lord, on my affliction,
  for the enemy has
    triumphed."

¹⁰The enemy laid hands
  on all her treasures;
she saw pagan nations
  enter her sanctuary—
those you had forbidden
  to enter your assembly.

¹¹All her people groan
  as they search for bread;
they barter their treasures for
    food
  to keep themselves alive.
"Look, Lord, and consider,
  for I am despised."

¹²"Is it nothing to you, all you
    who pass by?
  Look around and see.
Is any suffering like my
    suffering
  that was inflicted on me,
that the Lord brought on me
  in the day of his fierce anger?

¹³"From on high he sent fire,
  sent it down into my bones.
He spread a net for my feet
  and turned me back.
He made me desolate,
  faint all the day long.

14 "My sins have been bound into
         a yoke^a;
    by his hands they were
         woven together.
They have been hung on my
         neck,
    and the Lord has sapped my
         strength.
He has given me into the
         hands
    of those I cannot withstand.

15 "The Lord has rejected
    all the warriors in my
         midst;
he has summoned an army
         against me
    to^b crush my young men.
In his winepress the Lord has
         trampled
    Virgin Daughter Judah.

16 "This is why I weep
    and my eyes overflow with
         tears.
No one is near to comfort me,
    no one to restore my spirit.
My children are destitute
    because the enemy has
         prevailed."

17 Zion stretches out her hands,
    but there is no one to
         comfort her.
The LORD has decreed for
         Jacob
    that his neighbors become
         his foes;
Jerusalem has become
    an unclean thing among
         them.

18 "The LORD is righteous,
    yet I rebelled against his
         command.
Listen, all you peoples;
    look on my suffering.
My young men and young
         women
    have gone into exile.

19 "I called to my allies
    but they betrayed me.
My priests and my elders
    perished in the city
while they searched for food
    to keep themselves alive.

20 "See, LORD, how distressed
         I am!
    I am in torment within,
and in my heart I am
         disturbed,
    for I have been most
         rebellious.
Outside, the sword bereaves;
    inside, there is only death.

21 "People have heard my
         groaning,
    but there is no one to
         comfort me.
All my enemies have heard of
         my distress;
    they rejoice at what you have
         done.
May you bring the day you
         have announced
    so they may become like me.

22 "Let all their wickedness come
         before you;
    deal with them

---

^a 14 Most Hebrew manuscripts; many Hebrew manuscripts and Septuagint *He
kept watch over my sins*   ^b 15 Or *has set a time for me / when he will*

as you have dealt with me
    because of all my sins.
My groans are many
    and my heart is faint."

2 *a* How the Lord has covered
    Daughter Zion
    with the cloud of his anger*b*!
He has hurled down the
    splendor of Israel
from heaven to earth;
he has not remembered his
    footstool
    in the day of his anger.

2 Without pity the Lord has
    swallowed up
    all the dwellings of Jacob;
in his wrath he has torn down
    the strongholds of Daughter
    Judah.
He has brought her kingdom
    and its princes
    down to the ground in
    dishonor.

3 In fierce anger he has cut off
    every horn*c,d* of Israel.
He has withdrawn his right
    hand
    at the approach of the
    enemy.
He has burned in Jacob like a
    flaming fire
    that consumes everything
    around it.

4 Like an enemy he has strung
    his bow;
    his right hand is ready.

Like a foe he has slain
    all who were pleasing to the
    eye;
he has poured out his wrath
    like fire
    on the tent of Daughter Zion.

5 The Lord is like an enemy;
    he has swallowed up Israel.
He has swallowed up all her
    palaces
    and destroyed her
    strongholds.
He has multiplied mourning
    and lamentation
    for Daughter Judah.

6 He has laid waste his dwelling
    like a garden;
    he has destroyed his place of
    meeting.
The LORD has made Zion
    forget
    her appointed festivals and
    her Sabbaths;
in his fierce anger he has
    spurned
    both king and priest.

7 The Lord has rejected his altar
    and abandoned his
    sanctuary.
He has given the walls of her
    palaces
    into the hands of the enemy;
they have raised a shout in the
    house of the LORD
    as on the day of an
    appointed festival.

a This chapter is an acrostic poem, the verses of which begin with the successive
letters of the Hebrew alphabet.   *b* 1 Or *How the Lord in his anger / has treated
Daughter Zion with contempt*   *c* 3 Or *off / all the strength;* or *every king*
d 3 *Horn* here symbolizes strength.

8 The LORD determined to tear
      down
    the wall around Daughter
      Zion.
  He stretched out a measuring
      line
    and did not withhold his
      hand from destroying.
  He made ramparts and walls
      lament;
    together they wasted away.

9 Her gates have sunk into the
      ground;
    their bars he has broken and
      destroyed.
  Her king and her princes
      are exiled among the
      nations,
    the law is no more,
  and her prophets no longer
      find
    visions from the LORD.

10 The elders of Daughter Zion
    sit on the ground in silence;
  they have sprinkled dust on
      their heads
    and put on sackcloth.
  The young women of
      Jerusalem
    have bowed their heads to
      the ground.

11 My eyes fail from weeping,
    I am in torment within;
  my heart is poured out on the
      ground
    because my people are
      destroyed,
  because children and infants
      faint
    in the streets of the city.

12 They say to their mothers,
    "Where is bread and wine?"
  as they faint like the wounded
    in the streets of the city,
  as their lives ebb away
    in their mothers' arms.

13 What can I say for you?
    With what can I compare
      you,
    Daughter Jerusalem?
  To what can I liken you,
    that I may comfort you,
    Virgin Daughter Zion?
  Your wound is as deep as the
      sea.
    Who can heal you?

14 The visions of your prophets
    were false and worthless;
  they did not expose your sin
    to ward off your captivity.
  The prophecies they gave you
    were false and misleading.

15 All who pass your way
    clap their hands at you;
  they scoff and shake their
      heads
    at Daughter Jerusalem:
  "Is this the city that was called
    the perfection of beauty,
    the joy of the whole earth?"

16 All your enemies open their
      mouths
    wide against you;
  they scoff and gnash their
      teeth
    and say, "We have swallowed
      her up.
  This is the day we have waited
      for;
    we have lived to see it."

17 The LORD has done what he
planned;
he has fulfilled his word,
which he decreed long ago.
He has overthrown you
without pity,
he has let the enemy gloat
over you,
he has exalted the horn*a* of
your foes.

18 The hearts of the people
cry out to the Lord.
You walls of Daughter Zion,
let your tears flow like a
river
day and night;
give yourself no relief,
your eyes no rest.

19 Arise, cry out in the night,
as the watches of the night
begin;
pour out your heart like water
in the presence of the Lord.
Lift up your hands to him
for the lives of your children,
who faint from hunger
at every street corner.

20 "Look, LORD, and consider:
Whom have you ever treated
like this?
Should women eat their
offspring,
the children they have cared
for?
Should priest and prophet be
killed
in the sanctuary of the Lord?

21 "Young and old lie together
in the dust of the streets;
my young men and young
women
have fallen by the sword.
You have slain them in the day
of your anger;
you have slaughtered them
without pity.

22 "As you summon to a feast
day,
so you summoned against
me terrors on every side.
In the day of the LORD's
anger
no one escaped or survived;
those I cared for and reared
my enemy has destroyed."

3*b* I am the man who has seen
affliction
by the rod of the LORD's
wrath.
2 He has driven me away and
made me walk
in darkness rather than
light;
3 indeed, he has turned his
hand against me
again and again, all day
long.

4 He has made my skin and my
flesh grow old
and has broken my bones.
5 He has besieged me and
surrounded me
with bitterness and
hardship.

---

a 17 Horn here symbolizes strength.   *b* This chapter is an acrostic poem; the
verses of each stanza begin with the successive letters of the Hebrew alphabet,
and the verses within each stanza begin with the same letter.

⁶He has made me dwell in
darkness
like those long dead.

⁷He has walled me in so I
cannot escape;
he has weighed me down
with chains.
⁸Even when I call out or cry for
help,
he shuts out my prayer.
⁹He has barred my way with
blocks of stone;
he has made my paths
crooked.

¹⁰Like a bear lying in wait,
like a lion in hiding,
¹¹he dragged me from the path
and mangled me
and left me without help.
¹²He drew his bow
and made me the target for
his arrows.
¹³He pierced my heart
with arrows from his
quiver.
¹⁴I became the laughingstock of
all my people;
they mock me in song all day
long.
¹⁵He has filled me with bitter
herbs
and given me gall to drink.

¹⁶He has broken my teeth with
gravel;
he has trampled me in the
dust.
¹⁷I have been deprived of peace;
I have forgotten what
prosperity is.

¹⁸So I say, "My splendor is gone
and all that I had hoped
from the Lord."

¹⁹I remember my affliction and
my wandering,
the bitterness and the gall.
²⁰I well remember them,
and my soul is downcast
within me.
²¹Yet this I call to mind
and therefore I have hope:

²²Because of the Lord's
great love we are not
consumed,
for his compassions never
fail.
²³They are new every morning;
great is your faithfulness.
²⁴I say to myself, "The Lord is
my portion;
therefore I will wait for him."

²⁵The Lord is good to those
whose hope is in him,
to the one who seeks him;
²⁶it is good to wait quietly
for the salvation of the Lord.
²⁷It is good for a man to bear the
yoke
while he is young.

²⁸Let him sit alone in silence,
for the Lord has laid it on
him.
²⁹Let him bury his face in the
dust —
there may yet be hope.
³⁰Let him offer his cheek to one
who would strike him,
and let him be filled with
disgrace.

³¹ For no one is cast off
    by the Lord forever.
³² Though he brings grief, he will
        show compassion,
    so great is his unfailing love.
³³ For he does not willingly bring
        affliction
    or grief to anyone.

³⁴ To crush underfoot
    all prisoners in the land,
³⁵ to deny people their rights
    before the Most High,
³⁶ to deprive them of justice —
    would not the Lord see such
        things?

³⁷ Who can speak and have it
        happen
    if the Lord has not
        decreed it?
³⁸ Is it not from the mouth of the
        Most High
    that both calamities and
        good things come?
³⁹ Why should the living
        complain
    when punished for their
        sins?

⁴⁰ Let us examine our ways and
        test them,
    and let us return to the
        LORD.
⁴¹ Let us lift up our hearts and
        our hands
    to God in heaven, and say:
⁴² "We have sinned and rebelled
    and you have not forgiven.

⁴³ "You have covered yourself with
        anger and pursued us;
    you have slain without pity.

⁴⁴ You have covered yourself
        with a cloud
    so that no prayer can get
        through.
⁴⁵ You have made us scum and
        refuse
    among the nations.

⁴⁶ "All our enemies have opened
        their mouths
    wide against us.
⁴⁷ We have suffered terror and
        pitfalls,
    ruin and destruction."
⁴⁸ Streams of tears flow from my
        eyes
    because my people are
        destroyed.

⁴⁹ My eyes will flow unceasingly,
    without relief,
⁵⁰ until the LORD looks down
    from heaven and sees.
⁵¹ What I see brings grief to my
        soul
    because of all the women of
        my city.

⁵² Those who were my enemies
        without cause
    hunted me like a bird.
⁵³ They tried to end my life in a
        pit
    and threw stones at me;
⁵⁴ the waters closed over my
        head,
    and I thought I was about to
        perish.

⁵⁵ I called on your name, LORD,
    from the depths of the pit.
⁵⁶ You heard my plea: "Do not
        close your ears
    to my cry for relief."

⁵⁷You came near when I called
    you,
  and you said, "Do not fear."

⁵⁸You, Lord, took up my case;
  you redeemed my life.
⁵⁹Lord, you have seen the
    wrong done to me.
  Uphold my cause!
⁶⁰You have seen the depth of
    their vengeance,
  all their plots against me.

⁶¹Lord, you have heard their
    insults,
  all their plots against me —
⁶²what my enemies whisper and
    mutter
  against me all day long.
⁶³Look at them! Sitting or
    standing,
  they mock me in their
    songs.

⁶⁴Pay them back what they
    deserve, Lord,
  for what their hands have
    done.
⁶⁵Put a veil over their hearts,
  and may your curse be on
    them!
⁶⁶Pursue them in anger and
    destroy them
  from under the heavens of
    the Lord.

4ᵃ How the gold has lost its
    luster,
  the fine gold become dull!
  The sacred gems are scattered
    at every street corner.

²How the precious children of
    Zion,
  once worth their weight in
    gold,
  are now considered as pots of
    clay,
    the work of a potter's hands!

³Even jackals offer their breasts
    to nurse their young,
  but my people have become
    heartless
    like ostriches in the desert.

⁴Because of thirst the infant's
    tongue
  sticks to the roof of its
    mouth;
  the children beg for bread,
    but no one gives it to them.

⁵Those who once ate delicacies
  are destitute in the streets.
  Those brought up in royal
    purple
    now lie on ash heaps.

⁶The punishment of my people
  is greater than that of
    Sodom,
  which was overthrown in a
    moment
    without a hand turned to
    help her.

⁷Their princes were brighter
    than snow
  and whiter than milk,
  their bodies more ruddy than
    rubies,
    their appearance like lapis
    lazuli.

ᵃ This chapter is an acrostic poem, the verses of which begin with the successive
letters of the Hebrew alphabet.

⁸But now they are blacker than
  soot;
  they are not recognized in
    the streets.
Their skin has shriveled on
    their bones;
  it has become as dry as a
    stick.

⁹Those killed by the sword are
    better off
  than those who die of
    famine;
  racked with hunger, they
    waste away
  for lack of food from the
    field.

¹⁰With their own hands
    compassionate women
  have cooked their own
    children,
  who became their food
  when my people were
    destroyed.

¹¹The LORD has given full vent to
    his wrath;
  he has poured out his fierce
    anger.
He kindled a fire in Zion
  that consumed her
    foundations.

¹²The kings of the earth did not
    believe,
  nor did any of the peoples of
    the world,
  that enemies and foes could
    enter
  the gates of Jerusalem.

¹³But it happened because of the
    sins of her prophets
and the iniquities of her
    priests,
  who shed within her
  the blood of the righteous.

¹⁴Now they grope through the
    streets
  as if they were blind.
They are so defiled with
    blood
  that no one dares to touch
    their garments.

¹⁵"Go away! You are unclean!"
    people cry to them.
"Away! Away! Don't touch us!"
When they flee and wander
    about,
  people among the nations
    say,
  "They can stay here no
    longer."

¹⁶The LORD himself has
    scattered them;
  he no longer watches over
    them.
The priests are shown no
    honor,
  the elders no favor.

¹⁷Moreover, our eyes failed,
    looking in vain for help;
from our towers we watched
  for a nation that could not
    save us.

¹⁸People stalked us at every
    step,
  so we could not walk in our
    streets.
Our end was near, our days
    were numbered,
  for our end had come.

¹⁹Our pursuers were swifter
than eagles in the sky;
they chased us over the
mountains
and lay in wait for us in the
desert.

²⁰The LORD's anointed, our very
life breath,
was caught in their traps.
We thought that under his
shadow
we would live among the
nations.

²¹Rejoice and be glad, Daughter
Edom,
you who live in the land of Uz.
But to you also the cup will be
passed;
you will be drunk and
stripped naked.

²²Your punishment will end,
Daughter Zion;
he will not prolong your
exile.
But he will punish your sin,
Daughter Edom,
and expose your wickedness.

5 Remember, LORD, what has
happened to us;
look, and see our disgrace.
²Our inheritance has been
turned over to strangers,
our homes to foreigners.
³We have become fatherless,
our mothers are widows.
⁴We must buy the water we
drink;
our wood can be had only at
a price.

⁵Those who pursue us are at
our heels;
we are weary and find no
rest.
⁶We submitted to Egypt and
Assyria
to get enough bread.
⁷Our ancestors sinned and are
no more,
and we bear their
punishment.
⁸Slaves rule over us,
and there is no one to free us
from their hands.
⁹We get our bread at the risk of
our lives
because of the sword in the
desert.
¹⁰Our skin is hot as an oven,
feverish from hunger.
¹¹Women have been violated in
Zion,
and virgins in the towns of
Judah.
¹²Princes have been hung up by
their hands;
elders are shown no respect.
¹³Young men toil at the
millstones;
boys stagger under loads of
wood.
¹⁴The elders are gone from the
city gate;
the young men have stopped
their music.
¹⁵Joy is gone from our hearts;
our dancing has turned to
mourning.
¹⁶The crown has fallen from our
head.
Woe to us, for we have sinned!

¹⁷Because of this our hearts are
    faint,
  because of these things our
    eyes grow dim
¹⁸for Mount Zion, which lies
    desolate,
  with jackals prowling over it.

¹⁹You, LORD, reign forever;
  your throne endures from
    generation to generation.

²⁰Why do you always forget us?
  Why do you forsake us so
    long?
²¹Restore us to yourself, LORD,
  that we may return;
  renew our days as of old
²²unless you have utterly
    rejected us
  and are angry with us
    beyond measure.

Ezekiel

Introduction:

This book is named after the prophet Ezekiel, whose name means "God is strong." He wrote this message between the years 593 and 571 BC for his fellow exiles in Babylonian captivity.

Born in 623 BC to a priestly family, Ezekiel grew up in the surroundings of the temple in Jerusalem. In 597 BC he was included in a group of people taken as captives to Babylon. In 593 BC God called him in a divine revelation to be a prophet.

During the first part of his ministry, Ezekiel proclaimed a message similar to Jeremiah's — Jerusalem and the temple were doomed to destruction because of the sinfulness and idolatry of the people.

After the news reached Babylon that Jerusalem actually had been destroyed in 586 BC, Ezekiel proclaimed a new message of hope and restoration — God would re-gather the Israelites from the ends of the earth and re-establish them in their own land. The nations who challenged Israel's return would be defeated and judged.

Outline of contents:

Ezekiel's call (1:1–3:27)
Jerusalem's sinful condition and doom (4:1–24:27)
Foreign nations in prophecy (25:1–32:32)
Hopes for restoration (33:1–39:29)
Israel restored to Palestine (40:1–48:35)

Ezekiel's Inaugural Vision

1 In my thirtieth year, in the fourth month on the fifth day, while I was among the exiles by the Kebar River, the heavens were opened and I saw visions of God.

²On the fifth of the month — it was the fifth year of the exile of King Jehoiachin — ³the word of the LORD came to Ezekiel the priest, the son of Buzi, by the Kebar River in the land of the Babylonians.ᵃ There the hand of the LORD was on him.

⁴I looked, and I saw a windstorm coming out of the north — an immense cloud with flashing lightning and surrounded by brilliant light. The center of the

---

ᵃ 3 Or *Chaldeans*

fire looked like glowing metal, [5] and in the fire was what looked like four living creatures. In appearance their form was human, [6] but each of them had four faces and four wings. [7] Their legs were straight; their feet were like those of a calf and gleamed like burnished bronze. [8] Under their wings on their four sides they had human hands. All four of them had faces and wings, [9] and the wings of one touched the wings of another. Each one went straight ahead; they did not turn as they moved.

[10] Their faces looked like this: Each of the four had the face of a human being, and on the right side each had the face of a lion, and on the left the face of an ox; each also had the face of an eagle. [11] Such were their faces. They each had two wings spreading out upward, each wing touching that of the creature on either side; and each had two other wings covering its body. [12] Each one went straight ahead. Wherever the spirit would go, they would go, without turning as they went. [13] The appearance of the living creatures was like burning coals of fire or like torches. Fire moved back and forth among the creatures; it was bright, and lightning flashed out of it. [14] The creatures sped back and forth like flashes of lightning.

[15] As I looked at the living creatures, I saw a wheel on the ground beside each creature with its four faces. [16] This was the appearance and structure of the wheels: They sparkled like topaz, and all four looked alike. Each appeared to be made like a wheel intersecting a wheel. [17] As they moved, they would go in any one of the four directions the creatures faced; the wheels did not change direction as the creatures went. [18] Their rims were high and awesome, and all four rims were full of eyes all around.

[19] When the living creatures moved, the wheels beside them moved; and when the living creatures rose from the ground, the wheels also rose. [20] Wherever the spirit would go, they would go, and the wheels would rise along with them, because the spirit of the living creatures was in the wheels. [21] When the creatures moved, they also moved; when the creatures stood still, they also stood still; and when the creatures rose from the ground, the wheels rose along with them, because the spirit of the living creatures was in the wheels.

[22] Spread out above the heads of the living creatures was what looked something like a vault, sparkling like crystal, and awesome. [23] Under the vault their wings were stretched out one toward the other, and each had two wings covering its body. [24] When the creatures moved, I heard the sound of their wings, like the roar

of rushing waters, like the voice of the Almighty,[a] like the tumult of an army. When they stood still, they lowered their wings.

25 Then there came a voice from above the vault over their heads as they stood with lowered wings. 26 Above the vault over their heads was what looked like a throne of lapis lazuli, and high above on the throne was a figure like that of a man. 27 I saw that from what appeared to be his waist up he looked like glowing metal, as if full of fire, and that from there down he looked like fire; and brilliant light surrounded him. 28 Like the appearance of a rainbow in the clouds on a rainy day, so was the radiance around him.

This was the appearance of the likeness of the glory of the LORD. When I saw it, I fell facedown, and I heard the voice of one speaking.

Ezekiel's Call to Be a Prophet

2 He said to me, "Son of man,[b] stand up on your feet and I will speak to you." 2 As he spoke, the Spirit came into me and raised me to my feet, and I heard him speaking to me.

3 He said: "Son of man, I am sending you to the Israelites, to a rebellious nation that has rebelled against me; they and their ances-

tors have been in revolt against me to this very day. 4 The people to whom I am sending you are obstinate and stubborn. Say to them, 'This is what the Sovereign LORD says.' 5 And whether they listen or fail to listen — for they are a rebellious people — they will know that a prophet has been among them. 6 And you, son of man, do not be afraid of them or their words. Do not be afraid, though briers and thorns are all around you and you live among scorpions. Do not be afraid of what they say or be terrified by them, though they are a rebellious people. 7 You must speak my words to them, whether they listen or fail to listen, for they are rebellious. 8 But you, son of man, listen to what I say to you. Do not rebel like that rebellious people; open your mouth and eat what I give you."

9 Then I looked, and I saw a hand stretched out to me. In it was a scroll, 10 which he unrolled before me. On both sides of it were written words of lament and mourning and woe.

3 And he said to me, "Son of man, eat what is before you, eat this scroll; then go and speak to the people of Israel." 2 So I opened my mouth, and he gave me the scroll to eat.

3 Then he said to me, "Son of man, eat this scroll I am giving

---

[a] 24 Hebrew *Shaddai*   [b] 1 The Hebrew phrase *ben adam* means *human being*. The phrase *son of man* is retained as a form of address here and throughout Ezekiel because of its possible association with "Son of Man" in the New Testament.

you and fill your stomach with it." So I ate it, and it tasted as sweet as honey in my mouth.

⁴He then said to me: "Son of man, go now to the people of Israel and speak my words to them. ⁵You are not being sent to a people of obscure speech and strange language, but to the people of Israel— ⁶not to many peoples of obscure speech and strange language, whose words you cannot understand. Surely if I had sent you to them, they would have listened to you. ⁷But the people of Israel are not willing to listen to you because they are not willing to listen to me, for all the Israelites are hardened and obstinate. ⁸But I will make you as unyielding and hardened as they are. ⁹I will make your forehead like the hardest stone, harder than flint. Do not be afraid of them or terrified by them, though they are a rebellious people."

¹⁰And he said to me, "Son of man, listen carefully and take to heart all the words I speak to you. ¹¹Go now to your people in exile and speak to them. Say to them, 'This is what the Sovereign LORD says,' whether they listen or fail to listen."

¹²Then the Spirit lifted me up, and I heard behind me a loud rumbling sound as the glory of the LORD rose from the place where it was standing.ᵃ ¹³It was the sound of the wings of the living creatures brushing against each other and the sound of the wheels beside them, a loud rumbling sound. ¹⁴The Spirit then lifted me up and took me away, and I went in bitterness and in the anger of my spirit, with the strong hand of the LORD on me. ¹⁵I came to the exiles who lived at Tel Aviv near the Kebar River. And there, where they were living, I sat among them for seven days—deeply distressed.

Ezekiel's Task as Watchman

¹⁶At the end of seven days the word of the LORD came to me: ¹⁷"Son of man, I have made you a watchman for the people of Israel; so hear the word I speak and give them warning from me. ¹⁸When I say to a wicked person, 'You will surely die,' and you do not warn them or speak out to dissuade them from their evil ways in order to save their life, that wicked person will die forᵇ their sin, and I will hold you accountable for their blood. ¹⁹But if you do warn the wicked person and they do not turn from their wickedness or from their evil ways, they will die for their sin; but you will have saved yourself.

²⁰"Again, when a righteous person turns from their righteousness and does evil, and I put a stumbling block before them,

---

ᵃ 12 Probable reading of the original Hebrew text; Masoretic Text *sound—may the glory of the* LORD *be praised from his place*   ᵇ 18 Or *in*; also in verses 19 and 20 they will die. Since you did not warn them, they will die for their sin. The righteous things that person did will not be remembered, and I will hold you accountable for their blood. ²¹But if you do warn the righteous person not to sin and they do not sin, they will surely live because they took warning, and you will have saved yourself."

²²The hand of the LORD was on me there, and he said to me, "Get up and go out to the plain, and there I will speak to you." ²³So I got up and went out to the plain. And the glory of the LORD was standing there, like the glory I had seen by the Kebar River, and I fell facedown.

²⁴Then the Spirit came into me and raised me to my feet. He spoke to me and said: "Go, shut yourself inside your house. ²⁵And you, son of man, they will tie with ropes; you will be bound so that you cannot go out among the people. ²⁶I will make your tongue stick to the roof of your mouth so that you will be silent and unable to rebuke them, for they are a rebellious people. ²⁷But when I speak to you, I will open your mouth and you shall say to them, 'This is what the Sovereign LORD says.' Whoever will listen let them listen, and whoever will refuse let them refuse; for they are a rebellious people.

Siege of Jerusalem Symbolized

4 "Now, son of man, take a block of clay, put it in front of you and draw the city of Jerusalem on it. ²Then lay siege to it: Erect siege works against it, build a ramp up to it, set up camps against it and put battering rams around it. ³Then take an iron pan, place it as an iron wall between you and the city and turn your face toward it. It will be under siege, and you shall besiege it. This will be a sign to the people of Israel.

⁴"Then lie on your left side and put the sin of the people of Israel upon yourself.ᵃ You are to bear their sin for the number of days you lie on your side. ⁵I have assigned you the same number of days as the years of their sin. So for 390 days you will bear the sin of the people of Israel.

⁶"After you have finished this, lie down again, this time on your right side, and bear the sin of the people of Judah. I have assigned you 40 days, a day for each year. ⁷Turn your face toward the siege of Jerusalem and with bared arm prophesy against her. ⁸I will tie you up with ropes so that you cannot turn from one side to the other until you have finished the days of your siege.

⁹"Take wheat and barley, beans and lentils, millet and spelt; put them in a storage jar and use them to make bread for yourself. You

ᵃ 4 Or upon your side

are to eat it during the 390 days you lie on your side. **¹⁰**Weigh out twenty shekels*ᵃ* of food to eat each day and eat it at set times. **¹¹**Also measure out a sixth of a hin*ᵇ* of water and drink it at set times. **¹²**Eat the food as you would a loaf of barley bread; bake it in the sight of the people, using human excrement for fuel." **¹³**The LORD said, "In this way the people of Israel will eat defiled food among the nations where I will drive them."

¹⁴Then I said, "Not so, Sovereign LORD! I have never defiled myself. From my youth until now I have never eaten anything found dead or torn by wild animals. No impure meat has ever entered my mouth."

¹⁵"Very well," he said, "I will let you bake your bread over cow dung instead of human excrement."

¹⁶He then said to me: "Son of man, I am about to cut off the food supply in Jerusalem. The people will eat rationed food in anxiety and drink rationed water in despair, **¹⁷**for food and water will be scarce. They will be appalled at the sight of each other and will waste away because of*ᶜ* their sin.

God's Razor of Judgment

5 "Now, son of man, take a sharp sword and use it as a barber's razor to shave your head and your beard. Then take a set of scales and divide up the hair. **²**When the days of your siege come to an end, burn a third of the hair inside the city. Take a third and strike it with the sword all around the city. And scatter a third to the wind. For I will pursue them with drawn sword. **³**But take a few hairs and tuck them away in the folds of your garment. **⁴**Again, take a few of these and throw them into the fire and burn them up. A fire will spread from there to all Israel.

⁵"This is what the Sovereign LORD says: This is Jerusalem, which I have set in the center of the nations, with countries all around her. **⁶**Yet in her wickedness she has rebelled against my laws and decrees more than the nations and countries around her. She has rejected my laws and has not followed my decrees.

⁷"Therefore this is what the Sovereign LORD says: You have been more unruly than the nations around you and have not followed my decrees or kept my laws. You have not even*ᵈ* conformed to the standards of the nations around you.

⁸"Therefore this is what the Sovereign LORD says: I myself am against you, Jerusalem, and I will inflict punishment on you in the sight of the nations. **⁹**Because of

---

ᵃ **10** That is, about 8 ounces or about 230 grams   *ᵇ* **11** That is, about 2/3 quart or about 0.6 liter   *ᶜ* **17** Or *away in*   *ᵈ* **7** Most Hebrew manuscripts; some Hebrew manuscripts and Syriac *You have* all your detestable idols, I will do to you what I have never done before and will never do again. ¹⁰Therefore in your midst parents will eat their children, and children will eat their parents. I will inflict punishment on you and will scatter all your survivors to the winds. ¹¹Therefore as surely as I live, declares the Sovereign LORD, because you have defiled my sanctuary with all your vile images and detestable practices, I myself will shave you; I will not look on you with pity or spare you. ¹²A third of your people will die of the plague or perish by famine inside you; a third will fall by the sword outside your walls; and a third I will scatter to the winds and pursue with drawn sword.

¹³"Then my anger will cease and my wrath against them will subside, and I will be avenged. And when I have spent my wrath on them, they will know that I the LORD have spoken in my zeal.

¹⁴"I will make you a ruin and a reproach among the nations around you, in the sight of all who pass by. ¹⁵You will be a reproach and a taunt, a warning and an object of horror to the nations around you when I inflict punishment on you in anger and in wrath and with stinging rebuke. I the LORD have spoken. ¹⁶When I shoot at you with my deadly and destructive arrows of famine, I will shoot to destroy you. I will bring more and more famine upon you and cut off your supply of food. ¹⁷I will send famine and wild beasts against you, and they will leave you childless. Plague and bloodshed will sweep through you, and I will bring the sword against you. I the LORD have spoken."

Doom for the Mountains of Israel

6 The word of the LORD came to me: ²"Son of man, set your face against the mountains of Israel; prophesy against them ³and say: 'You mountains of Israel, hear the word of the Sovereign LORD. This is what the Sovereign LORD says to the mountains and hills, to the ravines and valleys: I am about to bring a sword against you, and I will destroy your high places. ⁴Your altars will be demolished and your incense altars will be smashed; and I will slay your people in front of your idols. ⁵I will lay the dead bodies of the Israelites in front of their idols, and I will scatter your bones around your altars. ⁶Wherever you live, the towns will be laid waste and the high places demolished, so that your altars will be laid waste and devastated, your idols smashed and ruined, your incense altars broken down, and what you have made wiped out. ⁷Your people will fall slain among you, and you will know that I am the LORD.

8 " 'But I will spare some, for some of you will escape the sword when you are scattered among the lands and nations. 9Then in the nations where they have been carried captive, those who escape will remember me — how I have been grieved by their adulterous hearts, which have turned away from me, and by their eyes, which have lusted after their idols. They will loathe themselves for the evil they have done and for all their detestable practices. 10And they will know that I am the LORD; I did not threaten in vain to bring this calamity on them.

11 " 'This is what the Sovereign LORD says: Strike your hands together and stamp your feet and cry out "Alas!" because of all the wicked and detestable practices of the people of Israel, for they will fall by the sword, famine and plague. 12One who is far away will die of the plague, and one who is near will fall by the sword, and anyone who survives and is spared will die of famine. So will I pour out my wrath on them. 13And they will know that I am the LORD, when their people lie slain among their idols around their altars, on every high hill and on all the mountaintops, under every spreading tree and every leafy oak — places where they offered fragrant incense to all their idols. 14And I will stretch out my hand against them and make the land a desolate waste from the desert to Diblah[a] — wherever they live. Then they will know that I am the LORD.' "

The End Has Come

7 The word of the LORD came to me: 2"Son of man, this is what the Sovereign LORD says to the land of Israel:

" 'The end! The end has come
    upon the four corners of the
    land!
3The end is now upon you,
    and I will unleash my anger
        against you.
I will judge you according to
        your conduct
    and repay you for all your
        detestable practices.
4I will not look on you with pity;
    I will not spare you.
I will surely repay you for your
        conduct
    and for the detestable
        practices among you.

" 'Then you will know that I am the LORD.'

5"This is what the Sovereign LORD says:

" 'Disaster! Unheard-of[b]
        disaster!
    See, it comes!
6The end has come!
    The end has come!

---

a 14 Most Hebrew manuscripts; a few Hebrew manuscripts *Riblah*   b 5 Most Hebrew manuscripts; some Hebrew manuscripts and Syriac *Disaster after*

It has roused itself against you.
See, it comes!
7 Doom has come upon you,
upon you who dwell in the
land.
The time has come! The day is
near!
There is panic, not joy, on
the mountains.
8 I am about to pour out my
wrath on you
and spend my anger against
you.
I will judge you according to
your conduct
and repay you for all your
detestable practices.
9 I will not look on you with
pity;
I will not spare you.
I will repay you for your
conduct
and for the detestable
practices among you.

" 'Then you will know that it is I
the LORD who strikes you.

10 " 'See, the day!
See, it comes!
Doom has burst forth,
the rod has budded,
arrogance has blossomed!
11 Violence has arisen,*a*
a rod to punish the wicked.
None of the people will be left,
none of that crowd —
none of their wealth,
nothing of value.
12 The time has come!
The day has arrived!

Let not the buyer rejoice
nor the seller grieve,
for my wrath is on the whole
crowd.
13 The seller will not recover
the property that was sold —
as long as both buyer and
seller live.
For the vision concerning the
whole crowd
will not be reversed.
Because of their sins, not one
of them
will preserve their life.

14 " 'They have blown the
trumpet,
they have made all things
ready,
but no one will go into battle,
for my wrath is on the whole
crowd.
15 Outside is the sword;
inside are plague and
famine.
Those in the country
will die by the sword;
those in the city
will be devoured by famine
and plague.
16 The fugitives who escape
will flee to the mountains.
Like doves of the valleys,
they will all moan,
each for their own sins.
17 Every hand will go limp;
every leg will be wet with
urine.
18 They will put on sackcloth
and be clothed with terror.

---

a 11 Or The violent one has become

Every face will be covered with
shame,
and every head will be
shaved.

19 " 'They will throw their silver
into the streets,
and their gold will be treated
as a thing unclean.
Their silver and gold
will not be able to deliver
them
in the day of the LORD's
wrath.
It will not satisfy their hunger
or fill their stomachs,
for it has caused them to
stumble into sin.
20 They took pride in their
beautiful jewelry
and used it to make their
detestable idols.
They made it into vile images;
therefore I will make it a
thing unclean for them.
21 I will give their wealth as
plunder to foreigners
and as loot to the wicked of
the earth,
who will defile it.
22 I will turn my face away from
the people,
and robbers will desecrate
the place I treasure.
They will enter it
and will defile it.

23 " 'Prepare chains!
For the land is full of
bloodshed,
and the city is full of
violence.

24 I will bring the most wicked of
nations
to take possession of their
houses.
I will put an end to the pride of
the mighty,
and their sanctuaries will be
desecrated.
25 When terror comes,
they will seek peace in
vain.
26 Calamity upon calamity will
come,
and rumor upon rumor.
They will go searching for a
vision from the prophet,
priestly instruction in the
law will cease,
the counsel of the elders will
come to an end.
27 The king will mourn,
the prince will be clothed
with despair,
and the hands of the people
of the land will tremble.
I will deal with them
according to their
conduct,
and by their own standards I
will judge them.

" 'Then they will know that I am
the LORD.' "

Idolatry in the Temple

8 In the sixth year, in the sixth
month on the fifth day, while
I was sitting in my house and the
elders of Judah were sitting before me, the hand of the Sovereign LORD came on me there. 2 I
looked, and I saw a figure like

that of a man.[a] From what appeared to be his waist down he was like fire, and from there up his appearance was as bright as glowing metal. ³He stretched out what looked like a hand and took me by the hair of my head. The Spirit lifted me up between earth and heaven and in visions of God he took me to Jerusalem, to the entrance of the north gate of the inner court, where the idol that provokes to jealousy stood. ⁴And there before me was the glory of the God of Israel, as in the vision I had seen in the plain.

⁵Then he said to me, "Son of man, look toward the north." So I looked, and in the entrance north of the gate of the altar I saw this idol of jealousy.

⁶And he said to me, "Son of man, do you see what they are doing—the utterly detestable things the Israelites are doing here, things that will drive me far from my sanctuary? But you will see things that are even more detestable."

⁷Then he brought me to the entrance to the court. I looked, and I saw a hole in the wall. ⁸He said to me, "Son of man, now dig into the wall." So I dug into the wall and saw a doorway there.

⁹And he said to me, "Go in and see the wicked and detestable things they are doing here." ¹⁰So I went in and looked, and I saw portrayed all over the walls all kinds of crawling things and unclean animals and all the idols of Israel. ¹¹In front of them stood seventy elders of Israel, and Jaazaniah son of Shaphan was standing among them. Each had a censer in his hand, and a fragrant cloud of incense was rising.

¹²He said to me, "Son of man, have you seen what the elders of Israel are doing in the darkness, each at the shrine of his own idol? They say, 'The LORD does not see us; the LORD has forsaken the land.'" ¹³Again, he said, "You will see them doing things that are even more detestable."

¹⁴Then he brought me to the entrance of the north gate of the house of the LORD, and I saw women sitting there, mourning the god Tammuz. ¹⁵He said to me, "Do you see this, son of man? You will see things that are even more detestable than this."

¹⁶He then brought me into the inner court of the house of the LORD, and there at the entrance to the temple, between the portico and the altar, were about twenty-five men. With their backs toward the temple of the LORD and their faces toward the east, they were bowing down to the sun in the east.

¹⁷He said to me, "Have you seen this, son of man? Is it a trivial matter for the people of Judah to do the detestable things they are doing here? Must they also fill

a 2 Or *saw a fiery figure*

the land with violence and continually arouse my anger? Look at them putting the branch to their nose! [18]Therefore I will deal with them in anger; I will not look on them with pity or spare them. Although they shout in my ears, I will not listen to them."

Judgment on the Idolaters

9 Then I heard him call out in a loud voice, "Bring near those who are appointed to execute judgment on the city, each with a weapon in his hand." [2]And I saw six men coming from the direction of the upper gate, which faces north, each with a deadly weapon in his hand. With them was a man clothed in linen who had a writing kit at his side. They came in and stood beside the bronze altar.

[3]Now the glory of the God of Israel went up from above the cherubim, where it had been, and moved to the threshold of the temple. Then the LORD called to the man clothed in linen who had the writing kit at his side [4]and said to him, "Go throughout the city of Jerusalem and put a mark on the foreheads of those who grieve and lament over all the detestable things that are done in it."

[5]As I listened, he said to the others, "Follow him through the city and kill, without showing pity or compassion. [6]Slaughter the old men, the young men and women, the mothers and children, but do not touch anyone who has the mark. Begin at my sanctuary." So they began with the old men who were in front of the temple.

[7]Then he said to them, "Defile the temple and fill the courts with the slain. Go!" So they went out and began killing throughout the city. [8]While they were killing and I was left alone, I fell facedown, crying out, "Alas, Sovereign LORD! Are you going to destroy the entire remnant of Israel in this outpouring of your wrath on Jerusalem?"

[9]He answered me, "The sin of the people of Israel and Judah is exceedingly great; the land is full of bloodshed and the city is full of injustice. They say, 'The LORD has forsaken the land; the LORD does not see.' [10]So I will not look on them with pity or spare them, but I will bring down on their own heads what they have done."

[11]Then the man in linen with the writing kit at his side brought back word, saying, "I have done as you commanded."

God's Glory Departs From the Temple

10 I looked, and I saw the likeness of a throne of lapis lazuli above the vault that was over the heads of the cherubim. [2]The LORD said to the man clothed in linen, "Go in among the wheels beneath the

cherubim. Fill your hands with burning coals from among the cherubim and scatter them over the city." And as I watched, he went in.

³Now the cherubim were standing on the south side of the temple when the man went in, and a cloud filled the inner court. ⁴Then the glory of the LORD rose from above the cherubim and moved to the threshold of the temple. The cloud filled the temple, and the court was full of the radiance of the glory of the LORD. ⁵The sound of the wings of the cherubim could be heard as far away as the outer court, like the voice of God Almighty*a* when he speaks.

⁶When the LORD commanded the man in linen, "Take fire from among the wheels, from among the cherubim," the man went in and stood beside a wheel. ⁷Then one of the cherubim reached out his hand to the fire that was among them. He took up some of it and put it into the hands of the man in linen, who took it and went out. ⁸(Under the wings of the cherubim could be seen what looked like human hands.)

⁹I looked, and I saw beside the cherubim four wheels, one beside each of the cherubim; the wheels sparkled like topaz. ¹⁰As for their appearance, the four of them looked alike; each was like a wheel intersecting a wheel.

¹¹As they moved, they would go in any one of the four directions the cherubim faced; the wheels did not turn about*b* as the cherubim went. The cherubim went in whatever direction the head faced, without turning as they went. ¹²Their entire bodies, including their backs, their hands and their wings, were completely full of eyes, as were their four wheels. ¹³I heard the wheels being called "the whirling wheels." ¹⁴Each of the cherubim had four faces: One face was that of a cherub, the second the face of a human being, the third the face of a lion, and the fourth the face of an eagle.

¹⁵Then the cherubim rose upward. These were the living creatures I had seen by the Kebar River. ¹⁶When the cherubim moved, the wheels beside them moved; and when the cherubim spread their wings to rise from the ground, the wheels did not leave their side. ¹⁷When the cherubim stood still, they also stood still; and when the cherubim rose, they rose with them, because the spirit of the living creatures was in them.

¹⁸Then the glory of the LORD departed from over the threshold of the temple and stopped above the cherubim. ¹⁹While I watched, the cherubim spread their wings and rose from the ground, and as they went, the wheels went

---

a 5 Hebrew *El-Shaddai*   *b 11* Or *aside*

with them. They stopped at the entrance of the east gate of the LORD's house, and the glory of the God of Israel was above them.

²⁰These were the living creatures I had seen beneath the God of Israel by the Kebar River, and I realized that they were cherubim. ²¹Each had four faces and four wings, and under their wings was what looked like human hands. ²²Their faces had the same appearance as those I had seen by the Kebar River. Each one went straight ahead.

God's Sure Judgment on Jerusalem

11 Then the Spirit lifted me up and brought me to the gate of the house of the LORD that faces east. There at the entrance of the gate were twenty-five men, and I saw among them Jaazaniah son of Azzur and Pelatiah son of Benaiah, leaders of the people. ²The LORD said to me, "Son of man, these are the men who are plotting evil and giving wicked advice in this city. ³They say, 'Haven't our houses been recently rebuilt? This city is a pot, and we are the meat in it.' ⁴Therefore prophesy against them; prophesy, son of man."

⁵Then the Spirit of the LORD came on me, and he told me to say: "This is what the LORD says: That is what you are saying, you leaders in Israel, but I know what is going through your mind. ⁶You have killed many people in this city and filled its streets with the dead.

⁷"Therefore this is what the Sovereign LORD says: The bodies you have thrown there are the meat and this city is the pot, but I will drive you out of it. ⁸You fear the sword, and the sword is what I will bring against you, declares the Sovereign LORD. ⁹I will drive you out of the city and deliver you into the hands of foreigners and inflict punishment on you. ¹⁰You will fall by the sword, and I will execute judgment on you at the borders of Israel. Then you will know that I am the LORD. ¹¹This city will not be a pot for you, nor will you be the meat in it; I will execute judgment on you at the borders of Israel. ¹²And you will know that I am the LORD, for you have not followed my decrees or kept my laws but have conformed to the standards of the nations around you."

¹³Now as I was prophesying, Pelatiah son of Benaiah died. Then I fell facedown and cried out in a loud voice, "Alas, Sovereign LORD! Will you completely destroy the remnant of Israel?"

The Promise of Israel's Return

¹⁴The word of the LORD came to me: ¹⁵"Son of man, the people of Jerusalem have said of your fellow exiles and all the other Israelites, 'They are far away from the LORD; this land was given to us as our possession.'

¹⁶ "Therefore say: 'This is what the Sovereign LORD says: Although I sent them far away among the nations and scattered them among the countries, yet for a little while I have been a sanctuary for them in the countries where they have gone.'

¹⁷ "Therefore say: 'This is what the Sovereign LORD says: I will gather you from the nations and bring you back from the countries where you have been scattered, and I will give you back the land of Israel again.'

¹⁸ "They will return to it and remove all its vile images and detestable idols. ¹⁹ I will give them an undivided heart and put a new spirit in them; I will remove from them their heart of stone and give them a heart of flesh. ²⁰ Then they will follow my decrees and be careful to keep my laws. They will be my people, and I will be their God. ²¹ But as for those whose hearts are devoted to their vile images and detestable idols, I will bring down on their own heads what they have done, declares the Sovereign LORD."

²² Then the cherubim, with the wheels beside them, spread their wings, and the glory of the God of Israel was above them. ²³ The glory of the LORD went up from within the city and stopped above the mountain east of it. ²⁴ The Spirit lifted me up and brought me to the exiles in Babylonia*ᵃ* in the vision given by the Spirit of God.

Then the vision I had seen went up from me, ²⁵ and I told the exiles everything the LORD had shown me.

The Exile Symbolized

12 The word of the LORD came to me: ²"Son of man, you are living among a rebellious people. They have eyes to see but do not see and ears to hear but do not hear, for they are a rebellious people.

³ "Therefore, son of man, pack your belongings for exile and in the daytime, as they watch, set out and go from where you are to another place. Perhaps they will understand, though they are a rebellious people. ⁴ During the daytime, while they watch, bring out your belongings packed for exile. Then in the evening, while they are watching, go out like those who go into exile. ⁵ While they watch, dig through the wall and take your belongings out through it. ⁶ Put them on your shoulder as they are watching and carry them out at dusk. Cover your face so that you cannot see the land, for I have made you a sign to the Israelites."

⁷ So I did as I was commanded. During the day I brought out my things packed for exile. Then in the evening I dug through the wall with my hands. I took my

---

ᵃ 24 Or *Chaldea*

belongings out at dusk, carrying them on my shoulders while they watched.

[8] In the morning the word of the LORD came to me: [9] "Son of man, did not the Israelites, that rebellious people, ask you, 'What are you doing?'

[10] "Say to them, 'This is what the Sovereign LORD says: This prophecy concerns the prince in Jerusalem and all the Israelites who are there.' [11] Say to them, 'I am a sign to you.'

"As I have done, so it will be done to them. They will go into exile as captives.

[12] "The prince among them will put his things on his shoulder at dusk and leave, and a hole will be dug in the wall for him to go through. He will cover his face so that he cannot see the land. [13] I will spread my net for him, and he will be caught in my snare; I will bring him to Babylonia, the land of the Chaldeans, but he will not see it, and there he will die. [14] I will scatter to the winds all those around him — his staff and all his troops — and I will pursue them with drawn sword.

[15] "They will know that I am the LORD, when I disperse them among the nations and scatter them through the countries. [16] But I will spare a few of them from the sword, famine and plague, so that in the nations where they go they may acknowledge all their detestable practices. Then they will know that I am the LORD."

[17] The word of the LORD came to me: [18] "Son of man, tremble as you eat your food, and shudder in fear as you drink your water. [19] Say to the people of the land: 'This is what the Sovereign LORD says about those living in Jerusalem and in the land of Israel: They will eat their food in anxiety and drink their water in despair, for their land will be stripped of everything in it because of the violence of all who live there. [20] The inhabited towns will be laid waste and the land will be desolate. Then you will know that I am the LORD.' "

There Will Be No Delay

[21] The word of the LORD came to me: [22] "Son of man, what is this proverb you have in the land of Israel: 'The days go by and every vision comes to nothing'? [23] Say to them, 'This is what the Sovereign LORD says: I am going to put an end to this proverb, and they will no longer quote it in Israel.' Say to them, 'The days are near when every vision will be fulfilled. [24] For there will be no more false visions or flattering divinations among the people of Israel. [25] But I the LORD will speak what I will, and it shall be fulfilled without delay. For in your days, you rebellious people, I will fulfill whatever I say, declares the Sovereign LORD.' "

²⁶The word of the LORD came to me: ²⁷"Son of man, the Israelites are saying, 'The vision he sees is for many years from now, and he prophesies about the distant future.'

²⁸"Therefore say to them, 'This is what the Sovereign LORD says: None of my words will be delayed any longer; whatever I say will be fulfilled, declares the Sovereign LORD.'"

False Prophets Condemned

13 The word of the LORD came to me: ²"Son of man, prophesy against the prophets of Israel who are now prophesying. Say to those who prophesy out of their own imagination: 'Hear the word of the LORD! ³This is what the Sovereign LORD says: Woe to the foolish*ᵃ* prophets who follow their own spirit and have seen nothing! ⁴Your prophets, Israel, are like jackals among ruins. ⁵You have not gone up to the breaches in the wall to repair it for the people of Israel so that it will stand firm in the battle on the day of the LORD. ⁶Their visions are false and their divinations a lie. Even though the LORD has not sent them, they say, "The LORD declares," and expect him to fulfill their words. ⁷Have you not seen false visions and uttered lying divinations when you say, "The LORD declares," though I have not spoken?

⁸"'Therefore this is what the Sovereign LORD says: Because of your false words and lying visions, I am against you, declares the Sovereign LORD. ⁹My hand will be against the prophets who see false visions and utter lying divinations. They will not belong to the council of my people or be listed in the records of Israel, nor will they enter the land of Israel. Then you will know that I am the Sovereign LORD.

¹⁰"'Because they lead my people astray, saying, "Peace," when there is no peace, and because, when a flimsy wall is built, they cover it with whitewash, ¹¹therefore tell those who cover it with whitewash that it is going to fall. Rain will come in torrents, and I will send hailstones hurtling down, and violent winds will burst forth. ¹²When the wall collapses, will people not ask you, "Where is the whitewash you covered it with?"

¹³"'Therefore this is what the Sovereign LORD says: In my wrath I will unleash a violent wind, and in my anger hailstones and torrents of rain will fall with destructive fury. ¹⁴I will tear down the wall you have covered with whitewash and will level it to the ground so that its foundation will be laid bare. When it*ᵇ* falls, you will be destroyed in it; and you will know that I am the LORD. ¹⁵So I will pour out

---

ᵃ 3 Or *wicked*   *ᵇ 14* Or *the city*

my wrath against the wall and against those who covered it with whitewash. I will say to you, "The wall is gone and so are those who whitewashed it, ¹⁶those prophets of Israel who prophesied to Jerusalem and saw visions of peace for her when there was no peace, declares the Sovereign LORD." '

¹⁷"Now, son of man, set your face against the daughters of your people who prophesy out of their own imagination. Prophesy against them ¹⁸and say, 'This is what the Sovereign LORD says: Woe to the women who sew magic charms on all their wrists and make veils of various lengths for their heads in order to ensnare people. Will you ensnare the lives of my people but preserve your own? ¹⁹You have profaned me among my people for a few handfuls of barley and scraps of bread. By lying to my people, who listen to lies, you have killed those who should not have died and have spared those who should not live.

²⁰" 'Therefore this is what the Sovereign LORD says: I am against your magic charms with which you ensnare people like birds and I will tear them from your arms; I will set free the people that you ensnare like birds. ²¹I will tear off your veils and save my people from your hands, and they will no longer fall prey to your power. Then you will know that I am the LORD. ²²Because you disheartened the righteous with your lies, when I had brought them no grief, and because you encouraged the wicked not to turn from their evil ways and so save their lives, ²³therefore you will no longer see false visions or practice divination. I will save my people from your hands. And then you will know that I am the LORD.' "

Idolaters Condemned

14 Some of the elders of Israel came to me and sat down in front of me. ²Then the word of the LORD came to me: ³"Son of man, these men have set up idols in their hearts and put wicked stumbling blocks before their faces. Should I let them inquire of me at all? ⁴Therefore speak to them and tell them, 'This is what the Sovereign LORD says: When any of the Israelites set up idols in their hearts and put a wicked stumbling block before their faces and then go to a prophet, I the LORD will answer them myself in keeping with their great idolatry. ⁵I will do this to recapture the hearts of the people of Israel, who have all deserted me for their idols.'

⁶"Therefore say to the people of Israel, 'This is what the Sovereign LORD says: Repent! Turn from your idols and renounce all your detestable practices!

⁷" 'When any of the Israelites or any foreigner residing in Israel separate themselves from me

and set up idols in their hearts and put a wicked stumbling block before their faces and then go to a prophet to inquire of me, I the LORD will answer them myself. **8** I will set my face against them and make them an example and a byword. I will remove them from my people. Then you will know that I am the LORD.

9 " 'And if the prophet is enticed to utter a prophecy, I the LORD have enticed that prophet, and I will stretch out my hand against him and destroy him from among my people Israel. **10** They will bear their guilt — the prophet will be as guilty as the one who consults him. **11** Then the people of Israel will no longer stray from me, nor will they defile themselves anymore with all their sins. They will be my people, and I will be their God, declares the Sovereign LORD.' "

Jerusalem's Judgment Inescapable

12 The word of the LORD came to me: **13** "Son of man, if a country sins against me by being unfaithful and I stretch out my hand against it to cut off its food supply and send famine upon it and kill its people and their animals, **14** even if these three men — Noah, Daniel[a] and Job — were in it, they could save only themselves by their righteousness, declares the Sovereign LORD.

15 "Or if I send wild beasts through that country and they leave it childless and it becomes desolate so that no one can pass through it because of the beasts, **16** as surely as I live, declares the Sovereign LORD, even if these three men were in it, they could not save their own sons or daughters. They alone would be saved, but the land would be desolate.

17 "Or if I bring a sword against that country and say, 'Let the sword pass throughout the land,' and I kill its people and their animals, **18** as surely as I live, declares the Sovereign LORD, even if these three men were in it, they could not save their own sons or daughters. They alone would be saved.

19 "Or if I send a plague into that land and pour out my wrath on it through bloodshed, killing its people and their animals, **20** as surely as I live, declares the Sovereign LORD, even if Noah, Daniel and Job were in it, they could save neither son nor daughter. They would save only themselves by their righteousness.

21 "For this is what the Sovereign LORD says: How much worse will it be when I send against Jerusalem my four dreadful judgments — sword and famine and wild beasts and plague — to kill its men and their animals! **22** Yet there will be some survivors — sons and daughters who will be

---

a 14 Or *Danel*, a man of renown in ancient literature; also in verse 20 brought out of it. They will come to you, and when you see their conduct and their actions, you will be consoled regarding the disaster I have brought on Jerusalem — every disaster I have brought on it. 23 You will be consoled when you see their conduct and their actions, for you will know that I have done nothing in it without cause, declares the Sovereign LORD."

Jerusalem as a Useless Vine

15 The word of the LORD came to me: 2 "Son of man, how is the wood of a vine different from that of a branch from any of the trees in the forest? 3 Is wood ever taken from it to make anything useful? Do they make pegs from it to hang things on? 4 And after it is thrown on the fire as fuel and the fire burns both ends and chars the middle, is it then useful for anything? 5 If it was not useful for anything when it was whole, how much less can it be made into something useful when the fire has burned it and it is charred?

6 "Therefore this is what the Sovereign LORD says: As I have given the wood of the vine among the trees of the forest as fuel for the fire, so will I treat the people living in Jerusalem. 7 I will set my face against them. Although they have come out of the fire,

the fire will yet consume them. And when I set my face against them, you will know that I am the LORD. 8 I will make the land desolate because they have been unfaithful, declares the Sovereign LORD."

Jerusalem as an Adulterous Wife

16 The word of the LORD came to me: 2 "Son of man, confront Jerusalem with her detestable practices 3 and say, 'This is what the Sovereign LORD says to Jerusalem: Your ancestry and birth were in the land of the Canaanites; your father was an Amorite and your mother a Hittite. 4 On the day you were born your cord was not cut, nor were you washed with water to make you clean, nor were you rubbed with salt or wrapped in cloths. 5 No one looked on you with pity or had compassion enough to do any of these things for you. Rather, you were thrown out into the open field, for on the day you were born you were despised.

6 "'Then I passed by and saw you kicking about in your blood, and as you lay there in your blood I said to you, "Live!"a 7 I made you grow like a plant of the field. You grew and developed and entered puberty. Your breasts had formed and your hair had grown, yet you were stark naked.

a 6 A few Hebrew manuscripts, Septuagint and Syriac; most Hebrew manuscripts repeat *and as you lay there in your blood I said to you, "Live!"*

8 "'Later I passed by, and when I looked at you and saw that you were old enough for love, I spread the corner of my garment over you and covered your naked body. I gave you my solemn oath and entered into a covenant with you, declares the Sovereign LORD, and you became mine.

9 "'I bathed you with water and washed the blood from you and put ointments on you. 10 I clothed you with an embroidered dress and put sandals of fine leather on you. I dressed you in fine linen and covered you with costly garments. 11 I adorned you with jewelry: I put bracelets on your arms and a necklace around your neck, 12 and I put a ring on your nose, earrings on your ears and a beautiful crown on your head. 13 So you were adorned with gold and silver; your clothes were of fine linen and costly fabric and embroidered cloth. Your food was honey, olive oil and the finest flour. You became very beautiful and rose to be a queen. 14 And your fame spread among the nations on account of your beauty, because the splendor I had given you made your beauty perfect, declares the Sovereign LORD.

15 "'But you trusted in your beauty and used your fame to become a prostitute. You lavished your favors on anyone who passed by and your beauty became his. 16 You took some of your garments to make gaudy high places, where you carried on your prostitution. You went to him, and he possessed your beauty.[a] 17 You also took the fine jewelry I gave you, the jewelry made of my gold and silver, and you made for yourself male idols and engaged in prostitution with them. 18 And you took your embroidered clothes to put on them, and you offered my oil and incense before them. 19 Also the food I provided for you — the flour, olive oil and honey I gave you to eat — you offered as fragrant incense before them. That is what happened, declares the Sovereign LORD.

20 "'And you took your sons and daughters whom you bore to me and sacrificed them as food to the idols. Was your prostitution not enough? 21 You slaughtered my children and sacrificed them to the idols. 22 In all your detestable practices and your prostitution you did not remember the days of your youth, when you were naked and bare, kicking about in your blood.

23 "'Woe! Woe to you, declares the Sovereign LORD. In addition to all your other wickedness, 24 you built a mound for yourself and made a lofty shrine in every public square. 25 At every street corner you built your lofty shrines and degraded your beauty, spreading your legs with in-

---

a 16 The meaning of the Hebrew for this sentence is uncertain.

creasing promiscuity to anyone who passed by. ²⁶You engaged in prostitution with the Egyptians, your neighbors with large genitals, and aroused my anger with your increasing promiscuity. ²⁷So I stretched out my hand against you and reduced your territory; I gave you over to the greed of your enemies, the daughters of the Philistines, who were shocked by your lewd conduct. ²⁸You engaged in prostitution with the Assyrians too, because you were insatiable; and even after that, you still were not satisfied. ²⁹Then you increased your promiscuity to include Babylonia,ᵃ a land of merchants, but even with this you were not satisfied.

³⁰" 'I am filled with fury against you,ᵇ declares the Sovereign LORD, when you do all these things, acting like a brazen prostitute! ³¹When you built your mounds at every street corner and made your lofty shrines in every public square, you were unlike a prostitute, because you scorned payment.

³²" 'You adulterous wife! You prefer strangers to your own husband! ³³All prostitutes receive gifts, but you give gifts to all your lovers, bribing them to come to you from everywhere for your illicit favors. ³⁴So in your prostitution you are the opposite of others; no one runs after you for your favors. You are the very opposite, for you give payment and none is given to you.

³⁵" 'Therefore, you prostitute, hear the word of the LORD! ³⁶This is what the Sovereign LORD says: Because you poured out your lust and exposed your naked body in your promiscuity with your lovers, and because of all your detestable idols, and because you gave them your children's blood, ³⁷therefore I am going to gather all your lovers, with whom you found pleasure, those you loved as well as those you hated. I will gather them against you from all around and will strip you in front of them, and they will see you stark naked. ³⁸I will sentence you to the punishment of women who commit adultery and who shed blood; I will bring on you the blood vengeance of my wrath and jealous anger. ³⁹Then I will deliver you into the hands of your lovers, and they will tear down your mounds and destroy your lofty shrines. They will strip you of your clothes and take your fine jewelry and leave you stark naked. ⁴⁰They will bring a mob against you, who will stone you and hack you to pieces with their swords. ⁴¹They will burn down your houses and inflict punishment on you in the sight of many women. I will put a stop to your prostitution, and you will no longer pay your lovers. ⁴²Then my

---

ᵃ 29 Or *Chaldea*   ᵇ 30 Or *How feverish is your heart,* wrath against you will subside and my jealous anger will turn away from you; I will be calm and no longer angry.

43 " 'Because you did not remember the days of your youth but enraged me with all these things, I will surely bring down on your head what you have done, declares the Sovereign LORD. Did you not add lewdness to all your other detestable practices?

44 " 'Everyone who quotes proverbs will quote this proverb about you: "Like mother, like daughter." 45 You are a true daughter of your mother, who despised her husband and her children; and you are a true sister of your sisters, who despised their husbands and their children. Your mother was a Hittite and your father an Amorite. 46 Your older sister was Samaria, who lived to the north of you with her daughters; and your younger sister, who lived to the south of you with her daughters, was Sodom. 47 You not only followed their ways and copied their detestable practices, but in all your ways you soon became more depraved than they. 48 As surely as I live, declares the Sovereign LORD, your sister Sodom and her daughters never did what you and your daughters have done.

49 " 'Now this was the sin of your sister Sodom: She and her daughters were arrogant, overfed and unconcerned; they did not help the poor and needy. 50 They were haughty and did detestable things before me. Therefore I did away with them as you have seen. 51 Samaria did not commit half the sins you did. You have done more detestable things than they, and have made your sisters seem righteous by all these things you have done. 52 Bear your disgrace, for you have furnished some justification for your sisters. Because your sins were more vile than theirs, they appear more righteous than you. So then, be ashamed and bear your disgrace, for you have made your sisters appear righteous.

53 " 'However, I will restore the fortunes of Sodom and her daughters and of Samaria and her daughters, and your fortunes along with them, 54 so that you may bear your disgrace and be ashamed of all you have done in giving them comfort. 55 And your sisters, Sodom with her daughters and Samaria with her daughters, will return to what they were before; and you and your daughters will return to what you were before. 56 You would not even mention your sister Sodom in the day of your pride, 57 before your wickedness was uncovered. Even so, you are now scorned by the daughters of Edom[a] and all

---

a 57 Many Hebrew manuscripts and Syriac; most Hebrew manuscripts, Septuagint and Vulgate *Aram* her neighbors and the daughters of the Philistines — all those around you who despise you. [58] You will bear the consequences of your lewdness and your detestable practices, declares the LORD.

[59] "'This is what the Sovereign LORD says: I will deal with you as you deserve, because you have despised my oath by breaking the covenant. [60] Yet I will remember the covenant I made with you in the days of your youth, and I will establish an everlasting covenant with you. [61] Then you will remember your ways and be ashamed when you receive your sisters, both those who are older than you and those who are younger. I will give them to you as daughters, but not on the basis of my covenant with you. [62] So I will establish my covenant with you, and you will know that I am the LORD. [63] Then, when I make atonement for you for all you have done, you will remember and be ashamed and never again open your mouth because of your humiliation, declares the Sovereign LORD.'"

Two Eagles and a Vine

17 The word of the LORD came to me: [2] "Son of man, set forth an allegory and tell it to the Israelites as a parable. [3] Say to them, 'This is what the Sovereign LORD says: A great eagle with powerful wings, long feathers and full plumage of varied colors came to Lebanon. Taking hold of the top of a cedar, [4] he broke off its topmost shoot and carried it away to a land of merchants, where he planted it in a city of traders.

[5] "'He took one of the seedlings of the land and put it in fertile soil. He planted it like a willow by abundant water, [6] and it sprouted and became a low, spreading vine. Its branches turned toward him, but its roots remained under it. So it became a vine and produced branches and put out leafy boughs.

[7] "'But there was another great eagle with powerful wings and full plumage. The vine now sent out its roots toward him from the plot where it was planted and stretched out its branches to him for water. [8] It had been planted in good soil by abundant water so that it would produce branches, bear fruit and become a splendid vine.'

[9] "Say to them, 'This is what the Sovereign LORD says: Will it thrive? Will it not be uprooted and stripped of its fruit so that it withers? All its new growth will wither. It will not take a strong arm or many people to pull it up by the roots. [10] It has been planted, but will it thrive? Will it not wither completely when the east wind strikes it — wither away in the plot where it grew?'"

[11] Then the word of the LORD came to me: [12] "Say to this rebellious people, 'Do you not know

what these things mean?' Say to them: 'The king of Babylon went to Jerusalem and carried off her king and her nobles, bringing them back with him to Babylon. ¹³Then he took a member of the royal family and made a treaty with him, putting him under oath. He also carried away the leading men of the land, ¹⁴so that the kingdom would be brought low, unable to rise again, surviving only by keeping his treaty. ¹⁵But the king rebelled against him by sending his envoys to Egypt to get horses and a large army. Will he succeed? Will he who does such things escape? Will he break the treaty and yet escape?

¹⁶" 'As surely as I live, declares the Sovereign LORD, he shall die in Babylon, in the land of the king who put him on the throne, whose oath he despised and whose treaty he broke. ¹⁷Pharaoh with his mighty army and great horde will be of no help to him in war, when ramps are built and siege works erected to destroy many lives. ¹⁸He despised the oath by breaking the covenant. Because he had given his hand in pledge and yet did all these things, he shall not escape.

¹⁹" 'Therefore this is what the Sovereign LORD says: As surely as I live, I will repay him for despising my oath and breaking my covenant. ²⁰I will spread my net for him, and he will be caught in my snare. I will bring him to Babylon and execute judgment on him there because he was unfaithful to me. ²¹All his choice troops will fall by the sword, and the survivors will be scattered to the winds. Then you will know that I the LORD have spoken.

²²" 'This is what the Sovereign LORD says: I myself will take a shoot from the very top of a cedar and plant it; I will break off a tender sprig from its topmost shoots and plant it on a high and lofty mountain. ²³On the mountain heights of Israel I will plant it; it will produce branches and bear fruit and become a splendid cedar. Birds of every kind will nest in it; they will find shelter in the shade of its branches. ²⁴All the trees of the forest will know that I the LORD bring down the tall tree and make the low tree grow tall. I dry up the green tree and make the dry tree flourish.

" 'I the LORD have spoken, and I will do it.' "

The One Who Sins Will Die

18 The word of the LORD came to me: ²"What do you people mean by quoting this proverb about the land of Israel:

" 'The parents eat sour grapes,
and the children's teeth are
set on edge'?

³"As surely as I live, declares the Sovereign LORD, you will no longer quote this proverb in Isra-

el. ⁴For everyone belongs to me, the parent as well as the child — both alike belong to me. The one who sins is the one who will die.

⁵ "Suppose there is a righteous man
　 who does what is just and right.
⁶ He does not eat at the mountain shrines
　 or look to the idols of Israel.
He does not defile his neighbor's wife
　 or have sexual relations with a woman during her period.
⁷ He does not oppress anyone,
　 but returns what he took in pledge for a loan.
He does not commit robbery
　 but gives his food to the hungry
　 and provides clothing for the naked.
⁸ He does not lend to them at interest
　 or take a profit from them.
He withholds his hand from doing wrong
　 and judges fairly between two parties.
⁹ He follows my decrees
　 and faithfully keeps my laws.
That man is righteous;
　 he will surely live,
　　　 declares the Sovereign Lord.

¹⁰ "Suppose he has a violent son, who sheds blood or does any of these other things^a ¹¹(though the father has done none of them):

"He eats at the mountain shrines.
He defiles his neighbor's wife.
¹² He oppresses the poor and needy.
He commits robbery.
He does not return what he took in pledge.
He looks to the idols.
He does detestable things.
¹³ He lends at interest and takes a profit.

Will such a man live? He will not! Because he has done all these detestable things, he is to be put to death; his blood will be on his own head.

¹⁴ "But suppose this son has a son who sees all the sins his father commits, and though he sees them, he does not do such things:

¹⁵ "He does not eat at the mountain shrines
　 or look to the idols of Israel.
He does not defile his neighbor's wife.
¹⁶ He does not oppress anyone
　 or require a pledge for a loan.
He does not commit robbery
　 but gives his food to the hungry
　 and provides clothing for the naked.

^a 10 Or *things to a brother*

17 He withholds his hand from
    mistreating the poor
and takes no interest or
    profit from them.
He keeps my laws and follows
    my decrees.

He will not die for his father's sin;
he will surely live. 18 But his father
will die for his own sin, because
he practiced extortion, robbed
his brother and did what was
wrong among his people.

19 "Yet you ask, 'Why does the
son not share the guilt of his father?' Since the son has done
what is just and right and has
been careful to keep all my decrees, he will surely live. 20 The
one who sins is the one who will
die. The child will not share the
guilt of the parent, nor will the
parent share the guilt of the child.
The righteousness of the righteous will be credited to them,
and the wickedness of the wicked will be charged against them.

21 "But if a wicked person turns
away from all the sins they have
committed and keeps all my decrees and does what is just and
right, that person will surely
live; they will not die. 22 None of
the offenses they have committed will be remembered against
them. Because of the righteous
things they have done, they will
live. 23 Do I take any pleasure in
the death of the wicked? declares
the Sovereign Lord. Rather, am I
not pleased when they turn from
their ways and live?

24 "But if a righteous person
turns from their righteousness
and commits sin and does the
same detestable things the wicked person does, will they live?
None of the righteous things that
person has done will be remembered. Because of the unfaithfulness they are guilty of and
because of the sins they have
committed, they will die.

25 "Yet you say, 'The way of the
Lord is not just.' Hear, you Israelites: Is my way unjust? Is it not
your ways that are unjust? 26 If
a righteous person turns from
their righteousness and commits
sin, they will die for it; because of
the sin they have committed they
will die. 27 But if a wicked person
turns away from the wickedness
they have committed and does
what is just and right, they will
save their life. 28 Because they
consider all the offenses they
have committed and turn away
from them, that person will surely live; they will not die. 29 Yet
the Israelites say, 'The way of the
Lord is not just.' Are my ways unjust, people of Israel? Is it not your
ways that are unjust?

30 "Therefore, you Israelites, I
will judge each of you according
to your own ways, declares the
Sovereign Lord. Repent! Turn
away from all your offenses;
then sin will not be your downfall. 31 Rid yourselves of all the offenses you have committed, and
get a new heart and a new spirit.

Why will you die, people of Israel? [32] For I take no pleasure in the death of anyone, declares the Sovereign LORD. Repent and live!

A Lament Over Israel's Princes

19 "Take up a lament concerning the princes of Israel [2] and say:

> "'What a lioness was your
>   mother
>   among the lions!
> She lay down among them
>   and reared her cubs.
> [3] She brought up one of her
>   cubs,
>   and he became a strong lion.
> He learned to tear the prey
>   and he became a man-eater.
> [4] The nations heard about
>   him,
>   and he was trapped in their
>   pit.
> They led him with hooks
>   to the land of Egypt.

> [5] "'When she saw her hope
>   unfulfilled,
>   her expectation gone,
> she took another of her
>   cubs
>   and made him a strong lion.
> [6] He prowled among the lions,
>   for he was now a strong lion.
> He learned to tear the prey
>   and he became a man-eater.
> [7] He broke down[a] their
>   strongholds
>   and devastated their towns.

> The land and all who were
>   in it
>   were terrified by his roaring.
> [8] Then the nations came against
>   him,
>   those from regions round
>   about.
> They spread their net for him,
>   and he was trapped in their
>   pit.
> [9] With hooks they pulled him
>   into a cage
>   and brought him to the king
>   of Babylon.
> They put him in prison,
>   so his roar was heard no
>   longer
>   on the mountains of Israel.

> [10] "'Your mother was like a vine
>   in your vineyard[b]
>   planted by the water;
> it was fruitful and full of
>   branches
>   because of abundant
>   water.
> [11] Its branches were strong,
>   fit for a ruler's scepter.
> It towered high
>   above the thick foliage,
> conspicuous for its height
>   and for its many branches.
> [12] But it was uprooted in fury
>   and thrown to the ground.
> The east wind made it shrivel,
>   it was stripped of its fruit;
> its strong branches withered
>   and fire consumed them.
> [13] Now it is planted in the desert,
>   in a dry and thirsty land.

---

[a] 7 Targum (see Septuagint); Hebrew *He knew* most Hebrew manuscripts *your blood*   [b] 10 Two Hebrew manuscripts;

¹⁴ Fire spread from one of its
main*ᵃ* branches
and consumed its fruit.
No strong branch is left on it
fit for a ruler's scepter.'

"This is a lament and is to be used
as a lament."

Rebellious Israel Purged

20 In the seventh year, in the fifth month on the tenth day, some of the elders of Israel came to inquire of the LORD, and they sat down in front of me.

² Then the word of the LORD came to me: ³ "Son of man, speak to the elders of Israel and say to them, 'This is what the Sovereign LORD says: Have you come to inquire of me? As surely as I live, I will not let you inquire of me, declares the Sovereign LORD.'

⁴ "Will you judge them? Will you judge them, son of man? Then confront them with the detestable practices of their ancestors ⁵ and say to them: 'This is what the Sovereign LORD says: On the day I chose Israel, I swore with uplifted hand to the descendants of Jacob and revealed myself to them in Egypt. With uplifted hand I said to them, "I am the LORD your God." ⁶ On that day I swore to them that I would bring them out of Egypt into a land I had searched out for them, a land flowing with milk and honey, the most beautiful of all lands. ⁷ And I said to them, "Each of you, get rid of the vile images you have set your eyes on, and do not defile yourselves with the idols of Egypt. I am the LORD your God."

⁸ "'But they rebelled against me and would not listen to me; they did not get rid of the vile images they had set their eyes on, nor did they forsake the idols of Egypt. So I said I would pour out my wrath on them and spend my anger against them in Egypt. ⁹ But for the sake of my name, I brought them out of Egypt. I did it to keep my name from being profaned in the eyes of the nations among whom they lived and in whose sight I had revealed myself to the Israelites. ¹⁰ Therefore I led them out of Egypt and brought them into the wilderness. ¹¹ I gave them my decrees and made known to them my laws, by which the person who obeys them will live. ¹² Also I gave them my Sabbaths as a sign between us, so they would know that I the LORD made them holy.

¹³ "'Yet the people of Israel rebelled against me in the wilderness. They did not follow my decrees but rejected my laws — by which the person who obeys them will live — and they utterly desecrated my Sabbaths. So I said I would pour out my wrath on them and destroy them in the wilderness. ¹⁴ But for the sake of my name I did what would keep it from being profaned in the eyes

---

ᵃ 14 Or *from under its*

of the nations in whose sight I had brought them out. **15** Also with uplifted hand I swore to them in the wilderness that I would not bring them into the land I had given them — a land flowing with milk and honey, the most beautiful of all lands — **16** because they rejected my laws and did not follow my decrees and desecrated my Sabbaths. For their hearts were devoted to their idols. **17** Yet I looked on them with pity and did not destroy them or put an end to them in the wilderness. **18** I said to their children in the wilderness, "Do not follow the statutes of your parents or keep their laws or defile yourselves with their idols. **19** I am the LORD your God; follow my decrees and be careful to keep my laws. **20** Keep my Sabbaths holy, that they may be a sign between us. Then you will know that I am the LORD your God."

21 " 'But the children rebelled against me: They did not follow my decrees, they were not careful to keep my laws, of which I said, "The person who obeys them will live by them," and they desecrated my Sabbaths. So I said I would pour out my wrath on them and spend my anger against them in the wilderness. **22** But I withheld my hand, and for the sake of my name I did what would keep it from being profaned in the eyes of the nations in whose sight I had brought them out. **23** Also with uplifted hand I swore to them in the wilderness that I would disperse them among the nations and scatter them through the countries, **24** because they had not obeyed my laws but had rejected my decrees and desecrated my Sabbaths, and their eyes lusted after their parents' idols. **25** So I gave them other statutes that were not good and laws through which they could not live; **26** I defiled them through their gifts — the sacrifice of every firstborn — that I might fill them with horror so they would know that I am the LORD.'

27 "Therefore, son of man, speak to the people of Israel and say to them, 'This is what the Sovereign LORD says: In this also your ancestors blasphemed me by being unfaithful to me: **28** When I brought them into the land I had sworn to give them and they saw any high hill or any leafy tree, there they offered their sacrifices, made offerings that aroused my anger, presented their fragrant incense and poured out their drink offerings. **29** Then I said to them: What is this high place you go to?' " (It is called Bamah[a] to this day.)

Rebellious Israel Renewed

30 "Therefore say to the Israelites: 'This is what the Sovereign LORD says: Will you defile your-

---

[a] 29 *Bamah* means *high place.*

selves the way your ancestors did and lust after their vile images? **31** When you offer your gifts — the sacrifice of your children in the fire — you continue to defile yourselves with all your idols to this day. Am I to let you inquire of me, you Israelites? As surely as I live, declares the Sovereign LORD, I will not let you inquire of me.

32 " 'You say, "We want to be like the nations, like the peoples of the world, who serve wood and stone." But what you have in mind will never happen. **33** As surely as I live, declares the Sovereign LORD, I will reign over you with a mighty hand and an outstretched arm and with outpoured wrath. **34** I will bring you from the nations and gather you from the countries where you have been scattered — with a mighty hand and an outstretched arm and with outpoured wrath. **35** I will bring you into the wilderness of the nations and there, face to face, I will execute judgment upon you. **36** As I judged your ancestors in the wilderness of the land of Egypt, so I will judge you, declares the Sovereign LORD. **37** I will take note of you as you pass under my rod, and I will bring you into the bond of the covenant. **38** I will purge you of those who revolt and rebel against me. Although I will bring them out of the land where they are living, yet they will not enter the land of Israel. Then you will know that I am the LORD.

39 " 'As for you, people of Israel, this is what the Sovereign LORD says: Go and serve your idols, every one of you! But afterward you will surely listen to me and no longer profane my holy name with your gifts and idols. **40** For on my holy mountain, the high mountain of Israel, declares the Sovereign LORD, there in the land all the people of Israel will serve me, and there I will accept them. There I will require your offerings and your choice gifts,*a* along with all your holy sacrifices. **41** I will accept you as fragrant incense when I bring you out from the nations and gather you from the countries where you have been scattered, and I will be proved holy through you in the sight of the nations. **42** Then you will know that I am the LORD, when I bring you into the land of Israel, the land I had sworn with uplifted hand to give to your ancestors. **43** There you will remember your conduct and all the actions by which you have defiled yourselves, and you will loathe yourselves for all the evil you have done. **44** You will know that I am the LORD, when I deal with you for my name's sake and not according to your evil ways and your corrupt practices, you people of Israel, declares the Sovereign LORD.' "

---

a 40 Or *and the gifts of your firstfruits*

Prophecy Against the South

45 The word of the LORD came to me: **46** "Son of man, set your face toward the south; preach against the south and prophesy against the forest of the southland. **47** Say to the southern forest: 'Hear the word of the LORD. This is what the Sovereign LORD says: I am about to set fire to you, and it will consume all your trees, both green and dry. The blazing flame will not be quenched, and every face from south to north will be scorched by it. **48** Everyone will see that I the LORD have kindled it; it will not be quenched.' "

49 Then I said, "Sovereign LORD, they are saying of me, 'Isn't he just telling parables?' "[a]

Babylon as God's Sword of Judgment

21 [b] The word of the LORD came to me: **2** "Son of man, set your face against Jerusalem and preach against the sanctuary. Prophesy against the land of Israel **3** and say to her: 'This is what the LORD says: I am against you. I will draw my sword from its sheath and cut off from you both the righteous and the wicked. **4** Because I am going to cut off the righteous and the wicked, my sword will be unsheathed against everyone from south to north. **5** Then all people will know that I the LORD have drawn my sword from its sheath; it will not return again.'

6 "Therefore groan, son of man! Groan before them with broken heart and bitter grief. **7** And when they ask you, 'Why are you groaning?' you shall say, 'Because of the news that is coming. Every heart will melt with fear and every hand go limp; every spirit will become faint and every leg will be wet with urine.' It is coming! It will surely take place, declares the Sovereign LORD."

8 The word of the LORD came to me: **9** "Son of man, prophesy and say, 'This is what the Lord says:

" 'A sword, a sword,
    sharpened and polished —
10 sharpened for the slaughter,
    polished to flash like
        lightning!

" 'Shall we rejoice in the scepter of my royal son? The sword despises every such stick.

11 " 'The sword is appointed to be
        polished,
    to be grasped with the hand;
it is sharpened and polished,
    made ready for the hand of
        the slayer.
12 Cry out and wail, son of man,
    for it is against my people;
    it is against all the princes of
        Israel.
They are thrown to the sword
    along with my people.
Therefore beat your breast.

---

[a] 49 In Hebrew texts 20:45-49 is numbered 21:1-5.   [b] In Hebrew texts 21:1-32 is numbered 21:6-37.

¹³ " 'Testing will surely come. And what if even the scepter, which the sword despises, does not continue? declares the Sovereign LORD.'

¹⁴ "So then, son of man, prophesy
and strike your hands
together.
Let the sword strike twice,
even three times.
It is a sword for slaughter —
a sword for great slaughter,
closing in on them from
every side.
¹⁵ So that hearts may melt with
fear
and the fallen be many,
I have stationed the sword for
slaughter ͣ
at all their gates.
Look! It is forged to strike like
lightning,
it is grasped for slaughter.
¹⁶ Slash to the right, you sword,
then to the left,
wherever your blade is
turned.
¹⁷ I too will strike my hands
together,
and my wrath will subside.
I the LORD have spoken."

¹⁸ The word of the LORD came to me: ¹⁹ "Son of man, mark out two roads for the sword of the king of Babylon to take, both starting from the same country. Make a signpost where the road branches off to the city. ²⁰ Mark out one road for the sword to come against Rabbah of the Ammonites and another against Judah and fortified Jerusalem. ²¹ For the king of Babylon will stop at the fork in the road, at the junction of the two roads, to seek an omen: He will cast lots with arrows, he will consult his idols, he will examine the liver. ²² Into his right hand will come the lot for Jerusalem, where he is to set up battering rams, to give the command to slaughter, to sound the battle cry, to set battering rams against the gates, to build a ramp and to erect siege works. ²³ It will seem like a false omen to those who have sworn allegiance to him, but he will remind them of their guilt and take them captive.

²⁴ "Therefore this is what the Sovereign LORD says: 'Because you people have brought to mind your guilt by your open rebellion, revealing your sins in all that you do — because you have done this, you will be taken captive.

²⁵ " 'You profane and wicked prince of Israel, whose day has come, whose time of punishment has reached its climax, ²⁶ this is what the Sovereign LORD says: Take off the turban, remove the crown. It will not be as it was: The lowly will be exalted and the exalted will be brought low. ²⁷ A ruin! A ruin! I will make it a ruin! The crown will not be restored until he to whom it rightfully belongs shall come; to him I will give it.'

ͣ 15 Septuagint; the meaning of the Hebrew for this word is uncertain.

28 "And you, son of man, prophesy and say, 'This is what the Sovereign LORD says about the Ammonites and their insults:

" 'A sword, a sword,
    drawn for the slaughter,
polished to consume
    and to flash like
        lightning!
29 Despite false visions
        concerning you
    and lying divinations about
        you,
it will be laid on the necks
    of the wicked who are to be
        slain,
whose day has come,
    whose time of punishment
        has reached its climax.

30 " 'Let the sword return to its
        sheath.
    In the place where you were
        created,
in the land of your ancestry,
    I will judge you.
31 I will pour out my wrath on
        you
    and breathe out my fiery
        anger against you;
I will deliver you into the
    hands of brutal men,
    men skilled in destruction.
32 You will be fuel for the
        fire,
    your blood will be shed in
        your land,
you will be remembered no
        more;
    for I the LORD have
        spoken.' "

Judgment on Jerusalem's Sins

22 The word of the LORD came to me:

2 "Son of man, will you judge her? Will you judge this city of bloodshed? Then confront her with all her detestable practices **3** and say: 'This is what the Sovereign LORD says: You city that brings on herself doom by shedding blood in her midst and defiles herself by making idols, **4** you have become guilty because of the blood you have shed and have become defiled by the idols you have made. You have brought your days to a close, and the end of your years has come. Therefore I will make you an object of scorn to the nations and a laughingstock to all the countries. **5** Those who are near and those who are far away will mock you, you infamous city, full of turmoil.

6 " 'See how each of the princes of Israel who are in you uses his power to shed blood. **7** In you they have treated father and mother with contempt; in you they have oppressed the foreigner and mistreated the fatherless and the widow. **8** You have despised my holy things and desecrated my Sabbaths. **9** In you are slanderers who are bent on shedding blood; in you are those who eat at the mountain shrines and commit lewd acts. **10** In you are those who dishonor their father's bed; in you are those who violate women during their period, when they are ceremonially unclean. **11**In you one man commits a detestable offense with his neighbor's wife, another shamefully defiles his daughter-in-law, and another violates his sister, his own father's daughter. **12**In you are people who accept bribes to shed blood; you take interest and make a profit from the poor. You extort unjust gain from your neighbors. And you have forgotten me, declares the Sovereign LORD.

13" 'I will surely strike my hands together at the unjust gain you have made and at the blood you have shed in your midst. **14**Will your courage endure or your hands be strong in the day I deal with you? I the LORD have spoken, and I will do it. **15**I will disperse you among the nations and scatter you through the countries; and I will put an end to your uncleanness. **16**When you have been defiled*a* in the eyes of the nations, you will know that I am the LORD.' "

17Then the word of the LORD came to me: **18**"Son of man, the people of Israel have become dross to me; all of them are the copper, tin, iron and lead left inside a furnace. They are but the dross of silver. **19**Therefore this is what the Sovereign LORD says: 'Because you have all become dross, I will gather you into Jerusalem. **20**As silver, copper, iron, lead and tin are gathered into a furnace to be melted with a fiery blast, so will I gather you in my anger and my wrath and put you inside the city and melt you. **21**I will gather you and I will blow on you with my fiery wrath, and you will be melted inside her. **22**As silver is melted in a furnace, so you will be melted inside her, and you will know that I the LORD have poured out my wrath on you.' "

23Again the word of the LORD came to me: **24**"Son of man, say to the land, 'You are a land that has not been cleansed or rained on in the day of wrath.' **25**There is a conspiracy of her princes*b* within her like a roaring lion tearing its prey; they devour people, take treasures and precious things and make many widows within her. **26**Her priests do violence to my law and profane my holy things; they do not distinguish between the holy and the common; they teach that there is no difference between the unclean and the clean; and they shut their eyes to the keeping of my Sabbaths, so that I am profaned among them. **27**Her officials within her are like wolves tearing their prey; they shed blood and kill people to make unjust gain. **28**Her prophets whitewash these deeds for them by false visions and lying divinations. They say, 'This is what the Sovereign LORD

---

a 16 Or *When I have allotted you your inheritance* *b 25* Septuagint; Hebrew *prophets* says' — when the LORD has not spoken. ²⁹The people of the land practice extortion and commit robbery; they oppress the poor and needy and mistreat the foreigner, denying them justice.

³⁰"I looked for someone among them who would build up the wall and stand before me in the gap on behalf of the land so I would not have to destroy it, but I found no one. ³¹So I will pour out my wrath on them and consume them with my fiery anger, bringing down on their own heads all they have done, declares the Sovereign LORD."

Two Adulterous Sisters

23 The word of the LORD came to me: ²"Son of man, there were two women, daughters of the same mother. ³They became prostitutes in Egypt, engaging in prostitution from their youth. In that land their breasts were fondled and their virgin bosoms caressed. ⁴The older was named Oholah, and her sister was Oholibah. They were mine and gave birth to sons and daughters. Oholah is Samaria, and Oholibah is Jerusalem.

⁵"Oholah engaged in prostitution while she was still mine; and she lusted after her lovers, the Assyrians — warriors ⁶clothed in blue, governors and commanders, all of them handsome young men, and mounted horsemen.

⁷She gave herself as a prostitute to all the elite of the Assyrians and defiled herself with all the idols of everyone she lusted after. ⁸She did not give up the prostitution she began in Egypt, when during her youth men slept with her, caressed her virgin bosom and poured out their lust on her.

⁹"Therefore I delivered her into the hands of her lovers, the Assyrians, for whom she lusted. ¹⁰They stripped her naked, took away her sons and daughters and killed her with the sword. She became a byword among women, and punishment was inflicted on her.

¹¹"Her sister Oholibah saw this, yet in her lust and prostitution she was more depraved than her sister. ¹²She too lusted after the Assyrians — governors and commanders, warriors in full dress, mounted horsemen, all handsome young men. ¹³I saw that she too defiled herself; both of them went the same way.

¹⁴"But she carried her prostitution still further. She saw men portrayed on a wall, figures of Chaldeans[a] portrayed in red, ¹⁵with belts around their waists and flowing turbans on their heads; all of them looked like Babylonian chariot officers, natives of Chaldea.[b] ¹⁶As soon as she saw them, she lusted after them and sent messengers to them in Chaldea. ¹⁷Then the

---

[a] 14 Or *Babylonians*   [b] 15 Or *Babylonia*; also in verse 16

Babylonians came to her, to the bed of love, and in their lust they defiled her. After she had been defiled by them, she turned away from them in disgust. ¹⁸When she carried on her prostitution openly and exposed her naked body, I turned away from her in disgust, just as I had turned away from her sister. ¹⁹Yet she became more and more promiscuous as she recalled the days of her youth, when she was a prostitute in Egypt. ²⁰There she lusted after her lovers, whose genitals were like those of donkeys and whose emission was like that of horses. ²¹So you longed for the lewdness of your youth, when in Egypt your bosom was caressed and your young breasts fondled.ᵃ

²²"Therefore, Oholibah, this is what the Sovereign LORD says: I will stir up your lovers against you, those you turned away from in disgust, and I will bring them against you from every side — ²³the Babylonians and all the Chaldeans, the men of Pekod and Shoa and Koa, and all the Assyrians with them, handsome young men, all of them governors and commanders, chariot officers and men of high rank, all mounted on horses. ²⁴They will come against you with weapons,ᵇ chariots and wagons and with a throng of people; they will take up positions against you on every side with large and small shields and with helmets. I will turn you over to them for punishment, and they will punish you according to their standards. ²⁵I will direct my jealous anger against you, and they will deal with you in fury. They will cut off your noses and your ears, and those of you who are left will fall by the sword. They will take away your sons and daughters, and those of you who are left will be consumed by fire. ²⁶They will also strip you of your clothes and take your fine jewelry. ²⁷So I will put a stop to the lewdness and prostitution you began in Egypt. You will not look on these things with longing or remember Egypt anymore.

²⁸"For this is what the Sovereign LORD says: I am about to deliver you into the hands of those you hate, to those you turned away from in disgust. ²⁹They will deal with you in hatred and take away everything you have worked for. They will leave you stark naked, and the shame of your prostitution will be exposed. Your lewdness and promiscuity ³⁰have brought this on you, because you lusted after the nations and defiled yourself with their idols. ³¹You have gone the way of your sister; so I will put her cup into your hand.

³²"This is what the Sovereign LORD says:

ᵃ 21 Syriac (see also verse 3); Hebrew *caressed because of your young breasts*
ᵇ 24 The meaning of the Hebrew for this word is uncertain.

"You will drink your sister's
cup,
a cup large and deep;
it will bring scorn and
derision,
for it holds so much.
³³You will be filled with
drunkenness and
sorrow,
the cup of ruin and
desolation,
the cup of your sister
Samaria.
³⁴You will drink it and drain it
dry
and chew on its pieces —
and you will tear your
breasts.

I have spoken, declares the Sovereign LORD.

³⁵"Therefore this is what the Sovereign LORD says: Since you have forgotten me and turned your back on me, you must bear the consequences of your lewdness and prostitution."

³⁶The LORD said to me: "Son of man, will you judge Oholah and Oholibah? Then confront them with their detestable practices, ³⁷for they have committed adultery and blood is on their hands. They committed adultery with their idols; they even sacrificed their children, whom they bore to me, as food for them. ³⁸They have also done this to me: At that same time they defiled my sanctuary and desecrated my Sabbaths. ³⁹On the very day they sacrificed their children to their idols, they entered my sanctuary and desecrated it. That is what they did in my house.

⁴⁰"They even sent messengers for men who came from far away, and when they arrived you bathed yourself for them, applied eye makeup and put on your jewelry. ⁴¹You sat on an elegant couch, with a table spread before it on which you had placed the incense and olive oil that belonged to me.

⁴²"The noise of a carefree crowd was around her; drunkards were brought from the desert along with men from the rabble, and they put bracelets on the wrists of the woman and her sister and beautiful crowns on their heads. ⁴³Then I said about the one worn out by adultery, 'Now let them use her as a prostitute, for that is all she is.' ⁴⁴And they slept with her. As men sleep with a prostitute, so they slept with those lewd women, Oholah and Oholibah. ⁴⁵But righteous judges will sentence them to the punishment of women who commit adultery and shed blood, because they are adulterous and blood is on their hands.

⁴⁶"This is what the Sovereign LORD says: Bring a mob against them and give them over to terror and plunder. ⁴⁷The mob will stone them and cut them down with their swords; they will kill their sons and daughters and burn down their houses.

⁴⁸ "So I will put an end to lewdness in the land, that all women may take warning and not imitate you. ⁴⁹ You will suffer the penalty for your lewdness and bear the consequences of your sins of idolatry. Then you will know that I am the Sovereign LORD."

Jerusalem as a Cooking Pot

24 In the ninth year, in the tenth month on the tenth day, the word of the LORD came to me: ² "Son of man, record this date, this very date, because the king of Babylon has laid siege to Jerusalem this very day. ³ Tell this rebellious people a parable and say to them: 'This is what the Sovereign LORD says:

> " 'Put on the cooking pot; put
> it on
> and pour water into it.
> ⁴ Put into it the pieces of
> meat,
> all the choice pieces — the
> leg and the shoulder.
> Fill it with the best of these
> bones;
> ⁵ take the pick of the flock.
> Pile wood beneath it for the
> bones;
> bring it to a boil
> and cook the bones in it.

⁶ " 'For this is what the Sovereign LORD says:

> " 'Woe to the city of bloodshed,
> to the pot now encrusted,
> whose deposit will not go
> away!

> Take the meat out piece by
> piece
> in whatever order it comes.

⁷ " 'For the blood she shed is in
> her midst:
> She poured it on the bare
> rock;
> she did not pour it on the
> ground,
> where the dust would cover
> it.
> ⁸ To stir up wrath and take
> revenge
> I put her blood on the bare
> rock,
> so that it would not be
> covered.

⁹ " 'Therefore this is what the Sovereign LORD says:

> " 'Woe to the city of bloodshed!
> I, too, will pile the wood
> high.
> ¹⁰ So heap on the wood
> and kindle the fire.
> Cook the meat well,
> mixing in the spices;
> and let the bones be
> charred.
> ¹¹ Then set the empty pot on the
> coals
> till it becomes hot and its
> copper glows,
> so that its impurities may be
> melted
> and its deposit burned
> away.
> ¹² It has frustrated all efforts;
> its heavy deposit has not
> been removed,
> not even by fire.

13 " 'Now your impurity is lewdness. Because I tried to cleanse you but you would not be cleansed from your impurity, you will not be clean again until my wrath against you has subsided.

14 " 'I the Lord have spoken. The time has come for me to act. I will not hold back; I will not have pity, nor will I relent. You will be judged according to your conduct and your actions, declares the Sovereign Lord.' "

Ezekiel's Wife Dies

15 The word of the Lord came to me: 16 "Son of man, with one blow I am about to take away from you the delight of your eyes. Yet do not lament or weep or shed any tears. 17 Groan quietly; do not mourn for the dead. Keep your turban fastened and your sandals on your feet; do not cover your mustache and beard or eat the customary food of mourners."

18 So I spoke to the people in the morning, and in the evening my wife died. The next morning I did as I had been commanded.

19 Then the people asked me, "Won't you tell us what these things have to do with us? Why are you acting like this?"

20 So I said to them, "The word of the Lord came to me: 21 Say to the people of Israel, 'This is what the Sovereign Lord says: I am about to desecrate my sanctuary—the stronghold in which you take pride, the delight of your eyes, the object of your affection. The sons and daughters you left behind will fall by the sword. 22 And you will do as I have done. You will not cover your mustache and beard or eat the customary food of mourners. 23 You will keep your turbans on your heads and your sandals on your feet. You will not mourn or weep but will waste away because of[a] your sins and groan among yourselves. 24 Ezekiel will be a sign to you; you will do just as he has done. When this happens, you will know that I am the Sovereign Lord.'

25 "And you, son of man, on the day I take away their stronghold, their joy and glory, the delight of their eyes, their heart's desire, and their sons and daughters as well— 26 on that day a fugitive will come to tell you the news. 27 At that time your mouth will be opened; you will speak with him and will no longer be silent. So you will be a sign to them, and they will know that I am the Lord."

A Prophecy Against Ammon

25 The word of the Lord came to me: 2 "Son of man, set your face against the Ammonites and prophesy against them. 3 Say to them, 'Hear the word of the Sovereign Lord. This is what the Sovereign Lord says: Because you said "Aha!"

[a] 23 Or away in

over my sanctuary when it was desecrated and over the land of Israel when it was laid waste and over the people of Judah when they went into exile, ⁴therefore I am going to give you to the people of the East as a possession. They will set up their camps and pitch their tents among you; they will eat your fruit and drink your milk. ⁵I will turn Rabbah into a pasture for camels and Ammon into a resting place for sheep. Then you will know that I am the LORD. ⁶For this is what the Sovereign LORD says: Because you have clapped your hands and stamped your feet, rejoicing with all the malice of your heart against the land of Israel, ⁷therefore I will stretch out my hand against you and give you as plunder to the nations. I will wipe you out from among the nations and exterminate you from the countries. I will destroy you, and you will know that I am the LORD.'"

A Prophecy Against Moab

⁸"This is what the Sovereign LORD says: 'Because Moab and Seir said, "Look, Judah has become like all the other nations," ⁹therefore I will expose the flank of Moab, beginning at its frontier towns—Beth Jeshimoth, Baal Meon and Kiriathaim—the glory of that land. ¹⁰I will give Moab along with the Ammonites to the people of the East as a possession, so that the Ammonites will not be remembered among the nations; ¹¹and I will inflict punishment on Moab. Then they will know that I am the LORD.'"

A Prophecy Against Edom

¹²"This is what the Sovereign LORD says: 'Because Edom took revenge on Judah and became very guilty by doing so, ¹³therefore this is what the Sovereign LORD says: I will stretch out my hand against Edom and kill both man and beast. I will lay it waste, and from Teman to Dedan they will fall by the sword. ¹⁴I will take vengeance on Edom by the hand of my people Israel, and they will deal with Edom in accordance with my anger and my wrath; they will know my vengeance, declares the Sovereign LORD.'"

A Prophecy Against Philistia

¹⁵"This is what the Sovereign LORD says: 'Because the Philistines acted in vengeance and took revenge with malice in their hearts, and with ancient hostility sought to destroy Judah, ¹⁶therefore this is what the Sovereign LORD says: I am about to stretch out my hand against the Philistines, and I will wipe out the Kerethites and destroy those remaining along the coast. ¹⁷I will carry out great vengeance on them and punish them in my wrath. Then they will know that I am the LORD, when I take vengeance on them.'"

A Prophecy Against Tyre

26 In the eleventh month of the twelfth[a] year, on the first day of the month, the word of the LORD came to me: ²"Son of man, because Tyre has said of Jerusalem, 'Aha! The gate to the nations is broken, and its doors have swung open to me; now that she lies in ruins I will prosper,' ³therefore this is what the Sovereign LORD says: I am against you, Tyre, and I will bring many nations against you, like the sea casting up its waves. ⁴They will destroy the walls of Tyre and pull down her towers; I will scrape away her rubble and make her a bare rock. ⁵Out in the sea she will become a place to spread fishnets, for I have spoken, declares the Sovereign LORD. She will become plunder for the nations, ⁶and her settlements on the mainland will be ravaged by the sword. Then they will know that I am the LORD.

⁷"For this is what the Sovereign LORD says: From the north I am going to bring against Tyre Nebuchadnezzar[b] king of Babylon, king of kings, with horses and chariots, with horsemen and a great army. ⁸He will ravage your settlements on the mainland with the sword; he will set up siege works against you, build a ramp up to your walls and raise his shields against you. ⁹He will direct the blows of his battering rams against your walls and demolish your towers with his weapons. ¹⁰His horses will be so many that they will cover you with dust. Your walls will tremble at the noise of the warhorses, wagons and chariots when he enters your gates as men enter a city whose walls have been broken through. ¹¹The hooves of his horses will trample all your streets; he will kill your people with the sword, and your strong pillars will fall to the ground. ¹²They will plunder your wealth and loot your merchandise; they will break down your walls and demolish your fine houses and throw your stones, timber and rubble into the sea. ¹³I will put an end to your noisy songs, and the music of your harps will be heard no more. ¹⁴I will make you a bare rock, and you will become a place to spread fishnets. You will never be rebuilt, for I the LORD have spoken, declares the Sovereign LORD.

¹⁵"This is what the Sovereign LORD says to Tyre: Will not the coastlands tremble at the sound of your fall, when the wounded groan and the slaughter takes place in you? ¹⁶Then all the princes of the coast will step down from their thrones and

---

a 1 Probable reading of the original Hebrew text; Masoretic Text does not have *month of the twelfth*. *b 7* Hebrew *Nebuchadrezzar,* of which *Nebuchadnezzar* is a variant; here and often in Ezekiel and Jeremiah lay aside their robes and take off their embroidered garments. Clothed with terror, they will sit on the ground, trembling every moment, appalled at you. **17** Then they will take up a lament concerning you and say to you:

> "'How you are destroyed, city
> of renown,
> peopled by men of the sea!
> You were a power on the seas,
> you and your citizens;
> you put your terror
> on all who lived there.
> **18** Now the coastlands tremble
> on the day of your fall;
> the islands in the sea
> are terrified at your
> collapse.'

19 "This is what the Sovereign LORD says: When I make you a desolate city, like cities no longer inhabited, and when I bring the ocean depths over you and its vast waters cover you, **20** then I will bring you down with those who go down to the pit, to the people of long ago. I will make you dwell in the earth below, as in ancient ruins, with those who go down to the pit, and you will not return or take your place[a] in the land of the living. **21** I will bring you to a horrible end and you will be no more. You will be sought, but you will never again be found, declares the Sovereign LORD."

A Lament Over Tyre

27 The word of the LORD came to me: **2** "Son of man, take up a lament concerning Tyre. **3** Say to Tyre, situated at the gateway to the sea, merchant of peoples on many coasts, 'This is what the Sovereign LORD says:

> "'You say, Tyre,
> "I am perfect in beauty."
> **4** Your domain was on the high
> seas;
> your builders brought your
> beauty to perfection.
> **5** They made all your
> timbers
> of juniper from Senir[b];
> they took a cedar from
> Lebanon
> to make a mast for you.
> **6** Of oaks from Bashan
> they made your oars;
> of cypress wood[c] from the
> coasts of Cyprus
> they made your deck,
> adorned with ivory.
> **7** Fine embroidered linen from
> Egypt was your sail
> and served as your
> banner;
> your awnings were of blue and
> purple
> from the coasts of Elishah.
> **8** Men of Sidon and Arvad were
> your oarsmen;
> your skilled men, Tyre, were
> aboard as your sailors.

---

a 20 Septuagint; Hebrew *return, and I will give glory*   *b* 5 That is, Mount Hermon   *c* 6 Targum; the Masoretic Text has a different division of the consonants.

⁹Veteran craftsmen of Byblos
were on board
as shipwrights to caulk your
seams.
All the ships of the sea and
their sailors
came alongside to trade for
your wares.

¹⁰ " 'Men of Persia, Lydia and Put
served as soldiers in your
army.
They hung their shields and
helmets on your walls,
bringing you splendor.
¹¹ Men of Arvad and Helek
guarded your walls on every
side;
men of Gammad
were in your towers.
They hung their shields
around your
walls;
they brought your beauty to
perfection.

¹² " 'Tarshish did business with
you because of your great wealth
of goods; they exchanged silver,
iron, tin and lead for your merchandise.
¹³ " 'Greece, Tubal and Meshek
did business with you; they traded human beings and articles of
bronze for your wares.
¹⁴ " 'Men of Beth Togarmah exchanged chariot horses, cavalry
horses and mules for your merchandise.

¹⁵ " 'The men of Rhodes[a] traded
with you, and many coastlands
were your customers; they paid
you with ivory tusks and ebony.
¹⁶ " 'Aram[b] did business with
you because of your many products; they exchanged turquoise,
purple fabric, embroidered work,
fine linen, coral and rubies for
your merchandise.
¹⁷ " 'Judah and Israel traded
with you; they exchanged wheat
from Minnith and confections,[c]
honey, olive oil and balm for your
wares.
¹⁸ " 'Damascus did business
with you because of your many
products and great wealth of
goods. They offered wine from
Helbon, wool from Zahar ¹⁹and
casks of wine from Izal in exchange for your wares: wrought
iron, cassia and calamus.
²⁰ " 'Dedan traded in saddle
blankets with you.
²¹ " 'Arabia and all the princes of
Kedar were your customers; they
did business with you in lambs,
rams and goats.
²² " 'The merchants of Sheba
and Raamah traded with you;
for your merchandise they exchanged the finest of all kinds of
spices and precious stones, and
gold.
²³ " 'Harran, Kanneh and Eden
and merchants of Sheba, Ashur and Kilmad traded with you.

---

[a] 15 Septuagint; Hebrew *Dedan*
manuscripts and Syriac *Edom*   [b] 16 Most Hebrew manuscripts; some Hebrew
uncertain.   [c] 17 The meaning of the Hebrew for this word is

²⁴In your marketplace they traded with you beautiful garments, blue fabric, embroidered work and multicolored rugs with cords twisted and tightly knotted.

²⁵ " 'The ships of Tarshish serve
  as carriers for your wares.
You are filled with heavy
    cargo
  as you sail the sea.
²⁶Your oarsmen take you
  out to the high seas.
But the east wind will break
    you to pieces
  far out at sea.
²⁷Your wealth, merchandise and
    wares,
  your mariners, sailors and
    shipwrights,
  your merchants and all your
    soldiers,
  and everyone else on board
  will sink into the heart of the
    sea
  on the day of your
    shipwreck.
²⁸The shorelands will quake
  when your sailors cry out.
²⁹All who handle the oars
  will abandon their ships;
  the mariners and all the
    sailors
  will stand on the shore.
³⁰They will raise their voice
  and cry bitterly over you;
  they will sprinkle dust on their
    heads
  and roll in ashes.
³¹They will shave their heads
    because of you
  and will put on sackcloth.

They will weep over you with
    anguish of soul
  and with bitter mourning.
³²As they wail and mourn over
    you,
  they will take up a lament
    concerning you:
"Who was ever silenced like
    Tyre,
  surrounded by the sea?"
³³When your merchandise went
    out on the seas,
  you satisfied many nations;
  with your great wealth and
    your wares
  you enriched the kings of the
    earth.
³⁴Now you are shattered by the
    sea
  in the depths of the waters;
  your wares and all your
    company
  have gone down with you.
³⁵All who live in the coastlands
  are appalled at you;
  their kings shudder with
    horror
  and their faces are distorted
    with fear.
³⁶The merchants among the
    nations scoff at you;
  you have come to a horrible
    end
  and will be no more.' "

A Prophecy Against the King of Tyre

28 The word of the LORD came to me: ²"Son of man, say to the ruler of Tyre, 'This is what the Sovereign LORD says:

" 'In the pride of your heart
  you say, "I am a god;
I sit on the throne of a god
  in the heart of the seas."
But you are a mere mortal and
  not a god,
  though you think you are as
  wise as a god.
³Are you wiser than Daniel[a]?
  Is no secret hidden from
  you?
⁴By your wisdom and
  understanding
you have gained wealth for
  yourself
and amassed gold and silver
  in your treasuries.
⁵By your great skill in trading
  you have increased your
  wealth,
and because of your wealth
  your heart has grown
  proud.

⁶" 'Therefore this is what the
Sovereign Lord says:

" 'Because you think you are
  wise,
  as wise as a god,
⁷I am going to bring foreigners
  against you,
  the most ruthless of
  nations;
they will draw their swords
  against your beauty and
  wisdom
  and pierce your shining
  splendor.

⁸They will bring you down to
  the pit,
  and you will die a violent
  death
  in the heart of the seas.
⁹Will you then say, "I am a god,"
  in the presence of those who
  kill you?
You will be but a mortal, not a
  god,
  in the hands of those who
  slay you.
¹⁰You will die the death of the
  uncircumcised
  at the hands of foreigners.

I have spoken, declares the Sovereign Lord.' "

¹¹The word of the Lord came
to me: ¹²"Son of man, take up a
lament concerning the king of
Tyre and say to him: 'This is what
the Sovereign Lord says:

" 'You were the seal of
  perfection,
  full of wisdom and perfect in
  beauty.
¹³You were in Eden,
  the garden of God;
every precious stone adorned
  you:
  carnelian, chrysolite and
  emerald,
  topaz, onyx and jasper,
  lapis lazuli, turquoise and
  beryl.[b]
Your settings and mountings[c]
  were made of gold;

---

[a] 3 Or *Danel*, a man of renown in ancient literature   [b] 13 The precise
identification of some of these precious stones is uncertain.   [c] 13 The meaning
of the Hebrew for this phrase is uncertain.

on the day you were created
 they were prepared.
¹⁴You were anointed as a
 guardian cherub,
 for so I ordained you.
 You were on the holy mount of
 God;
 you walked among the fiery
 stones.
¹⁵You were blameless in your
 ways
 from the day you were
 created
 till wickedness was found in
 you.
¹⁶Through your widespread
 trade
 you were filled with
 violence,
 and you sinned.
 So I drove you in disgrace from
 the mount of God,
 and I expelled you, guardian
 cherub,
 from among the fiery
 stones.
¹⁷Your heart became proud
 on account of your beauty,
 and you corrupted your
 wisdom
 because of your splendor.
 So I threw you to the earth;
 I made a spectacle of you
 before kings.
¹⁸By your many sins and
 dishonest trade
 you have desecrated your
 sanctuaries.
 So I made a fire come out from
 you,
 and it consumed you,

and I reduced you to ashes on
 the ground
 in the sight of all who were
 watching.
¹⁹All the nations who knew you
 are appalled at you;
 you have come to a horrible
 end
 and will be no more.'"

A Prophecy Against Sidon

²⁰The word of the LORD came to
me: ²¹"Son of man, set your face
against Sidon; prophesy against
her ²²and say: 'This is what the
Sovereign LORD says:

"'I am against you, Sidon,
 and among you I will display
 my glory.
You will know that I am the
 LORD,
 when I inflict punishment
 on you
 and within you am proved to
 be holy.
²³I will send a plague upon you
 and make blood flow in your
 streets.
The slain will fall within you,
 with the sword against you
 on every side.
Then you will know that I am
 the LORD.

²⁴"'No longer will the people of
Israel have malicious neighbors
who are painful briers and sharp
thorns. Then they will know that
I am the Sovereign LORD.

²⁵"'This is what the Sovereign
LORD says: When I gather the

people of Israel from the nations where they have been scattered, I will be proved holy through them in the sight of the nations. Then they will live in their own land, which I gave to my servant Jacob. **26** They will live there in safety and will build houses and plant vineyards; they will live in safety when I inflict punishment on all their neighbors who maligned them. Then they will know that I am the Lord their God.'"

A Prophecy Against Egypt

Judgment on Pharaoh

29 In the tenth year, in the tenth month on the twelfth day, the word of the Lord came to me: **2** "Son of man, set your face against Pharaoh king of Egypt and prophesy against him and against all Egypt. **3** Speak to him and say: 'This is what the Sovereign Lord says:

> "'I am against you, Pharaoh
>   king of Egypt,
>   you great monster lying
>   among your streams.
> You say, "The Nile belongs
>   to me;
>   I made it for myself."
> **4** But I will put hooks in your
>   jaws
>   and make the fish of your
>   streams stick to your
>   scales.

> I will pull you out from among
>   your streams,
>   with all the fish sticking to
>   your scales.
> **5** I will leave you in the desert,
>   you and all the fish of your
>   streams.
> You will fall on the open field
>   and not be gathered or
>   picked up.
> I will give you as food
>   to the beasts of the earth and
>   the birds of the sky.'

6 Then all who live in Egypt will know that I am the Lord.

"'You have been a staff of reed for the people of Israel. **7** When they grasped you with their hands, you splintered and you tore open their shoulders; when they leaned on you, you broke and their backs were wrenched.[a]

8 "'Therefore this is what the Sovereign Lord says: I will bring a sword against you and kill both man and beast. **9** Egypt will become a desolate wasteland. Then they will know that I am the Lord.

"'Because you said, "The Nile is mine; I made it," **10** therefore I am against you and against your streams, and I will make the land of Egypt a ruin and a desolate waste from Migdol to Aswan, as far as the border of Cush.[b] **11** The foot of neither man nor beast will pass through it; no one will

---

[a] 7 Syriac (see also Septuagint and Vulgate); Hebrew *and you caused their backs to stand*   [b] 10 That is, the upper Nile region

live there for forty years. **12** I will make the land of Egypt desolate among devastated lands, and her cities will lie desolate forty years among ruined cities. And I will disperse the Egyptians among the nations and scatter them through the countries.

13 " 'Yet this is what the Sovereign LORD says: At the end of forty years I will gather the Egyptians from the nations where they were scattered. **14** I will bring them back from captivity and return them to Upper Egypt, the land of their ancestry. There they will be a lowly kingdom. **15** It will be the lowliest of kingdoms and will never again exalt itself above the other nations. I will make it so weak that it will never again rule over the nations. **16** Egypt will no longer be a source of confidence for the people of Israel but will be a reminder of their sin in turning to her for help. Then they will know that I am the Sovereign LORD.' "

Nebuchadnezzar's Reward

17 In the twenty-seventh year, in the first month on the first day, the word of the LORD came to me: **18** "Son of man, Nebuchadnezzar king of Babylon drove his army in a hard campaign against Tyre; every head was rubbed bare and every shoulder made raw. Yet he and his army got no reward from the campaign he led against Tyre. **19** Therefore this is what the Sovereign LORD says: I am going to give Egypt to Nebuchadnezzar king of Babylon, and he will carry off its wealth. He will loot and plunder the land as pay for his army. **20** I have given him Egypt as a reward for his efforts because he and his army did it for me, declares the Sovereign LORD.

21 "On that day I will make a horn[a] grow for the Israelites, and I will open your mouth among them. Then they will know that I am the LORD."

A Lament Over Egypt

30 The word of the LORD came to me: **2** "Son of man, prophesy and say: 'This is what the Sovereign LORD says:

" 'Wail and say,
      "Alas for that day!"
3 For the day is near,
      the day of the LORD is near —
a day of clouds,
      a time of doom for the
            nations.
4 A sword will come against
            Egypt,
      and anguish will come upon
            Cush.[b]
When the slain fall in
            Egypt,
      her wealth will be carried
            away
      and her foundations torn
            down.

---

[a] *21 Horn* here symbolizes strength.
verses 5 and 9   [b] *4* That is, the upper Nile region; also in

5 Cush and Libya, Lydia and all Arabia, Kub and the people of the covenant land will fall by the sword along with Egypt.

6 " 'This is what the LORD says:

" 'The allies of Egypt will fall
    and her proud strength will
      fail.
From Migdol to Aswan
    they will fall by the sword
      within her,
            declares the Sovereign
              LORD.

7 " 'They will be desolate
    among desolate lands,
and their cities will lie
    among ruined cities.
8 Then they will know that I am
      the LORD,
    when I set fire to Egypt
    and all her helpers are
      crushed.

9 " 'On that day messengers will go out from me in ships to frighten Cush out of her complacency. Anguish will take hold of them on the day of Egypt's doom, for it is sure to come.

10 " 'This is what the Sovereign LORD says:

" 'I will put an end to the
        hordes of Egypt
    by the hand of
        Nebuchadnezzar king of
        Babylon.
11 He and his army — the most
      ruthless of nations —
    will be brought in to destroy
      the land.

They will draw their swords
      against Egypt
    and fill the land with the
      slain.
12 I will dry up the waters of the
      Nile
    and sell the land to an evil
      nation;
by the hand of foreigners
    I will lay waste the land and
      everything in it.

I the LORD have spoken.

13 " 'This is what the Sovereign LORD says:

" 'I will destroy the idols
    and put an end to the images
      in Memphis.
No longer will there be a
      prince in Egypt,
    and I will spread fear
      throughout the land.
14 I will lay waste Upper
      Egypt,
    set fire to Zoan
    and inflict punishment on
      Thebes.
15 I will pour out my wrath on
      Pelusium,
    the stronghold of Egypt,
    and wipe out the hordes of
      Thebes.
16 I will set fire to Egypt;
    Pelusium will writhe in
      agony.
Thebes will be taken by
      storm;
    Memphis will be in constant
      distress.
17 The young men of Heliopolis
    and Bubastis

will fall by the sword,
and the cities themselves
will go into captivity.
18 Dark will be the day at
Tahpanhes
when I break the yoke of
Egypt;
there her proud strength will
come to an end.
She will be covered with
clouds,
and her villages will go into
captivity.
19 So I will inflict punishment on
Egypt,
and they will know that I am
the LORD.' "

Pharaoh's Arms Are Broken

20 In the eleventh year, in the first month on the seventh day, the word of the LORD came to me: 21 "Son of man, I have broken the arm of Pharaoh king of Egypt. It has not been bound up to be healed or put in a splint so that it may become strong enough to hold a sword. 22 Therefore this is what the Sovereign LORD says: I am against Pharaoh king of Egypt. I will break both his arms, the good arm as well as the broken one, and make the sword fall from his hand. 23 I will disperse the Egyptians among the nations and scatter them through the countries. 24 I will strengthen the arms of the king of Babylon and put my sword in his hand, but I will break the arms of Pharaoh, and he will groan before him like a mortally wounded man. 25 I will strengthen the arms of the king of Babylon, but the arms of Pharaoh will fall limp. Then they will know that I am the LORD, when I put my sword into the hand of the king of Babylon and he brandishes it against Egypt. 26 I will disperse the Egyptians among the nations and scatter them through the countries. Then they will know that I am the LORD."

Pharaoh as a Felled Cedar of Lebanon

31 In the eleventh year, in the third month on the first day, the word of the LORD came to me: 2 "Son of man, say to Pharaoh king of Egypt and to his hordes:

" 'Who can be compared with
you in majesty?
3 Consider Assyria, once a cedar
in Lebanon,
with beautiful branches
overshadowing the
forest;
it towered on high,
its top above the thick
foliage.
4 The waters nourished it,
deep springs made it grow
tall;
their streams flowed
all around its base
and sent their channels
to all the trees of the
field.
5 So it towered higher
than all the trees of the
field;

its boughs increased
and its branches grew long,
spreading because of
abundant waters.
⁶All the birds of the sky
nested in its boughs,
all the animals of the wild
gave birth under its
branches;
all the great nations
lived in its shade.
⁷It was majestic in beauty,
with its spreading boughs,
for its roots went down
to abundant waters.
⁸The cedars in the garden of
God
could not rival it,
nor could the junipers
equal its boughs,
nor could the plane trees
compare with its branches —
no tree in the garden of God
could match its beauty.
⁹I made it beautiful
with abundant branches,
the envy of all the trees of
Eden
in the garden of God.

¹⁰ " 'Therefore this is what the Sovereign LORD says: Because the great cedar towered over the thick foliage, and because it was proud of its height, ¹¹I gave it into the hands of the ruler of the nations, for him to deal with according to its wickedness. I cast it aside, ¹²and the most ruthless of foreign nations cut it down and left it. Its boughs fell on the mountains and in all the val-leys; its branches lay broken in all the ravines of the land. All the nations of the earth came out from under its shade and left it. ¹³All the birds settled on the fallen tree, and all the wild animals lived among its branches. ¹⁴Therefore no other trees by the waters are ever to tower proudly on high, lifting their tops above the thick foliage. No other trees so well-watered are ever to reach such a height; they are all destined for death, for the earth below, among mortals who go down to the realm of the dead.

¹⁵ " 'This is what the Sovereign LORD says: On the day it was brought down to the realm of the dead I covered the deep springs with mourning for it; I held back its streams, and its abundant waters were restrained. Because of it I clothed Lebanon with gloom, and all the trees of the field withered away. ¹⁶I made the nations tremble at the sound of its fall when I brought it down to the realm of the dead to be with those who go down to the pit. Then all the trees of Eden, the choicest and best of Lebanon, the well-watered trees, were consoled in the earth below. ¹⁷They too, like the great cedar, had gone down to the realm of the dead, to those killed by the sword, along with the armed men who lived in its shade among the nations.

¹⁸ " 'Which of the trees of Eden can be compared with you in

splendor and majesty? Yet you, too, will be brought down with the trees of Eden to the earth below; you will lie among the uncircumcised, with those killed by the sword.

"'This is Pharaoh and all his hordes, declares the Sovereign LORD.'"

A Lament Over Pharaoh

32 In the twelfth year, in the twelfth month on the first day, the word of the LORD came to me: ² "Son of man, take up a lament concerning Pharaoh king of Egypt and say to him:

"'You are like a lion among the
nations;
you are like a monster in the
seas
thrashing about in your
streams,
churning the water with
your feet
and muddying the streams.

³ "'This is what the Sovereign
LORD says:

"'With a great throng of
people
I will cast my net over you,
and they will haul you up in
my net.
⁴ I will throw you on the
land
and hurl you on the open
field.
I will let all the birds of the sky
settle on you

and all the animals of the
wild gorge themselves on
you.
⁵ I will spread your flesh on the
mountains
and fill the valleys with your
remains.
⁶ I will drench the land with
your flowing blood
all the way to the mountains,
and the ravines will be filled
with your flesh.
⁷ When I snuff you out, I will
cover the heavens
and darken their stars;
I will cover the sun with a
cloud,
and the moon will not give
its light.
⁸ All the shining lights in the
heavens
I will darken over you;
I will bring darkness over
your land,
declares the Sovereign
LORD.
⁹ I will trouble the hearts of
many peoples
when I bring about your
destruction among the
nations,
among^a lands you have not
known.
¹⁰ I will cause many peoples to
be appalled at you,
and their kings will shudder
with horror because of
you
when I brandish my sword
before them.

---

^a 9 Hebrew; Septuagint *bring you into captivity among the nations, / to*

On the day of your downfall
each of them will tremble
every moment for his life.

¹¹ " 'For this is what the Sovereign LORD says:

" 'The sword of the king of
Babylon
will come against you.
¹²I will cause your hordes to
fall
by the swords of mighty
men—
the most ruthless of all
nations.
They will shatter the pride of
Egypt,
and all her hordes will be
overthrown.
¹³I will destroy all her cattle
from beside abundant
waters
no longer to be stirred by the
foot of man
or muddied by the hooves of
cattle.
¹⁴Then I will let her waters settle
and make her streams flow
like oil,
declares the Sovereign
LORD.
¹⁵When I make Egypt desolate
and strip the land of
everything in it,
when I strike down all who
live there,
then they will know that I
am the LORD.'

¹⁶"This is the lament they will
chant for her. The daughters of
the nations will chant it; for Egypt
and all her hordes they will chant
it, declares the Sovereign LORD."

Egypt's Descent Into the Realm of the Dead

¹⁷In the twelfth year, on the fifteenth day of the month, the word of the LORD came to me: ¹⁸"Son of man, wail for the hordes of Egypt and consign to the earth below both her and the daughters of mighty nations, along with those who go down to the pit. ¹⁹Say to them, 'Are you more favored than others? Go down and be laid among the uncircumcised.' ²⁰They will fall among those killed by the sword. The sword is drawn; let her be dragged off with all her hordes. ²¹From within the realm of the dead the mighty leaders will say of Egypt and her allies, 'They have come down and they lie with the uncircumcised, with those killed by the sword.'

²²"Assyria is there with her whole army; she is surrounded by the graves of all her slain, all who have fallen by the sword. ²³Their graves are in the depths of the pit and her army lies around her grave. All who had spread terror in the land of the living are slain, fallen by the sword.

²⁴"Elam is there, with all her hordes around her grave. All of them are slain, fallen by the sword. All who had spread terror in the land of the living went down uncircumcised to the

earth below. They bear their shame with those who go down to the pit. ²⁵A bed is made for her among the slain, with all her hordes around her grave. All of them are uncircumcised, killed by the sword. Because their terror had spread in the land of the living, they bear their shame with those who go down to the pit; they are laid among the slain.

²⁶"Meshek and Tubal are there, with all their hordes around their graves. All of them are uncircumcised, killed by the sword because they spread their terror in the land of the living. ²⁷But they do not lie with the fallen warriors of old,ᵃ who went down to the realm of the dead with their weapons of war — their swords placed under their heads and their shieldsᵇ resting on their bones — though these warriors also had terrorized the land of the living.

²⁸"You too, Pharaoh, will be broken and will lie among the uncircumcised, with those killed by the sword.

²⁹"Edom is there, her kings and all her princes; despite their power, they are laid with those killed by the sword. They lie with the uncircumcised, with those who go down to the pit.

³⁰"All the princes of the north and all the Sidonians are there; they went down with the slain in disgrace despite the terror caused by their power. They lie uncircumcised with those killed by the sword and bear their shame with those who go down to the pit.

³¹"Pharaoh — he and all his army — will see them and he will be consoled for all his hordes that were killed by the sword, declares the Sovereign LORD. ³²Although I had him spread terror in the land of the living, Pharaoh and all his hordes will be laid among the uncircumcised, with those killed by the sword, declares the Sovereign LORD."

Renewal of Ezekiel's Call as Watchman

33 The word of the LORD came to me: ²"Son of man, speak to your people and say to them: 'When I bring the sword against a land, and the people of the land choose one of their men and make him their watchman, ³and he sees the sword coming against the land and blows the trumpet to warn the people, ⁴then if anyone hears the trumpet but does not heed the warning and the sword comes and takes their life, their blood will be on their own head. ⁵Since they heard the sound of the trumpet but did not heed the warning, their blood will be on their own head. If they had

---

ᵃ 27 Septuagint; Hebrew *warriors who were uncircumcised*   ᵇ 27 Probable reading of the original Hebrew text; Masoretic Text *punishment* heeded the warning, they would have saved themselves. **6**But if the watchman sees the sword coming and does not blow the trumpet to warn the people and the sword comes and takes someone's life, that person's life will be taken because of their sin, but I will hold the watchman accountable for their blood.'

7"Son of man, I have made you a watchman for the people of Israel; so hear the word I speak and give them warning from me. **8**When I say to the wicked, 'You wicked person, you will surely die,' and you do not speak out to dissuade them from their ways, that wicked person will die for*a* their sin, and I will hold you accountable for their blood. **9**But if you do warn the wicked person to turn from their ways and they do not do so, they will die for their sin, though you yourself will be saved.

10"Son of man, say to the Israelites, 'This is what you are saying: "Our offenses and sins weigh us down, and we are wasting away because of*b* them. How then can we live?"' **11**Say to them, 'As surely as I live, declares the Sovereign LORD, I take no pleasure in the death of the wicked, but rather that they turn from their ways and live. Turn! Turn from your evil ways! Why will you die, people of Israel?'

12"Therefore, son of man, say to your people, 'If someone who is righteous disobeys, that person's former righteousness will count for nothing. And if someone who is wicked repents, that person's former wickedness will not bring condemnation. The righteous person who sins will not be allowed to live even though they were formerly righteous.' **13**If I tell a righteous person that they will surely live, but then they trust in their righteousness and do evil, none of the righteous things that person has done will be remembered; they will die for the evil they have done. **14**And if I say to a wicked person, 'You will surely die,' but they then turn away from their sin and do what is just and right— **15**if they give back what they took in pledge for a loan, return what they have stolen, follow the decrees that give life, and do no evil—that person will surely live; they will not die. **16**None of the sins that person has committed will be remembered against them. They have done what is just and right; they will surely live.

17"Yet your people say, 'The way of the Lord is not just.' But it is their way that is not just. **18**If a righteous person turns from their righteousness and does evil, they will die for it. **19**And if a wicked person turns away from their wickedness and does what is just and right, they will live by doing so. **20**Yet you Israelites say, 'The

---

a 8 Or *in*; also in verse 9   *b 10* Or *away in*

way of the Lord is not just.' But I will judge each of you according to your own ways."

Jerusalem's Fall Explained

²¹ In the twelfth year of our exile, in the tenth month on the fifth day, a man who had escaped from Jerusalem came to me and said, "The city has fallen!" ²² Now the evening before the man arrived, the hand of the LORD was on me, and he opened my mouth before the man came to me in the morning. So my mouth was opened and I was no longer silent.

²³ Then the word of the LORD came to me: ²⁴ "Son of man, the people living in those ruins in the land of Israel are saying, 'Abraham was only one man, yet he possessed the land. But we are many; surely the land has been given to us as our possession.' ²⁵ Therefore say to them, 'This is what the Sovereign LORD says: Since you eat meat with the blood still in it and look to your idols and shed blood, should you then possess the land? ²⁶ You rely on your sword, you do detestable things, and each of you defiles his neighbor's wife. Should you then possess the land?'

²⁷ "Say this to them: 'This is what the Sovereign LORD says: As surely as I live, those who are left in the ruins will fall by the sword, those out in the country I will give to the wild animals to be de-

voured, and those in strongholds and caves will die of a plague. ²⁸ I will make the land a desolate waste, and her proud strength will come to an end, and the mountains of Israel will become desolate so that no one will cross them. ²⁹ Then they will know that I am the LORD, when I have made the land a desolate waste because of all the detestable things they have done.'

³⁰ "As for you, son of man, your people are talking together about you by the walls and at the doors of the houses, saying to each other, 'Come and hear the message that has come from the LORD.' ³¹ My people come to you, as they usually do, and sit before you to hear your words, but they do not put them into practice. Their mouths speak of love, but their hearts are greedy for unjust gain. ³² Indeed, to them you are nothing more than one who sings love songs with a beautiful voice and plays an instrument well, for they hear your words but do not put them into practice.

³³ "When all this comes true — and it surely will — then they will know that a prophet has been among them."

The LORD Will Be Israel's Shepherd

34 The word of the LORD came to me: ² "Son of man, prophesy against the shepherds of Israel; prophesy and say to them: 'This is what the Sovereign LORD says: Woe to you shepherds of Israel who only take care of yourselves! Should not shepherds take care of the flock? ³You eat the curds, clothe yourselves with the wool and slaughter the choice animals, but you do not take care of the flock. ⁴You have not strengthened the weak or healed the sick or bound up the injured. You have not brought back the strays or searched for the lost. You have ruled them harshly and brutally. ⁵So they were scattered because there was no shepherd, and when they were scattered they became food for all the wild animals. ⁶My sheep wandered over all the mountains and on every high hill. They were scattered over the whole earth, and no one searched or looked for them.

⁷ "'Therefore, you shepherds, hear the word of the LORD: ⁸As surely as I live, declares the Sovereign LORD, because my flock lacks a shepherd and so has been plundered and has become food for all the wild animals, and because my shepherds did not search for my flock but cared for themselves rather than for my flock, ⁹therefore, you shepherds, hear the word of the LORD: ¹⁰This is what the Sovereign LORD says: I am against the shepherds and will hold them accountable for my flock. I will remove them from tending the flock so that the shepherds can no longer feed themselves. I will rescue my flock from their mouths, and it will no longer be food for them.

¹¹ "'For this is what the Sovereign LORD says: I myself will search for my sheep and look after them. ¹²As a shepherd looks after his scattered flock when he is with them, so will I look after my sheep. I will rescue them from all the places where they were scattered on a day of clouds and darkness. ¹³I will bring them out from the nations and gather them from the countries, and I will bring them into their own land. I will pasture them on the mountains of Israel, in the ravines and in all the settlements in the land. ¹⁴I will tend them in a good pasture, and the mountain heights of Israel will be their grazing land. There they will lie down in good grazing land, and there they will feed in a rich pasture on the mountains of Israel. ¹⁵I myself will tend my sheep and have them lie down, declares the Sovereign LORD. ¹⁶I will search for the lost and bring back the strays. I will bind up the injured and strengthen the weak, but the sleek and the strong I will destroy. I will shepherd the flock with justice.

¹⁷ "'As for you, my flock, this is what the Sovereign LORD says: I will judge between one sheep and another, and between rams and goats. ¹⁸Is it not enough for

you to feed on the good pasture? Must you also trample the rest of your pasture with your feet? Is it not enough for you to drink clear water? Must you also muddy the rest with your feet? ¹⁹Must my flock feed on what you have trampled and drink what you have muddied with your feet?

²⁰"'Therefore this is what the Sovereign Lord says to them: See, I myself will judge between the fat sheep and the lean sheep. ²¹Because you shove with flank and shoulder, butting all the weak sheep with your horns until you have driven them away, ²²I will save my flock, and they will no longer be plundered. I will judge between one sheep and another. ²³I will place over them one shepherd, my servant David, and he will tend them; he will tend them and be their shepherd. ²⁴I the Lord will be their God, and my servant David will be prince among them. I the Lord have spoken.

²⁵"'I will make a covenant of peace with them and rid the land of savage beasts so that they may live in the wilderness and sleep in the forests in safety. ²⁶I will make them and the places surrounding my hill a blessing.ᵃ I will send down showers in season; there will be showers of blessing. ²⁷The trees will yield their fruit and the ground will yield its crops; the people will be secure in their land. They will know that I am the Lord, when I break the bars of their yoke and rescue them from the hands of those who enslaved them. ²⁸They will no longer be plundered by the nations, nor will wild animals devour them. They will live in safety, and no one will make them afraid. ²⁹I will provide for them a land renowned for its crops, and they will no longer be victims of famine in the land or bear the scorn of the nations. ³⁰Then they will know that I, the Lord their God, am with them and that they, the Israelites, are my people, declares the Sovereign Lord. ³¹You are my sheep, the sheep of my pasture, and I am your God, declares the Sovereign Lord.'"

A Prophecy Against Edom

35 The word of the Lord came to me: ²"Son of man, set your face against Mount Seir; prophesy against it ³and say: 'This is what the Sovereign Lord says: I am against you, Mount Seir, and I will stretch out my hand against you and make you a desolate waste. ⁴I will turn your towns into ruins and you will be desolate. Then you will know that I am the Lord.

ᵃ 26 Or *I will cause them and the places surrounding my hill to be named in blessings* (see Gen. 48:20); or *I will cause them and the places surrounding my hill to be seen as blessed*

⁵ " 'Because you harbored an ancient hostility and delivered the Israelites over to the sword at the time of their calamity, the time their punishment reached its climax, ⁶therefore as surely as I live, declares the Sovereign LORD, I will give you over to bloodshed and it will pursue you. Since you did not hate bloodshed, bloodshed will pursue you. ⁷I will make Mount Seir a desolate waste and cut off from it all who come and go. ⁸I will fill your mountains with the slain; those killed by the sword will fall on your hills and in your valleys and in all your ravines. ⁹I will make you desolate forever; your towns will not be inhabited. Then you will know that I am the LORD.

¹⁰ " 'Because you have said, "These two nations and countries will be ours and we will take possession of them," even though I the LORD was there, ¹¹therefore as surely as I live, declares the Sovereign LORD, I will treat you in accordance with the anger and jealousy you showed in your hatred of them and I will make myself known among them when I judge you. ¹²Then you will know that I the LORD have heard all the contemptible things you have said against the mountains of Israel. You said, "They have been laid waste and have been given over to us to devour." ¹³You boasted against me and spoke against me without restraint, and I heard it. ¹⁴This is what the Sovereign LORD says: While the whole earth rejoices, I will make you desolate. ¹⁵Because you rejoiced when the inheritance of Israel became desolate, that is how I will treat you. You will be desolate, Mount Seir, you and all of Edom. Then they will know that I am the LORD.' "

Hope for the Mountains of Israel

36 "Son of man, prophesy to the mountains of Israel and say, 'Mountains of Israel, hear the word of the LORD. ²This is what the Sovereign LORD says: The enemy said of you, "Aha! The ancient heights have become our possession." ' ³Therefore prophesy and say, 'This is what the Sovereign LORD says: Because they ravaged and crushed you from every side so that you became the possession of the rest of the nations and the object of people's malicious talk and slander, ⁴therefore, mountains of Israel, hear the word of the Sovereign LORD: This is what the Sovereign LORD says to the mountains and hills, to the ravines and valleys, to the desolate ruins and the deserted towns that have been plundered and ridiculed by the rest of the nations around you — ⁵this is what the Sovereign LORD says: In my burning zeal I have spoken against the rest of the nations, and against all Edom,

for with glee and with malice in their hearts they made my land their own possession so that they might plunder its pastureland.' ⁶Therefore prophesy concerning the land of Israel and say to the mountains and hills, to the ravines and valleys: 'This is what the Sovereign LORD says: I speak in my jealous wrath because you have suffered the scorn of the nations. ⁷Therefore this is what the Sovereign LORD says: I swear with uplifted hand that the nations around you will also suffer scorn.

⁸"'But you, mountains of Israel, will produce branches and fruit for my people Israel, for they will soon come home. ⁹I am concerned for you and will look on you with favor; you will be plowed and sown, ¹⁰and I will cause many people to live on you—yes, all of Israel. The towns will be inhabited and the ruins rebuilt. ¹¹I will increase the number of people and animals living on you, and they will be fruitful and become numerous. I will settle people on you as in the past and will make you prosper more than before. Then you will know that I am the LORD. ¹²I will cause people, my people Israel, to live on you. They will possess you, and you will be their inheritance; you will never again deprive them of their children.

¹³"This is what the Sovereign LORD says: Because some say to you, "You devour people and deprive your nation of its children," ¹⁴therefore you will no longer devour people or make your nation childless, declares the Sovereign LORD. ¹⁵No longer will I make you hear the taunts of the nations, and no longer will you suffer the scorn of the peoples or cause your nation to fall, declares the Sovereign LORD.'"

Israel's Restoration Assured

¹⁶Again the word of the LORD came to me: ¹⁷"Son of man, when the people of Israel were living in their own land, they defiled it by their conduct and their actions. Their conduct was like a woman's monthly uncleanness in my sight. ¹⁸So I poured out my wrath on them because they had shed blood in the land and because they had defiled it with their idols. ¹⁹I dispersed them among the nations, and they were scattered through the countries; I judged them according to their conduct and their actions. ²⁰And wherever they went among the nations they profaned my holy name, for it was said of them, 'These are the LORD's people, and yet they had to leave his land.' ²¹I had concern for my holy name, which the people of Israel profaned among the nations where they had gone.

²²"Therefore say to the Israelites, 'This is what the Sovereign LORD says: It is not for your sake, people of Israel, that I am

going to do these things, but for the sake of my holy name, which you have profaned among the nations where you have gone. **23** I will show the holiness of my great name, which has been profaned among the nations, the name you have profaned among them. Then the nations will know that I am the LORD, declares the Sovereign LORD, when I am proved holy through you before their eyes.

24 " 'For I will take you out of the nations; I will gather you from all the countries and bring you back into your own land. **25** I will sprinkle clean water on you, and you will be clean; I will cleanse you from all your impurities and from all your idols. **26** I will give you a new heart and put a new spirit in you; I will remove from you your heart of stone and give you a heart of flesh. **27** And I will put my Spirit in you and move you to follow my decrees and be careful to keep my laws. **28** Then you will live in the land I gave your ancestors; you will be my people, and I will be your God. **29** I will save you from all your uncleanness. I will call for the grain and make it plentiful and will not bring famine upon you. **30** I will increase the fruit of the trees and the crops of the field, so that you will no longer suffer disgrace among the nations because of famine. **31** Then you will remember your evil ways and wicked deeds, and you will loathe yourselves for your

sins and detestable practices. **32** I want you to know that I am not doing this for your sake, declares the Sovereign LORD. Be ashamed and disgraced for your conduct, people of Israel!

33 " 'This is what the Sovereign LORD says: On the day I cleanse you from all your sins, I will resettle your towns, and the ruins will be rebuilt. **34** The desolate land will be cultivated instead of lying desolate in the sight of all who pass through it. **35** They will say, "This land that was laid waste has become like the garden of Eden; the cities that were lying in ruins, desolate and destroyed, are now fortified and inhabited." **36** Then the nations around you that remain will know that I the LORD have rebuilt what was destroyed and have replanted what was desolate. I the LORD have spoken, and I will do it.'

37 "This is what the Sovereign LORD says: Once again I will yield to Israel's plea and do this for them: I will make their people as numerous as sheep, **38** as numerous as the flocks for offerings at Jerusalem during her appointed festivals. So will the ruined cities be filled with flocks of people. Then they will know that I am the LORD."

The Valley of Dry Bones

37 The hand of the LORD was on me, and he brought me out by the Spirit of the LORD and set me in the middle of a valley; it was full of bones. ²He led me back and forth among them, and I saw a great many bones on the floor of the valley, bones that were very dry. ³He asked me, "Son of man, can these bones live?"

I said, "Sovereign LORD, you alone know."

⁴Then he said to me, "Prophesy to these bones and say to them, 'Dry bones, hear the word of the LORD! ⁵This is what the Sovereign LORD says to these bones: I will make breath*ᵃ* enter you, and you will come to life. ⁶I will attach tendons to you and make flesh come upon you and cover you with skin; I will put breath in you, and you will come to life. Then you will know that I am the LORD.'"

⁷So I prophesied as I was commanded. And as I was prophesying, there was a noise, a rattling sound, and the bones came together, bone to bone. ⁸I looked, and tendons and flesh appeared on them and skin covered them, but there was no breath in them.

⁹Then he said to me, "Prophesy to the breath; prophesy, son of man, and say to it, 'This is what the Sovereign LORD says: Come, breath, from the four winds and breathe into these slain, that they may live.'" ¹⁰So I prophesied as he commanded me, and breath entered them; they came to life

and stood up on their feet — a vast army.

¹¹Then he said to me: "Son of man, these bones are the people of Israel. They say, 'Our bones are dried up and our hope is gone; we are cut off.' ¹²Therefore prophesy and say to them: 'This is what the Sovereign LORD says: My people, I am going to open your graves and bring you up from them; I will bring you back to the land of Israel. ¹³Then you, my people, will know that I am the LORD, when I open your graves and bring you up from them. ¹⁴I will put my Spirit in you and you will live, and I will settle you in your own land. Then you will know that I the LORD have spoken, and I have done it, declares the LORD.'"

One Nation Under One King

¹⁵The word of the LORD came to me: ¹⁶"Son of man, take a stick of wood and write on it, 'Belonging to Judah and the Israelites associated with him.' Then take another stick of wood, and write on it, 'Belonging to Joseph (that is, to Ephraim) and all the Israelites associated with him.' ¹⁷Join them together into one stick so that they will become one in your hand.

¹⁸"When your people ask you, 'Won't you tell us what you mean by this?' ¹⁹say to them, 'This is what the Sovereign LORD says: I

ᵃ 5 The Hebrew for this word can also mean *wind* or *spirit* (see verses 6-14).

am going to take the stick of Joseph—which is in Ephraim's hand—and of the Israelite tribes associated with him, and join it to Judah's stick. I will make them into a single stick of wood, and they will become one in my hand.' **20** Hold before their eyes the sticks you have written on **21** and say to them, 'This is what the Sovereign LORD says: I will take the Israelites out of the nations where they have gone. I will gather them from all around and bring them back into their own land. **22** I will make them one nation in the land, on the mountains of Israel. There will be one king over all of them and they will never again be two nations or be divided into two kingdoms. **23** They will no longer defile themselves with their idols and vile images or with any of their offenses, for I will save them from all their sinful backsliding,*a* and I will cleanse them. They will be my people, and I will be their God.

24 "'My servant David will be king over them, and they will all have one shepherd. They will follow my laws and be careful to keep my decrees. **25** They will live in the land I gave to my servant Jacob, the land where your ancestors lived. They and their children and their children's children will live there forever, and David my servant will be their prince

forever. **26** I will make a covenant of peace with them; it will be an everlasting covenant. I will establish them and increase their numbers, and I will put my sanctuary among them forever. **27** My dwelling place will be with them; I will be their God, and they will be my people. **28** Then the nations will know that I the LORD make Israel holy, when my sanctuary is among them forever.'"

The LORD's Great Victory Over the Nations

38 The word of the LORD came to me: **2** "Son of man, set your face against Gog, of the land of Magog, the chief prince of*b* Meshek and Tubal; prophesy against him **3** and say: 'This is what the Sovereign LORD says: I am against you, Gog, chief prince of*c* Meshek and Tubal. **4** I will turn you around, put hooks in your jaws and bring you out with your whole army—your horses, your horsemen fully armed, and a great horde with large and small shields, all of them brandishing their swords. **5** Persia, Cush*d* and Put will be with them, all with shields and helmets, **6** also Gomer with all its troops, and Beth Togarmah from the far north with all its troops— the many nations with you.

7 "'Get ready; be prepared, you and all the hordes gathered about

---

a 23 Many Hebrew manuscripts (see also Septuagint); most Hebrew manuscripts *all their dwelling places where they sinned*   *b* 2 Or *the prince of Rosh,*   *c* 3 Or *Gog, prince of Rosh,*   *d* 5 That is, the upper Nile region you, and take command of them. ⁸After many days you will be called to arms. In future years you will invade a land that has recovered from war, whose people were gathered from many nations to the mountains of Israel, which had long been desolate. They had been brought out from the nations, and now all of them live in safety. ⁹You and all your troops and the many nations with you will go up, advancing like a storm; you will be like a cloud covering the land.

¹⁰ " 'This is what the Sovereign LORD says: On that day thoughts will come into your mind and you will devise an evil scheme. ¹¹You will say, "I will invade a land of unwalled villages; I will attack a peaceful and unsuspecting people — all of them living without walls and without gates and bars. ¹²I will plunder and loot and turn my hand against the resettled ruins and the people gathered from the nations, rich in livestock and goods, living at the center of the land.ᵃ" ¹³Sheba and Dedan and the merchants of Tarshish and all her villagesᵇ will say to you, "Have you come to plunder? Have you gathered your hordes to loot, to carry off silver and gold, to take away livestock and goods and to seize much plunder?" '

¹⁴ "Therefore, son of man, prophesy and say to Gog: 'This is what the Sovereign LORD says: In that day, when my people Israel are living in safety, will you not take notice of it? ¹⁵You will come from your place in the far north, you and many nations with you, all of them riding on horses, a great horde, a mighty army. ¹⁶You will advance against my people Israel like a cloud that covers the land. In days to come, Gog, I will bring you against my land, so that the nations may know me when I am proved holy through you before their eyes.

¹⁷ " 'This is what the Sovereign LORD says: You are the one I spoke of in former days by my servants the prophets of Israel. At that time they prophesied for years that I would bring you against them. ¹⁸This is what will happen in that day: When Gog attacks the land of Israel, my hot anger will be aroused, declares the Sovereign LORD. ¹⁹In my zeal and fiery wrath I declare that at that time there shall be a great earthquake in the land of Israel. ²⁰The fish in the sea, the birds in the sky, the beasts of the field, every creature that moves along the ground, and all the people on the face of the earth will tremble at my presence. The mountains will be overturned, the cliffs will crumble and every wall will fall to the ground. ²¹I will summon a sword against Gog on all my mountains,

---

ᵃ 12 The Hebrew for this phrase means *the navel of the earth.*   ᵇ 13 Or *her strong lions* declares the Sovereign Lord. Every man's sword will be against his brother. ²²I will execute judgment on him with plague and bloodshed; I will pour down torrents of rain, hailstones and burning sulfur on him and on his troops and on the many nations with him. ²³And so I will show my greatness and my holiness, and I will make myself known in the sight of many nations. Then they will know that I am the Lord.'

39 "Son of man, prophesy against Gog and say: 'This is what the Sovereign Lord says: I am against you, Gog, chief prince of*ᵃ* Meshek and Tubal. ²I will turn you around and drag you along. I will bring you from the far north and send you against the mountains of Israel. ³Then I will strike your bow from your left hand and make your arrows drop from your right hand. ⁴On the mountains of Israel you will fall, you and all your troops and the nations with you. I will give you as food to all kinds of carrion birds and to the wild animals. ⁵You will fall in the open field, for I have spoken, declares the Sovereign Lord. ⁶I will send fire on Magog and on those who live in safety in the coastlands, and they will know that I am the Lord.

⁷"'I will make known my holy name among my people Israel. I will no longer let my holy name

be profaned, and the nations will know that I the Lord am the Holy One in Israel. ⁸It is coming! It will surely take place, declares the Sovereign Lord. This is the day I have spoken of.

⁹"'Then those who live in the towns of Israel will go out and use the weapons for fuel and burn them up—the small and large shields, the bows and arrows, the war clubs and spears. For seven years they will use them for fuel. ¹⁰They will not need to gather wood from the fields or cut it from the forests, because they will use the weapons for fuel. And they will plunder those who plundered them and loot those who looted them, declares the Sovereign Lord.

¹¹"'On that day I will give Gog a burial place in Israel, in the valley of those who travel east of the Sea. It will block the way of travelers, because Gog and all his hordes will be buried there. So it will be called the Valley of Hamon Gog.*ᵇ*

¹²"'For seven months the Israelites will be burying them in order to cleanse the land. ¹³All the people of the land will bury them, and the day I display my glory will be a memorable day for them, declares the Sovereign Lord. ¹⁴People will be continually employed in cleansing the land. They will spread out across the land and, along with others,

ᵃ 1 Or *Gog, prince of Rosh,*   *ᵇ* 11 *Hamon Gog* means *hordes of Gog.*

they will bury any bodies that are lying on the ground.

"'After the seven months they will carry out a more detailed search. **15** As they go through the land, anyone who sees a human bone will leave a marker beside it until the gravediggers bury it in the Valley of Hamon Gog, **16** near a town called Hamonah.[a] And so they will cleanse the land.'

17 "Son of man, this is what the Sovereign LORD says: Call out to every kind of bird and all the wild animals: 'Assemble and come together from all around to the sacrifice I am preparing for you, the great sacrifice on the mountains of Israel. There you will eat flesh and drink blood. **18** You will eat the flesh of mighty men and drink the blood of the princes of the earth as if they were rams and lambs, goats and bulls — all of them fattened animals from Bashan. **19** At the sacrifice I am preparing for you, you will eat fat till you are glutted and drink blood till you are drunk. **20** At my table you will eat your fill of horses and riders, mighty men and soldiers of every kind,' declares the Sovereign LORD.

21 "I will display my glory among the nations, and all the nations will see the punishment I inflict and the hand I lay on them. **22** From that day forward the people of Israel will know that I am the LORD their God. **23** And the nations will know that the people of Israel went into exile for their sin, because they were unfaithful to me. So I hid my face from them and handed them over to their enemies, and they all fell by the sword. **24** I dealt with them according to their uncleanness and their offenses, and I hid my face from them.

25 "Therefore this is what the Sovereign LORD says: I will now restore the fortunes of Jacob[b] and will have compassion on all the people of Israel, and I will be zealous for my holy name. **26** They will forget their shame and all the unfaithfulness they showed toward me when they lived in safety in their land with no one to make them afraid. **27** When I have brought them back from the nations and have gathered them from the countries of their enemies, I will be proved holy through them in the sight of many nations. **28** Then they will know that I am the LORD their God, for though I sent them into exile among the nations, I will gather them to their own land, not leaving any behind. **29** I will no longer hide my face from them, for I will pour out my Spirit on the people of Israel, declares the Sovereign LORD."

The Temple Area Restored

40 In the twenty-fifth year of our exile, at the beginning of the year, on the tenth of

---

[a] 16 *Hamonah* means *horde.*   [b] 25 Or *now bring Jacob back from captivity*

the month, in the fourteenth year after the fall of the city — on that very day the hand of the LORD was on me and he took me there. [2] In visions of God he took me to the land of Israel and set me on a very high mountain, on whose south side were some buildings that looked like a city. [3] He took me there, and I saw a man whose appearance was like bronze; he was standing in the gateway with a linen cord and a measuring rod in his hand. [4] The man said to me, "Son of man, look carefully and listen closely and pay attention to everything I am going to show you, for that is why you have been brought here. Tell the people of Israel everything you see."

The East Gate to the Outer Court

[5] I saw a wall completely surrounding the temple area. The length of the measuring rod in the man's hand was six long cubits,[a] each of which was a cubit and a handbreadth. He measured the wall; it was one measuring rod thick and one rod high.

[6] Then he went to the east gate. He climbed its steps and mea-sured the threshold of the gate; it was one rod deep. [7] The alcoves for the guards were one rod long and one rod wide, and the projecting walls between the alcoves were five cubits[b] thick. And the threshold of the gate next to the portico facing the temple was one rod deep.

[8] Then he measured the portico of the gateway; [9] it[c] was eight cubits[d] deep and its jambs were two cubits[e] thick. The portico of the gateway faced the temple.

[10] Inside the east gate were three alcoves on each side; the three had the same measurements, and the faces of the projecting walls on each side had the same measurements. [11] Then he measured the width of the entrance of the gateway; it was ten cubits and its length was thirteen cubits.[f] [12] In front of each alcove was a wall one cubit high, and the alcoves were six cubits square. [13] Then he measured the gateway from the top of the rear wall of one alcove to the top of the opposite one; the distance was twenty-five cubits[g] from one parapet opening to the opposite one. [14] He measured along the faces of the projecting walls all around

---

[a] 5 That is, about 11 feet or about 3.2 meters; also in verse 12. The long cubit of about 21 inches or about 53 centimeters is the basic unit of measurement of length throughout chapters 40–48.   [b] 7 That is, about 8 3/4 feet or about 2.7 meters; also in verse 48   [c] 8,9 Many Hebrew manuscripts, Septuagint, Vulgate and Syriac; most Hebrew manuscripts *gateway facing the temple; it was one rod deep. [9] Then he measured the portico of the gateway; it*   [d] 9. That is, about 14 feet or about 4.2 meters   [e] 9 That is, about 3 1/2 feet or about 1 meter   [f] 11 That is, about 18 feet wide and 23 feet long or about 5.3 meters wide and 6.9 meters long   [g] 13 That is, about 44 feet or about 13 meters; also in verses 21, 25, 29, 30, 33 and 36

the inside of the gateway — sixty cubits.[a] The measurement was up to the portico[b] facing the courtyard.[c] **15** The distance from the entrance of the gateway to the far end of its portico was fifty cubits.[d] **16** The alcoves and the projecting walls inside the gateway were surmounted by narrow parapet openings all around, as was the portico; the openings all around faced inward. The faces of the projecting walls were decorated with palm trees.

The Outer Court

17 Then he brought me into the outer court. There I saw some rooms and a pavement that had been constructed all around the court; there were thirty rooms along the pavement. **18** It abutted the sides of the gateways and was as wide as they were long; this was the lower pavement. **19** Then he measured the distance from the inside of the lower gateway to the outside of the inner court; it was a hundred cubits[e] on the east side as well as on the north.

The North Gate

20 Then he measured the length and width of the north gate, leading into the outer court. **21** Its alcoves — three on each side — its projecting walls and its portico had the same measurements as those of the first gateway. It was fifty cubits long and twenty-five cubits wide. **22** Its openings, its portico and its palm tree decorations had the same measurements as those of the gate facing east. Seven steps led up to it, with its portico opposite them. **23** There was a gate to the inner court facing the north gate, just as there was on the east. He measured from one gate to the opposite one; it was a hundred cubits.

The South Gate

24 Then he led me to the south side and I saw the south gate. He measured its jambs and its portico, and they had the same measurements as the others. **25** The gateway and its portico had narrow openings all around, like the openings of the others. It was fifty cubits long and twenty-five cubits wide. **26** Seven steps led up to it, with its portico opposite them; it had palm tree decorations on the faces of the projecting walls on each side. **27** The inner court also had a gate facing south, and he measured from this gate to the outer gate on the south side; it was a hundred cubits.

The Gates to the Inner Court

28 Then he brought me into the inner court through the south gate, and he measured the south

---

[a] *14* That is, about 105 feet or about 32 meters   [b] *14* Septuagint; Hebrew *projecting wall*   [c] *14* The meaning of the Hebrew for this verse is uncertain.
[d] *15* That is, about 88 feet or about 27 meters; also in verses 21, 25, 29, 33 and 36
[e] *19* That is, about 175 feet or about 53 meters; also in verses 23, 27 and 47

gate; it had the same measurements as the others. **29**Its alcoves, its projecting walls and its portico had the same measurements as the others. The gateway and its portico had openings all around. It was fifty cubits long and twenty-five cubits wide. **30**(The porticoes of the gateways around the inner court were twenty-five cubits wide and five cubits deep.) **31**Its portico faced the outer court; palm trees decorated its jambs, and eight steps led up to it.

32Then he brought me to the inner court on the east side, and he measured the gateway; it had the same measurements as the others. **33**Its alcoves, its projecting walls and its portico had the same measurements as the others. The gateway and its portico had openings all around. It was fifty cubits long and twenty-five cubits wide. **34**Its portico faced the outer court; palm trees decorated the jambs on either side, and eight steps led up to it.

35Then he brought me to the north gate and measured it. It had the same measurements as the others, **36**as did its alcoves, its projecting walls and its portico, and it had openings all around. It was fifty cubits long and twenty-five cubits wide. **37**Its portico[a] faced the outer court; palm trees

decorated the jambs on either side, and eight steps led up to it.

The Rooms for Preparing Sacrifices

38A room with a doorway was by the portico in each of the inner gateways, where the burnt offerings were washed. **39**In the portico of the gateway were two tables on each side, on which the burnt offerings, sin offerings[b] and guilt offerings were slaughtered. **40**By the outside wall of the portico of the gateway, near the steps at the entrance of the north gateway were two tables, and on the other side of the steps were two tables. **41**So there were four tables on one side of the gateway and four on the other — eight tables in all — on which the sacrifices were slaughtered. **42**There were also four tables of dressed stone for the burnt offerings, each a cubit and a half long, a cubit and a half wide and a cubit high.[c] On them were placed the utensils for slaughtering the burnt offerings and the other sacrifices. **43**And double-pronged hooks, each a handbreadth[d] long, were attached to the wall all around. The tables were for the flesh of the offerings.

The Rooms for the Priests

44Outside the inner gate, within the inner court, were two rooms,

---

[a] 37 Septuagint (see also verses 31 and 34); Hebrew *jambs*   [b] 39 Or *purification offerings*   [c] 42 That is, about 2 2/3 feet long and wide and 21 inches high or about 80 centimeters long and wide and 53 centimeters high   [d] 43 That is, about 3 1/2 inches or about 9 centimeters

one[a] at the side of the north gate and facing south, and another at the side of the south[b] gate and facing north. **45**He said to me, "The room facing south is for the priests who guard the temple, **46**and the room facing north is for the priests who guard the altar. These are the sons of Zadok, who are the only Levites who may draw near to the LORD to minister before him."

47Then he measured the court: It was square — a hundred cubits long and a hundred cubits wide. And the altar was in front of the temple.

The New Temple

48He brought me to the portico of the temple and measured the jambs of the portico; they were five cubits wide on either side. The width of the entrance was fourteen cubits[c] and its projecting walls were[d] three cubits[e] wide on either side. **49**The portico was twenty cubits[f] wide, and twelve[g] cubits[h] from front to back. It was reached by a flight of stairs,[i] and there were pillars on each side of the jambs.

41 Then the man brought me to the main hall and measured the jambs; the width of the jambs was six cubits[j] on each side.[k] **2**The entrance was ten cubits[l] wide, and the projecting walls on each side of it were five cubits[m] wide. He also measured the main hall; it was forty cubits long and twenty cubits wide.[n]

3Then he went into the inner sanctuary and measured the jambs of the entrance; each was two cubits[o] wide. The entrance was six cubits wide, and the projecting walls on each side of it were seven cubits[p] wide. **4**And he measured the length of the inner sanctuary; it was twenty cubits, and its width was twenty cubits across the end of the main hall. He said to me, "This is the Most Holy Place."

5Then he measured the wall of the temple; it was six cubits thick, and each side room around the temple was four cubits[q] wide. **6**The side rooms were on three levels, one above another, thirty on each level. There were ledges all around the wall of the tem-

---

[a] 44 Septuagint; Hebrew *were rooms for singers, which were*   [b] 44 Septuagint; Hebrew *east*   [c] 48 That is, about 25 feet or about 7.4 meters   [d] 48 Septuagint; Hebrew *entrance was*   [e] 48 That is, about 5 1/4 feet or about 1.6 meters   [f] 49 That is, about 35 feet or about 11 meters   [g] 49 Septuagint; Hebrew *eleven*   [h] 49 That is, about 21 feet or about 6.4 meters   [i] 49 Hebrew; Septuagint *Ten steps led up to it*   [j] 1 That is, about 11 feet or about 3.2 meters; also in verses 3, 5 and 8   [k] 1 One Hebrew manuscript and Septuagint; most Hebrew manuscripts *side, the width of the tent*   [l] 2 That is, about 18 feet or about 5.3 meters   [m] 2 That is, about 8 3/4 feet or about 2.7 meters; also in verses 9, 11 and 12   [n] 2 That is, about 70 feet long and 35 feet wide or about 21 meters long and 11 meters wide   [o] 3 That is, about 3 1/2 feet or about 1.1 meters; also in verse 22   [p] 3 That is, about 12 feet or about 3.7 meters   [q] 5 That is, about 7 feet or about 2.1 meters

ple to serve as supports for the side rooms, so that the supports were not inserted into the wall of the temple. **7** The side rooms all around the temple were wider at each successive level. The structure surrounding the temple was built in ascending stages, so that the rooms widened as one went upward. A stairway went up from the lowest floor to the top floor through the middle floor.

8 I saw that the temple had a raised base all around it, forming the foundation of the side rooms. It was the length of the rod, six long cubits. **9** The outer wall of the side rooms was five cubits thick. The open area between the side rooms of the temple **10** and the priests' rooms was twenty cubits wide all around the temple. **11** There were entrances to the side rooms from the open area, one on the north and another on the south; and the base adjoining the open area was five cubits wide all around.

12 The building facing the temple courtyard on the west side was seventy cubits[a] wide. The wall of the building was five cubits thick all around, and its length was ninety cubits.[b]

13 Then he measured the temple; it was a hundred cubits[c] long, and the temple courtyard and the building with its walls were also a hundred cubits long. **14** The width of the temple courtyard on the east, including the front of the temple, was a hundred cubits.

15 Then he measured the length of the building facing the courtyard at the rear of the temple, including its galleries on each side; it was a hundred cubits.

The main hall, the inner sanctuary and the portico facing the court, **16** as well as the thresholds and the narrow windows and galleries around the three of them — everything beyond and including the threshold was covered with wood. The floor, the wall up to the windows, and the windows were covered. **17** In the space above the outside of the entrance to the inner sanctuary and on the walls at regular intervals all around the inner and outer sanctuary **18** were carved cherubim and palm trees. Palm trees alternated with cherubim. Each cherub had two faces: **19** the face of a human being toward the palm tree on one side and the face of a lion toward the palm tree on the other. They were carved all around the whole temple. **20** From the floor to the area above the entrance, cherubim and palm trees were carved on the wall of the main hall.

21 The main hall had a rectangular doorframe, and the one at the front of the Most Holy

---

a 12 That is, about 123 feet or about 37 meters   *b 12* That is, about 158 feet or about 48 meters   *c 13* That is, about 175 feet or about 53 meters; also in verses 14 and 15

Place was similar. ²²There was a wooden altar three cubits*a* high and two cubits square*b*; its corners, its base*c* and its sides were of wood. The man said to me, "This is the table that is before the LORD." ²³Both the main hall and the Most Holy Place had double doors. ²⁴Each door had two leaves—two hinged leaves for each door. ²⁵And on the doors of the main hall were carved cherubim and palm trees like those carved on the walls, and there was a wooden overhang on the front of the portico. ²⁶On the sidewalls of the portico were narrow windows with palm trees carved on each side. The side rooms of the temple also had overhangs.

The Rooms for the Priests

42 Then the man led me northward into the outer court and brought me to the rooms opposite the temple courtyard and opposite the outer wall on the north side. ²The building whose door faced north was a hundred cubits long and fifty cubits wide.*d* ³Both in the section twenty cubits*e* from the inner court and in the section opposite the pavement of the outer court, gallery faced gallery at the three levels. ⁴In front of the rooms was an inner passageway ten cubits wide and a hundred cubits*f* long.*g* Their doors were on the north. ⁵Now the upper rooms were narrower, for the galleries took more space from them than from the rooms on the lower and middle floors of the building. ⁶The rooms on the top floor had no pillars, as the courts had; so they were smaller in floor space than those on the lower and middle floors. ⁷There was an outer wall parallel to the rooms and the outer court; it extended in front of the rooms for fifty cubits. ⁸While the row of rooms on the side next to the outer court was fifty cubits long, the row on the side nearest the sanctuary was a hundred cubits long. ⁹The lower rooms had an entrance on the east side as one enters them from the outer court.

¹⁰On the south side*h* along the length of the wall of the outer court, adjoining the temple courtyard and opposite the outer wall, were rooms ¹¹with a passageway in front of them. These were like the rooms on the north; they had the same length and width, with similar exits and dimensions. Similar to the doorways on the north ¹²were the doorways of the rooms on the

---

a 22 That is, about 5 1/4 feet or about 1.5 meters   *b 22* Septuagint; Hebrew *long*
c 22 Septuagint; Hebrew *length*   *d 2* That is, about 175 feet long and 88 feet wide or about 53 meters long and 27 meters wide   *e 3* That is, about 35 feet or about 11 meters   *f 4* Septuagint and Syriac; Hebrew *and one cubit*   *g 4* That is, about 18 feet wide and 175 feet long or about 5.3 meters wide and 53 meters long
h 10 Septuagint; Hebrew *Eastward*

south. There was a doorway at the beginning of the passageway that was parallel to the corresponding wall extending eastward, by which one enters the rooms.

13 Then he said to me, "The north and south rooms facing the temple courtyard are the priests' rooms, where the priests who approach the Lord will eat the most holy offerings. There they will put the most holy offerings — the grain offerings, the sin offerings[a] and the guilt offerings — for the place is holy. 14 Once the priests enter the holy precincts, they are not to go into the outer court until they leave behind the garments in which they minister, for these are holy. They are to put on other clothes before they go near the places that are for the people."

15 When he had finished measuring what was inside the temple area, he led me out by the east gate and measured the area all around: 16 He measured the east side with the measuring rod; it was five hundred cubits.[b,c] 17 He measured the north side; it was five hundred cubits[d] by the measuring rod. 18 He measured the south side; it was five hundred cubits by the measuring rod. 19 Then he turned to the west side and measured; it was five hundred cubits by the measuring rod. 20 So he measured the area on all four sides. It had a wall around it, five hundred cubits long and five hundred cubits wide, to separate the holy from the common.

God's Glory Returns to the Temple

43 Then the man brought me to the gate facing east, 2 and I saw the glory of the God of Israel coming from the east. His voice was like the roar of rushing waters, and the land was radiant with his glory. 3 The vision I saw was like the vision I had seen when he[e] came to destroy the city and like the visions I had seen by the Kebar River, and I fell facedown. 4 The glory of the Lord entered the temple through the gate facing east. 5 Then the Spirit lifted me up and brought me into the inner court, and the glory of the Lord filled the temple.

6 While the man was standing beside me, I heard someone speaking to me from inside the temple. 7 He said: "Son of man, this is the place of my throne and the place for the soles of my feet. This is where I will live among the Israelites forever. The people of Israel will never again defile my holy name — neither they nor their kings — by their prostitution and the funeral of-

---

a 13 Or *purification offerings*   *b 16* See Septuagint of verse 17; Hebrew *rods*; also in verses 18 and 19.   *c 16* Five hundred cubits equal about 875 feet or about 265 meters; also in verses 17, 18 and 19.   *d 17* Septuagint; Hebrew *rods*   *e 3* Some Hebrew manuscripts and Vulgate; most Hebrew manuscripts *I* ferings[a] for their kings at their death.[b] [8]When they placed their threshold next to my threshold and their doorposts beside my doorposts, with only a wall between me and them, they defiled my holy name by their detestable practices. So I destroyed them in my anger. [9]Now let them put away from me their prostitution and the funeral offerings for their kings, and I will live among them forever.

[10]"Son of man, describe the temple to the people of Israel, that they may be ashamed of their sins. Let them consider its perfection, [11]and if they are ashamed of all they have done, make known to them the design of the temple — its arrangement, its exits and entrances — its whole design and all its regulations[c] and laws. Write these down before them so that they may be faithful to its design and follow all its regulations.

[12]"This is the law of the temple: All the surrounding area on top of the mountain will be most holy. Such is the law of the temple.

The Great Altar Restored

[13]"These are the measurements of the altar in long cubits,[d] that cubit being a cubit and a handbreadth: Its gutter is a cubit deep and a cubit wide, with a rim of one span[e] around the edge. And this is the height of the altar: [14]From the gutter on the ground up to the lower ledge that goes around the altar it is two cubits high, and the ledge is a cubit wide.[f] From this lower ledge to the upper ledge that goes around the altar it is four cubits high, and that ledge is also a cubit wide.[g] [15]Above that, the altar hearth is four cubits high, and four horns project upward from the hearth. [16]The altar hearth is square, twelve cubits[h] long and twelve cubits wide. [17]The upper ledge also is square, fourteen cubits[i] long and fourteen cubits wide. All around the altar is a gutter of one cubit with a rim of half a cubit.[e] The steps of the altar face east."

[18]Then he said to me, "Son of man, this is what the Sovereign LORD says: These will be the regulations for sacrificing burnt offerings and splashing blood

---

[a] 7 Or the memorial monuments; also in verse 9   [b] 7 Or their high places
[c] 11 Some Hebrew manuscripts and Septuagint; most Hebrew manuscripts regulations and its whole design   [d] 13 That is, about 21 inches or about 53 centimeters; also in verses 14 and 17. The long cubit is the basic unit for linear measurement throughout Ezekiel 40 – 48.   [e] 13,17 That is, about 11 inches or about 27 centimeters   [f] 14 That is, about 3 1/2 feet high and 1 3/4 feet wide or about 105 centimeters high and 53 centimeters wide   [g] 14 That is, about 7 feet high and 1 3/4 feet wide or about 2.1 meters high and 53 centimeters wide
[h] 16 That is, about 21 feet or about 6.4 meters   [i] 17 That is, about 25 feet or about 7.4 meters

against the altar when it is built: **19**You are to give a young bull as a sin offering[a] to the Levitical priests of the family of Zadok, who come near to minister before me, declares the Sovereign LORD. **20**You are to take some of its blood and put it on the four horns of the altar and on the four corners of the upper ledge and all around the rim, and so purify the altar and make atonement for it. **21**You are to take the bull for the sin offering and burn it in the designated part of the temple area outside the sanctuary.

22 "On the second day you are to offer a male goat without defect for a sin offering, and the altar is to be purified as it was purified with the bull. **23**When you have finished purifying it, you are to offer a young bull and a ram from the flock, both without defect. **24**You are to offer them before the LORD, and the priests are to sprinkle salt on them and sacrifice them as a burnt offering to the LORD.

25 "For seven days you are to provide a male goat daily for a sin offering; you are also to provide a young bull and a ram from the flock, both without defect. **26**For seven days they are to make atonement for the altar and cleanse it; thus they will dedicate it. **27**At the end of these days, from the eighth day on, the priests are to present your burnt offerings and fellowship offerings on the altar. Then I will accept you, declares the Sovereign LORD."

The Priesthood Restored

44 Then the man brought me back to the outer gate of the sanctuary, the one facing east, and it was shut. **2**The LORD said to me, "This gate is to remain shut. It must not be opened; no one may enter through it. It is to remain shut because the LORD, the God of Israel, has entered through it. **3**The prince himself is the only one who may sit inside the gateway to eat in the presence of the LORD. He is to enter by way of the portico of the gateway and go out the same way."

4Then the man brought me by way of the north gate to the front of the temple. I looked and saw the glory of the LORD filling the temple of the LORD, and I fell facedown.

5The LORD said to me, "Son of man, look carefully, listen closely and give attention to everything I tell you concerning all the regulations and instructions regarding the temple of the LORD. Give attention to the entrance to the temple and all the exits of the sanctuary. **6**Say to rebellious Israel, 'This is what the Sovereign LORD says: Enough of your detestable practices, people of Israel! **7**In addition to all your other detestable practices, you brought

---

[a] 19 Or *purification offering*; also in verses 21, 22 and 25

foreigners uncircumcised in heart and flesh into my sanctuary, desecrating my temple while you offered me food, fat and blood, and you broke my covenant. **8** Instead of carrying out your duty in regard to my holy things, you put others in charge of my sanctuary. **9** This is what the Sovereign Lord says: No foreigner uncircumcised in heart and flesh is to enter my sanctuary, not even the foreigners who live among the Israelites.

10 " 'The Levites who went far from me when Israel went astray and who wandered from me after their idols must bear the consequences of their sin. **11** They may serve in my sanctuary, having charge of the gates of the temple and serving in it; they may slaughter the burnt offerings and sacrifices for the people and stand before the people and serve them. **12** But because they served them in the presence of their idols and made the people of Israel fall into sin, therefore I have sworn with uplifted hand that they must bear the consequences of their sin, declares the Sovereign Lord. **13** They are not to come near to serve me as priests or come near any of my holy things or my most holy offerings; they must bear the shame of their detestable practices. **14** And I will appoint them to guard the temple for all the work that is to be done in it.

15 " 'But the Levitical priests, who are descendants of Zadok and who guarded my sanctuary when the Israelites went astray from me, are to come near to minister before me; they are to stand before me to offer sacrifices of fat and blood, declares the Sovereign Lord. **16** They alone are to enter my sanctuary; they alone are to come near my table to minister before me and serve me as guards.

17 " 'When they enter the gates of the inner court, they are to wear linen clothes; they must not wear any woolen garment while ministering at the gates of the inner court or inside the temple. **18** They are to wear linen turbans on their heads and linen undergarments around their waists. They must not wear anything that makes them perspire. **19** When they go out into the outer court where the people are, they are to take off the clothes they have been ministering in and are to leave them in the sacred rooms, and put on other clothes, so that the people are not consecrated through contact with their garments.

20 " 'They must not shave their heads or let their hair grow long, but they are to keep the hair of their heads trimmed. **21** No priest is to drink wine when he enters the inner court. **22** They must not marry widows or divorced women; they may marry only virgins of Israelite descent or widows of priests. **23**They are to teach my people the difference between the holy and the common and show them how to distinguish between the unclean and the clean.

24"'In any dispute, the priests are to serve as judges and decide it according to my ordinances. They are to keep my laws and my decrees for all my appointed festivals, and they are to keep my Sabbaths holy.

25"'A priest must not defile himself by going near a dead person; however, if the dead person was his father or mother, son or daughter, brother or unmarried sister, then he may defile himself. **26**After he is cleansed, he must wait seven days. **27**On the day he goes into the inner court of the sanctuary to minister in the sanctuary, he is to offer a sin offering[a] for himself, declares the Sovereign LORD.

28"'I am to be the only inheritance the priests have. You are to give them no possession in Israel; I will be their possession. **29**They will eat the grain offerings, the sin offerings and the guilt offerings; and everything in Israel devoted[b] to the LORD will belong to

them. **30**The best of all the firstfruits and of all your special gifts will belong to the priests. You are to give them the first portion of your ground meal so that a blessing may rest on your household. **31**The priests must not eat anything, whether bird or animal, found dead or torn by wild animals.

Israel Fully Restored

45 "'When you allot the land as an inheritance, you are to present to the LORD a portion of the land as a sacred district, 25,000 cubits[c] long and 20,000[d] cubits[e] wide; the entire area will be holy. **2**Of this, a section 500 cubits[f] square is to be for the sanctuary, with 50 cubits[g] around it for open land. **3**In the sacred district, measure off a section 25,000 cubits long and 10,000 cubits[h] wide. In it will be the sanctuary, the Most Holy Place. **4**It will be the sacred portion of the land for the priests, who minister in the sanctuary and who draw near to minister before the LORD. It will be a place for their houses as well as a holy place for the sanctuary. **5**An area 25,000 cubits long and 10,000 cubits wide will belong to the Levites, who serve in the tem-

---

[a] 27 Or *purification offering*; also in verse 29   [b] 29 The Hebrew term refers to the irrevocable giving over of things or persons to the LORD.   [c] 1 That is, about 8 miles or about 13 kilometers; also in verses 3, 5 and 6   [d] 1 Septuagint (see also verses 3 and 5 and 48:9); Hebrew *10,000*   [e] 1 That is, about 6 1/2 miles or about 11 kilometers   [f] 2 That is, about 875 feet or about 265 meters   [g] 2 That is, about 88 feet or about 27 meters   [h] 3 That is, about 3 1/3 miles or about 5.3 kilometers; also in verse 5

ple, as their possession for towns to live in.*a*

6 "'You are to give the city as its property an area 5,000 cubits*b* wide and 25,000 cubits long, adjoining the sacred portion; it will belong to all Israel.

7 "'The prince will have the land bordering each side of the area formed by the sacred district and the property of the city. It will extend westward from the west side and eastward from the east side, running lengthwise from the western to the eastern border parallel to one of the tribal portions. 8 This land will be his possession in Israel. And my princes will no longer oppress my people but will allow the people of Israel to possess the land according to their tribes.

9 "'This is what the Sovereign LORD says: You have gone far enough, princes of Israel! Give up your violence and oppression and do what is just and right. Stop dispossessing my people, declares the Sovereign LORD. 10 You are to use accurate scales, an accurate ephah*c* and an accurate bath.*d* 11 The ephah and the bath are to be the same size, the bath containing a tenth of a homer and the ephah a tenth of a homer; the homer is to be the standard measure for both. 12 The shekel*e* is to consist of twenty gerahs. Twenty shekels plus twenty-five shekels plus fifteen shekels equal one mina.*f*

13 "'This is the special gift you are to offer: a sixth of an ephah*g* from each homer of wheat and a sixth of an ephah*h* from each homer of barley. 14 The prescribed portion of olive oil, measured by the bath, is a tenth of a bath*i* from each cor (which consists of ten baths or one homer, for ten baths are equivalent to a homer). 15 Also one sheep is to be taken from every flock of two hundred from the well-watered pastures of Israel. These will be used for the grain offerings, burnt offerings and fellowship offerings to make atonement for the people, declares the Sovereign LORD. 16 All the people of the land will be required to give this special offering to the prince in Israel. 17 It will be the duty of the prince to provide the burnt offerings, grain offerings and drink offerings at the festivals, the New Moons and the Sabbaths — at all the appointed festivals of Israel. He will provide

---

a 5 Septuagint; Hebrew *temple; they will have as their possession 20 rooms*
b 6 That is, about 1 2/3 miles or about 2.7 kilometers   *c 10* An ephah was a dry measure having the capacity of about 3/5 bushel or about 22 liters.   *d 10* A bath was a liquid measure equaling about 6 gallons or about 22 liters.   *e 12* A shekel weighed about 2/5 ounce or about 12 grams.   *f 12* That is, 60 shekels; the common mina was 50 shekels. Sixty shekels were about 1 1/2 pounds or about 690 grams.   *g 13* That is, probably about 6 pounds or about 2.7 kilograms
h 13 That is, probably about 5 pounds or about 2.3 kilograms   *i 14* That is, about 2 1/2 quarts or about 2.2 liters

the sin offerings,[a] grain offerings, burnt offerings and fellowship offerings to make atonement for the Israelites.

18 "'This is what the Sovereign LORD says: In the first month on the first day you are to take a young bull without defect and purify the sanctuary. 19 The priest is to take some of the blood of the sin offering and put it on the doorposts of the temple, on the four corners of the upper ledge of the altar and on the gateposts of the inner court. 20 You are to do the same on the seventh day of the month for anyone who sins unintentionally or through ignorance; so you are to make atonement for the temple.

21 "'In the first month on the fourteenth day you are to observe the Passover, a festival lasting seven days, during which you shall eat bread made without yeast. 22 On that day the prince is to provide a bull as a sin offering for himself and for all the people of the land. 23 Every day during the seven days of the festival he is to provide seven bulls and seven rams without defect as a burnt offering to the LORD, and a male goat for a sin offering. 24 He is to provide as a grain offering an ephah for each bull and an ephah for each ram, along with a hin[b] of olive oil for each ephah.

25 "'During the seven days of the festival, which begins in the seventh month on the fifteenth day, he is to make the same provision for sin offerings, burnt offerings, grain offerings and oil.

46 "'This is what the Sovereign LORD says: The gate of the inner court facing east is to be shut on the six working days, but on the Sabbath day and on the day of the New Moon it is to be opened. 2 The prince is to enter from the outside through the portico of the gateway and stand by the gatepost. The priests are to sacrifice his burnt offering and his fellowship offerings. He is to bow down in worship at the threshold of the gateway and then go out, but the gate will not be shut until evening. 3 On the Sabbaths and New Moons the people of the land are to worship in the presence of the LORD at the entrance of that gateway. 4 The burnt offering the prince brings to the LORD on the Sabbath day is to be six male lambs and a ram, all without defect. 5 The grain offering given with the ram is to be an ephah,[c] and the grain offering with the lambs is to be as much as he pleases, along with a hin[d] of olive oil for each ephah. 6 On the day of the New Moon he is to offer a young bull, six lambs and a ram, all without defect. 7 He is

---

[a] 17 Or *purification offerings*; also in verses 19, 22, 23 and 25   [b] 24 That is, about 1 gallon or about 3.8 liters   [c] 5 That is, probably about 35 pounds or about 16 kilograms; also in verses 7 and 11   [d] 5 That is, about 1 gallon or about 3.8 liters; also in verses 7 and 11

to provide as a grain offering one ephah with the bull, one ephah with the ram, and with the lambs as much as he wants to give, along with a hin of oil for each ephah. **8** When the prince enters, he is to go in through the portico of the gateway, and he is to come out the same way.

9 " 'When the people of the land come before the LORD at the appointed festivals, whoever enters by the north gate to worship is to go out the south gate; and whoever enters by the south gate is to go out the north gate. No one is to return through the gate by which they entered, but each is to go out the opposite gate. **10** The prince is to be among them, going in when they go in and going out when they go out. **11** At the feasts and the appointed festivals, the grain offering is to be an ephah with a bull, an ephah with a ram, and with the lambs as much as he pleases, along with a hin of oil for each ephah.

12 " 'When the prince provides a freewill offering to the LORD — whether a burnt offering or fellowship offerings — the gate facing east is to be opened for him. He shall offer his burnt offering or his fellowship offerings as he does on the Sabbath day. Then he shall go out, and after he has gone out, the gate will be shut.

13 " 'Every day you are to provide a year-old lamb without defect for a burnt offering to the LORD; morning by morning you shall provide it. **14** You are also to provide with it morning by morning a grain offering, consisting of a sixth of an ephah*a* with a third of a hin*b* of oil to moisten the flour. The presenting of this grain offering to the LORD is a lasting ordinance. **15** So the lamb and the grain offering and the oil shall be provided morning by morning for a regular burnt offering.

16 " 'This is what the Sovereign LORD says: If the prince makes a gift from his inheritance to one of his sons, it will also belong to his descendants; it is to be their property by inheritance. **17** If, however, he makes a gift from his inheritance to one of his servants, the servant may keep it until the year of freedom; then it will revert to the prince. His inheritance belongs to his sons only; it is theirs. **18** The prince must not take any of the inheritance of the people, driving them off their property. He is to give his sons their inheritance out of his own property, so that not one of my people will be separated from their property.' "

19 Then the man brought me through the entrance at the side of the gate to the sacred rooms facing north, which belonged to the priests, and showed me a place at the western end. **20** He

---

a 14 That is, probably about 6 pounds or about 2.7 kilograms   *b* 14 That is, about 1 1/2 quarts or about 1.3 liters said to me, "This is the place where the priests are to cook the guilt offering and the sin offering[a] and bake the grain offering, to avoid bringing them into the outer court and consecrating the people."

²¹ He then brought me to the outer court and led me around to its four corners, and I saw in each corner another court. ²² In the four corners of the outer court were enclosed[b] courts, forty cubits long and thirty cubits wide;[c] each of the courts in the four corners was the same size. ²³ Around the inside of each of the four courts was a ledge of stone, with places for fire built all around under the ledge. ²⁴ He said to me, "These are the kitchens where those who minister at the temple are to cook the sacrifices of the people."

The River From the Temple

47 The man brought me back to the entrance to the temple, and I saw water coming out from under the threshold of the temple toward the east (for the temple faced east). The water was coming down from under the south side of the temple, south of the altar. ² He then brought me out through the north gate and led me around the outside to the outer gate facing east, and the water was trickling from the south side.

³ As the man went eastward with a measuring line in his hand, he measured off a thousand cubits[d] and then led me through water that was ankle-deep. ⁴ He measured off another thousand cubits and led me through water that was knee-deep. He measured off another thousand and led me through water that was up to the waist. ⁵ He measured off another thousand, but now it was a river that I could not cross, because the water had risen and was deep enough to swim in — a river that no one could cross. ⁶ He asked me, "Son of man, do you see this?"

Then he led me back to the bank of the river. ⁷ When I arrived there, I saw a great number of trees on each side of the river. ⁸ He said to me, "This water flows toward the eastern region and goes down into the Arabah,[e] where it enters the Dead Sea. When it empties into the sea, the salty water there becomes fresh. ⁹ Swarms of living creatures will live wherever the river flows. There will be large numbers of fish, because this water flows there and makes the salt water fresh; so where the river flows everything will live. ¹⁰ Fishermen will stand along the shore; from En Gedi to En

---

[a] 20 Or *purification offering*   [b] 22 The meaning of the Hebrew for this word is uncertain.   [c] 22 That is, about 70 feet long and 53 feet wide or about 21 meters long and 16 meters wide   [d] 3 That is, about 1,700 feet or about 530 meters   [e] 8 Or *the Jordan Valley*

Eglaim there will be places for spreading nets. The fish will be of many kinds — like the fish of the Mediterranean Sea. [11] But the swamps and marshes will not become fresh; they will be left for salt. [12] Fruit trees of all kinds will grow on both banks of the river. Their leaves will not wither, nor will their fruit fail. Every month they will bear fruit, because the water from the sanctuary flows to them. Their fruit will serve for food and their leaves for healing."

The Boundaries of the Land

[13] This is what the Sovereign LORD says: "These are the boundaries of the land that you will divide among the twelve tribes of Israel as their inheritance, with two portions for Joseph. [14] You are to divide it equally among them. Because I swore with uplifted hand to give it to your ancestors, this land will become your inheritance.

[15] "This is to be the boundary of the land:

"On the north side it will run from the Mediterranean Sea by the Hethlon road past Lebo Hamath to Zedad, [16] Berothah[a] and Sibraim (which lies on the border between Damascus and Hamath), as far as Hazer Hattikon, which is on the border of Hauran.

[17] The boundary will extend from the sea to Hazar Enan,[b] along the northern border of Damascus, with the border of Hamath to the north. This will be the northern boundary.

[18] "On the east side the boundary will run between Hauran and Damascus, along the Jordan between Gilead and the land of Israel, to the Dead Sea and as far as Tamar.[c] This will be the eastern boundary.

[19] "On the south side it will run from Tamar as far as the waters of Meribah Kadesh, then along the Wadi of Egypt to the Mediterranean Sea. This will be the southern boundary.

[20] "On the west side, the Mediterranean Sea will be the boundary to a point opposite Lebo Hamath. This will be the western boundary.

[21] "You are to distribute this land among yourselves according to the tribes of Israel. [22] You are to allot it as an inheritance for yourselves and for the foreigners residing among you and who have children. You are to consider them as native-born Israelites; along with you they are to be allotted an inheritance among the tribes of Israel. [23] In whatever tribe a foreigner resides, there

---

[a] 15,16 See Septuagint and 48:1; Hebrew *road to go into Zedad,* [16]*Hamath, Berothah.*   [b] 17 Hebrew *Enon,* a variant of *Enan*   [c] 18 See Syriac; Hebrew *Israel. You will measure to the Dead Sea.*

you are to give them their inheritance," declares the Sovereign LORD.

The Division of the Land

48 "These are the tribes, listed by name: At the northern frontier, Dan will have one portion; it will follow the Hethlon road to Lebo Hamath; Hazar Enan and the northern border of Damascus next to Hamath will be part of its border from the east side to the west side.

2 "Asher will have one portion; it will border the territory of Dan from east to west.

3 "Naphtali will have one portion; it will border the territory of Asher from east to west.

4 "Manasseh will have one portion; it will border the territory of Naphtali from east to west.

5 "Ephraim will have one portion; it will border the territory of Manasseh from east to west.

6 "Reuben will have one portion; it will border the territory of Ephraim from east to west.

7 "Judah will have one portion; it will border the territory of Reuben from east to west.

8 "Bordering the territory of Judah from east to west will be the portion you are to present as a special gift. It will be 25,000 cubits[a] wide, and its length from east to west will equal one of the tribal portions; the sanctuary will be in the center of it.

9 "The special portion you are to offer to the LORD will be 25,000 cubits long and 10,000 cubits[b] wide. 10 This will be the sacred portion for the priests. It will be 25,000 cubits long on the north side, 10,000 cubits wide on the west side, 10,000 cubits wide on the east side and 25,000 cubits long on the south side. In the center of it will be the sanctuary of the LORD. 11 This will be for the consecrated priests, the Zadokites, who were faithful in serving me and did not go astray as the Levites did when the Israelites went astray. 12 It will be a special gift to them from the sacred portion of the land, a most holy portion, bordering the territory of the Levites.

13 "Alongside the territory of the priests, the Levites will have an allotment 25,000 cubits long and 10,000 cubits wide. Its total length will be 25,000 cubits and its width 10,000 cubits. 14 They must not sell or exchange any of it. This is the best of the land and must not pass into other hands, because it is holy to the LORD.

15 "The remaining area, 5,000 cubits[c] wide and 25,000 cubits long, will be for the common use of the city, for houses and for pastureland. The city will be in the center of it 16 and will have these

---

<a> 8 That is, about 8 miles or about 13 kilometers; also in verses 9, 10, 13, 15, 20 and 21   <b> 9 That is, about 3 1/3 miles or about 5.3 kilometers; also in verses 10, 13 and 18   <c> 15 That is, about 1 2/3 miles or about 2.7 kilometers

measurements: the north side 4,500 cubits,[a] the south side 4,500 cubits, the east side 4,500 cubits, and the west side 4,500 cubits. [17]The pastureland for the city will be 250 cubits[b] on the north, 250 cubits on the south, 250 cubits on the east, and 250 cubits on the west. [18]What remains of the area, bordering on the sacred portion and running the length of it, will be 10,000 cubits on the east side and 10,000 cubits on the west side. Its produce will supply food for the workers of the city. [19]The workers from the city who farm it will come from all the tribes of Israel. [20]The entire portion will be a square, 25,000 cubits on each side. As a special gift you will set aside the sacred portion, along with the property of the city.

[21] "What remains on both sides of the area formed by the sacred portion and the property of the city will belong to the prince. It will extend eastward from the 25,000 cubits of the sacred portion to the eastern border, and westward from the 25,000 cubits to the western border. Both these areas running the length of the tribal portions will belong to the prince, and the sacred portion with the temple sanctuary will be in the center of them. [22]So the property of the Levites and the property of the city will lie in the center of the area that belongs to the prince.

The area belonging to the prince will lie between the border of Judah and the border of Benjamin.

[23] "As for the rest of the tribes: Benjamin will have one portion; it will extend from the east side to the west side.

[24] "Simeon will have one portion; it will border the territory of Benjamin from east to west.

[25] "Issachar will have one portion; it will border the territory of Simeon from east to west.

[26] "Zebulun will have one portion; it will border the territory of Issachar from east to west.

[27] "Gad will have one portion; it will border the territory of Zebulun from east to west.

[28] "The southern boundary of Gad will run south from Tamar to the waters of Meribah Kadesh, then along the Wadi of Egypt to the Mediterranean Sea.

[29] "This is the land you are to allot as an inheritance to the tribes of Israel, and these will be their portions," declares the Sovereign LORD.

The Gates of the New City

[30] "These will be the exits of the city: Beginning on the north side, which is 4,500 cubits long, [31]the gates of the city will be named after the tribes of Israel. The three gates on the north side will be the gate of Reuben, the gate of Judah and the gate of Levi.

---

[a] 16 That is, about 1 1/2 miles or about 2.4 kilometers; also in verses 30, 32, 33 and 34   [b] 17 That is, about 440 feet or about 135 meters

³²"On the east side, which is 4,500 cubits long, will be three gates: the gate of Joseph, the gate of Benjamin and the gate of Dan.

³³"On the south side, which measures 4,500 cubits, will be three gates: the gate of Simeon, the gate of Issachar and the gate of Zebulun.

³⁴"On the west side, which is 4,500 cubits long, will be three gates: the gate of Gad, the gate of Asher and the gate of Naphtali.

³⁵"The distance all around will be 18,000 cubits.*ƒ*

"And the name of the city from that time on will be:

THE LORD IS THERE."

ƒ 35 That is, about 6 miles or about 9.5 kilometers

Daniel

Introduction:

Daniel has traditionally been named the author of this book. The entire book tells of the experiences of Daniel and his friends as captives in Babylon and the divine revelation that came to Daniel in dreams and visions during his lifetime (about 605–530 BC).

Daniel was taken hostage from Jerusalem in 605 BC to the Babylonian court. After retelling and interpreting Nebuchadnezzar's dream Daniel was given a position of power. He wrote this book during Israel's captivity to encourage the people to trust in God who controls all of history.

In the last six chapters of this book, Daniel describes his visions of the rise and fall of earthly kingdoms and finally the rise of an everlasting kingdom.

Outline of contents:

Events during Nebuchadnezzar's reign (1:1–4:37)
The writing on the wall (5:1–30)
Daniel in the den of lions (5:31–6:28)
Visions during Belshazzar's reign (7:1–8:27)
Daniel's prayer and the seventy "sevens" (9:1–27)
Daniel's final revelation (10:1–12:13)

Daniel's Training in Babylon

1 In the third year of the reign of Jehoiakim king of Judah, Nebuchadnezzar king of Babylon came to Jerusalem and besieged it. ² And the Lord delivered Jehoiakim king of Judah into his hand, along with some of the articles from the temple of God. These he carried off to the temple of his god in Babylonia*a* and put in the treasure house of his god.

³ Then the king ordered Ashpenaz, chief of his court officials, to bring into the king's service some of the Israelites from the royal family and the nobility— ⁴ young men without any physical defect, handsome, showing aptitude for every kind of learning, well informed, quick to understand, and qualified to serve in the king's palace. He was to teach them the language and literature

a 2 Hebrew *Shinar*

of the Babylonians.*ᵃ* ⁵The king assigned them a daily amount of food and wine from the king's table. They were to be trained for three years, and after that they were to enter the king's service.

⁶Among those who were chosen were some from Judah: Daniel, Hananiah, Mishael and Azariah. ⁷The chief official gave them new names: to Daniel, the name Belteshazzar; to Hananiah, Shadrach; to Mishael, Meshach; and to Azariah, Abednego.

⁸But Daniel resolved not to defile himself with the royal food and wine, and he asked the chief official for permission not to defile himself this way. ⁹Now God had caused the official to show favor and compassion to Daniel, ¹⁰but the official told Daniel, "I am afraid of my lord the king, who has assigned your*ᵇ* food and drink. Why should he see you looking worse than the other young men your age? The king would then have my head because of you."

¹¹Daniel then said to the guard whom the chief official had appointed over Daniel, Hananiah, Mishael and Azariah, ¹²"Please test your servants for ten days: Give us nothing but vegetables to eat and water to drink. ¹³Then compare our appearance with that of the young men who eat the royal food, and treat your servants in accordance with what you see." ¹⁴So he agreed to this and tested them for ten days.

¹⁵At the end of the ten days they looked healthier and better nourished than any of the young men who ate the royal food. ¹⁶So the guard took away their choice food and the wine they were to drink and gave them vegetables instead.

¹⁷To these four young men God gave knowledge and understanding of all kinds of literature and learning. And Daniel could understand visions and dreams of all kinds.

¹⁸At the end of the time set by the king to bring them into his service, the chief official presented them to Nebuchadnezzar. ¹⁹The king talked with them, and he found none equal to Daniel, Hananiah, Mishael and Azariah; so they entered the king's service. ²⁰In every matter of wisdom and understanding about which the king questioned them, he found them ten times better than all the magicians and enchanters in his whole kingdom.

²¹And Daniel remained there until the first year of King Cyrus.

Nebuchadnezzar's Dream

2 In the second year of his reign, Nebuchadnezzar had dreams; his mind was troubled and he could not sleep. ²So the king summoned the magicians, enchanters, sorcerers and astrol-

---

ᵃ 4 Or *Chaldeans*   *ᵇ 10* The Hebrew for *your* and *you* in this verse is plural.

ogers[a] to tell him what he had dreamed. When they came in and stood before the king, [3]he said to them, "I have had a dream that troubles me and I want to know what it means.[b]"

[4]Then the astrologers answered the king,[c] "May the king live forever! Tell your servants the dream, and we will interpret it."

[5]The king replied to the astrologers, "This is what I have firmly decided: If you do not tell me what my dream was and interpret it, I will have you cut into pieces and your houses turned into piles of rubble. [6]But if you tell me the dream and explain it, you will receive from me gifts and rewards and great honor. So tell me the dream and interpret it for me."

[7]Once more they replied, "Let the king tell his servants the dream, and we will interpret it."

[8]Then the king answered, "I am certain that you are trying to gain time, because you realize that this is what I have firmly decided: [9]If you do not tell me the dream, there is only one penalty for you. You have conspired to tell me misleading and wicked things, hoping the situation will change. So then, tell me the dream, and I will know that you can interpret it for me."

[10]The astrologers answered the king, "There is no one on earth who can do what the king asks! No king, however great and mighty, has ever asked such a thing of any magician or enchanter or astrologer. [11]What the king asks is too difficult. No one can reveal it to the king except the gods, and they do not live among humans."

[12]This made the king so angry and furious that he ordered the execution of all the wise men of Babylon. [13]So the decree was issued to put the wise men to death, and men were sent to look for Daniel and his friends to put them to death.

[14]When Arioch, the commander of the king's guard, had gone out to put to death the wise men of Babylon, Daniel spoke to him with wisdom and tact. [15]He asked the king's officer, "Why did the king issue such a harsh decree?" Arioch then explained the matter to Daniel. [16]At this, Daniel went in to the king and asked for time, so that he might interpret the dream for him.

[17]Then Daniel returned to his house and explained the matter to his friends Hananiah, Mishael and Azariah. [18]He urged them to plead for mercy from the God of heaven concerning this mystery, so that he and his friends might not be executed with the rest of the wise men of Babylon. [19]Dur-

---

[a] 2 Or Chaldeans; also in verses 4, 5 and 10   [b] 3 Or was   [c] 4 At this point the Hebrew text has in Aramaic, indicating that the text from here through the end of chapter 7 is in Aramaic.

ing the night the mystery was revealed to Daniel in a vision. Then Daniel praised the God of heaven 20 and said:

"Praise be to the name of God
    for ever and ever;
    wisdom and power are his.
21 He changes times and
        seasons;
    he deposes kings and raises
        up others.
He gives wisdom to the wise
    and knowledge to the
        discerning.
22 He reveals deep and hidden
        things;
    he knows what lies in
        darkness,
    and light dwells with him.
23 I thank and praise you, God of
        my ancestors:
    You have given me wisdom
        and power,
    you have made known to me
        what we asked of you,
    you have made known to us
        the dream of the king."

Daniel Interprets the Dream

24 Then Daniel went to Arioch, whom the king had appointed to execute the wise men of Babylon, and said to him, "Do not execute the wise men of Babylon. Take me to the king, and I will interpret his dream for him."

25 Arioch took Daniel to the king at once and said, "I have found a man among the exiles from Judah who can tell the king what his dream means."

26 The king asked Daniel (also called Belteshazzar), "Are you able to tell me what I saw in my dream and interpret it?"

27 Daniel replied, "No wise man, enchanter, magician or diviner can explain to the king the mystery he has asked about, 28 but there is a God in heaven who reveals mysteries. He has shown King Nebuchadnezzar what will happen in days to come. Your dream and the visions that passed through your mind as you were lying in bed are these:

29 "As Your Majesty was lying there, your mind turned to things to come, and the revealer of mysteries showed you what is going to happen. 30 As for me, this mystery has been revealed to me, not because I have greater wisdom than anyone else alive, but so that Your Majesty may know the interpretation and that you may understand what went through your mind.

31 "Your Majesty looked, and there before you stood a large statue — an enormous, dazzling statue, awesome in appearance. 32 The head of the statue was made of pure gold, its chest and arms of silver, its belly and thighs of bronze, 33 its legs of iron, its feet partly of iron and partly of baked clay. 34 While you were watching, a rock was cut out, but not by human hands. It struck the statue on its feet of iron and clay and smashed them. 35 Then the iron,

the clay, the bronze, the silver and the gold were all broken to pieces and became like chaff on a threshing floor in the summer. The wind swept them away without leaving a trace. But the rock that struck the statue became a huge mountain and filled the whole earth.

³⁶ "This was the dream, and now we will interpret it to the king. ³⁷ Your Majesty, you are the king of kings. The God of heaven has given you dominion and power and might and glory; ³⁸ in your hands he has placed all mankind and the beasts of the field and the birds in the sky. Wherever they live, he has made you ruler over them all. You are that head of gold.

³⁹ "After you, another kingdom will arise, inferior to yours. Next, a third kingdom, one of bronze, will rule over the whole earth. ⁴⁰ Finally, there will be a fourth kingdom, strong as iron — for iron breaks and smashes everything — and as iron breaks things to pieces, so it will crush and break all the others. ⁴¹ Just as you saw that the feet and toes were partly of baked clay and partly of iron, so this will be a divided kingdom; yet it will have some of the strength of iron in it, even as you saw iron mixed with clay. ⁴² As the toes were partly iron and partly clay, so this kingdom will be partly strong and partly brittle. ⁴³ And just as you saw the iron mixed with baked clay, so the people will be a mixture and will not remain united, any more than iron mixes with clay.

⁴⁴ "In the time of those kings, the God of heaven will set up a kingdom that will never be destroyed, nor will it be left to another people. It will crush all those kingdoms and bring them to an end, but it will itself endure forever. ⁴⁵ This is the meaning of the vision of the rock cut out of a mountain, but not by human hands — a rock that broke the iron, the bronze, the clay, the silver and the gold to pieces.

"The great God has shown the king what will take place in the future. The dream is true and its interpretation is trustworthy."

⁴⁶ Then King Nebuchadnezzar fell prostrate before Daniel and paid him honor and ordered that an offering and incense be presented to him. ⁴⁷ The king said to Daniel, "Surely your God is the God of gods and the Lord of kings and a revealer of mysteries, for you were able to reveal this mystery."

⁴⁸ Then the king placed Daniel in a high position and lavished many gifts on him. He made him ruler over the entire province of Babylon and placed him in charge of all its wise men. ⁴⁹ Moreover, at Daniel's request the king appointed Shadrach, Meshach and Abednego administrators over the province of

Babylon, while Daniel himself remained at the royal court.

The Image of Gold and the Blazing Furnace

3 King Nebuchadnezzar made an image of gold, sixty cubits high and six cubits wide,*a* and set it up on the plain of Dura in the province of Babylon. ²He then summoned the satraps, prefects, governors, advisers, treasurers, judges, magistrates and all the other provincial officials to come to the dedication of the image he had set up. ³So the satraps, prefects, governors, advisers, treasurers, judges, magistrates and all the other provincial officials assembled for the dedication of the image that King Nebuchadnezzar had set up, and they stood before it.

⁴Then the herald loudly proclaimed, "Nations and peoples of every language, this is what you are commanded to do: ⁵As soon as you hear the sound of the horn, flute, zither, lyre, harp, pipe and all kinds of music, you must fall down and worship the image of gold that King Nebuchadnezzar has set up. ⁶Whoever does not fall down and worship will immediately be thrown into a blazing furnace."

⁷Therefore, as soon as they heard the sound of the horn, flute, zither, lyre, harp and all kinds of music, all the nations and peoples of every language fell down and worshiped the image of gold that King Nebuchadnezzar had set up.

⁸At this time some astrologers*b* came forward and denounced the Jews. ⁹They said to King Nebuchadnezzar, "May the king live forever! ¹⁰Your Majesty has issued a decree that everyone who hears the sound of the horn, flute, zither, lyre, harp, pipe and all kinds of music must fall down and worship the image of gold, ¹¹and that whoever does not fall down and worship will be thrown into a blazing furnace. ¹²But there are some Jews whom you have set over the affairs of the province of Babylon—Shadrach, Meshach and Abednego—who pay no attention to you, Your Majesty. They neither serve your gods nor worship the image of gold you have set up."

¹³Furious with rage, Nebuchadnezzar summoned Shadrach, Meshach and Abednego. So these men were brought before the king, ¹⁴and Nebuchadnezzar said to them, "Is it true, Shadrach, Meshach and Abednego, that you do not serve my gods or worship the image of gold I have set up? ¹⁵Now when you hear the sound of the horn, flute, zither, lyre, harp, pipe and all kinds of music, if you are ready to

---

a 1 That is, about 90 feet high and 9 feet wide or about 27 meters high and 2.7 meters wide   *b* 8 Or *Chaldeans* fall down and worship the image I made, very good. But if you do not worship it, you will be thrown immediately into a blazing furnace. Then what god will be able to rescue you from my hand?"

¹⁶Shadrach, Meshach and Abednego replied to him, "King Nebuchadnezzar, we do not need to defend ourselves before you in this matter. ¹⁷If we are thrown into the blazing furnace, the God we serve is able to deliver us from it, and he will deliver us*a* from Your Majesty's hand. ¹⁸But even if he does not, we want you to know, Your Majesty, that we will not serve your gods or worship the image of gold you have set up."

¹⁹Then Nebuchadnezzar was furious with Shadrach, Meshach and Abednego, and his attitude toward them changed. He ordered the furnace heated seven times hotter than usual ²⁰and commanded some of the strongest soldiers in his army to tie up Shadrach, Meshach and Abednego and throw them into the blazing furnace. ²¹So these men, wearing their robes, trousers, turbans and other clothes, were bound and thrown into the blazing furnace. ²²The king's command was so urgent and the furnace so hot that the flames of the fire killed the soldiers who took up Shadrach, Meshach and Abednego, ²³and these three men, firmly tied, fell into the blazing furnace.

²⁴Then King Nebuchadnezzar leaped to his feet in amazement and asked his advisers, "Weren't there three men that we tied up and threw into the fire?"

They replied, "Certainly, Your Majesty."

²⁵He said, "Look! I see four men walking around in the fire, unbound and unharmed, and the fourth looks like a son of the gods."

²⁶Nebuchadnezzar then approached the opening of the blazing furnace and shouted, "Shadrach, Meshach and Abednego, servants of the Most High God, come out! Come here!"

So Shadrach, Meshach and Abednego came out of the fire, ²⁷and the satraps, prefects, governors and royal advisers crowded around them. They saw that the fire had not harmed their bodies, nor was a hair of their heads singed; their robes were not scorched, and there was no smell of fire on them.

²⁸Then Nebuchadnezzar said, "Praise be to the God of Shadrach, Meshach and Abednego, who has sent his angel and rescued his servants! They trusted in him and defied the king's command and were willing to give up their lives rather than

---

a 17 Or *If the God we serve is able to deliver us, then he will deliver us from the blazing furnace and* serve or worship any god except their own God. ²⁹ Therefore I decree that the people of any nation or language who say anything against the God of Shadrach, Meshach and Abednego be cut into pieces and their houses be turned into piles of rubble, for no other god can save in this way."

³⁰ Then the king promoted Shadrach, Meshach and Abednego in the province of Babylon.

Nebuchadnezzar's Dream of a Tree

4 ᵃ King Nebuchadnezzar,

To the nations and peoples of every language, who live in all the earth:

May you prosper greatly!

² It is my pleasure to tell you about the miraculous signs and wonders that the Most High God has performed for me.

³ How great are his signs,
how mighty his
wonders!
His kingdom is an eternal
kingdom;
his dominion endures
from generation to
generation.

⁴ I, Nebuchadnezzar, was at home in my palace, contented and prosperous. ⁵ I had a dream that made me afraid. As I was lying in bed, the images and visions that passed through my mind terrified me. ⁶ So I commanded that all the wise men of Babylon be brought before me to interpret the dream for me. ⁷ When the magicians, enchanters, astrologers ᵇ and diviners came, I told them the dream, but they could not interpret it for me. ⁸ Finally, Daniel came into my presence and I told him the dream. (He is called Belteshazzar, after the name of my god, and the spirit of the holy gods is in him.)

⁹ I said, "Belteshazzar, chief of the magicians, I know that the spirit of the holy gods is in you, and no mystery is too difficult for you. Here is my dream; interpret it for me. ¹⁰ These are the visions I saw while lying in bed: I looked, and there before me stood a tree in the middle of the land. Its height was enormous. ¹¹ The tree grew large and strong and its top touched the sky; it was visible to the ends of the earth. ¹² Its leaves were beautiful, its fruit abundant, and on it was food for all. Under it the wild animals found shelter, and the birds lived in its branches; from it every creature was fed.

ᵃ In Aramaic texts 4:1-3 is numbered 3:31-33, and 4:4-37 is numbered 4:1-34.
ᵇ 7 Or *Chaldeans*

¹³"In the visions I saw while lying in bed, I looked, and there before me was a holy one, a messenger,ᵃ coming down from heaven. ¹⁴He called in a loud voice: 'Cut down the tree and trim off its branches; strip off its leaves and scatter its fruit. Let the animals flee from under it and the birds from its branches. ¹⁵But let the stump and its roots, bound with iron and bronze, remain in the ground, in the grass of the field.

"'Let him be drenched with the dew of heaven, and let him live with the animals among the plants of the earth. ¹⁶Let his mind be changed from that of a man and let him be given the mind of an animal, till seven timesᵇ pass by for him.

¹⁷"'The decision is announced by messengers, the holy ones declare the verdict, so that the living may know that the Most High is sovereign over all kingdoms on earth and gives them to anyone he wishes and sets over them the lowliest of people.'

¹⁸"This is the dream that I, King Nebuchadnezzar, had. Now, Belteshazzar, tell me what it means, for none of the wise men in my kingdom can interpret it for me. But you can, because the spirit of the holy gods is in you."

Daniel Interprets the Dream

¹⁹Then Daniel (also called Belteshazzar) was greatly perplexed for a time, and his thoughts terrified him. So the king said, "Belteshazzar, do not let the dream or its meaning alarm you."

Belteshazzar answered, "My lord, if only the dream applied to your enemies and its meaning to your adversaries! ²⁰The tree you saw, which grew large and strong, with its top touching the sky, visible to the whole earth, ²¹with beautiful leaves and abundant fruit, providing food for all, giving shelter to the wild animals, and having nesting places in its branches for the birds— ²²Your Majesty, you are that tree! You have become great and strong; your greatness has grown until it reaches the sky, and your dominion extends to distant parts of the earth.

²³"Your Majesty saw a holy one, a messenger, coming down from heaven and saying, 'Cut down the tree and destroy it, but leave the stump, bound with iron and bronze, in the grass of the

---

ᵃ 13 Or *watchman*; also in verses 17 and 23   ᵇ 16 Or *years*; also in verses 23, 25 and 32 field, while its roots remain in the ground. Let him be drenched with the dew of heaven; let him live with the wild animals, until seven times pass by for him.'

²⁴ "This is the interpretation, Your Majesty, and this is the decree the Most High has issued against my lord the king: ²⁵ You will be driven away from people and will live with the wild animals; you will eat grass like the ox and be drenched with the dew of heaven. Seven times will pass by for you until you acknowledge that the Most High is sovereign over all kingdoms on earth and gives them to anyone he wishes. ²⁶ The command to leave the stump of the tree with its roots means that your kingdom will be restored to you when you acknowledge that Heaven rules. ²⁷ Therefore, Your Majesty, be pleased to accept my advice: Renounce your sins by doing what is right, and your wickedness by being kind to the oppressed. It may be that then your prosperity will continue."

The Dream Is Fulfilled

²⁸ All this happened to King Nebuchadnezzar. ²⁹ Twelve months later, as the king was walking on the roof of the royal palace of Babylon, ³⁰ he said, "Is not this the great Babylon I have built as the royal residence, by my mighty power and for the glory of my majesty?"

³¹ Even as the words were on his lips, a voice came from heaven, "This is what is decreed for you, King Nebuchadnezzar: Your royal authority has been taken from you. ³² You will be driven away from people and will live with the wild animals; you will eat grass like the ox. Seven times will pass by for you until you acknowledge that the Most High is sovereign over all kingdoms on earth and gives them to anyone he wishes."

³³ Immediately what had been said about Nebuchadnezzar was fulfilled. He was driven away from people and ate grass like the ox. His body was drenched with the dew of heaven until his hair grew like the feathers of an eagle and his nails like the claws of a bird.

³⁴ At the end of that time, I, Nebuchadnezzar, raised my eyes toward heaven, and my sanity was restored. Then I praised the Most High; I honored and glorified him who lives forever.

His dominion is an eternal
    dominion;
  his kingdom endures from
    generation to generation.

35 All the peoples of the earth
    are regarded as nothing.
He does as he pleases
    with the powers of heaven
    and the peoples of the earth.
No one can hold back his hand
    or say to him: "What have
      you done?"

36 At the same time that my sanity was restored, my honor and splendor were returned to me for the glory of my kingdom. My advisers and nobles sought me out, and I was restored to my throne and became even greater than before. 37 Now I, Nebuchadnezzar, praise and exalt and glorify the King of heaven, because everything he does is right and all his ways are just. And those who walk in pride he is able to humble.

The Writing on the Wall

5 King Belshazzar gave a great banquet for a thousand of his nobles and drank wine with them. 2 While Belshazzar was drinking his wine, he gave orders to bring in the gold and silver goblets that Nebuchadnezzar his father*a* had taken from the temple in Jerusalem, so that the king and his nobles, his wives and his concubines might drink from them. 3 So they brought in the gold goblets that had been taken from the temple of God in Jerusalem, and the king and his nobles, his wives and his concubines drank from them. 4 As they drank the wine, they praised the gods of gold and silver, of bronze, iron, wood and stone.

5 Suddenly the fingers of a human hand appeared and wrote on the plaster of the wall, near the lampstand in the royal palace. The king watched the hand as it wrote. 6 His face turned pale and he was so frightened that his legs became weak and his knees were knocking.

7 The king summoned the enchanters, astrologers*b* and diviners. Then he said to these wise men of Babylon, "Whoever reads this writing and tells me what it means will be clothed in purple and have a gold chain placed around his neck, and he will be made the third highest ruler in the kingdom."

8 Then all the king's wise men came in, but they could not read the writing or tell the king what it meant. 9 So King Belshazzar became even more terrified and his face grew more pale. His nobles were baffled.

10 The queen,*c* hearing the voices of the king and his nobles, came into the banquet hall. "May the king live forever!" she said. "Don't be alarmed! Don't look so pale! 11 There is a man in

---

a 2 Or *ancestor*; or *predecessor*; also in verses 11, 13 and 18   *b 7* Or *Chaldeans*; also in verse 11   *c 10* Or *queen mother* your kingdom who has the spirit of the holy gods in him. In the time of your father he was found to have insight and intelligence and wisdom like that of the gods. Your father, King Nebuchadnezzar, appointed him chief of the magicians, enchanters, astrologers and diviners. ¹²He did this because Daniel, whom the king called Belteshazzar, was found to have a keen mind and knowledge and understanding, and also the ability to interpret dreams, explain riddles and solve difficult problems. Call for Daniel, and he will tell you what the writing means."

¹³So Daniel was brought before the king, and the king said to him, "Are you Daniel, one of the exiles my father the king brought from Judah? ¹⁴I have heard that the spirit of the gods is in you and that you have insight, intelligence and outstanding wisdom. ¹⁵The wise men and enchanters were brought before me to read this writing and tell me what it means, but they could not explain it. ¹⁶Now I have heard that you are able to give interpretations and to solve difficult problems. If you can read this writing and tell me what it means, you will be clothed in purple and have a gold chain placed around your neck, and you will be made the third highest ruler in the kingdom."

¹⁷Then Daniel answered the king, "You may keep your gifts for yourself and give your rewards to someone else. Nevertheless, I will read the writing for the king and tell him what it means.

¹⁸"Your Majesty, the Most High God gave your father Nebuchadnezzar sovereignty and greatness and glory and splendor. ¹⁹Because of the high position he gave him, all the nations and peoples of every language dreaded and feared him. Those the king wanted to put to death, he put to death; those he wanted to spare, he spared; those he wanted to promote, he promoted; and those he wanted to humble, he humbled. ²⁰But when his heart became arrogant and hardened with pride, he was deposed from his royal throne and stripped of his glory. ²¹He was driven away from people and given the mind of an animal; he lived with the wild donkeys and ate grass like the ox; and his body was drenched with the dew of heaven, until he acknowledged that the Most High God is sovereign over all kingdoms on earth and sets over them anyone he wishes.

²²"But you, Belshazzar, his son,ᵃ have not humbled yourself, though you knew all this. ²³Instead, you have set yourself up against the Lord of heaven. You had the goblets from his temple brought to you, and you and your

ᵃ 22 Or *descendant*; or *successor*

nobles, your wives and your concubines drank wine from them. You praised the gods of silver and gold, of bronze, iron, wood and stone, which cannot see or hear or understand. But you did not honor the God who holds in his hand your life and all your ways. [24] Therefore he sent the hand that wrote the inscription.

[25] "This is the inscription that was written:

MENE, MENE, TEKEL, PARSIN

[26] "Here is what these words mean:

Mene[a]: God has numbered the days of your reign and brought it to an end.

[27] Tekel[b]: You have been weighed on the scales and found wanting.

[28] Peres[c]: Your kingdom is divided and given to the Medes and Persians."

[29] Then at Belshazzar's command, Daniel was clothed in purple, a gold chain was placed around his neck, and he was proclaimed the third highest ruler in the kingdom.

[30] That very night Belshazzar, king of the Babylonians,[d] was slain, [31] and Darius the Mede took over the kingdom, at the age of sixty-two.[e]

Daniel in the Den of Lions

6[f] It pleased Darius to appoint 120 satraps to rule throughout the kingdom, [2] with three administrators over them, one of whom was Daniel. The satraps were made accountable to them so that the king might not suffer loss. [3] Now Daniel so distinguished himself among the administrators and the satraps by his exceptional qualities that the king planned to set him over the whole kingdom. [4] At this, the administrators and the satraps tried to find grounds for charges against Daniel in his conduct of government affairs, but they were unable to do so. They could find no corruption in him, because he was trustworthy and neither corrupt nor negligent. [5] Finally these men said, "We will never find any basis for charges against this man Daniel unless it has something to do with the law of his God."

[6] So these administrators and satraps went as a group to the king and said: "May King Darius live forever! [7] The royal administrators, prefects, satraps, advisers and governors have all agreed that the king should issue an edict

---

[a] 26 Mene can mean numbered or mina (a unit of money).   [b] 27 Tekel can mean weighed or shekel.   [c] 28 Peres (the singular of Parsin) can mean divided or Persia or a half mina or a half shekel.   [d] 30 Or Chaldeans   [e] 31 In Aramaic texts this verse (5:31) is numbered 6:1.   [f] In Aramaic texts 6:1-28 is numbered 6:2-29.

and enforce the decree that anyone who prays to any god or human being during the next thirty days, except to you, Your Majesty, shall be thrown into the lions' den. ⁸Now, Your Majesty, issue the decree and put it in writing so that it cannot be altered—in accordance with the law of the Medes and Persians, which cannot be repealed." ⁹So King Darius put the decree in writing.

¹⁰Now when Daniel learned that the decree had been published, he went home to his upstairs room where the windows opened toward Jerusalem. Three times a day he got down on his knees and prayed, giving thanks to his God, just as he had done before. ¹¹Then these men went as a group and found Daniel praying and asking God for help. ¹²So they went to the king and spoke to him about his royal decree: "Did you not publish a decree that during the next thirty days anyone who prays to any god or human being except to you, Your Majesty, would be thrown into the lions' den?"

The king answered, "The decree stands—in accordance with the law of the Medes and Persians, which cannot be repealed."

¹³Then they said to the king, "Daniel, who is one of the exiles from Judah, pays no attention to you, Your Majesty, or to the decree you put in writing. He still prays three times a day." ¹⁴When the king heard this, he was greatly distressed; he was determined to rescue Daniel and made every effort until sundown to save him.

¹⁵Then the men went as a group to King Darius and said to him, "Remember, Your Majesty, that according to the law of the Medes and Persians no decree or edict that the king issues can be changed."

¹⁶So the king gave the order, and they brought Daniel and threw him into the lions' den. The king said to Daniel, "May your God, whom you serve continually, rescue you!"

¹⁷A stone was brought and placed over the mouth of the den, and the king sealed it with his own signet ring and with the rings of his nobles, so that Daniel's situation might not be changed. ¹⁸Then the king returned to his palace and spent the night without eating and without any entertainment being brought to him. And he could not sleep.

¹⁹At the first light of dawn, the king got up and hurried to the lions' den. ²⁰When he came near the den, he called to Daniel in an anguished voice, "Daniel, servant of the living God, has your God, whom you serve continually, been able to rescue you from the lions?"

²¹Daniel answered, "May the king live forever! ²²My God sent

his angel, and he shut the mouths of the lions. They have not hurt me, because I was found innocent in his sight. Nor have I ever done any wrong before you, Your Majesty."

²³ The king was overjoyed and gave orders to lift Daniel out of the den. And when Daniel was lifted from the den, no wound was found on him, because he had trusted in his God.

²⁴ At the king's command, the men who had falsely accused Daniel were brought in and thrown into the lions' den, along with their wives and children. And before they reached the floor of the den, the lions overpowered them and crushed all their bones.

²⁵ Then King Darius wrote to all the nations and peoples of every language in all the earth:

"May you prosper greatly!

²⁶ "I issue a decree that in every part of my kingdom people must fear and reverence the God of Daniel.

"For he is the living God
 and he endures forever;
his kingdom will not be
  destroyed,
 his dominion will never
  end.
²⁷ He rescues and he saves;
 he performs signs and
  wonders
 in the heavens and on the
  earth.

He has rescued Daniel
 from the power of the lions."

²⁸ So Daniel prospered during the reign of Darius and the reign of Cyrus[a] the Persian.

Daniel's Dream of Four Beasts

7 In the first year of Belshazzar king of Babylon, Daniel had a dream, and visions passed through his mind as he was lying in bed. He wrote down the substance of his dream.

² Daniel said: "In my vision at night I looked, and there before me were the four winds of heaven churning up the great sea. ³ Four great beasts, each different from the others, came up out of the sea.

⁴ "The first was like a lion, and it had the wings of an eagle. I watched until its wings were torn off and it was lifted from the ground so that it stood on two feet like a human being, and the mind of a human was given to it.

⁵ "And there before me was a second beast, which looked like a bear. It was raised up on one of its sides, and it had three ribs in its mouth between its teeth. It was told, 'Get up and eat your fill of flesh!'

⁶ "After that, I looked, and there before me was another beast, one that looked like a leopard. And on its back it had four wings like those of a bird. This beast had

---

a 28 Or *Darius, that is, the reign of Cyrus*

four heads, and it was given authority to rule.

7 "After that, in my vision at night I looked, and there before me was a fourth beast—terrifying and frightening and very powerful. It had large iron teeth; it crushed and devoured its victims and trampled underfoot whatever was left. It was different from all the former beasts, and it had ten horns.

8 "While I was thinking about the horns, there before me was another horn, a little one, which came up among them; and three of the first horns were uprooted before it. This horn had eyes like the eyes of a human being and a mouth that spoke boastfully.

9 "As I looked,

"thrones were set in
        place,
    and the Ancient of Days took
        his seat.
His clothing was as white as
        snow;
    the hair of his head was
        white like wool.
His throne was flaming with
        fire,
    and its wheels were all
        ablaze.
10 A river of fire was flowing,
    coming out from before
        him.
Thousands upon thousands
        attended him;

ten thousand times ten
        thousand stood before
        him.
The court was seated,
    and the books were opened.

11 "Then I continued to watch because of the boastful words the horn was speaking. I kept looking until the beast was slain and its body destroyed and thrown into the blazing fire. 12 (The other beasts had been stripped of their authority, but were allowed to live for a period of time.)

13 "In my vision at night I looked, and there before me was one like a son of man,[a] coming with the clouds of heaven. He approached the Ancient of Days and was led into his presence. 14 He was given authority, glory and sovereign power; all nations and peoples of every language worshiped him. His dominion is an everlasting dominion that will not pass away, and his kingdom is one that will never be destroyed.

The Interpretation of the Dream

15 "I, Daniel, was troubled in spirit, and the visions that passed through my mind disturbed me. 16 I approached one of those standing there and asked him the meaning of all this.

"So he told me and gave me the interpretation of these things: 17 'The four great beasts are four

---

[a] 13 The Aramaic phrase *bar enash* means *human being*. The phrase *son of man* is retained here because of its use in the New Testament as a title of Jesus, probably based largely on this verse.

kings that will rise from the earth. ¹⁸But the holy people of the Most High will receive the kingdom and will possess it forever — yes, for ever and ever.'

¹⁹"Then I wanted to know the meaning of the fourth beast, which was different from all the others and most terrifying, with its iron teeth and bronze claws — the beast that crushed and devoured its victims and trampled underfoot whatever was left. ²⁰I also wanted to know about the ten horns on its head and about the other horn that came up, before which three of them fell — the horn that looked more imposing than the others and that had eyes and a mouth that spoke boastfully. ²¹As I watched, this horn was waging war against the holy people and defeating them, ²²until the Ancient of Days came and pronounced judgment in favor of the holy people of the Most High, and the time came when they possessed the kingdom.

²³"He gave me this explanation: 'The fourth beast is a fourth kingdom that will appear on earth. It will be different from all the other kingdoms and will devour the whole earth, trampling it down and crushing it. ²⁴The ten horns are ten kings who will come from this kingdom. After them another king will arise, different from the earlier ones; he will subdue three kings. ²⁵He will speak against the Most High and oppress his holy people and try to change the set times and the laws. The holy people will be delivered into his hands for a time, times and half a time.ᵃ

²⁶"'But the court will sit, and his power will be taken away and completely destroyed forever. ²⁷Then the sovereignty, power and greatness of all the kingdoms under heaven will be handed over to the holy people of the Most High. His kingdom will be an everlasting kingdom, and all rulers will worship and obey him.'

²⁸"This is the end of the matter. I, Daniel, was deeply troubled by my thoughts, and my face turned pale, but I kept the matter to myself."

Daniel's Vision of a Ram and a Goat

8 In the third year of King Belshazzar's reign, I, Daniel, had a vision, after the one that had already appeared to me. ²In my vision I saw myself in the citadel of Susa in the province of Elam; in the vision I was beside the Ulai Canal. ³I looked up, and there before me was a ram with two horns, standing beside the canal, and the horns were long. One of the horns was longer than the other but grew up later. ⁴I watched the ram as it charged toward the west and the north and

---

ᵃ 25 Or *for a year, two years and half a year*

the south. No animal could stand against it, and none could rescue from its power. It did as it pleased and became great.

⁵As I was thinking about this, suddenly a goat with a prominent horn between its eyes came from the west, crossing the whole earth without touching the ground. ⁶It came toward the two-horned ram I had seen standing beside the canal and charged at it in great rage. ⁷I saw it attack the ram furiously, striking the ram and shattering its two horns. The ram was powerless to stand against it; the goat knocked it to the ground and trampled on it, and none could rescue the ram from its power. ⁸The goat became very great, but at the height of its power the large horn was broken off, and in its place four prominent horns grew up toward the four winds of heaven.

⁹Out of one of them came another horn, which started small but grew in power to the south and to the east and toward the Beautiful Land. ¹⁰It grew until it reached the host of the heavens, and it threw some of the starry host down to the earth and trampled on them. ¹¹It set itself up to be as great as the commander of the army of the LORD; it took away the daily sacrifice from the LORD, and his sanctuary was thrown down. ¹²Because of rebellion, the LORD's people[a] and the daily sacrifice were given over to it. It prospered in everything it did, and truth was thrown to the ground.

¹³Then I heard a holy one speaking, and another holy one said to him, "How long will it take for the vision to be fulfilled — the vision concerning the daily sacrifice, the rebellion that causes desolation, the surrender of the sanctuary and the trampling underfoot of the LORD's people?"

¹⁴He said to me, "It will take 2,300 evenings and mornings; then the sanctuary will be reconsecrated."

The Interpretation of the Vision

¹⁵While I, Daniel, was watching the vision and trying to understand it, there before me stood one who looked like a man. ¹⁶And I heard a man's voice from the Ulai calling, "Gabriel, tell this man the meaning of the vision."

¹⁷As he came near the place where I was standing, I was terrified and fell prostrate. "Son of man,"[b] he said to me, "understand that the vision concerns the time of the end."

¹⁸While he was speaking to me, I was in a deep sleep, with my face to the ground. Then he touched me and raised me to my feet.

---

[a] 12 Or rebellion, the armies   [b] 17 The Hebrew phrase ben adam means human being. The phrase son of man is retained as a form of address here because of its possible association with "Son of Man" in the New Testament.

[19] He said: "I am going to tell you what will happen later in the time of wrath, because the vision concerns the appointed time of the end.[a] [20] The two-horned ram that you saw represents the kings of Media and Persia. [21] The shaggy goat is the king of Greece, and the large horn between its eyes is the first king. [22] The four horns that replaced the one that was broken off represent four kingdoms that will emerge from his nation but will not have the same power.

[23] "In the latter part of their reign, when rebels have become completely wicked, a fierce-looking king, a master of intrigue, will arise. [24] He will become very strong, but not by his own power. He will cause astounding devastation and will succeed in whatever he does. He will destroy those who are mighty, the holy people. [25] He will cause deceit to prosper, and he will consider himself superior. When they feel secure, he will destroy many and take his stand against the Prince of princes. Yet he will be destroyed, but not by human power.

[26] "The vision of the evenings and mornings that has been given you is true, but seal up the vision, for it concerns the distant future."

[27] I, Daniel, was worn out. I lay exhausted for several days. Then I got up and went about the king's business. I was appalled by the vision; it was beyond understanding.

Daniel's Prayer

9 In the first year of Darius son of Xerxes[b] (a Mede by descent), who was made ruler over the Babylonian[c] kingdom — [2] in the first year of his reign, I, Daniel, understood from the Scriptures, according to the word of the LORD given to Jeremiah the prophet, that the desolation of Jerusalem would last seventy years. [3] So I turned to the Lord God and pleaded with him in prayer and petition, in fasting, and in sackcloth and ashes.

[4] I prayed to the LORD my God and confessed:

"Lord, the great and awesome God, who keeps his covenant of love with those who love him and keep his commandments, [5] we have sinned and done wrong. We have been wicked and have rebelled; we have turned away from your commands and laws. [6] We have not listened to your servants the prophets, who spoke in your name to our kings, our princes and our ancestors, and to all the people of the land.

[7] "Lord, you are righteous, but this day we are covered

---

[a] 19 Or *because the end will be at the appointed time*   [b] 1 Hebrew *Ahasuerus*
[c] 1 Or *Chaldean*

with shame — the people of Judah and the inhabitants of Jerusalem and all Israel, both near and far, in all the countries where you have scattered us because of our unfaithfulness to you. **8**We and our kings, our princes and our ancestors are covered with shame, LORD, because we have sinned against you. **9**The Lord our God is merciful and forgiving, even though we have rebelled against him; **10**we have not obeyed the LORD our God or kept the laws he gave us through his servants the prophets. **11**All Israel has transgressed your law and turned away, refusing to obey you.

"Therefore the curses and sworn judgments written in the Law of Moses, the servant of God, have been poured out on us, because we have sinned against you. **12**You have fulfilled the words spoken against us and against our rulers by bringing on us great disaster. Under the whole heaven nothing has ever been done like what has been done to Jerusalem. **13**Just as it is written in the Law of Moses, all this disaster has come on us, yet we have not sought the favor of the LORD our God by turning from our sins and giving attention to your truth.

14The LORD did not hesitate to bring the disaster on us, for the LORD our God is righteous in everything he does; yet we have not obeyed him.

15"Now, Lord our God, who brought your people out of Egypt with a mighty hand and who made for yourself a name that endures to this day, we have sinned, we have done wrong. **16**Lord, in keeping with all your righteous acts, turn away your anger and your wrath from Jerusalem, your city, your holy hill. Our sins and the iniquities of our ancestors have made Jerusalem and your people an object of scorn to all those around us.

17"Now, our God, hear the prayers and petitions of your servant. For your sake, Lord, look with favor on your desolate sanctuary. **18**Give ear, our God, and hear; open your eyes and see the desolation of the city that bears your Name. We do not make requests of you because we are righteous, but because of your great mercy. **19**Lord, listen! Lord, forgive! Lord, hear and act! For your sake, my God, do not delay, because your city and your people bear your Name."

The Seventy "Sevens"

20While I was speaking and praying, confessing my sin and the sin of my people Israel and making my request to the LORD my God for his holy hill — ²¹while I was still in prayer, Gabriel, the man I had seen in the earlier vision, came to me in swift flight about the time of the evening sacrifice. ²²He instructed me and said to me, "Daniel, I have now come to give you insight and understanding. ²³As soon as you began to pray, a word went out, which I have come to tell you, for you are highly esteemed. Therefore, consider the word and understand the vision:

²⁴"Seventy 'sevens'ᵃ are decreed for your people and your holy city to finishᵇ transgression, to put an end to sin, to atone for wickedness, to bring in everlasting righteousness, to seal up vision and prophecy and to anoint the Most Holy Place.ᶜ

²⁵"Know and understand this: From the time the word goes out to restore and rebuild Jerusalem until the Anointed One,ᵈ the ruler, comes, there will be seven 'sevens,' and sixty-two 'sevens.' It will be rebuilt with streets and a trench, but in times of trouble. ²⁶After the sixty-two 'sevens,' the Anointed One will be put to death and will have nothing.ᵉ The people of the ruler who will come will destroy the city and the sanctuary. The end will come like a flood: War will continue until the end, and desolations have been decreed. ²⁷He will confirm a covenant with many for one 'seven.'ᶠ In the middle of the 'seven'ᶠ he will put an end to sacrifice and offering. And at the templeᵍ he will set up an abomination that causes desolation, until the end that is decreed is poured out on him.ʰ"ⁱ

Daniel's Vision of a Man

10 In the third year of Cyrus king of Persia, a revelation was given to Daniel (who was called Belteshazzar). Its message was true and it concerned a great war.ʲ The understanding of the message came to him in a vision.

²At that time I, Daniel, mourned for three weeks. ³I ate no choice food; no meat or wine touched my lips; and I used no lotions at all until the three weeks were over.

⁴On the twenty-fourth day of the first month, as I was standing on the bank of the great river, the Tigris, ⁵I looked up and there before me was a man dressed in linen, with a belt of fine gold from Uphaz around his waist. ⁶His body was like topaz, his face like lightning,

ᵃ 24 Or 'weeks'; also in verses 25 and 26   ᵇ 24 Or restrain   ᶜ 24 Or the most holy One   ᵈ 25 Or an anointed one; also in verse 26   ᵉ 26 Or death and will have no one; or death, but not for himself   ᶠ 27 Or 'week'   ᵍ 27 Septuagint and Theodotion; Hebrew wing   ʰ 27 Or it will come upon the wing of the abominable temple, until the end that is decreed is poured out on the desolated city   ʲ 1 Or true and burdensome his eyes like flaming torches, his arms and legs like the gleam of burnished bronze, and his voice like the sound of a multitude.

⁷I, Daniel, was the only one who saw the vision; those who were with me did not see it, but such terror overwhelmed them that they fled and hid themselves. ⁸So I was left alone, gazing at this great vision; I had no strength left, my face turned deathly pale and I was helpless. ⁹Then I heard him speaking, and as I listened to him, I fell into a deep sleep, my face to the ground.

¹⁰A hand touched me and set me trembling on my hands and knees. ¹¹He said, "Daniel, you who are highly esteemed, consider carefully the words I am about to speak to you, and stand up, for I have now been sent to you." And when he said this to me, I stood up trembling.

¹²Then he continued, "Do not be afraid, Daniel. Since the first day that you set your mind to gain understanding and to humble yourself before your God, your words were heard, and I have come in response to them. ¹³But the prince of the Persian kingdom resisted me twenty-one days. Then Michael, one of the chief princes, came to help me, because I was detained there with the king of Persia. ¹⁴Now I have come to explain to you what will happen to your people in the future, for the vision concerns a time yet to come."

¹⁵While he was saying this to me, I bowed with my face toward the ground and was speechless. ¹⁶Then one who looked like a man*a* touched my lips, and I opened my mouth and began to speak. I said to the one standing before me, "I am overcome with anguish because of the vision, my lord, and I feel very weak. ¹⁷How can I, your servant, talk with you, my lord? My strength is gone and I can hardly breathe."

¹⁸Again the one who looked like a man touched me and gave me strength. ¹⁹"Do not be afraid, you who are highly esteemed," he said. "Peace! Be strong now; be strong."

When he spoke to me, I was strengthened and said, "Speak, my lord, since you have given me strength."

²⁰So he said, "Do you know why I have come to you? Soon I will return to fight against the prince of Persia, and when I go, the prince of Greece will come; ²¹but first I will tell you what is written in the Book of Truth. (No one supports me against them except Michael, your prince. **11** ¹And in the first year of Darius the Mede, I took my stand to support and protect him.)

---

a 16 Most manuscripts of the Masoretic Text; one manuscript of the Masoretic Text, Dead Sea Scrolls and Septuagint *Then something that looked like a human hand*

The Kings of the South and the North

2 "Now then, I tell you the truth: Three more kings will arise in Persia, and then a fourth, who will be far richer than all the others. When he has gained power by his wealth, he will stir up everyone against the kingdom of Greece. 3 Then a mighty king will arise, who will rule with great power and do as he pleases. 4 After he has arisen, his empire will be broken up and parceled out toward the four winds of heaven. It will not go to his descendants, nor will it have the power he exercised, because his empire will be uprooted and given to others.

5 "The king of the South will become strong, but one of his commanders will become even stronger than he and will rule his own kingdom with great power. 6 After some years, they will become allies. The daughter of the king of the South will go to the king of the North to make an alliance, but she will not retain her power, and he and his power*a* will not last. In those days she will be betrayed, together with her royal escort and her father*b* and the one who supported her.

7 "One from her family line will arise to take her place. He will attack the forces of the king of the North and enter his fortress; he will fight against them and be victorious. 8 He will also seize their gods, their metal images and their valuable articles of silver and gold and carry them off to Egypt. For some years he will leave the king of the North alone. 9 Then the king of the North will invade the realm of the king of the South but will retreat to his own country. 10 His sons will prepare for war and assemble a great army, which will sweep on like an irresistible flood and carry the battle as far as his fortress.

11 "Then the king of the South will march out in a rage and fight against the king of the North, who will raise a large army, but it will be defeated. 12 When the army is carried off, the king of the South will be filled with pride and will slaughter many thousands, yet he will not remain triumphant. 13 For the king of the North will muster another army, larger than the first; and after several years, he will advance with a huge army fully equipped.

14 "In those times many will rise against the king of the South. Those who are violent among your own people will rebel in fulfillment of the vision, but without success. 15 Then the king of the North will come and build up siege ramps and will capture a fortified city. The forces of the South will be powerless to resist; even their best troops will not have the strength to stand. 16 The invader will do as he pleas-

a 6 Or *offspring*   *b 6* Or *child* (see Vulgate and Syriac) es; no one will be able to stand against him. He will establish himself in the Beautiful Land and will have the power to destroy it. **17** He will determine to come with the might of his entire kingdom and will make an alliance with the king of the South. And he will give him a daughter in marriage in order to overthrow the kingdom, but his plans*a* will not succeed or help him. **18** Then he will turn his attention to the coastlands and will take many of them, but a commander will put an end to his insolence and will turn his insolence back on him. **19** After this, he will turn back toward the fortresses of his own country but will stumble and fall, to be seen no more.

20 "His successor will send out a tax collector to maintain the royal splendor. In a few years, however, he will be destroyed, yet not in anger or in battle.

21 "He will be succeeded by a contemptible person who has not been given the honor of royalty. He will invade the kingdom when its people feel secure, and he will seize it through intrigue. **22** Then an overwhelming army will be swept away before him; both it and a prince of the covenant will be destroyed. **23** After coming to an agreement with him, he will act deceitfully, and with only a few people he will rise to power. **24** When the rich-

est provinces feel secure, he will invade them and will achieve what neither his fathers nor his forefathers did. He will distribute plunder, loot and wealth among his followers. He will plot the overthrow of fortresses — but only for a time.

25 "With a large army he will stir up his strength and courage against the king of the South. The king of the South will wage war with a large and very powerful army, but he will not be able to stand because of the plots devised against him. **26** Those who eat from the king's provisions will try to destroy him; his army will be swept away, and many will fall in battle. **27** The two kings, with their hearts bent on evil, will sit at the same table and lie to each other, but to no avail, because an end will still come at the appointed time. **28** The king of the North will return to his own country with great wealth, but his heart will be set against the holy covenant. He will take action against it and then return to his own country.

29 "At the appointed time he will invade the South again, but this time the outcome will be different from what it was before. **30** Ships of the western coastlands will oppose him, and he will lose heart. Then he will turn back and vent his fury against the holy covenant. He will return and show favor to those who forsake the holy covenant.

³¹ "His armed forces will rise up to desecrate the temple fortress and will abolish the daily sacrifice. Then they will set up the abomination that causes desolation. ³²With flattery he will corrupt those who have violated the covenant, but the people who know their God will firmly resist him.

³³ "Those who are wise will instruct many, though for a time they will fall by the sword or be burned or captured or plundered. ³⁴When they fall, they will receive a little help, and many who are not sincere will join them. ³⁵Some of the wise will stumble, so that they may be refined, purified and made spotless until the time of the end, for it will still come at the appointed time.

The King Who Exalts Himself

³⁶ "The king will do as he pleases. He will exalt and magnify himself above every god and will say unheard-of things against the God of gods. He will be successful until the time of wrath is completed, for what has been determined must take place. ³⁷He will show no regard for the gods of his ancestors or for the one desired by women, nor will he regard any god, but will exalt himself above them all. ³⁸Instead of them, he will honor a god of fortresses; a god unknown to his ancestors he will honor with gold and silver, with precious stones and costly gifts. ³⁹He will attack the mightiest fortresses with the help of a foreign god and will greatly honor those who acknowledge him. He will make them rulers over many people and will distribute the land at a price.ᵃ

⁴⁰ "At the time of the end the king of the South will engage him in battle, and the king of the North will storm out against him with chariots and cavalry and a great fleet of ships. He will invade many countries and sweep through them like a flood. ⁴¹He will also invade the Beautiful Land. Many countries will fall, but Edom, Moab and the leaders of Ammon will be delivered from his hand. ⁴²He will extend his power over many countries; Egypt will not escape. ⁴³He will gain control of the treasures of gold and silver and all the riches of Egypt, with the Libyans and Cushitesᵇ in submission. ⁴⁴But reports from the east and the north will alarm him, and he will set out in a great rage to destroy and annihilate many. ⁴⁵He will pitch his royal tents between the seas atᶜ the beautiful holy mountain. Yet he will come to his end, and no one will help him.

ᵃ 39 Or *land for a reward*   ᵇ 43 That is, people from the upper Nile region
ᶜ 45 Or *the sea and*

The End Times

12 "At that time Michael, the great prince who protects your people, will arise. There will be a time of distress such as has not happened from the beginning of nations until then. But at that time your people—everyone whose name is found written in the book—will be delivered. **2**Multitudes who sleep in the dust of the earth will awake: some to everlasting life, others to shame and everlasting contempt. **3**Those who are wise*a* will shine like the brightness of the heavens, and those who lead many to righteousness, like the stars forever and ever. **4**But you, Daniel, roll up and seal the words of the scroll until the time of the end. Many will go here and there to increase knowledge."

5Then I, Daniel, looked, and there before me stood two others, one on this bank of the river and one on the opposite bank. **6**One of them said to the man clothed in linen, who was above the waters of the river, "How long will it be before these astonishing things are fulfilled?"

7The man clothed in linen, who was above the waters of the river, lifted his right hand and his left hand toward heaven, and I heard him swear by him who lives forever, saying, "It will be for a time, times and half a time.*b* When the power of the holy people has been finally broken, all these things will be completed."

8I heard, but I did not understand. So I asked, "My lord, what will the outcome of all this be?"

9He replied, "Go your way, Daniel, because the words are rolled up and sealed until the time of the end. **10**Many will be purified, made spotless and refined, but the wicked will continue to be wicked. None of the wicked will understand, but those who are wise will understand.

11"From the time that the daily sacrifice is abolished and the abomination that causes desolation is set up, there will be 1,290 days. **12**Blessed is the one who waits for and reaches the end of the 1,335 days.

13"As for you, go your way till the end. You will rest, and then at the end of the days you will rise to receive your allotted inheritance."

---

a 3 Or *who impart wisdom*   *b* 7 Or *a year, two years and half a year*

Hosea

Introduction:

The prophet Hosea was a citizen of the northern kingdom, Israel, which he commonly called Ephraim. He probably began his ministry before King Jeroboam II died in 753 BC and may have given his messages shortly before the fall of Samaria in 722 BC.

Chapters 1–3 tell about Hosea's love for his unfaithful wife, Gomer. Her unfaithfulness is a picture of Israel's unfaithfulness in her covenant relationship with God. Instead of responding in thankfulness and love to God for all their blessings, the Israelites used their crops as offerings to idols. The injustice and mistreatment of others reflected their lack of love for God as well as for their fellow citizens.

Outline of contents:

Hosea's experience in family life (1:1–3:5)
Israel's sin (4:1–6:3)
Punishment for Israel (6:4–10:15)
God's judgment and mercy (11:1–14:9)

1 The word of the LORD that came to Hosea son of Beeri during the reigns of Uzziah, Jotham, Ahaz and Hezekiah, kings of Judah, and during the reign of Jeroboam son of Jehoash[a] king of Israel:

Hosea's Wife and Children

2 When the LORD began to speak through Hosea, the LORD said to him, "Go, marry a promiscuous woman and have children with her, for like an adulterous wife this land is guilty of unfaithfulness to the LORD." 3 So he married Gomer daughter of Diblaim, and she conceived and bore him a son.

4 Then the LORD said to Hosea, "Call him Jezreel, because I will soon punish the house of Jehu for the massacre at Jezreel, and I will put an end to the kingdom of Israel. 5 In that day I will break Israel's bow in the Valley of Jezreel."

6 Gomer conceived again and gave birth to a daughter. Then the LORD said to Hosea, "Call her Lo-Ruhamah (which means "not loved"), for I will no longer show love to Israel, that I should at all

---

[a] 1 Hebrew *Joash*, a variant of *Jehoash*

forgive them. ⁷Yet I will show love to Judah; and I will save them— not by bow, sword or battle, or by horses and horsemen, but I, the LORD their God, will save them."

⁸After she had weaned Lo-Ruhamah, Gomer had another son. ⁹Then the LORD said, "Call him Lo-Ammi (which means "not my people"), for you are not my people, and I am not your God.^a

¹⁰"Yet the Israelites will be like the sand on the seashore, which cannot be measured or counted. In the place where it was said to them, 'You are not my people,' they will be called 'children of the living God.' ¹¹The people of Judah and the people of Israel will come together; they will appoint one leader and will come up out of the land, for great will be the day of Jezreel.^b

2 ^c"Say of your brothers, 'My people,' and of your sisters, 'My loved one.'

Israel Punished and Restored

²"Rebuke your mother, rebuke her,
    for she is not my wife,
    and I am not her husband.
Let her remove the adulterous
    look from her face
    and the unfaithfulness from
    between her breasts.
³Otherwise I will strip her
    naked
    and make her as bare as on
    the day she was born;

I will make her like a desert,
    turn her into a parched land,
    and slay her with thirst.
⁴I will not show my love to her
    children,
    because they are the
    children of adultery.
⁵Their mother has been
    unfaithful
and has conceived them in
    disgrace.
She said, 'I will go after my
    lovers,
    who give me my food and my
    water,
    my wool and my linen, my
    olive oil and my
    drink.'
⁶Therefore I will block her path
    with thornbushes;
    I will wall her in so that she
    cannot find her way.
⁷She will chase after her lovers
    but not catch them;
    she will look for them but not
    find them.
Then she will say,
    'I will go back to my husband
    as at first,
    for then I was better off than
    now.'
⁸She has not acknowledged that
    I was the one
    who gave her the grain, the
    new wine and oil,
    who lavished on her the silver
    and gold—
    which they used for
    Baal.

^a 9 Or your I AM   ^b 11 In Hebrew texts 1:10,11 is numbered 2:1,2.   ^c In Hebrew texts 2:1-23 is numbered 2:3-25.

9 "Therefore I will take away my
   grain when it ripens,
   and my new wine when it is
   ready.
I will take back my wool and
   my linen,
   intended to cover her naked
   body.
10 So now I will expose her
   lewdness
   before the eyes of her
   lovers;
   no one will take her out of
   my hands.
11 I will stop all her celebrations:
   her yearly festivals, her New
   Moons,
   her Sabbath days — all her
   appointed festivals.
12 I will ruin her vines and her fig
   trees,
   which she said were her pay
   from her lovers;
I will make them a thicket,
   and wild animals will
   devour them.
13 I will punish her for the days
   she burned incense to the
   Baals;
   she decked herself with rings
   and jewelry,
   and went after her lovers,
   but me she forgot,"
                  declares the LORD.

14 "Therefore I am now going to
   allure her;
I will lead her into the
   wilderness
   and speak tenderly to her.

15 There I will give her back her
   vineyards,
   and will make the Valley of
   Achor*a* a door of hope.
There she will respond*b* as in
   the days of her youth,
   as in the day she came up
   out of Egypt.

16 "In that day," declares the
   LORD,
   "you will call me 'my
   husband';
   you will no longer call me
   'my master.'*c*
17 I will remove the names of the
   Baals from her lips;
   no longer will their names
   be invoked.
18 In that day I will make a
   covenant for them
   with the beasts of the field,
   the birds in the sky
   and the creatures that move
   along the ground.
Bow and sword and battle
   I will abolish from the
   land,
   so that all may lie down in
   safety.
19 I will betroth you to me
   forever;
   I will betroth you in*d*
   righteousness and
   justice,
   in*d* love and compassion.
20 I will betroth you in*d*
   faithfulness,
   and you will acknowledge
   the LORD.

a 15 Achor means *trouble.*   *b 15* Or *sing*   *c 16* Hebrew *baal*   *d 19,20* Or *with*

21 "In that day I will respond,"
        declares the LORD —
    "I will respond to the skies,
        and they will respond to the
            earth;
22 and the earth will respond to
            the grain,
        the new wine and the olive
            oil,
        and they will respond to
            Jezreel.*a*
23 I will plant her for myself in
            the land;
        I will show my love to the
            one I called 'Not my
            loved one.'*b*
    I will say to those called 'Not
            my people,*c*' 'You are my
            people';
        and they will say, 'You are
            my God.'"

Hosea's Reconciliation
With His Wife

3 The LORD said to me, "Go,
    show your love to your wife
again, though she is loved by another man and is an adulteress.
Love her as the LORD loves the Israelites, though they turn to other gods and love the sacred raisin
cakes."

²So I bought her for fifteen
shekels*d* of silver and about a
homer and a lethek*e* of barley.
³Then I told her, "You are to live
with me many days; you must
not be a prostitute or be intimate

with any man, and I will behave
the same way toward you."

⁴For the Israelites will live
many days without king or
prince, without sacrifice or sacred stones, without ephod or
household gods. ⁵Afterward the
Israelites will return and seek the
LORD their God and David their
king. They will come trembling
to the LORD and to his blessings
in the last days.

The Charge Against Israel

4 Hear the word of the LORD,
        you Israelites,
    because the LORD has a
            charge to bring
    against you who live in the
            land:
    "There is no faithfulness, no
            love,
        no acknowledgment of God
            in the land.
²There is only cursing,*f* lying
            and murder,
        stealing and adultery;
    they break all bounds,
        and bloodshed follows
            bloodshed.
³Because of this the land
            dries up,
        and all who live in it waste
            away;
    the beasts of the field, the
            birds in the sky
        and the fish in the sea are
            swept away.

---

a 22 Jezreel means *God plants.*   *b 23* Hebrew *Lo-Ruhamah* (see 1:6)
c 23 Hebrew *Lo-Ammi* (see 1:9)   *d 2* That is, about 6 ounces or about 170
grams   *e 2* A homer and a lethek possibly weighed about 430 pounds or about
195 kilograms.   *f 2* That is, to pronounce a curse on

4 "But let no one bring a charge,
    let no one accuse another,
  for your people are like those
    who bring charges against a priest.
5 You stumble day and night,
    and the prophets stumble with you.
  So I will destroy your mother—
6   my people are destroyed from lack of knowledge.

  "Because you have rejected knowledge,
    I also reject you as my priests;
  because you have ignored the law of your God,
    I also will ignore your children.
7 The more priests there were,
    the more they sinned against me;
  they exchanged their glorious God[a] for something disgraceful.
8 They feed on the sins of my people
    and relish their wickedness.
9 And it will be: Like people, like priests.
  I will punish both of them for their ways
    and repay them for their deeds.

10 "They will eat but not have enough;
  they will engage in prostitution but not flourish,
  because they have deserted the LORD
  to give themselves 11 to prostitution;
  old wine and new wine
    take away their understanding.
12 My people consult a wooden idol,
    and a diviner's rod speaks to them.
  A spirit of prostitution leads them astray;
    they are unfaithful to their God.
13 They sacrifice on the mountaintops
    and burn offerings on the hills,
  under oak, poplar and terebinth,
    where the shade is pleasant.
  Therefore your daughters turn to prostitution
    and your daughters-in-law to adultery.

14 "I will not punish your daughters
    when they turn to prostitution,
  nor your daughters-in-law
    when they commit adultery,

---

[a] 7 Syriac (see also an ancient Hebrew scribal tradition); Masoretic Text *me; / I will exchange their glory*

because the men themselves
consort with harlots
and sacrifice with shrine
prostitutes —
a people without
understanding will come
to ruin!

¹⁵ "Though you, Israel, commit
adultery,
do not let Judah become
guilty.

"Do not go to Gilgal;
do not go up to Beth Aven.*ᵃ*
And do not swear, 'As surely
as the LORD lives!'
¹⁶ The Israelites are stubborn,
like a stubborn heifer.
How then can the LORD
pasture them
like lambs in a meadow?
¹⁷ Ephraim is joined to idols;
leave him alone!
¹⁸ Even when their drinks are
gone,
they continue their
prostitution;
their rulers dearly love
shameful ways.
¹⁹ A whirlwind will sweep them
away,
and their sacrifices will
bring them shame.

Judgment Against Israel

5 "Hear this, you priests!
Pay attention, you Israelites!
Listen, royal house!
This judgment is against you:

You have been a snare at
Mizpah,
a net spread out on Tabor.
² The rebels are knee-deep in
slaughter.
I will discipline all of
them.
³ I know all about Ephraim;
Israel is not hidden
from me.
Ephraim, you have now turned
to prostitution;
Israel is corrupt.

⁴ "Their deeds do not permit
them
to return to their God.
A spirit of prostitution is in
their heart;
they do not acknowledge the
LORD.
⁵ Israel's arrogance testifies
against them;
the Israelites, even Ephraim,
stumble in their sin;
Judah also stumbles with
them.
⁶ When they go with their flocks
and herds
to seek the LORD,
they will not find him;
he has withdrawn himself
from them.
⁷ They are unfaithful to the
LORD;
they give birth to illegitimate
children.
When they celebrate their New
Moon feasts,
he will devour*ᵇ* their fields.

ᵃ 15 Beth Aven means house of wickedness (a derogatory name for Bethel, which means house of God). *ᵇ 7 Or Now their New Moon feasts / will devour them and*

8 "Sound the trumpet in
        Gibeah,
    the horn in Ramah.
  Raise the battle cry in Beth
        Aven[a];
    lead on, Benjamin.
9 Ephraim will be laid waste
    on the day of reckoning.
  Among the tribes of Israel
    I proclaim what is certain.
10 Judah's leaders are like
        those
    who move boundary
        stones.
  I will pour out my wrath on
        them
    like a flood of water.
11 Ephraim is oppressed,
    trampled in judgment,
    intent on pursuing idols.[b]
12 I am like a moth to Ephraim,
    like rot to the people of
        Judah.

13 "When Ephraim saw his
        sickness,
    and Judah his sores,
  then Ephraim turned to
        Assyria,
    and sent to the great king for
        help.
  But he is not able to cure you,
    not able to heal your sores.
14 For I will be like a lion to
        Ephraim,
    like a great lion to Judah.
  I will tear them to pieces and
        go away;
    I will carry them off, with no
        one to rescue them.

15 Then I will return to my lair
    until they have borne their
        guilt
    and seek my face —
  in their misery
    they will earnestly seek me."

Israel Unrepentant

6 "Come, let us return to the
        Lord.
  He has torn us to pieces
    but he will heal us;
  he has injured us
    but he will bind up our
        wounds.
2 After two days he will
        revive us;
    on the third day he will
        restore us,
  that we may live in his
        presence.
3 Let us acknowledge the
        Lord;
    let us press on to
        acknowledge him.
  As surely as the sun rises,
    he will appear;
  he will come to us like the
        winter rains,
    like the spring rains that
        water the earth."

4 "What can I do with you,
        Ephraim?
  What can I do with you,
        Judah?
  Your love is like the morning
        mist,
    like the early dew that
        disappears.

---

[a] 8 *Beth Aven* means *house of wickedness* (a derogatory name for Bethel, which
means *house of God*).   [b] 11 The meaning of the Hebrew for this word is uncertain.

⁵Therefore I cut you in pieces
  with my prophets,
  I killed you with the words of
    my mouth —
  then my judgments go forth
    like the sun.ᵃ
⁶For I desire mercy, not
    sacrifice,
  and acknowledgment of
    God rather than burnt
    offerings.
⁷As at Adam,ᵇ they have broken
    the covenant;
  they were unfaithful to me
    there.
⁸Gilead is a city of evildoers,
  stained with footprints of
    blood.
⁹As marauders lie in ambush
    for a victim,
  so do bands of priests;
  they murder on the road to
    Shechem,
  carrying out their wicked
    schemes.
¹⁰I have seen a horrible thing in
    Israel:
  There Ephraim is given to
    prostitution,
  Israel is defiled.

¹¹"Also for you, Judah,
  a harvest is appointed.

"Whenever I would restore the
    fortunes of my people,
7 ¹whenever I would heal
    Israel,
  the sins of Ephraim are
    exposed

and the crimes of Samaria
    revealed.
They practice deceit,
  thieves break into houses,
  bandits rob in the streets;
²but they do not realize
  that I remember all their evil
    deeds.
  Their sins engulf them;
  they are always before me.

³"They delight the king with
    their wickedness,
  the princes with their lies.
⁴They are all adulterers,
  burning like an oven
  whose fire the baker need not
    stir
  from the kneading of the
    dough till it rises.
⁵On the day of the festival of
    our king
  the princes become
    inflamed with wine,
  and he joins hands with the
    mockers.
⁶Their hearts are like an
    oven;
  they approach him with
    intrigue.
  Their passion smolders all
    night;
  in the morning it blazes like
    a flaming fire.
⁷All of them are hot as an
    oven;
  they devour their rulers.
  All their kings fall,
  and none of them calls
    on me.

ᵃ 5 The meaning of the Hebrew for this line is uncertain.   ᵇ 7 Or *Like Adam*; or
Like human beings

8 "Ephraim mixes with the
nations;
Ephraim is a flat loaf not
turned over.
9 Foreigners sap his strength,
but he does not realize it.
His hair is sprinkled with
gray,
but he does not notice.
10 Israel's arrogance testifies
against him,
but despite all this
he does not return to the LORD
his God
or search for him.

11 "Ephraim is like a dove,
easily deceived and
senseless —
now calling to Egypt,
now turning to Assyria.
12 When they go, I will throw my
net over them;
I will pull them down like
the birds in the sky.
When I hear them flocking
together,
I will catch them.
13 Woe to them,
because they have strayed
from me!
Destruction to them,
because they have rebelled
against me!
I long to redeem them
but they speak about me
falsely.
14 They do not cry out to me from
their hearts
but wail on their beds.

They slash themselves,[a]
appealing to their gods
for grain and new wine,
but they turn away from me.
15 I trained them and
strengthened their arms,
but they plot evil against me.
16 They do not turn to the Most
High;
they are like a faulty bow.
Their leaders will fall by the
sword
because of their insolent
words.
For this they will be ridiculed
in the land of Egypt.

Israel to Reap the Whirlwind

8 "Put the trumpet to your
lips!
An eagle is over the house of
the LORD
because the people have
broken my covenant
and rebelled against my law.
2 Israel cries out to me,
'Our God, we acknowledge
you!'
3 But Israel has rejected what is
good;
an enemy will pursue him.
4 They set up kings without my
consent;
they choose princes without
my approval.
With their silver and gold
they make idols for
themselves
to their own destruction.

a 14 Some Hebrew manuscripts and Septuagint; most Hebrew manuscripts *They
gather together*

⁵Samaria, throw out your calf-
idol!
My anger burns against
them.
How long will they be
incapable of purity?
⁶ They are from Israel!
This calf — a metalworker has
made it;
it is not God.
It will be broken in pieces,
that calf of Samaria.

⁷"They sow the wind
and reap the whirlwind.
The stalk has no head;
it will produce no flour.
Were it to yield grain,
foreigners would swallow it
up.
⁸Israel is swallowed up;
now she is among the
nations
like something no one
wants.
⁹For they have gone up to
Assyria
like a wild donkey
wandering alone.
Ephraim has sold herself to
lovers.
¹⁰Although they have sold
themselves among the
nations,
I will now gather them
together.
They will begin to waste away
under the oppression of the
mighty king.

¹¹"Though Ephraim built many
altars for sin offerings,

these have become altars for
sinning.
¹²I wrote for them the many
things of my law,
but they regarded them as
something foreign.
¹³Though they offer sacrifices as
gifts to me,
and though they eat the
meat,
the LORD is not pleased with
them.
Now he will remember their
wickedness
and punish their sins:
They will return to Egypt.
¹⁴Israel has forgotten their
Maker
and built palaces;
Judah has fortified many
towns.
But I will send fire on their
cities
that will consume their
fortresses."

Punishment for Israel

9 Do not rejoice, Israel;
do not be jubilant like the
other nations.
For you have been unfaithful
to your God;
you love the wages of a
prostitute
at every threshing floor.
²Threshing floors and
winepresses will not feed
the people;
the new wine will fail them.
³They will not remain in the
LORD's land;

Ephraim will return to Egypt
and eat unclean food in
Assyria.
⁴ They will not pour out wine
offerings to the LORD,
nor will their sacrifices
please him.
Such sacrifices will be to
them like the bread of
mourners;
all who eat them will be
unclean.
This food will be for
themselves;
it will not come into the
temple of the LORD.

⁵ What will you do on the day of
your appointed festivals,
on the feast days of the
LORD?
⁶ Even if they escape from
destruction,
Egypt will gather them,
and Memphis will bury
them.
Their treasures of silver will be
taken over by briers,
and thorns will overrun
their tents.
⁷ The days of punishment are
coming,
the days of reckoning are at
hand.
Let Israel know this.
Because your sins are so many
and your hostility so great,
the prophet is considered a
fool,
the inspired person a
maniac.

⁸ The prophet, along with my
God,
is the watchman over
Ephraim,ᵃ
yet snares await him on all his
paths,
and hostility in the house of
his God.
⁹ They have sunk deep into
corruption,
as in the days of Gibeah.
God will remember their
wickedness
and punish them for their
sins.

¹⁰ "When I found Israel,
it was like finding grapes in
the desert;
when I saw your ancestors,
it was like seeing the early
fruit on the fig tree.
But when they came to Baal
Peor,
they consecrated themselves
to that shameful idol
and became as vile as the
thing they loved.
¹¹ Ephraim's glory will fly away
like a bird —
no birth, no pregnancy, no
conception.
¹² Even if they rear children,
I will bereave them of every
one.
Woe to them
when I turn away from
them!
¹³ I have seen Ephraim, like Tyre,
planted in a pleasant place.

ᵃ 8 Or *The prophet is the watchman over Ephraim, / the people of my God*

But Ephraim will bring out
  their children to the slayer."

14 Give them, LORD —
  what will you give them?
Give them wombs that
  miscarry
  and breasts that are dry.

15 "Because of all their
  wickedness in Gilgal,
  I hated them there.
Because of their sinful
  deeds,
  I will drive them out of my
  house.
I will no longer love them;
  all their leaders are
  rebellious.
16 Ephraim is blighted,
  their root is withered,
  they yield no fruit.
Even if they bear children,
  I will slay their cherished
  offspring."

17 My God will reject them
  because they have not
  obeyed him;
  they will be wanderers
  among the nations.

10 Israel was a spreading
  vine;
  he brought forth fruit for
  himself.
As his fruit increased,
  he built more altars;
as his land prospered,
  he adorned his sacred
  stones.

2 Their heart is deceitful,
  and now they must bear
  their guilt.
The LORD will demolish their
  altars
  and destroy their sacred
  stones.

3 Then they will say, "We have
  no king
  because we did not revere
  the LORD.
But even if we had a king,
  what could he do for us?"
4 They make many promises,
  take false oaths
  and make agreements;
therefore lawsuits spring up
  like poisonous weeds in a
  plowed field.
5 The people who live in
  Samaria fear
  for the calf-idol of Beth
  Aven.ᵃ
Its people will mourn over it,
  and so will its idolatrous
  priests,
those who had rejoiced over its
  splendor,
  because it is taken from
  them into exile.
6 It will be carried to Assyria
  as tribute for the great king.
Ephraim will be disgraced;
  Israel will be ashamed of its
  foreign alliances.
7 Samaria's king will be
  destroyed,
  swept away like a twig on the
  surface of the waters.

ᵃ 5 Beth Aven means house of wickedness (a derogatory name for Bethel, which means house of God).

⁸The high places of
wickedness*ᵃ* will be
destroyed —
it is the sin of Israel.
Thorns and thistles will
grow up
and cover their altars.
Then they will say to the
mountains, "Cover us!"
and to the hills, "Fall
on us!"

⁹"Since the days of Gibeah, you
have sinned, Israel,
and there you have
remained.*ᵇ*
Will not war again overtake
the evildoers in Gibeah?
¹⁰When I please, I will punish
them;
nations will be gathered
against them
to put them in bonds for
their double sin.
¹¹Ephraim is a trained heifer
that loves to thresh;
so I will put a yoke
on her fair neck.
I will drive Ephraim,
Judah must plow,
and Jacob must break up the
ground.
¹²Sow righteousness for
yourselves,
reap the fruit of unfailing
love,
and break up your unplowed
ground;
for it is time to seek the
LORD,

until he comes
and showers his
righteousness on you.
¹³But you have planted
wickedness,
you have reaped evil,
you have eaten the fruit of
deception.
Because you have depended
on your own strength
and on your many
warriors,
¹⁴the roar of battle will rise
against your people,
so that all your fortresses
will be devastated —
as Shalman devastated Beth
Arbel on the day of
battle,
when mothers were dashed
to the ground with their
children.
¹⁵So will it happen to you,
Bethel,
because your wickedness is
great.
When that day dawns,
the king of Israel will be
completely destroyed.

God's Love for Israel

11 "When Israel was a child,
I loved him,
and out of Egypt I called my
son.
²But the more they were
called,
the more they went away
from me.*ᶜ*

ᵃ 8 Hebrew *aven,* a reference to Beth Aven (a derogatory name for Bethel); see
verse 5.   *ᵇ 9* Or *there a stand was taken*   *ᶜ 2* Septuagint; Hebrew *them*

They sacrificed to the Baals
    and they burned incense to
        images.
³It was I who taught Ephraim to
        walk,
    taking them by the arms;
but they did not realize
    it was I who healed them.
⁴I led them with cords of
        human kindness,
    with ties of love.
To them I was like one who
        lifts
    a little child to the cheek,
    and I bent down to feed
        them.

⁵"Will they not return to Egypt
    and will not Assyria rule
        over them
    because they refuse to
        repent?
⁶A sword will flash in their
        cities;
    it will devour their false
        prophets
    and put an end to their plans.
⁷My people are determined to
        turn from me.
    Even though they call me
        God Most High,
    I will by no means exalt
        them.

⁸"How can I give you up,
        Ephraim?
    How can I hand you over,
        Israel?
How can I treat you like
        Admah?

How can I make you like
        Zeboyim?
My heart is changed
        within me;
    all my compassion is
        aroused.
⁹I will not carry out my fierce
        anger,
    nor will I devastate Ephraim
        again.
For I am God, and not a man —
    the Holy One among you.
    I will not come against their
        cities.
¹⁰They will follow the LORD;
    he will roar like a lion.
When he roars,
    his children will come
        trembling from the west.
¹¹They will come from Egypt,
    trembling like sparrows,
    from Assyria, fluttering like
        doves.
I will settle them in their
        homes,"
    declares the LORD.

Israel's Sin

¹²Ephraim has surrounded me
        with lies,
    Israel with deceit.
And Judah is unruly against
        God,
    even against the faithful
        Holy One.ᵃ

12ᵇ ¹Ephraim feeds on the
        wind;
    he pursues the east wind all
        day

ᵃ 12 In Hebrew texts this verse (11:12) is numbered 12:1.   ᵇ In Hebrew texts 12:1-14 is numbered 12:2-15.

and multiplies lies and
violence.
He makes a treaty with
Assyria
and sends olive oil to
Egypt.
²The Lord has a charge to
bring against Judah;
he will punish Jacob*a*
according to his ways
and repay him according to
his deeds.
³In the womb he grasped his
brother's heel;
as a man he struggled with
God.
⁴He struggled with the angel
and overcame him;
he wept and begged for his
favor.
He found him at Bethel
and talked with him
there —
⁵the Lord God Almighty,
the Lord is his name!
⁶But you must return to your
God;
maintain love and justice,
and wait for your God
always.

⁷The merchant uses dishonest
scales
and loves to defraud.
⁸Ephraim boasts,
"I am very rich; I have
become wealthy.
With all my wealth they will
not find in me
any iniquity or sin."

⁹"I have been the Lord your God
ever since you came out of
Egypt;
I will make you live in tents
again,
as in the days of your
appointed festivals.
¹⁰I spoke to the prophets,
gave them many visions
and told parables through
them."

¹¹Is Gilead wicked?
Its people are worthless!
Do they sacrifice bulls in
Gilgal?
Their altars will be like piles
of stones
on a plowed field.
¹²Jacob fled to the country of
Aram*b*;
Israel served to get a wife,
and to pay for her he tended
sheep.
¹³The Lord used a prophet to
bring Israel up from
Egypt,
by a prophet he cared for
him.
¹⁴But Ephraim has aroused his
bitter anger;
his Lord will leave on him
the guilt of his bloodshed
and will repay him for his
contempt.

The Lord's Anger Against Israel

13 When Ephraim spoke,
people trembled;
he was exalted in Israel.

a 2 Jacob means *he grasps the heel*, a Hebrew idiom for *he takes advantage of* or *he deceives.*   *b 12* That is, Northwest Mesopotamia

But he became guilty of Baal
worship and died.
²Now they sin more and more;
they make idols for
themselves from their
silver,
cleverly fashioned images,
all of them the work of
craftsmen.
It is said of these people,
"They offer human
sacrifices!
They kiss*a* calf-idols!"
³Therefore they will be like the
morning mist,
like the early dew that
disappears,
like chaff swirling from a
threshing floor,
like smoke escaping through
a window.

⁴"But I have been the LORD
your God
ever since you came out of
Egypt.
You shall acknowledge no God
but me,
no Savior except me.
⁵I cared for you in the
wilderness,
in the land of burning heat.
⁶When I fed them, they were
satisfied;
when they were satisfied,
they became proud;
then they forgot me.
⁷So I will be like a lion to them,
like a leopard I will lurk by
the path.
⁸Like a bear robbed of her cubs,

I will attack them and rip
them open;
like a lion I will devour them —
a wild animal will tear them
apart.

⁹"You are destroyed, Israel,
because you are against me,
against your helper.
¹⁰Where is your king, that he
may save you?
Where are your rulers in all
your towns,
of whom you said,
'Give me a king and princes'?
¹¹So in my anger I gave you a
king,
and in my wrath I took him
away.
¹²The guilt of Ephraim is
stored up,
his sins are kept on record.
¹³Pains as of a woman in
childbirth come to him,
but he is a child without
wisdom;
when the time arrives,
he doesn't have the sense to
come out of the womb.

¹⁴"I will deliver this people from
the power of the grave;
I will redeem them from
death.
Where, O death, are your
plagues?
Where, O grave, is your
destruction?

"I will have no compassion,
¹⁵   even though he thrives
among his brothers.

---

a 2 Or *"Men who sacrifice / kiss*

An east wind from the LORD
will come,
blowing in from the desert;
his spring will fail
and his well dry up.
His storehouse will be
plundered
of all its treasures.
¹⁶ The people of Samaria must
bear their guilt,
because they have rebelled
against their God.
They will fall by the sword;
their little ones will be
dashed to the ground,
their pregnant women
ripped open."ᵃ

Repentance to Bring Blessing

14 ᵇ Return, Israel, to the
LORD your God.
Your sins have been your
downfall!
² Take words with you
and return to the LORD.
Say to him:
"Forgive all our sins
and receive us graciously,
that we may offer the fruit of
our lips.ᶜ
³ Assyria cannot save us;
we will not mount
warhorses.
We will never again say 'Our
gods'
to what our own hands have
made,
for in you the fatherless find
compassion."

⁴ "I will heal their waywardness
and love them freely,
for my anger has turned
away from them.
⁵ I will be like the dew to
Israel;
he will blossom like a lily.
Like a cedar of Lebanon
he will send down his roots;
⁶ his young shoots will grow.
His splendor will be like an
olive tree,
his fragrance like a cedar of
Lebanon.
⁷ People will dwell again in his
shade;
they will flourish like the
grain,
they will blossom like the
vine —
Israel's fame will be like the
wine of Lebanon.
⁸ Ephraim, what more have Iᵈ to
do with idols?
I will answer him and care
for him.
I am like a flourishing juniper;
your fruitfulness comes
from me."

⁹ Who is wise? Let them realize
these things.
Who is discerning? Let them
understand.
The ways of the LORD are
right;
the righteous walk in them,
but the rebellious stumble in
them.

ᵃ **16** In Hebrew texts this verse (13:16) is numbered 14:1. ᵇ In Hebrew
texts 14:1-9 is numbered 14:2-10. ᶜ **2** Or *offer our lips as sacrifices of bulls*
ᵈ **8** Or Hebrew; Septuagint *What more has Ephraim*

Joel

Introduction:

Although the name Joel was common in the Old Testament, nothing is known about this prophet beyond what the book says — he was the son of Pethuel.

In this book Joel describes in detail a severe locust plague that ravaged Palestine. In this event he saw a sign for the final judgment and warned the people to turn to God in repentance. Joel announced that the "day of the LORD" was coming, a day that would bring even greater judgment.

Outline of contents:

An invasion of locusts (1:1–12)
A call to repentance (1:13–20)
Warnings and God's promise (2:1–32)
God's final judgment and rule (3:1–21)

1 The word of the LORD that came to Joel son of Pethuel.

An Invasion of Locusts

2 Hear this, you elders;
    listen, all who live in the
        land.
Has anything like this ever
        happened in your days
    or in the days of your
        ancestors?
3 Tell it to your children,
    and let your children tell it to
        their children,
    and their children to the
        next generation.
4 What the locust swarm has left
    the great locusts have eaten;

what the great locusts have
        left
    the young locusts have
        eaten;
what the young locusts have
        left
    other locusts*a* have eaten.

5 Wake up, you drunkards, and
        weep!
    Wail, all you drinkers of
        wine;
wail because of the new wine,
    for it has been snatched from
        your lips.
6 A nation has invaded my
        land,
    a mighty army without
        number;

---

a 4 The precise meaning of the four Hebrew words used here for locusts is uncertain.

it has the teeth of a lion,
the fangs of a lioness.
⁷It has laid waste my vines
and ruined my fig trees.
It has stripped off their bark
and thrown it away,
leaving their branches
white.

⁸Mourn like a virgin in
sackcloth
grieving for the betrothed of
her youth.
⁹Grain offerings and drink
offerings
are cut off from the house of
the Lord.
The priests are in mourning,
those who minister before
the Lord.
¹⁰The fields are ruined,
the ground is dried up;
the grain is destroyed,
the new wine is dried up,
the olive oil fails.

¹¹Despair, you farmers,
wail, you vine growers;
grieve for the wheat and the
barley,
because the harvest of the
field is destroyed.
¹²The vine is dried up
and the fig tree is withered;
the pomegranate, the palm
and the apple*a* tree —
all the trees of the field — are
dried up.
Surely the people's joy
is withered away.

A Call to Lamentation

¹³Put on sackcloth, you priests,
and mourn;
wail, you who minister
before the altar.
Come, spend the night in
sackcloth,
you who minister before my
God;
for the grain offerings and
drink offerings
are withheld from the house
of your God.
¹⁴Declare a holy fast;
call a sacred assembly.
Summon the elders
and all who live in the
land
to the house of the Lord your
God,
and cry out to the Lord.

¹⁵Alas for that day!
For the day of the Lord is
near;
it will come like destruction
from the Almighty.*b*

¹⁶Has not the food been cut off
before our very eyes —
joy and gladness
from the house of our God?
¹⁷The seeds are shriveled
beneath the clods.*c*
The storehouses are in ruins,
the granaries have been
broken down,
for the grain has dried up.
¹⁸How the cattle moan!
The herds mill about

---

a 12 Or possibly *apricot*   *b* 15 Hebrew *Shaddai*   *c* 17 The meaning of the
Hebrew for this word is uncertain.

because they have no pasture;
even the flocks of sheep are
suffering.

¹⁹ To you, LORD, I call,
for fire has devoured
the pastures in the
wilderness
and flames have burned up
all the trees of the field.
²⁰ Even the wild animals pant for
you;
the streams of water have
dried up
and fire has devoured
the pastures in the
wilderness.

An Army of Locusts

2 Blow the trumpet in Zion;
sound the alarm on my holy
hill.

Let all who live in the land
tremble,
for the day of the LORD is
coming.
It is close at hand —
² a day of darkness and
gloom,
a day of clouds and
blackness.
Like dawn spreading across
the mountains
a large and mighty army
comes,
such as never was in ancient
times
nor ever will be in ages to
come.

³ Before them fire devours,
behind them a flame blazes.

Before them the land is like
the garden of Eden,
behind them, a desert
waste —
nothing escapes them.
⁴ They have the appearance of
horses;
they gallop along like
cavalry.
⁵ With a noise like that of
chariots
they leap over the
mountaintops,
like a crackling fire consuming
stubble,
like a mighty army drawn up
for battle.

⁶ At the sight of them, nations
are in anguish;
every face turns pale.
⁷ They charge like warriors;
they scale walls like soldiers.
They all march in line,
not swerving from their
course.
⁸ They do not jostle each other;
each marches straight
ahead.
They plunge through defenses
without breaking ranks.
⁹ They rush upon the city;
they run along the wall.
They climb into the houses;
like thieves they enter
through the windows.

¹⁰ Before them the earth shakes,
the heavens tremble,
the sun and moon are
darkened,
and the stars no longer
shine.

¹¹ The LORD thunders
    at the head of his army;
his forces are beyond
        number,
    and mighty is the army that
        obeys his command.
The day of the LORD is great;
    it is dreadful.
Who can endure it?

Rend Your Heart

¹² "Even now," declares the
    LORD,
    "return to me with all your
        heart,
    with fasting and weeping
        and mourning."

¹³ Rend your heart
    and not your garments.
Return to the LORD your
        God,
    for he is gracious and
        compassionate,
slow to anger and abounding
        in love,
    and he relents from sending
        calamity.
¹⁴ Who knows? He may turn and
        relent
    and leave behind a
        blessing—
grain offerings and drink
        offerings
    for the LORD your God.

¹⁵ Blow the trumpet in Zion,
    declare a holy fast,
    call a sacred assembly.
¹⁶ Gather the people,
    consecrate the assembly;

bring together the elders,
    gather the children,
    those nursing at the breast.
Let the bridegroom leave his
        room
    and the bride her chamber.
¹⁷ Let the priests, who minister
        before the LORD,
    weep between the portico
        and the altar.
Let them say, "Spare your
        people, LORD.
    Do not make your
        inheritance an object of
        scorn,
    a byword among the nations.
Why should they say among
        the peoples,
    'Where is their God?' "

The LORD's Answer

¹⁸ Then the LORD was jealous for
        his land
    and took pity on his people.

¹⁹ The LORD replied*a* to them:

"I am sending you grain, new
        wine and olive oil,
    enough to satisfy you fully;
never again will I make you
    an object of scorn to the
        nations.

²⁰ "I will drive the northern
        horde far from you,
    pushing it into a parched
        and barren land;
its eastern ranks will drown in
        the Dead Sea
    and its western ranks in the
        Mediterranean Sea.

---

a 18,19 Or LORD *will be jealous . . . / and take pity . . . / ¹⁹The* LORD *will reply*

And its stench will go up;
its smell will rise."

Surely he has done great
things!
21 Do not be afraid, land of
Judah;
be glad and rejoice.
Surely the LORD has done
great things!
22 Do not be afraid, you wild
animals,
for the pastures in the
wilderness are becoming
green.
The trees are bearing their
fruit;
the fig tree and the vine yield
their riches.
23 Be glad, people of Zion,
rejoice in the LORD your
God,
for he has given you the
autumn rains
because he is faithful.
He sends you abundant
showers,
both autumn and spring
rains, as before.
24 The threshing floors will be
filled with grain;
the vats will overflow with
new wine and oil.

25 "I will repay you for the years
the locusts have eaten —
the great locust and the
young locust,
the other locusts and the
locust swarm[a] —

my great army that I sent
among you.
26 You will have plenty to eat,
until you are full,
and you will praise the name
of the LORD your God,
who has worked wonders for
you;
never again will my people be
shamed.
27 Then you will know that I am
in Israel,
that I am the LORD your God,
and that there is no other;
never again will my people be
shamed.

The Day of the LORD

28 "And afterward,
I will pour out my Spirit on
all people.
Your sons and daughters will
prophesy,
your old men will dream
dreams,
your young men will see
visions.
29 Even on my servants, both
men and women,
I will pour out my Spirit in
those days.
30 I will show wonders in the
heavens
and on the earth,
blood and fire and billows of
smoke.
31 The sun will be turned to
darkness
and the moon to blood

---

[a] 25 The precise meaning of the four Hebrew words used here for locusts is uncertain.

before the coming of the
great and dreadful day of
the LORD.
³²And everyone who calls
on the name of the LORD will
be saved;
for on Mount Zion and in
Jerusalem
there will be deliverance,
as the LORD has said,
even among the survivors
whom the LORD calls.ᵃ

The Nations Judged

3ᵇ "In those days and at that
time,
when I restore the fortunes
of Judah and Jerusalem,
²I will gather all nations
and bring them down to the
Valley of Jehoshaphat.ᶜ
There I will put them on
trial
for what they did to my
inheritance, my people
Israel,
because they scattered my
people among the
nations
and divided up my land.
³They cast lots for my
people
and traded boys for
prostitutes;
they sold girls for wine to
drink.

⁴"Now what have you against
me, Tyre and Sidon and all you
regions of Philistia? Are you repaying me for something I have
done? If you are paying me back,
I will swiftly and speedily return
on your own heads what you have
done. ⁵For you took my silver and
my gold and carried off my finest
treasures to your temples.ᵈ ⁶You
sold the people of Judah and Jerusalem to the Greeks, that you
might send them far from their
homeland.

⁷"See, I am going to rouse them
out of the places to which you
sold them, and I will return on
your own heads what you have
done. ⁸I will sell your sons and
daughters to the people of Judah,
and they will sell them to the Sabeans, a nation far away." The
LORD has spoken.

⁹Proclaim this among the
nations:
Prepare for war!
Rouse the warriors!
Let all the fighting men draw
near and attack.
¹⁰Beat your plowshares into
swords
and your pruning hooks into
spears.
Let the weakling say,
"I am strong!"
¹¹Come quickly, all you nations
from every side,
and assemble there.

Bring down your warriors,
LORD!

ᵃ 32 In Hebrew texts 2:28-32 is numbered 3:1-5.   ᵇ In Hebrew texts 3:1-21 is
numbered 4:1-21.   ᶜ 2 *Jehoshaphat* means *the LORD judges*; also in verse 12.
ᵈ 5 Or *palaces*

12 "Let the nations be roused;
        let them advance into the
            Valley of Jehoshaphat,
    for there I will sit
        to judge all the nations on
            every side.
13 Swing the sickle,
        for the harvest is ripe.
    Come, trample the grapes,
        for the winepress is full
        and the vats overflow —
    so great is their
            wickedness!"

14 Multitudes, multitudes
        in the valley of decision!
    For the day of the LORD is
            near
        in the valley of decision.
15 The sun and moon will be
            darkened,
        and the stars no longer
            shine.
16 The LORD will roar from Zion
        and thunder from
            Jerusalem;
        the earth and the heavens
            will tremble.
    But the LORD will be a refuge
            for his people,
        a stronghold for the people
            of Israel.

Blessings for God's People

17 "Then you will know that I, the
            LORD your God,
        dwell in Zion, my holy hill.
    Jerusalem will be holy;
        never again will foreigners
            invade her.

18 "In that day the mountains
        will drip new wine,
    and the hills will flow with
            milk;
    all the ravines of Judah will
        run with water.
    A fountain will flow out of the
            LORD's house
    and will water the valley of
            acacias.ᵃ
19 But Egypt will be desolate,
        Edom a desert waste,
    because of violence done to
            the people of Judah,
        in whose land they shed
            innocent blood.
20 Judah will be inhabited forever
        and Jerusalem through all
            generations.
21 Shall I leave their innocent
            blood unavenged?
        No, I will not."

    The LORD dwells in Zion!

ᵃ 18 Or *Valley of Shittim*

Amos

Introduction:

The author's name, Amos, means "burden" or "burdenbearer." God called Amos, a shepherd, to be a prophet in the northern cities of Israel. During this time the people living in the northern kingdom were enjoying riches and wealth. Amos went to the people and announced God's judgment on them for turning away from God, for being cruel to the poor, and for living selfishly.

In a series of five visions, Amos saw the day of judgment coming soon. He warned the people to prepare themselves to meet God. For those who loved God, however, Amos had a word of hope. Some day the kingdom of David would be re-established and God's people would dwell in safety.

Outline of contents:

Judgment on Israel's neighbors (1:1–2:5)
Judgment on Israel (2:6–16)
Israel's guilt (3:1–6:14)
The five visions (7:1–9:10)
Israel's restoration (9:11–15)

1 The words of Amos, one of the shepherds of Tekoa — the vision he saw concerning Israel two years before the earthquake, when Uzziah was king of Judah and Jeroboam son of Jehoash[a] was king of Israel. ²He said:

> "The LORD roars from Zion
>   and thunders from
>   Jerusalem;
> the pastures of the shepherds
>   dry up,
>   and the top of Carmel
>   withers."

Judgment on Israel's Neighbors

³This is what the LORD says:

> "For three sins of Damascus,
>   even for four, I will not
>   relent.
> Because she threshed Gilead
>   with sledges having iron
>   teeth,
> ⁴I will send fire on the house of
>   Hazael
>   that will consume the
>   fortresses of Ben-Hadad.
> ⁵I will break down the gate of
>   Damascus;

---

a 1 Hebrew *Joash*, a variant of *Jehoash*

I will destroy the king who
is in*a* the Valley of
Aven*b*
and the one who holds the
scepter in Beth Eden.
The people of Aram will go
into exile to Kir,"
           says the LORD.

⁶This is what the LORD says:

"For three sins of Gaza,
even for four, I will not
relent.
Because she took captive
whole communities
and sold them to Edom,
⁷I will send fire on the walls of
Gaza
that will consume her
fortresses.
⁸I will destroy the king*c* of
Ashdod
and the one who holds the
scepter in Ashkelon.
I will turn my hand against
Ekron,
till the last of the Philistines
are dead,"
      says the Sovereign LORD.

⁹This is what the LORD says:

"For three sins of Tyre,
even for four, I will not
relent.
Because she sold whole
communities of captives
to Edom,
disregarding a treaty of
brotherhood,

¹⁰I will send fire on the walls of
Tyre
that will consume her
fortresses."

¹¹This is what the LORD says:

"For three sins of Edom,
even for four, I will not
relent.
Because he pursued his
brother with a sword
and slaughtered the women
of the land,
because his anger raged
continually
and his fury flamed
unchecked,
¹²I will send fire on Teman
that will consume the
fortresses of Bozrah."

¹³This is what the LORD says:

"For three sins of Ammon,
even for four, I will not
relent.
Because he ripped open the
pregnant women of
Gilead
in order to extend his borders,
¹⁴I will set fire to the walls of
Rabbah
that will consume her
fortresses
amid war cries on the day of
battle,
amid violent winds on a
stormy day.
¹⁵Her king*d* will go into exile,
he and his officials together,"
           says the LORD.

a 5 Or *the inhabitants of*   *b* 5 *Aven* means *wickedness.*   *c* 8 Or *inhabitants*
d 15 Or / *Molek*

2 This is what the LORD says:

"For three sins of Moab,
    even for four, I will not
       relent.
Because he burned to ashes
    the bones of Edom's king,
² I will send fire on Moab
    that will consume the
       fortresses of Kerioth.ᵃ
Moab will go down in great
       tumult
    amid war cries and the blast
       of the trumpet.
³ I will destroy her ruler
    and kill all her officials with
       him,"
                says the LORD.

⁴ This is what the LORD says:

"For three sins of Judah,
    even for four, I will not
       relent.
Because they have rejected the
    law of the LORD
    and have not kept his
       decrees,
because they have been led
    astray by false gods,ᵇ
    the godsᶜ their ancestors
       followed,
⁵ I will send fire on Judah
    that will consume the
       fortresses of Jerusalem."

Judgment on Israel

⁶ This is what the LORD says:

"For three sins of Israel,
    even for four, I will not
       relent.
They sell the innocent for
       silver,
    and the needy for a pair of
       sandals.
⁷ They trample on the heads of
       the poor
    as on the dust of the ground
    and deny justice to the
       oppressed.
Father and son use the same
       girl
    and so profane my holy
       name.
⁸ They lie down beside every
       altar
    on garments taken in
       pledge.
In the house of their god
    they drink wine taken as
       fines.

⁹ "Yet I destroyed the Amorites
    before them,
    though they were tall as the
       cedars
    and strong as the oaks.
I destroyed their fruit above
    and their roots below.
¹⁰ I brought you up out of Egypt
    and led you forty years in the
       wilderness
    to give you the land of the
       Amorites.

¹¹ "I also raised up prophets from
    among your children
    and Nazirites from among
       your youths.
Is this not true, people of
       Israel?"
               declares the LORD.

ᵃ 2 Or *of her cities*   ᵇ 4 Or *by lies*   ᶜ 4 Or *lies*

12 "But you made the Nazirites
  drink wine
and commanded the
  prophets not to
  prophesy.

13 "Now then, I will crush you
  as a cart crushes when
  loaded with grain.
14 The swift will not escape,
  the strong will not muster
  their strength,
and the warrior will not save
  his life.
15 The archer will not stand his
  ground,
  the fleet-footed soldier will
  not get away,
and the horseman will not
  save his life.
16 Even the bravest warriors
  will flee naked on that day,"
  declares the LORD.

Witnesses Summoned Against Israel

3 Hear this word, people of Israel, the word the LORD has
spoken against you — against the
whole family I brought up out of
Egypt:

2 "You only have I chosen
  of all the families of the
  earth;
therefore I will punish you
  for all your sins."

3 Do two walk together
  unless they have agreed to
  do so?
4 Does a lion roar in the thicket
  when it has no prey?

Does it growl in its den
  when it has caught nothing?
5 Does a bird swoop down to a
  trap on the ground
  when no bait is there?
Does a trap spring up from the
  ground
  if it has not caught anything?
6 When a trumpet sounds in a
  city,
  do not the people tremble?
When disaster comes to a city,
  has not the LORD caused it?

7 Surely the Sovereign LORD
  does nothing
without revealing his plan
  to his servants the prophets.

8 The lion has roared —
  who will not fear?
The Sovereign LORD has
  spoken —
  who can but prophesy?

9 Proclaim to the fortresses of
  Ashdod
  and to the fortresses of
  Egypt:
"Assemble yourselves on the
  mountains of Samaria;
  see the great unrest within
  her
  and the oppression among
  her people."

10 "They do not know how to
  do right," declares the
  LORD,
  "who store up in their
  fortresses
what they have plundered
  and looted."

¹¹ Therefore this is what the Sovereign LORD says:

"An enemy will overrun your
    land,
  pull down your strongholds
  and plunder your fortresses."

¹² This is what the LORD says:

"As a shepherd rescues from
    the lion's mouth
  only two leg bones or a piece
    of an ear,
so will the Israelites living in
    Samaria be rescued,
  with only the head of a
    bed
  and a piece of fabric*a* from a
    couch.*b*"

¹³ "Hear this and testify against the descendants of Jacob," declares the Lord, the LORD God Almighty.

¹⁴ "On the day I punish Israel for
    her sins,
  I will destroy the altars of
    Bethel;
  the horns of the altar will be
    cut off
  and fall to the ground.
¹⁵ I will tear down the winter
    house
  along with the summer
    house;
  the houses adorned with ivory
    will be destroyed

and the mansions will be
    demolished,"
        declares the LORD.

Israel Has Not Returned to God

4 Hear this word, you cows
    of Bashan on Mount
    Samaria,
  you women who oppress
    the poor and crush the
    needy
  and say to your husbands,
    "Bring us some drinks!"
² The Sovereign LORD has sworn
    by his holiness:
  "The time will surely come
when you will be taken away
    with hooks,
  the last of you with
    fishhooks.*c*
³ You will each go straight out
    through breaches in the
    wall,
  and you will be cast out
    toward Harmon,*d*"
        declares the LORD.
⁴ "Go to Bethel and sin;
  go to Gilgal and sin yet
    more.
  Bring your sacrifices every
    morning,
  your tithes every three
    years.*e*
⁵ Burn leavened bread as a
    thank offering
  and brag about your freewill
    offerings —

---

a 12 The meaning of the Hebrew for this phrase is uncertain. *b 12* Or *Israelites be rescued, / those who sit in Samaria / on the edge of their beds / and in Damascus on their couches.* *c 2* Or *away in baskets, / the last of you in fish baskets* *d 3* Masoretic Text; with a different word division of the Hebrew (see Septuagint) *out, you mountain of oppression* *e 4* Or *days*

boast about them, you
Israelites,
  for this is what you love
    to do,"
                declares the Sovereign
                  LORD.

6 "I gave you empty stomachs in
    every city
  and lack of bread in every
    town,
  yet you have not returned
    to me,"
                declares the LORD.

7 "I also withheld rain from you
    when the harvest was still
      three months away.
  I sent rain on one town,
    but withheld it from another.
  One field had rain;
    another had none and
      dried up.
8 People staggered from town to
    town for water
  but did not get enough to
    drink,
  yet you have not returned
    to me,"
                declares the LORD.

9 "Many times I struck your
    gardens and vineyards,
  destroying them with blight
    and mildew.
  Locusts devoured your fig and
    olive trees,
  yet you have not returned
    to me,"
                declares the LORD.

10 "I sent plagues among you
    as I did to Egypt.

I killed your young men with
    the sword,
  along with your captured
    horses.
I filled your nostrils with the
    stench of your camps,
  yet you have not returned
    to me,"
                declares the LORD.

11 "I overthrew some of you
    as I overthrew Sodom and
      Gomorrah.
  You were like a burning stick
    snatched from the fire,
  yet you have not returned
    to me,"
                declares the LORD.

12 "Therefore this is what I will
    do to you, Israel,
  and because I will do this to
    you, Israel,
  prepare to meet your God."

13 He who forms the mountains,
    who creates the wind,
  and who reveals his
    thoughts to mankind,
who turns dawn to darkness,
  and treads on the heights of
    the earth —
  the LORD God Almighty is
    his name.

A Lament and Call to Repentance

5 Hear this word, Israel, this
lament I take up concerning
you:

2 "Fallen is Virgin Israel,
  never to rise again,

deserted in her own land,
with no one to lift her up."

³This is what the Sovereign LORD says to Israel:

"Your city that marches out a
thousand strong
will have only a hundred
left;
your town that marches out a
hundred strong
will have only ten left."

⁴This is what the LORD says to Israel:

"Seek me and live;
⁵   do not seek Bethel,
do not go to Gilgal,
do not journey to Beersheba.
For Gilgal will surely go into
exile,
and Bethel will be reduced
to nothing.ᵃ"
⁶Seek the LORD and live,
or he will sweep through the
tribes of Joseph like a
fire;
it will devour them,
and Bethel will have no one
to quench it.

⁷There are those who turn
justice into bitterness
and cast righteousness to the
ground.

⁸He who made the Pleiades and
Orion,
who turns midnight into
dawn
and darkens day into night,

who calls for the waters of the
sea
and pours them out over the
face of the land—
the LORD is his name.
⁹With a blinding flash he
destroys the stronghold
and brings the fortified city
to ruin.

¹⁰There are those who hate the
one who upholds justice
in court
and detest the one who tells
the truth.

¹¹You levy a straw tax on the
poor
and impose a tax on their
grain.
Therefore, though you have
built stone mansions,
you will not live in them;
though you have planted lush
vineyards,
you will not drink their wine.
¹²For I know how many are your
offenses
and how great your sins.

There are those who oppress
the innocent and take
bribes
and deprive the poor of
justice in the courts.
¹³Therefore the prudent keep
quiet in such times,
for the times are evil.

¹⁴Seek good, not evil,
that you may live.

ᵃ 5 Hebrew *aven,* a reference to Beth Aven (a derogatory name for Bethel); see Hosea 4:15.

Then the Lord God Almighty
    will be with you,
    just as you say he is.
¹⁵ Hate evil, love good;
    maintain justice in the
        courts.
Perhaps the Lord God
    Almighty will have
    mercy
on the remnant of Joseph.

¹⁶ Therefore this is what the
Lord, the Lord God Almighty,
says:

"There will be wailing in all
    the streets
    and cries of anguish in every
        public square.
The farmers will be
        summoned to weep
    and the mourners to
        wail.
¹⁷ There will be wailing in all the
    vineyards,
    for I will pass through your
        midst,"
                        says the Lord.

The Day of the Lord

¹⁸ Woe to you who long
    for the day of the Lord!
Why do you long for the day of
    the Lord?
    That day will be darkness,
        not light.
¹⁹ It will be as though a man fled
    from a lion
    only to meet a bear,

as though he entered his house
    and rested his hand on the
        wall
    only to have a snake bite
        him.
²⁰ Will not the day of the Lord be
    darkness, not light —
    pitch-dark, without a ray of
        brightness?

²¹ "I hate, I despise your religious
    festivals;
    your assemblies are a stench
        to me.
²² Even though you bring me
        burnt offerings and grain
        offerings,
    I will not accept them.
Though you bring choice
        fellowship offerings,
    I will have no regard for
        them.
²³ Away with the noise of your
        songs!
    I will not listen to the music
        of your harps.
²⁴ But let justice roll on like a
        river,
    righteousness like a never-
        failing stream!

²⁵ "Did you bring me sacrifices
        and offerings
    forty years in the wilderness,
        people of Israel?
²⁶ You have lifted up the shrine
        of your king,
    the pedestal of your idols,
    the star of your god^a —

---

^a 26 Or lifted up Sakkuth your king / and Kaiwan your idols, / your star-gods;
Septuagint lifted up the shrine of Molek / and the star of your god Rephan, / their
idols

which you made for
yourselves.
²⁷Therefore I will send you into
exile beyond Damascus,"
says the LORD, whose name
is God Almighty.

Woe to the Complacent

6 Woe to you who are
complacent in Zion,
and to you who feel secure
on Mount Samaria,
you notable men of the
foremost nation,
to whom the people of Israel
come!
²Go to Kalneh and look at it;
go from there to great
Hamath,
and then go down to Gath in
Philistia.
Are they better off than your
two kingdoms?
Is their land larger than
yours?
³You put off the day of
disaster
and bring near a reign of
terror.
⁴You lie on beds adorned with
ivory
and lounge on your
couches.
You dine on choice lambs
and fattened calves.
⁵You strum away on your harps
like David
and improvise on musical
instruments.

⁶You drink wine by the bowlful
and use the finest lotions,
but you do not grieve over
the ruin of Joseph.
⁷Therefore you will be among
the first to go into exile;
your feasting and lounging
will end.

The LORD Abhors the Pride of Israel

⁸The Sovereign LORD has
sworn by himself—the LORD
God Almighty declares:

"I abhor the pride of Jacob
and detest his fortresses;
I will deliver up the city
and everything in it."

⁹If ten people are left in one
house, they too will die. ¹⁰And
if the relative who comes to carry the bodies out of the house
to burn them*a* asks anyone who
might be hiding there, "Is anyone
else with you?" and he says, "No,"
then he will go on to say, "Hush!
We must not mention the name
of the LORD."

¹¹For the LORD has given the
command,
and he will smash the great
house into pieces
and the small house into
bits.

¹²Do horses run on the rocky
crags?
Does one plow the sea*b* with
oxen?

---

a 10 Or *to make a funeral fire in honor of the dead* — *b 12* With a different word
division of the Hebrew; Masoretic Text *plow there*

But you have turned justice
into poison
and the fruit of
righteousness into
bitterness —
[13]you who rejoice in the
conquest of Lo Debar[a]
and say, "Did we not take
Karnaim[b] by our own
strength?"

[14]For the LORD God Almighty
declares,
"I will stir up a nation
against you, Israel,
that will oppress you all the
way
from Lebo Hamath to the
valley of the Arabah."

Locusts, Fire and a Plumb Line

7 This is what the Sovereign LORD showed me: He was preparing swarms of locusts after the king's share had been harvested and just as the late crops were coming up. [2]When they had stripped the land clean, I cried out, "Sovereign LORD, forgive! How can Jacob survive? He is so small!"

[3]So the LORD relented.

"This will not happen," the LORD said.

[4]This is what the Sovereign LORD showed me: The Sovereign LORD was calling for judgment by fire; it dried up the great deep and devoured the land. [5]Then I cried out, "Sovereign LORD, I beg you, stop! How can Jacob survive? He is so small!"

[6]So the LORD relented.

"This will not happen either," the Sovereign LORD said.

[7]This is what he showed me: The Lord was standing by a wall that had been built true to plumb,[c] with a plumb line[d] in his hand. [8]And the LORD asked me, "What do you see, Amos?"

"A plumb line," I replied.

Then the Lord said, "Look, I am setting a plumb line among my people Israel; I will spare them no longer.

[9]"The high places of Isaac will
be destroyed
and the sanctuaries of Israel
will be ruined;
with my sword I will rise
against the house of
Jeroboam."

Amos and Amaziah

[10]Then Amaziah the priest of Bethel sent a message to Jeroboam king of Israel: "Amos is raising a conspiracy against you in the very heart of Israel. The land cannot bear all his words. [11]For this is what Amos is saying:

"'Jeroboam will die by the
sword,

---

[a] 13 *Lo Debar* means *nothing.*   [b] 13 *Karnaim* means *horns; horn* here symbolizes strength.   [c] 7 The meaning of the Hebrew for this phrase is uncertain.   [d] 7 The meaning of the Hebrew for this phrase is uncertain; also in verse 8.

and Israel will surely go into
exile,
away from their native land.'"

¹²Then Amaziah said to Amos,
"Get out, you seer! Go back to the
land of Judah. Earn your bread
there and do your prophesying
there. ¹³Don't prophesy anymore
at Bethel, because this is the
king's sanctuary and the temple
of the kingdom."

¹⁴Amos answered Amaziah, "I
was neither a prophet nor the son
of a prophet, but I was a shepherd,
and I also took care of sycamore-
fig trees. ¹⁵But the LORD took me
from tending the flock and said
to me, 'Go, prophesy to my people Israel.' ¹⁶Now then, hear the
word of the LORD. You say,

" 'Do not prophesy against
Israel,
and stop preaching against
the descendants of
Isaac.'

¹⁷"Therefore this is what the
LORD says:

" 'Your wife will become a
prostitute in the city,
and your sons and daughters
will fall by the sword.
Your land will be measured
and divided up,
and you yourself will die in a
pagan*a* country.
And Israel will surely go into
exile,
away from their native
land.' "

A Basket of Ripe Fruit

8 This is what the Sovereign
LORD showed me: a basket
of ripe fruit. ²"What do you see,
Amos?" he asked.

"A basket of ripe fruit," I answered.

Then the LORD said to me, "The
time is ripe for my people Israel; I
will spare them no longer.

³"In that day," declares the
Sovereign LORD, "the songs in
the temple will turn to wailing.*b*
Many, many bodies—flung everywhere! Silence!"

⁴Hear this, you who trample the
needy
and do away with the poor of
the land,

⁵saying,

"When will the New Moon be
over
that we may sell grain,
and the Sabbath be ended
that we may market
wheat?"—
skimping on the measure,
boosting the price
and cheating with dishonest
scales,
⁶buying the poor with silver
and the needy for a pair of
sandals,
selling even the sweepings
with the wheat.

⁷The LORD has sworn by him-
self, the Pride of Jacob: "I will never forget anything they have done.

---

a 17 Hebrew *an unclean*   *b 3* Or *"the temple singers will wail*

8 "Will not the land tremble for
this,
and all who live in it mourn?
The whole land will rise like
the Nile;
it will be stirred up and then
sink
like the river of Egypt.

9 "In that day," declares the Sovereign LORD,

"I will make the sun go down
at noon
and darken the earth in
broad daylight.
10 I will turn your religious
festivals into mourning
and all your singing into
weeping.
I will make all of you wear
sackcloth
and shave your heads.
I will make that time like
mourning for an only
son
and the end of it like a bitter
day.

11 "The days are coming,"
declares the Sovereign
LORD,
"when I will send a famine
through the land —
not a famine of food or a thirst
for water,
but a famine of hearing the
words of the LORD.
12 People will stagger from sea to
sea
and wander from north to
east,

searching for the word of the
LORD,
but they will not find it.

13 "In that day

"the lovely young women and
strong young men
will faint because of thirst.
14 Those who swear by the sin of
Samaria —
who say, 'As surely as your
god lives, Dan,'
or, 'As surely as the god*a* of
Beersheba lives' —
they will fall, never to rise
again."

Israel to Be Destroyed

9 I saw the Lord standing by
the altar, and he said:

"Strike the tops of the pillars
so that the thresholds shake.
Bring them down on the heads
of all the people;
those who are left I will kill
with the sword.
Not one will get away,
none will escape.
2 Though they dig down to the
depths below,
from there my hand will take
them.
Though they climb up to the
heavens above,
from there I will bring them
down.
3 Though they hide themselves
on the top of Carmel,
there I will hunt them down
and seize them.

---

a 14 Hebrew *the way*

Though they hide from my eyes
at the bottom of the sea,
there I will command the
serpent to bite them.
⁴Though they are driven into
exile by their enemies,
there I will command the
sword to slay them.

"I will keep my eye on them
for harm and not for good."

⁵The Lord, the LORD
Almighty—
he touches the earth and it
melts,
and all who live in it mourn;
the whole land rises like the
Nile,
then sinks like the river of
Egypt;
⁶he builds his lofty palace*ᵃ* in
the heavens
and sets its foundation*ᵇ* on
the earth;
he calls for the waters of the
sea
and pours them out over the
face of the land—
the LORD is his name.

⁷"Are not you Israelites
the same to me as the
Cushites*ᶜ*?"
declares the LORD.
"Did I not bring Israel up from
Egypt,
the Philistines from
Caphtor*ᵈ*
and the Arameans from Kir?

⁸"Surely the eyes of the
Sovereign LORD
are on the sinful kingdom.
I will destroy it
from the face of the earth.
Yet I will not totally destroy
the descendants of Jacob,"
declares the LORD.
⁹"For I will give the
command,
and I will shake the people
of Israel
among all the nations
as grain is shaken in a sieve,
and not a pebble will reach
the ground.
¹⁰All the sinners among my
people
will die by the sword,
all those who say,
'Disaster will not overtake or
meet us.'

Israel's Restoration

¹¹"In that day

"I will restore David's fallen
shelter—
I will repair its broken walls
and restore its ruins—
and will rebuild it as it used
to be,
¹²so that they may possess the
remnant of Edom
and all the nations that bear
my name,*ᵉ*"
declares the LORD,
who will do these things.

ᵃ 6 The meaning of the Hebrew for this phrase is uncertain.   *ᵇ 6* The meaning
of the Hebrew for this word is uncertain.   *ᶜ 7* That is, people from the upper
Nile region   *ᵈ 7* That is, Crete   *ᵉ 12* Hebrew; Septuagint *so that the remnant
of people / and all the nations that bear my name may seek me*

¹³"The days are coming," declares the LORD,

"when the reaper will be
overtaken by the
plowman
and the planter by the one
treading grapes.
New wine will drip from the
mountains
and flow from all the hills,
¹⁴ and I will bring my people
Israel back from exile.ᵃ

"They will rebuild the ruined
cities and live in them.
They will plant vineyards
and drink their wine;
they will make gardens and
eat their fruit.
¹⁵I will plant Israel in their own
land,
never again to be uprooted
from the land I have given
them,"

says the LORD your God.

ᵃ 14 Or *will restore the fortunes of my people Israel*

Obadiah

Introduction:

The name Obadiah means "servant of the LORD." Nothing more is known about this prophet than this short book containing his prophecy.

Obadiah is a book of prophecy against the nation of Edom. This country had invaded and plundered Jerusalem at least four times, so Obadiah announced God's judgment against them and prophesied that their kingdom would be destroyed.

The Edomites are never heard of again in history after the destruction of Jerusalem in AD 70.

Outline of contents:

The doom of Edom (1–14)
Edom in the day of the LORD (15–21)

Obadiah's Vision

¹ The vision of Obadiah.

This is what the Sovereign LORD says about Edom—

We have heard a message from
   the LORD:
   An envoy was sent to the
     nations to say,
"Rise, let us go against her for
     battle"—

² "See, I will make you small
     among the nations;
   you will be utterly
     despised.
³ The pride of your heart has
     deceived you,
   you who live in the clefts of
     the rocks[a]

and make your home on the
     heights,
you who say to yourself,
   'Who can bring me down to
     the ground?'
⁴ Though you soar like the eagle
   and make your nest among
     the stars,
   from there I will bring you
     down,"
         declares the LORD.
⁵ "If thieves came to you,
   if robbers in the night—
oh, what a disaster awaits
     you!—
   would they not steal only as
     much as they wanted?
If grape pickers came to you,
   would they not leave a few
     grapes?

---

a 3 Or *of Sela*

⁶But how Esau will be
    ransacked,
  his hidden treasures
    pillaged!
⁷All your allies will force you to
    the border;
  your friends will deceive and
    overpower you;
  those who eat your bread will
    set a trap for you,ᵃ
  but you will not detect it.

⁸"In that day," declares the
    Lord,
  "will I not destroy the wise
    men of Edom,
  those of understanding in
    the mountains of Esau?
⁹Your warriors, Teman, will be
    terrified,
  and everyone in Esau's
    mountains
  will be cut down in the
    slaughter.
¹⁰Because of the violence
    against your brother
    Jacob,
  you will be covered with
    shame;
  you will be destroyed
    forever.
¹¹On the day you stood aloof
  while strangers carried off
    his wealth
  and foreigners entered his
    gates
  and cast lots for Jerusalem,
  you were like one of them.
¹²You should not gloat over your
    brother
  in the day of his misfortune,

nor rejoice over the people of
    Judah
  in the day of their
    destruction,
  nor boast so much
  in the day of their trouble.
¹³You should not march through
    the gates of my people
  in the day of their disaster,
  nor gloat over them in their
    calamity
  in the day of their disaster,
  nor seize their wealth
  in the day of their disaster.
¹⁴You should not wait at the
    crossroads
  to cut down their fugitives,
  nor hand over their survivors
  in the day of their trouble.

¹⁵"The day of the Lord is near
    for all nations.
  As you have done, it will be
    done to you;
  your deeds will return upon
    your own head.
¹⁶Just as you drank on my holy
    hill,
  so all the nations will drink
    continually;
  they will drink and drink
  and be as if they had never
    been.
¹⁷But on Mount Zion will be
    deliverance;
  it will be holy,
  and Jacob will possess his
    inheritance.
¹⁸Jacob will be a fire
  and Joseph a flame;

ᵃ 7 The meaning of the Hebrew for this clause is uncertain.

Esau will be stubble,
and they will set him on fire
and destroy him.
There will be no survivors
from Esau."
The LORD has spoken.

19 People from the Negev will
occupy
the mountains of Esau,
and people from the foothills
will possess
the land of the Philistines.
They will occupy the fields of
Ephraim and
Samaria,
and Benjamin will possess
Gilead.
20 This company of Israelite
exiles who are in Canaan
will possess the land as far
as Zarephath;
the exiles from Jerusalem who
are in Sepharad
will possess the towns of the
Negev.
21 Deliverers will go up on *a*
Mount Zion
to govern the mountains of
Esau.
And the kingdom will be the
LORD's.

Jonah

Introduction:

God called Jonah to be a prophet during the reign of King Jeroboam II (793–753 BC). His job was to warn a foreign nation that God would destroy them if they didn't admit they were sinful and start obeying God. But Jonah didn't want that job. He didn't want to be nice to the people of the city of Nineveh in Assyria since they were the enemy.

So Jonah ran away, taking a ship to a far-away country. His trip ended in disaster. After his adventure, Jonah obeyed God, went to Nineveh to preach and warned the people about God's judgment. Jonah learned, to his dismay, that God would forgive even a heathen city if the people were sorry for their sins.

Outline of contents:

Jonah flees from the Lord (1:1–17)
Jonah's prayer and deliverance (2:1–10)
Jonah goes to Nineveh (3:1–10)
Jonah's anger at the Lord's mercy (4:1–11)

Jonah Flees From the LORD

1 The word of the LORD came to Jonah son of Amittai: ² "Go to the great city of Nineveh and preach against it, because its wickedness has come up before me."

³ But Jonah ran away from the LORD and headed for Tarshish. He went down to Joppa, where he found a ship bound for that port. After paying the fare, he went aboard and sailed for Tarshish to flee from the LORD.

⁴ Then the LORD sent a great wind on the sea, and such a violent storm arose that the ship threatened to break up. ⁵ All the sailors were afraid and each cried out to his own god. And they threw the cargo into the sea to lighten the ship.

But Jonah had gone below deck, where he lay down and fell into a deep sleep. ⁶ The captain went to him and said, "How can you sleep? Get up and call on your god! Maybe he will take notice of us so that we will not perish."

⁷ Then the sailors said to each other, "Come, let us cast lots to find out who is responsible for this calamity." They cast lots and the lot fell on Jonah. ⁸ So they asked him, "Tell us, who is

responsible for making all this trouble for us? What kind of work do you do? Where do you come from? What is your country? From what people are you?"

⁹He answered, "I am a Hebrew and I worship the LORD, the God of heaven, who made the sea and the dry land."

¹⁰This terrified them and they asked, "What have you done?" (They knew he was running away from the LORD, because he had already told them so.)

¹¹The sea was getting rougher and rougher. So they asked him, "What should we do to you to make the sea calm down for us?"

¹²"Pick me up and throw me into the sea," he replied, "and it will become calm. I know that it is my fault that this great storm has come upon you."

¹³Instead, the men did their best to row back to land. But they could not, for the sea grew even wilder than before. ¹⁴Then they cried out to the LORD, "Please, LORD, do not let us die for taking this man's life. Do not hold us accountable for killing an innocent man, for you, LORD, have done as you pleased." ¹⁵Then they took Jonah and threw him overboard, and the raging sea grew calm. ¹⁶At this the men greatly feared the LORD, and they offered a sacrifice to the LORD and made vows to him.

Jonah's Prayer

¹⁷Now the LORD provided a huge fish to swallow Jonah, and Jonah was in the belly of the fish 2 ᵃ three days and three nights. ¹From inside the fish Jonah prayed to the LORD his God. ²He said:

"In my distress I called to the
  LORD,
  and he answered me.
From deep in the realm of the
    dead I called for help,
  and you listened to my cry.
³You hurled me into the
    depths,
  into the very heart of the
    seas,
  and the currents swirled
    about me;
  all your waves and breakers
    swept over me.
⁴I said, 'I have been banished
    from your sight;
  yet I will look again
    toward your holy temple.'
⁵The engulfing waters
    threatened me,ᵇ
  the deep surrounded me;
  seaweed was wrapped
    around my head.
⁶To the roots of the mountains I
    sank down;
  the earth beneath barred me
    in forever.
But you, LORD my God,
  brought my life up from the
    pit.

ᵃ In Hebrew texts 2:1 is numbered 1:17, and 2:1-10 is numbered 2:2-11.
ᵇ 5 Or *waters were at my throat*

7 "When my life was ebbing
away,
I remembered you, Lord,
and my prayer rose to you,
to your holy temple.

8 "Those who cling to worthless
idols
turn away from God's love
for them.
9 But I, with shouts of grateful
praise,
will sacrifice to you.
What I have vowed I will make
good.
I will say, 'Salvation comes
from the Lord.'"

10 And the Lord commanded
the fish, and it vomited Jonah
onto dry land.

Jonah Goes to Nineveh

3 Then the word of the Lord
came to Jonah a second time:
2 "Go to the great city of Nineveh
and proclaim to it the message I
give you."

3 Jonah obeyed the word of the
Lord and went to Nineveh. Now
Nineveh was a very large city; it
took three days to go through it.
4 Jonah began by going a day's
journey into the city, proclaiming, "Forty more days and Nineveh will be overthrown." 5 The
Ninevites believed God. A fast
was proclaimed, and all of them,
from the greatest to the least, put
on sackcloth.
6 When Jonah's warning reached
the king of Nineveh, he rose from

his throne, took off his royal robes,
covered himself with sackcloth
and sat down in the dust. 7 This
is the proclamation he issued in
Nineveh:

"By the decree of the king
and his nobles:

Do not let people or animals,
herds or flocks, taste anything;
do not let them eat or drink.
8 But let people and animals
be covered with sackcloth.
Let everyone call urgently on
God. Let them give up their
evil ways and their violence.
9 Who knows? God may yet relent and with compassion turn
from his fierce anger so that
we will not perish."

10 When God saw what they did
and how they turned from their
evil ways, he relented and did not
bring on them the destruction he
had threatened.

Jonah's Anger at the Lord's Compassion

4 But to Jonah this seemed
very wrong, and he became
angry. 2 He prayed to the Lord,
"Isn't this what I said, Lord,
when I was still at home? That is
what I tried to forestall by fleeing
to Tarshish. I knew that you are
a gracious and compassionate
God, slow to anger and abounding in love, a God who relents
from sending calamity. 3 Now,
Lord, take away my life, for it is
better for me to die than to live."

⁴But the LORD replied, "Is it right for you to be angry?"

⁵Jonah had gone out and sat down at a place east of the city. There he made himself a shelter, sat in its shade and waited to see what would happen to the city. ⁶Then the LORD God provided a leafy plant*ᵃ* and made it grow up over Jonah to give shade for his head to ease his discomfort, and Jonah was very happy about the plant. ⁷But at dawn the next day God provided a worm, which chewed the plant so that it withered. ⁸When the sun rose, God provided a scorching east wind, and the sun blazed on Jonah's head so that he grew faint. He wanted to die, and said, "It would be better for me to die than to live."

⁹But God said to Jonah, "Is it right for you to be angry about the plant?"

"It is," he said. "And I'm so angry I wish I were dead."

¹⁰But the LORD said, "You have been concerned about this plant, though you did not tend it or make it grow. It sprang up overnight and died overnight. ¹¹And should I not have concern for the great city of Nineveh, in which there are more than a hundred and twenty thousand people who cannot tell their right hand from their left — and also many animals?"

ᵃ 6 The precise identification of this plant is uncertain; also in verses 7, 9 and 10.

Micah

Introduction:

This book contains the writings of the prophet Micah who lived in the countryside of Judah during the reigns of Jotham, Ahaz and Hezekiah. Micah warned about God's judgment against the capital cities of both kingdoms, Jerusalem and Samaria, because of the sinfulness of their rulers, prophets and priests. The poor were oppressed and people's lives did not show that they belonged to a holy God.

But Micah promised the restoration of Zion and a kingdom of peace for those who trusted in God. He prophesied that a ruler born in Bethlehem would set up a kingdom that would last forever.

Outline of contents:

Judgment against Samaria and Jerusalem (1:1–16)
Leaders guilty of oppression (2:1–3:12)
Divine restoration (4:1–5:15)
Judgment and mercy (6:1–7:20)

1 The word of the LORD that came to Micah of Moresheth during the reigns of Jotham, Ahaz and Hezekiah, kings of Judah — the vision he saw concerning Samaria and Jerusalem.

2 Hear, you peoples, all of you,
listen, earth and all who live
in it,
that the Sovereign LORD may
bear witness against
you,
the Lord from his holy
temple.

Judgment Against Samaria and Jerusalem

3 Look! The LORD is coming
from his dwelling place;
he comes down and treads
on the heights of the
earth.
4 The mountains melt beneath
him
and the valleys split
apart,
like wax before the fire,
like water rushing down a
slope.
5 All this is because of Jacob's
transgression,
because of the sins of the
people of Israel.
What is Jacob's transgression?
Is it not Samaria?
What is Judah's high
place?
Is it not Jerusalem?

6 "Therefore I will make
   Samaria a heap of
   rubble,
 a place for planting
   vineyards.
 I will pour her stones into the
   valley
 and lay bare her
   foundations.
7 All her idols will be broken to
   pieces;
 all her temple gifts will be
   burned with fire;
 I will destroy all her
   images.
 Since she gathered her gifts
   from the wages of
   prostitutes,
 as the wages of prostitutes
   they will again be used."

Weeping and Mourning

8 Because of this I will weep and
   wail;
 I will go about barefoot and
   naked.
 I will howl like a jackal
 and moan like an owl.
9 For Samaria's plague is
   incurable;
 it has spread to Judah.
 It has reached the very gate of
   my people,
 even to Jerusalem itself.
10 Tell it not in Gath[a];
 weep not at all.
 In Beth Ophrah[b]
 roll in the dust.

11 Pass by naked and in shame,
 you who live in Shaphir.[c]
 Those who live in Zaanan[d]
 will not come out.
 Beth Ezel is in mourning;
 it no longer protects you.
12 Those who live in Maroth[e]
 writhe in pain,
 waiting for relief,
 because disaster has come
   from the LORD,
 even to the gate of
   Jerusalem.
13 You who live in Lachish,
 harness fast horses to the
   chariot.
 You are where the sin of
   Daughter Zion began,
 for the transgressions of
   Israel were found in you.
14 Therefore you will give parting
   gifts
 to Moresheth Gath.
 The town of Akzib[f] will prove
   deceptive
 to the kings of Israel.
15 I will bring a conqueror
   against you
 who live in Mareshah.[g]
 The nobles of Israel
 will flee to Adullam.
16 Shave your head in mourning
 for the children in whom you
   delight;
 make yourself as bald as the
   vulture,
 for they will go from you into
   exile.

---

a 10 Gath sounds like the Hebrew for tell.   b 10 Beth Ophrah means house of
dust.   c 11 Shaphir means pleasant.   d 11 Zaanan sounds like the Hebrew for
come out.   e 12 Maroth sounds like the Hebrew for bitter.   f 14 Akzib means
deception.   g 15 Mareshah sounds like the Hebrew for conqueror.

Human Plans and God's Plans

2 Woe to those who plan
 iniquity,
 to those who plot evil on
 their beds!
 At morning's light they carry it
 out
 because it is in their power
 to do it.
 ² They covet fields and seize
 them,
 and houses, and take them.
 They defraud people of their
 homes,
 they rob them of their
 inheritance.

³ Therefore, the LORD says:

"I am planning disaster
 against this people,
 from which you cannot save
 yourselves.
 You will no longer walk
 proudly,
 for it will be a time of
 calamity.
 ⁴ In that day people will ridicule
 you;
 they will taunt you with this
 mournful song:
 'We are utterly ruined;
 my people's possession is
 divided up.
 He takes it from me!
 He assigns our fields to
 traitors.'"

⁵ Therefore you will have no one
 in the assembly of the
 LORD
 to divide the land by lot.

False Prophets

⁶ "Do not prophesy," their
 prophets say.
 "Do not prophesy about
 these things;
 disgrace will not overtake
 us."
 ⁷ You descendants of Jacob,
 should it be said,
 "Does the LORD become*a*
 impatient?
 Does he do such things?"

"Do not my words do good
 to the one whose ways are
 upright?
 ⁸ Lately my people have risen up
 like an enemy.
 You strip off the rich robe
 from those who pass by
 without a care,
 like men returning from
 battle.
 ⁹ You drive the women of my
 people
 from their pleasant homes.
 You take away my blessing
 from their children forever.
 ¹⁰ Get up, go away!
 For this is not your resting
 place,
 because it is defiled,
 it is ruined, beyond all
 remedy.
 ¹¹ If a liar and deceiver comes
 and says,
 'I will prophesy for you
 plenty of wine and beer,'
 that would be just the
 prophet for this people!

---

a 7 Or *Is the Spirit of the LORD*

Deliverance Promised

12 "I will surely gather all of you,
Jacob;
I will surely bring together
the remnant of Israel.
I will bring them together like
sheep in a pen,
like a flock in its
pasture;
the place will throng with
people.
13 The One who breaks open the
way will go up before
them;
they will break through the
gate and go out.
Their King will pass through
before them,
the LORD at their head."

Leaders and Prophets Rebuked

3 Then I said,

"Listen, you leaders of
Jacob,
you rulers of Israel.
Should you not embrace
justice,
2 you who hate good and love
evil;
who tear the skin from my
people
and the flesh from their
bones;
3 who eat my people's flesh,
strip off their skin
and break their bones in
pieces;
who chop them up like meat
for the pan,
like flesh for the pot?"

4 Then they will cry out to the
LORD,
but he will not answer them.
At that time he will hide his
face from them
because of the evil they have
done.

5 This is what the LORD says:

"As for the prophets
who lead my people astray,
they proclaim 'peace'
if they have something to
eat,
but prepare to wage war
against anyone
who refuses to feed them.
6 Therefore night will come over
you, without visions,
and darkness, without
divination.
The sun will set for the
prophets,
and the day will go dark for
them.
7 The seers will be ashamed
and the diviners disgraced.
They will all cover their faces
because there is no answer
from God."

8 But as for me, I am filled with
power,
with the Spirit of the LORD,
and with justice and might,
to declare to Jacob his
transgression,
to Israel his sin.

9 Hear this, you leaders of Jacob,
you rulers of Israel,
who despise justice
and distort all that is right;

¹⁰who build Zion with
bloodshed,
and Jerusalem with
wickedness.
¹¹Her leaders judge for a bribe,
her priests teach for a price,
and her prophets tell
fortunes for money.
Yet they look for the LORD's
support and say,
"Is not the LORD among us?
No disaster will come
upon us."
¹²Therefore because of you,
Zion will be plowed like a
field,
Jerusalem will become a heap
of rubble,
the temple hill a mound
overgrown with thickets.

The Mountain of the LORD

4 In the last days

the mountain of the
LORD's temple will be
established
as the highest of the
mountains;
it will be exalted above the
hills,
and peoples will stream to it.

²Many nations will come and
say,

"Come, let us go up to the
mountain of the LORD,
to the temple of the God of
Jacob.
He will teach us his ways,
so that we may walk in his
paths."

The law will go out from Zion,
the word of the LORD from
Jerusalem.
³He will judge between many
peoples
and will settle disputes for
strong nations far and
wide.
They will beat their swords
into plowshares
and their spears into
pruning hooks.
Nation will not take up sword
against nation,
nor will they train for war
anymore.
⁴Everyone will sit under their
own vine
and under their own fig
tree,
and no one will make them
afraid,
for the LORD Almighty has
spoken.
⁵All the nations may walk
in the name of their gods,
but we will walk in the name
of the LORD
our God for ever and ever.

The LORD's Plan

⁶"In that day," declares the
LORD,

"I will gather the lame;
I will assemble the exiles
and those I have brought to
grief.
⁷I will make the lame my
remnant,
those driven away a strong
nation.

The LORD will rule over them
  in Mount Zion
    from that day and forever.
⁸As for you, watchtower of the
  flock,
    stronghold*ᵃ* of Daughter
      Zion,
  the former dominion will be
    restored to you;
  kingship will come to
    Daughter Jerusalem."

⁹Why do you now cry aloud —
  have you no king*ᵇ*?
Has your ruler*ᶜ* perished,
  that pain seizes you like that
    of a woman in labor?
¹⁰Writhe in agony, Daughter
  Zion,
  like a woman in labor,
for now you must leave the city
  to camp in the open field.
You will go to Babylon;
  there you will be rescued.
There the LORD will redeem
  you
  out of the hand of your
    enemies.

¹¹But now many nations
  are gathered against you.
They say, "Let her be defiled,
  let our eyes gloat over Zion!"
¹²But they do not know
  the thoughts of the LORD;
they do not understand his
  plan,
  that he has gathered them
    like sheaves to the
      threshing floor.

¹³"Rise and thresh, Daughter
  Zion,
  for I will give you horns of
    iron;
I will give you hooves of
  bronze,
  and you will break to pieces
    many nations."
You will devote their ill-gotten
  gains to the LORD,
  their wealth to the Lord of all
    the earth.

A Promised Ruler From Bethlehem

5*ᵈ* Marshal your troops now,
  city of troops,
    for a siege is laid against us.
They will strike Israel's
  ruler
    on the cheek with a rod.

²"But you, Bethlehem
  Ephrathah,
  though you are small among
    the clans*ᵉ* of Judah,
out of you will come for me
  one who will be ruler over
    Israel,
  whose origins are from of
    old,
    from ancient times."

³Therefore Israel will be
  abandoned
  until the time when she who
    is in labor bears a son,
and the rest of his brothers
  return
    to join the Israelites.

ᵃ 8 Or *hill*   *ᵇ 9* Or *King*   *ᶜ 9* Or *Ruler*   *ᵈ* In Hebrew texts 5:1 is numbered
4:14, and 5:2-15 is numbered 5:1-14.   *ᵉ 2* Or *rulers*

⁴He will stand and shepherd his
flock
in the strength of the LORD,
in the majesty of the name of
the LORD his God.
And they will live securely, for
then his greatness
will reach to the ends of the
earth.

⁵And he will be our peace
when the Assyrians invade
our land
and march through our
fortresses.
We will raise against them
seven shepherds,
even eight commanders,
⁶who will rule*a* the land of
Assyria with the
sword,
the land of Nimrod with
drawn sword.*b*
He will deliver us from the
Assyrians
when they invade our land
and march across our
borders.

⁷The remnant of Jacob will be
in the midst of many
peoples
like dew from the LORD,
like showers on the grass,
which do not wait for anyone
or depend on man.
⁸The remnant of Jacob will be
among the nations,
in the midst of many
peoples,

like a lion among the beasts of
the forest,
like a young lion among
flocks of sheep,
which mauls and mangles as it
goes,
and no one can rescue.
⁹Your hand will be lifted up
in triumph over your
enemies,
and all your foes will be
destroyed.

¹⁰"In that day," declares the
LORD,

"I will destroy your horses
from among you
and demolish your
chariots.
¹¹I will destroy the cities of your
land
and tear down all your
strongholds.
¹²I will destroy your
witchcraft
and you will no longer cast
spells.
¹³I will destroy your idols
and your sacred stones from
among you;
you will no longer bow down
to the work of your hands.
¹⁴I will uproot from among you
your Asherah poles*c*
when I demolish your cities.
¹⁵I will take vengeance in anger
and wrath
on the nations that have not
obeyed me."

a 6 Or *crush*   *b 6* Or *Nimrod in its gates*
goddess Asherah   *c 14* That is, wooden symbols of the

The LORD's Case Against Israel

6 Listen to what the LORD says:

"Stand up, plead my case
    before the mountains;
let the hills hear what you
    have to say.

2 "Hear, you mountains, the
    LORD's accusation;
listen, you everlasting
    foundations of the earth.
For the LORD has a case
    against his people;
he is lodging a charge
    against Israel.

3 "My people, what have I done
    to you?
How have I burdened you?
    Answer me.
4 I brought you up out of Egypt
    and redeemed you from the
        land of slavery.
I sent Moses to lead you,
    also Aaron and Miriam.
5 My people, remember
    what Balak king of Moab
        plotted
    and what Balaam son of Beor
        answered.
Remember your journey from
    Shittim to Gilgal,
    that you may know the
        righteous acts of the
        LORD."

6 With what shall I come before
    the LORD
    and bow down before the
        exalted God?
Shall I come before him with
    burnt offerings,
    with calves a year old?
7 Will the LORD be pleased with
    thousands of rams,
    with ten thousand rivers of
        olive oil?
Shall I offer my firstborn for
    my transgression,
    the fruit of my body for the
        sin of my soul?
8 He has shown you, O mortal,
    what is good.
And what does the LORD
    require of you?
To act justly and to love
    mercy
    and to walk humbly*a* with
        your God.

Israel's Guilt and Punishment

9 Listen! The LORD is calling to
    the city—
    and to fear your name is
        wisdom—
    "Heed the rod and the One
        who appointed it.*b*
10 Am I still to forget your ill-
    gotten treasures, you
        wicked house,
    and the short ephah,*c* which
        is accursed?
11 Shall I acquit someone with
    dishonest scales,
    with a bag of false weights?
12 Your rich people are violent;
    your inhabitants are liars
    and their tongues speak
        deceitfully.

a 8 Or *prudently*   *b 9* The meaning of the Hebrew for this line is uncertain.
c 10 An ephah was a dry measure.

¹³Therefore, I have begun to
destroy you,
to ruin*ᵃ* you because of your
sins.
¹⁴You will eat but not be
satisfied;
your stomach will still be
empty.*ᵇ*
You will store up but save
nothing,
because what you save*ᶜ* I will
give to the sword.
¹⁵You will plant but not harvest;
you will press olives but not
use the oil,
you will crush grapes but not
drink the wine.
¹⁶You have observed the statutes
of Omri
and all the practices of
Ahab's house;
you have followed their
traditions.
Therefore I will give you over
to ruin
and your people to derision;
you will bear the scorn of the
nations.*ᵈ*"

Israel's Misery

7 What misery is mine!
I am like one who gathers
summer fruit
at the gleaning of the
vineyard;
there is no cluster of grapes to
eat,
none of the early figs that I
crave.
²The faithful have been swept
from the land;
not one upright person
remains.
Everyone lies in wait to shed
blood;
they hunt each other with
nets.
³Both hands are skilled in
doing evil;
the ruler demands gifts,
the judge accepts bribes,
the powerful dictate what
they desire —
they all conspire together.
⁴The best of them is like a
brier,
the most upright worse than
a thorn hedge.
The day God visits you has
come,
the day your watchmen
sound the alarm.
Now is the time of your
confusion.
⁵Do not trust a neighbor;
put no confidence in a
friend.
Even with the woman who lies
in your embrace
guard the words of your
lips.
⁶For a son dishonors his
father,
a daughter rises up against
her mother,

ᵃ 13 Or *Therefore, I will make you ill and destroy you; / I will ruin*
ᵇ 14 The meaning of the Hebrew for this word is uncertain.   *ᶜ* 14 Or *You
will press toward birth but not give birth, / and what you bring to birth*
ᵈ 16 Septuagint; Hebrew *scorn due my people*

a daughter-in-law against her
  mother-in-law—
  a man's enemies are the
  members of his own
  household.

7 But as for me, I watch in hope
  for the LORD,
  I wait for God my Savior;
  my God will hear me.

Israel Will Rise

8 Do not gloat over me, my
  enemy!
  Though I have fallen, I will
  rise.
  Though I sit in darkness,
  the LORD will be my light.
9 Because I have sinned against
  him,
  I will bear the LORD's wrath,
  until he pleads my case
  and upholds my cause.
  He will bring me out into the
  light;
  I will see his righteousness.
10 Then my enemy will see it
  and will be covered with
  shame,
  she who said to me,
  "Where is the LORD your
  God?"
  My eyes will see her downfall;
  even now she will be
  trampled underfoot
  like mire in the streets.

11 The day for building your
  walls will come,
  the day for extending your
  boundaries.
12 In that day people will come to
  you
  from Assyria and the cities of
  Egypt,
  even from Egypt to the
  Euphrates
  and from sea to sea
  and from mountain to
  mountain.
13 The earth will become
  desolate because of its
  inhabitants,
  as the result of their deeds.

Prayer and Praise

14 Shepherd your people with
  your staff,
  the flock of your inheritance,
  which lives by itself in a forest,
  in fertile pasturelands.[a]
  Let them feed in Bashan and
  Gilead
  as in days long ago.

15 "As in the days when you came
  out of Egypt,
  I will show them my
  wonders."

16 Nations will see and be
  ashamed,
  deprived of all their power.
  They will put their hands over
  their mouths
  and their ears will become
  deaf.
17 They will lick dust like a snake,
  like creatures that crawl on
  the ground.
  They will come trembling out
  of their dens;

---

a 14 Or *in the middle of Carmel*

they will turn in fear to the
LORD our God
and will be afraid of you.
¹⁸Who is a God like you,
who pardons sin
and forgives the
transgression
of the remnant of his
inheritance?
You do not stay angry forever
but delight to show mercy.

¹⁹You will again have
compassion on us;
you will tread our sins
underfoot
and hurl all our iniquities
into the depths of the sea.
²⁰You will be faithful to Jacob,
and show love to Abraham,
as you pledged on oath to our
ancestors
in days long ago.

Nahum

Introduction:

Nahum was a prophet in the last half of the seventh century BC. He prophesied at the same time as Zephaniah, Jeremiah and Habakkuk.

Nahum is a book of prophecy against Nineveh, the capital of Assyria. The prophet describes the cruelty of the Assyrians as they conquered nation after nation. He predicts the siege and destruction of Nineveh and the end of the kingdom of Assyria.

Nahum's only advice to Judah was that they observe their religious festivals since the Assyrians would never again threaten Jerusalem.

Outline of contents:

The Lord's anger against Nineveh (1:1–15)
Nineveh's fall (2:1–13)
Misery to Nineveh (3:1–19)

1 A prophecy concerning Nineveh. The book of the vision of Nahum the Elkoshite.

The LORD's Anger Against Nineveh

²The LORD is a jealous and
    avenging God;
  the LORD takes vengeance
    and is filled with wrath.
The LORD takes vengeance on
    his foes
  and vents his wrath against
    his enemies.
³The LORD is slow to anger but
    great in power;
  the LORD will not leave the
    guilty unpunished.
His way is in the whirlwind
    and the storm,
  and clouds are the dust of
    his feet.

⁴He rebukes the sea and dries
    it up;
  he makes all the rivers run
    dry.
Bashan and Carmel wither
  and the blossoms of
    Lebanon fade.
⁵The mountains quake before
    him
  and the hills melt away.
The earth trembles at his
    presence,
  the world and all who live
    in it.
⁶Who can withstand his
    indignation?
  Who can endure his fierce
    anger?
His wrath is poured out like
    fire;
  the rocks are shattered
    before him.

7 The LORD is good,
    a refuge in times of trouble.
He cares for those who trust in
        him,
8   but with an overwhelming
        flood
he will make an end of
        Nineveh;
    he will pursue his foes into
        the realm of darkness.

9 Whatever they plot against the
        LORD
    he will bring*a* to an end;
    trouble will not come a
        second time.
10 They will be entangled among
        thorns
    and drunk from their wine;
    they will be consumed like
        dry stubble.*b*
11 From you, Nineveh, has one
        come forth
    who plots evil against the
        LORD
    and devises wicked plans.

12 This is what the LORD says:

"Although they have allies and
        are numerous,
    they will be destroyed and
        pass away.
Although I have afflicted you,
        Judah,
    I will afflict you no more.
13 Now I will break their yoke
        from your neck
    and tear your shackles
        away."

14 The LORD has given a
        command concerning
        you, Nineveh:
"You will have no
    descendants to bear your
        name.
I will destroy the images and
        idols
    that are in the temple of your
        gods.
I will prepare your grave,
    for you are vile."

15 Look, there on the mountains,
    the feet of one who brings
        good news,
    who proclaims peace!
Celebrate your festivals,
        Judah,
    and fulfill your vows.
No more will the wicked
        invade you;
    they will be completely
        destroyed.*c*

Nineveh to Fall

2   *d* An attacker advances
        against you, Nineveh.
Guard the fortress,
    watch the road,
    brace yourselves,
    marshal all your strength!

2 The LORD will restore the
        splendor of Jacob
    like the splendor of Israel,
though destroyers have laid
        them waste
    and have ruined their vines.

---

a **9** Or *What do you foes plot against the LORD? / He will bring it*   *b* **10** The meaning
of the Hebrew for this verse is uncertain.   *c* **15** In Hebrew texts this verse (1:15) is
numbered 2:1.   *d* In Hebrew texts 2:1-13 is numbered 2:2-14.

³The shields of the soldiers are red;
the warriors are clad in scarlet.
The metal on the chariots flashes
on the day they are made ready;
the spears of juniper are brandished.ᵃ
⁴The chariots storm through the streets,
rushing back and forth through the squares.
They look like flaming torches;
they dart about like lightning.

⁵Nineveh summons her picked troops,
yet they stumble on their way.
They dash to the city wall;
the protective shield is put in place.
⁶The river gates are thrown open
and the palace collapses.
⁷It is decreedᵇ that Nineveh
be exiled and carried away.
Her female slaves moan like doves
and beat on their breasts.
⁸Nineveh is like a pool
whose water is draining away.
"Stop! Stop!" they cry,
but no one turns back.
⁹Plunder the silver!
Plunder the gold!
The supply is endless,
the wealth from all its treasures!
¹⁰She is pillaged, plundered, stripped!
Hearts melt, knees give way,
bodies tremble, every face grows pale.

¹¹Where now is the lions' den,
the place where they fed their young,
where the lion and lioness went,
and the cubs, with nothing to fear?
¹²The lion killed enough for his cubs
and strangled the prey for his mate,
filling his lairs with the kill
and his dens with the prey.

¹³"I am against you,"
declares the LORD Almighty.
"I will burn up your chariots in smoke,
and the sword will devour your young lions.
I will leave you no prey on the earth.
The voices of your messengers will no longer be heard."

Woe to Nineveh

3 Woe to the city of blood,
full of lies,
full of plunder,
never without victims!
²The crack of whips,
the clatter of wheels,

ᵃ 3 Hebrew; Septuagint and Syriac *ready; / the horsemen rush to and fro.*
ᵇ 7 The meaning of the Hebrew for this word is uncertain.

galloping horses
and jolting chariots!
³Charging cavalry,
flashing swords
and glittering spears!
Many casualties,
piles of dead,
bodies without number,
people stumbling over the
corpses —
⁴all because of the wanton lust
of a prostitute,
alluring, the mistress of
sorceries,
who enslaved nations by her
prostitution
and peoples by her
witchcraft.

⁵"I am against you," declares
the LORD Almighty.
"I will lift your skirts over
your face.
I will show the nations your
nakedness
and the kingdoms your
shame.
⁶I will pelt you with filth,
I will treat you with
contempt
and make you a spectacle.
⁷All who see you will flee from
you and say,
'Nineveh is in ruins — who
will mourn for her?'
Where can I find anyone to
comfort you?"

⁸Are you better than Thebes,
situated on the Nile,
with water around her?

The river was her defense,
the waters her wall.
⁹Cush ͣ and Egypt were her
boundless strength;
Put and Libya were among
her allies.
¹⁰Yet she was taken captive
and went into exile.
Her infants were dashed to
pieces
at every street corner.
Lots were cast for her
nobles,
and all her great men were
put in chains.
¹¹You too will become drunk;
you will go into hiding
and seek refuge from the
enemy.

¹²All your fortresses are like fig
trees
with their first ripe fruit;
when they are shaken,
the figs fall into the mouth of
the eater.
¹³Look at your troops —
they are all weaklings.
The gates of your land
are wide open to your
enemies;
fire has consumed the bars
of your gates.

¹⁴Draw water for the siege,
strengthen your defenses!
Work the clay,
tread the mortar,
repair the brickwork!
¹⁵There the fire will consume
you;

ͣ 9 That is, the upper Nile region

the sword will cut you
down—
they will devour you like a
swarm of locusts.
Multiply like grasshoppers,
multiply like locusts!
16 You have increased the
number of your
merchants
till they are more numerous
than the stars in the sky,
but like locusts they strip the
land
and then fly away.
17 Your guards are like locusts,
your officials like swarms of
locusts
that settle in the walls on a
cold day—

but when the sun appears they
fly away,
and no one knows where.
18 King of Assyria, your
shepherds[a] slumber;
your nobles lie down to
rest.
Your people are scattered on
the mountains
with no one to gather them.
19 Nothing can heal you;
your wound is fatal.
All who hear the news about
you
clap their hands at your
fall,
for who has not felt
your endless cruelty?

a 18 That is, rulers

Habakkuk

Introduction:

Habakkuk was written as a dialogue or conversation between God and the prophet. Habakkuk saw that the leaders in Judah were oppressing the poor, so he asked God the question: Why do you allow wicked people to prosper? When God told him that the Babylonians would come to punish Judah, Habakkuk became more concerned. He did not understand how God could use the Babylonians, who were actually more wicked than the wicked Israelites, to bring judgment on God's chosen people. God's answer was that the just would live by faith in God and that they had the assurance that God was doing what was right. God told Habakkuk that eventually he would judge the Babylonians too and he would bring justice to his chosen people. Habakkuk ends his book with a prayer of praise.

Outline of contents:

Habakkuk's question and God's answer (1:1–11)
Habakkuk's second question and God's answer (1:12–2:20)
Habakkuk's prayer (3:1–19)

1

The prophecy that Habakkuk the prophet received.

Habakkuk's Complaint

² How long, LORD, must I call for
  help,
    but you do not listen?
  Or cry out to you,
    "Violence!"
  but you do not save?
³ Why do you make me look at
  injustice?
  Why do you tolerate
    wrongdoing?
  Destruction and violence are
    before me;

there is strife, and conflict
  abounds.
⁴ Therefore the law is paralyzed,
  and justice never prevails.
  The wicked hem in the
    righteous,
  so that justice is perverted.

The LORD's Answer

⁵ "Look at the nations and
    watch —
  and be utterly amazed.
  For I am going to do
    something in your days
  that you would not believe,
  even if you were told.

⁶I am raising up the
    Babylonians,ᵃ
  that ruthless and impetuous
    people,
 who sweep across the whole
    earth
  to seize dwellings not their
    own.
⁷They are a feared and dreaded
    people;
  they are a law to
    themselves
  and promote their own
    honor.
⁸Their horses are swifter than
    leopards,
  fiercer than wolves at dusk.
 Their cavalry gallops
    headlong;
  their horsemen come from
    afar.
 They fly like an eagle
    swooping to devour;
⁹ they all come intent on
    violence.
 Their hordesᵇ advance like a
    desert wind
  and gather prisoners like
    sand.
¹⁰They mock kings
  and scoff at rulers.
 They laugh at all fortified
    cities;
  by building earthen ramps
    they capture them.
¹¹Then they sweep past like the
    wind and go on —
  guilty people, whose own
    strength is their god."

Habakkuk's Second Complaint

¹²LORD, are you not from
    everlasting?
  My God, my Holy One, youᶜ
    will never die.
 You, LORD, have appointed
    them to execute
    judgment;
  you, my Rock, have ordained
    them to punish.
¹³Your eyes are too pure to look
    on evil;
  you cannot tolerate
    wrongdoing.
 Why then do you tolerate the
    treacherous?
 Why are you silent while the
    wicked
 swallow up those more
    righteous than
    themselves?
¹⁴You have made people like the
    fish in the sea,
  like the sea creatures that
    have no ruler.
¹⁵The wicked foe pulls all of
    them up with hooks,
  he catches them in his net,
 he gathers them up in his
    dragnet;
  and so he rejoices and is
    glad.
¹⁶Therefore he sacrifices to his
    net
  and burns incense to his
    dragnet,
 for by his net he lives in luxury
  and enjoys the choicest
    food.

ᵃ 6 Or *Chaldeans*   ᵇ 9 The meaning of the Hebrew for this word is uncertain.
ᶜ 12 An ancient Hebrew scribal tradition; Masoretic Text *we*

17 Is he to keep on emptying his
net,
destroying nations without
mercy?

2 I will stand at my watch
and station myself on the
ramparts;
I will look to see what he will
say to me,
and what answer I am to
give to this complaint.*a*

The LORD's Answer

2 Then the LORD replied:

"Write down the revelation
and make it plain on tablets
so that a herald*b* may run
with it.
3 For the revelation awaits an
appointed time;
it speaks of the end
and will not prove false.
Though it linger, wait for it;
it*c* will certainly come
and will not delay.

4 "See, the enemy is puffed up;
his desires are not upright —
but the righteous person
will live by his
faithfulness*d* —
5 indeed, wine betrays him;
he is arrogant and never at
rest.
Because he is as greedy as the
grave
and like death is never
satisfied,

he gathers to himself all the
nations
and takes captive all the
peoples.

6 "Will not all of them taunt him
with ridicule and scorn, saying,

" 'Woe to him who piles up
stolen goods
and makes himself wealthy
by extortion!
How long must this
go on?'
7 Will not your creditors
suddenly arise?
Will they not wake up and
make you tremble?
Then you will become their
prey.
8 Because you have plundered
many nations,
the peoples who are left will
plunder you.
For you have shed human
blood;
you have destroyed lands
and cities and everyone
in them.

9 "Woe to him who builds his
house by unjust gain,
setting his nest on high
to escape the clutches of
ruin!
10 You have plotted the ruin of
many peoples,
shaming your own house
and forfeiting your life.
11 The stones of the wall will cry
out,

a 1 Or and what to answer when I am rebuked   *b 2 Or so that whoever reads it*
c 3 Or Though he linger, wait for him; / he   *d 4 Or faith*

and the beams of the
woodwork will echo it.

12 "Woe to him who builds a city
with bloodshed
and establishes a town by
injustice!
13 Has not the LORD Almighty
determined
that the people's labor is only
fuel for the fire,
that the nations exhaust
themselves for nothing?
14 For the earth will be filled
with the knowledge of
the glory of the LORD
as the waters cover the
sea.

15 "Woe to him who gives drink
to his neighbors,
pouring it from the wineskin
till they are drunk,
so that he can gaze on their
naked bodies!
16 You will be filled with shame
instead of glory.
Now it is your turn! Drink
and let your nakedness
be exposed*a*!
The cup from the LORD's right
hand is coming around
to you,
and disgrace will cover your
glory.
17 The violence you have done to
Lebanon will overwhelm
you,
and your destruction of
animals will terrify you.

For you have shed human
blood;
you have destroyed lands
and cities and everyone
in them.

18 "Of what value is an idol
carved by a craftsman?
Or an image that teaches
lies?
For the one who makes
it trusts in his own
creation;
he makes idols that cannot
speak.
19 Woe to him who says to wood,
'Come to life!'
Or to lifeless stone, 'Wake
up!'
Can it give guidance?
It is covered with gold and
silver;
there is no breath in it."

20 The LORD is in his holy
temple;
let all the earth be silent
before him.

Habakkuk's Prayer

3 A prayer of Habakkuk the
prophet. On *shigionoth.*b

2 LORD, I have heard of your
fame;
I stand in awe of your deeds,
LORD.
Repeat them in our day,
in our time make them
known;
in wrath remember mercy.

---

a 16 Masoretic Text; Dead Sea Scrolls, Aquila, Vulgate and Syriac (see also
Septuagint) *and stagger*   *b* 1 Probably a literary or musical term

³God came from Teman,
the Holy One from Mount
Paran.ᵃ
His glory covered the heavens
and his praise filled the
earth.
⁴His splendor was like the
sunrise;
rays flashed from his hand,
where his power was hidden.
⁵Plague went before him;
pestilence followed his steps.
⁶He stood, and shook the earth;
he looked, and made the
nations tremble.
The ancient mountains
crumbled
and the age-old hills
collapsed—
but he marches on forever.
⁷I saw the tents of Cushan in
distress,
the dwellings of Midian in
anguish.

⁸Were you angry with the
rivers, Lᴏʀᴅ?
Was your wrath against the
streams?
Did you rage against the sea
when you rode your horses
and your chariots to victory?
⁹You uncovered your bow,
you called for many arrows.
You split the earth with rivers;
¹⁰   the mountains saw you and
writhed.
Torrents of water swept by;
the deep roared
and lifted its waves on high.

¹¹Sun and moon stood still in
the heavens
at the glint of your flying
arrows,
at the lightning of your
flashing spear.
¹²In wrath you strode through
the earth
and in anger you threshed
the nations.
¹³You came out to deliver your
people,
to save your anointed
one.
You crushed the leader of the
land of wickedness,
you stripped him from head
to foot.
¹⁴With his own spear you
pierced his head
when his warriors stormed
out to scatter us,
gloating as though about to
devour
the wretched who were in
hiding.
¹⁵You trampled the sea with
your horses,
churning the great waters.

¹⁶I heard and my heart
pounded,
my lips quivered at the
sound;
decay crept into my bones,
and my legs trembled.
Yet I will wait patiently for the
day of calamity
to come on the nation
invading us.

ᵃ 3 The Hebrew has *Selah* (a word of uncertain meaning) here and at the middle
of verse 9 and at the end of verse 13.

17 Though the fig tree does not bud
and there are no grapes on the vines,
though the olive crop fails
and the fields produce no food,
though there are no sheep in the pen
and no cattle in the stalls,
18 yet I will rejoice in the LORD,
I will be joyful in God my Savior.

19 The Sovereign LORD is my strength;
he makes my feet like the feet of a deer,
he enables me to tread on the heights.

For the director of music. On my stringed instruments.

Zephaniah

Introduction:

Zephaniah was a prophet during the reign of King Josiah (640–609 BC). He warned that the day of the Lord would bring judgment on Judah and Jerusalem and he called the people to return to God.

Zephaniah also predicted that God would destroy Judah's neighboring nations as well. With a note of hope, he promised that God would bring his people home.

Outline of contents:

God's judgment announced (1:1–2:3)
Judgment against the nations (2:4–15)
The future of Jerusalem (3:1–20)

1 The word of the LORD that came to Zephaniah son of Cushi, the son of Gedaliah, the son of Amariah, the son of Hezekiah, during the reign of Josiah son of Amon king of Judah:

Judgment on the Whole Earth in the Day of the LORD

2 "I will sweep away everything
    from the face of the earth,"
        declares the LORD.
3 "I will sweep away both man
    and beast;
  I will sweep away the birds
    in the sky
  and the fish in the sea —
  and the idols that cause the
    wicked to stumble."[a]

  "When I destroy all mankind
    on the face of the earth,"
        declares the LORD,

4 "I will stretch out my hand
    against Judah
  and against all who live in
    Jerusalem.
  I will destroy every remnant
    of Baal worship in this
    place,
  the very names of the
    idolatrous priests —
5 those who bow down on the
    roofs
  to worship the starry host,
  those who bow down and
    swear by the LORD
  and who also swear by
    Molek,[b]
6 those who turn back from
    following the LORD
  and neither seek the LORD
    nor inquire of him."

7 Be silent before the Sovereign
    LORD,

---

[a] 3 The meaning of the Hebrew for this line is uncertain.   [b] 5 Hebrew *Malkam*

for the day of the LORD is
near.
The LORD has prepared a
sacrifice;
he has consecrated those he
has invited.

⁸ "On the day of the LORD's
sacrifice
I will punish the
officials
and the king's sons
and all those clad
in foreign clothes.
⁹ On that day I will punish
all who avoid stepping on
the threshold,ᵃ
who fill the temple of their
gods
with violence and deceit.

¹⁰ "On that day,"
declares the LORD,
"a cry will go up from the Fish
Gate,
wailing from the New
Quarter,
and a loud crash from the
hills.
¹¹ Wail, you who live in the
market district;ᵇ
all your merchants will be
wiped out,
all who trade withᶜ silver will
be destroyed.
¹² At that time I will search
Jerusalem with lamps
and punish those who are
complacent,
who are like wine left on its
dregs,

who think, 'The LORD will do
nothing,
either good or bad.'
¹³ Their wealth will be
plundered,
their houses demolished.
Though they build houses,
they will not live in them;
though they plant vineyards,
they will not drink the wine."

¹⁴ The great day of the LORD is
near —
near and coming quickly.
The cry on the day of the LORD
is bitter;
the Mighty Warrior shouts
his battle cry.
¹⁵ That day will be a day of
wrath —
a day of distress and
anguish,
a day of trouble and ruin,
a day of darkness and gloom,
a day of clouds and
blackness —
¹⁶ a day of trumpet and battle
cry
against the fortified cities
and against the corner
towers.

¹⁷ "I will bring such distress on
all people
that they will grope about
like those who are blind,
because they have sinned
against the LORD.
Their blood will be poured out
like dust
and their entrails like dung.

ᵃ 9 See 1 Samuel 5:5.   ᵇ 11 Or *the Mortar*   ᶜ 11 Or *in*

[18]Neither their silver nor their
gold
will be able to save them
on the day of the LORD's
wrath."

In the fire of his jealousy
the whole earth will be
consumed,
for he will make a sudden end
of all who live on the earth.

Judah and Jerusalem Judged Along With the Nations

Judah Summoned to Repent

2 Gather together, gather
yourselves together,
you shameful nation,
[2]before the decree takes effect
and that day passes like
windblown chaff,
before the LORD's fierce anger
comes upon you,
before the day of the LORD's
wrath
comes upon you.
[3]Seek the LORD, all you humble
of the land,
you who do what he
commands.
Seek righteousness, seek
humility;
perhaps you will be
sheltered
on the day of the LORD's
anger.

Philistia

[4]Gaza will be abandoned
and Ashkelon left in ruins.

At midday Ashdod will be
emptied
and Ekron uprooted.
[5]Woe to you who live by the sea,
you Kerethite people;
the word of the LORD is against
you,
Canaan, land of the
Philistines.
He says, "I will destroy you,
and none will be left."
[6]The land by the sea will
become pastures
having wells for shepherds
and pens for flocks.
[7]That land will belong
to the remnant of the people
of Judah;
there they will find pasture.
In the evening they will lie
down
in the houses of Ashkelon.
The LORD their God will care
for them;
he will restore their
fortunes.[a]

Moab and Ammon

[8]"I have heard the insults of
Moab
and the taunts of the
Ammonites,
who insulted my people
and made threats against
their land.
[9]Therefore, as surely as I live,"
declares the LORD Almighty,
the God of Israel,
"surely Moab will become like
Sodom,

[a] 7 Or *will bring back their captives*

the Ammonites like
Gomorrah —
a place of weeds and salt
pits,
a wasteland forever.
The remnant of my people will
plunder them;
the survivors of my nation
will inherit their land."

¹⁰ This is what they will get in
return for their pride,
for insulting and mocking
the people of the LORD
Almighty.
¹¹ The LORD will be awesome to
them
when he destroys all the
gods of the earth.
Distant nations will bow down
to him,
all of them in their own
lands.

Cush

¹² "You Cushites,ᵃ too,
will be slain by my sword."

Assyria

¹³ He will stretch out his hand
against the north
and destroy Assyria,
leaving Nineveh utterly
desolate
and dry as the desert.
¹⁴ Flocks and herds will lie down
there,
creatures of every kind.
The desert owl and the screech
owl
will roost on her columns.

Their hooting will echo
through the windows,
rubble will fill the doorways,
the beams of cedar will be
exposed.
¹⁵ This is the city of revelry
that lived in safety.
She said to herself,
"I am the one! And there is
none besides me."
What a ruin she has become,
a lair for wild beasts!
All who pass by her scoff
and shake their fists.

Jerusalem

3 Woe to the city of
oppressors,
rebellious and defiled!
² She obeys no one,
she accepts no correction.
She does not trust in the LORD,
she does not draw near to
her God.
³ Her officials within her
are roaring lions;
her rulers are evening
wolves,
who leave nothing for the
morning.
⁴ Her prophets are unprincipled;
they are treacherous people.
Her priests profane the
sanctuary
and do violence to the law.
⁵ The LORD within her is
righteous;
he does no wrong.
Morning by morning he
dispenses his justice,

ᵃ 12 That is, people from the upper Nile region

and every new day he does
not fail,
yet the unrighteous know no
shame.

Jerusalem Remains Unrepentant

⁶ "I have destroyed nations;
their strongholds are
demolished.
I have left their streets
deserted,
with no one passing
through.
Their cities are laid waste;
they are deserted and empty.
⁷ Of Jerusalem I thought,
'Surely you will fear me
and accept correction!'
Then her place of refuge*a*
would not be destroyed,
nor all my punishments
come upon*b* her.
But they were still eager
to act corruptly in all they
did.
⁸ Therefore wait for me,"
declares the LORD,
"for the day I will stand up to
testify.*c*
I have decided to assemble the
nations,
to gather the kingdoms
and to pour out my wrath on
them —
all my fierce anger.
The whole world will be
consumed
by the fire of my jealous
anger.

Restoration of Israel's Remnant

⁹ "Then I will purify the lips of
the peoples,
that all of them may call on
the name of the LORD
and serve him shoulder to
shoulder.
¹⁰ From beyond the rivers of
Cush*d*
my worshipers, my scattered
people,
will bring me offerings.
¹¹ On that day you, Jerusalem,
will not be put to
shame
for all the wrongs you have
done to me,
because I will remove from
you
your arrogant boasters.
Never again will you be
haughty
on my holy hill.
¹² But I will leave within you
the meek and humble.
The remnant of Israel
will trust in the name of the
LORD.
¹³ They will do no wrong;
they will tell no lies.
A deceitful tongue
will not be found in their
mouths.
They will eat and lie down
and no one will make them
afraid."

¹⁴ Sing, Daughter Zion;
shout aloud, Israel!

---

a 7 Or *her sanctuary*   *b* 7 Or *all those I appointed over*   *c* 8 Septuagint and
Syriac; Hebrew *will rise up to plunder*   *d* 10 That is, the upper Nile region

Be glad and rejoice with all
your heart,
Daughter Jerusalem!
15 The LORD has taken away your
punishment,
he has turned back your
enemy.
The LORD, the King of Israel, is
with you;
never again will you fear any
harm.
16 On that day
they will say to Jerusalem,
"Do not fear, Zion;
do not let your hands hang
limp.
17 The LORD your God is with
you,
the Mighty Warrior who
saves.
He will take great delight in
you;
in his love he will no longer
rebuke you,
but will rejoice over you with
singing."

18 "I will remove from you
all who mourn over the
loss of your appointed
festivals,
which is a burden and
reproach for you.
19 At that time I will deal
with all who oppressed
you.
I will rescue the lame;
I will gather the exiles.
I will give them praise and
honor
in every land where they
have suffered shame.
20 At that time I will gather
you;
at that time I will bring you
home.
I will give you honor and
praise
among all the peoples of the
earth
when I restore your fortunes^a
before your very eyes,"
says the LORD.

---

^a 20 Or *I bring back your captives*

Haggai

Introduction:

Eighteen years had passed since Cyrus's decree in 538 BC had allowed the exiled Jews to return to Jerusalem. Because they were busy building their own homes, the people still had not finished building God's temple.

Haggai's message was that the time had come to build the house of the Lord. Under the leadership of Zerubbabel and Joshua and with Haggai's prodding, the temple was rebuilt during the years 520–515 BC.

Haggai told the people that the glory of the temple they were building would be greater than that of the former temple, even though the building itself would be less to look at. This temple would be greater because God would fill this house with his glory.

Outline of contents:

The call to rebuild the temple (1:1–15)
Hopes for the new temple (2:1–9)
Promised blessings (2:10–19)
God's final triumph (2:20–23)

A Call to Build the House of the Lord

1 In the second year of King Darius, on the first day of the sixth month, the word of the LORD came through the prophet Haggai to Zerubbabel son of Shealtiel, governor of Judah, and to Joshua son of Jozadak,[a] the high priest:

² This is what the LORD Almighty says: "These people say, 'The time has not yet come to rebuild the LORD's house.' "

³ Then the word of the LORD came through the prophet Haggai: ⁴ "Is it a time for you yourselves to be living in your paneled houses, while this house remains a ruin?"

⁵ Now this is what the LORD Almighty says: "Give careful thought to your ways. ⁶ You have planted much, but harvested little. You eat, but never have enough. You drink, but never have your fill. You put on clothes, but are not warm. You earn wages, only to put them in a purse with holes in it."

---

[a] 1 Hebrew *Jehozadak*, a variant of *Jozadak*; also in verses 12 and 14

⁷This is what the LORD Almighty says: "Give careful thought to your ways. ⁸Go up into the mountains and bring down timber and build my house, so that I may take pleasure in it and be honored," says the LORD. ⁹"You expected much, but see, it turned out to be little. What you brought home, I blew away. Why?" declares the LORD Almighty. "Because of my house, which remains a ruin, while each of you is busy with your own house. ¹⁰Therefore, because of you the heavens have withheld their dew and the earth its crops. ¹¹I called for a drought on the fields and the mountains, on the grain, the new wine, the olive oil and everything else the ground produces, on people and livestock, and on all the labor of your hands."

¹²Then Zerubbabel son of Shealtiel, Joshua son of Jozadak, the high priest, and the whole remnant of the people obeyed the voice of the LORD their God and the message of the prophet Haggai, because the LORD their God had sent him. And the people feared the LORD.

¹³Then Haggai, the LORD's messenger, gave this message of the LORD to the people: "I am with you," declares the LORD. ¹⁴So the LORD stirred up the spirit of Zerubbabel son of Shealtiel, governor of Judah, and the spirit of Joshua son of Jozadak, the high priest, and the spirit of the whole remnant of the people. They came and began to work on the house of the LORD Almighty, their God, ¹⁵on the twenty-fourth day of the sixth month.

The Promised Glory of the New House

In the second year of King Darius, ¹on the twenty-first day of the seventh month, the word of the LORD came through the prophet Haggai: ²"Speak to Zerubbabel son of Shealtiel, governor of Judah, to Joshua son of Jozadak,ᵃ the high priest, and to the remnant of the people. Ask them, ³'Who of you is left who saw this house in its former glory? How does it look to you now? Does it not seem to you like nothing? ⁴But now be strong, Zerubbabel,' declares the LORD. 'Be strong, Joshua son of Jozadak, the high priest. Be strong, all you people of the land,' declares the LORD, 'and work. For I am with you,' declares the LORD Almighty. ⁵'This is what I covenanted with you when you came out of Egypt. And my Spirit remains among you. Do not fear.'

⁶"This is what the LORD Almighty says: 'In a little while I will once more shake the heavens and the earth, the sea and the dry land. ⁷I will shake all nations, and what is desired by all nations will come, and I will fill this house with glory,' says the LORD

ᵃ 2 Hebrew *Jehozadak*, a variant of *Jozadak*; also in verse 4

Almighty. **⁸**'The silver is mine and the gold is mine,' declares the LORD Almighty. **⁹**'The glory of this present house will be greater than the glory of the former house,' says the LORD Almighty. 'And in this place I will grant peace,' declares the LORD Almighty."

Blessings for a Defiled People

¹⁰On the twenty-fourth day of the ninth month, in the second year of Darius, the word of the LORD came to the prophet Haggai: **¹¹**"This is what the LORD Almighty says: 'Ask the priests what the law says: **¹²**If someone carries consecrated meat in the fold of their garment, and that fold touches some bread or stew, some wine, olive oil or other food, does it become consecrated?'"

The priests answered, "No."

¹³Then Haggai said, "If a person defiled by contact with a dead body touches one of these things, does it become defiled?"

"Yes," the priests replied, "it becomes defiled."

¹⁴Then Haggai said, "'So it is with this people and this nation in my sight,' declares the LORD. 'Whatever they do and whatever they offer there is defiled.

¹⁵"'Now give careful thought to this from this day on*ᵃ* — consider how things were before one stone was laid on another in the LORD's temple. **¹⁶**When anyone came to a heap of twenty measures, there were only ten. When anyone went to a wine vat to draw fifty measures, there were only twenty. **¹⁷**I struck all the work of your hands with blight, mildew and hail, yet you did not return to me,' declares the LORD. **¹⁸**'From this day on, from this twenty-fourth day of the ninth month, give careful thought to the day when the foundation of the LORD's temple was laid. Give careful thought: **¹⁹**Is there yet any seed left in the barn? Until now, the vine and the fig tree, the pomegranate and the olive tree have not borne fruit.

"'From this day on I will bless you.'"

Zerubbabel the LORD's Signet Ring

²⁰The word of the LORD came to Haggai a second time on the twenty-fourth day of the month: **²¹**"Tell Zerubbabel governor of Judah that I am going to shake the heavens and the earth. **²²**I will overturn royal thrones and shatter the power of the foreign kingdoms. I will overthrow chariots and their drivers; horses and their riders will fall, each by the sword of his brother.

²³"'On that day,' declares the LORD Almighty, 'I will take you, my servant Zerubbabel son of Shealtiel,' declares the LORD, 'and I will make you like my signet ring, for I have chosen you,' declares the LORD Almighty."

ᵃ 15 Or *to the days past*

Zechariah

Introduction:

Zechariah's prophecies began two months after Haggai's first message (520 BC). In his opening message Zechariah told the people who had just begun rebuilding the temple that they needed to listen to God's message through the prophets. They also needed to keep a close relationship with God so that there would be no further judgment.

This opening message is followed by visions that encouraged the builders when they were ready to give up. Zechariah comforted them by telling them God had a long-range plan for Israel.

In chapters 7 and 8 Zechariah called the people to obey God by acting fairly and mercifully to one another. God wanted obedience in his relationship with them.

Chapters 9 through 14 tell of the coming Messiah, the last judgment and the long-range growth of the final kingdom.

Outline of contents:

The call to obedience (1:1–6)
Visions (1:7–6:15)
Obedience versus legalism (7:1–8:23)
Judgment on Israel's enemies (9:1–8)
The coming of Zion's king (9:9–14:21)

A Call to Return to the LORD

1 In the eighth month of the second year of Darius, the word of the LORD came to the prophet Zechariah son of Berekiah, the son of Iddo:

2 "The LORD was very angry with your ancestors. 3 Therefore tell the people: This is what the LORD Almighty says: 'Return to me,' declares the LORD Almighty, 'and I will return to you,' says the LORD Almighty. 4 Do not be like your ancestors, to whom the earlier prophets proclaimed: This is what the LORD Almighty says: 'Turn from your evil ways and your evil practices.' But they would not listen or pay attention to me, declares the LORD. 5 Where are your ancestors now? And the prophets, do they live forever? 6 But did not my words and my decrees, which I commanded my servants the prophets, overtake your ancestors?

"Then they repented and said, 'The LORD Almighty has done to us what our ways and practices deserve, just as he determined to do.'"

The Man Among the Myrtle Trees

7 On the twenty-fourth day of the eleventh month, the month of Shebat, in the second year of Darius, the word of the LORD came to the prophet Zechariah son of Berekiah, the son of Iddo.

8 During the night I had a vision, and there before me was a man mounted on a red horse. He was standing among the myrtle trees in a ravine. Behind him were red, brown and white horses.

9 I asked, "What are these, my lord?"

The angel who was talking with me answered, "I will show you what they are."

10 Then the man standing among the myrtle trees explained, "They are the ones the LORD has sent to go throughout the earth."

11 And they reported to the angel of the LORD who was standing among the myrtle trees, "We have gone throughout the earth and found the whole world at rest and in peace."

12 Then the angel of the LORD said, "LORD Almighty, how long will you withhold mercy from Jerusalem and from the towns of Judah, which you have been an-gry with these seventy years?"

13 So the LORD spoke kind and comforting words to the angel who talked with me.

14 Then the angel who was speaking to me said, "Proclaim this word: This is what the LORD Almighty says: 'I am very jealous for Jerusalem and Zion, 15 and I am very angry with the nations that feel secure. I was only a little angry, but they went too far with the punishment.'

16 "Therefore this is what the LORD says: 'I will return to Jerusalem with mercy, and there my house will be rebuilt. And the measuring line will be stretched out over Jerusalem,' declares the LORD Almighty.

17 "Proclaim further: This is what the LORD Almighty says: 'My towns will again overflow with prosperity, and the LORD will again comfort Zion and choose Jerusalem.'"

Four Horns and Four Craftsmen

18 Then I looked up, and there before me were four horns. 19 I asked the angel who was speaking to me, "What are these?"

He answered me, "These are the horns that scattered Judah, Israel and Jerusalem."

20 Then the LORD showed me four craftsmen. 21 I asked, "What are these coming to do?"

He answered, "These are the horns that scattered Judah so that no one could raise their head, but the craftsmen have come to terrify them and throw down these horns of the nations who lifted up their horns against the land of Judah to scatter its people."[a]

A Man With a Measuring Line

2 [b] Then I looked up, and there before me was a man with a measuring line in his hand. [2] I asked, "Where are you going?"

He answered me, "To measure Jerusalem, to find out how wide and how long it is."

[3] While the angel who was speaking to me was leaving, another angel came to meet him [4] and said to him: "Run, tell that young man, 'Jerusalem will be a city without walls because of the great number of people and animals in it. [5] And I myself will be a wall of fire around it,' declares the LORD, 'and I will be its glory within.'

[6] "Come! Come! Flee from the land of the north," declares the LORD, "for I have scattered you to the four winds of heaven," declares the LORD.

[7] "Come, Zion! Escape, you who live in Daughter Babylon!" [8] For this is what the LORD Almighty says: "After the Glorious One has sent me against the nations that have plundered you—for whoever touches you touches the apple of his eye— [9] I will surely raise my hand against them so that their slaves will plunder them.[c] Then you will know that the LORD Almighty has sent me.

[10] "Shout and be glad, Daughter Zion. For I am coming, and I will live among you," declares the LORD. [11] "Many nations will be joined with the LORD in that day and will become my people. I will live among you and you will know that the LORD Almighty has sent me to you. [12] The LORD will inherit Judah as his portion in the holy land and will again choose Jerusalem. [13] Be still before the LORD, all mankind, because he has roused himself from his holy dwelling."

Clean Garments for the High Priest

3 Then he showed me Joshua the high priest standing before the angel of the LORD, and Satan[d] standing at his right side to accuse him. [2] The LORD said to Satan, "The LORD rebuke you, Satan! The LORD, who has chosen Jerusalem, rebuke you! Is not this man a burning stick snatched from the fire?"

[3] Now Joshua was dressed in filthy clothes as he stood before the angel. [4] The angel said to those who were standing before him, "Take off his filthy clothes."

Then he said to Joshua, "See, I

---

[a] 21 In Hebrew texts 1:18-21 is numbered 2:1-4.   [b] In Hebrew texts 2:1-13 is numbered 2:5-17.   [c] 8,9 Or says after . . . eye: [9]"I . . . plunder them."
[d] 1 Hebrew satan means adversary.

have taken away your sin, and I will put fine garments on you."

⁵Then I said, "Put a clean turban on his head." So they put a clean turban on his head and clothed him, while the angel of the LORD stood by.

⁶The angel of the LORD gave this charge to Joshua: ⁷"This is what the LORD Almighty says: 'If you will walk in obedience to me and keep my requirements, then you will govern my house and have charge of my courts, and I will give you a place among these standing here.

⁸"'Listen, High Priest Joshua, you and your associates seated before you, who are men symbolic of things to come: I am going to bring my servant, the Branch. ⁹See, the stone I have set in front of Joshua! There are seven eyes*a* on that one stone, and I will engrave an inscription on it,' says the LORD Almighty, 'and I will remove the sin of this land in a single day.

¹⁰"'In that day each of you will invite your neighbor to sit under your vine and fig tree,' declares the LORD Almighty."

The Gold Lampstand and the Two Olive Trees

4 Then the angel who talked with me returned and woke me up, like someone awakened from sleep. ²He asked me, "What do you see?"

I answered, "I see a solid gold lampstand with a bowl at the top and seven lamps on it, with seven channels to the lamps. ³Also there are two olive trees by it, one on the right of the bowl and the other on its left."

⁴I asked the angel who talked with me, "What are these, my lord?"

⁵He answered, "Do you not know what these are?"

"No, my lord," I replied.

⁶So he said to me, "This is the word of the LORD to Zerubbabel: 'Not by might nor by power, but by my Spirit,' says the LORD Almighty.

⁷"What are you, mighty mountain? Before Zerubbabel you will become level ground. Then he will bring out the capstone to shouts of 'God bless it! God bless it!'"

⁸Then the word of the LORD came to me: ⁹"The hands of Zerubbabel have laid the foundation of this temple; his hands will also complete it. Then you will know that the LORD Almighty has sent me to you.

¹⁰"Who dares despise the day of small things, since the seven eyes of the LORD that range throughout the earth will rejoice when they see the chosen capstone*b* in the hand of Zerubbabel?"

¹¹Then I asked the angel, "What are these two olive trees on the right and the left of the lampstand?"

---

a 9 Or *facets*   *b* 10 Or *the plumb line*

¹²Again I asked him, "What are these two olive branches beside the two gold pipes that pour out golden oil?"

¹³He replied, "Do you not know what these are?"

"No, my lord," I said.

¹⁴So he said, "These are the two who are anointed to[a] serve the Lord of all the earth."

The Flying Scroll

5 I looked again, and there before me was a flying scroll.

²He asked me, "What do you see?"

I answered, "I see a flying scroll, twenty cubits long and ten cubits wide.[b]"

³And he said to me, "This is the curse that is going out over the whole land; for according to what it says on one side, every thief will be banished, and according to what it says on the other, everyone who swears falsely will be banished. ⁴The LORD Almighty declares, 'I will send it out, and it will enter the house of the thief and the house of anyone who swears falsely by my name. It will remain in that house and destroy it completely, both its timbers and its stones.'"

The Woman in a Basket

⁵Then the angel who was speaking to me came forward and said to me, "Look up and see what is appearing."

⁶I asked, "What is it?"

He replied, "It is a basket." And he added, "This is the iniquity[c] of the people throughout the land."

⁷Then the cover of lead was raised, and there in the basket sat a woman! ⁸He said, "This is wickedness," and he pushed her back into the basket and pushed its lead cover down on it.

⁹Then I looked up — and there before me were two women, with the wind in their wings! They had wings like those of a stork, and they lifted up the basket between heaven and earth.

¹⁰"Where are they taking the basket?" I asked the angel who was speaking to me.

¹¹He replied, "To the country of Babylonia[d] to build a house for it. When the house is ready, the basket will be set there in its place."

Four Chariots

6 I looked up again, and there before me were four chariots coming out from between two mountains — mountains of bronze. ²The first chariot had red horses, the second black, ³the third white, and the fourth dappled — all of them powerful. ⁴I asked the angel who was speaking to me, "What are these, my lord?"

---

[a] 14 Or *two who bring oil and*   [b] 2 That is, about 30 feet long and 15 feet wide or about 9 meters long and 4.5 meters wide   [c] 6 Or *appearance*   [d] 11 Hebrew *Shinar*

⁵The angel answered me, "These are the four spirits*a* of heaven, going out from standing in the presence of the Lord of the whole world. ⁶The one with the black horses is going toward the north country, the one with the white horses toward the west,*b* and the one with the dappled horses toward the south."

⁷When the powerful horses went out, they were straining to go throughout the earth. And he said, "Go throughout the earth!" So they went throughout the earth.

⁸Then he called to me, "Look, those going toward the north country have given my Spirit*c* rest in the land of the north."

A Crown for Joshua

⁹The word of the LORD came to me: ¹⁰"Take silver and gold from the exiles Heldai, Tobijah and Jedaiah, who have arrived from Babylon. Go the same day to the house of Josiah son of Zephaniah. ¹¹Take the silver and gold and make a crown, and set it on the head of the high priest, Joshua son of Jozadak.*d* ¹²Tell him this is what the LORD Almighty says: 'Here is the man whose name is the Branch, and he will branch out from his place and build the temple of the LORD. ¹³It is he who will build the temple of the LORD, and he will be clothed with maj-

esty and will sit and rule on his throne. And he*e* will be a priest on his throne. And there will be harmony between the two.' ¹⁴The crown will be given to Heldai,*f* Tobijah, Jedaiah and Hen*g* son of Zephaniah as a memorial in the temple of the LORD. ¹⁵Those who are far away will come and help to build the temple of the LORD, and you will know that the LORD Almighty has sent me to you. This will happen if you diligently obey the LORD your God."

Justice and Mercy, Not Fasting

7 In the fourth year of King Darius, the word of the LORD came to Zechariah on the fourth day of the ninth month, the month of Kislev. ²The people of Bethel had sent Sharezer and Regem-Melek, together with their men, to entreat the LORD ³by asking the priests of the house of the LORD Almighty and the prophets, "Should I mourn and fast in the fifth month, as I have done for so many years?"

⁴Then the word of the LORD Almighty came to me: ⁵"Ask all the people of the land and the priests, 'When you fasted and mourned in the fifth and seventh months for the past seventy years, was it really for me that you fasted? ⁶And when you were eating and drinking, were you not just feast-

---

a 5 Or *winds*   *b 6* Or *horses after them*   *c 8* Or *spirit*   *d 11* Hebrew *Jehozadak,* a variant of *Jozadak*   *e 13* Or *there*   *f 14* Syriac; Hebrew *Helem*
g 14 Or *and the gracious one, the*

ing for yourselves? ⁷Are these not the words the LORD proclaimed through the earlier prophets when Jerusalem and its surrounding towns were at rest and prosperous, and the Negev and the western foothills were settled?'"

⁸And the word of the LORD came again to Zechariah: ⁹"This is what the LORD Almighty said: 'Administer true justice; show mercy and compassion to one another. ¹⁰Do not oppress the widow or the fatherless, the foreigner or the poor. Do not plot evil against each other.'

¹¹"But they refused to pay attention; stubbornly they turned their backs and covered their ears. ¹²They made their hearts as hard as flint and would not listen to the law or to the words that the LORD Almighty had sent by his Spirit through the earlier prophets. So the LORD Almighty was very angry.

¹³"'When I called, they did not listen; so when they called, I would not listen,' says the LORD Almighty. ¹⁴'I scattered them with a whirlwind among all the nations, where they were strangers. The land they left behind them was so desolate that no one traveled through it. This is how they made the pleasant land desolate.'"

The LORD Promises to Bless Jerusalem

8 The word of the LORD Almighty came to me. ²This is what the LORD Almighty says: "I am very jealous for Zion; I am burning with jealousy for her."

³This is what the LORD says: "I will return to Zion and dwell in Jerusalem. Then Jerusalem will be called the Faithful City, and the mountain of the LORD Almighty will be called the Holy Mountain."

⁴This is what the LORD Almighty says: "Once again men and women of ripe old age will sit in the streets of Jerusalem, each of them with cane in hand because of their age. ⁵The city streets will be filled with boys and girls playing there."

⁶This is what the LORD Almighty says: "It may seem marvelous to the remnant of this people at that time, but will it seem marvelous to me?" declares the LORD Almighty.

⁷This is what the LORD Almighty says: "I will save my people from the countries of the east and the west. ⁸I will bring them back to live in Jerusalem; they will be my people, and I will be faithful and righteous to them as their God."

⁹This is what the LORD Almighty says: "Now hear these words, 'Let your hands be strong so that the temple may be built.' This is also what the prophets said who were present when the foundation was laid for the house of the LORD Almighty. ¹⁰Before

that time there were no wages for people or hire for animals. No one could go about their business safely because of their enemies, since I had turned everyone against their neighbor. **11** But now I will not deal with the remnant of this people as I did in the past," declares the LORD Almighty.

12 "The seed will grow well, the vine will yield its fruit, the ground will produce its crops, and the heavens will drop their dew. I will give all these things as an inheritance to the remnant of this people. **13** Just as you, Judah and Israel, have been a curse^a among the nations, so I will save you, and you will be a blessing.^b Do not be afraid, but let your hands be strong."

14 This is what the LORD Almighty says: "Just as I had determined to bring disaster on you and showed no pity when your ancestors angered me," says the LORD Almighty, **15** "so now I have determined to do good again to Jerusalem and Judah. Do not be afraid. **16** These are the things you are to do: Speak the truth to each other, and render true and sound judgment in your courts; **17** do not plot evil against each other, and do not love to swear falsely. I hate all this," declares the LORD.

18 The word of the LORD Almighty came to me.

19 This is what the LORD Almighty says: "The fasts of the fourth, fifth, seventh and tenth months will become joyful and glad occasions and happy festivals for Judah. Therefore love truth and peace."

20 This is what the LORD Almighty says: "Many peoples and the inhabitants of many cities will yet come, **21** and the inhabitants of one city will go to another and say, 'Let us go at once to entreat the LORD and seek the LORD Almighty. I myself am going.' **22** And many peoples and powerful nations will come to Jerusalem to seek the LORD Almighty and to entreat him."

23 This is what the LORD Almighty says: "In those days ten people from all languages and nations will take firm hold of one Jew by the hem of his robe and say, 'Let us go with you, because we have heard that God is with you.' "

Judgment on Israel's Enemies

9 A prophecy:

The word of the LORD is
        against the land of
        Hadrak
and will come to rest on
        Damascus —
for the eyes of all people and
        all the tribes of Israel
        are on the LORD — ^c

---

^a **13** That is, your name has been used in cursing (see Jer. 29:22); or, you have been regarded as under a curse.   ^b **13** Or *and your name will be used in blessings* (see Gen. 48:20); or *and you will be seen as blessed*   ^c **1** Or *Damascus. / For the eye of the LORD is on all people, / as well as on the tribes of Israel,*

2 and on Hamath too, which
    borders on it,
and on Tyre and Sidon,
    though they are very
    skillful.
3 Tyre has built herself a
    stronghold;
she has heaped up silver like
    dust,
and gold like the dirt of the
    streets.
4 But the Lord will take away her
    possessions
and destroy her power on
    the sea,
and she will be consumed by
    fire.
5 Ashkelon will see it and
    fear;
Gaza will writhe in
    agony,
and Ekron too, for her hope
    will wither.
Gaza will lose her king
    and Ashkelon will be
    deserted.
6 A mongrel people will occupy
    Ashdod,
and I will put an end to the
    pride of the Philistines.
7 I will take the blood from their
    mouths,
the forbidden food from
    between their teeth.
Those who are left will belong
    to our God
and become a clan in
    Judah,
and Ekron will be like the
    Jebusites.

8 But I will encamp at my temple
    to guard it against
    marauding forces.
Never again will an oppressor
    overrun my people,
for now I am keeping
    watch.

The Coming of Zion's King

9 Rejoice greatly, Daughter
    Zion!
Shout, Daughter Jerusalem!
See, your king comes to
    you,
righteous and victorious,
lowly and riding on a donkey,
    on a colt, the foal of a
    donkey.
10 I will take away the chariots
    from Ephraim
and the warhorses from
    Jerusalem,
and the battle bow will be
    broken.
He will proclaim peace to the
    nations.
His rule will extend from sea
    to sea
and from the River*a* to the
    ends of the earth.
11 As for you, because of the
    blood of my covenant
    with you,
I will free your prisoners
    from the waterless pit.
12 Return to your fortress, you
    prisoners of hope;
even now I announce that
    I will restore twice as
    much to you.

a 10 That is, the Euphrates

¹³ I will bend Judah as I bend my
bow
and fill it with Ephraim.
I will rouse your sons,
Zion,
against your sons, Greece,
and make you like a
warrior's sword.

The LORD Will Appear

¹⁴ Then the LORD will appear
over them;
his arrow will flash like
lightning.
The Sovereign LORD will
sound the trumpet;
he will march in the storms
of the south,
¹⁵ and the LORD Almighty will
shield them.
They will destroy
and overcome with
slingstones.
They will drink and roar as
with wine;
they will be full like a bowl
used for sprinkling^a the
corners of the altar.
¹⁶ The LORD their God will save
his people on that day
as a shepherd saves his
flock.
They will sparkle in his land
like jewels in a crown.
¹⁷ How attractive and beautiful
they will be!
Grain will make the young
men thrive,
and new wine the young
women.

The LORD Will Care for Judah

10 Ask the LORD for rain in
the springtime;
it is the LORD who sends the
thunderstorms.
He gives showers of rain to all
people,
and plants of the field to
everyone.
² The idols speak deceitfully,
diviners see visions that lie;
they tell dreams that are false,
they give comfort in vain.
Therefore the people wander
like sheep
oppressed for lack of a
shepherd.

³ "My anger burns against the
shepherds,
and I will punish the leaders;
for the LORD Almighty will
care
for his flock, the people of
Judah,
and make them like a proud
horse in battle.
⁴ From Judah will come the
cornerstone,
from him the tent peg,
from him the battle bow,
from him every ruler.
⁵ Together they^b will be like
warriors in battle
trampling their enemy into
the mud of the streets.
They will fight because the
LORD is with them,
and they will put the enemy
horsemen to shame.

^a 15 Or bowl, / like   ^b 4,5 Or ruler, all of them together. / ⁵They

6 "I will strengthen Judah
  and save the tribes of Joseph.
I will restore them
  because I have compassion
    on them.
They will be as though
  I had not rejected them,
for I am the LORD their God
  and I will answer them.
7 The Ephraimites will become
    like warriors,
  and their hearts will be glad
    as with wine.
Their children will see it and
    be joyful;
  their hearts will rejoice in
    the LORD.
8 I will signal for them
  and gather them in.
Surely I will redeem them;
  they will be as numerous as
    before.
9 Though I scatter them among
    the peoples,
  yet in distant lands they will
    remember me.
They and their children will
    survive,
  and they will return.
10 I will bring them back from
    Egypt
  and gather them from
    Assyria.
I will bring them to Gilead and
    Lebanon,
  and there will not be room
    enough for them.
11 They will pass through the sea
    of trouble;
  the surging sea will be
    subdued

and all the depths of the Nile
  will dry up.
Assyria's pride will be brought
    down
  and Egypt's scepter will pass
    away.
12 I will strengthen them in the
    LORD
  and in his name they will
    live securely,"
                declares the LORD.

11 Open your doors,
     Lebanon,
  so that fire may devour your
    cedars!
2 Wail, you juniper, for the cedar
    has fallen;
  the stately trees are ruined!
Wail, oaks of Bashan;
  the dense forest has been cut
    down!
3 Listen to the wail of the
    shepherds;
  their rich pastures are
    destroyed!
Listen to the roar of the lions;
  the lush thicket of the Jordan
    is ruined!

Two Shepherds

4 This is what the LORD my
God says: "Shepherd the flock
marked for slaughter. 5 Their
buyers slaughter them and go
unpunished. Those who sell
them say, 'Praise the LORD, I am
rich!' Their own shepherds do not
spare them. 6 For I will no longer
have pity on the people of the
land," declares the LORD. "I will
give everyone into the hands of

their neighbors and their king. They will devastate the land, and I will not rescue anyone from their hands."

⁷So I shepherded the flock marked for slaughter, particularly the oppressed of the flock. Then I took two staffs and called one Favor and the other Union, and I shepherded the flock. ⁸In one month I got rid of the three shepherds.

The flock detested me, and I grew weary of them ⁹and said, "I will not be your shepherd. Let the dying die, and the perishing perish. Let those who are left eat one another's flesh."

¹⁰Then I took my staff called Favor and broke it, revoking the covenant I had made with all the nations. ¹¹It was revoked on that day, and so the oppressed of the flock who were watching me knew it was the word of the LORD.

¹²I told them, "If you think it best, give me my pay; but if not, keep it." So they paid me thirty pieces of silver.

¹³And the LORD said to me, "Throw it to the potter"—the handsome price at which they valued me! So I took the thirty pieces of silver and threw them to the potter at the house of the LORD.

¹⁴Then I broke my second staff called Union, breaking the family bond between Judah and Israel.

¹⁵Then the LORD said to me, "Take again the equipment of a foolish shepherd. ¹⁶For I am going to raise up a shepherd over the land who will not care for the lost, or seek the young, or heal the injured, or feed the healthy, but will eat the meat of the choice sheep, tearing off their hooves.

¹⁷ "Woe to the worthless shepherd,
  who deserts the flock!
May the sword strike his arm
  and his right eye!
May his arm be completely withered,
  his right eye totally blinded!"

Jerusalem's Enemies to Be Destroyed

12 A prophecy: The word of the LORD concerning Israel.

The LORD, who stretches out the heavens, who lays the foundation of the earth, and who forms the human spirit within a person, declares: ² "I am going to make Jerusalem a cup that sends all the surrounding peoples reeling. Judah will be besieged as well as Jerusalem. ³On that day, when all the nations of the earth are gathered against her, I will make Jerusalem an immovable rock for all the nations. All who try to move it will injure themselves. ⁴On that day I will strike every horse with panic and its rider with madness," declares the LORD. "I will keep a watchful eye over Judah, but I will blind all the horses of the nations. **5**Then the clans of Judah will say in their hearts, 'The people of Jerusalem are strong, because the Lord Almighty is their God.'

6"On that day I will make the clans of Judah like a firepot in a woodpile, like a flaming torch among sheaves. They will consume all the surrounding peoples right and left, but Jerusalem will remain intact in her place.

7"The Lord will save the dwellings of Judah first, so that the honor of the house of David and of Jerusalem's inhabitants may not be greater than that of Judah. **8**On that day the Lord will shield those who live in Jerusalem, so that the feeblest among them will be like David, and the house of David will be like God, like the angel of the Lord going before them. **9**On that day I will set out to destroy all the nations that attack Jerusalem.

Mourning for the One They Pierced

10"And I will pour out on the house of David and the inhabitants of Jerusalem a spirit*a* of grace and supplication. They will look on*b* me, the one they have pierced, and they will mourn for him as one mourns for an only child, and grieve bitterly for him as one grieves for a firstborn son. **11**On that day the weeping in Jerusalem will be as great as the weeping of Hadad Rimmon in the plain of Megiddo. **12**The land will mourn, each clan by itself, with their wives by themselves: the clan of the house of David and their wives, the clan of the house of Nathan and their wives, **13**the clan of the house of Levi and their wives, the clan of Shimei and their wives, **14**and all the rest of the clans and their wives.

Cleansing From Sin

13 "On that day a fountain will be opened to the house of David and the inhabitants of Jerusalem, to cleanse them from sin and impurity.

2"On that day, I will banish the names of the idols from the land, and they will be remembered no more," declares the Lord Almighty. "I will remove both the prophets and the spirit of impurity from the land. **3**And if anyone still prophesies, their father and mother, to whom they were born, will say to them, 'You must die, because you have told lies in the Lord's name.' Then their own parents will stab the one who prophesies.

4"On that day every prophet will be ashamed of their prophetic vision. They will not put on a prophet's garment of hair in order to deceive. **5**Each will say, 'I am not a prophet. I am a farmer; the land has been my livelihood since my youth.*c*' **6**If someone

---

a 10 Or *the Spirit*   *b* 10 Or *to*   *c* 5 Or *farmer; a man sold me in my youth* asks, 'What are these wounds on your body*a*?' they will answer, 'The wounds I was given at the house of my friends.'

The Shepherd Struck, the Sheep Scattered

7 "Awake, sword, against my
    shepherd,
  against the man who is close
    to me!"
  declares the LORD Almighty.
"Strike the shepherd,
  and the sheep will be
    scattered,
  and I will turn my hand
    against the little ones.
8 In the whole land," declares
    the LORD,
  "two-thirds will be struck
    down and perish;
  yet one-third will be left in it.
9 This third I will put into the
    fire;
  I will refine them like silver
  and test them like gold.
They will call on my name
  and I will answer them;
I will say, 'They are my people,'
  and they will say, 'The LORD
    is our God.'"

The LORD Comes and Reigns

14 A day of the LORD is coming, Jerusalem, when your possessions will be plundered and divided up within your very walls.

2 I will gather all the nations to Jerusalem to fight against it; the city will be captured, the houses ransacked, and the women raped. Half of the city will go into exile, but the rest of the people will not be taken from the city. 3 Then the LORD will go out and fight against those nations, as he fights on a day of battle. 4 On that day his feet will stand on the Mount of Olives, east of Jerusalem, and the Mount of Olives will be split in two from east to west, forming a great valley, with half of the mountain moving north and half moving south. 5 You will flee by my mountain valley, for it will extend to Azel. You will flee as you fled from the earthquake*b* in the days of Uzziah king of Judah. Then the LORD my God will come, and all the holy ones with him.

6 On that day there will be neither sunlight nor cold, frosty darkness. 7 It will be a unique day — a day known only to the LORD — with no distinction between day and night. When evening comes, there will be light.

8 On that day living water will flow out from Jerusalem, half of it east to the Dead Sea and half of it west to the Mediterranean Sea, in summer and in winter.

9 The LORD will be king over the whole earth. On that day there

---

a 6 Or *wounds between your hands*   *b* 5 Or *⁵My mountain valley will be blocked and will extend to Azel. It will be blocked as it was blocked because of the earthquake* will be one LORD, and his name the only name.

¹⁰The whole land, from Geba to Rimmon, south of Jerusalem, will become like the Arabah. But Jerusalem will be raised up high from the Benjamin Gate to the site of the First Gate, to the Corner Gate, and from the Tower of Hananel to the royal winepresses, and will remain in its place. ¹¹It will be inhabited; never again will it be destroyed. Jerusalem will be secure.

¹²This is the plague with which the LORD will strike all the nations that fought against Jerusalem: Their flesh will rot while they are still standing on their feet, their eyes will rot in their sockets, and their tongues will rot in their mouths. ¹³On that day people will be stricken by the LORD with great panic. They will seize each other by the hand and attack one another. ¹⁴Judah too will fight at Jerusalem. The wealth of all the surrounding nations will be collected—great quantities of gold and silver and clothing. ¹⁵A similar plague will strike the horses and mules, the camels and donkeys, and all the animals in those camps.

¹⁶Then the survivors from all the nations that have attacked Jerusalem will go up year after year to worship the King, the LORD Almighty, and to celebrate the Festival of Tabernacles. ¹⁷If any of the peoples of the earth do not go up to Jerusalem to worship the King, the LORD Almighty, they will have no rain. ¹⁸If the Egyptian people do not go up and take part, they will have no rain. The LORD*a* will bring on them the plague he inflicts on the nations that do not go up to celebrate the Festival of Tabernacles. ¹⁹This will be the punishment of Egypt and the punishment of all the nations that do not go up to celebrate the Festival of Tabernacles.

²⁰On that day HOLY TO THE LORD will be inscribed on the bells of the horses, and the cooking pots in the LORD's house will be like the sacred bowls in front of the altar. ²¹Every pot in Jerusalem and Judah will be holy to the LORD Almighty, and all who come to sacrifice will take some of the pots and cook in them. And on that day there will no longer be a Canaanite*b* in the house of the LORD Almighty.

---

a 18 Or *part, then the LORD*   *b* 21 Or *merchant*

Malachi

Introduction:

This book records the messages of the prophet Malachi, who lived during the second half of the fifth century BC, after the temple had been rebuilt. The Jews had married foreign women, disobeyed God's rules for sacrifices, failed to give God what they should have, and forgotten God's covenant.

Malachi's chief concern was that the Israelites' relationship to God was not as it should be. They had forgotten God and treated him with dishonor. They failed to do what God required of them. Because of this, Malachi told the people God would judge them. But he also said that the God-fearing people did not need to worry because they would enjoy God's salvation forever.

Outline of contents:

God's love for Israel (1:1–5)
Israel insults God (1:6–2:16)
God's judgment and promise (2:17–4:6)

1 A prophecy: The word of the LORD to Israel through Malachi.[a]

Israel Doubts God's Love

² "I have loved you," says the LORD.

"But you ask, 'How have you loved us?'

"Was not Esau Jacob's brother?" declares the LORD. "Yet I have loved Jacob, ³ but Esau I have hated, and I have turned his hill country into a wasteland and left his inheritance to the desert jackals."

⁴ Edom may say, "Though we have been crushed, we will rebuild the ruins."

But this is what the LORD Almighty says: "They may build, but I will demolish. They will be called the Wicked Land, a people always under the wrath of the LORD. ⁵ You will see it with your own eyes and say, 'Great is the LORD — even beyond the borders of Israel!'

Breaking Covenant Through Blemished Sacrifices

⁶ "A son honors his father, and a slave his master. If I am a father, where is the honor due me?

---

[a] 1 *Malachi* means *my messenger.*

If I am a master, where is the respect due me?" says the LORD Almighty.

"It is you priests who show contempt for my name.

"But you ask, 'How have we shown contempt for your name?'
⁷"By offering defiled food on my altar.

"But you ask, 'How have we defiled you?'

"By saying that the LORD's table is contemptible. ⁸When you offer blind animals for sacrifice, is that not wrong? When you sacrifice lame or diseased animals, is that not wrong? Try offering them to your governor! Would he be pleased with you? Would he accept you?" says the LORD Almighty.

⁹"Now plead with God to be gracious to us. With such offerings from your hands, will he accept you?" — says the LORD Almighty.

¹⁰"Oh, that one of you would shut the temple doors, so that you would not light useless fires on my altar! I am not pleased with you," says the LORD Almighty, "and I will accept no offering from your hands. ¹¹My name will be great among the nations, from where the sun rises to where it sets. In every place incense and pure offerings will be brought to me, because my name will be great among the nations," says the LORD Almighty.

¹²"But you profane it by saying, 'The Lord's table is defiled,' and, 'Its food is contemptible.' ¹³And you say, 'What a burden!' and you sniff at it contemptuously," says the LORD Almighty.

"When you bring injured, lame or diseased animals and offer them as sacrifices, should I accept them from your hands?" says the LORD. ¹⁴"Cursed is the cheat who has an acceptable male in his flock and vows to give it, but then sacrifices a blemished animal to the Lord. For I am a great king," says the LORD Almighty, "and my name is to be feared among the nations.

Additional Warning to the Priests

2 "And now, you priests, this warning is for you. ²If you do not listen, and if you do not resolve to honor my name," says the LORD Almighty, "I will send a curse on you, and I will curse your blessings. Yes, I have already cursed them, because you have not resolved to honor me.

³"Because of you I will rebuke your descendants[a]; I will smear on your faces the dung from your festival sacrifices, and you will be carried off with it. ⁴And you will know that I have sent you this warning so that my covenant with Levi may continue," says the LORD Almighty. ⁵"My covenant was with him, a covenant of life

---

a 3 Or *will blight your grain*

and peace, and I gave them to him; this called for reverence and he revered me and stood in awe of my name. [6]True instruction was in his mouth and nothing false was found on his lips. He walked with me in peace and uprightness, and turned many from sin.

[7]"For the lips of a priest ought to preserve knowledge, because he is the messenger of the LORD Almighty and people seek instruction from his mouth. [8]But you have turned from the way and by your teaching have caused many to stumble; you have violated the covenant with Levi," says the LORD Almighty. [9]"So I have caused you to be despised and humiliated before all the people, because you have not followed my ways but have shown partiality in matters of the law."

Breaking Covenant Through Divorce

[10]Do we not all have one Father[a]? Did not one God create us? Why do we profane the covenant of our ancestors by being unfaithful to one another?

[11]Judah has been unfaithful. A detestable thing has been committed in Israel and in Jerusalem: Judah has desecrated the sanctuary the LORD loves by marrying women who worship a foreign god. [12]As for the man who does this, whoever he may be, may the LORD remove him from the tents of Jacob[b]—even though he brings an offering to the LORD Almighty.

[13]Another thing you do: You flood the LORD's altar with tears. You weep and wail because he no longer looks with favor on your offerings or accepts them with pleasure from your hands. [14]You ask, "Why?" It is because the LORD is the witness between you and the wife of your youth. You have been unfaithful to her, though she is your partner, the wife of your marriage covenant.

[15]Has not the one God made you? You belong to him in body and spirit. And what does the one God seek? Godly offspring.[c] So be on your guard, and do not be unfaithful to the wife of your youth.

[16]"The man who hates and divorces his wife," says the LORD, the God of Israel, "does violence to the one he should protect,"[d] says the LORD Almighty.

So be on your guard, and do not be unfaithful.

Breaking Covenant Through Injustice

[17]You have wearied the LORD with your words.

"How have we wearied him?" you ask.

---

[a] 10 Or *father*   [b] 12 Or [12]*May the LORD remove from the tents of Jacob anyone who gives testimony in behalf of the man who does this*   [c] 15 The meaning of the Hebrew for the first part of this verse is uncertain.   [d] 16 Or *"I hate divorce," says the LORD, the God of Israel, "because the man who divorces his wife covers his garment with violence,"*

By saying, "All who do evil are good in the eyes of the LORD, and he is pleased with them" or "Where is the God of justice?"

3 "I will send my messenger, who will prepare the way before me. Then suddenly the Lord you are seeking will come to his temple; the messenger of the covenant, whom you desire, will come," says the LORD Almighty.

² But who can endure the day of his coming? Who can stand when he appears? For he will be like a refiner's fire or a launderer's soap. ³ He will sit as a refiner and purifier of silver; he will purify the Levites and refine them like gold and silver. Then the LORD will have men who will bring offerings in righteousness, ⁴ and the offerings of Judah and Jerusalem will be acceptable to the LORD, as in days gone by, as in former years.

⁵ So I will come to put you on trial. I will be quick to testify against sorcerers, adulterers and perjurers, against those who defraud laborers of their wages, who oppress the widows and the fatherless, and deprive the foreigners among you of justice, but do not fear me," says the LORD Almighty.

Breaking Covenant by Withholding Tithes

⁶ "I the LORD do not change. So you, the descendants of Jacob, are not destroyed. ⁷ Ever since the time of your ancestors you have turned away from my decrees and have not kept them. Return to me, and I will return to you," says the LORD Almighty.

"But you ask, 'How are we to return?'

⁸ "Will a mere mortal rob God? Yet you rob me.

"But you ask, 'How are we robbing you?'

"In tithes and offerings. ⁹ You are under a curse — your whole nation — because you are robbing me. ¹⁰ Bring the whole tithe into the storehouse, that there may be food in my house. Test me in this," says the LORD Almighty, "and see if I will not throw open the floodgates of heaven and pour out so much blessing that there will not be room enough to store it. ¹¹ I will prevent pests from devouring your crops, and the vines in your fields will not drop their fruit before it is ripe," says the LORD Almighty. ¹² "Then all the nations will call you blessed, for yours will be a delightful land," says the LORD Almighty.

Israel Speaks Arrogantly Against God

¹³ "You have spoken arrogantly against me," says the LORD.

"Yet you ask, 'What have we said against you?'

¹⁴ "You have said, 'It is futile to serve God. What do we gain by carrying out his requirements and going about like mourners before the LORD Almighty? ¹⁵ But now we call the arrogant blessed. Certainly evildoers prosper, and

even when they put God to the test, they get away with it.'"

The Faithful Remnant

[16]Then those who feared the LORD talked with each other, and the LORD listened and heard. A scroll of remembrance was written in his presence concerning those who feared the LORD and honored his name.

[17]"On the day when I act," says the LORD Almighty, "they will be my treasured possession. I will spare them, just as a father has compassion and spares his son who serves him. [18]And you will again see the distinction between the righteous and the wicked, between those who serve God and those who do not.

Judgment and Covenant Renewal

4 [a] "Surely the day is coming; it will burn like a furnace. All the arrogant and every evildoer will be stubble, and the day that is coming will set them on fire," says the LORD Almighty. "Not a root or a branch will be left to them. [2]But for you who revere my name, the sun of righteousness will rise with healing in its rays. And you will go out and frolic like well-fed calves. [3]Then you will trample on the wicked; they will be ashes under the soles of your feet on the day when I act," says the LORD Almighty.

[4]"Remember the law of my servant Moses, the decrees and laws I gave him at Horeb for all Israel.

[5]"See, I will send the prophet Elijah to you before that great and dreadful day of the LORD comes. [6]He will turn the hearts of the parents to their children, and the hearts of the children to their parents; or else I will come and strike the land with total destruction."

---

[a] In Hebrew texts 4:1-6 is numbered 3:19-24.

The New Testament

Matthew

Introduction:

The book of Matthew tells of the good news that the long-awaited Messiah had come to save people — both Jews and Gentiles. Matthew, one of the twelve disciples, is believed to be the author of this book. It was probably written sometime before the Romans destroyed the temple in Jerusalem in AD 70.

Matthew uses much of the Gospel to show that Jesus is the promised Messiah of the Old Testament. Matthew frequently quotes the Old Testament and uses the phrase "kingdom of heaven." Because of this many people think he was writing his Gospel to Jewish people.

Matthew also presents Christ as the great teacher who helps us understand God's law and tells the people about the kingdom of God and what it is. Most of Christ's teachings are found in the following five places:

1. The Sermon on the Mount (5:1–7:27)
2. Instruction to the disciples (10:5–42)
3. Teaching through parables (13:3–52)
4. The meaning of discipleship (18:1–35)
5. Teachings about the end of time and the coming of the kingdom of heaven (24:4–25:46)

Outline of contents:

Background and preparation (1:1–4:25)
The Galilean ministry (5:1–18:35)
    The Sermon on the Mount (5:1–7:29)
    The ministry through miracles (8:1–10:42)
    Teaching through parables (11:1–13:52)
    Opposition and withdrawal (13:53–16:12)
    Jesus as the son of God (16:13–18:35)
The final period (19:1–28:20)
    Toward Jerusalem (19:1–20:34)
    The triumphal entry (21:1–17)
    Christ as teacher (21:18–25:46)
    Trial, death and burial (26:1–27:66)
    Resurrection and ascension (28:1–20)

The Genealogy of Jesus the Messiah

1 This is the genealogy[a] of Jesus the Messiah[b] the son of David, the son of Abraham:

2 Abraham was the father of Isaac,
Isaac the father of Jacob,
Jacob the father of Judah and his brothers,
3 Judah the father of Perez and Zerah, whose mother was Tamar,
Perez the father of Hezron,
Hezron the father of Ram,
4 Ram the father of Amminadab,
Amminadab the father of Nahshon,
Nahshon the father of Salmon,
5 Salmon the father of Boaz, whose mother was Rahab,
Boaz the father of Obed, whose mother was Ruth,
Obed the father of Jesse,
6 and Jesse the father of King David.

David was the father of Solomon, whose mother had been Uriah's wife,
7 Solomon the father of Rehoboam,
Rehoboam the father of Abijah,
Abijah the father of Asa,
8 Asa the father of Jehoshaphat,
Jehoshaphat the father of Jehoram,
Jehoram the father of Uzziah,
9 Uzziah the father of Jotham,
Jotham the father of Ahaz,
Ahaz the father of Hezekiah,
10 Hezekiah the father of Manasseh,
Manasseh the father of Amon,
Amon the father of Josiah,
11 and Josiah the father of Jeconiah[c] and his brothers at the time of the exile to Babylon.

12 After the exile to Babylon:
Jeconiah was the father of Shealtiel,
Shealtiel the father of Zerubbabel,
13 Zerubbabel the father of Abihud,
Abihud the father of Eliakim,
Eliakim the father of Azor,
14 Azor the father of Zadok,
Zadok the father of Akim,
Akim the father of Elihud,
15 Elihud the father of Eleazar,
Eleazar the father of Matthan,
Matthan the father of Jacob,

---

a 1 Or *is an account of the origin*   b 1 Or *Jesus Christ. Messiah* (Hebrew) and *Christ* (Greek) both mean *Anointed One*; also in verse 18.   c 11 That is, Jehoiachin; also in verse 12

¹⁶and Jacob the father of Joseph, the husband of Mary, and Mary was the mother of Jesus who is called the Messiah.

¹⁷Thus there were fourteen generations in all from Abraham to David, fourteen from David to the exile to Babylon, and fourteen from the exile to the Messiah.

Joseph Accepts Jesus as His Son

¹⁸This is how the birth of Jesus the Messiah came about[a]: His mother Mary was pledged to be married to Joseph, but before they came together, she was found to be pregnant through the Holy Spirit. ¹⁹Because Joseph her husband was faithful to the law, and yet[b] did not want to expose her to public disgrace, he had in mind to divorce her quietly.

²⁰But after he had considered this, an angel of the Lord appeared to him in a dream and said, "Joseph son of David, do not be afraid to take Mary home as your wife, because what is conceived in her is from the Holy Spirit. ²¹She will give birth to a son, and you are to give him the name Jesus,[c] because he will save his people from their sins."

²²All this took place to fulfill what the Lord had said through the prophet: ²³"The virgin will conceive and give birth to a son, and they will call him Immanuel"[d] (which means "God with us").

²⁴When Joseph woke up, he did what the angel of the Lord had commanded him and took Mary home as his wife. ²⁵But he did not consummate their marriage until she gave birth to a son. And he gave him the name Jesus.

The Magi Visit the Messiah

2 After Jesus was born in Bethlehem in Judea, during the time of King Herod, Magi[e] from the east came to Jerusalem ²and asked, "Where is the one who has been born king of the Jews? We saw his star when it rose and have come to worship him."

³When King Herod heard this he was disturbed, and all Jerusalem with him. ⁴When he had called together all the people's chief priests and teachers of the law, he asked them where the Messiah was to be born. ⁵"In Bethlehem in Judea," they replied, "for this is what the prophet has written:

⁶" 'But you, Bethlehem, in the
        land of Judah,
    are by no means least among
        the rulers of Judah;
    for out of you will come a ruler
        who will shepherd my
        people Israel.'[f]"

---

[a] 18 Or *The origin of Jesus the Messiah was like this*   [b] 19 Or *was a righteous man and*   [c] 21 *Jesus* is the Greek form of *Joshua*, which means *the LORD saves*.   [d] 23 Isaiah 7:14   [e] 1 Traditionally *wise men*   [f] 6 Micah 5:2,4

⁷Then Herod called the Magi secretly and found out from them the exact time the star had appeared. ⁸He sent them to Bethlehem and said, "Go and search carefully for the child. As soon as you find him, report to me, so that I too may go and worship him."

⁹After they had heard the king, they went on their way, and the star they had seen when it rose went ahead of them until it stopped over the place where the child was. ¹⁰When they saw the star, they were overjoyed. ¹¹On coming to the house, they saw the child with his mother Mary, and they bowed down and worshiped him. Then they opened their treasures and presented him with gifts of gold, frankincense and myrrh. ¹²And having been warned in a dream not to go back to Herod, they returned to their country by another route.

The Escape to Egypt

¹³When they had gone, an angel of the Lord appeared to Joseph in a dream. "Get up," he said, "take the child and his mother and escape to Egypt. Stay there until I tell you, for Herod is going to search for the child to kill him."

¹⁴So he got up, took the child and his mother during the night and left for Egypt, ¹⁵where he stayed until the death of Herod. And so was fulfilled what the Lord had said through the prophet: "Out of Egypt I called my son."ᵃ

¹⁶When Herod realized that he had been outwitted by the Magi, he was furious, and he gave orders to kill all the boys in Bethlehem and its vicinity who were two years old and under, in accordance with the time he had learned from the Magi. ¹⁷Then what was said through the prophet Jeremiah was fulfilled:

¹⁸"A voice is heard in Ramah,
  weeping and great
    mourning,
  Rachel weeping for her
    children
  and refusing to be
    comforted,
  because they are no more."ᵇ

The Return to Nazareth

¹⁹After Herod died, an angel of the Lord appeared in a dream to Joseph in Egypt ²⁰and said, "Get up, take the child and his mother and go to the land of Israel, for those who were trying to take the child's life are dead."

²¹So he got up, took the child and his mother and went to the land of Israel. ²²But when he heard that Archelaus was reigning in Judea in place of his father Herod, he was afraid to go there. Having been warned in a dream, he withdrew to the district of Galilee, ²³and he went and lived in a town called Nazareth. So was fulfilled what was said through

ᵃ 15 Hosea 11:1   ᵇ 18 Jer. 31:15

the prophets, that he would be called a Nazarene.

John the Baptist Prepares the Way

3 In those days John the Baptist came, preaching in the wilderness of Judea ²and saying, "Repent, for the kingdom of heaven has come near." ³This is he who was spoken of through the prophet Isaiah:

"A voice of one calling in the wilderness,
'Prepare the way for the Lord,
    make straight paths for
        him.'"ᵃ

⁴John's clothes were made of camel's hair, and he had a leather belt around his waist. His food was locusts and wild honey. ⁵People went out to him from Jerusalem and all Judea and the whole region of the Jordan. ⁶Confessing their sins, they were baptized by him in the Jordan River.

⁷But when he saw many of the Pharisees and Sadducees coming to where he was baptizing, he said to them: "You brood of vipers! Who warned you to flee from the coming wrath? ⁸Produce fruit in keeping with repentance. ⁹And do not think you can say to yourselves, 'We have Abraham as our father.' I tell you that out of these stones God can raise up children for Abraham. ¹⁰The ax is already at the root of the trees, and every tree that does not produce good fruit will be cut down and thrown into the fire.

¹¹"I baptize you withᵇ water for repentance. But after me comes one who is more powerful than I, whose sandals I am not worthy to carry. He will baptize you withᵇ the Holy Spirit and fire. ¹²His winnowing fork is in his hand, and he will clear his threshing floor, gathering his wheat into the barn and burning up the chaff with unquenchable fire."

The Baptism of Jesus

¹³Then Jesus came from Galilee to the Jordan to be baptized by John. ¹⁴But John tried to deter him, saying, "I need to be baptized by you, and do you come to me?"

¹⁵Jesus replied, "Let it be so now; it is proper for us to do this to fulfill all righteousness." Then John consented.

¹⁶As soon as Jesus was baptized, he went up out of the water. At that moment heaven was opened, and he saw the Spirit of God descending like a dove and alighting on him. ¹⁷And a voice from heaven said, "This is my Son, whom I love; with him I am well pleased."

Jesus Is Tested in the Wilderness

4 Then Jesus was led by the Spirit into the wilderness to be temptedᶜ by the devil. ²After fasting forty days and forty

---

ᵃ 3 Isaiah 40:3   ᵇ 11 Or in   ᶜ 1 The Greek for tempted can also mean tested.

nights, he was hungry. ³The tempter came to him and said, "If you are the Son of God, tell these stones to become bread."

⁴Jesus answered, "It is written: 'Man shall not live on bread alone, but on every word that comes from the mouth of God.'ᵃ"

⁵Then the devil took him to the holy city and had him stand on the highest point of the temple. ⁶"If you are the Son of God," he said, "throw yourself down. For it is written:

" 'He will command his angels
    concerning you,
and they will lift you up in
    their hands,
so that you will not strike your
    foot against a stone.'ᵇ"

⁷Jesus answered him, "It is also written: 'Do not put the Lord your God to the test.'ᶜ"

⁸Again, the devil took him to a very high mountain and showed him all the kingdoms of the world and their splendor. ⁹"All this I will give you," he said, "if you will bow down and worship me."

¹⁰Jesus said to him, "Away from me, Satan! For it is written: 'Worship the Lord your God, and serve him only.'ᵈ"

¹¹Then the devil left him, and angels came and attended him.

Jesus Begins to Preach

¹²When Jesus heard that John had been put in prison, he with-drew to Galilee. ¹³Leaving Nazareth, he went and lived in Capernaum, which was by the lake in the area of Zebulun and Naphtali — ¹⁴to fulfill what was said through the prophet Isaiah:

¹⁵"Land of Zebulun and land of
    Naphtali,
    the Way of the Sea, beyond
        the Jordan,
    Galilee of the Gentiles —
¹⁶the people living in darkness
    have seen a great light;
on those living in the land of
    the shadow of death
    a light has dawned."ᵉ

¹⁷From that time on Jesus began to preach, "Repent, for the kingdom of heaven has come near."

Jesus Calls His First Disciples

¹⁸As Jesus was walking beside the Sea of Galilee, he saw two brothers, Simon called Peter and his brother Andrew. They were casting a net into the lake, for they were fishermen. ¹⁹"Come, follow me," Jesus said, "and I will send you out to fish for people." ²⁰At once they left their nets and followed him.

²¹Going on from there, he saw two other brothers, James son of Zebedee and his brother John. They were in a boat with their father Zebedee, preparing their nets. Jesus called them, ²²and

---

ᵃ 4 Deut. 8:3   ᵇ 6 Psalm 91:11,12   ᶜ 7 Deut. 6:16   ᵈ 10 Deut. 6:13
ᵉ 16 Isaiah 9:1,2

immediately they left the boat and their father and followed him.

Jesus Heals the Sick

23 Jesus went throughout Galilee, teaching in their synagogues, proclaiming the good news of the kingdom, and healing every disease and sickness among the people. 24 News about him spread all over Syria, and people brought to him all who were ill with various diseases, those suffering severe pain, the demon-possessed, those having seizures, and the paralyzed; and he healed them. 25 Large crowds from Galilee, the Decapolis,[a] Jerusalem, Judea and the region across the Jordan followed him.

Introduction to the Sermon on the Mount

5 Now when Jesus saw the crowds, he went up on a mountainside and sat down. His disciples came to him, 2 and he began to teach them.

The Beatitudes

He said:

3 "Blessed are the poor in spirit,
  for theirs is the kingdom of
    heaven.
4 Blessed are those who mourn,
  for they will be comforted.
5 Blessed are the meek,
  for they will inherit the
    earth.
6 Blessed are those who
  hunger and thirst for
    righteousness,
  for they will be filled.
7 Blessed are the merciful,
  for they will be shown
    mercy.
8 Blessed are the pure in heart,
  for they will see God.
9 Blessed are the peacemakers,
  for they will be called
    children of God.
10 Blessed are those who are
  persecuted because of
    righteousness,
  for theirs is the kingdom of
    heaven.

11 "Blessed are you when people insult you, persecute you and falsely say all kinds of evil against you because of me. 12 Rejoice and be glad, because great is your reward in heaven, for in the same way they persecuted the prophets who were before you.

Salt and Light

13 "You are the salt of the earth. But if the salt loses its saltiness, how can it be made salty again? It is no longer good for anything, except to be thrown out and trampled underfoot.

14 "You are the light of the world. A town built on a hill cannot be hidden. 15 Neither do people light a lamp and put it under a bowl. Instead they put it on its stand, and it gives light to everyone in

a 25 That is, the Ten Cities

the house. [16]In the same way, let your light shine before others, that they may see your good deeds and glorify your Father in heaven.

The Fulfillment of the Law

[17]"Do not think that I have come to abolish the Law or the Prophets; I have not come to abolish them but to fulfill them. [18]For truly I tell you, until heaven and earth disappear, not the smallest letter, not the least stroke of a pen, will by any means disappear from the Law until everything is accomplished. [19]Therefore anyone who sets aside one of the least of these commands and teaches others accordingly will be called least in the kingdom of heaven, but whoever practices and teaches these commands will be called great in the kingdom of heaven. [20]For I tell you that unless your righteousness surpasses that of the Pharisees and the teachers of the law, you will certainly not enter the kingdom of heaven.

Murder

[21]"You have heard that it was said to the people long ago, 'You shall not murder,[a] and anyone who murders will be subject to judgment.' [22]But I tell you that anyone who is angry with a brother or sister[b,c] will be subject to judgment. Again, anyone who says to a brother or sister, 'Raca,'[d] is answerable to the court. And anyone who says, 'You fool!' will be in danger of the fire of hell.

[23]"Therefore, if you are offering your gift at the altar and there remember that your brother or sister has something against you, [24]leave your gift there in front of the altar. First go and be reconciled to them; then come and offer your gift.

[25]"Settle matters quickly with your adversary who is taking you to court. Do it while you are still together on the way, or your adversary may hand you over to the judge, and the judge may hand you over to the officer, and you may be thrown into prison. [26]Truly I tell you, you will not get out until you have paid the last penny.

Adultery

[27]"You have heard that it was said, 'You shall not commit adultery.'[e] [28]But I tell you that anyone who looks at a woman lustfully has already committed adultery with her in his heart. [29]If your right eye causes you to stumble, gouge it out and throw it away. It is better for you to lose one part of your body than for your whole body to be thrown into hell.

---

[a] 21 Exodus 20:13   [b] 22 The Greek word for *brother or sister* (*adelphos*) refers here to a fellow disciple, whether man or woman; also in verse 23.   [c] 22 Some manuscripts *brother or sister without cause*   [d] 22 An Aramaic term of contempt   [e] 27 Exodus 20:14

³⁰And if your right hand causes you to stumble, cut it off and throw it away. It is better for you to lose one part of your body than for your whole body to go into hell.

Divorce

³¹"It has been said, 'Anyone who divorces his wife must give her a certificate of divorce.'ᵃ ³²But I tell you that anyone who divorces his wife, except for sexual immorality, makes her the victim of adultery, and anyone who marries a divorced woman commits adultery.

Oaths

³³"Again, you have heard that it was said to the people long ago, 'Do not break your oath, but fulfill to the Lord the vows you have made.' ³⁴But I tell you, do not swear an oath at all: either by heaven, for it is God's throne; ³⁵or by the earth, for it is his footstool; or by Jerusalem, for it is the city of the Great King. ³⁶And do not swear by your head, for you cannot make even one hair white or black. ³⁷All you need to say is simply 'Yes' or 'No'; anything beyond this comes from the evil one.ᵇ

Eye for Eye

³⁸"You have heard that it was said, 'Eye for eye, and tooth for tooth.'ᶜ ³⁹But I tell you, do not resist an evil person. If anyone slaps you on the right cheek, turn to them the other cheek also. ⁴⁰And if anyone wants to sue you and take your shirt, hand over your coat as well. ⁴¹If anyone forces you to go one mile, go with them two miles. ⁴²Give to the one who asks you, and do not turn away from the one who wants to borrow from you.

Love for Enemies

⁴³"You have heard that it was said, 'Love your neighborᵈ and hate your enemy.' ⁴⁴But I tell you, love your enemies and pray for those who persecute you, ⁴⁵that you may be children of your Father in heaven. He causes his sun to rise on the evil and the good, and sends rain on the righteous and the unrighteous. ⁴⁶If you love those who love you, what reward will you get? Are not even the tax collectors doing that? ⁴⁷And if you greet only your own people, what are you doing more than others? Do not even pagans do that? ⁴⁸Be perfect, therefore, as your heavenly Father is perfect.

Giving to the Needy

6 "Be careful not to practice your righteousness in front of others to be seen by them. If you do, you will have no reward from your Father in heaven.

²"So when you give to the needy, do not announce it with

ᵃ 31 Deut. 24:1   ᵇ 37 Or *from evil*   ᶜ 38 Exodus 21:24; Lev. 24:20; Deut. 19:21
ᵈ 43 Lev. 19:18

trumpets, as the hypocrites do in the synagogues and on the streets, to be honored by others. Truly I tell you, they have received their reward in full. **3**But when you give to the needy, do not let your left hand know what your right hand is doing, **4**so that your giving may be in secret. Then your Father, who sees what is done in secret, will reward you.

Prayer

5"And when you pray, do not be like the hypocrites, for they love to pray standing in the synagogues and on the street corners to be seen by others. Truly I tell you, they have received their reward in full. **6**But when you pray, go into your room, close the door and pray to your Father, who is unseen. Then your Father, who sees what is done in secret, will reward you. **7**And when you pray, do not keep on babbling like pagans, for they think they will be heard because of their many words. **8**Do not be like them, for your Father knows what you need before you ask him.

9"This, then, is how you should pray:

" 'Our Father in heaven,
  hallowed be your name,
10your kingdom come,
  your will be done,
    on earth as it is in heaven.

11Give us today our daily bread.
12And forgive us our debts,
  as we also have forgiven our
  debtors.
13And lead us not into
  temptation,*a*
  but deliver us from the evil
  one.*b*'

14For if you forgive other people when they sin against you, your heavenly Father will also forgive you. **15**But if you do not forgive others their sins, your Father will not forgive your sins.

Fasting

16"When you fast, do not look somber as the hypocrites do, for they disfigure their faces to show others they are fasting. Truly I tell you, they have received their reward in full. **17**But when you fast, put oil on your head and wash your face, **18**so that it will not be obvious to others that you are fasting, but only to your Father, who is unseen; and your Father, who sees what is done in secret, will reward you.

Treasures in Heaven

19"Do not store up for yourselves treasures on earth, where moths and vermin destroy, and where thieves break in and steal. **20**But store up for yourselves treasures in heaven, where moths and vermin do not destroy, and

---

a 13 The Greek for *temptation* can also mean *testing.*   *b 13* Or *from evil*; some late manuscripts *one, / for yours is the kingdom and the power and the glory forever. Amen.*

where thieves do not break in and steal. ²¹For where your treasure is, there your heart will be also.

²²"The eye is the lamp of the body. If your eyes are healthy,ᵃ your whole body will be full of light. ²³But if your eyes are unhealthy,ᵇ your whole body will be full of darkness. If then the light within you is darkness, how great is that darkness!

²⁴"No one can serve two masters. Either you will hate the one and love the other, or you will be devoted to the one and despise the other. You cannot serve both God and money.

Do Not Worry

²⁵"Therefore I tell you, do not worry about your life, what you will eat or drink; or about your body, what you will wear. Is not life more than food, and the body more than clothes? ²⁶Look at the birds of the air; they do not sow or reap or store away in barns, and yet your heavenly Father feeds them. Are you not much more valuable than they? ²⁷Can any one of you by worrying add a single hour to your lifeᶜ?

²⁸"And why do you worry about clothes? See how the flowers of the field grow. They do not labor or spin. ²⁹Yet I tell you that not even Solomon in all his splendor was dressed like one of these. ³⁰If that is how God clothes the grass of the field, which is here today and tomorrow is thrown into the fire, will he not much more clothe you — you of little faith? ³¹So do not worry, saying, 'What shall we eat?' or 'What shall we drink?' or 'What shall we wear?' ³²For the pagans run after all these things, and your heavenly Father knows that you need them. ³³But seek first his kingdom and his righteousness, and all these things will be given to you as well. ³⁴Therefore do not worry about tomorrow, for tomorrow will worry about itself. Each day has enough trouble of its own.

Judging Others

7 "Do not judge, or you too will be judged. ²For in the same way you judge others, you will be judged, and with the measure you use, it will be measured to you.

³"Why do you look at the speck of sawdust in your brother's eye and pay no attention to the plank in your own eye? ⁴How can you say to your brother, 'Let me take the speck out of your eye,' when all the time there is a plank in your own eye? ⁵You hypocrite, first take the plank out of your own eye, and then you will see clearly to remove the speck from your brother's eye.

⁶"Do not give dogs what is sacred; do not throw your pearls to

---

ᵃ 22 The Greek for *healthy* here implies *generous*.   ᵇ 23 The Greek for *unhealthy* here implies *stingy*.   ᶜ 27 Or *single cubit to your height* pigs. If you do, they may trample them under their feet, and turn and tear you to pieces.

Ask, Seek, Knock

7 "Ask and it will be given to you; seek and you will find; knock and the door will be opened to you. 8 For everyone who asks receives; the one who seeks finds; and to the one who knocks, the door will be opened.

9 "Which of you, if your son asks for bread, will give him a stone? 10 Or if he asks for a fish, will give him a snake? 11 If you, then, though you are evil, know how to give good gifts to your children, how much more will your Father in heaven give good gifts to those who ask him! 12 So in everything, do to others what you would have them do to you, for this sums up the Law and the Prophets.

The Narrow and Wide Gates

13 "Enter through the narrow gate. For wide is the gate and broad is the road that leads to destruction, and many enter through it. 14 But small is the gate and narrow the road that leads to life, and only a few find it.

True and False Prophets

15 "Watch out for false prophets. They come to you in sheep's clothing, but inwardly they are ferocious wolves. 16 By their fruit you will recognize them. Do people pick grapes from thornbushes, or figs from thistles? 17 Like-wise, every good tree bears good fruit, but a bad tree bears bad fruit. 18 A good tree cannot bear bad fruit, and a bad tree cannot bear good fruit. 19 Every tree that does not bear good fruit is cut down and thrown into the fire. 20 Thus, by their fruit you will recognize them.

True and False Disciples

21 "Not everyone who says to me, 'Lord, Lord,' will enter the kingdom of heaven, but only the one who does the will of my Father who is in heaven. 22 Many will say to me on that day, 'Lord, Lord, did we not prophesy in your name and in your name drive out demons and in your name perform many miracles?' 23 Then I will tell them plainly, 'I never knew you. Away from me, you evildoers!'

The Wise and Foolish Builders

24 "Therefore everyone who hears these words of mine and puts them into practice is like a wise man who built his house on the rock. 25 The rain came down, the streams rose, and the winds blew and beat against that house; yet it did not fall, because it had its foundation on the rock. 26 But everyone who hears these words of mine and does not put them into practice is like a foolish man who built his house on sand. 27 The rain came down, the streams rose, and the winds blew and beat against that house, and it fell with a great crash."

²⁸When Jesus had finished saying these things, the crowds were amazed at his teaching, ²⁹because he taught as one who had authority, and not as their teachers of the law.

Jesus Heals a Man With Leprosy

8 When Jesus came down from the mountainside, large crowds followed him. ²A man with leprosy*a* came and knelt before him and said, "Lord, if you are willing, you can make me clean."

³Jesus reached out his hand and touched the man. "I am willing," he said. "Be clean!" Immediately he was cleansed of his leprosy. ⁴Then Jesus said to him, "See that you don't tell anyone. But go, show yourself to the priest and offer the gift Moses commanded, as a testimony to them."

The Faith of the Centurion

⁵When Jesus had entered Capernaum, a centurion came to him, asking for help. ⁶"Lord," he said, "my servant lies at home paralyzed, suffering terribly."

⁷Jesus said to him, "Shall I come and heal him?"

⁸The centurion replied, "Lord, I do not deserve to have you come under my roof. But just say the word, and my servant will be healed. ⁹For I myself am a man under authority, with soldiers under me. I tell this one, 'Go,' and he goes; and that one, 'Come,' and he comes. I say to my servant, 'Do this,' and he does it."

¹⁰When Jesus heard this, he was amazed and said to those following him, "Truly I tell you, I have not found anyone in Israel with such great faith. ¹¹I say to you that many will come from the east and the west, and will take their places at the feast with Abraham, Isaac and Jacob in the kingdom of heaven. ¹²But the subjects of the kingdom will be thrown outside, into the darkness, where there will be weeping and gnashing of teeth."

¹³Then Jesus said to the centurion, "Go! Let it be done just as you believed it would." And his servant was healed at that moment.

Jesus Heals Many

¹⁴When Jesus came into Peter's house, he saw Peter's mother-in-law lying in bed with a fever. ¹⁵He touched her hand and the fever left her, and she got up and began to wait on him.

¹⁶When evening came, many who were demon-possessed were brought to him, and he drove out the spirits with a word and healed all the sick. ¹⁷This was to fulfill what was spoken through the prophet Isaiah:

---

a 2 The Greek word traditionally translated *leprosy* was used for various diseases affecting the skin.

"He took up our infirmities
and bore our diseases."[a]

The Cost of Following Jesus

¹⁸When Jesus saw the crowd around him, he gave orders to cross to the other side of the lake. ¹⁹Then a teacher of the law came to him and said, "Teacher, I will follow you wherever you go."

²⁰Jesus replied, "Foxes have dens and birds have nests, but the Son of Man has no place to lay his head."

²¹Another disciple said to him, "Lord, first let me go and bury my father."

²²But Jesus told him, "Follow me, and let the dead bury their own dead."

Jesus Calms the Storm

²³Then he got into the boat and his disciples followed him. ²⁴Suddenly a furious storm came up on the lake, so that the waves swept over the boat. But Jesus was sleeping. ²⁵The disciples went and woke him, saying, "Lord, save us! We're going to drown!"

²⁶He replied, "You of little faith, why are you so afraid?" Then he got up and rebuked the winds and the waves, and it was completely calm.

²⁷The men were amazed and asked, "What kind of man is this? Even the winds and the waves obey him!"

Jesus Restores Two Demon-Possessed Men

²⁸When he arrived at the other side in the region of the Gadarenes,[b] two demon-possessed men coming from the tombs met him. They were so violent that no one could pass that way. ²⁹"What do you want with us, Son of God?" they shouted. "Have you come here to torture us before the appointed time?"

³⁰Some distance from them a large herd of pigs was feeding. ³¹The demons begged Jesus, "If you drive us out, send us into the herd of pigs."

³²He said to them, "Go!" So they came out and went into the pigs, and the whole herd rushed down the steep bank into the lake and died in the water. ³³Those tending the pigs ran off, went into the town and reported all this, including what had happened to the demon-possessed men. ³⁴Then the whole town went out to meet Jesus. And when they saw him, they pleaded with him to leave their region.

Jesus Forgives and Heals a Paralyzed Man

9 Jesus stepped into a boat, crossed over and came to his own town. ²Some men brought to him a paralyzed man, lying on a mat. When Jesus saw their faith, he said to the man, "Take heart, son; your sins are forgiven."

---

[a] 17 Isaiah 53:4 (see Septuagint)   [b] 28 Some manuscripts Gergesenes; other manuscripts Gerasenes

³At this, some of the teachers of the law said to themselves, "This fellow is blaspheming!"

⁴Knowing their thoughts, Jesus said, "Why do you entertain evil thoughts in your hearts? ⁵Which is easier: to say, 'Your sins are forgiven,' or to say, 'Get up and walk'? ⁶But I want you to know that the Son of Man has authority on earth to forgive sins." So he said to the paralyzed man, "Get up, take your mat and go home." ⁷Then the man got up and went home. ⁸When the crowd saw this, they were filled with awe; and they praised God, who had given such authority to man.

The Calling of Matthew

⁹As Jesus went on from there, he saw a man named Matthew sitting at the tax collector's booth. "Follow me," he told him, and Matthew got up and followed him.

¹⁰While Jesus was having dinner at Matthew's house, many tax collectors and sinners came and ate with him and his disciples. ¹¹When the Pharisees saw this, they asked his disciples, "Why does your teacher eat with tax collectors and sinners?"

¹²On hearing this, Jesus said, "It is not the healthy who need a doctor, but the sick. ¹³But go and learn what this means: 'I desire mercy, not sacrifice.'ᵃ For I have not come to call the righteous, but sinners."

ᵃ 13 Hosea 6:6

Jesus Questioned About Fasting

¹⁴Then John's disciples came and asked him, "How is it that we and the Pharisees fast often, but your disciples do not fast?"

¹⁵Jesus answered, "How can the guests of the bridegroom mourn while he is with them? The time will come when the bridegroom will be taken from them; then they will fast.

¹⁶"No one sews a patch of unshrunk cloth on an old garment, for the patch will pull away from the garment, making the tear worse. ¹⁷Neither do people pour new wine into old wineskins. If they do, the skins will burst; the wine will run out and the wineskins will be ruined. No, they pour new wine into new wineskins, and both are preserved."

Jesus Raises a Dead Girl and Heals a Sick Woman

¹⁸While he was saying this, a synagogue leader came and knelt before him and said, "My daughter has just died. But come and put your hand on her, and she will live." ¹⁹Jesus got up and went with him, and so did his disciples.

²⁰Just then a woman who had been subject to bleeding for twelve years came up behind him and touched the edge of his cloak. ²¹She said to herself, "If I only touch his cloak, I will be healed."

22 Jesus turned and saw her. "Take heart, daughter," he said, "your faith has healed you." And the woman was healed at that moment.

23 When Jesus entered the synagogue leader's house and saw the noisy crowd and people playing pipes, 24 he said, "Go away. The girl is not dead but asleep." But they laughed at him. 25 After the crowd had been put outside, he went in and took the girl by the hand, and she got up. 26 News of this spread through all that region.

Jesus Heals the Blind and the Mute

27 As Jesus went on from there, two blind men followed him, calling out, "Have mercy on us, Son of David!"

28 When he had gone indoors, the blind men came to him, and he asked them, "Do you believe that I am able to do this?"

"Yes, Lord," they replied.

29 Then he touched their eyes and said, "According to your faith let it be done to you"; 30 and their sight was restored. Jesus warned them sternly, "See that no one knows about this." 31 But they went out and spread the news about him all over that region.

32 While they were going out, a man who was demon-possessed and could not talk was brought to Jesus. 33 And when the demon was driven out, the man who had been mute spoke. The crowd was amazed and said, "Nothing like this has ever been seen in Israel."

34 But the Pharisees said, "It is by the prince of demons that he drives out demons."

The Workers Are Few

35 Jesus went through all the towns and villages, teaching in their synagogues, proclaiming the good news of the kingdom and healing every disease and sickness. 36 When he saw the crowds, he had compassion on them, because they were harassed and helpless, like sheep without a shepherd. 37 Then he said to his disciples, "The harvest is plentiful but the workers are few. 38 Ask the Lord of the harvest, therefore, to send out workers into his harvest field."

Jesus Sends Out the Twelve

10 Jesus called his twelve disciples to him and gave them authority to drive out impure spirits and to heal every disease and sickness.

2 These are the names of the twelve apostles: first, Simon (who is called Peter) and his brother Andrew; James son of Zebedee, and his brother John; 3 Philip and Bartholomew; Thomas and Matthew the tax collector; James son of Alphaeus, and Thaddaeus; 4 Simon the Zealot and Judas Iscariot, who betrayed him.

5 These twelve Jesus sent out with the following instructions:

"Do not go among the Gentiles or enter any town of the Samaritans. **6** Go rather to the lost sheep of Israel. **7** As you go, proclaim this message: 'The kingdom of heaven has come near.' **8** Heal the sick, raise the dead, cleanse those who have leprosy,[a] drive out demons. Freely you have received; freely give.

9 "Do not get any gold or silver or copper to take with you in your belts— **10** no bag for the journey or extra shirt or sandals or a staff, for the worker is worth his keep. **11** Whatever town or village you enter, search there for some worthy person and stay at their house until you leave. **12** As you enter the home, give it your greeting. **13** If the home is deserving, let your peace rest on it; if it is not, let your peace return to you. **14** If anyone will not welcome you or listen to your words, leave that home or town and shake the dust off your feet. **15** Truly I tell you, it will be more bearable for Sodom and Gomorrah on the day of judgment than for that town.

16 "I am sending you out like sheep among wolves. Therefore be as shrewd as snakes and as innocent as doves. **17** Be on your guard; you will be handed over to the local councils and be flogged in the synagogues. **18** On my account you will be brought before governors and kings as witnesses to them and to the Gentiles. **19** But when they arrest you, do not worry about what to say or how to say it. At that time you will be given what to say, **20** for it will not be you speaking, but the Spirit of your Father speaking through you.

21 "Brother will betray brother to death, and a father his child; children will rebel against their parents and have them put to death. **22** You will be hated by everyone because of me, but the one who stands firm to the end will be saved. **23** When you are persecuted in one place, flee to another. Truly I tell you, you will not finish going through the towns of Israel before the Son of Man comes.

24 "The student is not above the teacher, nor a servant above his master. **25** It is enough for students to be like their teachers, and servants like their masters. If the head of the house has been called Beelzebul, how much more the members of his household!

26 "So do not be afraid of them, for there is nothing concealed that will not be disclosed, or hidden that will not be made known. **27** What I tell you in the dark, speak in the daylight; what is whispered in your ear, proclaim from the roofs. **28** Do not be afraid of those who kill the body but cannot kill the soul. Rather, be afraid of the One who can destroy both soul and body in hell. **29** Are not two sparrows sold for a penny? Yet not

---

[a] 8 The Greek word traditionally translated *leprosy* was used for various diseases affecting the skin.

one of them will fall to the ground outside your Father's care.*[a]* **30** And even the very hairs of your head are all numbered. **31** So don't be afraid; you are worth more than many sparrows.

32 "Whoever acknowledges me before others, I will also acknowledge before my Father in heaven. **33** But whoever disowns me before others, I will disown before my Father in heaven.

34 "Do not suppose that I have come to bring peace to the earth. I did not come to bring peace, but a sword. **35** For I have come to turn

" 'a man against his father,
a daughter against her
mother,
a daughter-in-law against her
mother-in-law —
36 a man's enemies will be the
members of his own
household.'*[b]*

37 "Anyone who loves their father or mother more than me is not worthy of me; anyone who loves their son or daughter more than me is not worthy of me. **38** Whoever does not take up their cross and follow me is not worthy of me. **39** Whoever finds their life will lose it, and whoever loses their life for my sake will find it.

40 "Anyone who welcomes you welcomes me, and anyone who welcomes me welcomes the one who sent me. **41** Whoever welcomes a prophet as a prophet will receive a prophet's reward, and whoever welcomes a righteous person as a righteous person will receive a righteous person's reward. **42** And if anyone gives even a cup of cold water to one of these little ones who is my disciple, truly I tell you, that person will certainly not lose their reward."

Jesus and John the Baptist

11 After Jesus had finished instructing his twelve disciples, he went on from there to teach and preach in the towns of Galilee.*[c]*

2 When John, who was in prison, heard about the deeds of the Messiah, he sent his disciples **3** to ask him, "Are you the one who is to come, or should we expect someone else?"

4 Jesus replied, "Go back and report to John what you hear and see: **5** The blind receive sight, the lame walk, those who have leprosy*[d]* are cleansed, the deaf hear, the dead are raised, and the good news is proclaimed to the poor. **6** Blessed is anyone who does not stumble on account of me."

7 As John's disciples were leaving, Jesus began to speak to the crowd about John: "What did you go out into the wilderness to see? A reed swayed by the wind? **8** If not, what did you go out to see? A man dressed in fine clothes? No,

---

a 29 Or *will*; or *knowledge*   *b* 36 Micah 7:6   *c* 1 Greek *in their towns*
d 5 The Greek word traditionally translated *leprosy* was used for various diseases affecting the skin.

those who wear fine clothes are in kings' palaces. ⁹Then what did you go out to see? A prophet? Yes, I tell you, and more than a prophet. ¹⁰This is the one about whom it is written:

" 'I will send my messenger
    ahead of you,
  who will prepare your way
    before you.'ᵃ

¹¹Truly I tell you, among those born of women there has not risen anyone greater than John the Baptist; yet whoever is least in the kingdom of heaven is greater than he. ¹²From the days of John the Baptist until now, the kingdom of heaven has been subjected to violence,ᵇ and violent people have been raiding it. ¹³For all the Prophets and the Law prophesied until John. ¹⁴And if you are willing to accept it, he is the Elijah who was to come. ¹⁵Whoever has ears, let them hear.

¹⁶"To what can I compare this generation? They are like children sitting in the marketplaces and calling out to others:

¹⁷" 'We played the pipe for you,
    and you did not dance;
  we sang a dirge,
    and you did not mourn.'

¹⁸For John came neither eating nor drinking, and they say, 'He has a demon.' ¹⁹The Son of Man came eating and drinking, and they say, 'Here is a glutton and a drunkard, a friend of tax collectors and sinners.' But wisdom is proved right by her deeds."

Woe on Unrepentant Towns

²⁰Then Jesus began to denounce the towns in which most of his miracles had been performed, because they did not repent. ²¹"Woe to you, Chorazin! Woe to you, Bethsaida! For if the miracles that were performed in you had been performed in Tyre and Sidon, they would have repented long ago in sackcloth and ashes. ²²But I tell you, it will be more bearable for Tyre and Sidon on the day of judgment than for you. ²³And you, Capernaum, will you be lifted to the heavens? No, you will go down to Hades.ᶜ For if the miracles that were performed in you had been performed in Sodom, it would have remained to this day. ²⁴But I tell you that it will be more bearable for Sodom on the day of judgment than for you."

The Father Revealed in the Son

²⁵At that time Jesus said, "I praise you, Father, Lord of heaven and earth, because you have hidden these things from the wise and learned, and revealed them to little children. ²⁶Yes, Father, for this is what you were pleased to do.

²⁷"All things have been committed to me by my Father. No

ᵃ 10 Mal. 3:1   ᵇ 12 Or been forcefully advancing   ᶜ 23 That is, the realm of the dead one knows the Son except the Father, and no one knows the Father except the Son and those to whom the Son chooses to reveal him.

28 "Come to me, all you who are weary and burdened, and I will give you rest. 29 Take my yoke upon you and learn from me, for I am gentle and humble in heart, and you will find rest for your souls. 30 For my yoke is easy and my burden is light."

Jesus Is Lord of the Sabbath

12 At that time Jesus went through the grainfields on the Sabbath. His disciples were hungry and began to pick some heads of grain and eat them. 2 When the Pharisees saw this, they said to him, "Look! Your disciples are doing what is unlawful on the Sabbath."

3 He answered, "Haven't you read what David did when he and his companions were hungry? 4 He entered the house of God, and he and his companions ate the consecrated bread — which was not lawful for them to do, but only for the priests. 5 Or haven't you read in the Law that the priests on Sabbath duty in the temple desecrate the Sabbath and yet are innocent? 6 I tell you that something greater than the temple is here. 7 If you had known what these words mean, 'I desire mercy, not sacrifice,'[a] you would

not have condemned the innocent. 8 For the Son of Man is Lord of the Sabbath."

9 Going on from that place, he went into their synagogue, 10 and a man with a shriveled hand was there. Looking for a reason to bring charges against Jesus, they asked him, "Is it lawful to heal on the Sabbath?"

11 He said to them, "If any of you has a sheep and it falls into a pit on the Sabbath, will you not take hold of it and lift it out? 12 How much more valuable is a person than a sheep! Therefore it is lawful to do good on the Sabbath."

13 Then he said to the man, "Stretch out your hand." So he stretched it out and it was completely restored, just as sound as the other. 14 But the Pharisees went out and plotted how they might kill Jesus.

God's Chosen Servant

15 Aware of this, Jesus withdrew from that place. A large crowd followed him, and he healed all who were ill. 16 He warned them not to tell others about him. 17 This was to fulfill what was spoken through the prophet Isaiah:

18 "Here is my servant whom I
       have chosen,
    the one I love, in whom I
       delight;
I will put my Spirit on him,
    and he will proclaim justice
       to the nations.

a 7 Hosea 6:6

¹⁹He will not quarrel or cry out;
  no one will hear his voice in
    the streets.
²⁰A bruised reed he will not
    break,
  and a smoldering wick he
    will not snuff out,
  till he has brought justice
    through to victory.
²¹ In his name the nations will
    put their hope."^a

Jesus and Beelzebul

²²Then they brought him a demon-possessed man who was blind and mute, and Jesus healed him, so that he could both talk and see. ²³All the people were astonished and said, "Could this be the Son of David?"

²⁴But when the Pharisees heard this, they said, "It is only by Beelzebul, the prince of demons, that this fellow drives out demons."

²⁵Jesus knew their thoughts and said to them, "Every kingdom divided against itself will be ruined, and every city or household divided against itself will not stand. ²⁶If Satan drives out Satan, he is divided against himself. How then can his kingdom stand? ²⁷And if I drive out demons by Beelzebul, by whom do your people drive them out? So then, they will be your judges. ²⁸But if it is by the Spirit of God that I drive out demons, then the kingdom of God has come upon you.

²⁹"Or again, how can anyone

enter a strong man's house and carry off his possessions unless he first ties up the strong man? Then he can plunder his house. ³⁰"Whoever is not with me is against me, and whoever does not gather with me scatters. ³¹And so I tell you, every kind of sin and slander can be forgiven, but blasphemy against the Spirit will not be forgiven. ³²Anyone who speaks a word against the Son of Man will be forgiven, but anyone who speaks against the Holy Spirit will not be forgiven, either in this age or in the age to come.

³³"Make a tree good and its fruit will be good, or make a tree bad and its fruit will be bad, for a tree is recognized by its fruit. ³⁴You brood of vipers, how can you who are evil say anything good? For the mouth speaks what the heart is full of. ³⁵A good man brings good things out of the good stored up in him, and an evil man brings evil things out of the evil stored up in him. ³⁶But I tell you that everyone will have to give account on the day of judgment for every empty word they have spoken. ³⁷For by your words you will be acquitted, and by your words you will be condemned."

The Sign of Jonah

³⁸Then some of the Pharisees and teachers of the law said to him, "Teacher, we want to see a sign from you."

^a 21 Isaiah 42:1-4

39 He answered, "A wicked and adulterous generation asks for a sign! But none will be given it except the sign of the prophet Jonah. **40** For as Jonah was three days and three nights in the belly of a huge fish, so the Son of Man will be three days and three nights in the heart of the earth. **41** The men of Nineveh will stand up at the judgment with this generation and condemn it; for they repented at the preaching of Jonah, and now something greater than Jonah is here. **42** The Queen of the South will rise at the judgment with this generation and condemn it; for she came from the ends of the earth to listen to Solomon's wisdom, and now something greater than Solomon is here.

43 "When an impure spirit comes out of a person, it goes through arid places seeking rest and does not find it. **44** Then it says, 'I will return to the house I left.' When it arrives, it finds the house unoccupied, swept clean and put in order. **45** Then it goes and takes with it seven other spirits more wicked than itself, and they go in and live there. And the final condition of that person is worse than the first. That is how it will be with this wicked generation."

Jesus' Mother and Brothers

46 While Jesus was still talking to the crowd, his mother and brothers stood outside, wanting to speak to him. **47** Someone told him, "Your mother and brothers are standing outside, wanting to speak to you."

48 He replied to him, "Who is my mother, and who are my brothers?" **49** Pointing to his disciples, he said, "Here are my mother and my brothers. **50** For whoever does the will of my Father in heaven is my brother and sister and mother."

The Parable of the Sower

13 That same day Jesus went out of the house and sat by the lake. **2** Such large crowds gathered around him that he got into a boat and sat in it, while all the people stood on the shore. **3** Then he told them many things in parables, saying: "A farmer went out to sow his seed. **4** As he was scattering the seed, some fell along the path, and the birds came and ate it up. **5** Some fell on rocky places, where it did not have much soil. It sprang up quickly, because the soil was shallow. **6** But when the sun came up, the plants were scorched, and they withered because they had no root. **7** Other seed fell among thorns, which grew up and choked the plants. **8** Still other seed fell on good soil, where it produced a crop—a hundred, sixty or thirty times what was sown. **9** Whoever has ears, let them hear."

10 The disciples came to him and asked, "Why do you speak to the people in parables?"

[11] He replied, "Because the knowledge of the secrets of the kingdom of heaven has been given to you, but not to them. [12] Whoever has will be given more, and they will have an abundance. Whoever does not have, even what they have will be taken from them. [13] This is why I speak to them in parables:

"Though seeing, they do not
    see;
  though hearing, they do not
    hear or understand.

[14] In them is fulfilled the prophecy of Isaiah:

" 'You will be ever hearing but
    never understanding;
  you will be ever seeing but
    never perceiving.
[15] For this people's heart has
    become calloused;
  they hardly hear with their
    ears,
  and they have closed their
    eyes.
Otherwise they might see with
    their eyes,
  hear with their ears,
  understand with their hearts
  and turn, and I would heal
    them.'[a]

[16] But blessed are your eyes because they see, and your ears because they hear. [17] For truly I tell you, many prophets and righteous people longed to see what you see but did not see it, and to hear what you hear but did not hear it.

[18] "Listen then to what the parable of the sower means: [19] When anyone hears the message about the kingdom and does not understand it, the evil one comes and snatches away what was sown in their heart. This is the seed sown along the path. [20] The seed falling on rocky ground refers to someone who hears the word and at once receives it with joy. [21] But since they have no root, they last only a short time. When trouble or persecution comes because of the word, they quickly fall away. [22] The seed falling among the thorns refers to someone who hears the word, but the worries of this life and the deceitfulness of wealth choke the word, making it unfruitful. [23] But the seed falling on good soil refers to someone who hears the word and understands it. This is the one who produces a crop, yielding a hundred, sixty or thirty times what was sown."

The Parable of the Weeds

[24] Jesus told them another parable: "The kingdom of heaven is like a man who sowed good seed in his field. [25] But while everyone was sleeping, his enemy came and sowed weeds among the wheat, and went away. [26] When the wheat sprouted and formed heads, then the weeds also appeared.

[27] "The owner's servants came

[a] 15 Isaiah 6:9,10 (see Septuagint)

to him and said, 'Sir, didn't you sow good seed in your field? Where then did the weeds come from?'

28 " 'An enemy did this,' he replied.

"The servants asked him, 'Do you want us to go and pull them up?'

29 " 'No,' he answered, 'because while you are pulling the weeds, you may uproot the wheat with them. 30 Let both grow together until the harvest. At that time I will tell the harvesters: First collect the weeds and tie them in bundles to be burned; then gather the wheat and bring it into my barn.' "

The Parables of the Mustard Seed and the Yeast

31 He told them another parable: "The kingdom of heaven is like a mustard seed, which a man took and planted in his field. 32 Though it is the smallest of all seeds, yet when it grows, it is the largest of garden plants and becomes a tree, so that the birds come and perch in its branches."

33 He told them still another parable: "The kingdom of heaven is like yeast that a woman took and mixed into about sixty pounds[a] of flour until it worked all through the dough."

34 Jesus spoke all these things to the crowd in parables; he did not say anything to them without using a parable. 35 So was fulfilled what was spoken through the prophet:

"I will open my mouth in
     parables,
I will utter things hidden
     since the creation of the
     world."[b]

The Parable of the Weeds Explained

36 Then he left the crowd and went into the house. His disciples came to him and said, "Explain to us the parable of the weeds in the field."

37 He answered, "The one who sowed the good seed is the Son of Man. 38 The field is the world, and the good seed stands for the people of the kingdom. The weeds are the people of the evil one, 39 and the enemy who sows them is the devil. The harvest is the end of the age, and the harvesters are angels.

40 "As the weeds are pulled up and burned in the fire, so it will be at the end of the age. 41 The Son of Man will send out his angels, and they will weed out of his kingdom everything that causes sin and all who do evil. 42 They will throw them into the blazing furnace, where there will be weeping and gnashing of teeth. 43 Then the righteous will shine like the sun in the kingdom of their Father. Whoever has ears, let them hear.

---

[a] 33 Or about 27 kilograms   [b] 35 Psalm 78:2

The Parables of the Hidden Treasure and the Pearl

44 "The kingdom of heaven is like treasure hidden in a field. When a man found it, he hid it again, and then in his joy went and sold all he had and bought that field.

45 "Again, the kingdom of heaven is like a merchant looking for fine pearls. 46 When he found one of great value, he went away and sold everything he had and bought it.

The Parable of the Net

47 "Once again, the kingdom of heaven is like a net that was let down into the lake and caught all kinds of fish. 48 When it was full, the fishermen pulled it up on the shore. Then they sat down and collected the good fish in baskets, but threw the bad away. 49 This is how it will be at the end of the age. The angels will come and separate the wicked from the righteous 50 and throw them into the blazing furnace, where there will be weeping and gnashing of teeth.

51 "Have you understood all these things?" Jesus asked.

"Yes," they replied.

52 He said to them, "Therefore every teacher of the law who has become a disciple in the kingdom of heaven is like the owner of a house who brings out of his storeroom new treasures as well as old."

A Prophet Without Honor

53 When Jesus had finished these parables, he moved on from there. 54 Coming to his hometown, he began teaching the people in their synagogue, and they were amazed. "Where did this man get this wisdom and these miraculous powers?" they asked. 55 "Isn't this the carpenter's son? Isn't his mother's name Mary, and aren't his brothers James, Joseph, Simon and Judas? 56 Aren't all his sisters with us? Where then did this man get all these things?" 57 And they took offense at him.

But Jesus said to them, "A prophet is not without honor except in his own town and in his own home."

58 And he did not do many miracles there because of their lack of faith.

John the Baptist Beheaded

14 At that time Herod the tetrarch heard the reports about Jesus, 2 and he said to his attendants, "This is John the Baptist; he has risen from the dead! That is why miraculous powers are at work in him."

3 Now Herod had arrested John and bound him and put him in prison because of Herodias, his brother Philip's wife, 4 for John had been saying to him: "It is not lawful for you to have her." 5 Herod wanted to kill John, but he was afraid of the people, because they considered John a prophet.

⁶On Herod's birthday the daughter of Herodias danced for the guests and pleased Herod so much ⁷that he promised with an oath to give her whatever she asked. ⁸Prompted by her mother, she said, "Give me here on a platter the head of John the Baptist." ⁹The king was distressed, but because of his oaths and his dinner guests, he ordered that her request be granted ¹⁰and had John beheaded in the prison. ¹¹His head was brought in on a platter and given to the girl, who carried it to her mother. ¹²John's disciples came and took his body and buried it. Then they went and told Jesus.

Jesus Feeds the Five Thousand

¹³When Jesus heard what had happened, he withdrew by boat privately to a solitary place. Hearing of this, the crowds followed him on foot from the towns. ¹⁴When Jesus landed and saw a large crowd, he had compassion on them and healed their sick.

¹⁵As evening approached, the disciples came to him and said, "This is a remote place, and it's already getting late. Send the crowds away, so they can go to the villages and buy themselves some food."

¹⁶Jesus replied, "They do not need to go away. You give them something to eat."

¹⁷"We have here only five loaves of bread and two fish," they answered.

¹⁸"Bring them here to me," he said. ¹⁹And he directed the people to sit down on the grass. Taking the five loaves and the two fish and looking up to heaven, he gave thanks and broke the loaves. Then he gave them to the disciples, and the disciples gave them to the people. ²⁰They all ate and were satisfied, and the disciples picked up twelve basketfuls of broken pieces that were left over. ²¹The number of those who ate was about five thousand men, besides women and children.

Jesus Walks on the Water

²²Immediately Jesus made the disciples get into the boat and go on ahead of him to the other side, while he dismissed the crowd. ²³After he had dismissed them, he went up on a mountainside by himself to pray. Later that night, he was there alone, ²⁴and the boat was already a considerable distance from land, buffeted by the waves because the wind was against it.

²⁵Shortly before dawn Jesus went out to them, walking on the lake. ²⁶When the disciples saw him walking on the lake, they were terrified. "It's a ghost," they said, and cried out in fear.

²⁷But Jesus immediately said to them: "Take courage! It is I. Don't be afraid."

²⁸"Lord, if it's you," Peter replied, "tell me to come to you on the water."

29 "Come," he said.

Then Peter got down out of the boat, walked on the water and came toward Jesus. 30 But when he saw the wind, he was afraid and, beginning to sink, cried out, "Lord, save me!"

31 Immediately Jesus reached out his hand and caught him. "You of little faith," he said, "why did you doubt?"

32 And when they climbed into the boat, the wind died down. 33 Then those who were in the boat worshiped him, saying, "Truly you are the Son of God."

34 When they had crossed over, they landed at Gennesaret. 35 And when the men of that place recognized Jesus, they sent word to all the surrounding country. People brought all their sick to him 36 and begged him to let the sick just touch the edge of his cloak, and all who touched it were healed.

That Which Defiles

15 Then some Pharisees and teachers of the law came to Jesus from Jerusalem and asked, 2 "Why do your disciples break the tradition of the elders? They don't wash their hands before they eat!"

3 Jesus replied, "And why do you break the command of God for the sake of your tradition? 4 For God said, 'Honor your father and mother'ᵃ and 'Anyone who curses their father or mother is to be put to death.'ᵇ 5 But you say that if anyone declares that what might have been used to help their father or mother is 'devoted to God,' 6 they are not to 'honor their father or mother' with it. Thus you nullify the word of God for the sake of your tradition. 7 You hypocrites! Isaiah was right when he prophesied about you:

8 " 'These people honor me with
        their lips,
    but their hearts are far
        from me.
9 They worship me in vain;
    their teachings are merely
        human rules.'ᶜ"

10 Jesus called the crowd to him and said, "Listen and understand. 11 What goes into someone's mouth does not defile them, but what comes out of their mouth, that is what defiles them."

12 Then the disciples came to him and asked, "Do you know that the Pharisees were offended when they heard this?"

13 He replied, "Every plant that my heavenly Father has not planted will be pulled up by the roots. 14 Leave them; they are blind guides.ᵈ If the blind lead the blind, both will fall into a pit."

15 Peter said, "Explain the parable to us."

16 "Are you still so dull?" Jesus asked them. 17 "Don't you see that whatever enters the mouth

---

ᵃ 4 Exodus 20:12; Deut. 5:16   ᵇ 4 Exodus 21:17; Lev. 20:9   ᶜ 9 Isaiah 29:13
ᵈ 14 Some manuscripts blind guides of the blind

goes into the stomach and then out of the body? **18** But the things that come out of a person's mouth come from the heart, and these defile them. **19** For out of the heart come evil thoughts — murder, adultery, sexual immorality, theft, false testimony, slander. **20** These are what defile a person; but eating with unwashed hands does not defile them."

The Faith of a Canaanite Woman

21 Leaving that place, Jesus withdrew to the region of Tyre and Sidon. **22** A Canaanite woman from that vicinity came to him, crying out, "Lord, Son of David, have mercy on me! My daughter is demon-possessed and suffering terribly."

23 Jesus did not answer a word. So his disciples came to him and urged him, "Send her away, for she keeps crying out after us."

24 He answered, "I was sent only to the lost sheep of Israel."

25 The woman came and knelt before him. "Lord, help me!" she said.

26 He replied, "It is not right to take the children's bread and toss it to the dogs."

27 "Yes it is, Lord," she said. "Even the dogs eat the crumbs that fall from their master's table."

28 Then Jesus said to her, "Woman, you have great faith! Your request is granted." And her daughter was healed at that moment.

Jesus Feeds the Four Thousand

29 Jesus left there and went along the Sea of Galilee. Then he went up on a mountainside and sat down. **30** Great crowds came to him, bringing the lame, the blind, the crippled, the mute and many others, and laid them at his feet; and he healed them. **31** The people were amazed when they saw the mute speaking, the crippled made well, the lame walking and the blind seeing. And they praised the God of Israel.

32 Jesus called his disciples to him and said, "I have compassion for these people; they have already been with me three days and have nothing to eat. I do not want to send them away hungry, or they may collapse on the way."

33 His disciples answered, "Where could we get enough bread in this remote place to feed such a crowd?"

34 "How many loaves do you have?" Jesus asked.

"Seven," they replied, "and a few small fish."

35 He told the crowd to sit down on the ground. **36** Then he took the seven loaves and the fish, and when he had given thanks, he broke them and gave them to the disciples, and they in turn to the people. **37** They all ate and were satisfied. Afterward the disciples picked up seven basketfuls of broken pieces that were left over. **38** The number of those who ate was four thousand men, besides

Zaccheus
LUKE 19:1–10

The Triumphal Entry (Palm Sunday)
MATTHEW 21:1–11

What to Read When . . .

THINGS ARE GOING WELL
Luke 12:13–21; 1 Timothy 6:3–19; Hebrews 13:5

YOU ARE ANGRY
Matthew 5:21–22; Matthew 18:21–35; Ephesians 4:25–27; James 1:19–20

YOU ARE JEALOUS
Numbers 12:1–15; 16:1–35; Galatians 5:13–15, 19–21; James 3:13–18

YOU ARE LONELY
1 Kings 19:1–18; Psalm 41; Matthew 26:36–46; 2 Timothy 4:16–18

YOU ARE PROUD
Mark 10:35–45; Romans 12:3; Philippians 2:1–11

YOU ARE SAD
Isaiah 12; Isaiah 40:1–11; Jeremiah 31:10–13; 2 Corinthians 1:3–7; 7:6–13

YOU ARE SELFISH
Luke 12:13–21; 2 Corinthians 9:6–15; 1 John 3:16–18

YOU ARE STRUGGLING TO BE HONEST
Proverbs 12:17; Proverbs 12:22; Ephesians 4:25

YOU ARE STRUGGLING WITH LAZINESS
Proverbs 6:6–11, 10:4–5; Ephesians 5:15–16; 2 Thessalonians 3:6–15

YOU ARE WORRIED
Luke 12:22–34; Philippians 4:4–9; Hebrews 13:5–6

YOU HAVE BEEN FIGHTING WITH SOMEONE
Proverbs 15:18; Matthew 5:5; Colossians 3:15; James 3:17

YOU HAVE BEEN JUDGING OTHERS
Matthew 7:1–5; 1 Corinthians 4:1–5; James 2:1–13; 4:11–12

YOU NEED ASSURANCE OF SALVATION
Psalm 91:14–16; Micah 7:18–20; John 3:1–21; Acts 16:31

YOU NEED HOPE
Psalm 42; 130; Romans 5:1–11; Colossians 1:3–27; 1 Peter 1:3–9

YOU WANT TO LEARN TO PRAY
Matthew 6:5–15; Mark 11:22–25; Luke 18:9–14

What the Bible has to say about . . .

ANGER
Psalm 4:4; Proverbs 16:32; Ephesians 4:25–5:2

CARING/COMPASSION
Psalm 116:5–6; Micah 6:8; 2 Corinthians 1:3–7

CHILDREN
Psalm 78:1–7; Matthew 18:1–9; Mark 10:13–16; Ephesians 6:1–4

DEATH
Psalm 116:15–16; Isaiah 57:1–2; John 12:23–26; Romans 6:1–23

ETERNAL LIFE
Psalm 23; John 3:1–21

FRIENDSHIP
Proverbs 17:17; 26:6; John 14:23–15:17; Colossians 3:12–17

GIVING
Deuteronomy 15:7–11; Malachi 3:10–12; Matthew 6:1–4

HAPPINESS
Psalm 33; Isaiah 12; 52:7–10; Matthew 5:1–12; Philippians 4:4–9

HEAVEN
Matthew 6:19–21; 25:31–44; Revelation 21

HELL
Luke 16:22–24; Matthew 10:27–29; Mark 9:42–49

JOY
Isaiah 12; 52:7–10; Luke 15; James 1:2–18; 1 Peter 4:12–19

LOVE
Deuteronomy 6:1–5; 1 Corinthians 13; 1 John 4:7–21

THE POOR
Deuteronomy 15:1–11; Amos 5:11–15; James 2:1–13

REVENGE
Proverbs 25:21–22; Matthew 5:38–47; Romans 12:17–21

STEWARDSHIP
1 Chronicles 29:1–9; Matthew 25:14–30; Luke 12:35–48

SWEARING/PROFANITY
Exodus 20:7; Ephesians 4:29–32; James 3:1–12

women and children. **39**After Jesus had sent the crowd away, he got into the boat and went to the vicinity of Magadan.

The Demand for a Sign

16 The Pharisees and Sadducees came to Jesus and tested him by asking him to show them a sign from heaven.

2He replied, "When evening comes, you say, 'It will be fair weather, for the sky is red,' **3**and in the morning, 'Today it will be stormy, for the sky is red and overcast.' You know how to interpret the appearance of the sky, but you cannot interpret the signs of the times.*a* **4**A wicked and adulterous generation looks for a sign, but none will be given it except the sign of Jonah." Jesus then left them and went away.

The Yeast of the Pharisees and Sadducees

5When they went across the lake, the disciples forgot to take bread. **6**"Be careful," Jesus said to them. "Be on your guard against the yeast of the Pharisees and Sadducees."

7They discussed this among themselves and said, "It is because we didn't bring any bread."

8Aware of their discussion, Jesus asked, "You of little faith, why are you talking among yourselves about having no bread?

9Do you still not und Don't you remember loaves for the five thousa how many basketfuls yo ered? **10**Or the seven loa the four thousand, and how basketfuls you gathered? **11**H it you don't understand that I not talking to you about bre But be on your guard against yeast of the Pharisees and Sa ducees." **12**Then they understoo that he was not telling them to guard against the yeast used in bread, but against the teaching of the Pharisees and Sadducees.

Peter Declares That Jesus Is the Messiah

13When Jesus came to the region of Caesarea Philippi, he asked his disciples, "Who do people say the Son of Man is?"

14They replied, "Some say John the Baptist; others say Elijah; and still others, Jeremiah or one of the prophets."

15"But what about you?" he asked. "Who do you say I am?"

16Simon Peter answered, "You are the Messiah, the Son of the living God."

17Jesus replied, "Blessed are you, Simon son of Jonah, for this was not revealed to you by flesh and blood, but by my Father in heaven. **18**And I tell you that you are Peter,*b* and on this rock I will build my church, and the gates of

a 2,3 Some early manuscripts do not have *When evening comes . . . of the times.*
b 18 The Greek word for *Peter* means *rock.*

...erstand? ...the five ...nd, and ...gath- ...es for ...many ...ow is ...was ...ad? ...he ...d- ...d

soul? **27** For the Son of Man is going to come in his Father's glory with his angels, and then he will reward each person according to what they have done.

28 "Truly I tell you, some who are standing here will not taste death before they see the Son of Man coming in his kingdom."

...s His Death

...at time on Jesus be... ...xplain to his disciples ...must go to Jerusalem and ...many things at the hands ...e elders, the chief priests ...d the teachers of the law, and ...at he must be killed and on the third day be raised to life.

22 Peter took him aside and began to rebuke him. "Never, Lord!" he said. "This shall never happen to you!"

23 Jesus turned and said to Peter, "Get behind me, Satan! You are a stumbling block to me; you do not have in mind the concerns of God, but merely human concerns."

24 Then Jesus said to his disciples, "Whoever wants to be my disciple must deny themselves and take up their cross and follow me. **25** For whoever wants to save their life[c] will lose it, but whoever loses their life for me will find it. **26** What good will it be for someone to gain the whole world, yet forfeit their soul? Or what can anyone give in exchange for their

The Transfiguration

17 After six days Jesus took with him Peter, James and John the brother of James, and led them up a high mountain by themselves. **2** There he was transfigured before them. His face shone like the sun, and his clothes became as white as the light. **3** Just then there appeared before them Moses and Elijah, talking with Jesus.

4 Peter said to Jesus, "Lord, it is good for us to be here. If you wish, I will put up three shelters — one for you, one for Moses and one for Elijah."

5 While he was still speaking, a bright cloud covered them, and a voice from the cloud said, "This is my Son, whom I love; with him I am well pleased. Listen to him!"

6 When the disciples heard this, they fell facedown to the ground, terrified. **7** But Jesus came and touched them. "Get up," he said. "Don't be afraid." **8** When they looked up, they saw no one except Jesus.

---

[a] 18 That is, the realm of the dead word means either *life* or *soul*; also in verse 26.   [b] 19 Or *will have been*   [c] 25 The Greek

⁹As they were coming down the mountain, Jesus instructed them, "Don't tell anyone what you have seen, until the Son of Man has been raised from the dead."

¹⁰The disciples asked him, "Why then do the teachers of the law say that Elijah must come first?"

¹¹Jesus replied, "To be sure, Elijah comes and will restore all things. ¹²But I tell you, Elijah has already come, and they did not recognize him, but have done to him everything they wished. In the same way the Son of Man is going to suffer at their hands." ¹³Then the disciples understood that he was talking to them about John the Baptist.

Jesus Heals a Demon-Possessed Boy

¹⁴When they came to the crowd, a man approached Jesus and knelt before him. ¹⁵"Lord, have mercy on my son," he said. "He has seizures and is suffering greatly. He often falls into the fire or into the water. ¹⁶I brought him to your disciples, but they could not heal him."

¹⁷"You unbelieving and perverse generation," Jesus replied, "how long shall I stay with you? How long shall I put up with you? Bring the boy here to me." ¹⁸Jesus rebuked the demon, and it came out of the boy, and he was healed at that moment.

¹⁹Then the disciples came to Jesus in private and asked, "Why couldn't we drive it out?"

²⁰He replied, "Because you have so little faith. Truly I tell you, if you have faith as small as a mustard seed, you can say to this mountain, 'Move from here to there,' and it will move. Nothing will be impossible for you." [21] a

Jesus Predicts His Death a Second Time

²²When they came together in Galilee, he said to them, "The Son of Man is going to be delivered into the hands of men. ²³They will kill him, and on the third day he will be raised to life." And the disciples were filled with grief.

The Temple Tax

²⁴After Jesus and his disciples arrived in Capernaum, the collectors of the two-drachma temple tax came to Peter and asked, "Doesn't your teacher pay the temple tax?"

²⁵"Yes, he does," he replied.

When Peter came into the house, Jesus was the first to speak. "What do you think, Simon?" he asked. "From whom do the kings of the earth collect duty and taxes — from their own children or from others?"

²⁶"From others," Peter answered.

"Then the children are exempt," Jesus said to him. ²⁷"But so that we may not cause offense, go to

---

a 21 Some manuscripts include here words similar to Mark 9:29.

the lake and throw out your line. Take the first fish you catch; open its mouth and you will find a four-drachma coin. Take it and give it to them for my tax and yours."

The Greatest in the Kingdom of Heaven

18 At that time the disciples came to Jesus and asked, "Who, then, is the greatest in the kingdom of heaven?"

2 He called a little child to him, and placed the child among them. **3** And he said: "Truly I tell you, unless you change and become like little children, you will never enter the kingdom of heaven. **4** Therefore, whoever takes the lowly position of this child is the greatest in the kingdom of heaven. **5** And whoever welcomes one such child in my name welcomes me.

Causing to Stumble

6 "If anyone causes one of these little ones — those who believe in me — to stumble, it would be better for them to have a large millstone hung around their neck and to be drowned in the depths of the sea. **7** Woe to the world because of the things that cause people to stumble! Such things must come, but woe to the person through whom they come! **8** If your hand or your foot causes you to stumble, cut it off and throw it away. It is better for you to enter life maimed or crippled than to have two hands or two feet and be thrown into eternal fire. **9** And if your eye causes you to stumble, gouge it out and throw it away. It is better for you to enter life with one eye than to have two eyes and be thrown into the fire of hell.

The Parable of the Wandering Sheep

10 "See that you do not despise one of these little ones. For I tell you that their angels in heaven always see the face of my Father in heaven. [11] *a*

12 "What do you think? If a man owns a hundred sheep, and one of them wanders away, will he not leave the ninety-nine on the hills and go to look for the one that wandered off? **13** And if he finds it, truly I tell you, he is happier about that one sheep than about the ninety-nine that did not wander off. **14** In the same way your Father in heaven is not willing that any of these little ones should perish.

Dealing With Sin in the Church

15 "If your brother or sister *b* sins, *c* go and point out their fault, just between the two of you. If they listen to you, you have won them over. **16** But if they will not listen, take one or two others along, so that 'every matter may be estab-

---

a 11 Some manuscripts include here the words of Luke 19:10.   *b* 15 The Greek word for *brother or sister* (*adelphos*) refers here to a fellow disciple, whether man or woman; also in verses 21 and 35.   *c* 15 Some manuscripts *sins against you* lished by the testimony of two or three witnesses.'[a] [17] If they still refuse to listen, tell it to the church; and if they refuse to listen even to the church, treat them as you would a pagan or a tax collector.

[18] "Truly I tell you, whatever you bind on earth will be[b] bound in heaven, and whatever you loose on earth will be[b] loosed in heaven.

[19] "Again, truly I tell you that if two of you on earth agree about anything they ask for, it will be done for them by my Father in heaven. [20] For where two or three gather in my name, there am I with them."

The Parable of the Unmerciful Servant

[21] Then Peter came to Jesus and asked, "Lord, how many times shall I forgive my brother or sister who sins against me? Up to seven times?"

[22] Jesus answered, "I tell you, not seven times, but seventy-seven times.[c]

[23] "Therefore, the kingdom of heaven is like a king who wanted to settle accounts with his servants. [24] As he began the settlement, a man who owed him ten thousand bags of gold[d] was brought to him. [25] Since he was not able to pay, the master ordered that he and his wife and his children and all that he had be sold to repay the debt.

[26] "At this the servant fell on his knees before him. 'Be patient with me,' he begged, 'and I will pay back everything.' [27] The servant's master took pity on him, canceled the debt and let him go.

[28] "But when that servant went out, he found one of his fellow servants who owed him a hundred silver coins.[e] He grabbed him and began to choke him. 'Pay back what you owe me!' he demanded.

[29] "His fellow servant fell to his knees and begged him, 'Be patient with me, and I will pay it back.'

[30] "But he refused. Instead, he went off and had the man thrown into prison until he could pay the debt. [31] When the other servants saw what had happened, they were outraged and went and told their master everything that had happened.

[32] "Then the master called the servant in. 'You wicked servant,' he said, 'I canceled all that debt of yours because you begged me to. [33] Shouldn't you have had mercy on your fellow servant just as I had on you?' [34] In anger his master handed him over to the jailers to be tortured, until he should pay back all he owed.

[35] "This is how my heavenly Father will treat each of you unless you forgive your brother or sister from your heart."

---

[a] 16 Deut. 19:15   [b] 18 Or *will have been*   [c] 22 Or *seventy times seven*
[d] 24 Greek *ten thousand talents*; a talent was worth about 20 years of a day laborer's wages.   [e] 28 Greek *a hundred denarii*; a denarius was the usual daily wage of a day laborer (see 20:2).

Divorce

19 When Jesus had finished saying these things, he left Galilee and went into the region of Judea to the other side of the Jordan. ²Large crowds followed him, and he healed them there.

³Some Pharisees came to him to test him. They asked, "Is it lawful for a man to divorce his wife for any and every reason?"

⁴"Haven't you read," he replied, "that at the beginning the Creator 'made them male and female,'ᵃ ⁵and said, 'For this reason a man will leave his father and mother and be united to his wife, and the two will become one flesh'ᵇ? ⁶So they are no longer two, but one flesh. Therefore what God has joined together, let no one separate."

⁷"Why then," they asked, "did Moses command that a man give his wife a certificate of divorce and send her away?"

⁸Jesus replied, "Moses permitted you to divorce your wives because your hearts were hard. But it was not this way from the beginning. ⁹I tell you that anyone who divorces his wife, except for sexual immorality, and marries another woman commits adultery."

¹⁰The disciples said to him, "If this is the situation between a husband and wife, it is better not to marry."

¹¹Jesus replied, "Not everyone can accept this word, but only those to whom it has been given. ¹²For there are eunuchs who were born that way, and there are eunuchs who have been made eunuchs by others—and there are those who choose to live like eunuchs for the sake of the kingdom of heaven. The one who can accept this should accept it."

The Little Children and Jesus

¹³Then people brought little children to Jesus for him to place his hands on them and pray for them. But the disciples rebuked them.

¹⁴Jesus said, "Let the little children come to me, and do not hinder them, for the kingdom of heaven belongs to such as these." ¹⁵When he had placed his hands on them, he went on from there.

The Rich and the Kingdom of God

¹⁶Just then a man came up to Jesus and asked, "Teacher, what good thing must I do to get eternal life?"

¹⁷"Why do you ask me about what is good?" Jesus replied. "There is only One who is good. If you want to enter life, keep the commandments."

¹⁸"Which ones?" he inquired.

Jesus replied, "'You shall not murder, you shall not commit adultery, you shall not steal, you shall not give false testimony, ¹⁹honor your father and mother,'ᶜ

ᵃ 4 Gen. 1:27   ᵇ 5 Gen. 2:24   ᶜ 19 Exodus 20:12-16; Deut. 5:16-20 and 'love your neighbor as your-self.'^a"

20 "All these I have kept," the young man said. "What do I still lack?"

21 Jesus answered, "If you want to be perfect, go, sell your posses-sions and give to the poor, and you will have treasure in heaven. Then come, follow me."

22 When the young man heard this, he went away sad, because he had great wealth.

23 Then Jesus said to his disci-ples, "Truly I tell you, it is hard for someone who is rich to enter the kingdom of heaven. 24 Again I tell you, it is easier for a camel to go through the eye of a needle than for someone who is rich to enter the kingdom of God."

25 When the disciples heard this, they were greatly aston-ished and asked, "Who then can be saved?"

26 Jesus looked at them and said, "With man this is impossi-ble, but with God all things are possible."

27 Peter answered him, "We have left everything to follow you! What then will there be for us?"

28 Jesus said to them, "Truly I tell you, at the renewal of all things, when the Son of Man sits on his glorious throne, you who have followed me will also sit on twelve thrones, judging the twelve tribes of Israel. 29 And everyone who has left houses or brothers or sis-ters or father or mother or wife^b or children or fields for my sake will receive a hundred times as much and will inherit eternal life. 30 But many who are first will be last, and many who are last will be first.

The Parable of the Workers in the Vineyard

20 "For the kingdom of heaven is like a land-owner who went out early in the morning to hire workers for his vineyard. 2 He agreed to pay them a denarius^c for the day and sent them into his vineyard.

3 "About nine in the morning he went out and saw others standing in the marketplace doing noth-ing. 4 He told them, 'You also go and work in my vineyard, and I will pay you whatever is right.' 5 So they went.

"He went out again about noon and about three in the afternoon and did the same thing. 6 About five in the afternoon he went out and found still others standing around. He asked them, 'Why have you been standing here all day long doing nothing?'

7 "'Because no one has hired us,' they answered.

"He said to them, 'You also go and work in my vineyard.'

8 "When evening came, the owner of the vineyard said to his

---

^a 19 Lev. 19:18   ^b 29 Some manuscripts do not have or wife.   ^c 2 A denarius was the usual daily wage of a day laborer.

foreman, 'Call the workers and pay them their wages, beginning with the last ones hired and going on to the first.'

9 "The workers who were hired about five in the afternoon came and each received a denarius. 10 So when those came who were hired first, they expected to receive more. But each one of them also received a denarius. 11 When they received it, they began to grumble against the landowner. 12 'These who were hired last worked only one hour,' they said, 'and you have made them equal to us who have borne the burden of the work and the heat of the day.'

13 "But he answered one of them, 'I am not being unfair to you, friend. Didn't you agree to work for a denarius? 14 Take your pay and go. I want to give the one who was hired last the same as I gave you. 15 Don't I have the right to do what I want with my own money? Or are you envious because I am generous?'

16 "So the last will be first, and the first will be last."

Jesus Predicts His Death a Third Time

17 Now Jesus was going up to Jerusalem. On the way, he took the Twelve aside and said to them, 18 "We are going up to Jerusalem, and the Son of Man will be delivered over to the chief priests and the teachers of the law. They will condemn him to death 19 and will hand him over to the Gentiles to be mocked and flogged and crucified. On the third day he will be raised to life!"

A Mother's Request

20 Then the mother of Zebedee's sons came to Jesus with her sons and, kneeling down, asked a favor of him.

21 "What is it you want?" he asked.

She said, "Grant that one of these two sons of mine may sit at your right and the other at your left in your kingdom."

22 "You don't know what you are asking," Jesus said to them. "Can you drink the cup I am going to drink?"

"We can," they answered.

23 Jesus said to them, "You will indeed drink from my cup, but to sit at my right or left is not for me to grant. These places belong to those for whom they have been prepared by my Father."

24 When the ten heard about this, they were indignant with the two brothers. 25 Jesus called them together and said, "You know that the rulers of the Gentiles lord it over them, and their high officials exercise authority over them. 26 Not so with you. Instead, whoever wants to become great among you must be your servant, 27 and whoever wants to be first must be your slave— 28 just as the Son of Man did not come to be served, but to serve, and to give his life as a ransom for many."

Two Blind Men Receive Sight

²⁹As Jesus and his disciples were leaving Jericho, a large crowd followed him. ³⁰Two blind men were sitting by the roadside, and when they heard that Jesus was going by, they shouted, "Lord, Son of David, have mercy on us!"

³¹The crowd rebuked them and told them to be quiet, but they shouted all the louder, "Lord, Son of David, have mercy on us!"

³²Jesus stopped and called them. "What do you want me to do for you?" he asked.

³³"Lord," they answered, "we want our sight."

³⁴Jesus had compassion on them and touched their eyes. Immediately they received their sight and followed him.

Jesus Comes to Jerusalem as King

21 As they approached Jerusalem and came to Bethphage on the Mount of Olives, Jesus sent two disciples, ²saying to them, "Go to the village ahead of you, and at once you will find a donkey tied there, with her colt by her. Untie them and bring them to me. ³If anyone says anything to you, say that the Lord needs them, and he will send them right away."

⁴This took place to fulfill what was spoken through the prophet:

⁵"Say to Daughter Zion,
  'See, your king comes to you,
gentle and riding on a donkey,
  and on a colt, the foal of a
  donkey.' "ᵃ

⁶The disciples went and did as Jesus had instructed them. ⁷They brought the donkey and the colt and placed their cloaks on them for Jesus to sit on. ⁸A very large crowd spread their cloaks on the road, while others cut branches from the trees and spread them on the road. ⁹The crowds that went ahead of him and those that followed shouted,

"Hosannaᵇ to the Son of
  David!"

"Blessed is he who comes in
  the name of the Lord!"ᶜ

"Hosannaᵇ in the highest
  heaven!"

¹⁰When Jesus entered Jerusalem, the whole city was stirred and asked, "Who is this?"

¹¹The crowds answered, "This is Jesus, the prophet from Nazareth in Galilee."

Jesus at the Temple

¹²Jesus entered the temple courts and drove out all who were buying and selling there. He overturned the tables of the money changers and the benches of those selling doves. ¹³"It is written," he said to them, " 'My

---

ᵃ 5 Zech. 9:9   ᵇ 9 A Hebrew expression meaning "Save!" which became an exclamation of praise; also in verse 15   ᶜ 9 Psalm 118:25,26 house will be called a house of prayer,'*a* but you are making it 'a den of robbers.'*b*"

¹⁴The blind and the lame came to him at the temple, and he healed them. ¹⁵But when the chief priests and the teachers of the law saw the wonderful things he did and the children shouting in the temple courts, "Hosanna to the Son of David," they were indignant.

¹⁶"Do you hear what these children are saying?" they asked him.

"Yes," replied Jesus, "have you never read,

"'From the lips of children and infants
you, Lord, have called forth your praise'*c*?"

¹⁷And he left them and went out of the city to Bethany, where he spent the night.

Jesus Curses a Fig Tree

¹⁸Early in the morning, as Jesus was on his way back to the city, he was hungry. ¹⁹Seeing a fig tree by the road, he went up to it but found nothing on it except leaves. Then he said to it, "May you never bear fruit again!" Immediately the tree withered.

²⁰When the disciples saw this, they were amazed. "How did the fig tree wither so quickly?" they asked.

²¹Jesus replied, "Truly I tell you, if you have faith and do not doubt, not only can you do what was done to the fig tree, but also you can say to this mountain, 'Go, throw yourself into the sea,' and it will be done. ²²If you believe, you will receive whatever you ask for in prayer."

The Authority of Jesus Questioned

²³Jesus entered the temple courts, and, while he was teaching, the chief priests and the elders of the people came to him. "By what authority are you doing these things?" they asked. "And who gave you this authority?"

²⁴Jesus replied, "I will also ask you one question. If you answer me, I will tell you by what authority I am doing these things. ²⁵John's baptism—where did it come from? Was it from heaven, or of human origin?"

They discussed it among themselves and said, "If we say, 'From heaven,' he will ask, 'Then why didn't you believe him?' ²⁶But if we say, 'Of human origin'—we are afraid of the people, for they all hold that John was a prophet."

²⁷So they answered Jesus, "We don't know."

Then he said, "Neither will I tell you by what authority I am doing these things.

The Parable of the Two Sons

²⁸"What do you think? There was a man who had two sons. He

a 13 Isaiah 56:7   *b* 13 Jer. 7:11   *c* 16 Psalm 8:2 (see Septuagint) went to the first and said, 'Son, go and work today in the vineyard.'

²⁹ "'I will not,' he answered, but later he changed his mind and went.

³⁰ "Then the father went to the other son and said the same thing. He answered, 'I will, sir,' but he did not go.

³¹ "Which of the two did what his father wanted?"

"The first," they answered.

Jesus said to them, "Truly I tell you, the tax collectors and the prostitutes are entering the kingdom of God ahead of you. ³²For John came to you to show you the way of righteousness, and you did not believe him, but the tax collectors and the prostitutes did. And even after you saw this, you did not repent and believe him.

The Parable of the Tenants

³³ "Listen to another parable: There was a landowner who planted a vineyard. He put a wall around it, dug a winepress in it and built a watchtower. Then he rented the vineyard to some farmers and moved to another place. ³⁴When the harvest time approached, he sent his servants to the tenants to collect his fruit.

³⁵ "The tenants seized his servants; they beat one, killed another, and stoned a third. ³⁶Then he sent other servants to them, more than the first time, and the tenants treated them the same

way. ³⁷Last of all, he sent his son to them. 'They will respect my son,' he said.

³⁸ "But when the tenants saw the son, they said to each other, 'This is the heir. Come, let's kill him and take his inheritance.' ³⁹So they took him and threw him out of the vineyard and killed him.

⁴⁰ "Therefore, when the owner of the vineyard comes, what will he do to those tenants?"

⁴¹ "He will bring those wretches to a wretched end," they replied, "and he will rent the vineyard to other tenants, who will give him his share of the crop at harvest time."

⁴²Jesus said to them, "Have you never read in the Scriptures:

" 'The stone the builders
    rejected
  has become the cornerstone;
the Lord has done this,
  and it is marvelous in our
    eyes'ᵃ?

⁴³ "Therefore I tell you that the kingdom of God will be taken away from you and given to a people who will produce its fruit. ⁴⁴Anyone who falls on this stone will be broken to pieces; anyone on whom it falls will be crushed."ᵇ

⁴⁵When the chief priests and the Pharisees heard Jesus' parables, they knew he was talking about them. ⁴⁶They looked for a

---

ᵃ 42 Psalm 118:22,23   ᵇ 44 Some manuscripts do not have verse 44.

way to arrest him, but they were afraid of the crowd because the people held that he was a prophet.

The Parable of the Wedding Banquet

22 Jesus spoke to them again in parables, saying: ² "The kingdom of heaven is like a king who prepared a wedding banquet for his son. ³ He sent his servants to those who had been invited to the banquet to tell them to come, but they refused to come.

⁴ "Then he sent some more servants and said, 'Tell those who have been invited that I have prepared my dinner: My oxen and fattened cattle have been butchered, and everything is ready. Come to the wedding banquet.'

⁵ "But they paid no attention and went off — one to his field, another to his business. ⁶ The rest seized his servants, mistreated them and killed them. ⁷ The king was enraged. He sent his army and destroyed those murderers and burned their city.

⁸ "Then he said to his servants, 'The wedding banquet is ready, but those I invited did not deserve to come. ⁹ So go to the street corners and invite to the banquet anyone you find.' ¹⁰ So the servants went out into the streets and gathered all the people they could find, the bad as well as the good, and the wedding hall was filled with guests.

¹¹ "But when the king came in to see the guests, he noticed a man there who was not wearing wedding clothes. ¹² He asked, 'How did you get in here without wedding clothes, friend?' The man was speechless.

¹³ "Then the king told the attendants, 'Tie him hand and foot, and throw him outside, into the darkness, where there will be weeping and gnashing of teeth.'

¹⁴ "For many are invited, but few are chosen."

Paying the Imperial Tax to Caesar

¹⁵ Then the Pharisees went out and laid plans to trap him in his words. ¹⁶ They sent their disciples to him along with the Herodians. "Teacher," they said, "we know that you are a man of integrity and that you teach the way of God in accordance with the truth. You aren't swayed by others, because you pay no attention to who they are. ¹⁷ Tell us then, what is your opinion? Is it right to pay the imperial tax[a] to Caesar or not?"

¹⁸ But Jesus, knowing their evil intent, said, "You hypocrites, why are you trying to trap me? ¹⁹ Show me the coin used for paying the tax." They brought him a denarius, ²⁰ and he asked them, "Whose image is this? And whose inscription?"

²¹ "Caesar's," they replied.

Then he said to them, "So give

ᵃ 17 A special tax levied on subject peoples, not on Roman citizens back to Caesar what is Caesar's, and to God what is God's."

²²When they heard this, they were amazed. So they left him and went away.

Marriage at the Resurrection

²³That same day the Sadducees, who say there is no resurrection, came to him with a question. ²⁴"Teacher," they said, "Moses told us that if a man dies without having children, his brother must marry the widow and raise up offspring for him. ²⁵Now there were seven brothers among us. The first one married and died, and since he had no children, he left his wife to his brother. ²⁶The same thing happened to the second and third brother, right on down to the seventh. ²⁷Finally, the woman died. ²⁸Now then, at the resurrection, whose wife will she be of the seven, since all of them were married to her?"

²⁹Jesus replied, "You are in error because you do not know the Scriptures or the power of God. ³⁰At the resurrection people will neither marry nor be given in marriage; they will be like the angels in heaven. ³¹But about the resurrection of the dead—have you not read what God said to you, ³²'I am the God of Abraham, the God of Isaac, and the God of Jacob'ᵃ? He is not the God of the dead but of the living."

³³When the crowds heard this, they were astonished at his teaching.

The Greatest Commandment

³⁴Hearing that Jesus had silenced the Sadducees, the Pharisees got together. ³⁵One of them, an expert in the law, tested him with this question: ³⁶"Teacher, which is the greatest commandment in the Law?"

³⁷Jesus replied: "'Love the Lord your God with all your heart and with all your soul and with all your mind.'ᵇ ³⁸This is the first and greatest commandment. ³⁹And the second is like it: 'Love your neighbor as yourself.'ᶜ ⁴⁰All the Law and the Prophets hang on these two commandments."

Whose Son Is the Messiah?

⁴¹While the Pharisees were gathered together, Jesus asked them, ⁴²"What do you think about the Messiah? Whose son is he?"

"The son of David," they replied.

⁴³He said to them, "How is it then that David, speaking by the Spirit, calls him 'Lord'? For he says,

⁴⁴"'The Lord said to my Lord:
  "Sit at my right hand
until I put your enemies
  under your feet."'ᵈ

⁴⁵If then David calls him 'Lord,' how can he be his son?" ⁴⁶No one

---

ᵃ 32 Exodus 3:6   ᵇ 37 Deut. 6:5   ᶜ 39 Lev. 19:18   ᵈ 44 Psalm 110:1

could say a word in reply, and from that day on no one dared to ask him any more questions.

A Warning Against Hypocrisy

23 Then Jesus said to the crowds and to his disciples: ²"The teachers of the law and the Pharisees sit in Moses' seat. ³So you must be careful to do everything they tell you. But do not do what they do, for they do not practice what they preach. ⁴They tie up heavy, cumbersome loads and put them on other people's shoulders, but they themselves are not willing to lift a finger to move them.

⁵"Everything they do is done for people to see: They make their phylacteries*ᵃ* wide and the tassels on their garments long; ⁶they love the place of honor at banquets and the most important seats in the synagogues; ⁷they love to be greeted with respect in the marketplaces and to be called 'Rabbi' by others.

⁸"But you are not to be called 'Rabbi,' for you have one Teacher, and you are all brothers. ⁹And do not call anyone on earth 'father,' for you have one Father, and he is in heaven. ¹⁰Nor are you to be called instructors, for you have one Instructor, the Messiah. ¹¹The greatest among you will be your servant. ¹²For those who exalt themselves will be humbled, and those who humble themselves will be exalted.

Seven Woes on the Teachers of the Law and the Pharisees

¹³"Woe to you, teachers of the law and Pharisees, you hypocrites! You shut the door of the kingdom of heaven in people's faces. You yourselves do not enter, nor will you let those enter who are trying to. [14]ᵇ

¹⁵"Woe to you, teachers of the law and Pharisees, you hypocrites! You travel over land and sea to win a single convert, and when you have succeeded, you make them twice as much a child of hell as you are.

¹⁶"Woe to you, blind guides! You say, 'If anyone swears by the temple, it means nothing; but anyone who swears by the gold of the temple is bound by that oath.' ¹⁷You blind fools! Which is greater: the gold, or the temple that makes the gold sacred? ¹⁸You also say, 'If anyone swears by the altar, it means nothing; but anyone who swears by the gift on the altar is bound by that oath.' ¹⁹You blind men! Which is greater: the gift, or the altar that makes the gift sacred? ²⁰Therefore, anyone who swears by the altar swears by it and by everything on it. ²¹And anyone who swears by the temple swears by it and by the one who dwells in

ᵃ 5 That is, boxes containing Scripture verses, worn on forehead and arm
ᵇ 14 Some manuscripts include here words similar to Mark 12:40 and Luke 20:47.

it. [22] And anyone who swears by heaven swears by God's throne and by the one who sits on it.

[23] "Woe to you, teachers of the law and Pharisees, you hypocrites! You give a tenth of your spices — mint, dill and cumin. But you have neglected the more important matters of the law — justice, mercy and faithfulness. You should have practiced the latter, without neglecting the former. [24] You blind guides! You strain out a gnat but swallow a camel.

[25] "Woe to you, teachers of the law and Pharisees, you hypocrites! You clean the outside of the cup and dish, but inside they are full of greed and self-indulgence. [26] Blind Pharisee! First clean the inside of the cup and dish, and then the outside also will be clean.

[27] "Woe to you, teachers of the law and Pharisees, you hypocrites! You are like whitewashed tombs, which look beautiful on the outside but on the inside are full of the bones of the dead and everything unclean. [28] In the same way, on the outside you appear to people as righteous but on the inside you are full of hypocrisy and wickedness.

[29] "Woe to you, teachers of the law and Pharisees, you hypocrites! You build tombs for the prophets and decorate the graves of the righteous. [30] And you say, 'If we had lived in the days of our ancestors, we would not have tak-

en part with them in shedding the blood of the prophets.' [31] So you testify against yourselves that you are the descendants of those who murdered the prophets. [32] Go ahead, then, and complete what your ancestors started!

[33] "You snakes! You brood of vipers! How will you escape being condemned to hell? [34] Therefore I am sending you prophets and sages and teachers. Some of them you will kill and crucify; others you will flog in your synagogues and pursue from town to town. [35] And so upon you will come all the righteous blood that has been shed on earth, from the blood of righteous Abel to the blood of Zechariah son of Berekiah, whom you murdered between the temple and the altar. [36] Truly I tell you, all this will come on this generation.

[37] "Jerusalem, Jerusalem, you who kill the prophets and stone those sent to you, how often I have longed to gather your children together, as a hen gathers her chicks under her wings, and you were not willing. [38] Look, your house is left to you desolate. [39] For I tell you, you will not see me again until you say, 'Blessed is he who comes in the name of the Lord.'[a]"

The Destruction of the Temple and Signs of the End Times

24 Jesus left the temple and was walking away when his disciples came up to him to

[a] 39 Psalm 118:26

call his attention to its buildings. [2]"Do you see all these things?" he asked. "Truly I tell you, not one stone here will be left on another; every one will be thrown down."

[3]As Jesus was sitting on the Mount of Olives, the disciples came to him privately. "Tell us," they said, "when will this happen, and what will be the sign of your coming and of the end of the age?"

[4]Jesus answered: "Watch out that no one deceives you. [5]For many will come in my name, claiming, 'I am the Messiah,' and will deceive many. [6]You will hear of wars and rumors of wars, but see to it that you are not alarmed. Such things must happen, but the end is still to come. [7]Nation will rise against nation, and kingdom against kingdom. There will be famines and earthquakes in various places. [8]All these are the beginning of birth pains.

[9]"Then you will be handed over to be persecuted and put to death, and you will be hated by all nations because of me. [10]At that time many will turn away from the faith and will betray and hate each other, [11]and many false prophets will appear and deceive many people. [12]Because of the increase of wickedness, the love of most will grow cold, [13]but the one who stands firm to the end will be saved. [14]And this gospel of the kingdom will be preached in the whole world as a testimony to all nations, and then the end will come.

[15]"So when you see standing in the holy place 'the abomination that causes desolation,'[a] spoken of through the prophet Daniel—let the reader understand— [16]then let those who are in Judea flee to the mountains. [17]Let no one on the housetop go down to take anything out of the house. [18]Let no one in the field go back to get their cloak. [19]How dreadful it will be in those days for pregnant women and nursing mothers! [20]Pray that your flight will not take place in winter or on the Sabbath. [21]For then there will be great distress, unequaled from the beginning of the world until now—and never to be equaled again.

[22]"If those days had not been cut short, no one would survive, but for the sake of the elect those days will be shortened. [23]At that time if anyone says to you, 'Look, here is the Messiah!' or, 'There he is!' do not believe it. [24]For false messiahs and false prophets will appear and perform great signs and wonders to deceive, if possible, even the elect. [25]See, I have told you ahead of time.

[26]"So if anyone tells you, 'There he is, out in the wilderness,' do not go out; or, 'Here he is, in the inner rooms,' do not believe it. [27]For as lightning that comes from the east is visible even in the west, so will be the coming of the

[a] 15 Daniel 9:27; 11:31; 12:11

Son of Man. **28** Wherever there is a carcass, there the vultures will gather.

29 "Immediately after the distress of those days

" 'the sun will be darkened,
and the moon will not give
its light;
the stars will fall from the sky,
and the heavenly bodies will
be shaken.'[a]

30 "Then will appear the sign of the Son of Man in heaven. And then all the peoples of the earth[b] will mourn when they see the Son of Man coming on the clouds of heaven, with power and great glory.[c] **31** And he will send his angels with a loud trumpet call, and they will gather his elect from the four winds, from one end of the heavens to the other.

32 "Now learn this lesson from the fig tree: As soon as its twigs get tender and its leaves come out, you know that summer is near. **33** Even so, when you see all these things, you know that it[d] is near, right at the door. **34** Truly I tell you, this generation will certainly not pass away until all these things have happened. **35** Heaven and earth will pass away, but my words will never pass away.

The Day and Hour Unknown

36 "But about that day or hour no one knows, not even the angels in heaven, nor the Son,[e] but only the Father. **37** As it was in the days of Noah, so it will be at the coming of the Son of Man. **38** For in the days before the flood, people were eating and drinking, marrying and giving in marriage, up to the day Noah entered the ark; **39** and they knew nothing about what would happen until the flood came and took them all away. That is how it will be at the coming of the Son of Man. **40** Two men will be in the field; one will be taken and the other left. **41** Two women will be grinding with a hand mill; one will be taken and the other left.

42 "Therefore keep watch, because you do not know on what day your Lord will come. **43** But understand this: If the owner of the house had known at what time of night the thief was coming, he would have kept watch and would not have let his house be broken into. **44** So you also must be ready, because the Son of Man will come at an hour when you do not expect him.

45 "Who then is the faithful and wise servant, whom the master has put in charge of the servants in his household to give them their food at the proper time? **46** It will be good for that servant whose master finds him doing so when he returns. **47** Truly I tell you, he will put him in charge of all his possessions. **48** But suppose that

---

[a] 29 Isaiah 13:10; 34:4   [b] 30 Or *the tribes of the land*   [c] 30 See Daniel 7:13-14.
[d] 33 Or *he*   [e] 36 Some manuscripts do not have *nor the Son*.

servant is wicked and says to himself, 'My master is staying away a long time,' ⁴⁹and he then begins to beat his fellow servants and to eat and drink with drunkards. ⁵⁰The master of that servant will come on a day when he does not expect him and at an hour he is not aware of. ⁵¹He will cut him to pieces and assign him a place with the hypocrites, where there will be weeping and gnashing of teeth.

The Parable of the Ten Virgins

25 "At that time the kingdom of heaven will be like ten virgins who took their lamps and went out to meet the bridegroom. ²Five of them were foolish and five were wise. ³The foolish ones took their lamps but did not take any oil with them. ⁴The wise ones, however, took oil in jars along with their lamps. ⁵The bridegroom was a long time in coming, and they all became drowsy and fell asleep.

⁶"At midnight the cry rang out: 'Here's the bridegroom! Come out to meet him!'

⁷"Then all the virgins woke up and trimmed their lamps. ⁸The foolish ones said to the wise, 'Give us some of your oil; our lamps are going out.'

⁹"'No,' they replied, 'there may not be enough for both us and you. Instead, go to those who sell oil and buy some for yourselves.'

¹⁰"But while they were on their way to buy the oil, the bridegroom arrived. The virgins who were ready went in with him to the wedding banquet. And the door was shut.

¹¹"Later the others also came. 'Lord, Lord,' they said, 'open the door for us!'

¹²"But he replied, 'Truly I tell you, I don't know you.'

¹³"Therefore keep watch, because you do not know the day or the hour.

The Parable of the Bags of Gold

¹⁴"Again, it will be like a man going on a journey, who called his servants and entrusted his wealth to them. ¹⁵To one he gave five bags of gold, to another two bags, and to another one bag,ᵃ each according to his ability. Then he went on his journey. ¹⁶The man who had received five bags of gold went at once and put his money to work and gained five bags more. ¹⁷So also, the one with two bags of gold gained two more. ¹⁸But the man who had received one bag went off, dug a hole in the ground and hid his master's money.

¹⁹"After a long time the master of those servants returned and settled accounts with them. ²⁰The man who had received five bags of gold brought the other five. 'Master,' he said, 'you en-

---

ᵃ 15 Greek *five talents . . . two talents . . . one talent*; also throughout this parable; a talent was worth about 20 years of a day laborer's wage.

trusted me with five bags of gold. See, I have gained five more.'

21 "His master replied, 'Well done, good and faithful servant! You have been faithful with a few things; I will put you in charge of many things. Come and share your master's happiness!'

22 "The man with two bags of gold also came. 'Master,' he said, 'you entrusted me with two bags of gold; see, I have gained two more.'

23 "His master replied, 'Well done, good and faithful servant! You have been faithful with a few things; I will put you in charge of many things. Come and share your master's happiness!'

24 "Then the man who had received one bag of gold came. 'Master,' he said, 'I knew that you are a hard man, harvesting where you have not sown and gathering where you have not scattered seed. 25 So I was afraid and went out and hid your gold in the ground. See, here is what belongs to you.'

26 "His master replied, 'You wicked, lazy servant! So you knew that I harvest where I have not sown and gather where I have not scattered seed? 27 Well then, you should have put my money on deposit with the bankers, so that when I returned I would have received it back with interest.

28 " 'So take the bag of gold from him and give it to the one who has ten bags. 29 For whoever has will be given more, and they will have an abundance. Whoever does not have, even what they have will be taken from them. 30 And throw that worthless servant outside, into the darkness, where there will be weeping and gnashing of teeth.'

The Sheep and the Goats

31 "When the Son of Man comes in his glory, and all the angels with him, he will sit on his glorious throne. 32 All the nations will be gathered before him, and he will separate the people one from another as a shepherd separates the sheep from the goats. 33 He will put the sheep on his right and the goats on his left.

34 "Then the King will say to those on his right, 'Come, you who are blessed by my Father; take your inheritance, the kingdom prepared for you since the creation of the world. 35 For I was hungry and you gave me something to eat, I was thirsty and you gave me something to drink, I was a stranger and you invited me in, 36 I needed clothes and you clothed me, I was sick and you looked after me, I was in prison and you came to visit me.'

37 "Then the righteous will answer him, 'Lord, when did we see you hungry and feed you, or thirsty and give you something to drink? 38 When did we see you a stranger and invite you in, or needing clothes and clothe you?

[39] When did we see you sick or in prison and go to visit you?'

[40] "The King will reply, 'Truly I tell you, whatever you did for one of the least of these brothers and sisters of mine, you did for me.'

[41] "Then he will say to those on his left, 'Depart from me, you who are cursed, into the eternal fire prepared for the devil and his angels. [42] For I was hungry and you gave me nothing to eat, I was thirsty and you gave me nothing to drink, [43] I was a stranger and you did not invite me in, I needed clothes and you did not clothe me, I was sick and in prison and you did not look after me.'

[44] "They also will answer, 'Lord, when did we see you hungry or thirsty or a stranger or needing clothes or sick or in prison, and did not help you?'

[45] "He will reply, 'Truly I tell you, whatever you did not do for one of the least of these, you did not do for me.'

[46] "Then they will go away to eternal punishment, but the righteous to eternal life."

The Plot Against Jesus

26 When Jesus had finished saying all these things, he said to his disciples, [2] "As you know, the Passover is two days away — and the Son of Man will be handed over to be crucified."

[3] Then the chief priests and the elders of the people assembled in the palace of the high priest, whose name was Caiaphas, [4] and they schemed to arrest Jesus secretly and kill him. [5] "But not during the festival," they said, "or there may be a riot among the people."

Jesus Anointed at Bethany

[6] While Jesus was in Bethany in the home of Simon the Leper, [7] a woman came to him with an alabaster jar of very expensive perfume, which she poured on his head as he was reclining at the table.

[8] When the disciples saw this, they were indignant. "Why this waste?" they asked. [9] "This perfume could have been sold at a high price and the money given to the poor."

[10] Aware of this, Jesus said to them, "Why are you bothering this woman? She has done a beautiful thing to me. [11] The poor you will always have with you,[a] but you will not always have me. [12] When she poured this perfume on my body, she did it to prepare me for burial. [13] Truly I tell you, wherever this gospel is preached throughout the world, what she has done will also be told, in memory of her."

Judas Agrees to Betray Jesus

[14] Then one of the Twelve — the one called Judas Iscariot — went to the chief priests [15] and asked, "What are you willing to give me

[a] 11 See Deut. 15:11.

if I deliver him over to you?" So they counted out for him thirty pieces of silver. **16** From then on Judas watched for an opportunity to hand him over.

The Last Supper

17 On the first day of the Festival of Unleavened Bread, the disciples came to Jesus and asked, "Where do you want us to make preparations for you to eat the Passover?"

18 He replied, "Go into the city to a certain man and tell him, 'The Teacher says: My appointed time is near. I am going to celebrate the Passover with my disciples at your house.' " **19** So the disciples did as Jesus had directed them and prepared the Passover.

20 When evening came, Jesus was reclining at the table with the Twelve. **21** And while they were eating, he said, "Truly I tell you, one of you will betray me."

22 They were very sad and began to say to him one after the other, "Surely you don't mean me, Lord?"

23 Jesus replied, "The one who has dipped his hand into the bowl with me will betray me. **24** The Son of Man will go just as it is written about him. But woe to that man who betrays the Son of Man! It would be better for him if he had not been born."

25 Then Judas, the one who would betray him, said, "Surely you don't mean me, Rabbi?"

Jesus answered, "You have said so."

26 While they were eating, Jesus took bread, and when he had given thanks, he broke it and gave it to his disciples, saying, "Take and eat; this is my body."

27 Then he took a cup, and when he had given thanks, he gave it to them, saying, "Drink from it, all of you. **28** This is my blood of the[a] covenant, which is poured out for many for the forgiveness of sins. **29** I tell you, I will not drink from this fruit of the vine from now on until that day when I drink it new with you in my Father's kingdom."

30 When they had sung a hymn, they went out to the Mount of Olives.

Jesus Predicts Peter's Denial

31 Then Jesus told them, "This very night you will all fall away on account of me, for it is written:

" 'I will strike the shepherd,
   and the sheep of the flock
     will be scattered.'[b]

32 But after I have risen, I will go ahead of you into Galilee."

33 Peter replied, "Even if all fall away on account of you, I never will."

34 "Truly I tell you," Jesus answered, "this very night, before the rooster crows, you will disown me three times."

35 But Peter declared, "Even if I have to die with you, I will never

---

[a] 28 Some manuscripts *the new*   [b] 31 Zech. 13:7

disown you." And all the other disciples said the same.

Gethsemane

36 Then Jesus went with his disciples to a place called Gethsemane, and he said to them, "Sit here while I go over there and pray." **37** He took Peter and the two sons of Zebedee along with him, and he began to be sorrowful and troubled. **38** Then he said to them, "My soul is overwhelmed with sorrow to the point of death. Stay here and keep watch with me."

39 Going a little farther, he fell with his face to the ground and prayed, "My Father, if it is possible, may this cup be taken from me. Yet not as I will, but as you will."

40 Then he returned to his disciples and found them sleeping. "Couldn't you men keep watch with me for one hour?" he asked Peter. **41** "Watch and pray so that you will not fall into temptation. The spirit is willing, but the flesh is weak."

42 He went away a second time and prayed, "My Father, if it is not possible for this cup to be taken away unless I drink it, may your will be done."

43 When he came back, he again found them sleeping, because their eyes were heavy. **44** So he left them and went away once more and prayed the third time, saying the same thing.

45 Then he returned to the disciples and said to them, "Are you still sleeping and resting? Look, the hour has come, and the Son of Man is delivered into the hands of sinners. **46** Rise! Let us go! Here comes my betrayer!"

Jesus Arrested

47 While he was still speaking, Judas, one of the Twelve, arrived. With him was a large crowd armed with swords and clubs, sent from the chief priests and the elders of the people. **48** Now the betrayer had arranged a signal with them: "The one I kiss is the man; arrest him." **49** Going at once to Jesus, Judas said, "Greetings, Rabbi!" and kissed him.

50 Jesus replied, "Do what you came for, friend."[a]

Then the men stepped forward, seized Jesus and arrested him. **51** With that, one of Jesus' companions reached for his sword, drew it out and struck the servant of the high priest, cutting off his ear.

52 "Put your sword back in its place," Jesus said to him, "for all who draw the sword will die by the sword. **53** Do you think I cannot call on my Father, and he will at once put at my disposal more than twelve legions of angels? **54** But how then would the Scriptures be fulfilled that say it must happen in this way?"

55 In that hour Jesus said to the crowd, "Am I leading a rebel-

---

[a] 50 Or *"Why have you come, friend?"*

lion, that you have come out with swords and clubs to capture me? Every day I sat in the temple courts teaching, and you did not arrest me. ⁵⁶But this has all taken place that the writings of the prophets might be fulfilled." Then all the disciples deserted him and fled.

Jesus Before the Sanhedrin

⁵⁷Those who had arrested Jesus took him to Caiaphas the high priest, where the teachers of the law and the elders had assembled. ⁵⁸But Peter followed him at a distance, right up to the courtyard of the high priest. He entered and sat down with the guards to see the outcome.

⁵⁹The chief priests and the whole Sanhedrin were looking for false evidence against Jesus so that they could put him to death. ⁶⁰But they did not find any, though many false witnesses came forward.

Finally two came forward ⁶¹and declared, "This fellow said, 'I am able to destroy the temple of God and rebuild it in three days.'"

⁶²Then the high priest stood up and said to Jesus, "Are you not going to answer? What is this testimony that these men are bringing against you?" ⁶³But Jesus remained silent.

The high priest said to him, "I charge you under oath by the living God: Tell us if you are the Messiah, the Son of God."

⁶⁴"You have said so," Jesus replied. "But I say to all of you: From now on you will see the Son of Man sitting at the right hand of the Mighty One and coming on the clouds of heaven."[a]

⁶⁵Then the high priest tore his clothes and said, "He has spoken blasphemy! Why do we need any more witnesses? Look, now you have heard the blasphemy. ⁶⁶What do you think?"

"He is worthy of death," they answered.

⁶⁷Then they spit in his face and struck him with their fists. Others slapped him ⁶⁸and said, "Prophesy to us, Messiah. Who hit you?"

Peter Disowns Jesus

⁶⁹Now Peter was sitting out in the courtyard, and a servant girl came to him. "You also were with Jesus of Galilee," she said.

⁷⁰But he denied it before them all. "I don't know what you're talking about," he said.

⁷¹Then he went out to the gateway, where another servant girl saw him and said to the people there, "This fellow was with Jesus of Nazareth."

⁷²He denied it again, with an oath: "I don't know the man!"

⁷³After a little while, those standing there went up to Peter and said, "Surely you are one of them; your accent gives you away."

⁷⁴Then he began to call down

[a] 64 See Psalm 110:1; Daniel 7:13.

curses, and he swore to them, "I don't know the man!"

Immediately a rooster crowed. [75]Then Peter remembered the word Jesus had spoken: "Before the rooster crows, you will disown me three times." And he went outside and wept bitterly.

Judas Hangs Himself

27 Early in the morning, all the chief priests and the elders of the people made their plans how to have Jesus executed. [2]So they bound him, led him away and handed him over to Pilate the governor.

[3]When Judas, who had betrayed him, saw that Jesus was condemned, he was seized with remorse and returned the thirty pieces of silver to the chief priests and the elders. [4]"I have sinned," he said, "for I have betrayed innocent blood."

"What is that to us?" they replied. "That's your responsibility."

[5]So Judas threw the money into the temple and left. Then he went away and hanged himself.

[6]The chief priests picked up the coins and said, "It is against the law to put this into the treasury, since it is blood money." [7]So they decided to use the money to buy the potter's field as a burial place for foreigners. [8]That is why it has been called the Field of Blood to this day. [9]Then what was spoken by Jeremiah the prophet was fulfilled: "They took the thirty pieces of silver, the price set on him by the people of Israel, [10]and they used them to buy the potter's field, as the Lord commanded me."[a]

Jesus Before Pilate

[11]Meanwhile Jesus stood before the governor, and the governor asked him, "Are you the king of the Jews?"

"You have said so," Jesus replied.

[12]When he was accused by the chief priests and the elders, he gave no answer. [13]Then Pilate asked him, "Don't you hear the testimony they are bringing against you?" [14]But Jesus made no reply, not even to a single charge — to the great amazement of the governor.

[15]Now it was the governor's custom at the festival to release a prisoner chosen by the crowd. [16]At that time they had a well-known prisoner whose name was Jesus[b] Barabbas. [17]So when the crowd had gathered, Pilate asked them, "Which one do you want me to release to you: Jesus Barabbas, or Jesus who is called the Messiah?" [18]For he knew it was out of self-interest that they had handed Jesus over to him.

[19]While Pilate was sitting on the judge's seat, his wife sent him this message: "Don't have any-

[a] 10 See Zech. 11:12,13; Jer. 19:1-13; 32:6-9. [b] 16 Many manuscripts do not have *Jesus*; also in verse 17.

thing to do with that innocent man, for I have suffered a great deal today in a dream because of him."

20 But the chief priests and the elders persuaded the crowd to ask for Barabbas and to have Jesus executed.

21 "Which of the two do you want me to release to you?" asked the governor.

"Barabbas," they answered.

22 "What shall I do, then, with Jesus who is called the Messiah?" Pilate asked.

They all answered, "Crucify him!"

23 "Why? What crime has he committed?" asked Pilate.

But they shouted all the louder, "Crucify him!"

24 When Pilate saw that he was getting nowhere, but that instead an uproar was starting, he took water and washed his hands in front of the crowd. "I am innocent of this man's blood," he said. "It is your responsibility!"

25 All the people answered, "His blood is on us and on our children!"

26 Then he released Barabbas to them. But he had Jesus flogged, and handed him over to be crucified.

The Soldiers Mock Jesus

27 Then the governor's soldiers took Jesus into the Praetorium and gathered the whole company of soldiers around him. **28** They stripped him and put a scarlet robe on him, **29** and then twisted together a crown of thorns and set it on his head. They put a staff in his right hand. Then they knelt in front of him and mocked him. "Hail, king of the Jews!" they said. **30** They spit on him, and took the staff and struck him on the head again and again. **31** After they had mocked him, they took off the robe and put his own clothes on him. Then they led him away to crucify him.

The Crucifixion of Jesus

32 As they were going out, they met a man from Cyrene, named Simon, and they forced him to carry the cross. **33** They came to a place called Golgotha (which means "the place of the skull"). **34** There they offered Jesus wine to drink, mixed with gall; but after tasting it, he refused to drink it. **35** When they had crucified him, they divided up his clothes by casting lots. **36** And sitting down, they kept watch over him there. **37** Above his head they placed the written charge against him: THIS IS JESUS, THE KING OF THE JEWS.

38 Two rebels were crucified with him, one on his right and one on his left. **39** Those who passed by hurled insults at him, shaking their heads **40** and saying, "You who are going to destroy the temple and build it in three days, save yourself! Come down from the cross, if you are the Son of God!" ⁴¹In the same way the chief priests, the teachers of the law and the elders mocked him. ⁴²"He saved others," they said, "but he can't save himself! He's the king of Israel! Let him come down now from the cross, and we will believe in him. ⁴³He trusts in God. Let God rescue him now if he wants him, for he said, 'I am the Son of God.'" ⁴⁴In the same way the rebels who were crucified with him also heaped insults on him.

The Death of Jesus

⁴⁵From noon until three in the afternoon darkness came over all the land. ⁴⁶About three in the afternoon Jesus cried out in a loud voice, *"Eli, Eli,ᵃ lema sabachthani?"* (which means "My God, my God, why have you forsaken me?").ᵇ

⁴⁷When some of those standing there heard this, they said, "He's calling Elijah."

⁴⁸Immediately one of them ran and got a sponge. He filled it with wine vinegar, put it on a staff, and offered it to Jesus to drink. ⁴⁹The rest said, "Now leave him alone. Let's see if Elijah comes to save him."

⁵⁰And when Jesus had cried out again in a loud voice, he gave up his spirit.

⁵¹At that moment the curtain of the temple was torn in two from top to bottom. The earth shook, the rocks split ⁵²and the tombs broke open. The bodies of many holy people who had died were raised to life. ⁵³They came out of the tombs after Jesus' resurrection andᶜ went into the holy city and appeared to many people.

⁵⁴When the centurion and those with him who were guarding Jesus saw the earthquake and all that had happened, they were terrified, and exclaimed, "Surely he was the Son of God!"

⁵⁵Many women were there, watching from a distance. They had followed Jesus from Galilee to care for his needs. ⁵⁶Among them were Mary Magdalene, Mary the mother of James and Joseph,ᵈ and the mother of Zebedee's sons.

The Burial of Jesus

⁵⁷As evening approached, there came a rich man from Arimathea, named Joseph, who had himself become a disciple of Jesus. ⁵⁸Going to Pilate, he asked for Jesus' body, and Pilate ordered that it be given to him. ⁵⁹Joseph took the body, wrapped it in a clean linen cloth, ⁶⁰and placed it in his own new tomb that he had cut out of the rock. He rolled a big stone in front of the entrance to the tomb and went away. ⁶¹Mary Magdalene and the other Mary were sitting there opposite the tomb.

ᵃ 46 Some manuscripts *Eloi, Eloi*   ᵇ 46 Psalm 22:1   ᶜ 53 Or *tombs, and after Jesus' resurrection they*   ᵈ 56 Greek *Joses*, a variant of *Joseph*

The Guard at the Tomb

62The next day, the one after Preparation Day, the chief priests and the Pharisees went to Pilate. **63**"Sir," they said, "we remember that while he was still alive that deceiver said, 'After three days I will rise again.' **64**So give the order for the tomb to be made secure until the third day. Otherwise, his disciples may come and steal the body and tell the people that he has been raised from the dead. This last deception will be worse than the first."

65"Take a guard," Pilate answered. "Go, make the tomb as secure as you know how." **66**So they went and made the tomb secure by putting a seal on the stone and posting the guard.

Jesus Has Risen

28 After the Sabbath, at dawn on the first day of the week, Mary Magdalene and the other Mary went to look at the tomb.

2There was a violent earthquake, for an angel of the Lord came down from heaven and, going to the tomb, rolled back the stone and sat on it. **3**His appearance was like lightning, and his clothes were white as snow. **4**The guards were so afraid of him that they shook and became like dead men.

5The angel said to the women, "Do not be afraid, for I know that you are looking for Jesus, who was crucified. **6**He is not here; he has risen, just as he said. Come and see the place where he lay. **7**Then go quickly and tell his disciples: 'He has risen from the dead and is going ahead of you into Galilee. There you will see him.' Now I have told you."

8So the women hurried away from the tomb, afraid yet filled with joy, and ran to tell his disciples. **9**Suddenly Jesus met them. "Greetings," he said. They came to him, clasped his feet and worshiped him. **10**Then Jesus said to them, "Do not be afraid. Go and tell my brothers to go to Galilee; there they will see me."

The Guards' Report

11While the women were on their way, some of the guards went into the city and reported to the chief priests everything that had happened. **12**When the chief priests had met with the elders and devised a plan, they gave the soldiers a large sum of money, **13**telling them, "You are to say, 'His disciples came during the night and stole him away while we were asleep.' **14**If this report gets to the governor, we will satisfy him and keep you out of trouble." **15**So the soldiers took the money and did as they were instructed. And this story has been widely circulated among the Jews to this very day.

The Great Commission

16Then the eleven disciples went to Galilee, to the mountain where Jesus had told them to go. [17]When they saw him, they worshiped him; but some doubted. [18]Then Jesus came to them and said, "All authority in heaven and on earth has been given to me. [19]Therefore go and make disciples of all nations, baptizing them in the name of the Father and of the Son and of the Holy Spirit, [20]and teaching them to obey everything I have commanded you. And surely I am with you always, to the very end of the age."

Mark

Introduction:

Mark, the author of this Gospel, probably was the first to write down the events of Jesus' life. It is believed that he is the same person who worked for many years as a missionary with Paul and Barnabas.

The book of Mark, which stresses facts and actions rather than themes or topics, is the most exciting account of the life of Christ among the Gospels. Although it is the shortest of the four Gospels, it is often the most detailed. From the beginning Mark tells the stories of Christ's ministry, especially his miracles.

Mark shows Jesus as a man of action and authority. He spends one third of the book telling the events of Christ's last week on earth, ending with the Savior's death and resurrection.

Outline of contents:

Background and preparation (1:1–13)
Ministry of healing and teaching (1:14–8:26)
Jesus and his disciples (8:27–10:45)
Jericho and Jerusalem (10:46–13:37)
Passion and death of Christ (14:1–15:47)
The resurrected Christ and his followers (16:1–20)

John the Baptist Prepares the Way

1 The beginning of the good news about Jesus the Messiah,[a] the Son of God,[b] 2 as it is written in Isaiah the prophet:

"I will send my messenger
    ahead of you,
who will prepare your
    way"[c]—
3 "a voice of one calling in the
    wilderness,

'Prepare the way for the
    Lord,
make straight paths for
    him.' "[d]

4 And so John the Baptist appeared in the wilderness, preaching a baptism of repentance for the forgiveness of sins. 5 The whole Judean countryside and all the people of Jerusalem went out to him. Confessing their sins, they were baptized by him in the

---

[a] 1 Or *Jesus Christ. Messiah* (Hebrew) and *Christ* (Greek) both mean *Anointed One.*
[b] 1 Some manuscripts do not have *the Son of God.*   [c] 2 Mal. 3:1   [d] 3 Isaiah 40:3

Jordan River. **6**John wore clothing made of camel's hair, with a leather belt around his waist, and he ate locusts and wild honey. **7**And this was his message: "After me comes the one more powerful than I, the straps of whose sandals I am not worthy to stoop down and untie. **8**I baptize you with*a* water, but he will baptize you with*a* the Holy Spirit."

The Baptism and Testing of Jesus

9At that time Jesus came from Nazareth in Galilee and was baptized by John in the Jordan. **10**Just as Jesus was coming up out of the water, he saw heaven being torn open and the Spirit descending on him like a dove. **11**And a voice came from heaven: "You are my Son, whom I love; with you I am well pleased."

12At once the Spirit sent him out into the wilderness, **13**and he was in the wilderness forty days, being tempted*b* by Satan. He was with the wild animals, and angels attended him.

Jesus Announces the Good News

14After John was put in prison, Jesus went into Galilee, proclaiming the good news of God. **15**"The time has come," he said. "The kingdom of God has come near. Repent and believe the good news!"

Jesus Calls His First Disciples

16As Jesus walked beside the Sea of Galilee, he saw Simon and his brother Andrew casting a net into the lake, for they were fishermen. **17**"Come, follow me," Jesus said, "and I will send you out to fish for people." **18**At once they left their nets and followed him.

19When he had gone a little farther, he saw James son of Zebedee and his brother John in a boat, preparing their nets. **20**Without delay he called them, and they left their father Zebedee in the boat with the hired men and followed him.

Jesus Drives Out an Impure Spirit

21They went to Capernaum, and when the Sabbath came, Jesus went into the synagogue and began to teach. **22**The people were amazed at his teaching, because he taught them as one who had authority, not as the teachers of the law. **23**Just then a man in their synagogue who was possessed by an impure spirit cried out, **24**"What do you want with us, Jesus of Nazareth? Have you come to destroy us? I know who you are — the Holy One of God!"

25"Be quiet!" said Jesus sternly. "Come out of him!" **26**The impure spirit shook the man violently and came out of him with a shriek.

27The people were all so amazed that they asked each

---

a 8 Or *in*   *b* 13 The Greek for *tempted* can also mean *tested*.

other, "What is this? A new teaching—and with authority! He even gives orders to impure spirits and they obey him." **28**News about him spread quickly over the whole region of Galilee.

Jesus Heals Many

29As soon as they left the synagogue, they went with James and John to the home of Simon and Andrew. **30**Simon's mother-in-law was in bed with a fever, and they immediately told Jesus about her. **31**So he went to her, took her hand and helped her up. The fever left her and she began to wait on them.

32That evening after sunset the people brought to Jesus all the sick and demon-possessed. **33**The whole town gathered at the door, **34**and Jesus healed many who had various diseases. He also drove out many demons, but he would not let the demons speak because they knew who he was.

Jesus Prays in a Solitary Place

35Very early in the morning, while it was still dark, Jesus got up, left the house and went off to a solitary place, where he prayed. **36**Simon and his companions went to look for him, **37**and when they found him, they exclaimed: "Everyone is looking for you!"

38Jesus replied, "Let us go somewhere else—to the nearby villages—so I can preach there also. That is why I have come." **39**So he traveled throughout Galilee, preaching in their synagogues and driving out demons.

Jesus Heals a Man With Leprosy

40A man with leprosy[a] came to him and begged him on his knees, "If you are willing, you can make me clean."

41Jesus was indignant.[b] He reached out his hand and touched the man. "I am willing," he said. "Be clean!" **42**Immediately the leprosy left him and he was cleansed.

43Jesus sent him away at once with a strong warning: **44**"See that you don't tell this to anyone. But go, show yourself to the priest and offer the sacrifices that Moses commanded for your cleansing, as a testimony to them." **45**Instead he went out and began to talk freely, spreading the news. As a result, Jesus could no longer enter a town openly but stayed outside in lonely places. Yet the people still came to him from everywhere.

Jesus Forgives and Heals a Paralyzed Man

2 A few days later, when Jesus again entered Capernaum, the people heard that he had come home. **2**They gathered in such large numbers that there was no room left, not even outside the

---

[a] 40 The Greek word traditionally translated *leprosy* was used for various diseases affecting the skin.   [b] 41 Many manuscripts *Jesus was filled with compassion*

door, and he preached the word to them. ³Some men came, bringing to him a paralyzed man, carried by four of them. ⁴Since they could not get him to Jesus because of the crowd, they made an opening in the roof above Jesus by digging through it and then lowered the mat the man was lying on. ⁵When Jesus saw their faith, he said to the paralyzed man, "Son, your sins are forgiven."

⁶Now some teachers of the law were sitting there, thinking to themselves, ⁷"Why does this fellow talk like that? He's blaspheming! Who can forgive sins but God alone?"

⁸Immediately Jesus knew in his spirit that this was what they were thinking in their hearts, and he said to them, "Why are you thinking these things? ⁹Which is easier: to say to this paralyzed man, 'Your sins are forgiven,' or to say, 'Get up, take your mat and walk'? ¹⁰But I want you to know that the Son of Man has authority on earth to forgive sins." So he said to the man, ¹¹"I tell you, get up, take your mat and go home." ¹²He got up, took his mat and walked out in full view of them all. This amazed everyone and they praised God, saying, "We have never seen anything like this!"

Jesus Calls Levi and Eats With Sinners

¹³Once again Jesus went out beside the lake. A large crowd came to him, and he began to teach them. ¹⁴As he walked along, he saw Levi son of Alphaeus sitting at the tax collector's booth. "Follow me," Jesus told him, and Levi got up and followed him.

¹⁵While Jesus was having dinner at Levi's house, many tax collectors and sinners were eating with him and his disciples, for there were many who followed him. ¹⁶When the teachers of the law who were Pharisees saw him eating with the sinners and tax collectors, they asked his disciples: "Why does he eat with tax collectors and sinners?"

¹⁷On hearing this, Jesus said to them, "It is not the healthy who need a doctor, but the sick. I have not come to call the righteous, but sinners."

Jesus Questioned About Fasting

¹⁸Now John's disciples and the Pharisees were fasting. Some people came and asked Jesus, "How is it that John's disciples and the disciples of the Pharisees are fasting, but yours are not?"

¹⁹Jesus answered, "How can the guests of the bridegroom fast while he is with them? They cannot, so long as they have him with them. ²⁰But the time will come when the bridegroom will be taken from them, and on that day they will fast.

²¹"No one sews a patch of unshrunk cloth on an old garment. Otherwise, the new piece will

pull away from the old, making the tear worse. ²²And no one pours new wine into old wineskins. Otherwise, the wine will burst the skins, and both the wine and the wineskins will be ruined. No, they pour new wine into new wineskins."

Jesus Is Lord of the Sabbath

²³One Sabbath Jesus was going through the grainfields, and as his disciples walked along, they began to pick some heads of grain. ²⁴The Pharisees said to him, "Look, why are they doing what is unlawful on the Sabbath?"

²⁵He answered, "Have you never read what David did when he and his companions were hungry and in need? ²⁶In the days of Abiathar the high priest, he entered the house of God and ate the consecrated bread, which is lawful only for priests to eat. And he also gave some to his companions."

²⁷Then he said to them, "The Sabbath was made for man, not man for the Sabbath. ²⁸So the Son of Man is Lord even of the Sabbath."

Jesus Heals on the Sabbath

3 Another time Jesus went into the synagogue, and a man with a shriveled hand was there. ²Some of them were looking for a reason to accuse Jesus, so they watched him closely to see if he would heal him on the Sabbath. ³Jesus said to the man with the shriveled hand, "Stand up in front of everyone."

⁴Then Jesus asked them, "Which is lawful on the Sabbath: to do good or to do evil, to save life or to kill?" But they remained silent.

⁵He looked around at them in anger and, deeply distressed at their stubborn hearts, said to the man, "Stretch out your hand." He stretched it out, and his hand was completely restored. ⁶Then the Pharisees went out and began to plot with the Herodians how they might kill Jesus.

Crowds Follow Jesus

⁷Jesus withdrew with his disciples to the lake, and a large crowd from Galilee followed. ⁸When they heard about all he was doing, many people came to him from Judea, Jerusalem, Idumea, and the regions across the Jordan and around Tyre and Sidon. ⁹Because of the crowd he told his disciples to have a small boat ready for him, to keep the people from crowding him. ¹⁰For he had healed many, so that those with diseases were pushing forward to touch him. ¹¹Whenever the impure spirits saw him, they fell down before him and cried out, "You are the Son of God." ¹²But he gave them strict orders not to tell others about him.

Jesus Appoints the Twelve

¹³Jesus went up on a mountainside and called to him those he

wanted, and they came to him. [14]He appointed twelve[a] that they might be with him and that he might send them out to preach [15]and to have authority to drive out demons. [16]These are the twelve he appointed: Simon (to whom he gave the name Peter), [17]James son of Zebedee and his brother John (to them he gave the name Boanerges, which means "sons of thunder"), [18]Andrew, Philip, Bartholomew, Matthew, Thomas, James son of Alphaeus, Thaddaeus, Simon the Zealot [19]and Judas Iscariot, who betrayed him.

Jesus Accused by His Family and by Teachers of the Law

[20]Then Jesus entered a house, and again a crowd gathered, so that he and his disciples were not even able to eat. [21]When his family[b] heard about this, they went to take charge of him, for they said, "He is out of his mind."

[22]And the teachers of the law who came down from Jerusalem said, "He is possessed by Beelzebul! By the prince of demons he is driving out demons."

[23]So Jesus called them over to him and began to speak to them in parables: "How can Satan drive out Satan? [24]If a kingdom is divided against itself, that kingdom cannot stand. [25]If a house is divided against itself, that house cannot stand. [26]And if Sa-tan opposes himself and is divided, he cannot stand; his end has come. [27]In fact, no one can enter a strong man's house without first tying him up. Then he can plunder the strong man's house. [28]Truly I tell you, people can be forgiven all their sins and every slander they utter, [29]but whoever blasphemes against the Holy Spirit will never be forgiven; they are guilty of an eternal sin."

[30]He said this because they were saying, "He has an impure spirit."

[31]Then Jesus' mother and brothers arrived. Standing outside, they sent someone in to call him. [32]A crowd was sitting around him, and they told him, "Your mother and brothers are outside looking for you."

[33]"Who are my mother and my brothers?" he asked.

[34]Then he looked at those seated in a circle around him and said, "Here are my mother and my brothers! [35]Whoever does God's will is my brother and sister and mother."

The Parable of the Sower

4 Again Jesus began to teach by the lake. The crowd that gathered around him was so large that he got into a boat and sat in it out on the lake, while all the people were along the shore at the water's edge. [2]He taught

---

[a] 14 Some manuscripts *twelve — designating them apostles —*   [b] 21 Or *his associates*

them many things by parables, and in his teaching said: ³"Listen! A farmer went out to sow his seed. ⁴As he was scattering the seed, some fell along the path, and the birds came and ate it up. ⁵Some fell on rocky places, where it did not have much soil. It sprang up quickly, because the soil was shallow. ⁶But when the sun came up, the plants were scorched, and they withered because they had no root. ⁷Other seed fell among thorns, which grew up and choked the plants, so that they did not bear grain. ⁸Still other seed fell on good soil. It came up, grew and produced a crop, some multiplying thirty, some sixty, some a hundred times."

⁹Then Jesus said, "Whoever has ears to hear, let them hear."

¹⁰When he was alone, the Twelve and the others around him asked him about the parables. ¹¹He told them, "The secret of the kingdom of God has been given to you. But to those on the outside everything is said in parables ¹²so that,

" 'they may be ever seeing but
never perceiving,
and ever hearing but never
understanding;
otherwise they might turn and
be forgiven!'ᵃ"

¹³Then Jesus said to them, "Don't you understand this parable? How then will you understand any parable? ¹⁴The farmer sows the word. ¹⁵Some people are like seed along the path, where the word is sown. As soon as they hear it, Satan comes and takes away the word that was sown in them. ¹⁶Others, like seed sown on rocky places, hear the word and at once receive it with joy. ¹⁷But since they have no root, they last only a short time. When trouble or persecution comes because of the word, they quickly fall away. ¹⁸Still others, like seed sown among thorns, hear the word; ¹⁹but the worries of this life, the deceitfulness of wealth and the desires for other things come in and choke the word, making it unfruitful. ²⁰Others, like seed sown on good soil, hear the word, accept it, and produce a crop—some thirty, some sixty, some a hundred times what was sown."

A Lamp on a Stand

²¹He said to them, "Do you bring in a lamp to put it under a bowl or a bed? Instead, don't you put it on its stand? ²²For whatever is hidden is meant to be disclosed, and whatever is concealed is meant to be brought out into the open. ²³If anyone has ears to hear, let them hear."

²⁴"Consider carefully what you hear," he continued. "With the measure you use, it will be measured to you—and even more. ²⁵Whoever has will be given

ᵃ 12 Isaiah 6:9,10

more; whoever does not have, even what they have will be taken from them."

The Parable of the Growing Seed

²⁶ He also said, "This is what the kingdom of God is like. A man scatters seed on the ground. ²⁷ Night and day, whether he sleeps or gets up, the seed sprouts and grows, though he does not know how. ²⁸ All by itself the soil produces grain — first the stalk, then the head, then the full kernel in the head. ²⁹ As soon as the grain is ripe, he puts the sickle to it, because the harvest has come."

The Parable of the Mustard Seed

³⁰ Again he said, "What shall we say the kingdom of God is like, or what parable shall we use to describe it? ³¹ It is like a mustard seed, which is the smallest of all seeds on earth. ³² Yet when planted, it grows and becomes the largest of all garden plants, with such big branches that the birds can perch in its shade."

³³ With many similar parables Jesus spoke the word to them, as much as they could understand. ³⁴ He did not say anything to them without using a parable. But when he was alone with his own disciples, he explained everything.

Jesus Calms the Storm

³⁵ That day when evening came, he said to his disciples, "Let us go over to the other side." ³⁶ Leaving the crowd behind, they took him along, just as he was, in the boat. There were also other boats with him. ³⁷ A furious squall came up, and the waves broke over the boat, so that it was nearly swamped. ³⁸ Jesus was in the stern, sleeping on a cushion. The disciples woke him and said to him, "Teacher, don't you care if we drown?"

³⁹ He got up, rebuked the wind and said to the waves, "Quiet! Be still!" Then the wind died down and it was completely calm.

⁴⁰ He said to his disciples, "Why are you so afraid? Do you still have no faith?"

⁴¹ They were terrified and asked each other, "Who is this? Even the wind and the waves obey him!"

Jesus Restores a Demon-Possessed Man

5 They went across the lake to the region of the Gerasenes.[a] ² When Jesus got out of the boat, a man with an impure spirit came from the tombs to meet him. ³ This man lived in the tombs, and no one could bind him anymore, not even with a chain. ⁴ For he had often been chained hand and foot, but he tore the chains apart and broke the irons on his feet. No one was strong enough to subdue him. ⁵ Night and day among the tombs and in the hills he would cry out and cut himself with stones.

[a] 1 Some manuscripts *Gadarenes*; other manuscripts *Gergesenes*

⁶When he saw Jesus from a distance, he ran and fell on his knees in front of him. ⁷He shouted at the top of his voice, "What do you want with me, Jesus, Son of the Most High God? In God's name don't torture me!" ⁸For Jesus had said to him, "Come out of this man, you impure spirit!"

⁹Then Jesus asked him, "What is your name?"

"My name is Legion," he replied, "for we are many." ¹⁰And he begged Jesus again and again not to send them out of the area.

¹¹A large herd of pigs was feeding on the nearby hillside. ¹²The demons begged Jesus, "Send us among the pigs; allow us to go into them." ¹³He gave them permission, and the impure spirits came out and went into the pigs. The herd, about two thousand in number, rushed down the steep bank into the lake and were drowned.

¹⁴Those tending the pigs ran off and reported this in the town and countryside, and the people went out to see what had happened. ¹⁵When they came to Jesus, they saw the man who had been possessed by the legion of demons, sitting there, dressed and in his right mind; and they were afraid. ¹⁶Those who had seen it told the people what had happened to the demon-possessed man — and told about the pigs as well. ¹⁷Then the people began to plead with Jesus to leave their region.

¹⁸As Jesus was getting into the boat, the man who had been demon-possessed begged to go with him. ¹⁹Jesus did not let him, but said, "Go home to your own people and tell them how much the Lord has done for you, and how he has had mercy on you." ²⁰So the man went away and began to tell in the Decapolis[a] how much Jesus had done for him. And all the people were amazed.

Jesus Raises a Dead Girl and Heals a Sick Woman

²¹When Jesus had again crossed over by boat to the other side of the lake, a large crowd gathered around him while he was by the lake. ²²Then one of the synagogue leaders, named Jairus, came, and when he saw Jesus, he fell at his feet. ²³He pleaded earnestly with him, "My little daughter is dying. Please come and put your hands on her so that she will be healed and live." ²⁴So Jesus went with him.

A large crowd followed and pressed around him. ²⁵And a woman was there who had been subject to bleeding for twelve years. ²⁶She had suffered a great deal under the care of many doctors and had spent all she had, yet instead of getting better she grew worse. ²⁷When she heard about Jesus, she came up behind him in the crowd and touched his cloak, ²⁸because she thought,

_____

[a] 20 That is, the Ten Cities

"If I just touch his clothes, I will be healed." ²⁹Immediately her bleeding stopped and she felt in her body that she was freed from her suffering.

³⁰At once Jesus realized that power had gone out from him. He turned around in the crowd and asked, "Who touched my clothes?"

³¹"You see the people crowding against you," his disciples answered, "and yet you can ask, 'Who touched me?' "

³²But Jesus kept looking around to see who had done it. ³³Then the woman, knowing what had happened to her, came and fell at his feet and, trembling with fear, told him the whole truth. ³⁴He said to her, "Daughter, your faith has healed you. Go in peace and be freed from your suffering."

³⁵While Jesus was still speaking, some people came from the house of Jairus, the synagogue leader. "Your daughter is dead," they said. "Why bother the teacher anymore?"

³⁶Overhearing*a* what they said, Jesus told him, "Don't be afraid; just believe."

³⁷He did not let anyone follow him except Peter, James and John the brother of James. ³⁸When they came to the home of the synagogue leader, Jesus saw a commotion, with people crying and wailing loudly. ³⁹He went in and said to them, "Why all this commotion and wailing? The child is not dead but asleep." ⁴⁰But they laughed at him.

After he put them all out, he took the child's father and mother and the disciples who were with him, and went in where the child was. ⁴¹He took her by the hand and said to her, *"Talitha koum!"* (which means "Little girl, I say to you, get up!"). ⁴²Immediately the girl stood up and began to walk around (she was twelve years old). At this they were completely astonished. ⁴³He gave strict orders not to let anyone know about this, and told them to give her something to eat.

A Prophet Without Honor

6 Jesus left there and went to his hometown, accompanied by his disciples. ²When the Sabbath came, he began to teach in the synagogue, and many who heard him were amazed.

"Where did this man get these things?" they asked. "What's this wisdom that has been given him? What are these remarkable miracles he is performing? ³Isn't this the carpenter? Isn't this Mary's son and the brother of James, Joseph,*b* Judas and Simon? Aren't his sisters here with us?" And they took offense at him.

⁴Jesus said to them, "A prophet is not without honor except in his own town, among his relatives and in his own home." ⁵He could not do any miracles there, except

---

a 36 Or *Ignoring*   *b 3* Greek *Joses*, a variant of *Joseph* lay his hands on a few sick people and heal them. **6**He was amazed at their lack of faith.

Jesus Sends Out the Twelve

Then Jesus went around teaching from village to village. **7**Calling the Twelve to him, he began to send them out two by two and gave them authority over impure spirits.

8These were his instructions: "Take nothing for the journey except a staff—no bread, no bag, no money in your belts. **9**Wear sandals but not an extra shirt. **10**Whenever you enter a house, stay there until you leave that town. **11**And if any place will not welcome you or listen to you, leave that place and shake the dust off your feet as a testimony against them."

12They went out and preached that people should repent. **13**They drove out many demons and anointed many sick people with oil and healed them.

John the Baptist Beheaded

14King Herod heard about this, for Jesus' name had become well known. Some were saying,[a] "John the Baptist has been raised from the dead, and that is why miraculous powers are at work in him."

15Others said, "He is Elijah."

And still others claimed, "He is a prophet, like one of the prophets of long ago."

16But when Herod heard this, he said, "John, whom I beheaded, has been raised from the dead!"

17For Herod himself had given orders to have John arrested, and he had him bound and put in prison. He did this because of Herodias, his brother Philip's wife, whom he had married. **18**For John had been saying to Herod, "It is not lawful for you to have your brother's wife." **19**So Herodias nursed a grudge against John and wanted to kill him. But she was not able to, **20**because Herod feared John and protected him, knowing him to be a righteous and holy man. When Herod heard John, he was greatly puzzled[b]; yet he liked to listen to him.

21Finally the opportune time came. On his birthday Herod gave a banquet for his high officials and military commanders and the leading men of Galilee. **22**When the daughter of[c] Herodias came in and danced, she pleased Herod and his dinner guests.

The king said to the girl, "Ask me for anything you want, and I'll give it to you." **23**And he promised her with an oath, "Whatever you ask I will give you, up to half my kingdom."

24She went out and said to her mother, "What shall I ask for?"

"The head of John the Baptist," she answered.

[a] 14 Some early manuscripts *He was saying did many things*   [b] 20 Some early manuscripts *he*   [c] 22 Some early manuscripts *When his daughter*

²⁵At once the girl hurried in to the king with the request: "I want you to give me right now the head of John the Baptist on a platter."

²⁶The king was greatly distressed, but because of his oaths and his dinner guests, he did not want to refuse her. ²⁷So he immediately sent an executioner with orders to bring John's head. The man went, beheaded John in the prison, ²⁸and brought back his head on a platter. He presented it to the girl, and she gave it to her mother. ²⁹On hearing of this, John's disciples came and took his body and laid it in a tomb.

Jesus Feeds the Five Thousand

³⁰The apostles gathered around Jesus and reported to him all they had done and taught. ³¹Then, because so many people were coming and going that they did not even have a chance to eat, he said to them, "Come with me by yourselves to a quiet place and get some rest."

³²So they went away by themselves in a boat to a solitary place. ³³But many who saw them leaving recognized them and ran on foot from all the towns and got there ahead of them. ³⁴When Jesus landed and saw a large crowd, he had compassion on them, because they were like sheep without a shepherd. So he began teaching them many things.

³⁵By this time it was late in the day, so his disciples came to him. "This is a remote place," they said, "and it's already very late. ³⁶Send the people away so that they can go to the surrounding countryside and villages and buy themselves something to eat."

³⁷But he answered, "You give them something to eat."

They said to him, "That would take more than half a year's wages[a]! Are we to go and spend that much on bread and give it to them to eat?"

³⁸"How many loaves do you have?" he asked. "Go and see."

When they found out, they said, "Five — and two fish."

³⁹Then Jesus directed them to have all the people sit down in groups on the green grass. ⁴⁰So they sat down in groups of hundreds and fifties. ⁴¹Taking the five loaves and the two fish and looking up to heaven, he gave thanks and broke the loaves. Then he gave them to his disciples to distribute to the people. He also divided the two fish among them all. ⁴²They all ate and were satisfied, ⁴³and the disciples picked up twelve basketfuls of broken pieces of bread and fish. ⁴⁴The number of the men who had eaten was five thousand.

Jesus Walks on the Water

⁴⁵Immediately Jesus made his disciples get into the boat and

---

a 37 Greek *take two hundred denarii*

go on ahead of him to Bethsaida, while he dismissed the crowd. [46]After leaving them, he went up on a mountainside to pray.

[47]Later that night, the boat was in the middle of the lake, and he was alone on land. [48]He saw the disciples straining at the oars, because the wind was against them. Shortly before dawn he went out to them, walking on the lake. He was about to pass by them, [49]but when they saw him walking on the lake, they thought he was a ghost. They cried out, [50]because they all saw him and were terrified.

Immediately he spoke to them and said, "Take courage! It is I. Don't be afraid." [51]Then he climbed into the boat with them, and the wind died down. They were completely amazed, [52]for they had not understood about the loaves; their hearts were hardened.

[53]When they had crossed over, they landed at Gennesaret and anchored there. [54]As soon as they got out of the boat, people recognized Jesus. [55]They ran throughout that whole region and carried the sick on mats to wherever they heard he was. [56]And wherever he went—into villages, towns or countryside—they placed the sick in the marketplaces. They begged him to let them touch even the edge of his cloak, and all who touched it were healed.

That Which Defiles

7 The Pharisees and some of the teachers of the law who had come from Jerusalem gathered around Jesus [2]and saw some of his disciples eating food with hands that were defiled, that is, unwashed. [3](The Pharisees and all the Jews do not eat unless they give their hands a ceremonial washing, holding to the tradition of the elders. [4]When they come from the marketplace they do not eat unless they wash. And they observe many other traditions, such as the washing of cups, pitchers and kettles.[a])

[5]So the Pharisees and teachers of the law asked Jesus, "Why don't your disciples live according to the tradition of the elders instead of eating their food with defiled hands?"

[6]He replied, "Isaiah was right when he prophesied about you hypocrites; as it is written:

"'These people honor me with
  their lips,
 but their hearts are far from
  me.
[7]They worship me in vain;
 their teachings are merely
  human rules.'[b]

[8]You have let go of the commands of God and are holding on to human traditions."

[9]And he continued, "You have a fine way of setting aside the

---

[a] 4 Some early manuscripts *pitchers, kettles and dining couches*   [b] 6,7 Isaiah 29:13

commands of God in order to observe[a] your own traditions! **10** For Moses said, 'Honor your father and mother,'[b] and, 'Anyone who curses their father or mother is to be put to death.'[c] **11** But you say that if anyone declares that what might have been used to help their father or mother is Corban (that is, devoted to God) — **12** then you no longer let them do anything for their father or mother. **13** Thus you nullify the word of God by your tradition that you have handed down. And you do many things like that."

14 Again Jesus called the crowd to him and said, "Listen to me, everyone, and understand this. **15** Nothing outside a person can defile them by going into them. Rather, it is what comes out of a person that defiles them." [16][d]

17 After he had left the crowd and entered the house, his disciples asked him about this parable. **18** "Are you so dull?" he asked. "Don't you see that nothing that enters a person from the outside can defile them? **19** For it doesn't go into their heart but into their stomach, and then out of the body." (In saying this, Jesus declared all foods clean.)

20 He went on: "What comes out of a person is what defiles them. **21** For it is from within, out of a person's heart, that evil thoughts come — sexual immorality, theft, murder, **22** adultery, greed, malice, deceit, lewdness, envy, slander, arrogance and folly. **23** All these evils come from inside and defile a person."

Jesus Honors a Syrophoenician Woman's Faith

24 Jesus left that place and went to the vicinity of Tyre.[e] He entered a house and did not want anyone to know it; yet he could not keep his presence secret. **25** In fact, as soon as she heard about him, a woman whose little daughter was possessed by an impure spirit came and fell at his feet. **26** The woman was a Greek, born in Syrian Phoenicia. She begged Jesus to drive the demon out of her daughter.

27 "First let the children eat all they want," he told her, "for it is not right to take the children's bread and toss it to the dogs."

28 "Lord," she replied, "even the dogs under the table eat the children's crumbs."

29 Then he told her, "For such a reply, you may go; the demon has left your daughter."

30 She went home and found her child lying on the bed, and the demon gone.

Jesus Heals a Deaf and Mute Man

31 Then Jesus left the vicinity of Tyre and went through Sidon,

---

[a] 9 Some manuscripts *set up*   [b] 10 Exodus 20:12; Deut. 5:16   [c] 10 Exodus 21:17; Lev. 20:9   [d] 16 Some manuscripts include here the words of 4:23.
[e] 24 Many early manuscripts *Tyre and Sidon*

down to the Sea of Galilee and into the region of the Decapolis.[a] [32] There some people brought to him a man who was deaf and could hardly talk, and they begged Jesus to place his hand on him.

[33] After he took him aside, away from the crowd, Jesus put his fingers into the man's ears. Then he spit and touched the man's tongue. [34] He looked up to heaven and with a deep sigh said to him, *"Ephphatha!"* (which means "Be opened!"). [35] At this, the man's ears were opened, his tongue was loosened and he began to speak plainly.

[36] Jesus commanded them not to tell anyone. But the more he did so, the more they kept talking about it. [37] People were overwhelmed with amazement. "He has done everything well," they said. "He even makes the deaf hear and the mute speak."

Jesus Feeds the Four Thousand

8 During those days another large crowd gathered. Since they had nothing to eat, Jesus called his disciples to him and said, [2] "I have compassion for these people; they have already been with me three days and have nothing to eat. [3] If I send them home hungry, they will collapse on the way, because some of them have come a long distance."

[4] His disciples answered, "But where in this remote place can anyone get enough bread to feed them?"

[5] "How many loaves do you have?" Jesus asked.

"Seven," they replied.

[6] He told the crowd to sit down on the ground. When he had taken the seven loaves and given thanks, he broke them and gave them to his disciples to distribute to the people, and they did so. [7] They had a few small fish as well; he gave thanks for them also and told the disciples to distribute them. [8] The people ate and were satisfied. Afterward the disciples picked up seven basketfuls of broken pieces that were left over. [9] About four thousand were present. After he had sent them away, [10] he got into the boat with his disciples and went to the region of Dalmanutha.

[11] The Pharisees came and began to question Jesus. To test him, they asked him for a sign from heaven. [12] He sighed deeply and said, "Why does this generation ask for a sign? Truly I tell you, no sign will be given to it." [13] Then he left them, got back into the boat and crossed to the other side.

The Yeast of the Pharisees and Herod

[14] The disciples had forgotten to bring bread, except for one loaf they had with them in the boat.

[a] 31 That is, the Ten Cities

¹⁵ "Be careful," Jesus warned them. "Watch out for the yeast of the Pharisees and that of Herod."

¹⁶ They discussed this with one another and said, "It is because we have no bread."

¹⁷ Aware of their discussion, Jesus asked them: "Why are you talking about having no bread? Do you still not see or understand? Are your hearts hardened? ¹⁸ Do you have eyes but fail to see, and ears but fail to hear? And don't you remember? ¹⁹ When I broke the five loaves for the five thousand, how many basketfuls of pieces did you pick up?"

"Twelve," they replied.

²⁰ "And when I broke the seven loaves for the four thousand, how many basketfuls of pieces did you pick up?"

They answered, "Seven."

²¹ He said to them, "Do you still not understand?"

Jesus Heals a Blind Man at Bethsaida

²² They came to Bethsaida, and some people brought a blind man and begged Jesus to touch him. ²³ He took the blind man by the hand and led him outside the village. When he had spit on the man's eyes and put his hands on him, Jesus asked, "Do you see anything?"

²⁴ He looked up and said, "I see people; they look like trees walking around."

²⁵ Once more Jesus put his hands on the man's eyes. Then his eyes were opened, his sight was restored, and he saw everything clearly. ²⁶ Jesus sent him home, saying, "Don't even go into*a* the village."

Peter Declares That Jesus Is the Messiah

²⁷ Jesus and his disciples went on to the villages around Caesarea Philippi. On the way he asked them, "Who do people say I am?"

²⁸ They replied, "Some say John the Baptist; others say Elijah; and still others, one of the prophets."

²⁹ "But what about you?" he asked. "Who do you say I am?"

Peter answered, "You are the Messiah."

³⁰ Jesus warned them not to tell anyone about him.

Jesus Predicts His Death

³¹ He then began to teach them that the Son of Man must suffer many things and be rejected by the elders, the chief priests and the teachers of the law, and that he must be killed and after three days rise again. ³² He spoke plainly about this, and Peter took him aside and began to rebuke him.

³³ But when Jesus turned and looked at his disciples, he rebuked Peter. "Get behind me, Satan!" he said. "You do not have in mind the concerns of God, but merely human concerns."

a 26 Some manuscripts *go and tell anyone in*

The Way of the Cross

³⁴Then he called the crowd to him along with his disciples and said: "Whoever wants to be my disciple must deny themselves and take up their cross and follow me. ³⁵For whoever wants to save their life*ᵃ* will lose it, but whoever loses their life for me and for the gospel will save it. ³⁶What good is it for someone to gain the whole world, yet forfeit their soul? ³⁷Or what can anyone give in exchange for their soul? ³⁸If anyone is ashamed of me and my words in this adulterous and sinful generation, the Son of Man will be ashamed of them when he comes in his Father's glory with the holy angels."

9 And he said to them, "Truly I tell you, some who are standing here will not taste death before they see that the kingdom of God has come with power."

The Transfiguration

²After six days Jesus took Peter, James and John with him and led them up a high mountain, where they were all alone. There he was transfigured before them. ³His clothes became dazzling white, whiter than anyone in the world could bleach them. ⁴And there appeared before them Elijah and Moses, who were talking with Jesus.

⁵Peter said to Jesus, "Rabbi, it is good for us to be here. Let us put up three shelters—one for you, one for Moses and one for Elijah." ⁶(He did not know what to say, they were so frightened.)

⁷Then a cloud appeared and covered them, and a voice came from the cloud: "This is my Son, whom I love. Listen to him!"

⁸Suddenly, when they looked around, they no longer saw anyone with them except Jesus.

⁹As they were coming down the mountain, Jesus gave them orders not to tell anyone what they had seen until the Son of Man had risen from the dead. ¹⁰They kept the matter to themselves, discussing what "rising from the dead" meant.

¹¹And they asked him, "Why do the teachers of the law say that Elijah must come first?"

¹²Jesus replied, "To be sure, Elijah does come first, and restores all things. Why then is it written that the Son of Man must suffer much and be rejected? ¹³But I tell you, Elijah has come, and they have done to him everything they wished, just as it is written about him."

Jesus Heals a Boy Possessed by an Impure Spirit

¹⁴When they came to the other disciples, they saw a large crowd around them and the teachers of the law arguing with them. ¹⁵As soon as all the people saw Jesus, they were overwhelmed with wonder and ran to greet him.

ᵃ 35 The Greek word means either *life* or *soul*; also in verses 36 and 37.

¹⁶"What are you arguing with them about?" he asked.

¹⁷A man in the crowd answered, "Teacher, I brought you my son, who is possessed by a spirit that has robbed him of speech. ¹⁸Whenever it seizes him, it throws him to the ground. He foams at the mouth, gnashes his teeth and becomes rigid. I asked your disciples to drive out the spirit, but they could not."

¹⁹"You unbelieving generation," Jesus replied, "how long shall I stay with you? How long shall I put up with you? Bring the boy to me."

²⁰So they brought him. When the spirit saw Jesus, it immediately threw the boy into a convulsion. He fell to the ground and rolled around, foaming at the mouth.

²¹Jesus asked the boy's father, "How long has he been like this?"

"From childhood," he answered. ²²"It has often thrown him into fire or water to kill him. But if you can do anything, take pity on us and help us."

²³"'If you can'?" said Jesus. "Everything is possible for one who believes."

²⁴Immediately the boy's father exclaimed, "I do believe; help me overcome my unbelief!"

²⁵When Jesus saw that a crowd was running to the scene, he rebuked the impure spirit. "You deaf and mute spirit," he said, "I command you, come out of him and never enter him again."

²⁶The spirit shrieked, convulsed him violently and came out. The boy looked so much like a corpse that many said, "He's dead." ²⁷But Jesus took him by the hand and lifted him to his feet, and he stood up.

²⁸After Jesus had gone indoors, his disciples asked him privately, "Why couldn't we drive it out?"

²⁹He replied, "This kind can come out only by prayer.ᵃ"

Jesus Predicts His Death a Second Time

³⁰They left that place and passed through Galilee. Jesus did not want anyone to know where they were, ³¹because he was teaching his disciples. He said to them, "The Son of Man is going to be delivered into the hands of men. They will kill him, and after three days he will rise." ³²But they did not understand what he meant and were afraid to ask him about it.

³³They came to Capernaum. When he was in the house, he asked them, "What were you arguing about on the road?" ³⁴But they kept quiet because on the way they had argued about who was the greatest.

³⁵Sitting down, Jesus called the Twelve and said, "Anyone who wants to be first must be the very last, and the servant of all."

ᵃ 29 Some manuscripts *prayer and fasting*

36 He took a little child whom he placed among them. Taking the child in his arms, he said to them, **37** "Whoever welcomes one of these little children in my name welcomes me; and whoever welcomes me does not welcome me but the one who sent me."

Whoever Is Not Against Us Is for Us

38 "Teacher," said John, "we saw someone driving out demons in your name and we told him to stop, because he was not one of us."

39 "Do not stop him," Jesus said. "For no one who does a miracle in my name can in the next moment say anything bad about me, **40** for whoever is not against us is for us. **41** Truly I tell you, anyone who gives you a cup of water in my name because you belong to the Messiah will certainly not lose their reward.

Causing to Stumble

42 "If anyone causes one of these little ones — those who believe in me — to stumble, it would be better for them if a large millstone were hung around their neck and they were thrown into the sea. **43** If your hand causes you to stumble, cut it off. It is better for you to enter life maimed than with two hands to go into hell, where the fire never goes out. **[44]** *a* **45** And if your foot causes you to stumble, cut it off. It

is better for you to enter life crippled than to have two feet and be thrown into hell. **[46]** *a* **47** And if your eye causes you to stumble, pluck it out. It is better for you to enter the kingdom of God with one eye than to have two eyes and be thrown into hell, **48** where

> " 'the worms that eat them do not die,
> and the fire is not quenched.' *b*

49 Everyone will be salted with fire.

50 "Salt is good, but if it loses its saltiness, how can you make it salty again? Have salt among yourselves, and be at peace with each other."

Divorce

10 Jesus then left that place and went into the region of Judea and across the Jordan. Again crowds of people came to him, and as was his custom, he taught them.

2 Some Pharisees came and tested him by asking, "Is it lawful for a man to divorce his wife?"

3 "What did Moses command you?" he replied.

4 They said, "Moses permitted a man to write a certificate of divorce and send her away."

5 "It was because your hearts were hard that Moses wrote you this law," Jesus replied. **6** "But at the beginning of creation God

a 44,46 Some manuscripts include here the words of verse 48.   *b 48* Isaiah 66:24

'made them male and female.'[a] [7]'For this reason a man will leave his father and mother and be united to his wife,[b] [8]and the two will become one flesh.'[c] So they are no longer two, but one flesh. [9]Therefore what God has joined together, let no one separate."

[10]When they were in the house again, the disciples asked Jesus about this. [11]He answered, "Anyone who divorces his wife and marries another woman commits adultery against her. [12]And if she divorces her husband and marries another man, she commits adultery."

The Little Children and Jesus

[13]People were bringing little children to Jesus for him to place his hands on them, but the disciples rebuked them. [14]When Jesus saw this, he was indignant. He said to them, "Let the little children come to me, and do not hinder them, for the kingdom of God belongs to such as these. [15]Truly I tell you, anyone who will not receive the kingdom of God like a little child will never enter it." [16]And he took the children in his arms, placed his hands on them and blessed them.

The Rich and the Kingdom of God

[17]As Jesus started on his way, a man ran up to him and fell on his knees before him. "Good teacher," he asked, "what must I do to inherit eternal life?"

[18]"Why do you call me good?" Jesus answered. "No one is good — except God alone. [19]You know the commandments: 'You shall not murder, you shall not commit adultery, you shall not steal, you shall not give false testimony, you shall not defraud, honor your father and mother.'[d]"

[20]"Teacher," he declared, "all these I have kept since I was a boy."

[21]Jesus looked at him and loved him. "One thing you lack," he said. "Go, sell everything you have and give to the poor, and you will have treasure in heaven. Then come, follow me."

[22]At this the man's face fell. He went away sad, because he had great wealth.

[23]Jesus looked around and said to his disciples, "How hard it is for the rich to enter the kingdom of God!"

[24]The disciples were amazed at his words. But Jesus said again, "Children, how hard it is[e] to enter the kingdom of God! [25]It is easier for a camel to go through the eye of a needle than for someone who is rich to enter the kingdom of God."

[26]The disciples were even more amazed, and said to each other, "Who then can be saved?"

---

[a] 6 Gen. 1:27   [b] 7 Some early manuscripts do not have *and be united to his wife.*   [c] 8 Gen. 2:24   [d] 19 Exodus 20:12-16; Deut. 5:16-20   [e] 24 Some manuscripts *is for those who trust in riches*

27 Jesus looked at them and said, "With man this is impossible, but not with God; all things are possible with God."

28 Then Peter spoke up, "We have left everything to follow you!"

29 "Truly I tell you," Jesus replied, "no one who has left home or brothers or sisters or mother or father or children or fields for me and the gospel 30 will fail to receive a hundred times as much in this present age: homes, brothers, sisters, mothers, children and fields — along with persecutions — and in the age to come eternal life. 31 But many who are first will be last, and the last first."

Jesus Predicts His Death a Third Time

32 They were on their way up to Jerusalem, with Jesus leading the way, and the disciples were astonished, while those who followed were afraid. Again he took the Twelve aside and told them what was going to happen to him. 33 "We are going up to Jerusalem," he said, "and the Son of Man will be delivered over to the chief priests and the teachers of the law. They will condemn him to death and will hand him over to the Gentiles, 34 who will mock him and spit on him, flog him and kill him. Three days later he will rise."

The Request of James and John

35 Then James and John, the sons of Zebedee, came to him.

"Teacher," they said, "we want you to do for us whatever we ask."

36 "What do you want me to do for you?" he asked.

37 They replied, "Let one of us sit at your right and the other at your left in your glory."

38 "You don't know what you are asking," Jesus said. "Can you drink the cup I drink or be baptized with the baptism I am baptized with?"

39 "We can," they answered.

Jesus said to them, "You will drink the cup I drink and be baptized with the baptism I am baptized with, 40 but to sit at my right or left is not for me to grant. These places belong to those for whom they have been prepared."

41 When the ten heard about this, they became indignant with James and John. 42 Jesus called them together and said, "You know that those who are regarded as rulers of the Gentiles lord it over them, and their high officials exercise authority over them. 43 Not so with you. Instead, whoever wants to become great among you must be your servant, 44 and whoever wants to be first must be slave of all. 45 For even the Son of Man did not come to be served, but to serve, and to give his life as a ransom for many."

Blind Bartimaeus Receives His Sight

46 Then they came to Jericho. As Jesus and his disciples, together

with a large crowd, were leaving the city, a blind man, Bartimaeus (which means "son of Timaeus"), was sitting by the roadside begging. **47** When he heard that it was Jesus of Nazareth, he began to shout, "Jesus, Son of David, have mercy on me!"

48 Many rebuked him and told him to be quiet, but he shouted all the more, "Son of David, have mercy on me!"

49 Jesus stopped and said, "Call him."

So they called to the blind man, "Cheer up! On your feet! He's calling you." **50** Throwing his cloak aside, he jumped to his feet and came to Jesus.

51 "What do you want me to do for you?" Jesus asked him.

The blind man said, "Rabbi, I want to see."

52 "Go," said Jesus, "your faith has healed you." Immediately he received his sight and followed Jesus along the road.

Jesus Comes to Jerusalem as King

11 As they approached Jerusalem and came to Bethphage and Bethany at the Mount of Olives, Jesus sent two of his disciples, **2** saying to them, "Go to the village ahead of you, and just as you enter it, you will find a colt tied there, which no one has ever ridden. Untie it and bring it here.

3 If anyone asks you, 'Why are you doing this?' say, 'The Lord needs it and will send it back here shortly.' "

4 They went and found a colt outside in the street, tied at a doorway. As they untied it, **5** some people standing there asked, "What are you doing, untying that colt?" **6** They answered as Jesus had told them to, and the people let them go. **7** When they brought the colt to Jesus and threw their cloaks over it, he sat on it. **8** Many people spread their cloaks on the road, while others spread branches they had cut in the fields. **9** Those who went ahead and those who followed shouted,

"Hosanna!*a*"

"Blessed is he who comes in the name of the Lord!"*b*

10 "Blessed is the coming kingdom of our father David!"

"Hosanna in the highest heaven!"

11 Jesus entered Jerusalem and went into the temple courts. He looked around at everything, but since it was already late, he went out to Bethany with the Twelve.

Jesus Curses a Fig Tree and Clears the Temple Courts

12 The next day as they were leaving Bethany, Jesus was hun-

---

a 9 A Hebrew expression meaning "Save!" which became an exclamation of praise; also in verse 10   *b* 9 Psalm 118:25,26 gry. ¹³Seeing in the distance a fig tree in leaf, he went to find out if it had any fruit. When he reached it, he found nothing but leaves, because it was not the season for figs. ¹⁴Then he said to the tree, "May no one ever eat fruit from you again." And his disciples heard him say it.

¹⁵On reaching Jerusalem, Jesus entered the temple courts and began driving out those who were buying and selling there. He overturned the tables of the money changers and the benches of those selling doves, ¹⁶and would not allow anyone to carry merchandise through the temple courts. ¹⁷And as he taught them, he said, "Is it not written: 'My house will be called a house of prayer for all nations'ᵃ? But you have made it 'a den of robbers.'ᵇ"

¹⁸The chief priests and the teachers of the law heard this and began looking for a way to kill him, for they feared him, because the whole crowd was amazed at his teaching.

¹⁹When evening came, Jesus and his disciplesᶜ went out of the city.

²⁰In the morning, as they went along, they saw the fig tree withered from the roots. ²¹Peter remembered and said to Jesus, "Rabbi, look! The fig tree you cursed has withered!"

²²"Have faith in God," Jesus answered. ²³"Trulyᵈ I tell you, if anyone says to this mountain, 'Go, throw yourself into the sea,' and does not doubt in their heart but believes that what they say will happen, it will be done for them. ²⁴Therefore I tell you, whatever you ask for in prayer, believe that you have received it, and it will be yours. ²⁵And when you stand praying, if you hold anything against anyone, forgive them, so that your Father in heaven may forgive you your sins." [26] ᵉ

The Authority of Jesus Questioned

²⁷They arrived again in Jerusalem, and while Jesus was walking in the temple courts, the chief priests, the teachers of the law and the elders came to him. ²⁸"By what authority are you doing these things?" they asked. "And who gave you authority to do this?"

²⁹Jesus replied, "I will ask you one question. Answer me, and I will tell you by what authority I am doing these things. ³⁰John's baptism — was it from heaven, or of human origin? Tell me!"

³¹They discussed it among themselves and said, "If we say, 'From heaven,' he will ask, 'Then why didn't you believe him?' ³²But if we say, 'Of human

---

ᵃ 17 Isaiah 56:7   ᵇ 17 Jer. 7:11   ᶜ 19 Some early manuscripts *came, Jesus*
ᵈ 22,23 Some early manuscripts *"If you have faith in God," Jesus answered,* ²³*"truly*
ᵉ 26 Some manuscripts include here words similar to Matt. 6:15.

origin' . . ." (They feared the people, for everyone held that John really was a prophet.)

³³ So they answered Jesus, "We don't know."

Jesus said, "Neither will I tell you by what authority I am doing these things."

The Parable of the Tenants

12 Jesus then began to speak to them in parables: "A man planted a vineyard. He put a wall around it, dug a pit for the winepress and built a watchtower. Then he rented the vineyard to some farmers and moved to another place. ² At harvest time he sent a servant to the tenants to collect from them some of the fruit of the vineyard. ³ But they seized him, beat him and sent him away empty-handed. ⁴ Then he sent another servant to them; they struck this man on the head and treated him shamefully. ⁵ He sent still another, and that one they killed. He sent many others; some of them they beat, others they killed.

⁶ "He had one left to send, a son, whom he loved. He sent him last of all, saying, 'They will respect my son.'

⁷ "But the tenants said to one another, 'This is the heir. Come, let's kill him, and the inheritance will be ours.' ⁸ So they took him and killed him, and threw him out of the vineyard.

⁹ "What then will the owner of the vineyard do? He will come and kill those tenants and give the vineyard to others. ¹⁰ Haven't you read this passage of Scripture:

" 'The stone the builders rejected
    has become the cornerstone;
¹¹ the Lord has done this,
    and it is marvelous in our eyes'ᵃ?"

¹² Then the chief priests, the teachers of the law and the elders looked for a way to arrest him because they knew he had spoken the parable against them. But they were afraid of the crowd; so they left him and went away.

Paying the Imperial Tax to Caesar

¹³ Later they sent some of the Pharisees and Herodians to Jesus to catch him in his words. ¹⁴ They came to him and said, "Teacher, we know that you are a man of integrity. You aren't swayed by others, because you pay no attention to who they are; but you teach the way of God in accordance with the truth. Is it right to pay the imperial taxᵇ to Caesar or not? ¹⁵ Should we pay or shouldn't we?"

But Jesus knew their hypocrisy. "Why are you trying to trap me?" he asked. "Bring me a denarius

---

ᵃ 11 Psalm 118:22,23   ᵇ 14 A special tax levied on subject peoples, not on Roman citizens and let me look at it." **16**They brought the coin, and he asked them, "Whose image is this? And whose inscription?"

"Caesar's," they replied.

17Then Jesus said to them, "Give back to Caesar what is Caesar's and to God what is God's."

And they were amazed at him.

Marriage at the Resurrection

18Then the Sadducees, who say there is no resurrection, came to him with a question. **19**"Teacher," they said, "Moses wrote for us that if a man's brother dies and leaves a wife but no children, the man must marry the widow and raise up offspring for his brother. **20**Now there were seven brothers. The first one married and died without leaving any children. **21**The second one married the widow, but he also died, leaving no child. It was the same with the third. **22**In fact, none of the seven left any children. Last of all, the woman died too. **23**At the resurrection*a* whose wife will she be, since the seven were married to her?"

24Jesus replied, "Are you not in error because you do not know the Scriptures or the power of God? **25**When the dead rise, they will neither marry nor be given in marriage; they will be like the angels in heaven. **26**Now about the dead rising—have you not read in the Book of Moses, in the account of the burning bush, how God said to him, 'I am the God of Abraham, the God of Isaac, and the God of Jacob'*b*? **27**He is not the God of the dead, but of the living. You are badly mistaken!"

The Greatest Commandment

28One of the teachers of the law came and heard them debating. Noticing that Jesus had given them a good answer, he asked him, "Of all the commandments, which is the most important?"

29"The most important one," answered Jesus, "is this: 'Hear, O Israel: The Lord our God, the Lord is one.*c* **30**Love the Lord your God with all your heart and with all your soul and with all your mind and with all your strength.'*d* **31**The second is this: 'Love your neighbor as yourself.'*e* There is no commandment greater than these."

32"Well said, teacher," the man replied. "You are right in saying that God is one and there is no other but him. **33**To love him with all your heart, with all your understanding and with all your strength, and to love your neighbor as yourself is more important than all burnt offerings and sacrifices."

34When Jesus saw that he had answered wisely, he said to him, "You are not far from the kingdom of God." And from then on

---

a 23 Some manuscripts *resurrection, when people rise from the dead,*
b 26 Exodus 3:6   *c 29* Or *The Lord our God is one Lord*   *d 30* Deut. 6:4,5
e 31 Lev. 19:18

no one dared ask him any more questions.

Whose Son Is the Messiah?

³⁵While Jesus was teaching in the temple courts, he asked, "Why do the teachers of the law say that the Messiah is the son of David? ³⁶David himself, speaking by the Holy Spirit, declared:

> " 'The Lord said to my Lord:
> "Sit at my right hand
> until I put your enemies
> under your feet." ' ᵃ

³⁷David himself calls him 'Lord.' How then can he be his son?"

The large crowd listened to him with delight.

Warning Against the Teachers of the Law

³⁸As he taught, Jesus said, "Watch out for the teachers of the law. They like to walk around in flowing robes and be greeted with respect in the marketplaces, ³⁹and have the most important seats in the synagogues and the places of honor at banquets. ⁴⁰They devour widows' houses and for a show make lengthy prayers. These men will be punished most severely."

The Widow's Offering

⁴¹Jesus sat down opposite the place where the offerings were put and watched the crowd putting their money into the temple treasury. Many rich people threw in large amounts. ⁴²But a poor widow came and put in two very small copper coins, worth only a few cents.

⁴³Calling his disciples to him, Jesus said, "Truly I tell you, this poor widow has put more into the treasury than all the others. ⁴⁴They all gave out of their wealth; but she, out of her poverty, put in everything—all she had to live on."

The Destruction of the Temple and Signs of the End Times

13 As Jesus was leaving the temple, one of his disciples said to him, "Look, Teacher! What massive stones! What magnificent buildings!"

²"Do you see all these great buildings?" replied Jesus. "Not one stone here will be left on another; every one will be thrown down."

³As Jesus was sitting on the Mount of Olives opposite the temple, Peter, James, John and Andrew asked him privately, ⁴"Tell us, when will these things happen? And what will be the sign that they are all about to be fulfilled?"

⁵Jesus said to them: "Watch out that no one deceives you. ⁶Many will come in my name, claiming, 'I am he,' and will deceive many. ⁷When you hear of wars and rumors of wars, do not be alarmed.

ᵃ 36 Psalm 110:1

Such things must happen, but the end is still to come. **8** Nation will rise against nation, and kingdom against kingdom. There will be earthquakes in various places, and famines. These are the beginning of birth pains.

9 "You must be on your guard. You will be handed over to the local councils and flogged in the synagogues. On account of me you will stand before governors and kings as witnesses to them. **10** And the gospel must first be preached to all nations. **11** Whenever you are arrested and brought to trial, do not worry beforehand about what to say. Just say whatever is given you at the time, for it is not you speaking, but the Holy Spirit.

12 "Brother will betray brother to death, and a father his child. Children will rebel against their parents and have them put to death. **13** Everyone will hate you because of me, but the one who stands firm to the end will be saved.

14 "When you see 'the abomination that causes desolation'[a] standing where it[b] does not belong—let the reader understand—then let those who are in Judea flee to the mountains. **15** Let no one on the housetop go down or enter the house to take anything out. **16** Let no one in the field go back to get their cloak. **17** How dreadful it will be in those days for pregnant women and nursing mothers! **18** Pray that this will not take place in winter, **19** because those will be days of distress unequaled from the beginning, when God created the world, until now—and never to be equaled again.

20 "If the Lord had not cut short those days, no one would survive. But for the sake of the elect, whom he has chosen, he has shortened them. **21** At that time if anyone says to you, 'Look, here is the Messiah!' or, 'Look, there he is!' do not believe it. **22** For false messiahs and false prophets will appear and perform signs and wonders to deceive, if possible, even the elect. **23** So be on your guard; I have told you everything ahead of time.

24 "But in those days, following that distress,

> " 'the sun will be darkened,
>   and the moon will not give
>   its light;
> **25** the stars will fall from the sky,
>   and the heavenly bodies will
>   be shaken.'[c]

26 "At that time people will see the Son of Man coming in clouds with great power and glory. **27** And he will send his angels and gather his elect from the four winds, from the ends of the earth to the ends of the heavens.

28 "Now learn this lesson from the fig tree: As soon as its twigs get tender and its leaves come out, you know that summer is

---

[a] 14 Daniel 9:27; 11:31; 12:11   [b] 14 Or *he*   [c] 25 Isaiah 13:10; 34:4

near. ²⁹Even so, when you see these things happening, you know that it[a] is near, right at the door. ³⁰Truly I tell you, this generation will certainly not pass away until all these things have happened. ³¹Heaven and earth will pass away, but my words will never pass away.

The Day and Hour Unknown

³²"But about that day or hour no one knows, not even the angels in heaven, nor the Son, but only the Father. ³³Be on guard! Be alert[b]! You do not know when that time will come. ³⁴It's like a man going away: He leaves his house and puts his servants in charge, each with their assigned task, and tells the one at the door to keep watch.

³⁵"Therefore keep watch because you do not know when the owner of the house will come back—whether in the evening, or at midnight, or when the rooster crows, or at dawn. ³⁶If he comes suddenly, do not let him find you sleeping. ³⁷What I say to you, I say to everyone: 'Watch!'"

Jesus Anointed at Bethany

14 Now the Passover and the Festival of Unleavened Bread were only two days away, and the chief priests and the teachers of the law were scheming to arrest Jesus secretly and kill him. ²"But not during the festival," they said, "or the people may riot."

³While he was in Bethany, reclining at the table in the home of Simon the Leper, a woman came with an alabaster jar of very expensive perfume, made of pure nard. She broke the jar and poured the perfume on his head.

⁴Some of those present were saying indignantly to one another, "Why this waste of perfume? ⁵It could have been sold for more than a year's wages[c] and the money given to the poor." And they rebuked her harshly.

⁶"Leave her alone," said Jesus. "Why are you bothering her? She has done a beautiful thing to me. ⁷The poor you will always have with you,[d] and you can help them any time you want. But you will not always have me. ⁸She did what she could. She poured perfume on my body beforehand to prepare for my burial. ⁹Truly I tell you, wherever the gospel is preached throughout the world, what she has done will also be told, in memory of her."

¹⁰Then Judas Iscariot, one of the Twelve, went to the chief priests to betray Jesus to them. ¹¹They were delighted to hear this and promised to give him money. So he watched for an opportunity to hand him over.

The Last Supper

¹²On the first day of the Festival of Unleavened Bread, when it was

---

[a] 29 Or he   [b] 33 Some manuscripts *alert and pray*   [c] 5 Greek *than three hundred denarii*   [d] 7 See Deut. 15:11.

customary to sacrifice the Passover lamb, Jesus' disciples asked him, "Where do you want us to go and make preparations for you to eat the Passover?"

¹³ So he sent two of his disciples, telling them, "Go into the city, and a man carrying a jar of water will meet you. Follow him. ¹⁴ Say to the owner of the house he enters, 'The Teacher asks: Where is my guest room, where I may eat the Passover with my disciples?' ¹⁵ He will show you a large room upstairs, furnished and ready. Make preparations for us there."

¹⁶ The disciples left, went into the city and found things just as Jesus had told them. So they prepared the Passover.

¹⁷ When evening came, Jesus arrived with the Twelve. ¹⁸ While they were reclining at the table eating, he said, "Truly I tell you, one of you will betray me — one who is eating with me."

¹⁹ They were saddened, and one by one they said to him, "Surely you don't mean me?"

²⁰ "It is one of the Twelve," he replied, "one who dips bread into the bowl with me. ²¹ The Son of Man will go just as it is written about him. But woe to that man who betrays the Son of Man! It would be better for him if he had not been born."

²² While they were eating, Jesus took bread, and when he had given thanks, he broke it and gave it to his disciples, saying, "Take it; this is my body."

²³ Then he took a cup, and when he had given thanks, he gave it to them, and they all drank from it.

²⁴ "This is my blood of the*ᵃ* covenant, which is poured out for many," he said to them. ²⁵ "Truly I tell you, I will not drink again from the fruit of the vine until that day when I drink it new in the kingdom of God."

²⁶ When they had sung a hymn, they went out to the Mount of Olives.

Jesus Predicts Peter's Denial

²⁷ "You will all fall away," Jesus told them, "for it is written:

> "'I will strike the shepherd,
>   and the sheep will be
>   scattered.'ᵇ

²⁸ But after I have risen, I will go ahead of you into Galilee."

²⁹ Peter declared, "Even if all fall away, I will not."

³⁰ "Truly I tell you," Jesus answered, "today — yes, tonight — before the rooster crows twiceᶜ you yourself will disown me three times."

³¹ But Peter insisted emphatically, "Even if I have to die with you, I will never disown you." And all the others said the same.

Gethsemane

³² They went to a place called Gethsemane, and Jesus said to

ᵃ 24 Some manuscripts *the new*   ᵇ 27 Zech. 13:7   ᶜ 30 Some early manuscripts do not have *twice*.

his disciples, "Sit here while I pray." ³³He took Peter, James and John along with him, and he began to be deeply distressed and troubled. ³⁴"My soul is overwhelmed with sorrow to the point of death," he said to them. "Stay here and keep watch."

³⁵Going a little farther, he fell to the ground and prayed that if possible the hour might pass from him. ³⁶"*Abba,*^a Father," he said, "everything is possible for you. Take this cup from me. Yet not what I will, but what you will."

³⁷Then he returned to his disciples and found them sleeping. "Simon," he said to Peter, "are you asleep? Couldn't you keep watch for one hour? ³⁸Watch and pray so that you will not fall into temptation. The spirit is willing, but the flesh is weak."

³⁹Once more he went away and prayed the same thing. ⁴⁰When he came back, he again found them sleeping, because their eyes were heavy. They did not know what to say to him.

⁴¹Returning the third time, he said to them, "Are you still sleeping and resting? Enough! The hour has come. Look, the Son of Man is delivered into the hands of sinners. ⁴²Rise! Let us go! Here comes my betrayer!"

Jesus Arrested

⁴³Just as he was speaking, Judas, one of the Twelve, appeared. With him was a crowd armed with swords and clubs, sent from the chief priests, the teachers of the law, and the elders.

⁴⁴Now the betrayer had arranged a signal with them: "The one I kiss is the man; arrest him and lead him away under guard." ⁴⁵Going at once to Jesus, Judas said, "Rabbi!" and kissed him. ⁴⁶The men seized Jesus and arrested him. ⁴⁷Then one of those standing near drew his sword and struck the servant of the high priest, cutting off his ear.

⁴⁸"Am I leading a rebellion," said Jesus, "that you have come out with swords and clubs to capture me? ⁴⁹Every day I was with you, teaching in the temple courts, and you did not arrest me. But the Scriptures must be fulfilled." ⁵⁰Then everyone deserted him and fled.

⁵¹A young man, wearing nothing but a linen garment, was following Jesus. When they seized him, ⁵²he fled naked, leaving his garment behind.

Jesus Before the Sanhedrin

⁵³They took Jesus to the high priest, and all the chief priests, the elders and the teachers of the law came together. ⁵⁴Peter followed him at a distance, right into the courtyard of the high priest. There he sat with the guards and warmed himself at the fire.

⁵⁵The chief priests and the

^a *36* Aramaic for *father*

whole Sanhedrin were looking for evidence against Jesus so that they could put him to death, but they did not find any. ⁵⁶Many testified falsely against him, but their statements did not agree.

⁵⁷Then some stood up and gave this false testimony against him: ⁵⁸"We heard him say, 'I will destroy this temple made with human hands and in three days will build another, not made with hands.'" ⁵⁹Yet even then their testimony did not agree.

⁶⁰Then the high priest stood up before them and asked Jesus, "Are you not going to answer? What is this testimony that these men are bringing against you?" ⁶¹But Jesus remained silent and gave no answer.

Again the high priest asked him, "Are you the Messiah, the Son of the Blessed One?"

⁶²"I am," said Jesus. "And you will see the Son of Man sitting at the right hand of the Mighty One and coming on the clouds of heaven."

⁶³The high priest tore his clothes. "Why do we need any more witnesses?" he asked. ⁶⁴"You have heard the blasphemy. What do you think?"

They all condemned him as worthy of death. ⁶⁵Then some began to spit at him; they blindfolded him, struck him with their fists, and said, "Prophesy!" And the guards took him and beat him.

Peter Disowns Jesus

⁶⁶While Peter was below in the courtyard, one of the servant girls of the high priest came by. ⁶⁷When she saw Peter warming himself, she looked closely at him.

"You also were with that Nazarene, Jesus," she said.

⁶⁸But he denied it. "I don't know or understand what you're talking about," he said, and went out into the entryway.ᵃ

⁶⁹When the servant girl saw him there, she said again to those standing around, "This fellow is one of them." ⁷⁰Again he denied it.

After a little while, those standing near said to Peter, "Surely you are one of them, for you are a Galilean."

⁷¹He began to call down curses, and he swore to them, "I don't know this man you're talking about."

⁷²Immediately the rooster crowed the second time.ᵇ Then Peter remembered the word Jesus had spoken to him: "Before the rooster crows twiceᶜ you will disown me three times." And he broke down and wept.

Jesus Before Pilate

15 Very early in the morning, the chief priests, with

ᵃ 68 Some early manuscripts *entryway and the rooster crowed*   ᵇ 72 Some early manuscripts do not have *the second time.*   ᶜ 72 Some early manuscripts do not have *twice.*

the elders, the teachers of the law and the whole Sanhedrin, made their plans. So they bound Jesus, led him away and handed him over to Pilate.

² "Are you the king of the Jews?" asked Pilate.

"You have said so," Jesus replied.

³ The chief priests accused him of many things. ⁴ So again Pilate asked him, "Aren't you going to answer? See how many things they are accusing you of."

⁵ But Jesus still made no reply, and Pilate was amazed.

⁶ Now it was the custom at the festival to release a prisoner whom the people requested. ⁷ A man called Barabbas was in prison with the insurrectionists who had committed murder in the uprising. ⁸ The crowd came up and asked Pilate to do for them what he usually did.

⁹ "Do you want me to release to you the king of the Jews?" asked Pilate, ¹⁰ knowing it was out of self-interest that the chief priests had handed Jesus over to him. ¹¹ But the chief priests stirred up the crowd to have Pilate release Barabbas instead.

¹² "What shall I do, then, with the one you call the king of the Jews?" Pilate asked them.

¹³ "Crucify him!" they shouted.

¹⁴ "Why? What crime has he committed?" asked Pilate.

But they shouted all the louder, "Crucify him!"

¹⁵ Wanting to satisfy the crowd, Pilate released Barabbas to them. He had Jesus flogged, and handed him over to be crucified.

The Soldiers Mock Jesus

¹⁶ The soldiers led Jesus away into the palace (that is, the Praetorium) and called together the whole company of soldiers. ¹⁷ They put a purple robe on him, then twisted together a crown of thorns and set it on him. ¹⁸ And they began to call out to him, "Hail, king of the Jews!" ¹⁹ Again and again they struck him on the head with a staff and spit on him. Falling on their knees, they paid homage to him. ²⁰ And when they had mocked him, they took off the purple robe and put his own clothes on him. Then they led him out to crucify him.

STOP

The Crucifixion of Jesus   STOP

²¹ A certain man from Cyrene, Simon, the father of Alexander and Rufus, was passing by on his way in from the country, and they forced him to carry the cross. ²² They brought Jesus to the place called Golgotha (which means "the place of the skull"). ²³ Then they offered him wine mixed with myrrh, but he did not take it. ²⁴ And they crucified him. Dividing up his clothes, they cast lots to see what each would get.

²⁵ It was nine in the morning when they crucified him. ²⁶ The written notice of the charge against him read: THE KING OF THE JEWS.

[27] They crucified two rebels with him, one on his right and one on his left. [28] a [29] Those who passed by hurled insults at him, shaking their heads and saying, "So! You who are going to destroy the temple and build it in three days, [30] come down from the cross and save yourself!" [31] In the same way the chief priests and the teachers of the law mocked him among themselves. "He saved others," they said, "but he can't save himself! [32] Let this Messiah, this king of Israel, come down now from the cross, that we may see and believe." Those crucified with him also heaped insults on him.

The Death of Jesus

[33] At noon, darkness came over the whole land until three in the afternoon. [34] And at three in the afternoon Jesus cried out in a loud voice, *"Eloi, Eloi, lema sabachthani?"* (which means "My God, my God, why have you forsaken me?"). b

[35] When some of those standing near heard this, they said, "Listen, he's calling Elijah."

[36] Someone ran, filled a sponge with wine vinegar, put it on a staff, and offered it to Jesus to drink. "Now leave him alone. Let's see if Elijah comes to take him down," he said.

[37] With a loud cry, Jesus breathed his last.

[38] The curtain of the temple was torn in two from top to bottom. [39] And when the centurion, who stood there in front of Jesus, saw how he died, c he said, "Surely this man was the Son of God!"

[40] Some women were watching from a distance. Among them were Mary Magdalene, Mary the mother of James the younger and of Joseph, d and Salome. [41] In Galilee these women had followed him and cared for his needs. Many other women who had come up with him to Jerusalem were also there.

The Burial of Jesus

[42] It was Preparation Day (that is, the day before the Sabbath). So as evening approached, [43] Joseph of Arimathea, a prominent member of the Council, who was himself waiting for the kingdom of God, went boldly to Pilate and asked for Jesus' body. [44] Pilate was surprised to hear that he was already dead. Summoning the centurion, he asked him if Jesus had already died. [45] When he learned from the centurion that it was so, he gave the body to Joseph. [46] So Joseph bought some linen cloth, took down the body, wrapped it in the linen, and placed it in a tomb cut out of rock. Then he rolled a stone against the entrance of the tomb. [47] Mary Magdalene and Mary the mother of Joseph saw where he was laid.

---

a 28 Some manuscripts include here words similar to Luke 22:37.   b 34 Psalm 22:1   c 39 Some manuscripts *saw that he died with such a cry*   d 40 Greek *Joses,* a variant of *Joseph;* also in verse 47

Jesus Has Risen

16 When the Sabbath was over, Mary Magdalene, Mary the mother of James, and Salome bought spices so that they might go to anoint Jesus' body. ²Very early on the first day of the week, just after sunrise, they were on their way to the tomb ³and they asked each other, "Who will roll the stone away from the entrance of the tomb?"

⁴But when they looked up, they saw that the stone, which was very large, had been rolled away. ⁵As they entered the tomb, they saw a young man dressed in a white robe sitting on the right side, and they were alarmed.

⁶"Don't be alarmed," he said. "You are looking for Jesus the Nazarene, who was crucified. He has risen! He is not here. See the place where they laid him. ⁷But go, tell his disciples and Peter, 'He is going ahead of you into Galilee. There you will see him, just as he told you.'"

⁸Trembling and bewildered, the women went out and fled from the tomb. They said nothing to anyone, because they were afraid. *ᵃ*

[The earliest manuscripts and some other ancient witnesses do not have verses 9–20.]

⁹*When Jesus rose early on the first day of the week, he appeared first to Mary Magdalene, out of whom he had driven seven demons.* ¹⁰*She went and told those who had been with him and who were mourning and weeping.* ¹¹*When they heard that Jesus was alive and that she had seen him, they did not believe it.*

¹²*Afterward Jesus appeared in a different form to two of them while they were walking in the country.* ¹³*These returned and reported it to the rest; but they did not believe them either.*

¹⁴*Later Jesus appeared to the Eleven as they were eating; he rebuked them for their lack of faith and their stubborn refusal to believe those who had seen him after he had risen.*

¹⁵*He said to them, "Go into all the world and preach the gospel to all creation.* ¹⁶*Whoever believes and is baptized will be saved, but whoever does not believe will be condemned.* ¹⁷*And these signs will accompany those who believe: In my name they will drive out demons; they will speak in new tongues;* ¹⁸*they will pick up snakes with their hands; and when they drink deadly poison, it will not hurt them at all; they will place their hands on sick people, and they will get well."*

¹⁹*After the Lord Jesus had spoken to them, he was taken up into heaven and he sat at the right hand of God.* ²⁰*Then the disciples went out and preached everywhere, and the Lord worked with them and confirmed his word by the signs that accompanied it.*

ᵃ 8 Some manuscripts have the following ending between verses 8 and 9, and one manuscript has it after verse 8 (omitting verses 9-20): *Then they quickly reported all these instructions to those around Peter. After this, Jesus himself also sent out through them from east to west the sacred and imperishable proclamation of eternal salvation. Amen.*

Luke

Introduction:

Luke, the longest of the Gospels, was written by the same author as the book of Acts. Luke's writing shows him to be a highly educated man, who wrote from a Greek background and viewpoint.

In this Gospel Luke shows that Jesus loved all kinds of people. He often wrote about and identified by name the women Christ met and spoke to. He also gave more attention to children than any other Gospel writer. In the parables especially, he wrote about the poor and oppressed. Jesus is portrayed as an actual person in history who "came to seek and to save the lost" (19:10).

The theme of joy is felt throughout this book — from the song of Mary and later the angels at Jesus' birth to the disciples who "returned to Jerusalem with great joy" after Christ's ascension. It is obvious that Luke wanted to tell others that Christ's coming brought joy as well as hope and salvation to a sinful world.

Outline of contents:

Introduction (1:1–4)
The birth and childhood of John the Baptist
   and Jesus (1:5–2:52)
Ministry of John the Baptist (3:1–20)
Jesus' baptism and temptation (3:21–4:12)
Jesus' teaching and healing ministry (4:13–9:50)
Jesus' mission (9:51–18:30)
Suffering and crucifixion of Jesus (18:31–23:56)
Resurrection and ascension (24:1–53)

Introduction

1 Many have undertaken to draw up an account of the things that have been fulfilled[a] among us, ²just as they were handed down to us by those who from the first were eyewitnesses and servants of the word. ³With this in mind, since I myself have carefully investigated everything from the beginning, I too decided to write an orderly account for you, most excellent Theophilus, ⁴so that you may know the

---

[a] 1 Or been surely believed

certainty of the things you have been taught.

The Birth of John the Baptist Foretold

⁵ In the time of Herod king of Judea there was a priest named Zechariah, who belonged to the priestly division of Abijah; his wife Elizabeth was also a descendant of Aaron. ⁶ Both of them were righteous in the sight of God, observing all the Lord's commands and decrees blamelessly. ⁷ But they were childless because Elizabeth was not able to conceive, and they were both very old.

⁸ Once when Zechariah's division was on duty and he was serving as priest before God, ⁹ he was chosen by lot, according to the custom of the priesthood, to go into the temple of the Lord and burn incense. ¹⁰ And when the time for the burning of incense came, all the assembled worshipers were praying outside.

¹¹ Then an angel of the Lord appeared to him, standing at the right side of the altar of incense. ¹² When Zechariah saw him, he was startled and was gripped with fear. ¹³ But the angel said to him: "Do not be afraid, Zechariah; your prayer has been heard. Your wife Elizabeth will bear you a son, and you are to call him John. ¹⁴ He will be a joy and delight to you, and many will rejoice because of his birth, ¹⁵ for he will be great in the sight of the Lord. He is never to take wine or other fermented drink, and he will be filled with the Holy Spirit even before he is born. ¹⁶ He will bring back many of the people of Israel to the Lord their God. ¹⁷ And he will go on before the Lord, in the spirit and power of Elijah, to turn the hearts of the parents to their children and the disobedient to the wisdom of the righteous — to make ready a people prepared for the Lord."

¹⁸ Zechariah asked the angel, "How can I be sure of this? I am an old man and my wife is well along in years."

¹⁹ The angel said to him, "I am Gabriel. I stand in the presence of God, and I have been sent to speak to you and to tell you this good news. ²⁰ And now you will be silent and not able to speak until the day this happens, because you did not believe my words, which will come true at their appointed time."

²¹ Meanwhile, the people were waiting for Zechariah and wondering why he stayed so long in the temple. ²² When he came out, he could not speak to them. They realized he had seen a vision in the temple, for he kept making signs to them but remained unable to speak.

²³ When his time of service was completed, he returned home. ²⁴ After this his wife Elizabeth became pregnant and for five months remained in seclusion. ²⁵ "The Lord has done this for me," she said. "In these days he has shown his favor and taken away my disgrace among the people."

The Birth of Jesus Foretold

26In the sixth month of Elizabeth's pregnancy, God sent the angel Gabriel to Nazareth, a town in Galilee, **27**to a virgin pledged to be married to a man named Joseph, a descendant of David. The virgin's name was Mary. **28**The angel went to her and said, "Greetings, you who are highly favored! The Lord is with you."

29Mary was greatly troubled at his words and wondered what kind of greeting this might be. **30**But the angel said to her, "Do not be afraid, Mary; you have found favor with God. **31**You will conceive and give birth to a son, and you are to call him Jesus. **32**He will be great and will be called the Son of the Most High. The Lord God will give him the throne of his father David, **33**and he will reign over Jacob's descendants forever; his kingdom will never end."

34"How will this be," Mary asked the angel, "since I am a virgin?"

35The angel answered, "The Holy Spirit will come on you, and the power of the Most High will overshadow you. So the holy one to be born will be called*a* the Son of God. **36**Even Elizabeth your relative is going to have a child in her old age, and she who was said to be unable to conceive is in her sixth month. **37**For no word from God will ever fail."

38"I am the Lord's servant," Mary answered. "May your word to me be fulfilled." Then the angel left her.

Mary Visits Elizabeth

39At that time Mary got ready and hurried to a town in the hill country of Judea, **40**where she entered Zechariah's home and greeted Elizabeth. **41**When Elizabeth heard Mary's greeting, the baby leaped in her womb, and Elizabeth was filled with the Holy Spirit. **42**In a loud voice she exclaimed: "Blessed are you among women, and blessed is the child you will bear! **43**But why am I so favored, that the mother of my Lord should come to me? **44**As soon as the sound of your greeting reached my ears, the baby in my womb leaped for joy. **45**Blessed is she who has believed that the Lord would fulfill his promises to her!"

Mary's Song

46And Mary said:

"My soul glorifies the Lord
47   and my spirit rejoices in God
        my Savior,
48for he has been mindful
    of the humble state of his
        servant.
From now on all generations
    will call me blessed,
49   for the Mighty One has done
        great things for me—
holy is his name.
50His mercy extends to those
    who fear him,

---

a 35 Or So the child to be born will be called holy,

from generation to
generation.
⁵¹ He has performed mighty
deeds with his arm;
he has scattered those who
are proud in their inmost
thoughts.
⁵² He has brought down rulers
from their thrones
but has lifted up the humble.
⁵³ He has filled the hungry with
good things
but has sent the rich away
empty.
⁵⁴ He has helped his servant Israel,
remembering to be merciful
⁵⁵ to Abraham and his
descendants forever,
just as he promised our
ancestors."

⁵⁶ Mary stayed with Elizabeth
for about three months and then
returned home.

The Birth of John the Baptist

⁵⁷ When it was time for Elizabeth to have her baby, she gave
birth to a son. ⁵⁸ Her neighbors
and relatives heard that the Lord
had shown her great mercy, and
they shared her joy.

⁵⁹ On the eighth day they came
to circumcise the child, and they
were going to name him after his
father Zechariah, ⁶⁰ but his mother spoke up and said, "No! He is to
be called John."

⁶¹ They said to her, "There is no
one among your relatives who
has that name."

⁶² Then they made signs to his
father, to find out what he would
like to name the child. ⁶³ He asked
for a writing tablet, and to everyone's astonishment he wrote, "His
name is John." ⁶⁴ Immediately his
mouth was opened and his tongue
set free, and he began to speak,
praising God. ⁶⁵ All the neighbors
were filled with awe, and throughout the hill country of Judea people were talking about all these
things. ⁶⁶ Everyone who heard this
wondered about it, asking, "What
then is this child going to be?" For
the Lord's hand was with him.

Zechariah's Song

⁶⁷ His father Zechariah was
filled with the Holy Spirit and
prophesied:

⁶⁸ "Praise be to the Lord, the God
of Israel,
because he has come to his
people and redeemed
them.
⁶⁹ He has raised up a horn ᵃ of
salvation for us
in the house of his servant
David
⁷⁰ (as he said through his holy
prophets of long ago),
⁷¹ salvation from our enemies
and from the hand of all who
hate us —
⁷² to show mercy to our ancestors
and to remember his holy
covenant,
⁷³ the oath he swore to our
father Abraham:

ᵃ 69 *Horn* here symbolizes a strong king.

74 to rescue us from the hand of
    our enemies,
and to enable us to serve
    him without fear
75   in holiness and righteousness
    before him all our days.

76 And you, my child, will be
    called a prophet of the
    Most High;
for you will go on before the
    Lord to prepare the way
    for him,
77 to give his people the
    knowledge of salvation
through the forgiveness of
    their sins,
78 because of the tender mercy of
    our God,
by which the rising sun will
    come to us from heaven
79 to shine on those living in
    darkness
and in the shadow of death,
to guide our feet into the path
    of peace."

80 And the child grew and became strong in spirit[a]; and he lived in the wilderness until he appeared publicly to Israel.

The Birth of Jesus

2 In those days Caesar Augustus issued a decree that a census should be taken of the entire Roman world. 2 (This was the first census that took place while[b] Quirinius was governor of Syria.) 3 And everyone went to their own town to register.

4 So Joseph also went up from the town of Nazareth in Galilee to Judea, to Bethlehem the town of David, because he belonged to the house and line of David. 5 He went there to register with Mary, who was pledged to be married to him and was expecting a child. 6 While they were there, the time came for the baby to be born, 7 and she gave birth to her firstborn, a son. She wrapped him in cloths and placed him in a manger, because there was no guest room available for them.

8 And there were shepherds living out in the fields nearby, keeping watch over their flocks at night. 9 An angel of the Lord appeared to them, and the glory of the Lord shone around them, and they were terrified. 10 But the angel said to them, "Do not be afraid. I bring you good news that will cause great joy for all the people. 11 Today in the town of David a Savior has been born to you; he is the Messiah, the Lord. 12 This will be a sign to you: You will find a baby wrapped in cloths and lying in a manger."

13 Suddenly a great company of the heavenly host appeared with the angel, praising God and saying,

14 "Glory to God in the highest
    heaven,
and on earth peace to those
    on whom his favor rests."

a 80 Or in the Spirit   b 2 Or This census took place before

15When the angels had left them and gone into heaven, the shepherds said to one another, "Let's go to Bethlehem and see this thing that has happened, which the Lord has told us about."

16So they hurried off and found Mary and Joseph, and the baby, who was lying in the manger. 17When they had seen him, they spread the word concerning what had been told them about this child, 18and all who heard it were amazed at what the shepherds said to them. 19But Mary treasured up all these things and pondered them in her heart. 20The shepherds returned, glorifying and praising God for all the things they had heard and seen, which were just as they had been told.

21On the eighth day, when it was time to circumcise the child, he was named Jesus, the name the angel had given him before he was conceived.

Jesus Presented in the Temple

22When the time came for the purification rites required by the Law of Moses, Joseph and Mary took him to Jerusalem to present him to the Lord 23(as it is written in the Law of the Lord, "Every firstborn male is to be consecrated to the Lord"a), 24and to offer a sacrifice in keeping with what is said in the Law of the Lord: "a pair of doves or two young pigeons."b

25Now there was a man in Jerusalem called Simeon, who was righteous and devout. He was waiting for the consolation of Israel, and the Holy Spirit was on him. 26It had been revealed to him by the Holy Spirit that he would not die before he had seen the Lord's Messiah. 27Moved by the Spirit, he went into the temple courts. When the parents brought in the child Jesus to do for him what the custom of the Law required, 28Simeon took him in his arms and praised God, saying:

29"Sovereign Lord, as you have promised,
    you may now dismissc your
        servant in peace.
30For my eyes have seen your
        salvation,
31   which you have prepared in
        the sight of all nations:
32a light for revelation to the
        Gentiles,
    and the glory of your people
        Israel."

33The child's father and mother marveled at what was said about him. 34Then Simeon blessed them and said to Mary, his mother: "This child is destined to cause the falling and rising of many in Israel, and to be a sign that will be spoken against, 35so that the thoughts of many hearts will be revealed. And a sword will pierce your own soul too."

36There was also a prophet, Anna, the daughter of Penuel, of

a 23 Exodus 13:2,12   b 24 Lev. 12:8   c 29 Or promised, / now dismiss the tribe of Asher. She was very old; she had lived with her husband seven years after her marriage, **37** and then was a widow until she was eighty-four.*ᵃ* She never left the temple but worshiped night and day, fasting and praying. **38** Coming up to them at that very moment, she gave thanks to God and spoke about the child to all who were looking forward to the redemption of Jerusalem.

39 When Joseph and Mary had done everything required by the Law of the Lord, they returned to Galilee to their own town of Nazareth. **40** And the child grew and became strong; he was filled with wisdom, and the grace of God was on him.

The Boy Jesus at the Temple

41 Every year Jesus' parents went to Jerusalem for the Festival of the Passover. **42** When he was twelve years old, they went up to the festival, according to the custom. **43** After the festival was over, while his parents were returning home, the boy Jesus stayed behind in Jerusalem, but they were unaware of it. **44** Thinking he was in their company, they traveled on for a day. Then they began looking for him among their relatives and friends. **45** When they did not find him, they went back to Jerusalem to look for him. **46** After three days they found him in the temple courts, sitting among the teachers, listening to them and asking them questions. **47** Everyone who heard him was amazed at his understanding and his answers. **48** When his parents saw him, they were astonished. His mother said to him, "Son, why have you treated us like this? Your father and I have been anxiously searching for you."

49 "Why were you searching for me?" he asked. "Didn't you know I had to be in my Father's house?"*ᵇ* **50** But they did not understand what he was saying to them.

51 Then he went down to Nazareth with them and was obedient to them. But his mother treasured all these things in her heart. **52** And Jesus grew in wisdom and stature, and in favor with God and man.

John the Baptist Prepares the Way

3 In the fifteenth year of the reign of Tiberius Caesar — when Pontius Pilate was governor of Judea, Herod tetrarch of Galilee, his brother Philip tetrarch of Iturea and Traconitis, and Lysanias tetrarch of Abilene — **2** during the high-priesthood of Annas and Caiaphas, the word of God came to John son of Zechariah in the wilderness. **3** He went into all the country around the Jordan, preaching a baptism of repentance for the forgiveness of sins. **4** As it is written in the book of the words of Isaiah the prophet:

ᵃ 37 Or *then had been a widow for eighty-four years.* *ᵇ 49* Or *be about my Father's business*

"A voice of one calling in the
wilderness,
'Prepare the way for the Lord,
make straight paths for him.
⁵Every valley shall be filled in,
every mountain and hill
made low.
The crooked roads shall
become straight,
the rough ways smooth.
⁶And all people will see God's
salvation.'"ᵃ

⁷John said to the crowds coming out to be baptized by him, "You brood of vipers! Who warned you to flee from the coming wrath? ⁸Produce fruit in keeping with repentance. And do not begin to say to yourselves, 'We have Abraham as our father.' For I tell you that out of these stones God can raise up children for Abraham. ⁹The ax is already at the root of the trees, and every tree that does not produce good fruit will be cut down and thrown into the fire."

¹⁰"What should we do then?" the crowd asked.

¹¹John answered, "Anyone who has two shirts should share with the one who has none, and anyone who has food should do the same."

¹²Even tax collectors came to be baptized. "Teacher," they asked, "what should we do?"

¹³"Don't collect any more than you are required to," he told them.

¹⁴Then some soldiers asked him, "And what should we do?"

He replied, "Don't extort money and don't accuse people falsely — be content with your pay."

¹⁵The people were waiting expectantly and were all wondering in their hearts if John might possibly be the Messiah. ¹⁶John answered them all, "I baptize you withᵇ water. But one who is more powerful than I will come, the straps of whose sandals I am not worthy to untie. He will baptize you withᵇ the Holy Spirit and fire. ¹⁷His winnowing fork is in his hand to clear his threshing floor and to gather the wheat into his barn, but he will burn up the chaff with unquenchable fire." ¹⁸And with many other words John exhorted the people and proclaimed the good news to them.

¹⁹But when John rebuked Herod the tetrarch because of his marriage to Herodias, his brother's wife, and all the other evil things he had done, ²⁰Herod added this to them all: He locked John up in prison.

The Baptism and Genealogy of Jesus

²¹When all the people were being baptized, Jesus was baptized too. And as he was praying, heaven was opened ²²and the Holy Spirit descended on him in bodily form like a dove. And a voice came from heaven: "You are my Son, whom I love; with you I am well pleased."

²³Now Jesus himself was about

ᵃ 6 Isaiah 40:3-5   ᵇ 16 Or in

thirty years old when he began his ministry. He was the son, so it was thought, of Joseph,

the son of Heli, ²⁴the son of Matthat,

the son of Levi, the son of Melki,

the son of Jannai, the son of Joseph,

²⁵the son of Mattathias, the son of Amos,

the son of Nahum, the son of Esli,

the son of Naggai, ²⁶the son of Maath,

the son of Mattathias, the son of Semein,

the son of Josek, the son of Joda,

²⁷the son of Joanan, the son of Rhesa,

the son of Zerubbabel, the son of Shealtiel,

the son of Neri, ²⁸the son of Melki,

the son of Addi, the son of Cosam,

the son of Elmadam, the son of Er,

²⁹the son of Joshua, the son of Eliezer,

the son of Jorim, the son of Matthat,

the son of Levi, ³⁰the son of Simeon,

the son of Judah, the son of Joseph,

the son of Jonam, the son of Eliakim,

³¹the son of Melea, the son of Menna,

the son of Mattatha, the son of Nathan,

the son of David, ³²the son of Jesse,

the son of Obed, the son of Boaz,

the son of Salmon,^{*a*} the son of Nahshon,

³³the son of Amminadab, the son of Ram,^{*b*}

the son of Hezron, the son of Perez,

the son of Judah, ³⁴the son of Jacob,

the son of Isaac, the son of Abraham,

the son of Terah, the son of Nahor,

³⁵the son of Serug, the son of Reu,

the son of Peleg, the son of Eber,

the son of Shelah, ³⁶the son of Cainan,

the son of Arphaxad, the son of Shem,

the son of Noah, the son of Lamech,

³⁷the son of Methuselah, the son of Enoch,

the son of Jared, the son of Mahalalel,

the son of Kenan, ³⁸the son of Enosh,

the son of Seth, the son of Adam,

the son of God.

---

a 32 Some early manuscripts *Sala*   *b 33* Some manuscripts *Amminadab, the son of Admin, the son of Arni*; other manuscripts vary widely.

Jesus Is Tested in the Wilderness

4 Jesus, full of the Holy Spirit, left the Jordan and was led by the Spirit into the wilderness, [2] where for forty days he was tempted[a] by the devil. He ate nothing during those days, and at the end of them he was hungry.

[3] The devil said to him, "If you are the Son of God, tell this stone to become bread."

[4] Jesus answered, "It is written: 'Man shall not live on bread alone.'[b]"

[5] The devil led him up to a high place and showed him in an instant all the kingdoms of the world. [6] And he said to him, "I will give you all their authority and splendor; it has been given to me, and I can give it to anyone I want to. [7] If you worship me, it will all be yours."

[8] Jesus answered, "It is written: 'Worship the Lord your God and serve him only.'[c]"

[9] The devil led him to Jerusalem and had him stand on the highest point of the temple. "If you are the Son of God," he said, "throw yourself down from here. [10] For it is written:

"'He will command his angels
    concerning you
  to guard you carefully;
[11] they will lift you up in their
    hands,

so that you will not strike
    your foot against a
    stone.'[d]"

[12] Jesus answered, "It is said: 'Do not put the Lord your God to the test.'[e]"

[13] When the devil had finished all this tempting, he left him until an opportune time.

Jesus Rejected at Nazareth

[14] Jesus returned to Galilee in the power of the Spirit, and news about him spread through the whole countryside. [15] He was teaching in their synagogues, and everyone praised him.

[16] He went to Nazareth, where he had been brought up, and on the Sabbath day he went into the synagogue, as was his custom. He stood up to read, [17] and the scroll of the prophet Isaiah was handed to him. Unrolling it, he found the place where it is written:

[18] "The Spirit of the Lord is on
    me,
  because he has anointed me
  to proclaim good news to the
    poor.
He has sent me to proclaim
    freedom for the
    prisoners
  and recovery of sight for the
    blind,
to set the oppressed free,
[19]   to proclaim the year of the
    Lord's favor."[f]

---

[a] 2 The Greek for *tempted* can also mean *tested*.   [b] 4 Deut. 8:3   [c] 8 Deut. 6:13
[d] 11 Psalm 91:11,12   [e] 12 Deut. 6:16   [f] 19 Isaiah 61:1,2 (see Septuagint);
Isaiah 58:6

²⁰Then he rolled up the scroll, gave it back to the attendant and sat down. The eyes of everyone in the synagogue were fastened on him. ²¹He began by saying to them, "Today this scripture is fulfilled in your hearing."

²²All spoke well of him and were amazed at the gracious words that came from his lips. "Isn't this Joseph's son?" they asked.

²³Jesus said to them, "Surely you will quote this proverb to me: 'Physician, heal yourself!' And you will tell me, 'Do here in your hometown what we have heard that you did in Capernaum.' "

²⁴"Truly I tell you," he continued, "no prophet is accepted in his hometown. ²⁵I assure you that there were many widows in Israel in Elijah's time, when the sky was shut for three and a half years and there was a severe famine throughout the land. ²⁶Yet Elijah was not sent to any of them, but to a widow in Zarephath in the region of Sidon. ²⁷And there were many in Israel with leprosy*a* in the time of Elisha the prophet, yet not one of them was cleansed — only Naaman the Syrian."

²⁸All the people in the synagogue were furious when they heard this. ²⁹They got up, drove him out of the town, and took him to the brow of the hill on which the town was built, in order to throw him off the cliff. ³⁰But he walked right through the crowd and went on his way.

Jesus Drives Out an Impure Spirit

³¹Then he went down to Capernaum, a town in Galilee, and on the Sabbath he taught the people. ³²They were amazed at his teaching, because his words had authority.

³³In the synagogue there was a man possessed by a demon, an impure spirit. He cried out at the top of his voice, ³⁴"Go away! What do you want with us, Jesus of Nazareth? Have you come to destroy us? I know who you are — the Holy One of God!"

³⁵"Be quiet!" Jesus said sternly. "Come out of him!" Then the demon threw the man down before them all and came out without injuring him.

³⁶All the people were amazed and said to each other, "What words these are! With authority and power he gives orders to impure spirits and they come out!" ³⁷And the news about him spread throughout the surrounding area.

Jesus Heals Many

³⁸Jesus left the synagogue and went to the home of Simon. Now Simon's mother-in-law was suffering from a high fever, and they asked Jesus to help her. ³⁹So he bent over her and rebuked the

---

a 27 The Greek word traditionally translated *leprosy* was used for various diseases affecting the skin.

fever, and it left her. She got up at once and began to wait on them.

⁴⁰At sunset, the people brought to Jesus all who had various kinds of sickness, and laying his hands on each one, he healed them. ⁴¹Moreover, demons came out of many people, shouting, "You are the Son of God!" But he rebuked them and would not allow them to speak, because they knew he was the Messiah.

⁴²At daybreak, Jesus went out to a solitary place. The people were looking for him and when they came to where he was, they tried to keep him from leaving them. ⁴³But he said, "I must proclaim the good news of the kingdom of God to the other towns also, because that is why I was sent." ⁴⁴And he kept on preaching in the synagogues of Judea.

Jesus Calls His First Disciples

5 One day as Jesus was standing by the Lake of Gennesaret,ᵃ the people were crowding around him and listening to the word of God. ²He saw at the water's edge two boats, left there by the fishermen, who were washing their nets. ³He got into one of the boats, the one belonging to Simon, and asked him to put out a little from shore. Then he sat down and taught the people from the boat.

⁴When he had finished speaking, he said to Simon, "Put out into deep water, and let down the nets for a catch."

⁵Simon answered, "Master, we've worked hard all night and haven't caught anything. But because you say so, I will let down the nets."

⁶When they had done so, they caught such a large number of fish that their nets began to break. ⁷So they signaled their partners in the other boat to come and help them, and they came and filled both boats so full that they began to sink.

⁸When Simon Peter saw this, he fell at Jesus' knees and said, "Go away from me, Lord; I am a sinful man!" ⁹For he and all his companions were astonished at the catch of fish they had taken, ¹⁰and so were James and John, the sons of Zebedee, Simon's partners.

Then Jesus said to Simon, "Don't be afraid; from now on you will fish for people." ¹¹So they pulled their boats up on shore, left everything and followed him.

Jesus Heals a Man With Leprosy

¹²While Jesus was in one of the towns, a man came along who was covered with leprosy.ᵇ When he saw Jesus, he fell with his face to the ground and begged him, "Lord, if you are willing, you can make me clean."

¹³Jesus reached out his hand and touched the man. "I am will-

---

ᵃ 1 That is, the Sea of Galilee   ᵇ 12 The Greek word traditionally translated *leprosy* was used for various diseases affecting the skin.

ing," he said. "Be clean!" And immediately the leprosy left him.

¹⁴Then Jesus ordered him, "Don't tell anyone, but go, show yourself to the priest and offer the sacrifices that Moses commanded for your cleansing, as a testimony to them."

¹⁵Yet the news about him spread all the more, so that crowds of people came to hear him and to be healed of their sicknesses. ¹⁶But Jesus often withdrew to lonely places and prayed.

Jesus Forgives and Heals a Paralyzed Man

¹⁷One day Jesus was teaching, and Pharisees and teachers of the law were sitting there. They had come from every village of Galilee and from Judea and Jerusalem. And the power of the Lord was with Jesus to heal the sick. ¹⁸Some men came carrying a paralyzed man on a mat and tried to take him into the house to lay him before Jesus. ¹⁹When they could not find a way to do this because of the crowd, they went up on the roof and lowered him on his mat through the tiles into the middle of the crowd, right in front of Jesus. ²⁰When Jesus saw their faith, he said, "Friend, your sins are forgiven."

²¹The Pharisees and the teachers of the law began thinking to themselves, "Who is this fellow who speaks blasphemy? Who can forgive sins but God alone?"

²²Jesus knew what they were thinking and asked, "Why are you thinking these things in your hearts? ²³Which is easier: to say, 'Your sins are forgiven,' or to say, 'Get up and walk'? ²⁴But I want you to know that the Son of Man has authority on earth to forgive sins." So he said to the paralyzed man, "I tell you, get up, take your mat and go home." ²⁵Immediately he stood up in front of them, took what he had been lying on and went home praising God. ²⁶Everyone was amazed and gave praise to God. They were filled with awe and said, "We have seen remarkable things today."

Jesus Calls Levi and Eats With Sinners

²⁷After this, Jesus went out and saw a tax collector by the name of Levi sitting at his tax booth. "Follow me," Jesus said to him, ²⁸and Levi got up, left everything and followed him.

²⁹Then Levi held a great banquet for Jesus at his house, and a large crowd of tax collectors and others were eating with them. ³⁰But the Pharisees and the teachers of the law who belonged to their sect complained to his disciples, "Why do you eat and drink with tax collectors and sinners?"

³¹Jesus answered them, "It is not the healthy who need a doctor, but the sick. ³²I have not come to call the righteous, but sinners to repentance."

Jesus Questioned About Fasting

³³They said to him, "John's disciples often fast and pray, and so do the disciples of the Pharisees, but yours go on eating and drinking."

³⁴Jesus answered, "Can you make the friends of the bridegroom fast while he is with them? ³⁵But the time will come when the bridegroom will be taken from them; in those days they will fast."

³⁶He told them this parable: "No one tears a piece out of a new garment to patch an old one. Otherwise, they will have torn the new garment, and the patch from the new will not match the old. ³⁷And no one pours new wine into old wineskins. Otherwise, the new wine will burst the skins; the wine will run out and the wineskins will be ruined. ³⁸No, new wine must be poured into new wineskins. ³⁹And no one after drinking old wine wants the new, for they say, 'The old is better.'"

Jesus Is Lord of the Sabbath

6 One Sabbath Jesus was going through the grainfields, and his disciples began to pick some heads of grain, rub them in their hands and eat the kernels. ²Some of the Pharisees asked, "Why are you doing what is unlawful on the Sabbath?"

³Jesus answered them, "Have you never read what David did when he and his companions were hungry? ⁴He entered the house of God, and taking the consecrated bread, he ate what is lawful only for priests to eat. And he also gave some to his companions." ⁵Then Jesus said to them, "The Son of Man is Lord of the Sabbath."

⁶On another Sabbath he went into the synagogue and was teaching, and a man was there whose right hand was shriveled. ⁷The Pharisees and the teachers of the law were looking for a reason to accuse Jesus, so they watched him closely to see if he would heal on the Sabbath. ⁸But Jesus knew what they were thinking and said to the man with the shriveled hand, "Get up and stand in front of everyone." So he got up and stood there.

⁹Then Jesus said to them, "I ask you, which is lawful on the Sabbath: to do good or to do evil, to save life or to destroy it?"

¹⁰He looked around at them all, and then said to the man, "Stretch out your hand." He did so, and his hand was completely restored. ¹¹But the Pharisees and the teachers of the law were furious and began to discuss with one another what they might do to Jesus.

The Twelve Apostles

¹²One of those days Jesus went out to a mountainside to pray, and spent the night praying to God. ¹³When morning came, he called his disciples to him and chose twelve of them, whom he also designated apostles: ¹⁴Simon (whom he named Peter),

his brother Andrew, James, John, Philip, Bartholomew, ¹⁵Matthew, Thomas, James son of Alphaeus, Simon who was called the Zealot, ¹⁶Judas son of James, and Judas Iscariot, who became a traitor.

Blessings and Woes

¹⁷He went down with them and stood on a level place. A large crowd of his disciples was there and a great number of people from all over Judea, from Jerusalem, and from the coastal region around Tyre and Sidon, ¹⁸who had come to hear him and to be healed of their diseases. Those troubled by impure spirits were cured, ¹⁹and the people all tried to touch him, because power was coming from him and healing them all.

²⁰Looking at his disciples, he said:

"Blessed are you who are poor,
for yours is the kingdom of God.
²¹Blessed are you who hunger now,
for you will be satisfied.
Blessed are you who weep now,
for you will laugh.
²²Blessed are you when people hate you,
when they exclude you and insult you
and reject your name as evil,
because of the Son of Man.

²³"Rejoice in that day and leap for joy, because great is your reward in heaven. For that is how their ancestors treated the prophets.

²⁴"But woe to you who are rich,
for you have already received your comfort.
²⁵Woe to you who are well fed now,
for you will go hungry.
Woe to you who laugh now,
for you will mourn and weep.
²⁶Woe to you when everyone speaks well of you,
for that is how their ancestors treated the false prophets.

Love for Enemies

²⁷"But to you who are listening I say: Love your enemies, do good to those who hate you, ²⁸bless those who curse you, pray for those who mistreat you. ²⁹If someone slaps you on one cheek, turn to them the other also. If someone takes your coat, do not withhold your shirt from them. ³⁰Give to everyone who asks you, and if anyone takes what belongs to you, do not demand it back. ³¹Do to others as you would have them do to you.

³²"If you love those who love you, what credit is that to you? Even sinners love those who love them. ³³And if you do good to those who are good to you, what credit is that to you? Even sinners do that. ³⁴And if you lend to those from whom you expect repayment, what credit is that to you? Even

sinners lend to sinners, expecting to be repaid in full. **35** But love your enemies, do good to them, and lend to them without expecting to get anything back. Then your reward will be great, and you will be children of the Most High, because he is kind to the ungrateful and wicked. **36** Be merciful, just as your Father is merciful.

Judging Others

37 "Do not judge, and you will not be judged. Do not condemn, and you will not be condemned. Forgive, and you will be forgiven. **38** Give, and it will be given to you. A good measure, pressed down, shaken together and running over, will be poured into your lap. For with the measure you use, it will be measured to you."

39 He also told them this parable: "Can the blind lead the blind? Will they not both fall into a pit? **40** The student is not above the teacher, but everyone who is fully trained will be like their teacher.

41 "Why do you look at the speck of sawdust in your brother's eye and pay no attention to the plank in your own eye? **42** How can you say to your brother, 'Brother, let me take the speck out of your eye,' when you yourself fail to see the plank in your own eye? You hypocrite, first take the plank out of your eye, and then you will see clearly to remove the speck from your brother's eye.

A Tree and Its Fruit

43 "No good tree bears bad fruit, nor does a bad tree bear good fruit. **44** Each tree is recognized by its own fruit. People do not pick figs from thornbushes, or grapes from briers. **45** A good man brings good things out of the good stored up in his heart, and an evil man brings evil things out of the evil stored up in his heart. For the mouth speaks what the heart is full of.

The Wise and Foolish Builders

46 "Why do you call me, 'Lord, Lord,' and do not do what I say? **47** As for everyone who comes to me and hears my words and puts them into practice, I will show you what they are like. **48** They are like a man building a house, who dug down deep and laid the foundation on rock. When a flood came, the torrent struck that house but could not shake it, because it was well built. **49** But the one who hears my words and does not put them into practice is like a man who built a house on the ground without a foundation. The moment the torrent struck that house, it collapsed and its destruction was complete."

The Faith of the Centurion

7 When Jesus had finished saying all this to the people who were listening, he entered Capernaum. **2** There a centurion's servant, whom his master valued highly, was sick and about to die.

³The centurion heard of Jesus and sent some elders of the Jews to him, asking him to come and heal his servant. ⁴When they came to Jesus, they pleaded earnestly with him, "This man deserves to have you do this, ⁵because he loves our nation and has built our synagogue." ⁶So Jesus went with them.

He was not far from the house when the centurion sent friends to say to him: "Lord, don't trouble yourself, for I do not deserve to have you come under my roof. ⁷That is why I did not even consider myself worthy to come to you. But say the word, and my servant will be healed. ⁸For I myself am a man under authority, with soldiers under me. I tell this one, 'Go,' and he goes; and that one, 'Come,' and he comes. I say to my servant, 'Do this,' and he does it."

⁹When Jesus heard this, he was amazed at him, and turning to the crowd following him, he said, "I tell you, I have not found such great faith even in Israel." ¹⁰Then the men who had been sent returned to the house and found the servant well.

Jesus Raises a Widow's Son

¹¹Soon afterward, Jesus went to a town called Nain, and his disciples and a large crowd went along with him. ¹²As he approached the town gate, a dead person was being carried out — the only son of his mother, and she was a widow. And a large crowd from the town was with her. ¹³When the Lord saw her, his heart went out to her and he said, "Don't cry."

¹⁴Then he went up and touched the bier they were carrying him on, and the bearers stood still. He said, "Young man, I say to you, get up!" ¹⁵The dead man sat up and began to talk, and Jesus gave him back to his mother.

¹⁶They were all filled with awe and praised God. "A great prophet has appeared among us," they said. "God has come to help his people." ¹⁷This news about Jesus spread throughout Judea and the surrounding country.

Jesus and John the Baptist

¹⁸John's disciples told him about all these things. Calling two of them, ¹⁹he sent them to the Lord to ask, "Are you the one who is to come, or should we expect someone else?"

²⁰When the men came to Jesus, they said, "John the Baptist sent us to you to ask, 'Are you the one who is to come, or should we expect someone else?'"

²¹At that very time Jesus cured many who had diseases, sicknesses and evil spirits, and gave sight to many who were blind. ²²So he replied to the messengers, "Go back and report to John what you have seen and heard: The blind receive sight, the lame walk, those who have leprosy*a*

---

a 22 The Greek word traditionally translated *leprosy* was used for various diseases affecting the skin.

are cleansed, the deaf hear, the dead are raised, and the good news is proclaimed to the poor. ²³Blessed is anyone who does not stumble on account of me."

²⁴After John's messengers left, Jesus began to speak to the crowd about John: "What did you go out into the wilderness to see? A reed swayed by the wind? ²⁵If not, what did you go out to see? A man dressed in fine clothes? No, those who wear expensive clothes and indulge in luxury are in palaces. ²⁶But what did you go out to see? A prophet? Yes, I tell you, and more than a prophet. ²⁷This is the one about whom it is written:

> " 'I will send my messenger
>   ahead of you,
>   who will prepare your way
>   before you.'ᵃ

²⁸I tell you, among those born of women there is no one greater than John; yet the one who is least in the kingdom of God is greater than he."

²⁹(All the people, even the tax collectors, when they heard Jesus' words, acknowledged that God's way was right, because they had been baptized by John. ³⁰But the Pharisees and the experts in the law rejected God's purpose for themselves, because they had not been baptized by John.)

³¹Jesus went on to say, "To what, then, can I compare the people of this generation? What are they like? ³²They are like children sitting in the marketplace and calling out to each other:

> " 'We played the pipe for you,
>   and you did not dance;
>   we sang a dirge,
>   and you did not cry.'

³³For John the Baptist came neither eating bread nor drinking wine, and you say, 'He has a demon.' ³⁴The Son of Man came eating and drinking, and you say, 'Here is a glutton and a drunkard, a friend of tax collectors and sinners.' ³⁵But wisdom is proved right by all her children."

Jesus Anointed by a Sinful Woman

³⁶When one of the Pharisees invited Jesus to have dinner with him, he went to the Pharisee's house and reclined at the table. ³⁷A woman in that town who lived a sinful life learned that Jesus was eating at the Pharisee's house, so she came there with an alabaster jar of perfume. ³⁸As she stood behind him at his feet weeping, she began to wet his feet with her tears. Then she wiped them with her hair, kissed them and poured perfume on them. ³⁹When the Pharisee who had invited him saw this, he said to himself, "If this man were a prophet, he would know who is touching him and what kind of woman she is—that she is a sinner."

ᵃ 27 Mal. 3:1

40 Jesus answered him, "Simon, I have something to tell you."

"Tell me, teacher," he said.

41 "Two people owed money to a certain moneylender. One owed him five hundred denarii,[a] and the other fifty. **42** Neither of them had the money to pay him back, so he forgave the debts of both. Now which of them will love him more?"

43 Simon replied, "I suppose the one who had the bigger debt forgiven."

"You have judged correctly," Jesus said.

44 Then he turned toward the woman and said to Simon, "Do you see this woman? I came into your house. You did not give me any water for my feet, but she wet my feet with her tears and wiped them with her hair. **45** You did not give me a kiss, but this woman, from the time I entered, has not stopped kissing my feet. **46** You did not put oil on my head, but she has poured perfume on my feet. **47** Therefore, I tell you, her many sins have been forgiven—as her great love has shown. But whoever has been forgiven little loves little."

48 Then Jesus said to her, "Your sins are forgiven."

49 The other guests began to say among themselves, "Who is this who even forgives sins?"

50 Jesus said to the woman, "Your faith has saved you; go in peace."

The Parable of the Sower

8 After this, Jesus traveled about from one town and village to another, proclaiming the good news of the kingdom of God. The Twelve were with him, **2** and also some women who had been cured of evil spirits and diseases: Mary (called Magdalene) from whom seven demons had come out; **3** Joanna the wife of Chuza, the manager of Herod's household; Susanna; and many others. These women were helping to support them out of their own means.

4 While a large crowd was gathering and people were coming to Jesus from town after town, he told this parable: **5** "A farmer went out to sow his seed. As he was scattering the seed, some fell along the path; it was trampled on, and the birds ate it up. **6** Some fell on rocky ground, and when it came up, the plants withered because they had no moisture. **7** Other seed fell among thorns, which grew up with it and choked the plants. **8** Still other seed fell on good soil. It came up and yielded a crop, a hundred times more than was sown."

When he said this, he called out, "Whoever has ears to hear, let them hear."

9 His disciples asked him what this parable meant. **10** He said, "The knowledge of the secrets of the kingdom of God has been

---

[a] *41* A denarius was the usual daily wage of a day laborer (see Matt. 20:2).

given to you, but to others I speak in parables, so that,

" 'though seeing, they may not
see;
though hearing, they may
not understand.'[a]

11 "This is the meaning of the parable: The seed is the word of God. 12 Those along the path are the ones who hear, and then the devil comes and takes away the word from their hearts, so that they may not believe and be saved. 13 Those on the rocky ground are the ones who receive the word with joy when they hear it, but they have no root. They believe for a while, but in the time of testing they fall away. 14 The seed that fell among thorns stands for those who hear, but as they go on their way they are choked by life's worries, riches and pleasures, and they do not mature. 15 But the seed on good soil stands for those with a noble and good heart, who hear the word, retain it, and by persevering produce a crop.

A Lamp on a Stand

16 "No one lights a lamp and hides it in a clay jar or puts it under a bed. Instead, they put it on a stand, so that those who come in can see the light. 17 For there is nothing hidden that will not be disclosed, and nothing concealed that will not be known or brought out into the open.

18 Therefore consider carefully how you listen. Whoever has will be given more; whoever does not have, even what they think they have will be taken from them."

Jesus' Mother and Brothers

19 Now Jesus' mother and brothers came to see him, but they were not able to get near him because of the crowd. 20 Someone told him, "Your mother and brothers are standing outside, wanting to see you."

21 He replied, "My mother and brothers are those who hear God's word and put it into practice."

Jesus Calms the Storm

22 One day Jesus said to his disciples, "Let us go over to the other side of the lake." So they got into a boat and set out. 23 As they sailed, he fell asleep. A squall came down on the lake, so that the boat was being swamped, and they were in great danger.

24 The disciples went and woke him, saying, "Master, Master, we're going to drown!"

He got up and rebuked the wind and the raging waters; the storm subsided, and all was calm. 25 "Where is your faith?" he asked his disciples.

In fear and amazement they asked one another, "Who is this? He commands even the winds and the water, and they obey him."

a 10 Isaiah 6:9

Jesus Restores a Demon-Possessed Man

²⁶They sailed to the region of the Gerasenes,ᵃ which is across the lake from Galilee. ²⁷When Jesus stepped ashore, he was met by a demon-possessed man from the town. For a long time this man had not worn clothes or lived in a house, but had lived in the tombs. ²⁸When he saw Jesus, he cried out and fell at his feet, shouting at the top of his voice, "What do you want with me, Jesus, Son of the Most High God? I beg you, don't torture me!" ²⁹For Jesus had commanded the impure spirit to come out of the man. Many times it had seized him, and though he was chained hand and foot and kept under guard, he had broken his chains and had been driven by the demon into solitary places.

³⁰Jesus asked him, "What is your name?"

"Legion," he replied, because many demons had gone into him. ³¹And they begged Jesus repeatedly not to order them to go into the Abyss.

³²A large herd of pigs was feeding there on the hillside. The demons begged Jesus to let them go into the pigs, and he gave them permission. ³³When the demons came out of the man, they went into the pigs, and the herd rushed down the steep bank into the lake and was drowned.

³⁴When those tending the pigs saw what had happened, they ran off and reported this in the town and countryside, ³⁵and the people went out to see what had happened. When they came to Jesus, they found the man from whom the demons had gone out, sitting at Jesus' feet, dressed and in his right mind; and they were afraid. ³⁶Those who had seen it told the people how the demon-possessed man had been cured. ³⁷Then all the people of the region of the Gerasenes asked Jesus to leave them, because they were overcome with fear. So he got into the boat and left.

³⁸The man from whom the demons had gone out begged to go with him, but Jesus sent him away, saying, ³⁹"Return home and tell how much God has done for you." So the man went away and told all over town how much Jesus had done for him.

Jesus Raises a Dead Girl and Heals a Sick Woman

⁴⁰Now when Jesus returned, a crowd welcomed him, for they were all expecting him. ⁴¹Then a man named Jairus, a synagogue leader, came and fell at Jesus' feet, pleading with him to come to his house ⁴²because his only daughter, a girl of about twelve, was dying.

As Jesus was on his way, the crowds almost crushed him.

ᵃ 26 Some manuscripts *Gadarenes*; other manuscripts *Gergesenes*; also in verse 37

⁴³And a woman was there who had been subject to bleeding for twelve years,ᵃ but no one could heal her. ⁴⁴She came up behind him and touched the edge of his cloak, and immediately her bleeding stopped.

⁴⁵"Who touched me?" Jesus asked.

When they all denied it, Peter said, "Master, the people are crowding and pressing against you."

⁴⁶But Jesus said, "Someone touched me; I know that power has gone out from me."

⁴⁷Then the woman, seeing that she could not go unnoticed, came trembling and fell at his feet. In the presence of all the people, she told why she had touched him and how she had been instantly healed. ⁴⁸Then he said to her, "Daughter, your faith has healed you. Go in peace."

⁴⁹While Jesus was still speaking, someone came from the house of Jairus, the synagogue leader. "Your daughter is dead," he said. "Don't bother the teacher anymore."

⁵⁰Hearing this, Jesus said to Jairus, "Don't be afraid; just believe, and she will be healed."

⁵¹When he arrived at the house of Jairus, he did not let anyone go in with him except Peter, John and James, and the child's father and mother. ⁵²Meanwhile, all the people were wailing and mourning for her. "Stop wailing," Jesus said. "She is not dead but asleep."

⁵³They laughed at him, knowing that she was dead. ⁵⁴But he took her by the hand and said, "My child, get up!" ⁵⁵Her spirit returned, and at once she stood up. Then Jesus told them to give her something to eat. ⁵⁶Her parents were astonished, but he ordered them not to tell anyone what had happened.

Jesus Sends Out the Twelve

9 When Jesus had called the Twelve together, he gave them power and authority to drive out all demons and to cure diseases, ²and he sent them out to proclaim the kingdom of God and to heal the sick. ³He told them: "Take nothing for the journey — no staff, no bag, no bread, no money, no extra shirt. ⁴Whatever house you enter, stay there until you leave that town. ⁵If people do not welcome you, leave their town and shake the dust off your feet as a testimony against them." ⁶So they set out and went from village to village, proclaiming the good news and healing people everywhere.

⁷Now Herod the tetrarch heard about all that was going on. And he was perplexed because some were saying that John had been raised from the dead, ⁸others that Elijah had appeared, and still others that one of the prophets of long ago

ᵃ 43 Many manuscripts *years, and she had spent all she had on doctors* had come back to life. **⁹**But Herod said, "I beheaded John. Who, then, is this I hear such things about?" And he tried to see him.

Jesus Feeds the Five Thousand

¹⁰When the apostles returned, they reported to Jesus what they had done. Then he took them with him and they withdrew by themselves to a town called Bethsaida, **¹¹**but the crowds learned about it and followed him. He welcomed them and spoke to them about the kingdom of God, and healed those who needed healing.

¹²Late in the afternoon the Twelve came to him and said, "Send the crowd away so they can go to the surrounding villages and countryside and find food and lodging, because we are in a remote place here."

¹³He replied, "You give them something to eat."

They answered, "We have only five loaves of bread and two fish—unless we go and buy food for all this crowd." **¹⁴**(About five thousand men were there.)

But he said to his disciples, "Have them sit down in groups of about fifty each." **¹⁵**The disciples did so, and everyone sat down. **¹⁶**Taking the five loaves and the two fish and looking up to heaven, he gave thanks and broke them. Then he gave them to the disciples to distribute to the people. **¹⁷**They all ate and were satisfied, and the disciples picked up twelve basketfuls of broken pieces that were left over.

Peter Declares That Jesus Is the Messiah

¹⁸Once when Jesus was praying in private and his disciples were with him, he asked them, "Who do the crowds say I am?"

¹⁹They replied, "Some say John the Baptist; others say Elijah; and still others, that one of the prophets of long ago has come back to life."

²⁰"But what about you?" he asked. "Who do you say I am?"

Peter answered, "God's Messiah."

Jesus Predicts His Death

²¹Jesus strictly warned them not to tell this to anyone. **²²**And he said, "The Son of Man must suffer many things and be rejected by the elders, the chief priests and the teachers of the law, and he must be killed and on the third day be raised to life."

²³Then he said to them all: "Whoever wants to be my disciple must deny themselves and take up their cross daily and follow me. **²⁴**For whoever wants to save their life will lose it, but whoever loses their life for me will save it. **²⁵**What good is it for someone to gain the whole world, and yet lose or forfeit their very self? **²⁶**Whoever is ashamed of me and my words, the Son of Man will be ashamed of them when he comes in his glory and in the glory of the Father and of the holy angels.

²⁷ "Truly I tell you, some who are standing here will not taste death before they see the kingdom of God."

The Transfiguration

²⁸ About eight days after Jesus said this, he took Peter, John and James with him and went up onto a mountain to pray. ²⁹ As he was praying, the appearance of his face changed, and his clothes became as bright as a flash of lightning. ³⁰ Two men, Moses and Elijah, appeared in glorious splendor, talking with Jesus. ³¹ They spoke about his departure,ᵃ which he was about to bring to fulfillment at Jerusalem. ³² Peter and his companions were very sleepy, but when they became fully awake, they saw his glory and the two men standing with him. ³³ As the men were leaving Jesus, Peter said to him, "Master, it is good for us to be here. Let us put up three shelters — one for you, one for Moses and one for Elijah." (He did not know what he was saying.)

³⁴ While he was speaking, a cloud appeared and covered them, and they were afraid as they entered the cloud. ³⁵ A voice came from the cloud, saying, "This is my Son, whom I have chosen; listen to him." ³⁶ When the voice had spoken, they found that Jesus was alone. The disciples kept this to themselves and did not tell anyone at that time what they had seen.

Jesus Heals a Demon-Possessed Boy

³⁷ The next day, when they came down from the mountain, a large crowd met him. ³⁸ A man in the crowd called out, "Teacher, I beg you to look at my son, for he is my only child. ³⁹ A spirit seizes him and he suddenly screams; it throws him into convulsions so that he foams at the mouth. It scarcely ever leaves him and is destroying him. ⁴⁰ I begged your disciples to drive it out, but they could not."

⁴¹ "You unbelieving and perverse generation," Jesus replied, "how long shall I stay with you and put up with you? Bring your son here."

⁴² Even while the boy was coming, the demon threw him to the ground in a convulsion. But Jesus rebuked the impure spirit, healed the boy and gave him back to his father. ⁴³ And they were all amazed at the greatness of God.

Jesus Predicts His Death a Second Time

While everyone was marveling at all that Jesus did, he said to his disciples, ⁴⁴ "Listen carefully to what I am about to tell you: The Son of Man is going to be de-

ᵃ 31 Greek *exodos*

livered into the hands of men." ⁴⁵But they did not understand what this meant. It was hidden from them, so that they did not grasp it, and they were afraid to ask him about it.

⁴⁶An argument started among the disciples as to which of them would be the greatest. ⁴⁷Jesus, knowing their thoughts, took a little child and had him stand beside him. ⁴⁸Then he said to them, "Whoever welcomes this little child in my name welcomes me; and whoever welcomes me welcomes the one who sent me. For it is the one who is least among you all who is the greatest."

⁴⁹"Master," said John, "we saw someone driving out demons in your name and we tried to stop him, because he is not one of us."

⁵⁰"Do not stop him," Jesus said, "for whoever is not against you is for you."

Samaritan Opposition

⁵¹As the time approached for him to be taken up to heaven, Jesus resolutely set out for Jerusalem. ⁵²And he sent messengers on ahead, who went into a Samaritan village to get things ready for him; ⁵³but the people there did not welcome him, because he was heading for Jerusalem. ⁵⁴When the disciples James and John saw this, they asked, "Lord, do you want us to call fire down from heaven to destroy them*ᵃ*?" ⁵⁵But Jesus turned and rebuked them. ⁵⁶Then he and his disciples went to another village.

The Cost of Following Jesus

⁵⁷As they were walking along the road, a man said to him, "I will follow you wherever you go."

⁵⁸Jesus replied, "Foxes have dens and birds have nests, but the Son of Man has no place to lay his head."

⁵⁹He said to another man, "Follow me."

But he replied, "Lord, first let me go and bury my father."

⁶⁰Jesus said to him, "Let the dead bury their own dead, but you go and proclaim the kingdom of God."

⁶¹Still another said, "I will follow you, Lord; but first let me go back and say goodbye to my family."

⁶²Jesus replied, "No one who puts a hand to the plow and looks back is fit for service in the kingdom of God."

Jesus Sends Out the Seventy-Two

10 After this the Lord appointed seventy-two*ᵇ* others and sent them two by two ahead of him to every town and place where he was about to go. ²He told them, "The harvest is plentiful, but the workers are few. Ask the Lord of the harvest, therefore, to send out workers into his

ᵃ 54 Some manuscripts *them, just as Elijah did* also in verse 17   *ᵇ 1* Some manuscripts *seventy;*

harvest field. ³Go! I am sending you out like lambs among wolves. ⁴Do not take a purse or bag or sandals; and do not greet anyone on the road.

⁵"When you enter a house, first say, 'Peace to this house.' ⁶If someone who promotes peace is there, your peace will rest on them; if not, it will return to you. ⁷Stay there, eating and drinking whatever they give you, for the worker deserves his wages. Do not move around from house to house.

⁸"When you enter a town and are welcomed, eat what is offered to you. ⁹Heal the sick who are there and tell them, 'The kingdom of God has come near to you.' ¹⁰But when you enter a town and are not welcomed, go into its streets and say, ¹¹'Even the dust of your town we wipe from our feet as a warning to you. Yet be sure of this: The kingdom of God has come near.' ¹²I tell you, it will be more bearable on that day for Sodom than for that town.

¹³"Woe to you, Chorazin! Woe to you, Bethsaida! For if the miracles that were performed in you had been performed in Tyre and Sidon, they would have repented long ago, sitting in sackcloth and ashes. ¹⁴But it will be more bearable for Tyre and Sidon at the judgment than for you. ¹⁵And you, Capernaum, will you be lifted to the heavens? No, you will go down to Hades.ᵃ

¹⁶"Whoever listens to you listens to me; whoever rejects you rejects me; but whoever rejects me rejects him who sent me."

¹⁷The seventy-two returned with joy and said, "Lord, even the demons submit to us in your name."

¹⁸He replied, "I saw Satan fall like lightning from heaven. ¹⁹I have given you authority to trample on snakes and scorpions and to overcome all the power of the enemy; nothing will harm you. ²⁰However, do not rejoice that the spirits submit to you, but rejoice that your names are written in heaven."

²¹At that time Jesus, full of joy through the Holy Spirit, said, "I praise you, Father, Lord of heaven and earth, because you have hidden these things from the wise and learned, and revealed them to little children. Yes, Father, for this is what you were pleased to do.

²²"All things have been committed to me by my Father. No one knows who the Son is except the Father, and no one knows who the Father is except the Son and those to whom the Son chooses to reveal him."

²³Then he turned to his disciples and said privately, "Blessed are the eyes that see what you see. ²⁴For I tell you that many prophets and kings wanted to see what you see but did not see

ᵃ 15 That is, the realm of the dead

it, and to hear what you hear but did not hear it."

The Parable of the Good Samaritan

²⁵On one occasion an expert in the law stood up to test Jesus. "Teacher," he asked, "what must I do to inherit eternal life?"

²⁶"What is written in the Law?" he replied. "How do you read it?"

²⁷He answered, " 'Love the Lord your God with all your heart and with all your soul and with all your strength and with all your mind'ᵃ; and, 'Love your neighbor as yourself.'ᵇ"

²⁸"You have answered correctly," Jesus replied. "Do this and you will live."

²⁹But he wanted to justify himself, so he asked Jesus, "And who is my neighbor?"

³⁰In reply Jesus said: "A man was going down from Jerusalem to Jericho, when he was attacked by robbers. They stripped him of his clothes, beat him and went away, leaving him half dead. ³¹A priest happened to be going down the same road, and when he saw the man, he passed by on the other side. ³²So too, a Levite, when he came to the place and saw him, passed by on the other side. ³³But a Samaritan, as he traveled, came where the man was; and when he saw him, he took pity on him. ³⁴He went to

him and bandaged his wounds, pouring on oil and wine. Then he put the man on his own donkey, brought him to an inn and took care of him. ³⁵The next day he took out two denariiᶜ and gave them to the innkeeper. 'Look after him,' he said, 'and when I return, I will reimburse you for any extra expense you may have.'

³⁶"Which of these three do you think was a neighbor to the man who fell into the hands of robbers?"

³⁷The expert in the law replied, "The one who had mercy on him."

Jesus told him, "Go and do likewise."

At the Home of Martha and Mary

³⁸As Jesus and his disciples were on their way, he came to a village where a woman named Martha opened her home to him. ³⁹She had a sister called Mary, who sat at the Lord's feet listening to what he said. ⁴⁰But Martha was distracted by all the preparations that had to be made. She came to him and asked, "Lord, don't you care that my sister has left me to do the work by myself? Tell her to help me!"

⁴¹"Martha, Martha," the Lord answered, "you are worried and upset about many things, ⁴²but few things are needed—or indeed

---

ᵃ 27 Deut. 6:5   ᵇ 27 Lev. 19:18   ᶜ 35 A denarius was the usual daily wage of a day laborer (see Matt. 20:2).

only one.[a] Mary has chosen what is better, and it will not be taken away from her."

Jesus' Teaching on Prayer

11 One day Jesus was praying in a certain place. When he finished, one of his disciples said to him, "Lord, teach us to pray, just as John taught his disciples."

[2] He said to them, "When you pray, say:

" 'Father,[b]
hallowed be your name,
your kingdom come.[c]
[3] Give us each day our daily
bread.
[4] Forgive us our sins,
for we also forgive everyone
who sins against us.[d]
And lead us not into
temptation.[e] '"

[5] Then Jesus said to them, "Suppose you have a friend, and you go to him at midnight and say, 'Friend, lend me three loaves of bread; [6] a friend of mine on a journey has come to me, and I have no food to offer him.' [7] And suppose the one inside answers, 'Don't bother me. The door is already locked, and my children and I are in bed. I can't get up and give you anything.' [8] I tell you, even though he will not get up and give you the bread because of friendship, yet because of your shameless audacity[f] he will surely get up and give you as much as you need.

[9] "So I say to you: Ask and it will be given to you; seek and you will find; knock and the door will be opened to you. [10] For everyone who asks receives; the one who seeks finds; and to the one who knocks, the door will be opened.

[11] "Which of you fathers, if your son asks for[g] a fish, will give him a snake instead? [12] Or if he asks for an egg, will give him a scorpion? [13] If you then, though you are evil, know how to give good gifts to your children, how much more will your Father in heaven give the Holy Spirit to those who ask him!"

Jesus and Beelzebul

[14] Jesus was driving out a demon that was mute. When the demon left, the man who had been mute spoke, and the crowd was amazed. [15] But some of them said, "By Beelzebul, the prince of demons, he is driving out demons." [16] Others tested him by asking for a sign from heaven.

[17] Jesus knew their thoughts and said to them: "Any kingdom divided against itself will be ruined, and a house divided against itself will fall. [18] If Satan is divided against himself, how can his

---

[a] 42 Some manuscripts *but only one thing is needed*   [b] 2 Some manuscripts *Our Father in heaven*   [c] 2 Some manuscripts *come. May your will be done on earth as it is in heaven.*   [d] 4 Greek *everyone who is indebted to us*   [e] 4 Some manuscripts *temptation, but deliver us from the evil one*   [f] 8 Or *yet to preserve his good name*   [g] 11 Some manuscripts *for bread, will give him a stone? Or if he asks for*

kingdom stand? I say this because you claim that I drive out demons by Beelzebul. **19** Now if I drive out demons by Beelzebul, by whom do your followers drive them out? So then, they will be your judges. **20** But if I drive out demons by the finger of God, then the kingdom of God has come upon you.

21 "When a strong man, fully armed, guards his own house, his possessions are safe. **22** But when someone stronger attacks and overpowers him, he takes away the armor in which the man trusted and divides up his plunder.

23 "Whoever is not with me is against me, and whoever does not gather with me scatters.

24 "When an impure spirit comes out of a person, it goes through arid places seeking rest and does not find it. Then it says, 'I will return to the house I left.' **25** When it arrives, it finds the house swept clean and put in order. **26** Then it goes and takes seven other spirits more wicked than itself, and they go in and live there. And the final condition of that person is worse than the first."

27 As Jesus was saying these things, a woman in the crowd called out, "Blessed is the mother who gave you birth and nursed you."

28 He replied, "Blessed rather are those who hear the word of God and obey it."

The Sign of Jonah

29 As the crowds increased, Jesus said, "This is a wicked generation. It asks for a sign, but none will be given it except the sign of Jonah. **30** For as Jonah was a sign to the Ninevites, so also will the Son of Man be to this generation. **31** The Queen of the South will rise at the judgment with the people of this generation and condemn them, for she came from the ends of the earth to listen to Solomon's wisdom; and now something greater than Solomon is here. **32** The men of Nineveh will stand up at the judgment with this generation and condemn it, for they repented at the preaching of Jonah; and now something greater than Jonah is here.

The Lamp of the Body

33 "No one lights a lamp and puts it in a place where it will be hidden, or under a bowl. Instead they put it on its stand, so that those who come in may see the light. **34** Your eye is the lamp of your body. When your eyes are healthy,[a] your whole body also is full of light. But when they are unhealthy,[b] your body also is full of darkness. **35** See to it, then, that the light within you is not darkness. **36** Therefore, if your whole body is full of light, and no part of it dark, it will be just as full of light as when a lamp shines its light on you."

---

[a] *34* The Greek for *healthy* here implies *generous*.   [b] *34* The Greek for *unhealthy* here implies *stingy*.

Woes on the Pharisees and the Experts in the Law

37When Jesus had finished speaking, a Pharisee invited him to eat with him; so he went in and reclined at the table. **38**But the Pharisee was surprised when he noticed that Jesus did not first wash before the meal.

39Then the Lord said to him, "Now then, you Pharisees clean the outside of the cup and dish, but inside you are full of greed and wickedness. **40**You foolish people! Did not the one who made the outside make the inside also? **41**But now as for what is inside you — be generous to the poor, and everything will be clean for you.

42"Woe to you Pharisees, because you give God a tenth of your mint, rue and all other kinds of garden herbs, but you neglect justice and the love of God. You should have practiced the latter without leaving the former undone.

43"Woe to you Pharisees, because you love the most important seats in the synagogues and respectful greetings in the marketplaces.

44"Woe to you, because you are like unmarked graves, which people walk over without knowing it."

45One of the experts in the law answered him, "Teacher, when you say these things, you insult us also."

46Jesus replied, "And you experts in the law, woe to you, because you load people down with burdens they can hardly carry, and you yourselves will not lift one finger to help them.

47"Woe to you, because you build tombs for the prophets, and it was your ancestors who killed them. **48**So you testify that you approve of what your ancestors did; they killed the prophets, and you build their tombs. **49**Because of this, God in his wisdom said, 'I will send them prophets and apostles, some of whom they will kill and others they will persecute.' **50**Therefore this generation will be held responsible for the blood of all the prophets that has been shed since the beginning of the world, **51**from the blood of Abel to the blood of Zechariah, who was killed between the altar and the sanctuary. Yes, I tell you, this generation will be held responsible for it all.

52"Woe to you experts in the law, because you have taken away the key to knowledge. You yourselves have not entered, and you have hindered those who were entering."

53When Jesus went outside, the Pharisees and the teachers of the law began to oppose him fiercely and to besiege him with questions, **54**waiting to catch him in something he might say.

Warnings and Encouragements

12 Meanwhile, when a crowd of many thousands had gathered, so that they were trampling on one another, Jesus began to speak first to his disciples, saying: "Be*a* on your guard against the yeast of the Pharisees, which is hypocrisy. ²There is nothing concealed that will not be disclosed, or hidden that will not be made known. ³What you have said in the dark will be heard in the daylight, and what you have whispered in the ear in the inner rooms will be proclaimed from the roofs.

⁴"I tell you, my friends, do not be afraid of those who kill the body and after that can do no more. ⁵But I will show you whom you should fear: Fear him who, after your body has been killed, has authority to throw you into hell. Yes, I tell you, fear him. ⁶Are not five sparrows sold for two pennies? Yet not one of them is forgotten by God. ⁷Indeed, the very hairs of your head are all numbered. Don't be afraid; you are worth more than many sparrows.

⁸"I tell you, whoever publicly acknowledges me before others, the Son of Man will also acknowledge before the angels of God. ⁹But whoever disowns me before others will be disowned before the angels of God. ¹⁰And everyone who speaks a word against the Son of Man will be forgiven, but anyone who blasphemes against the Holy Spirit will not be forgiven.

¹¹"When you are brought before synagogues, rulers and authorities, do not worry about how you will defend yourselves or what you will say, ¹²for the Holy Spirit will teach you at that time what you should say."

The Parable of the Rich Fool

¹³Someone in the crowd said to him, "Teacher, tell my brother to divide the inheritance with me."

¹⁴Jesus replied, "Man, who appointed me a judge or an arbiter between you?" ¹⁵Then he said to them, "Watch out! Be on your guard against all kinds of greed; life does not consist in an abundance of possessions."

¹⁶And he told them this parable: "The ground of a certain rich man yielded an abundant harvest. ¹⁷He thought to himself, 'What shall I do? I have no place to store my crops.'

¹⁸"Then he said, 'This is what I'll do. I will tear down my barns and build bigger ones, and there I will store my surplus grain. ¹⁹And I'll say to myself, "You have plenty of grain laid up for many years. Take life easy; eat, drink and be merry."'

²⁰"But God said to him, 'You fool! This very night your life will be demanded from you. Then who will get what you have prepared for yourself?'

²¹"This is how it will be with whoever stores up things for themselves but is not rich toward God."

Do Not Worry

²²Then Jesus said to his disciples: "Therefore I tell you, do not worry

---

a 1 Or *speak to his disciples, saying: "First of all, be* about your life, what you will eat; or about your body, what you will wear. ²³For life is more than food, and the body more than clothes. ²⁴Consider the ravens: They do not sow or reap, they have no storeroom or barn; yet God feeds them. And how much more valuable you are than birds! ²⁵Who of you by worrying can add a single hour to your life*? ²⁶Since you cannot do this very little thing, why do you worry about the rest?

²⁷"Consider how the wild flowers grow. They do not labor or spin. Yet I tell you, not even Solomon in all his splendor was dressed like one of these. ²⁸If that is how God clothes the grass of the field, which is here today, and tomorrow is thrown into the fire, how much more will he clothe you—you of little faith! ²⁹And do not set your heart on what you will eat or drink; do not worry about it. ³⁰For the pagan world runs after all such things, and your Father knows that you need them. ³¹But seek his kingdom, and these things will be given to you as well.

³²"Do not be afraid, little flock, for your Father has been pleased to give you the kingdom. ³³Sell your possessions and give to the poor. Provide purses for yourselves that will not wear out, a treasure in heaven that will never fail, where no thief comes near and no moth destroys. ³⁴For where your treasure is, there your heart will be also.

Watchfulness

³⁵"Be dressed ready for service and keep your lamps burning, ³⁶like servants waiting for their master to return from a wedding banquet, so that when he comes and knocks they can immediately open the door for him. ³⁷It will be good for those servants whose master finds them watching when he comes. Truly I tell you, he will dress himself to serve, will have them recline at the table and will come and wait on them. ³⁸It will be good for those servants whose master finds them ready, even if he comes in the middle of the night or toward daybreak. ³⁹But understand this: If the owner of the house had known at what hour the thief was coming, he would not have let his house be broken into. ⁴⁰You also must be ready, because the Son of Man will come at an hour when you do not expect him."

⁴¹Peter asked, "Lord, are you telling this parable to us, or to everyone?"

⁴²The Lord answered, "Who then is the faithful and wise manager, whom the master puts in charge of his servants to give them their food allowance at the proper time? ⁴³It will be good for that servant whom the master finds doing so when he returns. ⁴⁴Truly I tell you, he will put him in charge of

---

a 25 Or *single cubit to your height*

all his possessions. **45** But suppose the servant says to himself, 'My master is taking a long time in coming,' and he then begins to beat the other servants, both men and women, and to eat and drink and get drunk. **46** The master of that servant will come on a day when he does not expect him and at an hour he is not aware of. He will cut him to pieces and assign him a place with the unbelievers.

47 "The servant who knows the master's will and does not get ready or does not do what the master wants will be beaten with many blows. **48** But the one who does not know and does things deserving punishment will be beaten with few blows. From everyone who has been given much, much will be demanded; and from the one who has been entrusted with much, much more will be asked.

Not Peace but Division

49 "I have come to bring fire on the earth, and how I wish it were already kindled! **50** But I have a baptism to undergo, and what constraint I am under until it is completed! **51** Do you think I came to bring peace on earth? No, I tell you, but division. **52** From now on there will be five in one family divided against each other, three against two and two against three. **53** They will be divided, father against son and son against father, mother against daughter and daughter against mother, mother-in-law against daughter-in-law and daughter-in-law against mother-in-law."

Interpreting the Times

54 He said to the crowd: "When you see a cloud rising in the west, immediately you say, 'It's going to rain,' and it does. **55** And when the south wind blows, you say, 'It's going to be hot,' and it is. **56** Hypocrites! You know how to interpret the appearance of the earth and the sky. How is it that you don't know how to interpret this present time?

57 "Why don't you judge for yourselves what is right? **58** As you are going with your adversary to the magistrate, try hard to be reconciled on the way, or your adversary may drag you off to the judge, and the judge turn you over to the officer, and the officer throw you into prison. **59** I tell you, you will not get out until you have paid the last penny."

Repent or Perish

13 Now there were some present at that time who told Jesus about the Galileans whose blood Pilate had mixed with their sacrifices. **2** Jesus answered, "Do you think that these Galileans were worse sinners than all the other Galileans because they suffered this way? **3** I tell you, no! But unless you repent, you too will all perish. **4** Or those eighteen who died when the tower in Siloam fell on them—do you think they were more guilty than all the others living in Jerusalem? ⁵I tell you, no! But unless you repent, you too will all perish."

⁶Then he told this parable: "A man had a fig tree growing in his vineyard, and he went to look for fruit on it but did not find any. ⁷So he said to the man who took care of the vineyard, 'For three years now I've been coming to look for fruit on this fig tree and haven't found any. Cut it down! Why should it use up the soil?'

⁸"'Sir,' the man replied, 'leave it alone for one more year, and I'll dig around it and fertilize it. ⁹If it bears fruit next year, fine! If not, then cut it down.'"

Jesus Heals a Crippled Woman on the Sabbath

¹⁰On a Sabbath Jesus was teaching in one of the synagogues, ¹¹and a woman was there who had been crippled by a spirit for eighteen years. She was bent over and could not straighten up at all. ¹²When Jesus saw her, he called her forward and said to her, "Woman, you are set free from your infirmity." ¹³Then he put his hands on her, and immediately she straightened up and praised God.

¹⁴Indignant because Jesus had healed on the Sabbath, the synagogue leader said to the people, "There are six days for work. So come and be healed on those days, not on the Sabbath."

¹⁵The Lord answered him, "You hypocrites! Doesn't each of you on the Sabbath untie your ox or donkey from the stall and lead it out to give it water? ¹⁶Then should not this woman, a daughter of Abraham, whom Satan has kept bound for eighteen long years, be set free on the Sabbath day from what bound her?"

¹⁷When he said this, all his opponents were humiliated, but the people were delighted with all the wonderful things he was doing.

The Parables of the Mustard Seed and the Yeast

¹⁸Then Jesus asked, "What is the kingdom of God like? What shall I compare it to? ¹⁹It is like a mustard seed, which a man took and planted in his garden. It grew and became a tree, and the birds perched in its branches."

²⁰Again he asked, "What shall I compare the kingdom of God to? ²¹It is like yeast that a woman took and mixed into about sixty pounds^a of flour until it worked all through the dough."

The Narrow Door

²²Then Jesus went through the towns and villages, teaching as he made his way to Jerusalem. ²³Someone asked him, "Lord, are only a few people going to be saved?"

He said to them, ²⁴"Make every effort to enter through the

---

^a 21 Or about 27 kilograms

narrow door, because many, I tell you, will try to enter and will not be able to. ²⁵Once the owner of the house gets up and closes the door, you will stand outside knocking and pleading, 'Sir, open the door for us.'

"But he will answer, 'I don't know you or where you come from.'

²⁶"Then you will say, 'We ate and drank with you, and you taught in our streets.'

²⁷"But he will reply, 'I don't know you or where you come from. Away from me, all you evildoers!'

²⁸"There will be weeping there, and gnashing of teeth, when you see Abraham, Isaac and Jacob and all the prophets in the kingdom of God, but you yourselves thrown out. ²⁹People will come from east and west and north and south, and will take their places at the feast in the kingdom of God. ³⁰Indeed there are those who are last who will be first, and first who will be last."

Jesus' Sorrow for Jerusalem

³¹At that time some Pharisees came to Jesus and said to him, "Leave this place and go somewhere else. Herod wants to kill you."

³²He replied, "Go tell that fox, 'I will keep on driving out demons and healing people today and tomorrow, and on the third day I will reach my goal.' ³³In any case, I must press on today and tomorrow and the next day—for surely no prophet can die outside Jerusalem!

³⁴"Jerusalem, Jerusalem, you who kill the prophets and stone those sent to you, how often I have longed to gather your children together, as a hen gathers her chicks under her wings, and you were not willing. ³⁵Look, your house is left to you desolate. I tell you, you will not see me again until you say, 'Blessed is he who comes in the name of the Lord.'ᵃ"

Jesus at a Pharisee's House

14 One Sabbath, when Jesus went to eat in the house of a prominent Pharisee, he was being carefully watched. ²There in front of him was a man suffering from abnormal swelling of his body. ³Jesus asked the Pharisees and experts in the law, "Is it lawful to heal on the Sabbath or not?" ⁴But they remained silent. So taking hold of the man, he healed him and sent him on his way.

⁵Then he asked them, "If one of you has a childᵇ or an ox that falls into a well on the Sabbath day, will you not immediately pull it out?" ⁶And they had nothing to say.

⁷When he noticed how the guests picked the places of honor at the table, he told them this parable: ⁸"When someone invites you to a wedding feast, do not take the place of honor, for a person more

---

ᵃ 35 Psalm 118:26   ᵇ 5 Some manuscripts *donkey*

distinguished than you may have been invited. ⁹ If so, the host who invited both of you will come and say to you, 'Give this person your seat.' Then, humiliated, you will have to take the least important place. ¹⁰ But when you are invited, take the lowest place, so that when your host comes, he will say to you, 'Friend, move up to a better place.' Then you will be honored in the presence of all the other guests. ¹¹ For all those who exalt themselves will be humbled, and those who humble themselves will be exalted."

¹² Then Jesus said to his host, "When you give a luncheon or dinner, do not invite your friends, your brothers or sisters, your relatives, or your rich neighbors; if you do, they may invite you back and so you will be repaid. ¹³ But when you give a banquet, invite the poor, the crippled, the lame, the blind, ¹⁴ and you will be blessed. Although they cannot repay you, you will be repaid at the resurrection of the righteous."

The Parable of the Great Banquet

¹⁵ When one of those at the table with him heard this, he said to Jesus, "Blessed is the one who will eat at the feast in the kingdom of God."

¹⁶ Jesus replied: "A certain man was preparing a great banquet and invited many guests. ¹⁷ At the time of the banquet he sent his servant to tell those who had been invited, 'Come, for everything is now ready.'

¹⁸ "But they all alike began to make excuses. The first said, 'I have just bought a field, and I must go and see it. Please excuse me.'

¹⁹ "Another said, 'I have just bought five yoke of oxen, and I'm on my way to try them out. Please excuse me.'

²⁰ "Still another said, 'I just got married, so I can't come.'

²¹ "The servant came back and reported this to his master. Then the owner of the house became angry and ordered his servant, 'Go out quickly into the streets and alleys of the town and bring in the poor, the crippled, the blind and the lame.'

²² " 'Sir,' the servant said, 'what you ordered has been done, but there is still room.'

²³ "Then the master told his servant, 'Go out to the roads and country lanes and compel them to come in, so that my house will be full. ²⁴ I tell you, not one of those who were invited will get a taste of my banquet.' "

The Cost of Being a Disciple

²⁵ Large crowds were traveling with Jesus, and turning to them he said: ²⁶ "If anyone comes to me and does not hate father and mother, wife and children, brothers and sisters — yes, even their own life — such a person cannot be my disciple. ²⁷ And whoever does not carry their cross and follow me cannot be my disciple.

28 "Suppose one of you wants to build a tower. Won't you first sit down and estimate the cost to see if you have enough money to complete it? 29 For if you lay the foundation and are not able to finish it, everyone who sees it will ridicule you, 30 saying, 'This person began to build and wasn't able to finish.'

31 "Or suppose a king is about to go to war against another king. Won't he first sit down and consider whether he is able with ten thousand men to oppose the one coming against him with twenty thousand? 32 If he is not able, he will send a delegation while the other is still a long way off and will ask for terms of peace. 33 In the same way, those of you who do not give up everything you have cannot be my disciples.

34 "Salt is good, but if it loses its saltiness, how can it be made salty again? 35 It is fit neither for the soil nor for the manure pile; it is thrown out.

"Whoever has ears to hear, let them hear."

The Parable of the Lost Sheep

15 Now the tax collectors and sinners were all gathering around to hear Jesus. 2 But the Pharisees and the teachers of the law muttered, "This man welcomes sinners and eats with them."

3 Then Jesus told them this parable: 4 "Suppose one of you has a hundred sheep and loses one of them. Doesn't he leave the ninety-nine in the open country and go after the lost sheep until he finds it? 5 And when he finds it, he joyfully puts it on his shoulders 6 and goes home. Then he calls his friends and neighbors together and says, 'Rejoice with me; I have found my lost sheep.' 7 I tell you that in the same way there will be more rejoicing in heaven over one sinner who repents than over ninety-nine righteous persons who do not need to repent.

The Parable of the Lost Coin

8 "Or suppose a woman has ten silver coins[a] and loses one. Doesn't she light a lamp, sweep the house and search carefully until she finds it? 9 And when she finds it, she calls her friends and neighbors together and says, 'Rejoice with me; I have found my lost coin.' 10 In the same way, I tell you, there is rejoicing in the presence of the angels of God over one sinner who repents."

The Parable of the Lost Son

11 Jesus continued: "There was a man who had two sons. 12 The younger one said to his father, 'Father, give me my share of the estate.' So he divided his property between them.

13 "Not long after that, the younger son got together all he had, set off for a distant country and there

a 8 Greek ten drachmas, each worth about a day's wages

squandered his wealth in wild living. ¹⁴After he had spent everything, there was a severe famine in that whole country, and he began to be in need. ¹⁵So he went and hired himself out to a citizen of that country, who sent him to his fields to feed pigs. ¹⁶He longed to fill his stomach with the pods that the pigs were eating, but no one gave him anything.

¹⁷"When he came to his senses, he said, 'How many of my father's hired servants have food to spare, and here I am starving to death! ¹⁸I will set out and go back to my father and say to him: Father, I have sinned against heaven and against you. ¹⁹I am no longer worthy to be called your son; make me like one of your hired servants.' ²⁰So he got up and went to his father.

"But while he was still a long way off, his father saw him and was filled with compassion for him; he ran to his son, threw his arms around him and kissed him.

²¹"The son said to him, 'Father, I have sinned against heaven and against you. I am no longer worthy to be called your son.'

²²"But the father said to his servants, 'Quick! Bring the best robe and put it on him. Put a ring on his finger and sandals on his feet. ²³Bring the fattened calf and kill it. Let's have a feast and celebrate. ²⁴For this son of mine was dead and is alive again; he was lost and is found.' So they began to celebrate.

²⁵"Meanwhile, the older son was in the field. When he came near the house, he heard music and dancing. ²⁶So he called one of the servants and asked him what was going on. ²⁷'Your brother has come,' he replied, 'and your father has killed the fattened calf because he has him back safe and sound.'

²⁸"The older brother became angry and refused to go in. So his father went out and pleaded with him. ²⁹But he answered his father, 'Look! All these years I've been slaving for you and never disobeyed your orders. Yet you never gave me even a young goat so I could celebrate with my friends. ³⁰But when this son of yours who has squandered your property with prostitutes comes home, you kill the fattened calf for him!'

³¹"'My son,' the father said, 'you are always with me, and everything I have is yours. ³²But we had to celebrate and be glad, because this brother of yours was dead and is alive again; he was lost and is found.'"

The Parable of the Shrewd Manager

16 Jesus told his disciples: "There was a rich man whose manager was accused of wasting his possessions. ²So he called him in and asked him, 'What is this I hear about you? Give an account of your management, because you cannot be manager any longer.'

³"The manager said to himself, 'What shall I do now? My master is taking away my job. I'm not strong enough to dig, and I'm ashamed to beg — ⁴I know what I'll do so that, when I lose my job here, people will welcome me into their houses.'

⁵"So he called in each one of his master's debtors. He asked the first, 'How much do you owe my master?'

⁶"'Nine hundred gallons*ᵃ* of olive oil,' he replied.

"The manager told him, 'Take your bill, sit down quickly, and make it four hundred and fifty.'

⁷"Then he asked the second, 'And how much do you owe?'

"'A thousand bushels*ᵇ* of wheat,' he replied.

"He told him, 'Take your bill and make it eight hundred.'

⁸"The master commended the dishonest manager because he had acted shrewdly. For the people of this world are more shrewd in dealing with their own kind than are the people of the light. ⁹I tell you, use worldly wealth to gain friends for yourselves, so that when it is gone, you will be welcomed into eternal dwellings.

¹⁰"Whoever can be trusted with very little can also be trusted with much, and whoever is dishonest with very little will also be dishonest with much. ¹¹So if you have not been trustworthy in handling worldly wealth, who will trust you with true riches? ¹²And if you have not been trustworthy with someone else's property, who will give you property of your own?

¹³"No one can serve two masters. Either you will hate the one and love the other, or you will be devoted to the one and despise the other. You cannot serve both God and money."

¹⁴The Pharisees, who loved money, heard all this and were sneering at Jesus. ¹⁵He said to them, "You are the ones who justify yourselves in the eyes of others, but God knows your hearts. What people value highly is detestable in God's sight.

Additional Teachings

¹⁶"The Law and the Prophets were proclaimed until John. Since that time, the good news of the kingdom of God is being preached, and everyone is forcing their way into it. ¹⁷It is easier for heaven and earth to disappear than for the least stroke of a pen to drop out of the Law.

¹⁸"Anyone who divorces his wife and marries another woman commits adultery, and the man who marries a divorced woman commits adultery.

The Rich Man and Lazarus

¹⁹"There was a rich man who was dressed in purple and fine linen and lived in luxury every

ᵃ 6 Or about 3,000 liters   *ᵇ 7* Or about 30 tons

day. **20** At his gate was laid a beggar named Lazarus, covered with sores **21** and longing to eat what fell from the rich man's table. Even the dogs came and licked his sores.

22 "The time came when the beggar died and the angels carried him to Abraham's side. The rich man also died and was buried. **23** In Hades, where he was in torment, he looked up and saw Abraham far away, with Lazarus by his side. **24** So he called to him, 'Father Abraham, have pity on me and send Lazarus to dip the tip of his finger in water and cool my tongue, because I am in agony in this fire.'

25 "But Abraham replied, 'Son, remember that in your lifetime you received your good things, while Lazarus received bad things, but now he is comforted here and you are in agony. **26** And besides all this, between us and you a great chasm has been set in place, so that those who want to go from here to you cannot, nor can anyone cross over from there to us.'

27 "He answered, 'Then I beg you, father, send Lazarus to my family, **28** for I have five brothers. Let him warn them, so that they will not also come to this place of torment.'

29 "Abraham replied, 'They have Moses and the Prophets; let them listen to them.'

30 " 'No, father Abraham,' he said,

'but if someone from the dead goes to them, they will repent.'

31 "He said to him, 'If they do not listen to Moses and the Prophets, they will not be convinced even if someone rises from the dead.' "

Sin, Faith, Duty

17 Jesus said to his disciples: "Things that cause people to stumble are bound to come, but woe to anyone through whom they come. **2** It would be better for them to be thrown into the sea with a millstone tied around their neck than to cause one of these little ones to stumble. **3** So watch yourselves.

"If your brother or sister*a* sins against you, rebuke them; and if they repent, forgive them. **4** Even if they sin against you seven times in a day and seven times come back to you saying 'I repent,' you must forgive them."

5 The apostles said to the Lord, "Increase our faith!"

6 He replied, "If you have faith as small as a mustard seed, you can say to this mulberry tree, 'Be uprooted and planted in the sea,' and it will obey you.

7 "Suppose one of you has a servant plowing or looking after the sheep. Will he say to the servant when he comes in from the field, 'Come along now and sit down to eat'? **8** Won't he rather say, 'Prepare my supper, get yourself ready and wait on me while I

a 3 The Greek word for *brother or sister* (*adelphos*) refers here to a fellow disciple, whether man or woman.

eat and drink; after that you may eat and drink'? ⁹Will he thank the servant because he did what he was told to do? ¹⁰So you also, when you have done everything you were told to do, should say, 'We are unworthy servants; we have only done our duty.'"

Jesus Heals Ten Men With Leprosy

¹¹Now on his way to Jerusalem, Jesus traveled along the border between Samaria and Galilee. ¹²As he was going into a village, ten men who had leprosy*a* met him. They stood at a distance ¹³and called out in a loud voice, "Jesus, Master, have pity on us!"

¹⁴When he saw them, he said, "Go, show yourselves to the priests." And as they went, they were cleansed.

¹⁵One of them, when he saw he was healed, came back, praising God in a loud voice. ¹⁶He threw himself at Jesus' feet and thanked him — and he was a Samaritan.

¹⁷Jesus asked, "Were not all ten cleansed? Where are the other nine? ¹⁸Has no one returned to give praise to God except this foreigner?" ¹⁹Then he said to him, "Rise and go; your faith has made you well."

The Coming of the Kingdom of God

²⁰Once, on being asked by the Pharisees when the kingdom of God would come, Jesus replied, "The coming of the kingdom of God is not something that can be observed, ²¹nor will people say, 'Here it is,' or 'There it is,' because the kingdom of God is in your midst."*b*

²²Then he said to his disciples, "The time is coming when you will long to see one of the days of the Son of Man, but you will not see it. ²³People will tell you, 'There he is!' or 'Here he is!' Do not go running off after them. ²⁴For the Son of Man in his day*c* will be like the lightning, which flashes and lights up the sky from one end to the other. ²⁵But first he must suffer many things and be rejected by this generation.

²⁶"Just as it was in the days of Noah, so also will it be in the days of the Son of Man. ²⁷People were eating, drinking, marrying and being given in marriage up to the day Noah entered the ark. Then the flood came and destroyed them all.

²⁸"It was the same in the days of Lot. People were eating and drinking, buying and selling, planting and building. ²⁹But the day Lot left Sodom, fire and sulfur rained down from heaven and destroyed them all.

³⁰"It will be just like this on the day the Son of Man is revealed. ³¹On that day no one who is on

---

a 12 The Greek word traditionally translated *leprosy* was used for various diseases affecting the skin.   *b 21* Or *is within you*   *c 24* Some manuscripts do not have *in his day.*

the housetop, with possessions inside, should go down to get them. Likewise, no one in the field should go back for anything. ³²Remember Lot's wife! ³³Whoever tries to keep their life will lose it, and whoever loses their life will preserve it. ³⁴I tell you, on that night two people will be in one bed; one will be taken and the other left. ³⁵Two women will be grinding grain together; one will be taken and the other left." [36]*a*

³⁷"Where, Lord?" they asked.

He replied, "Where there is a dead body, there the vultures will gather."

The Parable of the Persistent Widow

18 Then Jesus told his disciples a parable to show them that they should always pray and not give up. ²He said: "In a certain town there was a judge who neither feared God nor cared what people thought. ³And there was a widow in that town who kept coming to him with the plea, 'Grant me justice against my adversary.'

⁴"For some time he refused. But finally he said to himself, 'Even though I don't fear God or care what people think, ⁵yet because this widow keeps bothering me, I will see that she gets justice, so that she won't eventually come and attack me!' "

⁶And the Lord said, "Listen to what the unjust judge says. ⁷And will not God bring about justice for his chosen ones, who cry out to him day and night? Will he keep putting them off? ⁸I tell you, he will see that they get justice, and quickly. However, when the Son of Man comes, will he find faith on the earth?"

The Parable of the Pharisee and the Tax Collector

⁹To some who were confident of their own righteousness and looked down on everyone else, Jesus told this parable: ¹⁰"Two men went up to the temple to pray, one a Pharisee and the other a tax collector. ¹¹The Pharisee stood by himself and prayed: 'God, I thank you that I am not like other people — robbers, evildoers, adulterers — or even like this tax collector. ¹²I fast twice a week and give a tenth of all I get.'

¹³"But the tax collector stood at a distance. He would not even look up to heaven, but beat his breast and said, 'God, have mercy on me, a sinner.'

¹⁴"I tell you that this man, rather than the other, went home justified before God. For all those who exalt themselves will be humbled, and those who humble themselves will be exalted."

The Little Children and Jesus

¹⁵People were also bringing babies to Jesus for him to place his hands on them. When the disci-

---

a 36 Some manuscripts include here words similar to Matt. 24:40.

ples saw this, they rebuked them. 16 But Jesus called the children to him and said, "Let the little children come to me, and do not hinder them, for the kingdom of God belongs to such as these. 17 Truly I tell you, anyone who will not receive the kingdom of God like a little child will never enter it."

The Rich and the Kingdom of God

18 A certain ruler asked him, "Good teacher, what must I do to inherit eternal life?"

19 "Why do you call me good?" Jesus answered. "No one is good — except God alone. 20 You know the commandments: 'You shall not commit adultery, you shall not murder, you shall not steal, you shall not give false testimony, honor your father and mother.'*a*"

21 "All these I have kept since I was a boy," he said.

22 When Jesus heard this, he said to him, "You still lack one thing. Sell everything you have and give to the poor, and you will have treasure in heaven. Then come, follow me."

23 When he heard this, he became very sad, because he was very wealthy. 24 Jesus looked at him and said, "How hard it is for the rich to enter the kingdom of God! 25 Indeed, it is easier for a camel to go through the eye of a needle than for someone who is rich to enter the kingdom of God."

26 Those who heard this asked, "Who then can be saved?"

27 Jesus replied, "What is impossible with man is possible with God."

28 Peter said to him, "We have left all we had to follow you!"

29 "Truly I tell you," Jesus said to them, "no one who has left home or wife or brothers or sisters or parents or children for the sake of the kingdom of God 30 will fail to receive many times as much in this age, and in the age to come eternal life."

Jesus Predicts His Death a Third Time

31 Jesus took the Twelve aside and told them, "We are going up to Jerusalem, and everything that is written by the prophets about the Son of Man will be fulfilled. 32 He will be delivered over to the Gentiles. They will mock him, insult him and spit on him; 33 they will flog him and kill him. On the third day he will rise again."

34 The disciples did not understand any of this. Its meaning was hidden from them, and they did not know what he was talking about.

A Blind Beggar Receives His Sight

35 As Jesus approached Jericho, a blind man was sitting by the roadside begging. 36 When he heard the crowd going by, he asked what was happening.

a 20 Exodus 20:12-16; Deut. 5:16-20

37 They told him, "Jesus of Nazareth is passing by."

38 He called out, "Jesus, Son of David, have mercy on me!"

39 Those who led the way rebuked him and told him to be quiet, but he shouted all the more, "Son of David, have mercy on me!"

40 Jesus stopped and ordered the man to be brought to him. When he came near, Jesus asked him, **41** "What do you want me to do for you?"

"Lord, I want to see," he replied.

42 Jesus said to him, "Receive your sight; your faith has healed you." **43** Immediately he received his sight and followed Jesus, praising God. When all the people saw it, they also praised God.

Zacchaeus the Tax Collector

19 Jesus entered Jericho and was passing through. **2** A man was there by the name of Zacchaeus; he was a chief tax collector and was wealthy. **3** He wanted to see who Jesus was, but because he was short he could not see over the crowd. **4** So he ran ahead and climbed a sycamore-fig tree to see him, since Jesus was coming that way.

5 When Jesus reached the spot, he looked up and said to him, "Zacchaeus, come down immediately. I must stay at your house today." **6** So he came down at once and welcomed him gladly.

7 All the people saw this and began to mutter, "He has gone to be the guest of a sinner."

8 But Zacchaeus stood up and said to the Lord, "Look, Lord! Here and now I give half of my possessions to the poor, and if I have cheated anybody out of anything, I will pay back four times the amount."

9 Jesus said to him, "Today salvation has come to this house, because this man, too, is a son of Abraham. **10** For the Son of Man came to seek and to save the lost."

The Parable of the Ten Minas

11 While they were listening to this, he went on to tell them a parable, because he was near Jerusalem and the people thought that the kingdom of God was going to appear at once. **12** He said: "A man of noble birth went to a distant country to have himself appointed king and then to return. **13** So he called ten of his servants and gave them ten minas.[a] 'Put this money to work,' he said, 'until I come back.'

14 "But his subjects hated him and sent a delegation after him to say, 'We don't want this man to be our king.'

15 "He was made king, however, and returned home. Then he sent for the servants to whom he had given the money, in order to find out what they had gained with it.

16 "The first one came and said,

---

a 13 A mina was about three months' wages.

'Sir, your mina has earned ten more.'

¹⁷ " 'Well done, my good servant!' his master replied. 'Because you have been trustworthy in a very small matter, take charge of ten cities.'

¹⁸ "The second came and said, 'Sir, your mina has earned five more.'

¹⁹ "His master answered, 'You take charge of five cities.'

²⁰ "Then another servant came and said, 'Sir, here is your mina; I have kept it laid away in a piece of cloth. ²¹ I was afraid of you, because you are a hard man. You take out what you did not put in and reap what you did not sow.'

²² "His master replied, 'I will judge you by your own words, you wicked servant! You knew, did you, that I am a hard man, taking out what I did not put in, and reaping what I did not sow? ²³ Why then didn't you put my money on deposit, so that when I came back, I could have collected it with interest?'

²⁴ "Then he said to those standing by, 'Take his mina away from him and give it to the one who has ten minas.'

²⁵ " 'Sir,' they said, 'he already has ten!'

²⁶ "He replied, 'I tell you that to everyone who has, more will be given, but as for the one who has nothing, even what they have will be taken away. ²⁷ But those enemies of mine who did not want me to be king over them—bring them here and kill them in front of me.' "

Jesus Comes to Jerusalem as King

²⁸ After Jesus had said this, he went on ahead, going up to Jerusalem. ²⁹ As he approached Bethphage and Bethany at the hill called the Mount of Olives, he sent two of his disciples, saying to them, ³⁰ "Go to the village ahead of you, and as you enter it, you will find a colt tied there, which no one has ever ridden. Untie it and bring it here. ³¹ If anyone asks you, 'Why are you untying it?' say, 'The Lord needs it.' "

³² Those who were sent ahead went and found it just as he had told them. ³³ As they were untying the colt, its owners asked them, "Why are you untying the colt?"

³⁴ They replied, "The Lord needs it."

³⁵ They brought it to Jesus, threw their cloaks on the colt and put Jesus on it. ³⁶ As he went along, people spread their cloaks on the road.

³⁷ When he came near the place where the road goes down the Mount of Olives, the whole crowd of disciples began joyfully to praise God in loud voices for all the miracles they had seen:

³⁸ "Blessed is the king who comes
in the name of the Lord!"ᵃ

ᵃ 38 Psalm 118:26

"Peace in heaven and glory in the highest!"

³⁹Some of the Pharisees in the crowd said to Jesus, "Teacher, rebuke your disciples!"

⁴⁰"I tell you," he replied, "if they keep quiet, the stones will cry out."

⁴¹As he approached Jerusalem and saw the city, he wept over it ⁴²and said, "If you, even you, had only known on this day what would bring you peace—but now it is hidden from your eyes. ⁴³The days will come upon you when your enemies will build an embankment against you and encircle you and hem you in on every side. ⁴⁴They will dash you to the ground, you and the children within your walls. They will not leave one stone on another, because you did not recognize the time of God's coming to you."

Jesus at the Temple

⁴⁵When Jesus entered the temple courts, he began to drive out those who were selling. ⁴⁶"It is written," he said to them, "'My house will be a house of prayer'ᵃ; but you have made it 'a den of robbers.'ᵇ"

⁴⁷Every day he was teaching at the temple. But the chief priests, the teachers of the law and the leaders among the people were trying to kill him. ⁴⁸Yet they could not find any way to do it, because all the people hung on his words.

The Authority of Jesus Questioned

20 One day as Jesus was teaching the people in the temple courts and proclaiming the good news, the chief priests and the teachers of the law, together with the elders, came up to him. ²"Tell us by what authority you are doing these things," they said. "Who gave you this authority?"

³He replied, "I will also ask you a question. Tell me: ⁴John's baptism—was it from heaven, or of human origin?"

⁵They discussed it among themselves and said, "If we say, 'From heaven,' he will ask, 'Why didn't you believe him?' ⁶But if we say, 'Of human origin,' all the people will stone us, because they are persuaded that John was a prophet."

⁷So they answered, "We don't know where it was from."

⁸Jesus said, "Neither will I tell you by what authority I am doing these things."

The Parable of the Tenants

⁹He went on to tell the people this parable: "A man planted a vineyard, rented it to some farmers and went away for a long time. ¹⁰At harvest time he sent a servant to the tenants so they would give him some of the fruit of the vineyard. But the tenants beat him and sent him away empty-

---

ᵃ 46 Isaiah 56:7   ᵇ 46 Jer. 7:11

handed. **11**He sent another servant, but that one also they beat and treated shamefully and sent away empty-handed. **12**He sent still a third, and they wounded him and threw him out.

13 "Then the owner of the vineyard said, 'What shall I do? I will send my son, whom I love; perhaps they will respect him.'

14 "But when the tenants saw him, they talked the matter over. 'This is the heir,' they said. 'Let's kill him, and the inheritance will be ours.' **15**So they threw him out of the vineyard and killed him.

"What then will the owner of the vineyard do to them? **16**He will come and kill those tenants and give the vineyard to others."

When the people heard this, they said, "God forbid!"

17Jesus looked directly at them and asked, "Then what is the meaning of that which is written:

" 'The stone the builders rejected
has become the cornerstone'*a*?

18Everyone who falls on that stone will be broken to pieces; anyone on whom it falls will be crushed."

19The teachers of the law and the chief priests looked for a way to arrest him immediately, because they knew he had spoken this parable against them. But they were afraid of the people.

Paying Taxes to Caesar

20Keeping a close watch on him, they sent spies, who pretended to be sincere. They hoped to catch Jesus in something he said, so that they might hand him over to the power and authority of the governor. **21**So the spies questioned him: "Teacher, we know that you speak and teach what is right, and that you do not show partiality but teach the way of God in accordance with the truth. **22**Is it right for us to pay taxes to Caesar or not?"

23He saw through their duplicity and said to them, **24** "Show me a denarius. Whose image and inscription are on it?"

"Caesar's," they replied.

25He said to them, "Then give back to Caesar what is Caesar's, and to God what is God's."

26They were unable to trap him in what he had said there in public. And astonished by his answer, they became silent.

The Resurrection and Marriage

27Some of the Sadducees, who say there is no resurrection, came to Jesus with a question. **28** "Teacher," they said, "Moses wrote for us that if a man's brother dies and leaves a wife but no children, the man must marry the widow and raise up offspring for his brother. **29**Now there were seven brothers. The first one married a woman and died childless. **30**The second

---

a 17 Psalm 118:22

³¹and then the third married her, and in the same way the seven died, leaving no children. ³²Finally, the woman died too. ³³Now then, at the resurrection whose wife will she be, since the seven were married to her?"

³⁴Jesus replied, "The people of this age marry and are given in marriage. ³⁵But those who are considered worthy of taking part in the age to come and in the resurrection from the dead will neither marry nor be given in marriage, ³⁶and they can no longer die; for they are like the angels. They are God's children, since they are children of the resurrection. ³⁷But in the account of the burning bush, even Moses showed that the dead rise, for he calls the Lord 'the God of Abraham, and the God of Isaac, and the God of Jacob.'ᵃ ³⁸He is not the God of the dead, but of the living, for to him all are alive."

³⁹Some of the teachers of the law responded, "Well said, teacher!" ⁴⁰And no one dared to ask him any more questions.

Whose Son Is the Messiah?

⁴¹Then Jesus said to them, "Why is it said that the Messiah is the son of David? ⁴²David himself declares in the Book of Psalms:

" 'The Lord said to my Lord:
   "Sit at my right hand

⁴³until I make your enemies
   a footstool for your feet." 'ᵇ

⁴⁴David calls him 'Lord.' How then can he be his son?"

Warning Against the Teachers of the Law

⁴⁵While all the people were listening, Jesus said to his disciples, ⁴⁶"Beware of the teachers of the law. They like to walk around in flowing robes and love to be greeted with respect in the marketplaces and have the most important seats in the synagogues and the places of honor at banquets. ⁴⁷They devour widows' houses and for a show make lengthy prayers. These men will be punished most severely."

The Widow's Offering

21 As Jesus looked up, he saw the rich putting their gifts into the temple treasury. ²He also saw a poor widow put in two very small copper coins. ³"Truly I tell you," he said, "this poor widow has put in more than all the others. ⁴All these people gave their gifts out of their wealth; but she out of her poverty put in all she had to live on."

The Destruction of the Temple and Signs of the End Times

⁵Some of his disciples were remarking about how the temple was adorned with beautiful

ᵃ 37 Exodus 3:6   ᵇ 43 Psalm 110:1

stones and with gifts dedicated to God. But Jesus said, **6** "As for what you see here, the time will come when not one stone will be left on another; every one of them will be thrown down."

7 "Teacher," they asked, "when will these things happen? And what will be the sign that they are about to take place?"

8 He replied: "Watch out that you are not deceived. For many will come in my name, claiming, 'I am he,' and, 'The time is near.' Do not follow them. **9** When you hear of wars and uprisings, do not be frightened. These things must happen first, but the end will not come right away."

10 Then he said to them: "Nation will rise against nation, and kingdom against kingdom. **11** There will be great earthquakes, famines and pestilences in various places, and fearful events and great signs from heaven.

12 "But before all this, they will seize you and persecute you. They will hand you over to synagogues and put you in prison, and you will be brought before kings and governors, and all on account of my name. **13** And so you will bear testimony to me. **14** But make up your mind not to worry beforehand how you will defend yourselves. **15** For I will give you words and wisdom that none of your adversaries will be able to resist or contradict. **16** You will be betrayed even by parents, brothers and sisters, relatives and friends, and they will put some of you to death. **17** Everyone will hate you because of me. **18** But not a hair of your head will perish. **19** Stand firm, and you will win life.

20 "When you see Jerusalem being surrounded by armies, you will know that its desolation is near. **21** Then let those who are in Judea flee to the mountains, let those in the city get out, and let those in the country not enter the city. **22** For this is the time of punishment in fulfillment of all that has been written. **23** How dreadful it will be in those days for pregnant women and nursing mothers! There will be great distress in the land and wrath against this people. **24** They will fall by the sword and will be taken as prisoners to all the nations. Jerusalem will be trampled on by the Gentiles until the times of the Gentiles are fulfilled.

25 "There will be signs in the sun, moon and stars. On the earth, nations will be in anguish and perplexity at the roaring and tossing of the sea. **26** People will faint from terror, apprehensive of what is coming on the world, for the heavenly bodies will be shaken. **27** At that time they will see the Son of Man coming in a cloud with power and great glory. **28** When these things begin to take place, stand up and lift up your heads, because your redemption is drawing near."

29 He told them this parable: "Look at the fig tree and all the trees. **30** When they sprout leaves, you can see for yourselves and know that summer is near. ³¹Even so, when you see these things happening, you know that the kingdom of God is near.

³²"Truly I tell you, this generation will certainly not pass away until all these things have happened. ³³Heaven and earth will pass away, but my words will never pass away.

³⁴"Be careful, or your hearts will be weighed down with carousing, drunkenness and the anxieties of life, and that day will close on you suddenly like a trap. ³⁵For it will come on all those who live on the face of the whole earth. ³⁶Be always on the watch, and pray that you may be able to escape all that is about to happen, and that you may be able to stand before the Son of Man."

³⁷Each day Jesus was teaching at the temple, and each evening he went out to spend the night on the hill called the Mount of Olives, ³⁸and all the people came early in the morning to hear him at the temple.

Judas Agrees to Betray Jesus

22 Now the Festival of Unleavened Bread, called the Passover, was approaching, ²and the chief priests and the teachers of the law were looking for some way to get rid of Jesus, for they were afraid of the people. ³Then Satan entered Judas, called Iscariot, one of the Twelve. ⁴And Judas went to the chief priests and the officers of the temple guard and discussed with them how he might betray Jesus. ⁵They were delighted and agreed to give him money. ⁶He consented, and watched for an opportunity to hand Jesus over to them when no crowd was present.

The Last Supper

⁷Then came the day of Unleavened Bread on which the Passover lamb had to be sacrificed. ⁸Jesus sent Peter and John, saying, "Go and make preparations for us to eat the Passover."

⁹"Where do you want us to prepare for it?" they asked.

¹⁰He replied, "As you enter the city, a man carrying a jar of water will meet you. Follow him to the house that he enters, ¹¹and say to the owner of the house, 'The Teacher asks: Where is the guest room, where I may eat the Passover with my disciples?' ¹²He will show you a large room upstairs, all furnished. Make preparations there."

¹³They left and found things just as Jesus had told them. So they prepared the Passover.

¹⁴When the hour came, Jesus and his apostles reclined at the table. ¹⁵And he said to them, "I have eagerly desired to eat this Passover with you before I suffer. ¹⁶For I tell you, I will not eat it again until it finds fulfillment in the kingdom of God."

¹⁷After taking the cup, he gave thanks and said, "Take this and

divide it among you. ¹⁸For I tell you I will not drink again from the fruit of the vine until the kingdom of God comes."

¹⁹And he took bread, gave thanks and broke it, and gave it to them, saying, "This is my body given for you; do this in remembrance of me."

²⁰In the same way, after the supper he took the cup, saying, "This cup is the new covenant in my blood, which is poured out for you.^a ²¹But the hand of him who is going to betray me is with mine on the table. ²²The Son of Man will go as it has been decreed. But woe to that man who betrays him!" ²³They began to question among themselves which of them it might be who would do this.

²⁴A dispute also arose among them as to which of them was considered to be greatest. ²⁵Jesus said to them, "The kings of the Gentiles lord it over them; and those who exercise authority over them call themselves Benefactors. ²⁶But you are not to be like that. Instead, the greatest among you should be like the youngest, and the one who rules like the one who serves. ²⁷For who is greater, the one who is at the table or the one who serves? Is it not the one who is at the table? But I am among you as one who serves. ²⁸You are those who have stood by me in my trials. ²⁹And I confer on you a kingdom, just as my Father conferred one on me, ³⁰so that you may eat and drink at my table in my kingdom and sit on thrones, judging the twelve tribes of Israel.

³¹"Simon, Simon, Satan has asked to sift all of you as wheat. ³²But I have prayed for you, Simon, that your faith may not fail. And when you have turned back, strengthen your brothers."

³³But he replied, "Lord, I am ready to go with you to prison and to death."

³⁴Jesus answered, "I tell you, Peter, before the rooster crows today, you will deny three times that you know me."

³⁵Then Jesus asked them, "When I sent you without purse, bag or sandals, did you lack anything?"

"Nothing," they answered.

³⁶He said to them, "But now if you have a purse, take it, and also a bag; and if you don't have a sword, sell your cloak and buy one. ³⁷It is written: 'And he was numbered with the transgressors'^b; and I tell you that this must be fulfilled in me. Yes, what is written about me is reaching its fulfillment."

³⁸The disciples said, "See, Lord, here are two swords."

"That's enough!" he replied.

Jesus Prays on the Mount of Olives

³⁹Jesus went out as usual to the Mount of Olives, and his disciples followed him. ⁴⁰On reaching the

---

^a 19,20 Some manuscripts do not have *given for you . . . poured out for you.*
^b 37 Isaiah 53:12

place, he said to them, "Pray that you will not fall into temptation." ⁴¹He withdrew about a stone's throw beyond them, knelt down and prayed, ⁴²"Father, if you are willing, take this cup from me; yet not my will, but yours be done." ⁴³An angel from heaven appeared to him and strengthened him. ⁴⁴And being in anguish, he prayed more earnestly, and his sweat was like drops of blood falling to the ground.^a

⁴⁵When he rose from prayer and went back to the disciples, he found them asleep, exhausted from sorrow. ⁴⁶"Why are you sleeping?" he asked them. "Get up and pray so that you will not fall into temptation."

Jesus Arrested

⁴⁷While he was still speaking a crowd came up, and the man who was called Judas, one of the Twelve, was leading them. He approached Jesus to kiss him, ⁴⁸but Jesus asked him, "Judas, are you betraying the Son of Man with a kiss?"

⁴⁹When Jesus' followers saw what was going to happen, they said, "Lord, should we strike with our swords?" ⁵⁰And one of them struck the servant of the high priest, cutting off his right ear.

⁵¹But Jesus answered, "No more of this!" And he touched the man's ear and healed him.

⁵²Then Jesus said to the chief priests, the officers of the temple guard, and the elders, who had come for him, "Am I leading a rebellion, that you have come with swords and clubs? ⁵³Every day I was with you in the temple courts, and you did not lay a hand on me. But this is your hour — when darkness reigns."

Peter Disowns Jesus

⁵⁴Then seizing him, they led him away and took him into the house of the high priest. Peter followed at a distance. ⁵⁵And when some there had kindled a fire in the middle of the courtyard and had sat down together, Peter sat down with them. ⁵⁶A servant girl saw him seated there in the firelight. She looked closely at him and said, "This man was with him."

⁵⁷But he denied it. "Woman, I don't know him," he said.

⁵⁸A little later someone else saw him and said, "You also are one of them."

"Man, I am not!" Peter replied.

⁵⁹About an hour later another asserted, "Certainly this fellow was with him, for he is a Galilean."

⁶⁰Peter replied, "Man, I don't know what you're talking about!" Just as he was speaking, the rooster crowed. ⁶¹The Lord turned and looked straight at Peter. Then Peter remembered the word the Lord had spoken to him: "Before the rooster crows today, you will

---

^a *43,44* Many early manuscripts do not have verses 43 and 44.

disown me three times." ⁶²And he went outside and wept bitterly.

The Guards Mock Jesus

⁶³The men who were guarding Jesus began mocking and beating him. ⁶⁴They blindfolded him and demanded, "Prophesy! Who hit you?" ⁶⁵And they said many other insulting things to him.

Jesus Before Pilate and Herod

⁶⁶At daybreak the council of the elders of the people, both the chief priests and the teachers of the law, met together, and Jesus was led before them. ⁶⁷"If you are the Messiah," they said, "tell us."

Jesus answered, "If I tell you, you will not believe me, ⁶⁸and if I asked you, you would not answer. ⁶⁹But from now on, the Son of Man will be seated at the right hand of the mighty God."

⁷⁰They all asked, "Are you then the Son of God?"

He replied, "You say that I am."

⁷¹Then they said, "Why do we need any more testimony? We have heard it from his own lips."

23 Then the whole assembly rose and led him off to Pilate. ²And they began to accuse him, saying, "We have found this man subverting our nation. He opposes payment of taxes to Caesar and claims to be Messiah, a king."

³So Pilate asked Jesus, "Are you the king of the Jews?"

"You have said so," Jesus replied.

⁴Then Pilate announced to the chief priests and the crowd, "I find no basis for a charge against this man."

⁵But they insisted, "He stirs up the people all over Judea by his teaching. He started in Galilee and has come all the way here."

⁶On hearing this, Pilate asked if the man was a Galilean. ⁷When he learned that Jesus was under Herod's jurisdiction, he sent him to Herod, who was also in Jerusalem at that time.

⁸When Herod saw Jesus, he was greatly pleased, because for a long time he had been wanting to see him. From what he had heard about him, he hoped to see him perform a sign of some sort. ⁹He plied him with many questions, but Jesus gave him no answer. ¹⁰The chief priests and the teachers of the law were standing there, vehemently accusing him. ¹¹Then Herod and his soldiers ridiculed and mocked him. Dressing him in an elegant robe, they sent him back to Pilate. ¹²That day Herod and Pilate became friends — before this they had been enemies.

¹³Pilate called together the chief priests, the rulers and the people, ¹⁴and said to them, "You brought me this man as one who was inciting the people to rebellion. I have examined him in your presence and have found no basis for your charges against him. ¹⁵Neither has Herod, for he sent him back to us; as you can see, he has done nothing to deserve

death. [16]Therefore, I will punish him and then release him." [17]*a*

[18]But the whole crowd shouted, "Away with this man! Release Barabbas to us!" [19](Barabbas had been thrown into prison for an insurrection in the city, and for murder.)

[20]Wanting to release Jesus, Pilate appealed to them again. [21]But they kept shouting, "Crucify him! Crucify him!"

[22]For the third time he spoke to them: "Why? What crime has this man committed? I have found in him no grounds for the death penalty. Therefore I will have him punished and then release him."

[23]But with loud shouts they insistently demanded that he be crucified, and their shouts prevailed. [24]So Pilate decided to grant their demand. [25]He released the man who had been thrown into prison for insurrection and murder, the one they asked for, and surrendered Jesus to their will.

The Crucifixion of Jesus

[26]As the soldiers led him away, they seized Simon from Cyrene, who was on his way in from the country, and put the cross on him and made him carry it behind Jesus. [27]A large number of people followed him, including women who mourned and wailed for him. [28]Jesus turned and said to them, "Daughters of Jerusalem, do not weep for me; weep for yourselves and for your children. [29]For the time will come when you will say, 'Blessed are the childless women, the wombs that never bore and the breasts that never nursed!' [30]Then

" 'they will say to the
mountains, "Fall on us!"
and to the hills, "Cover us!" ' *b*

[31]For if people do these things when the tree is green, what will happen when it is dry?"

[32]Two other men, both criminals, were also led out with him to be executed. [33]When they came to the place called the Skull, they crucified him there, along with the criminals — one on his right, the other on his left. [34]Jesus said, "Father, forgive them, for they do not know what they are doing." *c* And they divided up his clothes by casting lots.

[35]The people stood watching, and the rulers even sneered at him. They said, "He saved others; let him save himself if he is God's Messiah, the Chosen One."

[36]The soldiers also came up and mocked him. They offered him wine vinegar [37]and said, "If you are the king of the Jews, save yourself."

[38]There was a written notice above him, which read: THIS IS THE KING OF THE JEWS.

[39]One of the criminals who hung there hurled insults at him: "Aren't you the Messiah? Save yourself and us!"

---

a 17 Some manuscripts include here words similar to Matt. 27:15 and Mark 15:6.
b 30 Hosea 10:8   *c 34* Some early manuscripts do not have this sentence.

[40]But the other criminal rebuked him. "Don't you fear God," he said, "since you are under the same sentence? [41]We are punished justly, for we are getting what our deeds deserve. But this man has done nothing wrong."

[42]Then he said, "Jesus, remember me when you come into your kingdom.[a]"

[43]Jesus answered him, "Truly I tell you, today you will be with me in paradise."

The Death of Jesus

[44]It was now about noon, and darkness came over the whole land until three in the afternoon, [45]for the sun stopped shining. And the curtain of the temple was torn in two. [46]Jesus called out with a loud voice, "Father, into your hands I commit my spirit."[b] When he had said this, he breathed his last.

[47]The centurion, seeing what had happened, praised God and said, "Surely this was a righteous man." [48]When all the people who had gathered to witness this sight saw what took place, they beat their breasts and went away. [49]But all those who knew him, including the women who had followed him from Galilee, stood at a distance, watching these things.

The Burial of Jesus

[50]Now there was a man named Joseph, a member of the Council, a good and upright man, [51]who had not consented to their decision and action. He came from the Judean town of Arimathea, and he himself was waiting for the kingdom of God. [52]Going to Pilate, he asked for Jesus' body. [53]Then he took it down, wrapped it in linen cloth and placed it in a tomb cut in the rock, one in which no one had yet been laid. [54]It was Preparation Day, and the Sabbath was about to begin.

[55]The women who had come with Jesus from Galilee followed Joseph and saw the tomb and how his body was laid in it. [56]Then they went home and prepared spices and perfumes. But they rested on the Sabbath in obedience to the commandment.

Jesus Has Risen

24 On the first day of the week, very early in the morning, the women took the spices they had prepared and went to the tomb. [2]They found the stone rolled away from the tomb, [3]but when they entered, they did not find the body of the Lord Jesus. [4]While they were wondering about this, suddenly two men in clothes that gleamed like lightning stood beside them. [5]In their fright the women bowed down with their faces to the ground, but the men said to them, "Why do you look for the living among the dead? [6]He is not here; he has risen! Remember

---

[a] 42 Some manuscripts *come with your kingly power*   [b] 46 Psalm 31:5

how he told you, while he was still with you in Galilee: [7] 'The Son of Man must be delivered over to the hands of sinners, be crucified and on the third day be raised again.' " [8] Then they remembered his words.

[9] When they came back from the tomb, they told all these things to the Eleven and to all the others. [10] It was Mary Magdalene, Joanna, Mary the mother of James, and the others with them who told this to the apostles. [11] But they did not believe the women, because their words seemed to them like nonsense. [12] Peter, however, got up and ran to the tomb. Bending over, he saw the strips of linen lying by themselves, and he went away, wondering to himself what had happened.

On the Road to Emmaus

[13] Now that same day two of them were going to a village called Emmaus, about seven miles[a] from Jerusalem. [14] They were talking with each other about everything that had happened. [15] As they talked and discussed these things with each other, Jesus himself came up and walked along with them; [16] but they were kept from recognizing him.

[17] He asked them, "What are you discussing together as you walk along?"

They stood still, their faces downcast. [18] One of them, named Cleopas, asked him, "Are you the only one visiting Jerusalem who does not know the things that have happened there in these days?"

[19] "What things?" he asked.

"About Jesus of Nazareth," they replied. "He was a prophet, powerful in word and deed before God and all the people. [20] The chief priests and our rulers handed him over to be sentenced to death, and they crucified him; [21] but we had hoped that he was the one who was going to redeem Israel. And what is more, it is the third day since all this took place. [22] In addition, some of our women amazed us. They went to the tomb early this morning [23] but didn't find his body. They came and told us that they had seen a vision of angels, who said he was alive. [24] Then some of our companions went to the tomb and found it just as the women had said, but they did not see Jesus."

[25] He said to them, "How foolish you are, and how slow to believe all that the prophets have spoken! [26] Did not the Messiah have to suffer these things and then enter his glory?" [27] And beginning with Moses and all the Prophets, he explained to them what was said in all the Scriptures concerning himself.

[28] As they approached the village to which they were going, Jesus continued on as if he were going farther. [29] But they urged

---

[a] 13 Or about 11 kilometers

him strongly, "Stay with us, for it is nearly evening; the day is almost over." So he went in to stay with them.

³⁰When he was at the table with them, he took bread, gave thanks, broke it and began to give it to them. ³¹Then their eyes were opened and they recognized him, and he disappeared from their sight. ³²They asked each other, "Were not our hearts burning within us while he talked with us on the road and opened the Scriptures to us?"

³³They got up and returned at once to Jerusalem. There they found the Eleven and those with them, assembled together ³⁴and saying, "It is true! The Lord has risen and has appeared to Simon." ³⁵Then the two told what had happened on the way, and how Jesus was recognized by them when he broke the bread.

Jesus Appears to the Disciples

³⁶While they were still talking about this, Jesus himself stood among them and said to them, "Peace be with you."

³⁷They were startled and frightened, thinking they saw a ghost. ³⁸He said to them, "Why are you troubled, and why do doubts rise in your minds? ³⁹Look at my hands and my feet. It is I myself! Touch me and see; a ghost does not have flesh and bones, as you see I have."

⁴⁰When he had said this, he showed them his hands and feet. ⁴¹And while they still did not believe it because of joy and amazement, he asked them, "Do you have anything here to eat?" ⁴²They gave him a piece of broiled fish, ⁴³and he took it and ate it in their presence.

⁴⁴He said to them, "This is what I told you while I was still with you: Everything must be fulfilled that is written about me in the Law of Moses, the Prophets and the Psalms."

⁴⁵Then he opened their minds so they could understand the Scriptures. ⁴⁶He told them, "This is what is written: The Messiah will suffer and rise from the dead on the third day, ⁴⁷and repentance for the forgiveness of sins will be preached in his name to all nations, beginning at Jerusalem. ⁴⁸You are witnesses of these things. ⁴⁹I am going to send you what my Father has promised; but stay in the city until you have been clothed with power from on high."

The Ascension of Jesus

⁵⁰When he had led them out to the vicinity of Bethany, he lifted up his hands and blessed them. ⁵¹While he was blessing them, he left them and was taken up into heaven. ⁵²Then they worshiped him and returned to Jerusalem with great joy. ⁵³And they stayed continually at the temple, praising God.

John

Introduction:

The fourth Gospel was written by John, one of Jesus' twelve disciples. He is referred to as "the disciple whom Jesus loved." John wrote this Gospel sometime between AD 90 and 100 so that "you may believe that Jesus is the Messiah, the Son of God, and that by believing you may have life in his name" (John 20:31).

Although the book of John gives a general outline of the life and work of Jesus Christ, it is very different from the other three Gospels. John reports five miracles that are not reported by the other authors. Only two miracles reported in the other Gospels are reported in John. This book contains no parables and stresses Jesus' relationships with individuals.

The purpose of this Gospel is to report the signs (called miracles in the other Gospels) that prove Christ is God and has supernatural powers. John focuses on proving that Jesus is the Son of God, but also shows that Jesus was human by including stories about Jesus being tired, sad, hungry and thirsty.

Outline of contents:

Prologue and theme (1:1–18)
Introduction of Jesus (1:19–4:54)
Jesus' ministry as God's Son (5:1–10:42)
Crises in Jerusalem (11:1–12:50)
Jesus with his disciples (13:1–17:26)
Trial, death and burial (18:1–19:42)
Resurrection and conclusion (20:1–21:25)

The Word Became Flesh

1 In the beginning was the Word, and the Word was with God, and the Word was God. ²He was with God in the beginning. ³Through him all things were made; without him nothing was made that has been made. ⁴In him was life, and that life was the light of all mankind. ⁵The light shines in the darkness, and the darkness has not overcome[a] it.

⁶There was a man sent from God whose name was John. ⁷He came as a witness to testify concerning that light, so that through

---

ᵃ 5 Or *understood*

him all might believe. [8]He himself was not the light; he came only as a witness to the light.

[9]The true light that gives light to everyone was coming into the world. [10]He was in the world, and though the world was made through him, the world did not recognize him. [11]He came to that which was his own, but his own did not receive him. [12]Yet to all who did receive him, to those who believed in his name, he gave the right to become children of God— [13]children born not of natural descent, nor of human decision or a husband's will, but born of God.

[14]The Word became flesh and made his dwelling among us. We have seen his glory, the glory of the one and only Son, who came from the Father, full of grace and truth.

[15](John testified concerning him. He cried out, saying, "This is the one I spoke about when I said, 'He who comes after me has surpassed me because he was before me.' ") [16]Out of his fullness we have all received grace in place of grace already given. [17]For the law was given through Moses; grace and truth came through Jesus Christ. [18]No one has ever seen God, but the one and only Son, who is himself God and[b] is in closest relationship with the Father, has made him known.

John the Baptist Denies Being the Messiah

[19]Now this was John's testimony when the Jewish leaders[b] in Jerusalem sent priests and Levites to ask him who he was. [20]He did not fail to confess, but confessed freely, "I am not the Messiah."

[21]They asked him, "Then who are you? Are you Elijah?"

He said, "I am not."

"Are you the Prophet?"

He answered, "No."

[22]Finally they said, "Who are you? Give us an answer to take back to those who sent us. What do you say about yourself?"

[23]John replied in the words of Isaiah the prophet, "I am the voice of one calling in the wilderness, 'Make straight the way for the Lord.' "[c]

[24]Now the Pharisees who had been sent [25]questioned him, "Why then do you baptize if you are not the Messiah, nor Elijah, nor the Prophet?"

[26]"I baptize with[d] water," John replied, "but among you stands one you do not know. [27]He is the one who comes after me, the straps of whose sandals I am not worthy to untie."

[a] 18 Some manuscripts *but the only Son, who*   [b] 19 The Greek term traditionally translated *the Jews* (*hoi Ioudaioi*) refers here and elsewhere in John's Gospel to those Jewish leaders who opposed Jesus; also in 5:10, 15, 16; 7:1, 11, 13; 9:22; 18:14, 28, 36; 19:7, 12, 31, 38; 20:19.   [c] 23 Isaiah 40:3   [d] 26 Or *in*; also in verses 31 and 33 (twice)

28 This all happened at Bethany on the other side of the Jordan, where John was baptizing.

John Testifies About Jesus

29 The next day John saw Jesus coming toward him and said, "Look, the Lamb of God, who takes away the sin of the world! **30** This is the one I meant when I said, 'A man who comes after me has surpassed me because he was before me.' **31** I myself did not know him, but the reason I came baptizing with water was that he might be revealed to Israel."

32 Then John gave this testimony: "I saw the Spirit come down from heaven as a dove and remain on him. **33** And I myself did not know him, but the one who sent me to baptize with water told me, 'The man on whom you see the Spirit come down and remain is the one who will baptize with the Holy Spirit.' **34** I have seen and I testify that this is God's Chosen One."[a]

John's Disciples Follow Jesus

35 The next day John was there again with two of his disciples. **36** When he saw Jesus passing by, he said, "Look, the Lamb of God!"

37 When the two disciples heard him say this, they followed Jesus. **38** Turning around, Jesus saw them following and asked, "What do you want?"

They said, "Rabbi" (which means "Teacher"), "where are you staying?"

39 "Come," he replied, "and you will see."

So they went and saw where he was staying, and they spent that day with him. It was about four in the afternoon.

40 Andrew, Simon Peter's brother, was one of the two who heard what John had said and who had followed Jesus. **41** The first thing Andrew did was to find his brother Simon and tell him, "We have found the Messiah" (that is, the Christ). **42** And he brought him to Jesus.

Jesus looked at him and said, "You are Simon son of John. You will be called Cephas" (which, when translated, is Peter[b]).

Jesus Calls Philip and Nathanael

43 The next day Jesus decided to leave for Galilee. Finding Philip, he said to him, "Follow me."

44 Philip, like Andrew and Peter, was from the town of Bethsaida. **45** Philip found Nathanael and told him, "We have found the one Moses wrote about in the Law, and about whom the prophets also wrote — Jesus of Nazareth, the son of Joseph."

46 "Nazareth! Can anything good come from there?" Nathanael asked.

"Come and see," said Philip.

---

[a] 34 See Isaiah 42:1; many manuscripts *is the Son of God.* [b] 42 *Cephas* (Aramaic) and *Peter* (Greek) both mean *rock.*

47 When Jesus saw Nathanael approaching, he said of him, "Here truly is an Israelite in whom there is no deceit."

48 "How do you know me?" Nathanael asked.

Jesus answered, "I saw you while you were still under the fig tree before Philip called you."

49 Then Nathanael declared, "Rabbi, you are the Son of God; you are the king of Israel."

50 Jesus said, "You believe[a] because I told you I saw you under the fig tree. You will see greater things than that." **51** He then added, "Very truly I tell you,[b] you[b] will see 'heaven open, and the angels of God ascending and descending on'[c] the Son of Man."

Jesus Changes Water Into Wine

2 On the third day a wedding took place at Cana in Galilee. Jesus' mother was there, **2** and Jesus and his disciples had also been invited to the wedding. **3** When the wine was gone, Jesus' mother said to him, "They have no more wine."

4 "Woman,[d] why do you involve me?" Jesus replied. "My hour has not yet come."

5 His mother said to the servants, "Do whatever he tells you."

6 Nearby stood six stone water jars, the kind used by the Jews for ceremonial washing, each holding from twenty to thirty gallons.[e]

7 Jesus said to the servants, "Fill the jars with water"; so they filled them to the brim.

8 Then he told them, "Now draw some out and take it to the master of the banquet."

They did so, **9** and the master of the banquet tasted the water that had been turned into wine. He did not realize where it had come from, though the servants who had drawn the water knew. Then he called the bridegroom aside **10** and said, "Everyone brings out the choice wine first and then the cheaper wine after the guests have had too much to drink; but you have saved the best till now."

11 What Jesus did here in Cana of Galilee was the first of the signs through which he revealed his glory; and his disciples believed in him.

12 After this he went down to Capernaum with his mother and brothers and his disciples. There they stayed for a few days.

Jesus Clears the Temple Courts

13 When it was almost time for the Jewish Passover, Jesus went up to Jerusalem. **14** In the temple courts he found people selling cattle, sheep and doves, and others sitting at tables exchanging money. **15** So he made a whip out of cords, and drove all from the temple courts, both sheep and cattle; he scattered the coins of

---

[a] 50 Or Do you believe . . . ?   [b] 51 The Greek is plural.   [c] 51 Gen. 28:12
[d] 4 The Greek for Woman does not denote any disrespect.   [e] 6 Or from about 75 to about 115 liters

the money changers and over-turned their tables. **16**To those who sold doves he said, "Get these out of here! Stop turning my Father's house into a market!" **17**His disciples remembered that it is written: "Zeal for your house will consume me."*a*

18The Jews then responded to him, "What sign can you show us to prove your authority to do all this?"

19Jesus answered them, "Destroy this temple, and I will raise it again in three days."

20They replied, "It has taken forty-six years to build this temple, and you are going to raise it in three days?" **21**But the temple he had spoken of was his body. **22**After he was raised from the dead, his disciples recalled what he had said. Then they believed the scripture and the words that Jesus had spoken.

23Now while he was in Jerusalem at the Passover Festival, many people saw the signs he was performing and believed in his name.*b* **24**But Jesus would not entrust himself to them, for he knew all people. **25**He did not need any testimony about mankind, for he knew what was in each person.

Jesus Teaches Nicodemus

3 Now there was a Pharisee, a man named Nicodemus who was a member of the Jewish rul-ing council. **2**He came to Jesus at night and said, "Rabbi, we know that you are a teacher who has come from God. For no one could perform the signs you are doing if God were not with him."

3Jesus replied, "Very truly I tell you, no one can see the kingdom of God unless they are born again.*c*"

4"How can someone be born when they are old?" Nicodemus asked. "Surely they cannot enter a second time into their mother's womb to be born!"

5Jesus answered, "Very truly I tell you, no one can enter the kingdom of God unless they are born of water and the Spirit. **6**Flesh gives birth to flesh, but the Spirit*d* gives birth to spirit. **7**You should not be surprised at my saying, 'You*e* must be born again.' **8**The wind blows wherever it pleases. You hear its sound, but you cannot tell where it comes from or where it is going. So it is with everyone born of the Spirit."*f*

9"How can this be?" Nicodemus asked.

10"You are Israel's teacher," said Jesus, "and do you not understand these things? **11**Very truly I tell you, we speak of what we know, and we testify to what we have seen, but still you people do not accept our testimony. **12**I have spoken to you of earthly things and you do not believe; how then will you believe if I speak of heavenly things? ¹³No one has ever gone into heaven except the one who came from heaven—the Son of Man.ᵃ ¹⁴Just as Moses lifted up the snake in the wilderness, so the Son of Man must be lifted up,ᵇ ¹⁵that everyone who believes may have eternal life in him."ᶜ

¹⁶For God so loved the world that he gave his one and only Son, that whoever believes in him shall not perish but have eternal life. ¹⁷For God did not send his Son into the world to condemn the world, but to save the world through him. ¹⁸Whoever believes in him is not condemned, but whoever does not believe stands condemned already because they have not believed in the name of God's one and only Son. ¹⁹This is the verdict: Light has come into the world, but people loved darkness instead of light because their deeds were evil. ²⁰Everyone who does evil hates the light, and will not come into the light for fear that their deeds will be exposed. ²¹But whoever lives by the truth comes into the light, so that it may be seen plainly that what they have done has been done in the sight of God.

John Testifies Again About Jesus

²²After this, Jesus and his disciples went out into the Judean countryside, where he spent some time with them, and baptized. ²³Now John also was baptizing at Aenon near Salim, because there was plenty of water, and people were coming and being baptized. ²⁴(This was before John was put in prison.) ²⁵An argument developed between some of John's disciples and a certain Jew over the matter of ceremonial washing. ²⁶They came to John and said to him, "Rabbi, that man who was with you on the other side of the Jordan—the one you testified about—look, he is baptizing, and everyone is going to him."

²⁷To this John replied, "A person can receive only what is given them from heaven. ²⁸You yourselves can testify that I said, 'I am not the Messiah but am sent ahead of him.' ²⁹The bride belongs to the bridegroom. The friend who attends the bridegroom waits and listens for him, and is full of joy when he hears the bridegroom's voice. That joy is mine, and it is now complete. ³⁰He must become greater; I must become less."ᵈ

³¹The one who comes from above is above all; the one who is from the earth belongs to the earth, and speaks as one from the earth. The one who comes from heaven is above all. ³²He testifies to what he has seen and heard, but no one accepts his testimony.

ᵃ 13 Some manuscripts *Man, who is in heaven*   ᵇ 14 The Greek for *lifted up* also means *exalted*.   ᶜ 15 Some interpreters end the quotation with verse 21.
ᵈ 30 Some interpreters end the quotation with verse 36.

33Whoever has accepted it has certified that God is truthful. 34For the one whom God has sent speaks the words of God, for God*a* gives the Spirit without limit. 35The Father loves the Son and has placed everything in his hands. 36Whoever believes in the Son has eternal life, but whoever rejects the Son will not see life, for God's wrath remains on them.

Jesus Talks With a Samaritan Woman

4 Now Jesus learned that the Pharisees had heard that he was gaining and baptizing more disciples than John — 2although in fact it was not Jesus who baptized, but his disciples. 3So he left Judea and went back once more to Galilee.

4Now he had to go through Samaria. 5So he came to a town in Samaria called Sychar, near the plot of ground Jacob had given to his son Joseph. 6Jacob's well was there, and Jesus, tired as he was from the journey, sat down by the well. It was about noon.

7When a Samaritan woman came to draw water, Jesus said to her, "Will you give me a drink?" 8(His disciples had gone into the town to buy food.)

9The Samaritan woman said to him, "You are a Jew and I am a Samaritan woman. How can you ask me for a drink?" (For Jews do not associate with Samaritans.*b*)

10Jesus answered her, "If you knew the gift of God and who it is that asks you for a drink, you would have asked him and he would have given you living water."

11"Sir," the woman said, "you have nothing to draw with and the well is deep. Where can you get this living water? 12Are you greater than our father Jacob, who gave us the well and drank from it himself, as did also his sons and his livestock?"

13Jesus answered, "Everyone who drinks this water will be thirsty again, 14but whoever drinks the water I give them will never thirst. Indeed, the water I give them will become in them a spring of water welling up to eternal life."

15The woman said to him, "Sir, give me this water so that I won't get thirsty and have to keep coming here to draw water."

16He told her, "Go, call your husband and come back."

17"I have no husband," she replied.

Jesus said to her, "You are right when you say you have no husband. 18The fact is, you have had five husbands, and the man you now have is not your husband. What you have just said is quite true."

19"Sir," the woman said, "I can see that you are a prophet. 20Our ancestors worshiped on this

---

a 34 Greek *he*   *b* 9 Or *do not use dishes Samaritans have used* mountain, but you Jews claim that the place where we must worship is in Jerusalem."

²¹ "Woman," Jesus replied, "believe me, a time is coming when you will worship the Father neither on this mountain nor in Jerusalem. ²² You Samaritans worship what you do not know; we worship what we do know, for salvation is from the Jews. ²³ Yet a time is coming and has now come when the true worshipers will worship the Father in the Spirit and in truth, for they are the kind of worshipers the Father seeks. ²⁴ God is spirit, and his worshipers must worship in the Spirit and in truth."

²⁵ The woman said, "I know that Messiah" (called Christ) "is coming. When he comes, he will explain everything to us."

²⁶ Then Jesus declared, "I, the one speaking to you — I am he."

The Disciples Rejoin Jesus

²⁷ Just then his disciples returned and were surprised to find him talking with a woman. But no one asked, "What do you want?" or "Why are you talking with her?"

²⁸ Then, leaving her water jar, the woman went back to the town and said to the people, ²⁹ "Come, see a man who told me everything I ever did. Could this be the Messiah?" ³⁰ They came out of the town and made their way toward him.

³¹ Meanwhile his disciples urged him, "Rabbi, eat something."

³² But he said to them, "I have food to eat that you know nothing about."

³³ Then his disciples said to each other, "Could someone have brought him food?"

³⁴ "My food," said Jesus, "is to do the will of him who sent me and to finish his work. ³⁵ Don't you have a saying, 'It's still four months until harvest'? I tell you, open your eyes and look at the fields! They are ripe for harvest. ³⁶ Even now the one who reaps draws a wage and harvests a crop for eternal life, so that the sower and the reaper may be glad together. ³⁷ Thus the saying 'One sows and another reaps' is true. ³⁸ I sent you to reap what you have not worked for. Others have done the hard work, and you have reaped the benefits of their labor."

Many Samaritans Believe

³⁹ Many of the Samaritans from that town believed in him because of the woman's testimony, "He told me everything I ever did." ⁴⁰ So when the Samaritans came to him, they urged him to stay with them, and he stayed two days. ⁴¹ And because of his words many more became believers.

⁴² They said to the woman, "We no longer believe just because of what you said; now we have heard for ourselves, and we know that this man really is the Savior of the world."

Jesus Heals an Official's Son

⁴³After the two days he left for Galilee. ⁴⁴(Now Jesus himself had pointed out that a prophet has no honor in his own country.) ⁴⁵When he arrived in Galilee, the Galileans welcomed him. They had seen all that he had done in Jerusalem at the Passover Festival, for they also had been there.

⁴⁶Once more he visited Cana in Galilee, where he had turned the water into wine. And there was a certain royal official whose son lay sick at Capernaum. ⁴⁷When this man heard that Jesus had arrived in Galilee from Judea, he went to him and begged him to come and heal his son, who was close to death.

⁴⁸"Unless you people see signs and wonders," Jesus told him, "you will never believe."

⁴⁹The royal official said, "Sir, come down before my child dies."

⁵⁰"Go," Jesus replied, "your son will live."

The man took Jesus at his word and departed. ⁵¹While he was still on the way, his servants met him with the news that his boy was living. ⁵²When he inquired as to the time when his son got better, they said to him, "Yesterday, at one in the afternoon, the fever left him."

⁵³Then the father realized that this was the exact time at which Jesus had said to him, "Your son will live." So he and his whole household believed.

⁵⁴This was the second sign Jesus performed after coming from Judea to Galilee.

The Healing at the Pool

5 Some time later, Jesus went up to Jerusalem for one of the Jewish festivals. ²Now there is in Jerusalem near the Sheep Gate a pool, which in Aramaic is called Bethesda*ᵃ* and which is surrounded by five covered colonnades. ³Here a great number of disabled people used to lie — the blind, the lame, the paralyzed. [4] *ᵇ* ⁵One who was there had been an invalid for thirty-eight years. ⁶When Jesus saw him lying there and learned that he had been in this condition for a long time, he asked him, "Do you want to get well?"

⁷"Sir," the invalid replied, "I have no one to help me into the pool when the water is stirred. While I am trying to get in, someone else goes down ahead of me."

⁸Then Jesus said to him, "Get up! Pick up your mat and walk." ⁹At once the man was cured; he picked up his mat and walked.

The day on which this took place was a Sabbath, ¹⁰and so the Jewish leaders said to the man

---

ᵃ 2 Some manuscripts *Bethzatha*; other manuscripts *Bethsaida*   *ᵇ 3,4* Some manuscripts include here, wholly or in part, *paralyzed — and they waited for the moving of the waters. ⁴From time to time an angel of the Lord would come down and stir up the waters. The first one into the pool after each such disturbance would be cured of whatever disease they had.*

who had been healed, "It is the Sabbath; the law forbids you to carry your mat."

¹¹ But he replied, "The man who made me well said to me, 'Pick up your mat and walk.' "

¹² So they asked him, "Who is this fellow who told you to pick it up and walk?"

¹³ The man who was healed had no idea who it was, for Jesus had slipped away into the crowd that was there.

¹⁴ Later Jesus found him at the temple and said to him, "See, you are well again. Stop sinning or something worse may happen to you." ¹⁵ The man went away and told the Jewish leaders that it was Jesus who had made him well.

The Authority of the Son

¹⁶ So, because Jesus was doing these things on the Sabbath, the Jewish leaders began to persecute him. ¹⁷ In his defense Jesus said to them, "My Father is always at his work to this very day, and I too am working." ¹⁸ For this reason they tried all the more to kill him; not only was he breaking the Sabbath, but he was even calling God his own Father, making himself equal with God.

¹⁹ Jesus gave them this answer: "Very truly I tell you, the Son can do nothing by himself; he can do only what he sees his Father doing, because whatever the Father does the Son also does. ²⁰ For the Father loves the Son and shows him all he does. Yes, and he will

show him even greater works than these, so that you will be amazed. ²¹ For just as the Father raises the dead and gives them life, even so the Son gives life to whom he is pleased to give it. ²² Moreover, the Father judges no one, but has entrusted all judgment to the Son, ²³ that all may honor the Son just as they honor the Father. Whoever does not honor the Son does not honor the Father, who sent him.

²⁴ "Very truly I tell you, whoever hears my word and believes him who sent me has eternal life and will not be judged but has crossed over from death to life. ²⁵ Very truly I tell you, a time is coming and has now come when the dead will hear the voice of the Son of God and those who hear will live. ²⁶ For as the Father has life in himself, so he has granted the Son also to have life in himself. ²⁷ And he has given him authority to judge because he is the Son of Man.

²⁸ "Do not be amazed at this, for a time is coming when all who are in their graves will hear his voice ²⁹ and come out—those who have done what is good will rise to live, and those who have done what is evil will rise to be condemned. ³⁰ By myself I can do nothing; I judge only as I hear, and my judgment is just, for I seek not to please myself but him who sent me.

Testimonies About Jesus

³¹ "If I testify about myself, my testimony is not true. ³² There is another who testifies in my favor,

and I know that his testimony about me is true.

³³ "You have sent to John and he has testified to the truth. ³⁴ Not that I accept human testimony; but I mention it that you may be saved. ³⁵ John was a lamp that burned and gave light, and you chose for a time to enjoy his light.

³⁶ "I have testimony weightier than that of John. For the works that the Father has given me to finish — the very works that I am doing — testify that the Father has sent me. ³⁷ And the Father who sent me has himself testified concerning me. You have never heard his voice nor seen his form, ³⁸ nor does his word dwell in you, for you do not believe the one he sent. ³⁹ You study[a] the Scriptures diligently because you think that in them you have eternal life. These are the very Scriptures that testify about me, ⁴⁰ yet you refuse to come to me to have life.

⁴¹ "I do not accept glory from human beings, ⁴² but I know you. I know that you do not have the love of God in your hearts. ⁴³ I have come in my Father's name, and you do not accept me; but if someone else comes in his own name, you will accept him. ⁴⁴ How can you believe since you accept glory from one another but do not seek the glory that comes from the only God[b]?

⁴⁵ "But do not think I will accuse you before the Father. Your accuser is Moses, on whom your hopes are set. ⁴⁶ If you believed Moses, you would believe me, for he wrote about me. ⁴⁷ But since you do not believe what he wrote, how are you going to believe what I say?"

Jesus Feeds the Five Thousand

6 Some time after this, Jesus crossed to the far shore of the Sea of Galilee (that is, the Sea of Tiberias), ² and a great crowd of people followed him because they saw the signs he had performed by healing the sick. ³ Then Jesus went up on a mountainside and sat down with his disciples. ⁴ The Jewish Passover Festival was near.

⁵ When Jesus looked up and saw a great crowd coming toward him, he said to Philip, "Where shall we buy bread for these people to eat?" ⁶ He asked this only to test him, for he already had in mind what he was going to do.

⁷ Philip answered him, "It would take more than half a year's wages[c] to buy enough bread for each one to have a bite!"

⁸ Another of his disciples, Andrew, Simon Peter's brother, spoke up, ⁹ "Here is a boy with five small barley loaves and two small fish, but how far will they go among so many?"

¹⁰ Jesus said, "Have the people sit down." There was plenty of grass in that place, and they sat

---

[a] 39 Or ³⁹Study   [b] 44 Some early manuscripts *the Only One*   [c] 7 Greek *take two hundred denarii*

down (about five thousand men were there). [11] Jesus then took the loaves, gave thanks, and distributed to those who were seated as much as they wanted. He did the same with the fish.

[12] When they had all had enough to eat, he said to his disciples, "Gather the pieces that are left over. Let nothing be wasted." [13] So they gathered them and filled twelve baskets with the pieces of the five barley loaves left over by those who had eaten.

[14] After the people saw the sign Jesus performed, they began to say, "Surely this is the Prophet who is to come into the world." [15] Jesus, knowing that they intended to come and make him king by force, withdrew again to a mountain by himself.

Jesus Walks on the Water

[16] When evening came, his disciples went down to the lake, [17] where they got into a boat and set off across the lake for Capernaum. By now it was dark, and Jesus had not yet joined them. [18] A strong wind was blowing and the waters grew rough. [19] When they had rowed about three or four miles,[a] they saw Jesus approaching the boat, walking on the water; and they were frightened. [20] But he said to them, "It is I; don't be afraid." [21] Then they were willing to take him into the boat, and immediately the boat

reached the shore where they were heading.

[22] The next day the crowd that had stayed on the opposite shore of the lake realized that only one boat had been there, and that Jesus had not entered it with his disciples, but that they had gone away alone. [23] Then some boats from Tiberias landed near the place where the people had eaten the bread after the Lord had given thanks. [24] Once the crowd realized that neither Jesus nor his disciples were there, they got into the boats and went to Capernaum in search of Jesus.

Jesus the Bread of Life

[25] When they found him on the other side of the lake, they asked him, "Rabbi, when did you get here?"

[26] Jesus answered, "Very truly I tell you, you are looking for me, not because you saw the signs I performed but because you ate the loaves and had your fill. [27] Do not work for food that spoils, but for food that endures to eternal life, which the Son of Man will give you. For on him God the Father has placed his seal of approval."

[28] Then they asked him, "What must we do to do the works God requires?"

[29] Jesus answered, "The work of God is this: to believe in the one he has sent."

[30] So they asked him, "What

---

[a] 19 Or about 5 or 6 kilometers

sign then will you give that we may see it and believe you? What will you do? **31** Our ancestors ate the manna in the wilderness; as it is written: 'He gave them bread from heaven to eat.'*ᵃ*

32 Jesus said to them, "Very truly I tell you, it is not Moses who has given you the bread from heaven, but it is my Father who gives you the true bread from heaven. **33** For the bread of God is the bread that comes down from heaven and gives life to the world."

34 "Sir," they said, "always give us this bread."

35 Then Jesus declared, "I am the bread of life. Whoever comes to me will never go hungry, and whoever believes in me will never be thirsty. **36** But as I told you, you have seen me and still you do not believe. **37** All those the Father gives me will come to me, and whoever comes to me I will never drive away. **38** For I have come down from heaven not to do my will but to do the will of him who sent me. **39** And this is the will of him who sent me, that I shall lose none of all those he has given me, but raise them up at the last day. **40** For my Father's will is that everyone who looks to the Son and believes in him shall have eternal life, and I will raise them up at the last day."

41 At this the Jews there began to grumble about him because he said, "I am the bread that came down from heaven." **42** They said, "Is this not Jesus, the son of Joseph, whose father and mother we know? How can he now say, 'I came down from heaven'?"

43 "Stop grumbling among yourselves," Jesus answered. **44** "No one can come to me unless the Father who sent me draws them, and I will raise them up at the last day. **45** It is written in the Prophets: 'They will all be taught by God.'*ᵇ* Everyone who has heard the Father and learned from him comes to me. **46** No one has seen the Father except the one who is from God; only he has seen the Father. **47** Very truly I tell you, the one who believes has eternal life. **48** I am the bread of life. **49** Your ancestors ate the manna in the wilderness, yet they died. **50** But here is the bread that comes down from heaven, which anyone may eat and not die. **51** I am the living bread that came down from heaven. Whoever eats this bread will live forever. This bread is my flesh, which I will give for the life of the world."

52 Then the Jews began to argue sharply among themselves, "How can this man give us his flesh to eat?"

53 Jesus said to them, "Very truly I tell you, unless you eat the flesh of the Son of Man and drink his blood, you have no life in you. **54** Whoever eats my flesh and drinks my blood has eternal life,

---

ᵃ 31 Exodus 16:4; Neh. 9:15; Psalm 78:24,25   *ᵇ 45* Isaiah 54:13

and I will raise them up at the last day. ⁵⁵ For my flesh is real food and my blood is real drink. ⁵⁶ Whoever eats my flesh and drinks my blood remains in me, and I in them. ⁵⁷ Just as the living Father sent me and I live because of the Father, so the one who feeds on me will live because of me. ⁵⁸ This is the bread that came down from heaven. Your ancestors ate manna and died, but whoever feeds on this bread will live forever." ⁵⁹ He said this while teaching in the synagogue in Capernaum.

Many Disciples Desert Jesus

⁶⁰ On hearing it, many of his disciples said, "This is a hard teaching. Who can accept it?"

⁶¹ Aware that his disciples were grumbling about this, Jesus said to them, "Does this offend you? ⁶² Then what if you see the Son of Man ascend to where he was before! ⁶³ The Spirit gives life; the flesh counts for nothing. The words I have spoken to you—they are full of the Spirit^a and life. ⁶⁴ Yet there are some of you who do not believe." For Jesus had known from the beginning which of them did not believe and who would betray him. ⁶⁵ He went on to say, "This is why I told you that no one can come to me unless the Father has enabled them."

⁶⁶ From this time many of his disciples turned back and no longer followed him.

⁶⁷ "You do not want to leave too, do you?" Jesus asked the Twelve.

⁶⁸ Simon Peter answered him, "Lord, to whom shall we go? You have the words of eternal life. ⁶⁹ We have come to believe and to know that you are the Holy One of God."

⁷⁰ Then Jesus replied, "Have I not chosen you, the Twelve? Yet one of you is a devil!" ⁷¹ (He meant Judas, the son of Simon Iscariot, who, though one of the Twelve, was later to betray him.)

Jesus Goes to the Festival of Tabernacles

7 After this, Jesus went around in Galilee. He did not want^b to go about in Judea because the Jewish leaders there were looking for a way to kill him. ² But when the Jewish Festival of Tabernacles was near, ³ Jesus' brothers said to him, "Leave Galilee and go to Judea, so that your disciples there may see the works you do. ⁴ No one who wants to become a public figure acts in secret. Since you are doing these things, show yourself to the world." ⁵ For even his own brothers did not believe in him.

⁶ Therefore Jesus told them, "My time is not yet here; for you any time will do. ⁷ The world cannot hate you, but it hates me because I testify that its works are evil. ⁸ You go to the festival. I am not^c going up to this festival,

^a 63 Or *are Spirit*; or *are spirit*   ^b 1 Some manuscripts *not have authority*
^c 8 Some manuscripts *not yet*

because my time has not yet fully come." ⁹After he had said this, he stayed in Galilee.

¹⁰However, after his brothers had left for the festival, he went also, not publicly, but in secret. ¹¹Now at the festival the Jewish leaders were watching for Jesus and asking, "Where is he?"

¹²Among the crowds there was widespread whispering about him. Some said, "He is a good man."

Others replied, "No, he deceives the people." ¹³But no one would say anything publicly about him for fear of the leaders.

Jesus Teaches at the Festival

¹⁴Not until halfway through the festival did Jesus go up to the temple courts and begin to teach. ¹⁵The Jews there were amazed and asked, "How did this man get such learning without having been taught?"

¹⁶Jesus answered, "My teaching is not my own. It comes from the one who sent me. ¹⁷Anyone who chooses to do the will of God will find out whether my teaching comes from God or whether I speak on my own. ¹⁸Whoever speaks on their own does so to gain personal glory, but he who seeks the glory of the one who sent him is a man of truth; there is nothing false about him. ¹⁹Has not Moses given you the law? Yet not one of you keeps the law. Why are you trying to kill me?"

²⁰"You are demon-possessed," the crowd answered. "Who is trying to kill you?"

²¹Jesus said to them, "I did one miracle, and you are all amazed. ²²Yet, because Moses gave you circumcision (though actually it did not come from Moses, but from the patriarchs), you circumcise a boy on the Sabbath. ²³Now if a boy can be circumcised on the Sabbath so that the law of Moses may not be broken, why are you angry with me for healing a man's whole body on the Sabbath? ²⁴Stop judging by mere appearances, but instead judge correctly."

Division Over Who Jesus Is

²⁵At that point some of the people of Jerusalem began to ask, "Isn't this the man they are trying to kill? ²⁶Here he is, speaking publicly, and they are not saying a word to him. Have the authorities really concluded that he is the Messiah? ²⁷But we know where this man is from; when the Messiah comes, no one will know where he is from."

²⁸Then Jesus, still teaching in the temple courts, cried out, "Yes, you know me, and you know where I am from. I am not here on my own authority, but he who sent me is true. You do not know him, ²⁹but I know him because I am from him and he sent me."

³⁰At this they tried to seize him, but no one laid a hand on him, because his hour had not

yet come. ³¹Still, many in the crowd believed in him. They said, "When the Messiah comes, will he perform more signs than this man?"

³²The Pharisees heard the crowd whispering such things about him. Then the chief priests and the Pharisees sent temple guards to arrest him.

³³Jesus said, "I am with you for only a short time, and then I am going to the one who sent me. ³⁴You will look for me, but you will not find me; and where I am, you cannot come."

³⁵The Jews said to one another, "Where does this man intend to go that we cannot find him? Will he go where our people live scattered among the Greeks, and teach the Greeks? ³⁶What did he mean when he said, 'You will look for me, but you will not find me,' and 'Where I am, you cannot come'?"

³⁷On the last and greatest day of the festival, Jesus stood and said in a loud voice, "Let anyone who is thirsty come to me and drink. ³⁸Whoever believes in me, as Scripture has said, rivers of living water will flow from within them."ᵃ ³⁹By this he meant the Spirit, whom those who believed in him were later to receive. Up to that time the Spirit had not been given, since Jesus had not yet been glorified.

⁴⁰On hearing his words, some of the people said, "Surely this man is the Prophet."

⁴¹Others said, "He is the Messiah."

Still others asked, "How can the Messiah come from Galilee? ⁴²Does not Scripture say that the Messiah will come from David's descendants and from Bethlehem, the town where David lived?" ⁴³Thus the people were divided because of Jesus. ⁴⁴Some wanted to seize him, but no one laid a hand on him.

Unbelief of the Jewish Leaders

⁴⁵Finally the temple guards went back to the chief priests and the Pharisees, who asked them, "Why didn't you bring him in?"

⁴⁶"No one ever spoke the way this man does," the guards replied.

⁴⁷"You mean he has deceived you also?" the Pharisees retorted. ⁴⁸"Have any of the rulers or of the Pharisees believed in him? ⁴⁹No! But this mob that knows nothing of the law — there is a curse on them."

⁵⁰Nicodemus, who had gone to Jesus earlier and who was one of their own number, asked, ⁵¹"Does our law condemn a man without first hearing him to find out what he has been doing?"

⁵²They replied, "Are you from Galilee, too? Look into it, and you will find that a prophet does not come out of Galilee."

ᵃ 37,38 Or me. And let anyone drink ³⁸who believes in me." As Scripture has said, "Out of him (or them) will flow rivers of living water."

[The earliest manuscripts and many other ancient witnesses do not have John 7:53 — 8:11. A few manuscripts include these verses, wholly or in part, after John 7:36, John 21:25, Luke 21:38 or Luke 24:53.]

8 ⁵³*Then they all went home,* ¹*but Jesus went to the Mount of Olives.* ²*At dawn he appeared again in the temple courts, where all the people gathered around him, and he sat down to teach them.* ³*The teachers of the law and the Pharisees brought in a woman caught in adultery. They made her stand before the group* ⁴*and said to Jesus, "Teacher, this woman was caught in the act of adultery.* ⁵*In the Law Moses commanded us to stone such women. Now what do you say?"* ⁶*They were using this question as a trap, in order to have a basis for accusing him.*

But Jesus bent down and started to write on the ground with his finger. ⁷*When they kept on questioning him, he straightened up and said to them, "Let any one of you who is without sin be the first to throw a stone at her."* ⁸*Again he stooped down and wrote on the ground.*

⁹*At this, those who heard began to go away one at a time, the older ones first, until only Jesus was left, with the woman still standing there.* ¹⁰*Jesus straightened up and asked her, "Woman, where are they? Has no one condemned you?"*

¹¹*"No one, sir," she said.*

"Then neither do I condemn you," Jesus declared. "Go now and leave your life of sin."

Dispute Over Jesus' Testimony

¹²When Jesus spoke again to the people, he said, "I am the light of the world. Whoever follows me will never walk in darkness, but will have the light of life."

¹³The Pharisees challenged him, "Here you are, appearing as your own witness; your testimony is not valid."

¹⁴Jesus answered, "Even if I testify on my own behalf, my testimony is valid, for I know where I came from and where I am going. But you have no idea where I come from or where I am going. ¹⁵You judge by human standards; I pass judgment on no one. ¹⁶But if I do judge, my decisions are true, because I am not alone. I stand with the Father, who sent me. ¹⁷In your own Law it is written that the testimony of two witnesses is true. ¹⁸I am one who testifies for myself; my other witness is the Father, who sent me."

¹⁹Then they asked him, "Where is your father?"

"You do not know me or my Father," Jesus replied. "If you knew me, you would know my Father also." ²⁰He spoke these words while teaching in the temple courts near the place where the offerings were put. Yet no one seized him, because his hour had not yet come.

Dispute Over Who Jesus Is

²¹Once more Jesus said to them, "I am going away, and you will look for me, and you will die

in your sin. Where I go, you cannot come."

22 This made the Jews ask, "Will he kill himself? Is that why he says, 'Where I go, you cannot come'?"

23 But he continued, "You are from below; I am from above. You are of this world; I am not of this world. **24** I told you that you would die in your sins; if you do not believe that I am he, you will indeed die in your sins."

25 "Who are you?" they asked.

"Just what I have been telling you from the beginning," Jesus replied. **26** "I have much to say in judgment of you. But he who sent me is trustworthy, and what I have heard from him I tell the world."

27 They did not understand that he was telling them about his Father. **28** So Jesus said, "When you have lifted up[a] the Son of Man, then you will know that I am he and that I do nothing on my own but speak just what the Father has taught me. **29** The one who sent me is with me; he has not left me alone, for I always do what pleases him." **30** Even as he spoke, many believed in him.

Dispute Over Whose Children Jesus' Opponents Are

31 To the Jews who had believed him, Jesus said, "If you hold to my teaching, you are really my disciples. **32** Then you will know the truth, and the truth will set you free."

33 They answered him, "We are Abraham's descendants and have never been slaves of anyone. How can you say that we shall be set free?"

34 Jesus replied, "Very truly I tell you, everyone who sins is a slave to sin. **35** Now a slave has no permanent place in the family, but a son belongs to it forever. **36** So if the Son sets you free, you will be free indeed. **37** I know that you are Abraham's descendants. Yet you are looking for a way to kill me, because you have no room for my word. **38** I am telling you what I have seen in the Father's presence, and you are doing what you have heard from your father.[b]"

39 "Abraham is our father," they answered.

"If you were Abraham's children," said Jesus, "then you would[c] do what Abraham did. **40** As it is, you are looking for a way to kill me, a man who has told you the truth that I heard from God. Abraham did not do such things. **41** You are doing the works of your own father."

"We are not illegitimate children," they protested. "The only Father we have is God himself."

42 Jesus said to them, "If God were your Father, you would love me, for I have come here from God.

---

[a] 28 The Greek for *lifted up* also means *exalted*. [b] 38 Or *presence. Therefore do what you have heard from the Father.* [c] 39 Some early manuscripts *"If you are Abraham's children," said Jesus, "then*

I have not come on my own; God sent me. ⁴³Why is my language not clear to you? Because you are unable to hear what I say. ⁴⁴You belong to your father, the devil, and you want to carry out your father's desires. He was a murderer from the beginning, not holding to the truth, for there is no truth in him. When he lies, he speaks his native language, for he is a liar and the father of lies. ⁴⁵Yet because I tell the truth, you do not believe me! ⁴⁶Can any of you prove me guilty of sin? If I am telling the truth, why don't you believe me? ⁴⁷Whoever belongs to God hears what God says. The reason you do not hear is that you do not belong to God."

Jesus' Claims About Himself

⁴⁸The Jews answered him, "Aren't we right in saying that you are a Samaritan and demon-possessed?"

⁴⁹"I am not possessed by a demon," said Jesus, "but I honor my Father and you dishonor me. ⁵⁰I am not seeking glory for myself; but there is one who seeks it, and he is the judge. ⁵¹Very truly I tell you, whoever obeys my word will never see death."

⁵²At this they exclaimed, "Now we know that you are demon-possessed! Abraham died and so did the prophets, yet you say that whoever obeys your word will never taste death. ⁵³Are you greater than our father Abraham? He died, and so did the prophets. Who do you think you are?"

⁵⁴Jesus replied, "If I glorify myself, my glory means nothing. My Father, whom you claim as your God, is the one who glorifies me. ⁵⁵Though you do not know him, I know him. If I said I did not, I would be a liar like you, but I do know him and obey his word. ⁵⁶Your father Abraham rejoiced at the thought of seeing my day; he saw it and was glad."

⁵⁷"You are not yet fifty years old," they said to him, "and you have seen Abraham!"

⁵⁸"Very truly I tell you," Jesus answered, "before Abraham was born, I am!" ⁵⁹At this, they picked up stones to stone him, but Jesus hid himself, slipping away from the temple grounds.

Jesus Heals a Man Born Blind

9 As he went along, he saw a man blind from birth. ²His disciples asked him, "Rabbi, who sinned, this man or his parents, that he was born blind?"

³"Neither this man nor his parents sinned," said Jesus, "but this happened so that the works of God might be displayed in him. ⁴As long as it is day, we must do the works of him who sent me. Night is coming, when no one can work. ⁵While I am in the world, I am the light of the world."

⁶After saying this, he spit on the ground, made some mud with the saliva, and put it on the man's eyes. ⁷"Go," he told him, "wash in the Pool of Siloam" (this word means "Sent"). So the man

went and washed, and came home seeing.

8 His neighbors and those who had formerly seen him begging asked, "Isn't this the same man who used to sit and beg?" **9** Some claimed that he was.

Others said, "No, he only looks like him."

But he himself insisted, "I am the man."

10 "How then were your eyes opened?" they asked.

11 He replied, "The man they call Jesus made some mud and put it on my eyes. He told me to go to Siloam and wash. So I went and washed, and then I could see."

12 "Where is this man?" they asked him.

"I don't know," he said.

The Pharisees Investigate the Healing

13 They brought to the Pharisees the man who had been blind. **14** Now the day on which Jesus had made the mud and opened the man's eyes was a Sabbath. **15** Therefore the Pharisees also asked him how he had received his sight. "He put mud on my eyes," the man replied, "and I washed, and now I see."

16 Some of the Pharisees said, "This man is not from God, for he does not keep the Sabbath."

But others asked, "How can a sinner perform such signs?" So they were divided.

17 Then they turned again to the blind man, "What have you to say about him? It was your eyes he opened."

The man replied, "He is a prophet."

18 They still did not believe that he had been blind and had received his sight until they sent for the man's parents. **19** "Is this your son?" they asked. "Is this the one you say was born blind? How is it that now he can see?"

20 "We know he is our son," the parents answered, "and we know he was born blind. **21** But how he can see now, or who opened his eyes, we don't know. Ask him. He is of age; he will speak for himself." **22** His parents said this because they were afraid of the Jewish leaders, who already had decided that anyone who acknowledged that Jesus was the Messiah would be put out of the synagogue. **23** That was why his parents said, "He is of age; ask him."

24 A second time they summoned the man who had been blind. "Give glory to God by telling the truth," they said. "We know this man is a sinner."

25 He replied, "Whether he is a sinner or not, I don't know. One thing I do know. I was blind but now I see!"

26 Then they asked him, "What did he do to you? How did he open your eyes?"

27 He answered, "I have told you already and you did not listen. Why do you want to hear it again? Do you want to become his disciples too?"

28 Then they hurled insults at him and said, "You are this fellow's disciple! We are disciples of Moses! 29 We know that God spoke to Moses, but as for this fellow, we don't even know where he comes from."

30 The man answered, "Now that is remarkable! You don't know where he comes from, yet he opened my eyes. 31 We know that God does not listen to sinners. He listens to the godly person who does his will. 32 Nobody has ever heard of opening the eyes of a man born blind. 33 If this man were not from God, he could do nothing."

34 To this they replied, "You were steeped in sin at birth; how dare you lecture us!" And they threw him out.

Spiritual Blindness

35 Jesus heard that they had thrown him out, and when he found him, he said, "Do you believe in the Son of Man?"

36 "Who is he, sir?" the man asked. "Tell me so that I may believe in him."

37 Jesus said, "You have now seen him; in fact, he is the one speaking with you."

38 Then the man said, "Lord, I believe," and he worshiped him.

39 Jesus said,[a] "For judgment I have come into this world, so that the blind will see and those who see will become blind."

40 Some Pharisees who were with him heard him say this and asked, "What? Are we blind too?"

41 Jesus said, "If you were blind, you would not be guilty of sin; but now that you claim you can see, your guilt remains.

The Good Shepherd and His Sheep

10 "Very truly I tell you Pharisees, anyone who does not enter the sheep pen by the gate, but climbs in by some other way, is a thief and a robber. 2 The one who enters by the gate is the shepherd of the sheep. 3 The gatekeeper opens the gate for him, and the sheep listen to his voice. He calls his own sheep by name and leads them out. 4 When he has brought out all his own, he goes on ahead of them, and his sheep follow him because they know his voice. 5 But they will never follow a stranger; in fact, they will run away from him because they do not recognize a stranger's voice." 6 Jesus used this figure of speech, but the Pharisees did not understand what he was telling them.

7 Therefore Jesus said again, "Very truly I tell you, I am the gate for the sheep. 8 All who have come before me are thieves and robbers, but the sheep have not listened to them. 9 I am the gate; whoever enters through me will be saved.[b]

a 38,39 Some early manuscripts do not have *Then the man said . . . 39Jesus said,*
b 9 Or *kept safe*

They will come in and go out, and find pasture. ¹⁰The thief comes only to steal and kill and destroy; I have come that they may have life, and have it to the full.

¹¹"I am the good shepherd. The good shepherd lays down his life for the sheep. ¹²The hired hand is not the shepherd and does not own the sheep. So when he sees the wolf coming, he abandons the sheep and runs away. Then the wolf attacks the flock and scatters it. ¹³The man runs away because he is a hired hand and cares nothing for the sheep.

¹⁴"I am the good shepherd; I know my sheep and my sheep know me— ¹⁵just as the Father knows me and I know the Father—and I lay down my life for the sheep. ¹⁶I have other sheep that are not of this sheep pen. I must bring them also. They too will listen to my voice, and there shall be one flock and one shepherd. ¹⁷The reason my Father loves me is that I lay down my life— only to take it up again. ¹⁸No one takes it from me, but I lay it down of my own accord. I have authority to lay it down and authority to take it up again. This command I received from my Father."

¹⁹The Jews who heard these words were again divided. ²⁰Many of them said, "He is de-mon-possessed and raving mad. Why listen to him?"

²¹But others said, "These are not the sayings of a man pos-sessed by a demon. Can a demon open the eyes of the blind?"

Further Conflict Over Jesus' Claims

²²Then came the Festival of Dedication[a] at Jerusalem. It was winter, ²³and Jesus was in the temple courts walking in Solo-mon's Colonnade. ²⁴The Jews who were there gathered around him, saying, "How long will you keep us in suspense? If you are the Messiah, tell us plainly."

²⁵Jesus answered, "I did tell you, but you do not believe. The works I do in my Father's name testify about me, ²⁶but you do not believe because you are not my sheep. ²⁷My sheep listen to my voice; I know them, and they follow me. ²⁸I give them eternal life, and they shall never perish; no one will snatch them out of my hand. ²⁹My Father, who has given them to me, is greater than all[b]; no one can snatch them out of my Father's hand. ³⁰I and the Father are one."

³¹Again his Jewish opponents picked up stones to stone him, ³²but Jesus said to them, "I have shown you many good works from the Father. For which of these do you stone me?"

³³"We are not stoning you for any good work," they replied, "but for blasphemy, because you, a mere man, claim to be God."

---

a 22 That is, Hanukkah   *b* 29 Many early manuscripts *What my Father has given me is greater than all*

[34] Jesus answered them, "Is it not written in your Law, 'I have said you are "gods"'[a]? [35] If he called them 'gods,' to whom the word of God came—and Scripture cannot be set aside— [36] what about the one whom the Father set apart as his very own and sent into the world? Why then do you accuse me of blasphemy because I said, 'I am God's Son'? [37] Do not believe me unless I do the works of my Father. [38] But if I do them, even though you do not believe me, believe the works, that you may know and understand that the Father is in me, and I in the Father." [39] Again they tried to seize him, but he escaped their grasp.

[40] Then Jesus went back across the Jordan to the place where John had been baptizing in the early days. There he stayed, [41] and many people came to him. They said, "Though John never performed a sign, all that John said about this man was true." [42] And in that place many believed in Jesus.

The Death of Lazarus

11 Now a man named Lazarus was sick. He was from Bethany, the village of Mary and her sister Martha. [2] (This Mary, whose brother Lazarus now lay sick, was the same one who poured perfume on the Lord and wiped his feet with her hair.) [3] So the sisters sent word to Jesus, "Lord, the one you love is sick."

[4] When he heard this, Jesus said, "This sickness will not end in death. No, it is for God's glory so that God's Son may be glorified through it." [5] Now Jesus loved Martha and her sister and Lazarus. [6] So when he heard that Lazarus was sick, he stayed where he was two more days, [7] and then he said to his disciples, "Let us go back to Judea."

[8] "But Rabbi," they said, "a short while ago the Jews there tried to stone you, and yet you are going back?"

[9] Jesus answered, "Are there not twelve hours of daylight? Anyone who walks in the daytime will not stumble, for they see by this world's light. [10] It is when a person walks at night that they stumble, for they have no light."

[11] After he had said this, he went on to tell them, "Our friend Lazarus has fallen asleep; but I am going there to wake him up."

[12] His disciples replied, "Lord, if he sleeps, he will get better." [13] Jesus had been speaking of his death, but his disciples thought he meant natural sleep.

[14] So then he told them plainly, "Lazarus is dead, [15] and for your sake I am glad I was not there, so that you may believe. But let us go to him."

[16] Then Thomas (also known as Didymus[b]) said to the rest of the disciples, "Let us also go, that we may die with him."

---

[a] 34 Psalm 82:6   [b] 16 *Thomas* (Aramaic) and *Didymus* (Greek) both mean *twin*.

Jesus Comforts the Sisters of Lazarus

17 On his arrival, Jesus found that Lazarus had already been in the tomb for four days. **18** Now Bethany was less than two miles*a* from Jerusalem, **19** and many Jews had come to Martha and Mary to comfort them in the loss of their brother. **20** When Martha heard that Jesus was coming, she went out to meet him, but Mary stayed at home.

21 "Lord," Martha said to Jesus, "if you had been here, my brother would not have died. **22** But I know that even now God will give you whatever you ask."

23 Jesus said to her, "Your brother will rise again."

24 Martha answered, "I know he will rise again in the resurrection at the last day."

25 Jesus said to her, "I am the resurrection and the life. The one who believes in me will live, even though they die; **26** and whoever lives by believing in me will never die. Do you believe this?"

27 "Yes, Lord," she replied, "I believe that you are the Messiah, the Son of God, who is to come into the world."

28 After she had said this, she went back and called her sister Mary aside. "The Teacher is here," she said, "and is asking for you." **29** When Mary heard this, she got up quickly and went to him. **30** Now Jesus had not yet entered the village, but was still at the place where Martha had met him. **31** When the Jews who had been with Mary in the house, comforting her, noticed how quickly she got up and went out, they followed her, supposing she was going to the tomb to mourn there.

32 When Mary reached the place where Jesus was and saw him, she fell at his feet and said, "Lord, if you had been here, my brother would not have died."

33 When Jesus saw her weeping, and the Jews who had come along with her also weeping, he was deeply moved in spirit and troubled. **34** "Where have you laid him?" he asked.

"Come and see, Lord," they replied.

35 Jesus wept.

36 Then the Jews said, "See how he loved him!"

37 But some of them said, "Could not he who opened the eyes of the blind man have kept this man from dying?"

Jesus Raises Lazarus From the Dead

38 Jesus, once more deeply moved, came to the tomb. It was a cave with a stone laid across the entrance. **39** "Take away the stone," he said.

"But, Lord," said Martha, the sister of the dead man, "by this time there is a bad odor, for he has been there four days."

a 18 Or about 3 kilometers

⁴⁰Then Jesus said, "Did I not tell you that if you believe, you will see the glory of God?"

⁴¹So they took away the stone. Then Jesus looked up and said, "Father, I thank you that you have heard me. ⁴²I knew that you always hear me, but I said this for the benefit of the people standing here, that they may believe that you sent me."

⁴³When he had said this, Jesus called in a loud voice, "Lazarus, come out!" ⁴⁴The dead man came out, his hands and feet wrapped with strips of linen, and a cloth around his face.

Jesus said to them, "Take off the grave clothes and let him go."

The Plot to Kill Jesus

⁴⁵Therefore many of the Jews who had come to visit Mary, and had seen what Jesus did, believed in him. ⁴⁶But some of them went to the Pharisees and told them what Jesus had done. ⁴⁷Then the chief priests and the Pharisees called a meeting of the Sanhedrin.

"What are we accomplishing?" they asked. "Here is this man performing many signs. ⁴⁸If we let him go on like this, everyone will believe in him, and then the Romans will come and take away both our temple and our nation."

⁴⁹Then one of them, named Caiaphas, who was high priest that year, spoke up, "You know nothing at all! ⁵⁰You do not realize that it is better for you that

one man die for the people than that the whole nation perish."

⁵¹He did not say this on his own, but as high priest that year he prophesied that Jesus would die for the Jewish nation, ⁵²and not only for that nation but also for the scattered children of God, to bring them together and make them one. ⁵³So from that day on they plotted to take his life.

⁵⁴Therefore Jesus no longer moved about publicly among the people of Judea. Instead he withdrew to a region near the wilderness, to a village called Ephraim, where he stayed with his disciples.

⁵⁵When it was almost time for the Jewish Passover, many went up from the country to Jerusalem for their ceremonial cleansing before the Passover. ⁵⁶They kept looking for Jesus, and as they stood in the temple courts they asked one another, "What do you think? Isn't he coming to the festival at all?" ⁵⁷But the chief priests and the Pharisees had given orders that anyone who found out where Jesus was should report it so that they might arrest him.

Jesus Anointed at Bethany

12 Six days before the Passover, Jesus came to Bethany, where Lazarus lived, whom Jesus had raised from the dead. ²Here a dinner was given in Jesus' honor. Martha served, while Lazarus was among those reclining at the table with him.

³Then Mary took about a pint*ᵃ* of pure nard, an expensive perfume; she poured it on Jesus' feet and wiped his feet with her hair. And the house was filled with the fragrance of the perfume.

⁴But one of his disciples, Judas Iscariot, who was later to betray him, objected, ⁵"Why wasn't this perfume sold and the money given to the poor? It was worth a year's wages.*ᵇ*" ⁶He did not say this because he cared about the poor but because he was a thief; as keeper of the money bag, he used to help himself to what was put into it.

⁷"Leave her alone," Jesus replied. "It was intended that she should save this perfume for the day of my burial. ⁸You will always have the poor among you,*ᶜ* but you will not always have me."

⁹Meanwhile a large crowd of Jews found out that Jesus was there and came, not only because of him but also to see Lazarus, whom he had raised from the dead. ¹⁰So the chief priests made plans to kill Lazarus as well, ¹¹for on account of him many of the Jews were going over to Jesus and believing in him.

Jesus Comes to Jerusalem as King

¹²The next day the great crowd that had come for the festival heard that Jesus was on his way to Jerusalem. ¹³They took palm branches and went out to meet him, shouting,

"Hosanna!*ᵈ*"

"Blessed is he who comes in
    the name of the Lord!"*ᵉ*

"Blessed is the king of Israel!"

¹⁴Jesus found a young donkey and sat on it, as it is written:

¹⁵"Do not be afraid, Daughter
    Zion;
  see, your king is coming,
    seated on a donkey's colt."*ᶠ*

¹⁶At first his disciples did not understand all this. Only after Jesus was glorified did they realize that these things had been written about him and that these things had been done to him.

¹⁷Now the crowd that was with him when he called Lazarus from the tomb and raised him from the dead continued to spread the word. ¹⁸Many people, because they had heard that he had performed this sign, went out to meet him. ¹⁹So the Pharisees said to one another, "See, this is getting us nowhere. Look how the whole world has gone after him!"

Jesus Predicts His Death

²⁰Now there were some Greeks among those who went up to worship at the festival. ²¹They came to Philip, who was from Bethsaida in Galilee, with a request. "Sir," they

---

ᵃ 3 Or about 0.5 liter   *ᵇ 5* Greek *three hundred denarii*   *ᶜ 8* See Deut. 15:11.
ᵈ 13 A Hebrew expression meaning "Save!" which became an exclamation of praise   *ᵉ 13* Psalm 118:25,26   *ᶠ 15* Zech. 9:9

said, "we would like to see Jesus." [22]Philip went to tell Andrew; Andrew and Philip in turn told Jesus.

[23]Jesus replied, "The hour has come for the Son of Man to be glorified. [24]Very truly I tell you, unless a kernel of wheat falls to the ground and dies, it remains only a single seed. But if it dies, it produces many seeds. [25]Anyone who loves their life will lose it, while anyone who hates their life in this world will keep it for eternal life. [26]Whoever serves me must follow me; and where I am, my servant also will be. My Father will honor the one who serves me.

[27]"Now my soul is troubled, and what shall I say? 'Father, save me from this hour'? No, it was for this very reason I came to this hour. [28]Father, glorify your name!"

Then a voice came from heaven, "I have glorified it, and will glorify it again." [29]The crowd that was there and heard it said it had thundered; others said an angel had spoken to him.

[30]Jesus said, "This voice was for your benefit, not mine. [31]Now is the time for judgment on this world; now the prince of this world will be driven out. [32]And I, when I am lifted up[a] from the earth, will draw all people to myself." [33]He said this to show the kind of death he was going to die.

[34]The crowd spoke up, "We have heard from the Law that the Messiah will remain forever, so how can you say, 'The Son of Man must be lifted up'? Who is this 'Son of Man'?"

[35]Then Jesus told them, "You are going to have the light just a little while longer. Walk while you have the light, before darkness overtakes you. Whoever walks in the dark does not know where they are going. [36]Believe in the light while you have the light, so that you may become children of light." When he had finished speaking, Jesus left and hid himself from them.

Belief and Unbelief Among the Jews

[37]Even after Jesus had performed so many signs in their presence, they still would not believe in him. [38]This was to fulfill the word of Isaiah the prophet:

"Lord, who has believed our
    message
  and to whom has the arm of
      the Lord been revealed?"[b]

[39]For this reason they could not believe, because, as Isaiah says elsewhere:

[40]"He has blinded their eyes
    and hardened their hearts,
  so they can neither see with
      their eyes,
    nor understand with their
      hearts,
    nor turn—and I would heal
      them."[c]

---

[a] 32 The Greek for *lifted up* also means *exalted*.   [b] 38 Isaiah 53:1
[c] 40 Isaiah 6:10

⁴¹Isaiah said this because he saw Jesus' glory and spoke about him.

⁴²Yet at the same time many even among the leaders believed in him. But because of the Pharisees they would not openly acknowledge their faith for fear they would be put out of the synagogue; ⁴³for they loved human praise more than praise from God.

⁴⁴Then Jesus cried out, "Whoever believes in me does not believe in me only, but in the one who sent me. ⁴⁵The one who looks at me is seeing the one who sent me. ⁴⁶I have come into the world as a light, so that no one who believes in me should stay in darkness.

⁴⁷"If anyone hears my words but does not keep them, I do not judge that person. For I did not come to judge the world, but to save the world. ⁴⁸There is a judge for the one who rejects me and does not accept my words; the very words I have spoken will condemn them at the last day. ⁴⁹For I did not speak on my own, but the Father who sent me commanded me to say all that I have spoken. ⁵⁰I know that his command leads to eternal life. So whatever I say is just what the Father has told me to say."

Jesus Washes His Disciples' Feet

13 It was just before the Passover Festival. Jesus knew that the hour had come for him to leave this world and go to the Father. Having loved his own who were in the world, he loved them to the end.

²The evening meal was in progress, and the devil had already prompted Judas, the son of Simon Iscariot, to betray Jesus. ³Jesus knew that the Father had put all things under his power, and that he had come from God and was returning to God; ⁴so he got up from the meal, took off his outer clothing, and wrapped a towel around his waist. ⁵After that, he poured water into a basin and began to wash his disciples' feet, drying them with the towel that was wrapped around him.

⁶He came to Simon Peter, who said to him, "Lord, are you going to wash my feet?"

⁷Jesus replied, "You do not realize now what I am doing, but later you will understand."

⁸"No," said Peter, "you shall never wash my feet."

Jesus answered, "Unless I wash you, you have no part with me."

⁹"Then, Lord," Simon Peter replied, "not just my feet but my hands and my head as well!"

¹⁰Jesus answered, "Those who have had a bath need only to wash their feet; their whole body is clean. And you are clean, though not every one of you." ¹¹For he knew who was going to betray him, and that was why he said not every one was clean.

¹²When he had finished washing their feet, he put on his clothes and returned to his place. "Do you

understand what I have done for you?" he asked them. **13** "You call me 'Teacher' and 'Lord,' and rightly so, for that is what I am. **14** Now that I, your Lord and Teacher, have washed your feet, you also should wash one another's feet. **15** I have set you an example that you should do as I have done for you. **16** Very truly I tell you, no servant is greater than his master, nor is a messenger greater than the one who sent him. **17** Now that you know these things, you will be blessed if you do them.

Jesus Predicts His Betrayal

18 "I am not referring to all of you; I know those I have chosen. But this is to fulfill this passage of Scripture: 'He who shared my bread has turned*a* against me.'*b*

19 "I am telling you now before it happens, so that when it does happen you will believe that I am who I am. **20** Very truly I tell you, whoever accepts anyone I send accepts me; and whoever accepts me accepts the one who sent me."

21 After he had said this, Jesus was troubled in spirit and testified, "Very truly I tell you, one of you is going to betray me."

22 His disciples stared at one another, at a loss to know which of them he meant. **23** One of them, the disciple whom Jesus loved, was reclining next to him. **24** Simon Peter motioned to this disciple and said, "Ask him which one he means."

25 Leaning back against Jesus, he asked him, "Lord, who is it?"

26 Jesus answered, "It is the one to whom I will give this piece of bread when I have dipped it in the dish." Then, dipping the piece of bread, he gave it to Judas, the son of Simon Iscariot. **27** As soon as Judas took the bread, Satan entered into him.

So Jesus told him, "What you are about to do, do quickly." **28** But no one at the meal understood why Jesus said this to him. **29** Since Judas had charge of the money, some thought Jesus was telling him to buy what was needed for the festival, or to give something to the poor. **30** As soon as Judas had taken the bread, he went out. And it was night.

Jesus Predicts Peter's Denial

31 When he was gone, Jesus said, "Now the Son of Man is glorified and God is glorified in him. **32** If God is glorified in him,*c* God will glorify the Son in himself, and will glorify him at once.

33 "My children, I will be with you only a little longer. You will look for me, and just as I told the Jews, so I tell you now: Where I am going, you cannot come.

34 "A new command I give you: Love one another. As I have loved you, so you must love one another. **35** By this everyone will know that you are my disciples, if you love one another."

---

a 18 Greek *has lifted up his heel*   *b 18* Psalm 41:9   *c 32* Many early manuscripts do not have *If God is glorified in him.*

36 Simon Peter asked him, "Lord, where are you going?"

Jesus replied, "Where I am going, you cannot follow now, but you will follow later."

37 Peter asked, "Lord, why can't I follow you now? I will lay down my life for you."

38 Then Jesus answered, "Will you really lay down your life for me? Very truly I tell you, before the rooster crows, you will disown me three times!

Jesus Comforts His Disciples

14 "Do not let your hearts be troubled. You believe in God*a*; believe also in me. **2** My Father's house has many rooms; if that were not so, would I have told you that I am going there to prepare a place for you? **3** And if I go and prepare a place for you, I will come back and take you to be with me that you also may be where I am. **4** You know the way to the place where I am going."

Jesus the Way to the Father

5 Thomas said to him, "Lord, we don't know where you are going, so how can we know the way?"

6 Jesus answered, "I am the way and the truth and the life. No one comes to the Father except through me. **7** If you really know me, you will know*b* my Father as well. From now on, you do know him and have seen him."

8 Philip said, "Lord, show us the Father and that will be enough for us."

9 Jesus answered: "Don't you know me, Philip, even after I have been among you such a long time? Anyone who has seen me has seen the Father. How can you say, 'Show us the Father'? **10** Don't you believe that I am in the Father, and that the Father is in me? The words I say to you I do not speak on my own authority. Rather, it is the Father, living in me, who is doing his work. **11** Believe me when I say that I am in the Father and the Father is in me; or at least believe on the evidence of the works themselves. **12** Very truly I tell you, whoever believes in me will do the works I have been doing, and they will do even greater things than these, because I am going to the Father. **13** And I will do whatever you ask in my name, so that the Father may be glorified in the Son. **14** You may ask me for anything in my name, and I will do it.

Jesus Promises the Holy Spirit

15 "If you love me, keep my commands. **16** And I will ask the Father, and he will give you another advocate to help you and be with you forever — **17** the Spirit of truth. The world cannot accept him, because it neither sees him nor knows him. But you know him, for he lives with you and will be*c*

---

a 1 Or *Believe in God*   *b* 7 Some manuscripts *If you really knew me, you would know*   *c* 17 Some early manuscripts *and is* in you. **18**I will not leave you as orphans; I will come to you. **19**Before long, the world will not see me anymore, but you will see me. Because I live, you also will live. **20**On that day you will realize that I am in my Father, and you are in me, and I am in you. **21**Whoever has my commands and keeps them is the one who loves me. The one who loves me will be loved by my Father, and I too will love them and show myself to them."

22Then Judas (not Judas Iscariot) said, "But, Lord, why do you intend to show yourself to us and not to the world?"

23Jesus replied, "Anyone who loves me will obey my teaching. My Father will love them, and we will come to them and make our home with them. **24**Anyone who does not love me will not obey my teaching. These words you hear are not my own; they belong to the Father who sent me.

25"All this I have spoken while still with you. **26**But the Advocate, the Holy Spirit, whom the Father will send in my name, will teach you all things and will remind you of everything I have said to you. **27**Peace I leave with you; my peace I give you. I do not give to you as the world gives. Do not let your hearts be troubled and do not be afraid.

28"You heard me say, 'I am going away and I am coming back to you.' If you loved me, you would be glad that I am going to the Father, for the Father is greater than I. **29**I have told you now before it happens, so that when it does happen you will believe. **30**I will not say much more to you, for the prince of this world is coming. He has no hold over me, **31**but he comes so that the world may learn that I love the Father and do exactly what my Father has commanded me.

"Come now; let us leave.

The Vine and the Branches

15 "I am the true vine, and my Father is the gardener. **2**He cuts off every branch in me that bears no fruit, while every branch that does bear fruit he prunes*a* so that it will be even more fruitful. **3**You are already clean because of the word I have spoken to you. **4**Remain in me, as I also remain in you. No branch can bear fruit by itself; it must remain in the vine. Neither can you bear fruit unless you remain in me.

5"I am the vine; you are the branches. If you remain in me and I in you, you will bear much fruit; apart from me you can do nothing. **6**If you do not remain in me, you are like a branch that is thrown away and withers; such branches are picked up, thrown into the fire and burned. **7**If you remain in me and my words remain in you, ask whatever you wish, and it will be done for you. **8**This is to my Father's glory, that

---

a 2 The Greek for *he prunes* also means *he cleans.*

you bear much fruit, showing yourselves to be my disciples.

9 "As the Father has loved me, so have I loved you. Now remain in my love. 10 If you keep my commands, you will remain in my love, just as I have kept my Father's commands and remain in his love. 11 I have told you this so that my joy may be in you and that your joy may be complete. 12 My command is this: Love each other as I have loved you. 13 Greater love has no one than this: to lay down one's life for one's friends. 14 You are my friends if you do what I command. 15 I no longer call you servants, because a servant does not know his master's business. Instead, I have called you friends, for everything that I learned from my Father I have made known to you. 16 You did not choose me, but I chose you and appointed you so that you might go and bear fruit — fruit that will last — and so that whatever you ask in my name the Father will give you. 17 This is my command: Love each other.

The World Hates the Disciples

18 "If the world hates you, keep in mind that it hated me first. 19 If you belonged to the world, it would love you as its own. As it is, you do not belong to the world, but I have chosen you out of the world. That is why the world hates you. 20 Remember what I told you: 'A servant is not greater than his master.'[a] If they persecuted me, they will persecute you also. If they obeyed my teaching, they will obey yours also. 21 They will treat you this way because of my name, for they do not know the one who sent me. 22 If I had not come and spoken to them, they would not be guilty of sin; but now they have no excuse for their sin. 23 Whoever hates me hates my Father as well. 24 If I had not done among them the works no one else did, they would not be guilty of sin. As it is, they have seen, and yet they have hated both me and my Father. 25 But this is to fulfill what is written in their Law: 'They hated me without reason.'[b]

The Work of the Holy Spirit

26 "When the Advocate comes, whom I will send to you from the Father — the Spirit of truth who goes out from the Father — he will testify about me. 27 And you also must testify, for you have been with me from the beginning.

16 "All this I have told you so that you will not fall away. 2 They will put you out of the synagogue; in fact, the time is coming when anyone who kills you will think they are offering a service to God. 3 They will do such things because they have not known the Father or me. 4 I have told you this, so that when their time comes you will remember that I warned you about them. I did not tell you

a 20 John 13:16   b 25 Psalms 35:19; 69:4

this from the beginning because I was with you, **5** but now I am going to him who sent me. None of you asks me, 'Where are you going?' **6** Rather, you are filled with grief because I have said these things. **7** But very truly I tell you, it is for your good that I am going away. Unless I go away, the Advocate will not come to you; but if I go, I will send him to you. **8** When he comes, he will prove the world to be in the wrong about sin and righteousness and judgment: **9** about sin, because people do not believe in me; **10** about righteousness, because I am going to the Father, where you can see me no longer; **11** and about judgment, because the prince of this world now stands condemned.

12 "I have much more to say to you, more than you can now bear. **13** But when he, the Spirit of truth, comes, he will guide you into all the truth. He will not speak on his own; he will speak only what he hears, and he will tell you what is yet to come. **14** He will glorify me because it is from me that he will receive what he will make known to you. **15** All that belongs to the Father is mine. That is why I said the Spirit will receive from me what he will make known to you."

The Disciples' Grief Will Turn to Joy

16 Jesus went on to say, "In a little while you will see me no more, and then after a little while you will see me."

17 At this, some of his disciples said to one another, "What does he mean by saying, 'In a little while you will see me no more, and then after a little while you will see me,' and 'Because I am going to the Father'?" **18** They kept asking, "What does he mean by 'a little while'? We don't understand what he is saying."

19 Jesus saw that they wanted to ask him about this, so he said to them, "Are you asking one another what I meant when I said, 'In a little while you will see me no more, and then after a little while you will see me'? **20** Very truly I tell you, you will weep and mourn while the world rejoices. You will grieve, but your grief will turn to joy. **21** A woman giving birth to a child has pain because her time has come; but when her baby is born she forgets the anguish because of her joy that a child is born into the world. **22** So with you: Now is your time of grief, but I will see you again and you will rejoice, and no one will take away your joy. **23** In that day you will no longer ask me anything. Very truly I tell you, my Father will give you whatever you ask in my name. **24** Until now you have not asked for anything in my name. Ask and you will receive, and your joy will be complete.

25 "Though I have been speaking figuratively, a time is coming when I will no longer use this kind of language but will tell you plainly about my Father. **26** In that day you will ask in my name. I am not saying that I will ask the Father on your behalf. **27**No, the Father himself loves you because you have loved me and have believed that I came from God. **28**I came from the Father and entered the world; now I am leaving the world and going back to the Father."

29Then Jesus' disciples said, "Now you are speaking clearly and without figures of speech. **30**Now we can see that you know all things and that you do not even need to have anyone ask you questions. This makes us believe that you came from God."

31"Do you now believe?" Jesus replied. **32**"A time is coming and in fact has come when you will be scattered, each to your own home. You will leave me all alone. Yet I am not alone, for my Father is with me.

33"I have told you these things, so that in me you may have peace. In this world you will have trouble. But take heart! I have overcome the world."

Jesus Prays to Be Glorified

17 After Jesus said this, he looked toward heaven and prayed:

"Father, the hour has come. Glorify your Son, that your Son may glorify you. **2**For you granted him authority over all people that he might give eternal life to all those you have given him. **3**Now this is eternal life: that they know you, the only true God, and Jesus Christ, whom you have sent. **4**I have brought you glory on earth by finishing the work you gave me to do. **5**And now, Father, glorify me in your presence with the glory I had with you before the world began.

Jesus Prays for His Disciples

6"I have revealed you[a] to those whom you gave me out of the world. They were yours; you gave them to me and they have obeyed your word. **7**Now they know that everything you have given me comes from you. **8**For I gave them the words you gave me and they accepted them. They knew with certainty that I came from you, and they believed that you sent me. **9**I pray for them. I am not praying for the world, but for those you have given me, for they are yours. **10**All I have is yours, and all you have is mine. And glory has come to me through them. **11**I will remain in the world no longer, but they are still in the world, and I am coming to you. Holy Father, protect them by the power of[b] your name, the name you gave me, so that they may be one as we are one. **12**While I was with them, I protected them and kept them safe by[a] that name you gave me. None has been lost except the one doomed to destruction so that Scripture would be fulfilled.

¹³ "I am coming to you now, but I say these things while I am still in the world, so that they may have the full measure of my joy within them. ¹⁴ I have given them your word and the world has hated them, for they are not of the world any more than I am of the world. ¹⁵ My prayer is not that you take them out of the world but that you protect them from the evil one. ¹⁶ They are not of the world, even as I am not of it. ¹⁷ Sanctify them by[b] the truth; your word is truth. ¹⁸ As you sent me into the world, I have sent them into the world. ¹⁹ For them I sanctify myself, that they too may be truly sanctified.

Jesus Prays for All Believers

²⁰ "My prayer is not for them alone. I pray also for those who will believe in me through their message, ²¹ that all of them may be one, Father, just as you are in me and I am in you. May they also be in us so that the world may believe that you have sent me. ²² I have given them the glory that you gave me, that they may be one as we are one— ²³ I in them and you in me— so that they may be brought to complete unity. Then the world will know that you sent me and have loved them even as you have loved me.

²⁴ "Father, I want those you have given me to be with me where I am, and to see my glory, the glory you have given me because you loved me before the creation of the world.

²⁵ "Righteous Father, though the world does not know you, I know you, and they know that you have sent me. ²⁶ I have made you[c] known to them, and will continue to make you known in order that the love you have for me may be in them and that I myself may be in them."

Jesus Arrested

18 When he had finished praying, Jesus left with his disciples and crossed the Kidron Valley. On the other side there was a garden, and he and his disciples went into it.

² Now Judas, who betrayed him, knew the place, because Jesus had often met there with his disciples. ³ So Judas came to the garden, guiding a detachment of soldiers and some officials from the chief priests and the Pharisees. They were carrying torches, lanterns and weapons.

---

[a] 12 Or *kept them faithful to*   [b] 17 Or *them to live in accordance with*
[c] 26 Greek *your name*

4 Jesus, knowing all that was going to happen to him, went out and asked them, "Who is it you want?"

5 "Jesus of Nazareth," they replied.

"I am he," Jesus said. (And Judas the traitor was standing there with them.) **6** When Jesus said, "I am he," they drew back and fell to the ground.

7 Again he asked them, "Who is it you want?"

"Jesus of Nazareth," they said.

8 Jesus answered, "I told you that I am he. If you are looking for me, then let these men go." **9** This happened so that the words he had spoken would be fulfilled: "I have not lost one of those you gave me."[a]

10 Then Simon Peter, who had a sword, drew it and struck the high priest's servant, cutting off his right ear. (The servant's name was Malchus.)

11 Jesus commanded Peter, "Put your sword away! Shall I not drink the cup the Father has given me?"

12 Then the detachment of soldiers with its commander and the Jewish officials arrested Jesus. They bound him **13** and brought him first to Annas, who was the father-in-law of Caiaphas, the high priest that year. **14** Caiaphas was the one who had advised the Jewish leaders that it would be good if one man died for the people.

Peter's First Denial

15 Simon Peter and another disciple were following Jesus. Because this disciple was known to the high priest, he went with Jesus into the high priest's courtyard, **16** but Peter had to wait outside at the door. The other disciple, who was known to the high priest, came back, spoke to the servant girl on duty there and brought Peter in.

17 "You aren't one of this man's disciples too, are you?" she asked Peter.

He replied, "I am not."

18 It was cold, and the servants and officials stood around a fire they had made to keep warm. Peter also was standing with them, warming himself.

The High Priest Questions Jesus

19 Meanwhile, the high priest questioned Jesus about his disciples and his teaching.

20 "I have spoken openly to the world," Jesus replied. "I always taught in synagogues or at the temple, where all the Jews come together. I said nothing in secret. **21** Why question me? Ask those who heard me. Surely they know what I said."

22 When Jesus said this, one of the officials nearby slapped him in the face. "Is this the way you answer the high priest?" he demanded.

23 "If I said something wrong,"

Jesus replied, "testify as to what is wrong. But if I spoke the truth, why did you strike me?" **24** Then Annas sent him bound to Caiaphas the high priest.

Peter's Second and Third Denials

25 Meanwhile, Simon Peter was still standing there warming himself. So they asked him, "You aren't one of his disciples too, are you?"

He denied it, saying, "I am not."

26 One of the high priest's servants, a relative of the man whose ear Peter had cut off, challenged him, "Didn't I see you with him in the garden?" **27** Again Peter denied it, and at that moment a rooster began to crow.

Jesus Before Pilate

28 Then the Jewish leaders took Jesus from Caiaphas to the palace of the Roman governor. By now it was early morning, and to avoid ceremonial uncleanness they did not enter the palace, because they wanted to be able to eat the Passover. **29** So Pilate came out to them and asked, "What charges are you bringing against this man?"

30 "If he were not a criminal," they replied, "we would not have handed him over to you."

31 Pilate said, "Take him yourselves and judge him by your own law."

"But we have no right to execute anyone," they objected.

32 This took place to fulfill what Jesus had said about the kind of death he was going to die.

33 Pilate then went back inside the palace, summoned Jesus and asked him, "Are you the king of the Jews?"

34 "Is that your own idea," Jesus asked, "or did others talk to you about me?"

35 "Am I a Jew?" Pilate replied. "Your own people and chief priests handed you over to me. What is it you have done?"

36 Jesus said, "My kingdom is not of this world. If it were, my servants would fight to prevent my arrest by the Jewish leaders. But now my kingdom is from another place."

37 "You are a king, then!" said Pilate.

Jesus answered, "You say that I am a king. In fact, the reason I was born and came into the world is to testify to the truth. Everyone on the side of truth listens to me."

38 "What is truth?" retorted Pilate. With this he went out again to the Jews gathered there and said, "I find no basis for a charge against him. **39** But it is your custom for me to release to you one prisoner at the time of the Passover. Do you want me to release 'the king of the Jews'?"

40 They shouted back, "No, not him! Give us Barabbas!" Now Barabbas had taken part in an uprising.

Jesus Sentenced to Be Crucified

19 Then Pilate took Jesus and had him flogged. [2] The soldiers twisted together a crown of thorns and put it on his head. They clothed him in a purple robe [3] and went up to him again and again, saying, "Hail, king of the Jews!" And they slapped him in the face.

[4] Once more Pilate came out and said to the Jews gathered there, "Look, I am bringing him out to you to let you know that I find no basis for a charge against him." [5] When Jesus came out wearing the crown of thorns and the purple robe, Pilate said to them, "Here is the man!"

[6] As soon as the chief priests and their officials saw him, they shouted, "Crucify! Crucify!"

But Pilate answered, "You take him and crucify him. As for me, I find no basis for a charge against him."

[7] The Jewish leaders insisted, "We have a law, and according to that law he must die, because he claimed to be the Son of God."

[8] When Pilate heard this, he was even more afraid, [9] and he went back inside the palace. "Where do you come from?" he asked Jesus, but Jesus gave him no answer. [10] "Do you refuse to speak to me?" Pilate said. "Don't you realize I have power either to free you or to crucify you?"

[11] Jesus answered, "You would have no power over me if it were not given to you from above. Therefore the one who handed me over to you is guilty of a greater sin."

[12] From then on, Pilate tried to set Jesus free, but the Jewish leaders kept shouting, "If you let this man go, you are no friend of Caesar. Anyone who claims to be a king opposes Caesar."

[13] When Pilate heard this, he brought Jesus out and sat down on the judge's seat at a place known as the Stone Pavement (which in Aramaic is Gabbatha). [14] It was the day of Preparation of the Passover; it was about noon.

"Here is your king," Pilate said to the Jews.

[15] But they shouted, "Take him away! Take him away! Crucify him!"

"Shall I crucify your king?" Pilate asked.

"We have no king but Caesar," the chief priests answered.

[16] Finally Pilate handed him over to them to be crucified.

The Crucifixion of Jesus

So the soldiers took charge of Jesus. [17] Carrying his own cross, he went out to the place of the Skull (which in Aramaic is called Golgotha). [18] There they crucified him, and with him two others — one on each side and Jesus in the middle.

[19] Pilate had a notice prepared and fastened to the cross. It read: JESUS OF NAZARETH, THE KING OF THE JEWS. [20] Many of the Jews read this sign, for the place where Jesus was crucified was near the city, and the sign was written in

Aramaic, Latin and Greek. **21** The chief priests of the Jews protested to Pilate, "Do not write 'The King of the Jews,' but that this man claimed to be king of the Jews."

22 Pilate answered, "What I have written, I have written."

23 When the soldiers crucified Jesus, they took his clothes, dividing them into four shares, one for each of them, with the undergarment remaining. This garment was seamless, woven in one piece from top to bottom.

24 "Let's not tear it," they said to one another. "Let's decide by lot who will get it."

This happened that the scripture might be fulfilled that said,

"They divided my clothes
 among them
and cast lots for my
 garment."*a*

So this is what the soldiers did.

25 Near the cross of Jesus stood his mother, his mother's sister, Mary the wife of Clopas, and Mary Magdalene. **26** When Jesus saw his mother there, and the disciple whom he loved standing nearby, he said to her, "Woman,*b* here is your son," **27** and to the disciple, "Here is your mother." From that time on, this disciple took her into his home.

The Death of Jesus

28 Later, knowing that everything had now been finished, and so that Scripture would be fulfilled, Jesus said, "I am thirsty." **29** A jar of wine vinegar was there, so they soaked a sponge in it, put the sponge on a stalk of the hyssop plant, and lifted it to Jesus' lips. **30** When he had received the drink, Jesus said, "It is finished." With that, he bowed his head and gave up his spirit.

31 Now it was the day of Preparation, and the next day was to be a special Sabbath. Because the Jewish leaders did not want the bodies left on the crosses during the Sabbath, they asked Pilate to have the legs broken and the bodies taken down. **32** The soldiers therefore came and broke the legs of the first man who had been crucified with Jesus, and then those of the other. **33** But when they came to Jesus and found that he was already dead, they did not break his legs. **34** Instead, one of the soldiers pierced Jesus' side with a spear, bringing a sudden flow of blood and water. **35** The man who saw it has given testimony, and his testimony is true. He knows that he tells the truth, and he testifies so that you also may believe. **36** These things happened so that the scripture would be fulfilled: "Not one of his bones will be broken,"*c* **37** and, as another scripture says, "They will look on the one they have pierced."*d*

---

a 24 Psalm 22:18   *b 26* The Greek for *Woman* does not denote any disrespect.
c 36 Exodus 12:46; Num. 9:12; Psalm 34:20   *d 37* Zech. 12:10

The Burial of Jesus

38 Later, Joseph of Arimathea asked Pilate for the body of Jesus. Now Joseph was a disciple of Jesus, but secretly because he feared the Jewish leaders. With Pilate's permission, he came and took the body away. **39** He was accompanied by Nicodemus, the man who earlier had visited Jesus at night. Nicodemus brought a mixture of myrrh and aloes, about seventy-five pounds.*ᵃ* **40** Taking Jesus' body, the two of them wrapped it, with the spices, in strips of linen. This was in accordance with Jewish burial customs. **41** At the place where Jesus was crucified, there was a garden, and in the garden a new tomb, in which no one had ever been laid. **42** Because it was the Jewish day of Preparation and since the tomb was nearby, they laid Jesus there.

The Empty Tomb

20 Early on the first day of the week, while it was still dark, Mary Magdalene went to the tomb and saw that the stone had been removed from the entrance. **2** So she came running to Simon Peter and the other disciple, the one Jesus loved, and said, "They have taken the Lord out of the tomb, and we don't know where they have put him!"

3 So Peter and the other disciple started for the tomb. **4** Both were running, but the other disciple outran Peter and reached the tomb first. **5** He bent over and looked in at the strips of linen lying there but did not go in. **6** Then Simon Peter came along behind him and went straight into the tomb. He saw the strips of linen lying there, **7** as well as the cloth that had been wrapped around Jesus' head. The cloth was still lying in its place, separate from the linen. **8** Finally the other disciple, who had reached the tomb first, also went inside. He saw and believed. **9** (They still did not understand from Scripture that Jesus had to rise from the dead.) **10** Then the disciples went back to where they were staying.

Jesus Appears to Mary Magdalene

11 Now Mary stood outside the tomb crying. As she wept, she bent over to look into the tomb **12** and saw two angels in white, seated where Jesus' body had been, one at the head and the other at the foot.

13 They asked her, "Woman, why are you crying?"

"They have taken my Lord away," she said, "and I don't know where they have put him." **14** At this, she turned around and saw Jesus standing there, but she did not realize that it was Jesus.

15 He asked her, "Woman, why are you crying? Who is it you are looking for?"

ᵃ 39 Or about 34 kilograms

Thinking he was the gardener, she said, "Sir, if you have carried him away, tell me where you have put him, and I will get him."

¹⁶ Jesus said to her, "Mary."

She turned toward him and cried out in Aramaic, "Rabboni!" (which means "Teacher").

¹⁷ Jesus said, "Do not hold on to me, for I have not yet ascended to the Father. Go instead to my brothers and tell them, 'I am ascending to my Father and your Father, to my God and your God.'"

¹⁸ Mary Magdalene went to the disciples with the news: "I have seen the Lord!" And she told them that he had said these things to her.

Jesus Appears to His Disciples

¹⁹ On the evening of that first day of the week, when the disciples were together, with the doors locked for fear of the Jewish leaders, Jesus came and stood among them and said, "Peace be with you!" ²⁰ After he said this, he showed them his hands and side. The disciples were overjoyed when they saw the Lord.

²¹ Again Jesus said, "Peace be with you! As the Father has sent me, I am sending you." ²² And with that he breathed on them and said, "Receive the Holy Spirit. ²³ If you forgive anyone's sins, their sins are forgiven; if you do not forgive them, they are not forgiven."

Jesus Appears to Thomas

²⁴ Now Thomas (also known as Didymus[a]), one of the Twelve, was not with the disciples when Jesus came. ²⁵ So the other disciples told him, "We have seen the Lord!"

But he said to them, "Unless I see the nail marks in his hands and put my finger where the nails were, and put my hand into his side, I will not believe."

²⁶ A week later his disciples were in the house again, and Thomas was with them. Though the doors were locked, Jesus came and stood among them and said, "Peace be with you!" ²⁷ Then he said to Thomas, "Put your finger here; see my hands. Reach out your hand and put it into my side. Stop doubting and believe."

²⁸ Thomas said to him, "My Lord and my God!"

²⁹ Then Jesus told him, "Because you have seen me, you have believed; blessed are those who have not seen and yet have believed."

The Purpose of John's Gospel

³⁰ Jesus performed many other signs in the presence of his disciples, which are not recorded in this book. ³¹ But these are written that you may believe[b] that Jesus is the Messiah, the Son of God, and that by believing you may have life in his name.

---

[a] 24 *Thomas* (Aramaic) and *Didymus* (Greek) both mean *twin*.   [b] 31 Or *may continue to believe*

Jesus and the Miraculous Catch of Fish

21 Afterward Jesus appeared again to his disciples, by the Sea of Galilee.[a] It happened this way: [2] Simon Peter, Thomas (also known as Didymus[b]), Nathanael from Cana in Galilee, the sons of Zebedee, and two other disciples were together. [3] "I'm going out to fish," Simon Peter told them, and they said, "We'll go with you." So they went out and got into the boat, but that night they caught nothing.

[4] Early in the morning, Jesus stood on the shore, but the disciples did not realize that it was Jesus.

[5] He called out to them, "Friends, haven't you any fish?"

"No," they answered.

[6] He said, "Throw your net on the right side of the boat and you will find some." When they did, they were unable to haul the net in because of the large number of fish.

[7] Then the disciple whom Jesus loved said to Peter, "It is the Lord!" As soon as Simon Peter heard him say, "It is the Lord," he wrapped his outer garment around him (for he had taken it off) and jumped into the water. [8] The other disciples followed in the boat, towing the net full of fish, for they were not far from shore, about a hundred yards.[c]

[9] When they landed, they saw a fire of burning coals there with fish on it, and some bread.

[10] Jesus said to them, "Bring some of the fish you have just caught." [11] So Simon Peter climbed back into the boat and dragged the net ashore. It was full of large fish, 153, but even with so many the net was not torn. [12] Jesus said to them, "Come and have breakfast." None of the disciples dared ask him, "Who are you?" They knew it was the Lord. [13] Jesus came, took the bread and gave it to them, and did the same with the fish. [14] This was now the third time Jesus appeared to his disciples after he was raised from the dead.

Jesus Reinstates Peter

[15] When they had finished eating, Jesus said to Simon Peter, "Simon son of John, do you love me more than these?"

"Yes, Lord," he said, "you know that I love you."

Jesus said, "Feed my lambs."

[16] Again Jesus said, "Simon son of John, do you love me?"

He answered, "Yes, Lord, you know that I love you."

Jesus said, "Take care of my sheep."

[17] The third time he said to him, "Simon son of John, do you love me?"

Peter was hurt because Jesus

---

[a] 1 Greek *Tiberias*   [b] 2 *Thomas* (Aramaic) and *Didymus* (Greek) both mean *twin.*   [c] 8 Or about 90 meters

asked him the third time, "Do you love me?" He said, "Lord, you know all things; you know that I love you."

Jesus said, "Feed my sheep. ¹⁸Very truly I tell you, when you were younger you dressed yourself and went where you wanted; but when you are old you will stretch out your hands, and someone else will dress you and lead you where you do not want to go." ¹⁹Jesus said this to indicate the kind of death by which Peter would glorify God. Then he said to him, "Follow me!"

²⁰Peter turned and saw that the disciple whom Jesus loved was following them. (This was the one who had leaned back against Jesus at the supper and had said, "Lord, who is going to betray you?") ²¹When Peter saw him, he asked, "Lord, what about him?"

²²Jesus answered, "If I want him to remain alive until I return, what is that to you? You must follow me." ²³Because of this, the rumor spread among the believers that this disciple would not die. But Jesus did not say that he would not die; he only said, "If I want him to remain alive until I return, what is that to you?"

²⁴This is the disciple who testifies to these things and who wrote them down. We know that his testimony is true.

²⁵Jesus did many other things as well. If every one of them were written down, I suppose that even the whole world would not have room for the books that would be written.

Acts

Introduction:

The book of Acts is a record of the acts of the apostles, and is often called by that name. It can also be called "The Acts of the Holy Spirit" because it teaches about the coming and work of the Spirit in the early Christian church. Acts is the second part of Luke's history. It was written so we would have the true story of how the Christian church began and grew.

This book focuses on the work of two of the apostles — Peter and Paul. Peter is the central person involved in beginning the church in Jerusalem. Paul is the important missionary who traveled to nearby countries to tell others about Christ.

The book of Acts teaches three things about the early church: (1) what the message of the early church was; (2) how the Jews rejected this message and how God sent the apostles to the Gentiles, who accepted the gospel; and (3) how the early church was treated by the local and Roman governments.

Outline of contents:

Christ's parting instructions (1:1–11)
The church in Jerusalem (1:12–8:1)
Expansion in Palestine (8:2–12:25)
Paul's first missionary journey (13:1–14:28)
The council of Jerusalem (15:1–35)
Paul's second missionary journey (15:36–18:22)
Paul's third missionary journey (18:23–19:41)
Paul in Jerusalem and Caesarea (20:1–26:32)
Paul's mission in Rome (27:1–28:31)

Jesus Taken Up Into Heaven

1 In my former book, Theophilus, I wrote about all that Jesus began to do and to teach ²until the day he was taken up to heaven, after giving instructions through the Holy Spirit to the apostles he had chosen. ³After his suffering, he presented himself to them and gave many convincing proofs that he was alive. He appeared to them over a period of forty days and spoke about the kingdom of God. ⁴On one occasion, while he was eating with them, he gave them this

command: "Do not leave Jerusalem, but wait for the gift my Father promised, which you have heard me speak about. **5** For John baptized with[a] water, but in a few days you will be baptized with[a] the Holy Spirit."

6 Then they gathered around him and asked him, "Lord, are you at this time going to restore the kingdom to Israel?"

7 He said to them: "It is not for you to know the times or dates the Father has set by his own authority. **8** But you will receive power when the Holy Spirit comes on you; and you will be my witnesses in Jerusalem, and in all Judea and Samaria, and to the ends of the earth."

9 After he said this, he was taken up before their very eyes, and a cloud hid him from their sight.

10 They were looking intently up into the sky as he was going, when suddenly two men dressed in white stood beside them. **11** "Men of Galilee," they said, "why do you stand here looking into the sky? This same Jesus, who has been taken from you into heaven, will come back in the same way you have seen him go into heaven."

Matthias Chosen to Replace Judas

12 Then the apostles returned to Jerusalem from the hill called the Mount of Olives, a Sabbath day's walk[b] from the city. **13** When they arrived, they went upstairs to the room where they were staying. Those present were Peter, John, James and Andrew; Philip and Thomas, Bartholomew and Matthew; James son of Alphaeus and Simon the Zealot, and Judas son of James. **14** They all joined together constantly in prayer, along with the women and Mary the mother of Jesus, and with his brothers.

15 In those days Peter stood up among the believers (a group numbering about a hundred and twenty) **16** and said, "Brothers and sisters,[c] the Scripture had to be fulfilled in which the Holy Spirit spoke long ago through David concerning Judas, who served as guide for those who arrested Jesus. **17** He was one of our number and shared in our ministry."

18 (With the payment he received for his wickedness, Judas bought a field; there he fell headlong, his body burst open and all his intestines spilled out. **19** Everyone in Jerusalem heard about this, so they called that field in their language Akeldama, that is, Field of Blood.)

20 "For," said Peter, "it is written in the Book of Psalms:

---

[a] *5* Or *in*   [b] *12* That is, about 5/8 mile or about 1 kilometer   [c] *16* The Greek word for *brothers and sisters* (*adelphoi*) refers here to believers, both men and women, as part of God's family; also in 6:3; 11:29; 12:17; 16:40; 18:18, 27; 21:7, 17; 28:14, 15.

" 'May his place be deserted;
　let there be no one to dwell
　　in it,'[a]

and,

" 'May another take his place
　of leadership.'[b]

21 Therefore it is necessary to choose one of the men who have been with us the whole time the Lord Jesus was living among us, 22 beginning from John's baptism to the time when Jesus was taken up from us. For one of these must become a witness with us of his resurrection."

23 So they nominated two men: Joseph called Barsabbas (also known as Justus) and Matthias. 24 Then they prayed, "Lord, you know everyone's heart. Show us which of these two you have chosen 25 to take over this apostolic ministry, which Judas left to go where he belongs." 26 Then they cast lots, and the lot fell to Matthias; so he was added to the eleven apostles.

The Holy Spirit Comes at Pentecost

2 When the day of Pentecost came, they were all together in one place. 2 Suddenly a sound like the blowing of a violent wind came from heaven and filled the whole house where they were sitting. 3 They saw what seemed to be tongues of fire that separated and came to rest on each of them. 4 All of them were filled with the Holy Spirit and began to speak in other tongues[c] as the Spirit enabled them.

5 Now there were staying in Jerusalem God-fearing Jews from every nation under heaven. 6 When they heard this sound, a crowd came together in bewilderment, because each one heard their own language being spoken. 7 Utterly amazed, they asked: "Aren't all these who are speaking Galileans? 8 Then how is it that each of us hears them in our native language? 9 Parthians, Medes and Elamites; residents of Mesopotamia, Judea and Cappadocia, Pontus and Asia,[d] 10 Phrygia and Pamphylia, Egypt and the parts of Libya near Cyrene; visitors from Rome 11 (both Jews and converts to Judaism); Cretans and Arabs — we hear them declaring the wonders of God in our own tongues!" 12 Amazed and perplexed, they asked one another, "What does this mean?"

13 Some, however, made fun of them and said, "They have had too much wine."

Peter Addresses the Crowd

14 Then Peter stood up with the Eleven, raised his voice and addressed the crowd: "Fellow Jews and all of you who live in Jerusalem, let me explain this to you;

---

[a] 20 Psalm 69:25   [b] 20 Psalm 109:8   [c] 4 Or languages; also in verse 11
[d] 9 That is, the Roman province by that name

listen carefully to what I say. [15] These people are not drunk, as you suppose. It's only nine in the morning! [16] No, this is what was spoken by the prophet Joel:

[17] " 'In the last days, God says,
   I will pour out my Spirit on
      all people.
   Your sons and daughters will
      prophesy,
   your young men will see
      visions,
   your old men will dream
      dreams.
[18] Even on my servants, both
      men and women,
   I will pour out my Spirit in
      those days,
   and they will prophesy.
[19] I will show wonders in the
      heavens above
   and signs on the earth
      below,
   blood and fire and billows of
      smoke.
[20] The sun will be turned to
      darkness
   and the moon to blood
   before the coming of the
      great and glorious day of
      the Lord.
[21] And everyone who calls
   on the name of the Lord will
      be saved.' [a]

[22] "Fellow Israelites, listen to this: Jesus of Nazareth was a man accredited by God to you by miracles, wonders and signs, which God did among you through him, as you yourselves know. [23] This man was handed over to you by God's deliberate plan and foreknowledge; and you, with the help of wicked men, [b] put him to death by nailing him to the cross. [24] But God raised him from the dead, freeing him from the agony of death, because it was impossible for death to keep its hold on him. [25] David said about him:

" 'I saw the Lord always
      before me.
   Because he is at my right
      hand,
   I will not be shaken.
[26] Therefore my heart is glad and
      my tongue rejoices;
   my body also will rest in
      hope,
[27] because you will not abandon
      me to the realm of the
      dead,
   you will not let your holy one
      see decay.
[28] You have made known to me
      the paths of life;
   you will fill me with joy in
      your presence.' [c]

[29] "Fellow Israelites, I can tell you confidently that the patriarch David died and was buried, and his tomb is here to this day. [30] But he was a prophet and knew that God had promised him on oath that he would place one of his descendants on his throne. [31] Seeing what was to come, he spoke of the resurrection of the

---

a 21 Joel 2:28-32   *b 23* Or *of those not having the law* (that is, Gentiles)
c 28 Psalm 16:8-11 (see Septuagint)

Messiah, that he was not abandoned to the realm of the dead, nor did his body see decay. ³²God has raised this Jesus to life, and we are all witnesses of it. ³³Exalted to the right hand of God, he has received from the Father the promised Holy Spirit and has poured out what you now see and hear. ³⁴For David did not ascend to heaven, and yet he said,

> " 'The Lord said to my Lord:
> "Sit at my right hand
> ³⁵until I make your enemies
>   a footstool for your feet." ' ^a

³⁶"Therefore let all Israel be assured of this: God has made this Jesus, whom you crucified, both Lord and Messiah."

³⁷When the people heard this, they were cut to the heart and said to Peter and the other apostles, "Brothers, what shall we do?" ³⁸Peter replied, "Repent and be baptized, every one of you, in the name of Jesus Christ for the forgiveness of your sins. And you will receive the gift of the Holy Spirit. ³⁹The promise is for you and your children and for all who are far off—for all whom the Lord our God will call."

⁴⁰With many other words he warned them; and he pleaded with them, "Save yourselves from this corrupt generation." ⁴¹Those who accepted his message were baptized, and about three thousand were added to their number that day.

The Fellowship of the Believers

⁴²They devoted themselves to the apostles' teaching and to fellowship, to the breaking of bread and to prayer. ⁴³Everyone was filled with awe at the many wonders and signs performed by the apostles. ⁴⁴All the believers were together and had everything in common. ⁴⁵They sold property and possessions to give to anyone who had need. ⁴⁶Every day they continued to meet together in the temple courts. They broke bread in their homes and ate together with glad and sincere hearts, ⁴⁷praising God and enjoying the favor of all the people. And the Lord added to their number daily those who were being saved.

Peter Heals a Lame Beggar

3 One day Peter and John were going up to the temple at the time of prayer—at three in the afternoon. ²Now a man who was lame from birth was being carried to the temple gate called Beautiful, where he was put every day to beg from those going into the temple courts. ³When he saw Peter and John about to enter, he asked them for money. ⁴Peter looked straight at him, as did John. Then Peter said, "Look at us!" ⁵So the man gave them his attention, expecting to get something from them.

⁶Then Peter said, "Silver or gold I do not have, but what I do have I give you. In the name of Jesus

---

^a 35 Psalm 110:1

Christ of Nazareth, walk." **7**Taking him by the right hand, he helped him up, and instantly the man's feet and ankles became strong. **8**He jumped to his feet and began to walk. Then he went with them into the temple courts, walking and jumping, and praising God. **9**When all the people saw him walking and praising God, **10**they recognized him as the same man who used to sit begging at the temple gate called Beautiful, and they were filled with wonder and amazement at what had happened to him.

Peter Speaks to the Onlookers

11While the man held on to Peter and John, all the people were astonished and came running to them in the place called Solomon's Colonnade. **12**When Peter saw this, he said to them: "Fellow Israelites, why does this surprise you? Why do you stare at us as if by our own power or godliness we had made this man walk? **13**The God of Abraham, Isaac and Jacob, the God of our fathers, has glorified his servant Jesus. You handed him over to be killed, and you disowned him before Pilate, though he had decided to let him go. **14**You disowned the Holy and Righteous One and asked that a murderer be released to you. **15**You killed the author of life, but God raised him from the dead. We are witnesses of this. **16**By faith in the name of Jesus, this man whom you see and know was made strong. It is Jesus' name and the faith that comes through him that has completely healed him, as you can all see.

17"Now, fellow Israelites, I know that you acted in ignorance, as did your leaders. **18**But this is how God fulfilled what he had foretold through all the prophets, saying that his Messiah would suffer. **19**Repent, then, and turn to God, so that your sins may be wiped out, that times of refreshing may come from the Lord, **20**and that he may send the Messiah, who has been appointed for you — even Jesus. **21**Heaven must receive him until the time comes for God to restore everything, as he promised long ago through his holy prophets. **22**For Moses said, 'The Lord your God will raise up for you a prophet like me from among your own people; you must listen to everything he tells you. **23**Anyone who does not listen to him will be completely cut off from their people.'[a]

24"Indeed, beginning with Samuel, all the prophets who have spoken have foretold these days. **25**And you are heirs of the prophets and of the covenant God made with your fathers. He said to Abraham, 'Through your offspring all peoples on earth will be blessed.'[b] **26**When God raised up his servant, he sent him first to

---

[a] 23 Deut. 18:15,18,19   [b] 25 Gen. 22:18; 26:4

you to bless you by turning each of you from your wicked ways."

Peter and John Before the Sanhedrin

4 The priests and the captain of the temple guard and the Sadducees came up to Peter and John while they were speaking to the people. [2] They were greatly disturbed because the apostles were teaching the people, proclaiming in Jesus the resurrection of the dead. [3] They seized Peter and John and, because it was evening, they put them in jail until the next day. [4] But many who heard the message believed; so the number of men who believed grew to about five thousand.

[5] The next day the rulers, the elders and the teachers of the law met in Jerusalem. [6] Annas the high priest was there, and so were Caiaphas, John, Alexander and others of the high priest's family. [7] They had Peter and John brought before them and began to question them: "By what power or what name did you do this?"

[8] Then Peter, filled with the Holy Spirit, said to them: "Rulers and elders of the people! [9] If we are being called to account today for an act of kindness shown to a man who was lame and are being asked how he was healed, [10] then know this, you and all the people of Israel: It is by the name of Jesus Christ of Nazareth, whom

you crucified but whom God raised from the dead, that this man stands before you healed. [11] Jesus is

" 'the stone you builders
    rejected,
  which has become the
    cornerstone.'[a]

[12] Salvation is found in no one else, for there is no other name under heaven given to mankind by which we must be saved."

[13] When they saw the courage of Peter and John and realized that they were unschooled, ordinary men, they were astonished and they took note that these men had been with Jesus. [14] But since they could see the man who had been healed standing there with them, there was nothing they could say. [15] So they ordered them to withdraw from the Sanhedrin and then conferred together. [16] "What are we going to do with these men?" they asked. "Everyone living in Jerusalem knows they have performed a notable sign, and we cannot deny it. [17] But to stop this thing from spreading any further among the people, we must warn them to speak no longer to anyone in this name."

[18] Then they called them in again and commanded them not to speak or teach at all in the name of Jesus. [19] But Peter and John replied, "Which is right in God's eyes: to listen to you, or

a 11 Psalm 118:22

to him? You be the judges! **20**As for us, we cannot help speaking about what we have seen and heard."

21After further threats they let them go. They could not decide how to punish them, because all the people were praising God for what had happened. **22**For the man who was miraculously healed was over forty years old.

The Believers Pray

23On their release, Peter and John went back to their own people and reported all that the chief priests and the elders had said to them. **24**When they heard this, they raised their voices together in prayer to God. "Sovereign Lord," they said, "you made the heavens and the earth and the sea, and everything in them. **25**You spoke by the Holy Spirit through the mouth of your servant, our father David:

"'Why do the nations rage
    and the peoples plot in vain?
26The kings of the earth rise up
    and the rulers band together
  against the Lord
    and against his anointed
      one.[a][b]

27Indeed Herod and Pontius Pilate met together with the Gentiles and the people of Israel in this city to conspire against your holy servant Jesus, whom you anointed. **28**They did what your power and will had decided beforehand should happen. **29**Now, Lord, consider their threats and enable your servants to speak your word with great boldness. **30**Stretch out your hand to heal and perform signs and wonders through the name of your holy servant Jesus."

31After they prayed, the place where they were meeting was shaken. And they were all filled with the Holy Spirit and spoke the word of God boldly.

The Believers Share Their Possessions

32All the believers were one in heart and mind. No one claimed that any of their possessions was their own, but they shared everything they had. **33**With great power the apostles continued to testify to the resurrection of the Lord Jesus. And God's grace was so powerfully at work in them all **34**that there were no needy persons among them. For from time to time those who owned land or houses sold them, brought the money from the sales **35**and put it at the apostles' feet, and it was distributed to anyone who had need.

36Joseph, a Levite from Cyprus, whom the apostles called Barnabas (which means "son of encouragement"), **37**sold a field he owned and brought the money and put it at the apostles' feet.

---

[a] 26 That is, Messiah or Christ   [b] 26 Psalm 2:1,2

Ananias and Sapphira

5 Now a man named Ananias, together with his wife Sapphira, also sold a piece of property. ²With his wife's full knowledge he kept back part of the money for himself, but brought the rest and put it at the apostles' feet.

³Then Peter said, "Ananias, how is it that Satan has so filled your heart that you have lied to the Holy Spirit and have kept for yourself some of the money you received for the land? ⁴Didn't it belong to you before it was sold? And after it was sold, wasn't the money at your disposal? What made you think of doing such a thing? You have not lied just to human beings but to God."

⁵When Ananias heard this, he fell down and died. And great fear seized all who heard what had happened. ⁶Then some young men came forward, wrapped up his body, and carried him out and buried him.

⁷About three hours later his wife came in, not knowing what had happened. ⁸Peter asked her, "Tell me, is this the price you and Ananias got for the land?"

"Yes," she said, "that is the price."

⁹Peter said to her, "How could you conspire to test the Spirit of the Lord? Listen! The feet of the men who buried your husband are at the door, and they will carry you out also."

¹⁰At that moment she fell down at his feet and died. Then the young men came in and, finding her dead, carried her out and buried her beside her husband. ¹¹Great fear seized the whole church and all who heard about these events.

The Apostles Heal Many

¹²The apostles performed many signs and wonders among the people. And all the believers used to meet together in Solomon's Colonnade. ¹³No one else dared join them, even though they were highly regarded by the people. ¹⁴Nevertheless, more and more men and women believed in the Lord and were added to their number. ¹⁵As a result, people brought the sick into the streets and laid them on beds and mats so that at least Peter's shadow might fall on some of them as he passed by. ¹⁶Crowds gathered also from the towns around Jerusalem, bringing their sick and those tormented by impure spirits, and all of them were healed.

The Apostles Persecuted

¹⁷Then the high priest and all his associates, who were members of the party of the Sadducees, were filled with jealousy. ¹⁸They arrested the apostles and put them in the public jail. ¹⁹But during the night an angel of the Lord opened the doors of the jail and brought them out. ²⁰"Go, stand in the temple courts," he said, "and tell the people all about this new life."

²¹ At daybreak they entered the temple courts, as they had been told, and began to teach the people.

When the high priest and his associates arrived, they called together the Sanhedrin — the full assembly of the elders of Israel — and sent to the jail for the apostles. ²² But on arriving at the jail, the officers did not find them there. So they went back and reported, ²³ "We found the jail securely locked, with the guards standing at the doors; but when we opened them, we found no one inside." ²⁴ On hearing this report, the captain of the temple guard and the chief priests were at a loss, wondering what this might lead to.

²⁵ Then someone came and said, "Look! The men you put in jail are standing in the temple courts teaching the people." ²⁶ At that, the captain went with his officers and brought the apostles. They did not use force, because they feared that the people would stone them.

²⁷ The apostles were brought in and made to appear before the Sanhedrin to be questioned by the high priest. ²⁸ "We gave you strict orders not to teach in this name," he said. "Yet you have filled Jerusalem with your teaching and are determined to make us guilty of this man's blood."

²⁹ Peter and the other apostles replied: "We must obey God rather than human beings! ³⁰ The God of our ancestors raised Jesus from the dead — whom you killed by hanging him on a cross. ³¹ God exalted him to his own right hand as Prince and Savior that he might bring Israel to repentance and forgive their sins. ³² We are witnesses of these things, and so is the Holy Spirit, whom God has given to those who obey him."

³³ When they heard this, they were furious and wanted to put them to death. ³⁴ But a Pharisee named Gamaliel, a teacher of the law, who was honored by all the people, stood up in the Sanhedrin and ordered that the men be put outside for a little while. ³⁵ Then he addressed the Sanhedrin: "Men of Israel, consider carefully what you intend to do to these men. ³⁶ Some time ago Theudas appeared, claiming to be somebody, and about four hundred men rallied to him. He was killed, all his followers were dispersed, and it all came to nothing. ³⁷ After him, Judas the Galilean appeared in the days of the census and led a band of people in revolt. He too was killed, and all his followers were scattered. ³⁸ Therefore, in the present case I advise you: Leave these men alone! Let them go! For if their purpose or activity is of human origin, it will fail. ³⁹ But if it is from God, you will not be able to stop these men; you will only find yourselves fighting against God."

⁴⁰ His speech persuaded them. They called the apostles in and

had them flogged. Then they ordered them not to speak in the name of Jesus, and let them go.

41 The apostles left the Sanhedrin, rejoicing because they had been counted worthy of suffering disgrace for the Name. **42** Day after day, in the temple courts and from house to house, they never stopped teaching and proclaiming the good news that Jesus is the Messiah.

The Choosing of the Seven

6 In those days when the number of disciples was increasing, the Hellenistic Jews*a* among them complained against the Hebraic Jews because their widows were being overlooked in the daily distribution of food. **2** So the Twelve gathered all the disciples together and said, "It would not be right for us to neglect the ministry of the word of God in order to wait on tables. **3** Brothers and sisters, choose seven men from among you who are known to be full of the Spirit and wisdom. We will turn this responsibility over to them **4** and will give our attention to prayer and the ministry of the word."

5 This proposal pleased the whole group. They chose Stephen, a man full of faith and of the Holy Spirit; also Philip, Procorus, Nicanor, Timon, Parmenas, and Nicolas from Antioch, a convert to Judaism. **6** They presented these men to the apostles, who prayed and laid their hands on them.

7 So the word of God spread. The number of disciples in Jerusalem increased rapidly, and a large number of priests became obedient to the faith.

Stephen Seized

8 Now Stephen, a man full of God's grace and power, performed great wonders and signs among the people. **9** Opposition arose, however, from members of the Synagogue of the Freedmen (as it was called) — Jews of Cyrene and Alexandria as well as the provinces of Cilicia and Asia — who began to argue with Stephen. **10** But they could not stand up against the wisdom the Spirit gave him as he spoke.

11 Then they secretly persuaded some men to say, "We have heard Stephen speak blasphemous words against Moses and against God."

12 So they stirred up the people and the elders and the teachers of the law. They seized Stephen and brought him before the Sanhedrin. **13** They produced false witnesses, who testified, "This fellow never stops speaking against this holy place and against the law. **14** For we have heard him say that this Jesus of Nazareth will destroy this place and change the customs Moses handed down to us."

a 1 That is, Jews who had adopted the Greek language and culture

¹⁵All who were sitting in the Sanhedrin looked intently at Stephen, and they saw that his face was like the face of an angel.

Stephen's Speech to the Sanhedrin

7 Then the high priest asked Stephen, "Are these charges true?"

²To this he replied: "Brothers and fathers, listen to me! The God of glory appeared to our father Abraham while he was still in Mesopotamia, before he lived in Harran. ³'Leave your country and your people,' God said, 'and go to the land I will show you.'ᵃ

⁴"So he left the land of the Chaldeans and settled in Harran. After the death of his father, God sent him to this land where you are now living. ⁵He gave him no inheritance here, not even enough ground to set his foot on. But God promised him that he and his descendants after him would possess the land, even though at that time Abraham had no child. ⁶God spoke to him in this way: 'For four hundred years your descendants will be strangers in a country not their own, and they will be enslaved and mistreated. ⁷But I will punish the nation they serve as slaves,' God said, 'and afterward they will come out of that country and worship me in this place.'ᵇ ⁸Then he gave Abraham the covenant of circumci-

sion. And Abraham became the father of Isaac and circumcised him eight days after his birth. Later Isaac became the father of Jacob, and Jacob became the father of the twelve patriarchs.

⁹"Because the patriarchs were jealous of Joseph, they sold him as a slave into Egypt. But God was with him ¹⁰and rescued him from all his troubles. He gave Joseph wisdom and enabled him to gain the goodwill of Pharaoh king of Egypt. So Pharaoh made him ruler over Egypt and all his palace.

¹¹"Then a famine struck all Egypt and Canaan, bringing great suffering, and our ancestors could not find food. ¹²When Jacob heard that there was grain in Egypt, he sent our forefathers on their first visit. ¹³On their second visit, Joseph told his brothers who he was, and Pharaoh learned about Joseph's family. ¹⁴After this, Joseph sent for his father Jacob and his whole family, seventy-five in all. ¹⁵Then Jacob went down to Egypt, where he and our ancestors died. ¹⁶Their bodies were brought back to Shechem and placed in the tomb that Abraham had bought from the sons of Hamor at Shechem for a certain sum of money.

¹⁷"As the time drew near for God to fulfill his promise to Abraham, the number of our people in Egypt had greatly increased. ¹⁸Then 'a new king, to whom Joseph meant nothing, came to power in

ᵃ 3 Gen. 12:1   ᵇ 7 Gen. 15:13,14

Egypt.'ᵃ ¹⁹He dealt treacherously with our people and oppressed our ancestors by forcing them to throw out their newborn babies so that they would die.

²⁰"At that time Moses was born, and he was no ordinary child.ᵇ For three months he was cared for by his family. ²¹When he was placed outside, Pharaoh's daughter took him and brought him up as her own son. ²²Moses was educated in all the wisdom of the Egyptians and was powerful in speech and action.

²³"When Moses was forty years old, he decided to visit his own people, the Israelites. ²⁴He saw one of them being mistreated by an Egyptian, so he went to his defense and avenged him by killing the Egyptian. ²⁵Moses thought that his own people would realize that God was using him to rescue them, but they did not. ²⁶The next day Moses came upon two Israelites who were fighting. He tried to reconcile them by saying, 'Men, you are brothers; why do you want to hurt each other?'

²⁷"But the man who was mistreating the other pushed Moses aside and said, 'Who made you ruler and judge over us? ²⁸Are you thinking of killing me as you killed the Egyptian yesterday?'ᶜ ²⁹When Moses heard this, he fled to Midian, where he settled as a foreigner and had two sons.

³⁰"After forty years had passed, an angel appeared to Moses in the flames of a burning bush in the desert near Mount Sinai. ³¹When he saw this, he was amazed at the sight. As he went over to get a closer look, he heard the Lord say: ³²'I am the God of your fathers, the God of Abraham, Isaac and Jacob.'ᵈ Moses trembled with fear and did not dare to look.

³³"Then the Lord said to him, 'Take off your sandals, for the place where you are standing is holy ground. ³⁴I have indeed seen the oppression of my people in Egypt. I have heard their groaning and have come down to set them free. Now come, I will send you back to Egypt.'ᵉ

³⁵"This is the same Moses they had rejected with the words, 'Who made you ruler and judge?' He was sent to be their ruler and deliverer by God himself, through the angel who appeared to him in the bush. ³⁶He led them out of Egypt and performed wonders and signs in Egypt, at the Red Sea and for forty years in the wilderness.

³⁷"This is the Moses who told the Israelites, 'God will raise up for you a prophet like me from your own people.'ᶠ ³⁸He was in the assembly in the wilderness, with the angel who spoke to him on Mount Sinai, and with our ancestors; and he received living words to pass on to us.

³⁹"But our ancestors refused to obey him. Instead, they rejected

---

ᵃ 18 Exodus 1:8   ᵇ 20 Or *was fair in the sight of God*   ᶜ 28 Exodus 2:14
ᵈ 32 Exodus 3:6   ᵉ 34 Exodus 3:5,7,8,10   ᶠ 37 Deut. 18:15

him and in their hearts turned back to Egypt. **40** They told Aaron, 'Make us gods who will go before us. As for this fellow Moses who led us out of Egypt — we don't know what has happened to him!'*a* **41** That was the time they made an idol in the form of a calf. They brought sacrifices to it and reveled in what their own hands had made. **42** But God turned away from them and gave them over to the worship of the sun, moon and stars. This agrees with what is written in the book of the prophets:

" 'Did you bring me sacrifices
    and offerings
  forty years in the wilderness,
    people of Israel?
43 You have taken up the
    tabernacle of Molek
  and the star of your god
    Rephan,
  the idols you made to
    worship.
Therefore I will send you into
    exile'*b* beyond Babylon.

44 "Our ancestors had the tabernacle of the covenant law with them in the wilderness. It had been made as God directed Moses, according to the pattern he had seen. **45** After receiving the tabernacle, our ancestors under Joshua brought it with them when they took the land from the nations God drove out before them. It remained in the land until the time of David, **46** who enjoyed God's favor and asked that he might provide a dwelling place for the God of Jacob.*c* **47** But it was Solomon who built a house for him.

48 "However, the Most High does not live in houses made by human hands. As the prophet says:

49 " 'Heaven is my throne,
    and the earth is my footstool.
  What kind of house will you
      build for me?
              says the Lord.
    Or where will my resting
        place be?
50 Has not my hand made all
      these things?'*d*

51 "You stiff-necked people! Your hearts and ears are still uncircumcised. You are just like your ancestors: You always resist the Holy Spirit! **52** Was there ever a prophet your ancestors did not persecute? They even killed those who predicted the coming of the Righteous One. And now you have betrayed and murdered him — **53** you who have received the law that was given through angels but have not obeyed it."

The Stoning of Stephen

54 When the members of the Sanhedrin heard this, they were furious and gnashed their teeth at him. **55** But Stephen, full of the Holy Spirit, looked up to heaven

---

a 40 Exodus 32:1   *b 43* Amos 5:25-27 (see Septuagint)   *c 46* Some early manuscripts *the house of Jacob*   *d 50* Isaiah 66:1,2 and saw the glory of God, and Jesus standing at the right hand of God. **56**"Look," he said, "I see heaven open and the Son of Man standing at the right hand of God."

57At this they covered their ears and, yelling at the top of their voices, they all rushed at him, **58**dragged him out of the city and began to stone him. Meanwhile, the witnesses laid their coats at the feet of a young man named Saul.

59While they were stoning him, Stephen prayed, "Lord Jesus, receive my spirit." **60**Then he fell on his knees and cried out, "Lord, do not hold this sin against them." When he had said this, he fell asleep.

8 And Saul approved of their killing him.

The Church Persecuted and Scattered

On that day a great persecution broke out against the church in Jerusalem, and all except the apostles were scattered throughout Judea and Samaria. **2**Godly men buried Stephen and mourned deeply for him. **3**But Saul began to destroy the church. Going from house to house, he dragged off both men and women and put them in prison.

Philip in Samaria

4Those who had been scattered preached the word wherever they went. **5**Philip went down to a city in Samaria and proclaimed the Messiah there. **6**When the crowds heard Philip and saw the signs he performed, they all paid close attention to what he said. **7**For with shrieks, impure spirits came out of many, and many who were paralyzed or lame were healed. **8**So there was great joy in that city.

Simon the Sorcerer

9Now for some time a man named Simon had practiced sorcery in the city and amazed all the people of Samaria. He boasted that he was someone great, **10**and all the people, both high and low, gave him their attention and exclaimed, "This man is rightly called the Great Power of God." **11**They followed him because he had amazed them for a long time with his sorcery. **12**But when they believed Philip as he proclaimed the good news of the kingdom of God and the name of Jesus Christ, they were baptized, both men and women. **13**Simon himself believed and was baptized. And he followed Philip everywhere, astonished by the great signs and miracles he saw.

14When the apostles in Jerusalem heard that Samaria had accepted the word of God, they sent Peter and John to Samaria. **15**When they arrived, they prayed for the new believers there that they might receive the Holy Spirit, **16**because the Holy Spirit had not yet come on any of them; they had simply been baptized in the name of the Lord Jesus. **17**Then Peter and John placed their hands on them, and they received the Holy Spirit.

[18] When Simon saw that the Spirit was given at the laying on of the apostles' hands, he offered them money [19] and said, "Give me also this ability so that everyone on whom I lay my hands may receive the Holy Spirit."

[20] Peter answered: "May your money perish with you, because you thought you could buy the gift of God with money! [21] You have no part or share in this ministry, because your heart is not right before God. [22] Repent of this wickedness and pray to the Lord in the hope that he may forgive you for having such a thought in your heart. [23] For I see that you are full of bitterness and captive to sin."

[24] Then Simon answered, "Pray to the Lord for me so that nothing you have said may happen to me."

[25] After they had further proclaimed the word of the Lord and testified about Jesus, Peter and John returned to Jerusalem, preaching the gospel in many Samaritan villages.

Philip and the Ethiopian

[26] Now an angel of the Lord said to Philip, "Go south to the road — the desert road — that goes down from Jerusalem to Gaza." [27] So he started out, and on his way he met an Ethiopian[a] eunuch, an important official in charge of all the treasury of the Kandake (which means "queen of the Ethiopians"). This man had gone to Jerusalem to worship, [28] and on his way home was sitting in his chariot reading the Book of Isaiah the prophet. [29] The Spirit told Philip, "Go to that chariot and stay near it."

[30] Then Philip ran up to the chariot and heard the man reading Isaiah the prophet. "Do you understand what you are reading?" Philip asked.

[31] "How can I," he said, "unless someone explains it to me?" So he invited Philip to come up and sit with him.

[32] This is the passage of Scripture the eunuch was reading:

"He was led like a sheep to the
        slaughter,
    and as a lamb before its
        shearer is silent,
    so he did not open his
        mouth.
[33] In his humiliation he was
        deprived of justice.
    Who can speak of his
        descendants?
    For his life was taken from
        the earth."[b]

[34] The eunuch asked Philip, "Tell me, please, who is the prophet talking about, himself or someone else?" [35] Then Philip began with that very passage of Scripture and told him the good news about Jesus.

[36] As they traveled along the

---

[a] 27 That is, from the southern Nile region   [b] 33 Isaiah 53:7,8 (see Septuagint)

road, they came to some water and the eunuch said, "Look, here is water. What can stand in the way of my being baptized?" [37] *a* [38] And he gave orders to stop the chariot. Then both Philip and the eunuch went down into the water and Philip baptized him. [39] When they came up out of the water, the Spirit of the Lord suddenly took Philip away, and the eunuch did not see him again, but went on his way rejoicing. [40] Philip, however, appeared at Azotus and traveled about, preaching the gospel in all the towns until he reached Caesarea.

Saul's Conversion

9 Meanwhile, Saul was still breathing out murderous threats against the Lord's disciples. He went to the high priest [2] and asked him for letters to the synagogues in Damascus, so that if he found any there who belonged to the Way, whether men or women, he might take them as prisoners to Jerusalem. [3] As he neared Damascus on his journey, suddenly a light from heaven flashed around him. [4] He fell to the ground and heard a voice say to him, "Saul, Saul, why do you persecute me?"

[5] "Who are you, Lord?" Saul asked.

"I am Jesus, whom you are persecuting," he replied. [6] "Now get up and go into the city, and you will be told what you must do."

[7] The men traveling with Saul stood there speechless; they heard the sound but did not see anyone. [8] Saul got up from the ground, but when he opened his eyes he could see nothing. So they led him by the hand into Damascus. [9] For three days he was blind, and did not eat or drink anything.

[10] In Damascus there was a disciple named Ananias. The Lord called to him in a vision, "Ananias!"

"Yes, Lord," he answered.

[11] The Lord told him, "Go to the house of Judas on Straight Street and ask for a man from Tarsus named Saul, for he is praying. [12] In a vision he has seen a man named Ananias come and place his hands on him to restore his sight."

[13] "Lord," Ananias answered, "I have heard many reports about this man and all the harm he has done to your holy people in Jerusalem. [14] And he has come here with authority from the chief priests to arrest all who call on your name."

[15] But the Lord said to Ananias, "Go! This man is my chosen instrument to proclaim my name to the Gentiles and their kings and to the people of Israel. [16] I will show him how much he must suffer for my name."

[17] Then Ananias went to the

a 37 Some manuscripts include here *Philip said, "If you believe with all your heart, you may." The eunuch answered, "I believe that Jesus Christ is the Son of God."*

house and entered it. Placing his hands on Saul, he said, "Brother Saul, the Lord—Jesus, who appeared to you on the road as you were coming here—has sent me so that you may see again and be filled with the Holy Spirit." ¹⁸Immediately, something like scales fell from Saul's eyes, and he could see again. He got up and was baptized, ¹⁹and after taking some food, he regained his strength.

Saul in Damascus and Jerusalem

Saul spent several days with the disciples in Damascus. ²⁰At once he began to preach in the synagogues that Jesus is the Son of God. ²¹All those who heard him were astonished and asked, "Isn't he the man who raised havoc in Jerusalem among those who call on this name? And hasn't he come here to take them as prisoners to the chief priests?" ²²Yet Saul grew more and more powerful and baffled the Jews living in Damascus by proving that Jesus is the Messiah.

²³After many days had gone by, there was a conspiracy among the Jews to kill him, ²⁴but Saul learned of their plan. Day and night they kept close watch on the city gates in order to kill him. ²⁵But his followers took him by night and lowered him in a basket through an opening in the wall.

²⁶When he came to Jerusalem, he tried to join the disciples, but they were all afraid of him, not believing that he really was a disciple. ²⁷But Barnabas took him and brought him to the apostles. He told them how Saul on his journey had seen the Lord and that the Lord had spoken to him, and how in Damascus he had preached fearlessly in the name of Jesus. ²⁸So Saul stayed with them and moved about freely in Jerusalem, speaking boldly in the name of the Lord. ²⁹He talked and debated with the Hellenistic Jews,ᵃ but they tried to kill him. ³⁰When the believers learned of this, they took him down to Caesarea and sent him off to Tarsus.

³¹Then the church throughout Judea, Galilee and Samaria enjoyed a time of peace and was strengthened. Living in the fear of the Lord and encouraged by the Holy Spirit, it increased in numbers.

Aeneas and Dorcas

³²As Peter traveled about the country, he went to visit the Lord's people who lived in Lydda. ³³There he found a man named Aeneas, who was paralyzed and had been bedridden for eight years. ³⁴"Aeneas," Peter said to him, "Jesus Christ heals you. Get up and roll up your mat." Immediately Aeneas got up. ³⁵All those who lived in Lydda and Sharon saw him and turned to the Lord.

³⁶In Joppa there was a disci-

ᵃ 29 That is, Jews who had adopted the Greek language and culture ple named Tabitha (in Greek her name is Dorcas); she was always doing good and helping the poor. ³⁷About that time she became sick and died, and her body was washed and placed in an upstairs room. ³⁸Lydda was near Joppa; so when the disciples heard that Peter was in Lydda, they sent two men to him and urged him, "Please come at once!"

³⁹Peter went with them, and when he arrived he was taken upstairs to the room. All the widows stood around him, crying and showing him the robes and other clothing that Dorcas had made while she was still with them.

⁴⁰Peter sent them all out of the room; then he got down on his knees and prayed. Turning toward the dead woman, he said, "Tabitha, get up." She opened her eyes, and seeing Peter she sat up. ⁴¹He took her by the hand and helped her to her feet. Then he called for the believers, especially the widows, and presented her to them alive. ⁴²This became known all over Joppa, and many people believed in the Lord. ⁴³Peter stayed in Joppa for some time with a tanner named Simon.

Cornelius Calls for Peter

10 At Caesarea there was a man named Cornelius, a centurion in what was known as the Italian Regiment. ²He and all his family were devout and God-fearing; he gave generously to those in need and prayed to

God regularly. ³One day at about three in the afternoon he had a vision. He distinctly saw an angel of God, who came to him and said, "Cornelius!"

⁴Cornelius stared at him in fear. "What is it, Lord?" he asked.

The angel answered, "Your prayers and gifts to the poor have come up as a memorial offering before God. ⁵Now send men to Joppa to bring back a man named Simon who is called Peter. ⁶He is staying with Simon the tanner, whose house is by the sea."

⁷When the angel who spoke to him had gone, Cornelius called two of his servants and a devout soldier who was one of his attendants. ⁸He told them everything that had happened and sent them to Joppa.

Peter's Vision

⁹About noon the following day as they were on their journey and approaching the city, Peter went up on the roof to pray. ¹⁰He became hungry and wanted something to eat, and while the meal was being prepared, he fell into a trance. ¹¹He saw heaven opened and something like a large sheet being let down to earth by its four corners. ¹²It contained all kinds of four-footed animals, as well as reptiles and birds. ¹³Then a voice told him, "Get up, Peter. Kill and eat."

¹⁴"Surely not, Lord!" Peter replied. "I have never eaten anything impure or unclean."

[15] The voice spoke to him a second time, "Do not call anything impure that God has made clean."

[16] This happened three times, and immediately the sheet was taken back to heaven.

[17] While Peter was wondering about the meaning of the vision, the men sent by Cornelius found out where Simon's house was and stopped at the gate. [18] They called out, asking if Simon who was known as Peter was staying there.

[19] While Peter was still thinking about the vision, the Spirit said to him, "Simon, three[a] men are looking for you. [20] So get up and go downstairs. Do not hesitate to go with them, for I have sent them."

[21] Peter went down and said to the men, "I'm the one you're looking for. Why have you come?"

[22] The men replied, "We have come from Cornelius the centurion. He is a righteous and God-fearing man, who is respected by all the Jewish people. A holy angel told him to ask you to come to his house so that he could hear what you have to say." [23] Then Peter invited the men into the house to be his guests.

Peter at Cornelius's House

The next day Peter started out with them, and some of the believers from Joppa went along. [24] The following day he arrived in Caesarea. Cornelius was expecting them and had called together his relatives and close friends. [25] As Peter entered the house, Cornelius met him and fell at his feet in reverence. [26] But Peter made him get up. "Stand up," he said, "I am only a man myself."

[27] While talking with him, Peter went inside and found a large gathering of people. [28] He said to them: "You are well aware that it is against our law for a Jew to associate with or visit a Gentile. But God has shown me that I should not call anyone impure or unclean. [29] So when I was sent for, I came without raising any objection. May I ask why you sent for me?"

[30] Cornelius answered: "Three days ago I was in my house praying at this hour, at three in the afternoon. Suddenly a man in shining clothes stood before me [31] and said, 'Cornelius, God has heard your prayer and remembered your gifts to the poor. [32] Send to Joppa for Simon who is called Peter. He is a guest in the home of Simon the tanner, who lives by the sea.' [33] So I sent for you immediately, and it was good of you to come. Now we are all here in the presence of God to listen to everything the Lord has commanded you to tell us."

[34] Then Peter began to speak: "I now realize how true it is that God does not show favoritism [35] but accepts from every nation the one who fears him and does what

---

[a] 19 One early manuscript *two*; other manuscripts do not have the number.

is right. **36**You know the message God sent to the people of Israel, announcing the good news of peace through Jesus Christ, who is Lord of all. **37**You know what has happened throughout the province of Judea, beginning in Galilee after the baptism that John preached— **38**how God anointed Jesus of Nazareth with the Holy Spirit and power, and how he went around doing good and healing all who were under the power of the devil, because God was with him.

39"We are witnesses of everything he did in the country of the Jews and in Jerusalem. They killed him by hanging him on a cross, **40**but God raised him from the dead on the third day and caused him to be seen. **41**He was not seen by all the people, but by witnesses whom God had already chosen—by us who ate and drank with him after he rose from the dead. **42**He commanded us to preach to the people and to testify that he is the one whom God appointed as judge of the living and the dead. **43**All the prophets testify about him that everyone who believes in him receives forgiveness of sins through his name."

44While Peter was still speaking these words, the Holy Spirit came on all who heard the message. **45**The circumcised believers who had come with Peter were astonished that the gift of the Holy Spirit had been poured out even on Gentiles. **46**For they heard them speaking in tongues*a* and praising God.

Then Peter said, **47**"Surely no one can stand in the way of their being baptized with water. They have received the Holy Spirit just as we have." **48**So he ordered that they be baptized in the name of Jesus Christ. Then they asked Peter to stay with them for a few days.

Peter Explains His Actions

11 The apostles and the believers throughout Judea heard that the Gentiles also had received the word of God. **2**So when Peter went up to Jerusalem, the circumcised believers criticized him **3**and said, "You went into the house of uncircumcised men and ate with them."

4Starting from the beginning, Peter told them the whole story: **5**"I was in the city of Joppa praying, and in a trance I saw a vision. I saw something like a large sheet being let down from heaven by its four corners, and it came down to where I was. **6**I looked into it and saw four-footed animals of the earth, wild beasts, reptiles and birds. **7**Then I heard a voice telling me, 'Get up, Peter. Kill and eat.'

8"I replied, 'Surely not, Lord! Nothing impure or unclean has ever entered my mouth.'

9"The voice spoke from heaven a second time, 'Do not call

a 46 Or *other languages*

anything impure that God has made clean.' ¹⁰This happened three times, and then it was all pulled up to heaven again.

¹¹"Right then three men who had been sent to me from Caesarea stopped at the house where I was staying. ¹²The Spirit told me to have no hesitation about going with them. These six brothers also went with me, and we entered the man's house. ¹³He told us how he had seen an angel appear in his house and say, 'Send to Joppa for Simon who is called Peter. ¹⁴He will bring you a message through which you and all your household will be saved.'

¹⁵"As I began to speak, the Holy Spirit came on them as he had come on us at the beginning. ¹⁶Then I remembered what the Lord had said: 'John baptized with^a water, but you will be baptized with^a the Holy Spirit.' ¹⁷So if God gave them the same gift he gave us who believed in the Lord Jesus Christ, who was I to think that I could stand in God's way?"

¹⁸When they heard this, they had no further objections and praised God, saying, "So then, even to Gentiles God has granted repentance that leads to life."

The Church in Antioch

¹⁹Now those who had been scattered by the persecution that broke out when Stephen was killed traveled as far as Phoenicia, Cyprus and Antioch, spreading the word only among Jews. ²⁰Some of them, however, men from Cyprus and Cyrene, went to Antioch and began to speak to Greeks also, telling them the good news about the Lord Jesus. ²¹The Lord's hand was with them, and a great number of people believed and turned to the Lord.

²²News of this reached the church in Jerusalem, and they sent Barnabas to Antioch. ²³When he arrived and saw what the grace of God had done, he was glad and encouraged them all to remain true to the Lord with all their hearts. ²⁴He was a good man, full of the Holy Spirit and faith, and a great number of people were brought to the Lord.

²⁵Then Barnabas went to Tarsus to look for Saul, ²⁶and when he found him, he brought him to Antioch. So for a whole year Barnabas and Saul met with the church and taught great numbers of people. The disciples were called Christians first at Antioch.

²⁷During this time some prophets came down from Jerusalem to Antioch. ²⁸One of them, named Agabus, stood up and through the Spirit predicted that a severe famine would spread over the entire Roman world. (This happened during the reign of Claudius.) ²⁹The disciples, as each one was able, decided to provide help for the brothers and

^{a} 16 Or in

sisters living in Judea. ³⁰This they did, sending their gift to the elders by Barnabas and Saul.

Peter's Miraculous Escape From Prison

12 It was about this time that King Herod arrested some who belonged to the church, intending to persecute them. ²He had James, the brother of John, put to death with the sword. ³When he saw that this met with approval among the Jews, he proceeded to seize Peter also. This happened during the Festival of Unleavened Bread. ⁴After arresting him, he put him in prison, handing him over to be guarded by four squads of four soldiers each. Herod intended to bring him out for public trial after the Passover.

⁵So Peter was kept in prison, but the church was earnestly praying to God for him.

⁶The night before Herod was to bring him to trial, Peter was sleeping between two soldiers, bound with two chains, and sentries stood guard at the entrance. ⁷Suddenly an angel of the Lord appeared and a light shone in the cell. He struck Peter on the side and woke him up. "Quick, get up!" he said, and the chains fell off Peter's wrists.

⁸Then the angel said to him, "Put on your clothes and sandals." And Peter did so. "Wrap your cloak around you and follow me," the angel told him. ⁹Peter followed him out of the prison, but he had no idea that what the angel was doing was really happening; he thought he was seeing a vision. ¹⁰They passed the first and second guards and came to the iron gate leading to the city. It opened for them by itself, and they went through it. When they had walked the length of one street, suddenly the angel left him.

¹¹Then Peter came to himself and said, "Now I know without a doubt that the Lord has sent his angel and rescued me from Herod's clutches and from everything the Jewish people were hoping would happen."

¹²When this had dawned on him, he went to the house of Mary the mother of John, also called Mark, where many people had gathered and were praying. ¹³Peter knocked at the outer entrance, and a servant named Rhoda came to answer the door. ¹⁴When she recognized Peter's voice, she was so overjoyed she ran back without opening it and exclaimed, "Peter is at the door!"

¹⁵"You're out of your mind," they told her. When she kept insisting that it was so, they said, "It must be his angel."

¹⁶But Peter kept on knocking, and when they opened the door and saw him, they were astonished. ¹⁷Peter motioned with his hand for them to be quiet and described how the Lord had brought him out of prison. "Tell James and the other brothers and

sisters about this," he said, and then he left for another place.

¹⁸In the morning, there was no small commotion among the soldiers as to what had become of Peter. ¹⁹After Herod had a thorough search made for him and did not find him, he cross-examined the guards and ordered that they be executed.

Herod's Death

Then Herod went from Judea to Caesarea and stayed there. ²⁰He had been quarreling with the people of Tyre and Sidon; they now joined together and sought an audience with him. After securing the support of Blastus, a trusted personal servant of the king, they asked for peace, because they depended on the king's country for their food supply.

²¹On the appointed day Herod, wearing his royal robes, sat on his throne and delivered a public address to the people. ²²They shouted, "This is the voice of a god, not of a man." ²³Immediately, because Herod did not give praise to God, an angel of the Lord struck him down, and he was eaten by worms and died.

²⁴But the word of God continued to spread and flourish.

Barnabas and Saul Sent Off

²⁵When Barnabas and Saul had finished their mission, they returned from*a* Jerusalem, taking with them John, also called

13 Mark. ¹Now in the church at Antioch there were prophets and teachers: Barnabas, Simeon called Niger, Lucius of Cyrene, Manaen (who had been brought up with Herod the tetrarch) and Saul. ²While they were worshiping the Lord and fasting, the Holy Spirit said, "Set apart for me Barnabas and Saul for the work to which I have called them." ³So after they had fasted and prayed, they placed their hands on them and sent them off.

On Cyprus

⁴The two of them, sent on their way by the Holy Spirit, went down to Seleucia and sailed from there to Cyprus. ⁵When they arrived at Salamis, they proclaimed the word of God in the Jewish synagogues. John was with them as their helper.

⁶They traveled through the whole island until they came to Paphos. There they met a Jewish sorcerer and false prophet named Bar-Jesus, ⁷who was an attendant of the proconsul, Sergius Paulus. The proconsul, an intelligent man, sent for Barnabas and Saul because he wanted to hear the word of God. ⁸But Elymas the sorcerer (for that is what his name means) opposed them and tried to turn the proconsul from the faith. ⁹Then Saul, who

a 25 Some manuscripts *to*

was also called Paul, filled with the Holy Spirit, looked straight at Elymas and said, [10]"You are a child of the devil and an enemy of everything that is right! You are full of all kinds of deceit and trickery. Will you never stop perverting the right ways of the Lord? [11]Now the hand of the Lord is against you. You are going to be blind for a time, not even able to see the light of the sun."

Immediately mist and darkness came over him, and he groped about, seeking someone to lead him by the hand. [12]When the proconsul saw what had happened, he believed, for he was amazed at the teaching about the Lord.

In Pisidian Antioch

[13]From Paphos, Paul and his companions sailed to Perga in Pamphylia, where John left them to return to Jerusalem. [14]From Perga they went on to Pisidian Antioch. On the Sabbath they entered the synagogue and sat down. [15]After the reading from the Law and the Prophets, the leaders of the synagogue sent word to them, saying, "Brothers, if you have a word of exhortation for the people, please speak."

[16]Standing up, Paul motioned with his hand and said: "Fellow Israelites and you Gentiles who worship God, listen to me! [17]The God of the people of Israel chose our ancestors; he made the people prosper during their stay in Egypt; with mighty power he led them out of that country; [18]for about forty years he endured their conduct[a] in the wilderness; [19]and he overthrew seven nations in Canaan, giving their land to his people as their inheritance. [20]All this took about 450 years.

"After this, God gave them judges until the time of Samuel the prophet. [21]Then the people asked for a king, and he gave them Saul son of Kish, of the tribe of Benjamin, who ruled forty years. [22]After removing Saul, he made David their king. God testified concerning him: 'I have found David son of Jesse, a man after my own heart; he will do everything I want him to do.'

[23]"From this man's descendants God has brought to Israel the Savior Jesus, as he promised. [24]Before the coming of Jesus, John preached repentance and baptism to all the people of Israel. [25]As John was completing his work, he said: 'Who do you suppose I am? I am not the one you are looking for. But there is one coming after me whose sandals I am not worthy to untie.'

[26]"Fellow children of Abraham and you God-fearing Gentiles, it is to us that this message of salvation has been sent. [27]The people of Jerusalem and their rulers did not recognize Jesus, yet in condemning him they fulfilled the

---

[a] 18 Some manuscripts *he cared for them*

words of the prophets that are read every Sabbath. **28**Though they found no proper ground for a death sentence, they asked Pilate to have him executed. **29**When they had carried out all that was written about him, they took him down from the cross and laid him in a tomb. **30**But God raised him from the dead, **31**and for many days he was seen by those who had traveled with him from Galilee to Jerusalem. They are now his witnesses to our people.

32"We tell you the good news: What God promised our ancestors **33**he has fulfilled for us, their children, by raising up Jesus. As it is written in the second Psalm:

> " 'You are my son;
>   today I have become your
>   father.'[a]

34God raised him from the dead so that he will never be subject to decay. As God has said,

> " 'I will give you the holy and
>   sure blessings promised
>   to David.'[b]

35So it is also stated elsewhere:

> " 'You will not let your holy one
>   see decay.'[c]

36"Now when David had served God's purpose in his own generation, he fell asleep; he was buried with his ancestors and his body decayed. **37**But the one whom God raised from the dead did not see decay.

38"Therefore, my friends, I want you to know that through Jesus the forgiveness of sins is proclaimed to you. **39**Through him everyone who believes is set free from every sin, a justification you were not able to obtain under the law of Moses. **40**Take care that what the prophets have said does not happen to you:

41" 'Look, you scoffers,
>   wonder and perish,
> for I am going to do something
>   in your days
>   that you would never
>   believe,
>   even if someone told you.'[d]"

42As Paul and Barnabas were leaving the synagogue, the people invited them to speak further about these things on the next Sabbath. **43**When the congregation was dismissed, many of the Jews and devout converts to Judaism followed Paul and Barnabas, who talked with them and urged them to continue in the grace of God.

44On the next Sabbath almost the whole city gathered to hear the word of the Lord. **45**When the Jews saw the crowds, they were filled with jealousy. They began to contradict what Paul was saying and heaped abuse on him.

46Then Paul and Barnabas answered them boldly: "We had

---

a 33 Psalm 2:7   *b 34* Isaiah 55:3   *c 35* Psalm 16:10 (see Septuagint)
d 41 Hab. 1:5

to speak the word of God to you first. Since you reject it and do not consider yourselves worthy of eternal life, we now turn to the Gentiles. **47** For this is what the Lord has commanded us:

" 'I have made you*a* a light for
the Gentiles,
that you*a* may bring
salvation to the ends
of the earth.'*b* "

48 When the Gentiles heard this, they were glad and honored the word of the Lord; and all who were appointed for eternal life believed.

49 The word of the Lord spread through the whole region. **50** But the Jewish leaders incited the God-fearing women of high standing and the leading men of the city. They stirred up persecution against Paul and Barnabas, and expelled them from their region. **51** So they shook the dust off their feet as a warning to them and went to Iconium. **52** And the disciples were filled with joy and with the Holy Spirit.

In Iconium

14 At Iconium Paul and Barnabas went as usual into the Jewish synagogue. There they spoke so effectively that a great number of Jews and Greeks believed. **2** But the Jews who refused to believe stirred up the other Gentiles and poisoned

their minds against the brothers. **3** So Paul and Barnabas spent considerable time there, speaking boldly for the Lord, who confirmed the message of his grace by enabling them to perform signs and wonders. **4** The people of the city were divided; some sided with the Jews, others with the apostles. **5** There was a plot afoot among both Gentiles and Jews, together with their leaders, to mistreat them and stone them. **6** But they found out about it and fled to the Lycaonian cities of Lystra and Derbe and to the surrounding country, **7** where they continued to preach the gospel.

In Lystra and Derbe

8 In Lystra there sat a man who was lame. He had been that way from birth and had never walked. **9** He listened to Paul as he was speaking. Paul looked directly at him, saw that he had faith to be healed **10** and called out, "Stand up on your feet!" At that, the man jumped up and began to walk.

11 When the crowd saw what Paul had done, they shouted in the Lycaonian language, "The gods have come down to us in human form!" **12** Barnabas they called Zeus, and Paul they called Hermes because he was the chief speaker. **13** The priest of Zeus, whose temple was just outside the city, brought bulls and wreaths to the city gates because

---

a 47 The Greek is singular.   *b* 47 Isaiah 49:6

he and the crowd wanted to offer sacrifices to them.

[14] But when the apostles Barnabas and Paul heard of this, they tore their clothes and rushed out into the crowd, shouting: [15] "Friends, why are you doing this? We too are only human, like you. We are bringing you good news, telling you to turn from these worthless things to the living God, who made the heavens and the earth and the sea and everything in them. [16] In the past, he let all nations go their own way. [17] Yet he has not left himself without testimony: He has shown kindness by giving you rain from heaven and crops in their seasons; he provides you with plenty of food and fills your hearts with joy." [18] Even with these words, they had difficulty keeping the crowd from sacrificing to them.

[19] Then some Jews came from Antioch and Iconium and won the crowd over. They stoned Paul and dragged him outside the city, thinking he was dead. [20] But after the disciples had gathered around him, he got up and went back into the city. The next day he and Barnabas left for Derbe.

The Return to Antioch in Syria

[21] They preached the gospel in that city and won a large number of disciples. Then they returned to Lystra, Iconium and Antioch, [22] strengthening the disciples and encouraging them to remain true to the faith. "We must go through many hardships to enter the kingdom of God," they said. [23] Paul and Barnabas appointed elders[a] for them in each church and, with prayer and fasting, committed them to the Lord, in whom they had put their trust. [24] After going through Pisidia, they came into Pamphylia, [25] and when they had preached the word in Perga, they went down to Attalia.

[26] From Attalia they sailed back to Antioch, where they had been committed to the grace of God for the work they had now completed. [27] On arriving there, they gathered the church together and reported all that God had done through them and how he had opened a door of faith to the Gentiles. [28] And they stayed there a long time with the disciples.

The Council at Jerusalem

15 Certain people came down from Judea to Antioch and were teaching the believers: "Unless you are circumcised, according to the custom taught by Moses, you cannot be saved." [2] This brought Paul and Barnabas into sharp dispute and debate with them. So Paul and Barnabas were appointed, along with some other believers, to go up to Jerusalem to see the apostles and elders about this question. [3] The church sent them on

---

[a] 23 Or *Barnabas ordained elders*; or *Barnabas had elders elected*

their way, and as they traveled through Phoenicia and Samaria, they told how the Gentiles had been converted. This news made all the believers very glad. **4**When they came to Jerusalem, they were welcomed by the church and the apostles and elders, to whom they reported everything God had done through them.

5Then some of the believers who belonged to the party of the Pharisees stood up and said, "The Gentiles must be circumcised and required to keep the law of Moses."

6The apostles and elders met to consider this question. **7**After much discussion, Peter got up and addressed them: "Brothers, you know that some time ago God made a choice among you that the Gentiles might hear from my lips the message of the gospel and believe. **8**God, who knows the heart, showed that he accepted them by giving the Holy Spirit to them, just as he did to us. **9**He did not discriminate between us and them, for he purified their hearts by faith. **10**Now then, why do you try to test God by putting on the necks of Gentiles a yoke that neither we nor our ancestors have been able to bear? **11**No! We believe it is through the grace of our Lord Jesus that we are saved, just as they are."

12The whole assembly became silent as they listened to Barnabas and Paul telling about the signs and wonders God had done among the Gentiles through them. **13**When they finished, James spoke up. "Brothers," he said, "listen to me. **14**Simon*a* has described to us how God first intervened to choose a people for his name from the Gentiles. **15**The words of the prophets are in agreement with this, as it is written:

16 " 'After this I will return
    and rebuild David's fallen
      tent.
  Its ruins I will rebuild,
    and I will restore it,
17that the rest of mankind may
      seek the Lord,
  even all the Gentiles who
      bear my name,
  says the Lord, who does these
      things'*b*—
18 things known from long ago.*c*

19"It is my judgment, therefore, that we should not make it difficult for the Gentiles who are turning to God. **20**Instead we should write to them, telling them to abstain from food polluted by idols, from sexual immorality, from the meat of strangled animals and from blood. **21**For the law of Moses has been preached in every city from the

---

a 14 Greek *Simeon*, a variant of *Simon*; that is, Peter   *b* 17 Amos 9:11,12 (see Septuagint)   *c* 17,18 Some manuscripts *things' — / *18*the Lord's work is known to him from long ago* earliest times and is read in the synagogues on every Sabbath."

The Council's Letter to Gentile Believers

²²Then the apostles and elders, with the whole church, decided to choose some of their own men and send them to Antioch with Paul and Barnabas. They chose Judas (called Barsabbas) and Silas, men who were leaders among the believers. ²³With them they sent the following letter:

The apostles and elders, your brothers,

To the Gentile believers in Antioch, Syria and Cilicia:

Greetings.

²⁴We have heard that some went out from us without our authorization and disturbed you, troubling your minds by what they said. ²⁵So we all agreed to choose some men and send them to you with our dear friends Barnabas and Paul— ²⁶men who have risked their lives for the name of our Lord Jesus Christ. ²⁷Therefore we are sending Judas and Silas to confirm by word of mouth what we are writing. ²⁸It seemed good to the Holy Spirit and to us not to burden you with anything beyond the following requirements: ²⁹You are to abstain from food sacrificed to idols, from blood, from the meat of strangled animals and from sexual immorality. You will do well to avoid these things.

Farewell.

³⁰So the men were sent off and went down to Antioch, where they gathered the church together and delivered the letter. ³¹The people read it and were glad for its encouraging message. ³²Judas and Silas, who themselves were prophets, said much to encourage and strengthen the believers. ³³After spending some time there, they were sent off by the believers with the blessing of peace to return to those who had sent them. ^[34]^a ³⁵But Paul and Barnabas remained in Antioch, where they and many others taught and preached the word of the Lord.

Disagreement Between Paul and Barnabas

³⁶Some time later Paul said to Barnabas, "Let us go back and visit the believers in all the towns where we preached the word of the Lord and see how they are doing." ³⁷Barnabas wanted to take John, also called Mark, with them, ³⁸but Paul did not think it wise to take him, because he had deserted them in Pamphylia and had not continued with them in the work. ³⁹They had

---

^a 34 Some manuscripts include here *But Silas decided to remain there.*

such a sharp disagreement that they parted company. Barnabas took Mark and sailed for Cyprus, [40]but Paul chose Silas and left, commended by the believers to the grace of the Lord. [41]He went through Syria and Cilicia, strengthening the churches.

Timothy Joins Paul and Silas

16 Paul came to Derbe and then to Lystra, where a disciple named Timothy lived, whose mother was Jewish and a believer but whose father was a Greek. [2]The believers at Lystra and Iconium spoke well of him. [3]Paul wanted to take him along on the journey, so he circumcised him because of the Jews who lived in that area, for they all knew that his father was a Greek. [4]As they traveled from town to town, they delivered the decisions reached by the apostles and elders in Jerusalem for the people to obey. [5]So the churches were strengthened in the faith and grew daily in numbers.

Paul's Vision of the Man of Macedonia

[6]Paul and his companions traveled throughout the region of Phrygia and Galatia, having been kept by the Holy Spirit from preaching the word in the province of Asia. [7]When they came to the border of Mysia, they tried to enter Bithynia, but the Spirit of Jesus would not allow them to. [8]So they passed by Mysia and went down to Troas. [9]During the night Paul had a vision of a man of Macedonia standing and begging him, "Come over to Macedonia and help us." [10]After Paul had seen the vision, we got ready at once to leave for Macedonia, concluding that God had called us to preach the gospel to them.

Lydia's Conversion in Philippi

[11]From Troas we put out to sea and sailed straight for Samothrace, and the next day we went on to Neapolis. [12]From there we traveled to Philippi, a Roman colony and the leading city of that district[a] of Macedonia. And we stayed there several days.

[13]On the Sabbath we went outside the city gate to the river, where we expected to find a place of prayer. We sat down and began to speak to the women who had gathered there. [14]One of those listening was a woman from the city of Thyatira named Lydia, a dealer in purple cloth. She was a worshiper of God. The Lord opened her heart to respond to Paul's message. [15]When she and the members of her household were baptized, she invited us to her home. "If you consider me a believer in the Lord," she said, "come and stay at my house." And she persuaded us.

---

[a] 12 The text and meaning of the Greek for *the leading city of that district* are uncertain.

Paul and Silas in Prison

16 Once when we were going to the place of prayer, we were met by a female slave who had a spirit by which she predicted the future. She earned a great deal of money for her owners by fortune-telling. 17 She followed Paul and the rest of us, shouting, "These men are servants of the Most High God, who are telling you the way to be saved." 18 She kept this up for many days. Finally Paul became so annoyed that he turned around and said to the spirit, "In the name of Jesus Christ I command you to come out of her!" At that moment the spirit left her.

19 When her owners realized that their hope of making money was gone, they seized Paul and Silas and dragged them into the marketplace to face the authorities. 20 They brought them before the magistrates and said, "These men are Jews, and are throwing our city into an uproar 21 by advocating customs unlawful for us Romans to accept or practice."

22 The crowd joined in the attack against Paul and Silas, and the magistrates ordered them to be stripped and beaten with rods. 23 After they had been severely flogged, they were thrown into prison, and the jailer was commanded to guard them carefully. 24 When he received these orders, he put them in the inner cell and fastened their feet in the stocks.

25 About midnight Paul and Silas were praying and singing hymns to God, and the other prisoners were listening to them. 26 Suddenly there was such a violent earthquake that the foundations of the prison were shaken. At once all the prison doors flew open, and everyone's chains came loose. 27 The jailer woke up, and when he saw the prison doors open, he drew his sword and was about to kill himself because he thought the prisoners had escaped. 28 But Paul shouted, "Don't harm yourself! We are all here!"

29 The jailer called for lights, rushed in and fell trembling before Paul and Silas. 30 He then brought them out and asked, "Sirs, what must I do to be saved?"

31 They replied, "Believe in the Lord Jesus, and you will be saved—you and your household." 32 Then they spoke the word of the Lord to him and to all the others in his house. 33 At that hour of the night the jailer took them and washed their wounds; then immediately he and all his household were baptized. 34 The jailer brought them into his house and set a meal before them; he was filled with joy because he had come to believe in God—he and his whole household.

35 When it was daylight, the magistrates sent their officers to the jailer with the order: "Release those men." 36 The jailer told Paul, "The magistrates have ordered that you and Silas be released. Now you can leave. Go in peace."

³⁷ But Paul said to the officers: "They beat us publicly without a trial, even though we are Roman citizens, and threw us into prison. And now do they want to get rid of us quietly? No! Let them come themselves and escort us out."

³⁸ The officers reported this to the magistrates, and when they heard that Paul and Silas were Roman citizens, they were alarmed. ³⁹ They came to appease them and escorted them from the prison, requesting them to leave the city. ⁴⁰ After Paul and Silas came out of the prison, they went to Lydia's house, where they met with the brothers and sisters and encouraged them. Then they left.

In Thessalonica

17 When Paul and his companions had passed through Amphipolis and Apollonia, they came to Thessalonica, where there was a Jewish synagogue. ² As was his custom, Paul went into the synagogue, and on three Sabbath days he reasoned with them from the Scriptures, ³ explaining and proving that the Messiah had to suffer and rise from the dead. "This Jesus I am proclaiming to you is the Messiah," he said. ⁴ Some of the Jews were persuaded and joined Paul and Silas, as did a large number of God-fearing Greeks and quite a few prominent women.

⁵ But other Jews were jealous; so they rounded up some bad characters from the marketplace, formed a mob and started a riot in the city. They rushed to Jason's house in search of Paul and Silas in order to bring them out to the crowd.ᵃ ⁶ But when they did not find them, they dragged Jason and some other believers before the city officials, shouting: "These men who have caused trouble all over the world have now come here, ⁷ and Jason has welcomed them into his house. They are all defying Caesar's decrees, saying that there is another king, one called Jesus." ⁸ When they heard this, the crowd and the city officials were thrown into turmoil. ⁹ Then they made Jason and the others post bond and let them go.

In Berea

¹⁰ As soon as it was night, the believers sent Paul and Silas away to Berea. On arriving there, they went to the Jewish synagogue. ¹¹ Now the Berean Jews were of more noble character than those in Thessalonica, for they received the message with great eagerness and examined the Scriptures every day to see if what Paul said was true. ¹² As a result, many of them believed, as did also a number of prominent Greek women and many Greek men.

¹³ But when the Jews in Thessalonica learned that Paul was

ᵃ 5 Or *the assembly of the people*

preaching the word of God at Berea, some of them went there too, agitating the crowds and stirring them up. ¹⁴The believers immediately sent Paul to the coast, but Silas and Timothy stayed at Berea. ¹⁵Those who escorted Paul brought him to Athens and then left with instructions for Silas and Timothy to join him as soon as possible.

In Athens

¹⁶While Paul was waiting for them in Athens, he was greatly distressed to see that the city was full of idols. ¹⁷So he reasoned in the synagogue with both Jews and God-fearing Greeks, as well as in the marketplace day by day with those who happened to be there. ¹⁸A group of Epicurean and Stoic philosophers began to debate with him. Some of them asked, "What is this babbler trying to say?" Others remarked, "He seems to be advocating foreign gods." They said this because Paul was preaching the good news about Jesus and the resurrection. ¹⁹Then they took him and brought him to a meeting of the Areopagus, where they said to him, "May we know what this new teaching is that you are presenting? ²⁰You are bringing some strange ideas to our ears, and we would like to know what they mean." ²¹(All the Athenians and the foreigners who lived there spent their time doing nothing but talking about and listening to the latest ideas.)

²²Paul then stood up in the meeting of the Areopagus and said: "People of Athens! I see that in every way you are very religious. ²³For as I walked around and looked carefully at your objects of worship, I even found an altar with this inscription: TO AN UNKNOWN GOD. So you are ignorant of the very thing you worship—and this is what I am going to proclaim to you.

²⁴"The God who made the world and everything in it is the Lord of heaven and earth and does not live in temples built by human hands. ²⁵And he is not served by human hands, as if he needed anything. Rather, he himself gives everyone life and breath and everything else. ²⁶From one man he made all the nations, that they should inhabit the whole earth; and he marked out their appointed times in history and the boundaries of their lands. ²⁷God did this so that they would seek him and perhaps reach out for him and find him, though he is not far from any one of us. ²⁸'For in him we live and move and have our being.'[a] As some of your own poets have said, 'We are his offspring.'[b]

²⁹"Therefore since we are God's offspring, we should not think that the divine being is like gold or silver or stone—an image made

[a] 28 From the Cretan philosopher Epimenides   [b] 28 From the Cilician Stoic philosopher Aratus

by human design and skill. [30]In the past God overlooked such ignorance, but now he commands all people everywhere to repent. [31]For he has set a day when he will judge the world with justice by the man he has appointed. He has given proof of this to everyone by raising him from the dead."

[32]When they heard about the resurrection of the dead, some of them sneered, but others said, "We want to hear you again on this subject." [33]At that, Paul left the Council. [34]Some of the people became followers of Paul and believed. Among them was Dionysius, a member of the Areopagus, also a woman named Damaris, and a number of others.

In Corinth

18 After this, Paul left Athens and went to Corinth. [2]There he met a Jew named Aquila, a native of Pontus, who had recently come from Italy with his wife Priscilla, because Claudius had ordered all Jews to leave Rome. Paul went to see them, [3]and because he was a tentmaker as they were, he stayed and worked with them. [4]Every Sabbath he reasoned in the synagogue, trying to persuade Jews and Greeks.

[5]When Silas and Timothy came from Macedonia, Paul devoted himself exclusively to preaching, testifying to the Jews that Jesus was the Messiah. [6]But when they opposed Paul and became abusive, he shook out his clothes in protest and said to them, "Your blood be on your own heads! I am innocent of it. From now on I will go to the Gentiles."

[7]Then Paul left the synagogue and went next door to the house of Titius Justus, a worshiper of God. [8]Crispus, the synagogue leader, and his entire household believed in the Lord; and many of the Corinthians who heard Paul believed and were baptized.

[9]One night the Lord spoke to Paul in a vision: "Do not be afraid; keep on speaking, do not be silent. [10]For I am with you, and no one is going to attack and harm you, because I have many people in this city." [11]So Paul stayed in Corinth for a year and a half, teaching them the word of God.

[12]While Gallio was proconsul of Achaia, the Jews of Corinth made a united attack on Paul and brought him to the place of judgment. [13]"This man," they charged, "is persuading the people to worship God in ways contrary to the law."

[14]Just as Paul was about to speak, Gallio said to them, "If you Jews were making a complaint about some misdemeanor or serious crime, it would be reasonable for me to listen to you. [15]But since it involves questions about words and names and your own law — settle the matter yourselves. I will not be a judge of such things." [16]So he drove them off. [17]Then the crowd there turned on Sosthenes the synagogue leader and

beat him in front of the proconsul; and Gallio showed no concern whatever.

Priscilla, Aquila and Apollos

[18] Paul stayed on in Corinth for some time. Then he left the brothers and sisters and sailed for Syria, accompanied by Priscilla and Aquila. Before he sailed, he had his hair cut off at Cenchreae because of a vow he had taken. [19] They arrived at Ephesus, where Paul left Priscilla and Aquila. He himself went into the synagogue and reasoned with the Jews. [20] When they asked him to spend more time with them, he declined. [21] But as he left, he promised, "I will come back if it is God's will." Then he set sail from Ephesus. [22] When he landed at Caesarea, he went up to Jerusalem and greeted the church and then went down to Antioch.

[23] After spending some time in Antioch, Paul set out from there and traveled from place to place throughout the region of Galatia and Phrygia, strengthening all the disciples.

[24] Meanwhile a Jew named Apollos, a native of Alexandria, came to Ephesus. He was a learned man, with a thorough knowledge of the Scriptures. [25] He had been instructed in the way of the Lord, and he spoke with great fervor[a] and taught about Jesus accurately, though he knew only the baptism of John. [26] He began to speak boldly in the synagogue. When Priscilla and Aquila heard him, they invited him to their home and explained to him the way of God more adequately.

[27] When Apollos wanted to go to Achaia, the brothers and sisters encouraged him and wrote to the disciples there to welcome him. When he arrived, he was a great help to those who by grace had believed. [28] For he vigorously refuted his Jewish opponents in public debate, proving from the Scriptures that Jesus was the Messiah.

Paul in Ephesus

19 While Apollos was at Corinth, Paul took the road through the interior and arrived at Ephesus. There he found some disciples [2] and asked them, "Did you receive the Holy Spirit when[b] you believed?"

They answered, "No, we have not even heard that there is a Holy Spirit."

[3] So Paul asked, "Then what baptism did you receive?"

"John's baptism," they replied.

[4] Paul said, "John's baptism was a baptism of repentance. He told the people to believe in the one coming after him, that is, in Jesus." [5] On hearing this, they were baptized in the name of the Lord Jesus. [6] When Paul placed his hands on them, the Holy Spirit came on them, and they spoke in

[a] 25 Or *with fervor in the Spirit*   [b] 2 Or *after*

tongues[a] and prophesied. [7]There were about twelve men in all.

[8]Paul entered the synagogue and spoke boldly there for three months, arguing persuasively about the kingdom of God. [9]But some of them became obstinate; they refused to believe and publicly maligned the Way. So Paul left them. He took the disciples with him and had discussions daily in the lecture hall of Tyrannus. [10]This went on for two years, so that all the Jews and Greeks who lived in the province of Asia heard the word of the Lord.

[11]God did extraordinary miracles through Paul, [12]so that even handkerchiefs and aprons that had touched him were taken to the sick, and their illnesses were cured and the evil spirits left them.

[13]Some Jews who went around driving out evil spirits tried to invoke the name of the Lord Jesus over those who were demon-possessed. They would say, "In the name of the Jesus whom Paul preaches, I command you to come out." [14]Seven sons of Sceva, a Jewish chief priest, were doing this. [15]One day the evil spirit answered them, "Jesus I know, and Paul I know about, but who are you?" [16]Then the man who had the evil spirit jumped on them and overpowered them all. He gave them such a beating that they ran out of the house naked and bleeding.

[17]When this became known to the Jews and Greeks living in Ephesus, they were all seized with fear, and the name of the Lord Jesus was held in high honor. [18]Many of those who believed now came and openly confessed what they had done. [19]A number who had practiced sorcery brought their scrolls together and burned them publicly. When they calculated the value of the scrolls, the total came to fifty thousand drachmas.[b] [20]In this way the word of the Lord spread widely and grew in power.

[21]After all this had happened, Paul decided[c] to go to Jerusalem, passing through Macedonia and Achaia. "After I have been there," he said, "I must visit Rome also." [22]He sent two of his helpers, Timothy and Erastus, to Macedonia, while he stayed in the province of Asia a little longer.

The Riot in Ephesus

[23]About that time there arose a great disturbance about the Way. [24]A silversmith named Demetrius, who made silver shrines of Artemis, brought in a lot of business for the craftsmen there. [25]He called them together, along with the workers in related trades, and said: "You know, my friends, that we receive a good income from this business. [26]And you see and hear how this fellow Paul has convinced and led

---

[a] 6 Or *other languages*   [b] 19 A drachma was a silver coin worth about a day's wages.   [c] 21 Or *decided in the Spirit*

astray large numbers of people here in Ephesus and in practically the whole province of Asia. He says that gods made by human hands are no gods at all. **27** There is danger not only that our trade will lose its good name, but also that the temple of the great goddess Artemis will be discredited; and the goddess herself, who is worshiped throughout the province of Asia and the world, will be robbed of her divine majesty."

28 When they heard this, they were furious and began shouting: "Great is Artemis of the Ephesians!" **29** Soon the whole city was in an uproar. The people seized Gaius and Aristarchus, Paul's traveling companions from Macedonia, and all of them rushed into the theater together. **30** Paul wanted to appear before the crowd, but the disciples would not let him. **31** Even some of the officials of the province, friends of Paul, sent him a message begging him not to venture into the theater.

32 The assembly was in confusion: Some were shouting one thing, some another. Most of the people did not even know why they were there. **33** The Jews in the crowd pushed Alexander to the front, and they shouted instructions to him. He motioned for silence in order to make a defense before the people. **34** But when they realized he was a Jew, they all shouted in unison for about two hours: "Great is Artemis of the Ephesians!"

35 The city clerk quieted the crowd and said: "Fellow Ephesians, doesn't all the world know that the city of Ephesus is the guardian of the temple of the great Artemis and of her image, which fell from heaven? **36** Therefore, since these facts are undeniable, you ought to calm down and not do anything rash. **37** You have brought these men here, though they have neither robbed temples nor blasphemed our goddess. **38** If, then, Demetrius and his fellow craftsmen have a grievance against anybody, the courts are open and there are proconsuls. They can press charges. **39** If there is anything further you want to bring up, it must be settled in a legal assembly. **40** As it is, we are in danger of being charged with rioting because of what happened today. In that case we would not be able to account for this commotion, since there is no reason for it." **41** After he had said this, he dismissed the assembly.

Through Macedonia and Greece

20 When the uproar had ended, Paul sent for the disciples and, after encouraging them, said goodbye and set out for Macedonia. **2** He traveled through that area, speaking many words of encouragement to the people, and finally arrived in Greece, **3** where he stayed three months. Because some Jews had plotted against him just as he was about to sail for Syria, he decided to go back through Macedonia. [4]He was accompanied by Sopater son of Pyrrhus from Berea, Aristarchus and Secundus from Thessalonica, Gaius from Derbe, Timothy also, and Tychicus and Trophimus from the province of Asia. [5]These men went on ahead and waited for us at Troas. [6]But we sailed from Philippi after the Festival of Unleavened Bread, and five days later joined the others at Troas, where we stayed seven days.

Eutychus Raised From the Dead at Troas

[7]On the first day of the week we came together to break bread. Paul spoke to the people and, because he intended to leave the next day, kept on talking until midnight. [8]There were many lamps in the upstairs room where we were meeting. [9]Seated in a window was a young man named Eutychus, who was sinking into a deep sleep as Paul talked on and on. When he was sound asleep, he fell to the ground from the third story and was picked up dead. [10]Paul went down, threw himself on the young man and put his arms around him. "Don't be alarmed," he said. "He's alive!" [11]Then he went upstairs again and broke bread and ate. After talking until daylight, he left. [12]The people took the young man home alive and were greatly comforted.

Paul's Farewell to the Ephesian Elders

[13]We went on ahead to the ship and sailed for Assos, where we were going to take Paul aboard. He had made this arrangement because he was going there on foot. [14]When he met us at Assos, we took him aboard and went on to Mitylene. [15]The next day we set sail from there and arrived off Chios. The day after that we crossed over to Samos, and on the following day arrived at Miletus. [16]Paul had decided to sail past Ephesus to avoid spending time in the province of Asia, for he was in a hurry to reach Jerusalem, if possible, by the day of Pentecost.

[17]From Miletus, Paul sent to Ephesus for the elders of the church. [18]When they arrived, he said to them: "You know how I lived the whole time I was with you, from the first day I came into the province of Asia. [19]I served the Lord with great humility and with tears and in the midst of severe testing by the plots of my Jewish opponents. [20]You know that I have not hesitated to preach anything that would be helpful to you but have taught you publicly and from house to house. [21]I have declared to both Jews and Greeks that they must turn to God in repentance and have faith in our Lord Jesus.

[22]"And now, compelled by the Spirit, I am going to Jerusalem, not knowing what will happen to me there. [23]I only know that in every

city the Holy Spirit warns me that prison and hardships are facing me. **24** However, I consider my life worth nothing to me; my only aim is to finish the race and complete the task the Lord Jesus has given me—the task of testifying to the good news of God's grace.

25 "Now I know that none of you among whom I have gone about preaching the kingdom will ever see me again. **26** Therefore, I declare to you today that I am innocent of the blood of any of you. **27** For I have not hesitated to proclaim to you the whole will of God. **28** Keep watch over yourselves and all the flock of which the Holy Spirit has made you overseers. Be shepherds of the church of God,*ᵃ* which he bought with his own blood.*ᵇ* **29** I know that after I leave, savage wolves will come in among you and will not spare the flock. **30** Even from your own number men will arise and distort the truth in order to draw away disciples after them. **31** So be on your guard! Remember that for three years I never stopped warning each of you night and day with tears.

32 "Now I commit you to God and to the word of his grace, which can build you up and give you an inheritance among all those who are sanctified. **33** I have not coveted anyone's silver or gold or clothing. **34** You yourselves know that these hands of mine

have supplied my own needs and the needs of my companions. **35** In everything I did, I showed you that by this kind of hard work we must help the weak, remembering the words the Lord Jesus himself said: 'It is more blessed to give than to receive.'"

36 When Paul had finished speaking, he knelt down with all of them and prayed. **37** They all wept as they embraced him and kissed him. **38** What grieved them most was his statement that they would never see his face again. Then they accompanied him to the ship.

On to Jerusalem

21 After we had torn ourselves away from them, we put out to sea and sailed straight to Kos. The next day we went to Rhodes and from there to Patara. **2** We found a ship crossing over to Phoenicia, went on board and set sail. **3** After sighting Cyprus and passing to the south of it, we sailed on to Syria. We landed at Tyre, where our ship was to unload its cargo. **4** We sought out the disciples there and stayed with them seven days. Through the Spirit they urged Paul not to go on to Jerusalem. **5** When it was time to leave, we left and continued on our way. All of them, including wives and children, accompanied us out of the city, and there on the beach we knelt to pray. **6** After saying goodbye to

---

ᵃ 28 Many manuscripts *of the Lord*   *ᵇ 28* Or *with the blood of his own Son.*

each other, we went aboard the ship, and they returned home.

⁷We continued our voyage from Tyre and landed at Ptolemais, where we greeted the brothers and sisters and stayed with them for a day. ⁸Leaving the next day, we reached Caesarea and stayed at the house of Philip the evangelist, one of the Seven. ⁹He had four unmarried daughters who prophesied.

¹⁰After we had been there a number of days, a prophet named Agabus came down from Judea. ¹¹Coming over to us, he took Paul's belt, tied his own hands and feet with it and said, "The Holy Spirit says, 'In this way the Jewish leaders in Jerusalem will bind the owner of this belt and will hand him over to the Gentiles.'"

¹²When we heard this, we and the people there pleaded with Paul not to go up to Jerusalem. ¹³Then Paul answered, "Why are you weeping and breaking my heart? I am ready not only to be bound, but also to die in Jerusalem for the name of the Lord Jesus." ¹⁴When he would not be dissuaded, we gave up and said, "The Lord's will be done."

¹⁵After this, we started on our way up to Jerusalem. ¹⁶Some of the disciples from Caesarea accompanied us and brought us to the home of Mnason, where we were to stay. He was a man from Cyprus and one of the early disciples.

Paul's Arrival at Jerusalem

¹⁷When we arrived at Jerusalem, the brothers and sisters received us warmly. ¹⁸The next day Paul and the rest of us went to see James, and all the elders were present. ¹⁹Paul greeted them and reported in detail what God had done among the Gentiles through his ministry.

²⁰When they heard this, they praised God. Then they said to Paul: "You see, brother, how many thousands of Jews have believed, and all of them are zealous for the law. ²¹They have been informed that you teach all the Jews who live among the Gentiles to turn away from Moses, telling them not to circumcise their children or live according to our customs. ²²What shall we do? They will certainly hear that you have come, ²³so do what we tell you. There are four men with us who have made a vow. ²⁴Take these men, join in their purification rites and pay their expenses, so that they can have their heads shaved. Then everyone will know there is no truth in these reports about you, but that you yourself are living in obedience to the law. ²⁵As for the Gentile believers, we have written to them our decision that they should abstain from food sacrificed to idols, from blood, from the meat of strangled animals and from sexual immorality."

²⁶The next day Paul took the men and purified himself along

with them. Then he went to the temple to give notice of the date when the days of purification would end and the offering would be made for each of them.

Paul Arrested

27When the seven days were nearly over, some Jews from the province of Asia saw Paul at the temple. They stirred up the whole crowd and seized him, **28**shouting, "Fellow Israelites, help us! This is the man who teaches everyone everywhere against our people and our law and this place. And besides, he has brought Greeks into the temple and defiled this holy place." **29**(They had previously seen Trophimus the Ephesian in the city with Paul and assumed that Paul had brought him into the temple.)

30The whole city was aroused, and the people came running from all directions. Seizing Paul, they dragged him from the temple, and immediately the gates were shut. **31**While they were trying to kill him, news reached the commander of the Roman troops that the whole city of Jerusalem was in an uproar. **32**He at once took some officers and soldiers and ran down to the crowd. When the rioters saw the commander and his soldiers, they stopped beating Paul.

33The commander came up and arrested him and ordered him to be bound with two chains. Then he asked who he was and what he had done. **34**Some in the crowd shouted one thing and some another, and since the commander could not get at the truth because of the uproar, he ordered that Paul be taken into the barracks. **35**When Paul reached the steps, the violence of the mob was so great he had to be carried by the soldiers. **36**The crowd that followed kept shouting, "Get rid of him!"

Paul Speaks to the Crowd

37As the soldiers were about to take Paul into the barracks, he asked the commander, "May I say something to you?"

"Do you speak Greek?" he replied. **38**"Aren't you the Egyptian who started a revolt and led four thousand terrorists out into the wilderness some time ago?"

39Paul answered, "I am a Jew, from Tarsus in Cilicia, a citizen of no ordinary city. Please let me speak to the people."

40After receiving the commander's permission, Paul stood on the steps and motioned to the crowd. When they were all silent, he said to them in Aramaic[a]: **1**"Brothers and fathers, listen now to my defense."

2When they heard him speak to them in Aramaic, they became very quiet.

Then Paul said: **3**"I am a Jew,

22

---

a 40 Or possibly *Hebrew*; also in 22:2

born in Tarsus of Cilicia, but brought up in this city. I studied under Gamaliel and was thoroughly trained in the law of our ancestors. I was just as zealous for God as any of you are today. ⁴I persecuted the followers of this Way to their death, arresting both men and women and throwing them into prison, ⁵as the high priest and all the Council can themselves testify. I even obtained letters from them to their associates in Damascus, and went there to bring these people as prisoners to Jerusalem to be punished.

⁶"About noon as I came near Damascus, suddenly a bright light from heaven flashed around me. ⁷I fell to the ground and heard a voice say to me, 'Saul! Saul! Why do you persecute me?'

⁸" 'Who are you, Lord?' I asked.

" 'I am Jesus of Nazareth, whom you are persecuting,' he replied. ⁹My companions saw the light, but they did not understand the voice of him who was speaking to me.

¹⁰" 'What shall I do, Lord?' I asked.

" 'Get up,' the Lord said, 'and go into Damascus. There you will be told all that you have been assigned to do.' ¹¹My companions led me by the hand into Damascus, because the brilliance of the light had blinded me.

¹²"A man named Ananias came to see me. He was a devout observer of the law and highly respected by all the Jews living there. ¹³He stood beside me and said, 'Brother Saul, receive your sight!' And at that very moment I was able to see him.

¹⁴"Then he said: 'The God of our ancestors has chosen you to know his will and to see the Righteous One and to hear words from his mouth. ¹⁵You will be his witness to all people of what you have seen and heard. ¹⁶And now what are you waiting for? Get up, be baptized and wash your sins away, calling on his name.'

¹⁷"When I returned to Jerusalem and was praying at the temple, I fell into a trance ¹⁸and saw the Lord speaking to me. 'Quick!' he said. 'Leave Jerusalem immediately, because the people here will not accept your testimony about me.'

¹⁹" 'Lord,' I replied, 'these people know that I went from one synagogue to another to imprison and beat those who believe in you. ²⁰And when the blood of your martyr*ᵃ* Stephen was shed, I stood there giving my approval and guarding the clothes of those who were killing him.'

²¹"Then the Lord said to me, 'Go; I will send you far away to the Gentiles.'"

Paul the Roman Citizen

²²The crowd listened to Paul until he said this. Then they raised their voices and shouted,

ᵃ 20 Or *witness*

"Rid the earth of him! He's not fit to live!"

23 As they were shouting and throwing off their cloaks and flinging dust into the air, 24 the commander ordered that Paul be taken into the barracks. He directed that he be flogged and interrogated in order to find out why the people were shouting at him like this. 25 As they stretched him out to flog him, Paul said to the centurion standing there, "Is it legal for you to flog a Roman citizen who hasn't even been found guilty?"

26 When the centurion heard this, he went to the commander and reported it. "What are you going to do?" he asked. "This man is a Roman citizen."

27 The commander went to Paul and asked, "Tell me, are you a Roman citizen?"

"Yes, I am," he answered.

28 Then the commander said, "I had to pay a lot of money for my citizenship."

"But I was born a citizen," Paul replied.

29 Those who were about to interrogate him withdrew immediately. The commander himself was alarmed when he realized that he had put Paul, a Roman citizen, in chains.

Paul Before the Sanhedrin

30 The commander wanted to find out exactly why Paul was being accused by the Jews. So the next day he released him and ordered the chief priests and all the members of the Sanhedrin to assemble. Then he brought Paul and had him stand before them.

23 Paul looked straight at the Sanhedrin and said, "My brothers, I have fulfilled my duty to God in all good conscience to this day." 2 At this the high priest Ananias ordered those standing near Paul to strike him on the mouth. 3 Then Paul said to him, "God will strike you, you whitewashed wall! You sit there to judge me according to the law, yet you yourself violate the law by commanding that I be struck!"

4 Those who were standing near Paul said, "How dare you insult God's high priest!"

5 Paul replied, "Brothers, I did not realize that he was the high priest; for it is written: 'Do not speak evil about the ruler of your people.'*a*"

6 Then Paul, knowing that some of them were Sadducees and the others Pharisees, called out in the Sanhedrin, "My brothers, I am a Pharisee, descended from Pharisees. I stand on trial because of the hope of the resurrection of the dead." 7 When he said this, a dispute broke out between the Pharisees and the Sadducees, and the assembly was divided. 8 (The Sadducees say that there is no resurrection, and that there are neither angels nor spirits, but

a 5 Exodus 22:28

the Pharisees believe all these things.)

⁹There was a great uproar, and some of the teachers of the law who were Pharisees stood up and argued vigorously. "We find nothing wrong with this man," they said. "What if a spirit or an angel has spoken to him?" ¹⁰The dispute became so violent that the commander was afraid Paul would be torn to pieces by them. He ordered the troops to go down and take him away from them by force and bring him into the barracks.

¹¹The following night the Lord stood near Paul and said, "Take courage! As you have testified about me in Jerusalem, so you must also testify in Rome."

The Plot to Kill Paul

¹²The next morning some Jews formed a conspiracy and bound themselves with an oath not to eat or drink until they had killed Paul. ¹³More than forty men were involved in this plot. ¹⁴They went to the chief priests and the elders and said, "We have taken a solemn oath not to eat anything until we have killed Paul. ¹⁵Now then, you and the Sanhedrin petition the commander to bring him before you on the pretext of wanting more accurate information about his case. We are ready to kill him before he gets here."

¹⁶But when the son of Paul's sister heard of this plot, he went into the barracks and told Paul.

¹⁷Then Paul called one of the centurions and said, "Take this young man to the commander; he has something to tell him." ¹⁸So he took him to the commander.

The centurion said, "Paul, the prisoner, sent for me and asked me to bring this young man to you because he has something to tell you."

¹⁹The commander took the young man by the hand, drew him aside and asked, "What is it you want to tell me?"

²⁰He said: "Some Jews have agreed to ask you to bring Paul before the Sanhedrin tomorrow on the pretext of wanting more accurate information about him. ²¹Don't give in to them, because more than forty of them are waiting in ambush for him. They have taken an oath not to eat or drink until they have killed him. They are ready now, waiting for your consent to their request."

²²The commander dismissed the young man with this warning: "Don't tell anyone that you have reported this to me."

Paul Transferred to Caesarea

²³Then he called two of his centurions and ordered them, "Get ready a detachment of two hundred soldiers, seventy horsemen and two hundred spearmen[a] to

a 23 The meaning of the Greek for this word is uncertain.

go to Caesarea at nine tonight. 24 Provide horses for Paul so that he may be taken safely to Governor Felix."

25 He wrote a letter as follows:

26 Claudius Lysias,

To His Excellency, Governor Felix:

Greetings.

27 This man was seized by the Jews and they were about to kill him, but I came with my troops and rescued him, for I had learned that he is a Roman citizen. 28 I wanted to know why they were accusing him, so I brought him to their Sanhedrin. 29 I found that the accusation had to do with questions about their law, but there was no charge against him that deserved death or imprisonment. 30 When I was informed of a plot to be carried out against the man, I sent him to you at once. I also ordered his accusers to present to you their case against him.

31 So the soldiers, carrying out their orders, took Paul with them during the night and brought him as far as Antipatris. 32 The next day they let the cavalry go on with him, while they returned to the barracks. 33 When the cavalry arrived in Caesarea, they delivered the letter to the governor and handed Paul over to him. 34 The governor read the letter and asked what province he was from. Learning that he was from Cilicia, 35 he said, "I will hear your case when your accusers get here." Then he ordered that Paul be kept under guard in Herod's palace.

Paul's Trial Before Felix

24 Five days later the high priest Ananias went down to Caesarea with some of the elders and a lawyer named Tertullus, and they brought their charges against Paul before the governor. 2 When Paul was called in, Tertullus presented his case before Felix: "We have enjoyed a long period of peace under you, and your foresight has brought about reforms in this nation. 3 Everywhere and in every way, most excellent Felix, we acknowledge this with profound gratitude. 4 But in order not to weary you further, I would request that you be kind enough to hear us briefly.

5 "We have found this man to be a troublemaker, stirring up riots among the Jews all over the world. He is a ringleader of the Nazarene sect 6 and even tried to desecrate the temple; so we seized him. [7]a 8 By examining him yourself you will be able to

---

a 6-8 Some manuscripts include here *him, and we would have judged him in accordance with our law.* 7 *But the commander Lysias came and took him from us with much violence,* 8 *ordering his accusers to come before you.*

learn the truth about all these charges we are bringing against him."

⁹The other Jews joined in the accusation, asserting that these things were true.

¹⁰When the governor motioned for him to speak, Paul replied: "I know that for a number of years you have been a judge over this nation; so I gladly make my defense. ¹¹You can easily verify that no more than twelve days ago I went up to Jerusalem to worship. ¹²My accusers did not find me arguing with anyone at the temple, or stirring up a crowd in the synagogues or anywhere else in the city. ¹³And they cannot prove to you the charges they are now making against me. ¹⁴However, I admit that I worship the God of our ancestors as a follower of the Way, which they call a sect. I believe everything that is in accordance with the Law and that is written in the Prophets, ¹⁵and I have the same hope in God as these men themselves have, that there will be a resurrection of both the righteous and the wicked. ¹⁶So I strive always to keep my conscience clear before God and man.

¹⁷"After an absence of several years, I came to Jerusalem to bring my people gifts for the poor and to present offerings. ¹⁸I was ceremonially clean when they found me in the temple courts doing this. There was no crowd with me, nor was I involved in any disturbance. ¹⁹But there are some Jews from the province of Asia, who ought to be here before you and bring charges if they have anything against me. ²⁰Or these who are here should state what crime they found in me when I stood before the Sanhedrin— ²¹unless it was this one thing I shouted as I stood in their presence: 'It is concerning the resurrection of the dead that I am on trial before you today.'"

²²Then Felix, who was well acquainted with the Way, adjourned the proceedings. "When Lysias the commander comes," he said, "I will decide your case." ²³He ordered the centurion to keep Paul under guard but to give him some freedom and permit his friends to take care of his needs.

²⁴Several days later Felix came with his wife Drusilla, who was Jewish. He sent for Paul and listened to him as he spoke about faith in Christ Jesus. ²⁵As Paul talked about righteousness, self-control and the judgment to come, Felix was afraid and said, "That's enough for now! You may leave. When I find it convenient, I will send for you." ²⁶At the same time he was hoping that Paul would offer him a bribe, so he sent for him frequently and talked with him.

²⁷When two years had passed, Felix was succeeded by Porcius Festus, but because Felix wanted to grant a favor to the Jews, he left Paul in prison.

Paul's Trial Before Festus

25 Three days after arriving in the province, Festus went up from Caesarea to Jerusalem, ²where the chief priests and the Jewish leaders appeared before him and presented the charges against Paul. ³They requested Festus, as a favor to them, to have Paul transferred to Jerusalem, for they were preparing an ambush to kill him along the way. ⁴Festus answered, "Paul is being held at Caesarea, and I myself am going there soon. ⁵Let some of your leaders come with me, and if the man has done anything wrong, they can press charges against him there."

⁶After spending eight or ten days with them, Festus went down to Caesarea. The next day he convened the court and ordered that Paul be brought before him. ⁷When Paul came in, the Jews who had come down from Jerusalem stood around him. They brought many serious charges against him, but they could not prove them.

⁸Then Paul made his defense: "I have done nothing wrong against the Jewish law or against the temple or against Caesar."

⁹Festus, wishing to do the Jews a favor, said to Paul, "Are you willing to go up to Jerusalem and stand trial before me there on these charges?"

¹⁰Paul answered: "I am now standing before Caesar's court, where I ought to be tried. I have not done any wrong to the Jews, as you yourself know very well. ¹¹If, however, I am guilty of doing anything deserving death, I do not refuse to die. But if the charges brought against me by these Jews are not true, no one has the right to hand me over to them. I appeal to Caesar!"

¹²After Festus had conferred with his council, he declared: "You have appealed to Caesar. To Caesar you will go!"

Festus Consults King Agrippa

¹³A few days later King Agrippa and Bernice arrived at Caesarea to pay their respects to Festus. ¹⁴Since they were spending many days there, Festus discussed Paul's case with the king. He said: "There is a man here whom Felix left as a prisoner. ¹⁵When I went to Jerusalem, the chief priests and the elders of the Jews brought charges against him and asked that he be condemned.

¹⁶"I told them that it is not the Roman custom to hand over anyone before they have faced their accusers and have had an opportunity to defend themselves against the charges. ¹⁷When they came here with me, I did not delay the case, but convened the court the next day and ordered the man to be brought in. ¹⁸When his accusers got up to speak, they did not charge him with any of the crimes I had expected. ¹⁹Instead, they had some points of dispute with him about their own

religion and about a dead man named Jesus who Paul claimed was alive. ²⁰I was at a loss how to investigate such matters; so I asked if he would be willing to go to Jerusalem and stand trial there on these charges. ²¹But when Paul made his appeal to be held over for the Emperor's decision, I ordered him held until I could send him to Caesar."

²²Then Agrippa said to Festus, "I would like to hear this man myself."

He replied, "Tomorrow you will hear him."

Paul Before Agrippa

²³The next day Agrippa and Bernice came with great pomp and entered the audience room with the high-ranking military officers and the prominent men of the city. At the command of Festus, Paul was brought in. ²⁴Festus said: "King Agrippa, and all who are present with us, you see this man! The whole Jewish community has petitioned me about him in Jerusalem and here in Caesarea, shouting that he ought not to live any longer. ²⁵I found he had done nothing deserving of death, but because he made his appeal to the Emperor I decided to send him to Rome. ²⁶But I have nothing definite to write to His Majesty about him. Therefore I have brought him before all of you, and especially before you, King Agrippa, so that as a result of this investigation I may have some-

thing to write. ²⁷For I think it is unreasonable to send a prisoner on to Rome without specifying the charges against him."

26

Then Agrippa said to Paul, "You have permission to speak for yourself."

So Paul motioned with his hand and began his defense: ²"King Agrippa, I consider myself fortunate to stand before you today as I make my defense against all the accusations of the Jews, ³and especially so because you are well acquainted with all the Jewish customs and controversies. Therefore, I beg you to listen to me patiently.

⁴"The Jewish people all know the way I have lived ever since I was a child, from the beginning of my life in my own country, and also in Jerusalem. ⁵They have known me for a long time and can testify, if they are willing, that I conformed to the strictest sect of our religion, living as a Pharisee. ⁶And now it is because of my hope in what God has promised our ancestors that I am on trial today. ⁷This is the promise our twelve tribes are hoping to see fulfilled as they earnestly serve God day and night. King Agrippa, it is because of this hope that these Jews are accusing me. ⁸Why should any of you consider it incredible that God raises the dead?

⁹"I too was convinced that I ought to do all that was possible to oppose the name of Jesus of Nazareth. ¹⁰And that is just what I did

in Jerusalem. On the authority of the chief priests I put many of the Lord's people in prison, and when they were put to death, I cast my vote against them. **11** Many a time I went from one synagogue to another to have them punished, and I tried to force them to blaspheme. I was so obsessed with persecuting them that I even hunted them down in foreign cities.

12 "On one of these journeys I was going to Damascus with the authority and commission of the chief priests. **13** About noon, King Agrippa, as I was on the road, I saw a light from heaven, brighter than the sun, blazing around me and my companions. **14** We all fell to the ground, and I heard a voice saying to me in Aramaic,*ª* 'Saul, Saul, why do you persecute me? It is hard for you to kick against the goads.'

15 "Then I asked, 'Who are you, Lord?'

" 'I am Jesus, whom you are persecuting,' the Lord replied. **16** 'Now get up and stand on your feet. I have appeared to you to appoint you as a servant and as a witness of what you have seen and will see of me. **17** I will rescue you from your own people and from the Gentiles. I am sending you to them **18** to open their eyes and turn them from darkness to light, and from the power of Satan to God, so that they may receive forgiveness of sins and a

place among those who are sanctified by faith in me.'

19 "So then, King Agrippa, I was not disobedient to the vision from heaven. **20** First to those in Damascus, then to those in Jerusalem and in all Judea, and then to the Gentiles, I preached that they should repent and turn to God and demonstrate their repentance by their deeds. **21** That is why some Jews seized me in the temple courts and tried to kill me. **22** But God has helped me to this very day; so I stand here and testify to small and great alike. I am saying nothing beyond what the prophets and Moses said would happen — **23** that the Messiah would suffer and, as the first to rise from the dead, would bring the message of light to his own people and to the Gentiles."

24 At this point Festus interrupted Paul's defense. "You are out of your mind, Paul!" he shouted. "Your great learning is driving you insane."

25 "I am not insane, most excellent Festus," Paul replied. "What I am saying is true and reasonable. **26** The king is familiar with these things, and I can speak freely to him. I am convinced that none of this has escaped his notice, because it was not done in a corner. **27** King Agrippa, do you believe the prophets? I know you do."

28 Then Agrippa said to Paul, "Do you think that in such a short

ª 14 Or *Hebrew*

time you can persuade me to be a Christian?"

²⁹ Paul replied, "Short time or long — I pray to God that not only you but all who are listening to me today may become what I am, except for these chains."

³⁰ The king rose, and with him the governor and Bernice and those sitting with them. ³¹ After they left the room, they began saying to one another, "This man is not doing anything that deserves death or imprisonment."

³² Agrippa said to Festus, "This man could have been set free if he had not appealed to Caesar."

Paul Sails for Rome

27 When it was decided that we would sail for Italy, Paul and some other prisoners were handed over to a centurion named Julius, who belonged to the Imperial Regiment. ²We boarded a ship from Adramyttium about to sail for ports along the coast of the province of Asia, and we put out to sea. Aristarchus, a Macedonian from Thessalonica, was with us.

³ The next day we landed at Sidon; and Julius, in kindness to Paul, allowed him to go to his friends so they might provide for his needs. ⁴ From there we put out to sea again and passed to the lee of Cyprus because the winds were against us. ⁵ When we had sailed across the open sea off the coast of Cilicia and Pamphylia, we landed at Myra in Lycia. ⁶ There the centurion found an Alexandrian ship sailing for Italy and put us on board. ⁷ We made slow headway for many days and had difficulty arriving off Cnidus. When the wind did not allow us to hold our course, we sailed to the lee of Crete, opposite Salmone. ⁸ We moved along the coast with difficulty and came to a place called Fair Havens, near the town of Lasea.

⁹ Much time had been lost, and sailing had already become dangerous because by now it was after the Day of Atonement.ᵃ So Paul warned them, ¹⁰ "Men, I can see that our voyage is going to be disastrous and bring great loss to ship and cargo, and to our own lives also." ¹¹ But the centurion, instead of listening to what Paul said, followed the advice of the pilot and of the owner of the ship. ¹² Since the harbor was unsuitable to winter in, the majority decided that we should sail on, hoping to reach Phoenix and winter there. This was a harbor in Crete, facing both southwest and northwest.

The Storm

¹³ When a gentle south wind began to blow, they saw their opportunity; so they weighed anchor and sailed along the shore of Crete. ¹⁴ Before very long, a wind of hurricane force, called the

ᵃ 9 That is, Yom Kippur

Northeaster, swept down from the island. [15]The ship was caught by the storm and could not head into the wind; so we gave way to it and were driven along. [16]As we passed to the lee of a small island called Cauda, we were hardly able to make the lifeboat secure, [17]so the men hoisted it aboard. Then they passed ropes under the ship itself to hold it together. Because they were afraid they would run aground on the sandbars of Syrtis, they lowered the sea anchor[a] and let the ship be driven along. [18]We took such a violent battering from the storm that the next day they began to throw the cargo overboard. [19]On the third day, they threw the ship's tackle overboard with their own hands. [20]When neither sun nor stars appeared for many days and the storm continued raging, we finally gave up all hope of being saved.

[21]After they had gone a long time without food, Paul stood up before them and said: "Men, you should have taken my advice not to sail from Crete; then you would have spared yourselves this damage and loss. [22]But now I urge you to keep up your courage, because not one of you will be lost; only the ship will be destroyed. [23]Last night an angel of the God to whom I belong and whom I serve stood beside me [24]and said, 'Do not be afraid, Paul. You must stand trial before Caesar; and God has graciously given you the lives of all who sail with you.' [25]So keep up your courage, men, for I have faith in God that it will happen just as he told me. [26]Nevertheless, we must run aground on some island."

The Shipwreck

[27]On the fourteenth night we were still being driven across the Adriatic[b] Sea, when about midnight the sailors sensed they were approaching land. [28]They took soundings and found that the water was a hundred and twenty feet[c] deep. A short time later they took soundings again and found it was ninety feet[d] deep. [29]Fearing that we would be dashed against the rocks, they dropped four anchors from the stern and prayed for daylight. [30]In an attempt to escape from the ship, the sailors let the lifeboat down into the sea, pretending they were going to lower some anchors from the bow. [31]Then Paul said to the centurion and the soldiers, "Unless these men stay with the ship, you cannot be saved." [32]So the soldiers cut the ropes that held the lifeboat and let it drift away.

[33]Just before dawn Paul urged them all to eat. "For the last fourteen days," he said, "you have been in constant suspense and have gone without food—you haven't eaten anything. [34]Now I urge you to take some food. You

---

[a] 17 Or the sails   [b] 27 In ancient times the name referred to an area extending well south of Italy.   [c] 28 Or about 37 meters   [d] 28 Or about 27 meters

need it to survive. Not one of you will lose a single hair from his head." ³⁵After he said this, he took some bread and gave thanks to God in front of them all. Then he broke it and began to eat. ³⁶They were all encouraged and ate some food themselves. ³⁷Altogether there were 276 of us on board. ³⁸When they had eaten as much as they wanted, they lightened the ship by throwing the grain into the sea.

³⁹When daylight came, they did not recognize the land, but they saw a bay with a sandy beach, where they decided to run the ship aground if they could. ⁴⁰Cutting loose the anchors, they left them in the sea and at the same time untied the ropes that held the rudders. Then they hoisted the foresail to the wind and made for the beach. ⁴¹But the ship struck a sandbar and ran aground. The bow stuck fast and would not move, and the stern was broken to pieces by the pounding of the surf.

⁴²The soldiers planned to kill the prisoners to prevent any of them from swimming away and escaping. ⁴³But the centurion wanted to spare Paul's life and kept them from carrying out their plan. He ordered those who could swim to jump overboard first and get to land. ⁴⁴The rest were to get there on planks or on other pieces of the ship. In this way everyone reached land safely.

Paul Ashore on Malta

28 Once safely on shore, we found out that the island was called Malta. ²The islanders showed us unusual kindness. They built a fire and welcomed us all because it was raining and cold. ³Paul gathered a pile of brushwood and, as he put it on the fire, a viper, driven out by the heat, fastened itself on his hand. ⁴When the islanders saw the snake hanging from his hand, they said to each other, "This man must be a murderer; for though he escaped from the sea, the goddess Justice has not allowed him to live." ⁵But Paul shook the snake off into the fire and suffered no ill effects. ⁶The people expected him to swell up or suddenly fall dead; but after waiting a long time and seeing nothing unusual happen to him, they changed their minds and said he was a god.

⁷There was an estate nearby that belonged to Publius, the chief official of the island. He welcomed us to his home and showed us generous hospitality for three days. ⁸His father was sick in bed, suffering from fever and dysentery. Paul went in to see him and, after prayer, placed his hands on him and healed him. ⁹When this had happened, the rest of the sick on the island came and were cured. ¹⁰They honored us in many ways; and when we were ready to sail, they furnished us with the supplies we needed.

Paul's Arrival at Rome

11 After three months we put out to sea in a ship that had wintered in the island — it was an Alexandrian ship with the figurehead of the twin gods Castor and Pollux. **12** We put in at Syracuse and stayed there three days. **13** From there we set sail and arrived at Rhegium. The next day the south wind came up, and on the following day we reached Puteoli. **14** There we found some brothers and sisters who invited us to spend a week with them. And so we came to Rome. **15** The brothers and sisters there had heard that we were coming, and they traveled as far as the Forum of Appius and the Three Taverns to meet us. At the sight of these people Paul thanked God and was encouraged. **16** When we got to Rome, Paul was allowed to live by himself, with a soldier to guard him.

Paul Preaches at Rome Under Guard

17 Three days later he called together the local Jewish leaders. When they had assembled, Paul said to them: "My brothers, although I have done nothing against our people or against the customs of our ancestors, I was arrested in Jerusalem and handed over to the Romans. **18** They examined me and wanted to release me, because I was not guilty of any crime deserving death.

19 The Jews objected, so I was compelled to make an appeal to Caesar. I certainly did not intend to bring any charge against my own people. **20** For this reason I have asked to see you and talk with you. It is because of the hope of Israel that I am bound with this chain."

21 They replied, "We have not received any letters from Judea concerning you, and none of our people who have come from there has reported or said anything bad about you. **22** But we want to hear what your views are, for we know that people everywhere are talking against this sect."

23 They arranged to meet Paul on a certain day, and came in even larger numbers to the place where he was staying. He witnessed to them from morning till evening, explaining about the kingdom of God, and from the Law of Moses and from the Prophets he tried to persuade them about Jesus. **24** Some were convinced by what he said, but others would not believe. **25** They disagreed among themselves and began to leave after Paul had made this final statement: "The Holy Spirit spoke the truth to your ancestors when he said through Isaiah the prophet:

26 " 'Go to this people and say,
  "You will be ever hearing but
    never understanding;
  you will be ever seeing but
    never perceiving."

27 For this people's heart has
   become calloused;
 they hardly hear with their
   ears,
 and they have closed their
   eyes.
  Otherwise they might see with
   their eyes,
  hear with their ears,
  understand with their hearts
 and turn, and I would heal
   them.'*a*

28 "Therefore I want you to know that God's salvation has been sent to the Gentiles, and they will listen!" **[29]** *b*

30 For two whole years Paul stayed there in his own rented house and welcomed all who came to see him. **31** He proclaimed the kingdom of God and taught about the Lord Jesus Christ — with all boldness and without hindrance!

---

a 27 Isaiah 6:9,10 (see Septuagint) *b* 29 Some manuscripts include here *After he said this, the Jews left, arguing vigorously among themselves.*

Romans

Introduction:

This letter was written by Paul to the church in Rome in AD 56 or 57 as he was finishing his third missionary journey. Since Paul hoped to go to Jerusalem and then to Rome and Spain, he probably wrote this letter in preparation for his visit.

The theme of this letter is righteousness. Paul teaches in this letter that: (1) no human being is righteous; (2) Jesus Christ is perfectly righteous; (3) if we have faith in Jesus, we are freed from the power of sin, given a new life, and returned to a right relationship with God; (4) we should live Christian lives that are "holy and pleasing to God."

Outline of contents:

Introduction (1:1–17)
No one is righteous (1:18–3:20)
Righteousness through faith (3:21–8:39)
Israel in God's plan (9:1–11:36)
Christian living and relationships (12:1–15:13)
Conclusion and greetings (15:14–16:27)

1 Paul, a servant of Christ Jesus, called to be an apostle and set apart for the gospel of God— ²the gospel he promised beforehand through his prophets in the Holy Scriptures ³regarding his Son, who as to his earthly life*a* was a descendant of David, ⁴and who through the Spirit of holiness was appointed the Son of God in power*b* by his resurrection from the dead: Jesus Christ our Lord. ⁵Through him we received grace and apostleship to call all the Gentiles to the obedience that comes from*c* faith for his name's sake. ⁶And you also are among those Gentiles who are called to belong to Jesus Christ.

⁷To all in Rome who are loved by God and called to be his holy people:

Grace and peace to you from God our Father and from the Lord Jesus Christ.

Paul's Longing to Visit Rome

⁸First, I thank my God through Jesus Christ for all of you, because your faith is being reported all over the world. ⁹God, whom I

---

a 3 Or *who according to the flesh*   *b* 4 Or *was declared with power to be the Son of God*   *c* 5 Or *that is* serve in my spirit in preaching the gospel of his Son, is my witness how constantly I remember you ¹⁰in my prayers at all times; and I pray that now at last by God's will the way may be opened for me to come to you.

¹¹I long to see you so that I may impart to you some spiritual gift to make you strong— ¹²that is, that you and I may be mutually encouraged by each other's faith. ¹³I do not want you to be unaware, brothers and sisters,ᵃ that I planned many times to come to you (but have been prevented from doing so until now) in order that I might have a harvest among you, just as I have had among the other Gentiles.

¹⁴I am obligated both to Greeks and non-Greeks, both to the wise and the foolish. ¹⁵That is why I am so eager to preach the gospel also to you who are in Rome.

¹⁶For I am not ashamed of the gospel, because it is the power of God that brings salvation to everyone who believes: first to the Jew, then to the Gentile. ¹⁷For in the gospel the righteousness of God is revealed—a righteousness that is by faith from first to last,ᵇ just as it is written: "The righteous will live by faith."ᶜ

God's Wrath Against Sinful Humanity

¹⁸The wrath of God is being revealed from heaven against all the godlessness and wickedness of people, who suppress the truth by their wickedness, ¹⁹since what may be known about God is plain to them, because God has made it plain to them. ²⁰For since the creation of the world God's invisible qualities — his eternal power and divine nature — have been clearly seen, being understood from what has been made, so that people are without excuse.

²¹For although they knew God, they neither glorified him as God nor gave thanks to him, but their thinking became futile and their foolish hearts were darkened. ²²Although they claimed to be wise, they became fools ²³and exchanged the glory of the immortal God for images made to look like a mortal human being and birds and animals and reptiles.

²⁴Therefore God gave them over in the sinful desires of their hearts to sexual impurity for the degrading of their bodies with one another. ²⁵They exchanged the truth about God for a lie, and worshiped and served created things rather than the Creator — who is forever praised. Amen.

²⁶Because of this, God gave them over to shameful lusts. Even their women exchanged natural sexual relations for unnatural ones. ²⁷In the same way the men also abandoned natural

---

ᵃ 13 The Greek word for *brothers and sisters* (*adelphoi*) refers here to believers, both men and women, as part of God's family; also in 7:1, 4; 8:12, 29; 10:1; 11:25; 12:1; 15:14, 30; 16:14, 17. ᵇ 17 Or *is from faith to faith* ᶜ 17 Hab. 2:4

relations with women and were inflamed with lust for one another. Men committed shameful acts with other men, and received in themselves the due penalty for their error.

²⁸ Furthermore, just as they did not think it worthwhile to retain the knowledge of God, so God gave them over to a depraved mind, so that they do what ought not to be done. ²⁹ They have become filled with every kind of wickedness, evil, greed and depravity. They are full of envy, murder, strife, deceit and malice. They are gossips, ³⁰ slanderers, God-haters, insolent, arrogant and boastful; they invent ways of doing evil; they disobey their parents; ³¹ they have no understanding, no fidelity, no love, no mercy. ³² Although they know God's righteous decree that those who do such things deserve death, they not only continue to do these very things but also approve of those who practice them.

God's Righteous Judgment

2 You, therefore, have no excuse, you who pass judgment on someone else, for at whatever point you judge another, you are condemning yourself, because you who pass judgment do the same things. ² Now we know that God's judgment against those who do such things is based on truth. ³ So when you, a mere human being, pass judgment on them and yet do the same things, do you think you will escape God's judgment? ⁴ Or do you show contempt for the riches of his kindness, forbearance and patience, not realizing that God's kindness is intended to lead you to repentance?

⁵ But because of your stubbornness and your unrepentant heart, you are storing up wrath against yourself for the day of God's wrath, when his righteous judgment will be revealed. ⁶ God "will repay each person according to what they have done."ᵃ ⁷ To those who by persistence in doing good seek glory, honor and immortality, he will give eternal life. ⁸ But for those who are self-seeking and who reject the truth and follow evil, there will be wrath and anger. ⁹ There will be trouble and distress for every human being who does evil: first for the Jew, then for the Gentile; ¹⁰ but glory, honor and peace for everyone who does good: first for the Jew, then for the Gentile. ¹¹ For God does not show favoritism.

¹² All who sin apart from the law will also perish apart from the law, and all who sin under the law will be judged by the law. ¹³ For it is not those who hear the law who are righteous in God's sight, but it is those who obey the law who will be declared righteous. ¹⁴ (Indeed, when Gentiles, who do not have the law, do by

nature things required by the law, they are a law for themselves, even though they do not have the law. [15] They show that the requirements of the law are written on their hearts, their consciences also bearing witness, and their thoughts sometimes accusing them and at other times even defending them.) [16] This will take place on the day when God judges people's secrets through Jesus Christ, as my gospel declares.

The Jews and the Law

[17] Now you, if you call yourself a Jew; if you rely on the law and boast in God; [18] if you know his will and approve of what is superior because you are instructed by the law; [19] if you are convinced that you are a guide for the blind, a light for those who are in the dark, [20] an instructor of the foolish, a teacher of little children, because you have in the law the embodiment of knowledge and truth — [21] you, then, who teach others, do you not teach yourself? You who preach against stealing, do you steal? [22] You who say that people should not commit adultery, do you commit adultery? You who abhor idols, do you rob temples? [23] You who boast in the law, do you dishonor God by breaking the law? [24] As it is written: "God's name is blasphemed among the Gentiles because of you."[a]
[25] Circumcision has value if you

observe the law, but if you break the law, you have become as though you had not been circumcised. [26] So then, if those who are not circumcised keep the law's requirements, will they not be regarded as though they were circumcised? [27] The one who is not circumcised physically and yet obeys the law will condemn you who, even though you have the[b] written code and circumcision, are a lawbreaker.

[28] A person is not a Jew who is one only outwardly, nor is circumcision merely outward and physical. [29] No, a person is a Jew who is one inwardly; and circumcision is circumcision of the heart, by the Spirit, not by the written code. Such a person's praise is not from other people, but from God.

God's Faithfulness

3 What advantage, then, is there in being a Jew, or what value is there in circumcision? [2] Much in every way! First of all, the Jews have been entrusted with the very words of God.

[3] What if some were unfaithful? Will their unfaithfulness nullify God's faithfulness? [4] Not at all! Let God be true, and every human being a liar. As it is written:

"So that you may be proved
    right when you speak
and prevail when you
    judge."[c]

---

[a] 24 Isaiah 52:5 (see Septuagint); Ezek. 36:20,22   [b] 27 Or who, by means of a
[c] 4 Psalm 51:4

⁵But if our unrighteousness brings out God's righteousness more clearly, what shall we say? That God is unjust in bringing his wrath on us? (I am using a human argument.) ⁶Certainly not! If that were so, how could God judge the world? ⁷Someone might argue, "If my falsehood enhances God's truthfulness and so increases his glory, why am I still condemned as a sinner?" ⁸Why not say — as some slanderously claim that we say — "Let us do evil that good may result"? Their condemnation is just!

No One Is Righteous

⁹What shall we conclude then? Do we have any advantage? Not at all! For we have already made the charge that Jews and Gentiles alike are all under the power of sin. ¹⁰As it is written:

"There is no one righteous, not
    even one;
¹¹   there is no one who
        understands;
    there is no one who seeks
        God.
¹²All have turned away,
    they have together become
        worthless;
    there is no one who does good,
        not even one."ᵃ
¹³"Their throats are open graves;
    their tongues practice
        deceit."ᵇ

"The poison of vipers is on
    their lips."ᶜ
¹⁴   "Their mouths are full of
        cursing and bitterness."ᵈ
¹⁵"Their feet are swift to shed
        blood;
¹⁶   ruin and misery mark their
        ways,
¹⁷and the way of peace they do
        not know."ᵉ
¹⁸   "There is no fear of God
        before their eyes."ᶠ

¹⁹Now we know that whatever the law says, it says to those who are under the law, so that every mouth may be silenced and the whole world held accountable to God. ²⁰Therefore no one will be declared righteous in God's sight by the works of the law; rather, through the law we become conscious of our sin.

Righteousness Through Faith

²¹But now apart from the law the righteousness of God has been made known, to which the Law and the Prophets testify. ²²This righteousness is given through faith inᵍ Jesus Christ to all who believe. There is no difference between Jew and Gentile, ²³for all have sinned and fall short of the glory of God, ²⁴and all are justified freely by his grace through the redemption that came by Christ Jesus. ²⁵God presented Christ as a sacrifice of

ᵃ 12 Psalms 14:1-3; 53:1-3; Eccles. 7:20   ᵇ 13 Psalm 5:9   ᶜ 13 Psalm 140:3
ᵈ 14 Psalm 10:7 (see Septuagint)   ᵉ 17 Isaiah 59:7,8   ᶠ 18 Psalm 36:1
ᵍ 22 Or through the faithfulness of

atonement,[a] through the shedding of his blood — to be received by faith. He did this to demonstrate his righteousness, because in his forbearance he had left the sins committed beforehand unpunished — [26]he did it to demonstrate his righteousness at the present time, so as to be just and the one who justifies those who have faith in Jesus.

[27]Where, then, is boasting? It is excluded. Because of what law? The law that requires works? No, because of the law that requires faith. [28]For we maintain that a person is justified by faith apart from the works of the law. [29]Or is God the God of Jews only? Is he not the God of Gentiles too? Yes, of Gentiles too, [30]since there is only one God, who will justify the circumcised by faith and the uncircumcised through that same faith. [31]Do we, then, nullify the law by this faith? Not at all! Rather, we uphold the law.

Abraham Justified by Faith

4 What then shall we say that Abraham, our forefather according to the flesh, discovered in this matter? [2]If, in fact, Abraham was justified by works, he had something to boast about — but not before God. [3]What does Scripture say? "Abraham believed God, and it was credited to him as righteousness."[b]

[4]Now to the one who works, wages are not credited as a gift but as an obligation. [5]However, to the one who does not work but trusts God who justifies the ungodly, their faith is credited as righteousness. [6]David says the same thing when he speaks of the blessedness of the one to whom God credits righteousness apart from works:

[7]"Blessed are those
     whose transgressions are
          forgiven,
     whose sins are covered.
[8]Blessed is the one
     whose sin the Lord will
          never count against
          them."[c]

[9]Is this blessedness only for the circumcised, or also for the uncircumcised? We have been saying that Abraham's faith was credited to him as righteousness. [10]Under what circumstances was it credited? Was it after he was circumcised, or before? It was not after, but before! [11]And he received circumcision as a sign, a seal of the righteousness that he had by faith while he was still uncircumcised. So then, he is the father of all who believe but have not been circumcised, in order that righteousness might be credited to them. [12]And he is then also the father of the circumcised who not only are circumcised but

---

[a] 25 The Greek for *sacrifice of atonement* refers to the atonement cover on the ark of the covenant (see Lev. 16:15,16).   [b] 3 Gen. 15:6; also in verse 22
[c] 8 Psalm 32:1,2

who also follow in the footsteps of the faith that our father Abraham had before he was circumcised.

¹³ It was not through the law that Abraham and his offspring received the promise that he would be heir of the world, but through the righteousness that comes by faith. ¹⁴ For if those who depend on the law are heirs, faith means nothing and the promise is worthless, ¹⁵ because the law brings wrath. And where there is no law there is no transgression.

¹⁶ Therefore, the promise comes by faith, so that it may be by grace and may be guaranteed to all Abraham's offspring — not only to those who are of the law but also to those who have the faith of Abraham. He is the father of us all. ¹⁷ As it is written: "I have made you a father of many nations."ᵃ He is our father in the sight of God, in whom he believed — the God who gives life to the dead and calls into being things that were not.

¹⁸ Against all hope, Abraham in hope believed and so became the father of many nations, just as it had been said to him, "So shall your offspring be."ᵇ ¹⁹ Without weakening in his faith, he faced the fact that his body was as good as dead — since he was about a hundred years old — and that Sarah's womb was also dead. ²⁰ Yet he did not waver through unbelief regarding the promise of God, but was strengthened in his faith and gave glory to God, ²¹ being fully persuaded that God had power to do what he had promised. ²² This is why "it was credited to him as righteousness." ²³ The words "it was credited to him" were written not for him alone, ²⁴ but also for us, to whom God will credit righteousness — for us who believe in him who raised Jesus our Lord from the dead. ²⁵ He was delivered over to death for our sins and was raised to life for our justification.

Peace and Hope

5 Therefore, since we have been justified through faith, weᶜ have peace with God through our Lord Jesus Christ, ² through whom we have gained access by faith into this grace in which we now stand. And weᵈ boast in the hope of the glory of God. ³ Not only so, but weᵈ also glory in our sufferings, because we know that suffering produces perseverance; ⁴ perseverance, character; and character, hope. ⁵ And hope does not put us to shame, because God's love has been poured out into our hearts through the Holy Spirit, who has been given to us.

⁶ You see, at just the right time, when we were still powerless, Christ died for the ungodly. ⁷ Very rarely will anyone die for a righteous person, though for a good person someone might possi-

---

ᵃ 17 Gen. 17:5   ᵇ 18 Gen. 15:5   ᶜ 1 Many manuscripts *let us*   ᵈ 2,3 Or *let us* bly dare to die. [8]But God demonstrates his own love for us in this: While we were still sinners, Christ died for us.

[9]Since we have now been justified by his blood, how much more shall we be saved from God's wrath through him! [10]For if, while we were God's enemies, we were reconciled to him through the death of his Son, how much more, having been reconciled, shall we be saved through his life! [11]Not only is this so, but we also boast in God through our Lord Jesus Christ, through whom we have now received reconciliation.

Death Through Adam, Life Through Christ

[12]Therefore, just as sin entered the world through one man, and death through sin, and in this way death came to all people, because all sinned—

[13]To be sure, sin was in the world before the law was given, but sin is not charged against anyone's account where there is no law. [14]Nevertheless, death reigned from the time of Adam to the time of Moses, even over those who did not sin by breaking a command, as did Adam, who is a pattern of the one to come.

[15]But the gift is not like the trespass. For if the many died by the trespass of the one man, how much more did God's grace and the gift that came by the grace of the one man, Jesus Christ, overflow to the many! [16]Nor can the gift of God be compared with the result of one man's sin: The judgment followed one sin and brought condemnation, but the gift followed many trespasses and brought justification. [17]For if, by the trespass of the one man, death reigned through that one man, how much more will those who receive God's abundant provision of grace and of the gift of righteousness reign in life through the one man, Jesus Christ!

[18]Consequently, just as one trespass resulted in condemnation for all people, so also one righteous act resulted in justification and life for all people. [19]For just as through the disobedience of the one man the many were made sinners, so also through the obedience of the one man the many will be made righteous.

[20]The law was brought in so that the trespass might increase. But where sin increased, grace increased all the more, [21]so that, just as sin reigned in death, so also grace might reign through righteousness to bring eternal life through Jesus Christ our Lord.

Dead to Sin, Alive in Christ

6 What shall we say, then? Shall we go on sinning so that grace may increase? [2]By no means! We are those who have died to sin; how can we live in it any longer? [3]Or don't you know that all of us who were baptized into Christ Jesus were baptized into his death? [4]We were therefore

buried with him through baptism into death in order that, just as Christ was raised from the dead through the glory of the Father, we too may live a new life.

⁵For if we have been united with him in a death like his, we will certainly also be united with him in a resurrection like his. ⁶For we know that our old self was crucified with him so that the body ruled by sin might be done away with,ᵃ that we should no longer be slaves to sin— ⁷because anyone who has died has been set free from sin.

⁸Now if we died with Christ, we believe that we will also live with him. ⁹For we know that since Christ was raised from the dead, he cannot die again; death no longer has mastery over him. ¹⁰The death he died, he died to sin once for all; but the life he lives, he lives to God.

¹¹In the same way, count yourselves dead to sin but alive to God in Christ Jesus. ¹²Therefore do not let sin reign in your mortal body so that you obey its evil desires. ¹³Do not offer any part of yourself to sin as an instrument of wickedness, but rather offer yourselves to God as those who have been brought from death to life; and offer every part of yourself to him as an instrument of righteousness. ¹⁴For sin shall no longer be your master, because you are not under the law, but under grace.

Slaves to Righteousness

¹⁵What then? Shall we sin because we are not under the law but under grace? By no means! ¹⁶Don't you know that when you offer yourselves to someone as obedient slaves, you are slaves of the one you obey—whether you are slaves to sin, which leads to death, or to obedience, which leads to righteousness? ¹⁷But thanks be to God that, though you used to be slaves to sin, you have come to obey from your heart the pattern of teaching that has now claimed your allegiance. ¹⁸You have been set free from sin and have become slaves to righteousness.

¹⁹I am using an example from everyday life because of your human limitations. Just as you used to offer yourselves as slaves to impurity and to ever-increasing wickedness, so now offer yourselves as slaves to righteousness leading to holiness. ²⁰When you were slaves to sin, you were free from the control of righteousness. ²¹What benefit did you reap at that time from the things you are now ashamed of? Those things result in death! ²²But now that you have been set free from sin and have become slaves of God, the benefit you reap leads to holiness, and the result is eternal life. ²³For the wages of sin is death, but the gift of God is eternal life inᵇ Christ Jesus our Lord.

ᵃ 6 Or *be rendered powerless*   ᵇ 23 Or *through*

Released From the Law, Bound to Christ

7 Do you not know, brothers and sisters — for I am speaking to those who know the law — that the law has authority over someone only as long as that person lives? **2** For example, by law a married woman is bound to her husband as long as he is alive, but if her husband dies, she is released from the law that binds her to him. **3** So then, if she has sexual relations with another man while her husband is still alive, she is called an adulteress. But if her husband dies, she is released from that law and is not an adulteress if she marries another man.

4 So, my brothers and sisters, you also died to the law through the body of Christ, that you might belong to another, to him who was raised from the dead, in order that we might bear fruit for God. **5** For when we were in the realm of the flesh,[a] the sinful passions aroused by the law were at work in us, so that we bore fruit for death. **6** But now, by dying to what once bound us, we have been released from the law so that we serve in the new way of the Spirit, and not in the old way of the written code.

The Law and Sin

7 What shall we say, then? Is the law sinful? Certainly not! Nevertheless, I would not have known what sin was had it not been for the law. For I would not have known what coveting really was if the law had not said, "You shall not covet."[b] **8** But sin, seizing the opportunity afforded by the commandment, produced in me every kind of coveting. For apart from the law, sin was dead. **9** Once I was alive apart from the law; but when the commandment came, sin sprang to life and I died. **10** I found that the very commandment that was intended to bring life actually brought death. **11** For sin, seizing the opportunity afforded by the commandment, deceived me, and through the commandment put me to death. **12** So then, the law is holy, and the commandment is holy, righteous and good.

13 Did that which is good, then, become death to me? By no means! Nevertheless, in order that sin might be recognized as sin, it used what is good to bring about my death, so that through the commandment sin might become utterly sinful.

14 We know that the law is spiritual; but I am unspiritual, sold as a slave to sin. **15** I do not understand what I do. For what I want to do I do not do, but what I hate I do. **16** And if I do what I do not want to do, I agree that the law is good. **17** As it is, it is no longer I myself who do it, but it is sin living in me. **18** For I know that good

[a] 5 In contexts like this, the Greek word for *flesh* (*sarx*) refers to the sinful state of human beings, often presented as a power in opposition to the Spirit.
[b] 7 Exodus 20:17; Deut. 5:21

itself does not dwell in me, that is, in my sinful nature.[a] For I have the desire to do what is good, but I cannot carry it out. [19] For I do not do the good I want to do, but the evil I do not want to do — this I keep on doing. [20] Now if I do what I do not want to do, it is no longer I who do it, but it is sin living in me that does it.

[21] So I find this law at work: Although I want to do good, evil is right there with me. [22] For in my inner being I delight in God's law; [23] but I see another law at work in me, waging war against the law of my mind and making me a prisoner of the law of sin at work within me. [24] What a wretched man I am! Who will rescue me from this body that is subject to death? [25] Thanks be to God, who delivers me through Jesus Christ our Lord!

So then, I myself in my mind am a slave to God's law, but in my sinful nature[b] a slave to the law of sin.

Life Through the Spirit

8 Therefore, there is now no condemnation for those who are in Christ Jesus, [2] because through Christ Jesus the law of the Spirit who gives life has set you[c] free from the law of sin and death. [3] For what the law was powerless to do because it was weakened by the flesh,[d] God did by sending his own Son in the likeness of sinful flesh to be a sin offering.[e] And so he condemned sin in the flesh, [4] in order that the righteous requirement of the law might be fully met in us, who do not live according to the flesh but according to the Spirit.

[5] Those who live according to the flesh have their minds set on what the flesh desires; but those who live in accordance with the Spirit have their minds set on what the Spirit desires. [6] The mind governed by the flesh is death, but the mind governed by the Spirit is life and peace. [7] The mind governed by the flesh is hostile to God; it does not submit to God's law, nor can it do so. [8] Those who are in the realm of the flesh cannot please God.

[9] You, however, are not in the realm of the flesh but are in the realm of the Spirit, if indeed the Spirit of God lives in you. And if anyone does not have the Spirit of Christ, they do not belong to Christ. [10] But if Christ is in you, then even though your body is subject to death because of sin, the Spirit gives life[f] because of righteousness. [11] And if the Spirit of him who raised Jesus from the dead is living in you, he who raised Christ from the dead will also give life to your mortal bod-

---

[a] 18 Or *my flesh*   [b] 25 Or *in the flesh*   [c] 2 The Greek is singular; some manuscripts *me*   [d] 3 In contexts like this, the Greek word for *flesh* (*sarx*) refers to the sinful state of human beings, often presented as a power in opposition to the Spirit; also in verses 4-13.   [e] 3 Or *flesh, for sin*   [f] 10 Or *you, your body is dead because of sin, yet your spirit is alive*

ies because of[a] his Spirit who lives in you.

[12] Therefore, brothers and sisters, we have an obligation — but it is not to the flesh, to live according to it. [13] For if you live according to the flesh, you will die; but if by the Spirit you put to death the misdeeds of the body, you will live.

[14] For those who are led by the Spirit of God are the children of God. [15] The Spirit you received does not make you slaves, so that you live in fear again; rather, the Spirit you received brought about your adoption to sonship.[b] And by him we cry, *"Abba,[c] Father."* [16] The Spirit himself testifies with our spirit that we are God's children. [17] Now if we are children, then we are heirs — heirs of God and co-heirs with Christ, if indeed we share in his sufferings in order that we may also share in his glory.

Present Suffering and Future Glory

[18] I consider that our present sufferings are not worth comparing with the glory that will be revealed in us. [19] For the creation waits in eager expectation for the children of God to be revealed. [20] For the creation was subjected to frustration, not by its own choice, but by the will of the one who subjected it, in hope [21] that[d] the creation itself will be liberated from its bondage to decay and brought into the freedom and glory of the children of God.

[22] We know that the whole creation has been groaning as in the pains of childbirth right up to the present time. [23] Not only so, but we ourselves, who have the firstfruits of the Spirit, groan inwardly as we wait eagerly for our adoption to sonship, the redemption of our bodies. [24] For in this hope we were saved. But hope that is seen is no hope at all. Who hopes for what they already have? [25] But if we hope for what we do not yet have, we wait for it patiently.

[26] In the same way, the Spirit helps us in our weakness. We do not know what we ought to pray for, but the Spirit himself intercedes for us through wordless groans. [27] And he who searches our hearts knows the mind of the Spirit, because the Spirit intercedes for God's people in accordance with the will of God.

[28] And we know that in all things God works for the good of those who love him, who[e] have been called according to his purpose. [29] For those God foreknew he also predestined to be

---

[a] 11 Some manuscripts *bodies through* [b] 15 The Greek word for *adoption*
to sonship is a term referring to the full legal standing of an adopted male heir in Roman culture; also in verse 23.   [c] 15 Aramaic for *father*
[d] 20,21 Or *subjected it in hope.* [21]*For*   [e] 28 Or *that all things work together for good to those who love God, who*; or *that in all things God works together with those who love him to bring about what is good — with those who*

conformed to the image of his Son, that he might be the first-born among many brothers and sisters. [30]And those he predestined, he also called; those he called, he also justified; those he justified, he also glorified.

More Than Conquerors

[31]What, then, shall we say in response to these things? If God is for us, who can be against us? [32]He who did not spare his own Son, but gave him up for us all — how will he not also, along with him, graciously give us all things? [33]Who will bring any charge against those whom God has chosen? It is God who justifies. [34]Who then is the one who condemns? No one. Christ Jesus who died — more than that, who was raised to life — is at the right hand of God and is also interceding for us. [35]Who shall separate us from the love of Christ? Shall trouble or hardship or persecution or famine or nakedness or danger or sword? [36]As it is written:

"For your sake we face death
    all day long;
  we are considered as sheep
    to be slaughtered."[a]

[37]No, in all these things we are more than conquerors through him who loved us. [38]For I am convinced that neither death nor life, neither angels nor demons,[b] neither the present nor the future, nor any powers, [39]neither height nor depth, nor anything else in all creation, will be able to separate us from the love of God that is in Christ Jesus our Lord.

Paul's Anguish Over Israel

9 I speak the truth in Christ — I am not lying, my conscience confirms it through the Holy Spirit — [2]I have great sorrow and unceasing anguish in my heart. [3]For I could wish that I myself were cursed and cut off from Christ for the sake of my people, those of my own race, [4]the people of Israel. Theirs is the adoption to sonship; theirs the divine glory, the covenants, the receiving of the law, the temple worship and the promises. [5]Theirs are the patriarchs, and from them is traced the human ancestry of the Messiah, who is God over all, forever praised![c] Amen.

God's Sovereign Choice

[6]It is not as though God's word had failed. For not all who are descended from Israel are Israel. [7]Nor because they are his descendants are they all Abraham's children. On the contrary, "It is through Isaac that your offspring will be reckoned."[d] [8]In other words, it is not the children by physical descent who are God's children, but it is the children of

---

[a] 36 Psalm 44:22   [b] 38 Or *nor heavenly rulers*   [c] 5 Or *Messiah, who is over all. God be forever praised! Or Messiah. God who is over all be forever praised!*
[d] 7 Gen. 21:12

the promise who are regarded as Abraham's offspring. ⁹For this was how the promise was stated: "At the appointed time I will return, and Sarah will have a son."ᵃ

¹⁰Not only that, but Rebekah's children were conceived at the same time by our father Isaac. ¹¹Yet, before the twins were born or had done anything good or bad — in order that God's purpose in election might stand: ¹²not by works but by him who calls — she was told, "The older will serve the younger."ᵇ ¹³Just as it is written: "Jacob I loved, but Esau I hated."ᶜ

¹⁴What then shall we say? Is God unjust? Not at all! ¹⁵For he says to Moses,

"I will have mercy on whom I
        have mercy,
    and I will have compassion
        on whom I have
        compassion."ᵈ

¹⁶It does not, therefore, depend on human desire or effort, but on God's mercy. ¹⁷For Scripture says to Pharaoh: "I raised you up for this very purpose, that I might display my power in you and that my name might be proclaimed in all the earth."ᵉ ¹⁸Therefore God has mercy on whom he wants to have mercy, and he hardens whom he wants to harden.

¹⁹One of you will say to me: "Then why does God still blame us? For who is able to resist his will?" ²⁰But who are you, a human being, to talk back to God? "Shall what is formed say to the one who formed it, 'Why did you make me like this?'"ᶠ ²¹Does not the potter have the right to make out of the same lump of clay some pottery for special purposes and some for common use?

²²What if God, although choosing to show his wrath and make his power known, bore with great patience the objects of his wrath — prepared for destruction? ²³What if he did this to make the riches of his glory known to the objects of his mercy, whom he prepared in advance for glory — ²⁴even us, whom he also called, not only from the Jews but also from the Gentiles? ²⁵As he says in Hosea:

"I will call them 'my people'
        who are not my people;
    and I will call her 'my loved
        one' who is not my loved
        one,"ᵍ

²⁶and,

"In the very place where it was
        said to them,
    'You are not my people,'
    there they will be called
        'children of the living
        God.'"ʰ

²⁷Isaiah cries out concerning Israel:

ᵃ 9 Gen. 18:10,14   ᵇ 12 Gen. 25:23   ᶜ 13 Mal. 1:2,3   ᵈ 15 Exodus 33:19
ᵉ 17 Exodus 9:16   ᶠ 20 Isaiah 29:16; 45:9   ᵍ 25 Hosea 2:23   ʰ 26 Hosea 1:10

"Though the number of the
    Israelites be like the sand
    by the sea,
  only the remnant will be
    saved.
28 For the Lord will carry out
  his sentence on earth with
    speed and finality."[a]

29 It is just as Isaiah said previously:

"Unless the Lord Almighty
  had left us descendants,
we would have become like
  Sodom,
  we would have been like
    Gomorrah."[b]

Israel's Unbelief

30 What then shall we say? That the Gentiles, who did not pursue righteousness, have obtained it, a righteousness that is by faith; **31** but the people of Israel, who pursued the law as the way of righteousness, have not attained their goal. **32** Why not? Because they pursued it not by faith but as if it were by works. They stumbled over the stumbling stone. **33** As it is written:

"See, I lay in Zion a stone that
    causes people to
    stumble
  and a rock that makes them
    fall,
  and the one who believes
    in him will never be put
    to shame."[c]

10 Brothers and sisters, my heart's desire and prayer to God for the Israelites is that they may be saved. **2** For I can testify about them that they are zealous for God, but their zeal is not based on knowledge. **3** Since they did not know the righteousness of God and sought to establish their own, they did not submit to God's righteousness. **4** Christ is the culmination of the law so that there may be righteousness for everyone who believes.

5 Moses writes this about the righteousness that is by the law: "The person who does these things will live by them."[d] **6** But the righteousness that is by faith says: "Do not say in your heart, 'Who will ascend into heaven?'"[e] (that is, to bring Christ down) **7** "or 'Who will descend into the deep?'"[f] (that is, to bring Christ up from the dead). **8** But what does it say? "The word is near you; it is in your mouth and in your heart,"[g] that is, the message concerning faith that we proclaim: **9** If you declare with your mouth, "Jesus is Lord," and believe in your heart that God raised him from the dead, you will be saved. **10** For it is with your heart that you believe and are justified, and it is with your mouth that you profess your faith and are saved. **11** As Scripture says, "Anyone who believes in him will never be put to shame."[h] **12** For

---

[a] 28 Isaiah 10:22,23 (see Septuagint)
28:16   [d] 5 Lev. 18:5   [e] 6 Deut. 30:12
[h] 11 Isaiah 28:16 (see Septuagint)

[b] 29 Isaiah 1:9   [c] 33 Isaiah 8:14;
[f] 7 Deut. 30:13   [g] 8 Deut. 30:14

there is no difference between Jew and Gentile—the same Lord is Lord of all and richly blesses all who call on him, [13]for, "Everyone who calls on the name of the Lord will be saved."[a]

[14]How, then, can they call on the one they have not believed in? And how can they believe in the one of whom they have not heard? And how can they hear without someone preaching to them? [15]And how can anyone preach unless they are sent? As it is written: "How beautiful are the feet of those who bring good news!"[b]

[16]But not all the Israelites accepted the good news. For Isaiah says, "Lord, who has believed our message?"[c] [17]Consequently, faith comes from hearing the message, and the message is heard through the word about Christ. [18]But I ask: Did they not hear? Of course they did:

"Their voice has gone out into
    all the earth,
  their words to the ends of the
    world."[d]

[19]Again I ask: Did Israel not understand? First, Moses says,

"I will make you envious by
    those who are not a
    nation;
  I will make you angry by
    a nation that has no
    understanding."[e]

[20]And Isaiah boldly says,

"I was found by those who did
    not seek me;
  I revealed myself to those
    who did not ask for me."[f]

[21]But concerning Israel he says,

"All day long I have held out
    my hands
  to a disobedient and
    obstinate people."[g]

The Remnant of Israel

11 I ask then: Did God reject his people? By no means! I am an Israelite myself, a descendant of Abraham, from the tribe of Benjamin. [2]God did not reject his people, whom he foreknew. Don't you know what Scripture says in the passage about Elijah—how he appealed to God against Israel: [3]"Lord, they have killed your prophets and torn down your altars; I am the only one left, and they are trying to kill me"[h]? [4]And what was God's answer to him? "I have reserved for myself seven thousand who have not bowed the knee to Baal."[i] [5]So too, at the present time there is a remnant chosen by grace. [6]And if by grace, then it cannot be based on works; if it were, grace would no longer be grace.

[7]What then? What the people of Israel sought so earnestly they did not obtain. The elect among

[a] 13 Joel 2:32   [b] 15 Isaiah 52:7   [c] 16 Isaiah 53:1   [d] 18 Psalm 19:4
[e] 19 Deut. 32:21   [f] 20 Isaiah 65:1   [g] 21 Isaiah 65:2   [h] 3 1 Kings 19:10,14
[i] 4 1 Kings 19:18

them did, but the others were hardened, **8**as it is written:

"God gave them a spirit of
stupor,
eyes that could not see
and ears that could not hear,
to this very day."*a*

9And David says:

"May their table become a
snare and a trap,
a stumbling block and a
retribution for them.
10May their eyes be darkened so
they cannot see,
and their backs be bent
forever."*b*

Ingrafted Branches

11Again I ask: Did they stumble so as to fall beyond recovery? Not at all! Rather, because of their transgression, salvation has come to the Gentiles to make Israel envious. **12**But if their transgression means riches for the world, and their loss means riches for the Gentiles, how much greater riches will their full inclusion bring!

13I am talking to you Gentiles. Inasmuch as I am the apostle to the Gentiles, I take pride in my ministry **14**in the hope that I may somehow arouse my own people to envy and save some of them. **15**For if their rejection brought reconciliation to the world, what will their acceptance be but life from the dead? **16**If the part of the dough offered as firstfruits is holy, then the whole batch is holy; if the root is holy, so are the branches.

17If some of the branches have been broken off, and you, though a wild olive shoot, have been grafted in among the others and now share in the nourishing sap from the olive root, **18**do not consider yourself to be superior to those other branches. If you do, consider this: You do not support the root, but the root supports you. **19**You will say then, "Branches were broken off so that I could be grafted in." **20**Granted. But they were broken off because of unbelief, and you stand by faith. Do not be arrogant, but tremble. **21**For if God did not spare the natural branches, he will not spare you either.

22Consider therefore the kindness and sternness of God: sternness to those who fell, but kindness to you, provided that you continue in his kindness. Otherwise, you also will be cut off. **23**And if they do not persist in unbelief, they will be grafted in, for God is able to graft them in again. **24**After all, if you were cut out of an olive tree that is wild by nature, and contrary to nature were grafted into a cultivated olive tree, how much more readily will these, the natural branches, be grafted into their own olive tree!

All Israel Will Be Saved

25I do not want you to be ignorant of this mystery, brothers and

---

a 8 Deut. 29:4; Isaiah 29:10   *b 10* Psalm 69:22,23

sisters, so that you may not be conceited: Israel has experienced a hardening in part until the full number of the Gentiles has come in, ²⁶and in this way^a all Israel will be saved. As it is written:

"The deliverer will come from Zion;
he will turn godlessness away from Jacob.
²⁷And this is^b my covenant with them
when I take away their sins."^c

²⁸As far as the gospel is concerned, they are enemies for your sake; but as far as election is concerned, they are loved on account of the patriarchs, ²⁹for God's gifts and his call are irrevocable. ³⁰Just as you who were at one time disobedient to God have now received mercy as a result of their disobedience, ³¹so they too have now become disobedient in order that they too may now^d receive mercy as a result of God's mercy to you. ³²For God has bound everyone over to disobedience so that he may have mercy on them all.

Doxology

³³Oh, the depth of the riches
of the wisdom and^e
knowledge of God!
How unsearchable his judgments,
and his paths beyond tracing out!

³⁴"Who has known the mind of the Lord?
Or who has been his counselor?"^f
³⁵"Who has ever given to God, that God should repay them?"^g
³⁶For from him and through him and for him are all things.
To him be the glory forever! Amen.

A Living Sacrifice

12 Therefore, I urge you, brothers and sisters, in view of God's mercy, to offer your bodies as a living sacrifice, holy and pleasing to God—this is your true and proper worship. ²Do not conform to the pattern of this world, but be transformed by the renewing of your mind. Then you will be able to test and approve what God's will is—his good, pleasing and perfect will.

Humble Service in the Body of Christ

³For by the grace given me I say to every one of you: Do not think of yourself more highly than you ought, but rather think of yourself with sober judgment, in accordance with the faith God has distributed to each of you. ⁴For just as each of us has one body with many members, and these members do not all have the

---

^a 26 Or *and so*   ^b 27 Or *will be*   ^c 27 Isaiah 59:20,21; 27:9 (see Septuagint); Jer. 31:33,34   ^d 31 Some manuscripts do not have *now.*   ^e 33 Or *riches and the wisdom and the*   ^f 34 Isaiah 40:13   ^g 35 Job 41:11

same function, [5] so in Christ we, though many, form one body, and each member belongs to all the others. [6] We have different gifts, according to the grace given to each of us. If your gift is prophesying, then prophesy in accordance with your[a] faith; [7] if it is serving, then serve; if it is teaching, then teach; [8] if it is to encourage, then give encouragement; if it is giving, then give generously; if it is to lead,[b] do it diligently; if it is to show mercy, do it cheerfully.

Love in Action

[9] Love must be sincere. Hate what is evil; cling to what is good. [10] Be devoted to one another in love. Honor one another above yourselves. [11] Never be lacking in zeal, but keep your spiritual fervor, serving the Lord. [12] Be joyful in hope, patient in affliction, faithful in prayer. [13] Share with the Lord's people who are in need. Practice hospitality.

[14] Bless those who persecute you; bless and do not curse. [15] Rejoice with those who rejoice; mourn with those who mourn. [16] Live in harmony with one another. Do not be proud, but be willing to associate with people of low position.[c] Do not be conceited.

[17] Do not repay anyone evil for evil. Be careful to do what is right in the eyes of everyone. [18] If it is possible, as far as it depends on you, live at peace with everyone.

[19] Do not take revenge, my dear friends, but leave room for God's wrath, for it is written: "It is mine to avenge; I will repay,"[d] says the Lord. [20] On the contrary:

> "If your enemy is hungry, feed him;
> if he is thirsty, give him something to drink.
> In doing this, you will heap burning coals on his head."[e]

[21] Do not be overcome by evil, but overcome evil with good.

Submission to Governing Authorities

13 Let everyone be subject to the governing authorities, for there is no authority except that which God has established. The authorities that exist have been established by God. [2] Consequently, whoever rebels against the authority is rebelling against what God has instituted, and those who do so will bring judgment on themselves. [3] For rulers hold no terror for those who do right, but for those who do wrong. Do you want to be free from fear of the one in authority? Then do what is right and you will be commended. [4] For the one in authority is God's servant for your good. But if you do wrong, be afraid, for rulers do not bear the sword for no reason. They are God's servants, agents of wrath to

---

[a] 6 Or the [b] 8 Or to provide for others
[d] 19 Deut. 32:35 [e] 20 Prov. 25:21,22
[c] 16 Or willing to do menial work

bring punishment on the wrong-doer. **5**Therefore, it is necessary to submit to the authorities, not only because of possible punishment but also as a matter of conscience.

6This is also why you pay taxes, for the authorities are God's servants, who give their full time to governing. **7**Give to everyone what you owe them: If you owe taxes, pay taxes; if revenue, then revenue; if respect, then respect; if honor, then honor.

Love Fulfills the Law

8Let no debt remain outstanding, except the continuing debt to love one another, for whoever loves others has fulfilled the law. **9**The commandments, "You shall not commit adultery," "You shall not murder," "You shall not steal," "You shall not covet,"*a* and whatever other command there may be, are summed up in this one command: "Love your neighbor as yourself."*b* **10**Love does no harm to a neighbor. Therefore love is the fulfillment of the law.

The Day Is Near

11And do this, understanding the present time: The hour has already come for you to wake up from your slumber, because our salvation is nearer now than when we first believed. **12**The night is nearly over; the day is almost here. So let us put aside the deeds of darkness and put on the armor of light. **13**Let us behave decently, as in the daytime, not in carousing and drunkenness, not in sexual immorality and debauchery, not in dissension and jealousy. **14**Rather, clothe yourselves with the Lord Jesus Christ, and do not think about how to gratify the desires of the flesh.*c*

The Weak and the Strong

14 Accept the one whose faith is weak, without quarreling over disputable matters. **2**One person's faith allows them to eat anything, but another, whose faith is weak, eats only vegetables. **3**The one who eats everything must not treat with contempt the one who does not, and the one who does not eat everything must not judge the one who does, for God has accepted them. **4**Who are you to judge someone else's servant? To their own master, servants stand or fall. And they will stand, for the Lord is able to make them stand.

5One person considers one day more sacred than another; another considers every day alike. Each of them should be fully convinced in their own mind. **6**Whoever regards one day as special does so to the Lord. Whoever eats meat does so to the Lord, for they give thanks to God; and whoever abstains does so to the Lord and gives

---

a 9 Exodus 20:13-15,17; Deut. 5:17-19,21   *b* 9 Lev. 19:18   *c* 14 In contexts like this, the Greek word for *flesh* (*sarx*) refers to the sinful state of human beings, often presented as a power in opposition to the Spirit.

thanks to God. **7** For none of us lives for ourselves alone, and none of us dies for ourselves alone. **8** If we live, we live for the Lord; and if we die, we die for the Lord. So, whether we live or die, we belong to the Lord. **9** For this very reason, Christ died and returned to life so that he might be the Lord of both the dead and the living.

10 You, then, why do you judge your brother or sister*a*? Or why do you treat them with contempt? For we will all stand before God's judgment seat. **11** It is written:

" 'As surely as I live,' says the Lord,
'every knee will bow before me;
every tongue will acknowledge God.' "*b*

12 So then, each of us will give an account of ourselves to God.

13 Therefore let us stop passing judgment on one another. Instead, make up your mind not to put any stumbling block or obstacle in the way of a brother or sister. **14** I am convinced, being fully persuaded in the Lord Jesus, that nothing is unclean in itself. But if anyone regards something as unclean, then for that person it is unclean. **15** If your brother or sister is distressed because of what you eat, you are no longer acting in love. Do not by your eating destroy someone for whom Christ died. **16** Therefore do not let what you know is good be spoken of as evil. **17** For the kingdom of God is not a matter of eating and drinking, but of righteousness, peace and joy in the Holy Spirit, **18** because anyone who serves Christ in this way is pleasing to God and receives human approval.

19 Let us therefore make every effort to do what leads to peace and to mutual edification. **20** Do not destroy the work of God for the sake of food. All food is clean, but it is wrong for a person to eat anything that causes someone else to stumble. **21** It is better not to eat meat or drink wine or to do anything else that will cause your brother or sister to fall.

22 So whatever you believe about these things keep between yourself and God. Blessed is the one who does not condemn himself by what he approves. **23** But whoever has doubts is condemned if they eat, because their eating is not from faith; and everything that does not come from faith is sin.*c*

15 We who are strong ought to bear with the failings of the weak and not to please ourselves. **2** Each of us should please our neighbors for their good, to build them up. **3** For even Christ did not please himself but, as it is written: "The insults of those who insult you have fallen on me."*d*

---

a 10 The Greek word for *brother or sister* (*adelphos*) refers here to a believer, whether man or woman, as part of God's family; also in verses 13, 15 and 21.
b 11 Isaiah 45:23   *c 23* Some manuscripts place 16:25-27 here; others after 15:33.   *d 3* Psalm 69:9

⁴For everything that was written in the past was written to teach us, so that through the endurance taught in the Scriptures and the encouragement they provide we might have hope.

⁵May the God who gives endurance and encouragement give you the same attitude of mind toward each other that Christ Jesus had, ⁶so that with one mind and one voice you may glorify the God and Father of our Lord Jesus Christ.

⁷Accept one another, then, just as Christ accepted you, in order to bring praise to God. ⁸For I tell you that Christ has become a servant of the Jews*a* on behalf of God's truth, so that the promises made to the patriarchs might be confirmed ⁹and, moreover, that the Gentiles might glorify God for his mercy. As it is written:

"Therefore I will praise you
    among the Gentiles;
I will sing the praises of your
    name."*b*

¹⁰Again, it says,

"Rejoice, you Gentiles, with his
    people."*c*

¹¹And again,

"Praise the Lord, all you
    Gentiles;
let all the peoples extol him."*d*

¹²And again, Isaiah says,

"The Root of Jesse will
    spring up,

one who will arise to rule
    over the nations;
in him the Gentiles will
    hope."*e*

¹³May the God of hope fill you with all joy and peace as you trust in him, so that you may overflow with hope by the power of the Holy Spirit.

Paul the Minister to the Gentiles

¹⁴I myself am convinced, my brothers and sisters, that you yourselves are full of goodness, filled with knowledge and competent to instruct one another. ¹⁵Yet I have written you quite boldly on some points to remind you of them again, because of the grace God gave me ¹⁶to be a minister of Christ Jesus to the Gentiles. He gave me the priestly duty of proclaiming the gospel of God, so that the Gentiles might become an offering acceptable to God, sanctified by the Holy Spirit.

¹⁷Therefore I glory in Christ Jesus in my service to God. ¹⁸I will not venture to speak of anything except what Christ has accomplished through me in leading the Gentiles to obey God by what I have said and done — ¹⁹by the power of signs and wonders, through the power of the Spirit of God. So from Jerusalem all the way around to Illyricum, I have fully proclaimed the gospel of Christ. ²⁰It has always been

a 8 Greek *circumcision*   *b 9* 2 Samuel 22:50; Psalm 18:49   *c 10* Deut. 32:43
d 11 Psalm 117:1   *e 12* Isaiah 11:10 (see Septuagint)

my ambition to preach the gospel where Christ was not known, so that I would not be building on someone else's foundation. ²¹Rather, as it is written:

"Those who were not told
about him will see,
and those who have not
heard will understand."^a

²²This is why I have often been hindered from coming to you.

Paul's Plan to Visit Rome

²³But now that there is no more place for me to work in these regions, and since I have been longing for many years to visit you, ²⁴I plan to do so when I go to Spain. I hope to see you while passing through and to have you assist me on my journey there, after I have enjoyed your company for a while. ²⁵Now, however, I am on my way to Jerusalem in the service of the Lord's people there. ²⁶For Macedonia and Achaia were pleased to make a contribution for the poor among the Lord's people in Jerusalem. ²⁷They were pleased to do it, and indeed they owe it to them. For if the Gentiles have shared in the Jews' spiritual blessings, they owe it to the Jews to share with them their material blessings. ²⁸So after I have completed this task and have made sure that they have received this contribution, I will go to Spain and visit you on the way. ²⁹I know that when I come to you, I will come in the full measure of the blessing of Christ.

³⁰I urge you, brothers and sisters, by our Lord Jesus Christ and by the love of the Spirit, to join me in my struggle by praying to God for me. ³¹Pray that I may be kept safe from the unbelievers in Judea and that the contribution I take to Jerusalem may be favorably received by the Lord's people there, ³²so that I may come to you with joy, by God's will, and in your company be refreshed. ³³The God of peace be with you all. Amen.

Personal Greetings

16 I commend to you our sister Phoebe, a deacon^{b,c} of the church in Cenchreae. ²I ask you to receive her in the Lord in a way worthy of his people and to give her any help she may need from you, for she has been the benefactor of many people, including me.

³Greet Priscilla^d and Aquila, my co-workers in Christ Jesus. ⁴They risked their lives for me. Not only I but all the churches of the Gentiles are grateful to them.

^a 21 Isaiah 52:15 (see Septuagint)   ^b 1 Or *servant*   ^c 1 The word *deacon* refers here to a Christian designated to serve with the overseers/elders of the church in a variety of ways; similarly in Phil. 1:1 and 1 Tim. 3:8,12.   ^d 3 Greek *Prisca*, a variant of *Priscilla*

⁵Greet also the church that meets at their house.

Greet my dear friend Epenetus, who was the first convert to Christ in the province of Asia. ⁶Greet Mary, who worked very hard for you. ⁷Greet Andronicus and Junia, my fellow Jews who have been in prison with me. They are outstanding among*ᵃ* the apostles, and they were in Christ before I was. ⁸Greet Ampliatus, my dear friend in the Lord. ⁹Greet Urbanus, our co-worker in Christ, and my dear friend Stachys.

¹⁰Greet Apelles, whose fidelity to Christ has stood the test.

Greet those who belong to the household of Aristobulus. ¹¹Greet Herodion, my fellow Jew.

Greet those in the household of Narcissus who are in the Lord.

¹²Greet Tryphena and Tryphosa, those women who work hard in the Lord.

Greet my dear friend Persis, another woman who has worked very hard in the Lord. ¹³Greet Rufus, chosen in the Lord, and his mother, who has been a mother to me, too. ¹⁴Greet Asyncritus, Phlegon, Hermes, Patrobas, Hermas and the other brothers and sisters with them. ¹⁵Greet Philologus, Julia, Nereus and his sister, and Olympas and all the Lord's people who are with them.

¹⁶Greet one another with a holy kiss.

All the churches of Christ send greetings.

¹⁷I urge you, brothers and sisters, to watch out for those who cause divisions and put obstacles in your way that are contrary to the teaching you have learned. Keep away from them. ¹⁸For such people are not serving our Lord Christ, but their own appetites. By smooth talk and flattery they deceive the minds of naive people. ¹⁹Everyone has heard about your obedience, so I rejoice because of you; but I want you to be wise about what is good, and innocent about what is evil.

²⁰The God of peace will soon crush Satan under your feet.

The grace of our Lord Jesus be with you.

²¹Timothy, my co-worker, sends his greetings to you, as do Lucius, Jason and Sosipater, my fellow Jews.

²²I, Tertius, who wrote down this letter, greet you in the Lord.

²³Gaius, whose hospitality I and the whole church here enjoy, sends you his greetings.

Erastus, who is the city's director of public works, and our brother Quartus send you their greetings. [24]ᵇ

ᵃ 7 Or *are esteemed by*   *ᵇ* 24 Some manuscripts include here *May the grace of our Lord Jesus Christ be with all of you. Amen.*

25 Now to him who is able to establish you in accordance with my gospel, the message I proclaim about Jesus Christ, in keeping with the revelation of the mystery hidden for long ages past, 26 but now revealed and made known through the prophetic writings by the command of the eternal God, so that all the Gentiles might come to the obedience that comes from*a* faith — 27 to the only wise God be glory forever through Jesus Christ! Amen.

1 Corinthians

Introduction:

This letter was written by Paul to the church in Corinth, probably in the winter of AD 55. While he was in Ephesus Paul sent this response to a letter he received from the Corinthian church.

The city of Corinth was a wealthy trading center located on the Mediterranean Sea. It was a city known throughout the Roman world for its wickedness. The new church in Corinth was having problems because the Christians struggled to act differently than the people around them.

The Christians in Corinth were not getting along with one another — they were taking sides. Some of them were living very sinful lives. Paul wrote this letter to scold them and teach them how Christians should act. He tried to teach the people practical lessons about the Christian life so they would know right from wrong.

Outline of contents:

Greetings and thanksgiving (1:1–9)
Divisions in the church (1:10–4:21)
Sexual immorality and lawsuits (5:1–6:20)
Marriage (7:1–40)
Christian rights and responsibility (8:1–11:1)
Christians in public worship (11:2–34)
Place and importance of spiritual gifts (12:1–14:40)
The resurrection of Christ and believers (15:1–58)
Conclusion (16:1–24)

1 Paul, called to be an apostle of Christ Jesus by the will of God, and our brother Sosthenes,

²To the church of God in Corinth, to those sanctified in Christ Jesus and called to be his holy people, together with all those everywhere who call on the name of our Lord Jesus Christ — their Lord and ours:

³Grace and peace to you from God our Father and the Lord Jesus Christ.

Thanksgiving

⁴I always thank my God for you because of his grace given you in Christ Jesus. ⁵For in him you have been enriched in every way — with all kinds of speech

and with all knowledge — [6]God thus confirming our testimony about Christ among you. [7]Therefore you do not lack any spiritual gift as you eagerly wait for our Lord Jesus Christ to be revealed. [8]He will also keep you firm to the end, so that you will be blameless on the day of our Lord Jesus Christ. [9]God is faithful, who has called you into fellowship with his Son, Jesus Christ our Lord.

A Church Divided Over Leaders

[10]I appeal to you, brothers and sisters,[a] in the name of our Lord Jesus Christ, that all of you agree with one another in what you say and that there be no divisions among you, but that you be perfectly united in mind and thought. [11]My brothers and sisters, some from Chloe's household have informed me that there are quarrels among you. [12]What I mean is this: One of you says, "I follow Paul"; another, "I follow Apollos"; another, "I follow Cephas[b]"; still another, "I follow Christ."

[13]Is Christ divided? Was Paul crucified for you? Were you baptized in the name of Paul? [14]I thank God that I did not baptize any of you except Crispus and Gaius, [15]so no one can say that you were baptized in my name. [16](Yes, I also baptized the household of Stephanas; beyond that,

I don't remember if I baptized anyone else.) [17]For Christ did not send me to baptize, but to preach the gospel — not with wisdom and eloquence, lest the cross of Christ be emptied of its power.

Christ Crucified Is God's Power and Wisdom

[18]For the message of the cross is foolishness to those who are perishing, but to us who are being saved it is the power of God. [19]For it is written:

"I will destroy the wisdom of
    the wise;
  the intelligence of the
    intelligent I will
    frustrate."[c]

[20]Where is the wise person? Where is the teacher of the law? Where is the philosopher of this age? Has not God made foolish the wisdom of the world? [21]For since in the wisdom of God the world through its wisdom did not know him, God was pleased through the foolishness of what was preached to save those who believe. [22]Jews demand signs and Greeks look for wisdom, [23]but we preach Christ crucified: a stumbling block to Jews and foolishness to Gentiles, [24]but to those whom God has called, both Jews and Greeks, Christ the power of God and the wisdom of God.

---

[a] 10 The Greek word for *brothers and sisters* (*adelphoi*) refers here to believers, both men and women, as part of God's family; also in verses 11 and 26; and in 2:1; 3:1; 4:6; 6:8; 7:24, 29; 10:1; 11:33; 12:1; 14:6, 20, 26, 39; 15:1, 6, 50, 58; 16:15, 20.
[b] 12 That is, Peter   [c] 19 Isaiah 29:14

²⁵For the foolishness of God is wiser than human wisdom, and the weakness of God is stronger than human strength.

²⁶Brothers and sisters, think of what you were when you were called. Not many of you were wise by human standards; not many were influential; not many were of noble birth. ²⁷But God chose the foolish things of the world to shame the wise; God chose the weak things of the world to shame the strong. ²⁸God chose the lowly things of this world and the despised things—and the things that are not—to nullify the things that are, ²⁹so that no one may boast before him. ³⁰It is because of him that you are in Christ Jesus, who has become for us wisdom from God—that is, our righteousness, holiness and redemption. ³¹Therefore, as it is written: "Let the one who boasts boast in the Lord."ᵃ

2 And so it was with me, brothers and sisters. When I came to you, I did not come with eloquence or human wisdom as I proclaimed to you the testimony about God.ᵇ ²For I resolved to know nothing while I was with you except Jesus Christ and him crucified. ³I came to you in weakness with great fear and trembling. ⁴My message and my preaching were not with wise and persuasive words, but with a demonstration of the Spirit's power, ⁵so that your faith might not rest on human wisdom, but on God's power.

God's Wisdom Revealed by the Spirit

⁶We do, however, speak a message of wisdom among the mature, but not the wisdom of this age or of the rulers of this age, who are coming to nothing. ⁷No, we declare God's wisdom, a mystery that has been hidden and that God destined for our glory before time began. ⁸None of the rulers of this age understood it, for if they had, they would not have crucified the Lord of glory. ⁹However, as it is written:

> "What no eye has seen,
>   what no ear has heard,
> and what no human mind has
>   conceived"ᶜ—
>   the things God has prepared
>   for those who love him—

¹⁰these are the things God has revealed to us by his Spirit.

The Spirit searches all things, even the deep things of God. ¹¹For who knows a person's thoughts except their own spirit within them? In the same way no one knows the thoughts of God except the Spirit of God. ¹²What we have received is not the spirit of the world, but the Spirit who is from God, so that we may understand what God has freely given us. ¹³This is what we speak, not in words taught us by human wisdom but in words

---

ᵃ 31 Jer. 9:24   ᵇ 1 Some manuscripts *proclaimed to you God's mystery*
ᶜ 9 Isaiah 64:4

taught by the Spirit, explaining spiritual realities with Spirit-taught words.[a] [14] The person without the Spirit does not accept the things that come from the Spirit of God but considers them foolishness, and cannot understand them because they are discerned only through the Spirit. [15] The person with the Spirit makes judgments about all things, but such a person is not subject to merely human judgments, [16] for,

> "Who has known the mind of
>   the Lord
>   so as to instruct him?"[b]

But we have the mind of Christ.

The Church and Its Leaders

3 Brothers and sisters, I could not address you as people who live by the Spirit but as people who are still worldly — mere infants in Christ. [2] I gave you milk, not solid food, for you were not yet ready for it. Indeed, you are still not ready. [3] You are still worldly. For since there is jealousy and quarreling among you, are you not worldly? Are you not acting like mere humans? [4] For when one says, "I follow Paul," and another, "I follow Apollos," are you not mere human beings?

[5] What, after all, is Apollos? And what is Paul? Only servants, through whom you came to believe — as the Lord has assigned to each his task. [6] I planted the seed, Apollos watered it, but God has been making it grow. [7] So neither the one who plants nor the one who waters is anything, but only God, who makes things grow. [8] The one who plants and the one who waters have one purpose, and they will each be rewarded according to their own labor. [9] For we are co-workers in God's service; you are God's field, God's building.

[10] By the grace God has given me, I laid a foundation as a wise builder, and someone else is building on it. But each one should build with care. [11] For no one can lay any foundation other than the one already laid, which is Jesus Christ. [12] If anyone builds on this foundation using gold, silver, costly stones, wood, hay or straw, [13] their work will be shown for what it is, because the Day will bring it to light. It will be revealed with fire, and the fire will test the quality of each person's work. [14] If what has been built survives, the builder will receive a reward. [15] If it is burned up, the builder will suffer loss but yet will be saved — even though only as one escaping through the flames.

[16] Don't you know that you yourselves are God's temple and that God's Spirit dwells in your midst? [17] If anyone destroys God's temple, God will destroy that person; for God's temple is sacred, and you together are that temple.

[18] Do not deceive yourselves.

[a] 13 Or *Spirit, interpreting spiritual truths to those who are spiritual*
[b] 16 Isaiah 40:13

If any of you think you are wise by the standards of this age, you should become "fools" so that you may become wise. [19]For the wisdom of this world is foolishness in God's sight. As it is written: "He catches the wise in their craftiness"[a]; [20]and again, "The Lord knows that the thoughts of the wise are futile."[b] [21]So then, no more boasting about human leaders! All things are yours, [22]whether Paul or Apollos or Cephas[c] or the world or life or death or the present or the future—all are yours, [23]and you are of Christ, and Christ is of God.

The Nature of True Apostleship

4 This, then, is how you ought to regard us: as servants of Christ and as those entrusted with the mysteries God has revealed. [2]Now it is required that those who have been given a trust must prove faithful. [3]I care very little if I am judged by you or by any human court; indeed, I do not even judge myself. [4]My conscience is clear, but that does not make me innocent. It is the Lord who judges me. [5]Therefore judge nothing before the appointed time; wait until the Lord comes. He will bring to light what is hidden in darkness and will expose the motives of the heart. At that time each will receive their praise from God.

[6]Now, brothers and sisters, I have applied these things to myself and Apollos for your benefit, so that you may learn from us the meaning of the saying, "Do not go beyond what is written." Then you will not be puffed up in being a follower of one of us over against the other. [7]For who makes you different from anyone else? What do you have that you did not receive? And if you did receive it, why do you boast as though you did not?

[8]Already you have all you want! Already you have become rich! You have begun to reign—and that without us! How I wish that you really had begun to reign so that we also might reign with you! [9]For it seems to me that God has put us apostles on display at the end of the procession, like those condemned to die in the arena. We have been made a spectacle to the whole universe, to angels as well as to human beings. [10]We are fools for Christ, but you are so wise in Christ! We are weak, but you are strong! You are honored, we are dishonored! [11]To this very hour we go hungry and thirsty, we are in rags, we are brutally treated, we are homeless. [12]We work hard with our own hands. When we are cursed, we bless; when we are persecuted, we endure it; [13]when we are slandered, we answer kindly. We have become the scum of the earth, the garbage of the world—right up to this moment.

---

a 19 Job 5:13   *b 20* Psalm 94:11   *c 22* That is, Peter

Paul's Appeal and Warning

14 I am writing this not to shame you but to warn you as my dear children. **15** Even if you had ten thousand guardians in Christ, you do not have many fathers, for in Christ Jesus I became your father through the gospel. **16** Therefore I urge you to imitate me. **17** For this reason I have sent to you Timothy, my son whom I love, who is faithful in the Lord. He will remind you of my way of life in Christ Jesus, which agrees with what I teach everywhere in every church.

18 Some of you have become arrogant, as if I were not coming to you. **19** But I will come to you very soon, if the Lord is willing, and then I will find out not only how these arrogant people are talking, but what power they have. **20** For the kingdom of God is not a matter of talk but of power. **21** What do you prefer? Shall I come to you with a rod of discipline, or shall I come in love and with a gentle spirit?

Dealing With a Case of Incest

5 It is actually reported that there is sexual immorality among you, and of a kind that even pagans do not tolerate: A man is sleeping with his father's wife. **2** And you are proud! Shouldn't you rather have gone into mourning and have put out of your fellowship the man who has been doing this? **3** For my part, even though I am not physically present, I am with you in spirit. As one who is present with you in this way, I have already passed judgment in the name of our Lord Jesus on the one who has been doing this. **4** So when you are assembled and I am with you in spirit, and the power of our Lord Jesus is present, **5** hand this man over to Satan for the destruction of the flesh,[a,b] so that his spirit may be saved on the day of the Lord.

6 Your boasting is not good. Don't you know that a little yeast leavens the whole batch of dough? **7** Get rid of the old yeast, so that you may be a new unleavened batch—as you really are. For Christ, our Passover lamb, has been sacrificed. **8** Therefore let us keep the Festival, not with the old bread leavened with malice and wickedness, but with the unleavened bread of sincerity and truth.

9 I wrote to you in my letter not to associate with sexually immoral people— **10** not at all meaning the people of this world who are immoral, or the greedy and swindlers, or idolaters. In that case you would have to leave this world. **11** But now I am writing to you that you must not associate with anyone who claims to be a brother or sister[c] but is sexually immoral or greedy, an idolater or slanderer,

---

[a] 5 In contexts like this, the Greek word for *flesh* (*sarx*) refers to the sinful state of human beings, often presented as a power in opposition to the Spirit. [b] 5 Or *of his body* [c] 11 The Greek word for *brother or sister* (*adelphos*) refers here to a believer, whether man or woman, as part of God's family; also in 8:11, 13.

a drunkard or swindler. Do not even eat with such people.

[12] What business is it of mine to judge those outside the church? Are you not to judge those inside? [13] God will judge those outside. "Expel the wicked person from among you."[a]

Lawsuits Among Believers

6 If any of you has a dispute with another, do you dare to take it before the ungodly for judgment instead of before the Lord's people? [2] Or do you not know that the Lord's people will judge the world? And if you are to judge the world, are you not competent to judge trivial cases? [3] Do you not know that we will judge angels? How much more the things of this life! [4] Therefore, if you have disputes about such matters, do you ask for a ruling from those whose way of life is scorned in the church? [5] I say this to shame you. Is it possible that there is nobody among you wise enough to judge a dispute between believers? [6] But instead, one brother takes another to court — and this in front of unbelievers!

[7] The very fact that you have lawsuits among you means you have been completely defeated already. Why not rather be wronged? Why not rather be cheated? [8] Instead, you yourselves cheat and do wrong, and you do this to your brothers and sisters. [9] Or do you not know that wrongdoers will not inherit the kingdom of God? Do not be deceived: Neither the sexually immoral nor idolaters nor adulterers nor men who have sex with men[b] [10] nor thieves nor the greedy nor drunkards nor slanderers nor swindlers will inherit the kingdom of God. [11] And that is what some of you were. But you were washed, you were sanctified, you were justified in the name of the Lord Jesus Christ and by the Spirit of our God.

Sexual Immorality

[12] "I have the right to do anything," you say — but not everything is beneficial. "I have the right to do anything" — but I will not be mastered by anything. [13] You say, "Food for the stomach and the stomach for food, and God will destroy them both." The body, however, is not meant for sexual immorality but for the Lord, and the Lord for the body. [14] By his power God raised the Lord from the dead, and he will raise us also. [15] Do you not know that your bodies are members of Christ himself? Shall I then take the members of Christ and unite them with a prostitute? Never! [16] Do you not know that he who unites himself with a prostitute is one with her in body? For it is said, "The two will become one

---

[a] 13 Deut. 13:5; 17:7; 19:19; 21:21; 22:21,24; 24:7   [b] 9 The words *men who have sex with men* translate two Greek words that refer to the passive and active participants in homosexual acts.

flesh."*a* ¹⁷But whoever is united with the Lord is one with him in spirit.*b*

¹⁸Flee from sexual immorality. All other sins a person commits are outside the body, but whoever sins sexually, sins against their own body. ¹⁹Do you not know that your bodies are temples of the Holy Spirit, who is in you, whom you have received from God? You are not your own; ²⁰you were bought at a price. Therefore honor God with your bodies.

Concerning Married Life

7 Now for the matters you wrote about: "It is good for a man not to have sexual relations with a woman." ²But since sexual immorality is occurring, each man should have sexual relations with his own wife, and each woman with her own husband. ³The husband should fulfill his marital duty to his wife, and likewise the wife to her husband. ⁴The wife does not have authority over her own body but yields it to her husband. In the same way, the husband does not have authority over his own body but yields it to his wife. ⁵Do not deprive each other except perhaps by mutual consent and for a time, so that you may devote yourselves to prayer. Then come together again so that Satan will not tempt you because of your lack of self-control. ⁶I say this as a concession, not as a command. ⁷I wish that all of you were as I am. But each of you has your own gift from God; one has this gift, another has that.

⁸Now to the unmarried*c* and the widows I say: It is good for them to stay unmarried, as I do. ⁹But if they cannot control themselves, they should marry, for it is better to marry than to burn with passion.

¹⁰To the married I give this command (not I, but the Lord): A wife must not separate from her husband. ¹¹But if she does, she must remain unmarried or else be reconciled to her husband. And a husband must not divorce his wife.

¹²To the rest I say this (I, not the Lord): If any brother has a wife who is not a believer and she is willing to live with him, he must not divorce her. ¹³And if a woman has a husband who is not a believer and he is willing to live with her, she must not divorce him. ¹⁴For the unbelieving husband has been sanctified through his wife, and the unbelieving wife has been sanctified through her believing husband. Otherwise your children would be unclean, but as it is, they are holy.

¹⁵But if the unbeliever leaves, let it be so. The brother or the sister is not bound in such circumstances; God has called us to live in peace. ¹⁶How do you know, wife, whether you will save your husband? Or, how do you know, husband, whether you will save your wife?

---

a 16 Gen. 2:24   *b* 17 Or *in the Spirit*   *c* 8 Or *widowers*

Concerning Change of Status

17 Nevertheless, each person should live as a believer in whatever situation the Lord has assigned to them, just as God has called them. This is the rule I lay down in all the churches. **18** Was a man already circumcised when he was called? He should not become uncircumcised. Was a man uncircumcised when he was called? He should not be circumcised. **19** Circumcision is nothing and uncircumcision is nothing. Keeping God's commands is what counts. **20** Each person should remain in the situation they were in when God called them.

21 Were you a slave when you were called? Don't let it trouble you — although if you can gain your freedom, do so. **22** For the one who was a slave when called to faith in the Lord is the Lord's freed person; similarly, the one who was free when called is Christ's slave. **23** You were bought at a price; do not become slaves of human beings. **24** Brothers and sisters, each person, as responsible to God, should remain in the situation they were in when God called them.

Concerning the Unmarried

25 Now about virgins: I have no command from the Lord, but I give a judgment as one who by the Lord's mercy is trustworthy. **26** Because of the present crisis, I think that it is good for a man to remain as he is. **27** Are you pledged to a woman? Do not seek to be released. Are you free from such a commitment? Do not look for a wife. **28** But if you do marry, you have not sinned; and if a virgin marries, she has not sinned. But those who marry will face many troubles in this life, and I want to spare you this.

29 What I mean, brothers and sisters, is that the time is short. From now on those who have wives should live as if they do not; **30** those who mourn, as if they did not; those who are happy, as if they were not; those who buy something, as if it were not theirs to keep; **31** those who use the things of the world, as if not engrossed in them. For this world in its present form is passing away.

32 I would like you to be free from concern. An unmarried man is concerned about the Lord's affairs — how he can please the Lord. **33** But a married man is concerned about the affairs of this world — how he can please his wife — **34** and his interests are divided. An unmarried woman or virgin is concerned about the Lord's affairs: Her aim is to be devoted to the Lord in both body and spirit. But a married woman is concerned about the affairs of this world — how she can please her husband. **35** I am saying this for your own good, not to restrict you, but that you may live in a right way in undivided devotion to the Lord.

36 If anyone is worried that he

might not be acting honorably toward the virgin he is engaged to, and if his passions are too strong[a] and he feels he ought to marry, he should do as he wants. He is not sinning. They should get married. **37** But the man who has settled the matter in his own mind, who is under no compulsion but has control over his own will, and who has made up his mind not to marry the virgin — this man also does the right thing. **38** So then, he who marries the virgin does right, but he who does not marry her does better.[b]

39 A woman is bound to her husband as long as he lives. But if her husband dies, she is free to marry anyone she wishes, but he must belong to the Lord. **40** In my judgment, she is happier if she stays as she is — and I think that I too have the Spirit of God.

Concerning Food Sacrificed to Idols

8 Now about food sacrificed to idols: We know that "We all possess knowledge." But knowledge puffs up while love builds up. **2** Those who think they know something do not yet know as they ought to know. **3** But whoever loves God is known by God.[c]

4 So then, about eating food sacrificed to idols: We know that "An idol is nothing at all in the world" and that "There is no God but one." **5** For even if there are so-called gods, whether in heaven or on earth (as indeed there are many "gods" and many "lords"), **6** yet for us there is but one God, the Father, from whom all things came and for whom we live; and there is but one Lord, Jesus Christ, through whom all things came and through whom we live.

7 But not everyone possesses this knowledge. Some people are still so accustomed to idols that when they eat sacrificial food they think of it as having been sacrificed to a god, and since their conscience is weak, it is defiled. **8** But food does not bring us near to God; we are no worse if we do not eat, and no better if we do.

9 Be careful, however, that the exercise of your rights does not become a stumbling block to the weak. **10** For if someone with a weak conscience sees you, with all your knowledge, eating in an idol's temple, won't that person

---

[a] 36 Or *if she is getting beyond the usual age for marriage* [b] 36-38 Or *36 If anyone thinks he is not treating his daughter properly, and if she is getting along in years (or if her passions are too strong), and he feels she ought to marry, he should do as he wants. He is not sinning. He should let her get married. 37 But the man who has settled the matter in his own mind, who is under no compulsion but has control over his own will, and who has made up his mind to keep the virgin unmarried — this man also does the right thing. 38 So then, he who gives his virgin in marriage does right, but he who does not give her in marriage does better.* [c] 2,3 An early manuscript and another ancient witness *think they have knowledge do not yet know as they ought to know. 3 But whoever loves truly knows.*

be emboldened to eat what is sacrificed to idols? ¹¹ So this weak brother or sister, for whom Christ died, is destroyed by your knowledge. ¹²When you sin against them in this way and wound their weak conscience, you sin against Christ. ¹³ Therefore, if what I eat causes my brother or sister to fall into sin, I will never eat meat again, so that I will not cause them to fall.

Paul's Rights as an Apostle

9 Am I not free? Am I not an apostle? Have I not seen Jesus our Lord? Are you not the result of my work in the Lord? ²Even though I may not be an apostle to others, surely I am to you! For you are the seal of my apostleship in the Lord.

³This is my defense to those who sit in judgment on me. ⁴Don't we have the right to food and drink? ⁵Don't we have the right to take a believing wife along with us, as do the other apostles and the Lord's brothers and Cephas*ᵃ*? ⁶Or is it only I and Barnabas who lack the right to not work for a living?

⁷Who serves as a soldier at his own expense? Who plants a vineyard and does not eat its grapes? Who tends a flock and does not drink the milk? ⁸Do I say this merely on human authority? Doesn't the Law say the same thing? ⁹For it is written in the Law of Moses: "Do not muzzle an ox while it is treading out the grain."*ᵇ* Is it about oxen that God is concerned? ¹⁰Surely he says this for us, doesn't he? Yes, this was written for us, because whoever plows and threshes should be able to do so in the hope of sharing in the harvest. ¹¹ If we have sown spiritual seed among you, is it too much if we reap a material harvest from you? ¹²If others have this right of support from you, shouldn't we have it all the more?

But we did not use this right. On the contrary, we put up with anything rather than hinder the gospel of Christ.

¹³Don't you know that those who serve in the temple get their food from the temple, and that those who serve at the altar share in what is offered on the altar? ¹⁴In the same way, the Lord has commanded that those who preach the gospel should receive their living from the gospel.

¹⁵But I have not used any of these rights. And I am not writing this in the hope that you will do such things for me, for I would rather die than allow anyone to deprive me of this boast. ¹⁶For when I preach the gospel, I cannot boast, since I am compelled to preach. Woe to me if I do not preach the gospel! ¹⁷If I preach voluntarily, I have a reward; if not voluntarily, I am simply discharging the trust committed to me.

ᵃ 5 That is, Peter   *ᵇ 9* Deut. 25:4

[18] What then is my reward? Just this: that in preaching the gospel I may offer it free of charge, and so not make full use of my rights as a preacher of the gospel.

Paul's Use of His Freedom

[19] Though I am free and belong to no one, I have made myself a slave to everyone, to win as many as possible. [20] To the Jews I became like a Jew, to win the Jews. To those under the law I became like one under the law (though I myself am not under the law), so as to win those under the law. [21] To those not having the law I became like one not having the law (though I am not free from God's law but am under Christ's law), so as to win those not having the law. [22] To the weak I became weak, to win the weak. I have become all things to all people so that by all possible means I might save some. [23] I do all this for the sake of the gospel, that I may share in its blessings.

The Need for Self-Discipline

[24] Do you not know that in a race all the runners run, but only one gets the prize? Run in such a way as to get the prize. [25] Everyone who competes in the games goes into strict training. They do it to get a crown that will not last, but we do it to get a crown that will last forever. [26] Therefore I do not run like someone running aim-lessly; I do not fight like a boxer beating the air. [27] No, I strike a blow to my body and make it my slave so that after I have preached to others, I myself will not be disqualified for the prize.

Warnings From Israel's History

10 For I do not want you to be ignorant of the fact, brothers and sisters, that our ancestors were all under the cloud and that they all passed through the sea. [2] They were all baptized into Moses in the cloud and in the sea. [3] They all ate the same spiritual food [4] and drank the same spiritual drink; for they drank from the spiritual rock that accompanied them, and that rock was Christ. [5] Nevertheless, God was not pleased with most of them; their bodies were scattered in the wilderness.

[6] Now these things occurred as examples to keep us from setting our hearts on evil things as they did. [7] Do not be idolaters, as some of them were; as it is written: "The people sat down to eat and drink and got up to indulge in revelry."[a] [8] We should not commit sexual immorality, as some of them did—and in one day twenty-three thousand of them died. [9] We should not test Christ,[b] as some of them did—and were killed by snakes. [10] And do not grumble, as some of them did—and were killed by the destroying angel.

---

[a] 7 Exodus 32:6   [b] 9 Some manuscripts *test the Lord*

¹¹These things happened to them as examples and were written down as warnings for us, on whom the culmination of the ages has come. ¹²So, if you think you are standing firm, be careful that you don't fall! ¹³No temptation*ᵃ* has overtaken you except what is common to mankind. And God is faithful; he will not let you be tempted*ᵃ* beyond what you can bear. But when you are tempted,*ᵃ* he will also provide a way out so that you can endure it.

Idol Feasts and the Lord's Supper

¹⁴Therefore, my dear friends, flee from idolatry. ¹⁵I speak to sensible people; judge for yourselves what I say. ¹⁶Is not the cup of thanksgiving for which we give thanks a participation in the blood of Christ? And is not the bread that we break a participation in the body of Christ? ¹⁷Because there is one loaf, we, who are many, are one body, for we all share the one loaf.

¹⁸Consider the people of Israel: Do not those who eat the sacrifices participate in the altar? ¹⁹Do I mean then that food sacrificed to an idol is anything, or that an idol is anything? ²⁰No, but the sacrifices of pagans are offered to demons, not to God, and I do not want you to be participants with demons. ²¹You cannot drink the cup of the Lord and the cup of demons too; you cannot have a part in both the Lord's table and the table of demons. ²²Are we trying to arouse the Lord's jealousy? Are we stronger than he?

The Believer's Freedom

²³"I have the right to do anything," you say—but not everything is beneficial. "I have the right to do anything"—but not everything is constructive. ²⁴No one should seek their own good, but the good of others.

²⁵Eat anything sold in the meat market without raising questions of conscience, ²⁶for, "The earth is the Lord's, and everything in it."*ᵇ*

²⁷If an unbeliever invites you to a meal and you want to go, eat whatever is put before you without raising questions of conscience. ²⁸But if someone says to you, "This has been offered in sacrifice," then do not eat it, both for the sake of the one who told you and for the sake of conscience. ²⁹I am referring to the other person's conscience, not yours. For why is my freedom being judged by another's conscience? ³⁰If I take part in the meal with thankfulness, why am I denounced because of something I thank God for?

³¹So whether you eat or drink or whatever you do, do it all for the glory of God. ³²Do not cause anyone to stumble, whether Jews, Greeks or the church of God—

ᵃ 13 The Greek for *temptation* and *tempted* can also mean *testing* and *tested.*
ᵇ 26 Psalm 24:1

³³even as I try to please everyone in every way. For I am not seeking my own good but the good of many, so that they may be saved.

11 ¹Follow my example, as I follow the example of Christ.

On Covering the Head in Worship

²I praise you for remembering me in everything and for holding to the traditions just as I passed them on to you. ³But I want you to realize that the head of every man is Christ, and the head of the woman is man,ᵃ and the head of Christ is God. ⁴Every man who prays or prophesies with his head covered dishonors his head. ⁵But every woman who prays or prophesies with her head uncovered dishonors her head — it is the same as having her head shaved. ⁶For if a woman does not cover her head, she might as well have her hair cut off; but if it is a disgrace for a woman to have her hair cut off or her head shaved, then she should cover her head.

⁷A man ought not to cover his head,ᵇ since he is the image and glory of God; but woman is the glory of man. ⁸For man did not come from woman, but woman from man; ⁹neither was man created for woman, but woman for man. ¹⁰It is for this reason that a woman ought to have authority over her ownᶜ head, because of the angels. ¹¹Nevertheless, in the Lord woman is not independent of man, nor is man independent of woman. ¹²For as woman came from man, so also man is born of woman. But everything comes from God.

¹³Judge for yourselves: Is it proper for a woman to pray to God with her head uncovered? ¹⁴Does not the very nature of things teach you that if a man has long hair, it is a disgrace to him, ¹⁵but that if a woman has long hair, it is her glory? For long hair is given to her as a covering. ¹⁶If anyone wants to be contentious about this, we have no other practice — nor do the churches of God.

Correcting an Abuse of the Lord's Supper

¹⁷In the following directives I have no praise for you, for your meetings do more harm than good. ¹⁸In the first place, I hear that when you come together as a church, there are divisions among you, and to some extent I believe it. ¹⁹No doubt there have to be differences among you to show which of you have God's approval. ²⁰So then, when you

---

ᵃ 3 Or *of the wife is her husband*   ᵇ 4-7 Or *⁴Every man who prays or prophesies with long hair dishonors his head. ⁵But every woman who prays or prophesies with no covering of hair dishonors her head — she is just like one of the "shorn women." ⁶If a woman has no covering, let her be for now with short hair; but since it is a disgrace for a woman to have her hair shorn or shaved, she should grow it again. ⁷A man ought not to have long hair*   ᶜ 10 Or *have a sign of authority on her*

Jesus Dies on the Cross
MARK 15:21–41

Jesus Returns to Heaven

ACTS 1:1–11

The ABCs of Becoming a Christian

Becoming a Christian (someone who follows Jesus Christ) is simple. Just follow the ABCs! Find the verses listed by using the table of contents in the front of this Bible. You can read the verses and talk to God right now, right where you are. He is always happy to listen.

A – ADMIT

Admit honestly to God that you are a sinner and have not obeyed him.

Romans 3:23 • Romans 6:23 • 1 John 1:9

B – BELIEVE

Believe that Jesus Christ is God's Son and died on the cross and became alive again. He died for your sins so you can be forgiven.

1 Corinthians 15:3–4 • John 3:16 • Acts 4:12 • Romans 5:8

C – CONFESS

Confess your faith in Jesus. Tell someone you know (like a pastor, parent, or other Christian). Then celebrate! If you don't already attend a church, try to find one. It is important to help you grow in your new life in Christ.

Romans 10:9–10 • Romans 10:13

If you followed these ABCs and decided to follow Jesus, we would love to hear from you! Write to:

Zonderkidz Bible Editors
Zondervan
5300 Patterson Avenue SE
Grand Rapids, MI 49530

Children from Every Nation

REVELATION 7:9–10

come together, it is not the Lord's Supper you eat, ²¹for when you are eating, some of you go ahead with your own private suppers. As a result, one person remains hungry and another gets drunk. ²²Don't you have homes to eat and drink in? Or do you despise the church of God by humiliating those who have nothing? What shall I say to you? Shall I praise you? Certainly not in this matter!

²³For I received from the Lord what I also passed on to you: The Lord Jesus, on the night he was betrayed, took bread, ²⁴and when he had given thanks, he broke it and said, "This is my body, which is for you; do this in remembrance of me." ²⁵In the same way, after supper he took the cup, saying, "This cup is the new covenant in my blood; do this, whenever you drink it, in remembrance of me." ²⁶For whenever you eat this bread and drink this cup, you proclaim the Lord's death until he comes.

²⁷So then, whoever eats the bread or drinks the cup of the Lord in an unworthy manner will be guilty of sinning against the body and blood of the Lord. ²⁸Everyone ought to examine themselves before they eat of the bread and drink from the cup. ²⁹For those who eat and drink without discerning the body of Christ eat and drink judgment on themselves. ³⁰That is why many among you are weak and sick, and a number of you have fallen

asleep. ³¹But if we were more discerning with regard to ourselves, we would not come under such judgment. ³²Nevertheless, when we are judged in this way by the Lord, we are being disciplined so that we will not be finally condemned with the world.

³³So then, my brothers and sisters, when you gather to eat, you should all eat together. ³⁴Anyone who is hungry should eat something at home, so that when you meet together it may not result in judgment.

And when I come I will give further directions.

Concerning Spiritual Gifts

12 Now about the gifts of the Spirit, brothers and sisters, I do not want you to be uninformed. ²You know that when you were pagans, somehow or other you were influenced and led astray to mute idols. ³Therefore I want you to know that no one who is speaking by the Spirit of God says, "Jesus be cursed," and no one can say, "Jesus is Lord," except by the Holy Spirit.

⁴There are different kinds of gifts, but the same Spirit distributes them. ⁵There are different kinds of service, but the same Lord. ⁶There are different kinds of working, but in all of them and in everyone it is the same God at work.

⁷Now to each one the manifestation of the Spirit is given for the common good. ⁸To one there is

given through the Spirit a message of wisdom, to another a message of knowledge by means of the same Spirit, [9]to another faith by the same Spirit, to another gifts of healing by that one Spirit, [10]to another miraculous powers, to another prophecy, to another distinguishing between spirits, to another speaking in different kinds of tongues,[a] and to still another the interpretation of tongues.[a] [11]All these are the work of one and the same Spirit, and he distributes them to each one, just as he determines.

Unity and Diversity in the Body

[12]Just as a body, though one, has many parts, but all its many parts form one body, so it is with Christ. [13]For we were all baptized by[b] one Spirit so as to form one body — whether Jews or Gentiles, slave or free — and we were all given the one Spirit to drink. [14]Even so the body is not made up of one part but of many.

[15]Now if the foot should say, "Because I am not a hand, I do not belong to the body," it would not for that reason stop being part of the body. [16]And if the ear should say, "Because I am not an eye, I do not belong to the body," it would not for that reason stop being part of the body. [17]If the whole body were an eye, where would the sense of hearing be? If the whole body were an ear, where would the sense of smell be? [18]But in fact God has placed the parts in the body, every one of them, just as he wanted them to be. [19]If they were all one part, where would the body be? [20]As it is, there are many parts, but one body.

[21]The eye cannot say to the hand, "I don't need you!" And the head cannot say to the feet, "I don't need you!" [22]On the contrary, those parts of the body that seem to be weaker are indispensable, [23]and the parts that we think are less honorable we treat with special honor. And the parts that are unpresentable are treated with special modesty, [24]while our presentable parts need no special treatment. But God has put the body together, giving greater honor to the parts that lacked it, [25]so that there should be no division in the body, but that its parts should have equal concern for each other. [26]If one part suffers, every part suffers with it; if one part is honored, every part rejoices with it.

[27]Now you are the body of Christ, and each one of you is a part of it. [28]And God has placed in the church first of all apostles, second prophets, third teachers, then miracles, then gifts of healing, of helping, of guidance, and of different kinds of tongues. [29]Are all apostles? Are all prophets? Are all teachers? Do all work miracles? [30]Do all have

---

[a] 10 Or languages; also in verse 28   [b] 13 Or with; or in

gifts of healing? Do all speak in tongues[a]? Do all interpret? [31] Now eagerly desire the greater gifts.

Love Is Indispensable

And yet I will show you the most excellent way.

13 If I speak in the tongues[b] of men or of angels, but do not have love, I am only a resounding gong or a clanging cymbal. [2] If I have the gift of prophecy and can fathom all mysteries and all knowledge, and if I have a faith that can move mountains, but do not have love, I am nothing. [3] If I give all I possess to the poor and give over my body to hardship that I may boast,[c] but do not have love, I gain nothing.

[4] Love is patient, love is kind. It does not envy, it does not boast, it is not proud. [5] It does not dishonor others, it is not self-seeking, it is not easily angered, it keeps no record of wrongs. [6] Love does not delight in evil but rejoices with the truth. [7] It always protects, always trusts, always hopes, always perseveres.

[8] Love never fails. But where there are prophecies, they will cease; where there are tongues, they will be stilled; where there is knowledge, it will pass away. [9] For we know in part and we prophesy in part, [10] but when completeness comes, what is in part disappears. [11] When I was a child, I talked like a child, I thought like a child, I reasoned like a child. When I became a man, I put the ways of childhood behind me. [12] For now we see only a reflection as in a mirror; then we shall see face to face. Now I know in part; then I shall know fully, even as I am fully known.

[13] And now these three remain: faith, hope and love. But the greatest of these is love.

Intelligibility in Worship

14 Follow the way of love and eagerly desire gifts of the Spirit, especially prophecy. [2] For anyone who speaks in a tongue[d] does not speak to people but to God. Indeed, no one understands them; they utter mysteries by the Spirit. [3] But the one who prophesies speaks to people for their strengthening, encouraging and comfort. [4] Anyone who speaks in a tongue edifies themselves, but the one who prophesies edifies the church. [5] I would like every one of you to speak in tongues,[e] but I would rather have you prophesy. The one who prophesies is greater than the one who speaks in tongues,[e] unless someone interprets, so that the church may be edified.

[6] Now, brothers and sisters, if I come to you and speak in tongues, what good will I be to you, unless I bring you some revelation

---

[a] 30 Or *other languages*   [b] 1 Or *languages*   [c] 3 Some manuscripts *body to the flames*   [d] 2 Or *in another language*; also in verses 4, 13, 14, 19, 26 and 27   [e] 5 Or *in other languages*; also in verses 6, 18, 22, 23 and 39

or knowledge or prophecy or word of instruction? [7] Even in the case of lifeless things that make sounds, such as the pipe or harp, how will anyone know what tune is being played unless there is a distinction in the notes? [8] Again, if the trumpet does not sound a clear call, who will get ready for battle? [9] So it is with you. Unless you speak intelligible words with your tongue, how will anyone know what you are saying? You will just be speaking into the air. [10] Undoubtedly there are all sorts of languages in the world, yet none of them is without meaning. [11] If then I do not grasp the meaning of what someone is saying, I am a foreigner to the speaker, and the speaker is a foreigner to me. [12] So it is with you. Since you are eager for gifts of the Spirit, try to excel in those that build up the church.

[13] For this reason the one who speaks in a tongue should pray that they may interpret what they say. [14] For if I pray in a tongue, my spirit prays, but my mind is unfruitful. [15] So what shall I do? I will pray with my spirit, but I will also pray with my understanding; I will sing with my spirit, but I will also sing with my understanding. [16] Otherwise when you are praising God in the Spirit, how can someone else, who is now put in the position of an inquirer,[a] say "Amen" to your thanksgiving, since they do not know what you are saying? [17] You are giving thanks well enough, but no one else is edified.

[18] I thank God that I speak in tongues more than all of you. [19] But in the church I would rather speak five intelligible words to instruct others than ten thousand words in a tongue.

[20] Brothers and sisters, stop thinking like children. In regard to evil be infants, but in your thinking be adults. [21] In the Law it is written:

"With other tongues
  and through the lips of
    foreigners
I will speak to this people,
  but even then they will not
    listen to me,
      says the Lord."[b]

[22] Tongues, then, are a sign, not for believers but for unbelievers; prophecy, however, is not for unbelievers but for believers. [23] So if the whole church comes together and everyone speaks in tongues, and inquirers or unbelievers come in, will they not say that you are out of your mind? [24] But if an unbeliever or an inquirer comes in while everyone is prophesying, they are convicted of sin and are brought under judgment by all, [25] as the secrets of their hearts are laid bare. So they will fall down and worship God, exclaiming, "God is really among you!"

---

[a] 16 The Greek word for *inquirer* is a technical term for someone not fully initiated into a religion; also in verses 23 and 24.   [b] 21 Isaiah 28:11,12

Good Order in Worship

²⁶ What then shall we say, brothers and sisters? When you come together, each of you has a hymn, or a word of instruction, a revelation, a tongue or an interpretation. Everything must be done so that the church may be built up. ²⁷ If anyone speaks in a tongue, two — or at the most three — should speak, one at a time, and someone must interpret. ²⁸ If there is no interpreter, the speaker should keep quiet in the church and speak to himself and to God.

²⁹ Two or three prophets should speak, and the others should weigh carefully what is said. ³⁰ And if a revelation comes to someone who is sitting down, the first speaker should stop. ³¹ For you can all prophesy in turn so that everyone may be instructed and encouraged. ³² The spirits of prophets are subject to the control of prophets. ³³ For God is not a God of disorder but of peace — as in all the congregations of the Lord's people.

³⁴ Women[a] should remain silent in the churches. They are not allowed to speak, but must be in submission, as the law says. ³⁵ If they want to inquire about something, they should ask their own husbands at home; for it is disgraceful for a woman to speak in the church.[b]

³⁶ Or did the word of God originate with you? Or are you the only people it has reached? ³⁷ If anyone thinks they are a prophet or otherwise gifted by the Spirit, let them acknowledge that what I am writing to you is the Lord's command. ³⁸ But if anyone ignores this, they will themselves be ignored.[c]

³⁹ Therefore, my brothers and sisters, be eager to prophesy, and do not forbid speaking in tongues. ⁴⁰ But everything should be done in a fitting and orderly way.

The Resurrection of Christ

15 Now, brothers and sisters, I want to remind you of the gospel I preached to you, which you received and on which you have taken your stand. ² By this gospel you are saved, if you hold firmly to the word I preached to you. Otherwise, you have believed in vain.

³ For what I received I passed on to you as of first importance[d]: that Christ died for our sins according to the Scriptures, ⁴ that he was buried, that he was raised on the third day according to the Scriptures, ⁵ and that he appeared to Cephas,[e] and then to the Twelve. ⁶ After that, he appeared to more than five hundred of the brothers and sisters at the same time, most of whom are still living, though some have

---

[a] 33,34 Or *peace. As in all the congregations of the Lord's people,* ³⁴*women*
[b] 34,35 In a few manuscripts these verses come after verse 40.   [c] 38 Some manuscripts *But anyone who is ignorant of this will be ignorant*   [d] 3 Or *you at the first*   [e] 5 That is, Peter

fallen asleep. [7] Then he appeared to James, then to all the apostles, [8] and last of all he appeared to me also, as to one abnormally born.

[9] For I am the least of the apostles and do not even deserve to be called an apostle, because I persecuted the church of God. [10] But by the grace of God I am what I am, and his grace to me was not without effect. No, I worked harder than all of them — yet not I, but the grace of God that was with me. [11] Whether, then, it is I or they, this is what we preach, and this is what you believed.

The Resurrection of the Dead

[12] But if it is preached that Christ has been raised from the dead, how can some of you say that there is no resurrection of the dead? [13] If there is no resurrection of the dead, then not even Christ has been raised. [14] And if Christ has not been raised, our preaching is useless and so is your faith. [15] More than that, we are then found to be false witnesses about God, for we have testified about God that he raised Christ from the dead. But he did not raise him if in fact the dead are not raised. [16] For if the dead are not raised, then Christ has not been raised either. [17] And if Christ has not been raised, your faith is futile; you are still in your sins. [18] Then those also who have fallen asleep in Christ are lost. [19] If only for this life we have hope in Christ, we are of all people most to be pitied.

[20] But Christ has indeed been raised from the dead, the firstfruits of those who have fallen asleep. [21] For since death came through a man, the resurrection of the dead comes also through a man. [22] For as in Adam all die, so in Christ all will be made alive. [23] But each in turn: Christ, the firstfruits; then, when he comes, those who belong to him. [24] Then the end will come, when he hands over the kingdom to God the Father after he has destroyed all dominion, authority and power. [25] For he must reign until he has put all his enemies under his feet. [26] The last enemy to be destroyed is death. [27] For he "has put everything under his feet."[a] Now when it says that "everything" has been put under him, it is clear that this does not include God himself, who put everything under Christ. [28] When he has done this, then the Son himself will be made subject to him who put everything under him, so that God may be all in all.

[29] Now if there is no resurrection, what will those do who are baptized for the dead? If the dead are not raised at all, why are people baptized for them? [30] And as for us, why do we endanger ourselves every hour? [31] I face death every day — yes, just as surely as I boast about you in Christ

Jesus our Lord. ³²If I fought wild beasts in Ephesus with no more than human hopes, what have I gained? If the dead are not raised,

"Let us eat and drink,
for tomorrow we die."ᵃ

³³Do not be misled: "Bad company corrupts good character."ᵇ ³⁴Come back to your senses as you ought, and stop sinning; for there are some who are ignorant of God—I say this to your shame.

The Resurrection Body

³⁵But someone will ask, "How are the dead raised? With what kind of body will they come?" ³⁶How foolish! What you sow does not come to life unless it dies. ³⁷When you sow, you do not plant the body that will be, but just a seed, perhaps of wheat or of something else. ³⁸But God gives it a body as he has determined, and to each kind of seed he gives its own body. ³⁹Not all flesh is the same: People have one kind of flesh, animals have another, birds another and fish another. ⁴⁰There are also heavenly bodies and there are earthly bodies; but the splendor of the heavenly bodies is one kind, and the splendor of the earthly bodies is another. ⁴¹The sun has one kind of splendor, the moon another and the stars another; and star differs from star in splendor.

⁴²So will it be with the resurrection of the dead. The body that is sown is perishable, it is raised imperishable; ⁴³it is sown in dishonor, it is raised in glory; it is sown in weakness, it is raised in power; ⁴⁴it is sown a natural body, it is raised a spiritual body.

If there is a natural body, there is also a spiritual body. ⁴⁵So it is written: "The first man Adam became a living being"ᶜ; the last Adam, a life-giving spirit. ⁴⁶The spiritual did not come first, but the natural, and after that the spiritual. ⁴⁷The first man was of the dust of the earth; the second man is of heaven. ⁴⁸As was the earthly man, so are those who are of the earth; and as is the heavenly man, so also are those who are of heaven. ⁴⁹And just as we have borne the image of the earthly man, so shall weᵈ bear the image of the heavenly man.

⁵⁰I declare to you, brothers and sisters, that flesh and blood cannot inherit the kingdom of God, nor does the perishable inherit the imperishable. ⁵¹Listen, I tell you a mystery: We will not all sleep, but we will all be changed— ⁵²in a flash, in the twinkling of an eye, at the last trumpet. For the trumpet will sound, the dead will be raised imperishable, and we will be changed. ⁵³For the perishable must clothe itself with the imperishable, and the mortal with immortality. ⁵⁴When the perishable has been clothed with the imperishable, and the mortal with

---

ᵃ 32 Isaiah 22:13   ᵇ 33 From the Greek poet Menander   ᶜ 45 Gen. 2:7
ᵈ 49 Some early manuscripts *so let us*

immortality, then the saying that is written will come true: "Death has been swallowed up in victory."[a]

55 "Where, O death, is your
           victory?
     Where, O death, is your
           sting?"[b]

56 The sting of death is sin, and the power of sin is the law. 57 But thanks be to God! He gives us the victory through our Lord Jesus Christ.

58 Therefore, my dear brothers and sisters, stand firm. Let nothing move you. Always give yourselves fully to the work of the Lord, because you know that your labor in the Lord is not in vain.

The Collection for the Lord's People

16 Now about the collection for the Lord's people: Do what I told the Galatian churches to do. 2 On the first day of every week, each one of you should set aside a sum of money in keeping with your income, saving it up, so that when I come no collections will have to be made. 3 Then, when I arrive, I will give letters of introduction to the men you approve and send them with your gift to Jerusalem. 4 If it seems advisable for me to go also, they will accompany me.

Personal Requests

5 After I go through Macedonia, I will come to you — for I will be going through Macedonia. 6 Perhaps I will stay with you for a while, or even spend the winter, so that you can help me on my journey, wherever I go. 7 For I do not want to see you now and make only a passing visit; I hope to spend some time with you, if the Lord permits. 8 But I will stay on at Ephesus until Pentecost, 9 because a great door for effective work has opened to me, and there are many who oppose me.

10 When Timothy comes, see to it that he has nothing to fear while he is with you, for he is carrying on the work of the Lord, just as I am. 11 No one, then, should treat him with contempt. Send him on his way in peace so that he may return to me. I am expecting him along with the brothers.

12 Now about our brother Apollos: I strongly urged him to go to you with the brothers. He was quite unwilling to go now, but he will go when he has the opportunity.

13 Be on your guard; stand firm in the faith; be courageous; be strong. 14 Do everything in love.

15 You know that the household of Stephanas were the first converts in Achaia, and they have devoted themselves to the service of the Lord's people. I urge you, brothers and sisters, 16 to submit to such people and to everyone who joins in the work and labors

---

[a] 54 Isaiah 25:8   [b] 55 Hosea 13:14

at it. [17] I was glad when Stephanas, Fortunatus and Achaicus arrived, because they have supplied what was lacking from you. [18] For they refreshed my spirit and yours also. Such men deserve recognition.

Final Greetings

[19] The churches in the province of Asia send you greetings. Aquila and Priscilla[a] greet you warmly in the Lord, and so does the church that meets at their house. [20] All the brothers and sisters here send you greetings. Greet one another with a holy kiss.

[21] I, Paul, write this greeting in my own hand.

[22] If anyone does not love the Lord, let that person be cursed! Come, Lord[b]!

[23] The grace of the Lord Jesus be with you.

[24] My love to all of you in Christ Jesus. Amen.[c]

---

[a] 19 Greek *Prisca*, a variant of *Priscilla*   [b] 22 The Greek for *Come, Lord* reproduces an Aramaic expression (*Marana tha*) used by early Christians.
[c] 24 Some manuscripts do not have *Amen*.

2 Corinthians

Introduction:

Paul wrote this second letter to the Corinthians soon after the first letter. The divisions and problems he addressed in 1 Corinthians were still in the church at Corinth. Paul may have visited Corinth, but left quickly because some of the members in the church refused to believe that he was an apostle of God.

After returning to Macedonia, Paul was encouraged when Titus brought him the good news that the people in the Corinthian church had recognized their problems and sins and were willing to change. Paul then wrote his second letter to the Corinthians.

In the first part of his letter Paul tells the Corinthians how happy and thankful he was when he heard that they were sorry for the way they had acted and were now trying to live the way God wanted them to.

In the second part of his letter, Paul defends himself against the people who were angry with him and who were saying untrue things about him.

Outline of contents:

Introduction (1:1–11)
Paul as God's messenger (1:12–7:16)
Generosity in giving (8:1–9:15)
Paul as an apostle (10:1–13:10)
Conclusion (13:11–14)

1 Paul, an apostle of Christ Jesus by the will of God, and Timothy our brother,

To the church of God in Corinth, together with all his holy people throughout Achaia:

²Grace and peace to you from God our Father and the Lord Jesus Christ.

Praise to the God of All Comfort

³Praise be to the God and Father of our Lord Jesus Christ, the Father of compassion and the God of all comfort, ⁴who comforts us in all our troubles, so that we can comfort those in any trouble with the comfort we ourselves receive from God. ⁵For just as we share abundantly in the sufferings of Christ, so also our comfort abounds through Christ. ⁶If we are distressed, it is for your comfort and salvation; if we are

comforted, it is for your comfort, which produces in you patient endurance of the same sufferings we suffer. [7] And our hope for you is firm, because we know that just as you share in our sufferings, so also you share in our comfort.

[8] We do not want you to be uninformed, brothers and sisters,[a] about the troubles we experienced in the province of Asia. We were under great pressure, far beyond our ability to endure, so that we despaired of life itself. [9] Indeed, we felt we had received the sentence of death. But this happened that we might not rely on ourselves but on God, who raises the dead. [10] He has delivered us from such a deadly peril, and he will deliver us again. On him we have set our hope that he will continue to deliver us, [11] as you help us by your prayers. Then many will give thanks on our behalf for the gracious favor granted us in answer to the prayers of many.

Paul's Change of Plans

[12] Now this is our boast: Our conscience testifies that we have conducted ourselves in the world, and especially in our relations with you, with integrity[b] and godly sincerity. We have done so, relying not on worldly wisdom but on God's grace. [13] For we do not write you anything you cannot read or understand. And I hope that, [14] as you have understood us in part, you will come to understand fully that you can boast of us just as we will boast of you in the day of the Lord Jesus.

[15] Because I was confident of this, I wanted to visit you first so that you might benefit twice. [16] I wanted to visit you on my way to Macedonia and to come back to you from Macedonia, and then to have you send me on my way to Judea. [17] Was I fickle when I intended to do this? Or do I make my plans in a worldly manner so that in the same breath I say both "Yes, yes" and "No, no"?

[18] But as surely as God is faithful, our message to you is not "Yes" and "No." [19] For the Son of God, Jesus Christ, who was preached among you by us — by me and Silas[c] and Timothy — was not "Yes" and "No," but in him it has always been "Yes." [20] For no matter how many promises God has made, they are "Yes" in Christ. And so through him the "Amen" is spoken by us to the glory of God. [21] Now it is God who makes both us and you stand firm in Christ. He anointed us, [22] set his seal of ownership on us, and put his Spirit in our hearts as a deposit, guaranteeing what is to come.

[23] I call God as my witness — and I stake my life on it — that it was in order to spare you that I did not return to Corinth. [24] Not that we

---

[a] 8 The Greek word for brothers and sisters (adelphoi) refers here to believers, both men and women, as part of God's family; also in 8:1; 13:11. [b] 12 Many manuscripts holiness [c] 19 Greek Silvanus, a variant of Silas

lord it over your faith, but we work with you for your joy, because it is by faith you stand firm. ¹So I made up my mind that I would not make another painful visit to you. ²For if I grieve you, who is left to make me glad but you whom I have grieved? ³I wrote as I did, so that when I came I would not be distressed by those who should have made me rejoice. I had confidence in all of you, that you would all share my joy. ⁴For I wrote you out of great distress and anguish of heart and with many tears, not to grieve you but to let you know the depth of my love for you.

Forgiveness for the Offender

⁵If anyone has caused grief, he has not so much grieved me as he has grieved all of you to some extent — not to put it too severely. ⁶The punishment inflicted on him by the majority is sufficient. ⁷Now instead, you ought to forgive and comfort him, so that he will not be overwhelmed by excessive sorrow. ⁸I urge you, therefore, to reaffirm your love for him. ⁹Another reason I wrote you was to see if you would stand the test and be obedient in everything. ¹⁰Anyone you forgive, I also forgive. And what I have forgiven — if there was anything to forgive — I have forgiven in the sight of Christ for your sake, ¹¹in order that Satan might not outwit us. For we are not unaware of his schemes.

Ministers of the New Covenant

¹²Now when I went to Troas to preach the gospel of Christ and found that the Lord had opened a door for me, ¹³I still had no peace of mind, because I did not find my brother Titus there. So I said goodbye to them and went on to Macedonia.

¹⁴But thanks be to God, who always leads us as captives in Christ's triumphal procession and uses us to spread the aroma of the knowledge of him everywhere. ¹⁵For we are to God the pleasing aroma of Christ among those who are being saved and those who are perishing. ¹⁶To the one we are an aroma that brings death; to the other, an aroma that brings life. And who is equal to such a task? ¹⁷Unlike so many, we do not peddle the word of God for profit. On the contrary, in Christ we speak before God with sincerity, as those sent from God.

³ Are we beginning to commend ourselves again? Or do we need, like some people, letters of recommendation to you or from you? ²You yourselves are our letter, written on our hearts, known and read by everyone. ³You show that you are a letter from Christ, the result of our ministry, written not with ink but with the Spirit of the living God, not on tablets of stone but on tablets of human hearts.

⁴Such confidence we have through Christ before God. ⁵Not that we are competent in ourselves to claim anything for

ourselves, but our competence comes from God. **6**He has made us competent as ministers of a new covenant—not of the letter but of the Spirit; for the letter kills, but the Spirit gives life.

The Greater Glory of the New Covenant

7Now if the ministry that brought death, which was engraved in letters on stone, came with glory, so that the Israelites could not look steadily at the face of Moses because of its glory, transitory though it was, **8**will not the ministry of the Spirit be even more glorious? **9**If the ministry that brought condemnation was glorious, how much more glorious is the ministry that brings righteousness! **10**For what was glorious has no glory now in comparison with the surpassing glory. **11**And if what was transitory came with glory, how much greater is the glory of that which lasts!

12Therefore, since we have such a hope, we are very bold. **13**We are not like Moses, who would put a veil over his face to prevent the Israelites from seeing the end of what was passing away. **14**But their minds were made dull, for to this day the same veil remains when the old covenant is read. It has not been removed, because only in Christ is it taken away. **15**Even to this day when Moses is read, a veil covers their hearts. **16**But whenev-

er anyone turns to the Lord, the veil is taken away. **17**Now the Lord is the Spirit, and where the Spirit of the Lord is, there is freedom. **18**And we all, who with unveiled faces contemplate*a* the Lord's glory, are being transformed into his image with ever-increasing glory, which comes from the Lord, who is the Spirit.

Present Weakness and Resurrection Life

4 Therefore, since through God's mercy we have this ministry, we do not lose heart. **2**Rather, we have renounced secret and shameful ways; we do not use deception, nor do we distort the word of God. On the contrary, by setting forth the truth plainly we commend ourselves to everyone's conscience in the sight of God. **3**And even if our gospel is veiled, it is veiled to those who are perishing. **4**The god of this age has blinded the minds of unbelievers, so that they cannot see the light of the gospel that displays the glory of Christ, who is the image of God. **5**For what we preach is not ourselves, but Jesus Christ as Lord, and ourselves as your servants for Jesus' sake. **6**For God, who said, "Let light shine out of darkness,"*b* made his light shine in our hearts to give us the light of the knowledge of God's glory displayed in the face of Christ.

a 18 Or *reflect*   *b* 6 Gen. 1:3

⁷But we have this treasure in jars of clay to show that this all-surpassing power is from God and not from us. ⁸We are hard pressed on every side, but not crushed; perplexed, but not in despair; ⁹persecuted, but not abandoned; struck down, but not destroyed. ¹⁰We always carry around in our body the death of Jesus, so that the life of Jesus may also be revealed in our body. ¹¹For we who are alive are always being given over to death for Jesus' sake, so that his life may also be revealed in our mortal body. ¹²So then, death is at work in us, but life is at work in you.

¹³It is written: "I believed; therefore I have spoken."ᵃ Since we have that same spirit ofᵇ faith, we also believe and therefore speak, ¹⁴because we know that the one who raised the Lord Jesus from the dead will also raise us with Jesus and present us with you to himself. ¹⁵All this is for your benefit, so that the grace that is reaching more and more people may cause thanksgiving to overflow to the glory of God.

¹⁶Therefore we do not lose heart. Though outwardly we are wasting away, yet inwardly we are being renewed day by day. ¹⁷For our light and momentary troubles are achieving for us an eternal glory that far outweighs them all. ¹⁸So we fix our eyes not on what is seen, but on what is unseen, since what is seen is temporary, but what is unseen is eternal.

Awaiting the New Body

5 For we know that if the earthly tent we live in is destroyed, we have a building from God, an eternal house in heaven, not built by human hands. ²Meanwhile we groan, longing to be clothed instead with our heavenly dwelling, ³because when we are clothed, we will not be found naked. ⁴For while we are in this tent, we groan and are burdened, because we do not wish to be unclothed but to be clothed instead with our heavenly dwelling, so that what is mortal may be swallowed up by life. ⁵Now the one who has fashioned us for this very purpose is God, who has given us the Spirit as a deposit, guaranteeing what is to come.

⁶Therefore we are always confident and know that as long as we are at home in the body we are away from the Lord. ⁷For we live by faith, not by sight. ⁸We are confident, I say, and would prefer to be away from the body and at home with the Lord. ⁹So we make it our goal to please him, whether we are at home in the body or away from it. ¹⁰For we must all appear before the judgment seat of Christ, so that each of us may receive what is due us for the things done while in the body, whether good or bad.

The Ministry of Reconciliation

¹¹Since, then, we know what it is to fear the Lord, we try to per-

ᵃ 13 Psalm 116:10 (see Septuagint)   ᵇ 13 Or Spirit-given

suade others. What we are is plain to God, and I hope it is also plain to your conscience. ¹²We are not trying to commend ourselves to you again, but are giving you an opportunity to take pride in us, so that you can answer those who take pride in what is seen rather than in what is in the heart. ¹³If we are "out of our mind," as some say, it is for God; if we are in our right mind, it is for you. ¹⁴For Christ's love compels us, because we are convinced that one died for all, and therefore all died. ¹⁵And he died for all, that those who live should no longer live for themselves but for him who died for them and was raised again.

¹⁶So from now on we regard no one from a worldly point of view. Though we once regarded Christ in this way, we do so no longer. ¹⁷Therefore, if anyone is in Christ, the new creation has come:ᵃ The old has gone, the new is here! ¹⁸All this is from God, who reconciled us to himself through Christ and gave us the ministry of reconciliation: ¹⁹that God was reconciling the world to himself in Christ, not counting people's sins against them. And he has committed to us the message of reconciliation. ²⁰We are therefore Christ's ambassadors, as though God were making his appeal through us. We implore you on Christ's behalf: Be reconciled to God. ²¹God made him who had no sin to be sinᵇ for

us, so that in him we might become the righteousness of God.

6 As God's co-workers we urge you not to receive God's grace in vain. ²For he says,

"In the time of my favor I
   heard you,
and in the day of salvation I
   helped you."ᶜ

I tell you, now is the time of God's favor, now is the day of salvation.

Paul's Hardships

³We put no stumbling block in anyone's path, so that our ministry will not be discredited. ⁴Rather, as servants of God we commend ourselves in every way: in great endurance; in troubles, hardships and distresses; ⁵in beatings, imprisonments and riots; in hard work, sleepless nights and hunger; ⁶in purity, understanding, patience and kindness; in the Holy Spirit and in sincere love; ⁷in truthful speech and in the power of God; with weapons of righteousness in the right hand and in the left; ⁸through glory and dishonor, bad report and good report; genuine, yet regarded as impostors; ⁹known, yet regarded as unknown; dying, and yet we live on; beaten, and yet not killed; ¹⁰sorrowful, yet always rejoicing; poor, yet making many rich; having nothing, and yet possessing everything.

¹¹We have spoken freely to you, Corinthians, and opened wide our

---

ᵃ 17 Or *Christ, that person is a new creation.*   ᵇ 21 Or *be a sin offering*
ᶜ 2 Isaiah 49:8

hearts to you. [12]We are not with-holding our affection from you, but you are withholding yours from us. [13]As a fair exchange — I speak as to my children — open wide your hearts also.

Warning Against Idolatry

[14]Do not be yoked together with unbelievers. For what do righ-teousness and wickedness have in common? Or what fellowship can light have with darkness? [15]What harmony is there between Christ and Belial[a]? Or what does a believer have in common with an unbeliever? [16]What agreement is there between the temple of God and idols? For we are the temple of the living God. As God has said:

"I will live with them
    and walk among them,
and I will be their God,
    and they will be my people."[b]

[17]Therefore,

"Come out from them
    and be separate,
            says the Lord.
Touch no unclean thing,
    and I will receive you."[c]

[18]And,

"I will be a Father to you,
    and you will be my sons and
        daughters,
        says the Lord Almighty."[d]

7 Therefore, since we have these promises, dear friends,
let us purify ourselves from ev-erything that contaminates body and spirit, perfecting holiness out of reverence for God.

Paul's Joy Over the Church's Repentance

[2]Make room for us in your hearts. We have wronged no one, we have corrupted no one, we have exploited no one. [3]I do not say this to condemn you; I have said before that you have such a place in our hearts that we would live or die with you. [4]I have spo-ken to you with great frankness; I take great pride in you. I am great-ly encouraged; in all our troubles my joy knows no bounds.

[5]For when we came into Mace-donia, we had no rest, but we were harassed at every turn — conflicts on the outside, fears within. [6]But God, who comforts the downcast, comforted us by the coming of Ti-tus, [7]and not only by his coming but also by the comfort you had given him. He told us about your longing for me, your deep sorrow, your ardent concern for me, so that my joy was greater than ever.

[8]Even if I caused you sorrow by my letter, I do not regret it. Though I did regret it — I see that my let-ter hurt you, but only for a little while — [9]yet now I am happy, not because you were made sorry, but because your sorrow led you to repentance. For you became sor-rowful as God intended and so

---

[a] 15 Greek *Beliar*, a variant of *Belial*   [b] 16 Lev. 26:12; Jer. 32:38; Ezek. 37:27
[c] 17 Isaiah 52:11; Ezek. 20:34,41   [d] 18 2 Samuel 7:14; 7:8

were not harmed in any way by us. [10]Godly sorrow brings repentance that leads to salvation and leaves no regret, but worldly sorrow brings death. [11]See what this godly sorrow has produced in you: what earnestness, what eagerness to clear yourselves, what indignation, what alarm, what longing, what concern, what readiness to see justice done. At every point you have proved yourselves to be innocent in this matter. [12]So even though I wrote to you, it was neither on account of the one who did the wrong nor on account of the injured party, but rather that before God you could see for yourselves how devoted to us you are. [13]By all this we are encouraged.

In addition to our own encouragement, we were especially delighted to see how happy Titus was, because his spirit has been refreshed by all of you. [14]I had boasted to him about you, and you have not embarrassed me. But just as everything we said to you was true, so our boasting about you to Titus has proved to be true as well. [15]And his affection for you is all the greater when he remembers that you were all obedient, receiving him with fear and trembling. [16]I am glad I can have complete confidence in you.

The Collection for the Lord's People

8 And now, brothers and sisters, we want you to know about the grace that God has given the Macedonian churches. [2]In the midst of a very severe trial, their overflowing joy and their extreme poverty welled up in rich generosity. [3]For I testify that they gave as much as they were able, and even beyond their ability. Entirely on their own, [4]they urgently pleaded with us for the privilege of sharing in this service to the Lord's people. [5]And they exceeded our expectations: They gave themselves first of all to the Lord, and then by the will of God also to us. [6]So we urged Titus, just as he had earlier made a beginning, to bring also to completion this act of grace on your part. [7]But since you excel in everything—in faith, in speech, in knowledge, in complete earnestness and in the love we have kindled in you[a]—see that you also excel in this grace of giving.

[8]I am not commanding you, but I want to test the sincerity of your love by comparing it with the earnestness of others. [9]For you know the grace of our Lord Jesus Christ, that though he was rich, yet for your sake he became poor, so that you through his poverty might become rich.

[10]And here is my judgment about what is best for you in this matter. Last year you were the first not only to give but also to have the desire to do so. [11]Now finish the work, so that your eager willingness to do it may be matched by your completion of it, according

---

[a] 7 Some manuscripts *and in your love for us*

to your means. ¹²For if the willingness is there, the gift is acceptable according to what one has, not according to what one does not have.

¹³Our desire is not that others might be relieved while you are hard pressed, but that there might be equality. ¹⁴At the present time your plenty will supply what they need, so that in turn their plenty will supply what you need. The goal is equality, ¹⁵as it is written: "The one who gathered much did not have too much, and the one who gathered little did not have too little."[a]

Titus Sent to Receive the Collection

¹⁶Thanks be to God, who put into the heart of Titus the same concern I have for you. ¹⁷For Titus not only welcomed our appeal, but he is coming to you with much enthusiasm and on his own initiative. ¹⁸And we are sending along with him the brother who is praised by all the churches for his service to the gospel. ¹⁹What is more, he was chosen by the churches to accompany us as we carry the offering, which we administer in order to honor the Lord himself and to show our eagerness to help. ²⁰We want to avoid any criticism of the way we administer this liberal gift. ²¹For we are taking pains to do what is right, not only in the eyes of the Lord but also in the eyes of man.

²²In addition, we are sending with them our brother who has often proved to us in many ways that he is zealous, and now even more so because of his great confidence in you. ²³As for Titus, he is my partner and co-worker among you; as for our brothers, they are representatives of the churches and an honor to Christ. ²⁴Therefore show these men the proof of your love and the reason for our pride in you, so that the churches can see it.

9 There is no need for me to write to you about this service to the Lord's people. ²For I know your eagerness to help, and I have been boasting about it to the Macedonians, telling them that since last year you in Achaia were ready to give; and your enthusiasm has stirred most of them to action. ³But I am sending the brothers in order that our boasting about you in this matter should not prove hollow, but that you may be ready, as I said you would be. ⁴For if any Macedonians come with me and find you unprepared, we — not to say anything about you — would be ashamed of having been so confident. ⁵So I thought it necessary to urge the brothers to visit you in advance and finish the arrangements for the generous gift you had promised. Then it will be ready as a generous gift, not as one grudgingly given.

---

[a] 15 Exodus 16:18

Generosity Encouraged

6 Remember this: Whoever sows sparingly will also reap sparingly, and whoever sows generously will also reap generously. **7** Each of you should give what you have decided in your heart to give, not reluctantly or under compulsion, for God loves a cheerful giver. **8** And God is able to bless you abundantly, so that in all things at all times, having all that you need, you will abound in every good work. **9** As it is written:

"They have freely scattered
their gifts to the poor;
their righteousness endures
forever."*a*

10 Now he who supplies seed to the sower and bread for food will also supply and increase your store of seed and will enlarge the harvest of your righteousness. **11** You will be enriched in every way so that you can be generous on every occasion, and through us your generosity will result in thanksgiving to God.

12 This service that you perform is not only supplying the needs of the Lord's people but is also overflowing in many expressions of thanks to God. **13** Because of the service by which you have proved yourselves, others will praise God for the obedience that accompanies your confession of the gospel of Christ, and for your generosity in sharing with them and with every-

one else. **14** And in their prayers for you their hearts will go out to you, because of the surpassing grace God has given you. **15** Thanks be to God for his indescribable gift!

Paul's Defense of His Ministry

10 By the humility and gentleness of Christ, I appeal to you — I, Paul, who am "timid" when face to face with you, but "bold" toward you when away! **2** I beg you that when I come I may not have to be as bold as I expect to be toward some people who think that we live by the standards of this world. **3** For though we live in the world, we do not wage war as the world does. **4** The weapons we fight with are not the weapons of the world. On the contrary, they have divine power to demolish strongholds. **5** We demolish arguments and every pretension that sets itself up against the knowledge of God, and we take captive every thought to make it obedient to Christ. **6** And we will be ready to punish every act of disobedience, once your obedience is complete.

7 You are judging by appearances.*b* If anyone is confident that they belong to Christ, they should consider again that we belong to Christ just as much as they do. **8** So even if I boast somewhat freely about the authority the Lord gave us for building you up rather than tearing you down, I will not be ashamed of it. **9** I do not want to

---

a 9 Psalm 112:9   *b* 7 Or *Look at the obvious facts*

seem to be trying to frighten you with my letters. ¹⁰For some say, "His letters are weighty and forceful, but in person he is unimpressive and his speaking amounts to nothing." ¹¹Such people should realize that what we are in our letters when we are absent, we will be in our actions when we are present.

¹²We do not dare to classify or compare ourselves with some who commend themselves. When they measure themselves by themselves and compare themselves with themselves, they are not wise. ¹³We, however, will not boast beyond proper limits, but will confine our boasting to the sphere of service God himself has assigned to us, a sphere that also includes you. ¹⁴We are not going too far in our boasting, as would be the case if we had not come to you, for we did get as far as you with the gospel of Christ. ¹⁵Neither do we go beyond our limits by boasting of work done by others. Our hope is that, as your faith continues to grow, our sphere of activity among you will greatly expand, ¹⁶so that we can preach the gospel in the regions beyond you. For we do not want to boast about work already done in someone else's territory. ¹⁷But, "Let the one who boasts boast in the Lord."[a] ¹⁸For it is not the one who commends himself who is approved, but the one whom the Lord commends.

Paul and the False Apostles

11 I hope you will put up with me in a little foolishness. Yes, please put up with me! ²I am jealous for you with a godly jealousy. I promised you to one husband, to Christ, so that I might present you as a pure virgin to him. ³But I am afraid that just as Eve was deceived by the serpent's cunning, your minds may somehow be led astray from your sincere and pure devotion to Christ. ⁴For if someone comes to you and preaches a Jesus other than the Jesus we preached, or if you receive a different spirit from the Spirit you received, or a different gospel from the one you accepted, you put up with it easily enough.

⁵I do not think I am in the least inferior to those "super-apostles."[b] ⁶I may indeed be untrained as a speaker, but I do have knowledge. We have made this perfectly clear to you in every way. ⁷Was it a sin for me to lower myself in order to elevate you by preaching the gospel of God to you free of charge? ⁸I robbed other churches by receiving support from them so as to serve you. ⁹And when I was with you and needed something, I was not a burden to anyone, for the brothers who came from Macedonia supplied what I needed. I have kept myself from being a burden to you in any way, and will continue to do so. ¹⁰As surely as the truth of Christ is

---

[a] 17 Jer. 9:24   [b] 5 Or *to the most eminent apostles*

in me, nobody in the regions of Achaia will stop this boasting of mine. ¹¹Why? Because I do not love you? God knows I do!

¹²And I will keep on doing what I am doing in order to cut the ground from under those who want an opportunity to be considered equal with us in the things they boast about. ¹³For such people are false apostles, deceitful workers, masquerading as apostles of Christ. ¹⁴And no wonder, for Satan himself masquerades as an angel of light. ¹⁵It is not surprising, then, if his servants also masquerade as servants of righteousness. Their end will be what their actions deserve.

Paul Boasts About His Sufferings

¹⁶I repeat: Let no one take me for a fool. But if you do, then tolerate me just as you would a fool, so that I may do a little boasting. ¹⁷In this self-confident boasting I am not talking as the Lord would, but as a fool. ¹⁸Since many are boasting in the way the world does, I too will boast. ¹⁹You gladly put up with fools since you are so wise! ²⁰In fact, you even put up with anyone who enslaves you or exploits you or takes advantage of you or puts on airs or slaps you in the face. ²¹To my shame I admit that we were too weak for that!

Whatever anyone else dares to boast about — I am speaking as a fool — I also dare to boast about. ²²Are they Hebrews? So am I. Are they Israelites? So am I. Are they Abraham's descendants? So am I. ²³Are they servants of Christ? (I am out of my mind to talk like this.) I am more. I have worked much harder, been in prison more frequently, been flogged more severely, and been exposed to death again and again. ²⁴Five times I received from the Jews the forty lashes minus one. ²⁵Three times I was beaten with rods, once I was pelted with stones, three times I was shipwrecked, I spent a night and a day in the open sea, ²⁶I have been constantly on the move. I have been in danger from rivers, in danger from bandits, in danger from my fellow Jews, in danger from Gentiles; in danger in the city, in danger in the country, in danger at sea; and in danger from false believers. ²⁷I have labored and toiled and have often gone without sleep; I have known hunger and thirst and have often gone without food; I have been cold and naked. ²⁸Besides everything else, I face daily the pressure of my concern for all the churches. ²⁹Who is weak, and I do not feel weak? Who is led into sin, and I do not inwardly burn?

³⁰If I must boast, I will boast of the things that show my weakness. ³¹The God and Father of the Lord Jesus, who is to be praised forever, knows that I am not lying. ³²In Damascus the governor under King Aretas had the city of the Damascenes guarded in order to arrest me. ³³But I was lowered in a

basket from a window in the wall and slipped through his hands.

Paul's Vision and His Thorn

12 I must go on boasting. Although there is nothing to be gained, I will go on to visions and revelations from the Lord. [2]I know a man in Christ who fourteen years ago was caught up to the third heaven. Whether it was in the body or out of the body I do not know—God knows. [3]And I know that this man—whether in the body or apart from the body I do not know, but God knows— [4]was caught up to paradise and heard inexpressible things, things that no one is permitted to tell. [5]I will boast about a man like that, but I will not boast about myself, except about my weaknesses. [6]Even if I should choose to boast, I would not be a fool, because I would be speaking the truth. But I refrain, so no one will think more of me than is warranted by what I do or say, [7]or because of these surpassingly great revelations. Therefore, in order to keep me from becoming conceited, I was given a thorn in my flesh, a messenger of Satan, to torment me. [8]Three times I pleaded with the Lord to take it away from me. [9]But he said to me, "My grace is sufficient for you, for my power is made perfect in weakness." Therefore I will boast all the more gladly about my weaknesses, so that Christ's power may rest on me. [10]That is why,

for Christ's sake, I delight in weaknesses, in insults, in hardships, in persecutions, in difficulties. For when I am weak, then I am strong.

Paul's Concern for the Corinthians

[11]I have made a fool of myself, but you drove me to it. I ought to have been commended by you, for I am not in the least inferior to the "super-apostles,"[a] even though I am nothing. [12]I persevered in demonstrating among you the marks of a true apostle, including signs, wonders and miracles. [13]How were you inferior to the other churches, except that I was never a burden to you? Forgive me this wrong!

[14]Now I am ready to visit you for the third time, and I will not be a burden to you, because what I want is not your possessions but you. After all, children should not have to save up for their parents, but parents for their children. [15]So I will very gladly spend for you everything I have and expend myself as well. If I love you more, will you love me less? [16]Be that as it may, I have not been a burden to you. Yet, crafty fellow that I am, I caught you by trickery! [17]Did I exploit you through any of the men I sent to you? [18]I urged Titus to go to you and I sent our brother with him. Titus did not exploit you, did he? Did we not walk in the same footsteps by the same Spirit?

---

a 11 Or *the most eminent apostles*

[19] Have you been thinking all along that we have been defending ourselves to you? We have been speaking in the sight of God as those in Christ; and everything we do, dear friends, is for your strengthening. [20] For I am afraid that when I come I may not find you as I want you to be, and you may not find me as you want me to be. I fear that there may be discord, jealousy, fits of rage, selfish ambition, slander, gossip, arrogance and disorder. [21] I am afraid that when I come again my God will humble me before you, and I will be grieved over many who have sinned earlier and have not repented of the impurity, sexual sin and debauchery in which they have indulged.

Final Warnings

13 This will be my third visit to you. "Every matter must be established by the testimony of two or three witnesses."[a] [2] I already gave you a warning when I was with you the second time. I now repeat it while absent: On my return I will not spare those who sinned earlier or any of the others, [3] since you are demanding proof that Christ is speaking through me. He is not weak in dealing with you, but is powerful among you. [4] For to be sure, he was crucified in weakness, yet he lives by God's power. Likewise, we are weak in him, yet by God's power we will live with him in our dealing with you.

[5] Examine yourselves to see whether you are in the faith; test yourselves. Do you not realize that Christ Jesus is in you—unless, of course, you fail the test? [6] And I trust that you will discover that we have not failed the test. [7] Now we pray to God that you will not do anything wrong—not so that people will see that we have stood the test but so that you will do what is right even though we may seem to have failed. [8] For we cannot do anything against the truth, but only for the truth. [9] We are glad whenever we are weak but you are strong; and our prayer is that you may be fully restored. [10] This is why I write these things when I am absent, that when I come I may not have to be harsh in my use of authority—the authority the Lord gave me for building you up, not for tearing you down.

Final Greetings

[11] Finally, brothers and sisters, rejoice! Strive for full restoration, encourage one another, be of one mind, live in peace. And the God of love and peace will be with you.

[12] Greet one another with a holy kiss. [13] All God's people here send their greetings.

[14] May the grace of the Lord Jesus Christ, and the love of God, and the fellowship of the Holy Spirit be with you all.

a 1 Deut. 19:15

Galatians

Introduction:

Paul wrote this letter to the Christian churches in the Roman province of Galatia. False teachers called Judaizers were confusing the Galatians by teaching that Gentile Christians were not really saved unless they obeyed all the Jewish laws — such as being circumcised, eating special foods, and celebrating Jewish feast days. This group also said that Paul did not have God's authority and, therefore, was not to be listened to.

Paul begins the letter by telling the Galatians what gospel it is that he preaches and that his authority is from God. He continues by stating that we cannot be saved from our sins by obeying the law; we are saved only by believing in Jesus Christ. Christians are free to live by the law of love, not the Law of Moses. Faith, Paul says, must be shown in love and believers must live by the Spirit.

Outline of contents:

Introduction (1:1–10)
Paul's authority from God (1:11–2:21)
Legalism versus God's grace (3:1–4:31)
The gospel in practice (5:1–6:16)
Conclusion (6:17,18)

1 Paul, an apostle — sent not from men nor by a man, but by Jesus Christ and God the Father, who raised him from the dead — ² and all the brothers and sisters^a with me,

To the churches in Galatia:

³Grace and peace to you from God our Father and the Lord Jesus Christ, ⁴who gave himself for our sins to rescue us from the present evil age, according to the will of our God and Father, ⁵to whom be glory for ever and ever. Amen.

No Other Gospel

⁶I am astonished that you are so quickly deserting the one who called you to live in the grace of Christ and are turning to a different gospel — ⁷which is really no gospel at all. Evidently some people are throwing you into confu-

^a 2 The Greek word for *brothers and sisters* (*adelphoi*) refers here to believers, both men and women, as part of God's family; also in verse 11; and in 3:15; 4:12, 28, 31; 5:11, 13; 6:1, 18.

sion and are trying to pervert the gospel of Christ. **8**But even if we or an angel from heaven should preach a gospel other than the one we preached to you, let them be under God's curse! **9**As we have already said, so now I say again: If anybody is preaching to you a gospel other than what you accepted, let them be under God's curse!

10Am I now trying to win the approval of human beings, or of God? Or am I trying to please people? If I were still trying to please people, I would not be a servant of Christ.

Paul Called by God

11I want you to know, brothers and sisters, that the gospel I preached is not of human origin. **12**I did not receive it from any man, nor was I taught it; rather, I received it by revelation from Jesus Christ.

13For you have heard of my previous way of life in Judaism, how intensely I persecuted the church of God and tried to destroy it. **14**I was advancing in Judaism beyond many of my own age among my people and was extremely zealous for the traditions of my fathers. **15**But when God, who set me apart from my mother's womb and called me by his grace, was pleased **16**to reveal his Son in me so that I might preach him among the Gentiles, my immediate response was not to consult any human be-

ing. **17**I did not go up to Jerusalem to see those who were apostles before I was, but I went into Arabia. Later I returned to Damascus.

18Then after three years, I went up to Jerusalem to get acquainted with Cephas*a* and stayed with him fifteen days. **19**I saw none of the other apostles — only James, the Lord's brother. **20**I assure you before God that what I am writing you is no lie.

21Then I went to Syria and Cilicia. **22**I was personally unknown to the churches of Judea that are in Christ. **23**They only heard the report: "The man who formerly persecuted us is now preaching the faith he once tried to destroy." **24**And they praised God because of me.

Paul Accepted by the Apostles

2 Then after fourteen years, I went up again to Jerusalem, this time with Barnabas. I took Titus along also. **2**I went in response to a revelation and, meeting privately with those esteemed as leaders, I presented to them the gospel that I preach among the Gentiles. I wanted to be sure I was not running and had not been running my race in vain. **3**Yet not even Titus, who was with me, was compelled to be circumcised, even though he was a Greek. **4**This matter arose because some false believers had infiltrated our ranks to spy on the freedom we have in

a 18 That is, Peter

Christ Jesus and to make us slaves. **5** We did not give in to them for a moment, so that the truth of the gospel might be preserved for you.

6 As for those who were held in high esteem—whatever they were makes no difference to me; God does not show favoritism—they added nothing to my message. **7** On the contrary, they recognized that I had been entrusted with the task of preaching the gospel to the uncircumcised,*a* just as Peter had been to the circumcised.*b* **8** For God, who was at work in Peter as an apostle to the circumcised, was also at work in me as an apostle to the Gentiles. **9** James, Cephas*c* and John, those esteemed as pillars, gave me and Barnabas the right hand of fellowship when they recognized the grace given to me. They agreed that we should go to the Gentiles, and they to the circumcised. **10** All they asked was that we should continue to remember the poor, the very thing I had been eager to do all along.

Paul Opposes Cephas

11 When Cephas came to Antioch, I opposed him to his face, because he stood condemned. **12** For before certain men came from James, he used to eat with the Gentiles. But when they arrived, he began to draw back and separate himself from the Gentiles because he was afraid of those who belonged to the circumcision group. **13** The other Jews joined him in his hypocrisy, so that by their hypocrisy even Barnabas was led astray.

14 When I saw that they were not acting in line with the truth of the gospel, I said to Cephas in front of them all, "You are a Jew, yet you live like a Gentile and not like a Jew. How is it, then, that you force Gentiles to follow Jewish customs?

15 "We who are Jews by birth and not sinful Gentiles **16** know that a person is not justified by the works of the law, but by faith in Jesus Christ. So we, too, have put our faith in Christ Jesus that we may be justified by faith in*d* Christ and not by the works of the law, because by the works of the law no one will be justified.

17 "But if, in seeking to be justified in Christ, we Jews find ourselves also among the sinners, doesn't that mean that Christ promotes sin? Absolutely not! **18** If I rebuild what I destroyed, then I really would be a lawbreaker.

19 "For through the law I died to the law so that I might live for God. **20** I have been crucified with Christ and I no longer live, but Christ lives in me. The life I now live in the body, I live by faith in the Son of God, who loved me and gave himself for me. **21** I do not set aside the grace of God, for if righteousness could be gained through the law, Christ died for nothing!"*e*

---

a 7 That is, Gentiles   *b 7* That is, Jews; also in verses 8 and 9   *c 9* That is, Peter; also in verses 11 and 14   *d 16* Or *but through the faithfulness of . . . justified on the basis of the faithfulness of*   *e 21* Some interpreters end the quotation after verse 14.

Faith or Works of the Law

3 You foolish Galatians! Who has bewitched you? Before your very eyes Jesus Christ was clearly portrayed as crucified. [2]I would like to learn just one thing from you: Did you receive the Spirit by the works of the law, or by believing what you heard? [3]Are you so foolish? After beginning by means of the Spirit, are you now trying to finish by means of the flesh?[a] [4]Have you experienced[b] so much in vain — if it really was in vain? [5]So again I ask, does God give you his Spirit and work miracles among you by the works of the law, or by your believing what you heard? [6]So also Abraham "believed God, and it was credited to him as righteousness."[c]

[7]Understand, then, that those who have faith are children of Abraham. [8]Scripture foresaw that God would justify the Gentiles by faith, and announced the gospel in advance to Abraham: "All nations will be blessed through you."[d] [9]So those who rely on faith are blessed along with Abraham, the man of faith.

[10]For all who rely on the works of the law are under a curse, as it is written: "Cursed is everyone who does not continue to do everything written in the Book of the Law."[e] [11]Clearly no one who relies on the law is justified before God, because "the righteous will live by faith."[f] [12]The law is not based on faith; on the contrary, it says, "The person who does these things will live by them."[g] [13]Christ redeemed us from the curse of the law by becoming a curse for us, for it is written: "Cursed is everyone who is hung on a pole."[h] [14]He redeemed us in order that the blessing given to Abraham might come to the Gentiles through Christ Jesus, so that by faith we might receive the promise of the Spirit.

The Law and the Promise

[15]Brothers and sisters, let me take an example from everyday life. Just as no one can set aside or add to a human covenant that has been duly established, so it is in this case. [16]The promises were spoken to Abraham and to his seed. Scripture does not say "and to seeds," meaning many people, but "and to your seed,"[i] meaning one person, who is Christ. [17]What I mean is this: The law, introduced 430 years later, does not set aside the covenant previously established by God and thus do away with the promise. [18]For if the inheritance depends on the law, then it no longer depends on the promise; but God in his grace gave it to Abraham through a promise.

[19]Why, then, was the law given at all? It was added because of

---

[a] 3 In contexts like this, the Greek word for *flesh* (*sarx*) refers to the sinful state of human beings, often presented as a power in opposition to the Spirit. [b] 4 Or *suffered* [c] 6 Gen. 15:6 [d] 8 Gen. 12:3; 18:18; 22:18 [e] 10 Deut. 27:26 [f] 11 Hab. 2:4 [g] 12 Lev. 18:5 [h] 13 Deut. 21:23 [i] 16 Gen. 12:7; 13:15; 24:7

transgressions until the Seed to whom the promise referred had come. The law was given through angels and entrusted to a mediator. ²⁰A mediator, however, implies more than one party; but God is one.

²¹Is the law, therefore, opposed to the promises of God? Absolutely not! For if a law had been given that could impart life, then righteousness would certainly have come by the law. ²²But Scripture has locked up everything under the control of sin, so that what was promised, being given through faith in Jesus Christ, might be given to those who believe.

Children of God

²³Before the coming of this faith,[a] we were held in custody under the law, locked up until the faith that was to come would be revealed. ²⁴So the law was our guardian until Christ came that we might be justified by faith. ²⁵Now that this faith has come, we are no longer under a guardian.

²⁶So in Christ Jesus you are all children of God through faith, ²⁷for all of you who were baptized into Christ have clothed yourselves with Christ. ²⁸There is neither Jew nor Gentile, neither slave nor free, nor is there male and female, for you are all one in Christ Jesus. ²⁹If you belong to Christ, then you are Abraham's seed, and heirs according to the promise.

4 What I am saying is that as long as an heir is underage, he is no different from a slave, although he owns the whole estate. ²The heir is subject to guardians and trustees until the time set by his father. ³So also, when we were underage, we were in slavery under the elemental spiritual forces[b] of the world. ⁴But when the set time had fully come, God sent his Son, born of a woman, born under the law, ⁵to redeem those under the law, that we might receive adoption to sonship.[c] ⁶Because you are his sons, God sent the Spirit of his Son into our hearts, the Spirit who calls out, "Abba,[d] Father." ⁷So you are no longer a slave, but God's child; and since you are his child, God has made you also an heir.

Paul's Concern for the Galatians

⁸Formerly, when you did not know God, you were slaves to those who by nature are not gods. ⁹But now that you know God — or rather are known by God — how is it that you are turning back to those weak and miserable forces[e]? Do you wish to be enslaved by them all over again? ¹⁰You are observing special days and months and seasons and years!

---

[a] 22,23 Or *through the faithfulness of Jesus . . .* ²³*Before faith came*   [b] 3 Or *under the basic principles*   [c] 5 The Greek word for *adoption to sonship* is a legal term referring to the full legal standing of an adopted male heir in Roman culture.
[d] 6 Aramaic for *Father*   [e] 9 Or *principles*

[11] I fear for you, that somehow I have wasted my efforts on you.

[12] I plead with you, brothers and sisters, become like me, for I became like you. You did me no wrong. [13] As you know, it was because of an illness that I first preached the gospel to you, [14] and even though my illness was a trial to you, you did not treat me with contempt or scorn. Instead, you welcomed me as if I were an angel of God, as if I were Christ Jesus himself. [15] Where, then, is your blessing of me now? I can testify that, if you could have done so, you would have torn out your eyes and given them to me. [16] Have I now become your enemy by telling you the truth?

[17] Those people are zealous to win you over, but for no good. What they want is to alienate you from us, so that you may have zeal for them. [18] It is fine to be zealous, provided the purpose is good, and to be so always, not just when I am with you. [19] My dear children, for whom I am again in the pains of childbirth until Christ is formed in you, [20] how I wish I could be with you now and change my tone, because I am perplexed about you!

Hagar and Sarah

[21] Tell me, you who want to be under the law, are you not aware of what the law says? [22] For it is written that Abraham had two sons, one by the slave woman and the other by the free woman. [23] His son by the slave woman was born according to the flesh, but his son by the free woman was born as the result of a divine promise.

[24] These things are being taken figuratively: The women represent two covenants. One covenant is from Mount Sinai and bears children who are to be slaves: This is Hagar. [25] Now Hagar stands for Mount Sinai in Arabia and corresponds to the present city of Jerusalem, because she is in slavery with her children. [26] But the Jerusalem that is above is free, and she is our mother. [27] For it is written:

"Be glad, barren woman,
  you who never bore a child;
shout for joy and cry aloud,
  you who were never in labor;
because more are the children
  of the desolate woman
than of her who has a
  husband."[a]

[28] Now you, brothers and sisters, like Isaac, are children of promise. [29] At that time the son born according to the flesh persecuted the son born by the power of the Spirit. It is the same now. [30] But what does Scripture say? "Get rid of the slave woman and her son, for the slave woman's son will never share in the inheritance with the free woman's son."[b] [31] Therefore, brothers and sisters, we are not children of the slave woman, but of the free woman.

[a] 27 Isaiah 54:1   [b] 30 Gen. 21:10

Freedom in Christ

5 It is for freedom that Christ has set us free. Stand firm, then, and do not let yourselves be burdened again by a yoke of slavery.

2 Mark my words! I, Paul, tell you that if you let yourselves be circumcised, Christ will be of no value to you at all. **3** Again I declare to every man who lets himself be circumcised that he is obligated to obey the whole law. **4** You who are trying to be justified by the law have been alienated from Christ; you have fallen away from grace. **5** For through the Spirit we eagerly await by faith the righteousness for which we hope. **6** For in Christ Jesus neither circumcision nor uncircumcision has any value. The only thing that counts is faith expressing itself through love.

7 You were running a good race. Who cut in on you to keep you from obeying the truth? **8** That kind of persuasion does not come from the one who calls you. **9** "A little yeast works through the whole batch of dough." **10** I am confident in the Lord that you will take no other view. The one who is throwing you into confusion, whoever that may be, will have to pay the penalty. **11** Brothers and sisters, if I am still preaching circumcision, why am I still being persecuted? In that case the offense of the cross has been abolished. **12** As for those agitators, I wish they would go the whole way and emasculate themselves!

Life by the Spirit

13 You, my brothers and sisters, were called to be free. But do not use your freedom to indulge the flesh[a]; rather, serve one another humbly in love. **14** For the entire law is fulfilled in keeping this one command: "Love your neighbor as yourself."[b] **15** If you bite and devour each other, watch out or you will be destroyed by each other.

16 So I say, walk by the Spirit, and you will not gratify the desires of the flesh. **17** For the flesh desires what is contrary to the Spirit, and the Spirit what is contrary to the flesh. They are in conflict with each other, so that you are not to do whatever[c] you want. **18** But if you are led by the Spirit, you are not under the law.

19 The acts of the flesh are obvious: sexual immorality, impurity and debauchery; **20** idolatry and witchcraft; hatred, discord, jealousy, fits of rage, selfish ambition, dissensions, factions **21** and envy; drunkenness, orgies, and the like. I warn you, as I did before, that those who live like this will not inherit the kingdom of God.

22 But the fruit of the Spirit is love, joy, peace, forbearance, kindness, goodness, faithfulness, **23** gentleness and self-con-

---

a 13 In contexts like this, the Greek word for *flesh* (*sarx*) refers to the sinful state of human beings, often presented as a power in opposition to the Spirit; also in verses 16, 17, 19 and 24; and in 6:8. *b 14* Lev. 19:18 *c 17* Or *you do not do what* trol. Against such things there is no law. ²⁴Those who belong to Christ Jesus have crucified the flesh with its passions and desires. ²⁵Since we live by the Spirit, let us keep in step with the Spirit. ²⁶Let us not become conceited, provoking and envying each other.

Doing Good to All

6 Brothers and sisters, if someone is caught in a sin, you who live by the Spirit should restore that person gently. But watch yourselves, or you also may be tempted. ²Carry each other's burdens, and in this way you will fulfill the law of Christ. ³If anyone thinks they are something when they are not, they deceive themselves. ⁴Each one should test their own actions. Then they can take pride in themselves alone, without comparing themselves to someone else, ⁵for each one should carry their own load. ⁶Nevertheless, the one who receives instruction in the word should share all good things with their instructor.

⁷Do not be deceived: God cannot be mocked. A man reaps what he sows. ⁸Whoever sows to please their flesh, from the flesh will reap destruction; whoever sows to please the Spirit, from the Spirit will reap eternal life.

⁹Let us not become weary in doing good, for at the proper time we will reap a harvest if we do not give up. ¹⁰Therefore, as we have opportunity, let us do good to all people, especially to those who belong to the family of believers.

Not Circumcision but the New Creation

¹¹See what large letters I use as I write to you with my own hand! ¹²Those who want to impress people by means of the flesh are trying to compel you to be circumcised. The only reason they do this is to avoid being persecuted for the cross of Christ. ¹³Not even those who are circumcised keep the law, yet they want you to be circumcised that they may boast about your circumcision in the flesh. ¹⁴May I never boast except in the cross of our Lord Jesus Christ, through which[a] the world has been crucified to me, and I to the world. ¹⁵Neither circumcision nor uncircumcision means anything; what counts is the new creation. ¹⁶Peace and mercy to all who follow this rule — to[b] the Israel of God.

¹⁷From now on, let no one cause me trouble, for I bear on my body the marks of Jesus.

¹⁸The grace of our Lord Jesus Christ be with your spirit, brothers and sisters. Amen.

---

[a] 14 Or *whom*   [b] 16 Or *rule and to*

Ephesians

Introduction:

Ephesus was a large, important city that naturally became the center for the Christian churches in the area. Paul wrote this letter to the Ephesians during his two-year imprisonment in Rome (about AD 60). This letter was sent to all the Christian churches near Ephesus, not just to the church in the city.

One of Paul's themes in Ephesians is that of unity and God's purpose "to bring unity to all things in heaven and on earth under Christ." Because of this unity, Paul writes, all Christians are one family in Christ and should love each other. He gives believers instructions on how to live a life of love by addressing the husband-wife, parent-children, and slave-master relationships.

In this letter Paul also writes about the church — not a church building in a certain place but the church that is made up of all Christians who have ever lived — the universal church. He compares Christ's relationship with the church to the human body, a building and a wife.

Outline of contents:

Greetings (1:1,2)
Christ and the church (1:3 – 3:21)
Conduct of the believer (4:1 – 6:9)
The Christian's warfare (6:10 – 20)
Conclusion (6:21 – 24)

1 Paul, an apostle of Christ Jesus by the will of God,

To God's holy people in Ephesus,[a] the faithful in Christ Jesus:

[2] Grace and peace to you from God our Father and the Lord Jesus Christ.

Praise for Spiritual Blessings in Christ

[3] Praise be to the God and Father of our Lord Jesus Christ, who has blessed us in the heavenly realms with every spiritual blessing in Christ. [4] For he chose us in him before the creation of the world to be

---

[a] 1 Some early manuscripts do not have *in Ephesus.*

holy and blameless in his sight. In love [5]he[a] predestined us for adoption to sonship[b] through Jesus Christ, in accordance with his pleasure and will — [6]to the praise of his glorious grace, which he has freely given us in the One he loves. [7]In him we have redemption through his blood, the forgiveness of sins, in accordance with the riches of God's grace [8]that he lavished on us. With all wisdom and understanding, [9]he[c] made known to us the mystery of his will according to his good pleasure, which he purposed in Christ, [10]to be put into effect when the times reach their fulfillment — to bring unity to all things in heaven and on earth under Christ.

[11]In him we were also chosen,[d] having been predestined according to the plan of him who works out everything in conformity with the purpose of his will, [12]in order that we, who were the first to put our hope in Christ, might be for the praise of his glory. [13]And you also were included in Christ when you heard the message of truth, the gospel of your salvation. When you believed, you were marked in him with a seal, the promised Holy Spirit, [14]who is a deposit guaranteeing our inheritance until the redemption of those who are God's possession — to the praise of his glory.

Thanksgiving and Prayer

[15]For this reason, ever since I heard about your faith in the Lord Jesus and your love for all God's people, [16]I have not stopped giving thanks for you, remembering you in my prayers. [17]I keep asking that the God of our Lord Jesus Christ, the glorious Father, may give you the Spirit[e] of wisdom and revelation, so that you may know him better. [18]I pray that the eyes of your heart may be enlightened in order that you may know the hope to which he has called you, the riches of his glorious inheritance in his holy people, [19]and his incomparably great power for us who believe. That power is the same as the mighty strength [20]he exerted when he raised Christ from the dead and seated him at his right hand in the heavenly realms, [21]far above all rule and authority, power and dominion, and every name that is invoked, not only in the present age but also in the one to come. [22]And God placed all things under his feet and appointed him to be head over everything for the church, [23]which is his body, the fullness of him who fills everything in every way.

Made Alive in Christ

2 As for you, you were dead in your transgressions and sins, [2]in which you used to live

---

[a] 4,5 Or *sight in love.* [5]*He*   [b] 5 The Greek word for *adoption to sonship* is a legal term referring to the full legal standing of an adopted male heir in Roman culture.
[c] 8,9 Or *us with all wisdom and understanding.* [9]*And he*   [d] 11 Or *were made heirs*   [e] 17 Or *a spirit*

when you followed the ways of this world and of the ruler of the kingdom of the air, the spirit who is now at work in those who are disobedient. ³All of us also lived among them at one time, gratifying the cravings of our flesh*a* and following its desires and thoughts. Like the rest, we were by nature deserving of wrath. ⁴But because of his great love for us, God, who is rich in mercy, ⁵made us alive with Christ even when we were dead in transgressions—it is by grace you have been saved. ⁶And God raised us up with Christ and seated us with him in the heavenly realms in Christ Jesus, ⁷in order that in the coming ages he might show the incomparable riches of his grace, expressed in his kindness to us in Christ Jesus. ⁸For it is by grace you have been saved, through faith—and this is not from yourselves, it is the gift of God— ⁹not by works, so that no one can boast. ¹⁰For we are God's handiwork, created in Christ Jesus to do good works, which God prepared in advance for us to do.

Jew and Gentile Reconciled Through Christ

¹¹Therefore, remember that formerly you who are Gentiles by birth and called "uncircumcised" by those who call themselves "the circumcision" (which is done in the body by human hands)— ¹²remember that at that time you were separate from Christ, excluded from citizenship in Israel and foreigners to the covenants of the promise, without hope and without God in the world. ¹³But now in Christ Jesus you who once were far away have been brought near by the blood of Christ.

¹⁴For he himself is our peace, who has made the two groups one and has destroyed the barrier, the dividing wall of hostility, ¹⁵by setting aside in his flesh the law with its commands and regulations. His purpose was to create in himself one new humanity out of the two, thus making peace, ¹⁶and in one body to reconcile both of them to God through the cross, by which he put to death their hostility. ¹⁷He came and preached peace to you who were far away and peace to those who were near. ¹⁸For through him we both have access to the Father by one Spirit.

¹⁹Consequently, you are no longer foreigners and strangers, but fellow citizens with God's people and also members of his household, ²⁰built on the foundation of the apostles and prophets, with Christ Jesus himself as the chief cornerstone. ²¹In him the whole building is joined together and rises to become a holy temple in the Lord. ²²And in him you too are being built together to

---

a 3 In contexts like this, the Greek word for *flesh* (*sarx*) refers to the sinful state of human beings, often presented as a power in opposition to the Spirit.

become a dwelling in which God lives by his Spirit.

God's Marvelous Plan for the Gentiles

3 For this reason I, Paul, the prisoner of Christ Jesus for the sake of you Gentiles —

²Surely you have heard about the administration of God's grace that was given to me for you, ³that is, the mystery made known to me by revelation, as I have already written briefly. ⁴In reading this, then, you will be able to understand my insight into the mystery of Christ, ⁵which was not made known to people in other generations as it has now been revealed by the Spirit to God's holy apostles and prophets. ⁶This mystery is that through the gospel the Gentiles are heirs together with Israel, members together of one body, and sharers together in the promise in Christ Jesus.

⁷I became a servant of this gospel by the gift of God's grace given me through the working of his power. ⁸Although I am less than the least of all the Lord's people, this grace was given me: to preach to the Gentiles the boundless riches of Christ, ⁹and to make plain to everyone the administration of this mystery, which for ages past was kept hidden in God, who created all things. ¹⁰His intent was that now, through the church, the manifold wisdom of God should be made known to the rulers and authorities in the heavenly realms, ¹¹according to his eternal purpose that he accomplished in Christ Jesus our Lord. ¹²In him and through faith in him we may approach God with freedom and confidence. ¹³I ask you, therefore, not to be discouraged because of my sufferings for you, which are your glory.

A Prayer for the Ephesians

¹⁴For this reason I kneel before the Father, ¹⁵from whom every family[a] in heaven and on earth derives its name. ¹⁶I pray that out of his glorious riches he may strengthen you with power through his Spirit in your inner being, ¹⁷so that Christ may dwell in your hearts through faith. And I pray that you, being rooted and established in love, ¹⁸may have power, together with all the Lord's holy people, to grasp how wide and long and high and deep is the love of Christ, ¹⁹and to know this love that surpasses knowledge — that you may be filled to the measure of all the fullness of God.

²⁰Now to him who is able to do immeasurably more than all we ask or imagine, according to his power that is at work within us, ²¹to him be glory in the church and in Christ Jesus throughout all generations, for ever and ever! Amen.

---

a 15 The Greek for *family* (*patria*) is derived from the Greek for *father* (*pater*).

Unity and Maturity in the Body of Christ

4 As a prisoner for the Lord, then, I urge you to live a life worthy of the calling you have received. ²Be completely humble and gentle; be patient, bearing with one another in love. ³Make every effort to keep the unity of the Spirit through the bond of peace. ⁴There is one body and one Spirit, just as you were called to one hope when you were called; ⁵one Lord, one faith, one baptism; ⁶one God and Father of all, who is over all and through all and in all.

⁷But to each one of us grace has been given as Christ apportioned it. ⁸This is why it*ᵃ* says:

"When he ascended on high,
    he took many captives
    and gave gifts to his people."*ᵇ*

⁹(What does "he ascended" mean except that he also descended to the lower, earthly regions*ᶜ*? ¹⁰He who descended is the very one who ascended higher than all the heavens, in order to fill the whole universe.) ¹¹So Christ himself gave the apostles, the prophets, the evangelists, the pastors and teachers, ¹²to equip his people for works of service, so that the body of Christ may be built up ¹³until we all reach unity in the faith and in the knowledge of the Son of God and become mature, attaining to the whole measure of the fullness of Christ.

¹⁴Then we will no longer be infants, tossed back and forth by the waves, and blown here and there by every wind of teaching and by the cunning and craftiness of people in their deceitful scheming. ¹⁵Instead, speaking the truth in love, we will grow to become in every respect the mature body of him who is the head, that is, Christ. ¹⁶From him the whole body, joined and held together by every supporting ligament, grows and builds itself up in love, as each part does its work.

Instructions for Christian Living

¹⁷So I tell you this, and insist on it in the Lord, that you must no longer live as the Gentiles do, in the futility of their thinking. ¹⁸They are darkened in their understanding and separated from the life of God because of the ignorance that is in them due to the hardening of their hearts. ¹⁹Having lost all sensitivity, they have given themselves over to sensuality so as to indulge in every kind of impurity, and they are full of greed.

²⁰That, however, is not the way of life you learned ²¹when you heard about Christ and were taught in him in accordance with the truth that is in Jesus. ²²You were taught, with regard to your former way of life, to put off your old self, which is being corrupted by its deceitful desires; ²³to be made new in the attitude of your

---

ᵃ 8 Or *God*   *ᵇ* 8 Psalm 68:18   *ᶜ* 9 Or *the depths of the earth* minds; ²⁴and to put on the new self, created to be like God in true righteousness and holiness.

²⁵Therefore each of you must put off falsehood and speak truthfully to your neighbor, for we are all members of one body. ²⁶"In your anger do not sin"^a: Do not let the sun go down while you are still angry, ²⁷and do not give the devil a foothold. ²⁸Anyone who has been stealing must steal no longer, but must work, doing something useful with their own hands, that they may have something to share with those in need.

²⁹Do not let any unwholesome talk come out of your mouths, but only what is helpful for building others up according to their needs, that it may benefit those who listen. ³⁰And do not grieve the Holy Spirit of God, with whom you were sealed for the day of redemption. ³¹Get rid of all bitterness, rage and anger, brawling and slander, along with every form of malice. ³²Be kind and compassionate to one another, forgiving each other, just as in Christ God forgave you.

¹Follow God's example, therefore, as dearly loved children ²and walk in the way of love, just as Christ loved us and gave himself up for us as a fragrant offering and sacrifice to God.

³But among you there must not be even a hint of sexual immorality, or of any kind of impurity, or of greed, because these are improper for God's holy people. ⁴Nor should there be obscenity, foolish talk or coarse joking, which are out of place, but rather thanksgiving. ⁵For of this you can be sure: No immoral, impure or greedy person — such a person is an idolater — has any inheritance in the kingdom of Christ and of God.^b ⁶Let no one deceive you with empty words, for because of such things God's wrath comes on those who are disobedient. ⁷Therefore do not be partners with them.

⁸For you were once darkness, but now you are light in the Lord. Live as children of light ⁹(for the fruit of the light consists in all goodness, righteousness and truth) ¹⁰and find out what pleases the Lord. ¹¹Have nothing to do with the fruitless deeds of darkness, but rather expose them. ¹²It is shameful even to mention what the disobedient do in secret. ¹³But everything exposed by the light becomes visible — and everything that is illuminated becomes a light. ¹⁴This is why it is said:

"Wake up, sleeper,
  rise from the dead,
  and Christ will shine on you."

¹⁵Be very careful, then, how you live — not as unwise but as wise, ¹⁶making the most of every opportunity, because the days are evil. ¹⁷Therefore do not be foolish, but understand what the Lord's will is. ¹⁸Do not get drunk

---

^a 26 Psalm 4:4 (see Septuagint)   ^b 5 Or *kingdom of the Messiah and God*

on wine, which leads to debauchery. Instead, be filled with the Spirit, [19] speaking to one another with psalms, hymns, and songs from the Spirit. Sing and make music from your heart to the Lord, [20] always giving thanks to God the Father for everything, in the name of our Lord Jesus Christ.

Instructions for Christian Households

[21] Submit to one another out of reverence for Christ.

[22] Wives, submit yourselves to your own husbands as you do to the Lord. [23] For the husband is the head of the wife as Christ is the head of the church, his body, of which he is the Savior. [24] Now as the church submits to Christ, so also wives should submit to their husbands in everything.

[25] Husbands, love your wives, just as Christ loved the church and gave himself up for her [26] to make her holy, cleansing[a] her by the washing with water through the word, [27] and to present her to himself as a radiant church, without stain or wrinkle or any other blemish, but holy and blameless. [28] In this same way, husbands ought to love their wives as their own bodies. He who loves his wife loves himself. [29] After all, no one ever hated their own body, but they feed and care for their body, just as Christ does the church — [30] for we are members of his body.

[31] "For this reason a man will leave his father and mother and be united to his wife, and the two will become one flesh."[b] [32] This is a profound mystery — but I am talking about Christ and the church. [33] However, each one of you also must love his wife as he loves himself, and the wife must respect her husband.

6 Children, obey your parents in the Lord, for this is right. [2] "Honor your father and mother" — which is the first commandment with a promise — [3] "so that it may go well with you and that you may enjoy long life on the earth."[c]

[4] Fathers,[d] do not exasperate your children; instead, bring them up in the training and instruction of the Lord.

[5] Slaves, obey your earthly masters with respect and fear, and with sincerity of heart, just as you would obey Christ. [6] Obey them not only to win their favor when their eye is on you, but as slaves of Christ, doing the will of God from your heart. [7] Serve wholeheartedly, as if you were serving the Lord, not people, [8] because you know that the Lord will reward each one for whatever good they do, whether they are slave or free.

[9] And masters, treat your slaves in the same way. Do not threaten them, since you know that he who is both their Master and yours is in heaven, and there is no favoritism with him.

---

[a] 26 Or *having cleansed*   [b] 31 Gen. 2:24   [c] 3 Deut. 5:16   [d] 4 Or *Parents*

The Armor of God

[10] Finally, be strong in the Lord and in his mighty power. [11] Put on the full armor of God, so that you can take your stand against the devil's schemes. [12] For our struggle is not against flesh and blood, but against the rulers, against the authorities, against the powers of this dark world and against the spiritual forces of evil in the heavenly realms. [13] Therefore put on the full armor of God, so that when the day of evil comes, you may be able to stand your ground, and after you have done everything, to stand. [14] Stand firm then, with the belt of truth buckled around your waist, with the breastplate of righteousness in place, [15] and with your feet fitted with the readiness that comes from the gospel of peace. [16] In addition to all this, take up the shield of faith, with which you can extinguish all the flaming arrows of the evil one. [17] Take the helmet of salvation and the sword of the Spirit, which is the word of God.

[18] And pray in the Spirit on all occasions with all kinds of prayers and requests. With this in mind, be alert and always keep on praying for all the Lord's people. [19] Pray also for me, that whenever I speak, words may be given me so that I will fearlessly make known the mystery of the gospel, [20] for which I am an ambassador in chains. Pray that I may declare it fearlessly, as I should.

Final Greetings

[21] Tychicus, the dear brother and faithful servant in the Lord, will tell you everything, so that you also may know how I am and what I am doing. [22] I am sending him to you for this very purpose, that you may know how we are, and that he may encourage you.

[23] Peace to the brothers and sisters,[a] and love with faith from God the Father and the Lord Jesus Christ. [24] Grace to all who love our Lord Jesus Christ with an undying love.[b]

---

[a] 23 The Greek word for *brothers and sisters* (*adelphoi*) refers here to believers, both men and women, as part of God's family.   [b] 24 Or *Grace and immortality to all who love our Lord Jesus Christ.*

Philippians

Introduction:

The letter to the Philippians was written by Paul while he was in prison in Rome about AD 60. The church in Philippi had sent Epaphroditus to Paul with a gift. While Epaphroditus was in Rome, he became sick, and the Philippian Christians were worried about him. After he was better, Paul sent him back to Philippi with this letter.

Paul reveals his love for the Philippians throughout this letter, the most personal one of all his letters written to a church. Paul thanks the Philippians for their love and helpfulness.

Even though Paul was writing from prison this letter is full of joy. The words "joy" or "rejoice" are used thirteen times. Paul gives his own testimony to the meaning of his present life when he writes "For to me, to live is Christ and to die is gain" (1:21).

As in his other letters Paul encourages the people and instructs them to live in harmony with others and in obedience to God.

Outline of contents:

Introduction (1:1–11)
Paul's circumstances and concern (1:12–30)
Imitating Christ's humility (2:1–18)
Paul's messengers (2:19–30)
Warnings and advice (3:1–4:20)
Conclusion (4:21–23)

1 Paul and Timothy, servants of Christ Jesus,

To all God's holy people in Christ Jesus at Philippi, together with the overseers and deacons[a]:

² Grace and peace to you from God our Father and the Lord Jesus Christ.

Thanksgiving and Prayer

³ I thank my God every time I remember you. ⁴ In all my prayers for all of you, I always pray with joy ⁵ because of your partnership in the gospel from the first day until now, ⁶ being confident of this, that he who began a good work in you will carry it

[a] 1 The word *deacons* refers here to Christians designated to serve with the overseers/elders of the church in a variety of ways; similarly in Romans 16:1 and 1 Tim. 3:8,12.

on to completion until the day of Christ Jesus.

[7] It is right for me to feel this way about all of you, since I have you in my heart and, whether I am in chains or defending and confirming the gospel, all of you share in God's grace with me. [8] God can testify how I long for all of you with the affection of Christ Jesus.

[9] And this is my prayer: that your love may abound more and more in knowledge and depth of insight, [10] so that you may be able to discern what is best and may be pure and blameless for the day of Christ, [11] filled with the fruit of righteousness that comes through Jesus Christ — to the glory and praise of God.

Paul's Chains Advance the Gospel

[12] Now I want you to know, brothers and sisters,[a] that what has happened to me has actually served to advance the gospel. [13] As a result, it has become clear throughout the whole palace guard[b] and to everyone else that I am in chains for Christ. [14] And because of my chains, most of the brothers and sisters have become confident in the Lord and dare all the more to proclaim the gospel without fear.

[15] It is true that some preach Christ out of envy and rivalry, but others out of goodwill. [16] The latter do so out of love, knowing that I am put here for the defense of the gospel. [17] The former preach Christ out of selfish ambition, not sincerely, supposing that they can stir up trouble for me while I am in chains. [18] But what does it matter? The important thing is that in every way, whether from false motives or true, Christ is preached. And because of this I rejoice.

Yes, and I will continue to rejoice, [19] for I know that through your prayers and God's provision of the Spirit of Jesus Christ what has happened to me will turn out for my deliverance.[c] [20] I eagerly expect and hope that I will in no way be ashamed, but will have sufficient courage so that now as always Christ will be exalted in my body, whether by life or by death. [21] For to me, to live is Christ and to die is gain. [22] If I am to go on living in the body, this will mean fruitful labor for me. Yet what shall I choose? I do not know! [23] I am torn between the two: I desire to depart and be with Christ, which is better by far; [24] but it is more necessary for you that I remain in the body. [25] Convinced of this, I know that I will remain, and I will continue with all of you for your progress and joy in the faith, [26] so that through my being with you again your boasting in Christ Jesus will abound on account of me.

---

[a] 12 The Greek word for *brothers and sisters* (*adelphoi*) refers here to believers, both men and women, as part of God's family; also in verse 14; and in 3:1, 13, 17; 4:1, 8, 21. [b] 13 Or *whole palace* [c] 19 Or *vindication*; or *salvation*

Life Worthy of the Gospel

²⁷Whatever happens, conduct yourselves in a manner worthy of the gospel of Christ. Then, whether I come and see you or only hear about you in my absence, I will know that you stand firm in the one Spirit,ᵃ striving together as one for the faith of the gospel ²⁸without being frightened in any way by those who oppose you. This is a sign to them that they will be destroyed, but that you will be saved — and that by God. ²⁹For it has been granted to you on behalf of Christ not only to believe in him, but also to suffer for him, ³⁰since you are going through the same struggle you saw I had, and now hear that I still have.

Imitating Christ's Humility

2 Therefore if you have any encouragement from being united with Christ, if any comfort from his love, if any common sharing in the Spirit, if any tenderness and compassion, ²then make my joy complete by being like-minded, having the same love, being one in spirit and of one mind. ³Do nothing out of selfish ambition or vain conceit. Rather, in humility value others above yourselves, ⁴not looking to your own interests but each of you to the interests of the others.

⁵In your relationships with one another, have the same mindset as Christ Jesus:

⁶Who, being in very natureᵇ
   God,
   did not consider equality
      with God something
      to be used to his own
      advantage;
⁷rather, he made himself
      nothing
   by taking the very natureᶜ of
      a servant,
   being made in human
      likeness.
⁸And being found in
      appearance as a man,
   he humbled himself
   by becoming obedient to
      death —
      even death on a cross!

⁹Therefore God exalted him to
      the highest place
   and gave him the name that
      is above every name,
¹⁰that at the name of Jesus every
      knee should bow,
   in heaven and on earth and
      under the earth,
¹¹and every tongue acknowledge
      that Jesus Christ is Lord,
   to the glory of God the Father.

Do Everything Without Grumbling

¹²Therefore, my dear friends, as you have always obeyed — not only in my presence, but now much more in my absence — continue to work out your salvation with fear and trembling, ¹³for it is God who works in you to will and to act in order to fulfill his good purpose.

ᵃ 27 Or *in one spirit*   ᵇ 6 Or *in the form of*   ᶜ 7 Or *the form*

[14] Do everything without grumbling or arguing, [15] so that you may become blameless and pure, "children of God without fault in a warped and crooked generation."[a] Then you will shine among them like stars in the sky [16] as you hold firmly to the word of life. And then I will be able to boast on the day of Christ that I did not run or labor in vain. [17] But even if I am being poured out like a drink offering on the sacrifice and service coming from your faith, I am glad and rejoice with all of you. [18] So you too should be glad and rejoice with me.

Timothy and Epaphroditus

[19] I hope in the Lord Jesus to send Timothy to you soon, that I also may be cheered when I receive news about you. [20] I have no one else like him, who will show genuine concern for your welfare. [21] For everyone looks out for their own interests, not those of Jesus Christ. [22] But you know that Timothy has proved himself, because as a son with his father he has served with me in the work of the gospel. [23] I hope, therefore, to send him as soon as I see how things go with me. [24] And I am confident in the Lord that I myself will come soon.

[25] But I think it is necessary to send back to you Epaphroditus, my brother, co-worker and fellow soldier, who is also your messenger, whom you sent to take care of my needs. [26] For he longs for all of you and is distressed because you heard he was ill. [27] Indeed he was ill, and almost died. But God had mercy on him, and not on him only but also on me, to spare me sorrow upon sorrow. [28] Therefore I am all the more eager to send him, so that when you see him again you may be glad and I may have less anxiety. [29] So then, welcome him in the Lord with great joy, and honor people like him, [30] because he almost died for the work of Christ. He risked his life to make up for the help you yourselves could not give me.

No Confidence in the Flesh

3 Further, my brothers and sisters, rejoice in the Lord! It is no trouble for me to write the same things to you again, and it is a safeguard for you. [2] Watch out for those dogs, those evildoers, those mutilators of the flesh. [3] For it is we who are the circumcision, we who serve God by his Spirit, who boast in Christ Jesus, and who put no confidence in the flesh — [4] though I myself have reasons for such confidence.

If someone else thinks they have reasons to put confidence in the flesh, I have more: [5] circumcised on the eighth day, of the people of Israel, of the tribe of Benjamin, a Hebrew of Hebrews; in regard to the law, a Pharisee; [6] as for zeal, persecuting the church; as for righteousness based on the law, faultless.

[7] But whatever were gains to me I now consider loss for the sake of Christ. [8] What is more, I consider everything a loss because of the surpassing worth of knowing Christ Jesus my Lord, for whose sake I have lost all things. I consider them garbage, that I may gain Christ [9] and be found in him, not having a righteousness of my own that comes from the law, but that which is through faith in[a] Christ — the righteousness that comes from God on the basis of faith. [10] I want to know Christ — yes, to know the power of his resurrection and participation in his sufferings, becoming like him in his death, [11] and so, somehow, attaining to the resurrection from the dead.

[12] Not that I have already obtained all this, or have already arrived at my goal, but I press on to take hold of that for which Christ Jesus took hold of me. [13] Brothers and sisters, I do not consider myself yet to have taken hold of it. But one thing I do: Forgetting what is behind and straining toward what is ahead, [14] I press on toward the goal to win the prize for which God has called me heavenward in Christ Jesus.

Following Paul's Example

[15] All of us, then, who are mature should take such a view of things. And if on some point you think differently, that too God will make clear to you. [16] Only let us live up to what we have already attained.

[17] Join together in following my example, brothers and sisters, and just as you have us as a model, keep your eyes on those who live as we do. [18] For, as I have often told you before and now tell you again even with tears, many live as enemies of the cross of Christ. [19] Their destiny is destruction, their god is their stomach, and their glory is in their shame. Their mind is set on earthly things. [20] But our citizenship is in heaven. And we eagerly await a Savior from there, the Lord Jesus Christ, [21] who, by the power that enables him to bring everything under his control, will transform our lowly bodies so that they will be like his glorious body.

Closing Appeal for Steadfastness and Unity

4 Therefore, my brothers and sisters, you whom I love and long for, my joy and crown, stand firm in the Lord in this way, dear friends!

[2] I plead with Euodia and I plead with Syntyche to be of the same mind in the Lord. [3] Yes, and I ask you, my true companion, help these women since they have contended at my side in the cause of the gospel, along with Clement and the rest of my coworkers, whose names are in the book of life.

---

[a] 9 Or *through the faithfulness of*

Final Exhortations

[4] Rejoice in the Lord always. I will say it again: Rejoice! [5] Let your gentleness be evident to all. The Lord is near. [6] Do not be anxious about anything, but in every situation, by prayer and petition, with thanksgiving, present your requests to God. [7] And the peace of God, which transcends all understanding, will guard your hearts and your minds in Christ Jesus.

[8] Finally, brothers and sisters, whatever is true, whatever is noble, whatever is right, whatever is pure, whatever is lovely, whatever is admirable — if anything is excellent or praiseworthy — think about such things. [9] Whatever you have learned or received or heard from me, or seen in me — put it into practice. And the God of peace will be with you.

Thanks for Their Gifts

[10] I rejoiced greatly in the Lord that at last you renewed your concern for me. Indeed, you were concerned, but you had no opportunity to show it. [11] I am not saying this because I am in need, for I have learned to be content whatever the circumstances. [12] I know what it is to be in need, and I know what it is to have plenty. I have learned the secret of being content in any and every situation, whether well fed or hungry, whether living in plenty or in want. [13] I can do all this through him who gives me strength.

[14] Yet it was good of you to share in my troubles. [15] Moreover, as you Philippians know, in the early days of your acquaintance with the gospel, when I set out from Macedonia, not one church shared with me in the matter of giving and receiving, except you only; [16] for even when I was in Thessalonica, you sent me aid more than once when I was in need. [17] Not that I desire your gifts; what I desire is that more be credited to your account. [18] I have received full payment and have more than enough. I am amply supplied, now that I have received from Epaphroditus the gifts you sent. They are a fragrant offering, an acceptable sacrifice, pleasing to God. [19] And my God will meet all your needs according to the riches of his glory in Christ Jesus.

[20] To our God and Father be glory for ever and ever. Amen.

Final Greetings

[21] Greet all God's people in Christ Jesus. The brothers and sisters who are with me send greetings. [22] All God's people here send you greetings, especially those who belong to Caesar's household.

[23] The grace of the Lord Jesus Christ be with your spirit. Amen.[a]

[a] 23 Some manuscripts do not have *Amen*.

Colossians

Introduction:

Colossians is the third letter Paul wrote from prison in Rome (about AD 60). Epaphras traveled from Colossae to Rome to tell Paul that false teachers were convincing the people that the Christian faith was incomplete. They were teaching the Colossians to worship angels and to follow special rules and ceremonies.

Paul wrote to the Colossians to oppose these false teachers. He reminded them that Jesus is supreme over everything, that Christ's death is all we need to be saved from our sins, and that through Christ we are free from man-made rules.

Outline of contents:

Greetings and appreciation (1:1–8)
Christ and the believer (1:9–2:5)
Dangerous rules (2:6–23)
Rules for holy living (3:1–4:6)
Greetings and conclusion (4:7–18)

1 Paul, an apostle of Christ Jesus by the will of God, and Timothy our brother,

²To God's holy people in Colossae, the faithful brothers and sisters*a* in Christ:

Grace and peace to you from God our Father.*b*

Thanksgiving and Prayer

³We always thank God, the Father of our Lord Jesus Christ, when we pray for you, ⁴because we have heard of your faith in Christ Jesus and of the love you have for all God's people — ⁵the faith and love that spring from the hope stored up for you in heaven and about which you have already heard in the true message of the gospel ⁶that has come to you. In the same way, the gospel is bearing fruit and growing throughout the whole world — just as it has been doing among you since the day you heard it and truly understood God's grace. ⁷You learned it from Epaphras, our dear fellow servant,*c* who is a

---

a 2 The Greek word for *brothers and sisters* (*adelphoi*) refers here to believers, both men and women, as part of God's family; also in 4:15.   *b* 2 Some manuscripts *Father and the Lord Jesus Christ*   *c* 7 Or *slave* faithful minister of Christ on our[a] behalf, [8]and who also told us of your love in the Spirit.

[9]For this reason, since the day we heard about you, we have not stopped praying for you. We continually ask God to fill you with the knowledge of his will through all the wisdom and understanding that the Spirit gives,[b] [10]so that you may live a life worthy of the Lord and please him in every way: bearing fruit in every good work, growing in the knowledge of God, [11]being strengthened with all power according to his glorious might so that you may have great endurance and patience, [12]and giving joyful thanks to the Father, who has qualified you[c] to share in the inheritance of his holy people in the kingdom of light. [13]For he has rescued us from the dominion of darkness and brought us into the kingdom of the Son he loves, [14]in whom we have redemption, the forgiveness of sins.

The Supremacy of the Son of God

[15]The Son is the image of the invisible God, the firstborn over all creation. [16]For in him all things were created: things in heaven and on earth, visible and invisible, whether thrones or powers or rulers or authorities; all things have been created through him and for him. [17]He is before all things, and in him all things hold together. [18]And he is the head of the body, the church; he is the beginning and the firstborn from among the dead, so that in everything he might have the supremacy. [19]For God was pleased to have all his fullness dwell in him, [20]and through him to reconcile to himself all things, whether things on earth or things in heaven, by making peace through his blood, shed on the cross.

[21]Once you were alienated from God and were enemies in your minds because of[d] your evil behavior. [22]But now he has reconciled you by Christ's physical body through death to present you holy in his sight, without blemish and free from accusation — [23]if you continue in your faith, established and firm, and do not move from the hope held out in the gospel. This is the gospel that you heard and that has been proclaimed to every creature under heaven, and of which I, Paul, have become a servant.

Paul's Labor for the Church

[24]Now I rejoice in what I am suffering for you, and I fill up in my flesh what is still lacking in regard to Christ's afflictions, for the sake of his body, which is the church. [25]I have become its servant by the commission God gave

---

[a] 7 Some manuscripts *your*   [b] 9 Or *all spiritual wisdom and understanding*
[c] 12 Some manuscripts *us*   [d] 21 Or *minds, as shown by*

me to present to you the word of God in its fullness — [26] the mystery that has been kept hidden for ages and generations, but is now disclosed to the Lord's people. [27] To them God has chosen to make known among the Gentiles the glorious riches of this mystery, which is Christ in you, the hope of glory.

[28] He is the one we proclaim, admonishing and teaching everyone with all wisdom, so that we may present everyone fully mature in Christ. [29] To this end I strenuously contend with all the energy Christ so powerfully works in me.

2 I want you to know how hard I am contending for you and for those at Laodicea, and for all who have not met me personally. [2] My goal is that they may be encouraged in heart and united in love, so that they may have the full riches of complete understanding, in order that they may know the mystery of God, namely, Christ, [3] in whom are hidden all the treasures of wisdom and knowledge. [4] I tell you this so that no one may deceive you by fine-sounding arguments. [5] For though I am absent from you in body, I am present with you in spirit and delight to see how disciplined you are and how firm your faith in Christ is.

Spiritual Fullness in Christ

[6] So then, just as you received Christ Jesus as Lord, continue to live your lives in him, [7] rooted and built up in him, strengthened in the faith as you were taught, and overflowing with thankfulness.

[8] See to it that no one takes you captive through hollow and deceptive philosophy, which depends on human tradition and the elemental spiritual forces[a] of this world rather than on Christ.

[9] For in Christ all the fullness of the Deity lives in bodily form, [10] and in Christ you have been brought to fullness. He is the head over every power and authority. [11] In him you were also circumcised with a circumcision not performed by human hands. Your whole self ruled by the flesh[b] was put off when you were circumcised by[c] Christ, [12] having been buried with him in baptism, in which you were also raised with him through your faith in the working of God, who raised him from the dead.

[13] When you were dead in your sins and in the uncircumcision of your flesh, God made you[d] alive with Christ. He forgave us all our sins, [14] having canceled the charge of our legal indebtedness, which stood against us and condemned us; he has taken it away, nailing it to the cross. [15] And hav-

---

[a] 8 Or *the basic principles*; also in verse 20   [b] 11 In contexts like this, the Greek word for *flesh* (*sarx*) refers to the sinful state of human beings, often presented as a power in opposition to the Spirit; also in verse 13.   [c] 11 Or *put off in the circumcision of*   [d] 13 Some manuscripts *us*

ing disarmed the powers and authorities, he made a public spectacle of them, triumphing over them by the cross.*ᵃ*

Freedom From Human Rules

¹⁶Therefore do not let anyone judge you by what you eat or drink, or with regard to a religious festival, a New Moon celebration or a Sabbath day. ¹⁷These are a shadow of the things that were to come; the reality, however, is found in Christ. ¹⁸Do not let anyone who delights in false humility and the worship of angels disqualify you. Such a person also goes into great detail about what they have seen; they are puffed up with idle notions by their unspiritual mind. ¹⁹They have lost connection with the head, from whom the whole body, supported and held together by its ligaments and sinews, grows as God causes it to grow.

²⁰Since you died with Christ to the elemental spiritual forces of this world, why, as though you still belonged to the world, do you submit to its rules: ²¹"Do not handle! Do not taste! Do not touch!"? ²²These rules, which have to do with things that are all destined to perish with use, are based on merely human commands and teachings. ²³Such regulations indeed have an appearance of wisdom, with their self-imposed worship, their false humility and their harsh treatment of the body, but they lack any value in restraining sensual indulgence.

Living as Those Made Alive in Christ

3 Since, then, you have been raised with Christ, set your hearts on things above, where Christ is, seated at the right hand of God. ²Set your minds on things above, not on earthly things. ³For you died, and your life is now hidden with Christ in God. ⁴When Christ, who is your*ᵇ* life, appears, then you also will appear with him in glory.

⁵Put to death, therefore, whatever belongs to your earthly nature: sexual immorality, impurity, lust, evil desires and greed, which is idolatry. ⁶Because of these, the wrath of God is coming.*ᶜ* ⁷You used to walk in these ways, in the life you once lived. ⁸But now you must also rid yourselves of all such things as these: anger, rage, malice, slander, and filthy language from your lips. ⁹Do not lie to each other, since you have taken off your old self with its practices ¹⁰and have put on the new self, which is being renewed in knowledge in the image of its Creator. ¹¹Here there is no Gentile or Jew, circumcised or uncircumcised, barbarian, Scythian, slave or free, but Christ is all, and is in all.

ᵃ 15 Or *them in him*   *ᵇ* 4 Some manuscripts *our*   *ᶜ* 6 Some early manuscripts *coming on those who are disobedient*

¹²Therefore, as God's chosen people, holy and dearly loved, clothe yourselves with compassion, kindness, humility, gentleness and patience. ¹³Bear with each other and forgive one another if any of you has a grievance against someone. Forgive as the Lord forgave you. ¹⁴And over all these virtues put on love, which binds them all together in perfect unity.

¹⁵Let the peace of Christ rule in your hearts, since as members of one body you were called to peace. And be thankful. ¹⁶Let the message of Christ dwell among you richly as you teach and admonish one another with all wisdom through psalms, hymns, and songs from the Spirit, singing to God with gratitude in your hearts. ¹⁷And whatever you do, whether in word or deed, do it all in the name of the Lord Jesus, giving thanks to God the Father through him.

Instructions for Christian Households

¹⁸Wives, submit yourselves to your husbands, as is fitting in the Lord.

¹⁹Husbands, love your wives and do not be harsh with them.

²⁰Children, obey your parents in everything, for this pleases the Lord.

²¹Fathers,*a* do not embitter your children, or they will become discouraged.

²²Slaves, obey your earthly masters in everything; and do it, not only when their eye is on you and to curry their favor, but with sincerity of heart and reverence for the Lord. ²³Whatever you do, work at it with all your heart, as working for the Lord, not for human masters, ²⁴since you know that you will receive an inheritance from the Lord as a reward. It is the Lord Christ you are serving. ²⁵Anyone who does wrong will be repaid for their wrongs, and there is no favoritism.

4 Masters, provide your slaves with what is right and fair, because you know that you also have a Master in heaven.

Further Instructions

²Devote yourselves to prayer, being watchful and thankful. ³And pray for us, too, that God may open a door for our message, so that we may proclaim the mystery of Christ, for which I am in chains. ⁴Pray that I may proclaim it clearly, as I should. ⁵Be wise in the way you act toward outsiders; make the most of every opportunity. ⁶Let your conversation be always full of grace, seasoned with salt, so that you may know how to answer everyone.

Final Greetings

⁷Tychicus will tell you all the news about me. He is a dear brother, a faithful minister and

a 21 Or *Parents*

fellow servant[a] in the Lord. [8]I am sending him to you for the express purpose that you may know about our[b] circumstances and that he may encourage your hearts. [9]He is coming with Onesimus, our faithful and dear brother, who is one of you. They will tell you everything that is happening here.

[10]My fellow prisoner Aristarchus sends you his greetings, as does Mark, the cousin of Barnabas. (You have received instructions about him; if he comes to you, welcome him.) [11]Jesus, who is called Justus, also sends greetings. These are the only Jews[c] among my co-workers for the kingdom of God, and they have proved a comfort to me. [12]Epaphras, who is one of you and a servant of Christ Jesus, sends greetings. He is always wrestling in prayer for you, that you may stand firm in all the will of God, mature and fully assured. [13]I vouch for him that he is working hard for you and for those at Laodicea and Hierapolis. [14]Our dear friend Luke, the doctor, and Demas send greetings. [15]Give my greetings to the brothers and sisters at Laodicea, and to Nympha and the church in her house.

[16]After this letter has been read to you, see that it is also read in the church of the Laodiceans and that you in turn read the letter from Laodicea.

[17]Tell Archippus: "See to it that you complete the ministry you have received in the Lord."

[18]I, Paul, write this greeting in my own hand. Remember my chains. Grace be with you.

---

[a] 7 Or *slave*; also in verse 12   [b] 8 Some manuscripts *that he may know about your*   [c] 11 Greek *only ones of the circumcision group*

1 Thessalonians

Introduction:

Paul started the church at Thessalonica on his second missionary journey. He taught there for about three weeks. Then the Jews opposed him so strongly he had to leave. On hearing from Timothy about the conditions in Thessalonica, Paul wrote this letter from Corinth to encourage the Thessalonians and to teach them more about Christianity (AD 51).

Paul praises the Thessalonians for being brave and not giving up their faith "in the midst of severe suffering" (1:6). He instructs them "how to live in order to please God" (4:1). And he teaches them about Jesus' second coming. He explains that the time of Jesus' coming is secret, so they should continue working until he comes.

Outline of contents:

Introduction and thanksgiving (1:1–10)
Paul's ministry in the church (2:1–3:13)
Instructions on the Lord's coming (4:1–5:11)
Conclusion (5:12–28)

1 Paul, Silas[a] and Timothy,

To the church of the Thessalonians in God the Father and the Lord Jesus Christ:

Grace and peace to you.

Thanksgiving for the Thessalonians' Faith

2 We always thank God for all of you and continually mention you in our prayers. **3** We remember before our God and Father your work produced by faith, your labor prompted by love, and your endurance inspired by hope in our Lord Jesus Christ.

4 For we know, brothers and sisters[b] loved by God, that he has chosen you, **5** because our gospel came to you not simply with words but also with power, with the Holy Spirit and deep conviction. You know how we lived among you for your sake. **6** You became imitators of us and of the Lord, for you welcomed the message in the midst of severe

---

[a] 1 Greek *Silvanus*, a variant of *Silas*   [b] 4 The Greek word for *brothers and sisters* (*adelphoi*) refers here to believers, both men and women, as part of God's family; also in 2:1, 9, 14, 17; 3:7; 4:1, 10, 13; 5:1, 4, 12, 14, 25, 27.

suffering with the joy given by the Holy Spirit. ⁷And so you became a model to all the believers in Macedonia and Achaia. ⁸The Lord's message rang out from you not only in Macedonia and Achaia — your faith in God has become known everywhere. Therefore we do not need to say anything about it, ⁹for they themselves report what kind of reception you gave us. They tell how you turned to God from idols to serve the living and true God, ¹⁰and to wait for his Son from heaven, whom he raised from the dead — Jesus, who rescues us from the coming wrath.

Paul's Ministry in Thessalonica

2 You know, brothers and sisters, that our visit to you was not without results. ²We had previously suffered and been treated outrageously in Philippi, as you know, but with the help of our God we dared to tell you his gospel in the face of strong opposition. ³For the appeal we make does not spring from error or impure motives, nor are we trying to trick you. ⁴On the contrary, we speak as those approved by God to be entrusted with the gospel. We are not trying to please people but God, who tests our hearts. ⁵You know we never used flattery, nor did we put on a mask to cover up greed — God is our witness. ⁶We were not looking for praise from people, not from you or any-

one else, even though as apostles of Christ we could have asserted our authority. ⁷Instead, we were like young children*a* among you.

Just as a nursing mother cares for her children, ⁸so we cared for you. Because we loved you so much, we were delighted to share with you not only the gospel of God but our lives as well. ⁹Surely you remember, brothers and sisters, our toil and hardship; we worked night and day in order not to be a burden to anyone while we preached the gospel of God to you. ¹⁰You are witnesses, and so is God, of how holy, righteous and blameless we were among you who believed. ¹¹For you know that we dealt with each of you as a father deals with his own children, ¹²encouraging, comforting and urging you to live lives worthy of God, who calls you into his kingdom and glory.

¹³And we also thank God continually because, when you received the word of God, which you heard from us, you accepted it not as a human word, but as it actually is, the word of God, which is indeed at work in you who believe. ¹⁴For you, brothers and sisters, became imitators of God's churches in Judea, which are in Christ Jesus: You suffered from your own people the same things those churches suffered from the Jews ¹⁵who killed the Lord Jesus and the prophets and

a 7 Some manuscripts *were gentle*

also drove us out. They displease God and are hostile to everyone [16]in their effort to keep us from speaking to the Gentiles so that they may be saved. In this way they always heap up their sins to the limit. The wrath of God has come upon them at last.[a]

Paul's Longing to See the Thessalonians

[17]But, brothers and sisters, when we were orphaned by being separated from you for a short time (in person, not in thought), out of our intense longing we made every effort to see you. [18]For we wanted to come to you — certainly I, Paul, did, again and again — but Satan blocked our way. [19]For what is our hope, our joy, or the crown in which we will glory in the presence of our Lord Jesus when he comes? Is it not you? [20]Indeed, you are our glory and joy.

3 So when we could stand it no longer, we thought it best to be left by ourselves in Athens. [2]We sent Timothy, who is our brother and co-worker in God's service in spreading the gospel of Christ, to strengthen and encourage you in your faith, [3]so that no one would be unsettled by these trials. For you know quite well that we are destined for them. [4]In fact, when we were with you, we kept telling you that we would be persecuted. And it turned out that way, as you well know. [5]For this reason, when I could stand it no longer, I sent to find out about your faith. I was afraid that in some way the tempter had tempted you and that our labors might have been in vain.

Timothy's Encouraging Report

[6]But Timothy has just now come to us from you and has brought good news about your faith and love. He has told us that you always have pleasant memories of us and that you long to see us, just as we also long to see you. [7]Therefore, brothers and sisters, in all our distress and persecution we were encouraged about you because of your faith. [8]For now we really live, since you are standing firm in the Lord. [9]How can we thank God enough for you in return for all the joy we have in the presence of our God because of you? [10]Night and day we pray most earnestly that we may see you again and supply what is lacking in your faith.

[11]Now may our God and Father himself and our Lord Jesus clear the way for us to come to you. [12]May the Lord make your love increase and overflow for each other and for everyone else, just as ours does for you. [13]May he strengthen your hearts so that you will be blameless and holy in the presence of our God and Father when our Lord Jesus comes with all his holy ones.

---

[a] 16 Or *them fully*

Living to Please God

4 As for other matters, brothers and sisters, we instructed you how to live in order to please God, as in fact you are living. Now we ask you and urge you in the Lord Jesus to do this more and more. ²For you know what instructions we gave you by the authority of the Lord Jesus.

³It is God's will that you should be sanctified: that you should avoid sexual immorality; ⁴that each of you should learn to control your own body*a* in a way that is holy and honorable, ⁵not in passionate lust like the pagans, who do not know God; ⁶and that in this matter no one should wrong or take advantage of a brother or sister.*b* The Lord will punish all those who commit such sins, as we told you and warned you before. ⁷For God did not call us to be impure, but to live a holy life. ⁸Therefore, anyone who rejects this instruction does not reject a human being but God, the very God who gives you his Holy Spirit.

⁹Now about your love for one another we do not need to write to you, for you yourselves have been taught by God to love each other. ¹⁰And in fact, you do love all of God's family throughout Macedonia. Yet we urge you, brothers and sisters, to do so more and more,

¹¹and to make it your ambition to lead a quiet life: You should mind your own business and work with your hands, just as we told you, ¹²so that your daily life may win the respect of outsiders and so that you will not be dependent on anybody.

Believers Who Have Died

¹³Brothers and sisters, we do not want you to be uninformed about those who sleep in death, so that you do not grieve like the rest of mankind, who have no hope. ¹⁴For we believe that Jesus died and rose again, and so we believe that God will bring with Jesus those who have fallen asleep in him. ¹⁵According to the Lord's word, we tell you that we who are still alive, who are left until the coming of the Lord, will certainly not precede those who have fallen asleep. ¹⁶For the Lord himself will come down from heaven, with a loud command, with the voice of the archangel and with the trumpet call of God, and the dead in Christ will rise first. ¹⁷After that, we who are still alive and are left will be caught up together with them in the clouds to meet the Lord in the air. And so we will be with the Lord forever. ¹⁸Therefore encourage one another with these words.

---

a 4 Or *learn to live with your own wife*; or *learn to acquire a wife*   *b* 6 The Greek word for *brother or sister* (*adelphos*) refers here to a believer, whether man or woman, as part of God's family.

The Day of the Lord

5 Now, brothers and sisters, about times and dates we do not need to write to you, ²for you know very well that the day of the Lord will come like a thief in the night. ³While people are saying, "Peace and safety," destruction will come on them suddenly, as labor pains on a pregnant woman, and they will not escape.

⁴But you, brothers and sisters, are not in darkness so that this day should surprise you like a thief. ⁵You are all children of the light and children of the day. We do not belong to the night or to the darkness. ⁶So then, let us not be like others, who are asleep, but let us be awake and sober. ⁷For those who sleep, sleep at night, and those who get drunk, get drunk at night. ⁸But since we belong to the day, let us be sober, putting on faith and love as a breastplate, and the hope of salvation as a helmet. ⁹For God did not appoint us to suffer wrath but to receive salvation through our Lord Jesus Christ. ¹⁰He died for us so that, whether we are awake or asleep, we may live together with him. ¹¹Therefore encourage one another and build each other up, just as in fact you are doing.

Final Instructions

¹²Now we ask you, brothers and sisters, to acknowledge those who work hard among you, who care for you in the Lord and who admonish you. ¹³Hold them in the highest regard in love because of their work. Live in peace with each other. ¹⁴And we urge you, brothers and sisters, warn those who are idle and disruptive, encourage the disheartened, help the weak, be patient with everyone. ¹⁵Make sure that nobody pays back wrong for wrong, but always strive to do what is good for each other and for everyone else.

¹⁶Rejoice always, ¹⁷pray continually, ¹⁸give thanks in all circumstances; for this is God's will for you in Christ Jesus.

¹⁹Do not quench the Spirit. ²⁰Do not treat prophecies with contempt ²¹but test them all; hold on to what is good, ²²reject every kind of evil.

²³May God himself, the God of peace, sanctify you through and through. May your whole spirit, soul and body be kept blameless at the coming of our Lord Jesus Christ. ²⁴The one who calls you is faithful, and he will do it.

²⁵Brothers and sisters, pray for us. ²⁶Greet all God's people with a holy kiss. ²⁷I charge you before the Lord to have this letter read to all the brothers and sisters.

²⁸The grace of our Lord Jesus Christ be with you.

2 Thessalonians

Introduction:

Paul was in Corinth when he sent his second letter to the Thessalonians a few months after the first letter. Some people had misunderstood Paul's teaching on the second coming and were sure Jesus was coming very soon. In fact, they had stopped working and were just waiting for Jesus.

Paul writes the Thessalonians again and describes what Jesus' second coming will be like. He also reminds them to keep working hard until Jesus comes and to use their time wisely.

Outline of contents:

Paul's personal concern (1:1–12)
Conditions for the Lord's coming (2:1–17)
Strong advice and a blessing (3:1–18)

1 Paul, Silas[a] and Timothy,

To the church of the Thessalonians in God our Father and the Lord Jesus Christ:

[2] Grace and peace to you from God the Father and the Lord Jesus Christ.

Thanksgiving and Prayer

[3] We ought always to thank God for you, brothers and sisters,[b] and rightly so, because your faith is growing more and more, and the love all of you have for one another is increasing. [4] Therefore, among God's churches we boast about your perseverance and faith in all the persecutions and trials you are enduring.

[5] All this is evidence that God's judgment is right, and as a result you will be counted worthy of the kingdom of God, for which you are suffering. [6] God is just: He will pay back trouble to those who trouble you [7] and give relief to you who are troubled, and to us as well. This will happen when the Lord Jesus is revealed from heaven in blazing fire with his powerful angels. [8] He will punish those who do not know God and do not obey the gospel of our Lord Jesus. [9] They will be punished with everlasting destruction and shut

---

[a] 1 Greek *Silvanus*, a variant of *Silas*   [b] 3 The Greek word for *brothers and sisters* (*adelphoi*) refers here to believers, both men and women, as part of God's family; also in 2:1, 13, 15; 3:1, 6, 13.

out from the presence of the Lord and from the glory of his might [10] on the day he comes to be glorified in his holy people and to be marveled at among all those who have believed. This includes you, because you believed our testimony to you.

[11] With this in mind, we constantly pray for you, that our God may make you worthy of his calling, and that by his power he may bring to fruition your every desire for goodness and your every deed prompted by faith. [12] We pray this so that the name of our Lord Jesus may be glorified in you, and you in him, according to the grace of our God and the Lord Jesus Christ.[a]

The Man of Lawlessness

2 Concerning the coming of our Lord Jesus Christ and our being gathered to him, we ask you, brothers and sisters, [2] not to become easily unsettled or alarmed by the teaching allegedly from us — whether by a prophecy or by word of mouth or by letter — asserting that the day of the Lord has already come. [3] Don't let anyone deceive you in any way, for that day will not come until the rebellion occurs and the man of lawlessness[b] is revealed, the man doomed to destruction. [4] He will oppose and will exalt himself over everything that is called God or is worshiped, so that he sets himself up in God's temple, proclaiming himself to be God.

[5] Don't you remember that when I was with you I used to tell you these things? [6] And now you know what is holding him back, so that he may be revealed at the proper time. [7] For the secret power of lawlessness is already at work; but the one who now holds it back will continue to do so till he is taken out of the way. [8] And then the lawless one will be revealed, whom the Lord Jesus will overthrow with the breath of his mouth and destroy by the splendor of his coming. [9] The coming of the lawless one will be in accordance with how Satan works. He will use all sorts of displays of power through signs and wonders that serve the lie, [10] and all the ways that wickedness deceives those who are perishing. They perish because they refused to love the truth and so be saved. [11] For this reason God sends them a powerful delusion so that they will believe the lie [12] and so that all will be condemned who have not believed the truth but have delighted in wickedness.

Stand Firm

[13] But we ought always to thank God for you, brothers and sisters loved by the Lord, because God chose you as firstfruits[c] to

---

[a] 12 Or *God and Lord, Jesus Christ*   [b] 3 Some manuscripts *sin*   [c] 13 Some manuscripts *because from the beginning God chose you*

be saved through the sanctifying work of the Spirit and through belief in the truth. ¹⁴He called you to this through our gospel, that you might share in the glory of our Lord Jesus Christ.

¹⁵So then, brothers and sisters, stand firm and hold fast to the teachings*a* we passed on to you, whether by word of mouth or by letter.

¹⁶May our Lord Jesus Christ himself and God our Father, who loved us and by his grace gave us eternal encouragement and good hope, ¹⁷encourage your hearts and strengthen you in every good deed and word.

Request for Prayer

3 As for other matters, brothers and sisters, pray for us that the message of the Lord may spread rapidly and be honored, just as it was with you. ²And pray that we may be delivered from wicked and evil people, for not everyone has faith. ³But the Lord is faithful, and he will strengthen you and protect you from the evil one. ⁴We have confidence in the Lord that you are doing and will continue to do the things we command. ⁵May the Lord direct your hearts into God's love and Christ's perseverance.

Warning Against Idleness

⁶In the name of the Lord Jesus Christ, we command you, broth-

ers and sisters, to keep away from every believer who is idle and disruptive and does not live according to the teaching*b* you received from us. ⁷For you yourselves know how you ought to follow our example. We were not idle when we were with you, ⁸nor did we eat anyone's food without paying for it. On the contrary, we worked night and day, laboring and toiling so that we would not be a burden to any of you. ⁹We did this, not because we do not have the right to such help, but in order to offer ourselves as a model for you to imitate. ¹⁰For even when we were with you, we gave you this rule: "The one who is unwilling to work shall not eat."

¹¹We hear that some among you are idle and disruptive. They are not busy; they are busybodies. ¹²Such people we command and urge in the Lord Jesus Christ to settle down and earn the food they eat. ¹³And as for you, brothers and sisters, never tire of doing what is good.

¹⁴Take special note of anyone who does not obey our instruction in this letter. Do not associate with them, in order that they may feel ashamed. ¹⁵Yet do not regard them as an enemy, but warn them as you would a fellow believer.

Final Greetings

¹⁶Now may the Lord of peace himself give you peace at all

---

a 15 Or *traditions*   *b* 6 Or *tradition*

times and in every way. The Lord be with all of you.

[17]I, Paul, write this greeting in my own hand, which is the distinguishing mark in all my letters. This is how I write. [18]The grace of our Lord Jesus Christ be with you all.

1 Timothy

Introduction:

First and Second Timothy and Titus are commonly called the pastoral letters because they deal with the qualifications and duties of pastors. Paul wrote these letters to the young leaders in the Christian church.

Timothy was born at Lystra and had a Greek father and a Jewish mother (who taught him the Scriptures from childhood). He went with Paul on his second missionary journey and from then on helped Paul in his work. At the time Paul wrote this letter, Timothy was working as the teacher and leader of the church at Ephesus.

Timothy was quite young to have the important job of leading a church, so Paul wrote this very personal letter to him. In this letter Paul gives him help and advice for his work. He warns him of false teachers and their teachings that are opposite God's commands. Because of Paul's deep care for Timothy he offers him advice on how to be a man of God.

Outline of contents:

Introduction (1:1–17)

Instructions for the church (1:18–3:16)

Personal instructions for Timothy (4:1–6:21)

1 Paul, an apostle of Christ Jesus by the command of God our Savior and of Christ Jesus our hope,

² To Timothy my true son in the faith:

Grace, mercy and peace from God the Father and Christ Jesus our Lord.

Timothy Charged to Oppose False Teachers

³ As I urged you when I went into Macedonia, stay there in Ephesus so that you may command certain people not to teach false doctrines any longer ⁴ or to devote themselves to myths and endless genealogies. Such things promote controversial speculations rather than advancing God's work—which is by faith. ⁵ The goal of this command is love, which comes from a pure heart and a good conscience and a sincere faith. ⁶ Some have departed from these and have turned to meaningless talk. ⁷ They want to be teachers of the

law, but they do not know what they are talking about or what they so confidently affirm.

⁸We know that the law is good if one uses it properly. ⁹We also know that the law is made not for the righteous but for lawbreakers and rebels, the ungodly and sinful, the unholy and irreligious, for those who kill their fathers or mothers, for murderers, ¹⁰for the sexually immoral, for those practicing homosexuality, for slave traders and liars and perjurers— and for whatever else is contrary to the sound doctrine ¹¹that conforms to the gospel concerning the glory of the blessed God, which he entrusted to me.

The Lord's Grace to Paul

¹²I thank Christ Jesus our Lord, who has given me strength, that he considered me trustworthy, appointing me to his service. ¹³Even though I was once a blasphemer and a persecutor and a violent man, I was shown mercy because I acted in ignorance and unbelief. ¹⁴The grace of our Lord was poured out on me abundantly, along with the faith and love that are in Christ Jesus.

¹⁵Here is a trustworthy saying that deserves full acceptance: Christ Jesus came into the world to save sinners—of whom I am the worst. ¹⁶But for that very reason I was shown mercy so that in me, the worst of sinners, Christ Jesus might display his immense patience as an example for those who would believe in him and receive eternal life. ¹⁷Now to the King eternal, immortal, invisible, the only God, be honor and glory for ever and ever. Amen.

The Charge to Timothy Renewed

¹⁸Timothy, my son, I am giving you this command in keeping with the prophecies once made about you, so that by recalling them you may fight the battle well, ¹⁹holding on to faith and a good conscience, which some have rejected and so have suffered shipwreck with regard to the faith. ²⁰Among them are Hymenaeus and Alexander, whom I have handed over to Satan to be taught not to blaspheme.

Instructions on Worship

2 I urge, then, first of all, that petitions, prayers, intercession and thanksgiving be made for all people— ²for kings and all those in authority, that we may live peaceful and quiet lives in all godliness and holiness. ³This is good, and pleases God our Savior, ⁴who wants all people to be saved and to come to a knowledge of the truth. ⁵For there is one God and one mediator between God and mankind, the man Christ Jesus, ⁶who gave himself as a ransom for all people. This has now been witnessed to at the proper time. ⁷And for

this purpose I was appointed a herald and an apostle—I am telling the truth, I am not lying—and a true and faithful teacher of the Gentiles.

[8] Therefore I want the men everywhere to pray, lifting up holy hands without anger or disputing. [9] I also want the women to dress modestly, with decency and propriety, adorning themselves, not with elaborate hairstyles or gold or pearls or expensive clothes, [10] but with good deeds, appropriate for women who profess to worship God.

[11] A woman[a] should learn in quietness and full submission. [12] I do not permit a woman to teach or to assume authority over a man;[b] she must be quiet. [13] For Adam was formed first, then Eve. [14] And Adam was not the one deceived; it was the woman who was deceived and became a sinner. [15] But women[c] will be saved through childbearing—if they continue in faith, love and holiness with propriety.

Qualifications for Overseers and Deacons

3 Here is a trustworthy saying: Whoever aspires to be an overseer desires a noble task. [2] Now the overseer is to be above reproach, faithful to his wife, temperate, self-controlled, respectable, hospitable, able to teach, [3] not given to drunkenness, not violent but gentle, not quarrelsome, not a lover of money. [4] He must manage his own family well and see that his children obey him, and he must do so in a manner worthy of full[d] respect. [5] (If anyone does not know how to manage his own family, how can he take care of God's church?) [6] He must not be a recent convert, or he may become conceited and fall under the same judgment as the devil. [7] He must also have a good reputation with outsiders, so that he will not fall into disgrace and into the devil's trap.

[8] In the same way, deacons[e] are to be worthy of respect, sincere, not indulging in much wine, and not pursuing dishonest gain. [9] They must keep hold of the deep truths of the faith with a clear conscience. [10] They must first be tested; and then if there is nothing against them, let them serve as deacons.

[11] In the same way, the women[f] are to be worthy of respect, not malicious talkers but temperate and trustworthy in everything.

[12] A deacon must be faithful to his wife and must manage his children and his household well. [13] Those who have served well

---

[a] 11 Or *wife*; also in verse 12   [b] 12 Or *over her husband*   [c] 15 Greek *she*
[d] 4 Or *him with proper*   [e] 8 The word *deacons* refers here to Christians designated to serve with the overseers/elders of the church in a variety of ways; similarly in verse 12; and in Romans 16:1 and Phil. 1:1.   [f] 11 Possibly deacons' wives or women who are deacons

gain an excellent standing and great assurance in their faith in Christ Jesus.

Reasons for Paul's Instructions

[14] Although I hope to come to you soon, I am writing you these instructions so that, [15] if I am delayed, you will know how people ought to conduct themselves in God's household, which is the church of the living God, the pillar and foundation of the truth. [16] Beyond all question, the mystery from which true godliness springs is great:

He appeared in the flesh,
was vindicated by the
Spirit,[a]
was seen by angels,
was preached among the
nations,
was believed on in the world,
was taken up in glory.

4 The Spirit clearly says that in later times some will abandon the faith and follow deceiving spirits and things taught by demons. [2] Such teachings come through hypocritical liars, whose consciences have been seared as with a hot iron. [3] They forbid people to marry and order them to abstain from certain foods, which God created to be received with thanksgiving by those who believe and who know the truth. [4] For everything God created is good, and nothing is to be rejected if it is received with thanksgiving, [5] because it is consecrated by the word of God and prayer.

[6] If you point these things out to the brothers and sisters,[b] you will be a good minister of Christ Jesus, nourished on the truths of the faith and of the good teaching that you have followed. [7] Have nothing to do with godless myths and old wives' tales; rather, train yourself to be godly. [8] For physical training is of some value, but godliness has value for all things, holding promise for both the present life and the life to come. [9] This is a trustworthy saying that deserves full acceptance. [10] That is why we labor and strive, because we have put our hope in the living God, who is the Savior of all people, and especially of those who believe.

[11] Command and teach these things. [12] Don't let anyone look down on you because you are young, but set an example for the believers in speech, in conduct, in love, in faith and in purity. [13] Until I come, devote yourself to the public reading of Scripture, to preaching and to teaching. [14] Do not neglect your gift, which was given you through prophecy when the body of elders laid their hands on you.

[15] Be diligent in these matters; give yourself wholly to them, so

---

[a] 16 Or *vindicated in spirit* [b] 6 The Greek word for *brothers and sisters* (*adelphoi*) refers here to believers, both men and women, as part of God's family.

that everyone may see your progress. [16]Watch your life and doctrine closely. Persevere in them, because if you do, you will save both yourself and your hearers.

Widows, Elders and Slaves

5 Do not rebuke an older man harshly, but exhort him as if he were your father. Treat younger men as brothers, [2]older women as mothers, and younger women as sisters, with absolute purity.

[3]Give proper recognition to those widows who are really in need. [4]But if a widow has children or grandchildren, these should learn first of all to put their religion into practice by caring for their own family and so repaying their parents and grandparents, for this is pleasing to God. [5]The widow who is really in need and left all alone puts her hope in God and continues night and day to pray and to ask God for help. [6]But the widow who lives for pleasure is dead even while she lives. [7]Give the people these instructions, so that no one may be open to blame. [8]Anyone who does not provide for their relatives, and especially for their own household, has denied the faith and is worse than an unbeliever.

[9]No widow may be put on the list of widows unless she is over sixty, has been faithful to her husband, [10]and is well known for her good deeds, such as bringing up children, showing hospitality, washing the feet of the Lord's people, helping those in trouble and devoting herself to all kinds of good deeds.

[11]As for younger widows, do not put them on such a list. For when their sensual desires overcome their dedication to Christ, they want to marry. [12]Thus they bring judgment on themselves, because they have broken their first pledge. [13]Besides, they get into the habit of being idle and going about from house to house. And not only do they become idlers, but also busybodies who talk nonsense, saying things they ought not to. [14]So I counsel younger widows to marry, to have children, to manage their homes and to give the enemy no opportunity for slander. [15]Some have in fact already turned away to follow Satan.

[16]If any woman who is a believer has widows in her care, she should continue to help them and not let the church be burdened with them, so that the church can help those widows who are really in need.

[17]The elders who direct the affairs of the church well are worthy of double honor, especially those whose work is preaching and teaching. [18]For Scripture says, "Do not muzzle an ox while it is treading out the grain,"[a] and

[a] 18 Deut. 25:4

"The worker deserves his wages."[a] [19] Do not entertain an accusation against an elder unless it is brought by two or three witnesses. [20] But those elders who are sinning you are to reprove before everyone, so that the others may take warning. [21] I charge you, in the sight of God and Christ Jesus and the elect angels, to keep these instructions without partiality, and to do nothing out of favoritism.

[22] Do not be hasty in the laying on of hands, and do not share in the sins of others. Keep yourself pure.

[23] Stop drinking only water, and use a little wine because of your stomach and your frequent illnesses.

[24] The sins of some are obvious, reaching the place of judgment ahead of them; the sins of others trail behind them. [25] In the same way, good deeds are obvious, and even those that are not obvious cannot remain hidden forever.

6 All who are under the yoke of slavery should consider their masters worthy of full respect, so that God's name and our teaching may not be slandered. [2] Those who have believing masters should not show them disrespect just because they are fellow believers. Instead, they should serve them even better because their masters are dear to them as fellow believers and are devoted to the welfare[b] of their slaves.

False Teachers and the Love of Money

These are the things you are to teach and insist on. [3] If anyone teaches otherwise and does not agree to the sound instruction of our Lord Jesus Christ and to godly teaching, [4] they are conceited and understand nothing. They have an unhealthy interest in controversies and quarrels about words that result in envy, strife, malicious talk, evil suspicions [5] and constant friction between people of corrupt mind, who have been robbed of the truth and who think that godliness is a means to financial gain.

[6] But godliness with contentment is great gain. [7] For we brought nothing into the world, and we can take nothing out of it. [8] But if we have food and clothing, we will be content with that. [9] Those who want to get rich fall into temptation and a trap and into many foolish and harmful desires that plunge people into ruin and destruction. [10] For the love of money is a root of all kinds of evil. Some people, eager for money, have wandered from the faith and pierced themselves with many griefs.

Final Charge to Timothy

[11] But you, man of God, flee from all this, and pursue righteousness, godliness, faith, love, endurance and gentleness. [12] Fight the good fight of the faith. Take hold

---

[a] 18 Luke 10:7   [b] 2 Or *and benefit from the service*

of the eternal life to which you were called when you made your good confession in the presence of many witnesses. [13] In the sight of God, who gives life to everything, and of Christ Jesus, who while testifying before Pontius Pilate made the good confession, I charge you [14] to keep this command without spot or blame until the appearing of our Lord Jesus Christ, [15] which God will bring about in his own time — God, the blessed and only Ruler, the King of kings and Lord of lords, [16] who alone is immortal and who lives in unapproachable light, whom no one has seen or can see. To him be honor and might forever. Amen.

[17] Command those who are rich in this present world not to be arrogant nor to put their hope in wealth, which is so uncertain, but to put their hope in God, who richly provides us with everything for our enjoyment. [18] Command them to do good, to be rich in good deeds, and to be generous and willing to share. [19] In this way they will lay up treasure for themselves as a firm foundation for the coming age, so that they may take hold of the life that is truly life.

[20] Timothy, guard what has been entrusted to your care. Turn away from godless chatter and the opposing ideas of what is falsely called knowledge, [21] which some have professed and in so doing have departed from the faith.

Grace be with you all.

2 Timothy

Introduction:

Paul probably was arrested sometime after writing 1 Timothy and Titus, so he wrote his second letter to Timothy from Rome where he was a prisoner.

In this letter Paul seems to know that he will never be released from prison and that he will soon die. This is why he writes to Timothy.

Paul expresses his desire to see Timothy again and encourages Timothy to continue the missionary work after his death. He gives Timothy more instructions on how to lead a church and warns him to stay away from false teachers. He urges Timothy to be faithful to true Christian teachings.

Outline of contents:

Greeting (1:1,2)
Encouragement to be faithful (1:3–2:13)
The false and the true way (2:14–3:9)
Paul's charge to Timothy (3:10–4:8)
Conclusion (4:9–22)

1 Paul, an apostle of Christ Jesus by the will of God, in keeping with the promise of life that is in Christ Jesus,

²To Timothy, my dear son:

Grace, mercy and peace from God the Father and Christ Jesus our Lord.

Thanksgiving

³I thank God, whom I serve, as my ancestors did, with a clear conscience, as night and day I constantly remember you in my prayers. ⁴Recalling your tears, I long to see you, so that I may be filled with joy. ⁵I am reminded of your sincere faith, which first lived in your grandmother Lois and in your mother Eunice and, I am persuaded, now lives in you also.

Appeal for Loyalty to Paul and the Gospel

⁶For this reason I remind you to fan into flame the gift of God, which is in you through the laying on of my hands. ⁷For the Spirit God gave us does not make us timid, but gives us power, love and self-discipline. ⁸So do not be ashamed of the testimony about

our Lord or of me his prisoner. Rather, join with me in suffering for the gospel, by the power of God. ⁹He has saved us and called us to a holy life — not because of anything we have done but because of his own purpose and grace. This grace was given us in Christ Jesus before the beginning of time, ¹⁰but it has now been revealed through the appearing of our Savior, Christ Jesus, who has destroyed death and has brought life and immortality to light through the gospel. ¹¹And of this gospel I was appointed a herald and an apostle and a teacher. ¹²That is why I am suffering as I am. Yet this is no cause for shame, because I know whom I have believed, and am convinced that he is able to guard what I have entrusted to him until that day.

¹³What you heard from me, keep as the pattern of sound teaching, with faith and love in Christ Jesus. ¹⁴Guard the good deposit that was entrusted to you — guard it with the help of the Holy Spirit who lives in us.

Examples of Disloyalty and Loyalty

¹⁵You know that everyone in the province of Asia has deserted me, including Phygelus and Hermogenes.

¹⁶May the Lord show mercy to the household of Onesiphorus, because he often refreshed me and was not ashamed of my chains. ¹⁷On the contrary, when he was in Rome, he searched hard for me until he found me. ¹⁸May the Lord grant that he will find mercy from the Lord on that day! You know very well in how many ways he helped me in Ephesus.

The Appeal Renewed

2 You then, my son, be strong in the grace that is in Christ Jesus. ²And the things you have heard me say in the presence of many witnesses entrust to reliable people who will also be qualified to teach others. ³Join with me in suffering, like a good soldier of Christ Jesus. ⁴No one serving as a soldier gets entangled in civilian affairs, but rather tries to please his commanding officer. ⁵Similarly, anyone who competes as an athlete does not receive the victor's crown except by competing according to the rules. ⁶The hardworking farmer should be the first to receive a share of the crops. ⁷Reflect on what I am saying, for the Lord will give you insight into all this.

⁸Remember Jesus Christ, raised from the dead, descended from David. This is my gospel, ⁹for which I am suffering even to the point of being chained like a criminal. But God's word is not chained. ¹⁰Therefore I endure everything for the sake of the elect, that they too may obtain the

salvation that is in Christ Jesus, with eternal glory. **11** Here is a trustworthy saying:

If we died with him,
    we will also live with him;
12 if we endure,
    we will also reign with him.
If we disown him,
    he will also disown us;
13 if we are faithless,
    he remains faithful,
    for he cannot disown
        himself.

Dealing With False Teachers

14 Keep reminding God's people of these things. Warn them before God against quarreling about words; it is of no value, and only ruins those who listen. **15** Do your best to present yourself to God as one approved, a worker who does not need to be ashamed and who correctly handles the word of truth. **16** Avoid godless chatter, because those who indulge in it will become more and more ungodly. **17** Their teaching will spread like gangrene. Among them are Hymenaeus and Philetus, **18** who have departed from the truth. They say that the resurrection has already taken place, and they destroy the faith of some. **19** Nevertheless, God's solid foundation stands firm, sealed with this inscription: "The Lord knows those who are his," and, "Everyone who confesses the name of the Lord must turn away from wickedness."

20 In a large house there are articles not only of gold and silver, but also of wood and clay; some are for special purposes and some for common use. **21** Those who cleanse themselves from the latter will be instruments for special purposes, made holy, useful to the Master and prepared to do any good work.

22 Flee the evil desires of youth and pursue righteousness, faith, love and peace, along with those who call on the Lord out of a pure heart. **23** Don't have anything to do with foolish and stupid arguments, because you know they produce quarrels. **24** And the Lord's servant must not be quarrelsome but must be kind to everyone, able to teach, not resentful. **25** Opponents must be gently instructed, in the hope that God will grant them repentance leading them to a knowledge of the truth, **26** and that they will come to their senses and escape from the trap of the devil, who has taken them captive to do his will.

3 But mark this: There will be terrible times in the last days. **2** People will be lovers of themselves, lovers of money, boastful, proud, abusive, disobedient to their parents, ungrateful, unholy, **3** without love, unforgiving, slanderous, without self-control, brutal, not lovers of the good, **4** treacherous, rash, conceited, lovers of pleasure rather than lovers of God— **5** having a form of godliness but denying its power. Have nothing to do with such people.

⁶They are the kind who worm their way into homes and gain control over gullible women, who are loaded down with sins and are swayed by all kinds of evil desires, ⁷always learning but never able to come to a knowledge of the truth. ⁸Just as Jannes and Jambres opposed Moses, so also these teachers oppose the truth. They are men of depraved minds, who, as far as the faith is concerned, are rejected. ⁹But they will not get very far because, as in the case of those men, their folly will be clear to everyone.

A Final Charge to Timothy

¹⁰You, however, know all about my teaching, my way of life, my purpose, faith, patience, love, endurance, ¹¹persecutions, sufferings—what kinds of things happened to me in Antioch, Iconium and Lystra, the persecutions I endured. Yet the Lord rescued me from all of them. ¹²In fact, everyone who wants to live a godly life in Christ Jesus will be persecuted, ¹³while evildoers and impostors will go from bad to worse, deceiving and being deceived. ¹⁴But as for you, continue in what you have learned and have become convinced of, because you know those from whom you learned it, ¹⁵and how

from infancy you have known the Holy Scriptures, which are able to make you wise for salvation through faith in Christ Jesus. ¹⁶All Scripture is God-breathed and is useful for teaching, rebuking, correcting and training in righteousness, ¹⁷so that the servant of God*a* may be thoroughly equipped for every good work.

4 In the presence of God and of Christ Jesus, who will judge the living and the dead, and in view of his appearing and his kingdom, I give you this charge: ²Preach the word; be prepared in season and out of season; correct, rebuke and encourage—with great patience and careful instruction. ³For the time will come when people will not put up with sound doctrine. Instead, to suit their own desires, they will gather around them a great number of teachers to say what their itching ears want to hear. ⁴They will turn their ears away from the truth and turn aside to myths. ⁵But you, keep your head in all situations, endure hardship, do the work of an evangelist, discharge all the duties of your ministry.

⁶For I am already being poured out like a drink offering, and the time for my departure is near. ⁷I have fought the good fight, I have finished the race, I have kept the faith. ⁸Now there is in store for me the crown of righteousness,

a 17 Or *that you, a man of God,*

which the Lord, the righteous Judge, will award to me on that day—and not only to me, but also to all who have longed for his appearing.

Personal Remarks

[9]Do your best to come to me quickly, [10]for Demas, because he loved this world, has deserted me and has gone to Thessalonica. Crescens has gone to Galatia, and Titus to Dalmatia. [11]Only Luke is with me. Get Mark and bring him with you, because he is helpful to me in my ministry. [12]I sent Tychicus to Ephesus. [13]When you come, bring the cloak that I left with Carpus at Troas, and my scrolls, especially the parchments.

[14]Alexander the metalworker did me a great deal of harm. The Lord will repay him for what he has done. [15]You too should be on your guard against him, because he strongly opposed our message.

[16]At my first defense, no one came to my support, but everyone deserted me. May it not be held against them. [17]But the Lord stood at my side and gave me strength, so that through me the message might be fully proclaimed and all the Gentiles might hear it. And I was delivered from the lion's mouth. [18]The Lord will rescue me from every evil attack and will bring me safely to his heavenly kingdom. To him be glory for ever and ever. Amen.

Final Greetings

[19]Greet Priscilla[a] and Aquila and the household of Onesiphorus. [20]Erastus stayed in Corinth, and I left Trophimus sick in Miletus. [21]Do your best to get here before winter. Eubulus greets you, and so do Pudens, Linus, Claudia and all the brothers and sisters.[b]

[22]The Lord be with your spirit. Grace be with you all.

---

[a] 19 Greek *Prisca*, a variant of *Priscilla*   [b] 21 The Greek word for *brothers and sisters* (*adelphoi*) refers here to believers, both men and women, as part of God's family.

Titus

Introduction:

Titus was another friend and helper of Paul's. He had traveled with Paul on several missionary journeys, and was working as the leader of the church on the island of Crete. This letter is similar to the two letters Paul wrote to Timothy.

The church in Crete was an unorganized church, made up of people who needed much instruction in being Christians. Paul tells Titus and the church how God's people should behave. He tells Titus to teach the people the truth of God and instructs him in how to be a good church leader.

Outline of contents:

Introduction (1:1–4)
Duties of elders and deacons (1:5–16)
Duties of a pastor (2:1–3:11)
Conclusion (3:12–15)

1 Paul, a servant of God and an apostle of Jesus Christ to further the faith of God's elect and their knowledge of the truth that leads to godliness — ²in the hope of eternal life, which God, who does not lie, promised before the beginning of time, ³and which now at his appointed season he has brought to light through the preaching entrusted to me by the command of God our Savior,

⁴To Titus, my true son in our common faith:

Grace and peace from God the Father and Christ Jesus our Savior.

Appointing Elders Who Love What Is Good

⁵The reason I left you in Crete was that you might put in order what was left unfinished and appoint*a* elders in every town, as I directed you. ⁶An elder must be blameless, faithful to his wife, a man whose children believe*b* and are not open to the charge of being wild and disobedient. ⁷Since an overseer manages God's household, he must be blameless — not overbearing, not quick-tempered, not given to drunkenness, not violent, not pursuing dishonest gain. ⁸Rather, he must be hospitable, one who loves what is good,

a 5 Or *ordain*   *b* 6 Or *children are trustworthy*

who is self-controlled, upright, holy and disciplined. [9]He must hold firmly to the trustworthy message as it has been taught, so that he can encourage others by sound doctrine and refute those who oppose it.

Rebuking Those Who Fail to Do Good

[10]For there are many rebellious people, full of meaningless talk and deception, especially those of the circumcision group. [11]They must be silenced, because they are disrupting whole households by teaching things they ought not to teach — and that for the sake of dishonest gain. [12]One of Crete's own prophets has said it: "Cretans are always liars, evil brutes, lazy gluttons."[a] [13]This saying is true. Therefore rebuke them sharply, so that they will be sound in the faith [14]and will pay no attention to Jewish myths or to the merely human commands of those who reject the truth. [15]To the pure, all things are pure, but to those who are corrupted and do not believe, nothing is pure. In fact, both their minds and consciences are corrupted. [16]They claim to know God, but by their actions they deny him. They are detestable, disobedient and unfit for doing anything good.

Doing Good for the Sake of the Gospel

2 You, however, must teach what is appropriate to sound doctrine. [2]Teach the older men to be temperate, worthy of respect, self-controlled, and sound in faith, in love and in endurance.

[3]Likewise, teach the older women to be reverent in the way they live, not to be slanderers or addicted to much wine, but to teach what is good. [4]Then they can urge the younger women to love their husbands and children, [5]to be self-controlled and pure, to be busy at home, to be kind, and to be subject to their husbands, so that no one will malign the word of God.

[6]Similarly, encourage the young men to be self-controlled. [7]In everything set them an example by doing what is good. In your teaching show integrity, seriousness [8]and soundness of speech that cannot be condemned, so that those who oppose you may be ashamed because they have nothing bad to say about us.

[9]Teach slaves to be subject to their masters in everything, to try to please them, not to talk back to them, [10]and not to steal from them, but to show that they can be fully trusted, so that in every way they will make the teaching about God our Savior attractive.

[11]For the grace of God has appeared that offers salvation to all people. [12]It teaches us to say "No" to ungodliness and worldly passions, and to live self-controlled, upright and godly lives in this present age, [13]while we wait for

[a] 12 From the Cretan philosopher Epimenides

the blessed hope — the appearing of the glory of our great God and Savior, Jesus Christ, ¹⁴who gave himself for us to redeem us from all wickedness and to purify for himself a people that are his very own, eager to do what is good.

¹⁵These, then, are the things you should teach. Encourage and rebuke with all authority. Do not let anyone despise you.

Saved in Order to Do Good

3 Remind the people to be subject to rulers and authorities, to be obedient, to be ready to do whatever is good, ²to slander no one, to be peaceable and considerate, and always to be gentle toward everyone.

³At one time we too were foolish, disobedient, deceived and enslaved by all kinds of passions and pleasures. We lived in malice and envy, being hated and hating one another. ⁴But when the kindness and love of God our Savior appeared, ⁵he saved us, not because of righteous things we had done, but because of his mercy. He saved us through the washing of rebirth and renewal by the Holy Spirit, ⁶whom he poured out on us generously through Jesus Christ our Savior, ⁷so that, having been justified by his grace, we might become heirs having

the hope of eternal life. ⁸This is a trustworthy saying. And I want you to stress these things, so that those who have trusted in God may be careful to devote themselves to doing what is good. These things are excellent and profitable for everyone.

⁹But avoid foolish controversies and genealogies and arguments and quarrels about the law, because these are unprofitable and useless. ¹⁰Warn a divisive person once, and then warn them a second time. After that, have nothing to do with them. ¹¹You may be sure that such people are warped and sinful; they are self-condemned.

Final Remarks

¹²As soon as I send Artemas or Tychicus to you, do your best to come to me at Nicopolis, because I have decided to winter there. ¹³Do everything you can to help Zenas the lawyer and Apollos on their way and see that they have everything they need. ¹⁴Our people must learn to devote themselves to doing what is good, in order to provide for urgent needs and not live unproductive lives.

¹⁵Everyone with me sends you greetings. Greet those who love us in the faith.

Grace be with you all.

Philemon

Introduction:

Philemon was a leader of the church at Colossae and a friend of Paul's. Philemon's slave, Onesimus, had stolen money from him and had run away to Rome. While he was there he met Paul and became a Christian.

Paul sends Onesimus back to Philemon with this letter. He begs Philemon to forgive Onesimus and to treat him as a brother in Christ instead of as a runaway slave.

This short letter, along with Ephesians, Colossians and Philippians are often called the prison letters because they were written while Paul was in prison in Rome (about AD 59–61).

Outline of contents:

Greetings (1–3)
Paul's concern and love (4–7)
Paul's plea for Onesimus (8–22)
Farewell (23–25)

¹Paul, a prisoner of Christ Jesus, and Timothy our brother,

To Philemon our dear friend and fellow worker — ²also to Apphia our sister and Archippus our fellow soldier — and to the church that meets in your home:

³Grace and peace to you*a* from God our Father and the Lord Jesus Christ.

Thanksgiving and Prayer

⁴I always thank my God as I remember you in my prayers, ⁵because I hear about your love for all his holy people and your faith in the Lord Jesus. ⁶I pray that your partnership with us in the faith may be effective in deepening your understanding of every good thing we share for the sake of Christ. ⁷Your love has given me great joy and encouragement, because you, brother, have refreshed the hearts of the Lord's people.

Paul's Plea for Onesimus

⁸Therefore, although in Christ I could be bold and order you to do what you ought to do, ⁹yet I

a 3 The Greek is plural; also in verses 22 and 25; elsewhere in this letter "you" is singular.

prefer to appeal to you on the basis of love. It is as none other than Paul—an old man and now also a prisoner of Christ Jesus— ¹⁰that I appeal to you for my son Onesimus,ᵃ who became my son while I was in chains. ¹¹Formerly he was useless to you, but now he has become useful both to you and to me.

¹²I am sending him—who is my very heart—back to you. ¹³I would have liked to keep him with me so that he could take your place in helping me while I am in chains for the gospel. ¹⁴But I did not want to do anything without your consent, so that any favor you do would not seem forced but would be voluntary. ¹⁵Perhaps the reason he was separated from you for a little while was that you might have him back forever— ¹⁶no longer as a slave, but better than a slave, as a dear brother. He is very dear to me but even dearer to you, both as a fellow man and as a brother in the Lord.

¹⁷So if you consider me a partner, welcome him as you would welcome me. ¹⁸If he has done you any wrong or owes you anything, charge it to me. ¹⁹I, Paul, am writing this with my own hand. I will pay it back—not to mention that you owe me your very self. ²⁰I do wish, brother, that I may have some benefit from you in the Lord; refresh my heart in Christ. ²¹Confident of your obedience, I write to you, knowing that you will do even more than I ask.

²²And one thing more: Prepare a guest room for me, because I hope to be restored to you in answer to your prayers.

²³Epaphras, my fellow prisoner in Christ Jesus, sends you greetings. ²⁴And so do Mark, Aristarchus, Demas and Luke, my fellow workers.

²⁵The grace of the Lord Jesus Christ be with your spirit.

ᵃ 10 *Onesimus* means *useful*.

Hebrews

Introduction:

Although the author of Hebrews is unknown, this book was probably written in the late AD 60s. During this time persecution was a real problem for the church in Rome. This letter was most likely written to the Jewish Christians in either Palestine or Rome who were ready to give up their faith and return to the Jewish beliefs because of persecution.

The book of Hebrews was written to teach Jewish Christians that Christ is from God and is better than angels, Moses, Joshua or any priest. He is the ultimate high priest "designated by God to be high priest in the order of Melchizedek" (5:10). The author states that after Christ's death, the Old Testament sacrifices were no longer needed because Christ made the final sacrifice for all sin by dying himself.

Chapter 11 is the famous chapter that summarizes the lives of men and women of faith in the Old Testament. These summaries reminded the people of their heritage and gave the persecuted Christians great hope. The author encourages his readers to "hold firmly to the faith we profess" (4:14) and to trust in God.

Outline of contents:

Christ — God's complete revelation (1:1–3)
Christ — superior to the angels (1:4–2:18)
Christ — superior to Moses and Joshua (3:1–4:13)
Christ — the superior intercessor or priest (4:14–7:28)
Christ's superior covenant and sacrifice (8:1–10:18)
The practical appeal (10:19–12:29)
Concluding advice (13:1–25)

God's Final Word: His Son

1 In the past God spoke to our ancestors through the prophets at many times and in various ways, ²but in these last days he has spoken to us by his Son, whom he appointed heir of all things, and through whom also he made the universe. ³The Son is the radiance of God's glory and the exact representation of his being, sustaining all things by his powerful word. After he had provided purification for sins,

he sat down at the right hand of the Majesty in heaven. **4** So he became as much superior to the angels as the name he has inherited is superior to theirs.

The Son Superior to Angels

5 For to which of the angels did God ever say,

> "You are my Son;
>> today I have become your Father"*a*?

Or again,

> "I will be his Father,
>> and he will be my Son"*b*?

6 And again, when God brings his firstborn into the world, he says,

> "Let all God's angels worship him."*c*

7 In speaking of the angels he says,

> "He makes his angels spirits,
>> and his servants flames of fire."*d*

8 But about the Son he says,

> "Your throne, O God, will last for ever and ever;
>> a scepter of justice will be the scepter of your kingdom.
> **9** You have loved righteousness and hated wickedness;

therefore God, your God, has set you above your companions by anointing you with the oil of joy."*e*

10 He also says,

> "In the beginning, Lord, you laid the foundations of the earth,
> and the heavens are the work of your hands.
> **11** They will perish, but you remain;
>> they will all wear out like a garment.
> **12** You will roll them up like a robe;
>> like a garment they will be changed.
> But you remain the same,
>> and your years will never end."*f*

13 To which of the angels did God ever say,

> "Sit at my right hand
>> until I make your enemies a footstool for your feet"*g*?

14 Are not all angels ministering spirits sent to serve those who will inherit salvation?

Warning to Pay Attention

2 We must pay the most careful attention, therefore, to what we have heard, so that we do not drift away. **2** For since the

---

a 5 Psalm 2:7   *b 5* 2 Samuel 7:14; 1 Chron. 17:13   *c 6* Deut. 32:43 (see Dead Sea Scrolls and Septuagint)   *d 7* Psalm 104:4   *e 9* Psalm 45:6,7
f 12 Psalm 102:25-27   *g 13* Psalm 110:1

message spoken through angels was binding, and every violation and disobedience received its just punishment, ³how shall we escape if we ignore so great a salvation? This salvation, which was first announced by the Lord, was confirmed to us by those who heard him. ⁴God also testified to it by signs, wonders and various miracles, and by gifts of the Holy Spirit distributed according to his will.

Jesus Made Fully Human

⁵It is not to angels that he has subjected the world to come, about which we are speaking. ⁶But there is a place where someone has testified:

"What is mankind that you are
      mindful of them,
   a son of man that you care
      for him?
⁷You made them a little*ᵃ* lower
      than the angels;
   you crowned them with
      glory and honor
⁸   and put everything under
      their feet."*ᵇ,ᶜ*

In putting everything under them,*ᵈ* God left nothing that is not subject to them.*ᵈ* Yet at present we do not see everything subject to them.*ᵈ* ⁹But we do see

Jesus, who was made lower than the angels for a little while, now crowned with glory and honor because he suffered death, so that by the grace of God he might taste death for everyone.

¹⁰In bringing many sons and daughters to glory, it was fitting that God, for whom and through whom everything exists, should make the pioneer of their salvation perfect through what he suffered. ¹¹Both the one who makes people holy and those who are made holy are of the same family. So Jesus is not ashamed to call them brothers and sisters.*ᵉ* ¹²He says,

"I will declare your name to
      my brothers and sisters;
   in the assembly I will sing
      your praises."*ᶠ*

¹³And again,

"I will put my trust in him."*ᵍ*

And again he says,

"Here am I, and the children
      God has given me."*ʰ*

¹⁴Since the children have flesh and blood, he too shared in their humanity so that by his death he might break the power of him who holds the power of death — that is, the devil — ¹⁵and free those who

---

ᵃ 7 Or *them for a little while*   *ᵇ 6-8* Psalm 8:4-6   *ᶜ 7,8* Or *⁷You made him a little lower than the angels;/ you crowned him with glory and honor/ ⁸and put everything under his feet."*   *ᵈ 8* Or *him*   *ᵉ 11* The Greek word for *brothers and sisters* (*adelphoi*) refers here to believers, both men and women, as part of God's family; also in verse 12; and in 3:1, 12; 10:19; 13:22.   *ᶠ 12* Psalm 22:22
ᵍ 13 Isaiah 8:17   *ʰ 13* Isaiah 8:18

all their lives were held in slavery by their fear of death. ¹⁶For surely it is not angels he helps, but Abraham's descendants. ¹⁷For this reason he had to be made like them,ᵃ fully human in every way, in order that he might become a merciful and faithful high priest in service to God, and that he might make atonement for the sins of the people. ¹⁸Because he himself suffered when he was tempted, he is able to help those who are being tempted.

Jesus Greater Than Moses

3 Therefore, holy brothers and sisters, who share in the heavenly calling, fix your thoughts on Jesus, whom we acknowledge as our apostle and high priest. ²He was faithful to the one who appointed him, just as Moses was faithful in all God's house. ³Jesus has been found worthy of greater honor than Moses, just as the builder of a house has greater honor than the house itself. ⁴For every house is built by someone, but God is the builder of everything. ⁵"Moses was faithful as a servant in all God's house,"ᵇ bearing witness to what would be spoken by God in the future. ⁶But Christ is faithful as the Son over God's house. And we are his house, if indeed we hold firmly to our confidence and the hope in which we glory.

Warning Against Unbelief

⁷So, as the Holy Spirit says:

"Today, if you hear his voice,
⁸   do not harden your
      hearts
as you did in the rebellion,
      during the time of testing in
      the wilderness,
⁹where your ancestors tested
      and tried me,
      though for forty years they
      saw what I did.
¹⁰That is why I was angry with
      that generation;
   I said, 'Their hearts are
      always going astray,
   and they have not known my
      ways.'
¹¹So I declared on oath in my
      anger,
   'They shall never enter my
      rest.' "ᶜ

¹²See to it, brothers and sisters, that none of you has a sinful, unbelieving heart that turns away from the living God. ¹³But encourage one another daily, as long as it is called "Today," so that none of you may be hardened by sin's deceitfulness. ¹⁴We have come to share in Christ, if indeed we hold our original conviction firmly to the very end. ¹⁵As has just been said:

"Today, if you hear his voice,
   do not harden your hearts
      as you did in the rebellion."ᵈ

ᵃ 17 Or *like his brothers*   ᵇ 5 Num. 12:7   ᶜ 11 Psalm 95:7-11
ᵈ 15 Psalm 95:7,8

¹⁶Who were they who heard and rebelled? Were they not all those Moses led out of Egypt? ¹⁷And with whom was he angry for forty years? Was it not with those who sinned, whose bodies perished in the wilderness? ¹⁸And to whom did God swear that they would never enter his rest if not to those who disobeyed? ¹⁹So we see that they were not able to enter, because of their unbelief.

A Sabbath-Rest for the People of God

4 Therefore, since the promise of entering his rest still stands, let us be careful that none of you be found to have fallen short of it. ²For we also have had the good news proclaimed to us, just as they did; but the message they heard was of no value to them, because they did not share the faith of those who obeyed.ᵃ ³Now we who have believed enter that rest, just as God has said,

"So I declared on oath in my anger,
   'They shall never enter my rest.' "ᵇ

And yet his works have been finished since the creation of the world. ⁴For somewhere he has spoken about the seventh day in these words: "On the seventh day God rested from all his works."ᶜ ⁵And again in the passage above he says, "They shall never enter my rest."

⁶Therefore since it still remains for some to enter that rest, and since those who formerly had the good news proclaimed to them did not go in because of their disobedience, ⁷God again set a certain day, calling it "Today." This he did when a long time later he spoke through David, as in the passage already quoted:

"Today, if you hear his voice,
   do not harden your hearts."ᵈ

⁸For if Joshua had given them rest, God would not have spoken later about another day. ⁹There remains, then, a Sabbath-rest for the people of God; ¹⁰for anyone who enters God's rest also rests from their works,ᵉ just as God did from his. ¹¹Let us, therefore, make every effort to enter that rest, so that no one will perish by following their example of disobedience.

¹²For the word of God is alive and active. Sharper than any double-edged sword, it penetrates even to dividing soul and spirit, joints and marrow; it judges the thoughts and attitudes of the heart. ¹³Nothing in all creation is hidden from God's sight. Everything is uncovered and laid

ᵃ 2 Some manuscripts *because those who heard did not combine it with faith*   ᵇ 3 Psalm 95:11; also in verse 5   ᶜ 4 Gen. 2:2   ᵈ 7 Psalm 95:7,8   ᵉ 10 Or *labor* bare before the eyes of him to whom we must give account.

Jesus the Great High Priest

[14] Therefore, since we have a great high priest who has ascended into heaven,[a] Jesus the Son of God, let us hold firmly to the faith we profess. [15] For we do not have a high priest who is unable to empathize with our weaknesses, but we have one who has been tempted in every way, just as we are — yet he did not sin. [16] Let us then approach God's throne of grace with confidence, so that we may receive mercy and find grace to help us in our time of need.

5 Every high priest is selected from among the people and is appointed to represent the people in matters related to God, to offer gifts and sacrifices for sins. [2] He is able to deal gently with those who are ignorant and are going astray, since he himself is subject to weakness. [3] This is why he has to offer sacrifices for his own sins, as well as for the sins of the people. [4] And no one takes this honor on himself, but he receives it when called by God, just as Aaron was.

[5] In the same way, Christ did not take on himself the glory of becoming a high priest. But God said to him,

"You are my Son;
today I have become your
Father."[b]

[6] And he says in another place,

"You are a priest forever,
in the order of
Melchizedek."[c]

[7] During the days of Jesus' life on earth, he offered up prayers and petitions with fervent cries and tears to the one who could save him from death, and he was heard because of his reverent submission. [8] Son though he was, he learned obedience from what he suffered [9] and, once made perfect, he became the source of eternal salvation for all who obey him [10] and was designated by God to be high priest in the order of Melchizedek.

Warning Against Falling Away

[11] We have much to say about this, but it is hard to make it clear to you because you no longer try to understand. [12] In fact, though by this time you ought to be teachers, you need someone to teach you the elementary truths of God's word all over again. You need milk, not solid food! [13] Anyone who lives on milk, being still an infant, is not acquainted with the teaching about righteousness. [14] But solid food is for the mature, who by constant use have trained themselves to distinguish good from evil.

6 Therefore let us move beyond the elementary teachings about Christ and be taken

---

[a] 14 Greek *has gone through the heavens* [b] 5 Psalm 2:7 [c] 6 Psalm 110:4

forward to maturity, not laying again the foundation of repentance from acts that lead to death,[a] and of faith in God, [2]instruction about cleansing rites,[b] the laying on of hands, the resurrection of the dead, and eternal judgment. [3]And God permitting, we will do so.

[4]It is impossible for those who have once been enlightened, who have tasted the heavenly gift, who have shared in the Holy Spirit, [5]who have tasted the goodness of the word of God and the powers of the coming age [6]and who have fallen[c] away, to be brought back to repentance. To their loss they are crucifying the Son of God all over again and subjecting him to public disgrace. [7]Land that drinks in the rain often falling on it and that produces a crop useful to those for whom it is farmed receives the blessing of God. [8]But land that produces thorns and thistles is worthless and is in danger of being cursed. In the end it will be burned.

[9]Even though we speak like this, dear friends, we are convinced of better things in your case — the things that have to do with salvation. [10]God is not unjust; he will not forget your work and the love you have shown him as you have helped his people and continue to help them. [11]We want each of you to show this same diligence to the very end, so that what you hope for may be fully realized. [12]We do not want you to become lazy, but to imitate those who through faith and patience inherit what has been promised.

The Certainty of God's Promise

[13]When God made his promise to Abraham, since there was no one greater for him to swear by, he swore by himself, [14]saying, "I will surely bless you and give you many descendants."[d] [15]And so after waiting patiently, Abraham received what was promised.

[16]People swear by someone greater than themselves, and the oath confirms what is said and puts an end to all argument. [17]Because God wanted to make the unchanging nature of his purpose very clear to the heirs of what was promised, he confirmed it with an oath. [18]God did this so that, by two unchangeable things in which it is impossible for God to lie, we who have fled to take hold of the hope set before us may be greatly encouraged. [19]We have this hope as an anchor for the soul, firm and secure. It enters the inner sanctuary behind the curtain, [20]where our forerunner, Jesus, has entered on our behalf. He has become a high priest forever, in the order of Melchizedek.

---

[a] 1 Or *from useless rituals*   [b] 2 Or *about baptisms*   [c] 6 Or *age,* [6]*if they fall*
[d] 14 Gen. 22:17

Melchizedek the Priest

7 This Melchizedek was king of Salem and priest of God Most High. He met Abraham returning from the defeat of the kings and blessed him, [2]and Abraham gave him a tenth of everything. First, the name Melchizedek means "king of righteousness"; then also, "king of Salem" means "king of peace." [3]Without father or mother, without genealogy, without beginning of days or end of life, resembling the Son of God, he remains a priest forever.

[4]Just think how great he was: Even the patriarch Abraham gave him a tenth of the plunder! [5]Now the law requires the descendants of Levi who become priests to collect a tenth from the people — that is, from their fellow Israelites — even though they also are descended from Abraham. [6]This man, however, did not trace his descent from Levi, yet he collected a tenth from Abraham and blessed him who had the promises. [7]And without doubt the lesser is blessed by the greater. [8]In the one case, the tenth is collected by people who die; but in the other case, by him who is declared to be living. [9]One might even say that Levi, who collects the tenth, paid the tenth through Abraham, [10]because when Melchizedek met Abraham, Levi was still in the body of his ancestor.

Jesus Like Melchizedek

[11]If perfection could have been attained through the Levitical priesthood — and indeed the law given to the people established that priesthood — why was there still need for another priest to come, one in the order of Melchizedek, not in the order of Aaron? [12]For when the priesthood is changed, the law must be changed also. [13]He of whom these things are said belonged to a different tribe, and no one from that tribe has ever served at the altar. [14]For it is clear that our Lord descended from Judah, and in regard to that tribe Moses said nothing about priests. [15]And what we have said is even more clear if another priest like Melchizedek appears, [16]one who has become a priest not on the basis of a regulation as to his ancestry but on the basis of the power of an indestructible life. [17]For it is declared:

"You are a priest forever,
    in the order of
        Melchizedek."[a]

[18]The former regulation is set aside because it was weak and useless [19](for the law made nothing perfect), and a better hope is introduced, by which we draw near to God.

[20]And it was not without an oath! Others became priests without any oath, [21]but he

[a] 17 Psalm 110:4

became a priest with an oath when God said to him:

"The Lord has sworn
  and will not change his mind:
  'You are a priest forever.'"[a]

²²Because of this oath, Jesus has become the guarantor of a better covenant.

²³Now there have been many of those priests, since death prevented them from continuing in office; ²⁴but because Jesus lives forever, he has a permanent priesthood. ²⁵Therefore he is able to save completely[b] those who come to God through him, because he always lives to intercede for them.

²⁶Such a high priest truly meets our need—one who is holy, blameless, pure, set apart from sinners, exalted above the heavens. ²⁷Unlike the other high priests, he does not need to offer sacrifices day after day, first for his own sins, and then for the sins of the people. He sacrificed for their sins once for all when he offered himself. ²⁸For the law appoints as high priests men in all their weakness; but the oath, which came after the law, appointed the Son, who has been made perfect forever.

The High Priest of a New Covenant

8 Now the main point of what we are saying is this: We do have such a high priest, who sat down at the right hand of the throne of the Majesty in heaven, ²and who serves in the sanctuary, the true tabernacle set up by the Lord, not by a mere human being.

³Every high priest is appointed to offer both gifts and sacrifices, and so it was necessary for this one also to have something to offer. ⁴If he were on earth, he would not be a priest, for there are already priests who offer the gifts prescribed by the law. ⁵They serve at a sanctuary that is a copy and shadow of what is in heaven. This is why Moses was warned when he was about to build the tabernacle: "See to it that you make everything according to the pattern shown you on the mountain."[c] ⁶But in fact the ministry Jesus has received is as superior to theirs as the covenant of which he is mediator is superior to the old one, since the new covenant is established on better promises.

⁷For if there had been nothing wrong with that first covenant, no place would have been sought for another. ⁸But God found fault with the people and said[d]:

"The days are coming,
    declares the Lord,
  when I will make a new
    covenant
with the people of Israel
  and with the people of
    Judah.

---

[a] 21 Psalm 110:4   [b] 25 Or *forever*   [c] 5 Exodus 25:40   [d] 8 Some manuscripts may be translated *fault and said to the people.*

⁹ It will not be like the covenant
    I made with their ancestors
when I took them by the hand
    to lead them out of Egypt,
because they did not remain
      faithful to my covenant,
  and I turned away from
      them,
          declares the Lord.
¹⁰ This is the covenant I will
      establish with the people
      of Israel
  after that time, declares the
      Lord.
I will put my laws in their
      minds
  and write them on their
      hearts.
I will be their God,
  and they will be my people.
¹¹ No longer will they teach their
      neighbor,
  or say to one another, 'Know
      the Lord,'
because they will all know me,
  from the least of them to the
      greatest.
¹² For I will forgive their
      wickedness
  and will remember their sins
      no more."[a]

¹³ By calling this covenant "new," he has made the first one obsolete; and what is obsolete and outdated will soon disappear.

Worship in the Earthly Tabernacle

9 Now the first covenant had regulations for worship and also an earthly sanctuary. ² A tabernacle was set up. In its first room were the lampstand and the table with its consecrated bread; this was called the Holy Place. ³ Behind the second curtain was a room called the Most Holy Place, ⁴ which had the golden altar of incense and the gold-covered ark of the covenant. This ark contained the gold jar of manna, Aaron's staff that had budded, and the stone tablets of the covenant. ⁵ Above the ark were the cherubim of the Glory, overshadowing the atonement cover. But we cannot discuss these things in detail now.

⁶ When everything had been arranged like this, the priests entered regularly into the outer room to carry on their ministry. ⁷ But only the high priest entered the inner room, and that only once a year, and never without blood, which he offered for himself and for the sins the people had committed in ignorance. ⁸ The Holy Spirit was showing by this that the way into the Most Holy Place had not yet been disclosed as long as the first tabernacle was still functioning. ⁹ This is an illustration for the present time, indicating that the gifts and sacrifices being offered were not able to clear the conscience of the worshiper. ¹⁰ They are only a matter of food and drink and various ceremonial washings — external

---

a 12 Jer. 31:31-34

regulations applying until the time of the new order.

The Blood of Christ

¹¹But when Christ came as high priest of the good things that are now already here,ᵃ he went through the greater and more perfect tabernacle that is not made with human hands, that is to say, is not a part of this creation. ¹²He did not enter by means of the blood of goats and calves; but he entered the Most Holy Place once for all by his own blood, thus obtainingᵇ eternal redemption. ¹³The blood of goats and bulls and the ashes of a heifer sprinkled on those who are ceremonially unclean sanctify them so that they are outwardly clean. ¹⁴How much more, then, will the blood of Christ, who through the eternal Spirit offered himself unblemished to God, cleanse our consciences from acts that lead to death,ᶜ so that we may serve the living God!

¹⁵For this reason Christ is the mediator of a new covenant, that those who are called may receive the promised eternal inheritance — now that he has died as a ransom to set them free from the sins committed under the first covenant.

¹⁶In the case of a will,ᵈ it is necessary to prove the death of the one who made it, ¹⁷because a will is in force only when somebody has died; it never takes effect while the one who made it is living. ¹⁸This is why even the first covenant was not put into effect without blood. ¹⁹When Moses had proclaimed every command of the law to all the people, he took the blood of calves, together with water, scarlet wool and branches of hyssop, and sprinkled the scroll and all the people. ²⁰He said, "This is the blood of the covenant, which God has commanded you to keep."ᵉ ²¹In the same way, he sprinkled with the blood both the tabernacle and everything used in its ceremonies. ²²In fact, the law requires that nearly everything be cleansed with blood, and without the shedding of blood there is no forgiveness.

²³It was necessary, then, for the copies of the heavenly things to be purified with these sacrifices, but the heavenly things themselves with better sacrifices than these. ²⁴For Christ did not enter a sanctuary made with human hands that was only a copy of the true one; he entered heaven itself, now to appear for us in God's presence. ²⁵Nor did he enter heaven to offer himself again and again, the way the high priest enters the Most

---

ᵃ 11 Some early manuscripts *are to come*   ᵇ 12 Or *blood, having obtained*
ᶜ 14 Or *from useless rituals*   ᵈ 16 Same Greek word as *covenant*; also in verse 17
ᵉ 20 Exodus 24:8

Holy Place every year with blood that is not his own. ²⁶Otherwise Christ would have had to suffer many times since the creation of the world. But he has appeared once for all at the culmination of the ages to do away with sin by the sacrifice of himself. ²⁷Just as people are destined to die once, and after that to face judgment, ²⁸so Christ was sacrificed once to take away the sins of many; and he will appear a second time, not to bear sin, but to bring salvation to those who are waiting for him.

Christ's Sacrifice Once for All

10 The law is only a shadow of the good things that are coming—not the realities themselves. For this reason it can never, by the same sacrifices repeated endlessly year after year, make perfect those who draw near to worship. ²Otherwise, would they not have stopped being offered? For the worshipers would have been cleansed once for all, and would no longer have felt guilty for their sins. ³But those sacrifices are an annual reminder of sins. ⁴It is impossible for the blood of bulls and goats to take away sins.

⁵Therefore, when Christ came into the world, he said:

"Sacrifice and offering you did
    not desire,
    but a body you prepared
    for me;

⁶with burnt offerings and sin
    offerings
    you were not pleased.
⁷Then I said, 'Here I am—it is
    written about me in the
    scroll—
I have come to do your will,
    my God.' "ᵃ

⁸First he said, "Sacrifices and offerings, burnt offerings and sin offerings you did not desire, nor were you pleased with them"—though they were offered in accordance with the law. ⁹Then he said, "Here I am, I have come to do your will." He sets aside the first to establish the second. ¹⁰And by that will, we have been made holy through the sacrifice of the body of Jesus Christ once for all.

¹¹Day after day every priest stands and performs his religious duties; again and again he offers the same sacrifices, which can never take away sins. ¹²But when this priest had offered for all time one sacrifice for sins, he sat down at the right hand of God, ¹³and since that time he waits for his enemies to be made his footstool. ¹⁴For by one sacrifice he has made perfect forever those who are being made holy.

¹⁵The Holy Spirit also testifies to us about this. First he says:

¹⁶"This is the covenant I will
    make with them
    after that time, says the
    Lord.

ᵃ 7 Psalm 40:6-8 (see Septuagint)

I will put my laws in their
hearts,
and I will write them on
their minds."[a]

[17]Then he adds:

"Their sins and lawless acts
I will remember no more."[b]

[18]And where these have been forgiven, sacrifice for sin is no longer necessary.

A Call to Persevere in Faith

[19]Therefore, brothers and sisters, since we have confidence to
enter the Most Holy Place by the
blood of Jesus, [20]by a new and living way opened for us through the
curtain, that is, his body, [21]and
since we have a great priest over
the house of God, [22]let us draw
near to God with a sincere heart
and with the full assurance that
faith brings, having our hearts
sprinkled to cleanse us from a
guilty conscience and having our
bodies washed with pure water.
[23]Let us hold unswervingly to
the hope we profess, for he who
promised is faithful. [24]And let us
consider how we may spur one
another on toward love and good
deeds, [25]not giving up meeting
together, as some are in the habit of doing, but encouraging one
another — and all the more as
you see the Day approaching.

[26]If we deliberately keep on sinning after we have received the
knowledge of the truth, no sacrifice for sins is left, [27]but only a
fearful expectation of judgment
and of raging fire that will consume the enemies of God. [28]Any-
one who rejected the law of Moses
died without mercy on the testimony of two or three witnesses.
[29]How much more severely do
you think someone deserves to be
punished who has trampled the
Son of God underfoot, who has
treated as an unholy thing the
blood of the covenant that sanctified them, and who has insulted the Spirit of grace? [30]For we
know him who said, "It is mine to
avenge; I will repay,"[c] and again,
"The Lord will judge his people."[d]
[31]It is a dreadful thing to fall into
the hands of the living God.

[32]Remember those earlier days
after you had received the light,
when you endured in a great
conflict full of suffering. [33]Some-
times you were publicly exposed
to insult and persecution; at other times you stood side by side
with those who were so treated.
[34]You suffered along with those
in prison and joyfully accepted
the confiscation of your property,
because you knew that you yourselves had better and lasting possessions. [35]So do not throw away
your confidence; it will be richly
rewarded.

[36]You need to persevere so that
when you have done the will of
God, you will receive what he has
promised. [37]For,

---

[a] 16 Jer. 31:33   [b] 17 Jer. 31:34   [c] 30 Deut. 32:35   [d] 30 Deut. 32:36; Psalm 135:14

"In just a little while,
    he who is coming will come
    and will not delay."[a]

[38] And,

"But my righteous[b] one will
    live by faith.
And I take no pleasure
    in the one who shrinks
    back."[c]

[39] But we do not belong to those who shrink back and are destroyed, but to those who have faith and are saved.

Faith in Action

11 Now faith is confidence in what we hope for and assurance about what we do not see. [2] This is what the ancients were commended for.

[3] By faith we understand that the universe was formed at God's command, so that what is seen was not made out of what was visible.

[4] By faith Abel brought God a better offering than Cain did. By faith he was commended as righteous, when God spoke well of his offerings. And by faith Abel still speaks, even though he is dead.

[5] By faith Enoch was taken from this life, so that he did not experience death: "He could not be found, because God had taken him away."[d] For before he was taken, he was commended as one who pleased God. [6] And without faith it is impossible to please God, because anyone who comes to him must believe that he exists and that he rewards those who earnestly seek him.

[7] By faith Noah, when warned about things not yet seen, in holy fear built an ark to save his family. By his faith he condemned the world and became heir of the righteousness that is in keeping with faith.

[8] By faith Abraham, when called to go to a place he would later receive as his inheritance, obeyed and went, even though he did not know where he was going. [9] By faith he made his home in the promised land like a stranger in a foreign country; he lived in tents, as did Isaac and Jacob, who were heirs with him of the same promise. [10] For he was looking forward to the city with foundations, whose architect and builder is God. [11] And by faith even Sarah, who was past childbearing age, was enabled to bear children because she[e] considered him faithful who had made the promise. [12] And so from this one man, and he as good as dead, came descendants as numerous as the stars in the sky and as countless as the sand on the seashore.

---

[a] 37 Isaiah 26:20; Hab. 2:3   [b] 38 Some early manuscripts *But the righteous*
[c] 38 Hab. 2:4 (see Septuagint)   [d] 5 Gen. 5:24   [e] 11 Or *By faith Abraham, even though he was too old to have children — and Sarah herself was not able to conceive — was enabled to become a father because he*

¹³All these people were still living by faith when they died. They did not receive the things promised; they only saw them and welcomed them from a distance, admitting that they were foreigners and strangers on earth. ¹⁴People who say such things show that they are looking for a country of their own. ¹⁵If they had been thinking of the country they had left, they would have had opportunity to return. ¹⁶Instead, they were longing for a better country—a heavenly one. Therefore God is not ashamed to be called their God, for he has prepared a city for them.

¹⁷By faith Abraham, when God tested him, offered Isaac as a sacrifice. He who had embraced the promises was about to sacrifice his one and only son, ¹⁸even though God had said to him, "It is through Isaac that your offspring will be reckoned."ᵃ ¹⁹Abraham reasoned that God could even raise the dead, and so in a manner of speaking he did receive Isaac back from death.

²⁰By faith Isaac blessed Jacob and Esau in regard to their future.

²¹By faith Jacob, when he was dying, blessed each of Joseph's sons, and worshiped as he leaned on the top of his staff.

²²By faith Joseph, when his end was near, spoke about the exodus of the Israelites from Egypt and gave instructions concerning the burial of his bones.

²³By faith Moses' parents hid him for three months after he was born, because they saw he was no ordinary child, and they were not afraid of the king's edict.

²⁴By faith Moses, when he had grown up, refused to be known as the son of Pharaoh's daughter. ²⁵He chose to be mistreated along with the people of God rather than to enjoy the fleeting pleasures of sin. ²⁶He regarded disgrace for the sake of Christ as of greater value than the treasures of Egypt, because he was looking ahead to his reward. ²⁷By faith he left Egypt, not fearing the king's anger; he persevered because he saw him who is invisible. ²⁸By faith he kept the Passover and the application of blood, so that the destroyer of the firstborn would not touch the firstborn of Israel.

²⁹By faith the people passed through the Red Sea as on dry land; but when the Egyptians tried to do so, they were drowned.

³⁰By faith the walls of Jericho fell, after the army had marched around them for seven days.

³¹By faith the prostitute Rahab, because she welcomed the spies, was not killed with those who were disobedient.ᵇ

³²And what more shall I say? I do not have time to tell about Gideon, Barak, Samson and Jephthah, about David and Samuel and the

---

ᵃ 18 Gen. 21:12   ᵇ 31 Or *unbelieving*

prophets, ³³who through faith conquered kingdoms, administered justice, and gained what was promised; who shut the mouths of lions, ³⁴quenched the fury of the flames, and escaped the edge of the sword; whose weakness was turned to strength; and who became powerful in battle and routed foreign armies. ³⁵Women received back their dead, raised to life again. There were others who were tortured, refusing to be released so that they might gain an even better resurrection. ³⁶Some faced jeers and flogging, and even chains and imprisonment. ³⁷They were put to death by stoning;[a] they were sawed in two; they were killed by the sword. They went about in sheepskins and goatskins, destitute, persecuted and mistreated — ³⁸the world was not worthy of them. They wandered in deserts and mountains, living in caves and in holes in the ground.

³⁹These were all commended for their faith, yet none of them received what had been promised, ⁴⁰since God had planned something better for us so that only together with us would they be made perfect.

12 Therefore, since we are surrounded by such a great cloud of witnesses, let us throw off everything that hinders and the sin that so easily entangles. And let us run with perseverance the race marked out for us, ²fixing our eyes on Jesus, the pioneer and perfecter of faith. For the joy set before him he endured the cross, scorning its shame, and sat down at the right hand of the throne of God. ³Consider him who endured such opposition from sinners, so that you will not grow weary and lose heart.

God Disciplines His Children

⁴In your struggle against sin, you have not yet resisted to the point of shedding your blood. ⁵And have you completely forgotten this word of encouragement that addresses you as a father addresses his son? It says,

"My son, do not make light of
　the Lord's discipline,
and do not lose heart when
　he rebukes you,
⁶because the Lord disciplines
　the one he loves,
and he chastens everyone he
　accepts as his son."[b]

⁷Endure hardship as discipline; God is treating you as his children. For what children are not disciplined by their father? ⁸If you are not disciplined — and everyone undergoes discipline — then you are not legitimate, not true sons and daughters at all. ⁹Moreover, we have all had human fathers who disciplined us and we respected them for it. How much more should we submit to the Father of spirits and

---

[a] 37 Some early manuscripts *stoning; they were put to the test;*
[b] 5,6 Prov. 3:11,12 (see Septuagint)

live! [10]They disciplined us for a little while as they thought best; but God disciplines us for our good, in order that we may share in his holiness. [11]No discipline seems pleasant at the time, but painful. Later on, however, it produces a harvest of righteousness and peace for those who have been trained by it.

[12]Therefore, strengthen your feeble arms and weak knees. [13]"Make level paths for your feet,"[a] so that the lame may not be disabled, but rather healed.

Warning and Encouragement

[14]Make every effort to live in peace with everyone and to be holy; without holiness no one will see the Lord. [15]See to it that no one falls short of the grace of God and that no bitter root grows up to cause trouble and defile many. [16]See that no one is sexually immoral, or is godless like Esau, who for a single meal sold his inheritance rights as the oldest son. [17]Afterward, as you know, when he wanted to inherit this blessing, he was rejected. Even though he sought the blessing with tears, he could not change what he had done.

The Mountain of Fear and the Mountain of Joy

[18]You have not come to a mountain that can be touched and that is burning with fire; to darkness, gloom and storm; [19]to a trumpet blast or to such a voice speaking words that those who heard it begged that no further word be spoken to them, [20]because they could not bear what was commanded: "If even an animal touches the mountain, it must be stoned to death."[b] [21]The sight was so terrifying that Moses said, "I am trembling with fear."[c]

[22]But you have come to Mount Zion, to the city of the living God, the heavenly Jerusalem. You have come to thousands upon thousands of angels in joyful assembly, [23]to the church of the firstborn, whose names are written in heaven. You have come to God, the Judge of all, to the spirits of the righteous made perfect, [24]to Jesus the mediator of a new covenant, and to the sprinkled blood that speaks a better word than the blood of Abel.

[25]See to it that you do not refuse him who speaks. If they did not escape when they refused him who warned them on earth, how much less will we, if we turn away from him who warns us from heaven? [26]At that time his voice shook the earth, but now he has promised, "Once more I will shake not only the earth but also the heavens."[d] [27]The words "once more" indicate the removing of what can be shaken — that is, created things — so that what cannot be shaken may remain.

[a] 13 Prov. 4:26   [b] 20 Exodus 19:12,13   [c] 21 See Deut. 9:19.   [d] 26 Haggai 2:6

²⁸Therefore, since we are receiving a kingdom that cannot be shaken, let us be thankful, and so worship God acceptably with reverence and awe, ²⁹for our "God is a consuming fire."ᵃ

Concluding Exhortations

13 Keep on loving one another as brothers and sisters. ²Do not forget to show hospitality to strangers, for by so doing some people have shown hospitality to angels without knowing it. ³Continue to remember those in prison as if you were together with them in prison, and those who are mistreated as if you yourselves were suffering.

⁴Marriage should be honored by all, and the marriage bed kept pure, for God will judge the adulterer and all the sexually immoral. ⁵Keep your lives free from the love of money and be content with what you have, because God has said,

"Never will I leave you;
    never will I forsake you."ᵇ

⁶So we say with confidence,

"The Lord is my helper; I will
    not be afraid.
What can mere mortals do
    to me?"ᶜ

⁷Remember your leaders, who spoke the word of God to you. Consider the outcome of their way of life and imitate their faith.

⁸Jesus Christ is the same yesterday and today and forever. ⁹Do not be carried away by all kinds of strange teachings. It is good for our hearts to be strengthened by grace, not by eating ceremonial foods, which is of no benefit to those who do so. ¹⁰We have an altar from which those who minister at the tabernacle have no right to eat.

¹¹The high priest carries the blood of animals into the Most Holy Place as a sin offering, but the bodies are burned outside the camp. ¹²And so Jesus also suffered outside the city gate to make the people holy through his own blood. ¹³Let us, then, go to him outside the camp, bearing the disgrace he bore. ¹⁴For here we do not have an enduring city, but we are looking for the city that is to come.

¹⁵Through Jesus, therefore, let us continually offer to God a sacrifice of praise — the fruit of lips that openly profess his name. ¹⁶And do not forget to do good and to share with others, for with such sacrifices God is pleased.

¹⁷Have confidence in your leaders and submit to their authority, because they keep watch over you as those who must give an account. Do this so that their work will be a joy, not a burden, for that would be of no benefit to you.

¹⁸Pray for us. We are sure that we have a clear conscience and

ᵃ 29 Deut. 4:24   ᵇ 5 Deut. 31:6   ᶜ 6 Psalm 118:6,7

desire to live honorably in every way. ¹⁹I particularly urge you to pray so that I may be restored to you soon.

Benediction and Final Greetings

²⁰Now may the God of peace, who through the blood of the eternal covenant brought back from the dead our Lord Jesus, that great Shepherd of the sheep, ²¹equip you with everything good for doing his will, and may he work in us what is pleasing to him, through Jesus Christ, to whom be glory for ever and ever. Amen.

²²Brothers and sisters, I urge you to bear with my word of exhortation, for in fact I have written to you quite briefly.

²³I want you to know that our brother Timothy has been released. If he arrives soon, I will come with him to see you.

²⁴Greet all your leaders and all the Lord's people. Those from Italy send you their greetings.

²⁵Grace be with you all.

James

Introduction:

The book of James may be the earliest of the New Testament letters, written about AD 48. This letter was written by James, the brother of Jesus, who was one of the leaders of the church in Jerusalem. The letter is addressed to Christians everywhere. Seven books of the New Testament, James through Jude, are called the general letters because they are addressed to Christians in general and not to a specific church.

James wrote this letter to teach Christians how to live Christ-like lives. He insists that if we have real faith, we will show it by acting like Christians. He gives practical advice on things like anger and quarreling, showing favoritism, controlling the tongue, boasting, patience and prayer.

Outline of contents:

The heart of true religion (1:1–27)
True faith in practice (2:1–3:12)
True wisdom in practice (3:13–5:12)
The prayer of faith (5:13–20)

1 James, a servant of God and of the Lord Jesus Christ,

To the twelve tribes scattered among the nations:

Greetings.

Trials and Temptations

²Consider it pure joy, my brothers and sisters,[a] whenever you face trials of many kinds, ³because you know that the testing of your faith produces perseverance. ⁴Let perseverance finish its work so that you may be mature and complete, not lacking anything. ⁵If any of you lacks wisdom, you should ask God, who gives generously to all without finding fault, and it will be given to you. ⁶But when you ask, you must believe and not doubt, because the one who doubts is like a wave of the sea, blown and tossed by the wind. ⁷That person

---

[a] 2 The Greek word for *brothers and sisters* (*adelphoi*) refers here to believers, both men and women, as part of God's family; also in verses 16 and 19; and in 2:1, 5, 14; 3:10, 12; 4:11; 5:7, 9, 10, 12, 19.

should not expect to receive anything from the Lord. **8** Such a person is double-minded and unstable in all they do.

9 Believers in humble circumstances ought to take pride in their high position. **10** But the rich should take pride in their humiliation — since they will pass away like a wild flower. **11** For the sun rises with scorching heat and withers the plant; its blossom falls and its beauty is destroyed. In the same way, the rich will fade away even while they go about their business.

12 Blessed is the one who perseveres under trial because, having stood the test, that person will receive the crown of life that the Lord has promised to those who love him.

13 When tempted, no one should say, "God is tempting me." For God cannot be tempted by evil, nor does he tempt anyone; **14** but each person is tempted when they are dragged away by their own evil desire and enticed. **15** Then, after desire has conceived, it gives birth to sin; and sin, when it is full-grown, gives birth to death.

16 Don't be deceived, my dear brothers and sisters. **17** Every good and perfect gift is from above, coming down from the Father of the heavenly lights, who does not change like shifting shadows. **18** He chose to give us birth through the word of truth, that we might be a kind of firstfruits of all he created.

Listening and Doing

19 My dear brothers and sisters, take note of this: Everyone should be quick to listen, slow to speak and slow to become angry, **20** because human anger does not produce the righteousness that God desires. **21** Therefore, get rid of all moral filth and the evil that is so prevalent and humbly accept the word planted in you, which can save you.

22 Do not merely listen to the word, and so deceive yourselves. Do what it says. **23** Anyone who listens to the word but does not do what it says is like someone who looks at his face in a mirror **24** and, after looking at himself, goes away and immediately forgets what he looks like. **25** But whoever looks intently into the perfect law that gives freedom, and continues in it — not forgetting what they have heard, but doing it — they will be blessed in what they do.

26 Those who consider themselves religious and yet do not keep a tight rein on their tongues deceive themselves, and their religion is worthless. **27** Religion that God our Father accepts as pure and faultless is this: to look after orphans and widows in their distress and to keep oneself from being polluted by the world.

Favoritism Forbidden

2 My brothers and sisters, believers in our glorious Lord Jesus Christ must not show favoritism. **2**Suppose a man comes into your meeting wearing a gold ring and fine clothes, and a poor man in filthy old clothes also comes in. **3**If you show special attention to the man wearing fine clothes and say, "Here's a good seat for you," but say to the poor man, "You stand there" or "Sit on the floor by my feet," **4**have you not discriminated among yourselves and become judges with evil thoughts?

5Listen, my dear brothers and sisters: Has not God chosen those who are poor in the eyes of the world to be rich in faith and to inherit the kingdom he promised those who love him? **6**But you have dishonored the poor. Is it not the rich who are exploiting you? Are they not the ones who are dragging you into court? **7**Are they not the ones who are blaspheming the noble name of him to whom you belong?

8If you really keep the royal law found in Scripture, "Love your neighbor as yourself,"*a* you are doing right. **9**But if you show favoritism, you sin and are convicted by the law as lawbreakers. **10**For whoever keeps the whole law and yet stumbles at just one point is guilty of breaking all of it. **11**For he who said, "You shall not commit adultery,"*b* also said, "You shall not murder."*c* If you do not commit adultery but do commit murder, you have become a lawbreaker.

12Speak and act as those who are going to be judged by the law that gives freedom, **13**because judgment without mercy will be shown to anyone who has not been merciful. Mercy triumphs over judgment.

Faith and Deeds

14What good is it, my brothers and sisters, if someone claims to have faith but has no deeds? Can such faith save them? **15**Suppose a brother or a sister is without clothes and daily food. **16**If one of you says to them, "Go in peace; keep warm and well fed," but does nothing about their physical needs, what good is it? **17**In the same way, faith by itself, if it is not accompanied by action, is dead.

18But someone will say, "You have faith; I have deeds."

Show me your faith without deeds, and I will show you my faith by my deeds. **19**You believe that there is one God. Good! Even the demons believe that — and shudder.

20You foolish person, do you want evidence that faith without deeds is useless*d*? **21**Was not our father Abraham considered righteous for what he did when he offered his son Isaac on the altar? **22**You see that his faith and

---

a 8 Lev. 19:18   *b 11* Exodus 20:14; Deut. 5:18   *c 11* Exodus 20:13; Deut. 5:17
d 20 Some early manuscripts *dead*

his actions were working together, and his faith was made complete by what he did. ²³And the scripture was fulfilled that says, "Abraham believed God, and it was credited to him as righteousness,"^a and he was called God's friend. ²⁴You see that a person is considered righteous by what they do and not by faith alone.

²⁵In the same way, was not even Rahab the prostitute considered righteous for what she did when she gave lodging to the spies and sent them off in a different direction? ²⁶As the body without the spirit is dead, so faith without deeds is dead.

Taming the Tongue

3 Not many of you should become teachers, my fellow believers, because you know that we who teach will be judged more strictly. ²We all stumble in many ways. Anyone who is never at fault in what they say is perfect, able to keep their whole body in check.

³When we put bits into the mouths of horses to make them obey us, we can turn the whole animal. ⁴Or take ships as an example. Although they are so large and are driven by strong winds, they are steered by a very small rudder wherever the pilot wants to go. ⁵Likewise, the tongue is a small part of the body, but it makes great boasts. Consider what a great forest is set on fire by a small spark. ⁶The tongue also is a fire, a world of evil among the parts of the body. It corrupts the whole body, sets the whole course of one's life on fire, and is itself set on fire by hell.

⁷All kinds of animals, birds, reptiles and sea creatures are being tamed and have been tamed by mankind, ⁸but no human being can tame the tongue. It is a restless evil, full of deadly poison.

⁹With the tongue we praise our Lord and Father, and with it we curse human beings, who have been made in God's likeness. ¹⁰Out of the same mouth come praise and cursing. My brothers and sisters, this should not be. ¹¹Can both fresh water and salt water flow from the same spring? ¹²My brothers and sisters, can a fig tree bear olives, or a grapevine bear figs? Neither can a salt spring produce fresh water.

Two Kinds of Wisdom

¹³Who is wise and understanding among you? Let them show it by their good life, by deeds done in the humility that comes from wisdom. ¹⁴But if you harbor bitter envy and selfish ambition in your hearts, do not boast about it or deny the truth. ¹⁵Such "wisdom" does not come down from heaven but is earthly, unspiritual, demonic. ¹⁶For where you have envy and

^a 23 Gen. 15:6

selfish ambition, there you find disorder and every evil practice. ¹⁷But the wisdom that comes from heaven is first of all pure; then peace-loving, considerate, submissive, full of mercy and good fruit, impartial and sincere. ¹⁸Peacemakers who sow in peace reap a harvest of righteousness.

Submit Yourselves to God

4 What causes fights and quarrels among you? Don't they come from your desires that battle within you? ²You desire but do not have, so you kill. You covet but you cannot get what you want, so you quarrel and fight. You do not have because you do not ask God. ³When you ask, you do not receive, because you ask with wrong motives, that you may spend what you get on your pleasures.

⁴You adulterous people,ᵃ don't you know that friendship with the world means enmity against God? Therefore, anyone who chooses to be a friend of the world becomes an enemy of God. ⁵Or do you think Scripture says without reason that he jealously longs for the spirit he has caused to dwell in usᵇ? ⁶But he gives us more grace. That is why Scripture says:

> "God opposes the proud
>   but shows favor to the
>   humble."ᶜ

⁷Submit yourselves, then, to God. Resist the devil, and he will flee from you. ⁸Come near to God and he will come near to you. Wash your hands, you sinners, and purify your hearts, you double-minded. ⁹Grieve, mourn and wail. Change your laughter to mourning and your joy to gloom. ¹⁰Humble yourselves before the Lord, and he will lift you up.

¹¹Brothers and sisters, do not slander one another. Anyone who speaks against a brother or sisterᵈ or judges them speaks against the law and judges it. When you judge the law, you are not keeping it, but sitting in judgment on it. ¹²There is only one Lawgiver and Judge, the one who is able to save and destroy. But you — who are you to judge your neighbor?

Boasting About Tomorrow

¹³Now listen, you who say, "Today or tomorrow we will go to this or that city, spend a year there, carry on business and make money." ¹⁴Why, you do not even know what will happen tomorrow. What is your life? You are a mist that appears for a little while and then vanishes. ¹⁵Instead, you ought to say, "If it is the Lord's will, we will live and do this or that." ¹⁶As it is, you boast in your arrogant schemes. All such boasting is evil. ¹⁷If anyone,

---

ᵃ 4 An allusion to covenant unfaithfulness; see Hosea 3:1.   ᵇ 5 Or that the spirit he caused to dwell in us envies intensely; or that the Spirit he caused to dwell in us longs jealously   ᶜ 6 Prov. 3:34   ᵈ 11 The Greek word for brother or sister (adelphos) refers here to a believer, whether man or woman, as part of God's family.

then, knows the good they ought to do and doesn't do it, it is sin for them.

Warning to Rich Oppressors

5 Now listen, you rich people, weep and wail because of the misery that is coming on you. ²Your wealth has rotted, and moths have eaten your clothes. ³Your gold and silver are corroded. Their corrosion will testify against you and eat your flesh like fire. You have hoarded wealth in the last days. ⁴Look! The wages you failed to pay the workers who mowed your fields are crying out against you. The cries of the harvesters have reached the ears of the Lord Almighty. ⁵You have lived on earth in luxury and self-indulgence. You have fattened yourselves in the day of slaughter.ᵃ ⁶You have condemned and murdered the innocent one, who was not opposing you.

Patience in Suffering

⁷Be patient, then, brothers and sisters, until the Lord's coming. See how the farmer waits for the land to yield its valuable crop, patiently waiting for the autumn and spring rains. ⁸You too, be patient and stand firm, because the Lord's coming is near. ⁹Don't grumble against one another, brothers and sisters, or you will be judged. The Judge is standing at the door!

¹⁰Brothers and sisters, as an example of patience in the face of suffering, take the prophets who spoke in the name of the Lord. ¹¹As you know, we count as blessed those who have persevered. You have heard of Job's perseverance and have seen what the Lord finally brought about. The Lord is full of compassion and mercy.

¹²Above all, my brothers and sisters, do not swear — not by heaven or by earth or by anything else. All you need to say is a simple "Yes" or "No." Otherwise you will be condemned.

The Prayer of Faith

¹³Is anyone among you in trouble? Let them pray. Is anyone happy? Let them sing songs of praise. ¹⁴Is anyone among you sick? Let them call the elders of the church to pray over them and anoint them with oil in the name of the Lord. ¹⁵And the prayer offered in faith will make the sick person well; the Lord will raise them up. If they have sinned, they will be forgiven. ¹⁶Therefore confess your sins to each other and pray for each other so that you may be healed. The prayer of a righteous person is powerful and effective.

¹⁷Elijah was a human being, even as we are. He prayed earnestly that it would not rain, and it did not rain on the land for

ᵃ 5 Or *yourselves as in a day of feasting*

three and a half years. [18]Again he prayed, and the heavens gave rain, and the earth produced its crops.

[19]My brothers and sisters, if one of you should wander from the truth and someone should bring that person back, [20]remember this: Whoever turns a sinner from the error of their way will save them from death and cover over a multitude of sins.

1 Peter

Introduction:

Peter, one of Jesus' twelve disciples, wrote this letter to the Christians who lived in the northern part of Asia Minor. These Christians were being persecuted for their faith, so Peter wrote to encourage them.

He urges them to remember how much Jesus suffered for them and to follow his example by trusting God to care for them. Because God chose them to be his people and his Son Jesus suffered and died for them, they should live holy lives. Peter also tells them how to handle suffering, live as Christians in this sinful world, and have hope for the future.

Outline of contents:

Greetings (1:1,2)
Praise to God for salvation (1:3–12)
Holy living (1:13–2:12)
Conduct of the believer (2:13–4:11)
Ministry through suffering (4:12–5:11)
Conclusion (5:12–14)

1 Peter, an apostle of Jesus Christ,

To God's elect, exiles scattered throughout the provinces of Pontus, Galatia, Cappadocia, Asia and Bithynia, ²who have been chosen according to the foreknowledge of God the Father, through the sanctifying work of the Spirit, to be obedient to Jesus Christ and sprinkled with his blood:

Grace and peace be yours in abundance.

Praise to God for a Living Hope

³Praise be to the God and Father of our Lord Jesus Christ! In his great mercy he has given us new birth into a living hope through the resurrection of Jesus Christ from the dead, ⁴and into an inheritance that can never perish, spoil or fade. This inheritance is kept in heaven for you, ⁵who through faith are shielded by God's power until the coming of the salvation that is ready to be revealed in the last time. ⁶In all this you greatly rejoice, though now for a little while you may have had to suffer grief in all kinds of trials. ⁷These have come so that the proven genuineness of your faith — of greater worth than gold, which perishes even though refined by fire — may

result in praise, glory and honor when Jesus Christ is revealed. **8**Though you have not seen him, you love him; and even though you do not see him now, you believe in him and are filled with an inexpressible and glorious joy, **9**for you are receiving the end result of your faith, the salvation of your souls.

10Concerning this salvation, the prophets, who spoke of the grace that was to come to you, searched intently and with the greatest care, **11**trying to find out the time and circumstances to which the Spirit of Christ in them was pointing when he predicted the sufferings of the Messiah and the glories that would follow. **12**It was revealed to them that they were not serving themselves but you, when they spoke of the things that have now been told you by those who have preached the gospel to you by the Holy Spirit sent from heaven. Even angels long to look into these things.

Be Holy

13Therefore, with minds that are alert and fully sober, set your hope on the grace to be brought to you when Jesus Christ is revealed at his coming. **14**As obedient children, do not conform to the evil desires you had when you lived in ignorance. **15**But just as he who called you is holy, so be holy in all you do; **16**for it is written: "Be holy, because I am holy."[a]

17Since you call on a Father who judges each person's work impartially, live out your time as foreigners here in reverent fear. **18**For you know that it was not with perishable things such as silver or gold that you were redeemed from the empty way of life handed down to you from your ancestors, **19**but with the precious blood of Christ, a lamb without blemish or defect. **20**He was chosen before the creation of the world, but was revealed in these last times for your sake. **21**Through him you believe in God, who raised him from the dead and glorified him, and so your faith and hope are in God.

22Now that you have purified yourselves by obeying the truth so that you have sincere love for each other, love one another deeply, from the heart.[b] **23**For you have been born again, not of perishable seed, but of imperishable, through the living and enduring word of God. **24**For,

"All people are like grass,
　　and all their glory is like the
　　　　flowers of the field;
the grass withers and the
　　　　flowers fall,
25　but the word of the Lord
　　　　endures forever."[c]

And this is the word that was preached to you.

---

[a] 16 Lev. 11:44,45; 19:2　　[b] 22 Some early manuscripts *from a pure heart*
[c] 25 Isaiah 40:6-8 (see Septuagint)

2 Therefore, rid yourselves of all malice and all deceit, hypocrisy, envy, and slander of every kind. [2] Like newborn babies, crave pure spiritual milk, so that by it you may grow up in your salvation, [3] now that you have tasted that the Lord is good.

The Living Stone and a Chosen People

[4] As you come to him, the living Stone — rejected by humans but chosen by God and precious to him — [5] you also, like living stones, are being built into a spiritual house[a] to be a holy priesthood, offering spiritual sacrifices acceptable to God through Jesus Christ. [6] For in Scripture it says:

"See, I lay a stone in Zion,
  a chosen and precious
    cornerstone,
and the one who trusts in him
  will never be put to shame."[b]

[7] Now to you who believe, this stone is precious. But to those who do not believe,

"The stone the builders
    rejected
has become the
    cornerstone,"[c]

[8] and,

"A stone that causes people to
    stumble
  and a rock that makes them
    fall."[d]

They stumble because they disobey the message — which is also what they were destined for.

[9] But you are a chosen people, a royal priesthood, a holy nation, God's special possession, that you may declare the praises of him who called you out of darkness into his wonderful light. [10] Once you were not a people, but now you are the people of God; once you had not received mercy, but now you have received mercy.

Living Godly Lives in a Pagan Society

[11] Dear friends, I urge you, as foreigners and exiles, to abstain from sinful desires, which wage war against your soul. [12] Live such good lives among the pagans that, though they accuse you of doing wrong, they may see your good deeds and glorify God on the day he visits us.

[13] Submit yourselves for the Lord's sake to every human authority: whether to the emperor, as the supreme authority, [14] or to governors, who are sent by him to punish those who do wrong and to commend those who do right. [15] For it is God's will that by doing good you should silence the ignorant talk of foolish people. [16] Live as free people, but do not use your freedom as a cover-up for evil; live as God's slaves. [17] Show proper respect to every-

[a] 5 Or *into a temple of the Spirit*   [b] 6 Isaiah 28:16   [c] 7 Psalm 118:22
[d] 8 Isaiah 8:14

one, love the family of believers, fear God, honor the emperor.

¹⁸Slaves, in reverent fear of God submit yourselves to your masters, not only to those who are good and considerate, but also to those who are harsh. ¹⁹For it is commendable if someone bears up under the pain of unjust suffering because they are conscious of God. ²⁰But how is it to your credit if you receive a beating for doing wrong and endure it? But if you suffer for doing good and you endure it, this is commendable before God. ²¹To this you were called, because Christ suffered for you, leaving you an example, that you should follow in his steps.

²²"He committed no sin,
and no deceit was found in
his mouth."ᵃ

²³When they hurled their insults at him, he did not retaliate; when he suffered, he made no threats. Instead, he entrusted himself to him who judges justly. ²⁴"He himself bore our sins" in his body on the cross, so that we might die to sins and live for righteousness; "by his wounds you have been healed." ²⁵For "you were like sheep going astray,"ᵇ but now you have returned to the Shepherd and Overseer of your souls.

3 Wives, in the same way submit yourselves to your own husbands so that, if any of them do not believe the word, they may be won over without words by the behavior of their wives, ²when they see the purity and reverence of your lives. ³Your beauty should not come from outward adornment, such as elaborate hairstyles and the wearing of gold jewelry or fine clothes. ⁴Rather, it should be that of your inner self, the unfading beauty of a gentle and quiet spirit, which is of great worth in God's sight. ⁵For this is the way the holy women of the past who put their hope in God used to adorn themselves. They submitted themselves to their own husbands, ⁶like Sarah, who obeyed Abraham and called him her lord. You are her daughters if you do what is right and do not give way to fear.

⁷Husbands, in the same way be considerate as you live with your wives, and treat them with respect as the weaker partner and as heirs with you of the gracious gift of life, so that nothing will hinder your prayers.

Suffering for Doing Good

⁸Finally, all of you, be likeminded, be sympathetic, love one another, be compassionate and humble. ⁹Do not repay evil with evil or insult with insult. On the contrary, repay evil with blessing, because to this you were called so that you may inherit a blessing. ¹⁰For,

---

ᵃ 22 Isaiah 53:9   ᵇ 24,25 Isaiah 53:4,5,6 (see Septuagint)

"Whoever would love life
and see good days
must keep their tongue from
evil
and their lips from deceitful
speech.
¹¹They must turn from evil and
do good;
they must seek peace and
pursue it.
¹²For the eyes of the Lord are on
the righteous
and his ears are attentive to
their prayer,
but the face of the Lord is
against those who do
evil."ᵃ

¹³Who is going to harm you if you are eager to do good? ¹⁴But even if you should suffer for what is right, you are blessed. "Do not fear their threats*ᵇ*; do not be frightened."ᶜ ¹⁵But in your hearts revere Christ as Lord. Always be prepared to give an answer to everyone who asks you to give the reason for the hope that you have. But do this with gentleness and respect, ¹⁶keeping a clear conscience, so that those who speak maliciously against your good behavior in Christ may be ashamed of their slander. ¹⁷For it is better, if it is God's will, to suffer for doing good than for doing evil. ¹⁸For Christ also suffered once for sins, the righteous for the unrighteous, to bring you to

God. He was put to death in the body but made alive in the Spirit. ¹⁹After being made alive,ᵈ he went and made proclamation to the imprisoned spirits — ²⁰to those who were disobedient long ago when God waited patiently in the days of Noah while the ark was being built. In it only a few people, eight in all, were saved through water, ²¹and this water symbolizes baptism that now saves you also — not the removal of dirt from the body but the pledge of a clear conscience toward God.ᵉ It saves you by the resurrection of Jesus Christ, ²²who has gone into heaven and is at God's right hand — with angels, authorities and powers in submission to him.

Living for God

4 Therefore, since Christ suffered in his body, arm yourselves also with the same attitude, because whoever suffers in the body is done with sin. ²As a result, they do not live the rest of their earthly lives for evil human desires, but rather for the will of God. ³For you have spent enough time in the past doing what pagans choose to do — living in debauchery, lust, drunkenness, orgies, carousing and detestable idolatry. ⁴They are surprised that you do not join them in their

---

ᵃ *12* Psalm 34:12-16   ᵇ *14* Or *fear what they fear*   ᶜ *14* Isaiah 8:12
ᵈ *18,19* Or *but made alive in the spirit,* ¹⁹*in which also*   ᵉ *21* Or *but an appeal to God for a clear conscience*

reckless, wild living, and they heap abuse on you. ⁵But they will have to give account to him who is ready to judge the living and the dead. ⁶For this is the reason the gospel was preached even to those who are now dead, so that they might be judged according to human standards in regard to the body, but live according to God in regard to the spirit.

⁷The end of all things is near. Therefore be alert and of sober mind so that you may pray. ⁸Above all, love each other deeply, because love covers over a multitude of sins. ⁹Offer hospitality to one another without grumbling. ¹⁰Each of you should use whatever gift you have received to serve others, as faithful stewards of God's grace in its various forms. ¹¹If anyone speaks, they should do so as one who speaks the very words of God. If anyone serves, they should do so with the strength God provides, so that in all things God may be praised through Jesus Christ. To him be the glory and the power for ever and ever. Amen.

Suffering for Being a Christian

¹²Dear friends, do not be surprised at the fiery ordeal that has come on you to test you, as though something strange were happening to you. ¹³But rejoice inasmuch as you participate in the sufferings of Christ, so that you may be overjoyed when his glory is revealed. ¹⁴If you are insulted because of the name of Christ, you are blessed, for the Spirit of glory and of God rests on you. ¹⁵If you suffer, it should not be as a murderer or thief or any other kind of criminal, or even as a meddler. ¹⁶However, if you suffer as a Christian, do not be ashamed, but praise God that you bear that name. ¹⁷For it is time for judgment to begin with God's household; and if it begins with us, what will the outcome be for those who do not obey the gospel of God? ¹⁸And,

"If it is hard for the righteous
  to be saved,
 what will become of the
  ungodly and the
  sinner?"ᵃ

¹⁹So then, those who suffer according to God's will should commit themselves to their faithful Creator and continue to do good.

To the Elders and the Flock

5 To the elders among you, I appeal as a fellow elder and a witness of Christ's sufferings who also will share in the glory to be revealed: ²Be shepherds of God's flock that is under your care, watching over them—not because you must, but because you are willing, as God wants you to be; not pursuing dishonest gain, but eager to serve; ³not lording it

---

ᵃ 18 Prov. 11:31 (see Septuagint)

over those entrusted to you, but being examples to the flock. [4]And when the Chief Shepherd appears, you will receive the crown of glory that will never fade away.

[5]In the same way, you who are younger, submit yourselves to your elders. All of you, clothe yourselves with humility toward one another, because,

> "God opposes the proud
>   but shows favor to the
>   humble."[a]

[6]Humble yourselves, therefore, under God's mighty hand, that he may lift you up in due time. [7]Cast all your anxiety on him because he cares for you.

[8]Be alert and of sober mind. Your enemy the devil prowls around like a roaring lion looking for someone to devour. [9]Resist him, standing firm in the faith, because you know that the family of believers throughout the world is undergoing the same kind of sufferings.

[10]And the God of all grace, who called you to his eternal glory in Christ, after you have suffered a little while, will himself restore you and make you strong, firm and steadfast. [11]To him be the power for ever and ever. Amen.

Final Greetings

[12]With the help of Silas,[b] whom I regard as a faithful brother, I have written to you briefly, encouraging you and testifying that this is the true grace of God. Stand fast in it.

[13]She who is in Babylon, chosen together with you, sends you her greetings, and so does my son Mark. [14]Greet one another with a kiss of love.

Peace to all of you who are in Christ.

---

[a] 5 Prov. 3:34   [b] 12 Greek *Silvanus*, a variant of *Silas*

2 Peter

Introduction:

Peter wrote this second letter about AD 66 to the same Christians he had written to earlier. They were living in the northern part of Asia Minor. These Christians were no longer being persecuted but were now in danger of being confused by false teachers.

Peter reminds the Christians that the best way to resist false teachers is to grow in the knowledge and practice of the Christian faith. He assures them that God will destroy the false teachers. Because Jesus will certainly keep his promise to come again, Peter reminds these Christians to live "holy and godly lives" (3:11).

Outline of contents:

Introduction (1:1,2)
True knowledge (1:3–21)
False teachers and their destruction (2:1–22)
The day of the Lord (3:1–18)

1 Simon Peter, a servant and apostle of Jesus Christ,

To those who through the righteousness of our God and Savior Jesus Christ have received a faith as precious as ours:

2 Grace and peace be yours in abundance through the knowledge of God and of Jesus our Lord.

Confirming One's Calling and Election

3 His divine power has given us everything we need for a godly life through our knowledge of him who called us by his own glory and goodness. 4 Through these he has given us his very great and precious promises, so that through them you may participate in the divine nature, having escaped the corruption in the world caused by evil desires.

5 For this very reason, make every effort to add to your faith goodness; and to goodness, knowledge; 6 and to knowledge, self-control; and to self-control, perseverance; and to perseverance, godliness; 7 and to godliness, mutual affection; and to mutual affection, love. 8 For if you possess these qualities in increasing measure, they will keep you from being ineffective and unproductive in your knowledge

of our Lord Jesus Christ. ⁹But whoever does not have them is nearsighted and blind, forgetting that they have been cleansed from their past sins.

¹⁰Therefore, my brothers and sisters,ᵃ make every effort to confirm your calling and election. For if you do these things, you will never stumble, ¹¹and you will receive a rich welcome into the eternal kingdom of our Lord and Savior Jesus Christ.

Prophecy of Scripture

¹²So I will always remind you of these things, even though you know them and are firmly established in the truth you now have. ¹³I think it is right to refresh your memory as long as I live in the tent of this body, ¹⁴because I know that I will soon put it aside, as our Lord Jesus Christ has made clear to me. ¹⁵And I will make every effort to see that after my departure you will always be able to remember these things.

¹⁶For we did not follow cleverly devised stories when we told you about the coming of our Lord Jesus Christ in power, but we were eyewitnesses of his majesty. ¹⁷He received honor and glory from God the Father when the voice came to him from the Majestic Glory, saying, "This is my Son, whom I love; with him I am well pleased."ᵇ ¹⁸We ourselves heard this voice that came from heaven when we were with him on the sacred mountain.

¹⁹We also have the prophetic message as something completely reliable, and you will do well to pay attention to it, as to a light shining in a dark place, until the day dawns and the morning star rises in your hearts. ²⁰Above all, you must understand that no prophecy of Scripture came about by the prophet's own interpretation of things. ²¹For prophecy never had its origin in the human will, but prophets, though human, spoke from God as they were carried along by the Holy Spirit.

False Teachers and Their Destruction

2 But there were also false prophets among the people, just as there will be false teachers among you. They will secretly introduce destructive heresies, even denying the sovereign Lord who bought them — bringing swift destruction on themselves. ²Many will follow their depraved conduct and will bring the way of truth into disrepute. ³In their greed these teachers will exploit you with fabricated stories. Their condemnation has long been hanging over them, and their destruction has not been sleeping.

ᵃ 10 The Greek word for *brothers and sisters* (*adelphoi*) refers here to believers, both men and women, as part of God's family.   ᵇ 17 Matt. 17:5; Mark 9:7; Luke 9:35

⁴For if God did not spare angels when they sinned, but sent them to hell,ᵃ putting them in chains of darknessᵇ to be held for judgment; ⁵if he did not spare the ancient world when he brought the flood on its ungodly people, but protected Noah, a preacher of righteousness, and seven others; ⁶if he condemned the cities of Sodom and Gomorrah by burning them to ashes, and made them an example of what is going to happen to the ungodly; ⁷and if he rescued Lot, a righteous man, who was distressed by the depraved conduct of the lawless ⁸(for that righteous man, living among them day after day, was tormented in his righteous soul by the lawless deeds he saw and heard)— ⁹if this is so, then the Lord knows how to rescue the godly from trials and to hold the unrighteous for punishment on the day of judgment. ¹⁰This is especially true of those who follow the corrupt desire of the fleshᶜ and despise authority.

Bold and arrogant, they are not afraid to heap abuse on celestial beings; ¹¹yet even angels, although they are stronger and more powerful, do not heap abuse on such beings when bringing judgment on them fromᵈ the Lord. ¹²But these peo-ple blaspheme in matters they do not understand. They are like unreasoning animals, creatures of instinct, born only to be caught and destroyed, and like animals they too will perish.

¹³They will be paid back with harm for the harm they have done. Their idea of pleasure is to carouse in broad daylight. They are blots and blemishes, reveling in their pleasures while they feast with you.ᵉ ¹⁴With eyes full of adultery, they never stop sinning; they seduce the unstable; they are experts in greed—an accursed brood! ¹⁵They have left the straight way and wandered off to follow the way of Balaam son of Bezer,ᶠ who loved the wages of wickedness. ¹⁶But he was rebuked for his wrongdoing by a donkey—an animal without speech—who spoke with a human voice and restrained the prophet's madness.

¹⁷These people are springs without water and mists driven by a storm. Blackest darkness is reserved for them. ¹⁸For they mouth empty, boastful words and, by appealing to the lustful desires of the flesh, they entice people who are just escaping from those who live in error. ¹⁹They promise them freedom, while they themselves are slaves of depravity—for

---

ᵃ 4 Greek *Tartarus*   ᵇ 4 Some manuscripts *in gloomy dungeons*   ᶜ 10 In contexts like this, the Greek word for *flesh* (*sarx*) refers to the sinful state of human beings, often presented as a power in opposition to the Spirit; also in verse 18.
ᵈ 11 Many manuscripts *beings in the presence of*   ᵉ 13 Some manuscripts *in their love feasts*   ᶠ 15 Greek *Bosor*

"people are slaves to whatever has mastered them." ²⁰ If they have escaped the corruption of the world by knowing our Lord and Savior Jesus Christ and are again entangled in it and are overcome, they are worse off at the end than they were at the beginning. ²¹ It would have been better for them not to have known the way of righteousness, than to have known it and then to turn their backs on the sacred command that was passed on to them. ²² Of them the proverbs are true: "A dog returns to its vomit,"[a] and, "A sow that is washed returns to her wallowing in the mud."

The Day of the Lord

3 Dear friends, this is now my second letter to you. I have written both of them as reminders to stimulate you to wholesome thinking. ² I want you to recall the words spoken in the past by the holy prophets and the command given by our Lord and Savior through your apostles.

³ Above all, you must understand that in the last days scoffers will come, scoffing and following their own evil desires. ⁴ They will say, "Where is this 'coming' he promised? Ever since our ancestors died, everything goes on as it has since the beginning of creation." ⁵ But they deliberately forget that long ago by God's word the heavens came into being and the earth was formed out of water and by water. ⁶ By these waters also the world of that time was deluged and destroyed. ⁷ By the same word the present heavens and earth are reserved for fire, being kept for the day of judgment and destruction of the ungodly.

⁸ But do not forget this one thing, dear friends: With the Lord a day is like a thousand years, and a thousand years are like a day. ⁹ The Lord is not slow in keeping his promise, as some understand slowness. Instead he is patient with you, not wanting anyone to perish, but everyone to come to repentance.

¹⁰ But the day of the Lord will come like a thief. The heavens will disappear with a roar; the elements will be destroyed by fire, and the earth and everything done in it will be laid bare.[b]

¹¹ Since everything will be destroyed in this way, what kind of people ought you to be? You ought to live holy and godly lives ¹² as you look forward to the day of God and speed its coming.[c] That day will bring about the destruction of the heavens by fire, and the elements will melt in the heat. ¹³ But in keeping with his promise we are looking forward to a new heaven and a new earth, where righteousness dwells.

---

[a] 22 Prov. 26:11   [b] 10 Some manuscripts *be burned up*   [c] 12 Or *as you wait eagerly for the day of God to come*

[14]So then, dear friends, since you are looking forward to this, make every effort to be found spotless, blameless and at peace with him. [15]Bear in mind that our Lord's patience means salvation, just as our dear brother Paul also wrote you with the wisdom that God gave him. [16]He writes the same way in all his letters, speaking in them of these matters. His letters contain some things that are hard to understand, which ig-norant and unstable people dis-tort, as they do the other Scrip-tures, to their own destruction.

[17]Therefore, dear friends, since you have been forewarned, be on your guard so that you may not be carried away by the error of the lawless and fall from your se-cure position. [18]But grow in the grace and knowledge of our Lord and Savior Jesus Christ. To him be glory both now and forever! Amen.

1 John

Introduction:

First, Second and Third John were written by John, Jesus' beloved disciple, who also wrote the fourth Gospel. All four books may have been written about the same time, probably about AD 90.

The first letter of John was written to warn Christians about dangerous false teachers who were trying to mislead them. These teachers were teaching that the man Jesus was not the Christ, the Son of God. They said that God did not become a man. John tells the Christians he is writing because it is very important for them to know and believe that Jesus Christ is both God and man.

John also encourages these Christians to keep their faith in Christ strong and to continue loving one another. He says Christians can know they are God's children if they love one another and if they obey God's commands.

Outline of contents:

Introduction (1:1–4)
Walking in the light (1:5–2:29)
Love must fill our life (3:1–4:21)
Faith and freedom from doubts (5:1–12)
Conclusion (5:13–21)

The Incarnation of the Word of Life

1 That which was from the beginning, which we have heard, which we have seen with our eyes, which we have looked at and our hands have touched — this we proclaim concerning the Word of life. ²The life appeared; we have seen it and testify to it, and we proclaim to you the eternal life, which was with the Father and has appeared to us. ³We proclaim to you what we have seen and heard, so that you also may have fellowship with us. And our fellowship is with the Father and with his Son, Jesus Christ. ⁴We write this to make our*a* joy complete.

Light and Darkness, Sin and Forgiveness

⁵This is the message we have heard from him and declare to you: God is light; in him there is

a 4 Some manuscripts *your*

no darkness at all. ⁶If we claim to have fellowship with him and yet walk in the darkness, we lie and do not live out the truth. ⁷But if we walk in the light, as he is in the light, we have fellowship with one another, and the blood of Jesus, his Son, purifies us from all^a sin.

⁸If we claim to be without sin, we deceive ourselves and the truth is not in us. ⁹If we confess our sins, he is faithful and just and will forgive us our sins and purify us from all unrighteousness. ¹⁰If we claim we have not sinned, we make him out to be a liar and his word is not in us.

2 My dear children, I write this to you so that you will not sin. But if anybody does sin, we have an advocate with the Father—Jesus Christ, the Righteous One. ²He is the atoning sacrifice for our sins, and not only for ours but also for the sins of the whole world.

Love and Hatred for Fellow Believers

³We know that we have come to know him if we keep his commands. ⁴Whoever says, "I know him," but does not do what he commands is a liar, and the truth is not in that person. ⁵But if anyone obeys his word, love for God^b

is truly made complete in them. This is how we know we are in him: ⁶Whoever claims to live in him must live as Jesus did.

⁷Dear friends, I am not writing you a new command but an old one, which you have had since the beginning. This old command is the message you have heard. ⁸Yet I am writing you a new command; its truth is seen in him and in you, because the darkness is passing and the true light is already shining.

⁹Anyone who claims to be in the light but hates a brother or sister^c is still in the darkness. ¹⁰Anyone who loves their brother and sister^d lives in the light, and there is nothing in them to make them stumble. ¹¹But anyone who hates a brother or sister is in the darkness and walks around in the darkness. They do not know where they are going, because the darkness has blinded them.

Reasons for Writing

¹²I am writing to you, dear
   children,
   because your sins have been
     forgiven on account of
     his name.
¹³I am writing to you, fathers,
   because you know him who
     is from the beginning.

---

^a 7 Or every   ^b 5 Or word, God's love (adelphos) refers here to a believer, whether man or woman, as part of God's family; also in verse 11; and in 3:15, 17; 4:20; 5:16.   ^c 9 The Greek word for brother or sister   ^d 10 The Greek word for brother and sister (adelphos) refers here to a believer, whether man or woman, as part of God's family; also in 3:10; 4:20, 21.

I am writing to you, young
men,
    because you have overcome
        the evil one.

¹⁴I write to you, dear children,
    because you know the
        Father.
I write to you, fathers,
    because you know him who
        is from the beginning.
I write to you, young men,
    because you are strong,
    and the word of God lives in
        you,
    and you have overcome the
        evil one.

On Not Loving the World

¹⁵Do not love the world or anything in the world. If anyone loves
the world, love for the Father*ᵃ* is
not in them. ¹⁶For everything in
the world — the lust of the flesh,
the lust of the eyes, and the pride
of life — comes not from the Father but from the world. ¹⁷The
world and its desires pass away,
but whoever does the will of God
lives forever.

Warnings Against Denying the Son

¹⁸Dear children, this is the last
hour; and as you have heard that
the antichrist is coming, even
now many antichrists have come.
This is how we know it is the last
hour. ¹⁹They went out from us,
but they did not really belong to
us. For if they had belonged to

they would have remained with
us; but their going showed that
none of them belonged to us.

²⁰But you have an anointing
from the Holy One, and all of you
know the truth.*ᵇ* ²¹I do not write
to you because you do not know
the truth, but because you do
know it and because no lie comes
from the truth. ²²Who is the liar?
It is whoever denies that Jesus is
the Christ. Such a person is the
antichrist — denying the Father
and the Son. ²³No one who denies the Son has the Father; whoever acknowledges the Son has
the Father also.

²⁴As for you, see that what you
have heard from the beginning
remains in you. If it does, you
also will remain in the Son and
in the Father. ²⁵And this is what
he promised us — eternal life.

²⁶I am writing these things to
you about those who are trying to
lead you astray. ²⁷As for you, the
anointing you received from him
remains in you, and you do not
need anyone to teach you. But as
his anointing teaches you about
all things and as that anointing
is real, not counterfeit — just as
it has taught you, remain in him.

God's Children and Sin

²⁸And now, dear children, continue in him, so that when he appears we may be confident and
unashamed before him at his
coming.

ᵃ 15 Or *world, the Father's love*   *ᵇ 20* Some manuscripts *and you know all things*

²⁹If you know that he is righteous, you know that everyone who does what is right has been born of him.

3 See what great love the Father has lavished on us, that we should be called children of God! And that is what we are! The reason the world does not know us is that it did not know him. ²Dear friends, now we are children of God, and what we will be has not yet been made known. But we know that when Christ appears,ᵃ we shall be like him, for we shall see him as he is. ³All who have this hope in him purify themselves, just as he is pure.

⁴Everyone who sins breaks the law; in fact, sin is lawlessness. ⁵But you know that he appeared so that he might take away our sins. And in him is no sin. ⁶No one who lives in him keeps on sinning. No one who continues to sin has either seen him or known him.

⁷Dear children, do not let anyone lead you astray. The one who does what is right is righteous, just as he is righteous. ⁸The one who does what is sinful is of the devil, because the devil has been sinning from the beginning. The reason the Son of God appeared was to destroy the devil's work. ⁹No one who is born of God will continue to sin, because God's seed remains in them; they cannot go on sinning, because they have been born of God. ¹⁰This is how we know who the children of God are and who the children of the devil are: Anyone who does not do what is right is not God's child, nor is anyone who does not love their brother and sister.

More on Love and Hatred

¹¹For this is the message you heard from the beginning: We should love one another. ¹²Do not be like Cain, who belonged to the evil one and murdered his brother. And why did he murder him? Because his own actions were evil and his brother's were righteous. ¹³Do not be surprised, my brothers and sisters,ᵇ if the world hates you. ¹⁴We know that we have passed from death to life, because we love each other. Anyone who does not love remains in death. ¹⁵Anyone who hates a brother or sister is a murderer, and you know that no murderer has eternal life residing in him.

¹⁶This is how we know what love is: Jesus Christ laid down his life for us. And we ought to lay down our lives for our brothers and sisters. ¹⁷If anyone has material possessions and sees a brother or sister in need but has no pity on them, how can the love of God be in that person? ¹⁸Dear

---

ᵃ 2 Or *when it is made known*   ᵇ 13 The Greek word for *brothers and sisters* (*adelphoi*) refers here to believers, both men and women, as part of God's family; also in verse 16.

children, let us not love with words or speech but with actions and in truth.

¹⁹This is how we know that we belong to the truth and how we set our hearts at rest in his presence: ²⁰If our hearts condemn us, we know that God is greater than our hearts, and he knows everything. ²¹Dear friends, if our hearts do not condemn us, we have confidence before God ²²and receive from him anything we ask, because we keep his commands and do what pleases him. ²³And this is his command: to believe in the name of his Son, Jesus Christ, and to love one another as he commanded us. ²⁴The one who keeps God's commands lives in him, and he in them. And this is how we know that he lives in us: We know it by the Spirit he gave us.

On Denying the Incarnation

4 Dear friends, do not believe every spirit, but test the spirits to see whether they are from God, because many false prophets have gone out into the world. ²This is how you can recognize the Spirit of God: Every spirit that acknowledges that Jesus Christ has come in the flesh is from God, ³but every spirit that does not acknowledge Jesus is not from God. This is the spirit of the antichrist, which you have heard is coming and even now is already in the world.

⁴You, dear children, are from God and have overcome them, because the one who is in you is greater than the one who is in the world. ⁵They are from the world and therefore speak from the viewpoint of the world, and the world listens to them. ⁶We are from God, and whoever knows God listens to us; but whoever is not from God does not listen to us. This is how we recognize the Spirit*a* of truth and the spirit of falsehood.

God's Love and Ours

⁷Dear friends, let us love one another, for love comes from God. Everyone who loves has been born of God and knows God. ⁸Whoever does not love does not know God, because God is love. ⁹This is how God showed his love among us: He sent his one and only Son into the world that we might live through him. ¹⁰This is love: not that we loved God, but that he loved us and sent his Son as an atoning sacrifice for our sins. ¹¹Dear friends, since God so loved us, we also ought to love one another. ¹²No one has ever seen God; but if we love one another, God lives in us and his love is made complete in us.

¹³This is how we know that we live in him and he in us: He has given us of his Spirit. ¹⁴And we have seen and testify that the Father has sent his Son to be the

---

a 6 Or *spirit*

Savior of the world. ¹⁵If anyone acknowledges that Jesus is the Son of God, God lives in them and they in God. ¹⁶And so we know and rely on the love God has for us.

God is love. Whoever lives in love lives in God, and God in them. ¹⁷This is how love is made complete among us so that we will have confidence on the day of judgment: In this world we are like Jesus. ¹⁸There is no fear in love. But perfect love drives out fear, because fear has to do with punishment. The one who fears is not made perfect in love.

¹⁹We love because he first loved us. ²⁰Whoever claims to love God yet hates a brother or sister is a liar. For whoever does not love their brother and sister, whom they have seen, cannot love God, whom they have not seen. ²¹And he has given us this command: Anyone who loves God must also love their brother and sister.

Faith in the Incarnate Son of God

5 Everyone who believes that Jesus is the Christ is born of God, and everyone who loves the father loves his child as well. ²This is how we know that we love the children of God: by loving God and carrying out his commands. ³In fact, this is love for God: to keep his commands.

And his commands are not burdensome, ⁴for everyone born of God overcomes the world. This is the victory that has overcome the world, even our faith. ⁵Who is it that overcomes the world? Only the one who believes that Jesus is the Son of God.

⁶This is the one who came by water and blood — Jesus Christ. He did not come by water only, but by water and blood. And it is the Spirit who testifies, because the Spirit is the truth. ⁷For there are three that testify: ⁸the*a* Spirit, the water and the blood; and the three are in agreement. ⁹We accept human testimony, but God's testimony is greater because it is the testimony of God, which he has given about his Son. ¹⁰Whoever believes in the Son of God accepts this testimony. Whoever does not believe God has made him out to be a liar, because they have not believed the testimony God has given about his Son. ¹¹And this is the testimony: God has given us eternal life, and this life is in his Son. ¹²Whoever has the Son has life; whoever does not have the Son of God does not have life.

Concluding Affirmations

¹³I write these things to you who believe in the name of the Son of God so that you may know that you have eternal life. ¹⁴This

---

a 7,8 Late manuscripts of the Vulgate *testify in heaven: the Father, the Word and the Holy Spirit, and these three are one.* ⁸*And there are three that testify on earth: the* (not found in any Greek manuscript before the fourteenth century) is the confidence we have in approaching God: that if we ask anything according to his will, he hears us. ¹⁵And if we know that he hears us — whatever we ask — we know that we have what we asked of him.

¹⁶If you see any brother or sister commit a sin that does not lead to death, you should pray and God will give them life. I refer to those whose sin does not lead to death. There is a sin that leads to death. I am not saying that you should pray about that. ¹⁷All wrongdoing is sin, and there is sin that does not lead to death.

¹⁸We know that anyone born of God does not continue to sin; the One who was born of God keeps them safe, and the evil one cannot harm them. ¹⁹We know that we are children of God, and that the whole world is under the control of the evil one. ²⁰We know also that the Son of God has come and has given us understanding, so that we may know him who is true. And we are in him who is true by being in his Son Jesus Christ. He is the true God and eternal life.

²¹Dear children, keep yourselves from idols.

2 John

Introduction:

John wrote this letter "to the lady chosen by God and to her children." He might have meant either a Christian woman and her family or a church and its members.

In this letter John writes how important it is for Christians to love one another. He says that to love means to obey God's commandments, and God's commandments tell us to live lives of love.

John again emphasizes the importance of the doctrine that Jesus is God's Son and a human being. Christians should separate themselves from those who teach that Jesus is not God's Son.

Outline of contents:

Greeting (1–3)
Advice and warning (4–11)
Conclusion (12,13)

[1] The elder,

To the lady chosen by God and to her children, whom I love in the truth — and not I only, but also all who know the truth — [2] because of the truth, which lives in us and will be with us forever:

[3] Grace, mercy and peace from God the Father and from Jesus Christ, the Father's Son, will be with us in truth and love.

[4] It has given me great joy to find some of your children walking in the truth, just as the Father commanded us. [5] And now, dear lady, I am not writing you a new command but one we have had from the beginning. I ask that we love one another. [6] And this is love: that we walk in obedience to his commands. As you have heard from the beginning, his command is that you walk in love.

[7] I say this because many deceivers, who do not acknowledge Jesus Christ as coming in the flesh, have gone out into the world. Any such person is the deceiver and the antichrist. [8] Watch out that you do not lose what we[a] have worked for, but that you may be rewarded fully. [9] Anyone who runs ahead and does not continue in the teaching of Christ does not have God; whoever continues

[a] 8 Some manuscripts *you*

in the teaching has both the Father and the Son. **10** If anyone comes to you and does not bring this teaching, do not take them into your house or welcome them. **11** Anyone who welcomes them shares in their wicked work.

12 I have much to write to you, but I do not want to use paper and ink. Instead, I hope to visit you and talk with you face to face, so that our joy may be complete.

13 The children of your sister, who is chosen by God, send their greetings.

3 John

Introduction:

John wrote this letter to his friend Gaius, a leader in the church. A man named Diotrephes in Gaius's church refused to welcome God's messengers. John writes this letter to praise and thank Gaius for his help and to scold Diotrephes for not cooperating. John promises to come to this church soon to deal with this matter himself.

Outline of contents:

Greeting (1–4)
Encouragement for Gaius (5–8)
A scolding for Diotrephes (9,10)
Praise for Demetrius (11,12)
Conclusion (13–15)

¹ The elder,

To my dear friend Gaius, whom I love in the truth.

² Dear friend, I pray that you may enjoy good health and that all may go well with you, even as your soul is getting along well. ³ It gave me great joy when some believers came and testified about your faithfulness to the truth, telling how you continue to walk in it. ⁴ I have no greater joy than to hear that my children are walking in the truth.

⁵ Dear friend, you are faithful in what you are doing for the brothers and sisters,ᵃ even though they are strangers to you. ⁶ They have told the church about your love. Please send them on their way in a manner that honors God. ⁷ It was for the sake of the Name that they went out, receiving no help from the pagans. ⁸ We ought therefore to show hospitality to such people so that we may work together for the truth.

⁹ I wrote to the church, but Diotrephes, who loves to be first, will not welcome us. ¹⁰ So when I come, I will call attention to what he is doing, spreading malicious nonsense about us. Not satisfied with that, he even refuses to welcome other believers. He also stops those who want to do so and puts them out of the church.

¹¹ Dear friend, do not imitate what is evil but what is good.

ᵃ 5 The Greek word for *brothers and sisters* (*adelphoi*) refers here to believers, both men and women, as part of God's family.

Anyone who does what is good is from God. Anyone who does what is evil has not seen God. [12] Demetrius is well spoken of by everyone — and even by the truth itself. We also speak well of him, and you know that our testimony is true.

[13] I have much to write you, but I do not want to do so with pen and ink. [14] I hope to see you soon, and we will talk face to face.

Peace to you. The friends here send their greetings. Greet the friends there by name.

Jude

Introduction:

Jude, like James, was a brother of Jesus. He wrote to warn Christians about the same false teachers Peter wrote about in his second letter. These false teachers were not only teaching that Jesus was not the Son of God; they were also leading the people to live sinful lives. Jude warns that God will punish and destroy these false teachers just as he had punished sinners in the Old Testament.

Outline of contents:

Introduction (1,2)
Warnings against false teachers (3–16)
Warning and conclusion (17–25)

¹Jude, a servant of Jesus Christ and a brother of James,

To those who have been called, who are loved in God the Father and kept for*ᵃ* Jesus Christ:

²Mercy, peace and love be yours in abundance.

The Sin and Doom of Ungodly People

³Dear friends, although I was very eager to write to you about the salvation we share, I felt compelled to write and urge you to contend for the faith that was once for all entrusted to God's holy people. ⁴For certain individuals whose condemnation was written about*ᵇ* long ago have secretly slipped in among you. They are ungodly people, who pervert the grace of our God into a license for immorality and deny Jesus Christ our only Sovereign and Lord.

⁵Though you already know all this, I want to remind you that the Lord*ᶜ* at one time delivered his people out of Egypt, but later destroyed those who did not believe. ⁶And the angels who did not keep their positions of authority but abandoned their proper dwelling—these he has kept in darkness, bound with everlasting chains for judgment on the great Day. ⁷In a similar way, Sodom and Gomorrah and the surrounding towns gave themselves up to sexual immorality and perversion. They serve

---

ᵃ 1 Or *by*; or *in*   *ᵇ* 4 Or *individuals who were marked out for condemnation*
ᶜ 5 Some early manuscripts *Jesus*

as an example of those who suffer the punishment of eternal fire.

⁸In the very same way, on the strength of their dreams these ungodly people pollute their own bodies, reject authority and heap abuse on celestial beings. ⁹But even the archangel Michael, when he was disputing with the devil about the body of Moses, did not himself dare to condemn him for slander but said, "The Lord rebuke you!"ᵃ ¹⁰Yet these people slander whatever they do not understand, and the very things they do understand by instinct—as irrational animals do—will destroy them.

¹¹Woe to them! They have taken the way of Cain; they have rushed for profit into Balaam's error; they have been destroyed in Korah's rebellion.

¹²These people are blemishes at your love feasts, eating with you without the slightest qualm— shepherds who feed only themselves. They are clouds without rain, blown along by the wind; autumn trees, without fruit and uprooted—twice dead. ¹³They are wild waves of the sea, foaming up their shame; wandering stars, for whom blackest darkness has been reserved forever.

¹⁴Enoch, the seventh from Adam, prophesied about them: "See, the Lord is coming with thousands upon thousands of his holy ones ¹⁵to judge everyone, and to convict all of them of all the ungodly acts they have committed in their ungodliness, and of all the defiant words ungodly sinners have spoken against him."ᵇ ¹⁶These people are grumblers and faultfinders; they follow their own evil desires; they boast about themselves and flatter others for their own advantage.

A Call to Persevere

¹⁷But, dear friends, remember what the apostles of our Lord Jesus Christ foretold. ¹⁸They said to you, "In the last times there will be scoffers who will follow their own ungodly desires." ¹⁹These are the people who divide you, who follow mere natural instincts and do not have the Spirit.

²⁰But you, dear friends, by building yourselves up in your most holy faith and praying in the Holy Spirit, ²¹keep yourselves in God's love as you wait for the mercy of our Lord Jesus Christ to bring you to eternal life.

²²Be merciful to those who doubt; ²³save others by snatching them from the fire; to others show mercy, mixed with fear— hating even the clothing stained by corrupted flesh.ᶜ

ᵃ 9 Jude is alluding to the Jewish *Testament of Moses* (approximately the first century A.D.). ᵇ 14,15 From the Jewish *First Book of Enoch* (approximately the first century B.C.) ᶜ 22,23 The Greek manuscripts of these verses vary at several points.

Doxology

24 To him who is able to keep you from stumbling and to present you before his glorious presence without fault and with great joy— 25 to the only God our Savior be glory, majesty, power and authority, through Jesus Christ our Lord, before all ages, now and forevermore! Amen.

Revelation

Introduction:

The apostle John wrote the book of Revelation during his exile on the island of Patmos. John's purpose in writing this book was to give hope and encouragement to the Christians who were suffering severe persecution for their faith in Jesus Christ. These Christians needed to know that God controls everything that happens here on earth.

Through imagery and symbols, John makes one thing very clear: Jesus Christ is the Lord and ruler over everyone and everything — even powerful human governments. Christ is clearly in control and will someday judge and punish what is evil, even Satan. He will also establish an everlasting kingdom with a new heaven and a new earth.

Outline of contents:

Christ reveals himself to John (1:1–20)
Letters to the seven churches (2:1–3:22)
The heavenly throne (4:1–5:14)
The seven seals (6:1–8:5)
The seven trumpets (8:6–11:19)
Seven more signs (12:1–14:20)
The bowls of wrath (15:1–16:21)
Babylon judged (17:1–19:10)
Beast and false prophet judged (19:11–21)
Satan judged (20:1–3)
Thousand-year reign (20:4–6)
Rebellion and final judgment (20:7–15)
New heaven, new earth, new Jerusalem (21:1–22:5)
Conclusion (22:6–21)

Prologue

1 The revelation from Jesus Christ, which God gave him to show his servants what must soon take place. He made it known by sending his angel to his servant John, ²who testifies to everything he saw — that is, the word of God and the testimony of Jesus Christ. ³Blessed is the one who reads aloud the words of this prophecy, and blessed are those who hear it and take to heart what is written in it, because the time is near.

Greetings and Doxology

[4]John,

To the seven churches in the province of Asia:

Grace and peace to you from him who is, and who was, and who is to come, and from the seven spirits[a] before his throne, [5]and from Jesus Christ, who is the faithful witness, the firstborn from the dead, and the ruler of the kings of the earth.

To him who loves us and has freed us from our sins by his blood, [6]and has made us to be a kingdom and priests to serve his God and Father — to him be glory and power for ever and ever! Amen.

[7]"Look, he is coming with the
    clouds,"[b]
  and "every eye will see him,
  even those who pierced him";
  and all peoples on earth
    "will mourn because of
    him."[c]

        So shall it be! Amen.

[8]"I am the Alpha and the Omega," says the Lord God, "who is, and who was, and who is to come, the Almighty."

John's Vision of Christ

[9]I, John, your brother and companion in the suffering and kingdom and patient endurance that are ours in Jesus, was on the island of Patmos because of the word of God and the testimony of Jesus. [10]On the Lord's Day I was in the Spirit, and I heard behind me a loud voice like a trumpet, [11]which said: "Write on a scroll what you see and send it to the seven churches: to Ephesus, Smyrna, Pergamum, Thyatira, Sardis, Philadelphia and Laodicea."

[12]I turned around to see the voice that was speaking to me. And when I turned I saw seven golden lampstands, [13]and among the lampstands was someone like a son of man,[d] dressed in a robe reaching down to his feet and with a golden sash around his chest. [14]The hair on his head was white like wool, as white as snow, and his eyes were like blazing fire. [15]His feet were like bronze glowing in a furnace, and his voice was like the sound of rushing waters. [16]In his right hand he held seven stars, and coming out of his mouth was a sharp, double-edged sword. His face was like the sun shining in all its brilliance.

[17]When I saw him, I fell at his feet as though dead. Then he placed his right hand on me and said: "Do not be afraid. I am the First and the Last. [18]I am the Living One; I was dead, and now look, I am alive for ever and ever! And I hold the keys of death and Hades.

[a] 4 That is, the sevenfold Spirit   [b] 7 Daniel 7:13   [c] 7 Zech. 12:10   [d] 13 See Daniel 7:13.

19 "Write, therefore, what you have seen, what is now and what will take place later. 20 The mystery of the seven stars that you saw in my right hand and of the seven golden lampstands is this: The seven stars are the angels[a] of the seven churches, and the seven lampstands are the seven churches.

To the Church in Ephesus

2 "To the angel[b] of the church in Ephesus write:

These are the words of him who holds the seven stars in his right hand and walks among the seven golden lampstands. 2 I know your deeds, your hard work and your perseverance. I know that you cannot tolerate wicked people, that you have tested those who claim to be apostles but are not, and have found them false. 3 You have persevered and have endured hardships for my name, and have not grown weary.

4 Yet I hold this against you: You have forsaken the love you had at first. 5 Consider how far you have fallen! Repent and do the things you did at first. If you do not repent, I will come to you and remove your lampstand from its place. 6 But you have this in your favor: You hate the practices of the Nicolaitans, which I also hate.

7 Whoever has ears, let them hear what the Spirit says to the churches. To the one who is victorious, I will give the right to eat from the tree of life, which is in the paradise of God.

To the Church in Smyrna

8 "To the angel of the church in Smyrna write:

These are the words of him who is the First and the Last, who died and came to life again. 9 I know your afflictions and your poverty — yet you are rich! I know about the slander of those who say they are Jews and are not, but are a synagogue of Satan. 10 Do not be afraid of what you are about to suffer. I tell you, the devil will put some of you in prison to test you, and you will suffer persecution for ten days. Be faithful, even to the point of death, and I will give you life as your victor's crown.

11 Whoever has ears, let them hear what the Spirit says to the churches. The one who is victorious will not be hurt at all by the second death.

To the Church in Pergamum

12 "To the angel of the church in Pergamum write:

These are the words of him who has the sharp, double-

---

[a] 20 Or *messengers*   [b] 1 Or *messenger*; also in verses 8, 12 and 18

edged sword. ¹³I know where you live—where Satan has his throne. Yet you remain true to my name. You did not renounce your faith in me, not even in the days of Antipas, my faithful witness, who was put to death in your city—where Satan lives.

¹⁴Nevertheless, I have a few things against you: There are some among you who hold to the teaching of Balaam, who taught Balak to entice the Israelites to sin so that they ate food sacrificed to idols and committed sexual immorality. ¹⁵Likewise, you also have those who hold to the teaching of the Nicolaitans. ¹⁶Repent therefore! Otherwise, I will soon come to you and will fight against them with the sword of my mouth.

¹⁷Whoever has ears, let them hear what the Spirit says to the churches. To the one who is victorious, I will give some of the hidden manna. I will also give that person a white stone with a new name written on it, known only to the one who receives it.

To the Church in Thyatira

¹⁸"To the angel of the church in Thyatira write:

These are the words of the Son of God, whose eyes are like blazing fire and whose feet are like burnished bronze. ¹⁹I know your deeds, your love and faith, your service and perseverance, and that you are now doing more than you did at first.

²⁰Nevertheless, I have this against you: You tolerate that woman Jezebel, who calls herself a prophet. By her teaching she misleads my servants into sexual immorality and the eating of food sacrificed to idols. ²¹I have given her time to repent of her immorality, but she is unwilling. ²²So I will cast her on a bed of suffering, and I will make those who commit adultery with her suffer intensely, unless they repent of her ways. ²³I will strike her children dead. Then all the churches will know that I am he who searches hearts and minds, and I will repay each of you according to your deeds.

²⁴Now I say to the rest of you in Thyatira, to you who do not hold to her teaching and have not learned Satan's so-called deep secrets, 'I will not impose any other burden on you, ²⁵except to hold on to what you have until I come.'

²⁶To the one who is victorious and does my will to the end, I will give authority over the nations— ²⁷that one 'will rule them with an iron

scepter and will dash them to pieces like pottery'[a] — just as I have received authority from my Father. [28]I will also give that one the morning star. [29]Whoever has ears, let them hear what the Spirit says to the churches.

To the Church in Sardis

3 "To the angel[b] of the church in Sardis write:

These are the words of him who holds the seven spirits[c] of God and the seven stars. I know your deeds; you have a reputation of being alive, but you are dead. [2]Wake up! Strengthen what remains and is about to die, for I have found your deeds unfinished in the sight of my God. [3]Remember, therefore, what you have received and heard; hold it fast, and repent. But if you do not wake up, I will come like a thief, and you will not know at what time I will come to you.

[4]Yet you have a few people in Sardis who have not soiled their clothes. They will walk with me, dressed in white, for they are worthy. [5]The one who is victorious will, like them, be dressed in white. I will never blot out the name of that person from the book of life, but will acknowledge that name before my Father and his angels. [6]Whoever has ears, let them hear what the Spirit says to the churches.

To the Church in Philadelphia

[7]"To the angel of the church in Philadelphia write:

These are the words of him who is holy and true, who holds the key of David. What he opens no one can shut, and what he shuts no one can open. [8]I know your deeds. See, I have placed before you an open door that no one can shut. I know that you have little strength, yet you have kept my word and have not denied my name. [9]I will make those who are of the synagogue of Satan, who claim to be Jews though they are not, but are liars — I will make them come and fall down at your feet and acknowledge that I have loved you. [10]Since you have kept my command to endure patiently, I will also keep you from the hour of trial that is going to come on the whole world to test the inhabitants of the earth.

[11]I am coming soon. Hold on to what you have, so that no one will take your crown. [12]The one who is victorious I will make a pillar in the temple of my God. Never again

---

[a] 27 Psalm 2:9   [b] 1 Or *messenger*; also in verses 7 and 14   [c] 1 That is, the sevenfold Spirit

will they leave it. I will write on them the name of my God and the name of the city of my God, the new Jerusalem, which is coming down out of heaven from my God; and I will also write on them my new name. ¹³Whoever has ears, let them hear what the Spirit says to the churches.

To the Church in Laodicea

¹⁴"To the angel of the church in Laodicea write:

These are the words of the Amen, the faithful and true witness, the ruler of God's creation. ¹⁵I know your deeds, that you are neither cold nor hot. I wish you were either one or the other! ¹⁶So, because you are lukewarm—neither hot nor cold—I am about to spit you out of my mouth. ¹⁷You say, 'I am rich; I have acquired wealth and do not need a thing.' But you do not realize that you are wretched, pitiful, poor, blind and naked. ¹⁸I counsel you to buy from me gold refined in the fire, so you can become rich; and white clothes to wear, so you can cover your shameful nakedness; and salve to put on your eyes, so you can see.

¹⁹Those whom I love I rebuke and discipline. So be earnest and repent. ²⁰Here I am! I stand at the door and knock. If anyone hears my voice and opens the door, I will come in and eat with that person, and they with me.

²¹To the one who is victorious, I will give the right to sit with me on my throne, just as I was victorious and sat down with my Father on his throne. ²²Whoever has ears, let them hear what the Spirit says to the churches."

The Throne in Heaven

4 After this I looked, and there before me was a door standing open in heaven. And the voice I had first heard speaking to me like a trumpet said, "Come up here, and I will show you what must take place after this." ²At once I was in the Spirit, and there before me was a throne in heaven with someone sitting on it. ³And the one who sat there had the appearance of jasper and ruby. A rainbow that shone like an emerald encircled the throne. ⁴Surrounding the throne were twenty-four other thrones, and seated on them were twenty-four elders. They were dressed in white and had crowns of gold on their heads. ⁵From the throne came flashes of lightning, rumblings and peals of thunder. In front of the throne, seven lamps were blazing. These are the seven spirits*ᵃ* of God. ⁶Also in front

---

ᵃ 5 That is, the sevenfold Spirit

of the throne there was what looked like a sea of glass, clear as crystal.

In the center, around the throne, were four living creatures, and they were covered with eyes, in front and in back. [7] The first living creature was like a lion, the second was like an ox, the third had a face like a man, the fourth was like a flying eagle. [8] Each of the four living creatures had six wings and was covered with eyes all around, even under its wings. Day and night they never stop saying:

"'Holy, holy, holy
is the Lord God Almighty,'[a]
who was, and is, and is to come."

[9] Whenever the living creatures give glory, honor and thanks to him who sits on the throne and who lives for ever and ever, [10] the twenty-four elders fall down before him who sits on the throne and worship him who lives for ever and ever. They lay their crowns before the throne and say:

[11] "You are worthy, our Lord and God,
to receive glory and honor and power,
for you created all things,
and by your will they were created
and have their being."

The Scroll and the Lamb

5 Then I saw in the right hand of him who sat on the throne a scroll with writing on both sides and sealed with seven seals. [2] And I saw a mighty angel proclaiming in a loud voice, "Who is worthy to break the seals and open the scroll?" [3] But no one in heaven or on earth or under the earth could open the scroll or even look inside it. [4] I wept and wept because no one was found who was worthy to open the scroll or look inside. [5] Then one of the elders said to me, "Do not weep! See, the Lion of the tribe of Judah, the Root of David, has triumphed. He is able to open the scroll and its seven seals."

[6] Then I saw a Lamb, looking as if it had been slain, standing at the center of the throne, encircled by the four living creatures and the elders. The Lamb had seven horns and seven eyes, which are the seven spirits[b] of God sent out into all the earth. [7] He went and took the scroll from the right hand of him who sat on the throne. [8] And when he had taken it, the four living creatures and the twenty-four elders fell down before the Lamb. Each one had a harp and they were holding golden bowls full of incense, which are the prayers of God's people. [9] And they sang a new song, saying:

---

[a] 8 Isaiah 6:3   [b] 6 That is, the sevenfold Spirit

"You are worthy to take the
scroll
and to open its seals,
because you were slain,
and with your blood you
purchased for God
persons from every tribe and
language and people and
nation.
[10] You have made them to be a
kingdom and priests to
serve our God,
and they will reign[a] on the
earth."

[11] Then I looked and heard the voice of many angels, numbering thousands upon thousands, and ten thousand times ten thousand. They encircled the throne and the living creatures and the elders. [12] In a loud voice they were saying:

"Worthy is the Lamb, who was
slain,
to receive power and
wealth and wisdom and
strength
and honor and glory and
praise!"

[13] Then I heard every creature in heaven and on earth and under the earth and on the sea, and all that is in them, saying:

"To him who sits on the throne
and to the Lamb
be praise and honor and
glory and power,
for ever and ever!"

[14] The four living creatures said, "Amen," and the elders fell down and worshiped.

The Seals

6 I watched as the Lamb opened the first of the seven seals. Then I heard one of the four living creatures say in a voice like thunder, "Come!" [2] I looked, and there before me was a white horse! Its rider held a bow, and he was given a crown, and he rode out as a conqueror bent on conquest.

[3] When the Lamb opened the second seal, I heard the second living creature say, "Come!" [4] Then another horse came out, a fiery red one. Its rider was given power to take peace from the earth and to make people kill each other. To him was given a large sword.

[5] When the Lamb opened the third seal, I heard the third living creature say, "Come!" I looked, and there before me was a black horse! Its rider was holding a pair of scales in his hand. [6] Then I heard what sounded like a voice among the four living creatures, saying, "Two pounds[b] of wheat for a day's wages,[c] and six pounds[b] of barley for a day's wages,[d] and do not damage the oil and the wine!"

[7] When the Lamb opened the fourth seal, I heard the voice of

---

[a] 10 Some manuscripts *they reign*   [b] 6 Or about 1 kilogram   [c] 6 Greek *a*
denarius   [d] 6 Or about 3 kilograms

the fourth living creature say, "Come!" [8]I looked, and there before me was a pale horse! Its rider was named Death, and Hades was following close behind him. They were given power over a fourth of the earth to kill by sword, famine and plague, and by the wild beasts of the earth.

[9]When he opened the fifth seal, I saw under the altar the souls of those who had been slain because of the word of God and the testimony they had maintained. [10]They called out in a loud voice, "How long, Sovereign Lord, holy and true, until you judge the inhabitants of the earth and avenge our blood?" [11]Then each of them was given a white robe, and they were told to wait a little longer, until the full number of their fellow servants, their brothers and sisters,[a] were killed just as they had been.

[12]I watched as he opened the sixth seal. There was a great earthquake. The sun turned black like sackcloth made of goat hair, the whole moon turned blood red, [13]and the stars in the sky fell to earth, as figs drop from a fig tree when shaken by a strong wind. [14]The heavens receded like a scroll being rolled up, and every mountain and island was removed from its place.

[15]Then the kings of the earth, the princes, the generals, the rich, the mighty, and everyone else, both slave and free, hid in caves and among the rocks of the mountains. [16]They called to the mountains and the rocks, "Fall on us and hide us[b] from the face of him who sits on the throne and from the wrath of the Lamb! [17]For the great day of their[c] wrath has come, and who can withstand it?"

144,000 Sealed

7 After this I saw four angels standing at the four corners of the earth, holding back the four winds of the earth to prevent any wind from blowing on the land or on the sea or on any tree. [2]Then I saw another angel coming up from the east, having the seal of the living God. He called out in a loud voice to the four angels who had been given power to harm the land and the sea: [3]"Do not harm the land or the sea or the trees until we put a seal on the foreheads of the servants of our God." [4]Then I heard the number of those who were sealed: 144,000 from all the tribes of Israel.

[5]From the tribe of Judah 12,000 were sealed,
  from the tribe of Reuben 12,000,
  from the tribe of Gad 12,000,

---

[a] 11 The Greek word for *brothers and sisters* (*adelphoi*) refers here to believers, both men and women, as part of God's family; also in 12:10; 19:10. [b] 16 See Hosea 10:8. [c] 17 Some manuscripts *his*

⁶from the tribe of Asher
12,000,

from the tribe of Naphtali
12,000,

from the tribe of Manasseh
12,000,

⁷from the tribe of Simeon
12,000,

from the tribe of Levi 12,000,

from the tribe of Issachar
12,000,

⁸from the tribe of Zebulun
12,000,

from the tribe of Joseph
12,000,

from the tribe of Benjamin
12,000.

The Great Multitude in White Robes

⁹After this I looked, and there before me was a great multitude that no one could count, from every nation, tribe, people and language, standing before the throne and before the Lamb. They were wearing white robes and were holding palm branches in their hands. ¹⁰And they cried out in a loud voice:

"Salvation belongs to our God,
who sits on the throne,
and to the Lamb."

¹¹All the angels were standing around the throne and around the elders and the four living creatures. They fell down on their faces before the throne and worshiped God, ¹²saying:

"Amen!
Praise and glory
and wisdom and thanks and
honor
and power and strength
be to our God for ever and
ever.
Amen!"

¹³Then one of the elders asked me, "These in white robes — who are they, and where did they come from?"

¹⁴I answered, "Sir, you know."

And he said, "These are they who have come out of the great tribulation; they have washed their robes and made them white in the blood of the Lamb. ¹⁵Therefore,

"they are before the throne of
God
and serve him day and night
in his temple;
and he who sits on the throne
will shelter them with his
presence.
¹⁶'Never again will they hunger;
never again will they thirst.
The sun will not beat down on
them,'ᵃ
nor any scorching heat.
¹⁷For the Lamb at the center of
the throne
will be their shepherd;
'he will lead them to springs of
living water.'ᵃ
'And God will wipe away
every tear from their
eyes.'ᵇ"

ᵃ 16,17 Isaiah 49:10   ᵇ 17 Isaiah 25:8

The Seventh Seal and the Golden Censer

8 When he opened the seventh seal, there was silence in heaven for about half an hour.

² And I saw the seven angels who stand before God, and seven trumpets were given to them.

³ Another angel, who had a golden censer, came and stood at the altar. He was given much incense to offer, with the prayers of all God's people, on the golden altar in front of the throne. ⁴ The smoke of the incense, together with the prayers of God's people, went up before God from the angel's hand. ⁵ Then the angel took the censer, filled it with fire from the altar, and hurled it on the earth; and there came peals of thunder, rumblings, flashes of lightning and an earthquake.

The Trumpets

⁶ Then the seven angels who had the seven trumpets prepared to sound them.

⁷ The first angel sounded his trumpet, and there came hail and fire mixed with blood, and it was hurled down on the earth. A third of the earth was burned up, a third of the trees were burned up, and all the green grass was burned up.

⁸ The second angel sounded his trumpet, and something like a huge mountain, all ablaze, was thrown into the sea. A third of the sea turned into blood, ⁹ a third of the living creatures in the sea died, and a third of the ships were destroyed.

¹⁰ The third angel sounded his trumpet, and a great star, blazing like a torch, fell from the sky on a third of the rivers and on the springs of water — ¹¹ the name of the star is Wormwood.[a] A third of the waters turned bitter, and many people died from the waters that had become bitter.

¹² The fourth angel sounded his trumpet, and a third of the sun was struck, a third of the moon, and a third of the stars, so that a third of them turned dark. A third of the day was without light, and also a third of the night.

¹³ As I watched, I heard an eagle that was flying in midair call out in a loud voice: "Woe! Woe! Woe to the inhabitants of the earth, because of the trumpet blasts about to be sounded by the other three angels!"

9 The fifth angel sounded his trumpet, and I saw a star that had fallen from the sky to the earth. The star was given the key to the shaft of the Abyss. ² When he opened the Abyss, smoke rose from it like the smoke from a gigantic furnace. The sun and sky were darkened by the smoke from the Abyss. ³ And out of the smoke locusts came down on the earth and were given power like that of scorpions of the earth.

---

¹ Wormwood is a bitter substance.

[4] They were told not to harm the grass of the earth or any plant or tree, but only those people who did not have the seal of God on their foreheads. [5] They were not allowed to kill them but only to torture them for five months. And the agony they suffered was like that of the sting of a scorpion when it strikes. [6] During those days people will seek death but will not find it; they will long to die, but death will elude them.

[7] The locusts looked like horses prepared for battle. On their heads they wore something like crowns of gold, and their faces resembled human faces. [8] Their hair was like women's hair, and their teeth were like lions' teeth. [9] They had breastplates like breastplates of iron, and the sound of their wings was like the thundering of many horses and chariots rushing into battle. [10] They had tails with stingers, like scorpions, and in their tails they had power to torment people for five months. [11] They had as king over them the angel of the Abyss, whose name in Hebrew is Abaddon and in Greek is Apollyon (that is, Destroyer).

[12] The first woe is past; two other woes are yet to come.

[13] The sixth angel sounded his trumpet, and I heard a voice coming from the four horns of the golden altar that is before God. [14] It said to the sixth angel who had the trumpet, "Release the four angels who are bound at the great river Euphrates." [15] And the four angels who had been kept ready for this very hour and day and month and year were released to kill a third of mankind. [16] The number of the mounted troops was twice ten thousand times ten thousand. I heard their number.

[17] The horses and riders I saw in my vision looked like this: Their breastplates were fiery red, dark blue, and yellow as sulfur. The heads of the horses resembled the heads of lions, and out of their mouths came fire, smoke and sulfur. [18] A third of mankind was killed by the three plagues of fire, smoke and sulfur that came out of their mouths. [19] The power of the horses was in their mouths and in their tails; for their tails were like snakes, having heads with which they inflict injury.

[20] The rest of mankind who were not killed by these plagues still did not repent of the work of their hands; they did not stop worshiping demons, and idols of gold, silver, bronze, stone and wood — idols that cannot see or hear or walk. [21] Nor did they repent of their murders, their magic arts, their sexual immorality or their thefts.

The Angel and the Little Scroll

10 Then I saw another mighty angel coming down from heaven. He was robed in a cloud, with a rainbow above his head; his face was like the sun, and his legs were like fiery pillars. ²He was holding a little scroll, which lay open in his hand. He planted his right foot on the sea and his left foot on the land, ³and he gave a loud shout like the roar of a lion. When he shouted, the voices of the seven thunders spoke. ⁴And when the seven thunders spoke, I was about to write; but I heard a voice from heaven say, "Seal up what the seven thunders have said and do not write it down."

⁵Then the angel I had seen standing on the sea and on the land raised his right hand to heaven. ⁶And he swore by him who lives for ever and ever, who created the heavens and all that is in them, the earth and all that is in it, and the sea and all that is in it, and said, "There will be no more delay! ⁷But in the days when the seventh angel is about to sound his trumpet, the mystery of God will be accomplished, just as he announced to his servants the prophets."

⁸Then the voice that I had heard from heaven spoke to me once more: "Go, take the scroll that lies open in the hand of the angel who is standing on the sea and on the land."

⁹So I went to the angel and asked him to give me the little scroll. He said to me, "Take it and eat it. It will turn your stomach sour, but 'in your mouth it will be as sweet as honey.'ᵃ" ¹⁰I took the little scroll from the angel's hand and ate it. It tasted as sweet as honey in my mouth, but when I had eaten it, my stomach turned sour. ¹¹Then I was told, "You must prophesy again about many peoples, nations, languages and kings."

The Two Witnesses

11 I was given a reed like a measuring rod and was told, "Go and measure the temple of God and the altar, with its worshipers. ²But exclude the outer court; do not measure it, because it has been given to the Gentiles. They will trample on the holy city for 42 months. ³And I will appoint my two witnesses, and they will prophesy for 1,260 days, clothed in sackcloth." ⁴They are "the two olive trees" and the two lampstands, and "they stand before the Lord of the earth."ᵇ ⁵If anyone tries to harm them, fire comes from their mouths and devours their enemies. This is how anyone who wants to harm them must die. ⁶They have power to shut up the heavens so that it will not rain during the time they are prophesying; and they have power to turn the waters into blood and to strike the earth with every kind of plague as often as they want.

⁷Now when they have finished their testimony, the beast that

Ezek. 3:3   ᵇ 4 See Zech. 4:3,11,14.

comes up from the Abyss will attack them, and overpower and kill them. **8** Their bodies will lie in the public square of the great city — which is figuratively called Sodom and Egypt — where also their Lord was crucified. **9** For three and a half days some from every people, tribe, language and nation will gaze on their bodies and refuse them burial. **10** The inhabitants of the earth will gloat over them and will celebrate by sending each other gifts, because these two prophets had tormented those who live on the earth.

11 But after the three and a half days the breath*a* of life from God entered them, and they stood on their feet, and terror struck those who saw them. **12** Then they heard a loud voice from heaven saying to them, "Come up here." And they went up to heaven in a cloud, while their enemies looked on.

13 At that very hour there was a severe earthquake and a tenth of the city collapsed. Seven thousand people were killed in the earthquake, and the survivors were terrified and gave glory to the God of heaven.

14 The second woe has passed; the third woe is coming soon.

The Seventh Trumpet

15 The seventh angel sounded his trumpet, and there were loud voices in heaven, which said:

> "The kingdom of the world has become
> the kingdom of our Lord and of his Messiah,
> and he will reign for ever and ever."

16 And the twenty-four elders, who were seated on their thrones before God, fell on their faces and worshiped God, **17** saying:

> "We give thanks to you, Lord God Almighty,
> the One who is and who was,
> because you have taken your great power
> and have begun to reign.
> **18** The nations were angry,
> and your wrath has come.
> The time has come for judging the dead,
> and for rewarding your servants the prophets
> and your people who revere your name,
> both great and small —
> and for destroying those who destroy the earth."

19 Then God's temple in heaven was opened, and within his temple was seen the ark of his covenant. And there came flashes of lightning, rumblings, peals of thunder, an earthquake and a severe hailstorm.

The Woman and the Dragon

12 A great sign appeared in heaven: a woman clothed

a 11 Or *Spirit* (see Ezek. 37:5,14)

with the sun, with the moon under her feet and a crown of twelve stars on her head. **2** She was pregnant and cried out in pain as she was about to give birth. **3** Then another sign appeared in heaven: an enormous red dragon with seven heads and ten horns and seven crowns on its heads. **4** Its tail swept a third of the stars out of the sky and flung them to the earth. The dragon stood in front of the woman who was about to give birth, so that it might devour her child the moment he was born. **5** She gave birth to a son, a male child, who "will rule all the nations with an iron scepter."*a* And her child was snatched up to God and to his throne. **6** The woman fled into the wilderness to a place prepared for her by God, where she might be taken care of for 1,260 days.

7 Then war broke out in heaven. Michael and his angels fought against the dragon, and the dragon and his angels fought back. **8** But he was not strong enough, and they lost their place in heaven. **9** The great dragon was hurled down — that ancient serpent called the devil, or Satan, who leads the whole world astray. He was hurled to the earth, and his angels with him.

10 Then I heard a loud voice in heaven say:

"Now have come the salvation
  and the power
 and the kingdom of our God,

and the authority of his
  Messiah.
For the accuser of our brothers
  and sisters,
 who accuses them before
  our God day and night,
 has been hurled down.
11 They triumphed over him
  by the blood of the Lamb
 and by the word of their
  testimony;
 they did not love their lives so
  much
 as to shrink from death.
12 Therefore rejoice, you heavens
  and you who dwell in them!
But woe to the earth and the
  sea,
 because the devil has gone
  down to you!
He is filled with fury,
 because he knows that his
  time is short."

13 When the dragon saw that he had been hurled to the earth, he pursued the woman who had given birth to the male child. **14** The woman was given the two wings of a great eagle, so that she might fly to the place prepared for her in the wilderness, where she would be taken care of for a time, times and half a time, out of the serpent's reach. **15** Then from his mouth the serpent spewed water like a river, to overtake the woman and sweep her away with the torrent. **16** But the earth helped the woman by opening its mouth and swallowing the river that the dragon had spewed out of his mouth. ¹⁷Then the dragon was enraged at the woman and went off to wage war against the rest of her offspring—those who keep God's commands and hold fast their testimony about Jesus.

The Beast out of the Sea

13 The dragon^a stood on the shore of the sea. And I saw a beast coming out of the sea. It had ten horns and seven heads, with ten crowns on its horns, and on each head a blasphemous name. ²The beast I saw resembled a leopard, but had feet like those of a bear and a mouth like that of a lion. The dragon gave the beast his power and his throne and great authority. ³One of the heads of the beast seemed to have had a fatal wound, but the fatal wound had been healed. The whole world was filled with wonder and followed the beast. ⁴People worshiped the dragon because he had given authority to the beast, and they also worshiped the beast and asked, "Who is like the beast? Who can wage war against it?"

⁵The beast was given a mouth to utter proud words and blasphemies and to exercise its authority for forty-two months. ⁶It opened its mouth to blaspheme God, and to slander his name and his dwelling place and those who live in heaven. ⁷It was given power to wage war against God's holy people and to conquer them. And it was given authority over every tribe, people, language and nation. ⁸All inhabitants of the earth will worship the beast— all whose names have not been written in the Lamb's book of life, the Lamb who was slain from the creation of the world.^b

⁹Whoever has ears, let them hear.

¹⁰"If anyone is to go into
captivity,
into captivity they will go.
If anyone is to be killed^c with
the sword,
with the sword they will be
killed."^d

This calls for patient endurance and faithfulness on the part of God's people.

The Beast out of the Earth

¹¹Then I saw a second beast, coming out of the earth. It had two horns like a lamb, but it spoke like a dragon. ¹²It exercised all the authority of the first beast on its behalf, and made the earth and its inhabitants worship the first beast, whose fatal wound had been healed. ¹³And it performed great signs, even causing fire to come down from heaven to

^a 1 Some manuscripts *And I*   ^b 8 Or *written from the creation of the world in the book of life belonging to the Lamb who was slain*   ^c 10 Some manuscripts *anyone kills*   ^d 10 Jer. 15:2

the earth in full view of the people. **14** Because of the signs it was given power to perform on behalf of the first beast, it deceived the inhabitants of the earth. It ordered them to set up an image in honor of the beast who was wounded by the sword and yet lived. **15** The second beast was given power to give breath to the image of the first beast, so that the image could speak and cause all who refused to worship the image to be killed. **16** It also forced all people, great and small, rich and poor, free and slave, to receive a mark on their right hands or on their foreheads, **17** so that they could not buy or sell unless they had the mark, which is the name of the beast or the number of its name.

18 This calls for wisdom. Let the person who has insight calculate the number of the beast, for it is the number of a man.[a] That number is 666.

The Lamb and the 144,000

14 Then I looked, and there before me was the Lamb, standing on Mount Zion, and with him 144,000 who had his name and his Father's name written on their foreheads. **2** And I heard a sound from heaven like the roar of rushing waters and like a loud peal of thunder. The sound I heard was like that of harpists playing their harps.

3 And they sang a new song before the throne and before the four living creatures and the elders. No one could learn the song except the 144,000 who had been redeemed from the earth. **4** These are those who did not defile themselves with women, for they remained virgins. They follow the Lamb wherever he goes. They were purchased from among mankind and offered as firstfruits to God and the Lamb. **5** No lie was found in their mouths; they are blameless.

The Three Angels

6 Then I saw another angel flying in midair, and he had the eternal gospel to proclaim to those who live on the earth — to every nation, tribe, language and people. **7** He said in a loud voice, "Fear God and give him glory, because the hour of his judgment has come. Worship him who made the heavens, the earth, the sea and the springs of water."

8 A second angel followed and said, " 'Fallen! Fallen is Babylon the Great,'[b] which made all the nations drink the maddening wine of her adulteries."

9 A third angel followed them and said in a loud voice: "If anyone worships the beast and its image and receives its mark on their forehead or on their hand, **10** they, too, will drink the wine of God's fury, which has been poured full

---

[a] Or *is humanity's number*   [b] 8 Isaiah 21:9

strength into the cup of his wrath. They will be tormented with burning sulfur in the presence of the holy angels and of the Lamb. [11] And the smoke of their torment will rise for ever and ever. There will be no rest day or night for those who worship the beast and its image, or for anyone who receives the mark of its name." [12] This calls for patient endurance on the part of the people of God who keep his commands and remain faithful to Jesus.

[13] Then I heard a voice from heaven say, "Write this: Blessed are the dead who die in the Lord from now on."

"Yes," says the Spirit, "they will rest from their labor, for their deeds will follow them."

Harvesting the Earth and Trampling the Winepress

[14] I looked, and there before me was a white cloud, and seated on the cloud was one like a son of man[a] with a crown of gold on his head and a sharp sickle in his hand. [15] Then another angel came out of the temple and called in a loud voice to him who was sitting on the cloud, "Take your sickle and reap, because the time to reap has come, for the harvest of the earth is ripe." [16] So he who was seated on the cloud swung his sickle over the earth, and the earth was harvested.

[17] Another angel came out of the temple in heaven, and he too had a sharp sickle. [18] Still another angel, who had charge of the fire, came from the altar and called in a loud voice to him who had the sharp sickle, "Take your sharp sickle and gather the clusters of grapes from the earth's vine, because its grapes are ripe." [19] The angel swung his sickle on the earth, gathered its grapes and threw them into the great winepress of God's wrath. [20] They were trampled in the winepress outside the city, and blood flowed out of the press, rising as high as the horses' bridles for a distance of 1,600 stadia.[b]

Seven Angels With Seven Plagues

15 I saw in heaven another great and marvelous sign: seven angels with the seven last plagues — last, because with them God's wrath is completed. [2] And I saw what looked like a sea of glass glowing with fire and, standing beside the sea, those who had been victorious over the beast and its image and over the number of its name. They held harps given them by God [3] and sang the song of God's servant Moses and of the Lamb:

"Great and marvelous are your deeds,
    Lord God Almighty.
Just and true are your ways,
    King of the nations.[c]

---

[a] 14 See Daniel 7:13.   [b] 20 That is, about 180 miles or about 300 kilometers
[c] 3 Some manuscripts *ages*

⁴Who will not fear you, Lord,
    and bring glory to your
        name?
For you alone are holy.
All nations will come
    and worship before you,
for your righteous acts have
        been revealed."ᵃ

⁵After this I looked, and I saw in heaven the temple — that is, the tabernacle of the covenant law — and it was opened. ⁶Out of the temple came the seven angels with the seven plagues. They were dressed in clean, shining linen and wore golden sashes around their chests. ⁷Then one of the four living creatures gave to the seven angels seven golden bowls filled with the wrath of God, who lives for ever and ever. ⁸And the temple was filled with smoke from the glory of God and from his power, and no one could enter the temple until the seven plagues of the seven angels were completed.

The Seven Bowls of God's Wrath

16 Then I heard a loud voice from the temple saying to the seven angels, "Go, pour out the seven bowls of God's wrath on the earth."

²The first angel went and poured out his bowl on the land, and ugly, festering sores broke out on the people who had the mark of the beast and worshiped its image.

³The second angel poured out his bowl on the sea, and it turned into blood like that of a dead person, and every living thing in the sea died.

⁴The third angel poured out his bowl on the rivers and springs of water, and they became blood. ⁵Then I heard the angel in charge of the waters say:

"You are just in these
        judgments, O Holy One,
    you who are and who were;
⁶for they have shed the blood
        of your holy people and
        your prophets,
    and you have given them
        blood to drink as they
        deserve."

⁷And I heard the altar respond:

"Yes, Lord God Almighty,
    true and just are your
        judgments."

⁸The fourth angel poured out his bowl on the sun, and the sun was allowed to scorch people with fire. ⁹They were seared by the intense heat and they cursed the name of God, who had control over these plagues, but they refused to repent and glorify him. ¹⁰The fifth angel poured out his bowl on the throne of the beast, and its kingdom was plunged into darkness. People gnawed

⁴ 4 Phrases in this song are drawn from Psalm 111:2,3; Deut. 32:4; Jer. 10:7;
ᵃ ... 86:9; 98:2.

their tongues in agony [11] and cursed the God of heaven because of their pains and their sores, but they refused to repent of what they had done.

[12] The sixth angel poured out his bowl on the great river Euphrates, and its water was dried up to prepare the way for the kings from the East. [13] Then I saw three impure spirits that looked like frogs; they came out of the mouth of the dragon, out of the mouth of the beast and out of the mouth of the false prophet. [14] They are demonic spirits that perform signs, and they go out to the kings of the whole world, to gather them for the battle on the great day of God Almighty.

[15] "Look, I come like a thief! Blessed is the one who stays awake and remains clothed, so as not to go naked and be shamefully exposed."

[16] Then they gathered the kings together to the place that in Hebrew is called Armageddon.

[17] The seventh angel poured out his bowl into the air, and out of the temple came a loud voice from the throne, saying, "It is done!" [18] Then there came flashes of lightning, rumblings, peals of thunder and a severe earthquake. No earthquake like it has ever occurred since mankind has been on earth, so tremendous was the quake. [19] The great city split into three parts, and the cities of the nations collapsed. God remembered Babylon the Great and gave her the cup filled with the wine of the fury of his wrath. [20] Every island fled away and the mountains could not be found. [21] From the sky huge hailstones, each weighing about a hundred pounds,[a] fell on people. And they cursed God on account of the plague of hail, because the plague was so terrible.

Babylon, the Prostitute on the Beast

17 One of the seven angels who had the seven bowls came and said to me, "Come, I will show you the punishment of the great prostitute, who sits by many waters. [2] With her the kings of the earth committed adultery, and the inhabitants of the earth were intoxicated with the wine of her adulteries."

[3] Then the angel carried me away in the Spirit into a wilderness. There I saw a woman sitting on a scarlet beast that was covered with blasphemous names and had seven heads and ten horns. [4] The woman was dressed in purple and scarlet, and was glittering with gold, precious stones and pearls. She held a golden cup in her hand, filled with abominable things and the filth of her adulteries. [5] The name written on her forehead was a mystery:

---

a 21 Or about 45 kilograms

BABYLON THE GREAT
THE MOTHER OF PROSTITUTES
AND OF THE ABOMINATIONS OF
THE EARTH.

⁶I saw that the woman was drunk with the blood of God's holy people, the blood of those who bore testimony to Jesus.

When I saw her, I was greatly astonished. ⁷Then the angel said to me: "Why are you astonished? I will explain to you the mystery of the woman and of the beast she rides, which has the seven heads and ten horns. ⁸The beast, which you saw, once was, now is not, and yet will come up out of the Abyss and go to its destruction. The inhabitants of the earth whose names have not been written in the book of life from the creation of the world will be astonished when they see the beast, because it once was, now is not, and yet will come.

⁹"This calls for a mind with wisdom. The seven heads are seven hills on which the woman sits. ¹⁰They are also seven kings. Five have fallen, one is, the other has not yet come; but when he does come, he must remain for only a little while. ¹¹The beast who once was, and now is not, is an eighth king. He belongs to the seven and is going to his destruction.

¹²"The ten horns you saw are ten kings who have not yet received a kingdom, but who for one hour will receive authority as kings along with the beast. ¹³They have one purpose and will give their power and authority to the beast. ¹⁴They will wage war against the Lamb, but the Lamb will triumph over them because he is Lord of lords and King of kings — and with him will be his called, chosen and faithful followers."

¹⁵Then the angel said to me, "The waters you saw, where the prostitute sits, are peoples, multitudes, nations and languages. ¹⁶The beast and the ten horns you saw will hate the prostitute. They will bring her to ruin and leave her naked; they will eat her flesh and burn her with fire. ¹⁷For God has put it into their hearts to accomplish his purpose by agreeing to hand over to the beast their royal authority, until God's words are fulfilled. ¹⁸The woman you saw is the great city that rules over the kings of the earth."

Lament Over Fallen Babylon

18 After this I saw another angel coming down from heaven. He had great authority, and the earth was illuminated by his splendor. ²With a mighty voice he shouted:

"'Fallen! Fallen is Babylon the Great!'ᵃ
She has become a dwelling
for demons

and a haunt for every impure
spirit,
a haunt for every unclean
bird,
a haunt for every unclean
and detestable animal.
³For all the nations have drunk
the maddening wine of her
adulteries.
The kings of the earth
committed adultery with
her,
and the merchants of the
earth grew rich from her
excessive luxuries."

Warning to Escape Babylon's Judgment

⁴Then I heard another voice
from heaven say:

" 'Come out of her, my people,'ᵃ
so that you will not share in
her sins,
so that you will not receive
any of her plagues;
⁵for her sins are piled up to
heaven,
and God has remembered
her crimes.
⁶Give back to her as she has
given;
pay her back double for what
she has done.
Pour her a double portion
from her own cup.
⁷Give her as much torment and
grief
as the glory and luxury she
gave herself.

In her heart she boasts,
'I sit enthroned as queen.
I am not a widow;ᵇ
I will never mourn.'
⁸Therefore in one day her
plagues will overtake
her:
death, mourning and
famine.
She will be consumed by fire,
for mighty is the Lord God
who judges her.

Threefold Woe Over Babylon's Fall

⁹"When the kings of the earth
who committed adultery with
her and shared her luxury see
the smoke of her burning, they
will weep and mourn over her.
¹⁰Terrified at her torment, they
will stand far off and cry:

" 'Woe! Woe to you, great city,
you mighty city of Babylon!
In one hour your doom has
come!'

¹¹"The merchants of the earth
will weep and mourn over her
because no one buys their cargoes anymore — ¹²cargoes of
gold, silver, precious stones and
pearls; fine linen, purple, silk
and scarlet cloth; every sort of
citron wood, and articles of every
kind made of ivory, costly wood,
bronze, iron and marble; ¹³car-
goes of cinnamon and spice, of
incense, myrrh and frankincense, of wine and olive oil, of

ᵃ 4 Jer. 51:45   ᵇ 7 See Isaiah 47:7,8.

fine flour and wheat; cattle and sheep; horses and carriages; and human beings sold as slaves.

14 "They will say, 'The fruit you longed for is gone from you. All your luxury and splendor have vanished, never to be recovered.' 15 The merchants who sold these things and gained their wealth from her will stand far off, terrified at her torment. They will weep and mourn 16 and cry out:

> " 'Woe! Woe to you, great city,
> dressed in fine linen, purple and scarlet,
> and glittering with gold,
> precious stones and pearls!
> 17 In one hour such great wealth has been brought to ruin!'

"Every sea captain, and all who travel by ship, the sailors, and all who earn their living from the sea, will stand far off. 18 When they see the smoke of her burning, they will exclaim, 'Was there ever a city like this great city?' 19 They will throw dust on their heads, and with weeping and mourning cry out:

> " 'Woe! Woe to you, great city,
> where all who had ships on the sea
> became rich through her wealth!
> In one hour she has been brought to ruin!'

20 "Rejoice over her, you heavens!
Rejoice, you people of God!
Rejoice, apostles and prophets!
For God has judged her with the judgment she imposed on you."

The Finality of Babylon's Doom

21 Then a mighty angel picked up a boulder the size of a large millstone and threw it into the sea, and said:

> "With such violence
> the great city of Babylon will be thrown down,
> never to be found again.
> 22 The music of harpists and musicians, pipers and trumpeters,
> will never be heard in you again.
> No worker of any trade
> will ever be found in you again.
> The sound of a millstone
> will never be heard in you again.
> 23 The light of a lamp
> will never shine in you again.
> The voice of bridegroom and bride
> will never be heard in you again.
> Your merchants were the world's important people.
> By your magic spell all the nations were led astray.
> 24 In her was found the blood of prophets and of God's holy people,

of all who have been
    slaughtered on the
    earth."

Threefold Hallelujah Over Babylon's Fall

19 After this I heard what sounded like the roar of a great multitude in heaven shouting:

"Hallelujah!
Salvation and glory and power
    belong to our God,
2   for true and just are his
        judgments.
He has condemned the great
    prostitute
    who corrupted the earth by
        her adulteries.
He has avenged on her the
    blood of his servants."

3 And again they shouted:

"Hallelujah!
The smoke from her goes up
    for ever and ever."

4 The twenty-four elders and the four living creatures fell down and worshiped God, who was seated on the throne. And they cried:

"Amen, Hallelujah!"

5 Then a voice came from the throne, saying:

"Praise our God,
    all you his servants,
you who fear him,
    both great and small!"

6 Then I heard what sounded like a great multitude, like the roar of rushing waters and like loud peals of thunder, shouting:

"Hallelujah!
For our Lord God Almighty
    reigns.
7 Let us rejoice and be glad
    and give him glory!
For the wedding of the Lamb
    has come,
    and his bride has made
        herself ready.
8 Fine linen, bright and clean,
    was given her to wear."
(Fine linen stands for the righteous acts of God's holy people.)

9 Then the angel said to me, "Write this: Blessed are those who are invited to the wedding supper of the Lamb!" And he added, "These are the true words of God."

10 At this I fell at his feet to worship him. But he said to me, "Don't do that! I am a fellow servant with you and with your brothers and sisters who hold to the testimony of Jesus. Worship God! For it is the Spirit of prophecy who bears testimony to Jesus."

The Heavenly Warrior Defeats the Beast

11 I saw heaven standing open and there before me was a white horse, whose rider is called Faithful and True. With justice he judges and wages war. 12 His eyes are like blazing fire, and on his head are many crowns. He has a name written on him that no

one knows but he himself. [13] He is dressed in a robe dipped in blood, and his name is the Word of God. [14] The armies of heaven were following him, riding on white horses and dressed in fine linen, white and clean. [15] Coming out of his mouth is a sharp sword with which to strike down the nations. "He will rule them with an iron scepter."[a] He treads the winepress of the fury of the wrath of God Almighty. [16] On his robe and on his thigh he has this name written:

KING OF KINGS AND LORD
OF LORDS.

[17] And I saw an angel standing in the sun, who cried in a loud voice to all the birds flying in midair, "Come, gather together for the great supper of God, [18] so that you may eat the flesh of kings, generals, and the mighty, of horses and their riders, and the flesh of all people, free and slave, great and small."

[19] Then I saw the beast and the kings of the earth and their armies gathered together to wage war against the rider on the horse and his army. [20] But the beast was captured, and with it the false prophet who had performed the signs on its behalf. With these signs he had deluded those who had received the mark of the beast and worshiped its image. The two of them were thrown alive into the fiery lake of burning sulfur. [21] The rest were killed with the sword coming out of the mouth of the rider on the horse, and all the birds gorged themselves on their flesh.

The Thousand Years

20 And I saw an angel coming down out of heaven, having the key to the Abyss and holding in his hand a great chain. [2] He seized the dragon, that ancient serpent, who is the devil, or Satan, and bound him for a thousand years. [3] He threw him into the Abyss, and locked and sealed it over him, to keep him from deceiving the nations anymore until the thousand years were ended. After that, he must be set free for a short time.

[4] I saw thrones on which were seated those who had been given authority to judge. And I saw the souls of those who had been beheaded because of their testimony about Jesus and because of the word of God. They[b] had not worshiped the beast or its image and had not received its mark on their foreheads or their hands. They came to life and reigned with Christ a thousand years. [5] (The rest of the dead did not come to life until the thousand years were ended.) This is the first resurrection. [6] Blessed and holy are those who share in the first resurrection. The second death has no

Psalm 2:9   [b] 4 Or God; I also saw those who

power over them, but they will be priests of God and of Christ and will reign with him for a thousand years.

The Judgment of Satan

[7] When the thousand years are over, Satan will be released from his prison [8] and will go out to deceive the nations in the four corners of the earth — Gog and Magog — and to gather them for battle. In number they are like the sand on the seashore. [9] They marched across the breadth of the earth and surrounded the camp of God's people, the city he loves. But fire came down from heaven and devoured them. [10] And the devil, who deceived them, was thrown into the lake of burning sulfur, where the beast and the false prophet had been thrown. They will be tormented day and night for ever and ever.

The Judgment of the Dead

[11] Then I saw a great white throne and him who was seated on it. The earth and the heavens fled from his presence, and there was no place for them. [12] And I saw the dead, great and small, standing before the throne, and books were opened. Another book was opened, which is the book of life. The dead were judged according to what they had done as recorded in the books. [13] The sea gave up the dead that were in it, and death and Hades gave up the dead that were in them, and each person was judged according to what they had done. [14] Then death and Hades were thrown into the lake of fire. The lake of fire is the second death. [15] Anyone whose name was not found written in the book of life was thrown into the lake of fire.

A New Heaven and a New Earth

21 Then I saw "a new heaven and a new earth,"[a] for the first heaven and the first earth had passed away, and there was no longer any sea. [2] I saw the Holy City, the new Jerusalem, coming down out of heaven from God, prepared as a bride beautifully dressed for her husband. [3] And I heard a loud voice from the throne saying, "Look! God's dwelling place is now among the people, and he will dwell with them. They will be his people, and God himself will be with them and be their God. [4] 'He will wipe every tear from their eyes. There will be no more death'[b] or mourning or crying or pain, for the old order of things has passed away."

[5] He who was seated on the throne said, "I am making everything new!" Then he said, "Write this down, for these words are trustworthy and true."

[6] He said to me: "It is done. I am the Alpha and the Omega, the

---

[a] 1 Isaiah 65:17   [b] 4 Isaiah 25:8

Beginning and the End. To the thirsty I will give water without cost from the spring of the water of life. **7** Those who are victorious will inherit all this, and I will be their God and they will be my children. **8** But the cowardly, the unbelieving, the vile, the murderers, the sexually immoral, those who practice magic arts, the idolaters and all liars — they will be consigned to the fiery lake of burning sulfur. This is the second death."

The New Jerusalem, the Bride of the Lamb

9 One of the seven angels who had the seven bowls full of the seven last plagues came and said to me, "Come, I will show you the bride, the wife of the Lamb." **10** And he carried me away in the Spirit to a mountain great and high, and showed me the Holy City, Jerusalem, coming down out of heaven from God. **11** It shone with the glory of God, and its brilliance was like that of a very precious jewel, like a jasper, clear as crystal. **12** It had a great, high wall with twelve gates, and with twelve angels at the gates. On the gates were written the names of the twelve tribes of Israel. **13** There were three gates on the east, three on the north, three on the south and three on the west. **14** The wall of the city had twelve foundations, and on them were the names of the twelve apostles of the Lamb.

15 The angel who talked with me had a measuring rod of gold to measure the city, its gates and its walls. **16** The city was laid out like a square, as long as it was wide. He measured the city with the rod and found it to be 12,000 stadia*a* in length, and as wide and high as it is long. **17** The angel measured the wall using human measurement, and it was 144 cubits*b* thick.*c* **18** The wall was made of jasper, and the city of pure gold, as pure as glass. **19** The foundations of the city walls were decorated with every kind of precious stone. The first foundation was jasper, the second sapphire, the third agate, the fourth emerald, **20** the fifth onyx, the sixth ruby, the seventh chrysolite, the eighth beryl, the ninth topaz, the tenth turquoise, the eleventh jacinth, and the twelfth amethyst.*d* **21** The twelve gates were twelve pearls, each gate made of a single pearl. The great street of the city was of gold, as pure as transparent glass.

22 I did not see a temple in the city, because the Lord God Almighty and the Lamb are its temple. **23** The city does not need the sun or the moon to shine on it, for the glory of God gives it light,

---

a 16 That is, about 1,400 miles or about 2,200 kilometers   *b 17* That is, about 200 feet or about 65 meters   *c 17* Or *high*   *d 20* The precise identification of some of these precious stones is uncertain.

and the Lamb is its lamp. ²⁴The nations will walk by its light, and the kings of the earth will bring their splendor into it. ²⁵On no day will its gates ever be shut, for there will be no night there. ²⁶The glory and honor of the nations will be brought into it. ²⁷Nothing impure will ever enter it, nor will anyone who does what is shameful or deceitful, but only those whose names are written in the Lamb's book of life.

Eden Restored

22 Then the angel showed me the river of the water of life, as clear as crystal, flowing from the throne of God and of the Lamb ²down the middle of the great street of the city. On each side of the river stood the tree of life, bearing twelve crops of fruit, yielding its fruit every month. And the leaves of the tree are for the healing of the nations. ³No longer will there be any curse. The throne of God and of the Lamb will be in the city, and his servants will serve him. ⁴They will see his face, and his name will be on their foreheads. ⁵There will be no more night. They will not need the light of a lamp or the light of the sun, for the Lord God will give them light. And they will reign for ever and ever.

John and the Angel

⁶The angel said to me, "These words are trustworthy and true. The Lord, the God who inspires the prophets, sent his angel to show his servants the things that must soon take place."

⁷"Look, I am coming soon! Blessed is the one who keeps the words of the prophecy written in this scroll."

⁸I, John, am the one who heard and saw these things. And when I had heard and seen them, I fell down to worship at the feet of the angel who had been showing them to me. ⁹But he said to me, "Don't do that! I am a fellow servant with you and with your fellow prophets and with all who keep the words of this scroll. Worship God!"

¹⁰Then he told me, "Do not seal up the words of the prophecy of this scroll, because the time is near. ¹¹Let the one who does wrong continue to do wrong; let the vile person continue to be vile; let the one who does right continue to do right; and let the holy person continue to be holy."

Epilogue: Invitation and Warning

¹²"Look, I am coming soon! My reward is with me, and I will give to each person according to what they have done. ¹³I am the Alpha and the Omega, the First and the Last, the Beginning and the End.

¹⁴"Blessed are those who wash their robes, that they may have the right to the tree of life and

may go through the gates into the city. ¹⁵Outside are the dogs, those who practice magic arts, the sexually immoral, the murderers, the idolaters and everyone who loves and practices falsehood.

¹⁶"I, Jesus, have sent my angel to give you*a* this testimony for the churches. I am the Root and the Offspring of David, and the bright Morning Star."

¹⁷The Spirit and the bride say, "Come!" And let the one who hears say, "Come!" Let the one who is thirsty come; and let the one who wishes take the free gift of the water of life.

¹⁸I warn everyone who hears the words of the prophecy of this scroll: If anyone adds anything to them, God will add to that person the plagues described in this scroll. ¹⁹And if anyone takes words away from this scroll of prophecy, God will take away from that person any share in the tree of life and in the Holy City, which are described in this scroll.

²⁰He who testifies to these things says, "Yes, I am coming soon."

Amen. Come, Lord Jesus.

²¹The grace of the Lord Jesus be with God's people. Amen.

a The Greek is plural.

Table of Weights and Measures

	Biblical Unit	Approximate American Equivalent	Approximate Metric Equivalent
Weights	talent (60 minas)	75 pounds	34 kilograms
	mina (50 shekels)	1 1/4 pounds	560 grams
	shekel (2 bekas)	2/5 ounce	11.5 grams
	pim (2/3 shekel)	1/4 ounce	7.8 grams
	beka (10 gerahs)	1/5 ounce	5.7 grams
	gerah	1/50 ounce	0.6 gram
	daric	1/3 ounce	8.4 grams
Length	cubit	18 inches	45 centimeters
	span	9 inches	23 centimeters
	handbreadth	3 inches	7.5 centimeters
	stadion (pl. stadia)	600 feet	183 meters
Capacity *Dry Measure*	cor [homer] (10 ephahs)	6 bushels	220 liters
	lethek (5 ephahs)	3 bushels	110 liters
	ephah (10 omers)	3/5 bushel	22 liters
	seah (1/3 ephah)	7 quarts	7.5 liters
	omer (1/10 ephah)	2 quarts	2 liters
	cab (1/18 ephah)	1 quart	1 liter
Liquid Measure	bath (1 ephah)	6 gallons	22 liters
	hin (1/6 bath)	1 gallon	3.8 liters
	log (1/72 bath)	1/3 quart	0.3 liter

The figures of the table are calculated on the basis of a shekel equaling 11.5 grams, a cubit equaling 18 inches and an ephah equaling 22 liters. The quart referred to is either a dry quart (slightly larger than a liter) or a liquid quart (slightly smaller than a liter), whichever is applicable. The ton referred to in the footnotes is the American ton of 2,000 pounds. These weights are calculated relative to the particular commodity involved. Accordingly, the same measure of capacity in the text may be converted into different weights in the footnotes.

This table is based upon the best available information, but it is not intended to be mathematically precise; like the measurement equivalents in the footnotes, it merely gives approximate amounts and distances. Weights and measures differed somewhat at various times and places in the ancient world. There is uncertainty particularly about the ephah and the bath; further discoveries may shed more light on these units of capacity.

Dictionary-Concordance

A

Aaron — the brother of Moses; he served as Moses' spokesman before Pharaoh (Ex 4:14–16, 27–31; 7:1–2); he was Israel's first high priest (Ex 28:1; Nu 17; Heb 5:1–4).

abandon — to leave completely; to desert.

Abba — the word for *father* in Aramaic, one of the three languages Jesus spoke.

> Ro 8:15 And by him we cry, "*A*, Father."
> Gal 4:6 the Spirit who calls out, "*A*, Father."

Abel — the second son of Adam (Ge 4:2); he offered a pleasing sacrifice to God (Ge 4:4; Heb 11:4) but was murdered by his brother Cain (Ge 4:8; Mt 23:35; 1Jn 3:12).

abhor — to hate or to turn away from.

> Ps 26:5 I *a* the assembly of evildoers
> Am 6:8 "I *a* the pride of Jacob

Abigail — the wife of Nabal; she helped save David's life (1Sa 25:14–35) and later became his wife (1Sa 25:36–42).

abolish — to destroy completely; to put an end to.

abomination — a thing to be hated.

abound — to be more than enough; to overflow.

> Ex 34:6 slow to anger, *a* in love
> Php 1:9 that your love may *a* more

Abraham — the father of the Jewish nation and of all believers. God promised that he would make a mighty nation of Abraham's children and would give them the land of Canaan (Ge 15; 17; 22; Ro 4; Heb 6:13–15). As a test, God told him to offer his son Isaac as a sacrifice (Ge 22; Heb 11:17–19) but withdrew this command when Abraham showed that he would trust God and obey him.

Absalom — a son of David (2Sa 3:3); he plotted to take David's throne. He died when his long hair became tangled in an oak tree and Joab, David's commander, plunged javelins into his heart (2Sa 14–18).

abstain — to keep from doing something.

abundance, abundant — having plenty; more than enough.

> Jude 2 Mercy, peace and love be yours in *a*.

Abyss — the place of the dead; the place where evil spirits live.

Achan — an Israelite who kept spoil from the conquest of Jericho for himself; as a result of Achan's stealing what belonged to God, the Israelites were defeated at Ai and he and his family were stoned to death (Jos 7; 22:20).

acknowledge — to know and to say that something is true; to recognize.

> Mt 10:32 I will also *a* before my Father in heaven.
> 1Jn 4:3 spirit that does not *a* Jesus is not from God.

acts — deeds.

> Ps 150:2 Praise him for his *a* of power
> Isa 64:6 all our righteous *a* are like filthy rags

Adam — the first person God created (Ge 1:26–2:25); he sinned by disobeying God (Ge 3) and in that way brought all people under the curse of sin (Ro 5:12–21).

admonish — to give warning or advice in a caring way.

adorn — to make more beautiful.

adultery — having sexual relations with someone other than one's husband or wife. Spiritual adultery means being unfaithful to God (Jer 3).

> Ex 20:14 You shall not commit *a*.
> Mt 5:28 lustfully has already committed *a*

adversary — enemy; opponent.

advice — an opinion given about a decision to be made.

> 1Ki 12:14 he followed the *a* of the young men
> Pr 20:18 Plans are established by seeking *a*;

advocate — 1. (*v.*) to speak in favor of; 2. (*n.*) someone who speaks in another person's defense; 3. (*n.*) another name for the Holy Spirit.

> Jn 14:16 he will give you another *a* to help you
> Jn 14:26 But the *A*, the Holy Spirit,
> Jn 15:26 "When the *A* comes, whom I will

affliction — trouble or pain that lasts a long time.

> Ro 12:12 patient in *a*, faithful in prayer.

agony — extreme pain of mind or body.

Ahab — a wicked king of Israel; the husband of Jezebel (1Ki 16:31). He caused

Israel to worship Baal rather than God (1Ki 16:31–33) and was opposed by God's prophet Elijah (1Ki 17:1; 18; 21).

alabaster — a hard marble like material that can be made into jars, vases or sculptures.

alienate — to make unfriendly; to turn a person's interest or affection away from another person or thing.

allot — to divide and give away in parts. In Old Testament times the land of Canaan was allotted to the twelve tribes of Israel.

Almighty — a name used to show how strong and powerful God is.

Ge 17:1 "I am God *A*; walk before me

Isa 6:3 "Holy, holy, holy is the LORD *A*;

altar — a raised platform made of stones, metal, dirt or wood, on which sacrifices were made.

ambush — the act of hiding in order to attack by surprise.

Amen — Hebrew word that means "so be it" or "let it become true."

Amos — a prophet of Israel who lived about the same time as Hosea and Jonah; he spoke about God's justice and righteousness.

Ananias — 1. the husband of Sapphira; he was struck dead for lying to God (Ac 5:1–11); 2. the disciple who baptized Saul (Ac 9:10–19); 3. the high priest before whom Paul was tried in Jerusalem (Ac 22:30–24:1).

ancestor — a person from whom someone is descended.

Ps 78:5 commanded our *a* to teach their children,

ancient — very old.

Andrew — one of the twelve apostles; the brother of Peter (Mt 4:18; 10:2; Ac 1:13).

angel — a heavenly being.

Ps 34:7 The *a* of the LORD encamps

Heb 1:14 Are not all *a* ministering spirits

Heb 2:7 made them a little lower than the *a*;

1Pe 1:12 Even *a* long to look

anger — a strong feeling of displeasure; rage; fury.

Ps 103:8 slow to *a*, abounding in love.

Jas 1:20 human *a* does not produce the righteousness

anguish — extreme pain or distress of mind or body.

Jer 49:24 *a* and pain have seized her;

annihilate — to destroy completely.

anoint — to pour oil on a person's head, either for a physical benefit (Jas 5:14) or to set someone apart for service to God (Ex 28:41).

antichrist — a person who is against Christ.

1Jn 2:18 you have heard that the *a* is coming,

1Jn 2:22 Such a person is the *a*

·iety — worry.

5:7 Cast all your *a* on him

Apollos — a Christian from Alexandria who knew the Scriptures well (Ac 18:24–28) and helped Paul to minister in Corinth (Ac 19:1; 1Co 1:12).

apostle — 1. any of the twelve men Jesus chose to work with him during his earthly ministry; after being equipped by the Holy Spirit, they were sent out to preach about Jesus; 2. later, someone who had been with Jesus, had seen his miracles and then taught others about him.

Mt 10:2 These are the names of the twelve *a*:

1Co 12:28 God has placed in the church first of all *a*,

1Co 15:9 For I am the least of the *a*

appalled — overcome with shock or horror.

appeal — to make an earnest request.

1Pe 5:1 I *a* as a fellow elder

appoint — to assign someone officially to a job or position.

Aquila — the husband of Priscilla; Aquila and Priscilla were co-workers with Paul in Corinth (Ac 18; Ro 16:3).

Aramaic — the language that was commonly spoken in the countries east of the Mediterranean Sea during Jesus' earthly ministry.

ark of the covenant law — also called the ark of the covenant; a large gold-covered box, which contained the Ten Commandments (tablets of the covenant law), a jar of manna and Aaron's staff, and was kept inside the Most Holy Place in the tabernacle (tent of meeting). It was a reminder to the Israelites of God's presence with them.

armor — protective clothing worn in battle, usually made of metal.

Eph 6:11 Put on the full *a* of God

aroma — an odor or smell, usually pleasant.

arouse — to excite; to stir to action.

arrest — to officially or lawfully make a prisoner of someone.

arrogant — proud; conceited.

arrow — See bow.

ascend — to go up. Jesus ascended to heaven to return to God the Father.

ascribe — to think of as caused by, coming from or belonging to.

1Ch 16:28 *a* to the LORD glory and strength,

Ashera poles — wooden poles honoring Ashera, the Canaanite goddess of love and war.

Dt 12:3 burn their *A* in the fire;

assemble — to bring a group of people together; to meet together.

Assyria — one of the powerful nations of Biblical times; it often attacked the Israelites; its capital was Nineveh.

astray — mistaken; not on the right path; lost.

Isa 53:6 We all, like sheep, have gone *a*,

atone — to make right, by paying the penalty, the relationship between God and humans that was broken through sin. In the Old Testament people atoned symbolically for their sins by offering sacrifices to God. In the New Testament Jesus corrected the relationship between God and people once and for all by dying to take away sins.

atonement — the payment that corrects the relationship between God and humans that was broken through sin.

> Lev 17:11 it is the blood that makes *a*
> Lev 23:27 this seventh month is the Day of *A*.
> Ro 3:25 God presented Christ as a sacrifice of *a*,
> Heb 2:17 that he might make *a* for the sins

attack — to set upon with force, as in a battle.

authority — the right and power to give orders.

> Mt 9:6 the Son of Man has *a* on earth
> Mt 28:18 "All *a* in heaven and on earth has
> Ro 13:1 for there is no *a* except that which
> Heb 13:17 your leaders and submit to their *a*,

avenge — to get back at or punish someone who has done wrong.

> Dt 32:35 It is mine to *a*; I will repay.

avoid — to keep away from.

> Pr 20:19 *a* anyone who talks too much.

awe — respect and wonder; a holy fear of God because of his great power.

> Ps 65:8 earth is filled with *a* at your wonders;

B

Baal — the name of many false gods in Canaan.

> 1Ki 18:25 Elijah said to the prophets of *B*,

Babel — a tower built soon after the flood; the builders were attempting to reach up to God, but God confused their language so that the building was stopped.

Babylon — the beautiful capital of Babylonia; it was a powerful and influential city in the Near East from the eighteenth to the sixth centuries B.C. In the New Testament, Babylon represents the godless city.

> Ps 137:1 By the rivers of *B* we sat and wept
> Rev 14:8 Fallen is *B* the Great,

Balaam — a seer who tried to curse Israel during their journey to the promised land, but God would not allow it (Nu 22 – 24).

balm — a skin cream used to heal sores and relieve pain.

> Jer 8:22 Is there no *b* in Gilead?

banish — to force a person away from a place.

banquet — a formal meal, usually for a large group of people.

baptize — a religious ceremony in which water is used as a symbol of cleansing from sin. Churches today baptize by sprinkling or pouring or immersing in water. Baptism is a sign that sin is washed away.

> Mk 1:9 and was *b* by John in the Jordan.
> Ac 1:5 but in a few days you will be *b*
> Ac 2:38 "Repent and be *b*, every one of you,

Barabbas — the Jews chose this criminal, rather than Jesus, to be released by Pilate (Mt 27:26).

Barnabas — an apostle; he was a co-worker with Paul on his first missionary journey (Ac 9:27; Ac 13 – 15).

barren — 1. unable to have children; 2. unable to produce crops.

Bartholomew — one of the twelve apostles (Mt 10:3; Ac 1:13). He was also probably known as Nathanael (Jn 1:45 – 49; 21:2).

Bathsheba — the wife of Uriah; she committed adultery with David and later became his wife (2Sa 11); she was the mother of Solomon (2Sa 12:24).

Beelzebul — the prince of demons; Satan.

> Lk 11:19 if I drive out demons by *B*,

Beersheba — an important town that marked the southern boundary of Judah.

believe — to accept as true; to trust; to have faith.

> Mk 1:15 Repent and *b* the good news!"
> Mk 9:24 "I do *b*; help me overcome my
> Jn 1:7 that through him all might *b*.
> Jn 3:18 does not *b* stands condemned
> Jn 20:27 Stop doubting and *b*."
> Ac 16:31 They replied, "*B* in the Lord Jesus,
> Ro 3:22 faith in Jesus Christ to all who *b*.
> 1Th 4:14 we *b* that Jesus died and rose again

Benjamin — the twelfth son of Jacob. Rachel was his mother, and he was the younger brother of Joseph (Ge 35:16 – 24; Ge 42 – 45).

besiege — to surround a city or town completely with an army, so that nothing can go in or out.

bestow — to give.

Bethlehem — the city in Judea where Jesus was born (Mt 2:1).

betray — to turn a friend over to his or her enemies; to be unfaithful to.

> Mt 27:3 When Judas, who had *b* him,
> 1Co 11:23 on the night he was *b*, took bread,

betroth — to promise to marry.

bewildered — confused; puzzled.

bind — 1. to tie with a rope or string; 2. to make tight or firm.

> Dt 6:8 and *b* them on your foreheads.
>
> Mt 16:19 whatever you *b* on earth will be

birthright — the special rights of the first-born son. In the Old Testament, after the father died, the oldest son received the father's power and right to make decisions for the entire family. He also got twice as much money and property as each of his brothers.

bitter — having harsh or hateful feelings.

> Eph 4:31 Get rid of all *b*, rage
>
> Heb 12:15 and that no *b* root grows up

blameless — without fault.

> Ge 17:1 walk before me faithfully and be *b*.
>
> 1Co 1:8 so that you will be *b* on the day

blaspheme — to speak carelessly, falsely or insultingly about God or holy things.

> Mk 3:29 whoever *b* against the Holy Spirit

blemish — a spot or mark that makes something imperfect.

> 1Pe 1:19 a lamb without *b* or defect.

bless — 1. to make holy; 2. to show favor to; 3. to ask God to show favor to.

> Ge 2:3 Then God *b* the seventh day
>
> Ge 12:3 I will *b* those who *b* you,
>
> Mt 5:3 "*B* are the poor in spirit
>
> Ro 12:14 *b* those who persecute you; *b*

blight — a disease in plants that makes them shrivel up and die.

blind — unable to see. Spiritual blindness is an inability to understand the things of God.

> Mt 11:5 The *b* receive sight, the lame walk,
>
> Jn 9:25 I was *b* but now I see!"

blood — as the life-giving fluid in the body, it represents life itself. In the Old Testament, the blood of sacrifices symbolized the giving of life for life. Through the blood of Jesus on the cross, believers are saved from death for their sins.

> Ex 12:13 and when I see the *b*, I will pass
>
> Lev 17:11 For the life of a creature is in the *b*,
>
> Mt 26:28 This is my *b* of the covenant,
>
> Eph 1:7 we have redemption through his *b*,
>
> Heb 9:12 once for all by his own *b*,

blot — to erase or get rid of.

> Ex 32:32 then *b* me out of the book you have
>
> Ps 51:1 *b* out my transgressions.

boast — to brag; to call attention to.

> Ps 44:8 In God we make our *b*
>
> Gal 6:14 May I never *b* except in the cross

Boaz — a wealthy man who lived in Bethlehem in the days of the judges; he married Ru (Ru 2; 4).

body — 1. physical part of a person; 2. a group working as a unit.

> Pr 3:8 This will bring health to your *b*
>
> Ro 12:1 to offer your *b* as a living sacrifice,
>
> 1Co 6:19 not know that your *b* are temples
>
> Eph 5:30 for we are members of his *b*.

bondage — slavery.

> Ezr 9:9 God has not forsaken us in our *b*.

born again — refers to the experience of salvation; entering God's family through faith in Christ.

> Jn 3:3 no one can see the kingdom of God unless they are *b*.
>
> 1Pe 1:23 For you have been *b*,

bow — a weapon made of a strip of flexible material with a cord connecting the two ends and holding the strip bent; used to shoot arrows.

branch — an extension of another body or system.

> Jer 33:15 I will make a righteous *B* sprout
>
> Jn 15:5 "I am the vine; you are the *b*.

bread — in Bible times the most important food in the diet.

> Dt 8:3 that man does not live on *b* alone
>
> Mt 6:11 Give us today our daily *b*.
>
> Jn 6:35 Jesus declared, "I am the *b* of life.

breastpiece — a decorated square of linen cloth worn by the high priest when he entered the Holy Place.

breastplate — a chest-covering made of metal or leather, worn by soldiers for protection.

bribe — money or favor given to influence judgment or conduct.

> Ex 23:8 "Do not accept a *b*,

bride — a woman who is about to get married. The church is called Jesus' bride.

bridegroom — a man who is about to get married. Christ is called the church's bridegroom.

bronze — a metal, the combination of copper and tin, used to make tools, weapons and ornamental articles.

brother — a male who has the same parents as another person.

> Ge 4:9 "Am I my *b* keeper?"
>
> Mt 18:15 "If your *b* or sister sins,
>
> 2Co 13:11 Finally, *b* and sisters, rejoice!

burden — a heavy load.

> Mt 11:30 my yoke is easy and my *b* is light.
>
> Gal 6:2 Carry each other's *b*,

burnt offering — in the Old Testament a sacrifice to the Lord that expressed devotion and complete surrender (Ge 8:20; Ex 29:18).

C

Caesar — the title of many Roman emperors.

Lk 2:1 In those days *C* Augustus

Mt 22:21 "Give back to *C* what is Caesar's,

Cain — Adam and Eve's firstborn son; he murdered his brother Abel (Ge 4:1 – 16).

calamity — a disaster, usually causing great loss and suffering.

Caleb — one of the twelve men who was sent to spy on Canaan. He came back with a positive report and encouraged the Israelites to take possession of Canaan (Nu 13:6 – 14:38; Dt 1:36).

call — 1. (*v.*) to ask to come; 2. to give a name to; 3. (*n.*) a summons for a particular purpose or job.

2Ch 7:14 if my people, who are *c*

Ps 145:18 near to all who *c* on him,

Mt 9:13 not come to *c* the righteous,

Ro 8:30 And those he predestined, he also *c*;

Ro 11:29 gifts and his *c* are irrevocable.

1Pe 2:9 of him who *c* you out of darkness

camel — a large animal, able to travel long distances and used for transportation of people and goods.

Canaan — 1. the land God promised to the nation of Israel; 2. the promised land.

capstone — the stone that holds two walls together; the stone that finishes a wall.

1Pe 2:7 has become the *c*,"

care — to show concern for.

Ps 8:4 human beings that you *c* for them?

1 Pe 5:7 on him because he *c* for you.

cavalry — a group of soldiers riding horses.

censer — a bowl or dish used for carrying hot coals or for burning incense.

census — a count of the population of a group of people.

centurion — a Roman army officer in charge of one hundred soldiers.

chaff — the seed covering of a grain such as wheat. In Bible times, the grain and chaff were separated by tossing the grain into the air so the wind could blow the chaff away.

Ps 1:4 They are like *c*

Mt 3:12 up the *c* with unquenchable fire."

chariot — a two-wheeled vehicle pulled by horses.

2Ki 6:17 and *c* of fire all around Elisha.

cheerful — full of joy; pleasant.

Pr 15:13 A happy heart makes the face *c*,

2Co 9:7 for God loves a *c* giver.

cherub (pl. cherubim) — an angel, with an appearance something like a human being.

children — sons and daughters.

Mt 19:14 "Let the little *c* come to me,

Eph 6:1 *C*, obey your parents in the Lord,

1Jn 3:1 that we should be called *c* of God!

choose (chosen) — to select.

Jos 24:15 then *c* for yourselves this day

Mt 22:14 "For many are invited, but few are *c*."

Jn 15:16 You did not *c* me,

Eph 1:4 he *c* us in him before the creation

1Pe 2:9 But you are a *c* people, a royal

Christ — the official title of Jesus, meaning "the Anointed One." It is a Greek word, and it means the same as the Hebrew word *Messiah.*

Jn 1:17 grace and truth came through Jesus *C.*

Ac 3:6 name of Jesus *C* of Nazareth, walk."

Ro 5:8 While we were still sinners, *C* died

Eph 5:23 as *C* is the head of the church,

Php 1:21 to live is *C* and to die is gain.

Christian — a believer in or follower of Christ.

Ac 11:26 The disciples were called *C* first

1Pe 4:16 as a *C*, do not be ashamed,

chronicles — a history of events in the order in which they took place.

church — the entire group of people who believe in Christ.

Mt 16:18 and on this rock I will build my *c*,

Eph 5:23 as Christ is the head of the *c*,

Col 1:24 the sake of his body, which is the *c*.

circumcision — the cutting off of the loose fold of skin at the end of the penis; it symbolized the agreement God made with the Israelites, and they came to be known as "the circumcision" (Eph 2:11).

Ge 17:10 Every male among you shall be *c.*

cistern — a pit dug into the ground for storing rainwater.

citadel — a tower or building, especially in a city, equipped for war.

city of refuge — one of six cities set aside by Moses and Joshua for those who had accidentally killed someone. Such people would be safe there until a fair trial could be held (Nu 35:9 – 15).

clan — a group of people belonging to the same extended family.

Ge 24:38 to my father's family and to my own *c*,

Zec 12:12 The land will mourn, each *c* by itself,

clean animals — animals God allowed the Israelites to sacrifice and eat.

cleanse — to make clean; to wash.

cloak — a loose-fitting coat without sleeves.

comfort — to relieve from distress; to console.

    Ps 23:4 rod and your staff, they *c* me.

    2Co 1:4 so that we can *c* those

commandment — an order given by God. God gave the Ten Commandments to the Israelites while they were encamped in the area of Mount Sinai.

    Ex 20:6 who love me and keep my *c*.

    Ecc 12:13 Fear God and keep his *c*.

    Mt 22:38 This is the first and greatest *c*.

commend — 1. to praise; 2. to hand over to someone for safekeeping.

    Ps 145:4 One generation *c* your works

companion — one who is a friend or associate or helper.

compassion (compassionate) — sympathy; pity.

    Ne 9:17 gracious and *c*, slow to anger

    Ps 103:4 and crowns you with love and *c*,

    Mt 9:36 When he saw the crowds, he had *c*

    Ro 9:15 and I will have *c* on whom I have *c*."

    Col 3:12 clothe yourselves with *c*, kindness,

conceive — 1. to become pregnant; 2. to think up or imagine.

    Mt 1:20 what is *c* in her is from the Holy

    1Co 2:9 no human mind has *c*

concubine — in Bible times, a woman who belonged to a man but did not have the rights of a wife. She was often one of the spoils of war, and her primary purpose was to bear children for the man.

condemn (condemnation) — to punish; to pronounce guilty.

    Jn 3:17 Son into the world to *c* the world,

    Ro 8:1 there is now no *c* for those who are

confess — 1. to say what you believe; 2. to tell your sins to someone.

    2Ti 2:19 "Everyone who *c* the name of the Lord

    1Jn 1:9 If we *c* our sins, he is faithful

conform — to agree with and try to be like someone; to do what others say to do.

    Ro 8:29 predestined to be *c* to the image

    1Pe 1:14 do not *c* to the evil desires you had

conscience — the sense of knowing if something is good or bad; a sense of right and wrong.

    Ro 2:15 their *c* also bearing witness,

    Tit 1:15 their minds and *c* are corrupted.

    Heb 9:14 cleanse our *c* from acts that lead

consecrate — to set aside or dedicate for God's use.

    13:2 "*C* to me every firstborn male.

    0:7 "*C* yourselves and be holy,

consider — to think about carefully.

    Ps 8:3 When I *c* your heavens,

console — to comfort.

conspire — to plan together to do wrong.

consult — to ask the advice or opinion of someone.

consume — 1. to use up or eat up; 2. to destroy completely.

    Jn 2:17 "Zeal for your house will *c* me."

    Heb 12:29 for our "God is a *c* fire."

contempt — lack of respect; looking down on someone or something as being worthless.

    Pr 14:31 Whoever oppresses the poor shows *c*

    1Th 5:20 Do not treat prophecies with *c*

contend — to struggle, as in a contest or against difficulties.

content — satisfied.

    Php 4:11 to be *c* whatever the circumstances.

    Heb 13:5 and be *c* with what you have,

contrite — to feel sorry for one's sins; to feel repentant.

    Ps 51:17 a broken and *c* heart,

    Isa 66:2 those who are humble and *c* in spirit,

convert — a person who has changed from one belief to another.

    1Ti 3:6 He must not be a recent *c*,

convict — 1. to prove one guilty; 2. to make a person feel sorrow.

    Jas 2:9 and are *c* by the law as lawbreakers.

copper — a common metal, easy to work with; often used to make coins.

Cornelius — a Roman to whom Peter preached the gospel; he became the first Gentile Christian (Ac 10).

cornerstone — the first or most important stone laid when constructing a building.

    Eph 2:20 with Christ Jesus himself as the chief *c*.

corrupt — 1. (*v.*) to change something from good to bad; 2. (*adj.*) wicked.

    Ge 6:11 Now the earth was *c* in God's sight

    1Co 15:33 "Bad company *c* good character."

counsel — to give advice to.

    Pr 15:22 Plans fail for lack of *c*,

covenant — 1. an agreement between two people or two groups of people, in which both usually make specific promises; 2. the promises of God for salvation.

    Ge 9:9 "I now establish my *c* with you

    Ex 19:5 if you obey me fully and keep my *c*,

    Jer 31:31 "when I will make a new *c*

    1Co 11:25 "This cup is the new *c* in my blood;

Heb 9:15 Christ is the mediator of a new *c*,

covet — to want for oneself something that belongs to another person.

Ex 20:17 "You shall not *c* your neighbor's

crafty — sly, clever.

Ge 3:1 Now the serpent was more *c*

crave — to desire strongly; to feel a deep need for.

1Pe 2:2 newborn babies, *c* pure spiritual

create — to make; to bring into being.

Ge 1:1 In the beginning God *c* the heavens

Ps 51:10 *C* in me a pure heart, O God,

Col 1:16 For in him all things were *c*:

Rev 10:6 who *c* the heavens and all that is

crime — an unlawful act.

criminal — someone who commits an unlawful act.

Lk 23:32 Two other men, both *c*,

cripple — a disabled person or animal.

cross — a tall beam with a crossbar on which a criminal was hung or tied to die.

Mt 10:38 Whoever does not take up their *c*

Gal 6:14 in the *c* of our Lord Jesus Christ,

Php 2:8 even death on a *c*!

Col 2:14 taken it away, nailing it to the *c*.

Heb 12:2 set before him he endured the *c*,

crown — a headpiece worn to symbolize glory, honor and victory.

1Co 9:25 it to get a *c* that will last forever.

2Ti 4:8 store for me the *c* of righteousness,

Rev 2:10 life as your victor's crown.

crucify — to put to death by nailing or tying a person's body to a cross.

Mt 27:22 They all answered, "*C* him!"

1Co 1:23 but we preach Christ *c*: a stumbling

Gal 2:20 I have been *c* with Christ

cruel — causing envy, grief or pain.

cubit — a measure of length in Bible times; about 18 inches.

cupbearer — an officer of considerable responsibility who tasted the king's food and wine before serving them to him (Ne 1:11).

curse — 1. (*v*.) to ask God to bring evil or injury to; 2. (*n*.) a prayer or desire that evil or injury come upon someone.

Lev 20:9 "Anyone who *c* their father or mother

Lk 6:28 bless those who *c* you, pray

Gal 3:13 "*C* is everyone who is hung on a pole."

custom — a practice common to a particular place or group of people.

Mk 15:6 Now it was the *c* at the festival

Ac 17:2 As was his *c*, Paul went into the synagogue

cymbals — a musical instrument; round metal disks either struck with a stick or struck together to produce a clanging sound.

cypress — an evergreen tree of the pine family.

D

Daniel — a young Jewish exile; he lived in Babylon during the reign of several kings, including Nebuchadnezzar. He prayed to God rather than obey an order to pray only to the king and was thrown into a lion's den (Da 1 – 6).

daughter — a female descendant.

Job 1:2 He had seven sons and three *d*,

David — the son of Jesse; anointed by Samuel to become king of Israel (1Sa 16:1 – 13); killed the giant Goliath (1Sa 17); during his reign Israel's place in the land of Canaan was made secure.

day — 1. the period of time between dawn and darkness; 2. a specified time.

Ge 1:5 God called the light "*d*,"

Ecc 12:1 Creator in the *d* of your youth,

Joel 2:31 and dreadful *d* of the LORD.

Mic 4:1 In the last *d*

Lk 11:3 Give us each *d* our daily bread.

Lk 18:33 On the third *d* he will rise

Heb 1:2 in these last *d* he has spoken to us

2Pe 3:8 With the Lord a *d* is like

deacon — a church officer whose qualifications are given in 1 Ti 3:8 – 13.

death — the end of physical life; also the penalty for sin (Ro 6:23).

Ecc 7:2 for *d* is the destiny of everyone;

Isa 25:8 he will swallow up *d* forever.

1Co 15:21 For since *d* came through a man,

1Co 15:55 Where, O *d*, is your sting?"

Rev 21:4 There will be no more *d*

debauchery — living an immoral life or a life without religion; living to please only oneself.

Deborah — a prophetess who led Israel to victory over the Canaanites (Jdg 4 – 5).

debt — something that one person owes another.

Mt 6:12 And forgive us our *d*,

deceive — to fool or trick; to lie.

Ge 3:13 "The serpent *d* me, and I ate."

Gal 6:7 Do not be *d*: God cannot be

1Jn 1:8 we *d* ourselves and the truth is not

declare — to make known formally; to state forcefully.

Ps 19:1 The heavens *d* the glory of God;

Eph 6:20 Pray that I may *d* it fearlessly,

decree — 1. (v.) to order or command; 2. (n.) an order or law given by someone with power and authority.

dedicate — to set apart for a special purpose, often for God's use.

defect — imperfection; fault.

defile — to make something that is good and pure into something impure or unclean.

defraud — to cheat someone by trickery.

Deity — God.

Col 2:9 of the *D* lives in bodily form,

delight — something that gives great pleasure.

Ps 119:47 for I *d* in your commands

Mt 12:18 the one I love, in whom I *d*;

deliver — to rescue; to set free.

demon — evil spirit. A demon-possessed person is one who is controlled by evil spirits.

Mk 5:15 possessed by the legion of *d*,

Jas 2:19 Good! Even the *d* believe that

denarius — a small Roman coin made of silver. During Jesus' earthly ministry, one denarius was the payment for about one day's work.

denounce — to say a person or thing is evil.

deposit — something pledged or given as part of the payment.

Eph 1:14 who is a *d* guaranteeing our

depraved (depravity) — evil or sinful.

2Ti 3:8 They are men of *d* minds,

2Pe 2:19 they themselves are slaves of *d*

deprive — to take something away from.

Am 5:12 and *d* the poor of justice

depths — the deepest part of a thing.

Ps 130:1 Out of the *d* I cry

La 3:55 from the *d* of the pit.

descendant — a member of a particular family line.

desecrate — to treat without respect or reverence.

desolate — not lived in; lonely; deserted.

despise — to look down on with contempt.

Pr 1:7 but fools *d* wisdom

Tit 2:15 Do not let anyone *d* you.

destiny — a predetermined course of events.

Php 3:19 Their *d* is destruction,

destitute — not having necessary things such as money and food.

destroy — to ruin completely.

detest — to hate.

devastate — to bring to ruin by violent action.

Jer 19:8 I will *d* this city

devil — the great enemy of God and tempter of people.

Lk 4:2 forty days he was tempted by the *d*.

Eph 6:11 stand against the *d* schemes.

2Ti 2:26 and escape from the trap of the *d*,

1:7 Resist the *d*, and he will flee

8 Your enemy the *d* prowls

devote — to set apart for a special person or for a special reason; to set apart for God's use.

devour — 1. to eat up greedily; 2. to destroy.

1Pe 5:8 looking for someone to *d*.

devout — religious; giving much time to prayer and worship.

die — 1. to lose life; 2. to become insensitive to, as to die to the law (Gal 2:19).

Ge 2:17 when you eat from it you will certainly *d*."

Ecc 3:2 a time to be born and a time to *d*,

Eze 18:4 one who sins is the one who will *d*.

Jn 11:26 by believing in me will never *d*.

1Co 15:22 in Adam all *d*, so in Christ all will

Php 1:21 to live is Christ and to *d* is gain.

diligence (diligent) — characterized by hard work or earnest effort.

disaster — a sudden event bringing great damage, loss or destruction.

Dt 31:29 *d* will fall on you

discern — to understand; to come to know the difference between two or more things.

Php 1:10 you may be able to *d* what is best

disciple — a follower or student, especially one who believes what the leader teaches. Anyone who believes in Jesus is his disciple.

Lk 14:27 and follow me cannot be my *d*.

Jn 13:35 everyone will know that you are my *d*,

discipline — 1. (v.) to correct; to teach what is right; 2. (n.) training that corrects, molds or perfects moral character.

Pr 29:17 *D* your children, and they will give you

Heb 12:6 the Lord *d* the one he loves,

Rev 3:19 Those whom I love I rebuke and *d*.

disgrace — to bring shame to.

disobey (disobedient) — to fail to obey.

1Pe 2:8 because they *d* the message

disown — to reject someone or something so completely that it no longer belongs to you.

Mt 26:34 you will *d* me three times."

2Ti 2:12 If we *d* him,

disperse — to scatter; to spread around.

dispute — to argue irritably.

dissension — disagreement; quarreling.

distress — suffering, misery, agony.

Ps 57:6 I was bowed down in *d*.

Ro 2:9 There will be trouble and *d*

divination — seeing into the future by magic.

Lev 19:26 "Do not practice *d* or seek omens.

divine — given by God; belonging to God.

Ro 1:20 his eternal power and *d* nature

divorce — to legally dissolve a marriage.
Mal 2:16 who hates and *d* his wife,"
Mt 19:3 for a man to *d* his wife for any
1Co 7:11 And a husband must not *d* his wife.

doctrine — teachings or beliefs about God.
1Ti 4:16 Watch your life and *d* closely.
Tit 2:1 what is appropriate to sound *d*.

dominion — power; rule.
Ps 22:28 for *d* belongs to the LORD
Eph 1:21 far above all rule and authority, power and *d*,

doom — 1. (*v.*) to make certain something will fail or be destroyed; 2. (*n.*) fate; condemnation; ruin.
Rev 18:10 In one hour your *d* has come!'

door — a barrier that can be opened and closed; Christians open the doors of their hearts to Jesus.
Mt 7:7 and the *d* will be opened to you.
Rev 3:20 I stand at the *d* and knock.

doubt — uncertainty.
Mt 21:21 if you have faith and do not *d*,
Mk 11:23 and does not *d* in their heart
Jas 1:6 you must believe and not *d*,

dread — great fear.

dream — thoughts, images or emotion occurring during sleep; God sometimes spoke to his people through dreams.
Da 2:4 Tell your servants the *d*,

dross — the impure scum that floats on the surface of molten metals; sometimes used as a picture of the wicked.
Ps 119:119 you discard like *d*;

drought — a long period of time without rain.

drunkard — a person who is often or usually drunk.
Pr 23:21 for *d* and gluttons become poor,

dwelling — place in which people live; house; in Scripture usually refers to the place where God lives.
1Ki 8:30 Hear from heaven, your *d* place,
Ps 84:1 How lovely is your *d* place,

E

earth — the place that God created for human beings to live.
Ge 1:1 God created the heavens and the *e*.
Ps 24:1 *e* is the LORD's, and everything
Mt 6:10 done, on *e* as it is in heaven.
Mt 24:35 Heaven and *e* will pass away,
Lk 2:14 on *e* peace to those
Php 2:10 in heaven and on *e* and under the *e*,
2Pe 3:13 to a new heaven and a new *e*,

Eden — the location of the beautiful garden God created for Adam and Eve.

edict — an order or law made by a person who has the power to enforce it.
Est 2:8 the king's order and *e*

edify — to teach someone to live a godly life, or to help someone to live in such a way.
1Co 14:4 but the one who prophesies *e* the church.

Egypt — one of the most powerful nations of ancient times, located in the northeast corner of Africa; the Israelites were captives in Egypt at the beginning of the book of Exodus.

elders — 1. the older men of a town or nation; they were the leaders of their community and made all the important decisions; 2. the leaders of the church.
1Ti 5:17 The *e* who direct the affairs
Tit 1:5 and appoint *e* in every town,

election — the choosing of Christians by God, as people who belong to him. Christians are called "the elect" (2Ti 2:10).
Ro 9:11 God's purpose in *e* might stand:
2Pe 1:10 to confirm your calling and *e*.

Eli — the high priest with whom Samuel spent the early years of his life (1Sa 2:11 – 26).

Elijah — a prophet of the Lord who predicted a famine in Israel (1Ki 17:1) and defeated the prophets of Baal in the test of whose God would set fire to the altar (1Ki 18:16 – 46).

Elisha — the prophet who succeeded Elijah. He was present when God took Elijah to heaven, and he took his place as prophet to Israel (2Ki 2:1 – 18).

Elizabeth — the mother of John the Baptist. Mary went to visit her when she found out she, too, was pregnant (Lk 1:5 – 58).

enchanter — a magician or snake charmer.

encourage — to inspire with courage or hope.
2Sa 19:7 Now go out and *e* your men.
1Th 4:18 Therefore *e* one another with these words.

endure — to continue; to keep on going; to bear something that is difficult or painful.
Ps 136:1 His love *e* forever.
Mal 3:2 who can *e* the day of his coming?
1Co 10:13 so that you can *e* it.

enemy — a person who opposes another person or a cause.
Mt 5:44 Love your *e* and pray
Php 3:18 many live as *e* of the cross of Christ.

enjoy — to take pleasure in.
Jdg 19:9 Stay and *e* yourself.
Jer 33:6 and will let them *e* abundant peace
3Jn 2 I pray that you may *e* good health

enmity — a feeling of antagonism, hostility or hatred.

Ge 3:15 put *e* between you and the woman,

Enoch — a man who "walked with God." Later in life, God "took him away" (Ge 5:18 – 24).

entice — to tempt or lure.

envoy — a person who represents one government in its dealings with another.

envy — to want for oneself something that belongs to another person.

1Co 13:4 It does not *e*, it does not boast,

ephod — a linen apron worn by a priest over his robe. It was decorated with gold, blue, purple and scarlet yarns.

Ephraim — 1. one of Joseph's sons; 2. the tribe of Israel whose members were descendants of Ephraim; 3. a name for the northern kingdom of Israel after the ten tribes of Israel and the two tribes of Judah separated from each other.

Esau — the firstborn son of Isaac and twin of Jacob (Ge 25:21 – 26). He sold his birthright to Jacob for a pot of stew (Ge 25:29 – 34) and was tricked out of his blessing by this same brother (Ge 27).

esteem — 1. (*v.*) to value; to consider important; 2. (*n.*) high regard or respect.

Pr 22:1 to be *e* is better than silver or gold.

Isa 53:3 and we held him in low *e*.

Esther — a Jewish woman who lived in Persia (Est 2:7) and became queen (Est 2:8 – 18). Upon being told of a plot to kill the Jews, she went to the king and pleaded for the Jewish people and thus saved them (Est 3 – 4; 7 – 9).

eternal — without beginning or end; forever; timeless.

Dt 33:27 The *e* God is your refuge,

Jn 3:16 him shall not perish but have *e* life.

Ro 6:23 but the gift of God is *e* life

1Jn 5:13 you may know that you have *e* life.

eunuch — a man whose sex organs have been removed so that he cannot produce children. Often in Bible times these men were important officials in royal palaces.

Eve — the first woman God created (Ge 2:20 – 24). Her name means "mother of all the living" (Ge 3:20).

everlasting — forever; without end.

Ps 90:2 from *e* to *e* you are God.

Isa 9:6 *E* Father, Prince of Peace.

Isa 55:3 I will make an *e* covenant with you,

2Th 1:9 punished with *e* destruction

‌**ᵃ‌**—wicked; doing things against God's

‌.9 of the knowledge of good and *e*.

Ps 23:4 I will fear no *e*,

Mt 6:13 but deliver us from the *e* one.

Ro 12:9 Hate what is *e*; cling

Ro 12:17 Do not repay anyone *e* for *e*.

Eph 6:16 all the flaming arrows of the *e* one.

exalt — to praise; to raise to an important position.

Ps 118:28 you are my God, and I will *e* you.

Ps 148:13 for his name alone is *e*;

Pr 14:34 Righteousness *e* a nation,

Mt 23:12 For those who *e* themselves

examine — to look over carefully; to test.

1Co 11:28 Everyone ought to *e* themselves

exclaim — to cry out or speak in sudden or strong emotion.

Lk 1:42 In a loud voice she *e*: "Blessed

exclude — to leave out.

execute — to put to death, especially as punishment for an illegal act.

Lk 23:32 were also led out with him to be *e*.

exile — 1. (*v.*) to force someone to leave his or her country or home; 2. (*n.*) forced removal from one's country or home.

Ezr 6:19 the *e* celebrated the Passover.

1Pe 1:1 To God's elect, *e* scattered

exodus — the departure of a large group of people from one place to go to another. The book of Exodus is the story of the Israelites' journey from Egypt to Canaan.

exploit — to take unfair advantage of.

Pr 22:22 Do not *e* the poor

extol — to praise.

Ps 34:1 I will *e* the LORD at all times;

Ps 95:2 and *e* him with music and song.

extortion — something gotten from a person by force or by using other illegal means.

Ezekiel — a priest who was called to be a prophet to the Jewish people when they were in exile in Babylon (Eze 1 – 3). He had many visions from the Lord (Eze 37; 40).

Ezra — a priest and teacher of the Law; he led a group of Jewish exiles back to Israel and helped them reestablish the temple of God and restore proper worship (Ezr 7 – 8).

F

fail — to be unsuccessful.

Ecc 6:6 but *f* to enjoy his prosperity.

1Co 13:8 Love never *f*.

faint — 1. (*adj.*) lacking courage; 2. (*v.*) to lose courage.

Ps 142:3 When my spirit grows *f* within me,

Lk 21:26 People will *f* from terror,

faith — belief and trust in God; knowing that God is real, even though one can't see him.

Mt 17:20 if you have *f* as small as a mustard

Lk 7:9 I have not found such great *f*

Ro 1:17 "The righteous will live by *f*."

Ro 3:22 given through *f* in Jesus Christ

1Co 13:2 and if I have a *f* that can move

2Co 5:7 we live by *f*, not by sight.

Eph 6:16 to all this, take up the shield of *f*,

1Ti 6:12 Fight the good fight of the *f*.

Heb 11:1 *f* is confidence in what we hope for

Heb 11:8 By *f* Abraham, when called to go

Heb 12:2 the pioneer and perfecter of *f*

Jas 2:26 so *f* without deeds is dead.

faithful (faithfulness) — trustworthy; loyal.

Ps 145:13 and *f* in all he does.

La 3:23 great is your *f*.

Mt 25:21 'Well done, good and *f* servant!

Ro 12:12 patient in affliction, *f* in prayer.

1Co 10:13 And God is *f*; he will not let you

1Jn 1:9 he is *f* and just and will forgive us

Rev 1:5 who is the *f* witness, the firstborn

false (falsehood) — a lie.

Ex 20:16 "You shall not give *f* testimony

family — a group of people who are related to each other.

Ps 68:6 God sets the lonely in *f*,

Lk 9:61 go back and say goodbye to my *f*."

1Ti 3:4 He must manage his own *f* well

famine — 1. a time when there is not enough food; 2. any severe shortage.

Am 8:11 but a *f* of hearing the words

Mt 24:7 There will be *f* and earthquakes

fast — 1. (*adj.*) firmly fixed; not movable; 2. (*v.*) to go without food for a period of time.

Ps 139:10 your right hand will hold me *f*.

Mt 6:16 "When you *f*, do not look somber

father — a male parent; God is also known as one's father.

Ge 2:24 why a man leaves his *f*

Ge 17:4 You will be the *f* of many nations.

Ex 20:12 "Honor your *f* and your mother,

Mt 6:9 "'Our *F* in heaven,

Lk 11:11 "Which of you *f*, if your son asks

Jn 10:30 I and the *F* are one."

Jn 14:6 No one comes to the *F*

favor — goodwill; a positive attitude toward another person.

1Sa 20:3 I have found *f* in your eyes,

fear — (*v.*) 1. to respect highly; to feel reverence and awe for; 2. to be afraid of; (*n.*) 1. profound reverence toward God; 2. anticipation or awareness of danger.

Dt 6:13 *F* the Lord your God, serve him

Ps 91:5 You will not *f* the terror of night,

Ps 111:10 *f* of the Lord is the beginning

Isa 41:10 So do not *f*, for I am with you;

Php 2:12 to work out your salvation with *f*

fellowship — companionship or friendship.

1Jn 1:6 claim to have *f* with him yet walk

1Jn 1:7 we have *f* with one another,

fertile — producing fruit in great quantities; productive.

Nu 13:20 How is the soil? Is it *f* or poor?

festival — a religious celebration.

Nu 29:12 Celebrate a *f* to the Lord

Ezr 6:22 with joy the *F* of Unleavened Bread,

Jn 4:45 in Jerusalem at the Passover *F*,

fig — 1. a brownish pear-shaped fruit that grows in countries near the Mediterranean Sea; 2. the tree that grows this fruit.

Joel 2:22 the *f* tree and the vine yield their riches.

firstborn — a family's first child. The firstborn son in an Israelite family became the head of the family when his father died, and he received twice as much money and property as each of his brothers.

Ex 11:5 Every *f* son in Egypt will die,

firstfruits — the first vegetables, fruits and grains harvested from the field.

Ex 23:19 "Bring the best of the *f* of your soil

flesh — 1. the soft parts of the bodies of humans and animals; 2. the believer's sinful nature.

Job 6:12 Is my *f* bronze?

Php 3:3 put no confidence in the *f*

Ro 8:13 live according to the *f*, you will die;

Ro 13:14 gratify the desires of the *f*.

flock — a collection of sheep under the care of a shepherd.

Ps 65:13 The meadows are covered with *f*

Isa 40:11 He tends his *f* like a shepherd:

flog — to beat with a stick or a whip.

flood — a large amount of water that covers the ground, as in the time of Noah (Ge 6–8).

foe — an enemy.

Ps 61:3 a strong tower against the *f*.

folly — foolishness; the lack of wisdom.

Pr 26:5 Answer a fool according to his *f*,

2Ti 3:9 their *f* will be clear to everyone.

fool — a person who is not wise.

Ps 14:1 The *f* says in his heart,

Lk 12:20 "But God said to him, 'You *f*!

forbearance — patient endurance; self-control; not enforcing a right.

Gal 5:22 love, joy, peace, *f*, kindness,

forefather — a male ancestor.

forever — for a limitless time.

Dt 32:40 As surely as I live *f*,

Ps 136:1 His love endures *f*.

forgive — to pardon or excuse; to no longer blame or be angry with someone who has done you wrong.

Mt 6:14 For if you *f* other people

Lk 23:34 Jesus said, "Father, *f* them,

Col 3:13 *F* as the Lord forgave you.

1Jn 1:9 and just and will *f* us our sins

forsake — to leave another completely alone; to abandon

Jos 1:5 I will never leave you nor *f* you.

Isa 55:7 Let the wicked *f* their ways

Mt 27:46 my God, why have you *f* me?"

fortified — to make strong, such as a town with a wall.

fortress — a city that is fortified.

fragrance (fragrant) — a sweet or pleasant odor.

SS 4:10 the *f* of your perfume

Php 4:18 They are a *f* offering.

free (freedom) — not bound; liberated.

Jn 8:32 and the truth will set you *f*."

Ro 6:18 You have been set *f* from sin

2Co 3:17 the Spirit of the Lord is, there is *f*.

friend — a person who loves and respects another person.

Pr 18:24 there is a *f* who sticks closer

Jn 15:13 to lay down one's life for one's *f*.

Jas 4:4 Anyone who chooses to be a *f*

fruitful — productive; yielding much fruit.

Ge 1:22 "Be *f* and increase in number

Jn 15:2 prunes so that it will be even more *f*.

fulfill (fulfillment) — to complete a promise or project.

Ps 116:14 I will *f* my vows to the LORD

Mk 14:49 But the Scriptures must be *f*."

Ro 13:10 Therefore love is the *f* of the law.

fury — intense anger.

Pr 6:34 jealousy arouses a husband's *f*,

G

Gabriel — the angel who announced the births of John the Baptist and Jesus (Lk 1:11–20, 26–38).

Galilee — the northern part of Palestine. Jesus grew up, preached and did most of his miracles there. Today this area is in northern Israel.

gall — 1. a plant with an extremely bitter-tasting fruit; 2. the liquid made by the liver.

Mt 27:34 mixed with *g*; but after tasting it,

genealogy — a list of a person's ancestors or descendants; a family tree.

generation — the entire number of people living at about the same time. . . . grandparents, parents and children are . . . different generations.

Ps 102:12 your renown endures through all *g*.

Lk 1:48 now on all *g* will call me blessed,

Gentile — anyone who is not a Jew.

Ro 3:9 and *G* alike are all under

Ro 11:13 as I am the apostle to the *G*,

Gideon — a judge who freed Israel from the rule and terror of the Midianites (Jdg 6–8). He asked for a sign from God, and God showed him his will by means of dew and a fleece (Jdg 6:36–40).

gift — 1. a present; 2. a talent or ability.

Ro 6:23 but the *g* of God is eternal life

1Co 12:4 There are different kinds of *g*,

2Co 9:15 be to God for his indescribable *g*!

glean — to pick up the grain or fruit left behind after harvesting; usually a way for the poor to get food.

Ruth 2:8 Don't go and *g* in another field

gloat — to look at or think about something or someone with malicious satisfaction.

Mic 7:8 Do not *g* over me, my enemy!

glorify — to praise and honor in worship.

Ps 34:3 *G* the LORD with me;

Jn 17:1 *G* your Son, that your Son may

glory — 1. honor; praise; 2. a source of pride or worthiness.

Ps 8:5 and crowned them with *g* and honor.

Ps 19:1 The heavens declare the *g* of God;

Lk 2:14 "*G* to God in the highest heaven,

Jn 1:14 We have seen his *g*, the *g* of the one

1Co 10:31 whatever you do, do it all for the *g*

Rev 4:11 to receive *g* and honor and power,

glutton — a person who eats too much.

Dt 21:20 He is a *g* and a drunkard."

gnash — to grind (one's teeth) together.

Mt 8:12 there will be weeping and *g* of teeth."

goat — an animal raised for its meat and milk; sometimes used in religious sacrifices.

God — the supreme creator and the powerful force of the universe; the one who is to be worshiped.

Ge 1:1 In the beginning *G* created

Ex 20:5 the LORD your *G*, am a jealous *G*,

Nu 23:19 *G* is not human, that he should lie,

Dt 6:4 LORD our *G*, the LORD is one.

Dt 6:5 Love the LORD your *G*

Ps 46:1 *G* is our refuge and strength,

Jn 1:18 ever seen *G*, but the one

Jn 3:16 For *G* so loved the world that he

Jn 4:24 *G* is spirit, and his worshipers must

1Jn 4:16 *G* is love.

Rev 4:8 holy is the Lord *G* Almighty,

godly — to be devoted and loving toward God, wanting to do his will.

1Ti 4:7 train yourself to be *g*.

2Pe 3:11 live holy and *g* lives

Golgotha — the hill outside Jerusalem where Jesus was hung on a cross.

Goliath — the Philistine giant who was killed by David (1Sa 17; 21:9).

gospel — 1. the good news that Jesus died for sins and rose again; 2. any of the first four books of the New Testament.

Ro 1:16 I am not ashamed of the *g*,

1Co 9:16 Woe to me if I do not preach the *g*!

1Co 15:2 By this *g* you are saved,

gossip — to talk too much about others, especially in a way that is hurtful.

2Co 12:20 slander, *g*, arrogance and disorder.

grace — an undeserved favor or gift; the undeserved forgiveness, kindness and mercy that God gives us.

Ro 3:24 all are justified freely by his *g*

Ro 5:20 where sin increased, *g* increased all

2Co 12:9 "My *g* is sufficient for you,

Eph 2:5 it is by *g* you have been saved.

Tit 3:7 having been justified by his *g*,

greed — selfish desire for more money or possessions than one needs.

Lk 12:15 on your guard against all kinds of *g*;

Col 3:5 evil desires and *g*, which is idolatry.

grieve — to cause someone pain or sorrow.

Jn 16:20 You will *g*, but your grief will turn

Eph 4:30 do not *g* the Holy Spirit of God,

guarantee — a pledge that something will take place.

Eph 1:14 who is a deposit *g* our inheritance

guardian-redeemer — in Old Testament times a close male relative who had the responsibility to marry a widow and buy her husband's property (Dt 25:5 – 6).

Ruth 3:9 since you are a *g* of our family.

guide — to direct or point out the way.

Ps 23:3 He *g* me along the right paths

guilty — deserving punishment for having broken a law or commandment.

Ex 34:7 does not leave the *g* unpunished;

Heb 10:22 to cleanse us from a *g* conscience

Jas 2:10 at just one point is *g* of breaking all

H

Hades — hell; the place where the spirits of the dead live.

Mt 16:18 the gates of *H* will not overcome it.

Hagar — a slave of Sarah and one of Abraham's wives; the mother of Ishmael (Ge 16:1 – 6; 25:12).

Haggai — a prophet who encouraged the Israelites returning from exile in Babylon to rebuild the temple (Ezr 5:1; Hag 1 – 2).

hallelujah — praise the Lord; a song of praise.

Rev 19:1 "*H*! Salvation and glory and power

hallowed — holy; sacred.

Mt 6:9 *h* be your name,

Ham — the youngest of Noah's three sons (Ge 5:32).

Hannah — she prayed for a son, and God gave her Samuel. She dedicated him to God; he lived in the temple as a boy and became a prophet and judge (1Sa 1 – 2).

harp — a musical instrument with twelve strings for strumming; frequently used in religious ceremonies.

Ps 71:22 I will praise you with the *h*

harvest — the season for gathering in crops.

Ge 8:22 "As long as the earth endures, seedtime and *h*,

hate — to detest, to have extreme dislike for.

Ps 5:5 You *h* all who do wrong;

Mk 13:13 Everyone will *h* you because of me,

haughty — proud.

Pr 16:18 a *h* spirit before a fall.

heal — to make well again.

Lk 8:43 but no one could *h* her.

Ac 28:27 and I would *h* them.'

heart — the center of a person's life, including the mind, the will and the emotions.

Dt 6:5 LORD your God with all your *h*

1Sa 16:7 but the LORD looks at the *h*."

Ps 51:10 Create in me a pure *h*, O God,

Ps 119:11 I have hidden your word in my *h*

Ps 139:23 Search me, O God, and know my *h*;

Eze 36:26 I will give you a new *h*

Mt 5:8 Blessed are the pure in *h*,

heaven — 1. the place where God lives; 2. the sky.

Ge 14:19 Creator of *h* and earth.

Mt 19:23 to enter the kingdom of *h*.

Lk 24:51 and was taken up into *h*.

Php 3:20 But our citizenship is in *h*.

Rev 21:1 Then I saw "a new *h* and a new earth,"

Hebrew — 1. another name for an Israelite; a descendant of Abraham; 2. the language spoken by the Jews. The Old Testament was written in Hebrew.

heir — someone who receives the property or blessings of a person who has died.

Ro 8:17 then we are *h* — *h* of God
Eph 3:6 gospel the Gentiles are *h* together

herd — a large number of animals of one kind kept together in a group.

Herod — the family name of five kings who ruled Palestine under the Roman emperor: Herod the Great (Mt 2:16); Herod Antipas (Mk 6:14 – 29); Herod Philip (Mt 14:3; Mk 6:17); Herod Agrippa I (Ac 12:1 – 4,19 – 23); Herod Agrippa II (Ac 23:35; 25:13 — 26:32).

Herodias — the wife of Herod Antipas; she persuaded her daughter to ask Antipas for the head of John the Baptist (Mk 6:17).

Hezekiah — a king of Judah; he restored the temple, reinstituted proper worship and sought the Lord's help against the Assyrians.

high priest — the chief religious official in the Jewish religion. In the Old Testament he offered the most important sacrifices to God in behalf of the people.

Heb 4:14 a great high *p* who has ascended
Heb 7:26 a high *p* truly meets our need

hinder — to hold back; to prevent; to delay.

Mt 19:14 come to me, and do not *h* them,

holy — set apart for God; belonging to God; pure; godly.

Ex 20:8 the Sabbath day by keeping it *h*.
Lev 11:44 and be *h*, because I am *h*.
Isa 6:3 "*H, h, h* is the Lord Almighty;
Ro 12:1 as a living sacrifice, *h* and pleasing
Rev 4:8 "*H, h, h* is the Lord God Almighty,

Holy Spirit — the third person of the Trinity; he lives and works in the hearts and minds of believers; he came at Pentecost in a powerful way (Ac 2). Other names are: the Spirit, Counselor and Comforter.

Ps 51:11 or take your *H* from me.
Jn 14:26 But the Advocate, the *H*,
Jn 20:22 and said, "Receive the *H*.
Ac 2:4 of them were filled with the *H*
Gal 5:22 But the fruit of the *S* is love, joy,

honor — to show respect to; to give credit to.

Ex 20:12 "*H* your father and your mother,
Ps 8:5 and crowned them with glory and *h*.

hope — the anticipation of something good.

Ps 42:5 Put your *h* in God,
Isa 40:31 but those who *h* in the Lord
Ro 8:24 But *h* that is seen is no *h* at all.
1Co 15:19 for this life we have *h* in Christ,
Heb 11:1 faith is confidence in what we *h* for

...les — a loosely organized or disorderly ...f people; usually committing harm-

Hab 1:9 Their *h* advance like a desert wind

horror — strong and painful fear or dread.

Jer 8:21 I mourn, and *h* grips me.

hosanna — a Hebrew word of praise meaning "save."

Mt 21:9 "*H* in the highest heaven!"

hospitality — welcoming people into one's home; sharing one's home and food with others.

Ro 12:13 Practice *h*.
1Pe 4:9 Offer *h* to one another

hostile — like an enemy; unfriendly.

human — like people rather than animals, in actions or thoughts or appearance.

humble — 1. (*v.*) to make lower; 2. (*adj.*) not proud; not pretending to be important.

Ps 147:6 The Lord sustains the *h*
Mt 23:12 who exalt themselves will be *h*,
Jas 4:10 *H* yourselves before the Lord,

humiliate — to make humble; to reduce to a lower position; to make ashamed.

1Co 11:22 by *h* those who have nothing?

humility — the absence of pride.

Php 2:3 but in *h* value others above
1Pe 5:5 clothe yourselves with *h*

hymn — a song of praise to God.

Eph 5:19 with psalms, *h*, and songs

hypocrite — a person who pretends to be better than he or she is.

Mt 6:5 when you pray, do not be like the *h*,
Mt 7:5 You *h*, first take the plank out

hyssop — a plant used to sprinkle water or blood for religious cleansing.

Ps 51:7 with *h*, and I will be clean;

I

idle — 1. lacking worth or basis; 2. lazy.

Dt 32:47 They are not just *i* words
1Th 5:14 warn those who are *i*

idol — a statue made by people and worshiped as if it had the power of a god; anything that takes the place of God in a person's life. Worshiping idols is called idolatry.

1Co 8:4 We know that "An *i* is nothing at all
Col 3:5 evil desires and greed, which is *i*.

image — likeness.

Ge 1:27 God created mankind in his own *i*,
Da 3:12 nor worship the *i* of gold you have set up."

Immanuel — a name for Jesus meaning "God with us."

Mt 1:23 and they will call him *I*"

immoral (immorality) — wicked; not living by right standards.

1Co 6:18 Flee from sexual *i*.
Eph 5:5 No *i*, impure or greedy person

immortal (immortality) — free from death; not able to die.

    1Co 15:53 and the mortal with *i*.

    1Ti 1:17 Now to the King eternal, *i*,

imperishable — not able to die or to be destroyed.

    1Pe 1:23 not of perishable seed, but of *i*,

impure — not pure; not clean.

    Ac 10:15 not call anything *i* that God has

    1Th 4:7 For God did not call us to be *i*,

incense — 1. spices burned to make a sweet-smelling smoke, as a way of worshiping God; 2. the sweet smell or the smoke of burning spices.

    Ps 141:2 my prayer be set before you like *i*;

    Rev 8:3 He was given much *i* to offer,

indignation — anger.

    Na 1:6 Who can withstand his *i*?

infirmity — physical weakness; disease.

    Lk 13:12 set free from your *i*."

inflict — to cause to be endured.

    Eze 5:8 I will *i* punishment on you

    2Co 2:6 The punishment *i* on him by

inhabitant — one who lives in a particular place.

    Nu 33:55 drive out all the *i* of the land

    Rev 6:10 the *i* of the earth and avenge

inherit — to receive money, property or keepsakes from a person after his or her death.

    Mt 5:5 for they will *i* the earth.

    Mk 10:17 "what must I do to *i* eternal life?"

inheritance — money, property or keepsakes received from a person after his or her death.

    Dt 4:20 to be the people of his *i*,

    1Pe 1:4 and into an *i* that can never perish,

iniquity — sin; wickedness.

    Ps 51:2 Wash away all my *i*

    Ps 103:10 or repay us according to our *i*.

    Isa 53:6 the *i* of us all.

injustice — unfairness.

    Pr 22:8 Whoever sows *i* reaps calamity,

inscription — 1. the writing on a coin; 2. a written title or message.

instruct — to give knowledge or information; to teach.

    Pr 9:9 *I* the wise and they will be wiser

    1Th 4:1 we *i* you how to live

instruction — the action of a teacher; a lesson.

    Ac 1:2 after giving *i* through the Holy Spirit

    2Ti 4:2 with great patience and careful *i*

insult — 1. (*v*.) to treat with contempt by word or action; to offend; 2. (*n*.) an act or speech of contempt.

    Ps 69:9 the *i* of those who *i* you have fallen

    Mt 5:11 "Blessed are you when people *i* you,

insurrection — revolt or rebellion against a government.

integrity — complete honesty.

    Ps 25:21 May *i* and uprightness protect me,

intercede — to beg or plead for another person.

    Ro 8:26 but the Spirit himself *i* for us

intercession — the plea made on behalf of another person.

    Isa 53:12 and made *i* for the transgressors.

intermarry — to marry someone from a different race or religion.

    Dt 7:3 Do not *i* with them.

interpret — to explain the meaning of.

    Mt 16:3 you cannot *i* the signs of the times.

    1Co 12:30 Do all speak in tongues? Do all *i*?

invoke — to call for help or support.

    Ac 19:13 to *i* the name of the Lord Jesus

Isaac — the promised son of Abraham and Sarah (Ge 17:19; 21:1 – 7); offered as a sacrifice by Abraham (Ge 22); married Rebekah (Ge 24) and was the father of Esau and Jacob (Ge 25).

Isaiah — a prophet called by God (Isa 6) to prophesy to Judah (Isa 1:1). Some of his prophesies were about the coming Messiah (Isa 53).

Ishmael — the son of Abraham and Hagar (Ge 16); he was not to be the son of the covenant (Ge 17:18 – 21).

Israel — 1. the new name God gave to Jacob (Ge 32:28); 2. the nation made up of descendants of the twelve sons of Jacob; 3. the northern ten tribes after they separated from Judah and Benjamin.

    Ge 37:3 Now *I* loved Joseph more than

    Dt 6:4 Hear, O *I*: The Lord our God,

    Lk 22:30 judging the twelve tribes of *I*.

    Eph 3:6 Gentiles are heirs together with *I*,

Israelites — the people of Israel.

    Ex 14:22 and the *I* went through the sea

    Ro 9:27 the number of the *I* be like the sand

J

Jacob — the son of Isaac and Rebekah; he was the twin brother of Esau (Ge 25:21 – 26); he bought Esau's birthright for a pot of stew (Ge 25:29 – 34); he wrestled with God, and his name was changed to Israel (Ge 32:22 – 32); the descendants of his twelve sons became the nation of Israel.

James — 1. one of the twelve apostles; the brother of John (Mt 4:21 – 22); 2. one of the twelve apostles; the son of Alphaeus (Mt 10:3); 3. the brother of Jesus (Mk 6:3); the author of the letter of James (Jas 1:1).

Japheth — one of the sons of Noah (Ge 5:32); he was blessed because he covered his father's nakedness (Ge 9:18 – 28).

jealous (jealousy) — 1. afraid of losing someone's love or affection; 2. angry or unhappy because of what someone else has; 3. careful to guard or keep what one has.

Joel 2:18 Then the LORD was *j* for his land

2Co 11:2 I am *j* for you with a godly *j*.

Gal 5:20 hatred, discord, *j*, fits of rage,

Jeremiah — a prophet called by God to prophesy to Judah (Jer 1:1 – 3). He is often referred to as the prophet of gloom, because he prophesied about the destruction of Judah.

Jericho — the ancient city destroyed by Joshua when the Hebrews entered Canaan (Jos 6).

Jeroboam — an official in Solomon's court; he rebelled and became the first king of the northern ten tribes of Israel (1Ki 11:26 – 40; 12:1 – 20).

Jerusalem — the political and religious center of the Jews; it was the site of many important events in the Bible; also called "Zion" and "the City of David."

2Ki 23:27 and I will reject *J*, the city I chose,

Ne 2:17 Come, let us rebuild the wall of *J*,

Ps 137:5 If I forget you, O *J*,

Jn 4:20 where we must worship is in *J*."

Rev 21:2 I saw the Holy City, the new *J*,

Jesse — the father of David, king of Israel (1Sa 16:10 – 13).

Jesus — The Son of God; the Savior of the world; the Messiah, through whom people can be saved.

Mt 1:21 you are to give him the name *J*,

Mk 11:22 "Have faith in God," *J* answered.

Php 2:10 name of *J* every knee should bow,

Jew — an Israelite; one of the chosen people of God; a descendant of Abraham through Jacob.

Mt 2:2 who has been born king of the *J*?

Ro 3:29 Or is God the God of *J* only?

Gal 3:28 There is neither *J* nor Gentile,

Jezebel — the wife of King Ahab (1Ki 16:31). She promoted Baal worship in Israel (1Ki 16:32 – 33), had many prophets of God killed (1Ki 18:4,13) and opposed the prophet Elijah (1Ki 19:1 – 2).

⸱⸱ab — the commander of the armies of ⸱ David.

⸱ the boy-king of Judah; he repaired ⸱⸱ple (2Ki 12).

Job — a wealthy man from the land of Uz who feared God (Job 1:1 – 5). His righteousness was tested by disaster (Job 1:6 – 22) and personal affliction (Job 2), but in the end God restored wealth and honor to him (Job 42).

John — 1. the Baptist (Mk 1:2 – 8); the son of Zechariah and Elizabeth (Lk 1). He preached in the desert, preparing the people for Jesus (Mt 3:11 – 12); baptized Jesus in the Jordan River (Mt 3:13 – 17); executed by Herod (Mk 6:14 – 29); 2. one of the twelve apostles; brother of the apostle James (Lk 5:1 – 10); wrote the Gospel of John, the letters of John (2Jn 1; 3Jn 1) and the book of Revelation (Rev 1:1; 22:8).

John Mark (see Mark, John).

Jonah — a prophet who was called to preach to Nineveh but instead fled to Tarshish (Jnh 1:1 – 3). While at sea a great storm arose because of his disobedience; he was thrown into the sea and was swallowed by a large fish (Jnh 1:4 – 17). He then repented and went to Nineveh and preached, telling the people to repent (Jnh 3).

Jonathan — a son of King Saul (1Sa 13:16) who had a close friendship with David (1Sa 18:1 – 4; 19 – 20; 23:16 – 18). When he was killed (1Sa 31) David mourned greatly for him (2Sa 1).

Joppa — an ancient walled town on the coast of Palestine.

Jordan — a river in Palestine that flows between the Sea of Galilee and the Dead Sea.

Jos 4:22 'Israel crossed the *J* on dry ground.'

Mt 3:6 baptized by him in the *J* River.

Joseph — 1. the son of Jacob and Rachel (Ge 30:24), who was favored by his father but hated by his brothers (Ge 37:3 – 4). He was sold into slavery (Ge 37:12 – 36), taken to Egypt and eventually given a high position under Pharaoh (Ge 41:41 – 57); 2. the husband of Mary and childhood father of Jesus (Mt 1:16 – 24; 2:13 – 19); 3. a disciple of Jesus from Arimathea; he gave his tomb for Jesus' burial (Mt 27:57 – 61); 4. the original name of Barnabas (Ac 4:36).

Joshua — 1. the son of Nun (Nu 13:8); Moses' aide and later his successor (Dt 31:1 – 18); he led the Israelites across the Jordan River into Canaan (Jos 3 – 4); was the commander in the conquest of Jericho (Jos 6), Ai (Jos 7 – 8), and a large part of Canaan (Jos 10 – 12); oversaw the dividing up of the promised land among the twelve tribes of Israel (Jos 13 – 22); 2. the high priest in Israel during the rebuilding of both the temple (Hag 1 – 2) and the altar (Ezr 3:2,8); also called Jeshua.

Josiah — godly king of Judah for thirty-one years shortly before the destruction of Jerusalem.

Judah — 1. Jacob's fourth son; 2. the tribe of Israel whose members were descendants of Judah; 3. a name for the southern kingdom after Judah and Benjamin separated from the northern ten tribes.

> Ge 29:35 So she named him *J.*
> Zec 10:4 From *J* will come the cornerstone,
> Mt 2:6 Bethlehem, in the land of *J,*
> Rev 5:5 See, the Lion of the tribe of *J,*

Judaism — the teachings of the Jewish religion.

Judas — 1. one of the twelve apostles (Lk 6:16; Ac 1:13); was probably also called Thaddaeus (Mt 10:3); 2. one of the brothers of Jesus (Mt 13:55); author of the last letter in the New Testament (Jude 1); 3. one of the twelve apostles, also called Iscariot; he betrayed Jesus (Mk 3:19; 14:10 – 50) and then hung himself (Mt 27:3 – 5).

Judea — the area of Palestine where the tribe of Judah lived after the exile.

> Mk 10:1 into the region of *J* and across the Jordan.
> Gal 1:22 to the churches of *J* that are in Christ.

judge — to decide if something is good or bad; to condemn.

> Ps 9:8 and *j* the peoples with equity.
> Mt 7:1 "Do not *j*, or you too will be judged.
> 2Ti 4:1 who will *j* the living and the dead,

judgment — 1. a decision or opinion; 2. a decision of guilt or innocence made by a judge in a court of law; punishment decided on by a court; 3. a decision from God, especially the final judgment when God will reward those who believe in him and condemn all others to hell.

> Dt 1:17 of anyone, for *j* belongs to God.
> Ps 119:66 Teach me knowledge and good *j,*
> Isa 66:16 the LORD will execute *j*
> Mt 5:21 who murders will be subject to *j.'*
> Mt 12:36 have to give account on the day of *j*
> Jn 5:22 but has entrusted all *j* to the Son,
> Ro 14:10 stand before God's *j* seat.
> 2Co 5:10 appear before the *j* seat of Christ,

just — righteous, legally correct.

> Ps 111:7 The works of his hands are faithful and *j;*
> Rev 16:7 true and *j* are your judgments."

justice — fairness.

> Isa 30:18 For the LORD is a God of *j.*
> Isa 61:8 "For I, the LORD, love *j;*
> Zec 7:9 'Administer true *j;* show mercy
> Lk 11:42 you neglect *j* and the love of God.

justify (justification) — to erase someone's sins; to declare righteous.

> Ac 13:39 a *j* you were not able to obtain
> Ro 3:24 and all are *j* freely by his grace
> Ro 4:25 and was raised to life for our *j.*
> Ro 5:1 since we have been *j* through faith,
> Gal 3:24 Christ came that we might be *j* by faith.

K

kind — considerate, loving.

> Eph 4:32 Be *k* and compassionate

king — ruler over a country or kingdom; Christ is often referred to as the King of kings.

> 1Ki 22:3 The *k* of Israel had said
> 1 Ti 6:15 the *K* of *k* and Lord of lords,

kingdom — an area or group of people headed by a king; God's kingdom, or the kingdom of heaven, is made up of all believers.

> Ex 19:6 you will be for me a *k* of priests
> Mt 3:2 "Repent, for the *k* of heaven has come
> Mt 5:3 for theirs is the *k* of heaven.
> Mt 6:33 But seek first his *k* and his
> Mt 16:19 the keys of the *k* of heaven;
> Jn 18:36 "My *k* is not of this world.
> 1Co 15:24 hands over the *k* to God the Father
> Rev 11:15 "The *k* of the world has become the *k*

Kish — the father of King Saul, the first king of Israel.

knowledge — possessing the facts, understanding.

> Pr 1:7 of the LORD is the beginning of *k,*
> Hos 4:6 are destroyed from lack of *k.*
> 1Co 8:1 *k* puffs up while love builds up.

L

Laban — the brother of Rebekah (Ge 24:29 – 51) and father of Rachel and Leah (Ge 29 – 31).

labor — 1. (*v.*) to work; 2. (*n.*) a task; 3. (*n.*) the time just before giving birth.

> Ge 5:29 the *l* and painful toil of our hands
> Ex 20:9 Six days you shall *l* and do all your work,
> Jer 13:21 like that of a woman in *l?*

lack — 1. (*v.*) to stand in need of; 2. (*n.*) the state of being in need of something.

> Ps 34:9 those who fear him *l* nothing.

lamb — a principal sacrificial animal in the Old Testament; since Jesus is the supreme sacrifice of God, he is called the "Lamb of God."

Isa 53:7 he was led like a *l* to the slaughter,

Jn 1:29 *L* of God, who takes away the sin

1Co 5:7 our Passover *l*, has been sacrificed.

Rev 5:6 Then I saw a *L*, looking

lament, **lamentation** — a cry of grief.

Ps 5:1 LORD, consider my *l*.

law — 1. God's rules, which help his people know what is right and wrong (the Ten Commandments are part of God's law); 2. (cap.) the first five books of the Bible, written by Moses.

Ps 1:2 and who meditates on his *l*

Ps 19:7 The *l* of the LORD is perfect,

Ps 119:97 Oh, how I love your *l*!

Mt 22:40 All the *L* and the Prophets hang

Ro 8:3 For what the *l* was powerless to do

Ro 13:10 love is the fulfillment of the *l*.

Gal 3:24 So the *l* was our guardian

Lazarus — 1. the poor man in one of Jesus' parables (Lk 16:19 – 31); 2. the brother of Mary and Martha; Jesus raised him from the dead (Jn 11:1 – 12:19).

Leah — the wife of Jacob; she had six sons and one daughter (Ge 29:16 — 30:21).

leprosy — a word used in the Bible for many different skin diseases and infections.

Mk 1:42 Immediately the *l* left him

Levite — a member of the tribe of Levi. The Levites took care of the temple. Only Levites could become priests, but not all Levites were priests.

lewd — indecent; wicked.

life — the total substance of a person's existence; can refer to both physical and spiritual existence.

Ge 2:7 into his nostrils the breath of *l*,

Jn 3:16 shall not perish but have eternal *l*.

Jn 11:25 "I am the resurrection and the *l*.

Jn 14:6 am the way and the truth and the *l*.

Ro 6:23 but the gift of God is eternal *l*

light — the form of energy that allows a person to see; in the Old Testament it symbolized life and blessing.

Ge 1:3 "Let there be *l*," and there was *l*.

Ps 27:1 The LORD is my *l* and my salvation

Ps 119:105 a *l* on my path.

Isa 9:2 have seen a great *l*;

Mt 5:16 let your *l* shine before others,

Jn 8:12 he said, "I am the *l* of the world.

1Jn 1:5 God is *l*; in him there is no

linen — cloth made from the fiber of flax ʾlants.

ʾ — to be alive; may refer to both physical ʾitual existence.

ʾ:12 so that you may *l* long

Ro 1:17 "The righteous will *l* by faith."

2Co 5:7 For we *l* by faith, not by sight.

Php 1:21 to *l* is Christ and to die is gain.

loathe — to feel disgust or hatred.

Job 10:1 "I *l* my very life;

locusts — a type of grasshopper. When they settle in a grain field, orchard or other cultivated area, they can destroy the crop.

Lord — refers to God as the master. (See also LORD.)

Mt 3:3 'Prepare the way for the *L*,

Lk 2:9 glory of the *L* shone around them,

Ac 16:31 replied, "Believe in the *L* Jesus,

Ro 10:13 on the name of the *L* will be saved."

Php 2:11 acknowledge that Jesus Christ is *L*,

2Pe 1:16 the coming of our *L* Jesus Christ,

Rev 17:14 he is *L* of lords and King of kings

Rev 22:20 Come, *L* Jesus.

LORD (Yahweh) — the intimate and personal name of God; it emphasizes his role as Israel's Redeemer and covenant Lord. (See also Lord.)

Ge 2:4 when the *L* God made the earth

Ex 20:2 "I am the *L* your God, who

Ps 23:1 The *L* is my shepherd, I lack

Ps 103:1 Praise the *L*, my soul;

Pr 1:7 The fear of the *L* is the beginning

Isa 6:3 "Holy, holy, holy is the *L* Almighty;

Isa 55:6 Seek the *L* while he may be found;

Lot — the nephew of Abraham (Ge 12:5). He chose to live in Sodom (Ge 13); Abraham pleaded with God for Lot's life when God was about to destroy Sodom (Ge 19:1 – 29).

lot — one of the ways used in Bible times to find out God's will about something. It is somewhat like drawing straws.

Mt 27:35 divided up his clothes by casting *l*.

Ac 1:26 Then they cast *l*, and the *l* fell

love — wanting good to come to another person; being concerned and willing to work for another person's benefit.

Ex 20:6 showing *l* to a thousand generations

Ps 23:6 Surely your goodness and *l* will follow

Ps 136:1 – 26 His *l* endures forever.

Mt 3:17 "This is my Son, whom I *l*;

Mt 5:44 *l* your enemies and pray

Mt 19:19 and '*l* your neighbor as yourself.' "

Jn 13:34 I give you: *L* one another.

Jn 15:13 Greater *l* has no one than this:

Ro 13:10 Therefore *l* is the fulfillment

Gal 5:22 But the fruit of the Spirit is *l*, joy,

Eph 1:4 – 5 In *l* he predestined us

1Jn 3:10 anyone who does not *l* their brother.

1Jn 3:16 This is how we know what *l* is:

1Jn 4:7 for *l* comes from God.

1Jn 4:10 This is *l*: not that we loved God,

1Jn 4:16 God is *l*.

Luke — a co-worker with Paul; he wrote the books of Luke and Acts (Col 4:14).

lust — a strong desire for something wrong.

Pr 6:25 Do not *l* in your heart

Ro 1:26 God gave them over to shameful *l*.

lyre — a small lap harp with three to twelve strings.

1Sa 18:10 David was playing the *l*,

M

Macedonia — a Roman province; the first part of Europe to receive Christianity.

Magi — men of Arabia and Persia who studied the stars. People thought they had the power to tell the meaning of dreams.

Mt 2:1 *M* from the east came to Jerusalem

maimed — crippled; having lost a part of one's body, such as an arm or leg.

majestic (majesty) — great and powerful.

Ex 15:6 was *m* in power.

Ps 8:1 how *m* is your name in all the earth!

Ps 111:3 Glorious and *m* are his deeds,

malice — hatred; wishing harm on someone else.

1Pe 2:1 rid yourselves of all *m*

Manasseh — 1. the older son of Joseph and the tribe descended from him (Ge 41:51; Nu 1:34); 2. one of the kings of Judah (2Ki 21:1).

manger — a feed box for cows or other animals.

Lk 2:7 placed him in a *m*, because there

maniac — an insane person; an overly enthusiastic person.

2Ki 9:20 he drives like a *m*."

manna — the special food God gave daily to the Israelites until they reached the promised land.

Ex 16:31 people of Israel called the bread *m*.

Jn 6:49 Your ancestors ate the *m*

Mark, John — the cousin of Barnabas (Col 4:10); a helper to Paul and Barnabas (Ac 13:5); later a co-worker with Barnabas (Ac 15:39) and then Paul (Phm 24); author of the second Gospel, according to early church tradition.

marriage — the joining together before God and other people of a man and a woman to form a new family.

Ge 29:26 younger daughter in *m* before the older

Mt 22:30 neither marry nor be given in *m*;

Heb 13:4 by all, and the *m* bed kept pure,

Martha — the sister of Mary and Lazarus, the man whom Jesus raised from the dead (Jn 11; 12:2).

marvelous — something that surprises, that fills one with wonder.

Ps 118:23 and it is *m* in our eyes.

Rev 15:3 "Great and *m* are your deeds,

Mary — 1. the mother of Jesus (Mt 1:16 – 25); 2. Mary Magdalene — a woman whom Jesus freed from demons (Lk 8:2), who was present at the cross (Mk 15:40) and who came on Easter morning to the tomb (Mt 27:61); 3. the sister of Martha and Lazarus; she washed Jesus' feet with expensive perfume (Jn 12:1 – 8).

master — one who rules over others.

Mt 6:24 "No one can serve two *m*.

Jn 13:16 no servant is greater than his *m*,

Matthew — a tax collector who became one of the twelve apostles (Mt 9:9 – 13); also called Levi (Mk 2:14 – 17).

mediator — one who makes peace between two people or two groups who are displeased and/or angry with each other. Jesus is the mediator between us and God.

1Ti 2:5 and one *m* between God and mankind,

Heb 9:15 For this reason Christ is the *m*

meditate — to think seriously and carefully.

Ps 1:2 who *m* on his law day and night.

Ps 119:15 I *m* on your precepts

medium — a person who can supposedly talk with the spirits of people who have died.

1Sa 28:7 "Find me a woman who is a *m*,

meek — patient; mild; gentle.

Ps 37:11 But the *m* will inherit the land

Mt 5:5 Blessed are the *m*,

Melchizedek — a priest and king of early Salem (Jerusalem); Jesus was said to be a priest like Melchizedek (Heb 5:6).

Mephibosheth — son of Jonathan and grandson of Saul; he lived out his life under King David's protection (2Sa 9:11).

mercy — kindness and forgiveness, especially when given to a person who doesn't deserve it.

Mic 6:8 To act justly and to love *m*

Ro 9:15 "I will have *m* on whom I have *m*,

1Pe 1:3 In his great *m* he has given us new

Messiah — the "Anointed One"; Christ; the one the Jews expected to come and be their king.

Lk 9:20 Peter answered, "God's *M*."

Jn 1:41 "We have found the *M*"

Methuselah — a man in early Bible times who lived 969 years (Ge 5:27).

Michal — daughter of Saul, wife of David, both of whom were kings of Israel.

midwives — women who helped with the birth of a baby.

Ex 1:17 The *m*, however, feared God

millstone — one of a pair of stones used to crush grain for flour.

Lk 17:2 sea with a *m* tied around their neck

minister — 1. (*v.*) to serve; to give care or attention to; 2. (*n.*) one who serves others as God directs.

2Co 3:6 as *m* of a new covenant
1Ti 4:6 you will be a good *m*

miracle — an unusual event, one that goes against the normal laws of nature. Miracles are done by the power of God.

Ps 77:14 You are the God who performs *m*;
Mk 6:2 What are these remarkable *m* he is
Ac 2:22 accredited by God to you by *m*,
Heb 2:4 it by signs, wonders and various *m*,

Miriam — the sister of Moses and Aaron (Nu 26:59); led the Israelites in praising God in dance and song after he had parted the waters of the Red Sea (Ex 15:20 – 21); later temporarily struck with leprosy because she criticized Moses (Nu 12).

Moab — 1. a son of Lot whose descendants became bitter enemies of the Israelites; 2. the land occupied by the Moabites, to the east of the Dead Sea.

money — a medium of exchange.

Ecc 5:10 Whoever loves *m* never has
Mt 6:24 You cannot serve both God and *m*.
1Co 16:2 set aside a sum of *m* in keeping
1Ti 6:10 For the love of *m* is a root

Mordecai — cousin of Esther, queen of Persia; he and Esther saved the Jews from a plot to put them all to death.

mortal — human; able to die.

Ps 9:20 the nations know they are only *m*.
Ps 103:15 The life of *m* is like grass,
1Co 15:53 and the *m* with immortality.

Moses — the leader of Israel in the exodus out of Egypt, ending in their passing through the Red Sea (Ex 12 – 14). He received the law of God at Sinai (Ex 19 – 23) and gave it to the people of Israel. Moses was allowed to view the land of Canaan from the top of Mount Nebo, but he died without entering it (Nu 20:1 – 13; Dt 34:5 – 12).

mother — the female parent.

Ge 2:24 and *m* and is united to his wife,
Dt 5:16 "Honor your father and your *m*,

ourn — to feel deep sorrow; to grieve.

5:4 Blessed are those who *m*,
— to kill someone illegally.
:13 "You shall not *m*.

muster — to gather together, especially to gather soldiers for war.

mute — unable to speak.

Mt 9:33 the man who had been *m* spoke.

myrrh — the sweet-smelling sap of the myrrh bush. It was used to make the sacred anointing oil.

Mt 2:11 gifts of gold, frankincense and *m*.

N

Nabal — a rich sheepherder in Judah who insulted David; when David planned to take revenge, Nabal's wife Abigail brought gifts to calm David; Nabal died shortly afterwards, and Abigail married David (1Sa 25:1 – 42).

Naboth — owner of a vineyard that King Ahab wanted and gained by having Naboth accused of blasphemy and stoned (1Ki 21:1 – 29).

Naomi — the mother-in-law of Ruth (Ru 1); she advised Ruth to seek marriage with Boaz (Ru 2 – 4).

Naphtali — a son of Jacob and father of the tribe of Naphtali (Nu 1:42 – 43).

nard — an expensive, pleasant-smelling oil from the spikenard, a plant that grew in India.

Mk 14:3 perfume, made of pure *n*.

Nathan — the prophet of God who exposed David's sin with Bathsheba, causing David to repent (2Sa 12:1 – 25).

Nathanael — one of the twelve apostles (Jn 1:45 – 49); was probably also called Bartholomew (Mt 10:3).

Nazarene — a person who lived in or came from the town of Nazareth in Galilee.

Mk 16:6 looking for Jesus the *N*,

Nazirite — a person who separated himself or herself by taking a vow to do special work for God. This included a promise not to cut one's hair and not to drink wine.

Jdg 16:17 I have been a *N* dedicated to God

Nebuchadnezzar — king of Babylon who took Judah into captivity.

Negev — the desert region south of Judea.

Ge 24:62 for he was living in the *N*.

Nehemiah — the Jewish cupbearer of King Artaxerxes of Persia (Ne 2:1); while in Jerusalem rebuilt the walls of the city (Ne 2 — 6) and with Ezra reestablished the worship of God there after the exile in Babylon (Ne 8).

neighbor — 1. someone who lives nearby; 2. any fellow human being.

Lev 19:18 but love your *n* as yourself.
Lk 10:36 of these three do you think was a *n*

Nicodemus — a Pharisee who visited Jesus at night (Jn 3) and learned about being born again.

Nile — the primary river in Egypt.

Nineveh — the city to which Jonah was sent to preach (Jnh 1:2); the ancient capital of Assyria.

Noah — "a righteous man" in early Bible times; he built an ark, as God commanded him (Ge 6–8). God made a covenant with him never again to cover the entire earth with a flood (Ge 9).

nullify — to make of no value; to make unimportant.

Mk 7:13 Thus you *n* the word of God

O

oath — a promise in which one asks God to witness that something is true.

Dt 10:20 take your *o* in his name.

obey (obedience) — to do as asked; to follow someone's commands or wishes.

Dt 6:3 careful to *o* so that it may go well

1Sa 15:22 To *o* is better than sacrifice,

Jn 14:23 who loves me will *o* my teaching.

Ac 5:29 "We must *o* God rather than human

Eph 6:1 Children, *o* your parents in the Lord,

offense — an act that makes someone angry by what was done.

offering — 1. something given to God as an act of worship; 2. the sacrifice of an animal to make the relationship between God and human beings right again. In the Old Testament, animals and grains were regularly used as offerings in an attempt to bring the people closer to God.

Ge 22:8 provide the lamb for the burnt *o*,

Isa 53:10 the LORD makes his life an *o*

Mk 12:33 is more important than all burnt *o*

Eph 5:2 as a fragrant *o* and sacrifice to God.

offspring — children.

Ge 3:15 and between your *o* and hers;

Ge 12:7 "To your *o* I will give this land."

oil — almost always refers to olive oil; used to anoint someone for a physical benefit or to set someone apart for service.

2Ki 9:6 prophet poured the *o* on Jehu's head

Lk 7:46 You did not put *o* on my head,

olive — a tree whose fruit gives olive oil, which was used for varied purposes.

oppress — to control people unfairly and cruelly by the use of one's power.

Isa 53:7 He was *o* and afflicted,

Zec 7:10 Do not *o* the widow

oracle — 1. a saying or answer; 2. the word of the Lord.

ordain — 1. to set apart for a specific office or duty; 2. to order or command.

Ps 111:9 he *o* his covenant forever

ordinance — 1. an official law; 2. a law made or commanded by God.

1Sa 30:25 a statute and *o* for Israel

ornate — elaborately decorated or adorned.

Ge 37:3 he made an *o* robe for him.

overseer — one of the terms used for leaders in the early church.

Ac 20:28 the Holy Spirit has made you *o*.

1Ti 3:2 Now the *o* is to be above reproach,

oxen — strong animals that were used in various ways in farming communities.

P

pagan — a person who does not worship God, especially someone who worships idols.

1Pe 2:12 such good lives among the *p* that,

papyrus — 1. a large water plant, similar to the reed, which grows in marshes and lakes. Moses' mother put him in a basket made from papyrus (Ex 2:3); 2. a paper made from this plant.

parable — a story that tells a special lesson or truth. Jesus told many parables.

paralyzed — unable to move certain parts of one's body.

Mk 2:3 bringing to him a *p* man,

parents — fathers and mothers.

Pr 17:6 and *p* are the pride of their children.

Eph 6:1 Children, obey your *p* in the Lord,

Col 3:20 obey your *p* in everything,

Passover — an annual holiday that still today reminds the Jewish people of how God freed them from slavery in Egypt. The Lord "passed over" the homes marked with the blood of a lamb on their doorframes, but he killed all the other firstborn in Egypt.

Ex 12:11 Eat it in haste; it is the LORD's *P*.

Passover lamb — the lamb killed on the Passover as a sacrifice. Jesus is our Passover lamb, because he was sacrificed for our deliverance from sin, in the same way a lamb was sacrificed when the Israelites were delivered from Egypt.

1Co 5:7 our *P* lamb, has been sacrificed.

pasture — a plot or section of grassy land used for grazing cattle.

patient (patience) — able to put up with problems or pain without complaining or becoming angry.

Ro 12:12 Be joyful in hope, *p* in affliction,

1Co 13:4 Love is *p*, love is kind.

Col 3:12 kindness, humility, gentleness and *p*.

patriarch — the father and ruler of a family; the head of a tribe.

Paul—a Pharisee from Tarsus (Ac 9:11); named Saul at birth (Ac 13:9). Jesus appeared to him on the road to Damascus (Ac 9:4–9), and he became a powerful apostle (Gal 1). His writings make up a large part of the New Testament, ranging from intricate theology to passionate letters to struggling churches.

peace—freedom from disturbance; calm.
Isa 9:6 Everlasting Father, Prince of *P.*
Lk 2:14 on earth *p* to those on whom his
Jn 14:27 *P* I leave with you; my *p*
Ro 5:1 we have *p* with God
Gal 5:22 joy, *p*, forbearance, kindness,

Pentecost—a Jewish feast celebrated fifty days after the Passover. Today the Christian church celebrates Pentecost because it was the day the Holy Spirit came to dwell with Christ's followers (Ac 2:1–4).

people—a collective group.
2Ch 7:14 if my *p*, who are called by my name,
1Pe 2:9 you are a chosen *p*,

perfect—flawless; without defect.
Mt 5:48 Be *p*, therefore, as your heavenly

perish—to spoil; to be destroyed.
Ps 102:26 They will *p*, but you remain;

persecute (persecution)—to continually treat someone cruelly and unfairly, even though that person has done nothing wrong. The early Christians were persecuted for believing in Jesus as the Son of God.
Jn 15:20 they *p* me, they will *p* you
Ac 26:14 'Saul, Saul, why do you *p* me?
Ro 12:14 Bless those who *p* you; bless

persevere (perseverance)—to refuse to give up; to keep on trying; to continue in one's actions or beliefs in spite of problems.
Ro 5:3 we know that suffering produces *p*;
Heb 10:36 You need to *p* so that
Heb 12:1 let us run with *p* the race

Persia—ancient geographical area and kingdom located north of the Persian Gulf.

pervert—to use wrongly; to turn from what is right.

pestilence—a plague; a disease that spreads quickly and kills many people.
Ps 91:3 snare and from the deadly *p.*

Peter—one of the twelve apostles; the brother of Andrew; also called Simon (Lk 6:14) and Cephas (Jn 1:42); he denied Jesus three times (Mk 14:66–72) but became a bold evangelist. He wrote the books of 1 and 2 Peter.

petition—to make a formal request.

pharaoh—the title given to the ruler of Egypt.

Pharisees—a group of Jews who obeyed strictly both God's laws and all their ... s about God's laws.
... 20 surpasses that of the *P*

Philip—1. one of the twelve apostles (Mt 10:3); 2. a deacon (Ac 6:1–7) and evangelist in Samaria; he witnessed to an Ethiopian (Ac 8:4–40).

Philistines—enemies of the Israelites throughout much of Old Testament history; they were especially powerful during the reigns of Saul and David.

Pilate—the governor of Judea who questioned Jesus (Lk 22:66—23:25) and then sent him to Herod (Lk 23:6–12). Pilate finally consented to Jesus' crucifixion when the crowds chose Barabbas rather than Jesus to be released (Lk 23:13–25).

pity—a sympathy or sorrow for the suffering of another.
Mk 9:22 take *p* on us and help us."

plague—1. a disease that kills many people, such as the plague of boils; 2. an event that causes much suffering or loss, such as the plague of locusts.

plead—to appeal earnestly; to beg.
Job 16:21 he *p* with God as one *p* for a friend.

pledge—a binding promise or agreement.
1Ti 5:12 they have broken their first *p.*

plot—to plan, usually secretly; to scheme.
Ps 83:5 With one mind they *p* together;

plowshare—the pointed part of the plow; it cuts into the soil to make rows.
Mic 4:3 will beat their swords into *p*

plunder—1. (*v.*) to loot or rob during a war; 2. (*n.*) property taken by plundering.

pomegranate—a reddish fruit about the size of an orange. It has many seeds and a juicy pulp.

poor—those who have little money.
Dt 15:4 there need be no *p* people
Isa 61:1 me to proclaim good news to the *p.*
Mt 26:11 The *p* you will always have
1Co 13:3 If I give all I possess to the *p*
2Co 8:9 yet for your sake he became *p*,

portico—a porch, usually at the front of a building.
2Ch 3:4 The *p* at the front of the temple

praise—1. (*v.*) to glorify; to say good things about someone or something; 2. (*n.*) approval; worship.
Ex 15:2 He is my God, and I will *p* him,
Ps 119:175 Let me live that I may *p* you,
Eph 1:12 might be for the *p* of his glory.

pray—to talk with God.
2Ch 7:14 will humble themselves and *p*
Mt 6:5 "And when you *p*, do not be like
Ro 8:26 do not know what we ought to *p*
1Th 5:16–17 Rejoice always, *p* continually,

preach—to tell the message of the gospel in public; to deliver a sermon.
Mt 11:1 and *p* in the towns of Galilee.

Ro 10:15 how can they *p* unless they are sent?

precept — command; law; rule.

Ps 19:8 The *p* of the LORD are right,

Ps 119:69 I keep your *p* with all my heart.

precious — valuable; of great worth.

Ps 139:17 How *p* to me are your thoughts,

predestine — to decide or decree ahead of time.

Ro 8:30 And those he *p*, he also called;

Eph 1:5 he *p* us for adoption

pregnant — carrying an unborn child within a woman's body.

Lk 1:24 his wife Elizabeth became *p*

prevail — to triumph or succeed.

pride — 1. (negative) the attitude that one is better than others; 2. (positive) a healthy self-respect or sense of satisfaction.

Pr 16:18 *P* goes before destruction,

Gal 6:4 they can take *p* in themselves

priest (priesthood) — a Levite who offered sacrifices and prayers to God for the people.

1Pe 2:9 you are a chosen people, a royal *p*,

prince — a male member of a royal family.

prison — a building where people are held, usually for committing a crime.

proclaim — to announce or declare.

1Ch 16:23 *p* his salvation day after day.

Ps 19:1 the skies *p* the work of his hands.

Isa 61:1 to *p* good news to the poor.

1Co 11:26 you *p* the Lord's death

profane — to make a holy thing impure by treating it with disrespect or irreverence.

Lev 22:32 Do not *p* my holy name,

prophecy — a message from God that a prophet brings to the people.

1Co 13:8 where there are *p*, they will cease;

2Pe 1:20 you must understand that no *p*

prophesy — to give the message of God to the people.

Joel 2:28 Your sons and daughters will *p*,

1Co 14:39 brothers and sisters, be eager to *p*,

prophet — a person who receives messages from God to tell to his people. A prophet is called by God to speak for him.

Dt 18:18 up for them a *p* like you

Lk 24:25 believe all that the *p* have spoken!

Ac 10:43 All the *p* testify about him that

Heb 1:1 through the *p* at many times

prosper — to succeed; achieve economic success.

Pr 11:25 A generous person will *p*;

prostitute — a person who lets someone use his or her body for sexual relations in exchange for money.

Jos 2:1 house of a *p* named Rahab

prostrate — lying facedown on the ground.

proud — to have pride.

Ro 12:16 Do not be *p*, but be willing

Jas 4:6 "God opposes the *p*

proverbs — 1. wise sayings; 2. (Proverbs) a book of the Bible that contains many wise sayings.

1Ki 4:32 He spoke three thousand *p*

provoke — to make angry; to cause trouble.

prudent — wise.

Pr 19:14 a *p* wife is from the LORD.

psalms — 1. poetry written to praise God; 2. (Psalms) a book of the Bible that contains many psalms.

Eph 5:19 speaking to one another with *p*,

punish (punishment) — to cause someone to suffer for doing wrong.

Ge 4:13 "My *p* is more than I can bear.

Ex 20:5 jealous God, *p* the children for the sin

pure — perfectly free from fault or blemish.

Ps 51:10 Create in me a *p* heart, O God,

purify — to make pure or clean.

1Jn 1:7 of Jesus, his Son, *p* us from all sin.

1Jn 1:9 and *p* us from all unrighteousness.

Purim — an annual Jewish holiday celebrating Queen Esther's rescue of the Jews when Haman plotted to destroy them.

pursue — 1. to follow in order to overtake; to chase; 2. to seek a goal.

Lev 26:7 You will *p* your enemies,

1Ti 6:11 and *p* righteousness, godliness,

Q

quail — a small spotted bird similar to the partridge; God provided quail and manna to the Israelites when they wandered in the wilderness.

Nu 11:32 people went out and gathered *q*.

quake — 1. (*v.*) to shake or tremble; 2. (*n.*) an earthquake.

Ps 75:3 the earth and all its people *q*,

Rev 16:18 so tremendous was the *q*.

queen — 1. the female ruler of a country; 2. the wife of a king.

R

Rabbi — a teacher of Jewish law.

Rachel — the daughter of Laban (Ge 29:16); she became Jacob's wife (Ge 29:28) and bore him two sons, Joseph and Benjamin (Ge 30:22–24; 35:16–24).

rage — a fit of anger.

Eph 4:31 Get rid of all bitterness, *r*

ram — a male sheep.

ransom — the price paid to get back a person who is held as a slave. Because peopl are slaves of sin, a ransom had to be paid, which was the death of the sinless one, Jesus.

Mt 20:28 and to give his life as a *r* for many."

Heb 9:15 as a *r* to set them free

reap — 1. to cut down grain at harvest time; to gather a crop together; 2. to get as a result or reward.

Gal 6:7 A man *r* what he sows.

Rebekah — Isaac's wife (Ge 24); the mother of Esau and Jacob (Ge 25:19 – 26). With her encouragement, Jacob tricked his father into giving him the blessing that belonged to Esau (Ge 27:1 – 17).

rebel — 1. (*v.*) to disobey and turn against those in authority; 2. (*n.*) a person who disobeys and flaunts authority.

Ro 13:2 whoever *r* against the authority

rebuke — to scold sharply.

2Ti 4:2 correct, *r* and encourage

Rev 3:19 Those whom I love I *r*

reconcile (reconciliation) — to return to friendship after a quarrel; human beings are "reconciled" to God through Christ.

Mt 5:24 First go and be *r* to them;

Ro 5:10 we were *r* to him through the death

2Co 5:18 and gave us the ministry of *r*.

redeem (redemption) — 1. to free from evil by paying a price (Gal 3:13); 2. to buy back.

Ex 21:30 the owner may *r* his life

Gal 3:13 Christ *r* us from the curse

Eph 1:7 In him we have *r* through his blood,

Col 1:14 in whom we have *r*, the forgiveness

Red Sea — the body of water the Israelites crossed in a miraculous way when they were escaping from slavery in Egypt.

refuge — a place of shelter and safety.

Ps 46:1 God is our *r* and strength,

regard — to pay attention to.

Ps 41:1 Blessed are those who have *r* for the weak;

regulations — rules dealing with procedure or ceremony.

Rehoboam — the son of Solomon; he became king after his father's death (1Ki 11:43). Because of his harsh treatment of the people, Israel was divided into two kingdoms (1Ki 12:1 – 24; 14:21 – 31).

reign — the time during which a king or other official rules.

rejoice — to express joy or gladness.

Ps 118:24 let us *r* today be glad.

Lk 1:47 and my spirit *r* in God my Savior,

Php 4:4 *R* in the Lord always.

␣␣␣ant — a small part remaining; a small ␣ group.

␣:21 A *r* will return,

repent (repentance) — to turn away from sin; to be sorry for what one has done and to promise not to do it again.

Mt 4:17 "*R*, for the kingdom of heaven

Lk 3:8 Produce fruit in keeping with *r*.

Ac 2:38 Peter replied, "*R* and be baptized,

reproach — 1. (*v.*) to blame or accuse; 2. (*n.*) something for which one can be blamed or criticized.

Job 27:6 my conscience will not *r* me

require (requirement) — to demand as necessary.

1Ki 8:31 is *r* to take an oath

Zec 3:7 obedience to me and keep my *r*,

rescue — to save or deliver.

Ps 140:1 *R* me, LORD from evildoers;

respect — to look up to or hold in high esteem.

1Pe 2:17 Show proper *r* to everyone,

restitution — to restore or pay back for damage, loss or injury.

Nu 5:7 must make full *r* for the wrong

restore — to bring back; to return something to its former condition.

Ps 51:12 *R* to me the joy of your salvation

Ac 3:21 time comes for God to *r* everything,

resurrection — the act of coming back to life after being dead.

Jn 11:25 Jesus said to her, "I am the *r*

Ro 1:4 in power by his *r* from the dead:

1Co 15:12 some of you say that there is no *r*

retribution — punishment for doing wrong.

Jer 51:56 For the LORD is a God of *r*;

Reuben — oldest son of Jacob and founder of the tribe of the same name.

revelation — the act of making known or telling about.

Gal 1:12 I received it by *r* from Jesus Christ.

Rev 1:1 *r* from Jesus Christ, which God gave

revenge — to hurt or punish a person who has wronged you; to get back at someone who has hurt you.

Lev 19:18 " 'Do not seek *r* or bear a grudge

Ro 12:19 Do not take *r*, my dear friends,

reverence (revere) — a deep respect, honor and awe.

Ps 5:7 in *r* I bow down

Col 3:22 of heart and *r* for the Lord.

reward — 1. (*v.*) to repay with good for something someone has done; 2. (*n.*) the gift one receives for good behavior or character.

Ps 127:3 offspring a *r* from him.

Jer 17:10 to *r* each person according to

Mt 5:12 because great is your *r* in heaven,

Mt 6:5 they have received their *r* in full.

righteous (righteousness) — being in a right relationship to God; not guilty before God.

Isa 64:6 and all our *r* acts are like filthy rags;

Ro 3:10 "There is no one *r*, not even one;

Rome — 1. the empire that controlled much of the known world at the time of Christ; 2. the capital city of the Roman Empire, located in Italy.

royal — of or belonging to the ruler of a country and his family.

Ruth — a Moabite widow who went with her mother-in-law Naomi to Bethlehem (Ru 1). There she gathered the gleanings from the field of Boaz (Ru 2), whom she later married (Ru 3:1 – 4:12). She was an ancestor of David (Ru 4:13 – 22) and of Jesus (Mt 1:5).

ruthless — merciless; cruel.

Ps 54:3 *r* people are trying to kill me

Hab 1:6 that *r* and impetuous people,

S

Sabbath — the seventh day of the week; the Jewish day of rest and worship. It extended from Friday sunset until Saturday sunset.

Ex 20:8 "Remember the *S* day

sackcloth — a rough cloth, usually woven from goats' hair. Clothing made of sackcloth was worn as a sign of mourning for the dead or as a sign that a person was sorry for his or her sins.

sacred — holy; set apart for God in a special way.

1Co 3:17 God's temple is *s*,

sacrifice — 1. (*v.*) to offer something as a gift to God; 2. (*n.*) an offering given to God. In the Old Testament God commanded the people to pay for their sins by sacrificing the blood of cattle, lambs, goats, doves or pigeons. These sacrifices were pictures of Jesus' coming as a once-for-all sacrifice for sinners.

Ex 12:27 'It is the Passover *s* to the LORD,

1Sa 15:22 To obey is better than *s*,

Ro 12:1 to offer your bodies as a living *s*,

Heb 9:28 so Christ was *s* once

1Jn 2:2 He is the atoning *s* for our sins,

Sadducees — a group of Jewish leaders, many of them priests. Unlike the Pharisees, the Sadducees did not believe in a resurrection of the dead, but they agreed with the Pharisees in their hatred of Jesus.

Mk 12:18 *S*, who say there is no resurrection,

salvation — deliverance from the guilt and power of sin. By his death and resurrection, Jesus brings salvation to people who believe in him.

Ps 27:1 The LORD is my light and my *s*

Lk 2:30 For my eyes have seen your *s*,

Ac 4:12 *S* is found in no one else,

2Co 7:10 brings repentance that leads to *s*

Php 2:12 to work out your *s* with fear

Heb 2:3 escape if we ignore so great a *s*?

Samaritan — a person who lived in or came from Samaria. Because the Samaritans were only partly Jewish and worshiped God differently from the Jews, Jews from Judea and Galilee hated the Samaritans. They would go out of their way to travel around Samaria (Lk 10:30 – 37).

Samson — an Israelite judge who was known for his great strength. He was betrayed by Delilah but in the end was used by God to punish the Philistines (Jdg 16).

Samuel — often called the last of Israel's judges and the first of Israel's prophets (see also Heb 11:32). His birth was earnestly prayed for by his mother Hannah (1Sa 1:10 – 18), and when he was old enough, she brought him to the temple and he was dedicated to the Lord (1Sa 1:21 – 28). There he was raised by Eli (1Sa 2:11; 18 – 26) and was called to be a prophet (1Sa 3).

sanctify (sanctification) — to make holy; sanctification is the ongoing work of the Holy Spirit in the hearts of believers.

Ro 15:16 to God, *s* by the Holy Spirit.

1Th 5:23 *s* you through and through.

2Th 2:13 through the *s* work of the Spirit

sanctuary — a place where God is worshiped; a holy place.

Ps 150:1 Praise God in his *s*;

Sanhedrin — the ruling council of the Jews in Jesus' time. It was made up of seventy men, and the leader was the high priest. The Sanhedrin could decide whether someone was innocent or guilty of breaking a Jewish law, but it could not put anyone to death without the permission of the Roman governor.

Mk 14:55 the whole *S* were looking for evidence

Sarah — the wife of Abraham and mother of Isaac; first called Sarai (Ge 11:29 – 31). God promised her that, though she had been barren throughout her life, she would give birth to a son in her old age (Ge 17:15 – 21; 18:10 – 15).

Satan — the devil; the leader of the fallen spirits; the most powerful enemy of God and humans.

Mk 4:15 *S* comes and takes away the word

2Co 11:14 for *S* himself masquerades

Rev 12:9 serpent called the devil, or *S*,

satisfy — 1. to please, to make happy; 2. to fulfill a condition.

Ps 103:5 who *s* your desires with good things

satrap — the governor of a province in ancient Persia.

Saul — 1. the first king of Israel (1Sa 9 — 10). He was anointed by Samuel but was later rejected by God because of disobedience; David was chosen to be his successor; 2. see Paul.

saved — 1. (*v.*) rescued from danger; 2. (*n.*) people who acknowledge that by Jesus' death they have been rescued from the punishment of death that their sins deserve.

Ro 10:13 on the name of the Lord will be *s.*"

Eph 2:8 For it is by grace you have been *s,*

Savior — a name for Jesus that means he saves his people from sin.

Lk 1:47 and my spirit rejoices in God my *S,*

1Ti 4:10 who is the *S* of all people,

1Jn 4:14 Son to be the *S* of the world.

scarlet — the color bright red.

scepter — a rod or stick held by a king or queen as a sign of royal power and authority.

Ge 49:10 The *s* will not depart from Judah,

scoff — to mock or sneer at.

Ps 2:4 the Lord *s* at them.

scorn — to despise, to reject with anger or contempt.

Ps 69:20 *S* has broken my heart

scorpion — a spider-like animal with a poisonous stinger at the end of its tail.

scoundrel — a mean, worthless person; a villain.

Pr 16:27 A *s* plots evil,

scourge — to whip.

2Ch 10:11 My father *s* you with whips;

scribe — a person with the important task of copying letters, books and legal papers.

Scripture — all or part of the Bible. When the Bible uses this word it means the Old Testament, since the New Testament had not yet been written. Today we call the Old and New Testaments the Bible or Scripture.

Jn 10:35 and *S* cannot be set aside

2Ti 3:16 All *S* is God-breathed

2Pe 1:20 that no prophecy of *S* came about

scroll — a book made of a long piece of leather or paper that was rolled around a stick at both ends.

Jos 18:9 They wrote its description on *s,*

a tool with a design raised on it into it; 2. the mark made by pressing

this tool onto wax, paper or other soft material. A seal was used to close a letter or legal paper or to prove the authority of the paper.

2Co 1:22 set his *s* of ownership on us,

Rev 5:2 "Who is worthy to break the *s*

sect — a group of people who hold one or more beliefs in common; especially, a small religious group that has separated from a larger group.

seer — a prophet; a person who, with God's help, can see what will happen in the future.

1Sa 9:19 "I am the *s,*" Samuel replied.

self-control — the ability to control one's own actions and feelings.

Gal 5:23 gentleness and *s.*

2Pe 1:6 and to knowledge, *s;* and to *s,*

selfish — centered on oneself; not interested in others.

Php 2:3 Do nothing out of *s* ambition

Sennacherib — an Assyrian king who raided Judah during the time of Hezekiah.

sexual immorality — using sex in ways God says are wrong.

1Co 6:13 body, however, is not meant for *s,*

1Th 4:3 that you should avoid *s;*

shame — a painful emotion caused by an awareness of guilt or shortcoming.

Pr 19:26 a child who brings *s* and disgrace.

1Co 15:34 I say this to your *s.*

sheep — the animal most often mentioned in Scripture, probably because it was the animal most often raised in Bible times; used for meat, for cloth, and for religious sacrifice.

Isa 53:6 We all, like *s,* have gone astray,

shekel — a specific weight of silver, used as money.

Shem — one of the three sons of Noah (Ge 5:32). He, along with his brother Japheth, covered his father when he was naked (Ge 9:21 – 31). Abraham was one of his descendants (Ge 11:10 – 32).

shepherd — someone who takes care of a flock of sheep. It is often used in the Bible as a figure of speech for anyone who cares for a group of people.

Ps 23:1 The Lord is my *s,* I lack nothing.

Jer 31:10 will watch over his flock like a *s.*'

Jn 10:11 The good *s* lays down his life

Ac 20:28 Be *s* of the church of God,

shield — a piece of defensive armor, usually carried on the arm; often a figure of speech in the Bible used to describe God's protection of his people.

Ps 7:10 My *s* is God Most High,

shrine — a dwelling for a god.

sickle—a tool with a long, curved blade and a short handle, used for cutting grain.

siege—see besiege.

signet—a ring with a design on it. The design was stamped in wax to seal a letter or legal paper. Signet rings were usually worn by people in authority.

Silas—a member of the church in Jerusalem; he traveled with Paul.

Simon—1. see Peter; 2. one of the twelve apostles; also called the Zealot (Mt 10:4; Ac 1:13); 3. a sorcerer in Samaria who had great influence on the Samaritan people during the early days of the church; he was severely rebuked by Peter (Ac 8:9–24) for attempting to buy the power of the Holy Spirit.

sin—1. (v.) to break the law of God; 2. (n.) the act of not doing what God wants.

> Nu 32:23 be sure that your s will find you
> Ps 51:2 and cleanse me from my s.
> Ps 119:11 that I might not s against you.
> Isa 1:18 "Though your s are like scarlet,
> Mt 1:21 he will save his people from their s."
> Lk 11:4 Forgive us our s,
> Jn 1:29 who takes away the s of the world!
> Ro 3:23 for all have s and fall short
> Ro 6:23 For the wages of s is death,
> 2Co 5:21 God made him who had no s to be s
> 1Jn 1:9 If we confess our s, he is faithful

Sinai, **Mount**—the mountain where Moses received the Ten Commandments (Ex 19—20).

sinner—a person who breaks the law of God.

> Ps 1:1 or stand in the way that s take
> Mt 9:13 come to call the righteous, but s."
> Lk 15:7 in heaven over one s who repents
> Lk 18:13 'God, have mercy on me, a s.'
> Ro 5:8 While we were still s, Christ died

slander—1. (v.) saying untrue things about another person in order to hurt him or her; 2. (n.) false charges or misrepresentations about another person.

> Lev 19:16 " 'Do not go about spreading s
> Titus 3:2 to s no one, to be peaceable

slaughter—1. the butchering of livestock for food; 2. the killing of great numbers of human beings, as in a battle.

slave—1. a person who is owned by another; 2. a person who is dominated or controlled by an outside force.

> Ro 7:14 I am unspiritual, sold as a s to sin.
> Gal 3:28 s nor free, male nor female,

slay, **slain**—to kill violently or in great numbers.

sluggard—a lazy person.

> Pr 19:24 A s buries his hand in the dish;

slumber—to sleep.

snare—a trap; something risky that tempts or endangers a person.

snatch—to grab suddenly, often without permission or right.

Sodom and Gomorrah—the two cities destroyed by God because the people were so wicked.

> Ge 19:24 rained down burning sulfur on S

Solomon—the son of David and Bathsheba (2Sa 12:24). He became king of Israel after David died (1Ki 1). He asked God for wisdom and was given it (1Ki 3), and he built the temple (1Ki 5–7). His many foreign wives turned his heart away from God (1Ki 11:1–13).

son—a male descendant.

> Pr 10:1 A wise s brings joy to his father,
> Joel 2:28 Your s and daughters will prophesy,
> 2Co 6:18 you will be my s and daughters,
> Heb 2:10 many s and daughters to glory,
> 1Jn 4:9 only S into the world that we might

Son of Man—a title Jesus used for himself to show his humanity as distinct from his divinity. It was also a reference to the Messiah prophesied about in Daniel 7:13.

> Mt 20:18 and the S will be delivered
> Mk 14:62 you will see the S sitting
> Lk 19:10 For the S came to seek
> Jn 3:14 so the S must be lifted up,

sorcery—the use of magic and supernatural powers that are evil; witchcraft.

> Dt 18:10 practices divination or s,

soul—the spiritual part of a person; the part of a person that does not die.

> Dt 6:5 with all your s and with all your
> Ps 23:3 he refreshes my s.
> Mt 10:28 kill the body but cannot kill the s.
> Mt 11:29 and you will find rest for your s.
> Mt 16:26 yet forfeit their s? Or what can
> Mt 22:37 with all your s and with all your

sovereign—having authority over everything; often used in Scripture as a descriptive title for God, "Sovereign LORD."

sow—to plant seeds. In Jesus' time seeds were sown by scattering them by hand over the ground.

> Job 4:8 and those who s trouble reap it.
> Mk 4:3 A farmer went out to s his seed.
> Gal 6:7 A man reaps what he s.

spear—a weapon with a long handle and a sharp point, usually thrown.

spirit—1. the part of a person that is not the body; the soul; 2. a being who does not have a body; 3. (cap.) see Holy Spirit.

Ps 31:5 Into your hands I commit my *s*;
Eze 36:26 you a new heart and put a new *s*
Mt 5:3 "Blessed are the poor in *s*,
Mt 26:41 *s* is willing, but the flesh is weak."
1Jn 4:1 Dear friends, do not believe every *s*,

splendor — something magnificent or splendid.

spoils — booty or plunder taken from an enemy in war.

springs — a source of water coming up from the ground.

Dt 8:7 streams, and deep *s* gushing out
Rev 7:17 lead them to *s* of living water.

staff — a stick used to lean on; a rod used by a shepherd.

Ps 23:4 your rod and your *s*,

starry hosts — the stars and other heavenly bodies.

2Ki 21:3 He bowed down to all the *s*

statutes — established rules or laws.

Ps 19:7 *s* of the LORD are trustworthy,

steadfast — settled; not changing or wavering.

Ps 51:10 and renew a *s* spirit within me.

steal — to rob; to take what belongs to someone else.

Ex 20:15 "You shall not *s*.
Eph 4:28 must *s* no longer,

stench — a terrible smell.

Stephen — one of the first seven men to serve the Jerusalem church (Ac 6:5); he became the first Christian martyr (Ac 7:60).

stiff-necked — stubborn.

Ac 7:51 "You *s* people!

stone — to kill or to try to kill someone by throwing rocks or stones.

strength — power; forcefulness.

Ex 15:2 "The LORD is my *s* and my defense;
Dt 6:5 all your soul and with all your *s*.
Ps 46:1 God is our refuge and *s*,
Isa 40:31 will renew their *s*.
Php 4:13 through him who gives me *s*.

strife — bitter and sometimes violent conflict.

Pr 30:33 stirring up anger produces *s*."

stronghold — a fortified place; a place of security.

1Sa 24:22 David and his men went up to the *s*.
Ps 27:1 The LORD is the *s* of my life

subdue — to bring under control; to conquer.

Ps 81:14 how quickly I would *s* their enemies

submission — humbleness; obedience.

14:34 but must be in *s*, as the law

11 learn in quietness and full *s*.

submit — to willingly yield to another.

Pr 3:6 in all your ways *s* to him,
Eph 5:21 *S* to one another out of reverence
Col 3:18 Wives, *s* yourselves to your husbands,
Jas 4:7 *S* yourselves, then, to God.

succeed — 1. to turn out well; 2. to follow another as heir or successor of a title or rank.

suffer — to bear or endure something painful.

Mk 8:31 the Son of Man must *s* many things
Lk 24:26 the Messiah have to *s* these things
1Co 12:26 If one part *s*, every part *s* with it;

suffering — the experience of enduring pain.

Isa 53:3 of *s*, and familiar with *pain.*
Ac 5:41 worthy of *s* disgrace for the Name.
Ro 8:17 share in his *s* in order that we may
2Ti 1:8 Rather, join with me in *s* for the gospel,

summon — to issue a call to come together; to send for.

Isa 43:1 I have *s* you by name; you are mine.

sustain — to give support; to help; to comfort.

Ps 18:35 and your right hand *s* me;
Ps 146:9 and *s* the fatherless and the widow,

swear — to promise forcefully or earnestly.

1Sa 30:15 "*S* to me before God that you will

swindler — someone who cheats another person out of money or other possessions.

1Co 6:10 nor *s* will inherit the kingdom

sword — a weapon with a long blade for cutting or thrusting.

symbol — an object or action that stands for or suggests something else. The cross is a symbol of Jesus' death.

synagogue — the Jewish place of worship and religious teaching.

Lk 4:16 the Sabbath day he went into the *s*,
Ac 17:2 his custom, Paul went into the *s*,

T

tabernacle — the tent used by the Israelites for meeting with God; the place where God chose to show his presence. The tabernacle was made by God's command and according to his plans. It is described in detail in Exodus 26. Also call the tent of meeting.

Ex 40:34 the glory of the LORD filled the *t.*

talent — a large amount of silver or gold, worth very much money.

Ex 25:39 A *t* of pure gold is to be used

tax — money a government requires its citizens to pay.

Mt 22:19 the coin used for paying the *t.*"

teach — to instruct; to help someone learn.

Ex 33:13 *t* me your ways so I may know you

Ps 90:12 *T* us to number our days,

Lk 11:1 said to him, "Lord, *t* us to pray,

Jn 14:26 will *t* you all things and will remind

tempest — a violent storm.

temple — 1. the place where the Jewish people worshiped and sacrificed in Jerusalem; the first temple was built by King Solomon as a house for God; 2. any place of worship. In this sense, the human body is referred to as a temple (1Co 6:19).

1Ki 8:27 How much less this *t* I have built!

Ac 17:24 not live in *t* built by human hands.

2Co 6:16 For we are the *t* of the living God.

tempt (temptation) — trying to get someone to do wrong.

Mt 4:1 the wilderness to be *t* by the devil.

1Co 10:13 No *t* has overtaken you except

tenant — one who rents land or a house from a landlord.

testimony — a statement made by a witness to prove that something is true.

Lk 18:20 not give false *t,* honor your father

tetrarch — a ruler over one-fourth of a kingdom.

Thaddaeus — one of the twelve apostles (Mk 3:18); son of James and probably also known as Judas (Lk 6:16; Ac 1:13).

thanks — the expression of gratitude.

1Ch 16:34 Give *t* to the LORD, for

Ps 100:4 give *t* to him and praise his name.

1Co 15:57 *t* be to God! He gives us the victory

2Co 9:15 *T* be to God for his indescribable

1Th 5:18 give *t* in all circumstances;

thanksgiving — recognizing and thanking the one who has provided a gift.

Ps 100:4 Enter his gates with *t*

Php 4:6 by prayer and petition, with *t,*

Thomas — one of the twelve apostles (Lk 6:15; Ac 1:13); at first he doubted Jesus' resurrection, but when he saw Jesus, he believed (Jn 20:24 – 28).

thrive — to grow vigorously.

Thummim — see Urim.

threshing floor — the place where grain was trampled by oxen or beaten with a stick to separate it from the stalk.

Ru 3:6 So she went down to the *t*

Timothy — fellow-traveler and official representative of the apostle Paul. He joined Paul on his second missionary journey (Ac 16 – 20), and at one point in this journey Paul sent him to minister to the church at Corinth (1Co 4:17; 16:10). He was the leader of the church at Ephesus (1Ti 1:3) and a co-writer with Paul (1Th 1:1; 2Th 1:1; Phm 1).

tithe — the giving to God of one-tenth of what one earns.

Lev 27:30 " 'A *t* of everything from the land,

Mal 3:10 the whole *t* into the storehouse,

Titus — a Gentile co-worker with Paul (Gal 2:1 – 3; 2Ti 4:10). Paul sent him to Corinth to help solve some of the problems there (2Co 2:13; 7 – 8; 12:18).

toil — 1. (*n.*) strenuous and tiring work; 2. (*v.*) to work long and hard.

Ecc 3:9 What do workers gain from their *t?*

tomb — a burial place. In Bible times, a tomb was often either a cave or a cavity dug into a stone cliff, with a large stone rolled in front to close it.

Mt 27:65 make the *t* as secure as you know

Lk 24:2 the stone rolled away from the *t,*

Jn 11:17 been in the *t* for four days.

tongue — 1. the organ of speech in the mouth; 2. a language.

Ps 39:1 and keep my *t* from sin;

Ac 2:4 and began to speak in other *t*

Php 2:11 every *t* acknowledge that Jesus

Jas 1:26 do not keep a tight rein on their *t*

torment — extreme pain or anguish; agony.

2Co 12:7 a messenger of Satan, to *t* me.

tradition — the handing down of information and beliefs from one generation to another.

Mt 15:2 break the *t* of the elders?

trample — to walk heavily causing injury or damage.

Ps 60:12 he will *t* down our enemies.

transfigure — to change the appearance of; to make bright and glorious.

Mt 17:2 There he was *t* before them.

transgression — sin; disobeying the law of God.

Ps 32:1 whose *t* are forgiven,

Isa 53:5 But he was pierced for our *t,*

Eph 2:1 you were dead in your *t* and sins,

treacherous — untrustworthy, unreliable, faithless.

tread — to step or walk on or over.

Job 24:11 they *t* the winepresses,

treasure — 1. (*n.*) wealth that is stored up or hidden away; 2. (*v.*) to hold or keep something precious, something of value; to cherish.

Mt 6:21 your *t* is, there your heart will be also.

treaty — an agreement between two people or groups or nations.

Ex 34:12 Be careful not to make a *t*

trespass — sin; wrongdoing.

Ro 5:17 For if, by the *t* of the one man,

tribe — a social group made up of a particular branch of a family.

tribute — payment by one ruler or nation to another as an act of submission or in order to guarantee protection.

Isa 16:1 Send lambs as *t* to the ruler

triumph — a victory; a notable success.

Pr 28:12 the righteous *t*, there is great elation;

true — certain; exactly right.

Ps 119:160 All your words are *t*;

Jn 17:3 the only *t* God, and Jesus Christ,

Ro 3:4 Let God be *t*, and every human

Php 4:8 whatever is *t*, whatever is noble,

trust — firm belief or faith in another.

Ps 37:3 *T* in the LORD and do good;

Pr 3:5 *T* in the LORD with all your heart

Isa 26:3 because they *t* in you.

Isa 30:15 in quietness and *t* is your strength,

1Co 4:2 been given a *t* must prove faithful.

trustworthy — deserving of trust; reliable.

Ps 19:7 The statutes of the LORD are *t*,

1Ti 1:15 Here is a *t* saying that deserves full

truth — that which conforms to the facts.

Ps 145:18 to all who call on him in *t*.

Zec 8:16 are to do: Speak the *t* to each other,

Jn 8:32 know the *t*, and the *t*

Jn 14:6 I am the way and the *t* and the life.

Ro 1:25 They exchanged the *t* about God

1Co 13:6 in evil but rejoices with the *t*.

Eph 4:15 Instead, speaking the *t* in love,

Heb 10:26 received the knowledge of the *t*,

1Jn 1:6 we lie and do not live out the *t*.

1Jn 1:8 deceive ourselves and the *t* is not

tunic — a long shirt worn by men in Bible times.

Ezr 9:3 When I heard this, I tore my *t*

turban — a head-covering made by winding a cloth around the head.

unbeliever — one who does not believe in Jesus.

2Co 6:14 Do not be yoked together with *u*.

unclean — morally or spiritually impure; unclean animals were those which the Israelites were not allowed to sacrifice or to eat.

unity — being one.

Ps 133:1 God's people live together in *u*!

Col 3:14 them all together in perfect *u*.

unleavened bread — bread made without yeast. It is usually flat, like a pancake or cracker.

Ex 12:17 "Celebrate the Festival of *U*,

uphold — to give support to.

Ps 37:17 the LORD *u* the righteous.

upright — honest; doing what is right and good.

Urim and Thummim — objects that were placed on the vest of the high priest; used to determine God's will for the nation of Israel.

utter — to pronounce, to speak.

Ps 78:2 I will *u* hidden things,

Jer 15:19 if you *u* worthy, not worthless, words,

utterly — completely, totally.

V

vain — worthless; unsuccessful; foolish. "In vain" means without success or result.

valiant — courageous.

vast — very great in size or amount; huge.

vault — the atmosphere or sky as seen from the earth.

Ge 1:8 God called the *v* "sky."

vengeance — hurt or punishment done to another person who has done something wrong against another.

Isa 34:8 For the LORD has a day of *v*,

vigor — strength and health in the body and its growth.

Job 20:11 The youthful *v* that fills his bones

vile — disgusting, evil.

Rev 22:11 let the *v* person continue to be *v*;

vindicate — to defend; to provide justice for; to set free.

Ps 135:4 For the LORD will *v* his people

violate — 1. to rape; 2. to make something unholy; 3. to fail to obey.

viper — 1. a venomous snake; 2. a treacherous or vicious person.

virgin — a woman or girl who has never had sexual intercourse.

Isa 7:14 The *v* will conceive

Mt 1:23 "The *v* will conceive

vision — a dream from God.

Nu 12:6 reveal myself to them in *v*,

Joel 2:28 your young men will see *v*.

— doubt.

:24 help me overcome my *u*!"

Ac 26:19 disobedient to the *v* from heaven.

vow — a solemn promise made before God or to God.

Jdg 11:30 Jephthah made a *v* to the Lord:

Ps 116:14 I will fulfill my *v* to the Lord

W

wages — payment received for work completed.

Ro 6:23 For the *w* of sin is death,

wail — to cry loudly.

walk — to follow a certain course.

Ps 1:1 who does not *w* in step

Isa 2:5 let us *w* in the light of the Lord.

Mic 6:8 and to *w* humbly with your God.

2Jn 6 his command is that you *w* in love.

wander — to move about without a fixed course.

Nu 32:13 he made them *w* in the wilderness

Jas 5:19 if one of you should *w* from the truth

warn — to give notice beforehand of danger or evil.

warrior — a soldier.

Isa 9:3 as *w* rejoice when dividing

wash — to clean.

Ps 51:7 *w* me, and I will be whiter

Ac 22:16 be baptized and *w* your sins away,

watch — to be on the lookout for someone or something.

Jer 31:10 will *w* over his flock like a shepherd.'

Mt 26:41 "*W* and pray so that you will not fall

way — the means of getting somewhere; the path.

2Sa 22:31 "As for God, his *w* is perfect:

Ps 1:1 or stand in the *w* that sinners

Ps 37:5 Commit your *w* to the Lord;

Isa 53:6 each of us has turned to our own *w*;

Jn 14:6 "I am the *w* and the truth

1Co 12:31 will show you the most excellent *w*.

wean — to help a child or animal begin to eat solid food rather than his or her mother's milk.

weapon — an object used for fighting.

weary — 1. tired; 2. having one's patience or tolerance exhausted.

Dt 25:18 When you were *w* and worn out,

Zec 11:8 and I grew *w* of them

weep, wept — to cry.

Jn 11:35 Jesus *w*.

welcome — 1. to greet a person pleasantly; 2. to make a person feel at home.

Jdg 19:20 "You are *w* at my house,"

wholehearted — sincere; devoted without holding anything back.

wicked — sinful.

Ps 1:1 walk in step with the *w*

Isa 55:7 Let the *w* forsake their ways

widow — a woman whose husband has died.

will — desire; seeking God's will means looking for what God wants to be done.

Ps 143:10 Teach me to do your *w*,

Isa 53:10 Yet it was the Lord's *w*

Mt 6:10 your *w* be done,

Mt 26:39 Yet not as I *w*, but as you *w*."

Ro 12:2 and approve what God's *w* is

Eph 5:17 understand what the Lord's *w* is.

1Jn 5:14 we ask anything according to his *w*,

Rev 4:11 and by your *w* they were created

winepress — a vat or tub in which the juice of grapes is pressed out. Used in the Bible as a symbol for the anger of God against wickedness.

Rev 14:19 into the great *w* of God's wrath.

wisdom — the understanding that comes from God.

Lk 2:52 And Jesus grew in *w* and stature,

Jas 1:5 of you lacks *w*, you should ask God,

witchcraft — practices using evil spirits, magic, or sorcery.

Mic 5:12 I will destroy your *w*

wither — to dry or shrivel up, usually from a lack of moisture.

witness — one who personally sees an event take place.

Ac 22:15 You will be his *w* to all people

woe — great misery; distress.

Isa 6:5 "*W* to me!" I cried.

Lk 11:42 "*W* to you Pharisees, because you

womb — the organ within a woman's body where a child grows before birth.

Lk 1:44 the baby in my *w* leaped for joy.

word — 1. the means of expressing oneself through language; 2. the Bible, as God's written message to people; 3. (cap.) Jesus is the Word sent from God because his life on earth told the message of God.

Jn 1:14 The *W* became flesh and made his

Heb 4:12 For the *w* of God is alive

work — 1. (*n.*) employment; duty; 2. (*v.*) to bring about; to try to achieve a goal.

Ex 23:12 "Six days do your *w*,

Jn 9:4 we must do the *w* of him who sent

Php 2:12 continue to *w* out your salvation

2Ti 3:17 equipped for every good *w*.

world — 1. the earth and those who live in it; 2. the secular, as opposed to the spiritual or religious.

Mt 5:14 "You are the light of the *w.*

Jn 1:29 who takes away the sin of the *w!*

Jn 3:16 so loved the *w* that he gave his one

Jn 8:12 he said, "I am the light of the *w.*

Ro 12:2 Do not conform to the pattern of this *w,*

1Jn 2:15 not love the *w* or anything in the *w.*

worldly — loving the things of the world more than the things of God.

Tit 2:12 to ungodliness and *w* passions,

worry — to feel anxious and uneasy.

Mt 6:25 I tell you, do not *w* about your life,

worship — 1. (*v.*) to give praise, honor and respect to God; 2. (*n.*) reverence given to God.

Ps 95:6 Come, let us bow down in *w,*

Jn 4:24 his worshipers must *w* in the Spirit

worthy — having value; honorable; deserving.

1Ch 16:25 For great is the LORD and most *w*

Eph 4:1 to live a life *w* of the calling you

Rev 5:2 "Who is *w* to break the seals

wrath — great anger; the strong anger of God.

Pr 15:1 A gentle answer turns away *w,*

Ro 5:9 saved from God's *w* through him!

X

Xerxes — king of Persia; he made Esther, a young Jewess, his queen (Est 2:15 – 18).

Y

yearn — to long for; to want very much.

yeast — the ingredient that makes dough rise; sometimes a figure of speech for the influence someone has over others.

Mt 16:6 guard against the *y* of the Pharisees

Gal 5:9 little *y* works through the whole

yield — 1. to submit; 2. to grow or produce fruit.

Ps 67:6 The land *y* its harvest;

Isa 48:11 I will not *y* my glory to another.

yoke — 1. (*v.*) to join together; 2. (*n.*) a wooden bar that goes over the necks of two animals, usually oxen. The yoke holds the animals together as they pull an object, such as a plow or a cart.

Mt 11:29 Take my *y* upon you and learn

2Co 6:14 Do not be *y* together

youth — the time when a person is young.

Ecc 12:1 Creator in the days of your *y,*

Z

Zacchaeus — a tax collector who climbed a tree in order to see Jesus.

zeal — eagerness; strong desire.

Ro 12:11 Never be lacking in *z,*

Zealot — a member of the Jewish group that wanted to fight against and overthrow the Roman government.

Zechariah — a prophet and priest who returned to Jerusalem from the Babylonian captivity; he encouraged the Jews to rebuild the temple (Ezr 5:1; 6:14; Zec 1:1).

Zerubbabel — a descendant of David (1Ch 3:19); he led the return of the Jews from the Babylonian captivity (Ezr 1 – 3; Ne 7:7; Hag 1 – 2; Zec 4).

Zion — 1. the hill on which the city of Jerusalem first stood; David's royal palace and the temple were both built on Mount Zion; 2. the entire city of Jerusalem.

Jer 50:5 They will ask the way to *Z*

Ro 11:26 "The deliverer will come from *Z;*

WORLD OF THE PATRIARCHS

Caspian Sea

Araxes R.

Mt. Ararat

Lake Urmia

Black Sea

Troy

Aegean Sea

Knossos

Caphtor (Crete)

Mycenae

Kittim (Cyprus)

Mediterranean Sea (The Great Sea)

HITTITES

Hattusa

Taurus Mts.

Ugarit

Gebal aka Byblos

Damascus

Megiddo
Hazor
Dothan
Bethel
Gerar
Kadesh Barnea

Carchemish

Aleppo

Ebla

Shechem
Ai
Hebron
Zoar
Beersheba

PADDAN ARAM

Harran

Tadmor

Mari

ARABIA

BABYLONIANS

Nineveh

Ashur

Tigris R.

Euphrates R.

Nuzi

Babylon

Nippur
Uruk

Ur

Persian Gulf

Sinai

Red Sea

Nile R.

EGYPTIANS

Zoan
Sukkoth
Memphis
Heliopolis

Possible location of Biblical "Ur of the Chaldeans," where Abraham's migration began.

Possible location of Sodom and Gomorrah.

→ Abraham's Journey

0   100 km.
0   100 miles

10,000 ft — 3050 m
5000 ft — 1525 m
2000 ft — 610 m
1000 ft — 305 m
0 (sea level) — 0 (sea level)
-1640 ft — -500 m

Maps by International Mapping.
Copyright © 2008 by Zondervan. All rights reserved.

EXODUS AND CONQUEST OF CANAAN

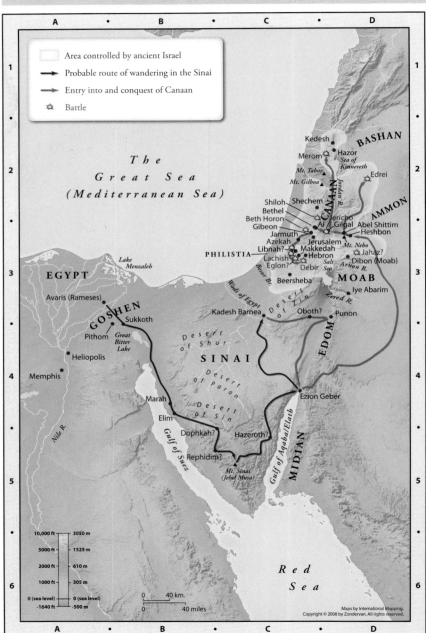

LAND OF THE TWELVE TRIBES

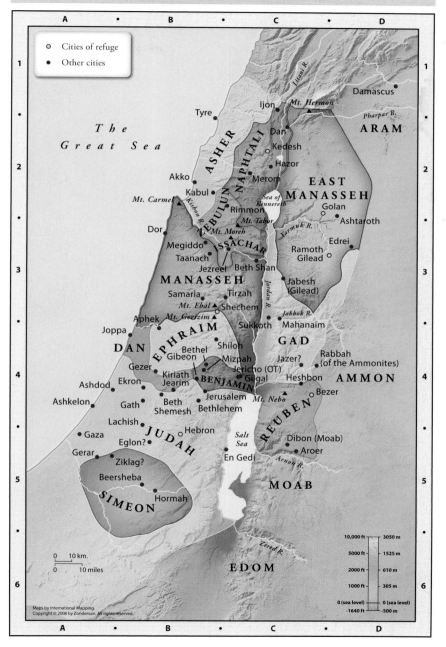

Cities of refuge

Other cities

A · B · C · D

The Great Sea

ASHER
NAPHTALI
ZEBULUN
ISSACHAR
MANASSEH
EPHRAIM
DAN
BENJAMIN
JUDAH
SIMEON
REUBEN
GAD
EAST MANASSEH
AMMON
MOAB
EDOM
ARAM

Damascus
Litani R.
Ijon
Mt. Hermon
Tyre
Pharpar R.
Dan
Kedesh
Hazor
Merom
Akko
Sea of Kinnereth
Golan
Ashtaroth
Kabul
Mt. Carmel
Kishon R.
Rimmon
Mt. Tabor
Dor
Mt. Moreh
Yarmuk R.
Megiddo
Edrei
Taanach
Ramoth Gilead
Jezreel
Beth Shan
Jordan R.
Samaria
Tirzah
Jabesh (Gilead)
Mt. Ebal
Shechem
Jabbok R.
Mt. Gerizim
Sukkoth
Mahanaim
Aphek
Joppa
Shiloh
Bethel
Gibeon
Mizpah
Jazer?
Rabbah (of the Ammonites)
Gezer
Kiriath Jearim
Jericho (OT)
Gilgal
Heshbon
Ashdod
Ekron
Jerusalem
Mt. Nebo
Bezer
Ashkelon
Gath
Beth Shemesh
Bethlehem
Lachish
Hebron
Salt Sea
Dibon (Moab)
Gaza
Eglon?
En Gedi
Aroer
Gerar
Ziklag?
Arnon R.
Beersheba
Hormah
Zered R.

0 10 km.
0 10 miles

10,000 ft — 3050 m
5000 ft — 1525 m
2000 ft — 610 m
1000 ft — 305 m
0 (sea level) — 0 (sea level)
-1640 ft — -500 m

Maps by International Mapping.
Copyright © 2008 by Zondervan. All rights reserved.

A · B · C · D

KINGDOM OF DAVID AND SOLOMON

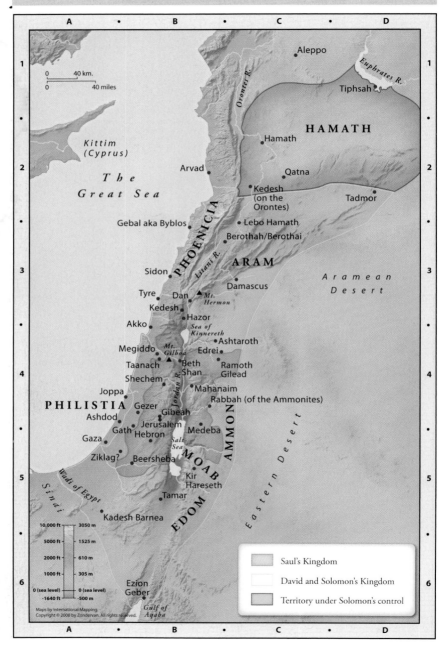

Aleppo

Euphrates R.

Tiphsah

0 — 40 km.
0 — 40 miles

*Kittim
(Cyprus)*

*The
Great Sea*

HAMATH

Hamath

Arvad

Qatna

Kedesh
(on the
Orontes)

Tadmor

Orontes R.

Gebal aka Byblos

Lebo Hamath

Berothah/Berothai

PHOENICIA

Litani R.

ARAM

*Aramean
Desert*

Sidon

Damascus

Tyre

Dan

▲ *Mt.
Hermon*

Kedesh

Hazor

Akko

*Sea of
Kinnereth*

Ashtaroth

Megiddo

▲ *Mt.
Gilboa*

Edrei

Taanach

Beth
Shan

Ramoth
Gilead

Shechem

Jordan R.

Joppa

Mahanaim

PHILISTIA

Gezer

Rabbah (of the Ammonites)

Ashdod

Gibeah

Gath

Jerusalem

Gaza

Hebron

Medeba

AMMON

Eastern Desert

*Salt
Sea*

Ziklag?

Beersheba

MOAB

Kir
Haresheth

Tamar

EDOM

Wadi of Egypt

Sinai

Kadesh Barnea

10,000 ft — 3050 m
5000 ft — 1525 m
2000 ft — 610 m
1000 ft — 305 m
0 (sea level) — 0 (sea level)
-1640 ft — -500 m

Ezion
Geber

*Gulf of
Aqaba*

Maps by International Mapping.
Copyright © 2008 by Zondervan. All rights reserved.

	Saul's Kingdom
	David and Solomon's Kingdom
	Territory under Solomon's control

JESUS' MINISTRY

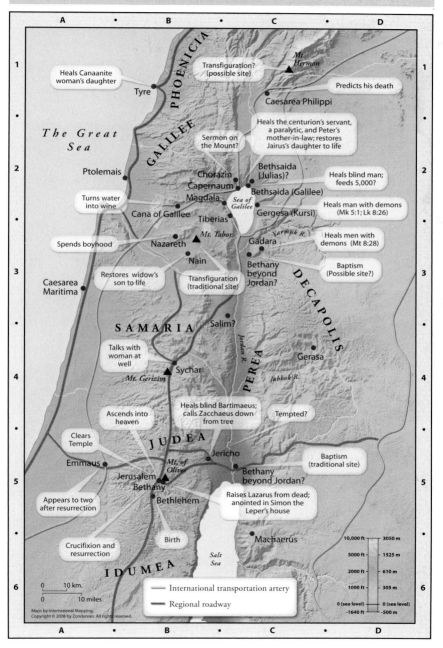

The Great Sea

- Heals Canaanite woman's daughter
- Tyre
- PHOENICIA
- Transfiguration? (possible site)
- Mt. Hermon
- Predicts his death
- Caesarea Philippi
- Heals the centurion's servant, a paralytic, and Peter's mother-in-law; restores Jairus's daughter to life
- GALILEE
- Sermon on the Mount?
- Ptolemais
- Chorazin
- Capernaum
- Bethsaida (Julias)?
- Heals blind man; feeds 5,000?
- Bethsaida (Galilee)
- Turns water into wine
- Magdala
- Sea of Galilee
- Cana of Galilee
- Tiberias
- Gergesa (Kursi)
- Heals man with demons (Mk 5:1; Lk 8:26)
- Spends boyhood
- Nazareth
- Mt. Tabor
- Gadara
- Yarmuk R.
- Heals men with demons (Mt 8:28)
- Nain
- Bethany beyond Jordan?
- DECAPOLIS
- Caesarea Maritima
- Restores widow's son to life
- Transfiguration (traditional site)
- Baptism (Possible site?)
- SAMARIA
- Salim?
- Talks with woman at well
- Sychar
- Mt. Gerizim
- PEREA
- Jordan R.
- Jabbok R.
- Gerasa
- Ascends into heaven
- Heals blind Bartimaeus; calls Zacchaeus down from tree
- Tempted?
- Clears Temple
- JUDEA
- Emmaus
- Jericho
- Baptism (traditional site)
- Jerusalem
- Mt. of Olives
- Bethany
- Bethany beyond Jordan?
- Appears to two after resurrection
- Bethlehem
- Raises Lazarus from dead; anointed in Simon the Leper's house
- Crucifixion and resurrection
- Birth
- Machaerus
- Salt Sea
- IDUMEA

10,000 ft	3050 m
5000 ft	1525 m
2000 ft	610 m
1000 ft	305 m
0 (sea level)	0 (sea level)
-1640 ft	-500 m

0   10 km.
0   10 miles

— International transportation artery
— Regional roadway

PAUL'S MISSIONARY JOURNEYS

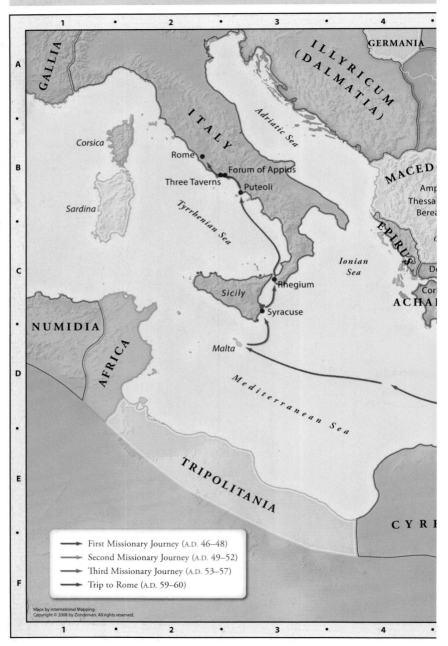

First Missionary Journey (A.D. 46–48)
Second Missionary Journey (A.D. 49–52)
Third Missionary Journey (A.D. 53–57)
Trip to Rome (A.D. 59–60)

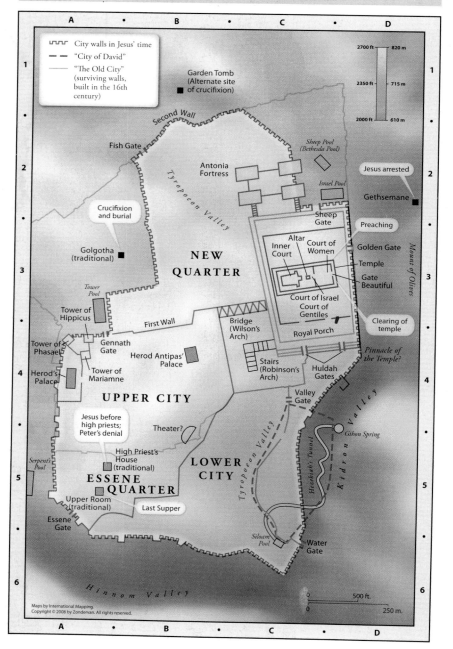

Maps by International Mapping.
Copyright © 2008 by Zondervan. All rights reserved.